Copyright © 1982, 1990, by John Wiley & Sons, Inc.

All rights reserved. Published simultaneously in Canada.

Reproduction or translation of any part of
this work beyond that permitted by Sections
107 and 108 of the 1976 United States Copyright
Act without the permission of the copyright
owner is unlawful. Requests for permission
or further information should be addressed to
the Permissions Department, John Wiley & Sons.

Library of Congress Cataloging in Publication Data:

The Handbook of school psychology / Terry B. Gutkin, Cecil R.
    Reynolds, editors.
        Includes bibliographical references.
        ISBN 0-471-01181-9
        1. Educational psychology—Handbooks, manuals, etc.   2. School
    psychology—Handbooks, manuals, etc.   I. Gutkin, Terry B., 1947–   .
    II.   Reynolds, Cecil R., 1952–   .
    LB1051.H2356   1990
    370.15—dc20   89-39299
                                                      CIP

Printed in the United States of America
10 9 8 7 6 5 4 3 2 1

THE HANDBOOK OF SCHOOL PSYCHOLOGY

SECOND EDITION

EDITORS

TERRY B. GUTKIN, Ph.D.

Department of Educational Psychology
University of Nebraska–Lincoln

CECIL R. REYNOLDS, Ph.D.

Department of Educational Psychology
Texas A & M University

WITHDRAWN

WILEY

JOHN WILEY & SONS
NEW YORK · CHICHESTER · BRISBANE · TORONTO · SINGAPORE

To my father, Harry Gutkin, and the memory of my mother, Rose Gutkin, whose lives taught me the values and integrity to which I will always aspire.

T.B.G.

To my mother, Daphne Reynolds, poet and teacher, and the memory of my father, Cecil Clayton Reynolds, career marine and dedicated father, for their insistence that I succeed and their compassionate modeling of service, the highest calling.

C.R.R.

LIST OF CONTRIBUTORS

Thomas M. Achenbach, Ph.D.
Professor, Department of Psychiatry
University of Vermont
Burlington, Vermont

Jack I. Bardon, Ph.D.
Excellence Foundation Professor
Director of the Collegium for the Advancement of
  Schools, Schooling, and Education
The University of North Carolina at Greensboro
Greensboro, North Carolina

David W. Barnett, Ph.D.
Professor of School Psychology and Counseling
University of Cincinnati
Cincinnati, Ohio

W. Louis Bashaw, Ph.D.
Professor of Educational Psychology
University of Georgia
Athens, Georgia

Mark J. Benson, Ph.D.
Assistant Professor of Family and Child Development
Virginia Polytechnic Institute and State University
Blacksburg, Virginia

John R. Bergan, Ph.D.
Professor of Educational Psychology
University of Arizona
Tucson, Arizona

Donald N. Bersoff, Ph.D., J.D.
Partner
Jenner & Block
Washington, D.C.

William E. Bickel, Ph.D.
Associate Professor, School of Education
Senior Scientist, Learning Research and Development
  Center
University of Pittsburgh
Pittsburgh, Pennsylvania

Douglas T. Brown, Ph.D.
Coordinator, School Psychology Program
Professor of Psychology
James Madison University
Harrisonburg, Virginia

Thomas P. Cafferty, Ph.D.
Associate Professor of Psychology
The University of South Carolina
Columbia, South Carolina

Charles D. Claiborn, Ph.D.
Associate Professor of Counselor Education and
  Counseling Psychology
The University of Iowa
Iowa City, Iowa

Carolyn T. Cobb, Ph.D.
Chief Consultant, Pupil Personnel Services
North Carolina Department of Public Instruction
Raleigh, North Carolina

Jane Close Conoley, Ph.D.
Professor of Educational Psychology and Buros Institute
  of Mental Measurements
University of Nebraska-Lincoln
Lincoln, Nebraska

Alice J. Corkill, Ph.D.
Assistant Professor of Psychology
University of Western Ontario
London, Ontario, Canada

Emory L. Cowen, Ph.D.
Professor of Psychology
University of Rochester
Rochester, New York

Michael J. Curtis, Ph.D.
Professor and Director of School Psychology
Department of School Psychology and Counseling
University of Cincinnati
Cincinnati, Ohio

Raymond S. Dean, Ph.D.
Distinguished Professor of Neuropsychology
Neuropsychology Laboratory
Ball State University
Muncie, Indiana

Tami F. Derr
Doctoral Candidate
Lehigh University
Bethlehem, Pennsylvania

Stephen N. Elliott, Ph.D.
Associate Professor
Department of Educational Psychology
University of Wisconsin-Madison
Madison, Wisconsin

Joseph L. French, Ed.D.
Professor of Educational Psychology
The Pennsylvania State University
University Park, Pennsylvania

Edward Gaughan, Ph.D.
Associate Professor of Psychology
Director, Child and Family Services Center
Alfred University
Alfred, New York

John A. Glover, Ed.D.
Research Professor in Education and Professor of
   Educational Psychology
Teachers College and Burris Laboratory School
Ball State University
Muncie, Indiana

Charles J. Golden, Ph.D.
Professor of Psychology
Drexel University
Philadelphia, Pennsylvania

Jeffrey W. Gray, Ph.D.
Tri-State Regional Rehabilitation Hospital
Evansville, Indiana

Rhonda Greenberg
Doctoral Candidate
Graduate School of Applied and Professional
   Psychology
Rutgers University
Piscataway, New Jersey

Terry B. Gutkin, Ph.D.
Professor of Educational Psychology
Coordinator of Doctoral Studies in Education
University of Nebraska-Lincoln
Lincoln, Nebraska

Ronald K. Hambleton, Ph.D.
Professor of Education and Psychology
University of Massachusetts
Amherst, Massachusetts

Patti L. Harrison, Ph.D.
Associate Professor of Behavioral Studies
Chair, School Psychology Program
The University of Alabama
Tuscaloosa, Alabama

Lawrence C. Hartlage, Ph.D.
Consulting Neuropsychologist
Augusta, Georgia

Julia A. Hickman, Ph.D.
Assistant Professor of Educational Psychology
The University of Texas at Austin
Austin, Texas

A. Dirk Hightower, Ph.D.
Senior Research Associate and Associate Director
Center for Community Study
University of Rochester
Rochester, New York

Paul T. Hofer, Ph.D., J.D.
Research Associate
Federal Judicial Center
Washington, D.C.

Jan N. Hughes, Ph.D.
Associate Professor of Educational Psychology
Texas A & M University
College Station, Texas

Robert J. Illback, Psy.D.
Executive Director, R.E.A.C.H., Inc.
Adjunct Professor of Psychology
Spalding University
Louisville, Kentucky

Robert F. Ittenbach, Ph.D.
Postdoctoral Fellow
University Affiliated Program on Developmental
   Disabilities
University of Minnesota
Minneapolis, Minnesota

John H. Jackson, Ph.D.
Senior Faculty
Wisconsin School of Professional Psychology
Milwaukee, Wisconsin

Roger P. Johanson, Ph.D.
Associate Professor of Teacher Education
Coe College
Cedar Rapids, Iowa

Steven Mills Kaiser, Ph.D.
Staff School Psychologist
Rome City School District
Rome, New York

Randy W. Kamphaus, Ph.D.
Associate Professor of Educational Psychology
University of Georgia
Athens, Georgia

Alan S. Kaufman, Ph.D.
Research Professor of Behavioral Studies
The University of Alabama
Tuscaloosa, Alabama

Ken Kavale, Ph.D.
Professor of Special Education
University of Iowa
Iowa City, Iowa

Barbara A. Kerr, Ph.D.
Associate Professor of Counselor Education
The University of Iowa
Iowa City, Iowa

Jack J. Kramer, Ph.D.
Associate Professor of Educational Psychology and
  Buros Institute of Mental Measurements
University of Nebraska-Lincoln
Lincoln, Nebraska

Thomas R. Kratochwill, Ph.D.
Professor of Educational Pyschology
University of Wisconsin—Madison
Madison, Wisconsin

Jennifer L. Lail, M.D.
Pediatrician, Chapel Hill Pediatrics, P.A.
Clinical Assistant Professor, Department of Pediatrics
University of North Carolina-Chapel Hill
Chapel Hill, North Carolina

Nadine M. Lambert, Ph.D.
Professor, School of Education
University of California
Berkeley, California

Charles A. Maher, Psy.D.
Professor of Psychology and Chair, Department of
  School Psychology
Director, Rutgers School Planning and Evaluation
  Center
Graduate School of Applied and Professional
  Psychology
Rutgers University
Piscataway, New Jersey

Douglas Marston, Ph.D.
School Psychologist
Minneapolis Public Schools
Minneapolis, Minnesota

Brian K. Martens, Ph.D.
Assistant Professor of Psychology and Education
Syracuse University
Syracuse, New York

Stephanie H. McConaughy, Ph.D.
Research Associate Professor
Department of Psychiatry
University of Vermont
Burlington, Vermont

Paul A. McDermott, Ph.D.
Professor of Measurement and Professional Psychology
Graduate School of Education
University of Pennsylvania
Philadelphia, Pennsylvania

William T. McKee, M.S.
Graduate Research Associate
Department of Psychology
Louisiana State University
Baton Rouge, Louisiana

Frederic J. Medway, Ph.D.
Professor of Psychology
School Psychology Training Program
The University of South Carolina
Columbia, South Carolina

Paul J. Meller, Ph.D.
Research Associate and Assistant Professor of
  Psychology
University of Rochester
Rochester, New York

Joel Meyers, Ph.D.
Professor and Director, Programs in School Psychology
State University of New York-Albany
Albany, New York

Thomas D. Overcast, J.D., Ph.D.
Attorney at Law
Edmonds, Washington

Kathleen D. Paget, Ph.D.
Department of Psychology
University of South Carolina
Columbia, South Carolina

Beeman N. Phillips, Ed.D.
Professor of Educational Psychology
Director, School Psychology Program
The University of Texas at Austin
Austin, Texas

Norman Pitt, Ph.D.
Assistant Director, University Counseling Center
Villanova University
Villanova, Pennsylvania

Walter B. Pryzwansky, Ed.D.
Associate Dean for Instruction and Research
School of Education
University of North Carolina
Chapel Hill, North Carolina

Cecil R. Reynolds, Ph.D.
Professor of Educational Psychology
Texas A & M University
College Station, Texas

Donal M. Sacken, J.D., Ph.D.
Associate Professor of Educational Administration
University of Arizona
Tucson, Arizona

Bruce D. Sales, J.D., Ph.D.
Professor of Psychology, Sociology, and Law
Director, Law-Psychology and Policy
University of Arizona
Tucson, Arizona

Richard A. Schmuck, Ph.D.
Professor of Educational Management and Psychology
University of Oregon
Eugene, Oregon

Carolyn S. Schroeder, Ph.D.
Pediatric Psychologist, Chapel Hill Pediatrics, P.A.
Clinical Professor, Departments of Pediatrics and
   Psychiatry
University of North Carolina-Chapel Hill
Chapel Hill, North Carolina

Edward S. Shapiro, Ph.D.
Associate Professor and Director
School Psychology Program
Lehigh University
Bethlehem, Pennsylvania

Susan M. Sheridan, Ph.D.
Assistant Professor of Educational Psychology
University of Utah
Salt Lake City, Utah

Matt Snapp, Ph.D.
Independent Practice
Austin, Texas

Stanley R. Strong, Ph.D.
Professor of Psychology
Virginia Commonwealth University
Richmond, Virginia

Deborah J. Tharinger, Ph.D.
Associate Professor of Educational Psychology
The University of Texas at Austin
Austin, Texas

Richard A. Weinberg, Ph.D.
Professor and Director, Institute of Child Development
University of Minnesota
Minneapolis, Minnesota

Joseph C. Witt, Ph.D.
Professor of Psychology
Department of Psychology
Louisiana State University
Baton Rouge, Louisiana

Frances F. Worchel, Ph.D.
Assistant Professor of Educational Psychology
Texas A & M University
College Station, Texas

Nükhet D. Yarbrough, Ph.D.
Assistant Professor of Psychology
Coe College
Cedar Rapids, Iowa

James E. Ysseldyke, Ph.D.
Professor of Educational Psychology
University of Minnesota
Minneapolis, Minnesota

Joseph E. Zins, Ed.D.
Professor of School Psychology
Department of School Psychology and Counseling
University of Cincinnati
Cincinnati, Ohio

FOREWORD

JACK I. BARDON

The University of North Carolina at Greensboro

In the Preface to the first edition of *The Handbook of School Psychology* published in 1982, the editors, Cecil R. Reynolds and Terry B. Gutkin, expressed their fervent hope that the *Handbook* would become a major reference work in school psychology. They also stated that the one major unifying theme of the *Handbook* was that the profession of school psychology had come of age. Since 1982 the *Handbook* has become one of the most widely used and often cited publications in school psychology. It is big (1284 pages) and comprehensive. It is used by students, practitioners, and scholars of professional psychology as a ready source of helpful, up-to-date information, providing evidence that the field is indeed active and that information and opinion related both to content and issues in school psychology are sufficiently different from content and issues in other specialties in psychology and education to warrant separate consideration.

The editor's decision to publish a second edition of the *Handbook* so soon after the publication of the original volume and to reconsider its organization and content suggests that school psychology continues to mature at a rapid pace. If the field has not yet come of age, it certainly is getting there. In the relatively short time between *Handbook* editions, school psychology has been influenced by new developments in both psychology and education. We know more now. We know more about how to apply our knowledge. We are faced with new problems not conceived of earlier. We are still concerned with long-standing problems calling for continuous reflection and consideration. A major indicator of the status of the field—its growing maturity—is the editors' recognition that the practice of school psychology emanates from a vast body of knowledge that is primarily psychological in con-

tent. Their decision to devote an entire section of the second edition to the scientific disciplines of psychology and their contributions to theory and practice in school psychology clearly distinguishes the second edition from the original *Handbook* and, in the process, helps elevate school psychology to the status of a true professional specialty. This edition demonstrates that practices in school psychology are not simply a collection of "things to do" to help people but are deeply rooted in psychological theory and research.

The second edition of the *Handbook* is more than it seems. In addition to being a useful source of information, it is a scholarly declaration of what the field has to say about itself; what it has to offer that sets it apart from other specialties in psychology and other professions. What is included and excluded and how knowledge and ideas are presented will serve to shape the field directly and in subtle ways. Analysis of the content of the second edition of the *Handbook* tells us a lot. We learn, as just stated, that school psychology is a product of the science of psychology. Although historically it has been more indebted to the psychology of individual differences and to abnormal psychology than to most other areas of psychology, that is no longer true. School psychology is now an applied, practitioner specialty that relies on a wonderful and rich amalgam of knowledge, theory, and methods touching virtually on the entire discipline. It is research based. It derives knowledge from theory tested by research and from empirical research findings. Its practitioners function as scientifically knowledgeable professionals whose methods in assessment and intervention are themselves research grounded. Practice is informed by knowing. Practice is cautious, as knowledge is cumulative and changing. No longer is it justifiable, as it might have been in the past, to say that all school psychologists can do is to operate as school technicians in a limited sphere of influence in a limited part of all that constitutes public education. This, in part, is what the revised *Handbook* has to tell us.

In addition, it informs us that the many ways in which assessment, intervention, and evaluation of the efficacy of both can be accomplished and the variety of problems to which school psychological knowledge and skills can be applied are almost overwhelming. To the extent that this revision of the *Handbook* is an accurate depiction of the field, and I believe it may well be, school psychology potentially has the ability to affect almost every aspect of education: the multiple ways in which children and youth, parents, and educators interact and influence one another. School psychology is concerned with persons, groups, and systems. It tries to work with children, parents, educators, administrators, programs, and organizations within the public schools and in other settings in which education takes place.

The vast array of possibilities for service presented in the *Handbook* illustrate the promise of the field and also some of its problems. The promise is that we have so much to offer. At least one problem is that no one school psychologist can offer it all or know it all. Another problem is that we are still struggling to figure out how to deliver what we have to offer. Knowledge, methods, and efficient systems of service delivery are not yet well integrated, nor are the contributions the field can make generally accepted by many who employ school psychologists or could employ them.

We also learn from this volume—with pleasure—that school psychology now has among its ranks scholars and researchers of a high order. Although not every author in this edition of the *Handbook* is primarily identified as a school psychologist, most are. It was unimaginable even two decades ago that school psychology could be characterized as a field in which most practitioners are sophisticated and well educated and that among its members are numbers of scholars and researchers in universities and school systems as well who contribute to the vibrancy of the specialty and whose works are cited by psychologists, mental health specialists, and educators across the world.

This second edition signals a coming of age, even more than did the first edition of the *Handbook*. When a handbook can reconceptualize its offerings with a firm base in the science and theory

of its discipline; and when it can detail and document the legal, ethical, and legislative issues, constraints, and regulations by which the field is governed and by which it choses to govern itself, it is arriving! This volume describes a reasonably self-confident specialty, much less self-conscious and timid than in the past. It speaks for school psychology without apology for what it borrows from other areas of psychology and education. Its contributors are appropriately critical of the field, as they should be, but throughout there is a sense of optimism for the future of school psychology even if there is not agreement on priorities and directions. All this we learn, directly and indirectly, from the revised *Handbook*.

School psychology probably will never have the clear, identifiable image it seeks; an identity or specific mission forevermore that sets it apart from all other specialties in psychology and education. In fact, it is working hard to overcome the too-often accepted specific mission of assessment confined to the classification of children for special education services. The more successful it is in overcoming this narrow mission, the more difficult it will be to pin down exactly what it *does*. Rather, it is more likely that school psychology will be recognized as having a central focus, with many ways in which this focus is addressed.

What is distinctive about the contents of this volume, more than anything else, in my opinion, is its concern in the main for how psychology influences people in the process of being educated, especially those working or learning in schools. In its overall description of how psychology can function to improve the lives of people who are teaching and learning, it comes as close as can be done at present to saying what school psychology is all about. Individuals representing the specialty will continue to try to shift it in one direction or another. Whatever worthwhile is happening in psychology— whatever are the new theories and research findings and popular ideas—will find their way into the schools, with school psychology serving as one of the major means by which these ideas and approaches can enter into the conduct of public education. It will continue to be a diverse and many faceted specialty. But increasingly, its educational orientation will serve as its reason for being.

School psychology, in retrospect, has benefited more than it has been harmed by its continuous dissatisfaction: its search for better ways to say what it is and what it wants to offer. The search will continue as the field grows and develops. This edition of the *Handbook* will undoubtedly serve as a benchmark to indicate where the field is now and also to stimulate research and creative practice in school psychological service delivery over at least the next decade.

Looking toward the future, what factors have influenced school psychology in the past, from which we can learn? Certainly, anyone working in education or concerned about it cannot doubt that what happens in schools is significally affected by policies, procedures, and events that derive from the political and cultural climate of the times. School psychology was created and has been sustained based on the needs of the public schools responding to mandated policies and procedures embedded in political and cultural imperatives. It has been promoted and at the same time hampered by its historical development; by an image problem fostered by legislation which relegated it to circumscribed and limited roles in special education; and further delimited by its inability to differentiate its contributions from those of others, the many pupil personnel specialties serving the schools and the other specialties in professional psychology, particularly clinical psychology. It has learned over the years that it must try to show that it is not a narrow specialty; that it is psychology in the service of schools and of education.

What factors may influence school psychology in the 1990s? The period between the two editions of the *Handbook* has been a time of special significance for education. A spate of national reports on public and higher education were issued and every sign suggests that education at all levels will continue to occupy national attention. For many reasons—ideological, economic, and political—attention has been centered on schools and on teacher preparation to an extent not known in our lifetime. Almost every state in the United States has instituted or is considering legislation to improve teachers' salaries, provide conditions purported to make teaching a more attractive profession, provide changes in basic curriculum at all levels of public education, and improve the quality of teaching through raising standards for entrance into teaching and through modifications in teacher preparation. Although some of these movements will not necessarily result in definitive action and major changes, they are part of an ongoing awareness that public education can and should be better and that schools are important places that require

national attention and public debate. For an indefinite period of time, people appear willing to support public education, to assign it a higher priority among the many national priorities. In the vernacular, education in the late 1980s and early 1990s is "in."

School psychology is not "in," nor is it especially "out." Rather, it is on the outside looking in, seeking a place for itself, as it has for many years, so that it too can participate in the current era of relative optimism and concern, popularity, and even controversy, all so much a part of education today. No reference to school psychology, so far, has been presented in any of the national reports on how to improve the schools. No specific reference to school psychology has been identified in any recent policy statements made about psychology, mental health, or the place of psychology in schools other than those made by groups representing the specialty itself: the American Psychological Association and the National Association of School Psychologists. The lack of national attention to how school psychology can contribute to the improvement of schools must be acknowledged by those of us who are involved in the field. We have a lot to offer. We have not been viewed by most in psychology or education as an important contributor or a useful potential contributor to mainstream education. We must continue to try to make our case.

Despite its relative inability to participate fully and directly in the educational changes taking place, school psychology has, nevertheless, been affected by them and has itself changed over time. In the first edition of the *Handbook,* I described the practice of school psychology as having moved over a period of about 50 years through three gradations of service provision best viewed as a continuum divided into levels. Level 1 includes basic psychometric services designed primarily to assist others with the identification and classification of children and youth in schools for the purpose of providing special education services, typically in segregated classrooms. Level 2 includes an expansion of Level 1 services involving more encompassing and complex assessment services for children and youth, not only in special education but throughout the school system, with test interpretation and recommendations for educational and mental health services offered by others. An advanced Level 2 developed along the continuum of school psychological services to include functions similar to those undertaken by child clinical psychologists, with special interest in how children fared in schools. Responsibilities at the advanced Level 2 most often include services related to alleviation of mental health problems: the treatment of pathological conditions and assistance with behavior problems. Still further along the continuum but at the same advanced Level 2, attention has increasingly been given to educational problems as well as mental health problems: to helping teachers and parents work with school and home concerns that impinge on classroom performance and learning. Level 3 was described as occurring more often in rhetoric than in actual practice. It involves school psychological services that affect school policies and practices through supervision, education and consultation, and research and evaluation at the system level.

As we begin the 1990s, the same levels of service offerings continue to occur in school psychology, but there are some changes. It is my impression that Level 1 functions are no longer modal. The beginning Level 2 operations continue to occupy the time of many school psychologists, but increasingly advanced Level 2 seems typical of the activities of school psychologists. Perhaps the most striking changes in how school psychological services are offered along the continuum is in interest and experimentation with advanced Level 2 services, with more attention than in the past given to academic performance and to the system factors that may influence how children perform and behave. Level 3 is still more talked about and wished for than offered. Recognition that school psychology is most often an indirect service delivery and that, when well done, it has a useful impact on the way others conduct their affairs seems to be well accepted by most practicing school psychologists.

The result of this gradual but forward movement along the service delivery continuum, again in my opinion, is leading to awareness by others that school psychological services are of a high quality and that school psychology can offer a wide range of options related to what school personnel and parents want children and youth in schools to accomplish. We appear to be involved in a process of professional development promoting new ways to assess and intervene in the lives of people in educational settings in order to increase their educational effectiveness and to improve the efficiency and productivity of the educational settings themselves. However, we have not yet arrived completely, nor are we yet well integrated into these educational systems.

While school psychology has not been centrally identified as a participant in the generally positive attention given to public education in recent years, it has continued to improve, to meet the needs of a changing public education system and to overcome some of the handicaps imposed on it by its own difficult-to-overcome image of being a limited service provider in education. Those of us involved in the field believe that progress has been made. School psychology is not what it used to be. It is better. Its practitioners are better prepared to practice at all levels of the service delivery continuum. There are more school psychologists available. What remains is the enormous task of convincing others that we ought to be more involved than we usually are in helping education move ahead.

This second edition of the *Handbook* brings together in one volume the best of what school psychology is and can be. In this respect alone, it is not just another book about the field. It is a document that can help show that the field is part of an established discipline of psychology with a strong base in knowledge and theory. It has many ways to offer its services and is broadly and creatively concerned with schooling; with how people teach, learn, and interact with one another in schools. It presents our state of the art and should serve us well until the time comes for the third edition, at the rate of current progress, probably in another six to eight years.

J.I.B.
August 1989

PREFACE

It is with the greatest sense of pride that we present the second edition of *The Handbook of School Psychology*. Eight years ago in the Preface to the first edition we wrote the following.

> *The Handbook of School Psychology* provides a comprehensive treatment of the body of knowledge on which school psychology was founded and on which it continues to grow. We fervently hope that *The Handbook* will become a major reference work that practicing school psychologists can consult for both current scientific knowledge and practical suggestions. The volume contains chapters ranging from scholarly presentation of theory and research to discussions of the nuts and bolts of daily practice. We intend to provide a single source within which can be found a massive—almost encyclopedic—array of information that meets the profession's current challenges and helps to shape its immediate future. (p. xiii)

Little has changed in this regard in the intervening eight years. Our goals for the second edition of the *Handbook* are virtually identical to those we held for the original work.

Despite the fact that our motivations for compiling the *Handbook* have remained the same since the early 1980s when it was first published, the field of school psychology has been anything but static. Whether one considers the nature of what school psychologists do or the settings within which they work, growth and diversity emerge as increasingly important themes for the field. In this second edition we have endeavored to capture these themes and the many other dynamic changes that have occurred during the last decade. To this end, the *Handbook* has been substantially reorganized and more than one half of the volume consists of new authors and/or new topics of interest, each of which was chosen carefully by the editors to capture a significant aspect of the "cutting edge" in school

psychology. Chapters retained from the first edition have all been updated and revised to provide the reader with a continuity of information from the original work as well as a contemporary view of the field.

Although it is nearly impossible to capture our many and varied thoughts about the second edition of the *Handbook* in these few brief paragraphs, the following idea emerges as the preeminent theme of the volume. *School psychology must first and foremost be built on the foundations of scientific psychology.* The addition of Section II (School Psychology and the Scientific Study of Behavior: Contributions of Theory and Practice) to this edition of the *Handbook* reflects our strong philosophical commitment to this position and our endorsement of the scientist-practitioner model it implies. As Reynolds notes in the beginning of his chapter in this and the previous volume, "In God we trust, all others must have data."

Naturally, for a book of this size and scope we are indebted to many people for their assistance throughout the publication process. Most importantly we acknowledge each of the chapter authors for their excellent work. Clearly, the *Handbook* embodies the thinking of many of the best minds in the field of school psychology. We are very excited about and grateful to the extraordinary collection of authors who have contributed to this volume. We also thank our respective department chairs, Toni Santmire (Department of Educational Psychology, University of Nebraska-Lincoln) and Mike Ash (Department of Educational Psychology, Texas A & M University), for providing the support and leadership necessary to encourage creative scholarship. We also express our thanks to the staff members of John Wiley & Sons, lead by Deborah Moore, the psychology editor, who have done an excellent job producing this volume: Deborah Herbert, Lucille Buonocore, Sandra Russell, Laura Nicholls, and Joan Kalkut.

Somehow our families managed once again to endure the experience of having us edit the *Hand-*

book. Although we may not have deserved their patience with us, we are deeply indebted for it. Our most heartfelt thanks are extended to our wives, Barbara Gutkin and Julia Hickman, as well as our children, Laura and Jeffrey Gutkin and Christopher Clark.

In closing we would like to express our belief that school psychology has the potential for being the most important of all the psychological specialties in terms of its impact on the mental health and education of our nation. Unfortunately, it is equally clear to us that the field has achieved only a very small fraction of our vision for it and remains, as of today, a "faint shadow" of what it might be. The second edition of *The Handbook of School Psychology* is intended to help bridge this gap. Although we harbor no delusions, we do believe that the ideas and perspectives presented in this volume can assist the field as it translates its current potential into its future reality.

Terry B. Gutkin
Cecil R. Reynolds

CONTENTS

SECTION III:
PSYCHOLOGICAL AND EDUCATIONAL ASSESSMENT
287

SECTION IV:
SCHOOL PSYCHOLOGICAL INTERVENTIONS: FOCUS ON CHILDREN
575

SECTION V:
SCHOOL PSYCHOLOGICAL INTERVENTIONS: FOCUS ON STAFF, PROGRAMS, AND ORGANIZATIONS
799

CURRENT PERSPECTIVES IN SCHOOL PSYCHOLOGY

1

HISTORY OF SCHOOL PSYCHOLOGY

JOSEPH L. FRENCH
Penn State University

And in the beginning there was school psychology!

In the first paragraph on page 1 of Volume 1 of the most influential journal for practicing psychologists in the first quarter of this century, Lightner Witmer, the acknowledged father of the clinical method in psychology, directed the focus of the clinical method to the mental development of children in schools: "During the last ten years the laboratory of psychology at the University of Pennsylvania has conducted, under my direction, what I have called 'a psychological clinic.' Children from the public schools of Philadelphia and adjacent cities have been brought to the laboratory by parents or teachers; these children had made themselves conspicuous because of an inability to progress in school work as rapidly as other children, or because of moral defects which rendered them difficult to manage under ordinary discipline" (Witmer, 1907, p. 1).

According to Witmer, the work of the psychological clinic began in March 1896 when Margaret T. Maguire, a teacher in the local schools and a student in psychology at the University of Pennsylvania, brought a 14-year-old boy to the laboratory to "ascertain the causes of a deficiency in spelling and to recommend the appropriate pedagogical treatment for its amelioration or cure" (p. 2). The previous year Witmer had worked with a college student who had "articulation . . . written discourse . . . and verbal audition . . . very deficient for a boy of his years," had lectured about him, and had conceptualized the clinical method of study and treatment. Later in the spring of 1896, Witmer worked with several other children whose progress was slower than expected.

In December 1896, Witmer described his work to the 4-year-old American Psychological Association (APA) as follows:

1. The investigation of the phenomena of mental development in school children, as manifested more particularly in mental and moral retardation, by means of the statistical and clinical methods.
2. A psychological clinic, supplemented by a training school in the nature of a hospital school, for the treatment of all classes of children suffering from retardation or physical defects interfering with school progress.
3. The offering of practical work to those engaged in the professions of teaching and medicine, and to those interested in social work, in the observation and training of normal and retarded children.

4. The training of students for a new profession—that of psychological expert, who should find his career in connection with the school system, through the examination and treatment of mentally and morally retarded children, or in connection with the practice of medicine (Witner, 1907, p. 5)

Witmer continued and expanded his clinical practice for most of the next 30 years. As a means of furthering clinical examination and treatment of children, Witmer founded the journal, *The Psychological Clinic* "to provide for the adequate publication of the results that are being obtained in this new field of psychological investigation . . ." (Witmer, 1907, p. 6). His early speeches to members of the APA had been criticized for their lack of scientific rigor and for extending too far the activities of the psychological laboratory. With a journal in which results of clinical studies could be published, he hoped to remedy the situation. In Volume 2, Witmer editorialized that it was created "to define a new field of research, to develop suitable methods of investigation, and at the same time to enlist the sympathy and active support of those who have not yet fully recognized the significance of the problem . . ." (Witmer, 1908, p. 1).

Two other psychologists started directing the application of psychology in laboratories at about the same time as Witmer. Each of their practices was more relevant than Witmer's to clinical psychology as it developed through the century. A laboratory was founded in the New York Pathological Institute in 1895 with Ira Van Gieson, a historical neurologist, as the first director, to develop knowledge of value to the New York state hospital system. In 1896, he employed Boris Sidis, who is known for his work concerning suggestibility, dissociation, and subconscious, "to represent psychology in this endeavor" (Popplestone & McPherson, 1984, p. 209). Van Gieson was dismissed in 1901 because he "refused to develop a program directly relevant to patient management" (p. 211), and the departure of Sidis shortly thereafter marked the beginning of a long interruption of psychological service at that institute. However, Sidis became director of another psychopathic hospital and laboratory, where he continued to publish on hallucinations and hypnosis.

The other early clinical laboratory in charge of a psychologist was also started in 1896, in the Fairbault (Minnesota) School for the Feeble-Minded. A. R. T. Wylie served "both as a druggist

and a psychologist" (Popplestone & McPherson, 1984, p. 228) for a short while, but the position of psychologist was vacant for several years until Fred Kuhlmann was appointed director of research in 1920. In the next 15 years Kuhlmann developed several adaptations of the Binet tests and his research on mental retardation during the first quarter of this century rivaled that of E. R. Johnstone, H. H. Goddard, and Edgar Doll at the Vineland training school in New Jersey.

Articles for psychologists appeared as early as 1894 in *The Pedagogical Seminary,* and two journals for practitioners preceded Witmer's. However, they were directed to those serving clients with abnormal or very retarded behavior. In 1896 Rogers became editor of the *Journal of Psychol-Asthenics,* a periodical that replaced the *Proceedings of the Association of Medical Officers of American Institutions for Idiots and Feeble-Minded Persons.* At Vineland E. R. Johnstone was Superintendent and editor of *The Training School,* which originated in 1904 as a house organ and was expanded for further distribution in 1907 (Popplestone and McPherson, 1984).

Witmer believed that the purpose of school was to develop the individual and thereby, to facilitate human progress. "The school must take its place as a social insitution second to none. . . . The school must go into many homes and make them worthy of the name. . . . If insufficient food and unhealthful environment make the progress of a child impossible, the school must bring these facts to the attention of the public, and must see that some satisfactory solution is offered" (Witmer, 1908, p. 3). He did not intend the journal to be "for the study of the *abnormal* child, but a journal for the study of the *individual* child" (p. 4). He believed the best material for study to be of those cases near the borderline between the pathological or abnormal and the normal. By Volume 8 the *Psychological Clinic* carried the subtitle, *A Journal of Orthogenics for the Normal Development of Every Child.*

Witmer did not refer to his practice as school psychology but referred to the clinical method and work in the "psychological clinic" which became a "regular part of the instruction offered to students in child psychology" (p. 4). He spoke of his qualifications being enhanced by his work as a "consulting psychologist with the Pennsylvania Training School for Feeble-Minded Children at Elwyn . . . the Haddonfield Training School and Miss Marvin's Home School in West Philadelphia"

(Witmer, 1907, p. 6). Later in this initial article, Witmer explained the title of his article "Clinical Psychology" as one he borrowed from medicine to indicate not a locality but the character of the method he used. His focus was "directly to children in the school room . . . and the next step in the child's mental and physical development" (p. 8). Perhaps because he used the title "Clinical Psychology" for his first article in *The Psychological Clinic* and/or perhaps because his work in the university psychology clinic proceeded without interruption for 40 years (and was continued by others after his retirement) and because his role as editor of *The Psychological Clinic* continued for 30 years, he is the acknowledged father of clinical psychology. It should be noted that the word "clinical" was not capitalized in the preceding sentence. Even as late as 1950 Witmer argued against the formation of school and clinical divisions in the Pennsylvania Psychological Association because he believed that sectioning . . . destroys unity" (Executive Committee, Pennsylvania Psychological Association, 1950, p. 3). As he predicted, forming sections in state associations (or forming separate state associations) helped divide clinical psychology into psychological specialties such as clinical, counseling, industrial, school, and others.

In 1914, J. E. Wallace Wallin published, through the Yale University Press, a book of 19 chapters, most of them reprints of earlier articles. The book title (or titles) and its dedication provide an indication of the times. *The Mental Health of the School Child* was the title in boldface print on the title page, but under it appear two other titles: *The Psycho-Educational Clinic in Relation to Child Welfare* and *Contributions to a New Science of Orthophrenics and Orthosomatics*. The volume was dedicated to G. Stanley Hall, founder of the modern child study movement and of the world's second psychological laboratory.

THE FIRST SCHOOL PSYCHOLOGICAL SERVICES

In 1892, the year the APA was founded with Hall as president, the editor of the *Journal of Education* referred to nationwide enthusiasm for Hall's child study movement (Winship, 1892). With strong encouragement from John Dewey, founder of the Laboratory School at the University of Chicago and APA's eighth president, the Chicago school board conducted a survey of the physical and mental characteristics of children in 1898 and demonstrated a need for a continuing survey. In 1899, Fred W. Smedley was appointed director of the Department of Child Study and Pedagogic Investigation with two assistants (Slater, 1980) and on April 4, 1900, he was "authorized to open a 'Psycho-physical laboratory' on Saturdays in the central office, since he and his staff were busy in the schools on other days" (Cutts, 1955, pp. 19–20). As reported by Cutts, Chicago's was the first public board of education, with the "possible exception of the Pedagogic Laboratory in Antwerp, Belgium" (p. 19) to establish such an operation under its juridiction.

The Binet-Simon tests were not published until 1905, 1908, and 1911 and they were not available in English until Elizabeth Kite helped Henry Goddard with the translation in 1910. In the Chicago school clinic and University of Chicago's Laboratory School they recognized brighter children as being taller and heavier than dull children. Following the advise of Hugo Munsterberg and Joseph Jastrow, APA's seventh and ninth presidents, they collected other anthropometric measurements, such as lung capacity, strength, endurance and visual and auditory acuity. Daniel P. MacMillan finished a Ph.D. at the University of Chicago in 1900, assisted in the Child Study Bureau for 2 years and became director of the Bureau in 1902. (While working full time as director, he obtained an M.D. degree in 1909.) Anthropological measurements were phased out in favor of newer, more psychological tests of perception, memory, association, attention, imagination, and judgment for prediction purposes (MacMillan, 1906). Perhaps because he pioneered the transition from anthropological to psychological tests in the schools he was called the first school psychologist by Garfield (1965), but he referred to himself as a child study specialist or an examiner. He held the post until 1935, when it was assumed by Grace Munson and in 1949 by Frances Mullen. All three contributed significantly to the development of school psychology (Mullen, 1981).

OTHER CLINICS SERVING CHILDREN

In the fall of 1923, Wallin (1914) sent a questionnaire to about 1,350 towns throughout the country to learn of their provisions for exceptional children. With repeated requests he was able to obtain a response from all (50) cities with a population of 100,000 and over, 96 (or 53%) from cities of 25,000 to 100,000, and 156 from towns of less than 25,000. He found special classes for exceptional children in all the large cities except Scranton, Pennsylvania; in 68% of the midsized cities responding; and in 37% of the small towns. He concluded that "in the vast majority of cases the psychological testing (and possibly also the diagnosis of mentally exceptional children in the schools is made by Binet testers—in other words, by amateurs" (Wallin, 1914, p. 395). According to Wallin, these amateurs were prepared by "having taken normal school [or] college . . . courses in . . . education and psychology," a summer course on testing and one on "feeble minded children," or "having taken a regular medical course and then reading literature on feeble minded . . . children . . ." (p. 395). It was his belief that "if it is possible . . . to prepare psycho-educational testers, the conclusion remains true: that such testers *are not expert psycho-educational diagnosticians,* and that to prepare expert psycho-educational diagnosticians requires *three or four years of technical training and clinical experience* (p. 395). (In the following 75 years we have not been able to speed up the process.)

Wallin believed that "the schools will not long be content with crude or amateurish psychological or psycho-educational clinics in the schools" (p. 397) and identified 20 school clinics which apparently he believed to be more than amateurish. With the dates of their founding they are: 1898, Chicago; 1907, Rochester; 1908, New York; 1911, Providence, Oakland, Hibbing (Minnesota), and Cincinnati; 1912, Grand Rapids, Seattle, Philadelphia, Springfield (Massachusetts), New Orleans, and Milwaukee; 1913, Buffalo, Washington, Albany, Los Angeles, and Trenton; and 1914, Detroit and St. Louis. (It should be remembered that his survey was started in 1913 and it was published in 1914, so additional professional clinics may have been started in 1914. He left the Psycho-Educational Clinic at the University of Pittsburgh to start a clinic in the St. Louis schools and Harris Teachers College when the book was published.)

In another study, Wallin (1914) found 17 acceptable clinics in the following colleges and universities: Cincinnati, Clark, Cornell, Girard, Iowa, Kansas, Minnesota, Missouri, New York, North Dakota, Oklahoma, Pennsylvania, Pitts-

burgh, Stanford, Tulane, Washington, and Yale. He listed 7 in medical schools: Georgetown, Harvard, Johns Hopkins, Michigan, New York Post, Rush (of Chicago), and Vanderbilt (of Columbia); 3 in normal schools: (Greeley) Colorado State Teachers College, Los Angeles State Normal School, and Mount Pleasant (Michigan) State Normal School (pp. 57–58); and 23 in other locations, such as institutions for the feebleminded or insane, correctional institutions, juvenile or criminal courts, and immigration stations (p. 399). Of the 70 psychological clinics recognized in 1913–1914, 20 were in the schools and the vast majority were serving children of school age.

JUVENILE COURTS

In the late nineteenth century, most children, especially adolescents, were school dropouts. Many were abandoned by their families. From 1850 to 1930 about 150,000 children were relocated from eastern cities to foster homes, mostly in the midwest (Jackson, 1986). Perhaps as a compliment to school personnel or perhaps as a cheap place to put them, schools were often called upon to establish ungraded classes for truants and incorrigibles (Cutts, 1955). Psychologists were often used by children's aid societies to assist with relocation of children in foster homes and by juvenile court judges who hoped to understand the causes of delinquency and remedies for it. Women were often the psychologists employed in these settings (French, 1988).

The Juvenile Psychopathic Institute in Chicago, which if not the first mental health clinic, has been cited most often as the model for those working with the courts. Organized in 1909 by William Healy, M.D., the institute used a psychiatrist, psychologist, and a social worker to study those brought before the court and to make recommendations to the judge. Initially, the psychologist with the Chicago Institute was Grace Fernald, but after developing one of the first performance tests with Healey, she moved to Los Angeles to direct the psychology department and laboratory (i.e., clinic) in the Los Angeles Normal School (later UCLA) and to specialize in reading. Her method of teaching poor readers to use auditory and kinesthetic as well as visual sense contributed more to her fame (G. M. Fernald, 1943) than did her work with Healy. Fernald was replaced by

August Bronner, who became director of psychology in 1914. Many attribute the Chicago model to Healy and Bronner, but perhaps that is because Bronner was a frequent speaker and author. She was one of the first to stress the influence of rapport in testing a child and to write about youth of average or higher intelligence who were thought to be retarded because they could not read. Many of her subjects had been labeled "delinquent." In 1917, Healy and Bronner moved to Boston to establish the Judge Baker Guidance Center, which further added to their prestige. (Few of the employed women psychologists were married. Bronner and Healy were not married until 1932. Maude Merrill, coauthor of the Stanford-Binet, who directed a psychological clinic for Stanford University and for the Juvenile Court of Palo Alto, married the presiding judge, William F. James, relatively late in life.)

During the December 1917 APA meeting, a committee of 10, at least half of whom were practicing psychology with schoolchildren, was appointed to develop a report on "the qualifications for psychological examiners and psychological experts" (Committee on the Qualifications of Psychological Examiners and Other Psychological Experts, 1919, p. 1). In its final report they recommended that a committee be established by a responsible agency to certify psychologists for practice. In its December 1921 meeting, the APA agreed to appoint a Committee on Certification of Consulting Psychologists to issue certificates that could be shown in court and displayed in one's office to indicate membership in a Section of Consulting Psychology (later called a Division)[1] and that the owner was qualified to make mental diagnoses (F. L. Wells, personal communication to B. T. Baldwin, January 6, 1922). The final action

was based on a petition to the APA by Helen Thompson Woolley (1920), an administrator of school psychological services in the Cincinnatti public schools since 1910, which was drafted as follows:

> The demand for mental examinations in the field of education of industry and of medicine has grown with great rapidity during the past few years. Particularly in the Public Schools, Clinics for mental diagnoses are constantly being organized. The State Education Congresses held in New York and Pennsylvania passed resolutions addressed to the State Departments of Education, recommending the employment of clinical psychologists by the departments for the service of the smaller communities which could not afford to maintain clinics of their own. Every State Teachers' Association and Educational Congress discusses the topic and reports on the work undertaken. . . .
>
> At present there is no constituted authority to which the public can appeal to find out what qualifications should be demanded of a person whose judgement is to be accepted in so vital and important a matter. The American Psychological Association is at present the only body competent to pass on the point. We, the undersigned, members of this Association, urge the Association to take action to formulate the requirements which should be made of those desiring to serve as clinical psychologists, and arrange to issue credentials to those who have met the requirements.

By 1922 the APA established a review committee consisting of Bird T. Baldwin, James McKeen Cattell, Edward K. Strong, F. L. Wells, and Woolley. Later, Cattell (who had recently been dismissed from Columbia University because of his views against U.S. involved in World War I) withdrew when it was decided that applicants would not be tested but would be issued certificates following a paper review and payment a fee of $35 for the initial evaluation and $1 each year for renewal. (The fees for the initial evaluation was 3.5% of the median income of APA members, that is, $1000.) Records in the APA archives in the Library of Congress illustrate that the paper review was based on endorsement of satisfactory practice

---

[1] The Section (and later the Division) of Consulting Psychologists were subunits of the American Psychological Association. Associations of Consulting Psychologists were developed as state and regional groups. A meeting was called by Edgar Doll on May 9, 1936, to try to facilitate the affiliation of the geographically diverse units with the APA in a fashion similar to that obtained by the Psychometric Society. Doll believed that "consulting interest is bound to have an extensive development, especially now that the academic field cannot provide employment, whereas the consulting field offers almost unlimited fields for further development" (E. A. Doll, personal communication to Donald Patterson, April 4, 1936, p. 1). State associations composed primarily of practitioners moved into the APA structure.

by a colleague and that while most applicants who were APA members were issued certificates, some applicants were not and that others obtained certificates only after lengthy correspondence and documentation. Included in the APA archives is a list of the first 25 applicants for the certificate. The first three were school psychologists: Woolley; Arnold Gessell, who had been employed by the state education agency to travel the state of Connecticut identifying children in need of special education; and A. H. Sutherland, director of the Department of Psychology and Educational Research in the Los Angeles city schools.

In a May 1922 meeting of the Committee on Certification of Consulting Psychologists it was agreed that membership in the Division of consulting Psychology be restricted to psychologists "dealing with adjustments of individuals in their personal relationships" (Committee, 1922, p. 1), that persons with a lower level of training than a Ph.D. be certified, and that sections of applied psychology such as industrial and educational be established "from time to time . . . as organizations parallel to the Section of Clinical Psychology" (p. 1). At least one third and probably one half of the clinical section was composed of psychologists who worked in clinics serving schoolchildren, and a special section for school psychologists was not considered at this time. Since most consulting psychologists of the 1920s were concerned with mental abilities, not personal adjustment, it is assumed that the restriction on membership to those dealing with "adjustments . . . in . . . personal relationships" was an attempt to broaden their role.

In the first third of this century physicians were the authorities primarily responsible for recommending to the courts those persons to be committed to or discharged from institutions for the feebleminded. Some physicians were using Binet tests, but many were making recommendations with very little direct observation of the individual of concern. By 1919, educators were so concerned with contemporary practice that the National Education Association (NEA) passed the following resolution: "The diagnosing of degrees of mental defect and the classification of children upon such diagnoses should be in the hands of highly qualified and certified psychologists only. The same standard should apply to those diagnosing physical handicaps" (NEA, 1920). An analysis of the laws in place in 1920 revealed that only seven states

mentioned psychologists in connection with professional services in mental institutions and that only in California and Illinois, where Healy and Bronner worked so effectively with Chicago's courts, could psychologists recommend a commitment without the concurring opinion of a physician. The California law was not clear about the status of psychologists. In Section 19, a judge could require the attendance of "a clinical psychologist and a reputable physician, or one of each, or two of either, to examine such person and testify as to his or her mentality" (p. 71). Pessimists might believe that only the presence of one reputable person was required. Optimists might assume that clinical was synonymous with reputable because in Section 42 we see that a "psychologist holding a Ph.D, and a physician qualified to serve under Section 19 of this Act" (p. 71) was required to recommend either release or discharge from an institution. Those states where courts could accept a recommendation from two physicians or a physician and a psychologist were Kansas, New York, Oregon, South Dakota, and Wisconsin (Hollingworth, 1922).

School Psychology in the Early 1930s
Psychological services in the 1930s were provided to children by a few individuals employed by the schools but most often by personnel in clinics sponsored by universities, teachers' colleges, social or governmental agencies, or foundations. Between January 1933 and June 1934 the clinical section of the American Psychological Association (Committee of the Clinical Section of the American Psychological Association [Committee of Clinical Section], 1935) engaged in an intensive effort to obtain descriptions of such clinics for publication as a Guide to Psychological Clinics in the United States in *The Psychological Clinic*. The committee obtained replies describing 87 psychological and 32 psychiatric clinics. The psychological clinics employed 311 psychologists, with 147 holding a doctorate. Many of the psychology clinics had a psychiatrist on the staff at least part time. A number of clinics listed several psychiatrists and/or physicians, but many did not list any. A few clinic directors, such as MacMillan in Chicago and Arnold Gessell at Yale, listed themselves as a psychologist (with a Ph.D. after their name) and on a different line as medical director (with an M.D. following their name). The guide listed 119 physicians, 98 social workers, and 21 remedial teachers.

Although Healy and Bronner consistently emphasized use of a psychiatrist, psychologist, and a social worker, in very few instances is the name of a social worker listed in this guide and in other sources. Where names of psychologists, physicians, teachers, and researchers were listed, names of social workers were often missing. After social work would be an entry such as "1" or "from a large staff." Witmer's disappointment in the small number of clinical teachers was evident in the editorial process: "Closely connected with unsatisfactory provision for social service is the scarcity of provision for remedial teaching in the clinics. . . . As clinical teaching is in a certain sense inseparable from clinical diagnosis, as for a large number of children clinical teaching must be continued over a period of time in order to arrive at a satisfactory diagnosis, it is clear that this phase of the work is much underdeveloped" (Witmer, 1935, pp. 19–20.) In the current era, Fuerstein (1979) continues to stress the need for clinical teaching in diagnosis.

Although many of the clinics announced services for infancy through adulthood, the vast majority of the clinics specialized in treating children with educational problems. Only a few clinics served adults either primarily or exclusively. One of these was the Ohio Bureau of Examination and Classification of Prisoners, which employed C. B. Rogers as director and chief psychiatrist, G. R. Mursell as chief psychologist, and Stanley S. Marzolf, M. A., as psychologist. Marzolf (1956) completed his Ph.D. 3 years later under Francis Maxfield (a student of Witmer's) at Ohio State and worked in school psychology the rest of his life, completing the second text for school psychologists in 1956 (French, 1987).

The names of the clinics provide a flavor of the services provided. There was only a little consistency in the use of terms Psychological Clinic, Psycho-Educational Clinic, and Bureau of Child Study. Among the more interesting titles were Traveling Child Guidance Clinic of the California Bureau of Juvenile Research, Juvenile Court Clinic, New England Home for Little Wanderers (an independent organization formed in Boston in 1915), Psychological Clinic of the Children's Aid and Society for the Prevention of Cruelty to Children of Erie (New York) County, House of Refuge (for persons 12 to 21), and the Vocational Adjustment Bureau for Girls.

Some of these clinics of the 1930s are notable today for the persons who worked in them, others for the types of services provided. Maude Merrill, coauthor of the 1937 and 1960 editions of the Stanford Binet, directed the Stanford University Psychological Clinic, where examinations were made on request for the Palo Alto public schools and the juvenile court. The Stanford clinic was established by Lewis Terman in 1912 as a training center for students in clinical methods, as were many of the university-based clinics in this period. The University of Denver Department of Research organized a clinic to train students in mental testing, with persons 3 to 18 under the direction of T. R. Garth. As will be noted elsewhere, research was often mentioned in association with clinical staff and function. (Perhaps this was because many of the psychologists held Ph.D.s, a research degree and wanted to emphasize the science of their work.)

Yale's director of the Clinic of Child Development was, by today's standards, overprepared for the position. Arnold Gesell held three doctorates: Ph.D., M.D., and D.Sc. As director, Gesell was listed as both a psychologist and a psychiatrist and may have been the first person to use the title "school psychologist" (Fagan, 1986a, 1987). The Yale clinic focused primarily on problems of neglect and placement but also attended to problems of education, guidance, and conduct of persons 4 weeks to 16 years of age. The clinic staff included not only Gessell as psychologist and psychiatrist but two psychologists, a clinical examiner, a physician, three researchers (two from medicine, one from psychology), a teacher-guidance worker, a clerk, and a part-time social worker.

In 1922, Stanley D. Porteus organized the Psychological and Psychopathic Clinic at the University of Hawaii under a legislative mandate associated with establishing a home for the feebleminded in Honolulu for persons 3 years to adult. The principal sources of referral were parents, school principals, juvenile courts, and social agencies. The Porteus Mazes and Goodenough drawings were the clinic's most used tests in the 1930s, but it should be noted that it was here as research assistant for 6 years that Russell G. Leiter developed the Leiter International Performance Scale, which he conceptualized while working as a special education teacher in Los Angeles from 1926 to 1930.

In 1934 the Chicago Bureau of Child Study celebrated its 35th anniversary, with psychologist and psychiatrist D. P. MacMillan continuing as director. Listed on the staff were 10 master's-level psychologists and 4 research workers, one of whom was Grace Munson, Ph.D., who later directed the bureau for 11 years. (In the APA *Directory* of 1965, Munson is listed as a school psychologist, 1918–1935; director of the Bureau of Child Study, 1935–1946; and assistant superintendent in charge of special education, 1946–1949. In the same directory Frances Mullen was listed as high school teacher, 1926–1929; school psychologist, Bureau of Child Study, 1939–1947; principal of Grahm elementary school, 1947–1949, director of the Bureau of Mentally Handicapped, 1949–1953; and assistant superintendent for special education, 1953–■.)

Paul Witty directed the Psycho-educational Clinic at Northwestern University serving children 3 to 19 years. In the 1934 guide the main clinic function was described as diagnosis of educational maladjustment. However, a little later Witty became much better known for selecting Quiz Kids for the famous radio show and for his writing about gifted children and how to teach reading.

The University of Indiana Psychological Clinic was directed by C. M. Louttit and served children 3 to 20. The 1934 guide listed as the tests most used as Binet-Simon, Witmer Formboard, Porteus Maze, and Merril Palmer. Today, Louttit is best known for his classic text (1936) *Clinical Psychology of Children's Behavior Problems*. Listed on his staff in 1934 was "psychologist" Gladys Firth, Ph.D., M.D., who later served as a school psychologist in South Bend, Indiana, for about 25 years.

The University of Iowa Psychological and Speech Clinic served as a model for many interdisciplinary clinics that followed. This clinic was located in the outpatient department of the Psychopathic Hospital in Iowa City under the university departments of psychology, psychiatry, and speech. Psychologist Lee Edward Travis was director, Wendell Johnson was the clinician in charge of stutterers, and Frank Robinson was the clinician in charge of reading disability cases. Other staff included three psychiatrists, three teachers, and two social workers. Services for children with speech or reading problems were recommended for many who were initially thought to be mentally retarded but who did not appear to be retarded when tested.

Harvard had a clinic from 1913 under the direction of W. F. Dearborn, M.D., Ph.D., to study educational problems of school children. The staff of eight psychologists, four teachers (one of whom was also a psychologist), and two consulting psychiatrists saw about 100 cases a year. Of the clients, about 90 presented educational problems. On the staff at this time was Psyche Cattell, who later developed an infant scale, and J. R. Hobson, whose reports about entrance to kindergarten on the basis of mental ability enabled many bright children to start formal schooling a year early.

With a history of more than 20 years at the time of the 1933–1934 survey, the Detroit (public school) psychological clinic was seeing about 5,000 children a year with a staff of two male and nine female psychologists and seven social workers under the direction of Harry J. Baker. (Members of his staff saw and closed more than 450 cases per year per psychologist.) More than half of the referrals were thought to need placement in programs for the mentally retarded, but 20% were referred because of conduct problems and nearly 20% were referred for other educational, placement, or guidance problems. Baker became the first president of the APA Division of School Psychologists in 1946–1947 and had been a subcommittee chairman for the 1930 White House Conference on Child Health and Protection and president of the Council for Exceptional Children from 1935 to 1937. He was author of the Detroit Learning Aptitude Test, first published in 1932 and widely used for decades, 20 other tests, and over 100 articles in educational and psychological journals.

The Psychological Corporation, a private organization, was among the 87 clinics listed in the guide. They offered psychological services of various types to the public for a fee. Among the 1933–1934 staff was Rose E. Anderson, director of the Child Adjustment and School Service Division, and Hazel Stanton of the Music Division. (Among the tests published by the Psychological Corporation were the Seashore Tests of Muscial Aptitude.) The Psychological Corporation had been in existence since founded by James McKeen Cattell in 1921. Instead of the publishing house it is today, it was first organized to serve as a broker for psychologist-stockholders who would consult with business, industries, schools, or individuals about psychological matters or use tests with designated persons. Half of the fee was to go to the psychologist and the other half to the corporation. Each psychologist had to promise to use half of his or her earnings for psychological research, and the corporation was to use its profits for grants for the advancement of scientific research. Many of the tests developed by the corporation for specific purposes were later entered in the general catalog. With this plan Cattell hoped to drive charlatans out of the market and to promote psychological research (Popplestone & McPherson, 1984).

In the early 1920s, David Wechsler was one of Psychological Corporation's part-time consultants. Among other things, he tested the intellectual ability of women in Ziegfeld's Follies for a reporter from the *New York World* and constructed tests for potential cab drivers of the Pittsburgh Yellow Cab Company, which included written portions on intelligence and performance sections on reaction time, mental alertness, and carefulness. After a short stint of consulting, he readily accepted work as a school psychologist with the New York Bureau of Child Guidance. The Bureau was partially financed by the Commonwealth Foundation to serve as a model program with the assumption that local communities would continue to finance programs that were successful. Wechsler joined the psychiatrist, psychologist, social worker team headed by psychiatrist Bernard Glueck, with Wechsler responsible for administration of intelligence, personality, and achievement tests. Based on data collected in this role, Wechsler (1926) published "the influence of education on intelligence as measured by the Binet-Simon tests" and concluded that Burt's version was better than Terman's. Upon completing his dissertation in 1925, Wechsler entered private practice and served as acting secretary of the Psychological Corporation. In 1932 he joined the Bellevue Psychiatric Hospital as chief psychologist. With Bellevue Hospital as his base, he authored three individual tests (and revisions of them) for measuring intelligence by school psychologists, the first of which did not appear until 1939 (Allen, 1974; Wechsler, 1938).

In the early 1930s at Columbia University, a Guidance Laboratory was formed in Teachers College to centralize the operation of a number of clinics under the direction of Esther Lloyd-Jones. Perhaps in no other setting were so many well-known psychologists involved in one organization. The consulting psychologists were Arthur I. Gates, Rudolph Pintner, Leta S. Hollingworth, Percival S. Symonds, G. B. Watson, Gertrude Hildreth, I. C. Sartorius, M. T. Whitley, and Meta Rust. Among

the consultants in education were Harry D. Kitson, Ruth Strang, and Elizabeth McDowell.

Meanwhile, 38 years after he started using clinical methods to study children, Witmer was still rolling along. His report for the University of Pennsylvania in the survey listed seven Ph.D. psychologists: Edwin B. Twitmyer as assistant director of the clinic and chief of the Corrective Speech Clinic, Mildred Loring Sylvester as executive officer and examining psychologist, and as examining psychologists, Robert A. Brotemarkle, Morris S. Viteles, Yale S. Nathanson, Miles Murphy, and Thomas J. Snee. In addition, he enumerated (but did not name) a social worker, a clinic teacher, a clerk, and a "professionally trained Keeper of Records" (Committee of Clinical Section, 1935, p. 117). Although Witmer recognized and preached about the need for social workers and clinical teachers, he hired more psychologists (and listed their names in surveys).

Of the clinics listed in the guide, only the New York University Psycho-Educational Clinic "was organized for the purpose of training students as school psychologists" (p. 97). Charles Benson was listed as director and Lloyd Yepsen as psychologist in a clinic that studied annually about 150 persons from infancy to adulthood and presented problems of conduct, education, guidance, mental defect, and abnormality. Specific mention of school psychologists in the statement of purpose of the clinic gives credence to the belief that New York University established the first collegiate program for the preparation of school psychologists in the late 1920s (Fagan, 1986a).

Rochester, New York, may have had the best ratio of psychologists to children in the 1930s when two clinics were serving children. A child study department was established by the Board of Education in 1906 "to aid in the selection of children who could not profit by the regular school work, for special education" (p. 98). Under the direction of Leila A. Martin in 1933 were 14 female school psychologists, 4 of whom had Ph.D..s. Also on the staff were a social worker and a psychiatric consultant (for one-half day each week). Also in Rochester, beginning in 1919, was a Child Study Department sponsored by the Society for the Prevention of Cruelty to Children. At the time of the 1933–1934 survey Carl R. Rogers was director of a staff that included three psychologists, two psychiatric consultants, and three physician consultants. Among the tests used by Rogers and his staff were the "Stanford Binet . . . Porteus Maze, Healy Pictorial, Kohs Block, Pintner-Patterson, [Bernreuter] Personality Inventory, Stanford Achievement, Goodenough Drawing, [and] Gates Reading" (p. 101). Rogers served an internship in the NYC Institute for Child Guidance (along with S. J. Beck) in 1927–1928, which prepared him for work with children. In Rochester he was a psychologist in 1928–1930 and for the next 10 years was psychologist and director of the clinic to prevent cruelty to children before moving to Ohio State University, University of Chicago, University of Wisconsin, and international fame as a professor and humanistic counselor.

Following the huge success of his books on *The Kallikak Family* and *FeebleMindedness: Its Causes and Consequences,* Henry H. Goddard (1912, 1914) left the Vineland Training school in 1918, worked 4 years in the Ohio Bureau of Juvenile Research, and then served as professor at Ohio State from 1922 until he retired in 1938. At Ohio State he directed the Psychological Clinic, which at the time of the 1933–1934 survey was staffed by chief clinician Francis Maxfield, two consulting psychologists, and assistant psychologist Marie Skodak. Whereas Goddard addressed the impact of heredity on intelligence through most of his life, Skodak moved from Ohio to the Iowa Child Welfare Research Station to study and report on the impact of environment in modifying IQs (see Skodak & Skells, 1949). In 1966–1969, Marie Skodak Crissey was a representative to the APA Council of Representatives from the Division of School Psychology and a member of the Divisions Executive Committee in 1959–1961.

Still another source of service delivery were clinics such as the one directed by Frank H. Reiter from the Pennsylvania Department of Public Instruction. Reiter, a student of Witmer, listed no staff in the survey but reported seeing annually 600 persons 6 to 16 years of age referred by schools and courts. As the need for special education grew throughout the country, many state education agencies started to provide help in the identification of children eligible (and not eligible) for special funding from the state.

THE EMERGING ROLE

R. B. W. Hutt (1923) was one of the first to write an article titled "The School Psychologist." He concluded that "the function of the psychologist [is] to discover the facts of mentality in the individual and to explain the deviations in behavior. It is his function to find, and occasionally apply the cure" (p. 51). A Ph.D. student of Witmer's, Hutt's article was based on his experiences in the Wynnewood, Pennsylvania, schools, where he worked before becoming a professor at Trinity College in Connecticut in 1927.

In the mid-1920s school psychologists were described more completely by Walter (1925), a director of psychological measurements in the New Rochelle schools, as persons who "bring to bear upon educational problems the knowledge and techniques which have been developed by the science of psychology" (p. 167). Walter identified six functions of school psychologists:

1. Direct all group testing within the system. Although teachers could give the tests and clerks could score them, Walters believed that psychologist were needed to select tests to be used and to interpret the data derived from them.

2. Diagnose problem cases through assessment of intellectual level, emotional reaction, and history from parents and teachers. He expected school psychologists to work with mentally and/or physically handicapped or mentally gifted children and adolescents, those with conduct disorders, and those with speech impairments.

3. Conduct therapy and establish a constructive mental hygiene program in the school.

4. Conduct research. Because they had opportunities, facilities, and techniques for collecting data and because they were prepared as scientists and knew how to analyze data, Walter believed that school psychologists should do so.

5. Bring a unique point of view to bear on educational problems. Because psychologists were prepared in a milieu different from teachers and school administrators and because of their familiarity with psychological theories, Walter believed that they had much to contribute to the study of students with learning problems.

6. Render contributions to the general theory and practice of education. Through formal presentations in staff meetings or work-

shops or through consultation with individual teachers, Walter believed that psychologists could help educators understand the effects of specific procedures on individuals and learn how to chart alternative courses of action. They would bring their psychological point of view to study not only the problem but also the solutions, which might help more than one problem child.

As described by Walter, the role was far from the anthropological measurements and surveys about educational achievement and school dropouts that had characterized much of the work at the turn of the century. The need of objective data for the placement of exceptional children in special programs, for the placement of children in foster homes, and for analyzing children with behavior problems and/or those classified as delinquents began to take all of the time that school psychologists had to spare. Readers of today may think that Walter was describing not just a school psychologist but a super psychologist.

Ten years later Ethel L. Cornell (1936), a psychologist in the Educational Research Division of the New York State Education Department, cut the list in half but had one that was just as inclusive. In the fifteenth yearbook for elementary principals she told them that school psychologists contribute to the educational process in three important ways: "(1) thru a special point of view in his approach to adjustment problems; (2) thru his special technics of diagnosis and analysis; and (3) thru his possibilities as a liaison officer" (p. 561). She believed that a school psychologist has "qualifications which distinguish him from the educational supervisor, on the one hand, and from the general clinical or academic psychologist on the other (p. 561).

In the first third of this century, psychologists were prepared by studying most of the graduate-level courses in psychology at a university and taking a selection of other courses recommended by the student's mentor. As psychology grew, more courses evolved and specialties within psychology began to develop. The split in psychology between the scientists with their laboratories and the practitioners with their clinics started with Witmer's transformation of a laboratory to a clinic, his advocacy of the clinical method of study, and his journal for publishing applied research.

CERTIFICATION BY STATE EDUCATION AGENCIES

By the mid-1930s certification standards were in place in Pennsylvania and New York. After Cornell shepherded certification standards for school psychologists through the New York Education Department, she wondered about certification of specialized groups of psychologists. "Should special groups of psychologists be certified before there is any general certification or will such an attempt retard the development of a general professonal group which has sufficient cohesion to make a profession" (Cornell, 1941, p. 62)? She justified governmental regulation of school psychologists because there was no "generally approved course of study for the preparation of psychologists [and] an acceptable type of preparation had to be adopted in the regulations" (p. 62).

The model for certification by state education agencies of school psychologists started in Pennsylvania when the State Council of Education passed the following resolution: "Resolved that the preparation standards for the certification of public school psychologists and public school psychological examiners be approved as of October 1, 1933, and that such persons as complete the preparation indicated . . . be certified by the superintedent of public instruction to designate pupils as candidates for special education [italics added] (State Council of Education, 1934, p. 27). Although the certification was for a specific purpose, designating children who were eligible for special education, the requirements were not very specific. They included 24 semester hours of theory, 12 of laboratory and practice and 12 of experience. The course in theory were further divided into subrequirements of educational psychology; clinical psychology, including exceptional children; psychology of childhood and adolescence; tests and measurements; statistics; and controlled electives. Subrequirements in laboratory and practice included credits in clinical methods, diagnostic teaching, social service, and individual research in educational psychology. The 12 semester hours of experience were for approved clinical work in diagnosis and treatment. The requirements for psychological examiners were half of those for psychologists in theory and laboratory. The requirements did not include a master's degree, and some persons with only a bachelor's degree were certified.

With the Thayer Conference and its report, school psychology had a clearly established professional identity. The terms "clinical," "applied," and "consulting" would not be used interchangeably much longer.

The identity of school as separate from clinical psychology was starting to be clear with the reorganization of the APA in 1945 and the formation of divisions. Evolution in the divisions for providers of services can be seen in division titles. Division 12 was initially known as the Division of Clinical and Abnormal Psychology, Division 17 as the Division of Counseling and Guidance Psychologists, and Division 16 as the Division of School Psychologists. Division 12 dropped the word "Abnormal" and Division 17 replaced "Guidance Psychologists" with "Psychology" while Division 16 was substituting "Psychology" for "Psychologists." These title changes suggest that personnel in Divisions 12 and 17 were getting closer together in role and function while Division 16 was broadening its title to include professors. Personnel in Divisions 12 ans 17 spent most of their time with adults and those in Division 16 with children and (to a lesser degree with) adolescents. During the 1940s and 1950s many members of Division 16 also belonged to Division 12. A smaller number of Division 16 members belonged to Division 17. Now there is little overlap except among retirees. Only recently have programs in "child clinical" and "applied developmental" psychology begun to emerge in other APA divisions as competitors for school psychologists in the child market.

INCREASED FUNDING FOR GRADUATE EDUCATION AND TRAINING

As the Soviets beat the Americans into space, in the late 1950s federal funding for education was increased greatly to help the United States catch up. Special funds were allocated for libraries, testing, and preparation of counselors and of teachers of math and science. Psychology was not ready for the great influx of money to prepare practitioners but was ready to prepare graduate students for college teaching.

Although accreditation by APA of psychology programs was begun in the late 1940s (Sears, 1947), for years the APA approved "clinical training facilities" without distinction by specialty. In the 1940s and 1950s most students in the accredited programs were interested in adults. From the 1957–1958 school year some students in APA accredited programs were awarded fellowships with funding from the National Institute for Mental Health NIMH). George Peabody College, Teachers College of Columbia University, University of Illinois, University of Michigan, and University of Minnesota were the institutions funded in the first wave, and their funding for school psychology students continued for many years. Later, other institutions received funding for students in school psychology but for shorter periods of time (S. P. Schneider, personal communication, October 15, 1981). Many of the graduate student recipients of NIMH support were employed in higher education, which, over time, helped produce psychologists for the schools.

In the 1960s, when federal money through the U.S. Office of Education was becoming available, school psychology was just coming into its own and was without strong advocacy groups in Washington. Funds from the Department of Education for training specialists to deal with learning problems went to special education and guidance, and much of that went to undergraduate and beginning graduate-level students. The APA advocated support of doctoral preparation of psychologists through the NIMH, which included school psychologists.

RAPIDLY INCREASING POSITIONS FOR PSYCHOLOGISTS IN THE SCHOOLS IN THE 1960S

The 1960s featured dramatic increases in employment opportunities for school psychologists. Passage of federal legislation about services for exceptional children sparked this demand even though school psychologists were not specifically mentioned in the landmark P.L. 94-142, the Education of All Handicapped Children Act. School psychologists were not specified because so few of them existed in many states and mention of the title would lead to a denial of service or provisions by psychologists inadequately prepared for work with children. (Even so, personnel with little graduate education [e.g., educational diagnosticians and learning disabilities specialists] filled positions that might have gone to qualified psychologists had enough been available.)

In 1965, Representative Sam M. Gibbons of the 19th district in Florida "concerned about the correlation between crime and education in our Country" (S. M. Gibbons, personal communication to Charles Gersoni of the APA, November 5, 1965, p. 1), had proposed a bill that would provide a "Good Start" program for "the early detection, correction, and prevention of learning disorders which at times results in delinquency and other disruptive behavior" (p. 1) and asked the APA for its views. In turn, the central staff polled leading preparers of school psychologists around the country but did not obtain much support for the preparation of specialists in child development at the nondoctoral level. Memos on file in the APA archives in the Library of Congress indicate that letters of strong support were written to the executive director by Eli Bower, James J. Gallagher, and Robert Sears; lukewarm support was received from Alan O. Ross, Boyd McCandless, and Ralph Tindall; and (six pages of) hard criticism came from Mary Alice White. The APA decided to provide positive but not strong support for the bill, which did not pass.

Between 1950 and 1970 the number of programs preparing school psychologist increased about 10 times and doubled again by the mid-1980s. According to Fagan (1986a) enrollment increased from about 1,000 students in the early 1960s to about 5,500 in the mid-1970s and perhaps as high as 7,300 in the mid-1980s. However, the number of part-time students enrolled by many institutions makes difficult the estimation of the number of full-time equivalent students. NASP estimated 20,000 school psychologists to be practicing in the mid-1980s (National Association of School Psychologists, 1984), but this does not account for all persons with graduate degrees in school psychology. Many who serve as school psychologist initially, step up the career ladder or move laterally to other positions in schools, in mental health agencies, or in private practice.

Accompanying the rapid growth of employment opportunities for school psychologists were journals with school psychology in the title. First, there was the *Journal of School Psychology* with Donald Smith as its editor in 1963. School psychologists in Ohio and leaders in Division 16 provided the impetus, but Samuel Bonham, director of the Bureau of Special Education in the Ohio education agency, may be thought of as the initial producer and William Farling as its business manager for decades. Jack I. Bardon, Beeman Phillips,

and Thomas Oakland had lengthy stints as editor. A year later *Psychology in the Schools* was started with William Hunt of Loyola of Chicago as its first editor and Gerald Fuller of Central Michigan serving as editor beginning in 1970. With the birth of the NASP in 1969 the *School Psychology Digest* was published for the membership. John Guidibaldi and Liam Grimley were its first two editors. When Daniel Reschley became editor the name was changed to *School Psychology Review*. Throughout this volume will be references to these and more recently developed journals for school psychologists.

After counseling was recognized as an accreditable specialty in 1958, leaders in school psychology started their campaign for identity (see Bonneau & Simmons, 1970). Strategically, the request for accreditation of school psychology programs by the APA was coupled with a request for recognition of the school specialty separate from clinical, counseling, and industrial/organizational by the American Board of (Examiners in) Professional Psychology (initially ABEPP and now ABPP). Eventually both groups (i.e., the APA through its Committee on Accreditation and ABPP) recognized school psychology in the late 1960s, but a program designated as school psychology was not accredited until 1971.

(For several decades the National Council for the Accreditation of Teacher Education [NCATE] has been accrediting programs under the jurisdiction of a university's director of teacher education, including those for the preparation of school psychologists. As is usually the case, the initial NCATE standards for accreditation of school psychology programs were minimal. NCATE standards were improved considerably after the NASP joined the NCATE and the NASP standards were adopted. During the late 1970s and 1980s the NASP/NCATE standards for program accreditation were similar in many ways to those used by the APA. Even so, as late as the mid-1980s, institutions with school psychology programs could receive NCATE accreditation under the old system [i.e., without meeting NASP standards]. In 1987, the NCATE changed its process to accredit institutions and the programs offered, not individual programs in institutions. Without accreditation of specific programs the value of NCATE accreditation has been reduced again.)

By the end of the 1960s the climate was ripe for the formation of the NASP as an organization separate from special education, guidance, and organized psychology. In special education and guidance, leaders were being developed in graduate programs for practitioners apart from psychology and the fields were developing their own identities. In the APA the belief continued that a fully qualified psychologist possessed a doctorate, yet school administrators sought and employed psychological personnel with less than a doctorate, for several reasons. There was a great need for psychometrists. In the vast majority of states, the requirements for an entry-level certificate from the SEA was at the master's or specialist level. Most of the school staff had little graduate education and it was thought to be appropriate to keep the level of pay for psychologists on the same scale as that of others on the staff.

The NASP was created by those who felt that existing organizations, such as the Council for Exceptional Children, American Personnel and Guidance Association (now the American Association for Counseling and Development), and American Psychological Association did not meet their needs. In its short history, the NASP has provided representation to education not provided by the APA. By developing standards for graduate education and for practice, the NASP has influenced SEA regulations and nondoctoral training far more than has the APA. However, the APA, far more than the NASP, has influenced state licensing boards in psychology and organizations associated with third-party payments for psychological service such as the National Register of Health Service Providers in Psychology. Although frequently looking over their shoulders at each other, the NASP and APA have independently developed guidelines for the practice of school psychology, accreditation standards, a separate literature, and national conventions. State affiliates of the APA may have divisions of school psychology in them, but the APA may have only one affiliate per state. The NASP, disagreeing with the APA on such sensitive issues as level of entry for independent practice and titles for practice, set out to establish strong state affiliates of their own and have done so in many state. The APA/NASP Inter Organizational Committee (IOC) was formed to play a facilitative role. The IOC was not designed to develop policy but to identify areas of mutual concern and to help both organizations work to improve psychological service to the constituencies of the schools and thereby to school psychology.

In the mid-1980s about three-fourths of all school psychologists did not hold a doctorate, but the percent with doctorates was climbing consistently and a majority of NASP members may have a doctorate in the not-too-distant future (Fagan, 1986b). Will this diminish the conflict over title and level of education required for private practice? It is unlikely.

Ninety years after the APA was formed, it had about 40 divisions and psychologists claimed many specialties. However, only the specialties of clinical, counseling, and school had programs of study accredited by the APA, and only clinical, counseling, industrial/organizational, and school had specialty guidelines approved by the APA. Within the APA, school psychology is clearly recognized as a specialty. Within education, school psychology has a clear identity through the NASP. From the beginning there was school psychology—and its future seems assured.

SUMMARY

1895–1915   Witmer conceptualized the clinical method for working with school children and helped get the method used across the United States by psychologists as the field moved from anthropological to psychological measurements.

1915–1930   An increasing number of practicing psychologists were employed across the country and clinics were established for the educational needs of children under the jurisdiction of various authorities, especially the public schools and teacher preparation institutions of higher education. Scores from Binet's tests, which were translated and adapted for use in the United States, provided the appearance of science in a society striving for orderliness.

1925   Water described the role of school psychologists to be much more inclusive than that of a psychometrist.

1930–1940   Professional psychology begins to split into specialties as the first governmental regulations on practice affect psychologists in the schools. Physicians fade from the schools, with psychologists taking over some of their functions.

1940–1955   Programs for preparing school psychologists appear more frequently in university catalogs. Professional psychology begins to formalize the split into specialties with the formation of divisions in the APA and the Boulder and Thayer conferences.

1960–1970 Federal legislation increases funding for education at all levels. Dramatic increases in employment for school psychologists drives the development of graduate programs for their preparation. School psychology identity in psychology fixed with standards for accreditation of doctoral programs by the APA and Diplomate status through the ABPP.

1970–1980 The NASP emerges as a powerful spokesperson for school psychology and greatly facilitates the impact of school psychology, especially in the education community.

1980– School psychologists in the NASP and APA become more cooperative in their work on behalf of the constituencies of the schools.

REFERENCES

Allen, A. J. (1974). *Selected papers of David Wechsler*. New York: Academic Press.

Bardon, J. I. (1983). Psychology applied to education: A specialty in search of an identity. *American Psychologist, 38,* 185–196.

Bardon, J. I. (1987). Past tense, present subjunctive, future imperfect: Reaction to Fagan's article. *School Psychology Review, 16,* 22–26.

Bonneau, A., & Simmons, W. (1970). APA accreditation: A status report. *American Psychologist, 25,* 581–584.

Committee of the Clinical Section of the American Psychological Association. (1935). Guide to psychological clinics in the United States. *The Psychological Clinic, 23,* 1–137.

Committee on Certification of Consulting Psychologists. (1922). Report (in the Archives of the APA in the Library of Congress).

Committee on the Qualifications of Psychological Examiners and Other Psychological Experts. (1919). Report (in the Archives of the APA in the Library of Congress).

Cornell, E. L. (1936). The school psychologist's contribution. *Elementary school principals' yearbook* (a portion of) *National Elementary Principal, 15,* 561–566.

Cornell, E. L. (1941). Certification of specialized groups of psychologists. *Journal of Consulting Psychology, 5,* 62–65.

Cutts, N. E. (Ed.). (1955). *School psychologists at mid-century.* Washington, DC: American Psychological Association.

Executive Committee, Pennsylvania Psychological Association. (1950). [Minutes of the May 5 meeting].

Fagan, T. K. (1986a). The historical origins and growth of programs to prepare school psychologists in the United States. *Journal of School Psychology, 24,* 9–22.

Fagan, T. K. (1986b). School psychology's dilemma: Reappraising solutions and directing attention to the future. *American Psychologist, 41,* 851–861.

Fagan, T. K. (1987). Gesell: The first school psychologist. Part I, The road to Connecticut. *School Psychology Review, 16,* 103–107.

Fernald, G. M. (1943). *Remedial techniques in basic school subjects.* New York: McGraw-Hill.

Fernald, W. E. (1922). The inauguration of a state-wide public school mental clinic in Massachusetts. *Mental Hygiene, 6,* 471–486.

French, J. L. (1984). On the conception, birth, and early development of school psychology with special reference to Pennsylvania. *American Psychologist, 39,* 976–986.

French, J. L. (1987). The first forty years of books in school psychology. *Professional School Psychology, 1,* 267–278.

French, J. L. (1988). Grandmothers I wish I knew: Contributions of women to the history of school psychology. *Professional School Psychology, 3,* 51–68.

French, J. L., Smith, D. C., & Cardon, B. W. (1968). Institutions offering graduate training and financial assistance in school psychology. *Journal of School Psychology, 6,* 261–267.

Furerstein, R. (1979). *The dynamic assessment of retarded performers: The learning potential assessment device, theory, instruments, and techniques.* Baltimore: University Park Press.

Garfield, S. L. (1965). Historical introduction. In B. B. Wolman (Ed.), *Handbook of clinical psychology.* New York: McGraw-Hill.

Gesell, A. (1952). Autobiography. In E. G. Boring, H. Werner, H. S. Langfeld, & R. M. Yerkes (Eds.), *A history of psychology in autobiography* (Vol. 4, pp. 123–142). Worcester, MA: Clark University Press.

Goddard, H. H. (1912). *The Kallikak family: A study in the heredity of feeble-mindedness.* New York: Macmillan.

Goddard, H. H. (1914). *Feeble-mindedness: Its causes and consequences.* New York: Macmillan.

Hilleboe, G. L. (1930). *Finding and teaching atypical children. Contributions to Education* (No. 423). New York: Bureau of Publications, Teachers College. Columbia University.

Hollingworth, L. S. (1922). Existing laws which authorize psychologists to perform professional services. *Journal of Criminal Law and Criminology, 13* (1), 70–73.

Hutt, R. B. W. (1923). The school psychologist. *Psychological Clinic, 15,* 48–51.

Louttit, C. M. (1936). *Clinical psychology of children's behavior problems.* New York: Harper & Brothers.

Jackson, D. D. (1986). It took trains to put street kids on the right track out of the slums. *Smithsonian, 17,* 95–102.

MacMillan, D. P. (1906). The physical and mental examinations of the public school pupils in Chicago.

Charities and Commons, 17, 529–535. (As reported in Mullen, 1981)

Marzolf, S. S. (1956). *Psychological diagnosis and counseling in the schools.* New York: Henry Holt.

Mullen, F. A. (1981). School psychology in the USA: Reminiscences of its origin. *Journal of School Psychology, 19,* 103–119.

National Association of School Psychologists. (1984). *Leaders of state school psychological associations 1984–85.* Olympia, WA: Author.

National Education Association. (1920, January). *NEA Bulletin, 8,* 23.

Popplestone, J. A., & McPherson, M. W. (1984). Pioneer psychological laboratories in clinical settings. In J. Brozek (Ed.), *Explorations in the history of psychology in the United States.* Lewisburg, PA: Buckness University Press.

Sears, R. R. (1947). Clinical training facilities: 1947. *American Psychologist, 2,* 199–205.

Skodak, M., & Skeels, H. M. (1949). A final follow-up of one hundred adopted children. *Journal of Genetic Psychology, 75,* 85–125.

Slater, R. (1980). The organizational origins of public school psychology. *Educational Studies, 2,* 1–12.

Smith, D. C. (1964–1965). Institutions offering graduate training in school psychology. *Journal of School Psychology, 3,* 58–66.

State Council of Education. (1934). *Items of business—Journals of meetings and annual reports* (pp. 23–27). Harrisburg, PA: Office of the State Board of Education.

Symonds, P. M. (1933, September 9). Every school should have a psychologist. *School and Society, 38,* (976) 322–329.

Symonds, P. M. (1942). The school psychologist—1942. *Journal of Consulting Psychology, 6,* 173–176.

Wallin, J. E. W. (1914). *Mental health of the school child.* New Heaven, CT: Yale University Press.

Walter, R. (1925). The functions of the school psychologist. *American Psychologist, 29,* 167–170.

Wechsler, D. (1926). On the influence of education on intelligence as measured by the Binet-Simon tests. *Journal of Educational Psychology, 17,* 248–257.

Wechsler, D. (1939). *The measurement of adult intelligence.* Baltimore: Williams & Wilkins.

Winship, A. E. (1892). Preliminary sketch of the history of child study in America. *Journal of Education, 36,* 141. (As reported in Mullen, 1981)

Witmer, L. (1907). Clinical Psychology. *The Psychological Clinic, 1,* 1–9.

Witmer, L. (1908). Retrospect and prospect: An editorial. *The Psychological Clinic, 2,* 1.

Woolley, H. T. (1920). To: The American Psychological Association, a petition dated November 18 and located in the Library of Congress Archives of the American Psychological Association.

2

CURRENT AND FUTURE PERSPECTIVES

OPINION 1
SCHOOL PSYCHOLOGY IN THE 1980s AND 1990s: A CONTEXT FOR CHANGE AND DEFINITION

CAROLYN T. COBB

North Carolina Department of Public Instruction—
Raleigh

School psychologists have deliberated about origin, identity, and appropriate roles throughout their brief history. The content and nature of school psychology practice have been variously defined, and their origins are not entirely clear. Lightner Witmer and his psychological clinic (Elliott & Witt, 1986; Fagan & Delugach, 1985; Magary, 1967) and the mental testing movement (Elliott & Witt, 1986; Tindall, 1979; Ysseldyke, 1978) are both cited as origins for school psychology. However, reference to the term *school psychologist* has been found as early as 1910 in Germany (Fagan & Delugah, 1985), which slightly predates Witmer. Apparently, the term was used without a conceptual reference to a specialty, but for psychological services—usually clinical—provided in a school setting.

Different orientations for school psychology have been proposed at different times in different places, including educational orientations (Gray, 1963; Reger, 1965; Vallett, 1963), mental health approaches (Bardon & Bennett, 1974; Caplan, 1970), and organizational development and program evaluation (Granger & Campbell, 1977; Granowsky & Davis, 1974; Maher, Illback, & Zins, 1984; Schein, 1969). School psychologists have received training in departments of psychology, as well as education (Brown, 1982). Although one can trace a gradual growth in and refinement of school psychology, its history is anything but orderly (Elliott & Witt, 1986). Bardon (1983) noted that school psychology has not developed but rather has accumulated.

As psychology in the schools has grown, attempts have been made to conceptualize practice and to exert some influence over the profession's direction. The Thayer Conference in 1954 (Cutts, 1955) represents the first national focus on school psychology as a specialty, followed almost 25 years later by the Spring Hill Symposium (Ysseldyke & Weinberg, 1981). However, influences on the development of the specialty typically have been external to it and were not designed to create a new specialty per se.

One major external influence has been the growth of special education. Although school psychologists already were well affiliated with psychoeducational testing and the identification of handicapped students, the passage of Public Law (P.L.) 94-142, the Education of All Handicapped Children Act (U.S. Congress, 1975), moved that identity to a most prominent level. While P.L. 94-142 has accomplished major educational goals for children who were previously unserved or underserved, it has dominated the direction of the specialty in the 1970s and 1980s (Ysseldyke, 1978). The dominant place of special education in school psychology was clearly evident in the scenarios developed and issues dealt with with at the Olympia Conference on the Future of School Psychology (Brown, Cardon, Coulter, & Meyers, 1982).

School psychology has had a rather random development. There was no early mandate for its existence as a specialty, and it has evolved in response to a series of events and expressed needs (Bardon, 1982; Grimley, 1985; Stern, 1911; Tindall, 1979). Of course, school psychology is now a recognized specialty within psychology with the requisite standards for training, credentialing, and the delivery of services. Nevertheless, we have spent an inordinate amount of time on our roles and functions and still have no cohesive theoretical base or objectives for our practice in schools (Bardon, 1983; Chovan, 1968; Reilly, 1973). Where can, and should, school psychology grow? Can it continue to mature as a profession, and how?

UNDERSTANDING SCHOOL PSYCHOLOGY AS A SYSTEM

Systems theory is a widely used concept to study almost any human or social organism. A systems approach may be used to understand anything from a business or political institution to a dysfunctional family and its treatment. In this chapter, I will describe the potential for school psychology's growth and future from the understanding of the systems in which it is embedded and through which it is influenced.

A systems view is useful for several reasons: (a) It helps to examine external influences from other systems over which we have little or no control; (b) it highlights the impact of our "outputs" and services; (c) it helps us see that we can behave in various ways—not only react helplessly —toward external influences; and (d) it emphasizes that in order to change any system component in a substantive way, the entire system must be considered and possibly altered (Katz & Kahn, 1978).

School psychology is embedded in various systems or contexts. These contexts influence us personally and professionally. Several major contexts for our practice include the political system, the structure of education, society, generic psychology, and the economy. In particular, current issues and forces impinging on education will, by definition, influence the direction of school psychology. Whether or not that direction is beneficial for children and to our professional liking will be determined in part by how we respond to these external influences.

Although we cannot control these systems or predict their futures exactly, there are certain likelihoods based on information collected about them. We must think and plan strategically to move our profession forward with the changing environment. Rather than acquiesce to external conditions, as seems to be most typical of our past, school psychologists must anticipate directions and needs, as well as analyze our own strengths and weaknesses, and make strategic decisions about our future.

The 1980s are a time of considerable social, economic, and educational upheaval. It is in this context of change that I see the opportunity to find the mandate for school psychology and to transform our practice. If we do not respond to the current system changes in meaningful and deliberate ways, our development may continue to be undefined and random—if it continues as school psychology at all.

CONTEXTS CREATING OPPORTUNITIES FOR CHANGE IN THE 1980s

The revolutionary pace of change in the 1980s in many aspects of our social, political, and professional lives is part of a fundamental and permanent redirection of the national economy from industrial to service and information. This economic shift creates a dislocation of people and expectations, and challenges the purposes and directions of education. These various contexts in turmoil cannot be ignored by education or school psychology as we choose our future course.

Societal Context

The last decade has seen a more conservative trend in the political and social arenas. This conservative orientation in education calls for a strict academic focus, avoidance of social and personal issues, and less support for ancillary services in schools. Child advocates generally agree that our society as a whole does not place children as a high priority (Children's Defense Fund, 1986; Howe, 1986; Packard, 1983). Government programs have been cut and seem to parallel efforts to restrict educational services. At the same time, there is increased awareness of changes in social and family contexts which are creating new dilemmas and stresses for both children and society (Elkind, 1981; Packard, 1983).

The very definition and nature of family are changing. Because of divorce, employment patterns, and the demise of the extended family, the number of adults in children's lives has decreased. Women have rapidly joined men in full-time jobs. More than 50% of mothers in two-parent families with children under age 6 work, and the percentages are higher for single-parent mothers and mothers with older children (B. Brophy, 1986). Thirteen million children in the United States, over 20%, are poor (Children's Defense Fund, 1986). Increased child poverty is associated with poorer nutrition and health, greater chance of physical abuse, greater likelihood of dropping out of school, and greater despair.

In addition to the economic and social pressures leading children to assume responsibility at earlier ages, some parental values emphasize success and achievement at earlier ages (Elkind, 1981). The level of stress and social pressures for children are indicated by the suicide rate for teenagers, substance abuse, and increased sexual involvement.

The extent of problems for children, as well as the long-term implications for society, may effectively counter those people who oppose government or public agency efforts to deal with these social issues. Widespread awareness of these problems and a shift toward more child-oriented attitudes are evident in a national survey of public attitudes toward children (Harris & Associates, 1986). Of the adults surveyed, three-fourths believed that children today are facing more severe problems than ever before. Less than half believed that children are happy, safe, or getting a good education. Almost two-thirds said that society and government do not do enough for children. Most respondents felt that schools could do better in meeting their responsibilities to children, indicating that they expect more than an academic education from schools. Most important, the majority of respondents were willing to pay more taxes to fund a wide variety of programs for children. Responses by nonparents were very similar to those of parents on these issues.

With decreased government support and the lack of more traditional family and community supports, schools are often being looked to as the institution that may have the greatest capability and opportunity to provide assistance in a number of areas. Children who are hungry, unhealthy, pressured, and unhappy are not likely to perform well academically. Many schools are developing before- and after-school care, increased crisis prevention and counseling efforts, in-school health clinics, substance abuse prevention programs, life planning skills curricula, and stress management programs for staff and children.

The Educational Context
  Educational Reform and
  School Effectiveness

Reform and effectiveness are key words in education for the 1980s. Educators have been confronted with a plethora of reports calling for significant reforms in educational practices (Adler, 1982; Carnegie Forum on Education and the Economy, 1986; Committee for Economic Development, 1985; Education Commission of the States, 1983; National Commission on Excellence, 1983; Peterson, 1983). Although highlighting the shortcomings of education, these reports have helped to place education in the forefront as a policy issue and have called for greater human and financial resources to be devoted to the schooling process. A number of themes run through these reform initiatives. Higher expectations and standards for all students are central to the recommendations, with a renewed emphasis on academic subjects.

Concern is also expressed for higher-level problem-solving and thinking skills, as well as increased technological literacy. More time spent on instruction is seen as essential, including longer school days and years and more emphasis on homework.

Concomitant with, and perhaps contributing to, these reform directives are results from research on effective schools, effective teaching, and educational productivity (Brookover, Brady, Flood, Schweitzer, & Weisenbaker, 1979; J. E. Brophy, 1979; Daugherty, 1981; Edmonds, 1979; Good & Brophy, 1984; Goodlad, 1984; Rosenshine, 1983; Rutter, Maughan, Mortimer, Ouston, & Smith, 1979; Walberg, 1984). Areas of emphasis in this effectiveness research include instructional leadership, shared goals, academic emphasis and opportunity to learn, allocation and use of time, uniform standards and high expectations, classroom management and structure, academic monitoring, relationships between what is taught and what is tested, classroom flexibility for individual students, and patterns of student/staff/parent involvement. We have moved dramatically toward a more empirical basis for teaching and schooling.

Accountability

New rigor in teacher preparation and accountability, as well as higher regard for teaching, is evident. Restructuring schools to give teachers more decision-making power is called for, along with proposals for higher salaries, master teachers, merit pay, career ladders, and more rigorous certification procedures. An outcomes measurement focus tends to be evident both for teachers and for student learning.

The emphasis on improving the quality of teachers and teaching and the related emphasis on accountability and educational outcomes also have implications for school psychology. Teachers, as well as students, are being asked to be accountable. An emphasis on career ladders and merit pay contributes to the notion of rewards based on competence and excellence. If teachers are to be evaluated based on specific practices (albeit narrow ones) shown to result in higher student achievement, how will psychologists be evaluated?

Consumers, taxpayers, and policymakers have a right to ask what they are getting for their money. I believe we are obligated to find ways to demonstrate that we are effective. It is important to struggle with defining our services in terms of outcomes, as well as processes, that are important to students, teachers, parents, and policymakers. Attention to evaluation and accountability may be essential not only to our survival, but also to our continued growth and development as a profession.

Categorical Programs Revisited

Given the increased emphasis on excellence and accountability, there is concern among some educators and student advocates that excellence be balanced with equity. As educational standards in regular education are being raised, criteria for special education placement and assistance have become tighter. Many students with special learning needs may not qualify for programs offering special help.

Although most of the reform reports note the need to provide special instruction and support for the educationally needy (e.g., handicapped, economically disadvantaged, slow learner), many advocates believe that the higher achievement initiatives may leave students with special needs further behind (Howe, 1986; National Assocaition of School Psychologists, 1985a; National Coalition of Advocates for Students, 1985). In addition, the report recommendations typically call for continued funding of special categorical programs or supplemental instruction rather than careful consideration of effective instructional and school paradigms for all students. It is reasonable to question whether excellence for all students can occur in the current educational system structure.

While regular education is inundated with reform efforts, special and remedial education programs have not gone without scrutiny (Wang, Reynolds, & Walberg, 1986). Lack of resources in regular education, as well as the lack of tolerance for diverse abilities and needs, has resulted in the overuse of special education to meet the needs of any student with special learning needs. But even the system of special education itself is besieged with controversy.

Although the accomplishments of P.L. 94-142 are important and acknowledged, many management and conceptual problems in the categorical system may inhibit providing the most effective education possible. The various categorical programs fragment services and reduce the ability to solve educational problems in a general way (Reynolds & Wang, 1983). These programs do not interact with each other or regular education and result in extreme disjointedness. Categorical labels assume a common etiology, as well as treatment strategies. However, the characteristics of children placed in special education categories are variable and inconsistent. There is no empirical basis for linking specific instructional approaches to these categories (Finn & Resnick, 1984; Reynolds & Wang, 1983). The extensive referral, assessment, and placement requirements lead to excessive proceduralism and expensive testing, which have little to do with determining instructional needs.

Disproportional placement of ethnic minorities in these programs has been perhaps the most compelling issue, resulting in significant professional controversy. Much of the debate has centered on the meaning of and implications of disproportionality. A comprehensive review of these issues, conducted by the National Research Council (NRC) at the request of the Office of Civil Rights (Heller, Holtzman, & Messick, 1982), concluded that disproportional placement was only symptomatic of deeper educational problems: (a) the validity of the referral and assessment procedures and (b) the quality of regular and special education instruction. Although the panel recognized the lack of empirical support for the current categorical service structure, their proposals fell short of total system reform. The NRC recommendations included the need to assess the quality of regular instruction, to conduct more functional assessments, and to place students in special programs that can be demonstrated to be effective. The panel noted that with these practices, disproportionality may not be eliminated but would not constitute inequity.

Emphasis on these practices has certainly increased. Better linkages with regular education are achieved through general education interventions prior to referral (Graden, Casey, & Bonstrom, 1985; Graden, Casey, & Christenson, 1985). Training in curriculum-based assessment (Gickling & Havetape, 1981; Tucker, 1985), as well as environmental assessment (Shapiro & Lentz, 1985; Ysseldyke & Christenson, 1986), provides more functional orientations to evaluation for academic interventions.

These practices are important for improved service delivery, but offering them as final solutions ignores fundamental issues regarding the system. Assuming that we can accurately evaluate the quality of students' previous instruction, validly assess and place them, and offer effective special programs, we will still have some students who have educational needs but who do not qualify for the available programs. Prasse (1985) also points out that regardless of assessment and program practices, disproportional placement is likely to be viewed by the courts as a problem and not merely a symptom. Even a statement by one of the NRC report authors (Messick, 1984) inadvertently highlights the intrinsic dilemma of the categorical system: "Only after deficiencies in the learning environment have been ruled out . . . should the child be exposed to the *risks of stigma and misclassification inherent in referral and individual assessment*" (p. 5; emphasis by author).

Thus, the special education subsystem of education, in which the life of most school psychologists is embedded, is under benevolent assault. Paired with the rapid changes in education as a whole, our profession is offered the opportunity to become an active participant in seeking effective solutions for children and a more effective and meaningful professional future.

The Professional Context

While we are contending with major and rapid changes in the societal and educational contexts, the professional context has not been static. The National Association of School Psychologists (NASP) and the Division of School Psychology (Division 16) of the American Psychological Association (APA) both purport to represent the interests of school psychology. They differ in numerous ways, including size, membership makeup, and general issue orientation.

The Evolution of NASP

The NASP was formed by practitioners out of the need to have their concerns better addressed, especially at the nondoctoral level. More than two thirds of NASP members are practitioners, and approximately 80% are nondoctoral (NASP, 1987). The NASP has become a visible, strong, and feasible professional representative for the school psychologist, with a membership of nearly 13,000 (NASP, 1988a) and a total budget of over $1 million (NASP, 1988b).

The NASP has a history of strong advocacy in professional and guild issues, including implementing national standards for training, accreditation, and credentialing; implementing activities and standards for training and practice at national and state levels; and assisting and consulting with states to promote professional and organizational growth. Enhancement of professional skills is emphasized through the NASP journal, *School Psychology Review,* as well as professional development products that are skill based and self-instructional. An aggressive plan to continue producing publications on emerging topics of importance to practitioners and the field has been initiated.

The establishment of a standing Children's Services Committee in 1985 moved the NASP forward in focusing on its primary client group (Cobb Myrick, 1985). Perhaps most significantly, the NASP has taken a leadership role in advocating for changes in the categorical service delivery structure in order to enhance the education of all students. Its related position statement (NASP, 1985a), developed jointly with the National Coalition of Advocates for Students, was the first official statement on this issue by any association and has enhanced liaison with other professional groups and federal education officials. Two major publications on alternative service delivery continue this priority (Canter, Dawson, Silverstein, Hale, & Zins, 1988; Graden, Zins, & Curtis, 1988).

In a major step forward in credentialing, the NASP has established a National Board of Certified School Psychologists. Although grandparenting provisions are included, national certification requires training consistent with the NASP sixth-year standards. Primary goals of this system are to further the high standards for school psychology nationally, to promote continuing professional development, and to enhance certification reciprocity among states (Batsche, 1988). Response to national certification has been strong, and thousands of applications arrived at the NASP office after the first mailing to members in May 1988 (G. Batsche, personal communication, June 1988).

An APA in Flux

Division 16 is a much smaller association of over 2,000 members (W. B. Pryzwansky, personal communication, April 3, 1987), and it has a higher representation of trainers. As NASP president during 1985–1986, I was an ad hoc member of the division's executive council. The extensive amount of time spent on internal matters, training issues, and position within the APA as a whole was notable. Few issues directly related to ongoing practice concerns of school psychologists (other than standards issues) were extensively discussed or acted upon. There were no practitioners on the

executive council, a correctable situation since they develop their own slate of candidates. Lest I sound too harsh, the small membership and budget might be cited as limitations on the possible activities of the division. However, one could argue circularly that more current and proactive stances might increase membership, especially of practitioners.

Certainly, the organizational structure of the APA constrains Division 16. Moving issues through the APA takes an inordinate amount of effort and time. The predominant orientation and control within the APA appear to be from clinically oriented health and human service providers. Neither academicians nor applied psychologists are satisfied with their representation within or level of service from the APA. In response to a clear gap in representation of school psychology and education, the APA has added a senior staff position of director for psychology in the schools. The ability of this position, housed in the Office of Professional Practice, to provide a strong voice for school psychology and its concerns is presently unknown.

Proposals to reorganize APA have been controversial, and the proper location for school psychology under different structures has been hotly debated. In discussions of an early reorganization proposal (Bardon, 1986) which offered two possible "homes" for school psychology (e.g., health and human service psychology or academic and applied psychology), I was surprised to observe that some Division 16 leaders felt that school psychology belonged in the health services provider area rather than the applied area. These views seem to represent what might be called first- and second-generation attitudes (Reilly, 1973). I do not believe they represent the most feasible opportunities for school psychology.

A revised APA restructuring plan submitted to the APA membership in the spring of 1988 was defeated (Fisher, 1988), and school psychologists within APA already are being solicited to join a new American Psychological Society (APS). The extent to which applied and academic/research psychologists may affiliate with the APS, allowing APA to be devoted to the promotion of clinical practice, is presently an open question. Similarly, the ability of the APA to accommodate and represent the needs of scientists as equally as clinicians is unknown.

The state of affairs in generic psychology's house and the seeming lack of a forceful vision for school psychology within the APA have contributed to NASP dominance as a primary representative of practicing school psychology. Incoming leadership in Division 16 may be bringing broader and newer visions for school psychology, including increased interest in children's issues (J. C. Conoley, personal communication, June 1988). If a shift in Division 16's emphases can be combined with an effective public policy voice in the new staff position, the APA may become a more powerful force in school psychology. Even if school psychology gains a better foothold in the APA, the NASP is growing stronger and will continue to be the primary organization representing psychology in the schools. Nevertheless, children and school psychology can best be served if they are strongly represented in both organizations.

The Doctoral/Nondoctoral Schism

The issue of doctoral/nondoctoral independent practice will continue to separate the two associations. I believe the eventual resolution of this issue will have little to do with who is competent at what level to do which things. It will be influenced by economic and market system forces beyond our easy control, such as increased competition and third-party insurers. Nondoctoral private practice may continue to exist, but not with a full array of services or the same status. I believe school psychologists will need to accept doctoral-level independent practice in the private sector at some time in the future.

A recent NASP survey of its practitioner members (Reschly, Genshaft, & Binder, 1987) showed that concern about and interest in nondoctoral licensure for private practice were still strong. However, the vast majority of respondents (73%) felt resolution of the independent practice issue with the APA was important, and they were divided equally over supporting a hypothetical resolution for doctoral entry to occur at a specified time in the future (e.g., 1995). These statements may reflect a beginning awareness of political and economic realities surrounding this issue. Perhaps it also represents the fact that the specialist level of training supported by the NASP is very close to doctoral standards, without the accompanying recognition.

By the same token, the APA should recognize that most services—even outside the schools—will be provided by nondoctoral practitioners and should attend to their needs as well. Nondoctoral independent practice will continue to be the standard in the schools. The factors controlling this direction emanate from need, supply and demand, policy control by educators, and competent services by nondoctoral psychologists. I do see increasing numbers of doctorally trained school psychologists in schools, especially as the nature of the specialty is better differentiated from clinical practice and career choices are made.

Related Services

Another aspect of the professional context is created by related service professionals (e.g., social workers, counselors) in the schools. These professionals often provide similar services in the social, personal, and family areas, and they are usually less expensive to employ. The terms we have used historically to define our services (e.g., assessment, consultation, intervention) can also be used by these specialties. How do we define our services as uniquely important? What makes us different? As we reshape the nature of our practice, we will need to delineate the unique applications of our knowledge base, while joining with those professionals who share some of our skills.

IMPLICATIONS OF THE CONTEXTS: THE NECESSARY TRANSFORMATION

The enormous social and personal pressures confronting the current and coming generations of students, the rapid economic changes and dislocations, the resulting priority on education and its outcomes and calls for broad restructuring, the advances in our instructional knowledge base, the turmoil within professional psychology, and the efforts to survive in the professional marketplace are factors that lead me to several conclusions regarding change within school psychology. The first is that we do, indeed, need to redefine the nature of our practice, and the time is now. Second, special education, as currently structured, is not our future. In fact, no particular educational program should define our future. Finally, and most important, we have some choice about how we change and thus can influence the direction in which we move.

Applied Psychology Orientation

Fundamental to moving beyond our various historical developments to a more defined specialty is the increasing shift from a mental health orientation to one of educational attainment and development, from clinical to instructional terminology, from a focus on the individual to increased systems interventions. It incorporates the expanding knowledge bases from cognitive and behavioral psychology. It recognizes that developmental needs of all students require support and nurturing. The scientific study of human behavior has provided the disciplinary base for educational practice (Glaser, 1982). Comprehensive education of children requires the use of knowledge that derives from psychology and which enhances cognitive, social, and personal development.

Our transformation means greater relevance to the instructional elements of schooling, including curriculum, teaching processes, and the environment in which learning occurs. Assessment must be linked to curriculum, instruction, and behavior rather than inferential characteristics that do not lead to relevant programming. Greater affiliation with educational psychology is essential (Bardon, 1983), especially with ongoing research in effective schooling and adaptive instruction. Schooling is fundamentally about instruction and teaching. To ignore these areas in our practice may mean that we eliminate ourselves from the most essential elements of education.

With the social and personal challenges confronting children, teaching basic life, social, and problem-solving skills is also essential. In addition to more traditional counseling and consultation interventions, an increased instructional orientation to developing these skills is necessary. Program development in areas such as latch-key children and preschool education is likely. In helping schools to meet the cognitive, social, and personal needs of youth, school psychologists will be among the best prepared to provide system-level interventions: program development, evaluation of programs, and organizational consultation.

Education System Restructuring: Rethinking Categorical Service Delivery

While redefining the nature of our practice is essential, the educational structure still has considerable influence over how we can practice. Basic reform of the categorical educational structure will be necessary. A less extreme approach calls for more regular education intervention, collaboration between special and general education, and bringing successful special education strategies to the regular program (Will, 1986). Lilly (1986), however, has questioned whether special education has demonstrated that it is more responsive and effective than general education.

Efforts to increase prereferral interventions and more functional assessments in addition to the eligibility assessments will certainly ameliorate some glaring weaknesses. But these improvements cannot remove the ultimate fragmentation of services to students who can be taught in similar ways, the disproportional representation, the hours spent on assessment without instructional use, the inherent stigma of the labeling process, or the child-deficit orientation of the categories. Nor will they relieve the school psychologist from the gatekeeper function of testing for placement.

The effective teaching literature, along with demonstrated effects of individualized, adaptive education (Wang, 1987; Waxman, Wang, Anderson, & Walberg, 1985), offers exciting possibilities for a system that can effectively meet diverse learning needs without the need to label and categorize students. However, these possibilities require more than a collaborative attitude between general and special education. Carefully monitored pilot programs that allow comingling of students previously served within categories and in general education are being advocated (NASP, 1985a; NCAS, 1985; Reynolds & Wang, 1983). Experimental programs such as the Adaptive Learning Environments Model (Wang & Birch, 1984) support the premise that mildly handicapped students, as well as gifted students, can be effectively instructed in the mainstream program—perhaps even more effectively than in the resource room (Wang & Baker, 1985).

Although many people in the special education community are resistant to these kinds of pilots (Teacher Education Division, 1986; Weintraub, 1986), I believe that the categorical system will eventually change. It will come slowly and with continued resistance, but the external forces are too strong. As economic pressures force more efficient utilization of funds, as equity concerns persist, as teachers learn more effective teaching strategies for all students, as caring advocates continue to insist on less denigrating ways to meet the needs of students, and particularly if research continues to show little support for the categorical model, the system will gradually change. This climate of change creates a prime opportunity for school psychologists to bring their knowledge and skills to the process of planning more effective educational structures, as well as for creating professional roles that have more relevance to the instructional lives of students and education as a whole.

An Emerging Consensus: Moving Beyond the 1980s

In order to transform the specialty, there must be some consensus about the nature of our practice, the roles we will perform, and the necessary educational structures. I believe that consensus is emerging and reflecting many of the directions I have cited. References supporting this conceptualization can be found increasingly in the school psychology literature, but a few key items warrant mention. Jack Bardon's article (1983) on the specialty's search for an identity was a major contribution in directing us toward an educational and applied orientation. The National School Psychology Inservice Training Network's document, *School Psychology: Blueprint for Training and Practice* (1984), identified the need for system change as essential to substantive changes in how children are served and how school psychologists practice. It also noted the need for an increase in school psychologists' applied skills in dealing with instructional, social, and affective areas. Reschly (1988) has noted the need for a revolution in school psychology which moves away from special education classification to assessment and interventions in natural settings.

The NASP (1985a) adopted a position statement calling for the piloting of alternative service delivery models, so that the educational attainment of all children may be maximized and the services better utilized. Long-range NASP priorities (NASP, 1985b) include (a) advocating alternative service delivery systems that will maximize educational attainment for all children; (b) promoting greater movement of practice into roles concerned with educational attainment of all children, including social/personal concerns and instructional processes; and (c) increasing acceptance and understanding of school psychology as a positive contributor to education by policymakers and consumers at all levels.

Intentional priorities are important in directing us beyond the 1980s, but collaborative strategic planning of relevant groups within the profession (e.g., trainers, professional associations, state departments of education) is essential in actually moving us toward this conceptualization. Shared goals provide the basis for developing action steps toward desired practice goals. We must all be going in the same direction, or we may end up nowhere in particular.

The NASP has already begun taking positions, targeting organizational priorities, beginning the long-term governmental and professional dialogues, communicating the vision to members, and promoting change in knowledge and skill through its publications and convention workshops. State associations can parallel these activities at the state level, perhaps with even more immediate impact. University programs must examine the content of their training. How can they begin to move toward an emphasis on more functional instructional assessment and applied educational psychology? Transformations in training and practice may be supported by actions of state departments of education by revising state standards for university program approval, offering staff development that reinforces these skills, and attempting to build school psychology into policies and programs in essential instructional areas as well as related support service areas.

Ultimately, individual practitioners can have the greatest influence by seeking out the necessary skills and being ready to apply them at every opportunity. Schools are presented with great challenges, and they will respond to those individuals or groups who can help find solutions. We cannot wait for the next generation of school psychologicsts to be trained.

The 1980s have been an exciting period for school psychology. The kinds of changes for children, society, and education have made our potential knowledge and skill more important than ever. The application of these skills to the challenges facing children and schools can directly influence how we become accountable and viable. The viability of school psychology beyond 1990 will depend on our ability to reconceptualize our practice and refine and reshape our skills accordingly. The contexts surrounding our practice are providing the opportunities for a school psychology practice that can have direct, positive impact on the lives of children and the restructing of education. Those of you reading this chapter in what is now the future will know if, indeed, we did accept the mandate for our practice.

REFERENCES

Adler, M. J. (1982). *The paideia proposal: An educational manifesto.* New York: Macmillan.

Bardon, J. I. (1982). The psychology of school psychology. In C. R. Reynolds & T. B. Gutkin (Eds.), *The handbook of school psychology* (pp. 3–14). New York: Wiley.

Bardon, J. I. (1983). Psychology applied to education: A

specialty in search of an identity. *American Psychologist, 38,* 185–196.

Bardon, J. I. (Chair). (1986). *Task force on the structure of APA: Third interim report.* Washington, DC: American Psychological Association.

Bardon, J. I., & Bennett, V. D. (1974). *School psychology.* Englewood Cliffs, NJ: Prentice-Hall.

Batsche, G. (1988, May). Questions and answers. *NASP Communiqué,* p. 1.

Brookover, W., Brady, C., Flood, P., Schweitzer, J., & Weisenbaker, J. (1979). *School social systems and student achievement: Schools can make a difference.* New York: Praeger.

Brophy, B. (1986, October). Children under stress. *U.S. News and World Report,* pp. 57–64.

Brophy, J. E. (1979). Teacher behavior and its effects. *Journal of Educational Psychology, 71,* 733–750.

Brown, D. T. (1982). Issues in the development of professional school psychology. In C. R. Reynolds & T. B. Gutkin (Eds.), *The handbook of school psychology* (pp. 14–23). New York: Wiley.

Brown, D. T., Cardon, B. W., Coulter, W. A., & Meyers, J. (Eds.). (1982). The Olympia proceedings [Entire issue]. *The School Psychology Review, 11.*

Canter, A., Dawson, P., Silverstein, J., Hale, L., & Zins, J. (1988). *NASP directory of alternative service delivery models.* Washington, DC: National Association of School Psychologists.

Caplan, G. (1970). *The theory and practice of mental health consultation.* New York: Basic Books.

Carnegie Forum on Education and the Economy. (1986). *A nation prepared: Teachers for the 21st century.* New York: Author.

Children's Defense Fund. (1986). *A children's defense budget: An analysis of the FY 1987 federal budget and children.* Washington, DC: Author.

Chovan, W. L. (1968). Some questions and imperatives concerning the territories of the school psychologist. *Journal of School Psychology, 6,* 267–271.

Cobb Myrick, C. (1985, September). Children: The first priority. *NASP Communiqué,* pp. 1, 3.

Committee for Economic Development. (1985). *Investing in our public schools: Business and the public schools.* Washington, DC: Author.

Cutts, W. (Ed.). (1955). *School psychologists at midcentury: A report of the Thayer conference on the functions, qualifications and training of school psychologists.* Washington, DC: American Psychological Association.

Daugherty, K. (1981). After the fall: Research on school effects since the Coleman report. *Harvard Educational Review, 51,* 301–308.

Edmonds, R. (1979). Effective schools for the urban poor. *Educational Leadership, 37,* 15–24.

Education Commission of the States. (1983). *Action for excellence: A comprehensive plan to improve our nation's schools.* Washington, DC: Author.

Elkind, D. (1981). *The hurried child.* Reading, MA: Addison-Wesley.

Elliott, S. N., & Witt, J. C. (1986). *The delivery of psychological services in schools: Concepts, processes, and issues.* Hillsdale, NJ: Lawrence Erlbaum.

Fagan, T. K., & Delugach, F. J. (1985). Literary origins of the term "school psychologist." In L. K. Grimley (Ed.), *Historical perspectives on school psychology.* Terre Haute, IN: Indiana State University, School of Education.

Finn, J. D., & Resnick, L. B. (1984). Issues in instruction of mildly mentally retarded children. *Educational Researcher, 13,* 9–11.

Fisher, K. (1988, September). GOR plan fails; Other avenues of unity sought. *APA Monitor,* pp. 1, 4–5.

Gickling, E. E., & Havertape, J. (1981). Curriculum-based assessment. In J. Tucker, *Non test-based assessment.* Minneapolis, MN: University of Minnesota, National Inservice Training Network for School Psychology.

Glaser, R. (1982). Instructional psychology: Past, present, and future. *American Psychologist, 37,* 292–305.

Good, T. L., & Brophy, J. E. (1984). *Looking in classrooms* (3rd ed.). New York: Harper & Row.

Goodlad, J. I. (1984). *A place called school: Prospects for the future.* New York: McGraw-Hill.

Graden, J. L., Casey, A., & Bonstrom, O. (1985). Implementing a prereferral intervention system: Part II. The data. *Exceptional Children, 51,* 487–496.

Graden, J. L., Casey, A., & Christenson, S. L. (1985). Implementing a prereferral intervention system: Part I. The model. *Exceptional Children, 51,* 377–384.

Graden, J. L., Zins, J. E., & Curtis, M. J. (1988). *Alternative educational delivery systems: Enhancing instructional options for all students.* Washington, DC: National Association of School Psychologists.

Granger, R. C., & Campbell, P. B. (1977). The school psychologist as program evaluator. *Journal of School Psychology, 15,* 174–183.

Granowsky, S., & Davis, L. T. (1974). Three alternative roles for the school psychologist. *Psychology in the Schools, 11,* 415–421.

Gray, S. W. (1963). *The psychologist in the schools.* New York: Holt, Rinehart and Winston.

Grimley, L. K. (1985). Mapping the territory for historical study of school psychology. In L. K. Grimley (Ed.), *Historical perspectives on school psychology.* Terre Haute, IN: Indiana State University, School of Education.

Harris, L., & Associates. (1986). *Children's needs and public responsibilities: A survey of American attitudes about the problems and prospects of American children* (Study No. 863009). New York: Author.

Heller, K. A., Holtzman, W. H., & Messick, S. (Eds.). (1982). *Placing children in special education: A strategy for equity.* Washington, DC: National Academy Press.

Howe, H. (1986). *The prospect for children in the United States.* Keynote address at the Annual Convention of the National Association of School Psychologists, Hollywood, FL.

Katz, D., & Kahn, R. (1978). *The social psychology of organizations* (2nd ed.). New York: Wiley.

Lilly, J. S. (1986, March). The relationship between general and special education: A new face on an old issue. *Counterpoint,* pp. 9–10.

Magary, J. F. (Ed.). (1967). *School psychological services in theory and practice: A handbook.* Englewood Cliffs, NJ: Prentice-Hall.

Maher, C. A., Illback, R. J., & Zins, J. E. (1984). *Organizational psychology in the schools: A handbook for professionals.* Springfield, IL: Charles C Thomas.

Messick, S. (1984). Assessment in context: Appraising student performance in relation to instructional quality. *Educational Researcher, 13,* 3–8.

National Association of School Psychologists. (1985a, June). Advocacy for appropriate educational services for all children: A position statement. *NASP Communiqué,* p. 9.

National Association of School Psychologists. (1985b, September). *Long range planning report: Five-year priorities.* Adopted by the Executive Board/ Delegate Assembly of the NASP.

National Association of School Psychologists. (1987). *Membership directory.* Kent, OH: Author.

National Association of School Psychologists. (1988a, June). *Paid membership report.* Report to the Executive Board of the NASP.

National Association of School Psychologists. (1988b, July). *Annual budget for 1988–89.* Approved by the Delegate Assembly of the NASP.

National Coalition of Advocates for Students. (1985). *Barriers to excellence: Our children at risk.* Boston: Author.

National Commission on Excellence in Education. (1983). *A nation at risk: The imperative for educational reform.* Washington, DC: Superintendent of Documents, U.S. Government Printing Office.

National School Psychology Inservice Training Network. (1984). *School psychology: A blueprint for training and practice.* Minneapolis, MN: Author.

Packard, V. O. (1983). *Our endangered children: Growing up in a changing world.* Boston: Little, Brown.

Peterson, P. E. (1983). *Making the grade: Report of the Twentieth Century Fund task force on federal elementary and secondary education policy.* New York: The Twentieth Century Fund.

Prasse, D. P. (1985). *Legal influence and educational policy in special education: Comments on the NAS report.* Paper presented at the Convention of the American Psychological Association, Los Angeles.

Reger, R. (1965). *School psychology.* Springfield, IL: Charles C Thomas.

Reilly, D. H. (1973). School psychology: View from the second generation. *Psychology in the schools, 10,* 151–155.

Reschly, D. (1988). Special education reform: School psychology revolution. *School Psychology Review, 17,* 459–475.

Reschly, D., Genshaft, J., & Binder, M. (1987). *The 1986 NASP survey: Comparison of practitioners, NASP leadership, and university faculty on key issues.* Washington, DC: National Association of School Psychologists.

Reynolds, M. C., & Wang, M. (1983). Restructuring special school programs: A position paper. *Policy Studies Review, 2,* 189–212.

Rosenshine, B. (1983). Teaching functions in instructional programs. *Elementary School Journal, 83,* 335–351.

Rutter, M., Maughan, B., Mortimer, P., Ouston, J., & Smith, A. (1979). *Fifteen thousand hours.* Cambridge, MA: Harvard University Press.

Schein, E. H. (1969). *Process consultation: Its role in organization development.* Reading, MA: Addison-Wesley.

Shapiro, E. S., & Lentz, F. E. (1985). Assessing academic behavior: A behavioral approach. *School Psychology Review, 14,* 325–338.

Stern W. (1911). The supernormal child: II. *Journal of Educational Psychology, 2,* 181–190.

Teacher Education Division, Council for Exceptional Children. (1986). *A statement on the regular education initiative.* Reston, VA: Author.

Tindall, R. H. (1979). School psychology: The development of a Profession. In G. D. Phye & D. J. Reschly (Eds.), *School psychology: Perspectives and issues.* New York: Academic Press.

Tucker, J. A. (Ed.). (1985). Curriculum-based assessment [Special issue]. *Exceptional Children, 51.*

U.S. Congress, Senate. (1975, June 2). *Education for all handicapped children act,* 5.6., 94th Congress, 1st Session (Report No. 94-168).

Vallett, R. E. (1963). *The practice of school psychology: Professional problems.* New York: Wiley.

Walberg, H. J. (1984). Improving the productivity of America's schools. *Educational Leadership, 41,* 19–30.

Wang, M. C. (1987). Individual differences and effective schooling. *Professional School Psychology, 2,* 53–66.

Wang, M. C., & Baker, E. T. (1985). Mainstreaming programs: Design and future effects. *Journal of Special Education, 19,* 503–521.

Wang, M. C., & Birch, J. W. (1984). Comparison of a full-time mainstreaming program and a resource room approach. *Exceptional Children, 51,* 33–40.

Wang, M. C., Reynolds, M. C., & Walberg, H. J. (1986). Rethinking special education. *Educational Leadership, 44,* 26–31.

Waxman, H. C., Wang, M. C., Anderson, K. A., & Walberg, H. J. (1985). Synthesis of research on the effects of adaptive education. *Educational Leadership, 43,* 26–29.

Weintraub, F. J. (1986, March). Maybe we don't need dragons any more. *Counterpoint,* pp. 10–11.

Will, M. (1986). *Educating students with learning problems—A shared responsibility: A report to the Secretary of Education.* Washington, DC: U.S. Department of Education.

Ysseldyke, J. (1978). Who's calling the plays in school psychology? *Psychology in the Schools, 15,* 373–378.

Ysseldyke, J., & Christenson, S. L. (1986). *The instructional environment scale.* Austin, TX: Pro-Ed Publications.

Ysseldyke, J., & Weinberg, R. (Eds.). (1981). The future of psychology in the schools: Proceedings of the Spring Hill symposium [Entire issue]. *School Psychology Review, 10.*

OPINION 2
SCHOOL PSYCHOLOGY IN THE NEXT DECADE: A PERIOD OF SOME DIFFICULT DECISIONS

WALTER B. PRYZWANSKY
University of North Carolina at Chapel Hill

Writing about the future is always "risky business" even if the targeted time span covers only five to ten years. It may be especially dangerous for me, if I am to take my wife's reservations about my prognostication ability to heart. Recently she reminded me that in the early 1960s I predicted the demise of professional football! I quickly owned up to that one but added the fact that I am now older (and maybe a little wiser) and appreciate the need for a data base. Here again, I was reminded that the data base may never be as complete as one needs, as noted by the tombstone inscription that read, "I told you I was sick." Nevertheless, despite the reservations I should have, the practice of regularly taking stock and projecting direction for the immediate future is a practice I deem valuable. If nothing else, it may energize efforts to proactively participate in shaping that direction.

There are some significant developments taking place currently in the fields of education and psychology that will need to be addressed by the school psychology specialty. Otherwise, those developments will still have their impact but in a more uncontrollable manner than we would choose. So having forewarned the reader and reminded myself of the precariousness of this assignment, I shall share my thoughts in a most humble way.

In this chapter, I discuss some of the developments taking place in the disciplines of psychology and education that have the most potential for affecting the specialty of school psychology in a direct way. Both disciplines were quite germane to the evolution of school psychology. Given the fact that much of our training background is in psychology, but the practice takes place primarily in educational settings, only these two disciplines were chosen. Interestingly, both of these disciplines are undergoing similar types of changes. These changes have been seen as guild versus discipline issues by their constituencies; consequently, I have kept that dichotomy to organize the material, but recognize that the lines may blur between the two.

I trust the reader will tolerate what at times may seem an arbitrary or even forced placement of topics and understand that it was done to emphasize a specific point. Finally, several rather comprehensive future writings have appeared in the literature (Conoley, 1987; Fagan, 1986; Meyers, 1988; National School Psychology Inservice Training Network, 1984). Readers are also advised to consult these references in their own deliberations about issues in the future.

THE PROFESSIONAL MOVEMENT

Psychology Guild Issues
The applied psychology area has probably received more attention and reflection by all psychologists during the last decade than in any previous period of time. While it is true that external factors contributed to that reexamination and the sense of urgency for decision making that was initiated, it is also equally valid to attribute the changes that took place to the developmental stage of the applied psychology area. One could argue, as some did, that training and credentialing reviews were long overdue. In some instances it was clear that there was no commonly agreed upon definition of a professional psychologist. As a result, the basic tasks of identifying common elements of training for applied psychologists and generating credentialing criteria have begun to take shape. School psychologists, through the American Psychological Association's (APA) Division of School Psychology and later the APA Task Force on Psychology in the Schools, have been afforded the oppportunity to participate in the discussions and decision-making bodies that lead the way in such undertakings within American psychology circles.

However, it is now my perception that "professional psychology" is embarking on a reexamination of its evolution, and in particular, the conceptualization of the applied branch of psychology as contrasted to its scientific arm. The logical question has been raised regarding the advisability of beginning the training for all professional psychologists with a generic applied training base. Already there is agreement on the psychological foundations training core, as noted by its inclusion in guidelines for professional practice of the four initial applied psychology specialties (APA, 1981). Also, the core seems to have been embraced by psychology credentialing (AASPB/National Register, 1987) and accreditation bodies (APA, 1986). Such a shift in training, as the generic–applied psychology training core idea implies, might lead to specialty's such as school psychology, or specializations such as psychoneurology, being emphasized in the latter stages of academic doctoral training or even at the predoctoral or postdoctoral internship phase. I suspect that the task of defining those common "applied" training elements would be a far easier task for some school psychologists than would embracing the implication that school psychologists are psychologists, and thus a specialty in psychology rather than a profession unto itself. Perhaps this identity question may not seem as threatening, then, until one addresses the issue of when, as well as how, a specialty gets defined.

Regardless of the dangers of dealing with such proposed changes in applied psychology, it seems that school psychology soon will need to decide publicly if it is part of professional psychology. Given a positive response, school psychology training then would resemble more and more of a psychology model, which seems to be a shift that is in fact taking place at the moment. Although one could argue that such changes have already taken place so that the identity with professional psychology is a given, two related developments have the potential for dramatically influencing the characteristics of school psychology.

First, the American Psychological Association is in the midst of a soul-searching exercise targeted on reorganization. As it appears now, psychologists who identify with the scientist role, the practitioner role, and the scientist-practitioner role, respectively, are coalescing into organization entities, which for convenience sake will be referred to simply as "societies" in this chapter. This reorganization movement will require that APA members and Divisions make choices regarding their preference for realignment. The fact that the practitioner society appears to be representing the health service provider emphasis should make the

significance of the reorganization obvious to the school psychology specialty. Clearly, some individual school psychologists may choose the scientist-practitioner emphasis, while others will adopt the practitioner "professional" emphasis with its clear clinical and mental health focus. Although most school psychologists can legitimately fit into one of those roles, few would seem qualified to claim both.

Second, a parallel development is taking place within the psychology licensing arena. A licensing bill (APA, 1987) has recently been recommended by the APA as a model for states to consider. In that proposal, all psychologists must hold the doctorate by 1995; however, presently "certified" school psychologists are exempt from this requirement as well as the remaining requirements, as long as their "certified" practice remains in settings under the purview of the State Board of Education.

There are several concomitant features associated with licensure that will affect school psychology directly. For example, defining a professional psychologist as a health service practitioner would no doubt disenfranchise some school psychologists. Similarly, a more likely credentialing approach stressing specialization might have equally disruptive effects on the specialty.

In the first scenario, licensure as a health service provider would be associated with doctorate training and traditional clinical practice objectives. On the other hand, specialty credentialing would require further definition and delineation of school psychology "practice," and it is doubtful that the very heterogeneous description of contemporary school psychology would continue. For one thing, the current practices delineating school psychology training would be inconsistent with a model equating specialties with skills gained at the predoctoral or even doctoral level. Also, it would not be unreasonable to base specialty definitions on skill/practice variables rather than setting orientation. For some in the school psychology specialty, an understanding of setting specific variables is all that differentiates them from other psychology specialties.

It goes without saying that the applied psychologists, for whom psychology licensure is not relevant to their practice, would probably pay less attention to the credentialing nomenclature being derived and its myriad implications. But it is hard to imagine a situation where the role and function of that applied psychologist based on similar training would not resemble the role and function of the licensed psychologist. One objective of professional movements such as these credentialing changes involves the reduction of confusion in the public understanding of the profession, so that such a similarity would defeat that goal.

Psychology Discipline Issues

In the introductory section, psychology guild-related issues have been addressed along with their potential impact on school psychology in the last decade of this century. It is important that we address internal developments that have the potential to influence the future as well.

We have witnessed such a proliferation of emphases in school psychology practice that an objective reviewer of journal articles would have difficulty identifying the unique service provided by the school psychologist. At the same time, the specialist-trained school psychologist (see NASP Standards, 1986) has become the norm among practitioners, with great pressure put on the specialist to be a clearly credible practitioner. That expectation has led to assertions that where practice is concerned, sixth-year specialist training is equal to and even better and more relevant than doctoral training within either the school psychology specialty or generic psychology. The notion of the psychologist working in the schools, when combined with these forces, is leading to a potentially dangerous outcome for the specialty.

The specialist-trained school psychologist is becoming the standard for the practitioner in the schools, with doctoral training relegated to research functions and, in some instances, evaluation responsibilities. However, the specialist may, in fact, be coming to be trained increasingly as a technician who can demonstrate competency on this or that test, while at the same time striving to serve a wider age range of students and deal with a variety of problems. Commonly, then, we have come to think of the school psychologist as competent in a variety of roles and techniques.

Increasingly, we are training the specialists to be competent in carrying out a variety of specific tasks rather than bringing skills to bear on solving problems. For example, in the assessment area the question should not be, "Does the student qualify for the program?" but rather, "How can we better understand the student so that appropriate intervention can be offered?" Clearly, the prevalence and impact of federal legislation influencing services for handicapped children have imposed certain contingencies for funding to take place and, as such, contributed to the prescribed functions and tasks orientation that exists in the schools. However, we may have allowed that set of circumstances to influence priorities in didactic as well as field aspects of training to an alarming degree. School psychology seems to have moved from the goal of training professionals (problem solvers) to preparing people to serve a set of circumscribed functions. A technician "set" can be said to have come unwittingly to influence many school psychology programs. To the extent that the doctoral program is conceptualized as primarily an extension of the specialist training level into the research area, the doctoral program orientation remains at that level as well.

The evolution of the models of school psychological service also warrants our reflection. We continue to hang on to the idea (or act as if we do) that one school psychologist will provide all services to X number of pupils or X number of schools. It is no wonder that school staff are still not our strongest advocates; there are so many needs to fill and we must be able to assess all types of exceptionalities, provide direct behavioral and academic interventions from dealing with suicidal ideation to autism to deafness to the teaching of writing skills. As long as we think of replicating the ideal school psychologist with each graduate, we will be encouraged in preservice and continuing education training to master all tests and interventions while being forced into the technician mold noted above. The evaluation of the effectiveness of school psychological services rests on the evaluation of individual school psychologists. Where the match is right, for whatever reason, such as personalities, interest, or even politics, the reception of the administration and certain staff will be positive. Otherwise, the best we can hope for is a mild, positive reaction.

In another publication (Pryzwansky, 1987), it was argued that we should begin to consider alternatives to the definition of school psychological services from the perspective of a unit designed to deploy individuals. For example, we could think of the school psychology staff as representing a range of expertise that could be called upon in any one situation. Similarly, continuity of service to students and parents throughout their schooling needs consideration, as does the integrity of the services unit. These ideas are not stated unmindful of the realities in the school systems that support the current deployment practices, but rather, as a challenge to examine alternatives and/or variations to service.

Education Guild Issues

Similar to what applied psychology has recently experienced, the teacher education group is undergoing a reexamination and redefinition of itself as a profession. The issue of entry into the profession has loomed most prominent in those discussions along with the encouragement of professional tier arrangements where supervisory/master/mentor teachers are expected to assume more of a leadership role in the instructional area. It is not the place of this chapter to review all of the recent reports that are contributing to this atmosphere of reform. The reader is encouraged to examine other important works (Carnegie Forum on Education and the Economy, 1986; Holmes Group, 1986; National Commission Excellence in Education, 1983).

In some circles, most notably schools of education, these developments have led to a discussion of the defining characteristics of the "discipline," or profession, of education. What are the core knowledge areas that all educators should possess, from both an acculturation and a practice orientation? The next step is for the education profession to be considered in terms of its specialties, and it is at this point that school psychology's place comes under scrutiny. From a resource allocation standpoint, educational specialties, and the programs that train for those specialties, would have the greatest priority in schools of education. Presumably, school psychology would have to be considered further removed from the core specialties (teacher education, school administration, school counseling) in most conceptual frameworks even though it has made great strides in terms of being accepted as an educational support service.

Two factors may account for the minimum attention currently being paid to school psychology's "fit" within the education training framework. First, perhaps, an overwhelming preoccupation with teacher education is consuming most of the energy in the schools of education for the time being. Second, it may be that the school psychology program in many schools of education is among the stronger programs when criteria such as faculty research, productivity, and quality of students are used to evaluate programs. Therefore,

the degree of "fit" may not be as relevant a consideration as the prestige the program helps bring to the school.

Nevertheless, we must be sensitive to the real possibility that the forces being brought to bear on teaching preparation programs, in the form of defining teaching as a profession, will probably move schools of education to a next logical conceptualization of the education field. A large percentage of school psychology doctoral programs, as well as master's programs, are in schools of education. Quality may not be enough *if* the primary criterion for inclusion of a program in the school is conceptual fit. The specialty's role within the education discipline becomes a factor in such decision making, along with the mission statement of the school. School psychology training programs, particularly those within schools of education, need to wrestle with the special demands and opportunities their unique placement in the university structure affords; they need to do that now. This does not necessarily mean divorcing ourselves from psychology, but does suggest that we increase our ties to education in visible and meaningful ways.

Barring some unexpected turn in the professionalism of the education movement, the questions posed in this section and others are just around the corner. For example, does school psychology have a responsibility in teacher education, and if so, what should the nature and amount of that input be? Of the eventual roles that school psychologists will be asked to fulfill in the school setting, what preservice experiences with education students would facilitate the effectiveness with which they will function?

School psychology can significantly enhance the educational experience of education majors through participation in the teacher education reform movement. Preservice contacts with school psychologists could serve as important experiences for educational professionals by contributing to their skills and perspectives while exposing them to a resource that they can utilize during their initial years in the profession as well as throughout their careers. Typically, teachers-in-training learn about school psychological services through a presentation on school support services in one of their courses; usually, that presentation also covers other resources, such as school counseling, special education, and social work, and the presentation is not made by a school psychologist. There may not be a better way to instill an appreciation of the range of knowledge and services available from school psychologists than through systematic early training contacts.

Just as psychology is struggling with defining specialities in terms of proficiencies in skills and techniques, the same questions are arising in the educational arena. As in psychology, it would seem reasonable to assume that all professional specialities would have training in a common foundation core and, furthermore, that each specialty's training core would be related to the discipline. The concept of a required education discipline core is not often discussed or given much consideration in school psychology circles, although it does receive some attention in the standards documents of APA and NASP. It certainly seems to be the prerogative of the education discipline and is variably defined from state to state or among schools of education.

The APA Specialty Guidelines (1981) refer to a core of academic experience in the basic psychology areas and training in the specialty areas of assessment, intervention, consultation, research, program development, and supervision, "with special emphasis on school-related problems or school settings" (p. 35). Coursework that is mentioned includes "social and philosophical bases of education, curriculum theory and practice, etiology of learning and behavior disorders, exceptional children, and special education . . . as well as organization theory and administrative practice" (p. 43). The NASP Standards lists educational foundations as one of four preparation areas with the following specific content included: education of exceptional learners; instructional and remedial techniques; and organization and operation of schools (NASP, 1986).

There seems to be less concern and controversy about the need for, as well as content of, the foundation core. The dilemma may arise when the instructional versus mental health core emphasis of the specialty is addressed. Although it could be argued that the school psychologist should bring a psychological background in each core area relevant to the schooling process, some still see the school psychologist primarily either as an applied educational psychologist or child clinical/developmental specialist rather than as the bridge between the two emphases. To the degree that the latter emphasis moves away from field-related training in schools, and the majority of graduates enter "school-related" settings and/or private

practice, program viability in a school of education becomes precarious. This observation is not meant to dismiss educators' priority on adjustment problems of students (e.g., discipline, teenage pregnancy, substance abuse, suicide, etc.), but simply to point out that where direct, school-related training and practice are not obvious, the program is seen as tangential (and sometimes it is seen that way regardless of obvious school setting connections). Also, to the extent that the school psychology specialty becomes nonacademically focused, such a mental health emphasis is questioned by faculty colleagues. But to deny that there is a need for such psychologists in the school disregards an area of need emphasized by educators.

However, the learning and/or instructional emphasis is not without its distraction, for it is in this area that other educational specialties lay claim to expertise and the interest in reconfiguration of the school psychology program with another education training program can arise. Personnel providing such assistance are typically viewed as adequately trained at the master's level, and in another sense, such a role could be conceptualized as a specialty within the teaching profession.

Education Discipline Issues

A discipline issue closely aligned to the education guild issues that have just been presented involves the research efforts of both faculty and students in the school psychology program, as well as those of the practitioner. As noted earlier, there are many student mental health problems that concern educators. It is unclear what degree of prioritization educators give to a service of prevention and intervention outside the classroom, as compared to their rating of the importance of how psychological factors interact with and affect cognition. Similarly unclear is the degree to which applied research, whether intervention based or not, needs to be educationally relevant both in training and application in the school system to have acceptance and credibility in those settings.

Arguments can be made from the perspective of the specialty that all research will eventually influence practice at some point. However, it seems now that the specialty needs to both articulate the wide-ranging research emphases that characterize its literature and explain why some psychology interests, which might be construed as clinical or experimental, hold importance for the specialty. For example, anorexia among college women, sexual practices, and the relation of cognition to phobic conditions are topics that may be difficult to justify in the context just described. The task for school psychologists is to demonstrate how a diverse research thrust is integrated into a relevant information base for learning and instruction. To not attempt this task contributes to the confusion regarding our uniqueness as a psychology specialty with a place in the educational setting. As always, this task needs to be done in such a way that it illustrates our uniqueness versus the perception that we are psychologists who are tangential and not part of the schooling process, or on the other hand, perform a service that should be the responsibility of an education specialty.

Credentialing of educational personnel, particularly teachers, is another professional area receiving a degree of attention comparable to that being experienced in psychology. The certification process, as it is referred to in education, seems to be flirting with a two-level system (i.e., an initial certification status that is followed by a level which may or may not signify permanent certification status). At the second level, various types of provisions for renewal may be included rather than a simple, permanent certification status. As a result of the teacher education reform movement of the past few years, the notion of a national certification examination has begun to take hold (Carnegie, 1986). This reconsideration of the concept and process of teacher education certification has led to pressure on educationally related specialties such as school counseling and social work to bring their credentialing efforts into line with the teacher certification model adopted in their respective states. For school psychology, this movement has meant the direction of effort to the development of state school psychology certification examinations, and no doubt these challenges have served as the impetus for the development of a national certification examination in school psychology endorsed by NASP ("Delegate assembly," 1988).

Although there seems to be no doubt that the credentialing efforts are as needed in education as they were in psychology, there is a dilemma for school psychologists. School psychologists can already be credentialed (Psychology Licensure), and the specialty is recognized at an advanced practice level (Diplomate in School Psychology from the American Board of Professional Psychology). Since the state departments of public instruction (SDPI) probably will not give up their authority to

credential educational professionals to work in the schools (and probably should not), a dual, parallel system of credentialing in psychology and education for school psychologists seems inescapable. Such a system, however, does not appear to be economically reasonable, and conceptually, it represents a potential disenfranchisement of doctoral-level school psychologists (Pryzwansky, 1989).

It is unfortunate that leaders in the school psychology area have not yet begun to address the credentialing dilemmas that are being fostered by such dual developments. One simple but conceptually sound first step may be the investigation of an integrated credentialing system that would avoid duplication and cognitive dissonance for our constituencies (Pryzwansky, 1987). Otherwise, to pursue the national certification examination alone, we could unwittingly and significantly de-emphasize our linkage to psychology, if not our claim to be psychologists.

The credentialing of school psychologists at the specialist level by SDPI also is not free of complications. The more that the specialty drifts to an alignment with teacher education where certification matters are concerned, the more likely that resolutions of related issues will be resolved similarly. Take, for example, the shortage of classroom teachers experienced in certain content areas and geographic locations, which is projected to be reflected generally in the teacher education profession very shortly. One commonly held resolution for these personnel needs involves on-the-job training (professional training) of people who hopefully have some related experience and background (i.e., lateral entry). If this model were applied to school psychology certification, what would be the equivalent of specialist training for those with a one-year master's degree in psychology? in social work? in school counseling? in special education? Who would determine acceptance into a lateral entry position and the criteria that must be met for certification eligibility? Has anyone asked if this is the appropriate model to deal with personnel shortages? What is done in other professions when shortages exist? Would there be pressure and/or interest in resurrecting the psychometrician level of certification?

The credentialing process has many other ramifications for school psychology, and the manner in which the current, rather basic decisions are made could serve as the road map for future, wide-ranging decisions regarding our evolution.

The question for the short-term future may not be will our standards rise (Fagan, 1986), but will we lower them?

The role of school psychologists has been a preoccupation of the specialty since its inception as a resource for the schools. It was noted earlier that the role has had a very service-oriented emphasis and has unquestionably been tied to assessment tasks. But as we provided more service, the demand for the service increased to the point where a cyclical pattern grew out of hand, especially during the early part of this decade, when schools were faced with dwindling resources. As argued earlier, there are realistic limits not only on the range of services that one school psychologist can offer, but also on the amount of service. Bardon (1983) articulated a professional model that lends itself to a resource or consultant conceptualization vis-á-vis the school setting. Given a professional definition, the number of school psychologists that are needed could be very different from a service-oriented role definition. Perhaps the schools need both types, but we might get along better and achieve our mutual goals if we step back and make our personnel decisions within a professional framework rather than a simple service-need framework.

Finally, we must begin to question the meaning of the drift of our school psychology graduates into settings other than the traditional K-12 school. While private practice has always remained an option, the number of school psychologists in full-time private practice has remained very small (5%), and even this practice could be conceptualized as remaining school oriented (Pryzwansky, 1989). Consequently, it is not private practice per se that is the source of this question, but rather the employment of school psychologists in university counseling centers, university-affiliated facilities, children's hospital units, child psychiatric facilities, family counseling centers, and mental health projects and centers. To applaud these developments is natural, for it signifies the credibility of the psychological training that takes place in the school psychology programs, while also serving as one type of recognition by our psychological colleagues that the specialty has matured. The realization of such opportunities is seductive, but it may bode negatively for the specialty, especially at the doctoral level, where there is some agreement that the number of students is growing and that it could eventually be the prevalent level of training (Fagan, 1987).

Is it possible that the specialty at this level may be becoming a pediatric/developmental/child psychology specialty? Although we could agree that a setting descriptor (i.e., school) may not be warranted for a specialty title, the "school" descriptor did at least suggest that the facilitation of the schooling process served as the prime interest and focus of the school psychologist. Of course, it is argued that the interest and focus of school psychologists remains the same regardless of setting, and that argument is true in some instances. Nevertheless, the specialty would still need to be alert if "specialized schooling" is what we are now focusing on. However, there are employment patterns where the alternative setting explanation is harder to justify within the traditional conceptualization of school psychology. Perhaps, in our enthusiasm to embrace the schooling concept (Bardon, 1983) and not be limited to the school institution emphasis, we have been pulled further and further away from the prime goal of facilitating learning. Again, in relationship to their organization's mission and state personnel needs, school of education graduate programs would seem to be in a dilemma when their graduates' employment patterns become so diverse.

CONCLUSIONS

Given the charge to write a "futures" chapter, the temptation to tackle specifics of the future for school psychologists was ever present. Although this type of reflection obviously needs to be an ongoing process, which itself should reflect ongoing changes, the emphasis on general guiding assumptions to plan must also be considered. A return to the issue discussed earlier, of professionalism versus the technician-oriented occupation, helps to illustrate this point. Competent, skill-oriented persons with integrity and commitment to do a job well are highly valued and needed in all segments of our society. Similarly, there is an expectation that their skills are constantly refined, added to, and expanded. However, there is a difference in their training and practice versus that of a professional, where the goal is problem resolution rather than task completion. The implications of this choice may be abstract, and not apparent in terms of specifics, but they are profound. So it is from this perspective that these comments are presented. In the fields of both psychology and education there are a number of challenges being addressed that impinge on the "directions" school psychology can take; these in turn, influence the assumptions we adopt or come to incorporate in a subtle and perhaps less intentional way.

In conclusion, there are at least four challenges that emerge from this reflection on the future for school psychology. Those challenges will be explored briefly and not necessarily in order of importance.

First, school psychologists need to become an integral part of the educational process at both the training and practice level. The fact that school psychologists are among the first to lose their positions in the face of shrinking resources may or may not be an indication of our current status. This goal may be inextricably tied to the accepted definition of public school education, but regardless, we must make that linkage. It does not seem that the definition of school psychology as an education specialty will resolve this challenge in the long run or that a switch from an identity with psychology needs to be considered. The current uniqueness of the school psychology specialty is what justifies our involvement in the educational process from preschool through postsecondary levels. We must operationalize that connection in both the training and practice areas.

Second, the progress that has been made toward the professionalism of school psychology needs to be enhanced in the next decade. The growth in accreditation from the APA and the efforts of the NASP to include specialist and doctoral programs in the National Council for the Accreditation of Teacher Education have been a powerful impetus in this direction. However, to become overly influenced by some setting needs, where certain responsibilities might more legitimately be handled by an educational specialist, may continue to reinforce a task-oriented definition of the school psychologist. Similarly, to allow guild issues or professional organizational issues to influence excessively the development of the specialty would be a serious detraction from the commitment to this goal.

Third, the diversity and/or heterogeneity that seems to characterize the specialty has often been noted as a quality attracting students to school psychology programs. It may be for the same reason that when we try to define ourselves, there is less agreement and clarity than we would like. Yet we seem to be promoting even more diversification of the specialty. A rationale for this state of affairs definitely needs to be considered and reflected in our service delivery models as well as our descriptions of the role of the individual school psychologist. Schools are responding to ever-expanding changes to deal with wide ranges of populations based on age, cultural background, and educational "problems." However, can this specialty be all things to all these school needs? We need to decide on what is common to all school psychologists, if not the setting in which they practice. Otherwise, we will continue to argue this definition as we have in the past because of the different assumptions that we make rather than the question of identity itself.

Finally, we must turn our attention to the task of attracting, and then keeping, the best and the brightest of the specialty as leaders in the nation's public schools and training programs. It would be ironic if we were to deemphasize this setting at a time in which there is educator interest in the specialty, and educators' priorities, in terms of their needs, fall within our bailiwick. The promise for school psychology, as one translator of the psychology knowledge base and vehicle for bringing a psychological perspective to bear in the education of the nation's children and youth, can truly become realized in the next decade. The opportunities to achieve that objective seem better than ever before. We can become a partner in the education reform movement, if that is where we want to specialize.

REFERENCES

American Association of State Psychology Boards and the National Register of Health Service Providers in Psychology. (1987). *Designated doctoral programs in psychology.* Washington, DC: Authors.

American Psychological Association. (1981). *Specialty guidelines for the delivery of services.* Washington, DC: Author.

American Psychological Association. (1986). *Accreditation handbook.* Washington, DC: Author.

American Psychological Association. (1987). Model act for state licensure of psychologists. *American Psychologist, 42,* 696–703.

Bardon, J. I. (1983). Psychology applied to education. *American Psychologist, 38,* 185–196.

Carnegie Forum on Education and the Economy. (1986). *A nation prepared: Teachers for the 21st century.* New York: Author.

Conoley, J. C. (1987). "Dr. Future, we presume," said school psychology. *Professional School Psychology, 2,* 173–180.

Delegate assembly adopts national certification system. (1988, May). *NASP Communiqué,* p. 14.

Fagan, T. K. (1986). School psychology's dilemma. *American Psychologist, 41,* 851–861.

Holmes Group, Inc. (1986). *Tomorrow's teachers: A report of the Holmes Group.* East Lansing, MI: Author.

Meyers, J. (1988). School psychology: The current state of practice and future practice of the specialty. *Professional School Psychology, 3,* 165–176.

National Association of School Psychologists. (1986). *Standards.* Washington, DC: Author.

National Commission on Excellence in Education. (1983). *A nation at risk: The imperative for educational reform.* Washington, DC: Superintendent of Documents, U.S. Government Printing Office.

National School Psychology Inservice Training Network. (1984). *School psychology: A blueprint for training and practice.* Minneapolis, MN: Author.

Pryzwansky, W. B. (1987). What type of licensure for school psychologists? *Professional Practice of Psychology, 8,* 1–6.

Pryzwansky, W. B. (1989). The private practice dimension of school psychology service delivery. In R. D. D'Amato & R. S. Dean. (Eds.), *The school psychologist in nontraditional settings: Integrating clients, services and settings* (pp. 67–85). Hillsdale, NJ: Lawrence Erlbaum.

OPINION 3
SCHOOL PSYCHOLOGY AFTER THE 1980s: ENVISIONING A POSSIBLE FUTURE

JOHN H. JACKSON
Milwaukee Board of School Directors

The opinions expressed in this chapter are premised on the assumption that school psychology in the 1980s has been a health care specialty and that its future will be the same. The author also assumes that school psychological services are and will continue to be provided within the overall educational enterprise. This is to say that school psychology functions to establish, enhance, and/or maintain the psychological well-being of individuals who are actively engaged in the conscious pursuit of studying and learning. The psychological well-being of the individual helps to facilitate the processes involved in the acts of studying and learning (e.g., attention, concentration, perception, retrieval, thinking, integration of ideas, abstracting, summarizing, drawing conclusions, and tolerating openness and the suspension of immediate judgment). Similarly, the psychological well-being of the individual has positive ramifications for feelings and emotions, the affect that fuels study and learning (e.g., self-regarding attitudes relative to scholarly activities, persistence, purpose, interpersonal relations, management of pressures and frustrations, and the general affect related to the self concept).

French (1985) has pointed out that earlier broadly defined roles for school psychologists had begun to narrow by the decades of the 1960s and 1970s. This was a time when psychologists were

counted on to test students and to inform classroom teachers how to instruct and otherwise work with the tested students on the basis of the test results. In those distant days, teachers, as a group, were not perceived as being broadly and deeply knowledgeable and understanding of how to teach children with learning problems (Brophy, 1982). That situation has changed over the years. Today, classroom teachers, as a whole, are perceived as being more sophisticated in these matters (Brophy, 1982). Nevertheless, there are yet numerous teachers who quite often indicate that they want someone else to take the child away and work with him or her elsewhere or to place him or her in a special education class for problem learners. Not all teachers have gained the modern sophistication, motivation, and skills necessary to teach troubled students. Individual teacher knowledge and understanding, although improved, is far from complete; what is important, however, is that as a group they see themselves as quite competent in terms of teaching their subject matter. The increase in teachers' knowledge base and heightened self-confidence are major factors in their relationship with school psychologists. Unfortunately, many who write and teach in the area of school psychology seem not to recognize these recent and dramatic changes.

The effectiveness of classroom teachers in the

teaching of subject matter has been reported in the literature. Eubanks and Levine (1983) and Harmon (1983) have discussed teacher effectiveness in two different teaching models in reporting on the effective schools movement and team teaching, respectively. Hunt (1981) has discussed earlier teacher disappointment with static school psychology reports that did not facilitate instruction, and his belief that *effective* teachers are also psychologists who, as such, can intuit and match student learning styles with instructional approaches for effective results. Perhaps this assessment of the *effective* teacher is justified to some extent, since teaching academics to students is the primary *raison d'être* for teachers.

In order to work harmoniously within this context, and effectively as partners with teachers in the service of children, the job of school psychologists is to help with student affect and emotions, especially with affect/emotion-impacted cognition and conation, rather than proposing to teach teachers how to teach their subject matter. Properly, the school psychologist's primary task is that of supporting the psychological health of the learner-as-learner.

SCHOOL PSYCHOLOGY AS A HEALTH CARE SPECIALTY WITHIN PSYCHOLOGY

School psychology is one of three psychological specialties recognized by the American Psychological Association (1983) as health care specialties, the others being clinical psychology and counseling psychology. These three psychological specialties, therefore, have much in common. For the most part, they deliver the same types of services: therapy, consultation, and diagnosis. Often they see the same types of recipients, who variously may be called patients, clients, and referred students, and who may be suffering from any number of psychological dysfunctions. Psychologists who are familiar with the work of the three specialties find it difficult to distinguish among them, except on the basis of the setting in which they typically work (Fox, Kovacs, & Graham, 1985). Job analysis of licensed psychologists document great overlap among the established specialties (Rosenfeld, Shimberg, & Thorton, 1984). Even employing the American Psychological Association (APA) criteria for the recognition of psychological specialties (APA, 1984), it has been

difficult to distinguish clearly among clinical, counseling, and school, again except by the setting in which services typically are delivered by each. Consequently, there are those who maintain that there are no real differences among the three specialties—that they all are clinical psychology with a little "c."

At the same time, there are those who will have no part of the idea of no difference among school, counseling, and clinical psychology. They hold out a number of reasons why the three health care specialties are different, one from the other. One such position is taken in the documentation prepared by Dyer (1984) at the request of the Division of School Psychology of the American Psychological Association, and promulgated by that division. These school psychologists especially are adamant in arguing that their specialty is broader than clinical and counseling—that service delivery within the educational enterprise is distinguishing.

The future relationship of school psychology with clinical and counseling psychology could take direction from one of the two positions portrayed immediately above. In those cases, school psychology would either be conceptualized as merely the practice of clinical psychology in the school setting or it would continue as a separate clinical (little "c") practice specialty. One alternative to these two possibilities will be considered in this chapter; it is a position that posits aspects of both the aforementioned positions.

THE CONCEPT OF GENERAL PRACTICE IN PSYCHOLOGY

Ordinarily, within a profession the first level of practice, the entry level, is that of general practice (e.g., medicine). This is a broad and general level of practice based on broad principles, knowledge, skills, and understandings; it serves the largest number of clients. Subsequent to admission to general practice, the practitioner is able, through further study, experience, and supervision, to qualify for specialty practice. This a more specialized and limited practice, based on a selected knowledge, skills, and experience base, and intended to serve a relatively smaller number of clients.

General practice in psychology, as used in this chapter, refers to the delivery of psychological services designed to alleviate psychological problems that are common to most individuals. Most of the time, general psychological practice would be the front-line practice. It would be that psychological service first sought out by individuals when they felt critical emotional distress, psychological discomfort, increasing tensions, and other indicators of psychological ill health. General psychological practitioners, as front-line service providers, would provide emergency services of a psychological nature.

Alpert (1985), in addressing change within a profession, has discussed what she calls the visionary future, which, in some ways, relates to the concept of general practice; her vision reveals further what general practice potentially might include. She speaks of community primary prevention, environmental primary prevention, and individual primary prevention. Subsumed under these primary preventions are, for example, programs assisting with decisions about becoming parents, an informational and referral registry, preparent and parent intervention programs, programs to help children cope with different environments, and facilitating the development of individual adaptive skills for personal problem solving.

General practitioners also would serve quite frequently as referral sources to other psychologists whose practices are limited to given specialty areas (e.g., clinical, school, and counseling). From time to time, the general psychological practitioner might find it appropriate to refer individuals to specialists outside the field of psychology; these other specialists would include but not be limited to neurologists and other physicians, speech pathologists, social workers, and educational specialists. The general practitioner presumably might work continually in some way with the person who has been referred to the specialist, and the specialist would continually provide information to the general practitioner that assists in the ongoing professional service delivery relationship between the client and general practitioner.

Education and training for service delivery as a general psychological practitioner would in part be separated from the education and training of those who are preparing for immediate entry into specialty practice. This necessarily would be the case, since both training and supervised experiences would be different for the two types of practitioners.

Psychology currently does not allow its students and practitioners the opportunity to pro-gress in the profession from general practice to specialty practice. *There is no general practice in psychology.* One studies and prepares in psychology from the beginning as a specialist, not as a generalist. Psychology courses at the undergraduate level and at the master's level are primarily in the science of psychology and not in the area of professional practice. Therefore, the psychology student who would practice in the profession prepares in clinical psychology, counseling psychology, industrial-organizational psychology, or school psychology according to the American Psychological Association, or in one of these four specialties or in clinical neuropsychology or forensic psychology according to the American Board of Professional Psychology.

A major shortcoming of the general practice vacuum in professional psychology is that the recognized specialties are relatively narrow and do not treat the overall individual. As a result of this limitation in the face of broad personal needs of the individual, the specialties have increasingly reached out to cover more and more of the person and thereby have increasingly overlapped in functioning or services delivered. Clinical, counseling, and school psychology provide counseling, therapy, consultation, psychological evaluation, assessment, and diagnosis. This confounds their status as separate psychological specialties, without giving the field a general psychological practice specialty.

The overlap among school, clinical, and counseling psychology, at least to some extent, causes additional shortcomings. Practitioners are in competition with each other. One specialty area may try to dominate or denigrate another. There is the continual quest for self-definition. A real need exists to be able to differentiate among the specialties fairly clearly in order to help set aside the confusion and internecine warfare that seems ever to be with us. The interposition of a field of general psychology practice would help to push the specialties of school, counseling, and clinical psychology back away from each other so that less confusion would exist and the so-called generic specialties of school, counseling, and clinical psychology could develop as true specialty areas.

Psychology takes pride in recognizing that it is a science and a profession that is based on that science. The practice of general psychology will rest on a base of research that subsumes the combined bases of school, clinical, and counseling.

Research from this broadened base could be expected to address a larger universe of especially relevant areas to general practice.

CONFLUENCE AND OVERLAP OF SCHOOL, COUNSELING, AND CLINICAL PSYCHOLOGY AS THE AREA OF GENERAL PRACTICE

The overlap is not insignificant or unimportant. This confluence of school, counseling, and clinical psychology is broad and deep. It seems obvious, at least to this writer, that the confluence of the three specialty areas, encompassing typical referral problems, together with the knowledge, skills, tools, and understandings relative thereto, may form the basis for the general practice of psychology.

The *problems* seen by the specialists, who today are school, clinical, and counseling psychologists, often are appropriate for general practice in psychology. They occur frequently and are not always severely debilitating. They are transient and ephemeral. They are acute. They are subject to recurring patterns and should be checked on and monitored routinely during the year. Some are so transparent that they are not really psychological problems at all and, therefore, deserve to be so identified and perhaps referred elsewhere—such as to a guidance counselor at the local school. The apparent problems of these individuals merely are reflecting the psychological problems of their families, their teachers, or others to whom they are closely related in some manner. For best results, these real but potentially short-term problems deserve to be dealt with by professionals whose training has specifically focused on them and on similar difficulties; their great frequency and the inconvenience they cause their victims, to say nothing of their chronic, nagging discomfort, call for providers who are especially trained to minister to them.

All too often specialists view behavior from a rather biased vantage point. They look for and seek psychopathology with every referral; thus they find it. Ysseldyke, Algozzine, Regan, and McGue (1981) have documented this type of behavior in populations they have studied. This phenomenon is readily seen when a child is referred as being possibly of superior ability. The referral is made to obtain an evaluation to determine the level of intellectual functioning and any potential psychological problems that might surface and become a stumbling block to academic achievement within a more pressure-filled learning situation than the regular classroom at school (e.g., a superior ability program). Although the child has evidenced no behavior or affect problems to date, quite often the specialist will assess the child and write a report that conveys a picture of psychopathology. One not knowing the child but reading the report would certainly conclude that the child had major problems, even though he or she had good psychological health, in fact. In actuality, the child of this nature needs to be served by a practitioner with a more balanced view. The usual view of the general practitioner in psychology would be that more balanced view—the view of the child from the more normal functioning perspective.

The *content or knowledge dimensions required* to practice successfully on the types of problems indicated above as appropriate to general psychological practice include such subareas as human development and growth, normal children and how they function, gray-area children or children at risk versus special education children, the nature and range of normal child and adolescent peer interaction, criteria required to document minimal psychopathology, normal intelligence and its variations and deviations, and how children in different ethnic groups express affect and emotions that are acceptable within their respective groups. Doubtless the general practitioner in psychology also will require knowledge, understanding, and skills in such usual content areas as psychopathology and differential diagnosis, assessment and intervention or treatment, and referral making for normal range and moderately involved children, adolescents, and adults.

For the problems identified previously, the general practitioner in psychology, as suggested earlier, will provide those psychological *services* found in the overlap area among school, counseling, and clinical psychology, such as assessment-evaluation-diagnosis, consultation, and treatment interventions, including various therapies. Services would include routine semiannual psychological checkups and monitoring. Also included would be preventive services such as treatment to prevent handicapping tensions (e.g., stress inoculation and behavioral rehearsal). This does not prevent psychological specialists from employing these services at their level with specialized problems.

Certain types of therapy probably would prove to be more feasible than other types for general practitioners, although no approach to therapy would be excluded arbitrarily. Long-term therapy would probably not be employed, or would be employed on a relatively infrequent basis, since long-term therapy most often is used with major or complicated psychological problems. Crisis counseling, time-limited therapy, and short-term therapies in general may prove to be therapies of choice for the types of problems suggested above as being appropriate to general practice; they can respond to the here-and-now problems, the more-surface-level problems, and/or the transient problems.

A large number, if not all, of the "nontherapy" interventions currently subsumed by school psychology can be expected to be useful at the level of general practice. This category includes, but is not limited to, supportive relationships, sensory-motor skills training, and preacademic skills training. As more attention is focused on these interventions, the number and type can be expected to increase.

At the general practice level, group therapy as well as individual therapy may be provided. Problems at this level may be related more to interpersonal than to intrapersonal matters and, therefore, may respond to group approaches. Long-term therapy most frequently would be reserved for use by specialists as they work with especially knotty problems, chronic problems, and problems that have been refractory to intervention efforts at the general practice level, all generally of an intrapersonal nature.

It may be that general practice in psychology will be *the* vehicle for consultation to become a viable form of intervention in the schools, which it is not at the present time. If the child or the adolescent has a mild or moderate problem, then, indeed, it may be realistic and helpful to intervene through consulting with the parent or teacher of the identified client. They might be effective in using the consultation of the general practitioner to work with the child or themselves when the problem is not intense, widespread, and/or chronic.

Psychological reports will need to describe individual functioning without necessarily presenting a picture of pathology. The general practitioner in psychology will need to feel secure enough to state, as may be true in a particular case, that "this child has not evidenced a psychological problem,"

regardless of whether the parents accept the evaluation or not. The general practitioner will not feel obligated to make a problem case out of a non-problem case simply because a referring person insists that the child has a psychological problem. Similarly, the general practitioner will not minimize a problem merely to avoid appropriately referring it to a psychological specialist, if such is needed.

In using consultation as a more workable form of intervention, the general practitioner may reduce the need to prepare the usual written psychological report. The briefest type of statement, if one is needed at all, might serve to transmit the information to the caretaker or to the client. If one assumes that quite frequently no psychological problem will be found, one may conclude that word of mouth could transmit this information in many instances.

When the school psychologists, clinical psychologicsts, and counseling psychologists treat the problems indicated above as being common to practice within the three specialty areas, they employ *skills, techniques,* and *tools* that also are common to the three specialty areas. Therefore, these skills, techniques, and tools would be appropriate to general practice in psychology. That is, their use could be *emphasized* in general practice. General practice would have no exclusive claim to them.

The skills and techniques that are referred to within this context include, but are not limited to, the following (each of which might be employed with either individuals or groups):

- Systematic observations: planned, controlled, unobtrusive, and measured observations of the client's overt behavior within a variety of situations at varying time points and for varying lengths of time
- Perceptive listening: listening to the client's overt and covert content and affective messages
- Surveying a general situation: determining visually or otherwise the overall characteristics and problems of the client's condition or the client in context
- Screening: determining client eligibility for specific tasks or assignments
- Monitoring within the natural environment: follow-through, unobtrusive checkups on the client within his or her natural habitat
- Data gathering and use: collecting and inter-

preting global, intrapersonal information on the client

- Matching interventions or treatments with evaluations: providing therapeutic intervention based on evaluation, assessment, or diagnosis of the client's broad range of complaints and problems
- Therapeutic interventions: providing individual, group, or child-in-family therapy for mild-to-moderate emotional disturbance

The tools referred to for use in general practice would include many of the tests, scales, schedules, interventions, and so on, currently used in school, clinical, and counseling psychology. The tools per se would not be as important as the way they would be used with the client. Administration, scoring, interpretation, and diagnosis appropriate to the level of problem at hand would be all-important. For example, the same intelligence test would be used in general practice as would be used in specialty practice, but the interpretations of data collected with the test would be relevant to the child, adolescent, or adult seeking general practice services for a mild-to-moderate problem rather than for a severe case.

Similar to the differential use of psychological tools for the general practice level would be the differential use of techniques for the general practice level. Client termination from counseling or therapy, for example, might be handled differently by specialists versus generalists. Ordinarily, the specialist would see a client and terminate the case when the targeted problem or condition goes into remission. On the other hand, the general practitioner would expect the client to return for appointments at regular intervals during the year and/or from year to year for general services. There would be mental health or psychological checkups on a recurring basis. Therefore, the general practitioner in psychology would not terminate the case. Rather, he or she would terminate a specific technique (e.g., brief therapy) with the client. The client would continue as a client of the general practitioner.

In general, skills, techniques, tools, and so on, that probably would prove to be most appropriate to the general practice level would be those that require a minimum amount of time and yield information about overall client functioning that the general practitioner could interpret clinically to yield hypotheses about relatively broad behaviors

or functions of the client. This would contrast with the narrower behavioral or functional concerns that the specialists in school psychology would have for his or her client. Needless to say, there would be overlap, since general and speciality practice are not mutually exclusive. To be more specific regarding criteria for selecting skills, tools, and techniques, one would expect the general practitioner to make more use of drawings, incomplete sentences, word association, and interviews than of major projective techniques for obtaining information on the personality and emotions of the client. One would expect more use in general practice of intelligence testing than of neuropsychological testing. Presumably, there would be more use of assessment tools that employ specific questions, answers, and scores than of those requiring clinical interpretation.

RELATIONSHIP OF GENERAL PRACTICE OF PSYCHOLOGY AND SCHOOL PSYCHOLOGY AS A PSYCHOLOGICAL SPECIALTY

The general practice of psychology would interface, as private general practice or institutional general practice, with the new specialty of school psychology in at least three ways. First, general practice would be a source of referrals for the new specialty of school psychology. Second, general practitioners would use the new school psychology specialists as consultants on specific, difficult problems. Third, general practitioners would use school psychology specialists for inservice training on relatively narrow areas of functioning.

The new specialty of school psychology, to be defined below, understandably would have within it certain components of general practice in psychology. This is the new school psychologist and the general practitioner would have certain things in common. There would be no discontinuities between these two types of psychologists. The school psychologist would have trained at the general practice level before entering specialty practice or would have trained *and practiced* at the general practice level before specialty practice. Thus, the specialist would have knowledge, skills, and techniques, as well as tools, appropriate to service delivery in general practice as a foundation upon which specialty practice would be based, although these might be employed differently. Because the specialty practice would be much narrower than general practice, the specialist would be knowledgeable in general practice but not practicing it. The true advantage of having the general practice knowledge or background would be that the specialist would not operate in a vacuum outside the mainstream of psychology and end up treating one narrow aspect of the client, actually fragmenting the client, but would treat the client within a holistic context.

THE NEW SCHOOL PSYCHOLOGY SPECIALTY

Basic Characteristics

The new school psychology specialty would be specifically and generically related to and involved with the schools and education in its very broadest sense. It would have some very clear-cut characteristics that would ensure this type of specific and generic relationship to the schools and education. First, it would facilitate academic learning across the life span. It would begin at the prenatal level of training for both child and parents, proceed to the preschool level, to kindergarten, to primary school, to elementary school, to the middle school, to the high school, to continuation school, to the junior college, to the four-year college, to the university, to schools of professional and vocational training, to the armed services, and to business, industry, professional, and other settings where induction, inservice, continuing education, and retirement training are conducted. In other words, the school psychological specialist would operate over the life span in tandem with the general practitioner in psychology, as general practitioners relate to the full range of the educational enterprise. The specialist might be centrally housed within a school system, while the general practitioner might be housed in individual school buildings, in other institutions, or in private practice.

Second, the specialty of school psychology would facilitate the inner life or affective learning of students or learners by addressing the most serious, hard-core emotional problems that have failed to yield to interventions at the general practice level or that have come to be recognized clearly as more appropriate to the level of the specialist than to the level of the general practitioner. London (1987) has called these types of problems "the 'psychosocial epidemics' that affect millions of U.S. school children" (p. 668). The services of the school

psychological specialist could go a long way to effect the "damage control" called for by London (1987, p. 672).

The school psychologist specialist would place emphasis on tough, affective, emotional and behavioral problems that affect functioning in the school setting or more generally in the educational setting. Recognizing that the individual cannot be compartmentalized, the specialist would not work, for example, only with *school emotions;* he or she would focus on recalcitrant emotional problems as they manifest themselves in the school community or educational setting, but with full knowledge that the treatment or overall interventions may have ramifications for the peer group, family, or larger community. Thus, the school psychology specialist would be allowed wide latitude in the treatment of intrasigent problems that would be referred to him or her.

Third, the school psychology specialist would facilitate cognitive development and coping strategies in students and learners where failure to learn is persistent and resistive to general practice interventions, and where coping strategies have persistently failed to prove effective. This function of the school psychology specialist is very important since it addresses *directly* the primary responsibility of the educational enterprise, the facilitation of learning. Although the position of the school psychology specialist does not move school psychology from a mental health focus to a focus on education as advocated by Bardon (1983), it recognizes the equal partnership of education and psychology in the school or learning setting, where either can be emphasized as required by the particular case.

Fourth, to best deliver effective, specialized school psychological services within educational systems, the specialist in school psychology probably would need to develop and market their programs proactively. This approach would be in great contrast to sitting back and waiting for individual student referrals, which now is the usual case. In fact, this might generate groups or clusters of similar referrals.

Organized, Systematic, Programmatic Service Delivery

The specialist in the new school psychology would provide organized, systematic, and programmatic service delivery. These organized programs could include student clients at the early phases of their problem syndrome or even at the proactive, preventive phases of their problematic syndromes for those difficulties that come to be recognized as initially appropriate for the specialist rather than for the general practitioner. Most of the programmatic service delivery probably would be secondary or tertiary prevention.

Examples of problem areas for such organized, systematic service delivery include those of child and adolescent suicide, violent behavior in the schools and its management, anti-child-abuse strategies, and alcohol an other drug abuse interventions. These are areas which generate problems that cannot be treated successfully by providing individual programs for referred students. Other players are involved in the problem or are dragged into it, often unwittingly. For example, a completed student suicide can involve much of the staff and the entire student body of several thousand in a particular school building (Jackson, 1987).

Another example is the area of violence reduction. This is the type of problem that involves destructive behavior by both school staff and students. This problem is especially complicated when it occurs within a multicultural setting such as a large urban school, which is reflected in programs in Boston (Prothrow-Stith, 1987) and Milwaukee (Milwaukee Board of School Directors, 1988).

Service Beyond P.L. 94-142 and Special Education

Public Law 94-142 in some ways regressed the institutional practice of present-day school psychology back from its gains under P.L. 89-10, the Elementary and Secondary Education Act of 1965—Title I, to a type of practice that existed in earlier times. Tindall (1983) has commented on P.L. 94-142 services, stating: "Unfortunately, the type of psychological services desired was chiefly that of classification and categorization so that the school system could qualify for funds" (p. 88). Consequently, the serious problems of 90% of a school's students, the non-special-education (regular education) students, have gone unmet. It is important that current efforts (Will, 1986) to modify this situation succeed if all students are to be recipients of services that are well qualified and adaptable to them.

In delivering services to these non-special-education students, the work of the school psychology specialist, the general practitioner in psy-

chology, and other supportive staff would be highly coordinated. For example, a student might be seeing the general practitioner in psychology for individual psychoeducational therapy and at the same time be in the program on violence reduction conducted by the specialist jointly with the full supportive services staff or the school social worker. This group of providers would jointly plan for the student or initiate evaluation of the student, articulate interventions, monitor the student, assess the results for the student, and review the program of offerings.

Range and Complexity of Tasks to Be Performed Within the Programmatic Services

The range and complexity of tasks to be performed within the programmatic services that are provided by the new school psychologists would be enormous. The range of tasks would incldue all of the following major tasks, plus a number of minor tasks:

- Conducting needs assessment: This involves planning with school administrators, defining the problem(s), designing tentative approaches to the problem(s), convincing the administrator, as necessary, of the possible efficacy of the approaches, selecting and/or preparing instruments to be used, surveying the target population, collecting data, analyzing the data, writing reports, and disseminating the information.

- Development of new products to suit the extant problem: Programs that have a successful impact on major student problems and staff problems within the school do not really exist today. A number of existing or commercial programs may have something to offer and can be used to trigger planning. The new school psychologist would have the important task of selecting the particular program to address the problem or problems, modifying a particular program or developing a new program especially fitted to the problem situation at hand, and orchestrating appropriate input from relevant school groups.

- Marketing the program or programs within a school system or to an individual school: The program selected, modified, or developed for use would need to be sold to the administrators and supervisors in the central administration and/or in the individual school, who would need to be convinced of the actual or potential effectiveness of the program. Since this may mean competing with a proposed program from a community group, a broad range of marketing skills might be needed.

- Implementing and monitoring the piloting and implementation of the program or programs: Important considerations in piloting and conducting the full-fledged program or programs would necessarily include staffing the program(s), planning logistical matters, providing ongoing checkups on staff confidence and morale and whether the promised program is actually being provided, providing support to program staff, and readying recipients of the program.
- Evaluation and redesigning: Progress reports can be especially helpful in keeping school administrators informed of what is happening. Hopefully, this will reassure them that the money is being well spent. Monitoring during the pilot phase may indicate the need to modify the program in some of its aspects. Final evaluation and monitoring, together with debriefing of involved staff, may indicate the need to redesign the program before it is rerun in the building, and especially before it is marketed elsewhere in the system or to other schools outside the system.

As with the range of the tasks listed above, the complexities of the tasks are enormous, made all the more so by the background of the present-day school psychologist. The enormity of the task stems from a number of sources. First, many of the skills explicitly or implicitly called for in the delineation above are not in the armamentarium of today's modal school psychologist. Second, the needed skills are skill clusters; that is, the clusters comprise many subskills that must be mastered and then combined. Third, the needed skills often require both formal instruction and supervised practice as well as time to achieve mastery. Fourth, the needed skills require a specific mental set that, generally speaking, has not been a part of the thinking of the average school psychologist in the field.

Greater Ties to the Larger Community

The new school psychology specialist is likely to have greater ties to the larger community in the conduct of his or her work than traditionally has existed for school psychologists in the past. That is, the new school psychology specialist is more likely than in the past to work with the community context of institutions and schools in terms of discussing and sizing up the problem of concern, framing the problem as questions to be answered, developing programs to fit the problem, reviewing outcomes, and delineating specific ways in which various parts of the community (e.g., agencies and other governmental units) can work collaboratively with those who are recipients of the program services.

The reason for the greater involvement of the contextual community is that the types of problems on which the new school psychology specialist will work will be those of greatest visibility, negative impact on the community, politicization, attraction for the police, and so on. With regard to these types of problems, the community demands real accomplishment and change in the school.

WHAT THE NEW SCHOOL PSYCHOLOGIST REQUIRES OF UNIVERSITY TRAINING PROGRAMS

University training programs in school psychology will need to change dramatically to adapt to the needs of the new school psychologist. While essentials of current training programs will be necessary, much more will be required in addition.

University training programs will need to emphasize what they have not heretofore. This includes truly understanding the school setting as a unique environment, placing special emphasis on the urban school. It also includes intense study of the "people problems" of the school beyond poor academic achievement and individual emotional problems. Understanding the essentials to successful approaches for addressing broad, group problems, together with packaging and marketing programmatic approaches, will be extremely important. A prerequisite to program building will be an understanding of the psychology of groups and the facilitation/management of group processes. As never before, there will be the need for intimate understanding of ethnic and racial groups per se and interactions within, between, and among these within the school setting.

The training program staff will in all likelihood need augmenting. Programs will need to add staff members who have the necessary perceptions and skills to deal with the day-to-day realities of the schools and who can successfully teach these and supervise programs in the schools.

EVENTS IN THE SCHOOLS THAT WILL HELP SHAPE THE NEW SCHOOL PSYCHOLOGY

There are a number of new administrative arrangements and instructional models recently initiated within the schools that potentially will have great influence on both general practice of psychology in the schools and the new specialty of school psychology. The new "effective schools" model within regular education for service to minority, at-risk, and gray-area children, and the clinical teacher model within special education and at the interface of special education and regular education emphasize the classroom teacher (supported by the administration, instructional materials, and curriculum guides) and what is needed for student learning. No special provisions are made for regular and routine psychological services.

Increasingly, one hears talk of the schools obtaining psychological and other servies from community-based organizations (CBOs), especially for those types of problems that would be appropriate for the new school psychologist. This is not contracting; it is simply the idea that CBOs should budget for service delivery to schools, gratis. Presumably, funding would come from state and federal governmental sources, and possibly from the United Way.

Decentralization, or the individual, school-based management (SBM) movement, especially in large urban areas, is empowering the school principal, teachers and other staff. Under this movement, each school has its own budget, goals, and instructional models for resolving its problems and instructing its students. Where SBM exists, the individual schools, not the central office, will probably make the decision to buy or not buy the program or programs being marketed by the specialist.

These administrative arrangements and instructional models reinforce the strong feelings of professional competence to teach subject matter that modern *teachers as a group* have, and which was referred to in the early part of the chapter. Thus, advising on the teaching of subject matter is not the future for psychology or school psychology. School psychology's focus must be squarely on cognitive, conative, and emotional blocks to individual and group learning, for which the new instructional models to not provide. School psychologist's focus must be on the psychological health of the learner-as-learner, in which they, and not CBO personnel, are the experts.

REFERENCES

Alpert, J. L. (1985). Change within a profession: Change, future, prevention, and school psychology. *American Psychologist, 40,* 1112–1121.

American Psychological Association. (1983). *Psychology as a health care profession.* Washington, DC: Author.

American Psychological Assocation. (1984). *Specialization in psychology: Principles.* Washington, DC: Author.

Bardon, J. I. (1983). Psychology applied to education: specialty in search of an identity. *American Psychologist, 38,* 185–196.

Brophy, J. (1982). Successful teaching strategies for the inner-city child. *Phi Delta Kappan, 63,* 527–530.

Dyer, C. (1984). *Application for the identification and continued recognition of a new specialty in psychology* (Division of School Psychology model application). Washington, DC: American Psychology Association.

Eubanks, E. E., & Levin, D. U. (1983). A first look at effective schools projects in New York City and Milwaukee. *Phi Delta Kappan, 64,* 697–702.

Fox, R. E., Kovacs, A. L., & Graham, S. R. (1985). Proposals for a revolution in the preparation and regulation of professional psychologists. *American Psychologist, 40,* 1042–1050.

French, J. L. (1985). An essay on becoming a school psychologist when school psychology was becoming. *Journal of School Psychology, 23,* 1–12.

Harmon, S. B. (1983). Teaming: A concept that works. *Phi Delta Kappan, 64,* 366–367.

Hunt, D. E. (1981). Learning style and the interdependence of practice and theory. *Phi Delta Kappan, 62,* 647.

Jackson, J. H. (1987, August). *Student suicide prevention: Comprehensive school programs and school psychologists' proficiencies.* Division of School Psychology Distinguished Service Award address prepared for presentation at the national convention of the American Psychological Association, New York.

London, P. (1987). Character education and clinical

intervention: A paradigm shift for U.S. schools. *Phi Delta Kappan, 68,* 667–673.

Milwaukee Board of School Directors. (1988). *Reduction of violent behavior in the Milwaukee Public Schools: A proposal.* Milwaukee, WI: Author.

Prothrow-Stith, D. (1987). *Violence prevention curriculum for adolescents.* Boston: Education Development Center, Inc.

Rosenfeld, M., Shimberg, D., & Thornton, R. (1984). Job analysis of licensed psychologists. *Professional Practice of Psychology, 5,* 1–20.

Tindall, R. (1983). I didn't aspire to be a school psychologist: Reflections. *Journal of School Psychology, 21,* 79–89.

Will, M. (1986). *Educating students with learning problems—A shared responsibility.* Washington, DC: U.S. Department of Education.

Ysseldyke, J., Algozzine, B., Regan, R., & McGue, M. (1981). The influence of test scores and naturally-occurring pupil characteristics on psychoeducational decision making with children. *Journal of School Psychology, 19,* 167–177.

SCHOOL PSYCHOLOGY AND THE SCIENTIFIC STUDY OF BEHAVIOR: CONTRIBUTIONS OF THEORY AND PRACTICE

3

READING, EVALUATING, AND APPLYING RESEARCH IN SCHOOL PSYCHOLOGY[1]

BEEMAN N. PHILLIPS
The University of Texas at Austin

Exploring avenues through which research can have an impact on the quality of psychological services to children, schools, and families is a central mission of this chapter. Yet advocates of more and better practical applications of psychological science are faced with a dilemma; despite a strong commitment to this endeavor, practical application itself is not fully understood. For some, practical application is applied research carried out in natural rather than laboratory environments. For others, it is addressing the questions generated by those working directly with children, schools, and families. For still others, practical application consists of interpreting basic theory or research as in the question: What does B. F. Skinner have to say to school psychologists? Finally, there are those who view practical application primarily in terms of communication between researchers and those responsible for programs and policy affecting children, schools, and families.

In this chapter, I address this dilemma and attempt to resolve it by giving practical application a more adequate definition and a clearer mission. In this process, I also seek to establish functional links between research and practice and to speak to research issues of major concern to practitioners who work with children, schools, and families.

This chapter is also predicated on the proposition that the interface between psychological science and professional practice must be strengthened, and that it is important to promote conceptualizations of this interface that have the potential to increase contributions of science to practice. A corollary of this proposition is that although the world of application of science is the stage, the script is not Shakespeare's *As You Like It*. It is, instead, a constructionist view of science that, in turn, provides part of the framework for this chapter. A second corollary is that in bridging the gap between science and practice, a gap that in school psychology is much too wide, the pivotal role of the practitioner must be recognized.

It is important, however, to realize that the predicament of the practitioner is that in the variations of professional practice, there is the high, hard ground where the practitioner can readily

---

[1] Portions of this chapter are based on invited addresses at the American Psychological Association Convention in 1986 and 1988 (see Phillips, 1987, 1989).

make use of research-based theory and technique, and there is the swampy lowland where situations are perplexing and messy and incapable of straightforward technical solution (Schon, 1983). The problem for the school psychologist practitioner, therefore, is to practice good psychological science in the swamp, where many of the most important and challenging school practice issues are, as well as on the high, hard ground.

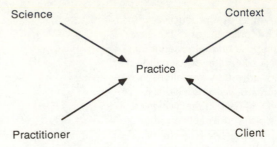

Figure 1.   Some coordinates of criteria for reading and evaluating research.

SOME COORDINATES OF CRITERIA FOR READING AND EVALUATING RESEARCH IN SCHOOL PSYCHOLOGY

Five elements in the total practice situation can be discriminated and appraised. First, there is *practice* itself; and since this is a human product, the second element is the *practitioner*. Third, practice is taken to have grounding in psychological *science*—to be about, signify, or reflect something that bears some relation to the psychological and educational sciences. There also is a historical, sociocultural, and institutional *context*. For the final element, we have the *client*: the students, teachers, parents, or others to whom the practice is addressed.

On this framework, I wish to spread out for analysis various criteria for reading, evaluating, and utilizing research. To emphasize the artificiality of the device, and at the same time make it easier to visualize analyses, let us arrange the five coordinates in a convenient pattern. A quadrangle will do, with practice in the center (see Figure 1).

Although any reasonably adequate set of criteria takes some account of all five elements, the criteria I present, as we shall see, exhibit a discernible orientation toward criteria that the practitioner would use. However, to use these coordinates to identify criteria by which to assess the value of scientific facts and principles to practice is only the beginning. For one thing, criteria identified in this way are not constants, but variables; they differ in significance according to the theory of practical application of science in which they are embedded. Take what I have called "scientific evaluation" (see Figure 2) as an example. In reflector or mirror theory (to be discussed later), practical application is guided by a deliberate attempt to import the truths of psychological science into the practice realm, and through these efforts the practitioner sets himself or herself up to emulate the scientist, and the resulting practice is itself comparable to a mirror presenting a selected and ordered image of science. There is, therefore, a conspicuous parallelism here, and the value of scientific studies to practice is ultimately judged by the results of scientific evaluation.

In contrast, in a radiant projector or lamp theory of practical application (to be discussed later), the practitioner is seen to unite and reconcile science and practice. There is not only a partnership, but a union, and the best practice is the

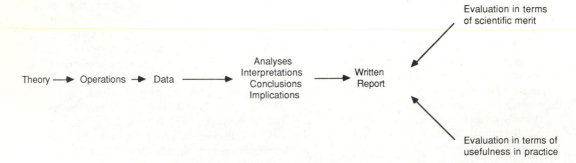

Figure 2.   A scientific research paradigm and evaluation perspective.

product of a productive tension between research and practice, and the practitioner's assimilative purpose and informed judgment. That is, practice is a projection of scientific facts and principles that includes transformations in form, nature, or structure, as well as additions to that which is given, and in engaging in practical application the practitioner is pictured as active rather than merely receptive. Thus practice is lawful without being scientifically legislated, and scientific evaluation is assigned a less determinate function than in mirror theory.

The criteria also are conditioned by the systemic character of both science and practice. Both have their own cultures, and the idea of culture turns our attention to the total pattern of behavior of scientists and practitioners. Some research criteria are, therefore, necessarily grounded in contextual information, and apart from the need to appraise scientific characteristics of research, there is the need for ecologically oriented criteria such as those presented in Table 1. They improve appraisal of the overall value of psychological science to practice.

Client-related research criteria also need to be examined. The distinction between group outcomes and those for individuals is one focus. For example, the standard practice of reporting research outcomes in terms of group means loses sight of the individual and does not take account of what proportion, and what types of individuals, actually improved as a result of the treatment. The assessment of consumer satisfaction and other aspects of social validation is another focus. These procedures, which can be adapted to a variety of research studies, are discussed at length by Kratochwill, Feld, and Van Somersen (1986).

NATURE OF PSYCHOLOGICAL SCIENCE

Trying to understand practical application is a matter, however, that turns on other fundamental issues. Of central importance is the revolution that is brewing in the behavioral and social sciences, although psychology has been slow to respond to it (Lawler et al., 1985; Rorer & Widiger, 1983). According to these writers, as well as others, much of the edifice of psychology is based on a few methodological underpinnings that are largely constructed out of the raw materials of logical positivism. Operationally, those underpinnings include faith in experimentalism, careful measurement, and sophisticated statistical techniques. But a variety of compromises do occur in the realities of doing research, although such departures from scientific rigor result in the sacrifice of both precision and confidence in the validity of the results.

A basic message of this chapter is that this model of research is plainly in need of augmentation, and that newer methods such as action research, "thick description," and "contextualism" (Lawler et al., 1985), which are suffused with constructionist tenets (see e.g., Gergen, 1985; Manicus & Secord, 1983), need to be adopted. Although less well codified and harder to defend as being truly rigorous, they offer the promise of

---

TABLE 1   Some School System Factors Influencing the Application of Research

1. Accommodation (i.e., making applications fit the system) is usually more effective than assimilation (i.e., making the system fit applications).
2. Applications usually are not accepted on research merit alone, since cost, availability, and degree of difficulty of usage are considerations.
3. Stability-maintaining conditions (e.g., a large proportion of tenured teachers and hierarchically arranged subsystems) work against applications.
4. Potential users assess applications in terms of consequences to them and others they are concerned about.
5. Application specialists need to be internally effective, highly involved, and committed, with a well established peer communication network and support system.
6. Spokespersons for bringing research to bear on complex issues, decisions, or other matters of policy need to open up communication channels, organize special groups to aid in implementation, teach others to use their applications, and at times introduce change-inducing changes by using outside consultants, citizen's groups, and so on.

psychological research that is less distant from, and more useful to, practice.

This view of psychological science is articulated well by Scarr (1985), and this elegant work is relied on heavily in portions of this and other sections. In essence, she adopts a constructionist position, believing that constructionism is a means for understanding the processes of psychological science that also invites the development of alternative criteria for evaluating psychological research. For example, one of the tenets of constructionism is that scientists have their own realities of which they try to persuade others, and scientific facts do not exist independently, being created within theoretical systems. Theory not only guides inquiry through the questions raised, it also influences the framework of research studies and the interpretation of results. Scientists seek to find "facts" to assimilate into their own world views and are biased toward "facts" that are concurrent with these prior beliefs. The realization that reality is a construction of the human (scientist's) mind does not of course deny its value; much of science is admirably useful. But there is no one set of facts, theory-guided in their invention, that are absolute and real.

In this view, there are other important distinctions. Science is a set of agreed-upon procedures or rules of knowing, not constructs or theories. The preference in much of psychology for proximal, rather than distal variables and causal explanations also is recognized; and this nearsightedness questioned. But science does evolve, although scientific knowledge is not necessarily cumulative in nature. It undergoes metamorphoses at times, and is influenced by sociocultural and historical context, these being major determinants of the most plausible and persuasive scientific ideas in a given era (Kuhn, 1970).

There also is the realization that the real world is a "cloud of correlated events" and interacting persons and environments. As researchers, one constructs a theory about relations among these events, persons, and environments. Investigators select a few elements, put them into studies, and in doing this eliminate other variables a priori from possible analysis.

A constructionist view also highlights the problems of causal inference. Both experimental and correlational designs have virtues and deficiencies in making direct and indirect causal inferences (Cook & Campbell, 1979; Feldman & Haas,

1970; Scarr, 1985). But problems of causal inference still exist even when both experimental and correlational approaches are utilized because behaviors in the real world are intrinsically confounded.

Finally, constructionist theory persuades one to think about the practitioner's role in implementation and application in a different way. To explicate the differences, two metaphors are useful, one comparing the practitioner to a mirror or reflector, the other to a lamp or a radiant projector. Under the assumptions of normative science, the practitioner is like a mirror, practice is viewed as imitation of science, and practical application is a reassembly of images and replicas of scientific facts and principles. It follows, from this view, that practical application is "brick and mortar" thinking in which science is mechanically associated with practice. In the alternative, constructionist view of science, the practitioner, seen as a lamp, is more of an architect of professional practice. In this view, the practitioner's informed judgment has command and authority over the utilization of science in practice, and practical application is a synthetic and blending activity in which scientific facts and principles are assimilated into practice. To get to the heart of the matter, the use of science in mirror theory involves only the practitioner's understanding of the action, practice, or art of mimicry. But in lamp theory, practical application is organic, having its source in practice itself, and such applications are the produce of an amassing power of the practitioner.

THE INTERSECTION BETWEEN RESEARCH AND PRACTICE IN SCHOOL PSYCHOLOGY

A related matter that requires special attention is the nature of the interface between research and practice in school psychology. It is assumed that research contributes to practice, directly and indirectly, and that the contribution of research to practice will be greatest where researchers adjust their priorities to reflect practice-relevant issues. Such readjustment should reduce the disaffection of practitioners with research and increase the proportion of researchers that have some interest and concern in matters of practice.

It should be noted, however, that school psychological practice is broad and not precisely definable and embraces the range of things that school psychologists actually or should do (see, e.g., the Specialty Guidelines, APA, 1981b). It is similarly difficult to define psychological research in any precise way, and nonspecificity will be embraced in dealing with issues confronting the interface of research and practice in school psychology.

It also is improtant to designate a working definition of the term *relevance*. This term will be used to designate aspects of research that bear an obvious relation to practice. But basic and applied research constitute a single continuum. In one sense, therefore, all psychological research is relevant to school psychological practice, although the relevance of some research is more apparent than that of other research.

The bidirectionality of the relationship between research and practice is a further point. The approach used here for construing this relationship is to consider the origin of research and practice. In the typology proposed in Figure 3, basic research is endogenous. It is "knowledge driven" and formu-

lated in terms of contemporary theory and research concerning questions, issues, or hypotheses relevant to the discipline, with little regard for broader societal or practice ramifications (Masters, 1984). Applied research, on the other hand, is exogenous, stemming from a consideration of societal issues, technological problems, or practice matters.

In a similar vein, one can trace the source of some professional practice to applied and basic research. That is, some aspects of practice are exogenous, being a product of science. In contrast, an endogenic perspective can be adopted for other aspects of professional practice. In this case, practice arises out of practice experiences, education and training, the practitioner's own psychodynamics, and other internal considerations.

To be sure, all research can be relevant to school psychological practice, and practice can serve to identify significant scientific questions. It would be a mistake, therefore, to construe practice

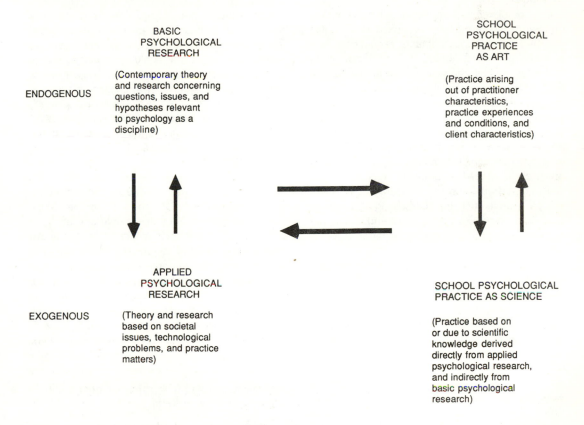

Figure 3. Endogenous/exogenous and bidirectional aspects of the relation of research to practice.

relevance narrowly or to overlook the ways that practice can influence research.

THE RANGE OF FUNCTIONS OF RESEARCH IN PRACTICE

Another challenge of the constructionist movement is essentially that of grappling with a broader conception of the role of research in practice. To appreciate this point, it should be realized that practitioners construct their own practice, and that they approach each practice problem with a particular viewpoint, implicit or explicit, that influences the questions raised about the problem, the framework of subsequent inquiry, and interpretations and application of the results. Practitioners thus are biased by this tendency to seek "facts" that are congruent with prior beliefs about problems. Although these biases may be personal, they frequently are preferences shared with professional colleagues.

As one example, practitioners have a distinct preference for proximal, as opposed to distal, variables even though many researchers and scholars have urged expanded views of context, as in the case of children who have a family and the contexts of school, neighborhood, and community, and whose school behavior and learning has genetic, ethological, neurobiological, and evolutionary bases. Different levels of analysis of practice problems need to be kept straight therefore, and taken into account in applications of research to practice. As a case in point, if practitioners see causes of a problem in child-centered terms, there will be a preference for child-changing interventions, in contrast to a system focus and an emphasis on system-changing intervention (Phillips, 1983).

A further implication of a constructionist perspective is that the facts, principles, and scientific theories are judged by their persuasive power in the community of practitioners, as well as the community of scientists. But scientists and practitioners operate in different worlds that reflect two different cultures, and C. P. Snow (1964) has made the case most compellingly, in the generic sense. Psychology also has its two cultures divided along the lines of researchers versus practitioners (Frank, 1984; Kimble, 1984). Nonetheless, if one goes beyond these philosophical, value, and attitudinal differences, there are some generally hopeful

conclusions that can be made. There is a shared experience and similarity of views, especially when practitioners are part of a highly professionalized field. In psychology, for example, many practitioners have doctoral degrees and training in a university setting where they were exposed to research, did some research, and so on, so that psychological science and research have become a language of discourse, a way to define problems, and so on. This is less true of school psychology of course, which may help to explain the size and scope of the gap between research and practice in this field (Block, 1982; Lambert, 1983).

However, even under those more promising conditions there still seems to be a difference in definition of "usefulness." Scientists see research as providing clear-cut, practical prescriptions that practitioners are likely to follow (see, e.g., Weiss & Weiss, 1981). Thus they focus, in their definition, on research used in direct, instrumental ways, and research as a basis for making particular practice choices.

In contrast, practitioners see a more diverse set of research characteristics and environmental factors contributing to usefulness. For example, raising new issues is a highly important aspect of useful research, and high-quality, objective research is useful even when it challenges conventional wisdom or the political status quo. Overall, their definition of usefulness includes the scientists' problem-solving definition, but it extends to the more comprehensive range of functions summarized in Figure 4.

In summary, scientists are right that practitioners rarely use research directly and instrumentally, as specific solutions to particular problems. But practitioners believe this is only one of many ways in which research evidence and scientific ideas can contribute to practice. The uses that practitioners see as important raise questions about the misuse of scientific research and ideas, however, and create further dilemmas for the scientist interested in the utilization of scientific knowledge (see, e.g., Bazelon, 1982; Gerard, 1983; Phillips, 1981, pp. 37–39; Robinson, 1984).

CONTRIBUTION OF DIFFERENT RESEARCH STRATEGIES TO PRACTICE

Definitive assessment of the boundaries of the research that can contribute to practice is also very

| Professional knowledge, i.e. keeping up with developments in fields related to one's job | + | Definition of problem, i.e. framing or conceptualizing practice problems | + | Advocacy, i.e. bringing new ideas to public attention; legitimating budget allocations; attacking established policies; and lobbying for new programs | + | Problem solving, i.e. providing clearcut practical prescriptions for on-the-job actions and decisions |

Figure 4. Range of functions of "useful" research. (Derived from Phillips, 1986.)

difficult because, in addition to the wide range of functions of research in practice, the knowledge base of school psychology has greatly expanded. Also, much of that vast literature is potentially relevant because of the expanded role of schools and the more comprehensive functions of school psychologists. As a consequence, ways to prioritize that total body of research are much needed.

As a place to begin, some form of intervention is at the core of school psychologists' functions, and research should inform their actions. One might therefore assign the highest priority to research that has the greatest potential benefits to intervention. In addition, it is important to recognize the inherent characteristics of research paradigms and the knowledge they generate.

"Main Effects" Research as the Starting Point
One way to respond to this situation is to order the models of behavior that underlie research and that determine the nature of research results and their implications for practice. For example, "main effects" research constitutes one useful basis for assessment and intervention activities, educational planning and policy development, and decisions by school psychologists (see Figure 5).

However, there are inherent limitations to "main effects" research insofar as practical application is concerned. Using an example provided by Rorer and Widiger (1983), if one considers the typical psychological or educational experimental study, there is one group that is subjected to some experimental manipulation, and another, the control group, that is not. At the end of the experiment, the mean scores of the groups are compared, and if they differ in a statistically significant sense it is concluded that the intervention caused the subjects to change in whatever outcome was measured.

But it should be noted that *group* data are being used to infer a *within-individual* effect, and that the intervention is applied *to the group as a whole* and is used to infer a causal effect that has its interconnections within the individual. The inference that is involved is questionable, therefore, because in the treated group some subjects' scores increased significantly, many others did not significantly increase or decrease, and a few were significantly lower. As a consequence, there is no constant effect for which the intervention can be said to be the cause. One can only say that the intervention caused some individuals to increase, a few to decrease, and most to stay the same on the outcome measure, and to extract further benefit from such research, one would need to set about examining those individual differences.

Going Beyond Main Effects to Interaction Effects Research
Such efforts would start of course with the premise that interactions do exist and are important to practice. However, in attending to interactions, the analysis of behavior is considerably extended, and conceptual status of individual differences variables, and the differences between interventions, becomes crucial. A significant consequence is that few reliable and replicable interactions have been demonstrated up to now (Cronbach & Snow, 1977; Phillips, 1985); although there are still other reasons for the lack of significant interactions. One factor is that such research has been methodologically weak, so that the presence of interactions could not be fully determined. Another is the inadequacy of theories guiding such research, including theoretically weak conceptions of interventions.

The search must go on, however, not only because of the high potential value of interactions,

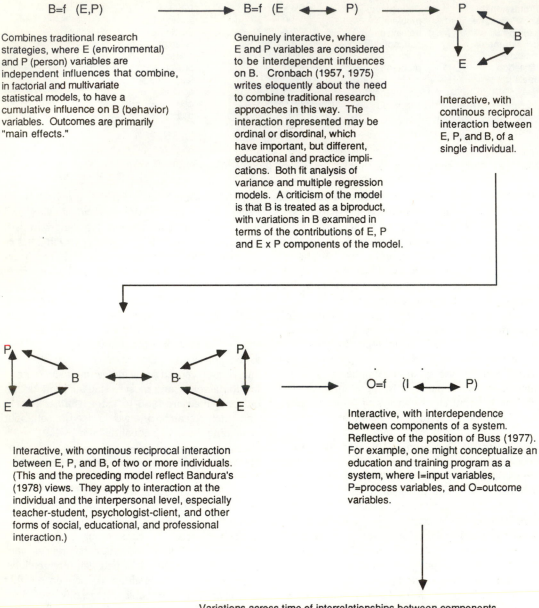

$B=f\ (E,P)$ ⟶ $B=f\ (E ⟷ P)$ ⟶

Combines traditional research strategies, where E (environmental) and P (person) variables are independent influences that combine, in factorial and multivariate statistical models, to have a cumulative influence on B (behavior) variables. Outcomes are primarily "main effects."

Genuinely interactive, where E and P variables are considered to be interdependent influences on B. Cronbach (1957, 1975) writes eloquently about the need to combine traditional research approaches in this way. The interaction represented may be ordinal or disordinal, which have important, but different, educational and practice implications. Both fit analysis of variance and multiple regression models. A criticism of the model is that B is treated as a biproduct, with variations in B examined in terms of the contributions of E, P and E x P components of the model.

Interactive, with continous reciprocal interaction between E, P, and B, of a single individual.

Interactive, with continous reciprocal interaction between E, P, and B, of two or more individuals. (This and the preceding model reflect Bandura's (1978) views. They apply to interaction at the individual and the interpersonal level, especially teacher-student, psychologist-client, and other forms of social, educational, and professional interaction.)

$O=f\ (I ⟷ P)$

Interactive, with interdependence between components of a system. Reflective of the position of Buss (1977). For example, one might conceptualize an education and training program as a system, where I=input variables, P=process variables, and O=outcome variables.

Variations across time of interrelationships between components of behavior, i.e., the times as a source of interactions, leading to the intergenerational hypothesis. For example, the effects of particular teacher characteristics and teaching behaviors on teaching effectiveness probably cannot be generalized across generations, say during the 1950's and 1980's.

Figure 5. Theoretical models of behavior and related strategies, arranged on a continuum of potential significance for practitioners and educational decision makers.

but because "main effects" interventions account for only small proportions of the variance in outcomes to which they are applied. The goal, of course, should be improved knowledge about individual differences that are important in the design of psychological and educational interventions with the aim of reaching an optimum fit of students or clients and inteventions or treatments (R. E. Snow, 1986). One avenue for such research is the Aptitude-Treatment Interaction concept (Cronbach & Snow, 1977; Phillips, 1985), and an alternative is the case study research model (Kratochwill, 1985). Both have the potential for studying individual differences and individuality at a sufficient level of complexity so as to be generalizable to the problems of school psychological practice.

APPLYING RESEARCH TO PRACTICE: SCHOOL CLASS SIZE RESEARCH AS AN EXEMPLAR

The goal of effectively applying research to practice is now pursued more directly, starting with school class size research, which provides a productive way to view the promise and the problems of practical application. In Glass, Cahen, Smith, and Filby's (1982) widely publicized review of research on class size and policy implications of the results, the research question was: Does class size affect pupil achievement and pupils' and teachers' attitudes? They located and analyzed the results for 77 studies on class size and pupil achievement, and 59 studies of affective and instructional effects of class size. Then they synthesized and summarized this accumulated knowledge using a meta-analysis. In this meta-analysis they used 725 statistical comparisons from the 77 studies, and 371 comparisons from the 59 studies. After the main analysis, they did subanalyses to see if overall findings represented results for good versus poor research studies, and studies of different subject-matter areas, different IQ levels, and so on. In all analyses, they compared very small versus small classes, small versus medium classes, medium versus large classes, and large versus very large classes.

What they found, for pupil achievement especially, is that (a) very small classes are *much better* than small classes, (b) small classes are *better* than large classes, and (c) large classes are *better* than very large classes. Using the small number of

studies that investigated how class process changed when class size was reduced in the middle of the year, they also suggest a plausible explanation for the effect of class size. In essence, teachers were better able to monitor individual pupils, keep them on task, and provide effective feedback when class size was *dramatically reduced*.

To concretize these results and give them additional meaning one should closely scrutinize the procedures used to analyze the research to date. For example, in combining the results of the studies, the authors *assumed* that class size and achievement are related exponentially. That is, the drop in learning as class size goes from 1 to 2 pupils is greater than 2 to 3, and so on. In addition, there were a substantial number of studies included that compared a class size of "1" with large class sizes of 20 to 35 (see their Table A.1 on p. 141). Also, most of the effect of class size, scaled in terms of percentile rank, occurred between a class size of 1 and 10 (see their Figure 2.1 on p. 49).

But the research question is not simply whether reducing class size improves achievement. There are two additional questions of relevance to school psychologists: Does reducing class size affect achievement enough to justify the extra cost? And are there better ways to achieve the same end? As to the first question, adding or subtracting 1 or 2 pupils from the average class size of a large school district will cost or save a million dollars but have very little effect on pupil achievement. Furthermore, adding pupils to large classes has very little negative impact, and this negative effect decreases with size of class. Thus, greatly reducing average class size (e.g., from 20 to 10) is consistently better but much more expensive, with such a change approximately doubling costs. On the other hand, increasing average class size (e.g., from 20 to 30) has very little impact on achievement but great impact on lowering costs.

As an example of the second question, assuming that one's goal is to increase the achievement of minority pupils, a comparison would be needed between the effects of busing, adding teacher aides, and so on, or spending the same amount on reducing the size of minority classes. Clearly, educational policy and decisions are not simply based on what works. Even if there is agreement on the importance of a goal such as to improve achievement, there is still the economic question of which of several alternative uses of limited resources will achieve this end most efficiently.

There also are other factors to consider beyond the question of what works and how cost-effective it is. Educational decisions involve politics, pressure groups, and limited resources as well as different perspectives based on values, opinions, beliefs, allegiances, personal status, and so on. For example, one would be likely to find such differences on the issue of class size in talking to a school board member, a principal, a school psychologist, a classroom teacher, a representative of an educational/psychological organization, a legislator, and a governor. Therefore, in fostering recognition of the value of supporting research that is an integral partner in the psychological and educational enterprise, claims about what scientific research can provide directly for the implementation of practice and policy must be cautiously made.

In this particular example, the cost factor in reducing class size is the most important consideration. However, a more general application of psychological science issue is also involved. A number of writers (e.g., Cohen, 1977; Howard and Conway, 1986; Koch, 1981) have emphasized that psychology has been largely unsuccessful in influencing behavior. The proportion of variance accounted for, which is one acceptable means of expressing psychological intervention results, brings home the reality of how little influence the best documented psychological or educational interventions actually have. For such interventions, the upper limit of variance accounted for is about 25%, which is another way of saying that when even the best interventions are applied, only a small proportion of those receiving them will benefit appreciably. This adds to the importance, therefore, of evaluating research results in terms of a broad spectrum of utilitarian as well as scientific criteria.

METHODS FOR REVIEWING AND INTEGRATING RESEARCH FINDINGS

I now examine ways to ascertain the current state of knowledge on a particular issue, problem, or topic—which is the first step in creating a knowledge base for practice. In the past, there has been insufficient attention to methods, procedures, and techniques for conducting such reviews. For example, books on research methodology seldom go beyond matters like use of card catalogs, indexes to periodicals, note taking, and so on. A consequence of this lack of attention is that the accumulation of knowledge from previous research has been slowed down. Another is that there is a lack of standards for judging the quality of reviews that one uses.

The focus and purpose of reviews, of course, varies. One might be interested in theory verification and development, or in sizing up new theoretical, methodological, or empirical developments. Another purpose might be to suggest directions for future reviews of a topic. Other purposes more closely related to the use of research in school psychology are to determine the efficacy of a particular intervention or make recommendations for practice or policy.

One can conceptualize methods of conducting reviews in terms of a continuum that is anchored at one end by narrative reviewing, which involves individualized judgment, analysis, interpretation, and generalization. Quantitative reviewing, as in meta-analysis, is at the other end, and it involves applying scientific methodology to the review process. But regardless of method, a review involves six basic tasks, as shown in Table 2.

Problems with Traditional Procedures

School psychologists who are overloaded with the demands of their applied work often rely on research reviews for scientific information relevant to practice problems, and the procedure they most often rely on is the traditional narrative approach characterized by separate description of related

---

TABLE 2   Basic Tasks in Reviewing
Research Studies

---

1. *Selecting* the purpose and focus of the review (i.e., the question, issue, problem, hypothesis, etc.).
2. *Sampling* available research studies in the literature.
3. *Representing* the characteristics of the studies and their findings, including the adequacy of the studies.
4. *Analyzing* the findings in the studies.
5. *Making interpretations and generalizations* about the findings.
6. *Reporting* the review (i.e., writing it up).

---

studies and intuitive integration of the results. But when a large number of studies are involved, narrative description and intuitive synthesis of results can be untrustworthy. Therefore, reviews of this kind need to be carefully evaluated, and practitioners who use them need to be aware of their potential problems. According to Cooper (1982) and Jackson (1980), these include:

1. Reviewers frequently fail to examine critically the evidence, methods, and conclusions of previous reviews of the topic.
2. Reviewers often focus their discussion and analysis on only a few of the full set of studies they find.
3. Reviewers frequently use crude and misleading representations of the findings of the studies (one procedure, for example, is to classify studies according to statistical significance, which is criticizable).
4. Reviewers sometime fail to recognize that random sampling error can play a part in variable findings.
5. Reviewers frequently fail to assess possible relationships between the characteristics of studies and findings (i.e., to look for interaction effects of this type).
6. Reviewers usually report so little about their methods of reviewing that readers cannot judge the validity of the conclusions.
7. There is much room for reviewer bias in the form of (a) selection of purpose in terms of preconceptions, (b) nonrepresentative sampling of studies, (c) selective use of findings, (4) distorted interpretations of findings, (e) overstating/understating generalizations, and (f) inappropriate advocacy in relation to practice and policy formulation.

Meta-Analysis: A Viable Alternative to Traditional Reviews?

Meta-analysis has been offered as an alternative to traditional review procedures, and for school psychologists interested in the efficacy of interventions, or in influencing policy through the creation of unequivocal, easy-to-understand summary statements, it is the review method of choice. However, there are several different versions of it. The Glass, McGraw, and Smith model (1981) emphasizes the estimation of effect sizes that are then interpreted using traditional inferential procedures. Other investigators (see, e.g., Hunter, Schmidt, & Jackson, 1982; Rosenthal & Rubin, 1982) use similar measures of effect size but prefer nontraditional inferential procedures that take into account sampling error, unreliability in measures, and range variation in arriving at the magnitude of the effect itself. With these developments, meta-analysis methodology has become increasingly sophisticated, and analyses such as these assume a large degree of expertise that goes considerably beyond elementary statistics.

However, meta-analysis and other forms of quantitative reviewing have obvious value. One value of quantitative reviews is that they are an efficient way to summarize a large literature. They also are, or can be, more objective than the traditional review process. Statistical analyses applied in quantitative reviews can also find relationships and trends too subtle to be seen by the "naked eye." This approach also enhances one's ability to look for interactions in the data and to examine possibilities never studied in the individual studies.

Nevertheless, there are pertinent practical issues that need to be addressed in addition to this promise. According to Green and Hall (1984), some of these issues are:

1. Should only studies that are the same in certain respects be aggregated?
2. Should one make a distinction between "good" and "bad" research studies? For example, can many weak studies add up to a strong conclusion, as in the case of smoking and lung cancer? Among weak studies, some may be weak in internal validity, others in external validity. But what is important depends on purpose; for example, in school intervention the significance of weaknesses depends on the interplay of causal interpretation and application. That is, causal interpretation requires high internal validity. But there are two levels of causal interpretation: knowing that an intervention works, and being able to explain why it works (theory). On the other hand, application requires high external validity. Thus with a school intervention one wants to know if it works (but not necessarily why), and then if it has applicability (i.e., to what kinds of problems, for

what types of pupils, and under what conditions).

3. The lack of independence when multiple results are analyzed from single studies presents a problem because nonindependence reduces reliability and increases systematic bias.

4. One can assess only direct evidence on a problem. Sometimes a problem of importance has not been studied but there are studies with indirect evidence that can be woven together. For example, will substance X reduce chronic depression in children? No studies have been done. But there are studies of the effects of X on chronic depression of adults, and studies of the similarities of the effects of some drugs on children and adults.

5. We also cannot determine whether characteristics of studies that relate to outcomes are causes of these effects. For example, if level of intelligence is a personal characteristic related to intervention outcome, is it a cause?

6. For every construct there are alternative measures, which may not have equivalent metrics. For example, what is described as upper middle SES on one measure may be described as middle SES on another.

7. Characteristics of outcome variables influence results. For example, the effects of an intervention may vary with type of effects measured (as in higher-order versus lower-order intellectual skills as outcomes), and with how effects are measured (i.e., characteristics of the tests used and conditions under which testing occurs).

8. In addition, almost all effect sizes use calculations based on estimates. Also, there are many characteristics of studies that are coded, which provides many opportunities to go wrong (in making classifications).

Entire studies also are ignored because they do not fit the classification scheme. Quantitative reviews also focus mainly on main effects, ignoring interaction effects, which involves oversimplifying the research domain.

9. In general, the most frequent criticism of quantitative reviews is that findings are combined uncritically. Instead, all of the ways that studies vary need to be subjected to analysis.

In summary, reading and evaluating statistical-quantitative as well as intuitive-narrative syntheses of the research literature are admittedly difficult. In recognition of this, an attempt was made to present an overview of review methods and to give advice that would be useful in doing and interpreting such reviews and in improving judgment calls in applying the results.

SCIENTIFIC EVALUATION OF INDIVIDUAL RESEARCH STUDIES

In this section, criteria for evaluation of the scientific merit of individual research studies are considered, and in this case two types of criteria can be applied. One is conceptual and technical analysis, where validity is the fundamental concern. The other consists of general criteria for evaluating research as a process and product. In both cases the source of the criteria are the rules and principles established by scientists, and a summary of these scientific evaluation procedures is provided in Figure 6.

Conceptual and Technical Analysis
Validity is the major issue in evaluating research where the focus is on research design. Campbell and Stanley (1963) initially identified two kinds of validity. These are: internal, which concerns the

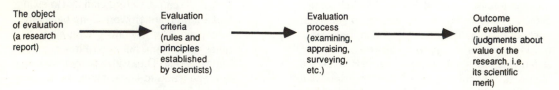

Figure 6. Steps in scientific evaluation.

inference that the relationship between two variables is causal, and external, which involves the inference that this causal relationship can be generalized across persons, situations, and so on.

More recently, Cook and Campbell (1979) proposed four types of validity, although they recognized that other types (beyond the four) could be identified. They further pointed out that this rationale corresponds to the four major decisions that the applied researcher, or anyone evaluating a research study, faces. Stated in the form of questions, these are:

1. Is there a relationship between the two operational variables? (This is statistical conclusion validity.)
2. If there is, the question is whether the relationship between those two operational variables is a causal relationship? (This is internal validity.)
3. If this is determined satisfactorily, there is a need to consider whether the cause-and-effect operations adequately represent the abstract constructs involved in the relationship? (This is construct validity.)
4. In addition to representativeness, the applied researcher or evaluator has the further interest in generalizing the relationship across persons, situations, times, and so on. (This is external validity.)

The purpose of research design is to produce unambiguous answers to these questions and to probe hypotheses about a variety of basic and applied research issues. Each research design has strengths and limitations of course, and threats to validity can be assessed and classified. This is done with an eye on quasi-experimental designs in Table 3. In general, experimental designs are the least vulnerable, followed by quasi-experimental (i.e., equivalent groups) designs. Others, such as one-group designs and causal modeling techniques, are the most vulnerable.

There are objections, however, to the Cook and Campbell type of distinctions between internal and external validity (Wortman, 1983). For example, the claim that random assignment rules out all threats to internal validity might be considered suspect. A treatment is embedded in a context, so it is not possible to know for sure that the treatment is the cause. The primacy of internal validity over external validity is also criticizable since no validity type can logically have precedence over another. In addition, one cannot reject inductive inference while basing external validity on inductive inference. That is, all generalization is presumptive.

Another issue is: How can one have validity internal to an experiment when propositions being tested are phrased in terms external to the experiment? That is, all research tests propositions that are general and universal in nature, and sampling is only the means by which one approximates representing general constructs.

Ecological validity is a special issue in relation to external validity, especially for practitioners. Brunswick (1955) introduced the concept to psychology. He opposed classic experimental designs that control and manipulate a limited set of variables through only a restricted range of values, and argued that many such experimental studies shed light on nothing more than narrow phenomena studied under specific conditions. Even if replicated, there is no evidence that results have wider validity. Results like this do not faithfully mirror real behavior of real people in a real world. Brunswick also advocated representative sampling of subjects and situations. Classic procedures, he argued, exaggerate the impact of proximal factors and minimize the significance of surrounding distal factors.

Berkowitz and Donnerstein (1982) have made analyses, however, which indicate that ecological validity is a minus as well as a plus. For example, if a researcher is interested primarily in testing the implication of a theoretical proposition, then systematic experimentation is necessary. In this case, the experimenter is interested in causal relations among general constructs, and the subject sample is an arbitrary group from the general universe. Thus greater weight is given to systematic experimental designs than to representativeness of subjects and settings.

The generalizability of experimental research is also an empirical question. In some areas of research, experimental (laboratory) and naturalistic methods produce similar results. For example, Dipboye and Flanagen (1979) examined 200 laboratory and 200 field studies in industrial/organizational psychology and concluded that there is little difference in the degree to which one can generalize. It is also important to recognize that demographic characteristics of the sample, and superficial characteristics of settings, may not be crucial to generalizability.

TABLE 3   Threats to Validity, Especially of Quasi-Experimental Research

Threats to Statistical Conclusion Validity
1. Small samples that lead to incorrect no-difference conclusions
2. Violations of assumptions of statistical tests (e.g., in analysis of covariance, regression of posttest on covariate should be homogeneous) and groups compared should be equivalent (e.g., on pretest means); in addition, the robustness of statistical tests needs to be considered
3. Multiple comparisons in "fishing" expeditions.
4. Measures with low reliability cannot detect true changes
5. Reliability of treatment implementation
6. Problems in logically proving the null hypothesis (e.g., true difference not detected because of lack of power of treatment or statistical test), extraneous sources of variance correlated with dependent variable, and factors related to threats above
7. Unnecessarily large error variance can be reduced by:
   a. Using subject as own control (i.e., serves in more than one experimental group)
   b. Selecting homogeneous samples
   c. Collecting pretest measures
   d. Matching on basis of variable correlated with posttest
   e. Covarying out variable correlated with posttest
   f. Increasing reliability of dependent variable

Threats to Internal Validity
1. History (i.e., event taking place between pretest and posttest)
2. Testing (e.g., familiarity with test used as dependent variable)
3. Instrumentation (i.e., change in measurements between pretest and posttest)
4. Statistical regression (i.e., among high pretest scores there are a disproportionate number with larger positive error components, while among low pretest scores there are a disproportionate number with larger negative error components)
5. Selection, especially in quasi-experimental groups
6. Mortality (i.e., different types of subjects drop out)
7. Interaction of selection with factors above (e.g., selection and instrumentation when different groups score at different mean positions on a test whose intervals are not equal)
8. Diffusion, compensatory equalization, compensatory rivalry, and resentful demoralization in relation to treatments/no treatments applied in the same field settings
9. Randomization rules out most of these threats, except mortality and inequities, and so on, identified in number 8

Threats to Construct Validity
1. Inadequate preoperational explication of constructs (e.g., trait is defined as stable predisposition to respond), and such "stability" usually includes consistency across modes of responding (i.e., affective, cognitive, and behavioral), and consistency across time or situations
2. Lack of multiple operationalizations of a construct; applies to both treatment and (especially) dependent variable
3. Hypothesis guessing within treatments, by subjects
4. Evaluation apprehension of subjects
5. Experimenter expectancies
6. To improve construct validity we should:
   a. Think through how construct should be defined
   b. Differentiate it from related constructs
   c. Decide which manipulations (for treatment) or measures (for dependent variable) can be used to operationalize the construct
   d. Have multiple measures or manipulations, which will improve "fit" between construct and operations

TABLE 3   *(continued)*

Threats to External Validity
1. Interaction of selection and treatment
2. Interaction of setting and treatment (e.g., can causal relationship obtained in elementary school be obtained in other settings)
3. Interaction of history and treatment; in many instances, researchers have target populations they want to generalize to, and so sample appropriately from these populations of persons, settings, or times
4. In the final analysis, external validity is a matter of replication, both within and across studies

Source. Derived from Cook and Campbell (1979), Chap. 2.

General Criteria for Evaluating Scientific Problem Solving

The other approach to scientific evaluation emphasizes more global aspects of research as process and product. But there are no ready-made sources of such criteria, as is the case for conceptual and technical analysis. One source, however, is experts who do evaluations of research studies on a regular basis for research-oriented journals (see, e.g., Gottfredson, 1978; Thomas, 1980). One thing we know from such studies is that reviewers as a group are highly credible, visible experts. Another is that there is considerable commonality in terms of the underlying evaluative factors that they use and that these factors can be meaningfully structured.

An example of such a taxonomy is presented in Figure 7. In this model, which is derived in part from Phillips (1982), there are two levels of scientific evaluation. In the first, formative evaluation, a research study is evaluated as a process using psychological science's agreed-upon set of research procedures as criteria. In this instance, the evaluator concentrates on the way a research study was given form or shape and was performed and reported.

In the other phase of scientific evaluation the impact or effect of a research study on the discipline is assessed. This amounts to summative evaluation, or a summing up of a study's probable contribution to the field. However, this higher level of evaluation does not compete with or supplant formative evaluation. That is, formative evaluation is a constituent of the higher level but can in no sense account for it.

Scientific Evaluation and Usefulness

These criteria for scientific evaluation are of primary concern to the research psychologist. But research that is to be shared with practitioners must, of course, be useful as well as scientifically meritorious. To be most effective, aspects of scientific evaluation that are critical requirements of usefulness need to be singled out, and this is done in Table 4.

To consider these characteristics further, note that essentially they represent factors of varying degrees of abstraction and concreteness that, in turn, reflect research and practice interrelationships. To take the first example, "readily available," if we take into account the limited access of practitioners to the literature, usefulness depends on the likelihood that practitioners will locate relevant research studies and on the dissemination activities of researchers. Another example, "has direct implications for action," emphasizes that the meaning of research results needs to be readily grasped, and that in writing up research reports it is important for researchers to make the meaning of results clear.

SPECIAL PROBLEMS IN EVALUATING APTITUDE-TREATMENT INTERACTION RESEARCH

The purpose of Aptitude-Treatment Interaction (ATI) research is to find the psychological or educational intervention for each student that maximizes his or her performance. This scientific as well as practical goal recognizes that the capacity for school learning cannot be conceived in the abstract. It is always a capacity to learn in a particular school environment, and the child who learns well under one condition may not learn well under another. Applied to school psychological practice, the bottom line is that to maximize prac-

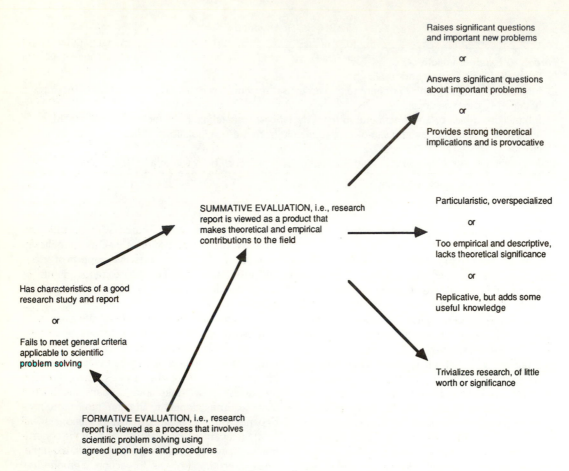

Figure 7. A model of scientific evaluation of research reports.

TABLE 4. Characteristics of Research Studies That Are Important to Their Usefulness to Practitioners

---

Readily available
Understandably written, not overly technical
Relevance to particular problem, issue
Conceptualizes problem, issue well
Examines manipulable variables
Studies population of particular interest
Sample appropriately drawn
Adequate information on methods, subjects, definitions, and so on
Objective, unbiased interpretation of results
Findings consistent, unambiguous
Recommendations supported by data
Adequate replication or follow-up of results
Has direct implications for action
Adds to practical knowledge

---

tical payoff, one has to determine both the best general psychological and educational interventions (i.e., the best interventions in a "main effects" sense) and the best allocation of students to those interventions (i.e., in an "interaction effects" sense). In addition, it is necessary to take interventions apart and reconstitute them to see whether the parts and pieces and newly constituted interventions affect the learning of individuals differently.

However, there are special problems with the dominant style of past ATI research, and new directions for ATI research have been put forward by Phillips (1985), Cronbach and Snow (1977), and others. For example, we cannot place the usual emphasis on the statistical significance of results. Confidence limits do preserve researchers and practitioners (and readers) from premature closure, but closure in the end will have to come from the theoretical and/or practical coherence of the results rather than from statistics alone. The costs of experimentation and the need to generalize also make it not possible to rely on statistics alone. Ultimately, we also have to recognize the probabilistic nature of scientific truths. To illustrate these points, Cronbach and Snow (1977) show that for research to be directly useful in school diagnostic-intervention decisions, investigators need to find fourth-order interactions of this type: Age × Ability × Subject Matter × Treatment × Outcome.

Past ATI research also has typically regarded individuals as independent and ignored socio-psychological effects. For example, disordinal in-

teractions have been used to match individual students and treatments, in contrast to determining classroom-based interaction effects and matching classes to treatments (see Figure 8). Experimental classes, groups, and so on, are, of course, formed according to some policy or practice, and findings would apply only to actual classes, groups, and so on, formed in the same way.

Most intervention studies, including ATI studies, also are too brief since such results are educationally significant only if they apply throughout an extended intervention. For example, complex school-related knowledge and skills, such as those in reading, take years to acquire. In addition, most

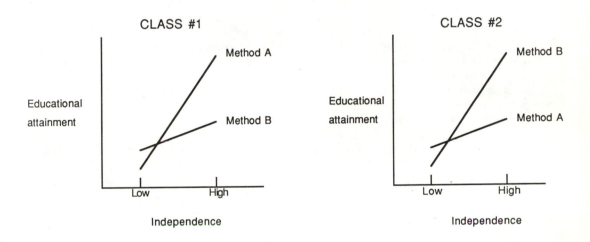

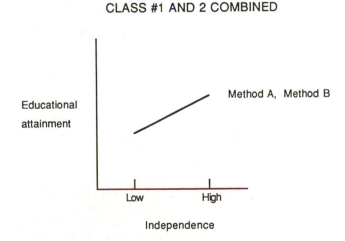

Figure 8. Example of how not taking classroom group effects into account misses important ATIs.

ATI research involves naive subjects who are having their first encounter with the task and experimental situation and have little opportunity to learn to learn. In contrast, children are "tuned" to the school learning situation.

ATI research also has emphasized learning through practice rather than learning through instruction. That is, "repeated trials" is the typical approach to learning (in learning experiments), and learning outcomes are practice rather than instruction effects. The need to find out what actually happens in the course of intervention is also important, as is the need for educationally realistic experimental interventions.

Demographic classification of ATI research also needs to be augmented with process-oriented variables (R. E. Snow, 1986). Age, sex, social status, and so on, should not be regarded as *the* major aptitude variables. Variability within each demographic subgroup is enormous, and such variables might be better considered as "proxies" for more meaningful variables.

Two methodological factors should also receive special mention. Samples generally are too small. Interaction studies are especially sensitive to sample size, and Cronbach and Snow (1977) recommend a sample size of 100 as a minimum. They also advocate the use of regression rather than analysis-of-variance models for ATI research.

Finally, in research on aptitude and instruction the motivation of the learner is taken for granted. This is because such research is short-term, novel, intrinsically interesting, and makes use of the subject's desire to be a good subject. Although general ability is first in documented positive effects on classroom achievement, academic engaged time or time on task is a close second (Denham & Lieberman, 1980). But academic engaged time requires a *motivated* learner, and ATI research needs more focus on motivated learning in the classroom.

THE ETHICS OF RESEARCH AND PRACTICE

In its early years, psychology gave little explicit attention to ethics in research. This was partly because psychologists believed that research could or should be value free. But it is now recognized that the behavior of scientists affects the science they produce. In more extreme form, the sometimes questionable and even fraudulent ways that scientists perform and publish research is the issue,

as, for example, in the failure to preserve data for others to review, the publication of materials that one knew or should have known were false, or the description of experiments so as to make the results look more conclusive than is actually the case. The central question here is why scientists are sometimes willing to bend the rules.

To address these and other issues, the ethics of research is receiving serious attention. It is of special note, for example, that codes of ethics have been revised to reflect more adequately ethical issues in research, and that the federal government has stepped up its efforts to set guidelines and regulations that promote ethical research practices. The consensus at the present time among psychologists about the ethics of research is represented by *Ethical Principles in the Conduct of Research with Human Participants* (APA, 1982). In addition, the more general and comprehensive *Ethical Principles of Psychologists* (APA, 1981a) includes a number of references to research, as shown in Table 5.

There also are increasing numbers of scholarly and empirical investigations of the ethics of research practices. A good example is the book by Diener and Crandall (1978) in which the ethical dilemmas that arise in research are thoroughly discussed, and a wealth of examples from the literature are provided that illustrate and add meaning to the dilemmas. More recently, Adair, Dushenko, and Lindsay (1985) reviewed research documenting the impact of ethical procedures, such as informed consent, explicitly giving subjects the freedom to withdraw, deception, and debriefing on research results. According to the *Publication Manual of the American Psychological Association* (APA, 1983), such practices should be reported and described, but as these authors point out, descriptions of ethical practices generally are not included in published reports. This makes the methodological significance of ethical procedures difficult to assess and impedes the development of knowledge of the effects of ethical procedures, which is a matter of special concern for those applying the results of such research in their practice.

It is also necessary to look at ethical issues in practice that are intertwined with the ethics of research. For example, Tokunaga (1984) recently reviewed ethical issues in consultation, and it is clear that issues problematic to consultation practice overlap with ethical issues in research. Con-

TABLE 5   References to Research in the Ethical Principles of Psychologists

Principle 1. Responsibility, Section a, responsibilities in doing and disseminating research

Principle 2. Moral and legal standards, Section d, responsibility to know state and federal statutes

Principle 4. Public statements, Section g, presenting science results and their publication fairly

Principle 5. Confidentiality, Sections e and f, identity of research subjects, and so on

Principle 7. Professional relationships, Sections a–j

    a. In planning research, making evaluations of ethical acceptability

    b. Maintenance of acceptable practice by subordinates

    c. Inform participants of all features that might influence decision to participate

    d. Openness and honesty with subjects except where concealment and deception are necessary; afterward, explain and justify

    e. Respect subjects' freedom to decline before and during experiment; especially important when experimenter has power over participants

    f. Develop fair and equitable agreement with subjects; experimenter must keep promises

    g. Protect subjects from physical and mental harm; if risks exist, inform subjects and take all possible measures to minimize them

    h. Afterward, tell subjects nature of study; remove misconceptions

    i. When undersirable consequences to subjects occur, must detect and remove them

    j. Information obtained about subjects during study must remain confidential unless there is agreement in advance on sharing

Source. APA (1981a).

cern for the ethics of psychotherapeutic practice is another example for which Haas, Fennimore, & Warburton (1983) list 162 references published between 1970 and 1982 that address ethical (as well as legal) issues. Although the focus is not on research in psychotherapeutic practice per se, there are numerous mentions of research and its application. Applying research to practice, therefore, reflects conscious and explicit ethical considerations.

RESEARCHERS AND PRACTITIONERS: A VITAL BUT DIFFICULT PARTNERSHIP IN SCHOOL PSYCHOLOGY

In this chapter a critical task has been explored—how to use research to improve practice—and in the perspective and procedures outlined, the interests of researchers and practitioners coincide. This admittedly is a rather broad and ambitious purpose, but it is an objective that adheres to an underlying and fundamental truth: There is no laboratory in which to apply psychological science; the world of practice is its only home. In addition, effective adoption of research is more likely when researchers interact with practitioners and embrace

the whole messy world of practice, knowing that its boundaries do not respect those of their discipline.

This interdependence takes still other forms, the most important of which are: (a) Researchers will maintain continuing, close contacts with practitioners so as to be responsive to their changing needs; (b) researchers will not presume that they can construct better understandings of practice problems than practitioners; (c) practitioners have ways of accurately identifying their practice problems and realize that solving them may be dependent on their wanting information of a scientific nature about these problems and their possible solutions; (d) practitioners can identify practice problems that are the least and the most amenable to productive, research-based solutions; and (e) practitioners know how psychological knowledge is and is not effectively applied to influence practice and have an understanding of the nature of practical application so as to distinguish good from bad applications.

Finally, although an interactive, collaborative, and participatory approach has much to offer, efforts to apply psychological science to practice is also a gambling situation where practitioners, in coping with the many uncertainties, will need to gamble well, selecting research results that increase the likelihood of practice gains and minimize possibilities of practice losses. Ultimately, psychological science and practice make conflicting claims on practitioners, and practitioners must make the best constructions of practical application they can and then act on their implications. In essence, practitioners must think and choose and rely on their own resources, recognizing that any given set of scientific facts and principles, and the applications they launch, are of limited usefulness. Research psychologists also need to make more modest claims of ultimate truth and of the applicability of their facts and principles, which means that they will be less embarrassed when other theories, facts, and principles replace their own favorite ones, or the applications they recommend fail to work. Nonetheless, it is now reasonable for views of practical applications of psychological science to be given depth, breadth, and excitement.

REFERENCES

Adair, J. G., Dushenko, T. W., & Lindsay, R. C. L. (1985). Ethical regulations and their impact on research practice. *American Psychologist, 40,* 59–72.

American Psychological Association. (1981a). Ethical principles of psychologists. *American Psychologist, 36,* 633–638.

American Psychological Association, Committee on Professional Standards. (1981b). Speciality guidelines for the delivery of services by school psychologists. *American Psychologist, 36,* 670–681.

American Psychological Association. (1982). *Ethical principles in the conduct of research with human participants.* Washington, DC: Author.

American Psychological Association. (1983). *Publication manual of the American Psychological Association* (3rd ed.). Washington, DC: Author.

Bandura, A. (1978). The self-system in reciprocal determinism. *American Psychologist, 33,* 344–358.

Bazelon, D. L. (1982). Veils, values, and social responsibility. *American Psychologist, 37,* 115–121.

Berkowitz, L, & Donnerstein, E. (1982). External validity is more than skin deep: Some answers to criticisms of laboratory experiments. *American Psychologist, 37,* 245–257.

Block, K. K. (1982). The handbook of school psychology: An invitation to development and research [Review of C. R. Reynolds & T. B. Gutkin (Eds.), *The handbook of school psychology.* New York: Wiley, 1982]. *Contemporary Education Review, 1,* 174–178.

Brunswick, E. (1955). Representative design and probabilistic theory in a functional psychology. *Psychological Review, 62,* 193–217.

Buss, A. R. (1977). The trait–situation controversy and the concept of interaction. *Personality and Social Psychology Bulletin, 3,* 196–201.

Campbell, D. T., & Stanley, J. C. (1963). Experimental and quasi-experimental designs for research on teaching. In N. L. Gage (Ed.), *Handbook of research on teaching* (pp. 171–246). Skokie, IL: Rand McNally.

Cohen, J. (1977). *Statistical power analysis for the behavioral sciences.* New York: Academic Press.

Cook, T. D., & Campbell, D. T. (1979). *Quasi-experimentation: Design and analysis issues for field settings.* Skokie, IL: Rand McNally.

Cooper, H. M. (1982). Scientific guidelines for conducting integrative research reviews. *Review of Educational Research, 52,* 291–302.

Cronbach, L. J. (1957). The two disciplines of psychology. *American Psychologist, 12,* 671–684.

Cronbach, L. J. (1975). Beyond the two disciplines of scientific psychology. *American Psychologist, 30,* 116–125.

Cronbach, L. J., & Snow, R. E. (1977). *Aptitude and instructional methods: Handbook for research on interactions.* New York: Irvington.

Denham, C., & Lieberman, A. (Eds.). (1980). *Time to learn.* Washington, DC: National Institute of Education.

Diener, E., & Crandall, R. (1978). *Ethics in social and behavioral research.* Chicago: University of Chicago Press.

Dipboye, R. L., & Flanagan, M. F. (1979). Research settings in industrial and organizational psychology: Are findings in the field more generalizable than in the laboratory? *American Psychologist, 34,* 141–150.

Feldman, C., & Haas, W. (1970). Controls, conceptualization, and the interpretation between experimental and correlational research. *American Psychologist, 25,* 633–635.

Frank, G. (1984). The boulder model: History, rationale, and critique. *Professional Psychology: Research and Practice, 15,* 417–435.

Gerard, H. B. (1983). School desegregation: The social science role. *American Psychologist, 38,* 869–877.

Gergen, K. J. (1985). The social constructionist movement in modern psychology. *American Psychologist, 40,* 266–275.

Glass, G. V., Cahen, L. S., Smith, M. L., & Filby, N. N. (1982). *School class size: Research and policy.* Beverly Hills, CA: Sage.

Glass, G. V., McGraw, B., & Smith, M. L. (1981). *Meta-analysis in social research.* Beverly Hills, CA: Sage.

Gottfredson, S. D. (1978). Evaluating psychological research reports: Dimensions, reliability, and correlates of quality judgments. *American Psychologist, 33,* 920–934.

Green, B. F., & Hall, J. A. (1984). Quantitative methods for literature reviews. *Annual Review of Psychology, 35,* 37–53.

Haas, L. J., Fennimore, D., & Warburton, J. R. (1983). A bibliography on ethical and legal issues in psychotherapy, 1970–1982. *Professional Psychology: Research and Practice, 14,* 771–779.

Howard, G. S., & Conway, C. G. (1986). Can there be an empirical science of volitional action? *American Psychologist, 41,* 1241–1251.

Hunter, J. E., Schmidt, F. L., & Jackson, G. B. (1982). *Meta-analysis: Cumulating research findings across studies. Studying organizations: Innovations in methodology* (Vol. 4). Beverly Hills, CA: Sage.

Jackson, G. B. (1980). Methods for integrative reviews. *Review of Educational Research, 50,* 438–460.

Kimble, G. A. (1984). Psychology's two worlds. *American Psychologist, 39,* 833–839.

Koch, S. (1981). Psychology and its human clientele: Beneficiaries or victims? In R. A. Kasschau & F. S. Kessel (Eds.), *Psychology and society: In search of symbiosis* (pp. 24–47). New York: Wiley.

Kratochwill, T. R. (1985). Case study research in school psychology. *School Psychology Review, 14,* 204–215.

Kratochwill, T. R., Feld, J. K., & Van Someren, K. R. (1986). The effectiveness of school psychological services. In S. N. Elliott & J. C. Witt (Eds.), *The delivery of psychological services in schools: Concepts, processes, and issues* (pp. 249–303). Hillsdale, NJ: Lawrence Erlbaum.

Kuhn, T. S. (1970). *The structure of scientific revolutions* (2nd rev. ed.). Chicago: University of Chicago Press. (Original work published 1962)

Lambert, N. M. (1983). School psychology today [Review of C. R. Reynolds and T. B. Gutkins (Eds.), *The handbook of school psychology.* New York: Wiley, 1982]. *Contemporary Psychology, 28,* 346–349.

Lawler, E. E., III, Mohrman, A. M., Jr., Mohrman, S. A., Ledford, G. E., Cummings, T. G., & Associates (1985). *Doing research that is useful for theory and practice.* San Francisco: Jossey-Bass.

Manicas, P. T., & Secord, P. F. (1983). Implications for psychology of the new philosophy of science. *American Psychologist, 38,* 399–413.

Masters, J. C. (1984). Psychology, research, and social policy. *American Psychologist, 39,* 851–862.

Phillips B. N. (1981). School psychology in the 1980's: Some critical issues related to practice. In T. R. Kratochwill (Ed.), *Advances in school psychology* Vol. 1, (pp. 19–43). Hillsdale, NJ: Lawrence Erlbaum.

Phillips, B. N. (1982). Reading and evaluating research in school psychology. In C. R. Reynolds & T. B. Gutkin (Eds.), *The handbook of school psychology* (pp. 24–47). New York: Wiley.

Phillips, B. N. (1983). School problems of adolescence.

In C. E. Walker & M. C. Roberts (Eds.), *Handbook of clinical child psychology* (pp. 24–47). New York: Wiley.

Phillips, B. N. (1985). New directions in aptitude–treatment interaction research. In C. R. Reynolds & V. L. Willson, *Methodological and statistical advances in the study of individual differences* (pp. 241–273). New York: Plenum Press.

Phillips, B. N. (1986). The impact of education and training on school psychological services. In S. N. Elliott & J. C. Witt (Eds.), *The delivery of psychological services in schools: Concepts, processes, and issues* (pp. 329–348). Hillsdale, NJ: Lawrence Erlbaum.

Phillips, B. N. (1987). On science, mirrors, lamps, and professional practice. *Professional School Psychology, 2,* 221–229.

Phillips, B. N. (1989). Role of the practitioner in applying science to practice. *Professional Psychology: Research and Practice, 20,* 3–8.

Robinson, D. H. (1984). Ethics and advocacy. *American Psychology, 39,* 787–793.

Rorer, L. G., & Widiger, T. A. (1983). Personality structure and assessment. *Annual Review of Psychology, 34,* 431–463.

Rosenthal, R., & Rubin, D. B. (1982). Comparing effect sizes of independent studies. *Psychological Bulletin, 92,* 500–504.

Scarr, S. (1985). Constructing psychology: Making facts and fables for our times. *American Psychologist, 40,* 499–512.

Schon, D. A. (1983). *The reflective practitioner.* New York: Basic Books.

Snow, C. P. (1964). *The two cultures and a second look.* Cambridge: Cambridge University Press.

Snow, R. E. (1986). Individual differences and the design of educational programs. *American Psychologist, 41,* 1029–1039.

Thomas G. (1980). Manuscript characteristics influencing reviewers' decisions. *Canadian Psychology, 21,* 17–21.

Tokunaga, H. T. (1984). Ethical issues in consultation: An evaluative review. *Professional Psychology: Research and Practice, 15,* 811–821.

Weiss, J. A., & Weiss, C. H. (1981). Social scientists and decision makers look at the usefulness of mental health research. *American Psychologist, 36,* 837–847.

Wortman, P. M. (1983). Evaluation research: A methodological perspective. *Annual Review of Psychology, 34,* 223–260.

4

THE CONTRIBUTIONS OF DEVELOPMENTAL PSYCHOLOGY TO SCHOOL PSYCHOLOGY

DEBORAH J. THARINGER
The University of Texas–Austin
NADINE M. LAMBERT
University of California–Berkeley

Developmental psychology contributes to school psychology at three different levels. At the first level, understanding the theories and research findings of developmental psychology enables the school psychologist to describe the level of development of a particular child, to make inferences about the child's prior developmental achievements, to specify the next developmental hurdles to be mounted, and to speculate about the environmental circumstances that may promote development. At a second and higher level, knowledge of developmental theories and research empowers the school psychologist to provide explanations of behavior within a developmental framework and to share with others the probable reasons for a child's particular behavior at a given point in time. At the third and highest level, school psychologists who have integrated theories of development and research findings into a conceptual framework for understanding behavior can develop comprehensive assessment plans to appraise the developmental characteristics of a child and can propose interventions to further the child's developmental progress.

The status of developmental psychology as a means to describe and explain children's behavior, as well as to intervene to promote children's mental health, has evolved concomitantly with school psychologists' role evolution from efforts to measure and describe individual differences, to offer reasons for children's behavior, and to intervene comprehensively to promote the effective functioning of children in school. School psychologists have acquired a variety of methods for describing children's behavior, and many school psychologists rely intuitively on a developmental framework in describing their psychological knowledge of children to others. A developmental perspective in school psychology practice, however, provides not only knowledge, but the ability to *apply* developmental knowledge differentially to explanations and interventions in order to promote the educational and psychological needs of children.

The usefulness of theory and research from the field of developmental psychology to the practice of school psychology seems so obvious that for some the connection goes without saying. That is, it makes implicit sense that a specialty that systematically has studied the development of the individual, specifically the child, and has had as its overall goal the description and explanation of the developmental process would be invaluable to an applied specialty that has as its goal promoting the mental health and educational development of children in the context of the school. However, although some practicing school psychologists and school psychology training programs adhere to a developmental perspective formally and some intuitively, many others do not and may not realize the potential to be gained from such an approach. We propose that a developmental perspective is necessary but not sufficient for functioning competently as a school psychologist. It is hoped that the information presented in this chapter will break down some of the barriers that have prevented school psychology from taking full advantage of what developmental psychology has to offer and will encourage school psychologists and educators of school psychologists to integrate a developmental perspective into their practice and into their training models. As school psychologists function in expanding roles in the schools, such as providing intervention services, an understanding and application of developmental knowledge and principles are essential if the needs of children are to be met effectively.

In preparing to address the contributions of developmental psychology, a discussion of the relationship between science and practice is provided. Following, the history of developmental psychology and the essence of a developmental perspective are described. The historical and present relationship between school and developmental psychology is then analyzed, including both enduring ties and prominent obstacles. A discussion of the usefulness of theory and a brief review of major developmental theories follow, including key contributions from each theory for practice. In addition, an integrated, contemporary view of the developing child is presented. Next, areas of research in developmental psychology that are of particular interest to the school psychology practitioner are described briefly. Finally, the contributions of developmental psychology to school psychology practice, specifically assessment, direct intervention, and indirect intervention are illustrated.

THE RELATIONSHIP BETWEEN SCIENCE AND PRACTICE

The application of science to practice is complex, as professional practice is a correlated cloud of events that are intrinsically confounded (Scarr, 1985). Many practitioners feel that science has failed them because it has not yielded specific "answers" to individual problems in the field. Many practicing school psychologists have found grand theories and research findings, so dutifully studied in graduate school, of limited use when they are trying to help a particular child and her or his family understand and cope with, for example, a serious emotional disturbance. We propose that the contributions of science to practice are important but limited, and that the degree of frustration practitioners have felt reflects their model of the relationship between science and practice, their expectations for what science can offer them, and their awareness of their role in the application of science to practice.

Two major models of the relationship between science and practice have been described: the mechanistic model and the constructivist model (Phillips, 1987, and Chapter 3, this volume; Scarr, 1985). In the mechanistic view, the world is envisioned as a machine composed of discrete parts. It is a closed, predictable, controllable system. The belief from the mechanistic view is that science reflects exact truth and reality. The mechanistic model assumes a direct translation of science to practice and is referred to as a "mirror" view. In the mirror perspective there is a one-to-one relationship between science and practice in that the functions of science are direct and instrumental. In principle, exact prediction is possible because complete knowledge of the state and forces at one point in time allows the next state to be inferred. From this mirror perspective, the aim of the practitioner is to reflect the truths of science in practice. Practical application is the reassembly of ideas that are literal replicas of scientific facts and principles. A practitioner taking a mechanistic view would attempt to solve a problem by directly fitting specific knowledge discovered by science to an individual case.

From the constructivist view knowledge of all kinds, including scientific knowledge, is a construction of the human mind (Scarr, 1985). The human mind is constructed in a social context, and its knowledge is in part created by the social and cultural context in which it interacts with the world. Therefore, knowledge of the world always is constructed by the human mind into the working models of reality in the sciences. Scientific facts are not discovered; they are invented by individuals. Their usefulness depends both on shared perceptions of the "facts" and on whether they work for various purposes, some theoretical and some practical. The constructivist view uses as its metaphor the "lamp." From the constructivist or lamp perspective, the practitioner projects a light on scientific facts and principles, and for each individual case, finds a different illumination. In lamp theory, the practitioner is pictured as active rather than merely receptive; the practitioner is a constructor and creator, allowing for unique individual solutions. The relationship between science and practice is not precise, but depends on the practitioner's own processing of scientific information, and its elucidation for a particular case.

Many school psychologists have been trained on the mechanistic tradition and many have found the public schools to have a mechanistic world view. We maintain that the mechanistic perspective of the relationship between science and practice is reductionistic and illusionary. We also propose, as others have (Phillips, 1987, and Chapter 3, this volume; Scarr, 1985), that the constructionist view will increase the contributions of science to practice and will allow school psychologists to use science more creatively and effectively in constructing their solutions to problems. From the mechanistic view, the practitioner is lead to believe that reality can be known and that there are answers and absolute solutions to problems, setting up an "expert" model and a "technician" mind set. By taking a constructivist view, scientists can make more modest claims of ultimate truth and practitioners can be less surprised and embarassed when the interventions they attempt based on their favorite theories and principles are not very effective. Constructivist school psychologists acquire a healthy humility and learn to rely on creative problem solving. When an approach fails, they replace it with a new approach that may prove to be more useful. It is accepted that any given theory and the intervention it launches are of limited usefulness—limited by the sociocultural time and space in which they occur (Scarr, 1985). The constructivist view forces both scientists and practitioners to accept the limited usefulness of any given set of facts and principles and the practical applications that follow, and forces them constantly to propose new models, study new relationships, and seek new applications. By abandoning the overly simple mechanistic view and acquiring a constructivist approach, the school psychologist will have a fruitful strategy for applying the contributions of developmental psychology to the complexities of school practice.

DEVELOPMENTAL PSYCHOLOGY

Developmental psychology is the scientific study of how individuals change over time and of the factors that produce the changes. The basic task of developmental psychology is that of describing and explaining change. Developmentalists trace the transformations that take place within the individual over the periods of childhood, adolscence, and adulthood, and characterize the manner in which people remain identifiably the same but also change radically as they grow older. Whereas historically developmentalists centered their attention on normal development, and the bulk of their research addressed age-normative behavior of infants and children, the current interests of developmental psychology are much broader.

History of Developmental Psychology

A historical analysis identifies the periods when certain developmental theories and research findings became available for the practitioner and charts the rise and fall of major theoretical perspectives. The history of developmental psychology in this country has been reviewed by Cairns (1983). He describes 100 years, subdivided into the formative period (1882–1912), the period of fragmentation (1913–1946), and the period of modern growth and expansion (1947–1982). During the formative years the field of child development was a vigorous, multidisciplinary undertaking with new ideas, fresh approaches, and novel methods, and involved European and American psychologists, anatomists, pediatricians, child guidance workers, and statisticians. During the 1890s, the first developmental journal was published, the first research institute was established, the first developmental textbooks were published, the first professional organizations were begun, and the first psychological clinic treating children was set up by Witmer at the University of Pennsylvania, referred to as the first child guidance clinic in America. It is noteworthy that developmental, school, and child clinical psychology see the establishment of the Witmer clinic as part of their birthright.

Famous figures during the formative period included Binet, G. Stanley Hall, James Mark Baldwin, and S. Freud. The major contributions of this early period included the study of the ontogeny of consciousness and intelligence, the development of volition and intentionality, the study of moral development, the relations between ontogeny and phylogeny, nature versus nurture, the question of the enduring effects of early experience, and social policy issues, including the application of developmental principles to child-rearing practices, passage of child labor laws, and revision of school curriculum.

During the middle period (1913–1946) there was much institutionalization and fragmentation. During the prosperity of the 1920s, there was strong support for research in psychology. In developmental psychology, there was an immediate need to extend the methodological boundaries of the discipline to permit systematic observation of additional issues, including social, cognitive, language, and moral development, as well as psychobiological changes. There also was an explosion in empirical research. The enterprise of child and developmental psychology became segregated into separate arenas, topics, and theories. It was readily apparent that no single theoretical model was broad enough to encompass the interests of the field.

During this middle period child development institutes were established at Iowa, Merrill Palmer, Minnesota, and Berkeley for the study and improvement of child rearing. The Society for Research in Child Development was established in 1933, along with its journal *Child Development* Issues tackled included the study of intellectual development, the pursuit of longitudinal studies (e.g., at Fels and Berkeley), the examination of children's fears (e.g., Jersild, Markey, & Jersild, 1933), and the documentation of growth and physical maturation from a maturational-unfolding perspective (Gesell, 1928, 1940). Research methods included the use of systematic observation, drawings, and interviews. Of broad significance, behaviorism became rooted in research and practice during this time with J. B. Watson (1914, 1928), an experimental child psychologist, sprouting the "modern" scientific approach to child rearing of the 1920s and 1930s. Studies of social and personality developmental examined size and gender composition of groups by age, natural occurrence of aggression, and social exchange. Honesty, prosocial behavior, and moral development were pursued, for example, in Hartshorne and May's (1928) studies of experimentally manipulated groups and Piaget's (1932) documentation of the natural occurrence of rule making and moral judgments. The development of and relationship between language and thought was explored by Piaget (1926) and by Vigotsky (1939). Developmental psychobiology and ethology were investigated (Lorenz, 1935), resulting in the origins of the systems approach that is influential in psychology today. In addition, Biber (1934) proposed applications of developmental psychology in the emerging nursery school programs.

Theoretical trends during this middle period included behaviorism, classical psychoanalysis, post and neo-Freudian formulations, behaviorism reinterpreting psychoanalytic concepts—the original social learning theory (Dollard, Miller, Doob, Mowrer, & Sears, 1939), Piaget's theory of cognitive development (Piaget, 1950), symbolic interactionism (Mead, 1934), Lewinian field theory (Lewin, 1931), and ethology (Lorenz, 1935). In-depth perspectives on theory and research in child and adolescent psychology available at the end of this period are provided by Carmichael (1946) and Barker, Kounin, and Wright (1943). Although the grand theories of child psychology were vigorously studied and applied during this period, they basically ignored each other. Each new theory challenged a previous one and proposed an attractive alternative conception of development more than it refined the earlier theory. By the end of the middle period there was a large body of empirical work on many domains of child development, which can be depicted as description of the normal course of development. But there also was much fragmentation, and due to the competition among theories, there was no overall theoretical integration and no overall theory accounting for development.

The modern era (1947–1982) is characterized by expansion, invention, and maturation. During the first half of the modern era (1947–1962), the most visible early theoretical trend was the rise, domination, and passing of the general learning theories. Until their grip began to fall during the 1960s, the behavioral model of learning was equivalent with American psychology and aspects of child behavior and development were couched in behavioristic terms. Social learning theory was prominent. Sears (1944) explored psychoanalytic learning theory from a social learning perspective, looking at aggression and dependency—but let it go to pursue the bidirectionality and social interactions in families, a pursuit that remains active in the field today. Operant conditioning models were prominent. Modeling and vicarious reinforcement were introduced by Bandura (1969), and cognitive reformulations of learning theories and principles were proposed (Kendler & Kendler, 1962). The extensive work in the behavioral tradition laid the foundation for school psychology's current use of behavioral measures, behavior modification, and behavioral consultation. Many developmental researchers of this period, however, were not converted to operant and social learning principles and with the fall of behaviorism and mechanistic models, dynamic models again were pursued.

In the second half of the modern era (1962–1982), the reemergence of the cognitive developmental theory of Piaget as a central focus for thinking and research was the most visible development in the field (Flavell, 1963). Investigations of language development, thinking, sensation, and information processing in children flourished. The barrier between social development and cognitive development was transcended, as evidenced by the study of social cognition (Shantz, 1975). There also was a fresh look at the major issues of psychobiological and behavioral development, including the effects of early experience, whether the infant is especially sensitive or invulnerable, and the importance of attachment, represented by the work of Harlow (Harlow, 1958; Harlow & Harlow, 1965), Bowlby (1958, 1969), and Ainsworth (1969). In addition, there was a surge in interest in the study of infant development and in the view of the infant as an adaptive and adapting organism. Organismic models predominated the second half of the modern era, and continue to do so today.

Developmental psychology in the 1980s can be described by five conceptual features: (a) concern with explanations of developmental change, that is, with the specification of the causes or antecedents of development as opposed to just the description of development; (b) attention to theory

or model testing as opposed to mere generation of developmental norms; (c) an emphasis on continual, reciprocal relations between active organisms and active contexts and concern with these relations, that is, a dialectical, transactional view; (d) predominance of theoretical pluralism, or multiplicity of reasonable theoretical alternatives; and (e) attention to the understanding of maladaptive development and variables (e.g., maltreatment) that contribute to placing children at risk.

A Developmental Perspective

It is apparent from the historical review that there has never been a unitary view of the content or process of development. However, by focusing on how developmental theorists have studied change over time and factors that produce change, a developmental perspective, useful to the practitioner, can be described. A developmental perspective, as applied to school psychology practice, is best viewed as a way of conceptualizing problems rather than as a solution to the problems. A developmental approach poses questions about the developmental course of adaptive and maladaptive behaviors, and offers guidelines for answering these questions. The role of a developmental approach is to help explain and change troublesome behavior in light of the developmental tasks, sequences, and processes that characterize human growth (Achenbach, 1982).

A concern for developmental issues is essential for understanding the mental health of children and adults (Eisenberg, 1977). The processes of development enables one to better understand the crucial links between genetic determinants and environmental variables, between physiogenic and psychogenic causes, and between earlier experiences and present behavior. A developmental perspective requires that the continuities and discontinuities between infancy, childhood, and adult life be taken into account. The adjective *developmental* specifies a concern with the general course of psychological development, with the changes that take place with developmental progression, and with the processes and mechanisms that underlie developmental transitions. Thus, developmentalists question whether there are age-dependent variations in susceptibility to stress, such as parental divorce; whether the development of depression or delinquent activities at one age is dependent on prior occurrences at an earlier age; and whether there are points in development when personality qualities become stabilized to the extent that although behavior may change, personality can no longer be totally transformed. A developmental approach can shed light on all phases of the life cycle, but the dramatic changes occurring from birth to maturity make it especially crucial for understanding problems of childhood and adolescence, as change is so intense during these periods (Achenbach, 1982). This general developmental perspective, along with developmental norms and descriptions, theoretical models, and research findings, equips the school psychology practitioner with indespensible tools for constructing solutions to children's problems.

THE RELATIONSHIP BETWEEN SCHOOL AND DEVELOPMENTAL PSYCHOLOGY

Developmental and school psychology share common ground, both in placing their origins at the establishment of the Witmer clinic and in being influenced by events in the general history of the field of psychology. Both fields have focused primarily on children: developmental from a theoretical and research perspective and school from an applied perspective. Even with these commonalities, the relationship between developmental and school psychology is described accurately as undeveloped and discontinuous.

Some school psychologists and school psychology educators have integrated a developmental perspective into their practice and training programs and have applied developmental findings beyond the assessment role and its normative inferences into the areas of intervention (Lindberg & Egeland, 1987). However, only when professional roles besides assessment define the professional skill armamentarium of school psychologists will the vast theoretical and research literature from developmental psychology establish itself as a necessary foundation for the practice of school psychology. As school psychologists engage more extensively in individual and group child counseling, teacher consultation, parent education and training, family counseling, and prevention activities, the developmental literature will prove to be an essential resource.

Enduring Contributions
of Developmental Psychology
The best and most established example of the utilization of developmental information in school psychology practice is the formal and informal

assessment of children. Assessment, for the purposes of identifying and classifying children for special programs, has been and remains the major role for school psychologists. To address the question, "Are Julie's intellectual abilities, academic performance, behavior, thoughts, and feelings normal?" school psychologists for decades have been using tools and information provided by child and developmental psychologists. In their assessment of children and adolescents, school psychologists have sought out tests that are developmentally based, achievement and behavioral norms, and descriptions of the developmental progressions of normal thoughts, feelings, and behavior. In their formal assessment activities, school psychologists routinely use tests that were developed with developmental features in mind (e.g., the Stanford-Binet, WISC-R) and tests that specify developmental norms (e.g., the Bender, DTVMI, D-A-P). There also are newly developed behavior checklists, to be completed by parents and teachers, that yield specific age by gender norms (Achenbach & Edelbrock, 1983).

In informal assessment activities, school psychologists compare a child's functioning with normative knowledge they have of the child's expected cognitive, behavioral, language, emotional, and social development, obtained from study and experience. Classic examples, beyond the stage descriptions provided by Freud, Erikson, and Piaget, include the descriptive norms provided by Gesell and his colleagues on motor, adaptive, language, and personal-social behavior (Gesell, 1928, 1940), by Havighurst (1953) on physical skills, getting along with others, developing fundamental academic skills, values, personal independence, and attitudes toward social institutions and authority, and by Jersild et al. (1933) on children's fears. More recent examples include Greenspan's (1981) description of the affective and interpersonal development of children, Wallerstein and Kelly's work on how children at different developmental levels cope with parental divorce (Wallerstein, 1985; Wallerstein & Kelly, 1980), and Selman's (1980) and Shantz's (1983) descriptions of the development of social cognition.

Intuitively, school psychologists may all, perhaps unknowingly, be developmentalists, even without any formal developmental specialization. Aside from utilizing developmentally based tests, normative data, and knowledge of progressions of development, school psychologists conduct assessments in the school setting using implicit developmental norms. That is, the child being assessed is functioning in a natural environment where there are built-in developmental comparisons available in the immediate context. For example, the school psychologist who is observing in the classroom or on the playground has 30 or 100 other similarly aged children with whom to compare the target child. Thus, the question of "normality" in relationship to the interactions and behaviors of other children can be addressed. School psychologists have an advantage over child mental health practitioners who see only referred children in a private office, clinic, or hospital setting. School psychologists, because they are involved with a broad spectrum of individual differences, look through glasses tinted with normality and clearly identify pathology when it presents itself, whereas psychologists who wear glasses tinted with pathology may miss normality when it presents itself.

Obstacles to Overcome to Optimize the Contributions of Developmental Psychology

Eight obstacles, and how to overcome their legacy or present limitations, are examined. The first four are conceptual distinctions between the fields of developmental and school psychology which have incorrectly promoted the view that school psychology cannot profit greatly from developmental psychology. These distinctions are noted by recognizing that developmental psychology pursues basic knowledge by studying the normal development of groups of children, primarily from an organismic perspective of human nature. In contrast, school psychology is an applied specialty, practicing with individual, atypical children, often from a mechanistic perspective. The remaining four obstacles are issues that may have affected the ability of school psychology to make use of developmental information or hampered developmental psychology from producing information relevant to school psychology. These include the predominance of the assessment role in school psychology practice, the nondevelopmental approach of learning theories, the predominance of Piagetian thought in developmental psychology, and the tendency of child practitioners to adultmorphize.

Basic versus Applied

Developmental and school psychology often are on different ends of the continnum of basic and applied psychology and typically have different immediate goals. Developmental psychology largely is an academic specialty, existing in university psychology departments and institutes of child development. The major goals of developmental psychology are to describe and to explain the process of devationment by conducting basic and applied research, often by following a specific theoretical framework. The basic aims are to produce research that enhances scientific understanding of development and to deseminate the findings.

In contrast, school psychology is an applied speciality, practiced in the schools. The goals are to respond to the special needs of children in ways that will promote their education, development, and mental health. To meet their goals, school psychologists assess the intellectual, academic, emotional and social functioning of children to determine their needs; collaborate with groups of professionals to plan and obtain appropriate interventions for children; consult with teachers, parents, and involved systems to obtain and to affect interventions for children; educate teachers, parents, and others to enhance the understanding and fair treatment of children; intervene directly with children, parents, and families to facilitate the academic, social, and emotional growth of children; and make medical and mental health referrals to obtain additional information and service. The basic and important aim of school psychology is to make a positive difference in the everyday lives of children.

Overcoming the tendency to interpret this basic versus applied or research versus practice difference as an obstacle demands the acknowledgment that both perspectives are needed to be effective in understanding and promoting a more optimal world for children, as one supplies basic knowledge that the other applies, through creative, constructive means. It is essential for developmental psychologists to listen to the needs of school psychologists and to engage in basic and applied research that may produce information of value to them. It also is important for school psychologists to realize the important contribution that theory and research can make to practice but also to remember that to link theory and research to practice they will have to construct the application, as research findings can rarely be applied directly to practice.

Normal versus Atypical

Developmental psychologists traditionally have studied and chronicled the "normal" child, with the aim of understanding normal development.

Specifications of universals of development often have been the focus of theorizing and research, for example, Piaget's work. In contrast, school psychologists work primarily with atypical children, children with learning, emotional, social, behavioral, and physical problems, and children at risk for such problems. For the school psychologist, individual differences, or deviations from the *norm,* are the focus. The solution to overcoming this obstacle is not for the developmentalist to study only atypical children (although as is discussed below, developmental psychologists have begun active study of children with problems and children at risk for problems) or for the school psychologist to work with only normal, healthy children. The solution is for the practitioner to understand the progression and processes of normal development in order to understand and intervene with abnormal developmental manifestations and processes. Normal development informs the understanding of abnormal development, and vice versa (Cowan, 1978).

Group versus Individual
Developmental psychologists typically study groups of children, focusing on one domain of functioning at a time, such as cognitive problem solving, or the effects of a certain variable on a domain of functioning, such as the effects of parenting styles on children's cognitive development, controlling for other variables whenever possible. Developmentalists look for group age differences or group relationships between variables. These studies lead to an understanding of associations between variables and hypotheses about causality. In contrast, school psychologists typically study an individual child and integrate the child's domains of functioning into a view of the whole child, and are unable to control for (or control) the variety of forces and influences on a child's life.

The solution to applying research on group characteristics to an analysis of individual differences is not to ignore group research findings but rather for a school psychologist to realize that research findings from group data will not apply to *all* children. If practitioners take a constructivist view of the relationship between knowledge and practice, they can feel comfortable trying out ideas gained from a body of research to determine their applicability or usefulness to a certain child's needs, and they can feel comfortable trying another approach when certain information does not

fit or certain changes do not result. It is important for the practitioner to remember that research findings offer ideas and guidelines and provide the practitioner with hypotheses for practice. Research findings are not meant to be applied directly, as each child is an individual and has been affected by and has affected a unique environment. Each child with whom a school psychologist works, in assessment or intervention, can be viewed as an *N*-of-1 "research" study. It remains useful, however, to approach each child's case with as many hypotheses as possible that have been supported by group research, and to dismiss ideas that do not work in each individual case.

Distinct View of Human Nature
Developmental psychology and school psychology historically have been guided by distinct views of human nature. Developmentalists primarily have taken an organismic view of human nature, with the exception of the period in history when behaviorism dominated child psychology. From the organismic view, the child is viewed as an active, organized whole that is changing constantly, and self-initiated behavior and thought lead to changes in both the structure and content of the child's behavior and thought.

Many, though not all, school psychologists have taken a mechanistic view, partially because of the dominant historical influence of behaviorism and learning theory in the practice of school psychology and education. From the mechanistic view, development is seen as being caused by external forces and events that act on the passive, machinelike mind of the child. A mechanistic view of the child's development has been quite prominent in American education, and school psychologists have undoubtably been pressured to view the child from a mechanistic perspective and to apply science to their practice with a mechanistic stance. The mechanistic view has been appealing because it has offered the psychologist a great deal of *control* over explaining the behavior of the child and developing behavioral assessment and intervention techniques, which have met with moderate success, but it also has led to the exclusion of other equally valuable perspectives. Although a school psychologist who is open to an organismic view of child development and who encourages this acceptance in the school setting may be in a more ambiguous situation, the organismic approach offers richer assessment and intervention alternatives. Steps toward an organismic perspective already have been made, as few contemporary school psychology practitioners are radical behaviorists. Recent additions to the social learning perspective, especially those offered by Bandura (1977), and developments in the cognitive behavioral perspective (Kendall, 1985; Mahoney & Nezworski, 1985) have caused many practitioners of the behavioral persuasion to adopt a view of the child as active and interactive with the environment and to acknowledge that a child's behavior is organized.

Predominance of the Assessment Role in School Psychology

This obstacle accounts for much of the discontinuous application of developmental psychology to school psychology. School psychologists who function primarily in an assessment role have utilized developmentally based tests and developmental norms but have not had the opportunity to integrate a developmental perspective into intervention activities, as they typically have not been offering intervention services. School psychologists are needed who are encouraged to consult with teachers, educate parents, and provide direct intervention services for children. The means for overcoming this obstacle is obvious—school psychologists must continue to negotiate their roles to provide services beyond assessment and placement for special programs and must seek out knowledge to make them more effective in their broader roles, including knowledge of developmental psychology. In addition, university training programs need to examine their curriculum to determine how much exposure students are getting to developmental principles and must strive to provide students with opportunities to construct applications of developmental models and research findings into their assessment and intervention practices.

The Nondevelopmental Approach of Learning Theories

As mentioned above, learning theories and behavioral approaches have been influential and prominent in the practice of school psychology. Behavioral approaches to assessment, observation, interviewing, consultation, and direct intervention with children based on classical, operant, and social learning principles are utilized. For the learning theorist, learning allows for development while for the developmentalist, development allows for learning. These are two very distinct points of view with very different implications for educational and psychological intervention. Learning theorists historically, and for the most part presently, have not been interested in developmental principles. The objective of learning theorists has been to discover general principles of behavior that hold across ages. The behavioral approach has yielded moderately impressive techniques for managing the behavior of children with serious problems with aggression, impulsivity, autism, and mental retardation. However, formal knowledge of human development at best has not been systematically incorporated into their assessment or treatment approaches and at worst has been systematically ignored. Although some would argue that practitioners from a behavioral perspective implicitly incorporate information about children's developmental levels into intervention plans, systematic applications of developmental principles are observed rarely.

Fortunately, this obstacle seemingly is being overcome. Many contemporary learning theorists and behaviorists are beginning to recognize the importance of a child's developmental level. Recently, some behaviorists have suggested that developmental theory and empirical findings could make several potentially important contributions to behavioral psychology (Hartman, Roper, & Bradford, 1979; Kazdin, 1985; Mash & Terdal, 1981), specifically in the formulation of behavioral assessment and treatment plans. Behaviorists have begun to accept that developmental norms must be considered when judging whether a behavior's frequency is excessive or deficient. A particular type and rate of behavior may well be normal at one age but may be abnormal at another age. In addition, it has been suggested that a complete behavioral assessment must consider the child's developmental history (Ross, 1978) and that it is impossible to judge the adequacy of a child's social skills without taking the child's developmental level into account (Hops & Greenwood, 1981.) Furthermore, it has been proposed that developmental norms could help practitioners outline the correct progression of skills to present in a training program. Some cognitive behaviorists have gone even further, calling for the adoption of an underlying developmental process-oriented conceptualization to cognitive-behavioral approaches to children's problems (Mahoney & Nezworski, 1985). Thus, even behavioral approaches, which have been among the most resistant to a developmental perspective, have begun to integrate developmental findings and to acknowledge that developmental considerations have an important place in assessment and intervention activities.

Predominance of Piagetian Thought in Developmental Psychology

Piaget's dominance from 1960 to the late 1970s in developmental psychology may be viewed by some as having presented an obstacle to the application of developmental psychology to school psychology. The dominance of learning theories in developmental psychology and an overemphasis on behavior with a neglect of cognitive and emotional factors characterize the prior 20 years, 1940–1960. It is fair to describe the Piagetian era as overemphasizing cognition, with the neglect of emotion and behavior. As behavior problems bring most children to the attention of school psychologists, the dominance of a Piagetian approach, with its focus on cognition, may have been very frustrating to practitioners with a developmental orientation who were trying to change behavior. The error does not appear to rest with Piagetian thought, however, but rather with the expectations of practitioners. If practitioners were looking to Piagetian theory and research findings for exact methods to change the behavior of children in the classroom, such as the behavioral theories attempted to offer, it follows that they were disappointed. Piaget did not focus on the study of how the environment affects the individual child or on individual differences. Rather, Piaget focused on the importance of the child's interactions with the environment in the construction of cognitive structures and on universal stage sequences of cognitive development.

If practitioners were looking to Piagetian theory and research findings to understand more fully the workings of the unconscious and of emotions, to add a cognitive component to the contributions of psychoanalytic theorists, it again follows that they would be disappointed. Piaget's work was concentrated on the physical and logicomathematical domains. He himself focused very little on the social and emotional domains of development, which are of primary interest to many school psychologists. Although Piaget stressed the importance of peer interaction for cognitive development and described affectivity as the motivation for cognition (Piaget, 1970), he did not develop these ideas extensively. Developmental psychologists

who have been influenced by Piaget and interested in the social and emotional domains have tended to study social, moral, or psychological reasoning (Kohlberg, 1969; Selman, 1980; Turiel, 1983), which is cognition about social and individual phenomena, and does not directly address behavior. The theoretical and empirical bridges spanning cognition, behavior, and emotion remain in the infancy of their construction. We propose that school psychologists grounded in developmental psychology are in a good position to help construct these bridges in practice.

A major obstacle in creating applications of Piagetian developmental psychology is that many school practitioners wanted Piagetian theory to answer pragmatic questions that the theory had not addressed. When Piagetian theory did not generate specific answers to questions such as how to get Susan to behave in the classroom, many practitioners were left unconvinced of its value. The irony is that in terms of being able to offer developmental principles or guidelines to school psychology practice, Piagetian theory is the most purely developmental theory of all. Cognitive developmental theory proposes general mechanisms of change, and Piagetian research findings offer universal descriptions of development. The Piagetian-oriented school psychologist knows that children think, perceive, organize, and understand their physical, social, and personal worlds very differently at different stages in their development. In terms of assessment and intervention, this simple statement has profound implications for practice.

The Piagetian view of development offers a way of understanding children's thoughts and the development of their thoughts that has useful implications for assessment and intervention in the cognitive domain, and also in the social, emotional, and behavioral domains (see Rosen, 1984). Particular assessment methods, such as structured and unstructured interviews, reflect increasing sensitivity to cognitive developmental theory. In devising clinical techniques for use with children, most practitioners intuitively apply common knowledge about child development. Many child practitioners would agree that play is a better diagnostic and therapeutic vehicle for children younger than 7 years of age than is a formal interview (Gelfand & Peterson, 1985). However, few practitioners have consulted the cognitive developmental literature for clues on improving their interviewing strategies with young children. Some investigators have argued that traditional interview formats are inappropriate for children because of the method's reliance on verbal skills and on the ability to deal with abstractions. However, other practitioners suggest that a child interview can be very useful if the interview is structured with the child's developmental level in mind (Goodman, 1972; Greenspan, 1981; Reisman, 1973). Research on cognitive development provides many helpful guidelines for school psychologists interviewing children (Bierman, 1983). Several useful techniques for organizing interviews for children of differing developmental levels are offered by Kanfer, Eyberg, and Krahn (1983), including the differential use of description, reflection, praise, and open-ended statements. Excellent suggestions regarding the implications of developmental changes in cognitive development, language competence, psychosocial development, and social reasoning for interviewing and intervening children and adolescents are offered by Hughes (1986) and Worchel (1986). In addition, Rosen's (1984) work on Piagetian perspectives on psychopathology and psychotherapy is extremely valuable for the practitioner desiring an in-depth understanding of dysfunction for this perspective.

Adultmorphizing

Related to the prominent influence of learning theory in school psychology and to the failure of many school psychologists to adopt an explicit developmental approach is the tendency of school psychologists, along with many other child mental health providers, to adultmorphize children (Garber, 1984; Gefland & Peterson, 1985). That is, children are viewed as if they were little adults, especially in terms of psychopathology and direct intervention needs.

Adultmorphising has been supported tacitly by two grand psychological theories, psychoanalytic theory and learning theory. Early psychoanalytic writings did not stress the uniqueness of child clients and some practitioners may have formed the idea that an in-depth understanding of child development was not necessary because the same knowledge and techniques that are applied with adults can be applied to children and adolescents. In addition, as mentioned above, learning theories are not developmentally oriented. Furthermore, until recently, many school psychologists, along

with clinical psychologists, have been content to use theories of adult psychopathology and adult research findings to understand child disorders, and to apply techniques developed with adults to intervene with children.

There are multiple signs that adultmorphizing is becoming a phenomenon of the past. There is a considerable literature about the application of psychoanalytic methods to therapy with children (O'Connor, Lee, & Schaefer, 1983), and as was discussed above, more and more behaviorists are calling for an integration of a developmental perspective when applying learning principles to the understanding of childhood disorders and to intervention with children (Kazdin, 1985; Kendall, 1985; Mahoney & Nezworski, 1985). As discussed previously, cognitive developmental theory and research findings have much to offer to the practitioner's interviews and interventions with children. Furthermore, developmental psychopathologists have begun to investigate the development of children with maladaptive patterns. The new field of developmental psycholopathology (Cicchetti, 1984; Rutter & Garmezy, 1983; Sroufe & Rutter, 1984) asks questions and sets up research endeavors that may make adultmorphizing totally extinct. Although developmental psychopathology has borowed the methodology and rigor of developmental psychology, developmental psychopathology differs from the study of normal child development in its strong focus on individual differences. Developmental psychopathologists ask about the variations in the course of development and about individual differences in the developmental process (Rutter & Garmezy, 1983). Finally, the change in thinking away from applying adult methods to children has also been influenced by recent classification systems that utilize categories specific to the child's developmental level, for example, the Diagnostic and Statistical Manual of the American Psychiatric Association (APA, 1980, 1987) and the Child Behavior Checklist System (Achenbach & Edelbrock, 1983).

DEVELOPMENTAL THEORIES

Theory is necessary for the advancement of science because it organizes and gives meaning to facts, provides a framework for them, and assigns more importance to some facts than others. In addition, a theory serves as a heuristic device, a process that raises questions, guides observations, and generates new information. Psychological theory guides the behavior of psychologists doing research. It helps the psychologist formulate questions, choose what to study, and decide how to study a problem. Theory is useful to the practitioner because it provides heuristics to guide problem solving. Unique to psychological theories, developmental theory focuses on and attempts to explain changes over time. This concern with change has presented developmental theorists and researchers with the tasks of describing and explaining, describing changes within one or several areas of behavior, describing changes in the relationships among several areas of behavior, and explaining the course of development that has been described (Miller, 1983). As mentioned above, much of the early work in child psychology was concerned with description, including description of the change process, whereas recent work in developmental psychology is attempting to explain change.

To account for developmental change, most developmental theories have offered a set of general principles or rules for change. These principles specify necessary and sufficient antecedents for change and identify variables that modify or modulate the rate or nature of each change. These processes have been as diverse as dynamic equilibration in Piaget's theory, physical maturation in Freudian and ethological theory, and vicarious reinforcement and modeling in social learning theory. No one developmental theory has satisfactorily handled both description and explanation (Miller, 1983). This partially is due to the fact that the various developmental theories have studied different phenomena. The phenomena studied and the methods of investigation employed are tied to the level of analysis undertaken, a focus on structure (organization) or process (dynamic, functioning aspects of the system), what content is emphasized, for example, personality or cognition, and whether overt behavior or covert thought and personality is emphasized. The various theories attend to very different levels of behavior and select different content areas. The stage theories look at stage-defining characteristics and thus operate at a very general level. In their view, the most important developments are cognitive or personality structures. Other theorists focus on more specific acquisitions that often are limited to certain situations or types of stimulation. With respect to

content, the theories range from stressing social behaviors and personality to thinking. Some theories have focused on universal change and some on individual differences. For example, Piaget emphasized cognitive concepts acquired in all cultural groups and Freud described universal psychosexual development, whereas social learning theory emphasized differences in various children's behavior that derive from the particular models, feedback, and learning situations to which the children are exposed. The diverse emphases on what develops illustrate why an integration of developmental theories is so difficult.

Even though an integration of developmental theories presently is not available, a knowledge of developmental theories can prevent tunnel vision among practitioners working with children. A rigid perspective on children's behavior can be avoided if one incorporates several theories in an attempt to understand children's behavior. In addition, as cultural conditions change and new information about development comes to light, practitioners must select what is useful from the various theories and research findings and ignore the aspects that no longer are applicable. Combining and integrating Freud's concern with underlying motivations and emotions, Erikson's concern with the mastery of psychosocial crises, Piaget's concern with cognitive structures, learning theory's concern with performance in specific situations, Bowlby's concern with the quality of attachment and the impact of separation, and Bronfenbrenner's concern with transactions between the child and multiple environmental systems produces a powerful perspective for understanding children's behavior. Seven major developmental theories are described briefly, with an emphasis on what develops, the principles or mechanisms of development, and key contributions to practice. Extensive reviews of developmental theories are provided by Breger (1974), Langer (1969), Miller (1983), Mussen (1983), Salkind (1981), and Thomas (1985). An integrated, contemporary view of the developing child follows.

Freud's Psychoanalytic Theory
Psychoanalytic theory focuses on the motivational forces underlying behavior, emotional aspects of the personality, and the development of the psyche. According to this perspective, development is the process by which the child copes with an invariant sequence of conflicts or psychological

disturbances. Development occurs because of disturbances or conflicts between a child's drives and the social environment. The tension-reduction equilibration process that occurs as a result is the child's subsequent attempt to restore calm. What develops is the emergence and balance of psychological structures that channel, repress, and transform psychosexual energy. These structures—the id, ego, and superego—mediate between the drives and the behavior. The child's development through the psychosexual stages early in life lays the foundation of personality.

Principles of Development

Freud's theory is a "trouble" theory of development. Development proceeds because of disturbances or perturbations to the system. The factors that initiate change include maturational changes, external frustrations, internal conflicts, personal inadequacies, and anxieties (Hall, 1954). Maturational changes both propel the child into activity as she or he tries to satisfy the drives and move her or him from stage to stage as the bodily site of pleasure changes. External frustrations come from people or events that do not allow for the immediate expression of needs. These frustrations cause a painful buildup of tension and force the child to delay and detour her or his discharge of energy. Internal conflicts arise from battle among the id, ego, and superego or, more specifically, between drives and forces of repression. Personal inadequacies refer to certain skills, knowledge, expertise, or experience that the child needs but lacks. Anxieties are unpleasant feelings that occur when the child anticipates physical or psychological pain. It is the ego that has the primary responsibility for guiding the course of change initiated by the disturbances noted above and strives to maintain a balance between the needs of the id and the superego.

Key Contributions for Practice

Knowledge about the unconscious, defense mechanisms, transference, and the effects of early experiences are important for school psychology practice. Psychoanalytic theory is widely recognized for acknowledging and promoting the unconscious as a powerful shaper of development. The belief is that the antecedents of daily behavior often are beyond the realm of conscious awareness. Behavior is seen as neither haphazard nor random but has determinable causes and is goal directed, while on the surface it may appear irrational. Today

many psychologists accept that behavior is directed by powerful unconscious drives. Another major contribution of psychoanalytic theory is that of defense mechanisms. As the ego develops, it evolves techniques for accommodating the conflicting demands made on it. A strong, mature ego uses direct means to accomplish this. It admits the nature of the demands and proposes forthright, reasoned ways to effect a solution that satisfies each source of demand to an acceptable degree. But a less mature ego uses defense mechanisms, because it cannot solve the conflicts among the demands that confront it. The function of a defense mechanism is to avoid or terminate anxiety, and defenses are not necessarily pathological. They are a necessary means of control and some are characteristic of the mature adult. The extensive use of defense mechanisms to control inadequate psychological adjustment, however, can result in psychological disturbance.

The concept of transference also is of use to the child practitioner. Transference consists of children transferring feelings and reactions that they have had to other important figures in the past onto current important figures, such as a school counselor or classroom teacher. Although the interpretation of the transferences may be reserved for in-depth psychoanalytic treatment, understanding the dynamics of how the child acts with key adults at school provides diagnostic information to understand the child's needs. Finally, Freud developed the idea, so widely accepted today, that early experience is crucial to later development. According to Freud, a behavior can be understood only if one knows how it developed in the person's early history. Both normal behavior and abnormal behavior have their roots in the early years when the basic structure of the personality is laid down. The early interactions between children's drives and their social environment set the pattern for later learning, social adjustment, and coping with anxiety. Although today this notion has been broadened to include the cumulative effects of early experience and to recognize mediators that may buffer or challenge the effects of early experience, it remains a central construct in developmental psychology and is crucial to the practitioner.

Erikson's Psychosocial Theory

Psychosocial theory focuses on the development of ego identity and the healthy personality (Erikson, 1950). Human development consists of moving from nonego identity to ego identity. Erikson is known as one of the founders of ego psychology. This movement within psychoanalysis reaffirms the importance of the ego in everyday behavior and recognizes that overt behavior is not only the direct result of unconscious forces but that consciousness and the learned defenses against forces greatly affect one's activity. Ego psychology centers attention on adaptation in the normal course of development. Ego psychologists give the environment and culture a greater role in the shaping of personality and postulate that the ego did not originate from the id but had its own autonomous development. Ego psychology has affected therapeutic method in that the focus of attention is to the ego defenses against instinctual forces rather than on only the expression of id contents.

Principles of Development

According to Erikson's psychosocial theory, the mechanism of development is equated with the epigenetic principle. According to the epigenetic principle, physical maturation writes the general timetable for development and within these parameters, the child's culture pushes, pulls, nurtures, and harms. In Erikson's view, society exerts its influence on the developing child at many levels, ranging from society's abstract ideology down to a parent's caress. Development is a result of the resolution of conflict from opposing forces. Erikson's picture of the process features a description of conflicts, inner and outer, which the vital personality weathers, reemerging from each crisis with an increased sense of inner unity, an increase of good judgment, and an increase in the capacity "to do well" according to the individual's own standards and to the standards of those who are significant to her. Erikson also elaborates on play as a specific mechanism of development (Erikson, 1977). He uses play in a broad sense to mean the use of imagination to try out ways of mastering and adapting to the world, to express emotions, to recreate past situations or imagine future situations, and to develop new models of existence.

Key Contributions for Practice

Erikson's best known contribution is his model of the eight psychosocial stages of development (Erikson, 1950). Each stage centers on a psychosocial crisis that involves the interaction of maturational expectations and societal expectations and

must be resolved if the child is to move constructively and effectively to the next stages. Over the developmental progressions of the eight stages there is an expansion of the radius of significant relationships, from the maternal person at the trust versus mistrust stage, to the basic family at the initiative versus guilt stage, to peer groups at the identity versus identity diffusion stage. At each stage, the individual struggles with the question "Who am I?" and reworks the answer and awareness at each stage. Although each crisis is most evident at a particular stage in the life cycle, each earlier crisis appears in some form throughout development. Each stage builds on the previous stages and influences the form of the latter stages, but also adds a new dimension to the person's interactions with the self and the environment. If a stage is not handled satisfactorily, the person continues to fight earlier battles in later life. Erikson optimistically claims, however, that it is never too late to resolve any of the crises. Additional contributions from Erikson that are useful for practice include a focus on the fit between the child and the culture at different stages of development and the need to look at the structure of the social organization in which the child finds herself, as the child is a life cycle in a community of life cycles.

Piaget's Theory of Cognitive Development

Piaget spent a lifetime studying genetic epistemology, that is, pursuing the development of the construction of knowledge, to answer the question "How do we come to know?" Piaget proposes the construct of constructivism as being central; the child actively constructs knowledge, has an active part in the process of knowing, and contributes to the form knowledge takes (Piaget, 1950, 1970). Piaget also proposes the construct of structuralism: underlying organizational properties of knowledge. According to Piaget, it is the underlying logical structure that develops. Piaget is best known for his stage approach to cognitive development. Cognitive development proceeds through a series of stages, where a stage is a period of time in which the child's thinking and behavior in a variety of situations reflect a particular type of underlying logical structure. Various cognitive levels provide different ways of adapting to the environment.

Principles of Development

Piaget, who was educated as a biologist, takes the position that living things by definition require active interaction with the environment to adapt or they will die. For Piaget, intelligence is adaptation to the environment. In the case of human beings, one essential aspect of interaction is the processing of information. The child is kept in intellectual interaction with the environment in order to survive and in the process, the self-regulating balance (equilibration) between assimilation and accommodation produces intellectual growth. Assimilation is the process of fitting one's understanding of reality into one's current cognitive organization. Children apply what they know in order to understand properties and relationships between properties and events. Accommodation refers to adjustments in the cognitive organization as a result of the demands of reality. Accommodation occurs because of the failure of the current structures to interpret a particular object or event satisfactorily. The resulting reorganization of thought leads to a different and more satisfactory assimilation of the experience. Assimilation and accommodation are closely intertwined in every cognitive activity from birth to death. Attempts to assimilate reality necessarily involve slight changes in the cognitive structures as they adjust to the new elements. Assimilation and accommodation are so related that Piaget sometimes defines adaptation as equilibrium between assimilation and accommodation. In a state of equilibrium, neither assimilation or accommodation dominates. An excessive predominance of one over the other can result in grossly dysfunctional behavior.

Piaget defines the developmental process as the result of physical maturation, plus experience with the physical environment, plus social experience, regulated by the process of equilibration. For Piaget, equilibration is the critical mechanism for change and growth. With each newly achieved equilibrated balance a wider perspective is attained, the ability to coordinate more perspectives is possible, and a new view of the old perspective is acquired. Reequilibration occurs when the current structural organization no longer is adequate to a task it is facing. It cannot assimilate or resolve the problem at the current level of development. The individual is "stuck" in a state of disequilibrium and in moving beyond the impasse there will occur structural modification or the invention of new structure (accommodation). The varying degrees of discrepancy between current organizational structures and the experience at hand raise the issue of what the limitations are to accommo-

dations. Piaget's answer, which has implications for educational and therapeutic practice, is that only moderately discrepant events or characteristics can be accommodated; great leaps are not possible. If the reality being presented or perceived is too different from the child's current level of understanding, the child cannot bridge the gap. There can never be radical departures from the old. Thus, development necessarily proceeds in small steps.

Key Contributions for Practice

Piaget's theory provides many implications for practice that can be mentioned only briefly (see Cowan, 1978; Rosen, 1984). Piaget has described the child as an active constructor of knowledge, one who takes an active role in her development and learning. Also, knowledge is biased. Experience always is filtered through the child's current ways of understanding, which is determined by the child's stage or level of cognitive development and its underlying structure of logic. In addition, the child is motivated to seek equilibrium when disequilibrated, which results in change. Relatedly, the role of the teacher and the counselor is to promote moderate disequilibrium in the child, by presenting the child with ideas that are slightly above her or his current conceptual level. Furthermore, social interaction is key to the construction of knowledge, as it helps relinquish egocentrism, forcing the child to define, justify, and clarify her or his thoughts. Finally, assessment and intervention activities must be matched to the cognitive developmental level of the child.

Social Learning Theory

It is beyond the scope and charge of this chapter to review learning theories. Learning theories traditionally emphasize learned behaviors, the environment's control of behavior, a breakdown of behavior into simple units, observable behavior, and rigorous, experimental methodology (Miller, 1983). As mentioned earlier, learning theories historically have not been developmentally oriented or open to developmental principles. However, a contemporary view of social learning theory, which is the most developmental of the learning theories, merits attention.

Social learning theory began as an attempt to explain systematically psychoanalytic constructs (Dollard et al., 1939; Sears, 1944), but soon after became a direction of research that focused on the process of socialization and how children learn social behaviors in a social context (Bandura, 1969). Bandura introduced the concepts of learning complex repertoires of behaviors through observation or modeling, imitation, and vicarious reinforcement. His later work (Bandura, 1977) depicts the child as an active participant in learning, with the child's cognition as central mediator and organizer in learning. Bandura describes the entire learning context as consisting of the characteristics of the child, the person's specific behavior, the environment, and the resulting interactions. He called this process "reciprocal determinism." The result of these interactions is new behavior and information that is the result of new organization of behavior learned earlier. Bandura does not propose an underlying cognitive structure, as does Piaget. Interestingly, whereas other theories have as their aim of development the aquisition or resolution of higher stages of development, such as Piaget, Freud, and Erikson, there is no universal goal or endpoint to development from a social learning perspective. What is universally developed is a skilled ability to learn by observing or listening, which allows the child to acquire large chunks of new behavior.

Principles of Development

There is currently considerable controversy as to whether social learning theory or any current learning theory is truly a developmental theory. Questions that remain unanswered include: Are developmental changes the same as short-term changes accumulated over a longer period of time? Are the central laws of learning the same, regardless of the child's cognitive level? Social learning theory focuses on processes of change, in contrast to Piaget and Freud, who focus on structural changes as the child goes through the stages. However, Bandura's current model of observational learning, which proposes attentional, retention, motor, and motivational processes, identifies a number of developmental variables. They are physical maturation, experience with the social world, and cognitive development. Physical maturation is relevant in that a child may not have the physical maturity to reproduce certain observed motor patterns. Experience with the social world causes development in two ways; the child with increasing age has a larger and increasingly differentiated set of social behaviors and as children get older, they face different social environments. Finally, the child's attention, memory, and cognitive

organization undergo dramatic changes during development.

Key Contributions for Practice

Social learning theory goes beyond the associational principle of classical conditioning and the reinforcement, punishment, and extinction principles of operant conditioning and as a result offers much to the practitioner who works with children in complex social contexts. Social learning theory has demonstrated systematically that children learn by observation, imitation, and vicarious reinforcement. There is also the allowance that learning can occur without reinforcement, direct or vicarious, but that reinforcement has a powerful effect on performance. The child is also seen as an active organism, who interacts with the environment and whose processing of the environment is dependent on the cognitive abilities of attention and retention. Lacking, however, is an explicit integration of developmental principles and learning, for example, how developmental level affects the acquisition of social skills.

Bowlby's Attachment Theory

Bowlby's theory of attachment incorporates a great deal from psychoanalytic thinking but also adopts principles from ethological and cognitive theory (Bowlby, 1980). His theory provides a way to conceptualize the propensity of human beings to make strong affectional bonds to significant others and to explain many forms of emotional distress and personality disturbance, including anxiety, anger, depression, and emotional distachment, which are a result of unwilling separation and loss. According to Bowlby (1969, 1980), attachment behaviors are innate and promote survival of the species because they allow for adaptation of the environment. In addition, adults are biologically predisposed to develop attachment. Attachment figures allow the child a secure base from which to explore, afford the child safety when threats are encountered, and permit the child to learn to regulate her or his level of stress. Attachment behavior is conceived as any form of behavior that results in a person attaining or retaining proximity to some other differentiated and preferred individual. Attachment behavior contributes to the individual's survival by keeping her or him in touch with care givers, thereby reducing the risk of coming to harm. During the course of healthy development, attachment behaviors lead to the development of attachments which are present and active throughout the life cycle. How a child's attachment behaviors develop and the patterns they take affect the patterns of affectional bonds made throughout one's lifetime.

Principles of Development

Bowlby specifically claims that there is a strong causal relationship between an individual's experiences with one's parents and the later capacity to make affectional bonds. Bowlby attributes varitions to the capacity to make affectional bonds to variations in the ways that parents perform their roles (Bowlby, 1979). Parents need to provide their children with a secure base and need to encourage them to explore from it. Children who receive such conditions grow up to be secure and self-reliant, and to be trusting, cooperative, and helpful toward others. In contrast, children who do not and who experience pathogenic parenting instead may become anxious, insecure individuals, usually described as overdependent or immature. Under stress they are apt to develop neurotic symptoms, depression, or phobias. Children who have parents who had anxious attachment relationship with their own parents or their spouses are, according to Bowlby, even more at risk for pathogenic parenting. These children experience parents who are persistently unresponsive to their care-eliciting behavior or are actively rejecting, discontinuities of parenting including hospitalization, persistent threats by parents that they do not love the child, threats by parents to abandon the child, threats by one parent to commit suicide, and guilt inducements claiming that the child's behavior is or will be responsible for the parent's death or illness (Bowlby, 1979). In addition, if a young child's attachment behaviors are continually aroused but not responded to, she or he eventually excludes from awareness sights, thoughts, or feelings that normally would activate attachment behaviors. This process is called defensive exclusion and interferes with child's emotional and social development. Thus, the effects of parental behavior on the next generation are very powerful. For example, an abused child is more likely to abuse her own children or fail to protect them from abuse than is a child who was not abused (Bowlby, 1982).

Key Contributions for Practice

There is a growing body of evidence supporting Bowlby's theory of personality and emotional de-velopment. Abnormal infant attachment experiences have been linked to adult depression and loneliness, character disorders, and phobias (Bowlby, 1982). In addition, there is strong evidence that children who experience secure attachment as infants become more competent cognitively, emotionally, and socially (Campos, Barrett, Lamb, Goldsmith, & Stenberg, 1983) than do infants who experience anxious and insecure attachment relationships. According to Bowlby, adverse childhood experiences, such as insecure attachment, can have effects of at least two kinds. They make the individual more vulnerable to later adverse experiences and they make it more likely that the individual will meet with further such experiences. Later adverse experiences are likely to be partially the consequences of the child's own actions, actions that spring from those disturbances of personality to which the earlier experiences have given rise. However, there is also some evidence that secure attachment relationships in childhood and adolescence can offset adverse earlier experiences (Rutter, 1981). Child practitioners need to recognize the importance of early and ongoing attachment relationships, the possible adverse consequences of separation and loss, the negative effects of pathogenic parenting, the need to intervene with parents and families who have negative relational patterns dominating their interactions, the importance of promoting positive peer interactions, and the necessity of providing a secure base in counseling from which the child can explore the self and make changes.

Bronfenbrenner's Ecological Theory

Bronfrenbrenner (1979) provides a framework for viewing the development of the child in context. His notions of the ecology of human development lie at a point of convergence among the biological, psychological, and social sciences as they bear on the evolution of the individual in society. Bronfenrenner describes the ecological environment as a set of nested structures, each contained within the next, with the inner most level being the developing child. These structures include the microsystem, which is defined as the complex of relations between the developing person and the environment in an immediate setting containing that person (e.g., home, school); the mesosystem, which is defined as the interrelations among major settings containing the developing person at a particular point in her life (e.g., the relations between home and school); the exosystem, which is defined as an extension of the mesosystem embracing other specific social structures that do not themselves contain the developing person but impinge upon or encompass the immediate settings in which the child is found and thereby influence or delimit what goes on there (e.g., parent's work setting, school board); and the macrosystem, which is defined as the overarching institutional patterns of the culture or subculture, such as the economic, social, educational, legal, and political systems, of which micro-, meso-, and exosystems are the concrete manifestations. Development is defined as a lasting change in the way in which a person perceives and deals with the environment. The study of development focuses on what the person perceives, desires, fears, and thinks about and how the nature of this psychological material changes as a function of a person's exposure and interaction in the environment. Development is viewed as the person's evolving conception of the ecological environment and one's relation to it, as well as the person's growing capacity to discover, sustain, or alter its properties.

Principles of Development

Bronfenbrenner's theory is concerned with the progressive accommodation between a growing human organism and its immediate environment, and the ways in which these relations are mediated by forces emanating from more remote regions in the larger physical and social milieu. Bronfenbrenner's theory is a theory of environmental interconnections and their impact on the forces directly affecting the child's psychological growth. "The ecology of human development involves the scientific study of the progressive, mutual accommodation between an active, growing human being and the changing properties of the immediate settings in which the developing person lives, as this process is affected by relations between these settings, and by the larger contexts in which the settings are embedded" (Bronfenbrenner, 1979, p. 21).

Key Contributions for Practice

An ecological perspective provides a useful overall model for planning assessment and intervention activities (see later section, "Contributions of Developmental Psychology to School Psychology Practice"). It also provides a helpful orientation from which to conceptualize emotional disturbance and behavior or conduct disorders (Apter & Conoley, 1984; Hobbs 1966, 1982; Swap, 1974).

Most children who are judged to be "normal" are operating in a behavioral ecology that can be defined as congruent. That is, the individual's behavior is in harmony with the social norms of the environment. When such congruence does not exist, the child is likely to be considered deviant or incompetent. From an ecological approach, emotional disturbance and behavior disorders are seen as residing in the interaction between a child and critical aspects of the child's surrounding environment. Disturbance is viewed not as a disease located within the child, but rather as discordance, a lack of balance in the system, a failure to achieve a match between the child and her or his systems. The disturbance lies in the area of functional maladaptation between the individual and her or his environment. The disturbance is a reciprocal disruptive exchange between the child and the environment—most critically, significant others. It follows from this view of disturbance that the environment must be given intervention attention equal to that shown to the individual who has been singled out as "disturbed." Assessment and interventions must focus on these points of discordance and the resulting failure to match. Problems belong to a system, not to an individual child. The goal of intervention is to make the system function in a way that enhances the development and well-being of all its members.

An Organismic, Transactional View of Development

The organismic, transactional approach to development (Cicchetti & Sroufe, 1978; Sroufe, 1979a, 1979b)—also sometimes referred to as the "organizational" or "structural" approach—consists of a set of regulative principles that can guide theorizing and research concerning human behavior (Santostefano, 1978; Sroufe & Rutter, 1984). This view is congruent with the theoretical conceptualization of organismic theorists (Piaget, 1970; Reese and Overton, 1970; Sroufe, 1979a; H. Werner, 1948; White, 1976). According to the organizational approach, development may be conceived of as a series of qualitative reorganizations among and within behavioral systems, which take place by means of differentiation and hierarchical integration. Variables at many levels of analysis determine the character of these organizations: genetic, constitutional, neurobiological, biochemical, behavioral, psychological, environmental, and sociological. Moreover, these variables are conceived as being in dynamic transaction with one another.

Principles of Development

The organismic transactional model conceptualizes the environment and the child as mutually influencing each other. This perspective makes it plausible to view, for example, child maltreatment phenomena as expressions of underlying dysfunction in the parent-child-environment system rather than as solely the result of aberrant parental personality traits, environmental stress, or deviant child characteristics. Since the child and the environment are seen as reciprocally influencing each other, it follows that behavior at a later point reflects not only the quality of earlier adaptation but also the intervening environmental inputs and supports. As the child develops, the match between child and parent as well as salient parent and child characteristics may change. If a child demonstrates deviant development across time, it is assumed that the child has been involved in a continuous maladaptive process. The continued manifestation of maladaptation depends on environmental support, while the child's characteristics, reciprocally, partially determine the nature of the environment. Thus, maladapted children contribute to their own environment and may contribute to their own psychopathology.

Key Contributions for Practice

This perspective offers a new conceptualization of healthy and pathological development. Normal or healthy development is defined as structural changes among the child's behavioral systems that reflect the dynamic interactions of changing familial, social, and environmental variables and that allow the child to attain competence (Cicchetti & Schneider-Rosen, 1986). The competent child is defined as one who is able to use internal and external resources in order to attain a satisfactory developmental adaptation (Waters & Sroufe, 1983). Internal resources include both specific skills and broad characteristics of an individual, which would be subsumed under general constructs such as self-esteem. External resources include anything else that may serve to help the developing child coordinate affect, cognition, and behavior in order to attain short- and long-term adaptation (e.g., relations with others, appropriate imitation of models). Adaptation at a particular developmental level implies the successful resolution of the developmental task or tasks most salient for that period. It is part of Waters and Sroufe's conception of competence that early competence predicts later competence, given no irregularities in

development (e.g., changes in the quality of care the child receives, increased stress in the environment). Pathological development, in contrast, is conceived of as a lack of effective integration and organization of the social, emotional, and cognitive competencies that are important to achieving adaptation at a particular developmental level (Cicchetti & Schneider-Rosen, 1986). Pathological development leads to personal distress and cognitive, affective, or social incompetence. Because early structures often are incorporated into later structures, an early deviation or disturbance in functioning ultimately may cause a much larger disturbance to emerge later.

An Integrated, Contemporary View of the Developing Child

The descriptions offered above of the major developmental theories indicate the variety of ways and the richness of how the developmental process has been conceptualized. Each of these theoretical frameworks may be useful to the practitioner in carrying out assessments and planning and implementing interventions. It also is useful to generate a view of the developing child that draws from the numerous theoretical perspectives and attempts some integration. The following four general assumptions are offered as one conceptualization of a contemporary view of the developing child that may be of particular use to school psychologists.

The Active Child

First, all major developmental theories have addressed the basic nature of the child and have viewed the child in mechanistic or organismic terms. From the mechanistic view, development is seen as being caused by external forces and events that act on the passive, machinelike mind of the child. From the organismic view, the child is viewed as an active, organized whole that is changing constantly. Self-initiated behavior and thought lead to changes in both the structure and content of the child's behavior and thought. Development does not occur as a series of linear additions, but rather, development is characterized by reorganization of both old and new elements. Thus reorganized, even previously existing elements are transformed. The "same" behavior may have totally new meaning with development, just as it may have different meanings in different contexts. Although the various theories differ in the degree of organization or structure underlying development, all contemporary versions of developmental theories portray children as active agents in their own development. The child at birth is seen as active, involved, and competent. In addition, over time the child is seen as becoming an increasingly active shaper of the environment (Sroufe, 1979a). Later experience is not a random influence on children because they selectively perceive, respond to, and create experience based on all that has gone before. Thus, the activity of children themselves plays a part in their developmental process.

Both Qualitative and Quantitative Change
Second, each theory has taken a stand on whether development is quantitative or qualitative. Theories that have taken a mechanistic view have emphasized quantitative change, whereas those that have adapted the organismic approach have emphasized qualitative change. Qualitative changes refer to changes in kind or type. New phenomena or characteristics emerge that cannot be reduced to previous elements. Qualitative changes typically involve changes in structure or organization. In contrast, quantitative changes refer to changes in amount, frequency, or degree. In some cases, the behavior becomes more efficient or consistent. The change is gradual and occurs in small increments—bits and pieces of information, habits, and skills are acquired during development. At a general level, the issue of qualitative versus quantitative change becomes an issue of stage versus nonstage. When there are similarities in a number of abilities or behaviors during a period of time, a theorist often infers that the child is in a particular "stage" or level of development. Although there is debate as to the existence of stages and there is controversy as to which developmental changes are qualitative and which are quantitative, most developmentalists agree that both qualitative and quantitative changes occur and are necessary.

Interaction/Transaction within the Environment
Third, each major theory has addressed how nature and nurture contribute to development. The basic issue is whether knowledge and behavior are derived from one's genetic endowment or from experience in the world. Anastasi (1958) points out that the important question is how nature and nurture interact to produce development. Today nearly all developmentalists agree that the interaction of innate and environmental factors accounts for both the development of a trait or behavior in an individual and the variations in a trait or behavior among individuals. Nature and nurture are inextricably intertwined. In addition, a child's developmental outcomes are commonly accepted to have multiple historical and causal determinants rather than single-factor etiologies. It is useful to view development from a transactional model, where the multiple transactions among environmental forces, care-giver characteristics, and child characteristics are seen as dynamic, reciprocal contributions to the events and outcomes of child development. Furthermore, the meaning of a child's behavior can be determined only within the child's total psychological context. The child is embedded in a variety of social systems and settings in which members affect each others' development and behavior.

Dependence of Later Development on Earlier Development
Fourth, development proceeds in one direction only; what happens at any point in the process is dependent on what has occurred up to that point. Development is viewed as a process whereby each solution of a developmental task is built upon successful completion of a previous one. This assumption raises the issue of the relationship between early competence and later development. The relationship is complex, but in examining the competence of children at various stages of the life span, several principles are germane (Cichetti & Schneider-Rosen, 1986): (a) Competence at one developmental period exerts a positive influence toward achieving competence at the next period; (b) early competence also exerts a subtle influence toward adaptation throughout the life span since each developmental issue, although perhaps most salient at one developmental period, is of continuing importance throughout the life cycle; (c) the failure to achieve adaptation at one period makes adaptation more difficult at the next, and to some extent, more difficult throughout the life span since each issue continues to assume importance throughout the individual's development; and (d) there are many factors that may mediate between early and later adaptation or maladaptation that may permit alternative outcomes to occur; that is, early problems or deviations in the successful resolution of a developmental task may be countered by major changes in the child's

experience that could result in the successful negotiation of subsequent developmental tasks.

Furthermore, in examining mediating variables in the relationship between early events and later adaptation or maladaptation, Rutter (1981, 1986) has proposed a number of ways in which early experience might be connected to later disorder. These inlcude some rather direct connections, where (a) experience leads to disorder at the time, which then persists; (b) experience leads to bodily changes that influence later functioning; and (c) experience leads to altered patterns of behavior at the time, which only later take the form of disorder. Other connections are less direct, where (d) early experience may change the family circumstances, which in time produce disorder in the individual; (e) early experience leads to sensitivities to stress and the modification of coping styles in the individual, which then later "predispose" the person to disorder, or "buffer" the person against stress; (f) experiences alter the individual's self-concept or attitudes, which, in turn, influence the response to later situations; and (g) experience influences behavior through effects on the selection of environments or on the opening or closing down of opportunities.

RESEARCH FINDINGS IN DEVELOPMENTAL PSYCHOLOGY

In addition to theoretical formulations, much research, often guided by theoretical frameworks, has been produced in developmental psychology. It is entirely beyond the scope of this chapter to review the research in the field of developmental psychology. In the recent *Handbook of Child Psychology,* edited by Mussen (1983), four volumes and 4,000 pages were used in attempting such a review, in contrast to Carmichael's first volume, the *Manual of Child Psychology* (1946), which covered exactly 1,000 pages. Topics of particular interest to school psychology practitioners are mentioned, however, along with references that offer current reviews of research.

Domains of Child Development
Developmental researchers have long divided up the child to obtain knowledge of developmental functioning in specific domains. Thus, research literature is available on such topics as cognitive development (Gelman & Baillargeon, 1983), intellectual development (Sternberg & Powell, 1983),

social-cognitive development (Selman, 1980; Shantz, 1983; Turiel, 1983), achievement motivation (Dweck & Elliot, 1983), self-understanding (Harter, 1983), moral reasoning (Rest, 1983), emotional development (Campos, et al., 1983; Cicchetti & Hesse, 1982), social development (Damon, 1983), temperament (Campos et al., 1983; Lerner & Lerner, 1986), development of sex typing and gender identity (Huston, 1983), sexual development (Tharinger, 1987), aggression and regulation of behavior (Parke & Slaby, 1983), and development of prosocial behavior (Radke-Yarrow, Zahn-Waxler, & Chapman, 1983).

Socialization of the Child's Development
A great deal of research in developmental psychology has focused on socialization factors in the child's development. An excellent review of theory and research on socialization in the context of the family has been provided by Maccoby and Martin (1983). The father's role in the child's development has been depicted by Lamb (1981). Socialization of the child by peers is described by Berkowitz (1985) and Hartup (1983), and socialization of the child by school has been reviewed by Minuchin and Shapiro (1983). The roles of television as a socializer of aggression has been summarized by Parke & Slaby (1983).

Child's Reactions to Life Events as Stressors
There is a growing body of research findings on the effects of life events as stressors that negatively affect children's development (Felner, 1984; Garmezy & Rutter, 1983; Johnson, 1986), as well as what factors contribute to seemingly invulnerable children (E. E. Werner & Smith, 1982). Children who are having problematic reactions to life stressors often are brought to the attention of school psychologists. The literature on the effects of parental divorce on children's development (Hetherington, Cox, & Cox, 1978; Hodges, 1986; Wallerstein, 1985; Wallerstein & Kelly, 1980), as well as on the effects of parental death (Blom, Cheney, & Snoddy, 1986) are important resources offering useful perspectives for school psychologists. As more children experience a portion of their lives in single parent homes and with step parents, researchers are investigating the impact of each (Canong & Coleman, 1984 Carlson, 1987; Furstenberg & Spanier; Shinn, 1978; Weiss, 1979). In addition, conceptual models and research are available on the effects of maltreatment on children's development, including physical

abuse (Parke & Collmer, 1975), sexual abuse (Caterino, 1987; Vevier & Tharinger, 1986), psychological abuse (Brassard, Germain, & Hart, 1987; Garbarino, Guttman, & Seeley, 1986), and the effects of growing up in an alcoholic family (Tharinger & Koranek, 1988).

Developmental Course of Childhood Disorders

With the birth of the field of developmental psychopathology (Achenbach, 1982; Cicchetti, 1984; Rutter & Garmezy, 1983; Sroufe & Rutter, 1984), conceptual models and research findings are becoming available on the developmental course of childhood disorders. Progress appears to be more rapid in applying a developmental perspective to the study of internalizing disorders, for example, childhood depression (Cicchetti & Schneider-Rosen, 1986; Rutter, 1986) and childhood anxiety disorders (Campbell, 1986), than with the behavior disorders, that is, attention deficit disorders and conduct disorders. With time, more research findings can be expected that examine the developmental course of all childhood disorders.

CONTRIBUTIONS OF DEVELOPMENTAL PSYCHOLOGY TO SCHOOL PSYCHOLOGY PRACTICE

Keeping in mind the constructivist view of the relationship between science and practice, that is, that the practitioner actively constructs practice selecting useful elements from science, in this section we highlight the contributions of developmental psychology to school psychology practice. Specifically discussed is what a developmental approach offers to the processes of assessment, direct intervention (counseling), and indirect intervention (consultation).

The Assessment Process

The goal of the assessment process is to evaluate a child's functioning, to determine the child's needs. to respond to the referral questions, and to make recommendations, when appropriate, for interventions to address the child's needs. What does a developmental perspective offer to the assessment process? It offers general guidelines for selection of assessment procedures, a conceptual model for the assessment process, a means of matching assessment methods to the developmental level of the child, guidelines for planning a developmental and

family history, and reference points from which to evaluate normality.

General Developmental Guidelines for the Assessment Process

The following are important developmental guidelines to be kept in mind when evaluating a child.

1. A child is dependent on the environment to fulfill basic physiological and psychological needs.
2. A child's family is the most active shaper of her or his environment.
3. A child also is an active participant in shaping her or his environment.
4. A child's functioning is multiply and transactionally determined.
5. A child strives to adapt to her or his environment, independent of the health of the environment.
6. A child's motivations for her or his behavior may not be conscious.
7. A child's attachment, separations, and losses are very significant factors in her or his psychological development.
8. A child's current functioning must be evaluated in light of her or his past functioning.
9. A child's behavior can only be understood in relation to the current context and the influence of past contexts.
10. As a child develops, conflicts, tensions, and problems are inevitable and necessary. The important factor for assessment is how the child and significant others respond to these conflicts.
11. If a child's thoughts, behaviors, or feelings appear atypical, it is important to consider where, under what circumstances, and at what developmental level this thought pattern, behavior, or emotional expression would make sense.
12. Both the child and her significant environments (i.e., school and home) need to be assessed.

A Model of the Assessment Process

The model of assessment that a practitioner adopts profoundly affects the assessment process. The various developmental theories offer different perspectives concerning assessment. For example, a Piagetian approach centers on understanding the structure of cognition and how it affects the child's learning and behavior, whereas a psychoanalytic approach stresses determining the unconscious motivations underlying the child's behavior. Because most major theories of development concentrate on one domain of functioning (i.e., thought, emotion, or behavior), selecting only one theoretical approach to the process of assessment is not sufficient for the school psychologist. A combination of theoretical models, however, and their implications for assessment offers a solution. We propose that the most useful overriding developmental model for assessment for the school psychologist is an ecological model. It emphasizes development in context and the transactions among the child and her or his environment that lead to development in the various domains of functioning. The ecological model also allows for the integration of other development models. That is, the psychoanalytic, psychosocial, cognitive developmental, attachment, social learning approach, and the transactional, organismic perspective can be utilized under the umbrella framework of an ecological model. The practitioner does not need to discard useful knowledge from the other approaches, but rather can integrate them in order to understand the process of the whole child's development.

In evaluating the child's functioning from an ecological perspective, the practitioner must determine (a) the degree of normality of the child's current functioning in numerous domains, such as intellectual, cognitive, language, physical, academic, behavioral, emotional, and social functioning, and the resulting synchrony or lack of synchrony in functioning among the domains; (b) the child's functioning historically and the factors and events that appear to have contributed positively and negatively to the child's functioning; (c) the current family and school environmental factors that are contributing positively and negatively to the child's functioning; (d) the current health, resourcefulness, expectations, and motivation of the child's environments, especially family members and significant school personnel; (e) the current fit between the child, family, and school in relation to the child's functioning and adaptation; and (f) and the child's current educational and psychological needs.

A Means of Matching Assessment Methods to the Development Level of the Child

Every child has unique features and thus every child assessment is different. The child brings to the process an individual history and a particular way of responding to the environment. As part of the assessment process, the practitioner engages the child to explain what the process is about, to establish rapport, to conduct an interview, and to ask the child to perform a number of tests and other tasks. Each child will respond in her or his own way. To be prepared, it is essential for the practitioner to have a variety of methods of engaging with children of different ages and developmental levels. Although each child must be understood individually, developmental information and guidelines are useful. The practitioner must be able to ask children questions in ways that match their developmental level, must be aware of toys and games children of different developmental levels enjoy, must be aware of what typically motivates children at different developmental levels, must be aware of the basis of children's logic at different developmental levels, must be aware of typical themes in children's play and conversation at different developmental levels, and must be aware of how childen express and censor emotion at different developmental levels. Skilled practitioners gain this knowledge through the study of developmental norms and descriptions; through experience with and feedback from children, as children let the observing adult know when adults are not on target; and through actively staying in touch with children's worlds through the media, children's literature, and observing children in natural settings. In addition, naturalistic child observation often is undertaken as a beginning step in the assessment process and observation of the child continues throughout the assessment process. The practitioner strives to observe the child along multiple developmental lines (Greenspan, 1981), keeping in mind the age appropriateness of the child's functioning, the expectations of the environment, and how the child functions on different tasks and in different settings. In summary, the developmental school psychologist does not fit the child to the assessment process, but instead fits the assessment process to the child.

Guidelines for Planning a Developmental and Family History

Developmental theory and research findings have established that earlier events in the child's life and the family's life and how the child copes with them profoundly affect the child's later functioning. Obtaining a thorough and accurate developmental and family history enables the practitioner to understand the child's current functioning in relation to her or his past, to have some insight into how the child and her or his environments might respond to intervention, and to help decide what types of intervention would be most effective. In addition, a thorough understanding of a child's functioning to date helps the school psychologist determine if the child's current difficulties fit with or depart from earlier patterns.

In a developmental history, the school psychologist needs information on the child's physical, medical, educational, cognitive, social, and emotional development, including when the child met early developmental milestones, how the child formed early attachments, how the child responded to early separations, losses, and traumas, how the child mastered early developmental tasks, how the child has responded to and performed in school, and the quality of the child's family and peer relationships. In a family history, information is needed on how the family adjusted to the child's entry into the family; changes and significant stresses that the family has undergone since the child's birth, such as additional children, marital separation or divorce, economic changes, moves, hospitalizations, substance abuse, and deaths in the family and extended family; how the family has coped positively and negatively with the changes and stresses; and what individuals in the family have been a significant resource for the child.

A Means from Which to Evaluate Normality
Developmental psychology rests on a tradition of child psychology, child development, and contemporary developmental psychology that spans more than 100 years. As mentioned earlier, school psychologists traditionally have utilized developmentally based tests, explicit developmental norms, and broad descriptions of development in evaluating whether or not a child's functioning is "normal" for his or her age and developmental level. This practice of evaluating children's behavior in relation to that of other children will continue and will be broadened as developmentalists provide fuller descriptions of children's social and emotional development and as developmental psychopathologists trace the developmental course of children with childhood disorders.

Direct Intervention—The Counseling Process
School psychologists often are called upon to offer individual counseling. The goals of counseling are to alleviate the child's emotional and cognitive distress; to change the child's behavior; to get the child back on track developmentally, in terms of meeting the challenges of upcoming developmental tasks successfully; and ultimately, to facilitate a more positive fit between the child and her or his environments. What does a developmental perspective offer the counseling process? It offers general guidelines, it specifies models for the process of change, it suggests means for matching the counseling intervention to the developmental level of the child, and it offers a means for setting the therapeutic goals and evaluating progress.

General Developmental Guidelines for the Counseling Process
The practitioner should keep in mind several important developmental guidelines when counseling with a child. The principles specified above under guidelines for the assessment process also are applicable to the process of counseling.

1. Remember that counseling is a developmental process and involves the development of a relationship between the child and the counselor.
2. Keep in mind that although the child's development is the focus of counseling, the counselor also is developing and changing.
3. Accept that development is the goal of counseling for the child. Development involves the child changing and developing new behaviors that are more effective in the real world. It also requires changes in the child's ideas, beliefs, attitudes, emotions, and unconscious processes, as well as changes in the child's environment.
4. Provide a secure base from which the child can explore, trust, and change.
5. Maintain a sound measure of equilibrium, avoiding any protracted predominance of either assimilation or accommodation, but be willing to risk temporary disequillibrium.
6. Accept that earlier events affect current behavior. Also accept that in intervention, earlier events cannot be changed or undone, but if they are identified, the child has the opportunity to experience the feelings that accompanied them, to change perceptions and cognitions of oneself in relation to the events, and to change her or his behavior.

7. Be prepared that all children respond differently to counseling because of their histories, current needs, and current environments. The counseling intervention must match the child's individual needs and developmental levels (see below).

Models for the Process of Change

Models adopted to guide counseling usually correspond with the practitioner's explicit or implicit theories of developmental change. In addition, the model or models of change adopted must fit the needs of the child, must take into account the needs of significant others in the child's environment, and must respond to the relationship between the child and the practitioner. Each of the major developmental theories proposes a model of change that can be applied to the therapeutic process. From the psychoanalytic perspective, the goal is to promote emotional and behavior change by interpreting the child's defenses to allow for unconscious elements that have been impeding development to become conscious. From the psychosocial perspective the goal is to promote optimal resolution of psychosocial crises by supporting the child's struggles positively and by helping to secure healthy, supportive environments for the child. From the cognitive-developmental perspective the goal is to promote progression to higher stages of cognitive reasoning, thus allowing the child greater ego flexibility, a wider range of application of her or his new structural organization, the ability to coordinate more perspectives, and an increased capacity to handle new and previously unfamiliar problems. From the social learning and cognitive behavioral perspectives the goal is to promote behavior change directly by reinforcing desired behavior, by providing positive models and positive vicarious experiences, and by changing children's cognitions, for example, by helping a child learn cognitive mediation to control impulsive behavior or by helping a child alter negative self-evaluations. From the attachment perspective the goal is to promote interpersonal change by providing a secure base for exploration by establishing a positive relationship with the child and by aiding the child in understanding the quality of her or his earlier attachments and the significance of her or his losses. From the ecological and the transactional organismic perspectives the goal is to promote behavioral, cognitive, emotional, and interpersonal change in the child by affecting changes in the child (using the methods described earlier) and in the child's environment, especially parents (e.g., through parent consultation), family (e.g., through family therapy), teachers (e.g., through teacher consultation), and peers (e.g., through classroom interventions and group counseling).

Although each of the models of change above is applicable with children and will promote change if matched with the child's need and developmental levels, an integrated perspective provides the most flexible and comprehensive model for change in counseling with children in schools. The practitioner cannot effect change optimally by focusing on only one domain of functioning, be it emotional, cognitive, or behavioral. A counselor needs to work simultaneously on cognitive, emotional, and behavior change in the here and now. In addition, with few exceptions, the counselor needs to work with significant adults in the child's world, especially parents and teachers, to effect change in the child's environment.

A Means of Matching the Counseling Intervention to the Developmental Level of the Child

By taking advantage of developmental research findings and descriptive knowledge about children at different ages, a practitioner is equipped to match the counseling intervention to the developmental levels and needs of the child. The child and the counseling intervention must fit, and it is the responsibility of the school psychologist to do the fine tuning. The practitioner must provide a setting that is developmentally appropriate; must be aware of the developmental tasks with which the child is struggling and how she or he has mastered earlier tasks; must supply developmentally appropriate information, activities, feedback, and reinforcers; must respond to the child in ways that are understandable to the child; and must proceed at a developmentally and individually appropriate rate. Children often are not at the same developmental levels cognitively, socially, and emotionally, and therefore the school psychologist must be able to provide materials and ideas at different levels in different domains and to respond on different levels.

A Means of Setting Therapeutic Goals and Evaluating Progress

The developmental approach offers a general method for setting and evaluating counseling goals. By understanding normal developmental progressions and age and culturally designated developmental tasks, the practitioner can evaluate the child's developmental levels and can set as the goals for counseling progression to higher, more advanced, and mature levels of functioning and preparation for upcoming developmental tasks. The progress of counseling can be evaluated in terms of the child's reaching higher levels of functioning and being able to accomplish developmental tasks successfully.

Indirect Intervention—The Process of Consultation with Teachers

Many school psychologists provide indirect intervention services, that is, services designed to affect significant others or systems that influence children. The goal is to facilitate change in the significant others or the systems so that they can promote positive change in many children. Teacher consultation is an example of indirect intervention and has become a prominent role for many school psychologists. Teacher consultation typically involves a problem-solving process in which the school psychologist is the consultant, the classroom teacher is the consultee, and a child in the teacher's classroom is the target of change. The major task of teachers is to teach basic skills and to impart the learning of academic knowledge in particular subject areas, such as science and mathematics. Additional tasks are to promote age-appropriate self-regulation of behavior, to promote social development through peer cooperation and provision of social and cultural knowledge, and to promote age-appropriate emotional development. A teacher may seek the help of a consultant when a child is not functioning as expected academically, behaviorally, socially, or emotionally.

The goals of teacher consultation are to provide services for presenting problems and to improve the teacher's functioning so that she or he can prevent and respond more effectively to similar problems in the future (Reynolds, Gutkin, Elliott, & Witt, 1984). The school consultant engages in a problem-solving process with the teacher-consultee in order to facilitate change. For example, the process may involve helping the teacher understand the child differently or more fully, changing the teacher's attitude toward the child, helping the teacher plan and carry out a specific intervention program, or educating the teacher about the needs of the child because of special

difficulties the child has. A developmental perspective offers school psychologists engaged in consultation with teachers general developmental guidelines for the consultation process and content for consultation.

General Developmental Guidelines for the Consultation Process

There are two major developmental guidelines that are essential to carrying out a successful consultation intervention. First, just as a school psychologist assessing a child must match the assessment methods to the individual needs and developmental levels of the child, and just as a school psychologist conducting counseling with a child must match the counseling intervention to the individual needs and developmental levels of the child, a school psychologist consulting with a teacher must match the methods or processes of consultation to the individual needs and developmental levels of the teacher. That is, the language and conceptualizations used, the problem-solving approach attempted, and any agreed-upon direct intervention that the teacher will carry out must be understandable and amenable to the teacher and must fit with the teacher's implicit theory of human development and human behavior. By paying careful attention to the consultee's needs, what the consultee has to offer, and the consultee's reactions to the consultant's approach, questions, and suggestions, a fit may be reached. Second, any plan for intervention coming out of the consultation process that the teacher agrees to attempt must fit with the individual needs and developmental levels of the target child.

Content for Consultation

Consultation, as described above, is a problem-solving process. Although the consultation literature focuses on the process of consultation, content is necessary for most consultation interventions to be effective. Knowledge of developmental descriptions, models for change, and research findings provide content for the process of consultation. In helping the teacher understand the child differently or providing the teacher with information about the needs of the child because of special difficulties, for example, a recent parental divorce, developmental models and research findings are invaluable. In helping the teacher plan and carry out a specific intervention program, such as how to foster a child's social interactions, offering the teacher information about the various processes of change may allow the teacher to integrate and use the knowledge to construct her or his own direct interventions, thus broadening the teacher's own repertoire.

CONCLUSIONS AND FUTURE DIRECTIONS

Developmental psychology and a developmental perspective have much to offer the practice of school psychology. In this chapter, the usefulness of a constructivist view of the relationship between science and practice has been put forth and a constructivist view of applying the contributions of developmental psychology to school psychology practice has been illustrated. The history of developmental psychology and the essence of a developmental approach have been reviewed, and obstacles that have prevented school psychology from taking full advantage of what developmental psychology has to offer have been described, along with ways to overcome them. Major theories and research findings have been presented briefly, demonstrating that developmental psychology offers the school psychologist theoretical models that account for developmental change, explicit norms and descriptions of normal developmental progressions, and research findings on relationships between certain variables and developmental outcomes. Understanding the theories and research findings of developmental psychology enables the school psychologist to describe the level of development of a particular child, to make inferences about the child's prior developmental achievements, to specify the next developmental hurdles to be mounted, and to speculate about the environmental circumstances that may promote development. In addition, knowledge of developmental theories and research empowers the school psychologist to provide explanations of behavior within a developmental framework. Furthermore, school psychologists who have integrated theories of development and research findings into a conceptual framework for understanding behavior can develop comprehensive assessment plans to appraise the developmental characteristics of a child and can propose interventions to further the child's developmental progress. The usefulness of developmental knowledge to school psychology practice has been illustrated by demonstrating some features that a developmental perspective offers

the processes of assessment, counseling, and teacher consultation. We hope that the information presented in this chapter encourages school psychology practitioners to integrate a developmental perspective into their practice and influences school psychology educators to integrate a developmental approach into their training models.

REFERENCES

Achenbach, T. M. (1982). *Developmental psychopathology* (2nd ed.). New York: Wiley.

Achenbach, T. M., & Edelbrock, C. (1983). [Manual for the child behavior checklist and revised child behavior profile]. Burlington, VT: University of Vermont.

Ainsworth, M. D. S. (1969). Object relations, dependency, and attachment: A theoretical review of the infant-mother relationship. *Child Development, 40,* 969–1025.

American Psychiatric Association. (1980). *Diagnostic and statistical manual of mental disorders* (3rd ed.). Washington, DC: Author.

American Psychiatric Association. (1987). *Diagnostic and statistical manual of mental disorders* (3rd rev. ed.). Washington DC: Author.

Anastasi, A. (1958). Heredity, environment, and the question "How?" *Psychological Review, 65,* 197–208.

Apter, S. J., & Conoley, J. C. (1984). *Childhood behavior disorders and emotional disturbance.* Englewood Cliffs, NJ: Prentice-Hall.

Bandura, A. (1969). *Principles of behavior modification.* New York: Holt, Rinehart and Winston.

Bandura, A. (1977). *Social learning theory.* Englewood Cliffs, NJ: Prentice-Hall.

Barker, R. G., Kounin, J. S., & Wright, H. F. (1943). *Child behavior development.* New York: McGraw-Hill.

Berkowitz, M. W. (Ed.). (1985). Peer conflict and psychological growth. *New directions for child development* (No. 29). San Francisco: Jossey-Bass.

Biber, B. (1934). A nursery school puts psychology to work. *69 Bank Street, 1,* 1–11.

Bierman, K. L. (1983). Cognitive development and clinical interviews with children. In B. B. Lahey & A. E. Kazdin (Eds.), *Advances in clinical child psychology* (Vol. 6). New York: Plenum Press.

Blom, G. E., Cheney, B. D., & Snoddy, J. E. (1986). *Stress in childhood: An intervention model for teachers and other professionals.* New York: Teachers College Press.

Bowlby, J. (1958). The nature of the child's tie to his mother. *International Journal of Psychoanalysis, 39,* 350–373.

Bowlby, J. (1969). *Attachment and loss: Vol. 1. Attachment.* New York: Basic Books.

Bowlby, J. (1979). *The making and breaking of affectional bonds.* London: Tavistock Publications.

Bowlby, J. (1980). *Attachment and loss: Vol. 3. Loss.* New York: Basic Books.

Bowlby, J. (1982). Attachment and loss: Retrospect and prospect. *American Journal of Orthopsychiatry, 52,* 664–678.

Brassard, M. R., Germain, R., & Hart, S. N. (1987). *Psychological maltreatment of children and youth.* Elmsford, NY: Pergamon Press.

Breger, L. (1974). *From instinct to identity: The development of personality.* Englewood Cliffs, NJ: Prentice-Hall.

Bronfenbrenner, J. (1979). *The ecology of human development: Experiments by nature and design.* Cambridge, MA: Harvard University Press.

Cairns, R. B. (1983). The emergence of developmental psychology. In P. H. Mussen (Ed.), *Handbook of child psychology: Vol. I. History, theory, and methods.* New York: Wiley.

Campbell, S. (1986). Developmental issues in childhood anxiety. In R. Gittelman (Ed.), *Anxiety disorders of childhood.* New York: Guilford Press.

Campos, J. J., Barrett, K. C., Lamb, M. E., Goldsmith, H. H., & Stenberg, C. (1983). Socioemotional development. In P. H. Mussen (Ed.), *Handbook of child psychology: Vol. II. Infancy and developmental psychobiology.* New York: Wiley.

Canong, L. H., & Coleman, M. (1984). The effects of remarriage on children: A review of the literature. *Family Relations, 33,* 389–406.

Carlson, C. (1987). Children and single parent homes. In A. Thomas & J. Grimes (Eds.), *Children's needs: Psychological perspectives.* Kent, OH: National Association of School Psychologists.

Carmichael, L. (1946). *Manual of child psychology.* New York: J. Wiley.

Caterino, L. (1987). Children and sexual abuse. In A. Thomas & J. Grimes (Eds.), *Children's needs: Psychological perspectives.* Kent, OH: National Association of School Psychologists.

Cicchetti, D. (1984). The emergence of developmental psychopathology. *Child Development, 55,* 1–7.

Cicchetti, D., & Hesse, P. (Eds.). (1982). Emotional development. *New Directions for Child Development* (No. 16). San Francisco: Jossey-Bass.

Cicchetti, D., & Schneider-Rosen, K. (1986). An organizational approach to childhood depression. In M. Rutter, C. E. Izard, & P. B. Read (Eds.), *Depression in young people: Clinical and developmental perspectives.* New York: Guilford Press.

Cicchetti, D., & Sroufe, A. L. (1978). An organizational view of affect: Illustration from the study of Down's syndrome infants. In M. Lewis & L. Rosenblum (Eds.), *The development of affect.* New York: Plenum Press.

Cowan, P. (1978). *Piaget with feeling.* New York: Holt, Rinehart, and Winston.

Damon, W. (1983). *Social and personality development.* New York: W. W. Norton.

Dollard, J., Miller, N. E., Doob, L. W., Mowrer, O. H., & Sears, R. R. (1939). *Frustration and aggression.* New Haven, CT: Yale University Press.

Dweck, C. S., & Elliot, E. S. (1983). Achievement motivation. In P. H. Mussen (Ed.), *Handbook of child psychiatry: Vol. IV. Socialization, personality and social development.* New York: Wiley.

Eisenberg, L. (1977). Development as a unifying concept in psychiatry. *British Journal of Psychiatry, 3,* 225–237.

Erikson, E. (1950). *Childhood and society.* New York: W. W. Norton.

Erikson, E. (1977). *Toys and reasons.* New York: W. W. Norton.

Felner, R. D. (1984). Vulnerability in childhood: A preventative framework for understanding children's efforts to cope with life stress and transitions. In M. C. Roberts & L. Peterson (Eds.), *Prevention of problems in childhood.* New York: Wiley.

Flavell, J. (1963). *The developmental psychology of Jean Piaget.* Princeton, NJ: D. Van Nostrand.

Furstenberg, F. F., & Spanier, G. B. (1984). *Recycling the family: Remarriage after divorce.* Beverly Hills, CA: Sage.

Garbarino, J., Guttman, E. B. & Seeley, J. W. (1986). *The psychologically battered child.* San Francisco: Jossey-Bass.

Garber, J. (1984). Classification of Child psychopathology: A developmental perspective. *Child Development, 1,* 30–48.

Garmezy, N., & Rutter, M. (1983). *Stress, coping and development in children.* New York: McGraw-Hill.

Gelfand, D. M., & Peterson, L. (1985). *Child development and psychopathology.* Beverly Hills, CA: Sage.

Gelman, R., & Baillargeon, R. (1983). A review of some Piagetian concepts. In P. H. Mussen (Ed.), *Handbook of child psychology: Vol. III. Cognitive development.* New York: Wiley.

Gesell, A. L. (1928). *Infancy and human growth.* New York: Macmillan.

Gesell, A. L. (1940). *The first five years of life.* New York: Harper & Row.

Goodman, J. D. (1972). The psychiatric interview. In B. B. Wolman (Ed.), *Manual of child psychopathology.* New York: McGraw-Hill.

Greenspan, S. (1981). *The clinical interview of the child.* New York: McGraw-Hill.

Hall, C. S. (1954). *A primer of Freudian psychology.* New York: World Press.

Harlow, H. F. (1958). The nature of love. *American Psychologist, 13,* 673–685.

Harlow, H. F., & Harlow, M. K. (1965). The affectional systems. In A. M. Schier, H. F. Harlow, & F. Stollnitz (Eds.), *Behavior of nonhuman primates: Modern research trends* (Vol. 2). New York: Academic Press.

Harter, S. (1983). Developmental perspectives on the self system. In P. H. Mussen (Ed.), *Handbook of child psychology: Vol. IV. Socialization, personality and social development.* New York: Wiley.

Hartman, D. P., Roper, B. L., & Bradford, D. C. (1979). Some relationships between behavioral and a traditional assessment. *Journal of Behavioral Assessment, 1,* 3–21.

Hartshorne, H., & May, M. S. (1928). *Studies in the nature of character.* New York: Macmillan.

Hartup, W. (1983). Peer relations. In P. H. Mussen (Ed.), *Handbook of child psychology: Vol. IV. Socializa-*

tion, personality and social development. New York: Wiley.

Havighurst, R. J. (1953). Human development and education. New York: Longmans.

Hetherington, E. M., Cox, M., & Cox, R. (1978). The aftermath of divorce. In J. H. Stevens, Jr., & M. Mathews (Eds.), Mother-child, father-child relations. Washington, DC: National Association for the Education of Young People.

Hobbs, N. (1966). Helping disturbed children: Psychological and ecological strategies. American Psychologist, 27, 1105–1115.

Hobbs, N. (1982). The troubled and troubling child. San Francisco: Jossey-Bass.

Hodges, W. F. (1986). Interventions for children of divorce: Custody, access, and psychotherapy. New York: Wiley.

Hops, H., & Greenwood, G. R. (1981). Social skills deficits. In E. J. Mash & L. G. Terdel (Eds.), Intellectual and social deficiencies. New York: Gardner Press.

Hughes, J. N. (1986). Interviewing children. In J. Dillard & R. Reilley, Interviewing and communication skills. Columbus, OH: Charles E. Merrill.

Huston, A. C. (1983). Sex-typing. In P. H. Mussen (Ed.), Handbook of child psychology: Vol. IV. Socialization, personality and social development. New York: Wiley.

Jersild, A. T., Markey, F. V., & Jersild, C. L. (1933). Children's fears, dreams, wishes, daydreams, likes, dislikes, pleasant and unpleasant memories. A study by the interview method of 400 children aged 5 to 12. Child Development Monographs (No. 12). New York: Teachers College Press.

Johnson, J. H. (1986). Life events as stressors in childhood and adolescence. Beverly Hills, CA: Sage.

Kanfer, R., Eyberg, S., & Krahn, G. L. (1983). Interviewing strategies in child assessment. In C. E. Walker & M. C. Roberts (Eds.), Handbook of clinical child psychology. New York: Wiley.

Kazdin, A. E. (1985). Recent advances in child behavior therapy. In S. I. Pfeiffer (Ed.), Clinical child psychology. New York: Grune & Stratton.

Kendall, P. (1985). Toward a cognitive-behavioral model of child psychopathology and a critique of related interventions. Journal of Abnormal Child Psychology, 13(3), 357–372.

Kendler, H. H., & Kendler, T. S. (1962). Vertical and horizontal processes in problem solving. Psychological Review, 69, 1–16.

Kohlberg, L. (1969). Stage and sequence: The cognitive-developmental approach to socialization. In D. A. Goslin (Ed.), Handbook of socialization theory. Skokie, IL: Rand McNally.

Lamb, M. (Ed.). (1981). The role of the father in child development (2nd ed.). New York: Wiley.

Langer, J. (1969). Theories of development. New York: Holt, Rinehart and Winston.

Lerner, J. V., & Lerner, R. M. (Eds.). (1986). Temperament and social interaction in infants and children. New Directions for Child Development (No. 31). San Francisco: Jossey-Bass.

Lewin, K. (1931). Environmental forces in child behavior and development. In C. Murchison (Ed.), A handbook of child psychology. Worcester, MA: Clark University Press.

Lindberg, S., & Egeland, B. (1987). Psychology in the school training program at the University of Minnesota. Professional School Psychology, 2, 67–74.

Lorenz, K. Z. (1935). Der Kumpan in der Umvelt des Vogels. Journal für Ornithologie, 83, 137–213, 289–413.

Maccoby, E. E., & Martin, J. A. (1983). Socialization in the context of the family: Parent–child interaction. In P. H. Mussen (Ed.), Handbook of child psychology: Vol. IV. Socialization, personality and social development. New York: Wiley.

Mahoney, M. J., & Nezworski, M. T. (1985). Cognitive-behavioral approaches to children's problems. Journal of Abnormal Child Psychology, 13(3), 467–476.

Mash, E. J., & Terdal, L. G. (1981). Behavioral assessment of childhood disorders. New York: Guilford Press.

Mead, G. H. (1934). Mind, self, and society. Chicago: University of Chicago Press.

Miller, P. (1983). Theories of developmental psychology. San Francisco: W. H. Freeman.

Minuchin, P. P., & Shapiro, E. K. (1983). The school as a context for social development. In P. H. Mussen (Ed.), Handbook of child psychology: Vol. IV. Socialization, personality and social development. New York: Wiley.

Mussen, P. (Ed.). (1983). Handbook of child psychology (Vols. I–IV). New York: Wiley.

O'Connor, K., Lee, A. C., & Schaefer, C. E. (1983). Psychoanalytic psychotherapy with children. In M. Hersen, A. E. Kazdin, & A. S. Bellack (Eds.), The clinical psychology handbook. Elmsford, NY: Pergamon Press.

Parke, R. D., & Collmer, C. W. (1975). Child abuse: An interdisciplinary analysis. In E. M. Hetherington (Ed.), Review of Child Development Research, (Vol. 5, pp. 509–590). Chicago: University of Chicago Press.

Parke, R. D., & Slaby, R. G. (1983). The development of aggression. In P. H. Mussen (Ed.), Handbook of child psychology: Vol. IV. Socialization, personality and social development. New York: Wiley.

Phillips, B. (1987). On science, mirrors, lamps, and professional practice. Professional School Psychology, 2, 221–229.

Piaget, J. (1926). The language and thought of the child. New York: Harcourt, Brace.

Piaget, J. (1932). The moral judgment of the child. London: Kegan Paul.

Piaget, J. (1950). The psychology of intelligence. New York: Harcourt, Brace.

Piaget, J. (1970). Piaget's theory. In P. H. Mussen (Ed.), Carmichael's manual of child psychology (Vol. 1). New York: Wiley.

Radke-Yarrow, M., Zahn-Waxler, C., & Chapman, M. (1983). Children's prosocial dispositions and behavior. In P. H. Mussen (Ed.), Handbook of child *psychology: Vol. IV. Socialization, personality and social development.* New York: Wiley.

Reese, H., & Overton, W. (1970). Models of development and theories of development. In L. R. Goulet & P. Baltes (Eds.), *Life span developmental psychology: Research and theory.* New York: Academic Press.

Reisman, J. M. (1973). *Principles of psychotherapy with children.* New York: Wiley.

Rest, J. (1983). Morality. In P. H. Mussen (Ed.), *Handbook of child psychology: Vol. III. Cognitive development.* New York: Wiley.

Reynolds, C. R., Gutkin, T. B., Elliott, S. N., & Witt, J. C. (1984). *School psychology: Essentials of theory and practice.* New York: Wiley.

Rosen, H. (1984). *Piagetian dimensions of clinical relevance.* New York: Columbia University Press.

Ross, A. O. (1978). Behavior therapy with children. In S. L. Garfield & A. E. Bergin (Eds.), *Handbook of psychotherapy and behavior change: An empirical analysis.* New York: Wiley.

Rutter, M. (1981). Stress, coping, and development: Some issues and some questions. *Journal of Child Psychology and Psychiatry, 22,* 323–356.

Rutter, M. (1986). The developmental psychopathology of depression: Issues and perspectives. In M. Rutter, C. E. Izard, & P. B. Read (Eds.), *Depression in young people: Clinical and developmental perspectives.* New York: Guilford Press.

Rutter, M., & Garmezy, N. (1983). *Developmental psychopathology.* In P. H. Mussen (Eds.), *Handbook of child psychology: Vol. IV. Socialization, personality and social development.* New York: Wiley.

Salkind, N. (1981). *Theories of human development.* New York: D. Van Nostrand.

Santostefano, S. (1978). *A biodevelopmental approach to clinical child psychology.* New York: Wiley.

Scarr, S. (1985). Constructing psychology: Making facts and fables for our times. *American Psychologist, 40,* 499–512.

Sears, R. R. (1944). Experimental analysis of psychoanalytic phenomena. In J. McV. Hunt (Ed.), *Personality and the behavior disorders* (Vol. 1). New York: Ronald Press.

Selman, R. L. (1980). *The growth of interpersonal understanding: Developmental and clinical analyses.* New York: Academic Press.

Shantz, C. U. (1975). The development of social cognition. In E. M. Hetherington (Ed.), *Review of child development research* (Vol. 5). Chicago: University of Chicago Press.

Shantz, C. U. (1983). Social cognition. In P. H. Mussen (Ed.), *Handbook of child psychology: Vol. III. Cognitive development.* New York: Wiley.

Shinn, M. (1978). Father absence and children's cognitive development. *Psychological Bulletin, 85*(2), 295–324.

Sroufe, L. A. (1979a). The coherence of individual development. *American Psychologist, 34,* 834–841.

Sroufe, L. A. (1979b). Socioemotional development. In

J. Osofsky (Ed.), *Handbook of infant development.* New York: Wiley.

Sroufe, L. A., & Rutter, M. (1984). The domain of developmental psychopathology. *Child Development, 55,* 17–29.

Sternberg, R. J., & Powell, J. S. (1983). *The development of intelligence.* In P. H. Mussen (Ed.), *Handbook of child psychology: Vol. III. Cognitive development.* New York: Wiley.

Swap, S. M. (1974). Disturbing classroom behaviors: A developmental and ecological view. *Exceptional Children, 41,* 163–172.

Tharinger, D. (1987). Children and sexual interest. In A. Thomas & J. Grimes (Eds.), *Children's needs: Psychological perspectives.* Kent, OH: National Association of School Psychologists.

Tharinger, D., & Koranek, M. (1988). Children of alcoholics—At risk and unidentified: A review of research and the service roles of school psychologists. *School Psychology Review, 17,* 166–191.

Thomas, R. M. (1985). *Comparing theories of child development* (2nd ed.). Belmont, CA: Wadsworth.

Turiel, E. (1983). *The development of social knowledge: Morality and convention.* Cambridge: Cambridge University Press.

Vevier, E., & Tharinger, D. (1986). Child sexual abuse: A review and intervention framework for the school psychologist. *Journal of School Psychology, 24,* 293–311.

Vigotsky, L. S. (1939). Thought and speech. *Psychiatry, 2,* 29–54.

Wallerstein, J. S. (1985). Children of divorce: Preliminary report of a ten-year follow up of older children and adolescents. *Journal of the American Academy of Child Psychiatry, 24,* 545–553.

Wallerstein, J. S., & Kelly, J. B. (1980). *Surviving the breakup: How children and parents cope with divorce.* New York: Basic Books.

Waters, G., & Sroufe, L. A. (1983). Competence as a developmental construct. *Developmental Review, 3,* 79–97.

Watson, J. B. (1914). *Behavior: An introduction to comparative psychology.* New York: Holt.

Watson, J. B. (1928). *Psychological care of infant and child.* New York: W. W. Norton.

Weiss, R. (1979). Growing up a little faster: The experience of growing up in a single-parent household. *Journal of Social Issues, 35*(4), 97–111.

Werner, E. E., & Smith, R. S. (1982). *Vulnerable but invincible: A longitudinal study of resilient children and youths.* New York: McGraw-Hill.

Werner, H. (1948). *Comparative psychology of mental development.* New York: International Universities Press.

White, S. H. (1976). The active organism in the theoretical behaviorism. *Human Development, 19,* 99–107.

Worchel, F. (1986). Interviewing adolescents. In J. Dillard & R. Reilley (Eds.), *Interviewing and communication skills.* Columbus, OH: Charles E. Merrill.

5

THE IMPLICATIONS OF COGNITIVE PSYCHOLOGY FOR SCHOOL PSYCHOLOGY

JOHN A. GLOVER
Ball State University
ALICE J. CORKILL
University of Western Ontario

The study of cognition is one of the most rapidly growing and changing areas in psychology. The literature is now so vast that a single chapter focusing on the implications of cognitive psychology can do no more than scratch the surface. The sheer breadth and depth of cognitive psychology is such that this chapter cannot be inclusive. We made some very difficult decisions about those topics we could address and those that were best left to another volume. Prior to beginning the chapter proper, it seemed important that we share the reasoning behind our choices.

Because our target audience is made up primarily of school psychologists rather than other cognitive psychologists, because of the relative youth of the "new" cognitive psychology (J. R. Anderson, 1985, dates its emergence to about 1960), and because of the rapid changes the field has experienced in the past 20 years, we begin this chapter with an accounting of a general cognitive perspective. Next, because information

processing has been so central to the reemergence of cognitive psychology (DiVesta, 1987), we describe a basic model of human information processing. We recognize that many contemporary cognitive psychologists believe that the use of such a model gives an overly mechanistic flavor to discussions of cognition, but we have found such a model to be a valuable backdrop for discussions of applications, especially when individual differences are considered.

After we have provided a basic cognitive perspective and outlined an information processing model, we move on to two types of implications for school psychologists. First, we stress how research in cognition can aid school psychologists in consulting with teachers about instructional issues. The chapter is completed with a discussion of a cognitive framework for viewing individual differences in cognitive ability, especially as it concerns mental retardation. Throughout our chapter we attempt to provide the reader with both the specific citations for the research we describe and references to more general readings that can be consulted to amplify the points we make.

A COGNITIVE VIEW

The reemergence of a cognitive psychology in the 1960s was predicated on several developments outside psychology. Advances in linguistics provided a basic means of thinking about language and its structure. Information theory, an area in mathematics, made the measurement of units of information possible. Most important, though, was the development of the electronic computer (J. R. Anderson, 1985, DiVesta, 1987; Sanford, 1986). Early "mentalism" was unworkable for several reasons, but the most telling was an inability to develop models of thought processes. The electronic computer allowed the development of models of thought processes that could be tested against observations of people's actual performance and altered to fit the results of research. In cognitive psychology, the period from about 1960 to 1972 was dominated by computerlike models of human information processing in which the computer was seen as a fairly direct analog of human thought. However, the continued testing and refinement of these models led to an important change in focus during the early 1970s. That is, cognitive psychologists found the "executive" components of their models of human information processing (that part of the models in which decisions were made) taking on increasing importance (see Atkinson & Shiffrin, 1968) until, finally, the focus shifted away from computer analogs to the active, dynamic nature of thought. To paraphrase Jenkins (1974, pp. 793–794) cognition is not a set of boxes in a flow diagram. A person's cognitive processes in a given situation depend on the physical and psychological context, the knowledge and skills the person brings to the context, the situation in which we ask for evidence of cognition, and the relation of what the subject supplies as evidence to what the experimenter demands.

Although computer-based models of cognition are still important, especially in gaining an overall sense of the human processing system, the cognitive perspective on human beings emphasizes the context of thinking events. What is attended, what and how things are perceived, how informa-tion is handled, and the way in which information is stored depends in part on the information itself, but also on what the person does with that information. In the next section we examine an overall model of the human information processing system and then begin to explore the implications of such models for school psychology.

A MODEL OF HUMAN COGNITION

Picture a typical sixth-grade classroom. The students have just finished a brief quiz and they have traded papers with their seatmates. The teacher begins to go through the test, reading the correct answers, responding to students' questions, and explaining how difficult problems should have been worked. In this class, one girl hears the first answer, "514 miles." She looks at her seatmate's answer and puzzles over the first digits in the answer, trying to determine whether it is a "5" or a "3." Knowing her friend almost always does well in math, our student decides the digit is a "5" and marks the answer as correct. However, during her concentration on the decision, she did not hear the next answer. Realizing this, our student raises her hand and asks the teacher to repeat the answer. This time there is no confusion, as the paper clearly indicates "40 miles per hour," the correct answer.

At this point, a student who missed the problem asks the teacher to show him how it should have been worked. Our student quickly remembers how she solved the problem and tunes out the teacher's explanation, thinking instead about an upcoming spelling test. She is quickly brought back to the classroom by the boy behind her who asks for the answer to problem two. Our student starts to respond—after all, it has only been a couple minutes since she heard the answer—but she finds she cannot recall the answer without looking back at the paper she is grading. Our student *does* remember that the answer is correct.

After our student whispers the answer to the boy behind her, she again looks at the teacher, who is now ready to go on to problem three. This time, our student listens very carefully as the teacher explains each step in solving the problem. Our student got the item correct, but she was afraid she had not really understood the process involved in solving it. As she listens to the teacher she compares what she hears to what she remembers doing, verifying that she really did understand how to solve such problems.

The scene we described above is common. Situations like it occur every day in almost every classroom. Even so, we may employ the student we followed and her actions to provide the basic outline of a human information processing system.

The Sense Receptors

The starting place in a model of human information processing is the sense receptors (e.g., eyes, ears) (Rock, 1984). The student in the example we described above gained information about correct answers, how problems are solved, and student questions from the external environment. For her to compare the teacher's answer to a classmate's, she had to hear one answer and read another. Her knowledge of the specific language being used and the task she was to perform came from external sources as well.

Although contemporary cognitive psychology is not completely empiricist (in particular, elements of nativism are seen in theories focusing on language development), it is clear that the quality of the sense receptors determine, in large part, the quality of information entering the human information-processing system. For example, if the student in our example suffered a hearing loss, she easily could have misunderstood the teacher's comments and incorrectly graded the paper. Similarly, if she suffered from an uncorrected vision problem, she could have misread her friend's response. Indeed, research suggests that deaf and blind individuals vary considerably from the norm in terms of the characteristics of their information-processing systems (e.g., Morariu & Bruning, 1984).

The Sensory Stores

In the general information-processing view, perception is more than merely sensing some stimulus. Perception is defined as the assignment of meaning to incoming stimuli (Rock, 1984). The difference between sensing a stimulus and perceiving it is analogous to the difference between feeling something under the rug and knowing that what has been felt is the locket you thought had been lost.

Perception is not an instantaneous process (e.g., McBurney & Collings, 1984; Rivlin & Gravelle, 1985; but compare to Gibson & Spelke, 1983). Before a person can determine the meaning of a stimulus, several cognitive processes must be carried out and each of these processes take time. In brief, a stimulus must be attended to, thought about, matched to previous knowledge, and a decision must be made about the meaning of the stimulus. We are not often aware of the active nature of perception unless we are viewing ambiguous figures such as the unclear "5" the girl in our example puzzled over.

In any event, perception takes time and many stimuli last for only very brief durations. Consider the simple act of understanding a question. In our example at the beginning of this section, the boy sitting behind our student might have used the words, "What is the answer to number two?" There seems to be nothing at all remarkable about hearing and understanding such a simple question until we consider that the sound of a word lasts for only a very brief time and then is gone. By the time the boy got to the word "answer" all physical traces of the word "what" were gone. Clearly, for understanding to occur, a human information-processing system must have some means of briefly storing representations of external stimuli until they can be acted on—until perception has occurred.

The sensory registers (there apparently is one register for each of the senses) solve this problem because they serve as brief holding systems for maintaining representations of incoming stimuli so that cognitive activities can begin to be performed on them. The words "what," "was," "the," "answer," "to," "number," and "two" do not merely disappear before they can be perceived; the echoic (auditory) sensory register holds them as the processes of perception go on. By the time our student hears the last word in the sentence, that word and representations of the other words are still available for her to put them together and discover the meaning of the boy's sentence.

Each of the sensory registers has a limited capacity and can hold information only for very brief periods of time (e.g., the iconic or visual sensory register is estimated to hold information for up to about 0.5 second; the echoic store for as long as 2.5 seconds) (see Averbach & Coriell, 1961; Marr, 1982; McBurney & Collings, 1984; Rivlin & Gravelle, 1985; Rock, 1984; Sperling, 1960). As we will see later in the chapter, there are individual differences in the size and duration of the various sensory registers that have important implications for understanding student performance.

Working Memory

The third component of the model we present here is the working memory. The *working memory* is both a short-term repository of information (subsuming the short-term memory component of other models) and the system's executive. Although distinctions between the repository and executive functions of working memory are somewhat arbitrary (see Baddeley & Hitch, 1974; Puckett & Kausler, 1984), below we examine the two functions separately.

Short-Term Memory

The student in our example found that she could not remember the answer to a problem even though she had heard it only moments before. This phenomenon occurred because of the fragility of information in *short-term memory*. Short-term memory, like the sensory registers, has a limited duration, typically estimated at under 30 seconds (see Schweikert & Boruff, 1986). Under normal circumstances, once information reaches the short-term memory it has a very brief life. However, if the information is rehearsed (thought about), it may be maintained for a considerable period. Indeed, given the right kinds of rehearsal it may be passed on to long-term memory.

Short-term memory also has a very limited capacity (see Dempster, 1981; Schweikert & Boruff, 1986; Shiffrin, 1973) that is determined *not* by a fixed number of chunks or bits (but *see* Miller, 1956) but instead, is limited by its duration (Schweikert & Boruff, 1986). That is, short-term memory can hold as much as can be verbalized in about 30 seconds. Typically, this ends up being about five to nine chunks of information. The girl in our example had no reason or desire to rehearse the answer to the question the boy behind her asked. Because she did not rehearse the answer, it passed quickly from short-term memory and was lost.

As it turns out, there are individual differences in short-term memory that have important implications for our understanding of cognitive abilities (Hunt, 1988; Puckett & Kausler, 1984). In addition, the way in which students encode (take in and rehearse) new information directly influences its likelihood of being passed on to long-term memory. Later in the chapter we review briefly different methods of encoding and individual differences in short-term memory.

The Executive

The executive component of working memory is where decisions are made. One crucial decision is how attention will be allocated. Simply, those things that do not receive attention are much less likely to be picked up and processed by the system. Our hypothetical student, for example, decided not to attend to the teacher's explanation of how the second problem was solved. Instead, she shifted her processing resources to a consideration of an upcoming spelling test. Little, if any, of the teacher's explanation was processed.

Studies of attention indicate that deciding to focus on one source of input rather than another does not result in an all-or-none phenomenon. However, focusing attention on one source of information does drastically reduce the amount of information picked up from other sources (Rivlen & Gravelle, 1985). The importance of managing students' attention, especially for students we identify as having attention problems (e.g., "hyperactive") becomes especially clear when we consider how attention determines which sources of information will be processed.

Other decisions in working memory involve what to remember, assigning meaning to incoming stimuli, what to recall from long-term memory, and the generation of language, to name a few. As one can imagine, the executive functions of working memory involve the manipulation of information. Studies focusing on both the speed and amount of information manipulated in working memory have indicated substantial individual differences (e.g., Hunt, 1988). Later, we review some of the research in this area as a means of focusing on implications of individual differences in information processing.

Long-Term Memory

Long-term memory is a relatively permanent repository of information. The duration of long-term memory and the factors that influence it are understood in part (see Fiedler & Stroehm, 1986; Klatzky, 1984; Neisser, 1982; Rubin & Friendly, 1986), but real questions remain as to why some memories seem to last for nearly a lifetime (e.g., remembering the address of the first house a person lived in), while others seem unavailable only hours or days after they were last recalled (e.g., the material studied for a final examination in analytic chemistry). In any event, long-term memory is a crucial component of the information-processing system that guides attention, perception, and the quality of decisions made in working memory.

To return to the classroom example we presented at the outset for a last time, long-term memory guided the girl's cognition throughout. Her ability to understand language, her knowledge of paper-correcting situations, her knowledge of her friend's typical math performance, her ability to recall how she solved a problem, her choice of what to pay attention to, and her interest in the upcoming spelling test all were due directly to long-term memory. Even the amount of information that can be held in working memory is determined in part by long-term memory. Larger amounts of familiar, well-learned information can be held in working memory; smaller amounts of unfamiliar, novel information.

As we noted earlier, the way in which information is processed determines the likelihood of its being passed into long-term memory (Walker, 1986). Not surprisingly, there are age-related changes in how children rehearse information and individual differences among students of the same age (see Brainerd & Pressley, 1985; Kail, 1984).

There also seem to be individual differences in long-term memory, but research in this area has been very difficult because of problems associated in defining exactly what a long-term memory is and in controlling how often a long-term memory is retrieved and rehearsed in between the time the information was first learned and the time of test. There do, however, seem to be some clear individual differences in the accessibility of long-term memory.

INSTRUCTIONAL IMPLICATIONS OF A BASIC MODEL OF INFORMATION PROCESSING

In our view, there are manifold implications of viewing students as active, dynamic processors of information. In this section we review a set of implications germane to consulting with teachers and parents about the nature of the learning process. In the next section we focus specifically on individual differences in information processing.

Attention

Presumably, an important goal of education is helping students acquire information they do not already possess. From an information-processing perspective, several things must happen for new information to be passed to long-term memory. We begin our discussion with a brief review of attention.

Severe limits on an individual's capacity for attention exist (e.g, Britton & Tesser, 1982; Halpain, Glover, & Harvey, 1985). In a now classic study, Treisman and Geffin (1967) fitted subjects with headphones in which different messages (prose passages) were played to each ear. Subjects were asked to shadow the message (repeat aloud) coming to one ear while at the same time signaling the appearance of specific key words heard in either ear. The results indicated that subjects were able to identify nearly 90% of the key words in the shadowed ear but only about 8% of the key words in the unshadowed ear. The implications of such attention-sharing studies are direct. Students cannot listen to the stereo, watch television, eat a piece of cake, and do homework simultaneously without drastically reducing the quality of performance. Similarly, students cannot both talk to a neighbor and follow a teacher's explanation without suffering a reduction in performance. Luckily, there are several good classroom management techniques available for focusing students' attention (see Williams, 1987, for a critical review).

The issue of attention, unfortunately, is not as simple as it seems at first glance. Several factors influence the demands on students' attention. Generally speaking, as the difficulty and complexity of tasks increase, so does the need for attention. In fact, tasks may rather easily be constructed so as to overwhelm students' attention capacities (see Rivlin & Gravell, 1985). The attentional demands of tasks, however, are not uniform and depend on students' expertise and development of automatic cognitive operations. For example, word decoding is automatic in fluent readers, requiring only little in the way of attention. In contrast, beginning or poor readers must devote great amounts of attention to decoding, with the result that little attention is left for comprehension. Automatic cognitive processes, of course, develop slowly on the basis of considerable practice (see Just & Carpenter, 1986).

In consulting with teachers about attention-related issues, then, it is important to focus on more than classroom management procedures. Care should be taken to help teachers consider the attentional demands of the tasks they require of students and how best to present and pace different materials so that students' attentional capacities are not overwhelmed. In addition, teachers should give careful thought to the relative level of expertise of their students and the development of automatic cognitive processes.

One other important implication of the limits on attention is the use of a secondary task procedure to determine relative levels of attention necessary to complete different tasks (see, e.g., Britton & Tesser, 1982; Halpain et al., 1985; Reynolds & Anderson, 1982). That is, students engaged in a primary task (e.g., reading a text) can be asked to respond to a secondary task (e.g., pushing a key on a computer keyboard as rapidly as possible after the sound of a tone) during the performance of the primary task. The primary task may be varied in different ways (e.g., altering the level of difficulty of the reading materials, having students look for answers to questions during reading) and students' reactions to the secondary task may be monitored to determine if their reaction times to the secondary task change as a function of how the primary task has been changed. At this point, the data indicate that reaction times increase as the difficulty of reading materials increase, as the complexity of to-be-answered questions increases, and as the amount of information students must hold in working memory in order to complete a task increases. Such procedures have been used to validate test item complexity (Plake, Glover, & Kraft, 1984) and may well have uses in establishing the relative levels of difficulty and complexity of varying kinds of tasks (for reviews of this literature, the reader is referred to Britton & Tesser, 1982, and Halpain et al., 1985).

Perception

Although attention is a necessary component of new learning, it is not sufficient. A bright graduate student, for example, could attend a lecture on, say, bias in testing given by the top expert in Taiwan. No matter how carefully the student attends the lecture, however, if he/she does not understand Chinese, little learning is likely. In other words, if perception (the assignment of meaning to incoming stimuli) does not occur, new learning is unlikely.

Teachers need to understand that they guide students' perception. In simple terms, for students to be able to perceive new information, it must be at a level that allows a meaning to be assigned (contrast the likely effect of saying "in aqueous solution" with "mixed in water" in explaining a science demonstration to fourth graders). Put another way, new information is most likely to be learned when it is meaningful; when it can be related in a substantive way to previously known information. In consulting with teachers, the key is to focus on having them understand their student's knowledge and abilities such that new learning can build directly on prior learning. Meaning will not be assigned (or at least not the meaning intended) by students if they cannot find something in long-term memory to relate to the new information. Teachers can make a profound difference in students' perceptions by presenting information at the student's level (i.e., related to what is known and yet not boring) and by the context in which they present new information (see McKoon & Ratcliff, 1986).

Because perception is guided by previous knowledge, it is a highly individualistic phenomenon. That is, two people may see the same scene in very different ways because of prior knowledge. Since education is based on the transmission of shared knowledge, teachers are in the position of needing to provide contexts for learning that will ensure a common perception.

The influence of context on learning is very clearly exemplified by a now-classic study conducted by Pichert and Anderson (1977). As a part of one of their experiments, Pichert and Anderson provided the same story to subjects who had been assigned to three conditions. The conditions were varied by the context given the story. Subjects in one condition were told to read the story (in which a description of a house and its contents were featured as part of a narrative following two boys staying home to play hooky) from the perspective of a burglar who would return to the house that night. Subjects in a second condition were asked to read the story from the perspective of a potential buyer of the house. Subjects in the control condition read the story without being given a context. Later, subjects in all three conditions were tested via free recall.

The results of the study indicated significant differences in terms of which elements of the story were recalled. Subjects given the "burglar" context tended to remember where valuables were located in the house as well as means of entering and leaving the house without notice. Subjects given the "prospective buyer" context tended to remember things about the condition of the house (e.g., a leaky roof). Subjects not given a context primarily remembered the narrative events.

The results of Pichert and Anderson's (1977) study as well as more recent work (see R. C. Anderson, 1984; Mandler, 1984) have demonstrated the powerful effects of context on learning. In R. C. Anderson's (1984) terms, perception and the encoding of information are guided by the schema activated for the task. Schemata are knowledge structures in long-term memory that contain elements of related information and provide plans for gathering information (R. C. Anderson, 1984; Mandler, 1984; Rumelhart, 1980). In particular, activating a "burglar" schema in readers gave them plans for gaining information about valuables. In contrast, activating a "prospective buyer" schema provided plans for gathering information about the quality of the house described in the story.

What students attend to and remember from any instructional activity depends on the schemata their teachers help activate in setting a context. A well-developed, accurate context allows students to focus on elements of information specifically germane to the goals of instruction. In contrast, poorly formed or nonexistent contexts are likely to lead to wasted effort and learning not closely aligned with the teacher's goals. In this regard, when we consult with teachers, our emphasis is on broadening instructional planning to include assessments of students' current state of knowledge and on the development of contexts congruent with instructional objectives.

Encoding

Encoding refers to the operations students perform on information as it passes through the information processing system. The ways in which students encode information have a powerful influence on what they remember (Gagné, 1985; Klatzky, 1984). A vast amount of educationally relevant research has examined how different encoding procedures influence recall. The literature is too vast to review here in detail. We will, however, briefly identify some encoding procedures that have consistently received research support.

Mnemonics

Mnemonics are memory aids designed to facilitate the recall of new information by placing it in an already well learned framework. Several mnemonic techniques have been investigated in depth (see Bellezza, 1981; Higbee, 1979; Higbee & Kunihara, 1985; Paivio, 1971; Pressley, Levin, & Delaney, 1982, for reviews) with considerable promise found in the Yodai method, the pegword method, and the method of loci (Levin, 1985). Here we will focus on the mnemonic approach that has received the greatest amount of research attention in recent years, the keyword mnemonic.

The keyword mnemonic was originally developed to facilitate students' acquisition of vocabulary (Atkinson, 1975). The method, however, has been extended successfully to learning several different kinds of facts (Levin, 1981; Pressley et al., 1982) and the acquisition of concepts during reading (McCormick & Levin, 1984). The keyword mnemonic consists of two states: an acoustic link and an imagery link.

When a new vocabulary item is encountered, the student must first find a "keyword" that sounds like a part of the to-be-learned word—the acoustic link (Levin, 1981). For example, a good keyword for the word conflagration is flag. Flag is similar to the second syllable of conflagration. Further, flags readily are imagined, making the second stage of the process easy.

After a keyword has been chosen (ball in the Spanish word caballo; horse), the student links it to an image. Here the student must imagine a visual image of the keyword interacting with the meaning of the to-be-learned word (Levin, 1981). For example, a student could imagine a flag on fire or a horse balancing on a ball. Then, at the time of test, when the student sees the word (e.g., caballo), it should evoke the keyword (e.g., ball), which should then help the student remember the image (the horse balanced on the ball).

As simple as the keyword method is, research on its effectiveness has shown powerful effects. It is helpful in facilitating the acquisition of English and foreign language vocabulary among students of all ages (Levin, 1981, 1986; Pressley et al., 1982) and has also been shown to enhance significantly memory for names, dates, facts (the planets, names of rivers, etc.) and concepts presented in reading materials (Levin, 1986; McCormick & Levin, 1984). Especially intriguing has been the use of the keyword method in helping retarded students acquire information (Levin, 1986). However, despite the extremely positive resarch reports on the keyword method, it is not widely used. The technique is easy to teach to students, students enjoy using it, and they quickly understand the benefits of the keyword method (Levin, 1986). We can only presume that we have not been effective in communicating the utility of mnemonics to teachers.

Adjunct Aids

Adjunct aids are questions, objectives, organizers, and other devices designed to guide students' comprehension of reading materials. The research on each of the various adjunct aids is expansive and readers are referred to Hamilton (1985), Hamaker (1986), Derry (1984), and Dinnel and Glover (1985) for recent reviews and theoretical formulations. Our focus here will be restricted to two types of adjunct aids, advance organizers and questions.

Advance Organizers. The idea of advance organizers dates back to the work of Ausubel (1960). He defined them as "appropriately relevant and inclusive introductory materials . . . introduced in advance of learning . . . and presented at a higher level of abstraction, generality, and inclusiveness" (1968, p. 148). In Ausubel's view, advance organizers provided "ideational scaffolding for the stable incorporation and retention of the more detailed and differentiated material that follows" (1968, p. 148).

The concept of advance organizers has a great deal of intuitive appeal and fits well within a contemporary cognitive view of learning, especially schema theory. Any technique that can facilitate the tying together of new information with information already in memory should prove beneficial. The research on advance organizers, however, has received considerable criticism (e.g., Barnes & Clawson, 1975; Faw & Waller, 1976; Mayer, 1979), in large part because of methodological flaws in early research and because of difficulties in determining exactly what is and what is not an advance organizer.

More recently, however, research on advance organizers indicates that they indeed have a consistent effect in increasing student's memory for prose (Corkill, Glover, & Bruning, 1987; Derry, 1984; Dinnel & Glover, 1985; Mayer & Bromage, 1980). Effective advance organizers, however, have some specific properties rather different than what Ausubel (e.g., 1968) proposed.

First, effective advance organizers include one or more concrete examples that relate the upcoming text to what students already know (Dinnel & Glover, 1985). Second, they focus primarily on readying students for the first segments of upcoming text rather than on the entirety of an upcoming segment of prose (Corkill et al., 1987). Third, they must be well learned or used in ways that activate relevant schemata in students (Dinnel & Glover, 1985). When advance organizers have these properties, they enhance students' comprehension of and memory for prose.

In the narrow, technical sense, advance organizers are written devices. Although we have consulted with teachers who wrote advance organizers, we have had better success employing a broader approach that Pearson (1984, 1985) has referred to as "schema activation." Where advance organizers are written materials that presumably activate schemata appropriate to the upcoming reading materials and help students relate what is to be read to what is already known, schema activation is a broader process based on classroom discussion, examples, and the visual mapping of schemata related to an upcoming topic in reading, discussion, or lecture. For example, prior to a lesson on deciduous trees, fourth-grade students can be asked to describe the characteristics of trees in their yards and guided to those that are deciduous as a means of activating relevant schemata. Similarly, high school students preparing for a lesson on parliamentary forms of government can be asked to talk about their knowledge of different forms of government and their knowledge could be charted on the blackboard by types of government (e.g., facist, communist, democratic) in order to activate relevant schemata. Senior literature students, as a final example, can be led in a discussion of, say, their knowledge of the Great Depression prior to reading the *Grapes of Wrath*.

Advance organizers and schema activation are similar to the notion of context setting we addressed earlier, but the focus of schema activation is on relating new information to students' existing knowledge. Research on effective teachers indicates that they employ strategies such as schema activation to engage students in learning (see Evertson & Smylie, 1987). When teachers are adapting instruction to special needs students, methods such as schema activation and the use of advance organizers should be stressed.

Questions. The literature dealing with the effect of questions on student learning has grown to the point that a new journal, *The Questioning Exchange,* has been founded. In general, the work in this area can be separated into two areas: questions accompanying reading materials and oral questions asked of students. As the literature on questions associated with reading materials is more extensive and because the general results of research on questions associated with reading materials agrees with the results of research on oral questions, our focus here will be on questions accompanying reading materials.

Providing questions for students to answer while reading has some interesting effects depending on where the questions appear and the form of questions employed. In looking at the effects of questions on readers' memory, researchers typically examine intentional learning (the learning of information specified in the questions) and incidental learning (the learning of information *not* asked for in the questions). Another common procedure is to examine the influence of different levels of questions, typically with the levels defined on the basis of hierarchy of learning, such as the Bloom, Englehart, Furst, Hill, and Krathwohl (1956) taxonomy.

For questions preceding a passage, the research indicates that lower-order questions (i.e., knowledge or comprehension level on the Bloom et al. taxonomy) facilitate intentional learning at the expense of incidental learning. This result is best accounted for via a directed attention effect (see Halpain et al., 1985; Reynolds & Anderson, 1982). That is, measures of readers' inspection time and allocation of attention indicate a clear "posthole" effect in which readers carefully attend to segments of prose containing answers but skim the remaining material.

In contrast to lower-order questions, higher-order questions (i.e., analysis or above on the Bloom et al. taxonomy) enhance the learning of intentional material but have no attenuating effect on incidental learning. A directed attention effect also accounts for these results (see Halpain et al., 1985). Measures of readers' inspection times and allocation of attention indicate that readers give more attention to question-relevant segments of passages but that they read the remaining text fairly carefully as well. Presumably, this set of events occurs because the answers to higher-order questions tend to be lodged in several places and

because it is difficult for readers to predict where answer-relevant contents will be found.

The results described above hold whether questions are all presented together or whether they are interspersed through a passage. However, when lower-order questions are interspersed, the negative effect on incidental learning is reduced (Glover, Harvey & Halpain, 1985). A different pattern of results appears, however, when questions follow reading materials.

Lower-order questions following segments of prose tend to enhance intentional learning with no particular effect on incidental learning. Higher-order questions following segments of prose also enhance intentional learning and have a small but consistent positive effect on incidental learning. Interestingly, questions following prose do *not* have their effect as a result of increasing students' overall levels of arousal or attention (Halpain et al., 1985). The directed attention effect, of course, also cannot account for the results because students have no way of knowing how to allocate their attention without seeing the questions first. The best explanation seems to be a reprocessing hypothesis. That is, when students have completed reading and then answer questions, they must retrieve information from their long-term memories about the passage, review it, and formulate answers. All of these cognitive operations elaborate the information in memory, increasing the likelihood of forming a strong memory trace (Halpain et al., 1985).

A contrast of pre- and postreading questions generally indicates that intentional learning is best facilitated by prereading questions. This is a direct result of how students allocate their attention (Glover et al., 1985). However, if a teacher's goal is to enhance intentional learning without adversely affecting incidental learning, postreading questions should be employed.

When higher- and lower-order questions are contrasted, memory for overall content is greater when higher-order rather than when lower-order questions are employed. Higher-order questions enhance memory for content associated with questions without affecting recall of content not associated with questions. In fact, higher-order questions provided after reading enhance both intentional and incidental learning.

When we consult with teachers about the use of questions, we recognize the need for lower-order questions in the learning of facts, but encourage the use of higher-order questions, especially those that require decisions (see Benton, Glover, & Bruning, 1983) and those of moderate levels of difficulty (see Benton, Glover, Monkowski, & Shaughnessy, 1983). We also stress the need to teach students *how* to respond to higher-order questions. Although we have been able to obtain true analysis level thinking among normal fourth graders (Glover, 1979), we have found that practice with feedback for answering higher-order questions is a necessary component of changing the ways in which students process information (Glover, Zimmer, Filbeck, & Plake, 1982). Simply, many students at all levels have not had any experience in dealing with questions beyond the comprehension level of the Bloom et al. (1956) taxonomy and need to learn the requirements of more sophisticated questions.

The Spacing Effect

One of the most enduring findings of memory research is that recall of verbal material is superior when learning trials are spaced rather than massed (see Hintzman, 1974; Underwood, 1964). Although advising teachers to be aware of the "spacing" effect is still a good idea, spaced learning trials may not be as economical in terms of classroom time as when teachers are explaining a concept to students or when students are learning a brief set of directions. However, recent attempts to explain the superiority of spaced over massed learning trials have led to research that indicates that the spacing effect may be circumvented.

Explanations for the spacing effect may be placed into two categories. The first suggests that spaced learning trials are superior because increasing intervals between repetitions allow for independent encodings of the memory event. The most widely studied explanation of this sort is the "encoding variability" hypothesis, which posits that greater recall will result from spaced repetitions because the spacing is likely to result in the encoding of the memory event in different subjective contexts. In this view, as the number of encoding contexts for to-be-learned information increases, so should the probability of recall (see Postman & Knecht, 1983; B. H. Ross & Landauer, 1978, for discussions). Recent research testing the "encoding variability" hypothesis, however, has demonstrated that increasing the number of contexts in which an item is processed does not enhance memory as compared to when encoding context is

held constant, thus casting doubt on this hypothesis (Postman & Knecht, 1983).

A second category of explanations has focused on reduced processing as a result of massing trials. That is, this category of explanations posits that after the initial learning trial in a massed trials session, subsequent presentations of the to-be-learned material result in reduced processing of the information. Among the many variants of explanations falling into this category, an "accessibility" hypothesis recently has gained considerable attention (Cuddy & Jacoby, 1982; Jacoby, 1978; Rose, 1980; Rose & Rowe, 1976). From this perspective, when a second (or any subsequent) learning trial occurs, the learner tries to retrieve the previous encoding of that information. The availability of the initial encoding varies with the spacing between the learning trials. Hence, massed learning trials are less effective than spaced learning trials because only the first learning trial receives full processing. Spaced learning trials, on the other hand, result in the reduced availability of the prior encoding, which increases the likelihood that the new learning trial will require a full encoding process.

One important implication of the accessibility hypothesis "is that anything that increases the probability of full encoding should also improve recall" (Dellarosa & Bourne, 1985, p. 530). Spacing learning trials apart is one way to increase the probability of full encoding of the material on different trials, since forgetting is likely to occur between spaced trials. Another approach, at least in terms of students' memory for more complex materials, is to alter the surface structure of materials so that the material presented in trials subsequent to the first appear unfamiliar, hence increasing the likelihood of full encoding processes (Dellarosa & Bourne, 1985).

Unlike individual words and nonsense syllables usually used in research on the spacing effect, reading materials and brief lectures contain two types of information: surface information (wording, etc.) and semantic (meaning) information. Subjects' memory for these two types of information seem to be independent, with different memory representations for each (Begg, 1971; Kintsch, 1975). Typically, forgetting for surface and semantic information occurs at different rates, with memory for surface information decaying very rapidly (J. R. Anderson & Paulson, 1977; Garrod & Trabasso, 1973; Jarvella, 1971, 1973; Sachs, 1967; Wright, 1969).

In their study of the spacing effect in recall of sentences, Dellarosa and Bourne (1985) reasoned that altering the surface structure of to-be-learned sentences across repetitions would have very little effect on recall in spaced learning trials. That is, since only the gist of the to-be-learned sentences would be available in memory after a brief delay (one distractor sentence), Dellarosa and Bourne predicted that altering the surface structure of the to-be-learned sentence for its second presentation would have a minimal effect on memory. Further, they believed that sentences presented in spaced trials, whether repeated verbatim or repeated in different surface structure forms, would be remembered well because they would be "likely to enjoy a reinstatement of full encoding processes, having suffered a delay in repetition" (Dellarosa & Bourne, 1985, p. 530). In contrast, Dellarosa and Bourne predicted different outcomes for massed presentations of sentences. That is, they expected that since a sentence's surface structure was likely to be retained in memory when the sentence was presented in massed trials, there would be a high likelihood of a verbatim repetition of a sentence being identified as a repetition, resulting in the retrieval of that sentence's prior encoding. Thus, according to the accessibility hypothesis, only the first learning trial would receive full processing. Presenting different surface structures of the same sentence, however, "should hinder recognition of the item as a repetition. As a result, full encoding processes should be initiated" (Dellarosa & Bourne, 1985, p. 530). The "full encoding" of sentences with the same gist but with different surface structures in massed presentations was predicted to result in significantly greater recall than verbatim sentences presented in massed trials.

In general, Dellarosa and Bourne's (1985) results supported their predictions. That is, verbatim sentences repeated in massed trials were recalled (a) at significantly lower level than verbatim sentences repeated in spaced trials, (b) sentences altered in surface structure repeated in spaced trials, or (c) sentences altered in surface structure repeated in massed trials. When the surface structure of sentences was altered, massed repetition of learning trials was as effective as spaced repetitions of learning trials.

More recently, Glover and Corkill (1987) examined the accessibility hypothesis in terms of students' memory for brief segments of prose and oral explanations of concepts. The results con-

formed to those of Dellarosa and Bourne. That is, learning in massed trials was as good as learning in spaced trials when paraphrased versions of prose materials and brief lectures were provided to students.

Two general implications can be drawn from work on the spacing effect. First, increasing the number of contexts in which materials are studied does not seem to increase memorability (see Smith, 1986, for a countervailing argument). Second, teachers can make directions, explanations, brief lectures, and written materials far more memorable in massed practice sessions if they will employ paraphrased versions of the materials. As a simple example, when a teacher is explaining a procedure to students (e.g., how to solve a particular type of mathematics problem), his or her students will be far more likely to remember the explanation if the teacher employs a paraphrased version of it during a repetition rather than merely repeating verbatim what has been said. As another example, when a student asks for a clarification of a point in a lecture, the teacher should not give a verbatim repetition of the content but instead should use a different explanation or a different example.

The Generation Effect

Self-generated materials are remembered better than material that is simply read (Glisky & Rabinowitz, 1985; Rabinowitz & Craik, 1986). This phenomenon has been observed for a wide variety of stimulus materials and in several kinds of posttest situations (Donaldson & Bass, 1980; Graf, 1980; Jacoby, 1978; Kane & Anderson, 1978). The difference between self-generation and reading in study can be seen, for example, in the difference between covering a list of spelling words and generating them from memory versus merely reading them over and over.

In contrasting reading with generation during encoding, Glisky and Rabinowitz (1985, p. 194) suggested that

> in the case of reading, access may be automatic and effortless. In . . . generation . . . a more controlled form of processing is required, involving an interaction between the . . . [to-be-learned information] and the knowledge system [semantic memory]. The processes themselves may be stored as integral parts of the memory trace; the resulting

enriched description of the word-event could thereby become potentially more retrievable.

McElroy and Slamecka (1982) have divided explanations for the "generation" effect into two general categories: (a) those based in semantic memory (memory for facts; an hypothetical component of long-term memory devoted to names, dates, facts, figures, etc.) and (b) those that emphasize the generation process itself. However, research suggests that the effects of generation and semantic memory cannot be disentangled. If students do not have the to-be-generated information in semantic memory (as when, say they have not yet started to learn new vocabulary words), the generation process has no apparent effect. However, varying the difficulty of generation and reinstating generation at the time of retrieval both influence individuals' memory for the materials, suggesting that the act of generation itself is implicated in the enhanced memory.

Although the exact contributions of the generation process and access to semantic memory remain unclear, the generation effect itself is highly robust. "The act of generation augments the storage . . . of information. The information enhanced by generation on a particular occasion is the specific information used to guide the generation process" (Rabinowitz & Craik, 1986, p. 236).

Even though we cannot yet tease out the contributions of accessing semantic memory and the act of generation, two important implications can be drawn from research on the generation effect. First, rereading is not an especially effective means of rehearsing information. Second, having students rehearse information they are learning through some form of generation procedure will enhance their memory for the content. However, for generation to have any utility, the material must already be fairly well learned. It would seem that the generation effect is best suited for the last few trials on a spelling test, a vocabulary list, the main points in a story, and so on.

Storage
How is information stored in long-term memory? The answer to this question (at least the best answer now possible) would require its own handbook. Here we will not attempt a review of theories of how information is organized in long-term memory (the reader is referred to J. R. Anderson, 1983, Mandler, 1984, and Tulving, 1985, for detailed

readings in this area). Instead, we will focus on two well-known long-term memory phenomena that demonstrate some of the qualities of the organization of information in long-term memory.

Organization in Free Recall
One of the most widely cited papers dealing with organization of long-term memory is that authored by Bousfield (1953). Bousfield read his subjects a set of 60 nouns, one every 3 seconds. The subjects had been told to listen carefully and concentrate as much as possible because they would be tested on their ability to recall the words in the list. What Bousfield did not tell his subjects was that the list consisted of 15 nouns in each of four specific categories (professions, men's names, vegetables, animals) that had been placed in random order.

At the completion of the list reading, Bousfield's subjects were tested via free recall. Their recall was good, far superior to what usually is seen when subjects are given unrelated words to recall. As important as the quality of recall was the fact that Bousfield's subjects clustered their recalls (i.e., remembering the men's names together, the animals together, etc.). This result has been replicated several times (e.g., Cofer, Bruce, & Reicher, 1966; Corkill & Glover, 1987; Puff, 1970), with the additional finding that the better the materials are organized, the more facilitated is recall.

Subjective Organization
It seems fairly clear that if an organization is available at the time of encoding, students will employ that organization in long-term memory. But what happens when no organization is provided for students? Tulving investigated this question by giving students (run individually) 16 unrelated words, one at a time. After the first exposure to the list was complete, the subjects were tested via free recall. Following the first trial, the subjects were given the same list again and tested again for several trials. As would be expected, overall recall increased as a function of the number of trials, but so did clustering of the words. That is, words tended to be recalled in groups, a subjective organization imposed by the subjects.

Tulving (1983, 1985) has argued that the phenomenon of subjective organization resulted from each subject imposing some organization on a set of unrelated words. For example, if the words *clock, picture,* and *tree* tended to appear together over and over in a subject's recalls, it might be because the subject was linking them in some fashion, such as by imagining a picture of a clock under a tree. In any event, even though no obvious organization was present in the materials that Tulving presented to his subjects, the subjects ultimately imposed organizations.

Implications

No matter what theoretical perspective we take on organization in long-term memory (e.g., schema theory, network models, set-theoretic models), the two phenomena we described above indicate that long-term memory is well organized, that learners will employ an available organization to guide their construction of a memory, that organized information is more readily recalled than unorganized information, and that in the absence of a clear organization learners will impose their own.

These findings have important implications for consulting with teachers about instructional practices. The quality of students' memory for information will reflect the quality of organization provided by teachers. That is, poorly organized or unorganized information will be recalled less well than well organized information. In addition, if an organization is not provided by the teacher, the students will impose their own organization. Finally, organization cues provided students are likely to be used, thus assuring a consistency of student learning.

Retrieval

Retrieval refers to gaining access to information in long-term memory and bringing it into working memory. Reciting Boyle's law, remembering the address of a friend, and describing yesterday's lunch are all examples of retrieval. However, retrieval is not always as simple as it seems from the examples listed above. A common phenomenon is knowing that one knows something but being unable to extract it from long-term memory. The classic instance is not remembering the answer to an examination question until one leaves the room after turning in the test. Another phenomenon is remembering things seemingly without intent. For instance, when a forgotten song is heard on the radio, it may bring back a rush of memories that had not been thought about in years.

It turns out that several retrieval phenomena can be accounted for on the basis of the cues people have at the time of retrieval. In this section we focus on the principle of encoding specificity

and how a knowledge of encoding specificity can help school psychologists more effectively consult with teachers on the assessment of learning.

Encoding Specificity

The principle of encoding specificity was first described by Tulving (Tulving & Osler, 1968; Tulving & Thomson, 1973). In short, this principle holds that retrieval cues provide access to information about events in memory if and only if the cues were stored as a part of the original memory for events (see Tulving, 1983, 1985). In other words, cues given at the time of test are likely to be effective only if they were a part of what students learned in the first place.

Encoding specificity has been observed in recognition, cued recall, and even free recall (Tulving, 1985). However, the classic early research was performed in a cued-recall paradigm. For example, Tulving and Osler (1968) had subjects learn a list of 24 words. Half of the subjects studied each of the 24 words paired with a weak associate (e.g., lady-queen). The other half saw only the 24 to-be-learned words. Then, at the time test, half of the subjects in each condition were given the weak associates as retrieval cues, the other half were not. The results indicated that only those subjects who had the weak associates present at the time of encoding and at retrieval benefited from them. Not surprisingly, subjects in this condition recalled significantly more than subjects in any other condition, with no other contrasts reaching significance (Tulving & Osler, 1968).

The pattern of results reported by Tulving and Osler has been replicated on several occasions (see Tulving, 1985) with various kinds of materials. For example, R. C. Anderson and Ortony had subjects learn several different kinds of sentences, such as "The principal pounded the stake" and "The principal pounded the desk." At the time of recall, Anderson and Ortony found that congruent cues, those that best fit the context of encoding, resulted in significantly greater levels of recall. For example, the word "fist" worked well as a cue for "The principal pounded the desk" but not for "The principal pounded the stake." Similarly, the cue "hammer" worked well for the "The principal pounded the stake" but not for "The principal pounded the desk."

More recently, Rabinowitz and Craik (1986) found that when operations required at encoding (generation, in this case) were required at retrieval, memory for the target items was enhanced. Apparently, as more elements of the encoding context are present at retrieval, memory performance is enhanced. Cues provided at retrieval that were not present at or congruent with the context of encoding, however, seem to offer little or no benefit in enhancing memory performance.

Implications

If we presume that teacher-made tests have as a primary purpose the assessment of student learning, the principle of encoding specificity has some important implications. First, the nature of cues provided in tests has a direct effect on student's memory performance. As test items provide cues present at the time of encoding, as items better recapitulate the context present at encoding, as test items better represent a meaningful problem, student memory performance will be enhanced. Issues of difficulty, discriminability, and reliability aside, a good test item is one that provides students with a maximal opportunity to demonstrate what has been learned. This means, from our perspective, that multiple-choice items must be carefully chosen so that the stems reinstate relevant cues. In choosing multiple-choice items from teachers' manuals, teachers should select only those that fit the context of their instruction. In writing multiple-choice items, teachers should construct stems with cues present at the time of encoding. Short-answer and essay items similarly require care in construction so that at least some of the context of the original learning is reproduced.

A second general implication is a reemphasis on the importance of context. As we noted earlier in the chapter, context has powerful effects on student learning and teachers guide the context of learning in classroom situations. The principle of encoding specificity clearly is contextually bound. Not only is the context teachers set for learning important at the time of encoding, it is also important at the time of test. Having teachers focus on context is likely to improve learning in the first place, but it is also likely to improve the quality of their assessments of student learning.

A third implication to be drawn from the principle of encoding specificity relates to what may be referred to as one aspect of transfer. Presumably, much of what is taught in schools is not designed to be situation specific. That is, we expect that general world knowledge, mathematics skills, reading skills, and so on, will generalize to settings outside the school. A part of this generalization is the ability to remember information in settings outside the classroom. Hence, the development of context at the time of learning that is likely to be congruent with out-of-class situations will facilitate transfer.

Finally, the principle of encoding specificity lets us see why some examination questions are so frustrating. A student may know that he or she knows the content but cannot recall the specific answer because the retrieval cue is poor—not enough of the original encoding context is provided to allow for retrieval of the answer. In a contrasting situation, encoding specificity allows us to see why hearing an old song, visiting a long-neglected neighborhood, or seeing a person for the first time in years can bring forth a flood of old memories. Simply, these stimuli act as cues that reinstate the context of encoding.

In this section we reviewed selected aspects of cognitive psychology relevant to consulting with teachers. The word *selected* needs to be kept in mind because we have barely scratched the surface of cognitive psychology. The reader is referred to volumes by Gagné (1985), Glover, Ronning, and Bruning (1990), and J. R. Anderson (1985) for more detailed introductions to cognitive psychology. In the next section we stress a different perspective on the implications of cognitive psychology—understanding individual differences.

INDIVIDUAL DIFFERENCES

The existence of differences in children's cognitive abilities is such a frequently made observation that it hardly bears mention. Our purpose in this second major part of the chapter is not to reiterate the obvious. Instead, we present an information-processing perspective for understanding process differences among children. We begin with an overview of how differences in information processing are viewed, then review processing differences between normal and retarded individuals as a means of spotlighting important research findings.

Sources of Individual Differences

Studies of individual differences in information processing are based on the observation of "bottlenecks" in the processing system (Broadbent, 1958; Hunt, 1988; Hunt, Frost, & Lunneborg,

1973). For example, far more information in the environment is available than can be held in the sensory registers (see Sperling, 1960). In addition, only a portion of what is held in the sensory registers can be accessed by the working memory (Darwin, Turvey, & Crowder, 1972; Sperling, 1960; von Wright, 1972). As we have seen, working memory has a limited capacity (Miller, 1956; Murdock, 1961; Schweikert & Boruff, 1986; Simon, 1974) and only a fraction of the information held in working memory is passed on to long-term memory (see Klatzky, 1984). These "bottlenecks" in the processing system taken with the obvious differences in cognitive achievement led several theorists (e.g., Case, 1974, 1985; Ellis, 1970; Hunt, 1978, 1988; Sternberg, 1984b) to propose that differences in cognitive abilities could be accounted for on the basis of differences in individuals' information-processing systems.

In particular, Hunt and his colleagues (e.g., Hunt, 1978, 1988; Hunt, Lansman, & Davidson, 1981; Hunt et al., 1973) have posited three potential sources of individual differences in information processing: knowledge, mechanics of information processing, and elementary information-processing programs. Differences in knowledge influence what will be attended, what will be perceived, and the probability of passing new information into long-term memory. For example, a child faced with an elevation problem in a map skills unit who knows how to solve such problems probably will attend to important aspects of the problem, assign appropriate meanings to various aspects of the problem, and is very likely to append any new information to her already existing store of knowledge in long-term memory. In contrast, a child who does not know about such problems is unlikely to know what to focus on, will not assign appropriate meanings to several aspects of the problem, and will have little likelihood of relating his experience with the problem to relevant knowledge structures in long-term memory.

From Hunt's perspective, the second source of individual differences in cognition is the mechanics of information processing: the "hardware" component of the information processing system (but see Hunt, 1978, p. 128). Hunt suggested that there were (a) capacity and duration differences in the sensory registers, (b) capacity, duration, and speed of manipulation differences in working memory, and (c) differences in speed of access to long-term memory. Hunt (1978) also proposed,

however, that "hardware" differences had to be considered in light of differences among individuals' elementary information-processing programs. In Hunt's terms (1978, p. 128) humans must possess

> simple strategies that are used as steps in virtually every larger problem. Examples are the strategy of repeating names that are to be remembered or the strategy of checking an answer after it has been developed but before it is publicly enunciated. . . . Much of what we refer to as general intelligence is based on the facility with which one uses such general information processes.

Of the sources of cognitive ability differences Hunt identifies, knowledge has been the most frequently investigated in psychometric studies, although from a perspective very different from that of information processing. Below we emphasize information-processing-oriented research.

Individual Differences in Cognition

A survey of all the research on individual differences in information processing is beyond the scope of this chapter. Here we briefly recount general approaches to the area and then examine in greater detail work examining differences between retarded and normal children.

Two Approaches to Research

Two different approaches have developed for research on individual differences in cognition. The cognitive-developmental approach grows out of attempts to understand the process of cognitive development in terms of the development of human information-processing systems. In contrast, the "intelligence" approach is based on more traditional psychometric views of the assessment of intelligence and has emphasized identifying cognitive processes associated with individual differences in intelligence. We describe each below.

The Cognitive-Developmental Approach.
The cognitive-developmental approach (e.g., Case, 1984, 1985; Sternberg, 1984a, 1984b) has focused on differences in working memory—the very clear observation that children's working memory capacity increases with age. Case's emphasis (e.g., 1985) has been on the efficiency of elementary information-processing programs used

in working memory. In general, he has argued that the capacity of working memory does not increase with development. That is, he does not perceive a change in "hardware." Instead, children's executive processes become more and more efficient through practice and increased knowledge, requiring less and less space in working memory.

The analogy to computer programs is direct—highly efficient programs can perform the same task that inefficient programs can complete but require less working memory space and function more rapidly. In Case's view, changes in working memory capacity (and the resulting changes in the cognitive products children produce) result from the formation of more and more efficient elementary information-processing programs (see Case, 1974, 1978, 1984, 1985).

Sternberg's (1982, 1984b, 1984c, 1984d) developmental approach has also centered on working memory as the source of individual differences in cognition, although Sternberg is working on a more comprehensive theory of intelligence. To date, Sternberg's primary emphasis has been on his componential subtheory growing out of his larger "triarchic" theory of intelligence. In this subtheory, Sternberg stresses elementary information-processing programs. Similar to Case, Sternberg believes that cognitive development proceeds as a function of the formation of more and more efficient elementary information-processing programs.

The "Intelligence" Approach. In contrast to the cognitive-developmental approach, the "intelligence" approach arose from attempts to meld experimental cognitive psychology and psychometrics (Hunt, 1988; Jensen, 1988). Beginning with Cronbach's (1957) call for experimental and psychometric psychology to work together, this approach has emphasized identifying information-processing tasks related to psychometric measures.

For example, Hunt and his colleagues (e.g., 1978, 1988) usually identify diverse groups of subjects on the basis of psychometric instruments and then attempt to determine whether these groups also differ in their performance on information processing tasks. Overall, Hunt has found that groups differing on measures of verbal ability also differ significantly in the capacity of iconic register, the capacity of working memory, the speed with which information can be

manipulated in working memory, the duration of information in working memory, and the speed with which long-term memory can be accessed (see Hunt, 1988, for a review). Unlike the developmental approach, the "intelligence" approach has emphasized all elements of the information-processing system and, as we will see below, considerable emphasis has been devoted to "hardware"-"software" distinctions.

Contrasts of Retarded and Normal Individuals
Research examining processing differences between normal and retarded individuals has proceeded largely from the "intelligence" perspective (e.g., Butterfield & Belmont, 1975; Ellis, 1970; Krupski, 1980; T. Nettelbeck & Brewer, 1981). The usual method is to identify a retarded group and either an age-matched or a mental-age matched group of normal subjects and then to compare them on a series of information-processing tasks (e.g., Caruso, 1985). Most such research has been conducted on adults and adolescent retarded subjects, although recent work has begun to focus on children (e.g., Bos & Tierney, 1984).

The overall results of this line of research fit well with those described by Hunt in contrasts of normal and highly capable students (see 1978, 1988). For example, the size of the iconic register appears to be smaller in retarded than in normal subjects (Hornstein & Mosely, 1979; Libkuman, Velliky, & Freidrich, 1980; Pennington & Luszca, 1975; L. E. Ross & Ward, 1978; Saccuzzo, Kerr, Marcus, & Brown, 1979). Although the data are less clear, it also appears that the duration of ionic store is shorter among the retarded (Saccuzzo et al., 1979) and that the availability of information from iconic store is poorer (Libkuman et al., 1980; Saccuzo et al., 1979).

Differences in Iconic Store
Pennington and Luszca (1975), who contrasted the iconic register capabilities of normal and mildly retarded young adults in a series of four experiments, provide an excellent example of iconic register research. In their study, arrays of letters were presented to the subjects via a tachistoscope for 50 milliseconds. Subjects then reported the letters seen after varying delay intervals. Confirming Sperling (1960), normal subjects reported about four items per array. The retarded subjects,

however, consistently reported an average of about one less item per array.

The Pennington and Luszca (1975) study has served as a model of sensory register research contrasting normal and retarded individuals. The reliability with which iconic store processing deficits are observed in retarded individuals and the widely held belief that no executive processes operate at the level of sensory registers (see Averbach & Coriell, 1961; Sperling, 1960) have been frequently cited reasons for concluding that part of the information-processing deficit in retarded individuals is due to structural ("hardware") limitations (see Saccuzzo & Michael, 1984), perhaps located in the visual cortex.

Working Memory Differences

Processing deficits also have been observed in other components of the system, particularly in working memory. For instance, the capacity of working memory is smaller among retarded individuals than among normal persons (Brown, 1974; Spitz, 1973), the speed of information manipulation is slower (Saccuzzo & Michael, 1984), the availability of elementary information processing programs is more limited (e.g., Borkowski & Cavanaugh, 1979), access to long-term memory (Saccuzzo & Michael, 1984) is more restricted, and there seem to be more limits on specific executive processes (e.g., R. Nettlebeck, Hvions, & Wilson, 1985). Although the exact nature of the relationship of sensory register deficits to working memory functions is unclear, sensory register capabilities have a strong influence on working memory (Saccuzzo & Michael, 1984) and must be considered in conjunction with observed deficits in working memory.

Given the breadth of the field, it is difficult to identify a prototypical study among the many that have examined working memory differences. Here a study by Ellis, Deacon, and Wooldridge (1985) will be our example. In four separate experiments, Ellis et al. compared the performance of normal and mildly retarded young adults' ability to recall sets of pictures after 0, 1, 15, and 30 seconds with the use of an intervening task (counting backward) designed to eliminate executive processing (and thereby to reduce the possibility of executive processes influencing recall). The general results confirmed typical findings on studies of normal adults—recall decreased as the delay after encoding increased, indicating that executive processes

had been blocked. When retarded and normal subjects were compared, similar patterns of forgetting as delay time increased were seen. However, the normal group recalled significantly more pictures than the retarded group at each of the delay intervals.

Ellis et al. (1985) interpreted their results as confirming a structural deficit in working memory among the retarded and discussed the major controversy in information-processing abilities research—whether working memory deficits are due to shortcomings in elementary information-processing programs (executive functions) or to structural problems.

Research on cognitive processes has passed the stage at which the "bottlenecks" in retarded people's information-processing capabilities are disputed. It is evident that there are deficits at each point in the processing system, although interestingly, no work has been completed to determine if different people suffer different deficits at different points in their systems. Currently, the argument focuses not on whether or not there are information-processing deficits, but instead on why these deficits occur.

Early work on memory deficits in the mentally retarded assumed structural problems (see Ellis, 1963). By about 1970, though, the emphasis shifted toward inadequacies in executive processes (see Belmont & Butterfield, 1969, 1977; Detterman, 1979; Ellis, 1970). More recent work (e.g., Ellis et al., 1985) has again emphasized structural deficits. It seems to us that neither of the extreme positions (structure only or executive processes only) can be completely accurate. The results of research on iconic memory strongly suggest structural deficits, as do studies based on minimal strategy paradigms (e.g., Ellis & Meador, 1985). However, it also appears that there are very real executive control deficits (e.g., Bos & Tierney, 1984; Luftig & Johnson, 1982). In addition, the lack of research examining different potential sources of information-processing deficits among the retarded leave us without a data base from which we can draw a conclusion about relative "hardware"-"software" contributions. Given the current status of research in the area, it appears that a middle-ground position (e.g., Campoine & Brown, 1978; Fisher & Zeamon, 1973; Zeamon & House, 1979) will be most fruitful for future research and the development of practical applications.

SUMMARY

In this chapter we illustrated and outlined a basic model of human information processing. The sense receptors, sensory stores, working memory (composed of both short-term memory and executive processes), and long-term memory work together to aid individuals in their attempts to deal effectively with information from their environment. Two critical components of the information-processing model, with considerable consequences for learning, are attention and perception. An individual's ability to attend to several tasks simultaneously is directly related to the difficulty of the tasks. If an individual attempts to attend to too many tasks at once, little learning is likely. Similarly, individuals may attend carefully to incoming stimuli, but if perception does not occur, little learning is likely. Because perception is guided by previous knowledge, providing a context to learners will aid them in focusing on the critical elements of new information.

The research surrounding the processes of encoding, storage, and retrieval (as related to information processing) have vast implications particularly relevant to consulting with teachers and parents about instructional issues. Mnemonics and adjunct aids (e.g., advance organizers and questions) as well as the spacing effect and generation effect demonstrate how different encoding procedures greatly influence recall. Long-term memory (storage) is well organized either by structures provided to learners at the time of encoding or by structures produced by the learners themselves. Retrieval of information depends in part on cues that individuals have at the time of retrieval.

The identification of sources of individual differences in cognitive ability and the impact of research on individual differences once again stresses the active, dynamic, and individualistic nature of human information processing. Three potential sources of individual differences (knowledge, mechanics of information processing, and elementary information processing programs) were identified by Hunt and his colleagues and have been investigated by numerous others.

The cognitive-developmental approach to individual differences focuses on understanding cognitive development in terms of human information processing and the "intelligence" approach focuses on identifying cognitive processes associated with individual differences. The particularly relevant research of individual differences between mentally retarded and normal individuals demonstrates the importance of this research with respect to school psychologists.

As we stated at the outset, the vast amount of literature concerning cognitive psychology could not be covered in a single chapter. Our purpose was to provide a framework in cognitive psychology for the school psychologist and, further, to provide specific citations for research in relevant areas that can be consulted for additional information. If an overriding theme emerged from this chapter, it is that individuals are active, dynamic processors of information with differing levels of cognitive ability based on differences in the individual's information-processing system.

REFERENCES

Anderson, J. R. (1983). A spreading activation theory of memory. *Journal of Verbal Learning and Verbal Behavior, 22*, 261–295.

Anderson, J. R. (1985). *Cognitive psychology and its implications* (2nd ed.). New York: W. H. Freeman.

Anderson, J. R., & Paulson, R. (1977). Representation and retention of verbatim information. *Journal of Verbal Learning and Verbal Behavior, 16*, 439–451.

Anderson, R. C. (1984). Role of the reader's schema in comprehension, learning, and memory. In R. C. Anderson, J. Osborn, & R. J. Tierney (Eds.), *Learning to read in American schools*. Hillsdale, NJ: Lawrence Erlbaum.

Atkinson, R. C. (1975). Mnemotechnics in second-language learning. *American Psychologist, 30*, 821–828.

Atkinson, R. C., & Shiffrin, R. M. (1968). Human memory: A proposed system and its control processes. In K. Spence & J. Spence (Eds.), *The psychology of learning and motivation* (Vol. 2). New York: Academic Press.

Ausubel, D. P. (1960). The use of advance organizers in the learning and retention of meaningful verbal material. *Journal of Educational Psychology, 51*, 267–272.

Ausubel, D. P. (1968). *Educational psychology: A cognitive view*. New York: Holt, Rinehart and Winston.

Averbach, E., & Coriell, A. S. (1961). Short-term memory in vision. *Bell System Technical Journal, 40*, 309–328.

Baddeley, A. D., & Hitch, G. J. (1974). Working memory. In G. Bower (Ed.), *The psychology of learning and motivation* (Vol. 8). New York: Academic Press.

Barnes, B. R., & Clawson, E. V. (1975). Do advance organizers facilitate learning? Recommendations for further research based on an analysis of 32 studies. *Review of Educational Research, 45*, 637–660.

Begg, I. (1971). Recognition memory for sentence meaning and wording. *Journal of Verbal Learning and Verbal Behavior, 10,* 176–181.

Bellezza, F. S. (1981). Mnemonic devices: Classification, characteristics, and criteria. *Review of Educational Research, 51,* 247–275.

Belmont, J. M., & Butterfield, E. C. (1969). The relations of short-term memory to development and intelligence. In L. P. Sipsitt & H. W. Reese (Eds.), *Advances in child development and behavior* (Vol. 4), New York: Academic Press.

Belmont, J. M., & Butterfield, E. C. (1977). The instructional approach to developmental cognitive research. In R. V. Kail, Jr., & J. W. Hagen (Eds.), *Perspectives on the development of memory and cognition.* Hillsdale, NJ: Lawrence Erlbaum.

Benton, S. L., Glover, J. A., & Bruning, R. H. (1983). The effect of number of decisions on prose recall. *Journal of Educational Psychology, 75,* 382–390.

Benton, S. L., Glover, J. A., Monkowski, P. G., & Shaughnessy, M. (1983). Decision difficulty and recall of prose. *Journal of Educational Psychology, 75,* 727–742.

Bloom, B. S., Englehart, M. D., Furst, E. S., Hill, W. A., & Krathwohl, D. R. (1956). *Taxonomy of educational objectives. The classification of educational goals: Handbook I. Cognitive domain.* New York: David McKay.

Borkowski, J. G., & Cavanaugh, J. C. (1979). Maintenance and generalization of skills and strategies by the retarded. In N. R. Ellis (Ed.), *Handbook of mental deficiency.* Hillsdale. NJ: Lawrence Erlbaum.

Bos, C. S., & Tierney, R. J. (1984). Inferential reading abilities of mildly mentally retarded and nonretarded students. *American Journal of Mental Deficiency, 89,* 75–82.

Bousfield, W. A. (1953). The occurrence of clustering and the recall of randomly arranged associates. *Journal of General Psychology, 49,* 229–240.

Brainerd, C. J., & Pressley, M. (Eds.). (1985). *Basic processing in memory development.* New York: Springer-Verlag.

Britton, B. K., & Tesser, A. (1982). Effects of prior knowledge on use of cognitive capacity in three complex cognitive tasks. *Journal of Verbal Learning and Verbal Behavior, 21,* 421–436.

Broadbent, D. E. (1958). *Perception and communication.* Oxford: Pergamon Press.

Brown, A. L. (1974). The role of strategic behavior in retardate memory. In N. R. Ellis (Ed.), *International review of research in mental retardation* (Vol. 7). New York: Academic Press.

Butterfield, E. C., & Belmont, J. M. (1975). Assessing and improving the executive cognitive functions of mentally retarded people. In I. Bialer & M. Sternlicht (Eds.), *Psychological issues in mental retardation.* New York: Academic Press.

Campione, J. C., & Brown, A. L. (1978). Toward a theory of intelligence: Contributions from research with retarded children. *Intelligence, 2,* 279–304.

Caruso, D. R. (1985). Influence of item identification on the memory performance of mentally retarded and nonretarded adults. *Intelligence, 9,* 51–68.

Case, R. (1974). Structures and strictures: Some functional limitations on the course of cognitive growth. *Cognitive Psychology, 6,* 544–573.

Case, R. (1978). A developmentally based theory and technology of instruction. *Review of Educational Research, 48,* 439–463.

Case, R. (1984). The process of stage transition: A neo-Piagetian view. In R. J. Sternberg (Ed.), *Mechanisms of cognitive development.* New York: W. H. Freeman.

Case, R. (1985). *Intellectual development: A systematic reinterpretation.* New York: Academic Press.

Cofer, C. N., Bruce, D. R., & Reicher, G. M. (1966). Clustering in free recall as a function of certain methodological variations. *Journal of Experimental Psychology, 71,* 868–866.

Corkill, A. J., & Glover, J. A. (1987). Information processing differences among creative and non-creative students: Remembering what's not there. *Journal of Creative Behavior, 13,* 9–14.

Corkill, A. J., Glover, J. A., & Bruning, R. H. (1987). Advance organizers: Another name for schema activation? Unpublished manuscript, University of Nebraska, Center for the Study of Cognition in Education, Lincoln.

Cronbach, L. S. (1957). The two disciplines of scientific psychology. *American Psychologist, 12,* 671–684.

Cuddy, L. J., & Jacoby, L. L. (1982). When forgetting helps memory: An analysis of repetition effects. *Journal of Verbal Learning and Verbal Behavior, 21,* 451–467.

Darwin, C. T., Turvey, M. T., & Crowder, R. G. (1972). An auditory analogue of the Sperling partial report procedure: Evidence for brief auditory storage. *Cognitive Psychology, 3,* 255–267.

Dellarosa, D., & Bourne, L. E. (1985). Surface form and the spacing effect. *Memory & Cognition, 13,* 529–537.

Dempster, F. N. (1981). Memory space: Sources of individual and developmental differences. *Psychological Bulletin, 89,* 63–100.

Derry, S. (1984). Effects of an organizer on memory for prose. *Journal of Educational Psychology, 76,* 98–107.

Detterman, D. K. (1979). Memory in the mentally retarded. In N. R. Ellis (Ed.), *Handbook of mental deficiency.* Hillsdale, NJ: Lawrence Erlbaum.

Dinnel, D., & Glover, J. A. (1985). Advance organizers: Encoding manipulations. *Journal of Educational Psychology, 77,* 514–521.

DiVesta, F. J. (1987). The cognitive movement in education. In J. A. Glover and R. R. Ronning (Eds.), *Historical foundations of educational psychology.* New York: Plenum Press.

Donaldson, W., & Bass, M. (1980). Relational information and memory for problem solutions. *Journal of Verbal Learning and Verbal Behavior, 19,* 26–35.

Ellis, N. R. (1963). The stimulus trace and behavioral inadequacy. In N. R. Ellis (Ed.), *Handbook of mental deficiency.* New York: McGraw-Hill.

Ellis, N. R. (1970). Memory processes in retardates and normals. In N. R. Ellis (Ed.), *International review of research in mental retardation* (Vol. 4). New York: Academic Press.

Ellis, N. R., Deacon, J. R., & Wooldridge, P. W. (1985). Structural memory deficits of mental retarded persons. *American Journal of Mental Deficiency, 89,* 393–402.

Ellis, N. R., & Meador, D. M. (1985). Forgetting in retarded and nonretarded persons under conditions of minimal strategy use. *Intelligence, 9,* 87–96.

Evertson, C. M., & Smylie, M. A. (1987). Research on classroom procedures: Views from two perspectives. In J. A. Glover and R. R. Ronning (Eds.), *Historical foundations of educational psychology.* New York: Plenum Press.

Faw, H., & Waller, T. G. (1976). Mathemagenic behaviors and efficiency in learning from prose. *Review of Educational Research, 46,* 691–720.

Fiedler, K., & Stroehm, W. (1986). What kind of mood influences what kind of memory: The role of arousal and information structure. *Memory & Cognition, 14,* 181–190.

Fisher, M. A., & Zeamon, D. (1973). An attention-retention theory of retardate discrimination learning. In N. R. Ellis (Ed.), *International review of research in mental retardation* (Vol, 7). New York: Academic Press.

Gagné, E. (1985). *The cognitive psychology of school learning.* Boston: Little, Brown.

Garrod, S., & Trabasso, T. (1973). A dual-memory information processing interpretation of sentence comprehension. *Journal of Verbal Learning and Verbal Behavior, 12,* 155–167.

Gibson, E. J., & Spelke, E. S. (1983). The development of perception. In J. H. Flavell & E. M. Markman (Eds.), *Handbook of child psychology* (Vol. 3). New York: Wiley.

Glisky, E. L., & Rabinowitz, J. C. (1985). Enhancing the generation effect through repetition of operations. *Journal of Experimental Psychology: Learning, Memory, and Cognition, 11,* 193–205.

Glover, J. A. (1979). Procedures to enhance the creative writing of elementary school children. *The Journal of Applied Behavior Analysis, 12,* 483.

Glover, J. A., & Corkill, A. J. (1987). The spacing effect in memory for paragraphs and brief lectures. *Journal of Educational Psychology, 79,* 221–224.

Glover, J. A., Harvey, A., & Halpain, D. (1985, March). Attentional mechanisms in responding to higher order questions during reading. Paper presented at the annual meeting of the American Educational Research Association, Chicago.

Glover, J. A., Ronning, R. R., & Bruning, R. H. (1990). *Cognitive psychology for teachers.* New York: Macmillan.

Glover, J. A., Zimmer, J. W., Filbeck, R. W., & Plake, B. S. (1982). Training students to use adjunct reading aids. *Journal of General Psychology, 107,* 267–276.

Graf, P. (1980). Two consequences of generating: Increased inter- and intraword organization of sentences. *Journal of Verbal Learning and Verbal Behavior, 17,* 649–667.

Halpain, D., Glover, J. A., & Harvey, A. L. (1985). Differential effects of higher- and lower-order questions: Attention hypotheses. *Journal of Educational Psychology, 77,* 703–715.

Hamaker, C. (1986). The effects of adjunct questions on prose learning. *Review of Educational Research, 56,* 212–242.

Hamilton, R. J. (1985). Adjunct questions and objectives. *Review of Educational Research, 55,* 47–86.

Higbee, K. L. (1979). Recent research on visual mnemonics: Historical roots and educational fruits. *Review of Educational Research, 49,* 611–630.

Higbee, K. L., & Kunihira, S. (1985). Cross-cultural applications of yodai mnemonics in education. *Educational Psychologist, 20,* 57–64.

Hintzman, D. L. (1974). Theoretical implications of the spacing effect. In R. L. Solso (Ed.), *Theories of cognitive psychology: The Loyola Symposium.* Hillsdale, NJ: Lawrence Erlbaum.

Hornstein, H. A., & Mosley, J. L. (1979). Iconic-memory processing of unfamiliar stimuli by retarded and nonretarded individuals. *American Journal of Mental Deficiency, 84,* 40–48.

Hunt, E. (1978). Mechanics of verbal ability. *Psychological Review, 85,* 109–130.

Hunt, E. (1988). Science, technology, and intelligence. In R. R. Ronning, J. A. Glover, & J. Conoley (Eds.), *Cognitive psychology and measurement* (pp. 223–256). Hillsdale, NJ: Lawrence Erlbaum.

Hunt, E., Frost, N., & Lunneborg, C. (1973). Individual differences in cognition: A new approach to intelligence. In G. Bower (Ed.), *The psychology of learning and motivation* (Vol. 7). New York: Academic Press.

Hunt, E., Lansman, M., & Davidson, J. (1981). Individual differences in long-term memory access. *Memory & Cognition, 9,* 599–608.

Jacoby, L. L. (1978). On interpreting the effects of repetition: Solving a problem versus remembering a solution. *Journal of Verbal Learning and Verbal Behavior, 17,* 649–667.

Jarvella, R. J. (1971). Syntactic processing of connected speech. *Journal of Verbal Learning and Verbal Behavior, 10,* 409–416.

Jarvella, R. J. (1973). Coreference and short-term memory for discourse. *Journal of Experimental Psychology, 98,* 426–428.

Jenkins, J. J. (1974). Remember that old theory of memory? Well, forget it! *American Psychologist, 29,* 785–795.

Jensen, A. R. (1988). The *g* beyond factor analysis. In R. R. Ronning, J. A. Glover, & J. Conoley (Eds.), *Cognitive psychology and measurement* (pp. 3–72). Hillsdale, NJ: Lawrence Erlbaum.

Just, M., & Carpenter, P. A. (1986). *The psychology of reading and language comprehension.* Boston: Allyn and Bacon.

Kail, R. V. (1984). *The development of memory in children* (2nd ed.). New York: W. H. Freeman.

Kane, J. H., & Anderson, R. C. (1978). Depth of processing and interference effects in the learning and remembering of sentences. *Journal of Educational Psychology, 70,* 625–635.

Kintsch, W. (1975). Memory representation of text. In R. L. Soslo (Ed.), *Information processing and cognition,* Hillsdale, NJ: Lawrence Erlbaum.

Klatzky, R. L. (1984). *Human memory: Structures and processes* (2nd ed.). New York: W. H. Freeman.

Krupski, A. (1980). Attention processes: Research, theory and implications for special education. In B. K. Keogh (Ed.), *Advance in special education: Vol. I. Basic constructs and theoretical orientations.* Greenwich, CT: JAI Press.

Levin, J. R. (1981). The mnemonic '80s: Keywords in the classroom. *Educational Psychologist, 16,* 65–82.

Levin, J. R. (1985). Yodai features - mnemonic procedure: A commentary on Higbee and Kunihara. *Educational Psychologist, 20,* 73–76.

Levin, J. R. (1986). Educational applications of mnemonic pictures: Possibilities beyond your wildest imagination. In A. A. Sheikh (Ed.), *Imagery in the educational process.* Farmingdale, NY: Baywood.

Libkuman, T. M., Velliky, R. S., & Freidrich, D. D. (1980). Nonselective read-out from iconic memory in normal, borderline, and retarded adolescents. *Intelligence, 4,* 363–369.

Luftig, R., & Johnson, R. (1982). Identification and recall of structurally important units in prose by mentally retarded learners. *American Journal of Mental Deficiency, 86,* 495–502.

Mandler, J. M. (1984). *Stories, scripts, and scenes: Aspects of schema theory.* Hillsdale, NJ: Lawrence Erlbaum.

Marr, D. (1982). *Vision.* San Francisco: W. H. Freeman.

Mayer, R. E. (1979). Can advance organizers influence meaningful learning? *Review of Educational Research, 49,* 371–383.

Mayer, R. E., & Bromage, B. K. (1980). Different recall protocols for technical texts due to advance organizers. *Journal of Educational Psychology, 72,* 209–225.

McBurney, D. H., & Collings, V. B. (1984). *Introduction to sensation/perception* (2nd ed.). Englewood Cliffs, NJ: Prentice-Hall.

McCormick, C. B., & Levin, J. R. (1984). A comparison of different prose-learning variations of the mnemonic keyword method. *American Educational Research Journal, 21,* 379–398.

McElroy, L. A., & Slamecka, N. J. (1982). Memorial consequences of generating nonwords: Implications for semantic-memory interpretations of the generation effect. *Journal of Verbal Learning and Verbal Behavior, 21,* 249–259.

McKoon, G., & Ratcliff, R. (1986). Inference about predictable events. *Journal of Experimental Psychology: Learning, Memory, and Cognition, 12,* 82–91.

Miller, G. A. (1956). The magical number seven, plus or minus two: Some limits on our capacity for processing information. *Psychololological Review, 63,* 81–97.

Morariu, J., & Bruning, R. H. (1984). Cognitive processing by prelingual deaf students as a function of language context. *Journal of Educational Psychology, 76,* 844–856.

Murdock, B. B. (1961). The retention of individual items. *Journal of Experimental Psychology, 64,* 618–625.

Neisser, U. (1982). *Memory observed.* San Francisco: W. H. Freeman.

Nettlebeck, R., Hirons, J., & Wilson, C. (1985). Mental retardation, inspection time, and central attentional impairment. *Intelligence, 9,* 91–98.

Nettelbeck, T., & Brewer, N. (1981). Studies of mental retardation and timed performance. In N. R. Ellis (Ed.), *International review of research in mental retardation* (Vol. 10). New York: Academic Press.

Paivio, A. (1971). *Imagery and verbal processes.* New York: Holt, Rinehart and Winston.

Pearson, D. P. (1984). Guided reading: A response to Isabel Beck. In R. C. Anderson, J. Osborn, and R. J. Tierney (Eds.), *Learning to read in American schools.* Hillsdale, NJ: Lawrence Erlbaum.

Pearson, D. P. (1985). *The comprehension revolution* (Reading Education Report No. 57). Urbana: University of Illinois at Urbana-Champaign, Center for the Study of Reading.

Pennington, F. M., & Luszcz, M. A. (1975). Some functional properties of iconic storage in retarded and nonretarded subjects. *Memory & Cognition, 3,* 295–301.

Pichert, J. W., & Anderson, R. C. (1977). Taking different perspectives on a story. *Journal of Educational Psychology, 69,* 309–315.

Plake, B. S., Glover, J. A., & Kraft, R. G. (1984). Cognitive capacity usage in responding to test items. *Journal of Psychoeducational Assessment, 2,* 333–343.

Postman, L., & Knecht, K. (1983). Encoding variability and retention. *Journal of Verbal Learning and Verbal Behavior, 22,* 133–152.

Pressley, M., Levin, J. R., & Delaney, H. D. (1982). The mnemonic keyword method. *Review of Educational Research, 52,* 61–92.

Puckett, J. M., & Kausler, D. H. (1984). Individual differences and models of memory span: A role for memory search rate? *Journal of Experimental Psychology: Learning, Memory, and Cognition, 10,* 72–82.

Puff, C. R. (1970). Role of clustering in free recall. *Journal of Experimental Psychology, 86,* 384–386.

Rabinowitz, J. C., & Craik, F. I. M. (1986). Specific enhancement effects associated with word generation. *Journal of Memory and Language, 25,* 226–237.

Reynolds, R. E., & Anderson, R. C. (1982). Influence of questions on the allocation of attention during reading. *Journal of Educational Psychology, 74,* 623–632.

Rivlin, R., & Gravelle, K. (1985) *Deciphering the senses: The expanding world of human perception.* New York: Simon and Schuster.

Rock, I. (1984). *Perception* (2nd ed.). New York: W. H. Freeman.

Rose, R. J. (1980). Encoding variability, levels of processing, and the effects of spacing upon judgments of frequency. *Memory & Cognition, 18,* 84–93.

Rose, R. J., & Rowe, E. J. (1976). Effects of orienting task, spacing of repetitions, and list context on judgments of frequency. *Journal of Experimental Psychology: Human Learning & Memory, 2,* 142–152.

Ross, B. H., & Landauer, T. K. (1978). Memory for at

least one of two items: Test and failure of retrieval theories of spacing effects. *Journal of Verbal Learning and Verbal Behavior, 17,* 669–680.

Ross, L. E., & Ward, T. B. (1978). The processing of information from short-term visual store—Developmental and intellectual level differences. In N. R. Ellis (Ed.), *International review of research in mental retardation* (Vol. 9). New York: Academic Press.

Rubin, D. C., & Friendly, M. (1986). Predicting which words get recalled: Measures of free recall, availability, goodness, emotionality, and pronounciability for 925 nouns. *Memory & Cognition, 14,* 79–94.

Rumelhart, D. E. (1980). *An introduction to human information processing.* New York: Wiley.

Saccuzzo, D. P., Kerr, M., Marcus, A., & Brown, R. (1979). Input capability and speed of processing in mental retardation. *Journal of Abnormal Psychology, 88,* 341–345.

Saccuzzo, D. P., & Michael, B. (1984). Speed of information processing and structural limitations by mentally retarded and dual-diagnosed retarded-schizophrenic persons. *American Journal of Mental Deficiency, 89,* 187–194.

Sachs, J. S. (1967). Recognition memory for syntactic and semantic aspects of connected discourse. *Perception & Psychophysics, 2,* 437–442.

Sanford, A. J. (1986). *Cognition and cognitive psychology.* New York: Basic Books.

Schweikert, R., & Boruff, B. (1986). Short-term memory capacity: Magic number of magic spell? *Journal of Experimental Psychology: Learning, Memory, and Cognition, 12,* 419–425.

Shiffrin, R. M. (1973). Information persistence in short-term memory. *Journal of Experimental Psychology, 100,* 39–49.

Simon, H. A. (1974). How big is a chunk? *Science, 183,* 482–488.

Smith, S. M. (1986). Environmental context-dependent recognition memory using a short-term memory task for input. *Memory & Cognition, 14,* 347–354.

Sperling, G. (1960). The information available in brief visual presentations. *Psychological Monographs, 74,* 1–29.

Spitz, H. H. (1973). Consolidating facts in the schematized learning and memory system of educable retardates. In N. R. Ellis (Ed.), *International review of research in mental retardation* (Vol. 6). New York: Academic Press.

Sternberg, R. J. (1982). A componential approach to intellectual development. In R. J. Sternberg (Ed.), *Advances in the psychology of human intelligence* (Vol. 1). Hillsdale, NJ: Lawrence Erlbaum.

Sternberg, R. J. (1984a). What should intelligence tests test? Implications of a triarchic theory of intelligence for intelligence testing. *Educational Researcher, 13,* 5–15.

Sternberg, R. J. (1984b). Mechanisms of cognitive development: A componential approach. In R. J. Sternberg (Ed.), *Mechanisms of cognitive development.* New York: W. H. Freeman.

Sternberg, R. J. (1984c). Toward a triarchic theory of human intelligence. *The Behavioral and Brain Sciences, 7,* 269–315.

Sternberg, S. J. (1984d). *Beyond IQ—A triarchic theory of human intelligence.* New York: Cambridge University Press.

Triesman, A. M., & Geffen, G. (1967). Selective attention: Perception or response? *Quarterly Journal of Experimental Psychology, 19,* 1–17.

Tulving, E. (1983). *Elements of episodic memory.* New York: Oxford University Press.

Tulving, E. (1985). On the classification problem in learning and memory. In L. Nilsson and T. Archer (Eds.), *Perspective on learning and memory.* Hillsdale, NJ: Lawrence Erlbaum.

Tulving, E., & Osler, S. (1968). Effectiveness of retrieval cues in memory for words. *Journal of Experimental Psychology, 77,* 793–801.

Tulving, E., & Thomson, D. M. (1973). Encoding specificity and retrieval processes in episodic memory. *Psychological Review, 80,* 352–373.

Underwood, B. J. (1964). Laboratory studies of verbal learning. In E. R. Hilgard (Ed.), *Part I of the 63rd Yearbook of the National Society for the Study of Education.* Chicago: University of Chicago Press.

von Wright, J. M. (1972). On the problem of selection in iconic memory. *Scandinavian Journal of Psychology, 13,* 159–171.

Walker, N. (1986). Direct retrieval from elaborated memory traces. *Memory & Cognition, 14,* 321–328.

Williams, R. L. (1987). Classroom management. J. A. Glover and R. R. Ronning (Eds.), *Historical foundations of educational psychology.* New York: Plenum Press.

Wright, P. (1969). Transformations and the understanding of sentences. *Language & Speech, 1,* 156–166.

Zeamon, D., & House, B. J. (1979). A review of attention theory. In N. R. Ellis (Ed.), *Handbook of mental deficiency.* Hillsdale, NJ: Lawrence Erlbaum.

6

CONTRIBUTIONS OF BEHAVIORAL PSYCHOLOGY TO SCHOOL PSYCHOLOGY

JOHN R. BERGAN
The University of Arizona

School psychology has its origins in the attempt to apply psychologist principals to bring about positive changes in the learning and adjustment of children in school. From its inception the field has been intervention oriented. The aim was not only to understand the child, but also to bring about beneficial changes in the child's functioning. The early work of Lightner Witmer, who founded the field (Cutts, 1955), was based on the belief that psychological principles could be used to diagnose and treat learning problems manifested by schoolchildren. By 1896 Witmer's success led him to call for the development of a new profession, that of the psychologist applying psychological principles to diagnose and treat intellectual and emotional problems in schoolchildren. Forty years later, when the profession began to grow, the commitment to intervention lessened. Assessment became the dominant function of the school psychologist and it has remained a key role up to the present time (see, e.g., Ramage, 1979).

Behavioral psychology has been a major force in restoring the commitment to intervention that was present in Witmer's early vision of the field. The behavioral approach has provided a powerful technology for promoting children's learning and adjustment in educational settings. Moreover, that technology is firmly founded in a scientific approach that requires empirical validation of treatment programs, thereby providing a mechanism for the continual evaluation of treatment effectiveness.

Behavioral theory with its commitment to empirically validated intervention has had a marked effect on the practice of school psychology. It has had a significant influence on all of the major roles and functions of the school psychologist. Moreover, it has affected the scientific knowledge base that provides the foundation for practice in the field. In this chapter we examine the contributions of behaviorism to school psychology. The chapter addresses the influence of behavioral psychology on the roles and functions of the school psychologist. Finally, it looks at some possible futures arising from the continuing interaction of behavioral thought and the practice of psychology in schooling.

ASSESSMENT

As mentioned earlier, assessment has long been a major function of the school psychologist. In its broadest sense, assessment may be defined as the gathering of information as a basis for making decisions (Cancelli & Duley, 1985). School psychologists use assessment to screen children to determine whether or not further diagnosis of learning and/or adjustment problems is warranted. They use assessment to classify children to determine their eligibility for placement in a special program. They apply assessment procedures as basis for instructional planning. Finally, they use assessment techniques to evaluate student progress. Behavioral technology has contributed to all of these forms of assessment.

Criterion-Referenced Assessment

One of the major influences of behavioral psychology on assessment practice involves criterion-referenced assessment. Criterion-referenced assessment came on the scene in the early 1960s (Glaser, 1963). This form of assessment references test responses against well-defined criteria specifying acceptable performance. In the early days of criterion-referenced assessment, criteria for judging performance were detailed in the form of instructional or behavioral objectives (Hambleton, 1985; Popham, 1978). This is where behavioral psychology entered the picture. The specification of objectives has its origins in the behavioral tradition. Criterion-referenced tests used behavioral technology to formulate objectives. In particular, the behavior to be assessed was specified in observable terms so that examiners could reliably determine whether or not criteria had been met. The specification of objectives remains the cornerstone of the criterion-referenced approach. However, to ensure congruence between objectives and items, current developers of criterion-referenced instruments frequently use domain specifications in the construction of criterion-referenced test items (Hambleton, 1985). Domain specifications include objectives, but also contain other information to ensure that items developed will be congruent with objectives. For instance, a sample item is provided and a description of the limits within which item content and item responses must fall is included.

The linking of assessment to objectives firmly establishes a relationship between assessment and instructional intervention. The principal use of the criterion-referenced approach is in the planning of instructional interventions based on assessment information. Criterion-referenced assessment is designed to determine those objectives that have and have not been mastered by students. Teachers who have information from a criterion-referenced test are able to target instruction toward the achievement of objectives that have not yet been met. The direct link between assessment and instruction is one of the most attractive features of the criterion-referenced approach. As has been pointed out many times in the literature, traditional norm-referenced assessment technology, which references test performance to examinee position in a norm group, does not ensure a link between assessment and instruction (e.g., Popham, 1978). Knowing where a child stands in a norm group does not tell a teacher what that child needs to be taught.

It has been recognized for some time that criterion-referenced assessment may be used in program evaluation as well as in the planning of instructional interventions (e.g., Popham, 1978). Criterion-referenced technology affords an unambiguous account of what has been learned in the course of instruction. When criterion-referenced test scores are coupled with an appropriate evaluation design, the program evaluator using criterion-referenced technology is able to identify the specific skills that have been mastered as a result of instruction. This kind of unambiguous information about program effects can be useful in the design of instructional programs. The use of criterion-referenced assessment makes it possible to pinpoint the kinds of skills that a program is particularly effective in developing. Similarly, it can reveal instances in which there are no changes in skill acquisition. This kind of information can be useful in devising strategies to increase program effectiveness.

Criterion-referenced assessment can be used for screening. However, it is not often applied for this purpose. The typical approach used in screening is to use norm-referenced assessment to identify individuals at the lower extremes of the score distribution provided by a suitable norm group. These individuals are then selected for further evaluation. Although criterion-referenced assessment is not often used for screening, there is something to be said for applying it in the screening process. Insofar as criterion-referenced assessment technology affords an indication of the kinds of skills that a student possesses, it can be used to determine the match between the student and the instructional program in which the student has been placed. If the match is not good, that is, if there is little relationship between what the child knows and needs to learn and the kinds of skills that are being taught in the program, further examination is warranted to establish a learning environment that is appropriate for meeting the student's needs. On the other hand, if the match is good, additional diagnostic work may not be needed.

Criterion-referenced measures are rarely used in the classification of students for purposes of placement in special programs. Norm-referenced instruments have dominated assessment practice related to placement in the past, and there is every reason to believe that they will continue to do so in the years ahead. Yet criterion-referenced assessment can be useful for placement. The ability of the criterion-referenced approach to identify the match between an instructional program and the skills that a child has mastered could be applied effectively in determining program placements. The kinds of skills targeted for instruction in the program for which the child is being considered could be matched against the child's learning needs reflected in the kinds of skills that have and have not been mastered. If the program affords a learning environment representing the best available match with respect to the child's needs, placement could be considered.

Behavioral Assessment

A second form of assessment representing the behavioral perspective that has had a major influence on school psychology is behavioral assessment. Given its name, behavioral assessment might be regarded as a generic term covering all forms of assessment coming out of the behavioral perspective (including criterion-referenced assessment). However, the origins and methods of behavioral assessment are sufficiently different from criterion-referenced assessment as to warrant separate treatment.

The hallmark of behavioral assessment is the inclusion of conditions surrounding the occurrence of behavior as part of the assessment process Kratochwill (1982). Surrounding conditions are generally defined as those things that occur immediately prior to and immediately following a behavior. The inclusion of immediate antecedent and consequent conditions strengthens the link between assessment and intervention. Identifying those things that occur before and after a behavior can lead to the determination of environmental factors controlling behavior. Knowledge of these determinants provides a basis for establishing intervention plans to produce beneficial behavioral changes. The school psychology literature is replete with studies illustrating the application of behavioral assessment procedures eventuating in the identification of conditions controlling behavior, the formulation of intervention plans including controlling conditions, and the implementation of plans to produce beneficial behavioral outcomes.

The behavioral assessment paradigm evolved from the research methodology developed for use in applied behavior analysis (e.g., Baer, Wolf, & Risley, 1968). The typical application of the applied behavioral analysis approach involves repeated observations of one or a small number of behaviors over a relatively extended time span. For example, one might observe instances of aggressive behaviors such as hitting in a classroom setting over a period of days. Following baseline observations, an intervention is introduced within the context of an appropriate experimental design (see, e.g., Kratochwill, 1978). The effects of the intervention are evaluated by examining changes in behavior associated with the presence of the intervention.

Applications of the behavioral assessment paradigm generally involve direct observations of behaviors of interest by one or more observers. Moreover, during at least part of the assessment process, two or more observers chart behavior at the same time in order to assess the reliability of observations (see, e.g., Kratochwill, 1978). Direct observation provides an objective record of the occurrence of behaviors of interest. The school psychologist using direct observation has a record of behavior as it occurs in the natural environment. Records of this type provide meaningful information that may be used to change behavior in the environment in which it occurs. The benefits of direct observation are well recognized, and many investigators have called for increased use of direct observational methods in school psychology (Alessi 1980; Kratochwill, 1980a, 1980b).

Despite the obvious benefits to direct observation, there are disadvantages associated with this approach. One of these is that observation in and of itself may produce changes in behavior.

Moreover, observation may interact with an intervention program to produce behavioral change (Kazdin, 1979). If this kind of interaction goes undetected, one may be fooled into believing that the intervention was responsible for desired behavioral change, when in fact change resulted from the combination of the intervention and behavioral observation.

A second disadvantage to direct observation is its cost in time and personnel. In many instances it may not be practical to undertake direct observation because of the expense involved in this kind of assessment. This is most certainly the case in school psychology. School psychologists generally operate under stringent time constraints. Moreover, the teachers with whom they generally work have similar constraints. As a result, it is not always possible for school psychologists to employ direct observation.

A third problem associated with direct observation has to do with the complexity of developing effective observation procedures for use in educational settings. Complexity may arise from needs related to determining what to observe, how and when to observe, and what kinds of devices to use in observation. If what is to be recorded is not readily apparent, it may be necessary to develop a coding procedure to ensure reliable recording of behavior. Developing a coding procedure requires careful definition of behaviors to be recorded. Coming up with an appropriate definition for recording can be a difficult and time-consuming task. A method of recording must be selected. For example, one may elect to record every occurrence of a behavior. On the other hand, in those instances in which behaviors occur at a relatively high frequency, one may elect to use a time-sampling procedure in which behavior is charted at specified time intervals. A recording method that is excessively complex may make observation impractical in school settings. Recording forms and recording devices must be selected. The cost and availability of recording devices are limiting factors affecting the practicality of observation. Similarly, the complexity of recording forms needs to be considered in developing a direct observation assessment program.

The architects of behavioral assessment have incorporated a number of assessment strategies beyond observation that can be employed in situations in which observation is not feasible (see, e.g., Cone & Hawkins, 1977). One of these is interview assessment. School psychologists may obtain information about the incidence of behavior by interviewing individuals who have had the opportunity to observe behaviors of interest. A second approach involves self-observation. In some cases it may be possible for an individual to observe his or her own behavior. For example, a student might chart the number of times during a week that he or she completed homework assignments on time. A third approach is self-report. A person may report retrospectively on the incidence of a particular behavior. Finally, individuals may be asked to rate the occurrence of behaviors of interest. For example, a teacher might be asked to rate the incidence of disruptive behavior occurring in a classroom over a given time span.

Methods of behavioral assessment that do not involve direct observation add to the usefulness of the behavioral paradigm by expanding the situations in which behavioral assessment techniques can be used effectively. There is, however, a trade-off associated with the use of these methods that cannot be dismissed. The objectivity provided by direct observation is compromised when self-observation and retrospective reports of various kinds are used to assess behavior. The school psychologist using behavioral assessment procedures must balance the loss of objectivity against the advantages to be gained through retrospective reporting in selecting a method of assessing behavior.

Behavioral assessment has made a number of significant contributions to both research and practice in the field of school psychology. As mentioned above, the behavioral assessment paradigm grew out of the applied behavioral analysis tradition. The fundamental aim of applied behavioral analysis is to link research to the solution of problems occurring in applied settings. The behavioral assessment paradigm has made substantial contributions to this end. School psychologists using behavioral assessment have produced volumes of the research studies that have advanced the state of knowledge in the field of school psychology and at the same time have contributed to the solution of practical problems occuring in school settings. Behavioral research conducted in school psychology has advanced the state of knowledge in a number of areas, including the learning and adjustment of individual students (Carroll, 1985), and factors influencing the effectiveness of school-based consultation (Kratochwill & Van Someren, 1985).

Behavioral assessment techniques have also made significant contributions to the practice of school psychology. School psychologists have made use of behavioral assessment procedures in providing consultation services to teachers (e.g., Bergan, 1977). The use of behavioral assessment in consultation has made it possible for teachers to gain increased understanding of children through careful observation of behaviors of concern in the natural environment. Behavioral assessment procedures have also made it possible to establish objective goals for consultation services and to evaluate the attainment of those goals objectively. The teacher using behavioral assessment procedures has a concrete definition of behaviors that are targets for change in consultation. When concrete definitions are used, it is possible to specify the goals of consultation clearly and through assessment to determine when and if those goals have been reached.

Behavioral assessment plays a vital role in the development of intervention plans. When data are collected on behaviors of concern and on the conditions surrounding behavior, it is possible to develop an intervention plan that takes advantage of contingencies operating in the natural environment. For example, if one ascertains that disruptive classroom behavior is generally followed by some kind of peer reinforcement, it may be possible to develop a plan that makes peer reinforcement contingent upon desired behavior. Using contingencies in the natural environment can minimize the costs of intervention. Moreover, the use of natural contingencies may increase the probability of achieving lasting changes in behavior. When new contingencies are introduced into the environment, plans must be established either to keep those contingencies in effect or to allow contingencies already available in the environment to come into play. The complexities associated with introducing new contingencies are avoided when contingencies already present in the environment are used for intervention.

Behavioral assessment can play an important role in making placement decisions. Behavioral assessment information affords a direct record of those behaviors that suggest the need for placement. Information of this kind almost invariably enhances the validity of placement decisions. For example, consider the situation in which a school psychologist is involved in making a decision with respect to the placement of a child in a special education program for the learning disabled. Standardized assessment instruments can be used to get a general picture of the child's intellectual functioning as reflected in his or her position in a norm group. However, standardized instruments will not provide information on the child's intellectual functioning in the classroom. Behavioral assessment can provide this information. Behavioral assessment procedures can indicate the child's ability to perform specific academic skills in the academic environment. Information describing what the child actually does in the academic setting should provide the foundation for any placement decision. Information on what the child can do in the academic setting opens the way to assessing the match between the kinds of skills the child possesses and the objectives of the instructional programs into which the child might be placed.

Behavioral assessment is useful not only for purposes of determining placement, but also for aiding the instructional programming process following placement. Information on what the child can do can be useful in establishing instructional objectives for the child in the new learning environment. Information on environmental conditions affecting the child's academic performance can assist in establishing a learning environment that will stimulate learning in the new setting. Moreover, information of this kind can be useful in facilitating generalization of skills acquired in the new environment to the regular classroom environment. In many cases, the child will be in the new environment for only a portion of the instructional day. Procedures facilitating the application of newly acquired skills in the regular classroom setting establish a useful congruence between the special learning environment and the regular classroom environment.

Latent Trait Theory and Behavioral Approaches to Assessment

One of the hallmark's of behavioral approaches to assessment is that they do not assume that an underlying latent trait is being measured through the assessment process. For example, a behaviorist would surely *not* assert that performance on a criterion-referenced mathematics achievement test was determined by a student's mathematical ability. Rather, he or she would say that the student's performance reflected specific skills that the student had mastered. Behavioral theorists have long regarded latent traits with disdain, arguing that their use as explanatory constructs obscures the identification of factors determining behavior (see, e.g., Bandura, 1977).

Avoidance of the latent trait construct is directly linked to the major benefits of the behavioral approach. Focusing on behaviorally defined skills rather than on global traits opens the way for behavioral instruments to relate assessment to instruction. For example, a global achievement test score indicating that a child is achieving at the third-grade level does not provide information that is specific enough to be used in detailed instructional planning for the child. On the other hand, criterion-referenced assessment results indicating the specific skills that the child has and has not mastered provides a suitable foundation for detailed instructional planning.

While avoidance of the trait construct has been associated with the benefits of behavioral approaches to assessment, it is at the same time a major limitation to the approach. This is apparent in the longstanding debate over the relative merits of norm-referenced assessment and criterion-referenced assessment. Not too long ago criterion-referenced assessment was presented as an alternative to norm-referenced assessment. Today it is argued that both forms of assessment are useful and that each serves a different purpose (see, e.g., Hambleton, 1985). If one wishes to know the position of an examinee in a norm group, one uses a norm-referenced instrument. If the aim is to determine what objectives have been mastered, one uses a criterion-referenced instrument.

Although this may seem at first to be a reasonable resolution to a protracted argument, it raises serious educational problems. It results in a state of affairs in which fundamentally different instruments are used to plan instruction than are used to determine the overall results of instruction. For example, large numbers of school districts have developed or purchased for use in instruction criterion-referenced assessment instruments linked to their curriculums. These same school districts typically use state-mandated norm-referenced assessment instruments to evaluate the outcomes of instruction. Inevitably the question arises as to whether or not the selected norm-referenced assessment instrument measures what the school is trying to teach.

The debate over the relative merits of norm-referenced and criterion-referenced assessment focused mainly on the issue of providing information regarding position in a norm group as opposed to providing information about the mastery of objectives. However, a more fundamental difference between the two approaches is that one makes use of latent (unobservable) traits and the other does not. I shall now violate fundamental assumptions of behavioral psychology by arguing that there are advantages to be gained by using latent traits and that the latent trait construct could and should be incorporated into the behavioral perspective.

One reason that behaviorists have given for avoiding latent traits is that they are global constructs that are not directly linked to observable behaviors (Bandura, 1977). There is nothing inherent in the latent trait construct that requires that there be no link between a trait and observable behavior. Moreover, there are highly developed sets of statistical procedures widely used in the measurement field that directly relate latent traits to observable behaviors. I am referring to models generated under item response theory (Lord, 1980).

Item response theory holds that the probability of responding correctly to a particular test item is a function of a latent trait (ability) and characteristics of the item such as its difficulty. If one knows the ability of the child, the difficulty of the item and other characteristics, such as the discriminating power of the item, one can predict the performance of the child on the item. Thus, a direct link is established between ability and an observable item response. Item response theory does not reference ability to position in a norm group. Rather, it references ability to the specific competencies of the child. For example, a child's ability score on a math achievement test can be used to predict the probability that he or she will be able to perform specific mathematical tasks of varying difficulty. The ability score may indicate that the child has a high probability of being able to perform simple counting tasks such as counting to 10 correctly and a moderate probability of being able to add using blocks with sums less than 10, and a low probability of correctly performing simple paper-and-pencil subtraction tasks.

What advantages are to be gained by relating the ability construct to observable behavior? First, it represents a set of reasonable assumptions about the cognitive functioning of the individual. It is reasonable to assume that skills do not function in isolation from one another, but rather are linked to each other and applied in the performance of related tasks. For example, it is reasonable to assume that if one teaches a child to count to five there is a likelihood that he or she will also be able to count to four. Moreover, it is reasonable, and indeed it has been validated empirically, that counting skills are used by the child in learning to add (see, e.g., Bergan, Stone, & Feld, 1984).

Of course, behavioral psychology includes constructs that can account for the linking of skills. Generalization is the primary example of these. However, generalization and related behavioral constructs do not lend themselves well to the determination of constellations of related skills in assessment. For example, there is currently no provision for determining skill relationships in criterion-referenced assessment. Skills are often grouped into well-defined domains in criterion-referenced assessment. At one point there was even some thought of changing the name of criterion-referenced assessment to domain-referenced assessment. However, the grouping of skills into domains makes no assumptions about the way an examinee relates one skill to another cognitively. In the early days of criterion-referenced assessment, Hively, Patterson, and Page (1966) attempted to define domains from a behavioral perspective using the stimulus generalization construct. Their efforts to validate domains empirically using the generalization construct were promising but unsuccessful. Today, domains are an administrative convenience enabling instructors to group items together by subject matter categories.

Item response theory provides a way to empirically validate relations among specific skills. Item response technology can be used to determine whether or not a skill is part of an underlying latent trait. Recent advances in factor analysis make this possible (see, e.g., Bock & Aitkin, 1981). The capability to link observable competencies to a latent trait adds specificity to the definition of the trait. It is no longer necessary to think of a latent trait as a global construct lacking specific behavioral referents. Rather, traits may be defined by the competencies that are empirically determined to belong to them.

There are practical as well as theoretical reasons for using the latent trait construct. One of these involves efficiency in assessment. Consider the situation in which a large number of competencies reflect a single latent trait. For example, computational skill might be conceptualized as a latent

ability comprised of addition, subtraction, multiplication, and other computational skills. It is possible to get an estimate of an individual's position on a latent trait from a sample of items reflecting the trait. Thus, one could estimate computational ability from a sample of computational items. It would not be necessary to include all of the items reflecting computation in order to estimate ability. Given that ability has been determined, it is possible to estimate the probability that a student will perform a given skill reflecting the assessed trait even though that skill has not been tested directly. For example, one could estimate the probability that a child could count to 10 even though assessment may not have included a question directly assessing that competency. The capability to estimate the performance of a large number of specific competencies from a sample represents a potential savings both in the cost of assessment and in the time required for assessment.

Another practical advantage associated with the latent trait approach is that it can be used to determine the sequencing of skills and to identify the position of examinees in skill sequences. The latent trait approach makes it possible to reference a child's ability to his or her position in a developmental path or skill sequence. Path referencing identifies those skills that the child has mastered in the past and those skills that the child is ready to learn next (Bergan, 1981, 1988; Bergan, Stone, & Feld, 1985). The initial conceptualization of criterion-referenced assessment called for the development of assessment instruments reflecting skill sequences (Glaser, 1963). However, at the time that criterion-referenced assessment was developed, effective statistical procedures were not available to validate sequences (Bergan, 1980). Moreover, there were no adequate procedures for identifying the position of individual students in such sequences. Not surprisingly, the effort to develop criterion-referenced assessment devices including skill sequences diminished. The vast majority of criterion-referenced tests currently available do not assess sequenced skills.

A third practical advantage to the latent trait approach is that it provides a summary score that reduces the amount of information that needs to be considered to determine what a student knows. To take advantage of the specific information regarding skill mastery offered by criterion-referenced assessment, one must make a list of all the objectives that have and have not been mastered. In many instances, that is indeed a long list. Keeping track of all the objectives that students have and have not mastered can be a formidable clerical task, which has turned more than one teacher off. In this connection, it is worth noting that the idea of linking instruction to objectives was set forth and tried without success long before the criterion-referenced assessment movement. In the early part of this century Bobbitt (1918) advocated that school curriculums be specified in terms of specific objectives. Bobbitt's view attracted a wide following, and large numbers of curriculum objectives were formulated for different subject matter fields. Pendleton identified 1581 objectives for English. Giller spelled out over 300 objectives for elementary arithmetic, and Billings detailed 888 objectives for social studies (Bergan & Dunn, 1976). Bobbitt's movement quickly collapsed under its own weight because it was not possible for teachers to manage the large numbers of objectives specified for the curriculum.

It should be pointed out that criterion-referenced assessment technology includes provision for a summary score just as latent trait technology does (Hambleton, 1985). The summary score most widely advocated is the proportion of items answered correctly (Hambleton, 1985). This score reflects the probability that a student will be able to perform correctly any given skill belonging to the domain represented by the items in the test. This score makes no distinction between skills of high and low difficulty. It simply asserts that if one samples a skill from the domain, the probability that a student will be able to perform that skill correctly can be estimated by the proportion of items passed on the test. If one wishes more detailed information about a specific skill, one must look at the student's performance on that skill.

Latent Trait Theory and Behavioral Theory

In the preceding section we asserted that assessment practices based on a behavioral perspective could benefit from inclusion of latent variables such as traits and abilities. Constructs of this type have been widely attacked in the behavioral literature. The immediate question that arises from consideration of these attacks is whether or not the inclusion of the latent trait construct is feasible within a behavioral perspective. To answer this question, it will be useful to compare latent trait

and behavioral views regarding the determinants of behavior.

Item response theory, which may also be called latent trait theory (e.g., Embretson, 1985), holds that the probability of a given response to a test item is a function of a latent trait and item characteristics such as item difficulty and discrimination. Estimates of item characteristics and the latent trait are determined from the performance of large numbers of examinees emitting responses to large numbers of test items. The items are generally administered under standardized testing conditions. One of these conditions typically requires that there will be no feedback or reinforcement for correct responses.

The clearest statement regarding what determines the probability of a response from a behavioral perspective comes from the writings of Skinner (see, e.g., Skinner, 1974). Skinner asserts that the probability of occurrence of a response is a function of learning history. In experimental research, learning history is typically represented by a response repeated many times under a standard set of stimulus conditions. One of these conditions is often the giving of reinforcement contingent on a particular type of response.

There are two major differences between the behavioral approach outlined by Skinner and the latent trait approach. First, the latent trait approach collects data based on the performance of a variety of related tasks, whereas the behavioral approach utilizes data from a single task repeated a large number of times. Second, the latent trait approach typically does not allow reinforcement to occur during data collection, whereas the behavioral approach almost invariably does include reinforcement at various points during data collection.

Of course, the two theoretical perspectives use very different constructs to explain response probability. To say that the probability of a correct response is determined by a latent ability is not the same as saying that the probability of a correct response is determined by learning history. However, there is an important similarity between the two perspectives. Both explain response probability in terms of a latent variable. Learning history is a construct that defines a latent variable, not a behavioral phenomena. One cannot observe learning history directly any more than one can observe ability directly. Both are defined by the aggregation of information from many observed behaviors. In fact, learning history may be regarded as a special case of a latent trait. It is possible to quantify learning history using latent trait statistical procedures applied to large numbers of responses to a given task. Under these conditions, the latent trait score is a learning history score that can be used to predict response probability.

The real issue is whether one wishes to explain behavior in terms of a latent variable asserting that the causes of behavior are based solely on past interactions with the environment or whether one is willing to entertain the possibility that internal processes (e.g., cognitions) may affect behavior. Those adhering to the radical behaviorist perspective set forth by Skinner would probably have great difficulty with the idea that internal processes could determine behavior. On the other hand, those operating from a cognitive behavioral perspective (e.g., Bandura, 1969, 1977, 1986) might well be able to incorporate latent trait theory into their framework since they already admit the importance of internal cognitive and affective processes in determining behavior. However, behaviorists of all types have had some pretty nasty things to say about traits in the past. A considerable amount of rethinking of behavioral theory would be required to take advantage of the latent trait viewpoint within a behavioral perspective.

Given that such rethinking occurred, one might guess that the expected sequence of events would be that latent traits would be incorporated into the behavioral perspective. Then behavioral assessment practices would change in ways that reflected latent trait constructs. This, however, can not be the case. Latent trait techniques are already being used in assessment practices that have traditionally fallen within the purview of the behavioral perspective. For example, latent trait technology has been used in criterion-referenced assessment instruments on a number of occasions (Hambleton, 1985; Nitko, 1980). One instrument widely used by school psychologists that makes use of criterion-referenced assessment and latent trait technology is the Key Math Diagnostic Test (Connolly, Nachtman, & Pritchell, 1976).

This shows that current assessment practice is not theory driven. Yet there is a subtle sign of the theoretical conflict between the latent trait and behavioral viewpoints in contemporary assessment practice. Although latent trait theory is being used in criterion-referenced assessment, it is being applied without reference to the theoretical constructs that underlie it. For example, the term *latent trait* is rarely mentioned in test manuals, even in those instances in which latent trait techniques are being used to determine item characteristics.

In part, this may be traced to the manner in which latent trait theory has been presented to psychometricians. The latent trait perspective was initially formulated by Lazarsfeld (1950). Lazarsfeld made the latent trait construct a salient part of the theory. However, latent trait constructs were introduced to psychometricians by Lord (1952, 1980). Lord named the theory item-response theory, thereby reducing the saliency of the latent trait construct. It is worth noting that this name was given to the approach at a time when relations between psychometrics and psychological theory were distant. The number and quality of programs in psychometrics within psychology departments was in a period of decline and the influence of psychometrics on psychological theory had waned. Recently, there has been a welcome resurgence of interest in the relationship between psychometrics and psychological theory (see, e.g., Embretson, 1985). Latent trait theory is being called latent trait theory and latent trait techniques are being used in psychological research. What remains is to reconcile latent trait constructs to assessment practice. It makes no sense to apply latent trait constructs within criterion-referenced assessment if the theoretical underpinnings of that form of assessment do not include latent variables.

CONSULTATION

While assessment has been and continues to be the dominant role of the school psychologist, consultation has emerged in second place as a highly valued activity (Ramage, 1979). Consultation in school psychology generally takes the following form: A consultant (school psychologist) provides information and advice to a consultee (teacher or parent) who is concerned about the learning and/or adjustment of one or more children, who are the clients ultimately benefiting from consultation service. A major advantage to consultation is its efficiency. One psychologist can serve a number of teachers, each of whom may work with more than one student. Moreover, even in the many instances in which there is only one student receiving services, there is a substantial gain in efficiency because the consultee is generally responsible for implementing the intervention designed to assist the child. This frees the psychologist to serve other cases. The behavioral perspective has had far-reaching influences on the conduct of consultation by school psychologists. Moreover, a large number of research studies show that consultation offered from the behavioral perspective produces beneficial educational outcomes.

Behavioral Consultation as Problem Solving

One of the major contributions of the behavioral perspective to consultation has to do with the way in which consultee concerns about children are conceptualized in behavioral consultation. Within a behavioral framework, the consultee is guided to conceptualize concerns in terms of a problem-solving framework designed to produce desired changes in child behavior (Bergan, 1977). A problem is defined in consultation in terms of the discrepancy between current observable behavior and desired behavior. The problem is to produce changes in behavior that enable the child to achieve the desired state. This view of child problems is markedly different from the widely used medical model conceptualization that depicts a problem as a child characteristic or trait.

In behavioral consultation, the focus is on assisting the child to change in desired ways. The concept of improvement is built into the way in which the child is viewed. In the medical model approach, the way in which concerns are defined is separated from whatever steps may be taken to change behavior. The problem is an internal characteristic of the child. For example, the problem may be that the child is retarded or disabled. These are individual characteristics that do not necessarily imply an intervention to bring about change. They may accurately describe the child, but they do not direct attention in any systematic way to the formation and implementation of plans to improve the child's functioning. For example, to describe a child as retarded does not provide specific direction for educational programming for the child. By contrast, the behavioral perspective commits the consultant and consultee to a plan of action to bring about desired changes in child behavior.

Empiricism and Behavioral Consultation

A second contribution of the behavioral perspective to consultation is that it promotes an empirical approach to the rendering of consultation services. Behavioral consultation includes an emphasis on the measurement of behaviors of concern in the consultation process. Data are used to validate empirically the existence of a problem, to determine the effectiveness of intervention plans, and to determine whether or not the goals of consultation have been attained. In the early phases of consultation, baseline data are collected to determine whether or not a problem in fact exists. Baseline data may reveal that the child is functioning adequately and does not need further service, in which case consultation can be discontinued. Data collected during plan implementation afford the opportunity to observe the relationship between an intervention and desired behavioral change. When change does not occur as intended, the intervention plan can be revised. Finally, data facilitate an unambiguous evaluation of the outcomes of consultation. When behavioral consultation is implemented, the attainment of consultation goals are judged in terms of data collected on behaviors of concern. The consultant, consultee, and the child are provided with objective evidence indicating whether or not desired change has occurred.

Research and Behavioral Consultation

A third contribution of the behavioral perspective to consultation is that behavioral consultation is research based. Research has provided support for the effectiveness of consultation services. Medway (1979, 1982) conducted extensive reviews of the consultation literature, which provided general support for consultation interventions. However, few well-controlled studies have actually been conducted (Bergan & Kratochwill, in press). Nonetheless, the existing data do support the assumption that consultation produces beneficial outcomes. There is also evidence that teachers who participate in consultation value the experience and believe that their classroom skills have improved as a result of consultation services (Gutkin, 1980).

Research has contributed significantly to an understanding of the factors that influence the effectiveness of behavioral consultation. Based on an extensive review of the behavioral consultation research literature, Kratochwill and Van Someren (1985) identify six factors influencing behavioral consultation effectiveness. The first of these is the integrity of implementation. For consultation to be effective, it must be implemented in accordance with well-established procedures documented through research. For example, there are instances in which consultation occurs without the identification of a problem. When this happens, the likelihood that consultation will be pursued further decreases (Bergan & Tombari, 1976). Similarly, to develop an effective intervention plan, conversation during consultation generally must focus on the conditions surrounding behavior of interest (Bergan, 1977). When this does not occur, the planning process may be compromised. Kratochwill and Van Someren (1985) advocate the standardization of consultation procedures to ensure the integrity of implementation.

A second factor that may influence the effectiveness of consultation is the training of consultants. Several reviews have been published on the training of behavioral consultants (Bergan & Kratochwill, in press; Bernstein, 1982; Ford, 1979; Medway, 1979, 1982). The literature on training indicates that in most instances training programs have not adequately stressed applied skills. Moreover, there is a lack of attention to specific skills necessary for consultation effectiveness.

A third factor influencing consultation effectiveness is the training of consultees. There is a substantial body of literature demonstrating the usefulness of training teachers in child behavior management techniques (Allen & Formann, 1984, Bernstein, 1982; Kazdin, 1980). Teachers provided with this kind of training are in a better position to profit from consultation services than are those who lack training (Kratochwill & Van Someren, 1985).

A fourth factor influencing the effectiveness of consultation is the acceptability of suggested intervention procedures to the consultant, consultee, and client. Interventions under consideration in consultation may be deemed unacceptable for a variety of reasons. They may be questioned on ethical grounds, or they may be challenged in terms of probable effectiveness. In some instances, an intervention may be regarded as potentially effective, but impractical to implement. For example, in cost of materials required for implementation may be prohibitive.

The probability that a treatment program will be acceptable to a consultee or client can be increased by involving those who are to implement the treatment in the formation of the treatment plan (Kratochwill & Van Someren, 1985). One way to involve consultees in the formulation of intervention plans is for the consultant, based on his or her expert knowledge, to determine the general strategy that is most likely to be effective in

producing desired outcomes. The consultant may then elicit the specific tactics to be used in the intervention from the consultee (Bergan, 1977).

A fifth factor that may influence consultation effectiveness is the relationship between the consultant and the consultee. Behavioral psychologists have tended to downplay the importance of interpersonal relationships between the consultant and consultee, preferring instead to focus on the process of consultation. Thus, there has not been a great deal of behavioral research on consultant-consultee relationships. Nonetheless, there is evidence that consultant-consultee relationships do have an important influence on consultation (e.g., Alpert, Ludwig, & Weiner, 1979; Friedman, 1977; Mann, 1972; Morris & Magrath, 1983; Schowengerdt, Fine, & Poggio, 1976). For example, Morris and Magrath (1983) identified a number of relationship factors with the potential to influence consultation outcomes. Included among these were the extent to which the consultee views the consultant as one who possesses expert knowledge, the ability of the consultant to act as a model who can demonstrate potentially effective intervention strategies, and general personality characteristics such as personal warmth.

The sixth factor identified by Kratochwill and Van Someren (1985) as influencing consultation effectiveness is the identification of target behaviors. The typical strategy used in behavioral consultation is to determine target behaviors based on consultee concerns. During the problem identification phase of consultation, the consultee identifies those aspects of client behavior that will become the focus of the consultation process. The intervention will be designed to change these behaviors, and the outcomes of consultation will be evaluated in terms of whether or not desired behavioral change has been achieved. A question that is generally overlooked, but that is nonetheless extremely important, is whether the target behaviors identified are indeed the ones that should be the focus of consultation services.

A fundamental issue that must be addressed in determining whether or not appropriate target behaviors have been selected is the extent to which changes in those behaviors will have a beneficial influence on other aspects of the client's life. This issue was addressed earlier in the chapter in the discussion of the role of the ability construct in behavioral psychology. As was illustrated in the example of the boy whose addition skills were improved but who was subsequently retained in grade because of low math ability, it is quite possible to achieve impressive changes in the performance of specific behaviors only to find later that the overall functioning of the client continues to be poor.

The basic problem associated with the selection of appropriate target behaviors is that very little is known about the development of fundamental academic and social skills necessary to function effectively in contemporary society. For example, comprehensive theories based on empirical evidence are lacking concerning the sequencing of basic math and reading skills. Detailed information is available concerning the development of specific skills such as counting and addition, but these are islands of knowledge in a largely unchartered sea. As a consequence, curriculum developers are forced to rely on the speculations of authors who lack the needed empirical evidence to define the scope and sequence of curriculums in a scientifically sound manner. The situation is even worse in the area of social development. Very little is known about the relationships among social skills and the sequencing of those skills. Accordingly, it is not surprising that behavioral consultants spend a great deal of their time getting rid of undesirable behaviors as opposed to building new skills that will advance the social development of the student.

Clearly, there is a need for major advances in the state of knowledge regarding the sequencing of development with respect to both academic and social skills. Gagné and his associates did much to increase knowledge regarding the hierarchical sequencing of skills in the 1960s and 1970s (see, e.g., Gagné, 1977). Gradually, this work gave way to a large volume of research by cognitive scientists (see, e.g., Brown & Burton, 1978; Resnick & Ford, 1981) detailing the cognitive processes associated with the performance of academic tasks. Although this research has produced a great deal of highly useful information, it has not solved the problem addressed by Gagné of specifying hierarchical relationships among intellectual skills.

Behavioral psychologists generally recognize the importance of skill sequences. For example, behavioral texts generally include sections on the use of task analysis (see, e.g., Resnick, Wang, & Kaplan, 1973) to guide the formulation of hypothesized hierarchies. However, behavioral psychologists have focused greater attention on environmental factors controlling behavior than on the

developmental sequencing of cognitive and social skills. Skinner's thinking played a major role in establishing the environmental emphasis characteristic of the behavioral viewpoint. Skinner (e.g., 1953, 1974) championed the view that behavior is explained by the environment. Skinner argued cogently and demonstrated through a large number of well-designed studies that the environment can control behavior and that given a knowledge of the environment one can predict behavior. Explanation based on prediction and control is a hallmark of the scientific enterprise. Knowledge of the sequencing of skills is not generally regarded as offering an explanation of behavior within the behavioral perspective. Yet it is a fact that knowledge of skills accomplished in the past is an excellent predictor of what will be learned in the future. If there is to be an understanding of the manner in which the acquisition of specific behaviors contribute to the overall development of competency in a given area, the investigation of sequential relationships among skills have to be resumed with full vigor.

INTERVENTION

Undoubtedly, the most important contribution of behavioral psychology to school psychology is the knowledge that it has provided with respect to the development and implementation of intervention plans to achieve desired behavioral outcomes. In some cases behavioral interventions are carried out directly by school psychologists. In other instances, interventions are formulated as part of consultation with teachers or parents who are responsible for implementation. In some instances, interventions are implemented by students to change their own behavior or to change teacher behavior. Regardless of who carries out the intervention and whose behavior is targeted for change, the behavioral paradigm has proven itself to be a powerful tool in achieving desired outcomes.

A Knowledge Base for Interventions

Behavioral psychology has positively influenced school psychology interventions in three ways. First, it has provided a vast fund of scientific knowledge regarding the kinds of environmental factors that influence behavior. There is no need to detail the environmental factors revealed through laboratory research carried out from the behavioral perspective. Textbooks on behavioral psycholoy provide a thorough account of these variables. Of course, the large volume of research carried out by Skinner (e.g., 1953) and his colleagues establishing the controlling influence of reinforcement on behavior must be mentioned. Research determining the role of discriminative stimuli in signaling the occurrence of behavior also represented a major contribution to interventions in school psychology.

Cognitive behavioral research on modeling influences carried out by Bandura (e.g., 1969, 1977) and his colleagues must also be noted. Of particular importance for school psychologists is the work of Rosenthal and Zimmerman showing that children could acquire rules as a result of observing the behavior of a model. In an extensive series of studies (see Rosenthal & Zimmerman, 1978), these investigators demonstrated that imitation of modeled behavior was not mere mimicry, but rather that children could acquire complex cognitive rules through vicarious learning. They showed that children could learn language rules vicariously. They also demonstrated that children could learn conservation skills believed by Piagetians to be governed by developmental processes beyond the purview of direct learning. In so doing they revealed the important role that vicarious learning could play in the development of intellectual skills of importance in the school.

Work initiated during the 1970s on self-control of behavior (see, e.g., Mahoney & Thoresen, 1974) also played an important role in the formation of interventions in school psychology. This work revealed processes of self-control that have been used in large numbers of interventions to help students to help themselves achieve desired learning and adjustment outcomes.

Finally, the large body of research dealing directly with behavioral interventions involving academic skills must be mentioned. Behavioral research in this area has included the use of behavioral techniques to increase general academic performance as well as studies involving specific academic skills, including reading skills, mathematics skills, spelling skills, and written language. Shapiro (1987) has carried out an extensive review of behavioral research involving academic skills. Shapiro cites a large volume of research documenting the effectiveness of behavioral techniques in remediating academic deficits. However, he suggests the need for studies addressing issues of generalization and maintenance of skills acquired through behavioral interventions.

Applied Behavior Analysis and Interventions in Schools

The applied behavior analysis movement initiated in the late 1960s (Baer, Wolf, & Risely, 1968) comprises the second major contribution of behavioral research to school psychology interventions. This movement established principles and procedures for conducting behavioral research in the natural environment to solve real problems of importance to clients receiving services as they participated as experimental subjects. The architects of applied behavior analysis recognized that one could not always generalize from laboratory research to the natural environment and that as a consequence it was necessary to carry out studies in the natural environment to test hypotheses regarding controlling influences on behavior. Of course, there were those who doubted that leaving the controlled environment of the laboratory for the uncontrolled natural environment would yield fruitful outcomes. Nonetheless, the applied behavior analysis movement certainly must be regarded as a resounding success.

Applied behavioral research has contributed to school psychology interventions in four ways. First, countless numbers of studies dealing directly with academic and social behaviors of children have been published. One need only look through the index of the *Journal of Applied Behavior Analysis* for any year since its inception to document this fact. Second, applied behavioral researchers have established research designs and procedures for observing behavior in the natural environment (see, e.g., Kratochwill, 1978), making it possible for school psychologists to conduct applied research in school settings. Third, applied behavioral researchers have empirically validated large numbers of intervention "packages" involving the application of sets of environmental conditions designed to operate in a coordinated fashion to produce a desired behavioral outcome. Packages typically include the necessary materials so that a potential package user, such as a school psychologist, may employ them with little or no modification to achieve desired behavioral outcomes. Finally, applied behavioral researchers have demonstrated the importance of establishing the social validity of interventions in the natural environment (see, e.g., Kazdin, 1981). This initiative has led to a number of recent important studies on the acceptability of different kinds of interventions in school psychology (see, e.g., Elliot, Turco, & Gresham, 1987; Von Brock & Elliot, 1987).

School Psychology Interventions and the Functional Analysis of Behavior

The final contribution of the behavioral perspective to school psychology interventions is the functional analysis paradigm, which undergirds research stemming from the radical behavioral perspective set forth by Skinner (e.g., 1953, 1974). The functional analysis of behavior is initiated by an operational definition of the behavior of interest. Then antecedent and consequent conditions associated with the behavior are specified. These are invariably selected on the basis of the assumption that they may have some influence over behavior. However, in the initial phases of the functional analysis, antecedent and consequent conditions are devoid of controlling status. They are simply regarded as conditions occurring before and after behavior. The goal of the functional analysis is to establish a functional relation between consequent and antecedent conditions and behavior. This goal can only be achieved through empirical investigation. A functional relation exists when behavior changes in systematic ways in the presence of antecedent and consequent events. When a functional relation has been validated empirically, antecedent conditions are assigned the status of discriminative stimuli signaling the occurrence of behavior. Consequent conditions assume the status of reinforcers or punishers, the former increasing and the latter decreasing the probability of occurrence of behavior. There has been a long-standing disagreement between radical behaviorists and cognitive behaviorists regarding the role of antecedent stimuli in determining behavior, but this need not be of concern in the present discussion. It is sufficient simply to note that within the cognitive view antecedent conditions (modeling conditions in particular) are thought to influence learning directly without the need for reinforcement. Radical behaviorists take exception to this conceptualization of antecedent stimuli.

The important point to make here is that the functional analysis paradigm provides a useful way of thinking about interventions in school psychology. When school psychologists use this paradigm, they become scientist-practitioners testing hypotheses about conditions controlling behaviors of interest in educational settings. The hypothesis testing orientation provided through the functional analysis paradigm introduces a useful form of accountability into the services provided by school psychologists. The psychologist using the paradigm continually evaluates intervention effectiveness.

When an intervention is not working as anticipated, it can be changed or replaced by another approach.

SOME POSSIBLE FUTURES FOR THE BEHAVIORAL PERSPECTIVE IN SCHOOL PSYCHOLOGY

Behavioral psychology has made major contributions to the field of school psychology, and it will undoubtedly continue to do so in the years ahead. The behavioral paradigm has been particularly influential in the provision of services to individual students experiencing learning and adjustment problems in school. In some respects, this is not surprising. The behavioral approach is sensitive to the functioning of the individual. Behavioral research is often carried out with a small number of subjects. The unit of analysis in behavioral studies is often individual behavior observed over an extended time span. The focus of the behavioral approach on the individual is congruent with school psychology practice, which is also heavily oriented to services to individual students.

The behavioral paradigm has played a particularly important role in shifting the focus of school psychological services to the individual from diagnosis to intervention. School psychology has become an intervention-oriented discipline to a far greater extent than was once the case. As pointed out at the beginning of the chapter, when school psychological services began to be provided on a broad scale in this country, the focus of services was primarily on diagnosis. Assessment was the principal activity of the school psychologist. The principal goal was to determine the eligibility of students for placement in special programs. Although diagnosis continues to be the dominant activity in school psychology, other intervention-oriented services such as consultation have assumed a significant place in the field. There is every reason to believe that the intervention orientation fostered by the behavioral perspective will increase in the years ahead. Behavioral research, in all probability, will continue to produce new insights into the factors influencing behavior change. As a result, one can expect that interventions designed using behavioral principles will become increasingly effective. To the extent that this occurs, one can expect greater intervention emphasis in school psychology than is currently characteristic of the field.

Although behavioral psychology has a good chance of increasing the effectiveness of services to individual students manifesting learning and adjustment problems in the years ahead, there is little sign that the behavioral approach will have an increasing impact on the learning of large groups of students in the future. Behavioral principles are widely used in the design of learning environments for exceptional children (see, e.g., Harris, 1983; Harris & Handleman, 1987; Whitman & Johnston, 1987). However, the behavioral paradigm has had only a limited influence on general education. The widespread use of criterion-referenced assessment instruments in the schools is, perhaps, the major example of the general impact of behavioral thought on schools. While criterion-referenced assessment has been useful in clarifying objectives for learning and in directing instruction toward the accomplishment of objectives, it might be hoped that behavioral thought could have a more far-reaching influence on education. The greatest educational achievements of the behavioral paradigm involve the design of learning environments. Variables such as modeling and feedback could be incorporated systematically into the design of instructional programs for all children in a school. Although a number of demonstration projects have verified this fact, there has been little interest in the widespread application of behavioral principles in instructional design in schools. Moreover, there is no reason to believe that this will change in the future.

Given Skinner's (1954) prophetic insights into the potential usefulness of machines in instruction, one might have thought that with the widespread use of microcomputers in education there would be a resurgence of interest in applying behavioral principles in the design of learning environments. However, this has not been the case. Contemporary behavioral psychologists have shown little interest in computer-aided instruction. To the extent that present trends can be regarded as a guide to the future, one would have to conclude regrettably that behavioral psychology will not play a major role in computer-aided instruction in the years ahead.

The areas of influence of behavioral psychology on the schools are congruent with the influence of school psychology on education. School psychologists are not typically called upon to assist in the development and implementation of programs for all students in a school. Rather, the focus of their services is on the individual student manifesting programs. Advocates of organization development consultation (e.g., Schmuck, Runkel, Saturen, Martell, & Derr, 1972) made an attempt to focus school psychological services on the entire school, but the organizational development approach has not been applied widely in the provision of school psychology services.

Since school psychologists are the only professionals working in education who are trained as psychologists, it seems apparent that if the role of the school psychologist is not broadened to include the development and implementation of programs for all students, the direct impact of behavioral psychology and other forms of psychology will probably continue to be limited to the individual student and to groups of students with special needs. Of course, psychology will continue to influence education in various indirect ways, such as through its impact on teacher training, on the production of educational materials, on test development, and on the development of computer software. Nonetheless, it is unfortunate that behavioral psychology as well as other forms of psychological science do not have a direct effect on education through the provision of psychological services to all students. Yet, it does not seem likely that this state of affairs will change very soon. Changing the scope of school psychological services would require a change in public policy. To this point, there has been no concerted effort by school psychologists to bring about this kind of change. Psychological science has much to offer to education. It may be hoped that at some point in time school psychologists will take the necessary actions to change public policy to support the broad-based provision of psychological services in the schools.

REFERENCES

Alessi, G. J. (1980). Behavioral observation for the school psychologist: Responsive-discrepancy model. *School Psychology Review, 9,* 31–45.

Allen, C. T., & Forman, S. G. (1984). Efficacy of methods of training teachers in behavior modification. *School Psychology Review, 13,* 26–32.

Alpert, J. L., Ludwig, L. M., & Weiner, L. (1979). Selection of consultees in school mental health consultation. *Journal of School Psychology, 17,* 59–66.

Baer, D. M., Wolf, M. M., & Risley, T. R. (1968). Some current dimensions of applied behavior analysis. *Journal of Applied Behavior Analysis, 1,* 91–97.

Bandura, A. R. (1969). *Principles of behavior modification.* New York: Holt, Rinehart and Winston.

Bandura, A. R. (1977). *Social learning theory.* Englewood Cliffs, NJ: Prentice-Hall.

Bandura, A. R. (1986). *Social foundations of thought and action: A social cognitive theory.* Englewood Cliffs, NJ: Prentice-Hall.

Bergan, J. R. (1977). *Behavioral consultation.* Columbus, OH: Charles E. Merrill.

Bergan, J. R. (1980). The structural analysis of behavior: An alternative to the learning hierarchy model. *Review of Educational Research, 50,* 225–246.

Bergan, J. R. (1981). Path referenced assessment in school psychology. In T. R. Kratochwill (Ed.), *Advances in school psychology* (Vol. 1). Hillsdale, NJ: Lawrence Erlbaum.

Bergan, J. R. (1988). Latent variable techniques for measuring development. In R. Langeheine, & Rost, J. (Eds.), *Latent trait and latent class models.* New York: Plenum Press.

Bergan, J. R., & Dunn, J. A. (1976). *Psychology and education: A science for instruction.* New York: Wiley.

Bergan, J. R., & Kratochwill, T. R. (in press). *Behavioral consultation in applied settings.* New York: Plenum Press.

Bergan, J. R., Stone, C. A., & Feld, J. K. (1984). Rule replacement in the development of basic number skills. *Journal of Educational Psychology, 76,* 289–299.

Bergan, J. R., Stone, C. A., & Feld, J. K. (1985). Path-referenced assessment of individual differences. In C. R. Reynolds & V. L. Willson (Eds.), *Methodological and statistical advances in the study of individual differences.* New York: Plenum Press.

Bergan, J. R., & Tombari, M. J. (1976). Consultant skill and efficiency and the implementation and outcomes of consultation. *Journal of School Psychology, 14,* 3–14.

Bernstein, G. S. (1982). Training behavior change agents: A conceptual review. *Behavioral Therapy, 13,* 1–23.

Bobbit, J. F. (1918). *The curriculum.* Boston: Houghton Mifflin.

Bock, R. D., & Aitkin, M. (1981). Marginal maximum likelihood estimation of item parameters: Application of an algorithm. *Psychometrika, 46,* 443–459.

Brown, J. S., & Burton, R. R. (1978). Diagnostic models for procedural bugs in basic mathematical skills. *Cognitive Science, 2,* 155–192.

Cancelli, A., & Duley, S. (1985). The role of assessment in school psychology. In J. R. Bergan (Ed.), *School psychology in contemporary society: An introduction.* Columbus, OH: Charles E. Merrill.

Carroll, J. D. (1985). Strategies for behavioral interventions in school psychology. In J. R. Bergan (Ed.), *School psychology in contemporary society: An introduction.* Columbus, OH: Charles E. Merrill.

Cone, J. D., & Hawkins, R. P. (Eds.). (1977). *Behavioral assessment: New directions in clinical psychology.* New York: Brunner/Mazel.

Connolly, A. J., Nachtman, W., & Pritchell, E. M. (1976). *Key math diagnostic test.* Circle Pines, MN: American Guidance Service.

Cutts, N. E. (1955). *School psychologists at mid-century.* Washington, DC: American Psychological Association.

Elliott, S. N., Turco, T., & Gresham, F. M. (1987). Consumers' and clients' pretreatment acceptability ratings of classroom-based group contingencies. *Journal of School Psychology, 25,* 145–154.

Embretson, S. E. (1985). *Test design developments in psychology in psychometrics.* Orlando, FL: Academic Press.

Ford, J. D. (1979). Research on training counselors and clinicians. *Review of Educational Research, 49,* 87–130.

Friedman, M. (1977). *Mental health consultation with teachers: An analysis of process variables.* Unpublished doctoral dissertation, Temple University, Philadelphia.

Gagné, R. M. (1977). *The conditions of learning* (3rd ed.). New York: Holt, Rinehart and Winston.

Glaser, R. (1963). Instructional technology and the measurement of learning outcomes: Some questions. *American Psychologist, 18,* 519–521.

Gutkin, T. B. (1980). Teacher perceptions of consultation services provided by school psychologists. *Professional Psychology,* pp. 637–642.

Hambleton, R. K. (1985). Criterion-referenced assessment of individual differences. In C. R. Reynolds & V. L. Willson (Eds.), *Methodological and statistical advances in the study of individual differences.* New York: Plenum Press.

Harris, S. L. (1983). *Families of the developmentally disabled: A guide to behavioral intervention.* Elmsford, NY: Pergamon Press.

Harris, S. L., & Handleman, J. S. (1987). Autism. In M. Hersen & V. B. VanHasselt (Eds.), *Behavior therapy with children and adolescents: A clinical approach.* New York: Wiley.

Hively, W., Patterson, H. L., & Page, S. H. (1968). A "universe-defined" system of arithmetic achievement tests. *Journal of Educational Measurement, 5,* 275–290.

Kazdin, A. E. (1979). Fictions, factions, and functions of behavior therapy. *Behavior Therapy, 10,* 629–654.

Kazdin, A. E. (1980). *Behavior modification in applied settings* (2nd ed.). Homewood, IL: Dorsey Press.

Kazdin, A. E. (1981). Acceptability of child treatment techniques: The influence of treatment efficacy and adverse side effects. *Behavior Therapy, 12,* 453–506.

Kratochwill, T. R. (Ed.) (1978). *Single subject research: Strategies for evaluating change.* New York: Academic Press.

Kratochwill, T. R. (Ed.). (1980a). *Advances in school psychology.* Hillsdale, NJ: Lawrence Erlbaum.

Kratochwill, T. R. (1980b). Behavioral assessment of academic and social problems: Implications for the individual education program. *School Psychology Review, 9,* 199–206.

Kratochwill, T. R. (1982). Advances in behavioral assessment. In C. R. Reynolds & T. B. Gutkin (Eds.), *Handbook of school psychology.* New York: Wiley.

Kratochwill, T. R., & Van Someren, K. (1985). Barriers to treatment success in behavioral consultation: Current limitations and future directions. *Journal of School Psychology, 23,* 225–239.

Lazarsfeld, P. F. (1950). The interpretation and computation of some latent structures. In S. A. Stouffer et al. (Eds.), *Measurement and prediction.* Princeton, NJ: Princeton University Press.

Lord, F. M. (1952). A theory of test scores. *Psychometric Monograph* (Whole No. 7).

Lord, F. M (1980). *Applications of item response theory to practical testing problems.* Hillsdale, NJ: Lawrence Erlbaum.

Mahoney, J. J., & Thoresen, C. E. (1974). *Self-control: Power to the person.* Monterey, CA: Brooks/Cole.

Mann, P. A. (1972). Accessibility and organizational power in the entry phase of mental health consultation. *Journal of Consulting and Clinical Psychology, 38,* 215–218.

Medway, F. J. (1979). How effective is school consultation: A review of recent research. *Journal of School Psychology, 17,* 275–282.

Medway, F. J. (1982). School consultation research: Past trends and future directions. *Professional Psychology, 13,* 422–430.

Morris, R. J., & Magrath, K. H. (1983). The therapeutic relationship in behavior therapy: In M. J. Laniter (Ed.), *Psychotherapy and patient relationships* (pp. 154–189). Homewood, IL: Dorsey Press.

Nitko, A. J. (1980). Distinguishing the many varieties of criterion-referenced tests. *Review of Educational Research, 50,* 461–485.

Popham, W. J. (1978). *Criterion-referenced assessment.* Englewood Cliffs, NJ: Prentice-Hall.

Ramage, J. C. (1979). National survey of school psychologists: Update. *School Psychology Digest, 8,* 153–161.

Resnick, L. B., & Ford, W. W. (1981). *The psychology of mathematics for instruction.* Hillsdale, NJ: Lawrence Erlbaum.

Resnick, L. B., Wang, M. C., & Kaplan, J. (1973). Task analysis in curriculum designs: A hierarchically sequenced introductory mathematics curriculum. *Journal of Applied Behavioral Analysis, 6,* 679–710.

Schmuck, R. A., Runkel, P. J., Saturen, S. L., Martell, R. T., & Derr, C. B. (1972). *Handbook of organization development in schools.* Palo Alto, CA: National Press.

Schowengerdt, R. V., Fine, M. J., & Poggio, J. P. (1976). An examination of some bases of teacher satisfaction with school psychological services. *Psychology in the Schools, 13,* 269–275.

Shapiro, E. S. (1987). Academic problems. In M. Hersen & V. B. VanHasselt (Eds.), *Behavior therapy with children and adolescents: A clinical approach.* New York: Wiley.

Skinner, B. F. (1953). *Science and human behavior.* New York: Macmillan.

Skinner, B. F. (1954). The science of learning and the art of teaching. *Harvard Educational Review, 24,* 86–97.

Skinner, B. F. (1974). *About behaviorism.* New York: Alfred A. Knopf.

Von Brock, M. B., & Elliott, S. (1987). Influence of treatment effectiveness information on the acceptability of classroom interventions. *Journal of School Psychology, 25,* 131–142.

Whitman, T. L., & Johnston, M. G. (1987). Mental retardation. In M. Hersen & V. G. VanHasselt (Eds.), *Behavior therapy with children and adolescents: A clinical approach.* New York: Wiley.

7

CONTRIBUTIONS OF INSTRUCTIONAL PSYCHOLOGY TO SCHOOL PSYCHOLOGY

RANDY W. KAMPHAUS
University of Georgia
NÜKHET D. YARBROUGH AND ROGER P. JOHANSON
Coe College

The role of instructional psychology as a knowledge base for school psychology practice depends to some extent on how one conceptualizes the role of the school psychologist. While most writers on school psychology practice leave some room for considering knowledge of instructional psychology as important, more recent writers have put even more emphasis on this area of expertise (Bardon, 1983; National School Psychology Inservice Training Network, 1984). Bardon (1983), for example, maintains that school psychology should distinguish itself further from other psychological specialties (such as clinical and counseling psychology) by emphasizing educational psychology as its knowledge base. Consistent with this emphasis is the position of the Ysseldyke, Reynolds & Weinberg (1984), where a variety of duties are listed for school psychologists, many of which could not be performed adequately without familiarity with findings from instructional psychology. Examples of these duties include class management, interpersonal communication and consultation, basic academic skills, classroom organization and social structures, systems development and planning, individual differences in development and learning, instruction, and research. Hence, it is more than sensible to include a chapter on this topic in this volume; cognizance of instructional psychology principles is crucial for the expanding role of the school psychologist.

We have chosen to organize this chapter around three themes. The first topic is a consideration of teacher behavior during instruction. In this section we present the findings regarding several teacher variables that have been identified as important for maximizing student achievement. In the next section we summarize research on student cognitions that are related to instructional outcomes. Finally, a section on applications of computer technology to instruction is presented. While we do not intend to represent the entire domain of knowledge that could be considered instructional psychology, we think that these three areas at least serve as a good start for school psychologists who may be interested in doing more reading in the area. For the school psychologist interested in delving further into research on instruction, the most comprehensive treatise on the subject is the *Handbook of Research on Teaching* (Wittrock, 1986). This text provides an impressive overview of a variety of factors that have been identified as crucial to the study of educational effectiveness. Moreover, this volume gives the reader a much deeper appreciation of the complexity and richness of research on instruction than can be imparted in this brief overview.

EFFECTIVE TEACHER BEHAVIOR

The emphasis on this area of the research literature is on defining the teacher behaviors that foster student academic achievement. Brophy and Good (1986) define this area of research as process-product or process-outcome research aimed at defining the teacher behaviors that foster student academic achievement. Previous reviews of this area can be found in volumes by Rosenshine (1971) and Dunkin and Biddle (1974).

One aspect of this research that immediately strikes readers of reviews such as Brophy and Good's (1986) is that the vast majority of research in this area is correlational in nature. This fact should be kept clearly in mind by readers of this section because there is a danger that research on instruction may be oversold. In a sense, because of the lack of experimental studies on teaching, the amount of knowledge of the teaching and learning process that is currently available is somewhat illusory. There is a great need for cooperative experimental research between school districts and university research centers. Unfortunately, research on teaching does not have the same advantages as, for example, medical research, where research, clinical training, and service delivery are frequently provided in the same setting.

The scope of study of the teaching process is broad. Examples of the variety of teacher behaviors studied include opportunity to learn, teacher role expectation, student engaged time, consistency of student success, active teaching, large-versus small-group instruction, structuring of lessons, lesson sequencing, teacher clarity, enthu-

siasm, pacing, difficulty of teacher questions, cognitive level and clarity of questions, post-question wait time, selecting the respondent to a question, reacting to correct, partly correct, and incorrect student responses, handling seatwork and homework, and the effects of grade level, SES, ability, affect, and teacher's intentions (Brophy & Good, 1986). A few of these important variables will now be considered.

Instructional Pacing/Content Covered

One of the most enduring findings in this literature is on instructinal pacing. Englert (1984), for example, assessed the presentation rates of special education teachers from high-achieving and low-achieving special education classes. The crucial finding in this study was that student achievement was enhanced when teachers maintained a more brisk rate of presentation of new material.

Dunkin and Doeneu (1980) studied the relationship between teacher behavior in sixth-grade social studies classes and achievement. Content coverage emerged as the premier correlate with student achievement. Other factors, such as teacher structuring, pupil participation, and teacher reacting, were not significantly related to student achievement. Consistent with these findings, Larrivee and Algina (1983) found several behaviors that were associated with lower student achievement on the part of mainstreamed special education students. These behaviors included frequency of teacher correction for misconduct, and time spent in transitions.

In a similar manner, Brophy and Good (1986) conclude from their review that opportunity to learn is associated with higher student achievement. Said another way, perhaps the focus of attention in this area should be teacher, as opposed to student, time on task. School psychologists engaged in teacher consultation should consider the amount of instruction being conducted in a classroom as a potentially feasible hypothesis that may explain poor student achievement. School psychologists should think of research on instruction when they encounter a teacher who is disorganized, who spends a great deal of time dealing with nonacademic activities (e.g., collecting lunch money), or whose class is constantly being interrupted by the guidance counselor. It seems that a key variable in the teaching and learning process is the most obvious one.

Seatwork and Homework

Research also shows that students learn more in classrooms where teachers spend more time actively teaching and supervising the students than assigning the students seatwork (Brophy and Good, 1986). This is not to say that teachers should spend more time lecturing to students. The findings in this area merely emphasize the active role of the teacher in instruction. This activity includes frequent questioning, giving feedback, providing clarification, and other activities.

Keith (1982) and Keith and Page (1985) have studied the effects of amount of homework on the academic achievement of high school seniors, using a large national data base. Using path analysis procedures they found that after ability, homework was more important for school achievement than were such factors as race and family background. Does this mean that teachers should simply increase homework in order to improve achievement? The answer to this question is yes, to a point. That is because the highest levels of homework were associated with *lower* levels of student achievement. This finding was replicated by Walberg and Tsai (1984), who studied the influence of homework and other time variables on reading achievement using another large national data base. They found that the highest level of homework was associated with lower achievement than that of the preceding level. These results should give pause to the school psychologist observing a special education classroom where students are engaged primarily in seatwork and where homework is rarely, if ever, assigned.

Individual Differences as Moderator Variables

As alluded to in the preceding section, individual differences such as ability still loom large as variables affecting student achievement. A study by Lara and Medley (1987) is representative of some of the research efforts being made in this area. They conducted observations of 21 elementary grade classes in grades 1 through 8. Of these 21 classes 15 were reading classes and 6 were mathematics classes. They correlated expected student gains with 22 teacher behaviors that were identified as indicators of teacher competence. Most important, the researchers found an interaction between teacher behaviors, student ability, and subject area. With regard to arithmetic achievement, for example, they concluded the following.

In most respects, the patterns of teacher behavior that correlated with achievement gains were distinctly different for learners at different ability levels. Three indicators, providing opportunities for learners to meet success daily, giving learners a voice in decision making, and establishing one-to-one counseling or supportive relationships with learners, had opposite effects on the two types of learners. All three were positively related to gains of high-ability learners but negatively related to gains of low-ability learners. (p. 20)

Interestingly, the pattern of effective teacher behavior was quite different for reading. The authors concluded the following regarding effective teacher behavior in reading.

There was no one indicator of competent teaching of reading, that is, no single indicator that was effective with both kinds of learners. High-ability learners seemed to learn best when the teacher demonstrated proper listening skills, used nonverbal communication skills, and avoided using praise or rewards. Low-ability learners showed greatest gains when the teacher gave clear, explicit instructions, but did not afford the opportunity for individuals to speak. (p. 21)

These findings alert the school psychologist involved in consultation work with teachers to the necessity of considering individual differences between pupils when designing instructional interventions. Furthermore, psychologists must also consider individual differences between curricular areas. Apparently, what constitutes effective teaching depends, among other things, on the child's SES and the academic subject being taught.

Interpersonal and Affective Variables

Soar and Soar (1987) identify additional teacher and classroom variables that affect student achievement. One of these is emotional climate. Interestingly, students seem to learn less when more negative affect is displayed by the teacher in the classroom. This is not a surprising finding; however, it is noteworthy that even the effect of negative emotions in the classroom is moderated by SES. Soar and Soar (1987) note that the relationship between negative affect and student achievement is strongest for low-SES pupils. In fact, some negative affect may even enhance the performance of high-SES pupils. Socioeconomic status again is important as a "moderator" variable in instruction.

The display of positive affect in the classroom is a more complicated story. Medley (1977) found that while in a number of studies positive affect appears to enhance achievement, in a similarly large number of studies positive affect had a negative impact on pupil achievement. The contingent use of praise, for example, seems to enhance performance on rote learning activities and inhibit performance on higher-level cognitive activities.

The "More Is Better" Fallacy

Soar and Soar (1987) describe the relationship between a number of teacher behaviors and pupil achievement as inverted "U-shaped", or in other words, nonlinear functions. Said another way, for a number of classroom variables a moderate level is ideal. Examples of such functions include time on task, level of teacher questioning, and amount of teacher control over learning. Soar and Soar (1979), for example, found that the highest achievement gains occurred when teacher control over instruction was moderate. In other words, both high and low levels of teacher control inhibited learning. Brophy and Evertson (1976) found that learning was *less* effective with the highest levels of time on task behavior. The last example of this nonlinearity is in regard to the use of questions pitched at a high cognitive level. Medley (1977) found, contrary to conventional wisdom, that a greater frequency of high-level questions was associated with *less* pupil learning. These findings all make one cautious regarding the use of the "more is better" philosophy when consulting with classroom teachers.

CONCLUSION

Soar and Soar (1987) conclude their review of this literature with the following helpful summary statements for school psychologists.

> Applying these results is not easy. Research has found it necessary to separate these components, but application leaves it to the sensitivity and skill of school psychologists and classroom teachers to orchestrate them in

ways that are functional for students. Beyond this the "more is better" fallacy creates further difficulty for the orchestration, indicating that, like an ingredient in a recipe, some is necessary, but more is not better. The teachers must not only "put it altogether" but must know when enough is enough. Finally, the research has been based on comparisons among large numbers of teachers, but individual teachers, unlike other professionals, rarely have the opportunity to compare themselves with others. Thus, sources of feedback such as pupils, supervisors, or school psychologists are crucial for establishing effective classrooms. (p. 12)

STUDENT COGNITIONS

In the previous *Handbook of School Psychology,* Phillips (1982) stated: "and in the most fundamental sense, school psychologists exist to intervene. We, therefore, assign the highest priority to research that has the *greatest potential as the basis for school intervention*" (p. 27). In this section we present research on student cognitions as mediators of learning from instruction. This emerging field of study in instructional psychology has special significance for school psychologists because of the types of assessment and intervention it suggests.

During the past decade, research on the study of the effectiveness of instruction has shifted from the study of the direct link between the teaching process and product to the study of student learning and achievement (Doyle, 1977, 1980; Shuell, 1986; Winne, 1985; Winne & Marx, 1977, 1980; Wittrock, 1978, 1986). "Student cognitions" refers to the students' thought processes during instruction. These thought processes include students' attention, attitudes, attributions, beliefs, expectations, learning strategies, metacognitive processes, motivations, prior knowledge, memory, and understanding (Wittrock, 1986). There is nothing new about the study of these variables (e.g., attention, prior knowledge) as psychological phenomena (e.g., Bransford & Johnson, 1972; Schneider & Shiffrin, 1977) or as instructional variables (e.g., Ausubel, 1960, 1968; Marks, Doctorow, & Wittrock, 1974; Mayer, 1975, 1976). Neither is the significance of studying mediational phenomena rather than stimulus response bonds in school-aged children a recent invention (e.g., Bower & Trabasso, 1963; Kendler & Kendler, 1962; Levine, 1966; McKeachie, 1974; Thurstone, 1924). However, including measures of student cognitions as mediators of learning and achievement is a new approach in the study of the effectiveness of instruction. For example, earlier studies operationalized attention as time on task and investigated its effects on student achievement. As mentioned in the preceding section, recent studies question the validity of observed time on task as an indicator of student attention (Brophy & Evertson, 1976; Good, 1983; Peterson, Swing, Braverman, & Buss, 1982) and/or include student-reported attention in their designs (Peterson, 1987; Peterson et al., 1982; Peterson, Swing, Stark, & Waas, 1984; Winne & Marx, 1982, 1983).

From this more recent perspective, measures of achievement after instruction is completed are not considered valid evidence for the effectiveness of teaching (Winne, 1982, 1985). Teaching affects student thinking, and student thinking mediates achievement (see Wittrock, 1986). Thus the question is no longer whether instructional manipulations work or do not work, but *why* or *how* they work or do not work. Even though measures of student behavior such as time spent on task may give us indications of observable, mediating processes, they tell us nothing about what is going on inside a student's head during instruction (Peterson et al., 1982). Overt variables are regarded as useful, albeit overly imprecise measures of cognitive processes (Doyle, 1977; Mayer, 1987; Peterson et al., 1982). To understand and improve classroom instruction, we need to focus on "how teachers and students think and behave" in addition to describing the subject matter being studied (Good, 1983, p. 142).

In the following sections we describe two prominent frameworks for studying students' mediating cognitive processes in the classroom and summarize research findings on specific student cognitions from the cognitive domain and from the affective domain (attributions, expectations, motivations). Space does not permit a thorough review of all the literature on student cognitions. Rather, our purpose is to concentrate on selected studies illustrating the significance and application of this approach for school psychologists. For a longer and more extensive review, interested readers are referred to Wittrock (1986).

One methodology for studying students'

mediating thought processes relies on obtaining student's self-reports of their thoughts during instruction. These self-reports are used to build theoretical models for further experimental testing (e.g., Peterson et al., 1984). A second methodology functions by formulating theories and models about the cognitive processes and cognitive outcomes mediating instruction and fitting performance data to these models (e.g., Mayer, 1983).

Students' Perceptions of Their Thought Processes during Instruction

The typical data collection procedure for studying students' perceptions of their own thoughts during instruction is to videotape lessons and show students targeted segments of the videotaped lesson while asking them to recall their thought processes (see Bloom, 1954). In their studies of upper elementary school students' cognitive processes, Winne and Marx (1982, 1983) interviewed both the teachers and the students. Results suggested that "there was a noticeable lack of one-to-one correspondence between instructional stimuli that the teachers identified and the cognitive processing that these cued for students" (Winne & Marx, 1982, p. 513). Students were more likely to perceive the intended instructional stimulus when they were not overly taxed by the amount of material or processing intended for them (see Calfee, 1981). Consequently, their ability to perceive and execute the intended cognitive processing was a function of how well they had mastered the content to be processed and how well practiced their responses were. Also, even when teachers had no specific intentions, the students reported cognitive responses to perceived stimuli.

In addition to investigating fifth- and sixth-grade students' cognitive processes, Peterson and her colleagues (Peterson & Swing, 1982; Peterson et al., 1982) investigated interactions with their attitudes and abilities in mediating achievement and attitudes. Seventy-two students were randomly assigned to one of six classes obtained by crossing ability level (High, Medium, Low) in math by attitude (High versus Low) toward math. Students were taught a 2-day unit on probability. Using the stimulated-recall procedure, their responses to predetermined questions and prompts (shown in Figure 1) were audiotaped. Care was taken not to cue certain expectations, and students were assured that their responses would not be evaluated for correctness.

Instructions for videotape viewing: In a few minutes I am going to ask you some questions about what you were doing or thinking at different times during the math lesson. But, first, you will look at different parts of the videotape we just made. Try to remember what you were doing and thinking during the part of the lesson you will see on the videotape.

Instructions for student interview: Now I am going to ask you some questions. There are no right or wrong answers. Answer each question as completely and honestly as you can. Remember, tell me what you were thinking or doing when Mr. Knickerbocker was first teaching you the lesson.

1. What were you thinking about during the part of the math lesson that you just saw on the videotape? If you were thinking about several different things, tell me about all of them.

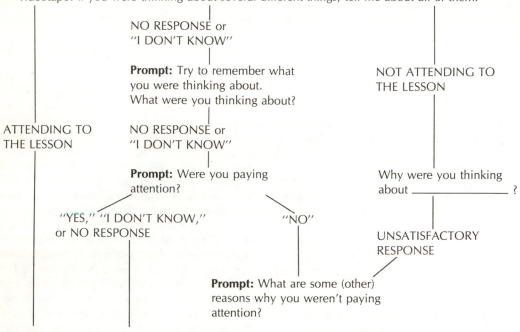

NO RESPONSE or
"I DON'T KNOW"

Prompt: Try to remember what you were thinking about.
What were you thinking about?

NOT ATTENDING TO
THE LESSON

ATTENDING TO
THE LESSON

NO RESPONSE or
"I DON'T KNOW"

Prompt: Were you paying attention?

Why were you thinking about _____ ?

"YES," "I DON'T KNOW,"
or NO RESPONSE

"NO"

UNSATISFACTORY
RESPONSE

Prompt: What are some (other) reasons why you weren't paying attention?

2. During the time Mr. Knickerbocker was teaching, were you understanding the part of the math lesson that you just saw?

"YES," NO RESPONSE, or
"I DON'T KNOW"

"NO"

What things did the teacher do to help you understand? **Prompt:** Tell me more about it or explain what you mean.

What did you have trouble understanding?
Prompt: Tell me more about it or explain what you mean.

What things were you doing or thinking that helped you understand? **Prompt:** Tell me more about it or explain what you mean.

Why were you having trouble understanding?

NO RESPONSE, "I DON'T KNOW," INCOMPLETE or UNSATISFACTORY RESPONSE

Prompt: Did the teacher do things that made it difficult for you to understand the math lesson? What were they?

What are some (other) reasons why you had trouble understanding the math lesson?

What things did you do or think about that should have helped you to understand?
Prompt: Tell me more about it or explain what you mean.

Note: Use each prompt only once.

Two independent coders transcribed the responses into five major categories: (a) attending during that segment of the lesson, (b) understanding that portion of the lesson, (c) students' reasons for not understanding, (d) students' cognitive strategies that helped the understanding of that portion of the lesson, and (e) students' perception of teacher behavior and strategies that helped him or her understand. Results indicated that students' reports of their understanding of the lesson (which was independent of ability) correlated significantly with achievement. Attending did not correlate with other variables due to a ceiling effect on the attending variable; that is, students were attending to the lesson almost all of the time ($M = 27.76$ out of 30), possibly due to the laboratory setting of the study. A later study by Peterson et al.(1984) conducted in a naturalistic setting with more diverse ethnic and socioeconomic groups of fifth graders found that observations of time on task were unrelated to students' reports of attention, and that student reports of attention were more valid indicators of learning. However, when the effects of mathematical ability were partialled out, the attending variable and the achievement scores were no longer related.

Results also indicated that students who reported using specific cognitive strategies did better on math achievement tests than did students who reported global strategies. These specific cognitive strategies included checking answers, applying information, going back and reworking problems, rereading directions, relating new information to prior knowledge, trying to understand the teacher or problem, asking for help, and motivating oneself. Global strategies reported were listening, remembering, and writing down information. Furthermore, Peterson and her colleagues found that higher-ability students more frequently reported using specific strategies than did lower-ability students. They engaged in these strategies more frequently than did lower-ability students and recognized teacher-provided overview as beneficial to their understanding. Lower ability students reported more general strategies and stated imprecise reasons for not understanding the lesson. Good explanations of *what* and *why* one did not understand were positively related to achievement test scores (Peterson et al., 1984).

These (Peterson et al., 1982, 1984) results are important for at least two reasons. First, they suggest that the inclination to attend is related to prior knowledge (cf. Winne & Marx, 1982). Second, these studies make clear the value of studying students' knowledge of content as well as content-specific strategies.

In the following sections we address students' attention, prior knowledge and metacognitive strategies, how they interact, and their role in learning and understanding.

Attention

Attention is a student thought process that mediates instruction and achievement. It helps explain the varied findings of studies with gifted, learning disabled (LD), hyperactive, or mentally retarded children (see Wittrock, 1986). Studies with gifted students indicate that gifted individuals are better able to direct their attention to relevant rather than irrelevant information than are nongifted individuals (Davidson & Sternberg, 1984). In a study designed to test the attention of intellectually gifted and nongifted sixth, seventh, and eighth graders to relevant and irrelevant novel and familiar information in solving analogy problems on a microcomputer, Marr and Sternberg (1986) found that nongifted students allocated as much time to irrelevant information as they did to relevant information, whereas the gifted students quickly dismissed the irrelevant information.

In the development of this kind of selective attention, learning-disabled children, on the other hand, lag 2 to 3 years behind normally developing children. Normally developing children from the ages of 5 to 15 show a large increase (largest at ages 12 and 13) in their ability to attend to and recall relevant information, and show no or little increase in attending to or recalling irrelevant (incidental) information (Wittrock, 1986). Being able to attend to relevant information and ignore

Figure 1. Stimulated-recall interview.
        Note. From "Students' Aptitudes and Their Reports of Cognitive Processes during Direct Instruction" by P. L. Peterson, S. R. Swing, M. T. Braverman, and R. Buss, 1982, *Journal of Educational Psychology, 74,* p. 538. Copyright 1982 by the American Psychological Association. Reprinted by permission.

the irrelevant is a very important factor in encoding new information for learning and problem solving. That information, however, is only relevant or irrelevant in relation to the learner. The incoming information is evaluated for relevancy in relation to the learner's prior knowledge.

For special students such as the learning disabled (LD), mentally retarded, and hyperkinetic learners, attentional disorder is a major impediment to learning both in and out of the classroom (see Krupski, 1980). Based mainly on memory studies, LD children have been described as lacking the use of attentional and mnemonic strategies (Hallahan, Kauffman, & Ball, 1973; Tarver, Hallahan, Kauffman, & Ball, 1976; Torgeson, 1977). Several attentional training programs have been developed to improve students' ability to attend, and in the case of hyperactive children to be able to remove some students from stimulant drug therapy (see Meichenbaum & Goodman, 1971). For instance, Douglas, Parry, Martin, and Garson (1976) successfully trained 7- and 8-year-old hyperkinetic children for 3 months in the use of self-talk to control attention. Measures of attention, oral and listening comprehension, planning, and analyzing detail suggested improved ability to attend. For further discussion of such cognitive training programs and their educational applications, see Meichenbaum and Asarnow (1979).

Especially since most of the problems with attention for learning disabled, mentally retarded, and behavior disordered students are traced to deficiencies in voluntary attention tasks rather than short-term involuntary attention tasks (Krupski, 1980; Zeamon & House, 1963), the success of the training depends in part on the students' ability to monitor their strategies and to give feedback about their appropriateness. In addition, it is important to note that the very groups who could benefit the most from training (i.e., lower-ability students, mentally retarded, learning-disabled students) may not be as aware of their own knowledge and understanding or possess the prior knowledge necessary to facilitate attention. Thus, the challenge for these children is to know when and where, and to what to pay attention.

A Model of Instruction Based on Students' Prior Knowledge

As stated earlier, the problem with traditional research in instruction has been that it did not provide the teacher with answers on *how* and *why* one approach works better than another. The stimulated-recall interview technique, where students are shown segments of target lessons and questioned about their thought processes, is one very important way of getting some answers about the mediating processes. Another powerful approach has been to develop theories of mediating cognitive processes and test them with appropriate operationalizations of cognitive outcome measures. For example, according to Mayer (1987), learning may involve actively relating what is presented with existing knowledge, integrating the two in working memory, and storing the result in long-term memory. The cognitive processes and states that mediate between the instructional methods and performance are (a) paying attention, (b) possessing prerequisite knowledge and strategies in long-term memory, (c) building internal connections (e.g., organizing the material around a topic), (d) building external connections (transferring relevant prerequisite knowledge from long-term memory to working memory, thus integrating new knowledge with the old), and (e) storing outcome in long-term memory. These processes and states make possible three cognitive outcomes that mediate performance. First, no learning occurs and presumably no change in performance if the learner fails to pay attention. Second, rote learning takes place if the learner pays attention but lacks the prerequisite knowledge. Since new information cannot be combined with preexisting information, student performance should improve, if at all, only on tests of verbatim retention. Third, integrated learning takes place if the learner pays attention and is able to build internal and external connections. New information is reorganized and integrated with existing knowledge enabling the learner to perform creative problem solving or transfer information to new learning situations (Mayer, 1987, p. 119).

Activating Prior Knowledge

For integrated learning to take place, the learner has to relate new information actively to existing knowledge, building external and internal connections. In this section we discuss some ways of building, activating, and organizing prior knowledge.

Advance Organizers

The use of advance organizers was one of the earliest researched instructional manipulations designed to facilitate learning by building or activating prior knowledge. The effect of receiving advance organizers versus no organizers was determined by performance on retention and comprehension tests. Ausubel (1960, 1968), the first to study the effects of advance organizers, described an advance organizer as providing "ideational scaffolding for the stable incorporation and retention of more detailed and differentiated material that follows" (Ausubel, 1968, p. 148). However, studies testing the effectiveness of advance organizers yielded mixed results (see Barnes & Clawson, 1975). It was not until later investigations taking into account the mediating cognitive processes and outcomes mentioned above that the phenomenon of advance organizers was better understood. In a series of studies on advance organizers, Mayer (1975, 1976, 1979, 1983) found that advance organizers promote learning and transfer only under certain conditions. For example, advance organizers are more effective with unfamiliar texts, where the students lack active prerequisite knowledge (Mayer, 1979; West & Fensham, 1976). Studies demonstrated that advance organizers increased learning significantly for students who lacked the background knowledge as assessed by a pretest on prior knowledge but not for students who scored high on the background test. Pretraining of the less knowledgeable students eliminated this interaction.

In addition, advance organizers promote transfer on creative problem-solving tasks (Mayer, 1979). Consistent with the mediating cognitive outcomes of integrated versus rote learning, the advance organizer group performed worse on verbatim retention than did the control group, but performed better on creative problem solving (Mayer, 1983), suggesting that the advance organizer served to increase integration and reorganization or material.

Finally, advance organizers are most effective when they provide the prerequisite knowledge to understand abstract material. Unlike Ausubel's initial conception of an advance organizer at a higher level of generality and abstraction, concrete advance organizers providing concrete analogies in physics facilitated learning and memory (Mayer, 1979, 1983; Royer & Cable, 1975, 1976; R. T. White & Mayer, 1980).

Building External Connections

In his model of generating learning, Wittrock (1981) describes comprehension as involving generation of relations among parts of the to-be-learned information and also between this information and the learners' knowledge base and experience. The effect of the external connection to the learner's knowledge base and experience on memory and comprehension has been demonstrated in studies where the amount and type of information depended on the experience or the perspective of the readers. For instance, Anderson, Reynolds, Schallert, and Goetz (1977) presented music majors and physical education majors with a passage that contained polysemous words, such as "notes," which could be interpreted in context either as note cards or musical notes, or "diamonds," as jewelry or shape on a playing card. Music students interpreted the passage as being about a music jam session and remembered information consistent with a music session. Physical education majors tended to interpret it as a card game and remembered information about the card game. In this and other similar studies readers' recall of a passage was influenced by the perspectives they took. For example, details such as where the coin collection was kept was more likely to be remembered by the students with a burglar versus a homebuyer perspective (Pichert & Anderson, 1977). In summary, building external connections to prior knowledge and experience enhance learning, memory, and comprehension.

Building Internal Connections

There is also empirical support for the effect on memory and comprehension of internal connections or relations among parts of the information (e.g., Doctorow, Wittrock, & Marks, 1978). For example, research on the instructional technique of "signaling" the conceptual structure of a passage by using headings, organizing sentences, and connecting words indicate that these techniques are the most effective for less able readers (Meyer, Brandt, & Bluth, 1980), possibly by directing their attention and prompting them to make internal connections.

An alternative to signaling is to get learners to make internal connections by instructing them to generate relations actively among the parts of a text, by writing headings and summaries, and by outlining or underlining main ideas (e.g., Dee-Lucas & DiVesta, 1980; Glynn & DiVesta, 1977. This instructional technique is shown to facilitate memory and comprehension for both low- and high-ability-level individuals (Doctorow et al., 1978; see also Wittrock, 1986). Underlining of important segments by students themselves lead to highest learning. Conversely, underlining directed at the irrelevant or structurally unimportant parts of a text reduces comprehension (Rickards & August, 1975). According to Wittrock (1986), underlining done by students lacking in prerequisite knowledge and ability may reduce comprehension, possibly by making it even more difficult to make internal connections. Thus, it seems that outlining assignments can aid or hinder retention depending on how well the outliner can identify relevant versus irrelevant content.

Deactivating Prior Knowledge

Up to this point, prior knowledge has been treated as the prerequisite knowledge necessary to facilitate new learning. The issue has been how to make the appropriate connections. Sometimes, however, prior knowledge hinders learning and problem solving. For example, the phenomena of problem solving set and functional fixedness (Duncker, 1945; Luchins, 1942; Luchins & Luchins, 1950) are instances where prior knowledge acts as a hindrance. Analogous to this phenomenon in problem solving, incorrect prior knowledge is demonstrated to persist even when children are taught otherwise (see Stein & Bransford, 1979). For example, elementary school children in three countries, New Zealand, Great Britain, and the United States, who have incorrect models of scientific events (such as the models of current flow between a light bulb and a battery) have been shown to persist in their incorrect beliefs even after demonstrations with ammeters which disprove their model. Interestingly, they often believe that the current flows the way the teacher thinks only in the classroom but not at home or outside the classroom (Osborne, 1981; Osborne & Wittrock, 1983; see also Wittrock, 1986). Possibly children who persist in their misconceptions do not know that they do not know (i.e., they lack metacognitive knowledge). For integrated learning and transfer to take place, students need to know how to monitor the use of their knowledge (see Glaser, 1984).

Metacognitive Processes

Metacognition refers to a person's thinking about the various subprocesses and strategies involved in one's own cognitive activities (i.e., it pertains to students' awareness of their own cognitions) (see Flavell, 1976). To the extent that one has metacognitive awareness of how one learns, thinks, and problem solves, one can begin to monitor cognitive activity (i.e., become aware of "executive

processes") (Belmont & Butterfield, 1977). Additionally, some writers discuss metacognition in children as including strategic procedural knowledge, regardless of whether the child is conscious or aware of it in any communicable way (see A. L. Brown 1978; Meichenbaum, Burland, Gruson, & Cameron, 1985). Some theorists separated the broad term *metacognition* into two activities: "knowledge about cognition" and "regulation of cognition" (A. L. Brown, 1975; Campione, Brown, & Ferrara, 1982). Knowledge about cognition refers to the stable and statable information about one's cognitive processes during any academic task. Regulation of cognition refers to self-regulatory executive control mechanisms, which include checking, planning, monitoring, testing, revising, and evaluating (Campione et al., 1982).

Our understanding of students' knowledge about their own cognitive processes is important for evaluating instruction as well as for diagnosing specific learning problems. Recent research on student cognitions using the stimulated-recall technique is uncovering students' knowledge of their own thought processes (see Peterson, 1987). As we saw earlier, Peterson and her colleagues' findings (Peterson & Swing, 1982; Peterson et al., 1982, 1984) suggest that students' general metacognitional knowledge (i.e., students' ability to judge, monitor, and diagnose their understanding, and their reported use of specific cognitive strategies) are related to their learning and achievement. However, these studies of student cognitions did not take into account students' prior knowledge of strategies (see Carpenter & Peterson, 1988). In a recent experiment, Peterson, Swing, and Stoiber (1986, cited in Peterson, 1987) taught fourth-grade mathematics students four cognitive strategies: (a) defining and describing, (b) comparing, (c) thinking of reasons, and (d) summarizing. The newly acquired knowledge of these strategies benefited low-ability students more than high-ability students, possibly by remediating a deficit in the knowledge of cognitive strategies. Moreover, low-ability students in the strategy group exhibited higher metacognitional knowledge of general cognitive strategies than did the control group.

The second type of metacognitive activity, in contrast to knowledge about one's own cognition, are self-regulatory mechanisms, which may be automatic and unconscious. If these self-regulatory mechanisms can be assessed (see Meichenbaum et al., 1985; Sternberg, 1985), they would contribute to the design, implementation, and monitoring of intervention programs for all students, and especially special students.

Metacognition versus Cognition

Most psychologists agree that the development of metacognitive processes is more likely to follow the development of prior knowledge (Armbruster, Echols, & Brown, 1983; see also Wittrock, 1986). Some have questioned whether cognition and metacognition are two separate constructs (see A. F. Brown, 1978; Cavanaugh & Perlmutter, 1982) asking the question: "Is knowing how to solve problems a different skill of ability from knowing that one knows how to solve problems?" (p. 441). Slife, Weiss, and Bell (1985) matched 24 learning-disabled elementary students with regular students on knowledge of mathematics based on their mathematics achievement scores and their performance on 10 math problems. The two groups did not differ on IQ scores. For the experimental task the two groups received regular classwork problems to look over and were asked to predict the number they would get correct. They were then asked to identify their problem solutions as right or wrong, and their identification accuracy and time were recorded. The LD group was less accurate in predicting their problem-solving performance and in identifying correct and incorrect responses. Their times for identification did not differ. Thus these results indicated that the learning-disabled subjects were less skilled in knowledge about their problem-solving skills and have less ability to monitor their problem-solving performance. Apart from providing initial evidence for the validity of metacognition as a separate construct from cognition, this study raised the question of why LD students of equivalent knowledge and ability who perform equally well on math problems would perform so poorly on the metacognitive task. In general, LD students show deficiencies in self-regulatory skills of planning, monitoring, and checking (Torgeson, 1977), and programs that teach these self-regulatory skills look promising. For a discussion of instruction in metacognitive processes, see the special issue of the *Journal of Topics in Learning and Learning Disabilities* on "Metacognition and Learning Disabilities" (1982).

General Metacognitive versus Specific Learning Strategies

Can some of these self-regulatory strategies be taught free of any specific content knowledge and be expected to transfer to different areas as needed? There is a growing body of evidence which indicates that students may have a number of strategies in their repertoires but fail to use them because they lack knowledge of when, where, and how to use them (see Borkowski, 1985; Flavell & Wellman, 1977).

Interaction of Knowledge and Metacognitive Strategies

Campione et al. (1982) explain that in the early and middle 1970s, the importance of strategies for mediating the performance of mentally retarded students was overstated. This panacea syndrome came about as a result of typical findings indicating that retarded children were less likely to employ task appropriate strategies (e.g., memory strategies) and that teaching retarded children to use relevant strategies improved their performance. Furthermore, priming studies in semantic memory demonstrated that the mentally retarded individuals did not lack a basic organization of memory as was once believed (Sperber, Ragain, & McCauley, 1976). However, as the role of the knowledge base was better understood in explaining developmental differences in memory (Chi, 1981) and problem solving (Siegler & Klahr, 1982; Siegler & Richards, 1982), the overemphasis on strategies gave way to an emphasis on prior knowledge. Since learning and retention depend on the amount of knowledge the learner already possesses, it was tempting to overemphasize inadequate knowledge as the major cause of the learning problems of retarded individuals. Campione and his colleagues argued for the importance of both prior knowledge and strategies: "Essentially we believe that the tendency to be strategic varies with intelligence and that the ability to execute a strategy efficiently in some domain depends upon the quantity and quality of the performer's knowledge of that domain. Without the appropriate knowledge, some strategies may be precluded; however, even when the knowledge is available, some individuals may not employ the strategies made possible by that knowledge" (Campione et al., 1982, p. 401).

Access of Knowledge

For a review and discussion of the teaching of general learning strategies for both basic and complex learning tasks, readers are referred to Weinstein and Mayer (1986). (See also the special issues of the *Educational Psychologist* on "Learning Strategies", Levin & Pressley, 1986.)

Teaching of some of the general learning strategies such as organizational strategies (Mayer, 1982, 1984) and metacognitive strategies such as comprehension monitoring (Malamuth, 1979; Meichenbaum & Asarnow, 1979; Wong & Jones, 1982) have been very effective for learning and comprehension tasks. However, acquiring relevant knowledge is not a guarantee that access will take place (see Bransford & Johnson, 1972; Bransford, Sherwood, Vye, & Rieser, 1986; Dooling & Lachman, 1971). It is possible for the knowledge of both content and strategies to remain inert (see Asch, 1969; Bereiter & Scardamalia, 1985; A. L. Brown, 1985; A. L. Brown & Campione, 1981; Gick & Holyoak, 1980; Perfetto, Bransford, & Franks, 1983; Simon & Hayes, 1976, 1977; Whitehead, 1929), particularly if students are not explicitly prompted to use them (A. L. Brown, Bransford, Ferrera, & Campione, 1983; A. L. Brown, Campione, & Day, 1981).

So far the evidence suggests that problem solving by diverse ability groups (mentally retarded students as well as college students) requires an understanding of how concepts and procedures can be applied for solving relevant problems. Bransford and his colleagues (1986) argue that many existing programs designed to teach thinking and problem solving involve an emphasis on general skills and strategies rather than specific knowledge, and that these programs can be made more effective by combining general metacognitive skills and domain-specific knowledge. They suggest, for instance, that students who have trouble differentiating the parts of a math problem situation that are numerically relevant from the parts that are not relevant to the solution may be asked to solve math word problems that involve such differentiations (see also Glaser, 1984, 1985).

Maybe the best statement explaining the interaction of prior knowledge, learning strategies, and metacognitive processes is a quote from Campione and his colleagues (1982): "Strategies can be beneficial only to the extent that learners anticipate their need, select from among them, oversee their operation, and understand their significance" (p. 434), which is only possible in relation to a body of content knowledge.

Motivational Thought Processes

In the past 20 years, cognitive theories of motivation that emphasize the role of mediating cognitions in initiating, directing, and sustaining behavior

have become increasingly more multidimensional, more sophisticated, and more refined (Clifford, 1986). Among those theories are learned helplessness (Abramson, Seligman, & Teasdale, 1978; Jones, Nation, & Massad, 1977; Miller & Norman, 1979; Seligman & Maier, 1967; Wortman & Brehm, 1975); locus of control (Rotter, 1954; 1966); many theories of intrinsic motivation, such as effectance motivation (Harter, 1978a, 1978b; R. W. White, 1959); personal causation (DeCharms, 1968, 1972, 1978); cognitive evaluation (Deci, 1971, 1972, 1975); overjustification (Greene & Lepper, 1974; Lepper & Greene, 1975, 1978; Lepper, Greene, & Nisbett, 1973); endogenous attribution (Kruglanski, 1975, 1978); and emergent motivation (Csikszentmihalyi, 1975, 1978). Many of these theories explain motivation in terms of attributions or causal interpretations of external constraints and rewards (e.g., Kruglanski, 1978; Lepper, 1973, 1980; Lepper & Greene, 1978). Many others have been modified and refined by including attributions (e.g., Abramson et al., 1978; Miller & Norman, 1979). In addition, integrative theories such as the achievement motivation theory (Atkinson, 1964; Atkinson & Litwin, 1960), which originally provided the impetus for the study of attributions, were also extended to include attributions (Diener & Dweck, 1978; Dweck, 1975, 1986, 1987; Nicholls, 1975, 1976, 1984; Weiner, Russell, & Lerman, 1978). Thus, although attribution theory is not the only motivational explanation of student learning, it is an important one.

Recent research on motivation in teaching has been focusing on students' attributions to explain not only students' perceptions of the causes of their successes and failures, and their effect on achievement, but also the effect of instruction on attributions that mediate achievement. Although there may be many reasons why students fail or succeed, such as fatigue, mood, and task interest, the most commonly reported causes are ability and effort (Bar-Tal & Baarom, 1979; Freize, 1976; see also Clifford, 1986).

Students' Attributions of Success and Failure
As children develop their concepts of effort and ability, the causes of their achievement become increasingly differentiated. Until about age 7 they do not even separate effort, ability, and achievement (Nichols, 1978). At age 7 or 8 they can discriminate between these concepts, but attribute

achievement to effort. It is not until they are about 11 years of age that they realize that both effort and ability can influence achievement. As children get older their locus of control also changes. Internality or their perceived competence in performing activities increases with age, but their perceived contingency or the perceived impact of their actions on external outcomes decreases (Lefcourt, 1982; Weisz & Stipek, 1982). These important findings imply that the training programs that teach children to attribute their successes and failures to effort need to take into account this developmental progression (see Wittrock, 1986).

According to attribution theory, how students interpret their successes and failures have different effects on their later achievement behavior. Whether they attribute their failures to unstable, modifiable causes such as effort or stable, unmodifiable causes such as ability influences their performance expectations and behaviors (see Weiner, 1979). Several research studies have repeatedly indicated that children who attribute their failure to lack of ability rather than lack of effort show decreased persistence and performance deficits when faced with difficulties (Andrews & Debus, 1978; Diener & Dweck, 1978; Dweck, 1975; Weiner, 1979).

Students' Goals

From a social-cognitive framework, Dweck (1986, 1987) shows that the particular goals that the children pursue on cognitive tasks not only determine their explanations of failure and success, but also influence their performance. According to Dweck, achievement situations present a choice of goals: (a) *learning goals,* where the goal is to increase competence, to understand or learn something new; and (b) *performance goals,* where the goal is to gain positive judgments and avoid negative judgments of one's competence (Dweck & Elliott, 1983; Nicholls, 1984). Even though they do not differ in intellectual ability, the goals that the children adopt predict their achievement pattern. Children with an adaptive ("mastery-oriented") pattern of achievement behavior seek challenges and exhibit high persistence, whereas children with a maladaptive ("helpless") pattern avoid challenges and display low persistence when faced with difficulty. Children's theories of intelligence appear to mediate their orientations to the two classes of goals. As can be seen in Table 1, children who believe that intelligence is fixed orient more toward

performance goals, and children who believe that intelligence is malleable orient more toward learning goals (see Dweck, 1987; Dweck & Elliott, 1983; see also Yussen & Kane, 1985). Children with performance goals are more likely to attribute their failures to a lack of ability (Ames, 1984; Ames, Ames, & Felker, 1977). They are also more likely to view expending effort as indicative of low ability (Leggett, 1986). Children with learning goals, in contrast, increase their effort and evaluate their strategies when confronted with obstacles (Ames, 1984; Ames et al., 1977; Diener & Dweck, 1978; Elliott & Dweck, 1985, reported in Dweck, 1986; Nicholls, 1984). Ames (1984) found that children who are put in competitive situations ("Let's see who is better at solving the puzzles? . . . Who will be the winner?") focused more on the question "Was I Smart?" Children who were put in an individual challenge situation ("Let's see how many of these puzzles you can solve . . . Try to solve as many as you can") focused more on effort attributions and used more self-instructions.

Sex Differences in Goals and Attributions

In her review, Dweck (1986) cites evidence that girls, particularly bright girls, are especially prone to the maladaptive motivational pattern. The recurrent finding in many studies is that girls more than boys attribute their high performances to effort and failures to lack of ability (Nicholls, 1975; see Licht & Dweck, 1983 for a review). Licht & Dweck (1984) found that even though high-achieving girls rated themselves bright, they still showed more helpless behavior after being exposed to a confusing condition. The brighter the girl was (as measured by IQ and self-rating), the harder it was for her to reach mastery after the confusion condition, whereas it was easier after the no-confusion condition. In a study of bright junior high school students, girls were more likely to think of intelligence as a fixed trait and choose performance goals that avoided challenge (Leggett, 1985). Sex differences in motivational patterns are largest among the brightest students. Bright girls compared to bright boys and less bright girls have lower confidence in their future success and less preference for novel and challenging tasks, make lack of ability attributions for their failures, and exhibit more helpless behavior when faced with failure or confusion (Licht & Dweck, 1983, 1984; Stipek & Hoffman, 1980). Based on this pattern of

TABLE 1   Achievement Goals and Achievement Behavior

Theory of Intelligence	Goal Orientation	Confidence in Present Ability	Behavior Pattern
Entity theory (Intelligence is fixed)	→ Performance goal (Goal is to gain positive judgments/avoid negative judgments of competence)	If high —→ but	Mastery-oriented High persistence
		If low —→	Helpless Avoid challenge Low persistence
Incremental theory (Intelligence is malleable)	→ Learning goal (Goal is to increase competence)	If high —→ or low —→	Mastery-oriented Seek challenge (that fosters learning) High persistence

Note. From ''Motivational Processes Affecting Learning'' by C.S. Dweck, 1986, *American Psychologist, 41*, p. 1041. Copyright 1986 by the American Psychological Association, Inc. Reprinted by permission.

156

results, Dweck (1986) argues for motivational influences on sex differences in mathematics achievement. After grade school, mathematics courses such as algebra, geometry, and calculus involve new skills and concepts and differ substantially from verbal areas in that the increments in difficulty in verbal tasks build gradually upon the familiar skills of reading and writing, whereas in math there are many more conceptual leaps. According to Dweck, the novel nature of mathematics makes it more compatible with challenge-seeking boys and less compatible with challenge-avoiding girls. The documented sex differences in course taking and achievement (Fennema & Sherman, 1977; Hilton & Berglund, 1974) can thus be predicted by motivational patterns of bright girls and bright boys (see also Fennema, 1985).

It is important to remember that actual competence or earlier success does not guarantee adaptive motivational patterns. Bright children, especially bright girls, may fall into the pattern of protecting the positive feedback they have been getting and avoiding challenging learning situations. Within a performance goal, students will choose challenging tasks only if they have confidence in their ability. "Yet the same focus on ability makes their confidence in their ability fragile—even the mere exertion of effort calls ability into question (Dweck, 1986, p. 1043).

The motivational intervention of ensuring success in small steps and delivering frequent praise builds the "fragile" confidence in a performance framework. What is needed is a learning goal orientation. So far, the few studies manipulating the goal orientations of students have produced desirable motivational patterns (Ames, 1984; Ames et al., 1977; Elliott & Dweck, 1985, reported in Dweck, 1986).

Motivational Interventions

Motivational intervention studies have been conducted mostly with underachievers. When students with learned helplessness were taught to attribute their failures to lack of effort, they improved or maintained their academic performance (Dweck, 1975). In elementary school, boys are criticized for nonintellectual acts such as their work being sloppy, whereas girls are criticized for intellectual matters, such as forgetting to carry the number over (Dweck, Davidson, Nelson, & Enna 1978). When this type of criticism is reversed in an experimental situation, both boys and girls who

receive the intellectual-type criticism end up attributing their failures to lack of ability (Dweck et al., 1978).

Since gifted children initially experience a high rate of success, it is especially easy for them to orient to performance goals rather than to learning goals, and to avoid situations that would compromise their ability. Research also indicates that college students who experienced 50% success show less performance deterioration following helplessness training where they are subjected to failure than did students who either experience 100% success or 100% failure (Jones et al., Massad, 1977). This almost perfect success rate does not allow students to gain control over the failure situations—to develop strategies to cope with failure (see Clifford, 1984). Schunk (1985) found that effort feedback for one's successes increases motivation, self-efficacy (perceived performance capability), and skills.

Learning disabled students are on the other extreme of the success–failure continuum. They experience repeated failures (see Licht, Kistner, Ozkaragoz, Shapiro, & Clausen, 1985), and research suggests that they are less likely to attribute these failures to insufficient effort (Butkowsky & Willows, 1980; Licht, 1983; Licht et al., 1985; Palmer, Drummond, Tollison, & Zinkgraff, 1982; Pearl, 1982; Pearl, Bryan, & Donahue, 1980, study 2). In addition, it has been suggested that LD students may blame the teacher's overall negative attitude, particularly if the teacher's feedback also includes criticisms of nonintellectual behaviors, such as being off task or disruptive (Licht et al., 1985). Since there is evidence that learning-disabled children are likely to have problems in these nonintellectual areas (Bryan, 1974; McKinney, McClure, & Feagans, 1982), and they do tend to blame external factors (Dweck, Goetz, & Strauss, 1980), it is not clear whether they attribute their failures to external factors or lack of ability. Licht and her colleagues (1985) designed a study including response options which clearly implicated the teacher, the task, and ability (e.g., "The story wasn't well written" rather than "The story was too difficult"). Their results showed that the tendency of the learning-disabled children to attribute their failures to insufficient ability versus external factors varied significantly with the sex of the child. The LD girls attributed their failures to insufficient ability more than did non-LD girls. The LD boys attributed their failures to external factors more than did non-LD boys. Consistently, LD girls, but not LD boys, were less persistent compared to their non-LD peers. The differential feedback that boys and girls receive may be one of the causes (see Licht et al., 1985). In contrast to these results, some other studies have found that LD boys are more likely to attribute their failures to lack of ability (Butkowsky, 1982; Butkowsky & Willows, 1980; Palmer et al., 1982). The results of a more recent study with seventh and eighth graders (Jacobsen, Lowery, & DuCette, 1986) showed that LD students used both effort and ability attributions, but used effort attributions more than did their normal-achieving peers (NA) in explaining failure. Interestingly, in this study, the LD group externalized success by attributing success to luck and task difficulty more than did the NA group. Jacobsen and her colleagues point out that the pattern of these results indicate that LD students may have doubts about their ability, and recommend exercising caution in interventions emphasizing effort attributions for failure with LD children: "The LD children we studied already presented an attributional pattern suggestive of less self-esteem, less certainty about the future, and more doubts about their ability than did their normally achieving counterparts. The addition of any potentially negative intervention must be carefully considered. Further, if the results of these investigations generalize to other LD children, attribution retraining of these children should occur only after study of their present attributions in real-life situations" (Jacobsen et al., 1986, p. 64; see also Covington & Omelich, 1981).

Despite the inconsistencies of their results on the attributions of failure of LD students, these studies taken together suggest that not all students are affected in the same way by repeated failures, that students' attributions should be measured more precisely, and that their sex, the difficulty of the task, and external influences be taken into account in designing intervention programs (see Jacobsen et al., 1986; Licht et al., 1985). For example, when students believe that a task is easy, prolonged effort feedback and praise signals low ability (Schunk, 1984; see Schunk & Cox, 1986; Weiner, Graham, Taylor, & Meyer, 1983). In a recent study with middle-school children who were classified as learning disabled in mathematics, Schunk and Cox (1986) found that LD students who were deficient in subtraction skills benefited from continuous verbalization and effort feedback

linking their successful problem solving with their efforts. They increased in their perceived performance as well as actual performance in math skills. One of the most important implications of this study is that "effort feedback is useful as an adjunct to a sound instructional program" (Schunk & Cox, 1986, p. 207).

The picture emerging from attribution research becomes even more complex when one considers the underlife in actual classrooms. Several important findings need consideration. Students would rather attribute their failures to insufficient effort than to insufficient ability and be perceived as lazy rather than unintelligent. Thus, they blame their failures on lack of effort to protect their self-worth (Beery, 1975; Covington & Beery, 1976). Regardless of their ability level, however, students who are perceived as trying hard are rewarded more for success and punished less for failure than are students who are viewed as not expending much effort (Eswara, 1972; Rest, Nierenberg, Weiner, & Heckhausen, 1973; Weiner & Kukla, 1970). So when students expend effort, which puts them in a favorable light with the teacher, they risk appearing incompetent to themselves and others. Covington and Omelich (1979) named this conflict involving effort a "doubled-edged sword in school achievement."

New Directions

Most retraining in attribution has focused on effort and ability. Wittrock (1986) commented: "For the future, research in motivation should study how attribution to cognitive strategies, rather than ability or effort, might influence learning and achievement. Strategy attribution might be effective with unsuccessful but hardworking students for whom training in effort attributions would make little sense (p. 306).

Studies that paired strategy instruction with effort attribution feedback reported increased self-efficacy and persistence (Schunk, 1983; Schunk & Cox, 1986; Short & Ryan, 1984). In addition to pairing effort attributions and strategy, McNabb (1987) also compared the effects of strategy attribution and effort attribution feedback on the attribution and motivation of students differing in their perceived math competence and their attitudes toward strategy and effort. Students with low perceived competence and those with negative attitudes toward strategy and effort (e.g., "sometimes it is better not to try your best") benefited more from strategy than from effort training.

Strategy attributions may provide one way of avoiding the "double-edged sword." Just like effort, strategy is unstable or modifiable and controllable. It also has an additional quality: "Strategy also implies ability, in that students who possess larger arsenals of strategies are better able to achieve success. Strategy, then, suggests a less immutable type of ability that is under the control of the student (McNabb, 1987, p. 19). It is possible that strategy attributions will orient students toward the learning goal orientation (Dweck, 1986, 1987) that we discussed earlier by encouraging students to increase their skills regardless of their ability levels. Even though a great deal more research is needed in this area for any specific recommendations, the pairing of strategy attributions rather than effort attributions with strategy training looks promising. The biggest challenge for school psychologists is to pinpoint the specific cognitive skill or knowledge that needs training.

Conclusion

In all of the student thought processes we have considered under the cognitive as well as the affective domain, *knowledge* has emerged as an interacting factor. Prior knowledge is required for new integrated learning. It influences the amount and type of information remembered. Prior knowledge refers not only to content specific facts, concepts, and relationships but also to content specific strategies and the student's awareness of and ability to monitor, alter, and adapt the strategies as well as to general cognitive strategies (such as the general problem-solving rules of thumb) and the student's awareness of and ability to monitor, alter, and adapt the strategies.

The better we understand the mechanisms by which knowledge is acquired, stored, and accessed, the more effective we will be in designing instruction and interventions. The stimulated interview technique, although very promising in revealing the cognitions of most students, might have limitations for special students because of its retroactive, thus reconstructive, nature (see Meichenbaum et al., 1985). Students with attentional disorders or memory impairment may find it more difficult to remember their thought processes. In addition, many students diagnosed as learning disabled may have a speech and language impairment (Wiig & Semel, 1973, 1974) and find it difficult to verbalize their thoughts. Future studies, which might use think-aloud protocols from students during wait time (Tobin, 1986; Tobin & Capie, 1983) inserted in videotaped lessons or actual classes behind a one-way mirror, may shed more light on the thought processes of special students. Clearly, considerable effort needs to be expended to confirm these findings and investigate the topic further with more effective methods.

The paradigm enhancement that occurred by including students' cognitions as mediators of achievement does not replace the process/product research or the ATI research in instructional psychology. Rather, it extends existing research findings by searching for more detailed understanding. The most important implication for school psychology is the type of intervention that this body of literature suggests. Future interventions need to focus on students' thought processes and utilize domain specific knowledge-based learning strategies. For the school psychologist this means that diagnoses should be based on assessments of what students know, as it always has been. However, our conception of what we mean by students' knowledge is changing rapidly, and we need assessment procedures that reflect these changes.

COMPUTER-ASSISTED INSTRUCTION

In this section we consider the potential contributions that computers can make to school-based instruction, with particular attention to issues that relate to the practice of school psychologists. No attempt will be made to provide a background in terminology. Resources that do so are widely available and too numerous to list. It is a measure of the rapidity of the computer revolution in education that although few consider themselves experts, most school personnel today are familiar with microcomputers and terms relating to hardware and software. Yet computer-assisted instruction (CAI) was not included in the first edition of the *Handbook of School Psychology,* and at the time of this release, few teachers, administrators, or school specialists would have been comfortable discussing instructional computing issues. The broad field of educational applications of computers has expanded remarkably in less than 10 years—since the advent of microcomputers.

Also excluded here are discussions of particular pieces of software or hardware. As just noted, change in this field is rapid. The best information regarding programs and computers will be current information. The reader seeking either additional background or more current information is referred to the journals listed in the December 1985 issue of the *Journal of Learning Disabilities* and the most current issue of courseware evaluations by EPIE/Consumer Reports. The monthly feature "Computers in the Schools" in the *Journal of Learning Disabilities,* and the resource lists in Budoff, Thormann, and Gras (1984), are also excellent references.

Instructional Uses of the Computer

A wide variety of instructional media have been hailed as major breakthroughs for education during this century. Films, filmstrips, overhead projectors, and television have all stirred the imaginations of educators. Yet "media research efforts have had inconsequential value for either theory or practice" (Clark and Angert, 1984, p. 11).

In recent years, computer technology has emerged as yet another innovation that may improve the ways we teach and our students learn. However, this time the possibility of change seems much more likely. Beginning with the large mainframe computers in the 1950s and continuing with the introduction of microcomputers in the late 1970s, research on educational applications of computers has been accumulating. The presence of computers in schools has increased dramatically. Even those who belittle its value must acknowledge that the computer is now a common reality in American education. The vast majority of schools in this country have acquired computers for instructional purposes (Becker, 1987a). One reason (for the optimism concerning instructional computing and the rapid adoption of this innovation), of course, is the versatility of the technology.

There are many ways in which we may utilize the considerable power of computers for school purposes. One helpful way of examining the variety of uses is to view the computer as taking on one of three potential roles: a "tutor," a "tool," or a "tutee" (Taylor, 1980). The most straightforward educational use of a computer is as a surrogate teacher. In the tutor mode, the computer serves as a delivery agent for instruction. Programmed instruction, drill and practice, and tutorials fall neatly within this category. The essential characteristic of the tutor mode is that the computer "teaches" the student. Also most naturally placed within this category are simulations and computer programs aimed at promoting problem solving and higher-order thinking. In general, these contain curricular intentions consistent with the tutorial image of a flow of instruction from the computer to the student.

The computer-as-tool model reflects uses that are common outside education. Here, it is implicit that some goal which could be accomplished without the aid of a computer has already been established. A computer is used simply as a tool to help accomplish that goal. Administrative duties common to school psychologists, such as record keeping, preparing reports, and communicating with colleagues are good examples. Direct instructional uses of the related tools should also be recognized. Students can productively use the computer for such tool uses as word processing, idea processing, preparing graphs and other "graphics," music or voice synthesis, data base management, spreadsheet analysis, and telecommunications.

The most controversial instructional computer use is the tutee mode. The image evoked (and from which the term originates) is that of the student "teaching" the computer (Papert, 1980). The computer starts out "dumb"; it "learns" by being carefully instructed (programmed) by the student. In this process of teaching, it is hypothesized, the student learns more than would be possible in a traditional receptive role. The programming language Logo was designed with this mode in mind. Research so far has failed to yield clear evidence of the validity of claims for Logo; debate over the value of the tutee mode continues (Clements, 1986; Johanson, 1988; Kurland et al., 1986; Linn, 1985; Papert, 1987).

Curricular Issues

To some extent, the debate just mentioned hinges on such larger issues as student autonomy, appropriate levels of directiveness in instruction, and conceptual-wholistic versus isolated skill development approaches. It has been noted that the greatest contribution of computer use in education may be the resultant impetus provided for reconsideration of our educational aims (Papert, 1987; Russell, 1986). Curricular questions—what are our instructional objectives, what content is most appropriate for this student, how should this content be structured and sequenced?—must always be paramount in planning instruction, whether or not a computer is to be utilized.

Several dangers must be noted. The computer may relieve us of the tedium of such instructional activities as skill drills, thus prompting us to engage students in these activities excessively. We (and our students) may be so impressed with the entertaining graphics or the invigorating competition or the sheer novelty of some piece of software that we incorporate it into our instruction despite its irrelevance to our objectives. We may feel compelled to use computers because of parental and societal pressure, settling for any use just to be sure that we are keeping up with modern technology.

The computer does not choose our goals and objectives. We must retain that task. The computer may help us to attain our goals, but it cannot replace policy planning and instructional decision making. On the instructional side, it is clear that computers do not replace the need for a human teacher (Carlson and Silverman, 1986). Computer instruction is a useful supplement, but it cannot be used effectively to the exclusion of regular instruction (Slesnick, 1984; Vinsonhaler and Bass, 1972).

While there is a danger of thoughtless acceptance of CAI, there is also the reverse danger that present school practice may be an obstacle to potentially beneficial reforms that the computer might bring about. Even the seemingly most compatible use, teaching basic skills on the computer, presents some problems. A recent study "documents the difficulty of integrating classroom-based microcomputer assisted instruction with current curriculum and instructional methods" (Bass, Ries, & Sharpe, 1986). Computers can encourage interactive learning and students' active involvement in building their own cognitive structures, but there are major constraints placed on us by our educational system (O'Brien, 1986). These include exclusionary emphasis on print, an orientation toward memorization and acquisition of "facts," and acceptance of the view of teacher as source and dispenser of knowledge. We must neither unquestioningly accept CAI nor allow current practice to place undue restrictions on educational innovations the computer may make possible.

Research Issues

The basic research question that arises concerning any instructional strategy is one of effectiveness.

With respect to CAI, much research has been done, but much is still needed (Waugh and Currier, 1986). The effects of CAI on various groups of students have been studied for about 30 years now. In recent years, meta-analyses of this research have been completed for the populations of secondary students (Bangert-Drowns, Kilik, & Kulik, 1985; Kulik, Bangert, & Williams, 1983), elementary students (Niemiec and Walberg, 1985), and exceptional children (Schmidt, Weinstein, Niemiec, & Walberg, 1985–1986). In general, results are rather encouraging.

In brief detail, the most prominent findings are as follows. CAI has a fairly consistent and significantly positive effect on student achievement (Bangert-Drowns et al., 1985; Schmidt et al., 1985–1986; Waugh and Currier, 1986). A variety of other findings are less broadly validated, but also significant. The computer's positive effects on educational achievement seem to be greatest at lower ability levels (Bangert-Drowns et al., 1985; Kulik et al., 1983; Niemiec and Walberg, 1985; Schmidt et al., 1985–1986). Another consistent finding is that students who learn using computers exhibit more positive attitudes toward their learning (Bangert-Drowns et al., 1985). However, there is some question about the focus of the improved attitudes. It is largely undisputed that attitudes toward the computer and instruction delivered by the computer have improved. It is not clear that the improvement of attitudes extends to the content itself (Kulik et al., 1983). In this aspect, the effect is at worst neutral. The computer does not contribute to negative feelings about the instructional content, but may not significantly improve such feelings either.

In at least two important areas, there are suggestions of possible negative effects of CAI. Some studies have suggested that long-term retention of learning may be inferior after CAI (Edwards, Norton, Taylor, Weiss, and Dusseldo, 1974; Waugh and Currier, 1986). This is not, however, a well-resolved question since other studies showed that retention was either not affected or was improved under the CAI condition (Kulik et al., 1983). Second, whereas CAI appears to be highly effective with disadvantaged and low-aptitude students (see Kulik et al., 1983; Niemiec and Walberg, 1985), there is no clear empirical evidence of the effectiveness of CAI with higher-ability students. The apparent conclusion is that CAI is actually less effective for high-ability students than it is for lower-ability students. It has been suggested that the structure often exerted by CAI is more appropriate for students whose limited understanding may reduce the amount of structure they can impose on the content themselves. However, three other explanations for this finding are possible. One is a simple ceiling effect, and/or a mismatch between the learners' needs and the instructional objectives of the CAI. Another possibility is that, as discussed below with respect to higher-order thinking, the specific objectives of software used with higher-ability students may simply have more broad and general objectives which are harder to measure, thus making it more difficult to *demonstrate* the effectiveness of the instruction. Third, Becker (1987b) cautions that most studies included in the major meta-analyses dealt with routine drill and practice on currently outdated systems. Such instruction would generally be inappropriate for high-achieving students and should not be expected to yield significant results.

Another general trend in the findings deserves note. More recent research on CAI has yielded stronger effects than those of older research studies (see Kulik et al., 1983; Schmidt et al., 1985–1986). The best hypothesis for this observation seems to be that CAI usage has become more sophisticated and perhaps more appropriate in its aims. More software is available and as a result, there is a larger pool of CAI materials that are judged as being high quality.

This review must end on a note of caution. It is suggested that the primary task now facing researchers completing meta-analyses may be to examine the quality of CAI usage (Schmidt et al., 1985–1986). That is, while it has generally been well shown that CAI yields advantages over traditional instruction on the tasks that have been studied, the reviews of research have not considered whether these instructional tasks were the most educationally significant ones available. Perhaps there are superior educational uses of computers that have not yet been adequately explored. Furthermore, research based on microcomputers is only now beginning to accumulate. Becker (1987b) notes that virtually all of the studies reviewed in the meta-analyses cited above involve mainframe or minicomputers. This important difference, as well as methodological concerns, suggest the need for microcomputer-based experimental studies.

Skill Development

Practice has long been a cornerstone of instruction. As many have noted, however, practice does not necessarily make perfect. Feedback, for modification of the practiced skill in the direction of perfection, is also required. Repetition of errors can simply further embed erroneous behavior in the learner's response hierarchy. Clearly, what many learners who require remedial assistance need is an individual tutor who can guide their practice. An appropriately programmed computer may be able to fill this role. Although it cannot be said that currently available software achieves the level of sophistication desired, progress in software design is clearly being made.

The general category of drill and practice constitutes the largest segment of educational software available. Similarly, drill and practice are reported as the most common use of computers in schools. Interestingly, this fact has been frequently lamented, yet it continues to be true each time that surveys are made. The computer is a natural choice for delivery or remedial instruction in basic skills areas. With a computer, each learner may work at an individually appropriate rate, receive immediate feedback (both corrective and reinforcing), have error patterns identified, and be guided "patiently."

Much research and theory in the area of skill development in recent years has promoted the concept of automaticity (see Bloom, 1986). To succeed at the higher-level tasks of reading comprehension or mathematical problem solving, it is theorized, a student must have achieved a degree of mastery of the lower-level tasks of word recognition or basic arithmetic computation. This should allow these lower-level tasks to be accomplished almost automatically so that the student's attention can be directed to the primary higher-level task. Because of the importance of basic skill development, its compatibility with regular individualized skill practice in the classroom, and the suitability of the computer to this task, this may well be the priority instructional use for computers, especially with learning-disabled children (Torgeson and Young, 1983).

Based on a review of the literature, concepts from information processing, and results of their own research, Goldman and Pellegrino (1987) identify several important considerations with respect to computer-based skill development: (a) "Disabled learners tend to exhibit exceptionally slow rates of learning" (p. 144). Individualized, computer-delivered instruction has the potential to provide some compensation for these slow rates. (b) the motivational advantage of computers to engage students in on-task activity is particularly important for ensuring that this needed practice will occur (see also Lepper, 1985). (c) Drill and practice must be preceded by instruction in the skill to be improved. That is, it is assumed that a sufficient level of learning has occurred that practice is possible. Some software does incorporate both tutorial and practice aspects. When errors in practice occur, some element of remediating instruction is probably necessary. (d) Alternatively, it may be a more realistic allocation of resources to allow a human teacher to introduce the skills and the computer to manage the practice. (e) When used with learning-handicapped students, gamelike aspects common to many drill and practice programs appear to be counterproductive. Attending to the relevant components of the instructional task tends to be a problem for some students. Rather than being motivational, game features simply provide undesirable additional distractions for such students. (f) The development of automaticity, which is indicated by stable skill performance at increased speeds of execution, can only be expected after a high level of accuracy has been achieved. CAI seems to aid development of both accuracy and speed. (g) It is important to remember that skill development is a facilitating objective. The ultimate intent is to promote higher-level cognition. It is a mistake to delay introducing complex tasks until automaticity of simpler skills is achieved.

Higher-Order Thinking

For many educators, part of the attraction of using computers in education has been a vision of revitalized schools in which such elusive goals as problem solving, independent thinking, personal expression, and creativity would become an integral part of the instructional process. Central to such goals is the conviction that learning is most effective and meaningful when the student is an active learner. It is a mistake to view these goals as appropriate only for gifted and talented children.

While expressing concern that instructional goals must not be too broad to be useful, Russell (1986) laments the excessive use of computers in special education for drill and practice. "The deficit model—identify the problem and fix it—can lead to an exclusive focus on students' difficulties, leaving little time or flexibility for developing students' strengths and interests" (p. 101). Her solution depends on incorporating enlarged goals, related to taking intellectual risks and communicating about content, into IEPs. Such goals, in turn, are then related to appropriate software beyond the drill and practice varieties. Doing so requires expanding to a view in which not only "measurable" but also "documentable" learning is accepted. Presumably, greater use of descriptive, individualized, anecdotal records of learning would be required. In a later section we suggest how computers may help teachers manage such records.

Pogrow and Buchanan (1985) have described a program for Chapter I students that used microcomputers to develop higher-order thinking. They argue that remedial programs often fail to help children develop basic skills, that higher-order thinking instruction can assist basic skill acquisition, and consequently, that it is a mistake to delay such instruction until basic skills have been mastered. Central to their program is the development of students' sense of competence. An interesting aspect of role reversal is built into the program by allowing the Chapter I students to bring friends into the computer lab to teach the non–Chapter I student how to use the computer. While reading was not an explicit teaching objective, students in the program did show reading score gains. This reciprocity between higher-order thinking and basic skills needs to be pursued.

The computer language Logo, although not really a software package, certainly belongs in the category of CAI aimed at the development of higher-order thinking. Recall that the term "tutee" was used earlier with respect to Logo. Papert (1980, 1984, 1987) outlines a radically different view of education using the computer and Logo. He designed the Logo instructional environment based on earlier years of study with Piaget. An important intent of Logo instruction is to allow each child to analyze his or her own thinking. In learning to program in Logo, children naturally encounter errors or "bugs" in their thinking. Logo provides an environment in which metacognitive activity can be promoted. Children are encouraged to consider their own thinking and to correct their errors.

While the claims for Logo have not been verified empirically (e.g., see Kurland et al., 1986), Logo instruction has been used with a full range of student populations. Weir, Russell, and Valente (1982) describe using Logo with disabled children. Papert (1987) has recently responded to critics, charging that they have engaged in "technocentric thinking" which limits the potential of educational computer usage. It should also be noted here that computer programming in languages other than Logo has been seen as a vehicle for promoting generalized cognitive growth. Older languages such as BASIC and Pascal have been studied extensively (e.g., see Linn, 1985). The newer declaration language, Prolog, also offers strong potential (Ennals and Briggs, 1985; Johanson, 1988).

Almost universal acceptance seems to have been granted to another category of CAI, simulations. Unfortunately, few good examples of such software have been developed. The basic idea of a simulation is that the computer models a real or imagined situation. Opportunities for interaction with this situation allow the student to gain experience that would otherwise be difficult, costly, time consuming, dangerous, or impossible. Perhaps the most widely known simulation is the Oregon Trail program available from MECC (Minnesota Educational Computing Consortium) and other sources. In this program, students are given the opportunity to take the place of settlers following the Oregon Trail west in the 19th century. They are required to make some decisions (which supplies to obtain, how much to eat, whether to stop at forts along the way, etc.) that would have confronted pioneers on the Oregon Trail. The computer then simulates the consequences of those decisions. The more detailed and realistic the simulation, the more likely it is to be educationally available. A principal purpose of simulations is often to stimulate the learner to form and revise hypotheses regarding the interaction of variables within the context of the situation modeled.

At the heart of software designed to promote higher-order thinking is the concept of interaction. Unlike books, television, and other educational media, computers can engage the student in a kind of ongoing dialogue. O'Brien (1986, p. 21) states the case well: "Fortunately, there is an increasing amount of software that enables students to act rather than merely to store, in which knowledge is constructed rather than copied, and in which coherence and meaning and generalizability rather than accumulation is the goal." Many software

companies have released lines of problem-solving programs dealing with concepts such as pattern recognition, deduction, inference, rule building, and planning. A primary problem with this software is that it is not clearly related to existing subject-oriented curricular priorities. Teachers may have a hard time incorporating this software into their regular instruction. The growing attention to and acceptance of teaching thinking skills and problem solving suggests that this is an area where professionals such as school psychologists can demonstrate leadership in revising educational goals. The increasingly sophisticated body of software available to facilitate these higher-order thinking objectives makes such a push more practical than it would have been 10 years ago.

One more area, applications software, deserves special attention while considering higher-order thinking. A variety of computer uses belong in the applications category. Among the most common uses for instructional purposes are word processing, data base management, and telecommunications. Recall that these are "tool"-mode uses of computers. They qualify as strategies for teaching higher-order thinking to the extent that they encourage students to use the computer as a tool for solving complex problems.

The importance of writing as a tool for thinking has been gaining widespread acceptance in many school subjects. At the same time, word processing has grown significantly as a primary use of microcomputers in schools. The tedium of rewriting, formatting, and producing neat work are all reduced by use of word processors. Data base software can be used to promote concepts of knowledge storage and retrieval. Categorical information (e.g., species and characteristics of plants, demographic data, or historical records) from the natural and social sciences lends itself easily to use in data bases. Careful researching and representing of the information stored may well lead students to deeper understanding and greater retention. Telecommunications—using the computer, a modem, and bulletin board services or other information networks—can promote a social context for learning. Students may link up with each other across a city or across the world to share their learning.

The potential instructional uses of computers are just beginning to be seen. Promoting higher-order thinking should not be overlooked as an appropriate goal of CAT.

Computers and Special Students

School psychologists are frequently involved in serving a variety of special needs groups. Computers have been employed to serve many of these students. Although other sections also apply, a brief overview of some considerations for using CAI with special students is presented here.

Physically handicapped students frequently have greater intellectual capabilities than they are able to demonstrate easily. Fortunately, a wide variety of technological innovations have been developed to assist them. For example, visually impaired students may benefit from large-print monitors, braille word processing systems, and hardware that scans print, converting it to a file which may then be transformed into computer-synthesized speech. If use of the computer keyboard is a physical problem, such modifications as joysticks and graphics pads; special keyboards with large, widely separated keys; head, mouth, foot, or eye movement controls; and increasingly sophisticated voice recognition systems are now available. Physical impairments need not deprive students of opportunities to benefit from CAI.

The learning disabled constitute a large and important category of special students. Kolich (1985) has reviewed the literature for microcomputer use with LD students and argues that existing software is generally limited and unaccommodating of differences in learning style. Skill development through drill and practice and individualized instruction have already been discussed. Isenberg (1985) suggests that cooperative learning strategies should be added to CAI for mainstreamed LD students. But several researchers have urged more use with these students of CAI that employs higher-order thinking. Mokros and Russell (1986) make a case for "learner-centered" software such as Logo, problem-solving software, and word processing. Their work includes a survey of 50 school districts' current CAI usage with LD and ED populations. Stearns (1986) argues for the use of problem-solving software with LD students. She claims that problem solving is not "supplementary" and that the computer is "an ideal medium for the teaching of problem solving" (p. 117). MacArthur and Schneiderman (1986)

promote the use of word processing with LD students and provide some insights into selecting and using appropriate software.

For behavior-disordered (BD) students, the primary advantages of CAI center on its affective consequences, especially student motivation. Manion (1986) reviewed the literature on the use of computers with BD students. The work she reviewed suggests that interaction with a computer is probably less personally threatening than interacting with a teacher, and that hyperactive students may engage in on-task behavior for a longer period of time when using computers.

Autistic students' social skills have been shown to improve when they interact with a computer (Panyan, 1984). For BD students in general, CAI seems to have benefits in the areas of school attendance, behavior, motivation, and self-esteem (Manion, 1986). A somewhat different use of CAI, for delivery of instruction to make a "time-out" strategy less punitive, is discussed in Johanson (1987).

Acceptance of instructional computer use with gifted and talented students is widespread. Articles describing such use are too numerous to mention. Smith (1985–1986) provides a useful annotated bibliography on this topic.

Management Assistance

Bennett and Maher (1984) assert that microcomputer technology is significantly altering the field of special education services. In addition to the instructional uses and the special adaptations for handicapped individuals already discussed, the computer can provide a variety of services directly to school psychologists and other special service providers. The most common of these are discussed below.

Anyone who spends a substantial amount of time preparing written materials can benefit from the use of a word processor. Software to allow microcomputers to function as word processors has increased in sophistication, availability, and ease of use while decreasing in cost over the past few years. It is rapidly becoming the case that ability to use a word processor is a requirement for effective school professionals. Educators who have not learned to use this valuable tool are simply denying themselves increased productivity.

Clearly, time saved in writing—a major portion of many specialists' time—can be devoted to actual delivery of services. Many letters, reports, and other documents have segments of text that can be reused with minor modification. A word processor makes it possible to combine and modify previously used documents with considerably less effort than simply rewriting each time.

With little doubt, the most common type of document used in the delivery of services to special students is the IEP. Computerized systems for preparation of IEPs are gaining wide usage. Such systems typically involved a bank of appropriate objectives keyed to particular student needs, subject areas, and assessment tools; the user selects from and organizes these in creating an IEP. Ryan and Rucker (1986) reviewed the use of computer-assisted IEP preparation and identified three major benefits: time savings of nearly one half, more positive attitudes of teachers toward the IEP, and decreased costs. Increased accessibility of these documents to teachers and administrators for periodic monitoring is another advantage. Hummel and Degnan (1986) have listed four basic options for computer-assisted IEP systems. One major caution must be noted—the potential for overly narrow IEPs exists when recommendations are drawn from a necessarily limited computer file. The possibility of adding items not listed must be available. A related problem often faced is the mediation of disagreements regarding IEPs. Parry and Hofmeister (1986) suggest that expert systems may be a valuable and comparatively inexpensive alternative to legal hearings over challenges to IEPs.

Testing is a major activity of most school psychologists. Computers can also assist in this process. One option is simple computer administration. Programs may also provide item analysis (e.g., identifying nondiscriminating items) and cumulative data on a group of students. Well-developed software would allow this information to be integrated into IEP programs. A variety of programs are available that assist in the development of teacher-made tests. Salend and Salend (1985) suggest guidelines for modifying presentation and response modes as well as motivational benefits when using such programs. Software is also available to assist in using various standardized tests such as the WISC-R, K-ABC, and Woodcock-Johnson. Such software is regularly reviewed in the *NASP Communiqué*.

A somewhat higher level of sophistication is available in programs that generate individual tests for students. The simplest option here is the type of program that selects items at random from a test item bank. But it is also possible for the item selection to be adaptive, that is, to be tailored to the performance of the testee. Considerable attention has recently been given to computerized adaptive testing (CAT). McBride (1985) has reviewed the uses of such testing procedures.

Record keeping can be facilitated by use of such computer tool programs as data base or file management systems, spreadsheets, and integrated packages that typically combine these with word processing and graphics preparation. Adequate description of these is beyond the scope of this chapter. Functions for which such programs might be used include maintaining individual records of services provided to students and progress made toward objectives; maintaining district records for use in meeting the reporting requirements of state and federal governments regarding P.L. 94-142, Chapter I, and other legislation; tabulating student statistics; and identifying all students who are currently using some instructional program, categorized as behavior disordered, or taking a given medication.

Conclusions

It seems clear that microcomputer technology has found a permanent place in our schools. School psychologists in particular are well advised to pursue to benefits that may result from using computers in their practice. Both instructional and administrative advantages have been discussed here. Furthermore, advances in research and development continue to be rapid. Microcomputers do not threaten to replace either teachers or school psychologists. But the potential that this new technology shows for improving educational practice is promising.

REFERENCES

Abramson, L. Y., Seligman, M. E. P., & Teasdale, J. D. (1978). Learned helplessness in humans: Critique and reformulation. *Journal of Abnormal Psychology, 87,* 49–74.

Ames, C. (1984). Achievement attributions and self-instructions under competitive and individualistic goal structures. *Journal of Educational Psychology, 76,* 478–487.

Ames, C., Ames, R., & Felker, D. W. (1977). Effects of competitive reward structure and valence of outcome on children's achievement attributions. *Journal of Educational Psychology, 69,* 1–8.

Anderson, R. C., Reynolds, R. E., Schallert, D. L., & Goetz, E. T. (1977). Frameworks for comprehending discourse. *American Educational Research Journal, 14,* 367–382.

Andrews, G. R., & Debus, R. L. (1978). Persistence and causal perceptions of failure: Modifying cognitive attributions. *Journal of Educational Psychology, 70,* 154–166.

Armbruster, B. B., Echols, C. H., & Brown, A. L. (1983, April). *The role of metacognition in reading to learn: A developmental perspective* (Reading Education Report No. 40). Urbana: University of Illinois at Urbana-Champaign, Center for the Study of Reading.

Asch, S. E. (1969). A reformulation of the problem of associations. *American Psychologist, 24,* 92–102.

Atkinson, J. W. (1964). *An introduction to motivation.* Princeton, NJ: D. Van Nostrand.

Atkinson, J. W., & Litwin, G. H. (1960). Achievement motive and test anxiety as motives to approach success and avoid failure. *Journal of Abnormal and Social Psychology, 60,* 52–63.

Ausubel, D. P. (1960). The use of advance organizers in the learning and retention of meaningful verbal material. *Journal of Educational Psychology, 51,* 267–272.

Ausubel, D. P. (1968). *Educational psychology: A cognitive view.* New York: Holt, Rinehart and Winston.

Bangert-Downs, R. L., Kilik, J. A., and Kulik, C. L. C. (1985). Effectiveness of computer-based education in secondary schools, *Journal of Computer-Based Instruction, 12*(3), 59–68.

Bardon, J. I. (1983). Psychology applied to education: A specialty in search of an identity. *American Psychologist, 38*(2), 185–196.

Barnes, B. R., & Clawson, E. U. (19750. Do advance organizers facilitate learning? Recommendations for further research based on an analysis of 32 studies. *Review of Educational Research, 45,* 637–659.

Bar-Tal, D., & Baarom, E. (1979). Pupils' attributions for success and failure. *Child Development, 50,* 264–267.

Bass, G., Ries, R., and Sharpe, W. (1986). Teaching basic skills through microcomputer assisted instruction. *Journal of Educational Computing Research, 2*(2), 207–219.

Becker, H. J. (1987a). Using computers for instruction. *BYTE, 12*(2), 149–162.

Becker, H. J. (1987b, April). The impact of computer use on children's learning: What research has shown and what it has not. Paper presented at the annual meeting of the American Educational Research Association, Washington, DC.

Beery, R. (1975). Fear of failure in the student experience. *Personnel and Guidance Journal, 54,* 190–203.

Belmont, J., & Butterfield, E. (1977). The instructional approach to developmental cognitive research. In R. Kail & J. Hagen (Eds.), *Perspectives on the development of memory and cognition* (pp. 437–481). Hillsdale, NJ: Lawrence Erlbaum.

Bennett, R. E., & Maher, C. A. (1984). *Microcomputers and exceptional children.* New York: The Haworth Press.

Bereiter, C., & Scardamalia, M. (1985). Cognitive coping strategies and the problem of "inert" knowledge. In S. Chipman, J. W. Segal, & R. Glaser (Eds.), *Thinking and learning skills: Current research and open questions* (Vol. 2, pp. 65–80). Hillsdale, NJ: Lawrence Erlbaum.

Bloom, B. S. (1954). The thought processes of students in discussion. In S. J. French (Ed.), *Accent on teaching: Experiments in general education* (pp. 23–46). New York: Harper.

Bloom, B. S. (1986). Automaticity: The hands and feet of genius. *Educational Leadership, 43*(5), 70–77.

Borkowski, J. G. (1985). Signs of intelligence: Strategy generalization and metacognition. In S. R. Yussen (Ed.), *The growth of reflection in children* (pp. 105–144). New York: Academic Press.

Bower, G. H., & Trabasso, T. R. (1963). Reversals prior to solution in concept identification. *Journal of Experimental Psychology, 66,* 409–418.

Bransford, J. D., & Johnson, M. K. (1972). Contextual prerequisites for understanding: Some investigations of comprehension and recall. *Journal of Verbal Learning and Verbal Behavior, 61,* 717–726.

Bransford, J. D., Sherwood, R., Vye, N., & Rieser, J. (1986). Teaching thinking and problem solving. *American Psychologist, 41,* 1078–1089.

Brophy, J. E., & Evertson, C. (1976). *Learning from teaching: A developmental perspective.* Boston: Allyn and Bacon.

Brophy, J., & Good, T. L. (1986). Teacher behavior and student achievement. In N. C. Wittrock (Ed.), *Handbook of research on teaching* (pp. 328–375). New York: Macmillan.

Brown, A. L. (1975). The development of memory: Knowing, knowing about knowing, and knowing how to know. In H. W. Reese (Ed.), *Advances in child development and behavior* (Vol. 10, pp. 103–152). New York: Academic Press.

Brown, A. L. (1978). Knowing when, where and how to remember: A problem of metacognition. In R. Glaser (Ed.), *Advances in instructional psychology* (pp. 77–165). Hillsdale, NJ: Lawrence Erlbaum.

Brown, A. L. (1985). Mental orthopedics, the training of cognitive skills: An interview with Alfred Binet. In S. Chipman, J. Segal, & R. Glaser (Eds.), *Thinking and learning skills* (Vol. 2, pp. 77–165). Hillsdale, NJ: Lawrence Erlbaum.

Brown, A. L., Bransford, J. D., Ferrera, R. A., & Campione, J. C. (1983). Learning, remembering, and understanding. In J. H. Flavell & E. M. Markman (Eds.), *Carmichael's manual of child psychology* (Vol. 1, pp. 77–166). New York: Wiley.

Brown, A. L., & Campione, J. C. (1981). Inducing flexible thinking: A problem of access. In M. Friedman, J. P. Das, & N. O'Connor (Eds.), *Intelligence and learning* (pp. 515–529). New York: Plenum Press.

Brown, A. L., Campione, J. C., & Day, J. D. (1981).

Learning to learn: On training students to learn from texts. *Educational Researcher, 10,* 14–21.

Brown, J. W. (1986). Some motivational issues in computer-based instruction. *Educational Technology, 26*(4), 27–29.

Bryan, T. S. (1974). Observational analysis of classroom behaviors of children with learning disabilities. *Journal of Learning Disabilities, 7,* 26–34.

Budoff, M., Thormann, J., & Gras, A. (1984). *Microcomputers in special education.* Cambridge, MA: Brookline Books.

Butkowsky, I. S. (1982, August). *The generality of learned helplessness in children with learning difficulties.* Paper presented at the annual convention of the American Psychological Association, Washington, DC.

Butkowsky, I. S., & Willows, D. M. (1980). Cognitive-motivational characteristics of children varying in reading ability: Evidence for learned helplessness in poor readers. *Journal of Educational Psychology, 72,* 408–422.

Calfee, R. (1981). Cognitive psychology and educational practice. In D. C. Berliner (Ed.), *Review of research in education* (Vol. 9, pp. 3–73). Washington, DC: American Educational Research Association.

Campione, J. C., Brown, A. L., & Ferrara, R. A. (1982). Mental retardation and intelligence. In R. J. Sternberg (Ed.), *Handbook of human intelligence* (pp. 392–490). New York: Cambridge University Press.

Carlson, S. A., and Silverman, R. (1986). Microcomputers and computer-assisted instruction in special classrooms: Do we need the teacher? *Learning Disability Quarterly, 9*(2), 105–110.

Carpenter, T. P., & Peterson, P. L. (Eds). (1988). Learning mathematics through instruction [Special issue]. *Educational Psychologist, 23,* 79–85.

Cavanaugh, J. C., & Perlmutter, M. (1982). Metamemory: A critical examination. *Child Development, 53,* 11–28.

Chi, M. T. H. (1981). Knowledge development and memory performance. In M. Friedman, J. P. Das, & N. O'Connor (Eds.), *Intelligence and learning.* New York: Plenum Press.

Clark, F. E., & Angert, J. F. (1984). Is there a light at the end of the tunnel vision? *Instructional Innovator, 29*(2), 10–14.

Clements, D. H. (1986). Effects of Logo and CAI environments on cognition and creativity. *Journal of Educational Psychology, 78*(4), 309–318.

Clifford, M. M. (1984). Thoughts of a theory of constructive failure. *Educational Psychologist, 19,* 108–120.

Clifford, M. M. (1986). *Human motivation.* Unpublished manuscript, University of Iowa, Iowa City, IA.

Covington, M. V., & Beery, R. G. (1976). *Self-worth and school learning.* New York: Holt, Rinehart and Winston.

Covington, M. V., & Omelich, C. L. (1979). Effort: The double-edged sword in school achievement. *Journal of Educational Psychology, 71,* 169–182.

Covington, M. V., & Omelich, C. L. (1981). As failures mount: Affective and cognitive consequences of ability demotion in the classroom. *Journal of Educational Psychology, 73,* 796–808.

Csikszentmihalyi, M. (1975). *Beyond boredom and anxiety,* San Francisco: Jossey-Bass.

Csikszentmihalyi, M. (1978). Intrinsic rewards and emergent motivation. In M. R. Lepper & D. Green (Eds.), *The hidden costs of reward.* Hillsdale, NJ: Lawrence Erlbaum.

Davidson, J. E., & Sternberg, R. J. (1984). The role of insight in intellectual giftedness. *Gifted Child Quarterly, 28,* 58–64.

DeCharms, R. (1968). *Personal causation: The internal affective determinants of behavior.* New York: Academic Press.

DeCharms, R. (1972). Personal causation training in the schools. *Journal of Applied Social Psychology, 2,* 95–113.

DeCharms, R. (1978). The origins of competence and achievement motivation in personal causation. In L. J. Fyans, Jr. (Ed.), *Achievement motivation* (pp. 22–33). New York: Plenum Press.

Deci, E. L. (1971). Effects of externally mediated rewards on intrinsic motivation. *Journal of Personality and Social Psychology, 18,* 105–115.

Deci, E. L. (1972). The effects of contingent and noncontingent rewards and controls on intrinsic motivation. *Organizational Behavior and Human Performance, 8,* 219–222.

Deci, E. L. (1975). *Intrinsic motivation.* New York: Plenum Press.

Dee-Lucas, D., & DiVesta, F. J. (1980). Learner generated organizational aids: Effects on learning from text. *Journal of Educational Psychology, 72,* 304–311.

Diener, C. I., & Dweck, C. S. (1978). An analysis of learned helplessness: Continuous changes in performance, strategy, and achievement cognitions following failure. *Journal of Personality and Social Psychology, 36,* 451–462.

Doctorow, M. J., Wittrock, M. C., & Marks, C. B. (1978). Generative processes in reading comprehension. *Journal of Educational Psychology, 70,* 109–118.

Dooling, D. J., & Lachman, R. (1971). Effects of comprehension on retention of prose. *Journal of Experimental Psychology, 88,* 216–222.

Douglas, V. I., Parry, P., Martin, P., & Garson, C. (1976). Assessment of a cognitive training program for hyperactive children. *Journal of Abnormal Child Psychology, 4,* 389–410.

Doyle, W. (1977). Paradigms for research on teacher effectiveness. In L. S. Schulman (Ed.), *Review of research in education* (Vol. 5, pp. 163–198). Itasca, IL: F. E. Peacock.

Doyle, W. (1980). *Student mediating responses in teaching effectiveness* (Final Report NIE-G-76-0099). Denton: North Texas State University.

Duncker, K. (1945). On problem solving (L. S. Lees, Trans.) *Psychological Monographs, 58* (Whole No. 270).

Dunkin, M., & Biddle, B. (1974). *The study of teaching.* New York: Holt, Rinehart and Winston.

Dunkin, M., & Doeneu, S. (1980). A replication study of unique and joint contributions to variance in student achievement. *Journal of Educational Psychology, 72,* 394–403.

Dweck, C. S. (1975). The role of expectations and

attributions in the alleviation of learned helplessness. *Journal of Personality and Social Psychology, 31,* 674–685.

Dweck, C. S. (1986). Motivational processes affecting learning. *American Psychologist, 41,* 1040–1048.

Dweck, C. S. (1987, April). *Children's theories of intelligence: Implications for motivation and learning.* Invited address presented at the meeting of the American Educational Research Association, Washington, DC.

Dweck, C. S., Davidson, W., Nelson, S., & Enna, B. (1978). Sex differences in learned helplessness: 2. The contingencies of evaluative feedback in the classroom: 3. An experiment analysis. *Developmental Psychology, 14,* 268–276.

Dweck, C. S., & Elliot, E. S. (1983). Achievement motivation. In E. M. Herrington (Ed.), *Socialization, personality, and social development* (pp. 643–691). New York: Wiley.

Dweck, C. S., Goetz, T. E., & Strauss, N. L. (1980). Sex differences in learned helplessness: IV. An experimental and naturalistic study of failure generalization and its mediators. *Journal of Personality and Social Psychology, 38,* 441–452.

Edwards, J., Norton, S., Taylor, S., Weiss, M., & Dusseldorp, R. (1975). How effective is CAI? A review of the research. *Educational Leadership, 33*(2), 147–153.

Englert, C. S. (1984). Effective direct instruction practices in special education settings. *Remedial & Special Education, 5*(2), 38–47.

Ennals, R., & Briggs, J. (1985). Fifth generation computing: Introducing micro-Prolog into the classroom. *Journal of Educational Computing Research, 11*(1), 97–111.

Eswara, H. S. (1972). Administration of reward and punishment in relation to ability, effort, and performance. *Journal of Social Psychology, 87,* 139–140.

Fennema, E. (1985). Attribution theory and achievement in mathematics. In S. R. Yussen (Ed.), *The growth of reflection in children* (pp. 245–265). Orlando, FL: Academic Press.

Fennema, E., & Sherman, J. (1977). Sex-related differences in mathematics achievement, spatial visualization and affective factors. *American Educational Research Journal, 14,* 51–71.

Flavell, J. H. (1976). Metacognitive aspects of problem solving. In L. B. Resnick (Ed.), *The nature of intelligence* (pp. 231–235). Hillsdale, NJ: Lawrence Erlbaum.

Flavell, J. H., & Wellman, H. M. (1977). Metamemory. In R. V. Kail, Jr., & J. W. Hagen (Eds.), *Perspectives on the development of memory and cognition* (pp. 3–33). Hillsdale, NJ: Lawrence Erlbaum.

Freize, I. H. (1976). Causal attributions and information seeking to explain success and failure. *Journal of Research in Personality, 10,* 293–305.

Gick, M. L., & Holyoak, K. J. (1980). Analogical problem solving. *Cognitive Psychology, 12,* 306–365.

Glaser, R. (1984). Education and thinking: The role of knowledge. *American Psychologist, 39,* 93–104.

Glaser, R. (1985). All's well that begins and ends with

both knowledge and process: A reply to Sternberg. *American Psychologist, 40,* 573–574.

Glynn, S. M., & DiVesta, F. J. (1977). Outline and hierarchical organization as aids for study and retrieval. *Journal of Educational Psychology, 69,* 89–95.

Goldman, S. R., & Pellegrino, J. W. (1987). Information processing and educational microcomputer technology: Where do we go from here? *Journal of Learning Disabilities, 20*(3), 144–154.

Good, T. L. (1983). Classroom research: A decade of progress. *Educational Psychologist, 18,* 127–144.

Greene, D., & Lepper, M. R. (1974). Effects of extrinsic rewards on children's subsequent intrinsic interest. *Child Development, 45,* 1141–1145.

Hallahan, D. P., Kauffman, J. M., & Ball, D. (1973). Selective attention and cognitive tempo of low-achieving and high-achieving sixth grade males. *Perceptual and Motor Skills, 36,* 579–583.

Harter, S. (1978a). Effectance motivation reconsidered: Toward a developmental model. *Human Development, 21,* 34–64.

Harter, S. (1987b). Pleasure derived from challenge and the effects of receiving grades on children's subsequent intrinsic interest. *Child Development, 49,* 788–799.

Hilton, T., & Berglund, G. (1974). Sex differences in mathematics achievement—A longitudinal study. *Journal of Education Research, 67,* 231–237.

Hummel, J. W., & Degnan, S. C. (1986). Options for technology-assisted IEPS. *Journal of Learning Disabilities, 19*(9), 562–566.

Isenberg, R. A. (1985). Computer-aided instruction and the mainstreamed learning disabled student. *Journal of Learning Disabilities, 18*(9), 557–558.

Jacobsen, B., Lowery, B., & DuCette, J. (1986). *Journal of Educational Psychology, 78,* 59–64.

Johanson, R. P. (1987). Disciplinary disincentives: Attendance and grading policies. *Proteus, 4*(1), 19–22.

Johanson, R. P. (1988). Computers, cognition and curriculum: Retrospect and prospect. *Journal of Educational Computing Research, 4*(1), 1–30.

Jones, S. L., Nation, J. R., & Massad, P. (1977). Immunization against learned helplessness in man. *Journal of Abnormal Psychology, 86,* 75–83.

Keith, T. Z. (1982). Time spent on homework and high school grades: A large-sample path analysis. *Journal of Educational Psychology, 74,* 248–253.

Keith, T. Z., & Page, E. B. (1985). Homework works at school: National evidence for policy changes. *School Psychology Review, 14*(3), 351–359.

Kendler, T. S., & Kendler, H. H. (1962). Inferential behavior as a function of subgoal constancy and age. *Journal of Experimental Psychology, 64,* 460–466.

Kolich, E. M. (1985). Microcomputer technology with the learning disabled: A review of the literature. *Journal of Learning Disabilities, 18*(7), 428–431.

Kruglanski, A. W. (1975). The endogenous–exogenous partition in attribution theory. *Psychological Review, 82,* 387–406.

Kruglanski, A. W. (1978). Issues in cognitive social psychology. In M. R. Lepper & D. Greene (Eds.),

The hidden costs of reward (pp. 19–29). Hillsdale, NJ: Lawrence Erlbaum.

Krupski, A. (1980). Attention processes: Research, theory, and implications for special education. In B. Keogh (Ed.), *Advances in special education* (Vol. 1, pp. 101–140). Greenwich, CT: JAI Press.

Kulik, J. A., Bangert, R. L., and Williams, G. W. (1983). Effects of computer-based teaching on secondary students. *Journal of Educational Psychology, 75*(1), 19–26.

Kurland, D. M., Pea, R. D., Clement, C., & Mawby, R. (1986). A study of the development of programming ability and thinking skills in high school students. *Journal of Educational Computing Research, 2*(4), 429–457.

Lara, A. V., & Medley, D. M. (1987). Effective teacher behavior as a function of learner ability. *Professional School Psychology, 2*(1), 15–23.

Lefcourt, H. M. (1982). *Locus of control: Current trends in theory and research* (2nd ed.). Hillsdale, NJ: Lawrence Erlbaum.

Leggett, E. (1985, March). *Children's entity and incremental theories of intelligence: Relationships to achievement behavior.* Paper presented at the meeting of the Eastern Psychological Association, Boston.

Leggett, E. (1986, April). *Individual differences in effort-ability inference rules: Implications for causal judgments.* Paper presented at the meeting of the Eastern Psychological Association, New York.

Lepper, M. R. (1973). Dissonance, self-perception, and honesty in children. *Journal of Personality and Social Psychology, 25,* 65–74.

Lepper, M. R. (1980). Intrinsic and extrinsic motivation in children: Detrimental effects of superfluous social control. In W. A. Collins (Ed.), *Aspects of the development of competence: The Minnesota symposium on child psychology* (Vol. 14). Hillsdale, NJ: Lawrence Erlbaum.

Lepper, M. R. (1985). Microcomputers in education: Motivational and social issues. *American Psychologist, 40*(1), 1–18.

Lepper, M. R., & Greene, D. (1975). Turning play into work: Effects of adult surveillance and extrinsic rewards on children's intrinsic motivation. *Journal of Personality and Social Psychology, 31,* 479–486.

Lepper, M. R., & Greene, D. (1978). Divergent approaches to the study of rewards. In M. R. Lepper & D. Greene (Eds.), *The hidden costs of reward* (pp. 217–244.) Hillsdale, NJ: Lawrence Erlbaum.

Lepper, M. R., Greene, D., & Nisbett, R. E. (1973). Undetermining children's intrinsic interest and extrinsic rewards: A test of the "overjustification" hypothesis. *Journal of Personality and Social Psychology, 23,* 129–137.

Levin, J. R., & Pressley, M. (Eds.). (1986). Learning strategies [Special issue]. *Educational Psychologist, 21* (1 and 2).

Levine, M. (1966). Hypothesis behavior by humans during discrimination learning. *Journal of Experimental Psychology, 71,* 331–338.

Licht, B. G. (1983). Cognitive-motivational factors that contribute to the achievement of learning disabled children. *Journal of Learning Disabilities, 8,* 483–490.

Licht, B. G., & Dweck, C. S. (1983). Sex differences in achievement orientations: Consequences for academic choices and attainments. In M. Marland (Ed.), *Sex differentiation and schooling* (pp. 72–97). London: Heinemann.

Licht, B. G., & Dweck, C. S. (1984). Determinants of academic achievement: The interactions of children's achievement orientations with skill area. *Developmental Psychology, 20,* 628–636.

Licht, B. S., Kistner, J. A., Ozkaragoz, T., Shapiro, S., & Clausen S. (1985). Causal attributions of learning disabled children: Individual differences and their implications for persistence. *Journal of Educational Psychology, 77,* 208–216.

Linn, M. C. (1985). The cognitive consequences of programming instruction in classrooms. *Educational Researcher, 14*(5), 14–16, 25–29.

Luchins, A. S. (1942). Mechanization in problem solving. *Psychological Monographs, 54* (Whole No. 248).

Luchins, A. S., & Luchins, E. H. (1950). New experimental attempts at providing mechanization in problem solving. *Journal of General Psychology, 42,* 279–297.

MacArthur, C. A., & Schneiderman, B. (1986). Learning disabled students' difficulties in learning to use a word processor: Implications for instruction and software evaluation. *Journal of Learning Disabilities, 19*(4), 248–253.

Malamuth, Z. (1979). Self-management training for children with reading problems: Effects on reading performance and sustained attention. *Cognitive Therapy and Research, 3,* 279–289.

Manion, M. H. (1986). Computers and behavior disordered students: A rationale and review of the literature. *Educational.Technology, 26*(7), 20–24.

Marks, C. B., Doctorow, M. J., & Wittrock, M. C. (1974). Word frequency in reading comprehension. *Journal of Educational Research, 67,* 259–262.

Marr, D. B., & Sternberg, R. J. (1986). Analogical reasoning with novel concepts: Differential attention of intellectually gifted and nongifted children to relevant and irrelevant stimuli. *Cognitive Development, 1,* 53–72.

Mayer, R. E. (1975). Different problem solving competencies established in learning computer programming with and without meaningful models. *Journal of Educational Psychology, 67,* 725–734.

Mayer, R. E. (1976). Some conditions of meaningful learning for computer programming: Advance organizers and subject control of frame sequencing. *Journal of Educational Psychology, 68,* 143–150.

Mayer, R. E. (1979). Twenty years of research on advance organizers: Assimilation theory is still the best predictor of results. *Instructional Science, 8,* 133–167.

Mayer, R. E. (1982). Instructional variables in text processing. In A. Flammer & W. Kintsch (Eds.), *Discourse processing.* Amsterdam: North-Holland.

Mayer, R. E. (1983). Can you repeat that? Qualitative and quantitative effects of repetition and advance organizers on learning from science prose. *Journal of Educational Psychology, 75,* 40–49.

Mayer, R. E. (1984). Aids to prose comprehension. *Educational Psychologist, 19,* 30–42.

Mayer, R. E. (1987). *Educational Psychology: A cognitive approach.* Boston: Little, Brown.

McBride, J. R. (1985). Computerized adaptive testing. *Educational Leadership, 43*(2), 25–28.

McKeachie, W. J. (1974). The decline and fall of the laws of learning. *Educational Researcher, 3,* 7–11.

McKinney, J. D., McClure, S., & Feagans, L. (1982). Classroom behavior of learning disabled children. *Learning Disability Quarterly, 5,* 45–52.

McNabb, T. F. (1987, April). *The effects of strategy and effort attribution training on the motivation of subjects differing in perceived math competence and attitude toward effort.* Paper presented at the meeting of the American Educational Research Association, Washington, DC.

Medley, D. (1977). *Teacher competency and teacher effectiveness: A review of process-product research.* Washington DC: American Association of Colleges for Teacher Education.

Meichenbaum, D., & Asarnow, J. (1979). Cognitive-behavior modification and metacognitive development: Implications for the classroom. In P. Kendall & S. Hollen (Eds.), *Cognitive-behavioral interventions: Theory, research, and procedures* (pp. 11–35). New York: Academic Press.

Meichenbaum, D., Burland, S., Gruson, L., & Cameron, R. (1985). Metacognitive assessment. In S. R. Yussen (Ed.), *The growth of reflection in children.* New York: Academic Press.

Meichenbaum, D., & Goodman, J. (1971). Training impulsive children to talk to themselves: A means of developing self-control. *Journal of Abnormal Psychology, 77,* 115–126.

Metacognition and Learning Disabilities [Special issue]. (1982). *Topics in Learning and Learning Disabilities, 2,* 1–107.

Meyer, B. J. F., Brandt, D. H., & Bluth, G. J. (1980). Use of top-level structure in text: Key for reading comprehension of ninth-grade students. *Reading Research Quarterly, 16,* 72–103.

Miller, I. W., & Norman, W. H. (1979). Learned helplessness in humans: A review and attribution theory model. *Psychological Bulletin, 86,* 93–118.

Mokros, J. R., & Russell, S. J. (1986). Learner-centered software: A survey of microcomputer use with special needs students. *Journal of Learning Disabilities, 19*(3), 185–189.

Nicholls, J. G. (1975). Causal attributions and other achievement related cognitions: Effects of task outcome, attainment value, and sex. *Journal of Personality and Social Psychology, 31,* 379–389.

Nicholls, J. G. (1976). Effort is virtuous but it's better to have ability: Evaluative responses to perceptions of effort and ability. *Journal of Research in Personality, 10,* 306–315.

Nicholls, J. G. (1978). The development of concepts of effort and ability, perception of academic attainment, and the understanding that difficult tasks require more ability. *Developmental Psychology, 49,* 800–814.

Nicholls, J. G. (1984). Conceptions of ability and achievement motivation. In R. Ames & C. Ames (Eds.), *Research on motivation in education* (Vol. 1, pp. 39–73). New York: Academic Press.

Niemiec, R. P., and Walberg, H. J. (1985). Computers and achievement in the elementary schools. *Journal of Educational Computing Research, 1*(4), 435–440.

O'Brien, T. C. (1986). Three anchors and computer-assisted learning. *NASSP Bulletin, 70*(489), 18–24.

Osborne, R. J. (1981). Children's ideas about electric current. *New Zealand Science Teacher, 29,* 12–19.

Osborne, R. J., & Wittrock, M. C. (1983). Learning science: A generative process. *Science Education, 67,* 489–508.

Palmer, D. J., Drummond, F., Tollison, P., & Zinkgraff, S. (1982). An attributional investigation of performance outcome for learning-disabled and normal-achieving pupils. *The Journal of Special Education, 16,* 207–219.

Panyan, M. V. (1984). Computer technology for autistic students. *Journal of Autism and Developmental Disorders, 14*(4), 375–382.

Papert, S. (1980). *Mindstorms: Children, computers and powerful ideas.* New York: Basic Books.

Papert, S. (1984). Tomorrow's classrooms. In M. Yazdani (Ed.), *New horizons in educational computing* (pp. 17–20). Chichester, West Sussex, England: Ellis Horwood.

Papert, S. (1987). Computer criticism vs. technocentric thinking. *Educational Researcher, 16*(1), 22–30.

Parry, J. D., and Hofmeister, A. M. (1986). Development and validation of an expert system for special educators. *Learning Disability Quarterly, 9*(2), 124–132.

Pearl, R. A. (1982). LD children's attributions for success and failure: A replication with a labeled LD sample. *Learning Disability Quarterly, 5,* 173–176.

Pearl, R. A., Bryan, T., & Donahue, M. (1980). Learning disabled children's strategy analyses under high and low success conditions. *Learning Disability Quarterly, 6,* 67–74.

Perfetto, G. A., Bransford, J. D., & Franks, J. J. (1983). Constraints on access in a problem solving context. *Memory and Cognition, 11,* 24–31.

Peterson, P. L. (1987, April). *Teachers' and students' cognitions as mediators of teaching effectiveness.* Invited address given at the annual meeting of the American Educational Research Association, Washington, DC.

Peterson, P. L., & Swing, S. R. (1982). Beyond time on task: Students' reports of their thought processes during classroom instruction. *Elementary School Journal, 82,* 481–491.

Peterson, P. L., Swing, S. R., Braverman, M. T., & Buss, R. (1982). Students' aptitudes and their reports of cognitive processes during direct instruction. *Journal of Educational Psychology, 74,* 535–547.

Peterson, P. L., Swing, S. R., Stark, K. D., & Waas, G. A. (1984). Students' cognition and time on task during mathematics instruction. *American Educational Research Journal, 21,* 487–515.

Phillips, B. N. (1982). Reading and evaluating research in school psychology. In C. R. Reynolds & T. B. Gutkin (Eds.), *The handbook of school psychology* (pp. 24–47). New York: Wiley.

Pichert, J. W., & Anderson, R. C. (1977). Taking different perspectives on a story. *Journal of Educational Psychology, 69,* 309–315.

Pogrow, S., & Buchanan, B. (1985). Higher order thinking for compensatory students. *Educational Leadership, 43*(1), 41–43.

Rest, S., Nierenberg, R., Weiner, B., & Heckhausen, H. (1973). Further evidence concerning the effects of perceptions of effort and ability on achievement evaluation. *Journal of Personality and Social Psychology, 28,* 187–191.

Richards, J. P., & August, G. J. (1975). Generative underlining strategies in prose recall. *Journal of Educational Psychology, 67,* 860–865.

Rosenshine, B. (1971). *Teaching behaviors and student achievement.* London: National Foundation for Educational Research.

Rotter, J. (1954). *Social learning and clinical psychology.* Englewood Cliffs, NJ: Prentice-Hall.

Rotter, J. (1966). Generalized expectancies for internal versus external control of reinforcement. *Psychological Monographs, 80,* 1–28.

Royer, J. M., & Cable, G. W. (1975). Facilitated learning in connected discourse. *Journal of Educational Psychology, 67,* 116–123.

Royer, J. M., & Cable, G. W. (1976). Illustrations, analogies, and facilitative transfer in prose learning. *Journal of Educational Psychology, 68,* 205–209.

Russell, S. J. (1986). But what are they learning? The dilemma of using microcomputers in special education. *Learning Disability Quarterly, 9*(2), 100–104.

Ryan, Lynne B., & Rucker, C. N. (1986). Computerized vs. noncomputerized individualized education programs: Teachers' attitudes, time and cost. *Journal of Special Education Technology, 8*(1), 5–12.

Salend, S. J., and Salend, S. M. (1985). Implications of using microcomputers in classroom testing. *Journal of Learning Disabilities, 18*(1), 51–53.

Schmidt, M., Weinstein, T., Niemic, R., and Walberg, H. J. (1985–1986). Computer-assisted instruction with exceptional children. *The Journal of Special Education, 19*(4), 493–501.

Schneider, W., & Shiffrin, R. M. (1977). Controlled and automatic information processing: I. Detection, search, and attention. *Psychological Review, 84,* 1–66.

Schunk, D. H. (1983). Ability vs. attributional feedback: Differential effects on self-efficacy and achievement. *Journal of Educational Psychology, 75,* 848–856.

Schunk, D. H. (1984). Sequential attributional feedback and children's achievement behaviors. *Journal of Educational Psychology, 76,* 1159–1169.

Schunk, D. H. (1985). Self-efficacy and classroom learning. *Psychology in the schools, 22,* 208–223.

Schunk, D. H., & Cox, P. D. (1986). Strategy training and attributional feedback with learning disabled students. *Journal of Educational Psychology, 78,* 201–209.

Seligman, M. E. P., & Maier, S. F. (1967). Failure to escape traumatic shock. *Journal of Experimental Psychology, 74,* 1–9.

Short, E. J., & Ryan, E. B. (1984). Metacognitive differences between skilled and less skilled readers: Remediating deficits through story grammar and attribution training. *Journal of Educational Psychology, 76,* 225–235.

Shuell, T. J. (1986). Cognitive conceptions of learning. *Review of Educational Research, 56,* 411–436.

Siegler, R. S., & Klahr, D. (1982). When do children learn? The relationship between existing knowledge and the acquisition of new knowledge. In R. Glaser (Ed.), *Advances in instructional psychology* (Vol. 2, pp. 121–211). Hillsdale, NJ: Lawrence Erlbaum.

Siegler, R. S., & Richards, D. D. (1982). The development of intelligence. In R. J. Sternberg (Ed.), *Handbook of human intelligence* (pp. 897–971). New York: Cambridge University Press.

Simon, H. A., & Hayes, J. R. (1976). The understanding process: Problem isomorphs. *Cognitive Psychology, 8,* 65–190.

Simon, H. A., & Hayes, J. R. (1977). Psychological differences among problem isomorphs. In N. J. Castelan, D. B. Pisoni, & G. R. Potts (Eds.), *Cognitive theory* (Vol. 2, pp. 21–41). Hillsdale, NJ: Lawrence Erlbaum.

Slesnick, T. (1984). Computer education research: A blinder for the misguided. *Proceedings of NECC '84: 6th Annual National Educational Computing Conference,* Dayton, OH.

Slife, B. D., Weiss, J., & Bell, T. (1985). Separability of metacognition and cognition: Problem solving of learning disabled and regular students. *Journal of Educational Psychology, 77,* 437–445.

Smith, R. L. (1985–1986). Computers and the gifted. *Journal of Computers in Mathematics and Science Teaching, 5*(2), 70–71.

Soar, R. S., & Soar, R. M. (1979). Emotional climate and man. In P. Peterson & H. Walberg (Eds.), *Research on teaching concepts, findings, and implications.* Berkeley, CA: McCutchan.

Soar, R. S., & Soar, R. M. (1987). Classroom management and affect expression. *Professional School Psychology, 2*(1), 3–14.

Sperber, R. D., Ragain, R. D., & McCauley, C. (1976). Reassessment of category knowledge in retarded individuals. *American Journal of Mental Deficiency, 81,* 227–234.

Stein, B. S., & Bransford, J. D. (1979). Constraints on effective elaboration: Effects of precision and subject generation. *Journal of Verbal Learning and Verbal Behavior, 18,* 769–777.

Sternberg, R. J. (1985). Review of Meichenbaum, Burland, Gruson, and Cameron's "Metacognitive Assessment". In S. R. Yussen (Ed.), *The growth of reflection in children.* Orlando, FL: Academic Press.

Stearns, P. H. (1986). Problem solving and the learning

disabled: Looking for answers with computers. *Journal of Learning Disabilities, 19*(2), 116–120.

Stipek, D. J., & Hoffman, J. (1980). Development of Children's performance-related judgments. *Child Development, 51,* 912–914.

Tarver, S. G., Hallahan, D. P., Kauffman, J. M., & Ball, D. W. (1976). Verbal rehearsal and selective attention in children with learning disabilities: A developmental lag. *Journal of Experimental Child Psychology, 22,* 375–385.

Taylor, R. (1980). *The computer in the school: Tutor, tool, tutee.* New York: Teachers College Press.

Thurstone, L. L. (1924). *The nature of intelligence.* New York: Harcourt, Brace.

Tobin, K. (1986). Effects of teacher wait time on discourse characteristics in mathematics and language arts classes. *American Educational Research Journal, 23,* 191–200.

Tobin, K., & Capie, W. (1983). The influence of wait time on classroom learning. *European Journal of Science Education, 5,* 35–48.

Torgeson, J. K. (1977). Memorization processes in reading-disabled children. *Journal of Educational Psychology, 69,* 571–578.

Torgeson, J. K., & Young, K. A. (1983). Priorities for the use of microcomputers with learning disabled children. *Journal of Learning Disabilities, 16*(4), 234–237.

Vinsonhaler, J. F., and Bass, R. K. (1972). A summary of ten major studies on CAI drill and practice. *Educational Technology, 12*(7), 29–32.

Walberg, H. J., & Tsai, S.-L. (1984). Reading achievement and diminishing returns to time. *Journal of Educational Psychology, 76*(3), 442–451.

Waugh, M. L., and Currier, D. (1986). Computer-based education: What we know and need to know. *Journal of Computers in Mathematics and Science Teaching, 5*(3), 13–15.

Weiner, B. (1979). A theory of motivation for some classroom experiences. *Journal of Educational Psychology, 71,* 3–25.

Weiner, B., Graham, S., Taylor, S., & Meyer, W. (1983). Social cognition in the classroom. *Educational Psychologist, 18,* 109–124.

Weiner, B., & Kukla, A. (1970). An attributional analysis of achievement motivation. *Journal of Personality and Social Psychology, 15,* 1–20.

Weiner, B., Russell, D., & Lerman, D. (1978). Affective consequences of causal ascriptions. In J. H. Harvey, W. J. Ickes, & R. F. Kidd (Eds.), *New directions in attribution research* (Vol. 2, pp. 59–90). Hillsdale, NJ: Lawrence Erlbaum.

Weinstein, C. F., & Mayer, R. F. (1986). The teaching of learning strategies. In M. C. Wittrock (Ed.), *Handbook of research on teaching* (3rd ed., pp. 297–314). New York: Macmillan.

Weir, S., Russel, S. J., and Valente, J. A. (1982). Logo: An approach to educating disabled children. *BYTE, 7*(9), 342–360.

Weisz, J. R., & Stipek, D. (1982). Competence, contingency, and the development of perceived control. *Human Development, 25,* 250–281.

West, L. H. T., & Fensham, P. J. (1976). Prior knowledge or advance organizers are affective variables in chemical learning. *Journal of Research in Science Teaching, 13,* 297–306.

White, R. T., & Mayer, R. E. (1980). Understanding intellectual skills. *Instructional Science, 9,* 101–107.

White, R. W. (1959). Motivation reconsidered: The concept of competence. *Psychological Review, 66,* 297–333.

Whitehead, A. N. (1929). *The aims of education.* New York: MacMillan.

Wiig, E. H., & Semel, E. M. (1973). Comprehension of linguistic concepts requiring logical operations by learning disabled children. *Journal of Speech and Learning Research, 16,* 627–636.

Wiig, E. H., & Semel, E. M. (1974). Development of comprehension and logico-grammatical sentences by grade school children. *Perceptual and Motor Skills, 38,* 171–176.

Winne, P. H. (1982). Minimizing the black box problem to enhance the validity of theories about instructional effects. *Instructional Science, 11,* 13–28.

Winne, P. H. (1985). Steps toward promoting cognitive achievements. *The Elementary School Journal, 85,* 673–693.

Winne, P. H., & Marx, R. W. (1977). Reconceptualizing research on teaching. *Journal of Educational Psychology, 69,* 668–678.

Winne, P. H., & Marx, R. W. (1980). Matching students' cognition responses to teaching skills. *Journal of Educational Psychology, 72,* 257–264.

Winne, P. H., & Marx, R. W. (1982). Students' and teachers' views of thinking processes involved in classroom learning. *Elementary School Journal, 82,* 493–518.

Winne, P. H., & Marx, R. W. (1983). *Students' cognitive processes while learning from teaching* (Final Report, NIE-G-0098). Burnaby, British Columbia: Simon Fraser University, Faculty of Education.

Wittrock, M. C. (1978). The cognitive movement in instruction. *Educational Psychologist, 13,* 15–30.

Wittrock, M. C. (1981). Reading comprehension. In F. J. Pirozzolo & M. C. Wittrock (Eds.), *Neuropsychological and cognitive processes of reading* (pp. 229–259). New York: Academic Press.

Wittrock, M. C. (1986). Students' thought processes. In M. C. Wittrock (Ed.), *Handbook of research on teaching* (3rd ed., pp. 297–314). New York: Macmillan.

Wong, B. Y. L., & Jones, W. (1982). Increasing metacomprehension in learning disabled and normally achieving students through self-questioning training. *Learning Disability Quarterly, 5,* 228–240.

Wortman, C. B., & Brehm, J. (1975). Responses to uncontrollable outcomes: An integration of reactance theory and the learned helplessness model. In L. Berkowitz (Ed.), *Advances in experimental social psychology* (Vol. 8, pp. 277–336). New York: Academic Press.

Ysseldyke, J. E., Reynolds, M. C., & Weinberg, R. A. (1984). *School psychology: A blueprint for training and practice.* Minneapolis, MN: National School Psychology Inservice Training Network.

Yussen, S. R., & Kane, P. T. (1985). Children's conception of intelligence. In S. R. Yussen (Ed.), *The growth of reflection in children* (pp. 207–241). New York: Academic Press.

Zeamon, D., & House, B. (1963). The role of attention in retardate discrimination learning. In N. Ellis (Ed.), *Handbook of mental deficiency* (pp. 159–223). New York: McGraw-Hill.

8

CONTRIBUTIONS OF SOCIAL PSYCHOLOGY TO SCHOOL PSYCHOLOGY

FREDERIC J. MEDWAY
THOMAS P. CAFFERTY
University of South Carolina

In 1897, Triplett published in the *American Journal of Psychology* the results of what is generally considered the first experiment in social psychology. The experiment concerned the effects of the presence of others on the performance of a simple motor task. For the majority of his subjects, Triplett found that performing in the presence of other people "positively stimulated," or facilitated, performance relative to performing in a solitary condition. Not only did Triplett investigate a process at the center of social psychology but it is particularly noteworthy, in light of this chapter's focus, that his sample was 40 children ranging in age from 8 to 17, drawn from schools around Indiana University. The results of the study and others following upon it had important implications for educational practices at the time. So it may be said that modern social psychology at its very inception was focused on issues and settings of interest to school psychology.

In the present chapter we define social psychology, briefly review historical developments in the area, and discuss selected areas of social psychology which in our opinion have particular relevance to school psychologists. Because of limitations on length, coverage of the topics will be more cursory than we would like. To remedy this, we try to give a concise review of some of the more traditional literature together with a few comprehensive references, followed by a more detailed discussion of some promising directions in the more recent literature.

THE FIELD OF SOCIAL PSYCHOLOGY

What Is Social Psychology?

Most social psychologists would accept G. Allport's definition of social psychology as "an attempt to understand and explain how the thought, feeling, and behavior of individuals are influenced by the actual, imagined, or implied presence of others" (1985, p. 3). As implied by the definition, social psychologists have a potentially unlimited array of topics that could be considered areas of study. For a variety of theoretical, historical, and practical reasons (Cartwright, 1979; Hendrick, 1977; Jones, 1985), the actual number of topics studied has been more modest, with most interest in recent years generated by such issues as (a) attitudes and attitude change, (b) attribution, (c) cognitive processes, (d) social and personal development, (e) attraction and affiliation, (f) sex roles, and (g) aggression (S. S. Smith, Richardson, & Hendrick, 1980).

In addition to the substantive areas just mentioned, social psychologists have conducted extensive research on the methodological issues involved in conducting experiments or field studies (see Rosenthal & Rosnow, 1985; Wuebben, Straits, & Schulman, 1974). These include experimental demand characteristics, subject roles, placebo effects, experimenter expectations, and other unintended influences. Social psychology also is the discipline that has developed the techniques and procedures used in group dynamics and program evaluation. Although most of the 4500 or so social psychologists in the United States (American Psychological Association Directory, 1986) are employed in higher education settings, it is not unusual to find many involved in evaluating programs such as Head Start, assisting in working out school integration plans, or providing interpersonal skills training in the community. Because of their particular skills and expertise and the contributions to school psychology, some have argued that schools should actually hire social psychologists to do organizational consultation and improve school learning environments (Lighthall, 1969; Medway, 1975).

The Development of Contemporary Social Psychology

If we take Triplett's study, described earlier, as the starting point for modern social psychology, the area is scarcely 90 years old. However, interest in understanding human social behavior can be traced back at least 2000 years, initially to early philosophers, later to sociologists, and subsequently to experimental psychologists. In this section we briefly review the contributions of the various disciplines as well as various historical events that shaped social psychology. A thorough view is offered by G. Allport (1985), and to a lesser extent in an overview of experimental social psychology by Hendrick (1977).

Contributions of Philosophy

Speculation about the origins and nature of social behavior existed long before the advent of an empirical social psychology. In Greek antiquity, Plato argued that social behavior was a manifestation of innate physiological characteristics of the members of a society. The type of social structure depended on the part of the body—head, heart, or stomach—that was dominant among the members of a society. Aristotle, while also something of a nativist, placed greater stress on the role of the environment in the production of social behavior (Sahakian, 1974). This "nature–nurture" or "organism–environment" dichotomy continues to be a basis for debate in the social sciences even in contemporary times, and appears most strongly in social psychology in alternative views of the bases for altruistic and aggressive behavior.

The era of social philosophizing that immediately preceded the emergence of modern social psychology was strongly influenced by scientific advances of the eighteenth and nineteenth centuries, especially Darwin's theory of evolution. This was an era marked by what G. Allport (1985) has termed "simple and sovereign theories," explanations for social behavior based on single overarching principles such as hedonism, egoism, sympathy, or imitation. One of the earliest social psychology texts, that of McDougall (1908), was based on a version of the imitation theory. Vestiges of these theories are found today across many subareas of psychology, and have become embedded in pedagogical theory as developed to provide the foundations for systems of universal education. It is often possible to trace back the fundamental assumptions about behavior that underlie various teacher training programs to these simple and sovereign theories. Although these theories continue to influence social psychology indirectly, social psychologists have by and large abandoned them in favor of what Merton (1957) has called "theories of the middle range," developed to deal with specific aspects of behavior or specific circumstances, such as helping behavior, aggression, social learning, social influence, interpersonal relations, and cooperation and competition (Hendrick, 1977).

Contributions of Sociology

While the term social psychology would seem to denote a synthesis of sociology and psychology, that synthesis has been rather incomplete. Early sociologists tended to study social behavior in the aggregate, viewing the group as an "organic whole"—a view perhaps best exemplified by Durkheim (1951), who studied the problem of suicide as a phenomenon that occurred for different reasons depending on societal circumstances. Psychologists, strongly influenced by their origins in physiology, tended to view the group as simply a collection of individuals behaving according to principles that could best be understood on the level of the individual. The most prominent spokesperson for this point of view was F. Allport (1924).

The scientific estrangement between sociology and psychology resulted in a failure among psychologists to appreciate and fully utilize the theoretical contributions of social psychologically oriented sociologists such as Simmel (1950), Cooley (1918), and Mead (1934). However, this oversight is rapidly being corrected, particularly as social psychologists revive interest in social development and in the self, acknowledging the major contributions of sociologists to this important area.

Emergence of Social Psychology

Returning to the origins of empirical social psychology, there are three aspects of Triplett's study that make it a harbinger of things to come in the field. First, it was solidly in the psychological tradition, with its focus on individual behavior in the group rather than on the group per se. As has already been discussed, social psychology would remain dominated by a psychological orientation in its development. Second, Triplett's study was a laboratory experiment. Despite some notable exceptions, the vast majority of social psychology studies would be conducted in the laboratory and use the experimental method for investigating phenomena of interest. The limitations on the generalizability and utility of such an approach have been widely discussed and debated (see Elms, 1975; Hovland, 1959; McGuire, 1967; Ring, 1967). Third, the study was conducted in the United States. Much of social psychology, then and now, has largely been an American enterprise and suffers from a lack of input from other cultures. While this limitation is being remedied by a growing worldwide interest in the field (see Moscovici, 1972), most of the subjects for social psychological research have been male college undergraduates. Thus, one must use

caution in interpreting and generalizing results from many traditional studies, a problem of clear concern to the school psychologist, whose clients include children, adults, males, and females, from diverse backgrounds and cultures.

Following Triplett's study, evidence that social psychology was becoming an area of considerable interest can be found in the publication of the first two textbooks bearing the title *Social Psychology* in 1908, although neither text was to become part of the mainstream of the area. One, by McDougall (1908), was based largely on his "hormic" or instinctive theories of behavior; while the other, by Ross (1908), was a sociology text with emphasis on group phenomena. More in the mainstream was the later textbook by F. Allport (1924), with its strong behaviorist flavor.

Most social psychologists, however, believe that the major developments of modern social psychology did not occur until the 1930s, with the greatest impetus provided by circumstances associated with World War II (see Cartwright, 1979; Hendrick, 1977; Jones, 1985). Many of these developments are summarized in Table 1. The main forces contributing to the upsurge of research in this period included technical advances in the measurement of attitudes through the use of self-report scales, demonstrations of the ability to investigate group norms in the laboratory, and an influx of European psychologists, such as Kurt Lewin, who initiated the systemic study of group dynamics.

Between World War II and the late 1950s, the field was dominated by the study of attitude change, group dynamics, and conformity. The two major theoretical orientations were the S-R tradition of behavioral psychology and the cognitive-perceptual orientation of the Gestalt psychologists from Europe. In 1957, Festinger published his theory of cognitive dissonance, which had been derived from the cognitive orientation. Although the theory applied to a variety of judgmental, attitudinal, and behavioral tasks, it was applied most strongly to the study of attitude change. Its simplicity and empirical support appealed to many social psychologists and made dissonance phenomena the dominant topic of interest for over a decade.

In the mid-1960s the field broadened in response to new theoretical developments and calls for more relevance. The calls for relevance stem-

TABLE 1   Landmarks in the History of Social Psychology

Date	Milestone
1897	Triplett conducts the first social psychological experiment.
1908	McDougall and Ross publish the first two social psychology texts.
1924	Allport publishes his behaviorist-oriented text in social psychology.
1928	L.L. Thurstone introduces the era of attitude measurement and assessment.
1936	Sherif introduces experimental methods for studying social norms.
1935–1939	Newcomb conducts longitudinal study of attitude development in the Bennington Study (Newcomb, 1943).
1939	Lewin et al. investigate the effect of leadership styles in performance.
1942–1945	World War II: The application of social psychological theory and methods to war-related applied problems.
1947	Clark and Clark publish the results of racial preferences in white and black children (Clark & Clark, 1965).
1947–1948	Hovland founds the Yale Communications–Persuasion Program. Lewin founds the research center for Group Dynamics at MIT.
1951	Asch publishes studies on conformity.
1954	Supreme Court announces *Brown* v. *Topeka* decision on desegregation, citing the Clark and Clark studies.
1957	Festinger publishes his "theory of cognitive dissonance."
1958	Heider offers another consistency model in his book *The Psychology of Interpersonal Relations,* which lays the foundation for attribution theory.
1958	Hollingshead and Redlich demonstrate the role of socioeconomic factors in mental illness.
1962	Schacter and Singer publish research on the social psychological determinants of emotional states.
1963	Milgram reports the first in a series of studies on obedience to authority.
1967	Kelley publishes "Attribution in Social Psychology"—one of the earliest works on attribution theory.
1970	Latane and Darley first report on their research on bystander intervention.
1970s	Calls for "relevance" in social psychology begin to bear fruit as social psychologists increasingly apply their skills and theories to problems in medicine, law, the environment, education, and other aspects of social life.
1980s	Attribution theory gives way to a new emphasis on the "cognitive" aspects of social behavior, and applied social psychology continues to grow in importance.

Source. Adapted with permission from Penrod (1983).

med from a new awareness of social ills in the United States, such as racial injustice, rising crime, public apathy to victims in distress, persistent conditions of poverty, environmental hazards, potential overpopulation, and public reaction to the dominant presence of the Vietnam conflict. Theoretical developments included Bandura's social learning theory (1965), the elaboration of attribution theory (Heider, 1958; Jones & Davis, 1965; Kelley, 1967), and the emergence of "theories of the middle range" (Merton, 1957) that were developed to explain social behavior in specific classes of situations. These theories or mini-theories have replaced the grand theories of the 1950s, proving more useful in attacking specific problems and suggesting research avenues in probing specific issues (Hendrick, 1977). At the same time the number of social psychological journals grew. These are listed in Table 2. The last decade has witnessed further expansion of both areas of research interest and theoretical development, especially the areas of social information processing and

TABLE 2   Major Journals in Social Psychology

Advances in Experimental Social Psychology
Applied Social Psychology Annual
Basic and Applied Social Psychology
European Journal of Social Psychology
Journal of Applied Social Psychology
Journal of Experimental Social Psychology
Journal of Personality and Social Psychology
Journal of Social Issues
Journal of Social Psychology
Personality and Social Psychology Bulletin
Review of Personality and Social Psychology

relationship development. There are also, however, some areas that appear to be fading in importance, despite the fact that there are still large gaps in our understanding. The study of basic group processes is one such area.

In summary, the social psychologists of the 1930s did not seem to concern themselves with research relevance. They worked in applied settings or on applied problems and incorporated those problems into their emerging theories or research programs without much self-consciousness. They worked in schools and therefore dealt with school problems and issues. They took the application of their findings by their colleagues in the applied fields for granted. Despite an increased concern for relevance by social psychologists today, the fragmentation and expansion of the field necessitates a chapter such as the present one to organize and interpret advances in the wide array of areas that currently comprise the field.

ATTITUDES AND ATTITUDE CHANGE

The study of attitudes has long held a major position in the field of social psychology. Indeed, at one time attitude issues virtually defined the field. Although this is no longer the case, attitude research remains a popular topic of study. McGuire (1985) estimated that studies of attitude change have been accumulating at the rate of over 1,200 per year, with over 7,000 publications appearing in the applied literature in the decade preceding his review.

For the school psychologist, attitude issues surface in a variety of contexts: public attitudes toward the profession; school staff attitudes toward psychological interventions in the schools; parental attitudes toward psychological services; and student attitudes toward each other, toward school in general, and toward specific subjects. It is not our intention to review the research on these and other topics, which would be prohibitive in any case. Rather, we will focus on the social psychological contributions to the study of attitudes. Those contributions involve (a) a definition of attitudes, (b) techniques for measuring them, (c) determining their relationship to behavior, and (d) strategies for changing them. For one looking for a general overview of attitude theory and research, McGuire's (1985) lengthy review is considered the classic in the area, but other summaries abound. Noteworthy among these for their general accessibility are Ajzen and Fishbein (1980), Oskamp (1977), Petty and Cacioppo (1981), and Zimbardo, Ebbesen, and Maslach (1977).

Definition of Attitudes

Upon even a brief acquaintance with the attitude literature, one becomes aware of differences and ambiguities in the definition of the term "attitude." This is more than a minor problem, as Fishbein and Ajzen (1975) point out, since a set of articles purportedly dealing with attitudes toward the same issue may actually be dealing with very different concepts. For instance, one study of teacher attitudes toward an instructional program may focus on whether the teachers *like or dislike* the program. Another study of the same purported topic may focus on teacher *beliefs* about the efficacy of such a program or the *ease* with which it can be implemented. Still another study may focus on the particular *behaviors* enacted by teachers to adopt the program in their classrooms.

Much of the confusion arises from the presence of single-component versus multicomponent definitions of attitude. Most theorists agree that the concept of attitude involves elements of cognition, affect, and behavior. However, the nature of the involvement and the nature of the elements constitute topics of some controversy. Problems arise when different researchers operate on implicit assumptions about how these components interact when designing attitude studies.

Fishbein and Ajzen (1975; Ajzen & Fishbein, 1980) have suggested a reformulation of the attitude concept that has proven very useful to researchers. This model of attitude research is depicted in Figure 1. They argue that the term "attitude" should be reserved for the affect felt by a person toward the object of interest. This attitude is determined by a set of the respondent's relevant "beliefs" about the object, weighted by his or her evaluation of each belief. These beliefs are what the person knows or predicts about the object (expressed in terms of likelihood statements). The evaluations are simple assignments of good–bad judgments to each belief. Thus, beliefs determine attitudes that then partially determine "behavioral intentions" of the person with respect to the object. Behavioral intentions also are determined in part by the person's perceptions of subjective norms (what others think that he or she should do) and by the person's motivation to comply with these norms. Behavioral intentions, in turn, most directly determine behavior. We will return to the links between attitudes and behavior in a later section.

In terms of the instructional program example above, teacher ideas about the likelihood that the program will produce certain outcomes or require certain efforts might constitute their set of relevant beliefs. These beliefs, each weighted by the teacher's evaluation on a good–bad dimension, should combine to produce an overall attitude. The attitude influences whether the teacher is willing to adopt the program for a student. The attitude is not the only influence on behavior, however, since the model suggests that the teacher's perceptions of what others think ought to be done and his or her motivation to comply with these experiences also influence intentions to behave. Finally, intentions to behave are realized in behavior itself, unless other events intervene to prevent its occurrence.

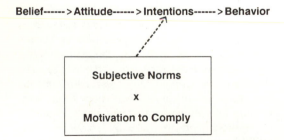

Figure 1. Fishbein–Ajzen model of attitude research.

Attitude Measurement

From a practical point of view, there are two related concerns that are usually raised about attitude measurement. The first is whether a good scale exists to measure some given attitude of interest. The second is how to construct such a scale if one does not.

With respect to the first concern, most attitude scales in use have been devised for purposes of a specific study and there is no central source for such scales. However, some scales in general use have been collected and critiqued in volumes by Robinson and Shaver (1973), Robinson, Athanasiou, and Head (1969), and Shaw and Wright (1967).

With respect to the second concern, methods for constructing attitude scales have constituted one of the major applications of social psychology. Guidelines for the construction and evaluation of scales are contained in a number of sources, including the collections of attitude scales referred to above. In addition, the interested reader should find helpful material in volumes by Selltiz, Wrightsman, and Cook (1976) and Rossi, Wright, and Anderson (1983). Original material concerning the theoretical background of many of the scaling techniques is contained in edited works by Fishbein (1967) and Summers (1970).

Attitudes and Behavior

Few issues in the attitude literature provoke as heated discussion as the relationship between attitudes, as measured by typical self-report scales, and actual behavior. Most attitude research has been conducted with the assumption that attitude has some implication for behavior, but a variety of studies have been conducted that demonstrate the statistical relationship is anything but satisfactory (see Wicker, 1969). Fishbein and Ajzen (1975) have used the model depicted in Figure 1 in an attempt to reconcile the different findings.

The most important implication of the model is the suggestion that the relationship between attitudes and behavior is mediated by *behavioral intentions,* which are dispositions to act in favorable or unfavorable ways toward the concept of interest. As indicated, these behavioral intentions are determined both by the attitude toward the object, and by the individual's perception of subjective norms regarding the behavior and his or her willingness to comply with them. So a child may have a positive attitude toward studying math, but the behavioral intention may be influenced by what he or she perceives as his or her friends' view of studying and by how important peer influence is to him or her.

Moreover, behavior is closely, but not perfectly, related to behavioral intentions. A variety of situational or temporal constraints may thwart intended behavior. Fishbein and Ajzen (1974) point out that any given behavior takes place in a specific place, at a specific time, with respect to a specific object, and involves a specific action. For instance, a child works in his or her room, after dinner, on a certain page in a math workbook, writing the answers to assigned problems. Behavior can be then generalized over any one or all of these components. According to Fishbein and Ajzen, attitude questionnaires will be more predictive of behavior if one tailors the generality or specificity of the questionnaire to the level of generality in the behavior we are trying to predict. For example, if one wants to predict if a child will exhibit undue anxiety during an examination, a specific measure of state test anxiety should be used. A more general measure of anxiety will be predictive across a wider variety of situations but less predictive than a specific measure in a given situation.

Attitude Change

Regardless of the nature of attitudes or their relation to behavior, there exists considerable interest in changing them. Several strategies have been suggested, depending on underlying assumptions about their nature. One of the earliest strategies was based on Hovland's view of attitudes as learned responses to stimuli inherent in communication settings (Hovland, Janis, & Kelley, 1953). According to this view, attitudes changed in response to a persuasive communication that could be analyzed in terms of a set of independent variables. These variables included features of the source (or communicator), the message, and the audience.

A second strategy for change is based on the view that humans seek cognitive consistency in their transactions with the world. This view underlies both balance and cognitive dissonance theories (Festinger, 1954). According to this view, attitude change occurs when one encounters inconsistencies in one's cognitions. The cognitions themselves may refer to behavior or to beliefs. One of the most powerful antecedents of attitude change is a perceived inconsistency between one's behavior and the beliefs salient to that behavior. A child who perceives himself or herself as an honest person, and who believes honest people do not cheat, should experience dissonance if he or she cheats on a test or assignment. The degree of dissonance or inconsistency should be a function of whether the behavior was seen as volitional and the degree of importance to the child of being honest and not cheating. One brings about attitude change, then, by arranging the environment so as to create an inconsistency in cognitions for the target.

This last notion has been applied directly to clinical practice by Brehm (1976) and Hughes (1983). These authors have suggested that in working with clients and consultees, psychologists should ask these individuals to freely choose courses of action with little external compensation, to choose actions that require effort, and to make public their commitment. Such actions are theoretically presumed to increase dissonance and thus result in greater behavioral compliance with therapy or consultation suggestions. However, at present, there is little empirical support for these recommendations.

A more recent view of the conditions necessary to produce attitude change has been developed by Fishbein and Ajzen. Consistent with their model, they propose a Theory of Reasoned Action, in which the beliefs underlying attitudes and behavior are of primary concern. They identify primary beliefs, which are the key beliefs determining behavior; proximal beliefs, which are closely linked to primary beliefs; target beliefs, which are those the attitude change agent seeks to change; and incidental beliefs, which are those related to the target beliefs but not to primary beliefs. Attitude change in the desired direction occurs when the change agent correctly identifies the primary beliefs and those proximal beliefs which are directly related to the primary beliefs. Under these conditions, the target beliefs specified by the change agent will in fact be those that produce desired change. Perhaps more important, desired attitude change often may not occur because the target beliefs identified by the change agent are not in fact those which are primary in the determination of the attitude.

One way of differentiating models of attitude change is to point out that some models are based on the assumption that change is basically a product of stimulus conditions and that if the conditions are right, change will occur. By contrast, other models are based on the idea that change is basically a product of relatively logical cognitive activity involving balancing of beliefs.

Recently, Petty and Caccioppo (1981) have suggested a model incorporating both sets of assumptions. They argue that attitudes may be changed through either central or peripheral routes. The central route involves controlled attentional processes and reasoning to reconcile belief differences in persuasive communications or in personal experience. Change is difficult to bring about through the central route, because the subject marshals his or her cognitive resources to defend the existing position. However, once change is achieved, it is relatively long-lasting, since it involves cognitive restructuring. On the other hand, the peripheral route involves relatively automatic processes without much conscious reasoning in achieving change. Pleasant sights, sounds, or associations bring about positive orientations to the target stimuli. For example, Hannah and Pliner (1983) concluded that teachers who have positive interactions with handicapped pupils are more likely to have positive attitudes toward them. However, change achieved through the peripheral route is of relatively short duration and is relatively superficial. At present, there is accumulating evidence supporting the validity of this model, and it seems to hold promise for future research.

SOCIAL PERCEPTION

Social psychology was one of the first disciplines to recognize that an adequate account of human behavior must take into account how people interpret social events and actions, how these interpretations are systematically influenced by variables associated with other people and situations, and how this interpretation affects behavior. Today, the importance of cognitions and beliefs is well established in numerous areas of educational, clinical, developmental, and experimental psychology.

Attribution Theories
General Attribution Theories
Understanding the cognitive and motivational processes used in assigning causes to events and behaviors is the goal of attribution theory (Harvey, Ickes, & Kidd, 1978). Unlike other psychological theories that are relatively well integrated, attribution theory involves a number of different prop-

ositions and conceptual frameworks that are related by a common purpose, to understand how people make causal explanations or ask questions beginning with "why" and to understand what they subsequently do with this information (Bem, 1967; Harvey & Weary, 1984; Heider, 1958; Jones & Davis, 1965; Kelley & Michela, 1980; Schachter, 1964).

The history of attribution theory begins with Heider's (1958) seminal writings on person perception. Heider believed that ordinary people attempt to make sense of things much like scientists do by explaining an action of another person as due to something about or within the person (personal causes) or something external to the person and associated with the environment (situational causes). For example, a teacher might see a child's school performance as due to their effort or the ease of the test.

Jones and Davis (1965) provided the second influential attribution statement by describing the conditions under which someone discounts environmental causes in favor of personal or trait explanations; simply, if someone does something unique or something not socially desirable (like resisting strong peer pressure) it tells us something about the person's internal character makeup. Subsequently, Kelley (1967) addressed the nature of cues used in deciding between personal and situational determinants. He noted that perceivers weigh information regarding an actor's *consistency* over time, over different circumstances (*distinctiveness*), and how many others act this way (*consensus*). Bem (1967), coming from the perspective of a radical behaviorist, noted that these same attributional cues are used to explain one's own behavior. He advanced the radical proposition (at the time) that people do not really know much more about why they do things than why another person does—they just look at their behavior for cues. According to Bem, if a school psychologist was doing much more testing than colleagues, it might be viewed as an indication of liking testing more than other professional duties.

Up through the early 1970s most attribution theorists wrote as if causal attribution depended exclusively on informational cues. Jones and Nisbett (1971) pointed out that often people view events in line with motivational biases or various selfish reasons. One of these biases, known as ego-defensive or egocentric attribution, holds that individuals are motivated to view the world in such a way that their self-image is enhanced or protected from threat. According to this view, people generally see themselves as the causes of positive events but deny personal responsibility for negative events. The so-called "fundamental attribution error" involves the tendency for attributors to underestimate the impact of situational factors in controlling others' behavior, especially in comparison to their own behavior. Such tendencies have been studied in numerous clinical settings relevant to school psychologists, including child abuse (Larrance & Twentyman, 1983) and marital conflict (Kyle & Falbo, 1985). For example, in high-stress marriages, partners are more likely to blame one another than to blame situational factors (Kyle & Falbo, 1985).

These writings constitute the major papers describing the general process of causal attribution. In addition to these, there have been several attribution models dealing with attributions for specific types of events. Two of these models hold particular relevance for school psychology and have generated considerable research over the last decade. They are Weiner's (1972, 1979) attributional theory of achievement motivation and Abramson, Seligman, and Teasdale's (1978) attributional formulation of learned helplessness.

Weiner's Attributional Theory of Achievement Motivation

Weiner's major contribution was that he took Heider's personal—environmental causal analysis and expanded it to include dimensions of stability (stable—variable) and controllability (potentially controllable or not). Additionally, he applied this analysis to understanding why individuals approach or avoid achievement-related tasks and make judgments about achievement behavior.

Weiner gives most emphasis to the locus of causality and stability dimensions and notes that people normally ascribe the causes of their achievement behavior to one of four causes: their ability, their effort or motivation, the ease or difficulty of the task, or luck. The former two causes are personal and the latter two are environmental. Ability and task difficulty are stable; effort and luck are variable. Research derived from Weiner's model has found that high achievers tend to attribute their success and failure to effort factors, whereas low achievers attribute their success to luck and failure to low ability. Of particular interest to school psychologists are findings indicating that the attributions of low achievers are similar

to those of clinically hyperactive and learning disabled students (Chaney & Bugental, 1982).

Abramson et al.'s Model of Learned Helplessness

Abramson et al. (1978) have argued that attributions serve as a mediator of learned helplessness, which, in severe cases, can lead to depression (Janoff-Bulman, 1979). Simply put, individuals who see no connection between their efforts and rewards are likely to see their failures as beyond their control or as a consequence of their low abilities. Such beliefs develop over time and appear to be reinforced by the statements of others, such as friends, teachers, and parents. Because this passive acceptance of failure resembles the behavior of animals and adults placed in unavoidable aversive situations it has been labeled learned helplessness.

The finding that learned helpless individuals do not believe that their effort is an important determinant of what happens to them led several researchers to wonder if this causal belief could be changed, and if so, would learned helplessness behaviors be ameliorated. This process, known as "attribution retraining," has been widely studied, especially with children. In these studies children are presented with a series of successes and failures on academic tasks (or a combination of the two) and, after each outcome, are given feedback from an adult that they were successful because they tried hard or that they were not successful because they did not try hard enough. These studies were reviewed by Cecil and Medway (1986), who concluded that effort feedback provided to learned helpless children and those who do not make spontaneous effort attributions can increase the task persistence and academic performance of such children, although long-standing attributions are resistant to change (Borkowski, Weyhing, & Carr, 1988). Attribution retraining is an easy procedure to carry out for children whose academic problems are due to poor motivation and self-defeating perceptions.

Other Applications of Attribution Theory to School Psychology

There are numerous areas in which a knowledge of attribution research has important implications for school psychologists. However, studies in two areas are especially relevant. These are studies of teachers' attributions for student performance and consultants' attributions for intervention outcomes.

Most school psychologists would acknowledge that it is very important to understand how teachers assign causation for student learning. This issue has been the focus of several studies which have asked actual teachers or undergraduates role-playing teachers to assign responsibility for the success or failure of a student (Bar-Tal, 1982). In some of these studies, the ratings of the teachers are compared with those of objective observers. The results of these studies have not, however, been entirely consistent and clear-cut. Most of this research indicates that professional teachers tend not to engage in egotistic attributions; rather, if they are familiar with the student, they tend to rate his or her ability, effort, preparation, and interest as more important determinants of success and less important determinants of failure than their own teaching. But if the teacher does not anticipate future interactions with the student, the teacher is more likely to blame them for failure and take credit for success. Medway (1979) found that teacher attributions were directly related to differential teaching strategies. In this study, teachers who attributed student problems to a lack of motivation were observed to criticize such students significantly more than they did comparison children.

A second relevant application of attribution theory to school psychology has involved work on consultants' attributions. Martin and Curtis (1981) asked a sample of school psychologists to recall their most and least successful consultation cases over a recent 5-year period and give a cause as to why the consultee was successful or not. As predicted by a motivational bias, consultees were held more responsible for consultation failures than successes. However, a follow-up study by D. K. Smith and Lyon (1986) indicated that the tendency to blame consultees for failure is much stronger among school consultants than is the tendency to blame oneself. Unfortunately, no study has directly compared teacher-psychologist perceptions or related these attributional tendencies to the success or failure of school consultation. Finally, since some of the most recent attribution work is being done in the areas of social relationships (Harvey & Weary, 1984), we might anticipate future extensions of attribution theory toward understanding the actual nature of communication acts between consultant and consultee.

Social Cognition

An attribution, as reviewed in the preceding section, is a discrete judgment. This judgment, however, is usually compared with or incorporated into new or existing impressions of an individual, group, or situation. Such impressions then guide further judgments and behavior. For instance, a parent may attribute a teacher's behavior (e.g., reporting a child to the principal) to a dispositional characteristic of the teacher (e.g., prejudice against members of certain racial, ethnic, or religious groups). The parent compares this attribution with other information about this teacher, other teachers in this school, or teachers in general. The attribution becomes encoded and stored with the relevant background information, perhaps to be recalled and utilized in future interactions between the parent and the teacher. The processes involved in this integration of social information are collectively termed social cognition, a topic of major interest among social psychologists today. General reviews of this emerging area are available in Fiske and Taylor (1984) and Markus and Zajonc (1985).

A discussion of some of the key issues and concepts in the field begins with the assumption that social information, like other forms of information, is encoded and stored in memory in meaningful structures. These structures allow access to the information for efficiently handling and responding to new information encountered in social interactions. Handling and responding to new information often involves inference processes, of which attribution is one. In the following sections we briefly examine the most common types of structures and inference processes proposed.

Structures

Three types of structures have received most attention: schema, prototype, and script. A schema can be defined as an internal representation that contains both a description of an object (a person, a group of persons, or situation) and a theory of how its components (traits, persons, or roles) operate (Markus & Zajonc, 1985). A schema allows one to go beyond the information given in a specific instance and generate hypotheses and additional items of information that may have important implications for behavior toward the object.

An area of interest to school psychologists, where the concept of schema has a potentially important application, is that of labeling (see Rolison & Medway, 1985). A label (EMR) may be said to invoke a schema in one for whom the label has meaning. Although the label is applied on the basis of a limited series of tests on specific aspects of intellectual functioning, the schema it invokes may have far broader implications. It may serve to focus attention on only certain aspects of the child's behavior that are expected within the schema. It may structure the interpretation of that behavior in ways that are consistent with the schema. It may influence the retrieval of information from memory when one is subsequently required to evaluate the child. And it may influence the kind of behavior displayed toward the child in such a way that behavior consistent with the schema is elicited from the child.

A second major structural concept is that of *prototype,* defined as an ideal case of a given social category (Cantor & Mischel, 1977). Essentially, prototypes come into play when one is trying to decide whether or not a social target is a member of a certain category. The target will be classified as a member of the category to the extent that its characteristics match those of the prototype. The closer the match, the more quickly and easily the categorization will be made. The concept has considerable relevance to a number of issues in school psychology involving assessment and placement decisions for children on the basis of an approximate match to various diagnostic categories (see McDermott, 1981).

The third structural concept, *script,* differs from the other two in that it involves a theory about a sequence of events or behavior as part of its content. The primary work in this area is credited to Abelson (Abelson, 1976; Langer & Abelson, 1972). Actual events or behavior are evaluated for their consistency with a preconceived script, and are considered informative to the extent that they are inconsistent. Like the other concepts, the script directs attention, facilitates interpretation of events, and affects the way such events are stored and recalled from memory. Scripts may exist for both situations and persons in situations. Thus, labeling a child EMR may initiate a script or expected sequence of behaviors pertaining to how the child might handle a challenging school task. To the extent that the child's performance matches the script, the use of the script is validated. Deviations from expectation may either trigger a change in the script for future use or force a change in the judgment of the child as diagnosed. Perhaps more important, the existence of the script may lead the perceiver to overlook important but not necessarily dramatic departures, thus maintaining the original and possibly incorrect judgment.

Inference Processes

We have indicated that schemata, prototypes, and scripts are assumed to have an effect on processes of social judgment. These processes have also become issues of research interest. An excellent and readable summary of work in this area is contained in a book by Nisbett and Ross (1980), who contend that humans have developed a variety of cognitive strategies to deal with the potentially overwhelming amount of information to which they are exposed. These strategies are normally functional in problem solving and decision making. They filter out unnecessary information and frequently result in efficient and speedy judgments. There are times, however, when these strategies operate to the detriment of the decision maker, resulting in the loss of, or incorrect assimilation of, important information, which in turn, may lead to a failure to adapt to new circumstances.

Probably the most important of the dynamic concepts is that of a *heuristic,* or shortcut decision rule. The study of heuristics in social cognition is heavily based on the work of Tverksy and Kahneman (1974), who suggested several types of heuristics that may be operating in general decision making. Two heuristics that have received attention in the psychological literature are the *representativeness heuristic* and the *availability heuristic* (Nisbett & Ross, 1980). According to the representativeness heuristic, people make judgments (such as diagnoses) based on the similarity of some characteristic of the target person to presumed characteristics of the class of interest. For instance, an otherwise normal child who has an undetected hearing disorder may be misjudged intellectually deficient by a teacher because the child exhibits behaviors (poor test performancce, inability to follow instructions, etc.) that "fit" the teacher's behavior expectations for intellectually deficient children.

Chapman and Chapman (1967, 1969) have demonstrated a similar process underlying what they call "illusory correlation" in diagnostic judgments of clinicians. In their studies, even experienced clinicians relied on invalid diagnostic signs in projective tests, primarily because the signs (e.g., large eyes in the Draw-A-Person test) seemed representative of the category of assignment (e.g., paranoia). Furthermore, belief in the validity of the signs was reinforced by selective attention to the co-occurrence of such signs and inattention to the occurrence of one sign without the other.

The availability heuristic operates when one judges the likelihood of an outcome based on the accessibility of that outcome in cognition. Accessibility refers to the ease with which such an outcome can be imagined, regardless of how likely it actually is to occur. Accessibility can be affected by such factors as recent experiences with the outcome, the dramatic impact of the outcome, and the personal salience of the outcome. In a school setting, a recent workshop may sensitize staff to problems that, although serious, occur with relatively low frequency. After the workshop, participants may be more likely to overestimate the prevalence of the problem and to detect the problem in those that do not have it.

INTERPERSONAL ATTRACTION

Why do we like some people and not others? And how can we get other people to change how much they like us? These issues are central to understanding human interaction and thus have been at the heart of social psychological research. This research was originated by Moreno (1934), who described the techniques of "sociometry" to measure patterns of attraction among group members. These techniques have been integral to measuring social behaviors and liking patterns in the classroom (Schmuck & Schmuck, 1971) and continue to be used in recent school psychology studies (Middleton, Zollinger, & Keene, 1986). Today there continues to be strong interest in the study of interpersonal attraction, its causes, consequences, and antecedents (Berscheid, 1985).

Early studies of attraction conceived of it as a unitary dimension that could be measured by a self-report scale with a "low" or "no attraction" anchor at one end and a "high attraction" at the other. This approach is commonly used in school psychology studies, such as studies of consumer satisfaction with psychologists and their services. However, some recent theorizing suggests that affective responses may involve both positive and negative components and that measurement should involve scales anchored with negative affect at one end and positive affect at the other. There

has also been an increase in the number of attraction studies that employ behavioral measures such as doing favors and expressing positive nonverbal behavior.

Theories of Attraction

There are several general social psychological theories that have been used to explain why people are attracted to one another. The cognitive consistency theories, which include Heider's (1958) balance theory and Festinger's (1957) cognitive dissonance theory, basically hold that we like those who like us, and vice versa (although people tend to like others more than to dislike them); that we like others who are similar to us, and vice versa; and that if harm befalls another person, people will tend to dislike the victim in order to restore consistency between the behavioral act and their attitude. The latter notion can be seen in Lerner's (1980) work on "just world" beliefs: namely, that good people deserve good things and bad people bad things. Lerner's work has numerous school applications, holding among other things, for example, that a child victim deserves his or her fate.

The second group of general attraction theories are the reinforcement theories. The simple idea here is that we like people who reward us in some way. However, since interpersonal relations involve two-way interaction, reinforcement notions of attraction have been modified to take into account how much an individual perceives that he or she has been rewarded relative to how much he or she has invested in the relationship (Adams, 1965), and relative awards received compared to other negative options inherent in terminating the relationship (Kelley & Thibaut, 1978). Kelley and Thibaut's theory has important implications for predicting the dissolution of close relationships such as divorce and giving up a child through adoption.

Recently, some social psychologists have turned their attention from studying attraction per se to investigating similarly intense emotions. Important work is being done on the study of love, rejection, and loneliness (see Berscheid, 1985).

Determinants of Attraction

Three factors have been found to be especially important in influencing attraction in initial and brief encounters. These are the physical attractiveness of the other, the similarity of the other to the individual, and to a lesser extent, social contact.

Physical Attractiveness

Across race, sex, age, and social class physically attractive people are liked more than less attractive people. Of particular importance to school psychologists are studies indicating a relationship between children's popularity and attractiveness (Huston & Levinger, 1978) and studies showing that teachers give attractive children better evaluations, more opportunities to perform, and treat them less harshly when they transgress (Berscheid, 1985). To some degree physical attractiveness itself is determined by nonverbal cues such as facial expression and smiling (Mueser, Grau, Sussman, & Rosen, 1984).

Similarity

Byrne (1969) noted an important quote from Aristotle who observed: "We like those who resemble us and are engaged in the same pursuits." Over the last 60 years there have been a host of studies showing that people like similar others. This basic notion has numerous implications for school psychologists, ranging from understanding the cohesion of groups of similar racial makeup to understanding why males tend to be referred for behavior problems by teachers, especially female teachers.

Social Contact

Numerous studies have indicated that social contact, familiarity, and physical proximity increase liking and attraction. Simply put, people tend to like others who live and work near them and with whom they interact frequently. There is, however, one important qualifier to this: The people involved must be treated as equals.

The social contact research has several important implications for school practices. One is the widely held belief that contact between ethnic groups will reduce prejudice. In 1954 the Supreme Court in *Brown* v. *Topeka Board of Education* ruled that segregated schools were inherently unequal and unconstitutional. Social psychologists such as Kenneth Clark and Stuart Cook who provided court testimony argued that school integration would (a) raise the self-esteem and school achievement of black children, and (b) reduce racial prejudice.

Subsequent research, however, has not indicated clear decreases in interracial prejudice following integration. Stephan (1978) noted that, at best, the existing studies were mixed; at worse,

there was some increase in white prejudice. The picture for improvements in achievement and self-esteem has been even less dramatic. What has appeared to go wrong was the failure to ensure equal status. Cook (1984) has noted that integration will work only if the parties are of equal status, if they are encouraged to cooperate, and if the surrounding community supports integrated schools.

A second important extension of the social contact hypothesis is in the area of mainstreaming. Here the research parallels that on school desegregation in indicating few real effects of this practice (or peer tutoring of the handicapped by nonhandicapped) on the social acceptance of distinctly different handicapped groups, such as retarded children (Gottlieb, Rose, & Lessen, 1983). While some have argued that the problems lie with needed curricular changes to support mainstreaming (Madden & Slavin, 1983), total acceptance of the handicapped by the nonhandicapped may be wishful thinking unless the two groups can cooperate on equal footing. We explore related extensions of the contact hypothesis in the next section.

INTERGROUP RELATIONS

Intergroup relations are processes of cooperation and competition between groups, including the antecedents and consequences of such processes. Much of the early work in this area was derived from Lewin's work on group dynamics, and consisted of analyzing intergroup situations in terms of forces or pressures arising from pursuit of incompatible goals (e.g., Deutsch, 1968). However, the landmark study in the area is Sherif's examination of conflict and cooperation in a boy's summer camp known as the Robber's Cave (Sherif, Harvey, White, & Sherif, 1961). In this study, the researchers placed boys arriving at a summer camp into one of two groups. Through a series of manipulations, they developed high cohesion within each group (by various cooperative exercises) and high conflict between groups (by competitive events and contrived confrontations). They then attempted to reduce intergroup hostility by encouraging friendly contact—an effort that proved unsuccessful. They eventually brought about a reduction in hostility through the introduction of "superordinate goals," conditions that required the groups to pool their efforts for the good of the camp (e.g., the formation of a joint baseball team to play another camp and the formation of a bucket brigade to supply water when the camp's system "failed"). The construction of the conflict situation and the use of superordinate goals to overcome intergroup hostility in the situation were major developments in the field, and have clear implications for the development of cooperation in school settings today.

Despite the success of Sherif's field study, there have been relatively few attempts at replication and extensions. Instead, much of the research on cooperation and competition has been conducted in the laboratory context of mixed-motive games. The term "game" here is meant in the technical sense of a rule-governed interaction between two or more parties. The parties are usually college student subjects who are seated in separate locations and briefed about the rules of the game by the researchers. Each party is told that they have a choice of actions (usually two) that they can take whenever it is their turn to play in the game. The actions available often consist of pressing one or another button on a keyboard or other console. The key to the game is that the outcome of any trial in the game is determined by the joint set of choices made by the players, so the outcome for any player is dependent on both his or her action and the action of the other player. By manipulating the set of outcomes for a game, psychologists have found that they can induce in subjects motivations to both cooperate and compete. This condition occurs when (a) each player wins a small amount if both players choose alternative A (e.g., by pressing a red button); (b) each player loses a modest amount if both players choose alternative B (e.g., by pressing a red button); and (c) a player loses a great deal if they choose alternative A when their partner chooses alternative B, but wins a great deal if they choose B when their partner chooses A. So both players have a motive to cooperate with each other to win a little at a time from the game. At the same time, however, there is the temptation to gain a competitive advantage over each other by exercising alternative B when the partner chooses alternative A. A game with this payoff structure is called a Prisoners' Dilemma game (from the situation of two prisoners suspected of a crime who each must decide whether to remain silent or to give testimony against the other in return for a light sentence), and has been used extensively to examine the circumstances under which cooperative

versus competitive choices are made (Rubin & Brown, 1975). Many of the principles of cooperation and competition applied to intergroup situations are based largely on this dyadic interaction.

One aspect of intergroup relations relevant to school psychologists is that concerned with prejudice and discrimination. Prejudice refers to an attitude toward members of another group based solely on their membership in that group, while discrimination refers to behaviors based on that attitude. Two themes in this area have been the focus of greatest recent attention. The first concerns the origins of prejudice and discrimination. G. Allport (1958) identified several personal, social, and economic sources of the problem. Basically, his view was that prejudice and discrimination arise from some defect in the person or the social system, and that the normal state of affairs is intergroup harmony. More recently, Tajfel offered convincing evidence that ingroup–outgroup distinctions and differences in allocation of reward arise whenever humans are divided into groups, no matter how arbitrary the basis of the division (Billig & Tajfel, 1973; Tajfel, 1970). The work of Tajfel and others has led to a revision of the earlier, more simplistic theories of ingroup–outgroup prejudice. The revision focuses on the idea that identification with a preferred ingroup enhances individual social identity, and the need for such enhancement is pervasive, as is the tendency to elevate the ingroup and denigrate the outgroup (Brown, 1986; Tajfel, 1978). Efforts at increasing intergroup harmony must operate to overcome this basic process as well as deal with the substantive problems underlying conflict.

The second theme of recent interest is the contact hypothesis, which in its simplest form suggests that one of the ways to reduce intergroup prejudice is by increasing intergroup contact. The early evidence pertaining to the validity of the hypothesis has been reviewed by a number of authors, most notably Amir (1969). This evidence was quite mixed, some studies indicating reduction, some no effect, and some increases in outgroup prejudice as a function of increased contact.

A reformulated hypothesis suggests that the effect of increased intergroup contact depends on the social context, the nature of contact activity, and the prior status of the participants. Support for this reformulation is found in a series of studies by Cook and his associates (Cook, 1969, 1978). The results from this program of studies led to efforts to apply the techniques developed to classroom settings involving multiracial and multiethnic classes. One set of such studies are those utilizing the "jigsaw" method (Aronson & Osherow, 1980; Aronson, Stephan, Sikes, Blaney, & Snapp, 1978). This method involves assembling multiracial or multiethnic groups of students from integrated classrooms. The material to be learned is divided into meaningful units and one unit is assigned to each child. The child must teach the assigned unit to the others in the group. All children are evaluated individually. This cooperative peer teaching technique results in improved intergroup attitudes, higher self-esteem, and positive attitudes toward school when the groups are ethnically balanced. Academic achievement does not suffer. Indeed, there is evidence that the students in the jigsaw groups outperform traditional classroom students, particularly minority students (Stephan, 1985).

A second set of studies derived from the contact hypothesis have been conducted by researchers at Johns Hopkins University examining the effectiveness of two cooperative learning techniques (DeVries, Edwards, & Slavin, 1978; DeVries & Slavin, 1978). The first, student-teams-achievement-division (STAD), involves multiracial peer teaching in small groups. Achievement is assessed in terms of individual prior performance or in terms of the performance of comparable students. The teams gain by improvement of members each at their own level, thus enhancing cooperation among team members. The second technique, teams-games-tournaments (TGT), also involves multiracial peer teaching, but achievement is assessed in tournaments among students of comparable achievement levels. It appears that these efforts generally decrease ingroup—outgroup hostility while increasing, or at least not affecting, academic achievement.

Although these and other cooperative learning techniques were developed to remedy school problems in the racially or ethnically desegregated classroom, the impressive gains in self-esteem and academic achievement in traditionally disadvantaged groups have led to further development of the techniques for adoption in a variety of educational settings. For instance, Warring, Johnson, Marayuma, and Johnson (1985) have demonstrated that a variant of the cooperative learning paradigm has proven effective in increasing not only cross-ethnic but cross-sex preferences in middle school students, a group notorious for the level of voluntary sex segregation in social activities. In another application, Johnson and Johnson (1982) have demonstrated the utility of a cooperative learning exercise in promoting sociometric preference for handicapped students, an outcome also reported by Slavin (1985) using a different technique. The implications for mainstreaming are obvious.

As implied in the discussion above, several cooperative learning techniques have been developed to meet a variety of needs, subject matter, and grade levels. These techniques have a great deal in common, but there are also important differences (Slavin, 1983). A very useful classification scheme for the practitioner has recently been published by Bohlmeyer and Burke (1987). They evaluated nine such techniques on the basis of subject matter, nature of student interdependence, intergroup interaction (cooperative, competitive, or independent), method of grouping, evaluation and reward system, and demands on the system for implementation. The appearance of this type of guide for the practitioner makes it clear that the techniques are rapidly moving out of controlled lab settings and becoming standard fare in primary and secondary schools.

AGGRESSION

Aggression may be defined as the intentional injury of another person. The aggressive act may be primarily a means toward some other end (e.g., a child hitting to get a toy or attention). This is known as *instrumental aggression*. Or, the aggression may be the end in itself (e.g., a child striking another with the sole intent to harm). This is known as *angry aggression*.

Causes of Aggression

There are three major views as to the causes of aggression. One perspective is that human aggression results from involuntary, biological instincts. Freud believed that every human being has an unconscious drive (the death instinct) toward destruction. Konrad Lorenz, the noted ethologist, also argued that all animal species have an inborn aggressive urge that is simply released by certain environmental conditions. The instinct model of aggression is dominant in Golding's (1954) *Lord of the Flies,* a novel about a group of schoolboys stranded on an island who resort to savagery and violence.

A second perspective, derived from drive theory, is the frustration–aggression hypothesis (Miller, 1941). Since this theory was first advanced, considerable research has accumulated indicating that individuals who are thwarted from reaching goals or placed in competitive settings often aggress. It will be recalled that in the "Robbers Cave" experiment by Sherif, two groups of male campers were brought into such competition with each other that fights and destructive raids on each others' cabins broke out.

It is the third view, however, derived from Bandura's social learning theory, that holds the most explanatory power and relevance for school psychologists. This model holds that there are certain antecedent or situational conditions that lead to emotional arousal that may, because of observational learning, reinforcement, or personality characteristics, lead to aggression or some alternative response. Below we describe in some detail the parameters of this model.

Antecedent Conditions

There are several antecedents that trigger emotional arousal. These include sex-role training that encourages boys to be more aggressive than girls, the presence of others that results in groups exhibiting more aggression than individuals alone, aggressive cues such as knives and guns, and characteristics of the target of aggression such as their gender and potential for retaliation. Some types of people are especially likely to be attacked, such as the handicapped and unattractive. For example, in one study (Berkowitz & Frodi, 1979) subjects delivered more punishment to a learner who was "funny looking" and stuttered than another with normal appearance even though all learners made the same number of mistakes. And finally, certain unpleasant environmental conditions, such as heat, crowding, invasions of personal space, and deindividuation, seem to trigger aggression. For instance, high school males have been found to be more competitive with one another in smaller rooms; certain places in buildings (elevators, stairwells, hallways) are especially likely vandalism targets. Such findings have implications for limiting school populations according to building size and for building design.

Mediating Conditions

According to social learning theory, the major conditions intervening between a potentially aggressive stimulus and aggressive response are (a) the degree of emotional arousal and (b) the anticipated consequences of aggression. Schachter (1964) has argued that individuals cannot clearly differentiate the nature of arousal; in fact, research suggests that erotic or drug-induced arousal may lead to aggression simply because the person may be unable to distinguish the internal signs of anger. Anticipated consequences refers to the reinforcement the person expects to obtain by being aggressive. Such reinforcement may be direct (e.g., peers encouraging two students to fight) or vicarious (e.g., someone observing that an aggressive other is rewarded).

Responses

Bandura's model holds that arousal (or anger) does not invariably result in aggression. Frustration and anger often lead to dependency, withdrawal, psychosomatic symptoms, constructive coping, or escape through drugs and alcohol, depending on the personality and learning history of the individual.

Sexual Aggression

Bandura's social learning theory has been used as a theoretical framework in understanding the nature of sexual aggression (Marshall & Barbaree, 1984), such as rape between acquaintances (so-called date rape) and child sexual abuse (Finkelhor, 1984). The importance of these theories for school psychologists rests on the fact that, unlike statements that designate types of people likely to abuse (e.g., based on a past abused history), these models stress multiple factors in an additive or interactive fashion. They highlight factors such as the motivation to commit the act, factors reducing aggression inhibitions, and factors reinforcing the opportunity to aggress. In one recent study, Malamuth (1986) showed that high levels of sexual aggression can be predicted from knowledge of males' hostility toward females, desire to dominate them, acceptance of force in sexual relationships, and prior aggression history. Social psychologists are showing that sexual aggression and child abuse must be conceptualized along a continuum encompassing a tendency to aggress rather than as an all-or-none phenomenon, and that searching for a primary causal factor of, or primary treatment strategy for, sexual and child abuse is likely to be futile.

Physical and Psychological Maltreatment

Social psychological models have recently been developed attempting to understand the nature of childhood abuse and neglect (Belsky, 1984). These models stress the interaction of parent, child, and environmental variables and hold greater promise for intervention effectiveness than models that focus on a single aspect.

Television and Aggression

In 1974, a 9-year-old girl was sexually assaulted in an incident similar to that shown 3 days earlier in a TV show called *Born Innocent.* In 1977, Ronny Zamora killed his neighbor during a burglary in a manner resembling a recently watched episode of the show "Kojak." And in 1981, John Hinckley Jr. shot President Reagan, admitting having identified with a character in the film *Taxi Driver.* Although these and other incidents make the headlines, there are numerous controlled studies indicating that children learn aggressive acts from both live and television models. Nearly all the major reviews of this issue have concluded that there is a correlation between viewing TV violence and subsequent aggression (Pearl, Bouthilet, & Lazar, 1982), especially when the viewers are preschool or young children who have difficulty judging intentionality and motive. The association is less strong for teenagers but still positive, although some have pointed out that aggressive young adults may favor violent shows (Freedman, 1984). The National Coalition of Television Violence cites recent studies showing that violent acts on cable TV and violent/sexually aggressive lyrics in rock videos and song lyrics have increased more than 50% over the last 10 years.

One important role for school psychologists now and in the future must be to assist in reducing violence in the schools, among children, and against them. We envision school psychologists working with certain children to modify viewing habits or their interpretation of violent events, to reduce those conditions that reinforce aggression, assisting national organizations and local PTAs in reducing violence on television, and assisting families to teach children the value of prosocial as compared to aggressive behavior.

ORGANIZATIONAL BEHAVIOR

In accordance with our definition of social psychology, most of the contributions to school psychology discussed thus far have applied to relatively simple social situations and interactions (e.g., student–teacher, teacher–psychologist, student–student). The school in which these situations and interactions occur, however, is a complex formal organization that to some extent determines and is affected by the interactions that take place. Organizational theory and research is a rapidly expanding interdisciplinary enterprise (Pfeffer, 1985), and a review of this literature is not within the scope of the present chapter. The related area of organizational development in the school is covered in another chapter in the present volume, while reviews of developments in several areas of organizational behavior can be found in editions of the *Annual Review of Psychology* (House & Singh, 1987; Schneider, 1985). However, social psychologists have contributed a perspective and research tradition to some aspects of the field, and continue to do so, particularly at the level of individual behavior in the organization.

One important tradition originated in the work of Lewin and his associates on leadership in groups (Lewin, Lippett, & White, 1939). Appropriately, this work was largely conducted in schools, with teachers serving in the role of leaders for their classes. The most famous of these studies concerned the role of the leader in creating a "climate" for the group. Autocratic, democratic, and laissez-faire styles of supervision were employed to create a so-called "climate" in which the groups of students worked. Demonstration that the democratic climate proved superior on overall criteria of performance ushered in a period of active research on leader behavior which received a considerable boost during World War II, with a focus on the training of effective leaders in military situations.

Subsequent work by Lewin's students and colleagues clarified the dimensions of leader behavior and established the validity of the socio-emotional versus task distinction in leader orientations. After a period of research on characteristics of effective leaders, this tradition culminated in Fiedler's development of the contingency theory of leadership effectiveness. According to Fiedler (1964), there is no one most effective leader across all situations. Instead, situations can be characterized as favorable or unfavorable to the leader based on characteristics such as the structure of the task, the preexisting leader–member relations, and the position power of the leader. For situations characterized as very favorable or unfavorable to the leader, those who are relatively task oriented are likely to prove most effective, whereas for situations between the extremes, those who are relatively human relations oriented are likely to prove most effective.

Fiedler and Garcia (1987) have recently proposed a second contingency-type theory to specify conditions under which a leader's cognitive resources will be effectively utilized in a leadership task. This cognitive resource utilization theory suggests that effective use can be made of cognitive resources when a leader is able to employ directive behavior, has task-relevant knowledge, has good leader–member relations, and is not under stress (House & Singh, 1987). Such contingency notions have important implications for the school environment, in terms of both principal–teacher and teacher–class interactions. The suggestion from this literature is that whether a given principal or teacher will be effective in their leadership position depends not only on their personal styles and resources, but on the nature of the environment in which such styles and resources are enacted.

A second research tradition developed by Lewin (1951) involves the study of group dynamics, the forces that develop in groups to encourage participation and change in their members, as well as commitment to group decisions. The first major study in this area was Lewin's project to change the shopping habits of midwestern homemakers to buy less desirable cuts of meat. Lewin first analyzed the forces on the homemakers influencing their current purchase decisions. He then set about to change these forces by a variety of discussion techniques, finding that active participation in discussion and group commitment brought about the greatest reported change. The power of group discussion to change behavior and the effectiveness of participatory management became cornerstones of the group dynamics movement as established by Lewin in the Center for Group Dynamics, first located at Massachusetts Institute of Technology and later moved to the University of Michigan. Some characteristics of effective small groups are listed in Table 3.

Whereas Lewin focused on the group as the unit of analysis for his work, a separate tradition developed from the view of an organization as a product of the interlocked behaviors of its members. Katz and Kahn (1978) argued, in their open-

TABLE 3   Characteristics of Effective Groups

Goals are clarified and changed so that the best possible match between individual goals and the group's goals may be achieved; goals are cooperatively structured.

Communication is two-way, and the open and accurate expression of both ideas and feelings is emphasized.

Participation and *leadership* are distributed among all group members; goal accomplishment, internal maintenance, and developmental change are underscored.

Ability and *information* determine influence and power; contracts are built to make sure that individuals' goals and needs are fulfilled; power is equalized and shared.

Decision-making procedures are matched with the situation; different methods are used at different times; consensus is sought for important decisions; involvement and group discussions are encouraged.

Controversy and *conflict* are seen as a positive key to members' involvement, the quality and originality of decisions, and the continuance of the group in good working conditions.

Interpersonal, group, and *intergroup* behaviors are stressed; cohesion is advanced through high levels of inclusion, affection, acceptance, support, and trust. Individuality is endorsed.

Problem-solving adequacy is high.

Members evaluate the effectiveness of the group and decide how to improve its functioning; goal accomplishment, internal maintenance, and development are all considered important.

Interpersonal effectiveness, self-actualization, and *innovation* are encouraged.

systems approach to organizational functioning, that the system processes of input, throughput, and output are accomplished through the interlocked, role-coordinated behavior of the individual members of the organization. Individual problems such as role strain, developing from competing demands on the occupants of various organizational roles, have been extensively examined in this research tradition.

The applicability of this approach to the school setting is apparent when the school is seen as an open system, with the environment providing inputs conceptualized in terms of student, teacher, parent, school board, and other concerns which must be recognized and effectively processed through interlocked behavior patterns. When these concerns demand conflicting behaviors, such as when teachers are faced with the need for collective action as members of a union while remaining concerned about their obligation to teach their students, role strain is likely to occur, with negative impact on the health and well-being of the teachers.

A more recent area where interests of social psychologists intersect with those of large organizations involves the process of performance appraisal, which refers to the (usually) periodic evaluation given by a supervisor of a subordinate based on recent job performance. These appraisals almost always involve some type of rating scale of the subordinate's traits or behaviors. Organizations use these appraisals to make decisions about raises, promotions, transfers, remedial training, or termination. There has, therefore, been a long-standing concern about the reliability and validity of such appraisals (Landy & Farr, 1980). Efforts to improve relatively poor reliability centered for some time on the form of the rating instrument itself, leading to innovations such as the Behaviorally Anchored Rating Scale. Later emphasis was placed on the training of raters to avoid common errors in the rating process. Both of these approaches, which produced improved—but far from ideal—ratings, assumed that the problems were mainly mechanical in nature. Recent work in social cognition, however, suggests that various rating problems may be the result of inherent information processing strategies that work quite well in nonrating contexts, where general impressions of others are quite sufficient (Landy & Farr, 1980).

The social cognition approach is derived from the recognition that performance appraisals are usually made from memory, and that they cover activities of the subordinate over a relatively long period of time (e.g., a year or 6 months). Under such conditions, a variety of factors that are now of interest to those in social cognition may play an important role in the appraisal process. For instance, general impressions of the subordinate may be formed early, based on salient behavior and various stereotype expectations. The early general impression forms the basis for a schema that in turn directs behavior toward the subordinate and information processing of the subordinate's behavior. Later appraisal of the subordinate is based on recall of information in the context of the schema. That recall of information may be biased in a number of ways; for example, information consistent with the schema may be more readily recalled than schema-inconsistent information, or negative information may be recalled more readily than positive information (DeNisi, Cafferty, & Meglino, 1984).

Work in this area takes on special significance for school situations, with increased emphasis on accountability and evaluation of teachers and administrative personnel. Better evaluation techniques must go beyond the creation of better observation forms and better objective indices of performance. They must take into account the information-processing characteristics and limitations of the raters.

CONCLUSION

The intent of this chapter was to provide a broad overview of contemporary social psychology and its applications to school psychology. As described in several texts devoted to the application of social psychology (e.g., Oskamp, 1984; Feldman, 1986), social psychology has at its roots field studies, survey research, group phenomenon, and action research. However, in recent years it has been heavily influenced by emerging work in cognitive psychology, artificial intelligence, and biopsychology. While the grand theories of the 1950s, such as dissonance, reactance, and social comparison, still hold explanatory power, it would be foolish for modern school psychologists to rely solely on these in attempting to understand issues of professional practice.

We strongly believe that a survey course in

social psychology is a basic prerequisite for any school psychologist. Clearly, we are all "social animals," bombarded daily by a myriad of stimuli directed at us by other individuals, groups, and organizations. And it is the recognition of this that makes salient the complexity of defining the client populations we serve (Stewart, 1986), identifying the nature of their schooling problems, and deciding on a choice of intervention strategy.

REFERENCES

Abelson, R. P. (1976). Script processing in attitude formation and decision making. In J. S. Carroll & J. W. Payne (Eds.), *Cognition and social behavior* (pp. 33–45). Hillsdale, NY: Lawrence Erlbaum.

Abramson, L. Y., Seligman, M. E. P., & Teasdale, J. D. (1978). Learned helplessness in humans: Critique and reformulation. *Journal of Abnormal Psychology, 87,* 49–75.

Adams, J. S. (1965). Inequity in social exchanges. In L. Berkowitz (Ed.), *Advances in experimental social psychology* (Vol. 2, pp. 267–299). New York: Academic Press.

Ajzen, I., & Fishbein, M. (1980). *Understanding attitudes and predicting social behavior.* Englewood Cliffs, NJ: Prentice-Hall.

Allport, F. (1924). *Social psychology.* Boston: Houghton Mifflin.

Allport, G. (1958). *The nature of prejudice.* Reading, MA: Addison-Wesley.

Allport, G. W. (1985). The historical background of social psychology. In G. Lindzey & E. Aronson (Eds.), *The handbook of social psychology* (3rd ed., Vol. 1, pp. 1–46). Hillsdale, NJ: Lawrence Erlbaum.

American Psychological Association. (1986). *Biographical directory of the American Psychological Association.* Arlington, VA: Author.

Amir, Y. (1969). Contact hypothesis in ethnic relations. *Psychological Bulletin, 71,* 319–342.

Aronson, E., & Osherow, N. (1980). Cooperation, prosocial behavior, and academic performance: Experiments in the desegregated classroom. In L. Bickman (Ed.), *Applied social psychology annual* (Vol. 1, pp. 163–196). Beverly Hills, CA: Sage.

Aronson, E., Stephan, C., Sikes, J., Blaney, N., & Snapp, M. (1978). *The jigsaw classroom.* Beverly Hills, CA: Sage.

Asch, S. E. (1951). Effects of group pressure upon the modification and distortion of judgments. In H. Guetzkow (Ed.), *Groups, leadership, and men* (pp. 177–190). Pittsburgh, PA: Carnegie Press.

Bandura, A. (1965). Vicarious processes: A case of no-trial learning. In L. Berkowitz (Ed.), *Advances in experimental social psychology* (Vol. 2, pp. 301–329). New York: Academic Press.

Bar-Tal, D. (1982). The effects of teachers' behavior on pupils' attributions: A review. In C. Antaki & C. Brewin (Eds.), *Attributions and psychological change: Applications of attributional theories to clinical and educational practice* (pp. 177–194). New York: Academic Press.

Belsky, J. (1984). The determinants of parenting: A process model. *Child Development, 55,* 83–96.

Bem, D. J. (1967). Self perception: An alternate explanation of cognitive dissonance phenomenon. *Psychological Bulletin, 74,* 183–200.

Berkowitz, L., & Frodi, A. (1979). Reactions to a child's mistakes as affected by his/her looks and speech. *Social Psychology Quarterly, 42,* 420–425.

Berscheid, E. (1985). Interpersonal attraction. In G. Lindzey & E. Aronson (Eds.), *Handbook of social psychology* (3rd ed., Vol. 2, pp. 413–484). Englewood Cliffs, NJ: Prentice-Hall.

Billig, M., & Tajfel, H. (1973). Social categorization and similarity in intergroup behavior. *European Journal of Social Psychology, 3,* 27–52.

Bohlmeyer, E. M., & Burke, J. P. (1987). Selecting cooperative learning techniques: A consultative strategy guide. *School Psychology Review, 16,* 36–49.

Borkowski, J. G., Weyhing, R. S., & Carr, M. (1988). Effects of attributional retraining on strategy-based reading comprehension in learning-disabled students. *Journal of Educational Psychology, 80,* 46–53.

Brehm, S. S. (1976). *The application of social psychology to clinical practice.* New York: Wiley.

Brown, R. (1986). *Social psychology: The second edition.* New York: Free Press.

Byrne, D. (1969). Attitudes and attraction. In L. Berkowitz (Ed.), *Advances in experimental social psychology* (Vol. 4, pp. 35–89). New York: Academic Press.

Cantor, N., & Mischel, W. (1977). Prototypes in person perception. In L. Berkowitz (Ed.), *Advances in experimental social psychology* (Vol. 12, pp 3–52). New York: Academic Press.

Cartwright, D. (1979). Contemporary social psychology in historical perspective. *Social Psychology Quarterly, 42,* 82–93.

Cecil, M., & Medway, F. J. (1986). Attribution retaining with low-achieving and learned helpless children. *Techniques: A Journal for Remedial Education and Counseling, 2,* 173–181.

Chaney, L. A., & Bugental, D. B. (1982). An attributional approach to hyperactive behavior. In C. Antaki & C. Brewin (Eds.), *Attributions and psychological change* (pp. 211–226). London: Academic Press.

Chapman, L. J., & Chapman, J. P. (1967). Genesis of popular but erroneous psychodiagnostic observations. *Journal of Abnormal Psychology, 72,* 193–204.

Chapman, L. J., & Chapman, J. P. (1969). Illusory correlation as an obstacle to the use of valid psychodiagnostic signs. *Journal of Abnormal Psychology, 74,* 271–280.

Clark, K. B., & Clark, M. P. (1965). Racial identification and preference in Negro children. In H. Proshansky & B. Seidenberg (Eds.), *Basic studies in social psychology* (pp. 308–317). New York: Holt, Rinehart and Winston.

Cook, S. W. (1969). Motives in a conceptual analysis of attitude-related behavior. In W. J. Arnold & D.

Levine (Eds.), *Nebraska symposium on motivation* (Vol. 17, pp. 179–235). Lincoln: University of Nebraska Press.

Cook, S. W. (1978). Interpersonal and attitudinal outcomes in cooperating interracial groups. *Journal of Research and Development in Education, 12,* 97–113.

Cook, S. W. (1984). The 1954 social science statement and school desegregation: A reply to Gerard. *American Psychologist, 39,* 819–832.

Cooley, C. H. (1918). *The social process.* New York: Charles Scribner's Sons.

DeNisi, A. S., Cafferty, T. P., & Meglino, B. M. (1984). A cognitive view of the performance appraisal process: A model and research propositions. *Organizational Behavior and Human Performance, 33,* 360–396.

Deutsch, M. (1968). The effects of cooperation and competition upon group process. In D. Cartwright & A. Zander (Eds.), *Group dynamics* (3rd ed., pp. 461–482). New York: Harper & Row.

DeVries, D. L., Edwards, K. J., & Slavin, R. E. (1978). Biracial learning teams and race relations in the classroom: Four field experiments using teams-games-tournaments. *Journal of Educational Psychology, 70,* 356–362.

DeVries, D. L., & Slavin, R. E. (1978). Teams-games-tournament (TGT): A review of ten classroom experiments. *Journal of Research and Development in Education, 12,* 28–38.

Durkheim, E. (1951). *Suicide.* Glencoe, IL: Free Press.

Elms, A. C. (1975). The crisis of confidence in social psychology. *American Psychologist, 30,* 967–976.

Feldman, R. S. (1986). *The social psychology of education: Current research and theory.* New York: Cambridge University Press.

Festinger, L. (1954). A theory of social comparison processes. *Human Relations, 7,* 117–140.

Festinger, L. (1957). *A theory of cognitive dissonance.* Stanford, CA: Stanford University Press.

Fiedler, F. E. (1964). A contingency model of leadership effectiveness. In L. Berkowitz (Ed.), *Advances in experimental social psychology* (Vol. 1, pp. 150–190). New York: Academic Press.

Fiedler, F. E., & Garcia, J. E. (1987). *New approaches to leadership: Cognitive resources and organizational performance.* New York: Wiley.

Finkelhor, D. (1984). *Child sexual abuse: New theory and research.* New York: Free Press.

Fishbein, M. (Ed.). (1967). *Readings in attitude theory and measurement.* New York: Wiley.

Fishbein, M., & Ajzen, I. (1974). Attitudes toward objects as predictors of single and multiple behavioral criteria. *Psychological Review, 81,* 59–74.

Fishbein, M., & Ajzen, I. (1975). *Belief, attitude, intention, and behavior: An introduction to theory and research.* Reading, MA: Addison-Wesley.

Fiske, S. T., & Taylor, S. E. (1984). *Social cognition.* Reading, MA: Addison-Wesley.

Freedman, J. L. (1984). Effects of television violence on aggressiveness. *Psychological Bulletin, 96,* 227–246.

Golding, W. (1954). *Lord of the flies.* New York: Coward-McCann.

Gottlieb, J., Rose, T., & Lessen, E. (1983). Mainstreaming. In K. Kerenau, M. Begab, & R. Edgerton (Eds.), *Environments and behavior: The adaption of mentally retarded persons* (pp. 195–212). Baltimore: University Park Press.

Hannah, M. E., & Pliner, S. (1983). Teacher attitudes toward handicapped children: A review and synthesis. *School Psychology Review, 12,* 12–25.

Harvey, J. H., Ickes, W., & Kidd, R. F. (Eds.). (1978). *New directions in attribution research* (Vol. 2). Hillsdale, NJ: Lawrence Erlbaum.

Harvey, J. H., & Weary, G. (1984). Current issues in attribution theory and research. *Annual Review of Psychology, 35,* 427–459.

Heider, F. (1958). *The psychology of interpersonal relations.* New York: Wiley.

Hendrick, C. (1977). Social psychology as an experimental science. In C. Hendrick (Ed.), *Perspectives on social psychology* (pp. 1–74). Hillsdale, NJ: Lawrence Erlbaum.

Hollingshead, A. B., & Redlich, F. C. (1958). *Social class and mental illness: A community study.* New York: Wiley.

House, R. J., & Singh, J. V. (1987). Organizational behavior: Some new directions for I/O psychology. *Annual Review of Psychology, 38,* 669–718.

Hovland, C. I. (1959). Reconciling results derived from experimental and survey studies of attitude change. *American Psychologist, 14,* 8–17.

Hovland, C. I., Janis, I. L., & Kelley, H. H. (1953). *Communication and persuasion.* New Haven, CT: Yale University Press.

Hughes, J. N. (1983). The application of cognitive dissonance to consultation. *Journal of School Psychology, 21,* 349–357.

Huston, T. L., & Levinger, G. (1978). Interpersonal attraction and relationships. *Annual Review of Psychology, 29,* 115–156.

Janoff-Bulman, R. (1979). Characterological versus behavioral self-blame: Inquiries into depression and rape. *Journal of Personality and Social Psychology, 37,* 1798–1809.

Johnson, D. W., & Johnson, R. T. (1982). The effects of cooperative and individualistic instruction on handicapped and nonhandicapped students. *Journal of Social Psychology, 118,* 257–268.

Jones, E. E. (1985). Major developments in social psychology during the past five decades. In G. Lindzey & E. Aronson (Eds.), *The handbook of social psychology* (3rd ed., Vol. 1, pp. 47–107). Hillsdale, NJ: Lawrence Erlbaum.

Jones, E. E., & Davis, K. E. (1965). From acts to dispositions: The attribution process in person perception. In L. Berkowitz (Ed.), *Advances in experimental social psychology* (Vol. 2, pp. 219–266). New York: Academic Press.

Jones, E. E., & Nisbett, R. E. (1971). *The actor and the observer: Divergent perceptions of behavior.* Morristown, NJ: General Learning Press.

Katz, D., & Kahn, R. L. (1978). *The social psychology of organizations* (2nd ed.). New York: Wiley.

Kelley, H. H. (1967). Attribution in social psychology. In D. Levine (Ed.), *Nebraska symposium on motiva-*

tion (pp. 192–238). Lincoln: University of Nebraska Press.

Kelley, H. H., & Michela, J. L. (1980). Attribution theory and research. *Annual Review of Psychology, 31,* 457–501.

Kelley, H. H., & Thibaut, J. W. (1978). *Interpersonal relations: A theory of independence.* New York: Wiley.

Kyle, S. O., & Falbo, T. (1985). Relationships between marital stress and attributional preferences for own and spouse behavior. *Journal of Social and Clinical Psychology, 3,* 339–351.

Landy, F. S., & Farr, J. L. (1980). Performance rating. *Psychological Bulletin, 87,* 72–107.

Langer, E., & Abelson, R. P. (1972). The semantics of asking a favor: How to succeed in getting help without really dying. *Journal of Personality and Social Psychology, 24,* 26–32.

Larrance, D. F., & Twentyman, C. T. (1983). Maternal attributions and child abuse. *Journal of Abnormal Psychology, 92,* 449–457.

Latane, B., & Darley, J. M. (1970). *The unresponsive bystander: Why doesn't he help?* New York: Appleton-Century-Crofts.

Lerner, M. J. (1980). *The belief in a just world: The fundamental illusion.* New York: Plenum Press.

Lewin, K. (1951). Psychological ecology. In D. Cartwright (Ed.), *Field theory in social science* (pp. 170–187). New York: Harper & Row.

Lewin, K., Lippett, R., & White, R. K. (1939). Patterns of aggressive behavior in experimentally created "social climates." *Journal of Social Psychology, 10,* 271–299.

Lighthall, F. F. (1969). A social psychologist for school systems. *Psychology in the Schools, 6,* 3–12.

Madden, N. A., & Slavin, R. E. (1983). Effects of cooperative learning on social acceptance of mainstreamed academically handicapped students. *Journal of Special Education, 17,* 171–182.

Malamuth, N. M. (1986). Predictors of naturalistic sexual aggression. *Journal of Personality and Social Psychology, 50,* 953–962.

Markus, H., & Zajonc, R. B. (1985). The cognitive perspective in social psychology. In G. Lindzey & E. Aronson (Eds.), *The handbook of social psychology* (3rd ed., Vol. 1, pp. 137–230). Hillsdale, NJ: Lawrence Erlbaum.

Marshall, W. L., & Barbaree, H. E. (1984). A behavioral view of rape. *International Journal of Law and Psychiatry, 7,* 51–77.

Martin, R. P., & Curtis, M. (1981). Consultants' perceptions of causality for success and failure of consultation. *Professional Psychology, 12,* 671–676.

McDermott, P. A. (1981). Sources of error in the psychoeducational diagnosis of children. *Journal of School Psychology, 19,* 31–44.

McDougall, W. (1908). *An introduction to social psychology.* London: Methuen.

McGuire, W. J. (1967). Some impending reorientations in social psychology: Some thoughts provoked by Kenneth Ring. *Journal of Experimental Social Psychology, 3,* 124–139.

McGuire, W. J. (1985). Attitudes and attitude change. In G. Lindzey & E. Aronson (Eds.), *The handbook of social psychology* (3rd ed., Vol. 2, pp. 233–346). Hillsdale, NJ: Lawrence Erlbaum.

Mead, G. H. (1934). *Mind, self, and society.* Chicago: University of Chicago Press.

Medway, F. J. (1975). A social psychological approach to internally based change in the schools. *Journal of School Psychology, 13,* 19–27.

Medway, F. J. (1979). Causal attributions for school-related problems: Teacher perceptions and teacher feedback. *Journal of Educational Psychology, 71,* 809–819.

Merton, R. K. (1957). *Social theory and social structure.* New York: Free Press.

Middleton, H., Zollinger, J., & Keene, R. (1986). Popular peers as change agents for the socially neglected child in the classroom. *Journal of School Psychology, 24,* 343–350.

Milgram, S. (1963). Behavioral study of obedience. *Journal of Abnormal and Social Psychology, 67,* 371–378.

Miller, N. E. (1941). The frustration-aggression hypothesis. *Psychological Review, 48,* 337–342.

Moreno, J. L. (1934). *Who shall survive?* (Monograph No. 58). Washington, DC: Nervous and Mental Disease Publishing.

Moscovici, S. (1972). Society and theory in social psychology. In J. Israel & H. Tajfel (Eds.), *The context of social psychology: A critical assessment* (pp. 17–68). New York: Academic Press.

Mueser, K. T., Grau, B. W., Sussman, S., & Rosen, A. J. (1984). You're only as pretty as you feel: Facial expression as a determinant of physical attractiveness. *Journal of Personality and Social Psychology, 46,* 468–478.

Newcomb, T. M. (1943). *Personality and social change.* New York: Dryden.

Nisbett, R. E., & Ross, L. (1980). *Human inference: Strategies and shortcomings in social judgment.* Englewood Cliffs, NJ: Prentice-Hall.

Oskamp, S. (1977). *Attitudes and opinions.* Englewood Cliffs, NJ: Prentice-Hall.

Oskamp, S. (1984). *Applied social psychology.* Englewood Cliffs, NJ: Prentice-Hall.

Pearl, D., Bouthilet, L., & Lazar, J. (Eds.). (1982). *Television and behavior: Ten years of scientific progress and implications for the eighties.* Washington, DC: U.S. Department of Health and Human Services.

Penrod, S. (1983). *Social psychology.* Englewood Cliffs, NJ: Prentice-Hall.

Petty, R. E., & Caccioppo, J. T. (1981). *Attitudes and persuasion: Classic and contemporary approaches.* Dubuque, IA: Wm. C. Brown.

Pfeffer, J. (1985). Organizations and organization theory. In G. Lindzey & E. Aronson (Eds.), *The handbook of social psychology* (3rd ed., Vol. 1, pp. 379–440). Hillsdale, NJ: Lawrence Erlbaum.

Ring, K. (1967). Experimental social psychology: Some sober questions about some frivolous values. *Journal of Experimental Social Psychology, 3,* 113–123.

Robinson, J. P., Athanasiou, R., & Head, K. B. (1969).

Measures of occupational attitudes and occupational characteristics. Ann Arbor, MI: Institute for Social Research.

Robinson, J. P., & Shaver, W. (1973). *Measures of social psychological attitudes*. Ann Arbor, MI: Institute of Social Relations.

Rolison, M. A., & Medway, F. J. (1985). Teacher expectations and attributions for student achievement: Effects of label, performance pattern, and special education intervention. *American Educational Research Journal, 22,* 561–573.

Rosenthal, R., & Rosnow, R. L. (1984). *Essentials of behavioral research: Methods and data analysis*. New York: McGraw-Hill.

Ross, E. A. (1908). *Social psychology: An outline and a source book*. New York: Macmillan.

Rossi, P. H., Wright, J. D.,, & Anderson, A. B. (Eds.). (1983). *Handbook of survey research*. New York: Academic Press.

Rubin, J. Z., & Brown, B. R. (1975). *The social psychology of bargaining and negotiation*. New York: Academic Press.

Sahakian, W. S. (1974). *Systematic social psychology*. New York: Chandler.

Schachter, S. (1964). The interaction of cognitive and physiological determinants of emotional state. In L. Berkowitz (Ed.), *Advances in experimental social psychology* (Vol. 1, pp. 49–80). New York: Academic Press.

Schachter, S., & Singer J (1962). Cognitive, social and physiological determinants of emotional state. *Psychological Review, 69,* 379–399.

Schmuck, R. A., & Schmuck, P. A. (1971). *Group processes in the classroom*. Dubuque, IA: Wm. C. Brown.

Schneider, B. (1985). Organizational behavior. *Annual Review of Psychology, 36,* 573–611.

Selltiz, C., Wrightsman, L. C., & Cook, S. W. (1976). *Research methods in social relations* (3rd ed.). New York: Holt, Rinehart and Winston.

Shaw, M. E., & Wright, J. M. (1967). *Scales for the measurement of attitudes*. New York: McGraw-Hill.

Sherif, M. (1936). *The psychology of social norms*. New York: Harper.

Sherif, M., Harvey, O. J., White, B. J., Hood, W. R., & Sherif, C. W. (1961). *Intergroup conflict and cooperation: The Robbers' Cave experiment*. Normal: University of Oklahoma Book Exchange.

Simmel, G. (1950) *The sociology of George Simmel* (K. H. Wolf, Ed. and Trans.). New York: Macmillan.

Slavin, R. E. (1983). *Cooperative learning*. New York: Longman.

Slavin, R. E. (1985). Team-assisted individualization: Combining cooperative learning and individualized instruction in mathematics. In R. E. Slavin, S. Sharon, S. Kagan, R. Hertz-Lazarowitz, C. Webb, & R. Schmuck (Eds.), *Learning to cooperate, coop-*

erating to learn (pp. 177–209). New York: Plenum Press.

Smith, D. K., & Lyon, M. A. (1986). School psychologists' attributions for success and failure in consultations with parents and teachers. *Professional Psychology: Research and Practice, 17,* 205–209.

Smith, S. S., Richardson, D., & Hendrick, C. (1980). Bibliography of journal articles in personality and social psychology. *Personality and Social Psychology Bulletin, 6,* 606–636.

Stephan, W. G. (1978). School desegregation: An evaluation of predictions made in Brown v. Board of Education. *Psychological Bulletin, 85,* 215–238.

Stephan, W. G. (1985). Intergroup relations. In G. Lindzey & E. Aronson (Eds.), *The handbook of social psychology* (3rd ed., Vol. 2, pp. 599–658). Hillsdale, NJ: Lawrence Erlbaum.

Stewart, K. J. (1986). Disentangling the complexities of clientage. In S. N. Elliott & J. C. Witt (Eds.), *The delivery of psychological services in the schools* (pp. 81–107). Hillsdale, NJ: Lawrence Erlbaum.

Summers, G. E. (Ed.). (1970). *Attitude measurement*. Skokie, IL: Rand McNally.

Tajfel, H. (1970). Experiments in intergroup discrimination. *Scientific American, 223,* 96–102.

Tajfel, H. (1978). *Differentiation between social groups*. London: Academic Press.

Thurstone, L. L. (1928). Attitudes can be measured. *American Journal of Sociology, 33,* 529–544.

Triplett, N. (1897). The dynamogenic factors in pacemaking and competition. *American Journal of Psychology, 9,* 507–533.

Tversky, A., & Kahneman, D. (1974). Judgment under uncertainty: Heuristics and biases. *Science, 185,* 1124–1131.

Warring, D., Johnson, D. W., Marayuma, G., & Johnson, R. (1985). Impact of different types of cooperative learning on cross-ethnic and cross-sex relationships. *Journal of Educational Psychology, 77,* 53–59.

Weiner, B. (1972). Attribution theory, achievement motivation, and the educational process. *Review of Educational Research, 42,* 203–215.

Weiner, B. (1979). A theory of motivation for some classroom experiences. *Journal of Educational Psychology, 71,* 3–25.

Wicker, A. (1969). Attitudes versus actions: The relationship of verbal and overt behavioral responses to attitude objects. *Journal of Social Issues, 25,* 41–78.

Wuebben, P. L., Straits, B. C., & Schulman, G. I. (Eds.). (1974). *The experiment as a social occasion*. Berkeley, CA: Glendessary Press.

Zimbardo, P. G, Ebbesen, E. B., & Maslach, C. (1977). *Influencing attitudes and changing behavior* (2nd ed.). Reading, MA: Addison-Wesley.

9

CONTRIBUTIONS OF COMMUNITY PSYCHOLOGY TO SCHOOL PSYCHOLOGY

JOEL MEYERS
EDWARD GAUGHAN
State University of New York at Albany
NORMAN PITT
Maxicare of Philadelphia

The specialty of school psychology predates the field of community psychology, yet in this chapter we consider the effects of community psychology on school psychology. Although it is difficult to establish conclusively just what effects one particular discipline has on another, there are a number of important factors associated with the development of community psychology which have also had important effects on training, practice, and research in the field of school psychology. The purpose of this chapter is to discuss these factors and to consider their effects on the field of school psychology.

Community Psychology: A Definition and Historical Overview

Community psychology emerged as a subdiscipline of psychology during the 1960s in a climate of political action, political unrest, and renewed attention to social issues. One important political factor at this time was the community mental health movement, which was initiated formally with the passage of the Community Mental Health Centers Act in 1965. This legislation marked a major shift in federal funding policy, emphasizing the delivery of mental health services in the local community and deemphasizing treatment provided in residential institutions.

In addition to these sociopolitical factors, the professional context for community psychology's evolution was the shift from clinical psychology's almost exclusive concern with the psychodynamic, intrapsychic factors that were thought to underlie the individual's behavior toward a focus on the social system. Community psychology is an approach that considers the application of psychological principles at the level of the community in an effort to resolve or prevent mental health problems of individuals in the community. As Spielberger and Iscoe (1970) noted: "Community psychology represents a new frontier in the study of human behavior, which is broadly concerned with clarifying the complex interrelationships between individuals and their environment" (p. 244).

Although it has been suggested that William Rhodes first used the term "community psychology" (e.g., Iscoe, Bloom, & Spielberger, 1977), this term began to be used consistently instead of "community mental health" at the Boston Conference on the Education of Psychologists for Community Mental Health in 1965. This conference emphasized the study and treatment of individuals in a community context and the need for evaluative research on consultation. It recognized, further, that traditional clinical approaches did not necessarily meet the mental health needs of low socioeconomic (SES) and minority group members.

The Division of Community Psychology in the American Psychological Association (Division 27) was formed in 1967 after the Boston conference. This was followed by the 1967 Symposium on Training in Community Psychology at Austin, Texas (Iscoe & Speilberger, 1970), which led to the National Conference on Training in Community Psychology, which also took place in Austin (Iscoe et al., 1977). This conference on training brought together most of the leaders in the field of community psychology, and it summarized historical events and the major issues confronting the field. Other important scholarly contributions that influenced the field from its inception in the mid-1960s are the books by Cowen, Gardner, and Zax (1967) and Sarason, Levine, Goldenberg, Cherlin, and Bennett (1966).

The Interface of Community Psychology and School Psychology: Historical Perspective

There has always been a natural, logical connection between school psychology and community psychology, since schools represent the one community agency in our society that maintains contact with the entire population of children and which has the potential for contact with the families of these children. Schools are one logical community agency to focus the efforts of community psychology toward children, and since school psychologists are regularly employed in school settings, they are one vehicle for providing psychological services to the community as a whole.

Some recent developments in both community psychology and school psychology have been attributable, in part, to criticisms concerning the medical model and the time demands associated with the diagnosis and treatment provided in individually based direct service models (e.g., Meyers, Parsons, & Martin, 1979). The time-consuming nature of these direct approaches to clinical treatment further exacerbates the unfortunate shortage of mental health professionals which was predicted by Albee (1959) based on a study he conducted for the Joint Commission on Mental Illness. He concluded: "The manpower demands projected over the next twenty years in the fields concerned with professional care of people with emotional disorders are so far beyond the probable supply of people available as to constitute a major national crisis" (Albee, 1967, p. 63). At the same time, popular literature, mass media, formal education about psychology and mental health problems, and legislation focused on problems of the mentally ill (e.g., the Community Mental Health Center's Act of 1965) have resulted in increased awareness of the potential offered by mental health services. While this has contributed to advances in applied professional psychology, it has also led to increased demands for services in the midst of the personpower shortage predicted by Albee.

Although training programs in professional psychology have produced increasingly larger numbers of professional psychologists since Albee's prediction, there remains a dramatic gap between the mental health needs in our society and the numbers of professionals available to provide these services (e.g., Meyers et al., 1979). Clinical psychology responded by developing the field of community psychology, and school psychology responded simultaneously by developing consultative, preventive and other indirect service delivery models. Meyers et al. (1979) noted a shift in focus toward approaches emphasizing: a community rather than a clinical perspective, prevention instead of therapy, experimentation with short-term remediation, new sources of personpower, a commitment to increased control by client and community, identification of environmental stressors, and indirect rather than direct service (Bloom, 1973). These forces created changes in the field of school psychology at the time that the field of community psychology developed.

Seymour Sarason's work emerged in this context, with particular implications for simultaneous developments in the fields of community and school psychology (i.e., Sarason et al., 1966; Sarason, 1972, 1974, 1976, 1982), and his Yale

Psycho-Educational Clinic, which was first planned in 1961, was particularly significant in this context. Unlike other clinics developed prior to that time, this clinic sought to provide services in the settings where problems were observed rather than at the clinic itself. By providing services in the appropriate environmental setting it was thought to be more likely that interventions would be successful and have broad environmental effects beyond the person referred. Thus, rather than provide services back at the clinic, the school setting was one focus of service delivery and the goal was to provide services in nontraditional ways directed at reaching a greater percentage of the population. Services were also provided at neighborhood employment centers, skill centers, regional centers for the mentally retarded, and day care centers. A crucial viewpoint underscored by the Yale Psycho-Educational Clinic was that psychological services must be provided by helping key settings such as the school change in an effort to benefit the people involved with those settings (e.g., students, teachers, parents). Initially, the professionals working for this clinic viewed themselves as clinical psychologists who sought to change settings through individuals. The radical shift symbolized by Sarason's work, however, was a focus on the community as a whole, in an effort to create organizational change rather than changes in individuals (Sarason, 1976). The ideas that form the basis for Sarason's clinic are still relevant for professional school psychologists.

Many of the contributions of community psychology to school psychology derive from preventive techniques and other indirect services, such as mental health consultation. Both disciplines, however, have also maintained an emphasis on the direct delivery of psychological services using techniques such as individual diagnostic testing and treatment. While various approaches to the delivery of diagnostic and treatment services have pervaded the school psychology literature, this approach in community psychology has been most apparent in the community mental health movement, which argued for the delivery of these direct services in the local community.

Models of Community Psychology Relevant to the Practice of School Psychology

The 1975 Austin Conference on Training in Community Psychology identified seven overlapping models (e.g., Iscoe et al. 1977). *Clinical Commu-* *nity Psychology* (Aponte, 1977) is an approach based on clinical training for work with individuals and groups, and the goal is to ameliorate symptoms associated with mental health problems. This model relies on clinical procedures to remediate individuals' problems. The *Community Clinical and Community Mental Health* model (Aponte, 1977) maintains some of the same clinical flavor as the first model, and adds a greater concern for mental health in the community. While mental health services might be provided to a broader range of the population through structures such as community mental health centers in these first two models, the primary focus of service delivery is direct psychological intervention. The third model discussed at the Austin conference was the *Community Development and Systems Approaches* (Lorion, 1977). This approach aims for a better quality of life for the community and emphasizes mental health, using procedures such as planning, management, and evaluation. Another model of community psychology is the *Interventive Preventive Systems* model (Dorr, 1977; Gerrard, 1977; Hodges, 1977). This model stresses techniques designed to build competence and modify systems, and it uses techniques such as evaluation and consultation while deemphasizing traditional clinical methods. The fifth model is the *Social Change Model,* emphasizing efforts to change institutions and society, and relying on a variety of techniques, including the political process (Gatz & Liem, 1977; Hassol, 1977). The *Social Ecology* model assesses community forces as a basis for planning multilevel interventions (Holahan, 1977). This model considers a variety of environmental factors, such as housing and population density. The last model mentioned at the Austin Conference was the *Applied Social Psychology and Urban Psychology Systems* model (Dohrenwend, 1977). Emphasizing external factors affecting people, particularly urban problems, this model uses evaluation and consultation as strategies geared to achieve social change for the well-being of humanity.

The issues underlying each of these models have had significant effects on the field of school psychology. There is, however, considerable overlap between these models, and their relationship to the field of school psychology can be understood most easily by considering four foundational elements: (a) the community mental health movement, (b) mental health consultation, (c) primary prevention of psychopathology, and (d) models of social change. These four factors provide the basis for considering the impact of community psychology on school psychology in the remainder of this chapter.

COMMUNITY MENTAL HEALTH MOVEMENT

The community mental health movement developed out of concern for a number of issues related to how care was being delivered to mentally and emotionaly disturbed people in this country. Fundamentally, it represented an attempt to make available comprehensive mental health services to the entire population at the local community level, and to develop mental health functions for society similar to those performed by general public health services. Two of the seven models discussed at the Austin conference on training (Iscoe et al., 1977) are closely related to the approaches most commonly associated with the community mental health movement: the clinical community psychology model (Aponte, 1977) and the community clinical and community mental health model (Aponte, 1977).

Historical Overview

With the passage in Congress of the Mental Retardation Facilities and Community Mental Health Centers Construction Act of 1963 (Public Law 88-164), the United States committed itself for the first time to a national policy of providing a system of community-based, comprehensive mental health services. This legislation marked a significant departure from previous policy in at least four major respects: (a) the federal government assumed a dominant policy and financial position in an area that had previously been left largely to state and local governments (Snow & Swift, 1985); (b) the focus of treatment was to be in the community, as contrasted to the mental health hospital (Iscoe and Spielberger, 1970); (c) the services envisioned at the federal level were to be more comprehensive than had previously been proposed by any policy or planning body; and (d) the federal initiative fostered the development of preventive programs (Felner, Jason, Moritsugu, & Farber, 1983). In large part, the particular form and emphasis of this legislation was an expression of the Zeitgeist of the 1960s, emphasizing the solution of social problems through the infusion of funds and expertise at a national level (Snow &

Swift, 1985) and community action at a local level (Jacobson, Ravlin, & Cooper, 1983). However, the major initiatives embodied in the Community Mental Health Center's Act actually had their roots in a variety of other developments that predate this legislation by two decades or more.

As a result of experiences in World War II, national concern about mental health issues increased greatly, resulting in significant policy shifts: The National Institute of Mental Health was established; millions of dollars were poured into development of Veterans Administration facilities; dissatisfaction with state hospitals increased; and a federal policy of block grants to states was established to encourage the development of community-based, outpatient psychiatric clinics (Buck, 1984). In 1955, Congress authorized the Joint Commission of Mental Illness and Mental Health to focus on and make recommendations regarding issues of resources and personpower in diagnosis, treatment, and rehabilitation of the mentally ill. The report of the Joint Commission served as the basis for the Mental Health Centers Act, with special urging from President Kennedy.

Funding for community mental health centers was appropriated explicitly for development and operation of community-based facilities, with funds being disbursed to qualified grantees who would each serve a population of 75,000 to 200,000 people (Buck, 1984). Programs were to be started on a "seed money" basis, with federal support to individual community mental health centers declining to zero in successive years. Five basic services were mandated: inpatient care, outpatient care, emergency services, partial hospitalization, and consultation and education. The concept of prevention was presumably embodied in the consultation and education function. In subsequent years community mental health centers have gone through major adjustments and changes as mandated services were altered and funding patterns changed drastically.

The most compelling changes came with the advent of Alcohol, Drug Abuse and Mental Health Administration (ADAMHA) Services Block Grants, whereby the state, rather than the community mental health center, became the recipients of federal funds. While these grants involve some stipulations for their use (e.g., five mandated services, preferential treatment for existing centers), the overall effect is to grant the state great discretion in setting their own priorities. To this extent, community mental health centers have ceased to be the primary vehicle for the influence of the federal government on mental health services (Buck, 1984). A number of studies have shown that at the level of the community mental health centers themselves, staffing and service changes have coincided with state priorities (Jerrell & Larsen, 1984; Vayda & Perlmutter, 1977).

Community Mental Health Centers and the Schools

It probably is fair to say that community mental health centers throughout the country have enjoyed their most consistent and most fully mutual relationship with the schools in their catchment areas. Community mental health centers and schools shared substantially in the day-to-day execution of their respective roles, and each benefitted significantly from the presence and activity of the other. It is interesting to note, moreover, that in their list of the "newer concepts" developed by community mental health (Ciarlo & Diamond, 1979), all have direct relevance to schools. Moreover, several authors have noted that schools are a logical focus for mental health center activities, in that access to school children and their families makes sense from a preventive or early intervention point of view (Anderson, 1976; Schultz, Harker, & Gardner, 1977; Vayda & Perlmutter, 1977). In that sense, community mental health centers, with their full range of services, can be viewed as a natural partner in the school's mission of socializing and educating a community's children.

Given the close contact between schools and community mental health centers, the frequent overlap in training provided for school psychologists and those employed by community mental health centers, the overlapping influence of professionals such as Gerald Caplan and Seymour Sarason, and the similar goals of providing psychological services to the largest possible proportion of the population in need of these services, the work of psychologists in community mental health centers has had a substantial impact on school psychology. These effects can be conceptualized most readily by considering three different aspects of the work provided in community mental health centers: direct service, consultative/ preventive services, and special collaborative programs. These three aspects are described below with reference to their impact on the practice of psychology in the schools.

Direct Service

As has been pointed out by a number of writers (e.g., Felner et al., 1983; Snow & Swift, 1985), community mental health centers have always been primarily direct service organizations. While this reality runs contrary to community mental health center ideology, the direct service orientation is easily demonstrated by a review of financial allocations; allocation of staff time (Snow & Swift, 1985); ideological and professional backgrounds of community mental health center staff; and even by the requirements of the original Community Mental Health Centers Act, according to which four of the five mandated services were explicitly direct service. This is particularly important in impoverished or rural communities, where the relationship to schools is essential because alternative private or public services might be inaccessible or actually nonexistent. Put quite simply, community mental health centers often have been the only realistic treatment option for disturbed children and/or their parents when the problems of the family or child became identified in the course of a child's education. The entire range of community mental health center services are pertinent to children, ranging from services for the mildly affected to the most profoundly impaired child, from the situationally distressed to the chronically psychotic parent. It also includes such disparate activities as coordinated case referral, collaboration on titration of psychoactive medication in children, emergency care for acute situations, and coordination of case management of mentally retarded children and parents.

There are instances when the direct service functions of the community mental health center can lead to an adversarial relationship with the school. These usually have to do with situations in which the clinic personnel are obliged by case circumstances to assume an advocacy role with regard to a client or class of clients. This would occur, for instance, when a community mental health center psychologist is asked for a second opinion concerning special educational placement, and then arrives at an opinion different from that of the school psychologist. Such adversial situations often can be managed with relative comfort in the context of an ongoing, mutually beneficial relationship between the school and the center. This is especially true when centers have been able to involve their clinicians directly in the school, not only as providers of direct service, but also as consultants and collaborators.

Consultative/Preventive Services

If schools and community mental health centers are highly compatible in the area of direct service, the complementarity of needs probably is most perfect in the areas of consultation and prevention. Children are logical targets of primary and secondary prevention efforts since they presumably are not affected, or are less permanently affected, than adults who have been exposed to adverse conditions over a longer period of time and whose personalities are more fully formed. In fact, schools have probably been the single most common location for consultation and education programs. One study of primary prevention efforts conducted by consultation and education units in Pennsylvania, Delaware, Maryland, Washington, DC, Virginia, and West Virginia found that consultation and education units rarely functioned in settings that did not deal with children, and that school personnel (i.e., teachers, school counselors, administrators, and boards of education) were the most frequent recipients of service (Vayda & Perlmutter, 1977). The varieties in form and context of consultative/preventive efforts have been virtually limitless and have simply been a part of the normal life of the school in many communities (Coles, Ciporen, Honigsberg, & Cohen, 1980; Jacobson et al., 1983; Tolan & Lounsbury, 1982; Waldron & Bolman, 1979). This is especially the case when one includes in these activities the ongoing case consultation, as an adjunct to direct service, that occurs between the community mental health center professionals and their counterparts in the school.

Special Collaborative Programs

There have been a variety of programs in which the educational system and the community mental health system have entered into relatively formal, long-term relationships whereby personnel from one system work within the facilities of the other system or at least within a consistent, multidisciplinary team of professionals. At times this has involved the community mental health system taking on educational activities normally provided by the school, or augmenting educational programs beyond what would normally be available (but often be inadequate) for exceptional subgroups of pupils. Such programs have been of considerable significance because the children served by them often would have been considered to be good candidates for residential care in their absence. Commonly, although not always, the children in these programs "would tend to be the more severe end of the diagnostic spectrum, including psychotic, autistic, brain damaged, schizoid, learning impaired, disinhibited and assaultive types of children" (Halpern, Kissel, & Gold, 1978, p. 320). As with other activities mentioned above, the particular form of these collaborative programs has varied widely, but the major categories are described below.

Day treatment programs for children and adolescents typically have operated wholly or primarily under the auspices of the community mental health center, although their format has been that of an educational institution for the most severely disturbed and/or disruptive children in a school system. Often the criterion for admission involved the primary determination that the child could not be accommodated within the regular or special educational settings in the normal school. Often the day treatment program offered the last-ditch effort to avoid hospitalization or long-term residential care. Conversely, they often were the means of transitioning an acutely disturbed young person back into the community after a period of hospitalization or residential care. Regardless of their particular configuration, the basic concept of these programs was that the child would be treated by a closely integrated team of educational and mental health professionals so that the pedagogical aspects of care were consistently and intensively intertwined with the mental health aspects.

Early intervention programs provide a category of collaborative programs involved with early identification of, and intervention with, high-risk children at the time of their entry into school. In many cases this consisted simply of assessments of identified children on school grounds preparatory to referral to appropriate programs at the community mental health center. Other innovative programs, however, involved a more truly collaborative effort. The Services to Young Children Program, for example, was operated in one of the most economically and socially disadvantaged public schools in Philadelphia. A full-time, clinical social worker employed by the community mental health center was housed in the school building itself, enabling him or her to enjoy a continuous collaborative relationship with a designated special teacher and aide employed by the school district. Their primary function was to operate a special class that accommodated a maximum of 20 children (10 in the morning and 10 in the afternoon) for intensive, compensatory educational input.

Children were referred by kindergarten and first-grade teachers in the home school and immediately neighboring schools; the primary basis for referral was evidence of a significant problem in any area of development or adjustment. Clinical and educational services were initiated by the three in-school workers. In addition, the community mental health center provided other appropriate supportive services during the course of the year, including psychiatric, psychological, pediatric, and speech and language services. By the end of the first-grade year a general, long-term intervention was planned for each child, where appropriate, including continued service at the community mental health center or referral to other specialized services.

Mention of a few other less intensive collaborative efforts should further illustrate the scope of possible arrangements. For a time, the Follow Through Program, a federally funded, compensatory education program, contracted with community mental health centers in Philadelphia to provide mental health services as a part of the program. Although the form of individual efforts varied greatly from year to year and from school to school, the on-going inclusion of a mental health professional in the program, over a period of years, fostered a range of collaborative efforts involving individual teachers, groups of teachers, counselors, building principals, parents, and other people relevant to the programs. Similarly, for a time, the School District of Philadelphia contracted with community mental health centers to provide psychiatric/mental health evaluations for children being considered for Socially and Emotionally Disturbed (SED) placement. This arrangement involved the community mental health center directly in the deliberations and decision-making function of the child study team. Not only did this foster valuable relationships with key school personnel, it also clearly positioned the community mental health center representatives to initiate appropriate and well-coordinated interventions in the cases of identified children.

Summary of Effects on School Psychology

The discipline of school psychology has been influenced by the ideology underlying the community mental health center movement: that it is important to provide mental health services to the general population at the community level. Schools represent a logical institutional site for this viewpoint, and since school psychology represents the field of mental health within the schools, its role has been influenced by this orientation. Community mental health centers, moreover, have implemented a variety of activities in schools focused on mental health through direct diagnosis and treatment, consultation, education, and prevention, and a variety of collaborative ventures. The presence of these mental health efforts has helped to demonstrate the range of services that can be provided by psychologists in schools, and this point has been underscored when school psychologists participated in these activities. Although mental health centers have modeled a variety of activities designed to remediate and prevent the mental health problems of students, most of these activities in schools have focused on diagnosis and remediation rather than consultation, education, and prevention. This has occurred because the vast majority of funding for mental health centers has been in support of such direct services.

MENTAL HEALTH CONSULTATION

Mental health consultation in schools is a process characterized by shared expertise between a mental health professional and an educational professional (i.e., Meyers et al., 1979). The goal of consultation is to help the educator solve a current work problem and to respond more effectively to similar problems in the future. It is a problem-solving process that occurs between a help-giver (the consultant) and a help-seeker (consultee) who has responsibility for another person (e.g., a student). Mental health consultation in the schools typically involves an educator as the consultee, while many school personnel (such as school psychologists and counselors), as well as some community mental health center staff, have served as consultants.

Historical Overview

Although school psychologists have had a long commitment to consultation for the delivery of school psychological services, this viewpoint has received particular attention during the past 30 years (e.g., see Meyers et al., 1979), coincident with the development and growth of the fields of community psychiatry (Caplan, 1951, 1955, 1961, 1964, 1974) and community psychology (Iscoe et al., 1977; Iscoe & Speilberger, 1970; Sarason, 1972, 1974, 1976; Sarason et al., 1966). The Thayer Conference (Cutts, 1955) described a variety of consultative services as important components of the school psychologist's role. These included helping to plan school curricula; helping to change attitudes of school staff, parents, and the community; and communicating effectively with school personnel (see Meyers et al., 1979).

Until the 1950s there had been little theory or practical guidelines for the practice of mental health consultation. The early influential writing in this field came particularly from the fields of community psychiatry, community psychology, and organization development. Sarason's influence came largely from his work at the Yale Psycho-Educational Clinic, and his emphasis on delivering services at the relevant community setting was delineated earlier in this chapter. The most important influence on mental health consultation from the field of community psychiatry was Gerald Caplan, who wrote a seminal article for the field of mental health consultation in 1963, which was followed by a now classic book entitled *The Theory and Practice of Mental Health Consultation* (Caplan, 1963, 1970).

Caplan's approach to mental health consultation began in 1948 when he was asked to supervise the mental health services for about 16,000 immigrant children in the state of Israel. Using a traditional direct service clinical model with a small group of psychologists and social workers he found that it was not possible to provide mental health services to the many children who needed these services. The result was a growing waiting list for clinical services, similar to what occurs in many of today's large urban school districts. At the same time he and his staff noted that certain institutions tended to refer particular types of clinical problems, and he reasoned that an approach to reduce the long waiting lists might be to develop techniques to help these institutions become more effective with the particular problems they referred most frequently. As a result, the amount of clinical staff time spent working directly with individuals was reduced and the time spent working with caretakers to improve their approaches with particular problems was increased. In this way consultation emerged as an approach designed to provide new techniques to caretakers for coping with

the problems they encountered on a daily basis with those children they served.

Although much of Caplan's work has had profound effects on the consultation literature and on the practice of psychology in the schools, three particular contributions stand out (Meyers et al., 1979). First, Caplan suggested that consultation must be a collaborative interchange between two professionals who each perceive the other as having particular strengths. Caplan believed that this could occur most readily between two professionals trained in different disciplines, and this may be an important key to the success of mental health consultation by school psychologists. Many teachers are used to receiving expert advice from supervisors, administrators, and curriculum specialists who tell them what to do, and this frequently leads to resistance. In contrast, school psychologists who practice mental health consultation consistent with Caplan's (1970) viewpoint develop collaborative and facilitative relationships with their educator/consultees, and the result is that educators generally support the consultative role for school psychologists (e.g., Curtis & Meyers, 1985).

Caplan's (1970) notions about confrontation have also received attention. Since his work derives from a psychodynamic perspective, Caplan argues that direct confrontation can be nonproductive because it breaks down the consultee's defenses. Since consultation is not the sort of long-term relationship provided in psychotherapy, he believes that the consultation relationship does not provide the opportunity to help build back the consultee's defenses. This viewpoint suggests that indirect confrontation techniques may be more valuable since they provide the message about the needed change in a more acceptable manner. Caplan (1970) suggests that indirect confrontation can be provided by keeping the focus of consultation on the client (i.e., the student) rather than on the consultee (i.e., the teacher). This approach was inconsistent with the traditional training of most psychodynamically oriented professionals at the time, and therefore, it represented a major shift in theroetical orientation to the delivery of psychological services. More recently, Meyers et al. (1979) have suggested that direct confrontation can also be provided constructively in the context of consultation.

The third major contribution was the conceptualization of four distinct types of mental health consultation (Caplan, 1963, 1970). These included client-centered case consultation, consultee-centered case consultation, program-centered administrative consultation, and consultee-centered administrative consultation. Client-centered case consultation focuses attention on the client by diagnosing the problem so that effective remedial plans can be developed, and it is assumed to result in some increased knowledge and skill for the consultee that may generalize to future work. Consultee-centered case consultation focuses on the consultee rather than the student who may have been referred. The goal is to improve the consultee's skill, objectivity, knowledge, or self-confidence. Program-centered administrative consultation and consultee-centered administrative consultation both focus on administrative problems of the organization. While program-centered administrative consultation attacks specific service delivery problems, consultee-centered administrative consultation considers more general administrative problems such as planning and maintaining programs for the prevention and control of mental disorders, or helping to manage interpersonal aspects of an organization's operations.

Another important influence on the practice of mental health consultation in the schools has been the work of organization development consultants (Fullan, Miles, & Taylor, 1979; Schein, 1969; Schmuck & Miles, 1971; Schmuck et al., 1972, 1977), whose approaches have been similar to Caplan's consultee-centered administrative consultation. Perhaps the most significant historical influence was Kurt Lewin, who, in 1946, initiated a meeting with community leaders to learn about group dynamics from firsthand experience. Members were placed in small groups, given group tasks to perform, and were provided feedback regarding their group behavior; this became known as a "T-group" because of its role as a training group. The National Training Laboratories grew out of this movement and offered training to a variety of organizations throughout the country to facilitate open feedback about group behavior, in an effort to improve communication and professional efficiency among organizational staff. T-group activities for schools and teachers began to be offered in the mid 1950s, and in 1961, the National Training Laboratories began to offer training especially designed for educators (Meyers et al., 1979). Since that time many systematic organization development efforts have been carried out in schools

focusing particularly on problems with communication, leadership, decision making, organizational roles, and problem-solving procedures. Efforts to implement these approaches in educational settings have been summarized (Fullan et al., 1979; Schmuck & Miles, 1971), and the organizational perspective emphasized by this approach to consultation is consistent with the systemic view of behavior offered generally by community psychology.

Major Issues in Mental Health Consultation and Their Implications for School Psychology
One result of the increased attention to consultation as an approach to the delivery of school psychological services has been a body of research demonstrating educators' preference for this approach compared to traditional testing and placement models (Curtis & Meyers, 1985), as well as beginning efforts to document the efficacy of consultation in educational settings (see research reviews by Alpert & Yammer, 1983; Curtis & Meyers, 1985; Fullan et al., 1980; Gutkin & Curtis, 1982; Mannino & Shore, 1975; Medway, 1979; Meyers, Pitt, Gaughan, & Freidman, 1978; see also Chapter 23 in this volume).

One important issue that has been addressed in recent research is the "preventive" value of consultation. Consultation has the potential to influence the behavior of the target child, as well as other children in the child's classroom, and similar children who the teacher may work with in the future. The potential value of consultation lies in its ability to have this sort of generalized effect since this allows the consultant to influence more children than would be possible with a model based on one-to-one delivery of service to the client. In this context, consultation has been found to result in improved professional skills for teachers; more accurate teacher attitudes regarding how serious children's problems are; improved teacher information and understanding of children's problems; improved teacher ability to provide concrete behavioral descriptions; and generalization of consultation benefits to other children in the same classroom (Curtis & Meyers, 1985). Despite these positive findings, there is a need for considerably more research on each of these questions, and general research on the outcome of consultation is a pressing need at the present time. Nevertheless, these results do suggest the preventive potential of consultation and help to demonstrate that a potentially effective technology does exist as a basis for the delivery of consultation services in schools.

Consultation can provide a pragmatic framework for the delivery of psychoeducational services to children in an indirect manner while emphasizing prevention of learning and adjustment problems rather than remediation and crisis intervention. Following Caplan's categorical system described earlier, consultation services can be focused at three distinct levels: the child, the teacher or classroom, and the school as a system (see Curtis & Meyers, 1985; Meyers et al., 1979). Traditional models have focused the attention of professionals on the first level (i.e., the child), while essentially ignoring the classroom and the school. As a result, school psychologists have not tapped the potential that exists to modify the school or classroom environment for the benefit of all children. A consultation model emphasizes service delivery to teachers and the school as a system rather than being limited to a search for pathology in the child, and this is compatible with the view of psychological service delivery emphasized in community psychology.

Mental health consultation has historical roots that tie this approach to community psychology. The work of Seymour Sarason, Gerald Caplan, and Kurt Lewin have been influential in the developing fields of community psychology and mental health consultation, and this work has had an important impact on the field of school psychology. This chapter has documented some of the influences of mental health consultation on the field of school psychology. In addition, this influence is noted in many recent publications (e.g., Alpert, 1982; Brown, Pryzwansky, & Schulte, 1987; Conoley, 1981; Curtis & Meyers, 1985; Gutkin & Curtis, 1982; Meyers et al., 1979; and chapter 23 in this volume). Surveys on the practice of school psychology suggest that a substantial part of the role of practicing school psychologists involves psychoeducational consultation (e.g., Goldwasser, Meyers, Christenson, & Graden, 1983; Martin & Meyers, 1980), and that consultation occupies a more central role in the training of school psychologists than was the case in the early 1970s (Meyers, Wurtz, & Flanagan, 1981). Moreover, while the initial literature on mental health consultation derived primarily from the fields of community psychology and community psychiatry, at this time the field of school psychology contributes at least as much to this literature

(e.g., Alpert, 1982; Alpert & Meyers, 1983; Bergan, 1977; Brown et al., 1987; Conoley, 1981; Meyers et al., 1979; Parsons & Meyers, 1984).

PRIMARY PREVENTION OF PSYCHOPATHOLOGY

The primary prevention of psychopathology has been closely associated with community psychology. Similar historical factors led to the development of both of these movements, and almost any general discussion of community psychology considers approaches for the primary prevention of psychopathology. Although perhaps to a lesser degree, the concepts associated with the primary prevention of psychopathology have also had an impact on school psychology.

Historical Overview

Albee (1980) believes that the primary prevention of psychopathology represents a paradigm shift (Kuhn, 1962) in applied psychology, and describes primary prevention as the fourth revolution in the delivery of psychological services. The first three "revolutions" had to do with the influence of Pinel, Freud, and the community mental health movement (see Albee, 1980).

Similar to the fields of community psychology and mental health consultation, one starting point for the primary prevention literature was Albee's (1959) predictions about the inadequate supply of professional personpower, along with his conclusion that direct service models could never be effective (Albee, 1967). In an early definition Cowen (1967) differentiated between primary, secondary, and tertiary prevention. Primary prevention involves preventive efforts provided before any indication of emotional problems, with these efforts being directed toward the entire population or toward particular at-risk groups (e.g., those from low SES backgrounds, single-parent homes). Secondary prevention focuses on populations or subgroups of the population showing early signs of disturbance, and this approach may involve early screening to detect at-risk groups, and preventive interventions to inhibit the emergent problems found in these groups. Tertiary prevention involves efforts to prevent the development of additional mental health problems in populations already experiencing serious mental health symptoms.

There is a growing body of literature on primary prevention with relevance to the practice of both community psychology and school psychology. Particularly noteworthy have been the contributions of Albee (Albee, 1978, 1980, 1981) and Cowen (Cowen, 1977, 1984; Cowen et al., 1967). An outgrowth of this work has been the series of Vermont Conferences on the Primary Prevention of Psychopathology under the leadership of George Albee which has brought together on an annual basis professionals from across the country with interests in primary prevention. The proceedings from each of these conferences have been published by the University Press of New England (e.g., Albee & Joffe, 1977; Bond & Joffe, 1982; Kent & Rolf, 1979; Kessler & Goldston, 1986), and these volumes summarize much of the thinking in primary prevention since the first conference was held in 1975. There have been numerous other recent books and articles in this field (e.g., Felner et al., 1983; Hermalin & Morell, 1987), there is a new publication devoted specifically to this topic (i.e., *The Journal of Primary Prevention*), and recently, the school psychology literature has begun to consider these issues (e.g., Alpert, 1983; Clarizio, 1979; Meyers & Parsons, 1987).

Major Issues in Primary Prevention and Their Implications for School Psychology

Before considering issues associated with primary prevention, it is important to conceptualize the impact of secondary prevention since these efforts may be implemented more frequently by school psychologists. Emory Cowen's Primary Mental Health Project (PMHP) developed in the Rochester schools is an excellent example of a secondary prevention program (Cowen, 1980; see also Cowen and Hightower's chapter in this volume, Chapter 31). This program used early screening to identify children at risk of developing serious emotional problems, and relied heavily on paraprofessionals to provide preventive treatments. A long-term evaluation has been implemented in a variety of school settings across the country, establishing the generalized efficacy of its specific procedures (Cowen, 1980; Cowen, Gesten & Wilson, 1979). PMHP has had and continues to have important effects on the delivery of psychological services in the schools.

There are two basic approaches to primary prevention in schools (Meyers & Parsons, 1987).

The first seeks to promote psychosocial health by developing competence in children using strategies designed to increase interpersonal skills, to foster self-esteem, and to develop other coping skills. The second approach to primary prevention in schools is to eliminate the causes or mediators of maladjustment by modifying the environment. This approach uses ecological, behavioral, and/or mental health principles as a basis for structuring the environment to reduce stress and to enhance interpersonal relationships.

Approaches to Build Competence

Meyers and Parsons (1987) have described three basic approaches to building competence which have particular relevance to the primary prevention of psychopathology in schools: (a) teaching interpersonal problem-solving skills, (b) using the school routine to build "strens," and (c) early education programs.

Interpersonal Problem-Solving Skills. Approaches to assess and teach social skills have important implications for school psychology, and the work of George Spivack and Myrna Shure (e.g., Spivack & Shure, 1974) is one example. They have demonstrated relationships between social problem-solving skills and mental health, and they have developed procedures and curriculum materials to teach children skills such as sensitivity to others, awareness of the causal effects of one's behavior, the perception of feelings, the development and use of alternative behavioral plans, and the awareness of means–ends relationships. Two particular cognitive skills relate to behavioral adjustment consistently: the ability to generate alternative action plans, and the ability to anticipate consequences of behavior. Improved interpersonal cognitive problem-solving skills, moreover, are followed by improved behavioral adjustment (Shure & Spivack, 1978; Spivack, Platt, & Shure, 1976; Spivak & Shure, 1974).

This research has profound implications for the practice of psychology in education. It suggests a concrete course of action directed toward preventive goals that can be initiated by psychologists in schools. Social skills training programs have been implemented by school psychologists and the results of these programs have been published in the school psychology literature (e.g., Alpert & Rosenfield, 1981; Gresham, 1985). The approaches to assess social skills (e.g., Gresham,

1981; Shure & Spivack, 1978), moreover, may be a productive addition to the assessment devices used by school psychologists. The use of assessment procedures derived from this preventive framework will increase the probability that school psychologists implement preventive interventions derived from this perspective.

Using the School Routine to Build Strens.

William Hollister (1965) coined the term *strens* to suggest that competence in reacting to stress can be built by providing successful exposure to minor stressful experiences (Phillips, Martin, & Meyers, 1972). The term was used to signify the individual's strength in dealing with stress and it is related to Janis's (1958) conception of psychological inoculation. Three particular issues have pragmatic implications for the development of strens in school children: coping with loss, conflict, and developmental crises. They each have important preventive implications for schools because the school experience is filled with repeated exposure to each type of stress, and teachers can work effectively to help children develop coping skills for each of these issues (Meyers & Parsons, 1987). For example, in the event of the death of a classroom pet (e.g., hamster), the teacher, can provide an opportunity for children to express their normal feelings of anger and sadness, provide an object lesson in the inevitability of loss and the appropriateness of the emotions accompanying loss, and help to reinforce the development of effective coping strategies.

Early Education Programs.

A variety of early education programs have been developed and implemented to provide educational enrichment, cognitive stimulation, and additional learning experiences. These programs have been offered, most frequently, to children in danger of educational failure, such as the economically disadvantaged. Many early-intervention programs have documented striking improvement in academic, social, and emotional indicators, and some studies have documented increased IQ scores. Early childhood education programs have substantial potential for preventive effects and it has been reported that there are fewer retentions, fewer children placed in special education, reduced costs of special education, higher earnings for graduates, fewer court convictions, and a lower birth rate for those who have been pupils in early childhood

education programs (e.g., Meyers & Parsons, 1987; Weber, Forster, & Weikart, 1978; Weikart, 1984).

Modifying the Environment

Until recently the mental health fields have generally ignored the potential of social systems. There is a growing body of evidence, however, indicating that social environments can have a profound impact on mental health (e.g. Moos, 1973, 1974, 1979). There are two basic approaches to modifying the environment: to improve the social climate in the class or school, and to reduce stress.

Improving Climate.

Barker and Gump (1964) were among the first to study systematically the effects of school environment, and at this point a large body of evidence suggests a variety of social, emotional, and academic effects associated with different components of school climate (e.g., Moos, 1979). The implications for prevention are that schools can promote positive adjustment and reduce mental health problems, while facilitating learning, by establishing environments which emphasize those dimensions that have been found to facilitate education. These include educational structures and procedures where there is an emphasis on interpersonal relationships, educational goals such as high achievement and competition, and the maintenance of classroom organization through clear structures and rules (Moos, 1979). The methods available to assess the climate of classrooms and schools, moreover, provide a useful addition to the assessment devices used typically by school psychologists (Moos, 1974a, 1974b, 1979).

Reducing Stress.

The environment can be modified to reduce or eliminate unnecessary stress by using cooperative learning principles that encourage children to work together (Johnson & Johnson, 1980). Stress can also be reduced through networks by providing after-school activities (Meyers & Parsons, 1987), peer and cross-age tutoring (e.g., Phillips et al., 1972), and scheduling procedures designed to maintain contact within a peer group (e.g., Felner, Ginter, & Primavera, 1982).

Modifying the school environment to reduce stress is a concept that has been in the school psychology literature for some time (e.g., see Phillips et al., 1972). A common feature of these approaches is that often they can be implemented realistically within the context of schools without requring dramatic increases in financial resources. Successful implementation of environmental modifications in schools, however, will inevitably require cooperation of the relevant educators.

Resistance to Primary Prevention

All of the primary prevention programs focused on building competence and modifying the environment have the potential to influence the practice of school psychology as more school psychologists implement these approaches in schools. These programs, however, require innovation, and as Sarason (1982) has documented, innovation is difficult to accomplish in public schools. The politics of schools often result in miscommunication between innovators and educators when each interprets the innovation as meeting their own needs without thinking clearly about the perspective of the other. Too often this process involves quick acceptance of the proposal without the careful planning that is necessary for success. Even though teachers are frequently the crucial personnel implementing primary prevention procedures, typically they are not consulted seriously during program development. As a result, preventive programs are often imposed on educators whose natural resistance to change within the educational system is exacerbated by this negative process.

School psychologists can help to prevent some of these problems by implementing principles designed to reduce resistance to primary prevention (Meyers & Parsons, 1987). For example, it is important to understand the culture of the school, and to negotiate directly with all relevant administrators, including the highest level of administrator in the organization that is relevant to the project. It is also important to spend the time necessary to be sure that all parties understand the proposed project, and teachers and other staff members must be actively involved in its planning and development. Finally, school psychologists implementing prevention programs will maximize their chances for success by drawing out resistance before implementation.

SOCIAL CHANGE

The social change model was delineated as a model of community psychology at the Austin conference on training (Gatz & Liem, 1977;

Hassol, 1977; Moore, 1977). It was described as an approach to change institutions and society in an effort to help all people, and it emphasized a variety of techniques, including the political process. From this perspective, effective change cannot occur by directing efforts toward the afflicted individual. Instead, it is assumed that the individual will receive meaningful help through strategies directed to broader issues (i.e., problems with agencies, institutions, or society in general) which may contribute to and perpetuate adversity for individuals.

The psychologist interested in social change needs broad-based training in various disciplines (psychology, sociology, economics, political science, labor relations, mass media) in order to have substantive and far-reaching effects on systems and on society as a whole (Sarason, 1976). Toward this end, the psychologist assumes an activist role, advocating for particular causes such as equal treatment for women, ethnic minority groups, handicapped people, and so on.

Historical Context

Just like community psychology, the roots of the social change movement can be traced to the disaffection and social activism of the late 1960s and early 1970s. At the time, mental health problems were viewed by some as a sane response to an insane society, and it was thought that they were caused, at least in part, by a society in which sociopolitical power was allocated on the basis of race, class, gender, and so on. The Austin Conference on Training in Community Psychology (Iscoe et al., 1977) underscored some of these issues by describing America as a society based on social class, where advancement of some was dependent on the exploitation of others. These sentiments resulted in the articulation of the social change model (Gatz & Liem, 1977; Hassol, 1977). Despite the discussion of social change models at this conference, this model of community psychology has not been well developed theoretically, and has probably had less impact, particularly in the schools, than the other models discussed in this chapter.

Issues and Ideology
The Goals of Social Change

The social change model seeks to alleviate the detrimental effects of systemic problems. Although ideally this would be accomplished by changing a system that is viewed as the source of pathology, in practice this is accomplished by modifying the environment to help individuals adjust to different aspects of society. While facilitating the adaptation of individuals may help in the short run, these approaches cannot remediate the systemic factors that caused the problems in the first place. Therefore, it is important to develop procedures to change key social structures.

The Question of Advocacy

It is common clinical thinking that a consultant should not advocate for a particular ideology, but must remain neutral to facilitate problem solving within the institution. But when a psychologist chooses not to express an opinion regarding the need for social change in a system, this inaction unwittingly provides support for the status quo (Goldenberg, 1983). Social change models suggest that the psychologist must advocate for a particular viewpoint.

The Professional's Values

Values affect professional judgment, professional decisions, and the practice of professional psychologists (Hassol, 1977). Although some professionals may try to avoid the impact of their own values, it is important to recognize their potential effects. For example, psychologists' views about the poor and minority groups may affect their practice. Those who believe that these oppressed subgroups are excluded from the American mainstream unfairly may be reluctant to facilitate access of group members to special education. Social change models suggest that psychologists must be aware of their own, as well as the organization's, professional values.

Conflict and Social Change

Conflict is an inevitable and normal part of social functioning within institutions, systems, and society. Rather than attempt to eliminate conflict, psychologists working with a social change model use conflict between subgroups to facilitate change (Chesler, Bryant, & Crowfoot, 1976). For example, when there is conflict between institutional subgroups such as teachers and students, the most effective way to facilitate social change is to create dialogue within the organization about this conflict. When the conflict is allowed to develop in this way, its potential for effecting change is enhanced. When conflict is suppressed or prematurely diminished, its underlying causes in the system are nurtured.

Professional Resistance to Social Change

Psychologists may be reluctant to implement social change models because they are not clearly psychological in nature. This perspective borrows from a variety of disciplines, such as political science, sociology, public policy, and so on, and the questions about whether this really constitutes a psychological approach might inhibit its practice by some psychologists. Further, as employees of an institution, school psychologists may be reluctant to implement this model because of concerns for job securtiy. Yet, psychologists generally, and school psychologists in particular, have witnessed public interest groups use social change models to create changes with profound implications for them, their clients, and the institutions they serve.

Controversy over the use of IQ tests by school psychologists presents an excellent example of the potential power of social change models. Concern over disproportionate placement of minority group children in special education classes for the retarded resulted in a variety of activities by public interest groups designed to change this practice (i.e., Larry P case, *Pace* v. *Hannon*). The *Pace* decision is particularly relevant for the present discussion since this was a case which eventually had an outcome that was similar to the Larry P case, even though the judge in this case reached a very different conclusion (i.e., that IQ tests were not biased). In the *Pace* decision, even though the school district had apparently won the legal battle, they responded to advocacy groups, settling out of court and agreeing to conditions that effectively barred the use of traditional IQ tests. Regardless of one's philosophical position regarding these cases, it should be clear that special interest groups can be powerfully effective using a social change model to influence the educational process.

A Model of Social Change Roles

The issues concerning social change and the related literature lead to a variety of potential roles that could be played by school psychologists or community psychologists. A conceptual model representing these potential roles is provided in Table 1 which consists of a $3 \times 2 \times 3$ matrix with three major dimensions: (a) the focus of intervention, (b) the internal/external dimension, and (c) the type of change agent. The first dimension, the focus of intervention, refers to the administrative level of the organization that is the focus of the intervention (i.e., top, middle, or bottom levels of administration). Interventions focused toward the top would be those directed to the highest administrative levels of the organization (e.g., principals, superintendents, school board members). Interventions directed toward the bottom would be those focused on the lowest administrative levels of the organization (i.e., students and their parents). The middle level includes the direct service providers of the institution, such as teachers in schools. Consider student rights and access to school records as an example. The psychologist could intervene at a systems level by advocating with the school board to enact better procedures to ensure confidentiality of records (i.e., the "top" as presented in Table 1). Or the psychologist could intervene at the individual level by educating the parents with whom he or she works regarding their due process rights (i.e., the "bottom" as presented in Table 1). Rather than changing the system at an administrative level, the latter approach seeks to "empower" the constituency group (Gesten & Jason, 1987; Glidewell, 1986; Rappaport, 1985a; 1985b).

The second dimension, the internal/external dimension, refers to the locus of the change agent with respect to the system. A psychologist employed by schools might be in a position to affect its structures, values, and priorities from within the system. A psychologist could also work from outside the school system (e.g., in a public interest research group) to marshal external pressures for systemic change in the schools. Those internal to the system have the advantage of knowing the system intimately, being proximate to those with influence in the system, and having established trust as a member of the system. It is often difficult, however, to facilitate social change as a member of the system given the numerous pressures that can be applied by others in the system. External change agents do not face the same systemic pressures that support the status quo, and they frequently have additional social power when they are viewed as the expert brought in from the outside. But external change agents do not have the advantages that characterize internal change agents. While it is possible to create social change as either an internal or external change agent, this dimension can have important implications for the process of creating change.

The third dimension, type of change agent, derives from Goldenberg's (1983) discussion of three different options for consultants. Type 1 refers to the "social technician;" a change agent who supports the status quo in a fundamental sense but takes action to calm the system when it is disrupted and to help the system's clients adapt to its "few" aversive aspects (Lorion, 1977). Type 2 refers to the "social broker," who views the system as flawed and in need of *some* change in order to minimize the oppression of the system and its structures on its constituents. From this perspective the change agent views the system as basically good but in need of some adjustment. Although the modifications sought may be fundamental, they do not require a revolutionary change in the basic system. Type 3 refers to the "social interventionist," who conceptualizes observed problems as deriving from fundamental flaws in the existing system, thus requiring radical change. This approach necessitates the most extreme change of the three types, and it would rely on social/political interventions which would create systemic disruption.

TABLE 1   Social Change Model for School Psychologists

| | Level of Management | | | | | |
| | Top | | Middle | | Bottom | |
	Internal	External	Internal	External	Internal	External
Social technician (Type 1)	TI 1	TE 1	MI 1	ME 1	BI 1	BE 1
Social broker (Type 2)	TI 2	TE 2	MI 2	ME 2	BI 2	BE 2
Social interventionist (Type 3)	TI 3	TE 3	MI 3	ME 3	BI 3	BE 3

While Types 1 and 2 might support some aspect of the status quo, Type 3 would agitate for wholesale change and/or dismantlement of existing social structures. All three types are included to underscore that the social change model can be a realistic option for many school psychologists. While Type 3 may be the most desirable when it is clear that major social change is needed, this role may be the most difficult for school psychologists to play. For those occasions when Type 3 is unrealistic, Types 1 and 2 may offer a more realistic approach to social change for school psychologists.

A careful consideration of the different cells of the model illustrates that a variety of approaches to change are possible. In some cells, the school psychologist's traditional skills may be required. For example, the internal change agent using the social technician (Type 1) approach to social change and working with the bottom levels of the system (cell BI-1) might need to use traditional psycho-educational diagnostic skills, as well as parent conferencing techniques, to initiate social change. A more expanded repertoire of skills might be required in some of the other cells of the model, such as consultation skills in cell MI-2 and social skills training in cell BI-2.

Other cells of the model would require skills which are less frequently conceptualized within the school psychologist's role, and this would be particularly true for those Type 3 change agents (social interventionists) working external to the school system (cells TE-3, ME-3, and BE-3). Those working within these dimensions of the model might need skills regarding political action, access to and knowledge of how to use print and media outlets, and connections to various advocacy networks (Chesler et al., 1976; Sarason, 1976). While school psychologists have functioned more frequently in some of the other cells of this model as noted above, there is a developing awareness that political sophistication can be appropriate to the work of some school psychologists. An excellent example of the use of these approaches to social action is the National Center for the Study of Corporal Punishment and Its Alternatives in the Schools, which uses advocacy to prevent the use of corporal punishment in school settings (Hyman & Wise, 1979). As similar approaches to social action are implemented more frequently, school psychologists may increase their opportunities to achieve the broader role that has been discussed

for years in the literature, rather than limiting their work to approaches designed to "adjust" individuals to an unhealthy system (Goldenberg, 1983; Reiff, 1977).

Summary

To summarize, the values and viewpoints of the social change model suggest that in ostensibly trying to help children, families, and schools, school psychologists may simultaneously be perpetuating the systems, values, and attitudes that have contributed to the problems in the first place. This is an ironic but intrinsic contradiction which is tied intricately to the school psychologist's traditional psychometric role. The contribution of community psychology and the social change model is that they provide an orientation which school psychologists could use in an effort to overcome some of these institutionalized problems.

A SUMMARY OF PAST AND FUTURE RELATIONSHIPS BETWEEN COMMUNITY PSYCHOLOGY AND SCHOOL PSYCHOLOGY

There is considerable overlap between the models of community psychology discussed in this chapter. Each evolved in reaction to concerns about the efficacy of traditional clinical models, especially in view of the apparent professional shortages that were predicted. Each is concerned with the mental health of the entire society, rather than being restricted to the clinical concerns for the well-being of afflicted individuals. Consistent with the entire community psychology movement, each evolved, in part, during the social and political activism that characterized the late 1960s and early 1970s. While mental health consultation is listed as one of the four foundational elements of community psychology, it is clear that consultation procedures are really an important element of each of the other three as well. Moreover, the primary prevention perspective and the social change model share a common philosophical base which suggests that mental health in society requires approaches that lead to empowerment for those who have suffered traditionally in our society.

Many of the ideas discussed in relation to each of the models and foundational elements of community psychology have important implications for the practice of school psychology. A core group of professionals writing about many of these ideas in the community psychology literature have facilitated the impact of these ideas on school psychology (i.e., George Albee, Gerald Caplan, Emory Cowen, Seymour Sarason, etc.). While the consultation model has probably had the greatest direct effect on the practice of school psychology, the others have also been significant. The social change model has been described, in particular, as a model that has had too little impact on the field of school psychology to date, and a framework is presented that may facilitate the use of this model by school psychologists in the future.

This chapter has reviewed the literature in community psychology to consider its implications for the practice of school psychology. The four foundational elements of community psychology discussed in this context were the community mental health center movement, mental health consultation, prevention of psychopathology, and social change models. Although these different elements are integrated through some of the common theoretical, philosophical, and historical factors reviewed throughout this chapter, there is no single theoretical perspective that clearly encompasses and makes sense of these approaches in their entirety. It is noted, moreover, that both disciplines of community psychology and school psychology are relatively young. There is a need for substantial conceptual work to provide the theoretical basis which might guide practice, research, and training, as well as providing the frame of reference needed to integrate these approaches and to facilitate the growing maturity of both disciplines.

Despite the conceptual immaturity of these fields, it is not surprising that community psychology can be described as a current and future influence on school psychology. In many ways, school psychologists were the first community psychologists. They have always practiced primarily in the prototypical community setting—the school. They are likely to have day-to-day contact with both clients (children) and their caretakers (teachers and parents), as well as with policymakers and administrators (principals, superintendents, school board members, department heads, etc.). With the reduction in monies allocated to community mental health centers generally, and to consultation and education units in particular, with the retrenchment of human service programs inherent in current conservative political ideology, and with the direct service emphasis of prepaid medical plans (i.e., HMOs), school psychology is one context where some of the ideas inherent in the community psychology literature can continue to be practiced in an effort to benefit society.

REFERENCES

Albee, G. W. (1959). *Mental health manpower trends.* New York: Basic Books.

Albee, G. W. (1967). The relation of conceptual models to manpower needs. In E. L. Cowen, E. A. Gardner, & M. Zax (Eds.), *Emergent approaches to mental health problems* (pp. 63–73). New York: Appleton-Century-Crofts.

Albee, G. W. (1978). Report of the task panel on prevention. In D. G. Forgays (Ed.), *Primary prevention of psychopathology* (Vol. 2). Hanover, NH: University Press of New England.

Albee, G. W. (1980). The fourth mental health revolution. *Journal of Prevention, 1,* 67–70.

Albee, G. W. (1981). Politics, power, prevention and social change. In J. M. Joffee & G. W. Albee (Eds.), *Prevention through political action and social change* (pp. 5–25). Hanover, NH: University Press of New England.

Albee, G. W., & Joffe, J. M. (Eds.). (1977).*Primary prevention of psychopathology: The issues.* Hanover, NH: University Press of New England.

Alpert, J. L. (1983 August). *Future, prevention, change, and school psychology.* Presidential address to Division 16 of the American Psychological Association at the annual convention, Annaheim, CA.

Alpert, J. L. (1982). *Psychological consultation in educational settings.* San Francisco: Jossey-Bass.

Alpert, J. L., & Meyers, J. (Eds.). (1983). *Training in consultation.* Springfield, IL: Charles C Thomas.

Alpert, J. L., & Rosenfield, S. (1981). Consultation and the introduction of social problem-solving groups in schools. *Personnel and Guidance Journal, 60,* 37–41.

Alpert, J. L., & Yammer, M. D. (1983). Research in school consultation: A content analysis of selected journals. *Professional Psychology, 14,* 604–612.

Anderson, L. S. (1976) The mental health center's role in school consultation: Toward a new model. *Community Mental Health Journal, 12,* 83–85.

Aponte, J. F. (1977). Clinical-community and community mental health models. In I. Iscoe, B. L. Bloom, & C. D. Spielberger (Eds.), *Community psychology in transition: Proceedings of the National Conference on Training in Community Psychology* (pp. 77–82). New York: Wiley.

Barker, R. G., & Gump, P. (1964). *Big school, small school.* Stanford, CA: Stanford University Press.

Bergan, J. R. (1977). *Behavioral consultation.* Columbus, OH: Charles E. Merrill.

Bloom, B. L. (1973). *Community mental health: A historical and critical analysis.* Morristown, NJ: General Learning Press.

Bond, L. A., & Joffe, J. M. (Eds.). (1982). *Facilitating infant and early childhood development.* Hanover, NH: University Press of New England.

Brown, D., Pryzwansky, W. B., & Schulte, A. C. (1987). *Psychological consultation: Introduction to theory and practice.* Boston: Allyn and Bacon.

Buck, J. A. (1984). Block grants and federal promotion of community mental health services. *Community Mental Health Journal, 20,* 236–247.

Caplan, G. (1951). A public health approach to child psychiatry. *Mental Hygiene, 35,* 235–249.

Caplan, G. (1955). *Emotional problems of early childhood.* New York: Basic Books.

Caplan, G. (Ed.). (1961). *Prevention of mental disorders in children.* New York: Basic Books.

Caplan, G. (1963). Types of mental health consultation. *American Journal of Orthopsychiatry, 3,* 470–481.

Caplan, G. (1964). *Principles of preventive psychiatry.* New York: Basic Books.

Caplan, G. (1970). *The theory and practice of mental health consultation.* New York: Basic Books.

Caplan, G. (1974). *Support systems and community mental health.* New York: Behavioral Publications.

Chesler, M. A., Bryant, B. I., & Crowfoot, J. E. (1976). Consultation in schools: Inevitable conflict, partisanship and advocacy. *Professional Psychology, 7,* 637–645.

Ciarlo, J. A., & Diamond, H. (1979). Editorial statement. *Community Mental Health Journal, 15,* 79–81.

Clarizio, H. F. (1979). Primary prevention of behavioral disorders in the schools. *School Psychology Digest, 8,* 434–445.

Coles, G. S., Ciporen, M. A., Honigsberg, R., & Cohen, B. (1980). Educational therapy in a community mental health center. *Community Mental Health Journal, 16,* 79–89.

Conoley, J. C. (1981). *Consultation in schools.* New York: Academic Press.

Cowen, E. L. (1967). Emergent approaches to mental health problems: An overview and directions for future work. In E. L. Cowen, A. Gardner, & M. L. Zax (Eds.), *Emergent approaches to mental health problems* (pp. 389–455). New York: Appleton-Century-Crofts.

Cowen, E. L. (1977). Baby steps toward primary prevention. *American Journal of Community Psychology, 5,* 1–22.

Cowen, E. L. (1980). The primary mental health project: Yesterday, today and tomorrow. *The Journal of Special Education, 14,* 133–154.

Cowen, E. L. (1984). A general structure model for primary prevention program development in mental health. *Personnel and Guidance Journal, 62,* 485–490.

Cowen, E. L., Gardner, A., & Zax, M. L. (1967). *Emergent approaches to mental health problems.* New York: Appleton-Century-Crofts.

Cowen, E. L., Gesten, E. L., & Wilson, A. B. (1979). The primary mental health project (PMHP): Evaluation of current program effectiveness. *American Journal of Community Psychology, 7,* 293–303.

Curtis, M. J., & Meyers, J. (1985). School-based consultation: Guidelines for effective practice. In J. Grimes

& A. Thomas (Eds.), *Best practices in school psychology* (pp. 79–94). Washington, DC: National Association of School Psychologists.

Cutts, N. (Ed.). (1955). *School psychologists at midcentury.* Washington, DC: American Psychological Association.

Dohrenwend, B. S. (1977). Applied social psychology. In I. Iscoe, B. L. Bloom, & C. D. Spielberger (Eds.), *Community psychology in transition: Proceedings of the National Conference on Training in Community Psychology* (pp. 127–132). New York: Wiley.

Dorr, D. (1977). Intervention and prevention: I. Preventive intervention. In I. Iscoe, B. L. Bloom, & C. D. Spielberger (Eds.), *Community psychology in transition: Proceedings of the National Conference on Training in Community Psychology* (pp. 87–93). New York: Wiley.

Felner, R. D., Ginter, M., & Primavera, J. (1982). Primary prevention during school transitions: Social support and environmental structure. *American Journal of Community Psychology, 10,* 277–290.

Felner, R. D., Jason, L. A., Moritsugu, J. N., & Farber, S. S. (Eds.). (1983). *Preventive psychology: Theory, research and practice.* Elmsford, NY: Pergamon Press.

Fullan, M., Miles, M. B., & Taylor, G. (1980). Organization development in schools: The state of the art. *Review of Educational Research, 50,* 121–183.

Gatz, M., & Liem, R. (1977). Social change: II. Systems analysis and intervention. In I. Iscoe, B. L. Bloom, & C. D. Spielberger (Eds.), *Community psychology in transition: Proceedings of the National Conference on Training in Community Psychology* (pp. 117–122). New York: Wiley.

Gerrard, M. (1977). Intervention and prevention: II. Systems analysis and organizational dynamics. In I. Iscoe, B. L. Bloom, & C. D. Spielberger (Eds.), *Community psychology in transition: Proceedings of the National Conference on Training in Community Psychology* (pp. 95–98). New York: Wiley.

Gesten, E. L., & Jason, L. A. (1987). Social and community interventions. *Annual Review of Psychology, 38,* 427–460.

Goldenberg, I. (1983). On values and advocacy in consultation. In J. Alpert & J. Meyers (Eds.), *Training in consultation* (pp. 213–220). Springfield, IL: Charles C Thomas.

Goldwasser, E., Meyers, J., Christenson, S., & Graden, J. (1983). The impact of PL 94-142 on the practice of school psychology. *Psychology in the Schools, 20,* 153–165.

Gresham, F. (1981). Assessment of children's social skills. *Journal of School Psychology, 19,* 120–133.

Gresham, F. (1985). Best practices in social skills training. In A. Thomas & J. Grimes (Eds.), *Best practices in school psychology* (pp. 181–192). Washington, DC: National Association of School Psychologists.

Gutkin, T. B., & Curtis, M. J. (1982). School-based consultation: Theory and techniques. In C. R. Reynolds & T. B. Gutkin (Eds.), *The handbook of school psychology* (pp. 519–561). New York: Wiley.

Halpern, W. I., Kissel, S., & Gold, J. (1978). Day

treatment as an aid to mainstreaming troubled children. *Community Mental Health Journal, 14,* 319–326.

Hassol, L. (1977). Social Change: I. Guidelines for social intervention. In I. Iscoe, B. L. Bloom, & C. D. Spielberger (Eds.), *Community psychology in transition: Proceedings of the National Conference on Training in Community Psychology* (pp. 109–116). New York: Wiley.

Hermalin, J., & Morell, J. A. (Eds.). (1987). *Prevention planning in mental health.* Newbury Park, CA: Sage.

Hodges, W. F. (1977). Intervention and prevention: III. Enhancement of competency. In I. Iscoe, B. L. Bloom, & C. D. Spielberger (Eds.), *Community psychology in transition: Proceedings of the National Conference on Training in Community Psychology* (pp. 99–107). New York: Wiley.

Holahan, C. J. (1977). Social ecology. In I. Iscoe, B. L. Bloom, & C. D. Spielberger (Eds.), *Community psychology in transition: Proceedings of the National Conference on Training in Community Psychology* (pp. 123–126). New York: Wiley.

Hollister, W. G. (1965). The concept of strens in preventive interventions and ego-strength building in the schools. In N. Lambert (Ed.), *The Protection and Promotion of Mental Health in Schools* (Mental Health Monograph 5, pp. 30–35). Washington, DC: U.S. Government Printing Office.

Hyman, I., & Wise, J. H. (Eds.). (1979). *Corporal punishment in American education: Readings in history, practice and alternatives.* Philadelphia: Temple University Press.

Iscoe, I., Bloom, B. L., & Spielberger, C. D. (Eds.). (1977). *Community psychology in transition: Proceedings of the National Conference on Training in Community Psychology.* New York: Wiley.

Iscoe, I., & Spielberger, C. D. (Eds.). (1970). *Community psychology: Perspectives in training and research.* New York: Appleton-Century-Crofts.

Jacobson, E., Ravlin, M., & Cooper, S. (1983). Issues in the training of mental health consultants in community mental health centers. In J. Alpert & J. Meyers (Eds.), *Training in Consultation.* (pp. 47–81). Springfield, IL: Charles C Thomas.

Janis, I. L. (1958). *Psychological stress.* New York: Wiley.

Jerrell, J. M., & Larsen, J. K. (1984). Policy shifts and organizational adaptation: a review of current developments. *Community Mental Health Journal, 20,* 282–293.

Johnson, D. W., & Johnson, R. (1980). Promoting constructive student–student relationships through cooperative learning. In M. R. Reynolds & R. Bentz (Eds.), *Extending the challenge: Working toward a common body of practice for teachers* (pp. 1–54). Minneapolis, MN: University of Minnesota, National Support Systems Project.

Kent, M. W., & Rolf, J. E. (Eds.). (1979). *Primary prevention of psychopathology: Social competence in children.* Hanover, NH: University Press of New England.

Kessler, M., & Goldston, S. E. (Eds.). (1986). *A decade of progress in primary prevention.* Hanover, NH: University Press of New England.

Kuhn, T. S. (1962). *The structure of scientific revolutions.* Chicago: University of Chicago Press.

Lorion, R. P. (1977). Community development and systems approaches. In I. Iscoe, B. L. Bloom, & C. D. Spielberger (Eds.), *Community psychology in transition: Proceedings of the National Conference on Training in Community Psychology* (pp. 83–86). New York: Wiley.

Mannino, F., & Shore, M. (1975). The effects of consultation: A review of empirical studies. *American Journal of Community Psychology, 3,* 1–21.

Martin, R. P., & Meyers, J. (1980). School psychologists and the practice of consultation. *Psychology in the Schools, 17,* 478–484.

Medway, F. J. (1979). How effective is school consultation: A review of recent research. *Journal of School Psychology, 17,* 275–282.

Meyers, J., Parsons, R. D., & Martin, R. (1979). *Mental health consultation in the schools.* San Francisco: Jossey-Bass.

Meyers, J., & Parsons, R. D. (1987). Prevention planning in the school system. In J. Hermalin and J. A. Morell (Eds.), *Prevention planning in mental health* (pp. 111–150). Newbury Park, CA: Sage.

Meyers, J., Pitt, N., Gaughan, E. J., & Freidman, M. P. (1978). A research model for consultation with teachers. *Journal of School Psychology, 16,* 137–145.

Meyers, J., Wurtz, R., & Flanagan, D. (1981). A national survey investigating consultation training occurring in school psychology programs. *Psychology in the Schools, 18,* 297–302.

Moore, T. (1977). Social change and community psychology. In I. Iscoe, B. L. Bloom, and C. D. Spielberger (Eds.), *Community psychology in transition: Proceedings of the National Conference on Training in Community Psychology* (pp. 257–266). New York: Wiley.

Moos, R. H. (1973). Conceptualization of human environments. *American Psychologist, 28,* 652–665.

Moos, R. H. (1974a). *Evaluating treatment environments: A social ecological approach.* New York: Wiley.

Moos, R. H. (1974b). *The social climate scales: An overview.* Palo Alto, CA: Consulting Psychologists Press.

Moos, R. H. (1979). *Evaluating educational environments.* San Francisco: Jossey-Bass.

Parsons, R. D., & Meyers, J. (1984). *Developing consultation skills.* San Francisco: Jossey-Bass.

Phillips, B. N., Martin, R. P., & Meyers, J. (1972). Interventions in relation to anxiety in school. In C. D. Spielberger (Ed.), *Anxiety: Current trends in theory and research* (Vol. 2, pp. 409–464). New York: Academic Press.

Rappaport, J. (1985a). *The death and resurrection of community mental health.* Presented at 93rd annual meetings of the American Psychological Association, Los Angeles.

Rappaport, J. (1985b). The power of empowerment language. *Social Policy, 16,* 15–21.

Reiff, R. (1977). Ya gotta believe. In I. Iscoe, B. L. Bloom, & C. D. Spielberger (Eds.), *Community psychology in transition: Proceedings of the Na-*

tional Conference on Training in Community Psychology (pp. 45–50). New York: Wiley.

Sarason, S. B. (1972). *The creation of settings and the future societies.* San Francisco: Jossey-Bass.

Sarason, S. B. (1974). *The psychological sense of community. Prospects for a community psychology.* San Francisco: Jossey-Bass.

Sarason, S. B. (1976). Community psychology, networks and Mr. Everyman. *American Psychologist, 13,* 317–328.

Sarason, S. B. (1982). *The culture of the school and the problem of change* (2nd ed.). Boston: Allyn and Bacon.

Sarason, S. B., Levine, M., Goldenberg, I. I., Cherlin, D. L., & Bennett, E. M. (1966). *Psychology in community settings.* New York: Wiley.

Schein, E. H. (1969). *Process consultation.* Reading, MA. Addison-Wesley.

Schmuck, R. A., & Miles, M. B. (Eds.). (1971). *Organizational development in the schools.* Palo Alto, CA: National Press Books.

Schmuck, R. A., et al. (1972). *Handbook of organization development in schools.* Palo Alto, CA: National Press Books.

Schmuck, R. A., et al. (1977). *The second handbook of organization development in schools.* Palo Alto, CA: Mayfield.

Schultz, C. L., Harker, P. C., & Gardner, J. M. (1977). In comparison of the community psychology and medical modes: Teaching attitudes toward deviance in high school students. *Community Mental Health Journal, 13,* 268–276.

Shure, M. B., & Spivack, G. (1978). *Problem solving techniques in childrearing.* San Francisco: Jossey-Bass.

Snow, D. L., & Swift, C. F. (1985). Consultation and education in community mental health: A historical analysis. *Journal of Primary Prevention, 6,* 3–30.

Spielberger, C. D., & Iscoe, I. (1970). The current status of training in community psychology. In I. Iscoe & C. D. Spielberger (Eds.), *Community psychology: Perspectives in training and research* (pp. 227–246). New York: Appleton-Century-Crofts.

Spivack, G., Platt, J. J., & Shure, M. B. (1976). *The problem solving approach to adjustment.* San Francisco: Jossey-Bass.

Spivack, G., & Shure, M. B. (1974). *Social adjustment of young children: A cognitive approach to solving real-life problems.* San Francisco: Jossey-Bass.

Tolan, P. H., & Lounsbury, J. W. (1982). Community mental health ideology presented in high school textbooks: A current analysis. *Community Mental Health Journal, 18,* 286–296.

Vayda, A. M., & Perlmutter, F. D. (1977). Primary prevention in community mental health centers: A survey of current activity. *Community Mental Health Journal, 13,* 343–335.

Waldron, J. A., & Bolman, W. M. (1979). Affective training for teachers of psychotic children. *Community Mental Health Journal, 15,* 229–236.

Weber, C. U., Foster, P. S., & Weikart, D. P. (1978). *An economic analysis of the Ypsilanti Perry Preschool Project* (Monograph of the High/Scope Educational Research Foundation, No. 5). Ypsilanti, MI: High/Scope Press.

Weikart D. (1984). *Early childhood education: Lessons for the prevention of mental health problems in children.* Address presented to the Fourth Annual Delaware Valley Conference on the Future of Psychology in the Schools, sponsored by Temple University, Department of School Psychology, Philadelphia.

10

CONTRIBUTIONS OF THE PSYCHOLOGY OF INDIVIDUAL DIFFERENCES TO SCHOOL PSYCHOLOGY: DIFFERENT DRUMMERS—ONE BEAT

MARK J. BENSON

Virginia Tech

RICHARD A. WEINBERG

University of Minnesota

We are interested in the child . . . as he comes to us—with his unique complex of ancestry, associates, home training, schooling, and physical and moral attributes. We are interested, not in finding out how he would have developed if he had had no environment at all; rather we wish to discover whether or not he can be made a more intelligent individual or a more learned one by improving conditions of his milieu within the limits found in reasonably good social communities

Lewis Terman (1928, pp. 2–3).

In 1776 a fledgling British colony boldly proclaimed its autonomy with the words, "We hold thee truths to be self-evident, that all men are created equal." Since then, equality of opportunity has matured into a dominant value of American culture (Gordon, 1972; Sampson, 1975; Spence, 1985). American egaliterianism and British individualism in the nineteenth century (Buss, 1976) combined to foster an ideology of "the individual" (Sampson, 1977; Spence, 1985), an ideology that has contributed to shaping American education. But a contrasting value has also shaped American education, the belief in America as a melting pot. Our melting pot ethic promotes a view of assimilation into American culture, and public education facilitates uniformity in acculturation. In fact, compulsory and mass education developed in part from the need to Americanize immigrant students (Kaplan & Kaplan, 1985). The conflicting values of conformity versus individuality present a continuing dilemma for educators.

The school psychologist confronts these dual values daily. As any educator, the school psychologist must weigh the merits of pluralism that the individualistic value implies against the merits of single standards that the acculturation value represents. Unlike other educators, however, school psychologists are more qualified to understand differences across individual students. Other professionals within schools are most often trained in acculturation models such as curriculum, teaching methods, and administration. In contrast, school psychologists are trained to evaluate and interpret individual differences. Although other educators may be interested in differences across their students, school psychologists are uniquely qualified to assess, conceptualize, and explain these differences. As unique scientists of individuality in the schools, the school psychologist's knowledge of differences enhances the effectiveness of placements, interventions, and systems decisions in schools.

HOW THE CHAPTER IS ORGANIZED

This chapter covers three principal areas:

1. History, definitions, and interpretations of differences
2. Domains of individual difference variation: general intelligence, specific cognitive skills, and personality development
3. A model for individual differences in school psychology

In the first section, the field of individual differences is traced from its founders to present thinkers. Traditional biases and historical prejudices concerning differences are clarified. The cornerstone concept, variation, is next discussed from statistical and theoretical perspectives. We then review variation from the vantage point of the school psychologist; we include not only differences in the traditional domain of general intelligence, but also variation in specific cognitive skills, domains of achievement, and personality development. This leads to a final section that presents a model of the domains of individual differences interacting with variation across situations. The model further implies alternative views on the placement of students and the role of school psychologists.

THE HISTORY OF INDIVIDUAL DIFFERENCES

During this century, three popular myths have become attached to the field of individual differences:

> Myth 1. Individual differences focus solely on heredity.
> Myth 2. Differences concern only IQ.
> Myth 3. Differences are pessimistic about education.

As with all myths, the actual history of individual differences has played a role in creating these myths. So we shall present a brief historical sketch of differential psychology by exploring these three myths.

Myth 1: Individual Differences Focus Solely on Heredity

Our historical review of individual differences could begin with references to the use of tests of differences by Chinese emperors to select workers in the twenty-third century B.C. (Dahlstrom, 1985) or with statements from Plato and Aristotle concerning eugenics, character differences, or environmental means of promoting the ideal character. Such departure points reveal the timeless and universal nature of the notion of differences across individuals. Indeed, the question as to whether behavior is preordained by *nature* or acquired by *nurture* has preoccupied thoughtful observers since antiquity. John Locke, the English philosopher, argued that at birth our minds are like blank slates (*tabula rasa*) and that as individuals, we are defined by learning.

As a branch of psychology the study of differential psychology actually begins with Darwin. Darwin's work, *The Origin of the Species* (1859/1958), ignited an upheaval in scientific communities that generated far-reaching effects, including the initiation of the *science* of individual differences. The central premise of Darwin's evolutionary theory was that more individuals are born to a species than can possibly survive, which results in a struggle for existence. To the extent that an individual varies from species members in a manner that is advantageous, that individual will have a better chance of surviving and reproducing. The constraints of the environment, then, dictate which members of the species will be naturally selected.

Darwin's cousin, Sir Francis Galton, was intrigued by evolutionary theory and undertook research on eminence in human families (1869/1962); it was he who coined the phrase "nature and nurture." He collected bibliographical and interview data on 1,000 men who had achieved prominence in their work. He found that these 1,000 men were descendants of only 300 families. Since the likelihood of eminence in a family was only 1 in 4,000, Galton concluded that eminence was a familial trait. He showed further the decreasing likelihood of eminence as relatives became less related to the eminent person. Galton's conclusions about the hereditary basis of genius have been criticized along several lines (see Schlesinger, 1985; Willerman, 1979). One major error of Galton's work, however, was the failure to control for environmental confounds, which renders his data just as easily interpretable from an environmental perspective as from the hereditary perspective.

Several other flawed investigations employing families were conducted in the early part of this century before rigorous designs became common. Research on the Stuarts versus the Tudors (Gun, 1930), the Kallikak clans (Goddard, 1912), and the Jukes (Estabrook, 1916) are significant examples. These studies inferred the hereditary conclusion to explain similarities observed within families.

From the foregoing it is clear that the historic roots of differential psychology spring from a hereditarian terrain of flawed research. More rigorous research in the latter half of this century has debunked these early conclusions and revealed instead that both heredity *and* environment contribute to differences across individuals. Moreover, for many variables heredity and environment are highly correlated with one another. This correlation reduces the issue of heredity *or* environment to the status of a fruitless question.

Myth 2: Individual Differences Concern Only IQ

Ironically, the contemporary measurement of individual differences began with astronomy rather than psychology. In estimating parallax times, investigators discovered that different observers recorded events at different rates. Several researchers began to examine these differences. One of them was Galton. His student, J. M. Cattell (1890), devised a series of 10 tasks that he called mental tests, primarily sensory and motor tasks. Cattell and Galton had limited success with their measures in predicting school achievement or other important variables. Another pair of researchers working at the same time, Binet and Simon (1905), discov-

ered a more effective set of mental tests. Binet's notion was to include tasks that tapped more complex problem-solving skills employing memory, judgment, and abstraction.

But intellectual assessment reflects only part of the history of individual differences. Research on differences across individuals can also be traced to differences in variables such as physical types and personality (Kretschmer, 1925; Sheldon & Stevens, 1946). Similarly, Freud (1950) promoted a differences approach in his notions of differential endowment of drive strength and differential effects of early experiences. Personality typologies such as the Freudian oral, anal, phallic, and genital personality types (Fenichel, 1945) or the Jungian (1933) dimensions of introversion, extroversion, thinking, feeling, sensing, and intuiting derive from a recognition of variance across individuals.

The actual assessment of individual differences extended beyond IQ assessment early in this century. The Rorschach Test (Rorschach, 1921) and the Thematic Apperception Test (Morgan & Murray, 1935; Murray et al., 1938) illustrate pioneering examples of the use of ambiguous stimuli to assess differences on a broad range of personality variables. The Personal Data Sheet (Woodworth, 1919), the Attitude Interest Blank (Terman & Miles, 1936), and the MMPI (Hathaway & McKinley, 1940/1980, 1942) reflect the use of self-report instruments to differentiate individuals across a variety of personality traits. Early career interest inventories Kuder, 1934; Strong, 1927, 1943) parallel this widening range of focus on human variation. Such examples depict the breadth of variables that may fall within the individual differences purview. Although the very early history of differential psychology centers on IQ, literally an infinite number of variables can fall within the purview of differential psychology.

Myth 3: Individual Differences Are Pessimistic About Education

Because heredity is associated with the past and because the past is unchangeable, we conclude through an associative process that heredity is unchangeable. Conversely, environment is associated with malleability or potential for change. Because educators are in the business of changing students, many educators identify with an environmental ideology and assume that hereditary explanations are pessimistic about education.

Actually, some heritable characteristics can be changed and some environmentally influenced characteristics are highly resistant to change, For example, phenylketonuria (PKU) is a heritable disease caused by a single recessive gene that results in severe mental retardation. Despite its heritability, modifications in the diet of young PKU patients can mitigate deleterious effects and actually improve IQs. Diabetes and heart disease also show a high level of heritability, but dietary and life-style interventions can dramatically alter outcomes. Even genes themselves can be altered by chemicals, x-rays, or temperature changes (Willerman, 1979). Some environmentally influenced conditions, conversely, are highly resistant to change. For example, prenatal malnutrition or cerebral brain damage can cause permanent mental retardation. Similarly, some acquired traits, such as alcoholism and cigarette addiction, can be highly resistant to interventions. Thus, despite the myth, the influence of heredity or environment clearly remains a separate issue from the malleability versus stability question.

Educators freed from these misleading associations can appreciate the potential for optimism despite marked individual differences. Influential educational theorists, such as Dewey (1916) and James (1958), understood the range of differences without pessimism. Assessing the level of the individual's understanding, guiding instruction using students' abilities, and providing environments for active student learning are basic postulates in these theories that reflect incisive understanding of individual differences. These theorists focused on understanding variations and tailoring instruction to respond to those differences. Some modern thinkers in differential psychology echo this emphasis on change. Tyler (1978) states that the important question is *not* heredity versus environment, but malleable versus unmalleable. Others stress that the important question is what we do about the differences (Gresham, 1986; Reynolds, 1986). Instead of pessimism, high heritability implies a need for specific interventions. A uniform environment inflates the heritability estimate, whereas highly varied or specific environments lessen the impact of heredity.

DEFINING, ASSESSING, AND INTERPRETING VARIATION

Theorists conceptualize variation across individuals as differences in types and differences in traits. Differences in types, such as oral or anal charac-

ters, contrast with trait differences which are continuous dimensions. Although the mean levels of these trait distributions are important, the variation from the mean occupies central significance for the differential psychologist. There are three ways to quantify the extent of this variation: standard deviation, the range, and the quartile range. The quartile range, half the magnitude between the 25th and 75th percentiles, and the range (endpoints on a continuum of scores) are unstable, due to their reliance on only two scores for determination. In contrast, the variance provides a stable index of dispersion through the use of each score, according to the variance formula:

$$\text{variance} = \frac{\Sigma(\text{mean of distribution} - \text{score})^2}{N}$$

Distributions also vary in their skewness, as illustrated by the positively and negatively skewed distributions in Figure 1. The kurtosis, that is, the flatness or peakedness, of a distribution also varies across distributions as illustrated in the platykurtic and leptokurtic distributions in Figure 1. The shapes of distributions of scores in a classroom can influence instruction decisions. For example, the negatively skewed distribution would suggest the need for special programming for children at the low end of the distribution, and a platykurtic distribution would imply the need for differential programming to meet the broad range of student skills. Distributions, however, reflect characteristics of the instrument and the sample characteristics. The shape of a distribution can therefore, be altered merely by changing the difficulty of the items.

Assessing Variance

The essential issue in assessing variance rests on the value judgment about what is important. Although differences in glucose levels, blood pressure, and hair coloration are largely irrelevant in the classroom, differences in achievement are paramount. Other differences, such as levels of perceptual skills, positive peer relations, conformity, appropriate behavior, self-esteem, motivation, and anxiety, however, vary in their importance across teachers and schools. Part of the dilemma of deciding which differences are important springs from the currently atheoretical orientation of the science of pedagogy (Glass, 1986). If we assume that achievement is the only educational goal of a school district, individual differences abound. The variation in reading level in a typical 7-grade

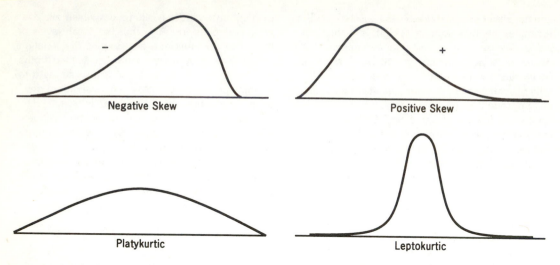

Figure 1. Types of distributions of scores.

classroom can range from a 4th-grade to a 12th-grade level. Put another way, if graduation from high school were based solely on achievement of a 12th-grade reading level, some students would graduate at age 10, while many 20-year-olds would never graduate.

The age grouping in schools is an expedient means for teaching to the developmental differences across the ages from 5 to 18. In an age grouping system, however, differences within an age group are essentially error variance. Indeed, some teachers may treat differences in achievement or other differences across students as a nuisance variable. Traditionally, differences in achievement within grade levels have been handled by tracking or special education.

This use of tracking to address differences derives from a single-dimensional approach to differences across students—the achievement dimension. Students are viewed as possessing more or less of this single variable. Tyler (1978) refers to this as a *vertical* approach to differences and argues instead for a *horizontal* approach in which many dimensions of difference are considered. In assessing variation, school psychologists often employ several dimensions, but the continued emphasis on achievement or ability differences in most evaluations perpetuates the vertical approach to differences. The screening and diagnostic roles that a school psychologist performs could be broadened by considering a myriad of other cogni-

tive, affective, and behavioral dimensions than have previously been employed. Including individual strengths and weaknesses in diagnostic evaluations has been found to be a valuable aspect of effective reports (Keogh, 1972; Rogers, 1977).

In addition, a differences approach need not be restricted to individual pupils. As Bardon (1982) describes, the clients of the school psychologist can include groups of students, groups of teachers, administrators, or the educational system. Just as teachers often treat individual differences across students as an error or nuisance variable, school psychologists may perceive teachers who vary from their expectations of receptive consultation as an error or nuisance factor. The psychologist who can assess individual differences in teachers, understand their causes, and predict their effects can present information in a manner that will motivate other school personnel to address the needs of the child.

Interpreting Variance

To motivate school personnel to move beyond seeing individual differences as error variance, interpretation of the differences is necessary. Reporting an achievement score that is significantly below average only identifies a difference; explaining the potential factors underlying the score promotes understanding. According to one position, a major component of effective assessment is the reduction of uncertainty or the explanation of the referring issues (Hayman, Raydner, Stenner, & Madey, 1979). The explanation of the uncertainty, or variance, is accomplished through a parsimonious formulation and understandable explanation of the observed variation in the data. Motivational, innate, temperamental, developmental, affective, cognitive, familial, or experiential constructs are examples of the causal dimensions that may be employed to explain variation. While remaining faithful to the data, the school psychologist should emphasize aspects of explanations that will promote positive change for the student. Individual needs of students and predictions of performance can be generated from the differences data. Decisions on placement, referral to other agencies, and formulation of recommendations should develop from these observations. Instructional recommendations might be more easily implemented in student-centered classrooms. Teacher-centered classrooms present a more challenging context within which to recommend instructional alternatives.

Because of our limited empirical base, recommendations are usually more of an art than a science. If aptitude-treatment interaction (ATI) research had yielded more robust findings, we could make scientifically verifiable recommendations. Part of the stalemate in ATI research has been due to the separation of two branches of psychology: experimental and correlational. Cronbach (1957) was the first to describe these two branches of psychology and to urge for their collaboration. The experimentalist branch focuses on controlling or manipulating independent variables. Subjects are assigned randomly to groups, and individual differences are treated as error variance. The other branch, correlational psychology, assesses variables in the situation and correlates them with one another. Correlational psychology focuses on explaining individual differences through observed associations. The meeting of these two branches is the discipline of ATI. In ATI research, the individual differences or aptitudes are subjected to different experimental treatments. To date, ATI research has had limited success, but substantial potential remains. By constructing individual difference measures that tie to outcomes (Hawkins, 1977) and systematically varying the dimensions, such as content, conditions, quantity, and modality (Jensen, 1964), ATI research may yield more fruitful results.

Studying Variation: The Complexity for the School Psychologist

The zygote, the cell that is formed from the uniting of the sperm and egg cells of the parents, contains the entire genetic material of the child. Half of the genetic material in the zygote derives from each of the parents. The nucleus of the zygote contains 23 pairs of chromosomes, which are strands of the complex molecule DNA that resemble a twisted ladder. The chromosomes carry the genes. There are some 5 to 10 million gene particles, and any gene may have several possible varieties or alleles. Consequently, the number of possible genotypes is astronomical. One estimate is 70 trillion (Gottesman, 1974). From the moment of conception then, each individual, literally, is unique.

This immense variation provides for efficient execution of the natural selection process. Genes that are endowed with a competitive advantage over others in the environment will more likely be maintained in the gene pool through the longevity and reproductivity of the organism. Thus, genetic diversity provides the foundation for the selection process to exert a powerful influence (Harris, 1966; Lewontin & Hubby, 1966; Mayr, 1970).

The process whereby this occurs is best understood with reference to the differences between genotype and phenotype. *Genotype* is the underlying genetic composition of the zygote or the organism. *Phenotype* is the visible or observable characteristic of the individual. Eye color, hair texture, height, intellectual skills, and aggressiveness are examples of phenotype variables. The phenotype at times may mask the characteristics of the genotype. For example, two parents with brown eyes, their phenotype, may contain a recessive gene for blue eyes in their genotype, which would result on average in one of their four children having blue eyes. If blue eyes were critically important to survival in our society, that child would be at a selective advantage and would be more likely to acquire the advantages that would increase her reproductive fitness, that is, reproduce others who would be at a selective advantage. Thus, it is through the phenotype that the genotypic selection process operates.

Eye color represents a rare example of the determination of phenotype by a single pair of genes. Most human characteristics are *polygenic,* that is, determined by more than one pair of genes. It was through studying phenotypes determined by one pair of genes, however, that Mendel discovered the genetic principles of dominance and recessiveness. Geneticists have since discovered that there are also intermediate types. The combination of levels of dominance and polygenic inheritance results in continuous phenotypic variables. In sufficiently large samples, variables such as height, weight, or intellectual ability approach the normal curve. Modern behavioral geneticists investigate these and innumerable other variables through a fairly well defined set of research strategies.

Research Strategies for Understanding Phenotypic Variation

There are four classes of techniques for investigating variation in behavioral genetics. First, there is the pedigree or lineage design, where the investigator selects a family line with a particular trait and compares the line with a control group. Galton's work on eminence mentioned earlier is an example (see also Goddard, 1912; Herber & Denver, 1970; Reed & Reed, 1965). A variation on this is the selection of a particular abnormality and evaluating the incidence in a family line (Haywood, Meyers, & Switsky, 1982).

A second research technique also employs family members but compares them to a target subject by their degree of genetic similarity. Because children derive half of their genetic material from each parent, they share 50% genetic overlap with each parent. Similarly, they share 50% with their siblings, who differ from them only in the probabilistic assortment of their parents genes. Children shares only 25% genetic overlap with their grandparents. Table 1 lists relatives and their degree of genetic similarity to a target subject.

Comparisons of correlations between various family members yield information on the heritability of a phenomenon under study. *Heritability* is a

statistical estimate of the proportion of variance in the distribution of a phenotype for a particular population that is accounted for by genetic or hereditary sources. Correlations that diverge widely from the percentage of overlap, either above or below, call the heritability hypothesis into question. Height and intelligence are variables that fit the expected correlations well. The correlation between heights of parents and their children or among siblings is estimated at $r = .50$ (Tyler, 1978). Similarly, the correlation between the IQs of parents and their children the IQs among siblings is approximately $r = .50$.

A third approach in behavioral genetics utilizes samples of identical and fraternal twins. Since identical twins originate with the splitting of the zygote, they are genetically identical; that is, there is 100% genetic overlap. Fraternal twins, which develop from separate eggs and separate sperm, are genetically no more alike than are nontwin siblings; they share only 50% genetic overlap. The fraternal twins provide an excellent control group for identical twins through the elimination of the age difference confound that occurs when comparing nontwin siblings. As an example, a recent review of 10 studies on personality traits in twins revealed an average $r = .47$ for identical twins and $r = .23$ for fraternal twins (Goldsmith, 1983). A central confound that continues to be debated is whether fraternal twins are treated in similar ways in their families (Plomin, 1986) or whether fraternal twins receive more differential treatment than do identical twins (Bronfenbrenner, 1975).

The foregoing methodologies share a common problem: observed similarities and differences are confounded by environments. To explain, consider the correlation between the IQs of siblings as $r = .50$. This coincides exactly with the genetic hypothesis of 50% overlap between siblings. As-

TABLE 1   Degree of Genetic Similarity by Relationship to a Child

Percent Overlap	Examples of Relatives	Degree
100	Identical twins	
50	Parent, sibling, fraternal twins	First
25	Uncle, grandparent, half-siblings	Second
12.5	Cousin, greataunt	Third

suming that siblings share the same environment, however, some of the relationship is due to environment. It is possible that the environments could be very similar such that a large part of the observed correlation between the siblings IQ is due to environmental factors.

The adoption design circumvents this problem by incorporating environmental as well as genetic differences. Adoptive children are compared with nonadoptive children or with siblings in the adoptive household. A variation on this is to sample twins who have been reared together with those who have been reared apart.

The adoption design varies environments, but typically does not directly assess environments. Willerman (1979) advocates fine-grained assessment of environments to explicate issues in behavioral genetics. Assessing environments is a complex task that has received systematic investigation only recently. The HOME (Caldwell & Bradley, 1978) is a promising example of a measure for assessing environments. The HOME utilizes observations and interviews to assess parental behavior through a 45-item, six-scale measure. Through the use of instruments for assessing environments, the persistent dilemma of identifying the sources of phenotypic variation may be unraveled.

Sources of Phenotypic Variation

Parents, teachers, and many school psychologists are tempted to reduce the sources of variation among students to the grand duo: genetics *or* environment. Actually, there are at least 11 sources of variation across students, as listed in Table 2. The term "main effect" in Table 2 refers to the influence of an independent variable on a dependent variable. For example, in a study on the effects of IQ and motivation on student achievement, we would expect a main effect for IQ. That is, we would predict that students with higher IQs would have greater achievement. We would also predict a main effect for motivation; that is, those with higher motivation would have higher achievement (see Figure 2). Although difficult to study, most educators agree that motivation represents a strong main effect on achievement.

In referring to the heritability of a characteristic, one is focusing on the genotype, which is inherited from the independent assortment of the randomly combined genes of the parents. But parents do not mate randomly. Instead, couples often share similar traits. This is assortative mating,

TABLE 2   Sources of Phenotypic Variation

Main effect: heredity
Assortative mating
Independent assortment of genes
Main effect: environment
Within family
Shared (siblings share family environment)
Nonshared (siblings treated differently)
Outside family
Nonsystematic (illness, accident)
Interaction
Covariation
Passive
Evocative
Active
Error variance
Unexplained variance

and variation across genotypes is inflated by this tendency. Actually, assortative mating should not logically be considered heritable variance, but we include it to highlight the common error of ignoring assortative mating, which results in inflated heritability estimates. Some investigators, however, do partial out assortative mating from their heritability estimates.

Turning to the main effects in the environment, we are met with a diversity of sources of variation. Rowe and Plomin (1981) distinguish between sources that are shared from those that are different across members of the family. Socioeconomic status (SES) illustrates a pervasive source of shared variance that influences school achievement. However, the variation that siblings experience separately in the environment can exert substantial influence (Plomin, 1986). These separate experiences can originate within the family because a parent or sibling interacts differently with the target student than with others in the family. Two investigations found, for example, that although parental control was not different across offspring, parents differed in their acceptance of the children within their family (Rowe, 1981, 1983). A more obvious source of difference is the variation that children from the same family experience outside their family context, such as among peers and teachers. Finally, there are also nonsystematic sources of variation among children in a family, such as accidents or illnesses (Rowe & Plomin, 1981).

So far we have discussed only the influence of heredity and environment as independent sources of variation. Interaction of heredity and environment is another class of variation. Interaction refers to the variance due to one level of variable operating differently at various levels of a second variable in affecting the outcome. This is illustrated graphically in Figure 2. As an example, consider two groups, a high-IQ and a low-IQ group. Add to this two environments, one that expects over-achievement and one that expects under-achievement, to produce the 2×2 design in Figure 2. If all groups perform at a moderate level of achievement, except for the low-IQ/overexpectation group, which performs at a low level, there is an interaction.

In behavior genetics the term *interaction* is often confused with interactionism. As seen from the example above, interaction is a statistical concept for reflecting variance due to differential operation of one variable within levels of a second variable. Interactionism, however, refers to a perspective (Bouchard & Segal, 1985; Rowe, 1987). The interactionism perspective conceptualizes two or more constructs as working together, separately, or interactively over time. An interactionism perspective on student misbehavior in a classroom, for example, would view misbehavior as a product of the reciprocal influences of the behaviors of the student, the teacher, and the peers operating to sustain the misbehavior.

There has been little evidence to date of any powerful interactions between heredity and environment in the behavioral genetics literature (Bouchard, 1976; Jinks & Fulker, 1970; Plomin,

1986). The reasons may rest with the difficulty of effectively assessing environments and the large samples needed to detect interactions. Another impediment masking interactions is the powerful *covariation* between heredity and environment.

Covariation Between Heredity and Environment

Covariation refers to the strength of association or correlation between variables. Heredity and environment are strongly associated for many important outcomes in cognitive and social development. At one level, parents not only pass on their genes, they also pass on aspects of their environments, such as parenting style, SES, and educational level. Three types of covariation between heredity and environment, including passive, evocative (or reactive), and active (Plomin, DeFries, & Loehlin, 1977), have been described. Passive covariation refers to associations where the child's role is that of a relatively passive recipient of the environment—receiving love or an enriched early educational environment. Evocative covariation occurs when the genotype elicits responses from the environment. Students with a hyperactivity genotype, for example, typically evoke reactions of frustration and punishment. Finally, covariation may also result from the individual's active selection in the environment. The student who chooses to major in logic may be expressing an underlying genotype for strong left-hemisphere dominance.

The inherent complexity in considering 11 sources of variance has led to difficulties in interpreting findings. It is widely accepted that beyond

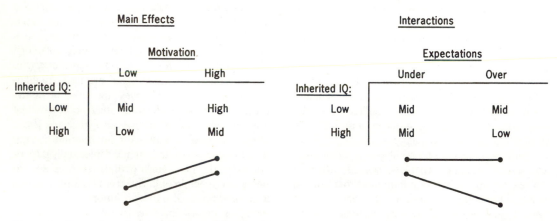

Figure 2. Examples of main effects and interactions.

broad parameters, investigators have reached different conclusions (Haywood & Switsky, 1986; Reynolds, 1986). Part of this is due to the assumptions necessary to execute a single behavioral genetic design, the reification of constructs, and the breadth of heritabilities, environments, and outcomes.

Heritability AND Environment

The 11 sources of variance presented here challenge the simplistic notion of explaining children's abilities or behaviors as either due simply to heredity *or* environment. Anastasi (1958, p. 197) has stressed the interdependence of heredity and environment in stating: "The organism is the product of its genes and its past environment." Both heredity and environment are necessary for the explanation of behavior. The misguided notion of pitting heredity and environment together to see which is more important is akin to asking whether word attack or reading comprehension is more important for reading skill. Both are necessary.

The interplay of genetics and environment begins even before the birth of the child. The prenatal environment has been shown to have profound influences on the development of the child. In addition to anomalies such as fetal alcohol syndrome, it has been shown that through hormonal action, the mother's emotionality can change the physiology of the fetus (Lubchenco, 1976). Even before the conception of the child, however, this interplay is activated. Through assortive mating, parents join together based on such factors as proximity, similarities in IQs, and social class. Once the zygote is formed, genes and environment continue an interplay even on the cellular level. Within the cell, chemicals within the cytoplasm inhibit or activate the gene. The same genes exposed to different cytoplasm will develop differently. Furthermore, for each cell the nearby cells constitute an environment.

Although current investigators often acknowledge the interplay of genetics and environment, some investigators paradoxically uphold the usefulness of heritability estimates. Scarr and Kidd (1983) identified semantic and mathematical ambiguities that attach to the notion of heritability estimation. There are different formulas for estimating heritability. Some double the difference between correlations of identical and fraternal twins. Others estimate either hereditary or environmental influence and then subtract from 100%. In general, heritability estimates assume that genetics and environment contribute additively. As illustrated earlier, there is often substantial covariation between heredity and environment. Accordingly, it is impossible to divide variation into that which is inherited and that which is acquired (Anastasi, 1965).

The metaphors that have been employed to describe the heredity–environment interplay are *canalization* and *reaction range*. *Canalization* (Waddington, 1962) presents the developing organism as a ball rolling down an incline that has various canals or grooves. Heredity defines the contours of the landscape and environment affects the lateral movement of the ball. The reification of canalization has misled investigators and laypersons alike. Canalization fails to capture the heredity–environment interplay because it presents heredity as preformed and unchanging. Actually, there is continual interplay between heredity and environment throughout development.

A second concept, *reaction range*, offers a quantifiable version of the canalization concept. According to this concept, the genotype sets parameters on phenotypic development. A range of phenotypes can develop from similar genotypes. Variation in the environments of individuals, then, broadens the genotypic variation. For a given genotype for intellectual ability, for example, investigators have estimated a 25-IQ-point reaction range (Scarr-Salapatek, 1975), based on the opportunities facilitated by certain environments. The interpretation of reaction range as set by heredity and influenced by environment ignores, however, the more dynamic interplay that occurs throughout development between heredity and environment.

Developmentalists, and most laypeople, have typically viewed heredity as playing an important role early in development and a decreasing role as the child matures. McCall (1981), for example, posits that until age 2, intelligence is largely controlled by genes, and that afterward heredity plays a less important role. Other theorists, however, argue that genes play an *increasing* role over the course of development. DeFries states that genes which affect IQ "make only a small contribution at first, but the effects are amplified throughout development" (Plomin, 1986, p. 59). One reason for the increasing role of heredity rests with the notion that children become increasingly more active in the selection of their environments as they develop. This niche-building increasingly resembles their genetic endowment (Scarr & McCartney, 1983).

The debate over the increasing versus decreasing role of heredity obscures the complexity of interplay between heredity and environment throughout development. Actually, the contributions of heredity and environment change over the course of development. For example, before and after puberty, genetic variation explains little of the variation in androgen or estrogen levels. During puberty, however, genetics powerfully influence variation in the hormone levels that affect the onset, termination, and duration of puberty. Huntington's chorea also exemplifies the changing influence of heredity over the course of development. Huntington's is caused by a single dominant gene that results in involuntary jerky movements. This hereditary disease typically remains dormant until about age 40. Thus, before age 20 genetic variation is irrelevant for the disease, but after age 50 or so, genetics predicts with nearly 100% accuracy.

What we have been referring to as the interplay between genetics and environment may be formulated as transactions between heredity and environment that change over the course of development. Some of the transactions may be due solely to heredity or solely to environment, or to a covariation between both, or an interaction between both. For a particular outcome, such as developmental competence, the relevant charactertistics of competence and the contributions of heredity and environment change over time.

Figure 3 presents a transactional model for developmental competence over the course of three stages of development. The figure illustrates the weakness of the role of interaction that has been documented in the literature. By contrast, the substantial role of covariation between heredity and environment is shown by the substantial open region. Previous theories on the interplay between heredity and environment have sometimes assumed that heredity and environment together could totally explain the observed variation. Because total explanation is virtually impossible, this model presents the more accurate view of explaining the variation that can truly be explained. This developmental model is extended to include situational variation and elaborated around the work of the school psychologist later in this chapter.

The figure presented above illustrates transactions for the hypothetical variable of developmental competence. Behavioral genetics research typically centers on the prediction of other variables, such as IQ, specific cognitive skills, temperament, criminality, mental disorders, and mental retardation. The prediction of IQ, however, has occupied a central place in the literature of behavioral genetics. It is the IQ domain to which we now turn.

DOMAINS OF VARIATION: OVERALL INTELLECTUAL FUNCTIONING

Measures of overall intellectual functioning were originally developed to predict which students would profit from schooling in France (Binet & Simon, 1905). IQ measures continue to be a good predictor of future achievement in school. Lower IQs are associated with lower school performance

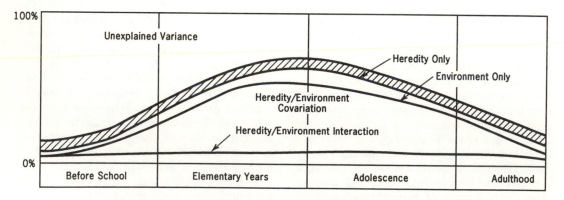

Figure 3. Transactional model of heredity and within-family environment across development.

(Cleary, Humphreys, Kendrick, & Wesman, 1975). Correlations with school grades center around .50 (Matarazzo, 1972; Willerman, 1979), with verbal IQs being better predictors of grades than performance IQs (.63 and .43, respectively) (Conroy & Plant, 1965). IQs are even better predictors for standardized achievement scores than they are for grades (Willerman, 1979). IQs also correlate highly with educational attainment among adults (.54 to .70; Duncan, 1968; Matarazzo, 1972) or in predicting future educational attainment of children (about .50; Bajema, 1968; Jencks, 1973). They are moderately correlated with occupational status or socioeconomic status (.40 to .50; Matarazzo, 1972). It is not surprising that many of these correlations cluster around .50 when we consider that socioeconomic status, income, and education correlate with one another above .80 (R. B. Cattell, 1942). Perhaps because of the restricted range, IQs are less effective in predicting "on the job" success (.20, Matarazzo, 1972). The effective prediction of outcomes over the long term distinguishes the IQ assessment from other measures. Although infant IQs are poor predictors of later IQs, the prediction of adult IQs from child IQs increases during early childhood (.40) to become highly predictive during the early school years (.70; Plomin & DeFries, 1981).

Because of its stability and power as a predictor, IQs have occupied center stage in the heritability–environment debate. Most investigators acknowledge that IQs are heritable, but the degree is hotly disputed (Herrnstein, 1973; Jensen, 1973; Kamin, 1974; Lewontin, 1970). Some authors have observed ironically that although the same literature is read, readers reach different conclusions (Haywood & Switsky, 1986; Reynolds, 1986).

Identical and Fraternal Twin Research

Some of the debate over the heritability of IQ derives from differences in correlations across studies, but most of the debate rests on the interpretation of the relationships among correlations. If IQ scores contained no error variance and were purely heritable, the identical twin correlation would be 1.00 for those reared together or apart rather than .86 and .72, respectively, as shown in Table 3. Nevertheless, these are the strongest correlations in families. Moreover, the magnitude of the reared-apart correlation suggests substantial heritability. Some authors have suggested that the reared-apart correlations may be inflated by artifacts—contact between the twins, placement bias, and common prenatal or postnatal environments.

Since fraternal twins are no more alike genetically than are nontwin siblings, a purely genetic basis for IQ variation would suggest correlations of .50 for siblings reared together or apart rather than the range of .24 to .60 as shown for sibling types in Table 3. Because assortive mating increases genetic similarity across siblings relative to others in the population, assortive mating for IQ ($r = .33$; Bouchard & McGee, 1981) would be expected to increase the sibling correlation above .50. This raises the philosophical issue, however, as to whether assortive mating is an environmental phenomenon or a heritable one.

Another approach to evaluating heritability is the difference between identical and fraternal twin correlations, which when doubled provides an estimate of heritability (Falconer, 1960). For example, recent studies of identical twins are reported in Table 4. The heritability estimates are simply the double of the difference between the identical and fraternal correlations. For the hereditarians, assortive mating and nonadditive sources of genetic variance artificially deflate the heritability estimates in Table 4. For environmentalists, the estimate would be inflated by interactions between heredity and environment and greater variation in the parental treatments of fraternal than of identical twins. Kamin (1974) argues, for example, that fraternal twins are treated more differentially than are identical twins, which exaggerates the correlational differences between identical and fraternal twins on IQ measures. Fraternal twins are typically compared instead of nontwin siblings, to control for time effects. Again, a philosophical question arises, however, as to whether time effects are essentially environmental or hereditary. It is an important question because substantial variation is observed in the difference between the fraternal twins and nontwin pairs (.60 and .47, respectively, as shown in Table 3).

The difference may also reflect a greater degree of differential perceptions and differential treatment of fraternal twins in comparison to nontwins. This may result from heightened *sibling deidentification* in nontwin pairs. Sibling deidentification is a process whereby siblings develop contrasting traits in order to mitigate against tension or rivalry in the family system (Schachter, 1985).

TABLE 3   Correlations Among Family Members

Familial Relationship	Number of Studies	Number of Pairings	Weighted Mean r^a
Monozygotic twins reared together	34	4,672	.86 (.88)
Monozygotic twins reared apart	3	65	.72 (.74)
Midparent–midoffspring reared together	3	410	.72
Dizygotic twins reared together	41	5,546	.60 (.53)
Midparent–offspring reared together	8	992	.50 (.52)
Siblings reared together	69	26,473	.47 (.49)
Parent–offspring reared together	32	8,433	.42
Adopted child–nonbiological adopted sib	6	369	.34
Half-siblings	2	200	.31
Adopted child–nonbiological sibling	5	345	.29 (.19)
Siblings reared apart	2	203	.24 (.46)
Adopting Midparent–offspring	6	758	.24
Adopting parent–offspring	6	1,397	.19 (.19)
Cousins	4	1,176	.15

[a]Correlations in parentheses are from an earlier meta-analysis by Erlenmeyer-Kimling and Jarwik (1963).
Source. Bouchard and McGee (1981).

Some might argue that the deidentification is a function of reactive and active genotype–environment covariation discussed earlier. That is, the child with a particular genotype may elicit differential responses from others which leads to the development of a particular set of traits and future choices. It is a philosophical question, however, whether this type of process is essentially hereditary, environmental, or both.

Parent–Child Research

Parent–offspring pairs have also received substantial attention in the heredity–environment debate. The midparent IQ, that is, the average of the parents' IQs, has been used increasingly in behavioral genetics research. For statistical as well as

polygenetic reasons, midparent correlations tend to be higher than single parent–offspring correlations (.50 versus .42), as shown in Table 3.

The adoption design has been a powerful technique for assessing the contributions of heredity and environment to IQs because it provides for assessment of both the biological family and adoptive families. As shown in Table 5, the correlations among family members raised in their biological families is consistently higher than the correlations of children with their adoptive parents. This corroborates the weighted averages from Table 3. These correlations are interpreted differently by hereditarians and environmentalists. The hereditarians argue that the significant correlations observed between adoptive children and their

TABLE 4   Identical and Fraternal Twin Correlations for Recent Investigations

Study	Twin Correlations		Heritability
	Identical	Fraternal	
Segal (1985)	.85	.42	.86
Wilson (1983) 9-year-olds	.83	.65	.36
Wilson (1983) 15-year-olds	.88	.54	.68
Tambs, Sundet, and Magnus (1984)	.88	.47	.82

TABLE 5   Adoptive and Biological Family Correlations for Recent Investigations

Study		Correlations between Child and Parent	
		Adoptive	Biological
Scarr and Weinberg (1976)	Fathers	.27	.39
	Mothers	.23	.34
Scarr and Weinberg (1978b)	Fathers	.15	.39
	Mothers	.04	.39
Horn, Loehlin, and Willerman (1979)	Fathers	.17	.42
	Mothers	.19	.23

parents are small. Moreover, they may be the result of selective placement, that is, the practice of placing children in adoptive families that are similar to their birth families. Selective placement estimates for the Scarr & Weinberg study (1977) were, for example, significant (.22 between the education of the biological and adoptive parent). Environmentalists argue that the adoptive correlations are attenuated because of the tendency in families to deidentify siblings. Adoptive families may experience more tension in our culture than do nonadoptive families, and consequently, these families may have more of a need for differentiating the traits of their children as means of reducing tension. Further, environmentalists add that the powerful differences in environment are *within* the family rather than across families. Rowe's (1981, 1983) investigations, for example, suggest that children within a family receive differential acceptance from their parents.

As should be obvious by this point, the question of heredity *or* environment is a naive question. Indeed, it is a case of a misplaced conjunction (Weinberg, 1983). The data clearly show that both heredity *and* environment contribute to IQ variation. The substantial covariation of heredity and environment, the issues of assortive mating, selective placement, reactive and active processes, deidentification among siblings, and the variation in heritability estimation point to the mutuality of heredity and environment rather than their competitive contribution. To drive the point further, regard this dilemma. It is known that individual differences in weight are highly heritable (Stunkard, Fock, & Hrubec, 1985). Without the environmental process of eating food, however,

people would not gain weight. Is that heredity or environment influencing differences in weight?

Environmental Variables

To complicate the picture further, let us add socioeconomic status (SES), income, parental education, and occupational status. These variables have typically been considered to be between-family environmental differences. In a meta-analysis of SES and IQ, White (1982) found an average correlation of .33. Associations between income and IQ are in the .20s and between education and IQs in the .30s (Bahr & Leigh, 1978; Mercy & Steelman, 1982). The similarity of these associations may be due in part to the high degree of interrelationship among SES, income, and education (above .80, Cattell, 1942). In contrast to the assumption that SES is an environmental variable to be partialed out, Scarr & Weinberg (in press) argue that SES is a heritable characteristic. The degree of heritability of SES is an indicator of mobility in a society. In a pure caste society, SES would be 100% heritable.

Plomin (1986) argues that the between-family differences pall, however, in comparison to the powerful within-family differences. The conventional differences of family size, offspring spacing, and birth order do not exert a powerful effect. Zajonc and his colleagues have suggested a confluence model to account for the finding that children who are later born and children from larger families have lower IQs (Zajonc, 1983; Zajonc & Markus, 1975; Zajonc, Markus, & Markus, 1979). The confluence model postulates that a child's environmental stimulation is the average intellectual level of those in the family.

Since younger children have lower intellectual levels than parents, they pull down the average intellectual level of the family. More children means a lower level. Later-born children are born into a family with a lower average intellectual level than are their older siblings. Wider spacing allows for improvement of the intellectual level of the family before the next child is born. Youngest children have an added decline in IQ because they lack the opportunity to be teachers to younger siblings. The model is elegant and accurately explains the data patterns for birth order, family size, and spacing as well as lower IQs obtained in father-absent families (Brackbill & Nichols, 1982) and lower IQs among triplets or twins than among singletons (Record, McKeown, & Edwards, 1970). But the overall variation in IQs that is explained by family size, spacing, and birth order is small. Moreover, after partialing out SES, family size and birth order explain only about 2% of the variance (Grotevant, Scarr, & Weinberg, 1977).

In comparison to birth order, spacing, and family size, measures of the home environment have shown substantial associations. But these associations are obtained when home environment variables are summed together. Wilson found that overall adequacy of the home environment, for example, was found to correlate at .55 with IQs. Summing across home environment scales achieved a multiple correlation with IQ of .72 (Majoribanks, 1972). Children who were malnourished before age 2 and later adopted into American families had lower IQs, lower achievement, lower weights, and lower heights at school age than those of similar adoptees who were not malnourished (Winick, Meyer, & Harris, 1975). Hereditarians challenge thee findings by indicating that home environment is confounded by parental IQ and parental education levels.

Such confounds should not show differential associations for boys and girls if the associations are purely hereditary. But Hanson (1975) found substantial sex differences. Averaging across family variables, the associations for boys between family variables and IQ were .23, but for girls, .45. For girls the highest associations were with freedom to engage in verbal expression ($r = .73$) and direct teaching of language behavior ($r = .69$). For boys the strongest associations were with parental involvement with the child ($r = .45$). Hyatt (1985) found that among girls, tension in intact families was associated with selected WPPSI subtests at the level of .40 to .60, but boys showed no such associations.

Bronfenbrenner (1985) argues that the most powerful environmental differences occur in the broader social context rather than in families. He presents data on identical twins reared apart but under similar or dissimilar conditions. The differences between twins reared in the same or different towns is low ($r = .83$ versus .67) or between twins reared in the same or different schools ($r = .87$ versus .66). But twins reared in the same or different communities have a marked difference (.86 versus .26). Bronfenbrenner echoes the claim of Coleman and his associates (1966) that it is not the specific setting, such as school, that has the greatest impact, but rather, the total social context reflected in the community.

The question of what creates individual differences in IQs remains a complex question. More important and direct questions involve how malleable IQs are and what are the antecedents of IQ change. Schooling contributes to changes in IQ, and Jencks and his colleagues (1972) estimate that each additional year of school boosts the IQ one point. Preschool enrichment programs tend to show immediate gains in IQ, but these gains fail to persist into the junior high school years. Because of its inherent stability and overdetermined nature, IQ may not be the most useful variable for assessing gains or change as a result of interventions.

SPECIFIC COGNITIVE DOMAINS

Unfortunately, specific cognitive domains prove to be not much better than IQs in assessing gains from interventions. This is because specific cognitive measures include substantial variance attributable to g. Consequently, specific cognitive measures are not better predictors of specific areas of achievement than are global cognitive measures. The residuals from partialing out g are sometimes employed, but the instability of these residuals limits their utility. Moreover, specific cognitive dimensions share a common home environment component (Loehlin & Vandenberg, 1968). Possibly due to these confounds, the heritability of specific skills is judged to be less, according to one reviewer (Tyler, 1978). Examining the Wechsler subtest correlations for identical and fraternal twins shows slightly reduced heritability in general for specific subtests than for overall IQs (Table 6).

TABLE 6   Identical and Fraternal Twin Correlations for Wechsler Scales

Subtest	Wilson (1975)		Segal (1985)		Tambs et al. (1984)	
	Identical	Fraternal	Identical	Fraternal	Identical	Fraternal
Information	.81	.51	.79	.38	.82	.46
Similarities	.73	.58	.76	.29	.71	.34
Arithmetic	.65	.52	.68	.28	.67	.27
Vocabulary	.71	.50	.78	.42	.87	.27
Comprehension	.80	.62	.65	.43	.81	.33
Picture Completion	.69	.26	.32	.42	.39	.30
Block Design	.68	.43	.61	.19	.69	.42
Picture Arrangement			.33	.25	.56	.26
Object Assembly			.54	.20	.69	.48
Coding/Digit Symbol			.68	.40	.80	.50
Animal House	.82	.40				
Mazes	.61	.45				
Geometric Designs	.72	.25				
Digit Span					.63	.33
Verbal IQ	.79	.51	.71	.34	.88	.42
Performance IQ	.79	.65	.87	.45	.79	.51

Using the adoption design, Scarr and Weinberg (1978b) found evidence for heritability of specific skills as well.

The Ravens Test has been widely used in behavior genetics research because of its assumed independence from cultural or experiential confounds. Actually, the heritability of Ravens scores is not higher than Wechsler subtests, and substantial inconsistency across studies has been reported (Canter, 1973; Foch & Plomin, 1980; Garfinkle & Vandenberg, 1981).

A flurry of research tested the hypothesis of sex-linked recessive inheritance of spatial skills (Bock & Kolakowski, 1973; Hartlage, 1970; Stafford, 1961; Yen, 1975). But later research has failed to show support for either sex-linked heritability or high heritability of spatial skills (Bouchard & McGee, 1977; Corley, DeFries, Kuse, & Vandenberg, 1980; DeFries, 1979; Loehlin, Sharon, & Jacoby, 1978).

As with spatial skills, reviewers sometimes point to several studies and imply that a particular cognitive skill is more heritable than most. Willerman (1979) concluded, for example, that verbal skills are highly heritable. Often, however, specific skills that at first seem highly heritable contain a substantial portion of g. It may be that the

quest for differential heritability of specific skills must begin with abilities that are independent of g. Alternatively, the heritability of specific skills may vary over the course of development. For example, the data in Table 6 show greater heritability for the performance IQ than for verbal IQ in the study of school-aged children (Segal, 1985). But the study of adults shows relatively greater heritability for verbal IQs (Tambs, Sundet, & Magnus, 1984).

INDIVIDUAL DIFFERENCES IN ACHIEVEMENT

Although behavioral genetics research has focused substantial attention on school-aged children, "Behavioral genetics studies have scarcely begun to consider school-related behavior" (Plomin, 1986). Plomin adds: "There is not a single twin study of achievement in the early school years" (p. 212). Although we know little about hereditary and environmental influences on achievement, some well-replicated findings relating achievement with other variables have been observed. As observed earlier, ability levels are good predictors of achievement, particulary verbal ability (Willerman, 1979). According to a recent review, achievement correlates moderately with parental income (.32), education of parents (.19), occupation of parents (.20), and with measures that sum across all three (.32) (White, 1982).

As with the specific cognitive skills, differential heritability for achievement in specific domains is difficult to replicate. Correlations for identical and fraternal twins are presented in Table 7. As seen from the across-domains correlations in Table 7, achievement is somewhat heritable, explaining about half of the variance (46%). Furthermore, achievement in school is important as a predictor of college grades (.56; Cleary et al., 1975) but not as a predictor of occupational success (Berg, 1970; McClelland, 1973).

The inheritance of disabilities is of central import to school psychologists, who are sometimes the first people to tell parents that their child has a disability. Because the base rates for many disabilities are low, the precise heritability is difficult to ascertain. Reading disabilities are found to run in families (Bakwin, 1973; DeFries, Volger, & LaBuda, 1985; Finucci, 1978), but the precise degree of concordance among family members varies with definitions, measures, and samples. Similarly, some levels of hereditary influence are associated with speech disabilities (Byrne, Willerman, & Ashmore, 1974), learning disabilities (Owen, Adams, Forrest, Stolz, & Fisher, 1971), and attention deficits or hyperactivity (Morrison & Stewart, 1973; Safer, 1973; Wender, 1971).

TABLE 7   Identical and Fraternal Twin Correlations for Achievement

Achievement Domain	Median Twin Correlations[a]	
	Identical	Fraternal
Reading	.86	.62
Written language	.74	.52
Mathematics	.73	.54
Social studies	.78	.51
Science	.66	.48
Across domains	.75	.52

[a]These median correlations are obtained from the following studies: Fischbein (1979); Husen (1959, 1960, 1963); Loehlin and Nichols (1976); Nichols (1965); and Schoenfeldt (1968).

GROUP DIFFERENCES

Because knowledge of group differences contributes to understanding the individual, group differences have become an important component in differential psychology. Differences, or variations, within groups are typically very broad compared to differences between groups. For example, gender *differences* have been observed in verbal fluency and spatial skills, with females performing better on verbal fluency and males performing better on spatial skills after the age of 8 (Maccoby & Jacklin, 1974). This corresponds to WAIS differences observed between men and women, men performing better on information, arithmetic, and picture completion, and women performing better on vocabulary, similarities, and digit span (Wechsler, 1958). Girls also achieve higher in elementary school than boys, but this narrows in adolescence (Grams & Waetjen, 1975). However, these differences are small, and large samples are needed to detect significant differences.

Sometimes these small, albeit significant differences are used erroneously as explanatory constructs. For example, a girl's spatial difficulties are "explained" by observing that boys are better than girls on spatial tasks. In addition to the small differences between groups, group membership is only a mediator of processes such as socialization or inheritance. Group membership itself cannot explain individual differences.

The error of "explaining" individual differences on the basis of group membership is particularly volatile in interpreting *race differences*. The best interpretation of race differences is as a mediating variable. Since race and SES are correlated in our society, race differences are sometimes due to SES differences. The average IQ for blacks is 15 points below the average IQ for whites (Jensen, 1985). The magnitude of this difference attenuates when SES is partialed out, but remains significant. Again, race differences are useless as explanatory constructs. Analysis of race as a mediating construct contributes more to understanding. For example, one study found that the relationship between SES of the parent and the IQ of the child is higher for whites (.38) than for blacks (.24) (Broman, Nichols, & Kennedy, 1975). This suggests that whereas family status may explain child IQs in white families, other variables are important in explaining the IQs of black children.

Along similar lines, one researcher found that

the heritability of IQ was greater for middle-income than for lower-income families (Scarr-Salapatek, 1971). Lower-income families may experience more environmental influences that interfere with processes that enhance IQs. *SES* is a significant context variable that correlates with many variables. In their review of individual differences in SES, Minton and Schneider (1980) concluded that higher SES is associated with higher IQs, higher achievement, higher educational attainment, higher occupational attainment, greater achievement motivation, better mental health, and more happiness. Although there is more to life than SES, SES appears to have a piece of all of it.

Age is such an automatic context for educational thinking that we almost forget that it as a group membership characteristic. Age differences in children are dramatic. Children begin rudimentary addition in first grade, and 8 years later they are solving simultaneous equations. The mental age construct from which IQs are derived assumes a linear increase in intelligence during childhood. Actually, the increase may be more akin to the growth curve during childhood, with the most dramatic increases in the early years of life, moderate increases in the middle years, and smaller changes during adolescence. A somewhat tired debate is whether this dramatic change is continuous, as most behaviorists or psychometrists would assert, or whether it is discontinuous, as Piagetians would argue. Clearly, there are qualitative changes in children's thinking, but the measurement issues and the differential generalization of new thought processes to all situations levels these changes.

PERSONALITY

Individual differences in the personalities of children have received less attention in the differential psychology literature than have personality differences in adults. This may be due in part to the recognition of childhood personalities as more plastic and more influenced by context and situation. Temperament research is an exception to this. Buss and Plomin (1975, 1984) have defined *temperament* as a genetically influenced set of personality traits that develop early. They delineate three central dimensions of temperament: emotionality, activity, and sociability. Other dimensions of temperament have been proposed: attention, self-

stimulation, excitatory thresholds, easy/difficult, slow to warm up, impulsivity, persistence, active/passive, and independent/dependent.

Moving into childhood, the study of personality becomes particularly cloudy. Much of this research is based on parental report rather than on behavioral observation or clinical interviews. Consequently, the findings may be more a reflection of the parents than of the children. Future research in childhood personality that employs child data through observation, interview, or developmentally appropriate self-report such as the Missouri Pictures may yield more promising findings. A major self-report, twin study on adolescent personality has been reported (Lochlin & Nichols, 1976). These authors administered a variety of personality, value, and behavioral self-report measures to 850 twins. They found remarkable consistency in the heritability across the variables, with identical twin correlations about .20 higher than fraternal twin correlations. On the California Psychological Inventory, for example, they obtained median correlations of .50 for identical twins and .32 for fraternal twins. These correlations are similar to the findings from a meta-analysis by Goldsmith (1983), who reviewed 10 studies of personality and values. Median correlations for these studies were .47 for identical twins and .23 for fraternal twins. The dissimilarity between these findings is the slightly greater heritability in the Goldsmith review.

A more thorough review of individual differences in personality is beyond the scope of this chapter. The reader is referred to various reviews regarding individual differences in schizophrenia (Gottesman & Shields, 1982), manic-depression (Nurnberger & Gershon, 1981), alcoholism (Gabrielli & Plomin, 1985; Pedersen, Fridberg, Floderus-Myrhed, McClearn, & Plomin, 1984), criminality (Pogue-Geile & Rose, 1985), neuroticism and extraversion (Eaves & Young, 1981; Loehlin, Willerman, & Horn, 1982; Scarr, Webber, Weinberg, & Wittig, 1981), and MMPI scales (Vandenberg, 1967).

A MODEL FOR SCHOOL PSYCHOLOGISTS

In the interest of integration, we present in this section a model of individual differences that provides a framework for the field of differential psychology, suggests future directions for research, and raises implications for the practice of psychology in the schools. The model begins with the cross-situations debate of the late 1960s and 1970s.

Cross-Situational Consistency

Mischel (1968) initiated the debate by criticizing individual-difference approaches to personality as explaining only a small part of the behavior of individuals across situations. He proposed, in fact, that traits were merely fictions that we believe in order to provide a sense of predictability. With its roots in behaviorism and behavior modification (Bandura & Walters, 1963), situationalism has come to focus on whether *some* individuals are consistent for *certain* traits (Bem & Allen, 1974; Kendrick & Stringfield, 1980). These data clearly show that some individuals vary across situations for certain behaviors. For the school psychologist this conclusion implies a need to examine the assumption of having tapped a representative sample of behavior, when a child is seen in a single testing situation. Frederiksen (1986) has shown, for example, that cognitive processes are strongly influenced by situational demands. Observation of children in different situations and settings at different times should produce more valid inferences and more effective interventions.

Toward this goal, a valuable aid would be a clearer understanding of the nature of situations. Unfortunately, although psychology has produced a plethora of trait theories, theory and research on situations are weak. Tyler (1978) has advocated the development of a typology of such situations. An important question that soon arises is: Which

situations are beneficial for school achievement? Brophy (1986) has reviewed a number of teacher variables that enhance children's achievement. A complete typology of situations, however, should probably begin with broadly applied situations that have powerful effects. Situations such as success versus failure, reward versus punishment, or high versus low expectations are examples of situational dimensions that relate to school performance.

Aptitude Treatment Interactions

The next question for the school psychologist is whether individuals react differently to different situations. Figure 4 presents a schemata for the interaction of individual differences and situations in affecting outcomes. Both path A and path B can contribute to effective schooling for children, but path C holds the greatest potential for understanding and intervention. Despite the lack of evidence for consistent aptitude-treatment interactions (Cronbach & Snow, 1977), interest in ATI persists. The reliance on aptitudes instead of more general traits may explain in part the failure of ATI to date. Anastasi (1986) points out that "situational variance is more conspicuous in the analyses of personality traits than in the analyses of ability." Indeed in one review, trait–situation interactions were more often observed to explain more of the variance than either the person or situation alone (Bowers, 1973). A shift to traits rather than abilities alone may enhance the ATI line of research. In addition, a focus on individual differences that are more directly tied to the situation may yield more powerful results (Benson, 1984; 1986). Dweck (1986) has observed that a shift from global con-

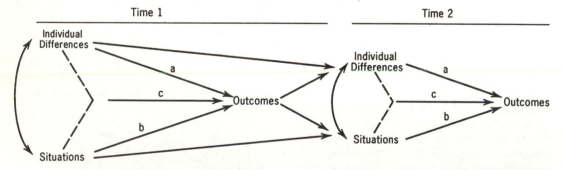

Figure 4. Trait × situation (aptitude × treatment) interactions over time. (*Note:* Path A concerns the line of research on student characteristics that affect achievement. Path B concerns the line of research on curricular or teacher characteristics that affect achievement. Path C concerns trait–situation or aptitude–treatment interaction research.)

cepts of locus of control to more specific constructs in social cognition, such as attributions, has generated stronger associations.

For the school psychologist who focuses on the interaction path, the issue of the cause of a referring problem becomes somewhat moot. The psychologist need not focus on whether the child or the teacher is to blame, but instead, search for the aspects of the current interaction that, when altered, would foster improvement. The task of the school psychologist becomes that of problem solver rather than of describer or classifier of individual differences. The assessment–intervention link becomes an integral aspect of the psychologist's work (Christenson, Abery, & Weinberg, 1986).

As seen from the model in Figure 4, differences in individuals, situations, and interactions are dynamic rather than stable entities. Change over time is expected. Reciprocal relationships are specified by the dashed lines. This transactional approach assumes that the ongoing transactions between individuals and situations alter future differences in individuals and situations. A crucial implication of the dynamic aspects of the model for a school psychologist is the need for systematic follow-up. The school psychologist becomes not just an assessor and recommender, but an ongoing evaluator and consultant. A second implication is that the school psychologist maintains a focus on the transactions between school personnel and the student. When observed over time, these transactions provide data not only on relationships, but also on the change in relationships.

Our discussion so far has centered on achievement as the outcome of interest. Actually, relevant outcomes are defined by the referral question. Acting out, withdrawal, off-task behavior, processing deficits, truancy, family problems, noncompliance and achievement delays are just a few types of outcomes that might be addressed in the referral. Rather than focusing strictly on standardized IQ or achievement outcomes, the school psychologist using this model would conduct the assessment with a focus on the outcome as specified in the referral question. The outcome diversity of this model implies a need for a wider net than that provided by standardized achievement measures. Standardized achievement is such an overdetermined variable that it is difficult to detect reliable changes from time 1 to time 2. Instead, criterion-referenced measures are more useful (Hambleton, 1982; Ysseldyke & Mirkin, 1982)

because of their greater sensitivity in detecting change and their relative freedom from practice effects. Task analyzing competence for specific outcomes, whether they be academic, behavioral, or social-emotional, can generate criterion-referenced tests that can facilitate ongoing assessment throughout the intervention period.

Influence of Context

The model as presented to this point has discussed individual differences as an independent variable interacting with situations to affect outcomes. The full model adds variation in contexts and genetics to understanding of the mediational role of individual differences in refluencing outcomes. (Because of the ambiguity associated with the term *environment*, the term *contexts* is used instead.) This conceptualization is somewhat different from the sources of phenotypic variation presented in Table 2.

Several of the contexts listed in Table 8 have received considerable attention in differential psychology. These include SES, race, age, and gender. As a context, age has probably received the greatest attention, with several major journals, and numerous books devoted solely to the topic of developmental change. Community is believed to be a powerful context which when measured effectively can explain a large degree of the variance (Bronfrenbrenner, 1985; Coleman et al., 1966). Zeitgeist is popularly assumed to be a powerful context, but the difficulty in conducting long-term longitudinal research makes it difficult to study. Schools have not been shown to have much impact on achievement once SES and community have been partialed out. Peers and family contexts

TABLE 8   Sources of Phenotypic Variation Due to Context

Broader than family contexts
   Shared (SES, race, community, Zeitgeist, school)
   [a] Nonshared (peers, age, gender)
Family contexts
   Shared (family style, parenting style)
      Nonshared (deidentification, differential treatment, differential perception)

---

[a]These contexts may sometimes be shared: that is, two siblings of the same sex, twins of the same age, or siblings sharing the same peers.

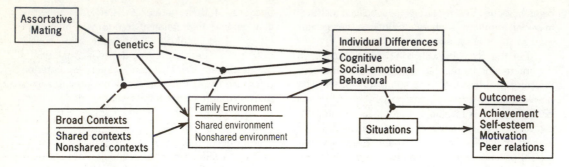

Figure 5. Contextual and situational model of individual differences.

are understudied areas as contributors to individual differences. The nonshared environment holds particular promise for innovative research. Several authors have concluded that nonshared environments contribute importantly to differences across individuals (Plomin, 1986; Scarr et al., 1981). These multiple contexts are introduced also in Figure 5.

Implications

The school psychologist who operates from this model recognizes the importance of context in influencing outcomes for particular children. Consequently, the initial approach suggested by the model is to work within prevailing contexts. A multidisciplinary approach is needed to address the variety in contexts. A home–school partnership is more likely to promote coordinated change for the child. Because of the importance of community context, the model implies the need for the school psychologist to be involved with the community. Differences in norms across communities suggest the increased importance of the school psychologist in conducting local research.

Regardless of their community, every school psychologist is confronted with questions from parents and teachers as to whether Johnny inherited his problems. Usually, people want to know if we are hereditarians *or* environmentalists. For the psychologist who understands the proposed model, a political paradox becomes evident. Assuming no error, if the environment is uniform for all children, heritability contributes 100% to the variance. When environments are more pluralistic, heritability exerts less influence. The heritability paradox is that if a trait is highly heritable, the solution is to stretch the environment to provide specific interventions that can produce change.

Conversely, if one wants a trait to become more heritable, the intervention would be the creation of highly standardized environments. If educators want to provide opportunities for all children, establishing a broad repertoire of options is indicated.

The school psychologist holds a unique position in the schools, as the professional most qualified to assess and interpret individual differences. The importance of the role is magnified by Willerman's (1979, p. 171) observation that "nowhere are individual differences more obvious than in the classroom." By understanding and interpreting those differences within contexts and situations across time, school psychologists can promote improvements in educational quality for all children.

REFERENCES

Anastasi, A. (1958). Heredity, environment, and the question "How?" *Psychological Review, 65,* 197–208.

Anastasi, A. (1965). *Differential psychology: Individual and group differences in behavior.* New York: Macmillan.

Anastasi, A. (1986). Evolving concepts of test validation. *Annual Review of Psychology, 37,* 1–15.

Bahr, S. J., & Leigh, G. K. (1978). Family size, intelligence, and expected education. *Journal of Marriage and the Family, 40,* 331–335.

Bajema, C. J. (1968). Relation of fertility to occupational status, IQ, educational attainment, and size of family of origin: A follow-up study of a male Kalamazoo public school population. *Eugenics Quarterly, 15,* 198–203.

Bakwin, H. (1973). Reading disability in twins. *Developmental Medicine and Child Neurology, 15,* 184–187.

Bandura, A., & Walters, R. H. (1963). *Social learning and personality development*. New York: Holt, Rinehart and Winston.

Bardon, J. I. (1982). The psychology of school psychology. In C. R. Reynolds & R. R. Gutkin (Eds.), *The handbook of school psychology*. New York: Wiley.

Bem, D. J., & Allen, A. (1974). On predicting some of the people some of the time: The search for cross-situational consistencies in behavior. *Psychological Review, 81,* 506–520.

Benson, M. (1984). *The effects of achievement attributions on self-evaluation, motivation, and anxiety*. Unpublished doctoral dissertation, University of Minnesota.

Benson, M. (1986). *Achievement attributions: The formation and effects among parents as observers and children as actors*. Paper presented at the biennial meeting of the Society for Research in Adolescence, Baltimore, MD.

Berg, I. (1970). *Education and jobs: The great train robbery*. New York: Praeger.

Binet, A., & Simon, T. (1961). The development of intelligence in children. In T. Shapley (Ed.), *Classics in psychology* (pp. 872–919). New York: Philosophical Library. (Reprinted from *L'Annee Psychologique*, 1905, *11,* 163–191).

Bock, R. D., & Kolakowski, D. (1973). Further evidence of sex-linked major-gene influence on human spatial visualizing ability. *American Journal of Human Genetics, 25,* 1–14.

Bouchard, T. J., Jr. (1976). Genetic factors in intelligence. In A. R. Kaplan (Ed.), *Human behavior genetics*. Springfield, IL: Charles C. Thomas.

Bouochard, T. J., Jr., & McGee, M. G. (1977). Sex differences in human spatial ability: Not an X-linked recessive gene effect. *Social Biology, 24,* 332–335.

Bouchard, T. J., Jr., & McGee, M. (1981). Familial studies of intelligence: A review. *Science, 212,* 1055–1059.

Bouchard, T. J., Jr., & Segal, N. L. (1985). Environment and IQ. In B. B. Wolman (Ed.), *Handbook of intelligence: Theories, measurements, and applications* (pp. 391–464). New York: Wiley.

Bowers, K. S. (1973). Situationism in psychology: An analysis and a critique. *Psychological Review, 80,* 307–336.

Brackbill, Y., & Nichols, P. L. (1982). A test of the confluence model of intellectual development. *Developmental Psychology, 18,* 192–198.

Broman, S. H., Nichols, P. L., & Kennedy, N. A. (1975). *Preschool IQ: Prenatal and early developmental correlates*. Hillsdale, NJ: Lawrence Erlbaum.

Bronfenbrenner, U. (1975). Nature with nurture: A reinterpretation of the evidence. In A. Montague (Ed.), *Race and IQ*. New York: Oxford University Press.

Bronfenbrenner, U. (1985). *Organism–environment interaction from an ecological perspective*. Paper presented at the biennial meeting of the Society for Research in Child Development, Toronto, Canada.

Brophy, J. (1986). Teacher influences on student achievement. *American Psychologist, 41*(10), 1069–1077.

Buss, A. H. (1976). Galton and the birth of differential psychology and eugenics: Social, political and economic forces. *Journal of the History of the Behavioral Sciences, 12,* 47–58.

Byrne, B. M., Willerman, L., & Ashmore, L. L. (1974). Severe and moderate language impairment: Evidence for distinctive etiologies. *Behavior Genetics, 4,* 331–345.

Caldwell, B. M., & Bradley, R. H. (1978). *Home observation for measurement of the environment*. Little Rock: University of Arkansas.

Canter, S. (1973). Personality traits in twins. In G. Claridge, S. Canter, & W. I. Hume (Eds.), *Personality differences and biological variations* (pp. 21–51). Elmsford, NY: Pergamon Press.

Cattell, J. M. (1890). Mental tests and measurements. *Mind, 15,* 373–380.

Cattell, R. B. (1942). The concept of social status. *Journal of Social Psychology, 15,* 293–308.

Christenson, S., Abery, B., & Weinberg, R. A. (1986). An alternative model for the delivery of psychological services in the school community. In S. N. Elliott & J. C. Witt (Eds.), *The delivery of psychological services in schools: Concepts, processes, and issues*. Hillsdale, NJ: Lawrence Erlbaum.

Cleary, T. A., Humphreys, L. G., Kendrick, S. A., & Wesman, A. (1975). Educational uses of tests with disadvantaged students. *American Psychologist, 30,* 15–41.

Coleman, J., Campbell, E., Hobson, C., McPartland, J., Mood, A., Weinfeld, F., & York, R. (1966). *Equality of educational opportunity*. Washington, DC: U.S. Government Printing Office.

Conroy, R., & Plant, W. T. (1965). WAIS and group test predictions of an academic success criterion: High school and college. *Educational and Psychological Measurement, 25,* 493–500.

Corley, R. P., DeFries, J. C., Kuse, A. R., & Vandenberg, S. G. (1980). Familial resemblance for the Identical Blocks Test of Spatial Ability: No evidence for X linkage. *Behaviior Genetics, 10,* 211–215.

Cronbach, L. J. (1957). The two disciplines of scientific psychology. *American Psychologist, 12,* 671–684.

Cronbach, L. J., & Snow, R. T. (1977). *Aptitudes and instructional methods*. New York: Irvington.

Dahlstrom, W. G. (1985). The development of psychological testing. In G. A. Kimble & K. Schlesinger, *Topics in the history of psychology,* (pp. 63–113). Hillsdale, NJ: Lawrence Erlbaum.

Darwin, C. (1958). *The origin of the species by means of natural selection of the preservation of favoured races in the struggle for life*. New York: New American Library. (Original work published 1859).

DeFries, J. C. (1979). Comment. In J. R. Royce & L. P. Mas (Eds.), *Theoretical advances in behavior genetics* (pp. 381–383). Alphen aan den Rijn, The Netherlands: Sijthoff en Noordhoff.

DeFries, J. C., Vogler, G. P. & LaBuda, M. L. (1985). Colorado Family Reading Study: An overview. In J. L. Fuller & E. L. Simmel (Eds.), *Behavior genetics: Principles and applications II*. Hillsdale, NJ: Lawrence Erlbaum.

Dewey, J. (1916). *Democracy and education.* New York: Macmillan.

Duncan, O. D. (1968). Ability and achievement. *Eugenics Quarterly, 15,* 1–11.

Dweck, C. S. (1986). Motivational processes affecting learning. *American Psychologist, 41*(10), 1040–1048.

Eaves, L. J., & Young, P. A. (1981). Genetical theory and personality differences. In R. Lynn (Ed.), *Dimensions of personality.* Oxford: Pergamon Press.

Erlenmeyer-Kimling, L., & Jarvik, L. F. (1963). Genetics and intelligence: A review. *Science, 142,* 1477–1479.

Estabrook, A. H. (1916). *The Jukes in 1915.* Washington, DC: Carnegie Institution.

Falconer, D. S. (1960). *Introduction to quantitative genetics.* Edinburgh: Oliver & Boyd.

Fenichel, O. (1945). *The psychoanalytic theory of neurosis.* New York: W. W. Norton.

Finucci, J. M. (1978). Genetic considerations in dyslexia. In H. R. Myklebust (Ed.), *Progress in learning disabilities* (Vol. 4, pp. 41–63). New York: Grune & Stratton.

Fischbein, S. (1979). *Heredity–environment influences on growth and development during adolescence: A longitudinal study of twins.* Lund, Sweden: CWK/Gleerup.

Foch, T. T., & Plomin, R. (1980). Specific cognitive abilities in 5-to-12-year-old twins. *Behavior Genetics, 10,* 507–520.

Frederiksen, N. (1986). Toward a broader conception of human intelligence. *American Psychologist, 41*(4), 445–452.

Freud, S. (1950). Analysis terminable and interminable. *Collected papers* (Vol. 5, pp. 316–357). London: Hogarth Press.

Gabrielli, W. F., & Plomin, R. (1985). Drinking behavior in the Colorado adoptee and twin sample. *Journal of Studies on Alcohol, 46,* 24–31.

Galton, F. (1962). *Hereditary genius: An inquiry into its laws and consequences.* (Original work published 1869) New York: World.

Garfinkle, A. S., & Vandenberg, S. G. (1981). Development of Piagetian logico-mathematical concepts and other specific cognitive abilities. In L. Gedda, P. Parisi, & W. T. Nance (Eds.), *Twin research: 3. Intelligence, personality, and development* (pp. 51–60). New York: Alan R. Liss.

Glass, G. V. (1986). Testing old, testing new: Schoolboy psychology and the allocation of intellectual resources. In B. S. Plake & J. C. Witt (Eds.), *The future of testing.* Hillsdale, NJ: Lawrence Erlbaum.

Goddard, H. H. (1912). *The Kallikak family.* New York: Macmillan.

Goldsmith, H. H. (1983). Genetic influences on personality from infancy to adulthood. *Child Development, 54,* 331–355.

Gordon, E. W. (1972). Toward defining equality of educational opportunity. In F. Mosteller & D. D. Moynihan (Eds.), *On equality of educational opportunity.* New York: Random House.

Gottesman, I. I. (1974). Developmental genetics and ontogenetic psychology: Overdue detente and propositions from a matchmaker. In A. D. Pick (Ed.), *Minnesota symposia on child psychology* (pp. 55–88). Minneapolis: University of Minnesota Press.

Gottesman, I. I., & Shields, J. (1982). *Schizophrenia: The epigenetic puzzle.* Cambridge: Cambridge University Press.

Grams, J. D., & Waetjen, W. B.(1975). *Sex: Does it make a difference?* North Scituate, MA: Duxbury.

Gresham, F. M. (1986). On the malleability of intelligence: Unnecessary assumptions, reifications, and occlusions. *School Psychology Review, 15*(2), 261–263.

Grotevant, H. D., Scarr, S., & Weinberg, R. A. (1977). Intellectual development in family constellations with adopted and natural children: A test of the Zajonc and Markus Model. *Child Development, 48,* 1699–1703.

Gun, W. T. J. (1930). The heredity of the Stewarts. *Eugeneics Review, 22,* 195–201.

Hambleton, R. K. (1982). Advances in criterion-referenced testing technology. In C. R. Reynolds & T. B. Gutkin (Eds.), *The handbook of school psychology.* New York: Wiley.

Hanson, R. A. (1975). Consistency and stability of home environmental measures related to IQ. *Child Development, 46,* 470–480.

Harris, H. (1966). Enzyme polymorphisms in man. *Proceedings of the Royal Society, 164,* 298–310.

Hartlage, L. C. (1970). Sex-linked inheritance of spatial ability. *Perceptual and Motor Skills, 31,* 610.

Hathaway, S. R., & McKinley, J. C. (1980). A multiphasic personality schedule (Minnesota): I. Construction of the schedule. In W. G. Dahlstrom & L. E. Dahlstrom (Eds.), *Basic readings on the MMPI.* Minneapolis: University of Minnesota Press. (Reprinted from *Journal of Psychology,* 1940, *10,* 249–254).

Hathaway, S. R., & McKinley, J. C. (1942). *The Minnesota Multiphasic Personality Schedule.* Minneapolis: University of Minnesota Press.

Hawkins, D. (1977). *The science and ethics of equality.* New York: Basic Books.

Hayman, J., Raydner, N., Stenner, A. J., & Madey, D. (1979). On aggregation, generalization, and utility in educational evaluation. *Educational Evaluation and Policy Analysis, 1,* 31–39.

Haywood, H. C., Meyers, L. E., & Switsky, H. N. (1982). Mental retardation. *Annual Review of Psychology, 33,* 309–342.

Haywood, H. C., & Switzky, H. N. (1986). The malleability of intelligence: Cognitive processes as a function of polygenic–experiential interaction. *School Psychology Review, 15*(2), 245–255.

Herber, R. F., & Denver, R. B. (1970). Researchon education and habilitation of the mentally retarded. In H. C. Haywood (Ed.), *Social-cultural aspects of mental retardation.* New York: Appleton-Century-Crofts.

Herrnstein, R. (1973). *IQ in the meritocracy.* Boston: Atlantic, Little, Brown.

Horn, J. M., Loehlin, J. C., & Willerman, L. (1979). Intellectual resemblance among adoptive and biological relatives: The Texas Adoption Project. *Behavior Genetics, 9,* 177–207.

Husen, T. (1959). *Psychological twin research: A methodological study.* Stockholm: Almqvist & Wiksell.

Husen, T. (1960). Abilities of twins. *Scandinavian Journal of Psychology, 1,* 125–135.

Husen, T. (1963). Intra-pair similarities in the school achievements of twins. *Scandinavian Journal of Psychology, 4,* 108–114.

Hyatt, A. (1985). *Effects of relationship tension on the early adjustment of children.* Unpublished doctoral dissertation, University of Minnesota.

James, W. (1958). *Talks with teachers.* New York: W. W. Norton.

Jencks, C. (1973). The methodology of inequality. *Sociology and Education, 46,* 451–470.

Jencks, C., Smith, M., Acland, H., Bane, M. J., Cohoen, B., Gintis, H., Heyns, B., & Michelson, S. (1972). *Inequality: A reassessment of the effects of family and schooling in America.* New York: Basic Books.

Jensen, A. R. (1973). *Educability and group differences.* New York: Basic Books.

Jensen, A. R. (1964). *Individual differences in learning: Interference factor.* (Cooperative Research Project No. 1867). Berkeley: University of California.

Jensen, A. R. (1985, April). *The g beyond factor analysis.* Paper presented at Buros–Nebraska symposium on measurement and testing, University of Nebraska, Lincoln.

Jinks, J. L., & Fulker, D. W. (1970). A comparison of the biometrical, genetical, MAVA, and classical approaches to the analysis of human behavior. *Psychological Bulletin, 73,* 311–349.

Jung, C. G. (1933). *Psychological types.* New York: Harcourt Brace & World.

Kamin, L. J. (1974). *The science and politics of IQ.* New York: Wiley.

Kaplan, M. S., & Kaplan, H. E. (1985). School psychology: Its educational and societal connections. *Journal of School Psychology, 23,* 319–325.

Kenrick, D. T., & Stringfield, D. O. (1980). Personality traits and the eye of the beholder: Crossing some traditional philosophical boundaries in the search for consistency in all of the people. *Psychological Review, 87,* 88–104.

Keogh, B. K. (1972). Psychological evaluations of exceptional children: Old hangups and new directions. *Journal of School Psychology, 10,* 131–145.

Kretschmer, E. (1925). *Physique and character.* New York Harcourt Brace.

Kuder, G. F. (1934). *Kuder Preference Record.* Chicago: Science Research Associates.

Lewontin, R. C. (1970). Race and intelligence. *Bulletin of the Atomic Scientists, 26,* 2–8.

Lewontin, R. C., & Hubby, J. L. (1966). A molecular approach to the study of genetic heterozygosity in natural populations of *Drosophila pseudoobscura. Genetics, 54,* 595–609.

Loehlin, J. C., & Nichols, R. C. (1976). *Heredity, environment, and personality.* Austin: University of Texas Press.

Loehlin, J. C., Sharon, S., & Jacoby, R. (1978). In pursuit of the "spatial gene": A family study. *Behavior Genetics, 8,* 27–41.

Loehlin, J. C., & Vandenberg, S. G. (1968). Genetic and enviornmental components in the covariation of cognitive abilities: An additive model. In S. G. Vandenberg (Ed.), *Progress in human behavior genetics* (pp. 261–285). Baltimore: Johns Hopkins University Press.

Loehlin, J. C., Willerman, L., & Horn, J. M. (1982). Personality resemblances between unwed mothers and their adopted-away offspring. *Journal of Personality and Social Psychology, 42,* 1089–1099.

Lubchenco, L. O. (1976). Classification of high risk infants by birth weight and gestational age: An overview. *Major problems in Clinical Pediatrics, 14,* 1–279.

Maccoby, E. E., & Jacklin, C. N. (1974). *The psychology of sex differences.* Stanford, CA: Stanford University Press.

Marjoribanks, K. (1972). Ethnic and environmental influences on mental abilities. *American Journal of Sociology, 78,* 323–337.

Matarazzo, J. D. (1972). *Wechsler's measurement and appraisal of adult intelligence* (5th ed.). Baltimore: Williams & Wilkins.

Mayr, E. (1970). *Population, species, and evolution.* Cambridge, MA: Harvard University Press–Belknap Press.

McCall, R. B. (1981). Nature–nurture and the two realms of development: A proposed integration with respect of mental development. *Child Development, 52,* 1–12.

McClelland, D. C. (1973). Testing for competence rather than for "intelligence.." *American Psychologist, 28,* 1–14.

Mercy, J. A., & Steelman, L. L. (1982). Familial influence on the intellectual attainment of children. *American Sociological Review, 47,* 532–542.

Minton, H. L., & Schneider, F. W. (1980). *Differential psychology.* Monterey, CA: Brooks/Cole.

Mischel, W. (1968). *Personality and assessment.* New York: Wiley.

Morgan, C. C., & Murray, H. A. (1935). A method for investigating fantasies: The Thematic Apperception Test. *Archives of Neurology and Psychiatry, 34,* 289–306.

Morrison, J. R., & Stewart, M. A. (1973). The psychiatric status of the legal families of adopted hyperactive children. *Archives of General Psychiatry, 28,* 888–891.

Murray, H. A., et al. (1938). *Explorations in personality: A clinical and experimental study of fifty men of college age.* New York: Oxford University Press.

Nichols, R. C. (1965). The National Merit Twin Study. In S. G. Vandenberg (Ed.), *Methods and goals in human behavior genetics* (pp. 231–244). New York: Academic Press.

Nurnberger, J. I., & Gershon, T. S. (1981). Genetics of affective disorders. In E. Friedman (Ed.), *Depression and antidepressants: Implications for courses and treatment.* New York: Raven Press.

Owen, F. W., Adams, P. A., Forrest, T., Stolz, L. M., & Fisher, S. (1971). Learning disorders in children:

Sibling studies. *Monographs of the Society for Research in Child Development, 36* (Whole No. 144).

Pedersen, N. L., Fridberg, L., Floderus-Myrhed, B., McClearn, G. E., & Plomin, R. (1984). Swedish early separated twins: Identification and characterization. *Acta Geneticae Medicae et Gemellologiae, 33,* 243–250.

Plomin, R. (1986). *Development, genetics, and psychology.* Hillsdale, NJ: Lawrence Erlbaum.

Plomin, R., & DeFries, J. C. (1981). Multivariate behavioral genetics and development: Twin studies. In L. Gedda, P. Parisi, & W. E. Nance (Eds.), *Twin research 3: Intelligence, personality, and development* (pp. 25–33). New York: Alan R. Liss.

Plomin, R., DeFries, J. C., & Loehlin, J. C. (1977). Genotype-environment interaction and correlation in the analysis of correlation in the analysis of human behavior. *Psychological Bulletin, 84,* 309–322.

Pogue-Geile, M. F., & Rose, R. J. (1985). Developmental genetic studies of adult personality. *Developmental Psychology, 21,* 547–557.

Record, R. G., McKeown, T., & Edwards, J. H. (1970). An investigation of the difference in measured intelligence between twins and single births. *Annals of Human Genetics, 34,* 11–20.

Reed, E. W., & Reed, S. C. (1965). *Mental retardation: A family study.* Philadelphia: W. B. Saunders.

Reynolds, C. R. (1986). Transactional models of intellectual development, yes. Deficit models of process remediation, no. *School Psychology Review, 15*(2), 256–260.

Rogers, G. W. (1977). Maximizing the practical contributions of psychological reports. *Journal of School Health, 47,* 104–105.

Rorschach, H. (1921). *Psychodiagnostic.* Berne: Birchen.

Rowe, D. C. (1981). Environmental and genetic influences on dimensions of perceived parenting: A twin study. *Developmental Psychology, 17,* 203–208.

Rowe, D. C. (1983). A biometrical analysis of perceptions of family environment: A study of twin and singleton sibling kinships. *Child Development, 54,* 416–423.

Rowe, D. C. (1987). Resolving the person-situation debate: Invitation to an interdisciplinary dialogue. *American Psychologist, 42*(3), 218–227.

Rowe, D. C., & Plomin, R. (1981). The importance of nonshared environmental influences in behavioral development. *Developmental Psychology, 17,* 517–531.

Safer, D. J. (1973). A familial factor in minimal brain dysfunction. *Behavior Genetics,* 175–186.

Sampson, E. E. (1975). Justice as equality. *Journal of Social Issues, 31*(3), 45–64.

Sampson, E. E. (1977). Psychology and the American ideal. *Journal of Personality and Social Psychology, 35,* 767–782.

Scarr, S., & Kidd, K. K. (1983). Developmental behaviour genetics. In P. H. Mussen (Ed.), *Handbook of child psychology: Vol. 2. Infancy and developmental psychobiology* (4th ed., pp. 345–433). New York: Wiley.

Scarr, S., & McCartney, K. (1983). How people make their own environments: A theory of genotype–environment effects. *Child Development, 54,* 424–435.

Scarr, S., Webber, P. L., Weinberg, R. A., & Wittig, M. A. (1981). Personality resemblance among adolescents and their parents in biologically related and adoptive families. *Journal of Personality and Social Psychology, 40,* 885–898.

Scarr, S., & Weinberg, R. A. (1976). IQ test performance of black children adopted by white families. *American Psychologist, 31,* 726–739.

Scarr, S., & Weinberg, R. A. (1977). Intellectual similarities within families of both adopted and biological children. *Intelligence, 1,* 170–191.

Scarr, S., & Weinberg, R. A. (1978a). Attitudes, interests, and IQ. *Human Nature, 1*(4), 29–36.

Scarr, S., & Weinberg, R. A. (1978b). The influence of "family background" on intellectual attainment. *American Sociological Review, 43,* 674–692.

Scarr, S., & Weinberg, R. A. (in press). The nature–nuture problem revisited: The Minnesota Adoption Studies.

Scarr-Salapatek, S. (1971). Race, social class, and IQ. *Science, 174,* 1285–1295.

Scarr-Salapatek, S. (1975). Genetics and the development of intelligence. In F. D. Horowitz (Ed.), *Review of child development research* (pp. 1–57). Chicago: University of Chicago Press.

Schachter, F. F. (1985). Sibling deidentification in the clinic: Devil vs. angel. *Family Process, 24,* 415–427.

Schlesinger, K. (1985). Behavioral genetics and the nature–nuture question. In G. A. Kimble & K. Schlesinger, *Topics in the history of psychology.* (pp. 63–113). Hillsdale, NJ: Lawrence Erlbaum.

Schoenfeldt, L. F. (1968). The hereditary components of the Project TALENT two-day test battery. *Measurement and Evaluation in Guidance, 1,* 130–140.

Segal, N. L. T. (1985). Monozygotic and dizygotic twins: A comparative analysis of mental ability profiles. *Child Development, 52,* 1051–1052.

Sheldon, W. H., & Stevens, S. S. (1946). *The varieties of temperament.* New York: Harper & Row.

Spence, J. T. (1985). Achievement American style: The rewards and costs of individualism. *American Psychologist, 85,* 1285–1295.

Stafford, R. E. (1961). Sex differences in spatial visualization as evidence of sex-linked inheritance. *Perceptual and Motor Skills, 13,* 428.

Strong, E. K. (1927). A vocational interest test. *The Educational Record, 8,* 197–121.

Strong, E. K. (1943). *Vocational interests of men and women.* Stanford, CA: Stanford University Press.

Stunkard, A. J., Foch, T. T., & Hrubec, Z. (1985). *Genetics and human obesity: I. Results of a twin study.* Manuscript submitted for publication.

Tambs, K., Sundet, J. M., & Magnus, P. (1984). Heritability analysis of the WAIS subtests: A study of twins. *Intelligence, 8,* 283–293.

Terman, L. M. (Ed.). (1928). *Nature and nurture: Their influences on intelligence* (27th Yearbook of the

National Society for the Study of Education, parts 1–2). Bloomington, IL: Public School Publications.

Terman, L. M., & Miles, C. C. (1936). *Sex and personality: Studies in masculinity and femininity.* New York: McGraw-Hill.

Tyler, L. E. (1978). *Individuality: Human possibilities and personal choice in the psychological development of men and women.* San Francisco: Jossey-Bass.

Vandenberg, S. G. (1967). Hereditary factors in normal personality traits as measured by inventories. In J. Wortis (Ed.), *Recent advances in biological psychialtry* (pp. 65–104). New York: Plenum Press.

Waddington, C. H. (1962). *New patterns in genetics and development.* New York: Columbia University Press.

Wechsler, D. (1958). *The measurement and appraisal of adult intelligence* (4th ed.). Baltimore: Williams & Wilkins.

Weinberg, R. A. (1983). A case of a misplaced conjunction: Nature or nurture? *Journal of School Psychology, 21,* 9–12.

Wender, P. H. (1971). *Minimal brain dysfunction in children.* New York: Wiley.

White, K. R. (1982). The relation between socioeconomic status and academic achievement. *Psychological Bulletin, 91,* 461–481.

Willerman, L. (1979). *The psychology of individual and group differences.* San Francisco: W. H. Freeman.

Wilson, R. S. (1975). Twins: Patterns of cognitive development as measured on the WPPSI. *Developmental Psychology, 11,* 126–139.

Wilson, R. S. (1983). The Louisville Twin Study: Developmental synchronies in behavior. *Child Development, 54,* 298–316.

Winick, M., Meyer, K. K., & Harris, R. C. (1975). Malnutrition and environmental enrichment by early adoption. *Science, 190,* 1173–1175.

Woodworth, R. S. (1919). Examination of emotional fitness for warfare. *Psychological Bulletin, 16,* 59–60.

Yen, W. M. (1975). Sex-linked major-gene influences on selected types of spatial performance. *Behavior Genetics, 5,* 281–298.

Ysseldyke, J. E., & Mirkin, P. K. (1982). The use of assessment information to plan instructional interventions: A review of the research. In C. R. Reynolds & T. B. Gutkin (Eds.), *The handbook of school psychology.* New York: Wiley.

Zajonc, R. B. (1983). Validating the confluence model. *Psychological Bulletin, 93,* 457–480.

Zajonc, R. B., & Markus, G. B. (1975). Birth order and intellectual development. *Psychological Review, 82,* 74–88.

Zajonc, R. B., Markus, H., & Markus, G. B. (1979). The birth order puzzle. *Journal of Personality and Social Psychology, 37,* 1325–1341.

11

CONTRIBUTIONS OF DEVELOPMENTAL PSYCHOPATHOLOGY TO SCHOOL SERVICES[1]

STEPHANIE H. MCCONAUGHY
THOMAS M. ACHENBACH

Department of Psychiatry, University of Vermont

In this chapter we discuss developmental psychopathology as a conceptual framework for understanding behavioral, emotional, and learning problems that fall within the purview of school psychologists. We begin by explaining developmental psychopathology as a general approach. We then outline its applications to school psychology in terms of normative-developmental guidelines, concepts of disorders, goals of services, and evaluations of outcomes. Thereafter, we present a model for empirically based assessment of disorders derived from developmental psychopathology, implications for administrative criteria for disorders, and practical applications to school psychology. For brevity, we use the term "children" to include ages 2 to 18 years.

[1]Preparation of this chapter was facilitated by Research Grant 84095284 from the W. T. Grant Foundation.

WHAT IS DEVELOPMENTAL PSYCHOPATHOLOGY?

Developmental psychopathology refers to the study of maladaptive behavioral and emotional deviance in relation to the developmental tasks, sequences, and processes that characterize human growth. It is not a theory or an explanation of *why* specific disorders occur. Instead, it is a way of thinking about problems that arise from many different causes, take different forms at different ages, and have different outcomes.

Children's problems have multiple causes, including constitutional vulnerabilities, temperament, family dynamics, stressful experiences, peer pressures, and cognitive characteristics. It is seldom possible to isolate all the factors contributing to a child's problems and even less possible to undo all the contributing factors. A developmental approach focuses on continuities between past, present, and future functioning. From this perspective, children's functioning is viewed not merely as an outcome of past events, but in relation to present and future developmental tasks, risks, assets, and liabilities. This means that children's needs must be judged in terms of helping them master developmental tasks, rather than attempting to restore previous levels of functioning by undoing the past.

School provides an especially crucial sequence of developmental tasks and challenges that must be mastered for successful adaptation in later life. The sequence of tasks is based partly on developmental processes—such as biological and cognitive maturation—and partly on social customs—such as mandatory schooling for ages 6 to 16, the teaching of reading in first grade, and more specialized teaching around the age of 11 or 12.

The sequences imposed by social customs do not always match the developmental timetables of individual children. There is evidence, for example, that some early reading difficulties reflect immaturity in aspects of perceptual development needed to acquire the reading skills taught in first grade (Hagin, Silver, & Kreeger, 1976). This perceptual immaturity is often only temporary. Yet, because it interferes with acquiring skills on the schedule dictated by school customs, children whose development lags in this one respect become increasingly handicapped as the school curriculum becomes increasingly dependent on reading. Such children may later be diagnosed as having specific reading disabilities and may develop emotional and behavioral problems in response to academic failure. Nevertheless, the initial problem was not a reading "disability" nor an emotional or behavioral disorder, but a temporary mismatch between perceptual development and the demands of the school curriculum.

An experimental study of first-graders manifesting perceptual lags showed that those who received ordinary academic tutoring in reading and those who received no intervention continued to have academic and behavioral problems (Arnold et al., 1977). By contrast, first-graders tutored in the perceptual skills that they lacked did not have later problems. Although all three groups eventually "outgrew" their perceptual lags, the presence of such lags at a crucial point in the school curriculum had continuing consequences for the pupils who did not receive perceptual training. These findings illustrate how particular developmental lags and mismatches with age-graded curricula can lead to continuing problems. A developmental perspective therefore compares children's functioning with that of their age-mates in order to identify areas in which deviance may be a source of trouble.

As applied to school psychology, developmental psychopathology has the following implications:

1. Children's functioning should be evaluated in relation to what is typical for normative samples of agemates.
2. Current maladaptive functioning should be viewed in relation to future developmental needs, rather than merely as an outcome of past influences that must be undone.
3. The causes for deviations from normative-developmental guidelines are diverse and can seldom be specifically pinpointed.
4. Interventions should be designed to facilitate mastery of important developmental tasks, especially the acquisition of academic and social skills needed for effective adaptation in later life.
5. The outcome of interventions should be evaluated in terms of improved progress toward specific developmental goals.

ASSESSMENT MODEL FOR DEVELOPMENTAL PSYCHOPATHOLOGY

Standardized measures of ability and achievement have long used age norms for assessing developmental progress. We will present an analogous normative-developmental approach to assessing behavioral/emotional problems. We feel that such an approach is especially needed to counteract the current tendency to view behavioral/emotional problems as disorders that exist in a categorical, all-or-none form. The tendency to impose categories has been fostered by efforts to make diagnostic criteria more precise, as in the American Psychiatric Association's (1980, 1987) *Diagnostic and Statistical Manual* Third Edition and Third Edition–Revised (DSM-III and DSM-III-R). In school settings, the tendency to view children's problems in terms of mutually exclusive categories has been fostered by administrative criteria for special services, such as those required by Public Law 94-142, the Education of the Handicapped Act

(1977). These criteria have been prompted by a need for rules for providing services. Yet they have been based more on administrative considerations than on the direct assessment of children.

Administrative definitions of disorders often require categorization of children according to diagnostic criteria or service distinctions that may not correspond to the children's needs. To receive special education services, for example, a child must meet the criteria for an eligibility category, such as specific learning disability or serious emotional disturbance. Even if the child has problems related to more than one category, administrative rules require determination of (a) which disorder is primary, and (b) whether the one that is primary meets the criteria for service within that category. Furthermore, the presence of other problems—such as "social maladjustment"—can disqualify the child for services altogether, even though it is clear that the child needs special help best rendered through the school.

We consider these issues in detail later. The important point here, however, is that assessing children only according to administrative categories does not provide a comprehensive and accurate picture of their problems, strengths, and needs. To provide a better basis for helping troubled children, we outline an approach to assessment based on normative-developmental principles for evaluating behavioral/emotional problems and competencies.

Multiple Sources of Data

Development proceeds along multiple pathways. Children are often more advanced in one area of functioning, such as cognition, than in another, such as social behavior. Their behavioral competencies and problems also vary from one situation and interaction partner to another. Because of these variations and because children cannot provide a full account of their own functioning, it is necessary to base assessment on multiple sources of data, such as reports by teachers, parents, and observers, self-reports, and psychological tests.

The different sources of data seldom converge on a single diagnostic construct. In fact, meta-analyses of many studies show correlations averaging only .28 between different types of informants rating children's behavioral/emotional problems under different conditions (e.g., teachers versus parents, teachers versus mental health workers, teachers versus observers). Correlations were even

lower—averaging only .22—between children's self-ratings and ratings of the children by others, including teachers, parents, and mental health workers (Achenbach, McConaughy, & Howell. 1987).

Although correlations averaged .60 between similar informants seeing children under generally similar conditions (e.g., pairs of teachers, pairs of parents, pairs of observers), it is clear that no one informant provides the same data as others would. It is therefore necessary to obtain data from multiple informants who interact with children under different conditions. Furthermore, it is unrealistic to expect that data from different sources will be adequately encapsulated in a single diagnostic category. Instead, the data obtained from different sources may reflect important differences in both the child's functioning and in the perceptions of different informants.

Multiaxial Empirically Based Assessment

Because assessment of children's behavioral/ emotional problems depends on the judgments of those who interact with the children, we will outline assessment procedures that make use of such judgments in a systematic way. These procedures employ *empirically based assessment,* which taps the ways in which children's functioning is experienced by particular informants.

Rather than imposing a priori categories on children's problems, empirically based assessment identifies syndromes of problems that actually occur together, as seen by particular informants. This has been accomplished by factor analyzing the behavioral/emotional problems of disturbed children and adolescents, as reported by parents, teachers, observers, and the subjects themselves. To provide normative/developmental reference points, data obtained for a particular child are compared with those obtained for normative samples of age-mates. The data obtained from each informant are scored on standardized profiles that provide age-based standard scores for each syndrome, as well as for competence and adaptive functioning.

To take account of variations across multiple domains of functioning, different assessment procedures are needed to identify inconsistencies as well as consistencies. This is especially true for designing the multifaceted interventions often needed to help children. Such interventions can be more effectively targeted and evaluated if we document how the child is seen in different contexts than if we must choose between different sources of data or view problems only in terms of diagnostic or administrative categories.

To highlight and preserve the variations in assessment data, we have proposed a model called *multiaxial empirically based assessment* (Achenbach, 1985; Achenbach & McConaughy, 1987; McConaughy & Achenbach, 1988). This model emphasizes that assessment should identify strengths and weaknesses in multiple areas via multiple standardized procedures. Because children's functioning may really differ from one area or situation to another, the goal is to use what each procedure reveals about needs for help in different contexts. In some cases, multiaxial assessment may reveal that certain interaction partners, such as a parent or teacher, need changing more than the child does. In other cases, multiaxial assessment may show that one type of intervention is needed for one context but a different type is needed for another context.

Table 1 outlines the following five axes relevant to assessment from preschool through high school: I. Parent Reports, II. Teacher Reports, III. Cognitive Assessment, IV. Physical Assessment, and V. Direct Assessment of the Child. Examples of assessment procedures are listed that have promising reliability, validity, and/or normative data, or for which such data are potentially available. The numerical ordering of the axes does not imply that the first axes take precedence over the later ones. Neither does it imply that assessment should always proceed from Axis I to Axis V. In referrals to school psychologists, for example, teacher reports (Axis II) would often be obtained first. The data to be obtained thereafter would depend on the referral problems and the practices of particular school systems. In some cases, parent reports (Axis I) or direct observations (Axis V) might be obtained second. In other cases, cognitive assessment (Axis III) or self-reports by the child (Axis V) might follow teacher reports. The specific procedures would also depend on the age of the child, the nature of the problems, and local conditions. Classroom observations, for example, may be more appropriate for preschool and elementary school levels than for the upper grades of high school. Self-report questionnaires, on the other hand, would be more appropriate for adolescents than for younger children.

EMPIRICALLY BASED PROCEDURES FOR ASSESSING BEHAVIORAL/EMOTIONAL PROBLEMS

We will briefly describe a family of empirically based standardized instruments for obtaining parent reports, teacher reports, self-reports, and direct observations of behavioral/emotional problems. Thereafter, we present applications of these procedures to special education. Details of the development, reliability, validity, and applications of these instruments are presented in manuals by Achenbach and Edelbrock (1983, 1986, 1987). Hand-scored and computer-scored profiles are available for all the instruments.

Child Behavior Checklist

The Child Behavior Checklist for Ages 4–16 (CBCL/4-16) is designed to obtain reports of the behavioral/emotional problems and competencies of 4- to 16-year-olds, as seen by their parents and parent surrogates. (A version designated as the CBCL/2-3 is also available for 2- and 3-year-olds.) The CBCL/4-16 includes 118 problem items, plus space to write in additional problems. The parent is asked to score 0 if an item is *not true* of the child, *1* if it is *somewhat or sometimes true,* and *2* if it is *very true or often true.* The standard instructions ask the parent to base ratings on the preceding 6 months, but this interval can be changed to suit the user's aims. Examples of items are: *Can't concentrate, can't pay attention for long; Gets in many fights;* and *Unhappy, sad, or depressed.* The CBCL/4-16 also has 20 competence items for reporting the quality and amount of participation in sports, other recreational activities, organizations, jobs, and chores; involvement with friends; how well the child gets along with siblings, other children, and parents; how well the child plays and works alone; and school functioning.

The CBCL/4-16 is scored on the Child Behavior Profile, which consists of problem scales derived from factor analyses of CBCLs completed for 2,300 4- to 16-year-olds referred for mental health services, plus competence scales designated as Activities, Social, and School. The scales are normed on 1,300 randomly selected nonreferred 4- to 16-year-olds. To reflect age and sex differences in the prevalence and patterning of problems, profiles are standardized separately for each sex at ages 4 to 5, 6 to 11, and 12 to 16. The profiles display scores for every problem and com-

TABLE 1   Examples of Multiaxial Assessment Procedures

Age Range	Axis I Parent Reports	Axis II Teacher Reports	Axis III Cognitive Assessment	Axis IV Physical Assessment	Axis V Direct Assessment of Child
2–5	CBCL/2-3 CBCL/4-16 History Parent interview	Preschool records Teacher interview	Ability tests Perceptual-motor tests Language tests	Height, weight Medical exam Neurological exam	Observation during play Interview
6–11	CBCL/4-16 History Parent interview	TRF School records Teacher interview	Ability tests Achievement tests Perceptual-motor tests Language tests	Height, weight Medical exam Neurological exam	DOF Semistructured clinical interview
12–18	CBCL/4-16 History Parent interview	TRF School records Teacher interview	Ability tests Achievement tests Language tests	Height, weight Medical exam Neurological exam	DOF YSR Clinical interview Self-concept measures Personality tests

Source. McConaughy and Achenbach (1988).

petence item, competence and problem scales, broad-band groupings of problems designated as Internalizing and Externalizing, and total scores for problems and competencies. *T* scores and percentiles are shown on the profile for various scale scores.

Teacher's Report Form

The Teacher's Report Form of the Child Behavior Checklist (TRF) has 118 problem items, 93 of which are the same as on the CBCL, plus 25 that are more apt to be observed by teachers than parents. Teachers are also asked to rate the pupil's performance in academic subjects, plus four adaptive characteristics, including how hard the pupil is working, how appropriately he or she is behaving, how much he or she is learning, and how happy he or she is.

The TRF is scored on the Teacher Version of the Child Behavior Profile. This profile consists of problem scales derived from factor analyses of TRFs completed for 1,700 6- to 16-year-olds referred for mental health or special school services for behavioral/emotional problems, plus scales for scoring adaptive functioning. Profiles are standardized separately for each sex at ages 6 to 11 and 12 to 16, with norms based on 1,100 randomly selected nonreferred pupils. The profiles display raw scores, *T* scores, and percentiles for all scales, Internalizing, Externalizing, and total problem and adaptive scores.

Youth Self-Report

The Youth Self-Report for Ages 11–18 (YSR) has most of the same items as the CBCL, but they are worded in the first person and modified where necessary to make them suitable for adolescents. Sixteen socially desirable items encourage adolescents to report their positive characteristics. The YSR Profile consists of problem scales derived from factor analyses of YSRs completed by 927 11- to 18-year-olds referred for mental health services, plus competence scales designated as Activities and Social. Profiles displaying raw scores, *T* scores, and percentiles are standardized separately for each sex, with norms based on 686 randomly selected nonreferred adolescents.

Direct Observation Form

The Direct Observation Form of the Child Behavior Checklist (DOF; Achenbach, 1986) is designed to score 96 problems similar to those on the TRF from observations of pupils in classrooms and other group settings, such as recess. In using the DOF, an observer writes a narrative description of a 10-minute observational sample of the target child's behavior, while also scoring on-task behavior at 1-minute intervals. At the end of the 10-minute sample, the observer scores the problem items on four-step scales. To obtain representative samples of behavior, it is recommended that the target child be observed for three to six 10-minute periods on different occasions, such as mornings and afternoons on different days. To provide a baseline for the behavior of other children in the same setting, it is also recommended that two control children be observed on the same occasions and that their scores be averaged for comparison with those of the target child.

Hand-scored and computer-scored profiles provide for averaging up to six observational sessions on the target child and two control children for on-task, total problems, Internalizing, and Externalizing. The computer-scored DOF profile also scores six scales derived from factor analyses of DOFs on 212 pupils referred for behavioral/emotional problems. Cutoff points for all problem scales, as well as *T* scores for the total problem score, are based on 287 randomly selected pupils observed in 45 elementary schools of 23 public and parochial school systems.

EMPIRICALLY BASED ASSESSMENT AND THE DSM-III-R

Several of the empirically derived syndromes have approximate counterparts among the child and adolescent disorders of the DSM-III-R (American Psychiatric Association, 1987), as summarized in Table 2. The similarities lie in the descriptive features found to co-occur in the empirically derived syndromes and the descriptive features selected by the committees that constructed the DSM categories. Some empirically derived syndromes have no clear counterparts in the DSM, however, while some DSM categories have not been borne out empirically.

The empirically derived syndromes are operationally defined in terms of specific assessment operations, and they are scored quantitatively to reflect gradations in the *degree to which* a child manifests their features. Norms based on randomly selected general population samples make it possi-

TABLE 2 Approximate Relations Between DSM-III-R and Empirically Derived Syndromes

DSM-111-R	CBCL	TRF	YSR	DOF
Solitary Aggressive Conduct Disorder } Oppositional Defiant Disorder	Aggressive	Aggressive	Aggressive	Aggressive
Group Delinquent Conduct Disorder	Delinquent	Delinquent	Delinquent	—
Attention Deficit–Hyperactivity Disorder	Hyperactive	Inattentive Nervous–Overactive	—	Hyperactive
Overanxious Disorder	Anxious–Obsessive Schizoid–Anxious	Anxious	—	Nervous–Obsessive
Gender Identity Disorder for Males	Sex Problems (boys 4-5)	—	Self-Destructive/ Identity Problems (boys only)	—
Schizoid Personality	Social Withdrawal	Social Withdrawal	—	—
Schizotypal Personality	Schizoid	—	Thought Disorder	—
Psychotic Disorders				
Somatization Disorder	Somatic Complaints	—	Somatic Complaints	—
Obsessive–Compulsive Disorder	Obsessive–Compulsive	Obsessive–Compulsive	—	—
Major Depression } Dysthymia	Depressed	Depressed (girls only)	Depressed	Depressed

Source. Achenbach and Edelbrock (1987).

ble to quantify the degree of deviance reported for individual children compared to their age-mates. The DSM categories, by contrast, are not based on specific assessment procedures. Furthermore, each descriptive feature and diagnosis listed in the DSM must be judged categorically as present versus absent, and there are no norms for determining whether what is reported for a child deviates from what typifies his or her peers.

The DSM diagnostic categories are in some respects like administrative categories that provide rules for matters such as third-party payment for services but that are not derived from actual assessment of children. The DSM recognizes the need for considering multiple aspects of functioning by providing axes for clinical syndromes, personality and developmental disorders, physical disorders, psychosocial stressors, and global assessment of functioning. Although the DSM's multiple axes acknowledge that there is more to diagnosis than clinical syndromes, they are designed mainly to elaborate on characteristics of individuals who are categorized in terms of clinical syndromes. They do not provide procedures for assessing functioning in different domains or for dealing with the variations often found between data from different sources.

EMPIRICALLY BASED ASSESSMENT AND SPECIAL EDUCATION CLASSIFICATIONS

With the passage of P.L. 94-142, the classification of children for special education services has become a major function of school psychologists. While a number of handicapping conditions were delineated by the federal law, the category of serious emotional disturbance (SED) relates most directly to identification of psychopathology. For this reason, we focus primarily on the SED category.

Serious Emotional Disturbance

P.L. 94-142 defines serious emotional disturbance as follows:

> (i) The term means a condition exhibiting one or more of the following characteristics over a long period of time and to a marked degree, which adversely affects educational performance: (a) an inability to learn which cannot be explained by intellectual, sensory, or health factors; (b) an inability to build or maintain

satisfactory interpersonal relationships with peers and teachers; (c) inappropriate types of behavior or feelings under normal circumstances; (d) a general pervasive mood of unhappiness or depression; or (e) a tendency to develop physical symptoms or fears associated with personal or school problems. (ii) The term includes children who are schizophrenic. The term does not include children who are socially maladjusted, unless it is determined that they are seriously emotionally disturbed. (Education of the Handicapped Act, 1977, p. 42478; amended 1981, p. 3866)

(For consistency, the term *seriously emotionally disturbed* is used throughout this chapter. It includes labels such as "severely emotionally disturbed," "emotionally disturbed," "socially and emotionally disturbed," "emotionally handicapped," and "behavior disordered," which appear in various state definitions and research studies.)

Variations in State Definitions

The federal law outlines the general characteristics of serious emotional disturbance (SED), but states vary considerably in their interpretation and application of the law. In a survey of 49 states, Epstein, Culligan, and Sabatino (1977) found that the majority of states agreed on general criteria for learning, behavioral/emotional, and interpersonal problems, but they were vague and inconsistent in specifying qualifying characteristics for SED. A major difference among states concerns whether externalizing behavior disorders (BD) are included in their definition of serious emotional disturbance. To address this problem, a special commission was mandated by Congress in 1983 to study the use of the SED term and determine whether a change in terminology was needed. The commission found large differences from state to state in the numbers and characteristics of children identified as SED/BD and served under that category. For example, the commission reported that in 1983-1984, one state classified only 3% of its handicapped populations as SED (.3% of its school-aged population), while another state classified and served 29% of its handicapped population as SED (3% of its school-aged population). The national averages of SED children in 1983-1984 were 8.4% of all handicapped and .92% of the school-aged population.

(over)

Despite such vast differences across states, no change in the federal definition was recommended (Tallmadge, Gamel, Munson, & Hanley, 1985).

Variations in Classification Systems

One attempt to clarify definitional issues in SED was Slenkovich's (1983) legal analysis of the relation between P.L. 94-142 and the DSM-III diagnostic system. Attorney Slenkovich presented a conservative interpretation of the federal law which excluded many of the diagnoses pertaining to externalizing behavior disorders, particularly Oppositional Disorder, Conduct Disorder, and Attention Deficit Disorder. She based her exclusion of these diagnoses on her interpretation of "inappropriate behavior or feelings under normal circumstances" as meaning bizarre or psychotic behavior, not socially unacceptable or problematic behavior. She also argued that diagnoses of Conduct Disorder, Oppositional Disorder, and Antisocial Personality were ruled out by the stipulation excluding socially maladjusted children unless they exhibit some other emotional condition defined by the law. In addition to the externalizing disorders, Slenkovich excluded certain internalizing disorders, such as Dysthymia, Major Depression—Single Episode, and Adjustment Disorders, because they failed to meet the requirement that the condition be exhibited over a long period of time. Other diagnoses, such as Eating Disorders, were excluded because they do not adversely affect educational performance, which Slenkovich interpreted as meaning academic achievement rather than broader social or developmental advancement.

Mental health professionals continue to differ considerably in their interpretation of the SED term and use of DSM-III diagnoses. In a survey of 120 school psychologists, Colegrove, Ostrander, Schwartz, and Daniels (1986) found that most adhered to their state definitions and approximately 70% did not use DSM-III diagnoses at all. Furthermore, school psychologists differed in whether they agreed with Slenkovich's interpretation of P.L. 94-142 concerning the DSM-III categories that qualify as SED. Most of the disagreement centered on whether externalizing behavior disorders should be included in the SED category. Significant differences were found among school psychologists concerning the eligibility of children with Attention Deficit Disorder and Conduct Disorder diagnoses, depending on whether their state definition included or excluded these behavior disorders. Other studies have also shown that contrary to Slenkovich's interpretation, Attention Deficit Disorder, Dysthymia,, and Conduct Disorders are among the most frequent diagnoses for SED children (Mattison, Humphrey, & Kales, 1986; Mattison, Humphrey, Kales, Hanford, Finkenbinder, & Hernit, 1986).

Differences in identification of psychopathology and special education eligibility also depend on whether children are classified by DSM-III diagnoses or empirically based procedures. Tharinger, Laurent, and Best (1986) compared the 94-142 criteria, DSM-III, and the CBCL system (Achenbach & Edelbrock, 1983, 1986) by having independent raters assign diagnoses to 6- to 12-year-old boys referred by their teachers for special education evaluations of emotional or behavioral problems. They found that the three systems classified different percentages of the sample, with unanimous agreement on only 29% of cases as having a disorder and 8% as having no disorder. The DSM-III was the most inclusive, classifying 82% as having an Axis I disorder, while the P.L. 94-142 criteria were the most exclusive, classifying 53% as seriously emotionally disturbed. The Teacher's Report Form of the CBCL fell between the other two systems, identifying 66% as having a significant behavior disorder. There was slightly higher agreement on identified children between the DSM-III and P.L. 94-142 (45%) than between the TRF and P.L. 94-142 (37%), although the total agreement on identified and nonidentified cases was the same for the DSM-III and TRF compared to P.L. 94-142 (55%). The lower agreement between the TRF and P.L. 94-142 on identified children, however, was probably because Tharinger et al. used a 98th percentile cutoff on the Internalizing and Externalizing scores rather than the 89th percentile cutoff specified in the TRF Manual (Achenbach & Edelbrock, 1986). The better agreement between DSM-III and P.L. 94-142 probably reflected a more liberal interpretation of the SED criteria than Slenkovich's, since 14 out of 20 cases had DSM-III diagnoses that would be excluded according to her interpretation (e.g., Attention Deficit Disorder, Oppositional Disorder, and Dysthymia). The overinclusiveness, vagueness, and poor reliability of the DSM-III diagnoses, however, led Tharinger et al. to question the validity of DSM-III for determining special education SED eligibility. Empirically based methods such as the CBCL and TRF, on the other hand, were recommended because of their higher reli-

(continue)

ability and validity, more clearly defined syndromes, normative data, and greater sensitivity and specificity in multimethod approaches to assessment (see also Gresham, 1985, and Mattison, Humphrey, & Kales, 1986, for similar conclusions).

Relations between Empirically Based Methods and Serious Emotional Disturbance
Without presupposing any particular interpretation of P.L. 94-142, we have illustrated various ways in which empirically based procedures can be useful in determining special education eligibility for serious emotional disturbance (Achenbach & McConaughy, 1987; McConaughy & Achenbach, 1989). Table 3 summarizes relations between the P.L. 94-142 SED definition and our multiaxial empirically based procedures. Nine general components of the federal definition are listed, together with the empirically derived syndromes and other features that apply most clearly to special education SED classification. Each empirically derived syndrome is listed next to the P.L. 94-142 characteristic that it most clearly represents, although a syndrome could include behaviors covering more than one characteristic. The syndromes in parentheses are also relevant if externalizing behavior disorders are included in the interpretation of SED.

Beside the empirically derived syndromes, Table 4 lists three general requirements specified in P.L. 94-142 for SED eligibility. The requirement that problems have existed for a *long period of time* is not specifically assessed by the empirically based measures, since the instructions for 6-month ratings on the CBCL and YSR and 2-month ratings on the TRF do not mean that a problem has been evident over the entire rating period. Further information from parent and teacher interviews and school records is required to assess duration. The item on the TRF asking how long the teacher has known the child and the section for the teacher to add open-ended comments, however, could easily include information on how long problems have existed. Follow-up evaluations using any of the four instruments could also be useful to document the continuation of problems over the follow-up period.

The norms and clinical cutoffs on the empirically based scales are particularly useful for determining whether problems exist to a *marked degree*. Comparisons to normative data indicate the degree of deviance in total problems, as well as in broad- and narrow-band syndromes. If a child's total problem score and/or Externalizing or Internalizing scores are above the clinical cutoffs, along with one or more scores on the relevant narrow-band scales, this provides strong evidence for problems existing to a marked degree. The ratings by parents and teachers, a youth's self-ratings, and direct observations thus provide quantitative indices of behavioral deviance beyond what is typically assessed by interviews or personality tests.

The criterion that a child's emotional disturbance *adversely affects educational performance* is not so clearly judged from the empirically based procedures alone, but requires information from other sources, particularly cognitive and achievement tests. The clinical cutoffs on the CBCL School scale and the TRF School Performance and Adaptive Functioning scales, however, can be useful for determining adverse educational effects. Information from parent and teacher interviews, the child's report card, and the open-ended comments of the teacher on the TRF can further supplement the findings of the cognitive assessment.

Finally, the requirement that an SED child *not be socially maladjusted* may rule out cases where the only scores in the clinical range are on the Delinquent scales of the CBCL, TRF, or YSR. A high score on only the Delinquent scale or a very high intraclass correlation with the Delinquent profile type could thus argue against SED classification, if there is no evidence of any other behavioral/emotional problems. However, the differences among state interpretations of whether externalizing behavior disorders are covered by SED make it difficult to formulate a general rule for using empirically based measures to rule out social maladjustment in SED determinations.

Serious Emotional Disturbance versus Learning Disabilities
While federal and state laws define general characteristics for specific learning disabilities and serious emotional disturbance, the overlap between learning and behavioral/emotional problems makes such absolute distinctions difficult. In the Isle of Wight study, for example, Rutter, Tizard, and Whitmore (1970) found that 25% of children experiencing academic underachievement were also rated by teachers as showing antisocial behavior. In a later study of disadvantaged London children, 47% with reading problems showed behavioral deviance (Rutter & Yule, 1975).

TABLE 3   Applications of Empirically Based Assessment to PL 94–142 Criteria for Serious Emotional Disturbance

PL 94–142 Components of SED	CBCL	TRF	YSR	DOF
Inability to learn	—	Inattentive	—	Withdrawn–Inattentive
Inability to build or maintain relationships	Social Withdrawal Hostile Withdrawal	Social Withdrawal Unpopular	Unpopular	—
Inappropriate types of behavior or feelings	Schizoid Schizoid–Anxious Schizoid–Obsessive Obsessive–Compulsive (Aggressive) (Hyperactive)	Self-Destructive Obsessive–Compulsive (Nervous–Overactive) (Aggressive)	Thought Disorder Self-Destructive/ Identity Problems (Aggressive)	Nervous-Obsessive Attention–Demanding (Aggressive) (Hyperactive)
General pervasive mood of unhappiness	Depressed Depressed–Withdrawal	Depressed	Depressed	Depressed
Tendency to develop physical symptoms or fears	Somatic Complaints Schizoid–Anxious Anxious–Obsessive	Anxious	Somatic Complaints	—
Schizophrenic	Schizoid	—	Thought Disorder	—
Long period of time	Follow-up evaluations	Follow-up evaluations	Follow-up evaluations	Follow-up evaluations
Marked degree	Total, Internalizing, or Externalizing scores >90th %ile Narrow-band scores >98th %ile	Total, Internalizing, or Externalizing scores >89th %ile Narrow-band scores >98th %ile	Total, Internalizing, or Externalizing scores >89th %ile Narrow-band scores >98th %ile	Total score >93rd %ile Narrow-band scores >98th %ile
Adversely affects educational performance	School scale <2nd %ile	School performance <2nd %ile Adaptive functioning <13th %ile	—	Low on-task score

Source. Achenbach and Edelbrock (1987).

Numerous other studies have shown an association between academic underachievement and behavioral/emotional problems. In one of the first studies of learning-disabled children's adjustment, Fabian (1955) found that 83% of problem readers were seriously maladjusted in social and/or personal domains. Since then, other researchers have reported more differentiated problems in LD children, such as feelings of insecurity (Owen, Adams, Forrest, Stolz, & Fisher, 1971), low self-confidence (Hunter & Johnson, 1971), low self-esteem (Blalock, 1981; Rosenberg & Gaier, 1977), depression (Klein & Seligman, 1976; Seligman, 1974), poor social skills (Rosenberg & Gaier, 1977; Pihl & McLarnon, 1984), and unpopularity among peers (Bruininks, 1978; Bryan, 1974, 1978; Bryan, Donahue, & Pearl, 1981; Rosenberg & Gaier, 1977; Wong & Wong, 1980).

Studies of behavioral problems among older LD youths have shown a preponderance of externalizing problems (Griffin, 1971; Siegel, 1974) and more antisocial and rebellious patterns than among non-LD youth (Blalock, 1981; Bryan, Werner, & Pearl, 1982). This type of evidence has led several researchers to suggest a link between learning disabilities and delinquency (Bryan, 1978; Jacobson, 1974; Keldgord, 1969; Mauser, 1974; Meltzer, Levine, Karniski, Palfrey, & Clarke, 1984; Morgan, 1979; Underwood, 1976; Zinkus, Gottlieb, & Zinkus, 1979). Retrospective studies of troubled children have also revealed high rates of learning disabilities among those diagnosed as antisocial (Sabatino & Mauser, 1978), socially withdrawn (Bryan & Bryan, 1977; Ritter, 1978; Sipperstein, Bopp & Bak, 1978), and delinquent (Keldgord, 1969; Morgan, 1979; Mulligan, 1969).

In view of the overlap between learning and behavioral/emotional problems, researchers have attempted to identify the characteristics that distinguish learning-disabled (LD) and educable mentally retarded children (EMR) from seriously emotionally disturbed children (SED). This research has shown that educators tend to associate poor academic performance with learning disabilities and mental retardation, whereas they associate behavior problems with emotional disturbance. Keogh, Tchir, and Windeguth-Behn (1974), for example, found that elementary school teachers generally described SED children (including both behaviorally disordered and emotionally disturbed) as having more behavior and personality problems (hyperactivity, aggression, lack of re-

spect, etc.) and EMR children as having more learning and academic problems (poor recall, short attention, poor reasoning, poor coordination). Ysseldyke and Algozzine (1981) showed further that the bias toward viewing behavioral problems as indicators of emotional disturbance was so strong that school professionals diagnosed computer-simulated cases as SED rather than LD on the basis of referral information alone, ignoring similar standardized test data for both types of cases.

Other studies have generally shown that it is easier to distinguish educable mentally retarded or normal children from either learning-disabled or seriously emotionally disturbed children, whereas the differences between learning-disabled and seriously emotionally disturbed children are more subtle. In a study of clinically referred and public school children, Hicks, Johansson, Heinze, and Halscott (1981) maintained that their Developmental Checklist discriminated children with learning disabilities, hyperactivity, and emotional problems from normal children, and was "somewhat successful" in separating attitudinal problems from hyperactivity and learning disability. However, examination of their data revealed considerable overlap between behavioral/emotional and learning problems in their sample of public school children receiving remedial instruction. Mild to severe scores were obtained on the Activity scale (measuring attention problems and overactivity) by 46% of the remedial group from parent ratings and by 59% from teacher ratings. Mild to severe scores on the Attitudinal scale (measuring emotional and motivational problems) were obtained by 45% of the remedial group from parent ratings and by 57% from teacher ratings. Low correlations between parent and teacher ratings for the remedial group further indicated considerable variation in their problems across home and school situations.

Fuller and Rankin (1984) reported that LD and SED children differed more from normal students than from each other on a self-report personality measure. The characteristics that did distinguish LD from SED children showed SED children to be less conscientious and compliant with rules, less reflective and internally restrained, but more shrewd than LD children. Gajar (1980) found that SED children had higher scores than both EMR and LD children on behavior rating scales of conduct disorder, personality problems, and immaturity/inadequacy. Wynne and Brown (1984) also found that behavior rating scales and measures of sustained attention and impulse control discriminated between SED and LD children better than did a variety of other instruments. SED children had higher total problem scores, more externalizing behavior, greater impulsivity, and poorer attention than LD children.

Findings have been mixed with respect to cognitive test differences between LD and SED children. Dean (1978, 1984a) argued that LD children show greater perceptual deficits on IQ tests than SED children, but other researchers have found few or no differences on cognitive measures (Coolidge, 1983; Gajar, 1980; Wynne & Brown, 1984).

EMPIRICALLY BASED ASSESSMENT OF LD AND SED CHILDREN

Because behavior rating scales have been particularly good discriminators between LD and SED children, a comparison of studies using the same empirically based measures can highlight similarities and differences between these two groups, as well as provide normative comparisons with non-handicapped children. Four recent studies have used Achenbach and Edelbrock's (1983, 1986) rating scales with LD and SED groups. McConaughy and Ritter (1986) and McConaughy (1986) used the Child Behavior Checklist to obtain parents' ratings of LD boys aged 6 to 11 and 12 to 16 years. They found significantly poorer social competence and more behavioral problems in both age groups of LD boys than in Achenbach and Edelbrock's (1983) normative samples of the same age range. Both groups of LD boys had significantly higher total problem, Internalizing, and Externalizing scores than did normal boys. The 6- to 11-year-old LD boys had particularly high scores on the Depressed, Uncommunicative, Obsessive-Compulsive, Social Withdrawal, Hyperactive, Aggressive, and Delinquent scales of the CBCL. The 12- to 16-year-old LD boys scored high on the Immature, Hostile–Withdrawal, Aggressive, and Hyperactive scales. Compared with Achenbach and Edelbrock's clinical samples, the younger LD boys had higher proportions with a hyperactive profile type and a lower proportion with the depressed–social withdrawal–aggressive type. The distribution of profile types among the

older LD boys was more similar to the clinically referred samples, with the exception of a lower proportion with the uncommunicative–delinquent type.

Mattison, Humphrey, and Kales (1986) used the Child Behavior Checklist to obtain parents' ratings of 6- to 12-year-old boys referred by their teachers for possible placement in SED classrooms. [Mattison et al. scored the 12-year-old boys on Achenbach and Edelbrock's (1986) 6- to 11-year scales to maintain consistency across the entire sample.] All of the boys referred had high total problem scores on the CBCL, as well as high Internalizing and Externalizing scores. The 63% of the sample who were identified as SED by basic staffing teams had significantly higher scores than did the non-SED boys on the Externalizing, Hyperactive, Aggressive, and Delinquent scales of the CBCL. The SED boys also had high scores on the Social Withdrawal scale, but so did the non-SED boys. Scores on the Connors Teacher Rating Scale (Goyette, Conners, & Ulrich, 1978) did not discriminate the SED from the non-SED boys as well as the parent ratings on the CBCL, since both groups obtained high Connors scores for conduct problems and asocial behaviors. However, the SED boys did obtain higher Connors scores than did non-SED boys on hyperactivity.

To compare the results of the two studies of 6- to 11-year-old boys, Table 4 shows the mean *T* scores on the CBCL for McConaughy and Ritter's (1986) 123 LD boys and Mattison et al.'s (1986) 50 SED boys, as well as the mean *T* score from Achenbach and Edelbrock's (1983) normative sample of 300 nonreferred boys. Table 4 shows that both LD and SED boys had scores well above the normative samples on all of the CBCL scales. The total problem scores for both LD and SED boys were in the clinical range (above 90th percentile). The SED boys showed more severe problems, however, with scores in the clinical range on the broad-band Internalizing and Externalizing scales (above 90th percentile), as well as on several narrow-band scales (above 98th percentile). The SED boys had significantly higher scores than the LD boys on the Schizoid–Anxious, Uncommunicative, Somatic Complaints, Social Withdrawal, Aggressive, and Delinquent scales. The LD and SED boys were generally comparable on the Depressed, Obsessive–Compulsive, and Hyperactive scales.

Harris, King, Reifler, and Rosenberg (1984)

TABLE 4   Mean *T* Scores on the Child Behavior Checklist for Learning Disabled (LD), Seriously Emotionally Disturbed (SED), and Normative Samples of 6 to 11-Year-Old Boys

CBCL Scales	LD[a] (N = 123)	SED[a] (N = 50)	Normative Sample (N = 300)
Broad-Band Scales			
Total Problems	63.2[c]	73.0[b,c]	50.5
Internalizing	60.5	66.9[b,c]	51.2
Externalizing	62.5	70.9[b,c]	51.0
Narrow-band Scales			
Schizoid–Anxious	61.5	65.5[b]	57.7
Depressed	62.0	62.4	57.3
Uncommunicative	65.1	69.0[b]	57.9
Obsessive–Compulsive	63.2	64.3	57.4
Somatic Complaints	61.6	66.8[b]	57.9
Social Withdrawal	64.4	71.5[b,c]	57.9
Hyperactive	68.5	69.4	57.6
Aggressive	63.2	71.0[b,c]	57.1
Delinquent	63.2	71.4[b,c]	57.7

[a]All *T* scores > normative sample, $p < .05$. LD sample from McConaughy and Ritter (1986); SED sample from Mattison et al. (1986); normative sample from Achenbach and Edelbrock (1983).
[b]*T* score in clinical range: A *T* score > 63 is in the clinical range (above 90th percentile) for the Total Problem, Internalizing, and Externalizing scales; a *T* score > 70 is in the clinical range (above 98th percentile) on the narrow-band scales.
[c]SED > LD, $p < .05$.

also compared LD and SED 6- to 12-year-old boys, using the Teacher's Report Form of the CBCL (Achenbach & Edelbrock, 1986; Edelbrock & Achenbach, 1984). Table 5 shows the mean *T* scores from their sample of 30 LD and 30 SED boys, along with mean *T* scores from Achenbach and Edelbrock's (1986) normative samples of 6- to 11-year-old boys. (Like Mattison et al., 1986, Harris et al. scored the 12-year-old boys on the 6- to 11-year scales to maintain consistency across scales.) Table 5 shows that both LD and SED boys had significantly higher scores on the TRF compared to the normative samples, with total problem, Internalizing, and Externalizing scores in the clinical range (above 89th percentile). As with the parent ratings, teacher ratings showed more severe problems for SED than for LD boys. The SED boys scored significantly higher than LD boys on total problems, Internalizing, and Externalizing, as well as higher on the Social Withdrawal, Self-Destructive, Inattentive, and Nervous–Overactive narrow-band scales. Although SED boys scored highest on the Aggressive scale, this scale did not distinguish them from LD boys, who also showed high aggression.

The findings on the empirically based measures summarized in Tables 4 and 5 clearly show that both LD and SED boys exhibit a wide range of behavioral/emotional problems at levels well above those found for normal boys of the same age. For those identified as SED by federal/state criteria, both parents and teachers report more total problems, more problems of an internalizing and externalizing nature, and more social withdrawal than reported for LD boys. SED boys appear to be more aggressive and delinquent than LD boys, according to their parents, and more self-destructive, overactive, and inattentive in school, according to their teachers. The finding that LD and SED boys showed equally high hyperactivity reported by parents and equally high aggression reported by teachers highlights the difficulty of differentiating between these two groups on the basis of psychiatric diagnoses such as Attention Deficit Disorder with Hyperactivity or Conduct Disorder. The lack of significant differences on the

TABLE 5   Mean *T* Scores on the Teacher's Report Form for Learning Disabled (LD), Seriously Emotionally Disturbed (SED), and Normative Samples of 6 to 11-Year-Old Boys

TRF Scales	LD[a] (N = 30)	SED[a] (N = 30)	Normative Sample (N = 300)
Broad-Band Scales			
Total Problems	65.4	71.1[b,c]	51.5
Internalizing	63.7	67.7[b,c]	52.3
Externalizing	64.3	70.4[b,c]	52.2
Narrow-Band Scales			
Anxious	62.4	64.4	57.3
Social Withdrawal	65.0	71.3[b,c]	58.0
Unpopular	64.4	69.7	57.6
Self-Destructive	63.5	68.4[b]	58.0
Obsessive–Compulsive	62.4	64.7	57.9
Inattentive	61.3	66.5[b]	57.7
Nervous–Overactive	62.2	67.7[b]	57.8
Aggressive	66.9	72.1[c]	57.6

[a]All *T* scores > normative sample, *p* < .05. LD and SED samples from Harris et al. (1984); normative sample from Achenbach and Edelbrock (1986).
[b]SED < LD, *p* < .05.
[c]*T* score in clinical range: A *T* score > 63 is in the clinical range (above 89th percentile) for the Total Problem, Internalizing, and Externalizing scales; a *T* score > 70 is in the clinical range (above 98th percentile) on the narrow-band scales.

CBCL Depressed and the TRF Anxious scales also highlights the difficulty of differentiating SED from LD boys on affective dimensions. We are currently conducting research using empirically based procedures to evaluate differences between LD and SED children. At the same time, the present findings illustrate a wide range of behavioral/ emotional problems for both LD and SED children. Such evidence supports the need of both groups for special education services addressing behavioral/emotional as well as learning problems regardless of their classification (Chandler & Jones, 1983a, 1983b; Dean, 1984b).

As with all classification systems, the final determination of whether a child meets LD or SED criteria for special education requires integration of information across all axes of assessment. The empirically based measures provide objectively scored, standardized information on the nature and severity of a child's behavioral/emotional functioning. This information must be integrated with cognitive assessment and other findings using the multiaxial approach outlined earlier in Table 1. The meta-analyses (Achenbach et al., 1987) dis-

cussed earlier demonstrated that agreement on descriptions of children's behavioral/emotional problems depends on the similarity between informants in their relationships with children and the situations in which they interact with them. The low correlations between different types of informants demonstrate the variability of children's behavior across diverse situations. This variability limits generalizability across situations for classifying children as behavior disordered (Gresham, 1985). Having presented the concepts of developmental psychopathology and empirically based assessment, we now address applications to school psychology practice.

IMPLEMENTING EMPIRICALLY BASED ASSESSMENT

Several authors have argued that empirically based measures provide valuable information in school-based assessments of children (Edelbrock, 1983; Gresham, 1983; McConaughy, 1985; Quay, 1983). Such procedures have the following advantages for school psychologists:

1. The information obtained is quantifiable and therefore amenable to psychometric standards of reliability and validity.
2. Normative data enable the psychologist to judge a child's deviance in relation to large samples of nonreferred age-mates.
3. The large pool of items enables the psychologist to assess a broad range of potential problems rather than focusing only on the referral complaints or most salient problems at the time.
4. Competencies and problems are aggregated into broad-band and narrow-band syndromes, enabling the psychologist to organize information in a hierarchical fashion, if desired.
5. The empirically derived syndromes reflect the way in which problems actually covary among clinically referred children, as reported by particular types of informants.
6. The four related instruments make it possible to integrate information from multiple informants across a variety of situations.
7. The instruments provide a quick and economical means of obtaining information on a child's functioning, enabling the psychologist to devote more time to assessing identified problems, formulating conclusions, and designing interventions.

National surveys have shown that school psychologists have not used such procedures as a routine practice in the past (Goh, Teslow, & Fuller, 1981; Goh & Fuller, 1983). Perhaps this was because it was not clear how empirically based assessment could be incorporated into the various stages of case management. To demonstrate this approach, we will outline the roles of empirically based procedures in gathering data, integrating data, developing treatment plans, and evaluating outcomes. A case study of a 15-year-old boy referred to a school psychologist will be used to illustrate different types of information obtained in multiaxial assessment.

Gathering Data
Initial Referral

A typical data gathering sequence is shown in Figure 1, beginning with initial referral. Parents, teachers, and other referral agents often state the reasons for referral in global terms, such as "hyperactivity," "learning problems," or "doesn't get along with other children." Common complaints by teachers are that the child "doesn't pay attention," "doesn't listen," or "can't follow directions." In fact, Achenbach and Edelbrock (1986) reported that the TRF item *Difficulty following directions* does not discriminate well between referred and nonreferred children, since it was scored for 35 to 50% of nonreferred children aged 6 to 16 and 60 to 80% of referred children. When asked for details, parents and teachers often describe particular episodes that have upset them and led to the referral.

The case of *15-year-old Gary* illustrates a typical referral to the school psychologist. Two ninth-grade teachers requested an assessment because Gary was inattentive and disruptive in class, aggressive and disliked by peers, and off task much of the time. He was receiving poor or failing grades in several classes, particularly English and history. Three teachers completed the TRF. Gary's total adaptive functioning was in the clinical range on all three reports (below the 13th percentile), with low ratings for working hard, behaving appropriately,

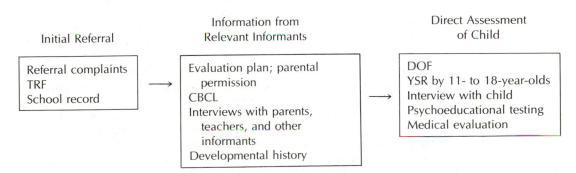

Initial Referral	Information from Relevant Informants	Direct Assessment of Child
Referral complaints TRF School record	Evaluation plan; parental permission CBCL Interviews with parents, teachers, and other informants Developmental history	DOF YSR by 11- to 18-year-olds Interview with child Psychoeducational testing Medical evaluation

Figure 1. Gathering data.

learning, and happiness. His score for school performance was also in the clinical range (below the 2nd percentile). Gary's total problem, Internalizing, and Externalizing scores from his English and history teachers were in the clinical range (above the 89th percentile), while scores from his industrial arts teacher (metal shop) were just below the clinical cutoff. On the narrow-band scales, scores were in the clinical range on one or more TRFs on the Social Withdrawal, Obsessive–Compulsive, Immature, Self-Destructive, Inattentive, and Aggressive scales (above 98th percentile). Two teachers scored him on the item *Strange behavior,* describing odd noises and facial expressions and hiding under furniture. The teachers commented that Gary seemed angry, unhappy, and withdrawn, in addition to having learning and behavior problems. The TRFs showed that his problems were most pronounced in the English and history class.

Information from Relevant Informants
Because of the severity of problems found on the TRFs, Gary's parents were contacted for permission for a comprehensive evaluation and were asked to complete the CBCL. Gary's total competence score on the CBCL completed by his mother was in the clinical range (below the 10th percentile). His scores on the Activities and Social scales were barely in the normal range, while his score on the School scale was in the clinical range (below the 2nd percentile). His total problem, Internalizing, and Externalizing scores were all in the clinical range (above the 90th percentile). Scores were in the clinical range on the Hostile–Withdrawal, Delinquent, Aggressive, and Hyperactive scales (above the 98th percentile), and at the clinical cutoff on the Obsessive–Compulsive scale.

School records showed that Gary had problems over much of his educational career, with poor grades and frequent detentions and suspensions for behavior problems. In the elementary grades, he had received special education services in reading as a learning disabled student, but was dropped from special education in seventh grade. His pediatrician had prescribed Ritalin for hyperactivity at age 8, which was used intermittently for several years. In an interview with the school psychologist, Gary's mother reported that he was the oldest of two children. Gary's parents were divorced and the mother had remarried, adding two stepbrothers to the family. The mother also reported the recent death of an uncle who was close to Gary.

Direct Assessment
After the TRF and CBCL have been scored and additional information has been obtained from relevant informants, the next step is usually direct assessment of the child. This involves several options that depend on the reason for referral, the age of the child, and the hypothesized nature of the problems. Use of the DOF for classroom observations would be appropriate for most school referrals, and could meet the requirement for direct observations required for special education evaluations by most states. Although norms for the total problem scores are limited to ages 5 to 14, the DOF can be used to record the on-task behavior and problems of older children in a systematic way. Use of the YSR would be appropriate if the child was at least 11 years old and not mentally retarded. An interview with the child is almost always included. Testing of cognitive ability, academic achievement, physical abnormalities, perceptual-motor skills, and speech and language functioning would depend on information already available and the referral complaints.

As part of the direct assessment, the school psychologist used the DOF to record observations of Gary in two classes. He was on-task only 25% of the time in English, in contrast to 85% in metal shop. Gary's total problem scores were substantially higher than those of two other "control" boys in the English class. The psychologist noted frequent talking, disturbing other students, restlessness, poor attention, and arguing with the teacher and peers about requirements. Prior to meeting with the psychologist, Gary completed the YSR. Gary's self-ratings produced a total competence score in the normal range, but total problem and Externalizing scores were in the clinical range (above 89th percentile). The score on the Thought Disorder scale was elevated into the clinical range (above 98th percentile). Gary scored as "sometimes true" the items, *I have thoughts that other people would think are strange* and *I do things other people think are strange,* as well as several other items on the same scale. His scores on all other scales, including the Aggressive scale, were in the normal range.

The TRF, CBCL, and YSR all showed that Gary was exhibiting behavioral/emotional problems well beyond normal limits. With this evidence in mind, the school psychologist interviewed Gary and conducted psychological and educational testing to probe further into the causes of his problems. An intelligence test showed average ability scores but below-average achievement in reading and written language. The clinical interview revealed extremely poor self-esteem, anger over the parents' divorce, problems getting along with the stepfather and stepbrothers, and unresolved grief over the death of the uncle. Gary appeared to have few friends and poor social problem-solving skills. Although Gary disliked school and was embarrassed about his poor reading ability, he was interested in vocational courses and wanted to complete high school.

Integrating Data
Comparing Data and
Formulating Conclusions

After the assessment data have been obtained, they must be integrated to form a plan of action, as shown in Figure 2. The first step is to compare data obtained from different sources via empirically based procedures. Although each instrument is tailored to a different type of informant, there are overlaps that facilitate comparisons between informants in terms of total scores, Internalizing and Externalizing scores, and scores on narrow-band scales. It may also be valuable to examine certain items across instruments, such as the items pertaining to strange behavior and strange ideas in the case of Gary. Comparisons across the various empirically based measures will identify similarities and differences. The findings from the empirically based measures must then be integrated with test results, the clinical interview, the child's history, and relevant aspects of the present environment.

After comparing data from the different sources to determine how the child appears from each perspective, the school psychologist formulates conclusions leading to an individualized conception of the child's functioning in relation to educational experience, family dynamics, and other important factors. The formulation should include hypotheses about causal factors involved in the case and the feasibility of various intervention options. Realistic goals for a treatment plan should emerge from the formulation, along with a determination by the basic staffing team as to whether the child is eligible for special education services.

The empirically based measures indicated that Gary could qualify for special education services according to the SED definition. As Table 6 shows, evidence supported several of the P.L. 94-142 criteria for SED classification:

1. Inability to learn was suggested by high scores on the Inattentive scale of the TRF.
2. Inability to build or maintain relationships was indicated by high scores on the Withdrawal scales of the CBCL and TRF.
3. Inappropriate types of behavior or feelings were indicated by the Obsessive–Compulsive, Hyperactive, Self-Destructive, and Aggressive scales of the CBCL and TRF, the Thought Disorder scale of the YSR, and strange behavior and strange ideas reported by Gary and his teachers.
4. Scores in the clinical range for total problems, Internalizing and/or Externalizing, and several narrow-band scales on the CBCL, TRF, and YSR showed problems to a marked degree of severity. The DOF total problem score was also greater for Gary than for other boys in his English class.
5. Low scores on the CBCL and TRF school scales, poor adaptive functioning on the TRF, and a low on-task score on the DOF provided evidence of adverse effects on educational performance.

Further information from parents and teachers indicated problems of hyperactivity and aggressive behavior for several years, adding evidence that Gary's problems had existed for a long period of time. Despite many attempts at behavior modification programs and prior special education services in reading, Gary was close to failing most of his academic subjects. The clinical interview between Gary and the school psychologist revealed personal and family issues in addition to Gary's more overt behavior problems. The past history and test results also suggested possible learning disabilities that certainly contributed to Gary's poor school performance. However, the test results did not meet state criteria for LD classification, and the preponderance of evidence pointed more heavily toward emotional disturbance. Gary's case thus illustrates the difficulty of separating learning and behavioral/emotional problems, particularly in the adolescent years.

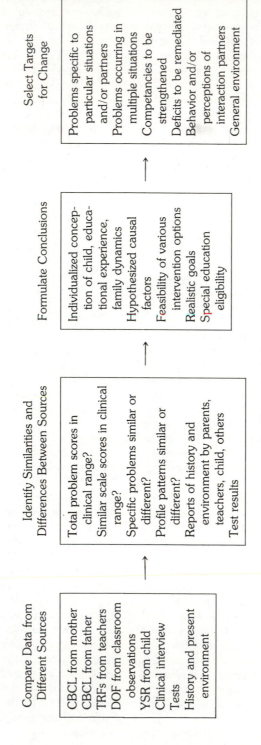

Figure 2. Integrating data.

TABLE 6 Findings of Empirically Based Assessment for the Case of Gary, Age 15

P.L. 94-142 Components of SED	CBCL	TRF	YSR	DOF
Inability to learn	—	Inattentive	—	—
Inability to build or maintain relationships	Hostile Withdrawal	Social Withdrawal	—	—
Inappropriate types of behavior or feelings	Obsessive–Compulsive Hyperactive Aggressive	Obsessive–Compulsive Self-Destructive Aggressive	Thought Disorder	—
General pervasive mood of unhappiness	—	—	—	—
Tendency to develop physical symptoms or fears	—	—	—	—
Schizophrenic	—	—	—	—
Long period of time	—	—	—	—
Marked degree	Total, Internalizing, and Externalizing scores >90th %ile Narrow-band scales >98th %ile	Total, Internalizing, and Externalizing scores >89th %ile Narrow-band scales >98th %ile	Total, Externalizing scores 89th %ile Narrow-band scales >98th %ile	Total Problem score controls
Adversely affects educational performance	School scale <2nd %ile	School scale <2nd %ile Adaptive functioning <13th %ile	—	Low on-task score

263

Selecting Targets for Change

Based on the case formulation, the school psychologist selects targets for change, such as problems occurring in relation to specific situations and/or interaction partners; problems occurring in multiple situations; competencies to be strengthened; deficits to be remediated; other people's behavior and/or perceptions that may be a source of trouble for the child; and aspects of the home and school environment that may need changing. In Gary's case, the TRFs revealed that his problems were most severe in his English and history classes, two areas that would be directly affected by his reading difficulties. He displayed fewer problems in vocational courses, on the other hand, where his interest was greater. The fact that his mother and teachers reported severe problems of hyperactivity, inattention, and poor social relations suggested that Gary continued to show clinical signs of Attention Deficit Disorder. The CBCL and clinical interview also revealed severe problems outside of school related to family dynamics and grief over the loss of a close relative. All these factors needed to be considered in the development of an appropriate treatment plan.

Implementing Interventions and Evaluating Outcomes

Selecting Interventions

Based on the integration of conclusions and selected targets for change, the next step is to develop an appropriate treatment plan. Figure 3 lists examples of interventions that are typically available to the school psychologist, although this is not meant to be an exhaustive list. The list of possible interventions highlights the fact that empirically based measures do not dictate particular placement decisions or types of treatments. Contrary to Gresham's view (1985), this an advantage rather than a disadvantage, because the results, of empirically based assessment can easily lead to different interventions, depending on the needs of the child and aspects of the environment in which an intervention takes place. Systematic selection of interventions is facilitated by empirically based assessment, as well as by advances in knowledge about the efficacy of different interventions for particular types of problems.

For Gary, an individualized education plan was developed by the basic staffing team addressing his learning problems and social-emotional needs. This included tutoring in reading and written work; emphasis on vocational training; regular consultation between the classroom teachers, special educator, and school psychologist; a behavior modification plan; social skills training; and renewal of medication for Attention Deficit Disorder. Gary was also referred to a clinical psychologist outside of school who specialized in work with adolescents and families.

Monitoring Effects

To monitor the effects of treatment, the empirically based procedures can be repeated after interventions have had time to produce results. More specialized monitoring of academic achievement and specific target behaviors and emotions may also be helpful, such as tabulations of on-task

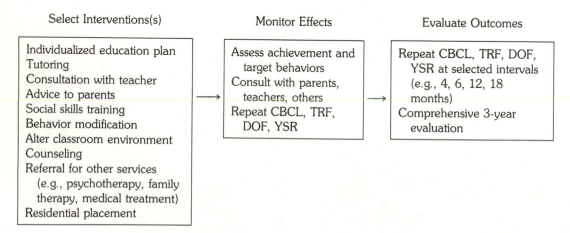

Figure 3. Implementing interventions and evaluating outcomes.

behaviors or targets of behavior modification plans, or use of scales measuring hyperactivity or depression (e.g. Goyette et al., 1978; Reynolds, Anderson, & Bartell, 1985; Reynolds, 1986). Yet if monitoring is confined to target variables, it will not reveal changes for better or worse in other areas. If the desired improvements do not occur, the interventions may need to be modified and the effects of revised approaches monitored.

Evaluating Outcomes

After the interventions have been in place for a reasonable time period or have been completed, evaluations of outcomes can be conducted at intervals such as 4, 6, 12, and 18 months. This can be done by repeating one or more of the empirically based procedures for comparison with previous assessments. In Gary's case, a follow-up was planned at the end of the school year, including TRFs from the three teachers involved in the initial referral and the newly assigned tutor, along with a CBCL from his mother. Gary's therapist also planned to obtain the YSR at the same time and summarize the results for the school psychologist. Follow-up evaluations are helpful not only to ensure that the pupil is indeed better off than before the intervention, but to help practitioners determine the typical effects of particular interventions in their caseload. For pupils in special education placements, a 3-year comprehensive reevaluation is required by law. The empirically based procedures can easily be incorporated into the reevaluation plan for comparison with results from the initial assessment.

behavioral/emotional problems and competencies. By focusing on quantitative, developmental, and situational variations in functioning, this model can help to counteract tendencies to view behavioral/emotional problems as disorders that exist in a categorical, all-or-none form. Designated as *multiaxial empirically based assessment,* the model emphasizes the importance of obtaining standardized data from multiple informants, including parents, teachers, observers, and children themselves, as well as from tests and medical diagnostic procedures. Rather than imposing a priori categories on children's problems, empirically based assessment identifies syndromes of problems that actually occur together, as seen by particular informants. The data obtained from each informant are scored on standardized profiles that provide age-based standard scores for each syndrome, as well as for competencies.

After presenting empirically based procedures for obtaining data from different sources, we outlined their relations to diagnostic categories of the DSM-III-R and the criteria for serious emotional disturbance prescribed by P.L. 94-142. We also considered overlaps between learning disabilities and behavioral/emotional problems. We demonstrated how empirically based assessment can aid in making eligibility determinations, as well as in implementing, monitoring, and evaluating the outcomes of interventions. A growing literature indicates that this approach to conceptualizing and assessing problems can improve our ways of helping children and can deal with dilemmas created by administrative criteria for eligibility.

SUMMARY AND CONCLUSIONS

We outlined an approach to behavioral, emotional, and learning problems known as "developmental psychopathology," which is the study of maladaptive deviance in relation to developmental tasks, sequences, and processes. This approach views children's functioning from the perspective of present and future developmental tasks, rather than merely as an outcome of past events. It compares children's functioning with that of their agemates in order to identify potential obstacles to development.

We presented an assessment model for developmental psychopathology that applies normative-developmental principles to the assessment of

REFERENCES

Achenbach, T. M. (1985). *Assessment and taxonomy of child and adolescent psychopathology.* Newbury Park, CA: Sage.

Achenbach, T. M. (1986). *Profile for the Direct Observation Form of the Child Behavior Checklist.* Burlington: University of Vermont, Department of Psychiatry.

Achenbach, T. M., & Edelbrock, C. (1983). *Manual for the Child Behavior Checklist and Revised Child Behavior Profile.* Burlington: University of Vermont, Department of Psychiatry.

Achenbach, T. M., & Edelbrock, C. (1986). *Manual for the Teacher's Report Form and Teacher Version of the Child Behavior Profile.* Burlington: University of Vermont, Department of Psychiatry.

Achenbach, T. M., & Edelbrock, C. (1987). *Manual for*

the Youth Self-Report and Profile. Burlington: University of Vermont, Department of Psychiatry.

Achenbach, T. M., & McConaughy, S. H. (1987). *Empirically-based assessment of child and adolescent psychopathology: Practical applications.* Newbury Park CA: Sage.

Achenbach, T. M., McConaughy, S. H., & Howell, C. (1987). Child/adolescent behavioral and emotional problems: Implications of cross-informant correlations for situational specificity. *Psychological Bulletin, 101,* 213–232.

American Psychiatric Association. (1980; 1987). *Diagnostic and statistical manual of mental disorders* (3rd ed., 1980; 3rd rev. ed., 1987). Washington, DC: Author.

Arnold, L. E., Barnebey, N., McManus, J., Smeltzer, D. J., Conrad, A., Winer, G., & Desgranges, L. (1977). Prevention by specific perceptual remediation for vulnerable first-graders. *Archives of General Psychiatry, 34,* 1279–1294.

Blalock, J. W. (1981). Persistent problems and concerns of young adults with learning disabilities. In W. Cruickshank and A. Silver (Eds.), *Bridges to tomorrow* (Vol. 2). Syracuse, NY: Syracuse University Press.

Bruininks, V. L. (1978). Peer status and personaity characteristics of learning disabled and nondisabled students. *Journal of Learning Disabilities, 11,* 484–489.

Bryan, T. H. (1974). Peer popularity of learning disabled children. *Journal of Learning Disabilities, 7,* 31–47.

Bryan, T. H. (1978). Social relationships and verbal interactions of learning disabled children. *Journal of Learning Disabilities, 11,* 107–115.

Bryan, T. H., & Bryan, J. H. (1977). The social-emotional side of learning disabilities. *Behavioral Disorders, 2,* 141–145.

Bryan, T., Donahue, M., & Pearl, R. (1981). Studies of learning disabled children's pragmatic competence. *Topics in Learning and Learning Disabilities, 1,* 29–30.

Bryan, T. H., Werner, M., & Pearl, R. (1982). Learning disabled students' conformity responses to prosocial and anti-social situations. *Learning Disability Quarterly, 5,* 344–352.

Chandler, H. N., & Jones, K. (1983a). Learning disabled or emotionally disturbed: Does it make any difference? Part I. *Journal of Learning Disabilities, 16,* 432–434.

Chandler, H. N., & Jones, K. E. (1983b). Learning disabled or emotionally disturbed: Does it make any difference? Part II. *Journal of Learning Disabilities, 16,* 561–564.

Colegrove, R., Ostrander, R., Schwartz, N., & Daniels, S. (1986, March). *Identification of emotional disturbance in children: A data-based model for schools.* Paper presented at the National Association of School Psychologists conference, Hollywood, FL.

Coolidge, F. L. (1983). WISC-R discrimination of learning-disabled and emotionally disturbed children: An intragroup and intergroup analysis. *Journal of Consulting and Clinical Psychology, 51,* 320.

Dean, R. S. (1978). Distinguishing learning-disabled and emotionally disturbed children on the WISC-R. *Journal of Consulting and Clinical Psychology, 46,* 381–382.

Dean, R. S. (1984a). Commentary on personality assessment in the schools: The special issue. *School Psychology Review, 13,* 95–98.

Dean, R. S. (1984b). On the multivariate analysis of clinical group profiles: Comment on Coolidge. *Journal of Consulting and Clinical Psychology, 52,* 306.

Edelbrock, C. (1983). Problems and issues in using rating scales to assess child personality and psychopathology. *School Psychology Review, 12,* 293–299.

Edelbrock, C., & Achenbach, T. M. (1984). The teacher version of the Child Behavior Profile: I. Boys aged 6–11. *Journal of Consulting and Clinical psychology, 52, 2,* 207–217.

Education of the Handicapped Act. (1977). *Federal Register, 42,* 42474–42518. (Amended 1981). *Federal Register, 46,* 3866.

Epstein, M., Culligan, D., & Sabatino, D. (1977). State definitions of behavior disorders. *Journal of Special Education, 11,* 417–425.

Fabian, A. A. (1955). Reading disabiity: An index of pathology. *American Journal of Orthopsychiatry, 25,* 319–326.

Fuller, G. B., & Rankin, R. E. (1984). Personality differences between learning disabled and emotionally impaired children. *School Psychology Review, 13,* 221–224.

Gajar, A. H. (1980). Characteristics across exceptional categories: EMR, LD, and ED. *Journal of Special Education, 14,* 165–173.

Goh, D. S., & Fuller, G. B. (1983). Current practices in the assessment of personality and behavior by school psychologists. *School Psychology Review, 12,* 240–243.

Goh, D. S., Teslow, C. J., & Fuller, G. B. (1981). The practice of psychological assessment among school psychologists. *Professional Psychology, 12,* 696–706.

Goyette, C. H., Conners, C. K., & Ulrich, R. F. (1978). Normative data on the Revised Conners Parent and Teacher Rating Scales. *Journal of Abnormal Child Psychology, 6,* 221–236.

Gresham, F. M. (1983). Multitrait–multimethod approach to multifactored assessment: Theoretical rationale and practical application. *School Psychology Review, 12,* 26–34.

Gresham, F. M. (1985). Behavior disorder assessment: Conceptual, definitional, and practical considerations. *School Psychology Review, 14,* 495–509.

Griffin, M. (1971). How does he feel? In E. Schloss (Ed.), *The educator's enigma: The adolescent with learning disabilities.* San Rafael, CA: Academic Therapy.

Hagin, R. A., Silver, A. A., & Kreeger, H. (1976). *TEACH: A preventive approach for potential learning disability.* New York: Walker.

Harris, J. C., King, S. L., Reifler, J. P., & Rosenberg, L. A. (1984). Emotional and learning disorders in 6–12-year-old boys attending special schools. *Jour-*

nal of the American Academy of Child Psychiatry, 23, 431–437.

Hicks, M. R., Johansson, C. B., Heinze, A. M., & Halscott, J. F. (1981). Teacher and parent checklist ratings with learning disabled, hyperactive, and emotionally disturbed children. Journal of Pediatric Psychology, 6, 43–60.

Hunter, E. J., & Johnson, L. C. (1971). Developmental and psychological differences between readers and non-readers. Journal of Learning Disabilities, 4, 572–577.

Jacobson, R. N. (1974). Learning disabilities and juvenile delinquency: A demonstrated relationship. In R. E. Weber (Ed.), Handbook on learning disabilities. Englewood Cliffs, NJ: Prentice-Hall.

Keldgord, R. (1969). Brain damage and delinquency. A question and a challenge. Academic Therapy, 4, 93–99.

Keogh, B. K., Tchir, C., & Windeguth-Behn, A. (1974). Teachers' perceptions of educationally high risk children. Journal of Learning Disabilities, 7, 43–50.

Klein, D. C., & Seligman, M. E. (1976). Reversal of performance deficits and perceptual deficits in learned helplessness and depression. Journal of Abnormal Psychology, 85, 11–26.

Mattison, R. E., Humphrey, F. J., & Kales, S. N. (1986). An objective evaluation of special class placement of elementary schoolboys with behavior problems. Journal of Abnormal Child Psychology, 14, 251–262.

Mattison, R. E., Humphrey, F. J., Kales, S. N., Hanford, H. A., Finkenbinder, R. L., & Hernit, R. C. (1986). Psychiatric background and diagnoses of children evaluated for special class placement. Journal of the American Academy of Child Psychiatry, 25, 514–520.

Mauser, A. J. (1974). Learning disabilities and delinquent youth. Academic Therapy, 6, 389–402.

McConaughy, S. H. (1985). Using the Child Behavior Checklist and related instruments in school-based assessments of children. School Psychology Review, 14, 479–494.

McConaughy, S. H. (1986). Social competence and behavioral problems of learning disabled boys aged 12–16. Journal of Learning Disabilities, 19, 101–106.

McConaughy, S. H., & Achenbach, T. M. (1988). Practical guide for the Child Behavior Checklist and related materials. Burlington: University of Vermont, Department of Psychiatry.

McConaughy, S. H., & Achenbach, T. M. (1989). Empirically based assessment of serious emotional disturbance. Journal of School Psychology, 27, 91–117.

McConaughy, S. H., & Ritter, D. (1986). Social competence and behavioral problems of learning disabled boys aged 6–11. Journal of Learning Disabilities, 19, 39–45.

Meltzer, L. J., Levine, M. D., Karniski, W., Palfrey, J. S., & Clarke, S. (1984). An analysis of the learning styles of adolescent delinquents. Journal of Learning Disabilities, 17, 600–608.

Morgan, D. I. (1979). Prevalence and types of handicapping conditions found in juvenile correctional insti-

tutions: A national survey. Journal of Special Education, 33, 283–295.

Mulligan, W. A. (1969). A study of dyslexia and delinquency. Academic Therapy, 4, 117–187.

Owen, F. W., Adams, P. A., Forrest, T., Stolz, L. J., & Fisher, S. (1971). Learning disorders in children: Sibling studies. Monographs of the Society for Research in Child Development, 36 (Serial No. 144).

Pihl, R. O., & McLarnon, L. D. (1984). Learning disabled children as adolescents. Journal of Learning Disabilities, 17, 96–100.

Quay, H. D. (1983). A dimensional approach to behavior disorder: The revised Behavior Problem Checklist. School Psychology Review, 12, 244–249.

Reynolds, W. M. (1986). A model for the screening and identification of depressed children and adolescents in school settings. Professional School Psychology, 1, 117–129.

Reynolds, W. M., Anderson, G., & Bartell, N. (1985). Measuring depression in children: A multimethod assessment investigation. Journal of Abnormal Child Psychology, 13, 513–526.

Ritter, D. R. (1978). Emotional development of children with specific learning disabilities. Paper presented at the annual meeting of the Vermont Association for Learning Disabilities, White River Junction, VT.

Rosenberg, B. S., & Gaier, E. L. (1977). The self concept of the adolescent with learning disabilities. Adolescence, 12, 489–498.

Rutter, M., Tizard, J., & Whitmore, K. (1970). Education, health, and behavior. London: Longman.

Rutter, M., & Yule, W. (1975). The concept of specific reading retardation. Journal of Child Psychology and Psychiatry, 16, 181–197.

Sabatino, D. A., & Mauser, A. J. (Eds.). (1978). Specialized education in today's secondary schools. Boston: Allyn and Bacon.

Seligman, M. E. (1974). Depression and learned helplessness. In R. J. Friedman & M. N. Katz (Eds.), The psychology of depression: Contemporary theory and research. Washington: Winston-Wiley.

Siegel, E. (1974). The exceptional child grows up. New York: E. P. Dutton.

Sipperstein, G. N., Bopp, M. J., & Bak, J. J. (1978). Social status of learning disabled children. Journal of Learning Disabilities, 11, 98–102.

Slenkovich, J. E. (1983). PL 94-142 as applied to DSM III diagnoses. Cupertino, CA: Kinghorn Press.

Tallmadge, G. K., Gamel, N. N., Munson, R. G., & Hanley, T. V. (1985). Special study on terminology (Report No. MV-85-01; SRA Technologies, Mountain View, CA, Contract No. 300-84-0144). Washington, DC: U.S. Department of Education.

Tharinger, D. J., Laurent, J., and Best, L. R. (1986). Classification of children referred for emotional and behavioral problems: A comparison of PL 94-142 SED criteria, DSM III, and the CBCL system. Journal of School Psychology, 24, 111–121.

Underwood, R. (1976). Learning disability as a predisposing cause of criminality. Canada's Mental Health, 24, 11–16.

Wong, B. Y. L., & Wong, R. (1980). Role-taking skills in

normal achieving and learning disabled children. *Learning Disability Quarterly, 3,* 11–18.

Wynne, M. E., & Brown, R. T. (1984). Assessment of high incidence learning disorders: Isolating measures with high discriminant ability. *School Psychology Review, 13,* 231–237.

Ysseldyke, J. E., & Algozzine, B. (1981). Diagnostic classification decisions as a function of referral information. *Journal of Special Education, 15,* 429–435.

Zinkus, P. O., Gottlieb, M. J., & Zinkus, C. B. (1979). The learning-disabled juvenile delinquent: A case for early intervention of perceptually handicapped children. *American Journal of Occupational Therapy, 33,* 180–184.

12

IMPLICATIONS OF NEUROPSYCHOLOGICAL RESEARCH FOR SCHOOL PSYCHOLOGY

JEFFREY W. GRAY

Ball State University

RAYMOND S. DEAN

Ball State University and
Indiana University School of Medicine

Our knowledge of the correspondence between the functioning of the human brain and behavior has increased more in the past two decades than in any other time in history (e.g., Dean, 1982b). A growing data base portraying a direct relationship between complex patterns of behavior and mechanisms of the brain has led a number of authors to argue for the utility of a neuropsychological perspective in school psychology (D'Amato, Gray, & Dean, in press; Gaddes, 1975; Hynd & Obrzut, 1981b; Hynd, 1981; Rourke, 1976; Strom, Gray, & Dean, & Fischer, in press). More generally, both the clinical research and the more basic study of underlying neuropsychological processes has implications for the practice of school psychology.

Consistent with research in the area, recent surveys suggest that school psychologists have become sensitive to the value of a neuropsycho-logical foundation (Hynd, Quackenbush, & Obrzut, 1980; Ramage, 1979). In conjunction with the school psychologist's strengths in assessment, learning, cognition, and educational intervention, neuropsychology offers a framework from which to integrate behavioral and educational information. Along these lines, a number of investigators have presented data favoring a neuropsychological approach in the differential diagnosis of cognitive disorders in school-aged children (Dean, 1982a; Fischer, Wenck, Schurr, & Ellen, 1985; Fisk & Rourke, 1979; Gaddes, 1975; Hynd, 1981; Hynd & Obrzut, 1981a).

A neuropsychological orientation may also provide the school psychologist with a means of reconciling psychoeducational assessment (Gaddes, 1975). Indeed, a neuropsychological framework, with its emphasis on brain–behavior relationships, has been shown to be of considerable value in integrating clinical information. Such an approach to assessment seems to hold unrealized potential with learning disordered children who present a unique challenge to school psychologists. Clearly, the nebulous placement categories in the schools linked with the rather primitive diagnostic criteria offer the school psychologist a meager foundation for practice (see Dean, 1977, 1983; Reynolds, 1981a, 1981b).

Neuropsychology has its roots in the fields of behavioral neurology and both clinical and experimental psychology (Boring, 1942; Reitan, 1976). This marriage between neurology and psychology is reflected in the assessment practices (Boring, 1942; Dean, 1978a; Reitan, 1976) and batteries (Golden, Hammeke, & Purisch, 1978; Reitan, 1969; Smith, 1975) used to infer neurological functioning. Indeed, most neuropsychological batteries assess a wide range of language, sensorimotor, perceptual, cognitive, and emotional factors (Boll, 1981; Reitan, 1974; Reitan & Davison, 1974). Dean (1985) has recently stressed the use of such a broad band of neuropsychological measures in the assessment of both childhood and adult neurological and psychiatric disorders. It seems clear that assumptions made on the basis of a single measure of organic functioning are tenuous at best (Reitan, 1966). Neuropsychological assessment has gone beyond the differential diagnosis of brain damage that gave birth to the speciality. It seems clear that the interpretation of neuropsychological data for an individual must be made within the context of patterns of strengths and weaknesses in conjunction with cutting scores of normal performance (Baron, 1978; Reitan, 1974).

Historically, neuropsychological assessment in the United States has focused on the identification and localization of cortical dysfunction (e.g., Boll, 1974; Dean, 1985; Reitan, 1974). Using standardized measures, the major objective of neuropsychological assessment continues to be to understand brain functioning from elements of behavior. Indeed, such an approach has been shown to be valuable both in diagnosing childhood neurological disorders and defining the behavioral effects of brain impairment (e.g., Rutter, 1982).

Neuropsychological assessment grew out of the medical communities' need to objectify the behavioral consequences of neurological dysfunction (Reitan, 1966). The post–World War II years offered a large patient population in which the behavioral effects of localized brain lesions could be studied and various measures validated as predictors of dysfunction. In general, this has been the paradigm used to portray the sensitivity of standardized measures to various types of brain damage (Halstead & Settlage, 1943; Hunt, 1943; Reitan, 1955). Clearly, the emphasis on predicting and localizing cortical damage has a rich historical base. Moreover, this early empirical/quantitative approach is reflected in most current neuropsychological batteries utilized in the United States. Indeed, the individual measures included in the most widely used neuropsychological battery (Halstead-Reitan Neuropsychological Battery; HRNB; Reitan, 1969) were included because of their ability to discriminate between normal controls and patients with documented neuropathology (Dean, 1985). Therefore, underlying functions measured by individual tests may often be obscure.

Many of the measures routinely administered by school psychologists (e.g., Wechsler Intelligence Scales, Minnesota Multiphasic Personality Inventory, Wide Range Achievement Test, etc.) are included as part of the neuropsychological examination. However, the neuropsychological interpretation of these data may differ drastically. The neuropsychological interpretation of these measures are based more on research that has examined the correspondence between these measures and the functional integrity of the brain than on school-based outcomes (Dean, 1979; Jortner, 1965; Pascal & Suttel, 1951). The interpretation of neuropsychological data with children must be made cautiously in light of the neurological differences between children and adults (Dean, 1985). Indeed, inferences drawn about specific cortical dysfunction for children are more tentative than those with adults because of the potential contributions of developmental and environmental variables (see Dean, 1985). Along these lines, it is important to note that a good deal of what we know about the neuropsychology of children comes from adult data. Thus, we must generalize adult findings to children with caution. With this caution in mind, the present chapter provides a focused review of clinical and basic research efforts in neuropsychology which hold implications for school psychology.

LEARNING DISABILITIES

It has become clear that children with learning disorders are a heterogeneous group (e.g., Rourke, 1975, 1978, 1983). This interpretation is consistent with a large corpus of data showing a lack of consistency in presenting symptoms for children identified as learning disabled (e.g., Rourke, 1975, 1978, 1983). Learning disability symptoms overlap with a number of other diagnostics. Indeed, research that has examined children diagnosed with various learning, behavioral, emotional, and neurological disorders has shown them to share many of the same symptoms (e.g., hyperactivity, attentional deficits, etc.) (Rattan & Dean, 1987). In addition, little evidence exists which implicates a single underlying cause for diverse learning problems (e.g., reading versus arithmetic, etc.). The general force of these data give one to question the utility of considering learning disabilities as a single syndrome (Rattan & Dean, 1987).

With its emphasis on cognitive–cortical relationships, neuropsychology has been proposed as an aid in understanding children's learning disorders (e.g., D'Amato et al., in press; Gaddes, 1983; Obrzut & Hynd, 1983; Rourke, 1981; Strom et al., in press). Consistent with this notion, it has been argued that a broad-band neuropsychological battery (e.g., Halstead–Reitan Neuropsychological Battery) allows consideration of a wider spectrum of functions than are accounted for in the typical psychoeducational assessment (Dean, 1982a, 1985, 1986b; Hynd & Obrzut, 1981b). From this point of view, neuropsychological assessment is seen to provide high-utility information that goes beyond the traditional approach of identifying children's learning problems.

Research which has examined the unique contribution of the Halstead–Reitan Neuropsychological Battery (HRNB) over that provided by a traditional psychoeducational assessment of children's learning problems has shown that only 10% of the functions measured by the HRNB were redundant with subtests of the Wechsler Intelligence Scale for Children–Revised (D'Amato et al., in press). The area of overlap between the two measures was attributed to a general cognitive reasoning component underlying each battery. In the same report, D'Amato et al. (in press) considered the unique contribution of the HRNB and WISC-R when subjected to factor analysis. In

accord with previous findings with adults (e.g., Russell, 1982), a six-factor solution emerged. Of interest to the present discussion, measures of the HRNB loaded on three unique factors involving spatial speed of operations, spatial memory, and neurological development. The combined findings of this investigation were seen as lending support to potential clinical and research utility of the HRNB when assessing learning disabled children in the schools.

In a related investigation, Strom et al. (in press) examined the incremental validity of the Halstead–Reitan over the Wechsler Intelligence Scale for Children–Revised (WISC-R) in predicting the Wide Range Achievement Test (WRAT) performance of children presenting with learning disorders. Subtests of the WISC-R alone and in combination with the Halstead–Reitan Neuropsychological Battery were regressed on each of the three WRAT subtests (Reading, Spelling, and Arithmetic). Results showed that the addition of the HRNB measures to information gleaned from subtests of the WISC-R significantly increased the amount of variability accounted for in each area of school achievement. Indeed, the addition of the HRNB to the WISC-R improved prediction of achievement as much as 30%. In an effort to examine school achievement overall, Strom et al. (in press) submitted these data to a canonical analysis. The results indicated that the HRNB overlapped with some 21% more of the WRAT achievement than did the WISC-R alone. It was apparent from these data that not only does the HRNB offer unique information over traditional psychoeducational assessment practices, but neuropsychological information also improves the school psychologists' ability to predict achievement in children referred for learning difficulties. Specifically, those HRNB tests purported to measure verbal auditory discrimination, nonverbal memory, mental flexibility, and manual dexterity of the nondominant hand were the most salient unique predictors of achievement.

With the recognition of the heterogeneous nature of our present learning disability classification and a growing concern for the diagnosis and treatment of these children have come attempts to subtype learning disorders with neuropsychological measures. More clearly defined subtypes would indeed improve the psychologists' ability to diagnose, treat, and consider individual children's prognosis (Denckla, 1972). With this in mind, a number of investigators have begun to embrace a neuropsychological approach in classifying learning disorders, (e.g., Denckla, 1972; Doehring & Hoshko, 1977; Fisk & Rourke, 1979; Mattis, French, & Rapin, 1975; Morris, Blashfield, & Satz, 1981). The majority of these studies have utilized a wide range of measures, most frequently tests of the HRNB have been augmented with other tests of specific function (Rattan & Dean, 1987). Generally speaking, the two major approaches used to identify specific subtypes of learning disorders have involved either clinical-rational or multivariate statistical techniques.

Based on a priori clinical criteria for inclusion, investigators have attempted to identify subtypes of learning disorders (e.g., Denckla, 1972; Mattis et al., 1975). In one early study, Mattis, French, and Rapin (1975) considered subtypes of learning deficits based on the primary area of impairment. Mattis et al. (1975) considered developmental language deficiencies, motor–speech difficulties with fine and grapho–motor disorders, and visual–spatial processing deficits to be the underlying impairment groups. Interestingly, 90% of the subjects met the clinical criteria for at least one of these three subtypes. A subsequent study aimed at statistical cross validation indicated that correct classification was achieved with 78% accuracy (Mattis, 1978). Consistent with the findings of Mattis et al. (1975), Denckla (1972) hypothesized three distinct clinical subtypes referred to as a specific language disability, specific visuospatial disability, and the dyscontrol syndrome. While the similarities in subtypes between these two studies is interesting, it is important to note that only 30% of a sample of learning disabled children met Denckla's (1972) criteria for one of the three groups. Thus, as many as 70% of the learning disabled children in this study could not be classified on the basis of the a priori criteria. These findings are reflective of the problems with clinical approaches to subtyping. Indeed, the reliability, validity, and generalizability of subtypes established through clinical means are often questionable. Moreover, these subtypes may be biased as a result of preexisting assumptions about specific deficits that accompany learning disabilities.

The identification of specific learning disability subtypes by empirical methods has relied on multivariate statistical procedures. Q-factor analytic procedure is one such method which allows the examination of the relationship between subjects rather than the analysis of correlations between tests. This data-driven classification method allows discrimination of groups on the basis of factor loadings of specific neuropsychological measures. One of the earliest investigations utilizing this procedure was conducted by Doehring and Hoshko (1977). Small sample size not withstanding, these investigators identified three subgroups of reading problem children composed of language disorders, phonological deficits, and intersensory integration difficulties. In an attempt to examine the stability of these subtypes, Doehring and Hoshko (1977) administered the same measures to groups of learning disabled and mentally retarded children. Results of this cross-validation attempt indicated that two of the three subtypes remained consistent across disability samples. Using larger samples and a broader band of neuropsychological measures, Petrauskas and Rourke (1979) identified three subtypes of impaired readers from those referred for neuropsychological assessment. The first group was characterized by impaired language abilities and normal visual–spatial processing and eye–hand coordination. A second subtype presented with sequencing difficulties and finger identification problems. The final group was identified by receptive and expressive language problems and impaired eye–hand coordination. Thus the results of the Doehring and Hoshko (1977) and the Fisk and Rourke (1979) studies suggest reliable subtypes of learning problems can be identified.

In an attempt to examine the developmental nature of these subtypes, Fisk and Rourke (1979) administered a neuropsychological battery to children at three different age levels (9–10 years, 11–12 years, and 13–14 years). Q-factor analysis of the children's performance produced three developmentally distinct subtypes. The subtype most indicative of the youngest group was characterized by problems in finger identification, difficulty in the perception of numbers written on the fingertips, and impaired auditory–verbal processing and psycholinguistic skills. A second group exhibited moderate to severe impairment in auditory–verbal processing with visual–perceptual and visual–spatial abilities within normal limits. The oldest subtype clearly portrayed a reading deficit similar to the first subtype but with more severe impairment in the perception of numbers written on the fingertips. In sum, 80% of the subjects met criteria for inclusion in one of the three groups. The results of this investigation suggest that childrens' learning problems differ as a function of chronological age and corresponding neurological development.

More recently has come the application of cluster analysis to the subtyping of children's learning disorders. Similar to a Q-factor procedure, cluster analysis attempts to match subjects according to their pattern of responses among measures so as to increase the homogenity within the groups and decrease the overlap between groups. Using this technique, Morris et al. (1981) reported five reliable clusters or subtypes of learning disabled children. A cross-validation indicated that less than 20% of the sample was misclassified when these clustering procedures were used. Interestingly, these cluster subgroups were similar to those found with Q-factoring techniques.

Of interest to the present discussion, there appears to be similarity in the learning disability subtypes across studies. Consistently, learning disabled children have been grouped on the basis of language deficiencies, visual–spatial processing deficits, and auditory processing deficits. Such consistency lends support to the generalizability of these learning disability subtypes.

Neuropsychological classification has also been attempted for children who present with specific academic deficits (e.g., reading or arithmetic disorders) (e.g., Rourke & Strang, 1983). For example, Rourke and Strang (1983) recently attempted to subtype children's arithmetical difficulties. The results of a Q-factor analysis with neuropsychological measures was interpreted as showing two distinct subtypes. The first group was characterized by normal visual–spatial and visual–perceptual abilities and impaired verbal and auditory–perceptual abilities. In contrast, the second group showed intact auditory–perceptual and verbal skills and deficits in visual–spatial and visual–perceptual processing. Thus, it appears that even within specific academic areas different patterns of neuropsychological impairment may underlie poor performance.

The findings of the investigations above, taken together, suggest that a number of consistent subtypes of learning disabilities may exist. Indeed, a number of impaired neuropsychological constellations have been shown to correspond to different learning problems. Clearly, such findings lead one to question the current diagnosis and treatment of learning disabilities as if it were a single nosological category. Future research must continue to address the changing neurological dysfunction that may be concomitant with development.

LATERALIZATION OF CEREBRAL FUNCTIONS

Scientists have long been interested in relating behavior to the functioning of specific areas of the brain. Indeed, as early as the nineteenth century, Jackson (1874) hypothesized that there were two different, yet interrelated modes of cognitive processing which followed hemispheric lines of the brain. In support of earlier neuroanatomical research, Jackson (1874) argued that language/verbal processing was served by the left hemisphere of the brain, whereas the right hemisphere was more adept at visual spatial processing. Consistent with these early arguments, recent research suggests that for most right-handed and many left-handed persons, linguistic functions are served by the left hemisphere (e.g., Gazzaniga, 1970), and functions of the right cerebral hemisphere of the brain are more adept at processing visual–spatial information (Sperry, Gazzaniga, & Bogen, 1969).

Investigations with normal subjects over the last two decades have further refined our understanding of the functioning of each cerebral hemisphere (Milner, 1971; Witelson,1 976). In general, it seems that the left hemisphere is better prepared to process information in the analytical, temporal, or sequential fashion necessary for the production and decoding of language (Gruber & Segalowitz, 1977). In contrast, the right hemisphere has been shown to be prepared to consider information of a holistic or simultaneous nature. This mode of processing has been shown to be of high utility in considering parallel information of a spatial nature (Bogen & Gazzaniga, 1965).

Concomitant with early findings of hemispheric differences came an interest in the relationship between children's learning problems and neurological abnormalities (Jackson, 1874/1932; Orton, 1937). Orton (1937) attributed a number of childhood language difficulties to a failure of one cerebral hemisphere to achieve dominance over the other. He argued that many of the processing problems these children suffer relate to the failure of one hemisphere to establish functional superiority for language. Although this early notion seems rather simplistic by present standards, numerous attempts have been made to portray the learning disabled child from this perspective (e.g., Dean, 1979; Hynd, Obrzut, Weed, & Hynd, 1979).

A number of techniques (e.g., dichotic listening and visual half-field paradigms) have been offered to assess language lateralization. Investigators have stressed the clinical utility of a dichotic listening paradigm in assessing cerebral laterality in children (e.g., Hynd & Obrzut, 1977). Within this model, subjects are presented with paired stimuli simultaneously to both ears. Subsequently, the subject is administered a memory task (recognition or recall) involving items that they heard previously. Ear dominance for a particular stimulus is determined on the basis of the number of items correctly remembered.

The utility of dichotic listening and split visual field assessment comes about because of the underlying physiology of the human visual and auditory systems. In general, the dominant hemisphere for a particular auditory or visual stimulus has been shown to produce faster and more accurate recognition than the other cerebral hemisphere (i.e., visual half field or auditory). This being the case, it is concluded that the cerebral hemisphere opposite the more proficient visual field or ear has a more specialized function for that type of stimulus. For example, a right-ear (REA) or right-visual-field (right VHF) advantage is expected for verbal stimuli if the left hemisphere is dominant for language.

Returning to Orton's (1937) early notions, it would be expected that children with reading and language difficulties would show less of the normal right-sided advantage (i.e., REA and right VHF) for verbal information if they lacked normal left-hemispheric dominance for language. This is the case, because language-related tasks are served by the left hemisphere of the brain. Contrary to this hypothesis, however, the majority of studies utilizing a dichotic listening paradigm have found the normal right-ear advantage for dyslexic (Sparrow & Satz, 1970; Witelson, 1977) and learning disabled children (e.g., Hynd et al., 1979). Taken together, these findings suggest that similar to normals, learning disabled children as a group have the left cerebral hemisphere specialized for language when presented auditorily.

A related line of research has examined the developmental aspects of ear asymmetry for learning disordered children compared to matched control groups (Bakker, 1973; Hynd et al., 1979; Satz, 1976; Satz, Rardin, & Ross, 1971; Sparrow & Satz, 1970). Again, these data suggest a right-ear advantage for both normal and learning disabled children. Moreover, little support exists for an interaction of ear advantage with the child's chronological age. Thus, these data do not support a developmental lag hypothesis in language lateralization for learning disabled children.

In contrast to findings with a dichotic listening paradigm, investigations examining the language lateralization for children with learning disorders have shown a less pronounced right-VHF advantage for language learning disabled children when compared to normal controls (Kershner, 1977; Marcel, Katz, & Smith, 1974; Marcel & Rajan, 1975; McKeever & VanDeventer, 1975). McKeever and VanDeventer (1975) compared the VHF performance of nine dyslexic children and a like number of normal cohorts. While under the unilateral presentation (i.e., stimuli presented either to the left or the right side but not both simultaneously) the learning disabled children showed a less consistent right-VHF advantage, they showed a normal right VHF advantage when stimuli were presented bilaterally (stimuli presented to the right and left sides simultaneously). At best, the findings cited thus far offer tentative support for a confused laterality of visually presented verbal material in learning disordered children.

In the same report as cited above, McKeever and VanDeventer (1975) also presented subjects with verbal stimuli via both a dichotic listening procedure and a visual half-field paradigm. Consistent with previous findings, subjects showed the normal right-ear advantage and a reduction in lateralization for stimuli presented visually. In a related investigation, Tomlinson-Keasey and Kelly (1979) replicated the finding of less consistent visual half-field performance for learning problem children. Taken together, these reports suggest a less consistent left-hemispheric specialization for linguistic material when presented visually.

Another avenue of research that has examined Orton's (1937) notions has focused on the relationship between learning problems and inconsistent laterality preference (e.g., handedness, etc.). Because the left hemisphere of the brain is dominant for language and motor functions right of midline are served by the same hemisphere, it had been suggested that the inconsistency in laterality preference for tasks may be a behavioral expression of the same confusion at the cortical level. With this overview as a back drop, numerous investigators have examined simple hand preference as a measure of cerebral laterality (see Dean, 1981, 1984). Although the simplicity of such a paradigm is appealing, simple handedness does not seem to relate directly to the lateralization of language (Dean, 1982a; Kinsbourne & Hiscock, 1977). Therefore, it is not surprising to find inconsistencies in investigations examining the concomitance between left-mixed handedness and children's learning problems. Indeed, Dunlop, Dunlop, and Fenelon (1973) found that simple handedness accounted for an insignificant portion of the variability in verbal dichotic listening performance.

Recently, a number of investigators have utilized a multifactor measure of lateral preference. Dean (1981, 1984) has argued that lateral preference is a complex multifactor variable and as such simple handedness may be an inadequate measure. In one investigation, Dean, Schwartz, and Smith (1981) reported a clear relationship between inconsistent lateralization of visually guided performance and childhood learning problems. However, when simple hand preference was examined in the same study, no significant difference existed between learning disabled children and normal controls. Similarly, Dean (1979) showed that learning disabled children with more salient verbal than nonverbal skills were more inconsistently lateralized than those children presenting with similar verbal and nonverbal abilities or verbal skills less than nonverbal functioning. Dean (1979) interpreted these results as supporting a deficit in the integration of visually based verbal strategies.

Recently, it has become clear that the relationship between children's learning problems and inconsistent lateralization of language is a most complex one (Dean, 1981). This is evident in the inconsistent findings across measurement paradigms. Indeed, present data support normal language lateralization for learning disabled children when measured in an auditory fashion, but less secure or confused language lateralization when stimuli are presented visually. Although these data appear contradictory, Beaumont and Rugg (1978) have interpreted such findings as reflecting a functional disassociation in visual and verbal systems which covary with the degree of hemispheric lateralization. Thus, many learning disabled children may experience problems in the integration of perceptual (visual) and verbal/cognitive strategies (Dean, 1979; Hines & Satz, 1974; Levy, 1969).

It appears that we are far from an agreement on the role that cerebral dominance plays in learning disabilities (Dean, 1981, 1984). Therefore, the inclusion of measures of cerebral laterality as a component of psychoeducational assessment with children referred for learning problems has less than empirical support. Clearly, it is important for the school psychologist to be aware of the many practical assessment and complex theoretical issues before considering such data in the assessment of children's learning disorders (Gray & Dean, in press).

CHILDREN'S PSYCHIATRIC DISORDERS

The major focus in the neuropsychological study of psychiatric disorders has centered around differential diagnosis (Dean, 1985). Indeed, the majority of referrals for neuropsychological examination in psychiatric settings seek to distinguish between functional and organic psychiatric disorders. However, this distinction is not as clear as was once assumed. Although functional psychiatric disorders have often been linked to psychosocial stressors, available evidence indicates that biochemical and structural (e.g., Andreasen, Olsen, Dennert, & Smith, 1982) neurological abnormalities exist for a number of functional psychiatric disorders.

Concomitant with an interest in the biomedical aspects of functional psychiatric disorders has come an interest in cognitive–neuropsychological aspects of specific adult and childhood disorders (Dean, 1985). Although a great majority of research in this area has focused on adult psychopathology, research has begun to implicate neuropsychological variables as contributing factors in childhood and adolescent psychiatric disorders (Hertzig & Birch, 1968; Seidel, Chadwick, & Rutter, 1975). Indeed, Hertzig and Birch (1968) reported that some 34% of a sample of adolescents presenting with psychiatric symptoms had some form of neuropsychological impairment.

More recently, Tramontana, Sherrets, and Golden (1980) reported that more than 60% of the child and adolescent psychiatric patients admitted to a large psychiatric hospital displayed impairment on the HRNB. Of interest, these psychiatric inpatients had a negative history for neurological symptoms as well as an unremarkable clinical neurological examinations. Consistent with these findings, Rutter (1977) also offered evidence of neuropsychological impairment for child psychiatric patients despite the fact that they had unremarkable neurological histories and examinations.

With the publication of more objective criteria for psychiatric diagnosis (American Psychiatric Association, 1980; Feighner, Robins, & Guze, 1972; Spitzer, Endicott, & Robins, 1977) and advances in the neurological understanding of functional mental disorders (Andreasen et al., 1982) investigators have begun to reexamine the neuropsychology of psychiatric disorders. Many of the studies in this area have focused on the utility of neuropsychological assessment in the differential diagnosis of various adult psychiatric disorders. Although problems exist in translating conclusions for adults to children, schizophrenic and primary affective disorders are considered as the same disorder without regard for the age at onset (e.g., DSM III, 1980). Moreover, criteria for nosological inclusion is the same for both adults and children (Dean, 1985).

The majority of the research in this area has focused on schizophrenia (e.g., Dean, Gray, & Seretny, 1987; Nasrallah, Keelor, VanSchroeder, & McCalley-Whitters, 1981; Piran, Bigler, & Cohen, 1982). Schizophrenic patients as a group have been shown to have diffuse neuropsychological dysfunction and a relatively greater impairment on measures of left frontotemporal functioning (Dean, 1985). Recently, Dean, Gray, and Seretny (1987) compared medical control patients with a like number of schizophrenics and primary affective depressives on the tests of the Wechsler Scale. Of interest, these data showed schizophrenic patients to have relative deficits in verbal abstraction, short-term memory for verbal information, and comprehension. Moreover, a profile analysis indicated that schizophrenics could be differentiated from medical and depressed patients on verbal subtests. Using a broad band of neuropsychological measures, Taylor and Abrams (1984) found similar impairments in patients presenting with schizophrenia. When taken together, these findings implicate dysfunction in the left temporal region of the brain (Milner, 1962). Interestingly, these results are consistent with previous research showing functional (e.g., Abrams & Taylor, 1982; Flor-Henry, 1976) and structural (Golden, Graber, Coffman, Berg, Newlin, & Bloch, 1981; Nasrallah, McCalley-Whitters, & Jacoby, 1982) central nervous system abnormalities in schizophrenia.

A more recent focus in the study of the neuropsychological foundations of psychiatric disorders has been on patients with primary affective disorders (depression). In a recent study, Dean et al. (1987) reported depressives to have relative deficits in long-term nonverbal memory and visual–spatial construction. Both of these cognitive functions have been considered to be sensitive to right temporal–parietal dysfunction of the brain. In a related investigation using the Halstead-Reitan Neuropsychological Battery, Gray, Rattan, & Dean (in press) found depressed patients to have right-hemispheric impairment. Such localized dysfunction was implicated in that depressed patients performed within normal limits and did not differ from normal controls on neuropsychological measures of left-hemispheric and general neuropsychological functioning. These studies are consistent with the often hypothesized right-hemispheric impairment in depressive disorders (Dean et al., 1987; Flor-Henry, 1976, 1977; Gray, Dean, Rattan, & Cramer, in press; Gray, Dean, D'Amato, & Rattan, in press; Gray, Rattan, & Dean, in press).

Importantly, it seems that the interpretation of right-hemisphere dysfunction for primary affective depressives seems to be consistent across instrumentation. For example, Flor-Henry (1976) reported a greater probability of an abnormal decrease in right-hemispheric electroencephalographic activity when depressed patients performed right-hemispheric tasks.

As mentioned above, neuropsychological assessment has often been seen as having utility in the differential diagnosis of functional psychiatric disorders. With this in mind, Gray et al. (in press) examined the utility of the HRNB in differential diagnosis. In this study, the HRNB was administered to primary affective depressives, undiagnosed psychiatric admissions, and normal controls. Contrasts between the groups showed that depressives differed from normals only on tasks seen to measure right-hemispheric functioning, while the mixed psychiatric patients differed from normals on all the HRNB measures. Further comparisons between psychiatric groups showed them to differ only on left-hemispheric measures, with the mixed psychiatric group performing more poorly than the depressives. Results from a stepwise discriminant analysis indicated that on the basis of neuropsychological information alone, depressives could be differentiated from normals and mixed psychiatric patients with clinical levels of accuracy. Gray et al. (in press) interpreted these results as lending support for the utility of neuropsychological measures as potential diagnostic markers of psychiatric disorders. Moreover, recent research suggests that neuropsychological results may hold implications for the treatment and prognosis of primary affective depression (Woods & Short, 1985).

A somewhat different line of research has suggested an overrepresentation of mixed lateral preference patterns in various groups of psychotics (e.g., Flor-Henry, 1977; Gur, 1977; Lishman & McMeekan, 1976; Nasrallah, McCalley-Whitters, & Kuperman, 1982; Walker & Birch, 1970).

Recently, Dean and Smith (1981) offered evidence of a correspondence between personality dimensions of the 16 PF and lateral preference patterns for normal young adults. In this two-study report, less stable, more left-oriented motoric preferences were related to higher levels of anxiety, emotional instability, and lower frustration tolerance. In a related investigation, Dean, Schwartz, and Hua (in press) offered evidence showing confused lateralization of schizophrenics on tasks requiring visually guided movement and visual preference. Interestingly, in both these studies general handedness accounted for little of the variability in emotional functioning.

Several investigations have offered tentative data favoring a relationship between confused lateralization and a number of childhood psychiatric disorders (Blau, 1977; Hicks & Pellegrini, 1978; Orme, 1970). Similar to findings with adults, higher levels of anxiety, emotional instability, and a lower tolerance for frustration were found concomitant with confused lateralization in children (Blau, 1977; Dean & Smith, 1981; Hicks & Pellegrini, 1978). Although these findings are interesting, conclusions regarding the etiological contribution of confused cerebral dominance in emotional disturbance are tenuous. This is true because a potential interaction exists between confused lateralization, aberrant behavior patterns, and perinatal brain insult (e.g., Satz, 1972). Indeed, Satz (1972) has argued that left handedness (inconsistent lateral preference) may result from either a genetic predisposition or perinatal insult. In the later case, Satz (1972) argued that trauma to the neonate may result in a pathological cerebral shift.

Although the majority of these findings are based on adult patients, it seems clear that a better understanding of the neuropsychology of psychiatric disorders will aid the psychologist in making diagnostic decisions and screening. Indeed, the school psychologist is often called upon to make a preliminary differential diagnosis. Research in the neuropsychology of psychiatric disorders would seem to have pertinence in both differential diagnosis and the future understanding of these disorders. For the school psychologist, using a neuropsychological approach may be useful in placement decisions and in the subsequent development of remedial programs with emotionally disturbed children.

HEAD INJURIES IN CHILDREN

With the prevalence of childhood head injuries increasing (as many as 1 million a year) (J. H. Field, 1976), it is important to understand the cognitive and emotional sequelae of such trauma. The complex relationship between emotional disturbance and neurological disorders is portrayed in investigations of childhood head injury (e.g., Dean, 1986a; Rutter, 1982; Rutter, Chadwick, & Shaffer, 1982). This line of research indicates that significantly greater numbers of psychiatric symptoms occur in children following head injury than seen in a normal population (G. Brown, Chadwick, Shaffer, Rutter, & Traub, 1981; Chadwick, Rutter, Brown, Shaffer, & Traub, 1981; Rutter, Chadwick, Shaffer, & Brown, 1980; Rutter et al., 1982; Shaffer, 1974). In a 2-year prospective study of children who suffered closed head injuries, Rutter and his colleagues (G. Brown et al., 1981; Chadwick et al., 1981; Rutter et al., 1980) found that some 50% of the children with severe head injuries developed a diagnosible psychiatric disorder. In contrast, children identified with more mild head injuries appeared to be at no greater risk of psychiatric morbidity than did a group of non-head-injured control patients. Of interest to the present discussion, a neuropsychological examination can provide information regarding the severity of the head injury and the probability of concomitant psychiatric disorders.

Dean (1986a) has recently argued that a twofold risk of psychiatric disorders exists following head injury. The first and most obvious relates to possible dysfunction resulting from the aberrations in brain structure and physiology concomitant with head injury. No less important are the patients' emotional reactions to perceived changes in neuropsychological functioning. In addition, it would seem that neurological damage may also lower the child's ability to cope with a premorbid emotional difficulty. From this point of view, both altered neurology and psychosocial stress may interact as etiological factors in post-head-injury psychiatric disorders.

Cognitive–neuropsychological deficits are also common sequelae of traumatic head injuries. Indeed, while controlling for premorbid intellectual abilities and severity of head injury, Rutter and his colleagues (G. Brown et al., 1981; Chadwick et al., 1981; Rutter et al., 1980) reported neuropsychological impairment to be concomitant with more severe head injury but not with mild head trauma. Generally speaking, the impairment was most salient immediately following the damage and became significantly less debilitating after 1 or 2 months. Neuropsychological assessment is valuable in establishing the degree of cognitive impairment as well as considering the prognosis for return to premorbid levels of functioning.

The cognitive–neuropsychological sequalae of head trauma is manifested differently in adults and children (Boll, 1974; Reed, Reitan, & Klove, 1965; Rutter, 1982; Rutter et al., 1982). While adult head-injured patients tend to present with localized deficits, children show more diffuse neuropsychological impairment following head injury. Some time ago, Ernhart, Graham, Eichman, Marshall, and Thurston (1963) showed that subtests of the Wechsler Intelligence Scales resistent to impairment in head-injured adults (e.g., vocabulary) were impaired for children following head injury. Similarly, Chadwick et al. (1981) and Shaffer, Chadwick, and Rutter (1975) portrayed a diffuse pattern of impaired cognitive–neuropsychological functions for children following head injury. Clearly, the effects of trauma are far more diffuse on a developing nervous system than that seen in adults. Neuropsychological differences between children and adults also may relate to the brain damage, which is more likely to be the result of falls and other accidents in children than in adults. Thus, other than differences in neurology between children and adults, the etiology of brain damage tends to differ for children.

A good deal of research with children suggests that the cognitive and behavioral effects of head injury are dependent on the severity of the trauma (Rutter, 1982; Rutter et al., 1982). Two measures of severity, the duration of unconsciousness and the degree of posttraumatic amnesia, have been shown to be efficient predictors of neuropsycho-

logical and psychiatric impairment 5 years following injury (Smith, 1981; Smith & Sugar, 1975).

Following mild head injuries, children may not experience unconsciousness or amnesia. However, this fact does not preclude impairment of cognitive functions. Chadwick, Rutter, Thompson, and Shaffer (1981) found that although mildly brain-injured subjects performed within normal limits on psychoeducational measures such as the Wechsler Intelligence Scale for Children–Revised, a large number of these children experienced other school-related problems (e.g., reading deficiencies). Thus, seemingly minor head injuries may not show up on traditional psychoeducational measures, but may have implications for classroom functioning. In such cases, neuropsychological measures may be of utility because they are more sensitive to minor dysfunction.

In light of the fact that the majority of children sustaining a head injury return to the schools, it seems important for the school psychologist to have a working knowledge of the neuropsychological results with this population. Clearly, the school psychologist is in a position to offer psychometric data relevant to the child's reintegration into the classroom. In more severe cases neuropsychological information has been shown to offer a method of educational prognosis.

PERINATAL COMPLICATIONS

Brain damage during the perinatal period is not an uncommon occurrence (Rutter, 1982). Indeed, as many as 8% of all live births encounter perinatal complications (Behrman, 1981). These complications involve problems during pregnancy, labor, and delivery. Although mental retardation, cerebral palsy, and epilepsy are well-known results of severe perinatal problems, a considerable data base exists which implicates perinatal difficulties in the etiology of less pervasive neuropsychological disorders (e.g., Commey & Fitzhardinge, 1979; T. M. Field, Dempsey, & Shuman, 1981; Gray, Dean, Strom, Wheeler, & Brockley, 1987; Pfeiffer, Heffernan, & Pfeiffer, 1985).

Methodological concerns not withstanding, research in this area suggests that children born with perinatal complications are more likely to present with developmental delays (Commey & Fitzhardinge, 1979; T. M. Field et al., 1981; Gray et al., 1987; Pfeiffer et al., 1985). For example, in a 4-year follow-up study of high-risk infants, Pfeiffer et al. (1985) reported a significantly higher morbidity rate for cognitive, neurodevelopmental, and behavioral disorders than found in the normal population. In a related study, high-risk infants experienced significantly more developmental delays, hyperactivity, speech difficulties, and attentional deficits 2 and 4 years postnatally then did a full-term control group. (Field, Dempsey, & Shuman, 1979, 1981).

Few investigations have examined the effects of perinatal complications beyond the preschool years. While controlling for socioeconomic factors, Gray et al. (1987) recently showed that developmentally disabled children were significantly more likely than a normal control group to have had risk factors occurring in the prenatal period as well as low birth weight and problems during labor and delivery. Similarly, Fitzhardinge and Steven (1972) found that although high-risk infants performed within normal limits on the Wechsler Intelligence Scale for Children, a larger-than-normal proportion of these children experienced speech disorders, attentional problems, and learning difficulties which required treatment.

Compared to the importance of perinatal complications, the amount of research in the area has been scant and plagued with methodological difficulties (see Gray, Dean, & Rattan, 1987a). Paramount among the methodological concerns has been the reliance on unstructured maternal reports as the major source of perinatal data. Problems with this approach relate to the reliability of the data (Robbins, 1963; Wenar, 1963). Indeed, researchers have reported errors of omission (Pollack & Woerner, 1966) as well as selective memory and/or confabulation (Rutt & Offord, 1971; Taft & Goldfarb, 1964) which threaten the veracity of maternal reports. Also problematic to the generalization of findings, most studies that have examined the behavioral impact of perinatal complications have focused on the preschool period of development. In light of the fact that most higher-level cognitive functions are not expected to be observed until the school-aged years, it seems important to follow the high-risk infant beyond the preschool years. Still another problem in such investigations concerns the focus on individual complications with little consideration for the potential interaction between risk factors. A more heuristic method in the study of the impact of such

perinatal problems would be the use of multivariate techniques.

With these methodological problems in mind, Dean and Gray (1985) developed a *Maternal Perinatal Scale* (MPS). Retrospective in nature, this instrument queries mothers systematically for information relating to the perinatal period. Such a format has been argued to be an economical and psychometrically verifiable method of identifying children who have suffered perinatal complications (Gray, Dean, & Rattan, 1987a, 1987b; Gray, Dean, Strom, Wheeler, & Brockley, 1987; Gray, Dean, Strom, Rattan, & Bechtel, 1987). Using a highly structured approach, this scale also allows the consideration of perinatal events in a multivariate fashion.

A number of studies have examined the reliability and validity of the MPS. Gray et al. (1987a) recently showed that more than 90% of the stability estimates for the 47 MPS items exceeded .90. Interestingly, intercorrelations between the items were consistent with previous obstetrical research (e.g., mother's length of labor was inversely related to the number of prior deliveries).

In a recent attempt to examine the validity of this self-report measure, Gray et al. (1987b) compared the accuracy of mother's self-report of perinatal information with the actual events as recorded in the hospital chart. Information assessed with the MPS proved to correspond highly with mother's hospital chart of the delivery. In this study, 91% of the correlations between mother's report and that same bit of information in the chart exceeded .90. In a further demonstration of its validity, Gray, Dean, Strom, Rattan, & Bechtal (1987) showed that a linear composite of MPS items accounted for a significant amount of the variability in three of five APGAR (a summary measure of the newborn's heart rate, respiratory effort, and reflex irritability) components at 1 minute and all five components at 5 minutes.

Although it appears that complications in the perinatal period place the infant at risk for various developmental and neuropsychological disorders, early intervention has been shown to improve the high-risk child's psychological and educational prognosis. When high-risk infants received continuous structured stimulation by the mother within the first few months following birth, they have been shown to perform within normal limits on a number of cognitive and developmental measures (Parmelee, Beckwith, Cohen, and Sigman (1983).

Parmelee et al. (1983) argued from these data that early intervention focusing on the interaction between the mother and child may be an effective treatment approach. Accordingly, it would seem that early identification is imperative if psychologists and educators are to meet the high-risk child's needs adequately. Thus, the establishment of a cost-effective and psychometrically sound screening process would seem to be the first step in the early intervention process. Moreover, school psychologists may play an integral role in this screening and intervention process. Clearly, research should continue to examine the complexities of the perinatal period of development. Moreover, a structured approach to the collection of perinatal data has utility for school psychologists who characteristically seek perinatal information from mothers of referred children.

COGNITIVE REHABILITATION WITH NEUROPSYCHOLOGICALLY IMPAIRED CHILDREN

Historically, clinical neuropsychology in the United States has focused on diagnosis. However, an increasing number of psychologists have begun to expand their practices to include some form of rehabilitation/remediation (Seretny, Dean, Gray, & Hartlage, 1985). It has become clear that neuropsychological data may go beyond diagnosis and serve as the foundation for developing rehabilitation strategies (Diller & Gordon, 1981; Golden et al., 1978; Gunnison, Kaufman, & Kaufman, 1982; Hartlage, 1975; Hartlage & Lucas, 1973a). Along these lines, it has been argued that the most effective approach with neuropsychologically impaired children may be one that focuses on individualized neuropsychological strengths (e.g., Hartlage & Lucas, 1973a, 1973b; Hartlage & Reynolds, 1981; Hartlage & Telzrow, 1983, 1984; Reynolds, 1981b; Telzrow, 1985).

In an effort to examine this strength model of teaching, Hartlage & Lucas (1973a) compared the word recognition of normal first-grade children after receiving traditional instruction to a group who had received reading instruction based on the child's neuropsychological strengths. The experimental group in which each subject's processing strengths was emphasized outperformed children taught using the traditional approach. The results of this investigation lend support to the utility of matching remedial strategies to information-processing strengths.

Citing a relatively large literature, Horton (1979a, 1979b, 1981) has argued in favor of a behavioral approach with neuropsychologically impaired children. Based on principles of programmed instruction, this approach focuses on the remediation of both lower-level (e.g., attention) and more complex (e.g., verbal–abstract reasoning) cognitive deficits. Children initially receive tasks requiring rudimentary cognitive skills and are presented with more complex exercises as they experience success. Each task is analyzed and broken down into its smallest component parts. After which, the child is guided through the tasks with the aid of progressively less explicit cues.

A number of behaviorally based techniques have been successfully employed with learning disabled children. For example, R. T. Brown and Alford (1984) used a self-instructional technique to treat both attentional deficits and academic difficulties in 20 learning disabled children. Following this behavioral instruction, the learning disabled children showed significant improvement on measures of learning aptitude, reading recognition, and impulsivity. Similarly, behavioral techniques have also been successfully employed with learning disabled children failing to utilize mnemonic strategies spontaneously (Hallahan & Sapona, 1983; Torgeson, 1979). These data suggest that a behavioral approach may be effective in organizing cognitive rehabilitation programs with learning disorders.

A number of computer-based programs have been developed for use with neurologically impaired children (e.g., Bracy, 1983). These clinically based programs focus on the remediation of selective and sustained attentional deficits, impaired verbal and nonverbal auditory and visual discrimination, and problems with stimulus differentiation and generalization. Other programs in the form of video games have been developed which focus on reading and math skills, memory, and visual–perceptual functioning (see Lynch, 1979, 1981 for a review). Game-like programs have also been developed which focus on motor coordination, planning, and visual scanning (Lynch, 1979, 1981). These rehabilitation programs are similar to available Atari games, which require the child to recognize and spell a wide variety of words and to add, subtract, multiply, and divide simple and complex groups of numbers.

A number of case studies suggest cognitive improvement in neuropsychologically impaired children who have been involved in such computer-based programs (Bracy, 1983). Similarly, a computer-based program has been advocated in the remediation of phonetic reading difficulties (Lynch, 1979); however, the crucial test of any cognitive retraining program comes with a comparison to gains made by untreated control subjects. Only with such controlled studies can the effects of computer retraining be separated from spontaneous recovery of functions which occurs following brain injury (Gray & Dean, in press). Although computer-based remediation may hold promise, at present the utility of such programs remains unsubstantiated.

A review of the available literature indicates that most cognitive remedial efforts are developed without specific concern for the child's behavior history and learned methods of coping with failure (e.g., Dean, 1978b). This is most interesting in light of the fact that a large number of children with neurological disorders also present with emotional problems (see Boll, 1981; Dean, 1985). Cognitive dysfunction and a concomitant emotional reaction to school-related tasks is portrayed quite clearly in children with chronic learning disorders (Bender, 1985; Dean & Rattan, 1986). Indeed, repeated failure in the schools may lead to what could be termed a phobic reaction to cognitive tasks (Dean & Rattan, 1986).

In a recent study in our laboratory, we tested a remedial approach that focuses on neuropsychological strengths while desensitizing the negative emotional reactions. Each learning disabled child was initially administered a complete neuropsychological battery. On the basis of these data, a hierarchy of remedial tasks was constructed for each child along an approach–avoidance continuum. Consistent with a behavioral focus, remedial sessions were structured using a task analytic approach. In this way, the cognitive deficit was approached through the use of a system that reinforced attempts, as well as successes, on an approach–avoidance hierarchy. Children were allowed to choose rewards that corresponded to the level of task difficulty from their individually prescribed learning hierarchy.

Following 8 months of treatment, children with chronic learning disorders showed significant gains in achievement, rated classroom behaviors, and were better able to cope with failure. Interest- ingly, although these children showed marked improvement in specific cognitive areas, they continued to present with neuropsychological impairment. Thus, it appears that the children may have learned methods of compensating for neuropsychological deficits. Clearly, these data stress the importance of considering emotional factors when treating learning disabled children.

The importance of cognitive rehabilitation with neuropsychologically impaired children is clear. Without such treatment these children often experience a vicious cycle of failure and avoidance. Although a number of rehabilitation techniques have been shown to be effective with neuropsychologically impaired children, further research is needed to delineate the clinical utility of such approaches more clearly.

CONCLUSIONS

Applied and basic research in neuropsychology will continue to hold implications for the practice of school psychology. This potential is portrayed in a common emphasis on differential diagnosis in both specialties. Although far from a panacea, neuropsychology provides school psychologists with a data base useful in the assessment, understanding, and remediation of children's cognitive and emotional problems. Clearly, the applied psychometric framework that both specialties cling to seems more consistent with diagnosis than with remediation. However, research common to both fields has begun to emphasize the understanding of children's deficits and early intervention.

The similarities between these fields highlights implications of neuropsychological research for school psychology. Indeed, neuropsychology with its emphasis on brain–behavior relationships offers data relevant to the understanding and assessment of a number of childhood disorders seen in the schools. Recent attempts to isolate neuropsychological constellations of specific subtypes of learning disorders have begun to pin down a nebulous school-related disorder. Moreover, data suggesting the unique contribution of neuropsychological measures in the diagnosis of learning disorders is equally encouraging. Investigations have also offered data portraying childhood head injuries and psychiatric disorders from a neuropsychological point of view. Such research has both diagnostic and treatment implications. Recent research focusing on the perinatal period of development suggests the utility of early identification and intervention with high-risk infants. Finally, and perhaps most important, data exist favoring a neuropsychological perspective which goes beyond diagnosis to the development of educational programs that maximize the child's inherent strengths. These results taken together suggest that neuropsychology may provide the psychologist with a useful framework from which to operate in the schools.

REFERENCES

Abrams, R., & Taylor, M. A. (1982). A comparison of unipolar and bipolar depressive illness. *American Journal of Psychiatry, 137,* 1084–1089.

American Psychiatric Association. (1980). *Diagnostic and statistical manual of mental disorders* (3rd ed.). Washington, DC: Author.

Andreason, N. C., Olsen, S. A., Dennert, J. W., & Smith, M. R. (1982). Ventricular enlargement in schizophrenia: Relationship to positive and negative symptoms. *American Journal of Psychiatry, 139,* 297–302.

Bakker, D. J. (1973). Hemispheric specialization and stages in the learning-to-read process. *Bulletin of the Orton Society, 23,* 15–27.

Baron, I. S. (1978). Neuropsychological assessment of neurological conditions. In P. R. Magrab (Ed.), *Psychological management of pediatric problems* (Vol. 2). Baltimore: University Park Press.

Beaumont, J. G., & Rugg, M. D. (1978). Neuropsychological laterality of function and dyslexia: A new hypothesis. *Dyslexia Review, 1,* 18–21.

Behrman, R. E. (1981). *Neonatal-perinatal medicine.* St. Louis, MO: C. V. Mosby.

Bender, W. N. (1985). Differences between learning disabled and non-learning disabled children in temperament and behavior. *Learning Disability Quarterly, 8,* 11–18.

Blau, T. H. (1977). Torque and schizophrenic vulnerability: As the world turns. *American Psychologist, 32,* 997–1005.

Bogen, J. E., & Gazzaniga, M. S. (1965). Cerebral commissurotoma in man: Minor hemisphere dominance for certain visuo-spatial functions. *Journal of Neuropsurgery, 23,* 394–399.

Boll, T. J. (1974). Behavioral correlates of cerebral damage in children aged 9 through 14. In R. M. Reitan & L. A. Davison (Eds.), *Clinical neuropsychology: Current status and applications.* Washington, DC: Hemisphere.

Boll, T. J. (1981). The Halstead-Reitan neuropsychological battery. In S. B. Filskov & T. J. Boll (Eds.), *Handbook of clinical neuropsychology.* New York: Wiley.

Boring, E. G. (1942). *Sensation and perception in the history of experimental psychology.* New York: Appleton-Century.

Bracy, O. L. (1983). Computer-based cognitive rehabilitation. *Cognitive Rehabilitation, 1,* 7–8, 18.

Brown, G., Chadwick, O., Shaffer, D., Rutter, M., & Traub, M. (1981). A prospective study of children with head injuries: III. Psychiatric sequelae. *Psychological Medicine, 11,* 63–78.

Brown, R. T., & Alford, N. K. (1984). Ameliorating attentional deficits and concomitant academic deficiencies in learning disabled children through cognitive training. *Journal of Learning Disabilities, 17,* 20–26.

Chadwick, O., Rutter, M., Brown, G., Shaffer, D., & Traub, M. (1981). A prospective study of children with head injuries: II. Cognitive sequelae. *Psychological Medicine, 11,* 49–61.

Chadwick, O., Rutter, M., Thompson, J., & Shaffer, D. (1981). Intellectual performance and reading skills after localized head injury in childhood. *Journal of Child Psychology and Psychiatry, 22,* 117–139.

Commey, J. O., & Fitzhardinge, P. M. (1979). Handicap in the preterm small-for-gestational age infant. *Journal of Pediatrics, 94,* 779–786.

D'Amato, R. C., Gray, J. W., & Dean, R. S. (1988). A comparison between intelligence and neuropsychological functioning. *Journal of School Psychology, 26,* 283–292.

Dean, R. S. (1977). Canonical analysis of a jangel fallacy. *Multivariate Experimental Clinical Research, 3,* 17–20.

Dean, R. S. (1978a). *Laterality preference schedule.* Madison: University of Wisconsin.

Dean, R. S. (1978b). The use of the WISC-R in distinguishing learning disabled and emotionally disturbed children. *Journal of Consulting and Clinical Psychology, 46,* 381–382.

Dean, R. S. (1979). Cerebral laterality and verbal-performance discrepancies in intelligence. *Journal of School Psychology, 17,* 145–150.

Dean, R. S. (1981). Cerebral dominance and childhood learning disorders: Theoretical perspectives. *School Psychology Review, 10,* 373–378.

Dean, R. S. (1982a). Assessing patterns of lateral preference. *Journal of Clinical Neuropsychology, 4,* 124–128.

Dean, R. S. (1982b). Neuropsychological assessment. In T. R. Kratochwill (Ed.), *Advances in school psychology* (Vol. 2). Hillsdale, NJ: Lawrence Erlbaum.

Dean, R. S. (1983). Intelligence–achievement discrepancies in diagnosing pediatric learning disabilities. *Clinical Neuropsychology, 3,* 58–62.

Dean, R. S. (1984). Functional lateralizatin of the brain. *Journal of Special Education, 18,* 240–256.

Dean, R. S. (1985). Neuropsychological assessment. In J. D. Cavenar, R. Michels, H. K. H. Brodie, A. M. Cooper, S. B. Guze, L. L. Judd, G. L. Klerman, & A. J. Solnit (Eds), *Psychiatry.* Philadelphia: J.B. Lippincott.

Dean, R. S. (1986a). Neuropsychological aspects of psychiatric disorders. In J. E. Obrzut and G. Hynd (Eds.), *Child neuropsychology* (Vol. 2). New York: Academic Press.

Dean, R. S. (1986b). Perspectives on the future of neuropsychological assessment. In B. S. Plake & J. C. Witt (Eds.), *Buros–Nebraska series on measurement and testing: Future testing and measurement*. Hillsdale, N.J.: Lawrence Erlbaum.

Dean, R. S., & Gray, J. W. (1985). *Maternal Perinatal Scale*. Muncie, IN: Ball State University.

Dean, R. S., Gray, J. W., & Seretny, M. L. (1987). Cognitive aspects of schizophrenia and primary affective depression. *International Journal of Clinical Neuropsychology, 9*, 33–36.

Dean, R. S., & Rattan, A. I. (1986). *Measuring the effects of failure with learning disabled children*. Paper presented at the annual convention of the National Academy of Neuropsychologistst, Las Vegas, NV.

Dean, R. S., Schwartz, N. H., & Hua, M. S. (in press). Lateral preference patterns in schizophrenia and affective disorders. *Journal of Consulting and Clinical Psychology*.

Dean, R. S., Schwartz, N. H., & Smith, L. S. (1981). Lateral preference patterns as a discriminator of learning difficulties. *Journal of Consulting and Clinical Psychology, 49*, 227–235.

Dean, R. S., & Smith, L. S. (1981). Personality and lateral preference patterns in children. *Clinical Neuropsychology, 4*, 22–28.

Denckla, M. B. (1972). Clinical syndromes in learning disabilities: The case for "splitting" vs. "lumping." *Journal of Learning Disabilities, 5*, 401–406.

Diller, L., & Gordon, W. A. (1981). Rehabilitation and clinical neuropsychology. In S. B. Filskov & T. J. Boll (Eds.), *Handbook of clinical neuropsychology*. New York: Wiley.

Doehring, D. G., & Hoshko, I. M. (1977). Classification of reading problems by the Q-technique of factor analysis. *Cortex, 13*, 281–294.

Dunlop, D. B., Dunlop, P., & Fenelon, B. (1973). Vision laterality analysis in children with reading disability: The results of new techniques of examination. *Cortex, 9*, 227–236.

Ernhart, C. G., Graham, F. K., Eichman, P. L., Marshall, J. M., & Thurston, D. (1963). Brain injury in the preschool child: Some developmental considerations. *Psychological Monographs, 77*, 17–33.

Feighner, J. P., Robins, E., & Guze, S. B. (1972). Diagnostic criteria for use in psychiatric research. *Archives of General Psychiatry, 26*, 57–63.

Field, J. H. (1976). *Epidemiology of head injury in England and Wales*. London: H.M. Stationery Office.

Field, T., Dempsey, J., & Shuman, H. H. (1979). Developmental assessments of infants surviving the respiratory distress syndrome. In T. Field, A. Sostek, S. Goldberg, & H. H. Shuman (Eds.), *Infants born at risk* (pp. 220–246). New York: Spectrum.

Field, T. M., Dempsey, J. R., & Shuman, H. H. (1981). Developmental follow-up of pre- and postterm infants. In S. L. Friedman & M. Sigman (Eds.), *Preterm birth and and psychological development* (pp. 299–312). New York: Academic Press.

Fischer, W. E., Wenck, L. S., Schurr, K. T., & Ellen, A. S. (1985). The moderating influence of gender, intelligence, and specific achievement deficiencies on the Bannatyne WISC-R recategorization. *Journal of Psychoeducational Assessment, 3*, 245–255.

Fisk, J. L., & Rourke, B. P. (1979). Identification of subtypes of learning-disabled children at three age levels: A neuropsychological, multivariate approach. *Journal of Clinical Neuropsychology, 1*, 289–310.

Fitzhardinge, P. M., & Steven, E. M. (1972). The small-for-date infant: Neurological and intellectual sequelae. *Pediatrics, 50*, 50–57.

Flor-Henry, P. (1976). Lateralized temporo-limbic dysfunction and psychopathology. *Annals of New York Academy of Science, 280*, 777.

Flor-Henry, P. (1977, March). *Increased incidence of sinistrality in the bipolar affective psychosis: Etiological implications*. Paper presented at a symposium entitled, The Sinistral Mind, by the University of California, Berkeley.

Gaddes, W. H. (1975). Neurological implications for learning. In W. M. Cruickshank & D. P. Hallahan (Eds.), *Perceptual and learning disability in children* (Vol. 2). Syracuse, NY: Syracuse University Press.

Gaddes, W. H. (1983). *Learning disabilities and brain function: A neuropsychological approach* (rev. ed.). New York: Springer-Verlag.

Gazzaniga, M. S. (1970). *The bisected brain*. New York: Appleton-Century-Crofts.

Golden, C. J., Graber, B., Coffman, J., Berg, R. A., Newlin, D. B., & Block, S. (1981). Structural brain deficits in schizophrenia. *Archives of General Psychiatry, 38*, 1014–1017.

Golden, C. J., Hammeke, T. A., & Purisch, A. D. (1978). Diagnostic validity of a standardized neuropsychological battery derived from Luria's neuropsychological tests. *Journal of Consulting and Clinical Psychology, 46*, 1258–1265.

Gray, J. W., & Dean, R. S. (in press). Approaches to the cognitive rehabilitation of children with neuropsychological impairment. In C. R. Reynolds (Ed.), *Child neuropsychology: Techniques of diagnosis and treatment*. New York: Plenum Press.

Gray, J. W., & Dean, R. S. (1988). Assessing functional laterality. In M. G. Tramontana & S. R. Hooper (Eds.), *Assessment issues in child neuropsychology* (pp. 205–223). New York: Plenum Press.

Gray, J. W., Dean, R. S., D'Amato, R. C., & Rattan, G. (1987). Differential diagnosis of primary affective depression using the Halstead–Reitan Neuropsychological Battery. *International Journal of Neuroscience, 35*, 43–50.

Gray, J. W., Dean, R. S., & Rattan, G. (1987a). Assessment of perinatal risk factors. *Psychology in the Schools, 24*, 15–21.

Gray, J. W., Dean, R. S., & Rattan, G. (1987b). *Mothers self-report of perinatal complications. Journal of Clinical Child Psychology, 17*, 242–247.

Gray, J. W., Dean, R. S., & Cramer, K. M. (1987). Neuropsychological aspects of primary affective depression. *International Journal of Neuroscience, 32*, 911–918.

Gray, J. W., Dean, R. S. Strom, D. A., Rattan, G., & Bechtel, B. A. (in press). *Maternal report of perinatal information as a predictor of cardiopulmonary functioning in the neonate. Pre- and Perinatal Psychology Journal.*

Gray, J. W., Dean R. S., Strom, D. A., Wheeler, T. E., & Brockley, M. (in press). *Perinatal complications as predictors of developmental disabilities. Developmental Neuropsychology.*

Gray, J. W., Rattan, A. I., & Dean, R. S. (1986). Differential diagnosis of dementia and depression in the elderly using neuropsychological methods. *Archives of Clinical Neuropsychology, 1,* 341–349.

Gruber, F. A., & Segalowitz, S. J. (1977). Some issues and methods in the neuropsychology of language. In S. J. Segalowitz and F. A. Gruber (Eds.), *Language development and neurological theory.* New York: Academic Press.

Gunnison, J., Kaufman, N., & Kaufman, A. (1982). Reading remediation based on sequential and simultaneous processing. *Academic Therapy, 17,* 297–307.

Gur, R. E. (1977). Motoric laterality imbalance in schizophrenia. *Archives of General Psychiatry, 34,* 33–37.

Hallahan, D. P., & Sapona, R. (1983). Self-monitoring of attention with learning disabled children: Past research and current issues. *Journal of Learning Disabilities, 16,* 616–620.

Halstead, W. L., & Settlage, P. H. (1943). Grouping behavior of normal persons and of persons with lesions of the brain. *Archives of Neurology and Psychiatry, 49,* 489–506.

Hartlage, L. C. (1975). Neuropsychological approaches to predicting outcome of remedial education strategies for learning disabled children. *Pediatric Psychology, 3,* 23–28.

Hartlage, L. C., & Lucas, D. G. (1973a). Group screening for reading disability in first grade children. *Journal of Learning Disabilities, 6,* 48–52.

Hartlage, L. C., & Lucas, D. G. (1973b). *Pre-reading expectancy screening scales.* Jacksonville, IL: Psychologists and Educators.

Hartlage, L. C., & Reynolds, C. R. (1981). Neuropsychological assessment and the individualization of instruction. In G. W. Hynd & J. E. Obrzut (Eds.), *Neuropsychological assessment and the school-age child: Issues and procedures.* New York: Grune & Stratton.

Hartlage, L. C., & Telzrow, C. F. (1983). The neuropsychological basis of educational intervention. *Journal of Learning Disabilities, 16,* 521–528.

Hartlage, L. C., & Telzrow, C. F. (1984). Rehabilitation of persons with learning disabilities. *Journal of Rehabilitation, 50,* 31–34.

Hertzig, M. E., & Birch, H. G. (1968). Neurological organization in psychiatrically disturbed adolescents. *Archives of General Psychiatry, 19,* 528–537.

Hicks, R. A., & Pellegrini, R. J. (1978). Handedness and anxiety. *Cortex, 14,* 119–121.

Hines, D., & Satz, P. (1974). Cross-model asymmetries in perception related to asymmetry in cerebral function. *Neuropsychologia, 12,* 239–247.

Horton, A. M., (1979a). Behavioral neuropsychology: A clinical case study. *Clinical Neuropsychology, 1*(3), 44–47.

Horton, A. M. (1979b). Behavioral neuropsychology: Rationale and research. *Clinical Neuropsychology, 1*(2), 20–23.

Horton, A. M., (1981). Behavioral neuropsychology in the schools. *School Psychology Review, 10,* 367–372.

Hunt, H. F. (1943). A practical clinical test for organic brain damage. *Journal of Applied Psychology, 27,* 375–386.

Hynd, G. W. (Ed.), (1981). Neuropsychology in the schools [Special issue]. *School Psychology Review, 10*(3).

Hynd, G. W., & Obrzut, J. E. (1977). Effects of grade level and sex on the magnitude of the dichotic ear advantage. *Neuropsychologia, 15,* 689–692.

Hynd, G. W., & Obrzut, J. E. (Eds.). (1981a). *Neuropsychological assessment and the school-age child: Issues and procedures.* New York: Grune & Stratton.

Hynd, G. W., & Obrzut, J. E. (1981b). School neuropsychology. *Journal of School Psychology, 19,* 45–50.

Hynd, G. W., Obrzut, J. E., Weed, W., & Hynd, C. R. (1979). Development of cerebral dominance: Dichotic listening asymmetry in normal and learning disabled children. *Journal of Experimental Child Psychology, 28,* 445–454.

Hynd, G. W., Quackenbush, R., & Obrzut, J. E. (1980). Training school psychologists in psychological assessment: Current practices and trends. *Journal of School Psychology, 18,* 148–153.

Jackson, J. H. (1932). On the duality of the brain. In J. Taylor (Ed.), *Selected writings of John Hughlings Jackson* (Vol. 2). London: Hodder and Stoughton. (Original work published 1874)

Jortner, S. (1965). A test of Hovey's MMPI scale for CNS disorders. *Journal of Clinical Psychology, 21,* 285.

Kershner, J. B. (1977). Cerebral dominance in disabled readers, good readers, and gifted children: Search for a valid model. *Child Development, 48,* 61–67.

Kinsbourne, M., & Hiscock, M. (1977). Does cerebral dominance develop? In S. J. Segalowitz & F. A. Gruber (Ed.), *Language development and neurological theory,* New York: Academic Press.

Levy, J. (1969). Possible basis for the evaluation of lateral specialization of the human brain. *Nature, 224,* 614–615.

Lishman, W. A., & McMeekan, E. R. L. (1976). Hand preference patterns in psychiatric patients. *British Journal of Psychiatry, 129,* 158–166.

Lynch, W. J. (1979). *A guide to Atari Videocomputer programs for rehabilitation settings.* Palo Alto, CA: Veterans Administration Medical Center.

Lynch, W. J. (1981). The use of electronic games in cognitive rehabilitation. In L. E. Trexler (Ed.), *Cognitive rehabilitation: Conceptualization and intervention.* New York: Plenum Press.

Marcel, T., Katz, L., & Smith, M. (1974). Laterality and reading proficiency. *Neuropsychologia, 12,* 131–139.

Marcel, T., & Rajan, P. I. (1975). Lateral specialization for recognition of words and faces in good and poor readers. *Neuropsychologia, 13,* 489–497.

Mattis, S. (1978). Dyslexia syndromes: A working hypothesis that works. In A. L. Benton & D. Pearl

(Eds.), *Dyslexia: An appraisal of current knowledge.* New York: Oxford University Press.

Mattis, S., French, J. H., & Rapin, I. (1975). Dyslexia in children and young adults: Three independent neuropsychological syndromes. *Developmental Medicine and Child Neurology, 17,* 150–163.

McKeever, W. F., & VanDeventer, A. D. (1975). Dyslexic adolescents: Evidence of impaired visual and auditory language processing associated with normal lateralization and visual responsivity. *Cortex, 11,* 361–378.

Milner, B. (1962). Laterality effects in audition. In O. V. B. Mountcastle (Ed.), *Interhemispheric relations and cerebral dominance,* Baltimore: Johns Hopkins University Press.

Morris, R., Blashfield, R., & Satz, P. (1981). Neuropsychology and cluster analysis: Potential problems. *Journal of Clinical Neuropsychology, 3,* 79–99.

Nasrallah, H. A., Keelor, K., VanSchroeder, C., & McCalley-Whitters, M. (1981). Motoric lateralization in schizophrenic males. *American Journal of Psychiatry, 138,* 1114–1115.

Nasrallah, H. A., McCalley-Whitters, M., & Jacoby, C. G. (1982). Cerebral ventricular enlargement in young manic males: A controlled CT study. *Journal of Affective Disorders, 4,* 15–19.

Nasrallah, H. A., McCalley-Whittersr, M., & Kuperman, S. (1982). Neurological differences between paranoid and nonparanoid schizophrenia part 1. Sensory-motor lateralization. *Journal of Clinical Psychiatry, 42,* 305–306.

Obrzut, J. E., & Hynd, G. W. (1983). The neurobiological and neuropsychological foundations of learning disabilities. *Journal of Learning Disabilities, 16,* 515–520.

Orme, J. E. (1970). Left-handedness ability and emotional instability. *British Journal of Social and Clinical Psychology, 9,* 87–88.

Orton, S. T. (1937). Specific reading disability-strephosymbolia. *Journal of the American Medical Association, 90,* 1095–1099.

Parmelee, A. H., Beckwith, L., Cohen, S. E., & Sigman, M. (1983). Early intervention: Experience with preterm infants. In T. B. Brazelton & B. M. Lester (Eds.), *New approaches to developmental screening of infants.* New York: Elsevier.

Pascal, G. R., & Suttel, B. J. (1951). *The Bender-Gestalt test: Quantification and validity for adults.* New York: Grune & Stratton.

Petrauskas, R., & Rourke, B. P. (1979). Identification of subgroups of retarded readers: A neuropsychological, multivariate approach. *Journal of Clinical Neuropsychology, 1,* 17–37.

Pfeiffer, S. I., Heffernan, L., & Pfeiffer, J. S. (1985). The prediction of possible learning disabilities in high risk infants. *International Journal of Clinical Neuropsychology, 7,* 49.

Piran, N., Bigler, E. D., & Cohen, D. (1982). Motoric laterality and eye dominance suggests unique patterns of cerebral organization in schizophrenia. *Archives of General Psychiatry, 39,* 1006–1010.

Pollack, M., & Woerner, M. G. (1966). Pre- and perinatal complications and "childhood schizophrenia:" A comparison of 5 controlled studies. *Journal of Child Psychology and Psychiatry and Allied Disciplines, 1,* 235–242.

Ramage, J. C. (1979). National survey of school psychologists: Update. *School Psychology Digest, 8,* 153–161.

Rattan, G., & Dean, R. S. (1987). The neuropsychology of children's learning disorders. In J. M. Williams and C. J. Long (Eds.), *The rehabilitation of cognitive disabilities.* New York: Plenum Press.

Reed, H. B. C., Reitan, R. H., & Klove, H. (1965). The influence of cerebral lesions on psychological test performance of older children. *Journal of Consulting Psychology, 29,* 247–251.

Reitan, R. M. (1955). An investigation of the validity of Halstead's measures of biological intelligence. *Archives of Neurology and Psychiatry, 73,* 28–35.

Reitan, R. M. (1966). Problems and prospects in studying the psychological correlates of brain lesions. *Cortex, 2,* 127–154.

Reitan, R. M. (1969). *Manual for administeration of neuropsychological test batteries for adults and children.* Indianapolis, IN: Author.

Reitan, R. M. (1974). Methodological problems in clinical neuropsychology. In R. M. Reitan and L. A. Davison (Eds.), *Clinical neuropsychology: Current status and applications.* New York: Wiley.

Reitan, R. M. (1976). Neurological and physiological bases of psychopathology. *Annual Review of Psychology, 27,* 189–216.

Reitan, R. M., & Davison, L. A. (1974). *Clinical neuropsychology: Current status and applications.* New York: Wiley.

Reynolds, C. R. (1981a). The falacy of two years below grade level for age as a diagnostic criteria for reading disorders. *Journal of School Psychology, 19,* 350–358.

Reynolds, C. R. (1981b). Neuropsychological assessment and the habilitation of learning: Considerations in the search for the aptitude x treatment interaction. *School Psychology Review, 10,* 343–349.

Robbins, L. C. (1963). The accuracy of parental recall of aspects of child development and of child rearing practices. *Journal of Abnormal and Social Psychology, 66,* 261–270.

Rourke, B. P. (1975). Brain–behavior relationships in children with learning disabilities: A research program. *American Psychologist, 30,* 911–920.

Rourke, B. P. (1976). Issues in the neuropsychological assessment of children with learning disabilities. *Canadian Psychological Review, 17,* 89–102.

Rourke, B. P. (1978). Reading, spelling, arithmetic disabilities: A neuropsychological perspective. In H. R. Myklebust (Ed.), *Progress in learning disabilities* (Vol. 4). New York: Grune & Stratton.

Rourke, B. P. (1981). Neuropsychological assessment of children with learning disabilities. In S. B. Filskov & T. J. Boll (Eds.), *Handbook of clinical neuropsychology.* New York: Wiley-Interscience.

Rourke, B. P. (1983). Reading and spelling disabilities: A developmental neuropsychological perspective. In U. Kirk (Ed.), *Neuropsychology of language, reading, and spelling.* New York: Academic Press.

Rourke, B. P., & Strang, J. D. (1983). Subtypes of

reading and arithmetic disabilities: A neuropsychological analysis. In M. Rutter (Ed.), *Developmental neuropsychiatry.* New York: Guilford Press.

Russell, E. W. (1982). Factor analysis of the revised Wechsler Memory Scale tests in a neuropsychological battery. *Perceptual and Motor Skills, 54,* 971–974.

Rutt, C. N., & Offord, D. R. (1971). Prenatal and perinatal complications in childhood schizophrenics and their siblings. *Journal of Nervous and Mental Disease, 152,* 324–331.

Rutter, M. (1977). Brain damage syndromes in childhood: Concepts and findings. *Journal of Child Psychology and Psychiatry, 18,* 1–21.

Rutter, M. (1982). Developmental neuropsychiatry: Concepts, issues, and prospects. *Journal of Clinical Neuropsychology, 4,* 91–115.

Rutter, M., Chadwick, O., & Shaffer, D. (1982). Head injury. In M. Rutter (Ed.), *Developmental neuropsychiatry.* New York: Guilford Press.

Rutter, M., Chadwick, O., Shaffer, D., & Brown's. (1980). A prospective study of children with head injuries: I. Design and methods. *Psychological Medicine, 10,* 633–645.

Satz, P. (1972). Pathological left-handedness: An explanatory model. *Cortex, 8,* 121–135.

Satz, P. (1976). Cerebral dominance and reading disabiity: An old problem revisited. In R. M. Knights and D. Bakker (Eds.), *The neuropsychology of learning disorders.* Baltimore: University Park Press.

Satz, P., Rardin, D., & Ross, J. (1971). An evaluation of a theory of specific developmental dyslexia. *Child Development, 42,* 2009–2021.

Seidel, V. P., Chadwick, O. F., & Rutter, M. (1975). Psychological disorders in crippled children: A comparative study of children with and without brain damage. *Developmental Medicine and Child Neurology, 17,* 563–575.

Seretny, M. L., Dean, R. S., Gray, J. W., & Hartlage L. C. (1986). The practice of clinical neuropsychology in the United States. *Archives of Clinical Neuropsychology, 1,* 90–94.

Shaffer, D. (1974). Psychiatric aspects of brain injury in childhood: A review. In S. Chess & A. Thomas (Eds.), *Annual progress in child psychiatry and child development.* New York: Brunner/Mazel.

Shaffer, D., Chadwick, O., & Rutter, M. (1975). Psychiatric outcome of localized head injury in children. In R. Porter & D. Fitzsimons (Eds.), *Outcome of severe damage to the central nervous system* (Ciba Foundation Symposium No. 34, new series). Amsterdam: Elsevier.

Smith, A. (1975). Neuropsychological testing in neurological disorders. In W. J. Friedlander (Ed.), *Advances in neurology* (Vol. 7). New York: Raven Press.

Smith, A. (1981). Principles underlying human brain functions in neuropsychological sequelae of different neuropathological processes. In S. B. Filskov &

T. J. Boll (Eds.), *Handbook of clinical neuropsychology.* New York: Wiley.

Smith, A., & Sugar, O. (1975). Development of above normal language and intelligence 21 years after left hemispherectomy. *Neurology, 25,* 812–818.

Sparrow, S., & Satz, P. (1970). Dyslexia, laterality, and neuropsychological development. In D. J. Bakker & P. Satz (Eds.), *Specific reading disability: Advances in theory and method.* Rotterdam: Rotterdam University Press.

Sperry, R. W., Gazzaniga, M. S., & Bogen, J. H. (1969). Interhemispheric relationships: The neocortical commissures: Syndromes of hemispheric disconnection. In P. Vinken & G. W. Bruyn (Eds.), *Handbook of Clinical Neurology* (Vol. 4, pp. 273–290). New York: Wiley.

Spitzer, R. L., Endicott, J., & Robins, E. (1977). *Research diagnostic criteria (RDC) for a selected group of functional disorders* (3rd ed.). New York: New York State Psychiatric Institute, *Biometries Research.*

Strom, D. A., Gray, J. W., Dean, R. S., & Fischer, W. E. (1987). Incremental validity of the Halstead–Reitan Neuropsychological Battery in predicting achievement for learning disabled children. *Journal of Psychoeducational Assessment, 5,* 32–40.

Taft, L. T., & Goldfarb, W. (1964). Prenatal and perinatal factors in childhood schizophrenia. *Developmental Medicine and Child Neurology, 6,* 32–40.

Taylor, M. A., & Abrams, R. (1984). Cognitive impairment in schizophrenia. *American Journal of Psychiatry, 141,* 196–201.

Telzrow, C. F. (1985). The science and speculation of rehabilitation in developmental neuropsychological disorders. In L. C. Hartlage & C. F. Telzrow (Eds.), *The neuropsychology of individual differences.* Elmsford, NY: Pergamon Press.

Tomlinson-Keasey, C., & Kelly, R. R. (1979). Is hemispheric specialization important to scholastic achievement? *Cortex, 15,* 97–101.

Torgesen, J. K. (1979). Factors related to poor performance on memory tasks in reading-disabled children. *Learning Disability Quarterly, 2,* 17–23.

Tramontana, M. G., Sherrets, S. D., & Golden, C. J. (1980). Brain dysfunction in youngsters with psychiatric disorders: Application of Selz–Reitan rules for neuropsychological diagnosis. *Clinical Neuropsychology, 2,* 118–123.

Walker, H. A., & Birch, H. G. (1970). Lateral preference and right-left awareness in schizophrenic children. *Journal of Nervous and Mental Disease, 15,* 341–351.

Wenar, C. (1963). The reliability of developmental histories. *Psychosomatic Medicine, 25,* 505–514.

Witelson, S. F. (1977). Developmental dyslexia: Two right hemispheres and none left. *Science, 195,* 309–311.

Woods, B. T., & Short, M. P. (1985). Neurological dimensions of psychiatry. *Biological Psychiatry, 20,* 192–198.

PSYCHOLOGICAL AND EDUCATIONAL ASSESSMENT

13

INTELLIGENCE TESTING IN THE SCHOOLS

ALAN S. KAUFMAN
PATTI L. HARRISON
RICHARD F. ITTENBACH

The University of Alabama

Since the publication of the first edition of the *Handbook of School Psychology* (Reynolds & Gutkin, 1982), intelligence testing in the schools has faced some dramatic changes. Although intelligence testing remains extremely popular, there is a sense of rebirth in the field (Harrison, 1986). The Wechsler Scales and Stanford-Binet have been the status quo of individual intelligence tests for many years. However, several new intelligence tests have been published recently, including the Woodcock-Johnson Tests of Cognitive Ability (Woodcock & Johnson, 1977), the Kaufman Assessment Battery for Children (Kaufman & Kaufman, 1983b), the fourth edition of the Stanford-Binet (Thorndike, Hagen, & Sattler, 1986), and new Detroit Tests of Learning Aptitude (Hammill, 1985). Several new tests are currently being developed, including the Kaufman Adolescent and Adult Intelligence Test (KAIT; see Harrison & Kaufman, 1986), the Das/Naglieri Cognitive Assessment System (see Naglieri & Das, 1986), and the Sternberg Multidimensional Abilities Test (see Trotter, 1986).

The new tests are typically based on various theoretical approaches to measuring cognitive ability and extensive research that was conducted before the tests were published. The split-brain research of Sperry (1968) and Levy and Trevarthon (1976) and the neuropsychological model of Luria (1966, 1970) have formed the basis for several of the tests. The theories and research of Sternberg (1985, 1986), Feuerstein (1979), Gardner (1983), and Cattell and Horn (Cattell, 1971; Horn, 1970) have also had an impact on intelligence testing.

Comprehensive assessment of cognitive abilities is being emphasized more and more. The new, as well as future, intelligence tests offer many ways to assess patterns of performance and conduct profile analysis. Clinical observations during testing and assessment of the environments in which children and adolescents display cognitive skills are other factors of comprehensive assessment that move school psychologists away from looking at a single IQ score.

Computerized testing is receiving a great deal of attention. Computerized scoring and reporting for individually administered intelligence tests is now common, and in the near future, school psychologists will probably administer intelligence tests via computer. Hopefully, however, computerized administration of tests will supplement, and not replace, assessment by trained individual examiners, since clinical observations of test behaviors are often more important than the test scores obtained (Kaufman, 1979).

In addition to changes in intelligence tests, school psychologists who use intelligence tests have changed and are much more than technicians. School psychologists have become better trained, as seen in the establishment of over 200 school psychology graduate programs in the last 20 years (Fagan, 1985). School psychologists have become more selective about the instruments they use and demand to see evidence of adequate norms, reliability, and validity before they use intelligence tests. For example, the fourth edition of the Stanford-Binet was the subject of much debate because the publisher failed to publish a technical manual when the test was initially released for use ("Stanford-Binet Draws," 1986).

Although intelligence testing appears to be going through a period of rebirth, the use of intelligence tests continues to be a controversial topic (Kaufman & Harrison, 1987). On one side, there is a call for the abolishment of intelligence tests, and on the other side, school psychologists must administer intelligence tests under unrealistic rules governing placement decisions that overemphasize the role of the obtained scores. Just as major legal cases differ on whether intelligence tests are fair (PASE) or unfair (Larry P), the professionals who use intelligence tests continue to disagree. It is likely that the future will hold arguments on the use of intelligence tests and calls to ban them; it is equally likely that new and revised intelligence tests will continue to be published.

A special issue of the Roeper Review in February 1986 contained articles that discussed the two sides of the IQ controversy. Some of the authors of the articles (e.g., Hatch & Gardner, 1986; Sternberg, 1986; Treffinger & Renzulli, 1986) argued against the use of intelligence tests, while others (Borland, 1986; Kaufman & Harrison, 1986; Robinson & Chamrad, 1986) argued for their continued use. Surprisingly, there were many similarities in the articles regardless of the point of view of the author(s), including discussions of misuses of tests, cautions for using them, and

conclusions that no intelligence test measures all aspects of cognitive ability. This special issue of the *Roeper Review* is just one example of the continued controversy surrounding intelligence testing; the special 1984 issue of the *Journal of Special Education* devoted to the K-ABC is another.

With the many issues in intelligence testing that school psychologists face, it was difficult to make a decision about the focus of this chapter. We elected to include the research conducted with two of the most widely used intelligence tests in schools: the Wechsler Intelligence Scale for Children–Revised (WISC-R) and the Kaufman Assessment Battery for Children (K-ABC). Space did not permit inclusion of the Woodcock-Johnson Psychoeducational Battery–Tests of Cognitive Ability, although this test has gained in popularity with school psychologists; readers are referred to McGrew's (1986) excellent new book on the interpretation of the Woodcock-Johnson.

Even for just the WISC-R and K-ABC, a systematic review of the many hundreds of research studies would have been impossible. Thus, our emphasis in this chapter is the research that we deem to be most valuable for test interpretation. For each test we selected several areas of research. Within each area of research, first the results of key research investigations are discussed, and then the implications of these results for test interpretation are explored.

WECHSLER INTELLIGENCE SCALE FOR CHILDREN–REVISED

The WISC-R (Wechsler, 1974) was the focus of a chapter by Alan S. Kaufman in the first edition of the *Handbook of School Psychology* (Reynolds & Gutkin, 1982). The purpose of this section of the current chapter is to update the earlier chapter using the wealth of research that has been conducted with the WISC-R in recent years. In the earlier chapter, Kaufman (1982) indicated that the WISC-R was the subject of an impressive variety of research investigation. This research continues forcefully today; our computer search of the literature yielded over 500 research articles on the WISC-R since 1977. The WISC-R will undoubtedly remain the subject of countless master's theses, doctoral dissertations, and research projects within the field of school psychology and related disciplines; however, a third edition of the test is much needed since the normative data, gathered in 1972, are half a generation old (and hence $4\frac{1}{2}$ points out of date; see Flynn, 1984).

In this section of the chapter we focus on research that has clear-cut and important implications for interpretation of the WISC-R. We have updated the chapter in the first edition of the *Handbook of School Psychology* in the following areas: verbal comprehension, perceptual organization, and freedom from distractibility factors; scatter; characteristic profiles; and assessment of minorities. We intended to include two new areas, namely treatment validity and neuropsychological research, based on Witt and Gresham's (1985) cogent arguments of the necessity of research in those two domains in order to support the WISC-R's validity. Unfortunately, we discovered virtually no empirical investigations in these areas warranting their exclusion for this chapter. Two areas that were included in the first chapter, subtest specificity and WISC-WISC-R discrepancies, are not discussed in the present chapter; the first topic has produced no new research of note, and the second topic is no longer clinically relevant!

Verbal Comprehension and Perceptual Organization Factors

Kaufman (1982) indicated that factor analytic investigations of the 1949 WISC did not provide clear-cut support for its construct validity. The research raised the possibility that the WISC Verbal and Performance IQs did not correspond to unitary abilities in children. Factor analytic research with the WISC-R has not produced equivocal results regarding the Verbal and Performance constructs; this finding, which is indeed a benefit to WISC-R examiners, is discussed as follows.

Research Results

Regardless of the factor-analytic technique employed, the age and ethnic background of the children tested, or the nature of the sample (normal versus exceptional), factor analysis of the WISC-R has yielded one consistent and recurrent finding: the emergence of robust verbal comprehension and perceptual organization factors. The verbal factor includes significant loadings by the five regularly administered verbal subtests (although Arithmetic is often a distant fifth), and the

TABLE 1   Comparability of WISC-R Factor Structures for White Children and Black Children in the Standardization Sample

	Verbal Comprehension		Perceptual Organization		Freedom from Distractibility	
	White	Black	White	Black	White	Black
Verbal						
Information	*63*	*58*	*26*	21	*35*	*42*
Similarities	*63*	*62*	32	28	26	28
Arithmetic	*37*	34	21	16	*55*	*68*
Vocabulary	*77*	*80*	22	21	31	33
Comprehension	*64*	*58*	26	33	18	23
Digit Span	18	23	10	23	*60*	57
Performance						
Picture Completion	31	*38*	*53*	55	09	13
Picture Arrangement	32	28	*44*	47	14	14
Block Design	23	19	*72*	67	30	32
Object Assembly	19	19	*66*	72	09	12
Coding	16	17	20	20	*36*	29
Mazes	09	10	*44*	*53*	20	19
Coefficient of congruence	99		99		99	

Source. Gutkin and Reynolds (1981).

Note. Decimal points are omitted. Loadings of .35 and above are italicized. Factor structures are based on 1868 white children and 305 black children, both groups ranging in age from $6\frac{1}{2}$ to $16\frac{1}{2}$ years.

nonverbal dimension has significant loadings by all performance subtests except Coding. When a hierarchical factor solution is employed, a general intelligence factor precedes the emergence of the verbal and perceptual factors (Vance & Wallbrown, 1978; Wallbrown, Blaha, Wallbrown, & Engin, 1975); when principal components of principal factor analysis is performed, verbal comprehension and perceptual organization factors emerge first, usually followed by a distractibility factor. Unlike the factors for the old WISC, the WISC-R factors do not seem to split apart but retain their integrity even when four or five factors are rotated (Kaufman, 1975).

The precise composition of the two major WISC-R factors is remarkably similar from group to group. This similarity was evident for the 11 age groups between 6½ and 16½ years in the standardized sample (Kaufman, 1975), and it also characterizes the variety of samples that have been factor analyzed by numerous investigators. The extreme congruence of the factor structures for blacks and whites was demonstrated empirically by Gutkin and Reynolds (1981), using data from the standardization sample (see Table 1). These authors also found highly congruent factors for males and females at two age levels (Reynolds & Gutkin, 1980) and for upper and lower socioeconomic

TABLE 2   Factor Loadings on the WISC-R Verbal Comprehensions Factor for a Variety of Normal and Clinical Samples

WISC-R Subtest	(1)	(2)	(3)	(4)	(5)	(6)	(7)	(8)	(9)	(10)	(11)	(12)	(13)	(14)	(15)	(16)	(17)	(18)
Verbal																		
Information	63	72	63	72	66	70	67	73	10	66	76	80	71	54	48	66	84	59
Similarities	64	78	59	66	67	59	61	61	72	61	68	46	69	71	50	63	77	69
Arithmetic	37	44	43	65	40	42	53	53	54	13	39	58	48	21	44	21	66	43
Vocabulary	72	83	74	76	67	74	80	71	81	75	76	76	70	65	77	76	82	81
Comprehension	64	69	64	74	61	71	62	71	62	64	56	85	55	64	65	63	82	77
Digit Span	18	29	35	46	33	31	26	30	48	—	—	—	14	—	—	13	38	28
Performance																		
Picture Completion	35	30	20	36	32	22	27	39	25	15	28	29	24	23	18	09	16	31
Picture Arrangement	33	16	20	39	17	23	38	34	38	07	23	48	18	16	16	21	48	30
Block Design	27	22	17	23	20	14	27	26	19	03	31	28	22	14	03	20	23	32
Object Assembly	21	08	07	09	14	09	10	15	24	04	−10	23	28	−01	−07	10	23	20
Coding	15	04	12	35	14	21	18	25	24	36	21	17	14	04	00	−04	07	20
Mazes	12	—	18	30	06	16	05	09	20	—	—	—	—	—	—	—	—	08

Note. Decimal points are omitted. Loadings of .35 and above are italicized. The groups are as follows:

1. Standardization sample, ages 6½–16½ (*N* = 2,200). Median loadings for 11 groups are as shown in table. *Source.* Kaufman (1975).
2. Normal children, ages 6 to 12 ½ (*N* = 212). *Source.* Kaufman and McLean (in press).
3. Normal white children, grades 1–9 (*N* = 252). *Source.* Reschly (1978).
4. Normal black children, grades 1–9 (*N* = 235). *Source.* Reschly (1978).
5. Normal Hispanic children, grades 1–9 (*N* = 223). *Source.* Reschly (1978).
6. Native-American Papago children, grades 1–9 (*N* = 240). *Source.* Reschly (1978).
7. Normal white children, ages 5–11 (*N* = 332). *Source.* Sandoval (1982).
8. Normal black children, ages 5–11 (*N* = 314). *Source.* Sandoval (1982).
9. Normal Hispanic children, ages 5–11 (*N* = 307). *Source.* Sandoval (1982).
10. Gifted children, ages 6–16 (*N* = 946). *Source.* Karnes and Brown (1980).
11. White referrals, mean age = 11 (*N* = 109). *Source.* Dean (1979a).
12. Hispanic referrals, mean age = 11.4 (*N* = 123). *Source.* Dean (1980).
13. Hispanic referrals, mean age = 10.5 (*N* = 142). *Source.* Gutkin and Reynolds (1980).
14. White referrals, ages 6–16 (*N* = 274). *Source.* Johnston and Bolen (1984).
15. Black referrals, ages 6–16 (*N* = 430). *Source.* Johnston and Bolen (1984).
16. Referrals, no problem found, grade 2–6 (*N* = 248). *Source.* Peterson and Hart (1979).
17. Predominantly Hispanic referrals, ages 6–13 (*N* = 106). *Source.* Stedman, Lawlis, Cortner, and Achterberg (1978).
18. Referrals, ages 7–16 (*N* = 164). *Source.* Swerdlik and Schweitzer (1978).

status groups in the standardization sample (Carlson, Reynolds, & Gutkin, 1983). Note in Table 1 that the congruence was found not only for the two major factors but also for the distractibility factor that is discussed in the next section of this chapter.

Table 2 summarizes the verbal comprehension factors isolated in principal components or principal factor analysis of the WISC-R, and Table 3 summarizes the perceptual organization factors identified in these same analyses. Space limits the inclusion of all pertinent analyses in these tables, but the ones shown represent the diversity of exceptional and normal populations from vari-

ous ethnic backgrounds that have been factor analyzed in the literature. As shown in Table 2, Information, Similarities, Vocabulary, and Comprehension generally had loadings in the .60s, .70s, and .80s on the Verbal Comprehension factor. The loadings for Arithmetic were steadily near .40, although even this subtest loaded above .60 in four studies. From Table 3 it can be seen that Block Design and Object Assembly are the best measures of the perceptual organization factor, but that Picture Completion, Picture Arrangement, and Mazes also bear an unequivocal and persistent relationship to this nonverbal dimension.

TABLE 2   (continued)

WISC-R Subtest	(19)	(20)	(21)	(22)	(23)	(24)	(25)	(26)	(27)	(28)	(29)	(30)	(31)	Median
Verbal														
Information	77	79	80	54	73	69	72	82	76	69	29	72	73	71
Similarities	77	84	73	72	65	70	67	75	54	73	41	56	67	67
Arithmetic	46	69	66	22	38	43	56	44	34	34	17	35	41	43
Vocabulary	83	88	86	79	80	82	75	82	76	80	95	87	57	77
Comprehension	80	80	77	76	74	72	61	65	69	67	36	56	53	65
Digit Span	—	—	—	13	05	—	34	23	44	—	30	12	46	30
Performance														
Picture Completion	29	34	38	16	20	29	16	30	17	22	13	21	16	24
Picture Arrangement	46	42	26	27	33	25	12	38	25	05	07	37	46	26
Block Design	33	12	19	25	18	20	24	37	22	−11	16	−25	27	22
Object Assembly	34	12	08	10	04	25	07	20	10	10	15	−03	04	10
Coding	−09	10	33	09	−07	11	30	27	−18	06	05	−17	26	14
Mazes	—	—	—	—	—	—	—	—	—	—	—	—	10	11

19. Referrals, ages 6–11 (N = 250). The WRAT was also included in the factor analysis but the factor loading for the WISC-R only are reported in Table X. *Source.* Wright & Dappen (1982).
20. Handicapped, middle-socioeconomic-status children, ages 7–12 (N = 107). *Source.* Hale (1983).
21. Handicapped, lower-socioeconomic-status children, ages 7–12 (N = 158). *Source.* Hale (1983).
22. Learning-disabled children, ages 6–14 (N = 198). *Source.* Kaufman and McLean (1986).
23. Learning-disabled and slow-learning children, grades 2–6 (N = 162). *Source.* Peterson and Hart (1979).
24. Learning-disabled children, mean age = 10½ (N = 275). *Source.* Schooler, Beebe, and Koepke (1978).
25. Learning-disabled Native-American, Navajo children, ages 6½–15. (N = 192). *Source.* Zarske, Moore, and Peterson (1981).
26. Psychiatrically impaired sample, ages 10½–16 (N = 100). *Source.* DeHorn and Klinge (1978).
27. Emotionally handicapped children, grades 2–6 (N = 147). *Source.* Peterson and Hart (1979).
28. Educable mentally retarded children, ages 12–15 (N = 95). *Source.* Cummins and Das (1980).
29. Low-IQ children, ages 9–11 (N = 107). *Source.* Groff and Hubble (1982).
30. Low-IQ children, ages 14–16 (N = 78). *Source.* Groff and Hubble (1982).
31. Mentally retarded children, ages 6–16½ (N = 80). *Source.* Van Hagen and Kaufman (1975).

TABLE 3   Factor Loadings on the WISC-R Perceptual Organization Factor for a Variety of Normal and Clinical Samples

WISC-R Subtest	(1)	(2)	(3)	(4)	(5)	(6)	(7)	(8)	(9)	(10)	(11)	(12)	(13)	(14)	(15)	(16)	(17)	(18)
Verbal																		
Information	25	25	32	32	20	26	18	23	*38*	12	09	−12	13	13	02	25	10	33
Similarities	34	28	26	30	15	34	25	20	20	07	*39*	−02	33	14	07	24	23	22
Arithmetic	20	28	26	*37*	13	*37*	26	*37*	*39*	09	−23	13	31	−01	05	−01	13	*39*
Vocabulary	24	08	23	19	26	14	17	24	29	03	22	24	27	18	13	23	30	23
Comprehension	30	34	22	16	20	13	23	16	28	03	−12	31	33	13	19	04	18	25
Digit Span	12	07	02	32	14	*36*	13	28	34	—	—	—	22	—	—	12	23	26
Performance																		
Picture Completion	*57*	*59*	*49*	*44*	*52*	*54*	*48*	*41*	*58*	*42*	*66*	*54*	*56*	*45*	*42*	*52*	*83*	*59*
Picture Arrangement	*41*	*59*	*53*	*47*	*38*	*43*	*42*	*53*	*41*	*50*	*59*	*44*	*72*	*42*	*37*	*40*	*31*	*52*
Block Design	*66*	*57*	*60*	*66*	*59*	*68*	*64*	*65*	*60*	*74*	*73*	*62*	*64*	*54*	*54*	*50*	*75*	*70*
Object Assembly	*65*	*69*	*59*	*57*	*58*	*56*	*77*	*65*	*54*	*74*	*69*	*79*	*51*	*70*	*66*	*52*	*68*	*76*
Coding	20	13	16	27	16	25	12	32	32	27	29	29	*37*	08	02	02	05	*44*
Mazes	*47*	—	*42*	*47*	*47*	*56*	32	*54*	*48*	—	—	—	—	—	—	—	—	*55*

Note. Decimal points are omitted. Loadings of .35 and above are italicized. See the note to Table 2 for a description of the groups and the data sources.

The obvious resemblance of the verbal comprehension and perceptual organization factors to Wechsler's dichotomous division of the WISC-R indicates that these factors might easily be assigned the labels verbal and performance, respectively. Factor analysis can be used to provide evidence of a test's construct validity (Anastasi, 1982), and the analyses of the WISC-R certainly support the validity of Wechsler's verbal and performance constructs. Furthermore, this validity applies not only to white children, but to black youngsters (Gutkin & Reynolds, 1981; Johnston & Bolen, 1984; Reschly, 1978; Sandoval, 1982; Vance & Wallbrown, 1978), Spanish-speaking children (Dean, 1979a, 1980; Gutkin & Reynolds, 1980; Reschly, 1978; Sandoval, 1982; Stedman, Lawlis, Cortner, & Achterberg, 1978), and Native Americans (Reschly, 1978; Zarske, Moore, & Peterson, 1981) as well. That is, the factor-analytic data suggest that the WISC-R is measuring the abilities it is supposed to be measuring for children from different ethnic backgrounds. The WISC-R's construct validity also extends to gifted (Karnes & Brown, 1980), mentally retarded (Cummins & Das, 1980; Groff & Hubble, 1982; Schooler, Beebe, & Koepke, 1978; Van Hagen & Kaufman, 1975), learning-disabled (Kaufman & McLean, 1986; Peterson & Hart, 1979; Schooler et al., 1978), emotionally disturbed (Peterson & Hart, 1979; Schooler et al., 1978), behavior-disordered (Finch, Kendall, Spirito, Entin, Montgomery, &

Schwartz, 1979), and psychiatric (DeHorn & Klinge, 1978) samples and to referrals to school and clinical psychologists (Dean, 1979a; Gutkin & Reynolds, 1980; Johnston & Bolen, 1984; Lombard & Riedel, 1978; Peterson & Hart, 1979; Stedman et al., 1978; Swerdlik & Schweitzer, 1978; Wright & Dappen, 1982).

Implications for Interpretation

The emergence of robust factors that closely resemble the verbal and performance scales of the WISC-R delivers a vital message to clinicians: Respect Wechsler's dichotomy and give much credence to the Verbal and Performance IQs. This suggestion is not intended to squelch profile interpretation but to set up a systematic, logical approach to the understanding of subtest fluctuations. Too many examiners seem to think of a Wechsler battery as a collection of 10 to 12 diverse subtests, each equipped to assess a certain segment of an individual's cognitive functioning. Some methods of interpretation (e.g., Banas & Wills, 1977, 1978; Flynn, Vitelli, & Goldblatt, 1978) openly advocate a fragmentation of the WISC-R into its component subtests as a first-line approach to profile attack. Even a table such as Wechsler's (1974, Table 12), which presents the differences between pairs of subtests required for statistical significance, can impel examiners to operate primarily from a subtest (rather than from a scale) orientation. Mueller, Mancini, and Short

TABLE 3   (continued)

WISC-R Subtest	(19)	(20)	(21)	(22)	(23)	(24)	(25)	(26)	(27)	(28)	(29)	(30)	(31)	Median
Verbal														
Information	29	18	27	18	19	11	09	29	21	−05	04	03	12	31
Similarities	20	17	20	16	00	30	30	45	24	−06	17	01	08	20
Arithmetic	43	29	28	20	32	37	30	40	07	−05	14	13	16	26
Vocabulary	23	12	20	18	08	23	09	31	27	16	15	02	27	22
Comprehension	25	21	19	21	27	15	24	38	32	33	11	09	48	21
Digit Span	—	—	—	14	05	—	48	10	−17	—	−12	41	06	14
Performance														
Picture Completion	64	59	57	61	42	47	48	68	49	64	55	66	83	55
Picture Arrangement	60	64	66	48	19	56	66	58	45	62	32	50	41	48
Block Design	73	86	80	65	75	70	29	71	66	78	55	71	62	66
Object Assembly	75	82	86	88	69	80	45	76	70	85	69	63	70	69
Coding	64	61	45	34	02	43	07	30	36	30	12	−01	45	27
Mazes	—	—	—	—	—	—	—	—	—	—	—	—	67	48

(1984) provided data indicating that more than half of all possible subtest comparisons were inappropriate and that the other comparisons varied according to age group. Clinicians who examine a subtest profile and immediately ponder the unique abilities assessed by apparently high and low scaled scores, and who rush to compute the significance of the difference between the child's 11 in Comprehension and 7 in Information, are putting the cart before the horse; they are ignoring the results of factor analysis.

If we respect the fact that large verbal and nonverbal factors exist for children of all ages, we should approach WISC-R profiles with some basic assumptions: (a) the most likely determinant of a child's score on any verbal subtest is his or her verbal comprehension ability, not the unique abilities associated with each subtest; (b) the most likely determinant of a score on any performance subtest is the child's perceptual organization ability; (c) fluctuations within the verbal scale should be treated as chance deviations from the child's overall verbal comprehension ability, unless statistical analysis proves otherwise; and (d) fluctuations within the performance scale should be treated as chance occurrences, pending statistical analysis.

These assumptions lead directly to a method of attacking WISC-R scaled-score profiles. Instead of treating each subtest as a measure of an isolated set of skills, or focusing on comparisons of subtests taken two at a time, each verbal scaled score should be compared to the child's own mean verbal score (which is a convenient estimate of his or her verbal comprehension ability). Then each performance scaled score should be compared to the child's performance mean to determine if the fluctuations are due to chance. When most of these comparisons are not statistically significant, we fall back on the original foregoing set of assumptions and therefore pay little or no attention to apparent fluctuations in the profile. Even though a child's scaled scores of 11 and 7 may differ significantly from each other, this finding is irrelevant and trivial if both of these scores do not differ significantly from the child's own mean. When a child's scaled scores do differ significantly from the verbal and/or performance means, only then do we have the right to speculate about strengths and weaknesses in abilities that are less global than verbal comprehension and perceptual organization.

The method described above derives from the results of factor analysis and clearly puts the verbal and performance scales in the forefront, relegating subtest analysis to the second line of attack. Sometimes prudent subtest analysis holds the key to understanding a child's profile because the verbal comprehension-perceptual organization dichotomy does not apply to that particular individual; however, factor-analytic research suggests that we begin with the assumption that the dichotomy is crucial for all children, even if subsequent statistical analysis leads us to reject this hypothesis. Fortunately, Davis (1959) developed formulas to permit statistical comparison of single scores with mean scores, Sattler (1982) applied some of these formulas to WISC-R data, and Silverstein (1981) amended the values required for significance by taking into account the errors that occur when multiple comparisons are made, and therefore, applying the Bonferroni correction. Whereas Sattler (1982) and Silverstein (1981) report the precise differences required for significance for each separate subtest, we feel that it is reasonable to use the following rule of thumb to determine significant discrepancies from a child's mean scores: ±3 points from a child's mean for all six Verbal subtests and Block Design; and ±4 points for the remaining five Performance tasks. The use of a simple rule of thumb reduces the examiner's dependency on a table and simplifies the clerical work, thereby facilitating the application of the interpretive procedure proposed here. For similar reasons, we do not ordinarily advocate the use of recomputed deviation quotients based on factor scores (Gutkin, 1978, 1979a; Sobotka & Black, 1978) for investigating relative strengths and weaknesses, except perhaps for examiners with statistical and psychometric expertise. Note that the rule of thumb proposed here differs from Kaufman's

(1979, 1982) suggestion of using ±3 points for all 12 subtests, because the previous rule was based on the available data *prior* to Silverstein's (1981) correction for multiple comparisons.

Freedom From Distractibility Factor

The freedom from distractibility factor was identified for the 1949 WISC, but its composition varied from group to group. For example, in Cohen's (1959) factor analysis of the WISC standardization sample, Digit Span loaded on the distractibility factor for all three age groups studied but Arithmetic loaded only at age 13½; furthermore, Digit Span was joined by Picture Arrangement at age 7½, and by Ojbect Assembly at age 10½. Indeed, when an objective criterion was used to determine the number of factors to rotate, the distractibility factor did not emerge at all (Silverstein, 1969). WISC-R factor analyses have produced different results.

Research Results

Analysis of the WISC-R standardization data produced a distractibility factor for each age group

TABLE 4   Factor Loadings on the WISC-R Freedom from Distractibility Factor for a Variety of Normal and Clinical Samples

WISC-R Subtest	(1)	(2)	(3)	(5)	(7)	(10)	(11)	(12)	(14)	(15)	(16)	(17)	(18)
Verbal													
Information	41	27	26	33	36	18	−19	−24	33	21	32	16	38
Similarities	28	09	26	22	24	09	−26	30	07	05	12	04	27
Arithmetic	58	46	45	45	37	81	52	63	98	41		40	49
Vocabulary	33	19	12	30	14	13	20	−20	22	−02	16	03	17
Comprehension	24	19	21	06	15	12	21	29	05	−16	−07	09	16
Digit Span	56	51	40	31	73	—	—	—	—	—	38	42	65
Performance													
Picture Completion	11	01	09	12	09	55	27	20	00	−02	08	01	19
Picture Arrangement	12	10	00	39	11	03	−17	22	15	−05	−01	21	43
Block Design	28	36	22	16	15	08	47	39	11	23	55	04	17
Object Assembly	12	20	18	09	20	05	24	26	04	02	48	36	12
Coding	42	54	40	37	30	27	44	38	15	39	25	94	19
Mazes	22	—	10	20	31	—	—	—	—	—	—	—	22

Note. Decimal points are omitted. Loadings of .35 and above are italicized. See the note to Table 2 for a description of the groups. Groups 4, 6, 8, 9, 13, 20, 21 are omitted from this table because a freedom from distractibility factor did not emerge for these samples. Group 24 is omitted because Schooler, Beebe, and Koepke (1978) did not investigate three-factor solutions.

between 6½ and 16½ (Kaufman, 1975), for black children and white children (Gutkin & Reynolds, in 1981; see Table 1), for boys and girls at two broadly defined age levels (Reynolds & Gutkin, 1980), and for high and low socioeconomic groups (Carlson et al., 1983). Digit Span and Arithmetic loaded substantially at all age levels, and Coding was also closely associated with the factor across the age range. Although Information tended to load with this factor when the varimax rotation was used, its loadings were minimal when oblique rotations were employed; hence, the distractibility factor was composed of the Arithmetic-Digit Span-Coding triad. When Silverstein's (1969) objective criterion for assessing the number of factors was applied to WISC-R data, the freedom from distractibility dimension emerged as a significant factor for four age groups and barely fell short of significance for the remaining ages. Thus, unlike its WISC counterpart, the WISC-R distractibility factor is sufficiently large and stable from age to age to constitute an important force to be reckoned with during profile analyses. Although the technique of heirarchical factor analysis typically yields general, verbal, and performance factors (e.g., Wallbrown et al., 1975), even this method was found to yield a fourth factor composed of Arithmetic and Digit Span for mentally retarded (Vance, Wallbrown, & Fremont, 1978) and learning disabled (Blaha & Vance, 1979) populations.

Table 4 shows the various third factors that have emerged for numerous normal and exceptional populations. Of the 31 groups summarized in Tables 2 and 3, meaningful distractibility factors emerged 21 times, or in two thirds of the analyses. In most of the studies, the third factor consisted primarily of two or all three of the freedom from distractibility triad of Arithmetic, Coding, and Digit Span. In some of the studies, other subtests had small but significant loadings on the third factor. However, in studies 10, 14, and 27 (Karnes & Brown, 1980; Johnston & Bolen, 1984; and Peterson & Hart, 1979), the third factor consisted primarily of Arithmetic. Overall, the three so-called "distractibility" subtests *each* loaded .35 or more on only 5 of the 21 distractibility factors, but at least two of the subtests loaded .35 or more on 18 of the studies (86%). Since Digit Span was excluded from a number of the WISC-R factor-analytic studies (including seven that produced distractibility factors), these results give favorable—but not clear-cut or decisive—support for the existence and composition of the distractibility dimension.

TABLE 4   (continued)

WISC-R Subtest	(19)	(22)	(26)	(27)	(28)	(29)	(30)	(31)	Median
Verbal									
Information	22	40	14	15	33	05	−05	24	24
Similarities	14	27	22	18	24	08	03	23	18
Arithmetic	41	69	49	75	75	48	58	54	49
Vocabulary	21	20	17	07	13	−02	−10	02	14
Comprehension	09	06	45	−02	−25	14	04	12	12
Digit Span	—	48	37	14	—	79	20	29	41
Performance									
Picture Completion	11	14	−01	03	07	03	−27	12	09
Picture Arrangement	13	24	12	08	32	28	−18	45	12
Block Design	13	33	23	10	12	19	10	05	17
Object Assembly	02	03	13	−11	−13	06	10	09	10
Coding	41	26	57	21	74	31	42	43	39
Mazes	—	—	—	—	—	—	—	24	22

Implications for Interpretation

Since research evidence suggests that the third WISC-R factor is meaningful, real, and fairly stable in terms of content, it has to enter an examiner's approach when attacking a profile. However, since it is smaller in size than the first two WISC-R factors, does not always emerge in WISC-R analyses, and varies in its composition, the distractibility factor deserves to take a back seat to the verbal comprehension and perceptual organization factors and, hence, to the V-P dichotomy. Consequently, freedom from distractibility factor scores should not be computed routinely for each child tested. The method described above for determining which verbal and performance scaled scores deviate significantly from the child's own mean scores should be the first step in interpretation. Then the distractibility factor should be explored only if one or more of its component subtests (Arithmetic, Digit Span, Coding) deviates significantly from its respective mean. When Arithmetic and Digit Span are consistent with the child's Verbal mean, and Coding is consistent with the Performance mean, the distractibility factor is not a discrete entity and usually does not merit interpretation. Even if one of the three subtests does depart significantly from the child's mean scores, a second criterion should then be applied; Does the distractibility factor reflect a unique or unidimensional ability? If, for example, a child's scaled scores on the three subtests range from 4 on Digit Span to 15 on Coding, a factor score for freedom from distractibility will be meaningless because this factor does not correspond to a unique dimension for the particular youngster. Thus, in order to interpret the distractibility factor properly: (a) the three scaled scores should be similar in magnitude to justify calling the factor a single dimension, and (b) the scores should differ from scores on the verbal and/or perceptual factors to support its existence as a discrete ability or trait. Empirical guidelines for making these determinations appear elsewhere (Kaufman, 1979, Chap. 3).

In those instances where there is justification for interpreting the third WISC-R factor, examiners have to use their clinical acumen to interpret the meaning of the score. Just because the factor is labeled freedom from distractibility does not automatically imply that high scores reflect attention concentration and low scores mean distractibility or poor attention span. This behavioral explanation is plausible, but so is at least one other noncognitive interpretation: freedom from disruptive anxiety. Lutey (1977) noted that research results pinpoint Arithmetic, Digit Span, and Coding as the Wechsler subtests most vulnerable to anxiety—not the kind of anxiety associated with psychopathology but more of a state or test anxiety.

In contrast to these behavioral explanations of the third factor there are some sensible cognitive alternatives. According to Bannatyne (1971, 1974), Arithmetic, Digit Span, and Coding all require sequencing ability and might be grouped together on that basis alone; indeed, the dimension may reflect sequential processing, as assessed by the K-ABC (Kaufman & Kaufman, 1983a). From Guilford's structure-of-intellect model, Meeker (1969, 1975) has shown that Arithmetic, Digit Span, and Coding B are the only WISC-R subtests that are primarily measures of symbolic content; and Jensen (1984) typically interprets the third factor as a measure of memory. Consequently, interpretations of the third factor in the ability rather than the behavioral domain are plausible, with sequencing, symbolic skills, or short-term memory qualifying as reasonable explanations of high or low scores on the Arithmetic-Digit Span-Coding trilogy.

Since there are numerous potential meanings of the third WISC-R factor, it is evident that it cannot be interpreted in isolation. Conceivably, high or low scores on this dimension will mean different things for different children. A behavioral explanation requires clinical support from observations of the child's test behavior. It would indeed be foolish to attribute low scores on the third-factor subtests to distractibility or anxiety for a child who was observed to be attentive, absorbed by the tasks, and calm. Prudent examiners will study the nature of the child's incorrect responses, information about the child's background, and method of solving problems, along with their clinical observations of the child's behavior, before trying to explain scores on the so-called distractibility factor. Further details on this clinical approach to third-factor interpretation are provided in Kaufman (1979, Chap. 3).

In view of the potential multifaceted clinical and psychometric contributions of the third factor for thorough profile interpretation, one final implication of the research findings should be implicit: Administer Digit Span routinely, and do not think of this subtest as either optional or supplementary (Evans & Hamm, 1979; Kaufman, 1979, p. 116).

Scatter

Sizable V-P IQ discrepancies have frequently been associated with exceptionalities such as neurological impairment (e.g., Holroyd & Wright, 1965), and considerable subtest scatter is often deemed a significant correlate of learning disabilities or minimal brain dysfunction (e.g., Clements, 1966). Unfortunately, these assertions have commonly been made without reference to, or awareness of, the fluctuations characteristic of normal profiles. If a V-P IQ discrepancy or an amount of subtest scatter is found to occur frequently in a normal population, how can that same discrepancy or degree of scatter be used to help diagnose an abnormality?

Research Results

Analysis of WISC-R V-P IQ discrepancies for the standardization sample revealed that the average child had a discrepancy of 9.7 points (SD = 7.6), regardless of the direction of the discrepancy (Kaufman, 1976a). Whereas the average discrepancy was a function of socioeconomic status (mean = 10.7 for children of professionals, decreasing steadily to mean = 9.2 for children of unskilled workers), V-P IQ discrepancies were unrelated to the variables of age, sex, and race. From these data it was discovered that 1 out of 2 normal children have a discrepancy that is significant at the 15% level (9 or more points), 1 out of 3 have a discrepancy that is significant at the 5% level (12+ points), and 1 out of 4 have a discrepancy that is significant at the 1% level (15+ points). Thus, it is common for normal children to differ significantly in their verbal comprehension and perceptual organization abilities. Although analogous data were published for the 1949 WISC (Seashore, 1951), clinicians and researchers frequently do not seem to have internalized the findings.

Normal subtest scatter is a topic that was apparently ignored in the voluminous literature on the 1949 WISC. Yet despite a lack of data on what constitutes normal subtest scatter, stereotypes persisted that the WISC profiles of emotionally disturbed and learning disabled children are replete with considerable subtest scatter. A study with the WISC-R standardization sample suggests that these stereotypes may be false. Normal children aged 6½ to 16½ displayed considerable scatter in their subtest profiles (Kaufman, 1976b). Although two main indexes of scatter were analyzed, only one is discussed here: scaled-score range, which

equals the child's highest scaled score minus his or her lowest scaled score on either the Verbal, Performance, or Full Scales. The results showed that the average scaled-score range for the full scale (10 regular subtests) equaled the astounding value of 7 (SD = 2). Furthermore, the mean of 7 ± 2 was found to characterize each of the 11 age groups, males and females, blacks and whites, and children from different socioeconomic backgrounds.

Thus, the average child had a scaled-score range of about 6–13 or 7–14. Since values within one standard deviation of the mean are typically deemed normal, even a scaled-score range of 9 is a normal amount of scatter. From that vantage point, ranges such as 3–12 or 6–15 on the 10 subtests are normal and expected. How often have ranges such as these been perceived as indicative of scatter, and used to corroborate the diagnosis of an abnormality? The answer is: probably too frequently. Certainly, we know from personal contact that many experienced WISC-R clinicians were dumbfounded by the amount of scatter that characterizes the profiles of normal youngsters.

Implications for Interpretation

The existence of data on normal V-P IQ discrepancies and subtest scatter should be utilized by clinicians and researchers alike as a source of basal levels of such fluctuations. Frequency of occurrence is a common criterion for determining the existence of an abnormality such as mental retardation. It makes sense to use a similar criterion before deciding whether a discrepancy is abnormal. Statistical significance is important, but it is not sufficient. It is helpful to know whether profile fluctuations, either within a scale or between scales, are statistically significant (i.e., whether differences in scores are "real" or merely due to chance), but it is also essential to know how prevalent these fluctuations are. Table 5 indicates the size of V-P discrepancies, and of scaled-score ranges, that occur with different frequencies. For example, a V-P IQ discrepancy of at least 26 points occurs at a frequency of less than 5% in the normal population; so does a verbal scaled-score range of 9 points, a performance range of 11 points, and a full-scale range of 12 points. These values would be used to detect abnormally large V-P discrepancies and scaled-score ranges in children's profiles for examiners who feel that 5% represents a reasonable criterion of abnormality. Examiners

TABLE 5   Degree of Abnormality of WISC-R V-P Discrepancies and of an Index of Subtest Scatter

Frequency of Occurrence in Normal Population	V-P IQ Discrepancy (Regardless of Direction)	Scaled-score Range[a]		
		Verbal (5 Subtests)	Performance (5 Subtests)	Full Scale (10 Subtests)
Less than 15%	19	7	9	10
Less than 10%	22	8	10	11
Less than 5%	26	9	11	12
Less than 2%	30	10	12	13
Less than 1%	34	11	13	14

[a]Scaled-score range equals the child's highest scaled score minus his or her lowest-scaled score. This index of subtest scatter is computed separately for the verbal, performance, and full scales.

who choose other cutoff points can utilize the other values shown in the table; however, the decision about which criterion of abnormality to choose rests with each individual examiner and will often be a function of the purpose for which the information is to be used. The precise criterion is not as important as the fact that an examiner should always use an objective method of determining whether a V-P IQ discrepancy or the degree of fluctuation in a subtest profile is abnormally large when compared to basal levels of normal scatter.

It is thus apparent that diagnostic decisions should not be based, even partially, on a significant V-P discrepancy or on the existence of significant strengths and weaknesses in the subtest profile unless the fluctuations occur infrequently in the normal population. When V-P IQ discrepancies and/or scaled-score ranges are both significant and rare, the WISC-R profile can be used as one piece of evidence to help corroborate a diagnosis of learning disabilities or brain damage, for example. However, when WISC-R fluctuations cannot be considered unusual by any reasonable standard, the WISC-R profile should usually be treated as irrelevant to an ultimate diagnosis of an abnormality. That is not to imply that the fluctuations are useless. Quite the opposite, a V-P discrepancy of 17 points, although not unusual, is still large enough to suggest a difference in the child's verbal and nonverbal abilities; such differences often translate to important remedial suggestions. Similarly, a strength and a weakness in the subtest profile offer insight into the child's pattern of abilities and may tie in with important educational suggestions, even if the amount of scatter in the profile is clearly normal. In summary, significant

V-P discrepancies and strengths or weaknesses in the subtest profile have educational significance, but they do not have diagnostic significance as well unless the fluctuations occur infrequently in the normal population.

Actually, even the diagnostic significance of an unusually large V-P discrepancy or scaled-score range requires reevaluation and systematic analysis with numerous populations of exceptional children. Assumptions that brain-injured, learning-disabled, and emotionally disturbed children are characterized by scatter in their Wechsler profiles must be put to empirical test. The proportions of these youngsters with very large V-P discrepancies and scaled-score ranges need to be compared to normal proportions for a wide variety of homogeneously defined exceptional groups.

The results of several studies do not seem promising for differential diagnosis. In a study of 41 learning-disabled children, Anderson, Kaufman, and Kaufman (1976) found that this group had a mean V-P discrepancy of 12.5 points, which was significantly larger than the mean for normal children; however, the scaled-score ranges for the learning-disabled children did not differ significantly from the normative values. Kavale and Forness (1984), in a meta-analysis of 94 studies investigating WISC-R performance of learning-disabled children found that the average learning-disabled child has discrepancies that are neither significant nor unique and scaled score ranges that are not significantly greater than those for normal children.

Representative research with other normal and learning-disabled samples and with a variety of exceptional groups has produced similar findings, as summarized in Table 6. Whereas some studies have produced statistically significant differences when comparing indexes of WISC-R scatter for clinical samples with comparable data for the standardization sample (e.g., Gutkin, 1979b; Tabachnick, 1979), these differences have not been meaningful in a practical sense. Quite consistently, the distributions of scatter indexes have overlapped greatly for normal and abnormal populations—a finding that holds both for V-P discrepancies and subtest variability. The only major exception is Teeter, Moore, and Petersen's (1982) study with normal, educationally disadvantaged, and learning-disabled Native American children.

Interestingly, even though Naglieri (1979) found significantly more scatter in his learning-disabled group than in the normative sample, his learning-disabled population did not differ significantly from a local control group of normal children on V-P discrepancy or subtest scatter.

The failure of scatter in WISC-R profiles to distinguish, in a meaningful way, between normal and clinical samples mitigates against its value in diagnosis. Perhaps the msot damaging testimony in the case against the use of WISC-R scatter for differential diagnosis comes from Gutkin's (1979b) investigation of 101 special education students with various handicaps. He found that indexes of V-P and subtest scatter did not discriminate among groups of emotionally disturbed, learning-disabled, minimally brain injured, and educable mentally retarded children. Although Gutkin's groups were relatively small, and many of the studies reported above deal with samples of limited size and generalizability, the consistency of the results from study to study represents a pattern that may ultimately challenge existing stereotypes of marked scatter in the profiles of exceptional children. Many additional studies are still needed, however, to understand more fully the relationship of interscale and intrascale scatter to various abnormal conditions.

Characteristic Profiles

The perpetual search for characteristic profiles in groups of exceptional children has turned up some interesting consistencies for children with school-related problems. In studies of the 1949 WISC groups of mentally retarded children and consistently performed relatively well on Picture Completion, Object Assembly, and Block Design, and poorly on Information, Arithmetic, and Vocabulary (Silverstein, 1968). Reading disabled children

tended to do well on the same three subtests on which the retarded groups had success, but scored characteristically low on four subtests: Information, Arithmetic, Digit Span, and Coding (Rugel, 1974b). The latter four subtests also proved particularly troublesome for various groups of learning-disabled children (Ackerman, Dykman, & Peters, 1976). Findings with the WISC-R to date seem highly consistent with the foregoing trends.

Research Results

A number of WISC-R investigations have been conducted with learning-disabled, emotionally and behaviorally disturbed, and mentally retarded children. The results of representative selection of these studies are summarized in Tables 7, 8, and 9, respectively. Presented here are the mean IQs for the diverse groups, along with a rank ordering of their mean subtests scores from 1 to 10, where 1 signifies the easiest test and 10 the hardest. (Digit Span and Mazes were not always given in these studies.) Tables 7, 8, and 9 also present consensus rankings, which were obtained by determining the mean ranking for each subtest and rank-ordering the means.

The rank orderings show some remarkable consistency within the various clinical areas. For learning-disabled and emotionally disturbed children, Object Assembly, Picture Completion, and Picture Arrangement were usually ranked as the easiest subtests and Coding, Information, and Arithmetic as the most difficult. For mentally retarded children, Picture Completion and Object Assembly were usually the easiest subtests and Arithmetic, Information, and Vocabulary were usually the most difficult.

Implications for Interpretation

Examination of the characteristic WISC-R profiles for learning-disabled children (Table 7), emotionally disturbed children (Table 8), and mentally retarded children (Table 9), points to the necessity of going beyond the V-P distinction in many cases. The three-factor solution seems to be more effective than the V and P IQs in explaining the observed rankings. The perceptual organization subtests tended to be the easiest for the learning-disabled groups shown in Table 7 and the emotionally disturbed groups shown in Table 8, yet many of the samples had negligible V-P IQ discrepancies. One reason for the lack of sensitivity of the V-P discrepancy for the learning-disabled and

TABLE 6 Mean V-P and Subtest Scatter Indexes for the Standardization Sample, Groups of Learning-Disabled Children, and Other Cross-Validation Samples

Source	N	Description of Sample	Average V-P IQ Discrepancy (Regardless of Direction)	Average Scaled-Score Range		
				Verbal (5 Subtests)	Performance (5 Subtests)	Full Scale (10 Subtests)
Kaufman (1976a, 1976b)	2200	Normal standardization sample	9.7	4.5	5.5	7.0
Schmidt and Saklofske (1983)	85	Average ability	10.5	4.9	5.2	7.1
Naglieri (1979)	20	Normal control group	12.6	—	—	8.0
Taylor, Ziegler, and Partenio (1984)	184	Normal white	9.6	—	—	—
Taylor, Ziegler, and Partenio (1984)	187	Normal black	8.9	—	—	—
Taylor, Ziegler, and Partenio (1984)	184	Normal Hispanic	13.7	—	—	—
Teeter, Moore, and Petersen (1982)	113	Normal Native American	30.2	4.4	5.9	10.1
Teeter, Moore, and Petersen (1982)	189	Educationally disadvantaged Native American	34.2	4.2	6.2	10.6
Schmidt and Saklofske (1983)	94	High ability	9.8	4.8	5.6	7.2
Anderson, Kaufman, and Kaufman (1976)	41	Learning disabled	12.5	4.8	5.7	7.5

Study	n	Group				
Bloom and Raskin (1980)	100	Learning disabled	10.6	—	—	—
Gutkin (1979b)	51	Learning disabled	11.9	4.2	6.4	7.7
Naglieri (1979)	20	Learning disabled	13.6	—	—	8.5
Ryckman (1981)	100	Learning disabled	—	—	—	8.2
Schiff, Kaufman, and Kaufman (1981)	30	Learning disabled	18.6	5.9	6.1	9.3
Schmidt and Saklofske (1983)	74	Learning disabled	11.7	4.8	6.0	7.9
Stevenson (1979)	55	Learning disabled	10.1	—	5.4	7.2
Tabachnick (1979)	105	Learning disabled	2.6	—	6.1	7.7
Teeter, Moore, and Petersen (1982)	150	Learning disabled Native Americans	28.7	3.9	6.8	9.9
Thompson (1980)	64	Learning disabled	10.0	—	—	7.6
Gutkin (1979b)	10	Mentally retarded	8.5	3.7	5.3	6.0
Naglieri (1979)	20	Mentally retarded	9.6	—	—	6.6
Thompson (1980)	14	Mentally retarded	7.6	—	—	5.9
Schmidt and Saklofske (1983)	24	Low ability	9.9	4.4	5.7	7.3
Gutkin (1979b)	17	Emotionally disturbed	12.9	4.9	6.0	7.8
Thompson (1980)	51	Psychological or behavioral disorder	8.4	—	—	7.2
Gutkin (1979b)	23	Minimally brain injured	11.8	4.6	6.1	7.3
Ollendick (1979)	121	Juvenile delinquents	—	4.5	5.7	7.3
Weiner and Kaufman (1979)	46	Referrals for learning and/or behavior problems	9.2	4.4	5.8	7.3
Strithart and Love (1979)	40	Referrals for learning disabilities	9.8	5.3	5.7	7.3
Moore and Wielan (1981)	434	Referrals for reading difficulties	11.2	4.6	5.9	7.6

TABLE 7   Rank Ordering of WISC-R Subtest Means for Learning-Disabled Samples

Source	N	Description of Sample	Information	Similarities	Arithmetic	Vocabulary	Comprehension	Picture Completion	Picture Arrangement	Block Design	Object Assembly	Coding	Mean V IQ	Mean P IQ	Mean FS IQ
Anderson, Kaufman, and Kaufman (1976)	41	Learning disabled	8.5	10	7	8.5	2	1	4	5	3	6	82	89	84
Clarizio and Bernard (1981)	278	Learning disabled	8	7	10	6	4	1	2.5	5	2.5	9	86	92	88
Fischer, Wenck, Schurr, and Ellen (1985)	266	Learning disabled	9.5	5.5	9.5	8	5.5	3	1	4	2	7	88	98	92
Henry and Wittman (1981)	40	Learning disabled (full-time placement)	8	4	9.5	5	3	1	6	7	2	9.5	84	85	83
Henry and Wittman (1981)	40	Learning disabled (resource placement)	10	4	9	7	5	1	2	6	3	8	89	95	91
Kaufman and McLean (1986)	198	Learning disabled	9	4.5	10	6	2	2	2	7	4.5	8	93	96	94
Law, Box, and Moracco (1980)	41	Learning disabled	7	7	5	9	2.5	7	2.5	10	1	4	87	87	86
Mishra (1984a)	64	Hispanic learning disabled	10	8	6	9	7	1	2	3	4	5	79	94	83
Mishra (1984b)	46	Native American learning disabled	9	5	8	7	4	1	2	3	6	10	81	88	82
Reilly, Wheeler, and Ettinger (1985)	40	Learning disabled	9	8	7	10	6	3	1.5	4	1.5	5	72	84	76
Schiff, Kaufman, and Kaufman (1981)	30	High IQ learning disabled	3	1	9	2	4	8	5	6	7	10	128	113	123
Smith, Coleman, Dokecki, and Davis (1977a)	132	High IQ learning Disabled	10	6	9	7	5	2	3	4	1	8	90	100	93
Smith, Coleman, Dokecki, and Davis (1977a)	72	Low IQ learning disabled	10	6.5	8	6.5	5	2	4	3	1	9	76	80	76
Vance et al. (1975)	58	Learning disabled	8	5.5	10	4	3	2	5.5	7	1	9	91	91	91
Vance and Fuller (1983)	68	Learning disabled	8	6	9	5	2	4	3	7	1	10	98	99	99
Zingale and Smith (1978)	30	High SES learning disabled	10	7	9	6	5	2	3	4	1	8	90	98	93
Zingale and Smith (1978)	56	Middle SES learning disabled	9	5	10	6	7	2	3	4	1	8	87	96	90
Zingale and Smith (1978)	36	Low SES learning disabled	10	6	8	9	5	2	3	4	1	7	82	90	84
Consensus Rankings			10	6	9	7	4	2	3	5	1	8			

TABLE 8   Rank Ordering of WISC-R Subtest Means for Emotionally or Behaviorally Disturbed Samples

Source	N	Description of Sample	Information	Similarities	Arithmetic	Vocabulary	Comprehension	Picture Completion	Picture Arrangement	Block Design	Object Assembly	Coding	Mean VIQ	Mean PIQ	Mean FS IQ
													WISC-R Subtest		
Clarizio and Bernard (1981)	67	Emotionally disturbed	8.5	5.5	8.5	7	5.5	2.5	2.5	4	1	10	88	93	90
Dean (1977)	41	Emotionally disturbed	10	5	9	7	8	2	3	4	1	6	81	94	—
Fischer, Wenck, Schurr, and Ellen (1985)	61	Emotionally disturbed	9	5	8	7	6	3	1.5	4	1.5	10	85	91	87
Hale and Landino (1981)	14	Emotionally disturbed (conduct problems)	6	7	10	8	3	1	5	2	4	9	—	—	—
Hale and Landino (1981)	26	Emotionally disturbed (withdrawn)	9	8	10	6	7	4	3	1	2	5	—	—	—
Hale and Landino (1981)	26	Emotionally disturbed (mixed)	2	6	10	7	4	2	3	5	1	9	—	—	—
J. D. Morris, Evans, and Pearson (1978)	71	White emotionally disturbed	8	2	7	6	3	1	5	9	4	10	—	—	—
Henry and Wittman (1981)	40	Emotionally disturbed	8	4	9	7	5	2	3	6	1	10	87	91	88
J. D. Morris, Evans, and Pearson (1978)	42	Black emotionally disturbed	10	9	4	8	2	1	6	5	3	7	—	—	—
Reilly, Wheeler, and Etlinger (1985)	21	Emotionally disturbed	9	5	10	8	7	2	3.5	1	3.5	6	79	92	84
Roth and Nicholson (1984)	21	Emotionally disturbed (conduct disorder)	10	5	9	8	3	6	1	4	2	7	88	94	90
Vance and Fuller (1983)	67	Behaviorally disordered	10	4.5	8	6	1	4.5	3	7	2	9	90	90	89
Ollendick (1979)	121	Juvenile delinquents	9	7	6	10	5	1	3	4	2	8	82	90	85
Reilly, Wheeler, and Etlinger (1985)	40	Juvenile delinquents	10	8	5	9	7	1	2.5	4	2.5	6	73	82	76
Roth and Nicholson (1984)	20	Juvenile delinquents (conduct disorder)	8	5	7	9.5	6	1	3	4	2	9.5	80	85	81
Consensus rankings			10	6	8	7	5	2	3	4	1	9			

TABLE 9 Rank Ordering of WISC-R Subtest Means for Mentally Retarded Samples

Source	N	Description of Sample	Information	Similarities	Arithmetic	Vocabulary	Comprehension	Picture Completion	Picture Arrangement	Block Design	Object Assembly	Coding	Mean VIQ	Mean PIQ	Mean FS IQ
									WISC-R Subtest							
Clarizio and Bernard (1981)	141	Educable mentally retarded	8.5	8.5	7	10	5	1	3	4	2	6	68	74	68
Henry and Wittman (1981)	40	Educable mentally retarded	9	4	8	5	3	1	10	7	2	6	66	66	63
Kaufman and Van Hagen (1977)	80	Mentally retarded	6	4.5	9	10	4.5	1	7	2.5	2.5	8	54	56	51
Law, Box, and Moracco (1980)	30	Educable mentally retarded	10	6	5	8	2.5	1	7	9	4	2.5	68	71	66
Reilly, Wheeler, and Etlinger (1985)	20	Educable mentally retarded	7	8	6	9	5	1	2.5	10	2.5	4	59	63	58
Consensus rankings			9	6	8	10	3	1	5	7	2	4			

emotionally disturbed children is the disparity between the children's performance on Coding and the remainder of the Performance scale. In fact, Coding and Arithmetic are among the most difficult subtests for the learning-disabled and emotionally disturbed samples and these tasks are usually joined at the bottom of the pile by the third distractibility subtest (Digit Span) whenever this optional task is administered (e.g., Fischer, Wenck, Schurr, & Ellen, 1985; Henry & Wittman, 1981; Kaufman & McLean, 1986; Vance & Fuller, 1983). Consequently, it is reasonable to postulate strong ability for learning-disabled and emotionally disturbed children in perceptual organization, medium ability in verbal comprehension, and weak ability in whatever is measured by the third factor. Indeed, M. L. Smith (1979) found that the freedom from distractibility factor was more effective than the other two factors in discriminating between disabled and nondisabled readers in grade 2, and was also a significant discriminator between the two groups in grades 4 and 6.

However, the three-factor model does not account for the very poor performance by learning-disabled and emotionally disturbed children on the Information subtest; nor does it explain the characteristic profiles of mentally retarded youngsters who typically perform poorer on Vocabulary than Digit Span. Not surprisingly, researchers in this area have looked for alternative groupings of Wechsler subtests to explain the persistent profiles. The most popular alternative is Bannatyne's category system, an approach that has been applied to WISC data by Rugel (1974b), and to WISC-R data by numerous investigators (e.g., Decker & Corley, 1984; Gutkin, 1979a; M. D. Smith, Coleman, Dokecki, & Davis, 1977a, 1977b; Vance & Singer, 1979). From this framework, reading and learning-disabled children have strong spatial ability (Picture Completion, Object Assembly, Block Design), medium verbal conceptualization ability (Similarities, Vocabulary, Comprehension), weak sequencing ability (Arithmetic, Digit Span, Coding), and a limited fund of acquired knowledge (Information, Arithmetic, Vocabulary) (e.g., Decker & Corley, 1984; Fischer et al., 1985; Vance & Singer, 1979). In contrast, retarded youngsters have no deficit in sequencing ability but have a strength in spatial ability that is offset by an acquired-knowledge weakness (Clarizio & Bernard, 1981; Kaufman & Van Hagen, 1977). However, Clarizio and Bernard (1981) found that

Bannatyne's category system was not useful in discriminating between learning-disabled, emotionally disturbed, mentally retarded, and nonhandicapped children, and Henry and Wittman (1981) found that the categories did not discriminate between learning-disabled and emotionally disturbed children.

Gutkin (1979a) demonstrated the inadvisability of generalizing the characteristic Bannatyne profile to Mexican-American learning-disabled children. Whereas he found the spatial > conceptual > sequencing profile for white learning-disabled children, he found a spatial > sequencing > conceptual group profile for Hispanics. The low conceptual score is consistent with a bulk of research showing that Spanish-speaking children perform relatively poorly on verbal conceptual tasks (Kaufman, 1979, pp. 31–34), and Gutkin's finding was largely predictable. Mishra (1984a) found a similar pattern for a sample of Hispanic children, and McShane and Plas (1982) and Zarske and Moore (1982) reported comparable findings for samples of Native American children. These results underscore the need to understand better the interaction between type of exceptionality and ethnic background and to generalize cautiously from data-based validity and descriptive studies.

Models other than Bannatyne's are also plausible as explanations of profiles obtained by exceptional children. Keogh and Hall (1974) related Witkin's work on the field-independent/field-dependent cognitive style to the abilities of mentally retarded children, and Stevenson (1980) analyzed WISC-R data for learning-disabled children, and Paget (1982) for emotionally disturbed children, from the vantage point of Witkin's approach. The application of Witkin's research to the characteristic profiles is quite logical in view of the finding that individuals with field-independent cognitive styles perform quite well on the Picture Completion, Object Assembly, and Block Design subtests (i.e., the strong areas for mentally retarded, reading-disabled, and learning-disabled groups). Also pertinent are the various processing models stemming from neuropsychology. Cerebral specialization researchers (Bogen, 1969; Gazzaniga, 1975; Nebes, 1974, Ornstein, 1978) have distinguished between left-hemisphere and right-hemisphere functioning: the left brain processes stimuli analytically, logically, and sequentially, in contrast to the global, holistic, nonverbal processing style of the right brain. Das and his colleagues (Das, 1973; Das, Kirby, & Jarman, 1975; Kirby & Das, 1977) made similar distinctions between successive and simultaneous processing, although these investigators do not adhere to a left hemisphere—right hemisphere explanation of the dual processing modes. Regardless of the neuropsychological model employed, it seems evident from an examination of the characteristic profiles of reading- and learning-disabled children that as a group these youngsters tend to excel in holistic, nonverbal, simultaneous processing but are deficient in successive and sequential processing. This conclusion has been supported by Kaufman and McLean (1986).

Which approach best explains the data—the factor analysis, Bannatyne's regroupings, the field-independent cognitive style, the two modes of processing stimuli, or some other model not mentioned here? All are potential explanations, depending on the specific child being assessed. Group profiles are important, but they do not tell us about specific individuals within the group. We need to approach each profile as a specific interpretive challenge, to be understood in the context of that child's particular cultural background and test behaviors. What is important is that we come armed with up-to-date knowledge about different psychological theories, so that we can select the appropriate one to best fit the data and history of a given child. The results of factor analysis should impel us to begin interpretation from the vantage point of a verbal—nonverbal dichotomy. However, the findings from investigations of exceptional samples implore us to depart from the dichotomous model whenever this two-pronged approach is found to be unsatisfactory for an individual and try to locate a more pertinent model from the accumulated fund of psychological theory and research. Nonetheless, the apparent characteristic profiles for some exceptional populations should *not* be used for diagnostic purposes, since research on differential diagnosis has generally been unfavorable (Clarizio & Bernard, 1981; Henry & Wittman, 1981) and meta-analytic research has indicated slightly significant but not necessarily distinctive performance on recategorized groupings for learning-disabled children (Kavale & Forness, 1984). But like the recommendation regarding findings of marked subtest scatter, the occurrence of a distinct WISC-R profile for a handicapped child does have important implications for remedial intervention.

Examination of the recurring Wechsler profiles for certain exceptional groups raises another interesting issue—the distinction between ability and achievement. Retarded groups usually perform poorest on the three subtests in Bannatyne's acquired knowledge grouping, and reading- and learning-disabled populations score low on two of these subtests (Information and Arithmetic). Consequently, depressed V and F-S IQs may be a direct effect of poor school achievement and inadequate acquired learnings for these youngsters, thereby providing an incorrect estimate of their so-called ability, potential, capacity, and so on. Any definitions of learning or reading disorders that include the stipulation of normal intelligence as a prerequisite for classification are therefore suspect.

Assessment of Minorities

A number of investigations have been conducted using the WISC-R with minority group youngsters. Whereas the results cannot possibly resolve the thorny issues associated with this topic that are currently the subject of controversy, not to mention litigation and legislation, some of these studies are nevertheless worthy of discussion.

Research Results

As indicated previously, Reschly's (1978) factor-analytic investigation supported the construct validity of the WISC-R for blacks, Chicanos, and Native Americans. Additional evidence of construct validity was cited above for blacks (Gutkin & Reynolds, 1981; Johnston & Bolen, 1984; Vance & Wallbrown, 1978), Hispanics (Dean, 1979a, 1980; Gutkin & Reynolds, 1980; Sandoval, 1982; Stedman et al., 1978), and Native Americans (Zarske et al., 1981).

The three WISC-R IQs have also been shown to be as reliable for groups of Hispanic youngsters as they are for the standardization sample (Dean, 1977, 1979b), and the reliabilities of the separate subtests were found to be equivalent for samples of white, black, and Hispanic youngsters (Oakland & Feigenbaum, 1979). However, Elliott et al. (1985) found that the 3-year stability of the WISC-R was equal for whites and blacks, but significantly greater for whites than Hispanics. Explorations into the differential validity of the WISC-R for various ethnic groups has generally shown no bias against minority children when this definition of test bias is employed. Reynolds and Hartlage (1979) found

Full Scale IQs to correlate significantly with WRAT scores for both blacks and whites and further found no significant differences between the correlations or regression lines for these two ethnic groups. Similarly, Reschly and Reschly (1979) found WISC-R Full Scale IQs and factor scores to correlate significantly with the reading and mathematics portions of the Metropolitan Achievement Tests, and with teacher ratings of "academics," for whites, blacks, Hispanics, and Native American Papagos. These investigators found the coefficients for whites, blacks, and Hispanics to be comparable in magnitude, although the values for Native Americans were somewhat lower. Whereas differences in the regression lines for these groups were observed, these differences did not indicate bias against the minority groups (Reschly & Sabers, 1979). Similar findings of little or no difference in the ability of the WISC-R to predict achievement for majority versus minority children have been reported by Reynolds and Gutkin (1980), Oakland and Feigenbaum (1979) and Oakland (1983). Mishra (1983) and McCullough, Walker, and Diesnner (1985) found the WISC-R to be a significant predictor of achievement for Native American children and Naglieri and Hill (1981) found no differences beween the WISC-R/achievement regression lines for matched samples of black and white children. In addition to construct validity (factor analysis) and differential predictive validity, the rank ordering of item difficulties is also a suitable index of bias. Evidence of lack of bias according to the first two of these indexes was provided above; evidence of the unbiased nature of the WISC-R based on the third index is also available (Jensen, 1976; Lambert, 1978; Sandoval, 1979; Sandoval & Millie, 1979; Sandoval, Zimmerman, & Woo-Sam, 1983). However, Flaugher (1978) explained the intricacies of the test bias issue and argued cogently that many aspects of bias are not easily solved by empirical indexes. Consequently, the studies described here are seen as supportive of the notion that the WISC-R has some unbiased qualities, but there is no intention to imply that the issue is anywhere near closed or resolved.

Table 10 compares blacks and whites in the standardization sample, broken down by the variables of socioeconomic status, geographic region, and urban–rural residence. For both racial groups, IQs were a distinct function of socioeconomic background and were largely unrelated to urban versus rural residence. Interestingly, however, IQs were a clear function of geographic region for blacks but not for whites.

Implications for Interpretation

Research on construct validity suggests that the WISC-R measures the same basic abilities for minority groups as for whites, and the predictive validity data indicate that the IQs are equally effective for minorities and whites in performing the practical function of predicting school success. However, there are no available data to support the use of the WISC-R IQs for placement purposes, and intelligent testing demands that the WISC-R be supplemented by numerous additional measures before making educational decisions. The results do support the judicious use of the WISC-R with minority group members. Had the WISC-R been shown to predict achievement well for whites but not for minority group members, or had the factors for blacks and Hispanics borne no resemblance to Wechsler's verbal-performance dichotomy, the use of the WISC-R for these groups would have indeed been suspect. For additional discussion of this general topic, focusing on issues such as black dialect, research on bilingualism, and the nature of suggested supplements to the WISC-R, see Kaufman (1979, Chaps. 1, 2, 5).

The results of the analyses in Table 10 are particularly revealing because they show emphatically that one cannot make a general statement about how well blacks, as a group, perform on the WISC-R. Their performance is distinctly a function of two of the three variables explored in Table 10. Whereas the IQs of whites are not a function of geographic region, the 10-point discrepancy in F-S IQs for blacks from the northeast versus blacks from the south is striking. The mean V IQ of 95 for northeastern blacks, for example, is only slightly below the overall mean of 100 and is close to the mean IQs of whites from the north central and southern regions. In view of the fact that twice as many blacks as whites in the standardization sample and in the United States as a whole have parents in semiskilled and unskilled occupations (Wechsler, 1974, p. 22), the foregoing discrepancies for northeastern blacks are undoubtedly a function of socioeconomic background. The relationships between parental occupation and IQ depicted for both blacks and whites in Table 10 point to the importance of interpreting WISC-R IQs and scaled scores fully within the context of relevant background information regarding race, socioeconomic level, and subculture.

TABLE 10 Relationship of Background Variables to the Mean WISC-R IQs Earned by Blacks and Whites, Aged 6½–16½

Variables	Blacks			Whites			Total Group		
	V	P	F-S	V	P	F-S	V	P	F-S
Parental Occupation									
1. Professional and technical	92	91	91	110	107	109	109	106	108
2. Managerial, clerical, sales	92	91	90	104	104	104	103	103	103
3. Skilled	90	87	88	100	101	101	100	100	100
4. Semiskilled	87	87	86	98	99	98	96	97	96
5. Unskilled	83	83	82	92	93	92	-88	89	87
Geographic Region									
Northeast	95	92	93	104	103	104	103	101	102
North central	90	89	88	101	102	102	100	101	100
South	85	84	83	101	101	101	97	97	97
West	85	91	87	103	104	104	102	103	103
Residence									
Urban	89	88	87	103	103	103	101	100	101
Rural	84	85	84	100	101	100	98	99	99

Note. Data are from Tables 2, 3, and 4 in an article by Kaufman and Doppelt (1976). Data for nonwhites other than blacks (e.g., Orientals) are excluded from the computations for blacks but are included in the computations for the total group.

KAUFMAN ASSESSMENT BATTERY FOR CHILDREN (K-ABC)

The K-ABC (Kaufman & Kaufman, 1983b) is an intelligence and achievement battery for children $2\frac{1}{2}$ to $12\frac{1}{2}$ years of age and was developed from theory and research in cognitive psychology and neuropsychology. Intelligence is defined by the authors of the K-ABC as an individual's ability to process information. Two types of processing are identified on the K-ABC: sequential processing, which focuses on the serial or temporal order of stimuli to solve problems, and simultaneous processing, which focus on the gestalt-like, usually spatial integration of stimuli to solve problems. The K-ABC distinguishes intelligence from achievement in much the same way that Cattell and Horn (Cattell, 1971; Horn, 1968; Horn and Cattell, 1966) distinguish fluid and crystallized intelligence. On the K-ABC, achievement is measured with tasks that are traditionally assessed by verbal scales of intelligence (language, vocabulary, general information) and achievement tests (reading, arithmetic). Thus, the 16 subtests of the K-ABC are combined to form five global scales: Sequential Processing, Simultaneous Processing, Mental Processing Composite (the composite of Sequential and Simultaneous Processing), Achievement, and Nonverbal (a special "short form" consisting of Sequential and Simultaneous subtests that do not require verbal directions or verbal responses).

The K-ABC has been surrounded by controversy since its publication with much opposition as well as support. After what some professionals saw as an overly zealous advertising campaign prior to the publication of the K-ABC (Kamphaus & Reynolds, 1984), many reviews and research reports of the K-ABC were published which added fuel to the controversy when they criticized or praised many aspects of the K-ABC from its theoretical foundation to its psychometric characteristics. Probably the most notable example was the publication in October 1984 of a special issue of the *Journal of Special Education*. In this issue, noted researchers such as Jensen, Anastasi, Sternberg, and Das criticized and complimented the K-ABC, dealing with issues such as the validity of the K-ABC as an intelligence test, the theory and research in cognitive psychology and neuropsychology which formed the foundation of the K-ABC, the factor structure of the K-ABC, and the nature of black–white differences on the K-ABC.

For this chapter we have selected to present two areas of research on the K-ABC which have produced numerous publications and have important practical implications for using the K-ABC. Factor-analytic research of the K-ABC will be reviewed and the two general directions the research has taken will be discussed: unrotated loadings on *g*, or general intelligence, and rotated loadings on Sequential, Simultaneous, and Achievement factors. The neuropsychological research with the K-ABC will be summarized, focusing on studies that (a) related the K-ABC to the Luria-Nebraska, (b) examined sequential versus simultaneous processing for children with known neurological impairment, and (c) evaluated K-ABC scores for children with reading and learning disabilities.

Factor Analysis

As mentioned, factor-analytic research has taken two directions. First, the K-ABC as a measure of Spearman's (1927) idea of *g*, or general intelligence, has been investigated by determining the subtest loadings on the first, unrotated factor in factory analysis (*g*, according to Kaufman, 1975). Second, the validity of the organization of the K-ABC into Sequential, Simultaneous, and Achievement dimensions has been explored through rotated factor analysis.

Research Results

Table 11 presents the K-ABC subtest loadings on *g* found in seven studies. As seen in Table 11, the achievement subtests are consistently the highest, or among the highest, measures of *g*. The mental processing subtests that usually have the highest loadings on *g* are Photo Series, Triangles, Word Order, and Matrix Analogies. Gestalt Closure has the lowest loadings on *g*, with the exception of the study by Naglieri and Jensen (1987).

There have been three types of factor-analytic studies investigating the organization of the K-ABC. Two-factor solutions were used to determine the organization of the mental processing subtests into Sequential and Simultaneous scales. Three-factor solutions were used to determine the organization of *all* K-ABC subtests, both mental processing and achievement, into Sequential, Simultaneous, and Achievement scales. Joint factor analyses of the K-ABC and WISC-R were conducted to assess the degree to which the two

TABLE 11   Factor Loadings of the K-ABC Subtests on Unrotated First Factor (g)

K-ABC Subtest	(1)	(2)	(3)	(4)	(5)	(6)	(7)	Median
Sequential Processing								
Hand Movements	54	50	61	47	51	52	53	52
Number Recall	55	52	63	31	54	52	56	54
Word Order	64	68	79	36	55	59	62	62
Simultaneous Processing								
Gestalt Closure	47	47	52	42	16	32	47	47
Triangles	65	62	67	63	69	66	62	65
Matrix Analogies	62	54	63	65	61	52	62	62
Spatial Memory	56	50	58	45	44	45	56	50
Photo Series	67	70	74	45	61	55	69	67
Achievement								
Faces and Places	69	77	76	68	68	64	65	68
Arithmetic	*82*	*83*	*84*	*71*	*75*	*74*	*77*	*77*
Riddles	*78*	*83*	*77*	*81*	*74*	*74*	*75*	*77*
Reading Decoding	*79*	—	*75*	69	*73*	58	69	*71*
Reading Understanding	*71*	—	*80*	*71*	*80*	*70*	*70*	*71*

Note. Decimal points are omitted. Good measure of g (loadings of .70 or greater) are italicized. The groups are as follows:

1. Standardization sample, ages 2½ to 12½ (*N* = 2,000). *Source:* Jensen (1984).
2. Standardization sample, ages 5, 7, and 10 (*N* = 600). Median loadings for the three ages are shown in the table. Reading Decoding and Reading Understanding were not included in the analyses. *Source:* Keith and Dunbar (1984).
3. Standardization samples, ages 5, 7, and 10 (*N* = 600). Median loadings for the three ages are shown in the table. *Source:* Keith (1985).
4. A combination of matched samples of normal white and black children in the fourth and fifth grades (*N* = 172). *Source:* Naglieri and Jensen (1987).
5. Sample of normal children, ages 6 to 12½ (*N* = 212). *Source:* Kaufman and McLean (1987).
6. Sample of learning-disabled children, ages 6 to 12½ (*N* = 198). *Source:* Kaufman and McLean (1986).
7. Sample of referred children, ages 6 to 12½ (*N* = 585). *Source:* Keith (1986).

instruments measure the same constructs. It should be pointed out that the factor analyses summarized here are based on standardization data or on data collected after the publication of the K-ABC, but there was also considerable factor-analytic research conducted as part of the development of the K-ABC (Kaufman, Kaufman, Kamphaus, & Naglieri, 1982; Naglieri, Kaufman, Kaufman, & Kamphaus, 1981).

Kaufman and Kamphaus (1984) found that analysis of the mental processing subtests yield two significant factors for the K-ABC standardization sample of 2,000 children. The rotated factor loadings of the mental processing subtests on the two factors indicated clear sequential and simultaneous factors with the sequential subtests having the highest mean loadings across the 11 age groups on the sequential factors and the simultaneous sub-

tests having the highest mean loadings on the simultaneous factor. The Word Order and Number Recall subtests had the highest loadings on the sequential factor across the 11 age groups. Magic Window and Gestalt Closure had the highest loadings on the simultaneous factor for preschool children, but Triangles and Photo Series were the best measures of simultaneous processing for school-aged children. The only subtest that did not consistently have its highest loading on its designated factor across the age range was Hand Movements. For ages 2½ through 4, this subtest had its highest loading on the sequential factor, but after age 4, this subtest loaded about equally on both the sequential and simultaneous factors. Willson, Reynolds, Chatman, and Kaufman (1985) used confirmatory factor-analytic technique with the standardization data to support the organization of the sequential and Simultaneous scales and found clear evidence of strong loadings of the subtests on their designated factors, as well as independence of the two factors.

Keith (1985), used the 5-, 7-, and 10-year-olds from the standardization sample (200 in each age group), and again found that a two-factor solution was most appropriate for the mental processing subtests. The Hand Movements subtest had a significant loading only on the simultaneous factor for age 5 and like Kaufman and Kamphaus, had dual loadings at age 10. The Word Order subtest had dual loadings on the sequential and simultaneous factors at age 7. Keith (1985) also used confirmatory techniques to support the clear division of the K-ABC mental processing subtests into sequential and simultaneous factors.

Several studies have investigated the organization of all of the K-ABC subtests into sequential, simultaneous, and achievement dimensions. The results of these studies are summarized in Tables

12, 13, and 14. Table 12 contains the factor loadings of the subtests on the sequential factor, Table 13 for the simultaneous factor, and Table 14 for the achievement factor. The results of these three-factor solutions are not quite as clear as those of the two-factor solutions.

Kaufman and Kamphaus (1984), using all 11 age groups of the standardization sample, found what was generally replicated in all of the studies shown in Tables 12, 13, and 14: The sequential subtests had their highest loadings on the sequential factor, the simultaneous subtests on the simultaneous factor, and the achievement subtests on the achievement factor. Hand Movements again had dual loadings on the sequential and simultaneous factors. All of the six achievement subtests had meaningful secondary loadings on the sequential or simultaneous factors. Most notably, the latter finding is consistent with the philosophy of the K-ABC authors (Kaufman & Kaufman, 1983a) that sequential and simultaneous Processing are

TABLE 12   Factor Loadings of K-ABC Subtests on the Sequential Factor

K-ABC Subtests	(1)	(2)	(3)	(4)	(5)	Median
Sequential Processing						
Hand Movements	*43*	*34*	*40*	*47*	*43*	*43*
Number Recall	*71*	*66*	*88*	*80*	*77*	*77*
Word Order	*67*	*71*	*59*	*69*	*67*	*67*
Simultaneous Processing						
Gestalt Closure	04	15	−10	00	01	01
Triangles	19	19	28	26	13	19
Matrix Analogies	30	31	26	06	32	30
Spatial Memory	27	25	14	22	27	25
Photo Series	25	31	21	28	29	28
Achievement						
Faces and Places	17	17	15	20	16	17
Arithmetic	*42*	*38*	27	28	*36*	*36*
Riddles	31	34	15	23	22	23
Reading Decoding	*41*	32	24	10	26	26
Reading Understanding	*38*	24	17	15	20	20

Note. Decimal points are omitted. Loadings of .35 and above are italicized. The groups are as follows:

1. Standardization sample, ages 6 to 12½ (*N* = 1,300). Mean factor loadings are shown in the table. *Source:* Kaufman and Kamphaus (1984).
2. Standardization samples, ages 5, 7, and 10 (*N* = 600). Median factor loadings are shown in the table. *Source:* Keith (1985).
3. Sample of normal children, ages 6 to 12½ (*N* = 212). *Source:* Kaufman and McLean (1987).
4. Sample of learning-disabled children, ages 6 to 13 (*N* = 198). *Source:* Kaufman and McLean (1986).
5. Sample of referred children ages 6 to 12½ (*N* = 585). *Source:* Keith (1986).

TABLE 13   Factor Loadings of K-ABC Subtests on the Simultaneous Factor

K-ABC Subtests	(1)	(2)	(3)	(4)	(5)	Median
Sequential Processing						
Hand Movements	*37*	*34*	*36*	30	*34*	34
Number Recall	11	16	03	08	10	10
Word Order	20	25	13	18	25	20
Simultaneous Processing						
Gestalt Closure	*45*	*56*	29	*46*	*55*	46
Triangles	*65*	*65*	*65*	*63*	*69*	65
Matrix Analogies	*59*	*52*	*50*	*58*	*48*	52
Spatial Memory	*59*	*52*	*55*	*59*	*60*	59
Photo Series	*64*	*64*	*43*	*58*	*71*	64
Achievement						
Faces and Places	30	*38*	24	*29*	*41*	30
Arithmetic	*51*	*52*	30	*45*	*54*	51
Riddles	*41*	*43*	24	*44*	*52*	43
Reading Decoding	27	20	24	03	14	20
Reading Understanding	28	*31*	21	08	16	21

Note. Decimal points are omitted. Loadings of .35 and above are italicized. The groups are as follows:

1. Standardization sample, ages 6 to 12½ (N = 1,300). Mean factor loadings are shown in the table. *Source:* Kaufman and Kamphaus (1984).
2. Standardization samples, ages 5, 7, and 10 (N = 600). Median factor loadings are shown in the table. *Source:* Keith (1985).
3. Sample of normal children, ages 6 to 12½ (N = 212). *Source:* Kaufman and McLean (1987).
4. Sample of learning-disabled children, ages 6 to 13 (N = 198). *Source:* Kaufman and McLean (1986).
5. Sample of referred children ages 6 to 12½ (N = 585). *Source:* Keith (1986).

important aspects of school performance. Interestingly, Arithmetic related highly to the sequential factor for preschool children and the simultaneous factor for school-aged children; Riddles related to simultaneous processing for all-aged children; and Reading/Decoding and Reading Understanding related to sequential Processing for children ages 5 to 7 but equally well with sequential and simultaneous processing for ages 8 to 12½.

Willson et al. (1985) used confirmatory factor-analytic techniques to investigate the three-factor structure of the K-ABC using the standardization data. They found a lack of fit to an independent three-factor model. However, the highest loadings of the subtests were on their designated factors.

Keith (1985) used a three-factor solution for ages 5, 7, and 10 in the standardization sample but found what he called substantial departures from the scale structure of the K-ABC, referring to the loadings of achievement subtests on the sequential and simultaneous factors. He suggested that the three factors of the K-ABC might well be called verbal memory instead of sequential, nonverbal reasoning instead of simultaneous, and verbal reasoning instead of achievement. Keith (1985) utilized confirmatory techniques for the three-factor solution and, like Willson et al. (1985), did not find a good fit to the three-factor model. Keith and Dunbar (1984) conducted a confirmatory factor analysis for Keith's (1985) proposed alternative model of verbal memory, nonverbal reasoning, and verbal reasoning but only found a fairly good fit to that model.

Kaufman and McLean (1987) found the typical three factors of sequential, simultaneous, and achievement with a three-factor solution for 212 normal children. McCallum, Karnes, and Oshler-Stinnett (1985) found a three-factor solution similar to that of Kaufman and Kamphaus (1984) for a sample of gifted children, but their sample size of 54 was insufficient for reaching firm conclusions about the factor for gifted children. Clark (1984)

TABLE 14   Factor Loadings of K-ABC Subtests on the Achievement Factor

K-ABC Subtests	(1)	(2)	(3)	(4)	(5)	Median
Sequential Processing						
Hand Movements	16	31	20	17	22	20
Number Recall	25	21	17	13	22	21
Word Order	30	33	30	22	22	30
Simultaneous Processing						
Gestalt Closure	30	13	08	08	18	13
Triangles	27	24	32	25	17	25
Matrix Analogies	28	15	32	23	25	25
Spatial Memory	11	18	14	00	05	11
Photo Series	26	28	40	11	15	26
Achievement						
Faces and Places	*74*	*46*	*66*	*58*	*53*	*58*
Arithmetic	*48*	*54*	*64*	*54*	*42*	*54*
Riddles	*66*	*36*	*74*	*57*	*52*	*57*
Reading Decoding	*70*	*74*	*67*	*79*	*82*	*74*
Reading Understanding	*77*	*80*	*83*	*89*	*87*	*83*

Note. Decimal points are omitted. Loadings of .35 and above are italicized. The groups are as follows:

1. Standardization sample, ages 6 to 12½ ($N = 1,300$). Mean factor loadings are shown in the table. *Source:* Kaufman and Kamphaus (1984).
2. Standardization samples, ages 5, 7, and 10 ($N = 600$). Median factor loadings are shown in the table. *Source:* Keith (1985).
3. Sample of normal children, ages 6 to 12½ ($N = 212$). *Source:* Kaufman and McLean (1987).
4. Sample of learning-disabled children, ages 6 to 13 ($N = 198$). *Source:* Kaufman and McLean (1986).
5. Sample of referred children ages 6 to 12½ ($N = 585$). *Source:* Keith (1986).

factor-analyzed the K-ABC mental processing and achievement subtest scores for a sample of 293 normal children, but reported a two-factor solution, a simultaneous/achievement factor and a sequential/simultaneous/achievement factor. However, Clark failed to report a three-factor solution, so it is not possible to compare his results with other data on the K-ABC.

Keith (1986) factor analyzed the K-ABC mental processing and achievement subtest scores for a large sample of 585 children referred for psychoeducational evaluation. In a three-factor solution, he noted the three factors of sequential, simultaneous, and achievement but reported that the two reading subtests had much higher loadings than did the other achievement subtests on the achievement factor. He tried a four-factor solution and found a separate reading factor consisting of high loadings from the two reading subtests and suggeted that use of the K-ABC may be facilitated by this fourth factor. Kaufman and McLean (1986),

however, with a sample of 198 learning-disabled students, did not find evidence for Keith's (1986) four factors and found high coefficients of congruence between their three-factor solution and the three-factor solution reported by Kaufman and Kamphaus (1984).

In three studies, investigators conducted a joint factor analysis with the K-ABC and WISC-R. Kaufman and McLean (in press) found a rather clear three-factor solution for a sample of 212 normal children. The three factors were WISC-R verbal/K-ABC achievement, WISC-R perceptual organization/K-ABC simultaneous, and WISC-R freedom from distractibility/K-ABC sequential. Again, they did not find evidence to support Keith's (1986) fourth factor of reading.

Keith, Hood, Eberhart, and Pottebaum (1985) reported a joint factor analysis for the K-ABC and WISC-R for a sample of 568 referred children. They reported that a four-factor solution was most appropriate for this set of data. The four factors were named nonverbal reasoning (K-ABC simultaneous and WISC-R perceptual organization subtests), verbal reasoning (K-ABC achievement and WISC-R verbal comprehension subtests), verbal memory (K-ABC sequential and WISC-R freedom from distractibility subtests), and reading (K-ABC reading subtests).

Kaufman and McLean (1986) found that either a three-factor *or* a four-factor solution was appropriate for the joint factor analysis of K-ABC and WISC-R scores for a sample of 198 learning-disabled children. The three-factor solution corresponded to the one reported by Kaufman and McLean (in press) and the four-factor solution corresponded to the one reported by Keith et al. (1985).

Implications for Interpretation

The factor-analytic research with the K-ABC has several important implications for interpretation. First, the subtest factor loadings on the unrotated first afctor, the *g* loadings, were usually highest for the achievement subtests.

Keith and Dunbar (1984), Keith (1985), and Jensen (1984) argued that, on the whole, the achievement subtests are better measures of intelligences than the mental processing subtests, because of their higher loadings on *g*. Similarly, they argued that the mental processing subtests are poorer measures of *g* because of their lower loadings. In raising these arguments, they questioned both the validity of the K-ABC mental processing subtests as measures of intelligence *and* the validity of the intelligence/achievement distinction made on the K-ABC.

Kaufman (1984a) responded to the higher loadings of the achievement subtests with the counterargument that perhaps Spearman's (1927) concept of *g* is better called *general achievement* rather than general intelligence, especially if clear-cut achievement tests such as those on the K-ABC have the highest loadings on it. Kamphaus and Reynolds (1984) made an important point supporting Kaufman's (1984a) counterargument, stating that the K-ABC intelligence-achievement distinction "requires a different conceptualization of intelligence that not all have been able to grasp, still clinging to measures of achievement such as Arithmetic and Expressive Vocabulary as the best measure of 'intelligence' or *g*" (p. 216). Kaufman and McLean (1987), in a joint factor analysis of the K-ABC and WISC-R with a sample of 212 normal

children, found that the best measures of *g* were WISC-R Information and Comprehension subtests and K-ABC Reading/Understanding and Riddles subtests, all measure of acquired facts and school-related skills, as well as verbal ability. Furthermore, Kaufman and O'Neal (1987) in a factor analysis of the Woodcock-Johnson cognitive and achievement subtests with children from the standardization sample, found that the best measures of *g* were achievement subtests, including achievement measures such as science and social studies.

Kaufman's (1984a) notion that *g* is *general achievement* is given empirical support with the Kaufman and McLean (1987) and Kaufman and O'Neal (1987) studies. Kaufman and McLean indicated that calling subtests which obviously measure achievement, intelligence "simply because of high *g* loadings is not sensible." The higher *g* loadings of the achievement subtests is not seen as a threat to the validity of the K-ABC, but they do bring to light a need to reconsider the question "What is *g*?"

The factor-analytic studies investigating the structure of the K-ABC typically supported the Sequential, Simultaneous, and Achievement scales for samples of normal, referred, learning disabled, and gifted children. Thus, the basis for interpreting the K-ABC from its basic model has been validated several times. However, that does *not* mean that the Kaufmans' interpetation of the model is the only variable approach, or even that it is desirable to have but one way to interpret the data.

Alternative organizations, specifically Keith and Dunbar's (1984) verbal reasoning, verbal memory, and nonverbal reasoning factors, have received some support. As indicated by Kaufman (1984a), "one should always challenge the 'goodness of fit' of a test author's model to the profile fluctuations exhibited by any given child and one must be ready to replace the author's model with a new one (such as Keith and Dunbar's) whenever appropriate support can be mustered for the alternative approach" (p. 431). Interpretation of the K-ABC alternative models are similar to the alternative models (e.g., Bannatynes, Meeker's) that are often applied to the WISC-R. Kaufman (1979) indicated that for specific children the use of these alternative models with the WISC-R may be better for interpretation than the Verbal-Performance dichotomy.

In Chapter 6 of the K-ABC *Interpretative Manual* (Kaufman & Kaufman, 1983a), the

K-ABC authors supplied many alternative methods for interpreting the K-ABC in order to generate hypotheses about children's performance. Kaufman and Kaufman indicate that the models should be used *only* when a specific child's performance cannot be adequately explained using the sequential, simultaneous, achievement structure of the K-ABC. Similarly, Kamphaus and Reynolds (in press) offered the following alternative norms for use with the K-ABC: a reading composite (a combination of the Reading/Decoding and Reading/Understanding subtests), a verbal intelligence composite (a combination of the Expressive Vocabulary, Faces and Places, and Arithmetic subtests), and a global scale composite (a combination of the Sequential and Simultaneous scales and the verbal intelligence composite).

Kaufman and McLean (1987) indicated that personal orientation plays an important role in how the K-ABC is interpreted. For example, the K-ABC Achievement scale can be interpreted as achievement, as was intended by the K-ABC authors, or verbal intelligence, as suggested by Keith and Dunbar (1984), Keith et al. (1985), and Kamphaus and Reynolds (in press). Admirers of the traditional Wechsler model may favor a verbal IQ interpretation, whereas followers of the K-ABC may support an achievement rather than ability interpretation. As indicated by Kaufman and McLean (1986, 1987), the K-ABC can be interpreted from the three WISC-R factors of verbal comprehension, perceptual organization, and freedom from distractibility, and the WISC-R can be interpreted from the three K-ABC factors of sequential, simultaneous, and achievement.

The factor loadings of some specific subtests also provide useful information for interpretation, also summarized by Kaufman and Kaufman (1983a). Riddles is very much related to the simultaneous factor, especially below age 9. Thus, a child who has a relatively high score on the Simultaneous Processing scale may also have a Riddles score that is relatively high. Similarly, arithmetic is related to sequential processing for preschool children but simultaneous processing for school-aged children. Performance on Expressive Vocabulary and Faces & Places is related to simultaneous processing, especially for younger children. Finally, for school-aged children, Hand Movements is related to both sequential and simultaneous processing. Examiners who keep these factor-analytic findings firmly in mind will be able

to interpret K-ABC profiles intelligently, going well beyond a mere reporting of the global standard scores.

Neuropsychological Resarch

As indicated previously, the K-ABC was developed from a theoretical and research foundation, particularly in neuropsychology. One aspect of the K-ABC's foundation is the link to Luria's (1966) theory of how processing occurs in the higher cortical regions of the brain (Kaufman & Kaufman, 1983a). While the K-ABC is not intended to be a neuropsychological battery, the Sequential and Simultaneous Processing Scales were intended by the test authors to represent the two types of functioning identified by cerebral specialization researchers (Bogen, 1975; Gazzaniga, 1975, 1978; Kinsoburne, 1978).

Several studies have investigated the neuropsychological aspects of the K-ABC. Three types of studies are summarized here: the relationship between the K-ABC and neuropsychological batteries, K-ABC scores of neurologically impaired children, and K-ABC scores of disabled children who were not classified as neurologically impaired, but whose disabilities are generally linked to cortical dysfunctions. Kamphaus and Reynolds (1987) also reviewed some of this research and provided an in-depth discussion of the neuropsychological foundations of the K-ABC.

Research Results

Snyder, Leark, Golden, Grove, and Allison (1983) conducted one of the three studies investigating the relationship between the K-ABC and the Luria-Nebraska Children's Battery, an adaptation of the Luria-Nebraska Neuropsychological Battery. Snyder et al. (1983) reported a multiple regression analysis, with the 11 Luria-Nebraska subtests serving as predictors and the K-ABC global scales serving as criteria, for a sample of 46 children referred for learning problems. For the Sequential Processing scale, the five significant predictors, in order of their contribution to the multiple correlation of .71, were the Luria-Nebraska Intelligence, Rhythm, Receptive Speech, Motor, and Tactile subtests. The three significant predictors of Simultaneous Processing ($R = .70$) were the Ingelligence, Visual, and Motor Subtests. The three significant predictors of the Mental Processing Composite, with a multiple correlation of .74, were Ingelligence, Motor, and Visual. For the Achievement scale, the three significant predictors, with a multiple correlation of .70, were Arithmetic, Receptive Speech, Writing, and Memory. These patterns of multiple correlations are as expected. Sequential Processing, with its consecutive, verbal nature was best predicted by Intelligence, Rhythm, and Speech; Simultaneous Processing, with its visual-motor and spatial integration nature, was best predicted by Intelligence, Visual, and Motor. The Achievement Scale was best predicted by the Luria-Nebraska achievement and language subtests.

Naglieri and Pfeiffer (cited in Kaufman and Kaufman, 1983a) reported a similar study for a small sample of learning-disabled children, but the best predictors of each K-ABC scale differed from the Snyder et al. (1983) study. For Sequential Processing, the best predictors were Rhythm, Receptive Speech, Reading, Memory (multiple correlation of .81); for Simultaneous Processing, Intelligence, Writing, Tactile, and Receptive Speech (multiple correlation of .75) for Mental Processing Composite, Memory, Tactile, Rhythm, Intelligence, and Writing (multiple correlation of correlation of .73).

Leark, Snyder, Golden, Grove, and Allison (1983) conducted a study similar to the Snyder et al. (1983) study with a larger sample of 65 children. The Luria-Nebraska subtests Pathognomic, Intelligence, and Receptive had the highest correlations with the K-ABC Sequential Processing Scale (−.52 to −.60). The subtests with the highest correlations with Simultaneous Processing were Intelligence, Visual, and Pathognomic (−.47 to −.57). The subtests with the highest correlations with the mental Processing Composite were Intelligence, Pathognomic, and Receptive (−.48 to −.64) and the subtests with the highest correlation with the Achievement scale were Pathognomic, Memory, Reading, Expressive, and Arithmetic (−.61 to −.65).

Several studies investigated the K-ABC scores of neurologically impaired children. J. M. Morris and Bigler (1985) selected, from a group of 79 children, a sample of 25 children who were right-handed and neurologically impaired. The 25 children were further divided into three groups based on their K-ABC scores: One group had Sequential scores greater than Simultaneous scores, another group had Simultaneous scores greater than Sequential scores, and the third group had no significant differences between Sequential and Simulta-

neous. For the three groups, two neurological test scores were determined, a right-hemisphere composite and a left-hemisphere composite. A multivariate analysis of variance indicated a significant difference between the three groups on the two scores. Further analyses supported the lateralization of Sequential Processing to the left hemisphere and Simultaneous Processing to the right hemisphere.

Shapiro and Dotan (1985) investigated the K-ABC scores of a group of 13 children with soft neurological signs that were not unilateral in nature and 14 children that had lateralized deficits and either focal abnormalities on an EEG or structural damage on a CAT scan. Shapiro and Dotan found that six of the eight children who had significantly lower Sequential than Simultaneous scores, also had predominantly left-hemisphere deficits. Four of the six children who had significantly lower Simultaneous than Sequential scores also had predominantly right-hemisphere deficits. Also, Shapiro and Dotan (1985) found that of the 13 children with diffuse (not unilateral) neurological problems, only 3 had significant sequential-simultaneous discrepancies; however, all 14 with unilateral damage displayed significant differences in their processing style. As Reynolds (1986) reported, the mean sequential-simultaneous standard-score difference found by Shapiro and Dotan for the group with focal problems was 18.5 points, compared to only 7.7 points for the nonfocal group. The WPPSI and WISC-R did nto achieve that type of discrimination with V-P discrepancies, which were 13.4 for the focal group and 11.3 for the nonfocal sample.

Lewandowoski and De Rienzo (1985) investigated the K-ABC and WISC-R scores of three groups, each with 12 children: children with right-hemisphere damage, children with left-hemisphere damage, and a control group. Lewandowski and De Rienzo found that the group with right-hemisphere damage scored significantly lower on both the Mental Processing Composite and Full Scale IQ than the control group. As predicted, this group performed significantly greater on Sequential than Simultaneous Processing; however, contrary to prediction, they did not score significantly better on the WISC-R Verbal than Performance IQ. Neither the K-ABC nor the WISC-R dichotomy, however, produced significant discrepancies for the 12 children with left-hemisphere damage. Indeed, the left-brain-damaged group earned

Mental Processing Composite and Full Scale IQs that did not differ significantly from the values for the control group.

Hammack (1985) investigated two groups of learning disabled children; one group had soft neurological signs and the other did not. The group with soft neurological signs had a greater mean Mental Processing Composite/Achievement discrepancy and had significantly lower scores than the control group on all of the Achievement subtests. No significant patterns concerning Sequential and Simultaneous Processing were noted.

Four studies investigated the K-ABC scores of reading disabled children. Telzrow, Redmond, and Zimmerman (1984) looked at the K-ABC scores of 23 children classified into three of Boder's dyslexia subtypes (dysphonetics, dyseidetics, and mixed) and found a significant relationship between Boder classification and the pattern of Sequential/Simultaneous score differences. Specifically, they found that the dysphonetics were far more likely than the other two groups to have a significantly greater Simultaneous than Sequential score difference. Dysphonetic dyslexics would be predicted to be poor in the sequential processing of information because, by definition, they have symbol–sound integration difficulties and they tend to make semantic substitution errors when reading (Boder, 1973).

Telzrow, Century, Harris, and Redmond (1985) divided a group of 27 reading-disabled children into dysphonetics, dyseidetics, and mixed. Again, as anticipated, the dysphonetics had higher Simultaneous than Sequential scores. The results with the dyseidetic children were less clear, but a small number of children in this sample, as well as among reading-disabled children in general, have this particular problem.

Hooper and Hynd (1986) attempted to discriminate 55 dyslexic students from 30 normal readers using K-ABC scores. All Sequential Processing and Achievement subtests discriminated significantly between the groups, as opposed to only one of five Simultaneous Processing tasks (Matrix Analogies). Among the global scales, only Simultaneous Processing did not discriminate significantly between the two groups; on the Sequential and Achievement scales, the dyslexics scored about one standard deviation below the control group of normal readers. In a descriptive discriminant function analysis, one significant discriminant function was generated, accounting for about two

thirds of the variance between groups. Three Achievement subtests entered the discriminant function first, with two Sequential subtests (Number Recall, Word Order) entering fourth and fifth and adding significantly to the discrimination. When a predictive discriminant analysis was conducted, Hooper and Hynd (1986) found an exceptionally high overall "hit" rate of 91%, as the K-ABC subtests correctly classified 26 of 30 normal readers and 51 of 55 dyslexics. In a previous study, however, Hooper and Hynd (1985) found that the K-ABC was not effective in discrimination *among* the dyslexics when they were grouped in five Boder categories.

Stoiber, Bracken, and Gissal (1983) investigated the K-ABC scores of a sample of 32 reading-disabled children and a matched sample of 32 normal children. Their results indicated a significant Simultaneous > Sequential Processing discrepancy, for the reading-disabled children, consistent with findings of sequential problems in a wide variety of reading-disabled groups (Kaufman, 1979; Rugel, 1974a). The reading/disabled sample also had significantly lower scores on the Mental Processing Composite, Sequential Processing Scale, and reading subtests than did the control group; however, as anticipated, the groups did not differ significantly on the Simultaneous Processing Scale.

Implications for Interpretation

Overall, the neuropsychological research with the K-ABC provides encouraging support for the neuropsychological foundation that is claimed, by the test authors, for the battery, as well as for the use of the K-ABC as an adjunct measure, to be used along with neurological and neuropsychological tests. The K-ABC shows a close relationship with the Luria-Nebraska in several studies. The construct validity of the K-ABC is supported by the pattern of correlations between the individual K-ABC global scales and the Luria-Nebraska subtests; subtests on the Luria-Nebraska that should theoretically have higher relationships with specific K-ABC scales consistently emerged as the best predictors of each scale in multiple regression analysis. The studies investigating K-ABC scores of children with neurological impairment support the relationship of the K-ABC Sequential Scale to left-hemisphere impairment and of the Simultaneous scale to right-hemisphere impairment. The studies investigating the use of the K-ABC with dyslexic children support the finding that dysphonetic dyslexics are significantly low in Sequential Processing compared to other types of dyslexics, and they also show the Sequential Processing and Achievement scales to be excellent discriminators of normal and dyslexic children.

The various studies do not offer unequivocal support for all brain-related hypotheses that one might device from the K-ABC model, but that type of broad-based support is rare for any instrument, particularly with neurologically impaired *children*. As Lewandowski and De Rienzo (1985) point out, "studies of brain-damaged children, particularly those with early injuries, do not reveal the same patterns of deficit in cognitive functioning as seen in older children or adults" (p. 215). Not only is there much ambiguity about whether brain damage in the left hemisphere leads to language deficits in children, or whether right-hemisphere damage produces visual-spatial problems in children (Lewandowski & De Rienzo, 1985), but even so-called "focal" or localized brain injury in children may conceivably lead to diffuse intellectual deficits (Hebb, 1949).

Consequently, the results of studies using the K-ABC with brain-damaged and dyslexic children are unusually positive. Each study reported at least one significant finding consistent with the K-ABC model of sequential versus simultaneous processing. Furthermore, when both the WISC-R and K-ABC were included in the same study (which characterized most investigations summarized in the preceding section), the K-ABC Sequential-Simultaneous dichotomy was at least as effective as the WISC-R V-P discrepancy in relating, in predicted directions, to unilateral brain damage or type of dyslexia. Sometimes the K-ABC dichotomy was clearly superior to the WISC-R V-P discrepancy or to recategorized WISC-R scores (e.g., Shapiro & Dotan, 1985; Telzrow et al., 1984), but in no study to date was it clearly inferior.

The generally positive findings in neuropsychological investigations have important implications for clinicians. It is true that the K-ABC was constructed with neuropsychology firmly in mind: The underlying Sequential-Simultaneous split has roots in both Luria's theorizing and the findings of split-brain researchers; several subtests were selected, in part, because they resembled tasks that had proven utility in neuropsychological research or practice; the focus or process instead of product is consistent with the goals of neuropsychological

foundation; and so on (Kaufman & Kaufman, 1983a). However, the best intentions and rational arguments are inconsequential compared to hard data with brain-injured children and dyslexic youngsters, or via correlations between the K-ABC and neuropsychological instruments. Whereas the latter type of evidence was presented in the *K-ABC Interpretive Manual* (Kaufman & Kaufman, 1983a), the more recent investigations of dyslexic and brain-damaged children greatly enhance the validity of the K-ABC for use with these populations, along with the validity of the theoretical brain-related model that was intended to underlie the processing scales. The Sequential Processing Scale, which has been maligned by some (Sternberg, 1984), has emerged as a particularly valuable scale for neuropsychological and learning disabilities assessment based on the general results of the studies reported here.

Thus, the available neuropsychological data lend credence to the suggestions by the test authors and other researchers (Majovski, 1984; Snyder, Leark, Hynd, and Hayes, 1984) for the use of the K-ABC for neuropsychological assessment. Kaufman and Kaufman (1983a), Snyder, Leark, Hynd, and Hayes (1984), Majovski (1984) all propose that the K-ABC be included in neuropsychological batteries for the assessment of preschool and school-aged children, supplementing the information yielded by diverse other neurological, psychological, and neuropsychological instruments. Majovski (1984) stresses that the theoretical framework on which the K-ABC is based "has value for conducting neuropsychological assessment of children" (p. 263), and the battery "includes several tasks that help to better describe brain–behavior relationships. The profiles and clinical observations obtained by using the K-ABC can serve to pinpoint areas of functioning which may require follow-up testing" (p. 263).

Snyder et al. (1984) felt that the inclusion of an Achievement Scale in the K-ABC makes the battery valuable for neuropsychological assessment because (a) school learning is a necessary component of neuropsychological batteries, but existing individual achievement tests have questionable psychometric properties; and (b) many neuropsychologists (Halstead, 1947; Hebb, 1949) have likewise made a distinction between intelligence and acquired knowledge. They also see value in the K-ABC regarding the clinical utility of understanding children's strengths and weaknesses and translating them to the planning of individual educational programs.

All of these proposed uses of the K-ABC for neuropsychological evaluation are given added support by the positive results of the several relevant studies. However, as Kaufman and Kaufman (1983a), Majovski (1984), and Snyder et al. (1984) all emphasize, the K-ABC is neither a neurological nor a neuropsychological battery; but it does serve as an excellent measure for use in conjunction with such measures as part of a thorough neuropsychological evaluation.

CONCLUSIONS

The discussions of the WISC-R and K-ABC represent a condensation of the many areas of research conducted with the instruments. We discussed the particular areas of research because we felt they had the greatest impact for interpretation of the tests by school psychologists. For discussion of other areas of research, school psychologists should read *Assessment of Children's Intelligence and Special Abilities* (Sattler, 1982), *Intelligent Testing with the WISC-R* (Kaufman, 1979),and *Clinical and Research Applications of the K-ABC* (Kamphaus & Reynolds, 1987).

School psychologists are faced with a challenge, given the many advances in intelligence testing, the many new instruments available now and those that will be available in the near future, and the controversies surrounding intelligence testing. The following suggestions for using intelligence tests, summarized from Harrison (1986) and Kaufman and Flaitz (in press), are listed to help school psychologists meet the challenge.

1. School psychologists should be keenly aware of the strengths and limitations of the intelligence tests they use.
2. They should use intelligence tests only for the purposes for which they were designed and the purposes supported by research.
3. They should assume the role of detectives and scientists and use intelligence tests as tools to develop hypotheses.
4. They must be fully cognizant of the theories of intelligence and cognitive functioning and interpret intelligence test functioning in light of these theories.
5. They must be proficient with all of the new

and different intelligence tests available and must select and use the one appropriate for each child.
6. They must be adept at interpreting the results of intelligence tests in the context of clinical observations, background and environment assessment, and results from other types of tests.
7. They must make interpretations that include helpful interventions and go beyond mere labeling.

In conclusion, intelligence testing, despite its criticisms, limitations, and changes is a major aspect of the role of school psychologists in serving children. However, intelligence testing must be put in its proper perspective: The primary reason we use intelligence tests is to help children (Hobbs, 1975a, 1975b). Intelligence tests do not make decisions about children: people make decisions and we use intelligence tests to provide some of the information that we use in making decisions (Anastasi, 1982). As stated by Kaufman and Harrison (1986), "the basic principle of intelligence testing is that a child who is evaluated with an individual intelligence tests has special needs and it is the examiner's job to help meet them" (p. 159).

REFERENCES

Ackerman, P. T., Dykman, R. A., & Peters, J. E. (1976). Hierarchical factor patterns on the WISC as related to areas of learning deficit. *Perceptual and Motor Skills, 42,* 381–386.

Anastasi, A. (1982). *Psychological testing* (5th ed.). New York: Macmillan.

Anderson, M., Kaufman, A. S., & Kaufman, N. L. (1976). Use of the WISC-R with a learning disabled population: Some diagnostic implications. *Psychology in the Schools, 13,* 381–386.

Banas, N., & Willis, I. H. (1977). Prescriptions from WISC-R patterns. *Academic Therapy, 13,* 241–246.

Banas, N., & Wills, I. H. (1978). Prescriptions from WISC-R patterns. *Academic Therapy, 33,* 344–358.

Bannatyne, A. (1971). *Language, reading and learning disabilities.* Springfield, IL: Charles C Thomas.

Bannatyne, A. (1974). Diagnosis: A note on recategorization of the WISC scaled scores. *Journal of Learning Disabilities, 7,* 272–274.

Blaha, J., & Vance, H. (1979). The hierarchical factor structure of the WISC-R for learning disabled children. *Learning Disabilities Quarterly, 2,* 71–75.

Bloom, A. S., & Raskin, L. M. (1980). WISC-R Verbal-Performance IQ discrepancies: A comparison of learning disabled children to the normative sample. *Journal of Clinical Psychology, 36*(1), 322–323.

Boder, E. (1973). Developmental dyslexia: A diagnostic approach based on three atypical reading–spelling patterns. *Developmental Medicine and Child Neurology, 15,* 663–687.

Bogen, J. E. (1969). The other side of the brain: Parts I, II, and III. *Bulletin of the Los Angeles Neurological Society, 34,* 135–162, 191–203.

Bogen, J. E. (1975). Some educational aspects of hemispheric specialization. *UCLA Educator, 17,* 24–32.

Borland, J. H. (1986). IQ tests: Throwing out the bathwater, saving the baby. *Roeper Review, 8*(3), 163–167.

Carlson, L., Reynolds, C. R., & Gutkin, T. B. (1983). Consistency of the factorial validity of the WISC-R for upper and lower SES groups. *Journal of School Psychology, 21,* 319–326.

Cattell, R. B. (1971). *Abilities: Their structure, growth, and action.* Boston: Houghton Mifflin.

Clarizio, H., & Bernard, R. (1981). Recategorized WISC-R scores of learning disabled children and differential diagnosis. *Psychology in the Schools, 18,* 5–12.

Clark, R. D. (1984, April). *Research with the K-ABC and an Appalachian sample.* Paper presented at the meeting of the National Association of School Psychologists, Philadelphia.

Clements, S. D. (1966). Minimal brain dysfunction in children: Terminology and identification—Phase one (NINDB Monograph No. 3, U.S. Public Health Service Publication No. 1415.). Washington, DC: Department of Health, Education, and Welfare.

Cohen, J. (1959). The factorial structure of the WISC at ages 7–6, 10–6, and 13–6. *Journal of Consulting Psychology, 23,* 285–299.

Cummins, J. P., & Das, J. P. (1980). Cognitive processing, academic achievement, and WISC-R performance in EMR children. *Journal of Consulting and Clinical Psychology, 48*(6), 777–779.

Das, J. P. (1973). Structure of cognitive abilities: Evidence for simultaneous and successive processing. *Journal of Educational Psychology, 64,* 103–108.

Das, J. P., Kirby, J., & Jarman, R. F. (1975). Simultaneous and successive syntheses: An alternative model for cognitive abilities. *Psychological Bulletin, 82,* 87–103.

Davis, F. B. (1959). Interpretation of differences among averages and individual test scores. *Journal of Educational Psychology, 50,* 162–170.

Dean, R. S. (1977). Reliability of the WISC-R with Mexican-American children. *Journal of School Psychology, 15,* 267–268.

Dean, R. S. (1979a). *WISC-R factor structure for Anglo and Hispanic children.* Paper presented at the annual meeting of the American Psychological Association, New York.

Dean, R. S. (1979b). Distinguished patterns for Mexican-American children on the WISC-R. *Journal of Clinical Psychology, 35,* 790–794.

Dean, R. S. (1980). Factor structure of the WISC-R with Anglos and Mexican-Americans. *Journal of School Psychology, 18*(3), 234–239.

Decker, S. N., & Corley, R. P. (1984). Bannatyne's "genetic dyslexic" subtype: A validation study. *Psychology in the Schools, 21,* 300–304.

DeHorn, A., & Klinge, V. (1978). Correlations and factor analysis of the WISC-R and the Peabody Picture Vocabulary Test for an adolescent psychiatric sample. *Journal of Consulting and Clinical Psychology, 46,* 1160–1161.

Elliott, S. N., Piersel, W. C., Witt, J. C., Argulewicz, E. N., Gutkin, T. B., & Galvin, G. A. (1985). Three-year stability of WISC-R IQs for handicapped children from three racial/ethnic groups. *Journal of Psychoeducational Assessment, 3,* 233–244.

Evans, J. G., & Hamm, H. A. (1979). An argument for administering WISC-R Digit Span. *Perceptual and Motor Skills, 49,* 573–574.

Fagan, T. K. (1985). The quantitative growth of school psychology programs in the United States. *School Psychology Review, 14,* 121–123.

Feuerstein, R. (1979). *The dynamic assessment of retarded performers: The learning potential assessment device, theory, instruments, and techniques.* Baltimore: University Park Press.

Finch, A. J., Kendall, P. C., Spirito, A., Entin, A., Montgomery, L. E., & Schwartz, D. J. (1979). Short form and factor-analytic studies of the WISC-R with behavior problem children. *Journal of Abnormal Child Psychology, 7,* 337–344.

Fischer, W. E., Wenck, L. S., Schurr, K. T., & Ellen, A. S. (1985). The moderating influence of gender, intelligence, and specific achievement deficiencies on the Bannatyne WISC-R recategorization. *Journal of Psychoeducational Assessment, 3,* 245–255.

Flaugher, R. L. (1978). The many definitions of test bias. *American Psychologist, 33,* 671–679.

Flynn, J. R. (1984). The mean IQ of Americans: Massive gains 1932 to 1978. *Psychological Bulletin, 95,* 29–51.

Flynn, J. T., Vitelli, R. J., & Goldblatt, R. (1978, March). *The TARDOR interpretive system.* Paper presented at the annual meeting of the National Association of School Psychologists, New York.

Gardner, H. (1983). *Frames of mind: The theory of multiple intelligences.* New York: Basic Books.

Gazzaniga, M. S. (1975). Recent research of hemispheric lateralization of the human brain: Review of the split-brain. *UCLA Educator, 27,* 9–12.

Gazzaniga, M. S. (1978). Recent research on hemispheric lateralization of the human brain: Review of the split-brain. *UCLA Educator, 17,* 9–12.

Groff, M., & Hubble, L. (1982). WISC-R factor structures of younger and older youth with low IQs. *Journal of Consulting and Clinical Psychology, 50*(1), 148–149.

Gutkin, T. B. (1978). Some useful statistics for the interpretation of the WISC-R. *Journal of Consulting and Clinical Psychology, 46,* 1561–1563.

Gutkin, T. B. (1979a). The WISC-R Verbal Comprehension, Perceptual Organization and Freedom from Distractibility deviation quotients. Data for practitioners. *Psychology in the Schools, 16,* 356–360.

Gutkin, T. B. (1979b). WISC-R scatter indices: Useful information for differential diagnosis? *Journal of School Psychology, 17,* 368–371.

Gutkin, T. B., & Reynolds, C. R. (1980). Factorial similarity of the WISC-R for Anglos and Chicanos referred for psychological services. *Journal of School Psychology, 18,* 34–39.

Gutkin, T. B., & Reynolds, C. R. (1981). Factorial similarity of the WISC-R for white and black children from the standardization sample. *Journal of Educational Psychology, 73,* 227–231.

Hale, R. L. (1983). An examination for construct bias in the WISC-R across socioeconomic status. *Journal of School Psychology, 21,* 153–156.

Hale, R. L., & Landino, S. A. (1981). utility of WISC-R subtest analysis in discriminating among groups of conduct problem, withdrawn, mixed, and nonproblem boys. *Journal of Consulting and Clinical Psychology, 49*(1), 91–95.

Halstead, W. C. (1947). *Brain and intelligence.* Chicago: University of Chicago Press.

Hammack, C. B. (1985). The Kaufman Assessment Battery for Children as a discriminator of learning disabled children exhibiting neurological signs. *Dissertation Abstracts International, 45*(12-A), 3584.

Hammill, D. D. (1985). *Detroit tests of learning aptitude.* Austin, TX: PRO-ED.

Harrison, P. L. (1986). *Current trends in cognitive assessment.* Paper presented at the annual meeting of the Tennessee Association of School Psychologists, Fall Creek Park, TN.

Harrison, P. L., & Kaufman, A. S. (1986). Assessing intelligence with the Kaufman batteries. In G. J. Robertson (Chair), *Perspectives on intellectual assessment: 1986.* Symposium conducted at the 94th annual meeting of the American Psychological Association, Washington, DC.

Hatch, T. C., & Gardner, H. (1986). From testing intelligence to assessing competencies: A pluralistic view of intellect. *Roeper Review, 8*(3), 147–150.

Hebb, D. O. (1949). *The organization of behavior.* New York: Wiley.

Henry, S. A., & Wittman, R. D. (1981). Diagnostic implications of Bannatyne's recategorized WISC-R scores for learning disabled children. *Journal of Learning Disabilities, 14*(9), 517–520.

Hobbs, N. (Ed.). (1975a). *Issues in the classification of children* (Vol. 1). San Francisco: Jossey-Bass.

Hobbs, N. (Ed.). (1975b). *Issues in the classification of children* (Vol. 2). San Francisco: Jossey-Bass.

Holroyd, J., & Wright, F. (1965). Neurological implications of WISC Verbal-Performance discrepancies in a psychiatric setting. *Journal of Consulting Psychology, 29,* 206–212.

Hooper, S. R., & Hynd, G. W. (1985). Differential diagnosis of subtypes of developmental dyslexia with the Kaufman Assessment Battery for Children. *Journal of Clinical Child Psychology, 14,* 145–152.

Hooper, S. R., & Hynd, G. W. (1986). Performance of normal and dyslexic readers on the Kaufman Assessment Battery for Children (K-ABC): A discriminant analysis. *Journal of Learning Disabilities, 19*(4), 206–210.

Horn, J. L. (1968). Organization of abilities and the development of intelligence. *Psychological Review, 75.* 242–259.

Horn, J. L. (1970). Organization of data on life-span development of human abilities. In L. R. Goulet and P. B. Baltes (Eds.), *Life-span developmental psychology.* New York: Academic Press.

Horn, J. L., & Cattell, R. B. (1966). Refinement and test of the theory of fluid and crystallized intelligence. *Journal of Educational Psychology, 57,* 253–270.

Jensen, A. R. (1976). Test bias and construct validity. *Phi Delta Kappan, 58,* 340–346.

Jensen, A. R. (1984). The black–white difference on the K-ABC: Implications for future tests. *Journal of Special Education, 18*(3), 377–408.

Johnston, W. T., & Bolen, L. M. (1984). A comparison of the factor structure of the WISC-R for blacks and whites. *Psychology in the Schools, 21,* 42–44.

Kamphaus, R. W., & Reynolds, C. R. (1984). Development and structure of the Kaufman Assessment Battery for Children. *Journal of Special Education, 18*(3), 213–228.

Kamphaus, R. W., & Reynolds, C. R. (1987). *Clinical and research applications of the K-ABC.* Circle Pines, MN: American Guidance Service.

Karnes, F. A., & Brown, K. E. (1980). Factor analysis of the WISC-R for the gifted. Journal of Educational Psychology, 72(2), 197–199.

Kaufman, A. S. (1975). Factor analysis of the WISC-R at eleven age levels between $6\frac{1}{2}$ and $16\frac{1}{2}$ years. *Journal of Consulting and Clinical Psychology, 43,* 135–147.

Kaufman, A. S. (1976a). Verbal-performance IQ discrepancies on the WISC-R. *Journal of Consulting and Clinical Psychology, 44,* 739–744.

Kaufman, A. S. (1976b). A new approach to the interpretation of test scatter on the WISC-R. *Journal of Learning Disabilities, 9,* 160–168.

Kaufman, A. S. (1979). *Intelligent testing with the WISC-R.* New York: Wiley.

Kaufman, A. S. (1982). The impact of WISC-R research for school psychologists. In C. R. Reynolds & T. B. Gutkin (Eds.), *The handbook of school psychology* (pp. 156–177). New York: Wiley.

Kaufman, A. S. (1984a). K-ABC and controversy. *Journal of Special Education, 18*(3), 409–444.

Kaufman, A. S., & Doppelt, J. E. (1976). Analysis of WISC-R standardization data in terms of the stratification variables. *Child Development, 47,* 165–171.

Kaufman, A. S., & Flaitz, J. (in press). Intellectual growth. In V. B. Van Hasselt & M. Hersen (Eds.), *The handbook of adolescent psychology.* Elmsford, NY: Pergamon Press.

Kaufman, A. S., & Harrison, P. L. (1986). Intelligence tests and gifted assessment: What are the positives? *Roeper Review, 8*(3), 154–159.

Kaufman, A. S., & Harrison, P. L. (1987). Intelligence testing. In C. R. Reynolds & L. Mann (Eds.), *Encyclopedia of special education* (pp. 850–855). New York: Wiley.

Kaufman, A. S., & Kamphaus, R. W. (1984). Factor analysis of the Kaufman Assessment Battery for Children (K-ABC) for ages $2\frac{1}{2}$ through $12\frac{1}{2}$ years. *Journal of Educational Psychology, 76*(4), 623–637.

Kaufman, A. S., & Kaufman, N. L. (1983a). *Interpretive manual for the Kaufman Assessment Battery for Children (K-ABC)*. Circle Pines, MN: American Guidance Services.

Kaufman, A. S., & Kaufman, N. L. (1983b). *The Kaufman Assessment Battery for Children (K-ABC)*. Circle Pines, MN: American Guidance Services.

Kaufman, A. S., Kaufman, N. L., Kamphaus, R. W., & Naglieri, J. A. (1982). Sequential and simultaneous factors at ages 3–12½. *Neuropsychology, 4*(2), 74–81.

Kaufman, A. S., & McLean, J. E. (1986). K-ABC/WISC-R factor analysis for a learning disabled population. *Journal of Learning Disabilities, 19*(3), 145–153.

Kaufman, A. S., & McLean, J. E. (1987). Joint factor analysis of the K-ABC and WISC-R for normal children. *Journal of School Psychology, 25,* 105–118.

Kaufman, A. S., & O'Neal, M. R. (1988). Analysis of the cognitive, achievement, and general factors underlying the Woodcock-Johnson Psycho-educational Battery. *Journal of Clinical Child Psychology, 17,* 143–151.

Kaufman, A. S., & Van Hagen, J. (1977). Investigation of the WISC-R for use with retarded children: Correlation with the 1972 Stanford-Binet and comparison of WISC and WISC-R profiles. *Psychology in the Schools, 14,* 10–14.

Kavale, K. A., & Forness, S. R. (1984). A meta-analysis of the validity of Wechsler scale profiles and recategorizations: Patterns of parodies? *Learning Disability Quarterly, 7,* 136–156.

Keith, T. Z. (1985). Questioning the K-ABC: What does it measure? *School Psychology Review, 14*(1), 9–20.

Keith, T. Z. (1986). Factor structure of the K-ABC for referred school children. *Psychology in the Schools, 23,* 241–246.

Keith, T. Z., & Dunbar, S. B. (1984). Hierarchical factor analysis of the K-ABC: Testing alternate models. *Journal of Special Education, 18*(3), 367–375.

Keith, T. Z., Hood, C., Eberhart, S., & Pottebaum, S. M. (1985, April). *Factor structure of the K-ABC for referred school children.* Paper presented at the annual meeting of the National Association of School Psychologists, Las Vegas, NV.

Keogh, B. K., & Hall, R. J. (1974). WISC subtest patterns of educationally handicapped and educable mentally retarded pupils. *Psychology in the Schools, 11,* 296–300.

Kinsbourne, M. (Ed.). (1978). *Asymmetrical function of the brain.* Cambridge: Cambridge University Press.

Kirby, J. R., & Das, J. P. (1977). Reading achievement, IQ, and simultaneous and successive processing. *Journal of Educational Psychology, 69,* 564–570.

Lambert, L. M. (1978, August). *Legal challenges to testing—Larry P.: A case in point.* Paper presented at the annual meeting of the American Psychological Association, Toronto.

Law, J. G., Box, D., & Moracco, J. D. (1980). A validation study of recategorized WISC-R scores of learning disabled children. *Education, 101*(2), 195–199.

Leark, R. A., Snyder, T., Grove, T., Golden, C. J., & Allison, R. (1983, August). *Comparison of the K-ABC with standardized neuropsychological batteries: Preliminary results.* Paper presented at the annual meeting of the American Psychological Association, Anaheim, CA.

Levy, J., & Trevarthon, C. (1976). Metacontrol of hemispheric function in human split-brain patients. *Journal of Experimental Psychology: Human Perception and Performance, 2,* 299–312.

Lewandowski, L. R., & De Rienzo, P. J. (1985). WISC-R and K-ABC performances of hemiplegic children. *Journal of Psychoeducational Assessment, 3,* 215–221.

Lombard, T. J., & Riedel, R. G. (1978). An analysis of the factor structure of the WISC-R and the effect of color on the coding subtest. *Psychology in the Schools, 15,* 176–179.

Luria, A. R. (1966). *Higher cortical functions in man.* New York: Basic Books.

Luria, A. R. (1970). The functional organization of the brain. *Scientific American, 322,* 66–78.

Lutey, C. L. (1977). *Individual intelligence testing: A manual and source book* (2nd ed.). Greeley, CO: Carol L. Lutey.

Majovski, L. V. (1984). The K-ABC: Theory and applications for child neuropsychological assessment and research. *Journal of Special Education, 18*(3), 257–268.

McCallum, R. S., Karnes, F. A., & Oehler-Stinnett, J. (1985). Construct validity of the K-ABC for gifted children. *Psychology in the Schools, 22*(3), 254–259.

McCullough, C. S., Walker, J. L., & Diesnner, R. (1985). The use of Wechsler scales in the assessment of Native Americans of the Columbia River basin. *Psychology in the Schools, 22,* 23–28.

McGrew, K. (1986). *Clinical interpretation of the Woodcock-Johnson tests of cognitive ability.* Orlando, FL: Grune & Stratton.

McShane, D. A., & Plas, J. M. (1982). Wechsler scale performance patterns of American Indian children. *Psychology in the Schools, 15,* 176–179.

Meeker, M. (1969). *The structure of intellect: its interpretation and uses.* Columbus, OH: Charles E. Merrill.

Meeker, M. (1975). *WISC-R template for SOI analysis.* El Segundo, CA: SOI Institute.

Mishra, S. P. (1983). Validity of WISC-R IQs and factor scores in predicting achievement for Mexican-American children. *Psychology in the Schools, 20,* 442–444.

Mishra, S. P. (1984a). Recategorized WISC-R scores of learning-disabled children from the Mexican-American culture. *Journal of Clinical Psychology, 40*(6), 1485–1488.

Mishra, S. P. (1984b). WISC-R performance patterns of learning-disabled children from Papago culture. *Journal of Clinical Psychology, 40*(6), 1489–1492.

Moore, D. W., & Weilan, D. P. (1981). WISC-R scatter indexes of children referred for reaching diagnosis. *Journal of Learning Disabilities, 14*(9), 511–514.

Morris, J. D., Evans, J. G., & Pearson, D. R. (1978). The

WISC-R subtest profile of a sample of severely emotionally disturbed children. *Psychological Reports, 42,* 319–325.

Morris, J. M., & Bigler, E. D. (1985, January). *An investigation of the Kaufman Assessment Battery for Children (K-ABC) with neurologically impaired children.* Paper presented at the annual meeting of the International Neurological Society, San Diego.

Mueller, H. H., Mancini, G. J., & Short, R. H. (1984). An evaluation of the diagnostic efficiency of the Wechsler Intelligence Scale for Children–Revised. *The Alberta Journal of Educational Research, 30*(4), 299–310.

Naglieri, J. A. (1979). *A comparison of McCarthy GCI and WISC-R IQ scores for educable mentally retarded, learning disabled, and normal children.* Unpublished doctoral dissertation, University of Georgia.

Naglieri, J. A., & Das, J. P. (1986, August). *Validity of the Das/Neglieri cognitive assessment system experimental version.* Paper presented at the 94th annual meeting of the American Psychological Association, Washington, DC.

Naglieri, J. A., & Hill, D. S. (1981). Comparison of WISC-R and K-ABC regression lines for academic prediction with black and white children. *Journal of Clinical Child Psychology, 15*(4), 352–355.

Naglieri, J. A., & Jensen, A. R. (1987). Comparison of black/white differences on the WISC-R and the K-ABC: Spearman's hypothesis. *Intelligence, 11,* 21–43.

Naglieri, J. A., Kaufman, A. S., Kaufman, N. L., & Kamphaus, R. W. (1981). Cross-validation of Das simultaneous and successive processes with novel tasks. *Alberta Journal of Educational Research, 127*(3), 264–271.

Nebes, R. D. (1974). Hemispheric specialization in commisurotomized man. *Psychological Bulletin 81,* 1–14.

Oakland, T. (1983). Concurrent and predictive validity estimates for the WISC-R IQs and ELPs by racial-ethnic and SES groups. *School Psychology Review, 12*(1), 57–61.

Oakland, T., & Feigenbaum, D. (1979). Multiple sources of test bias on the WISC-R and the Bender-Gestalt Test. *Journal of Consulting and Clinical Psychology, 47,* 968–974.

Ollendick, T. H. (1979). Discrepancies between verbal and performance IQ's and subtest scatter on the WISC-R for juvenile delinquents. *Psychological Reports, 45,* 563–568.

Ornstein, R. (1978). The split and the whole brain. *Human Nature, 1*(5), 76–83.

Paget, K. D. (1982). Intellectual patterns of conduct problem children on the WISC-R. *Psychology in the Schools, 19,* 439–445.

Peterson, C. R., & Hart, D. H. (1979). Factor structure of the WISC-R for a clinical-referred population and specific subgroups. *Journal of Consulting and Clinical Psychology, 47,* 643–645.

Reilly, T. F., Wheeler, L. J., & Etlinger, L. E. (1985). Intelligence versus academic achievement: A comparison of juvenile delinquents and special education classifications. *Criminal Justice and Behavior, 12*(2), 193–208.

Reschley, D. (1978). WISC-R factor structures among Anglos, blacks, Chicanos, and Native-American Papagos. *Journal of Consulting and Clinical Psychology, 46,* 417–422.

Reschley, D., & Reschley, J. E. (1979). Validity of WISC-R factor scores in predicting achievement and attention for four sociocultural groups. *Journal of School Psychology, 17,* 355–361.

Reschley, D., & Sabers, D. L. (1979). Analysis of test bias in four groups with the regression definition. *Journal of Educational Measurement, 16,* 1–9.

Reynolds, C. R. (Ed.). (1986, March). *Information Edge, 2*(1), 1–5.

Reynolds, C. R., & Gutkin, T. B. (1980). Stability of the WISC-R factor structure across sex at two age levels. *Journal of Clinical Psychology, 36,* 775–777.

Reynolds, C. R., & Gutkin, T. B. (1982). *The handbook of school psychology.* New York: Wiley.

Reynolds, C. R., & Hartlage, L. C. (1979). Comparison of WISC and WISC-R regression lines for academic prediction with black and white referred children. *Journal of Consulting and Clinical Psychology, 47,* 589–591.

Robinson, N. M., & Chamrad, D. L. (1986). Appropriate uses of intelligence tests with gifted children. *Roeper Review, 8*(3), 160–162.

Roth, H., & Nicholson, C. L. (1984). Intellectual and educational characteristics of court-identified and school-identified violent and assaultive youth. *Diagnostique, 9,* 226–231.

Rugel, R. P. (1974a). The factor structure of the WISC in two populations of disabled readers. *Journal of Learning Disabilities, 7,* 581–585.

Rugel, R. P. (1974b). WISC subtest scores of disabled readers: A review with respect to Bannatyne's re-categorization. *Journal of Learning Disabilities, 7,* 48–55.

Ryckman, D. B. (1981). Searching for a WISC-R profile for learning disabled children: An inappropriate task? *Journal of Learning Disabilities, 14*(9), 508–511.

Sandoval, J. (1979). The WISC-R and internal evidence of test bias with minority groups. *Journal of Consulting and Clinical Psychology, 47,* 919–927.

Sandoval, J. (1982). The WISC-R factoral validity for minority groups and Spearman's hypothesis. *Journal of School Psychology, 20*(3), 198–204.

Sandoval, J., & Millie, M. (1979). *Accuracy judgments of WISC-R item difficulty for minority groups.* Paper presented at the annual meeting of the American Psychological Association, New York.

Sandoval, J., Zimmerman, I. L., & Woo-Sam, J. M. (1983). Cultural differences on WISC-R Verbal items. *Journal of School Psychology, 21,* 49–55.

Sattler, J. M. (1982). *Assessment of children's intelligence and special abilities.* Boston: Allyn and Bacon.

Schiff, M. M., Kaufman, A. S., & Kaufman, N. L. (1981).

Scatter analysis of WISC-R profiles for learning disabled children with superior intelligence. *Journal of Learning Disabilities, 14*(7), 400–404.

Schmidt, H. P. J., & Saklofske, D. H. (1983). Comparison of the WISC-R patterns of children of average and exceptional ability. *Psychological Reports, 53,* 539–544.

Schooler, D. L., Beebe, M. C., & Koepke, T. (1978). Factor analysis of WISC-R scores for children identified as learning disabled, educable mentally impaired, and emotionally impaired. *Psychology in the Schools, 15,* 478–485.

Seashore, H. (1951). Differences between verbal and performance IQs on the WISC. *Journal of Consulting Psychology, 15,* 62–67.

Shapiro, E., & Dotan, N. (1985, October). *Focal neurological findings and the Kaufman Assessment Battery for Children (K-ABC).* Paper presented at the annual meeting of the National Academy of Neurological Psychologists, Philadelphia.

Silverstein, A. B. (1968). WISC subtest patterns of retardates. *Psychological Reports, 23,* 1061–1062.

Silverstein, A. B. (1969). An alternative factor analytic solution for Wechsler's intelligence scales. *Educational and Psychological Measurement, 29,* 763–767.

Silverstein, A. B. (1981). Reliability and abnormality of test score differences. *Journal of Clinical Psychology, 37*(2), 392–394.

Smith, M. D., Coleman, J. M., Dokecki, P. R., & Davis, E. E. (1977a). Intellectual characteristics of school labeled learning disabled children. *Journal of Learning Disabilities, 10,* 437–443.

Smith, M. D., Coleman, J. M., Dokecki, P. R., & Davis, E. E. (1977b). Recategorized WISC-R scores of learning disabled children. *Journal of Learning Disabilities, 10,* 437–443.

Smith, M. L. (1979). *The use of Kaufman's factor analysis of the WISC-R in distinguishing able and disabled readers at three grade levels.* Unpublished doctoral dissertation, Oklahoma State University.

Snyder, T. J., Leark, R. A., Golden, C. J., Grove, T., & Allison, R. (1983, April). *Correlation of the K-ABC, WISC-R, and Luria-Nebraska Children's Battery for exceptional children.* Paper presented at the annual meeting of the National Association of School Psychologists, Detroit.

Snyder, T. J., Leark, R. A., Hynd, G. W., & Hayes, F. (1984, April). *Usefulness of the K-ABC in neuropsychological assessment.* Paper presented at the meeting of the National Association of School Psychologists, Philadelphia.

Sobotka, K. R., & Black, F. W. (1978). A procedure for the rapid computation of the WISC-R factor scores. *Journal of Clinical Psychology, 34,* 117–119.

Spearman, C. (1927). *The abilities of man.* New York: Macmillan.

Sperry, R. W. (1968). *Hemisphere deconnection and unity in conscious awareness. American Psychologist, 23,* 723–733.

Stanford-Binet draws board attention. (1986). *Communique, 15,* 1–2.

Stedman, J. M., Lawlis, G. F., Cortner, R. H., & Achterberg, G. (1978). Relationships between WISC-R factors, achievement, and visual-motor maturation in children referred for psychological evaluation. *Journal of Consulting and Clinical psychology, 46,* 869–872.

Sternberg, R. J. (1984). An information-processing analysis and critique. *Journal of Special Education, 18*(3), 269–280.

Sternberg, R. J. (1985). *Beyond IQ: A triarchic theory of human intelligence.* New York: Cambridge University Press.

Sternberg, R. J. (1986). Identifying the gifted through IQ: Why a little bit of knowledge is a dangerous thing. *Roeper Review, 8*(3), 143–147.

Stenvenson, L. P. (1980). WISC-R analysis: Implications for diagnosis and intervention. *Journal of Learning Disabilities, 13*(6), 60–63.

Stoiber, K. C., Bracken, B. A., & Gissal, T. J. (1983). Cognitive processing styles in reading-disabled and a matched group of normal children. *Journal of Psychoeducational Assessment, 1*(3), 219–223.

Strichart, S. S., & Love, E. (1979). WISC-R performance of children referred to a university center for learning disabilities. *Psychology in the Schools, 16,* 183–188.

Swerdlik, M. E., & Schweitzer, J. (1978). A comparison of factor structures of the WISC and WISC-R. *Psychology in the Schools, 15,* 166–172.

Tabachnick, B. G. (1979). Test scatter on the WISC-R. *Journal of Learning Disabilities, 12,* 626–628.

Taylor, R. L., Ziegler, E. W., & Partenio, I. (1984). An investigation of WISC-R Verbal-Performance differences as a function of ethnic status. *Psychology in the Schools, 21,* 437–441.

Teeter, A., Moore, C. L., & Petersen, J. D. (1982). WISC-R verbal and performance of Native American students referred for school learning problems. *Psychology in the Schools, 19,* 39–44.

Telzrow, C. F., Century, E., Harris, B., & Redmond, C. (1985, April). *Relationships between neuropsychological processing models.* Paper presented at the annual meeting of the National Association of School Psychologists, Las Vegas, NY.

Telzrow, C. F., Redmond, C., & Zimmerman, B. (1984, October). *Dyslexic subtypes: A comparison of Bannatyne, Boder, and Kaufman models.* Paper presented at the annual meeting of the National Academy on Neurological Psychologists, San Diego.

Thompson, R. J. (1980). The diagnostic utility of WISC-R measures with children referred to a developmental evaluaton center. *Journal of Consulting and Clinical Psychology, 48*(4), 440–447.

Thorndike, R. L., Hagen, E. P., & Sattler, J. M. (1986). *The Stanford-Binet intelligence scale: Fourth edition.* Chicago: Riverside.

Treffinger, D. J., & Renzulli, J. S. (1986). Giftedness as potential for creative productivity: Transcending IQ scores. *Roeper Review, 8*(3), 150–154.

Trotter, R. J. (1986, August). Three heads are better than one. *Psychology Today,* pp. 56–62.

Van Hagen, J., & Kaufman, A. S. (1975). Factor analysis of the WISC-R for a group of mentally retarded children and adolescents. *Journal of Consulting and Clinical Psychology, 43,* 661–667.

Vance, H. B., & Fuller, G. B. (1983). Discriminant function analysis of LD/BD children scores on the WISC-R. *Journal of Clinical Psychology, 39*(5), 749–753.

Vance, H. B., & Singer, M. G. (1979). Recategorization of the WISC-R subtest scaled scores for learning disabled children. *Journal of Learning Disabilities, 12,* 487–491.

Vance, H. B., & Wallbrown, F. H. (1978). The structure of intelligence for black children: A hierarchical approach. *Psychological Record, 28,* 31–39.

Vance, H. B., Wallbrown, F. H., & Fremont, T. S. (1978). The abilities of retarded students: Further evidence concerning the stimulus trace factor. *Journal of Psychology, 100,* 77–82.

Wallbrown, F. H., Blaha, J., Wallbrown, H., & Engin, A. (1975). The hierarchical factor structure of the Wechsler Intelligence Scale for Children–Revised. *Journal of Psychology, 89,* 223–235.

Wechsler, D. (1974). *Wechsler Intelligence Scale for Children–Revised.* San Antonio: Psychological Corporation.

Weiner, S. A., & Kaufman, A. S. (1979). WISC-R vs. WISC for black chileren suspected of learning or behavioral disorders. *Journal of Learning Disabilities, 12,* 100–105.

Willson, V. L., Reynolds, C. R., Chatman, S., & Kaufman, A. S. (1985). Confirmatory factor analysis of simultaneous, sequential, and achievement factors on the K-ABC at 11 age levels ranging from $2\frac{1}{2}$ to $12\frac{1}{2}$ years. *Journal of School Psychology, 23*(3), 261–269.

Witt, J. C., & Gresham, F. M. (1985). Review of Wechsler Intelligence Scale for Children–Revised. In J. V. Mitchell (Ed.), *Ninth mental measurement yearbook* (pp. 1716–1719). Lincoln: University of Nebraska Press.

Woodcock, R., & Johnson, B. (1977). *Woodcock-Johnson psycho-educational battery.* Boston: Teaching Resources.

Wright, D., & Dappen, L. (1982). Factor analysis of the WISC-R and the WRAT with a referral population. *Journal of School Psychology, 20*(4), 306–312.

Zarske, J. A., & Moore, C. L. (1982). Recategorized WISC-R scores of learning disabled Navajo Indian children. *Psychology in the Schools, 19,* 156–159.

Zarske, J. A., Moore, C. L., & Peterson, J. D. (1981). WISC-R factor structures for diagnosed learning disabled Navajo and Papago children. *Psychology in the Schools, 18,* 402–407.

Zingale, S. A., & Smith, M. D. (1978). WISC-R patterns for learning disabled children at three SES levels. *Psychology in the Schools, 15,* 199–204.

14

ADVANCES IN BEHAVIORAL ASSESSMENT

THOMAS R. KRATOCHWILL
SUSAN M. SHERIDAN
University of Wisconsin–Madison

Interest in behavioral assessment continues to grow since writing the first chapter on this topic for the *Handbook of School Psychology* (Kratochwill, 1982). Although traditionally there were relatively few works focusing on behavioral assessment of children, this picture has changed recently. There are now several books (e.g., Mash & Terdal, 1981, 1988a; Shapiro, 1987b; Shapiro & Kratochwill, 1988b) specifically devoted to the topic of behavioral assessment with children in schools and applied settings.

A number of factors account for the growing interest in behavioral assessment in the field school psychology. Certainly, the continuing success of behavior therapy across diverse settings, child populations, and target problems accounts for increased interest in applications in the schools (Kratochwill & Morris, in press; Morris & Kratochwill, 1984). Moreover, with the increasing diversity of behavior therapy, researchers and clinicians have found it necessary to spend time clarifying methodological and conceptual aspects of assessment. Indeed, it has never been easy to speak of commonality within the domain of behavior therapy, and within contemporary practice and theory it is

no longer possible to speak of one unifying characteristic. Debates over terminology and the areas of practice to be included within the general rubric of behavior therapy and assessment have existed for some time (e.g., Deitz, 1978; Greenspoon & Lamal, 1978). In this chapter we present an overview of behavioral assessment, focusing on its applications in the domain of academic and social problems in school psychology. We elucidate features of the behavioral approach to assessment and discuss its use in diagnosis and treatment of learning and behavior disorders.

SCOPE OF BEHAVIOR THERAPY

There is currently no single definition of behavioral assessment, but it generally refers to "the identification of meaningful response units and their controlling variables for the purposes of understanding and altering behavior" (Hayes, Nelson, & Jarrett, 1986, p. 464). Some writers characterize behavioral assessment of children as a problem-solving strategy for understanding behavior and its determinants (Mash & Terdal, 1988b). Although there is no single element that characterizes a particular assessment as behavioral, certain concepts, methods, and purposes can be identified with behavioral assessment as an assessment *approach* (as opposed to a set of techniques), with its own set of assumptions and goals (Barrios, 1988; Nelson, 1985).

Several different models of behavior therapy have developed, including applied behavior analysis, the neobehavioristic mediational S-R model, cognitive behavior modification, and social learning theory. Because each particular model differs in what is to be included in *behavior* (Kazdin, 1978), the focus of assessment varies considerably among the different models. A review of each of these various approaches is beyond the scope of this chapter. The reader is referred to Wilson and Franks (1982) as well as original sources in the volume for a more detailed presentation.

Common Characteristics

A number of characteristics are associated with what has recently been described as a prototypical view of behavioral assessment (Mash & Terdal, 1988b, pp. 9–11). These include the following:

1. Behavioral assessment approaches follow a conceptualization of human behavior that focuses on the client's feelings, thoughts, and behaviors as they occur in specific situations, rather than manifestations of underlying global personality dimensions.
2. Behavioral assessment tends to be predominantly idiographic and individualized.
3. Behavioral assessments emphasize the role of situational influences on behavior.
4. Behavioral approaches have emphasized the instability of behavior over time.
5. Behavioral assessments are by their nature systems oriented.
6. Behavioral approaches generally emphasize contemporaneous controlling variables rather than historical causes.
7. Behavioral approaches are more often concerned with behaviors, cognitions, and affect as direct samples of the assessment domains rather than a sign of underlying cause.

8. Behavioral approaches focus on obtaining data that are relevant to treatment.
9. Behavioral approaches rely on multimethod assessment strategies (i.e., emphasizing different informants and methodologies).
10. Behavioral approaches generally embrace a low level of inference in the assessment process.
11. Behavioral approaches typically involve onging or repeated measurement in the assessment process.
12. Behavioral assessments should be empirically based (i.e., derived from knowledge in the area focused on in assessment and treatment).[1]

Readers might wonder how some of these features of behavioral assessment differ from more traditional procedures used in the school psychology field. The answer is that some of these features may not differ! In fact, many measures that were once considered traditional are now used routinely in behavioral assessment. Although traditionally there are numerous conceptual and methodological differences between behavioral and traditional assessment, the major differences emanate from the underlying assumptions that each approach adheres to in characterizing human functioning (Nelson & Hayes, 1979). Generally, assessment within both traditional and behavioral assessment leads to hypotheses. Traditional measurement suggests hypotheses regarding underlying "structures" or "causes," while behavioral assessment suggests hypotheses about the environment or person–environment events that become the primary focus of intervention efforts.

---

[1]There is considerable disagreement over the assumption that behavior therapy and assessment always rely on basic research in psychology as a source of hypotheses about treatment and assessment. For example, in applied behavior analysis there has been a transition from emphasizing research on various social problems toward emphasizing solutions to social problems (see Deitz, 1978, for an overview). With this has come a trend toward technology (e.g., Azrin, 1977) rather than an applied science. Yet some empirical data may not be available to support such a technology. Similarly, in the area of behavior assessment, empirical data supporting certain assumptions and practices are not yet available (see Hartmann, Roper, & Bradford, 1979).

Applications of Behavioral Assessment in School Psychology

Three major applications of behavioral assessment include treatment, selection, and research (Goldfried & Linehan, 1977).

Treatment

Several unique features of behavioral assessment in the clinical treatment context are noteworthy. First, assessment is specific and tailored to the client's problem and is linked closely to the treatment plan implemented. In this regard, the behavioral assessor must know which dimensions of a problem to assess when presented with a child referral. That is, for example, there will be different procedures and devices to use in assessment of conduct disorder than when assessing a child experiencing mental retardation. The behavioral assessor should provide a direct link between assessment and intervention. The entire *process* of assessment is designed to develop intervention strategies that can be monitored continuously and systematically to determine the efficacy of treatment. The variables that are assessed (a) clearly and operationally describe the referral problem, (b) will be directly manipulated during an intervention, and (c) are capable of being assessed repeatedly throughout the duration of an intervention program.

Reconceptualization of common referral questions is necessary in behavioral assessment (Shapiro, 1987a). Thus, a referral question such as "What is the underlying cause of this child's learning problem?" may be rephrased as "What strategies can be developed to best resolve this child's difficulties?" and lead the assessment process directly to the development of strategies for academic and behavior change. Several advantages of this position for school psychologists are apparent. First, information pertaining directly to the development of individualized educational plans (IEPs) as mandated by Public Law 94-142 may be provided. Second, behavioral assessment allows the school psychologist to function in a much broader role than a traditional diagnostic model. Specifically, the psychologist can participate in treatment. Third, these procedures bring the school psychologist into frequent contact with the teacher and may help establish a positive working relationship between the two professionals. A fourth advantage of behavioral as-

sessment is that it offers individual analysis of behavior change programs and provides opportunities for accountability. Finally, behavioral assessment may assist decision making in a much broader ecological context where the school environment and family are considered important in the assessment process (Shapiro, 1987a).

Selection

A second use of behavioral assessment is for selection proposes. Using behavioral assessment in a selection context presumes that the results of assessment data are used to identify clients for treatment or assign them to diagnostic categories that have relevance for intervention. Although behavioral assessment has not been generally applied extensively in this area (see Goldfried & Linehan, 1977; Kazdin, 1983; Wiggins, 1973), there is increasing work in developing measures that allows prediction of treatment program success (Hayes et al., 1986). Issues in this area are delineated in later discussion on treatment utility.

Research

Along with treatment and selection purposes, research-related functions constitute a third main use of behavioral assessment. Assessment and design methodology have been identifying features of behavior therapy and its scientific basis (Deitz, 1978). The empirical foundation refers to the use of empirically validated principles and procedures and the systematic evaluation of clinical interventions. Although research using behavioral assessment strategies has been conducted through single-case experimental designs (see Hersen & Barlow, 1976; Kazdin, 1978; Kratochwill, 1978), single-case methodology is a major feature of research in applied behavior analysis and is not necessarily characteristics of other domains of behavior therapy. A major characteristic of single-case research is the repeated measurement of the target response (see Bijou, Peterson, & Ault, 1968). Measurement can occur in three content areas, including cognitive, motor, and physiological dimensions (discussed below). Moreover, there is a definite preference for direct measurement techniques (actual measures of the target response using observational assessment) rather than indirect measurement (e.g., projective tests, perceptual-motor scales, personality inventories).

Phases of Behavioral Assessment

Traditionally, and especially in the school psychology field, assessment has been thought of as something that occurs prior to and perhaps after the treatment program has been terminated. We again emphasize that behavioral assessment should be related directly to the design of a treatment program in that the assessment procedures should be used to design an intervention and then repeated over various phases of the intervention. In this regard, assessment can be conceptualized as a number of stages or phases (e.g., Bergan, 1977; Cone & Hawkins, 1977a, 1977b; Hawkins, 1986; Mash & Terdal, 1988b). Various names have been applied to phases of behavioral assessment. We use the phases developed for behavioral consultation that integrate both assessment and treatment. These phases include problem identification, problem analysis, plan implementation, plan evaluation, generalization, and follow-up. These six phases are certainly not discrete and often overlap in practice. The clinician may also cycle back to previous phases to clarify further the nature of the problem. Different assessment procedures and devices can be used during different phases of assessment and therapy.

Problem Identification

The primary focus of assessment during problem identification is a definition of the specific target problems/clients. Generally, assessment involves measures that help define the scope and nature of the target problem. Measures such as interviews and rating scales provide the opportunity for such probes. The clinician may be interested in knowing if the referral problem is indeed the primary target for intervention. For example, a teacher may refer a child for a reading problem. Based on the administration of a rating scale, the school psychologist and teacher may determine that the child is also quite withdrawn socially, and this may be related to the reading problem. Thus, both identified problems become the focus of further assessment.

Problem Analysis

During problem analysis, assessment is focused primarily on an analysis of the target behaviors identified during problem identification. In this phase an emphasis is placed on determining controlling events in the environment (broadly con-

ceived). More direct assessment procedures, such as self-monitoring, analog assessment, and direct observation can be helpful in establishing a baseline level of the target responses. The psychologist may request that the child record the incidence of reading assignments completed (i.e., self-monitor) and that the teacher record (observationally) the frequency of social interaction. In addition to the baseline levels of the target behaviors, the psychologist focuses on the analysis of these events (overt and covert) that may be related to the maintenance of the problem (e.g., skill deficits in reading, attention from the teacher for social behaviors, etc.).

Treatment Implementation

Given that previous phases have yielded information useful in the conceptualization of a treatment, a program is then implemented during this phase. Assessment procedures can be used to monitor "treatment integrity" (i.e., to determine that it is being implemented as intended). Components for treatment are developed from different areas of therapy. Treatment procedures are implemented to maximize therapeutic change and so may be "packaged" to produce large changes rapidly.

Treatment Evaluation

Once a plan has been implemented, it should be monitored to evaluate its effectiveness. Direct observational measures can be used to evaluate the treatment (process and outcome) and a high priority is usually placed on these "direct" samples. Indirect measures may be used to serve as a check on direct measures. For example, the psychologist can request that the teacher complete behavior checklists or rating scales.

Generalization

In behavioral research and treatment, generalization refers to the transfer of behavior change across situations, behaviors, and individuals. Typically, the psychologist is interested in documenting (i.e., assessing) the transfer of behavior improvement on dimensions of clinical interest. For example, an increase in social interaction in the classroom may also be displayed on the playground and in other social settings. Moreover, an intervention program that results in positive change in a significant target behavior may also result in changes in other behaviors. The positive effects of increasing social interactions may also transfer to improved academic behavior. Finally, it is also possible for the treatment effects to transfer to other people in the environment. Improving social skills in the target client may also result in improved social skills of others that he or she comes in contact with.

It is commonly accepted that generalization must be programmed specifically (see Drabman, Hammer, & Rosenbaum, 1979; Stokes & Baer, 1977, for a review of procedures used to program generalization). Drabman et al. (1979) provided a conceptual framework on which various generalized effects of behavior modification programs may be categorized into 16 different classes for further analyses. Since the treatment may have effects beyond the target behavior and/or client, these aspects should be assessed.

Follow-up

Follow-up on the intervention program and client is an extremely important assessment phase. Follow-up assessment is typically aimed at evaluation of generalization or maintenance of behavior across time. Follow-up assessment is most informative when direct measures of the target clients are gathered. However, realizing that time and cost considerations will be a primary factor in follow-up assessment, brief indirect measures (e.g., self-report) are often used. When possible, it is desirable to gather social validation data on both the intervention and the target client. Furthermore, "consumer satisfaction" indices can be obtained from rating scales completed by the client and various socialization agents (see Kazdin, 1977b; Wolf, 1978). For example, the socialization agents may provide positive ratings on client improvement but report that the treatment procedure was time consuming and costly. Such feedback to the psychologist should be considered in the design of further intervention programs.

A Conceptual Framework for Behavioral Assessment

With growing diversity in behavior therapy in general and behavioral assessment in particular, a conceptual framework for classifying behavioral measures was a welcome addition to the literature. Cone (1977, 1978) and Cone and Hawkins (1977b) proposed the *Behavioral Assessment Grid* (*BAG*), a taxonomy, based on the simultaneous consideration of three aspects of the assessment process: (a) the contents assessed, (b) the methods used to assess them, and (c) the types of generalizability (i.e., reliability and validity) established for scores on the measure being classified. The relations among these three aspects of assessment are presented in Figure 1.

Contents

Behavioral assessment is commonly conceptualized in three content areas (Cone, 1977; Cone & Hawkins, 1977b), systems (Lang, 1971, 1977), or channels (Paul & Bernstein, 1973). The contents are most commonly referred to as motor, physiological, and cognitive. Although there are some basic disagreements as to what is specifically included within these categories, we follow the scheme presented by Cone (1978).

Motor content is traditionally the area most commonly assessed by behavior therapists. Included are activities of the striate musculature typically observable without instrumentation, such as talking, walking, hitting, running, jumping, and so on. Physiological contents include activities of muscles and glands autonomically innervated, and tonic muscle activity (Lang, 1971). Some examples include muscle tension, heart rate, respiration, and galvanic skin response. Cognitive contents must be defined in the context of the particular referents used. While verbal behavior (self-report) can be categorized as motoric when referring to the speech act, the referents may be motor, cognitive, or physiological. When verbal behavior refers to private events (e.g., feelings, thoughts), the referents are cognitive, but when it refers to a publicly verifiable behavior, the referent is either physiological or motoric. For example, if a child reports that "My teacher doesn't like me" the referent is cognitive (a private thought or covert event). On the other hand, if a child reports "I talk in class," the referent is motoric (a publically verifiable overt act).

When conducting behavioral assessment, the clinician should be concerned about the relations among the three content areas. In a particular situation an individual may respond cognitively, motorically, and/or physiologically (e.g., in a situation where different stimulus and consequent variables are operating). Evidence suggests that the three content areas are not necessarily highly intercorrelated (Bellack & Hersen, 1977a, 1977b; Cone, 1979; Hersen & Bellack, 1976). Problems in research investigating the relations among the

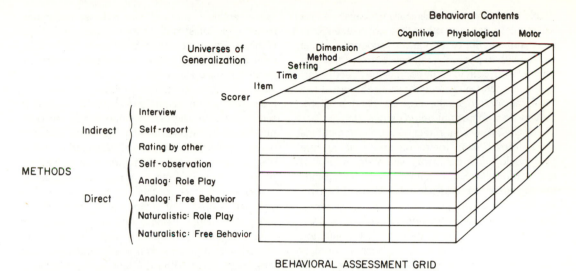

Figure 1. The Behavioral Assessment Grid (BAG), a taxonomy of behavioral assessment integrating contents, methods, and universes of generalization. (From "The Behavioral Assessment Grid (BAG): A Conceptual Framework and a Taxonomy" by J. D. Cone, 1978, *Behavior Therapy, 9,* pp. 882–888. Copyright © 1978 by Association for Advancement of Behavior Therapy. Reproduced by permission.)

three systems have been related to three issues: (a) lack of consensus regarding what is meant by each of the "modes," (b) concern over whether discussion of modes or channels is appropriate in behavioral psychology, and (c) methodological problems in existing research in this area (see Cone, 1979).

With regard to methodological problems, Cone and his associates (Cone, 1979; Cone & Hawkins, 1977a, 1977b) noted that comparisons of the three systems have sometimes confounded *method* of assessment with behavioral *content*. An example of this problem occurs when self-report measures of cognitive activities are compared to direct observation measures of motor behavior, as in assessment of anxiety (e.g., a child may be trembling but may report that he or she is not frightened). A low correlation between content areas may be due to content differences, method differences, or both.

A second methodological problem identified by Cone and Hawkins (1977a, 1977b) relates to definitions of the three response systems. Some people have based their definitions on hypothetical constructs. For example, when Lang (1971) dis-

cussed the three response systems in the context of measuring fear, the response was presumed to underlie a variety of behaviors such as escape and avoidance. In contrast to this view, Cone and his associates (Cone, 1977; 1978; Cone & Hawkins, 1977a, 1977b) examined each content area within the context of stimulus and consequent variables present in any given situation. Finally, some psychologists have expressed "discomfort" with using terms (i.e., channel, mode) that carry a construct connotation (see Cone, 1979).

Methods

A number of assessment methods are used to gather data across each of the three content areas. Cone (1977, 1978) ordered these methods along a continuum of directness representing the extent to which they (a) measure of the target behavior of clinical relevance, and (b) measure the target behavior at the time and place of its natural occurrence.

Methods are categorized on a continuum from direct to indirect assessment. Interview and self-report methods are at the indirect end of the continuum because the behavior is considered a verbal representation of clinically relevant activities taking place at some other time and place. Similarly, ratings by others are considered indirect because they typically involve retrospective descriptions of behavior. In contrast to direct observation, a rating of an event occurs subsequent to the behavior where the time of rating is far removed from the actual behavior occurrence.

Included within direct assessment methods are self-observation (or monitoring), analog: role play, analog: free behavior, naturalistic: role play, and naturalistic: free behavior. These dimensions are organized according to *who* does the observing, the *instructions given,* and *where* the observations occur. In self-monitoring the observer and the observee are the same person. Self-monitoring differs from self-report in that a person observes and records his or her own behavior at the time of its occurrence. Analog assessment refers to settings or situations that are analogous to, but not the same as the natural environment. In this type of assessment setting the client may be instructed to role play a particular behavior (role play) or act normally (free behavior), as if he or she were in the natural environment. Finally, assessment may be scheduled in the natural environment under either role play or completely naturalistic (free behavior) conditions. Specific assessment methods are discussed in more detail later.

Universes of Generalization

Once the various measures have been classified, they are indexed in terms of the different ways in which scores can be generalized. Generalizability theory can be used as the basis of this model (Cone, 1977, 1978; Cronbach, Glaser, Nanda, & Rajaratnam, 1972; Jones, Reid, & Patterson, 1974; Wiggins, 1973).

The various behavioral measures are generalized across six major universes: (a) scorer, (b) item, (c) time, (d) setting, (e) method, and (f) dimension (see Figure 1). *Scorer* generalization (or interrater agreement), refers to the extent to which data obtained by the scorer are comparable to the mean of the observations of all scorers that might have been observing the behavior. Essentially, this involves the match or agreement between clinicians on observations of a behavior. Where two people agree, scores are said to generalize across scorers. To determine if two observers agree, a measure of interobserver agreement is established on the target response. Ideally, a statistical index of this

agreement is computed that reflects true agreement and rules out chance agreement (e.g., Cohen's kappa coefficient) (Hartmann, 1982). *Item generalization* refers to the extent to which a given response (or set of responses) represents a larger universe of similar responses. In behavior assessment, item generalization could be used in self-report instruments, as when scores on odd-numbered items parallel those of even-numbered items. Similarly, in behavioral observation, odd–even scores might be compared during various phases of baseline and treatment. Generalization across *time* refers to the extent to which data collected at one point in time are representative of those that might have been collected at other times. Generally, behavioral assessors are concerned with the consistency of behavior across time, particularly within the context of stability in an intervention program. *Setting* generality refers to the extent to which data obtained in one situation are representative of those obtained in other situations. A behavioral assessor would be concerned with the degree of generality of a behavior across settings, such as from classroom A to classroom B. *Method* generality refers to the extent to which data from different methods of assessment produce consistent results. As Cone (1977) noted, "the method universe of generalization deals with the issue of the comparability of data produced from two or more ways of measuring the same behavioral content" (p. 420). For example, behavioral assessors would be concerned with the general correspondence between measures of self-report and direct observation of a behavior. Finally, *dimensions* generalization refers to the comparability of data on two or more different behaviors. When scores on a particular measure of one behavioral dimension relate to scores on other variables for the same clients, the scores are said to belong to a common universe.

METHODS OF BEHAVIORAL ASSESSMENT

Following the conceptual scheme presented above, the discussion will now center on the most common methods of behavioral assessment, including (a) behavioral interviews, (b) self-report, (c) problem checklists and rating scales, (d) analog measures, and (e) direct observation procedures. In addition, psychophysiological procedures, and traditional psychoeducational testing are discussed within the context of their use in behavioral assessment domains.[2]

Interview Assessment

Interview assessment methods are perhaps the most ubiquitous procedures for gathering clinical data (Burke & DeMers, 1979) and have been used widely in traditional psychotherapy and education and may, in fact, be the most frequently used assessment method in clinical and school settings (Gresham, 1984). Behavior therapists have also regarded the interview as an important clinical assessment technique (Gresham & Davis, 1988).

Relative to other areas of behavioral assessment there is a paucity of research on behavioral interviewing (Ciminero & Drabman, 1977; Hay, Hay, Angle, & Nelson, 1979; Linehan, 1977). Major concerns have been raised over the reliability and validity of the technique (Haynes & Jensen, 1979). Moreover, while some authors present a conceptual framework for the behavioral interview (e.g., Holland, 1970; Kanfer & Grimm, 1977; Kanfer & Saslow, 1969), few formal script guidelines are provided and the clinician does not have a rationale for what specific questions should be asked at what point during the intervention process.

One major behavioral system for interviewing clients and consultees is the behavioral consultation model, developed by Bergan, Kratochwill, and their associates (Bergan, 1977; Bergan & Kratochwill, in press; Kratochwill & Bergan, in press). The behavioral consultation model provides a systematic format to operationalize the verbal interactions occurring during behavioral interviewing. The problem-solving model originally developed by Bergan (1977) is designed to assist consultees (e.g., teachers, parents) to define various problems (e.g., academic social), to formulate and implement plans to solve problems (i.e., behavior therapy programs), and to evaluate various treatment goals (target of the interventions) and the effectiveness of therapeutic programs. Thus,

the major characteristics of the behavioral interview are the specification and definition of target behaviors, the identification and analysis of environmental conditions, and the use of interview data to plan, implement, and evaluate the outcomes of intervention. Behavioral consultation is procedurally operationalized through formal interviews in the problem identification, problem analysis, and problem evaluation stages.

The consultation model represents an interview assessment strategy within behavior therapy that links assessment to treatment. Since consultation involves a verbal interchange between a consultant and consultee and/or client, emphasis has been placed on the analysis of verbal behavior. Consultant control of verbal behavior during consultation necessitates not only recognition of the types of verbal utterances that occur during interviews, but also the ability to produce different kinds of verbalizations to meet specific interviewing objectives (Bergan, 1977). If a consultant wishes to elicit information about conditions controlling client behavior, he or she must be able to produce the type of verbal utterance most appropriate for that particular goal. Within this model, a sophisticated coding system has been developed to analyze verbal interactions occurring during interviews (Bergan & Tombari, 1975). In Chapter 23 in this volume, Gutkin and Curtis provide a further account of the behavioral consultation model.

The future will likely see increased sophistication and use of the interview assessment strategy. In recent reviews of the use of behavioral interviews, Gresham (1984) and Gresham and Davis (1988) provide psychometric evidence in terms of interrater reliability (scorer generality), criterion-related validity (method generality), and content validity. In the future we will probably see more problem-specific interview formats developed. The merits of this direction in interview development may be more systematic data gathering that increases reliability and validity (Mash & Terdal, 1988b).

Despite the recognized limitations of current interview procedures, several advantages over other assessment approaches can be identified (Linehan, 1977). First, the interview is a flexible system of obtaining data in that it can be used to gather both general information covering many areas of the client's functioning and detailed information in specific areas. Second, variations in the client's nonverbal and verbal behavior can be

---

[2]We have chosen to organize our presentation by *method* of assessment. Readers interested in the application of various assessment methods to *disorders* should review Mash and Terdal (1988a). The indirect–direct dimensions of behavioral assessment presented here are not to be confused with the indirect–direct distinctions commonly made between traditional and behavioral assessment (see, e.g., Hersen & Barlow, 1976, pp. 114–120).

examined in relation to the assessor's questions, thereby allowing analyses of responses and lines of further inquiry. Third, the interview provides an option for the development of a personal relationship between the therapist and the client (in contrast to such methods as direct observation, where there may be no interaction between therapist and client). An exception to this occurs when the therapist interviews a consultee rather than the client himself or herself. Currently, there is little research concerning children's abilities to report their own behaviors accurately, or the situational conditions surrounding their behaviors (including antecedents, consequences, and frequency or duration). It is assumed that several intellectual, developmental, and environmental variables may interact with a child's ability to verbalize accurate behavioral data in an interview, but this assumption has not been investigated extensively. Fourth, the interview allows for potentially greater confidentiality relative to some other assessment procedures (e.g., paper-and-pencil methods, direct observation). Fifth, interview assessment is an important method of gathering information from people who are unable to provide data through other means (e.g., those persons with limited communication skills, mental retardation). Finally, the interview allows the clinician to modify his or her questions and responses to fit the person's conceptual system and affords an opportunity for modification of the interviewee's verbal description. This advantage must be balanced against the potential disadvantage of a nonstandardized script that may promote subjective interpretations.

Self-Report, Behavior Checklists, and Rating Scales

A self-report is classified as an indirect assessment procedure because it, like the interview, represents a verbal description of clinically relevant behavior occurring at another time and place. Sometimes self-report assessment has been based on unreliable verbalizations in response to unstructured, open-ended questions. However, a variety of self-report inventories can be used to structure the situation (Bellack & Hersen, 1977a, 1977b). Examples of self-report assessment with parents and children are presented in Mash and Terdal (1988b) and a specific discussion of their use in schools is presented in Witt, Cavell, Heffer, Carey, and Martens (1988).

Behavior checklists and rating scales are con-

ceptually similar indirect behavior therapy assessment strategies. In these methods a person is asked to rate others (usually the client) based on past observations of that other's behavior. Due to the diversity of items that are typically included, the target behavior of actual clinical interest, such as social withdrawal, may or may not be involved. Moreover, a teacher or parent may be asked to rate a series of behaviors in addition to the social withdrawal problem (e.g., fear, aggression, academic work). Presumably, other relevant clinical problems may emerge from this assessment. Nevertheless, the identifying feature of checklist and rating scale assessment strategies is that the rating occurs subsequent to the actual behavior of clinical interest (Cone, 1977; Wiggins, 1973).

Self-Report

The growing emphasis on cognitive processes in behavior therapy focused attention on the need for self-report measurement. Due to the perceived problems inherent in subjective and unsystematic forms of self-report assessment, various inventories and schedules were developed. Also, as Tasto (1977) noted, in clinical practice *"the operational criteria for the existence of problems are self-reported verbalizations"* (p. 154).

Self-report inventories are potentially useful for at least two functions (Bellack & Hersen, 1977a). First, self-report measures can be useful in gathering data on motoric responses, physiological activity, and cognitions (see Figure 1). For example, one might ask a child the following questions that tap different contents: "How many math problems did you complete?" (motoric), "Do your palms sweat when you approach school?" (physiological), "Do you have negative thoughts about your teacher?" (cognitive). Assuming that an accurate assessment is provided, two of these questions, with the exception of cognitions, can be verified independently. A second function of self-report measures is to gather data about a client's subjective experience (or evaluation) of the three primary response systems. For example, one might ask a child "Do you like math?", "Are you afraid of school?", or "Do you dislike your teacher?". It can be observed that this second set of questions includes subjective components that are not objectively verifiable.

A number of variables may influence the type of data one obtains from self-report and their correspondence to the actual criterion measure.

Such factors as the source of the data (e.g., written or verbal report by the client), the form of the questions asked, the content of the questions, situational factors, and operational specification of terms will be important (Bellack & Hersen, 1977b; Haynes, 1978; Tasto, 1977). For example, during consultation interviews, a major tool of obtaining objective information is the verbal elicitor. The elicitor is a verbalization that calls for objective information and/or action from a listener (e.g., child, teacher). Thus, a question such as "What are some examples of the things you would have to do to complete your math assignment?" typically yields specific information about the problem.

Behavior Checklists and Rating Scales

A large variety of formal checklists and rating scales have been used in the clinical assessment with school-aged children. Walls, Werner, Bacon, and Zane (1977) provided a rather extensive catalog of available scales, as have other authors (e.g., Achenbach & Edelbrock, 1978; Edelbrock, 1988; Hoge, 1983; Spivack & Swift, 1973). In many cases, behavioral assessors use scales emanating from quite diverse sources and theoretical orientations. As noted previously, their use in behavioral assessment is premised on the nature of the data gathered and how such data are used in the development of a treatment program (i.e., treatment utility).

A comprehensive review of checklists and rating scales can be found in several sources (e.g., Edelbrock, 1988; Hoge, 1983; see specific chapters in Mash & Terdal, 1988b). Based on Hoge's review it was noted that rating measures supported a three-factor model that included personality adjustment, social adjustment, and academic competence. Hoge also reviewed aptitude measures and found less support for a three-factor model with this component.

A common device used in behavioral assessment includes the *Child Behavior Checklist* (CBCL) (Achenbach, 1978; Achenbach & Edelbrock, 1979; Edelbrock & Achenbach, 1984a, 1984b). Relative to other scales that are in common use in rating scale assessment, the *Child Behavior Checklist* (CBCL) has been used extensively to assess a wide range of children's behavior problems and adaptive behaviors (see Edelbrock, 1988, for a comprehensive review). A brief review of the CBCL is presented here to illustrate how it

might contribute to overall behavioral assessment options.

The CBCL can be completed by parents and includes 20 social competence items that assess school performance, social relations, and the amount of quality of participation in hobbies, activities, and sports. There are also 118 items covering specific behavior problems, and the parent rates each item on a 3-point scale (i.e., not true, somewhat or sometimes true, and very or often true). The CBCL is scored on a child behavior profile which provides a graphical representation of item responses across domains.

The psychometric adequacy of the CBCL is well documented. Normative data have been presented on 1300 randomly selected nonreferred children between the ages of 4 and 16 years. Reported test–retest and interrater reliability coefficients are good, and evidence for content, construct, and criterion-rated validity are reported.

A teacher version of the CBCL has also been developed (Edelbrock & Achenbach, 1984a, 1984b) and includes item content related to school settings, and can also be scored on a profile. All informants should be used whenever possible to provide cross-situational information from various sources.

Several positive features of checklists and rating scales have been identified (Ciminero & Drabman, 1977; Edelbrock, 1988). First, checklists are typically economical in cost, effort, and time relative to other assessment strategies such as direct observation. Second, many checklists are structured so that a relatively comprehensive picture of the problem can be obtained. For example, Hoge (1983) noted that a three-factor model consisting of personality adjustment, social adjustment, and academic competence was identified. Third, due to the diverse range of questions asked in typical checklists and rating scales, the clinician may be able to identify problems that were overlooked through other assessment methods such as direct observation and interviewing. In fact, these measures have been applied to a wide range of clinical disorders (Edelbrock, 1988). Fourth, data obtained from checklists and rating scales are usually relatively "easy" to quantify (as through factor analysis, multidimensional scaling). In this regard, they have been useful for classification of behavior disorders (see Kazdin, 1985). Fifth, checklists and rating scales frequently provide a useful measure for pre- and posttest evaluation of a therapy program. Sixth, they are frequently a convenient means of obtaining social validity data on therapeutic outcomes (Kazdin, 1977b; Wolf, 1978). Social validation refers broadly to the external evaluation of the goals, procedures, and results of therapeutic outcome. Finally, when populations of clients can be described accurately in terms of their response to checklist items, this information may assist in identifying the type of clients that were treated and how they responded to treatment. For example, general psychopathology scales are used extensively in evaluation of children's response to medication, and in the general area of childhood psychopharmacology for subject selection and sample description (see Conners, 1985 for a review of commonly used scales).

Conceptual and methodological issues have been raised for many years over the use of rating scales and checklists in both research and practice (e.g., Anastasi, 1976; Ciminero & Drabman, 1977; Evans & Nelson, 1977; Spivack & Swift, 1973; Walls et al., 1977). One major problem with these procedures is that they represent an indirect dimension of assessment. Since data are gathered retrospectively, their relation to actual occurrences of the target behavior in the natural environment remain less than perfect. A second issue relates to item selection. While it appears that rating scale developers have some criteria for generating items included in the scale, the rationale may not always be evident. Furthermore, an empirical item analysis is not always conducted. Third, it is frequently unclear under what conditions the scale should be administered. Fourth, there is sometimes no clear description or rationale for determining the presence or absence of a particular behavior. Fifth, the format of the rating scale differs considerably among the various published scales. Sixth, there is often considerable variation within particular scales with regard to the kinds of judgments required. Seventh, a large number of rating scales are constructed to detect the presence of negative behaviors (i.e., behavioral excesses and deficits) and less frequently focus on positive behaviors (assets). Finally, published scales vary widely on standards for reliability and standardization.

Rating scales and checklists will probably continue to be used extensively in behavioral assessment in schools and other applied settings. One reason for their popularity relates to the general ease with which such devices are adminis-

tered (but not necessarily interpreted). Nevertheless, the aforementioned conceptual and methodological considerations should be considered when using rating scales and checklists in behavioral assessment.

Self-Monitoring

Self-monitoring (SM) refers to an assessment technique in which a person observes and records his or her own behavior at the time of its occurrence. This procedure is regarded as a direct assessment procedure and is distinguished from self-report methods described above. While self-reports involve a reporting of events occurring at other times and/or places, SM involves an observation of the clinically relevant behavior at the time of its occurrence (Cone, 1977). Several authors have provided a review of the applications of SM (e.g., Gardner & Cole, 1988; Haynes, 1978; Mahoney, 1977; McFall, 1977b; Nelson, 1977a, 1977b) and the interested reader should consult these for greater detail. SM can be used for both assessment and treatment of various behaviors. In some cases, SM has been used as one component of a more complete system of behavioral self-control (Coates & Thoresen, 1979; Kanfer, 1979; Mace & West, 1986; Mahony & Arnkoff, 1978; S. G. O'Leary & Dubey, 1979; Rosenbaum & Drabman, 1979; Thoresen & Mahoney, 1974).

Self-Monitoring Assessment

When SM assessment is used, the client presents data on his or her own behavior to the clinician for at least two general reasons. First, the client may be requested to perform SM during the initial stages of assessment when attempting to identify specific problems. Baseline response levels help verify the existence of a problem as well as specific environmental factors related to the client's problem. Second, SM may be used to gather information on the success of an intervention program. The range of application of SM to various target behaviors has been quite extensive, including, for example, teachers' classroom behavior, academic behaviors (e.g., assignment completion; study activities; math, reading, and spelling performance; and time on task), dating behaviors, hand gestures, nail biting, respiration, sleep patterns, speech dysfluencies, face touching, swimming practice, lip and mouth biting, and a variety of unwanted repetitive behaviors.

Many different recording devices and methods have been used for SM assessment. Among the more common are record booklets, checklists, forms, counters, timers, meters, measures, scales, residual records (e.g., empty pop bottles), archival records (e.g., telephone bills), diaries, and many others. Table 1 presents an example of a SM form used for a child to record the number of assignments completed to a specific criterion over a 2-week period.

When used for assessment, a number of variables may influence the quality of self-monitoring. Both *accuracy* and *reactivity* have been identified as factors influencing the data. When considering the accuracy of SM the following factors should be noted (McFall, 1977b, pp. 200–201):

1. *Training:* Clients should be trained in the use of SM. Training a child in SM will generally result in better accuracy (see Mahoney, 1977, for an example of training).
2. *Systematic Methods:* Systematic SM methods, such as using the record form in Table 1, will typically result in more reliable and accurate outcomes than those methods that are more informal and non-systematic.
3. *Characteristics of the SM Device:* A SM device that is easy to use, allows simple data collection, and does not depend on the client's memory (e.g., wrist counter) usually provides more accurate data than when such a tool is not used.
4. *Timing:* Generally, a short time interval between the actual SM act and the occurrence of the target behavior is desirable for obtaining accurate data. In the exam-

ple above, the child should be directed to make a check each time an assignment is completed, rather than, for example, at the end of the day.

5. *Response Competition:* When a client is required to monitor concurrent responses, his or her attention is divided. This may cause interference and thereby reduce the accuracy of the SM data. In the example provided, the child has been instructed to record only one behavior—that of assignment completion—to reduce response competition.
6. *Response Effort:* The more time and energy the client must spend on the SM activity, the less accurate the data may be. Thus, dimensions of "time" and "energy" may prove to be aversive.
7. *Reinforcement:* Contingent positive reinforcement for accurate recording tends to increase accuracy. Some external criterion is usually established for accuracy. In the previous example, a teacher may be able to establish the accuracy of the SM assessment data as assignments are completed.
8. *Awareness of Accuracy Assessment:* The clinician should monitor the data and inform the client that accuracy is being monitored. Such client awareness will typically increase accuracy.
9. *Selection of Target Behaviors:* Since some behaviors are more salient, more easily discriminated, and/or more memorable, variations in accuracy will occur due to differences on these dimensions. Generally, higher levels of accuracy have

TABLE 1 Examples of a SM Form used by a 10-Year-Boy to Record Assignment Completion Over a 2-Week Period

	M	T	W	T	F	M	T	W	T	F
Total number assigned Total completed Percentage completed[a]										

[a]This is to be completed by the clinician.

been established on motor behaviors (e.g., nail biting) than verbal behaviors (e.g., number of times the person says "ah"), and positively valued behaviors are more accurately recorded than those that are negatively valued.

10. *Characteristics of Clients:* Some clients are more accurate recorders than others. One would generally expect young children to be less accurate than older children, adolescents, and adults. However, individual variations will occur within ages.

In SM assessment, reactivity is a problem when unintended or unwanted influences are the result of self-recording, and the data are not representative of data that would have occurred had SM not been used. McFall (1977b, pp. 202–204) presented the following eight variables that may influence the reactivity of SM.

1. *Motivation:* Clients who are motivated to change the behavior prior to engaging in SM are more likely to demonstrate reactive effects.

2. *Valence:* Depending on how clients value a particular SM behavior, it may or may not change. Generally, positively valued behaviors are likely to increase, negatively valued behaviors are likely to decrease, and neutral behaviors may not change.

3. *Target Behaviors:* The nature of target behaviors chosen for SM may influence reactivity.

4. *Goals, Reinforcement, and Feedback:* Specific performance goals, feedback, and reinforcement scheduled as part of SM could increase reactivity.

5. *Timing:* Reactivity may vary as a function of the timing of SM. For example, recording prior to a behavior may be more reactive than recording subsequent to its occurrence.

6. *Self-Monitoring Devices:* Generally, the more obtrusive the recording device, the more reactive it tends to be (e.g., a hand-held timer is more reactive than one that is out of sight and "awareness").

7. *Number of Target Behaviors:* As the number of target behaviors being monitored increases, reactivity may decrease.

8. *Schedule of Self-Monitoring:* Continuous SM may be more reactive than intermittent SM.

Positive Features of SM

Despite some potential methodological limitations, SM may be advantageous for behavioral assessment. First, it is a relatively cost-efficient means of assessment relative to such techniques as analogue and direct observational assessment. Second, SM may be the only assessment option, as in measurement of private behaviors (thoughts). Third, SM can minimize the potentially obtrusive effects of assessment that occur with other assessment procedures (e.g., interview, direct observation). Fourth, SM can help verify the existence of a problem in combination with other assessment methods. The aforementioned accuracy and reactivity variables may emerge in assessment. When SM is used as an intervention, somewhat different concerns must be considered (see Gardner & Cole, 1988, for a review).

Analog Assessment

An increasingly popular direct assessment procedure requires clients to respond to stimuli that simulate those found in the natural environment. In such assessment analog the client is usually requested to role play or perform as if he or she were in the natural environment. The most common analog assessment strategies are intellectual and psychoeducational tests. Analog assessment procedures have been used for many years within behavioral assessment, but it is only recently that systematic features have been outlined and advantages and disadvantages elucidated (see Gettinger, 1988; Haynes, 1978; Nay, 1977; Shapiro & Kratochwill, 1988a). Relative to direct naturalistic observational assessment, analog methods offer several positive contributions. First, especially in research, these measures permit increased opportunities for control of the situation. This feature may also emerge when analog assessment is being used for clinical and applied purposes. Many variables operating in the natural environment contaminate assessment efforts and analog procedures may reduce or eliminate these. Second, analog strategies may allow assessment of behaviors that are impossible to monitor in naturalistic settings (e.g., low-frequency events). Third, relative to direct observational assessment procedures, analog strategies may be less costly.

Fourth, analog assessment may help simplify and reduce complex constructs (e.g., intelligence). Through analog assessment clinicians may be able to control extraneous influences, isolate and manipulate specific variables, and reliably measure their effects. Finally, analog assessment procedures may help clinicians avoid certain ethical problems that emerge in naturalistic observation. For example, under analog assessment conditions the clinician may be able to test a procedure to learn about its characteristics prior to implementing it in the natural environment.

Domains of Analog Assessment

Nay (1977) identified five general categories of analog methods: paper-and-pencil analog, audiotape analog, videotape analogs, enactment analogs, and role-play analogs. Paper-and-pencil analog require the client to note how he or she would respond to a stimulus situation presented in written form. For example, teachers or parents may be asked to respond to a series of multiple-choice questions that depict different options to follow in implementing behavior management procedures. In paper-and-pencil analogs of this type, the stimulus situations are presented in a written mode with response options written, verbal, and/or physical. The client is usually presented with the stimulus and a cue for a response is made. The response made may be verbal and/or physical in that the client is asked to describe what he or she would do and/or physically respond as he or she typically would. While a major advantage of these procedures is that they can be administered to large numbers of clients at the same time and are easily quantified, the predictive utility of these procedures remains largely unknown. Moreover, this type of measure is limited because the clinician does not observe overt behavior in response to the actual stimulus.

Audiotape analog situations involve presentation of the stimulus items in an auditory format. Some characteristics of these procedures include a set of instructions to the client and a services of audio situations presented by the clinician. The client is typically required to make a verbal or other physical response. For example, the clinician may present audio transcripts of a teacher presenting information to a class of school-aged children. The child (client) may be requested to respond through role play or free behavior. Although the audio analog shares many of the advantages of the paper

and pencil analog, it still may not approach realistic stimulus conditions.

The videotape analog involves use of video technology to present a realistic scene for the client, one of its major advantages. In this regard it may approximate closely the naturalistic setting. Most often both audio and visual components are used. Video analogs can also be used for training intervention, as in the teaching of social skills, but cost and availability of the video equipment may represent major limitations of the procedure. Moreover, some child clients may have difficulty "getting into" the presentation.

Enactment analogs require the client to interact with relevant stimulus persons (or objects) typically present in the natural environment within the clinically contrived situation. Sometimes the therapist may bring relevant stimulus persons (e.g., peers, teachers) into the assessment setting to observe client responses, as has been done in assessment and treatment of elective mutism (e.g., Colligan, Colligan, & Dilliard, 1977). A major advantage of this approach is that stimuli can be arranged to be nearly identical to the natural environment. Of course, a limitation of this procedure is that the situation may still not duplicate the natural environment.

The final analog type, role play, can be used within the context of any of the aforementioned analog assessment procedures. Flexibility in format and option for direct measurement of the behavioral responses are major advantages of this procedure. For example, a script may be presented to the client, who is asked to rehearse covertly or enact overtly certain behaviors under various stimulus situations. A therapist may ask a high school student to role play asking someone for a date to assess various dating skills. The client may play himself or herself or another person and specific instructions may be present or absent. As is true of other analog assessment procedures, a major disadvantage is the potential lack of a match between the analog and the natural environment.

*Criterion-Referenced/Curriculum-
Based Assessment*

Criterion-referenced measures are a special form of analog assessment that has been aligned closely with, but not limited to, the behavioral paradigm (Bijou, 1976; Cancelli & Kratochwill, 1981). Since criterion-referenced tests were first introduced (Glaser & Klaus, 1962), continued clarification of the term as well as issues that must be addressed in their use have proliferated (see Hambleton, Swaminathan, Algina, & Coulson, 1978). In the early literature, criterion-referenced tests were considered precise measures of highly specific discrete behavior capabilities. Such behaviors were purported to be hierarchically sequenced, as derived through task analysis procedures (see Gagné, 1962, 1968; L. B. Resnick & Ford, 1978; L. D. Resnick, Wang, & Kaplan, 1973). Glaser (1971) provided the following definition of a criterion-referenced test:

> A criterion-referenced test is one that is deliberately constructed to yield measurements that are directly interpretable in terms of specified performance standards. Performance standards are generally specified by defining a class or domain of tasks that should be performed by the individual. Measurements are taken as representative samples of tasks drawn from the domain and such measurements are referenced directly to this domain for each individual. (p. 41)

Within this conceptualization, the term *domain-referenced test* has evolved. Thus, whether one prefers the term *criterion-referenced* (Hambleton et al., 1978) or *domain-referenced* (Subkoviak & Baker, 1977), it is generally assumed that the concept of "domain" is implied. Nevertheless, these notions have evolved outside a behavioral psychology orientation. It appears most useful to consider performance on a criterion-referenced test as a function of the immediate test situation and the previous interactions that comprise the history of the child (Bijou, 1976). Thus, specific responses to items on a criterion-referenced test are due to (a) the nature of the test items and (b) the setting factors in taking the test.

It should be noted that criterion-/domain-referenced tests are improved with an empirical validation of homogeneous item domains (e.g., Bergan, 1981, 1986). Procedures for establishing homogeneous item domains are available (e.g., latent structure analysis). With the development of procedures for empirically validating the scope and sequence of domains of homogeneous items, path-referenced assessment (Bergan, 1981) has been developed. This assessment procedure provides information about the learner that allows specific identification of skill and/or domain defi-

ciencies as well as the sequence (i.e., "path") of curriculum instruction that will lead most efficaciously to mastery of the task identified.

Curriculum-based assessment has grown in popularity in recent years and is affiliated with several approaches, including the Resource/ Consulting Teaching Model (e.g., Idol-Maestas, 1981), Vermont Consulting Teaching Models (Christie, McKenzie, & Burdett, 1972), Directive Teaching (Stephens, 1977), Exceptional Teaching (White & Haring, 1980), Precision Teaching (Lindsley, 1964), and Data-Based Program Modification (Deno, Marston, & Tindal, 1986; Deno & Mirkin, 1977). A common characteristic of all these approaches is that they involve direct and repeated measurement of child performance in the classroom curriculum. Depending on how this form of assessment is used, it might better be represented as a direct observational assessment method. The programs also typically involve a structured behaviorally based instructional program. Considerable work has been done on curriculum-based assessment in recent years and the range and scope of what is to be assessed has been expanded (see Lentz, 1988).

Criterion-/domain-referenced tests and curriculum-based measures have generally been used for three purposes within applied settings: (a) to diagnose problem behavior, (b) to monitor learning, and (c) to assess readiness for placement in a prescribed educational program. A central theme within these functions is that they allow measurement of a client's competence in a particular area of the curriculum and assist in the design of a specific instructional program. Yet several criticisms of these assessments have emerged related to the lack of normative data—a characteristic deemed desirable by many professionals.

In response to the issue of normative data, one must consider that norm-referenced and criterion-/domain-referenced tests are designed for different proposes. Items on a criterion-referenced test are randomly selected from each domain during test construction. On the other hand, psychometric theory (governing item selection for norm-referenced devices) suggests that to discriminate between good and poor learners, items that are passed by half of a sample of the population are desirable (Subkoviak & Baker, 1977).

People desiring normative information might consider the use of social validation as an alternative to psychometrically established norms (see

Kazdin, 1977b; Wolf, 1978). Social validation procedures have been developed to evaluate treatment outcomes in therapy research. Their use in assessment can occur in several ways. For example, the behavior of a client (e.g., addition skills) can be compared with that of his or her peers who are or not experiencing difficulties in the target skill. Also, subjective evaluations of the target behavior can be gathered from persons in the natural environment (e.g., teachers). While such information may be useful in establishing the degree of deviance among peers, it may not necessarily help design a better instructional program.

Traditional Assessment Devices in Behavioral Assessment

Behavioral writers, but not necessarily practitioners, have typically rejected various standardized tests of ability and have instead tended to favor the use of criterion-referenced tests, task analysis procedures, and curriculum-based assessment described above. However, there has been interest in the use of conventional tests, such as IQ scales (e.g., the Wechsler scales and the Stanford-Binet) and other norm-referenced tests as analog measures.

There are several reasons for the use of traditional tests within behavioral analog assessment (see Ciminero & Drabman, 1977; Evans & Nelson, 1986). In some states, traditional tests are legally required for diagnosis. The tests provide a sample of many school activities and skills, and standardized test taking is considered an important skill in school settings. Some standardized tests (e.g., IQ, achievement) include an assessment of knowledge not necessarily learned in school settings. Furthermore, instruments such as intelligence tests represent standardized measures of behavior and provide normative data that may help establish academic goals for remediation. Finally, the academic test provides the opportunity to view the child's performance on a standardized cognitive analog task.

While many traditional tests are generally reliable instruments with scores that may account for a moderate amount of variance in predicting school achievement (but not necessarily *school learning*), each of the aforementioned points should be examined critically. It is certainly true that tests are frequently mandated by institutional requirements or law. This is frequently based on the assumption that their use is critical to diagnosis and treatment. When it can be demonstrated that other assessment procedures are more relevant to the target problem, the reliance placed on such mandated measures may be minimized.

Second, the notion that traditional psycho-educational tests provide a sample of school-related skills is typically true, although they are an analog to classroom requirements. In this regard, most schoolchildren are required to know word definitions, assemble puzzles, and hold digits in memory as occurs in IQ testing. However, when tests are used on this premise, it is necessary to consider the correspondence between the skills assessed on the test and the ones that are the focus of the intervention. The degree to which a match occurs will relate to the usefulness for subsequent academic programming and have a bearing on the analog nature of the task.

Third, the standardized feature of testing is attractive to many psychologists. Indeed, such standardization can be a positive feature of behavioral analog assessment (Kratochwill, 1985). In this context, the clinician must attend to methodological considerations in analog assessment, with particular reference to the relation between test-sampled skills and the criterion behaviors of interest.

Fourth, normative data from traditional tests must be examined within the context of the skills sampled. For example, item content in IQ tests is based on the psychometric notion that these items should discriminate among individuals rather than among items within a domain for the target client (Cancelli & Kratochwill, 1981). When age norms are considered for remedial purposes it is difficult to determine the degree to which a score on one subtest must deviate before a serious deficiency is identified. Furthermore, remediation of the skill may not be apparent from the test item (Evans & Nelson, 1977).

Fifth, there is some validity to the notion that standardized tests contain item content that is not taught in school settings. For example, a comparison between IQ tests and tests of academic achievement may provide information helpful in the design of an instructional program. In this case it is again necessary to examine item content for its relevance to academic programming and for identifying prerequisite skill relations.

A final positive use of traditional tests, that of observing the child's performance on a standardized cognitive task, must be conducted with at least two considerations. To begin with, as noted above, use of the test for this purpose is still an analog assessment and should retain the cautions suggested for this assessment strategy. Second, it is again emphasized that observation of a child on a cognitive task may be less useful than observation of the child on an actual learning task reflecting curriculum content (Gettinger, 1988).

Considerations

The analog assessment procedure presents many behavior assessment options in school settings. Nevertheless, both reliability and validity issues need to be addressed when these procedures are used (Nay, 1977). People using these procedures should assess reliability data on target responses. A check on the validity of the analog is made by comparing the contrived assessment with the target behaviors occurring in the natural environment. This is usually accomplished through direct observation of the behaviors of concern. As is true of other assessment procedures, analog assessment may best be used as one of several techniques to assess behavior (Shapiro & Kratochwill, 1988a).

Direct Observational Assessment

Direct observational assessment represents one of the most widely used procedures in behavior therapy research and practice. Jones, Reid, and Patterson (1974) summarized three major characteristics of a "naturalistic observational system" that remain the hallmark of the approach. These include "recording of behavioral events in their natural settings at the time they occur, not retrospectively; the use of trained impartial observer-coders; and descriptions of behaviors which require little if any inference by observers to code the events" (p. 46). Such observations can occur under role play or free (naturally varying) conditions.

Although observational assessment strategies are commonly affiliated with behavior therapy approaches (e.g., Johnson & Bolstad, 1973; Jones et al., 1974; Kent & Foster, 1977; Lipinski & Nelson, 1974), they are clearly not limited to this orientation. Instead, they are used in rather diverse areas of psychology and education. The rather extensive literature in this area and the numerous methodological and conceptual issues militate against a thorough presentation here (see Hartmann, 1982, for more detailed coverage). When used in clinical assessment, many issues

emerge concerning the utility of direct observation. One major issue in its use in clinical assessment is the distinction between observational procedures and actual observational instruments (Kratochwill, Alper, & Cancelli, 1980). Most practicing school psychologists have used some type of observational procedure in their assessment work. This usually takes the form of direct observation of a child in a classroom, or having a parent or teacher record the occurrence of a child's behavior for some specified period of time. Although observational measurement may vary considerably on a number of dimensions (e.g., the person observing, the target response, the sophistication of the form), it is most commonly used as part of an assessment "battery" by school psychologists.

In contrast to such ubiquitous observational procedures, there are relatively few specific observational instruments in use in behavioral assessment. [We are excluding the rather large number of rating scales and checklists discussed in an earlier section of the chapter since these do not meet the criterion of direct observational assessment vis-à-vis the Cone (1977) and Jones et al. (1974) conceptualization.] The paucity of instruments for direct observational assessment may be due to the lack of attention to the development of these scales and typical requirements in applied settings to design situation-specific assessment forms.

Most instruments that have been developed focus on a rather specific range of behaviors (e.g., Alevizos, DeRisi, Liberman, Eckman, & Callahan, 1978; K. D. O'Leary, Romanczyk, Kass, Dietz, & Santogrossi, 1979; Patterson, Ray, Shaw, & Cobb, 1969; Wahler, House, & Stambaugh, 1976). These coding systems are used in different settings, including, for example, institutional program evaluation (Alevizos et al., 1978),[3] home (Patterson et al., 1969),[4] school (O'Leary et al., 1979; Saudargas, 1983),[5] and home and school (Wahler et al., 1976).[6] Each of these systems represents a

[3]The BOI is available from Dr. Peter N. Aleviazas, Department of Psychology, Straub Hall, University of Oregon, Eugene, OR 97403.

[4]The BCS is available through Research Press, Box 317741, Champaign, IL 61820.

[5]The O'Leary code is available from Dr. K. Daniel O'Leary, Department of Psychology, State University of New York at Stony Brook, Long Island, NY 11794.

[6]The Wahler code is available from Dr. Robert G. Wahler, Child Behavior Institute, the University of Tennessee at Knoxville, TN 37916.

promising observational instrument for assessment in research and practice (see Saudargas & Lentz, 1986, for a brief overview).

Recently, several specific codes have been used in school psychology research and practice.[7] One system designed by Alessi and Kaye (1983) provides the assessor with operational procedures to define and measure target behaviors. The assessment system is linked to a consultation model and is quite useful in focusing on specific target problems. As another alternative, Saudargas reports (see Saudargas, 1983; Saudargas & Lentz, 1986) a system called the *State-Event Classroom Observation System* (SECOS) that can be used for assessing multibehavior targets in school settings.[8] The system allows the assessor to gather data simultaneously on multiple behaviors in classrooms or for various research applications. Recently, Saudargas and Lentz (1986) provided a review of the SECOS, decision rules and

procedures for constructing standardized multiple observation systems, and procedures for obtaining reliability and validity data, as well as procedures for training observers in use of the code. Table 2 provides an overview of child and teacher behaviors that are included on the SECOS scale. In addition, Figure 2 provides the observation recording format used with the SECOS procedure. The code is very relevant in educational and psychological assessment generally, and can be used to assess a wide range of teacher and child behaviors (see Shapiro, 1987a; Shapiro & Lentz, 1986, for further discussion of the scale).

Direct observational measurement is a good method of assessment in research and practice, but a number of methodological issues have been raised in recent years that have made this assessment procedure complex (see Hartmann, 1984). Some recommendations have emerged from the research literature that can make this form of assessment more reliable and valid. First, persons functioning as observers should be trained prior to participating in observational sessions. Training should include samples of behavioral sequences and environmental settings that resemble closely the behaviors and settings in which data collection will occur. Performance should be monitored closely, and retraining should be conducted systematically to minimize observer drift from the original behavioral definition. Second, two or more observers should be involved in assessment efforts to establish interobserver agreement. Observers should be trained together, scores should be compared with a single formal criterion, and training should be long enough to ensure that there is agreement to a specified criterion on each code. This assessment of "reliability" is an important component of direct observational assessment and is recommended strongly for obtaining credible data. Third, the conditions for assessing observer agreement should be maintained to ensure consistent levels of agreement. Continuous overt monitoring and covert monitoring may help generate stable levels of agreement. Fourth, observer bias may be reduced by not communicating the specific treatment plan to the observer(s). Explicit instructions to the observer, indicating that the specific outcomes are unknown, may be preferable to complete avoidance of the topic. Fifth, standardized observational codes should be used when possible (e.g., SECOS). In the absence of instruments or coding sheets for a target problem,

---

[7]Emphasis on the observational assessment of environmental variables has led to the development of The Instructional Environmental Scale (TIES; Ysseldyke & Christenson, 1987). The TIEs is a qualitative observational scale used to gather descriptive information on the nature of a student's instructional environment. However, the TIES does not meet criteria for a direct observation procedure. Nevertheless, according to the authors, the major purposes of TIES include (a) the provision of a systematic description of the extent to which a student's academic or behavior problems are a function of factors in the instructional environment, and (b) the identification of starting points in designing appropriate instructional interventions for individual students. Twelve descriptive indicators of the student's learning environment are evaluated: instructional presentation (e.g., lesson development, clarity of directions, checking for student understanding); classroom environment (e.g., management, time-use, climate); teacher expectations; cognitive emphasis; motivational strategies; relevant practice (e.g., opportunity, task relevance, materials); academic engaged time (e.g., student involvement, maintenance); informed feedback (e.g., feedback, corrections); adaptive instruction; and progress evaluation (e.g., monitoring, follow-up planning).

Some preliminary psychometric support of TIES is reported by the authors. Interrater reliability coefficients, using intraclass correlation procedures, range from .83 to .96, with all but two exceeding .90. The authors also suggest evidence of content validity for the 12 components of TIES, and provide research-based support for the inclusion of each of the components. However, no evidence is provided to empirically support its validity.

[8]The SECOS is available from Dr. Richard A. Saudargas, Department of Psychology, University of Tennessee, Knoxville, TN 37996-0990.

TABLE 2   Child and Teacher Behaviors Included on the SECOS

State Behavior	Behavior Description
Schoolwork	The student has head and eyes oriented toward assigned schoolwork.
Out of seat	The student is out of his/her seat.
Looking around	The student is looking around and not engaged in any other activity.
Motor behavior	The student is engaged in repetitive, stereotyped body movements.
Play with object	The student is repetitive playing with an object.
Social interaction with child	The student is interacting with one or more other students.
Social interaction with teacher	The student is interacting with the classroom teacher.
Other activity	The student is engaged in an activity other than schoolwork

Event Behavior	Behavior Description
Raise hand	The student has his/her hand raised.
Call out	The student calls out to the teacher.
Out of seat	The student is out of his/her seat.
Object aggression	The student aggresses against an object.
Approach child	The student initiates a contact with the student being observed.
Teacher approach to schoolwork	The teacher initiates a contact with the student while the student is engaged in schoolwork.
Teacher approach to other activity	The teacher initiates a contact with the student while the student is not engaged in schoolwork.
Direction-opposition	The teacher gives a direction that is followed by student noncompliance.
Approval	The teacher praises the student's behavior.
Disapproval	Teacher disapproval of student behavior.

Figure 2. The observation recording form used in the Saudargas-Creed State-Event Class-room Observation System. (From "Estimating Percent of Time and Rate Via Direct Observation: A Suggested Observational Procedure and Format" by R. A. Saudargas and F. E. Lentz, 1986, *School Psychology Review, 15,* pp. 36–48. Copyright © 1986 by Reproduced by permission.)

Sandargas-Creed

Sheet #:_____

_____ (GR:)

Student

Date

M T W R F
Day (circle)

Start   End: Total:
Time

1. ISW:TPsnt   3. SmGp:Tled
2. ISW:TSmGp   4. LgGp:Tled

_____

School

Class Activity

_____

Ac. Beh

Teacher

Observer

Referral Problem

STATES	1	2	3	4	5	6	7	8	9	10	11	12	13	14	15	16	17	18	19	20	Σ	%
SW																						
OS																						
LK																						
M																						
PLO																						
SIC																						
SIT																						
OACT																						

EVENTS	1	2	3	4	5	6	7	8	9	10	11	12	13	14	15	16	17	18	19	20	Σ	Rate
RH																						
CAL																						
OS																						
OAG																						
AC																						
OCA																						

TEACHER	1	2	3	4	5	6	7	8	9	10	11	12	13	14	15	16	17	18	19	20	Σ	Rate
TA/SW																						
TA/OTH																						
DIR-OPP																						
DIR-C+																						
APP																						
DIS																						

COMMENTS: _____

_____

_____

specific observational codes should be developed so that behaviors can be scored easily. The clinician should typically be conservative in the number of codes that are to be rated at any one time (e.g., seven or less). Sixth, observations should be conducted in an unobtrusive fashion. To assist in the examination of obtrusiveness, data should be monitored for evidence of reactivity or bias. Eighth, measurement of the generality of observational data across different settings should be conducted. Although direct observations should occur in settings in which the target behavior has been identified, multiple assessment across behaviors and settings will elucidate further the extent of the problem and help monitor therapeutic effects. Finally, normative data are quite desirable in many cases and should be considered in observational assessment given adequate time and resources. Normative data may help identify objectively behavioral excesses and deficits in a given client (Hartmann, Roper, & Bradford, 1979; Nelson & Bowles, 1975). For example, behavioral assessors can record the behavior of both the target child and a "normal" or "typical" peer to compare their behavior. Such normative information may also be useful to validate a problem socially and help establish a successful treatment, as judged by peers or other socialization agents.

Although direct observational assessment will probably remain an important measurement procedure within school psychology practice, much work still remains to be done to make this form of assessment less expensive, less time consuming, and more versatile. Development of problem/disorder-specific instruments will be a high priority in the future. Fortunately, the increasing development of microcomputer technology may make this technology more useful in applied settings (see Kratochwill, Doll, & Dickson, 1986). Because observational assessment can involve less inference about a particular behavior relative to many traditional assessment practices, and because repeated assessment of the client across various phases of treatment is possible with the procedure, it should be used whenever possible.

Psychophysiological Assessment

Psychophysiological measures can be used across Cone's (1977) three domains of assessment discussed earlier in the chapter. We discuss psychophysiological assessment in a separate section because this measurement strategy involves a number of unique considerations. Behavioral researchers have increasingly focused on psychophysiological measures of behavior, but there is still little use of this technology in school psychology research and practice. Psychophysiological measurement can be defined as "the quantification of biological events as they relate to psychological variables" (Kallman & Feuerstein, 1977, p. 329). Growing interest in psychophysiological measures in child assessment may be due to increased sophistication in instrumentation, increased use of biofeedback and other behavior therapy procedures to treat psychophysiological disorders, and the finding that independent measures of physiological responding do not correlate perfectly with verbal reports and overt behavior, thus making it imperative that such measures be used directly.

Increased interest in psychophysiological assessment in behavior therapy has also occurred in part due to the increased interest in child health issues and the general growth in the area of behavioral medicine. It is beyond the scope of this chapter to provide a detailed overview of measures that might be used in this area (see Blake & Andrasik, 1988). However, it should be emphasized that psychophysiological assessment strategies have been used in a number of areas of child psychopathology for many years. For example, in the area of research on children's fears, phobias, and anxiety disorders, psychophysiological assessment has been more common over the past several years (see Barrios & Shigetomi, 1985, and Morris & Kratochwill, 1983, for reviews of the literature).

Domains of Psychophysiological Assessment

Psychophysiological assessment generally occurs in three domains: electromyographic, cardiovascular, and electrodermal measures (Nietzel & Bernstein, 1981). Electromyography (EMG) measurement involves assessment of the electrical activity generated when the skeletal muscles contract. The muscular tension is inferred from measurement of the muscle contraction and is usually recorded by attaching electrodes to the clients' skin. EMG levels have been found to be a sensitive measure of arousal but do not always correlate highly with other physiological measures. Nevertheless, there is little literature in this area with clinical treatment of children.

Cardiovascular activity involves assessment of heart rate, blood pressure, and peripheral blood flow, with heart rate being a common measure. Measures of blood flow through the peripheral arterials have been assessed with such instruments as strain gauges and plethysmography. Although these measures have also not been used extensively with children, heart rate measures have been used in some fear research. For example, heart rate has been found to increase when children have been asked to describe their most fearful experiences (Tal & Miklich, 1976). Some clinical researchers have used cardiovascular functions to measure outcome in phobic investigations. For example, Van Hasselt, Hersen, Bellack, Rosenblum, and Lamparski (1979) assessed an 11-year-old multiphobic child on motoric (ladder climb, blood behavioral avoidance test, and test taking), cognitive (*Target Complaint Scale*), and physiological measures. The physiological arousal on the ladder climb task was assessed by measuring the child's pulse rate 5 minutes prior to arrival and again immediately prior to ascending the ladder. The authors calculated a change score by subtracting the second reading from the first. Heart rate and finger pulse volume were also monitored throughout the behavior avoidance test and test-taking task. The authors found that there was a decrease in heart rate for the ladder climb task under relaxation treatment followed by a further decrease on this measure with implementation of a desensitization program. Interestingly, no change occurred on finger pulse volume or heart rate during the behavioral avoidance test and test-taking task.

Electrodermal measures are assessed through skin conductance and skin resistance. Usually, the assessment occurs by placing electrodes on the skin and passing electric current between them; results are displayed on a polygraph or meter. These measures have not been used extensively with children; however Melamed and her associates have used electrodermal measures in several studies (e.g., Melamed, Hawes, Heigy, & Glick, 1975).

Special Considerations in Psychophysiological Assessment

The use of psychophysiological assessment in schools and other settings necessitates consideration of several issues (Blake & Andrasik, 1988; Kallman & Feuerstein, 1977). First, due to their complexity and expense, physiological recordings should provide data that cannot be obtained as reliably and efficiently by other procedures. Second, within an applied context, psychophysiological assessment should provide the practitioner with information about the selection and evaluation of an intervention. Third, psychophysiological assessment procedures should possess adequate reliability and validity for their use in applied settings.

Several classes of problems have been identified when physiological measures are used, particularly in applied research. These concerns may also be apparent in practice and reduce the usefulness of this assessment. First, the equipment used to monitor physiological responses is sometimes subject to mechanical failure. Second, clients generally require variable amounts of time to adapt to the equipment during various phases of assessment. Here the issue of response reactivity is especially salient. Different measures will produce different degrees of reactivity. Electrodermal measures are apparently influenced greatly by procedural variations and environmental intrusions. Moreover, they appear to be quite sensitive to novel and interesting stimuli (see Nietzel & Bernstein, 1981, for a more detailed discussion). A third concern with physiological assessment concerns habituation and adaptation to the measures. When physiological responses are measured repeatedly, the effect of the treatment must be distinguished from mere habituation or adaptation to recording. Fourth, various clinician and contextual variables may interact with the physiological measures. Fifth, when various physiological response systems (e.g., GSR, heart rate, blood pressure) are used as indices of emotional arousal, the specific emotion experienced by the client cannot be assumed in the absence of a self-report confirmation.

As with other procedures, psychophysiological assessment can provide important information for the design of intervention programs. However, psychophysiological assessment is time consuming and costly, and its increased use of school settings has continued to be slow.

GENERAL ISSUES IN BEHAVIORAL ASSESSMENT

Behavioral assessment represents a growing and diverse range of procedures and techniques. The following general issues provide some of our final prespectives on advances in behavioral assessment in the schools.

1. There appears to be increased use of various behavioral assessment strategies in applied and school settings since the first edition of this chapter. However, this may be an artifact of the growing diversity of what is included in behavioral assessment. Some evidence is available to provide support for the notion that behavioral assessment as traditionally defined is not used extensively. For example, Klopfer and Toulbee's (1976) review of projective tests in the *Annual Review of Psychology* suggested that there were more than 500 journal articles pertaining to projective techniques during the period 1971 through 1974, not including the number of books published or revised. Three national surveys of psychological test practices from 1947 to 1971 suggested only minor changes in the top-ranking tests (Loutit & Brown, 1947; Lubin, Wallis, & Paine, 1971; Sandberg, 1961). Between 1961 and 1971, the Rorschach dropped in rank from first to second place, replaced by the Wechsler Adult Intelligence Scale (WAIS); the TAT moved from fourth place to tie with the Bender-Gestalt for third. Although some writers (Shemberg & Keeley, 1970; Thelen & Ewing, 1970, 1968) reported a general decline in testing training (especially among newer psychology training programs) and a shift from projective toward objective testing, surveys suggest that traditional testing continues to play a substantial role in applied settings (e.g., Anderson, Cancelli, & Kratochwill, 1979; Garfield & Kurtz, 1976; Goh, Teslow, & Fuller, 1981; Levy & Fox, 1975; Wade & Baker, 1977; Wade, Baker, & Hartmann, 1979; Wade, Baker, Morton, & Baker, 1978).

   Specific examinations of the assessment practices of behavior therapists suggests the extensive use of traditional assessment practices as well. Although behavior threapy grew to one of the most prominent therapeutic orientations in psychology (Garfield & Kurtz, 1976; Wade & Baker, 1977; Wade et al., 1978), traditional assessment procedures are still frequently used by behavior therapists. Wade et al. (1978) found that approximately half of their respondents (members of the Association for Advancement of Behavior Therapy) used traditional interviews and a substantial number of objective or projective tests. They provided three possible reasons to explain this finding: (a) agency requirements prescribed test use, (b) assessment involved labeling and classification, and (c) behavioral assessment was perceived as difficult in applied settings.

   These results generally correspond to assessment practices of school psychologists. Anderson et al. (1979) found that although the primary orientation of respondents (select members of the American Psychological Association Division 16 and the National Association of School Psychologists) were behaviorally oriented, traditional testing practices were salient. Goh et al. (1981) in their national survey of assessment practices of school psychologists found that "behavioral assessment has not become a frequent practice in the schools" (p. 705). Our perspective is that behavioral assessment is being used extensively in behavior *research*. Indeed, Shapiro (1987) found that of journals publishing articles on interventions with school-aged populations, the majority involved behavioral procedures. Nevertheless, a greater diversity of assessment practices are apparent in practice and will likely continue to be.

2. Selection of the specific behavior(s) in assessment and treatment has recently received much attention. The primary considerations include identifying the factors that are operative in selecting and defining target behaviors, and delineating how these factors contribute to an adequate and complete representation of clinical problems (Kratochwill, 1985).

   Several factors that contribute to the selection of target behaviors can be identified. Among these include the assessor's own theoretical and philosophical orientation, the manner in which adjustment/maladjustment is defined, and professional preferences regarding the enhancement of new, appropriate behaviors, versus the elimination of dysfunctional, inappropriate behaviors. Hawkins (1986) advocates a flexible constructional approach in target selection, and suggests that behavioral assessors "make every reasonable attempt to expand repertoires rather than contract them" (p. 352). His theoretical scheme illustrates the use of a functional analysis and its emphasis on setting events, potentiating variables, and consideration of several alternatives to remain "constructional."

Regardless of the approach selected by the assessor, a first important step in behavioral assessment is specifying and operationalizing the problem(s). In this process, specific procedures by which behaviors will be assessed are identified. Recent attention has focused on the extent to which the behaviors, as defined operationally, relate to the actual problems experienced by the client (Kazdin, 1985). Problems arise when the specific behaviors and the conditions under which they are assessed bear little relation to the problems identified by the client. Target behaviors and the conditions under which they are assessed are often selected for purposes of standardization, convenience, and "face validity," and are frequently inadequate and incomplete (Kazdin, 1985; Mash, 1985). Preassessment biases also contribute to the identification of behaviors that have a history of being addressed in child behavior therapy. The actual relation of the target behaviors to the client's statement of the problem or to functioning in everyday life is not typically established (Evans & Nelson, 1986).

A second critical issue in target selection concerns the specific behavior(s) to be assessed and treated. In selecting target behaviors in behavioral assessment, the possibility that a response may be part of a larger constellation of behaviors must be acknowledged. A constellation (or syndrome) refers to multiple characteristics that co-occur and encompasses different behaviors, affect, cognitions, and psychophysiological responses (Kazdin, 1983).

Assessment of only one area may fail to consider the complexity of the symptoms and their overall impact on a person's functioning. By selecting one or two target behaviors, narrowing the definition so that objective components can be assessed, and delineating the conditions under which it will be assessed, a clinical problem may be oversimplified (Kazdin, 1985).

A third issue in target selection is the degree of correspondence between the targets of treatment and the overall goals of treatment. Mash (1985) distinguishes between ultimate, instrumental, and intermediate treatment outcomes. Ultimate outcomes refer to the criteria for treatment success (e.g., goals). Instrumental outcomes are sufficient for the attainment of other outcomes without further intervention (e.g., targets). Intermediate outcomes refer to treatment targets that facilitate continued treatment, or are preconditions for a particular intervention. Unfortunately, a lack of sufficient attention is often given to (a) conceptualizing and developing measures of ultimate outcome, and (b) examining the relations between instrumental and ultimate outcomes (Mash, 1985).

There is a need in behavioral assessment research for establishing empirically the current and predictive validity of particular target behaviors (Kazdin, 1985). Of particular concern are studies that show a relation between the target behavior as defined and assessed and other measures of the client's problem. For example, Hoge and Andrews (1987) found validity for selecting academic performance targets, but not classroom behavior targets to facilitate academic achievement. If part of a syndrome, the target behaviors should be shown to correlate with other facets of the syndrome or with measures of the child's daily functioning. The target focus should also be examined in relation to general functioning in everyday life. Furthermore, it is important to show that change in a target behavior is associated with change in related behaviors. A validational assessment model as presented by Kazdin (1985) can address these and other research needs and serve as a basis for justifying the selection of target behaviors for treatment. Mash (1985) also suggests that target selection should be validated in relation to the resultant treatment. An appropriate selection is one that leads to generalizable and relevant therapeutic outcomes.

In a discussion of target selection in behavioral consultation, Kratochwill (1985) identified practical and operational constraints and offered a conceptual framework for assessment of target behaviors. Among the constraints identified are the verbal behaviors of the consultant and the verbal behavior in problem description by the consultee. The degree to which target behaviors are identified adequately depends partly on certain types of standardized questions asked by the consultant that elicit certain responses from the consultee. Because standardized implementation of behavioral consultation has begun only recently, it is difficult to evaluate this consideration. Nevertheless, a standardization approach to consultation is desirable to enhance treatment validity and permit replication (see below). Although standardized consultation procedures may be desirable, certain limitations are apparent. For example, such standardization may reduce the range and type of targets identified, and may support the identification and treatment of isolate behaviors. Also, reliable target behavior identification does not address the issue of whether the behaviors are important to the client.

3. Traditionally, behavioral assessment has focused primarily on contemporaneous behavior and controlling conditions. Behavioral influences were seen as proximal in time and in respect to the situation in which it occurred. Similarly, behavioral assessment of children tended to ignore some of the broader contextual variables that might be related to ongoing child behaviors (e.g., the family environment). Recently, however, behavioral assessors have recognized the importance of situationally and temporally remote variables as determinants of both child and family behavior and treatment outcomes (Mash & Terdal, 1988b).

As an example of work in the family intervention area, Wahler and his colleagues (e.g., Wahler, 1975; Wahler & Fox, 1981; Wahler & Graves, 1983) discuss the need to expand applied behavioral analysis to include the investigation of distal setting events. Defined as "environmental events that are temporally distant from the child behaviors and their stimulus contingencies" (Wahler & Graves, 1983; p. 19), setting events appear to exert control over stimulus–response interactions. Wahler and Fox (1981) suggest two crucial aspects of setting events:

First . . . at least some setting events are composed not simply of a durational condition or event but of both an environmental event and the person's response to that event. Secondly, the definition of setting events as the interaction of a stimulus and a response . . . admits into consideration setting events which occur wholly separate in space and time from the other, succeeding stimulus-response relationships which they influence. . . . [T]he onset and offset of some stimulus–response setting events may occur well before, yet still facilitate or inhibit, the occurrence of later interbehavioral relationships (p. 329).

4. Advances are also being made in the investigation of response covariation and interaction among behaviors. Response covariation refers to the correlations among several different responses. Behaviors may be organized into a pattern of "clusters," consisting of a variety of behaviors that covary systematically. This pattern is identified by concurrently assessing multiple behaviors and evaluating their relation and pattern of change over time.

Several important conditions have been suggested in the development of clusters of behaviors. Interactive, situational, or environmental variables, are relevant and may explain partially their development. Different situational cues may constitute a stimulus class based on their functional equivalence and serve as discriminative stimuli for particular response classes. Similarly, responses may form a single class of behavior because they serve similar functional proposes, rather than simply because they are topographically related to environmental events (Evans & Nelson, 1986). Modeling may also serve as an environmental influence in that it contributes to the organization of behavior in large segments or clusters (Kazdin, 1982).

Wahler (1975) suggested the concept of a "keystone behavior" in which a variety of different behaviors, although not related formally to each other, are all extensions of one or more basic responses. A given behavior might be the central response for a variety of different manifestations that do not appear to be related. However, it is often difficult to distinguish between a keystone behavior that is causal (the behavior structurally supports other behaviors) and one that is simply descriptive (Evans & Nelson, 1986).

Conceptualizing responses as covarying and interrelated has implications for behavioral assessment. Evans and Nelson (1986) suggest that the reciprocal interactions among behaviors necessitates a type of systems mapping as an appropriate assessment goal. They present Kanfer and Saslow's (1969) SORC model and Herbert's (1981) assessment procedures to obtain useful summaries of variables surrounding the behavior.

Kazdin (1982) also suggests an interactional model to examine the impact of person and situational variables and to provide a useful framework for systematic inquiry into response covariation patterns. An interactional approach can identify responses that covary within a given situation, variations in clusters of behaviors across situations, and unifying themes that account for such covariations. If the relations among situations and responses can be identified prior to treatment, they may serve as a basis for predicting the extent of the effect of change in specific aspects of behavior. Although clusters of responses may appear to be related by a central factor, this does not provide information regarding the manner in which behaviors initially become organized. Indeed, this and other aspects of response covariation await further research attention.

5. Major technological advances have occurred in the assessment process with the advent of computers, especially microcomputers. The use of computer technology in behavioral assessment is a relatively recent phenomenon (Kratochwill et al., 1986, in press; Romanczyk, 1986). Historically, behavioral assessment texts include little discussion of computer applications [Mash and Terdal (1988b) discuss computer developments briefly in their recent text]. In psychology and education, issues of journals have been devoted to computer applications in assessment and treatment (e.g., Bennett & Maher, 1984; McCullough & Wenck, 1984a) and these include some articles describing applications in the behavioral field.

Kratochwill et al. (in press) noted that developments in computer technology are important in behavioral assessment for the following reasons. To begin with, although many current applications of computer technology in psychology and education have focused on traditional testing (i.e., test administration, test scoring, and report generation), there is the potential for application of this technology across a wide range of behavioral measures on various adult and childhood behavior disorders (Reynolds, McNamara, Marion, & Tobin, 1985). Applications reviewed by Kratochwill et al. (in press) include interviews, checklists and rating scales, direct observation, self-monitoring, and psychophysiological measures. We suggest that computer technology may facilitate behavioral analysis and treatment design, and monitoring across behavioral measures.

Computers may also offer special benefits for behavior therapists in practice by reducing the time and cost of assessment. Although this may be considered an advantage of computer assessment applications generally, it is a special feature that should be considered by behavioral assessors because assessment has been considered very time consuming and costly for use in applied settings. As we noted above, surveys of practitioners who have enggaed in behavioral assessment practices have provided feedback suggesting time and cost as salient limitations.

Third, computer technology may help

standardize behavioral assessment on procedural and psychometric dimensions. As noted in this chapter, behavioral assessment has not been highly standardized, even though a movement in this direction could be positive (e.g., Cone & Hawkins, 1977b; Mash & Terdal, 1988b; Kratochwill, 1985). Computer programming requires researchers and clinicians to operationalize measures that remained previously at the conceptual level. Thus, this standardization could occur on both psychometric (accuracy, reliability, validity, norming) and procedural dimensions (protocol, instructions, coding) of various behavioral assessment computer strategies.

Fourth, microcomputer software programs can facilitate the dissemination of behavioral assessment strategies into diverse areas of practice. The range of applications from least to most influence of the psychologist in decision making and client care include the following (Hartman, 1986): (a) storage and retrieval of clinical records, (b) administration and storage of tests, (c) automated interviewing, (d) automated test interpretation, (e) integrated report writing/evaluations, and (f) treatment programming. Since increasing numbers of practitioners have access to microcomputers, the software programs provide a portable vehicle for assessment and treatment procedures, encouraging use in diverse settings.

Finally, computers in behavioral assessment may facilitate the link between assessment and treatment. Microcomputers have been used for both assessment and treatment of developmentally disabled children (e.g., Romanczyk, 1984, 1986), and may supplement conventional self-help or bibliotherapy formats in treatment (Reynolds et al., 1985). "Expert systems" may also facilitate the assessment treatment link (Kramer, 1985).

6. Over the years behavioral assessors have argued that the methods of behavioral assessment are directly relevant to treatment design and monitoring. Nevertheless, few empirical efforts were devoted to this assessment–treatment link. Behavioral assessors could document that certain behavioral assessment methods were used to evaluate treatment, but documenting how assessment leads to useful treatment planning remained unclear. Recently, behavioral assessors have proposed conceptual and methodological guidelines for defining treatment validity (Hayes et al., 1986; Nelson & Hayes, 1979) or treatment utility (Hayes, Nelson, & Jarrett, 1987). The term treatment utility is preferred and refers to "The degree to which assessment is shown to contribute to beneficial treatment outcome. An assessment device, distinction, or strategy has this kind of utility if it can be shown that the treatment outcome is positively influenced by this device, distinction, or strategy. The treatment utility of assessment deserves to be termed a type of utility because it relates closely to the functional thrust of that psychometric term" (Hayes et al., 1987, p. 963–964). The authors note that several different types of research questions can be addressed through treatment utility, including those related to target behaviors and classification, whether given assessment devices (e.g., functional analyses) are useful, and whether general assessment strategies are useful (e.g., self-monitoring, projective tests).

Hayes et al. (1987) developed a methodological typology that can be useful to researchers interested in research on treatment utility (see Table 3). In the table each row describes a specific kind of study, and the last three columns present methods appropriate to each research question. Of course, studies on treatment utility extend beyond those of interest to behavioral assessors. Nevertheless, the methodology for treatment utility studies is an important conceptual advance.

PERSPECTIVES ON BEHAVIORAL ASSESSMENT IN SCHOOL PSYCHOLOGY

Recently, a major transformation has been proposed in the way that psychology is practiced in the schools. A special task force of the National School Psychology Inservice Training Network (Ysseldyke, Reynolds, & Weinberg, 1984) encour-

TABLE 3   Types of Treatment Utility Studies, Questions Asked, and Methods Used

Type of Study	Question	Typical Group Comparison	Time Series (Single Case)	
			Main Question Between Subject	Main Question Within Subject
Post Hoc Studies				
	What is the relation between client characteristics and treatment outcome?	Pre-post correlational.	Time-series design, then correlational.	Not applicable.
A Priori Single-Dimension Studies				
Manipulated assessment	What is the effect of the administration of, or data from, different assessment devices or methods on treatment outcome?	Two or more groups randomly assigned. Assessment taken or made available differs. Use of information in treatment stays the same.	Two or more groups randomly assigned. Assessment taken or made available differs. Use of information in treatment stays the same. Treatment assessed in series of time-series designs.	Assessment taken or made available differs. Use of information in treatment stays the same. Treatments compared within subject using time-series designs.
Manipulated use	What is the effect of different uses of available assessment data on treatment outcome?	Two or more groups randomly assigned. Assessment the same. Use of assessment in treatment differs.	Two or more groups randomly assigned. Assessment the same. Use of assessment in treatment differs. Treatment assessed in series of time-series designs.	Assessment the same. Use of assessment in treatment differs. Treatments compared within subject using time-series designs.
Obtained differences	What is the relation between distinct patient types and treatment outcome?	Two or more known groups based on pretreatment differences. Same treatment.	Two or more known groups based on pretreatment differences. Treatment assessed in series of time-series designs.	Not applicable.

TABLE 3 (Continued)

Type of Study	Question	Typical Group Comparison	Time Series (Single Case) Main Question Between Subject	Main Question Within Subject
A Priori Multiple-Dimension Studies				
Manipulated assessment/ manipulated use	What is the effect of different assessment devices or methods when the information from them is used in different ways to design treatment?	Factorial groups randomly assigned. Assessment taken or made available differs. Use of assessment data in treatment differs.	Factorial groups randomly assigned. Assessment taken or made available differs. Use of assessment data in treatment differs. Treatment assessed in series of time-series designs.	Assessment taken or made available differs. Use of assessment data in treatment differs. Treatments based on different combinations of above compared within subject using time-series designs.
Manipulated assessment/obtained differences	What is the effect of different assessment devices or methods on treatment outcome for two or more distinct patient types?	Groups randomly assigned within known groups. Assessment taken or made available differs. Use of data in treatment stays the same.	Groups randomly assigned within known groups. Assessment taken or made available differs. Use of data in treatment stays the same. Treatment assessed in series of time-series designs.	Assessment taken or made available differs. Use of data in treatment stays the same. Treatments compared within subject using time-series designs in each of two or more known groups.
Manipulated use/obtained differences	What is the effect of different uses of available assessment data on treatment outcome for two or	Groups randomly assigned within known groups. Use of assessment data differs. Assessment	Groups randomly assigned within known groups. Use of assessment data differs. Treatment	Use of assessment data differs. Treatments compared within subject using

	more distinct patients types?	taken or made available stays the same.	assessed in series of time-series designs.	time-series designs in each of two or more known groups.
Manipulated assessment/ manipulated use/obtained differences	What is the effect of different types and uses of available assessment data on treatment outcome for two or more distinct patient types?	Groups randomly assigned within known groups. Use of assessment data differs. Assessment taken or made available differs.	Groups randomly assigned within known groups. Use of assessment data differs. Assessment taken or made available differs. Treatment assessed in series of time-series designs.	Nature and use of assessment data differs. Treatments compared within subject using time-series designs in each of two or more known groups.
Obtained differences/two or more treatments	What is the effect of different treatments on outcome for two or more distinct patient types?	Two or more known groups of subjects randomly assigned to two or more treatments.	Two or more known groups of subjects randomly assigned to two or more treatments. Treatment assessed in series of time-series designs. Each subject receives one type of treatment.	Two or more known groups of subjects. Two or more treatments compared within subject using time-series designs.

Source. From Hayes, S. C.., Nelson, R. O. & Garrett, R. B. (1987). The treatment utility of assessment: A functional approach to evaluating assessment quality. *American Psychologist, 42*, 963–974. Copyright 1987 by the American Psychological Association. Reprinted by permission.

aged a reconceptualization of psychological services in the schools, and school psychologists have been called to become an active part of the transformation. To break away from the role of school psychologists as "gatekeepers in an emerging nonsystem," this task force called for a broadening and qualitative shift in roles, to provide more effective and appropriate services to children. They propose that the major identification procedures be curriculum based, so that subsequent curricular interventions, instructional programs, and educational procedures can meet individual needs. In 1985, the Executive Board/Delegate Assembly of the National Association of School Psychologists (NASP) supported formally a position statement on the Advocacy for Appropriate Educational Services for All Children (NASP, 1988). Inadequate measurement technology, focusing on labels for placement rather than providing information for program development, was cited as a major problem in educational programming. Thus, NASP publicly supported the belief that

> psychological needs of children should be determined through a multi-dimensional, non-biased assessment process. This must evaluate the match between the learner and his or her educational environment, assessing the compatibility of curriculum and system as they interact with the child. . . . Referral to the assessment and placement process must always relate directly to services designed to meet psychoeducational needs. (p. 2)

Behavioral assessment is conceptually and functionally compatible with the transformation currently facing school psychologists. School psychologists are in a position to perform behavioral assessment more routinely than in the past and to engage in classroom consultation, and to link assessment results to effective behavioral programming to meet the needs of individual children. School psychologists must acknowledge this unique aspect of their roles and develop the skills and expertise necessary to deliver these services effectively.

Several models have been proposed that incorporate behavioral assessment and prereferral intervention procedures, aimed at remediating educational difficulties without classification and placement into special education (e.g., Graden, Casey, & Christenson, 1985; Lentz & Shapiro, 1985). The models incorporate methods that include both nontraditional and traditional diagnostic procedures.

A model suggested by Lentz and Shapiro (1985) consists of three distinct stages, called salients. At salient 1 (referral for evaluation), treatment strategies are developed and agreed upon through behavioral consultation between the teacher and parent. If the problem remains unresolved, salient 2 (individual assessment) is initiated. Salient 2 involves a more comprehensive behavioral assessment and incorporates decisions by the multidisciplinary team. Salient 3 (additional testing and placement recommendations) is involved when the results of salient 2 indicate assessment to determine eligibility for special education.

Graden and her colleagues (Graden, Casey, & Christenson, 1985; Graden, Casey, & Bonstrom, 1985) described and implemented a model very similar to that of Lentz and Shapiro (1985). Their model used a behavioral consultation approach in providing services. Prior to formal referral, consultation between the teacher and a consulting teacher or psychologist occurs to identify the problem and suggest prereferral strategies. A multidisciplinary team is involved if initial interviews and/or strategies are unsuccessful, and additional interviews are included as a result of team review or placement recommendation.

Graden, Casey, and Bonstrom (1985) reported the results of a study in which this prereferral model was implemented across six schools. In two schools, the model was followed only minimally, but in the remaining four schools, stricter adherence to the model was reported. The researchers suggested that the model resulted in a decreased number of children tested and placed in special education.

The models advanced by Lentz and Shapiro (1985), Graden, Casey, and Bonstrom (1985), and Graden, Casey, and Christenson (1985) offer an alternative conceptualization of service delivery for the school psychologist. However, certain limitations are apparent. Among these include the largely untested nature of the models, time constraints, and the necessity of change in perceptions of the role of the school psychologist on the part of both school psychologists and special educators. Nevertheless, potentially positive implications for the individual case, for administrative/systematic changes, and for program evaluation are apparent.

Furthermore, the aforementioned models allow the psychologist to utilize a variety of skills in schools, such as consultation, behavioral assessment, and intervention.

AUTHOR NOTES

The authors express appreciation to Ms. Karen Kraemer for her assistance in word processing the manuscript. Special appreciation is expressed to the late Marian F. Kratochwill for her editorial assistance on the manuscript.

REFERENCES

Achenbach, T. M. (1978). The Child Behavior Profile: I. Boys aged 6–11. *Journal of Consulting and Clinical Psychology, 46,* 478–488.

Achenbach, T. M., & Edelbrock, C. S. (1978). The classification of child psychopathology: A review and analysis of empirical efforts. *Psychological Bulletin, 85,* 1275–1301.

Achenbach, T. M., & Edelbrock, C. S. (1979). The Child Behavior Profile: II. Boys aged 12–16 and girls aged 6–11 and 12–16. *Journal of Consulting and Clinical Psychology, 47,* 223–233.

Alessi, G. J., & Kaye, J. H. (1983). *Behavior assessment for school psychologists.* Kent, OH: National Association of School Psychologists Professional Development Publications.

Alevizos, R., DeRisi, W., Liberman, R., Eckman, T., & Callahan, E. (1978). The behavior observation instrument: A method of direct observation for program evaluation. *Journal of Applied Behavior Analysis, 11,* 243–257.

Anastasi, A. (1976). *Psychological testing* (4th ed.). New York: Macmillan.

Anderson, T. S., Cancelli, A. A., & Kratochwill, T. R. (1979). Self-reported assessment practices of school psychologists: Implications for training and practice. *Journal of School Psychology, 22,* 17–29.

Azrin, N. H. (1977). A strategy for applied research: Learning based but outcome oriented. *American Psychologist, 32,* 140–149.

Barrios, B. A. (1988). On the changing nature of behavioral assessment. In A. S. Bellack and M. Herson (Eds.), *Behavioral assessment: A practical handbook* (3rd ed., pp. 3–41). Elmsford, NY: Pergamon Press.

Barrios, B. A., & Shigetomi, C. C. (1985). Assessment of children's fears: A critical review. In T. R. Kratochwill (Ed.), *Advances in school psychology* (Vol. 4, pp. 89–132). Hillsdale, NJ: Lawrence Erlbaum.

Bellack, A. S., & Hersen, M. (1977a). *Behavior modification: An introductory textbook.* Baltimore: Williams & Wilkins.

Bellack, A. S., & Hersen, M. (1977b). The use of self-report inventories in behavioral assessment. In J. D. Cone & R. P. Hawkins (Eds.), *Behavioral assessment: New directions in clinical psychology* (pp. 52–76). New York: Brunner/Mazel.

Bennett, R. E., & Maher, C. A. (Eds.). (1984). Microcomputers and exceptional children: An overview. *Special Services in the Schools, 1,* 3–5.

Bergan, J. R. (1977). *Behavioral consultation.* Columbus, OH: Charles E. Merrill.

Bergan, J. R. (1981). Path-referenced assessment. In T. R. Kratochwill (Ed.), *Advances in school psychology* (pp. 255–280). Hillsdale, NJ: Lawrence Erlbaum.

Bergan, J. R. (1986). Path-referenced assessment: A guide for instructional management. *Special Services in the Schools, 2,* 29–41.

Bergan, J. R., & Kratochwill, T. R. (in press). *Behavioral consultation in applied settings.* New York: Plenum Press.

Bergan, J. R., & Tombari, M. L. (1975). The analysis of verbal interactions occurring during consultation. *Journal of School Psychology, 13,* 109–226.

Bijou, S. (1976). *Child development: The basic stage of early childhood.* Englewood Cliffs, NJ: Prentice-Hall.

Bijou, S., Peterson, R. F., & Ault, M. H. (1968). A method to integrate descriptive and experimental field studies at the level of data and empirical concepts. *Journal of Applied Behavior Analysis, 1,* 175–191.

Blake, D. D., & Andrasik, F. (1988). Physiological and activity measures with educational problems. In E. S. Shapiro & T. R. Kratochwill (Eds.), *Behavioral assessment in schools* (pp. 161–205). New York: Guilford Press.

Burke, J. P., & DeMers, S. T. (1979). A paradigm for evaluating assessment interviewing techniques. *Psychology in the Schools, 16,* 51–60.

Cancelli, A. A., & Kratochwill, T. R. (1981). Criterion-referenced assessment. In T. R. Kratochwill (Ed.), *Advances in school psychology* Vol. 1, (pp. 217–254). Hillsdale, NJ: Lawrence Erlbaum.

Christie, L., McKenzie, H., & Burdett, C. (1972). The consulting teacher approach to special education: Inservice training for regular classroom teachers. *Focus on Exceptional Children, 5,* 1–10.

Ciminero, A. R., & Drabman, R. S. (1977). Current developments in the behavioral assessment of children. In B. B. Lahey & A. E. Kazdin (Eds.), *Advances in clinical child psychology* (Vol. 1, pp. 47–82). New York: Plenum Press.

Coates, T. J., & Thoresen, C. E. (1979). Behavioral self-control and educational practice or do we really need self control? In D. C. Berliner (Ed.), *Review of educational research* (Vol. 7, pp. 3–45). New York: American Educational Research Association.

Colligan, R. W., Colligan, R. C., & Dilliard, M. K. (1977). Contingency management in the classroom treatment of long-term elective mutism: A case report. *Journal of School Psychology, 15,* 9–17.

Cone, J. D. (1977). The relevance of reliability and validity for behavioral assessment. *Behavior Therapy, 8,* 411–426.

Cone, J. D. (1978). The behavioral assessment grid (BAG): A conceptual framework and a taxonomy. *Behavior Therapy, 9,* 882–888.

Cone, J. D. (1979). Confounded comparisons in triple response mode assessment research. *Behavioral Assessment, 1,* 85–95.

Cone, J. D., & Hawkins, R. P. (Eds.). (1977a). *Behavioral assessment: New directions in clinical psychology.* New York: Brunner/Mazel.

Cone, J. D., & Hawkins, R. P. (Eds.). (1977b). Current status and future directions in behavioral assessment. In J. D. Cone & R. P. Hawkins (Eds.), *Behavioral assessment: New directions in clinical psychology* (pp. 381–392). New York: Brunner/Mazel.

Conners, C. K. (1985). Methodological and assessment issues in pediatric psychopharmacology. In J. M. Wiener (Ed.), *Diagnosis and psychopharmacology of childhood and adolescent disorders* (pp. 69–110). New York: Wiley.

Cronbach, J., Glaser, G. S., Nanda, H., & Rajaratnam, N. (1972). *The dependability of behavioral measures.* New York: Wiley.

Deitz, S. M. (1978). Current status of applied behavior analysis: Science versus technology. *American Psychologist, 33,* 805–814.

Deno, S. L., Marston, D., & Tindall, G. (1986). Direct and frequent curriculum-based measurement: An alternative for educational decision-making. *Special Services in the Schools, 2,* 5–27.

Deno, S. L., & Mirkin, P. (1977). *Date-based program modification: A manual.* Minneapolis: University of Minnesota, Leadership Training Institute/Special Education.

Drabman, R. S., Hammer, D., & Rosenbaum, M. S. (1979). Assessing generalization in behavior modification with children: The generalization map. *Behavior Assessment, 1,* 203–219.

Edelbrock, C. (1988). Informant reports. In E. S. Shapiro & T. R. Kratochwill (Eds.), *Behavioral assessment in the schools* (pp. 351–383). New York: Guilford Press.

Edelbrock, C., & Achenbach, T. M. (1984a). The teacher version of the Child Behavior Profile: I. Boys aged 6–11. *Journal of Consulting and Clinical Psychology, 52,* 207–217.

Edelbrock, C., & Achenbach, T. M. (1984b). *The teacher version of the Child Behavior Profile: II. Boys aged 12–16 and girls aged 6–11 and 12–16.* Unpublished manuscript.

Evans, I. M., & Nelson, R. O. (1977). Assessment of child behavior problems. In A. R. Ciminero, K. S. Calhoun, & H. E. Adams (Eds.), *Handbook of behavioral assessment* (pp. 603–681). New York: Wiley.

Evans, I. M., & Nelson, R. O. (1986). Assessment of child behavior problems. In A. R. Ciminero, K. S. Calhoun, & H. E. Adams (Eds.), *Handbook of behavioral assessment* (pp. 603–681). New York: Wiley.

Gagné, R. M. (1962). The acquisition of knowledge. *Psychological Review, 69,* 355–365.

Gagné, R. M. (1968). Learning hierarchies. *Educational Psychologist, 6,* 1–9.

Gardner, W. I., & Cole, C. (1988). Self-monitoring. In E. S. Shapiro & T. R. Kratochwill (Eds.)., *Behavioral assessment in the schools* (pp. 206–246). New York: Guilford Press.

Garfield, S. L., & Kurtz, R. (1976). Clinical psychologists in the 1970's. *American Psychologist, 31,* 1–9.

Gettinger, M. (1988). Analogue measures. In E. S. Shapiro & T. R. Kratochwill (Eds.), *Behavioral assessment in the schools* (pp. 247–289). Hillsdale, NJ: Lawrence Erlbaum.

Glaser, R. (1971). A criterion-referenced test. In W. J. Popham (Ed.), *Criterion-referenced measurement: An introduction* (pp. 32–64). Englewood Cliffs, NJ: Educational Technology.

Glaser, R., & Klaus, D. J. (1962). Proficiency measurement: Assessing human performance. In R. M. Gagné (Ed.), *Psychological principles in systems development.* New York: Holt, Rinehart and Winston.

Goh, D. S., Teslow, C. J., & Fuller, G. B. (1981). The practice of psychological assessment among school psychologists. *Professional Psychology, 12,* 696–706.

Goldfried, M. R., & Linehan, M. M. (1977). Basic issues in behavioral assessment. In A. R. Ciminero, K. S. Calhoun, & H. E. Adam (Eds.), *Handbook of behavioral assessment* (pp. 15–46). New York: Wiley.

Graden, J. L., Casey, A., & Bonstrom, O. (1985). Implementing a prereferral intervention system: Part II. The data. *Exceptional Children, 51,* 487–496.

Graden, J. L., Casey, A., & Christenson, S. L. (1985). Implementing a prereferral intervention system: Part I. The model. *Exceptional Children, 51,* 377–384.

Greenspoon, J., & Lamal, P. A. (1978). Cognitive behavior modification—Who needs it? *The Psychological Record, 28,* 343–351.

Gresham, F. M. (1984). Behavioral interviews in school psychology: Issues in psychometric adequacy and research. *School Psychology Review, 13,* 17–25.

Gresham, F. M., & Davis, C. J. (1988). Behavioral interviews with teachers and parents. In E. S. Shapiro and T. R. Kratochwill (Eds.), *Behavioral assessment in schools* (pp. 455–493). New York: Guilford Press.

Hambleton, R. K., Swaminathan, H., Algina, J., & Coulson, D. B. (1978). Criterion-referenced testing and measurement: A review of technical issues and developments. *Review of Educational Research, 48,* 1–48.

Hartman, D. E. (1986). Artificial intelligence or artificial psychologist? Conceptual issues in clinical microcomputer use. *Professional Psychology: Research and Practice, 17,* 528–534.

Hartmann, D. P. (Ed.). (1982). *Using observers to study behavior: New directions for methodology of social and behavioral sciences.* San Francisco: Jossey-Bass.

Hartmann, D. P. (1984). Assessment strategies. In D. H. Barlow & M. Hersen (Eds.), *Single case experimental designs: Strategies for studying behavior change*

(2nd ed., pp. 107–139). Elmsford, Pergamon Press.

Hartmann, D. P., Roper, B. L., & Bradford, D. C. (1979). Some relationships between behavioral and traditional assessment. *Journal of Behavioral Assessment, 1,* 3–21.

Hawkins, R. P. (1986). Selection of target behaviors. In R. O. Nelson & S. C. Hayes (Eds.), *Conceptual foundations of behavioral assessment* (pp. 331–385). New York: Guilford Press.

Hay, W. H., Hay, L. R., Angle, H. V., & Nelson, R. O. (1979). The reliability of problem identification in the behavioral interview. *Behavioral Assessment, 1,* 107–118.

Hayes, S. C., Nelson, R. O., & Jarrett, R. B. (1986). Evaluating the quality of behavioral assessment. In R. O. Nelson & S. C. Hayes (Eds.), *Conceptual foundations of behavioral assessment* (pp. 463–503). New York: Guilford Press.

Hayes, S. C., Nelson, R. O., & Jarrett, R. B. (1987). The treatment utility of assessment: A functional approach to evaluating assessment quality. *American Psychologist, 42,* 963–974.

Haynes, S. N. (1978). *Principles of behavioral assessment.* New York: Gardner Press.

Haynes, S. N., & Jensen, B. J. (1979). The interview as a behavioral assessment instrument. *Behavioral Assessment, 1,* 97–106.

Hersen, M., & Barlow, D. H. (1976). *Single case experimental designs: Strategies for studying behavior change.* NY: Pergamon Press.

Hersen, M., & Bellack, A. S. (Eds.). (1976). *Behavioral assessment: A practical handbook.* Oxford: Pergamon Press.

Hoge, R. D. (1983). Psychometric properties of teacher-judgment measures of pupil aptitudes, classroom behaviors, and achievement levels. *Journal of Special Education, 17,* 401–429.

Hoge, R. D., & Andrews, D. A. (1987). Enhancing academic performance: Issues in target selection. *School Psychology Review, 16,* 228–238.

Holland, C. (1970). An interview guide for behavioral counseling with parents. *Behavior Therapy, 1,* 70–79.

Idol-Maestas, L. (1981). A teacher training model: The resource consulting teacher. *Behavioral Disorders, 6,* 108–121.

Johnson, S. M., & Bolstad, O. D. (1973). Methodological issues in naturalistic observation: Some problems and solutions for field research. In L. A. Hamerlynch, L. C. Handy, & E. J. Mash (Eds.), *Behavior change: Methodology, concepts, and practice* (pp. 7–67). Champaign, IL: Research Press.

Jones, R. R., Reid, J. B., & Patterson, G. B. (1974). Naturalistic observation in clinical assessment. In P. McReynolds (Ed.), *Advances in psychological assessment* (Vol. 3, pp. 42–95). San Francisco: Jossey-Bass.

Kallman, W. M., & Feuerstein, M. (1977). Psychophysiological procedures. In A. R. Ciminero, K. S. Calhoun, & H. E. Adams (Eds.), *Handbook of behavioral assessment* (pp. 329–364). New York: Wiley.

Kanfer, F. H. (1979). Personal control, social control, and altruism. Can society survive the age of individualism? *American Psychologist, 34,* 231–239.

Kanfer, F. H., & Grimm, L. G. (1977). Behavior analysis: Selecting target behaviors in the interview. *Behavior Modification, 1,* 7–28.

Kanfer, F. H., & Saslow, G. (1969). Behavioral diagnosis. In C. Franks (Ed.), *Behavior therapy: Appraisal and status* (pp. 417–444). New York: McGraw-Hill.

Kazdin, A. E. (1977b). Assessing the clinical or applied significance of behavior change through social validation. *Behavior Modification, 1,* 427–452.

Kazdin, A. E. (1978). *History of behavior modification.* Baltimore: University Park Press.

Kazdin, A. E. (1982). Symptom substitution, generalization, and response covariation: Implications for psychotherapy outcome. *Psychological Bulletin, 91,* 349–365.

Kazdin, A. E. (1983). Psychiatric diagnosis, dimensions of dysfunction, and child behavior therapy. *Behavior Therapy, 14,* 73–99.

Kazdin, A. E. (1985). Selection of target behaviors. The relationship of the treatment focus to clinical dysfunction. *Behavioral Assessment, 7,* 33–47.

Kent, R. N., & Foster, S. L. (1977). Direct observational procedures: Methodological issues in naturalistic settings. In A. R. Ciminero, K. S. Calhoun, & H. E. Adams (Eds.), *Handbook of behavioral assessment* (pp. 279–328). New York: Wiley.

Klopfer, W. E., & Toulbee, E. S. (1976). Projective tests. *Annual Review of Psychology, 27,* 543–567.

Kramer, J. J. (1985, August). *Computer-based test interpretation in psychoeducational assessment.* Paper presented at the 93rd Annual Convention of the American Psychological Association, Los Angeles, CA.

Kratochwill, T. R. (Ed.). (1978). *Single subject research: Strategies for evaluating change.* New York: Academic Press.

Kratochwill, T. R. (1982). Advances in behavioral assessment. In C. R. Reynolds & R. B. Gutkin (Eds.), *Handbook of school psychology* (pp. 314–350). New York: Wiley.

Kratochwill, T. R. (1985). Selection of target behaviors in behavioral consultation. *Behavioral Assessment, 7,* 59–61.

Kratochwill, T. R., Alper, S., & Cancelli, A. A. (1980). Nondiscriminatory assessment in psychology and education. In L. Mann & D. A. Sabatino (Eds.), *Fourth review of special education.* New York: Grune & Stratton.

Kratochwill, T. R., & Bergan, R. (in press). *Behavioral consultation in applied settings: An individual guide.* New York: Plenum Press.

Kratochwill, T. R., Doll, E. J., & Dickson, W. P. (1986). Microcomputers in behavioral assessment: Recent advances and remaining issues. *Computers in Human Behavior, 1,* 277–291.

Kratochwill, T. R., Doll, E. J., & Dickson, P. (in press). Use of computer technology in behavioral assessments. In T. B. Gutkin & S. Wise (Eds.), *Buros-Nebraska series on measurement and testing: Vol. 4. Computers and decision making processes.* Hillsdale, NJ: Lawrence Erlbaum.

Kratochwill, T. R., & Morris, R. J. (in press). *The practice of child therapy* (2nd ed.). Elmsford, NY: Pergamon Press.

Lang, P. J. (1971). The application of psychophysiological methods to the study of psychotherapy and behavior modification. In A. E. Bergin & S. L. Garfield (Eds.), *Handbook of psychotherapy and behavior change* (pp. 75–125). New York: Wiley.

Lang, P. J. (1977). Physiological assessment of anxiety and fear. In J. D. Cone & R. P. Hawkins (Eds.), *Behavioral assessment: New directions in school psychology* (pp. 178–195). New York: Brunner/Mazel.

Lentz, F. E., Jr. (1988). Direct observation and measurement of academic skills: A conceptual review. In E. S. Shapiro & T. R. Kratochwill (Eds.), *Behavioral assessment in schools* (pp. 76–120). New York: Guilford Press.

Lentz, F. E. J., & Shapiro, E. S. (1985). Behavioral school psychology: A conceptual model for the delivery of psychological services. In T. R. Kratochwill (Ed.), *Advances in school psychology* (Vol. 4, pp. 191–232). Hillsdale, NJ: Lawrence Erlbaum.

Levy, M. R., & Fox, H. M. (1975). Psychological testing is alive and well. *Professional Psychology, 6,* 420–424.

Lindsley, O. R. (1964). Direct measurement and prosthesis of retarded behavior. *Journal of Education, 147,* 62–81.

Linehan, M. M. (1977). Issues in behavioral interviewing. In J. D. Cone & R. P. Hawkins (Eds.), *Behavioral assessment: New directions in clinical psychology* (pp. 30–51). New York: Brunner/Mazel.

Lipinski, D. P., & Nelson, R. O. (1974). Problems in the use of naturalistic observation as a means of behavioral assessment. *Behavioral Therapy, 5,* 341–351.

Loutit, C. M., & Brown, C. G. (1947). Psychometric instruments in psychological clinics. *Journal of Consulting Psychology, 11,* 49–54.

Lubin, B., Wallis, R. R., & Paine, C. (1971). Patterns of psychological test usage in the United States: 1935–1969. *Professional Psychology, 1,* 70–74.

Mace, F. C., & West, B. J. (1986). Unresolved theoretical issues in self-management: Implications for research and practice. *Professional School Psychology, 1,* 149–163.

Mahoney, M. J. (1977). Some applied issues in self-monitoring. In J. D. Cone & R. P. Hawkins (Eds.), *Behavioral assessment: New directions in clinical psychology* (pp. 241–254). New York: Brunner/Mazel.

Mahoney, M. J., & Arnkoff, D. (1978). Cognitive and self-control therapies. In S. L. Garfield & A. E. Bergin (Eds.), *Handbook of psychotherapy and behavior change: An empirical analysis* (2nd ed., pp. 689–722). New York: Wiley.

Mash, E. J. (1985). Some comments on target selection in behavior therapy. *Behavioral Assessment, 7,* 63–78.

Mash, E. J., & Terdal, L. (Eds.). (1981). *Behavioral assessment of childhood disorders.* New York: Guilford Press.

Mash, E. J., & Terdal, L. G. (1988a). *Behavioral assessment of childhood disorders* (2nd ed.). New York: Guilford Press.

Mash, E. J., & Terdal, L. G. (1988b). Behavioral assessment of child and family disturbance. In E. J. Mash & L. G. Terdal (Eds.), *Behavioral assessment of childhood disorders* (2nd ed., pp. 3–65). New York: Guilford Press.

McCullough, C. S., & Wenck, L. S. (Eds.). (1984a). Computers in school psychology. *School Psychology Review, 13,* 421.

McFall, R. M. (1977b). Parameters of self-monitoring. In R. B. Stuart (Ed.), *Behavioral self-management: Strategies, techniques, and outcomes* (pp. 196–214). New York: Brunner/Mazel.

Melamed, B., Hawes, R. R., Heigy, E., & Glick, J. (1975). Use of filmed modeling to reduce uncooperative behavior of children during dental treatment. *Journal of Dental Research, 54,* 797–801.

Morris, R. J., & Kratochwill, T. R. (1983). *Treating children's fears and phobias: A behavioral approach.* Elmsford, NY: Pergamon Press.

Morris, R. J., & Kratochwill, T. R. (Eds.). (1984). *The practice of child therapy.* Elmsford, NY: Pergamon Press.

National Association of School Psychologists. (1988, October). Position statement on advocacy for appropriate educational services for all children. *Communique,* p. 20.

Nay, W. R. (1977). Analogue measures. In A. R. Ciminero, K. S. Calhoun, & H. E. Adams (Eds.), *Handbook of behavioral assessment* (pp. 233–277). New York: Wiley.

Nelson, R. O. (1977a). Assessment and therapeutic functions of self-monitoring. In M. Hersen, R. M. Eisler, & P. M. Miller (Eds.), *Progress in behavior modification* (Vol. 5, pp. 263–308). New York: Academic Press.

Nelson, R. O. (1977b). Methodological issues in assessment via self-monitoring. In J. D. Cone & R. P. Hawkins (Eds.), *Behavioral assessment: New directions in clinical psychology* (pp. 217–240). New York: Brunner/Mazel.

Nelson, R. O. (1985). Behavioral assessment in school psychology. In T. R. Kratochwill (Ed.), *Advances in school psychology* (Vol. 4, pp. 45–87). Hillsdale, NJ: Lawrence Erlbaum.

Nelson, R. O., & Bowles, P. E. (1975). The best of two worlds—Observation with norms. *Journal of School Psychology, 13,* 3–9.

Nelson, R. O., & Hayes, S. C. (1979). Some current dimensions of behavioral assessment. *Behavioral Assessment, 1,* 1–16.

Nietzel, M. T., & Bernstein, D. (1981). Assessment of anxiety and fear. In M. Hersen & A. S. Bellack (Eds.), *Behavioral assessment: A practical handbook* (2nd ed.). Elmsford, NY: Pergamon Press.

O'Leary, K. D., Romanczyk, R. G., Kass, R. E., Dietz, A., & Santogrossi, D. (1979). *Procedures for classroom observation of teachers and children.* Stony Brook: SUNY at Stony Brook, Psychology Department.

O'Leary, S. G., & Dubey, D. R. (1979). Applications of self-control procedures by children: A review. *Journal of Applied Behavior Analysis, 43,* 24–30.

Patterson, G. R., Ray, R. W., Shaw, D. A., & Cobb, J. A. (1969). *A manual for coding family interactions* (6th rev. ed.) (Document No. 01234). New York: ASIS National Auxiliary Publications Service, CCM Information Services.

Paul, G. L., & Bernstein, D. A. (1973). *Anxiety and clinical problems: Systematic desensitization and related techniques.* Morristown, NJ: General Learning Press.

Resnick, L. B., & Ford, W. W. (1978). The analysis of tasks for instruction: An information-processing approach. In A. C. Catania & T. A. Brigham (Eds.), *Handbook of applied behavior analysis: Social and instructional processes* (pp. 378–409). New York: Irvington.

Resnick, L. D., Wang, M. C., & Kaplan, J. (1973). Task analysis in curriculum. *Journal of Applied Behavior Analysis, 6,* 679–710.

Reynolds, R. V. C., McNamara, J. R., Marion, R. J., & Tobin, D. L. (1985). Computerized service delivery in clinical psychology. *Professional Psychology: Research and Practice, 16,* 339–353.

Romanczyk, R. G. (1984). Microcomputers and behavior therapy: A powerful alliance. *Behavior Therapist, 7,* 59–64.

Romanczyk, R. G. (1986). *Clinical utilization of microcomputer technology.* Elmsford, NY: Pergamon Press.

Rosenbaum, M. S., & Drabman, R. S. (1979). Self-control training in the classroom: A review and critique. *Journal of Applied Behavior Analysis, 12,* 467–485.

Sandberg, N. D. (1961). The practice of psychological testing in clinical services in the United States. *American Psychologist, 16,* 79–83.

Saudargas, R. A. (1983). *State-event classroom observation code.* Knoxville: University of Tennessee, Department of Psychology. (Available from author)

Saudargas, R. A., & Lentz, F. E. (1986). Estimating percent of time and rate via direct observation: A suggested observational procedure and format. *School Psychology Review, 15,* 36–48.

Shapiro, E. S. (1987a). *Behavioral assessment in school psychology.* Hillsdale, NJ: Lawrence Erlbaum.

Shapiro, E. S. (1987b). Intervention research methodology in school psychology. *School Psychology Review, 16,* 290–305.

Shapiro, E. S., & Kratochwill, T. R. (1988a). Analogue assessment: Methods for assessing emotional and behavioral problems. In E. S. Shapiro & T. R. Kratochwill (Eds.), *Behavioral assessment in schools* (pp. 290–321). New York: Guilford Press.

Shapiro, E. S., & Kratochwill, T. R. (Eds.). (1988b). *Behavioral assessment in schools.* New York: Guilford Press.

Shapiro, E. S., & Lentz, F. (1986). Behavioral assessment of academic skills. In T. R. Kratochwill (Ed.), *Advances in school psychology* (Vol. 5, pp. 87–139). Hillsdale, NJ: Lawrence Erlbaum.

Shemberg, K., & Keeley, S. (1970). Psychodiagnostic training in the academic setting: Past and present. *Journal of Consulting and Clinical Psychology, 34,* 205–221.

Spivack, G., & Swift, M. (1973). The classroom behavior of children: A critical review of teacher-administered rating scales. *Journal of Special Education, 7,* 55–89.

Stephens, T. (1977). *Teaching skills to children with learning and behavior disorders.* Columbus, OH: Charles E. Merrill.

Stokes, T. F., & Baer, D. M. (1977). An implicit technology of generalization. *Journal of Applied Behavior Analysis, 10,* 349–473.

Subkoviak, M., & Baker, F. B. (1977). Test theory. In L. S. Shulman (Ed.), *Review of research in education* (pp. 275–317). Itasca, IL: Peacock.

Tal, A., & Miklich, D. (1976). Emotionally induced decreases in pulmonary flow rates in asthmatic children. *Psychosomatic Medicine, 38,* 190–200.

Tasto, D. L. (1977). Self-report schedules and inventories. In A. R. Ciminero, K. S. Calhoun, & H. E. Adams (Eds.), *Handbook of behavioral assessment* (pp. 153–193). New York: Wiley.

Thelen, M. H., & Ewing, D. R. (1970). Roles, functions, and training in clinical psychology: A survey of academic clinicians. *American Psychologist, 25,* 550–554.

Thoresen, C. E., & Mahoney, M. J. (1974). *Behavioral self-control.* New York: Holt, Rinehart and Winston.

Van Hasselt, V. B., Hersen, M., Bellack, A. S., Rosenblum, N. D., & Lamparski, D. (1979). Tripartite assessment of the effects of systematic desensitization in a multi-phobic child: An experimental analysis. *Journal of Behavior Therapy and Experimental Psychiatry, 10,* 51–55.

Wade, T. C., & Baker, T. B. (1977). Opinions and use of psychological tests: A survey of clinical psychologists. *American Psychologist, 32,* 874–882.

Wade, T. C., Baker, T. B., & Hartmann, D. P. (1979). Behavior therapists' self-reported views and practices. *Behavior Therapist, 2,* 3–6.

Wade, T. C., Baker, T. B., Morton, T. L., & Baker, L. J. (1978). The status of psychological testing in clinical psychology: Relationships between test use and professional activities and orientations. *Journal of Personality Assessment, 42,* 3–10.

Wahler, R. G. (1975). Some structural aspects of deviant child behavior. *Journal of Applied Behavior Analysis, 8,* 27–42.

Wahler, R. G., & Fox, J. J. (1981). Setting events in applied behavior analysis: Toward a conceptual and methodological expansion. *Journal of Applied Behavior Analysis, 14,* 327–338.

Wahler, R. G., & Graves, M. G. (1983). Setting events in social networks: Ally or enemy in child behavior therapy? *Behavior Therapy, 14,* 19–36.

Wahler, R. G., House, A. E., & Stambaugh, E. E. (1976). *Ecological assessment of child problem behavior: A clinical package for home, school, and institutional setting.* Elmsford, NY: Pergamon Press.

Walls, R. T., Werner, T. J., Bacon, A., & Zane, T. (1977).

Behavior checklists. In J. D. Cone & R. P. Hawkins (Eds.), *Behavioral assessment: New directions in clinical psychology* (pp. 77–146). New York: Brunner/Mazel.

White, O., & Haring, N. (1980). *Exceptional teaching.* Columbus, OH: Charles E. Merrill.

Wiggins, J. S. (1973). *Personality and prediction: Principles of personality assessment.* Reading, MA: Addison-Wesley.

Wilson, G. T., & Franks, C. M. (Eds.). (1982). *Contemporary behavior therapy: Conceptual and empirical foundations.* New York: Guilford Press.

Witt, J. C., Cavell, T. A., Heffer, R. W., Carey, M. P., & Martens, B. K. (1988). Child self-report: Interviewing techniques and rating scales. In E. S. Shapiro and T. R. Kratochwill (Eds.), *Behavioral assessment in schools: Conceptual foundations and practical applications* (pp. 384–454). New York: Guilford Press.

Wolf, M. M. (1978). Social validity: The case for subjective measurement or how applied behavior analysis is finding its heart. *Journal of Applied Behavior Analysis, 11,* 203–214.

Ysseldyke, J. E., & Christenson, S. L. (1987). *The Instructional Environmental Scale. A comprehensive methodology for assessing an individual student's instruction.* Austin, TX: PRO-ED.

Ysseldyke, J. E., Reynolds, M. C., & Weinberg, R. A. (1984). *School psychology: A blueprint for training and practice.* Minneapolis, MN: National School Psychology Inservice Training Network.

15

CURRICULUM-BASED ASSESSMENT

EDWARD S. SHAPIRO
TAMI F. DERR
Lehigh University

Curriculum-based assessment (CBA) is a relatively new approach to educational assessment, although its basic idea is as old as education itself: using the curricula to assess student learning. CBA may be defined as a methodology whereby (a) assessment is linked to the curriculum and instruction, (b) educational success is evaluated by student progress in the curriculum, and (c) the purpose is to determine students' instructional needs. Therefore, instructional needs of students are based on their ongoing performance within existing course content. Unlike traditional assessment devices, CBA focuses not only on how to collect data and make diagnostic decisions, but also on how to interpret and use data to develop academic intervention strategies.

In this chapter, a brief overview of CBA is presented. After examining some basic assumptions and outcomes for CBA, the various models that have been described are presented. The methodology of one model (i.e., Shapiro & Lentz, 1985, 1986) is discussed in detail. Potential limitations and future concerns in using CBA are also given.

OVERVIEW AND RATIONALE

Problems of Test–Text Overlap

Academic performance has been assessed traditionally via standardized measures, such as norm-referenced achievement and intelligence tests. These measures, however, do not provide useful information related to instructional planning (Salmon-Cox, 1981). For example, while intelligence tests are supposed to diagnose the handicap of a student via standardized procedures and normative comparisons, and achievement tests provide data comparing the student's academic performance with that of a normative reference group, neither can determine a student's appropriate placement or progress within the curricula, nor are their results relevant to developing academic interventions (Deno, 1985). Standardized tests may not relate to what is being taught.

Evidence of the poor test–text overlap between standardized tests and various curricula has been cited by Jenkins and Pany (1978) and Shapiro and Derr (1987) for the academic area of reading. Shapiro and Derr (1987), replicating the

Jenkins and Pany (1978) study, compared the reading subtests of four widely used individual achievement tests (PIAT, WRAT-R, K-TEA, and Woodcock Reading Mastery) with the first-grade through fifth-grade levels of five popular reading curricula (Ginn-720; Scott, Foresman; Macmillan-R; Keys to Reading; and Scott, Foresman-Focus). Raw scores, grade equivalents, percentiles, and standard scores were reported that would be obtained if all words appearing in each grade level of the curriculum were mastered. The results showed that very little overlap exists between what is taught and what is tested. Furthermore, the degree of overlap varied considerably across tests and curricula, indicating that decisions based on these instruments are subject to the biases of the test administered as well as the curriculum being employed. It is important to note that both the Shapiro and Derr (1987) and Jenkins and Pany (1978) studies used data based on hypothetical cases and did not directly assess children and find the reported lack of test/text overlap. Good and Salvia (1988), however, found similar results with students actually assessed. What standardized achievement tests may actually be assessing are not the knowledge acquired by students, but instead, their ability to generalize from taught to untaught stimuli which are similar. For example, a student may be taught the words "sat" and "bat," but "cat" appears on the test. Whether the student can transfer their learned knowledge to a related but untaught stimulus may be more accurately what the test is assessing. While important, the test cannot be viewed as a valid measure of material *acquired* and certainly not a measure to assess progress in the curriculum across time. Other researchers have found similar lack of test–text overlap (Armbruster, Stevens, & Rosenshine, 1977; Leinhardt & Seewald, 1981).

Underlying Assumptions

The basis for the major distinctions between CBA and traditional measures lies within their respective underlying assumptions about behavior. Norm-referenced measures of achievement developed from a traditional model of assessment. Within this model, the learning process is conceptualized as a function of underlying psychological and neurological processes. Therefore, the causes of academic problems are viewed as either faulty information processing or poor skills within the cognitive domain. Either way, academic performance is seen as a skill residing *within* the learner. A somewhat

different view is taken by the behavioral model of assessment, of which CBA is a member. The behavioral model conceptualizs the learning process as an interaction between the environment and the developed skill repertoire of the learner. Therefore, the cause of an academic problem would be viewed as an interplay between the *environment* and the *skills* of the student. For example, poor instruction leading to low skill development or good instruction coupled with poor environmental contingencies would be likely interpretations for "causes" of academic problems within a behavioral framework.

Other important contrasting assumptions about behavior include the role of academic behavior, the role of history, and the consistency of behavior. The traditional assessment model views the role of academic behavior as an index of underlying dysfunction within the individual, whereas the behavioral model sees the role of academic behavior as only a sample of an individual's skills under the conditions observed. History plays an important but different role in the two models, in that history is often an explanation for observed dysfunctions in the traditional model, and reinforcement history is important behaviorally in examining the failure to acquire skills. Poor skills are viewed as pervasive across time in the traditional approach, whereas from the behavioral approach a lack of acquired behavior is viewed as a possible performance problem which may be situationally specific.

These opposing assumptions about behaviors have provided the impetus and rationale for the differing forms of academic assessment. From these assumptions, it is clear why standardized norm-referenced tests are primarily diagnostic (prescribing modes of instruction), indirect (involving moderate to high levels of inference), global tests which are conducted in a pretest/posttest fashion and yield nomothetic comparisons. Conversely, it is also clear why CBA operates as a direct, low-inference, ongoing method of assessment, targeting many variables across situations and settings, and resulting in idiographic comparison data used to target behavior, select interventions, and monitor/evaluate treatment.

Rationale for CBA

The rationale for using CBA measures, mentioned briefly before, is linked directly to all the disadvantages in using standardized norm-referenced assessment measures. In fact, CBA was developed in reaction to the many criticisms aimed at standardized norm-referenced tests. Some of these major criticisms include their curriculum bias (Good & Salvia, 1988; Jenkins & Pany, 1978; Shapiro & Derr, 1987), their inability to be used to monitor progress and/or evaluate treatment effects due to their insensitivity to short-term growth in student performance (Deno, 1985), their misclassification of nonhandicapped students (Ysseldyke, 1983), and their cultural and social biases (Gallagan, 1985).

In contrast, CBA, which measures individual student progress through the curriculum, has several advantages which address and control for the limitations of traditional assessment. First, the problem of poor test–text overlap is overcome partially because the student is tested directly on the material that he/she was expected to learn. Thus, failure by the student to master specific skills as evidenced on the assessment measures partially reflects true deficits in performance, rather than lack of exposure to tested material. Of course, test performance may also be influenced by other variables such as measurement error.

Second, the results of CBA are linked directly to instruction. The assessment results directly reflect which skills have not been mastered, and therefore indicate where in the curriculum instruction should begin. In addition, CBA has proven valuable in suggesting alternative instructional methods that help to improve student performance. In one study of 50 teachers who used CBA measures for 4 months, 90% stated that the measures were helpful in developing IEP objectives and goals and deciding when to change instructional techniques (Mirkin, Deno, Tindal, & Kuehnle, 1982).

Third, recent research indicates that CBA techniques provide valid and reliable measures of student performance in reading (Deno, 1985; Deno, Mirkin, & Chiang, 1982), spelling (Deno et al., 1982; Deno, Mirkin, Lowry, & Kuehnle, 1980; White & Haring, 1980), and writing (Deno, Marston, & Mirkin, 1982; Deno et al., 1982). Much of this research correlated CBA data with standardized achievement tests.

Fourth, by virtue of their ease in application and mode of development, CBA measures may be repeated frequently without practice effects and are highly sensitive to short-term and long-term change in performance (Deno, 1985). This methodology allows for ongoing assessment to monitor

and evaluate student progress and/or interventions.

Fifth, CBA has recently been used for making special education classification decisions. Prior to its inception, these decisions were made primarily using standardized norm-referenced measures. Although many of the commonly employed norm-referenced instruments are technically inadequate and produce considerable misclassification of mildly handicapped students (Ysseldyke, Thurlow, Graden, Wesson, Deno, & Algozzine, 1982), CBA measures have proven effective in discriminating between low-achieving and genuinely handicapped students (Deno, 1985). In addition, CBA has been used in making special education eligibility determinations in a number of large-scale programs (Coulter, 1985; German & Tindal, 1985; Marston & Magnusson, 1985). Finally, CBA's emphasis on curriculum performance and the development of instructional interventions render them potentially more racially and culturally neutral than most psychometric instruments (Gallagan, 1985).

In sum, the many advantages of CBA over more traditional assessment methods strongly suggest that CBA is a feasible alternative to current methods of academic assessment. Indeed, CBA can effectively provide a means for pre-placement evaluation, determine accuracy of student placements within curriculum materials, assist in the development of strategies for academic problem remediation, provide a means for setting IEP short- and long-term goals, provide a method for monitoring student progress and performance across time, provide an empirical method for determining intervention effectiveness, provide a potential strategy for screening students, and provide accountability for teachers and psychologists when making eligibility decisions.

It must be emphasized that CBA provides a methodology for different purposes than traditional psychodiagnostic assessments, and thus is not designed to replace them. For example, although CBA can greatly contribute to the decision-making process for eligibility, it should not be used in isolation for making these decisions when legal mandates require the administration of norm-referenced intelligence and/or achievement tests.

MODELS OF CBA

While the name *curriculum-based assessment* is recognized as a universal term for the assessment approach described above, in reality there are many different models falling under the rubric of CBA, each recognized by similar names. Examples include Idol, Nevin, and Paolucci-Whitcomb's (1986) model of curriculum-based assessment, Deno's model of curriculum-based measurement (1985), Gickling and Havertape's (1981) model of curriculum-based assessment, Blankenship's (1985) model of curriculum-based assessment, and Shapiro and Lentz's (1985, 1986) model of curriculum-based assessment (also named *behavioral assessment of academic skills*). While different in some respects, these models share a common ground. They all assess behavior directly from the curriculum and evaluate student progress within the curriculum. Thus, each of these models shares an assumption that student performance in the school curriculum provides the most relevant data for making instructional programming decisions. Given their similarities, a description of each of the aforementioned models is necessary to highlight the important and essential differences that make each model theoretically and/or methodologically unique.

CBA by Idol et al. (1986)

The model of curriculum-based assessment developed by Idol et al. (1986) defines CBA as tests that are (a) criterion-referenced, (b) teacher-constructed, and (c) designed to reflect curriculum content and directly measure student skill achievement within the specified curriculum. The major strength of this type of CBA is that as teachers develop the tests, they also formulate the primary goals and objectives of the school program. Thus, goal setting is a logical result of the process. By developing assessment tools that reflect what is being taught, teachers consequently gain an organized perspective of the program's goals.

In Idol et al.'s (1986) model, CBAs can be developed for various types of curricula: developmental, spiraling, or unestablished. Developmental curricula are, by definition, organized in a hierarchical fashion with each level containing prerequisite information necessary for mastery of subsequent levels. Examples of developmental curricula include basal reading, language arts, and spelling programs. Spiral curricula are also organized by level, although the concepts taught are repeated at subsequent levels. These concepts are not expected to be mastered fully at the level in which they are introduced, since more difficult applications appear in subsequent levels. Exam-

ples of spiral curricula include math, science, and social studies. Unestablished curricula are those which are developed by teachers to fit the needs of their students. Some examples of this type of curricula include written language, handwriting, and study skills. Thus, the Idol et al. (1986) model provides a comprehensive application of CBAs across all curricular areas, a feature that distinguishes this model from others.

The construction of CBAs within Idol et al.'s model (1986) follows the same general guidelines regardless of the type of curricula targeted. These steps include first selecting items from the curriculum, then ordering them by difficulty to be combined within a single test that is given on the first day of assessment. Two other forms of the same test are also constructed to be administered on the second and third days of testing. These three test days are used to control for any sporadic student responding that may occur.

The administration of CBAs includes testing students across several levels of curriculum. Students are typically measured for speed or proficiency in responding as well as for accuracy. Performance criteria are then established to determine acceptable levels of student performance or mastery. These criteria may be established in one of three ways. First, the classroom teacher and the consulting teacher or learning specialist function as a team to establish reasonable criteria based upon typical classroom performance. The second option is to incorporate some of the mastery criteria that are provided by Idol et al. (1986) based on actual practice. However, it is not recommended for the user to rely solely on these criteria since the criteria developed by Idol et al. (1986) may not be applicable to the particular population of students used in the assessment. The third option for establishing mastery criteria, the normative-sampling method, is the most cumbersome but most useful procedure (Idol-Maestas, 1983). This procedure involves taking samples of average and acceptable student performance within and across regular education classrooms, and sometimes across schools.

Once the mastery criteria have been established, the CBA may be administered to students individually or in groups. The CBA can be administered in its entirety, or sections of it may be given over time. If multiple forms have been developed, it is also possible to use the same probes over again, as a means of testing change in academic skills of students. It is suggested that teachers work together to develop CBAs that can be used by all teachers using the same curriculum, reducing the preparation time involved in CBA development.

Idol et al. (1986) list various advantages of their model of curriculum-based assessment, which include: (a) instruction becomes more streamlined; (b) students are offered instruction in unmastered areas without receiving repetitive instruction in previously mastered areas; (c) CBAs can be developed collaboratively with other teachers using the same curriculum; (d) CBAs can be used at the beginning of the school year or in segments during the course of the year; (e) CBAs may be used with individual students or groups of students; (f) multiple forms are developed; (g) CBAs may be used to monitor student progress over time; and (h) since CBA results are specific to the curriculum, they can easily be communicated to parents, teachers, and administrators.

Curriculum-Based Measurement by Deno (1985)

Deno's (1985) model of academic assessment, entitled curriculum-based measurement (CBM), was developed in an effort to decrease the separation between measurement and instruction, thus making data on student achievement more integral to daily decision making. CBM was designed primarily as a measurement and evaluation system that teachers could use routinely to monitor student progress and instructional effectiveness. Four major assumptions constitute the basis for this model. These are: (a) changes in instructional programs for individual students should be treated as hypotheses that must be empirically tested before their effectiveness can be evaluated; (b) time-series research designs are appropriate for monitoring and evaluating instructional program changes; (c) applying time-series designs requires the specification of data representing the "vital signs" of educational development which can be routinely obtained; and (d) the evaluation of program modifications requires well-trained professionals.

The conceptual framework of the CBM model is based on Deno and Mirkin's (1977) *Data-Based Program Modification* and includes five sets of decision-making areas and data-gathering phases. These areas and resultant phases are: (a) Problem Selection—Initial Needs Assessment, which includes computing the discrepancy ratio between expected and actual level of performance: (b) Program Selection—Program Planning, which includes developing long- and short-range goals and instructional strategies for achieving the goals; (c) Program Operationalization—Implementation Evaluation, which includes actually conducting the selected program and evaluating the integrity of its implementation; (d) Program Improvement—Program Evaluation, which includes appraisal progression of short-term and long-term goals and revisions of the program; and (e) Program Certification—Outcome Evaluation, which involves determining whether modifications have successfully eliminated the initial academic performance discrepancies.

Other features of this model include time-series data analysis, which permits conclusions to be drawn about the relation between changes in a student's program and the changes in his/her progress. In addition to evaluating specific program effects, time-series analysis allows student performance and treatment effects to be observed while the program is in progress, thus allowing continuous feedback. All performance data are charted in two basic graphs, progress and performance graphs, to display daily, weekly, and monthly data. Progress or mastery graphs are constructed to display the time it takes a student to master a set of instructional objectives; thus time is plotted along the abscissa and the objectives are plotted along the ordinate. Performance graphs, however, are designed to display how student behavior changes on a single task (e.g., addition facts). Thus, the abscissa again shows the time variables; however, the ordinate shows the level of performance on the targeted task on a day when the performance was measured. Both these graphs facilitate the visual description of progress/performance discrepancies and the estimate of required progress necessary for remediation. Specific calculations are also provided to determine progress/performance discrepancies numerically and to estimate progress/performance requirements.

The advantages of Deno's (1985) model of CBM include reliable and valid data, simple and efficient methods, understandable results, and inexpensive materials. First, the results of criterion validity studies revealed that all the curriculum-based measures were highly correlated with performance on standardized, norm-referenced tests, with correlations ranging from .70 to .95 (e.g., Deno, Marston, & Mirkin, 1982; Deno, Mirkin, &

Chiang, 1982). In addition, measures of oral reading, written expression, and spelling reliably discriminated between students who were in special education programs and those who were not, as well as growth throughout the elementary school years (Deno, 1985).

Second, Deno's model of CBM provides clear and effective communication of student performance, which is facilitated by the use of progress/performance graphs. The graphed data reflect student performance in the curriculum as defined by the dependent measure (e.g., words read correctly). These measures are easily depicted and understood by teachers, parents, and students. Thus, judgments about whether a student is benefiting from instruction can easily be made.

Third, the model is sensitive to growth in student performance over relatively short duration. Standardized achievement measures, in contrast, fail to show any student growth for up to 16 weeks (Marston, Fuchs, & Deno, 1986). The CBM data reveal change in performance within a short-term time frame (days, weeks) that allows teachers frequently to monitor and evaluate the effectiveness of interventions, helping to solve students' achievement problems more efficiently.

Fourth, since measures of student achievement may be obtained frequently, CBM improves the data base for making educational decisions. CBM requires only that a brief sample of curriculum-based performance be obtained regularly by the teacher. What results is a series of repeated measures that can be graphically displayed to describe the student's current level of performance in the curriculum and to estimate the rate of a student's increase in performance by computing the slope of the data (White & Haring, 1980). Thus, CBM yields a statistic (slope data) describing student growth which is unavailable when using standardized achievement tests.

Fifth, because of the simplicity in administering CBM procedures, it is possible to obtain local norms by sampling regular classroom peers. This can be performed for individual classes, schools, or entire school districts (Shinn, 1988). A students' performance could be determined reliably and regularly with peer-referenced comparisons between the performance of the target student and the average performance of his/her peers. The magnitude of this performance difference clearly represents the target student's degree of performance deficiency and is easily communicated to teachers and parents alike. Thus, peer referencing can serve as a basis for making educational decisions regarding student academic performance and growth.

Sixth, CBM procedures are cost-effective in that they do not require purchase of additional test materials. In addition, CBM is an efficient system, but only if teachers are carefully trained. If they are not, they come to believe that direct and frequent measurement of student performance in the curriculum takes too much time (Wesson, King, & Deno, 1984). When CBM is compared to standardized norm-referenced achievement tests along the cost-effectiveness dimension, CBM becomes the preferable choice. The time required to administer achievement tests varies, but most take approximately 1 hour. In contrast, only a few minutes are required to administer CBM. In fact, evidence exists that the time taken to frequently test student performance in the curriculum can actually lead to improved student achievement (Mirkin et al., 1981). In addition, commercially distributed achievement tests are far more expensive than CBM. More important is the issue of test effectiveness. Standardized achievement tests yield only norm-referenced scores that reflect the students' relative standing within some reference group. They do not yield any information regarding student competence within the curriculum being instructed, nor do they reflect student performance within the curriculum relative to the peer group. Similarly, achievement tests cannot generate data points frequently enough to establish actual rate of student growth.

Finally, CBM can be used to provide essential data for making special education programming decisions. Students can be screened with CBM and identified for service by the resulting discrepancy ratios between actual and expected performance. Current performance levels can be the basis for developing appropriate IEP goals, and progress can be evaluated that would facilitate needed and timely modifications in the program.

In sum, the concepts of frequent measurement, slope of improvement in the data, and curriculum, individual, and peer referencing provide a positive direction for CBM. The data that already exist on the effectiveness of CBM provide strong support for its continued use and importance in educational assessment.

Curriculum-Based Assessment by Gickling and Havertape (1981)

The model for curriculum-based assessment developed by Gickling and Havertape (1981) focuses on what children know and need in relationship to their curriculum assignments. The basic assumptions underlying this model are that (a) a curriculum scope and sequence exists for the area to be assessed; (b) perceptual and processing tasks are not prerequisites to academic tasks; (c) curricular materials can be assets or deterrents to learning; (d) assessment should be accurate, continuous, and lead to instructional improvement; and (e) assessment activities should be directly related to teaching activities.

Gickling and Havertape (1981) have labeled their target population the "curriculum casualty group." In other words, the curriculum has produced the problems of those students who do poorly. Only a portion of this group consists of handicapped students. The majority of these "casualties" are regular education students not receiving any special assistance.

The causes for the "casualties" stem from the nature of the curricular demand placed on students. Typically, curricula are designed to meet the needs of the average student. Expected progress in the curriculum does not differ across sudents and is usually evaluated by peer comparison. As a result, curricula fail to adapt to individual differences, move too fast, and demand too much in relation to existing skills for some students. Undoubtedly, these students fall further and further behind and become caught in a failure cycle, thus becoming "curriculum casualties." Uncorrected difficulties compound themselves and result in low-achieving students being graded more on their lack of prerequisite skills than on what they have learned. What is ultimately needed is the adjustment of the curriculum to fit individual needs. CBA enables teachers to do just that, by gaining control over the curriculum and matching it more effectively to the students' needs.

As a methodology, Gickling and Havertape (1981) have defined CBA as "a procedure for determining the instructional needs of a student based on the student's ongoing performance within existing course content." However, CBA is not just a process of data collection and interpretation. Rather, these two functions paired with application have a primary goal to facilitate the instructional decision-making process. Concern is placed on the acquisition of basic curriculum skills. Therefore, any data that do not have direct instructional application do not have any use in this model. The focus of each CBA is on (a) the student's entry skills relative to his or her coursework, (b) the instructional demands placed on the student from the course assignments, and (c) controlling the degree of task difficulty by modifying the tasks to match the abilities of the student, thereby using the curriculum appropriately to meet individual differences.

Control over the curriculum is first achieved by eliminating the instructional mismatch between the skills of students and the demands placed on them by the curricular assignments. This primary goal of CBA is approached first by determining the grade level on which the student functions and then choosing materials on a grade level appropriate for the student. This process breaks down for most low-achieving students because of their fragmented skills and because the curriculum fails to consider the variability in difficulty of curriculum assignments. Trying to match instructional tasks with students having fragmented skills does not solve their academic problems. In other words, it is not enough to individualize instruction for reading in general; one must alter the instruction task by task for each subskill taught within the reading curriculum.

To address the problem of control over curriculum variability, Gickling (1977) developed an Instructional Delivery Model, which provides a visual method for gauging the probability of task successes. It also provides a structure for controlling teacher difficulties in deciding what and how to teach. Gickling and Havertape (1981) list three basic advantages of this model: (a) its ease of application for the teacher, (b) its enhancement of teacher accountability, and (c) its basis for sound instructional principles. In this model, every instructional task is examined on three essential components: type of task, the number of items in the task, and the student's familiarity with the task items. These components provide information for measuring instructional decisions by the teacher, making daily instructional modifications, and delivering instruction systematically.

There are two types of tasks: reading and drill. Reading refers only to obtaining meaning from print. Drill includes all other assignments: for example, math, writing, spelling, and even subskill areas of reading, including word attack procedures. There are two types of items within each type of task: known items and challenging items. The ratio of known to challenging items comprises task difficulty. A known item is one for which the student can provide an immediate and correct response, while a challenging item is either an unknown or a hesitant response. These known/unknown ratios translate into three types of performance levels: instructional, independent, and frustrational. For reading tasks, the instructional level contains between 93 and 97% known items and 3 to 7% challenge items. For drill tasks, the instructional level is set at 70 to 85% known items with 15 to 30% challenge items. An independent level represents anything higher than the instructional ratios delineated above, whereas a frustrational level represents anything below. Students profit most when curricular materials are on an instructional level, yielding learning tasks that are familiar enough yet sufficiently challenging. At the independent level, neither assignment nor teacher assistance are used to full advantage; and obviously frustrational level assignments need to be avoided.

To use this strategy for CBA, it is critical to identify and control task difficulty relative to individual student needs across curricular assignments. This requires the evaluation of individual assignments and their appropriate modification to meet the ratios of known to challenging items per task. By evaluating the suitability of students' assignments with the criteria provided, teachers can identify the inappropriateness of some assignments before the assignment is given without penalizing the students with tasks that are too hard. This preassessment of assignments, including modifying, retaining, or discarding items when appropriate, helps to maintain an instructional level for low-achieving students. As such, a match results between instructional demands and the students' skills, thereby allowing students to consistently improve academically.

Gickling and Thompson (1985) provide six basic rules that if followed will facilitate the application of their model. These rules are: (a) maintain a high percentage of knowns to provide built-in reinforcement for the student; (b) keep new material within the margin of challenge, to decrease the probability of creating a frustrational task and an overload of instruction; (c) treat items of undeter-

mined status as unknowns to decrease the probability of jeopardizing an appropriate instructional ratio; (d) examine the planned content of the lesson before designing the drill work, so that the two tasks become coordinated and enhance the learning situation; (e) present the drill activities before the content of the lesson, in order to prepare the student for the task; and (f) take every task to a mastery level, which requires both independent performance and comprehension, so that no tasks are left at a submastery level.

As a direct classroom assessment approach, Gickling and Havertape's (1981) model of CBA provides a most readily available and useful source of information. CBA generates its own progress measurement with emphasis placed on the obtainable measures of rate of acquisition, rate of fluency, and knowledge and comprehension. CBA focuses on how to collect, interpret, and use these measures in order to affect instruction directly.

In sum, Gickling and Havertape's (1981) model of CBA provides teachers with the specifics of where to begin instruction and an instructional strategy for teaching specific children. CBA also provides a format for assessing the demands of students' learning tasks as well as a gauge for controlling the level of task difficulty. As a result, students are provided with more optimal learning experiences.

Curriculum-Based Assessment by Blankenship (1985)

The model of curriculum-based assessment developed by Blankenship (1985) is another variation of directly assessing academics through the curriculum. Blankenship defines CBA as ''the practice of obtaining direct and frequent measures of a student's performance on a series of sequentially arranged objectives derived from the curriculum used in the classroom'' (Blankenship & Lilly, 1981, p. 81). From this definition it is apparent that the essence of this approach, like the others, is the linking of assessment to curriculum and instruction. Within Blankenship's model, objective measures of performance are collected by the teacher on classroom-relevant skills and are used as a basis for making instructional decisions. The CBAs (this term is also used to refer to the instrument itself) are administered over a period of a few days to provide students with ample opportunities to respond to similar items on different occasions. This practice helps to ensure that assessment results reflect the typical performance of students.

CBAs are given at different times during the school year, corresponding to the different decision-making functions of the data. At the beginning of the school year, CBAs are administered to place students into curriculum materials and to identify students' specific skill deficits for instructional purposes. Following instruction, all or part of a CBA may be readministered to assess skill mastery and to determine whether additional instruction or practice is deemed necessary. After mastery is achieved, CBAs may be used periodically throughout the school year to measure long-term retention.

Blankenship's (1985) model resembles Idol et al's (1986) model of CBA, in that a CBA can be developed for any type of curriculum material. Similarly, the scope of each CBA developed depends on the number of skills a teacher wants to assess. The development of CBAs within this model does not follow a strict pattern, but instead, offers teachers flexibility in their construction. There are, however, general guidelines to follow for developing and using CBAs.

The goal when developing a CBA is to produce an assessment device to measure student performance and to develop a plan for administration and interpretation. Blankenship outlined 12 steps to meet this goal. The first nine steps are preinstruction guidelines, the tenth and eleventh steps are postinstruction guidelines, and the last step is a postmastery guideline. These steps are as follows:

1. List the skills that are presented in the selected curriculum materials. This helps to determine whether the skills presented match the teaching objectives.
2. Examine this list to check that all important skills are presented. If large gaps exist between skills or if skills are poorly sequenced, it is sometimes necessary to add to, delete from, or re-sequence the skills.
3. List the skills in a logical order.
4. Write an objective for each skill on the list. This requires the specification of the conditions under which a student is to perform a behavior, and the level of performance needed for mastery.
5. Prepare items to test each listed objective.

6. Prepare testing materials using these items. By writing objectives, the types of materials needed become apparent. A sufficient number of items must be included to assess each skill and alternate forms needed to be developed to allow for repeated measures across the school year.
7. Plan how the CBA will be given.
8. Administer the CBA prior to beginning instruction on a topic.
9. Study the results to determine (a) which students have already mastered the skills targeted for instruction, (b) which students possess sufficient prerequisite skills that render them ready to begin instruction, and (c) which students lack mastery of the prerequisite skills.
10. Readminister the CBA after instruction.
11. Study the results to determine (a) which students have mastered the skills and are ready to be instructed on a new topic, (b) which students are making sufficient progress but require more instruction or practice to achieve mastery, and (c) which students are making insufficient progress, thereby requiring instructional modifications.
12. Readminister the CBA periodically throughout the year to assess long-term retention.

Within Blankenship's (1985) model, CBAs requiring written responses are typically administered to an entire class at one time. Students are not required to complete all sections of a CBA during one sitting. One test session may last anywhere between 15 and 60 minutes, and greatly differs from the shorter timed probes used by other models (e.g., Deno, 1985; Idol et al, 1986; Shapiro & Lentz, 1985). CBAs that require oral responses are individually administered while the class is engaged in other activities. Blankenship (1985) also suggests that prior to CBA administration, students should be informed that (a) the purpose of the CBAs are to help the teacher identify the skills they need to learn; (b) many of the skills may be difficult, therefore, it is acceptable to leave unknown items blank; and (c) by doing well, students can avoid receiving instruction on already mastered skill areas. Students usually react favorably when they know they can avoid instruction on material they have already learned and can receive help in acquiring new skills.

Teachers are given a central role in the CBA process. Teachers develop and administer the CBAs and use CBA data to assist them in making academic decisions. As a result, teachers become necessary contributors during IEP meetings by (a) summarizing a student's present levels of performance, (b) suggesting appropriate goals and objectives, and (c) documenting pupil progress. Blankenship (1985) suggests that teachers work in pairs or teams within a school, to share the developmental responsibilities and exchange CBAs with their fellow teachers.

To summarize, Blankenship's model of CBA provides useful information at three stages in the teaching process: (a) prior to instruction, CBA data assist teachers in making decisions concerning student placement into curriculum materials; (b) immediately following instruction, CBA data assist teachers in adjusting instruction based on student performance; and (c) periodically throughout the school year, CBAs assess long-term retention and help to evaluate and communicate pupil progress to parents and school personnel. Blankenship maintains that CBA data can also provide the basis for making student referrals for special education services, identifying individualized education program (IEP) goals and objectives, and determining when reentrance into the regular classroom is appropriate for handicapped students.

Curriculum-Based Assessment by Shapiro and Lentz (1985, 1986)

The model of curriculum-based assessment devised by Shapiro and Lentz (1985, 1986) is a unique alternative for assessing academic skills. It is an assessment methodology designed to evaluate the critical variables that are related to a student's academic problems. The procedures employed in conducting the assessment involve collecting data that are as close as possible to the individual's behavior as it typically occurs in the classroom.

A critical and underlying assumption of the CBA is that a child's academic problem is a function of environmental and individual variables. As such, one cannot simply focus on the child's academic skills as the source of academic failure. It is equally important to examine events within the instructional environment that may be contributing

significantly to the child's problems. Careful examination of the teaching procedures, contingencies for performance, classroom structure, and other such instructional events may often suggest appropriate remediation strategies.

When academic skills are assessed, CBA requires that the child's academic behavior closest to actual classroom performance be evaluated. This requires that the assessment procedures are derived directly from the curriclum materials in which the child is being instructed. In this way, one is able to determine the degree to which a child has mastered what he or she have been expected to learn. Further, examination of permanent products (e.g., worksheets, homework assignments, etc.) may offer significant information about the child's academic problems.

CONDUCTING A CURRICULUM-BASED ASSESSMENT

Each of the models of curriculum-based assessment described so far requires a somewhat different set of procedures for actually conducting an evaluation. Space limitations obviously prevent extensive discussions of the various methodologies and interested readers are encouraged to examine materials published by each of the authors elaborating their particular models of curriculum-based assessment. For purposes of providing an illustration of the details on how a curriculum-based assessment can be conducted, the model described by Shapiro and Lentz (1985, 1986) will be presented. Given that this model incorporates elements to assess both the instructional environment and the child's individual academic skills, it may serve as a useful model for evaluating entire academic ecologies rather than just individual children's skills.

Overview of Assessment Methods

The CBA model described by Shapiro and Lentz (1985, 1986) follows a "funnel-shaped" assessment process beginning with a "wide" screening of a student's referred problems via teacher interview, and ending with a "narrow" identification of particular performance or skill problems, the environmental conditions related to the problems, and the delineation of specific targets for remediation (Figure 1). The CBA process produces data that are useful for a number of purposes, for

CURRICULUM BASED ASSESSMENT

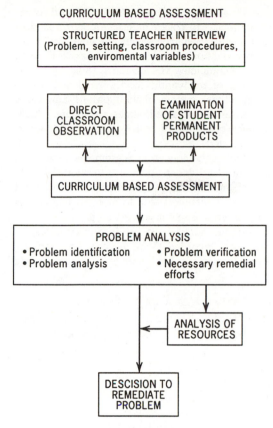

Figure 1. Flowchart model of Shapiro and Lentz's (1985, 1986) model of CBA.

example, reevaluation and placement of students in special education, as well as planning intervention. For all of these purposes, the sequence of activities is similar. This sequence is as follows: (a) teacher interview, analysis of interview data, and planning an assessment; (b) direct classroom observation and examination of student permanent products; and (c) administration of curriculum-based probes. Figure 1 illustrates this model of CBA.

Each of these methods of assessment is designed to evaluate particular variables which are known to be related to academic performance. Table 1 illustrates the relationship between variables assessed and the methods employed. It is evident from this table that several methods employed in the assessment process may be linked to evaluating the same variable. For example, allotted time is assessed through teacher interview but then confirmed through direct observation.

The Teacher Interview

A structured interview of the referring teacher is always the first step in CBA, and a successful interview is critical to the efficiency and success of the whole assessment sequence. Information gathered here will guide the other assessment efforts. Most of the data produced during the interview are related to the academic skills and performance of the referred student as well as understanding more about the instructional environment. Obviously, this form of assessment relies on teacher recollections. To ensure that the recollections are appropriate and accurate, it is strongly suggested that the

TABLE 1   Assessment Procedures for Achievement-Related Variables

Variable	Procedure
1. Actual placement of student in curriculum according to skill	Direct assessment, using skill probes, curriculum test, criteria-referenced tests
2. Expected placement	Teacher interview
3. Actual placement procedures used by teacher	Teacher interview, permanent products
4. Allotted time	Teacher interview, direct observation
5. Opportunities to respond	Direct observation/ permanent products
6. Student accuracy/ performance	Teacher interview, permanent products
7. Immediate contingencies	Direct observation
8. Competing behaviors	Direct observation teacher interview
9. Orientation to materials	Direct observation
10. Teacher feedback	Direct observation teacher interview
11. Teacher planning	Teacher interview

interviewer's questions are specific and directly related to the problem as seen by the teacher. During the interview, information should be gathered on (a) the exact nature of the problem; (b) the typical instructional procedures in the classroom, including grouping, how instruction occurs, time allotted for instruction, and the nature of individual seatwork; (c) the teachers' expectancies about acceptable student performance within the curriculum; (d) the student's behavior during instructional activities (e.g., on-task, accuracy, questions, etc.); (e) how the teacher evaluates student performance and the availability of any placement tests, mastery tests, and daily work; (f) the student's performance on daily work assignments; (g) the teacher arranged contingencies for student performance, including contingencies for accuracy/completion of classwork or homework; and (h) when instruction is scheduled (to facilitate observations). The format of the interview is based on the behavioral interviewing strategies discussed by Bergan (1977). Questions are asked directly in each area of basic academic skills which are of concern.

From the interview, one begins to plan the remainder of the assessment process. One must determine when and where it would be appropriate to conduct direct observations, what may be critical variables needed to be observed through direct observation methods, what permanent product data need to be examined, what may be the most important academic areas where skill deficiencies may be present, what are the appropriate places to conduct direct assessments of reading, math, and spelling, and what is the expected levels of student performance based on teacher report.

Direct Classroom Observation

Classroom observations yield direct information about the child's academic and academic-related behaviors and about how the environment may be affecting those behaviors. Shapiro and Lentz (1986) recommend that a standardized observational system be used. Many direct observation codes exist and almost any would be applicable for conducting a curriculum-based assessment. A few codes stand out as particularly useful for classroom observations (e.g., Alessi & Kaye, 1983; O'Leary, Romanczyk, Kass, Dietz, & Santogrossi, 1979). Shapiro and Lentz (1985, 1986) have been using the State-Event Classroom Observation System (SECOS) developed by Saudargas and asso-

ciates (Saudargas & Creed, 1980). This code offers opportunities to collect extensive data on student and teacher behavior which are very closely related to classroom academic performance. Figure 2 shows a completed SECOS form. Table 2 provides a listing of the various codes employed in the observational system. Two types of behavioral responses are obtained, states and events. Additionally, behaviors of both students and teachers are collected.

State behaviors provide estimates about what percent of an entire observation period the child was engaged in particular behavior. For the most part, these behaviors tend to be those that do not have discrete beginnings and endings and occur periodically throughout an instructional lesson. States are recorded as momentary time samples every 15 seconds. Each time an interval ends, the

TABLE 2   Saudargas Observation Code

Symbol	Behavior Cateogory
Student Behavior	
State	
SW	Schoolwork
OS	Out of seat
LK	Looking around
SIC	Social interaction with child
SIT	Social interaction with teacher
OACT	Other activity
Event	
RH	Raise hand
CAL	Call out to teacher
AC	Approach child
OAC	Other child approach
OS	Out of seat
Teacher Behavior	
TA/SW	Teacher approach to student doing SW
TA/OTH	Teacher approach to student doing other activity
APP	Teacher approval or praise of student behavior
DIS	Teacher disapproval of student behavior

Source. From *State-Event Classroom Observation Code,* by R. A. Saudargas and V. Creed, 1980, University of Tennessee, Department of Psychology, Knoxville, TN. Reprinted with permission.

Sandargas-Creed   Sheet #:_____

<u>T. W.</u>   (GR:)   M T W T F   Start Time: 9:00
Student   Date/yr   Day (circle)   End: 9:55   Total: 5 min.

                                  <u>**Reading**</u>   1. ISW: TPsnt   2. ISW: TSmGp
_____   Class Activity   ③ SmGp: Tled   4. LgGp: Tled
School
                                                                            /
<u>Mrs. C.</u>   <u>C.M.</u>   Referral: _____ (Ac.)   (Beh.)
Teacher   Observer

STATES	01	02	03	04	05	06	07	08	09	10	11	12	13	14	15	16	17	18	19	20	Σ	%
SW	1	1	1	1		1	1						1	1							8	40%
OS						1															1	5
LK				1										1	1	1					4	20
SIC			1	1									1								3	20
SIT			1	1									1								3	15
OACT								1	1												2	10

EVENTS	01	02	03	04	05	06	07	08	09	10	11	12	13	14	15	16	17	18	19	20	Σ	Rate
RH																	1	①			2	.4
CAL																						
AC																						
OCA																						
OS																						

TEACHER	01	02	03	04	05	06	07	08	09	10	11	12	13	14	15	16	17	18	19	20	Σ	Rate
TA/SW	1													g	g	g	g	1			6	1.2
TA/OTH	II											1									3	.6
APP												A									1	.2
DIS																						

COMMENTS:_____

_____

_____

Figure 2. Completed SECOS observation of T.W.

observer simply marks whether these behaviors are present at that instant. Certain rules do apply for which behaviors can and cannot be scored together, and interested readers are encouraged to obtain a copy of the SECOS before attempting to use this code. Further, state behaviors on the SECOS all involve behaviors targeting students directly.

Events consist of behaviors that have distinct beginning and ending parameters and are recorded by frequency counting. Each instance of these behaviors within the 15-second time interval are recorded. Both student and teacher directed behavior categories are included as events. Additionally, a number of behaviors (RH, CAL, AC, OCA, APP, DIS) have special coding rules involving the collection of data regarding student–student and student–teacher interactions, and whether teacher attention received by students is the result of individually or whole-classroom-directed teacher attention. Again, interested readers are encouraged to obtain a copy of the SECOS manual, which provides detailed explanations for each category of behavior.

Observations are conducted by alternating between state and event categories of behavior. When each interval begins, observers record any states evident at that moment. For the remainder of the 15-second interval, any events that occur are recorded. This procedure continues until the observation is completed.

States and events are scored differently. State behaviors are scored by calculating the percentage of intervals within which the behavior was found to occur. These data represent an estimate of the amount of time a particular behavior may be occurring. It is important to realize that these data represent *estimates* and are not actual percent time measures. Events are converted into rate data by dividing the frequencies of each behavior by the total time the behavior was observed. Figure 2 provides examples of these calculations for the completed data sheet.

One problem that affects the use of any observational system is when and how often to observe. The answers to these questions are based not on a set of rules but on good clinical skills. Observations should be planned during activities related to the child's referred problems. For example, if reading is a problem and teacher interview data indicate that the child's failure occurs in both small group and individual seatwork, then *at a*

minimum direct observation under both conditions would be valuable. Because these activities often occur consecutively in classrooms, one may be able to plan an observation time that covers both settings during a single visit to the classroom. Similarly, if during the teacher interview it is learned that the student is doing poorly in any individual seatwork activity compared to when the teacher is teaching directly, one would choose observation periods of individual seatwork across academic activities.

How often to observe is obviously related to the amount of time available to school psychologists as well as the variability of child behavior. Enough observations of the child need to be collected to provide an accurate picture of the referred child's behavior and the relevant environment. The teacher interview can provide some guidance for deciding observational frequency, if the interviewer solicits information regarding student variability. Comments from teachers suggesting that a student's behavior varies greatly day to day suggests that more observation needs to be done. A "best guess" recommendation is to observe for at least one full period where problems exist, and then portions of that period on one or two other days. If the data are still not stable across these observations, observers may need to schedule additional observations or interviews with the teacher to better understand the nature of the referral problem.

Interpretation of the data collected on the SECOS involves comparing data across different categories. The state behavior SW (Schoolwork) is viewed as an estimate of the rate of engaged time. SW levels are examined against the allocated time for instruction to obtain an estimate of the amount of time students spend engaged in academic tasks. For example, if a student is found to have a SW level of 50% during reading aggregated across observations and reading is allocated for a total of 60 minutes per day, one may conclude that the observed student was spending about 30 minutes per day engaged in reading. Likewise, permanent products (i.e., worksheets, scores on tests, writing samples) which were produced during the observation are examined against SW level. At times, students may show high SW levels, suggesting good on-task behavior, but reveal that they completed few problems on the given worksheet during the observation. Additionally, SW levels under varying conditions (i.e., group versus individual work periods) may show differential effects. The types and levels of non-SW behavior are also examined to determine how the student spent his or her nonengaged time.

Another useful analysis is to examine the intervals where SW and SIT (teacher interaction) are scored together. If there are many intervals where both SW and SIT are scored and few intervals where SW occurred alone, it may suggest that the student is only working when the teacher is assisting. This may provide information that the level of assigned work is too difficult, or that the student is highly reinforced by teacher attention. Additionally, the student may have learned that teacher proximity is a stimulus for working.

Events are interpreted in terms of the type and level of interactions occurring in the classroom. How the student contacts the teacher, how students contact each other, and how teachers contact students can all play an important part in the academic performance of students. Student contact of teachers is assessed on the SECOS through the RH (raise hand), OS (out of seat), and CAL (call out) categories. Student–student contact is directly assessed by the OCA (other child approach) and AC (approach child) categories. Teacher contact of students is also assessed directly by examining the categories of TA/SW (teacher-initiated approach when student engaged in schoolwork) and TA/OTH (teacher-initiated approach when student engaged in other activity). Additionally, levels of APP (approval) and DIS (disapproval) can be examined.

One other very useful procedure to assist interpretation of observational data is the collection of data on comparison children. Very often, the levels of behavior obtained on a referred student are important only when compared to peers in the same classrooms. These data can be collected at the same time that data are collected on the referred child. Several different procedures can be suggested for obtaining these data. First, teachers can be asked to refer a peer who represents an "average"-behaving student in his or her classroom. Second, the observer can randomly select a particular peer in the proximity of the target student. Third, the observer can randomly observe different peers during specified intervals across the observation. In each case, observation intervals in which the comparison child rather than the target child is observed are marked. On these intervals, data are obtained on the nonreferred child(ren)

and aggregated across the entire observation to provide a peer comparison. Among these methods, it may be safest to select different peers randomly for each observation interval, thus avoiding potential biases that may occur if a single student is observed as the peer comparison pupil.

Although the observation system described here, the SECOS, has been found to be a valuable and useful measure by the authors, and there appear to be data substantiating its usefulness for school psychologists (e.g., Saudargas & Lentz, 1986; Slate & Saudargas, 1986a, 1986b), any observation system which can accurately assess variables that affect academic performance would be acceptable. It is important to recognize that the assessment of academic problems must incorporate an evaluation of the instructional environment and the best way to examine this is through systematic, structured observation.

Assessing Individual Skills: Curriculum-Based Probes

Academic skills of students are assessed based on the model developed and elaborated by Deno and his associates (e.g., Deno, 1985). In reading, math, and spelling, the assessment procedures are derived directly from curriculum materials. In each case they are designed both to identify a student's instructional level within the curriculum, and to serve as a method of ongoing monitoring of academic progress. Similarly, assessments of written language are valuable for monitoring student progress, but are not directly derived from curriculum materials since such curricula rarely exist.

Reading

The assessment of reading skills involves the administration of short oral reading probes taken from the basal reading series in which the student is being instructed. Conducting an evaluation of reading has two major objectives. The first objective is to determine if the student is appropriately placed in the curriculum materials. Many times students fail to master material but are passed on through the reading series without any remedial efforts. The second objective is to establish baseline reading levels which can serve as comparison points for monitoring progress through the reading curriculum.

Reading probes are constructed by selecting three passages from each book of the basal reading series, one from the beginning third, middle third, and last third of the book. These passages should be 50 to 100 words for students in grades 1 to 3 and 150 to 200 words for grades 4+. Passages selected should not have a lot of dialogue, be text and not poetry or plays, and should not have many unusual or foreign words. Two copies of each probe are constructed, one for the child to read and one for the examiner. It is permissible to use the child's book; however, the physical limitation of always having easy access to the basal reading series may make this impossible. For each probe, a set of five to eight comprehension questions are developed. These questions should be of the who, what, why, where, and inference type.

Beginning with the book in which a child is currently placed, a child is instructed to read aloud the specified passages. If the examiner is planning to ask comprehension questions, the child is told before beginning to read that he or she will be asked a few questions about the passage when it is finished. The child is instructed to begin reading and the stopwatch is started. As the child reads, errors are marked for omissions, substitutions, additions, or pauses longer than 5 seconds. Repetitions or self-corrections are not scored as errors. The child is told to stop at the end of a minute unless comprehension questions are to be asked. In that case, the child finishes reading the passage and each of the comprehension questions are asked. The child is permitted to have the passage in front of him or her when the questions are asked.

The process is repeated for all three passages for each book of the reading series. The number of words read correctly per minute and the number of errors per minute are calculated for each passage,. along with the percentage of correct comprehension questions. *Median* scores across the three probes for each book represent the scores for that particular book (or level) of the series. Using the criteria for placement presented in Table 3, move either up or down the series and give the next set of three probes. If the child is within the instructional level, move up; if not, move down. Probes are given in this manner until the median scores for at least two sets of scores are instructional and the one above them is frustrational. The optimal pattern would look like this:

Level 7: Frustration
Level 6: Instructional

Level 5: Instructional
Level 4: Mastery

Often, this exact pattern will not emerge. Some children never reach a mastery level and will have a series of instructional levels. After three consecutive instructional levels, it is unnecessary to continue further. The child's placement is at the highest instructional level.

Significant controversy exists regarding the administration of comprehension questions. Although giving comprehension questions is certainly important, it does significantly add to the length of a reading assessment. For example, if a student reads at 50 words per minute, it would take 3 minutes to read a 150-word passage, 5 minutes for questions, and 2 minutes to prepare for the next probe. This means that assessing just one level of a series would take 30 minutes! Clearly, this amount of time would make such assessment unacceptable.

One way to handle this problem is to assess comprehension only when absolutely necessary. In clinical practice, it is recommended that comprehension be assessed only when oral reading rate data are discrepant with reasons for referral. For example, if a teacher refers a student for a reading problem but is found to be instructional or mastery at grade level, it may suggest that the real problem as seen by the teacher is in the area of comprehension. In such cases, one can reduce the number of probes given per level of the series.

The assessment of reading just described is designed to be the method employed for conducting an *initial* assessment. When assessing oral reading rates for ongoing progress monitoring, only a single passage is read from the level in which the child is being instructed. Usually, the passage read is taken from just ahead of the curriculum material the child is actually practicing in class. Thus, if a child is finishing a story on page 50, they may be asked to read from page 51. These probes should be taken at least three times every 2 weeks and can be graphed to provide a picture of the ongoing progress of student performance. These data can be displayed in graphic form, along with indications of goals, expected rates of performance (aimlines), and lines which indicate actual rates of performance. Such data displays can be very useful in making decisions regarding whether students are progressing at rates which

TABLE 3   Placement Criteria for Direct Reading Assessment

			Criterion		
			Median Words Correct per Minute	Median Words Incorrect per Minute	Median Comprehension (% Correct)
Deno and Mirkin (1977)	Grades 1–2	Frustration	29	8+	80
		Instructional	30–49	3–7	80
		Mastery	50+	2	80
	Grade 3+	Frustration	49	8+	80
		Instructional	50–99	3–7	80
		Mastery	100+	2	80
Lovitt and Hansen (1976)		[a] Instructional	45–65	4–8	50–75
Starlin (1982)		Frustration	69	11+	[b] Uses alternative procedure
		Instructional	70–149	6–10	
		Mastery	150+	5	

[a] Frustration and mastery levels defined as below and above instructional levels.
[b] See Starlin (1982) for full discussion.

Source. From "Behavioral assessment of academic skills" by E. S. Shapiro and F. E. Lentz, Jr., 1986, in T. R. Kratochwill (Ed.), *Advances in School Psychology* (Vol. 5, p. 120). Hillsdale, NJ: Erlbaum. Copyright © 1986 by Lawrence Erlbaum Associates. Reprinted by permission.

suggest they will meet goals that have been set for them.

Similar types of reading probes can also be developed for basal word lists as well as passages. These lists of words are taken from vocabulary lists derived from each book of the reading series or a standard list such as the Harris-Jacobson word list. Criteria for moving up or down the levels of the series are not the same as for reading passages. Interested readers are directed to Shinn's (1988) excellent description of how to develop this type of probe.

Math

The assessment of math begins by identifying the sequence of instruction for computational skills. If this is not available for a particular district, any available sequence for computational objectives will suffice (e.g., Deno & Mirkin, 1977). There should be little deviation from district to district and curriculum to curriculum in the order in which these skills are taught.

Math probes can be made for either the assessment of a single skill (such as two-digit regrouping in the tens column only) or for multiple skills (such as all addition and subtraction facts with results less than 10). Single-probe sheets are very useful for providing specific recommendations regarding mastered and deficient skills. These probes can be valuable in monitoring acquisition of newly taught skills. Multiple-probe sheets offer the advantage of assesing a broader range of skills at the same time and may be useful for exploring long-term progress across many instructional objectives.

In either case, probes are developed by creating a sheet of 30 to 35 problems taken from the same instructional objective(s). Two or three different probes based on the identical objective will be needed. A computer program published by the Minnesota Educational Computing Corporation (program A-151), available for Apple and Commodore, may be useful in developing these probes.

Choosing the probes to administer can be accomplished in a number of ways. One could examine recent end-of-level and end-of-book tests to determine which types of computational objectives the student has not mastered. Although this procedure is useful, it may not always be feasible since end-of-level and end-of-book tests may not be available. An alternative procedure, which is highly recommended, is to choose the particular objectives to be given based on the teacher interview. During the interview, one should have learned the current instructional and mastery levels of average performers as well as the current instructional, mastery, and frustrational level of the target student. Although these levels are all based on teacher perception, they can offer a framework for choosing the range of objectives that need to be assessed. For example, Table 4 displays tne computational skills mastery checklist for grades 1 to 3 in the Allentown School district. As noted on the table, the teacher interviewed indicated that the average performers in her third-grade class had mastered addition without regrouping and were being instructed in addition with regrouping. In contrast, the target student while mastering basic addition and subtraction facts, was having difficulty when any two-digit addition or subtraction was attempted, and was frustrational when regrouping was added. Given these findings during the interview, computational objectives would be chosen ranging from addition/subtraction facts (to assess mastery level), through addition/subtraction without regrouping (instructional level), to addition/subtraction with regrouping (frustration level).

Once the probes are chosen, students are instructed to work on the probe sheet for 1 or 2 minutes. Usually, 1 minute is used for simpler problems and 2 minutes for more complex operations such as two-digit multiplication. If the child's score is significantly below instructional level compared to the criteria provided in Table 5, only one additional probe of those skills is given. If the child's score is close to or within instructional/mastery levels, three probes of those same skills are usually administered.

Scoring of each probe is based on counting the separate digits in an answer. For addition and subtraction, only digits *below the answer line* are counted. For example, there is a possibility of three correct digits in the problem:

$$\begin{array}{r} 38 \\ +\ 65 \\ \hline 103 \end{array}$$

In this example the student would receive a score of 3. Notice that the digit added by the

TABLE 4   Allentown School District Elementary Math Whole Number Computational Skills Expected Mastery

Target	Class	
Grade 1		
M		1. Add two one-digit numbers: sums to 10
M		2. Subtract two one-digit numbers: combinations to 10
Grade 2		
M		3. Add two one-digit numbers: sums 11 to 19
		4. Add a one-digit number to a two-digit number—no regrouping
I		5. Add a two-digit number to a two-digit number—no regrouping
		6. Add a three-digit number to a three-digit number—no regrouping
		7. Subtract a one-digit number from a one- or two-digit number: combinations to 18
I		8. Subtract a one-digit number from a two-digit number—no regrouping
		9. Subtract a two-digit number from a two-digit number—no regrouping
		10. Subtract a three-digit number from a three-digit number—no regrouping
		11. Multiplication facts—0's, 1's, 2's
Grade 3		
		12. Add three or more one-digit numbers
		13. Add three or more two-digit numbers—no regrouping
	M	14. Add three or more three- and four-digit numbers—no regrouping
F		15. Add a one-digit number to a two-digit number with regrouping
		16. Add a two-digit number to a two-digit number with regrouping
	I	17. Add a two-digit number to a three-digit number with regrouping from the tens column only
		18. Add a two-digit number to a three-digit number with regrouping from the hundreds column only.
		19. Add a two-digit number to a three-digit number with regrouping from tens and hundreds columns
		20. Add a three-digit number to a three-digit number with regrouping from the tens column only
		21. Add a three-digit number to a three-digit number with regrouping from the hundreds column only
		22. Add a three-digit number to a three-digit number with regrouping from the tens and hundreds columns
		23. Add a four-digit number to a four-digit number with regrouping in one to three columns
		24. Subtract two four-digit numbers—no regrouping
		25. Subtract a one-digit number from a two-digit number with regrouping
		26. Subtract a two-digit number from a two-digit number with regrouping
		27. Subtract a two-digit number from a three-digit number with regrouping from tens column only
		28. Subtract a two-digit number from a three-digit number with regrouping from the hundreds column only

Note. M, mastery; I, instructional; F, frustrational.

Source. Reprinted by permission, Allentown School District, Allentown, Pennsylvania.

TABLE 5   Placement Criteria for Direct Assessment of Math

		Criterion	
		Median Digits Correct per Minute	Median Digits Incorrect per Minute
Grades 1–3	Frustration	0–9	8+
	Instructional	10–19	3–7
	Mastery	20+	≤2
Grade 4+	Frustration	0–19	8+
	Instructional	20–39	3–7
	Mastery	40+	52

Source. The data are from Deno and Mirkin (1977). The table is reproduced from "Behavioral assessment of academic skills" by E. S. Shapiro and F. E. Lentz, Jr., 1986, in T. R. Kratochwill (Ed.), *Advances in School Psychology* (Vol. 5, p. 124). Hillsdale, NJ: Erlbaum. Copyright 1986 by Lawrence Erlbaum Associates. Reprinted by permission.

student for regrouping (top of tens column) is not counted. Complex multiplication and long-division problems create special issues in scoring. All digits above and below the answer line are counted, but not digits written by students for regrouping. If a student multiplies incorrectly but then adds correctly, the digits added correctly are scored as correct, even though they obviously are not the right answer to the problem. Note the following two examples:

(a)	(b)
34	34
× 55	× 55
170	170
180	180
1970	1870

Example a has one digit incorrect, whereas b has two digits incorrect since in b the student multiplied incorrectly and then added incorrectly. The student's score for examples a and b would be 9 and 10, respectively. Thus, a student is not penalized for performing operations correctly but computations incorrectly. However, as seen in example b, if a student multiplies incorrectly and then adds incorrectly, the numbers that were not summed correctly are counted as errors. Also note that in multiplication, if correctly aligned, placeholders are counted as digits correct. Total digits correct and incorrect per minute are calculated.

As in reading, the procedures described for math are used in this way when conducting an initial assessment of math skills. Once the particular computational objectives in need of instruction are identified, repeated probes of this specific objective can be developed and administered to evaluate student progress toward mastering that objective.

Spelling

Assessment of spelling is similar to procedures employed for assessing basal word list reading. From the basal spelling text, three sets of 20 words each are taken randomly from each level of the series. Beginning at the level where a student is placed, words are dictated to the child at a rate of one every 7 seconds for 2 minutes. All three lists of words are administerd at each level of the series, using the median scores across the three probes to obtain a score for the level. Testing across levels continues either upward or downward until the student scores 20 to 39 letter sequences correct per 2 minutes if in grades 1 or 2, or 40 to 59 letter sequences correct per 2 minutes if in grades 3 to 6.

Two measures are obtained for spelling. One uses letters-in-a-sequence correct. The procedure for scoring spelling in this way is as follows. A "phantom" character is placed before and after each word. For example, the word ⎽ B U T T E R ⎽ has seven possible letter sequences. If the word BUTTER was spelled as:

⎽ B U T E R ⎽ it would have five letter sequences correct;

_ B U T T A R _ it would have five letter sequences correct;

_ B A T T A R _ it would have three letter sequences correct.

Students are given one point for each pair of correctly scored adjacent letters. The primary value of this form of scoring over percent words correct is the sensitivity that the measure has to changes in spelling behavior. In the example above, a student who first spells BUTTER as BATTAR, then as BUTER, and then correctly, clearly has made progress across spelling sessions. Yet a percent correct score would show no change across the first two sessions.

Although letters-in-a-sequence per minute are an important measure, it is suggested that percent words correct also be reported. Many times, it has been found that students show substantial improvements in letters-in-a-sequence but still fail to improve overall scores on weekly spelling tests. This is an important finding and may have implications for instructional programming.

Written Language

Unlike reading, math, and spelling, few schools have a particular curriculum for written language. As such, assessment of written language does not specifically emanate directly from curriculum materials. Written language can, however, be an indicator of many types of problems in areas such as grammar, spelling, handwriting, and so on. Given the ease of assessing this skill, it becomes a very useful and valuable part of the assessment of academic performance.

Written language is assessed by having students write a series of short stories in response to story starters. After giving the story starter to the student, they are asked to take a minute and think about what they will write. After 1 minute, the child is told to begin writing and is timed for 3 minutes. If they stop writing before the 3 minutes end, students are encouraged to continue until the time is up.

The number of words written correctly are counted. Correct is defined as words that can be recognized (even if misspelled). Capitalization and punctuation are ignored and the rate of words written correctly are calculated per 3 minutes. Criteria for performance can be compared to data reported from various sources reported in the literature; however, it may be just as easy to determine a local sample by administering the same probe to other children in a group format. The written language sample can also be scored for spelling, punctuation, capitalization, and grammatical usage.

USE OF DATA AND LIMITATIONS

Many of the ways in which data are collected from a curriculum-based assessment can and have been used have been discussed previously. Space limitations prohibit an exhaustive discussion of the literature which strongly supports the uses of CBA. Interested readers are directed to several resources which extensively discuss and describe these possibilities (e.g., Deno, 1985; Shapiro, 1987, 1989; Shinn, 1988, 1989). Despite the very positive and favorable reception that CBA has received in both the research literature as well as clinical practice, there are several limitations of the method that need to be recognized. These can be seen as problems that are conceptual, practical, and methodological.

In looking for a conceptual framework within which CBA can be placed, it seems most appropriately viewed as a behavioral approach to assessing academic skills. Shapiro (1989) draws a parallel between traditional and behavioral assessment for nonacademic problems (e.g., Hartmann, Roper, & Bradford, 1979), and norm-referenced and curriculum-based assessment of academic problems. Clearly, the focus on behavioral performance within the natural setting, observing actual behavior of student's academic problems rather then underlying constructs (such as perceptual skills), and remediation aimed at improving observable academic skills by concentrating on antecedent/consequent relationships, places CBA within a behavioral framework. Unfortunately, CBA has been validated primarily using traditional psychometric properties such as concurrent validity and test–retest reliability (e.g., Shinn, Tindal, & Stein, 1988). Although useful in providing social validation, the methodologies for evaluating behavioral assessment measures are quite different, concentrating primarily on how behavior differs when assessed across various aspects of the environment such as setting or person (see Cone, 1987, for a detailed discussion). There is currently little research which has carefully evaluated CBA in terms of its accuracy or generalizability across behavioral dimensions. Indeed, a recent study by Derr and Shapiro (1989) suggests that oral reading rates of third- and fourth-grade students may vary based on who assesses the student, where the assessment occurs, and whether students are aware they are being timed.

On the practical dimension, there are several problems of acceptability which have not been carefully examined. Just how accepted is this method by psychologists and teachers? To what degree will teachers view a brief oral reading rate measure as an indication of academic progress? How much responsibility will school psychologists have in assessing academic skills? In some settings, this role has been delegated to others, such as educational consultants. How acceptable will results based on these measures be to education professionals unfamiliar with assessment instruments that are not norm-referenced? Do these measures really lead to better intervention decisions? Again, all of these and many more questions are currently unanswered and in need of extensive research.

Finally, there are still methodological questions remaining about CBA. For example, the data base supporting mathematics is limited. Although Deno and his colleagues have provided extensive data for using the measures of reading, spelling, and written language, there has been little support for effective assessment of math. Procedures employed and described in this chapter have been useful in clinical practice; however, substantial research is needed to fully support how they are being employed. Additionally, the linkage of CBA assessment and intervention procedures is also in need of more extensive research. Despite positive outcome findings in two meta-analyses (Fuchs, & Fuchs, 1986a, 1986b), there remains limited research directly evaluating the treatment validity of CBA.

Like all new procedures, there are dangers of overacceptance and abuse. CBA appears to be here to stay. The methodology appears useful for prereferral intervention planning, it appears to be useful in providing a monitoring device for assessing the progress of students, and it may be useful in many other types of educational decision making. Caution is still suggested, however, and we need to proceed slowly in adopting and embracing CBA into the standard practices of school psychologists. With careful and measured enthusiasm, it is sincerely hoped that we will achieve the maximum value possible by integrating CBA methodology into current practices of school psychology.

REFERENCES

Alessi, G., & Kaye, J. H. (1983). *Behavioral assessment for school psychologists.* Kent, OH: National Association of School Psychologists.

Armbruster, B. B., Stevens, J. R., & Rosenshine, B. (1977). *Analyzing content coverage and emphasis: A study of three curricula and two tests* (Tech. Rep. No. 25). Urbana–Champaign: University of Illinois, Center for the Study of Reading.

Bergan, J. R. (1977). *Behavioral consultation.* Columbus, OH: Charles E. Merrill.

Blankenship, C. S. (1985). Using curriculum-based assessment data to make instructional decisions. *Exceptional Children, 52,* 233–238.

Blankenship, C. S., & Lilly, M. S. (1981). *Mainstreaming students with learning and behavior problems: Techniques for the classroom teacher.* New York: Holt, Rinehart and Winston.

Cone, J. (1987). Psychometric considerations and the multiple models of behavioral assessment. In M. Hersen & A. Bellack (Eds.), *Behavioral assessment: A practical handbook* (2nd ed., pp. 42–66). Elmsford, NY: Pergamon Press.

Coulter, W. A. (1985). Implementing curriculum-based assessment: Considerations for pupil appraisal professionals. *Exceptional Children, 52,* 277–281.

Deno, S. (1985). Curriculum-based measurement: The emerging alternative. *Exceptional Children, 52,* 219–232.

Deno, S. L., Marston, D., & Mirkin, P. (1982). Valid measurement procedures for continuous evaluation of written expression. *Exceptional Children, 48,* 368–371.

Deno, S., & Mirkin, P. K. (1977). *Data-based program modification: A manual.* Reston, VA: Council for Exceptional Children. Deno, S., Mirkin, P. K., & Chiang, B. (1982). Identifying valid measures of reading. *Exceptional Children, 49,* 36–45.

Deno, S., Mirkin, P., Lowry, L., & Kuehnle, K. (1980). *Relationships among simple measures of spelling and performance on standardized achievement tests* (Research Rep. No. 21). Minneapolis: University of Minnesota, Institute for Research on Learning Disabilities. (ERIC Document No. 197 508)

Derr, T. F., & Shapiro, E. S. (1989). A behavioral evaluation of curriculum-based assessment of reading. *Journal of Psychoeducational Assessment, 7,* 148–160.

Fuchs, L. S., & Fuchs, D. (1986a). Curriculum-based assessment of progress toward long-term and short-term goals. *Journal of Special Education, 20,* 69–82.

Fuchs, L. S., & Fuchs, D. (1986b). Effects of systematic formative evaluation: A meta-analysis. *Exceptional Children, 53,* 199–208.

Galagan, J. E. (1985). Psychoeducational testing: Turn

out the lights, the party's over. *Exceptional Children, 52,* 288–299.

German, G., & Tindal, G. (1985). An application of curriculum-based assessment: The use of direct and repeated measurement. *Exceptional Children, 52,* 244–265.

Gickling, E. E. (1977). Controlling academic and social performance using an instructional delivery model. *Programs for the emotionally handicapped: Administrative considerations.* Washington, DC: Coordination Office of Regional Resource Centers/Mideast Regional Resource Center.

Gickling, E. E., & Havertape, J. F. (1981). Curriculum-based assessment. In J. A. Tucker (Ed.), *Non-test based assessment.* Minneapolis: University of Minnesota, National School Psychology Inservice Network.

Gickling, E. E., & Thompson, V. P. (1985). A personal view of curriculum-based assessment. *Exceptional Children, 52,* 205–218.

Good, R. H., & Salvia, J. (1988). Curriculum bias in published, norm-referenced reading tests: Demonstrable effects. *School Psychology Review, 17,* 51–60.

Hartman, D. P., Roper, B. L., & Bradford, D. C. (1979). Some relationships between behavioral and traditional assessment. *Journal of Behavioral Assessment, 1,* 3–21.

Idol, L., Nevin, A., & Paolucci-Whitcomb, P. (1986). *Models of curriculum-based assessment.* Rockville, MD: Aspen.

Idol-Maestas, L. (1983). *Special educator's consultation handbook.* Rockville, MD: Aspen.

Jenkins, J., & Pany, D. (1978). Standardized achievement tests: How useful for special education? *Exceptional Children, 44,* 448–453.

Leinhardt, G., & Seewald, A. (1981). Overlap: What's tested, what's taught? *Journal of Educational Measurement, 18,* 85–96.

Lovitt, T., & Hansen, C. (1976). Round one—placing the child in the right reader. *Journal of Learning Disabilities, 9,* 347–353.

Marston, D., Fuchs, D., & Deno, S. (1986). Measuring pupil progress: A comparison of standardized achievement tests and curriculum-related measures. *Diagnostique, 11,* 77–90.

Marston, D., & Magnusson, D. (1985). Implementing curriculum-based measurement in special and regular education settings. *Exceptional Children, 52,* 266–276.

Mirkin, P., Deno, S., Tindal, G., & Kuehnle, K. (1982). Frequency of measurement and data utilization strategies as factors in standardized behavior assessment of academic skills. *Journal of Behavioral Assessment, 4* 361–370.

O'Leary, K. D., Romanczyk, R. G., Kass, R. E., Dietz, A., & Santogrossi, D. A. (1979). *Procedures for classroom observation of teachers and children.* Stony Brook: SUNY at Stony Brook, Psychology Department.

Salmon-Cox, L. (1981). Teachers and standardized achievement tests: What's really happening? *Phi Delta Kappan, 62,* 631–634.

Saudargas, R. A., & Creed, V. (1980). *State-event classroom observation system.* Knoxville: University of Tennessee, Department of Psychology.

Saudargas, R. A., & Lentz, F. E. (1986). Estimating percent of time and rate via direct observation: A suggested observational procedure and format. *School Psychology Review, 15,* 36–48.

Shapiro, E. S. (1987). *Behavioral assessment in school psychology.* Hillsdale, NJ: Lawrence Erlbaum.

Shapiro, E. S. (1989). *Academic skills problems: Direct assessment and intervention.* New York: Guilford Press.

Shapiro, E. S., & Derr, T. F. (1987). An examination of overlap between reading curricula and standardized achievement tests. *Journal of Special Education, 21,* 59–67.

Shapiro, E. S., & Lentz, F. E. (1985). Assessing academic behavior: A behavioral approach. *School Psychology Review, 14,* 325–338.

Shapiro, E. S., & Lentz, F. E. (1986). Behavioral assessment of academic behavior. In T. R. Kratochwill (Ed.), *Advances in school psychology* (Vol. 5, pp. 87–139). Hillsdale, NJ: Lawrence Erlbaum.

Shinn, M. (1988). Development of curriculum-based local norms for use in special education decision-making. *School Psychology Review, 17,* 61–80.

Shinn, M. (Ed.). (1989). *Curriculum-based measurement: Assessing special children.* New York: Guilford Press.

Shinn, M., Tindal, G. A. & Stein, S. (1988). Curriculum-based measurement and the identification of mildly handicapped students: A research review. *Professional School Psychology, 3,* 69–85.

Slate, J. R., & Saudargas, R. A. (1986a). Differences in learning disabled and average students' classroom behaviors. *Learning Disability Quarterly, 9,* 61–67.

Slate, J. R., & Saudargas, R. A. (1986b). Differences in the classroom behaviors of behaviorally disordered and regular class children. *Behavioral Disorders, 11,* 45–53.

Wesson, C., King, R. P., & Deno, S. L. (1984). Direct and frequent measurement of student performance: If it's good for us, why don't we use it? *Learning Disability Quarterly, 7,* 45–48.

White, O., & Haring, N. (1980). *Exceptional teaching* (2nd ed.). Columbus, OH; Charles E. Merrill.

Yesseldyke, J. E. (1983). Generalizations from five years of research on psychoeducational assessment and decision-making. *NASP Communique, 12*(1), 7.

Ysseldyke, J., Thrulow, M., Graden, J., Wesson, C., Deno, S., & Algozzine, B. (1982). Generalizations form five years of research on assessment and decision making. *Exceptional Education Quarterly, 4,* 75–93.

16

CRITERION-REFERENCED TESTING METHODS AND PRACTICES

RONALD K. HAMBLETON
University of Massachusetts at Amherst

Criterion-referenced testing is one type of testing that seems to be especially well suited for addressing many of the kinds of student assessments in which schools have an interest. In fact, many school districts are using criterion-referenced tests, and nearly all states have mandated criterion-referenced testing programs (sometimes referred to as "basic skills" or "competency" tests) (Jaeger, 1989). Because of the newness of the criterion-referenced testing area, however, and the proliferation of technical contributions, it has been difficult for test users to keep abreast of developments. This is especially true for professional groups such as school psychologists for whom the field of educational testing is only part of their responsibilities. Complicating matters for school psychologists is the fact that over its short history the field of criterion-referenced testing has been hampered by some confusing terminology and some faulty methodological contributions. At the same time, fortunately, substantial progress has been made toward the establishment of a practical and usable criterion-referenced testing technology (Berk, 1984; Hambleton, in press; Popham, 1978c). There is now sufficient technical knowledge (a) to build criterion-referenced tests, (b) to assess their

psychometric properties, and (c) to use and report test score information.

This chapter was prepared to provide school psychologists and others who work with tests in school settings with up-to-date information on the advances in criterion-referenced testing methods and practices. Except for one section in which norm-referenced achievement tests are compared to criterion-referenced achievement tests, norm-referenced tests are not considered in this chapter. No implicit criticism of norm-referenced achievement testing should be inferred. The two types of tests are designed to achieve different purposes; both purposes are important, and therefore both types of tests can play important roles in school testing programs.

DEFINITIONS, USES, AND INTERPRETATIONS

One of the first references to criterion-referenced testing appeared in a three-page paper by Robert Glaser in the *American Psychologist* in 1963. Over 900 papers have been published since 1963 on the topic and the face of educational testing has been changed dramatically. Glaser (1963), and later Popham and Husek (1969), were interested in an approach to testing that would provide information necessary for making a variety of individual and programmatic decisions arising in connection with specific objectives or competencies. Norm-referenced tests were seen as limited in terms of providing the desired kinds of information.

Standard procedures for testing and measurement within a norm-referenced framework are well known to educators, but these procedures are less appropriate when the question being asked concerns what examinees can and cannot do (Glaser, 1963; Hambleton & Novick, 1973; Popham & Husek, 1969). Norm-referenced tests are constructed, principally, to facilitate the comparison of individuals (or groups) with one another or with respect to a norm group on the trait measured by the test. Criterion-referenced tests (or, as they are sometimes called, "proficiency tests," "mastery tests," "competency tests," or "basic skills tests") are constructed to permit the interpretation of individual (and group) test scores in relation to a set of clearly defined objectives or competencies.

Many definitions of "criterion-referenced tests" have been proposed in the literature (see, e.g., Nitko, 1980; Popham, 1978c). In fact, Gray (1978) reported the existence of 57 different definitions! The one adopted in this chapter is a slight modification of a definition offered by Popham (1978c): "A criterion-referenced test is constructed to assess the performance levels of examinees in relation to a set of well-defined objectives (or competencies)." Popham's definition is probably the most widely accepted definition in the testing field. Four points about the definition require explanation. First, terms such as objectives, competencies, and skills can be used interchangeably. Second, each objective measured in a criterion-referenced test must be well defined. This means that the content or behaviors defining the objective must be clearly described. Well-defined objectives facilitate the process of writing test items and enhance the validity of test score interpretation. Item writing is improved because well-defined objectives provide a framework within which item writers and item reviewers can work. Validity is enhanced because of the clarity of the content or behavior domains to which test scores are referenced. The breadth and complexity of each domain of content or behaviors defining an objective can (and usually does) vary, but the domain must

be clearly defined. The purpose of the test will influence the appropriate breadth of domains. For example, diagnostic tests are organized around narrowly defined objectives. Year-end assessments, on the other hand, will normally be carried out with more broadly defined objectives.

Third, when more than one objective is measured in a criterion-referenced test, the test items are organized into nonoverlapping subtests corresponding to the objectives, and examinee performance is reported on each of the objectives. Fourth, the definition does not include a reference to a cutoff score or standard. It is common to set a standard of performance for each objective measured in the test and/or on the overall test score and interpret examinee performance in relation to it. But descriptive interpretations of scores such as "Student A answered correctly 70% of the items in the domain of content which addresses knowledge of capital cities of states" are also made and standards are not used in this type of score interpretation. That a standard need not be set on a criterion-referenced test may come as a surprise to some people who have mistakenly assumed that the word "criterion" in "criterion-referenced test" refers to a "standard" or "cutoff score." In fact, *criterion* is a word used by both Glaser (1963) and Popham and Husek (1969) to refer to the domain of content or behavior to which test scores are referenced.

A diagram representing a typical criterion-referenced test, examinee test scores, and associated mastery decisions is shown in Figure 1. Interestingly, the diagram appropriately describes several diverse applications: (a) the classroom teacher who wishes to make a diagnostic assessment of student performance, (b) a school district interested in year-end assessments, or (c) any schools that must certify students as qualified to receive high school diplomas. The differences among the three applications (and other applications as well) occur in the choice, breadth, and complexity of objectives, in the number of objectives and items included in tests, and in the minimum standards of examinee performance.

Figure 1 highlights three additional points about criterion-referenced tests:

1. The number of objectives measured in a criterion-referenced test will (in general) vary from one test to the next.
2. The number of test items measuring each

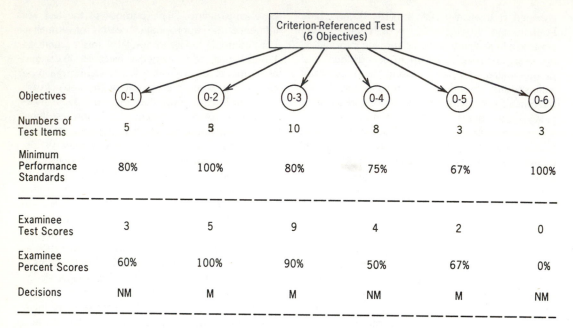

	0-1	0-2	0-3	0-4	0-5	0-6
Objectives	0-1	0-2	0-3	0-4	0-5	0-6
Numbers of Test Items	5	5	10	8	3	3
Minimum Performance Standards	80%	100%	80%	75%	67%	100%
Examinee Test Scores	3	5	9	4	2	0
Examinee Percent Scores	60%	100%	90%	50%	67%	0%
Decisions	NM	M	M	NM	M	NM

Figure 1. Diagram depicting a typical criterion-referenced test, examinee test scores and associated mastery decisions.

objective and the value of the minimum standard will (in general) vary from one objective to the next.

3. One method for making a mastery/nonmastery decision involves the comparison of an examinee's percent (or proportion-correct) score on the objective in question with the corresponding minimum standard. If an examinee's percent score is equal to or greater than the standard, the examinee is a "master (M)"; otherwise, the examinee is a "nonmaster (NM)."

Confusion has existed in the educational testing literature over the differences among three kinds of tests: criterion-referenced tests, domain-referenced tests, and objectives-referenced tests. The definition for a criterion-referenced test offered earlier is similar to one Millman (1974) and others proposed for a domain-referenced test. There are no essential differences between criterion-referenced and domain-referenced tests if Popham's definition (or a similar one) of a criterion-referenced test is adopted. However, the expression *domain-referenced test* is less likely to be misunderstood than the term *criterion-referenced test*. Why continue then to use the term *criterion-referenced test*? Popham (1978c), one of the leaders in the criterion-referenced testing field, offers one excellent reason. It is that there is considerable public support for "criterion-referenced tests" and therefore it would be undesirable and a waste of time if another campaign had to be initiated by educators for "domain-referenced tests."

Objectives-referenced tests are tests consisting of items that are matched to objectives. The primary distinction between criterion-referenced tests and objectives-referenced tests is as follows: In a criterion-referenced test the items are organized into clusters, with each cluster of items serving as a representative set of items from a clearly defined content domain measuring an objective. With an objectives-referenced test, no clear domain of content is specified, and items are not considered to be representative of a content domain. Differences between the two types of tests on the matter of "content domain specification" have one very important implication for the type of test score generalizations that can be made from each test. Since a criterion-referenced test consists of representative samples of items from well-defined domains of content, valid inferences about examinee performance in those domains can be made from examinee test performance. With objectives-referenced tests, domains of content are not clearly specified, so score interpretations must be in terms of the specific items included in the tests.

The primary purpose of norm-referenced tests and that of criterion-referenced tests differ substantially, so approaches to test development, test evaluation, and test score usage will differ as well. Some people have mistakenly argued that there is only one type of achievement test from which both norm-referenced and criterion-referenced interpretations are made. It cannot be disputed that norm-referenced interpretations may be drawn from scores on a criterion-referenced test. Also, "weak" criterion-referenced interpretations (interpretations without generalizations) or objectives-referenced interpretations can certainly be made with item scores from a norm-referenced test. But neither of these two interpretations is optimal. A criterion-referenced test is not built to produce a heterogeneous distribution of test scores (although it may result anyway), and therefore norm-referenced interpretations from a criterion-referenced test will be less stable (typically) than norm-referenced interpretations from a norm-referenced test. Similarly, a norm-referenced test is not built around objectives that are as carefully defined as objectives are with criterion-referenced tests. Also, it cannot be assumed, because of norm-referenced item selection strategies, that items on a norm-referenced test represent the domains from which they are sampled. Clearly, then, criterion-referenced score interpretations from norm-referenced tests will be less suitable than from criterion-referenced tests.

In summary, criterion-referenced tests can be used to make norm-referenced interpretations and norm-referenced tests can be used to make criterion-referenced interpretations, but neither use will be completely satisfactory. Norm-referenced and criterion-referenced interpretations are best made from tests constructed specifically to facilitate the desired kind of interpretations, that is, norm-referenced tests and criterion-referenced tests, respectively.

COMPARISON OF NORM-REFERENCED AND CRITERION-REFERENCED ACHIEVEMENT TESTS

Two points concerning the comparison are appropriate to highlight at the outset: (a) both criterion-referenced tests and norm-referenced tests have important roles to play in providing data for deci-

sion making; and (b) what differences exist are significant, but the two kinds of tests have much in common. On the latter point, it would be a rare person indeed who could label tests as criterion-referenced or norm-referenced from a review of the test items only. The fact is that the same item formats (e.g., multiple-choice, true-false, and matching) are used in both; both kinds of tests can be standardized (i.e., the conditions under which the tests are administered can be tightly defined or controlled); and test score norms can be produced for each type of test (Popham, 1976).

The results of a comparison of criterion-referenced tests and norm-referenced tests in seven areas are summarized in Table 1. It is clear from the table that there are differences in each of the areas, but several of these differences are especially important. First, a norm-referenced achievement test consists of test items that are from the content areas defined in the test blueprint *and* that contribute substantially to test score variability. Test scores are interpreted by comparing examinee test performance to the performance of examinees in clearly defined norm groups. A criterion-referenced test, on the other hand, consists of test items that sample, in a representative way, well-defined domains of content, and examinee test performance (often on an objective-by-objective basis) is interpreted in relation to the two endpoints on the percentage scale (0% and 100%) or, more commonly, in relation to a standard of performance or cutoff score on the test score (percentage) scale.

Second, both norm-referenced test and criterion-referenced test developers must prepare clear test blueprints. It is common for developers of both norm-referenced tests and criterion-referenced tests to prepare objectives to further define the content area of interest. But it is also true that the objectives for criterion-referenced tests must meet higher standards of clarity. Thus, in the area of content specifications, the difference between norm-referenced tests and criterion-referenced tests is in the degree to which content is clarified.

Finally, item statistics are used differently with the two types of tests. Norm-referenced test developers build tests to be content valid, but they also select items because of their desirable statistical characteristics. A heterogeneous distribution of examinee test scores is essential if a norm-referenced test is to serve its purpose, that is, produce reliable and valid norm-referenced inter-

TABLE 1 Comparison of Norm-Referenced and Criterion-Referenced Achievement Tests°

Area	Norm-Referenced Tests	Criterion-Referenced Tests
Purpose	A norm-referenced test is constructed specifically to facilitate comparisons among examinees on the content area measured by the test. Age-, grade-, percentile-, and standard-score norms are available to assist in the accomplishment of the purpose. In addition, since test items can be referenced to particular objectives, objective-referenced score interpretations are possible.	A criterion-referenced test is constructed to assess an examinee's level of performance in relation to each of a set of objectives or competencies measured by the test. Scores may be used (a) for descriptive purposes, (b) to make decisions, and (c) to evaluate program effectiveness. Examinees (or groups) can be compared with one another but this is *not* a primary use of the scores.
Test development	A test blueprint is prepared and items are written to fit the blueprint. An important factor in item selection is the statistical properties of the test items (item difficulty and discrimination). In general, items of moderate difficulty (*p* values in the range .30 to .70) and high discriminating power (point biserial correlations over .30) are the most likely to be selected for inclusion in a test because they contribute substantially to test score variance. Test reliability and validity will, generally, be higher when test score variance is high.	In addition to a test blueprint, very clear objective statements (sometimes called "domain specifications" or "expanded objectives") are prepared along with test items that are valid indicators of the objectives. Items are only deleted from the available item pool if they are *not* judged to measure the objective they were written to measure. "Representative" samples of test items are usually selected for inclusion in the test. Item statistics may be used to construct parallel tests or to design a test to optimally discriminate in the region of a standard of performance on the test score scale.
Measurement scales	The norm-referenced test score scale is anchored in the middle (the average level of group performance).	For criterion-referenced test score scales, the anchor points are two in number, and located at the ends of the scale (0% and 100%).

	Norm-referenced tests	Criterion-referenced tests
Test score generalizability	There is seldom interest in making generalizations from norm-referenced achievement test scores. Usually, the job is completed when test scores are compared to appropriate norms tables. Generalizations from examinee performance on aptitude and personality measures are, however, of considerably more interest than those from achievement tests (e.g., it is common to generalize from a WISC-R score to "intelligence"). Still, while generalizations from nonachievement test scores are of considerable interest and import, the primary basis for test score interpretations is normative.	With criterion-referenced test scores, the matter of generalizability is important. Seldom would anyone be content to interpret an examinee's score in terms of the *specific* items on a test. (Incidentally, this is all that can be appropriately done with scores obtained from *objectives-referenced tests*.) If the objective measured by a test is clear, and if items are selected to be representative of the content domain measuring the objective, examinee test performance on a set of items included in the test can be generalized to test performance in the larger domain of behaviors. *Strong* criterion-referenced test score interpretations of the kind just described are usually of interest to criterion-referenced test users.
Specificity of test score information	A norm-referenced test score provides a summary of a broadly defined area of achievement.	Users of criterion-referenced tests are endorsing the notion that important outcomes can be separated into discrete categories (referred to as objectives, skills, or competencies).
Reliability and validity	Test–retest, parallel-form, and internal consistency measures are useful ways for assessing score reliability. Approaches to validity depend on the intended uses of the scores.	Measures such as standard error of measurement and decision consistency are useful ways for assessing score reliability. Best methods for validity assessment depend on the intended uses of the scores. Since criterion-referenced test scores are used differently from norm-referenced scores, the kinds of validity investigations will differ also.
Norms	Essential for norm-referenced tests.	Norms can be of value when interpreting individual and group scores. For example, norms can be useful in setting realistic standards for examinee performance.

Note. All criterion-referenced tests are achievement tests. Some norm-referenced tests are too. The comparisons in this table are between norm-referenced and criterion-referenced *achievement* tests.

1. Preliminary considerations in building a test.
   (a) State test purposes.
   (b) Specify content areas (in the form of a test blueprint).
   (c) Identify the groups to be measured.
   (d) Specify the amount of time, money, and expertise necessary to complete the project.
   (e) Prepare a list of activities with a time frame and assign staff.

2. Preparation and review of objectives.

3. Additional test planning.
   (a) Select objectives to be measured in the test.
   (b) Determine the approximate test length and the number of test items per objective.
   (c) Identify item writers.

4. Preparation of test items to measure the objectives and initial item editing.

5. Assessment of content validity and reliability.
   (a) Use content and measurement specialists to assess:
       (i) Item-objective congruence.
       (ii) Technical quality of items.
       (iii) Item representativeness.
       (iv) Item bias.

(b) Field test the items to:
    (i) Detect flawed items.
    (ii) Check for bias.
    (iii) Determine item difficulty levels and discrimination indexes.
    (iv) Determine consistency of scores and/or decisions.

6. Revisions to test items.

7. Assembly of the test.
   (a) Determine the test length and number of items per objective.
   (b) Select items.
   (c) Assess item representativeness.
   (d) Prepare directions and practice questions.
   (e) Prepare layouts and test booklets.
   (f) Prepare scoring keys and answer sheets.

8. Selection and implementation of a standard-setting method.

9. Test administration.

10. Assessment of test score reliability and validity; compilation of test score norms (optional).

11. Preparation of a test administrator's manual and a technical manual.

12. Ongoing collection of additional technical information and technical manual updates.

Figure 2. Steps in building a criterion-referenced test.

pretations. The likelihood of the purpose being achieved is enhanced when items with moderate difficulty levels and moderate-to-high discrimination indices are selected. The criterion-referenced test developer, in contrast, uses item statistics mainly in the test development process to detect flawed items. Also, item statistics may be used in item selection when parallel forms of a test are being built or if a test is being constructed to discriminate optimally at a particular point (or points) on a test score scale. In the latter case, a more effective test is obtained when items are selected that maximally discriminate in the region on the test score scale where a standard is located

(see, e.g., Hambleton, 1989; Hambleton & de Gruijter, 1983). Readers are referred to Ebel (1978b), Mehrens and Ebel (1979), and Popham 1978b) for additional insights into the distinctions between norm-referenced tests and criterion-referenced tests.

TEST DEVELOPMENT

To provide a framework for reviewing the advances in criterion-referenced testing technology, a set of 12 steps are offered in this section for building criterion-referenced tests. The steps presented in Figure 2 are adapted from a model prepared by Hambleton and Simon (1980) and some earlier work by Hambleton and Eignor (1979). The care and attention with which each step is carried out should depend on the purpose of the test. For example, it would be unreasonable to expect a group of classroom teachers preparing a test for their own use to pursue each of the steps in depth. Too much time and money would be needed. On the other hand, when a test is to be used for determining high school graduation, for example, the steps should be carried out in considerable depth and the total process may take a year or more to complete properly.

Some brief remarks on each of the 12 steps follow:

Step 1. Test planning includes specifying test purposes; test content; groups to be assessed; time, money, and expertise available to construct the test; and a list of activities or steps for building the test.

Step 2. Individuals (or a committee) working from the general content guidelines prepared in Step 1 must prepare a set of well-defined objectives. Each objective description must clearly define the content or behavior domain if the description is to be of help to item writers and (later) test score users. After the objectives are drafted, they must be reviewed for clarity and completeness.

Step 3. If more objectives are available from Step 2 than can be measured in the test, a selection process may be implemented. Alternatively, some of the objectives can be combined to produce fewer more broadly defined objectives. Also, an estimate is needed of the number of items that should be written to measure each objective, and item writers must be located.

Step 4. Items are prepared to measure the objectives. Prior to sending them on for a formal review, it is useful for item writers to carry out an initial editing of their own work.

Step 5. A systematic review of the test items by content and measurement specialists is carried out and the test items are piloted with groups similar in characteristics to populations for whom the test is intended. A review of items for ethnic, racial, and sex bias and stereotyping is also carried out.

Step 6. Based on the data from Step 5, additional editing of the test items is carried out, and irreparably flawed items are discarded.

Step 7. Assembly of the test is carried out (or tests, if parallel forms are needed).

Step 8. A method for setting a minimum standard of performance on each objective (or on the overall test score) must be selected and implemented.

Step 9. The test is ready for administration.

Step 10. Reliability and validity information must be collected, and test score norms (if desired) are compiled on appropriately selected samples of examinees.

Step 11. Administration and technical manuals must be prepared for the more important tests. In the case of commercially available standardized criterion-referenced tests, the manuals are of considerable value in assessing test quality and test usefulness in particular settings.

Step 12. The psychometric properties of a test are not static and therefore it is important over time to continue to assess the technical characteristics of the test and the scores derived from it with groups of examinees for whom the test is intended.

Berk (1984), Hambleton (in press), Hambleton and Eignor (1979), Millman (1974), and Popham (1978c) provide additional details for building tests. Technical advances associated with several of the steps are considered in the next section.

TECHNICAL ADVANCES

Seven advances in criterion-referenced testing technology are considered in this section: objectives, content validity, reliability, item selection, test length, standard setting, and construct validity.

Objectives

Mager's (1962) classic book on preparing behavioral objectives had a tremendous impact on education in the 1960s and 1970s. Few of us at one time or another have not read the book or at least had the opportunity to write a few behavioral objectives. Teachers have been trained to write them; curricula have been defined by them and objectives-referenced tests have been constructed to measure them. Behavioral objectives are relatively easy to write and have contributed substantially to the organization of curricula, but they do *not* lead to unequivocal determination of the domains of content or behaviors that describe the objectives. For example, consider the following: "The student will identify the main ideas in passages at the second-grade readability level." Are passages on any topic acceptable? How long should the passages be? Should the passages be narrative, descriptive, or expository in nature? Consider another objective, "The student will identify the tone or emotion expressed in a paragraph." Whether someone planned to teach the objective or to write test items to measure it, several points would need to be clarified first. Which tones or emotions? How long should the paragraphs be? At what readability level should the paragraphs be written? Also, a test item writer might wonder about the "fineness" of discriminations that are to be required of a student. Popham (1974) referred to tests built from behavioral objectives as "cloud-referenced tests." This description is appropriate.

The production of test items to measure objectives cannot be handled efficiently when the content domains are unclearly defined. Also, when the domains of content are unclear, it is not possible to ensure that representative samples of test items from each item domain are drawn.

Domain specifications are one important new development in criterion-referenced testing (Popham, 1978c). A domain specification is prepared to clarify the intended content or behaviors specified by an objective. Test users find domain specifications helpful because the domains of content or behaviors to which test scores are referenced is

more clear. For the item writer, domain specifications provide much needed clarifications on appropriate content for preparing test items. Domains come in at least two varieties (Gray, 1978; Nitko, 1980). In an *ordered domain,* the subskills that describe an objective are arranged in some meaningful way, such as in a learning hierarchy. One of the advantages of an ordered domain is that statements of examinee performance in relation to the domain can be made from a test that may measure only a few of the subskills. In an *unordered domain,* and this is the more common of the two, the content or behaviors defining the domain are specified but relationships among the component parts are not specified.

Popham suggested four steps for the preparation of a domain specification. The first involves the preparation of a general description. The general description can be a behavioral objective, a detailed description of the objective, or a short cryptic descriptor. Next, a sample test item is prepared. The sample item will reveal the desired format and help to clarify the appropriate domain of test items. The third step is usually the most difficult. It is necessary to specify the content or behaviors included in a domain. Occasionally, for the purpose of clarification, it is also desirable to indicate which content or behaviors are not included in a domain specification. Characteristics of response alternatives or response limits are specified in the final step. An example of a domain specification in the mathematics area is shown in Figure 3. Work by IOX Associates in Los Angeles, the California Assessment Program, the Dallas Independent School District, and Educational Development Corporation, among others, shows clearly that domain specifications of a high quality can be prepared in a variety of subject areas for use at different grade levels by groups of individuals with varying degrees of content and technical expertise. Additional guidelines for preparing domain specifications and a variety of examples are provided by Hambleton (in press), Hambleton and Eignor (1979) and Popham (1978c, 1980).

To date, most of the domain specifications that have been prepared utilize objective item formats (e.g., multiple choice). Examples of domain specifications that are not are presented in Hambleton (in press). Two matters that require special attention when nonobjective item formats are used are (a) clear directions for administering the test and (b) a clearly developed plan for scoring examinee performance and/or products produced.

Objective

Given a number line with the endpoints labeled 0 and 1 as fractions with the same denominator, the student will be able to find the name of a point on the line.

Sample Item and Directions

Read the problem carefully and choose the best answer. Place the letter beside your answer on the answer sheet next to the number of the problem.

Find the numeral which correctly replaces the pointer in the number line above.

(a) 3   (b) $1\frac{3}{5}$ (c) $\frac{3}{5}$ (d) $\frac{1}{5}$

Content Section

1. The student is given a number line with the endpoints labeled 0 and 1 using rational numbers with the same denominator.
2. The divisions on the line shall be equally spaced.
3. The number of divisions on the line will be a multiple of the given denominator.
4. A pointer is used to identify the unknown point on the line.

Response Section

1. There is one correct and three incorrect responses.
2. The responses are given in ascending or descending order.
3. The distractors shall include:
   (a) The numeral that represents the ordinal position of the point in question.
   (b) The numeral that represents the length of each division on the number line.
   (c) The numeral that is one more than the correct response.

Figure 3. Example of a mathematics domain specification. It was prepared by Bob D'Ambrosio and is included in a criterion-referenced test battery that is published by Educational Development Corporation (reproduced with permission).

Content Validity

Test items can be written after the domain specifications have been prepared (see, e.g., Roid & Haladyna, 1982). Determination of content validity involves a consideration of three features of the test items: (a) item validities (i.e., the extent to which each test item measures some aspect of the content included in a domain specification), (b) technical quality, and (c) representativeness. These three factors are considered next.

Item Validity

The quality of criterion-referenced test items can be determined by the extent to which they reflect, in terms of their content, the domains from which they were derived. Unless one can say with a high degree of confidence that the items in a criterion-referenced test measure the intended objectives, any use of the test score information will be questionable.

There are two approaches that are currently used to establish the validity of criterion-referenced test items. The first approach requires content specialists to provide judgments of test items.

Several procedures have been suggested for obtaining judgmental data (Hambleton, Swaminathan, Algina, & Coulson, 1978; Rovinelli & Hambleton, 1977). For example, Hambleton (1984b) offered this set of directions:

First, read carefully through the lists of domain specifications and test items. Next, please indicate how well you feel each item reflects the domain specification it was written to measure. Judge a test item solely on the basis of the match between its content and the content defined by the domain specification that the test item was prepared to measure. Use the five-point rating scale shown below:

Poor	Fair	Good	Very Good	Excellent
1	2	3	4	5

Hambleton (1984b) described a second procedure for carrying out an item validity study. With the second procedure, reviewers are not told which domain specifications the items were written to measure:

Read carefully through the lists of domain specifications and test items. Your task is to indicate whether or not you feel each test item is a measure of one of the domain specifications. It is, if you feel examinee performance on the test item would provide an indication of an examinee's level of performance in a pool of test items measuring the domain specification. Beside each objective, write in the test item numbers corresponding to the test items that you feel measure the objective. In some instances you may feel that items do not measure any of the available domain specifications. Write these test item numbers in the space provided at the bottom of the rating form. (p. 116)

With either procedure, a measure of the perceived match between items and the objectives they were written to measure can be obtained along with an indication of the agreement among reviewers' ratings.

The second approach requires items to be pilot tested on a group of examinees similar in characteristics to those for whom the test is intended. The examinee item response data are analyzed to determine item difficulty levels and discrimination indices. An item that has a difficulty level that varies substantially from the difficulty levels of other items measuring the same domain specification must be studied carefully to determine if the variation is the result of a content or technical flaw. Items with very low or negative-valued discrimination indices should also be studied carefully for flaws. Readers are referred to Berk (1984), Hambleton (1985), Millman (1974), and Popham (1978c) for a discussion of additional item statistics and their usefulness in building criterion-referenced tests.

The use of item analytic techniques is important in the content-validation process. In situations where at least a moderate-sized sample of examinees is available and where the test constructor is interested in identifying aberrant items, not for elimination from the item pool but for correction, the use of an empirical approach to item validation will provide important information with regard to the assessment of item validity.

In sum, obtaining content specialists' ratings is the method to use for assessing item validities; empirical procedures should be used for the detection of aberrant items in need of correction. An excellent review of item statistics for use with criterion-referenced tests was prepared by Berk (1984).

Technical Adequacy of Test Items

The technical adequacy of test items can be established at the same time as test items are reviewed for the appropriateness of their content. Measurement specialists can be asked to review the test items to identify flaws in test items such as grammatical cues, poorly worded item stems, and non-random distribution of correct answers across the answer positions. Sample item technical review forms were presented by Hambleton (1984b; in press).

Representativeness of the Test Items

Reviewers can be asked to evaluate the representativeness of items measuring each objective. From a grid developed to describe the content or behaviors in a domain specification, reviewers can judge the degree of item representativeness. For example, a group of reviewers can be asked, "How well does the set of test items sample the domain of content or behaviors defining the objective?" When representativeness has not been achieved to some desired level, new test items must be added and/or items deleted to obtain a desired level of representativeness.

A second procedure is to carry out Cronbach's "duplication experiment." This experiment requires two teams of equally competent item writers and reviewers to work independently in preparing items for a criterion-referenced test. Each team is provided with the identical test specifications. These specifications were suggested by Cronbach (1971): "[The teams] would be aided by the same definition of relevant content, sampling rules, instructions to reviewers, and specifications for tryout and interpretation of the data . . ." (p. 456). If the domain specifications are clear, and if item samples for each objective are representative, the two measurements of each objective should be equivalent. Equivalence of forms can be checked by administering both tests to the same group of examinees and comparing the two sets of examinee test scores. One drawback to this type of study is the cost involved. The cost of preparing a test is approximately doubled. A second drawback is that the approach provides no protection against common blind spots in the domain specifications.

Reliability

Criterion-referenced test scores are used, principally, in two ways: (a) to make descriptions about examinee levels of performance and (b) to make mastery/nonmastery decisions based on examinee test performance (Traub & Rowley, 1980). With the first use, of interest to users is the precision with which domain scores are estimated.[1] Of interest with the second use is the test–retest decision consistency or parallel-form decision consistency. It is clear that the usual approaches to assessing test score reliability (test–retest reliability, parallel-form reliability, and corrected split-half reliability) do not address directly either use and therefore they are of limited value in the context of criterion-referenced measurement (Hambleton & Novick, 1973). It has been argued, incorrectly, that classical reliability indices are less useful with criterion-referenced tests because the scores often are fairly homogeneous, so classical reliability indices will be low. But if low reliability indices were the problem, the problem could be resolved by interpreting the indices more cautiously in light of homogeneous test score distributions or designing reliability studies to ensure more heterogeneous score distributions.

The extensive reliability literature pertaining to criterion-referenced tests is not reviewed here. The topic has probably received more attention from psychometricians than any other in the criterion-referenced testing field. The interested reader is referred to Hambleton et al. (1978) and Berk (1980) for reviews. In what follows, a few of the more practical contributions to the topic are considered.

Reliability of Domain Score Estimates

The standard error of measurement associated with domain score estimates can easily be calculated. It is useful in setting up confidence bands for examinee domain scores. Fortunately, it is not influenced to any considerable extent by the homogeneity of examinee domain scores (Lord & Novick, 1968).

Another approach for determining the consistency of domain score estimates was reported by Millman (1974) and by Hambleton et al. (1978). They suggested that the standard error of estima-

[1]An examinee domain score is the proportion of items in an item domain that he or she can answer correctly.

tion derived from the binomial test model given by the expression $\sqrt{\hat{\pi}(1 - \hat{\pi})/n}$, can be used to set up confidence bands around domain score estimates. In the expression, n is the number of items measuring an objective and $\hat{\pi}$ is the proportion-correct score for an examinee. For example, if an examinee answers 8 out of 10 test items correctly that measure an objective, $n = 10$, $\hat{\pi} = .80$, and the error associated with the domain score estimate is .13. Therefore, there is (approximately) a 68% chance that the examinee's domain score is somewhere in the interval .67 to .93 (i.e., $.8 \pm .13$).

Reliability of Mastery Classifications

Hambleton and Novick (1973) suggested that the reliability of mastery classification decisions should be defined in terms of the consistency of decisions from two administrations of the same test or parallel forms of a test. Suppose that examinees are to be classified into mastery states (e.g., "mastery" versus "nonmastery" or achievement levels, denoted A, B, C, D, and F), Hambleton and Novick suggested the formula below to measure the proportion of examinees who are consistently classified on the two administrations:

$$p_o = \sum_{j=1}^{m} p_{jj}$$

where p_{jj} is the proportion of examinees classified in the j th mastery state on the two administrations and m is the number of mastery states. In practice, m is usually equal to 2. The index p_o is the observed proportion of decisions that are in agreement. Among the factors affecting the value of p_o are test length, quality of test items, choice of cutoff score, group heterogeneity, and the closeness of the group mean performance to the cutoff score. The p_o statistic has considerable appeal and is easy to calculate. In the sample data reported in Table 2, the proportion of examinees classified in the same way on the two administrations is .82 ($p_o = .16 + .66$). In other words, in the sample of examinees who were administered the test items, 82% of the examinees were classified in the same way (either classified as masters or nonmasters on both administrations) on the basis of their performance on the two administrations.

Swaminathan, Hambleton, and Algina (1974) argued that the statistic p_o has one limitation: It does not take into account the proportion of agreement that occurs by chance alone. For example, suppose that examinees were assigned to one

TABLE 2   Summary of Mastery Classifications for a Group of Examinees on Two Test Administrations

Admin. 1	Admin. 2	Mastery State		Marginal Proportion
		Nonmaster	Master	
Mastery State	Nonmaster	.16	.04	.20
	Master	.14	.66	.80
Marginal Proportion		.30	.70	

of two mastery states based on "coin flips." Heads are "masters" and tails are "nonmasters." By chance alone, 50% of the examinees will be classified into the same mastery state on "two administrations." Decision consistency is assessed to be 50% and this is due to chance factors only! In assessing the consistency of decisions resulting from the use of a test, it would seem to be desirable to account in some way for the agreement due to chance. Therefore, Swaminathan et al. (1974) suggested using coefficient k (Cohen, 1960) as an index of decision consistency that is corrected for the agreement due to chance alone. This coefficient is defined as

$$k = \frac{p_o - p_c}{1 - p_c}$$

where

$$p_c = \sum_{j=1}^{m} p_j \cdot p_{\cdot j}$$

The symbols $p_{j \cdot}$ and $p_{\cdot j}$ represent the proportions of examinees assigned to mastery state j on the first and second administrations, respectively. The symbol p_c represents the proportion of agreement that would occur even if the classifications based on the two administrations were statistically independent. Thus, in a sense, it can be argued that k takes into account the composition of the group, and that in this sense it is more group independent than the simple proportion of agreement statistic, p_o. The statistic k can be thought of as a measure of decision consistency that is over and above the decision consistency due to chance alone. When the formula is applied to the results in Table 2, we obtain

$$p_o = .66 + .16$$
$$= .82$$
$$p_c = (.80 \times .70) + (.20 \times .30)$$
$$= .62$$
$$k = \frac{.82 - .62}{1 - .62}$$
$$= .53$$

The properties of k have been discussed in detail by Cohen (1960, 1968) and Fleiss, Cohen, and Everitt (1969) as well as by others. It is sufficient to note that the upper limit is $+1$ and can occur only when the marginal proportions for different administrations are equal. The lower limit is close to -1. The precise lower limit of k is unimportant in the context of criterion-referenced testing because negative values indicate considerable inconsistency and, therefore, highly unreliable decisions. Negative values, therefore, are unacceptable regardless of how close they are to the maximum.

The coefficient k depends on all factors that affect the decision-making procedure: the cutoff score, the heterogeneity of the group of examinees, and the method of assigning examinees to mastery states. Therefore, it is useful to report all of these factors when reporting k since this information contributes to its interpretation.

The concept of decision consistency is a useful one in the context of criterion-referenced measurement, but the approaches described above require the administration of a single test twice, or the administration of parallel forms of a test. In either case, testing time is doubled. Such approaches are often difficult to implement in practice because of limited testing time. With norm-referenced tests, one way to avoid the extra testing time in assessing reliability involves the use of the split-half method to determine the reliability of scores from a test that is one-half as long as the one of interest. Next, the Spearman-Brown formula is used along with the split-half reliability estimate to predict the reliability of scores with the test of interest. Unfortunately, the approach used with norm-referenced test scores cannot be applied to the problem of assessing consistency of decisions emanating from a single administration of a criterion-referenced test because the Spearman-Brown formula is not applicable. A rather different approach for estimating decision consistency from a single administration was developed by Subkoviak (1976). While the mathematical development of the formula is not comparable, Subkoviak's formula is the analog of the corrected split-half reliability index that is used with norm-referenced tests to estimate parallel-form reliability from a single test administration.

Subkoviak defined a coefficient of decision consistency for an examinee i, denoted $p_c^{(i)}$ as the probability of the examinee being consistently classified on two test administrations (with either the same test or parallel forms). For the case of two mastery states, this probability is given by

$$p_c^{(i)} = \text{Prob}(X_i \geq c, Y_i \geq c) + \text{Prob}(X_i < c, Y_i < c)$$

where c is the cutoff score on the objective and X_i and Y_i are the scores for the examinee on the two administrations. The two terms represent the probability of examinee i being consistently assigned to either a mastery or a nonmastery state. A measure of decision consistency for a group of N examinees is easily found:

$$p_o = \frac{\sum_{i=1}^{N} p_c^{(i)}}{N}$$

To determine p_o, it is necessary to estimate $p_c^{(i)}$, $i = 1, 2, \ldots, N$. Estimates can be obtained if two assumptions are made: (a) examinee scores on the two administrations are independently and identically distributed, and (b) for a fixed examinee, scores on the two parallel tests are binomially distributed. Of course, the appropriateness of the estimate of $p_c^{(i)}$ will depend on the validity of the two assumptions. The first assumption is quite reasonable. Assume that there exists a sampling distribution of possible test scores for an examinee

with a given true score. Variation in scores across occasions is due to errors of measurement. The first assumption is satisfied if the sampling distribution applies equally well to the examinee for both test administrations and if the scores are randomly drawn from the distribution. The second assumption is less reasonable because it cannot be true when item difficulties vary, and in general, they will. Fortunately, Subkoviak has shown that violations of this second assumption have only a modest effect on the results.

With only the two assumptions, Subkoviak showed that

$$p(X_i \geq c) = \sum_{X_i = c}^{n} \binom{n}{X_i} \pi_i^{X_i} (1 - \pi_i)^{n - X_i}$$

and

$$p_c^{(i)} = [p(X_i \geq c)]^2 + [1 - p(X_i \geq c)]^2$$

Once an estimate of an examinee's domain score (proportion-correct score), denoted $\hat{\pi}_i$, is obtained, $p(X_i \geq c)$ and $p_c^{(i)}$ can be obtained easily.

The average of $p_c^{(i)}$ for $i = 1, 2, \ldots, N$, is calculated next. The average serves as an estimate of the consistency of mastery decisions between two test administrations. The estimate is obtained from a single administration and depends on the chosen standard of performance. Subkoviak's estimate of decision consistency is very popular because the computational formula is straightforward and the assumptions on which it is based are reasonable.

It is also possible to obtain an estimate of k using Subkoviak's method. The only additional information needed is the proportion of examinees assigned to each mastery state on the single test administration. By making the reasonable assumption that these proportions would be the same on a retest or a parallel-form administration, the proportion of agreement expected by chance (p_c) can be obtained by the method introduced earlier ($p_c = p_1 p_{.1} + p_2 p_{.2}$). Therefore, if $p_1 = .20$ and $p_2 = .80$, then $p_{.1} = .20$ and $p_{.2} = .80$, and $p_c = .20^2 + .80^2 = .68$. With a value of p_c and with the p_o estimate from Subkoviak's method, k can quickly be calculated. It must be stressed that the proper reliability information (whether one is discussing domain scores or mastery classification decisions) needs to be reported on an objective-by-objective basis (Hambleton & Novick, 1973).

Item Selection

The item selection process is straightforward provided that the criterion-referenced test developer has been careful in defining objectives and in constructing test items. Larger domains require special attention to ensure that representative samples of test items are drawn. With large domains especially it helps to prepare a grid to organize the relevant content or behaviors. A test is usually constructed by taking either a random or a stratified random sample of items from each domain of interest.

The consistency of mastery/nonmastery decisions can be increased by selecting test items in a different fashion. Of course, increasing the number of test items is effective, but often it is not feasible to do so. When the primary purpose of a testing program is to make mastery/nonmastery decisions, a better test will result if test items are selected from the available pool of items measuring each objective on the basis of statistical properties. For example, suppose that a standard is set at 80% correct in the domain of test items measuring an objective. Test items that discriminate effectively in the region of the cutoff score on the test score scale will contribute most to decision consistency and validity (see, e.g., Hambleton & de Gruijter, 1983). A test constructed in this way will have maximum discriminating power in the region where decisions are to be made; therefore, more reliable and valid decisions will result. One possible drawback is that scores derived from the test cannot be used to make descriptive statements about examinee levels of performance because test items measuring each objective will not necessarily constitute a representative sample. There is at least one way to make descriptive statements about examinees' level of performance when nonrandom or nonrepresentative samples of test items are chosen: by introducing concepts and models from the field of item response theory (Hambleton, 1989; Hambleton & Swaminathan, 1985). Although the feasibility of such an approach has not been fully tested, the interested reader is referred to the chapter by Hambleton (1989) for a discussion of item response theory.

Test Length

A large body of literature exists on the topic of criterion-referenced test length (Hambleton, 1984a; Hambleton et al., 1978). Only a few of the more practical contributions are cited in this brief subsection.

When the primary use of the scores is description, a formula presented earlier for the precision of domain score estimates is useful:

$$\text{Precision} = \sqrt{\frac{\hat{\pi}(1 - \hat{\pi})}{n}}$$

By simple algebra, an expression for test length in terms of precision and domain scores can be obtained:

$$n = \frac{\hat{\pi}(1 - \hat{\pi})}{(\text{precision})^2}$$

By specifying a typical value for π (domain score estimate) in the group of examinees of interest, and the level of precision required of the domain score estimates, the appropriate test length can be found. Suppose that precision = .15 and $\pi = .75$. The value of n is 8.3. Therefore, 9 test items are needed to ensure the desired degree of precision in the domain score estimates. When in doubt about a typical value of π, set $\pi = .50$. This will ensure that a conservative test length is obtained, that is, a test length longer than one that will be needed is used.

When criterion-referenced test scores are to be used to make mastery/nonmastery decisions, there are a number of aids for selecting test lengths. Millman (1973) prepared a set of tables to predict the likelihood of examinees being misclassified as a function of domain score, test length, and cutoff score. Wilcox (1976) prepared tables that allow the user to study relationships among test lengths, cutoff scores, and minimum probabilities of correct classifications for examinees.

Eignor and Hambleton (1979) developed an approach in which test developers select a probable domain score distribution (from five that are available) for the group to be measured and then refer to tables that connect useful group test score summary statistics such as decision consistency, kappa, and decision accuracy (relation between decisions based on a test and decisions evolving from a criterion measure such as teacher ratings) to test length. (The tables are limited to cases where the standard is 80%.) The five probable domain score distributions are reported in Figure 4, and the relationship between test length and decision consistency is reported in Figure 5. (Eignor and Hambleton offer several other figures in their paper to represent other situations that may arise in practice.) Figures 4 and 5 are used in the following way: Suppose a test developer felt that distribution one in Figure 4 was the most probable for the group of

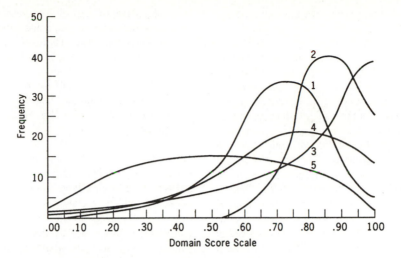

Figure 4. Graphical representation of five domain score distributions.

interest, and a minimum level of decision consistency of .70 was desired. From Figure 5, it can be determined that a test of nine items is required. Additional details on the approach are provided in Eignor and Hambleton (1979), Hambleton (1984a), Hambleton and Eignor (1979), and Hambleton, Mills, and Simon (1983).

Standard Setting

One of the primary purposes of criterion-referenced testing is to make decisions about indi-

viduals. This requires a standard or cutoff score on the test score scale to separate examinees into two categories, often labeled "masters" and "nonmasters." In some cases, examinees are divided into more than two mastery categories and so more than one cutoff score must be set.

At the outset it is essential to stress that *all* standard-setting methods involve judgment and are arbitrary. Some people have argued that arbitrary standards are not defensible and therefore they should not be used (Glass, 1978). Popham

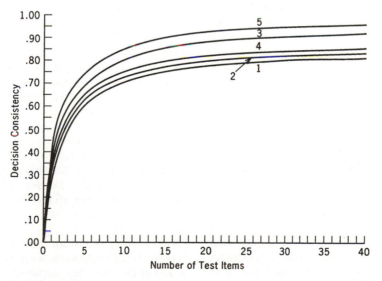

Figure 5. Relationship between decision consistency and test length with five test score distributions.

(1978a, 1978d) countered with the following response:

> Unable to avoid reliance on human judgment as the chief ingredient in standard-setting, some individuals have thrown up their hands in dismay and cast aside all efforts to set performance standards as arbitrary, hence unacceptable.
>
> But *Webster's Dictionary* offers us two definitions of arbitrary. The first of these is positive, describing arbitrary as an adjective reflecting choice or discretion, that is, "determinable by a judge or tribunal." The second definition, pejorative in nature, describes arbitrary as an adjective denoting capriciousness, that is, "selected at random and without reason." In my estimate, when people start knocking the standard-setting game as arbitrary, they are clearly employing *Webster's* second, negatively loaded definition.
>
> But the first definition is more accurately reflective of serious standard-setting efforts. They represent genuine attempts to do a good job in deciding what kinds of standards we ought to employ. That they are judgmental is inescapable. But to malign all judgmental operations as capricious is absurd. (p. 168)

Both Hambleton (1978) and Popham (1978a, 1978c, 1978d) stressed that many of the decisions that are made by society to regulate our lives are made arbitrarily, but in the positive sense of the word. For example, fire, health, environmental, and highway safety standards, to name just a few areas where standards are set, are set arbitrarily. In educational settings, arbitrary decisions are made by educators about such matters as curriculum and instructional methods. But what if a standard is set too high (or too low) on a test or if students are misclassified? Through experience and with careful evaluations of the test score results, standards that are not "in line" with others can be identified and revised. Ebel (1978a) makes a similar point:

> Pass—fail decisions on a person's achievement in learning trouble some measurement specialists a great deal. They know about errors of measurement. They know that some who barely pass do so only with the help of errors of measurement. They know that some who fail do so only with the hindrance of errors of measurement. For these, passing or failing does not depend on achievement at all. It depends on luck. That seems unfair, and indeed it is. But as any measurement specialist can explain, it is also entirely unavoidable. Make a better test and we reduce the number who will be passed or failed by error. But the number can never be reduced to zero. (p. 549)

The consequences of assigning a nonmaster to a mastery state (called a false-positive error) or a master to a nonmastery state (called a false-negative error) on a statewide basic skills test or a high school certification examination are, however, considerably more serious than errors made on classroom tests, so more attention must be given to the design of the more important testing programs.

Many of the available standard-setting methods have been described, compared, and critiqued in the literature (Berk, 1986; Glass, 1978; Hambleton & Eignor, 1979; Hambleton & Powell, 1983; Hambleton et al., 1978; Meskauskas, 1976; Millman, 1973; Shepard, 1984). Table 3 lists many of the methods. The methods are organized into three categories, labeled "judgmental," "empirical," and "combination." The judgmental methods require data from judges for setting standards, or require judgments to be made about the presence of variables (e.g., guessing) that influence the setting of a standard. The empirical methods require examinee test data to aid in the standard-setting process. The combination methods use both judgmental data and empirical data in the standard-setting process. Livingston and Zieky (1982) and Popham (1978d) have developed helpful guidelines for applying several of the methods. Several of the popular judgmental methods and combination methods are introduced next.

Judgmental Methods

In these methods, individual items are inspected, to judge how well the minimally competent person would perform on the test items. Judges are asked to assess how or to what degree a person who could be described as minimally competent would perform on each item.

Nedelsky Method. Judges are asked to identify distractors in multiple-choice test items that they feel the minimally competent student should be able to eliminate as incorrect. The minimum

TABLE 3   Classification of Methods for Setting Standards

Judgmental Methods	Empirical Methods	Combination Methods	
Item Content	Data-Criterion Measure	Judgmental-Empirical	Educational Consequences
Nedelsky (1954) Angoff (1971)	Livingston (1975) Livingston (1976)	Contrasting groups (Livingston & Zieky, 1982)	Block (1972)
Ebel (1972) Jaeger (1978)	Van der Linden & Mellenbergh (1977)	Borderline groups (Livingston & Zieky, 1982)	
	Decision-Theoretic Hambleton & Novick (1973)	Criterion groups (Berk, 1976)	
Guessing Millman (1973)	Bayesian Methods		
		Hambleton & Novick (1973) Schoon, Gullion, & Ferrara (1979)	

passing level for that item then becomes the reciprocal of the number of remaining alternatives. It is the "chance score" on the test item for the minimally competent student. The judges proceed with each test item in a like fashion, and on completion of the judging process each judge sums the minimum passing levels across the test items to obtain a standard. Individual judges' standards are averaged to obtain a standard for the set of test items.

Ebel's Method.   Judges rate test items along two dimensions: relevance and difficulty though other suitable dimensions could be substituted. There are four levels of relevance in Ebel's method: essential, important, acceptable, and questionable. Ebel uses three levels of difficulty: easy, medium, and hard. These levels form a 3×4 grid. The judges are asked to do two things:

1. Locate each of the test items in the proper cell, based on their relevance and difficulty.
2. Assign a percentage to each cell, that percentage being the percentage of items in the cell that the minimally qualified examinees should be able to answer.

The number of test items in each cell is multiplied by the appropriate percentage (agreed on by the judges), and the sum of all the cells, when divided by the total number of test items, yields the standard.

Angoff's Method.   When using Angoff's method, judges are asked to assign a probability to each test item directly, thus circumventing the analysis of a grid or the analysis of response alternatives. Each probability is to be an estimate of the likelihood of the minimally competent examinee answering the test item correctly. Individual judges' test score standards can then be averaged to obtain a standard for the set of test items.

Combination Methods

With these methods, judgments are made about the mastery status of a sample group of examinees from the population of interest. Choice of method determines the nature of the required judgments. Next, one or more groups for whom mastery determinations have been made are administered the test. Details are offered next for analyzing the judgmental data and the test scores.

Borderline-Group Method. This method requires that the judges first define what they would envision as minimally acceptable performance on the content area being assessed. The judges are then asked to submit a list of students whose performances would be so close to the borderline that they could not be reliably classified as masters or nonmasters. The test is administered to this group, and the median test score for the group may be taken as the standard. Alternatively, it may be decided to pass more or less than 50% of the minimally competent students. The situation is shown graphically in Figure 6. If a standard is set at .875 (7 items out of 8 items answered correctly), only 13.5% of the minimally competent students would be assigned to the "master" category.

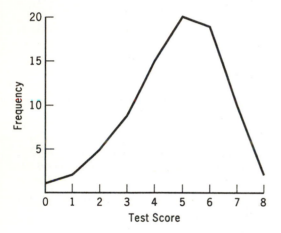

Effects of Varying the Cutoff Score

Test Score	Frequency	Cutoff Score	Percent Passing
8	2	8	2.50
7	9	7	13.50
6	18	6	36.25
5	20	5	61.25
4	15	4	80.00
3	8	3	90.00
2	5	2	96.25
1	2	1	98.75
0	1	0	100.00

Figure 6. Frequency polygon of criterion-referenced test scores for a group of individuals identified by judges as borderline or "minimally competent."

Contrasting Groups Method. Once judges have defined minimally acceptable performance for the domain specification being assessed, the judges are asked to identify those examinees they are certain are either masters or nonmasters in relation to the specified domain of content or behaviors. The test is administered to the groups and the score distributions for the two groups on an objective-by-objective basis are then plotted and the point of intersection is taken as the initial standard. In Figure 7, the point of intersection corresponds closest to a standard of 7 (out of 10). With a standard of 7, and using the test data in Figure 7, 20% of the masters and 20% of the nonmasters would be misclassified. The standard can be moved up to reduce the number of false-positive errors (examinees identified as masters by the test, but who have not adequately mastered the objectives) or down to reduce the number of false-negative errors (examinees identified as non-masters by the test, but who have adequately mastered the objectives). The direction to move the standard will depend on the relative seriousness of the two types of error. If the score distributions overlap completely, no decisions can be made reliably. The ideal situation would be one in which the two distributions did not overlap at all. The validity of this approach to standard setting depends on the appropriateness of the judges' classifications of examinees.

Construct Validity

It is essential to establish the validity of the descriptions and decisions made from the criterion-referenced test scores. Content validity evidence, however, is not sufficient since it pertains to the content of the test, whereas descriptions and decisions are made based on examinee *responses* to the test items. For example, a set of test items, on the basis of content considerations, may appear to be measuring "understanding" whereas they are actually measuring "recall of factual information." It is essential to establish the "content representativeness" of a set of test items, but the usefulness of a set of criterion-referenced test scores (or, for that matter, scores obtained from any test) must be determined by a carefully designed series of construct validation investigations. This point was brought to the attention of criterion-referenced test developers by Messick (1989) and Linn (1979). Messick (1975), for example, wrote:

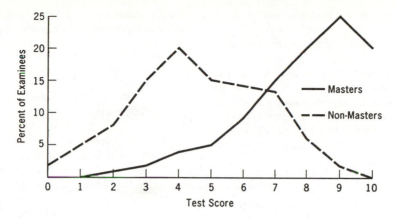

Distribution of Test Scores

Test Score	Percent of Masters	Percent of Nonmasters	Cutoff Score	False Failures	False Passes
10	20	0	10	80	0
9	25	2	9	55	2
8	20	6	8	35	8
7	15	12	7	20	20
6	8	14	6	12	34
5	5	16	5	7	50
4	4	20	4	3	70
3	2	15	3	1	85
2	1	8	2	0	93
1	0	5	1	0	98
0	0	2	0	0	100

Figure 7. Frequency polygons of criterion-referenced test scores for two groups (Masters and Non-masters of the content measured by the test as identified by judges).

The major problem. . .is that content validity. . .is focused upon test forms rather than measurements. Inferences in educational and psychological measurement are made from scores, and scores are a function of subject responses. Any concept of validity of measurement must include reference to empirical consistency. Content coverage is an important consideration in test construction and interpretation, to be sure, but in itself it does not provide validity. (pp. 960–961)

Messick (1975) also offered a useful definition of construct validation:

Construct validation is the process of marshalling evidence in the form of theoretically relevant empirical relations to support the inference that an observed response consistency has a particular meaning. (p. 955)

Fortunately, there is a wide assortment of methods (intratest, intertest, experimental, prediction) that can be used to provide validity evidence in relation to intended uses of a set of test scores (Hambleton, 1984b). Of course, accumulating construct validation evidence is a never-ending process. The amount of time and energy that is expended in the direction of construct validation must be consistent with the importance of the testing program. Criterion-referenced tests that are being used to monitor student progress in a curriculum on a day-to-day basis should demand less time, obviously, than tests that will be used to determine whether or not students graduate from high school.

Construct validation studies should begin with a statement of the purpose of the test scores. A clearly stated use will provide direction for the kind of evidence that is worth collecting. Later, when all of the data are collected and analyzed, a final conclusion as to the validity of the intended use (or uses) of the test scores can be offered. Several types of construct validation investigations are briefly considered next.

Factor Analysis

Factor analysis is a commonly employed procedure for the dimensional analysis of items in a norm-referenced test, or of scores derived from different norm-referenced tests, but it has rarely been used in construct validation studies of criterion-referenced test scores. One reason for its lack of use is that the usual input for factor analytic studies are correlations, and correlations are often low between items on a criterion-referenced test or between criterion-referenced test scores and other variables because score variability is often not very great. The problem can be resolved by choosing samples of examinees with a wide range of ability, for example, a group of masters and nonmasters. As many factors in a factor solution should be obtained as there are objectives covered in a test, and with items "loading" on only the factors (or objectives) that they were designed to measure.

Domain scores from many criterion-referenced tests can be factor analyzed and the resulting structure can be compared to a structure specifying a theoretical relationship among the objectives. Correlational studies among examinee scores on different objectives measured by a criterion-referenced test or among domain scores from other tests can be revealing.

Guttman Scalogram Analysis

Guttman scaling is a relevant procedure for the construct validation of criterion-referenced test scores in situations where the objectives can be organized into either a linear or a hierarchical sequence. First, the hierarchical structure of a set of objectives must be specified. To the extent that examinee domain scores in the hierarchy are predictable from a knowledge of the hierarchy, the evidence would support the construct validity of the domain scores. In situations where examinee domain scores are not predictable, one of the following three situations has occurred:

1. The hierarchy is incorrectly specified.
2. The domain scores are not valid indicators of the intended objectives.
3. A combination of the two explanations above is true.

Sources of Invalidity

There are many sources of error that can reduce the validity of an intended use of a set of criterion-referenced test scores. Suppose, for example, that an examinee was estimated to have an 80% level of performance on a test measuring "ability to identify the main idea in paragraphs." Is the test score valid for the intended interpretation? An answer depends on the answers to several other questions:

1. Were the test directions unclear to the student?
2. Did the student have a problem using the answer sheet?
3. Was the test administered under speeded testing conditions?
4. Was the student unmotivated to perform to the best of his or her ability?
5. Was the vocabulary in the passage at a suitable readability level?
6. Did test-taking skills play any role in the student's test performance?

The usefulness of the test scores is reduced if any of these (and many other) factors influence performance.

Experimental studies of potential sources of error to determine their effect on test scores are an important way to assess the construct validity of a set of test scores. Logical analyses and observations of testing methods and procedures can also be used to detect sources of invalidity in a set of test scores.

Criterion-Related Validity

Even if scores derived from criterion-referenced tests are descriptive of the objectives they are supposed to reflect, the usefulness of the scores as predictors of (say) "job success" or "success in the next unit of instruction" cannot be assured. Criterion-related validity studies of criterion-referenced test scores are no different in procedure from studies conducted with norm-referenced tests. Correlational, group-separation, and decision-accuracy methods are commonly used (Messick, 1989).

Decision Validity

Examinees are assumed to be "masters" if their test performance exceeds a minimum level of performance (referred to as a standard). The assessment of decision validity involves (a) the setting of a standard of test performance and (b) the comparison of test performance of two or more criterion groups in relation to the specified standard. Instructional decisions based on classroom criterion-referenced test scores can be validated by comparing the test performance, in relation to a standard of performance, of two criterion groups—those who have received instruction and those who have not. (Alternatively, two groups might be formed by asking teachers to identify students whom they are certain have an excellent grasp of the skills measured by the test under study and those who do not.) This situation is represented in Figure 7. Decision validity on each objective may be assessed by summing the number (a) of instructed examinees who exceed the performance standard and (b) of the uninstructed examinees who do not. The assumption is that these are the groups who are correctly classified by the testing procedure. Of course, the statement is not strictly true because some of the uninstructed examinees will have knowledge of the content covered by the test, and some of the examinees in the instructed group will not. The necessity of assuming that all uninstructed examinees are "nonmasters" and all instructed examinees are "masters" is one of the limitations of this approach for assessing decision validity.

The advantage of this procedure is that decision validity is reported in a readily interpretable way (number of correct decisions). Alternatively, the correlation between two dichotomous variables (group membership and the mastery decision) can be reported and used as an index of decision validity. Other possible statistics are reported by Berk (1976), Hambleton and Eignor (1979), Hambleton (in press), and Popham (1978c). Decision validity will depend on several important factors: (a) the quality of the test under investigation, (b) the appropriateness of the criterion groups, (c) the examinee group, and (d) the standard.

SUGGESTIONS FOR SELECTING AND EVALUATING CRITERION-REFERENCED TESTS

A study of Mitchell's Ninth *Mental Measurements Yearbook,* published in 1985, or the major test publishers' catalogs will reveal the existence of a large number of commercially available criterion-referenced tests. The tests, as might be expected, range considerably in the content they cover, the grade levels at which they are appropriate, special options, and technical quality (Hambleton & Eignor, 1978).

In this section we offer suggestions for selecting and evaluating criterion-referenced tests for use in school settings. Preliminary, practical, content, and technical considerations in the test evaluation and selection process are presented. Professional standards for evaluating criterion-referenced tests are given in the *Standards for Educational and Psychological Tests* (AERA, APA, & NCME, 1985).

Preliminary Considerations

Prior to initiating a search for a criterion-referenced test, it is essential to prepare a clear statement of the intended use(s) of the test score information. Information about the match between a test's purposes and the proposed uses is helpful in deciding whether to reject a test outright or retain it for additional review. Also, there are other preliminary considerations that can be used to reduce the pool of suitable tests: A specification of the variables of interest (e.g., prereading skills) or the curriculum areas provides a basis for excluding many tests from further consideration. Also, tests can be rejected if they are not suitable for administration to the examinee populations of interest. For example, some tests will be unsuitable for administration to examinees with certain types of handicaps. Tests that remain after a screening using the three preliminary considerations above can be reviewed further in relation to the practical, content, and technical requirements to be described next.

Practical Considerations

Costs

There is little point in reviewing a test for adoption if the cost of test booklets, answer sheets, and scoring exceeds the available budget. If the booklets are reusable, their cost can be amortized over several years. Also, money can sometimes be saved by scoring tests locally, but if the scoring is complicated or if a variety of summary reports are required (e.g., class, grade, school, and district test score summary reports), local test scoring and reporting will not usually be practical unless the testing program will be put in place for many years.

Availability and Number of Levels

When tests are to be used to monitor examinee progress over a number of years, a criterion-referenced test battery that includes a sequenced set of tests (varying in difficulty) is preferable to choosing a test from a different test publisher at each grade level. Within a particular test battery, there is uniformity of test directions, answer sheets, terminology, reporting scales, and norm groups, which greatly enhances the validity and usefulness of test score information.

Parallel Forms

The importance of this feature will depend on the intended uses of the test scores. Often teachers desire to monitor student progress over short periods of time (2 weeks, for example). It is better to pretest and posttest with parallel forms (rather than use the same form twice) to reduce the influence of memory on test performance. The impact of memory effects on test performance is reduced when the time between test administrations is increased but memory remains a factor, so whenever a test is to be used to monitor student growth or development, tests with parallel forms are preferable.

Item Formats

Item format is an important consideration because it influences the objectivity and speed of test scoring and the skills that can be measured by a test.

Administration Time

A test should not be adopted simply because it can, for example, be administered in a class period or a time period of interest. But to disregard time considerations completely would be a mistake. For example, tests that are very short require less time to administer but reliability and validity of test scores will, in general, be lower.

Qualifications of Administrators

Some tests can only be administered by people with special training. Ensure that a suitably trained administrator is available (or can be trained).

Types of Reports and Scores

It is essential to match the types of reports and test information needed with what is available with each test under consideration. For example, a district may want student, parent, teacher, building, and district reports of student performance or may need special reports for Chapter I. Another common request is for grade-level and out-of-level norms with criterion-referenced tests. Not all publishers provide the same types and amounts of test score information, so there is need to consider this very important area carefully.

Content and Technical Considerations

A list of questions is offered next that addresses important content and technical considerations in evaluating criterion-referenced tests. Many of the questions are self-explanatory. For the others, brief comments are provided.

1. Do the objectives measured in the test provide a comprehensive coverage of the area they purport to measure?

Often test developers promise more than they deliver. Content specialists must judge the match between the area covered by the test and the area that the test developer claims is being covered. For example, a set of objectives cannot comprehensively cover a K-8 mathematics curriculum if topics such as fractions, decimals, and measurement are excluded.

2. Does the set of objectives measured by the test have "curriculum relevance"?

When a curriculum is clearly described, a measure of overlap between the curriculum and the objectives measured in the test can be determined. Cronbach (1971) refers to this activity as determining the "curriculum relevance" of the test. When a test has several levels, the "curriculum relevance" of each level must be assessed.

It is important to identify the objectives in the test that do not overlap with the curriculum. If items are arranged into clusters corresponding to the objectives measured in the test, it is easy to exclude those items from the testing program. Often the test items are "scrambled" so that it is next to impossible to remove the unwanted ones from the test.

3. Are the objectives clearly written?

One of the differences between norm-referenced tests and criterion-referenced tests is the clarity with which item pools matched to objectives are defined. Objectives are properly written for use in criterion-referenced tests when the item domains are clearly defined. Domain specifications or something similar are essential for criterion-referenced tests.

4. Is it possible to "tailor" the test to meet local needs by selecting objectives that will be measured?
5. Is an acceptable justification provided for including each objective in the test?
6. Are the people who prepared the test blueprint, objectives, and test items suitably qualified?
7. Was the item review process carried out correctly?

Item quality is an essential characteristic of any good test. Therefore, information about the item review process is important to a test evaluator. Some of the questions requiring satisfactory answers are: How many item reviewers were involved, and what were their qualifications? What were the item reviewers asked to do? How many examinees were included in a pilot test of the items? Which item statistics were used, and were they interpreted correctly? Were the items checked for racial, sex, and ethnic bias and stereotyping? These questions require satisfactory answers if confidence in the item review process is to be justified.

8. Does the content of the test items match the content defined by the objectives they were written to measure?
9. Are the test items technically sound?
10. Is the chosen item format appropriate for providing valid test score information in relation to the objectives measured by the test?
11. Are the test items representative of the item domains they were drawn from? (If

not, is an acceptable explanation offered?)
12. Are the test items free of bias and stereotyping?

Test items that disadvantage a group of examinees because of their sex, ethnic background, or race are inappropriate in any kind of test. It is common practice to seek the views of appropriately selected groups in relation to the item bias question. Also, item bias can be studied by comparing the performance levels of contrasting groups (e.g., males and females) on particular items to the performance of the same groups on the total test. For example, suppose that average total test score performance for Group A is about 10% higher than for Group B. Special attention should be given to items where item performance levels differ sharply from 10% in the contrasting groups. In practice, somewhat more complex analyses are carried out (Hambleton & Swaminathan, 1985).

13. Was a suitable sample of examinees used to pilot test the items?

A suitable sample is one that is *not* too small and is representative of the populations in which the test will be used.

14. Were item statistics used correctly in building the test?

Some test publishers use item statistics like they would if they were building a norm-referenced test. Item statistics with criterion-referenced tests are especially helpful in the following situations: (a) detecting flawed items, (b) building parallel tests, and (c) conducting post-hoc reliability studies. Item statistics should not be used in item selection except when a test is being built to optimally discriminate at a particular point (or points) on a test score scale.

15. Do the test directions inform examinees about the test's purpose, time limits, marking answer sheets (or booklets), and scoring? Are sample questions available?
16. Are the answer sheets easy for examinees to use?
17. Are the test administrator's directions complete? (Do they provide step-by-step activities for the administrator? Do they

provide answers to typical student questions? Do they address matters pertaining to testing conditions such as lighting and ventilation?)

18. Are the responsibilities of the examiner before and after testing described clearly in the administrator's manual?

19. If hand scoring is possible, is it relatively easy to do?

20. How appropriate is the print size, quality of printing and pictures, and page layouts for the examinees who will be tested?

21. Are the samples of examinees included in any reliability studies of a suitable size, and representative of the population(s) in which the test will be used?

22. Are the correct kinds of reliability indices reported?

The kinds of reliability indices that are valuable are tied directly to the intended uses of the test scores. When scores are used for descriptive purposes, reliability indices that reflect degree of score precision (e.g., the standard error of measurement) are useful. When scores are used to assign examinees to mastery states, an indication of test–retest or parallel-form decision consistency will be informative. When average group performance is of central interest, some indication of the error associated with each mean would be desirable. Usual indices based on correlations such as parallel-form reliability and test–retest reliability are of limited value because they provide information that is *not* related directly to any of the common uses of criterion-referenced test scores.

23. Are the appropriate reliability indices high enough to justify the use of the test in the intended situation?

There are no established minimally acceptable reliability levels, nor are there likely ever to be any. What is clear is that reliability indices need to be higher for the more important uses, that is, uses that will have a longer and/or more important impact on the people involved.

24. Is a discussion of the factors that influence reliability indices provided in the technical manual?

25. Is an explanation offered in the technical manual for the selection of a standard-setting method? (Alternatively, is a pro-

cess described in the technical manual to help users select and apply a standard-setting method?)

There are many standard-setting methods, and these methods vary in their appropriateness with different types of tests and groups. It is important to evaluate the publisher's choice of a standard-setting method.

26. Was the standard-setting method implemented correctly?

27. Is evidence offered for the validity of the mastery classifications?

No matter how carefully standards are set, evidence for the validity of the resulting classifications is needed. For example, if a suitable external dichotomous criterion measure can be found, the extent of agreement in decisions from the test and the criterion measure is very helpful. It is also desirable for publishers to report the validity of classifications for several standards.

28. Is validity evidence offered for each intended use of the test scores?

29. Are the results of some meaningful validation studies reported in the technical manual?

30. Does the technical manual provide a discussion of factors that might influence the validity of test scores and decisions?

It is common for users to attach more significance to test scores than they deserve. In any suitable manual there should be a discussion of the effects of motivation, anxiety, coaching, poor health, and so on, on test performance.

31. Are the samples of examinees utilized in the preparation of norms described thoroughly?

32. Are the samples of examinees representative of the intended populations and large enough to produce stable norms?

33. Are the norms tables reported in convenient ways for users?

34. Are the norms up to date?

35. Are guidelines offered in the technical manual for interpreting test scores correctly?

36. Do the score report forms address the specific needs of users?

A criterion-referenced testing program is of limited value if the test score information is not reported in ways that meet the needs of users. For example, it is common to want student, teacher, building, and district reports. Are these reports available? Can test scores be summarized for special groups of students such as Chapter I children?

37. Are the score report forms convenient and understandable?
38. Are convenient score report forms available if people choose to score the test by hand?

The 38 questions above should be be helpful to school districts that wish to review comprehensively available commercial criterion-referenced tests.

Summary

A variety of considerations were suggested in this section of the chapter for selecting and evaluating tests. In any particular situation, the importance of each will likely vary. Nevertheless, some attention to each area of consideration will usually be desirable.

A possible set of steps for evaluating and selecting a test is offered below:

1. Select a committee to carry out the review process.
2. Specify the intended uses of the test, content areas of interest, and groups to be assessed.
3. Identify a set of tests that satisfy the preliminary considerations. The *Mental Measurements Yearbook,* measurement textbooks, and test catalogs will be helpful in locating tests.
4. Prepare test reviews by considering practical, content, and technical matters.
5. Specify both the essential and the most important characteristics of the desired test.
6. With the test reviews from step 4, and the information from step 5, identify the most suitable test.
7. Periodically review the suitability of the adopted test by interviewing users of the test and by conducting psychometric investigations of test scores.

CONCLUSIONS

The implementation of criterion-referenced testing programs in schools has reached substantial proportions. Furthermore, the establishment of minimum competency testing programs at district and state levels ensures that many schoolchildren will be affected by criterion-referenced test score results. In this chapter, current technology for constructing and evaluating these tests was discussed along with a comparison of norm- and criterion-referenced tests. Given the extensive use of criterion-referenced tests, it is fortunate that there now exists a well-developed technology for building criterion-referenced tests and evaluating test scores. On the other hand, because of the newness of the area and the rapidity of developments, the technology is not widely known or used, and as a result, many criterion-referenced tests do not achieve levels of quality that one might wish for (Hambleton, in press). But the situation has improved and will continue improving now that many of the important contributions have been identified (Berk, 1984), textbooks and instructional materials are becoming available (e.g., Berk, 1984; Hambleton, in press; Popham, 1978c), and there is a greater need for technical information among practitioners because of the wide use of criterion-referenced tests. It is worth repeating that the technology presented in this chapter, if followed carefully, can contribute substantially to the assessment of examinee knowledge and skills and the proper use of criterion-reference test score information.

REFERENCES

American Educational Research Association, American Psychological Association, and National Council on Measurement in Education. (1985). *Standards for Educational and Psychological Tests.* Washington, DC: APA.

Angoff, W. H. (1971). Scales, norms, and equivalent scores. In R. L. Thorndike (Ed.), *Educational measurement* (2nd ed.). Washington, DC: American Council on Education.

Berk, R. A. (1976). Determination of optimal cutting scores in criterion-referenced measurement. *Journal of Experimental Education, 45,* 4–9.

Berk, R. A. (1980). A consumer's guide to criterion-referenced test reliability. *Journal of Educational Measurement, 17,* 323–349.

Berk, R. A. (Ed.). (1984). *A guide to criterion-referenced test development.* Baltimore: Johns Hopkins University Press.

Berk, R. A. (1986). A consumer's guide to setting performance standards on criterion-referenced tests. *Review of Educational Research, 56,* 137–172.

Block, J. H. (1972). Student learning and the setting of mastery performance standards. *Educational Horizons, 50,* 183–190.

Cohen, J. (1960). A coefficient of agreement for nominal scales. *Educational and Psychological Measurement, 20,* 37–46.

Cohen, J. (1968). Weighted kappa: Nominal scale agreement with provision for scaled disagreement of partial credit. *Psychological Bulletin, 70,* 213–220.

Cronbach, L. J. (1971). Test validation. In R. L. Thorndike (Ed.), *Educational measurement* (2nd ed.). Washington, DC: American Council on Education.

Ebel, R. L. (1972). *Essentials of educational measurement.* Englewood Cliffs, NJ: Prentice-Hall.

Ebel, R. L. (1978a). A case for minimum competency testing. *Phi Delta Kappan, 59,* 546–549.

Ebel, R. L. (1978b). The case for norm-referenced measurements. *Educational Researcher, 7,* 3–5.

Eignor, D. R., & Hambleton, R. K. (1979). *Effects of test length and advancement score on several criterion-referenced test reliability and validity indices* (Laboratory of Psychometric and Evaluative Research Report No. 86). Amherst: University of Massachusetts, School of Education.

Fleiss, J. L., Cohen, J., & Everitt, B. S. (1969). Large sample standard errors of kappa and weighted kappa. *Psychological Bulletin, 72,* 323–327.

Glaser, R. (1963). Instructional technology and the measurement of learning outcomes. *American Psychologist, 18,* 519–521.

Glass, G. V. (1978). Standards and criteria. *Journal of Educational Measurement, 15,* 237–261.

Gray, W. M. (1978). A comparison of Piagetian theory and criterion-referenced measurement. *Review of Educational Research, 48,* 223–249.

Hambleton, R. K. (1978). On the use of cut-off scores with criterion-referenced tests in instructional settings. *Journal of Educational Measurement, 15,* 277–290.

Hambleton, R. K. (1984a). Determining test lengths. In R. A. Berk (Ed.), *A guide to criterion-referenced test construction.* Baltimore: Johns Hopkins University Press.

Hambleton, R. K. (1984b). Validating the test scores. In R. A. Berk (Ed.), *A guide to criterion-referenced test construction.* Baltimore: Johns Hopkins University Press.

Hambleton, R. K. (1985). Criterion-referenced assessment of individual differences. In C. Reynolds & V. L. Wilson (Eds.), *Methodologies and statistical advances in the study of individual differences.* New York: Plenum Press.

Hambleton, R. K. (1989). Principles and selected applications of item response theory. In R. L. Linn (Ed.), *Educational measurement* (3rd ed.). New York: Macmillan.

Hambleton, R. K. (in press). *A practical guide to criterion-referenced testing.* Norwell, MA: Kluwer Academic.

Hambleton, R. K., & de Gruijter, D. N. M. (1983). Application of item response models to criterion-referenced test item selection. *Journal of Educational Measurement, 20,* 355–367.

Hambleton, R. K., & Eignor, D. R. (1978). Guidelines for evaluating criterion-referenced tests and test manuals. *Journal of Educational Measurement, 15,* 321–327.

Hambleton, R. K., & Eignor, D. R. (1979). *A practitioner's guide to criterion-referenced test development, validation, and test score usage* (Laboratory of Psychometric and Evaluative Research Report No. 70). Amherst: University of Massachusetts, School of Education.

Hambleton, R. K., Mills, C. N., & Simon, R. (1983). Determining the lengths for criterion-referenced tests. *Journal of Educational Measurement, 20,* 27–28.

Hambleton, R. K., & Novick, M. R. (1973). Toward an integration of theory and method for criterion-referenced tests. *Journal of Educational Measurement, 10,* 159–170.

Hambleton, R. K., & Powell, S. (1983). A framework for viewing the process of standard-setting. *Evaluation and the Health Professions, 6,* 3–24.

Hambleton, R. K., & Simon, R. A. (1980, April). *Steps for constructing criterion-referenced tests.* Paper presented at the meeting of the American Educational Research Association, Boston.

Hambleton, R. K., & Swaminathan, H. (1985). *Item response theory: Principles and applications.* Norwell, MA: Kluwer Academic.

Hambleton, R. K., Swaminathan, H., Algina, J., & Coulson, D. B. (1978). Criterion-referenced testing and measurement: A review of technical issues and developments. *Review of Educational Research, 48,* 1–47.

Jaeger, R. M. (1978). *A proposal for setting a standard on the North Carolina High School Competency Test.* Paper presented at the meeting of the North Carolina Association for Research in Education, Chapel Hill.

Jaeger, R. M. (1989). Certification of student competence. In R. L. Linn (Ed.), *Educational measurement* (3rd ed.). New York: Macmillan.

Linn, R. L. (1979). Issues of validity in measurement for competency-based programs. In M. A. Bunda & J. R. Sanders (Eds.), *Practice and problems in competency-based measurement.* Washington, DC: National Council on Measurement in Education.

Livingston, S. A. (1975). *A utility-based approach to the evaluation of pass/fail testing decision procedures* (Report No. COPA-75-01). Princeton, NJ: Educational Testing Service, Center for Occupational and Professional Assessment.

Livingston, S. A. (1976). *Choosing minimum passing scores by stochastic approximation techniques* (Report No. COPA-76-02). Princeton, NJ: Educational Testing Service, Center for Occupational and Professional Assessment.

Livingston, S. A., & Zieky, M. J. (1982). *Passing scores: A manual for setting standards of performance on educational and occupational tests.* Princeton, NJ: Educational Testing Service.

Lord, F. M., & Novick, M. R. (1968). *Statistical theories of mental test scores.* Reading, MA: Addison-Wesley.

Mager, R. F. (1962). *Preparing instructional objectives.* San Francisco: Fearon.

Mehrens, W. A., & Ebel, R. L. (1979). Some comments on criterion-referenced and norm-referenced achievement tests. *NCME Measurement in Education, 10*(1), 1–8.

Meskauskas, J. A. (1976). Evaluation models for criterion-referenced testing: Views regarding mastery and standard-setting. *Review of Educational Research, 46,* 133–158.

Messick, S. A. (1975). The standard problem: Meaning and values in measurement and evaluation. *American Psychologist, 30,* 955–966.

Messick, S. A. (1989). Validity. In R. L. Linn (Ed.), *Educational measurement* (3rd ed., pp. 13–103). New York: Macmillan.

Millman, J. (1973). Passing scores and test lengths for domain-referenced measures. *Review of Educational Research, 43,* 205–216.

Millman, J. (1974). Criterion-referenced measurement. In W. J. Popham (Ed.), *Evaluation in education: Current applications.* Berkeley, CA: McCutchan.

Mitchell, J. (Ed.). (1985). *Mental measurements yearbook* (9th ed.). Highland Park, NJ: Gryphon Press.

Nedelsky, L. (1954). Absolute grading standards for objective tests. *Educational and Psychological Measurement, 14,* 3–19.

Nitko, A. J. (1980). Distinguishing the many varieties of criterion-referenced tests. *Review of Educational Research, 50,* 461–485.

Popham, W. J. (1974). An approaching peril: Cloud-referenced tests. *Phi Delta Kappan, 56,* 614–615.

Popham, W. J. (1976). Normative data for criterion-referenced tests. *Phi Delta Kappan, 58,* 593–594.

Popham, W. J. (1978a). As always, provocative. *Journal of Educational Measurement, 15,* 297–300.

Popham, W. J. (1978b). The case for criterion-referenced measurements. *Educational Researcher, 7,* 6–10.

Popham, W. J. (1978c). *Criterion-referenced measurement.* Englewood Cliffs, NJ: Prentice-Hall.

Popham, W. J. (1978d). *Setting performance standards.* Los Angeles: Instructional Objectives Exchange.

Popham, W. J. (1980). *Modern educational measurement.* Englewood Cliffs, NJ: Prentice-Hall.

Popham, W. J., & Husek, T. R. (1969). Implications of criterion-referenced measurement. *Journal of Educational Measurement, 6,* 1–9.

Roid, G. H., & Haladyna, T. M. (1982). *A technology for test-item writing.* New York: Academic Press.

Rovinelli, R. J., & Hambleton, R. K. (1977). On the use of content specialists in the assessment of criterion-referenced test item validity. *Tijdschrift voor Onderwijsresearch, 2,* 49–60.

Schoon, C. G., Gullion, C. M., & Ferrara, P. (1979). Bayesian statistics, credentialing examinations, and the determination of passing points. *Evaluation and the Health Professions, 2,* 181–201.

Shepard, L. A. (1984). Setting performance standards. In R. A. Berk (Ed.), *A guide to criterion-referenced test construction.* Baltimore: Johns Hopkins University Press.

Subkoviak, M. (1976). Estimating reliability from a single administration of a criterion-referenced test. *Journal of Educational Measurement, 13,* 265–275.

Swaminathan, H., Hambleton, R. K., & Algina, J. (1974). Reliability of criterion-referenced tests: A decision-theoretic formulation. *Journal of Educational Measurement, 11,* 263–268.

Traub, R. E., & Rowley, G. L. (1980). Reliability of test scores and decisions. *Applied Psychological Measurement, 4,* 517–546.

Van der Linden, W. J., & Mellenbergh, G. J. (1977). Optimal cutting scores using a linear loss function. *Applied Psychological Measurement, 1,* 593–599.

Wilcox, R. (1976). A note on the length and passing score of a mastery test. *Journal of Educational Statistics, 1,* 359–364.

17

PERSONALITY ASSESSMENT

FRANCES F. WORCHEL
Texas A & M University

While it is agreed that assessment is a predominant function of the school psychologist (Cancelli and Duley, 1985), the most valid and efficient method for conducting personality assessments remains controversial. The debate regarding effective assessment techniques is reflected in the lack of uniform training. Surveys indicate a wide variety of tests utilized: interviews, class observations, Bender-Gestalt, sentence completions, thematic stories, drawings, the Rorschach, and behavior rating scales (Goh, Teslow, & Fuller, 1981; Prout, 1983). However, lack of adequate training with these tests is cited as a crucial problem for school psychologists (Gresham, 1985). In a survey of NASP members, Ramage (1979) found assessment of emotionally disturbed children to be a major training need, with many school psychologists perceiving their abilities in this area to be inadequate (Barbarnel & Hoffenberg-Rutman, 1974).

A major training difficulty involves the lack of a widely accepted theoretical model for personality assessment. Models discussed in the literature include the medical model; psychoanalytic theory; trait theories; humanism; and neurobiological, cognitive developmental, behavioral, developmental psychopathology, pluralistic, ecological, and psychoeducational models (Cancelli & Duley, 1985; Knoff, 1986; Mercer & Ysseldyke, 1977).

The techniques presented in this chapter represent an integrated approach, probably best affiliated with the psychoeducational model. This model (Fagan, 1979; Knoff, 1986; Morse, 1975) considers both internal conflicts and environmental (particularly academic) influences. Thus, both traditional (e.g., projective) tests and more structured self-report measures will be reviewed.

In choosing among the numerous techniques that might be utilized in the personality assessment of a school-aged child, it was decided to focus on a fairly limited number, which, nonetheless, would provide a basic armament for the school psychologist. The techniques selected inlcude many of those most commonly used by the school psychologist in assessing emotional disturbance (Goh, Teslow, & Fuller, 1981; Prout, 1983). These are interview, Bender-Gestalt, the Child Behavior Checklist, depression inventories, sentence completions, thematic storytelling techniques, picture drawings, and the Rorschach. As there continues to be much debate over the validity and reliability of many of these measures, they will be critiqued for their suitability in conducting school-based personality assessments. Of course, many measures are not covered here; in particular, cognitive assessments, which are included in Chapter 13, and many of the excellent sources included in Chapter 14.

THE INTERVIEW

The interview should serve as the cornerstone for any comprehensive evaluation. Whether a structured interview is conducted as the first step in an assessment, or whether questioning continues informally throughout the assessment, a great deal of information will be gained merely by asking. In recent years, interviewing techniques have been marked by two major trends (Edelbrock & Costello, 1984). One, it has become more common to interview the child rather than the child's parents. Second, the interviews themselves have changed, becoming both more structured and more specialized. Thus, interviews are being developed which are geared toward a narrower age range or a specific behavioral problem. These changes were prompted by increasing concern that interviews were neither valid nor reliable. With the advent of the DSM III and clearer diagnostic categories, it has been possible to devise structured interviews with better psychometric properties. Currently, many structured interviews maintain test–retest reliabilities in the range .70 to .90 (Nuttall & Ivey, 1986). However, there remains concern over the validity of interviews. Nuttall and Ivey believe that most child interviews are inappropriate for judging specific personality traits or making fine discriminations between groups. However, structured interviews do seem valid for judging overall social-emotional functioning or in comparing groups of children (Paget, 1984).

Commonly used structured interviews for children and adolescents include the following:

Mental Health Assessment Form (MHAF) (Kestenbaum & Bird, 1978)

This is a semistructured screening interview for 7 to 12-year-olds; administration time—45 minutes. The interview consists of a general outline to be followed. Part I resembles a standard Mental Status exam, while Part II covers specific symptoms, interpersonal relationships, self-concept, and general levels of adaptation. Brief examples are included to facilitate scoring, but clinical knowledge is needed to determine whether a child deviates from normal behavior. A second form is being developed for 13 to 19-year-olds. The interrater reliability of this measure is somewhat low, due to the relatively unstructured format (Edelbrock & Costello, 1984). Paget (1984) rates concurrent validity as good, but cites a lack of evidence for predictive validity.

Kiddie Schedule for Affective Disorders and Schizophrenia (K-SADS) (Puig-Antich & Chambers, 1978)

This is a semistructured diagnostic interview for 6 to 17-year-olds; administration time—$1\frac{1}{2}$ hours. Parent and child are interviewed separately. The K-SADS covers background, specific symptoms, observations, and overall degree of impairment, and leads to RDC or DSM III diagnosis. The interviewer must have good clinical skills in order to score the K-SADS. Paget (1984) rates test–retest reliability as good; however, interrater reliability and validity studies suffer from small sample sizes.

The Child Screening Inventory (Langner et al., 1976)

This is a screening interview for 6- to 18-year-olds; administration time—15 to 20 minutes. The Child Screening Inventory can be used in conjunction with an extensive parent interview, including background, specific behaviors, marital relationship, and child rearing practices. The child interview yields seven factors: self-destructive tendencies, mentation problems, conflict with parents, regressive anxiety, delinquency, and isolation. Edelbrock and Costello (1984) report only fair validity for this instrument and recommend it only as a descriptive, rather than diagnostic, tool.

The Child Assessment Schedule (CAS) (Hodges, Kline, Stern, Cytryn, & Mcknew, 1982)

This is a structured interview for children aged 7 to 12; administration time—45 to 60 minutes. The CAS yields a total score indicating degree of pathology, content scores (e.g., family problems, self-image, school), and symptom complex scores related to DSM III diagnosis. Of the interviews reviewed here, the CAS appears to have the best psychometric properties. Reliabilities for total score and content areas are quite good, while numerous validation studies have yielded positive findings (Edelbrock & Costello, 1984).

The interviews reviewed here represent attempts to provide more structure and specificity to techniques which have in the past suffered from bias, lack of objectivity, and unreliability. Gains have clearly been made; however, Paget (1984) warns that most currently used interviews lack sufficient data on reliability and validity to warrant their usage in evaluating and diagnosing individual children. Structured interviews do not seem to be entirely appropriate for school-based assessments, as most of them are closely tied to DSM III symptomatology. Clearly, there is a need to develop interviews assessing criteria for emotional disturbance as outlined by P.L. 94-142. For example, a school-based interview would cover areas such as academic progress, relations with peers, feelings of depression or unhappiness, somatic complaints, and social maladjustment.

Regardless of which specific interviewing technique is being utilized, the school psychologist should be aware of the important information available from observing the child. In the course of the initial interview, the psychologist will be alert to the following:

1. *Child's Initial Reaction to the Interviewer:* Does the child willingly leave the classroom to go with the examiner? Does the child appear at ease, make spontaneous conversation, give answers without prompting, appear eager to begin structured testing? Is the child sullen, defensive, or view the examiner as a "threat"?

2. *Physical Appearance:* Is the child dressed neatly and appropriately? Does clothing reveal an overly advanced developmental level (i.e., the 8-year-old female with makeup, jewelry, and clothing more appropriate for an adolescent)? Does the child possess physical attributes (overweight, excess acne) that might result in teasing by peers?

3. *Fine and Gross Motor Skills:* Does the child appear clumsy? How does the child manipulate pencils and test materials? Are fine and gross motor skills equally developed?

4. *Interpersonal Relatedness:* Can the child converse with the examiner in an engaging manner, displaying social skills? How long does it take the child to "warm up" to the examiner?

5. *Resistance:* What types of resistance, if any, does the child display? Does the child avoid questions when particular areas are broached? Does the child use overt resistance (refusing to talk at all) or more passive actions (delay, changing the subject)? Does the child deny difficulties

("I don't know why I'm here. Everything is fine.")

6. *Mood and Affect:* What is the child's general affective state throughout the evaluation—lethargy, depression, anxiety, happiness? Is the child's mood congruent with behaviors? Is mood fairly stable, or does it vary wildly throughout the session?

7. *Ability to Stay on Task:* What is the child's tolerance for sustained effort? Does the child require frequent breaks or prompting? Does the child show persistence in attempting tasks or answering questions. Is the child impulsive, flighty? Can the child concentrate on a topic despite distractions?

8. *Response to Structure:* If the child begins to lose self-control, can he calm himself down? How does the child respond to the examiner's limit setting? How often does the examiner need to control the child? Are praise and encouragement effective? Are verbal commands effective? Does the child ever need physical restraint?

9. *Thematic Development:* Do particular themes develop during the interview: for example, need for nurturance, aggression and anger, need for structure?

10. *Overall Impression:* What overall impression does the examiner have of the child? Is this a child the examiner "would like to take home"? or does the examiner feel a sense of just having endured a whirlwind of activity and feel relief that the session is over? Does the examiner feel connected to the child, or feel that something was missing and that no real bond was formed with this child? This overall impression is likely to be quite predictive of how most other people relate to this child.

It is clear that an interview serves two important functions: providing verbal answers to specific content areas, and allowing the interviewer to observe the child's behaviors. During the interview the examiner should have begun the process of formulating and confirming hypotheses. At this point, a decision should be made as to what formal testing needs to be done. It is only after interacting with the child that a decision can be made as to whether structured questionnaires will be productive or whether more projective techniques need to be utilized.

THE BENDER-GESTALT TEST

Developed almost 50 years ago, the Bender-Gestalt remains one of the most widely used assessment techniques (Tolar & Brannigan, 1980; Vukovich, 1983). The test consists of nine cards with geometric designs which the child copies onto a piece of blank paper. Although it was developed as a test of visual motor integration for children aged 5 to 11, the Bender is frequently used both for this purpose and as a measure of emotional adjustment. The most frequently used scoring system for emotional indicators was developed by Koppitz (1963, 1975). This system uses items based on two criteria: ability to differentiate between groups of well adjusted and emotionally disturbed children, and lack of relationship to age and maturation in children aged 5 to 11. The following is a list of the 12 emotional indicators and their implications (Koppitz, 1982, p. 288).

1. *Confused Order (CA 8 or Older):* Lack of planning, poor organization, mental confusion.
2. *Wavy Line on Figures 1 or 2:* Poor motor coordination and/or emotional instability.
3. *Dashes Substituted for Circles on Figure 2:* Impulsivity or lack of interest.
4. *Increase in Size of Figures 1, 2, or 3:* Low frustration tolerance, explosiveness.
5. *Large Size:* Impulsivity, acting-out behavior.
6. *Small Size:* Anxiety, withdrawal, constriction, timidity.
7. *Fine Line:* Timidity, shyness, withdrawal.
8. *Careless Overwork, Reinforced Lines:* Impulsivity, aggressiveness, acting-out behavior.
9. *Second Attempt at Drawing Figures:* Impulsivity, anxiety, behavior problems.
10. *Expansiveness, Two or More Pages:* Acting-out behavior.
11. *Box Around One or More Figures:* Attempt to control impulsivity, weak inner control, need for outer limits and structure.

12. *Spontaneous Elaborations and/or Additions to Designs:* Very unusual, preoccupation with own thoughts, fears, anxieties, serious emotional problems.

Koppitz stresses that these indicators should be used cautiously. At least three are needed before one would consider a child to have emotional problems, and even this must be used only as a working hypothesis. Research regarding the psychometric properties of this method has been sparse. Gregory (1977) reported significant correlations between the Koppitz scores and 5 of the 17 factors on the Devereux Child Behavior Rating Scale (Spivack & Spotts, 1966), using elementary school children referred for psychological services. Tolar and Brannigan (1980) conclude that the Bender can differentiate between well-adjusted and maladjusted children, yet caution that it should not be used as a sole indicator of personality problems. Perhaps the single largest misuse of the Bender Gestalt involves the tendency to use it with adolescents, for whom the emotional indicators have not been normed.

CHILD BEHAVIOR CHECKLIST

The Child Behavior Checklist (CBCL) (Achenbach & Edelbrock, 1983) was developed to assess behavior disorders in children and adolescents using a developmental-normative perspective. In developing the test, the authors had three goals in mind: (a) to provide empirically based norms for different behaviors, (b) to determine patterns of behavior that occur at different ages, and (c) to study both stability and change in behaviors over time. The CBCL attempts to establish syndromes, or groups of behaviors that tend to co-occur (Edelbrock, 1984).

The CBCL is a checklist, filled out by the child's parent. Parents rate their children on 118 behavior problems, giving either a 1 (not true of the child), a 2 (somewhat or sometimes true), or a 3 (often true). The parents also rate their child on social competence items, which cover such areas as chores, activities, friendships, and schoolwork. Most parents can complete the checklist in about 15 minutes.

The CBCL yields different scales depending on the age and sex of the child. There are six separate scoring sheets, for boys and girls aged 4 to

5, 6 to 11, and 12 to 16. All forms have two broad band scales for Internalizing and Externalizing, as well as a Total Problem Score. The Social Competence items are broken into three scales: School, Activities, and Social. The 4–5 form is not scored for School. Depending on the age and sex of the child, either eight or nine behavioral syndromes are derived, such as depressed, obsessive compulsive somatic complaints, hyperactive, and aggressive (Achenbach & Edelbrock, 1983). All scales are scored using a normalized T, allowing for comparisons across scales.

The CBCL is most useful in identifying differences by age and clinical status. Of the 118 behavior problems, 84 showed significant age trends. For example, whining and fears occur in about 50% of nonreferred 4- to 5-year-olds but in only about 6% of nonreferred adolescents (Edelbrock, 1984). These age norms are invaluable in determining whether certain behaviors are developmentally appropriate. Similarly, 108 of the 118 behavior problems differentiate between nonreferred and clinic children. The best discriminator is the item "unhappy, sad, or depressed." This behavior is reported in 40 to 90% of referred children (depending on age and gender) but in only 10% of nonreferred children (Edelbrock, 1984). Thus, the CBCL should alert the school psychologist to certain behaviors that occur more frequently in disturbed children, versus those behaviors signifying more "normal" behavior.

The CBCL has quite good psychometric properties. In a study of content validity, 116 of the 118 behavior problems and all 20 social competence items were significantly associated with clinical status ($p < .01$). One week test–retest reliabilities for individual items revealed all intraclass correlations to be above .90, and the median Pearson correlation for scale scores was .89 (Edelbrock, 1984). Separate tests are now available for 2- to 3-year-olds, as well as a Teacher form for school-aged children. It is often quite informative to compare teacher and parent forms of the CBCL, and note discrepancies in any areas.

DEPRESSION AND ANXIETY MEASURES

In recent years there has been growing concern over the area of childhood depression. Among the many factors associated with depression in school-aged children are poor academic achievement, peer relationship problems, behavior problems, and in severe cases, suicide (Worchel, Nolan & Willson, 1987). Investigations of childhood depression have focused on such questions as whether childhood depression is similar to adult depression, whether "masked depression" actually exists and can be measured, whether there are differences in the manifestation of depression across sex and age, why self-reports of depression often differ from reports by others (e.g., teachers, parents), and what accurate prevalence figures are for child and adolescent depression. This growing concern with depression in school-aged children has prompted school psychologists to search for suitable measures to include in their assessment batteries. Although numerous new instruments have been developed, we review here only a limited number.

Children's Depression Inventory

The CDI (Kovacs, 1980/1981) is a 27-item self-report measure suitable for school-aged children and adolescents. The CDI is a downward extension of the Beck Depression Inventory (Beck, Ward, Mendelson, Mock, and Enbaugh, 1961). It includes both cognitive/affective and somatic items relating to schoolwork, interpersonal relations, mood, and affect. The child picks one of three responses to each item, describing the way that he or she has felt during the last 2 weeks. Administration and scoring take a total of about 15 to 20 minutes. The CDI may be administered individually or in groups. The CDI is currently the most widely used self-report measure of childhood depression (Kazdin & Petti, 1982) and has undergone numerous psychometric investigations. Kovacs (1980/1981) reports respectable internal consistency and statistically significant item-total correlations. Smucker, Craighead, Craighead, and Green (1986) report coefficient alphas of .83 to .89 and 1-year test–retest reliabilities of .41 for males and .69 for females. Validity has been established in several studies: Significant correlations have been established between the CDI and the Children's Depression Scale, the Children's Manifest Anxiety Scale–Revised, and the Children's Depression Rating Scale (Eason, Finch, Brasted, & Saylor, 1984; W. M. Reynolds, 1985). In addition, Lobovits and Handal (1985) compared children rated as either depressed or nondepressed based on DSM III criteria and found their CDI means to be significantly different.

Children's Depression Scale

The CDS (Lang & Tisher, 1978) is a 66-item self-report measure normed on children aged 9 through 16. Items focus on both depression and more positive experiences. The child places cards representing each item into one of five boxes, ranging from "very wrong" to "very right." The CDS yields the following six subscales: affective responses, social problems, self-esteem, preoccupation with own sickness/death, guilt, and pleasure. According to Tisher and Lang (1983), there is a tendency for girls to score higher than boys. In a study of validity the CDS discriminated well between regular schoolchildren, school refusers, and a clinic population.

Child Depression Scale

The CDS (Reynolds, 1980) is a 30-item self-report measure suitable for children aged 8 to 13. A four-point "almost never" to "all the time" response format is utilized. W. M. Reynolds, Anderson, and Bartell (1985) report good reliability for the CDS (coefficient alpha = .90). In addition, initial validity studies are promising; Reynolds reports significant correlations between the CDS and the Children's Depression Index and the Children's Manifest Anxiety Scale–Revised. A related measure, the Reynolds Adolescent Depression Scale (W. M. Reynolds, 1985), has also been developed for use with older youngsters.

Peer Nomination Inventory of Depression

The PNID (Lefkowitz & Tesiny, 1980) is a sociometric measure on which children select other children in their class who exhibit each of 20 characteristics (e.g., depression, happiness, popularity). For an average-sized class, the PNID takes about 15 minutes to administer and about an hour to score. Finch and Saylor (1984) rate the psychometric properties of this measure as excellent. Kazdin (1981) states that the PNID predicts school performance, self-concept, teacher ratings of work skills and social behavior, peer ratings of happiness and popularity, and locus of control.

Revised Children's Manifest Anxiety Scale

The RCMAS (C. R. Reynolds and Richmond, 1985) is a 37-item self-report measure of anxiety, appropriate for children aged 6 to 19. It may be administered individually or in groups, and requires about a third-grade reading level. Children answer "yes" or "no" to each statement, with the "yes" responses totaled to yield an anxiety score. Subscales include the following: physiological anxiety, worry, oversensitivity, social concerns, and concentration. A lie scale is also included as a measure of acquiescence, social desirability, or deliberate faking. C. R. Reynolds and Richmond (1985) caution that the RCMAS has the following limitations:

1. It should never be used as the sole measure of anxiety.
2. It is rather easy to understand the purpose of the test; thus social desirability responses or intentional faking are possibilities.
3. The RCMAS is not normed on diverse cultural groups.
4. The total score and scale scores should be used rather than individual items.

These cautions provided for the RCMAS appear relevant to all of the depression measures reviewed here. With the exception of the PNID, most self-report measures of depression are susceptible to "faking good." When diagnosing individual children, it seems prudent to use a depression scale as a screening device. Those children testing positive should be further evaluated with other measures.

SENTENCE COMPLETION METHODS

Sentence-completion methods have alternately been described as projective, semiprojective, or nonprojective techniques. This variability in description aptly denotes the numerous sentence-completion formats available. Most sentence-completion methods contain between 40 and 100 items and vary according to degree of structure, nature of the sentence stem, and content (Hart, 1986; Rabin & Zlotogorski, 1981).

Items range from very structured (The person my mother loves the most is . . .) to relatively unstructured (I am . . .). It is generally believed that the less structure inherent in the stem, the less directed the child is toward a particular response, and thus the test becomes more projective in nature. However, Koppitz (1982) contends that sentence completions fail to reveal any unconscious or involuntary information, and that pupils "give only answers they want to give." Hart (1986) refutes this, asserting that children often give atypical responses. However, these responses may result from a variety of sources: They may reflect atypical development and resulting psychology, an inadequate understanding of the requirements of the test, resistance or a lack of motivation on the part of the student, or poor rapport between student and examiner.

Items also vary regarding the use of first- and third-person referents. It is argued that a stem such as "I really hate . . ." may be threatening to some children and result in avoidance of a clinically relevant answer, whereas the stem "Most people hate . . ." might reveal more true feelings. Hart (1986) reviews studies supporting a mixture of first-, third-, and nonperson referents.

Finally, the content of the stems varies, depending on what type of information is being solicited. Many tests include items designed to measure feelings about one's self, relations with peers, school achievement, and family relationships.

Of the currently available sentence completion methods for school age children, only two will be reviewed here. Very few tests have been designed specifically for use with children, and fewer still have any sort of standardized scoring procedure with available normative data.

The HAAK Sentence Completion Test (Haak, 1976)

This test contains two forms: one for elementary school children (87 items), and a similar form for secondary school students (91 items). After the test is completed, the examiner transfers the responses onto an organization form, which groups items into a number of categories, as follows:

Coping: school tasks, peers, authority.
Attitudes: tasks, peers, authority.
Academic orientation: value, locus of control.
Relationships: father, mother, family unit, teacher, peers, self concept.
Emotional state: emotional language, sources of emotionality, stressors, fantasy content, solvers, comforters.
Aspirations
Openness to help

The advantages of this extremely comprehensive instrument are that it was designed specifically for school aged children and contains items related to a number of common concerns. The organization form facilitates interpretation, as similar items are clustered together to emphasize patterns of response. Unfortunately, interpretation is based on clinical skills. The competent examiner is assumed to have knowledge, based on experience, of a range of possible answers provided by normal and emotionally disturbed children. Although this instrument is quite promising, research on validity and reliability has yet to be presented.

The Hart Sentence Completion Test for Children

The HSCT (Hart, 1986) appears to be the most useful instrument currently available. This 40-item test, designed for ages 6 to 18, yields the following scales:

Perception of family.
Interaction with family.
Perception of peers.
Interactions with peers.
Perception of school.
Interaction with school.
Need orientation.
Personal evaluation.
Psychosexual awareness and future orientation.
General mental health.

Scoring of the HSCT involves two steps. First, each of the 10 scales is subjectively rated on a 5-point scale (negative versus positive). No criteria are given in making these ratings. Second, each individual item is rated as either negative or positive, with criteria given for judging each individual stem. These individual ratings are then summed to again form 10 scale ratings. Thus, the test produces two sets of scores for each of the HSCT scales. Both reliability and validity studies have been conducted on the HSCT. Ulman (1972) reported fair interrater reliabilities (.50 to .86), while Swanson (1975) reported stronger findings, with interrater reliabilities ranging from .90 to .99. In a validity investigation, Robyak (1975) demonstrated that five of the eight HSCT scales could distinguish between emotionally handicapped and typical schoolchildren. Those scales that did not significantly discriminate between groups were interaction with family, need orientation, and personal evaluation. Although Hart has not yet presented normative data for this test, work in this area is in progress and will hopefully provide a sentence-completion test with sound psychometric backing.

THEMATIC STORYTELLING TECHNIQUES

Thematic storytelling techniques are based on the projective hypothesis; since there is no "correct" answer, individuals are assumed to project their own needs, drives, anxieties, emotions, or conflicts onto the unstructured picture stimulus. Thus, pictures used as stimuli in these techniques are often selected to solicit particular thematic material.

Thematic Apperception Test

The TAT was the first widely used thematic technique, with most other methods being modifications of this test. Developed by Murray (1938, 1943), the TAT was presumed to reveal a person's needs (e.g., need for nurturance, need for achievement), presses from the environment (e.g., rejection by parents, medical illnesses), and themas. These themas, or themes, combine needs and presses into a pattern that is played out in the persons' story. For example, the need for nurturance and the press of paternal rejection may be portrayed in themes centering on children being left behind by parents. Thus, this theme might be expressed in various slightly different forms in response to a number of different cards. The job of the examiner is then to identify consistent themes that occur throughout the test.

The TAT consists of 20 cards, of which 10 are to be selected for each administration. Some of the cards are labeled as being more suitable for men, women, boys, or girls. Subjects are instructed to make up stories telling what is happening, what happened previously, how the people are feeling and thinking, and how the story ends. There is debate over how much and when the stories should be probed. In general, it is felt that questions tend to reduce the projective nature of the stories produced (Obrzut and Boliek, 1986). It is also recommended that stories be given verbally rather than written out by the subject. Written stories tend to be shorter and less detailed.

A variety of scoring systems have been devised for the TAT. In Murray's original system, stories or events are scored for the following: characteristics of the hero (main character); motives, needs, and feelings of the hero; environmental presses and their effect on the hero; outcomes, simple and complex themes; and interests or sentiments relating to the hero. Later systems have ranged from structured approaches with comprehensive rating scales to pure content analysis.

Karon (1981) contends that "there is no scoring scheme for the TAT which is both usable and sufficiently inclusive to be clinically relevant (p. 93)." Karon recommends a clinical approach whereby each story is examined individually in order to answer the question, "Why would a human being say that, out of all the possibilities that exist?" (p. 93). Specific guidelines recommended by Karon include the following (p. 97):

1. Disturbing material is probably more meaningful when contained in a short story than when embedded in a long, detailed story.
2. In general, bright people and healthy people give longer stories.
3. The less the content "fits" the card, the more meaningful it will be (e.g., a story about a man killing someone is more meaningful if the picture depicts a man sitting calmly on a chair).
4. A subject's behaviors are predicted by behaviors of the characters in the stories. A subject's verbalizations are predicted by characters who say things. A subject's thoughts are predicted by thoughts of characters (e.g., a story about a man who considers suicide is probably more predictive of *thinking* about suicide than of actually *attempting* suicide).

There does not appear to be a structured scoring technique for the TAT which is feasible in terms of complexity or time. Obrzut and Boliek (1986) concur with Karon's approach, suggesting that the best scoring technique involves inspection of the stories and observations of the subject's behaviors during the test administration. For a further review, the reader is referred to Bellak (1971) for a comprehensive discussion of typical themes elicited by each card.

Children's Apperception Test

The CAT was designed by Bellak and Bellak (1949) as a downward extension of the CAT suitable for children aged 3 to 10. The CAT consists of 10 pictures of animal characters. An alternative form, the CAT-H, contains human figures. Koppitz (1982) contends that the human forms are more appropriate for children over 6 or for brighter pupils. The CAT pictures were designed to elicit responses to typical childhood concerns, such as sibling rivalry, relations with parents, aggression, fear of being lonely at night, toilet behavior, and problems of growth. Interpretation of the CAT is similar to that for the TAT: analysis of heros, needs, drives, environmental forces, conflicts, and coping styles.

Roberts Apperception Test for Children

The RATC (McArthur & Roberts, 1982) is a recently developed storytelling technique designed for children aged 6 to 15. The RATC was intended as a projective test with a standardized scoring system. The test consists of 27 cards, 11 of which are parallel forms for males/females. Sixteen cards are administered during a testing, which takes about 20 to 30 minutes.

The RATC appears to have significant benefits over its predecessors (Worchel, 1987). The test manual includes comprehensive information on the RATC's psychometric properties, administration, and scoring, as well as a number of case studies. The pictures, clearly more modern than those in the TAT/CAT, depict scenes designed to elicit common concerns. For example, specific cards portray parent–child relationships, sibling relationships, aggression, mastery, parental disagreement and affection, observation of nudity, school, and peer relationships. The test has a standardized scoring system, with scores converted to normalized T's based on data from a sample of 200 well-adjusted children. The following scores may be obtained from the RATC:

1. *Adaptive Scales:* reliance on others, support others, support child, limit setting, problem identification, and resolution (three types).
2. *Clinical Scales:* anxiety, aggression, depression, rejection, unresolved.
3. *Critical Indicators:* atypical response, maladaptive outcome, refusal.
4. *Supplementary Measures:* ego functioning, aggression, levels of projection.

The scoring manual gives detailed instructions and examples for scoring each of these measures. It is possible to do a profile plot of the scores (about 20 to 30 minutes) without completing the more detailed and time-consuming Interpersonal Matrix.

A recent review of the RATC in the *Ninth Mental Measurements Yearbook* (Sines, 1985) cites validity data as being unimpressive. In perhaps the most substantial study to date, 200 well-adjusted children were compared with 200 children evaluated at guidance clinics. The normal children scored higher than the clinic children on all eight adaptive scales; however, the two groups could not be reliably differentiated on the clinical scales for aggression, anxiety, and depression.

McArthur and Roberts (1982) agree that current psychometric information is only a "first step" in establishing the RATC as a useful clinical tool. Overall, the RATC appears to be a well-designed, easy-to-use technique for children and young adolescents. The standardized scoring system, while admittedly lacking in validity evidence compared to more objective personality tests, appears to be relatively good compared to similar projective techniques (Worchel, 1987).

School Apperception Method

The SAM (Solomon & Starr, 1968) was developed for kindergarten through ninth graders to elicit stories concerning school-related problems. The 22 cards contain scenes such as a boy reading a book in class while other students watch him and form a line on the playground next to the monitor. Twelve cards are given during an administration. Scoring follows the guidelines given by Bellak (1947) for the TAT/CAT, and focuses on such themes as perception of teachers and peers, attitudes toward academics, punishment, frustration, aggression, and coping. The manual also provides questions to be used during the child's stories which are later scored qualitatively. In a review of the SAM, Obrzut and Boliek (1986) find the reliability, validity, and normative data to be unsubstantiated.

PICTURE DRAWINGS

Picture drawings are quite popular among school psychologists. In a recent survey (Prout, 1983), they were related as the third most frequently used technique, falling behind only the interview and classroom observations. The use of figure drawings to assess personality developed from earlier usage of these tests as a measure of cognitive abilities. The first tests to gain widespread usage as clinical tools were Machover's Draw-A-Person (1949) and Buck's House–Tree–Person (1948). Buck's is the more comprehensive sysem, and requires the child to complete pencil drawings of a house, a tree, a person, and then a person of the opposite sex. Next, the child is given crayons and asked to repeat the four drawings. Hammer (1981) recommends asking for additional drawings in pencil: the most unpleasant thing the subject can think of, a person in the rain, a family drawing, or an animal. Hammer states that this battery of at least eight drawings is mandatory for research purposes, and certainly advisable for clinical purposes. Hammer compares evaluating a child using only a single drawing to interpreting a Rorschach on the basis of just the first two cards. Koppitz (1982) takes a somewhat different approach. She suggests that a child should be asked to make a single drawing of a whole person. If an additional drawing is desired, a family drawing is recommended. Koppitz argues that the DAP becomes a portrait of the child's inner self, including his or her characteristics and attitudes. Thus, she believes that crayon or opposite sex drawings are unnecessary and do not justify the extra time needed.

Children's figure drawings are believed to yield several types of information. In addition to revealing a gross measure of intellectual functioning (Harris, 1963), drawings are assumed to contain nonverbal symbolic messages (Cummings, 1986). Cummings states that a figure drawing is a representation of the child's view of himself, and that the child will reveal conflicts, fears, family interactions, and perceptions of others through drawings. The emotionally disturbed child who has an inaccurate perception of the world will reveal these distortions in his or her pictures. Koppitz (1983) reaffirms this rationale, stating that drawings serve four functions with school-aged children (p. 422):

1. Human figure drawings reflect the child's personality and self-concept.
2. Family drawings show a child's perception of the family and their place within the family.
3. School drawings explore pupil's attitudes toward teachers and school.
4. Figure drawings can reveal student's attitudes toward social and cultural groups.

One of the most widely used interpretive systems for figure drawings has been developed by Koppitz (1968, 1982, 1983). Koppitz stresses the importance of behavioral observations while the child is producing his or her drawing. For example, it is important to observe what the child draws first. Koppitz maintains that most children draw a head

first; therefore, the observation that a child has drawn the feet first might be interpreted as that child having difficulties with interpersonal relations. After the drawing is completed, the following queries should be made: whether the person is real or made up, the age of the person, and what the person might be thinking or doing. Koppitz then recommends making a general, global assessment of the drawing, without looking at specific details or indicators. To make this global assessment, Koppitz suggests that the school psychologist obtain a large sample of drawings from the psychologist's school district, thus providing a reference group with which to compare clinical samples.

Next, the drawing is analyzed in terms of Koppitz's (1982) 30 emotional indicators (EIs). The EIs are grouped into five categories: impulsivity, insecurity, feelings of inadequacy, anxiety, shyness/timidity, and anger/aggressiveness. Included among the EIs are signs such as big figure, hands cut off, omission of eyes, short arms, teeth, and nude figure. A single EI is not clinically significant; three or more EIs suggest the possibility of emotional problems. Koppitz stresses that the EIs are not scores. They are simply indicators which occur more frequently on the drawings of emotionally disturbed children than on the drawings of normal children.

In an excellent review of figure drawing validation studies, Cummings (1986) finds varying results depending on the variable measured. His results might be summarized as follows:

1. *Body Image:* There is reasonable support for the hypothesis that children draw their concept of their own bodies.
2. *Gender Identity:* Caution should be used when making the interpretation that drawing a picture of the opposite sex implies problems with gender identity. The sex of the first-drawn picture is quite variable, and many children draw a different-sexed figure on alternate administrations.
3. *Size of Drawing:* There does not appear to be a systematic relationship between size of the drawing and self-concept.
4. *Anxiety:* There is some support for a relationship between anxiety and emotional indicators, particularly when the anxiety is experimentally manipulated.

Overall, Cummings' review appears to indicate a rationale for analyzing the total number of emotional indicators rather than attempting to relate specific indicators to specific characteristics. Cummings himself concludes that the greatest interpretive value of picture drawings is produced by observing the child's verbalizations and test-taking behaviors; the examiner should focus on the child's affective responses when drawing family members, attributions regarding success and failure, and spontaneous comments.

Hammner (1981) also discusses a number of contradictory studies relating characteristics of drawings to personality traits. Hammer provides several justifications for the lack of more positive findings. First, many studies attempt to use drawings to distinguish subjects with different psychiatric diagnoses. Hammer suggests that if the drawings appear unable to differentiate between these groups, it may be due to the unreliability of the psychiatric diagnoses. Second, many studies compare "normals" and clinical populations using group means. Thus, extremes tend to be canceled out. For example, anxiety may be indicated by either large body size or small body size. When this variable is analyzed as a group mean, significant results will be obscured. Overall, Hammer appears to advocate the clinical rather than the standardized approach to interpreting drawings. He applauds clinicians who use an "affective," "feeling" approach, who see the drawing as a "sensitive tool" and can interpret it with some "artistry" (p. 174).

In addition to the standard Draw-A-Person and House–Tree–Person, many school psychologists employ the following variations.

Kinetic Family Drawing

The KFD (Burns & Kaufman, 1972) was devised to gain information about the child's perceptions of his or her family and the relationships within the family. The instructions are as follows (p. 5): "Draw a picture of everyone in your family, including you, DOING something. Try to draw whole people, not cartoons or stick people. Remember, make everyone DOING something—some kind of actions." After the child has drawn the picture, the examiner may query as to who the different figures are and what they are doing. In general, family drawings are evaluated in terms of content.

- Who does the picture contain? Does a child whose parents have been divorced and/or remarried put both natural parents in the picture? Are step-parents included? In an intact family, are certain family members excluded? If so, it is likely that the child has some sort of difficulty with the excluded member.
- Are the family members interacting? In one of this author's cases, a 10-year-old boy with conduct problems was asked to do a KFD. The boy drew a table and four chairs, with a bare light bulb overhead. He described the picture as: "This is my family playing poker. Everyone's gone out for a drink." It soon became clear that this child felt very isolated and rejected by his parents.
- What are the relative sizes of the figures? Does the child view himself as very small and weak compared to other family members?
- What activity is the family engaged in? Fighting? Playing together? Despite explicit instructions, is the child unable to produce an interaction in the family?

Kinetic School Drawings

The KSD (Prout & Phillips, 1974) is similar to the KFD, with content interpretations aimed at issues concerning achievement and relations with peers and teachers. The following instructions are given: "I'd like you to draw a school picture. Put yourself, your teacher and a friend or two in the picture. Make everyone doing something. Try to draw whole people and make the best drawing you can. Remember, draw yourself, your teacher, and a friend or two, and make everyone doing something." Like the KFD, queries are used to further explore the picture.

Kinetic Drawing System

The KDS (Knoff & Proutt, 1985a, 1985b) is designed to examine the interactions between home and school relationships. For example, it is common for a child to do poorly at school because of conflicts at home. Alternatively, a child with a learning disability might develop a poor self-concept due to school failures, and subsequently act out at home due to the learning problems at school. With the KDS, both the KFD and the KSD are administered. Knoff and Proutt are in the process of developing an empirically based scoring and interpretation system for the KDS.

THE RORSCHACH

Of all the personality tests used to assess children and adolescents, the Rorschach is probably the most controversial. Koppitz (1982) dismisses it as not a useful tool for school settings, suggesting that the time and effort required make the Rorschach feasible only in clinical settings.

The Rorschach technique discussed here will be based on Exner's three-volume Comprehensive System (Exner, 1974, 1978, 1986; Exner & Weiner, 1982). In this system, 10 inkblots are shown to subjects, with the instructions: "Tell me what this might be." An extremely complex scoring system allows for 90 possible scores per response, divided into seven major categories (Exner, 1986), as follows:

1. *Location:* Responses are scored for their position on the card: Responses may use the whole card, common detail areas, detail areas rarely mentioned by the normative group, or areas involving white space.
2. *Determinants:* Movement, use of color, use of shape, or use of the shaded areas of the blot to imply depth, texture, or diffuse shading. This category also includes depth responses based only on form, pair responses (seeing two of something), and reflections.
3. *Organizational Activity:* Answers in which different areas of the blot are integrated in some sort of meaningful way. For example, the response "two bears" is not an integrated response. However, the response "two bears climbing a tree" is integrated.
4. *Populars:* Responses given quite frequently by the normative group, the criteria being an answer that is given at least once out of every three protocols.
5. *Contents:* All responses are scored for the type of content involved: for example, humans, animals, botany, sex.
6. *Special Scores:* Responses are coded when they contain unusual or bizarre characteristics, such as aggression, illogical thinking, redundancy, or perseveration.

In the Exner system, the Rorschach is considered primarily a cognitive-perceptual task and only secondarily a projective technique. Interpretations come from three different sources:

1. *The Structural Summary:* Data from the seven categories listed above are transformed into frequency counts (i.e., the number of color responses) and ratios (i.e., active movement/passive movement).
2. *The Sequence of Scores:* Scores on cards 1 to 10 are examined sequentially for patterns exhibited as the subject progresses through the test.
3. *Analysis of the Content:* Individual responses are examined for patterns, unusual contents, and projective material.

From the cognitive-perceptual framework, responses are considered a measure of the way in which individuals normally react in problem-solving situations. Interpretations based on structural data involve how the child scans the pictures, what the child sees, and what the child chooses to report. For example, the child who focuses on small details of the blots and gives numerous responses to each blot is assumed to approach other problem-solving tasks in a similar compulsive, pedantic way. Structural interpretations are empirically based, relying on normative tables. Separate indices are provided for schizophrenia, depression, and suicidal ideation.

After structural interpretations are made, the answers are also considered as a fantasy stimulus, and contents are analyzed. Using this approach, a child who identifies several cards as "two people with their back turned, running away from me" might lead to the interpretation that the child has difficulties with rejection. Naturally, interpretations based on content are more speculative than those based on structural data.

Given the complexity of the scoring system, there is legitimate concern that this technique is too time consuming to be useful for the school psychologist. Learning the Rorschach cannot really be done adequately without an entire graduate-level course devoted to the topic. Administration of the test averages about 45 minutes, and all but the very skilled clinician will require 1 to 2 hours to score and interpret the test. Exner has developed a computer scoring package that derives the structural summary and produces interpretive data, thus cutting down somewhat on scoring time.

The legitimacy of utilizing such a time-intensive instrument should be judged on the merits of the information produced by the test. Thus, the psychometric properties of the test, long an area of concern, are of primary importance. The developmental norms for children and adolescents are based on 1,870 nonpatient children aged 5 to 16, with between 105 and 150 protocols for each age level. According to Exner and Weiner (1982), the sample is roughly comparable to U.S. census data for proportions of males and females, white and minority youngsters, different socioeconomic groups, and urban, suburban, and rural areas. Although the adult standardization sample (age 17 and over) also contains norms for three clinical groups (schizophrenics, depressives, and character disordered), the current child norms are only for nonpatients.

In terms of reliability, Weiner (1986) reports interrater reliabilities of .85 or more for all the scoring codes, when trained examiners are used. Test–retest reliability is quite good for adults, with all but 2 of 19 variables showing 3-year correlations of .75 or higher. For children, particularly those 6 to 9 years old, test–retest reliabilities are substantially lower. Weiner (1986) explains this as being expected, given that the Rorschach measures cognitive perceptual abilities and patterns of coping, both of which should show developmental changes. When children are retested after short intervals (3 weeks), test–retest reliabilities are quite good.

In Exner and Weiner's (1982) volume on assessing children and adolescents, very little validity information is offered. It is generally assumed that interpretations based on adult data have the same meaning for children. However, they do include case studies of protocols from various nonpatients to demonstrate the efficacy of the Rorschach for a number of disorders (e.g., depression, schizophrenia, underachievement, behavior problems).

Overall, Exner's Comprehensive System for scoring and interpreting the Rorschach is psychometricaly superior to other systems and yields a great deal of clinically useful information. This may not be a feasible technique for the psychologist who conducts relatively few assessments. However, many school psychologists find themselves heavily committed to evaluation and, with practice, one can significantly reduce the time needed for scoring and interpretation.

CONCLUSIONS

The instruments reviewed in this chapter are not meant to be all-inclusive. Rather, it is intended that the reader have an idea of the types of tests that might be used together to form a solid battery for assessing emotional disturbance. Particularly when using projective techniques, it is important that the school psychologist use a rather extensive battery of tests. Many of the tests reviewed here have questionable validity when used alone. There seems to be growing consensus that more standardized, objective tests be used in diagnosis, while projective techniques be used as supplementary data, confirming hypotheses, describing individual differences in personality, and in making treatment recommendations.

Personality measures are often criticized as being too lengthy or time consuming to be useful to the school psychologist. This is a curious criticism, as it suggests that assessments of school-children are somehow less important than clinical cases, and not worthy of as much care in making diagnoses. Although it is certainty not true that longer tests are necessarily more valid or produce more information, the school psychologist should not reject a particular measure merely because of its length. A careful, comprehensive evaluation involves a matter of hours, or perhaps days. However, this assessment will probably affect a school child's progress for years to come.

Finally, in considering the current state of personality assessment, some general trends appear to be established:

1. It is important to assess the system, rather than just the individual child.
2. Assessment of behaviors will often be more valid and reliable than assessment of underlying traits; however, both can add useful information to a personality assessment.
3. Consideration must be made of developmental factors, with age norms needed for specific behaviors.
4. The school psychologist should be acutely aware of the most important step in the assessment process: formulating workable interventions.

REFERENCES

Achenbach, T., & Edelbrock, C. (1983). *Manual for the Child Behavior Checklist.* Burlington, VT: Queen City Printers.

Barbarnel, L., & Hoffenberg-Rutman, J. (1974). Attitudes toward job responsibilities and training satisfaction of school psychologists: A comparative study. *Psychology in the Schools, 11,* 425–429.

Beck, A. T., Ward, C. H., Mendelson, M., Mock, J., & Erbaugh, J. (1961). An inventory for measuring depression. *Archives of General Psychiatry, 4,* 561–571.

Bellak, L. (1947). *A guide to the interpretation of the Thematic Apperception Test.* New York: Psychological Corporation.

Bellak, L. (1971). *The TAT & CAT in Clinical Use.* New York: Grune & Stratton.

Bellak, L., & Bellak, S. (1949). *The Childrens Apperception Test.* New York: C. P. S.

Burns, R. C., & Kaufman, S. H. (1972). *Kinetic Family Drawing System (K-F-D): An introduction to understanding children through kinetic drawings.* New York: Brunner/Mazel.

Cancelli, A., & Duley, S. (1985). The role of assessment in school psychology. In J. Bergen (Ed.), *School psychology in contemporary society: An introduction* (pp. 119–139). Columbus, OH: Charles E. Merrill.

Cummings, J. A. (1986). Projective drawings. In H. Knoff (Ed.), *The assessment of child and adolescent personality* (pp. 199–244). New York: Guilford Press.

Eason, L. J., Finch, A. J., Brasted, W., & Saylor, C. F. (1985, Fall). The assessment of depression and anxiety in hospitalized pediatric patients. *Child Psychiatry and Human Development, 16*(1), 57–64.

Edelbrock, C. (1984). Developmental considerations. In T. Ollendick & M. Hersen (Eds.), *Child behavioral assessment: Principles and procedures* (pp. 20–37). Elmsford, NY: Pergamon Press.

Edelbrock, C., & Costello, A. (1984). Structurd psychiatric interviews for children and adolescents. In G. Goldstein & M. Herson (Eds.), *Handbook of psychological assessment* (pp. 276–290). Elmsford, NY: Pergamon Press.

Exner, J. E. (1974). *The Rorschach: A comprehensive system: Vol. 1. The Rorschach.* New York: Wiley.

Exner, J. (1978). *The Rorschach: A Comprehensive System: Vol. 2. Current research and advanced interpretation.* New York: Wiley.

Exner, J. (1986). *The Rorschach: A comprehensive system: Vol. 1.* (2nd. ed.). New York: Wiley.

Exner, J. E., & Weiner, I. B. (1982). *The Rorschach: A comprehensive system: Vol. 3. Assessment of children and adolescents.* New York: Wiley.

Fagan, S. A. (1979). Psychoeducational management and self-control. In D. Cullinan & M. Epstein (Eds.), *Special education for adolescents: Issues and perspectives* (pp. 235–272). Columbus, OH: Charles E. Merrill.

Finch, A. J., & Saylor, C. F. (1984). An overview of child depression. In W. Burns & J. Lavigne (Eds.), *Progress in pediatric psychology* (pp. 201–239). New York: Grune & Stratton.

Goh, D. S., Teslow, C. J., & Fuller, G. B. (1981). The practice of psychological assessment among school psychologists. *Professional Psychology, 12,* 1696–1706.

Gregory, M. K. (1977). Emotional indicators on the Bender-Gestalt and the Devereux Child Behavior Rating Scale. *Psychology in the Schools, 14,* 433–437.

Gresham, F. (1985). Behavior disorder assessment: Conceptual, definitional, and practical considerations. *School Psychology Review, 14*(4), 495–509.

Hammer, E. F. (1981). Projective drawings. In A. I. Rabin (Ed.), *Assessment with projective techniques.* New York: Springer.

Harris, D. B. (1963). *Children's drawings as a measure of intellectual maturity.* New York: Harcourt Brace & World.

Hart, D. H. (1986). The sentence completion techniques. In H. Knoff (Ed.), *The assessment of child and adolescent personality* (pp. 245–271). New York: Guilford Press.

Hodges, K., Kline, J., Stern, L., Cytryn, L., & McKnew, D. (1982). The development of the child assessment schedule for research and clinical use. *Journal of Abnormal Child Psychology, 10,* 173–189.

Karon, B. P. (1981). The Thematic Apperception Test. In A. I. Rabin (Ed.), *Assessment with projective techniques* (pp. 85–120). New York: Springer.

Kazdin, A. E. (1981). Assessment techniques for childhood depression. *Journal of the American Academy of Child Psychiatry, 20,* 358–375.

Kazdin, A. E., & Petti, T. (1982). Self report and interview measures of childhood and adolescent depression. *Journal of Childhood Psychology and Psychiatry, 23*(4), 437–457.

Kestenbaum, C., & Bird, H. (1978). A reliability study of the mental Health Assessment Form for school-age children. *Journal of the American Academy of Child Psychiatry, 7,* 338–347.

Knoff, H. (Ed.). (1986). *The assessment of child and adolescent personality.* New York: Guilford Press.

Knoff, H. M., & Prout, H. T. (1985a). *The Kinetic Drawing System: Family and School.* Los Angeles: Western Psychological Services.

Knoff, H. M., & Prout, H. T. (1985b). The Kinetic Drawing System: A review and integration of the Kinetic Family and School Drawing techniques. *Psychology in the Schools, 22,* 50–59.

Koppitz, E. M. (1963). *The Bender Gestalt Test for Young Children.* New York: Grune & Stratton.

Koppitz, E. M. (1968). *Psychological evaluation of children's human figure drawings.* New York: Grune & Stratton.

Koppitz, E. M. (1975). *The Bender Gestalt Test for Young Children* Vol. 2. New York: Grune & Stratton.

Koppitz, E. M. (1982). Personality assessment in the schools. In C. R. Reynolds & T. B. Gutkin, (Eds.), *The handbook of school psychology* (pp. 245–271). New York: Wiley.

Koppitz, E. M. (1983). Projective drawings with children and adolescents. *School Psychology Review, 12,* 421–427.

Kovacs, M. (1980–1981). Rating scales to assess depression in school-aged children. *Acta Paedopsychiatry, 46,* 305–315.

Lang, M., & Tisher, M. (1978). *Childrens Depression Scale.* Victoria: Australian Council for Educational Research.

Langner, T., Gersten, J., McCarthy, E., Eisenberg, J., Greane, E., Herson, J., & Jameson, J. (1976). A screening inventory for assessing psychiatric impairment in children 6–18. *Journal of Child Clinical Psychology, 44,* 286–296.

Lefkowitz, M. M., & Tesiny, E. P. (1980). Childhood depression: A critique of the concept. *Journal of Consulting and Clinical Psychology, 48,* 43–50.

Lobovits, D. A., & Handal, P. J. (1985). Childhood depression: Prevalence using DSM-III criteria and validity of parent and child depression scales. *Journal of Pediatric Psychology, 10*(1), 45–54.

McArthur, D. S., & Roberts, G. E. (1982). *Roberts Apperception Test for Children: Manual.* Los Angeles: Western Psychological Services.

Mercer, J., & Ysseldyke, J. (1977). Designing diagnostic-intervention programs. In T. Oakland (Ed.), *Psychological and educational assessment of minority children.* New York: Brunner/Mazel.

Morse, W. C. (1975). The education of socially maladjusted and emotionally disturbed children. In W. M. Cruickshank & G. O. Johnson (Eds.), *Education of exceptional children and youth,* (3rd ed., pp. 553–612). Englewood Cliffs, NJ: Prentice-Hall.

Murray, H. A. (1938). *Explorations in personality.* New York: Oxford University Press.

Murray, H. A. (1943). *Thematic Apperception Test Manual.* Boston: Harvard College.

Nuttall, E., & Ivey, A. (1986). The diagnostic interview process. In H. Knoff (Ed.), *The assessment of child and adolescent personality* (pp. 105–140). New York: Guilford Press.

Obrzut, J. E., & Boliek, C. A. (1986). Thematic approaches to personality assessment with children and adolescents. In H. Knoff (Ed.), *The assessment of child and adolescent personality* (pp. 173–198). New York: Guilford Press.

Paget, K. D. (1984). The structured association interview: A psychometric review. *Journal of School Psychology, 22,* 415–427.

Prout, H. (1983). School psychologists and social-emotional assessments techniques: Patterns in training and use. *School Psychology Review, 12,* 377–383.

Prout, H. T., & Phillips, P. D. (1974). A clinical note: The kinetic school drawing. *Psychology in the Schools, 11,* 303–306.

Puig-Antich, J., & Chambers, W. (1978). *The Schedule for Affective Disorders and Schizophrema for School Aged Children.* New York: New York State Psychiatric Institute.

Rabin, A. I., & Zlotogorski, Z. (1981). Completion methods: Word association, sentence and story completion. In A. I. Rabin (Ed.), *Assessment with projective techniques.* New York: Springer.

Ramage, J. (1979). National survey of school psychologists: Update. *School Psychology Digest, 8,* 153–161.

Reynolds, C. R., & Richmond, B. O. (1985). *Revised Children's Manifest Anxiety Scale: Manual.* Los Angeles: Western Psychological Services.

Reynolds, W. M. (1980). *Child Depression Scale.* Madison: University of Wisconsin.

Reynolds, W. M. (1985). Depression in childhood and adolescence: Diagnosis, assessment, intervention strategies and research. In T. Kratochwill (Ed.), *Advances in school psychology* (Vol. 4, pp. 133–189). Hillsdale, NJ: Lawrence Erlbaum.

Reynolds, W. M., Anderson, G., & Bartell, N. (1985). Measuring depression in children: A multimethod assessment investigation. *Journal of Abnormal Child Psychology, 13*(4), 513–526.

Robyak, S. L. (1975). *A validation study of the Hart Sentence Completion Test.* Unpublished master's thesis, University of Utah.

Sines, J. O. (1985). Review of the Roberts Apperception Test for Children. In J. Mitchell (Ed.), *The ninth mental measurements yearbook.* Lincoln, NE: Buros Institute.

Smucker, M. R., Craighead, W. E., Craighead, L. W., & Green B. J. (1986). Normative and reliability data for the Children's Depression Inventory. *Journal of Abnormal Child Psychiatry, 14*(1), 25–39.

Spivack, G., & Spotts, J. (1966). *Devereux Child Behavior (DCB) Rating Scale Manual.* Devon, PA: Devereux Press.

Swanson, C. H. (1975). *A validation study of the Hart Sentence Completion Test.* Unpublished master's thesis, University of Utah.

Tisher, M., & Lang, M. (1983). The Children's Depression Scale: Review and further developments. In D. Cantwell & G. Carlson (Eds.), *Affective disorders in childhood and adolescence: An update* (pp. 181–210). Engelwood Cliffs, NJ: Spectrum.

Tolor, A., & Brannigan, G. (1980). *Research and clinical applications of the Bender Gestalt Test.* Springfield, IL: Charles C. Thomas.

Ulman, J. E. (1972). *Inter-scorers reliability on the scoring system for the Hart Sentence Completion Test.* Unpublished master's thesis, University of Utah.

Vukovich, D. (1983). The use of projective assessments by school psychologists. *School Psychology Review, 12*(3), 358–365.

Weiner, I. (1986). Assessing children and adolescents with the Rorschach. In H. Knoff (Ed.), *The assessment of child and adolescent personality* (pp. 141–170). New York: Guilford Press.

Worchel, F. (1987). The Robert's Apperception Test for Children. In C. R. Reynolds & L. Mann (Eds.), *The encyclopedia of special education.* New York: Wiley.

Worchel, F., Nolan, B., & Willson, V. (1987). New perspectives on childhood depression. *Journal of School Psychology, 25,* 411–414.

18

NEUROPSYCHOLOGICAL ASSESSMENT TECHNIQUES

LAWRENCE C. HARTLAGE
CHARLES J. GOLDEN
University of Nebraska Medical Center

With the exception of a few reflex acts, almost all human adaptive behavior is mediated by the central nervous system. Higher levels of adaptive behavior, such as learning and information processing, are entirely dependent on the functional integrity of the central nervous system. Problems with learning and information processing, of the types commonly seen by school psychologists, thus reflect disorders within the central nervous system. The nonproblem areas in which school psychologists are sometimes involved, such as curriculum planning or vocational counseling, are to a considerable extent dependent on at least a tacit understanding of how the central nervous system processes information. A student with most efficient cortical functioning involving the nondominant central hemisphere, for example, will probably profit from action-oriented approaches to counseling; emphasis on curricular choices involving subjects with higher visuospatial and manipulative components than linguistic demands; and career planning to incorporate nondominant hemisphere strengths into an appropriate vocational area of emphasis.

The field of diagnosis and treatment of learning disabilities represents a special subsection of school psychology with unique dependence on knowledge of principles of neurological organization. The various disorders of receptive or expressive language and extraction of meaning from printed or graphic media each represent dysfunction involving specific cortical areas, and the essence of school psychological assessment of these problems involves a mapping of cortical assets and liabilities as a basis for developing recommendations for appropriate intervention.

Despite the heavy dependence of school psychology on a firm basis for understanding how the central nervous system works, the incidence of various types of disorders of the central nervous system, and the implications of these factors for daily school psychological practice, neurological components of most school psychology curricula occupy at best an insignificant part of the curriculum and in most training programs are totally neglected. To some extent, this neglect of neurological bases of learning has its roots in historical traditions, since the history of education in the

United States has been heavily behavioristic. Most educational programs have been based on the premise that given sufficient exposure to age-appropriate educational material, a student can be expected to develop more or less equal competence in such diverse areas as language, art, calculation, science, and history. Our experiences to the contrary, typified by repeated findings that even with equal exposure and emphasis some people do comparatively better in some subject areas than others, has been interpreted in behavioristic terms, such as "boys are expected to be better in math," rather than attempting to focus on intraindividual and interindividual patterns of uneven levels of neurological organization.

Another very important reason why neurological components have been lacking in school psychology training programs involves the simple nonavailability of people with sufficient neurological expertise to contribute to such programs. In the early 1970s, for example, there were fewer than 300 neurologists with special competence in children in the entire United States. Even among this small group of child neurologists, only a small percentage had sufficient knowledge of educational settings and school psychological needs to make much of a meaningful contribution. A knowledge of neurological diseases of childhood does not translate directly into the development of an appropriate individual educational program, or the determination for a given child whether an orthographic or phonetic approach would be the optimal reading instructional strategy.

Even when school psychologists in practice tried to relate school problems to neurological bases, the early results were far from promising. Categorization of children as minimal brain damaged represented one such approach, even though from the outset it was demonstrated to have little educational relevance (Reed, 1968). Another attempt to invoke neurological expertise in the management of school psychological problems involved the concept of hyperkinesis, which in its pure form represented a relatively well recognized entity. When attempted as a treatment approach in school psychology, the excesses involving both over-referral and over-treatment tended to mire the entire concept in controversy which has yet to be totally resolved.

THE CEREBRAL HEMISPHERES AND SCHOOL PSYCHOLOGICAL PRACTICE

Within the last decade, research in cerebral hemispheric specialization has resulted in findings with considerable importance for most aspects of school psychology practice. Before reviewing this research, it may be helpful to review the foundations on which this research was based.

Since the 1950s it has been recognized that in most adults the left cerebral hemisphere is specialized for language functions and the right cerebral hemisphere is more involved in processing spatial sorts of information (Reitan, 1955). Thus scores on verbal IQ tests (such as the majority of the Wechsler verbal subscales) generally reflect the functional level of the left cerebral hemisphere, while nonverbal IQ tests (e.g., Wechsler performance scales) measure more right-hemisphere-mediated abilities. In addition to processing verbal information, the left hemisphere is more specialized than the right for such cognitive tasks as logical, sequential, and analytic sorts of thinking; while the right hemisphere is more specialized for wholistic or gestalt types of information processing, music (Cohn, 1971; Gordon, 1975), and emotion (Schwartz, Davidson, & Maer, 1975). Anterior brain areas tend to be more concerned with planning and judgmental thinking, with more medially located brain areas involved in motor activities. In general, the motor strip of the brain enervates contralaterally; that is, the motor strip on the right side of the brain controls the left side of the body, and vice versa. Somewhat more posteriorly located brain areas deal with sensation and perception (e.g., the sensory strip), again with contralateral enervation, with purely visual functions located most posteriorly. Discrete brian areas have been known for many years to subserve discrete functions, along the general rules of hemispheric and anterior-to-posterior specialization described above. Thus the area for expressive speech (Broca, 1861) is located in the forward portions of the left hemisphere, with the area for receptive speech (Wernicke, 1974) located more posteriorly in the same hemisphere. Decoding meaning from printed words (manifested in such disorders as dyslexia) is even more posteriorly located, closer to the occipital lobe, on the left hemisphere.

Functions such as memory are similarly represented, according to the nature of material to be remembered. Thus verbal memory is more likely to involve the left hemisphere, while spatial memory is more dependent on the right hemisphere (Faglioni & Spinner, 1969; Ladavas, Vmilta, & Provinciali, 1979; Milner, 1971). Specifically, maze learning and form-board learning, for example, have been found to be impaired in patients with right-hemisphere dysfunctions (Corkin, 1965; De-Renzi, Faglioni, & Scotti, 1968), while verbal memory on the Wechsler Memory Scale was depressed with left hemisphere lesions (Schreiber, Golden, Kleinman, Goldfader, & Snow, 1976).

Although the greatest research emphasis involving consequences of brain dysfunction has focused on cognitive and information processing functions, there is evidence that personality factors are also involved. Hall and Hall (1968) has shown that impairment of the left cerebral hemisphere results in a limited and constricted approach to coping with the environment, while right-hemisphere impairment results in an expansive, uncritical, impulsive coping style. Historically, neurologists have referred to the adjustment of patients with right-hemisphere lesions as characterized by "la belle indifference"; while patients with left-hemisphere impairment demonstrate a classical "catastrophic reaction" equivalent of Hall's constricted approach (McFie & Zangwill, 1960).

Incidence and Educational Implications of Cerebral Asymmetry

More than 100 years ago, Heschl (1878) reported asymmetries in anatomical configurations of the two cerebral hemispheres, and 90 years later Geschwind and Levitsky (1968) compared the two hemispheres in autopsies on 100 human brains and found significant structural asymmetries in 76%. Similar findings have been supported from studies involving cerebral arteriographs (Lemay & Culebras, 1972). The incidence of structural asymmetry has been found to be approximately equal for both adults and children (Wada, 1973; Wada, Clarke, & Hame, 1975; Witelson & Pallie, 1973), and has in fact been found by the 34th week of fetal life (Chi, Dooling, & Gilles, 1977). Asymmetry of the two cerebral hemispheres has also been found in EEG patterns (Doyle, Ornstein, & Galin, 1974; Gardiner, Schulman, & Walter, 1973); a more prominent vein of Labbe in the dominant cerebral hemisphere contrasted with a more prominent vein of Trolard in the nondominant hemi-

sphere (DeChiro, 1962); in the thalamic distribution of norepinephrine (Oke, Keller, Mefford, & Adams, 1978); and in skull contour (Kinsbourne, 1972). Functional asymmetries have been reported in processing verbal material (Kimura, 1961) and in selective listening in young children (Hiscock & Kinsbourne, 1977).

There is reason to believe that this asymmetry of the cerebral hemispheres provides certain advantages in processing specialized types of information in an efficient manner (Kinsbourne, 1972). Conversely, however, if brain areas are specialized for certain types of tasks, the corresponding lack of brain specialization for other tasks may produce a handicap for the child who lacks specialization for processing information of a type considered crucial for his or her education. Indeed, the focus of educators on exposing all children of a given age to a common set of achievement expectancies tends to neglect all that is known about individual differences in human cerebral hemisphere specialization, and contributes in a major way to maximizing the likelihood that at any given age a number of children in a given classroom will be unable to process information at a rate sufficient for academic success. For the school psychologist who is knowledgeable about the educational implications of neurological organization, and who can assess an individual child's unique pattern of neurological organization, it is possible to maximize the potential of a given child's neuropsychological strengths to help the child achieve at the highest level possible.

In general, a conceptual model that is compatible with both current knowledge in clinical neurology and school psychology supports the following working assumptions:

1. Reading skill, especially involving auditory sequencing, phonics, synthesis of meaning, and comprehension, is dependent primarily on posterior portions of the dominant (almost always left) cerebral hemisphere.
a. Aquisition of some early reading skills, especially involving whole-word (traditional orthographic) and visual word-matching (flash card) types of instruction may involve posterior portions of the right hemisphere.
Implication: A youngster with right-hemisphere functioning somewhat more

efficient than left will be much more likely to profit from nonphonetic instruction, involving maximal utilization of visuospatial cues. Experience charts, basic word lists, word–picture matching, and drill with flash cards are examples of such techniques. Similarly and conversely, a child with comparatively stronger left-hemisphere functioning will be much more adept in processing reading instruction oriented toward phonetic approaches and reading for comprehension rather than individual word revisualization. Examples of optimal approaches for such children involve initial teaching alphabet or phonetic techniques for younger children, gradually shifting to more focus on synthesis and comprehension as the child acquires basic reading skills. For the young child with very deficient right-hemisphere function, aural comprehension approaches such as recording reading material onto tape are useful, since they use intact auditory sequencing and auditory memory abilities and nearly completely rule out any dependence on visuospatial recognition or memory facility.

2. Computation may involve either the right or left cerebral hemisphere, depending on the complexity of the material and the specific neuropsychological abilities required. For example, calculations involved in language contexts, such as WISC arithmetic or "modern math" questions involving sequential logic, require more left-hemisphere function, while visualization of two-dimensional problems (e.g., 237 × 49) involve somewhat greater reliance on the right hemisphere. At later ages, subjects such as algebra and computer programming, which tend to represent alternative language systems, are much more dependent on left-hemisphere function than plane geometry, which is more right-hemisphere dependent.

Implication: Mathematical instruction involving math concepts, language formulation, or sequential logic will be more effective with a student whose left hemisphere processes information well, while mathematical instruction involving working two-dimensional workbook problems, flash card multiplication tables, or similar visually oriented modes will be better with children whose right hemisphere is more efficient. Similarly, aural practice, language-embedded problems, or sequentially dependent math problems should be emphasized in students with stronger left- than right-hemisphere function. To meet academic curriculum requirements, concentrating on algebra and computer programming represent good approaches for strong left-hemisphere people, while more computational or geometric curricular foci may be more appropriate for students whose left hemisphere is comparatively weaker.

3. Spelling, being primarily an aspect of language, has strong dependence on the left cerebral hemisphere, although in very young children the acquisition of simple printing skills requires considerable right-hemisphere involvement. By the time that writing has replaced printing, the comparative involvement of right-hemisphere involvement has diminished to a considerable extent. The way in which spelling is taught has some importance on which hemisphere is involved; however, since spelling from "rules," such as those governing positional placements of the letters i and c, makes much more demand on the left hemisphere than does mere copying from a visual example.

Implication: For a strongly left hemisphere child, the early introduction of linguistic aids to spelling (e.g., "I before E, except after C, or when sounding like A, as in neighbor and weigh") will facilitate spelling skill acquisition. Conversely, for a strongly right-hemisphere child, the use of rote copying, visual aids, and using whole-word rather than sequential-letter approaches will be of value.

Research Relevance to Educational Implications

Neuropsychological profiles of school-aged children have consistently differentiated among children heterogeneously classified as learning disabled, on the basis of neuropsychological test findings relating hemisphere of dysfunction to specific patterns of impairment. Although abilities such as reading depend on a number of verbal, visuospatial, and general cognitive factors, there has been fairly consistent evidence that reading impairment involving difficulties with phonics, sound blending, and auditory sequencing in most cases can be traced to dysfunction of the left cerebral hemisphere (Rourke, 1976), while reading difficulty involving revisualization, visual imagery, and whole-word recognition is related to right-hemisphere dysfunction (Hartlage, 1975). Bannatyne was among the first to postulate this dichotomous model of reading disorder, classifying handicapped readers as verbal or spatial children (Bannatyne, 1968). Parallel research led Boder to classify similarly handicapped readers as dyseidetic or dysphonetic (Boder, 1973), and Hartlage to categorize them as type I and II reading disorders (Hartlage, Meader, & Lucas, 1976). Rourke and Finlayson (1978) found patterns of neuropsychological profiles supportive of this sort of conceptualization, with implications for other academic ability deficits involving spelling and arithmetic. Again in independent but parallel research, Farnham-Diggory (1978) developed a very similar model of arithmetic disorders postulated by Luria (1966), and Tarnopol and Tarnopol (1979) validated this model with nearly 300 students.

Relationship of Common Psychoeducational Tests to Neuropsychological Organization

Although there are comprehensive neuropsychological test batteries which can be of considerable importance for psychoeducational assessment and planning (Boll, 1977; Doehring, 1968; Filskov & Goldstein, 1974; Parsons, 1970; Reitan, 1974), these batteries require both a fairly extensive period for administration and considerable sophistication for adequate interpretation. Conversely, no single test can hope to assess the complex functioning of the central nervous system (Boll, 1974; Reitan, 1974), so in most applied school psychology settings some combination of tests is usually employed as a compromise between comprehensiveness and expediency (Hartlage, 1978). For the school psychologist to make a rational choice in determining what tests may be most applicable to the particular psychodiagnostic question at hand, it is of value to have at least a general knowledge of the neuropsychological correlates of psychometric tests in common use. Such a knowledge will enable the psychologist to evaluate the neuropsychological implications of tests which have been administered by others, as well as serve as a framework for deciding which tests are necessary to complete an adequate neuropsychological diagnostic profile for a specific child.

Wechsler Intelligence Scale for Children

Since the time of its introduction, the Wechsler Intelligence Scale for Children (Wechsler, 1949) has been recognized as being a most useful instrument for the detection of cerebral dysfunction (Beck & Lam, 1955; Belmont & Birch, 1960; Graham, 1952; Hartlage & Green, 1972; Holroyd, 1968; Hopkins, 1964; Horst, 1967; Jenkin, Spivack, Levine, & George, 1964; Lampel & Kaspar, 1972; Lansdell, 1962; Littell, 1960; Reed, 1967; Reed, Reitan, & Klove, 1965; Rourke, Young, & Flewelling, 1971; Rourke & Telegdy, 1971; Sattler, 1974; Schiffman, 1967; Seashore, 1951; Simensen & Sutherland, 1974).

In addition to its use as a measure of global mental ability against which to compare other scales as for use in determination of learning disorders (Hale, 1978; Hartlage & Steele, 1977; Schwarting & Schwarting, 1977), the multiscale nature of the instrument lends itself to a variety of interpretive strategies. Beyond using the verbal IQ as an estimate of level of functioning of the left cerebral hemisphere compared with the performance IQ as a measure of right-hemisphere function, it is possible to use groupings of sequential, conceptual, and spatial subtests (Bannatyne, 1968); categorization into verbal comprehension, perceptual organization, and freedom from distractability (Kaufman, 1975; Wallbrown, 1979); or other factor structures (Gutkin, 1978). Even greater refinement can be obtained by comparing individual subtests, such as comparing functional integrity of left and right temporal lobes by the Similarities versus Picture Arrangement subscales; or left- and right-parietal-lobe integrity by the Arithmetic versus Block Design subscales (Hartlage, 1976). Similarly, a given subtest can be compared against the global level of all subtests, to access the functional integrity of a given cortical area relative to general functional level. A special advantage of the Wechsler involves its common use and general recognition by educators, so that communication with teachers concerning neuropsychological status of children can be recognized as being related to the diagnostic work of the school psychologist (Moss, 1979; Reitan, 1966; Senf, 1979; Sollee, 1979). Indeed, it is not uncommon for special educators to expect Wechsler Scale substantiation for the diagnosis of the level and extent of learning deficit attributable to cerebral dysfunction (Rourke, 1975). Specific relationships between Wechsler variables and selected verbal, auditory-perceptual, visual-perceptual, and problem-solving abilities in children with learning disabilities have been reported (Boll, 1974; Hartlage, 1972; 1973a; Klonoff & Low, 1974; Rourke, Young, & Flewelling, 1971), to the point where this scale probably represents one of the necessary components of a neuropsychological evaluation.

Bender-Gestalt

Almost since its introduction, the Bender-Gestalt (Bender, Curran, & Shilder, 1938) has been the test instrument most commonly used for the assessment of cortical dysfunction (Schulberg & Tolor, 1961). This may be due at least partially to its ease of administration, its nonverbal characteristics, alleged freedom from cultural bias, and assumed validity for this purpose (Hartlage, 1966). A number of studies have tended to support at least some of these reasons for its popularity (Baroff, 1957; Bensberg, 1952; Bowland & Deabler, 1956; Feldman, 1952; Griffeth & Taylor, 1960; Hain, 1964; Nadler, Fink, Shontz, & Brink, 1959; Robinson, 1953; Tolor, 1956), despite the fact that the test samples relatively restricted aspects of brain function, restricted primarily to the nondominant cerebral hemisphere. Aside from its neglect of language aspects of neuropsychological function, a major problem with the use of the Bender-Gestalt in the assessment of learning problems possibly resultant from cortical dysfunction involves the differential involvement of the right cerebral hemisphere in school performance at varying ages. In early school grades, especially kindergarten and first grade, there is more involvement of non-language functions in the acquisition of academic skills than in later grades (Hartlage, 1979). This is probably due to the greater spatial components of letter and word recognition in early grades, which gradually declines as reading becomes more involved with comprehension and other left-hemisphere-mediated abilities in later years (Hartlage, 1973b). Findings that the Bender-Gestalt predicts first-grade reading achievement (Ackerman, Peters, & Dykman, 1971; Keogh, 1969; Koppitz, 1970) have been cited as support

for use of the Bender for early detection of possible neurological dysgenesis (Hartlage & Lucas, 1976), but follow-up studies of the predictive utility of the Bender-Gestalt for reading at ages 7 and 8 have shown decline of the relationship found with younger children (Edwards, Allery, & Snider, 1971; Hartlage & Lucas, 1971).

As a component of a comprehensive assessment battery, the Bender-Gestalt can be of some value in assessing the child's constructional praxic skills, as a means of comparing this level of performance with other abilities. Although an experimental scoring system for converting Bender scores to standard scores is available for a limited age range (Hartlage & Lucas, 1971), it is generally difficult to make direct comparisons of Bender performance with other measures to construct a profile of neuropsychological strengths and weaknesses. One of the Bender's advantages which is often not fully utilized is its potential for producing nonpsychometric insights about the nature of a dysfunction reflected in poor test performance, such as impaired performance due to poor planning, impulsivity, or compulsivity. From a strictly neuropsychological point of view, it may be possible to generate some initial hypotheses concerning likelihood of anterior versus posterior nondominant hemisphere contributors to poor performance. On a stimulus involving the integration of two discrete geometric figures (e.g., card A), for example, if the two figures are not properly integrated, rather than merely scoring the attempt as a failure, further questioning can be most useful for generating such hypotheses. Once the series of figures has been presented, inquiry about the adequacy of the reproduction can be initiated by asking the child to compare the stimulus and his reproduction of it. If the child responds that the figures are the same (even if different) a perceptual (i.e., posterior parietal right hemisphere) deficit may be involved, whereas if the child recognizes that the figures are different but cannot make them alike (given adequate mental ability), a motor (i.e., anterior) involvement is likely. Thus a broad category such as "perceptual-motor" can be reduced to component parts, each with more or less discrete neuroanatomical and functional implications, by the use of the Bender-Gestalt stimuli, using them as steps toward a clinical inference rather than as a definitive criterion measure.

During the past decade, there has been considerable research involving the use of the Bender with school-aged children, and one study (Buckley, 1978) has reviewed more than 100 reports of this research. In general, the Bender has not demonstrated a great deal of utility for predicting either school achievement or neurological impairment, and has been found to be influenced by cultural factors (Baker & Thurber, 1976; Hartlage & Lucas, 1976; Lambert, 1971; Schoolcraft, 1973). Nonetheless, its use in school psychological assessment continues high, and as recently as the Seventh Mental Measurements Yearbook (1972) was evaluated as necessary in every diagnosis of children above age 5 because of its perceived contributions to the evaluation of neurological impairment.

Somewhat more specific applications of Bender-Gestalt stimuli to educational settings have been reported by Fuller and his co-workers, who adapted the Gestalt designs to an administration and scoring system which permits more definitive differential diagnosis by etiological groups (Fuller, 1969; Fuller & Hawkins, 1968). The system, the Minnesota Perceptuo Diagnostic Test (Fuller and Laird, 1963), has been used with some success in screening involving general etiological bases of reading disorders (Fuller, 1964; Krippner, 1966; L'Abate, 1968; Wolf, 1968) and related to such external criteria as EEG findings (Zaler, 1968). As Fuller has pointed out (1969), a single-step interpretation of these sorts of data is not sufficient for identifying the locus or extent of brain dysfunction, but the data can be used as a part of a broader battery to provide information relative to specific areas of functioning.

Beery (1967) (a.k.a. Beery Developmental Form Sequence; Beery-Buktenica; Developmental Test of Visual Motor Integration)

This test differs from the Bender-Gestalt on two variables of neuropsychologicla consequence. Of special consequence for school psychologists is the younger mental age limit of the Beery, which can assess development below 2 years of age, while the Bender figures in general require mental development levels above 6 years of age. Also, the Beery Test requires the child to copy a figure in a predesignated area, omitting the element of planning but maximizing the focus of the test as a measure of constructional praxis. Its scoring system, with sex differences noted, is somewhat easier than the Bender to compare with other psychometric measures. Since the Beery is more readily convertible to standard scores, it may be less likely to fall victim to naive interpretation based on an absolute level of performance, since it is easy to compare Beery scores against the total configuration of other scores. Thus the Beery is not so likely as the Bender to generate false-positive identification of impairment of constructional praxis in persons of lower than average mental ability.

Hartlage and Lucas (1976) compared the Beery with the Bender for black and white children, and found that both scales had similar racial correlates with most other academic and intellectual measures, suggesting that the two scales may well produce data with comparable neuropsychological implications across at least these two ethnic groups.

Illinois Test of Psycholinguistic Abilities (ITPA)

This test (Kirk, McCarthy, & Kirk, 1968), a diagnostic tool based on Osgood's (1957) communication model, is oriented more toward specific teaching approaches than most psychometric instruments and so is often popular in school psychological settings. Studies of the factor structure of the revised ITPA (Smith & Marx, 1971) as well as of the experimental version (Haring & Ridgway, 1967; Myers, 1965; Weener, Barritt, & Semmel, 1967) have failed to document the functions and processes proposed by the authors, and others have found extremely high correlations between the ITPA and Stanford-Binet (Burns & Schaaf, 1974; Huizinga, 1973), suggesting that this instrument may assess abilities very similar to those assessed by standard intelligence tests (Carrol, 1972), and studies of the relationships of the WISC and ITPA have concluded that these two instruments generally do measure the same dimensions (Garms, 1970a; Leton, 1972). Similar relationships between the WISC and ITPA have been reported for severely emotionally disturbed children (Young & Cormack, 1974). Canonical analysis of the WISC and ITPA (Wakefield & Carlson, 1975) substantiated this conclusion, and further supported the suggestion of Garms (1970b) that the information in both instruments can be obtained by administering the WISC and three ITPA subscales (Visual Association, Verbal Expression, and Manual Expression).

A look at the content of the ITPA scales

suggests factorial impurity with respect to direct relationship with discrete neuropsychological functions. A look at some of the hypothesized channels, processes, and levels will illustrate this point. Such channels as auditory-vocal, for example, involve posterior portions of the language-dominant hemisphere, communication with the anterior portions of the same hemisphere, so that impairment of this ability does not have any specific neuropsychological localizing referent. Similarly, the visual-motor channel suggests involvement ranging across the nondominant hemisphere from frontal to occipital lobes, with important interactive parietal areas, so that poor performance involving this channel implies little more than a likelihood that some portions of the right hemisphere are dysfunctional. Processes such as reception imply probably posterior involvement, but the hemisphere and lobe of involvement are of course dependent on the components of the receptive process, and so depressed reception ability at best suggests possible posterior impairment of either hemisphere. Similarly, the hypothesized representational and automatic levels dependent to some interactive extent on content of information being received and the modality through which it is to be expressed, so that multiple neurological associative systems are likely to be recruited at stages of processing of information at the different levels.

Wide Range Achievement Test (Jastak and Jastak, 1965)

This is a very commonly used achievement test which has been the topic of considerable research with some neuropsychological implication. Hartlage and Hartlage (1977), for example, have demonstrated that a weighted formula for profiles of WRAT subscales relative to Wechsler scales can predict such phenomena as dysfunctions in the area of the supramarginal and angular gyri of the dominant hemisphere, and numerous studies have compared WRAT performance against discrete Wechsler scales (Brooks, 1977; Foster, 1965; Hartlage & Boone, 1972; Hartlage & Steele, 1977; Ryan, 1973; Schwarting & Schwarting, 1977). The Reading Subtest, involving both language reception and expression, has no unique localizing value by itself, but when used in combination with other scales for profile comparison can be useful in helping narrow possible loci of dysfunction. Thus uniquely low WRAT Reading scores, (with Spelling scores slightly lower), below expectancy for both

IQ and receptive language measures, with WRAT Arithmetic scores close to expectancy based on IQ, have been identified in children with suspected dysgenesis of dominant hemisphere temporal and parietal areas (Hartlage, 1978). While, of course, no autopsy or surgical validation is commonly available in such studies, genetic and dermatoglyphic validation criteria have been reported (Hartlage & Hartlage, 1973a, 1973b).

Perhaps one of the greatest values of the WRAT in school psychological assessment of neuropsychological function is as a "hold" item. In a child with suspected decline in mental function, or with failure to maintain academic progress at a previous rate, the use of WRAT standard scores can be of extreme value for identification and measurement of such problems. Such an approach has been demonstrated to be of value in the detection of brain tumor in a school-aged child referred for psychological evaluation (Hartlage & Hartlage, 1977), as well as for evaluation of effects of drug toxicity or impairment of learning secondary to treatment of a medical condition (Hartlage & Stovall, 1980). Another use of the WRAT as part of a battery involves its value for comparison of chronicity. In a youngster with fairly chronic school failure, a comparison of relationship between WRAT standard scores and Wechsler scores can help avoid needless referrals for neurological evaluation, since if the ratio appears to be fairly symmetrical for the two sets of scores, it is unlikely that neurological referral is indicated (Hartlage & Hartlage, 1978).

Peabody Picture Vocabulary Test (Dunn, 1959)

This has become a widely used test by school psychologists for assessment of verbal intelligence through the measurement of hearing vocabulary (Bochner, 1978). Although it has been found to produce slightly higher estimates of verbal ability than the Wechsler with mentally subnormal populations (Vance, Prichard & Wallbrown, 1978), a number of studies have reported significant correlations between Wechsler Verbal IQ and PPVT scores with such populations (Kimbrell, 1960; Thorne, Kaspar, & Schulman, 1965). However, the magnitude of the correlations has not been of sufficient magnitude as to suggest that the two scales are interchangeable (Sattler, 1974), and a look at the neuropsychological substrates of the tests clearly supports Sattler's conclusion. The nonequivalence of the two scales can be of value to the school psychologist in the assessment of language problems, since the very small loading of the PPVT on expressive language makes it a good basis for comparison with other verbal measures more dependent on expressive language as a way to help identify specific components of language disorders. Further, the good reliability of the scale (Bochner, 1978; Dunn, 1965; Kicklighter, Powell, & Parker, 1974; Raskin, Offenback, & Scoonover, 1971) is sufficient to support its use in comparison with such scales as the Wechsler for such purposes.

In the case of a child with good PPVT scores but relatively poor Wechsler vocabulary performance, the comparative efficiency of the language receptive mode contrasted with impaired performance on a test dependent on reception, association, and expression can help identify the level of dysfunction as being more anteriorly located than at the auditory receptive site. Conversely, if both PPVT and Wechsler vocabulary are similarly depressed, a posterior dysfunction is more likely involved, and apparent impairments in expressive language may be viewed in terms of difficulty with understanding the nature of the stimuli involved in the test.

Comprehensive Neuropsychological Test Batteries

Children's Versions of the Halstead-Reitan

The children's version of the Reitan-Indiana Neuropsychological Battery is designed for use with children aged 9 to 14 years, and there is another battery for children aged 5 to 8. The battery for older children is generally referred to as the Halstead Neuropsychological Test Battery for Children, while the battery for the younger children is called the Reitan-Indiana Neuropsychological Test Battery for Children.

This differential terminology reflects more of a gentlemen's agreement between Halstead and Reitan than any conceptual differences in the approaches to assessment, although there is some resultant confusion and inconsistency concerning the names of the batteries, which are often referred to as the Halstead-Reitan Battery. In any case, the battery was essentially derived from Halstead's 27 tests (Halstead, 1947), from which 10 were used to determine an impairment index. These 10 include Categories; Tactual Performance Test; Rhythm Test; Speech-Sounds Perception Test; Finger Oscillation Test; Time Sense Test, Critical Flicker

Frequency; and subparts of these tests. Other tests include a modification of the Halstead and Wepman Aphasia Screening Test (Halstead & Wepman, 1949); the Trail Making Test and Tests of Sensory-Perceptual Disturbances. The changes in the battery for older children mainly involve simplification of the Category, Tactual Performance, Speech-Sounds Perception, and Trail Making Tests, and omission of the Critical Flicker Fusion Test. The younger children's battery involves much more modification of old tests and the development of some entirely new tests, and so is in many respects different.

Although Reitan has been most diligent about providing workshops for both novice and advanced users of the battery, it is probably safe to say that those most qualified to make the levels of interpretation which the Battery will support are the relatively few neuropsychologists who have extensive supervised training, as is true of other neuropsychological batteries as well. Because the Battery itself is so comprehensive, many psychologists have felt that once they have access to the data it provides, they will be able to reach relevant diagnostic conclusions, without devoting the time and effort involved in first learning about both the central nervous system and the range of non-psychological conditions which can affect neuropsychological test scores (Givens & Hartlage, 1979). To some extent, this may be like buying a very fine stethoscope in hopes that the excellent quality of the instrument will make the user a qualified cardiologist.

Strengths of the test for properly trained users include its excellent fidelity, high degree of sensitivity for detecting subtle changes in the levels of function of discrete portions of the central nervous system, and widespread recognition and acceptance by both psychologists and physicians of the test as being the neuropsychological assessment battery of choice for refined, precise, and sophisticated measurement of cortical function. Its liability for use by school psychologists results not from any limitation of the test, but from the typical time pressures on psychologists and the general lack of school psychologists adequately trained in the use of the battery.

Luria-Nebraska Neuropsychological Battery

Although the work of Luria has been published in English and available in the United States for a number of years (Luria, 1932), it has only been in the past few years that his approach to diagnosis of neurological status has received increasing recognition. The most prominent manifestation of an interest in Luria has been the work of Golden and some of his co-workers in developing and promulgating the Luria technique (Golden, Hammeka, & Purisch, 1978; Golden, Purisch, & Hammeka, 1979). The main features of the technique involve the sampling of a great variety of behaviors related to cerebral function as compared with more traditional approaches which involve the sampling of a more highly intercorrelated series of behaviors (Hartlage & Haak, 1980).

The Luria-Nebraska, for example, is intended for adults 13 and older. It consists of 269 items, which include motor, rhythmic, tactile, writing, arithmetic, memory, and intelligence functions, which in turn have been factor analyzed into separate component factors (Hammeke, Golden, & Purisch, 1979; McKay & Golden, 19779). These factors do not necessarily measure specific areas of cortical integrity or dysfunction, although at least some of them (e.g., first arithmetic factor) do appear to assess functions which are reasonably discreetly localized (e.g., left posterior parietal). An additional benefit for the Luria technique is its relatively more comprehensive assessment of frontal-lobe integrity than is available from most other techniques.

While based almost entirely on Luria's theoretical formulations of brain function, the assessment techniques contain many of the sorts of items that are found in clinical neurological examinations. The fact that the items are arranged into sections corresponding to Luria's concepts helps systematize and standardize the data collection, and even if one does not accept Luria's concepts in toto, his system provides sufficient data to permit clinical inferences independent of Luria's theory. His breakdown of reading into automatic recognition and deliberate processing, for example, appears to be a distinction with clinical utility, whether or not one agrees with the theoretical concepts underlying the destination.

Many of the conclusions supported by the Luria Battery are ones that could be reached from other approaches. Luria (1973) has observed that the power of his testing lies in its ability to compare performance on patterns of items throughout the test. However, similar features are found in the Reitan-Indiana (Hartlage & Haak, 1979) and even from isolated subtests adapted from fairly common

scales (Hartlage & Hartlage, 1982). A special advantage of the Luria involves its flexibility to permit integration or even substitution of information from other tests into the Luria battery (Majovsky, 1979), while the Reitan-Indiana represents a more tightly organized and structured approach whose internal consistency and discriminative power may be attenuated by using only portions of the battery (e.g., Watson, Thomas, Anderson, & Felling, 1968).

It is of interest to note that in the hands of neuropsychologists trained and experienced in the use of one or the other Battery, the diagnostic conclusions are apt to be quite similar independent of which Battery was used. Vicente, for example (Vincente & Kennelly, 1979), has reported highly significant correlations among individual parts of the two Batteries, and Kane (1979) has reported similar comparisons of the two Batteries. Golden (1979) described a direct comparison of the two Batteries used with the same patients, with very similar diagnostic conclusions reached by investigators using each Battery.

Luria-Nebraska Children's Battery

For the past 7 years, researchers at the University of Nebraska and elsewhere have been attempting to develop objective neuropsychological test batteries for children that draw on some of the ideas and techniques employed by A. R. Luria. Development of the children's battery was heavily influenced by the earlier development of the adult Luria-Nebraska Neuropsychological Battery as well as the work done by Lawrence Majovski.

The original development of the battery was begun by administering the adult LNNB to children from ages 5 to 14. It was discovered that children ages 8 and up could do a majority of the procedures used in the adult battery. It was also found that those items in general corresponded to those that one would expect from Luria's theories on brain development. It was also found that below age 8, drastic changes were needed in the battery content to have a useful test. Thus, it was initially decided to develop a test down to age 8.

Similarly, it was found that 13- and 14-year-olds could perform perfectly normally on the adult battery (which was originally intended to extend down to age 15). At the 12-year-old level, children began to show difficulties with the adult battery (although above-average 12-year-olds can also perform perfectly normally). Thus it was decided that the adult battery could be used down to age 13 and that the new children's battery should aim at ages 8 to 12.

Items were deleted from the adult battery which appeared to be too difficult for initial normative youngsters in this age range. When possible, similar but easier items were substituted. We were also privileged to consult with Lawrence Majovski, who was working on developing a qualitative approach to the assessment of children based on his studies with Luria. We were able to adapt and add several additional items and areas of examination to the test from his suggestions. This initial work consisted of three successive versions of the test which were evaluated on groups of normal and impaired children until the fourth and recently published version was completed (Golden, 1986).

The final version of the children's battery consisted of 11 basic scales, just as the adult battery does, and 149 procedures. However, most of these procedures consist of numerous items, so that the actual number of items exceeds 500. Administration time takes about 1.0 to 3.0 hours, depending on levels of cooperation and levels of impairment.

This version was given to 125 children. The group consisted of 25 normal children at each of five age levels: 8, 9, 10, 11, and 12. From this group, each procedure was normed so that a score of 0 was set to mean a performance within one standard deviation of the median by adding up the scaled score on each procedure to yield a total raw score. Procedures were then correlated with each of the raw scores to ensure that procedures correlated highest with the scale they were assigned to, so that items could be reorganized when necessary.

After final scale assignments were determined, scale T scores were generated by first calculating the means and standard deviations of each of the original 125 normal subjects. An ANOVA for each scale score by age indicated no significant differences between the scale score by age indicated no significant differences between the scale mean scores for each age group, while F tests indicated no significant differences among group variances. As a result, the conversion of scale raw scores to T scores was done on the basis of all 125 patients rather than for each age group alone.

Each of the 11 scales is multifactorial in structure. This was done for several reasons. First,

each scale was conceived not as covering a specific skill but rather as a domain of skills in given areas (such as motor function). Second, this allowed the test to yield stable test scores (which is related to the number of items on the scale as well as the individual stabilities of the items) with fewer items in each skill area. This has the positive effect of allowing for a broader coverage of skills in a reasonable period of time. This has the drawback, however, of not covering any one area in as much detail as possible. This is remedied simply by following the LNNB performance. Thus, the LNNB can provide the general survey of skills needed, yet combined with more specific analysis when required.

In addition to the basic scales, the 149 items were factor analyzed in a population of 719 brain-damaged and normal children. The resulting factors were impressive in that few of the factor scales used items from multiple scales, suggesting that item placement was essentially correct. Some factor scales simply repeated what the regular scales already yielded, while some had too few to achieve reasonable stability. Those scales that were both stable and yielded new information were kept for further study.

A second analysis involved the factor analysis of each scale alone. Many of the resultant factors duplicated factors found in the first analysis and were discarded, as were factors that were insufficiently stable. At the end of this process, 11 additional scales were derived, two of which were cross-scale factors and 9 of which were intrascale. For each of these 11 scales, T-scores were derived on the basis of the performance of 240 normal children in the overall sample.

Of further interest to clinicians interested in the relationship between the Luria-Nebraska tests and the other tests commonly used was the effect of factor analyzing the original overall item factor analysis. The second analysis of the new factors yielded eight more general factors (achievement, motor speed, nonverbal auditory skills, visual skills, intelligence, tactile skills, memory, and language), while a further analysis of these scales yielded what were essentially verbal and nonverbal factors. This suggests, as did earlier work, that the domain of skills covered by the LNNB-CR is similar to the domain of skills covered by other tests, but that LNNB-CR at its basic level represents a more detailed breakdown of those basic skills. The need to use the LNNB-CR in any case may lie in the value to the examiner of such a detailed breakdown.

Other scales are also in the process of development as this is written, including scales to measure left- and right-hemisphere sensorimotor function and scales for the analysis of chronicity of disorders. However, there are no localization scales planned for the children's battery as with the adult battery since localized lesions do not generally cause consistent deficits in children because of the interaction of developmental processes with brain development and the time and location of the injury.

For those readers interested in the details of general research on the battery, the test manual (Golden, 1986) offers the most complete and detailed account of this work. Other reviews may be found in Plaisted, Gustavson, Wilkening, and Golden (1983). In general, research has examined the ability of the test to discriminate between brain-damaged and normal subjects (with hit rates of about 86%), while other studies have examined correlations between the LNNB and such tests as the PIAT and the WISC-R. As reported in the test manual, this work has generally confirmed the validity of the LNNB scales. Other work has evaluated the effectiveness of the test with such groups as children who are learning disabled or who have epilepsy.

New Innovations in Employing Luria's Approach

As this is being written, a new battery is being developed which represents a substantial expansion of the old battery. The new battery has been expanded to cover more heavily areas not well involved in Luria's original examination: more complex and detailed analysis of visual-spatial functions, more detailed analysis of various aspects of aphasia, reading comprehension, motor writing, complex memory functions, and higher intellectual skills. The new test combines items from both the children's and adult Luria-Nebraska battery, along with new items. A factor analysis of the items as a whole yielded 37 scales, which form the basis of the new test. In general, these scales are more like the factor scales, representing purer and somewhat more interrelated abilities.

The test differs in that instead of giving every item, items are given on the basis of the individual's abilities (as with the Stanford-Binet, for example). Within each area patients may get only very difficult, very easy, or moderately hard items, depending on their performance. This allows the test to contain items suitable from ages 3 through adulthood, and applicable to wide ranges of performance in brain-injured individuals. The giving of only a part of the item pool allows for a reasonable testing time in the 2- to 3-hour range.

The test will come in two versions, a paper-and-pencil version and a version primarily given by computer under the supervision of a technician or psychologist. The computer version has the advantage of ensuring that the test materials are given properly and timed properly, freeing the examiner to do more observation and analysis of the patient's performance. It is expected that the new version will be released for general use in about 3 years.

Other Issues in Neuropsychological Evaluation
Prior History

Regardless of what tests one uses, there are two general approaches that are necessary in any detailed neuropsychological examination. Of great importance is a detailed history. This can often identify factors important for the examination of disorders (such as idiopathic epilepsy) which may be missed upon standardized examinations. There are two theories on when history should be gathered and used: (a) knowing the history when the case begins and considering it all along in the diagnostic process, or (b) analyzing the case with a minimum of information and checking the detailed history afterward. (Doing any case blindly is not recommended.) Both techniques have their drawbacks. If too much history is known, one may be so biased that the inconsistencies between the history and data are overlooked or deemed unimportant.

Historical information and the conclusions made available by others prior to the neuropsychological assessment may be right or wrong. A lesion may exist as reported, or may not. The child's developmental history may be accurate or may contain serious errors. The relative accuracy of information depends on the source of that information as well as its nature. In all cases, however, it is important to double-check all such information.

Regardless of when one gathers the historical data, it is best to treat conclusions from the data as hypotheses to be confirmed or discarded. This leaves the clinician more flexibility to take his or her data seriously and to learn from those data all that is possible. If, at the end, discrepancies are found between history and neuropsychological findings, the clinician should investigate the history and the findings for errors that may cause this discrepancy, and look for conditions outside neuropsychology that may have affected one or the other source of data.

QUALITATIVE ANALYSIS

Another important part of an examination is qualitative analysis of the child's performance. Here, the interest is not in whether a child got a certain score on a certain item but rather *how* that score was achieved. While it is possible to interpret any test from only a quantitative or qualitative perspective, the use of only one technique does not yield the maximum amount of useful information in any given case. The two approaches complement one another and allow the examiner to enjoy the best of both methods, avoiding that continuing, yet ultimately futile argument over which approach is better or which approach should be the one employed.

In scoring qualitative errors, there are a wide range of possibilities aimed at gaining a better understanding of the "why" behind a child's error. Qualitative analysis can also aid in the evaluation of responses which are correct in terms of the quantitative scoring but still unusual, such as the child who reads a word properly but stutters in pronouncing it, or the child who can describe an object and its uses but is unable to give its name.

The disadvantage of qualitative inferences is the lack of formal scoring criteria and reliability across examiners. At present, there is no way in which such problems can be completely eliminated. Interpretation of qualitative information on more than a behavioral level is quite difficult. At present, all information on such interpretations is largely unsystematized in the sense that different clinicians or researchers use different definitions and different theoretical frameworks.

At present, learning to observe and interpret properly the qualitative aspects of behavior is done through clinical experience with children and the reading of such experiences reported in specific cases by clinicians such as Luria. An academic understanding of the qualitative aspects of behavior through reading and classes yields a basic framework from which later to approach supervised clinical experience. A standard examination, which allows the observation of the same basic behaviors across many diagnostic groups, is also an aid in making these clinical observations.

It is very important that the clinician learn to observe and record the child's approach to test items, especially if that approach differs from those seen in the normal child. (The examiner must have adequate experience with normals so that he or she can make this comparison.) This should be done even if the examiner does not understand the meaning of the behavior or its significance. Sometimes the significance becomes clear after the quantitative analysis is completed, or it may become clear upon consultation with one's supervisor or a consultant. By doing this on a systematic basis, the user will begin to appreciate the meaning of the child's behavior and to develop the ability to perform such analyses independently.

After a qualitative analysis has been made, it should be integrated with the quantitative analysis. It is our strong belief that neither form of data is inherently "superior" in any given case. In some cases, the qualitative data help to explain inconsistencies that cannot be resolved in the quantitative results. In other cases, the quantitative data suggest an alternative approach to an observation that clears up the interpretation of a qualitative aspect of behavior. Only when the two sets of data have been integrated has a fully effective initial evaluation been completed.

UTILITY OF DIFFERENT TESTS AND COMBINATIONS OF TESTS FOR ASSESSMENT OF NEUROLOGICAL ORGANIZATION

Although to a considerable extent the validity of any test or combination of tests depends on the skill of the user, an adequate battery for assessment of cortical function with implications for school psychology needs to meet at least two criteria. First, of course, is the need to sample a sufficiently broad variety of behaviors to permit inferences about levels of function of various cortical loci. Next, the battery must be one with relevance to the school setting; reasonably portable; not requiring excessive time or equipment; and involving tests that a reasonably well trained school psychologist can be expected to administer and interpret.

The following sample problem cases illustrate and demonstrate the neuropsychological implications of commonly available psychological tests and their relevance for school psychological practice. The only two measures with which some school psychologists may not be familiar (tapping and number writing) have been described elsewhere (Hartlage & Hartlage, 1977; Reitan, 1974) and can be performed without adding materially to the time, bulk, or equipment cost of a standard assessment battery. Similarly, norms at different ages, and for brain-impaired versus normal children, are available from a number of sources (Boll & Reitan, 1972; Doehring, 1968; Finlayson & Reitan, 1976; Hughes, 1976; Knights & Moule, 1967). Each case is presented with the presenting complaint, teacher comments if available, and such other information as might be available to school psychologists, followed by a synthesis and interpretation of the data, to involve the reader in a step-by-step analysis of the data. Each case was selected on the basis of its representativeness of a problem that might reasonably be expected to be encountered by all school psychologists.

Problem 1

Charles, a right-handed, white, 8-year-old male third-grade student from a lower-middle economic level school, was referred for chronic academic difficulties. Referral was deferred for 2 years since the first- and second-grade teachers, both of whom were well trained and experienced, felt that although his performance was

---

Charles   R Handed, Age 8 years 1 month

Test Findings   Standard Scores

Wechsler   Scaled Scores

Information	11	Picture Completion	9	Verbal IQ 99
Comprehension	10	Picture Arrangement	8	Performance IQ 87
Arithmetic	0	Block Design	7	Full Scale IQ 93

Wide Range Achievement Test   Grade Level

Reading	2.7	94
Spelling	2.4	90
Arithmetic	1.9	85

Constructional Praxis   89
(Beery VMI)

Receptive Language   102
(PPVT)

Motor (Rate of rapid finger oscillation per 10 seconds)
Right hand 39 taps average over 5 trials
Left hand 32 taps average over 5 trials

Sensory (Sum of correct identifications of numbers written on fingertips out of 20 presentations)
Sum of correctly perceived numbers written on right hand 19
Sum of correctly perceived numbers written on left hand 17

marginal, he seemed to have adequate comprehension and would be able to succeed when he got more mature. He had not repeated any grades. Interviews with the mother revealed that Charles had spoken his first words at 11 months, put words together at 18 months, ridden a tricycle at 4 to 5 years, and mastered the bicycle around the end of first grade. She mentioned that he had always been somewhat clumsy, but felt that this might have been due to his not taking time to pay attention to what he was doing. School readiness testing, mainly involving receptive language, was reported as normal.

This case represents one of the more common academic manifestations of central nervous system dysfunction. Reported developmental milestones suggest language development at approximate age expectancy, with nonlanguage at least a year delayed (Hartlage & Lucas, 1973), suggesting a fairly chronic superiority of left- over right-hemisphere function. Although not necessarily diagnostic, the impulsive behavior described by the mother is commonly found in children with relatively less well developed right-hemisphere function. Wechsler verbal IQ, although not dramatically higher than performance IQ, is compatible with chronic functional deficiency of the right hemisphere, and this asymmetry is further supported by the discrepancy between Peabody and Beery scores. Finally, the relatively better performance of the right hand on both motor and sensory functions, to an extent beyond what might be attributable to lateral preference, support functional deficiencies subserved by both anterior and posterior portions of the right cerebral hemisphere. Mastery of academic skills, reflected on Wide Range Achievement Test Scores, is essentially compatible with expectancies based on IQ levels, and thus further support a fairly long-standing condition. Educationally, the prognosis for this youngster is fairly good, since the increasing academic emphasis on his comparatively more efficient left hemisphere will enable him to perform at increasingly better levels. As an interim strategy, deemphasis of flash cards, othography, and other visuospatial instructional approaches may help ameliorate the difficulty to some extent, and in any case will help prevent the frustrations resultant from trying to process information that depends on the functional integrity of brain areas which for him are not adequate for this purpose.

Problem 2

Carol, a 9-year-old, fourth-oldest child of an upper-middle-class family, had been described as a good student in early school grades. She obeyed well, was quiet in class, and made a conscientious effort to do what she was told. She is now completing the third grade and has been referred for gradually increasing moodiness, occasional crying, and slowly declining performance school work. Whereas at the first-grade level she was an average-to-good student, her grades in second grade were fair to average, and this year have declined to fair to poor. She does not seem as motivated as she once was. She has been enrolled in an academically oriented private school which does not have access to school psychological services, so no prior testing has been done. She was referred for help in deciding whether to retain her or hire her a special tutor to help with school subjects. She was described by her mother as an unusually good child, not demanding much parental attention. Mother recollects that although Carol was always shy and quiet, she always played competitively with her preschool peers.

Findings show consistently lower language-mediated abilities compared with her nonlanguage skills. Her depressed language scores are not likely due to cultural impoverishment, and her private school experience has almost certainly provided her with good language stimulation, so that environmental factors are probably not contributory. Her developmental history, scanty though it is, describes the sorts of behaviors common to children with generally delayed left-hemisphere maturation, although some children obviously show the same behavior in the absence of any apparent neurological cause. Her very consistently lower scores on essentially all functions subserved by the left cerebral hemisphere, paired with comparatively poor right-hand performance compared with the left on both sensory and motor tasks, strongly supports an impression of mild impairment of left-hemisphere function. The fairly good congruence of WRAT reading and

Carol _____   R Handed, Age ___9___ years ___2___ months

Test Findings _____   _____ Standard Scores

Wechsler   Scaled Scores

Information	9	Picture Completion	12	Verbal IQ ___85___
Comprehension	7	Picture Arrangement	10	Performance IQ ___101___
Arithmetic	7	Block Design	11	Full Scale IQ ___92___
Similarities	8	Object Assembly	10	
Vocabulary	9	Coding	8	
Digit Span	6			

Wide Range Achievement Test   Grade Level

Reading	3.1	86
Spelling	3.0	85
Arithmetic	3.7	

Constructional Praxis   96
(Beery VMI)

Receptive Language   88
(PPVT)

Motor (Rate of rapid finger oscillation per 10 seconds)
Right hand 36 taps average over 5 trials
Left hand 37 taps average over 5 trials

Sensory (Sum of correct identification of numbers written on fingertips out of 20 presentations)
Sum of correctly perceived numbers written on right hand 16
Sum of correctly perceived numbers written on left hand 19

spelling scores with such other measures of language ability as Wechsler Verbal IQ and PPVT is further supportive of the chronicity of the condition.

Children with profiles similar to Carol's very often show very similar preschool and first-grade behaviors, characterized by limited language use and slightly above average responsiveness to approval by adults. If their level of right-hemisphere functioning is average or better, they can often make a good start in school, through successful utilization of the visuospatial cues typically provided children learning initial alphabet skills. As school shifts progressively more emphasis to language comprehension and conceptual synthesis, the left-hemisphere deficiency exerts an increasingly greater handicap onto school performance. Since increasing school grades require even more language facility, she will need both personal support and encouragement to keep trying, and help with using visuospatial cues to help as abreast as possible. Sometimes the highly language-dependent curricular focus in academically oriented private schools makes this problem more pronounced, and a transfer to a more technically oriented school curricular may be needed.

Problem 3

Gary, the 16-year-old of a pediatrician, had developed mentally at or above age expectancy across a wide variety of developmental milestones. His mother recalled that he was putting two and three words together at 15 months and rode his older brother's tricycle at 30 months, and his father reported that on the Denver Developmental Task (Frankenburg and Dodds, 1967) he was doing most tasks at the 4-year level when he was evaluated just after his third birthday. At age 6, after he had been in first grade for several weeks and was reportedly doing well, he suffered a closed head injury in an automobile accident which left him unconscious for 2 days. Recovery was quick and apparently complete, and he returned to school within 2 weeks. He got good (approximately B+ average) grades throughout most of his grade school career and planned to enroll in the engineering department of a state university after high school graduation. His high school aptitude and preentrance examinations showed him to be capable of college work, but he was on academic probation in high school on an intermittent basis during his first 2 years. After Gary failed a drafting course and an advanced geometry course the first quarter of his junior year, his father requested an evaluation.

Gary _____   R Handed, Age ___15___ years ___10___ months

Test Findings _____   ___ Standard Scores

Wechsler   Scaled Scores _____

Information	13	Picture Completion	8	Verbal IQ	110
Comprehension	12	Picture Arrangement	9	Performance IQ	85
Arithmetic	10	Block Design	7	Full Scale IQ	98
Similarities	12	Object Assembly	8		
Vocabulary	13	Coding	7		
Digit Span	10				

Wide Range Achievement Test	Grade Level	
Reading	11.4	112
Spelling	11.0	109
Arithmetic	8.1	92

| Constructional Praxis | 90 |
| (Bender "not significant") | |

| Receptive Language | 116 |
| (PPVT) | |

Motor (Rate of rapid finger oscillation per 10 seconds)
Right hand _49_ taps average over 5 trials
Left hand _41_ taps average over 5 trials

Sensory (Sum of correct identifications of numbers written on fingertips out of 20 presentations)
Sum of correctly perceived numbers written on right hand   _20_
Sum of correctly perceived numbers written on left hand   _15_

The developmental history strongly argues against any developmental delays, so it is probably fairly safe to attribute any possible neuropsychological deficit to the automobile accident. The Wechsler test profile suggests damage to posterior portions of the right cerebral hemisphere involving deficits of function of both temporal and parietal lobes. The comparatively poor performance on Block Design, Picture Completion, and Object Assembly is compatible with revisualization deficits; while motor impairment might depress functions on the B.D. and O.A. subtests, the motor-free P.C. subtest should be unaffected if motor impairments were all that showed deficit. The good left-hand tapping speed further rules out motor impairment, while the very poor recognition of numbers written on his left-hand fingertips strongly implicates the right parietal lobe. In light of his very good very skills, he is still probably capable of doing adequate college work—as predicted by his language-dependent college preentrance and aptitude tests—but definitely not in a right-hemisphere-dependent field such as engineering. Counseling with him and his parents to focus educational emphasis on his intact language hemisphere, such as concentrating on literature, humanities, social sciences, and languages, can turn his deficit areas into much less of an academic liability.

Problem 4

George was adopted at age 4, and no history was available for the prior years. His foster parents, both of whom were college graduates, recalled that when first adopted, George seemed withdrawn and shy. After some time with the parents, he eventually demonstrated signs of affection, but never discussed his feelings or shared his fears or concerns with them, although they frequently encouraged him to confide in them. They did not recollect any developmental milestones, other than that he quickly learned to ride the bicycle they had bought for his fifth birthday, and used to spend long periods riding around the neighborhood. He got along with neighborhood peers and enjoyed playing with them on the neighborhood playground, but he never sought them out and never got really close to any of them. Almost from the start his teacher spent home reports of his being a loner, although he never quarreled or started fights. His school work was marginal, but he was promoted to the third grade. From the first week of that year he seemed to be in a daze, and appeared to forget things immediately, although on some subjects he seemed to do fairly well. His teacher suspected that it was a motivation problem, since he did his best work on "easy" subjects such as art, music, and physical education, and he is occasionally good at some language arts tasks such as memorizing poetry or defining words.

Perhaps the most striking feature of his Wechsler profile is his uniquely depressed Similarities subtest. The relative isolation of this intellectual deficit is much more compatible with some sort of acquired insult to the left temporal area than to any generalized left-hemisphere deficit, and in fact the majority of other test measures are reasonably close to normal: Although we have no direct confirmation, the test data suggest that at some period George may have sustained an injury or other form of insult to the portion of his left cerebral hemisphere most involved with abstraction, conceptualizing relationships, and synthesis information. His reported memory problems may well arise from an inability to categorize or synthesize information. It is of interest that his right-hemisphere-mediated skills, such as art, music, and physical education, are reported as adequate, and he can process language tasks not requiring abstraction or synthesis. There is no way to be certain of the etiology of his reported social withdrawal, but it is reasonable to speculate that a lack of ability to synthesize his social experiences may have contributed to his apparent lack of interest in forming interpersonal relationships. As he grows older, George can probably function best in those subjects that do not require much abstract judgment or categorization, but which instead are fairly structured and routine. For children like George, learning that $3 + 4 = 7$ does not necessarily mean that he can then solve $4 + 3$, or $7 - 4$, so teachers need some counseling to help them understand that uneven performance may not indicate a lack of interest or motivation.

George _____   L Handed, Age __8__ years __9__ months

Test Findings _____   Standard Scores _____

Weschler   Scales Scores _____

Information	10	Picture Completion	11	Verbal IQ __94__
Comprehension	9	Picture Arrangement	8	Performance IQ __97__
Arithmetic	9	Block Design	11	Full Scale IQ __95__
Similarities	6	Object Assembly	10	
Vocabulary	9	Coding	8	
Digit Span	9			

Wide Range Achievement Test   Grade Level

Reading	3.0	94
Spelling	2.9	93
Arithmetic	3.0	94

Constructional Praxis   95
(Beery VMI)

Receptive Language   98
(PPVT)

Motor (Rate of rapid finger oscillation per 10 seconds)
Right hand _37_ taps average over 5 trials
Left hand _40_ taps average over 5 trials

Sensory (Sum of correct identifications of numbers written on fingertips out of 20 presentations)
Sum of correctly perceived numbers written on right hand _19_
Sum of correctly perceived numbers written on left hand _19_

Problem 5

Sam, the 10-year-old son of a musician father and artist mother, had been viewed by both parents as a child prodigy. Neither had any specific mental milestones to support this view, but were in strong agreement that he had been much smarter in all respects than similar-aged children of their neighbors and relatives. Sam had gone to kindergarten at 4 years, and parents reported he could have started school at age 5 but was small for his age so they waited until he was 6. He did well on his school readiness exam, scoring in the 50th percentile for beginning first-graders, and got very good grades in first grade. Second-grade performance was only average, and he was passed from third grade with some reservations by his teacher. He had been in fourth only a few days when his teacher requested a parent conference, stating that Sam refused to read. The parents talked with him with much effect, and then hired a retired teacher to help him with phonics, in which he seemed weak. After 3 months of this, on his tenth birthday, he was referred for evaluation of an apparent psychological block about reading. The school psy-chologist did all examinations listed below except for the fingertapping and number writing, which were done at the neuropsychology laboratory.

Sam_____   R Handed, Age ___10___ years, ___1___ month

Test Findings_____   _____Standard Scores

Wechsler   Scaled Scores_____

Information	12	Picture Completion	14		Verbal IQ 110
Comprehension	13	Picture Arrangement	10		Performance IQ 114
Arithmetic	10	Block Design	14		Full Scale IQ 113
Similarities	13	Object Assembly	13		
Vocabulary	12	Coding	9		
Digit Span	9				

Wide Range Achievement Test   Grade Level

Reading	3.1	84
Spelling	3.0	88
Arithmetic	4.9	99

Constructional Praxis   109
(Bender "not significant")

Receptive Language   112
(PPVT)

Motor (Rate of rapid finger oscillation per 10 seconds)
Right hand 40 taps average over 5 trials
Left hand 38 taps average over 5 trials

Sensory (Sum of correct identification of numbers written on fingertips out of 20 presentations)
Sum of correctly perceived numbers written on right hand 20
Sum of correctly perceived numbers written on left hand 20

This profile of Sam's Wechsler scores is a classic finding in congenital specific dyslexia, with subtests requiring sequencing usually showing the lowest scaled scores. In such cases, WRAT reading may be as much as 20 standard scores points or more lower than Full Scale IQ, with spelling equally low or even very slightly lower than reading, and arithmetic fairly close to an expectancy based on Full Scale IQ. Because of this profile, the parents were questioned closely concerning any other reading problems in the family, and the father eventually reluctantly disclosed that he had never really learned to read, and in fact rarely looked at a newspaper much beyond the comic strip.

The intact functions on tests such as the Bender, and on non-reading language tests such as the Peabody, help restrict possible constructional dyspraxia or receptive dysphasias as being etiologic in impaired spelling and writing achievement scores, respectively, and the intact and symmetrical performances on fingertapping and number writing further help rule out any significant dysfunction other than specific reading dysfunction. Ever since Hinschelwood first described the syndrome of specific dyslexia (1917), cases very similar to this have been reported with some regularity both in this country (Bannatyne, 1968; Hartlage, 1977; Hartlage & Hartlage, 1973a) and abroad (Critchley, 1966; Klassen, 1972). Although there is some variability among dyslexic children concerning prognosis, many children so handicapped profit from having at least some of their schoolwork recorded onto cassettes, so that they can acquire the information normally acquired by reading through another modality.

Problem 6

Donna is described as a well-behaved first-grader whom the teacher says acts "like the cat's got her tongue." Although the teacher reports that Donna seems to understand everything, she seems too bashful to speak up and answer, and always tries to avoid talking about her experiences or hobbies or interests to the class during "Show and Tell." According to the teacher, Donna's mother has indicated that she

---

Donna___   L Handed, Age __6__ years __6__ months

Test Findings___   ___ Standard Scores

Wechsler   Scaled Scores___

Information	8	Picture Completion	12	Verbal IQ	81
Comprehension	8	Picture Arrangement	11	Performance IQ	104
Arithmetic	10	Block Design	10	Full Scale IQ	96
Similarities	8	Object Assembly	11		
Vocabulary	6	Coding	9		
Digit Span	9				

Wide Range Achievement Test   Grade Level

Reading	Kg8	85
Spelling	Kg9	86
Arithmetic	1.5	97

Constructional Praxis   102
(Beery VMI)

Receptive Language   99
(PPVT)

Motor (Rate of rapid finger oscillation per 10 seconds)
Right hand _32_ taps average over 5 trials
Left hand _35_ taps average over 5 trials

Sensory (Sum of correct identifications of x's and o's written on fingertips out of 20 presentations)
Sum of correctly perceived x's and o's written on right hand _19_
Sum of correctly perceived x's and o's written on left hand _20_

sees nothing unusual in Donna's behavior and told the teacher that Donna comes from a family that just aren't big talkers. According to the father, who brought Donna to the examination, she had no history of any significant medical problems, and her developmental milestones were "generally about average." The father had worked nights during her first 3 years and had spent considerable time with her during this period. He had taken some developmental psychology courses and was motivated by them to keep fairly detailed records of her development. Careful questioning about milestones included following: She could recognize herself in a mirror, unwrap a piece of candy, and remove her coat unassisted and point to her hair, nose, and mouth at age 2; and at age 3, could put together short phrases like "I want that," copy a circle, button her coat, and pedal a tricycle.

She did approximately average on almost all tasks involving mental skills other than expressive language. This might have been predicted from the father's report of her developmental milestones since she was almost exactly at age expectancy on all tasks except putting together phrases, which was a full year delayed. The more receptive aspects of language, such as the Peabody, showed no evidence suggestive of posterior left-hemisphere impairment, and this was also supported by good performance on the right-hand fingertip symbol recognition. The right-hand rate of fingertapping, subserved by a cortical area close to that subserving spoken language, was the only other functional area involved, suggestive of either a fairly focal insult or a congenital dysphasia. In light of the teacher's comments about the mother, it was considered important to see her, since the father's obviously careful history had not indicated any apparent head trauma. When Donna's mother was tested, she was found to have a WAIS profile very similar to Donna's, with some response latency in formulating spoken answers and a tendency to speak in very short sentences. She admitted to having had severe difficulties in school and suffering a great deal of teasing concerning her speech, but reported no trouble in any mental tasks other than those involving expressive language. These data suggest dysphasia on a congenital basis, which will probably be extremely refractory to therapy, so that considerable caution must be exercised in pushing Donna to make progress beyond the level of limitations imposed by her central nervous system.

Overview

The six sample cases, reflecting relatively common school problems, afford an opportunity to track, on a test-by-test basis, the sorts of inferences supported by each test and to assess the interactive roles of the various test items in helping assess different areas of cortical function.

REFERENCES

Ackerman, P. T., Peters, J. E., & Dykman, R. A. (1971). Children with specific learning disabilities: Bender Gestalt findings and other signs. *Journal of Learning Disabilities, 4*(8), 35–44.

Baker, E. H., & Thurber, S. (1976). Bender Gestalt Test performances and the work recognition skills of disadvantaged children. *Journal of School Psychology, 14,* 64–66.

Bannatyne, A. (1968). Diagnosing learning disabilities and writing remedial prescriptions. *Journal of Learning Disabilities, 1*(4), 242–249.

Baroff, G. S. (1957). Bender Gestalt visuo-motor function in mental deficiency. *American Journal of Mental Deficiency, 61,* 753–760.

Beck, R. L., & Lam, H. S. (1955). Use of the WISC in predicting organicity. *Journal of Clinical Psychology, 11,* 155.

Beery, K. E. (1967). *Developmental test of visual motor integration: Manual.* Chicago: Follet.

Belmont, L., & Birch, H. (1960). The relation of time of life to behavioral consequences in brain damage: I. The performance of brain injured adults and the marble board test. *Journal of Nervous Mental Disabilities, 131,* 91–97.

Bender, L., Curran, F. J., & Shilder, P. (1938). Organization of memory traces in the Lorsakoff syndrome. *Archives of Neurological Psychiatry, 39,* 482–487.

Bensberg, G. J. (1952). Performance of brain injured and familial mental defectives on the Bender Gestalt Test. *Journal of Consulting Psychology, 16,* 61–64.

Bochner, S. (1978). Reliability of the Peabody Picture Vocabulary Test: A review of thirty-two selected research studies published between 1965 and 1974. *Psychology in the Schools, 15,* 302–325.

Boder, E. (1973). Developmental dyslexia: A diagnostic approach based on three atypical reading–spelling patterns. *Developmental Medicine and Child Neurology, 15,* 662–687.

Boll, T. (1974). Behavioral correlates of cerebral damage in children aged 9 through 14. In R. M. Reitan and L. A. Davison (Eds.), *Clinical neuropsychology: Current status and applications.* New York: Wiley.

Boll, T. J. (1977). A rationale for neuropsychological evaluation. *Professional Psychology,* 64–71.

Boll, T .J., & Reitan, R. M. (1972). Motor and tactile perceptuo deficits in brain-damaged children. *Perceptual and Motor Skills, 34,* 343–350.

Bowland, J., & Deabler, H. (1956). A Bender Gestalt diagnostic validity study. *Journal of Clinical Psychology, 12,* 82–84.

Broca, P. (1861). Perte de la parole, ramollissement chronique et destruction partielle du lobe antérieur gauche du cerveau. *Bulletin Société d'Anthropologie du Paris, 2,* 235–238.

Brooks, C. R. (1977). WISC, WISC-R, S-B, L&M, WRAT: Relationships and trends among children ages six to ten referred for psychological evaluation. *Psychology in the Schools, 14,* 30–33.

Buckley, P. (1978). The Bender Gestalt Test: A review of reported research with school age subjects, 1966–1977. *Psychology in the Schools, 15*(3), 327–338.

Burns, E., & Schaaf, S. (1974). The validity of ITPA composite psycholinguistic age and psycholinguistic quotient scores. *Psychology in the Schools, 11*(3), 308–309.

Carroll, J. B. (1972). Review of the ITPA. In O. K. Buros (Ed.), *The seventh mental measurements yearbook* (pp. 819–823). Highland Park, NJ: Gryphon Press.

Chi, J., Dooling, E., & Gilles, F. (1977). Gyral development of the human brain. *Annals of Neurology, 1*(1), 88–93.

Cohn, R. (1971). Differential cerebral processing of noise and verbal stimuli. *Science, 172,* 599–601.

Corkin, S. (1965). Tactually-guided maze learning in man: Effects of unilateral cortical excisions and bilateral hippocampal lesions. *Neuropsychologia, 3,* 339–351.

Critchley, M. (1966). *Developmental dyslexia.* London: Heinemann.

DeRenzi, E., Faglioni, P., & Scotti, G. (1968). Tactile spatial impairment and unilateral cerebral damage. *Journal of Nervous and Mental Disease, 146*(6), 468–475.

DeChiro, G. (1962). Angiographic patterns of cerebral convexity veins and superficial dural sinuses. *American Journal of Roentgenology, Radium Therapy and Nuclear Medicine, 87,* 308–321.

Doehring, D. (1968). *Patterns of impairments in specific reading disability.* Bloomington: Indiana University Press.

Doyle, J., Ornstein, R., & Galin, D. (1974). Lateral specialization of cognitive mode: II. EEG frequency analysis. *Psychophysiology, 11*(5), 567–578.

Dunn, L. M. (1959). *Peabody Picture Vocabulary Test: Manual of directions and norms:* Nashville, TN: American Guidance Service.

Dunn, L. M. (1965). *Peabody Picture Vocabulary Test expanded manual.* Minneapolis, MN: American Guidance Service.

Edwards, R. P., Allery, G. R., & Snider, W. (1971). Academic achievement and minimal brain dysfunction. *Journal of Learning Disabilities, 4*(3), 17–21.

Faglioni, P., & Spinner, H. (1969). Immediate and delayed recognition of nonsense figures in patients with unilateral hemispheric damage. *Journal of Learning Disabilities, 2,* 652–658.

Farnham-Diggory, S. (1978). *Learning disabilities.* Cambridge, MA: Harvard University Press.

Feldman, I. S. (1952). *Psychological differences among moron and borderline mental defectives as a function of etiology: I. Visual-motor functioning.* Unpublished doctoral dissertation, University of Pittsburgh.

Filskov, S. B., & Goldstein, S. G. (1974). Diagnostic validity of the Halstead-Reitan Neuropsychological Battery. *Journal of Consulting Clinical Psychology, 42,* 383–388.

Finlayson, M. A., & Reitan, R. M. (1976). Handedness in relation to measures of motor and tactile perceptual functions in normal children. *Perceptual and Motor Skills, 43,* 475–481.

Foster, J. B. (1965). Unpublished study noted in the *WRAT* by Jastak and Jastak. Wilmington, DE: Guidance Associates.

Frankenburg, W. K., & Dodds, J. B. (1967). The Denver Developmental Screening Test. *Journal of Pediatrics, 71,* 181–191.

Fuller, G. B. (1964). Perceptual consideration in children with a reading disability. *Psychology in the Schools, 1,* 314–317.

Fuller, G. B. (1969). *Perceptual behaviors and reading disability: Emphasis on the neurological impaired.* Paper presented at the 47th annual International CEC Convention, Houston.

Fuller, G. B., & Hawkins, W. F. (1968). *Differentiation of organic retarded children from nonorganic children.* Paper presented at the American Association on Mental Deficiency meeting, Washington, DC.

Fuller, G. B., & Laird, J. (1963). The Minnesota Percepto-Diagnostic Test. *Journal of Clinical Psychology, Monograph Supplement, 16,* 1–33.

Gardiner, M. F., Schulman, C., & Walter, D. O. (1973). Facultative EEG asymetries in infants and adults. *Cerebral Dominance, 34,* 37–40.

Garms, J. D. (1970a). Factor analysis of the WISC and ITPA. *Psychology, 7,* 30–31.

Garms, J. D. (1970b). A validation study of the ITPA. *Psychology, 7,* 9–12.

Geschwind, N., & Levitsky, W. (1968). Human brain, left–right asymmetries in temporal speech region. *Science, 161,* 186–187.

Givens, L. C., & Hartlage, L. C. (1979). *School psychology applies to medical college.* Paper presented at the American Psychological Association meeting, New York.

Golden, C. J. (1979). *Standardized Luria Neuropsychological evaluation: Further clinical and experimental results.* Paper presented at the American Psychological Association meeting, New York.

Golden, C. J. (1986). *Manual for the Luria-Nebraska Neuropsychological Battery: Children, Revision.* Los Angeles: Western Psychological Services.

Golden, C. J., Hammeke, T. A., & Purisch, A. D. (1978).

Diagnostic validity of a standardized neuropsychological battery derived from Luria's neuropsychological tests. *Journal of Consulting and Clinical Psychology, 46,* 1258–1265.

Golden, C. J., Purisch, A. D., & Hammeke, T. A. (1979). *The Luria-Nebraska Neuropsychological Battery.* Lincoln: University of Nebraska Press.

Gordon, H. (1975). Hemispheric asymmetry and musical performance. *Science, 189,* 68–69.

Graham, E. E. (1952). Wechsler Bellevue and WISC scattergrams of unsuccessful readers. *Journal of Consulting Psychology, 16,* 268–271.

Griffeth, R. M., & Taylor, V. H. (1960). Incidence of Bender Gestalt figure rotations. *Journal of Consulting Psychology, 24,* 189–190.

Gutkin, T. (1978). Some useful statistics for the interpretation of the WISC-R. *Journal of Consulting and Clinical Psychology, 46,* 1561–1563.

Hain, J. B. (1964). The Bender Gestalt test: A scoring method for identifying brain damage. *Journal of Consulting Psychology, 28,* 34–40.

Hale, R. (1978). The WISC-R as a predictor of WRAT performance. *Psychology in the Schools, 15,* 172–175.

Hall, M., & Hall, G. (1968). Ideation in patients with unilateral or bilateral midline brain lesions. *Journal of Abnormal Psychology, 73*(6), 526–531.

Halstead, W. C. (1947). *Brain and intelligence.* Chicago: University of Chicago Press.

Halstead, W. C., & Wepman, J. M. (1949). The Halstead-Wepman aphasia screening test. *Journal of Speech and Hearing Disorders, 14,* 9–15.

Hammeke, T. A., Golden, C. J., & Purisch, A. D. (1979). A standardized short, and comprehensive neuropsychological test battery based on the Luria Neuropsychological evaluation. *International Journal of Neuroscience, 9,* 1–9.

Haring, N. G., & Ridgway, R. W. (1967). Early identification of children with learning disabilities. *Exceptional Children, 33,* 387–395.

Hartlage, L. C. (1966). Common psychological tests applied to the assessment of brain damage. *Journal of Projective Technologies and Personality Assessment, 30*(4), 319–338.

Hartlage, L. C. (1972). *Differential academic behavioral, and psychological test profiles of three types of learning disabilities.* Paper presented at the National Association of School Psychologists meeting, San Francisco.

Hartlage, L. C. (1973a). Diagnostic profiles of four types of learning disabled children. *Journal of Clinical Psychology, 29*(4), 458–463.

Hartlage, L. C. (1973b). *Differential diagnosis and treatment of primary and secondary neurogenic learning problems.* Paper presented at the Council for Exceptional Children meeting, Houston.

Hartlage, L. C. (1975). *Technical aspects of diagnosis and treatment of learning disabilities in the U.S.* Paper presented at the International Federation on Learning Disabilities meeting, Brussels.

Hartlage, L. C. (1976). *Neurological determinants of common behavior patterns in children.* Paper presented at the Southeastern Psychological Association meeting, Atlanta.

Hartlage, L. C. (1977). Maturational variables in relation to learning disabilities. *Child Study Journal, 7*(1).

Hartlage, L. C. (1978). *Useful strategies for interpreting psychometric tests in MBD screening.* Paper presented at the National Association of School Psychologists meeting, Houston.

Hartlage, L. C. (1979). Management of common clinical problems: Learning disabilities. *School Related Health Care* (Ross Laboratories Monograph No. 9, pp. 28–33). Columbus, OH: Ross Laboratories.

Hartlage, L. C., & Boone, K. E. (1972). Correlates of the WISC and WISC-R. *Perceptual and Motor Skills, 45,* 1283–1286.

Hartlage, L. C. & Green, J. B. (1972). EEG abnormalities and WISC subtest differences. *Journal of Clinical Psychology, 28*(2), 170–171.

Hartlage, L. C., & Haak, R. (1979). *Evaluation of neurological assessment batteries in school settings.* Paper presented at the National Association of School Psychologists meeting, Chicago.

Hartlage, L. C., & Haak, R. (1980). *Reitan-Indiana Battery correlates of academic and developmental variables in learning disabled children.* Paper presented at the International Neuropsychological Society meeting, New York.

Hartlage, L. C., & Hartlage, P. L. (1973a). Comparison of hyperlexic and dyslexic children. *Neurology, 23*(4), 436–437.

Hartlage, L. C., & Hartlage, P. L. (1973b). *Relative contributions of neurology and neuropsychology in the diagnosis of learning disabilities.* Paper presented at the International Neuropsychological Society meeting, New Orleans.

Hartlage, L. C., & Hartlage, P. L. (1976).

Hartlage, L. C., & Hartlage, P. L. (1977). Relationship between neurological, behavioral, and academic variables. *Journal of Clinical Child Psychology, 6,* 52–53.

Hartlage, L. C., & Hartlage, P. L. (1978). Clinical consultation to Pediatric neurology and developmental pediatrics. *Journal of Clinical Child Psychology, 7*(1), 52–53.

Hartlage, L. C., & Hartlage, P. L. (1982). Psychological testing in neurological diagnosis. In J. R. Youmans (Ed.), *Neurological surgery* (2nd ed., chapt. 20). Philadelphia: W. B. Saunders.

Hartlage, L. C., & Lucas, D. G. (1971). Scaled score transformations of Bender Gestalt expectancy levels for young children. *Psychology in the Schools, 8,* 76–78.

Hartlage, L. C., & Lucas, D. G. (1973). *Mental Development Evaluation of the Pediatric Patient.* Springfield, IL, C.C. Thanblv.

Hartlage, L. C., & Lucas, T. (1976). Differential correlates of the Bender Gestalt and Beery Visual Motor Integration Test for black and white children. *Perceptual and Motor Skills, 43,* 1039–1042.

Hartlage, L. C., Meador, K., & Lucas, T. (1976, August). *Neurological and cultural fair assessment for psychoeducational diagnosis.* Paper presented at the annual meeting ot the International Congress of Psychology, Washington, DC.

Hartlage, L. C., & Steele, C. (1977). WISC and WISC-R correlates of academic achievement. *Psychology in the Schools, 14,* 15–18.

Hartlage, L. C., & Stovall, K. (1980). *Effects of serum anticonvulsant levels on neuropsychological test performance.* Paper presented at the International Neuropsychological Society meeting, New York.

Heschl, R. L. (1978). *Ueber die vordere quere Schläfenwindung des menschlichen Grosshirns.* Braumüller: Vienna.

Hinschelwood, J. (1917). *Congenital word-blindness,* London: H.K. Lewis.

Hiscock, M., & Kinsbourne, M. (1977). Selective listening asymmetry in preschool children. *Developmental Psychology, 13*(3), 217–224.

Holroyd, J. (1968). When WISC verbal IQ is low. *Journal of Clinical Psychology, 24,* 457.

Hopkins, K. D. (1964). An Empirical analysis of the efficacy of the WISC in the diagnosis of organicity in children of normal intelligence. *Journal of Genetic Psychology, 163,* 105.

Horst, M. (1967). *Psychological screening. Management of the child with learning disabilities: An interdisciplinary challenge.* Selected papers from the 4th annual conference of the Association for Children with Learning Disabilities, San Rafael, CA.

Hughes, H. E. (1976). Norms developed at the University of Chicago for the neuropsychological evaluation of children. *Journal of Pediatric Psychology, 1*(3), 11–15.

Huizinga, R. (1973). Relationship of the ITPA to the Standford-Binet from L-M and the WISC. *Journal of Learning Disabilities, 6,* 451–456.

Jastak, K. F., & Jastak, S. R. (1965). *Wide Range Achievement Test:* Wilmington, DE: Guidance Associates.

Jenkin, N., Spivack, G., Levine, M., & Savage, W. (1964). Wechsler profiles and academic achievement in emotionally disturbed boys. *Journal of Consulting Psychology, 28*(3), 290.

Kane, R. (1979). *Comparison of the Luria Neuropsychological Battery and the Halstead-Reitan.* Paper presented at the American Psychological Association meeting, New York.

Kaufman, A. S. (1975). Factor analysis of the WISC-R at eleven age levels between $6\frac{1}{2}$ and $16\frac{1}{2}$ years. *Journal of Consulting and Clinical Psychology, 43,* 135–147.

Keogh, B. (1969). The Bender Gestalt with children: Research implications. *Journal of Special Education, 3,* 15–22.

Kicklighter, R. H., Powell, J., & Parker, J. (1974). The Peabody Picture Vocabulary Test and naive versus trained examiners. *Journal of Experimental Education, 42,* 27–29.

Kimbrell, D. L. (1960). Comparison of Peabody, WISC, and academic achievement scores among educable mental defectives. *Psychological Reports, 7,* 502.

Kimura, D. (1961). Cerebral dominance and the perception of verbal stimuli. *Canadian Journal of Psychology, 15,* 166–171.

Kinsbourne, M. (1972). Eye-head turning indicates cerebral lateralization. *Science, 176,* 539–541.

Kirk, S. A., McCarthy, J. J., & Kirk, W. D. (1968). *Examiner's Manual: Illinois Test of Psycholinguistic Abilities.* Urbana: University of Illinois Press.

Klassen, E. (1972). *The syndrome of specific dyslexia.* Baltimore: University Park Press.

Klonoff, H., & Low, M. (1974). Disordered brain function in young children and early adolescents: Neuropsychological and electroencephalographic correlates. In R. M. Reitan & L. A. Davison (Eds.), *Clinical neuropsychology: Current status and applications.* New York: Wiley.

Knights, R. M., & Moule, A. D. (1967). Normative and reliability data on finger and foot tapping in children. *Perceptual and Motor Skills, 25,* 717–720.

Koppitz, E. M. (1970). Brain damage, reading disability, and the Bender Gestalt Test. *Journal of Learning Disabilities, 3,* 429–433.

Krippner, S. (1966). Diagnostic and remedial use of the Minnesota Perceptuo-diagnostic test in a reading clinic. *Psychology in the Schools, 3,* 171–175.

L'Abate, L. (1968). *Discussion for the symposium on the contribution of clinical testing to assessment of children with brain dysfunction and learning difficulties.* Paper presented at the meeting of the American Association on Mental Deficiency, Minneapolis, MN.

Ladavas, E., Umilta, C., & Provinciali, L. (1979). Hemisphere-dependent cognitive performances in epileptic patients. *Epilepsia, 20,* 493–502.

Lambert, N. (1971). Item analysis and validity investigation of BVMGT score items. *Psychology in the Schools, 8*(1), 78–85.

Lampel, A., & Kaspar, J. (1972). *Use of the WISC as a diagnostic tool in assessing brain damage in children.* Paper presented at the 80th annual convention of the American Psychological Association, Honolulu.

Lansdell, H. (1962). Laterality of verbal intelligence in the brain. *Science, 135,* 922–923.

Lemay, M., & Culebras, A. (1972). Human brain morphologic differences in the hemispheres demonstrable by carotid arteriography. *New England Journal of Medicine, 287*(4), 168–170.

Leton, D. A. (1972). A factor analysis of ITPA and WISC scores of learning disable pupils. *Psychology in the Schools, 9,* 31–36.

Littell, W. M. (1960). The Wechsler Intelligence Scale for Children: Review of a decade of research. *Psychological Bulletin, 57,* 155.

Luria, A. R. (1932). *The nature of human conflicts.* New York: Liveright.

Luria, A. R. (1966). *Higher cortical functions in man.* New York: Basic Books.

Luria, A. R. (1973). *The working brain.* New York: Basic Books.

Majofsky, L. V. (1979). *Luria's approach to neuropsychological assessment.* Workshop presented for

Owens Clinic and Clinical Neuropsychology, Madison, WI.

McFie, J., & Zangwill, O. L. (1960). Visual constructive disabilities associated with lesions of the left cerebral hemisphere. *Brain, 83,* 243–260.

McKay, S., & Golden, C. (1979). Empirical derivation of neuropsychological scales for the lateralization of brain damage using the Luria Nebraska Neuropsychological Test Battery. *Clinical Neuropsychology, 1*(2), 1–4.

Milner, B. (1971). Interhemispheric differences in the localization of psychological processes in man. *British Medical Bulletin, 27,* 272–277.

Moss, J. (1979). Neuropsychology: One way to go. *Journal of Special Education, 13*(1), 45–49.

Myers, P. (1965). A study of language disabilities in cerebral palsied children. *Journal of Speech and Hearing Research, 8,* 129–136.

Nadler, F. B., Fink, S. L., Shontz, F. C., & Brink, R. (1959). Objective scoring versus clinical evaluation of the Bender Gestalt. *Journal of Clinical Psychology, 15,* 39–41.

Oke, A., Keller, R., Mefford, I., and Adams, R. (1978). Lateralization of norepinephrine in human thalamus. *Science, 200,* 1411–1413.

Osgood, C. E. (1957). A behavioristic analysis of perception and language as cognitive phenomena. In the University of Colorado, Psychology Department, *Contemporary approaches to cognition.* Cambridge, MA: Harvard University Press.

Parsons, O. A. (1970). Clinical neuropsychology. In C. Speilburger (Ed.), *Current topics in clinical and community psychology* (Vol. 2). New York: Academic Press.

Plaisted, J. R., Gustavson, J. L., Wilkening, G. N., & Golden, C. J. (1983). The Luria-Nebraska Neuropsychological Battery–Children's Revision: Theory and current research findings. *Journal of Clinical Child Psychology, 12,* 13–21.

Raskin, L. M., Offenback, S., & Scoonover, D. (1971). A developmental study of PPVT temporal stability over two to six month intervals. *Psychological Reports, 28,* 501–502.

Reed, J. (1968). The ability deficits of good and poor readers. *Journal of Learning Disabilities, 2,* 134–239.

Reed, J., Reitan, R., & Klove, H. (1965). Influence of cerebral palsy lesions on psychological test performance of older children. *Journal of Consulting Psychology, 29,* 247–251.

Reed, J. C. (1967). Reading achievement as related to differences between WISC and performance IQ's. *Child Development, 38,* 835–840.

Reitan, R. M. (1955). Certain differential effects of left and right cerebral lesions in human adults. *Journal of Comparative and Physiological Psychology, 48,* 474–477.

Reitan, R. M. (1966). The needs of teachers for specialize information in the area of neuropsychology. In W. Cruickshank (Ed.), *The teacher of brain-injured children* (pp. 223–243). Syracuse, NY: Syracuse University Press.

Reitan, R. M. (1974). Psychological effects of cerebral lesions in children of early school age. In R. M. Reitan and L. A. Davison (Eds.), *Clinical neuropsychology: Current status and applications.* New York: Wiley.

Robinson, N. M. (1953). Bender Gestalt performance of schizophrenics and pametrics. *Journal of Clinical Psychology, 9,* 291–293.

Rourke, B. (1975). Brain–behavior relationships in children with learning disabilities. *American Psychologist, 30*(9), 291–293.

Rourke, B. (1976). Reading retardation in children: Developmental lag or deficit? In R. Knights and D. Bakkey (Eds.), *Neuropsychology of learning disorders: Theoretical approaches.* Baltimore: University Park Press.

Rourke, B., & Finlayson, M. (1978). Neuropsychological significance of variations in patterns of academic performance: Verbal and visual-spatial abilities. *Journal of Abnormal Child Psychology, 6*(1), 121–133.

Rourke, B., & Telegdy, G. (1971). Lateralizing significance of WISC verbal-performance discrepancies for older children with learning disabilities. *Perceptual and Motor Skills, 33,* 875–883.

Rourke, B., Young, G., & Flewelling, R. (1971). The relationships between WISC verbal-performance discrepancies and selected verbal, auditory-perceptual, visual-perceptual, and problem-solving abilities in children with learning disabilities. *Journal of Clinical Psychology, 27*(4), 475–479.

Ryan, L. (1973). An investigation of the relationship between the scores earned by selected Negro and white children on the WISC and WRAT. *Dissertation Abstracts International, 34,* 2398.

Sattler, J. (1974). *Assessment of children's intelligence.* Philadelphia: W.B. Saunders.

Schiffman, G. B. (1967). Diagnosing cases of reading disability with suggested neurological impairment. In J. Allen Figurel (Ed.), *Vistas in reading: Proceedings of the International Reading Association* (Fol. 2). Newark, DE: International Reading Association.

Schoolcraft, D. R. (1973). The effectiveness of the Bender Gestalt Test for children and the knowledge of letter names in the prediction of reading achievement with first grade children in a rural area. *Dissertation Abstracts International, 33,* 4988A.

Schreiber, D., Golden, H., Kleinman, K., Goldfader, P., & Snow, M. (1976). The relationship between independent neuropsychological and neurological detection and localization of cerebral impairment. *Journal of Nervous and Mental disease, 162*(5), 360–365.

Schulberg, H. C., & Tolor, A. (1961). The use of the Bender Gestalt Test in clinical practice. *Journal Project Technology, 25,* 347–351.

Schwarting, F., & Schwarting, K. (1977). The relationship of the WISC-R and WRAT: A study based upon a selected population. *Psychology in the Schools, 14*(4), 431–433.

Schwartz, G., Davidson, R., & Maer, F. (1975). Right hemisphere lateralization for emotion in the human brain: Interactions with cognition. *Science 190,* 286–288.

Seashore, H. G. (1951). Differences between verbal and performance IQ's on the WISC. *Journal of Consulting Psychology, 15,* 62–67.

Senf, G. (1979). Can neuropsychology really change the face of special education? *Journal of Special Education, 13*(1), 51–56.

Simensen, R., & Sutherland, J. (1974). Psychological assessment of brain damage: The Wechsler scales. *Academic Therapy, 10*(1), 69–81.

Smith, D., & Marx, R. (1971). The factor structure of the revised edition of the Illinois test of psycholinguistic abilities. *Psychology in the Schools, 8*(4), 349–356.

Sollee, N. (1979). *Recommendations for educational and psychological intervention.* Symposium on Neuropsychology Services in a Pediatric Hospital, American Psychological Association, New York.

Tarnopol, M., & Tarnopol, L. (1979). Brain function and arithmetic disability. *Focus on Learning Problems in Mathematics, 1*(3), 23–40.

Thorne, F. M., Kaspar, J. C., & Schulman, J. L. (1965). The Peabody Picture Vocabulary Test in comparison with other intelligence tests on an achievement test in a group of mentally retarded boys. *Educational and Psychological Measurement, 25,* 589–595.

Tolor, A. (1956). A comparison of the Bender Gestalt Test and the digit-span test as measures of recall. *Journal of Consulting Psychology, 20,* 305–309.

Vance, H., Prichard, K., & Wallbrown, F. (1978). Comparison of the WISC-R and PPVT for a group of mentally retarded students. *Psychology in the Schools, 15*(3), 349.

Vicente, P., & Kennelly, D. (1979). *Intercorrelations between the Luria-Neuropsychological Battery and the Halstead-Reitan.* Paper presented at the American Psychological Association meeting, New York.

Wada, J. (1973). Sharing and shift of cerebral speech dominance and morphological hemispheral asymmetry. *Excerpta Medicin International Congress Series, 296,* 252.

Wada, J., Clarke, R., & Hame, A. (1975). Cerebral hemisphere asymmetry in humans. *Archives of Neurology, 37,* 234–246.

Wakefield, J., & Carlson, R. (1975). Canonical analysis of the WISC and ITPA. *Psychology in the Schools, 12*(1), 14–20.

Wallbrown, F. (1979). *A factor analytic framework for the clinical interpretation of the WISC-R.* Paper presented at the National Association of School Psychologists meeting, Chicago.

Watson, C. G., Thomas, R. W., Anderson, D., and Felling, J. (1968). Differentiation of organics from schizophrenics at two chronicity levels by use of the Reitan-Halstead Organic Test Battery. *Journal of Consulting and Clinical Psychology, 32,* 679–684.

Wechsler, D. (1949). *Wechsler Intelligence Scale for Children: Manual.* New York: Psychological Corporation.

Weener, P., Barritt, L. S., & Semmel, M. L. (1967). A critical evaluation of the ITPA. *Exceptional Children, 33,* 373–380.

Wernicke, C. (1974). *Der aphasiche sumpomen Komplex.* Brevlaus, West Germany. Chn and Weigert.

Witelson, S., & Pallie, W. (1973). Left hemisphere specialization for language in the newborn. *Brain, 96,* 641–646.

Wolf, C. W. (1968). *Characteristics of specific dyslexia.* Paper presented at the American Association on Mental Deficiency meeting, Minneapolis, MN.

Young, I. L., & Cormack, P. H. (1974). The relationship of the WISC to the revised ITPA in emotionally disturbed children. *Psychology in the Schools, 11*(1), 47–50.

Zaler, G. (1968). Hemispheric lateralization: EEG focus and Gestalt separation. *Michigan Mental Health Research Bulletin, 2,* 31–37.

19

ASSESSMENT OF INFANTS, TODDLERS, PRESCHOOL CHILDREN, AND THEIR FAMILIES: EMERGENT TRENDS

KATHLEEN D. PAGET
University of South Carolina
DAVID W. BARNETT
University of Cincinnati

With the enactment of Public Law 99-457 (Education of the Handicapped Amendments of 1986), early intervention services have become increasingly important to school psychologists and other school personnel. Responsibilities to be assumed include child and family assessment within a multidisciplinary context, interagency coordination, family consultation and intervention, and program evaluation. Although these activities are familiar to school psychologists, they take on new meaning when applied to infant, toddler, and preschool circumstances.

The purpose of this chapter is twofold: (a) to present a framework for understanding relevant issues related to assessment practices with very young children and their families, and (b) to describe procedures of assessment for these populations. The authors must state explicitly that we do not conceptualize assessment as a process distinct from intervention. We borrow a definition from Almy and Genishi (1979) suggesting that assessment is a process of *ongoing* insight into how children and families think, interact, and behave. Thus, assessment is synonomous with intervention planning, and interventions that are attempted are forms of assessment as the behaviors of young children and their families are sampled continually from the time of referral.

The chapter is organized into six major sections. First, an overview of the most recent legislative initiatives relevant to very young children and their families is provided. This overview is followed by a rationale for an ecological model of assessment and a discussion of multidisciplinary team functioning. Next, guidelines for the assessment of family needs are detailed, followed by information pertinent to assessment of classroom settings. Finally, assessment procedures within the context of an individualized evaluation session are delineated.

OVERVIEW OF PUBLIC LAW 99-457

It is important to review the essential components of Public Law 99-457 in this section because the law provides a context for the remainder of the chapter. The law includes provisions for handicapped children of all ages; however, the most dramatic provisions relate to handicapped and "at risk" children between the ages of birth and 6 and their families. With respect to these populations, P.L. 99-457 establishes two federal programs. One program addresses 3- through 5-year-old handicapped children (Part B), and the other addresses handicapped and at-risk infants and toddlers from birth to age 3 (Part H). Detailed information regarding this law can be found in House Report 99-860 (1986).

The Preschool Grant Program (Part B)

P.L. 99-457 creates a new mandate for state education agencies to serve all 3-, 4-, and 5-year-old handicapped children by 1990–1991. This new preschool mandate was achieved by lowering the P.L. 94-142 mandate to age 3. The purpose of the Preschool Grant Program is to extend P.L. 94-142 rights to children from age 3, including all definitions and requirements. States participating under P.L. 99-142 must ensure a "free, appropriate public education" to all handicapped children beginning at age 3, by 1990–1991. Children who are 3, 4, and 5 years of age are eligible for services under this new program if they are handicapped according to one or more of the P.L. 94-142 diagnostic categories: deaf, deaf-blind, hard of hearing, mentally retarded, multihandicapped, orthopedically impaired, other health impaired, seriously emotionally disturbed, specific learning disability, speech impaired, and visually handicapped. However, Congress made an important distinction for these young children; that is, the documentation of children served as required by the federal government does not *have* to be a diagnostic category for this age group. This provision, according to traditional criteria, allows states to serve preschool children without labeling them.

Another way that P.L. 94-142 was changed for this young age group is that parental instruction is an allowable cost, in addition to services delivered directly to the child. This change reflects the important role that parents play in the lives of preschool-aged children. Finally, preschool services under P.L. 99-457 differ from school-aged requirements under Public Law 94-142 such that variations in length of day and service model (home-based, center-based, etc.) are encouraged. In addition, local education agencies are encouraged to contract with appropriate existing non-public school community preschool programs to provide a range of services and service models (e.g., the mainstreaming opportunities offered by Head Start).

The Preschool Grant Program has two channels of funds: (a) one for reimbursing school districts for children served in the previous year (served children); and (b) one for advance payment for the number of additional children the state reports they intend to serve the following year (unserved children). If a state does not ensure a free, appropriate, public education beginning at age 3 to all handicapped children by 1990–1991, it will lose all Preschool Grant Funds, all P.L. 94-142 dollars that were generated by the 3- to 5-year-olds, and all grants and contracts related to preschool special education funded under the Education of the Handicapped Act discretionary programs.

Handicapped Infants and Toddlers Program (Part H)

The second landmark program established by P.L. 99-457 is the Handicapped Infants and Toddlers Program. This section of the law creates a new federal program for handicapped and at-risk children from birth to age 3 years and their families. The purposes of this program are (a) to provide financial assistance to states to develop and implement a statewide, comprehensive, coordinated, multidisciplinary, interagency program of early intervention services; (b) to facilitate the coordination of early intervention resources from federal, state, local, and private sources (including private insurers); and (c) to enhance states' capacities to provide high-quality early intervention services.

The Program is directed to the needs of children, birth to their third birthday, who need early intervention because they are experiencing developmental delays in one or more of the following areas: cognitive, physical, language and speech, psychosocial, or self-help skills; have a physical or mental condition that has a high probability of resulting in delay (e.g., Down syndrome, cerebral palsy, etc.); or are at risk medically or environmentally for substantial developmental delays if early intervention is not provided. In addition, the infant and toddler's family must receive services under this program to facilitate their capacity to assist in the development of their child.

If a state applies for funds under this program, it must assure that it has adopted a policy that contains the following required components of a statewide system:

- A definition of the term "developmentally delayed"
- Timetables for ensuring services to all eligible children by the fifth year of participation
- Multidisciplinary evaluations of the functioning of all eligible children and the needs of their families to assist in the development of their child
- Provision for a written Individualized Family Service Plan (IFSP) for all children
- A comprehensive Child Find system, including a system for making referrals to providers. "Primary referral sources" must be included (e.g., hospitals, physicians, other health care providers and agencies, and day care facilities)
- A public awareness program focusing on early identification
- A central directory containing state resources, services, experts, and research and demonstration projects
- A comprehensive system of personnel development—including training of public and private service providers, primary referral sources, as well as preservice training
- A single line of authority in a lead agency designated or established by the governor to carry out the general administration, supervision, and monitoring of programs and activities
- A policy pertaining to the contracting or making of other arrangements with local providers
- A procedure for securing timely reimbursements of funds between state and local agencies
- Procedural safeguards with respect to the settlement of disagreements between parents and providers, the right to appeal, the right to confidentiality of information, the opportunity to examine records, assignment of surrogate parents, written prior notices to parents in their native language, and procedures to ensure the provision of services pending the resolution of complaints
- Policies and procedures relating to the establishment and maintenance of personnel training, hiring, and certification/licensing standards
- A system for compiling data on the early intervention programs

A key feature of this part of the law is the development of written IFSPs developed by a multidisciplinary team and the parents. Services provided must be designed to meet the developmental needs of the child and be in accordance with family needs. Services may include special education, speech and language pathology and audiology, occupational therapy, physical therapy, psychological services, parent and family training and counseling, transitions, medical services for diagnostic purposes, and health services necessary to enable the child to benefit from other early intervention services. Case management services must be provided for every eligible child and his or her parent.

All services must be provided at no cost to parents except where federal or state law provides for a system of payments by parents, including provision for a schedule of sliding fees. The IFSP must contain (a) a statement of the child's present levels of development (cognitive, speech/language, psychosocial, motor, and self-help); (b) a statement of the family's strengths and needs relating to enhancing the child's development; (c) a statement of major outcomes expected to be achieved for the child and family; (d) the criteria, procedures, and timelines for determining progress; (e) the specific early intervention services necessary to meet the unique needs of the child and family, including the method, frequency, and intensity of service; (f) the projected dates for the initiation of services and expected duration; (g) the name of the case manager; and (h) procedures for transition from early intervention into the preschool program. The IFSP must be evaluated at least once a year, and must be reviewed every 6 months or more often where appropriate. Because of the importance and novelty of family needs assessments and IFSPs, relevant issues and procedures are discussed in this chapter.

RATIONALE FOR AN ECOLOGICAL MODEL

Given the essential legislative components listed above, it is clear that an ecological model must guide the conceptualization of service delivery to infants, toddlers, and preschoolers. An ecological model can be considered in social systems terms (see Dunst, 1985) wherein one would expect both direct and indirect influences on child, parental, and family outcomes. Continual influences from family, school, and community contexts must be considered if our assessments and interventions are to be complete. Of central importance is that behavioral and learning difficulties are not viewed as deficits residing in the child or his or her parents; rather, such difficulties are viewed as variations resulting from ecological forces that affect parent, child, and family behavior.

For school-aged children (Reynolds, Gutkin, Elliott, & Witt, 1984), as well as children of preschool age (Adelman, 1982; Barnett, 1984; Lapides, 1977; Paget, 1985; Paget & Nagle, 1986; Thurman & Widerstrom, 1989), ecological models have been proposed as the most effective framework for special service delivery. With a focus on a child's roles within an entire ecological system, professionals using the model analyze the child's interactions with people and objects, as well as reactions to events. Direct observation and consultation with significant adults in various settings constitute major activities. Thus, an ecological approach is consistent with an indirect service delivery model that provides professionals access to a greater diversity and number of activities than is possible under direct service models (Barnett & Paget, 1988; Conoley & Gutkin, 1986). Moreover, of particular relevance to preschool children is the increased possibility that newly acquired skills will generalize across settings when services are delivered in a variety of natural contexts.

Lapides (1977) describes an ecological view of preschool services as one that is a proactive, seeking-out effort rather than a "reactive set of professional rituals" that result from the wait-for-referral approach (p. 185). Beyond this, an ecological model assumes that each child and family are unique and that no one technique or strategy is appropriate across all children and parents. These assumptions are entirely consistent with the necessary emphasis in early education on prevention and individualized intervention.

An ecological model proposed by Bandura (1978) stresses the interplay or reciprocal influence among personal characteristics, behavior, and environmental phenomena. We believe the model accommodates very well the rapid developmental changes, behavioral fluctuations, and emerging skills that characterize very young children. Using this model, professionals view learning and behavior problems as resulting from the interaction between a child's motivation and developmental status, specific situational factors, and differing approaches to socialization. In this regard, Bronfenbrenner (1974) observed that "the psychological development of the young child is enhanced through his/her involvement in progressively more complex, enduring patterns of reciprocal contingent interaction with persons with whom he/she has established a mutual and engaging attachment (p. 31). With this in mind, it is essential to assess salient features of family and classroom situations and how these features influence young children's development.

MULTIDISCIPLINARY ASSESSMENT

When conducting comprehensive, ecologically based assessments of young children and their families, professionals increasingly will be concerned with the effectiveness of multidisciplinary teams. Instruments to evaluate team functioning (e.g., Bagnato, 1984; Bailey, Helsel-DeWert, Thiele, & Ware, 1983) are emerging in response to criticism that multidisciplinary models do not take full advantage of the range of skills each person brings to a team (e.g., Holm & McCartin, 1978). Thus, alternative team approaches have been proposed and termed "interdisciplinary," implying role release and the crossing of discipline borders. In striving to be effective interventionists, we must have skills as synthesizers (Iacino & Bricker, 1978), seeking out and evaluating information from other professionals, and combining it with our own expertise. Ongoing information exchange and mutual support are vital aspects of the transdisciplinary approach and are congruent with the spirit of reciprocal influence advanced in this chapter and the spirit of P.L. 99-457.

Putting issues of terminology aside, Caldwell (1978) has argued that young children with handicaps and their families need professionals to "de-discipline themselves and cooperate in the task of answering basic questions and providing service" (p. xi). Professional synthesis of judgment and knowledge is essential at the preschool level, because developmental problems are multifaceted and often fall outside the expertise of any one profession. A severely multihandicapped child, for example, exhibits complex language, cognitive, self-care, and movement difficulties that require the expertise of medical, educational, psychological, and language specialists. Moreover, communication with the family of such a child from a well-coordinated team approach is more likely to be effective than the fragmentation resulting from each professional working alone (Dunst, Trivette, & Deal, 1988). Even with more subtle developmental disorders (i.e., language disorders), collaboration among team members often is essential to effective intervention (Paget, 1985).

ASSESSMENT OF FAMILY NEEDS

The roles played by families in early intervention programs are changing dramatically with the passage of P.L. 99-457, to the extent that family members are also team members. The expansion in family roles is particularly dramatic under Part H of P.L. 99-457 where early intervention services comprise newly-applied concepts such as the IFSP and case management. Concomitantly, roles played by professionals are shifting toward more emphasis on the assessment of family needs and strengths. Because these roles are new for many professionals, it is useful to discuss limitations of traditional practice and detail guidelines and procedures for assessing family needs.

The common practice of addressing only child needs has been the focus of recent criticism in the early childhood literature (Bristol & Gallagher, 1982; Dunst, 1985; Schultz, 1982; Wahler, 1980) even prior to passage of the law and the mandate to complete Individualized Family Service Plans. Traditionally, the major goal of early intervention programs has been to effect change in some aspect of the child's behavior or functioning ability, with family concerns seldom being addressed prior to or during interventions (A. P. Turnbull & Winton, 1984). Nevertheless, the scope of assessment and intervention practices has expanded enormously, from a strictly child focus to a focus on the family as a system within a child's broad-based ecology (Bronfenbrenner, 1974; Dunst, 1985; Paget, 1988). With the passage of P.L. 99-457, profes-

sionals face challenges associated with involvement of the family as a whole system, moving beyond the "parent" involvement mandates of P.L. 94-142.

Criticism also has focused on the practice of treating all parents or families as if they were homogeneous. Much of this criticism has been raised by family systems and ecobehavioral researchers (Crnic, Friedrich, & Greenberg, 1983; Dunst, 1985; A. P. Turnbull, Summers, & Brotherson, 1987) who recognize that families often differ in fundamental ways and consequently have different strengths and needs. Families vary in their structure, ethnic and cultural backgrounds, economic status, educational resources, ideologies, personal and mental health problems, and coping styles for dealing with problems (Bristol, 1987; Kaiser & Fox, 1986; Summers, 1988; A. P. Turnbull et al., 1987). In addition, important differences may exist *within* families, such as between a mother and father. Although the concept of family differences is generally *acknowledged,* it seldom has been *incorporated* into the design of early intervention programs. As a result, professionals have run the risk of treating all families and family members similarly, perhaps failing to modify treatment programs to respond to individual family needs.

The term family *needs assessment* has been used to describe a variety of assessments that (a) assess parents' desire for information (Sparling & Lowman, 1983), (b) assess the types of stress and reactions to stress that families encounter (Bristol, Donovan, & Harding, 1984; Dunst & Trivette, 1985; Holroyd, 1974), (c) evaluate program effectiveness (Berger & Fowlkes, 1980; Vincent et al., 1980), (d) assess parent strengths and family relationships (Schaefer & Edgerton, 1981), and (e) assess the home environment (Caldwell & Bradley, 1979). Despite how the term is applied to specific situations, the operative issue is that professionals must now develop family-focused intervention programs that are *responsive* to family needs and concerns (Dunst et al., 1988).

Assessment of family "needs" may focus on demographic and other descriptive information and fail to identify needs from the family's perspective. Parents may be asked about marital status, employment, family constellation, daily schedule, and the child's current level of functioning, and professionals may use this information to define the parent's level of participation and select goals for intervention. Nevertheless, professional expectations may not match the family's desired level of participation or the family's priorities for intervention. Knowledge that a mother works or that she is a single parent, for example, does not indicate the mother's concern or interest level with regard to involvement in an intervention plan. Thus, parent perspectives cannot be derived or assumed from traditional demographic and descriptive information, and such assessments, when used alone, are not useful in helping professionals understand what families say they want or need from an intervention program.

All professionals, including school psychologists, must begin to examine critically the types of assessments they conduct and how they interpret the results by asking questions such as whether the assessments evaluate needs from the family's perspective, help professionals and families understand each other's perspectives, and are helpful in developing family-focused interventions. Additionally, Wasik (1984) states that the administration of a needs assessment implies a promise to help and recommends that professionals consider the implications of this promise prior to obtaining information about family needs. Moreover, our assessments of family needs require careful ethical judgments, particularly with respect to confidentiality of information. Specific descriptions of measures that assess varied aspects of family needs and resources are provided in Bailey and Simeonsson (1988) and Dunst et al. (1988).

The Scope of Family Needs Assessments

Numerous writers have asserted that the scope of a needs assessment should be defined by the feasibility of intervention. Dunst et al. (1988) suggest that professionals assess family strengths (e.g., parenting skills; family–child interactions) prior to selecting intervention tasks and the resources available to the family for accomplishing the tasks. These authors suggest further that professionals identify "personal projects," where strengths within the family system as well as strengths of individual family members are recognized and used as a foundation for meeting needs. Fawcett, Seekins, Whang, Múiń, and Suarez de Balcazar (1982) use the term "improvement agenda" to suggest a similar process that can be used to assure that strengths are maintained during intervention. Bristol and Gallagher (1986) have developed assessment procedures related to mother and father perceptions of family needs, and Dunst et al. (1988) delineate a detailed family support model

of assessment and intervention. In addition, numerous examples of family assessment and measures specific procedures for structuring observations of parent–child interaction have been developed by Farran, Kasari, and Jay (1984), Fewell (1984, 1986), and Dunst (1986a, 1986b). When using any of these measures, it is important not to *assume* dysfunction among family members because of the presence of a developmentally disabled child.

In programs where parents or family members are expected to participate in intervention, it is important to assess their ability or desire to do so. In adhering to legal mandates, professionals run the risk of assuming that all families wish to be equally involved with their child's program and that all parents have the time and skills (or enthusiasm and abilities to learn the skills) required to be involved in their child's program. However, there is growing recognition that not all families want to be involved in their child's treatment program (Lynch & Stein, 1982; Schultz, 1982; Winton & Turnbull, 1981). Without family input, expectations regarding involvement may be unrealistic or unreasonable (H. R. Turnbull & A. P. Turnbull, 1982; Winton & Turnbull, 1981). Persons responsible for the parent or family components of early intervention programs should strive to involve parents and other family members according to the family needs and abilities. This may require looking beyond the immediate family to the extended family. In this respect, Vadasy, Fewell, Meyer, and Schnell (1984) have identified assessment and intervention procedures appropriate for use with grandparents.

Developing Family-Focused Interventions

The development of family-focused interventions may be approached by having families rank needs in order of importance, select several needs as highest priority, or indicate satisfaction or dissatisfaction with how the needs are currently being met. It is important when selecting intervention goals that the family and professionals consider the impact of interventions on the family in terms of time, finances, and skills, and overall quality of life (Chandler, Fowler, & Lubeck, 1986). If a parent agrees to work on physical therapy exercises at home, for example, the amount of time required to conduct therapy should be addressed as well as the extent to which the therapy may compete with other tasks or family interactions (Rainforth & Salisbury, 1988). Professionals may also need to limit the number of goals simultaneously addressed during intervention, although the design of a creative and responsive intervention plan may serve to address multiple goals (see Deal, Dunst, & Trivette, 1989).

In school-based programs where professionals and families jointly determine treatment goals, disagreements may arise regarding the choice of goals or the importance of different goals (Clarke-Stewert, 1981). Chandler et al. (1986) describe a situation where professionals recommend that a parent work on speech training, while the parents indicate a strong desire to work on toilet training. Although speech training may have been an important intervention goal, it was decided that training the child to toilet independently would reduce the time previously spent by the family on diapering, laundering, and so on, thus resulting in increased time for the family to work on speech needs and to engage in other family activities.

When incorporating the results of family needs assessments into goals on IFSPs, we must be careful to retain the spirit of the new law. According to Dunst et al. (1988), the potentially most damaging aspect of the IFSP has to do with the role the "case manager" is expected to play in implementing the plan. Rather than being responsible for implementing the plan, Dunst and associates assert that professionals should engage in roles that enable and empower the family in a manner that makes them better able to mobilize resources to meet their needs more self-sufficiently. In addition, they propose that fluid rather than static approaches must be taken wherein frequent modifications occur as a result of the many changes that occur within families. A 6-month review of family needs is not likely to be responsive to the many changes that occur in family life.

Family-Level Outcome Measures
When family needs are considered and when parent participation is expected, outcome measures will differ from those traditionally employed for assessing program efficacy. Obviously, benefits to family members from program participation cannot be assessed adequately by measuring child change on developmental assessments (Sheehan, 1982). Benefits to families must be measured in terms of impact on families in areas such as satisfaction, decreased time required in child care tasks, parent and family member interactions with the child, stress, and change in parenting abilities and practices. This process must be viewed as a continuous process, with changes made over time as reflected by family needs.

In summary, the implementation of assessment and intervention practices that are responsive to the needs of the families as well as the children requires changes in the ways that professionals and practitioners view families. Many of these changes reflect a number of considerations that professionals have begun to acknowledge and address, but are typically overlooked or neglected in designing family-focused interventions. This oversight can result in programs that lack social validity and receive little or no "consumer" support. Wolf (1978) cautions that consumers are the best evaluators of their own needs and satisfactions. He reminds us that "if participants don't like the treatment they may avoid, it, or complain loudly, and will be less likely to use our technology, no matter how potentially effective and efficient it might be" (p. 206). Thus, professionals in early education programs must assess and use families' perceptions of satisfaction as the primary guide to program development and individual educational program planning. Information from professionals should supplement what is provided by families rather than family information supplementing our perspectives. Certainly, family satisfaction with services and identification of needs are value judgements that families, not professionals, are most qualified to make.

ASSESSMENT OF PRESCHOOL CLASSROOMS

Considerable evidence indicates that preschool classrooms in addition to family settings have profound effects on the behavior of handicapped and nonhandicapped children (Carta, Sainato, & Greenwood, 1988; Moore, 1987, 1988; Rogers-Warren, 1982; Rogers-Warren & Wedel, 1980; Twardosz, 1984). Various characteristics of a preschool classroom settings influence children's social interactions (Wachs & Gruen, 1982), language production (Hart & Risley, 1980), engagement with the environment (Doke, 1975), and sense of competence (Olds, 1982). Collectively, the available evidence demonstrates that numerous child behavior characteristics are affected by the ecology of classroom environments. Because school psychologists increasingly serve as consultants to preschool teachers, knowledge of salient classroom features and their effects on children's behavior is essential.

Environmental Organization

The salient components of preschool classrooms include both human and physical features (Rogers-Warren & Wedel, 1980). These components can be conceptualized according to the physical environment, staff assignments and behaviors, classroom scheduling and transitions between activities, and types of instruction (Dunst, McWilliam, & Holbert, 1986).

The arrangement of the physical environment influences a number of different aspects of child behavior. Organization of the environment into "open spaces" and "learning zones" has been found to promote both high levels of child engagement (the amount of time a child spends interacting with the animate or inanimate environment in a developmentally appropriate manner) and smooth transitions between classroom activities (Twardosz & Risley, 1982). In turn, smooth transitions serve to decrease behavior problems when children do not have to wait in crowded situations for long periods of time (Fowler, 1982; Krantz & Risley, 1977).

The manner in which caregivers carry out their assigned duties has also been found to influence child outcomes. Having staff assigned responsibility for particular classroom areas ("zones") during transitions decreases non-engaged time compared to having staff assigned responsibility for individual children (LeLaurin & Risley, 1972). Similarly, B. O'Brien and Risley (1983) found that staff members who used facilitative and elaborative styles of interactions were more likely to encourage engagement with both the physical and social environment.

A set sequence of classroom activities for children has been shown to produce fewer disruptions and higher rates of task completion than a random sequence of classroom events (Fredericksen & Fredericksen, 1977). For example, Krantz and Risley (1977) found that when story time was preceded by a rest period (rather than an active period), transition times were shorter, disruptions less frequent, and attentional engagement to adults was higher. Doke and Risley (1972) investigated the effects of allowing 4- and 5-year olds to move individually from one classroom activity to the next, as opposed to waiting for a group transition, and found that individual transitions produced higher engagement levels than did group transitions.

Preschool programs vary considerably in the types of instruction employed. J. E. Johnson, Ershler, and Bell (1980) found preschools that used formal instructional methods produced more constructive play, but discovery-based programs produced higher levels of engagement. Highly structured, teacher-directed programs produce more attention to adults but less independence (Huston-Stein, Friedrich-Cofer, & Susman, 1977). In addition, engagement levels have been found to vary according to the formality of the activities (Doke, 1975) and teaching method (McWilliam, Trivette, & Dunst, 1985).

The use of incidental teaching and other naturalistic teaching techniques with young children is supported by numerous studies (Fabry, Mayhew, & Hanson, 1984; Hart & Risley, 1975, 1978, 1980; McGee, Krante, Mason, & McClannahan, 1983; M. O'Brien, Porterfield, Herbert-Jackson, & Risley, 1979). This type of teaching consists of a sequence of instructional steps that guide adult responsiveness to child-initiated interactions (Dunst & McWilliam, 1988). The procedure is designed to produce attentiveness, elaboration, and mastery of socially and culturally defined competencies. The use of incidental teaching has been found particularly effective in producing elaboration in language production (Hart & Risley, 1975, 1978, 1980).

Results from the studies described above have served as the foundation for the development of environment-based assessment tools that contribute to ecologically valid assessments, consultation with teachers, and intervention planning. These instruments are described briefly below.

Environment-Based Assessment Techniques

A number of assessment instruments have been developed to quantify the various components of preschool environments. Each assessment procedure described differs with respect to explicit attempts to specify the manner in which the environment can be expected to affect different aspects of child functioning.

An instrument called the *Planned Activity Check (PLA-Check)* (Risley & Cataldo, 1973, 1974) determines, for the number of persons present for a given activity, the percentage of children who are engaged and which materials, activities, people, or schedules generate the greatest amount of interest and participation. In contrast to *PLA-Check*, which measures group level of engagement, the *Caregiver Assessment of Child Engagement* (CACE; McWilliam & Galant, 1984) and the *Daily Engagement Rating Scale* (DERS; McWilliam, Galant, & Dunst, 1984) measure engagement levels for individual children. Both are rating scales that permit an assessment of different degrees of engagement. Two types (attentional and active) and three categories (adults, peers, and materials) of engagement are measured on each scale. The CACE measures engagement levels for specific classroom activities (e.g., group and snack times). The DERS provides a daily measure of engagement for all classroom activities taken together. PLA-Check and both the CACE and DERS were designed to assess the manner in which environments and their various components affect child outcomes.

The *Early Childhood Environment Rating Scale* (ECERS; Harms & Clifford, 1980) is designed to provide an overall picture of preschool settings, including the manner in which materials, space, child-level activities, classroom scheduling, and adult supervision are organized and used. The scale includes 37 items divided into seven subareas: (a) personal-care routines, (b) furnishings, and display, (c) language-reasoning experiences, (d) fine and gross motor activities, (e) creative activities, (f) social development, and (g) adult needs. Each ECERS item is scored on a 7-point scale ranging from inadequate to excellent provision of support. The scale was designed for use in classrooms serving preschool children primarily between 3 and 6 years of age.

The authors of the ECERS have developed two additional measures within the same framework for environmental assessment, which focus on two specific types of environments. The *Infant/ Toddler Environment Rating Scale (ITERS;* Harms, Cryer, & Clifford, 1989) is designed to assess the quality of care provided for children under age 30 months. The *Family Day Care Rating Scale (FDCRS;* Harms & Clifford, 1989) is designed to assess the quality of care provided in family/home day care. A comparison of subscales and items on the ECERS, ITERS, and FDCRS is provided by Bailey (1988).

The *Classroom Observation Instrument* (COI; Stallings, 1975) measures classroom arrangements and events considered conducive to educational performance. It is designed primarily for the assessment of prekindergarten, kindergarten, and early elementary school classroom environments. The scale includes 602 items divided into five categories: (a) classroom characteristics (e.g., number of teachers and children, adult-to-child ratio); (b) physical environment (e.g., work-group patterns and presence and use of materials; (c) classroom patterns (e.g., distribution of persons and type of activities), (d) person roles (e.g., type of roles that different persons are performing), and (e) child and adult behavior characteristics (e.g., types of interactions and forms of engagement). Behaviors in categories c, d, and e are coded using a time-sampling observation system. The scale is derived from a framework that specifically assesses the degree to which different aspects of the classroom environment affect child behavior. The six child-outcome measures obtained as part of the use of the COI are independence, task persistence, cooperation, verbal initiative, observed self-esteem, and question asking.

Rogers-Warren, Santos-Colond, Warren, & Hasselbring (1984, cited in Dunst, McWilliam, & Holbert, 1986) developed and validated an assessment tool *(Infant/Toddler Learning Project Observation System* (ITLP) that also explicitly considers the manner in which the classroom environment can be expected to influence levels of child engagement. The ITLP includes 34 items divided into seven categories: (a) physical environment, (b) classroom scheduling, (c) material availability, (d) appropriateness of learning activities, (e) behavior management, (f) child–care giver interactions, and (g) classroom safety. Each item is rated on a 5-point scale ranging from inadequate to adequate attention to the various dimensions of the classroom environment. The scale was specifically designed for use in classroom for children functioning under 2 years of age.

The *Preschool Assessment of the Classroom Environment Scale* (PACE; Dunst et al., 1986) is similar to the Rogers-Warren et al. (1984) instrument because both are based on a common set of assumptions (e.g., the importance of child engagement) and are derived from a common set of empirical investigations (e.g., Krantz & Risley, 1977; LeLaurin & Risley, 1972).

The PACE is a 70-item rating scale that assesses four broad categories of the classroom ecology: (a) program organization, (b) environmental organization, (c) methods of instruction, and (d) program outcomes. Each major category includes subcategories that assess specific components of the classroom environment. Each subcategory includes five individual items that assess specific aspects of each classroom component. Each item is scored on a 5-point rating scale in terms of the degree to which the classroom components and their specific aspects are consistent with variables found to optimize child functioning. The PACE was designed to be used in classrooms with children functioning from birth to 6 years of age.

Administration of the scale includes three steps: (a) observation of the classroom environment, (b) an interview with the person(s) responsible for the overall management of the classroom, and (c) a review of written materials (e.g., IEPs). The classroom observation generally takes about 2 to 4 hours to sample adequately the full range of activities, events, and routines that constitute the "typical" classroom environment. The interview permits an assessment of the degree to which classroom activities are consistent with program philosophy, policies, procedures, and so on. The review of written materials permits an assessment of the match between what is prescribed and what is actually occurring.

Dunst et al. (1986) outline five steps in translating assessment results from the PACE into intervention plans. First, a self-evaluation of the classroom environment is completed by a teacher/caregiver requesting consultation on one or more aspects of the classroom environment. The self-evaluation is made using an instrument called the *Needs Evaluation for Educators Of Developmentally Delayed Students* (NEEDS) (McWilliam & Dunst, 1985). The NEEDS includes the same 70 items that are on the PACE; however, the items are stated in terms of the degree to which the teacher/care giver would like help with improving one or more components of the classroom environment. Second, the PACE is completed by an independent observer in the manner described above. Third, the results from both the NEEDS and PACE are used to discuss those aspects of the environment that are both conducive and not conducive to optimal child functioning. Fourth, a technical assistance plan is developed and implemented to reinforce and strengthen the program activities that are "working" and to change or improve components that are less than optimal. Fifth, changes in child behavior and functioning are monitored relative to changes in the environment so as to establish the effectiveness of the intervention procedures. This five-step process provides the structure for both developing and implementing changes in the classroom ecology and determining the efficacy of these efforts.

From the information above, it is clear that careful assessment of preschool classroom environments can serve as a functional mechanism for understanding a child's functioning in the classroom context, consulting with preschool teachers, and designing interventions. By assessing preschool children individually and in groups within the classroom setting, naturally occurring teaching opportunities can be continued, adapted, or eliminated, depending on what is deemed most appropriate for the children.

INDIVIDUALLY ADMINISTERED ASSESSMENT MEASURES

In this section a variety of screening and assessment instruments and procedures are discussed which were designed to be used in individual assessment situations. As the reader peruses the following information, it should be kept in mind that the assessment methods presented are related to one another in complementary fashion. That is, they can be combined into assessment batteries to meet specified purposes, with each method eliciting unique information from the child. In doing this we must be mindful not to turn assessment into a mechanical procedure. Rather, the primary purpose of individualized assessment procedures should be to supplement information from family and classroom assessment to arrive at functional instructional targets for each child assessed.

Screening Instruments

When screening infants, toddlers, and preschool-aged children for developmental problems, the primary purpose is to identify within a given population those children who appear to need special services to help them achieve their maximum potential (Lichtenstein & Ireton, 1984). Thus, developmental screening programs should not be started unless interventions are to be provided to those who are found to have a problem or disability through subsequent diagnostic evaluations. In addition, screening instruments should not be used for diagnosis of developmental disabilities, development of specific interventions for children with developmental problems, or evaluation of the effectiveness of an intervention program. Scott and Hogan (1982) have identified several criteria that should be considered in selecting a screening instrument. Conditions for which screening is done should be well defined, instruments should have demonstrated reliability and predictive validity, data on the numbers of false positives and false negatives should be available, and the procedure should be acceptable to both the professional and lay communities. We would add to this list the caveat that screening procedures should not simply involve administration of a test; rather, careful observation of the child's behavior in home and school settings should be incorporated as well. Selected screening instruments are summarized in Table 1. For more detailed information regarding these instruments and the screening process in general, the reader is referred to excellent discussions in Lichtenstein and Ireton (1984).

Norm-Referenced Assessment Instruments
Standardized assessment tools normed on preschool-aged children provide the opportunity to compare a young child's performance with that of other children his or her age. Nevertheless, because these tests are administered in an individualized assessment situation at one point in time, results must be interpreted as a sampling of behavior within this context only. Some of the most popular instruments are described below, although the information does not comprise an exhaustive listing of available tests nor are in-depth reviews provided. Interested readers are referred to Buros (1989), Sattler (1988), Salvia and Ysseldyke (1988), and other compendia of test reviews for more in-depth information. In addition, Bracken (1988) provides an important framework for evaluating the technical adequacy of these instruments, and Zelazo (1982) and Shelton (1989) provide an excellent discussions of the limitations of norm-referenced instruments for handicapped infants and toddlers.

The Bayley Scales of Infant Development
The Bayley Scales (1969) have been used widely to evaluate the developmental status of low-functioning preschool-aged children and infants and toddlers between the ages of 1 and 36 months. A mental and motor index can be obtained, and an interpretive social behavior record can be completed as an adjunct to the mental and motor assessment portions. The scales were standardized carefully and reliability data are good, although their limited predictive value and need to be restandardized have long been recognized (Campbell, Siegel, Parr, & Ramey, 1986).

Other limitations of the Bayley Scales have been noted by a number of writers and researchers (e.g., Horowitz, 1982; Zelazo, 1982). These include: (a) unevenness in the depth of evaluation in different domains of functioning; (b) an assumption underlying the motor scale that intact neuromotor functioning reflects intact intellectual ability (which is valid in some but not all cases); (c) confounds in the results because of a child's peripheral handicaps (e.g., motoric impairment interfering with language production); and (d) the lack of norms for children with specific handicaps.

The Stanford-Binet Intelligence Scale
The 1972 version of the Stanford-Binet (Terman & Merrill, 1973) has been criticized for use with preschoolers because of its outdated norms, its high verbal content, and its emphasis on one global score (Reynolds & Clark, 1983; Salvia & Ysseldyke, 1988; Sattler, 1988). Despite this criticism, it has a long history of use for assessing preschool-aged children and evaluating the effects of programs, such as Head Start.

The fourth edition of the Stanford-Binet (Thorndike, Hagen, & Sattler, 1986) was devised using a theoretical model of intelligence. This three-level model of cognitive ability consists of a general reasoning component (g), which is subdivided into crystallized abilities, fluid-analytic abilities, and short-term memory. *Crystallized abilities* are measured by subtests that assess verbal and quantitative reasoning; *fluid-analytic abilities* involve visualization tasks; and *short-term memory* is assessed by separate items. A total of 15 subtests is on the new test, but only eight of these are given to children ages 2 through 5. These subtests are Vocabulary, Comprehension, Absurdities, Quantitative, Pattern Analysis, Copying, Bead Memory, and Memory for Sentences. The subtests are organized into subscales termed Verbal Reasoning, Abstract/Visual Reasoning, Quantitative Reasoning, and Short-Term Memory.

The new edition of the Stanford-Binet addresses many of the criticisms raised with respect to earlier versions of the test, adding items that are nonverbal in format and moving away from emphasis on a single score. Although it is still possible

TABLE 1   Selected Screening Instruments

Instrument	Administration	Standardization	Domains
Battelle Development Inventory Screening Test Newborg, Stock, Wanek, Guidubaldi, & Svinicki (1984)	Direct observation, naturalistic observation, or parent interview	Drawn from full-scale BDI standardized on 800 children, birth through 8 years, representative of general population	96 items; 5 domains: personal-social, adaptive, motor, communition, cognitive
Denver Developmental Screening Test Frankenburg, Dodds, Fandal, Kazuk, & Cohrs (1975)	Direct testing, some parent interview	Originally standardized on 1,036 children, ages 2 weeks to 6.4 years, all from the Denver area	105 items; 4 domains: gross motor, fine motor, adaptive language, personal, social
Developmental Profile II Alpern, Boll, & Shearer (1980)	Interview and some direct testing	Standardized on 3,008 children from birth to 9 years; underrepresentation of Oriental, Spanish-American, and mixed and rural backgrounds	186 items; 5 scales: physical, self-help, social, academic, and communication
Developmental Indicators for the Assessment of Learning–Revised Mardell-Czudnowski & Goldenberg (1983)	Requires a team to administer	Normed on 2,477 children ages 2 to 6 years	24 items in 3 domains (gross motor and fine motor, concepts, and language) plus 8 additional behavioral items
Minnesota Child Development Inventory (MCDI) Ireton & Thwing (1972)	Maternal report inventory	Standardized on 796 children from Minneapolis suburb, ages 1 to 6 years, not representative of general population	320 items; 8 scales: general development, gross motor, fine motor, expressive language, comprehension, conceptual situation comprehension, self-help, personal-social; all 320 items must be completed

Source.   From Multidimensional screening instruments by C. C. Robinson, J. Rose, and B. Jackson, 1986, *Diagnostique, 11*, 135–154. Reprinted by permission.

to obtain a score reflecting a "general" factor, the new edition recognizes the need for looking at different types of abilities. Nevertheless, preliminary factor analytic evidence suggests caution when interpreting the subscale scores (Reynolds, Kamphaus, & Rosenthal, 1988). From an ecological perspective, the new Binet represents an improved method for assessing preschoolers who have no school experience, by separating abilities that are influenced by school-like experiences from those thought to depend less on such experiences.

Kaufman Assessment Battery for Children (K-ABC)

The K-ABC (Kaufman & Kaufman, 1983) encompasses the age range from $2\frac{1}{2}$ through $12\frac{1}{2}$ years and thus has caught the interest of professionals who assess preschool-aged children. The technical sophistication of the K-ABC attests to the fact that much careful preparation and validation went into publication of the test. A major innovation in the development of the K-ABC is the application of Rasch-Wright latent trait methodology to the selection of items (Kamphaus & Reynolds, 1987).

The K-ABC battery yields a global score and subscale scores in four areas of functioning: Sequential Processing, Simultaneous Processing, a Mental Processing Composite (MPC), and Achievement. Unlike many intelligence tests, the K-ABC was developed from a theoretical foundation that focuses on the individual's information processing and problem-solving style. Also unlike the others, the global score (Mental Processing Composite), is obtained from tests that "minimize the role of language and verbal skills for successful performance, and include stimuli that are as fair as possible for children from diverse backgrounds" (Kaufman & Kaufman, 1983, p. 2). The inclusion of teaching items for problem-solving tasks on the test, the nonverbal nature of the items, and the "colorful, child-oriented, and game-like" nature of the test materials are appealing for use with preschoolers. Another useful feature of the test is that out-of-level testing is possible. That is, a gifted $4\frac{1}{2}$-year-old can be assessed using the school-age subtests of the K-ABC, while a delayed 5-year-old can be assessed using a younger level.

Recent research with the K-ABC raises some issues for consideration by preschool examiners. Using data from 5-year-olds in the standardization sample, Keith (1985) suggests that sequential-simultaneous interpretations may not apply to preschoolers. His factor analysis suggests that a one-factor solution (a simultaneous factor) may best explain the data for this age group. Keith indicates further that if a two-factor solution is allowed, factor one for 5-year-olds is a reasoning factor (primarily nonverbal reasoning) and factor two is a verbal memory factor. In addition, Bracken (1985) points out that the breadth of information attainable from the K-ABC for preschool-aged children may be limited, requiring administration of additional tests. Because of the extensive amount of research conducted with the K-ABC, it is essential that professionals educate themselves regarding the most effective uses of the K-ABC. An excellent synthesis of research and clinical applications of the K-ABC is provided in Kamphaus and Reynolds (1987), to which the reader is referred for detailed information.

McCarthy Scales of Children's Abilities

The McCarthy Scales were developed to measure "the general intellectual level of children as well as their strengths and weaknesses in important abilities" (McCarthy, 1972, p. 1). In addition to a global measure of cognitive ability (the General Cognitive Index, GCI), the test provides measures of specific abilities (Verbal, Perceptual-Performance, Quantitative, Memory, and Motor). The McCarthy Scales have been viewed as a major alternative to the Binet and WPPSI (Paget, 1986; Salvia & Ysseldyke, 1988). The test was carefully designed and standardized. Reported reliabilities for the GCI and the Verbal Scale are excellent, although those for the other scales are somewhat lower. Other strengths reported for the McCarthy are its useful profile of abilities, which may be relevant to developmental concerns, and its appeal to younger children (Sattler, 1988). In addition, the range of ages for which the test can be used ($2\frac{1}{2}$ to $8\frac{1}{2}$) is a positive feature for professionals who work with a broad spectrum of young children. Disadvantages of the McCarthy are the lack of provision for children's refusals and its limited floor, which requires the use of extrapolated GCIs (Harrison & Naglieri, 1978) with moderately and severely developmentally disabled children.

Validity studies of the McCarthy Scales have resulted in several noteworthy findings. Although the test offers a useful framework for diagnostic purposes because of the several different ability scales, factor-analytic studies (e.g., Kaufman, 1975) show that for 3- and 4-year olds, a quantitative factor does not appear, resulting in cautious interpretation of the Quantitative Scale for this age group. In addition, wider scatter between different scales has been shown to be common, suggesting that differences between subscale scores do not necessarily imply deficiencies. Kaufman and Kaufman (1977) provide useful guidelines for interpreting subtest scatter and scores on individual subtests.

With respect to the McCarthy's utility for assessing preschool children with handicaps, the manual asserts that it is useful for assessing children with mental retardation, sensory deficits, speech deficits, giftedness, and learning disabilities. Nevertheless, users should beware that none of these special groups were incorporated into the normative sample. In addition, studies have shown that McCarthy GCIs obtained on preschoolers may be significantly lower than IQs obtained on other norm-referenced tests. Gerken, Hancock, and Wade (1978) reported a mean difference of 10.5 between the GCI and Stanford-Binet IQ for a preschool sample, and Bracken (1981) found a mean difference of 15.7 for a sample of gifted preschool and primary children. Phillips, Pasewark, and Tindall (1978) found a difference of seven points between the GCI and WPPSI Full Scale IQ, with the WPPSI being higher. Although Kaufman and Kaufman (1977) have interpreted lower GCIs with learning-disabled children as evidence that the McCarthy more accurately predicts "learning disabilities" in young children, others have interpreted the differences as evidence that the McCarthy is measuring something other than intelligence (Bracken, 1981).

Wechsler, Preschool and Primary Scale of Intelligence (WPPSI)

The WPPSI (Wechsler, 1967) is a downward extension of the *Wechsler Intelligence Scale for Children,* and was designed to measure a child's global intellectual ability on verbal and performance tasks. The test is comprised of Verbal and Performance subscales and yields three Intelligence Quotients (Verbal, Performance, and Full Scale), each with a mean of 100 and standard deviation of 15. In devising the WPPSI, Wechsler wanted an instrument that would be continuous with the WISC and the WAIS; therefore, he deliberately chose items from the WISC and used the

same items or extensions of those items for the WPPSI. Thus, the items did not originate from an emphasis on the cognition of preschool-aged children.

Reviews of the WPPSI suggest that it is less than ideal for preschool assessment. The age range is restrictive (4 to $6\frac{1}{2}$ years). The test is extremely long (requires 1 to $1\frac{1}{2}$ hours), and some preschoolers find it difficult to attend to the tasks for that length of time. Proper administration is difficult, and scoring is subjective on some items (see Reynolds & Clark, 1983; Sattler, 1988). Strengths of the WPPSI are its excellent standardization sample and its statistical properties. Some professionals find that looking at the Verbal-Performance discrepancy provides useful information (see Sattler, 1988 for a review of related studies). Nevertheless, readers are cautioned that differences of 11 points between VIQ and PIQ are relatively common on the WPPSI and 12-point differences occur for one-out-of-four children (Reynolds & Gutkin, 1981).

Although good normative data, reliability, and validity of the WPPSI may make it useful for comparisons of an individual child's performance with that of age mates in the standardization sample, the following cautions should be noted. Studies suggest care in interpreting the WPPSI for black, Mexican-American, and low-SES children, because they tend to score lower than white children and have greater Verbal-Performance discrepancies (Kaufman, 1973). Another problem is the limited floor and ceiling of the WPPSI, which is especially problematic to age 4. The lowest possible Full Scale IQ for a 4-year-old is 55, making the results difficult to interpret for low-functioning children. The WPPSI recently was revised and awaits empirical validation.

Griffiths Mental Development Scales

The Griffiths scales are actually two separate instruments. The original scales were first published in 1954 and cover the period from birth to 2 years of age. The revised and extended scales were published in 1979 (Griffiths, 1979) and assess the performance of children ages birth to 8 years in the following areas: locomotor, personal-social, hearing and speech, hand and eye coordination, performance, and practical reasoning. Each scale has been developed so that it can be used separately, but the principal purpose of these scales is to provide a profile of an individual child's abilities in various domains. Unlike other instruments that lack an adequate floor, the Griffiths Scales provide useful information regarding the functioning of severely impaired children. A major disadvantage of the scales is that they were normed on children in Great Britain, requiring cautious interpretation of the results for American children.

Battelle Developmental Inventory

The Battelle Developmental Inventory (BDI; Newborg, Stock, Wnek, Guidubaldi, & Svinicki, 1984) is a standardized assessment instrument that evaluates children's development from birth through 8 years, across five domains: personal/social, adaptive, communication, motor, and cognitive. The test has advantages in its ability to evaluate a broad spectrum of functioning across a wide age range of children. Professionals, including special educators and preschool and day care staff, can administer separate portions of the test using domain-specific booklets.

A materials list is provided in the manual, but examiners must accumulate many of the materials themselves. Scoring of items is based on a 3-point system that provides indication of emerging skills. Items may be scored through structured test format, observation in a natural setting, and parent or teacher interview. The procedures in the BDI manual describe general and specific adaptations for the handicapped child (e.g., motor, visual, hearing, speech, and emotional impaired, and multiply handicapped). Although handicapped children were included in the standardization sample, separate norms are not available at this time.

A child's performance can be summarized with a percentile rank, standard score, and an age equivalent. The authors suggest that this information be used to monitor a child's progress, make placement and eligibility decisions, and develop and implement Individualized Education Plans. Recent evidence, however, suggests the need for much caution when interpreting the BDI because of age-related discontinuities (Boyd, 1989). Because the original item pool was selected to develop a normative test rather than a criterion-referenced assessment, it may have limited value for actual program planning, but may be most useful in identifying relative strengths and weaknesses from which to develop goals and objectives. For a more detailed review of the BDI, the reader is referred to Molitor and Kramer (1987).

Adaptations of Norm-Referenced Instruments

Recommended practice suggests the need to look beyond the end-product score from norm-referenced tests to observations of behavior so as to understand the process employed by children in arriving at responses. With preschoolers who have limited exposure to "testing situations" and those who have moderate to severe impairments, it is useful to administer tests under nonstandardized conditions, to modify test materials, and to accept nonstandard responses in an effort to obtain information about the conditions that elicit optimal performance. Because children with moderate to severe impairments are not represented in the standardization sample of norm-referenced tests and because their peripheral disabilities preclude valid assessment of other domains (e.g., language, social cognitive), adaptations of tests are essential to a true understanding of these children's strengths and weaknesses. Examiners must be flexible enough to involve the child's parent or caregiver to maximize the child's performance, to create the opportunity to observe care giver–child interventions, and to become involved in play with the child. In addition to these informal procedures, some professionals have "formalized" adaptations of standardized procedures for use with specific populations. DuBose (1981) and DuBose and Langley (1977) developed scales for use with deaf-blind children and other handicapped children by adapting items from various scales. Haeussermann (1958) also advocated this adaptive administration approach for young children with cerebral palsy. Although these adaptations are not norm-referenced, norms are not necessary when the objective is to understand the process whereby children learn rather than to document their scores. Nevertheless, results of test adaptations must be interpreted cautiously, and care should be taken when interpreting differences in performance under standardized and nonstandardized conditions to parents and teachers.

Piagetian-Based Scales

The developmental theory of Piaget has been popular for explaining intellectual development of normal children from birth onward. Ordinal scales have been developed from this theory to assess children's development in reference to Piagetian stages. Scales for assessing development in the first stage (sensorimotor) are used primarily for assessing infants (Escalona & Corman, 1969; Uzgiris & Hunt, 1975), although some people have advocated using these measures to assess the cognitive development of low-functioning preschoolers (e.g., Bricker & Bricker, cited in DuBose, 1981; S. J. Rogers, 1977). The *Concept Assessment Kit* (Goldschmidt & Bentley, 1968) is a commercially available instrument for assessing children ages 4 to 7, who are believed to be in Piaget's preoperational stage of cognitive development.

Because Piagetian-based tools often do not meet validity and reliability standards and are not norm-referenced in the traditional sense, they have not been used frequently for placement and classification decisions, although they have proven useful in instruction and programming for those who adhere to Piagetian or neo-Piagetian theory (Dunst, 1981). Nevertheless, proponents of Piagetian-based assessment have pointed out their dangers (Dunst & Gallagher, 1983; Dunst & Rheingrover, 1981; S. J. Rogers, 1982) and have asserted cautions in interpreting results. Recent evidence indicates that preschool-aged children can function better on certain cognitive tasks than Piaget's theory proposes, if these tasks are presented in a manner suited to preschoolers' interests (Gelman & Baillargeon, 1983). In addition, there is evidence that children may show more competence in one aspect of a cognitive developmental stage than another (Dunst & Rheingrover, 1981). Therefore, just as with measures discussed previously, Piagetian tasks, presented in the typical manner, may underestimate a child's true abilities.

Curriculum-Based Assessment
Instruments that are curriculum-based were developed to meet the need for assessment results that would transfer into useful recommendations for curriculum and intervention (Fewell, 1984; Neisworth & Bagnato, 1986). These tools often are checklists of items drawn from descriptions of normal child development and are very appropriate for program planning with preschool populations. Some require formal administration of items under standard conditions, while others can be administered informally by observing children and/or questioning parents or care givers.

Bagnato, Neisworth, and Capone (1986) developed a typology of curriculum-based assessment (CBA) measures. Such a typology is very useful because curriculum-based scales vary with respect to the theoretical basis of the items, inclusion of instructional strategies, modifications for handicap, and comprehensiveness. The typology includes five categories of CBA instruments: (a) normal-developmental, (b) adaptive, (c) handicap-specific, (d) strategy-matched, and (e) curriculum-referenced scales. Normal-developmental CBA scales are based on developmental milestones with nonhandicapped children as the reference group. Adaptive measures refer to developmentally sequenced objectives with structured accommodations for specific disabilities. Handicap-specific instruments address the unique needs of a particular impairment (e.g., visual or neuromotor disabilities). Strategy-matched materials suggest techniques for achieving the objectives (e.g., behavioral methods), and curriculum-referenced CBA measures are "hybrids" of norm- and criterion-referenced scales that are frequently standardized. The latter scales are not as precise as specific curriculum-embedded measures, although they do offer normative assessment of child status and estimate curriculum-entry points (Bagnato et al., 1986). Specific information about instruments in each category is summarized in Table 2.

Several cautions are in order regarding the use of curriculum-based instruments. Items from these scales do not always lead to legitimate or functional instructional goals that would improve children's abilities to function more independently in their ecologies. In addition, like some of the standardized assessment tools, many curriculum-based or criterion-referenced instruments have cognitive skill sequences that are not in true developmental progression for all children (Garwood, 1983). This issue may not pose major problems when making curriculum decisions regarding normal or mildly handicapped preschoolers, but it can be important in the assessment of children with moderate and severe handicaps. Moreover, as Strain (1984) has suggested, some criterion-referenced instruments are based on normal developmental milestones, are not referenced to handicapped children, and do not present validity or reliability indices. Thus, several of them are subject to many of the same criticisms as norm-referenced instruments. CBA measures represent an important advance in preschool assessment, and the reader interested in more detailed discussion is referred to Neisworth and Bagnato (1986), Bagnato et al. (1986), and Bagnato, Neisworth, & Munson (1989).

TABLE 2   Curriculum-Based Assessment Measures

Instrument	Domains/ Components	Age Range	Theoretical Base	Target Population	Important Features
Normal-Developmental					
Learning Accomplishment Profile (LAP) Sanford & Zelman, 1981	Fine and Gross Motor, Language, Cognition, Self-Help, Personal-Social	0–72 months	Developmental	Normal-developmentally delayed	Monitors child progress
Early Learning Accomplishment Profile (ELAP) Glover, Preminger, & Sanford, 1978	Fine and Gross Motor, Language, Cognition, Self-Help, Personal-Social	0–36 months	Developmental	Normal-developmentally delayed	Wider task analysis for infants
The Portage Curriculum Bluma, Shearer, Frohman, & Hillard, 1976	Infant Stimulation, Socialization, Language, Self-Help Cognitive, Motor	0–72 months	Developmental	Normal-developmentally delayed	Developmental-task approach useful for both home- and center-based programs
Early intervention Developmental Profile (EIDP) S. G. Rogers et al., 1981	Cognitive, Perceptual Fine Motor, Gross Motor, Social-Emotional, Self-Care, Language	0–36 months	Developmental	Mild-severe, handicapped infants-toddlers	Suggestions for altering response modes in order to circumvent sensory or motor deficits; allows for interdisciplinary team assessment
Carolina Curriculum for Handicapped Infants N. Johnson, Jens, & Attermeier, 1985	Cognitive, Communication, Language, Social Skills Adaptation, Self-Help, Fine and Gross Motor	0–24 months	Piagetian	Mildly delayed and multi-handicapped	Instructional adaptations for the blind and impaired

Instrument	Areas Assessed	Age Range	Standardization	Population	Comments
Developmental Activities Screening Inventory II Fewell & Langley, 1984	Fine Motor Coordination, Cause–Effect, Means–End Relationship, Association Number Concept, Size Discrimination, Seriation	0–60 months	Developmental	Handicapped; ideally suited for children with auditory or language problems	Adaptations for impairments includes teaching activities
The Haeussermann Educational Evaluation Haeussermann, 1958; Jedrysek, Klapper, Pope, & Wortis, 1972	Comprehension and Use of Language, Recognition of Pictorial Symbols, Discrimination of Colors and Amounts, Ability to Perceive Differences, Recall of Basic Symbols from Memory	24–72 months	Developmental	Cerebral-palsied preschoolers	Requires neither speech nor manipulation Combines clinical and quantitative
Handicap Specific					
Autism Screening Instrument for Educational Planning (ASEEP) Krug, Arick, & Almond, 1979	Vocal Behavior, Interaction Assessment, Educational Assessment of Functional Skills, Prognosis of Learning Rate	Preschool and school-aged	None	Severely handicapped, autistic	Normative data facilitate differentiation of autistic from normal functioning
Uniform Performance Assessment System (UPAS) Haring, White, Edgar, Affleck, & Hayden, 1981	Preacademic/Fine Motor, Communication Self-Help/Social, Gross Motor, Inappropriate Behaviors	0–72 months	Developmental	Moderate and severely handicapped	Special codes provided to identify purpose of an item so assessment procedures can be adapted; task analysis; unique capacity assesses

TABLE 2 (continued)

Instrument	Domains/Components	Age Range	Theoretical Base	Target Population	Important Features
					disabled/wheelchair needs, atypical behavior patterns, and reinforcement levels
Oregon Project for Visually Impaired and Blind D. Brown, Simmons, & Methvin, 1979	Fine-Gross Motor, Communication, Social-Emotional, Self-Help, Cognition	0–72 months	Developmental	Visually impaired/blind	Aids acquisition of first-grade skills orientation, mobility, Braille
Clark Early Language Program (CELP) Clark & Moores, 1979	Receptive Language, Expressive Language	30 months–adult	Developmental	Hearing impaired	Prepares for a traditional reading program
Individualized Assessment Treatment for Austistic and Developmentally Delayed Children Schopler, Lansing, Reichler, & Waters, 1979	Integrated Assessment and Curricular	0–8 years	Behavioral	Autistic, developmentally delayed	Inclusion of instructional and behavioral strategies
The Callier-Azusa Scale: Assessment of Deaf/Blind Children Stillman, 1974	Motor Development, Perceptual Development, Daily Living Skills, Cognition, Communication	0–9 years	Developmental	Deaf/blind, severely and profoundly handicapped	Particularly comprehensive at lower developmental levels; target treatments, goals

Sequenced Inventory of Communication Development (SICD) Hedrick, Prather, & Tobin, 1984	and Language, Social Development Expressive/Receptive Language: discrimination, awareness understanding, imitation oral motor, vocal, vocal responsiveness in initiating conversations with others	4–48 months	Developmental	Children with hearing communication disorders	Evaluation occurs in an informal play atmosphere; pragmatics
Strategy-Matched Hawaii Early Learning Profile Furuno, Inatsuka, Allman, & Zelsloft, 1979	Cognitive, Language, Gross and Fine Motor, Social-Emotional, Self-Help	0–36 months	Behavioral	Normal	Methods to shape or stimulate emergence of specific adaptive skills
Infant Learning: A Cognitive-Linguistic Intervention Strategy Dunst, 1981	Cognitive, Social Language	0–36 months	Piagetian	Infants	Matrix for use in designing instructional goals and techniques; based on Uzgiris-Hunt Scale
The HICOMP Preschool Curriculum Willoughby-Herb & Neisworth, 1982	Communication, Own-Care, Motor, Problem Solving	0–60 months	Behavioral–Developmental	Handicapped and nonhandicapped	Includes behavioral strategies to teach clusters of skills and a table for linking various developmental scales to the curriculum tasks

TABLE 2 *(continued)*

Instrument	Domains/ Components	Age Range	Theoretical Base	Target Population	Important Features
The Programmed Environments Curriculum (PEC) Tawney, Knapp, O'Reilly, & Pratt, 1979	Functional Living Skills, Cognitive Skills, Motor Skills, Self-Help Skills	0–36 months	Behavioral	Moderate, severe, and profound disabilities	Appropriate in either an individual or group setting; direct instruction model
Curriculum-Referenced Battelle Developmental Inventory (BDI) Newborg, Stock, Wnek, Guidubaldi, & Svinicki, 1984	Personal-Social, Adaptive, Motor, Communication, Cognitive	0–8 years	Behavioral	Normal/ handicapped	Modifications for administration to various handicapping conditions; includes abbreviated screening test to establish need for comprehensive assessment

Brigance Diagnostic Inventory of Early Development (BDIED) Brigance, 1978	Pre-speech, General Knowledge, Comprehension, Fine Motor, Preambulatory	0–7 years	Developmental	Normal/ handicapped	Allows for a variety of response styles to accommodate certain dysfunctions; matches to computerized IEP
Peabody Developmental Motor Scales, (PDMS) Folio & Fewell, 1983	Neuromotor Fine: grasping, hand use, eye–hand coordination, manual dexterity Gross: reflexes, balance, nonlocomotor, locomotor, receipt, propulsion of objects	0–83 months	Normal- developmental	Handicapped	Cards outline activities and training programs

Source. From Curriculum-Based assessment for the young exceptional child: Rationale and review, by S. J. Bagnato, J. T. Neisworth, and A. Capone, 1986, *Topics in Early Childhood Special Education, 6*, 97–110. Reprinted by permission

Process-Oriented Assessment Approaches

The main assumption of process assessment is that the identification of learning strategies is integral to any full explanation of children's performance (Sternberg, 1981). Fewell (1984) states that most process-oriented approaches have stemmed from human information-processing models that are based on performance of *normal* children. However, they are beginning to be used to understand handicapped children, because deficient information-processing mechanisms seem to be characteristic of certain handicapping conditions.

One technique appearing as a useful addition to traditional cognitive assessment tools is the test–teach–test paradigm. In this approach, assessment is not seen as static; rather, the examiner gives the child an opportunity to learn from the experience and apply that learning to solve the problems presented. The Haeussermann approach (1958) mentioned earlier and the *Learning Potential Assessment Device* (LPAD) (Feuerstein, Rand, & Hoffman, 1980) are examples of this technique. The LPAD technique yields information about a child's "cognitive map" and ability to learn and thus is seen as useful for intervention planning. Special adaptations of the LPAD for preschoolers have been made (Lidz, 1983). A. L. Brown and Ferrara (1985) discuss process-oriented techniques from research based on the theory of Vygotsky, whereby children are given a set of increasingly explicit hints toward solution of a problem until they are able to solve it. These techniques are reported to be useful as measures of less biased cognitive assessment of children from diverse cultures.

Although developed with infants, there are some experimental approaches to assessment that may prove useful for assessing severely and multiply impaired preschoolers. Examples include measures designed by Kearsley (1979), Lewis and Goldberg (1969), and Zelazo (1981) to assess a child's understanding of events based on his or her visual fixation, vocalization, and heart rate. An expectancy is established with the child by presenting the same stimulus or sequence several times followed by a discrepant event. The child's reaction to the discrepant event in terms of the aforementioned physiological measures provides an idea of his or her cognitive functioning. Kearsley (1979) has shown that multiply impaired children who evidence significant delays on standardized tests are more likely to perform at an age-appropriate level on these expectancy tests.

From the discussion above, it is clear that assessment of competence in young children is a complex process involving a multimeasure/multisource approach (Bagnato, Neisworth, & Munson, 1989). Assessors who attempt to glean an adequate amount of information from the use of one measure in isolation from others will discover the futility of this approach in deriving meaningful information about a child. Bagnato, Neisworth, & Munson (1989) provide elaboration of this point, and the reader is referred to their book for more detailed explanation.

SUMMARY AND CONCLUSIONS

In closing this chapter, it must be emphasized that the development of functional, developmentally appropriate goals for children and their families is the primary purpose of any assessment or "intervention planning" strategies. Goals can be developed only after a thorough assessment of the child's developmental skill level, his or her functioning in home and school environments, and the family's needs. The importance of setting goals that match the child's and family's needs and are attainable within the context of family and/or classroom routines cannot be overemphasized (see Rainforth & Salisbury, 1988). Collaborative partnerships among families, school psychologists, teachers, and other professionals set the stage for ecologically valid assessments and interventions. Beyond the mandates of legislation, we must view such partnerships as an essential ethical responsibility if we truly wish to be responsive to young children and their families.

REFERENCES

Adelman, H. S. (1982). Identifying learning problems at an early age: A critical appraisal. *Journal of Clinical Child Psychology, 11,* 255–261.

Almy, M., & Genishi, C. (1979). *Ways of studying children* (rev. ed.). New York: Teachers College Press.

Alpern, G., Boll, T., & Shearer, M. (1980). *Developmental Profile II manual.* Aspen, CO: Psychological Development.

Bagnato, S. J., (1984). Team congruence in developmental diagnosis and intervention: Comparing clinical judgment and child performance measures. *School Psychology Review, 13,* 7–16.

Bagnato, S. J., & Neisworth, J. T., & Munson, S. (1989). *Linking developmental assessment and early inter-*

vention: Curriculum based prescriptions (rev. ed.). Rockville, MD: Aspen.

Bagnato, S. J., Neisworth, J. T., & Capone, A. (1986). Curriculum-based assessment for the young exceptional child: Rationale and review. *Topics in Early Childhood Special Education, 6,* 97–110.

Bailey, D. B. (1988). Assessing environments. In D. B. Bailey and M. Wolery (Eds.), *Assessing infants and preschoolers with handicaps* (pp. 97–114). Columbus, OH: Charles E. Merrill.

Bailey, D. B., Helsel-DeWert, M., Thiele, J. R., & Ware, W. B. (1983). Measuring participation on the interdisciplinary team. *American Journal of Mental Deficiency, 88,* 247–254.

Bailey, D. B., & Simeonsson, R. J. (1988). *Family assessment in early intervention.* Columbus, OH: Charles E. Merrill.

Bandure, A. (1978). The self-esteem in reciprocal determinism. *American Psychologist, 33,* 344–358.

Barnett, D. W. (1984). An organizational approach to preschool services: Psychological screening, assessment, and intervention. In C. Maher, R. Illback, & J. Zins (Eds.), *Organizational psychology in the schools:* A handbook for practitioners (pp. 53–82). Springfield, IL: Charles C. Thomas.

Barnett, D. W., & Paget, K. D. (1988). Alternative service delivery in preschool settings: Practical and conceptual foundations. In J. Graden, J. Zins, & M. R. Curtis (Eds.), *Alternative educational systems: Enhancing instructional options for all students* (pp. 291–308). Washington, DC: National Association of School Psychologists.

Bayley, N. (1969). *Bayley scales of infant development.* New York: Psychological Corporation.

Berger, M., & Fowlkes, M. A. (1980). Family intervention project: A family network model for serving young handicapped children. *Young Children, 35,* 22–23.

Bluma, S. M., Shearer, M. S., Frohman, A. H., & Hillard, J. H. (1976). *Portage guide to early education.* Portage, WI: Portage Project.

Boyd, R. D. (1989). What a difference a day makes: Age-related discontinuities and the Battelle Developmental Inventory. *Journal of Early Intervention, 13,* 114–119.

Bracken, B. A. (1981). McCarthy Scales as a learning disability diagnostic aid: A closer look. *Journal of Learning Disabilities, 14,* 128–130.

Bracken, B. A. (1985). A critical review of the Kaufman Assessment Battery for Children (K-ABC). *School Psychology Review, 14,* 21–36.

Bracken, B. A. (1988). Limitations of preschool instruments and standards for minimal levels of technical adequacy. *Journal of Psychoeducational Assessment, 5,* 313–326.

Brigance, A. (1978). *The Brigance diagnostic inventory of early development.* North Billerica, MA: Curriculum Associates.

Bristol, M. M. (1987). Methodological caveats in the assessment of single-parent families of handicapped children. *Journal of the Division of Early Children, 11,* 135–142.

Bristol, M. M., Donovan, A., & Harding, A. (1984). *Assessing the broader impact of intervention Workshop on measuring stress and support.* Unpublished manuscript, University of North Carolina at Chapel Hill, Frank Porter Graham Child Development Center.

Bristol, M. M., & Gallagher, J. J. (1982). A famiy focus for intervention. In C. T. Ramey & P. Trohanis (Eds.), *Finding and educating the high risk and handicapped infant* (pp. 137–161). Baltimore: University Park Press.

Bristol, M. M., & Gallagher, J. J. (1986). Research on fathers of young handicapped children: Evolution, review, and some future directions. In J. J. Gallagher & P. M. Vietze (Eds.), *Families of handicapped persons: Research, programs, and policy issues* (pp. 81–100). Baltimore: Paul H. Brookes.

Bronfenbrenner, U. (1974). Is early intervention effective? *A report on longitudinal evaluations of preschool programs* (Vol. 2) (U.S. Department of Health, Education, and Welfare Publication No. 76-30035). Washington, DC: U.S. Government Printing Office.

Brown, A. L., & Ferrara, R. A. (1985). Diagnosing zones of proximal development. In J. Wertsch (Ed.), *Culture, communication, and cognition—Vygotskian perspectives* (p. 5). London: Cambridge University Press.

Brown, D., Simmons, V., & Methvin, J. (1979). *The Oregon project for visually impaired and blind preschool children.* Medford, OR: Jackson County Educational Service District.

Buros, O. (1989). *Tenth mental measurements yearbook.* Lincoln, NE: Buros Institute.

Caldwell, B. M. (1978). Foreword to K. E. Allen, V. A. Holm, and J. L. Schiefulbusch (Eds.), *Early intervention: A team approach.* Baltimore: University Park Press.

Caldwell, B., & Bradley, R. (1979). Manual for the *House Observation for Measurement of the Environment.* Little Rock: University of Arkansas.

Campbell, S. K., Siegel, E., Parr, C. A., & Ramey, C. T. (1986). Evidence for the need to renorm the Bayley Scales of Infant Development based on the performance of a population-based sample of 12 month-old infants. *Topics in Early Childhood Special Education, 6,* 83–96.

Carta, J. T., Sainato, D. M., & Greenwood, C. R. (1988). Advances in the ecological assessment of classroom instruction for young children with handicaps. In S. L. Odom & M. B. Karnes (Eds.), *Early intervention for infants and children with handicaps* (pp. 217–240). Baltimore: Paul H. Brookes.

Chandler, L. K., Fowler, S. A., & Lubeck, R. C. (1986). Assessing family needs: The first step in providing family-focused intervention. *Diagnostique, 11,* 233–245.

Clark, C. R., & Moores, D. F. (1979). *Clark early language development program.* Allen, TX: DLM Teaching Resources.

Clark-Stewart, A. K. (1981). Parent education in the 1970's. *Education and Policy Analysis, 3,* 47–58.

Conoley, J. C., & Gutkin, T. (1986). School psychology: A reconceptualization of service delivery realistics. In S. N. Elliott & J. C. Witt (Eds.), *The delivery of psychological services in schools*. Hillsdale, NJ: Lawrence Erlbaum.

Crnic, K. A., Friedrich, W. N., & Greenberg, M. T. (1983). Adaptation of families with mentally retarded children: A model of stress, coping, and family ecology. *American Journal of Mental Deficiency, 88,* 125–138.

Deal, A. G., Dunst, C. J., & Trivette, C. M. (1989). A flexible and functional approach to developing individualized Family Support Plans. *Infants and Young Children, 1,* 32–43.

Doke, L. A. (1975). The organization of day care environments: Formal versus informal activities. *Child Care Quarterly, 4,* 216–222.

Doke, L. A., & Risley, T. R. (1972). The organization of day-care environments: Required versus optimal activities. *Journal of Applied Behavioral Analysis, 5,* 405–420.

DuBose, R. (1981). Assessment of severely impaired young children: Problems and recommendations. *Topics in Early Childhood Special Education, 1,* 9–21.

DuBose, R., & Langley, B. (1977). *The developmental activities screening inventory.* Hingham, MA: Teaching Resources.

Dunst, C. J. (1981). *Infant learning: A cognitive-linguistic intervention strategy.* Hingham, MA: Teaching Resources.

Dunst, C. J. (1985). Rethinking early intervention. *Analysis and Intervention in Developmental Disabilities, 5,* 165–201.

Dunst, C. J. (1986a). *The caregiver styles of interaction scales.* Unpublished document, Human Development and Training Institute, Morganton, NC.

Dunst, C. J. (1986b). *A rating scale for assessing parent-child play opportunities.* Unpublished document, Human Development Research and Training Institute, Morganton, NC.

Dunst, C. J., & Gallagher, J. L. (1983). Piagetian approaches to infant assessment. *Topics in Early Childhood Special Education, 3,* 44–62.

Dunst, C. J., & McWilliam, R. A. (1988). Cognitive assessment of multiply handicapped young children. In T. Wachs & R. Sheehan (Eds.), *Assessment of developmentally disabled children* (pp. 105–130). New York: Plenum Press.

Dunst, C. J., McWilliam, R. A., & Holbert, K. (1986). Assessment of preschool classroom environments. *Diagnostique, 11,* 212–232.

Dunst, C. J., & Rheingrover, R. M. (1981). Discontinuity and instability in early development: Implications for assessment. *Topics in Early Childhood Special Education, 1,* 49–60.

Dunst, C. J., & Trivette, C. M. (1985). *A guide to measures of social support and family behaviors.* Chapel Hill, NC: Technical Assistance Development System.

Dunst, C. J., Trivette, C. M., & Deal, A. G. (1988). *Enabling and empowering families: Principles and guideliness for pactice.* Cambridge, MA: Brookline.

Escalona, S. K., & Corman, H. H. (1969). *Albert Einstein Scales of Sensorimotor Development.* New York: Albert Einstein College of Medicine of Yeshiva Univeristy.

Fabry, B. D. Mayhev, G. L., & Hanson, A. (1984). Incidental teaching of mentally retarded students within a token system. *American Journal of Mental Deficiency, 89,* 29–36.

Farran, D., Kasari, C., & Jay, S. (1984). *Parent-caregiver interaction scale: Training manual.* Chapel Hill, NC: Frank Porter Graham Child Development Center.

Fawcett, S. B., Seekins, T., Whang, P. L., Muiu, C., & Suarez de Balcazar, Y. (1982). Involving consumers in decision-making. *Social Policy, 12,* 36–41.

Feuerstein, R., Rand, Y., & Hoffman, M. (1980). *Instructional enrichment.* Baltimore: University Park Press.

Fewell, R. R. (1984). Assessment of preschool handicapped children. *Educational Psychologist, 19,* 172–179.

Fewell, R. R. (1986). A handicapped child in the family. In R. R. Fewell & P. F. Vadasy (Eds), *Families of handicapped children: Needs and supports across the life span* (pp. 3–34). Austin, TX: PRO-ED.

Fewell. R. R., & Langley, M. B. (1984). *Developmental activities screening inventory II.* Austin, TX: PROED.

Folio, M. R., & Fewell, R. R. (1983). *The Peabody developmental motor scales.* Allen, TX: DLM Teaching Resources.

Fowler, S. A. (1982). Transition from preschool to kindergarten for children with special needs. In K. E. Allen & E. M. Goetz (Eds.), *Problems in early childhood education* (pp. 309–330). Rockville, MD: Aspen.

Frankenburg, W., Dodds, J., Fandal, A., Kazuk, E., & Cohrs, M. (1975). *Denver Development Screening Test reference manual.* Denver, CO: Ladoca Project and Publishing Foundation.

Fredericksen, L. W., & Fredericksen, C. B. (1977). Experimental evaluation for classroom environments: Scheduling planned activities. *American Journal of Mental Deficiency, 81,* 421–427.

Furono, S., Inatsuka, T. T., Allman, T. L., & Zelsloft, B. (1979). *The Hawaii Early Learning Profile.* Palo Alto, CA: Vort Corporation.

Garwood, S. G. (1983). Intelligence and cognition. In S. G. Garwood & R. Fewell (Eds.), *Educating young handicapped children: A developmental approach* (pp. 149–201). Rockville, MD: Aspen.

Gelman, R., & Baillargeon, R. (1983). A review of some Piagetian concepts. In J. H. Flavell & E. M. Markman (Eds.), *Cognitive development* (pp. 167–230). New York: Wiley.

Gerken, K. C., Hancock, K. A., & Wade, T. H. (1978). Comparison of the Stanford-Binet Intelligence Scale and the McCarthy Scales of Children's Abilities with preschool children. *Psychology in the Schools, 15,* 468–472.

Glover, M. E., Preminger, J. L., & Sanford, A. R. (1978). *The Early Learning Accomplishment Profile.* Winston-Salem, NC: Kaplan School Supply.

Goldschmidt, M. J., & Bentler, P. M. (1968). *Manual: Concept Assessment Kit: Conservation.* San Diego: Educational & Industrial Testing Service.

Griffiths, R. (1979). *The abilities of young children.* London: Child Development Research Center.

Haeussermann, E. (1958). *Developmental potential of preschool children: An evaluation in intellectual, sensory, and emotional functioning.* New York: Grune & Stratton.

Haring, H. G., White, A. R., Edgar, E. B., Affleck, J. O., & Hayden, A. H. (1981). *Uniform performance assessment system.* Columbus, OH: Charles E. Merrill.

Harms, T., & Clifford, R. M. (1980). *Early childhood environment rating scale.* New York: Teachers College Press.

Harms, T., & Clifford, R. M. (1989). *The family day care rating scale.* New York: Teachers College Press.

Harms, T., Cryer, D., & Clifford, R. M. (1989). *Infant/toddler environment rating scale.* New York: Teachers College Press.

Harrison, P. L., & Naglieri, J. A. (1978). Extrapolated General Cognitive Indexes on the McCarthy Scales for gifted and mentally retarded children. *Psychological Reports, 43,* 1291–1296.

Hart, B., & Risley, T. R. (1975). Incidental teaching of language in the preschool. *Journal of Applied Behavior Analysis, 8,* 411–420.

Hart, B., & Risley, T. R. (1978). Promoting productive language through incidental teaching. *Education and Urban Society, 10,* 407–429.

Hart, B., & Risley, T. R. (1980). In vivo language intervention: Unanticipated general effects. *Journal of Applied Behavior Analysis, 13,* 407–432.

Hedrick, D. A., Prather, E. M., & Tobin, A. R. (1984). *Sequenced inventory of communication development.* Los Angeles: Western Psychological Services.

Holm, J. A., & McCartin, P. E. (1978). Interdisciplinary child development teams: Issues in training and interdisciplinariness. In K. E. Allen, V. A. Holm, and R. L. Schiefelbusch (Eds.), *Early intervention: A team approach.* Baltimore, University Park Press.

Holroyd, J. (1974). The questionnaire on resources and stress: An instrument to measure families' responses to a handicapped member. *Journal of Community Psychology, 2,* 92–94.

Horowitz, F. D. (1982). Methods of assessment for high-risk and handicapped infants. In C. T. Ramey & R. L. Trohanis (Eds.), *Finding and educating high-risk and handicapped infants* (pp. 101–118). Baltimore: University Park Press.

House of Representatives. (1986, September). *Education of the Handicapped Act Amendments of 1986* (Report No. 99-860). Washington, DC: U.S. Government Printing Office.

Huston-Stein, A., Friedrich-Cofer, L., & Susman, E. (1977). The relation of classroom structure to social behavior, imaginative play, and self-regulation of economically disadvantaged children. *Child Development, 48,* 908–916.

Iacino, R., & Bricker, B. B. (1978). A model for preparing personnel to work with the severely-profoundly handicapped. In E. N. Haring and D. Bricker (Eds.), *Teaching the severely handicapped* (Vol. 3). Columbus, OH: Special Press.

Ireton, H., & Thwing, E. (1972). *The Minnesota Child Development Inventory.* Minneapolis, MN: Behavior Science Systems.

Jedrysek, E., Klapper, Z., Pope, L., & Wortis, J. (1972). *Psychoeducational evaluation of the preschool child.* New York: Grune & Stratton.

Jenkins, J. R., & Pany, J. D. (1978). Standardized achievement tests: How useful for special education? *Exceptional Children, 44,* 448–458.

Johnson, J. E., Ershler, J., & Bell, C. (1980). Play behavior in a discovery-based and a formal-educational preschool program. *Child Development, 51,* 271–274.

Johnson, N., Jens, K., & Attermeier, B. (1985). *Carolina curriculum for handicapped infants.* Baltimore: Paul H. Brookes.

Kaiser, A. P., & Fox, J. J. (1986). Behavioral parent training research: Contributions to an ecological analysis of families of handicapped children. In J. J. Gallagher & P. M. Vietze (Eds.), *Families of handicapped persons: Research programs, and policy issues* (pp. 219–235). Baltimore: Paul H. Brookes.

Kamphaus, R. W., & Reynolds, C. R. (1987). *Clinical and research applications of the K-ABC.* Circle Pines, MN: American Guidance Service.

Kaufman, A. S. (1973). Comparison of the preformance of matched groups of black children and white children on the WPPSI. *Journal of Consulting and Clinical Psychology, 41,* 186–191.

Kaufman, A. S. (1975). Factor structure of the McCarthy Scales at five age levels between 2½ and 8½. *Educational and Psychological Measurement, 35,* 641–656.

Kaufman, A. S., & Kaufman, N. L. (1977). *Clinical evaluation of young children with the McCarthy Scales.* New York: Grune & Stratton.

Kaufman, A. S., & Kaufman, N. L. (1983). *Kaufman Assessment Battery for Children; Interpretive Manual.* Circle Pines, MN: American Guidance Service.

Kearsley, R. (1979). Iatrogenic retardation: A syndrome of learned incompetence. In R. Kearsley & I. Sigel (Eds.), *Infants at risk: Assessment of cognitive functioning* (pp. 153–180). Hillsdale, NJ: Lawrence Erlbaum.

Keith, T. Z. (1985). Questioning the K-ABC: What does it measure? *School Psychology Review, 14,* 9–20.

Krantz, P. J., & Risley, T. R. (1977). Behavioral ecology in the classroom. In K. D. O'Leary & S. G. O'Leary (Eds.), *Classroom management: The successful use of behavior modification* (pp. 349–367). Elmsford, NY: Pergamon Press.

Krug, D. A., Arick, J., & Almond, P. J. (1979). Autism screening instrument for educational planning. In J. Gilliam (Ed.), *Autism: Diagnosis, instruction, management, and research* (pp. 67–82). Austin: University of Texas Press.

Lapides, J. (1977). The school psychologist and early education: An ecological view. *Journal of School Psychology, 15,* 184–189.

LeLaurin, K., & Risley, T. R. (1972). The organization of day care environments: "Zone" versus "man-to-man" staff assignments. *Journal of Applied Behavior Analysis, 5,* 225–232.

Lewis, M., & Goldberg, S. (1969). The acquisition and

violation of expectancy: An experimental paradigm. *Experimental Child Psychology, 7,* 70–80.

Lichtenstein, R., & Ireton, H. (1984). *Preschool screening. Identifying young children with developmental and educational problems.* Orlando, FL: Grune & Stratton.

Lidz, C. S. (1983). Dynamic assessment and the preschool child. *Journal of Psychoeducational Assessment, 1,* 59–72.

Lynch, E. W., & Stein, R. (1982). Perspectives on parent participation in special education. *Exceptional Education Quarterly, 3,* 56–63.

Mardell-Czudnowski, C., & Goldenberg, D. (1983). Revision and restandardization of a preschool screening test: DIAL becomes DIAL-R. *Journal of the Division of Early Childhood, 8,* 149–156.

McCarthy, D. (1972). *Manual for the McCarthy Scales of Children's Abilities.* New York: Psychological Corporation.

McGee, G. Y., Krantz, P. J., Mason, D., & McClannahan, L. J. (1983). A modified incidental-teaching procedure for autistic youth: Acquisition and generalization of receptive object labels. *Journal of Applied Behavior Analysis, 16,* 329–338.

McWilliam, R. A., & Dunst, C. J. (1985). *Needs evaluation for educators of developmentally disabled students.* Unpublished rating scale, Family, Infant and Preschool Program, Western Carolina Center, Morganton, NC.

McWilliam, R. A., & Galant, K. (1984). *Caregiver assessment of child engagement.* Unpublished rating scale, Family, Infant and Preschool Program, Western Carolina Center, Morganton, NC.

McWilliam, R. A., Galant, K., & Dunst, C. J. (1984). *Daily engagement rating scale.* Unpublished rating scale, Family, Infant and Preschool Program, Western Carolina Center, Morganton, NC.

McWilliam, R. A., Trivette, C. M., & Dunst, C. J. (1985). Behavior engagement as a measure of the efficacy of early intervention. *Analysis and Intervention in Developmental Disabilities, 5,* 59–71.

Molitor, D. L., & Kramer, J. J. (1987). Battelle Developmental Inventory. *Journal of Psychoeducational Assessment, 5,* 287–291.

Moore, G. T. (1987). The physical environment and cognitive development in child-care centers. In C. S. Weinstein & T. G. David (Eds.), *Spaces for children: The build environment and child development* (pp. 41–72). New York: Plenum Press.

Moore, G. T. (1988). Theoretical perspectives on development and the environment: A paper in memory of Joachim Wohlwill. *Children's Environment Quarterly, 5,* 5–12.

Neisworth, J. T., & Bagnato, S. J. (1986). Curriculum-based developmental assessment: Congruence of testing and teaching. *School Psychology Review, 15,* 180–199.

Newborg, J., Stock, J. R., Wnek, L., Guidubaldi, J., & Svinicki, J. (1984). *The Battelle Developmental Inventory.* Allen, TX: DLM Teaching Resources.

O'Brien, B., & Risley, T. R. (1983). Infant-toddler day care: Practical considerations and applications to children with special needs. In E. M. Goetz & K. E. Allen (Eds.), *Early childhood education: Special environmental, policy, and legal considerations* (pp. 41–62). Rockville, MD: Aspen.

O'Brien, M., Porterfield, J., Herbert-Jackson, E., & Risley, T. R. (1979). *The toddler center: A practical guide to day care for 1- and 2-year olds.* Baltimore: University Park Press.

Olds, A. R. (1982). Designing play environments for children under 3. *Topics in Early Childhood Special Education, 2,* 87–95.

Paget, K. D. (1985). Preschool services in the schools: Issues and implications. *Special Services in the Schools, 2,* 3–25.

Paget, K. D. (1986). The McCarthy Scales of Children's Abilities. In J. V. Mitchell (Ed.), *Ninth mental measurement yearbook* (pp. 922–926). Lincoln, NE: Buros Institute.

Paget, K. D. (1988). Early intervention: Infants, preschool children, and families: In J. C. Witt, S. N. Elliott, & F. M. Gresham (Eds.), *Handbook of behavior therapy in education* (pp. 569–600). New York: Plenum Press.

Paget, K. D., & Nagle, R. J. (1986). A conceptual model of preschool assessment. *School Psychology Review, 15,* 154–165.

Phillips, B. L., Pasewark, R. A., & Tindall, R. C. (1978). Relationship among McCarthy Scales of children's abilities, WPPSI, and Columbia Mental Maturity Scale. *Psychology in the Schools, 15,* 352–256.

Rainforth, B., & Salisbury, C. L. (1988). Functional home programs: A model for therapists. *Topics in Early Childhood Special Education, 1,* 33–45.

Reynolds, C. R., & Clark, J. (1983). Assessment of cognitive abilities. In K. D. Paget & B. A. Bracken (Eds.), *The psychoeducational assessment of preschool children* (pp. 163–190). New York: Grune & Stratton.

Reynolds, C. R., & Gutkin, T. B. (1981). Test scatter on the WPPSI: Normative analyses of the standardization sample. *Journal of Learning Disabilities, 14,* 460–464.

Reynolds, C. R., Gutkin, T. B., Elliott, S. N., & Witt, J. C. (1984). *School psychology: Essentials of theory and practice.* New York: Wiley.

Reynolds, C. R., Kamphaus, R. W., & Rosenthal, B. L. (1988). Factor analysis of the Stanford-Binet Fourth Edition for ages 2 years through 23 years. *Measurement and Evaluation in Counseling and Development, 21,* 52–63.

Risley, T. R., & Cataldo, M. F. (1973). *Planned activity check: Materials for training observers.* Unpublished manual, Center for Applied Behavior Analysis, Lawrence, KS.

Risley, T. R., & Cataldo, M. F. (1974). *Evaluation of planned activities: The PLA Check measure of classroom participation.* Unpublished manual, Center for Applied Behavior Analysis, Lawrence, KS.

Robinson, C. C., Rose, J., & Jackson, B. (1986). Multidimensional screening instruments. *Dianostique, 11,* 134–154.

Rogers, S. J. (1977). Characteristics of the cognitive development of profoundly retarded children. *Child Development, 48,* 837–843.

Rogers, S. J. (1982). Assessment of cognitive development in the preschool years. In G. Ulrey & S. J. Rogers (Eds.), *Psychological assessment of handicapped infants and young children* (pp. 45–53). New York: Thieme-Stratton.

Rogers, S. G., Donovan, C. M. D'Eugenio, D. B., Brown, S. L., Lynch, E. W., Moersch, M. S., & Schafer, D. S. (1981). *Early intervention developmental profile.* Ann Arbor: University of Michigan Press.

Rogers-Warren, A. K. (1982). Behavior ecology in classrooms for young, handicapped children. *Topics in Early Childhood Special Education, 2*(1), 21–32.

Rogers-Warren, A. K., Santos-Colond, J., Warren, S. F., & Hasselbring, T. S. (1984, December). *Strategies and issues in quantifying early intervention.* Paper presented at the National Center for Clinical Infant Programs Conference, Washington, DC.

Rogers-Warren, A. K., & Wedel, J. W. (1980). The ecology of preschool classroom for the handicapped. *New Directions for Exceptional Children, 1,* 1–24.

Sanford, A., & Zelman, J. G. (1981). *The learning accomplishment profile.* Winston-Salem, NC: Kaplan School Supply.

Salvia, J., & Ysseldyke, J. E. (1988). *Assessment in special and remedial education* (4th ed.). Boston: Houghton Miffin.

Sattler, J. M. (1988). *Assessment of children.* San Diego, CA: Author.

Schaefer, E., & Edgerton, M. (1981). *Manual for the sibling inventory of behavior.* Unpublished manuscript, University of North Carolina at Chapel Hill, Department of Maternal and Child Health.

Schopler, E., Lansing, M., Reichler, R. J., & Waters, L. (1979). *Individualized assessment and treatment for autistic and developmentally disabled children.* Austin, TX: PRO-ED.

Schultz, J. (1982). A parent views parent participation. *Exceptional Education Quarterly, 3,* 17–24.

Scott, K., & Hogan, A. (1982). Methods for the identification of high-risk and handicapped infants. In C. Ramey & P. Trohanis (Eds.), *Finding and educating high-risk and handicapped infants.* Baltimore: University Park Press.

Sheehan, R. (1982). Issues in documenting early intervention with infants and parents. *Topics in Early Childhood Special Education, 1,* 67–75.

Shelton, T. L. (1989). The assessment of cognition/intelligence in infancy. *Infants and Young Children, 1,* 10–25.

Sparling, J., & Lowman, B. (1983). Parents' information needs as revealed through interests, problems, attitudes, and preferences. In R. Haskins & J. J. Gallagher (Eds.), *Parent education and public policy* (pp. 304–323). Norwood, NJ: Ablex.

Stallings, J. A. (1975). Implementation and child effects of teaching practices in Follow Through classrooms. *Monographs of the Society for Research in Child Development, 40*(7–8, Serial No. 163).

Sternberg, R. J. (1981). Testing and cognitive psychology. *American Psychologist, 36,* 1181–1189.

Stillman, R. D. (1974). *The Callier Azusa scale: Assessment of deaf/blind children.* Reston VA: Council for Exceptional Children.

Strain, P. S. (1984). Efficacy research with young handicapped children: A critique of the status quo. *Journal of the Division of Early Childhood, 9,* 4–10.

Summers, J. A. (1988). Family adjustment: Issues in research on families with developmentally disabled children. In V. B. Van Hasselt, P. S. Strain, & M. Hersen (Eds.), *Handbook of developmental and physical disabilities* (pp. 79–90). Elmsford, NY: Pergamon Press.

Tawney, J., Knap, D., O'Reilly, C., & Pratt, S. (1979). *Programmed environments curriculum.* Columbus, OH: Charles E. Merrill.

Terman, L. M., & Merrill, M. A. (1973). *Manual for the Third Revision (Form L-M) of the Stanford-Binet Intelligence Scale.* Boston: Houghton Miffin.

Thorndike, R. L., Hagen, E. P., & Sattler, J. M. (1986). *Stanford-Binet Intelligence Scale: Fourth Edition.* Chicago: Riverside.

Thurman, S. K., & Widerstrom, A. H. (1989). *Young children with special needs: A developmental and ecological approach* (Rev. Ed.) Boston: Allyn and Bacon.

Turnbull, A. P., Summers, J. A., & Brotherson, M. J. (1987). From parent involvement to family support. In S. M. Pueschell, C. Tingey, J. E. Pynders, A. C. Crocker, & D. M. Crutcher, (Eds.), *New perspectives on Down's syndrome.* Baltimore: Paul H. Brookes.

Turnbull, A. P., & Winton, P. J. (1984). Parent involvement policy and practice: Current research and implications for families of young severely handicapped children. In J. Blacher (Ed.), *Severely handicapped children and their families: Research in review* (pp. 337–397). New York: Academic Press.

Turnbull, H. R., & Turnbull, A. P. (1982). Parent involvement in the education of handicapped children: A critique. *Mental Retardation, 20,* 115–122.

Twardosz, S. (1984). Environmental organization: The physical, social, and programmatic context of behavior. In M. Hersen, R. M. Eisler, & P. M. Miller (Eds.), *Progress in behavior modification* (Vol. 18, pp. 123–161). New York: Academic Press.

Twardosz, S., & Risley, T. R. (1982). Behavioral-ecological consultation to day care centers. In A. Jeger & R. Slotnick (Eds.), *Community mental health and behavioral-ecology: A handbook of theory, research, and practice* (pp. 147–159). New York: Plenum Press.

Uzgiris, I. C., & Hunt, J. (1975). *Assessment in infancy: Ordinal scales of psychological development.* Urbana: University of Illinois Press.

Vadasy, P. F., Fewell, R. R., Meyer, D. J., & Schnell, G. (1984). Siblings of handicapped children: A developmental perspective on family interactions. *Family Relations, 33,* 155–167.

Vincent, L. J., Salisbury, C., Walters, G., Brown, P., Grunewald, L. J., & Powers, M. (1980). Program evaluation in early childhood/special education: Criteria of the next environment. In W. Sailor, B. Wilcox, & L. Brown (Eds.), *Methods of instruction* for severely handicapped students (pp. 303–328). Baltimore: Paul H. Brookes.

Wachs, R. D., & Gruen, G. E. (1982). Early experience and human development. New York: Plenum Press.

Wahler, R. G. (1980). The insular mother: Her problems in parent-child treatment. Journal of Applied Behavior analysis, 13, 207–219.

Wasik, B. H. (1984). Teaching parents effective problem solving: A handbook for professionals. Chapel Hill, NC: Robert Wood Johnson Foundation Infant Health and Development Programs.

Wechsler, D. (1967). Manual for the Wechsler Preschool & Primary Scale of Intelligence. New York: Psychological Corporation.

Willoughby-Herb, S. J., & Neisworth, J. T. (1982). HICOMP preschool curriculum. Columbus, OH: Charles E. Merrill.

Winton, P., & Turnbull, A. P. (1981). Parent involvement as viewed by parents of preschool handicapped children. Topics in Early Childhood Special Education, 1, 11–19.

Wolf, M. (1978). Social validity: A case for subjective measurement or how applied behavior analysis in finding its heart. Journal of Applied Behavior Analysis, 11, 203–214.

Zelazo, P. (1981). An information processing approach to infant cognitive assessment. In M. Lewis and L. Taft (Eds.), Developmental disabilities: Theory, assessment, and intervention (pp. 130–155). New York: S P Medical and Scientific Books.

Zelazo, P. (1982). Alternative assessment procedures for handicapped infants and toddlers: Theoretical and practical issues. In D. D. Bricker (Ed.), Intervention with at-risk and handicapped infants (pp. 107–127). Baltimore: University Park Press.

20

TEST BIAS IN PSYCHOLOGICAL ASSESSMENT

CECIL R. REYNOLDS
Texas A&M University
STEVEN M. KAISER
Utica Public Schools

In God We Trust
All Others Must Have Data
                    Unknown

The issue of bias in testing has been a recurring social embroglio throughout the history of mental measurement. Discussions pertaining to test bias are frequently accompanied by emotionally laden polemics decrying the use of mental tests with any minority group member who has not been exposed to the cultural and environmental circumstances of the white middle class. Yet it appears that the use of mental measures—in varying forms and for varying purposes—persists. Intertwined within the general issue of bias in tests and measures has been the use of intelligence tests for educational purposes. While scientific and societal discussion pertaining to differences between/among groups on measures of cognitive or intellectual functioning in no way fully encompasses the broader topic of bias in mental measurement, there is little doubt that the so-called "IQ controversy" has generated the lion's share of public scrutiny over the years. Witness the proliferation of publications in the more popular press (see Gould, 1981, or Jensen, 1980, Chap. 1) as well as court actions and legislation addressing the use of IQ tests within our schools and industry (e.g., *Diana v. California State Board of Education,* 1970; *Griggs v. Duke Power Company,* 1970; *Hobson v. Hansen,* 1967; *Larry P. v. Wilson Riles,* 1972). Further, the controversy has been fueled by actions taken by organizations such as the Association of Black Psychologists (ABP). ABP, at its annual meeting for the year 1969, adopted a policy statement that supported parents who refused achievement, aptitude, performance, and intellectual testing of their children for purposes related in any way to "labeling," to placement in "special" classes, to "tracking," and/or to the perpetuation of inferior educational opportunities for blacks.

In this chapter we maintain a focus on the empirical evaluation of test bias, with particular emphasis placed on statistical criteria and methods for investigating possible differential impact of mental measurements across groups. Brief discussions will also be presented related to the major historical developments leading up to the present subspecialty of bias research in testing as well as to examiner effects, to labeling, and to litigation pertaining to testing between/among populations. Contrary to the state of bias research two decades ago, a considerable body of research about and techniques to detect bias have been generated within the field.

GENERAL CONSIDERATIONS CONCERNING BIAS RESEARCH

The issue of bias in mental testing has been an important component to the study of individual differences and to social policy since Binet first offered a series of graduated intellectual tasks for evaluating cognitive development. Galton has been seen as the single most important precursor to the mental testing movement. He is, perhaps, best known for establishing the first anthropometric laboratory, where, for a small fee, persons could undergo various sensory and motor measures and be provided with some relative performance standing in relation to group data gathered during the course of his research. Galton and others of his era felt that human intelligence was built upon elementary sensations because sensations were, in effect, the gateway to the mind.

However, by the turn of the century attempts to validate a link between sensation and intellect proved discouraging. Independent estimates of intellectual ability (e.g., teacher's ratings, academic standing, occupational achievements, etc.) did not meld with acuity data (Heidbreder, 1933), and researchers such as Cattell gradually abandoned attempts to analyze intelligence via the senses in favor of tasks that demanded reasoning, problem solving, the acquisition of knowledge, "thinking" if you will, for successful execution. Regardless, Galton had a profound impact on the fields of differential psychology and mental measurement. He developed—and implemented—twin studies, questionnaire studies, and correlational studies in his investigations of human intellect, and as Fancher (1979) has noted: "Among his important contributions was the very idea that tests could be employed to measure psychological differences between people. . . . He thus elevated the scientific study of individual differences to the level of a major psychological specialty with important social implications" (p. 254).

In France in the 1890s, Binet also rejected the premise that lower-order sensory acuity measures could adequately reflect human thought processes.

He and his colleagues argued that individual differences in human intellect were more readily apparent with more complex functions, such as memory, verbal comprehension, reasoning ability, and the heuristically appealing notion of judgment.

The Binet-Simon scales were quickly translated and embellished throughout the world. The scales had a strong advocate in the United States in Goddard, who translated the scales into English, and by 1909, recommended to the American Association for the Study of the Feebleminded that scores from the scales be used to classify the mentally deficient. From the very beginnings, however, there is clear evidence of concern surrounding the differential impact of mental testing across groups.

Pintner and Keller (1922) collected data on numerous national and racial groups and reported a wide variation in median IQs. Further analysis was completed by separating those children whose parents did and did not speak English in the home. Results of testing with the Binet placed, on average, non-English-speaking-environment children 8 points below those whose families spoke English in the home. Further nonverbal intellectual testing served to increase the scores of non-English-home-environment children; and the authors concluded that "those children who hear a foreign language in their homes may suffer a serious handicap when tested only by the revisions of the Binet Test" (p. 222). While students of school psychology might regard the issue of test bias in general—and intellectual testing in particular—as a product of more recent social concern, educational and psychological literature from this earlier era (e.g., Kohs, 1923; Pintner, 1923; Pressey & Pressey, 1922) readily attests to the fact that scholars were concerned about factors other than innate intelligence affecting (and presumably biasing) mental measurement test performance. Freeman's (1926) text provides a fairly representative example of what psychologists and educators read then, and still read to a certain extent today. The position statement also illustrates the long-standing and rocky courtship between the practical uses of mental measurements and the theoretical exploration of environmental and genetic factors on intellectual development. Freeman summarized:

> The detailed examination of the scientific evidence which is at hand indicates the correctness of the moderate view as contrasted with

ethnic extreme. As was pointed out in the first chapter, one may regard intelligence tests as an entirely new and perfect instrument for detecting native capacity. At the other extreme he may discount them and regard them as merely somewhat improved instruments for measuring the results of teaching. The consideration of the historical development of tests, in common with an analysis of their results, shows that neither of these views is correct. Intelligence tests have made a marked advance toward the measurement of native capacity, but these scores are still influenced to a considerable degree by the effects of training, and in their interpretation this influence must always be taken into account. (pp. 474–475)

The Nature/Nurture Issue

Bond (1981) observes that there has been a strong pull by professionals and the lay public alike to formulate conclusions regarding the relative impact of genetic and environmental factors on test performance if mean differences between/among groups are disparate and those tests in use are shown not to be biased in a statistical sense. Bond goes on to point out that one reason that bias research and intelligence testing has apparently remained so volatile a social issue has been a result of ubiquitous discussion pertaining to race differences in intelligence. He asks the reader to consider the statement: "Test results indicate that white students, on the average, achieve higher levels of competence in most academic subjects than black students, on the average" (p. 56). The statement, viewed objectively, merely addresses a presumed result of past academic achievement and does not provide an etiology for the observed difference. However, consider: "Test results indicate that white students as a group possess greater aptitude for academic work than black students as a group" (p. 56). The seemingly minor change in language quickly elevates the statement into the realm of "genetic" or "innate" superiority of one group over another for most people and, understandably, triggers a decidedly emotional response.

It may surprise some readers to know that investigation of test bias can proceed unabated without attention being paid to the "nature–nurture" question. That is not to say that the relative impact of endowment and experience on human intellectual development is not a viable issue in the scientific arena. It is, but is also burdened with inadequate methodology at present for convincing conclusions to be made. The nature–nurture question has presumably been a part of our quest to understand our being since the time human being's were apparently able to formulate the question. Jensen (1980) has clearly stated that research on test bias ought not to be confused with potentially polemic discussion pertaining to genetic and environmental factors as they relate to individual differences. He further notes that data obtained from all test scores are measures of phenotypic and not genotypic expression. The idea of phenotype in scientific terminology refers to the detectable expression of the interaction of *both* genotype and the environment, which ultimately constitute the characteristics of an organism. Consequently, investigation of test bias is, by nature, investigation of possible bias in the measurement of phenotypes. If bias is not found in a purely statistical sense within a test, conclusions drawn concerning genetic differences between/among groups using the "nonbiased" measure are, simply put, another issue with a plethora of complicating factors.

While Jensen (1980) takes the stand that advancement in psychometric knowledge is a vital component to a better understanding of the reasons underlying individual and group differences, he concludes:

> The answers to questions about test bias surely need not await a scientific consensus on the so-called nature–nurture question. A proper assessment of test bias, on the other hand, is an essential step towards a scientific understanding of the observed differences in test scores as well as the observed differences in all the important educational, occupational, and social correlates of test scores. Test scores themselves are merely correlates, predictors, and indicators of other socially important variables, which would not be altered in the least if tests did not exist. The problem of individual differences and group differences would not be made to disappear by abolishing tests. One cannot treat a fever by throwing away the thermometer. (p. xi)

Jensen's often-cited comments in the *Harvard Educational Review* concerning the possible role of genetics as a causative factor for the consistent disparity reported (see Shuey, 1966) in mean IQs between blacks and whites seems an odd twist in comparison to the passage quoted above. Yet the two positions are not discordant if one is able to separate systematic investigation of bias in tests and measures from estimation of the relative impact of constitution and environment upon test scores. It is interesting to note that both "environmental proponents" and "genetic proponents" in the nature–nurture issue have defended their positions from essentially the same data. Loehlin, Lindzey, and Spuhler (1975, Chap. 10), in a major text in the field of differential psychology, conclude that the fact that data seemingly fall in favor of both camps suggests that resolution of the more extreme positions is in no way imminent. It is now generally agreed that heredity and environment operate interactively in determining traits with the influence of each depending on the action of the other (Minton & Schneider, 1980).

Tyler (1965) has suggested that the most important information to be gleaned from this domain of research is not the proportional contribution of nature and nurture in the making of traits or abilities, but how amenable traits or abilities are to change and how change can be effectively carried out. Minton and Schneider (1980) have taken Tyler's position, stressing that "genetic" does not automatically imply a low level of modifiability, nor does "environmental" signal that a trait or ability is easily changeable. The authors point out that certain genetically based disorders such as phenylketonuria can readily be prevented by the environmental adjustment of diet, whereas social workers, psychologists, and other social service providers frequently find it impossible to modify deviant behaviors generally assumed to be a direct function of environmental circumstances.

Mean Score Differences as Test Bias

As the notion that bias investigation can readily be divorced from the nature–nurture issue might be surprising to many readers, the fact that differences in mean levels of performance on cognitive or ability tasks between/among groups is not evidence of test bias might be more surprising still. A number of writers have mistakenly taken this position in recent times (Alley & Foster, 1978; Chinn, 1979; Hilliard, 1979; Jackson, 1975; Mercer, 1976; Williams, 1974; Wright & Isenstein, 1977). Those who support this definition of test bias correctly state that there is no valid a priori scientific reason to believe that intellectual or other cognitive performance levels should differ across race. It is the inference that tests demonstrating such a difference are inherently biased because there can in reality be no differences that is fallacious. Just as there is no a priori basis for deciding that differences exist, there is no a priori basis for deciding that differences do not exist. From the standpoint of the objective methods of science, a priori or premature acceptance of either hypothesis (differences exist versus differences do not exist) is untenable. Some adherents to the mean difference as bias definition also require that the distribution of test scores in each population or subgroup be identical prior to assuming that the test is fair, regardless of its validity. "Regardless of the purpose of a test or its validity for that purpose, a test should result in distributions that are statistically equivalent across the groups tested in order for it to be considered nondiscriminatory for those groups" (Alley & Foster, 1978, p. 2). Portraying a test as biased regardless of its purpose or validity conveys an inadequate understanding of the psychometric construct and issues of bias. The mean difference and equivalent distribution concepts of test bias have been the most uniformly rejected of all criteria of test bias examined by sophisticated psychometricians involved in investigating the problems of bias in assessment.

Jensen (1980) discussed the mean differences as bias definition in terms of the egalitarian fallacy. The egalitarian fallacy contends that all human populations are in fact identical on all mental traits or abilities. Any differences with regard to any aspect of the distribution of mental test scores indicates that something is wrong with the test itself. As Jensen points out, such an assumption is totally scientifically unwarranted. There are simply too many examples of specific abilities and even sensory capacities that have been shown unmistakably to differ across human populations. The result of the egalitarian assumption, then, is to remove the investigation of population differences in ability from the realm of scientific inquiry. Logically followed, this fallacy leads to other untenable conclusions as well. Torrance (1980), an adherent of the cultural-bias hypothesis, pointed out that disadvantaged black children occasionally earn higher scores on creativity tests—and therefore, have more creative ability—than many white children because their environment has forced them to learn to "make do" with less and with simple objects. The egalitarian assumption would hold that this is not true, but rather the content of the test is biased against white or high-SES children.

Culture-Free Tests, Culture Loading, and Culture Bias

A third area of bias investigation that has been confusing in both professional literature (e.g., Alley & Foster, 1978; Chinn, 1979) and literature for the public has been the interpretation of culture loading and culture bias. A test or test item can be culture loaded without being culturally biased. *Culture loading* refers to the degree of cultural specificity present in the test or individual items of the test. Certainly, the greater the cultural specificity of a test item, the greater the likelihood of the item being biased when used with people from other cultures. The test item "Who was the first president of the United States?" represents a culture-loaded item. However, the item is general enough to be considered useful with children in the United States. The cultural specificity of the item is too great, however, to allow the item to be used on an aptitude measure for 10-year-old children from Paraguay (but not as a measure of knowledge of U.S. history). Virtually all tests in current use are bound in some way by their cultural specificity. Culture loading must be viewed on a continuum from general (defining the culture in a broad, liberal sense) to specific (defining the culture in narrow, highly distinctive terms).

A variety of attempts have been made to develop a culture-free (sometimes referred to as culture-fair) intelligence test (Cattell, 1978). However, the reliability and validity of these tests are uniformly inadequate from a psychometric perspective (Anastasi, 1976; Ebel, 1979). The difficulty in developing a culture-free measure of intelligence lies in the tests being irrelevant to intellectual behavior within the culture under study. Intelligent behavior is defined within human society in a large part on the basis of behavior judged to be of value to the survival and improvement of the culture and the people within that culture. A test that is "culture blind" then cannot be expected to predict intelligent behavior within a variety of cultural settings. Once a test has been developed within a culture (a culture-loaded test) its generalizability to other cultures or subcultures within the dominant societal framework becomes a matter for empirical investigation.

Jensen (1980) admonishes that when investigating the psychometric properties of culture-loaded tests across differing societies or cultures, it cannot be assumed that content (or face validation) inspection will determine which tests or items are biased against those cultures or societies not represented in the test or item content. Tests or items that exhibit characteristics of being culturally loaded cannot be determined to be biased with any degree of certainty unless objective statistical inspection is completed. Jensen refers to the mistaken notion that anyone can judge tests and/or items as being "culturally unfair" on superficial inspection as the "culture-bound fallacy."

The Question of Labeling Effects

The relative impact of placing a label on a child's behavior or developmental status has been an issue also closely aligned with the field of psychometrics in general, and bias investigation in particular. The union has undoubtedly been a by-product to a larger extent of the practice of using intellectual measures for the determination of mental retardation. Although the issue of labeling effects is an important one, it requires consideration in bias research much the same as does the ongoing debate surrounding the nature–nurture question. In effect, the realm of bias investigation need not concern itself with labeling much the same as it can continue unabated whether or not the nature–nurture issue is addressed. However, there are some important considerations regarding bias in referral for services, diagnosis, and labeling that warrant consideration for any interested student of school psychology.

Rosenthal is the researcher most closely associated with the influence of labeling upon teacher and parent perceptions of a child's ability and potential. Even though his early studies had many difficulties, labeling effects have been shown in some subsequent experimental studies (e.g., Critchley, 1979; Foster & Ysseldyke, 1976; Jacobs, 1978), but not in others (e.g., MacMillan, Jones & Aloia, 1974; McCoy, 1976). However, these studies generally are of a very short-term nature under quite artificial circumstances. Not infrequently, participants are asked to rate the behavior or degree of pathology of a child seen on videotape. Categorical labels for the child are systematically varied while the observed behaviors remain constant. The demand characteristics of such a design are substantial. Long-term effects of labeling and special education placement have been examined less vigorously. Comparisons of the effects of formal, diagnostic labels with the informal, often cursory personal labeling process that occurs between teachers and children over the course of a school year that is subsequently passed on to the next grade via the teachers' lounge (Dworkin & Dworkin, 1979) need to be made. The strict behaviorist position (Ross, 1974, 1976) also contends that formal diagnostic procedures are unnecessary and potentially harmful due to labeling effects. However, whether or not there are detrimental effects on children due to the application of formal labels remains an open question (Hobbs, 1975).

Even without the application of formal, codified labels by psychologists or psychiatrists, the mental labeling, classification, and appraisal of individuals by the people with whom they come into contact is a common, constant occurrence (Reynolds, 1979c). Auerbach (1971) stated that adults often interpret early learning difficulties as a primary emotional disturbance, unrelated to learning problems. According to Bower (1970), children who start the first grade below the mean age of their classmates and are below average in the development of school readiness skills or have behavior problems are more likely to be regarded as emotionally disturbed by school staff and are more likely to be referred to residential placements than are their peers. (As with many other childhood disorders, this effect is noted to be more profound for boys than girls but not blacks versus whites.) The American Psychological Association (1970) recognized that such constant appraisal of individuals occurs at the informal level, and, in an official position statement, takes the stance that specialized, standardized, psychological techniques have been developed to supersede our informal, often casual approach to the appraisal of others. The specialized psychological techniques available to the trained examiner add validity and utility to the results of such appraisals. Quantification of behavior results, allowing systematic comparisons of the individuals' characteristics with those of a selected reference or norm group. It is not unreasonable to anticipate that the informal labeling of children so often indulged in by teachers and parents is substantially more harmful than accurate psychoeducational diagnostics intended to accrue beneficial activity toward the child. Should noncategorical funding for services to exceptional children become a reality (Gutkin & Tieger, 1979), or the use of normative assessment ultimately be banned, the informal labeling process will continue.

From the standpoint of test bias issues, then, the question of labeling children or not labeling children becomes moot. Test bias is concerned with the accuracy of such labels across some nominal grouping system (typically race, sex, or socioeconomic status have been the variables of interest). It is a question of whether race, sex, or any other demographic variable of interest influences the diagnostic process or the placement of a child in special programs independent of the child's cognitive, emotional, and behavioral status. However, a variety of well-designed studies have investigated the influence of race and socioeconomic status on the class placement recommendations (i.e., bias in test interpretation) of school psychologists. Some of these studies investigated teacher bias as well and are reviewed in the first edition of this work.

Early Bias Research
Jensen (1980) reports that first attempts to investigate bias in mental tests were restricted to the exploration of certain internal characteristics of items within any given measure. More specifically, emphasis was placed on the relative impact of social class differences on item performance. Earlier thinking in the mental test movement followed the logic that if mental tests did, in fact, measure some general trait presumed to be "within" the individual, items ought not strongly discriminate between/among social classes. Items most discriminating in this regard were considered suspect and, in essence, biased. Jensen further notes that this genre of research (in effect, the investigation of group X item interactions in modern statistical parlance) proved faulty and, consequently, inconclusive because, in part, percentage passing is not an interval scale and must be placed in a normalized index, because the influence of chronological age on the type of task under inspection requires control, and because content inspection of items reveals little information about an item's underlying factor structure. Concerning the latter, there is little or no scientific rationale behind the contention that highly discriminatory items are, by default, biased if it can be demonstrated that those items are tapping different (e.g., if those items load more highly on the general factor of intelligence) aspects of intellectual ability than items presumably less biased as determined by minimal group percent-

age differences across levels of SES. In effect, it can be argued that those high discrimination items under inspection are adequately measuring a unique aspect of intellectual functioning and not differing levels of economic status per se if those high discrimination items can be shown to exhibit unique psychometric properties.

Several doctoral dissertations completed at midcentury served to propel bias research into a new arena of sophistication. Both dissertations deserve special notice because they attempted to address directly the issue of cultural fairness of commonly used tests of the period, were ambitious in their scope, and served to demonstrate that an awkward, seemingly unruly research topic was amenable to systematic investigation.

Eells (see Eells, Davis, Havighurst, Herrick, & Typer, 1951) tested the hypothesis that the economic status of a child's environment was, on average, related to mean IQ differences because children were exposed to qualitatively different experiences in, for example, vocabulary spoken at home and discussion of topics that would seem to expand a youngster's general knowledge and reasoning skills. Eells postulated that the intellectual demands of various mental tests were more closely aligned to the environment of high-status than with low-status groups and consequently reflected in mean differences the extent to which any given youngster experienced a more "stimulating" environment. Eells proceeded with an ambitious project, including thousands of children, a lengthy battery of commonly used tests of the time, and demographic data related to family economic status. High, middle, and low groups were created from family economic/social data, and for the low-status group, further division was made along ethnic lines. Children were either 9, 10, 13, or 14 years of age.

Eells' data revealed sizable variation in terms of item difficulties across low- and high-status groups and age ranges tested. Although virtually all items investigated reflected superiority by the high-status group over the low-status group, magnitudes fluctuated as seen by discordant percentages of items that reached statistically significant levels among the differing age groupings. Eells also found that ethnic grouping did not appreciably influence test item performance as groups (Eells divided into an "ethnic" group and an "Old American" group) faired about as well on most items. Furthermore, the largest status differences were found to be greater on easier test items, defined as those items with less verbal and general informational content. This finding ran contrary to Eells' anticipated results, although he did find that status differences were, in general, greater with items that demanded stronger verbal skills and information presumably more accessible to high-status youngsters of the time. Finally, Eells examined patterns in the choice of multiple-choice distractors between high- and low-status groups. He found that high-status students tended to select with greater frequency more plausible distractors—ones closest to the correct answer—than did low-status students. By and large, low-status subjects appeared to guess as their overall patterns across items seemed more random in comparison.

Although Eells conceded that his data were less than consistent, he nonetheless became the first to advocate clearly and strongly the development and use of culture-fair tests. His research served to accelerate interest in the empirical aspects of bias investigation as well as to heighten sensitivity for those aspects of test items that might differentially impact between/among groups. Yet his main desire—to design culture-fair tests that would eliminate bias—failed in rather rapid order. A second dissertation from this period yielded more consistent data with regard to the issue of culture fairness and the culture-bound fallacy and also remains as a hallmark in bias research.

McGurk (1951) addressed the question as to whether items from commonly used intellectual tests could be determined by inspection from qualified persons to be culturally loaded. He enlisted 78 judges with presumed sensitivity (e.g., professors of psychology and sociology, teachers, counselors, etc.) with regard to the cultural content within tasks and asked each to rate selected items as being least cultural, neutral, or high in cultural content. McGurk's aim was to find those items from intellectual tests which consistently showed strong consensus among the judges as being most and least culturally loaded. Definition was left up to individual opinion, and ultimately, high and low cultural content was decided upon when a significant proportion of the judges made the same classification for individual items. What fell out from the first stage of the project was 103 items felt to be high on cultural loading and 81 items considered generally culture-free by expert opinion.

McGurk made comparisons of performances

by black and white high school seniors on the 184 items. He then selected 37 pairs of items from these data matched on the basis of difficulty (determined by percent passing) levels. In effect, each pair included a least and a most culturally loaded item, as determined by the judges, that black and white students had subsequently passed in similar numbers. The 37 pairs were then administered to a large sample of white students and a smaller sample of blacks in both Pennsylvania and New Jersey. Because McGurk has such a surplus of white students, he was then able to create black–white pairs who had had similar curriculum exposure and who had attended the same school district, including present placement at the time of testing. Pairings were also made so as to match for social and economic factors.

Results of McGurk's careful planning yielded some interesting results. First, mean differences on items characterized as least and most culturally loaded ran contrary to what one might expect if it was assumed on face value that whites would do better on more culturally bound tasks. In fact, black–white mean differences on the judged least loaded items were twice as great as differences on the presumed high-culture-content items. McGurk determined that blacks performed, relatively speaking, better on those items classified as more culturally loaded, even when item difficulty was held constant. Second, correlations between item difficulties showed similar magnitude between the low and high culture questions, providing strong evidence that blacks and whites showed similar patterns in the relative difficulties of items. Third, further analysis of selected low and high social/ economic groups revealed that whites showed greater differences between low- and high-SES groups on high-culture-content items as opposed to low-content items. However, blacks evidenced a pattern opposite to the white group. Black differences (i.e., between the low- and high-SES students) were found to be greatest within the least-culture items and relatively weaker with those items judged high in culture content.

Where Can Research Go?

Harrington (1975, 1976) has taken a quite different, experimentally oriented approach to the issue of test bias. His work bears mention lest we continue to view bias research as limited to psychometric tasks, subjects, and computerized statistical analyses. Whereas Eells' and McGurk's work provide witness to where bias investigation

has come from, Harrington perhaps shows the myriad of possible avenues of investigation for the future. In earlier research, Harrington (1968a, 1968b) suggested that the existence of genetic × environmental interactions in intelligence could affect item selection in the construction of intelligence tests in a manner resulting in bias (mean differences in total test scores) against minorities. Harrington is thus raising the issue of representation in the test development sample, yet from a slightly different perspective. The small actual number of minority children in the standardization sample are unable to exert any significant impact on the item analysis data, and the content of the test subsequently becomes biased against groups with less than majority representation. Although this argument is not new, Harrington's (1975, 1976) subsequent approach to researching this question is quite interesting and innovative. Harrington began by creating experimental populations with varying proportions of minority composition (group membership was defined on a genetic basis). For his experimental populations, Harrington used six species of rats from genetically homogeneous groups. Harrington then set out to develop six intelligence tests, using standard psychometric procedures. Six test development populations were developed with varying degrees of minority group representation. Items for use in test development for each population were the same and consisted of a large number of performance measures on black and/or white Hebb-Williams-type mazes (Hebb-Williams mazes being accepted standard tasks for the measure of rat intelligence).

After the administration of all items to each of the six populations, a test was constructed separately for each population. Following traditional psychometric practice, internal consistency analyses were undertaken, and items showing the greatest item-total correlations within each population were retained for the "IQ test" for that population. A total of 50 items were retained within each of the six populations. Harrington then hypothesized that if minority group representation in the population does not affect item selection, the six measures would be essentially equivalent forms (i.e., group performance should be independent of the test form employed). To test this hypothesis, Harrington randomly sampled each of the six test development populations and administered all six of the newly developed tests to the new grouping of subjects.

Significant positive correlations occurred between the group mean on any individual test and the degree of group representation in the population used to develop the test. For example, for Test A, group a had the greatest representation in the test development sample and the highest mean on the instrument subsequently developed. For Test B, group c had the greatest proportionate representation and the highest score on that instrument. Harrington concluded that "the greater the proportional representation of a homogeneous group in the test base population [the test development sample] the higher the mean score of the group on the test derived on that population." From some further analyses of this data set, Harrington concluded that it is not possible for tests developed and normed on a white majority to have equivalent predictive validity with blacks or any other minority group. Harrington also contends that the generalization of his results with animals to humans is direct and not analogical since his experiments are a direct, empirical test of common psychometric assumptions and practice. Harrington's comments on predictive validity are particularly crucial since, as will be seen, most definitions of test bias rely heavily on the differential prediction of some specified criterion (Anastasi, 1976; Bartlett & O'Leary, 1969; Cleary, 1968; Cleary, Humphreys, Kendrick, & Wesman, 1975; Cronbach, 1970; Darlington, 1971; Einhorn & Bass, 1971; Hunter & Schmidt, 1976; Hunter, Schmidt, & Hunter, 1979; Kallingal, 1971; Kennedy, 1978; Linn & Werts, 1971; Potthoff, 1966; Reynolds, 1978, 1980b, 1980c; Reynolds, Bossard, & Gutkin, 1980; Reynolds & Gutkin, 1980a).

While Harrington's (1975, 1976) results are impressive and seem to call into question certain of the basic psychometric assumptions underlying test construction (particularly as they apply to the development of intelligence tests), his generalizations fail on three major points. First, intelligence and other aptitude tests have been shown to have equivalent predictive validity across racial groupings in a variety of circumstances with a rather diverse set of criterion measures. Second, well-documented findings that Japanese-Americans, Chinese-Americans, and Jewish-Americans typically score as well or better than whites on traditional intelligence tests and tests of some specific aptitudes (M. Gross, 1967; Marjoribanks, 1972; Tyler, 1965; Willerman, 1979) are entirely contradictory to Harrington's (1975, 1976) results given their proportately small representation in the test development population of such instruments. Neither can Harrington's theory explain why African infants, with zero representation in the standardization samples of such instruments as the Bayley Scales of Infant Development (Bayley, 1969), consistently score at higher levels than do American infants (Gerber & Dean, 1957; Leiderman, Babu, Kagia, Kraemer, & Leiderman, 1973; Warren, 1972); nor can Harrington's theory explain why Canadian children of French descent and American children earn approximately equivalent scores on the WISC-R information subtest (Beauchamp, Samuels, & Griffore, 1979), or why native Eskimos and white Canadian children earn equivalent scores on Raven's Progressive Matrices (MacArthur, 1968). Again, such findings are in direct contradiction to predictions drawn from Harrington's results. Third, Harrington's theory of minority–majority group score differences cannot account for different patterns of cognitive performance between minority groups (Bogen, DeZure, Tenhouten, & Marsh, 1972; Dean, 1979a; Dershowitz & Frankel, 1975; Reynolds, McBride, & Gibson, 1979; Vance, Hankins, & McGee, 1979; Willerman, 1979).

Different patterns of performance under Harrington's model implies differential bias in item selection depending on the type of test involved. The degree of differential bias would also have to remain relatively constant across a number of different test batteries and test development samples with varying degrees of minority representation. This is at present an untenable assumption. Furthermore, there is evidence that socioeconomic class has its greatest relation to level of performance and race to pattern of performance (Willerman, 1979). How this type of differential effect on test scores by minority category could occur under the Harrington model is not clear. Nevertheless, considerable research remains to be conducted regarding Harrington's (1975, 1976) theory of group differences in mental test scores. Although most of his predictions concerning human minority performance do not hold, it is not at all clear why not.

OBJECTIONS TO TEST USE WITH MINORITIES

Many potentially legitimate objections to the use of educational and psychological tests with minorities have been raised by black and other minority psychologists. Too frequently, the objections of these groups are viewed as facts without a review of any empirical evidence (e.g., Council for Exceptional Children, 1978; Hilliard, 1979). The problems most often cited in the use of tests with minorities typically fall into the following categories (these categories have been drawn together with some modifications primarily from categories suggested in the writings of Clarizio, 1978; Reschly, 1980; Vandivier & Vandivier, 1979; and Wright & Isenstein, 1977):

1. *Inappropriate Content:* Black or other minority children have not been exposed to the material involved in the test questions or other stimulus materials. The tests are geared primarily toward white middle-class homes and values.

2. *Inappropriate Standardization Samples:* Ethnic minorities are underrepresented in the collection of normative reference group data. Williams (Wright & Isenstein, 1977) criticized the WISC-R (Wechsler, 1974) standardization sample for including blacks only in proportion to the total U.S. population. Out of 2200 children in the WISC-R standardization sample, 330 were minority. Williams contends that such small actual representation has no impact on the test. In earlier years, it was not unusual for standardization samples to be all white (e.g., the 1949 WISC).

3. *Examiner and Language Bias:* Since most psychologists are white and primarily speak only standard English, they intimidate black and other ethnic minorities. They are also unable to communicate accurately with minority children. Lower test scores for minorities then are said to reflect only this intimidation and difficulty in the communication process, not lowered ability levels.

4. *Inequitable Social Consequences:* As a result of bias in educational and psychological tests, minority group members, who are already at a disadvantage in the educational and vocational markets because of past discrimination, are disproportionately relegated to dead-end educational tracks and thought unable to learn. Labeling effects also fall under this category.

5. *Measurement of Different Constructs:* Related to (1) above, this position asserts that the tests are measuring significantly different attributes when used with children from other than the white middle-class culture. Mercer (1979), for example, contended that when IQ tests are used with minorities, they are measuring only the degree of Anglocentrism (adherence to white middle-class values) of the home.

6. *Differential Predictive Validity:* While tests may accurately predict a variety of outcomes for white middle-class children, they fail to predict at an acceptable level any relevant criteria for minority group members. Corollary to this objection are a variety of competing positions regarding the selection of an appropriate, common criterion against which to validate tests across cultural groupings. Scholastic or academic attainment levels are considered by a variety of black psychologists to be biased as criteria.

THE PROBLEM OF DEFINITION

The defining of test bias has produced considerable, as yet unresolved debate among measurement and assessment experts (Angoff, 1976; Bass, 1976; Bernal, 1975; Cleary et al., 1975; Cronbach, 1976; Darlington 1971, 1976, 1978; Einhorn & Bass, 1971; Flaugher, 1978; A. L. Gross & Su, 1975; Humphreys, 1973; Hunter & Schmidt, 1976, 1978; Linn, 1976; McNemar, 1975; Novick & Petersen, 1976; Petersen & Novick, 1976; Reschly, 1980; Reynolds, 1978; Sawyer, Cole, & Cole, 1976; Schmidt & Hunter, 1974; Thorndike, 1971). While the resulting debate has generated a number of selection models from which to examine bias, selection models focus on the decision-making system and not on the test itself. The various selection models are discussed at some length in Hunter and Schmidt (1976), Hunter, Schmidt, and Rauschenberger (1984), Jensen (1980), Petersen and Novick (1976), Ramsay (1979), and Reynolds and Brown (1984). The decision-making system chosen ultimately must be a societal decision (especially with regard to educational decision making) that will depend to a large extent on the value system and goals of the society. Thus, prior to choosing a model for test use in selection, it must be decided whether the ultimate goal is equality of opportunity, equality of outcome, or representative equality (these concepts are discussed in more detail in Nichols, 1978).

Equality of opportunity is a competitive model wherein selection is based on ability. As more eloquently stated by Lewontin (1970), under equality of opportunity: "True merit. . .will be the criterion of men's earthly reward" (p. 92). Equality of outcome is a selection model that is based on ability deficits. Compensatory and remedial education programs are typically constructed on the basis of the equality of outcome selection models. Children of low ability or believed to be at high risk for academic failure are selected for remedial, compensatory, or other special educational programs. In a strictly predictive sense, tests are used in a similar manner under both of these models. However, under equality of opportunity, selection is based on the prediction of a high level of criterion performance; under equality of outcome, selection is determined by the prediction of "failure" or a preselected low level of criterion performance. Interestingly, it is the failure of compensatory and remedial education programs to bring the disadvantaged learner to "average" levels of performance that has resulted in the charges of test bias now in vogue.

The representative equality model also relies on selection, but selection that is proportionate to numerical representation of subgroups in the population under consideration. Representative equality is typically thought to be independent of the level of ability within each group; however, models can be constructed that select from each subgroup the desired proportion of individuals based on relative ability level of the group, independent of group ability, or any gradient between these two positions. Even under the conditions of representative equality, it is imperative to employ a selection device (test) that will rank order individuals within groups in a reliable and valid manner. The best way to ensure fair selection under any of these models, then, is to employ tests that are equally reliable and equally valid for all groups concerned. The tests employed should also be the most reliable and most valid for all groups under consideration. The concept of test bias per se then resolves to a question of test validity. Test use (i.e., fairness) may be defined as biased or nonbiased only by the societal value system; at present this value system is leaning strongly toward some

variant of the representative equality selection model. As noted above, all models are facilitated by the use of a nonbiased test. That is, the use of a test with equivalent cross-group validities makes for the most parsimonious selection model, greatly simplifying the creation and application of the selection model that has been chosen.

This leads to the essential component of what exactly test bias is. Test bias refers in a global sense to the systematic error in the estimation of some "true" value for a group of individuals. The key word here is "systematic" error, as all measures contain error, assumed to be random unless shown to be otherwise. Bias investigation is a statistical inquiry which does not concern itself with culture loading, labeling effects, or test use/test fairness. Concerning the latter, Jensen (1980) comments: "Unbiased tests can be used unfairly and biased tests can be used fairly. Therefore, the concepts of bias and unfairness should be kept distinct. . .a number of different, and often mutually contradictory, criteria for fairness have been proposed, and no amount of statistical or psychometric reasoning per se can possibly settle any arguments as to which is best" (pp. 375–376).

There are basically three types of validity: content, construct, and predictive (or criterion-related). Test bias may exist under any or all of these categories of validity. Although no category of validity is completely independent of any other category, each is discussed separately here for the purposes of clarity and convenience. Frequently encountered in this area of research are the terms "single-group validity" and "differential validity." Single-group validity refers to the phenomenon of a test being valid for one group but not another. Differential validity refers to a condition where a test is valid for all groups concerned but the degree of validity varies as a function of group membership. Although these terms have most often been applied to predictive or criterion-related validity (validity coefficients are then examined for significance and compared across groups), the concepts of single-group and differential validity are equally applicable to content and construct validity.

RESEARCH STRATEGIES AND RESULTS

Bias in Content Validity
Bias in the item content of intelligence tests is one of the favorite topics of those who decry the use of

standardized tests with minorities (e.g., Hilliard, 1979; Williams, 1972; Wright & Isenstein, 1977). Typically, critics review the items of a test and single out specific items as being biased because (a) the items ask for information that minority or disadvantaged children have not had equal opportunity to learn, and/or (b) the scoring of the items is improper since the test author has arbitrarily decided on the only correct answer and minority children are inappropriately penalized for giving answers that would be correct in their own culture but not that of the test maker, and/or (c) the wording of the question is unfamiliar and even though a minority child may "know" the correct answer is unable to respond because he or she did not understand the question. Each of these three criticisms, when accurate, has the same basic empirical result; the item becomes relatively more difficult for minority group members than for the majority population. This leads directly to an empirically defined, testable definition of content bias for aptitude tests.

> An item or subscale of a test is considered to be *biased* in content when it is demonstrated to be relatively more difficult for members of one group than another when the general ability level of the groups being compared is held constant and no reasonable theoretical rationale exists to explain group differences on the item (or subscale) in question.

With regard to achievement tests, the issue of content bias is considerably more complex. Exposure to instruction, general ability level of the groups, and the accuracy and specificity of the sampling of the domain of items are all important variables in determining whether the content of an achievement test is biased (see Schmidt, 1983). Research into item (or content) bias with achievement tests has typically, and perhaps mistakenly, relied on methodology appropriate for determining item bias in aptitude tests. Nevertheless, research examining for content bias in both types of instruments has yielded quite comparable results.

One method of locating "suspicious" test items requires that item difficulties be determined separately for each group under consideration. If any individual item or series of items appears to be exceptionally difficult for the members of any group, relative to other items on the test, the item is considered potentially biased and removed from

the test. A more exacting and widespread approach to identifying biased items involves an analysis of variance procedure wherein the groups × items interaction term is of interest (e.g., Angoff & Ford, 1973; Cardall & Coffman, 1964; Cleary & Hilton, 1968; Plake & Hoover, 1979; Potthoff, 1966; Stanley, 1969).

The definition of content bias preferred above actually requires that the differences between groups (of unequal ability) be the same for every item on the test. Thus, in the analysis of variance procedure, the groups × items interaction should not yield a significant result. Whenever the differences in items are not uniform (a significant groups × items interaction does exist) one may contend that the item is biased, that it measures a different entity for each group. Earlier in this area of research, it was hoped that the empirical analysis of tests at the item level would result in the identification of a category of items having similar content as biased and that such items could then be avoided in future test development (Flaugher, 1978). Very little similarity among items determined to be biased has been found. No one has been able to identify those characteristics of an item that cause the item to be biased. It does seem that poorly written, sloppy, and ambiguous items tend to be identified as biased with greater frequency than those items typically encountered in a well-constructed standardized instrument. The variable at issue, then, may be the item reliability. Item reliabilities are typically not large and poorly written or ambiguous test items can easily have reliabilities approaching zero. Decreases in reliability are known to increase the probability of the occurrence of bias (Linn & Werts, 1971).

Once items have been identified as biased under the procedures above, attempts have been made to eliminate "test bias" by eliminating the offending items and rescoring the tests. As pointed out by Flaugher (1978) and Flaugher and Schrader (1978), however, little is gained by this tactic. Mean differences in performance between groups is affected only slightly and the test becomes more difficult for everyone involved since the items eliminated typically have moderate to low difficulty. When race × items interactions have been found, the interaction typically accounts for a very small proportion of variance. For example, in analyzing items on the WISC-R, Jensen (1976), Sandoval (1979), and Miele (1979) found the items × groups interaction to account for only 2 to

5% of the variance in performance. Using a similar technique with the Wonderlic Personnel Test, Jensen (1977) found the race × item interaction to account for only about 5% of the test score variance. Thus, the elimination of the offending items can be expected to have little, if any, significant effect. These analyses have been of a post-hoc nature (i.e., after the tests have been standardized), however, and the use of empirical methods for determining item bias during the test development phase (as with the recent revision of the Metropolitan Achievement Test) are to be encouraged.

With multiple-choice tests, another level of complexity can easily be added to the examination of content bias. With a multiple-choice question, typically three or four distractors are given in addition to the correct response. Distractors may be examined for their attractiveness (the relative frequency with which they are chosen) across groups. When distractors are found to be disproportionately attractive for members of any particular group, the item may be defined as biased. When items are constructed to have an equal distribution of responses to each distractor for the total test population, chi-square can be used to examine directly the distribution of choices for each distractor for each group (Burrill, 1975).

Jensen (1976) investigated the distribution of wrong responses for two multiple-choice intelligence tests, the Peabody Picture Vocabulary Test (PPVT) and Raven's Progressive Matrices (the Raven). Each of these two tests were individually administered to 600 white and 400 black children between the ages of 6 and 12. The analysis of incorrect responses for the PPVT indicated that the errors were distributed in a nonrandom fashion over the distractors for a large number of items. However, no racial bias in response patterns occurred since the disproportionate choice of distractors followed the same pattern for blacks and whites. For the Raven, blacks made different types of errors than whites, but only on a small number of items. Jensen followed up these items and compared the black response pattern to the response patterns of white children at a variety of age levels. For every item showing differences in black/white response patterns, the black response could be duplicated by the response patterns of whites approximately 2 years younger than the blacks.

More recently, Veale and Foreman (1983) have advocated inspection of multiple-choice tests

for bias in distractor or "foil" response distribution as a means of refining tests *before* they are finalized for the marketplace. The authors note that there are many instances whereby unbiased external criterion (such as achievement or ability) or culturally valid tests are not readily accessible for detecting bias in the measure under study. Veale and Foreman add that inspection of incorrect responses to distractor items can often lead to greater insight concerning cultural bias in any given question than would inspection of percentage of correct responses across groups. They conclude that significant differential response patterns (i.e., when groups disproportionately respond to differing distractors) may suggest that one of the distractors is, in fact, a correct response for a particular cultural group or may contain specific cultural content that serves to attract/detract one group to a greater extent than another. Veale and Foreman (1983) provide the statistical analyses for their *overpull probability model* along with procedures for measuring cultural variation and diagramming the source of bias within any given item.

Consider the following example provided by the authors:

> Pick out the correct sentence below:
> (A) Janie takes her work seriously.
> (B) Janie work take too much time.
> (C) Working with books are my favorite thing.
> (D) Things people likes to do is their business.

In this example, blacks are strongly attracted to distractor (D), while other groups are more inclined to pick (C) as seen by Veale and Foreman's *overpull* computations. The (D) distractor, at face value, may be differentially affecting black performance because of the "street" language presumably more common in the black culture. Upon further inspection, there is also the question of whether the stem of this particular item provides clear direction (i.e., correct *standard* English) to the testee. Knowledge of the differential response patterns across groups allows for item refinement, and subsequent statistical inspection can ensure that distractors are not overly attractive/distracting to one group over another in revised format.

Investigation of item bias during test development is certainly not restricted to multiple-choice items and methods such as those outlined by Veale and Foreman. There are a plethora (see Jensen, 1980, Chap. 9) of possibilities. For example, Scheuneman has more recently (1987) used the results of log-linear methodology on Graduate Record Examination Test (GRE) item data to show some interesting influences on black/white performance when item characteristics (e.g., vocabulary content, one true or one false answer to be selected, diagrams used or not used, use of antonym items, etc.) where uniformly investigated. While Scheuneman indicated that future research of this type should reduce the number of variables she had attempted to address (there were 16 hypotheses), results nonetheless suggested that basic item bias or content research across groups was a feasible way in which to answer whether differential effects "could be demonstrated through the manipulation of relatively stable characteristics of test items" (p. 116). Scheuneman (1987) presented pairs of items with the designated characteristic of a question format under study in one item and the characteristic absent or modified in the other. Paired experimental items were administered in the experimental section of the GRE General Test, given in December 1982. Results indicated that certain "item elements"—common in general form to a variety of questions—appeared to affect black and white performance differentially. For example, significant group-by-version interactions were seen for one correct true versus one correct false response and by adding/modifying prefixes/suffixes to the stimulus word in antonym items.

The question is then raised whether the items showing differential impact are measuring the content domain (e.g., verbal, quantitative, or analytical thinking) as opposed to an aspect of "element" within the presentation to some degree. Scheuneman concluded that more research along this line is needed in the future to move bias investigation into an arena whereby more systematic rules and procedures can be developed in test construction.

Another approach to the identification of biased items has been pursued by Jensen (1976). According to Jensen, if a test contains items that are disproportionately more difficult for one group of examinees than another, the correlation of P decrements between adjacent items will be low for the two groups. (P decrement refers to the difference in the difficulty index, P, from one item of a test to the next item. Typically, ability test items are arranged in ascending order of difficulty.) Jensen (1974, 1976) also contends that if a test contains biased items, the correlation between the rank order of item difficulties for one race with another will also be low. Jensen (1974, 1976, 1977) calculated cross-racial correlations of item difficulties for large samples of black and white children on five major intelligence tests: the Peabody Picture Vocabulary Test, Raven's Progressive Matrices, the Revised Stanford-Binet Intelligence Scale Form L-M, the Wechsler Intelligence Scale for Children—Revised, and the Wonderlic Personnel Test. Cross-racial correlations of P decrements were reported for several of the scales. Jensen's results are summarized in Table 1 along with the results of several other investigators also employing Jensen's methodology.

As is readily apparent in Table 1, little evidence to support any consistent content bias within any of the scales investigated was found. The consistently large magnitude of the cross-racial correlations of P decrements is impressive and indicates a general lack of content bias in the instruments as a whole. As noted previously, however, some individual items were identified as biased, yet they collectively accounted for only 2 to 5% of the variance in performance differences and showed no detectable pattern in item content.

A common practice in recent times has been the inclusion of expert testimony by professionals and members of minority groups in the development of new psychological and educational tests. The practice typically asks for an "armchair" inspection of individual items as a means of locating and expurgating biased components to the measure under development. Since, as previously noted, no detectable pattern or common characteristic of individual items statistically shown to be biased has been observed (given reasonable care in the item-writing stage), it seems reasonable to question the "armchair" or expert minority panel approach to determining biased items. The bulk of scientific data since the pioneering work of McGurk in 1951 has not supported the position that anyone can—upon surface inspection—detect the degrees to which any given item will differentially impact group performance (Shepard, 1982). Several researchers since McGurk's time have identified items as being disproportionately more difficult for minority group members than for members of the majority culture and subsequently compared their results with a panel of expert judges. Their data have provided some interesting results. However,

TABLE 1   Cross-Racial Analysis of Content Bias for Five Major Intelligence Scales

Scale	Cross-Racial Correlation of Rank Order of Item Difficulties[a]	
	Black–White Correlations[b]	White-Mexican American Correlations[b]
Peabody Picture Vocabulary Test (Jensen, 1974)	.99(.79),.98(.65)	.98(.78),.98(.66)
Raven's Progressive Matrices (Jensen, 1974)	.99(.98),.99(.96)	.99(.99),.99(.97)
Stanford-Binet Intelligence Scale (Jensen, 1976)	.96	
Wechsler Intelligence Scale for Children-Revised (Jensen, 1976)	.95	
(Sandoval, 1979)[c]	.98(.87)	.99(.91)
(Miele, 1979)(1949 WISC)	.96,.95	
Wonderlic Personnel Test (Jensen, 1977)	.94(.81)	

[a]Correlation of P decrements across race is included in paretheses if reported.
[b]Where two sets of correlations are presented, data were reported separately for males and females and are listed males first. The presence of a single correlation indicates that data were pooled across gender.
[c]Median values for the 10 WISC-R subtests excluding digit span and coding.

as will be discussed after the data are presented, participation by minority groups and other interested parties has grown to be considered as an integral part of test development (Tittle, 1982) for reasons other than "armchair" determination of bias.

After identifying the eight most racially discriminating and eight least racially discriminating items on the Wonderlic Personnel Test, Jensen (1976) asked panels of five black psychologists and five white psychologists to sort out the eight most and eight least discriminating items when only these 16 items were presented to them. The judges sorted the items at a no better than chance level. Sandoval and Miille (1979) conducted a somewhat more extensive analysis using items from the WISC-R. These two researchers had 38 black, 22 Mexican-American, and 40 white university students from Spanish, history, and education classes to identify items from the WISC-R that are more difficult for a minority child than a white child and items that are equally difficult for each group. A total of 45 WISC-R items were presented to each judge; these items included the 15 most difficult items for blacks as compared to whites, the 15

most difficult items for Mexican-Americans as compared to whites, and the 15 items showing the most nearly identical difficulty indexes for minority and white children. The judges were asked to read each question and determine whether they thought the item was (a) easier for minority than for white children, (b) easier for white than for minority children, or (c) of equal difficulty for white and minority children. Sandoval and Miille's (1979) results indicated that the judges were not able to differentiate accurately between items that were more difficult for minorities and items that were of equal difficulty across groups. The effects of the judge's ethnic background on the accuracy of item bias judgments were also considered. Minority and nonminority judges did not differ in their ability to identify accurately biased items, nor did they differ with regard to the type of incorrect identification they tended to make. Sandoval and Miille's (1979) two major conclusions were that "(1) judges are not able to detect items which are more difficult for a minority child than an Anglo child, and (2) the ethnic background of the judge makes no difference in accuracy of item selection for minority children" (p. 6).

Anecdotal evidence is also available to refute the accuracy of "armchair" analyses of test bias in item content. Far and away, the most widely cited example of a biased intelligence test item is item 6 of the WISC-R comprehension subtest: "What is the thing to do if a boy (girl) much smaller than yourself starts to fight with you?" This item is generally considered to be biased against black children in particular because of the scoring criteria. According to the item's critics, the most logical response for a black child is to "fight back," yet this is a zero-point response. The most correct, two-point response is to walk away and avoid fighting with the child, a response critics claim invites disaster in the black culture, where children are taught to fight back and would not "know" the "correct white response." Black responses to this item have been empirically investigated in several studies with the same basic results. The item is relatively easier for black children than for white children. When all items on the WISC-R are ranked separately according to difficulty level for blacks and whites, the item above is the forty-second least difficult item (where 1 represents the easiest item) for black children and the forty-seventh least difficult for white children (Jensen, 1976). Miele (1979) reached a similar conclusion, stating that this item "is relatively easier for blacks than it is for whites" (p. 163). The results of these empirical studies with large samples of black and white children is unequivocal. When matched for overall general intellectual skill, more black than white children will get this item correct (the very item most often singled out as a blatant example of the inherent bias of intelligence tests against blacks).

Even without empirical support for its validity, a number of prestigious writers support continued use of the "face validity" approach of using a panel of minority judges to identify "biased" test items (Anastasi, 1976; Kaufman, 1979b; Sandoval & Miille, 1979). Those who support the continued use of this technique see it as a method of gaining greater rapport with the public. As pointed out by Sandoval and Miille (1979), "public opinion, whether it is supported by empirical findings, or based on emotion, can serve as an obstacle to the use of a measurement instrument" (p. 7). The elimination of items that are offensive or otherwise objectionable to any substantive segment of the population for whom the test is intended seems an appropriate action that may aid in the public's acceptance of new and better psychological as-sessment tools. However, the subjective judgment approach should not be allowed to supplant the use of the more sophisticated empirical procedures in the determination of biased items. Rather, the subjective approach should serve as a supplemental procedure, and items identified through this method (provided that some interrater agreement can be obtained—an aspect of the subjective method yet to be well researched) as objectionable eliminated when a psychometrically equivalent (or better) item can be obtained as a replacement and the intent of the item kept intact (e.g., with a criterion-referenced measure, the new item must be designed to measure the same objective). The reliability, construct validity, and predictive validity of measures should not suffer any substantial losses for the purposes of increasing face validity.

Researchers such as Tittle (1982) have stressed that galvanization between statistical and face validity or judgmental camps in nonbiased test construction can occur with greater ease than one might think, given the above-cited research. Judgmental analysis allows for the *perception* of fairness in items, tests, and evaluations, and the perception should not be taken lightly. Tittle (1982) argues that "judgmental methods arise from a different, nonstatistical ground. In examining fairness or bias primarily on statistical grounds, we may again be witnessing a technical solution to a problem that is broader than the technical issues" (p. 34). Tests under construction should include definitive information concerning the nonbiased nature of the measure from a statistical standpoint in addition to support by minority groups or other interested parties who have had opportunity to inspect the test for perception of fairness. Tittle notes that Cronbach (1980) does not find the issue of fairness in the judgment sense to be outside the realm of test validation. Cronbach states: "The politicalization of testing ought not be surprising. Test data influences the fortunes of individuals and the support given to human service programs" (p. 100). Tittle (1975, 1982) argues that the general field of test development requires greater consensus regarding specific, multidimensional steps taken to formulating "fair" measures because "fairness" in testing will never be realistically viewed by the public from a unidimensional, statistical standpoint. She concludes:

In the test development setting there needs to be a closer examination and agreement on the test development process, the judgmental and statistical data that are to be developed and reported, and the decision rules used as the basis to identify the final set of test items. Such agreement would permit both users and developers to reach a conclusion as to whether a test is "fair" for a particular subgroup, e.g., minorities and women. (p. 33)

Berk (1982) has proposed a three-step process for test development that responds to many of the issues outlined by Tittle. Berk's conceptualization includes the following: (a) *judgmental review* to explore for content that is, for example, stereotypic, culture-specific, or offensive in language; (b) *statistical analyses* to detect performance discrepancies between/among groups; and (c) *posteriori analysis* of statistical data to determine whether item or test bias is present and, if so, to make appropriate adjustments. The author argues that both the way in which bias is perceived by society and the empirical methodologies used to detect bias require unification if an equitable and lasting solution to "fair" test development is to be realized.

Thus far in this section we have focused on the identificaton of biased items. Several other studies actually researching other hypotheses have provided data that are relevant to the issue of content bias of intelligence tests, specifically the WISC-R. Jensen and Figueroa (1975) investigated black–white differences in mental test scores as a function of differences in Level I (rote learning and memory) and Level II (complex cognitive processing) abilities. These researchers tested a large number of blacks and whites on the WISC-R digit-span subtest and then analyzed the data separately for digits forward and digits backward. The content of the digits forward and digits backward tasks is the same. Thus, if score differences are due only to bias in content validity, score differences across race should remain constant for the two tasks. On the other hand, since the information processing demands of the two tasks are quite different, the relative level of performance on the two tasks would not be the same if blacks and whites differ in their ability to process information according to the demands of the two tasks. Jensen and Figueroa (1975) found the latter. That is, the black—white score difference on digits backward was more than twice the magnitude of the difference for digits forward. Granted, this methodology can provide only indirect evidence regarding the content validity of an instrument; however,

its importance is in providing a different view of the issues and an alternative research strategy. Since the Jensen and Figueroa results are not indicative of any content bias in the digit-span subtest, they add to a growing body of literature that strongly suggests the lack of cultural bias in well-constructed, standardized tests.

Another study (Reynolds, 1980d) examined each of the 12 WISC-R subtests for cultural bias against blacks. Using a variation of the items by group ANOVA methodology, discussed earlier, Reynolds matched 270 black children with 270 white children from the WISC-R standardization sample on the basis of gender and WISC-R full-scale IQ. IQs were required to match within one standard error of measurement. When multiple matching cases were encountered, children were matched on the basis of socioeconomic status. Matching the two groups of children on the basis of the full-scale IQ essentially equates the two groups for overall general intellectual ability (g). By then examining black–white differences in performance on each subtest of the WISC-R, it is possible to determine which, if any, of the subtests are disproportionately difficult for blacks or whites. A significant F ratio in the multivariate analysis of variance for the 12 WISC-R subtests was followed with univariate F tests between black and white means on each of the 12 WISC-R subtests. A summary of Reynolds' (1980d) results is presented in Table 2. Blacks exceeded whites on two subtests: digit span and coding. Whites exceeded blacks in performance on three subtests: comprehension, object assembly, and mazes. A trend was apparent for blacks to perform at a higher level on the arithmetic subtest, while whites tended to exceed blacks on the picture arrangement subtest. While these results can be interpreted to indicate bias in several of the WISC-R subtests, the actual differences are very small (typically on the order of .10 to .15 standard deviations) and the amount of variance in performance associated with ethnic group membership is less than 5% in each case. The results are also reasonably consistent with Jensen's theory of mental test score differences and their relationship to Level I and Level II abilities. The digit-span and coding subtests are clearly the best measures of Level I abilities on the WISC-R, while comprehension, object assembly, and mazes are more closely associated with Level II abilities. Such findings are relatively constant across age (Reynolds, 1989).

Thus, from a large number of studies employing a wide range of methodology, a relatively clear

TABLE 2   Means, Standard Deviations, and Univariate Fs for Comparison of Performance on Specific WISC-R Subtests by Groups of Blacks and Whites Matched for WISC-R Full-Scale IQ[a]

WISC-R Variable	Blacks		Whites		D^b	F^c	p
	X	SD	X	SD			
Information	8.40	2.53	8.24	2.62	−.16	0.54	NS
Similarities	8.24	2.78	8.13	2.78	−.11	0.22	NS
Arithmetic	8.98	2.62	8.62	2.58	−.36	2.52	10
Vocabulary	8.21	2.61	8.27	2.58	+.06	.06	ns
Comprehension	8.14	2.40	8.58	2.47	+.44	4.27	.05
Digit span	9.51	3.09	8.89	2.83	+.62	6.03	.01
Picture completion	8.49	2.88	8.60	2.58	+.11	0.18	NS
Picture arrangement	8.45	2.92	8.79	2.89	+.34	1.78	.10
Block design	8.06	2.54	8.33	2.76	+.27	1.36	NS
Object Assembly	8.17	2.90	8.68	2.70	+.51	4.41	.05
Coding	9.14	2.81	8.65	2.80	−.49	4.30	.05
Mazes	8.69	3.14	9.19	2.98	+.50	3.60	.05
Verbal IQ	89.63	12.13	89.61	12.07	−.02	0.04	NS
Performance IQ	89.29	12.22	90.16	11.67	+.87	0.72	NS
Full scale IQ	88.61	11.48	88.96	11.35	+.35	0.13	NS

[a]From Reynolds (1980d).
[b]White X̄-black X̄.
[c]Degrees of freedom = 1,538.

picture emerges. Content bias in well-prepared standardized tests is irregular in its occurrence and no common characteristics of items that are found to be biased can be ascertained by expert judges (minority or nonminority). The variance in group score differences on mental tests associated with ethnic group membership when content bias has been found is relatively small (typically ranging from 2 to 5%). Even this small amount of bias has been seriously questioned as Hunter (1975) describes such findings basically as methodological artifacts. While the search for common "biased" item characteristics will continue and psychologists must pursue the public relations issue of face validity, armchair claims of cultural bias in aptitude tests have found no empirical support in a large number of actuarial studies contrasting the performance of a variety of racial groups on items and subscales of the most widely employed intelligence scales in the United States; neither differential nor single group validity has been demonstrated.

Bias in Construct Validity

There is no single method for the accurate determination of the construct validity of educational and psychological tests. The defining of bias in con-

struct validity then requires a general statement that can be researched from a variety of viewpoints with a broad range of methodology. The following rather persimonious definition is preferred: *Bias* exists in regard to construct validity when a test is shown to measure different hypothetical traits (psychological constructs) for one group than another or to measure the same trait but with differing degrees of accuracy.

As is befitting the concept of construct validity, many different methods have been employed to examine existing psychological tests and batteries of tests for potential bias in construct validity. One of the more popular and necessary empirical approaches to investigating construct validity is factor analysis (Anastasi, 1976; Cronbach, 1970). Factor analysis, as a procedure, identifies clusters of test items or clusters of subtests of psychological or educational tests that correlate highly with one another, and less so or not at all with other subtests or items. Factor analysis then allows one to determine patterns of interrelationships of performance among groups of individuals. For example, if several subtests of an intelligence scale load highly on (are members of) the same factor, then if a group of individuals score high on one of these subtests, they would be expected to score at a high level on other subtests that load highly on that factor. Psychologists attempt to determine through a review of the test content and correlates test(s) measures the same variable across populations.

Two basic approaches, each with a number of variations, have been employed to compare factor-analytic results across populations. The first approach asks how similar are the results for each group; the second, and less popular approach, asks whether the results show a statistically significant difference between groups. The most sophisticated approach to the latter question has been the work of Joreskog (1969, 1971) in simultaneous factor analysis in several populations. Joreskog employs the chi-square test for goodness of fit across the factor-analytic results for several groups to determine whether there is a "fit" or the results differ significantly across the groups. A full treatment of Joreskog's techniques are certainly beyond the scope and intent of this chapter. The computational procedure is quite complex and the comparison of factors very sensitive. Little has been done as yet in the bias literature with Joreskog's method. As computer programs for Joreskog's analyses become more available, his methodology will almost certainly be employed to compare factor structures in research on internal bias in educational and psychological tests.

Miele (1979) has demonstrated the use of a simpler method (actually developed by Jensen and presented in detail in Jensen, 1980) for testing the significance of the difference between factors for two populations that also employs the chi-square as the test statistic. In Miele's method, all factor loadings are converted to Fisher's z scores. The z scores for corresponding factors are paired by variable and then subtracted. The differences in factor loadings, now expressed as differences in z scores, are squared. The squared scores are summed and the mean derived. The mean of the squared differences is then divided by the following quantity:

$$\left(\frac{1}{N_1 - 3} + \frac{1}{N_2 - 3}\right)$$

where N_1 is the number of subjects in group 1 and N_2 is the number of subjects in group 2. This division yields the test statistic that is distributed as a chi-square with 1 degree of freedom. Miele's methodology has also received little use in the bias in assessment literature. As one part of a com-

prehensive internal analysis of test bias on the WISC, Miele (1979) compared the first principal component factor across race for blacks and whites at the preschool and first-, third-, and fifth-grade levels. This factor, often thought of as a measure of g, did not significantly differ across race at any age level. Miele's results with the WISC indicate that the factor loadings for g are essentially equivalent and that when score differences occur between groups, the differences reflect a difference on whatever is common to all variables that make up the test rather than to some personological or moderator variable that is specific to one group.

A number of techniques have been developed to measure the similarity of factors across groups. Katzenmeyer and Stenner (1977) described a technique based essentially on factor score comparisons. A factor score is a composite score derived by summing an individual's weighted scores on each variable that appears on a factor. Weights are derived from the factor analysis procedure and are directly related to the factor loadings of the variables. Katzenmeyer and Stenner proposed that factor scores be derived based on factor analysis of the combined groups of interest (e.g., factor analyze the scores of blacks and whites as a single, homogeneous groups). Then the scores of each group are factor analyzed separately and factor scores again determined. The correlation between the factor scores based on the total group analysis and the factor scores of the single group analysis is then used as an estimate of the factorial similarity of the test battery across groups. The method is actually somewhat more complex as described by Katzenmeyer and Stenner (1977) and has not been widely employed in the test bias literature, yet it is a practical technique with many utilitarian implications and should receive more attention in future literature.

The two most common methods of determining factorial similarity or factorial invariance involve the direct comparison of factor loadings across groups. The two primary techniques for this comparison are (a) to calculate a coefficient of congruence (Harman, 1976) between the loadings of corresponding factors for two groups, and (b) the simple calculation of a Pearson product-moment coefficient of correlation between the factor loadings of the corresponding factors. The latter technique, although used with some frequency, is less satisfactory than the use of the coefficient of congruence, since in the comparison of factor loadings, certain of the assumptions underlying the

Pearson r may be violated. When determining the degree of similarity of factors a value of .90 or greater is typically, though arbitrarily, taken to indicate equivalent factors (factorial invariance).

In contrast to Hilliard's (1979) strong statement that studies of factorial similarity across race have not been reported "in the technical literature," a number of such studies have appeared over the last decade, dealing with a number of different tests. The focus here will be primarily on reviewing studies comparing factor-analytic results across race for aptitude tests.

Since the WISC (Wechsler, 1949) and its successor, the WISC-R (Wechsler, 1974), have been the most widely employed individual intelligence tests with school-aged children, it is appropriate that the factor structure of these two instruments across race has received extensive investigation for normal and referral populations of children. Using a large, random sample, Reschly (1978) compared the factor structure of the WISC-R across four racially identifiable grous: whites, blacks, Mexican-Americans, and Native American Papagos, all from the southwestern United States. Consistent with the findings of prevous researchers with the 1949 WISC (Lindsey, 1967; Silverstein, 1973), Reschly (1978) reported substantial congruency of factors across race when the two-factor solutions were compared (the two-factor solution typically delineates Wechsler's a priori grouping of the subtests into a verbal and a performance, or nonverbal, scale). The 12 coefficients of congruence for comparisons of the two-factor solution across all combinations of racial groupings ranged only from .97 to .99, denoting factorial equivalence of this solution across groups. Reschly compared three-factor solutions also (three-factor solutions typically relinquish verbal comprehension, perceptual organization, and freedom from distractibility factors), finding congruence only between whites and Mexican-Americans. These findings are also consistent with previous research with the WISC (Semler & Iscoe, 1966). The g factor present in the WISC-R was shown to be congruent across race, also demonstrated by Miele (1979) for the WISC. Reschly concluded that the usual interpretation of the WISC-R full-scale IQ as a measure of overall, general intellectual ability appears to be equally appropriate for whites, blacks, Mexican-Americans, and Native American Papagos. More recently, Jensen (1985) has presented rather compelling data which argue that the black/white discrepancy seen in major tests of aptitude reflects primarily g factor abilities. Reschly also concluded that the verbal/performance scale distinction on the WISC-R is equally appropriate across race and that there is strong evidence for having confidence in the integrity of the construct validity of the WISC-R for a variety of populations.

Support for Reschly's (1978) conclusions is available from a variety of other factorial studies of the WISC and WISC-R. Applying a hierarchical factor-analytic method developed by Wherry and Wherry (1969), Vance and Wallbrown (1978) factor analyzed the intercorrelation matrix of the WISC-R subtests for 150 blacks from the Appalachian region of the United States, who had been referred to a psychoeducational clinic. The two-factor hierarchical solution determined for Vance and Wallbrown's (1978) blacks was highly similar to hierarchical factor solutions determined for the standardization sample of the WISC-R (Wallbrown, Blaha, Wallbrown, & Engin, 1975), the 1949 WISC (Blaha, Wallbrown, & Wherry, 1975), and other Weschsler scales. Vance and Wallbrown's (1978) results with the WISC-R are also consistent with a previous hierarchical factor analysis with the 1949 WISC for a group of disadvantaged blacks and whites (Vance, Huelsman, & Wherry, 1976).

Several other studies comparing the WISC-R factor structure across race for normal and referral populations of children have also provided increased support for the generality of Reschly's (1978) conclusions and rthe results of other investigators cited above. Oakland and Feigenbaum (1979) factor analyzed the 12 WISC-R subtests' intercorrelations separately for stratified (race, age, sex, SES) random samples of normal white, black, and Mexican-American children from a large urban school district of the southwestern United States. Pearson r's were calculated between corresponding factors for each group. For the g factor, the black–white correlation between factor loadings was .95, the Mexican American–White correlation was .97, and the black–Mexican American correlation was .96. Similar comparisons across all WISC-R variables produced correlations ranging only from .94 to .99. Oakland and Feigenbaum concluded that the results of their factor analyses "do not reflect bias with respect to construct validity for these three racial-ethnic . . . groups" (p. 973).

Gutkin and Reynolds (1981) determined the

factorial similarity of the WISC-R for groups of black and white children from the WISC-R standardization sample. This study is particularly important to examine in determining the construct validity of the WISC-R across race due to the sample employed in the investigation. The sample included 1868 white and 305 black children obtained in a stratified random sampling procedure designed to mimic the 1970 U.S. census data on the basis of age, sex, race, SES, geographic region of residence in the United States, and urban versus rural residence. Similarity of the WISC-R factor structure across race was investigated by comparing each of the following for the black and white groups for two- and three-factor solutions: (a) the magnitude of unique variances, (b) the pattern of subtest loadings on each factor, (c) the portion of total variance accounted for by common factor variance, and (d) the percentage of common factor variance accounted for by each factor. Coefficients of congruence comparing the unique variances, the g factor, the two-factor, and the three-factor solutions across race all achieved a value of .99. The portion of total variance accounted for by common factor variance varied negligibly for blacks and whites being 53% and 51%, respectively. The percentage of common factor variance accounted for by each factor in both the two- and three-factor solutions was also strikingly similar across these two racial groups. Gutkin and Reynolds (1981) concluded that for white and black children, the WISC-R factor structure was essentially invariant and that no evidence of single-group or differential construct validity could be found.

Reynolds and Harding (1983) examined the robustness of these conclusions under six different methods of factor comparison. Since a number of techniques are available and may not always get the same results when comparing factors across groups, Reynolds and Harding compared the factor structure derived by Gutkin and Reynolds (1981) using the most common measures of similarity. The robust nature of Gutkin and Reynolds (1981) conclusions is demonstrated clearly in Table 3. Regardless of the method of factor comparison, the structure of the WISC-R for blacks and for whites is judged to be invariant, justifying consistent interpretations of performance on these scales for blacks and whites.

Subsequent studies comparing the WISC-R factor structure for referral populations of white and Mexican-American children have also strongly

supported the construct validity of the WISC-R across race. Dean (1979b) compared three-factor WISC-R solutions across race for whites and Mexican-Americans referred due to learning problems in the regular classroom. Analyzing the 10 regular WISC-R subtests, Dean reported coefficients of congruence between corresponding factors of .84 for Factor 1 (verbal comprehension), .89 for Factor 2 (perceptual organization), and .88 for Factor 3 (freedom from distractibility). While not quite reaching the typical value of .90 required to indicate equivalent factors, Dean's results do indicate a high degree of similarity. The relative strength of the various factors was also highly consistent across race. Gutkin and Reynolds (1980) also compared two- and three-factor principal factor solutions to the WISC-R across race for referral populations of white and Mexican-American children. Gutkin and Reynolds (1980) made additional comparisons of the factor solutions derived with their referral sample to solutions derived by Reschly (1978; personal communication, 1979) and also with solutions from the WISC-R standardization sample. Coefficients of congruence for the Gutkin and Reynolds' two-factor solution for whites and Mexican-Americans were .98 and .91, respectively, for Factors 1 and 2. For the three-factor solution, the coefficients of congruence for Factors 1, 2, and 3 were .97, .85, and .91, respectively. The g factor showed a coefficient of congruence value of .99 across race. When Gutkin and Reynolds (1980) compared their solutions with those derived by Reschly (personal communication, 1979) for normal white, black, Mexican-American, and Papago children, and with results based on the WISC-R standardization sample, the coefficients of congruence all exceeded .90. When comparing three-factor solutions, the results were more varied but also supported the consistent similarity of WISC-R factor analytic results across race.

DeFries et al. (1974) administered 15 mental tests to large samples of Americans of Japanese ancestry and Americans of Chinese ancestry. After examining the pattern of intercorrelations among the 15 tests for each of these two ethnic groups, DeFries et al. concluded that the cognitive structure of the two groups was virtually identical. In reviewing this study, Willerman (1979) concluded that "the similarity in factorial structure [between the two groups] suggests that the manner in which the tests are construed by the subjects is similar regard-

TABLE 3   Indexes of Factorial Similarity for Three-Factor Solutions of the Wechsler Intelligence Scale for Children-Revised for Blacks and Whites

| | | | Index of Similarity | | | | | |
Factor	Coefficient of Congruence, Correlation Matrix	Coefficient of Congruence, Covariance Matrix	Pearson r, No Transformation	Pearson r, Fisher Transformation	Salient[a] Variable Similarity Index .10	.20	Factor[b] Score Correlation Blacks	Whites
1. Verbal Comprehension	.99	.99	.98	.98	.96	.88	.99	.99
2. Perceptual Organization	.99	.99	.95	.95	1.00	.91	.99	.99
3. Freedom from Distractibility	.99	.98	.96	.94	.91	.88	.98	.99

[a]Reported using two separate cutoff values to indicate salience, .10 as recommended by Cattell (1978) and .20 as suggested by Cattell when a conservative stance is taken.
[b]Correlations for blacks are reported between scores for each individual based on factor scores derived from formulas based on a black only analysis and scores from a total sample analysis. White correlations are from a white-only analysis compared to a total sample analysis.

less of ethnicity and that the tests are measuring the same mental abilities in the two groups" (p. 468).

At the adult level, Kaiser (1986) and Scholwinski (1985) have analyzed the WAIS-R (1981) and reported substantial similarity between factor structures for black and white samples obtained from the WAIS-R standardization data. Kaiser completed separate hierarchical analyses for all black subjects ($N = 192$) and white subjects ($N = 1664$) in the WAIS-R standardization sample and calculated coefficients of congruence of 0.999 for the general factor, 0.984 for the verbal factor, and 0.970 for the performance or nonverbal factor. Scholwinski selected 177 black and 177 white subjects from the standardization sample, closely matched on the basis of age, sex, and full-scale IQ. Separate factor analyses again showed nearly identical structures between groups. These data suggest that factor structures generated from the Wechsler format show strong similarity across black–white groups beyond childhood and adolescent levels of development.

At the preschool level, factor-analytic results also tend to show consistency of construct validity across race, although the results are less clear cut. In a comparison of separate factor analyses of the McCarthy Scales of Children's Abilities (McCarthy, 1972) for groups of black and white children, Kaufman and DiCuio (1975) concluded that the McCarthy scales showed a high degree of factorial similarity between the two races. The conclusion was not straightforward, however. Four factors were found for the blacks and three for the whites. Kaufman and DiCuio based their conclusion of factorial similarity on the finding that each "white" factor had a coefficient of congruence of .85 to .93 with one "black" factor. As has been noted, the customary, albeit arbitrary, cutoff value for indicating factorial equivalence by the coefficient of congruence is .90 (Harman, 1976; Mulaik, 1972). One black factor on the McCarthy scales had no white counterpart with a coefficient of congruence beyond .74 (the memory factor), and the black and white motor factors showed a coefficient of congruence of only .85.

When investigating the factor structure of the Weschler Preschool and Primary Scale of Intelligence (WPPSI) across race, blacks and whites showed greater consistent in factor structure than with the McCarthy scales. The two factors, essentially mirroring Wechsler's verbal and performance scales, were virtually identical between the races.

Both factors also appear closely related to the hierarchical factor solution presented by Wallbrown, Blaha, and Wherry (1973) for blacks and whites. When comparing factor analyses of the Goodenough-Harris Drawing Test scoring items, Merz (1970) found highly similar factor structures for blacks, whites, Mexican-American, and Native American Indians. Other investigators have found differences across race in the factor structures of several tests designed for preschool and primary-grade children. Goolsby and Frary (1970) factor analyzed the Metropolitan Readiness Test (MRT) and the Metropolitan Achievement Test (MAT) together for separate groups of blacks and whites, finding differences in the factor structure of this grouping of tests across race. When evaluating the experimental edition of the Illinois Test of Psycholinguistic Abilities (ITPA), Leventhal and Stedman (1970) noted differences in the factor structure of this battery for blacks and whites. Two more recent studies have clarified somewhat the issue of differential construct validity of preschool tests across race.

The MRT (Hildreth, Griffith, & McGauvran, 1969) is one of the most widely employed of all preschool screening measures and is composed of six subtests: word meaning, listening, matching, letter naming, numbers, and copying. Reynolds (1979a) had previously shown this to be essentially a one-factor (general readiness) instrument. In a subsequent study, Reynolds (1979b) compared the general factor making up the MRT across race (blacks and whites) and sex. When comparing the first principal component factor (and in this case, the only factor) of the MRT across race and sex, substantial congruency was noted. Coefficients of congruence across each pair of race/sex groupings ranged only from .92 to .99, with the lowest coefficient derived from the intraracial comparison for white females and white males. Eigenvalues and subsequently the proportion of variance accounted for by the factor were also highly similar across race and sex. Reynolds concluded that his findings supported the presence of a single general-readiness factor and the construct validity of the MRT across race and sex, indicating that the MRT measures the same abilities in the same manner for blacks, whites, males, and females. The lack of differential or single-group construct validity across sex has also been demonstrated with aptitude tests for school-aged children (Reynolds & Gutkin, 1980b).

In a more comprehensive study employing seven major preschool tests (McCarthy Draw-A-Design and Draw-A-Child, Lee-Clark Reading Readiness Tests, Tests of Basic Experiences in Language and in Math, Preschool Inventory-Revised Edition, and the MRT), Reynolds (1980a) reached a similar conclusion. A two-factor solution was determined with this battery for each of the four race/sex groups as above. Coefficients of congruence ranged only from .95 to .99 for the two-factors, and the average degree of intercorrelation was essentially the same for all groups, as were eigenvalues and the percent of variance accounted for by the factors. Reynolds (1980a) again concluded that the abilities being measured were invariant across race and that there was no evidence of differential or single-group construct validity of preschool tests across race or sex. The clear trend in studies of preschool tests' construct validity across race (and sex) is to uphold validity across groups. Such findings add support to the use of existing preschool screening measures with black and white children of both sexes in the very necessary process of early identification (Reynolds, 1979c) of potential learning and behavior problems.

As is appropriate for studies of construct validity, comparative factor analysis has not been the only method of determining whether single group or differential validity exists. Another method of investigation involves comparing internal consistency reliability estimates across groups. Internal consistency reliability is determined by the degree to which the items are all measuring a similar construct. The internal consistency reliability coefficient reflects the accuracy of measurement of the construct. To be unbiased with regard to construct validity, internal consistency estimates should be approximately equal across race. This characteristic of tests has been investigated for a number of popular aptitude tests for blacks, whites, and Mexican-Americans.

With groups of black and white adults, Jensen (1977) calculated internal consistency estimates (using the Kuder-Richardson formula 21) for the Wonderlic Personnel Test (a frequently used employment/aptitude test). KR values of .86 and .88 occurred, respectively, for blacks and whites. Using Hoyt's formula, Jensen (1974) determined internal consistency estimates of .96 on the Peabody Picture Vocabulary Test (PPVT) for each of three groups of children: blacks, whites, and Mexican-Americans. When broken down according to gender within each racial grouping, the values ranged only from .95 to .97. On Raven's colored matrices, internal consistency estimates were also quite similar across race and sex, ranging only from .86 to .91 for the six race/sex groupings. Thus, Jensen's (1974, 1977) research with three popular aptitude tests shows no signs of differential or single-group validity with regard to homogeneity of test content or accuracy of measurement across groups.

Sandoval (1979) and Oakland and Feigenbaum (1979) have extensively investigated internal consistency of the various WISC-R subtests (excluding digit span and coding, for which internal consistency analysis is inappropriate) for whites, blacks, and Mexican-Americans. Both of these studies included large samples of children, with Sandoval's (1979) including over 1000. Sandoval found internal consistency estimates to be within .04 of one another for all subtests except object assembly. This subtest was most reliable for blacks (.95), while being about equally reliable for whites (.79) and Mexican-Americans (.75). Oakland and Feigenbaum reported internal consistency estimates that never differed by more than .06 among the three groups except for object assembly again. In this instance, object assembly was most reliable for whites (.76), with about equal reliabilities for blacks (.64) and Mexican-Americans (.67). Oakland and Feigenbaum additionally compared reliabilities across sex finding highly similar values for males and females. Dean (1977) examined the internal consistency of the WISC-R for Mexican-American children tested by white examiners. Dean reported internal consistency reliability estimates consistent with, although slightly exceeding, values reported by Wechsler (1974) for the predominantly white standardization sample. The Bender-Gestalt Test has also been reported to have similar internal consistency estimates for whites (.84), blacks (.81), and Mexican-Americans (.72) and for males (.81) and females (.80) (Oakland & Feigenbaum, 1979).

Several other methods have also been used to determine the construct validity of popular psychometric instruments across race. Since intelligence is considered a developmental phenomenon, the correlation of raw scores with age has been viewed as one measure of construct validity for intelligence tests. Jensen (1976) reported that the correlation between raw scores on the PPVT and age are .79 for whites, .73 for blacks, and .67 for Mexican-Americans. For Raven's colored matrices, correlations of raw scores with age were .72

for whites, .66 for blacks, and .70 for Mexican-Americans. Thus, in regard to increases in scores with age, the tests behave in a highly similar manner for whites, blacks, and Mexican-Americans.

Another measure of differential construct validity is the comparability of items' discrimination indexes (item-total correlations, D) across groups. Correlations of D values across race and sex for the WISC-R and the Bender-Gestalt Test have been reported by Oakland and Feigenbaum (1979). For the WISC-R, D values correlated .79 between whites and blacks and .82 between whites and Mexican-Americans, which is similar to the correlation of .75 between blacks and Mexican-Americans. D values for the Bender-Gestalt correlated .95 for whites and blacks, .82 for whites and mexican-Americans, and .94 for blacks and Mexican-Americans. WISC-R D values correlated .88 across sex and the Bender values correlated .84 for males and females.

Construct validity of a large number of popular psychometric assessment instruments has been investigated across race and sex with a variety of populations of minority and white children and with a divergent set of methodologies. All roads have led to Rome. No consistent evidence of bias in construct validity has been found with any of the many tests investigated. This leads to the conclusion that psychological tests, especially aptitude tests, function in essentially the same manner across race and sex; test materials are perceived and reacted to in a similar manner; and tests measure the same construct with equivalent accuracy for blacks, whites, Mexican-Americans, and other American minorities for both sexes. Single-group and differential validity have not been found and likely are not an existing phenomenon with regard to well-constructed standardized psychological and educational tests. This means that test score differences across race are real and not an artifact of test bias. These differences cannot be ignored and, as Miele (1979) succinctly stated, "If this . . . difference [in test scores] is the result of genetic factors, acceptance of the cultural bias hypothesis would be unfortunate. If the difference is the result of environmental factors, such acceptance would be tragic" (p. 162).

Bias in Predictive or Criterion-Related Validity
Evaluating bias in predictive validity of educational and psychological tests is less related to the evaluation of group mental test score differences than to the evaluation of individual test scores in a more absolute sense. This is especially true for aptitude (as opposed to diagnostic) tests where the primary purpose of administration is the prediction of some specific future outcome or behavior. Internal analyses of bias (such as with content and construct validity) are less confounded than analyses of bias in predictive validity, however, due to the potential problems of bias in the criterion measure. Predictive validity is also strongly influenced by the reliability of criterion measures, which frequently is poor. The degree of relation between a predictor and a criterion is restricted as a function of the square root of the product of the reliabilities of the two variables.

Arriving at a consensual definition of bias in predictive validity is also a difficult task, as has already been discussed. Yet, from the standpoint of the practical applications of aptitude and intelligence tests, predictive validity is the most crucial form of validity in relation to test bias. Much of the discussion in professional journals concerning bias in predictive validity has centered around models of selection. These issues have been discussed previously in this chapter and are not reiterated here. Since this section is concerned with bias in respect to the test itself and not the social or political justifications of any one particular selection model, the Cleary et al. (1975) definition, with only slight restatement, provides a clear direct statement of test bias with regard to predictive validity: A test is considered biased with respect to predictive validity when the inference drawn from the test score is not made with the smallest feasible random error or if there is constant error in an inference or prediction as a function of membership in a particular group.

The foregoing definition of bias is a restatement of previous definitions by Cardall and Coffman (1964), Cleary (1968), and Potthoff (1966), and has been widely accepted (although certainly not without criticism: e.g., Bernal, 1975; Linn & Werts, 1971; Schmidt & Hunter, 1974; Thorndike, 1971). Oakland and Matuszek (1977) examined special education class placement procedures under a variety of models of bias in prediction and demonstrated that the smallest number of children are misplaced when the Cleary et al. conditions of fairness are met, although under legislative "quota" requirements, they favored the Thorndike (1971) conditions of selection. The Cleary regression definition is also apparently the definition espoused in government guidelines on testing and has been held in at least one recent court decision (*Cortez v. Rosen* 1975) to be the only historically, legally, and logically required condition of test fairness (Ramsay, 1979) (although apparently the judge in the Larry P. decision adopted the mean differences approach to defining bias). A variety of educational and psychological personnel have adopted the Cleary regression approach to bias, including (a) noted psychological authorities on testing (Anastasi, 1976; Cronbach, 1970; Humphreys, 1973), (b) educational and psychological researchers (Bossard, Reynolds, & Gutkin, 1980; Kallingal, 1971; Pfiefer & Sedlacek, 1971; Reynolds & Hartlage, 1978, 1979; Stanley & Porter, 1967; Wilson, 1969), (c) industrial/organizational psychologists (Bartlett & O'Leary, 1969; Einhorn & Bass, 1971; Gael & Grant, 1972; Grant & Bray, 1970; Ramsay, 1979; Tenopyr, 1967), and (d) even critics of educational and psychological testing (Goldman & Hartig, 1976a, 1976b; Kirkpatrick, 1970; Kirkpatrick, Gwen, Barrett, & Katzell, 1968).

The evaluation of bias in prediction under the Cleary et al. (1975) definition (the regression definition) is quite straightforward. With simple regressions, predictions take the form of $Y_i = aX_i + b$, where a is the regression coefficient and b is a constant. When this equation is graphed (forming a regression line), a represents the slope of the regression line and B the Y intercept. Since our definition of fairness in predictive validity requires errors in prediction to be independent of group membership, the regression line formed for any pair of variables must be the same for each group for whom predictions are to be made. Whenever the slope or the intercept differs significantly across groups, there is bias in prediction if one attempts to use a regression equation based on the combined groups. When the regression equations for two (or more) groups are equivalent, prediction is the same for all groups. This condition is referred to variously as homogeneity of regression across groups, simultaneous regression, or fairness in prediction. Homogeneity of regression across groups is illustrated in Figure 1. In this case, the single regression equation is appropriate with all groups, any errors in prediction being random with respect to group membership (i.e., residuals uncorrelated with group membership). When homogeneity of regression does not occur, for "fairness" in prediction to occur, separate regression equations must be used for each group.

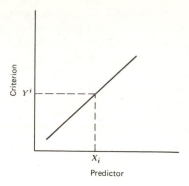

Figure 1. Equal slopes and intercepts result in homogeneity of regression that causes the regression lines for group *a*, group *b*, and the combined group *c* to be identical.

In fact, in actual clinical practice, regression equations are seldom generated for the prediction of future performance. Instead, some arbitrary, or perhaps statistically derived, cutoff score is determined, below which "failure" is predicted. For school performance, IQs two or more standard deviations below the test mean are used to infer a high probability of failure in the regular classroom if special assistance is not provided for the student in question. Essentially, then, clinicians are establishing mental prediction equations that are assumed to be equivalent across race, sex, and so on. While these mental equations cannot be readily tested across groups, the actual form of criterion prediction can be compared across groups in several ways. Errors in prediction must be independent of group membership. If regression equations are equal, this condition is met. To test the hypothesis of simultaneous regression, slopes and intercepts must both be compared. An alternative method is the direct examination of residuals through ANOVA or a similar design (Reynolds, 1980c).

In the evaluation of slope and intercept values, two basic techniques have been most often employed in the research literature. Gulliksen and Wilks (1965) described methods for separately testing regression coefficients and intercepts for significant differences across groups. Using separate, independent tests for these two values considerably increases the probability of a decision error and unnecessarily complicates the decision-making process. Potthoff (1966) has described a useful technique allowing one to test simultaneously the equivalence of regression coefficients and intercepts across K independent groups with a single F ratio. If a significant F results, the researcher may then test the slopes and intercepts separately if information concerning which value differs is desired. When homogeneity of regression does not occur, there are three basic conditions that can result: (a) intercept constants differ, (b) regression coefficients (slopes) differ, or (c) slopes and intercepts differ. These conditions are depicted pictorially in Figures 2, 3, and 4. The regression coefficient is related to the correlation coefficient between the two variables and is one measure of the strength of the relationship between two variables. When intercepts differ and regression coefficients do not, a situation such as that in Figure 2 results. Relative accuracy of prediction is the same for the two groups (a and b), yet the use of a regression equation derived by combining the two groups results in bias that works against the group with the higher mean criterion score. Since the slope of the regression line is the same for all groups, the degree of error in prediction remains constant and does not fluctuate as a function of a person's score on the independent variable. That is, regardless of group member b's score on the predictor, the degree of underprediction in performance on the criterion is the same. As illustrated in Figure 2, the use of the common regression equation results in the prediction of a criterion score of Y^c for a score of X. This score (Y^c) overestimates how well members of group a will perform and underestimates the criterion performance of members of group b.

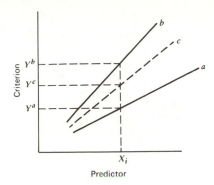

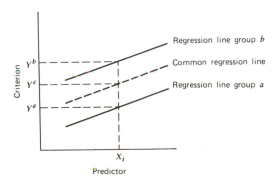

Figure 2. Equal slopes with differing intercepts result in parallel regression lines and a constant bias in prediction.

Figure 3. Equal intercepts and differing slopes result in nonparallel regression lines with the degree of bias dependent on the distance of the individual's score (x_i) from the origin.

Figure 3, nonparallel regression lines, illustrates the case where intercepts are constant across groups but the slope of the line is different for each group. Here too the group with the higher mean criterion score is typically underpredicted when a common regression equation is applied. The amount of bias is prediction that results from using the common regression line is not constant in this case but instead varies as a function of the distance of the score from the mean. The more difficult, complex case of bias is represented in Figure 4. Here we see the result of significant differences in slopes and intercepts. Not only does the amount of bias in prediction accruing from the use of a common equation vary in this instance, but the actual direction of bias can reverse, depending on the location of the individual's score in the distribution of the independent variable. Only in the case of Figure 4 do members of the group with the lower mean criterion score run the risk of having their performance on the criterion variable underpredicted by the application of a common regression equation.

A considerable body of literature has developed in recent years regarding the differential predictive validity of tests across race for employment selection and college admissions. In a recent review of 866 black–white test validity comparisons from 39 studies of test bias in personnel selection, Hunter, Schmidt, and Hunter (1979) concluded that there was no evidence to substantiate hypotheses of differential or single-group va-

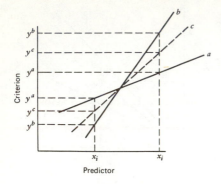

Figure 4. Differing slopes *and* intercepts result in the complex condition where the amount and the direction of the bias are a function of the distance of an individual's score from the origin.

lidity with regard to the prediction of job performance across race for blacks and whites. Other racial groupings were not examined by Hunter, Schmidt, and Hunter (1979). A similar conclusion was reached by O'Conner, Wexley, and Alexander (1975). A number of studies have also focused on differential validity of the Scholastic Aptitude Test (SAT) in the prediction of college performance (typically measured by grade-point average). In general, these studies have found either no difference in the prediction of criterion performance for blacks and whites or a bias (underprediction of the criterion) against Whites (Cleary, 1968; Cleary et al., 1975; Goldman & Hartig, 1976; Kallingal, 1971; Pfeifer & Sedlacek, 1971; Stanley, 1971; Stanley & Porter, 1967; Temp, 1971). When bias against whites has been found, the differences between actual and predicted criterion scores, while statistically significant, have been quite small. Thus far only one study has been found reporting bias against blacks in the prediction of college grade-point average from SAT scores. Bower (1970) reported that when disadvantaged black students were given special courses as freshmen, which were later included in the calculation of the college grade-point average, SAT scores significantly underpredicted these students' freshmen grade-point averages. Again, however, the actual differences turned out to be quite small even though grades earned in the special classes tended to be higher than in regular college courses. Several recent studies have investigated bias in the prediction of school performance for children.

Reschly and Sabers (1979) evaluated the validity of WISC-R IQs in the prediction of Metropolitan Achievement Test (MAT) performance (reading and math subtests) for whites, blacks, Mexican-Americans, and Native American Papagos. The choice of the MAT as a criterion measure in studies of predictive bias is particularly appropriate since item analysis procedures were employed (as described earlier) to eliminate racial bias in item content during the test construction phase. Anastasi (1976) pointed out the MAT as an exemplary model of an achievement test designed to reduce or eliminate cultural bias. The Reschly and Sabers' (1979) comparison of regression systems indicated bias in the prediction of the various achievement scores. Again, however, the bias produced generally significant underprediction of white performance when a common regression equation was applied. Achievement test performance of the Native American Papago group showed the greatest amount of overprediction of all nonwhite groups. Although some slope bias was evident, Reschly and Sabers typically found intercept bias resulting in parallel regression lines. Using similar techniques, but including teacher ratings, Reschly and Reschly (1979) also investigated the predictive validity of WISC-R factor scores with samples of white, black, Mexican-American, and Native American Papago children. A significant relationship occurred between the three WISC-R factors first delineated by Kaufman (1979a) and measures of achievement for the white and nonwhite groups with the exception of the Papagos. Significant correlations occurred between the WISC-R freedom from distractibility factor (Kaufman, 1979a) and teacher ratings of attention for all four groups. Reschly and Reschly concluded that "These data also again confirm the relatively strong relationship of WISC-R scores to achievement for most non-Anglo as well as Anglo groups" (p. 359).

Reynolds and Hartlage (1979) investigated the differential validity of full-scale IQs from the WISC-R and its 1949 predecessor, the WISC, in predicting reading and arithmetic achievement for black and for white children who had been referred by their teachers to psychological services in a rural, southern school district. Comparisons of correlations and a Potthoff analysis to test for identity of regression lines revealed no significant differences in the ability or function of the WISC or WISC-R to predict achievement for these two groups. Reynolds and Gutkin (1980b) replicated this study for the WISC-R with large groups of white and Mexican-American children from the southwest. Reynolds and Gutkin contrasted regression systems between WISC-R verbal, performance, and full-scale IQs and the "academic basics" of reading, spelling, and arithmetic. Only the regression equation between the WISC-R performance IQ and arithmetic achievement differed for the two groups. The difference in the two equations was due to an intercept bias that resulted in the overprediction of achievement for the Mexican-American children. Reynolds, Gutkin, Dappen, and Wright (1979) also failed to find differential validity in the prediction of achievement for males and females with the WISC-R.

In a related study, Hartlage, Lucas, and Godwin (1976) compared the predictive validity of what they considered to be a relatively culture-free test (the Raven matrices) with a more culture-loaded test (the 1949 WISC) for a group of low SES, disadvantaged rural children. Hartlage, Lucas, and Godwin found that the WISC had consistently larger correlations with measures of reading, spelling, arithmetic than did the Raven matrices. While not making the comparison with other groups that is necessary to draw firm conclusions, the study does support the validity of the WISC, which has been the target of many of the claims of bias in the prediction of achievement for low-SES, disadvantaged rural children. Henderson, Butler, and Goffeney (1969) also reported that the WISC and the Bender-Gestalt Test are equally effective in the prediction of reading and arithmetic achievement for white and nonwhite groups, although their study has a number of methodological difficulties, including heterogeneity of the nonwhite comparison group.

A study by Goldman and Hartig (1976b) produced quite different results with the WISC. These researchers report that when validities are calculated separately for the prediction of achievement for whites, blacks, and Mexican-Americans, the predictive validity of the WISC is good for white children but near zero for the nonwhite groups. A closer examination of the methodology of the study gives considerable insight into this unusual finding. The criterion measure, academic grade-point average, showed considerable restriction of range for the black and Mexican-American groups. Inexplicably, calculation of the academic grade-point average included, in addition to traditional academic subjects, grades from music, health, art, instrumental music, and physical education. It is clearly inappropriate to include inflated grades from such school activities in the calculation of "academic grade-point average." The use of academic grade-point average, especially in presecondary settings, is fraught with problems, including unreliability, questionable validity, and the lack of constant scaling. Teachers may be grading on some absolute scale of achievement, relative to other children in the classroom, relative to how well the teacher believes the child should be performing or on the basis of effort, motivation, or even attractiveness. Some parents will even demand stricter grading standards for their children than others. To confound the problems of academic grade-point average as a criterion, grading practices not only vary between classrooms and schools but within classrooms as well (the Goldman and Hartig children came from 14 different schools). When groups are to be combined across schools, and homogeneity of the new group then assumed, the equivalence of the schools regarding environments, academic standards, and grading practices must first be demonstrated empirically (Jensen, 1980). A variety of other problems are apparent. The predictive validities reported for white children in this study are also considerably lower than are typically reported for the WISC. Thus the contradictory nature of their study, as compared to a large number of other studies, must certainly be called into question. Studies with a number of other aptitude tests also contradict Goldman and Hartig (1976b).

Bossard et al. (1980) published the first regression analysis of test bias on the Stanford-Binet Intelligence Scale for separate groups of black and white children. Neither regression systems nor correlations differed at $p < .05$ for the prediction of the basic academic skills of reading, spelling, and arithmetic achievement for these two groups of referred children. An earlier study by Sewell (1979), while not comparing regression systems, also found no significant differences in validity coefficients for Stanford-Binet IQs predicting California Achievement Test scores for black and white first-grade children.

A series of studies comparing the predictive validity of group IQ measures across race has been reviewed by Jensen (1980) and Sattler (1974). Typically, regression systems have not been compared in these studies; instead, researchers have compared only the validity coefficients across race, a practice that tells only whether the tests can be used fairly, not whether the test is actually non-biased. The comparison of validity coefficients is nevertheless relevant since equivalence in predictive validities is a first step in evaluating differential validity. That is, if predictive validities differ, regression systems must differ, but not vice versa, since the correlation between two variables is a measure of the strength or magnitude of a relationship and does not dictate the form of a relationship. While the number of studies evaluating group IQ tests across race is small, they have typically employed extremely large samples. The Lorge-Thorndike verbal and nonverbal IQs have most often been investigated. Jensen (1980) and Sattler (1974) concluded that the few available studies suggest that standard IQ tests in current use have comparable validities for black and white children at the elementary school level.

Guterman (1979) reported on an extensive analysis of the predictive validity of the Ammons and Ammons Quick Test (QT) (a measure of verbal IQ) for children of different social classes. Social class was determined by a weighted combination of Duncan's socioeconomic index and the number of years of education of each parent. Three basic measures of scholastic attainment were employed as criterion measures: (1) the vocabulary test of the General Aptitude Test Battery (GATB), (2) the test of reading comprehension from the Gates Reading Survey, and (3) the arithmetic section of the GATB. School grades in academic subjects for grades 9, 10, and 12 were also used to examine for bias in prediction. Guterman reached similar conclusions with regard to all criterion measures across all social classes. Slopes and intercepts of regression lines did not differ across social class for the prediction of any of the criterion measures described above by the IQ derived from the QT. Several other social knowledge criterion measures were also examined. Again, slopes were constant across social class, and with the exception of sexual knowledge, intercepts were also constant. Guterman concluded that his data provide strong support for equivalent validity of IQ measures across social class. In reanalyzing the Guterman (1979) study, Gordon and Rudert (1979) reached even stronger conclusions. By analyzing the Guterman data by race within the various SES categories through a method of path analysis, Gordon and Rudert (1979) demonstrated that the QT was also not biased across race in the

prediction of academic attainment and that IQ (as determined on the QT) plays the same role in status attainment models for blacks and whites and has stronger direct effects on later status attainment than does SES. Certainly with school-aged children and adults, there is compelling evidence that differential and single-group predictive validity hypotheses must be rejected.

As with construct validity, at the preschool level the evidence is again less clear and convincing but points toward a lack of bias against minorities. Based on doubts expressed about the usefulness of customary readiness tests with students of certain racial and ethnic backgrounds and with low SES children, Mitchell (1967) investigated the predictive validity of two preschool readiness tests used in the USOE Cooperative First Grade Reading Study of 1964–1965. Chosen for study were the Metropolitan Readiness Tests, Form A (1964–1965 revision) and the Murphy-Durrell Reading Readiness Analysis (1964 revision). Mitchell's sample included 7,310 whites, 518 blacks, and 39 Mexican-Americans. Criterion measures chosen were the Stanford Achievement Test, 1963 revision, Primary I reading and spelling subtests. Mitchell's results do not support a hypothesis of lower predictive validity for nonwhites than whites on either readiness scale. Although some significant differences occurred in the obtained correlations with achievement for blacks and whites, 26 correlations were higher for blacks. Mitchell concluded that the two readiness tests perform their functions as well with black as with white children and that the general level of predictive validity was similar. This overstates the case somewhat, but since only validity coefficients and not regression systems were compared, Mitchell's (1967) study does support the predictive validity of these readiness tests across race.

Oakland (1978) recently investigated the differential predictive validity of six readiness tests (MRT, Tests of Basic Experiences Language and Concepts Subtests, Clymer-Barrett Prereading Battery, Slosson Intelligence Test, and the Slosson Oral Reading Test) across race (black, white, and Mexican-American) for middle- and lower-SES children. The Metropolitan Achievement Test (MAT), California Achievement TEST (CAT), and California Test of Mental Maturity (CTMM) served as criterion variables. Since the CTMM is an IQ test, prediction of CTMM scores by the various readiness tests is excluded from the following discussion. Although Oakland (1978) did not use any tests of statistical significance to compare the correlations between the independent- and dependent-variable pairs across race and SES, a clear pattern existed showing higher levels of prediction for white as opposed to nonwhite groups. Oakland also did not compare regression systems, limiting his study to the report of the various validity coefficients for each race/SES grouping. Oakland's (1978) results clearly indicate potential bias in the prediction of early school achievement by individual readiness or screening tests. The lower correlations for nonwhite groups, however, given their lower mean criterion scores, leads to anticipation of bias favoring nonwhites in the prediction of early school achievement.

To investigate this possibility, Reynolds (1978) conducted an extensive analysis of predictive bias for seven major preschool tests (the McCarthy Drawing Tests, Draw-A-Design, and Draw-A-Child; the Tests of Basic Experiences, Math and Language subtests; MRT; Preschool Inventory-Revised Edition; and the Lee-Clark Reading Readiness Test) across race and sex for large groups of blacks and whites. For each preschool test, validity coefficients, slopes, and intercepts were compared predicting performance on the four subtests of the Metropolitan Achievement Test as the criterion measure (word knowledge, word discrimination, reading, and arithmetic). The general advantages of the MAT as a criterion in external studies of bias was pointed out previously. In the Reynolds (1978) study, the MAT had the added advantage of being chosen by the teachers in the district where data were gathered from a large number of early achievement tests as the battery most closely measuring what was taught in their classrooms. Regression systems and validity coefficients were compared for each independent- and dependent-variable pair for white females (WF) versus white males (WM), black females (BF) versus black males (BM), WF versus BF, and WM versus BM, resulting in 112 comparisons of validity coefficients and 112 comparisons of regression systems. Mean performance on all criterion measures rank ordered WF > WM > BF > BM. The mean validity coefficients (by the Fisher z transformation) between the independent and dependent variables across the 12-month period from pre- to posttest were .59 for WF, .50 for WM, .43 for BF, and .30 for BM. Although the mean correlations were lower for blacks, the 112 comparisons of pairs of correlations revealed only three significant differences, a less-than-chance occurrence with

this number of comparisons (Sakoda, Cohen, & Beall, 1954). Using the Potthoff (1966) technique for comparing regression lines produced quite different results. Of the 112 comparisons of regression lines, 43 (38.4%) showed differences. For comparisons with race as the major variable (and sex controlled) 31 (55.2%) of the 56 comparisons showed significantly different regression lines. When race was controlled and sex comparisons conducted, 12 (21.2%) of the 56 comparisons showed significantly different regression lines. Clearly, racial bias was significantly more prevalent than sex bias ($p < .01$) in prediction. In comparing the various pretests, bias occurred most often with the Preschool Inventory and the Lee-Clark; none of the comparisons involving the MRT showed bias. Although race clearly influenced homogeneity of regression across groups, the bias in each case acted to overpredict performance of lower-scoring groups; thus the bias acted against whites and females and in favor of blacks and males. A follow-up study (Reynolds, 1980c) has indicated one potential method for avoiding bias in the prediction of early school achievement with readiness or screening measures.

Brief screening measures, especially at the preschool level, typically do not have the high level of reliability obtained by such instruments as the WISC-R or the Stanford-Binet. As discussed previously, Linn and Werts (1971) have demonstrated convincingly that poor reliability can lead to bias in prediction. Early screening measures as a rule also assess a very limited area of function rather than allowing the child to demonstrate his or her skills in a variety of areas of cognitive functioning. The one well-researched, reliable, broad-based readiness test, the MRT, has failed to show bias with regard to internal or external criteria. Comprehensive and reliable individual preschool instruments such as the WPPSI and the McCarthy scales, while showing no internal evidence of test bias, have not been researched with regard to predictive bias across race. Recently, Reynolds (1980c) examined the predictive validity of the seven preschool measures described previously when combined into a larger battery, thus increasing the scope and reliability of the assessment.

Since our definition of predictive bias requires that errors in prediction be independent of group membership, Reynolds directly examined residuals (a residual term is the remainder when the predicted score for an individual is subtracted from the person's obtained score) across race and sex when the seven-test battery was used to predict MAT scores in a multiple regression formula. Subsets of the seven-test battery were also examined. Results of a race-by-sex analysis of variance of residuals for each of the MAT subtests when the seven-test battery was employed revealed no significant differences in residuals across race and sex and no significant interactions occurred. When a subset of the larger battery was submitted to the same analysis, racial bias in prediction did not occur; however, a significant F value resulted for sex effects in the prediction of two of the four MAT subscores (word discrimination and word knowledge). Examination of the residuals for each group showed that the bias in prediction was again against the group with the higher mean criterion score; there was a consistent underprediction of performance for females. The magnitude of the effect was small, however, being on the order of .13 to .16 standard deviations. Thus at the preschool level, the only convincing evidence of bias in predictive validity is a sex, not a race effect. Although females would tend to be slightly over-identified through early screening, it is interesting to note that whereas special education classes are more blatantly sexist than racist in composition, it is boys who outnumber girls at a ratio of about 3.5 to 4 : 1. Few, if any, would argue that this disproportionate representation of males in special education is inappropriate or due to "test bias."

With regard to bias in predictive validity, the empirical evidence suggests conclusions similar to those regarding bias in content and construct validity. There is no strong evidence to support contentions of differential or single-group validity. Bias occurs infrequently and with no apparently observable pattern, except with regard to instruments of poor reliability and high specificity of test content. When bias occurs, it is consistently in the direction of favoring low-SES, disadvantaged ethnic minority children, or other low-scoring groups. Clearly, bias in predictive validity cannot account for the disproportionate number of minority group children diagnosed and placed in EMR or EMH settings.

CONCLUSION

Undoubtedly, the issue of bias in mental testing is an important one with strong historical precedence in the social sciences and, ultimately, formidable social consequences. As the history of mental measurement was at the onset closely wed to societal needs and expectations, testing in all forms has remained in the limelight, subjected to the crucible of social inspection, review, and, at times, condemnation. However, the fact that tests and measures of human aptitude and achievement continue in most modern cultures provides strong indication that the practice holds a value over and above the recurring maelstrom created over the years pertaining to test data interpretation. The ongoing controversy related to test bias and the "fair" use of measures will undoubtedly remain with the social sciences for at least as long as we intertwine the nature–nurture issue and affirm differences between/among groups in mean performance on standardized tests.

Numerous scholars in the field of psychometrics have been attempting to separate the nature–nurture issue and mean difference data from the more orderly, empirically driven specialty of bias investigation, but the separation will without doubt not be a clean one in the foreseeable future. Davis (1983) has noted that a sharp distinction has developed between the popular press and scientific literature with regard to the interpretation of mental measurement research. All too often, the former engenders thoughts of biased measures put into use for socially pernicious purposes (e.g., Gould, 1981); the latter has attempted to maintain balanced scientific analysis and inquiry in fields (i.e., psychology and education) often accused of courting political, social, and professional ideologies (Napoli, 1981; Samelson, 1974). The former appears to have created—at least—confusion in public opinion concerning the possibility of "fair" testing. The latter—reported in this chapter—has been demonstrating through a rather sizable body of data that the cultural test bias hypothesis is not a particularly strong one at present. In any event, societal scrutiny and ongoing sentiment about testing has without question served to force the psychometric community to further refine its definition of bias, to inspect practices in the construction of nonbiased measures, and to develop statistical procedures to detect bias when it is occurring. We can argue whether the social sciences have from the onset overstepped their bounds in implementing testing for social purposes before adequate data and methods were developed, but the resulting advancements made in bias technology in response to ongoing public inspection are undeniable.

Data from the empirical end of bias investigation do suggest several guidelines to follow to ensure equitable assessment. Points to consider include (a) investigation of possible referral source bias, as there is evidence that persons are not always referred for services based on impartial, objective rationales; (b) inspection of test developer data for evidence that sound statistical analyses for bias across groups to be evaluated with the measure have been completed; (c) assessment with the most reliable measure available; and (d) multiple abilities should be assessed. In other words, psychologists need to view multiple sources of accurately derived data prior to making decisions concerning children. Hopefully, this is not too far afield from what has actually been occurring in the practice of psychological assessment, although one continues to hear isolated stories of grossly incompetent placement decisions being made (Mason, 1979). This does not mean that psychologists should be blind to a child's environmental background. Information concerning the home, community, and school environment must all be evaluated in the individualized decision-making process. Exactly how this might be done is the topic of other chapters in this volume. Neither, however, can the psychologist ignore the fact that low-IQ ethnic, disadvantaged children are just as likely to fail academically as are white, middle-class, low-IQ children, provided that their environmental circumstances remain constant. Indeed, it is the purpose of the assessment process to beat the prediction, to provide insight into hypotheses for environmental interventions that prevent the predicted failure.

A philosophical perspective is emerging in the bias literature that is not only demanding test developers to demonstrate in publication whether their measures demonstrate differential content, construct, and predictive validity across groups prior to publication, but also incorporate in some form content analyses by interested groups to ensure that offending materials are omitted. Although there are no sound empirical data to suggest that persons can determine biased items from a statistical standpoint upon surface inspection, the synergistic relationship between test use and pure psychometrics must be acknowledged and accommodated in orderly fashion before tests gain greater acceptance within society. Ideally, a clear consensus on "fairness" (and steps taken to reach this end) is needed between those persons with more subjective concerns and those interested

in gathering objective bias data during and after test construction. Accommodation along this line would ultimately ensure that all parties interested in any given test are of the opinion that the measure in question is nonbiased and that the steps taken to achieve "fairness" could be held up to public scrutiny without reservation. Given the significant and reliable methods developed over the last several decades in bias research, it is untenable at this point to subjugate statistical analyses in favor of "armchair" determination of bias. Test authors and publishers need to demonstrate factorial invariance across all groups for whom the test is designed in order to make the instrument more readily interpretable. Comparisons of predictive validity across race and sex during the test development phase are also needed. With the exception of some recent achievement tests, this has not been common practice, yet it is at this stage where tests can be altered through a variety of item-analysis procedures to eliminate any apparent racial or sexual bias.

A variety of criteria must be explored further before the question of bias is empirically resolved. Many different achievement tests and teacher-made, classroom-specific tests need to be employed in future studies of predictive bias. The entire area of differential validity of tests in the affective domain is in need of exploration. With the exception of a few limited studies of differential construct validity (e.g., Katzenmeyer & Stenner, 1977; Ozehosky & Clark, 1971) little work has been done evaluating the validity of psychologists' interpretations of children's objective personality test data across race and sex. This is an important area for examination as more objective determinations of emotional disturbance are required. It will also be important to stay abreast of methodological advances that may make it possible to resolve some of the current issues and to identify common characteristics among those now seen as irregular or random infrequent findings of bias.

REFERENCES

Alley, G., & Foster, C. (1978). Nondiscriminatory testing of minority and exceptional children. *Focus on Exceptional Children, 9,* 1–14.

American Psychological Association. (1970). Psychological assessment and public policy. *American Psychologist, 31,* 264–266.

Anastasi, A. (1976). *Psychological testing* (4th ed.). New York: Macmillan.

Angoff, W. H. (1976). Group membership as a predictor variable: A comment on McNemar. *American Psychologist, 31,* 612.

Angoff, W. H., & Ford, S. R. (1973). Item-race interaction on a test of scholastic aptitude. *Journal of Educational Measurement, 10,* 95–106.

Auerbach, A. G. (1971). The social control of learning disabilities. *Journal of Learning Disabilities, 4,* 25–34.

Bartlett, C. J., & O'Leary, B. S. (1969). A differential prediction model to moderate the effect of heterogeneous groups in personnel selection. *Personnel Psychology, 22,* 1–18.

Bass, A. R. (1976). The "equal risk" model: A comment on McNemar. *American Psychologist, 31,* 611–612.

Bayley, N. (1969). *Bayley scales of infant development.* New York: Psychological Corporation.

Beauchamp, D. P., Samuels, D. D., & Griffore, R. J. (1979). WISC-R Information and Digit Span scores of American and Canadian children. *Applied Psychological Measurement, 3,* 231–236.

Berk, R. A. (ed.) (1982), *Handbook of methods for detecting test bias,* Baltimore, MD: Johns Hopkins University Press.

Bernal, E. M. (1975). A response to "Educational uses of tests with disadvantaged students." *American Psychologist, 30,* 93–95.

Blaha, J., Wallbrown, F., & Wherry, R. J. (1975). The hierarchial factor structure of the Wechsler Intelligence Scale for Children. *Psychological Reports, 35,* 771–778.

Bogen, J. E., DeZure, R., Tenhouten, N., & Marsh, J. (1972). The other side of the brain IV: The A/P ratio. *Bulletin of the Los Angeles Neurological Society, 37,* 49–61.

Bond, L. (1981). Bias in mental tests. In B. F. Green (Ed.), *Issues in testing: Coaching, disclosure, and ethnic bias.* San Francisco: Jossey-Bass.

Bossard, M. D., Reynolds, C. R., & Gutkin, T. B. (1980). A regression analysis of test bias on the Stanford-Binet Intelligence Scale. *Journal of Clinical Child Psychology, 9,* 52–54.

Bower, E. M. (1970). The three-pipe problem: Promotion of competent human beings through a pre-school, kindergarten, program and other sundry elementary matters. In G. J. Williams & S. Gordon (Eds.), *Clinical child psychology: Current practices and future perspectives.* New York: Behavioral Publications.

Burrill, L. E. (1975 December). *Statistical evidence of potential bias in items and tests assessing current educational status.* Paper presented at the annual meeting of the Southeastern Conference on Measurement in Education, New Orleans.

Cardall, C., & Coffman, W. E., (1964). *A method of comparing the performance of different groups on the items in a test* (Research Bulletin 64–61). Princeton, NJ: Educational Testing Service.

Cattell, R. B. (1978). Are culture fair intelligence tests possible and necessary? *Journal of Research and Development in Education, 12,* 3–13.

Chinn, P. C. (1979). The exceptional minority child: Issues and some answers. *Exceptional Children, 46,* 532–536.

Clarizio, H. F. (1978). Nonbiased assessment of minority group children. *Measurement and Evaluation in Guidance, 11,* 106–113.

Cleary, T. A. (1968). Test bias: Prediction of grades of Negro and white students in integrated colleges. *Journal of Educational Measurement, 5,* 118–124.

Cleary, T. A., & Hilton, T. L. (1968). An investigation of item bias. *Educational and Psychological Measurement, 28,* 61–75.

Cleary, T. A., Humphreys, L. G., Kendrick, S. A., & Wesman, A. (1975). Educational uses of tests with disadvantaged students. *American Psychologist, 30,* 15–41.

Cortez v. Rosen (1975). United States District Court of Northern District of California. (not reported in FEP).

Council for Exceptional Children. (1978). Minorities position policy statements. *Exceptional Children, 45,* 57–64.

Critchley, D. L. (1979). The adverse influence of psychiatric diagnostic labels on the observation of child behavior. *American Journal of Orthopsychiatry, 49,* 157–160.

Cronbach, L. J. (1970). *Essentials of psychological testing.* New York: Harper & Row.

Cronbach, L. J. (1976). Equity in selection—Where psychometrics and political philosophy meet. *Journal of Educational Measurement, 13,* 31–42.

Cronbach, L. J. (1980). Validity on parole: How can we go straight? In W. B. Schraeder (Ed.), *New directions for testing and measurement: No. 5—Measuring achievement: Progress over a decade.* San Francisco: Jossey-Bass.

Darlington, R. B. (1971). Another look at "cultural fairness." *Journal of Educational Measurement, 8,* 71–82.

Darlington, R. B. (1976). A defense of rational personnel selection, and two new methods. *Journal of Educational Measurement, 13,* 43–52.

Darlington, R. B. (1978). Cultural test bias: Comments on Hunter and Schmidt. *Psychological Bulletin, 85,* 673–674.

Dean, R. S. (1977). Reliability of the WISC-R with Mexican-American children. *Journal of School Psychology, 15,* 267–268.

Dean, R. S. (1979a). Distinguished patterns for Mexican-American children on the WISC-R. *Journal of Clinical Psychology, 35,* 790–794.

Dean, R. S. (1979b, September). *WISC-R factor structure for Anglo and Hispanic children.* Paper presented to the annual meeting of the American Psychological Association, New York.

DeFries, J. C., Vandenberg, S. G., McClearn, G. E., Kuse, A. R., Wilson, J. R., Ashton, G. C., & Johnson, R. C. (1974). Near identify of cognitive structure in two ethnic groups. *Science, 183,* 338–339.

Dershowitz, Z., & Frankel, Y. (1975). Jewish culture and the WISC and WAIS test patterns. *Journal of*

Consulting and Clinical Psychology, 43, 126–134.

Diana v. California State Board of Education, (F. Supp. N.D. Cal. 1970).

Dworkin, N., & Dworkin, Y. (1979). The legacy of Pygmalion in the classroom. *Phi Delta Kappan, 61,* 712–715.

Ebel, R. L. (1979). Intelligence: A skeptical view. *Journal of Research and Development in Education, 12,* 14–21.

Eells, K., Davis, A., Havighurst, R. J., Herrick, V. E., & Typer, R. W. (1951). *Intelligence and culture differences.* Chicago: University of Chicago Press.

Einhorn, H. J., & Bass, A. R. (1971). Methodological considerations relevant to discrimination in employment testing. *Psychological Bulletin, 75,* 261–269.

Fancher, R. E. (1979). *Pioneers of psychology.* New York: W. W. Norton.

Flaugher, R. L. (1978). The many definitions of test bias. *American Psychologist, 33,* 671–679.

Flaugher, R. L., & Schrader, W. B. (1978). *Eliminating differentially difficult items as an approach to test bias* (RB-78-4). Princeton, NJ: Educational Testing Service.

Foster, G., & Ysselkyke, J. (1976). Expectancy and halo effects as a result of artificially induced teacher bias. *Contemporary Educational Psychology, 1,* 37–45.

Freeman, F. N. (1926). *Mental tests: Their history, principles and applications.* Boston: Houghton Mifflin.

Gael, S., & Grant, D. L. (1972). Employment test validation for minority and non-minority telephone company service representatives. *Journal of Applied Psychology, 56,* 135–139.

Gerber, M., & Dean, R. F. (1957). Gesell tests on African children. *Pediatrics, 20,* 1055–1065.

Goldman, R. D., & Hartig, L. K. (1976a). Predicting the success of black, Chicano, Oriental, and white college students. *Journal of Educational Measurement, 13,* 107–117.

Goldman, R. D., & Hartig, L. K. (1976b). The WISC may not be a valid predictor of school performance for primary-grade minority children. *American Journal of Mental Deficiency, 80,* 583–587.

Goolsby, T. M., & Frary, R. B. (1970). Validity of the Metropolitan Readiness Test for white and Negro students in a southern city. *Educational and Psychological Measurement, 30,* 443–450.

Gordon, R. A., & Rupert, E. E. (1979). Bad news concerning IQ tests. *Sociology of Education, 52,* 174–190.

Gould, S. J. (1981). *The mismeasure of man.* New York: W.W. Norton.

Grant, D. L., & Bray, D. W. (1970). Validation of employment tests for telephone company installation and repair occupations. *Journal of Applied Psychology, 54,* 7–14.

Griggs et al. v. Duke Power Company, U.S. 124 (1970).

Gross, A. L., & Su, W. (1975). Defining a "fair" or "unbiased" selection model. *Journal of Applied Psychology, 60,* 345–351.

Gross, M. (1967). *Learning readiness in two Jewish groups.* New York: Center for Urban Education.

Gulliksen, H., & Wilks, S. S. ?1965). Regression tests for several samples. *Psychometrika, 15,* 91–114.

Guterman, S. S. (1979). IQ tests in research on social stratification: The cross-class validity of the tests as measures of scholastic aptitude. *Sociology of Education, 52,* 163–173.

Gutkin, T. B., & Reynolds, C. R. (1980). Factorial similarity of the WISC-R for Anglos and Chicanos referred for psychological services. *Journal of School Psychology, 18,* 34–39.

Gutkin, T. B., & Reynolds, C. R. (1981). Factorial similarity of the WISC-R for white and black children from the standardization sample. *Journal of Educational Psychology, 73,* 227–231.

Gutkin, T. B., & Tieger, A. G. (1979). Funding patterns for exceptional children: Current approaches and suggested alternatives. *Professional Psychology, 10,* 670–680.

Harman, H. (1976). *Modern factor analysis* (2nd ed.). Chicago: University of Chicago Press.

Harrington, G. M. (1968a). Genetic–environmental interaction in "intelligence:" I. Biometric genetic analysis of maze performance of *Rattus norvegicus. Developmental Psychobiology, 1,* 211–218.

Harrington, G. M. (1968b). Genetic–environmental interaction in "intelligence": II. Models of behavior, components of variance, and research strategy. *Developmental Psychobiology, 1,* 245–253.

Harrington, G. M. (1975). Intelligence tests may favour the majority groups in a population. *Nature, 258,* 708–709.

Harrington, G. M. (1976 September). *Minority test bias as a psychometric artifact: The experimental evidence.* Paper presented at the annual meeting of the American Psychological Association, Washington, DC.

Hartlage, L. C., Lucas, T., & Godwin, A. (1976). Culturally biased and culture fair tests correlated with school performance in culturally disadvantaged children. *Journal of Clinical Psychology, 32,* 235–237.

Heidbreder, E. (1933). *Seven psychologies.* Englewood Cliffs, NJ: Prentice-Hall.

Henderson, N. B., Butler, B. B., & Goffeney, B. (1969). Effectiveness of the WISC and Bender-Gestalt test in predicting arithmetic and reading achievement for white and non-white children. *Journal of Clinical Psychology, 25,* 268–271.

Hildreth, G. H., Griffith, N. L., & McGauvran, M. E. (1969). *Metropolitan Readiness Tests.* New York: Harcourt Brace Jovanovich.

Hilliard, A. G. (1979). Standardization and cultural bias as impediments to the scientific study and validation of "intelligence." *Journal of Research and Development in Education, 12,* 47–58.

Hobbs, N. R. (1975). *The future of children.* San Francisco: Jossey-Bass.

Hobson v. Hansen, 269 F. Supp. 401, (D.D.C. 1967).

Humphreys, L. G. (1973). Statistical definitions of test validity for minority groups. *Journal of Applied Psychology, 58,* 1–4.

Hunter, J. E. (1975 December), *A critical analysis of the use of item means and item-test correlations to determine the presence or absence of content bias in achievement test items.* Paper presented at the National Institute of Education Conference on Test Bias, Annapolis, MD.

Hunter, J. E., & Schmidt, F. L. (1976). Critical analysis of the statistical and ethical implications of various definitions of test bias. *Psychological Bulletin, 83,* 1053–1071.

Hunter, J. E., & Schmidt, F. L. (1978). Bias in defining test bias: Reply to Darlington. *Psychological Bulletin, 85,* 675–676.

Hunter, J. E., Schmidt, F. L., & Hunter, R. (1979). Differential validity of employment tests by race. A comprehensive review and analysis. *Psychological Bulletin, 86,* 721–735.

Hunter, J., Schmidt, F., & Rauschenberger, J. (1984). Methodological, statistical, and ethical issues in the study of bias in mental testing. In C. R. Reynolds & R. T. Brown (Eds.), *Perspectives on bias in mental testing* (pp. 41–101). New York: Plenum Press.

Jackson, G. D. (1975). Another psychological view from the Association of Black Psychologists. *American Psychologist, 30,* 88–93.

Jacobs, W. R. (1978). The effect of the learning disability label on classroom teachers' ability objectively to observe and interpret child behaviors. *Learning Disabilities Quarterly, 1,* 50–55.

Jensen, A. R. (1974). How biased are culture-loaded tests? *Genetic Psychology Monographs, 90,* 185–224.

Jensen, A. R. (1976). Test bias and construct validity. *Phi Delta Kappan, 58,* 340–346.

Jensen, A. R. (1977). An examination of culture bias in the Wonderlic Personnel Test. *Intelligence, 1,* 51–64.

Jensen, A. R. (1980). *Bias in mental testing.* New York: Free Press.

Jensen, A. R. (1985). The nature of the black–white difference on various tests: Spearman's hypothesis. *Behavioral and Brain Sciences, 8,* 193–263.

Jensen, A. R., & Figueroa, R. A. (1975). Forward and backward Digit-Span interaction with race and IQ. *Journal of Educational Psychology, 67,* 882–893.

Joreskog, K. G. (1969). A general approach to confirmatory maximum likelihood factor analysis. *Psychometrika, 34,* 183.

Joreskog, K. G. (1971). Simultaneous factor analysis in several populations. *Psychometrika, 36,* 409–426.

Kaiser, S. M. (1986). *Ability patterns of black and white adults on the Wechsler Adult Intelligence Scale—Revised independent of general intelligence and as a function of socioeconomic status.* Unpublished doctoral dissertation, Texas A & M University.

Kallingal, A. (1971). The prediction of grades for black and white students at Michigan State University. *Journal of Educational Measurement, 8,* 263–265.

Katzenmeyer, W. G., & Stenner, A. J. (1977). Estimation of the invariance of factor structures across sex and race with implications for hypothesis testing. *Educational and Psychological Measurement, 37,* 111–119.

Kaufman, A. S. (1979a). Cerebral specialization and intelligence testing. *Journal of Research and Development in Education, 12,* 96–108.

Kaufman, A. S. (1979b, October). *The future of psychological assessment and its relationship to school psychology.* Invited address to the 4th annual Midwestern Conference on Psychology in the Schools, Boys Town, NE.

Kaufman, A. S., & DiCuio, R. (1975). Separate factor analyses of the McCarthy Scales for groups of black and white children. *Journal of School Psychology, 13,* 10–18.

Kennedy, D. A. (1978). Rationality, emotionality, and testing. *Journal of School Psychology, 16,* 16–24.

Kirkpatrick, J. J. (1970, September). *The psychological testing establishement: Vested interest versus responsibility.* Paper presented at the annual meeting of the American Psychological Association, Miami Beach.

Kirkpatrick, J. J., Gwen, R. G., Barrett, R. S., & Katzell, R. A. *Testing and fair employment.* New York: New York University Press.

Kohs, S. C. (1923). *Intelligence measurement.* New York: Macmillan.

Larry, P. v. Riles, 343 F. Supp. 1306 (N.D. Cal. 1972) Aff'd 502 F.2d 963 (9th Cir. 1974); 495 F. Supp. 926.

Leiderman, P. H., Babu, B., Kagia, J., Kraemer, H. C., & Leiderman, F. G. (1973). African infant precocity and some social influences during the first year. *Nature, 242,* 247–249.

Leventhal, D. S., & Stedman, D. J. (1970). A factor analytic study of the Illinois Test of Psycholinguistic Abilities. *Journal of Clinical Psychology, 26,* 473–477.

Lewontin, R. C. (1970). Race and intelligence. *Bulletin of the Atomic Scientists, 26,* 2–8.

Lindsey, J. (1967). *The factorial organization of intelligence in children as related to the variables of age, sex, and subculture.* Unpublished doctoral dissertation, University of Georgia.

Linn, R. L. (1976). In search of fair selection procedures. *Journal of Educational Measurement, 13,* 53–58.

Linn, R. L., & Werts, C. E. (1971). Considerations for studies of test bias. *Journal of Educational Measurement, 8,* 1–4.

Loehlin, J., Lindzey, G., & Spuhler, J. N. (1975). *Race differences in intelligence.* San Francisco: W. H. Freeman.

MacArthur, R. S. (1968). Some differential abilities of northern Canadian youth. *International Journal of Psychology, 3,* 43–51.

MacMillan, D. L., Jones, R. L., & Aloia, G. F. (1974). The mentally retarded label: A theoretical analysis and review of research. *American Journal of Mental Deficinece, 79,* 241–261.

Marjoribanks, K. (1972). Ethnic and environmental influences on mental abilities. *American Journal of Sociology, 78,* 323–337.

Mason, E. J. (1979). A blessing dressed up like the plague? *School Psychologist, 35*(2), 6.

McCarthy, D. (1972). *McCarthy Scales of Children's Abilities.* New York: Psychological Corporation.

McCoy, S. A. (1976). Clinical judgements of normal childhood behaviors. *Journal of Consulting and Clinical Psychology, 44,* 710–714.

McGurk, F. V. J. (1951). *Comparison of the performance*

of Negro and white high school seniors on cultural and noncultural psychological test questions. Washington, DC: Catholic University of America Press.

McNemar, Q. (1975). On so-called test bias. *American Psychologist, 30,* 848–851.

Mercer, J. R. (1976, August). *Cultural diversity, mental retardation, and assessment: The case for non-labeling.* Paper presented at the 4th International Congress of the International Association for the Scientific Study of Mental Retardation, Washington, DC.

Mercer, J. R. (1979). In defense of racially and culturally nondiscriminatory assessment. *School Psychology Digest, 8,* 89–115.

Merz, W. R. (1970). *A factor analysis of the Good-enough-Harris drawing test across four ethnic groups.* Doctoral dissertation, University of Michigan, Ann Arbor. University Microfilms No. 70–19, 714)

Miele, F. (1979). Cultural bias in the WISC. *Intelligence, 3,* 149–164.

Minton, H. L., & Schneider, F. W. (1980). *Differential psychology.* Monterey, CA: Brooks/Cole.

Mitchell, B. C. (1967). Predictive validity of the Metropolitan Readiness Tests and the Murphy-Durrell Reading Analysis for white and for Negro pupils. *Educational and Psychological Measurement, 27,* 1047–1054.

Mulaik, S. A. (1972). *The foundation of factor analysis.* New York: McGraw-Hill.

Nichols, R. C. (1978). Policy implications of the IQ controversy. In L. S. Schulman (Ed.), *Review of research in education* (Vol. 6). Itasca, IL: Peacock.

Novick, M. R., & Petersen, N. S. (1976). Towards equalizing educational and employment opportunity. *Journal of Educational Measurement, 13,* 77–88.

Oakland, T. (1978). Predictive validity of readiness tests for middle and lower socioeconemic status Anglo, black and Mexican American children. *Journal of Educational Psychology, 70,* 574–582.

Oakland, T., & Feigenbaum, D. (1979). Multiple sources of test bias on the WISC-R and the Bender-Gestalt Test. *Journal of Consulting and Clinical Psychology, 47,* 968–974.

O'Conner, E. J., Wexlery, K. N., & Alexander, R. A. (1975). Single group validity: Fact or fallacy. *Journal of Applied Psychology, 60,* 352–355.

Ozehosky, R. J., & Clark, E. T. (1971). Verbal and nonverbal measures of self-concept among kindergarten boys and girls. *Psychological Reports, 28,* 195–199.

Petersen, N. S., & Novick, M. R., (1976). An evaluation of some models for culture fair selection, *Journal of Educational Measurement, 13,* 3–29.

Pfeifer, C. M., & Sedlacek, W. E. (1971). The validity of academic predictors for black and white students at a predominantly white university. *Journal of Educational Measurement, 8,* 253–261.

Pintner, R. (1923). *Intelligence testing.* New York: Holt.

Pintner, R., & Keller, R. (1922). Intelligence tests of foreign children. *Journal of Educational Psychology, 13,* 214–222.

Plake, B., & Hoover, H. (1979, September). A meth-odology for identifying biased achievement test items that removes the confounding in a items by groups interaction due to possible group differences in instructional level. Paper presented at the annual meeting of the American Educational Research Association, Toronto.

Potthoff, R. F. (1966). *Statistical aspects of the problem of biases in psychological tests* (Institutes of Statistics Mimeo Series No. 479). Chapel Hill, NC: University of North Carolina, Department of Statistics.

Pressey, S. L., & Pressey, L. L. (1922). *Introduction to the use of standardized tests.* Yonkers, NY: World.

Ramsay, R. T. (1979). *The testing manual: A guide to test administration and use.* Pittsburgh, PA: Author.

Reschly, D. J. (1978). WISC-R factor structures among Anglos, blacks, Chicanos, and Native American Papagos. *Journal of Consulting and Clinical Psychology, 46,* 417–422.

Reschly, D. J. (1980). Concepts of bias in assessment and WISC-R research with minorities. In H. Vance and F. Wallborwn (Eds.), *WISC-R: Research and interpretation.* Washington, DC: National Association of School Psychologists.

Reschly, D. J., & Reschly, J. E. (1979). Validity of WISC-R factor scores in predicting achievement and attention for four sociocultural groups. *Journal of School Psychology, 17,* 355–361.

Reschly, D. J., & Sabers, D. (1979). Analysis of test bias in four groups with the regression definition. *Journal of Educational Measurement, 16,* 1–9.

Reynolds, C. R. (1978). *Differential validity of several preschool assessment instruments for blacks, whites, males, and females.* Unpublished doctoral dissertation, University of Georgia, Athens.

Reynolds, C. R. (1979a). A factor analytic study of the Metropolitan Readiness Test. *Contemporary Educational Psychology, 4,* 315–317.

Reynolds, C. R. (1979b). The invariance of the factorial validity of the Metropolitan Readiness Tests for blacks, whites, males and females. *Educational and Psychological Measurement, 39,* 1047–1052.

Reynolds, C. R. (1979c). Should we screen pre-schoolers? *Contemporary Educational Psychology, 4,* 175–181.

Reynolds, C. R. (1980a). Differential construct validity of a preschool battery for blacks, whites, males and females. *Journal of School Psychology, 18,* 112–125.

Reynolds, C. R. (1980b, April). *Differential predictive validity of a preschool battery across race and sex.* Paper presented at the annual meeting of the American Educational Research Association, Boston.

Reynolds, C. R. (1980c). A examination for test bias in a preschool battery across race and sex. *Journal of Educational Measurement, 17,* 137–146.

Reynolds, C. R. (1980d, September). *Patterns of intellectual abilities among blacks and whites matched for "g."* Paper presented at the annual meeting of the American Psychological Association, Montreal.

Reynolds, C. R. (1989, August). *Are there racially identifiable ability patterns across the lifespan?* Invited address to the annual meeting of the Americal Psychological Association, New Orleans.

Reynolds, C. R., Bossard, M. D., & Gutkin, T. B. (1980, April). *A regression analysis of test bias on the Stanford-Binet Intelligence Scale.* Paper presented at the annual meeting of the American Educational Research Association, Boston.

Reynolds, C. R., & Brown, R. T. (Eds.). (1984). *Perspectives on bias in mental testing.* New York: Plenum Press.

Reynolds, C. R., & Gutkin, T. B. (1980a). A regression analysis of test bias on the WISC-R for Anglos and Chicanos referred to psychological services. *Journal of Abnormal Child Psychology, 8,* 237–243.

Reynolds, C. R., & Gutkin, T. B. (1980b). Stability of the WISC-R factor structure across sex at low age levels. *Journal of Clinical Psychology, 36,* 775–777.

Reynolds, C. R., Gutkin, T. B., Dappen, L., & Wright, D. (1979). Differential validity of the WISC-R for boys and girls referred for psychological services. *Perceptual and Motor Skills, 48,* 868–879.

Reynolds, C. R., & Harding, R. E. (1983). Outcome in two large sample studies of factorial similarity under six methods of comparison. *Educational and Psychological Measurement, 43*(3), 723–728.

Reynolds, C. R., & Hartlage, L. C. (1978, March). *Comparison of WISC and WISC-R racial regression lines.* Paper presented at the annual meeting of the Southeastern Psychological Association, Atlanta.

Reynolds, C. R., & Hartilage, L. C. (1979). Comparision of WISC and WISC-R regression lines for academic prediction with black and with white referred children. *Journal of Consulting and Clinical Psychology, 47,* 589–591.

Reynolds, C. R., McBride, R. D., & Gibson, L. J. (1979, March). *Black-Shite IQ discrepancies may be related to differencs in hemisphericity.* Paper presented at the annual meeting of the National Association of School Psychologists, San Diego.

Ross, A. O. (1974). A clinical child psychologist "examines" retarded children. In G. J. Williams and S. Gordon (Eds.), *Clinical child psychology: Current trends and future perspectives.* New York: Behavioral Publications.

Ross, A. O. (1976). *Psychological aspects of learning disabilities and reading disorders.* New York: McGraw-Hill.

Sakoda, J. M., Cohen, B. H., & Beall, G. (1954). Test of significance for a series of statistical tests. *Psychological Bulletin, 51,* 172–175.

Sandoval, J. (1979). The WISC-R and internal evidence of test bias with minority groups. *Journal of Consulting and Clinical Psychology, 47,* 919–927.

Sandoval, J., & Millie, M. (1979, September). *Accuracy judgements of WISC-R item difficulty for minority groups.* Paper presented at the annual meeting of the American Psychological Association, New York.

Sattler, J. M. (1974). *Assessment of children's intelligence.* Philadelphia: W. B. Saunders.

Sawyer, R. L., Cole, N. S., & Cole, J. W. (1976). Utilities and the issue of fairness in a decision theoretic model for selection. *Journal of Educational Measurement, 13,* 59–76.

Scheuneman, J. D. (1987). An experimental, exploratory study of causes of bias in test items. *Journal of Educational Measurement, 29,* 97–118.

Schmidt, F. L., & Hunter, J. E. (1974). Racial and ethnic bias in psychological tests: Divergent implications of two definitions of test bias. *American Psychologist, 29,* 1–8.

Schmidt, W. H. (1983). Content biases in achievement tests. *Journal of Educational Measurement, 20,* 165–178.

Scholwinski, E. J. (1985). *Ability patterns of white and black adults as determined by the subscales on the Wechsler Adult Intelligence Scale—Revised.* Unpublished doctoral dissertation, Texas A & M University.

Semler, I., & Iscoe, I. (1966). Structure of intelligence in Negro and white children. *Journal of Educational Psychology, 57,* 326–336.

Sewell, T. E. (1979). Intelligence and learning tasks as predictors of scholastic achievement in black and white first-grade children. Journal of School Psychology, 17, 325–332.

Shepard, L. A. (1982). Definitions of bias. In R. A. Berk (Ed.), *Handbook of methods for detecting test bias.* Baltimore: Johns Hopkins University Press.

Shuey, A. M. (1966). *The testing of Negro intelligence* (2nd ed.). New York: Social Science Press.

Silverstein, A. B. (1973). Factor structure of the Wechsler Intelligence Scale for children for three ethnic groups. *Journal of Educational Psychology, 65,* 408–410.

Stanley, J. C. (1969). Plotting ANOVA interactions for ease of visual interpretation. *Educational and Psychological Measurement, 29,* 793–797.

Stanley, J. C. (1971). Predicting college success of the educationally disadvantaged. *Science, 171,* 640–647.

Stanley, J. C., & Porter, A. C. (1967). Correlation of scholastic aptitude test scores with college grades for Negroes vs. whites. *Journal of Educational Measurement, 4,* 199–218.

Temp, G. (1971). Validity of the SAT for blacks and whites in thirteen integrated institutions. *Journal of Educational Measurements, 8,* 245–251.

Tenopyr, M. L. (1967, September). *Race and socioeconomic status as moderators in predicting machine-shop training success.* Paper presented at the annual meeting of the American Psychological Association, Washington, DC.

Thorndike, R. L. (1971). Concepts of culture-fairness. *Journal of Educational Measurement, 8,* 63–70.

Tittle, C. K. (1975). Fairness in educational achievement testing. *Education and Urban Society, 8,* 86–103.

Tittle, C. K. (1982). Use of judgemental methods in item bias studies. In R. A. Berk (ed.), *Handbook of methods for detecting test bias.* Baltimore: John Hopkins University Press.

Torrance, E. P., (1980). Psychology of gifted children and youth. In W. M. Cruickshank (Ed.), *Psychology of Exceptional Children and Youth,* Englewood Cliffs, NJ: Prentice-Hall.

Tyler, L. E. (1965). *The psychology of human differences* (2nd ed). New York: Appleton-Century-Crofts.

Vance, H. B., Hankins, N., & McGee, H. (1979). A preliminary study of black and white differences on the Revised Wechsler Intelligence Scale for Children. *Journal of Clinical Psychology, 35,* 815–819.

Vance, H. B., Huelsman, C. B., & Wherry, R. J. (1976).

The hierarchical factor structure of the Wechsler Intelligence Scale for Children as it relates to disadvantaged white and black children. *Journal of General Psychology, 95,* 287–293.

Vance, H. B., & Wallbrown, F. H., (1978). The structure of intelligence for black children: A hierarchical approach. *Psychological Record, 28,* 31–39.

Vandivier, P. L., & Vandivier, S. S. (1979). A nonbiased assessment of intelligence testing. *Educational Forum, 44,* 97–108.

Veale, J. R., & Foreman, D. I. (1983). Assessing cultural bias using foil response data: Cultural variation. *Journal of Educational Measurement, 20,* 249–258.

Wallbrown, F. H., Blaha, J., Wallbrown, J., & Engin, A. (1975). The hierarchical factor structure of the Wechsler Adult Intelligence Scale. *British Journal of Educational Psychology, 44,* 47–65.

Wallbrown, F. H., Blaha, J., & Wherry, R. J. (1973). The hierachical factor structure of the Wechsler Preschool and Primary Scale of Intelligence. *Journal of Consulting and Clinical Psychology, 41,* 356–362.

Warren, N. (1972). African infant precocity. *Psychological Bulletin, 78,* 535–367.

Wechsler, D. (1949). *Wechsler Intelligence Scale for Children.* New York: Psychological Corporation.

Wechsler, D. (1974). *Wechsler Intelligence Scale for Children—Revised.* New York: Psychological Corporation.

Wherry, R. J., & Wherry, R. J., Jr. (1969). WHEWH program. In R. J. Wherry (Ed.), *Psychology Department computer programs.* Ohio State University, Department of Psychology.

Willerman, L. (1979). *The psychology of individual and group differences.* San Francisco: W. H. Freeman.

Williams, R. L. (1972, September). *The BITCH-100: A culture specific test.* Paper presented at the annual meeting of the American Psychological Association, Honolulu.

Williams, R. L. (1974). From dehumanization to black intellectual genocide: A rejoinder. In G. J. Williams and S. Gordon (Eds.), *Clinical Child Psychology: Current practices and future perspectives.* New York: Behavioral Publications.

Wilson, K. M. (1969). *Black students entering CRC colleges: Their characteristics and their first year academic performance* (Research memo 69-1). Poughkeepsie, NY: College Research Center.

Wright, B. J., & Isenstein, V. R. (1977). *Psychological tests and minorities* (DHEW Publication No. ADM 78-482). Rockville, MD: National Institute of Mental Health. (Reprinted 1978)

21

APPLIED SYSTEMS—ACTUARIAL ASSESSMENT

PAUL A. MCDERMOTT

University of Pennsylvania

In the first edition of the *Handbook,* a chapter on actuarial assessment systems (McDermott, 1982) demonstrated the relative advantages of quantitative approaches to child assessment. The concept of *acturial* classification was introduced, where decisions flowed not so much from clinical impressions on a case-by-case basis, but from empirical probabilities as derived through experience with many case studies. The presentation considered applications of multivariate statistical methods that would enable us to predict likely outcomes for children, to develop feasible classifications for variations in child functioning, and to assign such classifications with improved accuracy. The chapter further explored the public and legal policies that would encourage the acturial approach in school psychological practice.

In most respects, the present chapter begins where the earlier one ended. It addresses more recent methodological advances, but does so in a manner that will not impede new readers unfamiliar with the earlier work. We shall concern ourselves less with the mathematical operations and assumptions underlying acturial assessment, and more with the systematic integration of those methods into a comprehensive model for child assessment—a model that will *apply* actuarial assessment as it is properly guided by expert clinical judgment and the more salient conventions of common psychological practice.

CONTRASTING METHODS OF ASSESSMENT

Contemporary approaches to child assessment derive primarily from inductive theory and deductive research on the dynamics of human development and behavior. They endeavor to appreciate the unique influences of genetics, environment, and their interactions in promoting a vast array of human differences. Thus, case referral information, developmental factors, contextual observations, and test results are collected and considered in order to produce meaningful descriptions of child functioning and to shed light on probable case etiology and prognosis.

Within this broader context, two major schools of child assessment have emerged—the clinical and the actuarial. Clinical assessment has been the more popular. It regards childhood normality as an absence of detectable pathology, where pathology is determined in the medical tradition by consensus within professional organizations or through the popularity of leading writers. Clinical method recognizes the import of diverse professional experience, intuition, common sense, and a variety of other human qualities that can be manifested by a given practitioner. The most distinguishing feature of clinical methodology is its reliance on competent human judgment in weighing the elements of any specific case study. Its popularity stems largely from the conviction that it enables psychologists to be more sensitive to the nuances of individual child circumstances, from the personal satisfaction experienced in judgments that rest upon acquired expertise, and from the convenience afforded by a method able to function in isolation from a rather more complicated universe of ever-evolving empirical knowledge.

Actuarial methods focus upon aspects of child functioning as they *actually* are known to vary among children. One begins with an extensive and representative set of data describing how children differ along certain dimensions of functioning (e.g., aptitude, attainment, or personality). The dimensions selected are those empirically demonstrated to influence successful adjustment or schooling, and eventual independent living. For any given dimension, the continuum of *natural* variation in human differences is observed and quantitative indicators are applied to denote the relative intensity (or severity) of the dimensional characteristic under study. Thereby, childhood normality is associated with levels of functioning that are typical or commonplace (with respect to age, education, etc.), and exceptionality (not necessarily pathology) is viewed as functioning that is truly rare or atypical. Given such an actuarial data base, assessments of the quality of child functioning for new case studies are guided by comparisons to the natural variations in functioning as they exist in the general child population.[1]

---

[1]It is suggested occasionally that because clinicians frequently use scores derived from tests that are standardized with representative national samples, such use constitutes actuarial rather than clinical assessment. The surmise is invalid inasmuch as conventional practice compels the clinician to *weigh* and *interpret* test data and to *integrate* them with anamnestic case information. The processes of weighing, interpreting, and integrating are essentially matters of clinical judgment and they tend to vary greatly even when precisely identical test and other case information are assessed by different clinicians (see, e.g., Achenbach & Edelbrock, 1978, Flor, 1978, and McDermott, 1981).

Specifically, actuarial assessment is designed to be sensitive to both prevailing and peculiar trends in the incidence of psychological phenomena and to deviations of phenomena from either a child's own general pattern or those patterns typified by age-mates or other peers. Most important, perhaps, it is both sensitive and accommodating to sources of error that plague clinical approaches, including inconsistency among psychological phenomena, accidental occurrences that mask themselves as significant, and redundant phenomena that otherwise appear separately important. Each decision is rendered in the light of the *probability* of its accuracy and is tempered by the degree of its probable error.

For either method it can be argued that its major source of strength is at once a major source of weakness. Clinical assessment is limited by its dependence on human judgment; actuarial assessment by the necessity for good data and the technical convenience to apply those data. For example, inasmuch as clinical assessment is carried out by many different persons for whom general expertise is more an assumption than an established fact, resulting decisions are too often unreliable; that is, the extent of skill demonstrated is too often no better than that expected by novice clinicians, naive laypersons, or random accident. This unfortunate circumstance has been shown empirically and with fair persistence among clinical child psychologists and psychiatrists (Beitchman, Dielman, Landis, Benson, & Kemp, 1978; Freeman, 1971; Spitzer & Fleiss, 1974), among school psychologists and special educators (Flor, 1978; McDermott, 1980b; Petersen & Hart, 1978; Thurlow, Ysseldyke, & Casey, 1984), and even among those attempting to apply the newer national and international classification systems designed for children (Achenbach, 1980; Rutter & Shaffer, 1980; Spitzer, Forman, & Nee, 1979). The ultimate consequence is grave indeed, for as Spitzer and his associates have emphasized, any such approach to assessment must be inherently "invalid" (Spitzer & Fleiss, 1974, p. 341). On the other hand, sound actuarial information is difficult

---

to obtain. It demands rather exhaustive and costly efforts to standardize and execute data-collection procedures. Moreover, the specialized knowledge ordinarily required in analyzing and applying such information often is regarded as too complicated or otherwise imposing in day-to-day practice.

Nevertheless, both clinical and actuarial strategies offer much promise. Whereas the future may find one approach transcending the other as the standard for best practice and scientific advance, neither is presently so perfect as to justify exclusion of the other. The more reasonable contemporary perspective is to regard clinical and actuarial processes as complementary, each mitigating the other's inherent weaknesses. Clinical method has the advantage whenever good actuarial information is unavailable. As examples, this would include all situations wherein psychologists must address the potential impact of unusual situational factors in children's lives, such as stressful social or physical environs, limited education, or unfamiliarity with the predominant culture, and unusual personal factors such as exceptional talent, sensory handicaps, language impairment, or poor health. Actuarial methods are best suited for treating information gathered through norm-based tests of ability and achievement, through standardized parent or teacher interview schedules, and through empirical measures of observed child behavior. Actuarial strategies are ideal as well for diagnostic decision making that engages specific standard criteria or for differential classification or criterion-referenced programming activities, which, by their nature, are either very time consuming or relatively confusing.

THE SYSTEMS-ACTUARIAL CONCEPT

A workable merger of the more salient features of actuarial and clinical assessment must satisfy several basic criteria. It must combine the strategies without having them interfere with one another; it must preclude endemic validity threats as associated with judgment bias, limited scope of knowledge, and unreliability affecting clinical processes (for specific examples, see Achenbach, 1978; Garfield, 1978; McDermott, 1981, 1988; Spitzer, Endicott, & Robins, 1975); and it must compensate for the practical constraints attendant upon specialized, quantitative, actuarial procedures. Moreover, the

ideal assessment system should be reasonably comprehensive. That is, unlike available systems in psychology and special education, it should not focus exclusively upon child psychopathology or disability, but should recognize with equal import all verifiable types and subtypes of normality and positive exceptionality. Nor should assessment be regarded simply as those activities that confirm or periodically reconfirm special education placement or psychological treatment; instead, comprehensive assessment must consider as well all the intervening processes by which specific programs of instruction or remediation are selected and individualized for children. All of this would call for a rather sophisticated, yet comprehensible model for child assessment.

To this end, we shall consider what is known as the systems-actuarial model (McDermott, 1981a, 1980d). It evolves partly from modern decision theory; specifically that application referred to as hierarchical systems logic. Through systems logic, we make a complicated problem more understandable by reordering the sequences in which component questions are asked and answered. Thus, one considers first those questions that are more fundamental, primary, and discriminating—much as in the game "Twenty Questions." For instance, in differential diagnosis of mental retardation, the question "Is the child's adaptive behavior deficient?" is deemed primary because mental retardation cannot exist in lieu of defective environmental adaptation (Grossman, 1983). Thereafter, secondary and clarifying questions are posed (e.g., those concerning the level or subtype of mental retardation). With each successive answer, substantial numbers of alternative questions are eliminated and others raised to importance.

Conventional systems logic, although decisively more efficient, is sometimes not discernibly more effective (i.e., accurate) than alternative methods. That is because it forces users to accept discrete "Yes" or "No" responses to questions and does not prescribe objective standards for accepting or rejecting either response. Once again considering the mental retardation question, we might imagine that there are nearly as many definitions of "deficient" adaptive behavior as there are child specialists, such that a "Yes" or "No" decision is more a consequence of personal preference than probable accuracy.

Alternatively, the *systems-actuarial* method,

while subscribing to the general theory of hierarchical *systems* logic, removes its more arbitrary elements by substituting objective criteria based on the best *actuarial* information pertaining to children. Hence, most decisions rest on the logical *and* statistical probability of their accuracy, having considered the probability of plausible alternatives. In turn, *expert clinical judgment* is applied to address the unique personal and situational factors that affect children, to determine the most appropriate sources of information for case study, to select among the various actuarial strategies available, and to qualify actuarial decisions that are found either limited or suspect.

A MODEL FOR APPLICATION

To apply the systems-actuarial concept, we must devise a model that is useful in school and clinical practice and in special education settings. The comprehensiveness and complexity of such a model will require that it be usable in a *computerized* form; this would solve as well the problem of convenience because the laborious maintenance of actuarial information and execution of complicated statistical procedures can be carried out automatically. Figure 1 presents the general structure for such a model. It is called the *multidimensional assessment* model and is applied through computer software known as M.MAC (from *McDermott Multidimensional Assessment of Children*, McDermott & Watkins, 1985, 1987). M.MAC is a comprehensive microcomputer system for use by school psychologists and other specialists in assessing the psychological and educational functioning of children aged 2 through 18 years. It works with computers such as the IBM PC and XT, Apple II, II+, III, //e, //c, and most compatibles. M.MAC performs actuarial analyses and interpretation of data derived from tests and standardized observations and interviews, and systematically integrates that information with child demography and expert clinical judgment. It does so for two main purposes: first, to produce objective *classifications* of childhood normality and exceptionality, and second, to design *individualized educational programs* (IEPs) based on actual performance in fundamental skill areas.

As shown in Figure 1, the multidimensional model has four main *levels:* Identification, Exceptionality, Classification, and Program Design. These correspond to the basic stages of child assessment, with the Identification and Exceptionality Levels serving as preparatory stages and the Classification and Program Design Levels as culminating stages devoted to classification and IEP design, respectively. The psychologist, having gathered basic case information, administered appropriate tests, and obtained necessary input from teachers and parents, begins assessment at the point marked "Enter System" and proceeds through the various levels as indicated by the directional arrows. At each level, M.MAC poses questions or requests entry of case data while the psychologist, in an interactive fashion, gives responses and selects the types of assessment to be carried out. Finally, the system independently processes all information and prints a 4- to 16-page Classification Record or IEP. All of this takes about 10 to 15 minutes, depending on the amount of case data and complexity of assessment procedures ordered.

It will be noted that the Classification and Program Design Levels are systematically linked within the model. This affirms the philosophy that, to be meaningful, assessment cannot end when children are diagnosed or placed. Valid assessment must continue through the stage that will provide *specific, potentially attainable,* and *verifiable* goals for instruction or intervention (Gough, 1971; McClung, 1973). Therefore, the Classification and Program Design Levels are integrated so that they may be used sequentially or independently. When used sequentially for a given case study, IEPs are designed immediately following classificatory assessment. In this way, all case information pertinent to both classification and educational program design is supplied only once. The psychologist may elect to undertake classificatory assessment on one occasion and later, having allowed time to elapse for gathering additional case information or for conferring with other child study specialists, design a more specific educational program. Alternatively, different types of specialists may concentrate on different levels of assessment; for example, the school psychologist carrying out classification work and a teacher developing IEPs.

We shall explore in the remaining sections of this chapter each level of the multidimensional model, beginning with the preparatory levels and proceeding to the main Classification and Program Design Levels of child assessment.

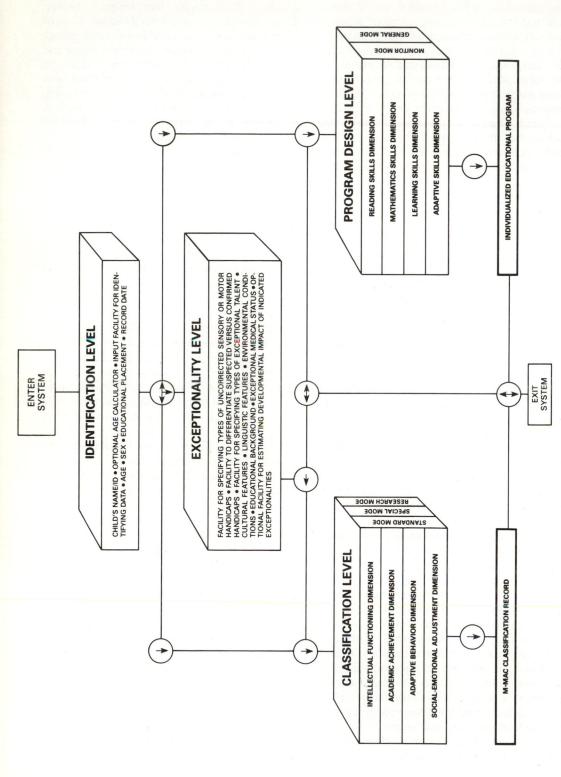

Figure 1. General structure of the multidimensional assessment model. (From the *Microcomputer systems manual for McDermott Multidimensional Assessment of Children* by P. A. McDermott and M. W. Watkins, 1985, 1987, San Antonio. Copyright 1985, 1987 by The Psychological Corporation. Reproduced by permission. All rights reserved.)

Preparatory Levels of Assessment

Basic Information

The *Identification Level* requests that the psychologist supply basic information concerning child demography and vital statistics. This information is used automatically thereafter to guide high-speed computerized search and retrieval of actuarial information that varies as a function of a child's age, educational placement and, sometimes, gender. Thus the M.MAC system stores within its memory 9,260 pieces of data describing psychological and educational phenomena as they exist among children. These include statistical parameters such as means, standard deviations, standard errors of measurement and prediction, reliability and validity coefficients, characteristics of normal and abnormal subpopulations already identified, and a wide variety of statistics describing the *prevalence* (i.e., predominance or rarity) of conditions as established in empirical research.

Special Information

Through the *Exceptionality Level*, the psychologist informs the system about unusual personal and situational factors concerning the child. These would include major sensory and other physical handicaps, talents, special language and cultural features, medical problems, environmental stresses, and inadequate education. The psychologist discriminates impairments of speech, hearing, vision, and physical coordination as either *confirmed* or *suspected*, where those considered confirmed must be a matter of medical record or clinical speech pathology and suspected impairments are those regarded possible or probable according to best clinical judgment.

This information serves several important purposes, as follows:

1. *Potential Validity Threats:* Each exceptional factor is regarded as a conceivable threat to the validity of formal assessment. Thus any factor may operate directly or indirectly to reduce the validity of information obtained through standardized tests or through standardized or clinical observations and interviews. A *direct* validity threat is any personal or situational factor commonly found to interfere directly with a child's performance on a standardized test (e.g., sensory or motor impairment, limited language, poor education, etc.). An *indirect* threat is any condition the knowledge of which may tend to bias or otherwise influence a psychologist's judgments or information provided by parents or teachers (e.g., knowledge of family problems or of the child's current inclusion in special education). Table 1 lists the various personal and situational factors and their roles as direct or indirect threats. For each standardized or clinical assessment procedure employed by the psychologist, the printed M.MAC Record posts cautionary notices specifying exceptional child factors and the potential threats posed directly or indirectly to valid interpretation of results.

2. *Developmental Impact and Coping:* In addition to reporting exceptional factors, the psychologist is given the opportunity to evaluate the developmental effects and coping related to each factor. This procedure is consistent with that advocated by the World Health Organization (Rutter, Shaffer, & Sheperd, 1975) and American Psychiatric Association (APA, 1980, pp. 26–30) for exercising clinical judgment in estimating the probable importance of unusual characteristics of the child or environment. The quality of coping for each factor is thus evaluated as "Good," "Unapparent," "Poor," or should the psychologist find evaluation difficult or inadvisable, as "Unspecified."

3. *Provisional Classifications:* As stated, one of the main functions of the multidimensional model is classification. If any personal or situational factors (excluding current special education placement) are reported and the system renders classifications of specific learning disabilities or developmental learning disorders, resulting classifications will have the term *Provisional* appended to them. This indicates that the learning disorder(s) may be secondary to the reported personal or situational factors, a circumstance which by classic theory (Bateman, 1965; Kirk & Bateman, 1962; Johnson & Myklebust, 1967) and contemporary law (C. D. Mercer, Forgnone, & Wolking, 1976; U.S. Department of Health, Education, and Welfare [USHEW], 1977a) may preclude the classification. Use of provisional classi-

TABLE 1   Exceptional Personal and Situational Factors Regarding Children That Pose Potential Threats to the Validity of Assessment Processes

Exceptional Factor	Type of Validity Threat	
	Direct	Indirect
Confirmed impairment of speech	×	×
Confirmed impairment of hearing	×	×
Confirmed impairment of vision	×	×
Confirmed physical coordination problem	×	×
Confirmed physical handicap other than major sensory or motor impairment		×
Suspected speech impairment		×
Suspected hearing impairment		×
Suspected vision impairment		×
Suspected physical coordination problem		×
Other possible physical handicap		×
Recently suffered acute medical condition(s)	×	×
Subject to chronic ill-health		×
Multi- or bilingual with English as primary language		×
English as secondary language	×	×
Limited facility in using the English language	×	×
Primarily nonEnglish communication in home		×
Member of a cultural or racial minority group		×
Limited opportunity to assimilate the prevailing culture	×	×
Markedly inconstant or stressful social environs (family, neighborhood, etc.)		×
Markedly inconstant or stressful physical environs (safety, warmth, toxicity, etc.)		×
Markedly disadvantageous economic environs (poverty, opportunity, etc.)		×
Comparatively little opportunity for formal education	×	×
Markedly inconstant or unresponsive educational background	×	×
Current placement in special education setting		×

Note.   Confirmation of major sensory, motor, and physical handicaps requires formal medical diagnosis. Speech impairment must be confirmed through medical or speech pathology.

fications to signify diagnostic uncertainty or need for additional information is recommended by the APA (1980, p. 25).

4. *Selection or Elimination of Ability Measures:* Wechsler intelligence scales are used often to assess children's ability. Consequently, it must be decided whether the Full Scale, Verbal, or Performance IQ is to serve as the principal indicator of intellectual functioning and as the best estimate of expected levels of academic achievement. The decision cannot be an arbitrary one, but is necessarily regulated by the relative construct viability, reliability, and predictive efficiency of the several measures.[2] In many instances the Full Scale IQ best satisfies these criteria. Frequently, however, Verbal and Performance IQs are

[2]Some psychologists commonly interpret Verbal-Performance IQ discrepancies to suggest that the higher IQ is a more valid estimate of a child's "true potential" or that the lower IQ is somehow of dubious verity. Also, administrative regulations or conventions of practice in some localities actually compel psychologists' acceptance of the Full Scale IQ as the principal indicator of intellectual functioning or expected achievement. These practices find no support in measurement theory or empirical research, and they will tend to introduce substantial and systematic error to assessment processes.

found significantly disparate and, to the extent that the contruct meaningfulness of the Full Scale IQ rests on the homogeniety of its Verbal and Performance components and because Verbal IQs are generally the best predictors of achievement, the Verbal IQ is selected. Such decisions are essentially actuarial and routinely handled by M.MAC.

Nevertheless, occasions arise for deferment to clinical judgment. Reports of major sensory or motor handicaps, or a child's limited facility in using English language, raise concern for the validity of specific Wechsler measures. Specifically, indications of confirmed or suspected impairments to speech, hearing, or language usage can justify the psychologist's decision not to administer the Verbal scale or a decided preference for the Performance IQ as principal indicator; conversely, indication of impairment to vision or physical coordination can argue for elimination of the Performance scale or preference for the Verbal IQ as principal indicator.[3] Therefore, the system provides for such options and prints a record of all decisons, justifications, and consequences.

5. *Interpretation of Disparity in Ability Measures:* Whenever differences between Wechsler Verbal and Performance IQs are found both reliable and rare, interpretations are guided by the best empirical evidence (see McDermott & Watkins, 1987, p. 160, for a reference list). Such interpretations suggest possible deviations in cognitive functioning, motivational issues, or unusual styles of learning or reactivity. However, the psychologist's suggestion of major sensory, motor, or language handicaps will alter more common interpretations in the light of the primary and more imposing handicaps.

[3]Note that theoretical and psychometric assumptions preclude arbitrary decisions to administer only the Verbal or Performance scale on Wechsler intelligence tests (e.g., see Piotrowski, 1976, and Wechsler, 1974, 1981).

CLASSIFICATION OF NORMALITY AND EXCEPTIONALITY

Classification is based on four principal dimensions of child functioning. As represented on the face of the Classification Level block in Figure 1, they are the Intellectual Functioning, Academic Achievement, Adaptive Behavior, and Social-Emotional Adjustment Dimensions. Various analyses are performed for each dimension, and decisions *across* dimensions are integrated to yield multidimensional classifications. All results are presented in a printed M.MAC Classification Record. Figure 2 enlarges the face of the Classification Level block to illustrate features associated with each dimension and the printed Record. Although a full discussion of features would not be possible within the scope of this chapter, more important aspects are summarized below as they relate to actuarial or clinical assessment.

General Actuarial Features

In proceeding through the successive classification dimensions, the psychologist indicates which standardized instruments were used for data collection. Selections are made among 12 of the finest individually administered intelligence and achievement tests, 4 parent interview schedules, and 9 behavior observation scales. Obtained scores are entered into the system and processed in the light of child population characteristics as reflected in normative statistics for the tests and other evaluation devices.

Comparability of Scaling

It is difficult to draw meaningful comparisons among scores obtained from different instruments. Scores appear in varied forms, some being standard scores based on a mean of 100 and standard deviation 15, others having a mean of 50 or standard deviation of 10 or 16, and many scales provide only raw scores with no consistent distribution of values. To remedy this, M.MAC uses the mixed categorical–dimensional approach to classification advocated by Cromwell, Blashfield, and Strauss (1975) whereby underlying standard score ranges are associated with terminology that describe *comparable* levels of functioning. For instruments not providing standard scores, standard scores are calculated automatically by the system.

Descriptive levels of intellectual, academic, and adaptive functioning are based on the popu-

CLASSIFICATION LEVEL

ALTERNATE ANALYSIS OF DATA FROM A SINGLE SCALE ONLY

INTELLECTUAL FUNCTIONING DIMENSION

SELECTION OF SCALES • BYPASS FOR UNADMINISTERED SUBSCALES • CORRECTION FOR SIMUL-
TANEOUS STATISTICAL TESTS • CONFIDENCE LIMITS FOR OBTAINED SCORES • SIGNIFICANCE AND
ESTIMATED PREVALENCE OF VERBAL-PERFORMANCE IQ DIFFERENCE • OPTIONAL CALCULATION OF
FACTOR DEVIATION QUOTIENTS • DEVIATIONS FROM CHILD'S AVERAGE FUNCTIONING LEVEL • RE-
LATIONSHIP TO SUSPECTED AND CONFIRMED SENSORY-MOTOR OR LANGUAGE IMPAIRMENTS •
QUALITATIVE LEVEL OF INTELLECTUAL FUNCTIONING • SUMMARY TABLES, INTERPRETATION, AND
VERBAL REPORT OF RESULTS • NOTICE OF DIRECT VALIDITY THREATS BY SITUATIONAL OR CHILD
EXCEPTIONALITY • DIMENSION SUMMARY

ACADEMIC ACHIEVEMENT DIMENSION

SELECTION OF SCALES • ADJUSTMENT FOR UNADMINISTERED SUBSCALES • AUTOMATIC BYPASS
FOR PRESCHOOL LEVEL CHILDREN • CORRECTION FOR SIMULTANEOUS STATISTICAL TESTS • CON-
FIDENCE LIMITS FOR OBTAINED SCORES • DEVIATIONS FROM CHILD'S AVERAGE ACHIEVEMENT LEVEL
• ALTERNATE REGRESSION OR ESTIMATED TRUE DIFFERENCE ANALYSES TO DETERMINE ACHIEVE-
MENT PROBLEMS • SIGNIFICANCE AND ESTIMATED PREVALENCE FOR DETECTED UNDER- AND
OVERACHIEVEMENT • POSTING OF COEFFICIENTS USED TO CALCULATE EXPECTED ACHIEVEMENT
• QUALITATIVE STATUS OF ACHIEVEMENT RELATIVE TO EXPECTANCY IN EACH SUBJECT AREA •
QUALITATIVE LEVELS OF ACHIEVEMENT RELATIVE TO AGE OR GRADE PLACEMENT • SUMMARY TA-
BLES AND VERBAL REPORT FOR EACH SUBJECT AREA • NOTICE OF DIRECT VALIDITY THREATS BY
SITUATIONAL OR CHILD EXCEPTIONALITY • DIMENSION SUMMARY

ADAPTIVE BEHAVIOR DIMENSION

SELECTION OF SCALES • ALTERNATE FACILITY FOR EVALUATION BASED ON PROFESSIONAL JUDG-
MENT AND/OR UNSPECIFIED INDICES • CORRECTION FOR SIMULTANEOUS STATISTICAL TESTS •
CONFIDENCE LIMITS FOR OBTAINED SCORES • DEVIATIONS FROM CHILD'S AVERAGE ADAPTATION
LEVEL • ALTERNATE ANALYSIS BY CUTTING-SCORE, DISCRIMINANT FUNCTION, OR GENERALIZED
DISTANCE TECHNIQUE FOR CERTAIN SCALES • INDEX OF PROFILE SIMILARITY TO EXISTING MR POP-
ULATIONS • AUTOMATIC CROSS-VALIDATION OF MULTIVARIATE GROUPING ANALYSES AGAINST
CONVENTIONAL CUTTING-SCORE ANALYSIS • QUALITATIVE LEVEL OF ADAPTATION RELATIVE TO
AGE FOR EACH SUBSKILL AREA • ALTERNATE FACILITY FOR CLINICAL DIAGNOSIS OF DEFICIENCY
AREAS UNDER AAMD GUIDELINES • SUMMARY TABLES AND VERBAL REPORT OF RESULTS • NO-
TICE OF INDIRECT VALIDITY THREATS BY SITUATIONAL OR CHILD EXCEPTIONALITY • DIMENSION
SUMMARY

SOCIAL-EMOTIONAL ADJUSTMENT DIMENSION

SELECTION OF SCALES • ALTERNATE FACILITY FOR EVALUATION BASED ON PROFESSIONAL JUDG-
MENT AND/OR UNSPECIFIED MEASURES • CALCULATION OF STANDARD SCORES • CONFIDENCE
LIMITS FOR STANDARD SCORES • ALTERNATE ANALYSIS BY CUTTING-SCORE OR SYNDROMIC PRO-
FILE TECHNIQUE FOR CERTAIN SCALES • INDEX OF PROFILE SIMILARITY TO EXISTING ADJUSTED
AND MALADJUSTED SUBPOPULATIONS • QUALITATIVE ADJUSTMENT LEVEL OR MALADJUSTMENT
SEVERITY LEVEL • ALTERNATE FACILITY FOR CLINICAL DIAGNOSIS OF PRIMARY AND SECONDARY
CHILDHOOD DISORDERS BY TYPE AND SUBTYPE UNDER DSM-III CRITERIA • SUMMARY TABLES AND
VERBAL REPORT OF RESULTS • NOTICE OF INDIRECT VALIDITY THREATS BY SITUATIONAL OR CHILD
EXCEPTIONALITY • DIMENSION SUMMARY

M·MAC CLASSIFICATION RECORD

CHILD'S NAME/ID • AGE • SEX • EDUCATIONAL PLACEMENT • RECORD DATE • ASSESSMENT METH-
ODS (SCALES, PROFESSIONAL JUDGMENT, ETC.) • OPERATIONS MODE • STATISTICAL CRITERIA •
ALTERED CUTTING-SCORES • NOTICE OF PARAMETER ALTERATIONS • NOTICE OF COMBINATIONS
OF DATA FROM TWO INFORMANTS OR OBSERVERS • TYPES OF SITUATIONAL AND CHILD EXCEP-
TIONALITY AND ESTIMATED DEVELOPMENTAL IMPACT • MULTIDIMENSIONAL CLASSIFICATION
SUMMARY • TYPES OF EXCEPTIONAL TALENT • INTELLECTUAL GIFTEDNESS • INTELLECTUAL
FUNCTIONING LEVEL • MENTAL RETARDATION LEVEL • EDUCATIONAL RETARDATION LEVEL • TYPES
OF COMMENSURATE ACHIEVEMENT • TYPES OF SPECIFIC LEARNING DISABILITIES • TYPES OF DE-
VELOPMENTAL LEARNING DISORDERS • TYPES OF PROVISIONAL LEARNING DISABILITIES OR DE-
VELOPMENTAL LEARNING DISORDERS • TYPES OF ACADEMIC OVERCOMPENSATION • POSSIBLE
VISUAL-MOTOR OR COMMUNICATION DISORDERS • SOCIAL-EMOTIONAL ADJUSTMENT LEVEL •
SEVERITY LEVEL OF SOCIAL-EMOTIONAL MALADJUSTMENT • MALADJUSTMENT TYPE BASED ON
EMPIRICAL CLASSIFICATION OR PRIMARY AND SECONDARY TYPES AND SUBTYPES BASED ON CLIN-
ICAL CLASSIFICATION • M·MAC REFERENCE CODE FOR EACH CLASSIFICATION • OPTIONAL RELATED
REFERENCE CODES FOR DSM-III AND WORLD HEALTH ORGANIZATION CLASSIFICATION SYSTEMS

TABLE 2   Descriptive Terminology, Standard Score Ranges, and Population Prevalence for Levels of Intellectual, Academic, and Adaptive Functioning

Level of Functioning	Standard Score Range	Estimated Prevalence
Very superior	≥ 2 SDs above M	2.3%
Superior	≥ 1.33 and < 2 SDs above M	6.9%
High average	$\geq .67$ and < 1.33 SDs above M	16.0%
Average	$\leq .67$ SDs below and $< .67$ SDs above M	49.7%
Low average	≤ 1.33 and $> .67$ SDs below M	16.0%
Borderline	≤ 2 and > 1.33 SDs below M	6.9%
Mildly deficient	≤ 3 and > 2 SDs below M	2.1%
Moderately deficient	≤ 4 and > 3 SDs below M	1 in 1,000
Severely deficient	≤ 5 and > 4 SDs below M	< 1 in 300,000 (extrapolated)
Profoundly deficient	> 5 SDs below M	< 1 in 3.3 million (extrapolated)

lar terminology used by Wechsler (1974) and the American Association on Mental Deficiency (AAMD) (Grossman, 1983). Standard score ranges and estimated population prevalence are given in Table 2. For example, a WISC-R IQ of 83 (where the test $M = 100$ and $SD = 15$; Wechsler, 1974) would be described as *low average* intellectual functioning, a Total Reading score of 38 on the *Woodcock Reading Mastery Tests* (where $M = 50$ and $SD = 10$; Woodcock, 1973) would indicate *low average* reading achievement, and an Average score of 31 on the *Adaptive Behavior Inventory for Children* (ABIC) ($M = 50$ and $SD = 15$; J.R. Mercer & Lewis, 1982) would indicate *low average* adaptive functioning.[4]

A parallel method is used for the social-

[4]Note that terms describing subnormal levels of intellectual functioning do not refer to or imply mental retardation. Mental retardation remains a multidimensional classification requiring evidence for both deficient intellectual functioning and adaptive behavior (APA, 1987; Grossman, 1983; USHEW, 1977b). Thus, in accord with AAMD recommendation (Grossman, 1983), a very low IQ can indicate no more than deficient intellectual functioning.

emotional adjustment area. Here, terms such as "superior" and "deficient" are inappropriate. Instead, M.MAC converts raw data to standard T-score form ($M = 50$ and $SD = 10$) consistent with the practice in maladjustment research (Edelbrock & Achenbach, 1980; McDermott, 1980c; Miller 1981) and assigns maladjustment terminology in accord with the APA (1980). Terminology and respective T-score ranges are listed in Table 3.

TABLE 3   Descriptive Terminology and Standard T-Score Ranges for Levels of Social-Emotional Adjustment and Maladjustment

Level of Functioning	T-Score Ranges
Well adjusted	< 60
Adequately adjusted	60–69
Mildly maladjusted	70–79
Moderately maladjusted	80–89
Severely maladjusted	90–99
Extremely maladjusted	> 99

Figure 2. Features of the Classification Level by dimensions. (From the *Microcomputer systems manual for McDermott Multidimensional Assessment of Children* by P. A. McDermott and M. W. Watkins, 1985, 1987, San Antonio. Copyright 1985, 1987 by The Psychological Corporation. Reproduced by permission. All rights reserved.)

Factorial Integrity

A major source of assessment error is the notion that tests and parts of tests measure what authors or publishers may claim (see Tryon, 1979, for a critique). The systems-actuarial model generally applies only those test scales, subscales, and other trait domains for which construct validity is established through factor- or cluster-analytic research. An exception is made for certain areas of academic achievement (reading comprehension, mathematics, etc.) because differential performance in those areas is recognized by public policy and can have a substantial impact on children's lives.

Statistical Inferences

Whereas derived standard scores are regularly reported and interpreted, along with upper and lower score limits reflecting confidence in reliability, certain scores are subjected to inferential analysis. Values representing unique and reliable aspects of intellectual functioning, achievement in different subject areas, or subareas of adaptive behavior are evaluated for possible deviations from *a child's own average levels of performance* (using Davis's, 1959, method). For each such analysis, the increased risk of error associated with multiple comparisons is controlled automatically through Bonferroni corrections (Silverstein, 1982). Moreover, corrections are adjusted appropriately whenever the psychologist decides to add or delete optional areas of assessment.

Discrepancies between Wechsler Verbal and Performance quotients, among WISC-R factor scores calculated by the system, and performance evaluations by different observers or informants are tested for statistical significance via the standard error of measurement for the difference between obtained scores (Davis, 1964).

Population Prevalence

Statistical significance is important because it indicates that observed performance deviations are probably not a consequence of measurement error. But observations that are statistically reliable need not be *clinically* meaningful. This is because most performance deviations are part of the natural variation of psychological and educational phenomena. In contrast, clinically remarkable or abnormal deviations are relatively rare. Therefore, interpretations of statistically significant performance deviations are guided whenever possible by actuarial knowledge of clinical rarity. Esti-

mated prevalence is calculated (applying Silverstein's 1981a, 1981b, formula) to reflect the percentage of children in the general population showing deviations as serious as those for the child under study. Consistent with the accepted standard defining prevalence for mental deficiency, giftedness, and maladjustment, deviations common to no more than 3% of the general population are deemed clinically significant.

General Clinical Features

We have considered already the importance of clinical discretion in selecting instrumentation, gathering data, and for detection and causal attribution regarding unusual characteristics of the child or environment. The model further invokes clinical expertise whenever conventional actuarial approaches are judged unnecessary or inappropriate.

Clinical Assessment of Adaptive Behavior

Psychologists are required to ensure that children diagnosed as mentally retarded manifest substantial deficiency for *both* intellectual functioning *and* environmental adaptation. The practice complies with the standard established by AAMD (Grossman, 1983), APA (1987), and the Committee on Child Psychiatry (1966), and with federal law regulating special education placement (USHEW, 1977b). At the conceptual level, the standard is widely accepted in specialty fields (Cromwell et al., 1975; Silverstein, 1973). However, due partly to the nonavailability of systematic means for applying both intellectual and adaptive aspects in classification, many specialists have tended to disregard adaptive behavior and rest decisions on intelligence indices alone (see Adams, 1973, and Peterson & Hart, 1978). Unfortunately, this overlooks the limited criterion validity of intelligence quotients (i.e., they are useful in predicting relative success or failure in *academic* endeavors) and overlooks the ability of adaptive measures to complement IQ (Adams, 1973; Zigler & Trickett, 1978) and assess functioning outside the school setting (Adams, McIntosh, & Weade, 1973; Doll, 1953; Grossman, 1977).

The systems-actuarial model requires that any effort to formally classify child functioning must consider current adaptive behavior. It resolves difficulties in integrating intellective and adaptive concepts through hierarchical logic (discussed below) and ordinarily encourages the use of standardized adaptive behavior inventories. Nevertheless, to the extent that questions about defective adaptation pertain more exclusively to classification of mental retardation, and because mental retardation is itself rather rare (less than 3% of the general population), it is unlikely that most casework will require more rigorous assessments of adaptive behavior. This is true for children thought gifted and for the preponderance of children referred for behavioral and learning problems. If a psychologist can readily determine the adequacy of adaptive behavior or finds available instrumentation inadequate for certain cases (e.g., more severely retarded children), classification should not require use of more time consuming or less appropriate standardized instruments.

Within this framework, the model supports alternate use of professional judgment in assessing adaptive behavior. The psychologist specifies whether general adaptation is "Good," "Adequate," or "Deficient" and whether judgment relies upon clinical observations of the child, interviews with parents or guardians, or a combination of these and other methods. If adaptation is judged "Deficient," the system will request that, if possible, the psychologist indicate specific areas of deficiency in accord with the criteria proposed by the AAMD (Grossman, 1977, 1983). Possible areas of deficiency include the development of sensory-motor skills, communication skills, self-help skills, prevocational skills, socialization, and use of appropriate reasoning and judgment in gaining mastery of the environment.

Clinical Assessment of Social-Emotional Adjustment

Although the rigor of empirical rating scales is usually preferred in assessing behavioral and emotional adjustment, circumstances may render clinical judgment the better alternative. With many children the possibility of social-emotional disturbance is remote so that more formal observations by teachers or parents may be regarded as unnecessary. Furthermore, empirical scales will tend to undervalue the import of solitary, although grave symptomatic behaviors (e.g., fire-setting) and can be less useful for differentiating among extraordinarily rare conditions such as autism and other childhood psychoses.

M.MAC thus alternatively supports clinical determination of social-emotional status. It asks the psychologist to specify whether the child is "Well Adjusted," "Adequately Adjusted," or "Maladjusted" and to indicate bases for the decision. If maladjustment is indicated, the system gives the psychologist the opportunity to diagnose both *primary* and *secondary* types and subtypes of disturbance according to the *Diagnostic and Statistical Manual of Mental Disorders,* 3rd edition (DSM-III) (APA, 1980) and its revision (DSM-III-R) (APA, 1987). These include variations of conduct; anxiety; attention deficit; adjustment, autistic, and pervasive developmental disorders; and schizoid, identity, and oppositional disorder of childhood or adolescence.

Clinical Assessment of Exceptional Talent

It will be recalled that the Exceptionality Level of the system asks the psychologist to indicate any special talents that a child may possess. Specifically, the psychologist may record that the child demonstrates (or probably demonstrates) (a) high skill in the performing arts, (b) high skill in the mechanical or manual arts, (c) high skill in the literary or fine arts, (d) very superior athletic skills, and/or (e) high inventive or scientific skill. This information evokes a formal classification of Exceptional Talent with specification of relevant skills.

Unidimensional Assessment

Whereas the model will preclude formal classification that does not consider each of the four assessment dimensions, a psychologist may use the system to evaluate child functioning under any single dimension. Such applications are helpful in screening and follow-up work, as well as research.

Systems-Actuarial Logic for Classification

The system produces 113 empirical and 35 clinical classifications. For a given child, at least one or as many as four classifications are rendered for each of the following areas: (a) cognitive functioning, (b) academic functioning, and (c) social-emotional functioning.

Each classification is accompanied by a two-letter mnemonic code for easy recall (e.g., AW for Anxiety-Withdrawal Disorder, LD for Specific Learning Disability, etc.). Most codes also include numerical values. Numbers to the *left* of letter codes indicate qualitative *level* of functioning (e.g., good, severe, etc.) and numbers to the *right* of letter codes indicate specific *types* (e.g., achievement in reading, in mathematics; attention deficit disorders with hyperactivity, without hyperactivity; etc.). A parenthetical (P) code signifies a provisional classification, as discussed previously.

In addition, the psychologist may elect to have corresponding codes for the DSM-III-R (APA, 1987) and its international counterpart, the *International Classification of Diseases,* 9th revision (ICD-9) (World Health Organization, 1978), published adjacent to M.MAC codes. This can be rather useful for compliance with government agencies and insurance carriers, or for studying relationships among major clinical and empirical classification systems (see McDermott, 1986; Quay, 1986).

Classification of Cognitive Functioning

Figure 3 summarizes basic logic for differential classification of cognitive functioning. A careful study of this information will make several factors apparent. First, classification is keyed initially to a value called the *Mild Mental Retardation cutting-score.* Ordinarily, this value is set at 2 SDs below *M* (e.g., a Wechsler IQ of 70). Second, IQs equal to or greater than the cutting-score preclude classifications of retardation and invite classifications of normal (NM) or Borderline Intellectual Functioning (BD)—the decision depending on the score range within which the IQ falls, as shown in Table 2.

Values falling below the cutting-score open the possibility of Mental Retardation, the exact severity level ordinarily determined under AAMD criteria, as shown in Table 4. Alternatively, Intellectual or Educational Retardation may be classified, the former a nosology recommended by the AAMD to denote deficient intellectual functioning coexisting with generally adequate environmental

adaptation, and the latter a term long used by educators to describe general intellectual and academic deficiency in a child who cannot be regarded as mentally retarded.

Intellectual Giftedness (not illustrated in Figure 3) is classified when (a) the IQ is equal to or greater than the value set for the *Intellectual Giftedness cutting-score* (ordinarily, 2 SDs above *M*; e.g., a Wechsler IQ of 130), and (b) no Specific Learning Disabilities are classified for the child. The latter criterion follows for theoretical reasons (see McDermott & Watkins, 1987) and to avoid clashes between academic supplementary enrichment or acceleration programs and remedial programs required for more fundamental learning disorders. However, the psychologist is able to eliminate the latter criterion.

The system enables psychologists to alter the cutting-score for Intellectual Giftedness, as well as cutting-scores associated with Mild, Moderate, Severe, and Profound retardation. This permits adjustments for research or local requirements, as when a school district serves disproportionate numbers of advantaged or disadvantaged children.

Classification of Academic Functioning

For each academic subject area considered, a child's current achievement is assessed from three perspectives; (a) qualitative level of performance (average, superior, etc., as indicated in Table 2) compared to that for children of similar age or at the same grade placement, (b) deviation from one's average level of performance across all subject areas, and (c) discrepancy between levels of expected and observed performance. The latter assessment forms the basis for classification, where *expectancy* is the level of performance that would be manifest if essential elements in a child's life

TABLE 4   Standard Cutting-Score Ranges for Classification of Mental, Intellectual, and Educational Retardation

Severity Level	Cutting-Score Range for Mental, Intellectual, and Educational Retardation	Wechsler IQ Equivalent
Mild	> 2 and ≤ 3 SDs below *M*	69–55
Moderate	> 3 and ≤ 4 SDs below *M*	.54–40
Severe	> 4 and ≤ 5 SDs below *M*	39–25
Profound	> 5 SDs below *M*	<25

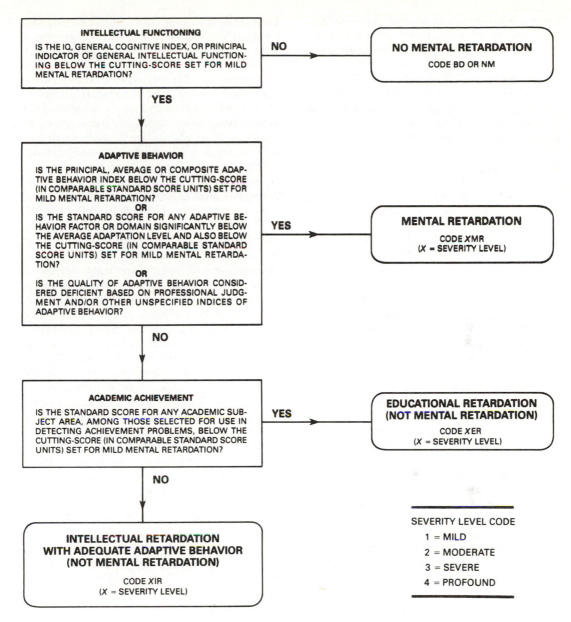

Figure 3. Systems-actuarial logic for the differential classification of mental proficiency and retardation. (From the *Microcomputer systems manual for McDermott Multidimensional Assessment of Children* by P. A. McDermott and M. W. Watkins, 1985, 1987, San Antonio. Copyright 1985, 1987 by The Psychological Corporation. Reproduced by permission. All rights reserved.)

(health, educational opportunity, family stability, etc.) were to remain relatively constant and the child did not receive extraordinary assistance or interference with learning.

Consistent with the seminal theory by Thorndike (1963), Bateman (1965), Kirk and Bateman (1962), and Johnson and Myklebust (1967), expected achievement is estimated through level of general intellectual functioning. Discrepancies between expected and observed achievement are thereafter examined either through *regression analysis* employing the standard error of discrepancies from prediction (Thorndike, 1963) to test statistical significance and the standard deviation of discrepancies from prediction (Salvia & Good, 1982; Thorndike, 1963) to discern prevalence, or through *estimated true difference analysis* using the standard error of measurement of estimated true differences (Stanley, 1971) to determine significance. Whereas the model generally prefers and conducts regression analysis, alternate estimated true difference analysis is applied wherever published research has failed to provide actuarial information necessary for regression procedures. (*Note:* M.MAC's memory stores such information for all major intelligence and achievement tests, and users can enter, store, and apply new information in unlimited quantities.)

Figure 4 presents portions of two M.MAC Records involving the same intelligence data (WISC-R Verbal IQ = 106) and standard scores for reading (93) and mathematics (76) on the BASIS achievement test (The Psychological Corporation [TPC], 1983). The Record on the left gives results based on regression and that on the right as based on estimated true differences. For each, the systems (or the psychologist) sets a criterion for accepting discrepancies from expected achievement as *abnormal* (these are posted at the bottom of the respective Records). The reader will notice that in each instance the discrepancy for reading achievement fails to meet the abnormality criterion, while that for mathematics satisfies the criterion. Since the mathematics discrepancy is negative (−27 or −28), we know that observed achievement is markedly *below* expectancy— hence, *underachievement*. Had the discrepancy been positive, *overachievement* would have been indicated. These important distinctions open the formal classificatory process, with performance in each subject area classified ultimately as Commensurate (with expectancy) or indicative of a Specific

Learning Disability, Developmental Learning Disorder, or Possible Academic Overcompensation, as per the decision logic given in Figure 5.[5]

Commensurate Achievement is classified when either (a) observed achievement is not abnormally discrepant from expected achievement, or (b) significant overachievement is detected but without evidence for consequent ill-effects (i.e., no significant underachievement in another area and no associated social-emotional maladjustment). Specific Learning Disabilities are differentiated in accordance with the legal standard prevailing throughout most of North America (C. D. Mercer et al., 1976; Ministry of Education, 1981; USHEW, 1977a), that is, a severe discrepancy between expected and observed achievement which is not primarily the result of a visual, hearing, or motor handicap; mental retardation; emotional disturbance; environmental, cultural, or economic disadvantage; or lack of appropriate learning experience. If the psychologist reports such unusual personal or situational factors through the Exceptionality Level, or maladjustment is classified through the Social-Emotional Adjustment Dimension, the classification Specific Learning Disability (Provisional) is made, with determination of whether the learning problem is causative or consequential remaining a matter of clinical judgment. Evidence for subnormal intellectual functioning precludes learning disability classification, as warranted under regulations affecting most educational institutions, but raises the possibility for classification of Developmental Learning Disorders, in accordance with the APA (1980, 1987) and World Health Organization (1978).

Educators rarely assess for overachievement. This stems primarily from the misconception that intelligence or expectancy is (or should be) a feasible measure of innate ability or *potential*, so naturally, to the degree that such a premise could

---

[5]The developers of the multidimensional model have expressed reservations about validity and utility for the learning disability concept (McDermott & Watkins, 1985, 1987, pp. 151–154). For example, Sabatino and Miller (1980) report the continued absence of convincing support for the assumption that children called learning disabled actually benefit by available remedial programs. The problem emits partly from unreliable methods of identifying learning disabled children (Achenbach, 1978; Garfield, 1978). The model includes learning disability classifications in order to provide the assessment reliability prerequisite to establishing assessment validity and utility.

ACADEMIC ACHIEVEMENT DIMENSION
BASIC ACHIEVEMENT SKILLS INDIVIDUAL SCREENER (BASIS)
DISCREPANCY BETWEEN EXPECTED & OBSERVED ACHIEVEMENT (REGRESSION ANALYSIS)

LEVEL OF ACHIEVEMENT	READING	MATH
EXPECTED	103	103
OBSERVED	93	76
DIS-CREPANCY	-10	-27
STAT. SIGNIF.	.05	.0001
ESTIMATED % PREVAL.	20	2.5
COEF-FICIENT	.58	.43

MAXIMUM OVERALL ESTIMATED PREVALENCE LEVEL FOR ACCEPTING ABNORMALITY OF DISCREPANCY FROM EXPECTED ACHIEVEMENT = 6%

ACADEMIC ACHIEVEMENT DIMENSION
BASIC ACHIEVEMENT SKILLS INDIVIDUAL SCREENER (BASIS)
DISCREPANCY BETWEEN EXPECTED & OBSERVED ACHIEVEMENT (ESTIMATED TRUE DIFF.)

LEVEL OF ACHIEVEMENT	READING	MATH
EXPECTED	106*	106*
OBSERVED	93*	78*
DIS-CREPANCY	-13*	-28*
STAT. SIGNIF.	.05	.0001

MAXIMUM PROBABILITY LEVEL FOR ACCEPTING ABNORMALITY OF DISCREPANCY FROM EXPECTED ACHIEVEMENT = .001

Figure 4. Examples of actuarially confirmed ability/achievement discrepancies based on regression analyses (left) and estimated true differences analyses (right).

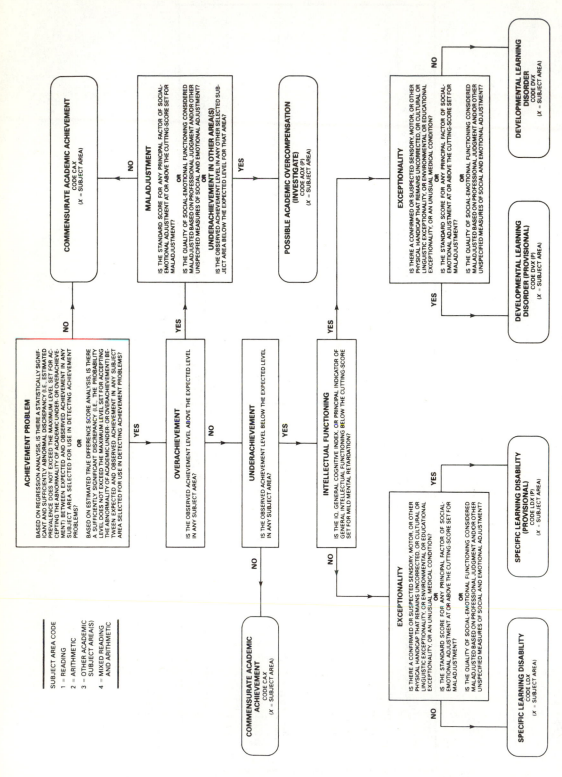

Figure 5. Systems-actuarial logic for the differential classification of academic functioning. (From the *Microcomputer systems manual for McDermott Multidimensional Assessment of Children* by P. A. McDermott and M. W. Watkins, 1985, 1987, San Antonio. Copyright 1985, 1987 by The Psychological Corporation. Reproduced by permission. All rights reserved.)

be true, one logically cannot accept the contradiction that a child might perform *better* than potential dictates. Of course, neither IQ nor expectancy (nor anything else we know of) reflects potential. Moreover, the same theoretical formulation that spawns the concept of underachievement and its attendant learning disorders tautologically compels us to recognize the existence of overachievement and its conceivably related learning disorders (see McDermott & Watkins, 1985; Thorndike, 1963). That is, just as appreciable underachievement would suggest that a child's learning is somehow inordinately *inhibited,* one is persuaded to accept the reciprocal argument that appreciable overachievement might suggest that learning is inordinately *induced.* Clinical psychologists have therefore recognized that strong and sustained pressure to achieve in some area can have harmful effects, such as social-emotional maladjustment or failure to achieve in other important areas. More commonly, clinicians tend to think of children *overcompensating* in one area for problems in others. As Figure 5 shows, Possible Academic Overcompensation is classified whenever substantial overachievement is accompanied by either classified maladjustment or substantial underachievement in another important academic area.

Classification of Social-Emotional Functioning

Social-emotional adjustment is assessed through clinical or empirical methods. Application and advantages of the clinical method were discussed previously. Empirical methods are rooted in standardized observation and normative comparison of behaviors and other verifiable phenomena. Child adjustment is a matter of social relativity, one that must be viewed in the context of natural social situations. Relevant behavior should be observed by those most familiar with and unobtrusive in specific social contexts, such as teachers in the school or parents in the home. Standardized behavior rating scales are ideal for this application and generally produce assessments more reliable and valid than those possible through conventional clinical approaches (Achenback & Edelbrock, 1978; McDermott, 1986; Quay, 1986).

Systems logic for differential between social-emotional adjustment and maladjustment is shown in Figure 6. When clinical judgment is used, functioning is classified as Good or Adequate Ad-

justment (AJ codes) or as Maladjusted (ML codes), the exact classification and code depending on which of the 33 primary and secondary maladjustment types and subtypes are selected from the DSM-III-R. When empirical rating scales are used, teacher or parent responses are associated with *factors* or syndromes of disturbance, each having standard *T*-score values that become higher as psychopathology increases. Adjustment and maladjustment are differentiated by comparing the highest *T* score among the various factors to the *Maladjustment cutting-score,* which usually is set at 70 (in compliance with international precident; Quay & Peterson, 1983; Trites, Dugas, Lynch, & Ferguson, 1979; Trites & Laprade, 1983).

As Table 3 indicated, a high *T* score below 60 is regarded Good Adjustment (1AJ) and one between 60 and 69 is regarded Adequate Adjustment (2AJ). Additionally, functioning initially determined Maladjusted is typed and subtyped based on the patterns of *T* scores falling above the cutting-score. Thus, if one factor falls in the maladjusted range and it measures acting-out and conduct disturbance, the Conduct Disorder (CD) classification is made. Similarly, classifications are made for Anxiety-Withdrawal Disorders (AW), Attention Deficit Disorders without Hyperactivity (AD1), Attention Deficit Disorders with Hyperactivity (AD2), and combinations of anxiety and conduct disorders called Disturbances of Emotions and Conduct (AW-CD). Finally, severity (mild to extreme, as listed in Table 3) and primacy of disturbance (e.g., Conduct Disorder primary to Attention Deficits, or vice versa) are determined by the range and order of *T* scores associated with maladjustment factors. (*Note:* M.MAC provides means for the psychologist to alter *T*-score values associated with levels of adjustment and severity of maladjustment, as may be required for regional subpopulations or research.)

Apart from the cutting-score procedure, systems-actuarial assessment makes possible considerably more sophisticated mathematical routines. Particularly helpful in differential classification of social-emotional functioning is what is known as *multivariate typing.* One of the empirical rating scales supported by M.MAC, the *Bristol Social Adjustment Guides* (BSAG) (Stott, 1981), produces scores on six syndromes of child behavior. Working with profiles over the six syndromes for each of the 2,527 children and adolescents in the BSAG normative sample, McDermott (1983)

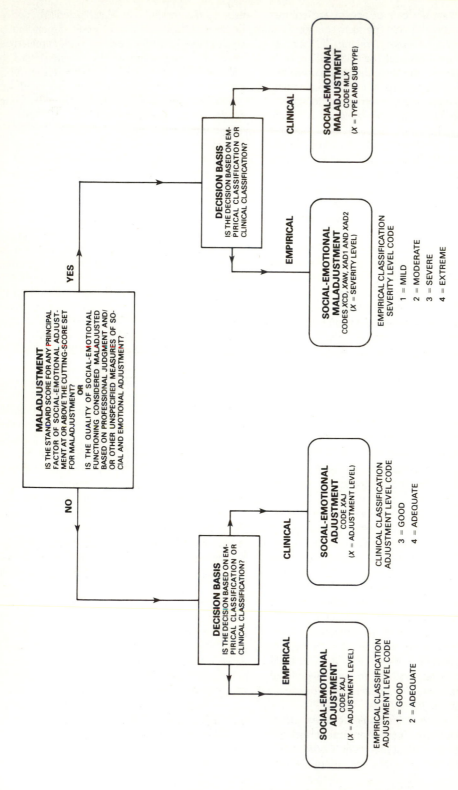

Figure 6. Systems-actuarial logic for the differential classification of social-emotional adjustment and maladjustment. (From the *Microcomputer systems manual for McDermott Multidimensional Assessment of Children* by P. A. McDermott and M. W. Watkins, 1985, 1987, San Antonio. Copyright 1985, 1987 by The Psychological Corporation. Reproduced by permission. All rights reserved.)

established through sequential clustering a *typology* of 16 syndromic profile types. Therefore, considering BSAG scores for any child newly assessed, M.MAC calculates the similarity of the child's profile to each of the 16 known types and classifies the child according to highest similarity.

Figure 7 shows a portion of a child's M.MAC Record presenting results from multivariate typing. Names of the 16 profile types appear on the upper left. On the right side a column headed "Group Membership Index" gives a value for each type. The values are adaptations of Tatsuoka's (1974) coefficient of similarity between individual and group profiles and they range from 0 to 20, where 20 would indicate a perfect match between a child's profile and the mean profile for a given type, and a value of less than 10 would indicate a similarity of no greater than chance (i.e., dissimilarity). With respect to the example in Figure 7, the highest index is for TP 11, Conduct Disorder with Attention Deficits. Reading the text that continues the sample Record, we find that this typing evokes a certain severity level, a description of children who constitute the type in the general population, and a statement of prevalence as estimated from the actuarial data.

Multivariate typing and a related classification procedure, discriminant function analysis, also are available under the Adaptive Behavior Dimension (for details on methods and assumptions for both procedures, refer to McDermott, 1982, pp. 257–265). In those instances, psychologists using the *AAMD Adaptive Behavior Scale–School Edition* (ABS-SE) (Lambert, 1981) benefit from research by Lambert and Hartsough (1981) defining patterns of adaptivity unique to children already identified as normal, educable mentally retarded, and trainable mentally retarded.

Expert System Options for Classification

The model as implemented through computer software actually comprises an *expert system*. Such expertise emanates from three sources: cumulative knowledge about children in general as gained from empirical research and population studies (the actuarial component), experiential knowledge as gathered by the psychologist in prior clinical work and the current case study (the clinical component), and knowledge of necessary and accepted standards of practice for child classification (the criterion or decision rule component). Whereas assessment reliability demands consistent application of all knowledge components, psychologists must have reasonable flexibility in choosing appropriate actuarial information and adjusting classificatory criteria for special circumstances.

Returning once more to Figure 1, the reader will notice that the Classification Level block shows partitions along its side labeled Standard Mode, Special Mode, and Research Mode. These *operations modes* enable the psychologist to alter assessment criteria and to change actuarial information bases as deemed appropriate. Figure 8 enlarges the Classification Level block to illustrate the options associated with each mode.

Standard Mode is recommended for typical casework. It requires no intervention by the psychologist and automatically applies general population norms; conventional cutting-scores for giftedness and severity of retardation and maladjustment; maximum 3% prevalence levels for accepting abnormality of IQ discrepancies, underachievement, and overachievement; and use of the maximum ($p < .05$) probability level as common to most foundation research in psychology and education. Since the mode functions much as an autopilot, it makes the most widely accepted standards for assessment also the most convenient, thereby increasing the likelihood of consistency across psychologists and settings. Assuming constancy among the 50 or so pieces of identifying, clinical, and psychometric data collected for any given child, resulting classifications will *never* vary, even though the child data are treated and interact in very complicated ways with hundreds of pieces of actuarial data stored in the system's memory.

The other operations modes open numerous options to the psychologist. *Special Mode* is intended mainly for periodic use in daily practice. Included are options, mentioned previously, that permit alteration of cutting-scores defining giftedness and levels of retardation, adjustment, and maladjustment. Additionally, psychologists may set different prevalence criteria for recognizing abnormality of ability/achievement discrepancies and IQ discrepancies, and select different combinations of academic subject areas to be considered in the classification of specific learning disabilities and developmental learning disorders.

One convenient actuarial feature enables psychologists to incorporate information independently obtained from *two* teachers or parents. We have emphasized the benefits wrought by standardized adaptive and social behavior scales.

SOCIAL-EMOTIONAL ADJUSTMENT DIMENSION

BRISTOL SOCIAL ADJUSTMENT GUIDES (BSAG)

ANALYSIS BY SYNDROMIC PROFILE METHOD:

SYNDROMIC PROFILE GROUP	GROUP MEMBERSHIP INDEX
TP 1. GOOD ADJUSTMENT	3.6
TP 2. ADEQUATE ADJUSTMENT WITH IMPULSIVITY	5
TP 3. ADEQUATE ADJUSTMENT WITH PEER CONFLICT	6.5
TP 4. ADEQUATE ADJUSTMENT WITH EMANCIPATORY TRAITS	7.5
TP 5. ADEQUATE ADJUSTMENT WITH DISTURBANCE OF CONDUCT	16
TP 6. ADEQUATE ADJUSTMENT WITH MOTIVATIONAL DEFICITS	6.9
TP 7. ADEQUATE ADJUSTMENT WITH WITHDRAWAL	6.6
TP 8. ADEQUATE ADJUSTMENT WITH DEPRESSED MOOD	8.2
TP 9. ATTENTION DEFICIT DISORDER WITH HYPERACTIVITY	11.1
TP 10. CONDUCT DISORDER (SOCIALIZED AGGRESSIVE)	17.6
TP 11. CONDUCT DISORDER WITH ATTENTION DEFICITS	18.3
TP 12. CONDUCT DISORDER (UNDERSOCIALIZED AGGRESSIVE)	16.4
TP 13. ANXIETY-WITHDRAWAL DISORDER (AVOIDANT)	5.5
TP 14. ANXIETY-WITHDRAWAL DISORDER (OPPOSITIONAL)	11.5
TP 15. ANXIETY-WITHDRAWAL DISORDER (SCHIZOID)	8.2
TP 16. ANXIETY-WITHDRAWAL DISORDER (DYSTHYMIC)	7.9

ACCORDING TO THE OVERALL CONFIGURATION OF OBSERVED STYLES OF BEHAVIOR, THE CHILD'S SOCIAL AND EMOTIONAL REACTIONS ARE CONSIDERED MODERATELY MALADJUSTED AT THIS TIME.

THE PATTERN AND LEVELS OF SYNDROME ELEVATIONS MOST CLOSELY RESEMBLE THE TYPICAL PROFILE FOR TP 11, CONDUCT DISORDER WITH ATTENTION DEFICITS AND HYPERACTIVITY.

A GENERAL SYNOPSIS OF BEHAVIORAL CHARACTERISTICS AND POPULATION PREVALENCE FOR THIS PROFILE TYPE IS AS FOLLOWS:

TP 11. A CLASS OF SERIOUS GENERAL OVERREACTIVE BEHAVIOR MARKED BY THOUGHTLESS AGGRESSIVENESS AND INTRUSIONS UPON OTHERS' RIGHTS; A VICIOUS CYCLE MAY BE EVIDENT, INVOLVING THE CHILD'S INITIAL LACK OF FORETHOUGHT, IMPULSIVE INTERFERENCE WITH OTHERS, CONSEQUENT REJECTION BY PEERS AND ADULTS AND, IN TURN, INDUCED HOSTILITY ON THE CHILD'S PART; DELINQUENT-LIKE BEHAVIOR, AT LEAST PARTIALLY REACTIVE; SEEN IN BOYS VS. GIRLS THREE-FOURTHS OF THE TIME; THE SPECIFIC SUBTYPE OF DISORDER MAY BE CONSIDERED UNDER-SOCIALIZED, AGGRESSIVE.

ESTIMATED POPULATION PREVALENCE = 1%

THIS ASSESSMENT IS BASED ON SUMMATIVE EVALUATIONS FOLLOWING OBSERVATION OF THE CHILD OVER TIME IN CERTAIN NATURAL SOCIAL SETTINGS. HOWEVER, THE GENERALITY OF THE OBSERVED BEHAVIOR STYLES CANNOT BE ASSUMED AUTOMATICALLY ACROSS ALL IMPORTANT AREAS OF THE CHILD'S SOCIAL AND EMOTIONAL FUNCTIONING. VERIFICATION SHOULD PROCEED THROUGH ADDITIONAL OBSERVATION AND INQUIRY.

Figure 7. Example of actuarial profile typing to classify social-emotional maladjustment.

However, their relative superiority can be compromised when parent informants or teacher observers inadvertently or deliberately distort information. The danger is greatest when faulty perspectives on environmental adaptivity may lead to classifications of mental deficiency or manifestations of contextually unique behavior (e.g., in one classroom or with one teacher only) may suggest maladjustment. Consequently, the model provides means for entry, comparison, and optional merger or selection of informant and observer information.

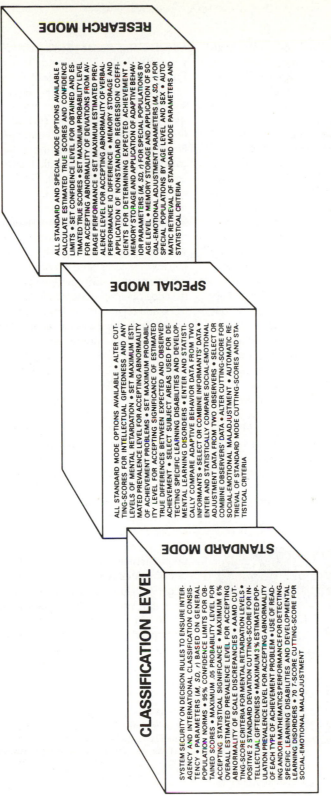

Figure 8. Features of the Classification Level by operations modes. (From the *Microcomputer systems manual for McDermott Multidimensional Assessment of Children* by P. A. McDermott and M. W. Watkins, 1985, 1987, San Antonio. Copyright 1985, 1987 by The Psychological Corporation. Reproduced by permission. All rights reserved.)

Figure 9 shows an M.MAC computer screen resulting from a psychologist's entry of ratings by two teachers on the *Vineland Adaptive Behavior Scales* (VABS) (Sparrow, Balla, & Cichetti, 1984). The display gives derived standard scores for the overall Composite and underlying factors of adaptivity as produced by each teacher. Moreover, it reports a "Similarity Coefficient" (Cattell, 1949) reflecting the degree of comparability between the teachers' evaluations both in terms of *levels* of functioning and profile *patterns* (where a coefficient of 1.0 would indicate perfect similarity, .40 reasonable similarity, and ≤ 0.0 dissimilarity). Also reported is the "Significance of Difference" (Davis, 1964) between the Composite scores produced by the teachers (where p values $\geq .10$ suggest reasonable similarity and $< .10$ dissimiliarity). Using this actuarial information, the psychologist discovers whether the teachers' evaluations confirm or contradict one another, whereupon the system is commanded either to apply one teacher's data and eliminate the other's or to combine both teachers' data mathematically. Data combinations can improve discernibly both the reliability and cross-situational validity of assessments. Similar analyses may be conducted in the adaptive behavior area using the ABIC, ABS-SE, *Vineland Social Maturity Scale-Revised* (Doll, 1965), and all versions of the VABS, and in the social-emotional adjustment area for the BSAG, *Conners Teacher Rating Scale* (CTRS) (Trites, Blovin & Laprade, 1982), *Louisville Behavior Checklist* (Miller, 1981), *Kohn*

Social Competence Scale and *Kohn Problem Checklist* (Kohn, 1988), and the *Revised Behavior Problem Checklist* (Quay & Peterson, 1983).

The *Research Mode* is reserved for unusual subpopulations or empirical inquiry. Psychologists may change criteria for all statistical tests. In addition to derived scores and associated confidence limits ordinarily generated, the system will calculate estimated true scores and their special confidence limits (Glutting, McDermott, & Stanley, 1987) that correct for measurement error within more extreme or unreliable performance indices. Most important are the facilities allowing psychologists to enter, store, and apply new or special actuarial data. Among the nearly 10,000 pieces of normative information stored in computer memory *matrices* [6], about 3,450 pieces can be changed to describe diverse subpopulations. For example, *M*s, *SD* s, and reliability coefficients can be stored for all scales and subscales of adaptive behavior and social-emotional adjustment, as might be desired for minority cultural or language groups or for regional or clinically distinct subsamples. Similarly, all statistics reflecting achievement expectancy relationships among intelligence tests and academic subject areas are alterable.

In this regard, Figure 10 shows one of 1,094 "Matrix Update" computer screens. It displays a matrix storing raw score *M*s on a factor called Hyperactivity from the CTRS, as obtained from a random sample of 4,806 male children aged 4 to 12 (Trites et al, 1982). By entering new values, the psychologist changes all subsequently derived *T* scores, confidence limits, statistical tests, and multidimensional classifications to reflect hyperactivity phenomena in a unique group. An unlimited number of values may be stored simultaneously, with original values preserved automatically. Thereafter, the psychological expert determines which set of values is proper for a given child, and high-speed computerized routines retrieve and apply those values as ordered.

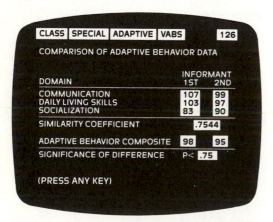

Figure 9. Example of actuarial tests for similarity of adaptive behavior assessments by two different teachers.

[6]A matrix is a location in software memory holding a set of related numerical values. For example, the values may be related because they pertain to the same subscale of a test, same combinations of subscales from different tests, or same gender within a population. Moreover, values that comprise a specific set are differentiated according to population segments, such as values for each age or educational level.

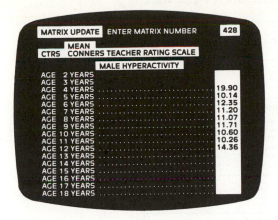

Figure 10. Example of an M.MAC computer screen for entering and storing actuarial information for new or special populations of children.

ASSESSMENT FOR INDIVIDUALIZED EDUCATIONAL PROGRAMS

Classificatory assessment is fundamental for distinguishing aspects of normal and exceptional child functioning. Once exceptionality is evident, primary focus shifts from questions of *how well* a child functions (compared to others) or *why* this may be so, to understanding exactly *what* a child knows or can do (irrespective of others) and *what* the necessary steps may be in promoting developmental or learning progress. Recognizing these goals, the Program Design Level of our model applies four dimensions of assessment: the Reading Skills, Mathematics Skills, Learning Skills, and Adaptive Skills Dimensions.

The psychologist or other child specialist begins by selecting one or more dimensions for programming. Ordinarily, choices would depend upon preceding classification results, although many specialists elect to use the Program Design Level independently or postpone use until more information is obtained or classification results are discussed with child study groups. For each skills dimension, the method used for data collection is indicated (i.e., tests, teacher's classroom observations, clinical observations, or parent interview) and pertinent data are entered. Computerized actuarial assessment commences, with unlimited opportunity for modification by the specialist, and the final IEP is printed. Figure 11 summarizes the

principal features associated with each skills dimension and the IEP.

General Program Design Features

Public policy on an international scales holds that special education and related intervention programs must be *explicitly stated* and *accomodating* to children's current levels of functioning: for example, Education Act of 1981, Eng., c. 60; Can. Rev. Stat. c., § 1 [1], para. 63, 1980; and 20 U.S.C. §§ 1401 (19), 1414(a)(5), 1977. Additionally, review of the theoretical and research literature suggests that several other qualities be required of any assessment procedures used in designing programs for special children.

Objectivity

Computer-based IEP generators have enjoyed recent popularity. They are a response to the labor and tedium involved in mandatory development and timely revision of detailed special education plans. However, *previous IEP generators, although computer-based, are not computer-guided.* They consist of more or less extensive libraries of instructional objectives or goals from which a specialist is expected to select, where the grounds for selecting given objectives and ignoring others invariably remain subjective and unspecified. Hence the most difficult and error-ridden element of manual IEP development (i.e., choosing objectives) finds no relief in popular IEP generators—they serve only to cure the more trivial clerical tasks that can be handled by a computer.

M.MAC contains within its memory 1,111 behavioral performance objectives. Each objective is matched in terms of *content meaning* to specific items, mastery levels, or psychometric response-difficulty criteria on the finest educational screening and diagnostic instruments. For the Reading Skills Dimension these include the *Woodcock Reading Mastery Tests* (WRMT) (Woodcock, 1973), all elementary- and secondary-school levels and alternate forms of the *Stanford Diagnostic Reading Tests* (Karlsen, Mdden, & Gardner, 1976), and the Reading components of the BASIS achievement test (TPC, 1983). The Mathematics Skills Dimension supports the *KeyMath Diagnostic Arithmetic Test* (KDAT) (Connolly, Wachtman, & Pritchett, 1976), all levels and forms of the *Stanford Diagnostic Mathematics Tests* (Beatty, Madden, Gardner, & Karlsen, 1976), and the Mathematics sections of BASIS. Children's Learning Skills are

PROGRAM DESIGN LEVEL

SELECT SINGLE OR COMBINATION OF SKILLS DIMENSIONS

READING SKILLS DIMENSION

SELECTION OF CRITERION-REFERENCED SCREENING OR DIAGNOSTIC SCALES • BEHAVIORAL OBJECTIVES KEYED TO CRITERION- AND/OR LEVEL-BASED PERFORMANCE • AUTOMATIC INTEGRATION OF CRITERION PERFORMANCE LEVELS ACROSS SUBSKILL AREAS • 6 SUBSKILL AREAS • LETTER IDENTIFICATION • WORD RECOGNITION • PHONETICS: CONSONANT SOUNDS • PHONETICS: VOWEL SOUNDS • WORD COMPREHENSION • PASSAGE COMPREHENSION

MATHEMATICS SKILLS DIMENSION

SELECTION OF CRITERION-REFERENCED SCREENING OR DIAGNOSTIC SCALES • BEHAVIORAL OBJECTIVES KEYED TO CRITERION-BASED PERFORMANCE • AUTOMATIC INTEGRATION OF CRITERION PERFORMANCE ACROSS SUBSKILL AREAS • 11 SUBSKILL AREAS • NUMERATION: WHOLE NUMBERS AND DECIMALS • NUMERATION: GEOMETRY, SYMBOLS AND SCALES • NUMERATION: RATIONAL NUMBERS • ADDITION OPERATIONS • ADDITION APPLICATIONS • SUBTRACTION OPERATIONS • SUBTRACTION APPLICATIONS • MULTIPLICATION OPERATIONS • MULTIPLICATION APPLICATIONS • DIVISION OPERATIONS • DIVISION APPLICATIONS

LEARNING SKILLS DIMENSION

SELECTION OF CRITERION- AND NORM-REFERENCED SCALES • BEHAVIORAL OBJECTIVES KEYED TO CRITERION- AND NORM-BASED PERFORMANCE LEVELS • 19 SUBSKILL AREAS • TASK INITIATIVE • SELF-DIRECTION • ASSERTIVENESS • ACCEPTANCE OF ASSISTANCE • GROUP LEARNING • CONCENTRATION • ATTENTION • TASK RELEVANCE • TASK PLANNING • PROBLEM SOLVING • CONSEQUENTIAL THINKING • LEARNING FROM ERROR • FLEXIBILITY • TASK COMPLETION • TASK COMPLIANCE • RESPONSE DELAY • WORK HABITS AND ORGANIZATION • RECOGNITION OF THE TEACHER • RECOGNITION OF OTHER LEARNERS

ADAPTIVE SKILLS DIMENSION

SKILL AREAS KEYED TO AAMD BEHAVIORAL CLASSIFICATION SYSTEM • SELECTION OF PERFORMANCE OBJECTIVES BASED ON PARENT INTERVIEW AND/OR CHILD OBSERVATION • 17 SUBSKILL AREAS • SELF HELP: EATING • SELF HELP: DRESSING • SELF HELP: TOILETING • SELF HELP: HYGIENE AND GROOMING • SELF HELP: TRAVELING • SELF HELP: MONEY MANAGING • COMMUNICATION: PREVERBAL • COMMUNICATION: VERBAL • COMMUNICATION: SYMBOL USE • SOCIALIZATION: PREGROUP ACTIVITY • SOCIALIZATION: GROUP ACTIVITY • SENSORY-MOTOR: PREWALKING • SENSORY-MOTOR: GROSS COORDINATION • SENSORY-MOTOR: FINE COORDINATION • OCCUPATION: SIMPLE TASKS • OCCUPATION: COMPLEX TASKS • OCCUPATION: FORMAL WORK

INDIVIDUALIZED EDUCATIONAL PROGRAM

CHILD'S NAME/ID • AGE • SEX • EDUCATIONAL PLACEMENT • RECORD DATE • ASSESSMENT METHODS (SCALES, PARENT INTERVIEW, ETC.) • OPERATIONS MODE • LIST OF BEHAVIORAL PERFORMANCE OBJECTIVES FOR EACH SUBSKILL AREA • OPTIONAL REFERENCE CODES FOR COMPUTER-ASSISTED INSTRUCTION AND COMPUTER-MANAGED INSTRUCTION PROGRAMS KEYED TO SPECIFIC PERFORMANCE OBJECTIVES IN READING AND MATHEMATICS assessed through standardized teacher-observation scales, the *Study of Children's Learning Behaviors* (SCLB) or *Learning Behaviors Scale* (LBS) (Stott, McDermott, Green, & Francis, 1988a, 1988b), the SCLB having been normed on 2,036 American prekindergarten through fourth-grade children and the LBS on an international sample of 1,227 American, Canadian, and Australian kindergarten and first-grade children. Finally, evaluations under the Adaptive Skills Dimension are based on standardized or clinical observations by a child specialist or interviews with parents or guardians, or on combinations thereof.

Consistent with the actuarial premise, assessment data must derive from measurement processes known to be suitably reliable and valid. In turn, the system's logic (to be discussed) automatically sorts through the otherwise confusing mixture of content within tests or scales, discerns levels and patterns of a child's *actual* performance, and objectively links measured performance to corresponding objectives for an IEP.

Moreover, recommended objectives always are stated in *behavioral* or operational form. This is not to imply that teachers and other specialists should adopt "behavioristic" strategies in remedial instruction or treatment; that decision must vary with specialists' theoretical orientation, competencies, and the context. Rather, learning and developmental objectives expressed in behavioral terms tend to be more universally understood. They are specific enough to avoid the pitfalls of vague or generic goals, and provide the explicit criteria necessary for judging whether or not prescribed objectives eventually are attained. Figure 12 illustrates portions of an M.MAC IEP and typical performance objectives for certain mathematical areas.

Hierarchy

The sheer volume and complexity of behavioral performance objectives within each skills dimension can be overwhelming. Order is needed if the programs designed are to make educational and psychological sense. For this reason the 1,111 objectives are distributed across 53 *subskill areas* (e.g., Phonetics-Consonant Sounds, Learning from Error, etc.). (Refer to Figure 11 for complete lists of subskill areas under each skills dimension.) Within subskill areas, objectives are ordered hierarchically so that foundation skills are considered first with more difficult or dependent skills following sequentially. (Observe in Figure 12 that objectives under the subskill area called Whole Numbers & Decimals are ordered hierarchically.) This approach is compatible with conventional curricula and particularly useful for specialists who wish to improve children's skills through step-by-step approximations.

In areas where the subskills themselves are interdependent (e.g., in mathematics, mastery of certain numeration concepts pertaining to fractions and ratios is prerequisite for mastery of certain division operations), the selection of objectives is integrated so that objectives chosen in one area do not outpace those in others.

Continuity

Assessment activities tend to become discontinuous after a child has been classified. Careful classification work by psychologists too often reaps little more than formal sanction for special education placement, with psychologists' discoveries or recommendations for the future somehow forestalled, filed, or otherwise unapparent in subsequent intervention programs. Several factors contribute, among them, difficulty adapting psychological information for educational applications, unfamiliarity with necessary theory and practice of educational sequencing and curriculum hierarchy, and some understandable reluctance to take on more work or to preempt the prerogatives of specialists outside professional psychology.

Nevertheless, valuable contributions by psychologists do not end with classification. In fact, psychologists can do much to ensure that the same rigor and care characterizing classificatory assessment extends through assessment intended for

Figure 11. Features of the Program Design Level by dimensions. (From the *Microcomputer systems manual for McDermott Multidimensional Assessment of Children* by P. A. McDermott and M. W. Watkins, 1985, 1987, San Antonio. Copyright 1985, 1987 by The Psychological Corporation. Reproduced by permission. All rights reserved.)

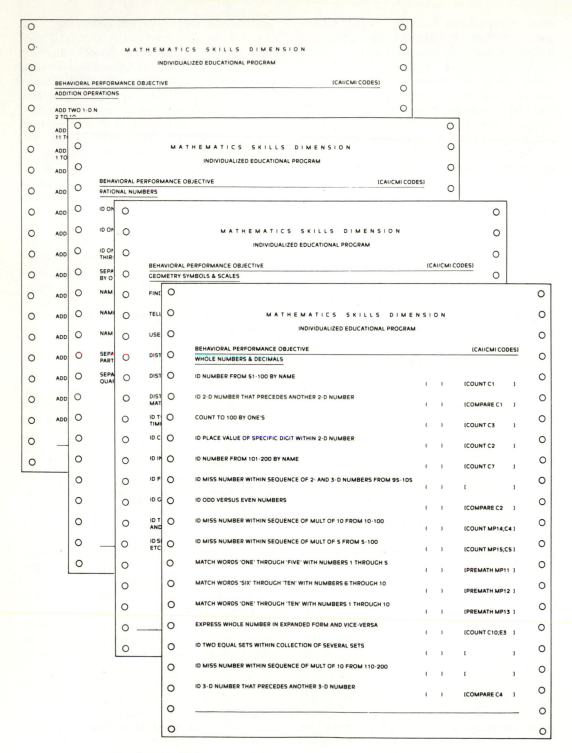

Figure 12. Example of an M.MAC-generated IEP.

developing educational programs. At the same time, psychologists can enhance appreciably their own knowledge of educational program design and of its relevance to foregoing classificatory information.

The multidimensional model fosters continuity of classification and program design, not merely by inclusion of both in one system that eliminates redundancy of investigation, but by enabling psychologists to apply information used differently for classification and program design. For example, whereas certain information from achievement tests such as the WRMT, KDAT, and BASIS might have been applied formerly in comparative classification, information from the same tests is used on criterion-referenced bases for producing detailed remedial plans. In similar fashion, information earlier gathered through parent interview or child observation can be effected in sequenced recommendations for improving personal, social, and other adaptive skills.

Individualization

It is generally assumed that individualized remedial programs are, in fact, *individualized*. The assumption often is unjustified. Programs intended to be child-oriented are too often teacher-, institution-, or placement-oriented. This is not necessarily the fault of educators or other treatment personnel. It sometimes reflects the fact that detailed assessment and its translation into workable, individually tailored programs are unattainable given available resources (e.g., see Shaw, Bensky, & Dixon, 1981; Weiskopf, 1980).

Nonetheless, IEPs that are inexact, "generic," or so common that they are duplicated within school or regional agencies must be regarded as improper. They thwart the philosophy of individualization and tend to defeat the intent of public policy and legislative mandate. The resource problem is resolved largely through computer-guided program design—an approach able to accomplish in minutes what would take a human specialist many hours per child. In addition, given the variety of assessment methods supported by the model, the quantity and diversity of possible program objectives, and the obvious differences among children themselves, the systems approach is unlikely to yield identical IEPs for different children at any time for the same child at different times.

Systems-Actuarial Logic for Educational Program Design

It seems clear from discussion thus far that unlike classification procedures addressing how well and why a child performs as compared to others, program design studies exactly what a child does and does not perform irrespective of others. What, then, defines program design as an actuarial process? To understand this, it will help to consider two concepts we refer to as structural logic and search logic.

Structural logic is the mechanism by which behavioral performance objectives within subskill areas are arranged in a hierarchy. That is, each objective, or the corresponding item or skill measured by tests or observation scales, retains a succinct difficulty or mastery level as determined through item analyses in standardization. Difficulty levels are based on the proportion of the general child population demonstrating mastery of any given skill. Subskill hierarchies are ordered according to progressive item/skill-response difficulty such that the structure of each hierarchy matches the actuarial hierarchy in the greater population. Once the actuarial base is set (as reflected in the structure of M.MAC's subskill hierarchies), performance measured for any new child may be assessed.

The *search logic* is applied when data for a new child are entered. Each objective within a hierarchy has an invisible *flag*. By means of high-speed search, flags are lowered when a child demonstrates mastery (by passing items or meeting performance thresholds) and raised when mastery is not demonstrated (items failed or thresholds unmet). The search proceeds to discover at what points in the hierarchy both stable success and failure are evident and commences to recommend objectives following the point of stable success, the quantity of objectives recommended having been set previously by the specialist. The recommended objectives include not only those pertaining directly to the child's earliest measured failure, but include as well those objectives representing graduated skills that bridge the gap between the child's highest level of success and earliest measured failure, thus promoting successive approximations in skill development as programs are eventually implemented.

Expert Systems Options for Educational Program Design

Professional discretion as exercised in classificatory work is no less vital when assessing for individual remedial needs. Any assessment method, even the most accurate and efficient, is imperfect at best and can benefit from the guidance of those having relevant expertise. For designing intervention plans, the systems-actuarial method looks to professional judgment in selecting assessment methods and defining the scope of resultant IEPs. In addition, specialists may apply the model under either of two operations modes: the Monitor Mode or the General Mode. Figure 13 partitions the Program Design Level by operations modes, summarizing options associated with each.

Monitor Mode allows the specialist to preview and change system-recommended IEPs *before they are printed*. For each subskill area involved in a particular case study, all available performance objectives are displayed on the computer screen. Objectives that were "flagged" as important for a child (based on the logic explained above) are highlighted, indicating that they will be printed if

the specialist agrees. The specialist is able to scroll up and down the hierarchy, accept or reject recommended objectives, and select others.

Figure 14 presents a typical monitoring screen. Shown are a number of objectives within the Rational Numbers hierarchy of the Mathematics Skills Dimension. Three objectives are highlighted, indicating that they are recommended as based on actual *measured* performance. Other objectives are recommended as well, and could be examined by scrolling further up the hierarchy. The specialist may decide that because of the child's history of repeated academic difficulty and disappointment, it would be better to move farther down the hierarchy, to select a number of easier (already measured) objectives that will guarantee continued success for several months, and to print the modified IEP. One can see then that the Monitor Mode is intended for design of IEPs that are (a) initially developed through objective criterion-referenced assessment, and (b) thereafter refined through professional judgment to meet the unique requirements of each child.

When the system is operated in *General*

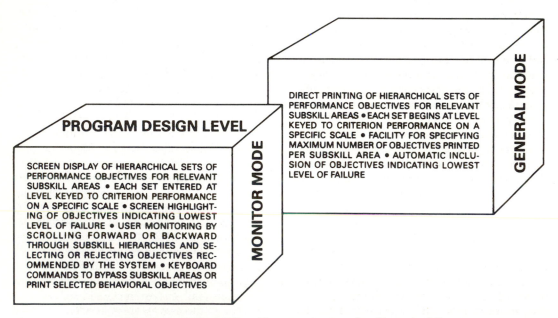

Figure 13. Features of the Program Design Level by operations modes. (From the *Microcomputer systems manual for McDermott Multidimensional Assessment of Children* by P. A. McDermott and M. W. Watkins, 1985, 1987, San Antonio. Copyright 1985, 1987 by The Psychological Corporation. Reproduced by permission. All rights reserved.)

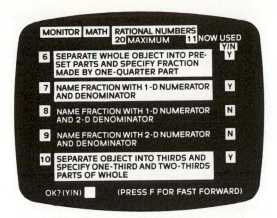

Figure 14. Example of an M.MAC computer screen for tailoring IEPs before printing.

Mode, there is no need to preview recommended objectives. Assessment moves directly from data analyses to printing an IEP. This procedure is considerably faster than monitoring, and it allows specialists to accept the IEP as final or to review it in the context of other program recommendations.

Both modes provide other features. The reader may recall that under the Learning Skills Dimension, remedial programs are drawn from standardized observations by teachers using the SCLB or LBS learning style scales. The scales are relatively brief (16 and 22 items, respectively) and provide information on *how* a child is inclined to learn (flexibility, assertiveness, considering consequences of actions, etc.). The system provides options for (a) item responses to be entered by the psychologist (as when a paper version of the SCLB or LBS was completed by the teacher), or for (b) items to be rated directly on the computer screen (as when the teacher prefers to use the system for this and other educational program development).

Returning to the sample IEP displayed in Figure 12, one will observe under the right-hand column headed "CAI/CMI Codes" a series of symbols associated with various mathematics objectives. The codes refer to specific drill and practice exercises provided by popular computer-assisted instruction (CAI) and computer-managed instruction (CMI) software programs. The programs include *The Reading Machine* (Watkins, Johnson, Adams, & Bloom, 1981), *PRISM:*

Reading (TPC, 1982b), *The Vocabulary Machine* (Watkins & Johnson, 1984), *The Math Machine* (Watkins, Johnson, & Bloom, 1985), *Math Wars* (Watkins, 1982), and *PRISM: Math* (TPC, 1982a). Most of the programs have built-in learning reinforcers and enable teachers to maintain reinforcement schedules and records of successes and errors for entire classrooms on a child-by-child basis. Thus, as an option in the reading and mathematics areas, it is possible for the same computer facilities to be used by the psychologist in assessing child functioning and by children who are actually engaging in the recommended instructional programs.

A FINAL NOTE

The discussion argues for a general model of child assessment that would merge the more salient features of actuarial and clinical methodology. Within this context, the concept of systems-actuarial assessment is introduced and a comprehensive model for its application is presented. Whereas such models have clear implications for improving accuracy and efficiency of psychological practice, they can be equally helpful in other applications. Those supervising professional preparation activities may find that prospective psychologists and educators benefit as they gain understanding of the systematic logic and varied outcomes of assessment processes. Empirical research can benefit also from the convenient contrasts made possible through flexible methods of child assessment and alterable criteria for decision making.

REFERENCES

Achenbach, T. M. (1978). Psychopathology of childhood: Research problems and issues. *Journal of Consulting and Clinical Psychology, 46,* 759–776.

Achenbach, T. M. (1980). DSM-III in light of empirical research on the classification of child psychopathology. *Journal of the American Academy of Child Psychiatry, 19,* 395–412.

Achenbach, T. M., & Edelbrock, C. S. (1978). The classification of child psychopathology: A review and analysis. *Psychological Bulletin, 85,* 1275–1301.

Adams, J. (1973). Adaptive behavior and measured intelligence in the classification of mental retardation. *American Journal of Mental Deficiency, 78,* 77–81.

Adams, J., McIntosh, E. I., & Weade, B. L. (1973). Ethnic background, measured intelligence, and adaptive behavior scores in mentally retarded children. *American Journal of Mental Deficiency, 78,* 1–6.

American Psychiatric Association. (1980). *Diagnostic and statistical manual of mental disorders* (3rd ed.). Washington, DC: Author.

American Psychiatric Association. (1987). *Diagnostic and statistical manual of mental disorders* (rev. 3rd ed.). Washington, DC: Author.

Bateman, B. (1965). An educator's view of a diagnostic approach to learning disorders. In J. Hullmuth (Ed.), *Learning disorders* (pp. 219–239). Seattle: Special Child Publications.

Beatty, L. S., Madden, B., Gardner, E. F., & Karlsen, B. (1976). *Stanford Diagnostic Mathematics Test* (Red, Green, and Brown levels). New York: Harcourt Brace Jovanovich.

Beitchman, J. H., Dielman, T. E., Landis, J. R., Benson, R. M., & Kemp, R. L. (1978). Reliability of the Group for the Advancement of Psychiatry diagnostic categories in child psychiatry. *Archives of General Psychiatry, 35,* 1461–1468.

Cattell, R. B. (1949). r_p and other coefficients of pattern similarity. *Psychometrika, 14,* 279–298.

Committee on Child Psychiatry. (1966). *Psychopathological disorders in childhood: Theoretical considerations and a proposed classification.* New York: Group for the Advancement of Psychiatry.

Connolly, A. J., Wachtman, W., & Pritchett, E. M. (1976). *KeyMath Diagnostic Arithmetic Test.* Circle Pines, MN: American Guidance Service.

Cromwell, R. L., Blashfield, R. K., & Strauss, J. S. (1975). Criteria for classification systems. In N. Hobbs (Ed.), *Issues in the classification of children* (Vol. 1, pp. 4–25). San Francisco: Jossey-Bass.

Davis, F. B. (1959). Interpretation of differences among average and individual test scores. *Journal of Educational Psychology, 50,* 162–170.

Davis, F. B. (1964). *Educational measurements and their interpretation.* Belmont, CA: Wadsworth.

Doll, E. A. (1953). *Measurement of social competence: A manual for the Vineland Social Maturity Scale.* Circle Pines, MN: American Guidance Service.

Doll, E. A. (1965). *Vineland Social Maturity Scale—Revised.* Circle Pines, MN: American Guidance Service.

Edlelbrock, C., & Achenbach, T. M. (1980). A typology of Child Behavior Profile patterns: Distribution and correlates for disturbed children aged 6–16. *Journal of Abnormal Child Psychology, 8,* 441–470.

Flor, J. E. (1978). Service provider agreement and special education reform. *Dissertation Abstracts International, 39,* 10A. (University Microfilms No. 79-8734)

Freeman, M. (1971). A reliability study of psychiatric diagnosis in childhood and adolescence. *Journal of Child Psychology and Psychiatry, 12,* 43–54.

Garfield, S. L. (1978). Research problems in childhood diagnosis. *Journal of Consulting and Clinical Psychology, 46,* 596–601.

Glutting, J. J., McDermott, P. A., & Stanley, J. C. (1987). Resolution of differences in establishing confidence limits for test scores. *Educational and Psychological Measurement, 47,* 607–614.

Gough, H. (1971). Some reflections on the meaning of psychodiagnosis. *American Psychologist, 26,* 161–167.

Grossman, H. J. (Ed.). (1977). *Manual on terminology and classification in mental retardation* (rev. ed.). Washington, DC: American Association on Mental Deficiency.

Grossman, H. J. (Ed.). (1983). *Classification in mental retardation.* Washington, DC: American Association on Mental Deficiency.

Johnson, D. J., & Myklebust, H. R. (1967). *Learning disabilities: Educational principles and practices.* New York: Grune & Stratton.

Karlsen, B., Madden, R., & Gardner, E. F. (1976). *Stanford Diagnostic Reading Tests* (Red, Green, and Brown levels). New York: Harcourt Brace Jovanovich.

Kirk, S. A., & Bateman, B. (1962). Diagnosis and remediation of learning disabilities. *Exceptional Children, 29,* 73–76.

Kohn, M. (1988). *Kohn Social Competence Scale and Problem Checklist.* San Antonio: Psychological Corporation.

Lambert, N. M. (1981). *AAMD Adaptive Behavior Scale—School Edition: Diagnostic and technical manual.* Monterey, CA: Publishers Test Service.

Lambert, N. M., & Hartsough, C. S. (1981). Development of a simplified diagnostic scoring method for the school version of the Adaptive Behavior Scale. *American Journal of Mental Deficiency, 86,* 138–147.

McClung, M. (1973). School classification: Some legal approaches to labels. *Inequity in Education, 14,* 17–57.

McDermott, P. A. (1980a). A computerized system for the classification of developmental, learning, and adjustment disorders in school children. *Educational and Psychological Measurement, 40,* 761–768.

McDermott, P. A. (1980b). Congruence and typology of diagnoses in school psychology: An empirical study. *Psychology in the Schools, 17,* 12–24.

McDermott, P. A. (1980c). Prevalence and constituency of behavioral disturbance taxonomies in the regular school population. *Journal of Abnormal Child Psychology, 8,* 523–536.

McDermott, P. A. (1980d). A systems-actuarial method for the differential diagnosis of handicapped children. *Journal of Special Education, 14,* 7–22.

McDermott, P. A. (1981). Sources of error in the psychoeducational diagnosis of children. *Journal of School Psychology, 19,* 31–44.

McDermott, P. A. (1982). Actuarial assessment systems for the grouping and classification of schoolchildren. In C. R. Reynolds & T. B. Gutkin (Eds.), *The handbook of school psychology* (pp. 243–272). New York: Wiley.

McDermott, P. A. (1983). A syndromic typology for analyzing school children's disturbed social behavior. *School Psychology Review, 12,* 250–259.

McDermott, P. A. (1986). The observation and classification of exceptional child behavior. In R. T. Brown & C. R. Reynolds (Eds.), *Psychological perspectives on childhood exceptionality: A handbook* (pp. 136–180). New York: Wiley-Interscience.

McDermott, P. A. (1988). Agreement among diagnosticians or observers: Its importance and determination. *Professional School Psychology, 3*, 225–240.

McDermott, P. A., & Watkins, M. W. (1985). *McDermott Multidimensional Assessment of Children: 1985 Apple II version.* San Antonio: The Psychological Corporation.

McDermott, P. A., & Watkins, M. W. (1987). *McDermott Multidimensional Assessment of Children: 1987 IBM version.* San Antonio: Psychological Corporation.

Mercer, C. D., Forgnone, C., & Wolking, W. D. (1976). Definitions of learning disabilities used in the United States. *Journal of Learning Disabilities, 9*, 376–386.

Mercer, J. R., & Lewis, J. F. (1982). *Adaptive Behavior Inventory for Children.* New York: Psychological Corporation.

Miller, L. C. (1981). *Louisville Behavior Checklist manual* (rev. ed.). Los Angeles: Western Psychological Services.

Ministry of Education. (1981). *Special education information handbook.* Toronto: Author.

Petersen, C. R., & Hart, D. H. (1978). Use of multiple discriminant function analysis in evaluation of a state-wide system for identification of educationally handicapped children. *Psychological Reports, 43*, 743–755.

Piotrowski, R. J. (1976). The effect of omitting a limited number of subtests on the Full Scale reliability of the WISC-R. *Psychology in the Schools, 13*, 298–301.

Psychological Corporation. (1982a). *PRISM: Math 1.* New York: Author.

Psychological Corporation. (1982b). *PRISM: Reading 1.* New York: Author.

Psychological Corporation. (1983). *Basic Achievement Skills Individual Screener.* New York: Author.

Quay, H. C. (1986). Classification. In H. C. Quay & J. S. Werry (Eds.), *Psychopathological disorders of childhood* (3rd ed., pp. 1–34). New York: Wiley.

Quay, H. C., & Peterson, D. R. (1983). *Interim manual for the Revised Behavior Problem Checklist.* Coral Gables, FL: Authors.

Rutter, M., & Shaffer, D. (1980). DSM-III: A step forward or back in terms of the classification of child psychiatric disorders? *Journal of the American Academy of Child Psychiatry, 19*, 371–394.

Rutter, M., Shaffer, D., & Shepherd, M. (1975) *A multi-axial classification of child psychiatric disorders.* Geneva: World Health Organization.

Sabatino, D. A., & Miller, T. L. (1980). The dilemma of diagnosis in learning disabilities: Problem and potential directions. *Psychology in the Schools, 17*, 76–86.

Salvia, J., & Good, R. (1982). Significant discrepancies in the classification of pupils: Differentiating the concept. In J. T. Neisworth (Ed.), *Assessment in special education* (pp. 77–82). Rockville, MD: Aspen.

Shaw, S. F., Bensky, J. M., & Dixon, B. (1981). *Stress and burnout: A primer for special education and special services personnel.* Reston, VA: Council for Exceptional Children.

Silverstein, A. B. (1973). Note on prevalence. *American Journal of Mental Deficiency, 77*, 380–382.

Silverstein, A. B. (1981a). Reliability and abnormality of test score differences. *Journal of Clinical Psychology, 37*, 392–394.

Silverstein, A. B. (1981b). Verbal-performance IQ discrepancies on the WISC-R: One more time. *Journal of Consulting and Clinical Psychology, 49*, 465–466.

Silverstein, A. B. (1982). Pattern analysis as simultaneous statistical inference. *Journal of Consulting and Clinical Psychology, 50*, 234–240.

Sparrow, S. S., Balla, D. A., & Cichetti, D. V. (1984). *Vineland Adaptive Behavior Scales.* Circle Pines, MN: American Guidance Service.

Spitzer, R. L., Endicott, J., & Robins, E. (1975). Clinical criteria for psychiatric diagnosis and DSM-III. *American Journal of Psychiatry, 132*, 187–192.

Spitzer, R. L., & Fleiss, J. L. (1974). A re-analysis of the reliability of psychiatric diagnosis. *British Journal of Psychiatry, 125*, 341–347.

Spitzer, R. L., Forman, J. B. W., & Nee, J. (1979). DSM-III field trials: 1. Initial interater diagnostic reliability. *American Journal of Psychiatry, 136*, 815–817.

Stanley, J. C. (1971). Reliability. In R. L. Thorndike, *Educational measurement* (2nd ed., pp. 356–442). Washington, DC: American Council on Education.

Stott, D. H. (1981). *Manual to the Bristol Social Adjustment Guides.* San Diego: Educational and Industrial Testing Service.

Stott, D. H., McDermott, P. A., Green, L. F., & Francis, J. M. (1988a). *Learning Behaviors Scale* (research ed.). San Antonio: Psychological Corporation.

Stott, D. H., McDermott, P. A., Green, L. F., & Francis, J. M. (1988b). *Study of Children's Learning Behaviors.* San Antonio: Psychological Corporation.

Tatsuoka, M. M. (1974). *Classification procedures: Profile similarity.* Champaign, IL: Institute for Personality and Ability Testing.

Thorndike, R. L. (1963). *The concepts of over- and underachievement.* New York: Teachers College Press.

Thurlow, M. L., Ysseldyke, J. E., & Casey, A. (1984). Teachers' perceptions of criteria for identifying learning disabled students. *Psychology in the Schools, 21*, 349–355.

Trites, R. L., Blouin, A. G., & Laprade, K. (1982). Factor analysis of the Conners Teacher Rating Scale based on a large normative sample. *Journal of Consulting and Clinical Psychology, 50*, 615–623.

Trites, R. L., Dugas, E., Lynch, G., & Ferguson, H. (1979). Prevalence of hyperactivity. *Journal of Pediatric Psychology, 4*, 179–188.

Trites, R. L., & Laprade K. (1983). Evidence for an independent syndrome of hyperactivity. *Journal of Child Psychology and Psychiatry, 24*, 573–586.

Tryon, W. W. (1979). The test-trait fallacy. *American Psychologist, 34*, 402–406.

U.S. Department of Health, Education, and Welfare. (1977a). Assistance to states for education of handicapped children. *Federal Register, 42,* 65082–65085.

U.S. Department of Health, Education, and Welfare. (1977b). Education of handicapped children. *Federal Register, 42,* 42474–42518.

Watkins, M. W. (1982). *Math wars.* Phoenix, AZ: SouthWest EdPsych Services.

Watkins, M. W., & Johnson, L. (1984). *The vocabulary machine.* Phoenix, AZ: SouthWest EdPsych Services.

Watkins, M. W., Johnson, L., Adams, S., & Bloom, L. (1981). *The reading machine.* Phoenix, AZ: SouthWest EdPsych Services.

Watkins, M. W., Johnson, L., & Bloom, L. (1985). *The math machine.* Phoenix, AZ: SouthWest EdPsych Services.

Wechsler, D. (1974). *Manual for the Wechsler Intelligence Scale for Children–Revised.* New York: Psychological Corporation.

Wechsler, D. (1981). *Wechsler Adult Intelligence Scale–Revised.* New York: Psychological Corporation.

Weiskopf, P. E. (1980). Burnout among teachers of exceptional children. *Exceptional Children, 47,* 18–23.

Woodcock, R. W. (1973). *Woodcock Reading Mastery Tests manual.* Circle Pines, MN: American Guidance Services.

World Health Organization. (1978). *Mental disorders: Glossary and guide to their classification in accordance with the ninth revision of the International Classification of Diseases.* Geneva: Author.

Zigler, E., & Trickett, P. K. (1978). IQ, social competence, and evaluation of early childhood intervention programs. *American Psychologist, 33,* 789–798.

22

EDUCATIONAL TESTING APPLICATIONS OF THE RASCH MODEL

W. LOUIS BASHAW

University of Georgia

This chapter concerns what are now standard measurement techniques in education and psychology. The general topic of item response models and the specific topic of "the Rasch model" have been heavily researched since the first edition of this *Handbook*. This chapter repeats much of the tutorial content of the corresponding chapter in the first edition and presents discussion of recent advances in this important area. The reasons for including this chapter in the *Handbook* have not changed. In fact, knowledge about this set of measurement tools is more important today than in 1982.

This chapter is about an approach to test construction and interpretation that continues to become increasingly important. The approach has several names, including latent test theory, item characteristic curve theory, and item response theory. (The latter term has become the preferred label due to the importance of Frederick Lord's contributions [Lord, 1980].) The body of theory and applied techniques has grown substantially since the last edition of the *Handbook* due partly to the improvement in computers and computer soft-

ware and largely to adoption of the techniques by test publishers. Today, most test publishers and most new statewide testing programs utilize item response theory to a large extent. The school psychologist cannot ignore this approach to testing since it has become so widely used.

One of the more popular item response models is the Rasch model, developed in the late 1950s by a Danish mathematician, Georg Rasch, and popularized in this country by Benjamin Wright of the University of Chicago. This particular model has been especially well used in school testing programs, and its widespread use is the reason for it being the subject of a *Handbook* chapter.

The school psychologist is normally the resident expert in all psychometric matters, if not in all quantitative matters. It is essential that school psychologists have at their fingertips information on any aspect of psychometrics that is likely to be needed.

This chapter is included because of the increasing use of this model and the work of researchers who have built upon Rasch's work. Test development, test interpretation, and item banking will so frequently involve what is now called the Rasch model that it is imperative that school psychologists have a working knowledge of Rasch's principles and of standard applications of his work.

Although Rasch's work is part of the psychometric literature called item response theory, it did not originate in the more general latent trait theories. His model leads to procedures that are more practical than is true of more complicated latent trait models. In particular, these procedures often require less data than do the other, more complicated models. However, since there are competing latent trait models, and since many experts prefer the more complicated models in some applications, you do need to know how Rasch's ideas differ from those of other item response theory protagonists, and should know something about the approaches to determining if the Rasch model or a competing model should be preferred in a particular application.

It is appropriate to start with an introduction to Rasch's thinking about measurement. Rasch's notion was that the test giver should have wide latitude in choosing test items without running into scaling problems; and furthermore, that tests ought to be readily interpretable without concern as to the characteristics of the sample chosen for norm development. This goal he formalized as "specific objectivity." His work was the development of a model for test construction that allows for this specific objectivity.

Specific objectivity can be described as a testing situation in which a specific domain of test tasks is defined, in which a specific population of examinees is defined, and which is characterized by two desirable features: person measurement is independent of the set of items used to measure a person, and item measurement (calibration of difficulty) is independent of the set of persons used in the calibration. That is, the test constructor and the test user both will have considerably more freedom than is generally the case in educational testing. In particular, the need for massive, representative norm groups is diminished considerably; the concepts of item banking, random generation of test forms, and tailored testing become highly feasible; the concepts of scaling can be joined with the concepts of criterion referencing in meaningful ways; and problems concerning comparability of multiple levels and forms can be resolved. Moreover, these gains can be accomplished without sacrificing any traditional techniques of interest to test users.

In 1960 Rasch published *Probabilistic Models for Some Intelligence and Attainment Tests* (Rasch, 1980/1960), in which he described several mathematical models for representing responses to test questions. One of these models, which he called the "simple item analysis model," popularly known as "the Rasch model," is discussed at length in this chapter. The chapter also includes information on other Rasch models that appeared in his 1960 work since some of these other models are gaining broader use. Moreover, there exist extensions of his work that have applications in modern intelligence testing theory, which is also of critical importance to the school psychologist.

While a smattering of research on the Rasch model appeared in this country between 1960 and 1967, it was not until the 1967 ETS Invitational Conference on Testing that a paper was presented that stirred the interest of the American measurement community. University of Chicago Professor Benjamin Wright's paper *Sample-free Test Calibration and Person Measurement,* presented at that conference, has probably served to popularize the Rasch model more than any other work. Research became highly active worldwide during the 1970s and continues to be a major topic in recent measurement journals. The series of training sessions by Benjamin Wright at American Educational Research Association annual meetings since 1969 has created a large, active American constituency for Rasch's work.

There are several texts available today that will give you extensive information on Rasch's work and on the other IRT models. Among the more important texts that present all models are Baker (1985); Hambleton (1983); Hambleton and Swaminathan (1985); Hulin, Drasgow, and Parsons (1983); and Lord (1980). The Birnbaum section of Lord and Novick (1968) will still impress readers with its scope. Among these works, a reader new to this topic might profit best by Baker's work, especially since it is accompanied by a microcomputer tutorial that is quite helpful in explaining many of the more complex ideas in IRT. Also, a reader would need to review the full issue of the *Journal of Educational Measurement* that is dedicated to IRT (Jaeger, 1977) and the full issue of *Applied Educational Measurement* concerning advances in IRT (Hambleton & van der Linden, 1982).

Among works focusing especially on Rasch's works are, of course, his famous 1960 book. Wright and Stone (1979) remains the best source of advice on implementation of the item response version of Rasch's work. Although it needs to be revised to include developments since 1979, there is little in it that cannot be used effectively today. Wright and Masters (1982) present rather full discussion of procedures for applying Rasch's work to a variety of types of rating scales. Andrich's (1988) monograph on the Rasch model is an excellent treatise on the model's development and its relationship to classical measurement models. He also gives full descriptions of estimation methods and tests of fit.

In this chapter we provide a brief description of George Rasch's background as it relates to his theoretical psychometric work, a formal description of the Rasch Model, a discussion of how the model should be used for the construction of test item pools, a discussion of how Rasch-calibrated item sets can be used and interpreted, and a brief comparison of the Rasch model to other choices of psychometric models.

GEORG RASCH

An analysis of Rasch's contributions can be better appreciated with a little knowledge of his personal history. Like Alfred Binet, Rasch's psychometric contributions arose out of the need to solve specific applied problems. These comments come from the preface of his book (Rasch, 1960/1980) and from a mimeographed sketch that was distributed when he visited the University of Georgia in the early 1970s.

Rasch was trained as a mathematician. He received a Ph.D. in 1930 at the University of Copenhagen on the basis of a thesis on matrix calculus. He became interested in statistics and spent the year of 1936 with R. A. Fisher at a time when Fisher was conceptualizing the concept of "sufficiency." He later spent time with John Tukey at Harvard while Tukey was concerned about "additivity." Both of these fundamental statistics concepts are central to Rasch's psychometric ideas.

Psychometrically, like Binet, Rasch was asked to participate in a project concerning the measurement of intelligence. However, Rasch's specific job was to standardize a group intelligence test for the Denmark Department of Defense. This was in the

period 1945–1948. The item analysis phase, he cites, led him to question traditional procedures as being too sample dependent. He was also concerned that the traditional person measurement was too dependent on the set of items that was chosen for a test form. Thus this was the period in which he defined the problem "of how to develop tests that yield specific objectivity."

In 1952 he was requested by the Denmark Department of Social Welfare to help assess the reading competency of retarded students. At that time, he developed two of the models discussed in his 1960 book. These models involved the use of oral reading of error counts as modeled by the Poisson process. (These "reading models" or "Rasch-Poisson models" are useful whenever one counts errors and expects the frequency of errors to the number of trials to be relatively small. In addition to reading, the models have been specifically adapted to analyzing writing samples [Andrich, 1973]. The Poisson version also has promise in the area of mastery testing, in which errors are supposed to be relatively rare.) Thus, by 1952, Rasch had essentially solved the problem of the unambiguous definition of person ability and task difficulty.

At the end of 1952, he reanalyzed the group intelligence test using what he called the model of simple conformity or model for the items of a test. This is the model that had become known as the Rasch model in this country and is the topic of this chapter.

The Danish Institute for Educational Research was established in 1955. In this institute Rasch was able to continue his theoretical work while applying them to "a wealth of problems requiring clarification, elaborations and extensions of the principles already laid down" (Rasch, 1960/1980, p. ix). The institute also published his book.

During the year that this book was released, 1960, Rasch visited the University of Chicago. Here he established a continuing close relationship with Benjamin Wright, who has been responsible for the growth of interest in Rasch's work in this country.

Thus the Rasch model (or models) was developed out of a strong theoretical mathematics and statistics background as applied to the multitude of problems facing an educational testing consultant. This range of problems in Rasch's life included reading, writing, psychological and biological development, mental ability, attitudes, social grouping, social interaction, demography, criminology, and bioassay.

THE RASCH MODEL

Models

The term *model* requires some explanation. Usage in this chapter refers to an equation that is intended to describe the interaction of an examinee with a test task. Mathematical equations used as models are simplifications of a more complex reality and are generally used for predictions. These simplifications are often in the form of model assumptions. Most of the equations of physics called laws are models of this type. The gravitational model

$$s = \tfrac{1}{2}gt^2$$

is an example. This model predicts the distance an object will fall in time *t*, where *g* is a gravitational constant. To predict accurately, the model requires the two assumptions, or conditions, that the object start at rest and that it exist and fall in a vacuum. The first of these assumptions can be avoided by adding to the model another term, or parameter, that indicates how far a dropping object has already fallen. The second assumption cannot be avoided. The model has proven quite useful to physicists without regard to whether or not a vacuum condition exists. Thus mathematical equations as models can sometimes be improved by adding extra parameters, but this addition brings with it the complexity of new parameters that must be estimated.

There will always be assumptions associated with models, and the effect of ignoring these assumptions must be studied. When a model is appropriate over a wide variety of possible violations of an assumption, it is said by statisticians to be "robust" with respect to the assumption. The study of statistical robustness is critical in the evaluation of competing models.

There are at least two general uses of models. One use is to describe rather accurately a complex phenomenon. The second is to be a guide in the development of a phenomenon. An example of the first use is the gravitational law.

This second use is of greater concern in this chapter. An example of the second use is a house blueprint. A blueprint for a new house is a model of an architect's concept of a building that does not exist. If a builder faithfully follows the blueprint plan, a house can be built that is similar to the architect's conceptualization. There are assumptions—such as that materials indicated by the architect will be obtained, that costs can be met without compromise, that an appropriate lot is used for construction, that competent builders will be used, and others.

The Rasch model is to a test constructor what blueprints are to a builder—it is a set of plans for designing a measurement process. If the plans are followed adequately, a measurement process is developed that has certain desirable properties, which Rasch called "specific objectivity." If the plans are not followed, these desirable features may not be obtained.

There is a concern by some psychometricians that the Rasch model is too simple, that it does not adequately predict test behavior. These psychometricians are concerned with the first use—the degree to which a model predicts examinee behavior on traditional, existing tests.

The second use of models is more appropriate in the study of Rasch's work. The primary use of the Rasch model is as a guide for test construction. Specifically, it is a guide for building a pool of test questions that can be used quite flexibly. Assumptions in the model are conditions that one tries to establish. Which of several competing latent trait models might "fit" given data best is of secondary concern. However, more general latent trait models are discussed at the end of this chapter.

STOCHASTIC MODELS

The Rasch model is a stochastic model rather than a deterministic model (see Lord and Novick, 1968, pp. 23–24). Deterministic models are used in physics where predictions are expected to be quite accurate. In behavioral sciences we know that our models do not include all possible causes, and predictions from them will be somewhat in error. Thus, we, in the behavioral sciences, normally make interval predictions and associate probabilities of accuracy with these intervals. For example, we might say that the client's intelligence is in the range of 100 to 110 (instead of saying 105), and we attach to this interval the probability of .68 or .95, or whatever our confidence level is.

In particular, the Rasch model and other latent trait models predict the *probability* of something happening. Formally, the model gives the probability of examinees answering a test question correctly.

Odds and Probability

As a background topic, it is useful to introduce the concept of odds. This term is used essentially in the betting sense. Formally, odds and probability are equivalent ways of expressing one's expectations of an event occurring. In particular, if odds are designated by O and probability is designated by P, the functional relationship between them is

$$P = \frac{O}{(1 + O)}$$

or, equivalently,

$$O = P + (1 - P)$$

Thus if the probability of a student passing a question is .20, the odds for a pass are .25. (A gambler might say "1 to 4," but decimal notation is appropriate here.) The probability of a fail is $Q = 1 - P$, or .80. The odds for failing are 4.0 (or 4 to 1).

The scale differences are important here. The scale for probability is 0 to 1, with 0 meaning impossible and 1 meaning certain. On the odds scale, impossible is zero, while certain is an undefined extremely large number (designated by "∞"). A probability of .5 translates into an odds value of 1.0. Thus events with less than a 50–50 chance have probabilities in the range 0 to .5, while odds are in the range 0 to 1.0. Events that are more likely than 50–50 have probabilities in the range .5 to 1.0 and odds in the range 1.0 to ∞.

Rasch Model in Odds Form

A simple way to express Rasch's item analysis model is in odds form. In analysis of variance methods we use multiplication to designate interactions. Here we will also. Consider the interaction of a person of ability A with a question of easiness E. We can model the odds for this person passing this item as

$$O = A \times E \tag{1}$$

This information can be meaningful if we measure person ability and item easiness on odds scales. That is, if $A = 0$, this person finds all questions impossibly difficult. If A is large, say 100, the person finds all but the most difficult questions extremely easy. Similar statements can be made about items. If $E = 0$, the item is impossibly hard for all examinees. If E is extremely large, most examinees will find the item very easy. If A and E are reciprocals, so that $A \times E = 1.0$, the item and person "match." The item and the person are equal in the sense that the item is exactly appropriate for the person's ability. The interaction form $O = A \times E$ can be rewritten as a simple additive equation by using logarithms. We have

$$\log O = \log A + \log E$$

Any logarithm base can be used. It is common in most statistical and mathematical work to use natural logarithms, where the base is the irrational number e, which is about 2.72. Natural logs are universally designated by "ln." So we have

$$\ln O = \ln A + \ln E$$

We can reverse our easiness scale into a difficulty scale by changing the plus sign to a minus sign. Letting $a = \ln A$ and $d = -\ln E$, we have

$$\ln \text{Odds} = a - d$$

where d is a difficulty index.

By measuring persons and items on log scales, the difference $a - d$ is a direct measure of the appropriateness of item difficulty to person ability. It is a useful index for constructing interpretive tables. The difference $a - d$ will be called "u."

Rasch Model in Probability Form

The simple odds equation $O = A \times E$ can be converted into probability form by the relationship $P = O/(1 + O)$. We have

$$P = \frac{AE}{1 + AE} \tag{2}$$

This formula can be converted to use a natural log scale for ability and difficulty by substituting

$$A = e^a \quad \text{and} \quad E = e^{-d}$$

The latter substitution converts easiness to difficulty. We have

$$p = \frac{e^{a-d}}{1 + e^{a-d}} \tag{3}$$

It is also useful to know a form for Q, the probability of failure. Since $Q=1-P$, we get

$$Q = \frac{1}{1 + AE} \quad \text{or} \quad Q = \frac{1}{1 + e^{a-d}} \quad (4)$$

The pieces of a model, P and Q, can be put together to form a model that relates probability to a test item score, x, where x is assigned 1 for correct and 0 for wrong. We can write

$$P(x) = \frac{(AE)^x}{1 + AE} = \frac{e^{x(a-d)}}{1 + e^{a-d}} \quad (5)$$

which equals equation (2) if $x=1$ and equals equation (4) if $x=0$ (see Lord & Novick, 1968, p. 362).

To make our model (equation [5]) more specific, we need to add a subscript (i) on A and x to indicate what person is involved and a different subscript (j) on E and x to indicate which item is involved. We have

$$P(x_{ij}) = \frac{(A_i E_j)^{x_{ij}}}{1 + A_i E_j} \quad (6)$$

which is the probability of a response x by person i to item j.

A graph of P versus a for any item is a sigmoid curve that looks like a cumulative distribution function. Such a graph is called an item characteristic curve.

The Rasch Model

A full statement of the Rasch Model is conveniently made in a standard "if-then" theorem form: "If you do certain things, then you get certain results." The desired results are the flexibility properties of specific objectivity. The "if" part of the statements are the model assumptions.

Consider a general symbol λ_{ij} as a parameter describing the situation of person i's response to task j, where responses can be "correct" or "wrong." Let P_{ij} be the probability of a "correct" response. Then *IF*

1. $P_{ij} = \dfrac{\lambda_{ij}}{1 + \lambda_{ij}}$
2. $\lambda_{ij} = A_i E_j$
3. persons respond independently of each other, and
4. items are not mutually interdependent,

THEN the resulting test will yield specific objectivity properties.

Condition 1 is a restatement of equation (5) in general terms. Condition 2 states that the situational parameter λ can be partitioned into two and only two parts, one dealing with the difficulty of the task and the other with the ability of the person. This separation of person and item parameters is central to Rasch scaling. Condition 3 says essentially that students should not cheat and Condition 4 says that items should not be written such that some items provide clues for other items.

There are several major implications of these "if" statements. There is only one ability and one easiness parameter. This means that we should attempt to assess only one trait at a time. Psychometricians have argued for some time that building unidimensional tests maximizes interpretability. The Rasch model formalizes this concept. Since there are no item parameters other than a difficulty parameter, it follows that the need for other parameters must be eliminated in test construction. In particular, there are no discrimination or guessing parameters. Therefore, we should choose items that are equally "good" in the discrimination sense so that this parameter will be unneeded. We should also write items that minimize guessing as a factor.

Other models that are used commonly include parameters for discrimination and/or guessing. That is, the more general IRT models appear to allow item pools that vary in discrimination and account for guessing. Many testing experts believe that these additional parameters are necessary. Issues related to the number of item parameters are presented in a subsequent section.

Let's take a better look at the "then" portion of our theorem, specific objectivity. The separation of person and item parameters leads to the condition that items can be compared and calibrated without a heavy regard for the nature of the calibration sample. Item calibration is said to be independent of the person sample. On the other hand, person comparisons, or measurement, is separated from the items, so that person measurement is largely independent of the set of items used. The limits of these independence claims are suggested by the word *specific*, namely, that these independence claims are restricted to specified item domains and person populations.

The construction of item pools which have equal discrimination values means that all items in the pool are similarly scaled quantitatively, and thus are interchangeable except for their difficulty. This allows us to give bright students difficult questions and slow students easy ones and still get comparable scores for them. This property solves the controversy of whether to test at grade or reading level. It also permits computerized adaptive testing (CAT), which is the use of computers to administer tests individually in an interactive mode. CAT can permit examinees to be tested quite efficiently by finding the most appropriate items for each examinee.

Here are some other applications implied by specific objectivity as listed by Wright (in Jaeger, 1977, pp. 107–114): linking test forms and levels, building test "networks," criterion referencing scores, norm referencing scores, discovering guessers or careless examinees, determining item bias (a direct consequence of the condition that different samples should yield similar calibrations), controlling measurement precision, and test tailoring. Many other applications are possible. The more general latent trait models also permit most of these applications, but these other models bring with them greater mathematical complexity and difficult estimation problems.

CONSTRUCTING RASCH ITEM POOLS

It is important for the reader to discriminate between "test construction" and "test use." For this reason, these topics are clearly separated in this chapter. In this section we discuss techniques for building test item pools according to Rasch model specifications. An "item pool" might be a single short instrument designed for a specific purpose; or a "pool" might be a large item bank from which specific tests are chosen for specific purposes. In particular, such item banks are generated so that new forms can easily be constructed each examination period. Also, such banks can be used in tailored testing schemes, like CAT, in which each examinee receives items unique to that examinee's ability level.

Types of Appropriate Tests

Latent trait models are most appropriately applied to measures of traits as constructs. That is, you ought to be able to conceptualize the construct to be measured as having a dimension along which you expect to find individual differences. Relevant variables are those which show developmental growth or growth as a result of training. Thus standard concerns for aptitudes and attitudes are

appropriate for Rasch scaling. Wright and Masters (1982) is an excellent text for attitude assessment methods.

Much attention has been given to normal achievement tests (e.g., the Oregon statewide testing programs). This writer has a concern that some applications to achievement testing might be inappropriate. In particular, high school–level sciences and social sciences possibly will not generate a "trait." Generic tests in areas such as these will possibly fail to be unidimensional to the point that Rasch scaling could be inappropriate. Achievement areas such as elementary-level reading and arithmetic, on the other hand, appear quite appropriate.

The dimensionality of a test is a serious concern with regard to all IRT models, but it has been ignored in many applications or the investigators decided that the concerns were not serious based on their results. One of the important areas of today's psychometric research is that of multidimensional models; see, for example, Embretson (1984), Whiteley (1980a, 1980b), or Stegelmann (1983). However, the user will more often be concerned with the construction of reasonably homogeneous single tests. Screening items for discrimination homogeneity, separating items by content or item format, and minimizing guessing will assist in obtaining unidimensional properties. Factor analysis can be used to assist in decisions concerning dimensionality, but there are problems in its use with individual item responses as data (Lord & Novick, 1968, pp. 381–382).

Item pools should not easily be classified into subgroups of items, especially if these subgroups can be associated with particular training programs unique to certain examinee subsamples. That is, do not have "new math" and "old math" items in the same test if examinees include some trained in "new math" and some not so trained. Such a situation calls clearly for two tests, as two clear traits are probably involved. Excellent suggestions as to how to subdivide tests into more homogeneous tests on rational rather than empirical bases have been made by Mislevy (1984) and Tatsuoka (1987). These suggestions include separating items by format and separating them by the cognitive tasks required in their solution as judged by subject experts.

Tests covering a broad range of skills, such as general intelligence, might work reasonably well since a general factor will dominate item interrelationships. The concern is the avoidance of tests measuring two or several distinct abilities, each assessed by distinct subsets of items or requiring distinct sets of cognitive skills. Each of these "common factors" needs to be tested separately.

Types of Items

The conditions of the model lead to concerns about item type. In particular, the need to deemphasize guessing and to create experimental independence among items can be considered in test planning.

The elimination of guessing is best done by not using formats that permit it (e.g., the *Woodcock Reading Mastery Test,* Woodcock, 1974). However, most test development and applied research has been done using multiple-choice tests. Some users believe that the evidence clearly supports the use of the multiple-choice format despite the apparent problems inherent in this item type. However, there is considerable objection to using models without a guessing factor for multiple-choice tests. In particular, see Divgi (1986). If one feels compelled to use multiple-choice item types, one ought to consider adding extra alternatives to decrease guessing. Another plausible approach is to borrow the "testlet" idea of Wainer and Kiely (1987), which they suggest in another context. That is, consider scoring small sets of items as if the set is a single item. An examinee might be required to pass all of a set (testlet) of three items before getting any credit; thus the probability of getting credit by guessing is reduced to an extremely small value. Moreover, multiple-choice item writers need necessarily to pay attention to traditional rules on how to generate meaningful distractors so that guessing is minimized by careful item writing and, subsequently, these writers should use distractor analysis as part of the item analysis phase of test development. However, this writer believes that the first attack on the issue of item type is the creative design of item types that reduce the possibilities of guessing to insignificance. For example, many tests can use free response item type and still be scored quickly by proper computer equipment and software.

Experimental independence among items can also be controlled somewhat by test constructors. In particular, items need to be written clearly so that the trait of interest is the reason for success or failure on the item. No items in the pool should provide clues to correct answers of other items.

Item Selection

Item selection is not highly different from the selection of items in traditional item analysis. There is a difference: namely, the test developer might choose to discard items with extremely high discrimination estimates in order to increase the homogeneity of discrimination estimates. However, traditional item analysis and Rasch item analysis will both identify many of the same items. That is, using a Rasch program will not lead to drastic redefinition of what constitutes a good item. In particular, any item analysis routine will lead to discarding poorly discriminating items. Discarding these poor items will lead to making discrimination values relatively homogeneous, whether or not items with high discrimination indexes are left in the pool. In general, however, the Rasch analysis should lead to a selection of items of relatively equal discrimination. Equivalent slopes can be translated roughly into slope values between .8 and 1.25. However, a wider range of slopes is typical and usually works well.

The usual discrimination indexes are the biserial and point-biserial correlations of each item with estimated ability and the item characteristic curve discrimination parameter (often called the slope parameter, as the discrimination parameter is proportional to the slope of the item characteristic curve at the point of steepest slope). Under the (implausible) assumption of joint normality of items with traits, all three of these indexes are functions of each other (Lord & Novick, 1968, p. 378).

A simple way to make a rough estimation of item slope for any item is to graph raw scores against $\ln (p/q)$. That is, for each raw score, calculate the natural log of the proportion of persons who both earned that score and passed the item (p) divided by $1-p$. This is done for each raw score. The graph consisting of the raw score as baseline and $\ln (p/q)$ as ordinate should give approximately straight lines. (Curves in the tails can be straightened out by changing the baseline from X to $\ln [X/(K-X]$.) The slopes of these straight lines can be determined directly from the graphs or by fitting a simple linear model to the points on the graph. After discordant items are deleted, a pool of items graphed on a common graph should be a set of nearly parallel lines. (This procedure is presented in detail by Rasch [1960/ 1980, pp. 76–107].) Although the procedure outlined is relatively simple, it would be quite time consuming to conduct without a computer; moreover, it does require large samples. If samples are not large, raw scores can be grouped (which is done in some of the available computer programs).

There is a direct test statistic called mean-square fit that is based on the similarity of data to the model. Basically, it is a chi-square test of whether or not proportions obtained match expected proportions. In general, this index has led to more confusion than help and possibly should be ignored even if it appears on computer output. In particular, it is highly affected by sample size and a user of it is likely to reject items that ought not be rejected. (Rentz & Bashaw, 1975, pp. 41–43). Most of the available computer routines provide some type of fit test.

Desired Statistics

A Rasch item pool needs only two statistics per item—the difficulty and its standard error. Keeping other item analysis data is not to be discouraged, however. In particular, traditional distractor analysis will always be helpful and many reviewers of testing programs will want to see traditional item analysis statistics. With these two indexes for each item, person scores, and accompanying standard errors, are readily calculable. Scoring tables for various forms and equating constants for linking forms are readily calculable.

Editing Data

A major concern is that data used for calibration be valid. Rasch analyses do not require extremely large samples; however, data used ought to be trustworthy. In particular, data gatherers ought to assure themselves that examinees are cooperating.

Moreover, data from students of overly low ability possibly should be excluded from calibration samples if multiple-choice exams are used. Such students introduce too much guessing behavior into the data.

Estimation of Parameters

Software for estimating abilities and item parameters using the Rasch model and the two- and three-parameter models has been made fully available. In this section we first provide a guide to some of today's software and then the logic of estimation for the Rasch model.

First, let's consider general principles. All models require the assumptions of local independence and of person independence. These assumptions are used to construct probability equations to estimate the probability of person response vectors and of full data sets. This is done by multiplying together the various terms that are assumed to be independent. These probabilities are called "likelihood functions," and these functions are used to make the estimations. One finds the estimates that make the data "maximally likely." These estimates are therefore, called, "maximum likelihood estimates." However, there exist a variety of estimation methods, all based to some degree on a likelihood function. We will not include a "consumer's guide" but will give some references to critical sources.

Software

There are programs for both microcomputers and full-framecomputers. Also, for the Rasch model there are ways to make estimates that do not require computers (Wright, in Jaeger, 1977, pp. 100–101, and Wright & Stone, 1979). The microcomputer programs available today include Bock's BILOG (PC BILOG (Mislevy & Bock, 1986), useful for all of the IRT models. Also, there is the most commonly used of the Rasch programs—Microscale (Wright & Linacre, 1984). Assessment Systems Corporation (1987) has RASCAL for the Rasch model and ASCAL for the more complicated models. These are packaged separately, and both are also packaged within MicroCAT, their full system for computerized test bank construction and computerized test administration.

Large computer software includes the most commonly used program, LOGIST (Wingersky, Barton, & Lord, 1982), for the several complex models developed at ETS under Lord's leadership. The most widely used Rasch program is BICAL (Wright & Mead, 1980). Mislevy and Bock (1984) have BILOG for several models.

The two- and three-parameter models require assumptions about the person population and require fairly large samples. These factors have led to interest in variations in estimating. There have been two directions—a Bayesian approach and a search for "robust" estimators. The Bayesian approach is discussed by Lord (1984), Mislevy (1986), and Swaminathan and Gifford (1985). It is available as an option in the MicroCAT and ASCAL routines of Assessment Systems Corporation (1987). The robust estimation approach is an attempt to find estimators that are not subject to sample fluctuations as are the estimations obtained in situations usually requiring large samples. For these, see, for example, Smith (1985) and Wainer and Wright (1980). The AMJACK procedure of Wainer and Wright is likely to get considerable use, especially if software is prepared for commercial use.

Logic of Rasch Estimation

The purpose of this section is to give an intuitive feeling for parameter estimation as it relates to traditional concepts. The basic equation (6) gives the probability of one person's response to one item. The independence assumptions provide a convenient way to write out the probability of a person's response to a set of items as the repeated product of item probabilities. Similarly, the probability of a set of responses of many persons to one item is the repeated product of (6) over persons. The double product of (6) over both persons and items yields the probability of a full matrix of person responses to the items. These equations can be solved to yield the maximum likelihood estimates of all parameters. One way to write out a partial solution is given in equations (7) and (8), which, when solved for the a and d parameters, give us our solutions.

$$X_i = \sum_{j=1}^{k} P_{ij} \qquad (7)$$

where X is the number of correct responses given by person i and k is the number of items.

$$p_j = \frac{1}{N} \sum_{i=1}^{N} P_{ij} \qquad (8)$$

where p is the proportion correct for question j and N is the person sample size.

Equations (7) and (8) can be solved fairly easily for the a's and d's by standard techniques. Equations (7) define one estimate of a for each possible score group from 1 to $k-1$, with abilities for scores of zero and k left undefined. Equations (8) define one estimate of each d for each item. Solving equations (7) requires knowing all d's; while solving equations (8) require knowing all a's. In initial calibration, the solution proceeds by guessing ability values and using the guesses to solve (8). The resulting difficulty estimates are used to solve (7). The new ability estimates are used again to re-solve (8). This process continues until a stable solution is obtained for both sets of a's and d's. (However, in test use, the d's are known from previous calibration. Thus, determining an ability estimate for one person when items have been calibrated previously is relatively easy.)

There is a standard initial guess. A look at this will provide some insight into the meaning of the estimates. If we assume temporarily that all items are equal in difficulty, we can substitute the average difficulty d for each d_i and (7) becomes

$$X_i = k\bar{P} = \frac{kA_i\bar{E}}{1 + A_i\bar{E}} \qquad (9)$$

the solution to which is

$$a_i = \ln \frac{X_i}{k-X_i} + \bar{d}$$

This simplified scoring rule, which can be calculated using most hand-held calculators, yields answers very near to final solutions to (7) and (8) determined by computer. It shows that Rasch ability estimates are very close to a simple function of the number of correct answers. Moreover, it clearly shows how the difficulty of items enters estimation. Namely, persons who answer hard questions (high positive d's) get bonus points depending on how hard were the questions attempted. Persons who take easy questions get penalty points taken away, since easy questions will have negative d values.

A parallel construction is possible for easinesses. We get

$$d_j = \bar{a} - \ln \frac{p_R}{p_w}$$

where p_R is the proportion of correct responses to question j and p_W is the proportion of incorrect responses. The log term will be negative if more persons miss than pass question j; therefore making d_j higher than the average ability. If more pass than fail, the log term is positive and is thus subtracted from the average a. So d is high and positive for hard questions and low for easy ones.

Standard computer routines usually set the average d to zero arbitrarily. This centers difficulty values for the item pool being calibrated. However, all d's and a's can be rescaled to any arbitrary center and unit. Users of tests constructed commercially should remember that the origin (zero point) and interval of measurement are arbitrarily chosen by the test developer.

This section must conclude on a reminder. Most users will use tests developed by others. These users will need only to get number-correct scores and use tables for scaling and interpreting just like they do now with standardized tests.

Standard Error Estimation

Standard errors of ability estimates and of item difficulties are estimated in several ways from complex to simple. In general, both standard errors are estimated fairly accurately by the square root of the reciprocal of the sum of PQ's. The standard error of ability is based on summing, for each possible raw score, over all items, whereas the standard error of difficulty is based on summing, for each item, over all persons. These estimates will be the normal output of any computer program.

However, very simple forms exist. Consider that since P and Q sum to 1.0, PQ must be between 0 and .25. Thus the minimum standard error of ability can be estimated to be $2/\sqrt{k}$, where k is the number of items. Also, the minimum standard error of difficulty can be estimated to be $2/\sqrt{N}$, where N is the size of the calibration person sample. These simple estimates clearly show the importance of the numbers of items for accurate person measurement and the person sample size for accurate item calibration. A fairly reasonable estimate of standard errors is $2.5/\sqrt{k}$ for ability and $2.5/\sqrt{N}$ for item difficulty.

Matching Items to Groups

General guides for constructing a group test from an item bank were developed by Wright and described in detail in Wright and Stone (1979, pp. 129–140). In general, the test construction model is a "3-D" model—the constructor must consider the "height," "width," and "length" of a test. Items should be chosen so that the average ability matches the average difficulty (i.e., $A=1/E$, or $a-d=0$). The width of a test is the range of difficulty values chosen. The range of item difficulty chosen should be based on the estimated person variance. That is, we want to choose a subset out of our item pool that will contain items that assess each of our examinees. If we have a bright group, it is a waste of time to include many easy items. If we have a heterogeneous group, we need some items that match each of our examinees. Wright and Stone (1979) suggest that a reasonable width is four times the expected standard deviation of ability (p. 139).

A general guide is to pick items such that you think that the average ability differs from the item estimates by less than two. Another guide, suggested by Wright for width, is that the hardest item should yield at least a probability of .2 for the least able person, whereas the easiest item should yield a probability of about .8 for the most capable person. Items outside these ranges would tend to be nonfunctioning for large numbers of examinees.

The length of the test must fit the desired accuracy. A guide for length is to choose k to be between $4/S^2$ and $9/S^2$, where S is the desired standard error of measurement. This choice of test length is appropriate if $a-d$ values are in the range -2 to $+2$ (Wright & Stone, 1979, p. 136). If you want the standard error to be about .5 of a ln unit, k should be between 16 and 36. The lower value is appropriate for homogeneous person samples when items fit them, whereas the higher value would be more appropriate for wider tests assessing heterogeneous person samples.

Interpretation of Probabilities

Table 1 presents a general table that can be widely used for score interpretation. It gives the probabilities for various person–item combinations. It is based on natural logarithms, although similar tables for other log bases are easily constructed with hand-held calculators. The table is used by comparing a person's ability estimate to an item difficulty by subtraction. For example, if a person's a exceeds an item's d by $+1$, the probability of this person passing this item is .73. The result, .73, can be interpreted semantically as a prediction that this person (or other persons of the same ability) will pass 73% of tasks having this particular easiness value. It can also be interpreted semantically as a prediction that among all persons of this ability, 73% of them will pass this task or another task of the same degree of difficulty.

Specific test questions can be identified as "standard tasks" for comparative purposes. These tasks can be, but do not need to be, part of a test used for ability estimation. The standard tasks do need to be calibrated on the same scale as all other tasks or items.

Tables can be constructed to show probabilities of passing standard tasks for persons of various ability estimates. Such tables can be validated by gathering appropriate data. Table 2 is an example of this type of table. It is based on data from the *Sequential Tests of Educational Progress* and gives probabilities for passing three specific items for students of five ability levels. If these items tested crucial objectives, this table would give a type of meaningful criterion referencing of the ability estimates (e.g., a person with a -2 has a 50–50 chance of success on questions like Task 1,

TABLE 1   General Rasch Probability Table

$u = a - d$	Probability	$u = a - d$	Probability
−4	.018	4	.982
−3	.047	3	.953
−2.5	.076	2.5	.924
−2	.119	2	.881
−1.8	.142	1.8	.858
−1.6	.168	1.6	.832
−1.4	.198	1.4	.802
−1.2	.231	1.2	.768
−1.0	.269	1.0	.731
−.8	.310	.8	.690
−.6	.354	.6	.646
−.4	.401	.4	.599
−.2	.450	.2	.550
−.1	.475	.1	.525
0	.500	0	.500

but little chance of success on questions on Tasks 2 and Task 3).

MODIFYING TEST BANKS

Items can easily be added to test banks. A set of calibrated items from the bank can be administered along with the new items. A computer analysis of the resulting data will yield easiness values centered on zero. Thus the set of original items will receive difficulty values differing from their item bank calibrations of difficulty. The average difference between the original and new difficulty values for the old items must be determined. This average must be added to each of the difficulties of the new items to yield difficulties for the new items that are on the same scale as all of the other items in the bank.

TABLE 2   Sample Probability Table

Log Ability	Task 1	Task 2	Task 3
+2	.98	.89	.52
+1	.95	.75	.29
0	.88	.52	.13
−1	.74	.29	.05
−2	.51	.13	.02

Preexisting test forms and levels can be tied together into large item banks. This was the topic of the Rentz and Bashaw paper in Jaeger (1977, pp. 161–180) and the Rentz and Bashaw (1975) reports.

Person "Misfit"

One of the ideas that has intrigued the profession since the preceding edition of the *Handbook* is that of testing whether or not a person is responding "properly." This means that the response pattern does not fit the order of item easiness—the person is missing easy questions, or passing overly difficulty questions, or both. Wright tried to label such persons as "guessers," "sleepers," "plodders," or "fumblers" (in Jaeger, 1977, p. 110). He suggested some ways to test the fit of persons to the model which paralleled the tests of fit of items to the model.

Procedures and issues are discussed in detail in Weiss (1983). The Trabin and Weiss chapter (pp. 83–108) is a good review and suggests looking at the person response curve, which is an analog to the item characteristic curve. Levine and Drasgow (1982, pp. 109–131) use the term *appropriateness measurement*, a term that has increased in its use.

There are two reasons for having a way to identify such testing behavior. The most important is that such a procedure can identify persons with unique educational histories or unique ability patterns. That is, there is diagnostic value in such a method.

The second purpose is to screen out bad data from calibration studies. However, the deleting of data creates some logic problems—essentially a decision problem of changing a target population in perhaps unknown ways.

In any case, most of the software listed will give some type of "person fit" statistic. Smith (1985) suggested that robust estimation procedures will lessen the effect of strange subject behavior (that is why such methods are called robust). But he warns that to hide the unique response patterns is to lose any diagnostic value of identifying such responses.

OTHER LATENT TRAIT MODELS

The development of the Rasch model was presented according to this writer's impression of how Rasch developed the model. That is, the development progressed from a simple statement of interaction (equation [1]), to a probability statement (equation [2]), to a log form of the probability statement (equation [3]). This form, when generalized to

$$\frac{e^u}{1 + e^u}$$

where u is a linear function of an ability, is the general form of the logistic function. This suggests a model where u contains a slope parameter, say $u = \beta(a - d)$. Such a model, having two item parameters (d for location and β for slope or discrimination), is an attractive alternative to the Rasch model, which has only a location parameter.

Another model, a modification of the two-item-parameter model, adds a parameter for the lower asymptote of the item characteristic curve. This three-item-parameter model is used commonly in trait research. The asymptote parameter is often characterized as a guessing parameter and is considered by some experts as necessary for multiple-choice items.

These models, and others, were compared analytically by Ronald Hambleton and Linda Cook in Jaeger (1977, pp. 75–96). Other comparisons are reported by Baker (1985, 1987), Lord (1980), Masters and Wright (1984), and others.

Explicating these alternatives and reviewing the arguments as to how many parameters there

should be were not among the purposes of this chapter. Proponents of these more complex models state that existing tests contain items that are too complex for the Rasch one-item-parameter model. However, the inclusion of the extra parameters leads to estimation problems according to Wright and Stone (1979, pp. ix and x).

The more complex models require more data. Specifically, each possible score *pattern* gets a different ability estimate using the two- or three-parameter models. Consider a 10-item test. A 10-item test yields 1,024 score patterns. You could have a sample of 1,000 without having two persons getting the same ability estimate. A 10-item test given to 1,000 students yields 10,000 bits of information. This information must be used, in the three-parameter model, to estimate 30 item parameters and 1,000 abilities. The two-parameter model would require the estimation of 20 item parameters and 1,000 abilities. The Rasch model would require estimates for only 19 parameters— 10 difficulties and the nine abilities corresponding to the possible scores of 1, 2, . . . , 9. Clearly, many fewer data are needed to get stable Rasch estimates.

The importance of sample size has been studied at length. Whereas the Rasch calibration can be conducted fairly reliably with a few hundred cases, if the test is appropriate in difficulty for the sample, at least one authority has said that to do a stable three-parameter calibration requires 10,000 cases (Wainer and Thissen, 1987). This is probably an overestimate since there are programs that reduce this "requirement" by either using Bayesian or robust methods to improve estimation. However, Lord has said that if samples are small, the Rasch model should be employed (in Weiss, 1983, pp. 51–62). Others who have studied this problem include Mislevy (1986) and Rigdon and Tsutakawa (1987).

The convenience of using a total-correct score ties Rasch scaling to traditional scaling. The total-correct score is proven by Rasch (1960/1980) to be a sufficient estimate for ability under his model. It is the only model with this property.

This final section is written in a style that shows the writer's bias. There are many prominent psychometricians who believe that the use of the more complicated models is necessary. The simplicity of applications of item banks using the Rasch model framework dictates, to this writer at least, that it is necessary to demonstrate considerable extra benefit from the more complex models before these models should be employed routinely. One's effort is probably best spent in developing appropriate item banks so that the Rasch model can be used and its benefits obtained.

REFERENCES

Andrich, D. (1973). *Latent trait psychometric theory in the measurement and evaluation of essay writing ability.* Unpublished doctoral dissertation, University of Chicago.

Andrich, D. (1988). *Rasch models for measurement.* Sage University Paper Series on Quantitative Applications in the Social Sciences (07–068). Newbury Park, CA: Sage.

Assessment Systems Corporation. (1987). *User's manual for the MicroCAT Testing System* (2nd ed.). St. Paul, MN: Author.

Baker, F. B. (1985). *The basics of item response theory.* Portsmouth, NH: Heinemann.

Baker, F. B. (1987). Methodology review: Item estimation under the one-, two-, and three-parameter logistic models. *Applied Psychological Measurement, 11,* 111–141.

Divgi, D. R. (1986). Does the Rasch model really work for multiple choice items? Not if you look closely. *Journal of Educational Measurement, 23,* 283–298.

Embretson (Whitely), S. E. (1984). A general latent trait model for response processes. *Psychometrika, 49,* 175–186.

Eyde, L. D. (1987, September). Computerised psychological testing [Special issue]. *Applied Psychology: An International Review, 36*(3 & 4).

Hambleton, R. K. (Ed.). (1983). *Applications of item response theory.* Vancouver: Educational Research Institute of British Columbia.

Hambleton, R. K., & Swaminathan, H. (1985). *Item response theory: Principles and applications.* Hingham, MA: Kluwer Nijhoff.

Hambleton, R. K., & van der Linden, W. J. (Eds.). (1982). Advances in item response theory and applications [Special issue]. *Applied Psychological Measurement, 6*(4).

Hulin, C. L., Drasgow, F., & Parsons, C. K. (1983). *Item response theory: Applications to psychological measurement.* Homewood, IL: Dow Jones–Irwin.

Jaeger, R. M. (1977). Applications of latent trait models. [Entire issue]. *Journal of Educational Measurement, 14*(2).

Levine, M. V., & Drasgow, F. (1982). Appropriateness measurement: Review, critique, and validating studies. *British Journal of Mathematical and Statistical Psychology, 35,* 42–56.

Lord, F. M. (1980). *Applications of item response theory to practical testing problems.* Hillsdale, NJ: Lawrence Erlbaum.

Lord, F. M. (1984). *Maximum likelihood and Bayesian parameter estimation in item response theory* (Research Report RR-84-30-ONR). Princeton, NJ: Educational Testing Service.

Lord, F. M., & Novick, M. R. (1968). *Statistical theories of mental test scores.* Reading, MA: Addison-Wesley.

Masters, G. N., & Wright, B. D. (1984). The essential process in a family of measurement models. *Psychometrika, 49,* 529–544.

Mislevy, R. J. (1986). Bayes modal estimation in item response models. *Psychometrika, 51,* 177–195.

Mislevy, R. J., & Bock, R. D. (1984). *BILOG I maximum likelihood item analysis and test scoring.* Mooresville, IN: Scientific Software.

Mislevy, R. J. & Bock, R. D. (1986). *PC-BILOG item analysis and test scoring with binary logistic models.* Mooresville, IN: Scientific Software.

Rasch, G. (1980). *Probabilistic models for some intelligence and attainment tests.* Chicago: University of Chicago Press. (Original work published 1960)

Rentz, R. R., & Bashaw, W. L. (1975). *Equating reading tests with the Rasch model* (2 vols.) (Final Report of the U.S. Department of Health, Education, and Welfare, Contract No. OEC-O-72-5237). Athens, GA: University of Georgia, College of Education, Educational Research Laboratory.

Rigdon, S. E., & Tsutakawa, R. K. (1987). Estimation for the Rasch model when both ability and difficulty parameters are random. *Journal of Educational Statistics, 12,* 76–86.

Smith, R. M. (1985). A comparison of Rasch person analysis and robust estimators. *Educational and Psychological Measurement, 45,* 433–444.

Stegelmann, W. (1983). Expanding the Rasch model to a general model having more than one dimension. *Psychometrika, 48,* 259–267.

Swaminathan, H., & Gifford, J. A. (1985). Bayesian estimation in the two parameter logistic model. *Psychometrika, 50,* 349–364.

Tatsuoka, K. K. (1987). Validation of cognitive sensitivity for item response curves. *Journal of Educational Psychology, 24,* 233–245.

Wainer, H., & Kiely, G. L. (1987) Item clusters and computerized testing: A case for testlets. *Journal of Educational Measurement, 24,* 185–202.

Wainer, H., & Thissen, D. (1987). Estimating ability with the wrong model. *Journal of Educational Statistics, 12,* 339–368.

Wainer, H., & Wright, B. D. (1980). Robust estimates of ability in the Rasch model. *Psychometrika, 45,* 373–380.

Weiss, D. J. (Ed.). (1983). *New horizons in testing.* New York: Academic Press.

Whitely, S. E. (1980a). Multicomponent latent trait models for ability tests. *Psychometrika, 45,* 479–494.

Whitley, S. E. (1980b). Latent trait models in the study of intelligence. *Intelligence, 4,* 97–132.

Wingersky, M. S., Barton, M. A., & Lord, F. M. (1982). *LOGIST user's guide: Logist, version 1.0.* Princeton, NJ: Educational Testing Service.

Woodcock, R. W. (1974). *Woodcock Reading Mastery Test.* Circle Pines, MN: American Guidance Service.

Wright, B. D. (1967). Sample-free test calibration and person measurement. *Proceedings: 1967 Invita-*

tional Conference on Testing Problems. Princeton, NJ: Educational Testing Service.

Wright, B. D., & Linacre, J. M. (1984). *MICROSCALE.* Boston: Mediax Interactive Technologies.

Wright, B. D., & Masters, G. N. (1982). *Rating scale analysis.* Chicago: MESA Press.

Wright, B. D., & Mead, R. J. (1980). *BICAL: Calibrating items and scales with the Rasch model* (Research Memorandum No. 23C). Chicago: University of Chicago, Department of Education, MESA Psychometric Laboratory.

Wright, B. D., & Stone, M. H. (1979). *Best test design.* Chicago: MESA Press.

SCHOOL PSYCHOLOGICAL INTERVENTIONS: FOCUS ON CHILDREN

23

SCHOOL-BASED CONSULTATION: THEORY, TECHNIQUES, AND RESEARCH

TERRY B. GUTKIN
University of Nebraska–Lincoln
MICHAEL J. CURTIS
University of Cincinnati

Over the last 10 to 20 years, school-based consultation has emerged as one of the professional activities most preferred by school psychologists, frequently being ranked by practitioners as *the* most desired role. Since the original publication of this chapter in the first edition of the *Handbook* (Gutkin & Curtis, 1982), a continuing stream of surveys, position statements, journal miniseries, books, and book chapters has appeared, attesting to the central role of school-based consultation in the eyes of both school psychologists and the recipients of their services (Alpert, 1984; Alpert & Associates, 1982; Alpert & Silverstein, 1985; Bergan & Kratochwill, in press; Brown, Pryzwansky, & Schulte, 1987; Conoley, 1981, 1986; Conoley & Conoley, 1982; Curtis & Meyers, 1985; Fisher, Jenkins, & Crumbley, 1986; Gallessich, 1983; Mannino, Trickett, Shore, Kidder, & Levin, 1986; Meyers, 1981, 1988; Piersel, 1985; Reschly, 1988; Rosenfield, 1987; Smith, 1984; Smith & Lyon, 1985; Wright & Gutkin, 1981; Ysseldyke et al., 1984). There is even a new journal, the *Journal*

of Educational and Psychological Consultation (edited by Howard Margolis and due to begin publication in the fall of 1989), devoted entirely to consultation theory and research. Supporting the positive attitudes reflected in these and other publications has been a series of research reviews and meta-analyses indicating that school-based consultation is, in fact, an effective means of service delivery (Mannino & Shore, 1985; Medway, 1979b; Medway & Updyke, 1985).

Although in the remainder of this chapter we discuss school-based consultative services primarily from the perspective of school psychologists, it is important to note they are not alone in their support for this approach to service delivery within educational settings. Among others, special educators (Idol & West, 1987; West, 1988; West & Idol, 1987), counseling psychologists (Bundy & Poppen, 1986; Gallessich, 1985; Kurpius, 1978; Meade, Hamilton, & Yuen, 1982), community psychologists (O'Neill & Trickett, 1982), and most recently, speech pathologists (Gallagher & Prutting, 1983; Warren & Rogers-Warren, 1985) also view consultative services as vital.

Despite the broad and growing interest among educational service providers in consultative services, there is still much confusion regarding what constitutes consultation per se. Part of the problem is the term "consultation" itself, which is used in so many contexts and in reference to so many different types of service relationships that it has practically become devoid of meaning. Barry (1970) observed: "Today almost everyone is a consultant. Every program has consultants. Sometimes it seems as if there are more consultants than consultees!" (p. 363). Although there is no single definition of consultation with universal support, Medway's (1979b) definition is used for the purposes of this chapter. Specifically, he defines consultation as a process of "collaborative problem-solving between a mental health specialist (the consultant) and one or more persons (the consultees) who are responsible for providing some form of psychological assistance to another (the client)" (p. 276).

CORE CHARACTERISTICS OF SCHOOL-BASED CONSULTATIVE SERVICES

Although there are many diverse approaches to consultation, two of which are detailed later in this chapter, there are a number of core elements that are common to virtually all models. These elements define the nature of interactions between consultants and consultees and thus serve to define operationally the consultative process. The most important of these core elements are described briefly below.[1]

---

[1] The reader should note that in this section of the chapter the authors are integrating ideas discussed previously in many, many prior publications. In most instances these concepts have become part of "accepted" consultation theory and it is difficult, if not impossible, to know who first presented each one. Space limitations also prohibit the presentation of a comprehensive citation list. Readers interested in further detail are referred to (1) Caplan (1970), generally considered to be the seminal theoretical work establishing the core characteristics of consultation services; (2) Kidder, Tinker, Mannino, and Trickett (1986), a comprehensive annotated bibliography covering 855 journal articles, books, book chapters, and doctoral dissertations from 1978 through 1984; and (3) Gutkin and Curtis (1982), the original version of this chapter, which includes a reasonably extensive reference list pertaining to the ideas presented in this section.

Indirect Service Delivery

The single most definitive characteristic of consultation is the indirect service delivery concept. In the more traditional system of direct service delivery, the psychologists's primary contact is with a client (or patient). Psychologists working from an indirect service delivery model, however, interact primarily with "care givers" (consultees), who work directly and intensively with clients, rather than with the clients themselves. In school-based consultation, the consultant is typically a school psychologist, the consultee is typically a teacher or parent, and the client is typically a student. Of course, other alignments are also possible, such as when principals, teacher aides, superintendents, or school bus drivers serve as consultees and/or clients. Regardless of the specific case, however, when functioning as a consultant, the psychologist provides indirect services to clients by working with consultees who have direct ongoing contact with clients. These relationships are illustrated in Figure 1.

Consultant–Consultee Relationship

In consultation, the psychologist's ability to deliver services to a child depends on meaningful collaboration with relevant consultees (e.g., teachers, parents). Regardless of how accurately a psychologist might diagnose a child's psychoeducational needs and how skillfully he or she might match those needs to treatment recommendations for that child, no psychological services will actually be delivered to that child unless consultees take action. As such, the establishment of an open, trusting relationship between the consultant and his or her consultees is of paramount importance.[2]

Coordinate Power Status

Among the most important aspects of the consultation relationship is the coordinate power status of the consultant and the consultee (Tyler, Pargament, & Gatz, 1983). It is believed that hierarchi-

---

[2] While it has long been recognized that the establishment of a positive relationship with teachers and parents is crucial for school psychologists serving as consultants, there has been too little attention paid to this critical variable for nonconsultative functions. Proposing what he termed "the paradox of school psychology," Gutkin (1988) has argued that it is necessary for school psychologists to focus the bulk of their professional time and energy on adults rather than on children if they hope to service children effectively, regardless of what type of service (e.g., consultation, assessment) is being provided by school psychologists.

Direct Service Delivery Model

Teacher $\xrightarrow{\text{referral}}$ Psychologist $\xrightarrow{\text{treatment}}$ Child

Indirect Service Delivery Model

Psychologist $\xleftarrow{\text{referral}}$ Teacher $\xrightarrow{\text{treatment}}$ Child
(consultant) $\xrightarrow{\text{consultation}}$ (consultee)

Figure 1. Direct and indirect service delivery models.

cal power relationships might restrict the free flow of communication and the development of rapport between consultants and consultees. The consultee is thus viewed as an equal to the consultant and as such has equivalent authority in the decision-making process. The consultation interaction is collaborative and places neither the consultant nor the consultee in either a superordinate or subordinate role. Supporting these assumptions have been a number of studies indicating that consultees prefer collaborative approaches to consultation (Babcock & Pryzwansky, 1983; Pryzwansky & White, 1983; Wenger, 1979).

Consultee's Right to Reject Consultant Suggestions

One concrete manifestation of the coordinate power relationship between the consultant and consultee is the explicit recognition of the consultee's right to reject any suggested treatment plan or other course of action offered by the consultant. Although Bowers (1971) humorously suggested a variety of ways in which psychologists can intimidate others into following their ideas, the fact is that school psychologists have neither the formal nor informal power to force consultees to take steps against their own will. As such, recognition of a consultee's right to reject consultant suggestions is less of a magnanimous gesture toward that consultee than it is a recognition of the realities that face consultants. As stated by Gutkin and Curtis (1981):

> Once the door to the classroom is closed, there is little that any of the educational specialists can do to insure the occurrence of any event that the teacher does not want to occur. . . . We must recognize that if a teacher decides that a remedial program is inappropriate, it is highly likely that the plan

will never be implemented. This would be true regardless of the actual quality of the particular program. (pp. 220–221)

Attempting to force a consultee to accept a consultant's suggestions typically results in a situation where either the consultee refuses to act on the recommendations, or the recommendations are carried out by the consultee in such a way as to ensure their failure. Displays of attempted force by the consultant also typically lead to power struggles with the consultee, resulting in damaged relationships and lowered probabilities of effective subsequent consultative interactions.

Consultees' *subjective* perceptions of consultants' treatment recommendations and suggestions are thus crucial. With this realization has come a recent and substantial body of research addressing treatment acceptability for teachers (Elliott, 1988; Reimers, Wacker, Koeppl, 1987). Based on this work, it is clear that teachers' decisions to accept or reject treatment recommendations are complex events based on a multitude of variables. The notion that consultees will implement treatment recommendations solely because consultants believe that they are likely to be effective is, unfortunately, naive and overly simplistic. As such, the task facing consultants as they work with consultees is to develop treatment recommendations that are sound both in terms of (a) objective criteria (i.e., they have been demonstrated to be effective in prior research and clinical practice), and (b) subjective criteria (i.e., they are judged by the consultee to be acceptable).

Neither the consultee's right to reject consultant suggestions nor the acceptability research, however, should lead consultants to abandon prematurely ideas they think are feasible, even though they are not to a consultee's liking. Consultants should, of course, consider a consultee's reasons for rejecting specific strategies and determine if these objections have merit. There may, in fact, be a sound basis for the consultee's judgment of the proposed strategy. Beyond this, however, consultants should use all their skills of persuasion, short of creating a win–lose power struggle, to help a consultee see the validity of the ideas proposed. If this fails, however, consultants will usually be better off to go along with a consultee's decision. This does not suggest a passive acceptance of an idea, but rather a bona fide effort to assist the consultee in the implementation of the strategy. If the consultee's alternative solutions prove to be effective, the presenting problem is solved and the consultation is deemed by all to be a success. If, on the other hand, despite the best efforts of both parties, the consultee's ideas do not produce the desired results and the relationship between the consultant and consultee has remained strong, the consultee may find himself or herself ready to reconsider the consultant's original suggestions.

One final point needs to be considered in relationship to the consultee's right to reject consultant suggestions. The consultant should not "negotiate" points of fact. For example, if a teacher believes that a child has been sexually abused, it would be necessary under most state laws for that teacher to report the suspected abuse to the proper authorities. This type of action would be necessary regardless of whether the consultee found it palatable. Similarly, a child who does not qualify for special education services under federal and state law could not be recommended by a psychologist for those services simply because the teacher does not want to deal with the student-related concerns in the regular classroom. From the perspective of consultation theory, the objective in both cases would be to motivate the consultee to take appropriate actions without endangering the consultant–consultee relationship and the consultee's coordinate status. Depending on the specifics of the situation, this can be a very difficult and subtle task.

Involvement of the Consultee in the Consultation Process

The active involvement of the consultee in the consultation process is seen as a crucial element in successful consultation. For one thing, it is believed that "the consultant can seldom learn enough about the classroom, teacher(s), or the various human ecological systems operating to 'really' know what a better course of action would be in order to improve a particular environment" (Pyle, 1977, p. 193). Furthermore, failure to involve the consultee in the consultation process might result in the consultee's failure to "own" resulting treatment plans and thus decrease the probability that agreed-on interventions will be carried out as they were intended. Reinking, Livesay, and Kohl (1978) have provided some empirical support for the latter assumption by demonstrating that consultee implementation of programs generated as a result of consultation is related directly to the degree of consultee involvement in the problem-solving process.

Unfortunately, the degree to which teachers wish to be active participants in consultative activities is not clear. Research in this area has produced mixed results. On the positive side, there is a rather long list of studies indicating that teachers and other school personnel typically indicate a preference for consultative approaches over more traditional service delivery models in which they typically serve a more passive role (Gutkin & Curtis, 1982). Supporting these studies are recent results reported by Gutkin (1986). In that study, 191 teachers working in 24 different schools with 24 different consultants generated an average rating of 4.7 on a 5-point scale (with 1 being "unimportant" and 5 being "important") when asked how important they felt it was for teachers to be involved in the development of remedial programs for students experiencing difficulties. On the negative side are studies reporting that "the teacher wants relief and wants to unload the problem on the consultant" (Lambert, 1976, p. 516) and the knowledge that most teachers are ill prepared to assume their responsibilities as consultees because they have received little, if any, training for this function (Bardon, 1977; Kratochwill & Van Someren, 1985). The most reasonable conclusion at this time is that we do not know just how much the "typical" teacher is predisposed to be an active participant in consultative interactions and that such inclinations probably vary with the specifics of particular circumstances.

It is entirely possible that the negative perspectives of many teachers are not altogether unjustified. Many service delivery systems are structured so that teachers are, in fact, "on their own" when facing student-related concerns. Because so many resources are invested in functions related to determining eligibility for special education, they are not available to assist and support classroom teachers. Consequently, the only options for the teachers are to refer a student for a suspected handicap, or face the situation alone.

There is research that provides at least some initial ideas regarding how negative consultee attitudes and ignorance of consultation processes might be addressed by school psychologists. Bandura's (1977, 1982) work in the area of self-efficacy, for example, is instructive. He found that

> the strength of people's convictions in their own effectiveness determines whether they

will even try to cope with difficult situations. . . . Efficacy expectations determine how much effort people expend, and how long they will persist in the face of obstacles and aversive experiences. (Bandura, 1977, pp. 79–80)

Building on Bandura's insights and the work of Brown and Schulte (1987), Gutkin and Hickman (1988) successfully increased teachers' preferences for consultative services by increasing their sense of self-efficacy and control in relationship to a hypothetical referral problem. Similarly, Gutkin and Ajchenbaum (1984) found a substantial positive correlation between teachers' perceptions of control over presenting problems and their preferences for consultative versus referral services when considering how to cope with these problems. Ponti and Curtis (1984) reported a significant increase in generalized teacher expectations for success in dealing with student problems after only 3 weeks of interactions with high-skilled consultants. Wehmann, Zins, and Curtis (1989) also reported findings in which teacher expectations for successful problem resolution significantly increased following 10 weeks of school psychological consultation. Regarding teachers' knowledge of consultation and their ability to use problem-solving processes, research indicates that both can be enhanced successfully using direct training (T. K. Anderson, Kratochwill, & Began, 1986; Chandy, 1974; Curtis & Metz, 1986; Epps & Lane, 1987) and modeling (Cleven & Gutkin, 1988; Revels & Gutkin, 1983) interventions.

Voluntary Nature of Consultation

Ideally, the consultation relationship should be initiated voluntarily by the consultee rather than at the request of the consultant or third parties. Consultee initiation is thought to be important because it generally indicates that two important factors are operative. First, the consultee recognizes that a problem exists. Second, the consultee is motivated to do something about this problem. Of course, the realities of school-based consultation do not always follow the preferences of theorists, and practicing school psychologists often find themselves engaged in consultation relationships that were not initiated by the consultee. Although not the preferred set of circumstances, consultation activities can still proceed successfully as long as the continuation of the relationship is voluntary.

Consultation that is neither initiated voluntarily nor continued voluntarily by the consultee is typically beset with problems. Simply stated, it is extremely difficult to "force" a teacher to serve as an effective consultee. Although school authorities can mandate that a teacher interact with a psychologist regarding a particular problem, they have few (if any) ways to ensure that this interaction will be productive. Given the nature of consultative activities, it is quite easy for either of the parties to sabotage the effort when they have a hidden agenda to do so. When forced to consult, teachers may wish to "prove" the ineffectiveness of the consultant's ideas. Consistent with this perspective, Hinkle, Silverstein, and Walton (1977) report retrospective data indicating that consultees' failure to adopt recommendations occurs most often when principals request teachers who do not want consultative assistance to obtain such help.

Confidentiality

Ensuring the confidentiality of consultee communications with a consultant is an essential element of successful consultation and one that is consistent with the ethical guidelines of our profession (Hughes, 1986). Unless consultees know that the information they share with consultants will be kept in confidence, they are unlikely to communicate openly and honestly during consultation interactions. Like clients in more clinical situations, consultees are unlikely to discuss their professional shortcomings and other sensitive matters if they feel that this information might eventually be revealed to third parties (Woods & McNamara, 1980).

Under certain circumstances, maintaining a consultee's confidentiality can become a difficult issue for school-based consultants. Principals, for example, often claim, perhaps legitimately, that since they are legally and administratively responsible for everything that transpires in their schools, they must be kept informed regarding student-related concerns. Fortunately, most principals seem to understand the importance of confidentiality once it is explained to them. Additionally, principal's information needs can usually be satisfied by discussing the products and decisions resulting from consultations rather than the specific content of communication per se. There should be no problem in informing a principal of the former (e.g., Johnny is going to be given stars as a reward for completing his math assignments), as long as the latter (e.g., Ms. Smith feels that her teaching skills in the area of third-grade mathematics are below par) remains confidential. A similar line of logic can be applied to sharing consultee information with parents and groups such as IEP teams.

At all points during a consultation, there should be a consensus between the consultant and the consultee as to which aspects of their relationship are public and which are confidential. Similarly, it is important for both the consultant and the consultee to understand the legal limits of the consultee's confidentiality, although these limits may often be difficult to discern with precision (Bersoff & Hofer, Chapter 38, this volume; Overcast, Sales, & Sacken, Chapter 39, this volume). For example, in those instances when the consultee is a teacher and the client under discussion is a child, it is unclear whether any information could be kept confidential from the child's parents if they were to request it. Similarly, a variety of state laws prohibit the maintenance of confidentiality for information pertaining to child abuse and/or the commission of a felony.

Focus of Consultation

First and foremost, consultative services are intended to address the needs of clients. Consultees' needs are considered only to the extent that they relate to client needs. In school-based consultation, this usually means that primary attention is devoted to the psychological and educational needs of children rather than to the personal needs of teachers. Although Tunnecliffe, Leach, and Tunnecliffe (1986) recently used consultation techniques successfully as a stress reduction technique for teachers, consultative services generally stand in sharp contrast with those of traditional psychotherapy.

Goals of Consultation

Every model of school-based consultation is intended to achieve both remedial and preventive goals. Remediation is operationalized by helping consultees "fix" current problems, while prevention is attained by increasing consultees' problem-solving skills and psychological knowledge so that they can function more effectively with their clients in the future. The degree of emphasis placed on remediation versus prevention varies across consultation models.

Most available research addresses the remedial rather than the preventive goal. That is, the bulk of the consultation literature examines whether consultants were able to bring about behavioral and attitudinal changes in consultees and clients in response to presenting problems. Although this body of research has been criticized on methodological grounds (e.g., Gresham & Kendell, 1987; Medway, 1982; Meyers, Pitt, Gaughan, & Friedman, 1978; Pryzwansky, 1986), there is consensus that school-based consultation services are effective from a remedial perspective (Mannino & Shore, 1975; Medway, 1979b; Medway & Updyke, 1985). In Medway and Updyke's (1985) meta-analysis, for example, it was reported that "consultees showed improvements greater than 71% and clients showed improvements greater than 66% of untreated comparable groups" (p. 489).

There is considerably less research available regarding the preventive outcomes of consultative services, although this literature is growing and virtually all the data that are available support the preventive efficacy of this approach. Representative of these findings are the following: (a) student referral rates drop dramatically after teachers are exposed to consultative services (Graden, Casey, & Bonstrom, 1985; Gutkin, Henning-Stout, & Piersel, 1988; Ponti, Zins, & Graden, 1988; Ritter, 1978); (b) client gains following consultation services have been found to generalize to other children in the same class as a result of increased teacher effectiveness (Jason & Ferone, 1978; Meyers, 1975); (c) underachieving children whose teachers and parents received consultation-type services during their fourth, fifth, and sixth grades achieved significantly better on several academic measures at the time of high school graduation than a control group of underachievers (Jackson, Cleveland, & Merenda, 1975); (d) teachers in schools having consultants found problems to be less serious than teachers in matched schools without consultants when presented with an identical list of child problems (Gutkin, Singer, & Brown, 1980); (e) teachers' problem-solving skills have been enhanced by exposing them to either live or modeled consultation interactions (Cleven & Gutkin, 1988; Curtis & Metz, 1986; Curtis & Watson, 1980; Revels & Gutkin, 1983); (f) teachers report increased professional skills as a result of consultation services (Gutkin, 1980, 1986; Hinkle et al., 1977; Zins, 1981); (g) following consultation services, teachers' attributions for the causation of student-related problems changed from internal-to-the-child to interactional in nature, recognizing the importance of ecological factors such as instructional methods and other students (Wehmann, Zins, & Curtis, 1989); (h) using psychologists in consultative roles, the Primary Mental Health Project successfully has provided prevention services for 30 years by modifying class environments to promote learning and psychological wellness, and teaching children adjustment and coping skills (Cowen & Hightower, Chapter 31, this volume); and (i) a variety of preventive outcomes have been achieved in community-based programs as a result of consultation services (Gonzales, 1986; Mann, 1986; Roberts & Thorsheim, 1986; Vincent, 1986) and the application of psychological knowledge (Price, Cowen, Lorion, & Ramos-McKay, 1988). Above and beyond these studies, a *School Psychology Review* (Zins & Forman, 1988) mini-series details how school psychologists might develop prevention programs for substance abuse, suicide, pregnancy, behavioral problems, injuries, academic failure, and sexual abuse (Davis, Sandoval, & Wilson, 1988; Elias & Branden, 1988; Forman & Linney, 1988; Paget, 1988; Peterson, 1988; Shapiro, 1988; Tharinger et al., 1988; Zins, Conyne, & Ponti, 1988). In each instance, these authors discuss either implicitly or explicitly the consultative roles that school psychologists might play in these programs. Finally, Curtis, Curtis, and Graden (1988) and Zins, Curtis, Graden, and Ponti (1988) discuss the preventive benefits of a comprehensive school-based intervention assistance program founded in a consultation model for service delivery.

Client Interventions

Assessment Process

Ideally, psychologists would like to gather all available data prior to decision making. Unfortunately, the range of facts and information that could be accumulated for any presenting problem is almost infinite. Reality thus dictates that sources of information be prioritized since time constraints never permit an exhaustive collection of data. For school-based consultants, information pertaining to the environment and the behavior of consultees and clients in that environment are most crucial.

Teacher and parent interviews are considered to be essential elements of the data-gathering process, since they are usually the persons most knowledgeable of the client's daily environment, as well as the way in which both they and the client interact within that environment. Teachers and

parents have had the opportunity to observe the client under a wide variety of circumstances and for protracted periods of time and thus typically have a wealth of invaluable information. It is important to note, however, that even in those instances when teacher and parent observations are less than completely accurate, these data will be critical since their *subjective* perceptions will influence their future behavior toward the client as well as their willingness to implement interventions for the client.

Direct observation is also among the primary sources of data for school-based consultants because it provides the psychologist with a first-hand look at the complex interaction between clients, consultees, and their daily environments (Wilczenski, Sulzer-Azaroff, Feldman, & Fajardo, 1987). It also gives them an opportunity to assess the validity of consultee observations, although it is important for consultants to remember that in those instances when their observations are not congruent with what has been reported by the consultee, it may be the consultee who is correct.

In those cases when the client is experiencing an academic problem, work samples and data gathered from curriculum-based assessment may be excellent sources of information (Deno, 1985; Rosenfield, 1987; Rosenfield & Rubinson, 1985; Shapiro & Derr, Chapter 15, this volume; Shinn, Tindal, & Stein, 1988). Traditional normative testing is thought to be less useful in most instances because these procedures usually provide too little direct insight into the design of treatment interventions (Galagan, 1985; Meyers, Pfeffer, & Erlbaum, 1985).

Interventions Resulting from Consultation

As per the indirect service delivery concept, interventions resulting from consultation should be those that can be, and will be, implemented by the consultee rather than by the consultant. Typically, these consist of some form of environmental manipulation since (a) there is a substantial body of research specifying what types of environments lead to effective teaching (Wittrock, 1986), effective parenting (Kramer, Chapter 27, this volume), and effective behavior change (Martens & Meller, Chapter 24, this volume); (b) all consultees routinely manipulate meaningful school and home environmental variables on a daily basis, thus demonstrating they are both capable and willing to undertake interventions of this nature; and

(c) nonenvironmental manipulations, such as psychotherapy, will probably be beyond the skills of most consultees (although Hattie, Sharpley, and Rogers' [1984] meta-analysis of the therapy literature indicates that paraprofessionals can be effective therapists if given the appropriate training and supervision).

The range of interventions commonly resulting from consultation services is quite vast and beyond the space limitations imposed by a chapter such as this. At best, it is possible to list a few of the major categories of environmental variables most often considered for manipulation. These are (a) reward and punishment contingencies, (b) curriculum content, (c) instructional techniques, (d) teacher behavior, (e) peer and sibling behavior, (f) parent behavior, (g) the physical arrangement of the classroom and home, and (h) school administrative policies.

Short-Term Follow-Up of Treatment Recommendations

Short-term follow-up (hereafter referred to simply as follow-up), ranging anywhere from one day to a few weeks after treatment implementation, is perhaps the most essential characteristic discriminating between effective and ineffective consultation services. Unfortunately, many problem-solving efforts seem to reflect a search for "the" solution. The truth is that no matter how much interviewing, observing, and/or testing a psychologist does on any particular case, there is no assurance that resulting treatment recommendations will be optimal, or even adequate. It is virtually impossible to determine the efficacy of any treatment plan until it is implemented and evaluated. For both children and adults, a technology that accurately relates a taxonomy of interventions to a taxonomy of either formal or informal diagnosis simply does not exist at this point in time (Arter & Jenkins, 1979; Dance & Neufeld, 1988, Ysseldyke & Marston, Chapter 26, this volume). As such, mechanisms for corrective feedback *must* be built into all consultation services. Treatment plans generated as a result of consultative interactions should be viewed as high-probability hypotheses, with the expectation that follow-up will be required to determine if refinement or replacement of the original intervention program will be necessary. To be effective, school-based consultation must be an iterative process.

There are numerous other reasons why follow-up contacts with consultees are thought to be so important. To quote an old and wise adage, "There are many slips twixt the cup and the lip." First, ideas that sound simple during the course of consultation may, in fact, require skills that the consultee does not possess to an adequate degree. Often, the consultee does not become aware of this fact until actually attempting to implement the strategy in question. At this point it may become painfully clear to the consultee that he or she does not really know how to carry out the treatment that was agreed on. For example, a teacher who has always depended on punishment strategies for class control may agree to institute a program of contingent social reinforcement for a child but have considerable difficulty because it runs counter to already well-ingrained teaching habits. Follow-up is needed in such cases to monitor implementation and either revise the treatment program or assist the consultee in acquiring the necessary skills.

Second, concepts the consultant believes that he or she has communicated clearly may have been misunderstood by the consultee. In these instances, the consultee attempts to implement the program incorrectly from the outset. For example, a teacher agrees to utilize a time-out program but fails to understand the appropriate time frame for such a procedure. Consequently, when the child in question exhibits inappropriate behaviors, the teacher proceeds to isolate him or her from the rest of the class for several hours at a time. Follow-up contacts give the consultant an opportunity to assess whether the program is being executed as intended. If it is not, the consultant can work with the consultee to make the necessary adjustments.

Third, the consultee may realize after attempting to implement the program that he or she lacks one or more prerequisite resources. Many psychoeducational interventions are complex and require a variety of materials and support to be administered effectively. Individualized instruction is perhaps one of the best examples. A teacher who attempts to implement such a program may be stymied by the lack of adequate curricular materials in the building, the absence of teacher aides, an excessively large number of other children in the classroom (many of whom also need considerable personal attention), or any of a wide variety of other similar problems. Follow-up contacts give the consultant an opportunity to work with the consultee for the purposes of either securing these necessary resources or redesigning the intervention so that it can be carried out effectively without the aid of these supports.

Fourth, there is evidence to indicate that teachers are often so busy that they are not aware of the nature of their own interactions with children (Martin & Keller, 1976). Jackson (1968), for example, reported that teachers may engage in up to 1000 interpersonal interchanges per day, a pace at which it is most difficult to recall accurately the details of each interaction. When this is the case, teachers may improperly implement interventions due to a lack of awareness of their own classroom behavior. In instances such as this, follow-up observations by the consultant, coupled with corrective feedback to the teacher, will be critical to the success of a planned intervention.

Fifth, when treatment proves to be successful, someone ought to provide reinforcement to the consultee for a job well done. As Sarason, Levine, Goldenberg, Cherlin, and Bennett (1966) point out, "teaching is a lonely profession" (p. 74) and teachers typically go without overt reinforcement from colleagues and superiors when everything is going well. This tends to sap consultee motivation for handling future problems. During follow-up, the consultant is in an excellent position to provide reinforcement to the consultee, and perhaps of equal importance, to receive some reinforcement for his or her own work. Consultant reinforcement of the consultee is also critical during that period of time after the intervention has been initiated and before treatment success or failure is evident. In those instances when interventions do not bring about the desired results, the consultant needs to be around to share the frustration, provide support, and join the consultee in "getting back to the drawing board." Given the lack of clear diagnosis—treatment relationships, unsuccessful outcomes are bound to occur despite everyone's best efforts and intentions. Follow-up permits the consultant to help the consultee learn to take failure in stride and to use information resulting from an unsuccessful program as input for the generation of a new intervention.

Last, but not least, follow-up facilitates the professional growth of both the consultee *and the consultant*. Recalling that all consultation interactions have both remedial and preventive goals, follow-up contacts provide the consultant with an opportunity to review effective interventions with the consultee and to determine the underlying reasons for the program's success. There is consid-

erable learning in this process for both the consultee and the consultant, and this knowledge can be used by either party for dealing with similar cases encountered in the future.

Consultant and Consultee Responsibilities During Consultation

First and foremost, consultants must be experts on how to go about solving problems (i.e., process expertise), even if they have little idea as to what the specific solution is for a particular problem (i.e., content expertise). It has long been thought that consultants can be effective even if they are consulting in an area about which they have little information, as long as they understand the process of problem solving and are able to steer the consultation interaction in directions that are consonant with this process. The authors believe that consultants generally can be effective in such situations only to a limited extent. Content expertise does increase the consultant's ability to ask questions that will generate relevant new information, and to clarify subtle, but perhaps critical elements of the consultee's perspective. Furthermore, content expertise is critical for a school psychologist's credibility with parents, teachers, and other educational personnel. Nevertheless, we do agree that *the major responsibility of the consultant during consultation is to maintain and direct the collaborative problem-solving process*. Supporting this conclusion, Wilcox (1977) found that consultees' attitudes toward a consultant and the consultation process correlated .88 and .83, respectively, with consultant process control in group consultation settings. Additionally, Curtis and Van Wagener (1988) demonstrated that despite very positive attitudinal evaluations of consultation by both consultant and consultee, the absence of problem solving during the interactive process resulted in no changes in the classroom in terms of either teacher or client behaviors.

Both the consultant and consultee are responsible for sharing their respective content expertise with each other during the consultation process. The psychologist is viewed as an expert in the area of human behavior, while the teacher is viewed as an expert in education. Parents also have important content information to contribute during the consultation interaction by virtue of their experience as parents and their understanding of the ecology of their home environment. By collaboratively combining these bodies of knowledge, the consultant and consultee can create a rich mix of ideas from which creative responses to presenting problems are likely to arise.

Above and beyond contributing content expertise, consultees are also responsible for providing treatment to the client. That is, consonant with the notion of indirect service, it is the consultee who must carry out the intervention plans collaboratively generated and agreed upon during the consultation process.

Finally, it is the joint responsibility of the consultant and consultee to continue working together until an effective solution is found to meet the presenting psychoeducational needs of the client. In response to the iterative requirements of the consultation process, both participants must be ready to review and revise treatment strategies on an ongoing basis.

THE BASIC RATIONALE FOR CONSULTATIVE SERVICES

Having discussed the core characteristics of school-based consultation, we turn now to an examination of the basic rationale underlying these services. In the original version of this chapter (Gutkin & Curtis, 1982), a fairly extensive historical review was presented to give the reader a sense of how the consultation model evolved. Some 10 years later it is safe to say that little has changed. The forces that lead to the creation of the consultation model are still operative, perhaps even more strongly now than ever before.

Problems Associated with Traditional Systems of School Psychological Service Delivery

Dominance of the Medical Model

The medical model, positing that psychoeducational problems are the result of disease states internal to individuals, traditionally has been (and continues to be) the dominant conceptual approach applied to assessment, diagnosis, and treatment. Although this conceptualization has long ago been called into serious question for persons of all ages (Szasz, 1960), it seems particularly inappropriate for children whose psychological and educational difficulties clearly result from interactions between the internal characteristics of the individual and the external characteristics of the environment (Saxe, Cross, & Silverman, 1988). One need only note the obvious relationships between variables such

as economic poverty and ethnic minority status on the one hand and psychoeducational dysfunction on the other hand to conclude that environmental factors are of great importance to the psychological and educational health of children. Services, such as traditional special education and psychotherapy, built largely on the foundation of the medical model are thus bound to be of limited effectiveness. Consistent with this conclusion are the findings of Bergan, Byrnes, and Kratochwill (1979) and Tomari and Bergan (1978) indicating that teachers are both less optimistic about interventions and less able to intervene successfully when consultants use medical rather than behavioral model cues and verbalizations.

Inadequacy of Traditional, Medical Model Special Education Services

Traditional special education services, and the school psychologist's role within them, have been severely criticized for decades. Almost 20 years ago, for example, Barclay (1971) concluded: "There is increasing evidence . . . that school psychology practice has been weighed in the balance and found wanting" (p. 257). More recently, a report from the National School Psychology Inservice Training Network (Ysseldyke et al., 1984) stated that "many school psychologists have become psychometric robots," serving as "gatekeepers" of a "non-system" (p. 8), while Reschly (1988) predicted the coming of "a revolution in the nature and purposes of school psychological services" (p. 459) in response to the current state of affairs in special education. Consonant with these analyses have been criticisms noting the inadequacies of commonly used special education: (a) assessment instruments, many of which are technically inadequate (W. M. Reynolds, 1979; Ysseldyke, Algozzine, Regan, & Potter, 1980) and largely irrelevant to the development of treatment programs (Galagan, 1985); (b) diagnostic procedures, many of which are based on invalidated approaches (Kavale & Forness, 1984; Kramer, Henning-Stout, Ullman, & Schellenberg, 1987) and lack adequate reliability and/or validity (Bus, 1989; McDermott, 1980, 1988; Tharinger, Laurent, Best, 1986; Vinsonhaler, Weinshank, Wagner, & Pollin, 1983; Ysseldyke et al., 1983); and (c) treatment programs, few, if any, of which have been shown to be differentially effective for children falling into different diagnostic categorizations (Arter & Jenkins, 1979; Dance & Neufeld, 1988,

Ysseldyke & Marston, Chapter 26, this volume) and most of which are of questionable overall effectiveness (Kavale & Glass, 1984).

In response to these problems, the National Association of School Psychologists and the National Coalition of Advocates for Students (NASP/NCAS, 1985) adopted an official position statement, "Advocacy for Appropriate Educational Services for All Children." In so doing, these organizations called for the development of alternatives to the current medical model orientation that is reflected in categorical systems of special education.

Inappropriate Focus of School Psychological Services

Through the dominance of the medical model, school psychological services have focused primarily on assessing, diagnosing and treating the internal pathologies of children. Traditionally, much less attention has been given to the environments in which children function (e.g., classrooms, homes) and the adults who populate those environments. In a number of recent works, however, several authors have pointed out the serious problems associated with this approach (Conoley & Gutkin, 1986a, 1986b; Gutkin, 1988; Hawryluk & Smallwood, 1986).

> Adults rather than children control the environments within which children function. Given that environmental factors play an important role in the development and maintenance of children's psychological and educational problems, it is usually essential that the treatment of children's problems include a strong environmental focus (Saxe, Cross, & Silverman, 1988). It makes little sense to "cure" the intrapersonal and intrapsychic problems of children only to return them to the environment that created (or at least facilitated the creation of) their problems in the first place.
>
> The primary environments within which children function are the home and school settings. The primary persons in control of these environments are parents and teachers. If school psychologists hope to bring about meaningful improvements in the lives of children they will have to function in such a way as to exert meaningful influence on parents and teachers. (Gutkin, 1988, pp. 12–13)

Gutkin (1988), in fact, described what he termed "the paradox of school psychology," that is, "to serve children effectively school psychologists must, first and foremost, concentrate their attention and professional expertise on adults" (p. 20).

The "Numbers Problem"

There are a staggering number of children in the United States who need immediate and intensified psychological and educational attention.

> At least 12%, or 7.5 million, of the nation's children suffer from emotional or other problems that warrant mental health treatment. Untold others—the 14 million children living in poverty; the 7 million children of alcoholic parents, and the 1 million who are neglected or abused—are at serious risk of developing mental health problems. Only 20% to 30% of these children may be getting appropriate mental health services. (Dougherty, 1988, p. 811).

A similar and equally disturbing picture is painted by the recent report "A Nation At Risk" (National Commission on Excellence in Education, 1983), in terms of children who are failing academically in our schools.

> If an unfriendly foreign power had attempted to impose on America the mediocre educational performance that exists today, we might well have viewed it as an act of war. As it stands, we have allowed this to happen to ourselves. We have even squandered the gains in student achievement made in the wake of the Sputnik challenge. Moreover, we have dismantled essential support systems which helped make those gains possible. We have, in effect, been committing an act of unthinking, unilateral educational disarmament. (p. 8)

The Commission goes on to cite a host of statistics supporting their conclusion, including the fact that

> some 23 million American adults are functionally illiterate by the simplest tests of everyday reading, writing, and comprehension. About 13 percent of all 17-year-olds in the United States can be considered functionally illiterate. Functional illiteracy among minority youth may run as high as 40 percent. (p. 11)

Albee's (1968) warning of 20 years ago remains prophetic. There are not now, nor will there ever be, enough psychologists and psychiatrists to treat all the children who could benefit from, or are in dire need of, such treatment.

School-Based Consultation:
A Feasible Solution

Although school-based consultation services are clearly not a panacea for all the complex problems facing children, education, and school psychology, they are responsive to the critical service delivery issues raised in this section. First, school-based consultation services are generally based on conceptualizations of human behavior that differ markedly from the medical model. Chief among these are the behavioral model (Bergan, 1977; Skinner, 1953), postulating that human behavior is primarily a function of environmental stimuli, and the ecological model (Bandura, 1978; Barker, 1965, 1968; Lewin, 1951), asserting that human behavior results from a complex interaction between environmental factors and the individual characteristics of people.

Second, school-based consultation offers a meaningful alternative to traditional special education services. By focusing psychologists' attention on the design of treatment programs rather than testing and labeling children, psychologists can bring to bear on client problems a massive body of validated intervention techniques (Martens & Meller, Chapter 24, this volume). Including the consultee as a coequal collaborator further enhances the information base for intervention design and increases the probability that the intervention will, in fact, be implemented by the consultee as planned. Perhaps most important, school-based consultation services incorporate short-term follow-up of treatment recommendations by the consultant, thus providing all concerned with the opportunity to refine, revise, and improve initial treatment hypotheses as dictated by the progress of the client.

Third, school-based consultation services are responsive to "the paradox of school psychology" identified by Gutkin (1988). Primary attention is paid to interacting with the significant adult care givers that populate and substantially affect children's lives. Appropriate changes in the behaviors and attitudes of these care givers (consultees), and the environments which they control (e.g., schools, homes), should lead to substantive, long-lasting positive outcomes for children with special needs.

Finally, school-based consultation also holds the potential for making meaningful progress with the "numbers problem." The keys to serving the enormous caseloads of children in need of additional psychological and educational assistance are to emphasize prevention and increase vastly the numbers and types of persons who can provide high-quality treatment. An "educational" rather than a "clinical" approach to school psychological services is needed (Bardon, 1983). Although not addressing his remarks to school psychology in particular, Miller was clearly making the same point in his 1969 presidential address to the American Psychological Association when he urged psychologists to "give psychology away" to nonpsychologists.

If a school psychologist works successfully with a child via direct service, he or she has served one child. If, on the other hand, a school psychologist can transmit via consultation new psychological and educational skills to a teacher with a 20-year career span and 25 students per year, he or she can affect as many as 500 children. If school psychologists stay with traditional services and a medical model conceptualization of human behavior, service providers are limited primarily to psychiatrists and doctoral psychologists because only persons with extensive postgraduate training will be allowed to "cure" the internal disease states of children. If, on the other hand, the field moves to school-based consultation and behavioral/ecological models of human behavior, the pool of potential service providers increases enormously since all those who can manipulate the environment (including teachers and parents) become empowered to provide treatment. In conjunction with this logic, it is important to note the existence of a substantial body of research indicating that with appropriate training, psychological paraprofessionals such as teachers and parents can use both behavioral (e.g, Allen & Forman, 1984; Epps & Lane, 1987; Kramer, Chapter 27, this volume; Martens & Meller, Chapter 24, this volume; O'Leary & O'Leary, 1977) and psychotherapeutic (Hattie, Sharpley & Rogers, 1984) interventions very effectively.

MAJOR APPROACHES TO SCHOOL-BASED CONSULTATION

Ecological Consultation

Issues Related to Terminology

In our original chapter (Gutkin & Curtis, 1982), problem-solving and behavioral consultation were presented as two distinct models. Since that time, however, we have come to believe that it is most reasonable to integrate them into a single system entitled "ecological consultation." A number of factors influenced our decision.

First and foremost, there is enormous similarity between the problem-solving and behavioral consultation models. On a practical level, one can see the clear congruence of the two models by comparing Gutkin and Curtis's (1982) seven-step problem-solving consultation sequence with Bergan's (1977) four-step and Goodwin and Coates's (1976) 12-step behavioral consultation sequences (see Table 1). Although the number of steps and the specific words differ, the underlying concepts are virtually identical. The problem-solving and behavioral consultation models are also highly compatible at a theoretical level (Rogers-Warren & Warren, 1977). For instance, Skinnerian approaches to behavioral psychology (Skinner, 1953), which postulate that human behavior varies as a function of antecedent and consequent stimuli, are encompassed by and entirely consistent with Bandura's (1978) ecologically oriented theory of reciprocal determinism, postulating continuous, mutual, and reciprocal interactions between environmental, behavioral, and personological factors. Recent suggestions to expand behavioral consultation theory to include concepts from ecological and systems theory further highlight the underlying compatibility of problem-solving and behavioral models of school-based consultation (Keller, 1981; Martens & Witt, 1988; Witt & Martens, 1988).

"Problem solving" and "behavioral consultation" were renamed "ecological consultation" also because neither of the traditional names are entirely appropriate (C. R. Reynolds, Gutkin, Elliott, & Witt, 1984). Since all consultation models have problem solving as a goal, it seems misleading to single out one particular approach and label that as "problem-solving consultation," implying incorrectly that problem-solving processes are somehow unique to this approach. The title "behavioral consultation" was also rejected because it incorrectly implied that users of this consultative methodology were rigidly limited to a behaviorist paradigm when assessing client problems and designing treatment programs (see Martens & Witt [1988] and Witt & Martens [1988] for examples of how behavioral consultants might wish to incorporate theory and techniques from nonbehavioral schools of thought). The term "ecological consultation," on the other hand, is broad enough to encompass both the problem-solving and behavioral consultation models while correctly communicating the notion that consultants using this approach focus on the *interaction* between persons, environments, and behaviors during the consultation process.

Problem-Solving Processes

Ecological consultation is a synthesis of the core characteristics of school-based consultation service delivery models, as described previously, and a problem-solving technology thought to maximize the probability of developing high-quality strategies for the solution of presenting problems. The specifics of this problem-solving process have been discussed by hundreds of authors (see Parnes, Noller, & Biondi [1977] for an extensive list of works on problem solving). Of specific interest to this chapter is the work of Osborn (1963), which sets forth most of the basic principles of the problem-solving process, and a growing body of literature relating these processes to meaningful clinical and consultative phenomena (e.g., Carkhuff, 1973; Dixon & Glover, 1984; D'Zurilla and Goldfried, 1971; Heppner, 1978; Heppner & Krauskopf, 1987; Matiland, Fine, & Tracy, 1985; Spivak, Platt, & Shure, 1976). For the purposes of this chapter, we will employ the problem-solving sequence proposed by Gutkin and Curtis (1982), which is a bit more detailed than Bergan's (1977) sequence and considerably broader than the one suggested by Goodwin and Coates (1976).

Although presented as specific sequences of events, actual problem solving rarely proceeds in the exact lockstep order depicted in Table 1. Movement back and forth between steps is quite frequent because (a) the verbal interaction between consultant and consultee cannot (and should not) be controlled to the point where their communications follow the theoretical sequence in a lockstep fashion, and (b) information that arises during any particular step may suggest a need to

TABLE 1   Problem-Solving Sequences Most Applicable to School-Based Consultation

Gutkin and Curtis (1982)	Bergan (1977)	Goodwin and Coates (1976)[a]
1. Define and clarify the problem	1. Problem identification	1. Define inappropriate behavior
		2. Define appropriate behavior
2. Analyze the forces impinging on the problem	2. Problem analysis	3. Analyze antecedents for inappropriate behavior
		4. Analyze consequences for inappropriate behavior
		5. Analyze antecedents for appropriate behavior
		6. Analyze consequences for appropriate behavior
3. Brainstorm alternative strategies		7. Design antecedents for appropriate behavior
		8. Design consequences for appropriate behavior
		9. Design a signal
		10. Design consequences for inappropriate behavior
4. Evaluate and choose among alternative strategies		
5. Specify consultee and consultant responsibilities		
6. Implement the chosen strategy	3. Plan implementation	11. Implement
7. Evaluate the effectiveness of the action and recycle if necessary	4. Problem evaluation	12. Follow-up

Source. From Gutkin and Curtis (1982) with slight modifications by the authors.

reinterpret material from a prior step. The ordering of steps presented in Table 1 should be viewed by the consultant as a set of flexible guidelines to be adhered to when the situation permits, rather than as a rigid sequence of events.

Step 1.   Define and Clarify the Problem: Defining and clarifying the presenting problem is a critical first step in the problem-solving process. Bergan and Tombari (1976) reported, for example, that "once consultative problem solving . . . was carried through problem identification, problem solution almost invariably resulted" (p. 12). It is generally believed that the manner in which a problem is defined during this initial step sets important parameters for the remainder of the consultation interaction (Witt & Elliott, 1983). In support of this assumption are findings by Tombari and Bergan (1978) indicating that the use of behavioral rather than medical model problem definitions and verbal cues positively affected consultee expectations for problem resolution.

Although the problem-definition stage appears on the surface to be quite simple, it is, in fact, one of the most difficult tasks facing the consultant. Inexperienced consultants tend to rush through this stage in an attempt to reach the solution-generation phase of the process. Curtis and

Watson (1980) have provided data that indicate that low-skill consultants may inadvertently reinforce consultee's tendencies to move too rapidly through problem definition and into the evaluation of problem solutions. Unfortunately, both consultants and consultees typically find the brainstorming of alternatives to be less than satisfactory under these conditions because of their failure to invest more effort and time in the problem-definition stage.

A useful problem definition is one that is stated in concrete, behaviorally descriptive terms. If at all possible, the identified problem behavior should be one that is both directly observable and amenable to quantification. Unfortunately, Lambert's (1976) study of elementary school teachers led her to conclude that teachers experience considerable difficulty when trying to specify pupil problems in this manner. She found that teachers tended to report student problems with general and vague statements (e.g., the child is poorly motivated, the student has low ability) rather than in terms that have clear implications for "operational changes in classroom practice" (p. 516). Research demonstrates, however, that teachers exposed to highly skilled consultants via direct interaction or modeling significantly improve in problem-clarification skills (Cleven & Gutkin, 1988; Curtis & Watson, 1980).

One of the consultant's first tasks, therefore, is to assist the consultee in arriving at a concrete, behavioral definition of the problem. One means for doing this is simply to ask the consultee for further specification of vague problem statements. For example, in a consultee states that the problem with Johnny is that he is "mean to other children," the consultant may ask the consultee, "Can you be more specific?" "What behaviors lead you to say that he is mean to other children?" "The last time Johnny was being mean to other children, what was he actually doing at that moment?" Often a series of questions such as these lead to a rapid clarification of the problem. It is also helpful to ask the consultee "open-ended" questions, that is, questions that require explanation or description in response. While "closed" questions can be answered "yes" or "no," open questions call upon the consultee to describe carefully the problem situation and its surrounding circumstances.

One common reason why consultees may be unable to provide a clear, behavioral definition of a problem is that they are trying to describe too many problems at once. Both experience and research (Saxe, Cross, & Silverman, 1988) tell us that children typically evidence multiple rather than singular difficulties. Social-adjustment problems, for example, often occur concomitantly with academic difficulties and family dysfunction. The range of difficulties with children such as these is so broad that a specific, behavioral definition of the problem situation is very difficult to develop. In such instances, the consultant should help the consultee divide the overall problem into its component parts, give priorities to each specific component part, and then work toward a behavioral definition for the most important component that has been identified. This procedure helps the consultee reduce the complexity of a problem so that he or she can avoid being overwhelmed and can work effectively toward the development of a useful problem statement.

A common error made by consulting psychologists at this point in the process is to assume that the consultee's first verbalization of a problem statement corresponds to the consultee's major concern. It is, however, not unusual for the consultee's initial problem statement to serve as either an intentional or an unintentional veil behind which to hide the real concern. In some instances, for example, the consultee may need to establish a strong sense of trust in the consultant prior to the sharing of highly sensitive information. In presenting a "safe" problem, the consultee may, in effect, be testing whether he or she can trust the consultant. The consultant's skills in maintaining a nonevaluative stance with such consultees should increase the probability that the consultee will eventually share potentially more threatening problems with the consultant.

In other instances, the consultee may be experiencing so many problems that he or she is genuinely confused as to what constitutes the essential versus the peripheral elements of the situation. In these cases, the initial problem presented by the consultee may be relatively insignificant in comparison with another aspect of the problem that may not emerge until later in the consultative process. In such situations, the consultant's listening skills and ability to help the consultee discuss and establish priorities for the component parts of the problem situation will be important. Focusing on the consultee's goals for the client will further facilitate this process (e.g., "If we replace behavior X with behavior Y, will you feel that we have solved the most pressing aspect of your concern for this child?'').

The most problematic situation for the consultant is when the consultee has a purposeful hidden agenda. For example, a teacher asks to consult with the psychologist concerning a child in his or her class who has previously been diagnosed as emotionally disturbed and who is currently being mainstreamed. The teacher is overtly asking for assistance in working with this child, but is covertly trying to undermine the consultation process and strengthen the argument with the principal that emotionally disturbed children cannot be handled effectively in regular education classes. Although consultee behavior will vary in this situation, the consultant should be sensitive to the possible presence of hidden agendas when the consultee resists working toward a concrete, behavioral problem definition or insists on unrealistic goals for the client. If the situation is extreme and other techniques fail, the consultant may have to confront the consultee in an attempt to bring the consultee's covert agenda to the surface.

Before leaving the problem-definition phase, the consultant should engage the consultee in an examination of goals for the client. It is critical for the remainder of the process that the consultee's expectations for client improvement be realistic. Lack of attention to this task may result in consultee and consultant perceptions of failure even when an effective intervention has been implemented. If, for example, a child engages in less than two social interactions with peers per day and a teacher's goal is to design an intervention that will make the child one of the most popular students in the class, the consultant would be remiss if he or she failed to help the consultee explore whether such a goal was realistic. Proceeding with the problem-solving process without the identification of a more realistic goal would almost certainly doom the entire process to failure.

Step 2.   Analyze the Forces Impinging on the Problem: The major tasks at this stage are to collect detailed information pertaining to the identified problem and to discern the ecological context within which this problem is occurring. What factors contribute to the problem or impede its resolution? How do these factors interrelate with each other and cause or support the continuation of the problem? Of equal relevance, but often overlooked by consultees, is the question of which resources are available that could be used to

facilitate the problem's resolution? Behavioral (Kratochwill & Sheridan, Chapter 14, this volume; Shapiro, 1987) and curriculum-based (Deno, 1985; Shapiro & Derr, Chapter 15, this volume; Shinn, Tindal, & Stein, 1988) assessment methodologies will often be particularly pertinent in responding to these types of questions, although data relating to behavior, environment, and person should be considered if needed.

Step 3.   Brainstorm Alternative Strategies: At this point in the process, the consultee and the consultant should have a clear understanding of the problem definition and the ecological context within which the problem occurs. Consequently, they are prepared to begin enumerating potential solutions.

Four rules of brainstorming should be followed whenever possible. First, at this point in the process, criticism of ideas is not allowed. Both the consultant and the consultee should refrain from evaluating the quality of the ideas that are generated. Second, freewheeling is encouraged. The consultant and consultee should let their imagination run loose. D'Zurilla and Goldfried (1971) caution participants, however, that they should engage in " limited-criteria thinking" rather than "free association." The consultant and consultee should limit their responses "so that they are clearly relevant to dealing with such-and-such a problem or situation" (p. 115). Total suspension of judgment is thus seen as inappropriate. Third, produce as many ideas as possible. It is presumed that the more strategies the consultant and consultee are able to produce, the more likely they are to design an ideal or high-quality solution. Fourth, combine and modify ideas generated earlier. The consultant and consultee may find that the revision and synthesis of individual ideas will result in a new strategy that is superior to the original.

Unfortunately, consultants often experience some difficulty in implementing the total brainstorming package. The "natural instincts" of many untrained problem solvers, which includes the vast majority of school-based personnel, run counter to deferring qualitative judgments and producing long lists of alternative solutions. Typically, consultees strive to generate "the best solution" as quickly as possible and are resistant to continue generating new ideas once they believe they have found "the answer." Because time is a most precious commodity for most teachers, they may consider brainstorming to be inefficient and a waste of the little spare time available to them. In coping with this issue, consultants must remain sensitive to the time constraints under which teachers and other school-based consultees usually operate and adjust their consulting style accordingly. This is not to imply that consultants must simply accept a "hurry up" approach to problem solving. Instead, the consultant should work with the consultee to clarify real time demands.

Step 4. Evaluate and Choose Among Alternative Strategies: After completing the brainstorming stage, the consultant and consultee must choose which strategy or strategies to implement. Unfortunately, individuals are often unable to recognize the best solution for a problem among a long list of alternatives. The consultant should strive to ensure that the choice of strategies to be used in response to the presenting problem is not made hastily and to help the consultee review each alternative from a variety of perspectives. The final choice of intervention techniques, however, rests with the consultee, who must, after all, carry out the treatment plan.

When reviewing the list of alternatives, the consultant and consultee should consider the ecological impact of each (Martens & Witt, 1988). That is, they must remember that classrooms are ecological systems. As such, changes in any one aspect of the system will result in changes in other aspects of the system as well. For example, if a teacher chooses to increase dramatically his or her level of attention to a particular child during reading lessons, will he or she have to decrease attention to other children by a corresponding amount? If so, what impact will this decreased attention have on the class as a whole or on other children who also require a great deal of attention during reading? Do the potential gains from this intervention outweigh the potential losses? Sarason (1982) provides a classic discussion of how failure to view change from an ecological perspective often results in unintended outcomes that directly undercut the most significant effects of a planned change. One technique that the authors have found to be effective in predicting the ecological effects of a proposed intervention is to return to the forces discussed in Step 2 of the problem-solving process and to consider the impact of the proposed intervention on each of these forces.

Step 5. Specify Consultee and Consultant Responsibilities: This is a crucial step that is often overlooked. Unless the issues inherent in this step are overtly discussed, the planned intervention may "fall between the cracks" and, to everyone's frustration, little will be accomplished. It is always a good idea to specify the "who," "when," "where," and "how" types of issues after the consultant and consultee agree on a course of action. For example, in a case where the consultee has chosen to establish a token economy for a first-grade class, who will be responsible for obtaining the god stars or other materials that will be needed to contingently reinforce children in the class? When will the intervention be started? Where will it be conducted (e.g., homeroom, reading class, lunchroom)? How will the consultee keep track of how many gold stars and points each child has accumulated? How often will backup reinforcers be distributed? Attention to these seemingly minor details can easily make the difference between an effective program and a return to the status quo. According to research conducted by Happe (1982) (as discussed by Gresham & Kendell [1987]), (a) providing explicit instructions to consultees for carrying out treatment plans is one of the methods most frequently cited by school-based consultants as leading to treatment implementation by consultees, although (b) only about "one-half of consultation plans that are verbally committed to by consultees are actually completed" (p. 311). Clearly, there are altogether too many cases where lack of attention to details has resulted in the failure of what otherwise might have been a highly effective intervention.

Step 6. Implement the Chosen Strategy: A consultant should never assume that a verbal agreement to implement a particular treatment program necessarily means that the program will be carried out. If the consultant has done a good job of involving the consultee in the design and selection of the proposed intervention, there should be relatively few instances of failure to enact a plan due to consultee resistance. There are, however, many legitimate problems that consultees encounter that reduce their motivation to carry through with a planned intervention. For example, the consultee may have tried the plan for a few days and have been disappointed with the results. The consultees may have been unaware of the length of time the plan would have to be in place before results would be realized. Or perhaps the consultee found the treatment to be more time consuming than was originally anticipated. Sometimes consultees will not realize that they are lacking prerequisite technical skills until they actually attempt to implement a program. In the harried worlds of many school-based personnel, it is not unusual for some unexpected (e.g., a child threatens suicide) or expected (e.g., parent–teacher conferences) events to temporarily distract a consultee's attention from the intervention plans agreed on with the consultant.

Step 7.   Evaluate the Effectiveness of the Action and Recycle If Necessary: As discussed earlier, short-term follow-up of treatment implementation is a crucial element of effective consultation. The consultant's role at this stage is to work with the consultee to evaluate the effectiveness of actions taken as a result of the consultation process. In those instances where intervention has either been unsuccessful or less than adequately effective, the consultant should encourage the consultee to join him or her in returning to an appropriate earlier point in the problem-solving process. Even when treatment has produced satisfactory results, the consultant should continue to check in with the consultee from time to time because the effectiveness of the planned intervention may not remain stable over time.

Caplanian Mental Health Consultation
Issues Related to Terminology

Prior to discussing the mental health consultation model, a brief word on terminology is in order. There is some confusion in the literature as to what specifically constitutes mental health consultation. Many writers (e.g., Meyers, Parsons, & Martin, 1979) use the term in a generic sense to refer to all types of consultation concerning mental health issues. This more general definition would include behavioral, problem-solving, and ecological consultation approaches among its components. For the purposes of this chapter, we use a more restricted definition of the term in order to facilitate an examination of the similarities and differences between specific consultation models. As such, the subsequent discussion of mental health consultation refers specifically to the concepts originally developed by Caplan (1970).

Problems-Solving Processes

Caplanian mental health consultation has a great deal in common with the ecological consultation model presented previously. In fact, most of the core characteristics of school-based consultation models that were discussed earlier in this chapter

were first articulated by Caplan (1963, 1964, 1970). Despite this overlap, however, there are enough unique aspects of Caplan's mental health consultation model to warrant its presentation as a distinct approach. In particular, Caplan and many of the earlier theoreticians in mental health consultation were psychiatrists rather than psychologists. Consequently, the mental health consultation model, as presented by these authors, had a clear psychoanalytic flavor. The early literature on mental health consultation is laced with references to ego states, pre- and subconscious motivations, and so forth. In this regard, mental health consultation is quite disparate from the more extrapersonal, situationally oriented perspectives of ecological consultation approaches.

Caplan (1963, 1970) discussed four overlapping types of mental health consultation: (a) client-centered case consultation, (b) consultee-centered case consultation, (c) program-centered administrative consultation, and (d) consultee-centered administrative consultation. These approaches differ according to whether the primary goal of consultation is prevention or remediation and whether the focus of consultation regards individual cases or programs. Unfortunately, space limitations preclude a discussion of each of these four types of Caplanian mental health consultation. Clearly, however, consultee-centered case consultation has been the centerpiece of Caplan's work and as such will be singled out for more detailed analysis here.

Consultee-centered case consultation, in which the primary goal of consultation is prevention and focus is upon individual cases, is described by Caplan (1970) as follows:

> The consultant's primary focus is upon elucidating and remedying the shortcomings in the consultee's professional functioning that are responsible for his difficulties with the case about which he is seeking help. . . . Improvement in this client is a side effect, welcome though it may be, and the primary goal is to improve the consultee's capacity to function effectively in this category of case, in order to benefit many similar clients in the future. Because of the educational emphasis, the consultant uses the discussion of the current case situation, not basically in order to understand the client, but in order to understand and remedy the consultee's work diffi-

culties, as manifested in this example. (Caplan, 1970, p. 125)

There are several subtle but significant differences between ecological consultation on the one hand, and consultee-centered case consultation on the other. In the former method, the consultant works with the consultee to delineate the causes of a client's presenting problem, as well as potential solutions. In consultee-centered case consultation, the consultant is only indirectly interested in the causes and solutions for the client's presenting problem. Instead, the primary focus is on determining why the consultee is having difficulties with a particular case and removing these difficulties for the consultee so that the consultee can proceed to handle the problem independently. For example, under the ecological consultation methodology, a consultant might work with a consultee to determine why a particular child is continuously hostile to his or her teacher and peers. The outcome of such a consultation would typically be a series of planned interventions that are designed to reduce the occurrence of the child's problem behaviors. With consultee-centered case consultation, however, the consultant's main concern is not with the causes of the child's behavior and potential solutions for it, but with (a) determining why the consultee cannot handle this particular problem more effectively, and (b) implementing strategies to improve the consultee's professional functioning in regard to such situations.

Caplan (1963, 1970) postulated four reasons for the work difficulties that underlie consultees' needs for consultee-centered case consultation. The first of these is consultee lack of knowledge of understanding. "The consultee's inability to handle the case may be due to his lack of knowledge about the psychosocial factors involved in such situations or he may not see the relevance of theoretical concepts he learned at school to the realities of the client's problems" (Caplan, 1970, p. 127). The principal tactic to resolve this type of consultee difficulty is for the consultant to supply the consultee with missing information. Considerable care is necessary, however, to avoid falling into a superior—subordinate relationship with the consultee that might jeopardize the coordinate nature of the consultation process.

A second consultee difficulty is lack of skill. Often, the teacher is quite knowledgeable about the factors that affect the teaching process. However, while being aware of the empirical literature on the subject and the relevant theory, a teacher might still lack the skill or ability to implement this knowledge effectively in the classroom. (Meyers, Parsons, & Martin, 1979, p. 122)

As the consultant works with a consultee who is experiencing a skill problem, a variety of possibilities present themselves. The consultant may simply try to teach the consultee a particular skill through either instruction or readings. However, this approach is often ineffective unless it is followed with some form of supervised practice. The consultant may also try to model effective behavior for the consultee; shape the consultee's behavior via observation, feedback, and contingent social reinforcement; or utilize behavioral rehearsal/role play experiences. If the consultant is not able to assist the consultee in obtaining the necessary skills, he or she should work along with the consultee to determine from whom such competency building experiences might be available.

Caplan (1970) warns again that the consultant must be careful at this point not to upset the coordinate professional relationship that he or she has established with the consultee. One way for the consultant to avoid this problem is to involve the consultee in the identification of skill deficits and ways to overcome them rather than unilaterally deciding on a course of action for the consultee. Another helpful approach is to generate a wide variety of alternative skills, behaviors, and methods for their acquisition, leaving the final choices for each to the consultee, rather than prescribing a single "correct" response.

Lack of self-confidence is a third reason why a consultee might benefit from consultee-centered case consultation. In such instances, Caplan (1970) recommends that the consultant "provide nonspecific ego support and . . . smooth the consultee's path to other supportive figures in the consultee organization" (p. 131). It would appear that a consultant's ability to listen nonjudgmentally to a consultee's dilemma, provide encouragement concerning consultee strengths, help a consultee realistically appraise his or her own weaknesses, and empathize with consultee feelings should all help to alleviate problems caused by a consultee's lack of self-confidence.

The final reason cited by Caplan as to why

consultees might be struggling with a particular case and thus seeking out consultee-centered case consultation is a lack of objectivity.

> The consultee's difficulty with his client is caused by defective judgment based upon a lack of professional objectivity and a loss of normal "professional distance." The consultee, as it were, gets either too close or too distant from one or more factors in the client's life drama so that he is not able to perceive them accurately enough to carry out his task. Another way of describing the situation is that personal subjective factors in the consultee invade his role functioning, distort his perceptions, and cloud his judgment, so that in this current case he behaves less effectively than is usual for him and thus is not able to utilize his existing knowledge and skills. (Caplan, 1970, pp. 131–132)

It is clear that Caplan considers lack of objectivity to be the most important of the four categories of consultee difficulties that lead to consultee-centered case consultation. He states, "In a well-organized institution or agency in which there is an effective personnel system, administrative control, and a well-developed supervisory network, most cases that present themselves for consultee-centered case consultation fall into this fourth category" (Caplan, 1970, p. 131). Do most consultee-centered case consultation contacts in school settings, in fact, concern consultee objectivity? Unfortunately, there is no definitive evidence either to support or refute Caplan's assumptions. Many school psychologists would argue with Caplan's conclusions, however, because the existence of an "effective personnel system, good administrative control, and a well-developed supervisory network" is a questionable reality in many school systems. The personal experiences of the authors and their colleagues, as well as preliminary research findings (Gutkin, 1981), all indicate that consultee lack of knowledge, skill, and self-confidence are more pervasive problems among school personnel than is the lack of objectivity.

Caplan (1970) went on to further detail the kinds of forces that typically cause a consultee to lose his or her sense of professional objectivity in regard to presenting case problems. He discussed (a) direct personal involvement of the consultee with the client, (b) simple identification of the consultee with the client, (c) transference of consultee experiences and psychic difficulties onto the client's case, (d) characterological distortions of perception and behavior on the part of the consultee in regards to the client, and (e) theme interference.

Because the last of these causes is a concept that Caplan stresses so heavily and one with which most school psychologists are not familiar, theme interference requires some additional explanation.

> The theme is a continuing representation of an unsolved problem or of an experienced defeat or important need frustration. . . . It also has a repetition compulsion quality. This usually takes a syllogistic form, involving an inevitable link between two items or statements: Statement A denotes a particular situation of condition that was characteristic of the original unsolved problem. Statement B denotes the unpleasant outcome. The syllogism takes the form, "All A inevitably leads to B." The implication is that whenever the person finds himself involved in situation or condition A, he is fated to suffer B, and that this generalization applies universally—that is, everyone who is involved in A inevitably suffers B. . . . For instance, if Statement A (Initial Category) is "A person who masturbates excessively" and Statement B (Inevitable Outcome) is "His nervous system will be damaged and his intelligence will be blunted," the syllogism takes the form "All people who masturbate excessively damage their nervous systems and blunt their intelligence." The theme may be a sequel to guilt-ridden conflicts over masturbation in the professional worker's childhood or adolescence. When, for a variety of reasons, there is a disequilibrium in the defenses against this old conflict and the deeper fantasies that underlie it, the situation is ripe. . . . The consultee unconsciously selects a client from his case load, and from certain cues in his statements or behavior, fits him into the Initial Category of "a person who masturbates excessively." This then arouses the expectations that "his nervous system will inevitably be damaged and his intelligence blunted." The worker becomes very upset by this foreboding and begins to make a number of abortive attempts to prevent or stave off the expected doom. . . . These remedial or

preventive efforts are usually panicky and inconsistent, and a realization of their obvious ineffectiveness confirms the consultee's certainty that the expected doom cannot be prevented. . . . Unconsciously, his consolation is that this time the catastrophe will occur to a client and not to himself. (Caplan, 1970, pp. 145–147)

Caplan (1970) proposed several techniques for helping reduce consultee theme interference. One strategy is to unlink the presenting problem from the theme by convincing the consultee that the client does not fit the Initial Category. For example, if the theme is, "All children who are not sufficiently disciplined by their parents will grow up without self-control and thus lead unproductive lives as adults," the consultant could attempt to show the consultee that in the current case the client is adequately disciplined by his or her parents. If successful with this intervention, the consultee will "unlink" this client from the theme and will return to his or her normal professional efficiency.

Although unlinking may resolve the presenting problem, Caplan (1970) argued against using this tactic because it leaves the consultee's theme intact. The situation has been resolved in regard to a specific client, but the generalized bias remains. Instead, Caplan proposed four techniques of theme interferences reduction, all of which are intended to weaken a consultee's theme and thus enable the consultee to cope effectively with the presenting problem and future problems of a similar nature.

> The goal of the consultant's intervention is to invalidate the obligatory link between the two categories that expresses the theme. The consultant accepts and supports the displacement of the theme onto the client's case and the definition of this case as a test case by concurring with the Initial Category in all its details that are personally meaningful to the consultee. The consultant engages the consultee in a joint examination of the link between the Initial Category and the Outcome Category and helps the consultee realize that this outcome is not inevitable. Since the syllogism formulates the connection as invariable, if we can demonstrate that on even one occasion in an authentic test case that meets all the consultee's unconscious requirements the con-

nection between the categories does not hold, we will dissipate or weaken the theme. (pp. 166–167)

The first of these strategies is called "verbal focus on the client." In this approach, the consultant verbally examines the presenting problem with the consultee. "The consultant demonstrates that although the Inevitable Outcome is one logical possibility, there are other possibilities too; and that the evidence indicates that one or more of these is more probable than the doom that the consultee envisages" (Caplan, 1970, p. 167).

The second approach is called "verbal focus on an alternate object—the parable." When the presence of a highly sensitive theme makes discussion of the client's problem emotionally upsetting to the consultee, Caplan (1970) recommends that the consultant direct the discussion away from the client's situation and onto a case that is superficially as different as possible from the presenting case but which retains the essential elements of the theme. Caplan hypothesizes that the use of a parable allows the consultant to weaken the theme while preventing the consultee's unconscious conflicts from becoming conscious.

Caplan's (1970) third tactic for theme interference reduction is termed "nonverbal focus on the case." The essence of this technique is for the consultant to remain calm and relaxed, thus nonverbally signaling the consultee that the expected Inevitable Outcome and the negative consequences associated with it are rather unlikely. When using this technique, Caplan suggests the following:

> This lack of tension and pressure for quick action by the consultant will have a theme reduction significance for the consultee only if he believes the consultant has a real understanding of the nature of the danger that the consultee perceives in the case. It is therefore essential that the consultant should have demonstrated his own involvement in elucidating the complexities of the case, and have indicated his awareness of both the Initial Category and the Inevitable Outcome. Only then will his lack of anxiety have an impact. Otherwise, the consultee will believe that the consultant's relaxed behavior means that he does not care about or does not understand what is likely to happen to the client. (p. 178)

The fourth and final approach to theme interference reduction is "nonverbal focus on the consultation relationship." Caplan (1970) hypothesizes that consultees will often express themes in the way they relate to the consultant and provides a case study involving the following theme: "A weak and helpless woman who builds a link with a big powerful man and becomes dependent upon him will inevitably be exploited and belittled by him" (p. 180). Caplan notes that the consultee was acting out this theme in her relationship with the consultant by being unnecessarily deferent to him and anticipating the consultant's belittling of her. The consultant dealt with this by taking on the role of a powerful male figure but then coupling this activity with a recognition of the consultee's professional expertise, power, and authority. The consultant thus helped the consultee weaken the presenting theme by manipulating his relationship with the consultee so as to invalidate the link between the Initial Category and the Inevitable Outcome.

Although the work of Caplan has been a milestone in the history and development of consultation theory, many argue that his approaches to the reduction of theme interference are too psychodynamic and without empirical support[3] at

[3]We make this statement despite the findings of Medway and Updyke's (1985) meta-analysis, in which they concluded that the effect sizes for mental health consultation were equivalent to those for ecological consultation (described as "behavioral consultation" in their article). We suspect strongly that their conclusion reflects the definitional difficulties noted at the beginning of our discussion of mental health consultation. Specifically, the mental health consultation studies reviewed in the Medway and Updyke meta-analysis did not appear to use theme interference reduction as an intervention tool and thus were probably not investigations of Caplanian mental health consultation per se. Rather, the major intervention tools for these studies were "instructing, modeling, questioning, observing, supporting, and relationship building" (p. 493), techniques that are as compatible with ecological consultation as they are with Caplanian mental health consultation. Supporting our observation, Gresham and Kendell (1987) concluded after reviewing the research literature that "there is no empirical support for the hypothesis that theme interference seriously impedes consultees' professional objectivity nor is there empirical support for the techniques suggested by Caplan to reduce theme interference" (p. 311). Similarly, we are aware of no empirical investigations of Caplanian mental health consultation in school settings since Gutkin (1981) published his data contradicting Caplan's assumption that lack of objectivity is the most common problem experienced by consultees seeking consultation.

this point in time (e.g., Gresham & Kendell, 1987; Meyers, Parsons, & Martin, 1979). The authors accept Caplan's assumptions that consultee effectiveness can be seriously impeded by the loss of professional objectivity, but seriously question the psychoanalytic line of logic put forth to account for this phenomenon. Alternative, situationally based explanations can adequately account for most consultee behaviors, including the loss of professional objectivity. Meyers, Friedman, and Gaughan (1975), for example, presented exploratory evidence that supports the use of direct confrontation techniques during consultee-centered case consultation, a technique frowned upon by Caplan for fear of elevating subconscious conflicts to the fore. The authors are in substantial agreement with Meyers, Parsons, and Martin (1979) when they conclude:

> More readily implemented and effective techniques might become apparent if the teacher's lack of objectivity were defined in more objective and behavioral terms. The resulting consultation techniques should be related directly to the problem definitions, and they should be more straightforward, and more readily understood by both consultant and consultee. This approach is more consistent with the idea that environmental factors influence behavior. Although consultants advocate this principle when helping teachers to understand environmental factors that can influence students' problems, this principle seems to be ignored in Caplan's ego-based conception of teacher problems. It needs to be made clear that the teacher's lack of objectivity can be helped, not only through intrapersonal clinical techniques and insight, but also through modifying the teacher's school environment. (p. 135)

CRITICAL CONTEMPORARY AND FUTURE ISSUES

Research Agendas

To improve the quality of school-based consultation services, it will be necessary to improve the body of empirical knowledge pertaining to this service delivery approach. Although the literature in school-based consultation continues to grow, it is not doing so at a fast enough pace (Duncan & Pryzwansky, 1988; C. R. Reynolds & Clark,

1984). Although comprehensive literature reviews (Mannino & Shore, 1975; Medway, 1979b) and a meta-analysis (Medway & Updyke, 1985) all find school-based consultation services to be effective, there has also been considerable dissatisfaction with the overall quality of consultation research (Gresham & Kendell, 1987; Medway, 1982; Meyers et al., 1978; Pryzwansky, 1986). Among the criticisms most commonly directed toward this body of research are the following: (a) an overreliance on large group rather than small-N designs, (b) inadequate use of control and comparison groups, (c) failure to conduct long-term follow-up of consultee and client behavior changes, (d) use of univariate rather than multivariate research methods, (e) inadequate assessment of treatment integrity, (f) focusing on narrow client behaviors rather than the total ecology of problem situations, (g) excessive reliance on graduate student consultants, (h) inadequate specification of consultation models and underlying assumptions, and (i) dependence on self-report and shifts in attitude rather than observed behavioral change.

Clearly, there is much important research work remaining to be done. The following two issues are among those we believe to be most crucial for the field.

The Technology of Communication

In the original version of this chapter published in the first edition of the *Handbook* (Gutkin & Curtis, 1982), considerable space was used to discuss "the technology of communication" (e.g., genuineness, listening and encouraging consultee verbalizations, empathy, paraphrasing, confrontation). At that time we stated: "At its most basic level, consultation is an interpersonal exchange. As such, the consultant's success is going to hinge largely on his or her communication and relationship skills" (p. 822). This statement is just as valid today as when it was written.

Unfortunately, our knowledge base regarding the technology of communication has advanced very little since that time. With some notable exceptions (T. K. Anderson et al., 1986; Cleven & Gutkin, 1988; Henning-Stout & Conoley, 1987; Kratochwill, 1985; Witt, Moe, Gutkin, & Andrews, 1984), a review of the school psychology journals reveals a sparsity of research directed at psychologists' communication processes with consultees and clients. Much of the relevant theoretical (Ber-

gan, 1977) and empirical (Bergan, Byrnes, & Kratochwill, 1979; Bergan & Tombari, 1975; Tombari & Bergan, 1978) work was published over a decade ago. Improving our understanding of the interpersonal communication processes that occur during school-based consultation interactions must become a high-priority research agenda for the 1990s and beyond.

Although there has been little new knowledge generated in this area during the last decade, increasing awareness of an important research tool is beginning to emerge (Benes & Gutkin, 1989; Bus & Kruizenga, in press; Saudargas, 1989). We are referring to lag sequential analysis (Gottman, Markman, & Notarius, 1977; Gottman & Notarius, 1978; Kratochwill, 1978), a statistical technique for testing the probabilities that "event A" is followed sequentially in time by "event B," "event C," or some other event. The chief advantage of this method over traditional ANOVA and regression approaches is that it provides the researcher with a "moving picture" rather than a "still photograph" of consultative interactions (K. M. Benes, personal communication, 1988). Rather than examining static and summative data such as the total frequency of specific types of verbalizations (e.g., How many "open" questions were asked by the consultant during the course of the consultation session?), lag sequential analysis can be used to address the sequential patterns of communication between consultants and consultees (e.g., When consultants use "open" questions, do consultees tend to respond with a long monologue? If so, do these consultee responses lead consultants to paraphrase or summarize consultee verbalizations?). Hopefully, the qualitatively superior insights that are possible with lag sequential analysis will spur researchers to examine the interactive processes of school-based consultation in substantially greater detail than has been the case up to this point in time.

The Social Psychology of Consultation

From a review of the school-based consultation research to date, it would seem that too little attention has been given to the social psychology of consultation interactions (Conoley & Gutkin, 1986a, 1986b; Gutkin, 1988; Medway & Cafferty, Chapter 8, this volume). As the branch of psychology devoted to studying "ways in which people (or groups of people) affect others and are in turn affected by them" (Raven & Rubin, 1983, p. 15), it would appear to hold a great deal of relevance to school-based consultants working within the context of an indirect service delivery model. Although it is not possible within the limited confines of this chapter to review all of the areas of social psychological research that would have important implications for school-based consultation, two of the most critical topics are presented below.

First, there is the area of interpersonal influence. Clearly, consultants working with consultees for the purposes of improving the psychological and educational circumstances of third parties (i.e., clients) must be concerned with this phenomena (Zins et al., 1988). In fact, a reasonable argument could be made that consultation is primarily a bidirectional process of interpersonal influence between the consultant and the consultee.[4] Although there has been some work in this area of direct relevance to school psychology consultants (e.g., Martin, 1978), to date the most relevant theory (Strong, 1968) and research (e.g., Beutler, Crago & Arizmendi, 1986; Strong & Dixon, 1971) have been done by counseling psychologists who have demonstrated that therapy outcomes can be influenced by manipulating variables pertaining to clients' perceptions of therapists (i.e., expertness, trustworthiness, and attraction). There can be no doubt that a parallel situation exists in school-based consultation. Specifically, the way in which the consultee and consultant perceive each other will affect their ability to influence each other and thus play a major role in shaping the outcomes of consultative interactions. Research is sorely needed to understand the mechanisms by which

this occurs and how school psychologists can use this information to improve the quality of their consultation interactions with their consultees.

Attribution theory (e.g., Helder, 1958) is another area of social psychology with direct implications for consulting school psychologists (Zins et al., 1988). By attributing the behaviors of others to either internal (i.e., a trait or characteristic of the person) or external (i.e., environmental and situation) causes, people form impressions of why other people behave as they do. "One of the most consistent findings coming out of attribution research is that people tend to use internal attributions (often in the forms of personality traits) to explain the behavior of others, but use external attributions when describing their own behavior" (Martin, 1983, p. 36). In light of Bandura's (1977, 1982) work in the area of self-efficacy, in which he postulates that people's motivation to intervene in a situation is largely dependent on their sense of being able to be effective in that situation, it becomes quite likely that both consultants' and consultees' attributions of each other's behaviors, as well as clients' behaviors, could have a major impact on the consultation process.

For example, a consultant's willingness to continue working with a consultee who fails to implement treatment recommendations could be affected by whether the consultant attributes that consultee's behavior to internal causes, over which the consultant may have little control (e.g., resistance), or external causes, which the consultant may be able to affect successfully (e.g., the treatment takes too much teacher time). Similarly, the willingness of a consultee to work with a consultant in regard to a problem student could be significantly affected by whether that consultee attributes the student's behavior to internal causes beyond his or her control (e.g., the child's behavior results from a neurological dysfunction) or external causes within his or her control (e.g., the child's behavior results from an inappropriate curriculum) (Ponti & Curtis, 1984). Unfortunately, research indicates that both consulting school psychologists and teachers alike seem to be prone to attributing the failures of others to internal rather than external factors (Martin & Curtis, 1981; Medway, 1979a; Short & Ringer, 1987; Smith & Lyon, 1986), succumbing to the "fundamental attribution error" (Martin, 1983, p. 37). The result of this is that consultants "blame" consultees for consultative

[4]Conceptualizing consultation in terms of interpersonal influence does not, in any way, imply that the process is noncollaborative in nature, as has been suggested by Stewart (1986). Rather, it simply recognizes that *both* the consultant and consultee have valid expertise and insights to share with each other and that each does so with the intent of influencing the thoughts and behaviors of the other party. After all, if the consultant and consultee had no intention of influencing each other, what would be the purpose of their interaction? As long as the consultant recognizes that the consultative exchange is between coequals and that the consultee has the final authority to either accept or reject intervention plans, there is no inconsistency between exerting interpersonal influence and interacting in a collaborative manner.

failures, reducing their motivation to continue consulting with consultees, and that consultees "blame" clients for their psychoeducational problems, reducing their motivation to consult with school psychologists about how to reduce and prevent children's problems in their classroom. Two studies (Ponti & Curtis, 1984; Wehmann et al., 1989) suggest that interactions with skilled consultants may positively influence teachers' attributions for student-related problems. On the other hand, research by Curtis, Zins, and Ponti (1988) indicates that the tendency of school psychology consultants to attribute consultation outcomes to consultee characteristics did not differ for those who had received formal training in consultation versus those who had not. Obviously, more research is needed to understand these important and complex phenomena, and to learn how we can modify them.

Practice Agendas

Again, space limitations preclude a thorough discussion of the many critical practice issues facing school-based consultants. The following are two issues we believe are of particular importance.

Closing the Gap Between Real and Ideal Job Roles

Although recent survey data indicate that an increasing proportion of school psychologists' time (approximately 20 to 30%) is being spent in consulting roles (Smith & Lyon, 1985; Wright & Gutkin, 1981), these and other surveys also show that practitioners desire to spend substantially more time as consultants than they are currently doing (Fisher et al., 1986; Smith, 1984; Smith & Lyon, 1985; Wright & Gutkin, 1981). Closing the gap between real and ideal functions has been, and (unfortunately) remains, a major problem for school psychologists.

In the original version of this chapter published in the first edition of the *Handbook* (Gutkin & Curtis, 1982), we listed time constraints, inadequate consultee training, funding legislation, and the novelty of consultation services as major obstacles to increased usage of consultation services in schools. Below we briefly review the progress that has been made in reference to each of these four issues.

1. Of the four obstacles identified in our earlier chapter, we believe that the time constraints of consultation services remain the most intractable problem. Intensive analyses of complex problems coupled with individualized intervention and meaningful follow-up takes more teacher time and effort than referring a child for testing, and thus may be less well received by teachers (Piersel & Gutkin, 1983; Witt & Martens, 1988). Of course, this is only true from a short-term perspective. Over the long haul, effective consultation that remedies presenting problems, prevents future problems from occurring and/or getting out of hand, and increases teachers' professional competencies requires *less* teacher time and effort than facing persistent and disturbing child problems on a daily basis. Thus, among the most important tasks facing school psychologists is that of getting consultees to attend to the long-term rather than only the short-term contingencies of referral versus consultation services. Given the well-known fact that short-term contingencies notoriously have a stronger impact on human behavior than do long-term contingencies (Masters, Burish, Hollon, & Rimm, 1987), this is no small challenge.

2. Although it remains true that few, if any, teachers receive preservice training as consultees, it appears that this may be less of a problem as we enter the 1990s because it now seems quite feasible to provide consultees with necessary skills via inservice and modeling experiences. Although not conclusive, there is research to support this assumption (T. K. Anderson et al., 1986; Chandy, 1974; Cleven & Gutkin, 1988; Curtis & Metz, 1986; Curtis & Watson, 1980; Epps & Lane, 1987; Revels & Gutkin, 1983), including "a large body of literature [that] demonstrates the efficacy of training teachers in childhood behavior management techniques" (Kratochwill & Van Someren, 1985, p. 229). Advances in parent-training interventions (Kramer, Chapter 27, this volume) and the development of empirically derived consultation competencies that could be used to train

either teachers or parents (West & Cannon, 1988) also provide fuel for some optimism along these lines.

3. In terms of funding issues, it remains difficult for school-based consultation services to compete with traditional testing in light of continuing federal and state laws that reinforce school districts financially for the identification of handicapped children (Gutkin & Tieger, 1979). Despite this, however, there may be an important change of direction coming about in the near future. A recent federal study (U.S. Department of Education, in press) documents the substantially higher costs of providing special versus regular education services, as well as the notable difference between students served through special education resource programs ($1,325 per student) versus through self-contained classes ($4,233 per student). Perhaps relatedly, there appears to be a shift of emphasis in many states and school districts toward prereferral intervention direct at minimizing the number of children placed unnecessarily in special education programs and in increased efforts to serve students through resource rather than pull-out programs. Consultative support by specialists, such as the school psychologist, for the regular class teacher is a fundamental element in such approaches (Graden, Casey, & Christenson, 1985). Thus, within the next decade we may see a significant increase in school-based consultation services driven (ironically) by funding factors in conjunction with the P.L. 94-142 mandate for least restrictive environment programming for all handicapped children.

4. Finally, we suspect the novelty of school-based consultation services is becoming less and less of a problem. We noted earlier that according to recent surveys of practicing school psychologists (Fisher, Jenkins, & Crumbley, 1986; Smith, 1984; Smith & Lyon, 1985; Wright & Gutkin, 1981), consultation services are on the rise and thus becoming more common. It would seem that the significance of this obstacle can only decrease with the passage of time.

Above and beyond the four points discussed above, two other issues suggest themselves as being particularly relevant to school psychologists' attempts to close the gap between real and ideal roles and thus increase their usage of school-based consultation services. First, it is essential to improve both the quantity and quality of consultation training that most school psychologists receive in graduate school (Kratochwill & Van Someren, 1985). Although the field appears to have made progress during recent years, there is still far too little emphasis placed on this service delivery approach in most graduate programs. A recent survey, for example, indicates that

> while 55% of the doctoral programs responding offer at least one course devoted solely to consultation, only 32% of the subdoctoral programs offer such a course. Also, 19% of the doctoral programs and only 1% of the subdoctoral programs offer more than one consultation course. Some programs have no courses with even a significant partial focus on consultation, and 17% of the doctoral programs, as well as 42% of the subdoctoral programs, fall in this category. (Meyers, Wurtz, & Flanagan, 1981)

It would seem to be self-evident that the field of school psychology will not be able to bring about a major change in service delivery models if graduate training programs are not preparing students to function under this model. In light of NASP standards requiring preparation in the area of consultation for all school psychology training programs, we are hopeful that this situation will improve in the near future. We are also pleased to note a number of books (Alpert & Meyers, 1983; Parsons & Meyers, 1984) and research studies (Carlson & Tombari, 1986; Curtis & Zins, 1988; McDougall, Reschly, & Corkery, 1988) addressing preservice and inservice training procedures for school psychologists that have appeared within the last few years.

Finally, to successfully close the gap between real and ideal job roles, school psychologists will have to adopt a systems orientation in their work. By focusing professional attention almost exclusively on individual children, teachers and parents instead of organizational and systems variables, school psychologists are failing to gain access to powerful administrative forces that could make a meaningful difference in their struggle. Additional detail on the utility and importance of a systems perspective is provided immediately below.

Systems Orientation

When viewed from a systems perspective (von Bertalanffy, 1967, 1968, 1974), it is quite obvious that children's problems do not occur in isolation. They occur as part of large and complex systems of interactions among a multitude of individuals, groups, and organizations. The key conceptual shortcoming of the medical model is the assumption that children's problems lie within the child. We agree with Knoff (1984), who concludes that "complex problems are referred to the school psychologist as child-centered problems when they are actually multifaceted, multisubsystem prob-

lems'' (p. 87). Figure 2 illustrates this perspective, delineating the micro, meso, exo, and macro systems affecting children at school.

To be successful, school psychologists, in general, and school-based consultants, in particular, must expand the systems orientation of services. Two of many possible examples are presented to highlight this point. First, in a series of studies, Ysseldyke and his colleagues have shown that the decision to refer a child for special education services is as much a function of the referring teacher as it is the referred child, and that once referred for a special education evaluation the odds are very high that a referred child will be diagnosed as needing special education (Ysseldyke, 1986). If we wish to understand and modify this phenomena, it will be necessary to consider characteristics of referring teachers and multidisciplinary teams, as well as district, state, and national guidelines pertaining to special education, in addition to those

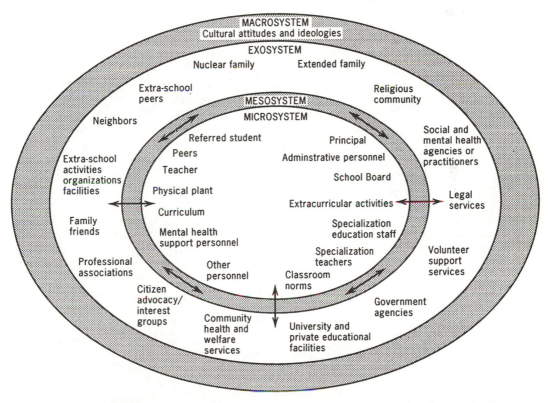

Figure 2. Ecomap showing micro, meso, exo, and macro systems for typical school child. (From Knoff, 1984; reprinted with permission.)

child characteristics that are traditionally examined. Second, there is evidence that organizational variables affect (a) whether school personnel use consultation services (Bossard & Gutkin, 1983), (b) how school personnel interact with school-based consultants (Gutkin, Clark, & Ajchenbaum, 1985), and (c) the attitudes of school personnel towards consultation services (Gutkin & Bossard, 1984).

A systems perspective will also be very important for school psychologists if they hope to change their contemporary roles to include a heavier emphasis on consultation services. As noted by Sarason (1982), it is always difficult to bring about real change in schools and it is nearly impossible if one relies primarily on a "psychology of individuals" rather than an understanding of organizations and systems. Whether examining national systems of credentialing, as detailed in all of its natural confusion by Fagan (1986) (Figure 3), or local systems in school districts (Conoley & Gutkin, 1986b) (Figure 4), it is

most clear that increased understanding of systems and how to intervene with them will be essential to bringing about meaningful change in the roles of school psychologists (Zins & Curtis, 1984).

To be optimistic, since the publication of the first edition of the *Handbook,* there is evidence of increasing theoretical and research interest in systems perspectives among school psychologists (e.g., C. Anderson, 1983; Burke & Ellison, 1985; Curtis & Metz, 1986; Dappen & Gutkin, 1986; Elliott & Witt, 1986; Ellison & Burke, 1987; Fine, 1985; Fish & Jain, 1988; Fleming & Fleming, 1983; Graden, Zins, & Curtis, 1988; Gutkin, 1988; Hobbs, 1978; Illback & Maher, 1984; Knoff, 1984; Martens & Witt, 1988; Piersel & Gutkin, 1983; Plas, 1986; Power & Bartholomew, 1985; Robinson, Cameron, & Raethel, 1985; Schmuck, Chapter 36, this volume); (Witt & Martens, 1988). Unfortunately, however, it would appear that professional practice has barely begun to scratch the surface in this area.

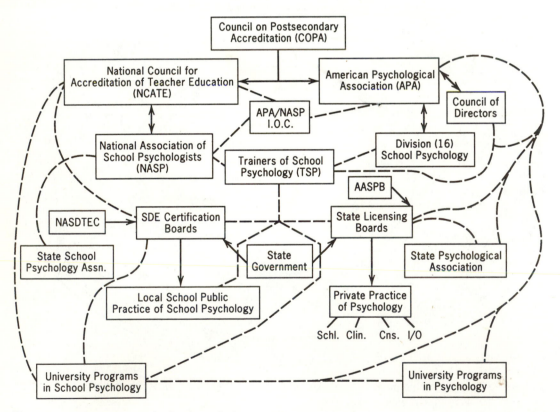

Figure 3. A systems view of school psychology at the national level. (From Fagan, 1986. Copyright 1986 by the American Psychological Association; reprinted with permission.)

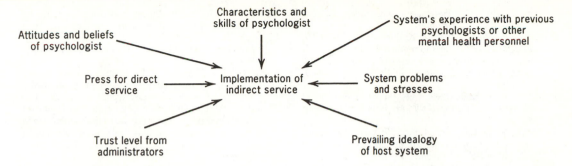

Figure 4. A systems view of school psychology at the local level. (From Conoley and Gutkin, 1986; reprinted with permission.)

CONCLUSION

We find ourselves very much in agreement with Alpert (1985), who argued that to change a profession, a clear, perhaps even utopian vision of the future is needed by those working in that profession. Based on our literature review, there is no doubt that school psychologists want to see major changes regarding their mode of practice (e.g., Alpert, 1985; Bardon, 1983; Graden, Zins, & Curtis, 1988; Reschly, 1988; Ysseldyke et al., 1984). We have tried in this chapter to provide readers with the theory, techniques, and research to build an alternative future for school psychology. We believe that school-based consultation provides an effective, meaningful, pragmatic, and exciting set of alternatives to traditional school psychological services.

REFERENCES

Albee, G. W. (1968). Conceptual models and manpower requirements in psychology. *American Psychologist, 23,* 317–320.

Allen, C. T., & Forman, S. G. (1984). Efficacy of methods of training teachers in behavior modification. *School Psychology Review, 13,* 26–32.

Alpert, J. L. (1984). School consultation. In J. E. Ysseldyke (Ed.), *School psychology: The state of the art* (pp. 167–181). Minneapolis; MN: National School of Psychology Inservice Training Network.

Alpert, J. L. (1985). Change within a profession: Change, future, prevention, and school psychology. *American Psychologist, 40,* 1112–1121.

Alpert, J. L., & Associates (1982). *Psychological consultation in educational settings.* San Francisco: Jossey-Bass.

Alpert, J. L., & Meyers, J. (Eds.). (1983). *Training in consultation.* Springfield, IL: Charles C Thomas.

Alpert, J. L., & Silverstein, J. (1985). Mental health consultation: Historical, present, and future perspectives. In J. R. Bergan (Ed.), *School psychology in contemporary society: An introduction* (pp. 281–315). Columbus, OH: Charles E. Merrill.

Anderson, C. (1983). An ecological developmental model for a family orientation in school psychology. *Journal of School Psychology, 21,* 179–189.

Anderson, T. K., Kratochwill, T. R., & Bergan, J. R. (1986). Training teachers in behavioral consultation and therapy: An analysis of verbal behaviors. *Journal of School Psychology, 24,* 229–241.

Arter, J. A., & Jenkins, J. R. (1979). Differential diagnosis-perspective teaching: A critical appraisal. *Review of Educational Research, 49,* 517–555.

Babcock, N. L., & Pryzwansky, W. B. (1983). Models of consultation: Preferences of educational professionals at five stages of service. *Journal of School Psychology, 21,* 359–366.

Bandura, A. (1977). *Social learning theory.* Englewood Cliffs, NJ: Prentice-Hall.

Bandura, A. (1978). The self-system in reciprocal determinism. *American Psychologist, 33,* 344–358.

Bandura, A. (1982). Self-efficacy mechanism in human agency. *American Psychologist, 37,* 122–147.

Barclay, J. R. (1971). Descriptive, theoretical, and behavioral characteristics of sub-doctoral school psychologists. *American Psychologist, 26,* 257–280.

Bardon, J. I. (1983). Psychology applied to education: A specialty in search of an identity. *American Psychologist, 38,* 185–196.

Bardon, J. I. (1977, August). *The consultee in consultation: Preparation and training.* Paper presented at the annual meeting of the American Psychological Association, San Francisco.

Barker, R. G. (1965). Explorations in ecological psychology. *American Psychologist, 20,* 1–14.

Barker, R. G. (1968). *Ecological psychology.* Stanford, CA: Stanford University Press.

Barry, J. R. (1970). Criteria in the evaluation of consultation. *Professional Psychology, 1,* 363–366.

Benes, K. M., & Gutkin, T. B. (1989, March). Functional analysis of communication behavior in the consultation environment. In J. J. Kramer (Chair), *Consultant/teacher/parent/child: A new look at old problems.* Symposium conducted at the annual meeting of the National Association of School Psychologists, Boston.

Bergan, J. R. (1977). *Behavioral consultation.* Columbus, OH: Charles E. Merrill.

Bergan, J. R., Byrnes, I. M., & Kratochwill, T. R. (1979). Effects of behavioral and medical models of consultation on teacher expectancies and instruction of a hypothetical child. *Journal of School Psychology, 17,* 306–316.

Bergan, J. R., & Kratochwill, T. R. (in press). *Behavioral consultation in applied settings.* New York: Plenum Press.

Bergan, J. R., & Tombari, M. L. (1975). The analysis of verbal interactions occurring during consultation. *Journal of School Psychology, 13,* 209–226.

Bergan, J. R., & Tombari, M. L. (1976). Consultant skill and efficiency and the implementation and outcomes of consultation. *Journal of School Psychology, 14,* 3–14.

Bertalanffy, von, L. (1967). *Robots, man and minds.* New York: Braziller.

Bertalanffy, von, L. (1968). *General systems theory.* New York: Braziller.

Bertalanffy, von, L. (1974). General systems theory and psychiatry. In S. Arieti (Ed.), *American handbook of psychiatry* (2nd ed. Vol. 1, pp. 1095–1117). New York: Basic Books.

Beutler, L. E., Crago, M., & Arizmendi, T. G. (1986). Research on therapist variables in psychotherapy. In S. L. Garfield & A. E. Bergin (Eds.), *Handbook of psychotherapy and behavior change* (3rd ed., pp. 257–310). New York: Wiley.

Bossard, M. D., & Gutkin, T. B. (1983). The relationship of consultant skill and school organizational characteristics with teacher use of school based consultation services. *School Psychology Review, 12,* 50–56.

Bowers, N. E. (1971). Some guidelines for the school psychologist in his attempts to intimidate the teacher during a conference. *Journal of School Psychology, 9,* 357–361.

Brown, D., Pryzwansky, W. B., & Schulte, A. C. (1987). *Psychological consultation: Introduction to theory and practice.* Boston: Allyn and Bacon.

Brown, D., & Schulte, A. C. (1987). A social learning model of consultation. *Professional Psychology: Research and Practice, 18,* 283–287.

Bundy, M. L., & Poppen, W. A. (1986). School counselors' effectiveness as consultants: A research review. *Elementary School Guidance and Counseling, 20,* 215–222.

Burke, J. P., & Ellison, G. C. (1985). School psychologists' participation in organization development: Prerequisite considerations. *Professional Psychology: Research and Practice, 16,* 521–528.

Bus, A. G. (1989). How are recommendations concerning reading and spelling disabilities arrived at and why do experts disagree? *Psychology in Schools, 26,* 54–61.

Bus, A. G., & Kruizenga, T. H. (in press). Diagnostic problem-solving behavior of expert practitioners in the field of learning disabilities. *Journal of School Psychology.*

Caplan, G. (1963). Types of mental health consultation. *American Journal of Orthopsychiatry, 33,* 470–481.

Caplan, G. (1964). *Principles of preventive psychology.* New York: Basic Books.

Caplan, G. (1970). *The theory and practice of mental health consultation.* New York: Basic Books.

Carkhuff, R. R. (1973). *The art of problem solving.* Amherst, MA: Human Resource Development Press.

Carlson, C. I., & Tombari, M. L. (1986). Multilevel school consultation training: Preliminary program evaluation. *Professional School Psychology, 1,* 89–104.

Chandy, J. (1974). *The effects of an inservice orientation on teacher perception and use of the mental health consultant.* Paper presented at the annual meeting of the American Psychological Association, New Orleans.

Cleven, C. A., & Gutkin, T. B. (1988). Cognitive modeling of consultation processes: A means for improving consultee's problem definition skills. *Journal of School Psychology, 26,* 379–389.

Conoley, J. C. (Ed.). (1981). *Consultation in schools: Theory, research, procedures.* New York: Academic Press.

Conoley, J. C. (Ed.). (1986). Mini-series on indirect service delivery. *School Psychology Review, 15,* 455–545.

Conoley, J. C., & Conoley, C. W. (1982). *School consultation: A guide to practice and training.* Elmsford, NY: Pergamon Press.

Conoley, J. C., & Gutkin, T. B. (1986a). Educating school psychologists for the real world. *School Psychology Review, 15,* 457–465.

Conoley, J. C., & Gutkin, T. B. (1986b). School psychology: A reconceptualization of service delivery realities. In S. N. Elliott & J. C. Witt (Eds.), *The delivery of psychological services in schools: Concepts, processes, and issues* (pp. 393–424). Hillsdale, NJ: Lawrence Erlbaum.

Curtis, M. J., Curtis, V. A., & Graden, J. L. (1988). Prevention and early intervention through intervention assistance programs. *School Psychology International, 9,* 257–264.

Curtis, M. J., & Metz, L. W. (1986). System level intervention in a school for handicapped children. *School Psychology Review, 15,* 510–518.

Curtis, M. J., & Meyers, J. (1985). Best practices in school-based consultation. In A. Thomas & J. Grimes (Eds.), *Best practices in school psychology* (pp. 79–94). Kent, OH: National Association of School Psychologists.

Curtis, M. J., & Van Wagener, E. (1988, April). *An analysis of failed consultation.* Paper presented at the annual meeting of the National Association of School Psychologists, Chicago.

Curtis, M. J., & Watson, K. (1980). Changes in consultee problem clarification skills following consultation. *Journal of School Psychology, 18,* 210–221.

Curtis, M. J., & Zins, J. E. (1988). Effects of training in consultation and instructor feedback on acquisition of consultation skills. *Journal of School Psychology, 26,* 185–190.

Curtis, M. J., Zins, J. E., & Ponti, C. R. (1988, August). *Consultants' attributions for success or failure as a function of training.* Paper presented at the annual meeting of the American Psychological Association, Atlanta.

Dance, K. A., & Neufeld, R. W. J. (1988). Aptitude-treatment interaction research in the clinical setting:

A review of attempts to dispel the "patient uniformity" myth. *Psychological Bulletin, 104*, 192–213.

Dappen, L. D., & Gutkin, T. B. (1986). Domain theory: Examining the validity of an organizational theory with public school personnel. *Professional School Psychology, 1*, 257–265.

Davis, J. M., Sandoval, J., & Wilson, M. P. (1988). Strategies for the primary prevention of adolescent suicide. *School Psychology Review, 17*, 559–569.

Deno, S. L. (1985). Curriculum-based measurement: The emerging alternative. *Exceptional Children, 52*, 219–232.

Dixon, D. N., & Glover, J. A. (1984). *Counseling: A problem solving approach.* New York: Wiley.

Dougherty, D. (1988). Children's mental health problems and services: Current federal efforts and policy implications. *American Psychologist, 43*, 808–812.

Duncan, C. F., & Pryzwansky, W. B. (1988). Consultation research: Trends in doctoral dissertations 1978–1985. *Journal of School Psychology, 26*, 107–119.

D'Zurilla, T. J., and Goldfried, M. R. (1971). Problem solving and behavior modification. *Journal of Abnormal and Social Psychology, 78*, 107–126.

Elias, M. J., & Branden, L. R. (1988). Primary prevention of behavioral and emotional problems in school-aged populations. *School Psychology Review, 17*, 581–592.

Elliott, S. N. (1988). Acceptability of behavioral treatments: Review of variables that influence treatment selection. *Professional Psychology: Research and Practice, 19*, 68–80.

Elliott, S. N., & Witt, J. C. (Eds.). (1986). *The delivery of psychological services in schools: Concepts, processes, and issues.* Hillsdale, NJ: Lawrence Erlbaum.

Ellison, G. C., & Burke, J. P. (1987). Strategy for selecting organization development interventions for schools. *Professional Psychology: Research and Practice, 18*, 385–390.

Epps, S., & Lane, M. P. (1987). Assessment and training of teacher interviewing skills to program common stimuli between special and general education environments. *School Psychology Review, 16*, 50–68.

Fagan, T. K. (1986). School psychology's dilemma: Reappraising solutions and directing attention to the future. *American Psychologist, 41*, 851–861.

Fine, M. J. (1985). Intervention from a systems-ecological perspective. *Professional Psychology: Research and Practice, 16*, 262–270.

Fish, M. C., & Jain, S. (1988). Using systems theory in school assessment and intervention: A structural model for school psychologists. *Professional School Psychology, 3*, 291–300.

Fisher, G. L., Jenkins, S. J., & Crumbley, J. D. (1986). A replication of a survey of school psychologists: Congruence between training, practice, preferred role, and competence. *Psychology in the Schools, 23*, 271–279.

Fleming, D. C., & Fleming, E. R. (1983). Consultation with multidisciplinary teams: A program of development and improvement of team functioning. *Journal of School Psychology, 21*, 367–376.

Forman, S. G., & Linney, J. A. (1988). School-based prevention of adolescent substance abuse: Programs, implementation and future directions. *School Psychology Review, 17*, 550–558.

Galagan, J. E. (1985). Psychoeducational testing: Turn out the lights, the party's over. *Exceptional Children, 52*, 288–299.

Gallagher, T., & Prutting, C. (Eds.). (1983). *Pragmatic assessment and intervention issues in language.* San Diego, CA: College-Hill Press.

Gallessich, J. (1983). *The profession and practice of consultation.* San Francisco: Jossey-Bass.

Gallessich, J. (1985). Toward a meta-theory of consultation. *The Counseling Psychologist, 13*, 336–354.

Gonzales, L. R. (1986). A community service for a rural high school. *Prevention in Human Services, 4*, 37–71.

Goodwin, D. L., & Coates, T. J. (1976). *Helping students help themselves.* Englewood Cliffs, NJ: Prentice-Hall.

Gottman, J. M., Markman, H., & Notarius, C. (1977). The topography of marital conflict: A sequential analysis of verbal and nonverbal behavior. *Journal of Marriage and the Family, 39*, 461–477.

Gottman, J. M., & Notarius, C. (1978). Sequential analysis of observational data using Markov chains. In T. R. Kratochwill (Ed.), *Single subject research* (pp. 237–285). New York: Academic Press.

Graden, J. L., Casey, A., & Bronstrom, O. (1985). Implementing a prereferral intervention system: Part II. The data. *Exceptional Children, 51*, 487–496.

Graden, J. L., Casey, A., & Christenson, S. L. (1985). Implementing a prereferral intervention system: Part I. The model. *Exceptional Children, 51*, 377–384.

Graden, J. L., Zins, J. E., & Curtis, M. J. (Eds.). (1988). *Alternative educational delivery systems: Enhancing instructional options for all students.* Washington, DC: National Association of School Psychologists.

Gresham, F. M., & Kendell, G. K. (1987). School consultation research: Methodological critique and future research directions. *School Psychology Review, 16*, 306–316.

Gutkin, T. B. (1980). Teacher perceptions of consultation services provided by school psychologists. *Professional Psychology, 11*, 637–642.

Gutkin, T. B. (1981). Relative frequency of consultee lack of knowledge, skill, confidence, and objectivity in school settings. *Journal of School Psychology, 19*, 57–61.

Gutkin, T. B. (1986). Consultees' perceptions of variables relating to the outcomes of school-based consultation interactions. *School Psychology Review, 15*, 375–382.

Gutkin, T. B. (1988). *Reconceptualization of service delivery realities.* Paper presented at the annual convention of the American Psychological Association, Atlanta.

Gutkin, T. B., & Ajchenbaum, M. (1984). Teachers' perceptions of control and preferences for consultative services. *Professional Psychology: Research and Practice, 15*, 565–570.

Gutkin, T. B., & Bossard, M. D. (1984). The impact of consultant, consultee, and organizational variables on teacher attitudes toward consultation services. *Journal of School Psychology, 22*, 251–258.

Gutkin, T. B., Clark, J. H., & Ajchenbaum, M. (1985). Impact of organizational variables on the delivery of school-based consultation services: A comparative case study approach. *School Psychology Review, 14,* 230–235.

Gutkin, T. B., & Curtis, M. J. (1981). School-based consultation: The indirect service delivery concept. In M. J. Curtis & J. E. Zins (Eds.), *The theory and practice of school consultation* (pp. 219–226). Springfield, IL: Charles C Thomas.

Gutkin, T. B., & Curtis, M. J. (1982). School-based consultation: Theory and techniques. In C. R. Reynolds & T. B. Gutkin (Eds.), *The handbook of school psychology* (pp. 796–828). New York: Wiley.

Gutkin, T. B., Henning-Stout, M., & Piersel, W. C. (1988). Impact of a district-wide behavioral consultation prereferral intervention service on patterns of school psychological service delivery. *Professional School Psychology, 3,* 301–308.

Gutkin, T. B., & Hickman, J. A. (1988). Teachers' perceptions of control over presenting problems and resulting preferences for consultation versus referral services. *Journal of School Psychology, 26,* 395–398.

Gutkin, T. B., Singer, J. H., & Brown, R. (1980). Teacher reactions to school-based consultation services: A multivariate analysis. *Journal of School Psychology, 18,* 126–134.

Gutkin, T. B., & Tieger, A. G. (1979). Funding patterns for exceptional children: Current approaches and suggested alternatives. *Professional Psychology, 10,* 670–680.

Happe, D. (1982). Behavioral intervention: It doesn't do any good in your briefcase. In J. Grimes (Eds.), *Psychological approaches to problems of children and adolescents* (pp. 15–41). Des Moines, IA: Iowa Department of Public Instruction.

Hattie, J. A., Sharpley, C. F., & Rogers, H. J. (1984). Comparative effectiveness of professional and paraprofessional helpers. *Psychological Bulletin, 95,* 534–541.

Hawryluk, M. K., & Smallwood, D. L. (1986). Assessing and addressing consultee variables in school-based behavioral consultation. *School Psychology Review, 15,* 519–528.

Helder, F. (1958). *The psychology of interpersonal relations.* New York: Wiley.

Henning-Stout, M., & Conoley, J. C. (1987). Consultation and counseling as procedurally divergent: Analysis of verbal behavior. *Professional Psychology: Research and Practice, 18,* 124–127.

Heppner, P. P. (1978). A review of the problem-solving literature and its relationship to counseling process. *Journal of Counseling Psychology, 25,* 366–375.

Heppner, P. P., & Krauskopf, C. J. (1987). An information-processing approach to personal problem solving. *The Counseling Psychologist, 15,* 371–447.

Hinkle, A., Silverstein, B., & Walton, D. M. (1977). A method for the evaluation of mental health consultation to the public schools. *Journal of Community Psychology, 5,* 262–265.

Hobbs, N. (1978). Families, schools and communities: An ecosystem for children. *Teachers College Record, 79,* 755–766.

Hughes, J. N. (1986). Ethical issues in school consultation. *School Psychology Review, 15,* 489–499.

Idol, L., & West, J. F. (1987). Consultation in special education: Part II. Training and practice. *Journal of Learning Disabilities, 20,* 474–494.

Illback, R. J., & Maher, C. A. (1984). The school psychologist as an organizational boundary role professional. *Journal of School Psychology, 22,* 63–72.

Jackson, R. M., Cleveland, J. C., & Merenda, P. F. (1975). The longitudinal effects of early identification and counseling of underachievers. *Journal of School Psychology, 13,* 119–128.

Jason, L. A., & Ferone, L. (1978). Behavioral versus process consultation interventions in school settings. *American Journal of Community Psychology, 6,* 531–543.

Kavale, K. A., & Forness, S. R. (1984). A meta-analysis of the validity of Wechsler scale profiles and recategorizations: Patterns or parodies? *Learning Disabilities Quarterly, 7,* 136–156.

Kavale, K. A., & Glass, G. V. (1984). Meta-analysis and policy decisions in special education. In B. K. Keogh (Ed.), *Advances in special education* (Vol. 4, pp. 195–247). Greenwich, CT: JAI Press.

Keller, H. R. (1981). Behavioral consultation. In J. C. Conoley (Ed.), *Consultation in schools: Theory, research, procedures* (pp. 59–99). New York: Academic Press.

Kidder, M. G., Tinker, M. B., Mannino, F. V., & Trickett, E.J. (1986). An annotated reference guide to the consultation literature, 1978–1984. In F. V. Mannino, E. J. Trickett, M. F. Shore, M. G. Kidder, & G. Levin (Eds.), *Handbook of mental health consultation* (pp. 521–796). Rockville, MD: National Institute of Mental Health.

Knoff, H. M. (1984). The practice of multimodal consultation: An integrating approach for consultation service delivery. *Psychology in the Schools, 21,* 83–91.

Kramer, J. J., Henning-Stout, M., Ullman, D. P., & Schellenberg, R. P. (1987). The viability of scatter analysis on the WISC-R and the SBIS: Examining a vestige. *Journal of Psychoeducational Assessment, 5,* 37–47.

Kratochwill, T. R. (1978). *Single subject research: Strategies for evaluating change.* New York: Academic Press.

Kratochwill, T. R. (1985). Selection of target behaviors in behavioral consultation. *Behavioral Assessment, 7,* 49–61.

Kratochwill, T. R., & Van Someren, K. R. (1985). Barriers to treatment success in behavioral consultation: Current limitations and future directions. *Journal of School Psychology, 23,* 225–239.

Kurpius, D. (Ed.). (1978). [Special issue]. *Personnel and Guidance Journal, 56* (6).

Lambert, N. M. (1976). Children's problems and classroom interventions from the perspective of classroom teachers. *Professional Psychology, 7,* 507–517.

Lewin, K. (1951). *Field theory in social science.* New York: Harper & Row.

Maitland, R. E., Fine, M. J., & Tracy, D. B. (1985). The effects of an interpersonally based problem-solving process on consultation outcome. *Journal of School Psychology, 23,* 337–345.

Mann, P. A. (1986). Prevention of child abuse: Two contrasting social support services. *Prevention in Human Services, 4,* 73–111.

Mannino, F. V., & Shore, M. F. (1975). Effecting change through consultation. In F. V. Mannino, B. W. MacLennan, & M. F. Shore (Eds.), *The practice of mental health consultation* (pp. 25–46). New York: Gardner Press.

Mannino, F. V., Trickett, E. J., Shore, M. F., Kidder, M. G., & Levin, G. (1986). *Handbook of mental health consultation.* Rockville, MD: National Institute of Mental Health.

Martens, B. K., & Witt, J. C. (1988). Expanding the scope of behavioral consultation: A systems approach to classroom behavior change. *Professional School Psychology, 3,* 271–281.

Martin, R. P. (1978). Expert and referent power: A framework for understanding and maximizing consultation effectiveness. *Journal of School Psychology, 16,* 49–55.

Martin, R. P. (1983). Consultant, consultee, and client expectations of each others behavior in consultation. *Psychology in the Schools, 12,* 35–41.

Martin, R. P., & Curtis, M. J. (1981). Consultants' perceptions of causality for success and failure of consultation. *Professional Psychology, 12,* 670–676.

Martin, R. P., and Keller, A. (1976). Teacher awareness of classroom dyadic interactions. *Journal of School Psychology, 14,* 47–55.

Masters, J. C., Burish, T. G., Hollon, S. D., & Rimm, D. C. (1987). *Behavior therapy: Techniques and empirical findings* (3rd ed.). San Diego, CA: Harcourt Brace Jovanovich.

McDermott, P. A. (1980). Congruence and typology of diagnoses in school psychology: An empirical study. *Psychology in the Schools, 17,* 12–24.

McDermott, P. A. (1988). Agreement among diagnosticians or observers: Its importance and determination. *Professional School Psychology, 3,* 225–240.

McDougall, L. M., Reschly, D. J., & Corkery, J. M. (1988). Changes in referral interviews with teachers after behavioral consultation training. *Journal of School Psychology, 26,* 225–232.

Meade, C. J., Hamilton, M. K., & Yuen, R. K.-W. (1982). Consultation research: The time has come the walrus said. *Counseling Psychologist, 10,* 39–51.

Medway, F. J. (1979a). Causal attributions for school-related problems: Teacher perceptions and teacher feedback. *Journal of Educational Psychology, 71,* 809–818.

Medway, F. J. (1979b). How effective is school consultation: A review of recent research. *Journal of School Psychology, 17,* 275–282.

Medway, F. J. (1982). School consultation research: Past trends and future directions. *Professional Psychology, 13,* 422–430.

Medway, F. J., & Updyke, J. F. (1985). Meta-analysis of consultation outcome studies. *American Journal of Community Psychology, 13,* 489–504.

Meyers, J. (1975). Consultee-centered consultation with a teacher as a technique in behavior management. *American Journal of Community Psychology, 3,* 111–121.

Meyers, J. (1981). Mental health consultation. In T. R. Kratochwill (Ed.), *Advances in school psychology* (Vol. 1, pp. 133–168). Hillsdale, NJ: Lawrence Erlbaum.

Meyers, J. (1988). School psychology: The current state of practice and future practice of the specialty. *Professional School Psychology, 3,* 165–176.

Meyers, J., Friedman, M. P., & Gaughan, E. J., Jr. (1975). The effects of consultee-centered consultation on teacher behavior. *Psychology in the Schools, 12,* 288–295.

Meyers, J., Parsons, R. D., & Martin, R. P. (1979). *Mental health consultation in the schools.* San Francisco: Jossey-Bass.

Meyers, J., Pfeffer, J., & Erlbaum, V. (1985). Process assessment: A model for broadening assessment. *Journal of Special Education, 19,* 73–89.

Meyers, J., Pitt, N. W., Gaughan, E. J., Jr., & Friedman, M. P. (1978). A research model for consultation with teachers. *Journal of School Psychology, 16,* 137–145.

Meyers, J., Wurtz, R., & Flanagan, D. (1981). A national survey investigating consultation training occurring in school psychology programs. *Psychology in the Schools, 18,* 297–302.

National Association of School Psychologists/National Coalition of Advocates for Students. (1985). *Advocacy for appropriate educational services for all children.* Washington, DC: Authors.

National Commission on Excellence in Education. (1983, April). *A nation at risk: The imperative for educational reform.* Washington, DC: U.S. Department of Education.

O'Leary, K. D., & O'Leary, S. G. (1977). *Classroom management: The successful use of behavior modification* (2nd ed.). Elmsford, NY: Pergamon Press.

O'Neill, P. O., & Trickett, E. J. (1982). *Community consultation.* San Francisco: Jossey-Bass.

Osborn, A. F. (1963). *Applied imagination.* (3rd ed.). New York: Charles Scribner's Sons.

Paget, K. D. (1988). Adolescent pregnancy: Implications for prevention strategies in educational settings. *School Psychology Review, 17,* 570–580.

Parnes, S. J., Noller, R. B., & Biondi, A. M. (1977). *Guide to creative action.* New York: Scribner.

Parsons, R. D., & Meyers, J. (1984). *Developing consultation skills.* San Francisco: Jossey-Bass.

Peterson, L. (1988). Preventing the leading killer of children: The role of the school psychologist in injury prevention. *School Psychology Review, 17,* 593–600.

Piersel, W. C. (1985). Behavioral consultation: An approach to problem solving in educational settings. In J. R. Bergan (Ed.), *School psychology in contemporary society: An introduction* (pp. 252–280). Columbus, OH: Charles E. Merrill.

Piersel, W. C., & Gutkin, T. B. (1983). Resistance to school-based consultation: A behavioral analysis of the problem. *Psychology in the Schools, 20,* 311–320.

Plas, J. M. (1986). *Systems psychology in the schools.* Elmsford, NY: Pergamon Press.

Ponti, C. R., & Curtis, M. J. (1984, August). *Effects of consultation on teachers' attributions for children's school problems.* Paper presented at the annual meeting of the American Psychological Association, Toronto.

Ponti, C. R., Zins, J. E., & Graden, J. L. (1988). Implementing a consultation-based service delivery system to decrease referrals for special education: A case study of organizational considerations. *School Psychology Review, 17,* 89–100.

Power, T. J., & Bartholomew, K. L. (1985). Getting uncaught in the middle: A case study in family-school system consultation. *School Psychology Review, 14,* 222–229.

Price, R. H., Cowen, E. L., Lorion, R. P., & Ramos-McKay, J. (Eds.). (1988). *Fourteen ounces of prevention: A casebook for practitioners.* Washington, DC: American Psychological Association.

Pryzwansky, W. B. (1986). Indirect service delivery: Considerations for future research in consultation. *School Psychology Review, 15,* 479–488.

Pryzwansky, W. B., & White, G. W. (1983). The influence of consultee characteristics on preferences for consultation approaches. *Professional Psychology: Research and Practice, 14,* 457–461.

Pyle, R. R. (1977). Mental health consultation: Helping teachers help themselves. *Professional Psychology, 8,* 192–198.

Raven, B. H., & Rubin, J. Z. (1983). *Social psychology* (2nd ed.). New York: Wiley.

Reimers, T. M., Wacker, D. P., & Koeppl, G. (1987). Acceptability of behavioral interventions: A review of the literature. *School Psychology Review, 16,* 212–227.

Reinking, R. H., Livesay, G., & Kohl, M. (1978). The effects of consultation style on consultee productivity. *American Journal of Community Psychology, 6,* 283–290.

Reschly, D. J. (1988). Special education reform: School psychology revolution. *School Psychology Review, 17,* 459–475.

Revels, O. H., & Gutkin, T. B. (1983). Effects of symbolic modeling procedures and model status on brainstorming behavior. *Journal of School Psychology, 21,* 311–318.

Reynolds, C. R., & Clark, J. H. (1984). Trends in school psychology research: 1974–1980. *Journal of School Psychology, 22,* 43–52.

Reynolds, C. R., Gutkin, T. B., Elliott, S. N., & Witt, J. C. (1984). *School psychology: Essentials of theory and practice.* New York: Wiley.

Reynolds, W. M. (1979). Clinical usage versus psychometric quality. *Professional Psychology, 10,* 324–329.

Ritter, D. R. (1978). Effects of a school consultation program upon referral patterns of teachers. *Psychology in the Schools, 15,* 239–243.

Roberts, B. R., & Thorsheim, H. I. (1986). A partnership approach to consultation: The process and results of a major primary prevention field experiment. *Prevention in Human Services, 4,* 151–186.

Robinson, V. M. J., Cameron, M. M., & Raethel, A. M. (1985). Negotiation of a consultative role for school psychologists: A case study. *Journal of School Psychology, 23,* 43–49.

Rogers-Warren, A., & Warren, S. F. (1977). *Ecological perspectives in behavior analysis.* Baltimore, MD: University Park Press.

Rosenfield, S. A. (1987). *Instructional consultation.* Hillsdale, NJ: Lawrence Erlbaum.

Rosenfield, S. A., & Rubinson, F. (1985). Introducing curriculum-based assessment through consultation. *Exceptional Children, 52,* 282–287.

Sarason, S. B. (1982). *The culture of the school and the problem of change* (2nd ed.). Boston: Allyn and Bacon.

Sarason, S. B., Levine, M., Goldenberg, I. I., Cherlin, D. L., & Bennett, E. (1966). *Psychology in community settings.* New York: Wiley.

Saudargas, R. A. (1989, March). Sequential analysis for understanding teacher-child interaction. In J. J. Kramer (Chair), *Consultant/teacher/parent/child: A new look at old problems.* Symposium conducted at the annual meeting of the National Association of School Psychologists, Boston.

Saxe, L., Cross, T., & Silverman, N. (1988). Children's mental health: The gap between what we know and what we do. *American Psychologist, 43,* 800–807.

Shapiro, E. S. (1987). *Behavioral assessment in school psychology.* Hillsdale, NJ: Lawrence Erlbaum.

Shapiro, E. S. (1988). Preventing academic failure. *School Psychology Review, 17,* 601–613.

Shinn, M. R., Tindal, G. A., & Stein, S. (1988). Curriculum-based measurement and the identification of mildly handicapped students: A research review. *Professional School Psychology, 3,* 69–85.

Short, R. J., & Ringer, M. M. (1987). Consultant experience and attributions in school consultation. *Professional School Psychology, 2,* 273–279.

Skinner, B. F. (1953). *Science and human behavior.* New York: Macmillan.

Smith, D. K. (1984). Practicing school psychologists: Their characteristics, activities, and populations served. *Professional Psychology: Research and Practice, 15,* 798–810.

Smith, D. K., & Lyon, M. A. (1985). Consultation in school psychology: Changes from 1981 to 1984. *Psychology in the Schools, 22,* 404–409.

Smith, D. K., & Lyon, M. A. (1986). School psychologists' attributions for success and failure in consultations with parents and teachers. *Professional Psychology: Research and Practice, 17,* 205–209.

Spivak, G., Platt, J. J., & Shure, M. B. (1976). *The problem solving approach to adjustment.* San Francisco: Jossey-Bass.

Stewart, K. J. (1986). Innovative practice of indirect service delivery: Realities and idealities. *School Psychology Review, 15,* 466–478.

Strong, S. R. (1968). Counseling: An interpersonal influence process. *Journal of Counseling Psychology, 15,* 215–224.

Strong, S. R., & Dixon, D. N. (1971). Expertness, attractiveness, and influence in counseling. *Journal of Counseling Psychology, 18,* 562–580.

Szasz, T. S. (1960). The myth of mental illness. *American Psychologist, 15,* 113–118.

Tharinger, D. J., Krivacska, J. J., Laye-McDonough, M., Jamison, L., Vincent, G. G., & Hedlund, A. D. (1988). Prevention of child sexual abuse: An analysis of issues, educational programs and research findings. *School Psychology Review, 17,* 614–634.

Tharinger, D. J., Laurent, J., & Best, L. R. (1986). Classification of children referred for emotional and behavioral problems: A comparison of Pl 94-132 SED criteria, DSM III, and the CBCL system. *Journal of School Psychology, 24,* 111–121.

Tombari, M. L., & Bergan, J. R. (1978). Consultant cues and teacher verbalizations, judgements, and expectancies concerning children's adjustment problems. *Journal of School Psychology, 16,* 212–219.

Tunnecliffe, M. R., Leach, D. J., & Tunnecliffe, L. P. (1986). Relative efficacy of using behavioral consultation as an approach to teacher stress management. *Journal of School Psychology, 24,* 123–131.

Tyler, F. B., Pargament, K. I., & Gatz, M. (1983). The resource collaborator role: A model for interactions involving psychologists. *American Psychologist, 38,* 388–398.

U.S. Department of Education, Office of Special Education Programs (in press). *Patterns of special education service delivery and cost.* Washington, DC: Author.

Vincent, T. A. (1986). Two into one: An ecological perspective on school consolidation. *Prevention in Human Services, 4,* 149.

Vinsonhaler, J. F., Weinshank, A. B., Wagner, C. C., & Polin, R. M. (1983). Diagnosing children with educational problems: Characteristics of reading and learning disabilities specialists, and classroom teachers. *Reading Research Quarterly, 18,* 134–164.

Warren, S. F., & Rogers-Warren, A. K. (Eds.). (1985). *Teaching functional language.* Baltimore, MD: University Park Press.

Wehmann, B. Zins, J., & Curtis, M. J. (1989, March). *Effects of consultation on teachers' perceptions of children's problems.* Paper presented at the annual meeting of the National Association of School Psychologists, Boston.

Wenger, R. D. (1979). Teacher response to collaborative consultation. *Psychology in the Schools, 16,* 127–131.

West, J. F. (Ed.). (1988). *School consultation: Interdisciplinary perspectives on theory, research, training, and practice.* Austin, TX: Association of Educational and Psychological Consultants.

West, J. F., & Cannon, G. S. (1988). Essential collaborative consultation competencies for regular and special educators. *Journal of Learning Disabilities, 21,* 56–63.

West, J. F., & Idol, L. (1987). School consultation: Part I. An interdisciplinary perspective on theory, models, and research. *Journal of Learning Disabilities, 20,* 388–408.

Wilcox, M. R. (1977, August). *Variables affecting group mental health consultation for teachers.* Paper presented at the annual meeting of the American Psychological Association, San Francisco.

Wilczenski, F. L., Sulzer-Azaroff, B., Feldman, R. S., & Fajardo, D. E. (1987). Feedback to teachers on student engagement as a consultation tool. *Professional School Psychology, 2,* 261–272.

Witt, J. C., & Elliott, S. N. (1983). Assessment in behavioral consultation: The initial interview. *School Psychology Review, 12,* 42–49.

Witt, J. C., & Martens, B. K. (1988). Problems with problem-solving consultation: A re-analysis of assumptions, methods, and goals. *School Psychology Review, 17,* 211–226.

Witt, J. C., Moe, G., Gutkin, T. B., & Andrews, L. (1984). The effect of saying the same thing in different ways: The problem of language and jargon in school-based consultation. *Journal of School Psychology, 22,* 361–367.

Wittrock, M. C. (Ed.). (1986). *Handbook of research on teaching* (3rd ed.). New York: Macmillan.

Woods, K. M., & McNamara, J. R. (1980). Confidentiality: Its effect on interviewee behavior. *Professional Psychology, 11,* 714–721.

Wright, D., & Gutkin, T. B. (1981). School psychologists' job satisfaction and discrepancies between actual and desired work functions. *Psychological Reports, 49,* 735–738.

Ysseldyke, J. E. (1986). Current practice in school psychology. In S. N. Elliott & J. C. Witt (Eds.). *The delivery of psychological services in schools: Concepts, processes, and issues.* Hillsdale, NJ: Lawrence Erlbaum.

Ysseldyke, J. E., Algozzine, B., Regan, R. R., & Potter, M. (1980). Technical adequacy of tests used in simulated decision making. *Psychology in the Schools, 17,* 202–209.

Ysseldyke, J. E., Reynolds, M. C., Weinberg, R. A., Bardon, J., Heaston, P., Hines, L., Ramage, J., Rosenfield, S., Schakel, J., & Taylor, J. (1984). *School psychology: A blueprint for training and practice.* Minneapolis, MN: National School Psychology Inservice Training Network.

Ysseldyke, J. E., Thurlow, M., Graden, J., Wesson, C., Algozzine, B., & Deno, S. (1983). Generalizations from five years of research on assessment and decision making: The University of Minnesota Institute. *Exceptional Children Quarterly, 4,* 75–93.

Zins, J. E. (1981). Using data-based evaluation in developing school consultation services. In M. J. Curtis & J. E. Zins (Eds.), *The theory and practice of school consultation* (pp. 261–269). Springfield, IL: Charles C Thomas.

Zins, J. E., Conyne, R., & Ponti, C. R. (1988). Primary prevention: Expanding the impact of psychological services in schools. *School Psychology Review, 17,* 542–549.

Zins, J. E., & Curtis, M. J. (1984). Building consultation into the educational services delivery system. In C. A. Maher, R. J. Illback, & J. E. Zins (Eds.), *Organizational psychology in the schools* (pp. 213–242). Springfield, IL: Charles C Thomas.

Zins, J. E., Curtis, M. J., Graden, J. L., & Ponti, C. R. (1988). *Helping students succeed in the regular classroom.* San Francisco: Jossey-Bass.

Zins, J. E., & Forman, S. G. (1988). Mini-series on primary prevention: From theory to practice. *School Psychology Review, 17,* 539–634.

24

THE APPLICATION OF BEHAVIORAL PRINCIPLES TO EDUCATIONAL SETTINGS

BRIAN K. MARTENS
Syracuse University
PAUL J. MELLER
University of Rochester

Structuring the classroom environment in order to maximize children's learning has long been of concern to educators and parents alike (Duke, 1978; Gallup, 1977). Principal components of the classroom environment through which the opportunities for learning occur are the various instructional and management practices of teachers (Gettinger, 1988; Lentz & Shapiro, 1986). Not surprising, it is here, in the relationship between teacher-directed events and children's classroom behavior, that focus has been placed on the application of behavioral principles to educational settings (Kazdin, 1982a; Sulzer-Azaroff & Mayer, 1977). The use of behavioral principles in school settings, or applied behavior analysis, has proven successful in response to a variety of discipline and instructional problems, ranging from the improvement in oral reading (Singh, Singh, & Winton, 1984) to reduction in disruptive school bus behavior (Greene, Bailey, & Barber, 1981).

The processes upon which applied behavior analysis are based are those of stimulus control,

positive and negative reinforcement, and punishment, all of which were first demonstrated in experimental operant research (Skinner, 1953). When antecedent events (e.g., teachers working sample problems on the chalkboard) increase the frequency with which behavior occurs (e.g., students successfully completing assigned work), and the frequency of behavior decreases in the absence of these events, stimulus control is present. Positive reinforcement occurs when consequent events increase the frequency of behavior (e.g., receiving free time contingent upon accurate work). Similarly, when the frequency of behavior increases but does so via the termination or avoidance of an aversive stimulus (e.g., completing assignments in class to prevent unsatisfactory reports to parents), the functional process is negative reinforcement. Finally, when consequent events *decrease* behavior (e.g., losing 5 minutes of recess time for disrupting others), punishment is in effect. These processes emerge in the instructional and management practices of teachers, and serve to support both appropriate and inappropriate student behavior.

In the present chapter we review the ways in which behavioral processes have been used formally to enhance children's academic and social functioning in educational settings. The chapter begins by identifying educationally relevant behavior that has been the frequent target of intervention in the literature. Next, procedures for manipulating behavioral antecedents are presented, followed by a discussion of strategies for altering behavioral consequences, in the form of either reinforcement or punishment. Finally, more complex strategies for altering children's classroom behavior are discussed which take into account the relationship between behavior and the environment at a systems level. In examining these strategies, the inherent difficulties in introducing new elements into the classroom instructional/management system are recognized, and procedures for facilitating the continuity of successful intervention effects are discussed.

SELECTION OF INTERVENTION TARGETS

A number of investigators have identified classes of educationally relevant and socially significant behavior that enable children to function adaptively in the classroom setting. Often termed academic survival skills (Hops, 1983), these include behavior such as complying with teacher requests, working cooperatively with peers, and asking and answering questions. For example, in their comprehensive attempt to identify empirically skills related to elementary school adjustment, McConnell, Strain, Kerr, Stagg, Lenkner, and Lambert (1984) collected information on 130 elementary schoolchildren from a total of 19 classrooms. The data obtained included teacher ratings of academic and social competence, group achievement test scores, students' self-reports of competence, and direct observations of classroom behavior. Results showed that children rated by teachers as making good adjustments to school were characterized by higher achievement test scores in reading and math, higher frequencies of academic engaged time (percent of total classroom time spent working on academic tasks), increased rates of compliance with teacher commands, and receipt of fewer negative social initiations from peers.

Studies similar to the McConnell et al. (1984) investigation have made it evident that a diverse array of skills are required of children for adaptive classroom functioning. To date, most applied behavior analytic research in school settings has focused on the subset of classroom behavior that *interferes* with effective learning, such as disruption, inattention to task, and noncompliance (e.g., Wilson, Robertson, Herlong, & Haynes, 1979). In recent years, however, there has been a growing body of research reporting the application of behavioral principles to the improvement in children's academic performance as well. Academic targets of behavioral interventions have included spelling (Harris, 1986; Shapiro & Goldberg, 1986); letter, number, and shape identification (Bradley-Johnson, Sunderman, & Johnson, 1983; Weeks & Gaylord-Ross, 1982); mathematics (McLaughlin, 1982; Simon, Ayllon, & Milan, 1982); oral reading (Singh et al., 1984); and handwriting (Trap, Milner-Davis, Joseph, & Cooper, 1978).

The application of behavioral principles to a wide range of intervention targets has resulted in the growing realization that classroom behavior occurs as an interrelated and often complex system (Martens & Witt, 1984; 1988a). As a result, observed changes in one behavior category (e.g., increases in academic performance) are frequently accompanied by changes in other categories (e.g., decreases in disruptive behavior), although the latter may not be explicitly targeted by treatment (Ayllon & Roberts, 1974; Center, Deitz, & Kaufman, 1982; Lentz, 1988a). Recognizing these complexities in children's classroom behavior, research in applied behavior analysis has made increasing use of multiple behavior categories in the evaluation of treatment impact (Evans, Meyer, Kurkjian, & Kishi, 1988).

An example of positive results from monitoring multiple behavior categories occurred in a study conducted by Witt, Hannafin, & Martens (1983). In their attempts to increase children's percent correct on daily reading assignments, these investigators simultaneously monitored the frequency of disruptive classroom behavior (e.g., making noise, hitting others). Results indicated that delivery of home-based reinforcement contingent upon academic performance only was accompanied by decreased frequencies of disruptive behavior.

Unfortunately, changes observed in children's classroom behavior that are not explicitly targeted by intervention can be maladaptive as well. For example, Sajwaj, Twardosz, and Burke (1972) found that extinction of a preschool child's frequent and inappropriate initiations of speech to the teacher was accompanied by collateral decreases in *appropriate* behavior during group academic activities.

MANIPULATING BEHAVIORAL ANTECEDENTS

The majority of behaviorally based strategies for improving children's academic and social functioning have involved the manipulation of behavioral consequences (Ruggles & LeBlanc, 1982; Weeks & Gaylord-Ross, 1981). As a result, a sizable body of research has evolved for improving children's classroom behavior by providing either contingent reinforcement or punishment.

However, the manipulation of consequences has not always proven successful as a means of altering children's behavior (Carr, Newsom, & Binkoff, 1976, 1980). For example, Carr et al. (1976) reported the case of an 8-year-old boy referred by teachers for frequent self-destructive behavior (i.e., hitting his head an average of 60 times per minute). Prior to the study, several treatment strategies involving the manipulation of consequences had been attempted, albeit unsuccessfully, including restraint, contingent electric shock, extinction, time-out, and differential reinforcement of incompatible behavior. The investigators found, however, that by couching teacher demands within a positive context (e.g., having the teacher relate a story to the child between requests), rates of the aberrant behavior decreased to near-zero levels.

In addition to questioning the effectiveness of strict contingency management, teachers may be unwilling to use elaborate reinforcement or punishment techniques, which they perceive as unacceptable or overly difficult to implement (Foxx & Shapiro, 1978; Martens, Peterson, Witt, & Cirone, 1986; Salend, Esquivel, & Pine, 1984; Witt, Martens, Elliott, 1984). As a result, the manipulation of behavioral *antecedents,* or setting events, has been suggested as an effective and time-efficient alternative to contingency management procedures (Center et al., 1982; Gaylord-Ross,

Weeks, & Lipner, 1980; Koegel, Dunlap, & Dyer, 1980; Wahler & Fox, 1981).

The manipulation of antecedents is based on the process of stimulus control demonstrated repeatedly in experimental operant research (Jenkins, 1965; Reynolds, 1975). Antecedent control in the classroom therefore represents a potentially powerful but relatively infrequently used intervention strategy in applied behavior analytic research. As stated by Knoff (1984):

> In the classroom, the teacher is one of the predominant antecedent stimuli which maintains stimulus control while facilitating appropriate student behavior. This paradigm develops as the teacher instructs and prompts, and then differentially reinforces, appropriate student behavior. Eventually, appropriate behavior occurs in the teacher's presence even though it is no longer continuously reinforced (p. 249).

For example, Hamlet, Axelrod, and Kuerschner (1984) utilized a stimulus control paradigm to investigate the effects of demanded eye contact between teachers and students as a setting event for compliance. Two 11-year-old children referred for high rates of noncompliant behavior were given various instructions throughout the school day (e.g., "Put your books away") under two conditions. During the baseline condition, the teacher simply called the student's name prior to giving instructions. In the experimental condition, the teacher called the student's name and then demanded eye contact with the statement, "Look at me," prior to making each request. Results indicated that mean percentages of compliance during conditions of demanded eye contact more than doubled those of baseline.

Educators have long been concerned with the relationship of children's behavior to the antecedent conditions of curriculum material and manner of task presentation (Bradley-Johnson et al., 1983; Gettinger, 1988; L'Abate & Curtis, 1975). Perhaps one of the most obvious setting events for academic performance is the difficulty level of the task (Center et al., 1982). Weeks and Gaylord-Ross (1981) investigated the relationship between task difficulty, number of errors, and self-injurious behavior in two severely handicapped children. It was hypothesized that presentation of a difficult task would serve as a discriminative stimulus for aberrant behavior, which in turn would be maintained by successful escape from the task demands. In contrast, the presentation of easy tasks contained no aversive properties from which to escape and thereby would not function as setting events for self-injury.

As predicted, near-zero rates of self-injurious behavior were observed during the baseline and easy conditions, with few or no errors. Presentation of the difficult task was accompanied by dramatic increases in errors as well as self-injurious behavior. Manipulating task difficulty through use of an errorless learning procedure returned frequencies of self-injurious behavior to near-zero rates.

In an attempt to improve children's oral reading through the manipulation of antecedents, Singh and Singh (1984) examined the effects of previewing passages on numbers of errors made as well as spontaneous self-corrections. Previewing consisted of the teacher and student discussing the background of the story, looking at accompanying pictures, and identifying the meanings of unknown words. Results of the study showed that the mean number of oral reading errors for each student was greatly reduced following preview of the target passage, but was virtually identical to the baseline condition when either an unrelated passage or no passage was previewed. In addition, spontaneous corrections of oral reading errors increased over baseline rates on days in which subjects previewed the target passage prior to reading.

INCREASING DESIRED BEHAVIOR

As mentioned previously, the majority of behaviorally based strategies for improving children's academic and social functioning have involved the manipulation of consequences. Most frequently, consequent events in the classroom have been arranged to *increase* behavior (Shapiro & Lentz, 1985), a process known as reinforcement. Reinforcement procedures have been applied effectively to a diverse array of educational and social goals, including social skills development (E. J. Barton, 1981; Odom, Hoyson, Jamieson, & Strain, 1985; Walker, Greenwood, Hops, & Todd, 1979), attention to task (Fantuzzo & Clement, 1981; Greer & Polirstok, 1982), classroom disruption (Fowler, 1986), school vandalism (Mayer, Butterworth, Nafpaktitis, & Sulzer-Azaroff, 1983), reading performance (Greer & Polirstok, 1982;

Griswold & Arnold, 1980; Schimek, 1983), verbal communication (Risley & Hart, 1968; Zwald & Gresham, 1982), and continence (Lyon, 1984).

Types of Reinforcers and Their Applications

Despite their common function of increasing behavior, the variety of reinforcing stimuli used in educational settings has been as diverse as their applications. Forness (1973) suggested that reinforcers may be ordered along a continuum of increasing abstractness and social relevance. Arranged in a hierarchy, this continuum of reinforcers includes edibles, tangibles, tokens or checks, contingent activities, social approval, receiving feedback, and acquiring competence. Because of its usefulness as a taxonomy of reinforcement alternatives, the hierarchy proposed for Forness has been used to organize the following discussion of reinforcers and their applications in school settings.

Edibles

Because food is a commonly used and potent reinforcer in experimental operant research, attempts have been made to apply it in the classroom as well. For example, L. E. Barton, Brulle, and Repp (1987) used edible rewards to reinforce activities incompatible with autistic-like behavior in severely handicapped children. After preselecting their own food rewards, subjects were reinforced on a fixed-interval schedule for performing any behavior other than the target. Results showed the frequencies of maladaptive behavior to be maintained at levels well below those of baseline.

Although food rewards have proven successful with young and severely disabled children, several factors limit their applicability to the classroom. First, edibles are more susceptible to effects of satiation than are many other commonly available rewards such as social approval (Sulzer-Azaroff & Mayer, 1977). Second, due to the relatively artificial nature of edibles as rewards in the classroom, their use over time and across settings may be difficult to arrange. Third, the distribution of edibles as reinforcers requires constant proximity between the teacher and the child, an arrangement that is not always possible given the demands on teacher time from other students. Finally, the selection of edibles for use in a reinforcement program may itself prove problematic. In choosing food rewards, consideration must be given to their nutritive properties, potential for allergic reactions, and parental preferences over what children ingest, in addition to reinforcement value.

Exchangeables

Exchangeable reinforcers include any item given contingent on a target behavior that may later be traded for another reinforcing item or event. Various exchangeables, such as tokens (e.g., Kazdin & Gessey, 1980;), points (e.g., Fantuzzo & Clement, 1981; Simon et al., 1982), and stickers (e.g., Vasta & Stirpe, 1979) have been used successfully in classroom reinforcement programs. In general, reinforcement programs that utilize exchangeable reinforcers are referred to as token economies.

Token economies have proven quite useful in educational settings because of the flexibility involved in their implementation. The distribution of tokens requires little time, and providing a child with an exchangeable reinforcer does not necessitate interrupting an ongoing activity (Kazdin, 1977a). Children's tolerance for delaying gratification may also be enhanced as a function of the delay between earning and exchanging points (Kalish, 1981). In addition, the flexibility in selecting backup reinforcers allows several students to be maintained on the program simultaneously without individual preferences for reward reducing treatment effectiveness. Similarly, the availability of multiple backup reinforcers decreases the probability of a child becoming satiated with a given item.

Although token economies have proven effective in a variety of applications, maintaining treatment effects over time continues to be a concern in their use, since the tokens themselves may acquire discriminative properties. In such cases, the desired behavior may occur only when tokens are employed as part of the reinforcement procedure (Kazdin, 1982c). Although this may have positive effects when tokens act as cues for teachers to praise students at rates above baseline, tokens, points, and other exchangeables are not typically found as naturally occurring reinforcers. To overcome the problem of maintenance, the final phase of implementing a token economy often involves transferring control of the child's behavior from the tokens to a stimulus that *is* commonly found in the classroom setting. This transition usually takes place by pairing the tokens with naturally occurring consequences such as letter grades or social approval (Kazdin, 1977a; Stokes & Baer, 1977).

A novel approach employed in withdrawal of a token economy enabled children to *earn* their way out of the program contingencies (Kazdin & Mascitelli, 1980). In this study, two mentally retarded elementary schoolchildren were placed on a token economy to increase attention to assigned tasks. The intervention procedures were in effect three time periods a day. Points earned during the first period could be traded for food rewards, such as gum, candy, ice cream, and soda. Points accumulated during the second period, however, could be used to earn oneself off the token economy program during the third period. The backup reinforcer of being off the program was strengthened by the social status and praise that accompanied reaching this level. Results showed both conditions to be effective in increasing students' attending behaviors. However, higher levels of attending were associated with the condition of being able to earn one's way off the program.

Activities and Privileges

The use of activities as reinforcers is based on the Premack Principle (Premack, 1965), which asserts that behavior with a high probability of occurring may be used to increase the rate of low-probability behavior. The large number of activities and special privileges available in the classroom make this setting highly conducive for use of the Premack Principle in behavioral programming. Particularly attractive to program administrators is the ready availability of activity reinforcers (Sulzer-Azaroff & Mayer, 1977), thus significantly decreasing the amount of time and expense required to initiate treatment (Eller, Idecker, & Holben, 1978). Perhaps of equal importance is the possibility of building into the program activities that supplement social and academic growth. For example, Schimek (1983) taught diagraph discrimination to an 8-year-old girl, using reading to younger students as a reinforcer for accurate performance.

Despite the many benefits of incorporating privileges and activities into a behavior program, several characteristics of these programs may hinder their implementation and effectiveness. First, an activity-oriented reinforcement program (e.g., contingent gym time) may be difficult to apply to a single child (Schmidt & Ulrich, 1969). Second, it may be difficult for teachers to maintain the on-task behavior of the class at large while working with a smaller group of students. Toward this goal,

Cowen, Jones, and Bellack (1979) devised a group-based intervention to increase on-task behavior while the teacher was involved with children in a separate activity. Following a baseline period, students were told that they would be required to complete 15 minutes of "good seatwork" in a 30-minute period. Once the class as a whole completed the required amount of work, the remainder of the period would be used for a preferred activity. Upon any classroom disruption, a timer that was set at the beginning of the period was stopped and students were informed of their misbehavior. The clock was restarted when all students were back on-task. The intervention proved effective in decreasing the mean frequency of disruptive behavior across five classrooms.

A third difficulty associated with the use of activities and privileges as reinforcers is the need to interrupt behavior to provide reward, or defer reinforcement, until a later time. Frequently, the structure of the school day allows for certain activities (e.g., art, gym, recess) to occur only at prescribed times. The reinforcing potential of these activities may be severely diminished as a function of their limited access. Scheduling problems may be minimized, however, by incorporating activities as backup reinforcers in a token economy (McLaughlin and Malaby, 1972).

Social Rewards

Among the most frequently used and effective types of reward in the classroom are social reinforcers (Drabman, 1976). Various forms of social reinforcement are routinely available in classroom settings, including teacher attention, smiling, verbal praise, peer approval, and "pats on the back." Because social reinforcers are easy to administer, naturally occurring, and potent in changing children's behavior (Derevensky & Rose, 1978), they have been employed in a variety of educational settings. For example, Darch and Gersten (1985) demonstrated the effectiveness of verbal praise for increasing reading accuracy in first-grade students. Conditions of rapid pace presentation (i.e., no pause), rapid pace plus praise, and praise only were instituted sequentially following a modified reversal design. All three experimental conditions were shown to increase students' reading accuracy above baseline. Further analyses indicated that praise alone was more effective at increasing students' performance than was increased rate of presentation. However, both interventions applied simultaneously provided the greatest gains.

Social reinforcement strategies have also been used to modify students' cognitive and affective processes. In an attempt to increase the self-esteem of elementary school children, Phillips (1984) directed teachers to reinforce students' positive self-referent statements (e.g., "I am happy about this"). No reinforcement was provided for similar statements made by students in a comparison group. A reversal design used with the experimental group indicated an increase in positive self-referent statements as a function of the intervention. In addition, contingent verbal reinforcement was successful in increasing students' self-esteem scores on a self-esteem inventory.

Feedback and Acquiring Competence

The next level of reinforcement as outlined by Forness (1973) is acquiring knowledge of the correctness of one's actions. The determination of answer correctness has often been provided through feedback, although the effectiveness of feedback alone remains questionable (Kazdin, 1982a). It is therefore recommended that feedback be paired with other procedures, such as modeling, rehearsal, and social reinforcement (Leger et al., 1979). Feedback paired with other rewards in this manner has proven effective in increasing such desired classroom behavior as group participation and time in-seat (Reitz, 1979; Schulman, Suran, Stevens, & Kupst, 1979).

An interesting case of feedback and its implicit social component is that of public posting. In this procedure, names or pictures of students who have attained the required level of performance are prominently displayed in the classroom. Blount and Stokes (1984) utilized public posting for promoting increased oral hygiene in second-grade students. In the initial phase of the intervention, students were provided feedback about where plaque was located, and praised if their plaque level was below criterion. The second phase of the program involved placing the child's picture on a posterboard at the front of the classroom contingent upon effective toothbrushing. The mean level of plaque was lower significantly during the public posting condition across two classrooms.

Alternative Systems of Reinforcement Delivery

The majority of behavioral interventions for improving children's classroom performance employ the teacher or other members of the teaching staff as monitors and implementors of contingent events. However, the time required of teachers in maintaining interventions may limit program effectiveness or preclude treatment use. In addition, teaching staff may not always be the most effective change agents. In response to these concerns, several methods of delivering reinforcement have been employed in which teacher involvement is decreased without compromising program effectiveness. Three such methods are self-monitoring/self-reinforcement, peer reinforcement, and home-based reinforcement.

Self-monitoring/Self-reinforcement

Self-monitoring strategies have been used effectively for remediating such classroom problems as maintaining on-task behavior (Christie, Hiss, & Lozanoff, 1984), reducing disruption (Rhode, Morgan, & Young, 1983), and increasing work completion (Piersel & Kratochwill, 1979). The ability of self-monitoring to sustain existing changes in behavior was demonstrated by Workman, Helton, and Watson (1982). The intervention in this study was designed to increase sustained work activity by a 4-year-old boy who was trained in self-monitoring via modeling, guided practice, and praise. Monitoring entailed a momentary time-sampling procedure in which the student noted whether he was on-task or off-task following an auditory cue. Multiple reversals indicated significant increases in the child's sustained schoolwork. Although not targeted, collateral increases in the frequency of compliance were also noted.

Peer Reinforcement

Just as peer approval may foster inappropriate classroom activities, it can be equally effective in maintaining productive school behavior (Greenwood, Carta, & Hall, 1988). Particularly well suited for peer dispensing are social reinforcers and feedback. For example, Greer and Polirstok (1982) recruited three ninth-grade students who had been experiencing academic and disciplinary problems as tutors for poor-reading eighth-grade students. Initially, tutors were given no special directions about how or when to provide social reinforcement. Following five training sessions, the tutors were placed on a token economy in which they were given points for using contingent praise with their tutees. The token economy was subsequently withdrawn to allow for free tutoring. The intervention proved successful at two levels. First, peer tutors' use of contingent approval statements sig-

nificantly increased tutees' reading comprehension scores, and these gains were greater than those generated by the mere introduction of the peer tutor. Second, the intervention yielded collateral changes in the tutors' behaviors. Specifically, increases where found for the tutors' own reading comprehension scores as well as time on-task in nontarget classrooms.

Home-Based Reinforcement

The ability of parents to act as agents of change and facilitators of growth in children has long been recognized (Cook, 1980; Leichter, 1977; Simpson & Poplin, 1981). The vast number of contingencies available to parents gives them an important role in structuring their children's environment. Programs that enlist parents in the use of these contingencies to alter school behavior are termed home-based interventions (e.g., Witt et al., 1983). Home-based interventions generally require teachers to provide feedback to the child's parents, who then act on the information by dispensing reinforcement or punishment. In such procedures, home-based contingencies are a special case of token economies since feedback from the teacher acts as a token, and parents' contingent reactions serve as backup reinforcers (Broughton, Barton, & Owen, 1981). Consequentially, home-based interventions share many of the advantages and pitfalls of more traditional token economies.

One unique advantage of home-based contingency programs is the diversity and number of reinforcers available to parents. In addition, home-based contingencies allow for efficient use of teacher time. The monitoring and reporting of behavior requires little time relative to classroom disruption, additional one-to-one attention, or dispensing reinforcers.

Home-based interventions have been successful in remediating a variety of school-related difficulties (Budd, Leibowitz, Riner, Mindell, & Goldfarb, 1981; Simpson, Swenson, & Thompson, 1980). For example, Blechman, Kotanchik, and Taylor (1981) developed a home-based contingency system for maintaining the academic performance of students considered at risk for failure. Students in this study were assigned to one of three groups as a function of variability in academic work demonstrated during baseline. Parents, in turn, provided the children with rewards contingent upon reports of accurate classwork. The intervention proved successful in increasing the accuracy *and* consistency of students' performance. Similar gains were not observed for the matched control groups.

Several features are necessary for the successful development of home-based interventions. First and foremost, parents must be receptive to the intervention and capable of high levels of follow-through. Broughton et al. (1981) found that depressed parents as well as spouses undergoing marital discord were poor agents of behavior change. Related to this issue, delivery of contingent reinforcement must be consistent to be effective. Second, to ensure appropriate implementation, parents must be given adequate training in the principles of behavior management and techniques for selecting appropriate and effective rewards, as well as guided practice through the intervention process (Witt et al., 1983). Finally, home-based systems necessitate an efficient mode of communication between the school and family.

Group Contingency Programs

When reinforcement of the entire class is provisional upon the performance of some subset of the class, a *dependent* group contingency is in effect. For example, Ascare and Axelrod (1973) provided target students with points for work completion. The entire class was allowed additional free time when points earned by the target children exceeded a predetermined limit.

Although poorly performing children are often selected for monitoring, this is not a critical feature of dependent group contingencies. Drabman, Spitalnik, and Spitalnik (1974) demonstrated equivalent decreases in target children's disruptive behavior through contingently rewarding the class based on performance of the most disruptive, least disruptive, and randomly selected students.

It has been suggested that maintaining the anonymity of monitored students may decrease the negative social consequences that can result from using dependent group contingencies. Speltz, Shimura, and McReynolds (1982), however, found that positive social interactions with peers were greater when the monitored child was preselected and known rather than randomly selected following the work period. In addition, equivalent class gains in worksheet performance were obtained with identified and unidentified target children.

Group contingency programs may also be implemented as a series of parallel individual contingencies in which each member of the class earns his or her own reward independent of the group. Individual contingency programs, such as token economies, that are applied to the group as a whole are considered *independent* group contingency programs. Independent contingency programs require continuous monitoring of each group member's level of performance, thereby requiring greater time involvement from the teacher.

In *interdependent* group contingency programs, rewards are provided to all students contingent upon the average group performance. A drawback of interdependent programs is the possibility of an unimproved student receiving reinforcement when the group average remains above criterion. However, this problem can be controlled by pairing interdependent and dependent contingencies in a single intervention (Crouch, Gresham, & Wright, 1985). Crouch et al. instituted an interdependent group system to increase on-task behavior of third-grade children. Concerns were voiced about the possibility of some students being reinforced by losing privileges for the rest of the class. Therefore, an independent contingency was simultaneously employed for disruptive behavior. If a student was disruptive four times a day, a response cost of lost recess the following day was administered. The program was effective at significantly increasing on-task behavior. Incidentally, implementation of the response-cost procedure was necessary only once throughout the 3 weeks of intervention.

One of the most common applications of interdependent group contingencies is the Good Behavior Game (Barish, Saunders, & Wolf, 1969). The program is arranged in a gamelike fashion in which teams of students compete against each other and a set criterion of appropriate classroom behavior. Students are given points for *inappropriate* behavior; thus low scores may be traded for subsequent rewards. A positive component of the game format was added by Darveaux (1984), who removed points earned for inappropriate behavior contingent upon accurate work completion. The program was highly effective at decreasing disruptive behavior *and* increasing assignment completion. The effectiveness of the Good Behavior Game has been demonstrated repeatedly for improving academic performance and classroom disruption (Bear & Richards, 1980; Saigh & Umar, 1983).

An interesting application of a group program involved a school-based dependent group contingency developed to eliminate destructive behavior at home (Gresham, 1983). An 8-year-old mildly retarded boy was referred for such destructive behavior as fire setting, vandalizing property, and loosening lug nuts on the family car. Following a 1-week baseline, the child's mother sent a note describing his behavior of the previous day to the teacher. If five good notes were received in a week, the entire class earned a party in honor of the target child. The target child was allowed to act as host of the party, dispensing food and prizes to his classmates. The program quickly facilitated a positive change in the student's home behavior.

DECREASING UNDESIRED BEHAVIOR

Aberrant student behavior can be particularly distressful to teachers because it limits opportunities for the academic engagement of all students. It is not surprising, then, that a large number of referrals presented to behavioral consultants are in response to student misbehavior. In the following section we discuss various intervention strategies that have been used in educational settings to reduce inappropriate student behavior. Subsumed under the heading of punishment, these strategies involve the application of events following behavior to reduce the frequency of behavior in the future (Van Houten, 1983).

Issues in the Use of Punishment
Ethical and Legal Concerns
Court rulings have regulated the use of punishment in school settings by mandating use of the least restrictive intervention still likely to produce positive outcomes (Feldman & Peay, 1982). In the spirit of Public Law 94-142, the least restrictive rule emphasizes development of balance between treatment efficacy and the restriction of student rights. For example, in the treatment of severe self-injurious behavior, the probability of harmful extinction bursts may justify a more restrictive punishment technique over a less restrictive (and less effective) extinction strategy (Macmillan, Forness, & Trumbull, 1973).

In admonishing applied behavior analysts for overly restricting children's classroom behavior, Winett and Winkler (1972) supported the legal position on punishment as sound ethical practice

also. According to Winett and Winkler (1972), the model student depicted in applied behavior analytic research is one who "stays glued to his seat and desk all day, continually looks at his teacher or his text/workbook, does not talk to or in fact look at other children, does not talk unless asked to by the teacher, hopefully does not laugh or sing (or at the wrong time), and assuredly passes silently in halls" (p. 501). Since effective learning may occur within a variety of social and behavioral contexts, these authors asserted a primary ethical concern in the use of punishment in the schools should be the extent to which such procedures contribute to the educational process.

Practical Considerations
In addition to ethical and legal concerns, several practical considerations must also be taken into account when deciding to punish. First, punishment techniques inform children of what *not* to do but provide little information concerning appropriate alternative methods of responding. Because children are always doing something according to the behavior stream notion (Schoenfeld & Farmer, 1970), eliminating one response will probably be accompanied by increases in another. Without specifying a more appropriate behavior either through instruction or differential reinforcement, the use of punishment may result in replacement of one maladaptive response with another equally inappropriate behavior.

Second, it may be necessary to use punishment in conjunction with reinforcement when responding to classroom behavior problems. Research concerning the acceptability of behavioral interventions has demonstrated a clear preference for positive over reductive techniques by both teachers and children (Elliott, Witt, Galvin, & Peterson, 1984; Kazdin, French, & Sherick, 1981; Witt, Martens, & Elliott, 1984; Witt & Robbins, 1985). The conjunctive use of punishment with reinforcement may also be necessary to generate reinforcement opportunities (Kalish, 1981). If a child is displaying aberrant behavior at high rates, little opportunity remains to respond appropriately and thereby receive reward. Pfiffner, Rosen, and O'Leary (1985) illustrated this by demonstrating that an all-positive approach to classroom management was effective *only* after high rates of appropriate responding were established using *both* reinforcement and punishment.

A third practical consideration in the use of

punishment concerns the numerous negative effects associated with such procedures. Maladaptive responses to punishment have included increased emotionality and aggression, avoidance of the punisher, negative self-statements, negative reactions to peers, and modeling of aggressive and punitive behaviors (Newsom, Favell, & Rincover, 1983; Sulzer-Azaroff & Mayer, 1977). Use of punishment in the classroom may also have negative effects on the teacher. Punishment by its very nature requires teachers to attend to inappropriate student activities. Research has suggested the expectation of select events can effectively bias perceptions of other events (Neisser, 1979). In the classroom, a teacher who is "set" to punish inappropriate responding may miss opportunities to reinforce appropriate behavior.

Finally, teachers may be negatively reinforced for punishing to the exclusion of other intervention methods because it rapidly decreases disruptive student behavior (Newsom et al., 1983). A cycle is entered whereby the student's behavior, which is only temporarily suppressed by punishment, acts as a negative reinforcer for the teacher's frequent use of punishment. The cycle becomes self-perpetuating and may lead to increased frustration for the teacher and student alike.

Types of Punishment and Their Applications
Verbal Reprimands

Perhaps the most common method of punishment involves the use of reprimands. Because reprimands are easy to administer and produce immediate effects, they often represent a primary tool for behavior management in the classroom. In fact, early research on the frequency of reprimands indicated their use by teachers far exceeded that of approval and praise (Heller & White, 1975; White, 1975). Although more recent investigations have not found as great a discrepancy, the mean frequency of reprimand use remains high (Nafpaktitis, Mayer, & Butterworth, 1985; Wyatt & Hawkins, 1987).

Several factors have been demonstrated to influence the use of reprimands in school settings. Principal among these have been grade level, educational context, and class ability. In a summary of 16 observational studies employing students from first through twelfth grade, White (1975) demonstrated that the use of teacher disapproval decreased as a function of student grade level. This trend was later replicated by Wyatt and

Hawkins (1987). In addition, White (1975) found that teachers reprimanded more frequently for classroom management than for educational instruction.

The influence of class ability level on teacher rates of reprimanding was demonstrating by Heller and White (1975), who studied teachers' use of contingent verbal responses with urban junior high school students. Subjects in the study were placed into high-ability and low-ability classes on the basis of Metropolitan Achievement Test scores. A comparison of the two groups revealed that teachers emitted fewer disapproving statements in the high-skill classes than in the low-skill classes. Further analyses of the data indicated that this discrepancy was accounted for by differences in the frequency of disapproval related to classroom management. Specifically, teachers used a greater number of reprimands for classroom management in the low-ability classes, but no differences were observed between classrooms for rates of disapproval related to academic instruction.

Although inconsistent results have been reported over the efficacy of reprimands (Van Houten & Doleys, 1983), the method by which reprimands are delivered does appear to affect treatment effectiveness. Van Houten, Mackenzie-Keating, Sameoto, and Colavecchia (1982) conducted a two-experiment study demonstrating the influence of joint verbal and nonverbal reprimands as well as teacher proximity on reducing disruptive behavior. Results of the first experiment showed significant decreases in disruptive behavior for both verbal and nonverbal (i.e., eye contact and a firm grasp) procedures. However, the magnitude of change was greater for the combined condition. Results of the second experiment showed that punishment delivered from 7 meters produced no significant changes in behavior. However, reprimands provided from 1 meter significantly reduced incidences of disruption. These results are consistent with the work of O'Leary, Kaufman, Kass, and Drabman (1970), who found praise plus soft reprimands to be more effective at decreasing disruptive behavior than praise plus loud reprimands delivered from across the room.

Overcorrection

Another frequently used strategy for reducing aberrant classroom behavior is overcorrection (Foxx & Azrin, 1972). Originally designed for use with severely disabled populations, overcorrection has been successfully applied to classroom behavior such as spelling (Foxx & Jones, 1978), attendance (Foxx, 1976), sharing (Barton & Osborne, 1978), and elective mutism (Matson, Esveldt-Dawson, & O'Donnell, 1979). In addition, combined positive practice overcorrection with reinforcement has been demonstrated to be effective in such areas as the acquisition of sign language (Linton & Singh, 1984), enhancing reading decoding (Singh, Singh, & Winton, 1984), and increasing spelling achievement (Matson, Esveldt-Dawson, & Kazdin, 1982; Ollendick, Matson, Esveldt-Dawson, & Shapiro, 1980).

Overcorrection is a punishment procedure in which an aversive activity contingently follows the undesired behavior. Unlike procedures that reinforce behavior with contingent activities, overcorrection requires the consequence to be topographically similar to the undesired response (Foxx & Bechtel, 1983). The consequences employed in overcorrection procedures are categorized either as restitutional or positive practice. Restitutional overcorrection requires the child to make amends for behavior by changing the environment to a state better than before the disruption occurred. For example, a student may be required to clean *and* paint a desk for drawing on the writing surface.

Fox and Bechtel (1983) suggested that three steps be followed in the development of a restitutional overcorrection program. First, all aspects of the disturbance consequent to the undesired response must be identified. Second, the sequence of steps necessary to restore and improve the environment must also be identified. Third, the student must be required to perform these corrective activities upon each occurrence of an undesired act. In so doing, responsibility for the consequences of misbehavior are shifted from other individuals to the child (Sulzer-Azaroff & Mayer, 1977).

Not all disruptive student behavior has a direct impact on the environment. For example, a student's use of an inaccurate algorithm in solving subtraction problems has little environmental affect. In such cases, positive practice overcorrection may be appropriate. Positive practice involves the repetitive rehearsal of an appropriate response. Similar to restitutional overcorrection, consequences of positive practice must be related to the initial response. Thus, positive practice for the math student described above may involve repeatedly vocalizing the appropriate algorithm (e.g.,

subtract the bottom number from the top) followed by practice trials.

In contrast to the other reductive techniques, a primary goal of positive practice overcorrection is the replacement of inappropriate behavior with more desired responses. Powers and Crowel (1985) illustrated such response substitution by replacing the stereotypical vocalizations of an 8-year-old autistic boy with socially appropriate responses. After each inappropriate vocalization, the child was administered a language drill consisting of five or more socially relevant questions. Positive practice overcorrection was demonstrated to decrease significantly the frequency of inappropriate vocalizations and increase appropriate social language use.

Response Cost

The punishment techniques described previously involve the contingent delivery of an aversive stimulus following an undesired behavior. Response cost, however, is an omission training procedure in which reinforcing stimuli are *removed* consequent to inappropriate responding (Pazulinec, Meyerrose, & Sajwaj, 1983). By definition, response cost techniques may only be applied in situations where students have ongoing access to reinforcement.

The requirement of ongoing access to reinforcement for successful initiation of response cost procedures has been accomplished with a variety of techniques (Pazulinec et al., 1983). First, settings may be selected that have a preexisting wealth of available reinforcers. In these situations, retention of the environment's reinforcing nature after the response cost is initiated must be avoided. Second, response cost may be instituted as an ancillary technique within a positive reinforcement program. Toward this end, response cost may be used in conjunction with token reinforcement. Third, points may be distributed noncontingently to students at the outset of an intervention period. Although students are not given the opportunity to earn additional tokens, they may lose points for inappropriate behavior.

In addition to enhancing the effectiveness of positive reinforcement procedures, response cost provides other benefits for the behavior manager. First, effects of response cost procedures tend to last over time. In fact, several investigations employing response cost procedures have been unable to return subjects to baseline levels of responding because of the longevity of treatment impact (Broughton & Lahey, 1978; Salend & Allen, 1985; Witt & Elliott, 1982). The potency of treatment effects is another benefit of response-cost procedures. For example, Rapport, Murphy, and Baily (1980) were able to produce significant gains in the on-task behavior of two elementary schoolboys diagnosed as attention deficit disorder that were superior to varying dosages of Ritalin.

Similar to token reinforcement programs, response-cost interventions may involve a time and resource commitment prohibitive to their use in school settings. However, modifications of response-cost procedures have increased their utility as classroom management tools (Salend & Allen, 1985). For example, Witt and Elliott (1982) developed a response-cost lottery program to decrease inappropriate behavior in three fourth-grade students. Following an explanation of the program, students were given four slips of paper with their name on each. After each infraction of the class rules, one slip of paper was taken away from the student. At the end of the class period the students were allowed to deposit the remaining slips of paper in a box. A single student's name was drawn from the box at the end of each week to receive a prize. The students were made aware that decreases in rule infractions would increase their chance of winning the prize. The procedure required little teacher time or expense for implementation, and was successful in reducing students' disruptive behavior.

Time-Out From Reinforcement

Time-out from reinforcement (time-out) is a form of omission training in which students are placed in a less reinforcing environment contingent upon misbehavior (Brantner & Doherty, 1983). Although commonly associated with seclusion, time-out procedures may also involve simply ignoring the student or requiring the observation of others. Common to all forms of time-out is the necessity for contingent delivery and a significant difference in the amount of reinforcement available during time-in and time-out periods (Harris, 1985). Time-out may be differentiated from response cost in that response cost involves the removal of previously earned rewards, whereas in time-out only the *opportunity* to earn reward is removed.

The most restrictive form of time-out, isolation, involves removing the child from the environment where the misbehavior occurred to an isolated room devoid of reinforcement opportunities (Harris, 1985). Because of its restrictiveness, however, isolation time-out has several disadvantages for use in the classroom. First, the procedure requires the availability of a room, devoid of reinforcing stimuli and available on a continuous basis, to be used as a time-out facility. In addition, difficulties may arise in attempting to place the child in the time-out room. Lentz (1988b) warns that unless a staff member is able to control a physical confrontation with the student, isolation time-out should not be considered. In addition to potential physical harm, the confrontation may itself prove reinforcing to the student, leading to an increase in undesired behavior. As a result, self-management of placement into the time-out room should be encouraged whenever possible (Pease & Tyler, 1979). Finally, the potential for abuse of isolation time-out is great. In attempts to curtail misuses of seclusion time-out, recent legislation has regulated the use of these procedures by institutional review boards (Brantener & Doherty, 1983).

Children need not be removed from the classroom in order to produce a time-out situation. Exclusion time-out refers to procedures in which the child is removed from the *area* of reinforcement (Brantener & Doherty, 1983). Application of exclusion time-out may simply involve placing a student in a corner facing the wall or in a separate designated area of the classroom.

In addition to effectively reducing the behavior of the target child, exclusion time-out has been demonstrated to alter the behavior of nontarget children as well. For example, an exclusion time-out procedure was instituted in a kindergarten class in an effort to decrease the frequency of aggressive behavior in a male student (Wilson et al., 1979). Contingent on an aggressive act, the student was placed in a small open booth that obscured his vision of the classroom for 5 minutes. Significant decreases were observed in aggressive acts by the target child as well as other boys in the class.

The least restrictive form of time-out is nonexclusionary time-out. This procedure does not require displacement of the student, but merely denies the child access to reinforcement (Harris, 1985). The practice of nonexclusionary time-out may include techniques such as contingent ignoring, denying participation in ongoing activities, or having the student face away from the rest of the class. As with all forms of time-out, the intervention period must provide less opportunity for reinforcement than time-in.

Perhaps the most frequently cited nonexclusionary time-out procedure is an intervention developed by Foxx and Shapiro (1978). Students in cottage-based special education class wore ribbons to signify availability of reinforcement. To create a contrast between time-out and time-in, a reinforcement procedures was instituted whereby each of five students received an edible reinforcer and praise every 2.5 minutes for not displaying disruptive behavior while wearing the ribbon. During the time-out phase, the reinforcement program was maintained but occurrences of disruption resulted in removal of the student's ribbon. This act signaled the start of a 3-minute period in which the child could view, but not participate in, classroom activities. The time-out ribbon plus reinforcement proved to be significantly more effective at reducing classroom disruption than reinforcement alone.

Several factors must be considered in deciding which form of time-out is most appropriate for a given problem. First, the implementation of time-out should follow the least restrictive treatment rule (Feldman & Peay, 1982). Therefore, positive techniques as well as less restrictive forms of time-out should be considered before implementing seclusion time-out. Research has suggested that less aversive techniques such as response cost may be as effective as time-out in reducing undesired behavior (Gresham, 1979). Along similar lines, the magnitude of inappropriate behavior must be severe to warrant seclusion time-out procedures.

Once the decision to implement a time-out procedure has been made, several logistical aspects of the program must also be resolved. Parameters to be considered include the duration of time-out (Barton et al., 1987), contingencies for release (Mace, Page, Ivancic, & O'Brien, 1986), and transition back to time-in. In addition, several situations may arise for which time-out may be contraindicated for reducing behavior. Among these are cases in which the behavioral excess takes the form of avoidance or self-stimulation. In these situations, time-out may act as a negative reinforcer or provide additional opportunities for the problem behavior to occur.

ALTERING BEHAVIOR INDIRECTLY

Honig (1966) summarized the methodological principles that are common to both applied behavior analysis and experimental operant research. These include (a) an emphasis on single-subject designs in the demonstration of treatment impact, (b) the recording over time of observable behavior, (c) the control of behavior via manipulation of behavior–environment relationships, and (d) the definition of treatment procedures in operational terms. An implicit, although pervasive characteristic of these common procedural requirements has been the influence of Watsonian elementism and its emphasis on single-order interactions between behavior and events in the environment (Martens & Witt, 1988a; Parrish, Cataldo, Kolko, Neef, & Egel, 1986). As a result of this influence, much of applied behavior analytic research in educational settings has focused on relatively simple behavior–environment relationships in the demonstration of treatment impact (Willems, 1974). As stated by Parrish et al. (1986):

> Early basic operant research included investigation of variables affecting relationships between responses and provided a knowledge base for analyzing complex cases of behavior (e.g., Skinner, 1935). Yet, in the subsequent five or so decades, applied research has focused primarily on more simple behavioral relationships, demonstrating their power and utility in resolving important problems. That applied behavior analysis should begin in the simplest way and build up to the complex, step by step, is characteristic of scientific analysis and the course by which scientific knowledge grows. (p. 241)

Within recent years, applied behavior analytic research has begun to expand its scope of inquiry to include more complex behavior–environment processes (Martens & Houk, 1989). In so doing, procedures for altering children's classroom behavior that affect multiple behavior categories or individuals simultaneously have emerged as alternatives to more traditional contingency management strategies.

Differential-Reinforcement-of-Other and Incompatible Behavior

Differential-reinforcement-of-other behavior (DRO) is a term referring to procedures in which reward is delivered contingent upon the *absence* rather than the presence of a target behavior (Sulzer-Azaroff & Mayer, 1977). DRO procedures are behavior *suppression* techniques because the rule by which reward is delivered calls for the child *not* to engage in some proscribed activity (Deitz, Repp, & Deitz, 1976).

As an example, Repp, Barton, and Brulle (1983) compared two frequently used variations of the DRO procedure for their effectiveness in reducing disruptive classroom behavior. In the first procedure, reward was delivered to subjects at 5-minute intervals for not engaging in disruptive behavior when the interval ended (momentary DRO). The second procedure called for the delivery of reward at 5-minute intervals if the children did not engage in disruptive behavior throughout the entire preceding 5-minute period (whole-interval DRO). In either procedure, engaging in the proscribed behavior reset the interval timer resulting in additional reinforcement delay. Results indicated that whole-interval DRO was more effective than momentary DRO in suppressing the target behavior. However, momentary DRO was effective in maintaining disruptive behavior at low levels once its frequency had already been reduced by the other procedure.

Because reward is postponed if the child engages in the proscribed behavior, DRO has been traditionally viewed as a behavior suppression technique. However, acknowledging that behavior occurs as a continuous stream suggests that DRO procedures must increase behavior also, although this "other" behavior, which is reinforced, remains unspecified. Specifically, a child who spends less time engaging in some target response as a result of DRO contingencies must occupy that time engaging in other activities for which they do receive reward. In fact, since the child is reinforced for engaging in *any* behavior other than the target, DRO procedures are likely to affect a variety of behavior categories (Poling & Ryan, 1982).

Rather than relying upon unknown contingencies in the classroom environment to determine which of these "other" behavior categories the child will engage in, several investigators have found that selective reinforcement of certain categories (e.g., academic performance) reliably produces collateral decreases in other categories (e.g., classroom disruption; Aaron & Bostow, 1978; Ayllon & Roberts, 1974). Termed as differential-reinforcement-of-incompatible behavior (DRI), this procedure is based on the principle that if children spend the majority of their time doing one thing, there will be little time remaining to do another. For example, Aaron and Bostow (1978)

monitored children's on-task behavior and six areas of academic performance. These investigators found both academic performance and time on-task increased when only correct academic performance was rewarded.

Although rewarding correct academic performance has been shown to increase time on-task, increased time on-task does not necessarily improve academic performance (Lentz, 1988a). This was demonstrated in a study by Harris (1986), who compared two variations of a self-monitoring procedure for improving children's spelling performance. In the first condition, children responded on a checksheet to the question, "Was I paying attention?" upon hearing a randomly emitted tone (self-monitoring of attention). In the second condition, subjects were instructed to count the number of spelling words written at the end of each monitoring period (self-monitoring of academic performance). Results showed both conditions to be equally effective in increasing on-task behavior. However, self-monitoring of productivity produced higher rates of academic performance than self-monitoring of attention in three of the four subjects participating in the study.

Response Class Procedures

The practice of incorporating multiple behavior categories in the evaluation of treatment impact has produced increased reports of intervention "side effects" in the application of behavioral principles to school settings. Intervention side effects refer to the occurrence of simultaneous changes in untargeted behavior following the manipulation of contingencies for a single response (Kazdin, 1982b; Russo, Cataldo, & Cushing, 1981; Voeltz & Evans, 1982).

Although generally viewed as second-order or side effects, collateral changes in untargeted behavior have been reported with such regularity that the label "side effects" may be inaccurate (Evans et al., 1988). Rather, as stated by Willems (1974):

> When we think in terms of environment–behavior *systems,* we can see that there is a fundamental misconception embedded in the term "side-effect." . . . What we so glibly call side effects no more deserve the adjective "side" than does the "principal" effect. They are all aspects of the interdependencies [of behavior in applied settings] that we need so badly to understand. (p. 155)

As anticipated by Willems and supported in subsequent research (Parrish et al., 1986; Simon et al., 1982), collateral changes in untargeted behavior can be *expected* to occur in complex behavior—environment systems such as the classroom. As a result, applied behavior analysts have begun to make use of these changes as a means of facilitating intervention effectiveness. An area of research that has emerged in these efforts has been the investigation of response covariation or the impact of treatment at the response class level (Evans et al., 1988; Kazdin, 1982b; Russo et al., 1981; Voeltz & Evans, 1982; Wahler, 1975).

A response class refers simply to two or more behaviors that are observed to change together either as a function of naturally occurring consequences or following treatment (Kazdin, 1982b). For example, Martens and Witt (1984) assessed naturally occurring patterns of covariation among five categories of classroom behavior over a 12-week period. Results of stepwise regression analyses indicated significant proportions of variance in a single category (e.g., responding to the teacher) could be explained by frequencies of covarying categories (e.g., being off-task) either alone or in combination. In addition, the behavior categories shown to covary, as well as their order of entry into the regression equations, varied across subjects.

To date, the most systematic investigation of intervention effects at the response class level has been conducted by Wahler and his associates (Kara & Wahler, 1977; Lichstein & Wahler, 1976; Wahler, 1975; Wahler & Fox, 1981). Characteristic of Wahler's research has been the analysis of multiple behavior categories as an interrelated *system* and the effects that behavioral interventions have on this system when only a single behavior category is targeted. For example, Wahler (1975) observed two children referred for disruption and noncompliance at home and at school over a 3-year period. Using an observational coding system that enabled the monitoring of 19 behavior categories, response classes were identified among the children's behavior via application of cluster analytic techniques. Following implementation of a combined time-out and contingent reward procedure, Wahler found that interrelationships among behavior categories during baseline were predictive of changes in untargeted behavior during the experimental phases.

Vicarious Reinforcement Effects

In addition to examining intervention effects on nontarget behavior, several investigators have also focused on the effects of reinforcement on nearby observers (Boyd, Keilbaugh, & Axelrod, 1981; Kazdin, 1977b, 1979; Witt & Adams, 1980). This line of research has demonstrated that reinforcement of a target child's behavior often "spreads" to influence the behavior of other children in the classroom, albeit indirectly.

Using a procedure in which reward was delivered to a target child while monitoring activities of both the target child and an adjacent peer, Kazdin (1973) demonstrated vicarious reinforcement effects on children's seat-work behavior. Target children were rewarded with praise contingent first upon attentive behavior (e.g., sitting quietly, working on assignments) and then inattentive behavior (e.g., talking without permission, playing with materials rather than working). Following reinforcement of the target children for attentive behavior, increased rates of attending were observed for both the target children and the nontarget peers as well. Rewarding the target children with praise following *inattentive* behavior, however, increased this aberrant behavior in the targets, but resulted in increased rates of attentive behavior in the adjacent peers. In explanation of these findings, Kazdin suggested that delivery of reward to the target child served as a cue to the adjacent peer that reward was available. Since the behavior targeted for reward was not identified explicitly to either child, it was suggested that the nontarget peer relied upon previous experience (i.e., children in the classroom are rewarded for being good) in the selection of behavior in which to engage.

Lest the reader become overly optimistic concerning the use of vicarious reinforcement to enhance children's classroom behavior, research subsequent to Kazdin's early work has suggested a somewhat different scenario than reported above. Specifically, changes in the behavior of nontarget peers typically occur in the same direction as those observed in the target child, and such changes are enhanced if reinforcement contingencies are made explicit or the target child's behavior becomes salient (Boyd et al., 1981; Witt & Adams, 1980). In addition, vicarious reinforcement effects, when they occur, are often shortlived (Kazdin, 1979) and may be followed by decrements in performance with continued feedback to the observer that engaging in the desired behavior fails to elicit reward (Ollendick, Dailey, & Shapiro, 1983).

SPECIAL TOPICS IN THE APPLICATION OF BEHAVIORAL PRINCIPLES

Classroom instruction and management practices that result in maladaptive student behavior often evolve over periods of months and years. Successful intervention, therefore, may require significant adults in the classroom setting (e.g., teachers, aides) to change what are often long-standing patterns in the way they interact with children. Because the use of behaviorally based interventions in schools requires teachers to change *their* behavior in order to change children's behavior, two issues become of paramount importance in treatment effectiveness. First, to what extent do these changes actually occur (e.g., are treatment procedures used or used correctly)? Second, do these changes occur over time and across situations (e.g., are the effects of treatment on children and teachers lasting)? These issues are examined in the following sections with discussion of the generalization and maintenance of treatment impact as well as the acceptability of treatment procedures.

Generalization and Maintenance of Treatment Impact

Generalization of treatment impact refers to changes in behavior similar to those observed during the treatment conditions that occur in times, settings, behavior, or individuals for which treatment contingencies are not operating (Baer, Wolf, & Risley, 1968; Wahler, Berland, & Coe, 1979). Previous discussion of response class procedures has suggested that treatment effects are *likely* to generalize to behavior categories other than those targeted, although the direction of these collateral changes may not always be desirable. Similarly, in the discussion of vicarious reinforcement effects it was suggested that treatment procedures may also influence nearby peers if either the delivery of reward or behavior of the target child can be readily observed. With regard to the generalization of treatment impact over time (maintenance) and across settings, however, there currently exists a consensus of opinion in applied behavior analytic research that these can occur only through their explicit programming (Stokes & Baer, 1977). Al-

though the parameters of generalization programming have yet to be fully uncovered, Wahler et al. (1979), in their review of generalization processes in child behavior therapy, stated: "Clearly, there is reason to voice doubts about the outcomes of mixing imposed (programmed) contingencies within the natural contingencies of environments" (p. 52). Voeltz and Evans (1982) have supported this view by suggesting that the effects of treatment may fail to generalize over time when treatment is ended because the target behavior resumes its status as a function of the maladaptive behavior–environment relationship that existed during baseline. The common point to both these assertions which flows from the basic tenets of operant research is that the generalization and maintenance of treatment *impact* is largely a function of the generalization and maintenance of treatment *procedures* (Kazdin, 1982b; Martens & Witt, 1988b). That is, changes in behavior observed during treatment have a greater probability of generalizing to other times or settings if the contingencies operating at those times or in those settings are similar to the ones employed during treatment.

In considering the generalization of treatment impact from one setting or time to another (e.g., different classrooms or workstations within a classroom), the operation of concurrent schedules of reinforcement has proven to be a useful heuristic (Martens & Witt, 1988a; McDowell, 1982; Simon et al., 1982). Fundamental to this process is the assumption that at any given time children have a choice of behavior in which to engage. According to Herrnstein's law of effect, this choice is guided by the amount of reinforcement contingent on the target behavior relative to all reinforcement available in the setting (McDowell, 1982). For example, Martens and Houk (1989) found that time on-task increased with increases in contingent teacher attention, but did so at a slower rate when reinforcement contingent on inappropriate behavior was also high.

In terms of generalization, Herrnstein's law of effect suggests that during the implementation of a treatment procedure (e.g., earning points to exchange for later free time), a great deal of reward is provided to the child contingent on one or more "appropriate" responses. In the most simple case, then, the child has a two-choice discrimination. He or she can continue responding in inappropriate ways and receive whatever reward is available for doing so (e.g., attention from peers, satisfaction from arguing with the teacher) or the child can behave appropriately and receive exchangeable points. Treatment is successful when the child selects the latter behavior because of its association with a richer reinforcement schedule.

In contrast, during generalization, when treatment conditions are no longer in effect, the schedule of reinforcement for appropriate behavior is likely to revert to the previous low or nonexistent level present at baseline. The child, again faced with a choice, is likely this time to opt for engaging in *inappropriate* behavior. Thus, if lasting changes in teacher-directed events that support desired behavior fail to occur in the classroom environment, maintenance of this behavior beyond the treatment phase will not be likely to occur either.

Intervention Acceptability

In recognizing the need for intervention procedures to function as integral components of the classroom instruction/management system, increased emphasis has been placed on perceptions of these procedures by people responsible for their use (Kazdin, 1980a, 1980b, 1981; Kazdin et al., 1981; Witt, Elliott, & Martens, 1984; Wolf, 1978). As stated by Witt (1986):

> It is time to examine not only the content of what we do about classroom management (i.e., the development of new, more effective interventions) but also the process by which we do what we do. As researchers it is no longer sufficient for us to develop classroom interventions that are effective within the confines of university-based research projects but are unlikely to be used again anywhere (except perhaps in the context of another special project). (p. 37)

Termed as treatment acceptability, research in this area has suggested that people are often unwilling to utilize techniques that they perceive as unfair, unreasonable or intrusive, or inconsistent with their notions of what treatment should be (Kazdin, 1980a). Research conducted by Witt and his associates (Martens, Witt, Elliott, & Darveaux, 1985; Witt, Elliott, & Martens, 1984; Witt & Robbins, 1985) has indicated that teacher judgments of intervention acceptability are based on consideration of the amount of time and skill required for implementation, potential risk to the target child, and effects of treatment on other children in the

classroom, in addition to intervention effectiveness. This line of research has suggested that treatment alternatives shown to be equally effective in application may be quite different in acceptability. As a result, certain intervention strategies may prove unsuccessful, not because of the strategy per se, but because its lack of acceptability precluded it from being used or being used correctly.

In an investigation into this issue, Martens et al. (1986) surveyed over 2000 teachers concerning their perceptions of various school-based intervention strategies (e.g., time-out, vicarious reinforcement, redirection with a prompt). Subjects in the study rated each procedure according to perceptions of its effectiveness and ease of use as well as its frequency of use using separate 5-point Likert-type scales. Following factor analyses of respondents' ratings, results indicated that the strategies rated as most effective, easiest to use, *and* most frequently used by both regular and special education teachers were manipulating antecedents through use of redirective prompts and manipulating contingent rewards. In contrast, time-out and other procedures involving punishment that were rated as difficult to use and ineffective were also rated as being used with the lowest frequency.

CONCLUSIONS

Experimental operant research (Skinner, 1953) has described a set of processes in behavior–environment relationships unsurpassed for their precision and power. It is not surprising, then, that these processes have enjoyed successful application to a variety of socially significant problems over the years subsequent to their identification. Notable among these areas of application has been the use of behavioral technology to enhance the educational experiences of children.

As in the application of any technology, the use of behavioral principles in educational settings has undergone a gradual evolution. Early efforts to utilize operant techniques in schools focused exclusively on demonstrating treatment efficacy. As prescribed by Baer et al. (1968) in their seminal paper concerning the mission of applied behavior analytic research: "If the application of behavioral techniques does not produce large enough effects for practical value, then application has failed. Its practical value [that of the treatment procedure], specifically its powers in altering behavior enough to be socially important, is the essential criterion"(p. 96). Through many years of demonstrating treatment efficacy, the extent to which operant principles *can* be applied in the schools has become apparent.

In recent years, however, emphasis has slowly turned from showcasing the effectiveness of behavioral technology to demonstrating that treatment procedures can function as integral components of the classroom instructional/management system. Toward this goal, issues concerning the generalization and maintenance of treatment impact as well as the "goodness of fit" between intervention procedures and educational practices have received increased attention. In addition, behavioral technology itself has changed in focus from the demonstration of treatment effectiveness in a univariate, sequential, and often contextually ignorant fashion to investigation of the systemlike interdependencies that together influence children's classroom behavior. These advances continue to build on the foundation of principles firmly established in experimental operant research. Together with efforts to increase our understanding of ways in which behavioral technology can be made to complement existing educational practice, it would appear that applied behavior analysis in the schools is coming of age. If the old adage is true that with maturity comes increased responsibility, research in this area should continue to be an important and exciting activity for years to come.

REFERENCES

Aaron, B. A., & Bostow, D. E. (1978). Indirect facilitation of on-task behavior produced by contingent free-time for academic productivity. *Journal of Applied Behavior Analysis, 11,* 197.

Ascare, D., & Axelrod, S. (1973). Use of a behavior modification procedure in four open classrooms. *Psychology in the Schools, 10,* 243–248.

Ayllon, T. & Roberts, M. D. (1974). Eliminating discipline problems by strengthening academic performance. *Journal of Applied Behavior Analysis, 7,* 71–76.

Baer, D. M., Wolf, M. M., & Risley, T. R. (1968). Some current dimensions of applied behavior analysis. *Journal of Applied Behavior Analysis, 1,* 91–97.

Barish, H., Saunders, M., & Wolf, M. (1969). Good behavior game: Effects of individual contingencies for group consequences on disruptive behavior in the classroom. *Journal of Applied Behavior Analysis, 2,* 119–124.

Barton, E. J. (1981). Developing sharing: An analysis of modeling and other behavior techniques. *Behavior Modification, 5*(3), 386–398.

Barton, E. S., & Osborne, J. G. (1978). The development of classroom by a teacher using positive practice. *Behavior Modification, 2,* 231–250.

Barton, L. E., Brulle, A. R., & Repp, A. C. (1987). Effects of differential scheduling of timeout to reduce maladaptive responding. *Exceptional Children, 53*(4), 351–356.

Bear, G. G., & Richards, H. C. (1980). An interdependent group-oriented contingency system for improving academic performance. *School Psychology Review, 9*(2), 190–193.

Blechman, E. A., Kotanchik, N. L., & Taylor, C. J. (1981). Families and school together: Early behavioral intervention with high risk children. *Behavior Therapy, 12,* 308–319.

Blount, R. L., & Stokes, T. F. (1984). Contingent public posting of photographs to reinforce dental hygiene: Promoting effective toothbrushing by elementary school children. *Behavior Modification, 8*(1), 79–92.

Boyd, L. A., Keilbaugh, W. S., & Axelrod, S. (1981). The direct and indirect effects of positive reinforcement on on-task behavior. *Behavior Therapy, 12,* 80–92.

Bradley-Johnson, S., Sunderman, P., & Johnson, C. M. (1983). Comparison of delayed prompting and fading for teaching preschoolers easily confused letters and numbers. *Journal of School Psychology, 21,* 327–335.

Brantner, J. P., & Doherty, M. A. (1983). A review of timeout: A conceptual and methodological analysis. In S. Axelrod & J. Apsche (Eds.), *The effects of punishment on human behavior* (pp. 87–132). New York: Academic Press.

Broughton, S. F., Barton, E. S., & Owen, P. R. (1981). Home based contingency systems for school problems. *School Psychology Review, 10*(1), 26–36.

Broughton, S. F., & Lahey, B. B. (1978). Direct and collateral effects of positive reinforcement, response cost, and mixed contingencies for academic performance. *Journal of School Psychology, 16*(2), 126–136.

Budd, K. S., Leibowitz, J. M., Riner, L. S., Mindell, C., & Goldfarb, A. L. (1981). Home-based treatment of severe disruptive behaviors: A reinforcement package for preschool and kindergarten children. *Behavior Modification, 5*(2), 273–298.

Carr, E. G., Newsom, C. D., & Binkoff, J. A. (1976). Stimulus control of self-destructive behavior in a psychotic child. *Journal of Abnormal Child Psychology, 4,* 139–153.

Carr, E. G., Newsom, C. D., & Binkoff, J. A. (1980). Escape as a factor in the aggressive behavior of two retarded children. *Journal of Applied Behavior Analysis, 13,* 101–117.

Center, D. B., Deitz, S. M., & Kaufman, M. E. (1982). Student ability, task difficulty, and inappropriate classroom behavior. *Behavior Modification, 6,* 355–374.

Christie, D. J., Hiss, M., & Lozanoff, B. (1984). Modification of inattentive classroom behavior: Hyperactive children's use of self recording with teacher guidance. *Behavior Modification, 8*(3), 391–406.

Cook, V. J. (1980). The influence of home and family on the development of literacy in children. *School Psychology Review, 9*(4), 369–373.

Cowen, R. J., Jones, F. H., & Bellack, A. S. (1979) Grandma's rule with group contingencies—A cost effective means of classroom management. *Behavior Modification, 3*(3), 397–418.

Crouch, P. L., Gresham, F. M., & Wright, W. R. (1985). Interdependent and independent group contingencies with immediate and delayed reinforcement for controlling classroom behavior. *Journal of School Psychology, 23,* 177–187.

Darch, C., & Gersten, R. (1985). The effects of teacher presentation rate and praise on LD students' oral reading performance. *British Journal of Educational Psychology, 55,* 295–303.

Darveaux, D. X. (1984). The good behavior game plus merit: Controlling disruptive behavior and improving student motivation. *School Psychology Review, 13*(4), 510–514.

Deitz, S. M., Repp, A. C., & Deitz, D. E. D. (1976). Reducing inappropriate classroom behavior of retarded students through three procedures of differential reinforcement. *Journal of Mental Deficiency Research, 20,* 155–170.

Derevensky, J. L., & Rose, M. I. (1978). Teacher preferences for various positive reinforcements. *Psychology in the Schools, 15*(4), 565–570.

Drabman, R. S., Spitalnik, R., & Spitalnik, K. (1974). Sociometric and disruptive behavior as a function of four types of token reinforcement programs. *Journal of Applied Behavior Analysis, 7,* 93–101.

Drabman, R. S. (1976). Behavior modification in the classroom. In W. E. Craighead, A. E. Kazdin, & M. J. Mahoney (Eds.), *Behavior modification principles, issues, and applications.* Boston: Houghton Mifflin.

Duke, D. L. (1978). How administrators view the crisis in school discipline. *Phi Delta Kappan, 59,* 323–331.

Eller, B. F., Ideker, J. S., & Holben, M. M. (1978). So you don't have money for your token economy. *Psychological Reports, 43,* 322.

Elliott, S. M., Witt, J. C., Galvin, G. A., & Peterson, R. (1984). Acceptability of positive and reductive behavioral interventions: Factors that influence teachers' decisions. *Journal of School Psychology, 22,* 353–360.

Evans, I. M., Meyer, L. H., Kurkjian, J. A., & Kishi, G. S. (1988). An evaluation of behavioral interrelationships in child behavior therapy. In J. C. Witt, S. N. Elliott, & F. M. Gresham, (Eds.), *Handbook of behavior therapy in education* (pp. 189–216). New York: Plenum Press.

Fantuzzo, J. W., & Clement, P. W. (1981). Generalization of the effects of teacher and self-administered token reinforcers to nontreated students. *Journal of Applied Behavior Analysis, 14,* 435–447.

Feldman, M. P., & Peay, J. (1982). Ethical and legal issues. In A. S. Bellack, M. Hersen, & A. E. Kazdin (Eds.), *International handbook of behavior modification and therapy* (pp. 231–261). New York: Plenum press.

Forness, S. R. (1973). The reinforcement hierarchy. *Psychology in the Schools, 10,* 168–177.

Fowler, S. A. (1986). Peer-monitoring and self-monitoring: Alternatives to traditional teacher management. *Exceptional Children, 52*(6), 573–581.

Foxx, R. M. (1976). Increasing a mildly mentally retarded women's attendance at self-help classes by overcorrection and instruction. *Behavior Therapy, 7,* 390–396.

Foxx, R. M., & Azrin, N. H. (1972). Restitution: A method of eliminating aggressive–disruptive behavior of retarded and brain damaged patients. *Behavior Research and Therapy, 10,* 15–27.

Foxx, R. M., & Bechtel, D. R. (1983). Overcorrection: A review and analysis. In S. Axelrod & J. Apsche (Eds.), *The effects of punishment on human behavior* (pp. 133–220). New York: Academic Press.

Foxx, R. M., & Jones, J. R. (1978). A remediation program for increasing spelling achievement of elementary and junior high school students. *Behavior Modification, 2,* 211–230.

Foxx, R. M., & Shapiro, S. T. (1978). The time-out ribbon: A nonexclusionary timeout procedure. *Journal of Applied Behavior Analysis, 11,* 125–136.

Gallup, G. H. (1977). Ninth annual Gallup Poll of the public's attitudes toward the public schools. *Phi Delta Kappan, 59,* 33–48.

Gaylord-Ross, R. J., Weeks, M., & Lipner, C. (1980). An analysis of antecedent, response, and consequence events in the treatment of self-injurious behavior. *Education and Training of the Mentally Retarded, 15,* 35–42.

Gettinger, M. (1988). Methods of proactive classroom management. *School Psychology Review, 17,* 277–242.

Greene, B. F., Bailey, J. S., & Barber, F. (1981). An analysis and reduction of disruptive behavior on school buses. *Journal of Applied Behavior Analysis, 14,* 177–192.

Greenwood, C. R., Carta, J. J., & Hall, R. V. (1988). The use of peer tutoring strategies in classroom management and educational instruction. *School Psychology Review, 17,* 258–275.

Greer, R. D., & Polirstok, S. R. (1982). Collateral gains and short-term maintenance in reading and on-task responses by inner-city adolescents as a function of their use of social reinforcement while tutoring. *Journal of Applied Behavior Analysis, 15,* 123–139.

Gresham, F. M. (1979). Comparison of response cost and timeout in a special education setting. *Journal of Special Education, 131*(2), 199–208.

Gresham, F. M. (1983). Use of a home-based dependent group contingency system in controlling destructive behavior: A case study. *School Psychology Review, 12*(2), 195–198.

Griswold, P. A., & Arnold, M. R. (1980). Rate and function of vowel recognition as a function of spoken reinforcers and age. *Journal of School Psychology, 18*(3), 256–262.

Hamlet, C. C., Axelrod, S., & Kuerschner, S. (1984). Eye contact as an antecedent to compliant behavior.

Journal of Applied Behavior Analysis, 17, 553–557.

Harris, K. R. (1985). Definitional, parametric and procedural considerations in timeout intervention and research. *Exceptional Children, 51*(4), 279–288.

Harris, K. R. (1986). Self-monitoring of attentional behavior versus self-monitoring of productivity: Effects on on-task behavior and academic response rate among learning disabled children. *Journal of Applied Behavior Analysis, 19,* 417–423.

Heller, M. S., & White, M. A. (1975). Rates of teacher verbal approval and disapproval to higher and lower ability classes. *Journal of Educational Psychology, 67*(6), 796–800.

Honig, W. K. (1966). Introductory remarks. In W. K. Honig (Ed.), *Operant behavior: Areas of research and application.* New York: Appleton-Century-Crofts.

Hops, H. (1983). Children's social competencies and skills: Current research practices and future directions. *Behavior Therapy, 14,* 3–18.

Jenkins, H. M. (1965). Measurement of stimulus control during discriminative operant conditioning. *Psychological Bulletin, 64,* 365–376.

Kalish, H. I. (1981). *From behavioral science to behavior modification.* New York: McGraw-Hill.

Kara, A., & Wahler, R. G. (1977). Organizational features of a young child's behavior. *Journal of Experimental Child Psychology, 24,* 24–39.

Kazdin, A. E. (1973). The effect of vicarious reinforcement on attentive behavior in the classroom. *Journal of Applied Behavior Analysis, 6,* 71–78.

Kazdin, A. E. (1977a). *The token economy. A review and evaluation.* New York: Plenum Press.

Kazdin, A. E. (1977b). Vicarious reinforcement and direction of behavior change in the classroom. *Behavior Therapy, 8,* 57–63.

Kazdin, A. E. (1979). Vicarious reinforcement and punishment in operant programs for children. *Child Behavior Therapy, 1,* 13–26.

Kazdin, A. E. (1980a). Acceptability of alternative treatments for deviant child behavior. *Journal of Applied Behavior Analysis, 13,* 259–297.

Kazdin, A. E. (1980b). Acceptability of time out from reinforcement procedures for disruptive child behavior. *Behavior Therapy, 11,* 329–344.

Kazdin, A. E. (1981). Acceptability of child treatment techniques: The influence of treatment efficacy and adverse side effects. *Behavior Therapy, 12,* 493–506.

Kazdin, A. E. (1982a). Applying behavioral principles in the schools. In C. R. Reynolds & T. B. Gutkin (Eds.), *The handbook of school psychology* (pp. 501–529). New York: Wiley.

Kazdin, A. E. (1982b). Symptom substitution, generalization and response covariation: Implications for psychotherapy outcome. *Psychological Bulletin, 91,* 349–365.

Kazdin, A. E. (1982c). The token economy: A decade later. *Journal of Applied Behavior Analysis, 15,* 331–346.

Kazdin, A. E., French, N. H., & Sherick, R. B. (1981). Acceptability of alternative treatments for children:

Evaluation of inpatient children, parents, and staff. *Journal of Consulting and Clinical Psychology, 49,* 900–907.

Kazdin, A. E., & Geesey, S. (1980). Enhancing classroom attentiveness by preselection of back-up reinforcers in a token economy. *Behavior Modification, 4*(1), 98–114.

Kazdin, A. E., & Mascitelli, S. (1980). The opportunity to earn oneself off a token system as a reinforcer for attentive behavior. *Behavior Therapy, 11,* 68–78.

Knoff, H. M. (1984). Stimulus control, paraprofessionals, and appropriate playground behavior. *School Psychology Review, 13,* 249–253.

Koegel, R. L., Dunlap, G., & Dyer, K. (1980). Intertrial interval duration and learning in autistic children. *Journal of Applied Behavior Analysis, 13,* 91–99.

L'Abate, L., & Curtis, L. T. (1975). *Teaching the exceptional child.* Philadelphia: W.B. Saunders.

Leger, H. J., Groff, D., Harris, V. W., Finfreck, L. R., Weaver, F. H., & Kratochwill, T. R. (1979). An instructional package to teach communication behavior in a classroom setting. *Journal of School Psychology, 17*(4), 339–346.

Leichter, H. J. (1977). *The family as educator.* New York: Teachers College Press.

Lentz, F. E. (1988a). On-task behavior; academic performance, and classroom disruptions: Untangling the target selection problem in classroom interventions. *School Psychology Review, 17,* 243–257.

Lentz, F. E. (1988b). Reductive procedures. In J. C. Witt, S. N. Elliott, & F. M. Gresham (Eds.), *Handbook of behavior therapy in education* (pp. 439–468). New York: Plenum Press.

Lentz, F. E., & Shapiro, E. S. (1986). Functional assessment of the academic environment. *School Psychology Review, 15,* 346–357.

Lichstein, K. L., & Wahler, R. G. (1976). The ecological assessment of an autistic child. *Journal of Abnormal Child Psychology, 4,* 31–54.

Linton, J. M., & Singh, N. N. (1984). Acquisition of sign language using positive practice overcorrection. *Behavior Modification, 8*(4), 553–566.

Lyon, M. (1984). Positive reinforcement and logical consequences in the treatment of classroom encopresis. *School Psychology Review, 13*(2), 238–243.

Mace, F. C., Page, T. J., Ivancic, M. T., & O'Brien, S. (1986). Effectiveness of brief time-out with and without contingent delay: A comparative Analysis. *Journal of Applied Behavior Analysis, 19,* 79–86.

MacMillan, D. L., Forness, S. R., & Trumbull, B. M. (1973). The role of punishment in the classroom. *Exceptional Children, 40,* 85–96.

Martens, B. K., & Houk, J. L. (1989). The application of Herrnstein's law of effect to disruptive and on-task behavior of a retarded adolescent girl. *Journal of the Experimental Analysis of Behavior, 51,* 17–27.

Martens, B. K., Peterson, R. L., Witt, J. C., & Cirone, S. (1986). Teacher perceptions of school based interventions. *Exceptional Children, 53,* 213–223.

Martens, B. K., & Witt, J. C. (1984). Assessment and prediction in an ecological system: Application of the general linear model to the response-class concept. *Journal of Behavioral Assessment, 6,* 197–206.

Martens, B. K., & Witt, J. C. (1988a). Ecological behavior analysis. In M. Hersen, R. M. Eisler, & P. M. Miller (Eds.), *Progress in behavior modification* (Vol. 22, pp. 115–140). Beverly Hills, CA: Sage.

Martens, B. K., & Witt, J. C. (1988b). On the ecological validity of behavior modification. In J. C. Witt, S. N. Elliott, & F. M. Gresham (Eds.), *The handbook of behavior therapy in education* (pp. 325–342). New York: Plenum Press.

Martens, B. K., Witt, J. C., Elliott, S. N., & Darveaux, D. X. (1985). Teacher judgements concerning the acceptability of school-based interventions. *Professional Psychology, 16,* 191–198.

Matson, J. L., Esveldt-Dawson, K., & Kazdin, A. E. (1982). Treatment of spelling deficits in mentally retarded children. *Mental Retardation, 20*(2), 76–81.

Matson, J. L., Esveldt-Dawson, K., & O'Donnell, D. (1979). Overcorrection, modeling and reinforcement, procedures for reinstating speech in a mute boy. *Child Behavior Therapy, 1,* 363–370.

Mayer, G. R., Butterworth, T., Nafpaktitis, M., & Sulzer-Azaroff, B. (1983). Preventing school vandalism and improving discipline: A three year study. *Journal of Applied Behavior Analysis, 16,* 355–369.

McConnell, S. R., Strain, P. S., Kerr, M. M., Stagg, V., Lenkner, D. A., & Lambert, D. L. (1984). An empirical definition of elementary school adjustment. *Behavior Modification, 8,* 451–473.

McDowell, J. J. (1982). The importance of Herrnstein's mathematical statement of the law of effect for behavior therapy. *American Psychologist, 37,* 771–779.

McLaughlin, J. F. (1981). The effects of a classroom token economy on math performance in an intermediate grade class. *Education and Treatment of Children, 4,* 139–147.

McLaughlin, T. F., & Malaby, J. (1972). Intrinsic reinforcers in a classroom token economy. *Journal of Applied Behavior Analysis, 5,* 263–270.

Nafpaktitis, M., Mayer, R. G., & Butterworth, T. (1985). Natural rates of teacher approval and disapproval and their relation to student behavior in intermediate school classrooms. *Journal of Educational Psychology, 77*(3), 362–367.

Neisser, V. (1979). The control of information pickup in selective looking. In A. D. Pick (Ed.), *Perception and its development* (pp. 201–219). Hillsdale, NJ: Lawrence Erlbaum.

Newsom, C., Favell, J. E., & Rincover, A. (1983). Side effects of punishment. In A. Axelrod & J. Apsche (Eds.), *The effects of punishment on human behavior.* New York: Academic Press.

Odom, S. L., Hoyson, M., Jamieson, B., & Strain, P. A. (1985). Increasing handicapped preschooler's peer social interactions: Cross-setting and component analysis. *Journal of Applied Behavior Analysis, 18,* 3–16.

O'Leary, K. D., Kaufman, K. F., Kass, R. E., & Drabman, R. S. (1970). The effects of loud and soft repri-

mands on the behavior of disruptive students. *Exceptional Children, 37,* 145–155.

Ollendick, T. H., Dailey, D., & Shapiro, E. S. (1983). Vicarious reinforcement: Expected and unexpected effects. *Journal of Applied Behavior Analysis, 16,* 485–491.

Ollendick, T. H., Matson, J. L., Esveldt-Dawson, K., & Shapiro, E. (1980). Increasing spelling achievement: An analysis of treatment procedures utilizing an alternating treatment design. *Journal of Applied Behavior Analysis, 13,* 645–654.

Parrish, J. M., Cataldo, M. F., Kolko, D. J., Neef, N. A., & Egel, A. L. (1986). Experimental analysis of response covariation among compliant and inappropriate behaviors. *Journal of Applied Behavior Analysis, 19,* 241–254.

Pazulinec, R., Meyerrose, M., & Sajwaj, T. (1983). Punishment via response cost. In S. Axelrod & J. Apsche (Eds.), *The effects of punishment on human behavior* (pp. 71–86). New York: Academic Press.

Pease, G. A., & Tyler, V. O. (1979). Self-regulation of timeout duration in the modification of disruptive classroom behavior. *Psychology in the Schools, 16*(1), 101–105.

Pfiffner, L. J., Rosen, L. A., & O'Leary, S. G. (1985). The efficacy of an all-positive approach to classroom management. *Journal of Applied Behavior Analysis, 18,* 257–261.

Phillips, R. H. (1984). Increasing positive self-referent statements to improve self-esteem in low-income elementary school children. *Journal of School Psychology, 22,* 155–163.

Piersel, W. C., & Kratochwill, T. R. (1979). Self-observation and behavior change: Applications to academic and adjustment problems through behavioral consultation. *Journal of School Psychology, 17*(2), 151–161.

Poling, A., & Ryan, C. (1982). Differential-reinforcement-of-other-behavior schedules. *Behavior Modification, 6,* 3–21.

Powers, M. D., & Crowel, R. L. (1985). The educative effects of positive practice overcorrection: Acquisition, generalization and maintenance. *School Psychology Review, 14*(3), 360–372.

Premack, D. (1965). Reinforcement theory. In D. Levine (Ed.), *Nebraska symposium on motivation* (pp. 123–188). Lincoln: University of Nebraska Press.

Rapport, M. D., Murphy, A., & Baily, J. S. (1980). The effects of response cost treatment tactic on hyperactive children. *Journal of School Psychology, 18*(2), 98–111.

Reitz, A. L. (1979). The use of feedback and delayed praise to increase participation in group activity. *Journal of School Psychology, 17*(3), 237–243.

Repp, A. C., Barton, L. E., & Brulle, A. R. (1983). A comparison of two procedures for programming the differential reinforcement of other behaviors. *Journal of Applied Behavior Analysis, 16,* 435–445.

Reynolds, G. S. (1975). *A primer of operant conditioning.* Glenview, IL: Scott, Foresman.

Rhode, G., Morgan, D. P., & Young, K. R. (1983). Generalization and maintenance of treatment gains of behaviorally handicapped students from resource rooms to regular classrooms using self-evaluation procedures. *Journal of Applied Behavior Analysis, 16,* 171–188.

Risley, T. R., & Hart, B. (1968). Developing correspondence between the non-verbal and verbal behavior of preschool children. *Journal of Applied Behavior Analysis, 1,* 267–281.

Ruggles, T. R., & LeBlanc, J. M. (1982). Behavior analysis procedures in classroom teaching. In A. S. Bellack, M. Hersen, & A. E. Kazdin (Eds.), *International handbook of behavior modification and therapy* (pp. 959–996). New York: Plenum Press.

Russo, D. C., Cataldo, M. F., & Cushing, P. J. (1981). Compliance training and behavioral covariation in the treatment of multiple behavior problems. *Journal of Applied Behavior Analysis, 14,* 209–222.

Saigh, P. A., & Umar, A. M. (1983). The effects of a good behavior game on the disruptive behavior of Sudanese elementary school students. *Journal of Applied Behavior Analysis, 16,* 339–344.

Sajwaj, T., Twardosz, S., & Burke, M. (1972). Side effects of extinction procedures in a remedial preschool. *Journal of Applied Behavior Analysis, 5,* 163–175.

Salend, S. J., & Allen, E. M. (1985). Comparative effects of externally managed and self-managed response costs systems on inappropriate classroom behavior. *Journal of School Psychology, 23,* 59–67.

Salend, S. J., Esquivel, L., & Pine, P. B. (1984). Regular and special education teachers' estimates of use of aversive contingencies. *Behavioral Disorders, 9,* 89–94.

Schimek, N. (1983). Errorless discrimination training of diagraphs with a learning disabled student. *School Psychology Review, 11*(1), 101–105.

Schmidt, G. W., & Ulrich, R. E. (1969). Effects of group contingent events upon classroom noise. *Journal of Applied Behavior Analysis, 2,* 171–179.

Schoenfeld, W. N., & Farmer, J. (1970). Reinforcement schedules and the "behavior stream" In W. N. Schoenfeld (Ed.), *The theory of reinforcement schedules.* New York: Appleton-Century-Crofts.

Schulman, J. L., Suran, B. G., Stevens, T. M., & Kupst, M. J. (1979). Instructions, feedback, and reinforcement in reducing activity levels in the classroom. *Journal of Applied Behavior Analysis, 12,* 441–447.

Shapiro, E. S., & Goldberg, R. (1986). A comparison of group contingencies for increasing spelling performance among sixth grade students. *School Psychology Review, 15,* 546–557.

Shapiro, E. S., & Lentz, F. E. (1985). A survey of school psychologists' use of behavior modification procedures. *Journal of School Psychology, 23,* 327–336.

Simon, S. J., Ayllon, T., & Milan, M. A. (1982). Behavioral compensation: Contrastlike effects in the classroom. *Behavior Modification, 6*(3), 407–420.

Simpson, R. L., & Poplin, M. S. (1981). Parents as agents of change. *School Psychology Review, 10*(1), 15–25.

Simpson, R. L., Swenson, C. R., & Thompson, T. N. (1980). Academic performance in the classroom as a function of a parent applied home management program with severely emotionally disturbed children. *Behavioral Disorders, 6*(1), 4–11.

Singh, N. N., & Singh, J. (1984). Antecedent control of oral reading errors and self-corrections by mentally retarded children. *Journal of Applied Behavior Analysis, 17,* 111–119.

Singh, N. N., Singh, J., & Winton, A. S. W. (1984). Positive practice overcorrection of oral reading errors. *Behavior Modification, 8,* 23–37.

Skinner, B. F. (1935). The generic nature of the concepts of stimulus and response. *Journal of General Psychology, 12,* 40–65.

Skinner, B. F. (1953). *Science and human behavior:* New York: Free Press.

Speltz, M. L., Shimura, J. W., & McReynolds, W. T. (1982). Procedural variations in group contingencies: Effects on children's academic and social behaviors. *Journal of Applied Behavior Analysis, 15,* 533–544.

Stokes, T. F., & Baer, D. M. (1977). An implicit technology of generalization. *Journal of Applied Behavior Analysis, 10,* 349–367.

Sulzer-Azaroff, B., & Mayer, G. R. (1977). *Applying behavior-analysis procedures with children and youth.* New York: Holt, Rinehart and Winston.

Trap, J. J., Milner-Davis, P., Joseph, S., & Cooper, J. D. (1978). The effects of feedback and consequences on transitional cursive letter formation. *Journal of Applied Behavior Analysis, 14,* 381–394.

Van Houten, R. (1983). Punishment: From the animal laboratory to the applied setting. In S. Axelrod & J. Apsche (Eds.), *The effects of punishment on human behavior* (pp. 13–44). New York: Academic Press.

Van Houten, R., & Doleys, D. M. (1983). Are social reprimands effective? In S. Axelrod & J. Apsche (Eds.), *The effects of punishment on human behavior* (pp. 45–70). New York: Academic Press.

Van Houten, R., Mackenzie-Keating, S. E., Sameoto, D., & Colavecchia, B. (1982). An analysis of some variables influencing the effectiveness of reprimands. *Journal of Applied Behavior Analysis, 15,* 65–83.

Vasta, R., & Stirpe, L. A. (1979). Reinforcement effects on three measures of children's interest in math. *Behavior Modification, 3*(2), 223–244.

Voeltz, L. M., & Evans, I. M. (1982). The assessment of behavioral interrelationships in child behavior therapy. *Behavioral Assessment, 4,* 131–165.

Wahler, R. G. (1975). Some structural aspects of deviant child behavior. *Journal of Applied Behavior Analysis, 8,* 27–42.

Wahler, R. G., Berland, R. M., & Coe, T. D. (1979). Generalization processes in child behavior change. In B. B. Lahey & A. E. Kazdin (Eds.), *Advances in clinical child psychology* (Vol. 2). New York: Plenum Press.

Wahler, R. G., & Fox, J. J. (1981). Setting events in applied behavior analysis: Toward a conceptual and methodological expansion. *Journal of Applied Behavior Analysis, 14,* 327–338.

Walker, H. M., Greenwood, C. R., Hops, H., & Todd, N. M. (1979). Differential effects of reinforcing topographic components of social interactions: Analysis and direct replication. *Behavior Modification, 3*(3), 291–321.

Weeks, M., & Gaylord-Ross, R. (1981). Task difficulty

and aberrant behavior in severely handicapped students. *Journal of Applied Behavior Analysis, 14,* 449–463.

White, M. A. (1975). Natural rates of teacher approval and disapproval in the classroom. *Journal of Applied Behavior Analysis, 8,* 367–372.

Willems, E. P. (1974). Behavioral technology and behavioral ecology. *Journal of Applied Behavior Analysis, 7,* 151–165.

Wilson, C. C., Robertson, S. J., Herlong, L. H., & Haynes, S. N. (1979). Vicarious effects of time-out in the modification of aggression in the classroom. *Behavior Modification, 3*(1), 97–111.

Winett, R. A., & Winkler, R. C. (1972). Current behavior modification in the classroom: Be still, be quiet, be docile. *Journal of Applied Behavior Analysis, 5,* 499–504.

Witt, J. C. (1986). Teacher's resistance to the use of school-based interventions. *Journal of School Psychology, 24,* 37–44.

Witt, J. C., & Adams, R. M. (1980). Direct and observed reinforcement in the classroom. *Behavior Modification, 4,* 321–336.

Witt, J. E., & Elliott, S. N. (1982). The response cost lottery: A time efficient and effective classroom intervention. *Journal of School Psychology, 20,* 155–161.

Witt, J. C., Elliott, S. N., & Martens, B. K. (1984). Acceptability of behavioral interventions used in classrooms: The influence of amount of teacher time, severity of behavior problem, and type of intervention. *Behavior Disorders, 9,* 204–209.

Witt, J. C., Hannafin, M. J., & Martens, B. K. (1983). Home based reinforcement: Behavioral covariation between academic performance and inappropriate behavior. *Journal of School Psychology, 21,* 337–348.

Witt, J. C., Martens, B. K., & Elliott, S. N. (1984). Factors affecting teachers' judgments of the acceptability of behavioral interventions: Time involvement, behavior problem severity, and type of intervention. *Behavior Therapy, 15,* 95–104.

Witt, J. C., Robbins, J. (1985). Acceptability of reductive interventions for the control of inappropriate child behavior. *Journal of Abnormal Child Psychology, 13,* 59–67.

Wolf, M. M. (1978). Social validity: The case for subjective measurement or how applied behavior analysis is finding its heart. *Journal of Applied Analysis, 11,* 203–214.

Workman, E. A., Helton, G. B., & Watson, P. J. (1982). Self-monitoring effects in a four-year-old child: An ecological behavior analysis. *Journal of School Psychology, 20*(1), 57–64.

Wyatt, W. J., & Hawkins, R. P. (1987). Rates of teachers'-verbal approval and disapproval: Relationship to grade level, classroom activity, student behavior, and teacher characteristics. *Behavior Modification, 11*(1), 27–51.

Zwald, L., & Gresham, F. M. (1982). Behavioral consultation in a secondary class: Using DRL to decrease negative verbal interactions. *School Psychology Review, 11*(4), 428–432.

25

INTERVENTION TECHNIQUES AND PROGRAMS FOR ACADEMIC PERFORMANCE PROBLEMS

STEPHEN N. ELLIOTT

University of Wisconsin–Madison

EDWARD S. SHAPIRO

Lehigh University

The fact that many children, handicapped and nonhandicapped alike, experience significant academic difficulties is readily apparent to anyone who has spent time in a classroom or is involved in schooling. These academic difficulties take many forms (e.g., word recognition, reading comprehension, mathematical reasoning, written communication problems) and can be influenced by many factors, but include primarily the interaction among children's cognitive abilities and behavior, teachers' instructional behaviors, and curricular materials. The central purpose of this chapter is to examine empirically validated teacher–student interventions that directly affect academic performance problems. We acknowledge potentially fruitful opportunities for interventions with parents and administrators, at both educational and legislative levels; however, such interventions are more indirect and are outside the focus of this chapter.

In the first edition of *The Handbook of School Psychology* (C. R. Reynolds & Gutkin, 1982), Ysseldyke and Mirkin (1982) provided an excellent

chapter entitled "The Use of Assessment Information to Plan Instructional Interventions." These authors provided a cogent review of research on the assessment-intervention process with respect to ability training and skill training. The ability training approach (also referred to as the diagnostic-prescriptive approach) is based on the premise that learning difficulties are the result of an internal process dysfunction. Following from this viewpoint, advocates (e.g., Barsch, 1965; Frostig, 1967; Kephart, 1971) recommended administering tests to identify within-child process disorders such as sequential memory deficits, figure–ground deficiencies, or visual association dysfunctions. Interventions, which amounted largely to practicing items such as those on the recommended tests (e.g., ITPA), were then designed to "cure" the underlying causative problems. The Ysseldyke and Mirkin (1982) review, coupled with an earlier review of diagnostic-prescriptive teaching by Arter and Jenkins (1979), provide strong conceptual and methodological criticisms that result in the sound rejection of the ability training approach. Ysseldyke and Mirkin suggested that an assessment-intervention approach that focused on a student's skills and measured learning behaviors directly and frequently would lead to more effective instructional interventions.

We concur with Ysseldyke and Mirkin's perspective, and therefore have elected to review several behaviorally oriented intervention techniques and programs that have been tested and found to be effective for improving students' academic performance. Two major classroom-based intervention programs, the *Adaptive Learning Environments Model* or ALEM (Wang, 1980a; Wang & Birch, 1984; Wang & Walberg, 1983) and *Direct Instruction* (Bereiter & Engelmann, 1966; Carnine & Silbert, 1979; Engelmann & Carnine, 1982) are featured in this examination of academic interventions. In addition to these rather comprehensive intervention packages, we examine self-management, peer tutoring and performance feedback, group interventions such as *Cooperative Learning* (Johnson & Johnson, 1975; Slavin, 1983a; Slavin, Sharan, Kagan, Lazarowitz, Webb, & Schmuck, 1985), and operant techniques for increasing important academic behaviors (engaged time, work completion, and accuracy). First, however, we believe it is important to discuss our conceptualization of academic problems and approach to planning interventions.

CONCEPTUALIZING ACADEMIC PROBLEMS AND PLANNING INTERVENTIONS

The research of individuals such as Centra and Potter (1980), Brophy (1986), and Keith (1982) provide a framework for the complex array of variables that influence students' academic performance. These variables include parents, peers, teachers, schools, and, of course, students themselves. No single study adequately has investigated the influence of all these variables at one time, although the structural model outlined (see Figure 1) by Centra and Potter provides a heuristic for conceptualizing the relationship among the many salient variables.

The Unit of Analysis

As illustrated by the interrelational model in Figure 1, teacher behavior and student behavior are the variables of central importance to academic performance. Thus, with academic problems, the *unit of analysis* for one's assessment *and* intervention should be the three-way interaction among a student, a teacher, and the materials to be learned. The Student × Teacher × Materials interaction occurs within the context of a *learning event*. A learning event takes place within a relatively short time period (e.g., 2 to 3 minutes for young students, 30 to 40 minutes with older students) and has three distinct phases: prelearning, learning, and postlearning. Basic and applied research from instructional psychology, human learning, and cognitive psychology has demonstrated that important prelearning activities for effective learning include attention to teacher or task, comprehension of directions, and motivation to learn, whereas important postlearning activities include reviewing and summarizing of information, self-questioning, and corrective feedback about performance.

Academic Performance and Skills Deficits

Reading and math, the most frequent academic areas targeted for assessment and intervention, cover large domains made up of numerous separate behaviors. Traditional educational thought and standardized tests espouse a *molecular* or subskill approach to assessment of reading and math behaviors. For example, a child who does not readily produce all the vowel sounds accurately would be provided a different type of treatment than would one who frequently reverses letters; thus, a molecular subskill assessment is designed to discriminate the different patterns of errors. Lahey (1979) and Lentz (1988) both provide evidence that a *molar* approach to assessment and treatment can be used successfully to treat academic behavior without being concerned with academic subskills or error patterns. For example, Lahey (1979) demonstrated it was possible to improve oral reading by reinforcing entirely correct readings without assessing the kinds of errors made. Thus, he showed that different children with different molecular problems in oral reading all reduced

Figure 1. Structural model of school and teacher variables influencing student learning outcomes. (From, "School and Teacher Effects: An Interrelational Model" by J. A. Centra and D. A. Potter, 1980, *Review of Educational Research, 50,* pp. 273–291. Copyright 1980 by Reprinted by permission.)

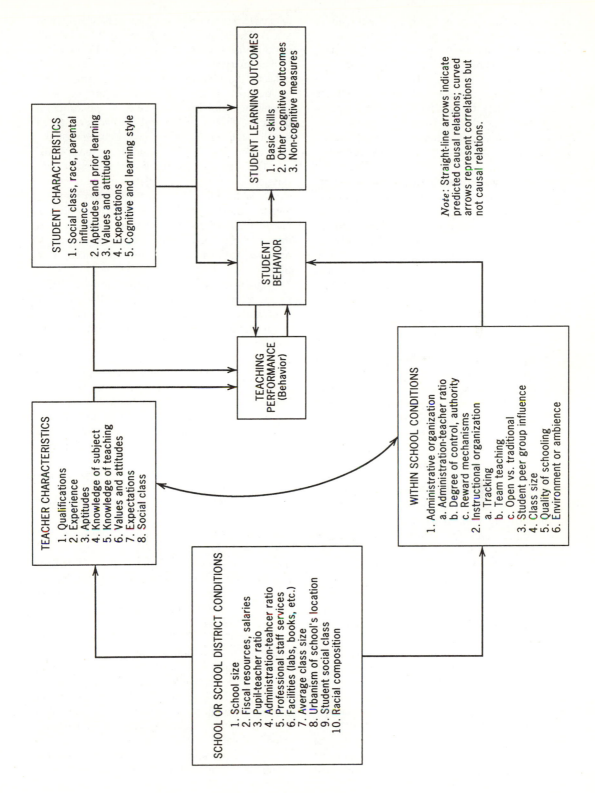

STUDENT CHARACTERISTICS

1. Social class, race, parental influence
2. Aptitudes and prior learning
3. Values and attitudes
4. Expectations
5. Cognitive and learning style

STUDENT LEARNING OUTCOMES

1. Basic skills
2. Other cognitive outcomes
3. Non-cognitive measures

STUDENT BEHAVIOR

TEACHING PERFORMANCE (Behavior)

TEACHER CHARACTERISTICS

1. Qualifications
2. Experience
3. Aptitudes
4. Knowledge of subject
5. Knowledge of teaching
6. Values and attitudes
7. Expectations
8. Social class

WITHIN SCHOOL CONDITIONS

1. Administrative organization
   a. Administration-teacher ratio
   b. Degree of control, authority
   c. Reward mechanisms
2. Instructional organization
   a. Tracking
   b. Team teaching
   c. Open vs. traditional
3. Student peer group influence
4. Class size
5. Quality of schooling
6. Environment or ambience

SCHOOL OR SCHOOL DISTRICT CONDITIONS

1. School size
2. Fiscal resources, salaries
3. Pupil-teacher ratio
4. Administration-teacher ratio
5. Professional staff services
6. Facilities (labs, books, etc.)
7. Average class size
8. Urbanism of school's location
9. Student social class
10. Racial composition

Note: Straight-line arrows indicate predicted causal relations; curved arrows represent correlations but not causal relations.

637

errors when the molar unit of correct oral reading was reinforced. The same kind of molar assessment and treatment has been shown effective for reading comprehension and handwriting (e.g., Lahey, McNess, & Brown, 1973).

The concepts of molar and molecular units for assessment interact pragmatically with the type of deficit experienced by a learner. It seems clear, based on the research on molar-level interventions for academic problems, that not all academic problems are the result of skills deficits. The major difference between a skills deficit and a performance deficit is that *skills deficits* may require the acquisition of new behaviors before progress can occur, whereas *performance deficits* require changing the level of performance of already acquired skills.

It has been our experience that many academic problems, particularly those primarily characterized by deficits in performance rather than deficits in skills, are due to a learner's or teacher's actions/interactions during either the prelearning or postlearning phases of a learning event. From an intervention perspective, the prelearning and postlearning phases involve more overt student and teacher behaviors than the learning phase. Thus, prelearning (antecedents) and postlearning (consequences) phases should serve as initial *target behavior zones* for both assessment and intervention.

Target Behaviors

Kazdin (1985) and Mash (1985) have stressed the importance of demonstrating that the targets of intervention are valid with respect to the ultimate goal of the intervention. With regard to academic performance deficits, two types of targets frequently have been selected for modification. The first type of target has concerned academic performance where the number of problems completed by a student or the level of task accuracy is the focus of change. The second type of target has been specific classroom behaviors that are assumed relevant to academic achievement. These behaviors typically include positive behaviors such as on-task, attentiveness to teacher or task, volunteering answers, and negative behaviors such as off-task or inappropriate interactions with peers.

Hoge and Andrews (1987) reviewed 22 experimental investigations in which the validity of the two types of target behaviors (i.e., academic performance and specific classroom behaviors)

relative to a criterion of academic achievement was tested. The results of manipulating the academic performance targets were positive in 11 out of 13 studies reviewed. These results substantiate a link between academic performance targets and achievement indices, and thus support efforts of practitioners to modify academic performance problems *directly*. Hoge and Andrew also noted significant increases in on-task behavior of the children involved in these academic interventions.

The results of the studies employing specific classroom behaviors as targets were much more equivocal than those using academic performance targets. According to Hoge and Andrews (1987), the interventions produced the desired changes in the target classroom behaviors in nearly all cases; however, the effects on achievement indices were mixed.

The results of the Hoge and Andrews (1987) review serve to raise questions about the validity of a student's classroom behavior as a target behavior when assessed in terms of its impact on academic performance. The selection of these target behaviors are more justified on grounds of social competence or classroom management rather than achievement. In sum, while functional links exist between student's classroom behaviors and academic performances, the behaviors and links to achievement are complex, and more research is needed before practitioners can use such targets confidently.

In addition to research by individual behavioral psychologists such as those cited by Hoge and Andrews (1987), Shapiro (1986) noted several large-scale, systematic efforts to determine predictors of academic performance have been conducted (e.g., Beginning Teacher Evaluation Study, Juniper Gardens Children's Project, Behavior Analysis Project Follow-Through). An examination of these projects indicates that two major factors influence academic performance: *content mastered* and *academic engaged time*.

Rosenshine (1979, 1981) defined content mastered as the amount of materials actually learned. Obviously, the more content mastered, the more information learned; however, the implication of having to increase a student's rate of progress through curriculum materials is difficult to address without increasing amount of time engaged in learning (Rosenshine, 1981). Thus, the variable of academic engaged time has become extremely important in predicting academic performance (Berliner, 1979; Fredrick, Walberg, & Rasher, 1979).

The development of the *Code for Instructional Structure and Student Academic Response* (CISSAR) by Stanley and Greenwood (1981) enhanced research on academic engaged time and many salient teacher and student instructional variables. Investigators consistently have reported that the academic engaged time of students with academic difficulties in regular education is very low (e.g., Hall, Delquadri, Greenwood, & Thurston, 1982; Stanley & Greenwood, 1983). A similar trend has been reported in classes for learning-disabled students (Thurlow, Ysseldyke, Graden, & Algozzine, 1984). In all these studies, direct relationships have been observed between task engagement rates and academic performance. Thus, increasing task engagement rates should be a goal of any intervention designed to improve students' academic performance.

LINKING ASSESSMENT TO INTERVENTION PROCEDURES

Choosing an appropriate remediation strategy should be based on a linkage between assessment and intervention; however, no explicit model or procedure has been developed for accomplishing such a linking with academic problems. Research in linking assessments to interventions for non-academic problems has been advanced by Nelson and Hayes (1986), who described three linking procedures: a functional analysis, the keystone behavior strategy, and the diagnostic strategy.

Functional Analysis

The purpose of functional analysis is to determine empirically the relationships between the variables controlling the target behavior and subsequently to modify these behaviors. In terms of selecting a treatment strategy, the identification of specific environmental variables related to behavior change would differentially lead to the selection of various treatment procedures. Hypothetically, choosing the strategy with functional relationships to the target behavior would result in improvement, whereas choosing those strategies without such functional relationships should not result in any change in the target response. Based on the work of Iwata, Dorsey, Slifer, Bauman, and Richman (1982), Mace and his colleagues, in a

series of studies, have provided several examples of the potential use of the functional analysis methodology. Mace, Yankanich, and West (in press) provided both a description and example of the application of this methodology to the treatment of stereotypic behavior in an 8-year-old profoundly mentally retarded girl. The method begins with the conducting of a problem identification interview with the referral source, followed by data collection to generate a series of potential hypotheses regarding variables that may be functioning to maintain the aberrant response. These hypotheses are then evaluated through the development of analog conditions, typically employed in an alternating treatments design. Data are graphed and examined to determine which variables are functionally related to the response and a relevant treatment procedure based on this knowledge is then generated, implemented, and evaluated. If the analysis was accurate, the aberrant behavior should be significantly altered once the appropriate treatment procedure is implemented.

Although there have not been studies that have applied this methodology directly to the selection of effective treatment strategies for academic problems, the procedures described by Mace et al. (in press) seem to have direct applicability to such problems. For example, hypotheses could be generated based on direct observation and interview data collected during the initial analysis phase. These hypotheses could be tested through analog conditions, and differential treatment procedures generated. From these data, one could determine the effective treatment and the functional variables related to academic performance. Thus, one student who is performing poorly in math may be found to be having problems related to competing contingencies (being drawn off-task by peers), while another student may need to have the level of difficulty reduced. Each of these cases would require differential interventions that could be evaluated and implemented systematically within the classroom setting.

Keystone Behavior Strategy

This procedure is based on the notion that one may be able to identify a group of responses that have been found to be linked to a particular disorder. Within this set of responses, a particular response is identified which, if changed, would result in significant and substantial change in the overall group of responses. Thus, one attempts to identify a key response that would be functionally related to all others. Nelson and Hayes (1986) note that the primary difference between functional analysis and the keystone behavior strategy is that functional analysis is based on stimulus–response relationships, whereas the keystone strategy is based on response–response interactions.

Although the keystone behavior strategy certainly has applicability to the selection of interventions for academic problems, no studies have been reported which have specifically examined this procedure. Jenkins, Larson, and Fleisher (1983), and M. Roberts and Smith (1980), however, conducted studies that would be analogous to a keystone strategy in the remediation of reading problems. In the Jenkins et al. (1983) study, the relationships between reading comprehension and two instructional strategies for correcting reading errors, word supply and word drill, were examined. Results showed that drill correction had substantially more impact on word recognition and comprehension than did word supply. Similarly, Roberts and Smith (1980) examined the effects of interventions aimed at either increasing oral reading rate or decreasing error rate on comprehension levels. Results suggested that improvements in rates (correct or error) did not effect comprehension. When comprehension was targeted, collateral changes did occur in both reading rates.

Diagnostic Strategy

The diagnostic strategy in choosing interventions is based on the traditional medical model premise that effective diagnosis leads to effective treatment. In this model, the diagnosis is determined from the assessment information and is based on a particularly nosology (e.g., DSM-III-R). The specific intervention plan is determined based on this diagnosis. Applications of this approach to academic problems are somewhat vague since educational settings do not use the same type of nosological classifications as clinicians. However, a child diagnosed as Attention Deficit Hyperactive Disorder may be viewed as a good candidate for pharmacological therapy to affect classroom performance. Similarly, a child with a conduct disorder who is having academic problems may be viewed as more likely to respond to contingency management aimed at the child's disruptive behavior rather than at the academic performance problem (Hoge & Andrews, 1987).

Little evidence exists that indicates effective diagnosis can be conducted adequately. For example, Felton and Nelson (1984) reported that six clinicians assessing the same clients had poor levels of agreement regarding controlling variables, yet had much higher levels of agreement on the treatment proposals. Clearly, the link between assessment and intervention was quite poor. Wilson and Evans (1983) reported low levels of agreement in identifying children's problems from written protocols.

In educational settings, children with academic problems are often considered for placement into special education. In a sense, the decision as to a child's eligibility for special education is a diagnostic decision, since eligibility is based on meeting the criteria for a specific classification (e.g., learning disabled, behavior disordered, educable mentally retarded). Yet these diagnostic labels have little to do with educational treatment. Indeed, there are substantial data which suggest that the instructional processes in classes for all mildly handicapped classrooms are not very different (e.g., M. C. Reynolds, 1984). Thus, the diagnostic-treatment link is equally weak for academic problems.

Template Matching Strategy

A final procedure called template matching that may have implications for selection of intervention strategies has been described and used by Cone (1987), Cone and Hoier (1986), and Hoier, McConnell, and Pallay (1987). Data are obtained on individuals deemed as possessing effective levels of the desired behaviors. These profiles or templates are compared against individuals who are targeted for remediation to identify the specific behaviors that need to be remediated. As described in Cone (1987), Hoier (1984) compared the social skills of third- and fourth-grade students against those considered exemplary in their behavior. Using primarily peer assessment data, discrepancies between examplary and other student behavior became targets for intervention. In a validation of the process, it was found that as a child's template approached the exemplary template, increases in peer interaction were evident.

Although designed primarily to identify behaviors for remediation, the procedure may have implications for choosing intervention strategies. For example, once specific behaviors are identified, one may decide on alternative treatments for differential templates. By matching the template to the treatment procedure, one may be able to make effective recommendations for interventions.

Conclusions and Summary

Despite the potential for the functional analysis, keystone behavior, or template matching strategies to be applied for remediating academic problems, the current methods for choosing an intervention strategy remain largely subjective. Typically, teachers are interviewed about the child's problem, the data are examined regarding potentially important variables that may affect academic performance, the research literature and/or one's clinical experiences are scanned to determine the variables critical to achievement, and recommendations are made for interventions. These recommendations often are based on the teacher's experiences with other students exhibiting similar problems, past successes and failures, the range of expertise offered by the teacher and consultant, the structure of the classroom, the time available for remediation, the resources offered by the setting, and other variables that may or may not have direct relationships to the problem at hand. Clearly, a more empirical analysis of these effects would be worthwhile. At present, the functional analysis methodology suggested by Mace et al. (in press) may have the most applicability. Still, significant work remains to demonstrate that the procedures described for assessing and treating aberrant behavior are also applicable for assessing and treating problems in skill acquisition. It is important to remember that the variables surrounding an academic ecology may be significantly more complex than those surrounding behaviors such as pica or stereotypic head weaving (Lentz & Shapiro, 1986). Further, moving the functional analysis methodology into school-based applications may require additional modifications of the procedure. Despite these cautions, this method appears to offer significant promise for making the assessment–intervention link an empirically based decision.

Substantial work needs to be done to bring the decision-making process for choosing intervention strategies in line with the assessment methodology employed. Conceptually, behavioral assessment is designed to offer this link. Although the empirical link is somewhat questionable at this time, behavioral assessment continues to offer the best opportunity for using the assessment data to make one's "best guess" as to the critical elements needed for an effective intervention. Now let's examine the content and efficacy of several intervention approaches.

GENERAL INTERVENTION TECHNIQUES

Numerous chapters have been written that document an array of behavioral (e.g., Ruggles & LeBlanc, 1982; Shapiro, 1987) and cognitive-behavioral (e.g., Hallahan, Lloyd, Kaufman, & Loper 1983) intervention techniques that have been used effectively with various types of academic problems. Space limitations preclude a discussion of each of these techniques. Rather, the purpose here is to provide a brief summary of a few of the most effective techniques, many of which are components of one of the intervention packages featured later in this chapter.

Self-Management

Over the past 10 years, there has been an increasing interest in the potential for self-management techniques in behavior change. Specifically, self-strategies involve teaching individuals to apply to themselves specified contingencies on the occurrence of behavior. These strategies have involved operant-based, contingency management procedures as well as cognitive-based, self-instruction strategies.

Conceptually, self-management has a number of advantages over more externally controlled behavioral interventions. First, because the individual controls the contingency himself or herself, there is a higher probability that behavior can be generalized across time and settings (e.g., Holman & Baer, 1979). Second, self-management potentially is more efficient than externally controlled contingencies since significant others are not necessary to conduct the intervention. A third major advantage of self-management is the crucial need to teach students responsibility for their behavior. By asking individuals to consider carefully their own behavior and its related consequences, students may begin to initiate behavior effectively prior to prompts from teachers and increase skills in independent living.

Kanfer (1971) has provided a conceptual model for self-management processes. His model contains three primary components: self-monitoring, self-evaluation, and self-reinforcement. Self-monitoring involves both the self-observation and self-recording of behavior. At times, this process alone may be reactive and result in behavior change (e.g., Nelson, 1977). Once behavior is monitored, the person must evaluate the behavior against a known criterion. At this point, a decision is made by the person as to whether the self-monitored behavior is in the desired direction of change. Finally, based on the self-evaluation of behavior, the person decides whether he or she has met the criterion for self-reinforcement, and if so, applies the appropriate rewards for behavior. Although there have been significant questions raised as to the explanatory mechanisms operating in self-management processes (e.g., Bandura, 1977; Mace & Kratochwill, 1985), Kanfer's model has fairly wide acceptance among researchers (Karoly, 1982).

Self-management procedures can be divided roughly into two types (R. N. Roberts & Dick, 1982). One set of procedures are based on contingency management and are designed to manipulate effectively consequences of behavior. These procedures usually involve self-monitoring of behavior and rewards for attaining specified criteria. Although the complexity of the procedures reported in the literature vary widely, most self-management procedures based on contingency management principles are similar.

The other type of self-management procedure involves the manipulation of cognitive variables and typically uses verbal mediation. Individuals are taught self-instruction as a mechanism to learn alternatives to inappropriate responding. Conceptually, the use of self-instruction is viewed as an attempt to modify cognitive events which are seen as antecedents to problem behavior. Again, although the operating mechanisms of self-instruction training are not fully understood (e.g., Friedling & O'Leary, 1979), the strategy does appear to be a useful self-management intervention.

An example of a self-management program based on contingency management as well as one based on cognitive change will be presented. These examples were selected to demonstrate how self-management strategies are derived and employed.

Contingency Management

Rhode, Morgan, and Young (1983) describe the use of a self-management program designed to achieve transfer and maintenance of behavior from a resource room setting to a regular education setting. Selecting six students identified as behaviorally disordered between first and fifth grades, training in self-management procedures was begun within the resource room setting alone while data were collected throughtout the study in both resource room and mainstreamed settings. Following a baseline period, a token reinforcement system was begun along with systematic verbal feedback. In this phase, teachers rated the students every 15 minutes during the 60-minute period in which the study was implemented. Ratings ranged from 0 to 5 and general guidelines were provided for the teachers to anchor their ratings. Students were rated on both academic performance and behavior every 15 minutes.

Results of the Rhode et al. (1983) program were impressive. All students showed immediate gains in the percentage of appropriate behavior when the teacher-controlled reinforcement system was implemented. These gains, however, were present only within the resource room setting where the self-management program was being conducted. No change was noted within the regular classroom setting until the self-management program was begun in that setting. In addition, appropriate behavior remained high as the program systematically was withdrawn from both classrooms. This study provides an excellent example of the numerous components of an effective self-management system. First, the study demonstrates the potential for transferring an intervention which initially is teacher centered to a self-management intervention. Second, the procedures demonstrate the power of teaching self-management in one setting and then using the technique, once mastered, in another setting. Third, and most important, the study clearly illustrates how such procedures can result in behavioral maintenance with effective and systematic withdrawal of the behavior change program.

Cognitive-Based Interventions

Procedures that have been developed for the modification of cognitions typically have employed varied forms of self-instruction. Originally described by Meichenbaum and Goodman (1971), self-instruction involves having individuals talk aloud as they perform a task. The self-instructions are designed to refocus the person's thoughts and teach effective problem solving. Although the technique was first described for reducing impulsive behavior in children (Meichenbaum & Goodman, 1971), the procedure has since been applied to many problems, including increasing on-task behavior (e.g., Bornstein & Quevillon, 1976), social skills (e.g., Cartledge & Milburn, 1983), and academic skills (e.g., Fox & Kendall, 1983).

Johnston, Whitman, and Johnson (1980) provided an excellent example of a typical self-instruction training program. Three children in classes for the educable mentally retarded were taught to add and subtract with regrouping by training them to make specific self-statements related to performing the task accurately. Training was conducted in a 20- to 30-minute session during which the children were given problems to complete. The instructor then modeled the use of self-instruction by asking and answering a series of questions (e.g., "What kind of problem is this? It's an add problem. I can tell by the sign. Now what do I do?"). The self-instruction training was conducted following guidelines established by Meichenbaum and Goodman (1971) and involved having (a) the trainer first solve the problems using the self-instructions while the subject watched; (b) the child perform the task while the trainer instructed aloud; (c) the child speak aloud while solving the problem with the help of the trainer; (d) the child perform the self-instructions aloud without trainer prompting; and finally, (e) the child perform the task using private speech. Results of this study demonstrated that self-instruction training can be an effective strategy for teaching such skills. Similar results were found in a follow-up study (Whitman & Johnston, 1983).

Effectiveness of Self-Management Interventions

Applications of self-management can be found for a wide variety of problems with a wide variety of populations (e.g., Karoly & Kanfer, 1982). This would include target behaviors such as on-task (e.g., Glynn, Thomas, & Shee, 1973), disruptive behavior (e.g., Turkewitz, O'Leary, & Ironsmith, 1975), reading (e.g., McLaughlin, Burgess, & Sackville-West, 1982), spelling (e.g., Childs, 1983), and aggressive behavior (Shapiro & Derr, 1987). Procedures have been used with mentally retarded children and adults (e.g., Ackerman & Shapiro, 1984; Shapiro, 1986), severely multi-handicapped children (e.g., Shapiro, Browder, & D'Huyvetters, 1984), emotionally disturbed ado-

lescents (e.g., Santogrossi, O'Leary, Romanczyk, & Kaufman, 1973), and learning-disabled children (e.g., Hallahan, Lloyd, Kosiewicz, Kauffman, & Graves, 1979).

A large number of summaries of investigations in the areas of self-management can be found in the literature (e.g., Karoly & Kanfer, 1982; R. N. Roberts & Dick, 1982; Shapiro, 1986). Overall, most studies have found that self-management can be an effective mechanism for behavior change. One point that remains unclear, however, is the exact mechanism that actually controls the behavior change process. As an example, there have been three different theoretical conceptualizations regarding the reactivity of self-monitoring (Nelson & Hayes, 1981). These include Rachlin's operant recording response model, Kanfer's cognitive-behavioral model, and a model suggested by Nelson and Hayes (1981) which is an integration of these hypotheses. Few empirical studies have actually investigated these explanations, but the results of those studies tend to question more cognitive explanations of behavior change (e.g., Mace & Kratochwill, 1985).

Another important issue evident from reviews of the literature is the idiosyncratic nature of self-management among some types of individuals. In a number of studies with mentally retarded children and adults, Shapiro and his colleagues (Ackerman & Shapiro, 1984; Browder & Shapiro, 1985; Browder, Shapiro, & Ambrogio, 1986; Shapiro & Ackerman, 1983) have found that although the overall effect of self-management appears positive, some individuals were unresponsive to part or all of the training procedures. Examination of nonresponders does not appear to yield any significant variables that result in these outcomes.

Examination of research on the use of self-management with academic problems suggests strongly that the procedures may be considered an effective intervention. In particular, self-monitoring and its variations (self-recording, self-graphing, self-assessment) have been used frequently as interventions for various types of academic problems (e.g., Hundert & Bucher, 1978; Stevenson & Fantuzzo, 1984).

Peer Tutoring

A procedure that frequently has been used to increase academic engaged time is peer tutoring. It is assumed that peer tutoring should result in significant increases in the frequency of academic responses. Instead of one teacher asking one question to 24 students and receiving one response, you have the possibility of 12 students asking the same question to 12 other students and receiving 12 responses all within the same time frame. Additionally, in line with research on instructional methods, error correction is often more prompt and efficient, questions are at lower cognitive levels, and the responses are given in the same modality as testing for mastery (e.g., writing of spelling words in practice instead of oral recitation).

Greenwood, Dinwiddie, Terry, Wade, Stanley, Thibadeau, and Delquadri (1984) reported three experiments which provide convincing evidence of the potential that peer tutoring has for modifying academic response rates. The study involved five teachers and 128 students in grades 3 through 6. The four lowest students in each class were identified and targeted for intensive observation as interventions were employed with the entire class. In the first experiment, data were obtained on academic response rates, weekly scores on spelling and vocabulary, and scores on standardized achievement tests. Following baseline, students were exposed to either a teacher-mediated procedure or classwide tutoring. In the teacher-mediated condition, teachers were instructed to design a lesson for the content to be taught, but not use peer tutoring. Suggestions were made for teachers to employ teacher–student discussion, media, readers, and paper/pencil tasks in that order. Classwide peer tutoring was conducted by having paired students read the item to his or her peer, have the tutee write the response, correct the response if incorrect, and award points for the correct response. These conditions were presented in a withdrawal design, counterbalancing the order of conditions across subjects. Results of this study were as predicted; academic response rates increased significantly and gains in spelling and vocabulary were substantially higher within the tutoring condition.

In the second experiment in this study, pretreatment baselines were compared to both the teacher-mediated and peer tutoring condition. Results again confirmed the findings of previous studies. Academic responding was highest during peer tutoring. Gains in achievement were evident during both procedures although were largest for peer tutoring. These gains were especially strong for spelling and vocabulary.

Finally, in the third experiment, Greenwood et al. (1984) described an attempted replication of previous findings. Of interest in this experiment was the unplanned deviation from peer tutoring procedures. Results of the study replicated other findings, with declines in academic performance evident when the teacher deviated from the peer tutoring approach.

This study, along with others conducted at Junipar Gardens (Greenwood, Delquadri, & Hall, 1984) provide strong and consistent evidence that peer tutoring can be an effective procedure for increasing academic response rates. Additionally, the procedure appears to result in significant improvements in academic performance. Other researchers have also found peer tutoring to have significant effects on academic performance in reading and math (McKenzie & Budd, 1981; Redd, Ullman, Stelle, & Roesch, 1979; Young, Hecimovic, & Salzberg, 1983).

It is important to recognize that all the peer tutoring studies reported here also included a contingent reinforcement component. The extent to which tutoring alone versus peer tutoring and contingent reinforcement would be effective has not been evaluated. Given the equally strong evidence supporting the use of contingent reinforcement in increasing academic response (e.g., Ruggles & LeBlanc, 1982), it is questionable whether tutoring alone would have the substantial effects it appears to have.

Performance Feedback

A simple, often effective technique for improving a variety of academic behaviors involves providing response contingent feedback about performance. Van Houten and Lai Fatt (1981) examined the impact of public posting of weekly grades on biology tests with 12th-grade high school students. Results of the first experiment found that the effects of public posting plus immediate feedback and praise increased accuracy from 55.7% to 73.2% correct across the 47 students in the study. In a replication of the study with 106 students, Van Houten and Lai Fatt (1981) showed that public posting alone with biweekly feedback increased student performance. These results were consistent with earlier studies which examined the use of explicit timing and public posting in increasing math and composition skills in regular elementary school students (Van Houten, Hill, & Parsons, 1975; Van Houten & Thompson, 1976).

These studies suggest that simply supplying

students immediate feedback with public recognition may be sufficient to alter some academic performance deficits. It is also important to note that these procedures were implemented with both elementary and secondary age students in regular education classrooms.

Group Contingencies and Cooperative Learning Strategies

The use of effective group interventions in the regular classroom setting for some teachers is becoming a matter of necessity as well as convenience. In this section we describe two similar intervention techniques, group contingencies and cooperative learning, and examine their effectiveness for improving the academic performances of children. These two behavior change strategies have developed separately, with the group contingency methods emanating from applied behavioral psychology, while the cooperative learning methods grew out of social psychological research and educational practices. Both intervention approaches have been documented to affect academic performance and a wide range of classroom behaviors, such as attitude toward learning and peer interactions.

Definitions, Advantages, and Disadvantages of Group Contingencies

Litlow and Pumroy (1975) identified three major types of group contingencies: (a) *dependent,* where the group's attainment of a reward depends on the performances of a target student or students meeting a specified criterion; (b) *interdependent,* where the group's attainment of a reward depends on every member of the group meeting a specified criterion or alternatively the group's average performance exceeding the criterion; and (c) *independent,* where each member of the group's attainment of the reward depends on his or her own performance meeting the specified criterion. Gresham and Gresham (1982) noted that the dependent and interdependent group contingencies have at least two advantages over other intervention methods. First, because students are organized into groups, the group contingency programs require less teacher time and attention in monitoring and charting behaviors and distributing rewards (e.g., Barrish, Saunders, & Wolf, 1969). Second, the fact that students in dependent and interdependent group contingencies are working in groups to attain good classroom behavior sets the

occasion for peers to act as behavior change agents.

Several disadvantages of group contingency treatments have also been identified. First, with dependent and interdependent group contingencies, the poor performance of a single student can prevent the entire group from obtaining a reward (Crouch, Gresham, & Wright, 1985). A second potential disadvantage of group contingencies is that once a group perceives that they have lost the reinforcement for a particular day, they may no longer be motivated to maintain their behavioral or academic efforts (Crouch et al., 1985). A third potential shortcoming of group contingencies is peer pressure (Axelrod, 1973; Packard, 1970; Shores, Apolloni, & Norman, 1976). The latter point is controversial in that several researchers indicate that group contingencies are facilitative (e.g., Pigott, Fantuzzo, Heggie, & Clement, 1984) to the academic environment, rather than detrimental. The direction and extent of classroom peer pressures are probably due to the social characteristics of the students and the nature of the task.

Effectiveness of Group Contingencies

Interventions employing a group contingency have most often been used to manage students' classroom social interactions (i.e., the Good Behavior Game of Barrish et al., 1969); however, several investigators have demonstrated that group contingencies improve academic performances above baseline levels (e.g., Chadwick & Day, 1971; Haring & Hauch, 1969; Hopkins, Schultz, & Garton, 1971; Lovitt, Guppy, & Blattner, 1969; McCarthy et al., 1977; McLaughlin, 1981; Shapiro & Goldberg, 1986; Wodarski, Hamblin, Buckholdt, & Ferritor, 1971).

A study of Shapiro and Goldberg (1986) provides a good example of a classroom group contingency intervention designed to increase academic performance. These authors selected two regular classrooms of sixth graders and focused on increasing spelling accuracy. Each day a spelling test was constructed by randomly selecting 10 words from a master list. An alternating treatments design was used to compare spelling accuracy across three group contingency conditions (i.e., independent, interdependent, and dependent). Following a baseline period, the treatment conditions were presented in counterbalanced fashion across days. Following the alternating treatment phase, the most effective treatment was implemented across the final 6 days of the study. The classrooms were managed by a token economy, so in the independent group contingency all students scoring a 90% or better on the spelling test received five token economy points. In the interdependent group contingency condition, the mean score for all students taking the test was calculated and if the mean of a group was 90% or better, all the students in the group received five token economy points regardless of their individual scores on the test. In the dependent group contingency condition, one student's test from each group was selected randomly and if the score was 90% or better, all the students from the same group received five token economy points. With the percentage of correctly spelled words as the dependent variable, Shapiro and Goldberg (1986) found that all three types of group contingencies improved spelling performance on daily tests and that there were no significant differences in effectiveness among the contingencies. Students' ratings of the acceptability of the three conditions, however, indicated that they significantly preferred the independent contingency over both the interdependent and the dependent contingencies.

As exemplified by the Shapiro and Goldberg (1986) study, no clear evidence exists in the literature which demonstrates that one type of group contingency is superior to the other types of group contingencies for improving academic performance (Allen et al., 1980; McCarthy et al., 1977; McLaughlin, 1981; Wodarski et al., 1971). Research on treatment acceptability, however, has demonstrated that the three types of group contingencies are differentially acceptable (Elliott, Turco, & Gresham, 1987; Shapiro & Goldberg, 1986). Specifically, Elliott et al. (1987) found that teachers and school psychologists evaluated dependent group contingencies as unacceptable, whereas independent and interdependent group contingencies were acceptable intervention approaches for dealing with classroom behavior problems. Students (fifth graders) rated all three forms of group contingencies as mildly acceptable.

Description of Cooperative Learning Strategies

The traditional classroom has a goal structure that emphasizes individualistic competition rather than group cooperation. Competitive goal structures have been criticized for discouraging students from helping one another learn (Johnson & Johnson, 1975), and for establishing a situation in which low achievers have little chance of success (Slavin, 1977). As a result, several educational researchers have designed academic management and incentive systems to increase the use of cooperative goal structures (e.g., Johnson & Johnson, 1975; Sharan & Sharan, 1976; Slavin, 1983a). These systems collectively have been called cooperative learning strategies and are characterized by having a small group of four to six mixed-ability students learning together. The reward to incentive structure of cooperative learning groups varies with the particular technique employed. Some cooperative learning techniques (e.g., Student-Teams-Achievement Divisions or STAD, Teams-Games-Tournament or TGT) provide a *group reward for individual learning,* whereas some techniques (e.g., Learning Together, Group-Investigation) provide a *group reward for a group product,* and at least one technique (i.e., Jigsaw) provides an *individual reward.*

Kagan (1985) identified six cooperative learning methods and provided a detail structural analysis of these methods. A close examination of Kagan's work suggests that there are four basic cooperative learning strategies: Student Team Learning, Jigsaw, Learning Together, and Group-Investigation. Although each of these basic approaches share the concept of a cooperative goal structure, they exhibit much diversity in terms of task structure (task specialization versus no task specialization) and incentive structure. Bohlmeyer and Burke (1987) provide a school psychologists' consultative guide for selecting cooperative learning strategies. A comprehensive analysis of these various cooperative learning approaches is beyond the scope of this chapter; however, a brief description of each of these basic approaches is in order.

Two specific interventions, Student Teams-Achievement Divisions (STAD) and Teams-Games-Tournament (TGT), both developed by Slavin (1980), are representative of *Student Team Learning.* In STAD, after a teacher presents a lesson, students work together in small teams (four to five members) to master a worksheet on the lesson. Once mastered, each student takes a quiz on the material. The scores that the students contribute to their team are based on the degree to which the students have improved over their individual past averages. The teams with the highest scores are recognized publicly. TGT is similar to STAD, except that students play academic games as representatives of their teams instead of taking quizzes. TGT requires more concern with ability matching across teams and seems to emphasize more individual competition than STAD. Both STAD and TGT employ a group study task structure and provide a group reward for individual learning. Thus, these interventions most closely resemble an interdependent group contingency.

Jigsaw (Aronson, 1978) was one of the first cooperative learning methods. In Jigsaw, each student in a group of five to six students is given some unique information on a topic the entire group is studying. After students study their unique information, they meet with their counterparts from other groups in an "expert group" to discuss the information further. Once the expert groups finish, students return to their learning groups to teach their teammates what they have learned. The entire class will eventually take a test for individual grades. Thus, although Jigsaw requires cooperation for academic success, it seems to stress the role of individual experts (task specialization) and individual accountability and in many ways is more like an independent group contingency than an interdependent group contingency.

Perhaps the method that stresses cooperation the most is *Learning Together* as developed by Johnson and Johnson (1975). In this approach to cooperative learning, students work together in small groups to complete a single worksheet. Students receive praise and rewards for completing the worksheet accurately. Thus, this approach stresses group study (no task specialization) and employs a group product incentive structure.

Sharan and Sharan (1976) developed a complicated strategy called *Group-Investigation*. Specifically, it requires small groups of students to take substantial responsibility for deciding what they will learn, how they will organize themselves to learn it, and how they will communicate what they have learned to their teacher and classmates. This method has the least in common with group contingencies and is more aptly characterized as an alternative educational philosophy than a cooperative learning strategy. It stresses task specialization and employs a group incentive structure. In addition, Group-Investigation appears best suited to students who are not having academic difficulties.

Potential Disadvantages of Cooperative Learning Strategies

The educational rationale for cooperative learning strategies emanated from socialization needs more than achievement needs. Consequently, when one examines cooperative learning strategies from an achievement perspective, several potential disadvantages are apparent. First, there is an inherent danger that the low-achieving students in heterogeneous teams may have little to contribute and that the high-achieving students may belittle the contributions of the low achievers (Slavin, 1985). This problem is averted in STAD and TGT since they make a group reward contingent on individual learning; however, the possibility for this problem exists in the Learning Together and Group-Investigation approaches since reinforcement is contingent on a single group product. Second, the importance of individualized education (especially for handicapped children) seems to be negated in some of the cooperative learning approaches. For example, in STAD, TGT, and Jigsaw there is no differentiation of learning objectives among students or teams. These potential disadvantages, however, are overshadowed by documented academic efficacy of cooperative learning methods.

Effectiveness of Cooperative Learning

Several reviews documenting the effectiveness of cooperative learning strategies have been published in major journals since 1980 (Johnson, Maruyama, Johnson, Nelson, & Skon, 1981; Sharan, 1980; Slavin, 1980, 1983b). In his 1983 review, Slavin identified 46 field experiments in elementary and secondary schools that examined the effects of cooperative learning on student learning in comparison to control groups. In all the studies examined, the cooperative learning intervention lasted a minimum of 2 weeks and most often at least 8 weeks. Slavin (1983a) concluded that a favorable effect on student achievement was found in 29 studies, no difference in achievement in 15, and in 2 studies there was a significant difference favoring the control group. Slavin observed that the most successful methods for increasing student achievement were the ones in which group scores were composed of the sum of individual achievements, or in which each member had a unique task for which he or she could be held accountable. Of the 27 studies in which all group members studied the same material and group rewards were provided based on the individual achievements of the groups members, 24 (89%) showed significantly positive effects on achievement in comparison with the control groups. In contrast, increased achievement was not observed in any of the nine studies in which all group members studied the same material and the group was rewarded based on a group product, or in which no group reward was given. Among the 10 studies in which each student had a unique task, 5 reported positive effects on achievement. Among these 5 studies, the most successful methods were those in which the groups were rewarded on the basis of the sum of individual test scores, such as Jigsaw II, or on the basis of a group product, as in Group-Investigation.

The pervasiveness of the effects of cooperative learning across settings and types of students was also documented in Slavin's (1983a) review. He concluded that the positive effects of cooperative learning methods on student achievement appeared just as frequently (a) in elementary and as in secondary schools; (b) in urban, suburban, and rural schools; (c) in academic subjects as diverse as math, language arts, social studies, and reading; (d) with high, average, and low achievers; and (e) with minority students as with white students.

With regard to handicapped children, several researchers have demonstrated that cooperative learning strategies improved academic performance and/or relationships between mainstreamed and nonmainstreamed students (Armstrong, Johnson, & Balow, 1981; Ballard, Corman, Gottlieb, & Kaufman, 1977; Madden & Slavin, 1983). Perhaps the best example of this research is the Slavin, Madden, and Leavey (1984) investigation, where they used Team Assisted Instruction (TAI: a math program that combines individualized instruction, cooperative learning teams, and direct instruction) for a 24-week period with 1371 third, fourth, and fifth graders of whom 113 were academically handicapped. Standardized mathematics computations, concepts, and applications scales served as dependent variables. The results indicated significant positive treatment effects favoring TAI for math computations only. No Treatment × Handicap interaction was found. The positive effects on the achievement of the mainstreamed academically handicapped students provided important confirmation of Madden and Slavin's (1983) conclusion that for mainstreaming to be maximally effective for the academically handicapped student, the regular class program must be designed to accomodate diverse instructional needs.

A causal perusal of school psychology's journals indicated only a handful of investigators employing group contingencies and no empirical reports of cooperative learning interventions! This is discouraging given the documented *effectiveness* and apparent *acceptability* of these interventions.

Summary and Conclusions

Taken together, the research reviewed in this section provides strong evidence that behavioral procedures such as contingent reinforcement, feedback, praise, self-recording, and group contingencies are all capable of affecting behavior change in academic performance. Additionally, procedures specifically targeted at increasing academic engagement, such as peer tutoring and cooperative learning, appear to be related to improvements in academic responding.

Although these procedures all seem to be effective, they have in common an underlying component of contingent reinforcement. Even peer tutoring, designed to affect academic performance indirectly, provides for the earning of points contingent upon correct academic responding. Given the strong effects that reinforcement has on behavior in general, it is likely that the inclusion of a reinforcement component is a critical variable for improving academic behavior. The procedures discussed in this section are applicable across types of academic skills. Numerous studies have been conducted employing these or some variation of these procedures in changing specific academic skills. For a detailed review of interventions for academic performance difficulties in reading, math, spelling, and other language arts, see Shapiro (1987), Hallahan et al. (1983), Kerr and Lambert (1982), Piersel (1987), and Slavin, Sharan, Kagan, Lazanowitz, Webb, and Schmuck (1985).

INTERVENTION PROGRAMS

Adaptive Learning Education Model

Description

The concept of adaptive education is founded on the principle that individual differences in student learning require educational programs to be matched to student characteristics (Wang & Walberg, 1983). Specifically, education is considered adaptive when instruction is altered depending on student background, abilities, past performance, interest, time to acquire new skills, and the types of competencies needed to learn the instructed skills. Indeed, the general concept of individualizing or adapting instruction for handicapped learners has been widely accepted (Wang, 1980a; Wang & Walberg, 1983).

Over the last 10 years, several major projects have demonstrated the implementation of adaptive education. One of the most systematic, wide-scale programs has been the Adaptive Education Learning Model (ALEM) (Wang, 1983). The ALEM is an instructional program developed at the University of Pittsburgh Learning Research and Development Center and evaluated across 10 sites and 156 classes between kindergarten through fourth grade. All implementation sites for the ALEM were part of the Nationl Follow Through Program or the Handicapped Children's Model Program. The primary goal of the original ALEM project was to demonstrate that children of varying education levels could be accommodated effectively within the context of regular classroom settings and that each student could acquire basic academic skills within that setting. Additionally, the ALEM was designed to teach students how to cope and adapt to the social demands of the classroom setting.

The ALEM consists of five major components: (a) a basic skills curriculum using highly structured and hierarchically arranged prescriptive activities, and an open-ended exploratory component allowing students to self-select activities based on individual learning needs and interests; (b) a self-management system designed to maximize instructional resources; (c) a family component incorporating extensive communication and reinforcement of skills between the school and home environments; (d) a flexible grouping and instructional team system within the classroom; and (e) a data-based staff development program (Wang & Walberg, 1983). The integration of the five components is a critical aspect of the ALEM, yet to date no attempt to examine the specific influences of the single components has been reported.

Basic Skills Curriculum Component.

Probably the heart of the adaption that occurred in the ALEM project was the development of a highly structured, prescriptive learning component. The curriculum used built-in diagnostic procedures using criterion-referenced tests to provide frequent feedback to teachers on student mastery. In this way, students neither repeated tasks they had mastered nor were being instructed on tasks for which they lacked prerequisite skills (Wang & Walberg, 1983). Steps within skills hierarchies

were purposely kept small to ensure success with even the least able students. Specific curricula materials varied, as some ALEM sites used materials developed at the University of Pittsburgh (e.g., Resnick, Wang, & Kaplan, 1973) and others adapted already exiting published curricula.

A variety of instructional procedures were used within the ALEM project. This included the use of paper-and-pencil tasks and manipulative materials within individual seatwork activities as well as individual and small-group teacher instruction. In addition, computerized data collection was employed successfully in some sites (Wang, 1980a).

Self-Management Component.

To maximize the time for learning, students were taught to be responsible for planning and completing their own tasks. Specifically, students used the Self-Schedule System (Wang, 1976, 1980a) to plan their daily instructional activities. An anticipated outcome of such a system was that teachers could devote more time to instruction and less to managing behavior and discipline (e.g., Borg & Ascione, 1982).

Family Involvement Component.

Although not viewed as important as other components of the model, the known relationship between parental interest in school and children's academic success made parental involvement within the ALEM critical. The specific type of involvement varied from site to site; however, at minimum parents were made aware of the child's academic activities, were informed about the curriculum, and were kept appraised of the child's progress (Wang, 1980a). The primary goal was to increase the communication between school and home.

Flexible Groupings Component.

Several types of instructional groupings were used in the ALEM. Cross-age groupings of children were common. This provided opportunities for flexible use of space, teaching resources, and materials. Students who were making unusually slow progress or who were accelerating through the materials could be accommodated easily. Use of ungraded classrooms with multiage groups also provided efficient use of teacher time as well as potential use of peer tutoring. There are substantial data, which we have already discussed, which suggest that the use of peer tutoring can provide effective increases in opportunities to respond as well as significant gains in both tutor and tutee academic skills (e.g., Young et al., 1983).

Team teaching was also employed exclusively in the ALEM. The instructional arrangement was able to meet the needs of individual students effectively while efficiently deploying teacher resources. Additionally, team teaching allowed teachers with interest and expertise to instruct in areas of specific interests (Wang, 1980a).

Data-Based Staff Development Component. The evaluative feedback included written plans and procedures for increasing the school staff's implementation of the ALEM with high degrees of treatment integrity. The extensive program involving criterion-referenced testing was also employed to provide teachers with the necessary information to determine if their instructional adaptations were consistent with the ALEM.

Effectiveness

Wang, Gennari, and Waxman (1985) and Wang and Walberg (1983) reported data on the integrity of the implementation of the ALEM across sites. The Implementation Assessment Battery for Adaptive Instruction (Wang, 1980b) was employed in 94 classrooms to assess whether specific domains, such as materials, space, facilities, time, and personnel, were being employed in ways consistent with the model. Results of this analysis demonstrated that the overall average integrity scores during Spring across all sites was 85%. Patterns of change in implementation across time suggested significant improvements in treatment integrity between Fall and Spring at all sites. Further studies examining differences between ALEM and non-ALEM classes clearly suggest that even in the low-implementation classes, significant and substantial differences existed between the ALEM and non-ALEM classrooms (Wang & Walberg, 1983).

A particularly important assumption of the ALEM model is the expected increase in student engaged time. Wang and Walberg (1983) investigated this relationship by obtaining data on the behavior of students and teachers through the Student Behavior Observation Schedule (SBOS) (Wang, 1984). The SBOS is a direct observation measure which was collected on every student in 72 classrooms. Results of this study showed that the higher the degree of implementation of the

ALEM, the greater the frequency of instructional interactions between students and teachers, the fewer disruptive peer interactions, and the less time spent in solitary work. Examination of the data also showed that students in the highest implementation classes spent the least time in individual nonacademic activities and more time in self-initiated learning activities.

Although the data obtained on treatment integrity clearly suggested that the ALEM was implemented with a high degree of success in most sites, the outcome of student achievement was most critical to an effective model. Data obtained on standardized achievement tests collected in the spring of each year found that ALEM students scored well above the estimated population norms for students from other non-ALEM classrooms which were also part of the National Follow-Through Program. Indeed, students in ALEM classes scored between the 46th and 58th percentiles in reading achievement and between the 44th and 66th percentiles in math. Further, significantly more ALEM students than predicted scored in the upper quartile, whereas significantly fewer ALEM students than predicted scored in the lowest quartile. Data were also provided on the mean objectives mastered in math and reading; however, no comparison data on non-ALEM classes were available.

ALEM and Mainstreaming. Another major purpose of the ALEM project was to demonstrate that identified exceptional students can receive all instruction within a fully mainstreamed, regular education environment. Wang and Birch (1984) reported a study conducted in 1980–1981 which compared the effectiveness of the ALEM program across 179 children between kindergarten and third grade. Students in the sample had been assigned randomly to ALEM or non-ALEM classes. Within the ALEM classes, handicapped students received all instruction within the regular classroom environment. Similar identified students in non-ALEM classes spent the morning sessions receiving reading and mathematics in a special education resource room. Data were obtained using the SBOS, standardized achievement test scores in reading and math, and the Perceived Competence Scale (PCS) (Harter, 1982) to assess student self-perception of cognitive, social, and physical competence. Program costs were also examined to determine the cost-effectiveness of the ALEM.

Examination of the data from the 11 handicapped students in the ALEM and non-ALEM classes indicated that when assessed in April, ALEM students were engaged in significantly more independent work, higher levels of on-task behavior, and significantly fewer teacher-directed activities than were non-ALEM students. Further, positive changes that occurred in the A.M. sessions for the behavior of ALEM students from September to April generalized to the P.M. sessions as well. In contrast, changes in the resource room students across this same period did not generalize to the mainstreamed settings.

Comparisons of scores on the Stanford Achievement Test in math and reading found that handicapped students in the ALEM classes made significant gains in reading and equivalent gains in math compared to non-ALEM students. Further, examination of the student attitude scale suggested that handicapped students in ALEM rated their own competence higher than non-ALEM students. Additionally, non-ALEM handicapped students showed lower self-ratings on all scales compared to regular non-ALEM students. In the ALEM classes, handicapped students' ratings equaled that of their peers.

An interesting analysis was completed regarding program costs. Despite a substantially higher start-up cost compared to regular education programs, the district saved almost $20,000 in costs by the third year of implementation due to the redeployment of current district special education resources within the mainstreamed settings.

Data from the ALEM classes suggest strongly the potential efficacy of a full-time, mainstreaming model for the education of handicapped pupils. These findings are consistent with other studies which have found that mainstreamed pupils outperform nonmainstreamed students in academic and social outcomes (Leinhardt & Pallay, 1982; Wang & Baker, 1985–1986).

Critical Analysis and Future Issues

Wang and her associates have presented a coherent and valuable model for adaptive education. Unfortunately, close examination of the outcome data is somewhat disappointing. For example, Berliner (1985), in a critique of the model, questioned the degree to which the model is really adaptive. In a path analysis reported by Wang et al. (1985), the relationship between classroom process (i.e., interaction between teachers,

students, and peers, instructional settings, types and initiation of activities) and instructional planning was negative. This suggested that less planning and management by teachers resulted in increased classroom process. Clearly, the ALEM would therefore not be related to behaviors such as time on-task, distraction, and other variables affecting academic performance. Berliner pointed out that other than adapting to differences in *rate* of learning, the ALEM does not appear to adapt to types of student needs, such as variations in responsiveness to instructional materials, types of feedback, need for structure, and so on.

Another point that is bothersome about the data reported on the ALEM is the failure to examine academic outcomes for individuals within the program. All data reported are aggregated from large groups of students and based on standardized achievement measures. It seems that the model would be ideally suited to the use of curriculum-based assessment (e.g., Shapiro, 1987; Shapiro & Lentz, 1986). Such data would provide more direct measurements of the impact of the ALEM on individual student achievement. Given the underlying philosophy of an adaptive education program, this approach seem logical. Although data reported by Wang and Walberg (1983) on the number of items mastered in the curriculum is in a positive direction, the failure to provide more individualized data of this nature as well as comparison data on non-ALEM students is a serious omission.

Although the research that supports the ALEM model has been questioned (e.g., Hallahan, Keller, McKinney, Lloyd, & Bryan, 1988), the ALEM offers a strong demonstration of the potential use of adaptive education. Its potential for affecting the education of academically handicapped students within the regular education system is currently untapped. Additional research is needed, however, to understand and document that the methodology has the desired impact at the individual student level.

Direct Instruction
Description
The term *direct instruction* has been applied in two related but different ways in the intervention literature. Rosenshine (1979) has used the term "direct instruction" (not capitalized) to refer to instructional strategies that enhance a student's academic engaged time. Specifically, he considers tech-

niques that result in frequent student responses, high-paced instruction, teacher control of material, and similar methods designed to increase engaged time as indicative of direct instruction. No emphasis is given to the specific curriculum materials.

Direct Instruction (capitalized) is the instructional approach conceptualized by Engelmann and his colleagues (e.g., Engelmann & Carnine, 1982) and implemented and evaluated through Project Follow Through in the late 1960s and 1970s. Although Direct Instruction contains all of the characteristics described by Rosenshine (1979), it also contains very specific curricular materials that contain explicit instructions for teaching.

The principle on which Direct Instruction materials have been developed is that for *all* students to learn, materials and teacher presentation must be clear and unambiguous (Gersten, Woodward, & Darch, 1986). Although this sounds simple, examinations of many instructional programs, particularly basal reading materials, have not been designed with sufficient precision to allow mildly handicapped students to succeed. Direct Instruction curricula have been developed so that students initially acquiring a skill are presented with questions for which there can be only one correct response. Additionally, materials are generated that offer simple but elegant strategies for application (Gersten et al., 1986). For example, after teaching students to discriminate short and long vowel sounds of three vowels (o, a, i), students would be taught a rule: "If the last letter is *e*, you'll hear a letter *name* in the word. You'll hear the name of the letter that is underlined." Practice using the rule is then implemented with students constantly being asked to recite the rule as the skill is mastered.

Development of the Direct Instruction model was based on two guiding principles: teach more in less time and control the details of what happens (Becker & Carnine, 1981). All instructional activities are designed to increase academic engaged time and to focus on teaching the general case. What the teacher is to say and do is written out within teaching manuals. Student progress is monitored using criterion-referenced progress tests and the methods for obtaining these data are written explicitly in the manuals.

Examination of the teaching techniques of the Direct Instruction model reveals variations based on the skill levels of the students (Becker & Carnine, 1981). Whereas initial acquisition of skills in reading relies heavily on small-group instruction and unison responding, later skills are instructed through more independent and large class instruction. Additionally, less reliance on unison responding occurs in later grades. Feedback mechanisms also change across grades, with children in the early grades receiving immediate feedback and older children getting delayed feedback. The overriding emphasis in the model is on mastery instruction. Students being instructed in small groups are not advanced until *all* students in the group achieve mastery on the skill taught. For example, Stein and Goldman (1980) compared the performance of learning-disabled students (ages 6 to 8) being instructed in either the Direct Instruction reading curriculum (DISTAR) or the Palo Alto series. Although the two series are very similar in content, a critical difference in the teaching strategy is the insistence of the DISTAR curriculum that mastery of skills by each student in the group be obtained before proceeding. By contrast, the Palo Alto curriculum allows teachers to proceed when most students have acquired the instructed skill. Results of their study showed that the mean gain for DISTAR was 15 months (over the 9-month period) compared to a gain of 7 months for the Palo Alto curriculum.

The Direct Instruction model contains at least seven basic teaching strategies. Each of these are presented briefly, because they serve to guide the development of academic interventions in general. Readers interested in more detailed descriptions of these techniques should see Engelmann and Carnine (1982).

Scripted Presentations. Each lesson is scripted for the teacher. The exact words to be used in presenting materials along with appropriate sequencing of teacher questions and responses to student performance is offered. Becker and Carnine (1981) note that this feature of the model is frequently criticized, noting that scripted lessons may stifle teacher creativity and initiative. They point out, however, that the use of scripts allows one to use a pretested strategy with proven effectiveness. Scripts also reduce the time needed for teachers to prepare lessons. Further, scripted lessons make the monitoring of student performance easier since student lessons are standardized.

Small-Group Instruction. Much of the teaching in the model, particularly at the lower grades, is done within small groups. This structure permits frequent student responses, more direct adult contact, teacher-controlled instruction, and opportunities for modeling by other students. These groups often consist of 5 to 10 students and occur throughout the instructional day. At higher grades, reliance on small groups is reduced and more independent instruction is employed.

Unison Responding. During the small-group instruction, students frequently are asked to respond in unison. This creates an atmosphere of high pace, high intensity, and active participation of students.

Signals. Another important component of the Direct Instruction model is the use of signals within the instructional process. Signals are used to help pace students through a lesson as to when responses should be given. For example, in sounding out a word, students might be told to say a sound aloud as long as the teacher touches it. This procedure would ensure that students blended correctly as the teacher moved from sound to sound across the word. Effective use of signals can also provide opportunities to allow students who need a few extra seconds to formulate a response not to be dominated by the more able students in a group.

Pacing. Through the use of signals, unison responding, and small-group instruction, the pacing of instruction is clearly controlled. Becker and Carnine (1981) point out that students are likely to be more attentive to fast-paced presentation. However, the use of a fast-paced instructional strategy does not mean that teachers rush students into giving responses when more time is needed to formulate answers. Carnine (1976) demonstrated that students answered correctly about 80% of the time when in a fast-paced condition (12 questions per minute) as compared to answering correctly 30% of the time in a slow rate condition (questions per minute).

Corrections. Correcting errors is an important part of the instructional process of Direct Instruction. Research on correcting errors, while limited, suggests the need for students to attend to the feedback and rehearse the corrected strategies for the results of error correction to be effective (Fink & Carnine, 1975). Additionally, modeling of correct responses can be effective, but the correction also needs to be applied in subsequent situations (Stromer, 1975).

Praise. Not surprisingly, the use of praise within the small-group, fast-paced instructional sessions is a critical component of the Direct Instruction model. The relationship of teacher attention to increasing student attentiveness is well documented (e.g., Cossairt, Hall, & Holman, 1973; Hall, Lund, & Jackson, 1968).

Effectiveness

The Direct Instruction model was one of the major models of compensatory education for low-functioning students evaluated through Project Follow Through in the 1970s. Although the evaluation conducted by the Abt Associates in 1977 has been considered controversial regarding the fairness of the measures employed, adequacy of the sample, and appropriateness of the analysis, the evaluation did provide direct comparisons of eight different models of compensatory education. Each model was based on a different instructional philosophy, ranging from emphases on increased children's self-esteem, language development, parent education, cognitive development, behavior analysis, or direct instruction. Comparisons were made using measures of basic skills (word knowledge, spelling, language, math computation), cognitive conceptual skills (reading, math concepts, math problem solving, Raven's Progressive Matrices), and affective measures (Coopersmith Self-Esteem Inventory and Intellectual Achievement Responsibility Scale). These measures were combined into a measure entitled the Index of Significant Outcomes (ISO).

Results of the Abt report are clear with regard to the comparison of approaches. Examination of overall ISO scores found that the Direct Instruction model ranked first across cognitive, affective, and basic skills measures. Additionally, in none of the subareas examined did Direct Instruction rank any less than third (Becker & Carnine, 1981).

The Abt report also compared the models on four subtests of the Metropolitan Achievement Tests: Total reading, Total math, Spelling, and Language. In all areas, students in the Direct Instruction model far outscored all others, with average scores across the four basic skill areas ranging from the 40th percentile in Reading to the

50th percentile in Spelling and Language. Math fell at the 48th percentile.

Data obtained by Becker and Engelmann (1978) at the Direct Instruction sites provide even stronger evidence of the success of the model. Scores obtained on the Wide Range Achievement Test given at the pre-kindergarten and third-grade periods found students at or above the 50th percentile in reading, arithmetic, and spelling. In a further follow-up, Becker and Gersten (1982) reported WRAT and MAT scores for all students who had been at the 3-year Direct Instruction sites who were now in the fifth and sixth grades. Results showed that these students outperformed a matched group of students who were not involved in Direct Instruction. These effects were particularly strong in reading, math problem solving, and spelling. Effects in MAT science, math concepts, math computation, and word knowledge were not significantly different. One curious finding of the follow-up study has been that compared to a national norm sample, the participants lose ground after Follow-Through ended. This suggests that without continued instruction using similar strategies, children may be unlikely to continue progressing at a rate commensurate with their peers.

Critical Analysis and Future Issues

Comparisons of the Direct Instruction model and the ALEM model previously described show apparently very different approaches to academic interventions with handicapped children. Indeed, where the basic principle underlying the ALEM is that instruction needs to be adapted to individual needs, the Direct Instruction model takes the opposite position—that the sequence of a teaching program is defined by *what is to be taught, not whom* (Becker & Carnine, 1981). In the Direct Instruction model, all children receive the identical sequence of instruction using identical teaching strategies. What is varied is the *entry level* of instruction and the trials to mastery.

Another major difference between the ALEM and Direct Instruction is the degree to which learning occurs independently. Within the ALEM model, as demonstrated in the extensive treatment integrity data reported by Wang and Walberg (1983), students spend much of their time engaged in individual assignments. In contrast, Direct Instruction places teachers in a direct, structured, and controlled teaching position. Becker and Carnine

(1981) argued strongly that controlling the sequences of instruction and providing systematic training is necessary for efficient learning to occur. Further, it is not just rote learning that can be acquired through Direct Instruction, but higher cognitive, problem-solving skills as well. As demonstrated by the ISO data, only the Direct Instruction model was successful in showing gains in cognitive-process objectives.

The results of the Abt studies and the strong showing of Direct Instruction should not be surprising. Indeed, significant research on the Follow-Through project has continued to demonstrate the superiority of Direct Instruction to other strategies for teaching basic skills to mildly handicapped learners. Further, the research on academic engaged time (Rosenshine, 1981; Rosenshine & Berliner, 1978), opportunities to respond (Greenwood et al., 1984), and other time variables related to educational gains (Gettinger, 1984) have demonstrated clearly that those educational processes which result in increased student engaged time will result in increased student performance.

Future research issues related to Direct Instruction do *not* need to center upon demonstrations of its effectiveness. These data exist and are convincing. More important, however, efforts need to be devoted to examining how these strategies can be adopted more widely into the educational system for handicapped students. It is unfortunate that the technology and resources exist for accelerating the academic performance of low-achieving youngsters, but continue to go relatively untapped.

CONCLUSIONS

In this chapter we reviewed a variety of instructional techniques and two major intervention programs designed to enhance children's academic performance. Most of the intervention procedures discussed had a decidedly behavioral orientation and a substantial empirical base. It was suggested that once learning content is adjusted to an appropriate entry level, students' academic performance can be influenced successfully. In fact, it was argued that observable target behaviors such as academic engaged time, work completion, and work accuracy were much preferred over internal process variables or general classroom behaviors. Intervention procedures based on the manipulation of antecedents, consequences, or both of these have been demonstrated to affect reading, math, spelling, and written language functioning. In addition, procedures such as peer tutoring or cooperative learning have also been shown to have a positive effect on students' social behaviors.

Although each of the techniques and intervention programs reviewed has a solid research base, we pointed out potential disadvantages and issues for future research. In general, the most pervasive issues for future research concern the generalization and maintenance of the effects from a particular intervention. School psychologists additionally are challenged to identify or develop interventions that are time and cost-efficient, appropriate for a group of students varying in ability, and which can readily be implemented by most teachers. Thus, interventions must be acceptable to consumers as well as effective. Some of the intervention procedures presented in this chapter have been found highly acceptable (i.e., cooperative learning); however, several powerful methods (i.e., Direct Instruction) apparently lack wide acceptability. Researchers and practitioners are challenged to understand resistance to such techniques and to identify ways to modify them without negatively affecting effectiveness.

In closing, we return to the issue of conceptualizing academic problems. When such problems are analyzed broadly to include the assessment and manipulation of student, teacher, and curriculum variables, we believe that many direct intervention techniques have been demonstrated to enhance the observable performance of learners of all ages and abilities.

References

Ackerman, A. M., & Shapiro, E. S. (1984). Self-monitoring and work productivity with mentally retarded adults. *Journal of Applied Behavior Analysis, 17,* 403–407.

Allen, G. J., Chinsky, J. M., Larsen, S. W., Lochman, J. E., & Selinger, H. V. (1976). Community psychology and the schools: A behaviorally oriented multilevel preventive approach. Hillsdale, NJ: Lawrence Erlbaum.

Armstrong, B., Johnson, D. W., & Balow, B. (1981). Effects of cooperative vs. individualistic learning experiences on interpersonal attraction between learning-disabled and normal-progress elementary school students. *Contemporary Educational Psychology, 6,* 102–109.

Aronson, E. (1978). *The Jigsaw classroom.* Beverly Hills, CA: Sage.

Arter, J. A., & Jenkins, J. R. (1979). Differential diagnosis—Prescriptive teaching: A critical appraisal. *Review of Educational Research, 49,* 517–555.

Axelrod, S. (1973). Comparisons of individual and group contingencies in two special classes. *Behavior Therapy, 4,* 83–90.

Ballard, M., Corman, L., Gottlieb, J., & Kaufman, M. (1977). Improving the social status of mainstreamed retarded children. *Journal of Educational Psychology, 69,* 605–611.

Bandura, A. (1977). Self-efficacy: Toward a unifying theory of behavioral change. *Psychological Review, 84,* 191–215.

Barrish, H. H., Saunders, M., & Wolf, M. M. (1969). Good behavior game: Effects of individual contingencies for group consequences on disruptive behavior in a classroom. *Journal of Applied Behavior Analysis, 2,* 119–124.

Barsch, R. H. (1965). *A novigenic curriculum.* Madison, WI: Bureau for Handicapped Children.

Becker, W. C., & Carnine, D. W. (1981). Direct instruction: A behavior theory model for comprehensive educational intervention with the disadvantaged. In S. W. Bijou & R. Ruiz (Eds.), *Behavior modification: Contributions to education* (pp. 145–210). Hillsdale, NJ: Lawrence Erlbaum.

Becker, W. C., & Engelmann, S. (1978). Systems for basic instruction: Theory and applications. In A. C. Catania & T. A. Brigham (Eds.), *Handbook of applied behavior research* (pp. 325–377). New York: Irvington.

Becker, W. C., & Gersten, R. (1982). A follow-up of Follow Through: The later effects of the Direct Instruction model on children in fifth and sixth grads. *American Educational Research Journal, 19,* 75–92.

Bereiter, C., & Engelmann, S. (1966). *Teaching disadvantaged children in the preshool.* Englewood Cliffs, NJ: Prentice-Hall.

Berliner, D. A. (1979). Tempus enducare. In P. L. Peterson & H. L. Walberg (Eds.), *Research on teaching* (pp. 120–135). Berkley, CA: McCutchan.

Berliner, D. A. (1985). How is adaptive education like water in Arizona? In M. C. Wang & J. Walberg (Eds.), *Adapting to individual differences* (pp. 298–312). Berkeley, CA: McCutchan.

Bohlmeyer, E. M., & Burke, J. P. (1987). Selecting cooperative learning techniques: A consultative strategy guide. *School Psychology Review, 16,* 36–49.

Borg, W. R., & Ascione, F. R. (1982). Classroom management in elementary mainstreaming classrooms. *Journal of Educational Psychology, 74,* 84–85.

Bornstein, P. H., & Quevillon, R. P. (1976). The effects of a self-instructional package on overactive preschool toys. *Journal of Applied Behavior Analysis, 9,* 179–188.

Brophy, J. (1986). Teacher influences on student achievement. *American Psychologist, 41,* 1069–1077.

Browder, D. M., & Shapiro, E. S. (1985). Applications of self-management to individuals with severe handicaps: A review. *Journal of the Association for Persons with Severe Handicaps, 10,* 200–208.

Browder, D. M., Shapiro, E. S., & Ambrogio, B. M. (1986). Movement training: When trainer initiated reinforcement and self-monitoring are not enough. *International Journal of Rehabilitation Research, 9,* 363–372.

Carnine, D. (1976). Effects of two teacher presentation rates on off-task behavior, answering correctly, and participation. *Journal of Applied Behavior Analysis, 9,* 199–206.

Carnine, D., & Silbert, J. (1979). *Direct instruction reading.* Columbus, OH: Charles E. Merrill.

Carledge, G., & Milburn, J. F. (1983). Social skill assessment and teaching in the schools. In T. R. Kratochwill (Ed.), *Advances in school psychology* (Vol. 3, pp. 175–236). Hillsdale, NJ: Lawrence Erlbaum.

Centra, J. A., & Potter, D. A. (1980). School and teacher effects: An interrelational model. *Review of Educational Research, 50,* 273–291.

Chadwick, B. A., & Day, R. C. (1971). Systematic reinforcement: Academic performance or underachieving students. *Journal of Applied Behavior Analysis, 4,* 311–319.

Childs, R. E. (1983). Teaching rehearsal strategies for spelling to mentally retarded children. *Education and Training of the Mentally Retarded, 18,* 318–320.

Cone, J. D. (1987). Behavioral assessment with children and adolescents. In M. Hersen & V. B. Van Hasslet (Eds.), *Behavior therapy with children and adolescents: A clinical approach* (pp. 29–49). New York: Wiley.

Cone, J. D., & Hoier, T. S. (1986). Assessing children: The radical behavioral perspective. In R. Prinz (Ed.), *Advances in behavioral assessment of children and families* (Vol. 2, pp. 155–179). Greenwich, CT: JAI Press.

Cossiart, A., Hall, R. V., & Holman, B. L. (1973). The effects of experimenter's instruction, feedback, and praise on teacher praise and student attending behavior. *Journal of Applied Behavior Analysis, 6,* 89–100.

Crouch, P. L., Gresham, F. M., & Wright, W. R. (1985). Interdependent and independent group contingencies with immediate and delayed reinforcement for controlling classroom behavior. *Journal of School Psychology, 23,* 177–187.

Elliott, S. N., Turco, T. L., & Gresham, F. M. (1987). Consumers' and clients' pretreatment acceptability ratings of classroom-based group contingencies. *Journal of School Psychology, 25,* 145–154.

Engelmann, S., & Carnine, D. W. (1982). *Theory of Instruction.* New York: Irvington.

Felton, J. L., & Nelson, R. O. (1984). Inter-assessor agreement on hypothesized controlling variables and treatment proposals. *Behavioral Assessment, 6,* 199–208.

Fink, T. W., & Carnine, D. W. (1975). Contol of arithmetic errors using informational feedback and errors. *Journal of Applied Behavior Analysis, 8,* 461.

Fox, D. E. C., & Kendall, P. C. (1983). Thinking through academic problems: Applications of cognitive behavior therapy to learning. In T. R. Kratochwill (Ed.), *Advances in school psychology* (Vol. 3, pp. 269–301). Hillsdale, NJ: Lawrence Erlbaum.

Fredrick, W. C., Walberg, H. J., & Rasher, S. P. (1979). Time, teacher comments, and achievement in urban high schools. *Journal of Educational Research, 73,* 63–65.

Friedling, C., & O'Leary, S. G. (1979). Effects of self-instruction on second and third grade hyperactive children: A failure to replicate. *Journal of Applied Behavior Analysis, 12,* 211–219.

Frostig, M. (1967). Testing as a basis for educational therapy. *Journal of Special Education, 2,* 15–34.

Gersten, R., Woodward, J., & Darch C. (1986). Direct Instruction: A research-based approach to curriculum design and teaching. *Exceptional Children, 53,* 17–31.

Gettinger, M. (1984). Achievement as a function of time spent in learning and time needed for learning. *American Educational Research Journal, 21,* 617–628.

Glynn, E. L., Thomas, J. D., & Shee, S. M. (1973). Behavioral self-control of on-task behavior in an elementary classroom. *Journal of Applied Behavior Analysis, 6,* 105–113.

Greenwood, C. R., Delquadri, J. C., & Hall, R. V. (1984). Opportunity to respond and student academic performance. In W. L. Heward, T. E. Heron, D. S. Hill, & J. Trap-Porter (Eds.), *Focus on behavior analysis in education.* Columbus, OH: Charles E. Merrill.

Greenwood, C. R., Dinwiddie, G., Terry, B., Wade, L., Stanley, S. O., Thibadeau, S., & Delquadri, J. C. (1984). Teacher versus peer-mediated instruction: An ecobehavioral analysis of achievement outcomes. *Journal of Applied Behavior Analysis, 17,* 521–538.

Gresham, F. M., & Gresham, G. N. (1982). Interdependent, dependent, and independent group contingencies for controlling disruptive behavior. *Journal of Special Education, 16,* 101–110.

Hall, R. V., Delquadri, J., Greenwood, C. R., & Thurston, L. (1982). The importance of opportunity to respond in children's academic success. In E. B. Edgar, N. G. Haring, J. R. Jenkins, & C. G. Pious (Eds.), *Mentally handicapped children: Education and training* (pp. 107–140). Baltimore: University Park Press.

Hall, R. V., Lund, D., & Jackson, D. (1968). Effects of teacher attention on study behavior. *Journal of Applied Behavior Analysis, 1,* 1–12.

Hallahan, D. P., Keller, C. E., McKinney, J. D., Lloyd, J. W., & Bryan, T. (1988). Examining the research base of the regular education initiative: Effeicacy studies and the adaptive learning environments model. *Journal of Learning Disabilities, 21,* 29–35.

Hallahan, D. P., Lloyd, J. W., Kaufman, J. M., & Loper, A. B. (1983). Academic problems. In R. Morris & T. R. Kratochwill (Eds.), *The practice of child behavior therapy* (pp. 113–141). Elmsford, NY: Pergamon Press.

Hallahan, D., Lloyd, J., Kosiewicz, M., Kauffman, J., & Graves, A. (1979). Self-monitoring of attention as a treatment for a learning disabled boys' off-task behavior. *Learning Disability Quarterly, 2,* 24–32.

Haring, N. C., & Hauck, M. (1969). Improved learning conditions in the establishment of reading skills with disabled readers. *Exceptional Children, 35,* 341–352.

Harter, S. (1982). The Perceived Competence Scale for children. *Child Development, 53,* 87–97.

Hoge, R. D., & Andrews, D. A. (1987). Enhancing academic performance: Issues in target selection. *School Psychology Review, 16,* 228–238.

Hoier, T. S., McConnell, S., & Pallay, A. G. (1987). Observational assessment for planning and evaluating educational transitions: An initial analysis of template matching. *Behavioral Assessment, 9,* 6–20.

Holman, J., & Baer, D. M. (1979). Facilitating generalization of on-task behavior through self-monitoring of academic tasks. *Journal of Autism and Developmental Disabilities, 9,* 429–446.

Hopkins, B. L., Schultz, R. C., & Garton, K. L. (1971). The effects of access to a playroom on the rate and quality of printing and writing of first and second grade students. *Journal of Applied Behavior Analysis, 10,* 121–126.

Hundert, J., & Bucher B. (1978). Pupils' self-scored arithmetic performance: A practical procedure for maintaining accuracy. *Journal of Applied Behavior Analysis, 11,* 304.

Iwata, B., Dorsey, M., Slifer, K., Bauman, K., & Richman, G. G. (1982). Toward a functional analysis of self-injury. *Analysis and Intervention in Developmental Disabilities, 2,* 3–20.

Jenkins, J. R., Larson, K., & Fleisher, L. (1983). Effects of error correction on ward recognition and reading comprehension. *Learning Disability Quarterly, 6,* 139–145.

Johnson, D. W., & Johnson, R. T. (1975). *Learning together and alone.* Englewood Cliffs, NJ: Prentice-Hall.

Johnson, D. W., & Johnson R. T. (1985). Cooperative learning and adaptive education. In M. C. Wang & H. J. Walbert (Eds.), *Adapting instruction to individual differences* (pp. 105–134). Berkely, CA: McCutchan.

Johnson, D. W., Maruyama, G., Johnson, R., Nelson, D., & Skon, L. (1981). The effects of cooperative, competitive, and individualistic goal structures on achievement: A meta-analysis. *Psychological Bulletin, 89,* 47–62.

Johnston, M. B., Whitman, T. L., & Johnson, M. (1980). Teaching addition and subtraction to mentally retarded children: A self-instructional program. *Applied Research in Mental Retardation, 1,* 141–160.

Kagan, S. (1985). dimensions of cooperative classroom structures. In R. E. Slavin, S. Sharan, S. Kagan, R. H. Lazarowitz, C. Webb, & R. Schmuck (Eds.), *Learning to cooperate, cooperating to learn* (pp. 67–96). New York: Plemun Press.

Kanfer, F. H. (1971). The maintenance of behavior by self-generated stimuli and reinforcement. In A. Jacobs & L. B. Sachs (Eds.), *The psychology of private events* (pp. 39–58). New York: Academic Press.

Karoly, P. (1982). Perspectives on self-management and behavior change. In P. Karoly & F. H. Kanfer (Eds.), *Self-management and behavior change: From theory to practice* (pp. 3–31). Elmsford, NY: Pergamon Press.

Karoly, P., & Kanfer, F. H. (Eds.). (1982). *Self-management and behavior change. From theory to practice.* Elmsford, NY: Pergamon Press.

Kazdin, A. E. (1985). Selection of target behaviors: The relationship of the treatment focus to clinical dysfunction. *Behavioral Assessment, 7,* 33–47.

Keith, T. Z. (1982). Time spent on homework and high school grades: A large-sample path analysis. *Journal of Educational Psychology, 74,* 248–253.

Kephart, N. C. (1971). *The slow learner in the classroom* (2nd ed). Columbus, OH: Charles E. Merrill.

Kerr, M. M., & Lambert, D. L. (1982). Behavior modification of children's written language. In M. Hersen, R. Eisler, & P. M. Miller (Eds.), *Progress in behavior modification* (Vol. 13, pp. 79–109). New York: Academic Press.

Lahey, B. B. (1979). *Behavior therapy with hyperactive and learning disabled children.* New York: Oxford University Press.

Lahey, B. B., McNess, M. P., & Brown, C. C. (1973). Modification of deficits in reading for comprehension. *Journal of Applied Behavior Analysis, 6,* 475–480.

Leinhardt, G., & Pallay, A. (1982). Restrictive educational settings: Exile or haven? *Review of Educational Research, 52,* 557–578.

Lentz, F. E., Jr. (1988). On-task behavior, academic performance, and classroom interventions. *School Psychology Review, 17,* 243–257.

Lentz, F. E., Jr., & Shapiro, E. S. (1986). Functional assessment of the academic environment. *School Psychology Review, 15,* 346–357.

Litlow, L., & Pumroy, D. K. (1975). A brief review of classroom group-oriented contingencies. *Journal of Applied Behavior Analysis, 8,* 341–347.

Lovitt, T. C., Guppy, T. E., & Blattner, J. E. (1969). The use of free time contingency with fourth graders to increase spelling accuracy. *Behavior Research and Therapy, 7,* 151–156.

Mace, F. C., & Kratochwill, T. R. (1985). Theories of reactivity in self-monitoring: A comparison of cognitive-behavioral and operant models. *Behavior Modification, 9,* 323–343.

Mace, F. C., Yankanich, M. A., & West, B. (in press). Toward a methodology of experimental analysis and treatment of aberrant classroom behaviors. *Special Services in the Schools.*

Madden, N. A., & Slavin, R. E. (1983). Cooperative learning and social acceptance of mainstreamed academically handicapped students. *Journal of Special Education, 17,* 171–182.

Mash, E. J. (1985). Some comments on target selection in behavior therapy. *Behavioral Assessment, 7,* 63–78.

McKenzie, M. L., & Budd, K. S. (1981). A peer tutoring package to increase mathematics performance: Examination of generalized changes in classroom behavior. *Education and Treatment of Children, 4,* 1–15.

McLaughlin, T. F. (1981). The effects of individual and group contingencies on reading performance of special education students. *Contemporary Educational Psychology, 6,* 76–79.

McLaughlin, T. F., Burgess, N., & Sackville-West, L. (1981). Effects of self-recording and self-recording + matching on academic performance. *Child Behavior Therapy, 3,* 17–27.

Meichenbaum, D., & Goodman, J. (1971). Training impulsive children to talk to themselves: A means of developing self-control. *Journal of Abnormal Psychology, 77,* 115–126.

Nelson, R. O. (1977). Assessment and therapeutic functions of self-monitoring. In M. Hersen, R. M. Eisler, & P. M. Miller (Eds.), *Progress in behavior modification* (Vol. 5, pp. 263–308). New York: Academic Press.

Nelson, R. O., & Hayes, S. C. (1981). Theoretical explanations for reactivity in self-monitoring. *Behavior Modification, 5,* 3–14.

Nelson, R. O., & Hayes, S. C. (1986). *Conceptual foundations of behavioral assessment.* New York: Guilford Press.

O'Leary, S. D., & Dubey, D. R. (1979). Applications of self-control procedures by children: A review. *Journal of Applied Behavior Analysis, 12,* 449–465.

O'Leary, S. D., & O'Leary K. D. (1976). Behavior modification in the school. In H. Leitenberg (Ed.), *Handbook of behavior modification and behavior therapy.* Englewood Cliffs, NJ: Prentice-Hall.

Packard, R. (1970). The control of "classroom attention:" A group contingency for complex behavior. *Journal of Applied Behavior Analysis, 3,* 13–28.

Pacquin, M. J. (1978). The effects of pupil self graphing on academic performance. *Education and Treatment of Children, 1,* 5–16.

Piersel, W. C. (1987). Basic skills education. In C. A. Maher & S. G. Forman (Eds.), *A behavioral approach to education of children and youth* (pp. 39–74). Hillsdale, NJ: Lawrence Erlbaum.

Pigott, H. E., Fantuzzo, J. W., Heggie, D. L., & Clement, P. W. (1984). A student-administered group-oriented contingency intervention: Its efficacy in a regular classroom. *Child & Family Behavior Therapy, 6,* 41–56.

Redd, W. H., Ullman, R. K., Stelle, C., & Roesch, P. (1979). A classroom incentive program instituted by tutors after school. *Education and Treatment of Children, 2,* 169–176.

Resnick, L. B., Wang, M. C., & Kaplan, J. (1973). Behavior analysis in curriculum design: A hierarchically sequenced introductory mathematics curriculum. *Journal of Applied Behavior Analysis, 6,* 679–710.

Reynolds, C. R. & Gutkin, T. B. (1982). *The Handbook of School Psychology.* New York: Wiley.

Reynolds, M. C. (1984). Classification of students with handicaps. In E. W. Gordon (Ed.), *Review of research in education* (pp. 145–179). Washington, DC: AERA.

Rhode, G., Morgan, D. P., & Young, K. R. (1983). Generalization and maintenance of treatment gains of behaviorally handicapped students from resource rooms to regular classrooms using self-evaluation procedures. *Journal of Applied Behavior Analysis, 16,* 171–188.

Roberts, M., & Smith, D. D. (1980). The relationship among correct and error oral reading rates and comprehension. *Learning Disability Quarterly, 3,* 54–63.

Roberts, R. N., & Dick, M. L. (1982). Self-control in the classroom: Theoretical issues and practical applications. In T. R. Kratochwill (Ed.), *Advances in school psychology* (Vol. 2, pp. 275–314). Hillsdale, NJ: Lawrence Erlbaum.

Rosenshine, B. V. (1979). Content, time, and direct instruciton. In P. L. Peterson, & H. J. Walberg (Eds.), *Research on teaching* (pp. 28–56). Berkeley, CA: McCutchan.

Rosenshine, B. V. (1981). Academic engaged time, content covered, and direct instruction. *Journal of Education, 3,* 38–66.

Rosenshine, B. V., & Berliner, D. C. (1978). Academic engaged time. *British Journal of Teacher Education, 4,* 3–16.

Ruggles, T. R., & LeBlanc, J. M. (1982). Behavior analysis procedures in classroom teaching. In A. S. Bellack, M. Hersen, & A. E. Kazdin (Eds.), *International handbook of behavior modification and therapy* (pp. 959–996). New York: Plenum Press.

Santogrossi, D. A., O'Leary, K. D., Romanczyk, R. G., & Kaufman, K. F. (1973). Self-evaluation by adolescents in a psychiatric hospital school taken program. *Journal of Applied Behavior Analysis, 6,* 277–287.

Shapiro, E. S. (1981). Self-control procedures with the mentally retarded. In M. Hersen, R. M. Eisler, & P. M. Miller (Eds.), *Progress in behavior modification* (Vol. 12, pp. 265–297). New York: Academic Press.

Shapiro, E. S. (1986). Behavior modification: Self-control and cognitive procedures. In R. P. Barrett (Ed.), *Severe behavior disorders in the mentally retarded* (pp. 61–97). New York: Plenum Press.

Shapiro, E. S. (1987). *Behavioral assessment in school psychology.* Hillsdale, NJ: Lawrence Erlbaum.

Shapiro, E. S., & Ackerman, A. (1983). Increasing productivity rates in adult mentally retarded clients: The failure of self-monitoring. *Applied Research in Mental Retardation, 4,* 163–181.

Shapiro, E. S., Browder, D. M., & D'Huyvetters, K. (1984). Increasing academic productivity of severely, multihandicapped children with self-management: Idiosyncratic effects. *Analysis and Intervention in Developmental Disabilities, 4,* 171–188.

Shapiro, E. S., & Derr, T. F. (1987). School interventions for aggression. *Special Services in the Schools, 21,* 59–67.

Shapiro, E. S., & Goldberg, R. (1986). A comparison of group contingencies in increased spelling performances among sixth grade students. *School Psychology Review, 15,* 546–559.

Shapiro, E. S., & Klein, R. D. (1980). Self-management of classroom behavior with retarded disturbed children. *Behavior Modification, 4,* 83–97.

Shapiro, E. S., & Lentz, F. E., Jr. (1986). Behavioral

assessment of academic skills. In T. R. Kratochwill (Ed.), *Advances in school psychology* (Vol. 5, pp. 87–139). Hillsdale, NJ: Lawrence Erlbaum.

Sharan, S. (1980). Cooperative learning in small groups: Recent methods and effects on achievement, attitudes, and ethnic relations. *Review of Educational Research, 50,* 241–271.

Sharan, S., & Sharan, Y. (1976). *Small-group teaching.* Englewood Cliffs, NJ: Educational Technology.

Shores, R. E., Apolloni, T., & Norman, C. W. (1976). Changes in peer verbalizations accompanying individual and group contingencies to modify on-task behavior. *Perceptual and Motor Skills, 43,* 1155–1162.

Slavin, R. E. (1977). Classroom reward structure: An analytic and practical review. *Review of Educational Research, 47,* 633–650.

Slavin, R. E. (1980). *Using student team learning* (rev. ed.). Baltimore: Johns Hopkins University, Center for Social Organization of Schools.

Slavin, R. E. (1983a). *Cooperative learning.* New York: Longman.

Slavin, R. E. (1983b). Team-assisted individualization: A cooperative learning solution for adaptive instruction in mathematics. In M. C. Wang & H. J. Walberg (Eds.), *Adapting instruction to individual differences* (pp. 236–253). Berkeley, CA: McCutchan.

Slavin, R. E. (1985). An introduction to cooperative learning research. In R. E. Slavin, S. Sharan, S. Kagan, R. H. Lazarowitz, C Webb, & R. Schmuck (Eds.), *Learning to cooperate, cooperating to learn* (pp. 5–16). New York: Plenum Press.

Slavin, R. E., Madden, N. A., & Leavey, M. (1984). Effects of team assisted individualization on the mathematics achievement of academically handicapped and nonhandicapped students. *Journal of Educational Psychology, 76,* 813–819.

Slavin, R. E., Sharan, S., Kagan, S., Lazarowitz, R. H., Webb, C., & Schmuck, R. (1985). *Learning to cooperate, cooperating to learn.* New York: Plenum Press.

Stanley, S. O., & Greenwood, C. R. (1981). *SCISSAR: Code for instructional structure and student academic response: Observer's manual.* Kansas City, KS: University of Kansas–Lawrence, Bureau of Child Research, Junipar Garden Children's Project.

Stanley, S. O., & Greenwood, C. R. (1983). How much "opportunity to respond" does the minority disadvantaged student receive in school? *Exceptional Children, 49,* 370–373.

Stein, C. L. E., & Goldman, J. (1980). Beginning reading instruction for children with minimal brain dysfunctions. *Journal of Learning Disabilities, 13,* 219–222.

Stevenson, H. C., & Fantuzzo, J. W. (1984). Application of the "Generalization Map" to a self-control intervention with school-aged children. *Journal of Applied Behavior Analysis, 17,* 203–212.

Stromer, R. (1975). Modifying letter and number reversals in elementary school children. *Journal of Applied Behavior Analysis, 8,* 211.

Thurlow, M. L., Ysseldyke, J. E., Graden, J., & Al-

gozzine, B. (1984). Opportunity to learn for LD students receiving different levels of special education services. *Learning Disabilities Quarterly, 7,* 55–67.

Turkewitz, H., O'Leary, K. D., & Ironsmith, M. (1975). Generalization and maintenance of appropriate behavior through self-control. *Journal of Consulting and Clinical Psychology, 43,* 577–583.

Van Houten, R., Hill, S., & Parsons, M. (1975). An analysis of a performance feedback system: The effects of timing and feedback, public posting, and praise upon academic performance and peer interaction. *Journal of Applied Behavior Analysis, 8,* 449–457.

Van Houten, R., & Lai Fatt, D. (1981). The effects of public posting on high school biology test performance. *Education and Treatment of Children, 4,* 217–226.

Van Houten, R., & Thompson, C. (1976). The effects of explicit timing on math performance. *Journal of Applied Behavior Analysis, 9,* 227–230.

Wang, M. C. (Ed.). (1976). *The Self-Schedule System for instructional-learning management in adaptive school learning environments* (LRDC Publication Series 1976/9). Pittsburgh, PA: University of Pittsburgh, Learning Research and Development Center.

Wang, M. C. (1980a). Adaptive instruction: Building on diversity. *Theory into Practice, 9,* 122–128.

Wang, M. C. (1980b). *The degree of implementation assessment for the Adaptive Learning Environments Model.* Pittsburgh, PA: University of Pittsburgh, Learning Research and Development Center.

Wang, M. C. (in press). Effective mainstreaming is possible—Provided that . . . . *Analysis and Intervention in Developmental Disabilities.*

Wang, M. C., & Baker, E. T. (1985–1986). Mainstreaming programs: Design features and effects. *Journal of Special Education, 19,* 503–521.

Wang, M. C., & Birch, J. W. (1984). Comparison of a full-time mainstreaming program and a resource room approach. *Exceptional Children, 51,* 33–40.

Wang, M. C., Gennari, P., & Waxman, H. C. (1985). The Adaptive Learning Environmental Model: Design, implementation, and effects. In M. C. Wang & H. J. Walberg (Eds.), *Adapting instruction to individual differences* (pp. 121–235). Berkeley, CA: McCutchan.

Wang, M. C., & Walberg, H. J. (1983). Adaptive instruction and classroom time. *American Educational Research Journal, 20,* 601–626.

Whitman, T., & Johnston, M. B. (1983). Teaching addition and subtraction with regrouping to educable mentally retarded children: A group self-instructional training program. *Behavior Therapy, 14,* 127–143.

Wilson, F. E., & Evans, I. M. (1983). The reliability of target behavior selection assessment. *Behavioral Assessment, 5,* 15–32.

Wodarski, J. S., Hamblin, R. L., Buckholdt, D. R., & Ferritor, D. E. (1971). The effects of low performance group and individual contingencies on cooperative behaviors exhibited by fifth graders. *Psychological Record, 22,* 359–368.

Young, C., Hecimovic, A., & Salzberg, C. L. (1983). Tutor-tutee behavior of disadvantaged kindergarten children during peer tutoring. *Education and Treatment of Children, 6,* 123–135.

Ysseldyke, J. E., & Mirkin, P. K. (1982). The use of assessment information to plan instructional interventions: A review of the research. In C. R. Reynolds & T. B. Gutkin (Eds.), *The Handbook of School Psychology* (pp. 395–409). New York: Wiley.

26

THE USE OF ASSESSMENT INFORMATION TO PLAN INSTRUCTIONAL INTERVENTIONS: A REVIEW OF THE RESEARCH

JAMES E. YSSELDYKE
University of Minnesota
DOUGLAS MARSTON
Minneapolis Public Schools

The development of individualized educational programs (IEPs) for all handicapped students is a requirement of federal and state legislation. In developing IEPs, local education agencies (LEAs) must engage in intensive and continuous efforts to locate and identify handicapped students and must assess them to identify their educational needs. In this chapter we examine alternative perspectives on the ways in which assessment information may be used to plan instructional interventions for students who are experiencing academic or learning difficulties, and we review empirical evidence on the efficacy of those alternative perspectives.

Efforts to use assessment information for the purpose of planning instructional interventions clearly have their roots in early laboratory research on individual differences. Educators and psychologists long have observed and reported differences

in the extent to which individuals profit from instruction. Researchers have endeavored to understand why this is true and to develop ways of identifying instructional interventions that will be differentially effective for different kinds of individuals.

Observed differences in task performance and achievement have characteristically been attributed to differences in "learning ability" (however broadly that term has been perceived). The notion of learning ability (or abilities), as conceptualized within the framework of modern learning theory, is abstracted or inferred from observations of the performance of individuals in learning situations.

Early efforts to identify correlates of observed differences in task performance, and to develop mechanisms for identification of individual and group differences in learning and learning style on laboratory experimental tasks, have led to efforts to identify assessment instruments that could be used to predict the effectiveness of specific instructional interventions. These efforts are best evidenced in attempts to identify interactions between pupil characteristics, traits, or abilities and the effectiveness of special instructional strategies. Interest among educators in assessment-intervention links is most often traced to Cronbach's (1957) APA presidential address, in which he urged psychologists from correlation disciplines, who were concerned with individual differences, and psychologists from experimental disciplines, who were concerned with treatment differences, to pool their efforts in attempts to observe experimental effects for subjects of differing characteristics and to conduct investigations designed to identify aptitude-treatment interactions.

Building on the early notion that different students learn in different ways, that these differences can be identified and considered in the planning of instructional interventions, and that different kinds of interventions will produce different degrees of academic and social gain in students with differing abilities, school psychologists have long endeavored to develop systematic means of using data derived form psychoeducational assessment to plan interventions. Within the past two decades we have observed a tremendous increase in efforts to identify assessment-intervention links and a significant increase in discussions of assessment-intervention links (cf. the special issue of *School Psychology Review,* 1986, *15*[3], on "Linking Assessment to Instructional Intervention.") The professional literature in school psychology contains numerous discussions and research reports under the general heading "diagnostic-prescriptive teaching." Interest in the topic has served as an impetus for the development of proposed diagnostic-prescriptive models (Bateman, 1967; Frostig, 1967; Ysseldyke & Sabatino, 1973), methodologies for differential interpretation of student's performance on tests, diagnostic-prescriptive "cookbooks," and considerable debate on the efficacy of specific approaches in using assessment data to plan instructional interventions (Algozzine & Ysseldyke, 1986; Deno, 1986; Fuchs & Fuchs, 1986; K. A. Howell, 1986; Kavale & Forness, 1986; Keogh, 1974; Lentz & Shapiro, 1986; Mann & Phillips, 1967; Newcomer, 1977; Smead, 1977; Ysseldyke, 1973; Ysseldyke, 1986; Ysseldyke & Christenson, 1987a; Ysseldyke & Marston, 1987; Ysseldyke & Salvia, 1974).

ALTERNATIVE CONCEPTIONS OF THE CAUSES OF EDUCATIONAL EXCEPTIONALITY

Those who assess and plan instructional programs for handicapped students employ a variety of competing approaches. They assess students, instructional tasks, learning environments, and pupil progress. Sometimes they use one approach; more often, approaches are used in some combination. The specific approaches and procedures that are used are best understood as direct consequences of the alternative perspectives professionals hold on the causes of educational exceptionality was provided by Quay (1973). He identified three viewpoints on how and why a child is educationally handicapped.

Quay (1973) reported that many educators and psychologists believe that exceptional children suffer from dysfunctions in processes that are crucial to learning. Generalized or specific processes *within* the child, such as sensory processes (e.g., auditory acuity), response processes (e.g., motor coordination), specific hypothesized internal processes (e.g., memory, attention, visual perception), or global hypothesized internal processes (e.g., intelligence, personality, motivation), are seen as impaired as dysfunctional and causative of learning problems. Those who adhere to this view, labeled by Quay as the process dysfunction view, "place the locus of the problem within the child, and assume that the dysfunction itself is unremediable and must be bypasses or, at best, be compensated for" (p. 166).

A second view about the nature of educational exceptionality has been labeled by Quay as the experiential defect view. According to this viewpoint, "while dysfunctions in the child's learning apparatus may be hypothesized (such as inadequate neurological organization), these dysfunctions are theorized to be due primarily to defects of experience (inadequate experience at crawling)" (p. 166). The distinguishing feature in this viewpoint is the belief that learning problems result from *defective* experience. The view is most prominent in conceptions of emotional disturbance and leads to diagnostic-intervention efforts designed to undo the harm caused by the experiential defect.

A third conception of exceptionality, labeled by Quay as the experience deficit notion, holds that while a student's learning apparatus may be intact, handicaps result from a limited behavioral repertoire. This third viewpoint leads directly to assessment and intervention efforts designed to identify experiential deficits and to provide remedial or compensatory instruction to alleviate or ameliorate those deficits.

Quay indicates that in practice all three viewpoints affect assessment and intervention efforts. He reports that strict application of any one viewpoint would be based on the assumption that categorical groupings of students evidence behavioral unities, but that in reality any handicap involves many dimensions. A fourth view of the nature of exceptionality, called an interactive view, is one in which it is recognized that learning problems may be the result of simultaneous occurrence of difficulties resulting from process dysfunctions, experience defects, and experience deficits.

Those who assess children and plan instructional programs might best operate from an interactive viewpoint of the nature of exceptionality. Review of practice and review of the literature in this area, however, generally reveals early on a strict adherence to one of three viewpoints, either the process dysfunction, experiential defect, or experiential deficit notion, but an increasing shift over time to an interactive perspective.

ALTERNATIVE PERSPECTIVES ON THE ASSESSMENT–INTERVENTION PROCESS

Diagnosing the Learner

Clearly, the approach used most often by school psychologists in response to referral of a student is one in which the psychologist administers a battery of tests for the purpose of finding out what is wrong with the learner. Yet within this approach, different strategies and activities are engaged in, and these are a function of the beliefs of psychologists about the nature of the causes of exceptionality. Within this perspective, assessment activities range along a continuum. At the one end of the continuum are those activities in which assessment or diagnosis is focused on discovery of process dysfunctions, identification of those within-pupil characteristics that are believed to cause academic and behavior difficulties. At the other end of the continuum, emphasis is on discovery of experiential deficits, gaps in the students' experience or learning of skills that act to impede future learning of more complex skills.

Psychological and educational literature is abundant with proposed diagnostic-prescriptive models in which there is an effort to identify process disorders or dysfunctions and prescribe remedial or compensatory programs to alleviate or ameliorate the underlying dysfunction. We have seen numerous proposals for optometric vision training and a number of proposed psycholinguistic training programs (Kirk & Kirk, 1971; Minskoff, Wiseman, & Minskoff, 1972). Similarly, numerous investigators have proposed diagnostic-prescriptive perceptual-motor training programs (Barsch, 1965; Frostig & Horne, 1964), training in sensory integration (Ayres, 1972), modality training (de Hirsch, Jansky, & Langford, 1966; Wepman, 1967), and training in rhythm and body balance (Rice, 1962).

All of the diagnostic-prescriptive approaches based on a process dysfunction conception of the nature of exceptionality operate similarly. When students experience academic difficulties it is presumed that the difficulties are caused by inner process dysfunctions or disorders. Tests are administered in an effort to identify the specific nature of the within-child disorder that is creating or contributing to learning difficulties. Disorders or deficits are test named (e.g., figure–ground deficiencies, auditory sequential memory deficits, body image problems, eye–hand coordination difficulties, visual association dysfunctions, and manual expression disorders). Specific interventions are developed to "cure" the underlying causative problems. When school psychologists focus their assessment activities on diagnosing the learner they typically gather data using norm-referenced tests. Yet data on process dysfunctions or experiential deficits can also be gathered by means of observation or interview (of students, teachers, or others in students' environments).

Diagnosing Instruction

A second perspective on the use of assessment information to plan instructional interventions is one in which the focus is on instructional diagnosis rather than on diagnosing the learner. Those who advocate instructional diagnosis recommend that assessment begin by task analyzing instruction and assessing the extent to which instruction is matched appropriately to the developmental level of the learner (Englemann, Granzin, & Severson, 1979). A recent advance in instructional diagnosis is the practice of curriculum-based assessment, "a procedure for determining the instructional needs of a student based upon the student's ongoing performance within existing course content" (Gickling, 1981, p. CBA/R4). According to Englemann et al. (1979), "The purpose of instructional diagnosis is to determine aspects of instruction that are inadequate, to find out precisely how they are inadequate, and to imply what must be done to correct their inadequacy" (p. 361).

Those who espouse a practice of instructional diagnosis generally believe that academic successes and failures are more likely a function of environmental factors than of within-student factors. Or, at the least, they recognize the significant contribution of environmental factors to learning (Bijou, 1977; K. W. Howell, Kaplan & O'Connell, 1979). Ysseldyke and Salvia (1974) and K. W. Howell et al. (1979) characterized this approach as a task-analytic or skills training approach to the assessment and treatment of children who experience academic difficulties. Within this model there is no search for ability or process dysfunctions or deficits. Assumptions about causality are regarded as irrelevant (Stephens, Hartman, & Lucas, 1978). Assessment is focused on trying to devise the best possible instructional program with the intention of improving the child's functioning on school-related tasks.

Just as there are many different approaches within the ability training paradigm, numerous models have been devised that advocate a skill training approach. Representative are programs such as Behavioral Assessment of Academic Skills (Shapiro & Lentz, 1985), Directive Teaching (Stephens, 1976), Direct Instruction (Carnine & Silbert, 1979), Direct Assessment (K. A. Howell, 1986), DISTAR (Becker & Englemann, 1969), Data Based Instruction (Fox, Egner, Paolucci, Perlman, & McKenzie, 1973), Data Based Program Modification (Deno & Mirkin, 1977), Formative Evaluation (Deno, 1986), Individual Instruction (Peter, 1972), and Precision Teaching (Lindsley, 1971). All are similar in their adherence to sequential, systematic, intensive, individualized, or small-group instruction on skills that are directly related to the academic and social requirements of the school program. They differ, however, along several critical dimensions that prevent viewing these approaches as a unitary system.

The conceptual framework for analysis of these differences, one that is of particular interest with respect to issues of assessment for purposes of

program planning, is provided by Van Etten and Van Etten (1976). They present a model of educational measurement that is conceptualized along two dimensions, frequency and directness, as shown in Table 1.

Frequency. On the frequency dimension, measures are designated as continuous and noncontinuous. Continuous measures are those in which a response is recorded every time it happens, providing a session-by-session record of change in pupil behavior. Noncontinuous measures are those that are administered at periodic intervals (e.g., every 6 weeks, every semester, at the completion of a unit of study once a year).

Directness. On this dimension measures are designated as either direct or indirect. Direct measures are those that measure precisely the same skills as have been taught and often use the same response mode as was employed in teaching the skills initially. Indirect measures are those in which test items are usually sampled from a larger domain and are not necessarily the items that have been taught. Success on the sampled items is viewed as indicative of mastery of the behaviors from which the samples were taken.

Application of the Van Etten Model. Nearly all measurement approaches mentioned as ability training approaches (i.e., those based on a process dysfunction viewpoint of the nature of excep-

TABLE 1   The Measurement Model

	Directness of Measurement	
	Type I Indirect and Noncontinuous	Type III Direct and Noncontinuous
Frequency of Measurement	Type II Indirect and Continuous	Type IV Direct and Continuous

Note. From "The Measurement of Pupil Progress and Selecting Instructional Materials" by G. Van Etten and G. Van Etten, 1976, *Journal of Learning Disabilities, 9*(8), pp. 469–480.

tionality) are indirect and noncontinuous, and would be identified within the Van Etten and Van Etten paradigm as of Type I. Evaluation of the assessment practices of the skills training approaches cited previously reveals that while none of them are appropriately classified as Type I or II category, several are characteristic of Type III measurement (i.e., DISTAR, Directive Teaching, Behavioral Assessment of Academic Skills, Direct Instruction), while others belong in the Type IV category (i.e., Precision Teaching, Exceptional Teaching, Formative Evaluation, Data Based Instruction, DBPM). What, if anything, is the significance of these differences?

Van Etten and Van Etten (1976) propose that different categories of measurement may be appropriate for different purposes. The closer the measurement system is to Type IV, however, "the more direct and the more continuous the data system becomes and the more precise the teaching learning process becomes" (p. 480).

When a noncontinuous measurement strategy is used, even if the measures are direct (i.e., Type III), data-based decisions can occur only at specified intervals. When direct and continuous measurement occurs (i.e., Type IV), there is the potential to make data-based decisions at every point in the student's program.

Those who propose direct and continuous measurement for purposes of program planning (Type IV) operate from the assumption that no matter how carefully assessment might have been done initially, at the present time educational program planners are unable to predict which interventions will consistently have certain effects. Making differential predictions about the extent to which treatments will be successful, and making such predictions prior to intervention, is therefore virtually impossible (Deno, Mirkin, & Shinn, 1978). Program plans are, at best, hypotheses that must be empirically tested to determine their effectiveness for an individual student. Morrissey and Semmel (1976) note that "the teacher's ability to make decisions, probably more than any other variable, affects how and what a child will learn" (p. 114). The assumption is made that the more direct and continuous the information is that is available to the teacher, the higher the probability the teacher will make better decisions, which in turn will lead to increased student achievement.

Other major advantages that are cited in support of direct and continuous measurement

approaches to program planning are the continuity in the type of assessment data collected throughout the program; prevention of "overteaching" and "underteaching" (Lovitt, 1977) through provision of precise information about when program objectives are achieved; and finally, not the least of the advantages is the accountability of current assessment information. This is of course particularly relevant with respect to the accountability and evaluation requirements of P.L. 94-142.

Deno's Formative Evaluation Model. It is argued that with the assistance of instructional diagnosis, educators gain much information about how to teach students who are experiencing difficulties. Deno's (1986) formative evaluation model is used here to illustrate the way in which assessment is linked to intervention. This Formative Evaluation model, a refinement of the Data-Based Program Modification Model (Deno & Mirkin, 1977), is based on four important assumptions.

Assumption 1.

At the present time we are unable to prescribe specific and effective changes in instruction for individual pupils with certainty. Therefore, changes in instructional programs which are arranged for an individual child can be treated only as hypotheses which must be empirically tested before a decision can be made on whether they are effective for that child.

What Deno and Mirkin (1977) are proposing is that we appreciate the unique qualities of each child we teach, and continually examine the effectiveness of our interventions on a case by case basis. Supporting this notion, Bijou and Grimm (1972) wrote: "Diagnosis involves arriving at a set of decisions . . . for designing a program that will meet a child's specific academic and social needs. The initial set of decisions is considered tentative and changing throughout the period of instruction as new findings are revealed" (pp. 23–24). Thus, initial diagnosis does not guide instruction for the duration of intervention. Rather, it is the interaction of initial diagnosis and initial instruction that determines pupil performance and provides the educator with a convenient stopping point at which a working hypothesis about how to teach a particular pupil can be reevaluated. As this assessment and instruction process continues, it is this iterative test–teach–test–teach process that contributes to the formative evaluation of instruction. It is argued that only in this way can assessment be truly linked to instruction.

Assumption 2.

Time series research designs are uniquely appropriate for testing instructional reforms (hypotheses) which are intended to improve individual performance.

Traditional approaches to measuring effectiveness are not successful due to problems related to use of technically inadequate tests, unreliability of the pre- and posttest design and inadequate behavior sampling (Marston & Magnusson, 1985). The time-series research design solves many of these problems with its reliance on direct observation, repeated measurement, and graphic display of student performance (Glass, Wilson, & Gottman, 1975; Kratochwill, 1978).

Assumption 3.

Special education is an intervention system, created to produce reforms in the educational programs of selected individuals, which can (and, now with due process requirements, must) be empirically tested.

In the past the placement of children in special education services often meant permanent assignment to this service delivery sytem. This "pull-out" mentality effectively created a one-way street where only 10% of those served in special education returned to mainstream services. However, given the guiding philosophy of P.L. 94-142 of providing handicapped pupils with the most appropriate education in the least restrictive environment, special education is seen as an untested intervention that must be documented as effective. Formative evaluation provides the means for empirically testing instructional interventions.

Assumption 4.

To apply time series designs to (special) educational reforms we need to specify the data representing the "vital signs" of educational development which can be routinely (frequently) obtained in and out of school.

The initial proposal of using Data-Based Program Modification or Formative Evaluation within the time-series framework met with the immediate dilemma of "what to measure." Referring to this data base as the "vital signs" of education, Deno and Mirkin (1977) first had to specify those observable behaviors that were in fact valid and reliable measures of reading, spelling, written expression, and other academic domains. Research on these academic domains is presented in a later section.

Presented in Figure 1 is a formative evaluation example in which Curriculum-Based Measurement (CBM) has been used to establish those instructional interventions that are working for a particular child. As can be seen in the first phase of instruction, the child has been instructed in a Merrill reader with little demonstrated improvement. In the ensuing instructional phase the teacher has introduced direct instruction procedures with much success. Phase three and four instructional changes are relatively minor adjustments. The data indicate that the addition of reinforcement contingencies and error practice contribute to further improvement.

Citing Deno and Mirkin (1977), Fuchs and Fuchs (1986) offer four reasons why formative evaluation may lead to more effective instructional programming for handicapped students.

> First, its inductive nature avoids reliance on initial diagnoses of learner characteristics when there are incomplete conceptualizations of the relation between students' abilities and educational treatments. Second, its measurement procedures have been shown to be psychometrically acceptable, whereas many ATI-related measures seem to be inadequate. Third, it requires repeated measurement by classroom teachers in familiar classroom settings, which appears more ecologically valid and less reactive than the use of traditional assessment procedures associated with typical ATI approaches. Finally, systematic formative evaluation's repeated use of technically adequate measurement procedures appears consonant with public demand for accountability in special education, as reflected in legislative action such as PL 94-142. (p. 319)

Diagnosing the Instructional Environment

For the most part, emphasis in the assessment activities in which school psychologists engage has

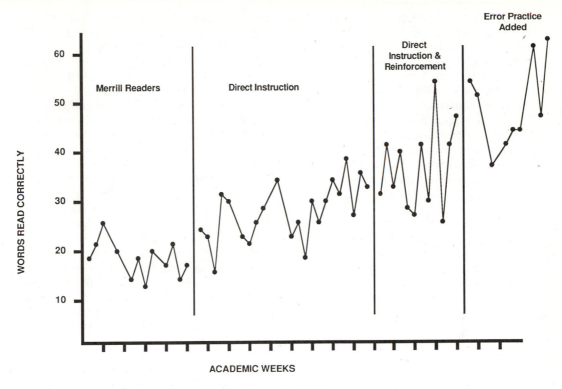

Figure 1. Example of instruction guided by Formative Evaluation.

been student-oriented. To a lesser extent, school psychologists engage in diagnosis of instruction. Within the past few years there has been a major increase in efforts to account for the extent to which instruction is appropriate for students. This increased interest in quality of instruction or in the qualitative nature of instruction has come about in response to two trends. First, there has been a general awakening of interest in the effectiveness of instruction for all students. This interest is evidenced in the publication of major national reports on excellence or examining the extent of excellence in our nations schools (Boyer, 1983; Goodlad, 1984; National Commission on Excellence in Education, 1983; Sizer, 1984). As a result, professionals have begun to ask serious questions both about the quality of instruction for handicapped students and the implications of the push for excellence on the education of handicapped students (Pugach, 1987; Sapon-Shevin, 1987; Shepard, 1987). Second, researchers have increasingly been reporting that elementary age students are actively engaged in instruction for only very limited amounts of time per day (Berliner, 1980; Borg, 1980; Frederick & Walberg, 1980; Good & Beckerman, 1978; Graden, Thurlow, & Ysseldyke, 1983; Rosenshine, 1980; Thurlow, Ysseldyke, Graden, & Algozzine, 1984). And they have begun to ask major questions about the extent to which there are differences in the quantitative and qualitative nature of instruction of mildly handicapped students (Ysseldyke, Thurlow, Christenson, & Weiss, in press). As questions of excellence are asked, and as researchers call attention to the limited amounts of time that mildly handicapped students are actively engaged in instruction, school psychologists have begun to take a more critical look at the nature of instruction for students who experience academic difficulties.

The notion that we ought to assess or in some way account for the nature of the instructional environment is not new. Major textbooks on psychoeducational assessment include statements on the importance of assessing the instructional environment as well as, or in addition to, assessing the student. Consider the following examples:

Behavior does not occur in a vacuum. The individual behaves in a particular environmental context, which in part determines the nature of his responses. The resulting behavior depends on the interaction of respondent and situational variables. The same individual will respond differently in different situations. Hence, the prediction of criterion performance from test scores or from earlier criterion behavior (such as school grades or performance on a previous job) can be materially improved by taking situational variables into account. (Anastasi, 1976, p. 578)

At a minimal level, the teacher should be prepared to assess pupil–teacher interaction, pupil–curriculum 'match,' peer relationships, school and classroom climate, and extraneous variables existing outside the school setting. Unless such evaluations are conducted, it is highly likely that whatever diagnostic and remedial efforts are employed with the child in isolation will be largely ineffective. (Wallace & Larsen, 1978, p. 102)

The argument that we ought to spend as much time assessing the instructional environment as we spend assessing the learner was supported recently when a National Academy of Science Panel on Equity in Special Education concluded that "Valid assessment of the learning environment is as critical as valid assessment of the individual" (Heller, Holtzman, & Messick, 1982, p. xi). Those who argue that we ought to be spending our time assessing instructional or learning environments state that the major purpose of any assessment ought to be intervention, and that since students' performance is a function of classroom variables, it is necessary to analyze the learning environment to design effective interventions. It is reasoned that educators should not categorize or label a student without first considering the role instructional factors play in the student's learning difficulties.

To date, efforts to assess the quality, effectiveness, or qualitative nature of the instructional environment have been nonsystematic and problematic (Ysseldyke & Christenson, 1987a). Instructional diagnosis has consisted primarily of analysis of the scope and sequence of the curriculum, or, less frequently, task analysis of complex academic skills or behaviors (sometimes within a formative evaluation or curriculum-based as-

sessment model). Data have been gathered primarily by nonsystematic observation, self-report, and checklist completion. Recently, Ysseldyke and Christenson (1987b) developed a methodology for describing and assessing systematically the qualitative nature of instruction for students.

In thinking about the nature of instruction, it is necessary to recognize that four major areas comprise the instructional process. A teacher must *plan* what he or she is going to do with students, selecting or establishing goals/objectives, setting mastery criteria, and planning ways to monitor progress toward completion of instructional goals. A teacher must *manage* both classrooms and instruction; he or she must establish rules of classroom conduct, motivate students, manage teaching, and so on. A teacher must *teach*; he or she must present information to students, monitor and adjust instruction, assign work, and adapt instruction to the needs of individual learners. Finally, a teacher must *monitor* instruction; he or she must engage in both formative and summative evaluation.

Ysseldyke and Christenson (1987b) developed a formal systematic procedure that can be used to gather data on the nature of the instructional environment for an individual student and that can be used in planning instructional interventions for individuals. Based on a comprehensive review of the literature on effective instruction, models of schooling, effective schools, teacher effectiveness, and instructional psychology, Ysseldyke and Christenson developed The Instructional Environment Scale (TIES). TIES is a system used by school psychologists or others to gather data on the extent to which 12 components of effective instruction are used in a student's instructional environment. The information is used to identify starting points in the development of instructional interventions for individual students. To date, though, there is no systematic evaluation of the effectiveness of TIES in improving quantity or quality of instruction for either handicapped or nonhandicapped students.

RESEARCH ON ABILITY TRAINING

In this section we review the research base for diagnostic-prescriptive approaches in which specific abilities are trained to either alleviate ability weaknesses or with the long-range goal of improving academic success. Nearly all of these assessment-intervention efforts spring from the view that learning problems result from either process dysfunctions or experiential defects.

In our review we simply cannot exhaust the myriad of investigations in which specific within-student processes and abilities have been assessed and trained. Rather, we have relied on earlier reviews of research and integrated these to provide a state of the art perspective regarding the research evidence to support such assessment–intervention efforts.

Ysseldyke (1973) identified three primary methodologies that characterize research on traditional diagnostic prescriptive approaches. We have organized this section of the chapter similarly, reviewing descriptive research, gain-score research, and aptitude–treatment interaction research.

Descriptive Research

Ysseldyke (1973) reported that "one of the chief factors causing educators to formulate and adhere to a diagnostic-prescriptive model has been the repeated finding that certain behavioral disabilities, or deficits, are correlated with academic difficulties" (p. 6). Three kinds of descriptive research served as the early basis for the generation of diagnostic-prescriptive models and procedures; similar research continues to go on. First, many investigators have attempted to gain a better understanding of learning difficulties and/or of categorical groups of students by administering tests and describing pupil performance. Second, others have tried to understand learning problems by contrasting the test performance of a priori-defined groups of students. Investigators have compared "normal" students with representatives of specific handicapped populations (e.g., learning disabled, mentally retarded); they have contrasted groups of handicapped students (e.g., comparisons of emotionally disturbed and learning disabled students), "good readers" and "poor readers"; and they have investigated differences between under-achievers and those labeled handicapped. A third kind of descriptive research is exhibited in the many correlational studies in which pupil performance on ability measures is compared in an effort to identify those characteristics associated with learning difficulties. The results of descriptive studies have led many to formulate theoretical reasons why students fail, and to develop assessment–

intervention programs based on presumed causes of difficulties. We review briefly the major summaries of descriptive research.

Perhaps the one area receiving most attention in reviews of the assessment–intervention process has been research on perceptual-motor assessment and training. Larsen and Hammill (1975) reviewed 60 published studies correlating performance on achievement tests with performance on measures of visual discrimination, spatial relations, visual memory, and auditory–visual integration. Larsen and Hammill used a criterion of a reported correlation greater than .35 as indicative of a significant relationship. Of the 600 correlation coefficients they found in the 60 studies, Larsen and Hammill report that none of the measures of visual discrimination, spatial relations, auditory–visual integration, and visual memory correlated on the average higher than .35 with measures of academic achievement. They concluded that "the combined results of the correlational research treated in this paper suggest that measured visual-perceptual skills are not sufficiently related to academic achievement to be particularly useful" (pp. 287–288).

Considerable debate has focused on the extent to which "good readers" and "poor readers" differ in their performance on visual perceptual measures. Several investigators have reported statistically significant differences between divergent groups of readers on visual perceptual measures, but Hammill, Larsen, Parker, Bagley, and Sanford (1974) report that all of these studies did not control for IQ differences in their samples. They reported the results of a contrast between "good," "average," and "poor" readers on visual-perceptual measures. Even without controlling for IQ, the visual-perceptual measures did not discriminate between groups.

Hammill and Larsen (1974b) reviewed 33 studies correlating auditory perceptual skills with reading ability. Specifically, they reviewed 292 correlations between pupil performance on criterion measures and performance on measures of auditory discrimination, auditory memory, blending, and auditory–visual integration. Hammill and Larsen concluded that auditory perceptual skills are not sufficiently related to reading to be particularly useful for school practice.

The relationship between performance on psycholinguistic measures and measures of academic performance has similarly received considerable attention. Newcomer and Hammill (1975) reviewed 28 studies correlating performance on the Illinois Test of Psycholinguistic Abilities (ITPA), either concurrently or predictively, with performance on measures of reading, spelling, and arithmetic. Using a standard of a .35 correlation between measures as indicative of a significant relationship, they reported that nine of 12 ITPA subtests lack validity for any aspect of achievement. In addition, Newcomer and Hammill (1975) reviewed 22 studies of the diagnostic validity of the ITPA for reading achievement, focusing on studies in which researchers attempted to differentiate between "divergent groups" of readers (usually defined variously as "good readers" and "bad readers," or "readers" and "nonreaders") using the ITPA. They reported that none of the ITPA subtests discriminate between divergent groups of readers. Thus, despite numerous textbook claims for the relationship between performance on measures of specific abilities and on measures of academic achievement, extensive reviews of the research indicate little empirical evidence for such claims.

Kavale and Forness (1987) conducted a meta-analysis of 39 studies searching for aptitude–treatment interactions in modality testing and teaching. They found that neither modality testing nor modality instruction were efficacious. Students who were taught by instructional methods matched to their modality preferences did not learn more, or more rapidly, than students taught by methods other than those "preferred." Kavale and Forness could not find support for the modality model.

Gain Score Research

One rationale for many of the existing assessment –intervention paradigms based on a process dysfunction viewpoint has been the presumption that students with deficits profit from remedial instruction and that remedial instruction is necessary to improve their chances of academic success. Ysseldyke (1973) identified two kinds of research designs that can be characterized as gain-score research and that have been used to support ability training efforts. The first kind is research in which deficits are presumed for entire groups of students (e.g., disadvantaged students), and special and "traditional" interventions are compared. The second is research in which students demonstrating specific deficits are first identified (e.g., by screen-

ing tests or diagnostic tests), interventions are prescribed, and gains in either the deficit area or in general academic functioning are observed following training. Hundreds of studies have used gain-score methodologies in an effort to demonstrate the efficacy of specific interventions.

The one area of research that has triggered the most controversy is psycholinguistic assessment and training. Hammill and Larsen (1974a) reviewed 38 studies using psycholinguistic training based on the model of the Illinois Test of Psycholinguistic Abilities (ITPA), using gain in performance on the ITPA as the outcome measure. They concluded that the effectiveness of psycholinguistic training had not been demonstrated. Minskoff (1975) challenged the conclusions reached by Hammill and Larsen, stating that the investigations reviewed were characterized by methodological problems and that psycholinguistic training had not been shown to be ineffective. Lund, Foster, and McCall-Perez (1978) reanalyzed the majority of the 28 studies reviewed by Hammill and Larsen, claiming that Hammill and Larsen had not properly analyzed the data, and that gains had indeed been demonstrated on many ITPA subtests. Hammill and Larsen (1978a) responded to the Minskoff criticism by reaffirming their initial position. While the effectiveness of psycholinguistic training has not been demonstrated, it is also true that most of the studies designed to test its adequacy were characterized by methodological flaws. Ysseldyke (1973) described the nature of methodological problems in gain-score research, calling attention to issues of failure to consider Hawthorne effects, regression effects, linearity across different levels, and lack of reliability for both diagnostic devices and outcome measures.

The efficacy of perceptual-motor assessment– intervention programs has been similarly challenged. While Mann (1970, 1971), Mann and Phillips (1967), and Ysseldyke (1978) based their criticisms on logical and theoretical arguments, others have systematically reviewed the research in this area. Hammill, Goodman, and Wiederholt (1974) analyzed 14 studies using the Frostig-Horne program and found that in 13 of the studies there was no demonstrated gain in reading. Wiederholt and Hammill (1971) systematically examined the efficacy of Frostig-Horne visual perceptual training for 130 kindergarten and first-grade students in Philadelphia. Students were randomly assigned to experimental and control groups and pretested on the Developmental Test of Visual Perception. Twenty-one experimental and 24 control group subjects had perceptual quotients below 90 and constituted, using Frostig's definition, the "perceptually handicapped" group. Experimental subjects received 16 weeks of training using the Frostig-Horne worksheets, while control group subjects received traditional instruction. Following training, experimental subjects scored no higher than controls on academic (selected subtests of the Metropolitan Achievement Test) and readiness (selected subtests of the Metropolitan Readiness Test) measures. Furthermore, nonperceptually handicapped students gained significantly on the Developmental Test of Visual Perception, while "perceptually handicapped" students did not.

We observed earlier that optometric vision training is a frequently proposed intervention for students who are experiencing academic difficulties. Keogh (1974) conducted an extensive review of optometric vision training programs. She concluded:

> Confusion within the available literature makes reasonable comparisons across studies difficult, if not impossible. Remedial methods differ markedly. Developmental vision training may include among other things gross motor activities, Delacato techniques, use of lenses, fine motor training, tachistoscopic and eye muscle training, use of Frostig materials, and reading tutors. Most programs have mixed together so many techniques that particular influences of a specific method are not retrievable from the data. (p. 226)

Aptitude–Treatment Interaction Research

Ysseldyke (1973) and Reynolds and Balow (1972) hailed aptitude–treatment interaction research designs as offering promise for establishment of empirical support for traditional assessment–intervention efforts. They indicated that considerable research was necessary establishing links between pupils' test performance and the effectiveness of specific interventions. They joined Cronbach's (1957) plea for research that would demonstrate that pupils who evidenced specific aptitudes would learn best under one instructional strategy, while those who exhibited different aptitudes would learn best when taught under different instructional strategies.

Efforts to demonstrate aptitude–treatment interactions (ATIs) have for the most part met with failure. Bracht (1970) reviewed 90 studies that used an ATI methodology. Eighty-five of the 90 studies produced only nonsignificant or ordinal interactions. Of five studies reported by Bracht that specifically involved handicapped learners, all produced nonsignificant or ordinal interactions. Ysseldyke (1973) reviewed five ATI studies with handicapped students. In all five there were no significant disordinal interactions.

Newcomer and Goodman (1975) conducted an investigation in which learners were assigned to treatment groups on the basis of their performance on the ITPA and a battery of 18 additional tests that measured the same psychological constructs as the ITPA. Four treatment groups were formed: a low auditory group, high auditory group, low visual group, and high visual group. Subjects were assigned to complete two learning conditions, a set of associative learning tasks, and a set of meaningful categorization tasks. The authors failed to identify evidence for an ATI.

Vandever and Neville (1974) conducted a similar investigation with 282 second graders. Six groups of subjects (visual strength, visual weakness, auditory strength, auditory weakness, kinesthetic strength, kinesthetic weakness) were assigned to classes in which instruction was tailored to either their strength or their weakness. Children taught to their strength did no better than those taught to their weakness.

Ysseldyke (1977) reported the results of an ATI investigation in which first-grade students were randomly assigned to five treatment groups: perceptual training, perceptual and language training, language conceptual training, Hawthorne, and control. A total of 240 F tests for nonparallelism of regression were computed, and 11 reached significance. Ysseldyke (1977) reported that the 11 significant ATIs "neither have practical meaning nor contribute to our general theoretical knowledge regarding diagnostic-prescriptive teaching" (p. 7).

Theoretically, the aptitude–treatment interaction design has considerable promise of providing empirical support for diagnostic-prescriptive teaching. To date, investigations using an ATI design have failed to provide support. While there are many different explanations for such failure, the explanation offered by Mann, Proger, and Cross (1973) is most cogent. They state, quite simply, that there are major methodological problems in the measurement of aptitude itself.

RESEARCH ON DIAGNOSING INSTRUCTION

In this section we review the research base on diagnosing instruction with direct and continuous assessment procedures. Howell, Kaplan, and O'Connell (1979) aptly articulate the philosophy that is characteristic of this approach, which is also known as formative evaluation.

> The model of educational evaluation which is most useful is the model that evaluates variables teachers can control. In order for an evaluative system to have high instructional utility, it must deal with instructional variables. It must test in areas which instruction can influence. (Howell, Kaplan, & O'Connell, p. 10)

Direct and continuous assessment approaches go beyond specification of instructional variables to view assessment as a dynamic process that begins when a problem is initially identified and continues through the entire program. Direct and continuous measurement and frequent analysis of data using time-series research designs are the basic methodology. Bijou and Grimm (1972) propose that

> diagnosing involves arriving at a set of decisions . . . for designing an academic program that will meet a child's specific and social needs. The *initial set of decisions is considered tentative and changing throughout the period of instruction* as new findings are revealed. (pp. 23–24)

They identify three sets of interrelated assessment procedures that are chronologically arranged to provide information for decisions with respect to treatment. The first set of assessments yield information about what the child can do in areas that are the targets of instruction and provide the basis for decisions concerning the starting place in the educational program. The second set of assessments provide running accounts of the adequacy of the programs (e.g., materials, consequences, context) and provide the basis for decisions about changing programs. The third set indicate the child's competencies at the end of instruction and provide the basis for decisions regarding the child's progress over the intervention period.

We turn now to a description of the research base for the formative evaluation model and its monitoring system, curriculum-based measurement. Included in our review is a description of the empirical data supporting the technical adequacy of this approach, its effectiveness in monitoring teacher interventions and actual implementation in school districts in the country.

Technical Adequacy

A necessary requisite for implementing formative evaluation systems in the educational arena is the specification of academic behaviors that educators could validly and reliably measure on a frequent basis. During the late 1970s and the early 1980s, Stanley Deno and Phyllis Mirkin devoted a significant portion of their research at the University of Minnesota's Institute for Research on Learning Disabilities (IRLD) to this question. This line of research focused on the vital signs of education of "What to Measure?" in the areas of reading, spelling, written expression, and math.

Reading. A critical CBM validity study in reading was conducted by Deno, Mirkin, and Chiang (1982). These authors identified five measures of reading that could potentially be employed within a formative evaluation framework: (a) asking the student to read aloud stories from the pupil's basal reader (Passage Reading); (b) asking the student to read aloud lists of words randomly selected from the pupil's basal reader (Isolated Word Lists); (c) asking the student to read aloud words underlined in a story from his or her basal reader (Reading in Context); (d) asking the student to supply words that had been deleted from stories from his or her basal reader (Cloze Comprehension Procedure); and (e) asking the student to give the meaning of words selected from the basal reader story (Word Meaning). These curriculum-based measures, which could be administered frequently, scored objectively, and graphed, were then correlated with accepted standardized tests of reading. Criterion measures selected for this criterion-related validity study were the Stanford Diagnostic Reading Test (Karlsen, Madden, & Gardner, 1975), the Woodcock Reading Mastery Test (Woodcock, 1973), and the Reading Comprehension subtest from the Peabody Individual

Achievement Test (Dunn & Markwardt, 1970). Deno et al. (1982) found that listening to a child read aloud from his or her basal reader for 1 minute was a valid measure of reading skill. Correlation coefficients ranged from .73 to .91, with most coefficients above .80. Further confirmation of this finding was provided by Deno, Marston, Shinn, and Tindal (1983), and by Marston and Magnusson (1985), who demonstrated that oral reading fluency correlated significantly with other standardized tests of reading.

In addition, Deno et al. (1983) established the discriminative validity of oral reading when they reliably differentiated LD and non-LD samples of students. This finding was replicated by Shinn and Marston (1985), who found that words read aloud differentiated regular education students, pupils served in Chapter I, and mildly handicapped students with learning disabilities. Marston, Tindal, and Deno (1982) demonstrated that CBM procedures predicted LD classification as well as traditional measures of aptitude—achievement discrepancy. However, the direct measures of student reading (CBM) required significantly less expenditure in cost and time.

The validation of the reading measure was also demonstrated in the study of sensitivity to growth. Marston, Fuchs, and Deno (1986) examined the short-term reading progress of students across 10-week and 16-week intervals with standardized reading tests and CBM procedures. While both approaches identified student improvement, the CBM procedures (1) delineated greater growth in the reading performance of students, and (2) correlated much higher with teacher perceptions of individual student improvement.

IRLD investigators also examined the reliability of CBM procedures. In the reading domain, test–retest reliability coefficients ranged from .80 to .90 for intervals of 1 day and 2 weeks. Examination of reading passages equated for reading difficulty provided parallel reliability coefficients that ranged from .80 to .90. Interscorer agreement coefficients of .80 to .90 were found when the scoring of reading samples was analyzed (Marston, 1982; Tindal, Marston, & Deno, 1983).

Spelling. In spelling, IRLD staff members conducted several studies documenting the technical adequacy of CBM measures for formative evaluation. In their study of brief, curriculum-based measures of spelling, Deno, Mirkin, Lowry, and

Kuehnle (1980) examined the extent to which words spelled correctly and incorrectly, and correct and incorrect letter sequences, a scoring procedure devised by White and Haring (1980), related with criteria such as the spelling subtest of the Stanford Achievement Test (Madden, Gardner, Rudman, Karlsen, & Merwin, 1973), the Test of Written Spelling (Larsen & Hammill, 1976), and the spelling subtest from the Peabody Individual Achievement Test (Dunn & Markwardt, 1970). These authors found that the most valid measures of spelling for formative evaluation systems were either words spelled correctly or correct letter sequences, where correlation coefficients ranged from .80 to .96. In addition, it was determined that 1-, 2-, and 3-minute-long samples were adequate samples of spelling.

The measurement of student growth in spelling was addressed by Deno et al. (1982) and by Marston, Lowry, Deno, and Mirkin (1981). In both studies student spelling performance as measured with CBM procedures showed significant growth across the school year for elementary students in regular education.

Reliability studies of the CBM spelling procedures provide a test–retest reliability of .92 for correct letter sequences and coefficients of .82 to .92 for alternative form reliability (Marston, 1982). The average interscorer reliability coefficient was .87.

Written Expression. The initial study of curriculum-based measures of written expression explored the validity of student compositions and the number of words written, the number of words spelled correctly, the number of mature word choices, the number of large words written, and Hunt's (1965) average length of t-units (Deno, Marston, & Mirkin, 1982). All five measures were correlated with the following criterion measures: the Test of Written Language (Hammill & Larsen, 1978b), the Developmental Sentence Scoring System (Lee & Canter, 1971), and the Language subtest of the Stanford Achievement Test (Madden et al., 1973). The results from this study indicated that the number of words written and spelled correctly were valid measures of written expression (coefficients ranged from .70 to .90); the compositions could be written using story starters, picture stimuli, or topic sentences, and the length of written samples could range from 2 to 5 minutes.

Student growth in written expression was

studied by Marston, Lowry, Deno, and Mirkin (1981) and by Deno, Marston, Mirkin, Lowry, Sindelar, and Jenkins (1982). In both studies elementary students in grades 1 through 6 from regular education significantly increased in total words written, total words written correctly, and number of correct letter sequences during the course of the academic school year. Examination of shorter-term progress over 10- and 16-week periods showed significant gains for total words written and total words written correctly (Marston et al., 1986).

Marston and Deno (1981) analyzed the reliability of written expression measures and determined that test–retest reliability was .81 to .92 for 1 day and .62 to .70 for 3 weeks. Alternate form reliability for story starters, picture stimuli, and topic sentences ranged from .74 to .87. Internal consistency coefficients, derived from examining performance at the end of 2, 3, 4, and 5 minutes, ranged from .70 to .99. Coefficients of .90 to .99 were found for interscorer reliability.

Math. Research on CBM measures of math was not conducted at the Minnesota IRLD, but in the Pine County Special Education Cooperative (Germann & Tindal, 1985) and the Minneapolis Public Schools (Skiba, Magnusson, Marston, & Erickson, 1986). In both studies the performance of elementary students on math probes composed of addition, subtraction, multiplication, and division problems specific to grade-level curricula was examined. Probes were scored for number of correct problems and correct digits written (White & Haring, 1981). Correlation coefficients with the California Achievement Test indicated that digits correct was a valid measure of math performance.

Data Utilization

While evidence of CBM's technical adequacy is essential for its use in educational decision making, research demonstrating its efficacy within the formative evaluation framework is also necessary. Referred to as "data utilization" research, a series of studies have been conducted to establish the extent to which utilization of CBM procedures in monitoring special education interventions is useful to teachers. In this section we review four major issues related to this topic: setting measurable IEP goals, use of data decision rules, use of graphs, and the effectiveness of formative evaluation. In addition, we will review what the current research using

CBM says about specific instructional strategies and how it affects teacher attitudes.

Setting Measurable IEP Goals

Of central importance in the Formative Evaluation model is the process of setting either short-term goals or long-term goals for the individual educational plan. The short-goal (STG) approach consists of identifying a series of objectives linked to the curriculum sequence in which the pupil is instructed. For example, a student might have six or seven short-term objectives over the course of an academic year. Small groups of items are specifically created for each objective and pupil progress is monitored frequently beginning with the first instructional objective. With the mastery of a specific set of items, short-term goal measurement is then shifted to the next objective in the curricular sequence.

Long-term goal (LTG) setting and measurement varies in that an annual goal is established at the outset of writing the IEP. The larger item pool used to measure pupil skills is pulled from the entire year-long curriculum. Progress is then assessed by frequently measuring pupil performance on probes consisting of items randomly drawn from the large item pool.

Fuchs (1986) states that while the short-term approach is more sensitive to current instruction and is easier for teachers to understand, the long-term approach has three distinct advantages. First, LTGs are more closely linked to the desired academic or behavioral performance. Second, in criterion validity studies LTG measurement procedures correlate higher with standardized tests of achievement than do STG measures. Third, the LTG approach is better suited to time-series data analysis because it involves longer instructional periods, whereas STG monitoring is implemented across brief and discrete instructional periods. As a result, in STG, where trends in the data vary from objective to objective, it is difficult to monitor the effectiveness of many instructional interventions. In terms of empirical data, the meta-analysis conducted by Fuchs and Fuchs (1986) suggests that improvement in student achievement is much greater when LTGs are set for handicapped children.

Use of Data Decision Rules

Once goals are established and progress monitoring has begun, the educator must begin to make sense of the time-series data that he or she is graphing. Fuchs (1986) notes that while teachers may collect pupil data on a frequent basis, they often do not use the data to alter and improve instructional programs. Such was the case in a study where special education resource teachers (SERTs) continued ineffective instructional interventions although formative evaluation data indicated that students were not progressing (Tindal, Fuchs, Mirkin, Christenson, & Deno, 1981).

Questions that typically arise when examining the time-series data include: What is adequate improvement? At what point do I make changes to my instructional plan? How much of a change must I make in the program? To answer these questions White and Haring (1980) have proposed the use of data decision rules, a set of formal rules used to analyze repeated measurement data that guide the educator's decisions concerning instruction.

Goal-Oriented Decision Rules. In the goal-oriented approach, decisions about instructional changes center on the IEP goal and the current level of performance. The analysis focuses on the IEP aimline, that line of progress on a graph that connects baseline performance with the specified goal or criterion. All evaluations of instructional effectiveness are based on looking forward to the prescribed goal and are described by whether performance is above or below the aimline. For example, in the initial stage of phase B of Figure 2

the pupil's performance is typically at or above the aimline, suggesting that the instructional regime is effective. However, later in phase B the pupil's performance has fallen below the aimline on four successive occasions. At this point, the Goal-Oriented decision rule indicates that a change in the instructional intervention should be implemented. A change, represented by the dark, vertical line, is illustrated in Figure 2. Phase C instruction is then initiated and data collection continues.

Treatment-Oriented Decision Rules. The reference point of the criterion is reversed in the treatment-oriented decision rule strategy. In this approach the current instructional plan is judged by comparing learning rate within this phase to the learning rate of the previous treatment. Effectiveness is evaluated by drawing the trend line or slope through 9 to 12 data points of the present phase. The slopes drawn by the special education resource teachers (SERTs) on the IEP graphs are calculated with White and Haring's (1981) Quarter-Intersect method. At this point the treatment-oriented approach offers two alternatives. If the rate of progress within the present instructional phase is higher than in the preceding period, minor modifications or additions to the program may be considered. However, if the slope indicates an undesirable rate of progress (e.g., a negative slope or slope lower than in the preceding phase), major changes or modifications in the intervention should be considered. In phase B of

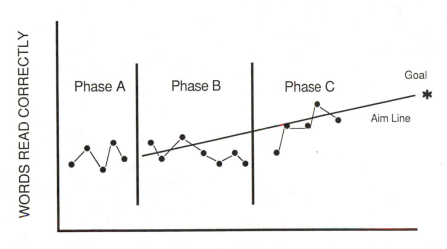

Figure 2. Goal-oriented decision rules.

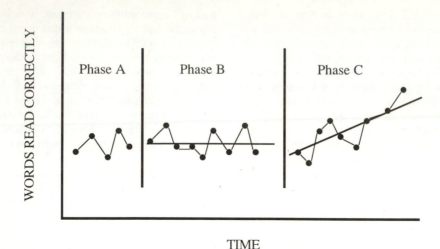

Figure 3. Treatment-oriented decision rules.

Figure 3, the flat trend line indicates that the instructional program is not successful and a major change is to be made in the next phase. The slope in phase C, however, is increasing significantly and suggests only minor modifications for the upcoming phase D.

Currently, there is relatively little evidence favoring either set of decision rules (Deno, 1986). Regardless of which approach is used, the need for decision rules was made abundantly clear when Fuchs and Fuchs (1986) demonstrated that no use of rules is correlated with a .5 standard deviation increase in student achievement, while implementation of a formal set of decision rules is associated with a mean effect size of .91.

Use of Graphs

For those implementing direct and repeated measurement procedures there exists two graphing options. The simplest option is the use of equal interval graph paper (Glass, Wilson, & Gottman, 1975) on which time is measured along the horizontal (abscissa) axis and performance is scaled along the vertical axis (ordinate). For both scales, measurement is incremented in equal interval units.

An alternative is using the Standard Behavior Chart, a graph on which the vertical axis measuring performance is based on a logarithmic scale (Pennypacker, Koenig, & Lindsley, 1972). Noting

that initial progress of handicapped students may be slow and misleading, proponents of the Standard Behavior Chart conclude that academic improvement increases proportionately and not arithmetically. As a result, the Standard Behavior Chart provides a truer picture of intervention effectiveness, thus improving the link between assessment and instruction.

Current evidence about the comparative effectiveness of both approaches is scant. Brandstetter and Mertz (1978) addressed the issue of the efficacy of both graphs and found higher rates of student achievement when data were charted when compared to a no-charting condition. The study failed, however, to compare the logarithmic approach to equal-interval graphs. Fuchs and Fuchs (1985) compared effect sizes for studies in which the Standard Behavior Chart and equal-interval graphs were used to analyze repeated measurement data. Their data show no statistically significant difference between the two graphing approaches. Marston (1988), however, examined trend lines on both types of graphs and found that prediction of student performance on the equal interval graph approach was significantly better than on the Standard Behavior Chart.

Effectiveness of Formative Evaluation

In an 18-week study of the effects of frequent curriculum-based measurement on student achievement, Fuchs, Deno, and Mirkin (1984) found that formative evaluation significantly improved the reading skills of handicapped children. The subjects who volunteered for the study were 39 special education teachers from the New York City Public Schools who each worked with three or four students for the project. Teachers in the experimental condition ($N = 18$) were first trained to write curriculum-based IEP goals and objectives in reading. Second, the teachers were trained to measure student performance on a twice-weekly basis in which they listened to their students read aloud, for 1 minute, from randomly selected stories from the IEP goal material. Third, the teachers learned how to graph the reading data, analyze learning trends, and utilize the information to make instructional changes in the pupil programs. The remaining teachers were assigned to the control group condition and were asked to set goals and monitor pupil progress as they would typically perform these tasks.

At the end of the project several trends concerning the use of formative evaluation were evident. First, special education students, whose instruction was guided by the CBA monitoring and decision rules, achieved significantly better than did their "control" counterparts on both standardized tests of reading and passage reading from the CBA materials. Second, the instructional techniques of the "experimental teachers" changed significantly. Specifically, those teachers increased the structure of their lessons and the learning environment. Third, the experimental teachers had a more valid perception about the improvement of their students and as a result could more accurately modify student goals. Finally, students in the "experimental condition" had more awareness of IEP goals and objectives. The authors note that there is increasing evidence that student knowledge of goals is related to improved performance.

Fuchs and Fuchs (1986) examined the effectiveness of formative evaluation by conducting a meta-analysis of 21 existing studies. In this investigation the authors analyzed 96 effect sizes related to pupil performance in reading, math, spelling and writing. The results demonstrated that the performance of handicapped students was significantly increased when their teachers implemented formative evaluation procedures. The data suggested that these students progressed a total of .7 standard deviation unit more than control subjects,

which is comparable to increasing from the 50th percentile to the 76th percentile. Further, teachers using formative evaluation with a specific set of decision rules were more effective than teachers utilizing formative evaluation but using teacher judgment as to when to make instructional changes.

RESEARCH ON ASSESSMENT OF STUDENTS' INSTRUCTIONAL ENVIRONMENTS

Research on the formal assessment of students' instructional environments is very recent, and there are few studies. Yet there clearly is an extensive knowledge base and considerable research on the nature of instruction. Research on teacher effectiveness, instructional psychology, instructional effectiveness, teacher decision making, and models of school learning set the stage for formal research on assessment of students' instructional environments. Ysseldyke and Christenson (1987a) described factors related to instructional outcomes for exceptional students. Ysseldyke, Christenson, and Thurlow (1987) reviewed the research on factors that influence student outcomes. On the basis of this delineation of factors, Ysseldyke and Christenson (1987b) developed The Instructional Environment Scale (TIES). TIES is a systematic methodology for collecting data on the qualitative nature of students' instruction. Data are gathered on 16 components of effective instruction: Instructional Presentation, Classroom Environment, Teacher Expectations, Cognitive Emphasis, Motivational Strategies, Relevant Practice, Academic Engaged Time, Informed Feedback, Adaptive Instruction, Progress Evaluation, Instructional Planning, and Student Understanding. Students' instructional environments are described following direct classroom observation, teacher interview, and student interview. Research using TIES is now being completed.

Algozzine, Morsink, and Algozzine (in press) completed a study of the nature of instruction provided in 40 self-contained special classrooms for students with different categorical labels. They found few differences in teacher communication patterns, learner involvement in instructional strategies, methods, or techniques in classes for different categories of students.

IMPLICATIONS FOR THE ROLE OF THE SCHOOL PSYCHOLOGIST

What is the potential impact of formative evaluation and assessment of instructional environments upon the role of the school psychologist? In the Minneapolis Public Schools where the implementation of curriculum-based assessment (CBA) has been primarily the responsibility of the special education resource teachers, not the psychologists, it appears that implementation of CBA, with its emphasis on a curricular based set of objective criteria for referrals and eligibility, has had some impact on the practices of school psychologists in the district. Canter (1986) compared the time psychologists were engaged in a variety of activities before the implementation of formative evaluation (1981) and after implementation (1986). Several significant findings emerged from this report. First, in the area of assessment, the amount of time psychologists tested was virtually the same in 1981 and 1986: about 35%. However, Minneapolis school psychologists were testing proportionately fewer students in 1986. Canter concluded that by reducing unnecessary testings psychologists can spend more time on those cases that demand comprehensive assessment. Second, there has been an increase in the time Minneapolis school psychologists spend in consultation activities with individual students and department programs. The increase went from 12% in 1981 to 35% in 1986. Third, the district psychologists are also engaged in more direct treatment activities, 1.5% in 1981 and 6% in 1986. In general, all three trends are viewed as improvements by a staff that prefers consultation and treatment activities to assessment. The extent to which these benefits can be directly attributed to the implementation of CBA remains an open question. What is not in doubt, however, is the fact that implementation of CBA has given the Student Support Teams, for the first time, an objective set of criteria for purposes of making psychoeducational decisions.

Reynolds (1982) writes that P.L. 94-142 has had a tremendous impact on education:

> Public education has changed: Student bodies have become more heterogeneous, new structures have begun to appear, and new functions and roles are demanded of teachers, building principals, school psychologists, and other specialists. Most of the changes derive from the mandated provision of services to populations that, heretofore, were considered marginal, that is, the handicapped, minority, economically disadvantaged, bilingual, migrant, and other children and youth who have been systematically set aside or excluded from the mainstreams of society and the schools. (p. 102)

Obviously, as education changes, there is an impact on the role of the school psychologist. Although the changes for school psychologists may be difficult, Reynolds suggests that this would be eased by "an in-depth analysis of the emerging rights of children and the new principles being applied to the education of "marginal" children" (p. 102). To move in this direction, Reynolds (1982) identified nine clusters of competencies that school psychologists must possess to make a successful transition: individualized assessment, consultation, diverse social structures, individualized instruction, deliberate psychological education, parent involvement, teaching basic skills, group management, and the law and judicial procedures. Although all clusters are critical to bettering services for handicapped students, it is individualized assessment of "marginal children" that receives significant emphasis.

> In general, assessment processes in the schools should be oriented to instructional decisions: that is, the assessments should help to design appropriate instructional programs for students. . . . Assessments should be mainly curriculum-based or behavioral. . . . In general, behavioral assessments should be based heavily on direct observations rather than on presumed predispositional or underlying traits. . . . Assessments of school progress should be highly specific to the domains of instruction and so designed that individuals have clear opportunities to become aware of their own progress. . . . (pp. 104–106)

We have included these remarks because moves to increase formative evaluation and assessment of instructional environments fit nicely with the model proposed by Reynolds. It is oriented to instruction, is data driven, relates to the curriculum, and is behaviorally based. We are in agreement with Reschly (in press), who states that the conventional testing model is inadequate. "The amount of time and energy now devoted to pre-placement and reevaluations in special education, which are dominated by determination of eligibility, represents excessively costly and ineffective use of resources." As school psychologists retreat from the "gate-keeper" status and move toward consultation and direct service, formative evaluation and assessment of instructional environments will help guide their decision making on pupil progress and intervention effectiveness. It is our belief that as the role of the school psychologist changes, attraction to formative evaluation and assessment of instructional environments will increase.

REFERENCES

Algozzine, B., Morsink, C., & Algozzine, K. (1988). "What's happening in self-contained special education classrooms. *Exceptional Children, 55,* 259–265.

Algozzine, B., & Ysseldyke, J. E. (1986). The future of the LD field: Screening and diagnosis. *Journal of Learning Disabilities, 19*(7), 394–398.

Anastasi, A. (1976). *Psychological testing* (4th ed.). New York: Macmillan.

Ayres, A. J. (1972). Improving academic scores through sensory integration. *Journal of Learning Disabilities, 5,* 336–343.

Barsch, R. H. (1965). *A movigenic curriculum.* Madison, WI: Bureau for Handicapped Children.

Bateman, B. (1967). Three approaches to diagnosis and remediation. *Academic Therapy Quarterly, 2,* 215–222.

Becker, W. C., & Engelmann, S. (1976). *Analysis of achievement data on six cohorts of low-income children from 20 school districts in the University of Oregon Direct Instruction Follow Through Model.* Eugene, OR: Bureau of School Systems.

Berliner, D. (1980). Allocated time, engaged time, and academic learning time in elementary school mathematics instruction. *Focus on Problems in Mathematics, 2,* 27–39.

Bijou, S. W. (1977). Practical implications of an interactional model of child development. *Exceptional Children, 44*(1), 6–15.

Bijou, S. W., & Grimm, J. A. (1972, October). *Behavioral diagnosis and assessment in teaching young handicapped children.* Washington, DC: Bureau of Education for the Handicapped, Division of Research.

Borg, W. R. (1980). Time and school learning. In C. Derham & A. Lieberman (Eds.), *Time to learn.* Washington, DC: National Institute of Education.

Boyer, E. L. (1983). *High school: A report on secondary education in American.* New York: Harper & Row.

Bracht, G. (1970). Experimental factors related to aptitude-treatment interactions. *Review of Educational Research, 40,* 627–646.

Brandstetter, G., & Mertz, C. (1978). Charting scores in precision teaching for skill acquisition. *Exceptional Children, 45,* 42–48.

Canter, A. (1986). *1986 time/task study.* Minneapolis, MN: Minneapolis Public Schools, Department of Special Education, Psychological Services.

Carnine, D., & Silbert, J. (1979). *Direct instruction reading.* Columbus, OH: Charles E. Merrill.

Cronbach, L. J. (1957). The two disciplines of scientific psychology. *American Psychologist, 12,* 671–684.

de Hirsch, K., Jansky, J. J., & Langford, W. S. (1966). *Predicting reading failure.* New York: Harper & Row.

Deno, S. L. (1986). Formative evaluation of individual student programs: A new role for school psychologists. *School Psychology Review, 15*(3), 358–374.

Deno, S. L., Marston, D., & Mirkin, P. (1982). Valid measurement procedures for continuous evaluation of written expression. *Exceptional Children, 48*(4), 368–371.

Deno, S. L., Marston, D., Mirkin, P., Lowry, L., Sindelar, P., & Jenkins, J. (1982). *The use of standard tasks to measure achievement in reading, spelling and written expression: A normative and developmental study* (Research Report No. 87). Minneapolis: University of Minnesota, Institute for Research on Learning Disabilities.

Deno, S. L., Marston, D., Shinn, M., & Tindal, J. (1983). Oral reading fluency: A simple datum for scaling reading disability. *Topics in Learning and Learning Disabilities, 2*(4), 53–59.

Deno, S. L., & Mirkin, P. (1977). *Data-based program modification: A manual.* Minneapolis: University of Minnesota, Leadership Training Institute/Special Education.

Deno, S. L., Mirkin, P. K., & Chiang, B. (1982). Identifying valid measures of reading. *Exceptional Children, 49,* 36–45.

Deno, S. L., Mirkin, P. K., Lowry, L., & Kuehnle, K. (1980). *Relationships among simple measures of spelling and performance on standardized achievement tests* (Research Report No. 21). Minneapolis: University of Minnesota, Institute for Research on Learning Disabilities.

Deno, S. L., Mirkin, P. K., & Shinn, M. (1979). *Behavioral perspectives on the assessment of learning disabled children* (Monograph No. 12). Minneapolis: University of Minnesota, Institute for Research on Learning Disabilities.

Dunn, L. M., & Markwardt, F. C. (1970). *Peabody individual achievement test.* Circle Pines, MN: American Guidance Service.

Englemann, S., Granzin, A., & Severson, H. (1979). Diagnosing instruction. *Journal of Special Education, 13,* 355–363.

Fox, W. L., Egner, A. N., Paolucci, P. E., Perlman, P. F., & McKenzie, H. S. (1973). An introduction to a regular classroom approach to special education. In E. Deno (Ed.), *Instructional alternatives for exceptional children.* Arlington, VA: Council for Exceptional Children.

Frederick, W., & Walberg, H. (1980). Learning as a function of time. *Journal of Educational Research, 73,* 183–194.

Frostig, M. (1967). Testing as a basis for educational therapy. *Journal of Special Education, 2,* 15–34.

Frostig, M., & Horne, D. (1964). *The Frostig program for development of visual perception.* Chicago: Fallett.

Fuchs, L. S. (1986). Monitoring progress of mildly handicapped pupils: Review of current practice and research. *Remedial and Special Education, 7,* 5–12.

Fuchs, L. S., Deno, S. L., & Mirkin, P. K. (1984). The effects of frequent curriculum-based measurement and evaluation on pedagogy, student achievement and student awareness of learning. *American Educational Research Journal, 21*(2), 449–460.

Fuchs, L. S., & Fuchs, D. (1986). *Effects of systematic formative evaluation: A meta analysis. Exceptional Children, 53*(3), 199–208.

Fuchs, L. S., & Fuchs, D. (1986). Linking assessment to instructional interventions: An overview. School Psychology Review, 15(3), 318–323.

Germann, G., & Tindal, G. (1985). An application of curriculum-based assessment: The use of direct and repeated measurement. *Exceptional Children, 52,* 244–265.

Gickling, E. (1981). Curriculum-based assessment. In J. Tucker (Ed.), *Non-test-based assessment: A training module* (pp. 17–104). Minneapolis, MN: National School Psychology Inservice Training Network.

Glass, G. V., Wilson, V. L., & Gottman, J. M. (1975). *Design and analysis of time-series experiments.* Boulder: University of Colorado Press.

Good, T., & Beckerman, T. (1978). Time on task: A naturalistic study in 6th grade classrooms. *Elementary School Journal, 78,* 192–201.

Goodlad, J. I. (1984). *A place called school.* New York: McGraw-Hill.

Graden, J. Thurlow, M. L., & Ysseldyke, J. E. (1983). Instructional ecology and academic responding time for students at three levels of teacher-perceived behavioral competence. *Journal of Experimental Child Psychology, 36,* 241–256.

Hammill, D., Goodman, L., & Wiederholt, J. L. (1974). Visual-motor processes: Can we train them? *The Reading Teacher, 27*(5), 469–478.

Hammill, D. D., & Larsen, S. C. (1974a). The effectiveness of psycholinguistic training. *Exceptional Children, 41,* 5–14.

Hammill, D. D., & Larsen, S. C. (1974b). The relationship of selected auditory perceptual skills and reading ability. Journal of Learning Disabilities, 1, 429–435.

Hammill, D. D., & Larsen, S. C. (1978a). The effectiveness of psycholinguistic training: A reaffirmation of position. *Exceptional Children, 44,* 402–417.

Hammill, D. D., & Larsen, S. C. (1978b). *The test of written language.* Austin, TX: PRO-ED.

Hammill, D. D., Larsen, S. C., Parker, R., Bagley, M. T., & Sanford, H. G. (1974). *Perceptual and conceptual correlates of reading.* Unpublished manuscript.

Heller, K. A., Holtzman, W., & Messick, S. (1982). *Placing children in special education: A strategy for equity.* Washington, DC: National Academy Press.

Howell, K. A. (1986). Direct assessment of academic performance. *School Psychology Review, 15*(3), 324–335.

Howell, K. W., Kaplan, J. S., & O'Connell, C. Y. (1979). *Evaluating exceptional children: A task analysis approach.* Columbus, OH: Charles E. Merrill.

Hunt, K. W. (1965). *Grammatical structures written at three grade levels* (Research Report No. 3). Champaign, IL: National Council of Teachers of English.

Karlsen, B., Madden, R., & Gardner, E. F. (1975). *Stanford diagnostic reading test.* New York: Harcourt Brace Jovanovich.

Kavale, K. A., & Forness, S. R. (1986). *The science of learning disabilities.* Boston: College-Hill Press.

Kavale, K. A., & Forness, S. R. (1987). A matter of substance over style: A quantitative synthesis assessing the efficacy of modality testing and teaching. *Exceptional Children, 54,* 228–240.

Keogh, B. K. (1974). Optometric vision training program for children with learning disabilities: Review of issues and research. *Journal of Learning Disabilities, 1,* 36–48.

Kirk, S. A., & Kirk, W. D. (1971). Psycholinguistic learning disabilities: Diagnosis and remediation. Urbana: University of Illinois Press.

Kratochwill, T. R. (1978). Foundations of time-series research. In T. R. Kratochwill (Ed.), *Single subject research: Strategies for evaluating change.* New York: Academic Press.

Larsen, S. C., & Hammill, D. D. (1975). The relationship of selected visual perceptual abilities to school learning. *Journal of Special Education, 9,* 281–291.

Larsen, S. C., & Hammill, D. D. (1976). *Test of written spelling.* Austin, TX: PRO-ED.

Lee, L., & Canter, S. (1971). Developmental sentence scoring: A clinical procedure for estimating syntactic development in children's spontaneous speech. *Journal of Speech and Hearing Disorders, 36,* 315–340.

Lentz, F. E., Jr., & Shapiro, E. S. (1986). Functional assessment of the academic environment. *School Psychology Review, 15*(3), 346–357.

Lindsley, O. R. (1971). Precision teaching in perspective: An interview with Ogden R. Lindsley. *Teaching Exceptional Children, 3*(3), 114–119.

Lovitt, T. C. (1977). *In spite of my resistance . . . I have learned from children.* Columbus, OH: Charles E. Merrill.

Lund, K. A., Foster, G. E., & McCall-Perez, F. C. (1978). The effectiveness of psycholinguistic training. A reevaluation. *Exceptional Children, 44,* 310–319.

Madden, R., Gardner, E. R., Rudman, H., Karlsen, B., & Merwin, J. C. (1973). *Stanford Achievement Test.* New York: Harcourt Brace Jovanovich.

Mann, L. (1970). Perceptual training: Misdirections and redirections. *American Journal of Orthopsychiatry, 40,* 30–38.

Mann, L. (1971). Perceptual training revisited: The training of nothing at all. *Rehabilitation Literature, 32,* 322–335.

Mann, L., & Phillips, W. A. (1967). Fractional practices in special education: A critique. *Exceptional Children, 42,* 136–144.

Mann, L., Proger, B., & Cross, L. (1973). *Aptitude-treatment interactions with handicapped children: A focus on the measurement of the aptitude com-*

ponent. Paper presented at the American Educational Research Association meeting, New Orleans. (ERIC Document Reproduction Service No. 075 510)

Marston, D. (1982). *The technical adequacy of direct, repeated measurement of academic skills in low achieving elementary students.* Unpublished doctoral dissertation, University of Minnesota.

Marston, D. (1988). Measuring academic progress of students with learning difficulties: A comparison of the semi-logarithmic chart and equal interval graph paper. *Exceptional Children, 55*(1), 38–44.

Marston, D., & Deno, S. L. (1981). *The reliability of simple, direct measures of written expression* (Research Report No. 50). Minneapolis: University of Minnesota, Institute for Research on Learning Disabilities.

Marston, D., Fuchs, L., & Deno, S. L. (1986). Measuring pupil progress: A comparison of standardized achievement tests and curriculum-related measures. *Diagnostique, 11,* 77–90.

Marston, D., Lowry, L., Deno, S. L., & Mirkin, P. K. (1981). *An analysis of learning trends in simple measures of reading, spelling, and written expression: A longitudinal study* (Research Report No. 49). Minneapolis: University of Minnesota, Institute for Research on Learning Disabilities.

Marston, D., & Magnusson, D. (1985). Implementing curriculum-based measurement in special and regular education settings. *Exceptional Children, 52*(3), 266–276.

Marston, D., Tindal, G., & Deno, S. L. (1982). *Predictive efficiency of direct, repeated measurement: An analysis of cost and accuracy in classification* (Research Report No. 104). Minneapolis: University of Minnesota, Institute for Research on Learning Disabilities.

Minskoff, E. (1975). Research on psycholinguistic training: Critique and guidelines. *Exceptional Children, 42,* 136–144.

Minskoff, E., Wiseman, D. E., & Minskoff, J. G. (1972). *The MWM program for developing language abilities.* Ridgewood, NJ: Educational Performance Associates.

Morrissey, P. A., & Semwel, M. I. (1976). Instructional models for the learning disabled. *Theory into Practice, 14*(2), 110–122.

National Commission on Excellence in Education. (1983). *A nation at risk: The imperative for educational reform.* Washington, DC: U.S. Department of Education.

Newcomer, P. L. (1977). Special education services for the "mildly handicapped": Beyond a diagnostic and remedial model. *Journal of Special Education, 11,* 153–165.

Newcomer, P. L., & Goodman, L. (1975). Effects of modality instruction on the learning of meaningful and nonmeaningful material by auditory and visual learners. *Journal of Special Education, 9,* 261–268.

Newcomer, P. L., & Hammill, D. D. (1975). The ITPA and academic achievement: A survey. *Reading Teacher, 28,* 731–741.

Pennypacker, H. S., Koenig, C. H., & Lindsley, O. R.

(1972). *Handbook of the Standard Behavior Chart.* Kansas City, KS: Precision Media.

Peter, L. J. (1972). *Individual instruction.* New York: McGraw-Hill.

Pugach, M. (1987). The national education reports and special education: Implications for teacher preparation. *Exceptional Children, 53*(4), 308–314.

Quay, H. C. (1973). Special education: Assumptions, techniques, and evaluative criteria. *Exceptional Children, 40,* 165–170.

Reschly, D. J. (1987). Learning characteristics of mildly handicapped students: Implications for classification, placement, and programming. In M. C. Wang, M. C. Reynolds, & H. J. Walberg (Eds.), *The handbook of special education: Research and practice.* Oxford: Pergamon Press.

Reynolds, M. C. (1982). The rights of children: A challenge to school psychologists. In T. R. Kratochwill (Ed.), *Advances in school psychology* (Vol. 2). Hillsdale, NJ: Lawrence Erlbaum.

Reynolds, M. C., & Balow, B. (1972). Categories and variables in special education. *Exceptional Children, 38,* 357–366.

Rice, A. (1962). Rhythmic training and board balancing prepares a child for formal learning. *Nations Schools, 6,* 72.

Rosenshine, B. (1980). How time is spent in elementary classrooms. In C. Denham & A. Lieberman (Eds.), *Time to learn* (pp. 107–126). Washington, DC: National Institute for Education.

Rosner, J. (1963). The philosophy of developmental vision. *Journal of the American Optometric Association, 34,* 550–556.

Sapon-Shevin, M. (1987). The national education reports and special education: Implications for students. *Exceptional Children, 53*(4), 300–306.

Shapiro, E. S., & Lentz, F. E. (1985). Behavioral assessment of academic skills. In T. R. Kratochwill (Ed.), *Advances in school psychology* (Vol. 5). Hillsdale, NJ: Lawrence Erlbaum.

Shepard, L. A. (1987). The new push for excellence: Widening the schism between regular and special education. *Exceptional Children, 53*(4), 327–329.

Shinn, M., & Marston, D. (1985). Assessing mildly handicapped, low achieving and regular education students: A curriculum-basd approach. *Remedial and Special Education, 6,* 31–38.

Sizer, T. R. (1984). *Horace's compromise: The dilemma of the American high school.* Boston: Houghton Mifflin.

Skiba, R., Magnusson, D., Marston, D., & Erickson, K. (1985). *The assessment of mathematics performance in special education: Achievement tests, proficiency tests, or formuative evaluation.* Minneapolis, MN: Minneapolis Public Schools.

Smead, V. S. (1977). Ability training and task analysis in diagnostic/prescriptive teaching. *Journal of Special Education, 11,* 113–115.

Stephens, T. M. (1976). *Directive teaching of children with learning and behavioral handicaps* (2nd ed.). Columbus, OH: Charles E. Merrill.

Stephens, T. M., Hartman, A. C., & Lucas, V. H. (1978).

Teaching children basic skills. Columbus, OH: Charles E. Merrill.

Thurlow, M. L., Ysseldyke, J. E., Graden, J., & Algozzine, B. (1984). Opportunity to learn for LD students receiving different levels of special education services. *Learning Disability Quarterly, 7,* 55–68.

Tindal, G., Fuchs, L. S., Mirkin, P. K., Christenson, S., & Deno, S. (1981). *The relationship between student achievement and teacher assessment of short- or long-term goals* (Research Report No. 61). Minneapolis: University of Minnesota, Institute for Research on Learning Disabilities. (ERIC Document Reproduction Service No. ED 218 846)

Tindal, G., Marston, D., & Deno, S. L. (1983). *The reliability of direct and repeated measurement* (Research Report No. 109). Minneapolis: University of Minnesota, Institute for Research on Learning Disabilities.

Vandever, T. R., & Neville, D. D. (1974). Modality aptitude and word recognition. *Journal of Reading Behavior, 6,* 195–201.

Van Etten, C., & Van Etten, G. (1976). The measurement of pupil progress and selecting instructional materials. *Journal of Learning Disabilities, 9*(8), 469–480.

Wallace, G., & Larsen, S. C. (1978). *Educational assessment of learning problems: Testing for teaching.* Boston: Allyn and Bacon.

Wepman, J. M. (1967). The perceptual basis for learning. In E. C. Frierson & W. B. Barbe (Eds.), *Educating children with learning disabilities: Selected readings.* New York: Appleton-Century-Crofts.

White, O. R., & Haring, N. G. (1980). *Exceptional teaching: A multi-media training package* (2nd ed.). Columbus, OH: Charles E. Merrill.

Wiederholt, J. L., & Hammill, D. E. (1971). Use of the Frostig Horne Visual Perception Program in urban schools. *Pschology in the Schools, 3,* 260–274.

Woodcock, R. W. (1973). *Woodcock reading mastery tests* (Form A). Circle Pines, MN: American Guidance Services.

Ysseldyke, J. E. (1973). Diagnostic-prescriptive teaching:

The search for aptitude–treatment interactions. In L. Mann & D. Sabatino (Eds.), *The first review of special education.* New York: Grune & Stratton.

Ysseldyke, J. E. (1977). Aptitude–treatment interaction research with first grade children. *Contemporary Educational Psychology, 2,* 1–9.

Ysseldyke, J. E. (1978). Remediation of ability deficits in adolescents: Some major questions. In L. Mann, L. Goodman, & J. L. Wiederholt (Eds.), *The learning disabled adolescent.* Boston: Houghton Mifflin.

Ysseldyke, J. E. (1986). The use of assessment information to make decisions about students. In R. J. Morris & B. Blatt (Eds.), *Perspectives in special education: The state of the art.* Elmsford, NY: Pergamon Press.

Ysseldyke, J. E. & Christenson, S. L. (1987a). Evaluating students' instructional environments. *Remedial and Special Education, 8,* 17–24.

Ysseldyke, J. E., & Christenson, S. L. (1987b). *The instructional environment scale (TIES).* Austin, TX: PRO-ED.

Ysseldyke, J. E., Christenson, S. & Thurlow, M. (1987). *Instructional factors that influence student achievement: An integrative review* (Monograph No. 7). Minneapolis: University of Minnesota, Instructional Alternatives Project.

Ysseldyke, J. E., & Marston, D. (1987). Issues in the psychological evaluation of children. In V. Van Hasselt, M. Hersen, & P. Strain (Eds.), *Handbook of development and physical disabilities.* Elmsford, NY: Pergamon Press.

Ysseldyke, J., & Sabatino, D. (1973). Toward validation of the diagnostic-prescriptive model. *Academic Therapy, 8,* 415–422.

Ysseldyke, J. E., & Salvia, J. A. (1974). Diagnostic prescriptive teaching: Two models. *Exceptional Children, 41,* 181–186.

Ysseldyke, J. E., Thurlow, M. L., Christenson, S. L., & Weiss, J. (1987). Time allocated to instruction of mentally retarded, learning disabled, emotionally disturbed, and non-handicapped elementary students. *Journal of Special Education, 21,* 43–55.

27

TRAINING PARENTS AS BEHAVIOR CHANGE AGENTS: SUCCESSES, FAILURES, AND SUGGESTIONS FOR SCHOOL PSYCHOLOGISTS

JACK J. KRAMER

University of Nebraska–Lincoln

Two goals have guided the development of this chapter. First and foremost, an attempt is made to review the research that has been completed during the past two decades evaluating the training of parents as behavior change agents. Both the successes and failures of this research are delineated with suggestions for future research provided. Second, an attempt is made to emphasize the importance of school psychologists becoming more involved with parents and families. Although the importance of family life in educational achievement has been recognized by both school psychologists (e.g., Paget, 1987) and other professionals (e.g., G. E. Greenwood, Ware, Gordon, & Rhine, 1981), psychological services in the schools have not generally included parents and families as critical elements in the behavior change process (e.g., Carlson & Sincavage, 1987). Failure to utilize parents and family systems to enhance learning is to squander valuable resources.

Although school psychologists have not spent much of their time focusing on parents and family systems, psychological service delivery has been conceptualized increasingly as systemic in nature. According to Martens and Witt (1988):

> Emphasis on the application of an ecological perspective in psychology has increased steadily over the past 10 years. Ecologically based models such as embedded systems theory and reciprocal determinism (Bandura, 1978) have been applied to a diverse array of topics ranging from normal and abnormal human development to the functioning of large organizations (Bronfenbrenner, 1979; Dunst, 1985; Paget & Nagle, 1986). Defined by Webster as the branch of science concerned with the interaction of organisms and their environment, ecology refers to the study of mutual adaptation and accommodation between an organism and its habitat (Willems, 1974). Borrowing from this biological sciences model, the emergent ecological perspective in psychology has resulted in a paradigm shift away from a molecular focus on single determinants of behavior toward a molar focus that

emphasizes behavior–environment interactions at both an organismic and systems level. (pp. 115–116)

As we will see in our review of the parent training literature, no body of research more clearly details the importance of understanding the interaction among the myriad of variables that affect family systems than does the last two decades of attempts to train parents as behavior change agents.

OVERVIEW: EVOLUTION AND CURRENT PERSPECTIVES

Many different people have traced the origins of attempts to provide parent education, with somewhat different outcomes (e.g., Beekman, 1977; Kramer, 1985; Polster & Dangel, 1984). However, most agree that it was not until the appearance of the so-called "child study movement" during the late 19th and early 20th centuries that there was sustained interest in the study of children's needs and subsequently, ways to teach parents to provide for these needs.

Although the child study movement began in earnest in Europe, it is clear that efforts in this country to understand more about parents' ability to have a positive impact on children can be traced to this movement. During the child study movement biographical and anecdotal records were used to study infant and child cognitive development as well as physical growth in young children. G. Stanley Hall and his graduate students Henry Goddard, Arnold Gesell, and Lewis Terman did much of the early child study work and maintained the momentum of the movement in America.

Related to the child study movement was the development of techniques and instruments that allowed for the examination of both the physical and mental growth of the child. Studies examined the development of a variety of intellectual, moral, and social concepts. Early attempts to map general patterns of growth with precise outlines failed, however, because these attempts neglected the importance of environmental influences. As a result, one of the broad conclusions of the child study movement was that while an understanding of biological development of the child was important, the environmental history of the child was also important in influencing the behavior of the child (Good & Teller, 1973).

Over the last 30 to 40 years many authors have advanced suggestions for improving parents' ability to have a positive impact on their children. Rarely have these suggestions been based on experimental evidence. "Authors often base their ideas on personal experience, untested assumptions, and social convention" (Polster and Dangel, 1984, p. 3). Both Polster and Dangel (1984) and Beekman (1977) have examined published materials targeted at parents and concluded that these materials have varied more as a function of the political climate in the United States than through advancement in scientific knowledge. This trend is not all that surprising given that very little research on training parents as behavior change agents was available until the 1970s.

During the two decades covered by this review, interest in and experimental analysis of parent–child interaction and the effects of environmental stimuli on parent and child behavior has grown extensively (Rogers-Weise & Kramer, 1988). Although most people working with parents would agree that training can improve parent effectiveness, much controversy has ensued regarding the "how" and "what" of such training.

As suggested above, parent education and training programs have had a variety of goals, including developing self-awareness, using effective teaching methods, improving communication and family life, and supplying child development information (among others). Not surprisingly, the instructional content and teaching methods used to accomplish these goals have often varied as a function of the theoretical perspective of the author of the program. Three perspecitves have dominated within the parent training area: humanistic approaches (e.g., *Between Parent and Child*, Ginott, 1969; *Parent Effectiveness Training* (PET), Gordon, 1970), Adlerian-based approaches (e.g., *Active Parenting*, Popkin, 1983; *Systematic Training for Effective Parenting* (STEP), Dinkmeyer & McKay, 1977; mother study groups), and behavioral approaches (e.g., *Parents Are Teachers*, Becker, 1971; *Solving Child Behavior Problems at Home & School*, Blechman, 1985).

Dembo, Sweitzer, and Lauritzen (1985) reviewed representative parent education research in the areas cited above (i.e., humanistic, Adlerian, and behavioral). In the humanistic area research evaluating *PET* was reviewed. The majority of research (15 of 18 studies reviewed) consists of unpublished master's theses and doctoral dissertations. Many of these projects were completed under the direction of the founder of PET, Thomas Gordon. Assessment of program effectiveness has focused primarily upon changes in parental child-rearing attitudes, with mixed results. Few investigations examined changes in parent and/or child behaviors; however, the available evidence indicated little or no apparent change in the behavior of targeted individuals. Other reviewers have reached similiar conclusions (e.g., W. J. Doherty & Puder, 1980).

Ten studies were examined in an attempt to assess the efficacy of Adlerian approaches to parent training. Most of the reviewed research involved mother-study groups. Parent attitude measures in these studies have indicated positive changes in child-rearing attitudes, but little evidence of change in children's behavior (Dembo et al., 1985). A recent dissertation (Weise, 1989) evaluated the effects of parent participation in an Adlerian-based training program (*Active Parenting,* Popkin, 1983). Multiple dependent measures were used within a Solomon four-group design. As with previous studies, participants tended to develop a more tolerant attitude toward their children and perceived themselves as better parents than did parents not participating in the parenting program. Parents did not improve their knowledge of behavior principles of child management following training. Nor did parental report of children's behavior or child report of self-concept change as a function of training.

By far the largest number of studies has been done with behavioral parent training. Dembo and his colleagues suggest that these studies appear to have fewer methodological flaws and to have utilized larger numbers of oucome variables than did the studies cited above. In general, these investigations appear to have shown that analysis of enviromental stimuli increases the ability to affect the behavior of parents and children.

Although the scarcity of data on humanistic and Adlerian programs makes it difficult to evaluate the long-term impact of these programs, there has been no shortage of research on behavioral parent training. There are, however, a variety of reasons other than just volume of research that argue for focusing our attention on behavioral parent training. The experimental analysis of behavior, which serves as the foundation for all attempts to apply behavior management principles to parents and childrne, has a long history of promoting the development of effective technologies for behavior change. The success of early

research in the experimental analysis of behavior (e.g., Skinner's work with operant conditioning [Skinner, 1938]) caused researchers to move out of the laboratory and into schools, clinics, and hospitals. Among the earliest demonstrations of the potential of these principles in an applied context involved investigations of teaching machines (e.g., Skinner, 1954), programmed instruction (e.g., Keller, 1968), and operant conditioning of severely impaired populations (e.g., Azrin, Rubin, O'Brien, Ayllon, & Roll, 1968). Buoyed by the success of these investigations, researchers began to look for new settings (e.g., homes) and populations (e.g., parents) to whom these methods could be applied. Although the ultimate impact of methods developed from humanistic and Adlerian approaches to parent training is unknown, the research examined herein will leave little question that application of the methods developed from the experimental analysis of behavior have done much to advance our understanding of the parenting process and its impact on children.

The point of view expressed in this chapter is similar to that advanced by Hawkins (1972):

> It is not a matter of whether parents will use behavior modification techniques to manipulate their children, but rather whether they will use these techniques unconsciously with an unknown, unchosen and unhappy result, or use them consciously, efficiently, and consistently to develop the qualities they choose for their children. (p. 38)

PARENT TRAINING: TWO DECADES OF ADVANCEMENT AND REFINEMENT

Parents have been a popular subject population for behavioral scientists. The many different reviews of the parent training literature appearing during the last two decades provide evidence of both the interest in the area and volume of research that has been completed (Berkowitz & Graziano, 1972; Bernstein, 1983; Budd & Fabray, 1985; Dangel & Polster, 1984a; Kramer, 1985; Moreland, Schwebel, Beck, & Wells, 1982; O'Dell, 1974; Resinger, Ora, & Frangia, 1976; Rogers-Weise & Kramer, 1988; Sanders & James, 1983). Obviously, many ways of categorizing or classifying this research have been advanced. The model proposed by Gail Bernstein (1983) will be used here to help organize the extensive research literature.

Although Bernstein's article was a description of a generic model for understanding the training of behavior change agents, the questions she poses have been adapted here to facilitate our understanding of parent training research over the last two decades. The questions, as well as answers provided by the behavioral literature, are detailed below.

What Problems Must Parents Be Able to Solve?

The notion here is that training must address problems that will be encountered in the real world. Or, as Bernstein (1983) succinctly states: "There is little point in teaching people to apply behavioral analysis to problems they will not be called upon to solve, and there is much to be gained from using frequently occurring problems as examples during training" (p. 7).

Behavioral scientists have studied the effects of using parents as agents of change for many different problems experienced by children. Examples include stealing (e.g., Stumphauzer, 1976), hyperactivity (e.g., Dubey, O'Leary, & Kaufman, 1983), language development (Muir & Milan, 1982), dining out (e.g., Bauman, Reiss, Rogers, & Bailey, 1983; R. B. Greene, Harrison, & Greene, 1984), extensive television watching (Wolfe, Mendes, & Factor, 1984), and others. Researchers have also been interested in studying the effects of parent training activities on improving harmful behavior in parents (e.g., abuse) that lead to problems with children (e.g., Sandler, VanDercar, & Milhoen, 1978; Wolfe & Sandler, 1981). The examples cited above merely scratch the surface of the many problems that researchers have addressed through parent training.

Two of the most widely researched problems areas in regard to parent training have been non-compliance and aggression in young children. When families experience serious interpersonal conflict, parents and children have developed dysfunctional social interaction patterns that result in children coercing reinforcers through some combination of disobedience, fighting, stealing, lying, crying and temper tantrums. Researchers such as Forehand and McMahon (1981), Patterson (1982), Wahler (1980), and their colleagues have spent years investigating these problems and have developed highly structured programs designed to help parents learn new skills and apply these skills in an effective manner. The systematic research

programs developed by these scientists have provided much of the available information about what works with parents. It should also be noted that when we examine some of the shortcomings of behavioral parent training, it will also be clear that it is the research on noncompliance and antisocial behavior that has provided the most information on factors that attenuate the effectiveness of training methods.

Regardless of whether one uses number of research articles (Rogers-Weise & Kramer, 1988) or parent-referral data (Forehand, 1977), researchers and parents have defined the major problems that parents have to deal with as noncompliance and aggression. Even when professionals have attempted to develop preventive rather than remedial programs, parents have typically been taught skills that would help them avoid the conflict caused by child noncompliance (Azrin & Foxx, 1974; B. F. Greene, Clark, & Risley, 1977; R. B. Greene et al., 1984).

One final note about the problems that confront parents in regard to their children. The work of Patterson and colleagues (e.g., Bank, Patterson, & Reid, 1987; Patterson, 1982) suggests that one of the best predictors of "delinquincy" are levels of noncompliance and conflict in families with young children. The addition of antisocial and aggressive acts to noncompliance increases the chances of significant, long-term problems. These data support the conclusions reached by Robins (1979) a decade ago. Children in homes with high rates of noncompliance and aversive control are at risk for serious problems as adolescents and adults if the problem of childhood noncompliance is not dealt with quickly and efficiently. Failure to teach parents skills to deal with these problems in early childhood appears to have long-term deleterious consequences for both children and parents. Results suggesting the types of skills that are most likely to lead to resolution of parent–child conflict are examined below.

What Skills Of Parents Lead to Problem Solution?

Do parents who have fewer problems with their children do things differently than parents with greater numbers of problems? If the process of studying parent behavior and the impact of environmental stimuli on parents and children is functional, we would expect the answer to this question to be "yes." In fact, the answer is "yes," and knowledge of the relative importance to parent and child behavior of differing skill levels has advanced significantly.

The method used most frequently to determine differences between functional and dysfunctional families has been to examine differences that exist between clinic-referred and non-clinic-referred children and families. This approach reveals that factors such as parents' perception of children's behavior, marital adjustment, parents' personal adjustment, and parents' extrafamilial relationships are among the best predictors of the severity of family distress (see McMahon and Forehand, 1984, for a review of this research). In a similar manner, qualitative research from outside the behavioral literature (Stinnett & DeFrain, 1985) has identified a number of characteristics of "strong" families, including commitment to the family, appreciation and acknowledgment of family members' contribution to the family, communication among family members, time together, spiritual wellness or commitment to some standard of behavior, and the ability to cope with stress. Although the information provided above is important, these kinds of global predictors and characteristics tell us little about either the specific environmental conditions or individual behaviors that distinguish effective from dysfunctional parenting. Or stated differently, it is important to know about an individual's "level of adjustment," but it is more important to understand the environmental stimuli functionally related to parental behavior and to know the behaviors that need to be taught or eliminated so that people are better "adjusted" or more "functional."

Researchers interested in a more molecular analysis of parenting skills related to child and family adjustment have indicated that skill deficits such as an inability to organize (e.g., G. Doherty, 1975), high frequency of verbal commands and a corresponding inability to code behavior appropriately (Wahler & Dumas, 1984), misperception of levels of misbehavior in chilren (Lobitz & Johnson, 1975), and inability to establish or maintain social relationships (Wahler, 1980) all contribute to parenting inefficiency. Longitudinal data from nonclinical populations suggest that "healthier" families tend to use more positive or prosocial teaching methods than do parents of clinic-referred children (Bank et al., 1987). It is also apparent from many training studies that parents who have learned or are able to learn to discuss, model, provide connective feedback, avoid or deescalate arguments, and consequate behavior appropriately are able to teach more efficiently and effectively (McMahon & Forehand, 1984; Moreland et al., 1982).

Data from nonclinical and "competent" families (Blechman, 1984) similar to that cited above has been rare. Answers to questions about "effective" parents in naturalistic settings and the differences between clinical and nonclinical populations has not been available. For example, research investigating parent–child interaction over long periods of time (e.g., weeks, months, years) in naturalistic settings has begun to appear only recently, although alternative methods for analyzing these types of data are becoming increasingly familiar to behavioral scientists (e.g., Bakeman & Gottman, 1986). It seems safe to conclude, at present, that we know a great deal about the characteristics that tend to define populations seeking services for noncompliant and disobediant children and we have learned about many different skills that when taught in clinic settings tend to improve parenting effectiveness. However, when it comes to describing optimal conditions in family systems, we know considerably less about the occurrence of specific behaviors and their frequency, duration, and sequence.

What Teaching Techniques Produce Acquisition of Behavior Change Skills In Parents?

If a family has a problem (e.g., high rates of arguments between parent and child) and we know one of the skills that will improve the situation (e.g., ability to avoid or deescalate arguments), how best do we teach parents the behaviors needed to reduce or eliminate the problem? As we will see, research has provided a good deal of information about the general procedures that promote learning in parents and we are beginning to understand more about the optimal ways to combine these procedures.

Unfortunately for most practitioners pressed for time, no studies can be found demonstrating that parents can learn behavior change skills through oral instruction. Talking, as an instructional tool for training behavior change agents, has not been shown to alter behavior in any significant manner (O'Dell, 1985; Ziarnik & Bernstein, 1982). However, research has been completed demonstrating that with well-defined, discrete problems, written instructions may assist *some* parents in improving their skill level. For example, both Johnson, Whitman, and Barloon-Noble (1978) and Green et al. (1976) were able to alter parent behavior through written instruction so that parents could reduce levels of inappropriate child behavior. It should also be noted that both studies cited above were characterized by minimal levels of therapist-delivered instruction. Researchers have shown that some parents can learn to reduce inappropriate mealtime behavior (McMahon & Forehand, 1978), reduce levels of enuresis (Besalal, Azrin, Thienes-Hontos, & McMorrow, 1980), and reduce children's fear of the dark (Giebenhain & O'Dell, 1984) through the use of written materials and without therapist contact.

However, the programs cited above were, for the most part, based on empirically developed training materials that provided considerable detail about interventions that would need to be undertaken by parents (O'Dell, 1985). Others have noted significant problems with many of the written materials available for parents (e.g., Glasgow & Rosen, 1978; McMahon & Forehand, 1980). Studies comparing the instructional effects of using different training procedures have generally found written materials to be among the least effective (e.g., Flanagan, Adams, & Forehand, 1979; Nay, 1975; O'Dell, Flynn, & Beniolo, 1977). The equivocal nature of much of the research on the effects of verbal instructions (both oral and written) and the lack of empirical data on many currently available published programs lead one to seriously question the use of such procedures in isolation.

There is no shortage of research demonstrating the effectiveness of procedures that more directly involve the client "in" the material to be learned. As in other instructional settings, procedures that require the client to be engaged (e.g., C. R. Greenwood, Delquadri, and Hall, 1984) in the material do better than those which require less involvement. Visual methods such as modeling (e.g., Nay, 1975; Webster-Stratton, 1981) and interactive methods such as role playing/behavioral rehearsal (e.g., Flanagan et al., 1979; O'Dell et al., 1977) have been shown to enhance learning. In addition to the importance of having an opportunity to practice overtly or covertly, the presence of corrective feedback generally enhances training effects (Bernal, Williams, Miller, & Reagor, 1972; Forehand & King, 1977). It is

beyond the scope of this review to examine the many different studies demonstrating the benefits of direct instruction of the skills to be learned. Suffice it to say, however, that these procedures have been shown to be effective in improving parents' behavior change skills, both when used alone and when combined with each other (Forehand & King, 1977; O'Dell, Mahoney, Horton, & Turner, 1979). Written materials may be a helpful adjunct to these more direct methods (O'Dell, Krug, Patterson, & Faustman, 1980), although much remains unknown about the optimal ways to combine procedures to maximize training effectiveness (O'Dell, 1985).

The training program described by Forehand and McMahon (1981) to train parents to reduce noncompliance in children incorporates many of the procedures described above.

> The parent training program employs a controlled learning environment in which to teach the parent to change maladaptive patterns of interactions with the child. Sessions are conducted in a clinic setting with individual families rather than in groups. Treatment occurs in clinic playrooms equipped with one-way mirrors for observation, sound systems, and bug-in-the-ear (Farrall Instruments) devices by which the therapist can unobtrusively communicate with the parent. A table, chairs, and several age-appropriate toys are in each playroom. A number of discrete parenting skills are taught in a systematic manner. The skills are taught to the parent by way of didactic interaction, modeling, and role playing. The parent also practices the skills in the clinic with the child while receiving prompting and feedback from the therapist by means of the bug-in-the-ear device. Finally, the parent employs these newly acquired skills in the home setting. (McMahon & Forehand, 1984, pp. 300)

Within this training program, parents are taught how to attend and describe the appropriate behavior of their children and to eliminate commands, questions, and criticisms. Handouts are given prior to the introduction of new skills (e.g., rewards, time-out), skills are modeled and practiced, homework is assigned in the form of daily 10-minute practice sessions, feedback is provided based on clinic observations of the parent–child dyad (typically, mother–child), and "competence" (based on stated behavioral and temporal criteria) must be demonstrated before a new skill is introduced. Most training programs that have demonstrated some degree of success combine training techniques in a manner similar to that described above, with written materials, modeling, behavioral rehearsal, and feedback included in most packages (Azrin & Foxx, 1974; Braukmann, Ramp, Tigner, & Wolf, 1984; Dangel & Polster, 1984b; Lutzker, 1984; Patterson, Reid, Jones, & Conger, 1975; Shearer & Loftin, 1984).

When one discusses effective training procedures with parents, the issue of obtained competence appears most deserving of our attention. Regardless of whether one works with individual clients or with groups (e.g., Eyberg & Matarazzo, 1980; Rickert et al., 1988), working with parents to achieve stated levels of competence is more effective than is time-limited or didactic training. Although it is important to know how to train parents *most* effectively, the ultimate goal of training is to ensure parental competence. Perhaps in our efforts to train parent as behavior change agents, the single most important step we can take toward assuring learning is to understand and operationalize the skills we want parents to learn and continue to provide training and feedback until parents achieve stated levels of competence. This process might be both expensive and time consuming, but what is the alternative—more cost-efficient training methods that don't work as well (or at all)?

As indicated at the beginning of this section on "teaching techniques," much has been learned about effective training and the impact of combining procedures into treatment packages. However, much remains unknown about how these combinations of procedures interact with factors such as parent characteristics and training content (O'Dell, 1985). Further, there is a great deal to learn about how to combine training procedures to minimize therapist time and maximize therapeutic outcome.

What Procedures Promote Generalization of Behavior Change Skills?

The conclusion of almost every review of the training literature with parents during the last 20 years, and there have been many, has been that generalization of behavior change skills by parents is not to be expected as a normal consequence of training (Berkowitz & Graziano, 1972; Bernstein, 1983; Budd & Fabray, 1985; Dangel & Polster,

1984a; Kramer, 1985; Moreland, Schwebel, Beck, & Wells, 1982; Resinger et al., 1976; Sanders & James, 1983). An overview of this research is provided below. Consistent with previous analyses (e.g., Dragman, Hammer, & Rosenbaum, 1978; Moreland et al., 1982; Sanders & James, 1983), generalization research in parent training is examined in four areas: temporal, setting, behavior, and sibling. In each of these four areas the primary concern is with transfer of *parent* skills rather than with child behavior, essentially because the ability of parents to generalize skills across time, setting, behavior, and individuals is a necessary prerequisite of behavior change in children. Of course, the ultimate test of generalization is change in child behavior, which is also discussed below.

The ability of parents to generalize trained skills over time (i.e., maintenance or temporal generalization) has received more attention than any other form of generalization. In an early and extensive test of temporal generality, Patterson (1974) found that approximately 50% of the families who had participated in training required further training in order to return skill levels to the point at which they had been immediately subsequent to training. Although more positive outcomes ranging from 6–12 months (Forehand et al., 1979) to 3–9 years (Strain, Steele, Ellis, and Timm, 1982) have been obtained, the failure of parents to maintain skills has been a consistent finding of many of the leading researchers in the area (O'Dell, 1982), with failure rates similar or even greater than that noted by Patterson (1974) above.

Although researchers have lamented difficulties in obtaining maintenance of results, many investigators have been innovative in devolping programs to assist in generalization across time. O'Dell (1985) has looked extensively at this research and suggested that therapist-delivered contingencies in search of maintenance have included, "in order of reported frequency, . . . social reinforcement, discussing benefits to the parent and child, contracting, making continuation in training contingent on parent completion of assignments, tangible rewards such as money or books, and contingent return of fees" (p. 89). Examination of this research reveals that these techniques have typically enhanced generalization, if in a somewhat modest fashion.

Setting generalization involves the transfer of skills from the treatment setting to some other place, such as home, school, or community. In general, these studies have yielded equivocal results. For example, many studies have been completed demonstrating that parents *can* transfer skills across settings (e.g., Budd, Pinkston, & Green, 1977). As with maintenance, the addition of therapist-controlled contingencies during (e.g., Eyberg & Johnson, 1974; Rinn, Vernon, & Wise, 1975) and following (e.g., Muir & Milan, 1982) training enhance setting generalization. However, when one goes beyond case study or small-*N* experimental research and examines broader attempts to provide parents with skills that can be maintained and transfered to new settings (McMahon & Forehand, 1984; Patterson, 1982; Wehler, 1980), the evidence is less convincing in regard to our ability to ensure setting generalization with large numbers of parents. As the number of problems beyond the parent–child conflict increase within the family system, our ability to foster generalization of skills to the natural environment decreases.

Studies of setting generalization of "target" child behavior from clinic to school following completion of training by the child's parents have also yielded conflicting results. Examples include decreases in inappropriate behaviors with concommitant increases in appropriate behavior (Cox & Matthews, 1977), no relationship between clinic improvements and school behavior (Forehand et al., 1979), and even increases in school problems following parent training (S. M. Johnson, Bolstad, & Lobitz, 1976).

Although much less research has been conducted on behavioral and sibling generalization, evidence does exist suggesting that parents can apply clinic-learned skills to behaviors that were not the focus of training (Koegel, Glahn, & Nieminen, 1978; Wells, Forehand, & Griest, 1980) and children who were not the "target" of trained skills (Eyberg & Robinson, 1982). Little data are available, but we suspect that just as in other areas, behavioral and sibling generalization will vary as a function of the extent to which the stimuli in the training and natural settings are similar and the number and strength of competing stimuli in the natural environment.

Our understanding of basic considerations in the study of generalization of training has advanced considerably in the last 20 years. Much remains unknown about the nature or manner in which to have an impact on the specific stimulus

conditions that exist in the natural environment of stressed parents, although analysis of these events appears at an ever-increasing rate (e.g., Wahler & Barnes, 1988). Until recently, it appears that researchers have spent more time studying how to train parents to learn new skills as opposed to how to implement these skills in the natural environment.

Summary: Where to From Here?

The importance of establishing the presence of training effects with parents has been the focus of this chapter up until this point. During the last decade, researchers (Kazdin, 1977; Wolf, 1978) have suggested the importance of establishing social validity as well as training efficacy. Social validity involves evaluating the extent to which therapeutic changes are "clinically or socially important for the client" (Kazdin, 1977, p. 429). Three distinct approaches to the assessment of social validity in the training of parents have emerged: social comparison (Forehand, Wells, & Griest, 1980; Patterson, 1974), consumer satisfaction (McMahon & Forehand, 1983, 1984; McMahon, Tiedemann, Forehand, & Griest, 1984; Patterson and Reid, 1983), and treatment acceptability (Calvert and McMahon, 1987; Kazdin, 1980a, 1980b, 1981; Reimers, Wacker, & Koeppl, 1987; Walle, Hobbs, & Caldwell, 1984).

The impact of training effectiveness on social validity and parent perception is unclear, although some evidence of parents ability to distinguish between programs of differing effectiveness is available (Dubey et al., 1983; McMahon et al., 1984). Although a relatively "late" entrant into the behavioral parent training literature, research on social validity has increased significantly during the last decade. Much has been learned, not only about whether training programs have impact on or are noticed by individuals in the child's natural environment, but also about the perceptions and feelings of parents regarding the interventions they are asked to use and the programs in which they participate.

As a result of the literature reviewed to this point, we can provide important information to parents that was not available just a few years ago. For example, the importance and potential benefits of early parental intervention and the potential danger of failed remediation efforts can be emphasized with more assurance and confidence. Although it is heartening to know that we have learned a great deal during the last two decades, there is much yet to be accomplished.

PARENT TRAINING RESEARCH: THE NEXT GENERATION

Much has been accomplished in a relatively short period. There have, however, been noteworthy "failures" within this body of research and, just as significantly, numerous areas that have escaped serious investigation. Some of these deficiencies have been alluded to above. Promising and needed research initiatives are identified below.

Systemic Considerations in Parent Training

The attenuating effects of factors such as low-socioeconomic status (e.g., Dumas & Wahler, 1983; McMahon, Forehand, Griest, & Wells, 1981), poor parental adjustment (e.g., Griest, Wells, & Forehand, 1979), and inaccurate parental perceptions of child behavior (e.g., Lobitz & Johnson, 1975) on training effectiveness are well established. The importance of social relationships and mother "insularity" on parent training are also well documented (e.g., Wahler, 1980; Wahler & Dumas, 1984). The presence of harsh, excessively punitive, and inconsistent father behavior (e.g., Patterson, 1982) within the family system appears to be a negative influence on child adjustment. Unfortunately, treatment for these parents who are most in need of services continues to be a significant problem for therapists interested in improving the quality of the parent–child relationship.

This is not to suggest, however, that we have not learned a great deal about family systems and the limitations of earlier conceptualizations of human behavior. Ongoing research programs offer increased hope for understanding the difficulties of changing behavior in complex behavioral ecosystems. At the beginning of this chapter Martens and Witt were quoted (1988) regarding the expanding conceptualizations of human behavior within psychology. The "figure-context interbehavioral model" proposed by Wahler and Dumas (in press) to account for attentional and coding deficits in dysfunctional mother-child dyads and the "antisocial behavior" model advanced by Patterson and colleagues (e.g., Bank et al., 1987; Patterson, 1986) both provide evidence of the increased importance that researchers attach to understanding the complex array of stimuli that constitute

family systems. Focus on a broader understanding of parent and child behavior as it exists in environmental ecosystems has led to a better understanding both of the importance of setting events (e.g., family and community) on behavior and the impact of long-term patterns of dysfunctional behavior (e.g., aggression) in analysis and remediation of parent–child functioning.

Finally with regard to family systems, there appears a need for more data describing behavioral interaction within natural settings and "healthy" families (e.g., Bank et al., 1987; Blechman, 1984; O'Dell, 1985). Increased knowledge of long-term behavioral patterns in families characterized by high levels of positive interaction would serve as useful comparison data to that already available on dysfunctional families. Measurement of the levels of family management constructs (i.e., discipline, monitoring, positive practices, problem solving, and parent involvement) advanced by Patterson and associates (Patterson, 1982; Patterson & Bank, 1986) appear a reasonable starting point for researchers interested in assessment of functional families. Descriptive data on the behavioral interactions of healthy families would seem an important precursor to the development of the next generation of programs targeted at improving the behavior change skills of parents.

Self-Help/Bibliotherapy

There is little available research that would suggest that self-help manuals or other self-administered instruction materials serve to promote the development of behavior change skills in parents or any other group. Although examples of training success are available (e.g., Giebienhain & O'Dell, 1984; McMahon & Foreland, 1978), verbal materials given to parents have less effect on skill development than do most other approaches. Unfortunately, this has not stopped authors and publishers from marketing materials that claim to help parents improve their skills.

Reviews of both self-help manuals (Bernal & North, 1978; McMahon & Forehand, 1980; O'Farrell & Keuthen, 1983) and general bibliotherapy approaches (e.g., Stevens & Pfost, 1982) suggest that the following conclusions are warranted with regard to these materials: (a) most commercially available products designed to be self-administered do not promote behavior change; (b) most published materials have not undergone experimental testing and provide no validation data related to parent or child behavior change; (c) although typically not of much help by themselves, self-help materials can be of assistance when combined with therapist contact (e.g., Butler, 1976; M. R. Johnson et al., 1978) or other training methods (e.g., Heifetz, 1977); and (d) published materials vary a great deal in readability and one cannot assume that the instructional level of these materials will be appropriate for all clients.

Although the evidence is not supportive of the use of self-help materials, it would seem that further experimental research is warranted. Clearly, the current state of the art suggests that bibliotherapy should not be expected to work as a matter of course. There is suggestive evidence that some parents (e.g., more schooling, higher SES) may be able to learn to manage discrete problems (e.g., Besalal and Azkin, 1980; Clark et al., 1977) with the use of well-designed materials (O'Dell, 1985). Given the evidence suggesting that the price of effective interventions spiral as parents become more stressed, we should not dismiss lightly the possibility that some groups may respond positively to less costly procedures. Many parents seek out information about parenting prior to the birth of a child and certainly before the appearance of problems. Perhaps information supplied to young parents and functional parent–child dyads should be considered a "first-order" level of intervention, with therapists progressing to other, more costly levels (e.g., modeling, rehearsal, role playing) only as needed. A similiar "multiple gating" approach for using resources to assess family functioning has been advanced elsewhere (e.g., Loeber, Dishion, & Patterson, 1984).

With increased availability of computer and video technology, there is increased likelihood that verbal instructional materials will be designed and marketed for parents. The appearance of new products, as well as other reasons suggested above, all argue for ongoing research to determine if verbal materials can be expected to work consistently and, if so, under what conditions and with what groups.

Short-term Workshops/Didactic Training

The research cited above makes it clear that information presented alone does not produce behavior change in parents or their children (if one assumes that parents read material provided to them). It also appears that even when didactic instruction is provided by an "expert," as in many short-term workshops, information does not lead to behavior change in individuals (Ziarnik & Bernstein, 1982).

The point has been made in many ways throughout different sections of this chapter—talking to parents about the principles and practice of effective parenting has consistently been shown to be one of the weaker instructional strategies for making parents better change agents (e.g., O'Dell, 1985). This appears true across different formats and content (e.g., Flanagan et al., 1979; Rickert et al., 1988). It is true that verbal instruction (both oral and written) can be effective in promoting increased knowledge in parents, but knowledge does not necessarily lead to behavior change (e.g., Flanagan et al., 1979; Nay, 1975).

One interesting feature of didactic parent training interactions is that parents often report feeling better about themselves and/or their child management skills following participation in the training. Consistent, positive changes in parental attitude following training have been demonstrated in both behavioral and other forms of parent training (e.g., Dembo et al., 1985). Although the precise meaning of this finding is unclear, it does appear that parents who complete training report that they like getting together, talking about their children, and reviewing different strategies for dealing with parent–child problems. If one's goal is to improve parental knowledge, it appears that didactic, group training is a cost-efficient method for obtaining this goal. Futhermore, parents completing the group will typically report the experience as being positive—no small accomplishment if one is concerned about parent's perception of their child's school and school system.

Training Parent Therapists

Differences in therpist skill level and the impact of such variablity on therapeutic outcome have been acknowledged by most of the leading researchers in the field. "Therapists must be experienced and trained clinicians who can deal with a variety of family problems, such as marital conflict, depression, and alcoholism, which may arise as issues during the course of the parent training" (Bank et al., 1987, p. 79). Unfortunately, of all the variables specific to parent training, it would appear that the least amount of research attention has been given to those variables related to the "parent trainer" or "therapist." Although research on general therapist effectiveness has been completed (see e.g., Garfield & Bergin, 1978; Gurman & Kniskern, 1981; Parloff, Waskow, & Wolfe, 1978), the variablility of the quality of this research provides little in the way of support for specific guidelines related to best practices for parent trainers.

Many commercially available training programs suggest only that the trainer be familiar with the materials or, if they so desire, complete a brief workshop (e.g., Popkin, 1983). Yet the difficulties encountered by therapists in training behavior change skills is significant. Chamberlain and Baldwin (1988) note the liklihood of resistance from as many as 30% of parents involved in a training program particulary when the training relates to specific techniques of discipline.

Investigators at the Oregon Social Learning Center have acknowledged the importance of therapists dealing effectively with client resistance (Bank et al., 1987; Chamberlain & Baldwin, 1988) as an important precursor to effective intervention. Wahler and Dumas (1984) have pointed out the benefits of parent therapists serving as effective listeners and assisting clients within the context of a "friendship" relationship. Clinical evidence from the laboratories cited above suggest that initially, troubled parents do not react positively to trainers who "tell" them what they have to do to change their behavior. Unfortunately, other than for anecdotal data, little evidence is available that has elucidated either the specific stimuli or the combinations of therapist behaviors that serve to promote effective interaction between therapist and client.

Some exceptions do exist. Issacs, Embry, and Baer (1982) have shown that graduate students of varying backgrounds can be trained to improve "instructing, informing, and praising" behavior with a few hours of training and feedback. Bergan and colleagues (e.g., Bergan, Kratochwill, & Luiten, 1980; Bergan & Tombari, 1976) have demonstrated the importance of problem definition in the resolution of problems experienced by teachers in school situations. Although this research dealt with consultations between psychologist and teacher, there are many similiarities between these consultations and that which occurs between psychologist and parent during problem definition (Bernstein, 1983). This research of Bergan and colleagues is important, not only as a result of findings in regard to problem identification, but because the research draws attention to

the verbal behavior of psychologists and the relationship of verbal behavior to problem definition, and ultimately, problem resolution.

While describing their attempts to increase generalization of parent training across settings (i.e., mand review), Wahler and Dumas (1984) had this to say about training therapists to serve as parent trainers:

> We cannot, however, provide clear rule descriptions of how the parent trainer responds to the mother's answers to the inquiries. . . . We know that some parent trainers are very good at this supplementary teaching and some are not—certainly an index of the "art vs. technology" status of mand review. (p. 403)

It is inevitable that parent training "interventions" will involve the trainer with children, parents, and the entire family system. It stands to reason that well-schooled and experienced trainers would be more effective at promoting skill development in parents and children. Specific knowledge about how such "experience" is manifested during and across sessions with clients is unknown. Empirical verification of the differential impact of trainer skill level on intervention effectiveness is not available. Clearly, further investigation of the effects of trainer characteristics and behavior on development *and* maintenance of effective skills in families is warranted.

Parents As Agents of Educational Change

The evidence that parents can be effective in advancing school achievement and behavior is clear and convincing. Whether monitoring a home–school communcation program (e.g., Imber, Imber, & Rothstein, 1979; Weiss et al., 1983), tutoring their children (e.g., C. R. Greenwood et al., 1984), or participating in a behavior management program (e.g., Pray, Kramer, & Lindskog, 1986), parents have been effective agents of change for a variety of school-related problems. Individual parents not experiencing significant stress can be trained to direct or assist the remediation of many different types of problems that occur at school (e.g., Allen, 1978; Atkeson & Forehand, 1978; Whorton et al., 1982). The extent to which schools (e.g., Skinner, 1984; Watkins, 1988) and school psychologists have been able to use this information (e.g., Carlson & Sincavage, 1987) is discouraging.

Even in the absence of professional assistance, however, parents have not stood still when it comes to the "preparedness" of their children for the schooling experience. There seems little debate about the fact that children come to school better prepared than was the case a generation ago. There has been a great deal of controversy, however, over "how" parents have prepared their children for schooling, with many believing that children have been placed at risk for a variety of behavioral and emotional problems as a result of parent pressure and expectations (e.g., Elkind, 1981). Based on the impressive parent–school research literature and the questions that society has about current parenting practices, the question isn't whether or not school psychologists should move to involve parents in education and schooling, but how? Most governmental mandates and system priorties have not encouraged the involvement of school psychologists with parents. Further, schools have not traditionally been involved with parents until after children have reached school age.

There is little to guide us in the development of specific strategies for school psychologists interested in working with parents. That is, there is little empirical evidence that tells us "better" or "best" ways for practitioners to become more involved with parents. We do know, however, that children can learn, that parents can teach, and that parents play an important role in children's perception about and development in school. In the final section of this chapter some tentative suggestions are offered for school psychologists interested in developing or improving parents' behavior change skills.

How to Make Groups as Effective as One-to-One Training

As with many other areas within the parent training literature, the evidence on group training is suggestive, but not definitive. Group training can be effective (Rinn et al., 1975), with some reports suggesting that group training is as effective as one-to-one training (Conte, 1979; Kovitz, 1976). However, the precise meaning of "as effective" is not clear given the methodologies and outcome measures used in published research. As with training in general, interactive instructional procedures used during group instruction are more

effective than are verbal instructions (e.g., Flanagan et al., 1979; Nay, 1975). Others have used group training in the clinic before proceeding to more intensive individualized competency training in the home (e.g., Wolfe, Sandler, & Kaufman, 1981). However, the specific factors responsible for the effectiveness of group instructional procedures and the relative contributions to effectiveness made by different instructional procedures (e.g., written materials, rehearsal, homework) when used in combination are unknown.

Although there is evidence that group training can be effective, there is little question that group size tends to have a negative effect on the learning of individual members of the group (e.g., Bloom, 1984). The impact of group size on training effectiveness with parents is unknown. Furthermore, the interactive effects of variables such as group size, subject characteristics, and training content have escaped serious investigation.

It is important to point out that didactic and group are not interchangeable terms, at least as it relates to parent training. As we have already seen, didactic training has not proven very successful. Outcomes of interactive group training are at least suggestive of the possibility that this form of training may reduce the cost of delivering behavior change training to parents (e.g., Kovitz, 1976; Brightman, Baker, Clark, & Ambrose, 1982). The work by Bloom and associates (e.g., Anania, 1983; Bloom, 1984; Burke, 1984) examining factors related to making groups as effective as one-to-one instruction serves as one example of how researchers interested in group training of parents may proceed in an attempt to find efficient, effective means of training parents.

Parent Training: Real-World Applications

In the final section of this chapter suggestions for school psychologists interested in working with parents are offered. Before proceeding, it is interesting to take note of the manner in which parent training is currently being provided. Although few objective data are available, the personal experience of this and other authors (e.g., O'Dell, 1985) suggests there is a significant gap between state-of-the-art research and current practice in schools and clinics.

In his review of the parent training literature, O'Dell (1985) identified three general types of training: (a) verbal, didactic methods using oral and written instructions; (b) verbal, didactic methods employing verbal and visual instruction; and (c) interactive methods such as rehearsal and role playing. Although it is suspected that most parents currently receive instruction of the first type cited, there would seem little question that the first two categories suggested by O'Dell account for almost all the variance in what constitutes "parent training" in the real world.

Numerous surveys of school psychologists suggest that these professionals have little time for activities such as parent training (e.g., Carlson & Sincavage; 1987; Kramer & Peters, 1985). In an attempt to collect data on the kind of practices falling under the heading of "parent training" throughout Nebraska, a small number of mental health workers were surveyed by this author and his graduate students. Although our current N is small (less than 30), our sample shows that trainers prefer prepackaged programs, with materials based on Adlerian psychology (e.g., Active Parenting, STEP) most frequently mentioned as instructional content. Professionals working within settings other than schools also report little time for these kinds of activities, especially in resource-poor areas such as rural settings (e.g., Childs & Melton, 1980). When opportunities to work with parents present themselves, would we expect most therapists working in applied settings appear to do anything other than rely on verbal instruction? Many prepackaged programs are available and take less time than do many of the other instructional methods discussed throughout this review. Group, didactic training allows for many parents to be reached with limited expenditure of resources. Whether or not it is reasonable to continue such practices is discussed below.

FINAL CONSIDERATIONS: IMPLICATIONS FOR PRACTICE

There is much to be excited about based on the current analysis of the parent training literature that has accumulated during the past 20 or more years. Our understanding of human behavior and the influences that individual characteristics, environmental stimuli, and systematic events have on our ability to train effective parenting skills has advanced positively. Many problems persist and much remains to be accomplished, as noted in the sections that appear immediately above.

As indicated in the introduction to this chapter, there is an opportunity for school psychologists to use the information learned during the last two decades to enhance the effectiveness of psychological services provided to children and their families. Just as parenting and parent training have been conceptualized from a systemic/ecological perspective, there is much need for school psychologists to move beyond the boundaries of school buildings and traditional modes of service delivery to provide services that have an impact on the total ecology. The suggestions offered by Paget (1985) show just how this ecological orientation could be implemented within a preschool service delivery model that involves parents as intrical elements in educational planning and service delivery.

Although the opportunity exists for much to be accomplished, the research presented to this point has not painted a totally positive picture. The analysis of the empirical literature also points out that in training parents as behavior change agents, the term "training" means very different things depending on the nature of the problem or problems presented and the pretraining skill level of the parent. School psychologists pressed for time must be aware of the costs of different levels of interventions with parents.

The goal of this chapter has not been and will not be to tell school psychologists how best to organize service delivery in their practice or exactly how much time to spend on parent interventions. For example, it is clear to most practicing school psychologists that legislative mandates requiring multidisciplinary planning and prereferral intervention teams provide mechanisms for contact with parents that have not always been available. We would, of course, be remiss if we follow this legislation blindly, meeting the letter but not the spirit of parent and family involvement embodied in such mandates. But how best to accomplish the goal of parent involvement? Solutions seem better left to individual practitioners and others concerned with modifying organizational behavior. Evidence of parent ability to alter children's behavior and the serious consequences of long-term patterns of dysfunctional behavior in families both argue, however, that school psychologists should consider making parents and families an essential part of service delivery.

What has been provided below is a hierarchy of decisions and strategies for the school psychologist interested in having an impact on parents' behavior change skills. The suggestions offered are tentative, but some attempt has been made to integrate the empirical literature with the realities of service delivery in most school settings. The quality of that integration is a determination left to others. The suggestions offered below are based on the assumption that increased interaction between parents and school psychologists is desirable.

1. Practitioners should decide how best they can be involved with parents and the delivery of behavior change training. At one level this involves knowing how much time they are willing and able to devote to working with parents to have an impact on behavior change skills. The answer to this question will help to determine what kinds of family situations can be handled by the school psychologist and which to refer to others. Some (perhaps the majority) school psychologists might see themselves as a "coordinator" of services. This person might function as an initial "screener" of problems and would work to see that individuals are matched to the correct service delivery option within the school and/or the community. This person might, or might not, be involved with direct service delivery to parents and families.

2. If an attempt is made to match behavior problems and service delivery options, it stands to reason that an assessment of family functioning must be made. Although assessment of family functioning has not been the target of this review, the importance of understanding general levels of family functioning and types of social interchanges in the family environment has been made clear. Mash and Terdal (1988) provide an excellent review of the many assessment approaches and tools available to practitioners interested in family assessment. Due to parental involvement in schooling and the mandate that parents be included in special education decision making, the school psychologist would appear to be in a better position to assess the interrelationship among child, parent, and family functioning than is any other mental health professional.

3. Prior to any assessment of child and family functioning, it seems clear that psychologist and parent should have as clear an understanding as possible of the "problem(s)." At one level, this involves a clear statement of "what" is expected to change. For most parents, the "what" means something that the child is or is not doing. And in many instances within schools, minor alterations in school or home environment may bring about change in children. It is quite another matter to help parents understand that some aspect of their behavior must change in order for their child's behavior to be altered. That is, it is often difficult to point out to parents that their behavior is "the problem." Whether an individual school psychologist takes on this task or refers the family to someone else, helping parents to decide on the nature of the problem has been shown to be an effective first step in problem resolution. It is important to reiterate that the school psychologist may not be able to function as the parent trainer in these cases. There are too many parents, too many problems, and too little time. However, school psychologists will be remiss if they have not investigated community resources and developed a network of possible referral sources.

4. At a minimum all school psychologists should have access to high-quality written materials that discuss basic skills and factual information about parent–child management and parent–child interaction. For example, handouts on effective use of specific procedures (e.g., rule setting, shaping and teaching new skills, time out) and examples of specific ways in which parents can facilitate school progress (e.g., attending parent-teacher conferences, tutoring) would all seem useful and cost-effective ways of getting information to parents.

5. In addition, videotaped materials that model important skills appear to be an effective means of teaching parents about behavior change and are certainly less expensive than direct training. Whether school psychologists have access to these materials in the schools or whether these

materials are available from other sources is irrelevant. However, the availability of videotaped materials would seem essential for school practitioners interested in the training of parents. Some authors have suggested (O'Dell, 1985) that with some parents, it may be sufficient to have parents view videotapes and read accompanying instructional materials with minimal therapist contact. The therapist can then monitor progress and determine if additional direct training is necessary. Materials of the type developed by Dangel and Polster (1984b) or those available from publishers such as Research Press may be used in the manner suggested above.

6. Direct intervention may be necessary for many parents. For some parents, direct intervention may mean not only direct instruction of parenting skills, but also some degree of "maintenance" support for parents as they attempt to implement skills in the natural environment. The data continue to suggest that direct intervention and shaping of skills is the best strategy for teaching parents behavior change skills. If we are truly interested in improving parenting skills, we must be interested in facilitating parents' abiity to implement these skills in their particular environmental ecology. We do a disservice to the parents most in need of services if we train skills in the clinic but fail to follow up on parents' ability to implement behavior change strategies in the natural evironment.

7. It is suggested that practitioners ask themselves questions about the reasons for conducting short-term, didactic workshops designed to improve behavior change skills with parents. In general, these workshops do not work, if "work" is defined as changing behavior in a reliable manner. However, these types of workshops may be useful as public relations tools and have been shown to improve parents' knowledge of the specific topics discussed within the group. The research available indicates that even in the absence of demonstrable behavior change, parents report postive feelings about the parent training experi-

ence. Although the use of materials that do not produce change is not advocated, the fact that parents feel good about the experience is an important point.

8. School psychologists should resist the temptation to pick up popular, commercially published materials that exist in the absence of any validity data. Although surely controversial, it is suggested that practitioners abandon the use of these materials. What if we were to seek out our physician for a particular ailment and she or he were to suggest the use of a treatment procedure for which there were no data indicating that this technique worked for our ailment. Our "treatment" would consist of two-and-a-half-hour sessions one night a week for 6 weeks and would cost $50. If we were to become aware of information indicating that the best we could hope for would be an increase in our knowledge of the disorder (but no "cure"), would we be upset? Would we demand to know the reason for our physician's behavior? Would we feel cheated and would we suggest incompetence on the part of our physician? At present, the most popular parent training programs (e.g., STEP, Active Parenting, PET) exist without any convincing data suggesting that they ever result in productive behavior change in either parents or children. What reasons can be advanced for the continued use of such procedures?

It is understood that there will be those who say that there is not enough time for school psychologists to implement the kinds of strategies suggested above—and in many instances these people would be correct. But there seems little excuse for school psychologists not seeking out others (e.g., private practitioners, social service workers, community agencies, mental health facilities) who do have the time. If the goal of our training efforts is to improve parental skills, the strategies suggested above are what it takes. To date, there is little evidence that shortcuts work. We delude ourselves if we believe that having parents read a book or attend a short-term workshop of 6 to 8 weeks will change their behavior.

In the words of O'Dell (1985):

> Some would suggest that the costs of such extensive intervention procedures are prohibitive. Fortunately, many families probably can be helped without employing all of these procedures. However, they could be a minority. It may turn out that successful intervention with most families which possess clinically significant problems is inherently expensive. If so, the price should be paid or the technology not applied. After all, what is the point of employing a brief and inexpensive intervention that is unlikely to work? (p. 98)

Finally, the literature that has accumulated in the parent training area may serve school psychologists in another manner. Perhaps there is something to be learned from our attempts to train parents as behavior change agents about how best to have an impact on teachers while we work in schools as behavioral consultants. First, the notion that our "verbal consultations" would be enough to change teachers behavior in anything more than a temporary fashion is unrealistic. Second, we must separate the problem identification phase of consultation from the implementation phase. Just as with parents, the fact that teachers may have the knowledge or have received "consultation" training does not mean that they will implement the learned strategies when they return to the classroom. In any case, no matter how practitioners make use of the last twenty years of parent training research, there is much that this literature has to offer. We can only hope that the next two decades prove to be as productive.

ACKNOWLEDGMENTS

The author gratefully acknowledges the assistance of a number of graduate students whose efforts have contributed to the completion of this chapter, including Deborah Barker, Scott Brase, Mary Ellen Sternitzke, Margaret Rogers-Weise, and Martin Weise.

REFERENCES

Allen, K. E. (1978). The teacher therapist: Teaching parents to help children through systematic contingency management. *Journal of Special Education, 2*, 47–55.

Anania, J. (1983). The influence of instructional conditions on student learning and achievement. *Evaluation in Education: An International Review Series, 7*, 1–92.

Atkeson, B. M., & Forehand, R. (1978). Parents as behavior change agents with school related problems. *Education and Urban Society, 10*, 521–539.

Azrin, N. H., & Foxx, R. M. (1974). *Toilet training in less than a day.* New York: Simon and Schuster.

Azrin, N. H., Rubin, H., O'Brien, R., Ayllon, T., & Roll, D. (1968). Behavioral engineering: Postural control by a portable operant apparatus. *Journal of Applied Behavior Analysis, 1*, 99–108.

Bakeman, R., & Gottman, J. M. (1986). *Observing interaction: An introduction to sequential analysis.* Cambridge: Cambridge University Press.

Bandura, A. (1978). The self-system in reciprocal determinism. *American Psychologist, 33*, 91–97.

Bank, L., Patterson, G. R., & Reid, J. B. (1987). Delinquency prevention through training parents in family management. *Behavior Analyst, 10*, 75–82.

Bauman, D. E., Reiss, M. L., Rogers, R. W., & Bailey, J. S. (1988). Dining out with children: Effectiveness of a parent advice package on pre-meal inappropriate behavior. *Journal of Applied Behavior Analysis, 16*, 55–68.

Becker, W. O. (1971). *Parents are teachers.* Champaign, IL: Research Press.

Beekman, D. (1977). *The mechanical baby: A popular history of the theory and practice of child raising.* Westport, CT: Lawrence Hill.

Bergan, J. R., Kratochwill, T. R., & Luiten, J. (1980). Competency-based training in behavioral consultation. *Journal of School Psychology, 18*, 91–97.

Bergan, J. R., & Tombari, M. L. (1976). Consultant skill and efficiency and the implementation and outcomes of consultation. *Journal of School Psychology, 14*, 3–14.

Berkowitz, B. P., & Graziano, A. M. (1972). Training parents as behavior therapists: A review. *Behavior Research and Therapy, 10*, 297–310.

Bernal, M. E., & North, J. A. (1978). A survey of parent training manuals. *Journal of Applied Behavior Analysis, 11*, 533–544.

Bernal, M. E., Williams, D. E., Miller, W. H., & Reagor, P. A. (1972). The use of videotape feedback and operant learning principles in training parents in management of deviant children. In R. D. Rubin, H. Fernstermacher, J. D. Henderson, & L. P. Ullman (Eds.), *Advances in behavior therapy* (pp. 149–176). New York: Academic Press.

Bernstein, G. S. (1983). Training behavioral change agents: A conceptual analysis. *Journal of Applied Behavior Analysis, 11*, 533–544.

Besalal, V. A., Azrin, N. H., Thienes-Hontos, P., & McMorrow, M. (1980). Evaluation of a parent's manual of training enuretic children. *Behaviour Research and Therapy, 13*, 358–360.

Blechman, E. A. (1984). Competent parent: competent children. Behavioral objectives of parent training. In R. F. Dangel & R. A. Polster (Eds.), *Parent training: Foundations of research and practice* (pp. 34–63). New York Guilford Press.

Blechman, E. A. (1985). *Solving child behavior problems at home and at school.* Champaign, IL: Research Press.

Bloom, B. (1984). The 2 sigma problem: The search for methods of group instruction as effective as one-to-one tutoring. *Educational Researcher, 13,* 4–16.

Braukmann, C. J., Ramp, K. K., Tigner, D. M., & Wolf, M. M. (1984). The teaching family approach to training group-home parents: Training procedures, validation research, and outcome findings. In R. F. Dangel & R. A. Polster (Eds.), *Parent training: Foundations of research and practice* (pp. 144–161). New York: Guilford Press.

Brightman, R. P., Baker, B. L., Clark, D. B., & Ambrose, S. A. (1982). Effectiveness of alternative parent training formats. *Journal of Behavior Therapy and Experimental Psychiatry, 13,* 113–117.

Bronfenbrenner, U. (1979). *The ecology of human development.* Cambridge, MA: Harvard University Press.

Budd, K. S., & Fabray, P. L. (1985). Parent and family training. In R. P. Barrett (Ed.), *Severe behavior disorders in the mentally retarded* (pp. 235–271). New York: Plenum Press.

Budd, K. S., Pinkston, E., & Green, D. R. (1977). *An analysis of two parent training packages for remediation of child aggression in laboratory and home settings.* Paper presented at the annual meeting of the American Psychological Association, Montreal.

Burke, A. J. (1984). Students' potential for learning contrasted under tutorial and group approaches to instruction. (Doctoral dissertation, University of Chicago, 1983). *Dissertation Abstracts International, 44,* 2025A.

Butler, J. F. (1976). The toilet training success of parents after reading *Toilet training in less than a day. Behavior Therapy, 7,* 185–191.

Calvert, S. C., & McMahon, R. J. (1987). The treatment acceptability of a behavioral parent training program and its components. *Behavior Therapy, 2,* 165–179.

Carlson, C. I., & Sincavage, J. (1987). Family-oriented school psychology practice: Results of a national survey of NASP members. *School Psychology Review, 16,* 519–526.

Childs, A. W., & Melton, G. B. (1983). *Rural psychology.* New York: Plenum Press.

Clark, H. B., Greene, B. F., Macrae, J. W., McNees, M. P., Davis, J. L., & Risley, T. R. (1977). A parent advice package for family shopping trips: Development and evaluation. *Journal of Applied Behavior Analysis,* 10, 605–624.

Conte, J. R. (1979). A review of the literature: Helping groups of parents change their children's behavior. *Child and Youth Services, 2,* 1–23.

Cox, W. D., & Matthews, C. O. (1977). Parent group education: What does it do for the children? *Journal of School Psychology, 15,* 358–361.

Dangel, R. F., & Polster, R. A. (Eds.). (1984a). *Parent training: Foundations of research and practice.* New York: Guilford Press.

Dangel, R. F., & Polster, R. A. (1984b). WINNING!: A systematic, empirical approach to parent training. In R. F. Dangel & R. A. Polster (Eds.), *Parent training: Foundations of research and practice* (pp. 162–201). New York: Guilford Press.

Dembo, M. H., Sweitzer, M., & Lauritzen, P. (1985). An evaluation of group parent education: Behavioral, PET, Adlerian programs. *Review of Educational Research, 55,* 155–200.

Dinkmeyer, D., & McKay, G. (1977). *Systematic training for effective parenting.* Circle Pines, MN: American Guidance Service.

Doherty, G. (1975). Basic life skills and parent effectiveness training with the mothers of acting-out adolescents. *Journal of Clinical Child Psychology, 31,* 3–6.

Doherty, W. J., & Ruder, R. G. (1980). Parent effectiveness training: Criticisms and comments. *Journal of Marital and Family Therapy, 11,* 263–270.

Drabman, R. S., Hammer, D., & Rosenbaum, M. S. (1979). Assessing generalization in behavior modification with children: The generalization map. *Behavioral Assessment, 1,* 203–219.

Dubey, D. R., O'Leary, S. G., & Kaufman, K. F. (1983). Training parents of hyperactive children in child management: A comparative outcome study. *Journal of Abnormal Child Psychology, 11,* 229–246.

Dumas, J. S., & Wahler, R. G. (1983). Predictors of treatment outcome in parent training: Mother insularity and socio-economic advantage. *Behavioral Assessment, 5,* 301–313.

Dunst, C. J. (1985). Rethinking early intervention. *Analysis and Intervention in Developmental Disabilities, 5,* 165–201.

Elkind, D. (1981). *The hurried child: Growing up too fast too soon.* Reading, MA: Addison-Wesley.

Eyberg, S. M., & Johnson, S. M. (1974). Multiple assessment of behavior modification with families. *Journal of Consulting and Clinical Psychology, 42,* 594–606.

Eyberg, S. M., & Matarazzo, R. G. (1980). Training parents as therapists: A comparison between individual parent–child interaction training and parent group didactic training. *Journal of Clinical Psychology, 36,* 492–499.

Eyberg, S. M., & Robinson, E. A. (1982). Parent–child interaction training: Effects on family functioning. *Journal of Clinical Child Psychology, 11,* 130–137.

Flanagan, S., Adams, H. E., & Forehand, R. (1979). A comparison of four instructional methods for teaching parents the use of time out. *Behavior Therapy, 10,* 94–102.

Forehand, R. (1977). Child noncompliance to parental requests: Behavioral analysis and treatment. In M. Hersen, R. M. Eisler, & P. M. Miller (Eds.), *Progress in behavior modification* (Vol. 5, pp. 111–147). New York: Academic Press.

Forehand, R., & Atkeson, B. M. (1977). Generality of treatment effects with parents as therapists: A review of assessment and implementation procedures. *Behavior Therapy, 8,* 575–593.

Forehand, R., & King, H. E. (1977). Noncompliant children: Effects of parent training on behavior and attitude change. *Behavior Modification, 1,* 93–108.

Forehand, R., & McMahon, R. J. (1981). *Helping the noncompliant child: A clinician's guide to parent training.* New York: Guilford Press.

Forehand, R., Sturgis, E. T., McMahon, R. J., Aguar, D., Gree, K., Wells, K. C., & Breiner, J. (1979). Parent behavioral training to modify child noncompliance:

Treatment generalization across time and from home to school. *Behavior Modification, 3,* 3–25.

Forehand, R., Wells, K. C., & Griest, D. L. (1980). An examination of the social validity of a parent training program. *Behavior Therapy, 11,* 488–502.

Garfield, S. L., & Bergin, A. E. (1978). *Handbook of psychotherapy and behavior change: An empirical analysis* (2nd ed.). New York: Wiley.

Giebenhain, J. E., & O'Dell, S. L. (1984). Evaluation of a parent training manual for reducing children's fear of the dark. *Journal of Applied Behavior Analysis, 17,* 121–125.

Ginott, H. G. (1969). *Between parent and child.* New York: Avon Books.

Glasgow, R. E., & Rosen, G. M. (1978). Behavioral bibliotherapy: A review or self-help behavior therapy manuals. *Psychological Bulletin, 35,* 1–23.

Good, H. G., & Teller, J. D. (1973). *A history of American education.* New York: Macmillan.

Gordon, T. (1970). *Parent effectiveness training.* New York: David McKay.

Green, D. R., Budd, K., Johnson, M., Lang, S., Pinkston, E., & Rudd, S. (1976). Training parents to modify problem child behaviors. In E. J. Mash, L. C. Handy, & L. A. Hamerlynck (Eds.), *Behavior modification approaches to parenting*)pp. 3–18). New York: Brunner/Mazel.

Greene, B. F., Clark, H. B., & Risley, T. (1977). *Shopping with children.* San Rafael, CA: Academic Therapy.

Greene, R. B., Harrison, W. L., & Greene, B. F. (1984). Turning the table on advice programs for parents: Using placemats to enhance family interaction at restaurants. *Journal of Applied Behavior Analysis, 17,* 497–508.

Greenwood, C. R., Delquadri, J. C., & Hall, R. V. (1984). Opportunity to respond and student academic achievement. In W. L. Heward, T. E. Heron, D. S. Hill, & J. Porter-Trap (Eds.), *Focus on behavior analysis in education* (pp. 58–88). Columbus, OH: Charles E. Merrill.

Greenwood, G. E., Ware, W. B., Gordon, I. J., & Rhine, W. R. (1981). Parent education model. In W. R. Rhine (Ed.), *Making schools more effective: New directions from follow-through* (pp. 49–94). New York: Academic Press.

Griest, D. L., Forehand, R., Wells, K. C., & McMahon, R. J. (1980). An examination of differences between nonclinic and behavior-problem clinic-referred children and their mothers. *Journal of Abnormal Psychology, 89,* 497–500.

Griest, D. L., Wells, K. C., & Forehand, R. (1979). An examination of predictors of maternal perceptions of maladjustment in normal and deviant children. *Journal of Abnormal Psychology, 88,* 277–281.

Gurman, A. S., & Kniskern, D. P. (1981). Family therapy outcome research: Knowns and unknowns. In A. S. Gurman & D. P. Kniskern (Eds.), *Handbook of family therapy* (pp. 742–775). New York: Brunner/Mazel.

Hawkins, R. P. (1972). How to conduct systematic behavior modification. *SALT: School Applications of Learning Theory, 4,* 12–17.

Heifetz, L. J. (1977). Behavioral training for parents and retarded children. *American Journal of Mental Deficiency, 82,* 194–203.

Imber, S. C., Imber, R. B., & Rothstein, C. (1979). Modifying independent work habits: An effective parent–teacher communication system. *Exceptional Children, 46,* 218–221.

Issacs, C. D., Embry, L. H., & Baer, D. M. (1982). Training family therapists: An experimental analysis. *Journal of Applied Behavior Analysis, 15,* 505–520.

Johnson, M. R., Whitman, T. L., & Barloon-Noble, R. (1978). A home-based program for a preschool behaviorally disturbed child with parents as therapists. *Journal of Behavior Therapy and Experimental Psychiatry, 9,* 65–70.

Johnson, S. M., Bolstad, O. D., & Lobitz, G. K. (1976). Generalization and contrast phenomena in behavior modification with children. In E. J. Mash, L. A. Hamerlynck, & L. C. Handy (Eds.), *Behavior modification and families* (pp. 113–129). New York: Brunner/Mazel.

Kazdin, A. E. (1977). Assessing the clinical or applied importance of behavior change through social validation. *Behavior Modification, 1,* 427–452.

Kazdin, A. E. (1980a). Acceptability of alternative treatments for deviant child behavior. *Journal of Applied Behavior Analysis, 13,* 259–273.

Kazdin, A. E. (1980b). Acceptability of time-out from reinforcement procedures for disruptive child behavior. *Behavior Therapy, 11,* 329–344.

Kazdin, A. E. (1981). Acceptability of child treatment techniques: The influence of treatment efficacy and adverse side effects. *Behavior Therapy, 12,* 493–506.

Kazdin, A. E., French, N. H., & Sherick, R. B. (1981). Acceptability of alternative treatments for children: Evaluations by inpatient children, parents, and staff. *Journal of Consulting and Clinical Psychology, 49,* 900–907.

Keller, F. S. (1968). Goodbye teacher. . . . *Journal of Applied Behavior Analysis, 1,* 79–89.

Kelley, M. L., Embry, L. H., & Baer, D. M. (1979). Skills for child management and family support. *Behavior Modification, 3,* 373–396.

Koegel, R. L., Glahn, T. J., & Nieminen, G. S. (1978). Generalization of parent training results. *Journal of Applied Behavior Analysis, 11,* 95–109.

Kovitz, K. E. (1976). Comparing group and individual methods for training parents in child management techniques. In E. J. Mash, L. C. Handy, & L. A. Hamerlynck (Eds.), *Behavior modification approaches to parenting* (pp. 124–140). New York: Brunner/Mazel.

Kramer, J. J. (1985). Best practices in parent training. In A. Thomas & J. Grimes (Eds.), *Best practices in school psychology.* Kent, OH: National Association of School Psychologists.

Kramer, J. J., & Peters, G. M. (1985). What we know about rural school psychology: A brief review and analysis. *School Psychology Review, 14,* 452–456.

Lobitz, G. K., & Johnson, S. M. (1975). Normal vs. deviant children: A multi-method comparison. *Journal of Abnormal Child Psychology, 3,* 353–374.

Loeber, R., Dishion, T. J., & Patterson, G. R. (1984).

Multiple gaiting: A multistage assessment procedure for identifying youths at risk for delinquincy. *Journal of Research in Crime and Delinquincy, 21,* 7–32.

Lutzker, J. R. (1984). Project 12-Ways: Treating child abuse and neglect from an ecobehavioral perspective. In R. F. Dangel & R. A. Polster (Eds.), *Parent training: Foundations of research and practice* (pp. 260–297). New York: Guilford Press.

Martens, B. K., & Witt, J. C. (1988). Ecological behavior analysis. In M. Hersen, R. M. Eisler, & P. M. Miller (Eds.), *Progress in behavior modification* (Vol. 22, pp. 115–140). Beverly Hills, CA: Sage.

Mash, E. J., & Terdal, L. G. (1988). Behavioral assessment of child and family disturbance. In E. J. Mash & L. G. Terdal (Eds.), *Behavioral assessment of childhood disorders: Selected core problems.* New York: Springer.

McMahon, R. J., & Forehand, R. (1978). Nonprescription behavior therapy: Effectiveness of a brochure in teaching mothers to correct their children's inappropriate mealtime behavior. *Behavior Therapy, 9,* 814–820.

McMahon, R. J., & Forehand, R. (1980). Self-help behavior therapies in parent training. In B. B. Lahey and A. E. Kazdin (Eds.), *Advances in clinical child psychology* (Vol. 3, pp. 149–176). New York: Plenum Press.

McMahon, R. J., & Forehand, R. (1983). Consumer satisfaction in behavioral treatment of children: Types, issues, and recommendations. *Behavior Therapy, 14,* 209–225.

McMahon, R. J., & Forehand, R. (1984). Parent training for the noncompliant child: Treatment outcome, generalization, and adjunctive therapy procedures. In R. F. Dangel & R. A. Polster (Eds.), *Parent training: Foundations of research and practice* (pp. 298–328). New York: Guilford Press.

McMahon, R. J., Forehand, R., Griest, D. L., & Wells, K. C. (1981). Who drops out of treatment during parent behavior training? *Behavioral Counseling Quarterly, 49,* 526–532.

McMahon, R. J., Tiedemann, G. L., Forehand, R., & Griest, D. L. (1984). Parental satisfaction with parent training to modify child noncompliance. *Behavior Therapy, 15,* 295–303.

Moreland, J. R., Schwebel, A. I., Beck, S., & Wells, R. (1982). Parents as therapists: A review of the behavior therapy parent training literature—1975 to 1981. *Behavior Modification, 6,* 250–276.

Muir, K. A., & Milan, M. A. (1982). Parent reinforcement of child achievement: The use of a lottery to mazimaize parent training effects. *Journal of Applied Behavior Analysis, 15,* 455–460.

Nay, W. R. (1975). A systematic comparison of instructional techniques for parents. *Behavior Therapy, 6,* 14–21.

O'Dell, S. L. (1974). Training parents in behavior modification: A review. *Psychological Bulletin, 81,* 418–438.

O'Dell, S. L. (1982). Enhancing parent involvement in training: A discussion. *Behavior Therapist, 5,* 9–13.

O'Dell, S. L. (1985). Progress in parent training. In M. Hersen, R. M. Eisler, & P. M. Miller (Eds.), *Progress in behavior modification* (Vol. 19, pp. 57–108). New York: Academic Press.

O'Dell, S. L., Flynn, J. M., & Beniolo, L. A. (1977). A comparison of parent training techniques in child behavior modification. *Journal of Behavior Therapy and Experimental Psychiatry, 8,* 261–268.

O'Dell, S. L., Krug, W. W., Patterson, J. N., & Faustman, W. O. (1980). An assessment of methods for training parents in the use of time-out. *Journal of Behavior Therapy and Experimental Psychiatry, 11,* 21–25.

O'Dell, S. L., Mahoney, N., Horton, W., & Turner, P. (1979). Media-assisted training: Alternative models. *Behavior Therapy, 13,* 103–110.

O'Farrell, T. J., & Keuthen, N. J. (1983). Readability of behavior therapy self-help manuals. *Behavior Therapy, 14,* 449–454.

Paget, K. D. (1985). Preschool services in the schools: Issues and implications. *Special Services in the Schools, 2,* 3–25.

Paget, K. D. (1987). Systemic family assessment: Concepts and strategies for school psychologists. *School Psychology Review, 16,* 429–442.

Paget, K. D., & Nagle, R. J. (1986). A conceptual model of preschool assessment. *School Psychology Review, 15,* 154–165.

Parloff, M. B., Waskow, I. E., & Wolfe, B. E. (1978). Research on therapist variables in relation to process and outcome. In S. L. Garfield & A. E. Bergin (Eds.), *Handbook of psychotherapy and behavior change: An empirical analysis* (2nd ed., pp. 233–282). New York: Wiley.

Patterson, G. R. (1974). Interventions for boys with conduct problems: Multiple settings, treatments, and criteria. *Journal of Consulting and Clinical Psychology, 42,* 471–481.

Patterson, G. R. (1982). *Coercive family process.* Eugene, OR: Castalia.

Patterson, G. R. (1986). Performance models for antisocial boys. *American Psychologist, 41,* 432–444.

Patterson, G. R., & Bank, L. (1986). Bootstrapping your way in the nomological thicket. *Behavioral Assessment, 8,* 49–73.

Patterson, G. R., & Guillion, M. E. (1968). *Living with children.* Champaign, IL: Research Press.

Patterson, G. R., & Reid, J. B. (1973). Intervention for families of aggressive boys: A replication study. *Behavior Research and Therapy, 11,* 383–394.

Patterson, G. R., Reid, J. B., Jones, R. R., & Conger, R. E. (1975). *A social learning approach to family intervention: Families with aggressive children* (Vol. 1). Eugene, OR: Castalia.

Polster, R. A., & Dangel, R. F. (1984). Behavioral parent training: Where it came from and where it's at. In R. F. Dangel & R. A. Polster (Eds.), *Parent training: Foundations of research and practice.* New York: Guilford Press.

Popkin, M. H. (1983). *Active parenting.* Atlanta: Active Parenting.

Pray, B. P., Jr., Kramer, J. J., & Lindskog, R. (1986). Assessment and treatment of tic behavior: A review and case study. *School Psychology Review, 15,* 418–429.

Reimers, T. M., Wacker, D. P., & Koepell, G. (1987).

Acceptability of behavioral interventions: A review of the literature. *School Psychology Review, 16,* 212–227.

Reisinger, J. J., Ora, J. P., & Frangia, G. W. (1976). Parents as change agents for their children: A review. *Journal of Community Psychology, 4,* 103–123.

Rickert, V. I., Sottolano, D. C., Parrish, J. M., Riley, A. W., Hunt, F. M., & Pelco, L. E. (1988). Training parents to become better behavior managers: The need for a competency-based approach. *Behavior Modification, 12,* 475–496.

Rinn, R. C., Vernon, J. C., & Wise, M. J. (1975). Training parents of behaviorally-disordered children in groups: A three years' program evaluation. *Behavior Therapy, 6,* 378–387.

Robins, L. N. (1979). Follow-up studies. In H. C. Quay & J. S. Werry (Eds.), *Psychopathological disorders of childhood* (2nd ed., pp. 414–446). New York: Academic Press.

Rogers-Weise, M. R., & Kramer, J. J. (1988). Parent training research: An analysis of the empirical literature 1975–1985. *Psychology in the Schools, 25,* 325–330.

Sanders, M. R., & James, J. E. (1983). The modification of parent behavior: A review of generalization and maintenance. *Behavior Modification, 7,* 3–27.

Sandler, J., VanDercar, C., & Milhoen, G. S. (1978). Training child abusers in the use of positive reinforcement practices. *Behavior Research and Therapy, 16,* 169–176.

Shearer, D. E., & Loftin, C. R. (1984). The Portage Project: Teaching parents to teach their preschool children in the home. In R. F. Dangel & R. A. Polster (Eds.), *Parent training: Foundations of research and practice* (pp. 93–126). New York: Guilford Press.

Skinner, B. F. (1938). *The behavior of organisms.* New York: Appleton-Century.

Skinner, B. F. (1954). The science of learning and the art of teaching. *Harvard Educational Review, 24,* 86–97.

Skinner, B. F. (1984). The shame of American education. *American Psychologist, 39,* 947–954.

Stevens, M. J., & Pfost, K. S. (1982). Bibliotherapy: Medicine for the soul? *Psychology, 79,* 21–25.

Stinnett, N., & DeFrain, J. (1985). *Secrets of strong families.* Boston: Little, Brown.

Strain, P. S., Steele, P., Ellis, T., and Timm, M. A. (1982). Long-term effects of oppositional child treatment with mothers as therapists and therapist trainers. *Journal of Applied Behavior Analysis, 15,* 163–169.

Stumphauzer, J. S. (1976). Elimination of stealing by self-reinforcement of alternative behavior and family contracting. *Journal of Behavior Therapy and Experimental Psychiatry, 7,* 265–268.

Wahler, R. G. (1980). The insular mother: Her problems in parent–child treatment. *Journal of Applied Behavior Analysis, 13,* 207–219.

Wahler, R. G., & Barnes, P. G. (1988). *Synthesis teaching to a supplement to parent training with troubled mothers.* Presented at the annual meeting of the Association for the Advancement of Behavior Therapy. New York.

Wahler, R. G., & Dumas, J. E. (1984). Changing the observational coding styles of insular andnoninsular mothers: A step towards maintenance of parent training effects. In R. F. Dangel & R. A. Polster (Eds.), *Parent training: Foundations of research and practice* (pp. 379–416). New York: Guilford Press.

Wahler, R. G., & Dumas, J. E. (in press). Attentional problems in dysfunctional mother–child interactions. An interbehavioral model. *Psychological Bulletin.*

Walle, D. L., Hobbs, S. A. & Caldwell, H. S. (1984). Sequence of parent training procedures: Effects on child noncompliance and treatment acceptability. *Behavior Modification, 8,* 540–552.

Watkins, C. L. (1988). Project Follow Through: A story of the identification and neglect of effective instruction. *Youth Policy, 10,* 7–11.

Webster-Stratton, C. (1981). Videotape modeling. A method of parent education. *Journal of Clinical Child Psychology, 10,* 93–98.

Weise, M. J. (1989). *Evaluation of an Adlerian parent training program with multiple outcome measures.* Unpublished doctoral dissertation. University of Nebraska–Lincoln.

Weiss, A. B., Cooke, N. L., Grossman, M. A., Heward, W. L., Heron, T. E., Hassett, M. E., & Ryno-Vrabel, M. (1983). *Implementing a telephone-managed home–school communications program.* Columbus, OH: Special Press.

Wells, K. C., Forehand, R., & Griest, D. L. (1980). Generality of treatment effects from treated to untreated behaviors resulting from a parent training program. *Journal of Clinical Child Psychology, 9,* 217–219.

Whorton, D., Sasso, G., Elliott, M., Hughes, V., Critchlow, W., Terry, B., Stanley, S. O., Greenwood, C. R., & Delquadri, J. (1982). Teaching formats that maximize the opportunity to respond: Peer and parent tutoring programs. *Education and Treatment of Children, 5,* 217–224.

Willems, E. P. (1974). Behavioral technology and behavioral ecology. *Journal of Applied Behavior Analysis, 7,* 151–165.

Wolf, M. M. (1978). Social validity: The case for subjective measurement or how applied behavior analysis is finding its heart. *Journal of Applied Behavior Analysis, 11,* 208–214.

Wolfe, D. A., Mendes, M. G., & Factor, D. F. (1984). A parent-administered program to reduce children's television viewing. *Journal of Applied Behavior Analysis, 17,* 267–273.

Wolfe, D. A., & Sandler, J. (1981). Training abusive parents in effective child management. *Behavior Modification, 5,* 320–355.

Wolfe, D. A., Sandler, J., & Kaufman, K. (1981). A competency-based parent training program for child abusers. *Journal of Consulting and Clinical Psychology, 49,* 633–640.

Ziarnik, J. P., & Bernstein, G. S. (1982). A critical examination of the effects of in service training on staff performance. *Mental Retardation, 20,* 109–114.

28

GROUP INTERVENTIONS
IN THE SCHOOLS[1]

CHARLES D. CLAIBORN
BARBARA A. KERR
The University of Iowa

STANLEY R. STRONG
Virginia Commonwealth University

Human beings are social animals. This is particularly true of schoolchildren and adolescents, who spend large shares of work and leisure time in group interactions. Families are groups that, because they are time unlimited and relatively closed, have rather special dynamics. Classes are large groups and contain subgroups defined by class tasks and social relationships. Clubs, teams, and committees provide abundant opportunities for students to take part in groups. Through participation in groups, students learn the essentials of adaptive social behavior: how to lead, follow, cooperate, negotiate, organize, and decide. Through repeated rehearsal, shaped unsystematically by interpersonal feedback, students develop ways to communicate ideas and feelings clearly, to listen perceptively and consider discerningly, and to interact strategically and persuasively.

The rationale for counseling students in groups stems from the pervasiveness of groups in their lives. A small group of one's peers is a familiar social setting where behavior is likely to be natural, spontaneous, and characteristic of behavior outside of counseling. If, as Glass (1973) pointed out, students regard themselves differently in a dyad with an adult than in a group with other students, the behavior and attitude change that the counselor seeks to effect might be obtained more easily in a group setting. In addition, problems that students face are often group related; they involve poor relationships and pressures, confusions of status and identity, and interactions with parents, teachers, and other adults. Dinkmeyer (1970) emphasized the importance of using the social setting of the group to deal with social and interpersonal problems of students. Since groups are natural and often attractive to students, they may provide an initial approachability to counter the stigmatizing

---

[1] This chapter incorporates information from the chapter on group counseling in the first edition of the *Handbook,* which two of us coauthored (Claiborn & Strong, 1982). The review has been updated and extended to include noncounseling group interventions.

connotations of seeking help from a counselor. It is perhaps easier to say (or to think) "I'm attending a group" than "I'm going to counseling," a distinction that could determine whether an individual seeks help at all. That other members of a group have sought help can counter a student's feelings of being peculiar and alone by virtue of having difficulties. Later in the life of a group the cohesiveness of the group—the attraction of members to each other and to the group—keeps the student in counseling until his or her goals have been achieved.

Counseling groups in the schools resemble adult counseling groups in their integration of group dynamics with the theoretical orientations of counseling to yield many distinct models. Thus, there are behavioral groups, encounter groups, structured group experiences, career awareness groups, play groups, and so on. Groups vary according to their purpose, as well as according to the orientation of the leader. Neither of these variables, however, provides a clear indication of what occurs in the group and how change results from it. For example, Lieberman, Yalom, and Miles (1973) found in their encounter group study that the expressed orientation of the groups leaders (the type of group they led) bore no relationship to their behavior in the group. Particular leader behaviors, however, were related to positive and negative outcomes. Thus, there is a case for examining group processes in a manner that cuts across counseling theories and provides basic principles of change applicable to a wide range of group procedures.

In this chapter we describe basic group processes, including the elements of change and the principles of group leadership and facilitation. The ways in which these change mechanisms and principles of leadership are applied to group counseling in the schools are then examined. A critical review of the wide variety of formats and interventions for group counseling will show the underlying commonalties and specific strengths of the various types of groups.

BASIC PROCESSES

Group counseling, as discussed here, does not include family counseling nor classroom guidance activities, although many of the techniques used to conduct groups can be employed to help families change or to facilitate discussions and structured experiences in the classroom. Group counseling is the meeting in several sessions over a limited period of time of a small number of clients, generally from 4 to 12, with one or two counselors to achieve client goals through changes in attitudes or behaviors. This loose definition does not include all of the features shared by most counseling groups, nor does it hint at the diversity of procedures that it includes. But it delimits the subject of this chapter to the common usage of the term among practitioners and researchers.

Each group has two purposes. The first is that of changing member attitudes or behaviors. The second purpose is to form the group into a change agent with the qualities and procedures necessary to effect those changes. The former task cannot be done until the latter is well under way. Bednar and Kaul (1978) summarized the features that make a group an agent of change. First, the group serves as a social microcosm. The relationships, roles, and interactions present in each person's social environment appear in the group, allowing a close examination of interpersonal issues that are important, and perhaps troublesome, in the member's life. Second, the group promotes social learning; modeling, behavioral experimentation, feedback, and consensual validation expand interpersonal awareness and facilitate the gradual alteration of interpersonal behavior. Third, the group permits members to be helpful to each other, a therapeutic experience in itself. To these, Yalom (1975) has added universality, the awareness that one is not unique in having certain concerns or difficulties, and cohesiveness, a quality that renders the group influential in the lives of its members. These features distinguish group from individual counseling, or at least function differently in group settings. If they can be considered the operative therapeutic factors in group counseling, they suggest not only basic reasons why people change in groups (a theoretical question), but what group procedures are indicated for particular clients and problem areas (a practical question). Bednar and Kaul (1978) stressed the need for research relating particular elements of counseling groups to outcome. This would help to sort out the puzzling phenomena of group processes into understandable and manipulable mechanisms of change. But at present, theoretical speculations about what causes people to change in groups must depend primarily on extrapolations from social psychology and individual counseling.

Change Mechanisms

The counseling group is the interpersonal context of change, and the group process—the interaction of the members—contains the forces promoting change. Although each group develops uniquely, certain processes are common to all groups and account for the changes in the members. These basic mechanisms are the subject of this section.

Norms

Norms are the group's values, "standardized generalizations concerning expected behavior in matters that are of some importance to the group" (Shaw, 1976, p. 250). Although members vary in the degree to which they accept the group's norms, norms exert considerable control over members' behavior. As interpersonal attraction among the members (group cohesiveness) increases, so does conformity to group norms (Shaw, 1976). Members are anxious to comply with the standards of a group they value. Group members also maintain norms through social reinforcement, and extinguish deviation from norms through selective inattention (Rose, 1972) and outright disapproval (MacLennan & Felsenfeld, 1968). Thus, in limiting some behaviors and encouraging others, norms profoundly affect group functioning. They act as change agents themselves and provide the means for other change mechanisms to operate.

Practitioners consider some norms generally important for an effective counseling group. Some of these involve behavior in the group. There is likely to be a norm concerning appropriate self-disclosure for the group: honest, intimate, but to a degree that does not threaten the person too greatly. A norm regarding how to request, give, and receive feedback is essential to interpersonal learning. Norms for active listening, offering support, and acknowledging the feelings expressed by one's own behavior are also important. Other norms are more philosophical and concern the group's values and attitudes rather than specifically what members should do. For example, MacLennan and Felsenfeld (1968), discussing group work with adolescents, stated that "groups concerned with individual change should emphasize the importance of facing reality, the importance of respecting oneself and others, the willingness to become involved with each other" (p. 15). Yalom (1975) noted that members should come to feel responsible for the group's functioning as active contributors to the process.

Many norms are specific to the group, dictated by its purpose, its composition, and the theoretical orientation of the counselor. An encounter group, for example, might have a norm promoting feeling statements and a here-and-now focus, thus discouraging discussions of experiences members have outside the group. A problem-solving group, by contrast, may concentrate on skill learning by role-playing situations brought into the group by members. Certainly, groups vary in the norms they have about physical contact.

Norms develop out of the group's interaction. Sometimes the counselor deliberately shapes the norms, while in other instances the norms are merely the product of the sequence of events. Individual member behaviors also contribute powerfully to norm formation. In any case, norms are the product of the group's behavior; they are not a set of procedures agreed on prior to group interaction. Norms are often held tacitly but may be made explicit for examination by the group. It is important for the group to be aware of how particular norms affect members' behavior; at times group members may choose to abandon or alter norms they deem unnecessary or undesirable. The group counselor, as an expert in group process, anticipates the development of untherapeutic norms, and uses his or her influence to promote norms most likely to be therapeutic; the counselor may also influence norm development by modeling appropriate behaviors in the group (Yalom, 1975).

Cohesiveness

Group cohesiveness has several definitions, but a prominent and useful one is based on the notion of interpersonal attraction (Lott & Lott, 1965). Cohesiveness may be considered the attraction of members to each other and to the group, although attraction to the group as a whole is not necessarily the same thing as liking of the members for each other (Ribner, 1974). This definition helps to account for the effects of cohesiveness on influence in groups. In social psychological experiments, when group attractiveness (cohesiveness) is increased, members exhibit greater conformity to group norms and compliance with other members' influence attempts (Shaw, 1976). In discussing therapy groups, Yalom (1975) considered cohesiveness analogous to the relationship in individual therapy, and acknowledged influence based on interpersonal attraction as the mechanism by which it operates. In a cohesive group, members are more likely to resolve cognitive discrepancies—such as between members' self-perceptions and others' perceptions of them—by modifying their own attitudes in the direction of viewpoints expressed in the group. Interpersonal influence may thus account for studies Yalom (1975) has cited linking high cohesiveness to positive outcomes in therapy and encounter groups. Cohesiveness is operationalized so variously and often so vaguely in such research, however, that it is not yet possible to specify the contribution of cohesiveness to change (Bednar & Kaul, 1978).

Leadership

While each member in a group has some ability to influence the others, the counselor is the primary influence agent in the group. The counselor's ability to influence others in the group—his or her social power—derives from expert, legitimate, and referent sources (Strong & Matross, 1973). The counselor is an expert in at least two areas, group process and the content area of the group (assertion, transactional analysis, career planning, and so on). Members of the group see the counselor as able to supply resources they need to profit from the group, and this gives his or her statements substantial credibility. The counselor is influential by virtue of occupying a particular role in and outside the group; this is legitimacy. Members are aware that the group counselor (or group leader) is a socially sanctioned helper, such as a guidance counselor, a school psychologist, or a social worker. They also acknowledge the counselor's role in initiating, conducting, and otherwise assuming responsibility in the group. Third, the counselor is a participating member of the group (more so in some cases than in others) and thereby has access to the influence potentially available to all members, that of a referent. Referent power is influence based on interpersonal attractiveness. If members perceive that the counselor likes them, or is similar to them in important ways (such as past experience or values), they are apt to consider the counselor's statements as particularly applicable to them. In most groups, the counselor emphasizes one or another of the sources of social power. In a behavioral group, for example, the counselor builds a warm relationship with the group members but otherwise stresses expertise in behavioral techniques (Varenhorst, 1976). Of course, when the counselor serves as a model, similarity cues are most important. The philosophy of an Adlerian group emphasizes "equality," and thus the counselor may exhibit some expertise but generally eschews the role of decision maker and focuses the group on intermember similarities (Sonstegard & Dreikurs, 1973). In client-centered and some encounter approaches, the counselor may reject expertness explicitly and participate in the group "as a person," emphasizing common values and understandings with members. Disregarding what the counselor chooses to emphasize and deemphasize, his or her ability to influence members stems from their perceptions of his or her expert, legitimate, and referent value.

Power and Control

Power in a group may be defined as one person's control over resources valued by another (Johnson & Johnson, 1982). All group members possess a certain kind of power in that each member is perceived by the group to control a valued personal resource, such as reinforcement, openness, trustworthiness, strength, or merely the ability to stay quiet. Resources are not all equally valued, however, and thus the power of the group is typically unbalanced. This is especially true at the beginning of a group, before members' resources are fully appreciated. Throughout the life of a group, members use their own resources in exercising power over others and are themselves susceptible to others' power over them. Power in this context takes the form of interpersonal influence, the ability of one person to shape (often subtly) the attitudes and behavior of others (Strong & Claiborn, 1982).

If power is the ability to influence, or have an impact on, others in the group, control may be considered the direction this influence takes. Strong and Claiborn (1982) conceptualize control as the impact that one person's behavior has on limiting the range of possible responses by the other person. Control is thus reciprocal; in an interaction, each person's behavior has the effect of controlling the other person's behavior in the sense of restricting its possibilities. In a group control does not flow in one direction only, but back and forth among the members as they interact. Control, like the power behind it, is usually subtle, although it can be overt. When it is subtle, it takes the form of relationship messages that always accompany content messages and indicate how—that is, in what kind of relationship—the content is to be received (Watzlawick, Beavin, & Jackson,

1967). For example, when a group member discloses feeling sad, this may have the controlling effect of prompting the group to offer support and withhold confrontation. The (stated) content message is "I feel sad," but the (unstated) relationship message might be "Be nice to me." Every content message carries with it some kind of relationship message, and thereby exercises some kind—and degree—of control over the behavior of others. When control is overt, this simply means that content and relationship messages are the same, as in "Listen to me! *I'm* talking."

An important feature of group counseling is that it gives members the opportunity to understand their power, their control over others, and others' control over them. This happens as processing in the group helps members focus on the relationship messages that accompany their content messages, something that is rarely done in everyday life. In addition, group counseling helps members develop more effective ways of establishing and exercising power, and of controlling and responding to the control of others. Thus, a bossy child may learn that others become more cooperative as his or her "I'm the boss" relationship messages are replaced by "I'm likable" relationship messages—in other words, as bossy behavior is replaced by cooperative behavior on the child's part.

Group Facilitation

The counselor serves essentially three functions in the group. The procedural function includes initiating the group, managing the group process through rules and limits, and terminating the group. The indirect intervention function refers to behaviors that render the group interaction therapeutic: establishing norms, structuring, focusing the group on its process and tasks, and shaping the feedback, disclosure, and helping skills of the members. The direct intervention function has to do with helping members in the group to change by offering support, feedback, and interpretations and through teaching and skill training. Particular counselor behaviors often perform several functions simultaneously.

Procedural Behaviors

The counselor not only creates the group and determines its membership, but maintains it throughout its existence, the term of which the counselor defines. Among procedural behaviors are determining group composition and screening; structuring the groups; and setting limits throughout the life of the group.

Group Composition and Screening. The particular combination of members in any group is a determinant of the group's interaction and its outcome. A key question is: To what extent should members of a group be alike (homogeneous composition) and to what extent different (heterogeneous composition) in order for the group to function effectively? To answer the question it is first necessary to specify the variable on which homogeneity is based. Research on task groups (see Shaw, 1976) has indicated that groups heterogeneous with regard to intellectual ability and personality perform more effectively than homogeneous groups. These variables are perhaps less relevant to the functioning of counseling groups than is interpersonal behavior. Concerning this variable, Yalom (1975) reported that homogeneous task groups (interpersonally compatible on the FIRO-B Scale) are more cohesive and effective than are heterogeneous (incompatible) groups. Task groups are not counseling groups, however, so one must be cautious in applying these findings to situations in which the "task" is the attitude and behavior change of the members. Yalom (1975) has contended that while it is important for therapeutic groups to provide the variety of viewpoints and role behaviors that would certainly result from a heterogeneous composition, homogeneity in the sense of interpersonal compatibility is more important, because it contributes to group cohesiveness. A group so composed, he asserted, is more likely to produce positive outcomes and, in any case, will not be without the diversity necessary for interpersonal learning and attitude change.

Compatibility of the members is one of two factors with regard to which counseling groups in the schools may be composed. The second factor is modeling. Ginott (1961) recommended a balance, in children's play groups, between compatibility and heterogeneity, the former preventing a very different child from receiving harmful ridicule, the latter promoting therapeutic identification (i.e., modeling) among the children. Behavioral groups often include among the members explicitly chosen models, students who already exhibit behaviors that other members need to acquire (e.g., Warner, Niland, & Maynard, 1971). Model-reinforcement groups are often homogeneous with respect to problem area, but the presence of models makes the members heterogeneous in behavioral repertoire. Rose (1972), recognizing the functions served by intermember compatibility and the presence of models, presented a behavioral composition scheme that builds in both. This scheme is based on ratings of prospective members on several behaviors relevant to the group. The scheme ensures that each member performs at a similar level to at least one other member on each behavior and, apart from this, allows for considerable differences in performance as well. The scheme is a very systematic way of achieving Ginott's (1961) balance.

Group composition is directly linked to screening, since the counselor can gather information during screening necessary to compose the group. The counselor can also exclude persons whose needs are inappropriate to the group's purpose and who might possibly be harmed from a group experience. Screening for an effective group composition is rarely done systematically. Most often, the counselor interviews or observes prospective members and chooses those whom the group is likely to help and who have something to offer the group. The most informative screening procedure is one that gives the counselor an idea of the person's in-group behavior. Since students are likely to behave quite differently in a one-to-one interview with the counselor than in a group of their peers, the group should not be composed on the basis of interview data alone. In a school setting, the counselor often has access to other information about students' interpersonal behavior, ranging from direct observation to discussions with teachers who have referred the students. If such information is gathered and considered objectively, it can be most helpful in composing the group. Rose's (1972) behavioral procedure is an example of such a device.

The counselor must be aware of the potential harm that accompanies the group procedures being used and communicate this to prospective members. The counselor is responsible to see that students who are not likely to benefit from the group are not admitted. Students who do not belong in the group are referred to a more appropriate group or to individual counseling. In doing this the counselor must take care not to communicate rejection but to emphasize that it is important for each student to receive the best services.

Screening procedures serve to inform prospective members as well as the counselor. As the counselor is learning about the student's needs, concerns, and interpersonal style during intake, the student is obtaining a description of the group. The counselor must communicate clearly (a) the group's purpose, (b) the nature of the group process, (c) specific behaviors and activities that members will perform, (d) potential risks of participating, and (e) the (hopefully) voluntary nature of participation. Examples of screening information to use with children and adolescents are found in Ohlsen (1973) and Gazda (1976b), respectively.

Structure. The group's structure refers to the extent to which the members are clear about what behaviors are expected of them in the group. Groups vary greatly in structure, and counselors rationalize the amount of structure they employ in terms of their theoretical orientation rather than empirical evidence. Thus, structure is considered by those who oppose it (e.g., MacLennan & Felsenfeld, 1968) to reduce spontaneity and personal responsibility, while those supporting the use of structure (e.g., Ohlsen, 1977) claim it contributes to the efficiency of group functioning.

Structuring can occur as part of preparation for participation before a group begins or it can occur during a group. Pregroup structuring communicates to prospective members what the group will be like and what will be expected of them as participants. Typically, this is done in an interview in which clients ask questions to clarify the behavioral requirements of the group (Yalom, 1975). Other media used to explain group functioning and relevant behaviors include hand puppets and slide shows (Dinkmeyer & Muro, 1971), classroom presentations (Ohlsen, 1973), and open-ended questionnaires involving self-disclosure of concerns and goals (Kochendofer, 1975).

Studies generally have found such structuring to be helpful and directly related to in-group behavior (Bednar & Kaul, 1978). Corder, Haizlip, Whiteside, and Vogel (1980) found that pretherapy training for adolescents, which included contracts, distribution of guidelines, and videotaped instruction and demonstration of appropriate group behavior, led to greater group cohesiveness, less irrelevant talk, increases in positive statements, fewer questions and conflicts, better feedback, and a lower dropout rate than comparison groups. Hunt and Smith (1980) presented group counseling in an involving manner for black female adolescents, linking group counseling to their cultural experiences and showing its relevance to students' personal situations. Their techniques resulted in a high placement rate in counseling groups over a period of two semesters.

Methods of structuring during the group range from counselor suggestions and instructions to structured group exercises. For children's groups, most writers contend that some structuring is vital. Kissiah (1975) stated that most children need direction in group interaction and recommended that early in the group the counselor help members know when to speak, how to listen, and how to pick out the main ideas in a discussion. Ohlsen (1973) stated that children need to understand how to behave in groups and require training in role behavior appropriate to group functioning, such as helper skills. Yet Ohlsen (1977) and Glass (1973) cautioned against overstructuring and emphasized that the counselor should supply structuring interventions only as they are needed in the group. Not all groups for children are structured. Those involving play rely less on group interaction and are relatively unstructured (Ginott, 1961). Structuring is required only if the behaviors to be performed are unfamiliar to group members.

Adolescents may also benefit from some structuring in the group. Gazda (1976a) recommended initial structuring to shape members' attitudes toward the group, especially expectancies of a positive experience and hard work. Structuring the activities of the group is probably best determined by members' need. If they are interpersonally sophisticated, less structuring is required and they are able to assume responsibility in the group more quickly (Glass, 1973). In support of this position, Bednar and Kaul (1978) noted that individuals exhibiting "higher levels of interpersonal functioning responded more favorably to lower structure demands" (p. 794).

Structuring accelerates the group process (Yalom, 1975). If the group is short-term, initial structuring of activities may be crucial to establishing a therapeutic level of functioning. This is often done with structured group exercises that require the members to interact according to a set of instructions and afterward to process the experience. Exercises can be valuable contributors to group functioning if they are conducted properly. If they are not, they produce confusion and disrupt the process of the group. Shapiro (1978) has proposed guidelines for using exercises in a group. First,

exercises should fit sensibly and comfortably into the group process, facilitating and not interfering with the group's development. Second, they should be voluntary. If members are unwilling to participate and processing their reluctance does not produce consent, the exercise should not be used. Third, the counselor should inform members of the purpose of the exercise before it begins; this requires that he or she be clear about its purpose before suggesting it. Fourth, the counselor should be willing to stop the exercise at any time to process reactions to it, even if it has not been completed. It is the impact of the experience on the group and not the exercise itself that is of value. For this reason, an exercise should always be processed; otherwise, very little learning can result. Handbooks of structured group exercises are available for children (e.g., Hawley & Hawley, 1972) and adults (e.g., Pfeiffer & Jones, 1969–1974). The choice of any exercise for group counseling should be dictated by personal knowledge of how well it works and whether it serves the purpose required by the group.

Many practitioners eschew not only structured exercises but structure itself, preferring instead for the group to develop as it will, limited only by the counselor's process comments and interpersonal feedback. More structure is presumed to reduce members' responsibility and freedom to develop a group that is genuinely and uniquely their own. However, Bednar, Melnick, and Kaul (1974) argued that early structuring promotes personal responsibility in the long run. Structuring, by which they meant instructions and exercises to clarify role expectations, allows for relatively high-risk behaviors (self-disclosure, feedback, and confrontation) under conditions of low responsibility. Members' personal responsibility is initially low because they are carrying out the instructions of the counselor. However, the increased cohesion resulting from increased risk taking creates a safe atmosphere within which members can become more aware of their own behavior and, ultimately, more responsible for it.

A member's sense of responsibility for his or her behavior in the group is influenced by how the counselor structures and processes the group. The counselor's comments can persuade members to attribute changes they make to their own resources (Strong, 1978). Thus, after initially structuring the group to produce the desired high-risk behaviors, the counselor may during the course of the group increase interpretations of personal responsibility and correspondingly decrease structuring. This might be expected to heighten the sense of responsibility that members feel for their interaction and progress in the group.

Setting Limits. Many groups for children and adolescents have specific rules and limits guiding members' behavior, and it is the counselor's job to communicate and enforce these rules and limits. Some rules concern the maintenance of the group. Gazda (12976a, p. 60) recommended a set of "ground rules" that concern such matters as confidentiality, attendance, and the authority of the counselor, in addition to clarifying appropriate in-group behaviors. These are communicated to members at the outset of the group. Other restrictions protect members by limiting certain behaviors. In play-group therapy, limits are firmly and clearly communicated to children as the need for them arises; if the child proposes to behave in an unacceptably harmful or destructive way, the counselor encourages the verbal expression of feelings and attempts to channel the behavioral expression into other forms of play (Ginott, 1961). Dinkmeyer and Muro (1971) also recognized the need of protecting members in verbal interaction. They recommended that when the group places too much pressure on an individual, the counselor should intervene, perhaps by redirecting the focus onto the source of the pressure. Restrictions on behavior should serve the beneficial functions described and not curb spontaneous interaction, arouse undue resistance, or place the counselor in the inaccessible position of an uncompromising authoritarian. Rules must be acceptable to the group; the reasons for having them and difficulties with compliance should be discussed in the group.

Indirect Intervention

The set of behaviors that most clearly differentiate counseling in a group from individual counseling are those that mold the group into a change agent. To the extent that the counselor is a participant in the group on a par with other members, he or she can model appropriate participatory behaviors. Members will observe closely how the counselor expresses feelings, receives negative feedback, supports other members, reacts to silence, and so on. The counselor can also draw attention to effective behavior by other members, point out its beneficial consequences, and reinforce it. Con-

versely, the counselor can extinguish ineffective or disruptive behavior by ignoring it.

Yalom's (1975) notion of a "self-reflective loop" (p. 122) is most helpful in relating the counselor's indirect interventions to interpersonal learning in the group. The first task of the counselor is to focus the attention of the group on its here-and-now interaction. This task is essential, because the initial tendency of members is to discuss issues external to the group and unrelated to its purpose. Members are also reluctant to disclose their immediate feelings and perceptions to the group. The counselor encourages the expression of feeling, prompts the sharing of interpersonal perceptions, and comments on the relationship implications of messages. As members learn to focus on these aspects of their interaction, and become more familiar with each other, they are said to function in the here-and-now. The counselor is then able to help the group reflect on their experience, through eliciting feedback, pointing out interactional patterns, and making interpretations. The counselor's function here is to enhance the capacity of the members to provide each other with new learning and opportunities to change. The counselor helps members to combine cognitive learning with emotional experience and thus derive meaning from their interaction. Specific indirect interventions include process commentary; giving, receiving, and guiding feedback; and facilitating self-disclosure.

Process Commentary. Much of the focus in an interactional group is on the relationship aspects of messages. Implications of each member's verbal and nonverbal behavior for the relationships with other members are brought to the level of verbal awareness in an activity known as "processing." This provides insight into interpersonal behavior: how one initiates a relationship, obtains help, expresses liking, responds to hostility, and so on.

Feedback. Feedback is a major source of interpersonal learning; it can modify self-perceptions and other socially based beliefs, and it can influence the direction of behavior change in the group. The effect of receiving feedback is often so profound that considerable care must be taken to see that members learn how to request, give, and receive it constructively.

To be effective, feedback must be credible. It must be perceived to come from accurate and trustworthy sources. Positive feedback is generally perceived to be more credible than negative feedback (e.g., Jacobs, Jacobs, Feldman, & Cavior, 1973), but negative feedback is as credible when accompanied by positive feedback (Jacobs et al., 1973; Schaible & Jacobs, 1975). In addition to valance, feedback varies in behavioral specificity. Behavioral feedback seems to be more effective than feedback with solely emotional content; this is particularly important if the feedback is negative (Jacobs et al., 1973). Of course, feedback needs to be communicated clearly in order to have appropriate impact. Quite often it is not, and the confusion that results becomes the focus of the group. The clarification of interpersonal perceptions, like the expression of feelings, is a difficult communication skill. Counselor process comments serve to sort out messages that are ambiguously sent, misinterpreted by the receiver, or both. The counselor's own feedback should be a model of clarity and specificity and should be delivered in a trustworthy, supportive manner.

Receiving feedback is as important a skill as sending it. It is a potentially threatening experience, and the use of some initial structuring can be beneficial in rehearsing nondefensive listening. Counselor instructions to group members usually include the notion that feedback does not demand a change but may be accepted or rejected. Each theory of group work contains a homily that states this in a clever way; it is only half true, of course, since the social power in the group gives feedback considerable weight. It is important for group members to have the illusion of choice; it promotes personal responsibility and reduces resistance. As MacLennan and Felsenfeld (1968) noted, the counselor's willingness to receive members' feedback, consider it carefully in front of the group, and admit mistakes now and then demonstrates and models to members a nondefensive posture for interacting in the group.

Feedback is so much a part of group counseling that it seems unnecessary to detail the many particular instances of its use. It is important to note that even in children's groups that emphasize unstructured play rather than verbal interaction, feedback via peer reactions is considered essential to learning (Ginott, 1961). Komechak (1971) stated that combined play with interaction creates the opportunity for children to receive immediate feedback regarding the interpersonal consequences of their behavior. In such groups, counselor interventions respond to behavior immediately and objectively and are limited largely to perceptions of the child's behavior and its consequences. This model also helps to shape the feedback children give each other.

Self-Disclosure. Self-disclosure is the communication of personal information that one would not normally reveal to others (Vander Kilk, 1985). As groups develop, self-disclosure increases in quantity and deepens in intimacy. Negative self-disclosures may lead to greater group cohesiveness because they increase vulnerability and social dependence. When negative self-disclosures meet with acceptance and support, therapeutic change is more likely. If, however, self-disclosures are met with disapproval or condemnation, subsequent risk taking is reduced (Orvis, Kelley & Butler, 1976; Passer, Kelley, & Mishela, 1978; Strong & Claiborn, 1982). Positive self-disclosures may have a therapeutic effect for the individual if they take place during high cohesiveness conditions in the group, usually during later stages. Otherwise, positive self-disclosures, if not given in the context of other "weaknesses" can actually lead to negative responses from group members (Jones & Gordon, 1972; Nelson-Jones & Strong, 1976). The counselor must encourage gradual self-disclosure from group members while carefully shaping the group's responses toward warmth and acceptance. The counselor may need to prevent premature negative or positive self-disclosure if the group is not yet ready to respond appropriately.

Therefore, how the counselor encourages and manages the self-disclosure of group members may have a great impact on the development of the group and positive change for the individuals. Counselor self-disclosures should always be deliberate and moderate, because unplanned, intense self-disclosure may lead to the members perceiving the counselor as overly needy (Weigel, Dinges, Dyer, & Straumfjord, 1972). Appropriate, discrete counselor self-disclosure can foster acceptance and trust (Vander Kolk, 1985) and lead to greater group cohesiveness.

Clearly, self-disclosure cannot be considered the all-powerful and completely beneficial element of group counseling is was once considered to be (Jourard, 1971). However, properly managed, it is a basic and potent mechanism for change.

Direct Intervention

Much of the group counseling literature implies that the use of indirect and direct interventions is inversely proportional. Some group orientations purport to rely more heavily on the interaction created by the process focus of the counselor to bring about desired changes, while other orientations appear to treat individuals in a group setting, with the counselor essentially applying one-to-one helping skills to each member. While most group orientations emphasize the use of indirect or direct interventions, it cannot be assumed that the techniques practitioners claim to employ are the exclusive change agents in their groups (Lieberman et al., 1973). Counselors have both an indirect and direct impact on the change individual members undergo, the proportion varying as a function of the counselor, the member, and the group, in addition to the theoretical rationale of the treatment.

Verbal Interventions. Communication on the content level is important to the cognitive learning of participants in group counseling. The counselor's verbal interventions, as well as everyone's feedback, effect changes in members' self-perceptions, beliefs, and ways of looking at the world. Over time, the group's communication provides members with a conceptual framework to understand their subjective experience and social reality. The counselor's interventions are instrumental to this process. Guided by his or her conceptual system, the counselor gives meaning to what happens in the group through selective responses, process comments, and interpretations. In a sense, the counselor is a teacher, and the members are learning a new language. Like psychological interpretation, the counselor's interventions and group facilitation provide new labels for members' experience and draw relationships between events that were not previously seen (Levy, 1963).

The theoretical orientation embodied in the counselor's interventions is less significant than the fact that the counselor does promote cognitive learning in the group. In other words, it makes little difference what language members learn, as long as they learn one. This is highlighted by Lieberman et al.'s finding that "Meaning-Attribution" (1973, p. 238), the counselor's use of conceptual, interpretive interventions, was positively correlated with successful outcome in encounter groups, indepen-

dent of the counselors' theoretical orientations. The meaning attribution function was the important element in members' change, not the particular meaning. Group counselors operate from diverse and contradictory frames of reference, and none are consistently more effective than others. However, it is important not to take this as evidence that what the counselor says has little to do with change, for it is likely that without cognitive learning, the effect of group interaction on members' behavior would be weakened considerably.

Verbal behavior in the group is often dissonance arousing (Mayer, Rohen, & Whitley, 1969). Feedback inevitably reveals discrepancies between self-perceptions and the perceptions of others or between beliefs and observations. To the extent that discrepant information is difficult to discount, the individual is likely to change his or her attitude in the direction of the discrepancy. The social power of the communicators, the cohesiveness of the group, and the degree of consensus regarding the feedback promote attitude change. Dissonant states can be distressing, especially if the discrepant cognitions are relevant to self-concept or deeply held values, as is frequently the case in group counseling. Heightened emotionality or confusion accompanying dissonance arousal motivates attitude change and renders the individual open to interpretations that resolve the discrepancy by reframing the situation. Attitude change in a group may be a simple shift in the direction of feedback, or a reconceptualization of events integrating the discrepant cognitions. The counselor's task is to promote the kind of attitude change most in keeping with the individual's goals.

Modeling, Rehearsal, and Reinforcement. Modeling, behavioral rehearsal, and reinforcement may be more systematically applied in behavioral group counseling, but other sorts of groups rely heavily on them to influence group functioning and to help members achieve goals.

In addition to being an expert, the counselor is a member of the group and uses that role to model behaviors relevant to the establishment of therapeutic norms: active listening, constructive feedback, intimate self-disclosure, and so on. The counselor also brings the group's attention to such behaviors exhibited by members, informally using them as models. Modeling not only allows members to acquire the interactional skills necessary for participation in the group, but exposes them to a greater repertoire of behaviors to use in working on problems. To the extent that members see others as similar to themselves and observe their behavior to lead to positive consequences, they will be encouraged to try out alternative behaviors themselves (Mayer, Rohen, & Rhitley, 1969). The use of peers as models, especially in school settings where peers are highly influential, is by itself a case for counseling students in groups (Hosford, 1973).

The group is also an excellent setting for behavioral rehearsal. Members learn to support and trust each other, creating a climate in which they may experiment with otherwise threatening behaviors and receive immediate, constructive feedback. Members may perform behaviors in the group interaction until they feel comfortable enough to try them outside the group. Or they may role-play situations to consider which of several alternative behaviors is most effective. In either case, the group provides an opportunity to attempt and refine interpersonal and problem-solving behaviors that are otherwise difficult to acquire.

Reinforcement in the group promotes vicarious learning (modeling) and the acquisition of skills through rehearsal. In addition, social reinforcement by the counselor shapes norms that are then maintained by social reinforcement from group members (Rose, 1972). Liberman (1971) reported that systematic social reinforcement in a group increases cohesiveness. Thus, reinforcement is pervasive in the functioning of a group, directly affecting the operation of several of the change mechanisms. The group counselor should recognize the power of his or her social reinforcement in producing a therapeutic interaction and should attend to the emerging contingencies by which members selectively reinforce and extinguish interactional behavior in the group.

Support. In the course of the group, the counselor establishes a relationship with each member that is basic to helping that member change. It is important that the counselor be supportive and communicate an attitude of caring (e.g., Gazda, 1978). This notion receives support both in individual counseling (see Mitchell, Bozarth, & Krauft, 1977) and in group counseling (Lieberman et al., 1973) research linking counselor warmth and acceptance to positive outcome. Offering support at difficult moments in the group can be crucial to a member's willingness to work through a conflict or to receive and consider negative feedback.

Children's Groups

Although the dynamics of children's groups are similar to those of adult groups with regard to the basic processes reviewed here, the methods are necessarily different (Vander Kolk, 1985). Groups for children are generally shorter in duration, with 30-minute sessions more common than the adult 1- to 2-hour group session. Children's groups are also smaller than the typical adult group of 8 to 12 individuals. More structured preparation may be necessary, and except in play therapy or insight therapy, more structured exercises may need to be used. Gazda (1976a) has emphasized that children's groups should emphasize the strengths of the members of the groups, and that the focus of group counseling for children should be on prevention of later problems. Gazda (1976a) also explains the necessity of linking the goals of group counseling to the appropriate developmental level of the members.

APPLICATIONS IN THE SCHOOLS

The same theories of helping underlie group counseling as individual counseling, although their implications for techniques are somewhat different as a function of the group setting. Theories of group work are theories of counseling and psychotherapy integrated with some knowledge of group dynamics. The group counselor's theoretical orientation is a cognitive tool for understanding the phenomena of the group; thus, it necessarily contains notions about communication and other interpersonal behavior and about group process variables—leadership, norms, cohesiveness, group development, and composition. The counselor's theory of group work also determines what the counselor attends to in the group, and what language he or she uses to describe it. The meaning-attribution function of the counselor, an interpretive activity that promotes cognitive learning based on experiences in the group, depends for its specific content on the counselor's cognitive framework or theoretical orientation.

The counselor's theory also affects the roles and techniques employed with the group, although there is not as clear a link between theory and practice as one might think. Theorists write as if their theory determines technique and techniques operate according to principles embodied in the theory. But there is little evidence for this, since group counselors of different orientations use similar techniques. The warm, helping relationship established by the behavioral counselor may be indistinguishable from that of the client-centered counselor. The use of reflection, process comments, encouragement, behavioral feedback, and even particular structuring techniques is common in groups based on a variety of theories. Conversely, practitioners of the same theory may differ in major ways with respect to technique. Two Reality Therapy leaders, for example, may offer very different degrees of support, or may challenge the client confrontively or humorously. Indeed, the theme of the first part of this chapter is that basic change processes in the group are independent of the theoretical content of the group. This idea is not only consistent with a unified theory of change, based on the social psychology of small-group behavior, but it is supported by encounter group research indicating that there is little correspondence between the theoretical orientation of group leaders and leader behaviors in the group (Lieberman et al., 1973).

In the present review we discuss the theoretical underpinnings of the various interventions, as well as research support for the application of these interventions to specific problem areas. It should be stated at the outset, however, that despite the great variety of group counseling interventions being used in the schools, relatively few appear with any frequency in the professional literature. While some of these may be effective and widely applicable, none have been very thoroughly researched. The evidence supporting the use of most interventions remains sketchy at best and often entirely anecdotal—as, indeed, it was in the first edition of this chapter.

In this review group interventions are organized partly by counseling approach and partly by problem focus, depending on which characteristic of the intervention is the more salient in the literature describing it. Although this may seem slightly irrational at first, it reflects the state of the field and should be the most helpful to readers who wish to go beyond this chapter to original sources. Thus, the first of the following sections describes counseling approaches that are distinct in terms of their theoretical base, the nature of their interventions, or both: play, activity, behavioral, drama/

role playing, and multimodal groups. In the next section we describe approaches defined by their focus on a particular client problem area: problem behaviors, personality and social adjustment, academic concerns, and career concerns. The final section has to do with the usefulness of parent and teacher groups for dealing with children's problems. Other issues, such as client or process variables affecting the use of the interventions, are raised within these sections, as appropriate.

Theoretically Based Approaches
Play Groups

Play group counseling for young children, based on the psychotherapies of Axline (1947) and Ginott (1961) among others, is unlike the other group procedures discussed in this chapter. While the interaction among children is considered the agent of change, little attempt is made, beyond group composition, to develop the group for therapeutic effect. Instead, the counselor is passively attentive to the children's play, responding to their remarks, reflecting the feelings expressed by their behavior, but not actively probing or interpreting. The counselor is not indifferent, but warm, accepting, and permissive (within limits), and communicates an attitude of respect for the child.

Two principles underlie this treatment and suggest change mechanisms which may be operating. The first regards the expressiveness of play: "Play is symbolic of the child's immediate experiencing as well as his life history. As the child interacts with play media or creates his own imaginary props, he communicates to others what he is experiencing. His play may be due to or have residuals of past experiences, but it is expressed in the immediate here-and-now context" (Bosdell, 1973, p. 29). Bosdell (1973) noted that play does not exclude verbal communication of attitudes, feelings, and tendencies to behave. Thus, the influence processes present in play group counseling may be expected to effect attitude and behavior change much as in groups where the communication is largely verbal. Interaction with other children and with the counselor introduces discrepant ideas, arouses dissonance, and changes meanings for the child, meanings that receive their strongest expression in play (Slavson & Schiffer, 1975).

The second principle of play group counseling is that the social and emotional context established by the counselor's behavior promotes change. Ginott (1961) stated that the presence of other children during play can suggest alternative behaviors to the child through identification, which is essentially a process of learning through imitation. The counselor's unobtrusive behavior conveys an attitude that contributes to interpersonal learning not only by allowing it to occur, but by emphasizing and respecting the child's choice to behave as he or she will. Occasionally, the counselor explicitly communicates this to the child. The group thus "provides a tangible social setting for discovering and experimenting with new and more satisfying modes of relating to peers [and] a milieu where new social techniques can be tested in terms of reality mastery and inter-individual relationships" (Ginott, 1961, p. 11). Changes in interpersonal behavior are supplemented and supported by changes in self-concept, as they are in all group counseling.

Gazda (1973) recommended play group counseling for children under 9. Group counseling for young children is indicated particularly when their interpersonal behavior is withdrawn, immature, or disruptive (Ginott, 1961), as both modeling and feedback processes during play provide experiences in which appropriate alternative behaviors may be learned. Inasmuch as the child's difficulties have an interpersonal component or may be resolved through altered interpersonal relationships, the play group may be beneficial. Care must be taken not to include children whose interpersonal behavior would disrupt group interactions irreparably. Ginott (1961) cited intense sibling rivalry, sociopathy, inappropriate sexuality, extreme aggressiveness, and severe reactions to stress as characteristics for which play group counseling is a poor treatment choice.

Regarding the selection of toys for play group counseling, Bosdell (1973) made the following recommendations: Toys should facilitate communication and the expression of feeling, provide experiences of mastery over the environment, and promote interaction among the children. She suggested toys that have multiple uses and thus do not restrict the child's range of behavior. In addition, toys that would elicit activity stressful to the counselor should be excluded. Play group counseling relies so much on the toys available to the children that the interpersonal implications of the toys—for the children and the counselor—must be considered carefully; the experience of each counselor

is probably the best judge, in the absence of other evidence.

A more recent variation of play group counseling is developmental play (Brody, 1978; Burt & Myrick, 1980). Here, adults and children together engage in structured exercises that involve close physical contact. The primary goal of developmental play is the building of positive emotional relationships with adults, within which children can explore alternative ways of interacting and trusting others. In contrast to traditional play group counseling, developmental play structures the environment more deliberately to stimulate children's emotional experiencing and behavioral exploration. In addition, its focus on adult–child relationships, rather than the peer relationships common to play group counseling, suggests that developmental play provides more of the nurturance and encouragement associated with effective parenting than do the interpersonal understandings one gets from peer interactions. The actual outcomes of development play, however, have yet to be established by research.

Research on play group interventions in school settings has produced mixed results. Moulin (1970) studied play as a treatment for underachieving first, second, and third graders. The counselor's role was characterized by "indirect influence" (p. 90), communicated essentially through client-centered verbal strategies. The aim of treatment was to enhance communication and thereby indirectly improve school performance. Group members did improve, as compared with controls, in psycholinguistic ability, but this did not affect school achievement. The procedures (and underlying assumptions) of the traditional play group have been investigated in two comparative studies with shy, friendless children. Thombs and Muro (1973) found play somewhat more effective than verbal group counseling in increasing peer preferences, measured sociometrically; both forms of counseling were superior to no treatment. This indirectly supports the idea that play can facilitate interpersonal learning among children. Clement and Milne (1967) compared a play group using verbal reinforcement only (a typical play group) with one also using tangible reinforcers to shape social approach behavior in young boys. Results indicated the tangible reinforcement group to be superior in improving the target behaviors in and out of counseling. Whereas the tangible group increased verbal communication, social play, and decreased problem behaviors, the traditional play group members actually showed a decrease in social play.

Play group interventions are based more in opinion than data. Not only is the traditional approach—unstructured play in the presence of a supportive but unobtrusive counselor—questionably effective, compared with more active interventions, but even less is known about *why* and *for whom* it is effective when it is. For very young children, play interventions may be more effective than verbal ones. But beyond this, only the study of reinforcement suggests a possible therapeutic mechanism. Until more systematic research on play groups is conducted in school settings, the usefulness of this famous counseling approach must remain a mystery.

Activity Groups

For children who are beyond the primary grades, play (or other activities) may be combined with verbal interaction in counseling. Activity-interview groups (Slavson & Schiffer, 1975) include a "working part," in which members engage in activities (usually games) appropriate to their age, and a "talking part," during which members gather in a circle and discuss problem behaviors and concerns. The activities of the group promote here-and-now interaction and provide material from the children's immediate experience with each other to apply to discussions of out-of-counseling behavior. The counselor, having observed the interaction of the group during the activity, facilitates the discussion with minimal structuring, focusing the group's attention on its task, eliciting self-disclosure, and shaping feedback. Cohesiveness is important in these groups, which employ the change mechanisms common to any interactional group.

A variation of activity-interview group counseling is the substitution of structured group exercises for the activity, in which case the processing of the exercise is the talking part of the group. The exercises serve to elicit a certain kind of interaction appropriate to the purpose of the group. A group focusing on clear communication, for example, might employ exercises demonstrating the roles played by different channels of communication, or how messages become distorted as they are passed from person to person. Groups for children employing structured group exercises are virtually indistinguishable from similar groups for adolescents and adults.

Most applications of activity groups found in the literature have been described rather than evaluated. Two examples of these will suffice. Komechak (1971) reported using activity groups as a broad-based counseling approach for elementary school children. For activities she drew mostly upon the arts. She then stimulated group discussions with uncritical behavioral comments. She claimed that the groups developed an effective means of exchanging feedback that in turn led to positive changes in the members' behavior. Hillman, Penczar, and Barr (1975) developed an approach to guidance called Activity Group Guidance (AGG), which they used to provide a wide a range of guidance services to elementary school students. The emphasis on guidance rather than counseling suggests an application to the developmental concerns of all students, rather than the remediation of problems in certain students. AGG uses various media from the arts, sciences, and physical education to achieve such guidance goals as effective problem solving and interpersonal relations. A typical session begins with the discussion of a topic, shifts to an activity, and ends by processing the activity in a way relevant to the topic. The activity is by far the longest part of the session, and the discussions are very brief. Leadership in the group, as in most play and activity groups, is rather nondirective, so that students can experience themselves as autonomous decision makers and see the consequences of their decisions. The authors' subjective evaluation of numerous AGG groups, run weekly over the course of the school year, indicated that they were effective in reducing the incidence of adjustment problems.

Hillman and Runion (1978) compared AGG groups with discussion only and control groups for fifth-grade Hispanic and white children. At the end of treatment, AGG children exhibited greater social power among their peers, measured sociometrically, than did children in either of the other groups. This suggests that activities, at least as combined with discussion, provide some opportunity for interpersonal learning that discussion alone does not. Another comparison of activity groups with alternative approaches concerned counseling rather than guidance. Barcai and Dremen (1976) compared art activity, involving minimal verbal interaction but emphasizing cooperation, with verbal counseling and remedial work for fourth- and fifth-grade underachievers. They found that art activity groups were more effective in improving school performance, but that the other approaches had a greater impact on non-school-related measures of intellectual ability.

As with play groups, the research support for activity groups is not commensurate with their popularity. Although they follow the familiar and much investigated cycle of experiential learning, specific information about the mechanisms of change, the appropriateness of particular activities for particular children, and the nature and amount of processing necessary for effective learning is clearly needed. Without such an understanding, it is difficult to argue for the efficiency, let alone the superiority, of activity group interventions, compared with traditional counseling.

Behavioral Groups

Behavioral interventions have proven to be quite effective in changing behavior in group settings. Behavioral groups emphasize the application of learning principles to changing in-group and out-of-counseling behavior. They use the group process and intermember relationships differently than do other group approaches, although norms, cohesiveness, and influence processes are acknowledged to be important (Rose, 1972). Not surprisingly, behavioral groups have stimulated more than the average amount of research, the discussion of which will serve to illustrate the techniques they employ.

Reinforcement alone can be effective in shaping interactional behavior in the group. Token or material reinforcers may be used initially, as is perhaps necessary with children, but social reinforcers are also quite potent in this regard. Rose (1972) presents a clear example of shaping an evenly distributed communication network in the group:

> Give each member a stopwatch and, if necessary, teach him how to use it. After all members demonstrate competence in the use of the watches, each measures the amount of time the neighbor on his right speaks. At the end of fifteen minutes, the therapist writes down the names and the times on the blackboard. . . . The group then has the task of equalizing the time spoken by dividing the fifteen minute period among [the number of people in the group]. The low participants, however, have to be given some help to participate. A brief discussion follows on what should be talked about, and members are

encouraged to take notes. With young children the therapist puts the notes or hints on the board. A brief practice session takes place, and then each member again times the neighbor on his right. Warnings are given when [a member's] limit is reached. If not member goes thirty seconds above or below the allotted amount, the group may be reinforced. . . . Regardless of initial success, multiple trials are essential in order to stabilize the new communication pattern. (pp. 174–175)

Several studies have examined the effects of in-group reinforcement on behavior change in and outside the group. In research described previously, Clement and Milne (1967) found tangible reinforcers to be an effective supplement to the verbal reinforcement already present in traditional play group counseling. The tangible reinforcement of social approach behaviors during play increased the social nature of the play and led to an improvement in problems outside of counseling. A replication of the study (Clement, Fazzone, & Goldstein, 1970) further supported the superiority of tangible over verbal reinforcement. As in the earlier study, members of the traditional play group actually exhibited less social approach behavior, on some measures, as a result of counseling.

Tosi, Swanson, and McLean (1970) studied the effect of social reinforcement on the verbal behavior of sixth graders who did not speak in class. Results showed that for the experimental group only, reinforcement of in-group verbalizations (or other unspecified aspects of the treatment) led to an increase in unsolicited verbal behavior in the classroom, a change that was present at follow-up. Hinds and Roehlke (1970) compared systematic reinforcement of appropriate classroom behaviors with an attention-placebo (discussion) group and a no-treatment control group to determine their relative effectiveness in changing behavior in class. Groups were comprised of third, fourth, and fifth graders, referred to counseling because of specific problem behaviors. The experimental treatment included discussions and role plays of classroom scenes, and behavior was shaped by successively more social reinforcers, a common practice in children's groups. The members first received points (redeemable for game playing at the end of the session), then were administered four subsequent phases of reinforcement: points plus verbal approval by the counselor; the opportunity to lose as well as obtain points, plus verbal approval; points plus verbal reinforcement by peers; and verbal reinforcement alone. Results, measured by ratings of classroom videotapes, indicated the superiority of the treatment group over the other two groups. This supported the contention that systematic reinforcement of specific behaviors—as opposed to the unsystematic reinforcers operating in any discussion—is a mechanism of change in behavioral counseling. Other studies of reinforcement in group counseling have supported its usefulness in decreasing truancy in high school students (Brooks, 1975) and increasing the performance of school tasks by elementary school underachievers (Silverman, 1976). Both of these studies employed material and verbal reinforcement and the principles of successive approximations to shape target behaviors.

The combination of modeling and reinforcement in group counseling has also proven effective. Krumboltz and Thoresen (1964) studied the contributions of these techniques to shaping information seeking behavior in high school juniors. They found that social reinforcement alone was as effective as social reinforcement preceded by a tape-recorded model in increasing the target behavior. Both were more effective than attention-placebo and no-treatment control groups. For males, however, the model-reinforcement group was superior to reinforcement only; this is perhaps attributable to the fact that the model was a male. In other studies, the models were group members who exhibited high levels of the target behaviors, but who were unaware that they were models. Hansen, Niland, and Zani (1969) used a model-reinforcement group to raise the sociometric status of low-status sixth graders. The model-reinforcement group combined high- and low-status children and the reinforcement group included only children of equivalent status. In both group, the counselor reinforced appropriate ideas in a discussion of how to get along with others. The model-reinforcement group produced greater change in sociometric scores than the reinforcement group, and change was sustained at follow-up.

A similar study was conducted with high school juniors who were "alienated" (Warner & Hansen, 1970). The focus of group discussions was on powerlessness, normlessness, and social isolation, and positive statements in these areas

were reinforced in the group. Nonalienated students (male and female) served as models in the model-reinforcement group; the reinforcement-only group was different only in not containing nonalienated students. While both groups were effective in reducing alienation, as compared with attention-placebo and control groups, they did not differ from each other in effectiveness. Data concerning group cohesiveness or the members' perceptions of the models might have suggested why the models were not especially influential. Warner, Niland, and Maynard (1971) used children with realistic academic goals as models in a group designed to make the goals of unrealistic children more realistic. Fifth and sixth graders who reported being satisfied only with A's and B's but who were getting C's or worse in their school work were the clients. The models were satisfied with C's. In group discussions of the students' needs, interests, abilities, and goals, the counselor reinforced realistic goal statements in models and clients. Although there was no control group, results indicated that unrealistic goals were reduced.

Hargrave and Hargrave (1979) combined modeling, role playing, and behavioral rehearsal in an activity group format to shape social skills in preadolescents. Group sessions began with a discussion phase, in which the behavioral interventions were used, then continued with a team sports phase, which gave the students an opportunity for natural social interaction. Sessions ended with a processing phase, in which the counselors commented on the students' behavior during the game; role playing might also be used in this phase to focus on a skill. Results of a comparison of this treatment with a no-treatment control indicated that the treatment was more effective in reducing classroom behavior problems. Bretzing and Caterino (1984) used model-reinforcement groups to address both behavior problems and low self-esteem in elementary students. Groups always included one peer without the relevant problems to serve as a positive role model, and the counselors developed a point system to reinforce group norms. Although there was no control group, teacher ratings indicated pre–post improvement in the students' classroom behavior.

At least three other behavioral interventions have been used in group counseling in the schools, as reported in the research literature. Amerikaner and Summerlin (1982) used relaxation training and positive feeling imagery with first- and second-grade learning-disabled students. The students in this group exhibited less acting out in the classroom than students in a "social skills" group (which actually focused on awareness of self and others) and a no-treatment control. However, students in the social skills group exhibited higher self-esteem following treatment. Maher and Barbrack (1982) developed a behavioral group counseling treatment for ninth-grade students showing a poor adjustment to school. The counselors were either school counselors or 12th-grade students. Counseling was conducted according to a problem-solving framework, but incorporated traditional behavioral interventions described by Rose (1972); the focus was on school attendance, grades, and classroom behavior. Compared with control group students, who received the school's regular counseling services, students in the behavioral groups showed improved attendance and grades, as well as reduced disciplinary problems and special education referrals; these changes were maintained at a 10-week follow-up. Whether the behavioral groups were led by counselors or older students made no difference in outcome. Huey (1983) reported an assertion training treatment for verbally or physically aggressive adolescents. In an evaluation of the program with black students (Huey, 1979), he found it to be superior to both a discussion group and a no-treatment control in reducing aggressive behavior.

Finally, in a well-designed experiment in a residential school, Thompson and Hudson (1982) compared the effects of behavioral group counseling, values clarification groups, placebo groups (unstructured discussion), and no treatment on students' maladaptive behaviors. Behavioral counseling was distinguished by the use of a behaviorally specific language to discuss problems and formulate goals. Three counselors administered each of the three treatments in nine separate groups. No changes were exhibited in ratings of the students' behavior (by school staff, blind to the particular treatments students received) during the 15 weeks the groups were run. However, in the 15 weeks following treatment, students in the two active counseling groups showed improvement in both maladaptive behavior and behavioral indicators of unhappiness. There was no difference between the active treatments on either measure. This study was less an investigation of behavioral interventions than of the use of a behavioral language to conceptualize and work on problems.

The study showed, as most studies comparing the effects of alternative theoretical frameworks show (see Claiborn, 1982), that the choice of a framework matters less than the presence of a framework. Thus, both treatments providing students with a new way of conceptualizing their problems—behavioral counseling and values clarification—were superior to the placebo treatment, which offered nothing new.

Behavioral groups emphasize the use of behavioral techniques, which seem effective, but they contain features common to all group counseling that may also contribute to their therapeutic value, such as the content of the discussion, interpersonal influence by the counselor and group members, self-disclosure, and feedback. Research in reinforcement and modeling that does not control the effects of these processes leaves open the possibility that other change mechanisms accounts for their effects. Researchers have done a good job, however, in beginning to isolate particular change agents in behavioral groups and have yielded information that is useful to all practitioners. It is clear that reinforcement in the group can affect the nature of the group interaction quite powerfully, in addition to increasing behaviors that are directly related to client goals. Deliberate, systematic use of reinforcement by the counselor can, at the very least, help to create desired interactional patterns in groups that would otherwise communicate poorly. The work on modeling suggests that groups may be more beneficial if members vary in the extent to which they perform group-relevant behaviors to maximize the opportunities for imitative learning. And finally, the use of a behavioral framework, such as the problem-solving sequence or a behaviorally specific focus on antecedents, behaviors, and consequences, would seem to be a useful way to conceptualize problems in a group setting. Although it is not demonstrably superior to other theoretical frameworks, a behavioral framework does lend itself to other important interventions, like group problem solving, role playing, and goal attainment outside the group.

Drama and Role Playing

Drama and role playing refer to the different functions of interventions more than to differences in procedure. Drama serves an expressive function and is used in group counseling as a means of self-disclosure. Role playing serves a rehearsal function and is used as a means of acquiring new behaviors. Both interventions, moreover, can be used by themselves as the sole means of treatment, but they are commonly used in combination with other interventions as the need arises.

As an expressive technique, drama heightens the actor's awareness of feelings and attitudes associated with particular roles and situations. Engaging in a dramatic exercise in counseling can bring into sharp focus attitude discrepancies and distorted conceptualizations that bear importantly on the client's behavior and that make attitude change possible and desirable. Feedback from observers and participants in the drama facilitates this process, so drama should always be followed by discussion (processing) to reflect on the experience and derive some learning from it.

Gazda (1973) discussed using drama in a play-interview format, so that coping behaviors could be examined and changed in the context of family and school situations re-created in the session. This could serve the role-playing function, too, when preceded by models (such as dolls and puppets), whose own dramatic situations stimulate the children to discuss and learn about alternative ways of coping. Hosford and Acheson (1976) have noted that through fantasizing situations in drama, children can learn how to make decisions by playing out their choices. The feelings and ideas that represent the child's tendencies to behave are translated into behavior. Future consequences of present choices are brought to bear on the child's current thinking. Learning can also result from planning the drama (Hosford & Acheson, 1976). The counselor suggests a general theme for the drama—a value important in the lives of the participants—and facilitates the discussion by which the group works out the particulars. Both the planning and the drama can serve as problem-solving activities.

Wells (1962) reported an unconventional use of drama in the elementary school. According to her experience, dramatic techniques may be used anywhere in the school as a device for demonstrating how an event (such as a fight) occurred and for expressing feelings in connection with the event. Role reversal, in which participants play each other's parts, is useful in enhancing interpersonal learning. She also proposed a form of role playing in the natural setting, in which children are placed in real positions that are contrary to their ordinary behavior. As examples, she cited the instances of a messy child given the role of getting the room

ready for the next class, and a troublemaker being sent to the office for commendable reasons.

Role playing can serve a variety of purposes in group counseling, as noted by Passmore (1973). It can (a) increase the involvement of members in the group, (b) clarify problem situations, (c) promote empathic understanding of others, (d) suggest new or alternative behaviors, (e) provide practice in performing behaviors, and (f) help members generalize behaviors to new situations. Like a structured group exercise (which it is), role playing should meet the needs of group members, who need to be clear about its purpose. The counselor's task is to introduce the role play, making sure that everyone understands what role to play and the context in which to play it. The counselor must also stop the role play at an appropriate point and facilitate the group in a discussion of what occurred.

Sometimes a role play is followed by other role plays in which the participants either take the same roles and attempt some alternative behaviors, or reverse the roles and examine the situation from another perspective. Each role play should be processed before moving on to the next one, for the interaction about the role play contributes so importantly to cognitive learning. Processing also provides suggestions about how to structure the subsequent role play so as to maximize its usefulness. Learning from role playing need not depend entirely on others' observation. Self-observation is possible with videotape, which can be played back after the role play. Videotape procedures are extremely useful in the group when members are learning fairly complex interpersonal skills, like helping, job interviewing, or participating in a group.

The use of a drama and role playing in school counseling has received some attention by researchers. Harth (1966) attempted to change attitudes toward school of failing third graders by having them play the roles of teacher, principal, and other school personnel. Attitude change was not obtained, but students' classroom behavior did improve. In a study by Reisman and Beyer (1973), underachieving second and third graders participated in dramatic techniques as a way of understanding the consequences of their poor school performance and the attitudes of parents and teachers toward them. Drama was only one of the techniques used, but students, with the help of counselor interpretations, reportedly gained greater insight into their own feelings and others' attitudes as a result of counseling.

Gibbons and Lee (1972) used drama in combination with problem-solving discussions with fifth-grade boys who exhibited inappropriate classroom behaviors. The group was relatively unstructured, with a focus on exchanging ideas and making decisions. The group became very cohesive, and the boys' classroom behavior improved. Altmann and Firnesz (1973) used role playing with fourth graders to increase their self-esteem, measured both behaviorally by teachers and with a self-report instrument. The role plays were done in response to stimulus stories that concerned self-esteem and that required students to make decisions as the characters in the stories. Role plays of alternative solutions were systematically reinforced by the counselor. Results indicated the treatment was effective in increasing self-esteem behaviors, but the attention-placebo (discussion) group also showed positive changes.

Other investigations of role playing in group counseling have been in the context of behavioral groups, where they are combined with other interventions, such as modeling, for skill acquisition purposes. These include the Hargrave and Hargrave (1979) and Huey (1979) studies described in the preceding section. It is difficult, in such studies, to specify the effects of these techniques in the absence of research isolating their application from other group procedures. More systematic investigations could not only begin to determine the effectiveness of drama and role playing in changing attitudes and behavior but also clarify their contribution to such features of the group process as cohesiveness, self-disclosure, and acceptance of others.

Multimodal Groups

Multimodal approaches represent a recent innovation in group counseling in the schools. "Multimodal" refers to a combination of interventions aimed at different aspects of psychological functioning. The approach most often used in the school counseling literature is identified by the acronym HELPING (Keat, 1979) and uses interventions to affect student Health (and its relationship to psychological well-being), Emotional awareness and expressiveness, Learning, Personal interaction (including social skills and interpersonal awareness), Imagery (including both positive self-concept and interests), Need to know (awareness

of one's own attitudes and beliefs), and Guidance (representing behavioral interventions applied by the counselor). Durbin (1982) used the HELPING model in group counseling for sixth-grade girls. The girls contracted for an activity in each of the seven "modes," as the areas of functioning are called, and received a reward for their accomplishments in each mode. The author's subjective evaluation of the group was simply that it increased the girls' positive and decreased their negative feelings about themselves. Green (1978) also used the HELPING model in group counseling for children of divorce. The children were exposed to a series of structured group exercises related to the seven modes and focusing on their adjustment to the divorce. Only subjective evaluative data were reported, and it suggested that the groups were well received. One wishes that both of these reports had been accompanied by a more objective assessment of their impact. Authors advocating a multimodal approach would seem obliged not only to provide an overall evaluation of the approach, but an evaluation of each component, as well.

Tyler and Pargament (1981) reported the results of a nationwide study of multimodal group counseling aimed generally at psychosocial competence. High school students in the groups, which were led by school counselors, worked on goals in four specific areas: career, education, interpersonal, and intrapersonal development. On outcome measures, students showed increased internal locus on control, trust, active coping, and system blame, and decreased social desirability orientation. Thus, the groups were clearly impactful with respect to the students' psychological functioning on a general level; however, as in the aforementioned nonstudies, the design of this otherwise sound study makes it impossible to tell how specific components of the multimodal approach contributed to outcome.

Goldstein, Sprafkin, Gershaw, and Klein (1980) have reported a multimodal "structured learning approach" to training adolescents in social skills, called Skillstreaming. Following their (well-supported) belief that "almost everything works—but only for certain youngsters" (pp. 9–10), they have combined such behavioral interventions as reinforcement, modeling, role playing, and problem solving with direct teaching and interpersonal processes such as feedback and influence to shape a variety of socially appropriate behaviors, depending on the needs of the group and individual members. Unlike most multimodal approaches, the Skillstreaming interventions are explicitly drawn from the research literature and carefully combined to achieve specific goals. Moreover, Goldstein et al. (1980) report considerable research on structured learning in a variety of settings, indicating that not only are the component interventions themselves empirically based, but that the structured learning approach to combining interventions for specific goals is as well. Without a doubt, Skillstreaming is an exemplary multimodal approach.

Until researchers employ a componential assessment of multimodal group approaches, as Goldstein et al. (1980) have done, such approaches will remain only an interesting idea. It is difficult to defend the multimodal concept without data showing the separate and interactive contributions of each mode. This methodological criticism is not exactly new, as it echoes almost exactly the summary comments of the preceding two sections. There is a sense in which all group approaches are multimodal—they combine interventions to affect different aspects of psychological functioning. Research on such complex approaches, teasing out the respective contribution of each component, is tricky to say the least. Still, for the sake of scientific understanding and the efficient delivery of services, it must be attempted.

Problem-Focused Approaches
Problem Behavior Groups

Counseling groups have been used to change a variety of problem behaviors relevant to participation and performance in school. Gibbons and Lee (1972) found an unstructured discussion format effective in reducing classroom behavior problems. Group members, fifth-grade boys, were able to develop their own rules for operating and to use the group to discuss concerns about school, exchange suggestions, and even decide on recommendations to make to their teachers and principal. Tidwell and Bachus (1977) reported the use of values-oriented counseling helpful in decreasing aggressive behavior in fourth-, fifth-, and sixth-grade boys. The group interaction allowed for mutual helping, cooperation, and empathic understanding as the boys participated in structured exercises concerning values and decision making. The counselor focused the group on awareness and learning of value concepts from the exercises, and emphasized recall of earlier learning.

Cobb and Richards (1983) found small group counseling to be as effective as classroom guidance in improving classroom climate and conduct in fourth and fifth graders, as evidenced by behavioral indicators of disruptiveness, anxiety, and attention seeking. Randolph and Hardage (1973) compared a client-centered group with classroom behavior management by the teacher and no treatment for their effectiveness in shaping classroom-related task behaviors. The group was not only less effective than the other two conditions but actually produced a decrease in the target behaviors of its members.

Myrick and Kelly (1971) examined the use of a communication triad to enhance the in-class attentiveness of one of the three children. The "group" was structured so that each child played the role of listener, speaker, and observer in discussions of feelings and school-related topics. Each session was processed with the help of the counselor. Results showed that the target child became progressively more attentive in class, as compared with baseline performance.

Junior high students with behavior problems were given unstructured group counseling in two studies. Caplan (1957) found that counseling, which included open discussions of problems and accomplishments in school, improved the behavior and self-concepts of the group members. These changes did not occur for students in the control condition. Webb and Eikenberry (1964) investigated a similar group and found it to improve classroom conduct of the students. They attributed these results to the identification of group members with the counselor, which they contended ought to have changed their attitudes toward other adults.

Using a preventive approach, Huey (1985) found that small-group interventions provided an effective orientation to high school. The groups, comprised of black eighth graders, were led by juniors from the school the students would be entering. Sessions focused on school attendance and appropriate conduct, and made use of such interventions as cohesiveness, modeling, effective communication, and stress management. Results comparing participating students with eighth graders from the previous year indicated a lower number of failing grades, absences, and conduct problems for the program participants.

Very different theoretical approaches have been found to be reasonably effective in changing problem behaviors, and with varying success. It is clear from the preceding discussion that verbal, nondirective approaches have been popular and occasionally effective. Despite the stereotype of such approaches as "middle class," nondirective counseling has been used quite effectively with poor inner-city students exhibiting problem behaviors (Barcai & Robinson, 1969). Behavioral interventions, either alone or in combination with verbal counseling, seem to have grown in popularity in the last decade and a half. Thus, Gumaer and Myrick (1974) combined client-centered counseling with behavioral interventions, particularly social reinforcement, to reduce disruptive behavior in elementary school students. The inclusion of behavioral interventions is not always successful, however. Kelly and Matthews (1971) studied the use of tangible and social reinforcement with a similar population, but found them to be ineffective in reducing disruptive classroom behavior. This seems to have been an exception rather than the rule, however. Our own review and that of others (see Howard & Zimpfer, 1972) finds fairly strong support for the application of behavioral interventions in shaping such specific behaviors as those discussed here.

Another factor that has been found to be useful in group counseling for problem behaviors is the use of peer counselors. Schweisheimer and Walberg (1976) investigated the use of peer counselors as small-group leaders for potential dropouts. High school juniors were trained in group dynamics, communication theory, and decision making, and then led groups of freshmen and sophomores, in which the focus was on goal setting and decision making. Results indicated that group members increased their school attendance and decisiveness more than control subjects. Group counseling as a part of a larger intervention project to improve school-related behaviors also employed older students as group leaders (Bradfield et al., 1975). These groups emphasized mutual support, discussion of concerns, and feedback. The language of treatment was behavioral and facilitated discussion of problem situations and solutions. The program as a whole was quite effective in reducing problem behavior, but the contribution of the group to this outcome was unspecified.

Finally, it is worth noting that peer counselors were found to be quite as effective as trained school counselors in the Maher and Barbrack (1982) study of behavioral groups, described above. Aside from the treatment itself, the use of peer counselors in problem behavior groups seems to be an effective strategy. This could be because of modeling, but also because older peers might be considered to have social power—and influence— as psychological referents. This referent power might more than compensate, in fact, for their lesser expertise.

In a long-range retrospective study of the use of group counseling for problem behaviors in the schools, Riester and Tanner (1980) contacted high school juniors and seniors who had received group counseling (of an unspecified type) in the third, fourth, or fifth grades. The students had originally had interpersonal problems or negative attitudes toward school. The students reported that the groups had been particularly helpful in their development of interpersonal skills and positive attitudes toward school. They also ranked Yalom's (1975) curative factors in terms of their importance in the group. Factors receiving a top rank from at least one-third of the students were interpersonal learning, cohesiveness, catharsis, guidance, and identification (modeling). Although the data are subjective and quite open to bias, they at least suggest that an intervention at one point in time— especially when it facilitates adaptation to an important environment like school—can have a significant impact for years to come.

Personality and Social Adjustment Groups
Many counseling groups focus more on personality and interpersonal issues—self-awareness, self-esteem, acceptance by peers, and the like—than on specific behaviors. This is evident not only in the group process, but in the outcome measures used by researchers. This section will not only describe the basic features of groups of this sort, but will illustrate their extraordinary variability. As one should realize having read the first part of this chapter, however, the essential features of these groups are functionally quite similar and their variability, on the whole, superficial.

Several studies have focused on a group counseling for self-concept concerns. McCurdy, Cincerich, and Walker (1977) provided human relations training to seventh-grade boys exhibiting problem behaviors and found it to improve their self-esteem. English and Higgins (1971) were unable to demonstrate the superiority of client-centered group counseling over an attention-placebo activity group in increasing students' self-acceptance. Krantzler, Mayer, Dyer, and Munger (1966) compared a client-centered group with teacher-led guidance and no treatment for fourth-grade students. They found both treatments to be more effective than no treatment in raising the students' sociometric status, but no different from each other; changes were maintained at follow-up. Payne and Dunn (1972) found differences among ethnic subgroups in response to (unspecified) group guidance activities designed to raise self-concept. Whereas Hispanic children improved their concept of self as subject (i.e., one's self-perceptions), black and white children improved their concept of self as object (oneself as perceived by others). No explanation for the differences was given, but they may not have been due to the treatment since the control subjects also showed concept changes.

One deviation from the basic group counseling format deserves mention. This is the occasional conversion of the class into a counseling group, as described by Grossman and Retish (1976). Here, the counselor used the class as the setting for weekly sessions designed to raise the self-concept of minority sixth graders. Underlying the approach were ideas concerning the class as a supportive community, the therapeutic benefits of helping others, and the importance of gaining control over one's own life. Discussions of school-related problems and role-playing alternative solutions were the techniques employed, and anecdotal evidence indicated that they were effective. Hawes (1973) also recommended the classroom as a setting for changing classroom and relationship behavior. Two kinds of meetings were described: "open-end meetings," with an interactional focus, and "planning meetings," consisting of problem-solving discussions. Based on the Reality Therapy philosophy of self-respect and personal responsibility, the procedures attempted to allow children to become involved as decision makers in their own education and to experience themselves as successful.

Other groups have had psychosocial adjustment as a goal. Mannarino, Christy, Durlak, and Magnussen (1982) identified first, second, and third graders who were showing such signs of school maladjustment as acting out or low mood, and administered social competence training to them in a group counseling format. The groups, lead by undergraduates, focused on interpersonal problem identification, generation of alternative solutions, and anticipation of consequences of solutions. Results indicated that compared with control subjects, group members had superior classroom adjustment, as rated by teachers, and greater peer acceptance, determined sociometrically. Janus and Podolec (1982) used group counseling to enhance self-awareness, social skills, and classroom cohesiveness in mentally retarded students. The group process consisted of developing appropriate norms of listening and speaking, as well as group problem solving. As subjectively evaluated by the leader, the moderately retarded older group (ages 17 to 22) worked very hard and showed considerable improvement, but the mildly retarded younger group (ages 10 to 12) had more difficulty conforming to group norms. An effective strategy for shaping listening and speaking norms in the latter group was "passing the mike," whereby it became rewarding to speak—and be heard, when the tape of the group was played—when only one child had the microphone.

Clark and Seals (1984) reported the use of group counseling for elementary students who were ridiculed by their peers. The group was Adlerian in orientation, emphasizing the self-worth of the students in terms of their importance to the group, correcting faulty beliefs that promote ineffective behavior, and increasing students' awareness of skills and confidence. Although the group was not evaluated, the authors reported that it was successful. Not only were students able to gain insight into the dynamics of ridicule and the role played by their own cognition, but they also learned effective strategies for making themselves a less desirable target for ridicule (modifying negative personal characteristics, for example) and for dealing with tormentors. Sheridan, Baker, and de Lissovoy (1984) studied the use of group counseling for children of changing families (e.g., divorce). Junior high school students participated either in group counseling, which consisted of a structured discussion of relevant topics, or a bibliotherapy group, which discussed assigned readings. Results indicated, however, that neither group differed from controls in school attendance, GPA, self-concept, or parent-rated behaviors.

Finally, two studies reported the use of group interventions for modifying gender-related beliefs in girls. Assessing outcome in terms of values, Deutsch and Wolleat (1981) found structured group counseling to be much more effective in expanding girls' sex-role options and broadening their sense of family responsibilities, compared with a control group. Simmons and Parson (1983) administered a Life Choices program to preadolescent girls in a small-group format. The goals of the program were to increase self-esteem, awareness of sex-role options, and internal control—all aspects of the overall goal of "empowerment." The groups made use of cohesion, decision making, and various adult role models. In a comparison of the effects of the program with a no-treatment control, there was no difference in locus of control, but several differences in values. Girls in the program indicated valuing career and service to society more than controls, while controls placed a greater value on having a house, husband, and children. In addition to focusing on gender issues, these studies illustrate how groups can serve important attitude change functions.

Because of the heterogeneity of groups described in this section, it is difficult to draw conclusions about their effectiveness or their mechanisms of change. Although studies are increasingly employing control groups for assessing treatment effects, the treatments themselves are often so complex, the dependent measures so diverse and noncomparable across studies, and the designs so completely concerned with outcome to the exclusion of process that it is difficult to generalize beyond specific applications. Still, these studies represent a good beginning—considerably ahead of the state of affairs reported in the first edition of this chapter. Hopefully, with successful outcome established for many groups, researchers can turn their attention in a programmatic way to basic change mechanisms underlying positive outcomes and to the generalization of outcomes beyond the specific population, problems focus, and setting of the original research.

Career Development Groups

One of the most effective means of providing career guidance is within the context of group counseling (Herr & Cramer, 1984). Attitudes toward work and occupational preferences begin to form early in elementary school. As Herr and Cramer point out, "Whether or not education and career guidance respond to this fact, the evidence shows that elementary students have already begun to assimilate perceptions and preferences that may be wholesome and meaningful or distorted and ultimately harmful to aspiration and achievement" (p. 216).

Career guidance in groups in elementary and junior high grades most frequently takes the form of career education, exploration, and the establishment of positive work attitudes and values. Hoyt (1982) summed up evaluations of career education activities in the United States. In a wide variety of cases, career education had positive effects, such as improved career awareness, increased career exploration, improved knowledge of individual interests, skills, and values related to work. Among reports of career group counseling with elementary students are Wellington and Olechowski's (1966) finding of increased occupational awareness as a result of interviews of workers and discussions of interviews; Goff's (1967) finding of increased vocational knowledge, occupational aspiration, and realism as a result of working through the process of making vocational choices; and Yabroff's (1969) finding of greater realism in academic planning as a result of career decision-making groups.

Junior high career development groups must add the dimension of exploration and overcoming of sex-role stereotypes because of the appearance at that age of sex differences in choices, work values, and career maturing differences (Crites, 1978; Pedro, Wolleat, & Fennema, 1980). Further differentiation of self-characteristics from those of others and greater depth of understanding of occupations are also goals for this age. Motsch (1980) was successful in increasing junior high girls' career exploration through a peer social modeling group in which girls received stimulus materials related to broadening their options, viewed videotaped models engaged in a wide variety of career options, and received positive reinforcement for discussion and exploration.

High school career counseling groups, in addition to further clarification of vocational interests, needs, and values, should help students link their education to the world of work (Herr & Cramer, 1984). Life-Planning Workshops (Brown, 1980), which include a wide variety of exploration, self-assessment, and goal-setting activities, have been among the most widely used and effective group counseling interventions for meeting these goals. A comprehensive Career Development Curriculum, used in small groups and including activities focusing on career awareness, self-awareness, and decision making, has been associated with increased career maturity (Mackin & Hansen, 1981). Meyer, Strowig, and Hosford (1970) demonstrated the effectiveness of reinforcing verbal career information-seeking behavior in a comprehensive career counseling setting for increasing students' career exploration.

Finally, guidance laboratories, which bring high school students in small groups to a university campus for life planning activities and class visitation, have been effective in promoting a number of the goals of career guidance, particularly with gifted students. Guidance laboratories have led to higher career aspirations for gifted girls (Kerr, 1983), more knowledge of the world of work (Perrone, Male, & Karshner, 1979), and increased discussion of career goals and career exploration (Kerr & Ghrist-Priebe, 1987).

Career counseling groups are not only effective in enhancing career development but also provide a nonstigmatizing avenue for young people to seek counseling about a wide variety of lifestyle issues which may only be tangentially related to career goals. It is this aspect that makes career counseling groups one of the most versatile vehicles for the provision of guidance to young people.

Academic Groups

Group counseling has been used in the treatment of a variety of academic problems, including study and work habits deficits, learning disabilities, and underachievement. Because study problems are frequently related to poor time management, test anxiety, and lack of organization, most group approaches have involved some combination of time management, relaxation training, and training in effective study techniques. Harris and Trujillo (1975) reported on a comparison of a behavioral self-management group and a small-group discussion of study habits and problems for junior high students who were poor readers and had below-average IQs. They found that both the self-management and discussion groups were associated with more improvement in grades than the control group over a 6-week period. The discussion group maintained gains over the controls at a semester follow-up. The self-management group reported increased study efficiency and confidence in their work. Cole (1979) provided a model of group guidance for study skills which combined discussion of study problems, training in time management and study skills, and goal setting, but did not report evaluative data.

Group counseling for learning disabled (LD) students has frequently focused on self-concept and self-esteem, because these students have often

suffered from others' misunderstanding and ridicule (Shaefer, Johnson, & Wherry, 1982). Ledebur (1977) presented a model for a group which explores topics of concern to LD children, such as special placement and ridicule and teaches problem-solving skills. Omizo and Omizo (1986) reported a decrease in "self-defeating behaviors" as a result of a similar group for LD students.

Underachievers present a great challenge to counselors. A sizable literature on the characteristics of underachievers and the wide variety of treatments for underachievement exists (Bricklin & Bricklin, 1967; Dowdall & Colangelo, 1982; Pringle, 1970; Roth & Meyersburg, 1963). However, these is little agreement about exact definitions or appropriate treatment strategies. Generally, underachievers are considered to be students whose observed performance is discrepant with their potential as measured by objective tests. A great many of the interventions designed to remedy underachievement are group counseling approaches which focus on improving self-concept and changing classroom behavior. Finney and Van Dalsem (1965) reported improved school attendance and attitudes toward school for underachievers who participated in intensive groups which were essentially unstructured "growth" groups. In addition, treatment group members improved on a number of personality variables, such as self-confidence and outgoingness, compared to control group members. However, the treatment did not improve academic performance. A small-group discussion of school problems with 5-, 8-, and 9-year-olds, reported by Mishne (1971), resulted in improved reading scores but no improvement in test anxiety.

Dowdall and Colangelo (1982) concluded after a review of interventions for underachieving gifted that most were consistently *ineffective* in the treatment of underachievement, and that short-term, superficial interventions were not worth the time or effort. According to these authors, only long-term, intensive, comprehensive programs combining counseling, classroom modifications, and case study work and beginning in the earliest grades like that of Whitmore (1980) hold much promise for improvement of the academic behavior of underachievers.

Parent and Teacher Groups

Participants in counseling groups in the schools need not be students. Even if the ultimate aim of the counselor is to change student attitudes or behavior, an indirect approach, by which changes are effected in significant adults in the students' lives, is a plausible alternative to direct counseling. Parent and teacher study groups were described by Granum (1976) as a combination of didactic learning and interactional group counseling. The members, either parents or teachers experiencing problems with students, read and discuss books relevant to their difficulties, following the topics on a syllabus. But the group also develops as a group: members share concerns, specify goals for change, and complete behavioral homework assignments. The counselor facilitates group interaction, including the development of cohesiveness and appropriate norms. A similar format for use with teachers has been described by Dinkmeyer and Muro (1971). It is called a C-group, for reasons obvious in its stated activities and characteristics.

1. The group collaborates and works together on mutual concerns.
2. The group consults. The interaction within the group helps the members develop new approaches to relationships with children.
3. The group clarifies for each member what it is he really believes and how congruent or incongruent his behavior is with what he believes.
4. The group confronts. The group expects each individual to see himself, his purposes and attitudes, and be willing to confront other members of the group.
5. The group is concerned and cares. It shows that it is involved with both children and group members.
6. The group is confidential insofar as personal material discussed in the group is not carried out of the group.
7. The group develops a commitment to change. Participants in the group are concerned with recognizing that they can really only change themselves. They are expected to develop a specific commitment, which involves an action they will take before the next C-group to change their approach to a problem. (pp. 272–273)

The authors have pointed out that the C-group, like parent and teacher study groups, is intended ultimately to help students, and the students' behavior is the focus of early group meetings. But the teachers, as members of the group, are the ones changing most directly as a function of the group experience, as evidenced by the development of the group to focus on the teachers' behavior in interaction with students.

Research has been generally supportive of the idea that group interventions with parents and teachers have an effective impact on the students. Mink (1964) suggested that a group of parents of underachieving students was perhaps as effective alone in altering students' behavior as the combined use of student and parent groups. The parents' group was largely informational and included discussions of such issues as interests, values, aptitudes, and intelligence, about which the parents displayed considerable misunderstanding. The parent group investigated by Esterson, Feldman, Krigsman, and Warsaw (1975) focused on the relationship between parents in an experiential format, with a school psychologist as the group leader. The treatment was based on the notion that a better interpersonal environment at home would contribute to children's greater involvement in school. Results indicated that the children whose parents were in the group showed improved reading scores, as compared with controls. Math scores did not show improvement.

Behavioral group counseling for students and communication skills training for parents were compared in a study by Hayes, Cunningham, and Robinson (1977) to determine their effects on the involvement of underachieving children in school. Only the children of the counseled parents, not children counseled directly, were superior to no-treatment controls in self-esteem and motivation; they showed reduced anxiety, as well. Taylor and Hoedt (1974) investigated the use of Adlerian group counseling with mothers and with teachers of children with classroom behavior problems. Both forms of treatment were more effective in reducing the children's problem behavior than was group counseling with the children themselves. A school psychologist worked with the adults, however, and a school guidance counselor with the children. Counseling for inattentive students was the subject of a study by Randolph and Wallin (1973), which compared a model reinforcement group with the training of teachers to use classroom contingency management. Both treatments were effective in improving students' classroom-related behavior and grades, but in this case the direct approach was much more effective.

Lewis (1986) found group counseling for parents of children with behavior problems to be more effective than no treatment in altering the children's behavior. In this study, however, the children themselves received no counseling. Finally, Wantz and Recor (1984) found that Adlerian group counseling for parents was more useful when accompanied by a parallel group for children. Conducting parent and child groups together resulted in higher parent attendance and greater improvement in children's behavior, as compared with earlier studies of parent groups alone.

Although these studies do not point clearly to the superiority of either the direct or indirect approaches, they do illustrate reasonable alternatives to counseling students through the use of groups. School personnel should be alert to the variety of possibilities for group counseling, including that of changing students through changing their parents or teachers.

REFERENCES

Altmann, H. A., & Firnesz, K. M. (1973). A role playing approach to influencing behavioral change and self-esteem. *Elementary School Guidance and Counseling, 7*, 276–281.

Amerikaner, M., & Summerlin, M. L. (1982). Group counseling with learning disabled children: Effects of social skills and relaxation training on self-concept and classroom behavior. *Journal of Learning Disabilities, 15*, 340–343.

Axline, V. (1947). *Play therapy.* Boston: Houghton Mifflin.

Barcai, A., & Dremen, S. D. (1976). A comparison of three approaches to underachieving children: Eleven school related tests. *Acta Paedopsychiatrica, 42*, 60–67.

Barcai, A., & Robinson, E. H. (1969). Conventional group therapy with preadolescent children. *International Journal of Group Psychotherapy, 19*, 334–345.

Bednar, R. L., & Kaul, T. J. (1978). Experiential group research: Current perspectives. In S. L. Garfield & A. E. Bergin (Eds.), *Handbook of psychotherapy and behavior change: An empirical analysis* (2nd ed.). New York: Wiley.

Bednar, R. L., Melnick, J., & Kaul, T. J. (1974). Risk, responsibility and structure: A conceptual framework for initiating group counseling and psychotherapy. *Journal of Counseling Psychology, 21*, 31–37.

Bosdell, B. J. (1973). Counseling children with play media. In M. M. Ohlsen (Ed.), *Counseling children in groups: A forum.* New York: Holt, Rinehart and Winston.

Bradfield, R. H., Hilliard, A., Palmer, B., Jones, L.,

Wofford, J., & Gray, B. (1975). Project B.E.A.M.: An experiment in intervention. *Journal of Negro Education, 44*, 34–41.

Bretzing, B. H., & Caterino, L. C. (1984). Group counseling with elementary students. *School Psychology Review, 13*, 515–518.

Bricklin, B., & Bricklin, P. (1967). *Bright child, poor grades.* New York: Delacorte.

Brody, V. (1978). Developmental play: A relationship-focused program for children. *Child Welfare, 57*, 591–599.

Brooks, B. D. (1975). Contingency management as a means of reducing school truancy. *Education, 95*, 206–211.

Brown, D. A. (1980). Life planning workshop for high school students. *School Counselor, 29*, 77–83.

Burt, M., & Myrick, R. D. (1980). Developmental play: What is it all about? *Elementary School Guidance and Counseling, 15*, 14–21.

Caplan, S. W. (1957). The effect of group counseling on junior high school boys' concepts of themselves in school. *Journal of Counseling Psychology, 4*, 124–128.

Claiborn, C. D. (1982). Interpretation and change in counseling. *Journal of Counseling Psychology, 29*, 439–453.

Claiborn, C. D., & Strong, S. R. (1982). Group counseling in the schools. In C. R. Reynolds & T. B. Gutkin (Eds.), *Handbook of school psychology.* New York: Wiley.

Clark, A. J., & Seals, J. M. (1984). Group counseling for ridiculed children. *Journal for Specialists in Group Work, 9*, 157–162.

Clement, P., Fazzone, R., & Goldstein, B. (1970). Tangible reinforcers and child group therapy. *Journal of the American Academy of Child Psychiatry, 9*, 409–427.

Clement, P., & Milne, D. C. (1967). Group play therapy and tangible reinforcers used to modify the behavior of 8-year-old boys. *Behavior Research and Therapy, 5*, 301–312.

Cobb, H. C., & Richards, H. C. (1983). Efficacy of counseling services in decreasing behavior problems of elementary school children. *Elementary School Guidance and Counseling, 17*, 180–187.

Cole, C. G. (1979). A group guidance approach to improving students' study skills. *School Counselor, 27*, 29–33.

Corder, B., Haizlip, T., Whiteside, R., & Vogel, M. (1980). Pre-therapy training for adolescents in group psychotherapy: Contracts, guidelines, and pre-therapy preparation. *Adolescence, 15*, 699–706.

Crites, J. O. (1978). *Theory and research handbook for the career maturity inventory.* Monterey, CA: CTB/McGraw-Hill.

Deutsch, R., & Wolleat, P. L. (1981). Dispelling the forced-choice myth. *Elementary School Guidance and Counseling, 16*, 112–120.

Dinkmeyer, D., & Muro, J. J. (1971). *Group counseling: Theory and practice.* Itaska, IL: Peacock.

Dowdall, C. B., & Colangelo, N. (1982). Underachieving gifted students: Review and implications. *Gifted Child Quarterly, 26*, 179–184.

Durbin, D. M. (1982). Multimodal group sessions to enhance self-concept. *Elementary School Guidance and Counseling, 16,* 288–295.

English, R. W., & Higgins, T. E. (1971). Client-centered group counseling with pre-adolescents. *Journal of School Health, 41,* 507–509.

Esterson, H., Feldman, C., Krigsman, N., & Warsaw, S. (1975). Time limited group counseling with parents of preadolescent underachievers: A pilot program. *Psychology in the Schools, 12,* 79–84.

Finney, B. C., & Van Dalsem, E. (1969). Group counseling for gifted underachieving high school graduates. *Journal of Counseling Psychology, 16,* 87–94.

Gazda, G. M. (1973). Group procedures with children: A developmental approach. In M. M. Ohlsen (Ed.), *Counseling children in groups: A forum.* New York: Holt, Rinehart and Winston.

Gazda, G. M. (1976a). Group counseling: A developmental approach. In G. M. Gazda (Ed.), *Theories and methods of group counseling in the schools* (2nd ed.). Springfield, IL: Charles C Thomas.

Gazda, G. M. (1976b). Guidelines for ethical practice in group counseling and related group work. In G. M. Gazda (Ed.), *Theories and methods of group counseling in the schools* (2nd ed.). Springfield, IL: Charles C Thomas.

Gazda, G. M. (1978). *Group counseling: A developmental approach* (2nd ed.). Boston: Allyn and Bacon.

Gibbons, T. J., & Lee, M. K. (1972). Group counseling: Impetus to learning. *Elementary School Guidance and Counseling, 6,* 163–169.

Ginott, H. G. (1961). *Group psychotherapy with children: The theory and practice of play-therapy.* New York: McGraw-Hill.

Glass, S. D. (1973). Practical considerations in group counseling. In M. M. Ohlsen (Ed.), *Counseling children in groups: A forum.* New York: Holt, Rinehart and Winston.

Goff, W. H. (1967). *Vocational guidance in elementary schools: A report of Project P.A.C.E.* Paper presented at the annual meeting of the American Vocational Association, Cleveland.

Goldstein, A. P., Sprafkin, R. P., Gershaw, N. J., & Klein, P. (1980). *Skillstreaming the adolescent.* Champaign, IL: Research Press.

Granum, R. A. (1976). Adlerian group counseling. In G. M. Gazda (Ed.), *Theories and methods of group counseling in the schools* (2nd ed.). Springfield, IL: Charles C Thomas.

Green, B. J. (1978). HELPING children of divorce. *Elementary School Guidance and Counseling, 13,* 31–45.

Grossman, F., & Retish, P. M. (1976). Classroom counseling: An approach to improve student self-concept. *Counseling and Values, 21,* 64–66.

Gumaer, J., & Myrick, R. (1974). Behavioral group counseling with disruptive children. *School Counselor, 21,* 313–317.

Hansen, J. C., Niland, T. M., & Zani, L. P. (1969). Model reinforcement in group counseling with elementary school children. *Personnel and Guidance Journal, 47,* 741–744.

Hargrave, G. E., & Hargrave, M. L. (1979). A peer group socialization therapy program in the school: An outcome investigation. *Psychology in the Schools, 16,* 546–550.

Harris, M. B., & Trujillo, A. E. (1975). Improving study habits of junior high school students through self-management versus group discussion. *Journal of Counseling Psychology, 22,* 513–517.

Harth, R. (1966). Changing attitudes toward school, classroom behavior, and reaction to frustration of emotionally disturbed children through role playing. *Exceptional Children, 33,* 119–120.

Hawes, R. M. (1973). Getting along in the classroom. In M. M. Ohlsen (Ed.), *Counseling children in groups: A forum.* New York: Holt, Rinehart and Winston.

Hawley, R. C., & Hawley, I. L. (1972). *A handbook of personal growth activities for classroom use.* Amherst, MA: Education Research Associates.

Hayes, E. J., Cunningham, G. K., & Robinson, J. B. (1977). Counseling focus: Are parents necessary? *Elementary School Guidance and Counseling, 12,* 8–14.

Herr, E. L., & Cramer, S. H. (1984). *Career guidance and counseling through the lifespan.* Boston: Little, Brown.

Hillman, B. W., Penczar, J. T., & Barr, R. (1975). Activity group guidance: A developmental approach. *Personnel and Guidance Journal, 53,* 761–767.

Hillman, B. W., & Runion, K. B. (1978). Activity group guidance: Process and results. *Elementary School Guidance and Counseling, 13,* 104–111.

Hinds, W. C., & Roehlke, H. J. (1970). A learning theory approach to group counseling with elementary school children. *Journal of Counseling Psychology, 17,* 49–55.

Hosford, R. E. (1973). Behavioral group counseling with elementary school children. In M. M. Ohlsen (Ed.), *Counseling children in groups: A forum.* New York: Holt, Rinehart and Winston.

Hosford, P. M., & Acheson, E. (1976). Child drama for group guidance and counseling. In G. M. Gazda (Ed.), *Theories and methods of group counseling in the schools* (2nd ed.). Springfield, IL: Charles C Thomas.

Howard, W., & Zimpfer, D. G. (1972). The findings of research on group approaches in elementary guidance and counseling. *Elementary School Guidance and Counseling, 6,* 163–167.

Hoyt, K. B. (1982). Federal and state participation in career education: Past, present, and future. *Journal of Career Education, 9,* 5–15.

Huey, W. C. (1979). The comparative effects of counselor-led and peer-led group assertive training on aggression in black adolescents. *Dissertation Abstracts International, 40,* 3121A.

Huey, W. C. (1983). Reducing adolescent aggression through group assertive training. *School Counselor, 30,* 193–203.

Huey, W. C. (1985). Information-processing groups: A peer-led orientation approach. *School Counselor, 33,* 3–8.

Hunt, P., & Smith, J. P. (1980). Initiation of group counseling with minority female adolescents. *School Counselor, 27,* 193–197.

Jacobs, A., Jacobs, M., Feldman, G., & Cavior, N. (1973). Feedback II—The credibility gap: Delivery of positive and negative emotional and behavioral feedback in groups. *Journal of Consulting and Clinical Psychology, 41,* 215–223.

Janus, N. G., & Podolec, M. (1982). Counseling mentally retarded students in the public school. *School Psychology Review, 11,* 453–458.

Johnson, P. W., & Johnson, F. P. (1982). *Joining together: Group theory and group skills.* Englewood Cliffs, NJ: Prentice-Hall.

Jones, E. E., & Gordon, E. M. (1972). Timing of self-disclosure and its effects on personal attraction. *Journal of Personality and Social Psychology, 24,* 358–365.

Jourard, S. (1971). *The transparent self.* New York: Van Nostrand Rheinhold.

Keat, D. B. (1979). *Multimodal therapy with children.* Elmsford, NY: Pergamon Press.

Kelly, E. W., & Matthews, D. B. (1971). Group counseling with discipline-problem children at the elementary school level. *School Counselor, 18,* 273–278.

Kerr, B. A. (1983). Raising the career aspirations of gifted girls. *Vocational Guidance Quarterly, 32,* 37–44.

Kerr, B. A., & Ghrist-Priebe, S. L. (1988). Intervention for multipotentiality: Effects of a career counseling laboratory for gifted high school students. *Journal of Counseling and Development, 66,* 366–369.

Kissiah, R. K. (1975). Beginning group counseling: A practical approach. *Elementary School Guidance and Counseling, 10,* 14–20.

Kochendofer, S. A. (1975). Group preparation: Interview vs. questionnaire. *School Counselor, 23,* 38–42.

Komechak, M. G. (1971). The activity-interaction group: A process for short-term counseling with elementary school children. *Elementary School Guidance and Counseling, 6,* 13–20.

Krantzler, G. D., Mayer, G. R., Dyer, C. O., & Munger, P. F. (1966). Counseling with elementary school children: An experimental study. *Personnel and Guidance Journal, 44,* 944–949.

Krumboltz, J. D., & Thoresen, C. E. (1964). The effect of behavioral counseling in group and individual settings on information-seeking behavior. *Journal of Counseling Psychology, 11,* 324–333.

Ledebur, G. W. (1977). The elementary learning disability process group and the school psychologist. *Psychology in the Schools, 14,* 62–66.

Levy, L. H. (1963). *Psychological interpretation.* New York: Holt, Rinehart and Winston.

Lewis, W. M. (1986). Group training for parents of children with behavior problems. *Journal for Specialists in Group Work, 11,* 194–199.

Liberman, R. (1971). Reinforcement of cohesiveness in group therapy. *Archives of General Psychiatry, 25,* 168–177.

Lieberman, M. A., Yalom, I. D., & Miles, M. B. (1973). *Encounter groups: First facts.* New York: Basic Books.

Lott, A. J., & Lott, B. E. (1965). Group cohesiveness as interpersonal attraction: A review of relationships with antecedent and consequent variables. *Psychological Bulletin, 64,* 349–352.

Mackin, R. K., & Hansen, L. S. (1981). A theory-based career development course: A plant in the garden. *School Counselor, 28,* 325–334.

MacLenna, B. W., & Felsenfeld, N. (1968). *Group counseling and psychotherapy with adolescents.* New York: Columbia University Press.

Maher, C. A., & Barbrack, C. R. (1982). Preventing high school maladjustment: Effectiveness of professional and cross-age behavioral group counseling. *Behavior Therapy, 13,* 259–270.

Mannarino, A. P., Christy, M., Durlak, J. A., & Magnussen, M. G. (1982). Evaluation of social competence training in the schools. *Journal of School Psychology, 20,* 11–19.

Mayer, G. R., Rohen, T. M., & Whitley, A. D. (1969). Group counseling with children: A cognitive-behavioral approach. *Journal of Counseling Psychology, 16,* 142–149.

McCurdy, B., Ciucevich, M., & Walker, B. (1977). Human relations training with seventh grade boys identified as behavior problems. *School Counselor, 24,* 248–252.

Meyer, J. B., Strowig, W., & Hosford, R. E. (1970). Behavioral-reinforcement counseling with rural high school youth. *Journal of Counseling Psychology, 17,* 127–132.

Mink, O. G. (1964). Multiple counseling with underachieving junior high school pupils of bright-normal and higher ability. *Journal of Educational Research, 58,* 31–34.

Mishne, J. (1971). Group therapy in elementary school. *Social Casework, 21,* 18–25.

Mitchell, K. M., Bozarth, J. D., & Krauft, C. C. (1977). A reapprisal of the therapeutic effectiveness of accurate empathy, nonpossessive warmth, and genuineness. In A. S. Gurman & A. M. Razin (Eds.), *Effective psychotherapy: A handbook of research.* Elmsford, NY: Pergamon Press.

Motsch, P. (1980). Peer social modeling: A tool for assisting girls with career exploration. *Vocational Guidance Quarterly, 12,* 229–236.

Moulin, E. K. (1970). The effects of client centered group counseling using play media on the intelligence, achievement, and psycholinguistic abilities of underachieving primary school children. *Elementary School Guidance and Counseling, 5,* 85–95.

Myrick, R. D., & Kelly, F. D. (1971). Group counseling with primary school-age children. *Journal of School Psychology, 9,* 137–143.

Nelson-Jones, R., & Strong, S. R. (1976). Positive and negative self-disclosure, timing, and personal attraction. *British Journal of Social and Clinical Psychology, 15,* 323–325.

Ohlsen, M. M. (1973). Counseling children. In M. M. Ohlsen (Ed.), *Counseling children in groups: A forum.* New York: Holt, Rinehart and Winston.

Ohlsen, M. M. (1977). *Group counseling* (2nd ed.). New York: Holt, Rinehart and Winston.

Omizo, C., & Omizo, D. (1986). Group counseling: It works. *Academic Therapy, 21,* 367–368.

Orvis, B. R., Kelley, H. H., & Butler, D. (1976). Attributional conflict in young couples. In J. Harvey, W. Ickes, & R. Kidd (Eds.), *New directions in attribution research* (Vol. 1). Hillsdale, NJ: Lawrence Erlbaum.

Passer, M. W., Kelley, H. H., & Mishela, J. L. (1978). Multidimensional scaling of the causes for negative interpersonal behavior. *Journal of Personality and Social Psychology, 36,* 951–962.

Passmore, J. L. (1973). Role playing: A therapeutic adjunct to group counseling. In M. M. Ohlsen (Ed.), *Counseling children in groups: A forum.* New York: Holt, Rinehart and Winston.

Payne, B. F., & Dunn, C. J. (1972). An analysis of the change in self-concept by racial descent. *Journal of Negro Education, 41,* 156–163.

Pedro, J. O., Wolleat, P., & Fennema, E. (1980). Sex differences in the relationship of career interests and mathematics plans. *Vocational Guidance Quarterly, 29,* 25–34.

Perrone, P. A., Male, R. A., & Karshner, W. W. (1979). Career development needs of talented students: A perspective for counselors. *School Counselor, 27,* 16–23.

Pfeiffer, J. W., & Jones, J. E. (1969–1974). *A handbook of structured experiences for human relations training* (Vols. 1–5). La Jolla, CA: University Associates.

Pringle, M. L. (1970). *Able misfits.* London: Longman Group.

Randolph, D. L., & Hardage, N. C. (1973). Behavioral consultation and group counseling with potential dropouts. *Elementary School Guidance and Counseling, 7,* 204–209.

Randolph, D. L., & Wallin, K. R. (1973). A comparison of behavioral consultation and behavioral consultation with model-reinforcement group counseling for children who are consistently off-task. *Journal of Educational Research, 67,* 103–107.

Reisman, E. R., & Beyer, L. M. (1973). Group counseling in an elementary school setting. *Child Welfare, 52,* 192–195.

Ribner, N. G. (1974). Effects of an explicit group contract on self-disclosure and group cohesiveness. *Journal of Counseling Psychology, 21,* 116–120.

Riester, A. E.,. & Tanner, D. L. (1980). Group counseling: Follow-up viewpoints. *Elementary School Guidance and Counseling, 14,* 222–230.

Rose, S. D. (1972). *Treating children in a group.* San Francisco: Jossey-Bass.

Roth, R. M., & Meyersburg, A. H. (1963). The non-achievement syndrome. *Personnel and Guidance Journal, 61,* 535–540.

Schaefer, C. E., Johnson, L., & Wherry, J. N. (1982). *Group therapies for children and youth.* San Francisco: Jossey-Bass.

Schaible, T., & Jacobs, A. (1975). Feedback III—Sequence effects: Enhancement of feedback acceptance and group attractiveness by manipulation of the sequence and valence of feedback. *Small Group Behavior, 6,* 151–173.

Schweisheimer, W., & Walberg, H. J. (1976). A peer counseling experiment: High school students as small group leaders. *Journal of Counseling Psychology, 23,* 398–401.

Shapiro, J. L. (1978). *Methods of group psychotherapy and encounter: A tradition of innovation.* Itaska, IL: Peacock.

Shaw, M. E. (1976). *Group dynamics: The psychology of small group behavior* (2nd ed.). New York: McGraw-Hill.

Sheridan, J. T., Baker, S. B., & de Lissovoy, V. (1984). Structured group counseling and explicit bibliotherapy as in-school strategies for preventing problems in youth of changing families. *School Counselor, 32,* 134–141.

Silverman, M. (1976). The achievement motivation group: A counselor-directed approach. *Elementary School Guidance and Counseling, 11,* 100–106.

Simmons, C. H., & Parson, R. J. (1983). Empowerment for role alternatives in adolescence. *Adolescence, 18,* 193–200.

Slavson, S. R., & Schiffer, M. (1975). *Group psychotherapies for children: A textbook.* New York: International Universities Press.

Sonstegard, M. A., & Dreikurs, R. (1973). The Adlerian approach to group counseling of children. In M. M. Ohlsen (Ed.), *Counseling children in groups: A forum.* New York: Holt, Rinehart and Winston.

Strong, S. R. (1978). Social psychological approach to psychotherapy research. In S. L. Garfield & A. E. Bergin (Eds.), *Handbook of psychotherapy and behavior change: An empirical analysis* (2nd ed.). New York: Wiley.

Strong, S. R., & Claiborn, C. D. (1982). *Change through interaction: The social psychology of counseling and psychotherapy.* New York: Wiley.

Strong, S. R., & Matross, R. P. (1973). Change processes in counseling and psychotherapy. *Journal of Counseling Psychology, 20,* 25–37.

Taylor, W. F., & Hoedt, K. C. (1974). Classroom related behavior problems: Counsel parents, teachers, or children? *Journal of Counseling Psychology, 21,* 3–8.

Thombs, M. R., & Muro, J. J. (1973). Group counseling and the sociometric status of second grade children. *Elementary School Guidance and Counseling, 7,* 194–197.

Thompson, D. G., & Hudson, G. R. (1982). Values clarification and behavioral group counseling with ninth-grade boys in a residential school. *Journal of Counseling Psychology, 29,* 394–399.

Tidwell, R., & Bachus, V. A. (1977). Group counseling for aggressive school children. *Elementary School Guidance and Counseling, 12,* 2–7.

Tosi, D. J., Swanson, D., & McLean, P. (1970). Group counseling with nonverbalizing elementary school children. *Elementary School Guidance and Counseling, 4,* 260–266.

Tyler, F. B., & Pargament, K. I. (1981). Racial and personal factors and the complexities of competence-oriented changes in a high school group counseling program. *American Journal of Community Psychology, 9,* 697–714.

Vander Kolk, C. J. (1985). Introduction to group counseling and psychotherapy. Columbus, OH: Charles E. Merrill.

Varenhorst, B. B. (1976). Behavioral group counseling. In G. M. Gazda (Ed.), *Theories and methods of group counseling in the schools* (2nd ed.). Springfield, IL: Charles C Thomas.

Wantz, R. A., & Recor, R. D. (1984). Simultaneous parent–child group intervention. *Elementary School Guidance and Counseling, 19,* 126–131.

Warner, R. W., & Hansen, J. C. (1970). Verbal-reinforcement and model-reinforcement group counseling with alienated students. *Journal of Counseling Psychology, 17,* 168–172.

Warner, R. W., Niland, T. M., & Maynard, P. E. (!971). Model reinforcement group counseling with elementary school children. *Elementary School Guidance and Counseling, 5,* 248–255.

Watzlawick, P., Beavin, J. H., & Jackson, D. D. (1967). Pragmatic of human communication: A study of interactional patterns, pathologies, and paradoxes. New York: W. W. Norton.

Webb, A. P., & Eikenberry, J. (1964). A group counseling approach to the acting-out preadolescent. *Psychology in the Schools, 1,* 395–400.

Weigel, R. G., Dinges, N., Dyer, R., & Straumfjord, A. A. (1972). Perceived self-disclosure, mental health, and who is liked in group treatment. *Journal of Counseling Psychology, 19,* 47–52.

Wellington, J. A., & Olechowski, N. (1966). Attitudes toward the world of work in elementary school. *Vocational Guidance Quarterly, 14,* 160–162.

Wells, C. G. (1962). Psychodrama and creative counseling in the elementary school. *Group Psychotherapy, 15,* 244–252.

Whitmore, J. R. (1980). *Giftedness, conflict, and under-achievement.* Boston: Allyn and Bacon.

Yabroff, W. (1969). Learning decision-making. In J. D. Krumboltz & C. E. Thoresen (Eds.), *Behavioral counseling: Cases and techniques.* New York: Holt, Rinehart and Winston.

Yalom, I. D. (1975). *The theory and practice of group psychotherapy* (2nd ed.). New York: Basic Books.

29

BRIEF PSYCHOTHERAPIES

Jan N. Hughes

Texas A&M University

DEFINITIONAL AND CONCEPTUAL ISSUES

School psychologists providing therapy to children and their families frequently work under time and resource constraints that necessitate focused, time-limited psychotherapy. Of concern is the effectiveness of brief therapy approaches, as compared to long-term psychotherapy. In this regard, if time-limited psychotherapy were just less of the same transactions that occur in traditional psychotherapy, school psychologists would be providing second-rate therapy. In fact, time-limited therapies differ in several important ways from traditional psychotherapy, as detailed below. Furthermore, studies comparing the effectiveness of brief and traditional psychotherapy have found no evidence of differential outcome effectiveness (e.g., Fisher, 1980; Kinston & Bentovim, 1981; Phillips & Johnston, 1973; Weakland, Fisch, Watzlawick, & Bodin, 1974).

Psychotherapy is one of several interventions available to school psychologists. Academic skills training, behavioral consultation, and parent education are among the other therapeutic interventions employed by school psychologists. Psychotherapy differs from those interventions in its reliance on the therapeutic relationship and its concern with clients' emotional as well as behavioral adjustment.

The central defining characteristic of brief psychotherapy is time. Whereas traditional therapy is open-ended with respect to time, brief therapy imposes time constraints. Although there is no consensus on the number of sessions that fall within the limits of brief therapy, a 10-to-12 session limit is most typical (de Shazer, 1985, Fisher, 1984; Weakland et al., 1974). While some therapists place a definite session limit on therapy, other therapists emphasize the short-term nature of therapy without setting a specific number of sessions. In all instances, the time-limited nature of therapy is explained to clients at the first session, if not in the telephone contact.

Because a majority of psychotherapy clients across the board terminate therapy after between 6 and 10 sessions (Gurman, 1981), it is important to define brief psychotherapy other than in terms of time. Compared to traditional psychotherapy, brief psychotherapy (a) is more directed, (b) goals are more specific and clearly articulated, (c) fewer data on the client's overall personality functioning and history are collected, (d) the data collected bear directly on the presenting problem, (e) the client assumes a more active role, and (f) interventions are focused on the articulated goals (de Shazer, 1985). The time constraints foster an expectation on the part of the clients that improvement will occur quickly, and this positive expectation is assumed to facilitate therapy.

Brief therapy has a preventive orientation in that the brief therapist assumes that a focused intervention for a relatively mild problem can establish or reinforce adaptive coping responses that will strengthen the client's overall coping ability. The identified problem area is viewed as a leverage for intervening in a client or family system, helping the client or family learn more adaptive ways of functioning in the future. For example, parents may react to noncompliance in their 6-year-old daughter by increasing their aversive control, perpetuating a reciprocally determined, coercive cycle of parent–child interactions (Patterson, 1975). An early, focused intervention could prevent the solidification of a parent–child relationship characterized by reciprocal aversive control.

Brief therapy and crisis theory share certain concepts. The concepts of equilibrium, time, and change are essential both to crisis theory (Jacobson, 1980) and to brief psychotherapy (Ewing, 1978). Caplan (1961) defines a crisis as a state

> provoked when a person faces an obstacle to important life goals that is for a time insurmountable through the utilization of customary methods of problem solving. A period of disorganization ensues, a period of upset during which many different abortive attempts at a solution are made. Eventually some kind of adaptation is achieved which may or may not be in the best interest of that person or his fellows. (p. 18)

Thus, a crisis results from the disturbance of an existing equilibrium as a result of rapidly occurring significant changes in forces affecting that equilibrium. During this disturbance, the individual's or system's usual way of functioning is upset. After the crisis, the individual's or system's level of functioning will be the same as, higher than, or lower than the state existing before the crisis. During the disequilibrium, the system is most susceptible to the influence of external forces. Both the crisis interventionist and the brief psychotherapist take advantage of the disequilibrium to influence the system to adopt healthier ways of functioning.

Brief Psychotherapy and the School Psychologist

Brief psychotherapy is an appropriate therapy model for school psychologists for several reasons. An obvious reason is the considerable time constraints under which psychologists in the school's work. It is important to note that time constraints are also often important when providing therapy outside schools. Since most clients tend to stay in therapy for 6 to 10 sessions, regardless of the therapist's plan (de Shazer, 1985), it is important to accomplish what can be done within these few sessions. Second, brief therapy's focus on a specific problem area is more compatible with a school's philosophy and purposes than traditional psychotherapy's focus on global changes in a child's personality. Third, brief therapies tend to recognize the importance of changing the family and school systems in order to change the child. Because the school psychologist typically works with parents and school systems, he or she is in a good position to intervene in these systems in a systematic and coordinated fashion. Fourth, child problems often come to the attention of school psychologists before the problem is of sufficient magnitude for the family voluntarily to seek psychotherapy outside the school or for external pressure (e.g., the juvenile court) to require the family enter therapy. Thus, the school psychologist can intervene earlier in the problem, when brief therapy is likely to be most helpful.

Models of Brief Psychotherapy

Brief psychotherapy cannot be characterized by a single theoretical orientation. Early in its development, brief therapy employed primarily behavioral approaches (Goldstein, 1978; Werry & Wollersheim, 1973). As behavior therapists expanded their techniques and theoretical bases to include cognitively oriented therapies, brief cognitive-behavior interventions were developed. Also, family-oriented therapists applied family therapy models and concepts to brief therapy. Despite the variety of theoretical approaches applied in brief psychotherapy with children, a unifying assumption is it is important to include parents, family, and teachers as both agents and targets of change when working with a child client. Thus, the brief psychotherapist takes an ecological view of a child's behavior and attempts to change these external influences on the child to promote healthier child functioning.

Setting the Treatment Focus

One of the most difficult and important tasks in brief psychotherapy is identifying the treatment focus. In traditional psychotherapy, a treatment focus is determined after completion of a comprehensive child evaluation, including an extensive social and developmental history, medical evaluation, personality and intellectual evaluation, and evaluation of important support systems (e.g., family, peer group, and school). This evaluation is often completed by a multidisciplinary team and results in a diagnosis and a treatment plan that specifics the problem areas that need to be addressed in therapy. Treatment goals are stated in nonspecific terms, such as meeting dependency needs in ways that respect others' rights or developing a positive self-concept. In contrast, brief psychotherapy assessment is less comprehensive and more focused on the problem area. The goal of the assessment is the formulation of a "focal hypothesis" (Kinston & Bentovim, 1981). A focal hypothesis "refers to an 'ad hoc' clinical theory developed to clarify or bring into focus a large number of disparate and apparently unrelated phenomena" (Kinston & Bentovim, 1981, p. 367). For example, an 8-year-old girl is referred for therapy due to her refusal to eat all but a limited number of foods. Despite the parents' urging, cajoling, and bribes, the girl refuses to eat any meats or vegetables and is significantly underweight. The parents view the child as sick and are extremely protective of her. During the family session, both parents defer to the daughter. The therapist hypothesizes that the food refusal is caused by a breakdown in the executive control of the parental subsystem and reframes the food refusal as disobedience rather than as sickness. When the parents view the food refusal as disobedience, they are able to exert appropriate controls over eating. The therapist's intervention did not require a psychological evaluation of the child or an extensive family history.

A second example of developing a focal hypothesis concerns a 4-year-old girl who has temper outbursts and wets the bed. The mother's attempts to discipline the child are undermined by the father, who is in an alliance with the daughter against the mother. The therapist instructs the father to change the bed sheets, thereby lessening the alliance between the daughter and father and strengthening the parental subsystem.

These two case examples illustrate the importance of developing a focal hypothesis that organizes diverse pieces of information into a mini-theory that both explains the creation of the problem and points to solutions.

Brief Therapy Approaches

Brief psychotherapy is not the model of choice for all clients. In the absence of empirical evidence that certain clients are more likely to benefit from long-term therapy than from brief therapy, the school psychologist must decide which clients are likely candidates for brief therapy and which clients should be referred for long-term therapy. Brief therapy may not be the therapy of choice for psychotic children, children who have multiple and chronic problems, and children who have relatively few areas of strength that can be utilized to resolve problem areas.

There are as many theoretical orientations to brief therapy as there are to long-term therapy. In this chapter we discuss brief psychotherapy approaches that are especially relevant to working with children and their families: behavior therapy, cognitive-behavior therapy, social skills training, and family therapy. The theoretical basis and therapy methods for each approach are briefly summarized. In addition, case studies illustrate each therapy approach.

BRIEF BEHAVIOR THERAPY

Behavior therapy is a broad term, encompassing a wide variety of therapeutic techniques. Indeed, a basic tenet of behavior therapy is that different client problems require different treatments. In behavior therapy the selection of a specific intervention is based on empirical studies of the effectiveness of that intervention with similar cases. Although a variety of techniques are subsumed under the term "behavior therapy," these techniques are tied together by a set of shared assumptions. The following brief discussion of these assumptions is based on Rimm and Masters (1974) and Ross (1981). A primary assumption is psychological disorders are forms of behavior that have been acquired or modified, to a considerable degree, through the lawful operation of psychological principles of development, learning, perception, cognition, and social interaction (Ross, 1981). A corollary assumption is that these same principles can be applied productively to bring about changes in the maladaptive behavior. Second, behavior therapists assume that the presenting problem is important in its own right and not just as a symptom of some underlying cause that exists in the client's intrapsychic life. Third, behavior therapists focus on the present events rather than on the historical antecedents of problems. Finally, behavior therapy entails continuous evaluation of specific, objectively defined behaviors. This ongoing assessment of treatment procedures is critical to the evaluation of their effectiveness. Behavior therapists use techniques that have been subjected to empirical verification and found effective.

In recent years, behavior therapists have increasingly considered the role of cognitive variables in the development and treatment of maladaptive behavior. Contemporary behavior therapists recognize that a person's behavior is mediated by cognitive events (i.e., thoughts, perceptions, images, expectancies, and beliefs) and view cognitions as appropriate targets for change in therapy.

Because behavior therapy applies psychological principles derived from all of experimental psychology, a comprehensive review of the theoretical basis of behavior therapy is beyond the limits and goals of this chapter. Excellent discussions of the theoretical basis of behavior therapy are found in Mahoney (1974) and Rimm and Masters (1974). A listing of those psychological principles most frequently applied in behavior therapy includes principles of operant conditioning, classical conditioning, social learning theory, and cognition.

Behavior therapy includes many of the approaches discussed in Martens' and Meller's chapter in this volume (Chapter 24). To minimize overlap with that chapter, in the present chapter we focus on child problems likely to result in a referral for psychotherapy. Thus, the focus is on problems that involve the psychologist working directly with the child and his or her family rather than on problems that involve the psychologist working indirectly with the child through consultation with school personnel.

Steps in Behavior Therapy

Typically, the behavior therapist proceeds through four steps in a systematic and structured approach to the problem behavior. First, specific and objectively defined behaviors are selected as targets for treatment. The behavior therapist helps the child and parents state problems in specific, behavioral terms. For example, the parents refer their 7-year-old daughter for excessive shyness. The therapist asks questions about the behavioral referents of shyness: "What about your daughter's behavior leads you to believe she is shy? If her shyness improved, what changes in her behavior would you expect to see?" As a result of this interviewing procedure, the target behavior might be stated as playing alone, and the desired behavior as playing with other children. The second step is to assess the identified target behaviors. In the example of the shy girl, the therapist might observe the girl at recess or lunchtime and count the number of times she interacts with other children. These behavioral observations are the hallmark of behavioral assessment. Often, the assistance of teachers or others is enlisted in obtaining the behavioral observations. The assessment includes a determination of those antecedents events in the environment that are present when the girl plays with others as well as the consequences of her interacting with others. Thus, the observation data would address questions such as: Are there certain children she is more likely to play with? What entry approaches does she exhibit? Does the size of the group or the type of activity predict her playing with others? Does the teacher's proximity or instructions predict her playing alone versus playing with others? How do the other children respond to her when she plays alone and plays with others? In addition to observing the child, the therapist might administer a self-report questionnaire, such as the Revised Manifest Anxiety Scale (Reynolds & Richmond, 1978), to determine the extent to which anxiety might interfere with the girl's social participation. The therapist might also use behavior checklists and rating scales completed by the child's parents or teacher to assess the severity of the behavior or to assess specific social skills or interfering problem behaviors. At the third step, the therapist designs and implements a treatment plan based on the behavioral assessment. In this example, the treatment plan might involve teaching the girl social skills necessary for social participation. For example, the therapist might discuss with the child social participation skills (e.g., conversational skills, joining in, initiating skills), model these skills in role plays or present filmed models, provide the child with practice opportunities through role plays or structured play sessions, provide performance feedback to the child, and assign practice exercises. To lessen the girl's anxiety about social participation, the therapist might gradually expose her to increasingly active play situations, rewarding her attempts to participate. At the fourth step, the therapist assesses the effects of treatment by analyzing the continuously collected data on the target behaviors. In addition, teacher or parent ratings of the child's participation could be used to evaluate the treatment.

BRIEF COGNITIVE BEHAVIOR THERAPY

The "cognitivization" of psychology has been the topic of much scholarly writing in the last 15 years (Bandura, 1977; Mahoney, 1974, Meichenbaum, 1977, Ornstein, 1972). Research in such processes as attention, memory, problem solving, imagery, self-referent speech, beliefs, attributions, and motivation that began in the 1960s continues unabated today, affecting every area of psychology. The rigor of research conducted by experimental and cognitive psychologists and the demonstrated effectiveness of cognitively oriented therapeutic approaches encouraged behavior therapists to broaden their theoretical framework, allowing a dual focus on cognition and behavior.

Today the term "cognitive behavior therapy" identifies a diverse assemblage of models and strategies that share two primary assumptions. First, cognitive mediating events affect behavior. A corollary assumption is that a specific focus on a person's cognitions is an effective strategy for changing behavior. The second assumption is that individuals are active participants in their own learning. Thus, cognitive behaviorism is not a unified theory but a set of models and strategies that are loosely tied together by these two assumptions.

The empricial evidence for the effectiveness of the cognitive behavior approach is impressive. Self-instructinal training (Meichenbaum, 1975), problem-solving therapy (Spivack, Platt, & Shure, 1976; Spivack & Shure, 1974), self-control ther-

apy (Kanfer, 1980), and cognitive therapy (Beck, 1976; Ellis, 1962) are examples of cognitive-behavioral approaches that have been subjected to empirical test and found to be effective with certain problems.

In this chapter we describe briefly three cognitive behavioral therapies with children and adolescents; rational-emotive therapy, self-control therapies, and problem-solving therapies. Although each of these therapies recognizes the reciprocal relationships among cognition, behavior, and the environment, these different approaches vary in their focus on central mediating processes. Thus, rational-emotive therapy (RET) focuses directly on cognitions (beliefs and perceptions), whereas self-control therapies emphasize overt behavior and view thoughts as covert responses to which principles of learning can be applied. Problem-solving therapies focus on specific cognitive skills thought to mediate healthy adjustment.

Rational-Emotive Therapy

Rational-emotive therapy (RET) was developed by Albert Ellis, a clinical psychologist and psychotherapist. Since Ellis published his theory of personality and abnormal behavior in 1957, scores of books and articles on RET with adults and, more recently, with children have appeared.

The central assumption of RET is that people's emotional reactions (e.g., hostility, depression) are the result of their interpretations of events, not the result of the events themselves. Ellis's ABC formula of human functioning expresses the relationship between an activating event (A), the client's beliefs (B), and the client's emotional and behavioral consequences (C). Thus, RET runs counter to operant theories of human functioning that stress the relationship between environmental conditions and human responses. According to RET, whether a particular emotional or behavioral consequence follows a given environmental event depends on the individual's interpretation, or appraisal of that event. In RET theory, it is not the stimuli, or activating events, that are crucial to a person's reaction, but the person's perceptions and interpretations of events.

The core idea in RET is that individuals make themselves emotionally healthy or emotionally upset by the way they process the many activating events in their lives. Moreover, people differ in their tendency to process events according to a rational belief system versus an irrational belief system. Rational belief systems are logical, empirical, nonabsolute, and undemanding, while irrational beliefs are illogical, nonempirical, absolute, and demanding. Irrational thinking leads to emotional upsets that, in turn, interfere with adaptive performance.

The therapist's task is to help the client discover and analyze rational and irrational thought statements that activate emotional upsets, using the ABC model. The goal of therapy is to teach clients to replace irrational beliefs with rational ones without the continued assistance of the therapist.

Steps in Rational-Emotive Therapy
First the steps in RET with adults and older children are outlined. Next, modifications in this approach necessary when working with younger children are discussed.

1. *Problem Identification and Assessment:* "The goal of a RET problem assessment is for the practitioner to identify the specific emotions and behaviors which are problematic and to become aware of the client's irrational thoughts and beliefs which underlie the problems" (Bernard & Joyce, 1984, p. 64). First the therapist identifies the emotional responses (e.g., depression, hostility, or anxiety) that cause the client's subjective discomfort and lead to maladaptive behavioral responss. At this step, the therapist attempts to link the emotional responses to the behavioral responses. For example, a child's anger leads to aggressive outbursts, or a child's depression leads to social withdrawal and underachievement. Next, the therapist attempts to identify the antecedent event that precipitated the emotional and behavioral consequences. For example, the client's latest episode of depression followed a failing grade on an important exam. At this step, the therapist attempts to determine the client's perceptions of the event as well as the client's thoughts, both rational and irrational, about the event. The therapist employs a variety of techniques to assess the antecedent events and the client's beliefs about those events, including inter-

viewing, self-monitoring procedures, and objective tests (see Bernard & Joyce, 1984, for a discussion of these techniques).

2. *Disputation:* The therapist uses a set of direct, verbally persuasive strategies for convincing clients of the irrationality of their beliefs. Specific disputation techniques include didactic presentation of RET theory, humor and exaggeration, cognitive modeling, bibliotherapy, socratic dialoguing, and questioning. The therapist attempts to convince clients of the errors in their thinking and teach them how to identify their own errors and how to subject them to logical analysis. In addition to verbal persuasion, the therapist might employ rational-emotive imagery or behavioral disputation to help clients think and feel differently. In rational-emotive imagery, the therapist asks clients to imagine themselves in the problematic situation but feeling better and behaving more adaptively. The therapist asks the client to verbalize the self-statements accompanying this positive image. In behavioral disputation, the therapist asks clients to expose themselves to situations they find very fearsome or anxiety provoking. For example, asking an 11-year-old boy who cannot postpone gratification to practice delaying gratification or asking a 9-year-old girl who cannot tolerate being messy to make a big mess are examples of behavioral disputation strategies.

3. *Practice and Application:* The client is asked to practice rational thinking outside the therapy session. A common homework assignment is writing down upsetting events, along with the emotional and behavioral consequences. The client also records self-statements about the event. Next, the client detects irrational self-statements, replacing them with rational ones.

RET with Children
Bernard and Joyce (1984) propose that different irrational belief systems underlie two major classifications of childhood psychopathology, internalizers and externalizers. Internalizers blame themselves for failure and disappointments. Internalizers say things to themselves like "I should have done

better''; ''I am so dumb''; ''It is awful that I never get things right.'' Internalizers feel depressed and anxious and may behave in a shy, withdrawn, or depressed manner. The two basic beliefs that internalizers seem to hold are, first, that to be worthwhile they must be loved and approved of by all significant people in their lives. Second, one must be thoroughly competent, adequate, and achieving in all pursuits in order to be worthwhile. Externalizers blame others for disappointments and failures. Externalizers turn their preferences into absolute demands, believing that others should not behave in ways that interfere with their goals. Externalizers demand that others change their behavior and believe they cannot stand it when they do not get what they want.

Children are different from adults in many ways that have implications for conducting RET. Compared to adults, children's language competence and abilities to engage in abstract thought, to simultaneously consider several aspects of a problem situation, and to engage in hypothetical-deductive reasoning are limited. Because RET with adults relies heavily on verbal persuasive strategies, including philosophical analysis and deductive reasoning, RET with children requires substantial modifications. Moreover, children may interpret the confrontational questions common in RET with adults as scolding (Knaus, 1977).

Bernard and Joyce (1984) discuss modifications necessary in applying RET with children. These modifications include concrete examples, role play, imaginal and pictoral presentations of verbal concepts, and teaching specific self-statements rather than disputing general beliefs. Examples of these modifications follow.

Because children do not have as well developed a vocabulary of feelings, the therapist might employ special materials to help children express their feelings. The feeling thermometer, feeling charts, emotional flashcards, games (e.g., Talking, Feeling, and Doing Game; Gardner, 1973), and sentence completion forms are among the techniques used to assess the child's emotional reactions. Because children are often not able to report their own self-talk, special techniques are suggested for eliciting a child's self-talk. Puppets, guided imagery, storytelling procedures, self-monitoring procedures, and labeling are among the techniques recommended by Bernard & Joyce (1984, pp. 190–207). Direct questioning is combined with a variety of less direct techniques to help the child verbalize and become aware of his or her self-talk. Thus, the therapist might ask: ''What were you thinking when _____ happened? Picture yourself back in class, and tell me what you were thinking when _____.'' Older children may be asked to self-monitor their thinking, using the Happening-Thought-Feeling-Reaction (HTFR) Form (Bernard & Joyce, 1984, p. 204).

The RET child therapist employs didactic teaching as well as stories and exercises to help children understand the basic tenet of RET (i.e., that thoughts, not events, cause feelings). Knaus (1974) makes this basic point with a story about a boy getting bumped and feeling angry. Then the child discovers that the person who bumped him is blind, and he feels guilty. The therapist asks why the boy feels angry and then guilty about the same event.

Young (1983) describes a variety of techniques to help children and adolescents learn RET principles. For example, the therapist provides a child with a list of rational and irrational thoughts and asks the child to place an × next to the thoughts that are irrational (i.e., absurd and false rather than sensible and true). To help a child make the distinction between failing something and being a failure, the therapist might draw a large circle on a piece of paper and tell the child that the circle represents the child. The therapist draws little circles inside the self-circle, representing various traits, characteristics, and performances of the child. The therapist points out that one bad feature does not make the self all bad. This same point might be made with an analogy. For example, it is silly to junk a car because it has a bad tire. Similarly, it is silly to junk yourself when you do such and such (Young, 1983).

Another RET approach with young children is teaching them to apply specific rational self-statements in the upsetting situation. This strategy makes minimal demands on the child's abilities to abstract and generalize. In one of the rare experimental studies of specific self-statements, Kanfer, Karoly and Newman (1975) instructed 5- and 6-year-old children who were afraid of the dark to rehearse brave statements, such as ''I am a brave boy (girl), I can take care of myself in the dark.'' These children remained in the dark longer and tolerated a lower level of illumination than children in the control groups.

Coping self-talk has been successfully combined with other procedures, such as relaxation training, token economies, and visual imagery in several studies on fear reduction (e.g., Graziano, Mooney, Huber, & Ignasiak, 1979; Peterson & Shigitomi, 1981). Unfortunately, the relative contribution of the coping self-talk to fear reduction cannot be determined from these multicomponent studies.

Evaluation of RET with Children

There is very little empirical research on the effectiveness of standard, or formal, RET with children. Formal RET refers to disputational training aimed at changing the philosophical belief system of the individual. There is some empirical evidence that approaches that Ellis refers to as nonspecific, or general RET approaches, are effective in the treatment of children's fears and anxieties. These nonspecific approaches run the gamut of cognitive behavioral approaches and include self-instructional training and problem-solving therapy. Because these approaches are derived from different theoretical and empirical bases, lumping them together under the term "general RET" does not promote scientific investigation and is, therefore, scientifically untenable.

Self-Instructional Training

Self-instructional training has its roots in Luria's (1961) and Vygotsky's (1962) theories regarding the internalization of language in the control of behavior. Luria proposes that young children first learn to conform their behavior to the verbal instructions of others. Next, young children learn to guide their behavior by talking aloud to themselves. The 3-year-old boy who says "go slow" while walking with a glass of milk is using overt speech to regulate behavior. Finally, children use silent, or internal, speech to guide their behavior. These covert self-instructions enable the child to think about a situation before reacting to it. In addition to a shift in self-instruction from external control to internal control, Luria hypothesized a shift in the type of self-statements from statements whose function is to slow down behavior to statements whose function is to guide behavior through semantic control.

In an often-cited study, Meichenbaum and Goodman (1971) taught impulsive second-grade children how to use self-instructions to slow themselves down and to think through problems. Their program consists of five stages. First, an adult model performs a task, such as completing a maze or coloring a design, while instructing himself or herself aloud. The self-statements include identifying the problem, labeling alternative solutions, evaluating solutions, choosing one solution, monitoring implementation of the solution, correcting errors, and providing self-reinforcement. In the second stage, the child performs the task while receiving verbal instructions from the adult. In the third and fourth stages, the child performs the task, first pronouncing the self-statements aloud and then whispering them. Finally, the child performs the task while using covert self-instructions. Training begins with simple perceptual tasks and proceeds to more complex tasks as the child masters self-instructions.

In the Meichenbaum and Goodman (1971) study, subjects who received self-instructional training for four 30-minute sessions improved on tests of cognitive impulsivity and on measures of task performance; however, no improvement in classroom behavior was found.

In a lengthy review of 15 years of research on self-instructional training for impulsive and hyperactive children, Kendall and Braswell (1985) conclude that SIT utilizing interactive teaching methods and behavioral contingencies produces significant treatment effects on measures of cognitive impulsivity and classroom behavior. Furthermore, many of the training programs reviewed consist of fewer than 12 sessions. Because applications of SIT for classroom problems are reviewed by Elliott in Chapter 25 of this volume, applications of SIT outside the classroom with children referred for problems other than impulsivity are reviewed herein.

Graziano and Mooney (1980) taught 17 children between the ages of 6 and 13 years of age to use self-instructions to reduce their severe nighttime fears. These fears were described by the parents as highly disruptive and of long duration (i.e., 3 to 6 years). Treatment took place over five sessions, and children and parents were seen in separate groups. Children were taught self-relaxation, positive imagery, and coping self-statements ("I am brave. I can take care of myself in the dark.") Children received a bravery token from their parents for practicing the skills and for being brave during the night. The child monitored his or her token earnings and could exchange tokens for special privileges. Parents were instructed in how to administer the token system and in the use of social reinforcement. In addition, parents completed home observation sheets for 7 days before and after the intervention. Compared to children in a waiting list control group, treated children were rated by their parents as significantly less fearful. At follow-up observation 2 months after treatment, 14 of the 17 experimental subjects met the behavioral criterion of success, set at 10 consecutive fearless nights. Six months following treatment, 11 of the 13 waiting list control subjects met the behavioral criterion. Although this study demonstrates the effectiveness of SIT in combination with behavioral contingencies, it does not permit an evaluation of SIT alone.

SIT has been applied to aggressive children, with mixed evidence of its effectiveness (Kendall & Braswell, 1985). SIT with aggressive children typically combines problem-solving training with self-statements to "slow down" and "stop and think" (Camp, Blom, Hebert, & van Doorninck, 1977; Coats, 1979; Urbain & Kendall, 1980).

Schneider (1974; Robin, Schneider, & Dolnick, 1976; Schneider & Robin, 1976) developed a SIT procedure called the turtle technique to help emotionally disturbed, aggressive children to inhibit aggressive reponses. Children are taught the "turtle response" of pulling in one's limbs and lowering the head to withdraw from a provoking situation. Next, children are taught relaxation skills they can use while "doing the turtle." While studies present evidence that the turtle results in a reduction in aggressive behavior, the lack of an attention control group and the improbability that classroom observers were blind to subjects' condition (i.e., doing the turtle is a noticeable activity) limit confidence in these findings.

A case example of SIT with an aggressive child demonstrates the effectiveness of a relatively brief (12 sessions) intervention that combines relaxation training, rational-emotive therapy, and SIT. The author was the therapist for Julie, a 12-year-old Caucasian girl of average intelligence who was referred by the school counselor to an outpatient psychotherapy clinic for aggressive outbursts. Julie frequently had temper tantrums at school when frustrated, fought with her classmates, and used foul language. On two occasions during the first two months of the school year, Julie physically assaulted her teacher. Julie's mother stated that she and her husband could not control Julie when she had one of her "fits" and that they were ready

to "send Julie to a home for bad girls." Julie's father, a recovering alcoholic, worked on an oil rig in a city a 3-hour drive from home, and was home only 2 days a week. Because Julie's parents frequently argued and were considering divorcing for the second time, family therapy was not considered a good choice.

Julie received 12 one-hour sessions twice a week. During the first session, the therapist interviewed Julie and her mother and stated the treatment goals as teaching Julie ways to control her temper and alternatives to aggressive behavior. To increase Julie's motivation to learn anger control skills, the disadvantages of Julie's temper were discussed. The therapist saw Julie individually for the sessions; however, the therapist spent approximately 15 minutes with Julie's mother at the beginning of each hour session, explaining the treatment, obtaining information regarding Julie's behavior at home and at school, and teaching parent management approaches. During sessions 2 to 4, Julie learned relaxation skills using progressive muscle relaxation and positive visual imagery. Julie received a notebook in which she recorded her relaxation practices at home, and the therapist rewarded her with a grab bag of toys for completing relaxation homework. During sessions 3 and 4, Julie completed an anger hierarchy, indicating on an anger thermometer how angry she felt when different things happened. Body cues associated with angry feelings were identified. The items for the anger hierarchy were obtained from Julie's diary of anger-arousing situations as well as from teacher and parent reports. During sessions 5 and 6, Julie learned coping self-statements to help her stay cool when starting to feel angry (e.g., "Relax, calm down"; "I can feel angry without blowing up"; "Blowing up will not help me get what I want"; "I am in control of me. I do not have to fight"; "I can solve this problem if I think it out"). Julie continued practicing relaxation at home and in the sessions. During session 7, Julie was instructed to relax and then to imagine an incident low on the anger hierarchy. If she started to feel tense and angry, she was instructed to practice coping self-statements and to relax until she no longer felt tense and angry. During sessions 7 to 9, Julie practiced coping self-statements and relaxation while imagining increasingly arousing situations. Specific coping self-statements that were most helpful in reducing angry feelings were identified. In addition, Julie was given a notebook in which she recorded her use of relaxation and coping self-statements in anger-arousing situations outside the clinic. She recorded the situation, her use of coping statements and relaxation, and the outcomes (What happened? How did I feel? What did I do? What happened next?) Beginning during session 8 and continuing through session 12, Julie practiced social problem-solving steps. Specifically, the therapist taught Julie to think of different ways she could solve problems (alternative thinking) and to anticipate the consequences of different solutions (consequential thinking). These problem-solving steps were incorporated into the coping self-statements. Julie continued to record her use of the skills taught and received rewards for bringing the recordings to each session.

At posttreatment and at 3-month follow-up, Julie's teacher reported an improvement in Julie's disruptive behaviors, according to the Conner's Teacher Rating Questionnaire (Goyette, Conners, & Ulrich 1978). Fortunately, the teacher had kept frequency counts of Julie's aggressive behaviors for a 6-week period just prior to treatment and, at the therapist's request, continued to count aggressive behaviors until 6 weeks after treatment. The number of aggressive behaviors at posttreatment was 23% of the pretreatment level and 28% of the pretreatment level at 6 week follow-up. Julie's parents also reported a noticeable improvement. Near the end of treatment, Julie proudly told the therapist about provocations during the week to which she had responded "cool as a cucumber."

Evidence of the effectiveness of SIT provided by these two case studies is bolstered by results of a group anger-control intervention study (Feindler, Marriott, & Iwata, 1984). Thirty-six adolescents attending a junior high school behavior modification program for multisuspended delinquents were randomly assigned to one or two treatment groups or to a no-treatment control group. Training occurred over 10 hour-long sessions and consisted of relaxation training, self-control training, and problem-solving training. Compared to nontreated controls, trained subjects improved on measures of self-control and problem solving and reduced their disruptive and severely aggressive behaviors in school.

In summary, SIT combined with other cognitive-behavioral interventions with aggressive children provide at least modest support for the effectiveness of such short-term cognitive behavioral approaches with aggressive children.

Problem-Solving Therapy

The most extensive research program to date on the assessment and treatment of children's interpersonal cognitive problem-solving (ICPS) skills has been conducted by George Spivack and Myrna Shure and their colleagues at the Hahnemann Community Mental Health Center in Philadelphia (Shure & Spivack, 1978; Spivack, Platt, & Shure, 1976; Spivack & Shure, 1974). This research has demonstrated relationships between ICPS skills and social adjustment in preschool children (Shure, 1981; Spivack & Shure, 1974), elementary-aged children (Shure & Spivack, 1972), and adolescents (Platt, Spivack, Altman, Altman, & Peizer, 1974; Siegel, Platt, & Peizer, 1976). Three ICPS skills have shown the strongest and most consistent relationship to adjustment: alternative thinking, consequential thinking, and means–end thinking. Alternative thinking is the ability to generate multiple alternatives to a given interpersonal problem situation. Consequential thinking is the ability to predict the consequences of a particular alternative and to use this information in decision making. Means–end thinking is the ability to plan in a step-by-step way the actions needed to attain a specific goal, to recognize potential obstacles to reaching the goal, and to use a realistic time frame in implementing a means to a goal. Spivack and Shure and their associates as well as other researchers have developed programs to teach ICPS skills to children and adolescents. In a review of 14 studies of social-cognitive problem-solving interventions with children, Urbain and Kendall (1980) concluded that the evidence of the effectiveness of such training is encouraging.

Although problem-solving training programs differ somewhat in instructional procedures, typical procedures include direct verbal instructions to the child, modeling, discussion of hypothetical problem situations, behavior rehearsal, and self-instructional training (Ladd & Mize, 1983; Urbain & Kendall, 1980). Some school-based programs are quite lengthy. For example, in the Spivack and Shure (1974) program, preschool teachers taught children social-problem-solving skills in 46 half-hour sessions. Furthermore, many social-problem-solving programs have been conducted with nonclinical populations (Olexa & Forman, 1984; Spivack & Shure, 1974; Weissberg et al., 1981; Zahavi & Asher, 1978).

Nevertheless, a few studies have taught social-problem-solving skills to clinically defined populations in a brief therapy format, providing evidence of the effectiveness of brief problem-solving therapy. Urbain and Kendall (cited in Kendall & Braswell, 1985) taught impulsive-aggressive third-grade children ICPS skills during twelve 50-minute sessions over a 6-week period. Although training resulted in improvement on measures of social cognitive problem solving, no improvement on teachers' ratings of impulsive-aggressive behaviors resulted. Mannario, Christy, Durlak, and Magnussen (1982) taught ICPS skills to 32 first through third graders who had behavior problems. Children in the 14-week intervention program made significant gains in classroom adjustment and peer acceptance, compared to children in a control group. Although the evidence for the effectiveness of brief social problem-solving training with clinical populations of children in promising, additional research investigations are needed to establish its effectiveness with different groups as well as to establish the durability of treatment gains.

SOCIAL SKILLS TRAINING THERAPY

An extensive body of literature demonstrates the relationship between peer rejection and isolation in childhood and a wide range of learning and adjustment difficulties both in childhood and in later years (see Asher & Hymel, 1981, for a review). Furthermore, studies of behavioral and cognitive correlates of peer acceptance have suggested specific skills that might underlie the unpopular child's peer relationship difficulties (Putallaz & Gottman, 1982). The past 10 years have seen an explosion of social skills training programs that attempt to teach specific cognitive and behavioral social skills to rejected and socially isolated children (for reviews, see Gresham & Lemanek, 1983; Hughes, 1986). Although these training programs differ in length, procedures, and skills taught, most can be grouped into one of two training types: behavioral skill training and training based on social learning theory. The behavioral skills training programs (e.g., Bornstein, Bellack, & Hersen, 1977, 1980) use role plays (modeling, behavior rehearsal, performance feedback) to teach specific behavioral skills (e.g., eye contact, body posture, assertive communication). For example, Bornstein, Bellack, and Hersen (1980) taught four hospitalized aggressive children specific assertion skills (i.e., eye contact, nonhostile tone, requests for new behavior). Children received nine treatment sessions in a multiple baseline design across behaviors. Al-

though treatment resulted in improvement in assertive behaviors in novel role plays, evidence that the children generalized the taught skills to interactions outside the treatment setting is inconclusive. Franco, Christoff, Crimmins, and Kelly (1983) taught conversational skills to an extremely shy 14-year-old male, using modeling, behavior rehearsal, and performance feedback in the context of role plays. Treatment sessions lasted 20 to 30 minutes and were conducted twice weekly for a 15-week period. Treatment resulted in improvements in conversational skills as measured by observation of unstructured conversations with unfamiliar partners as well as parent, teacher, and self-reports of conversational effectiveness. In yet another case study, Matson et al. (1980) used role plays to teach specific assertion skills to four hospitalized emotionally disturbed children between the ages of 9 and 11. Training resulted in improvements in behavior ratings of ward staff, who were not blind to the treatment status of children.

In conclusion, behavioral social skill training results in improvement in role play performance of taught skills, but evidence of generalization of training across settings and tasks is inconsistent (for reviews, see Gresham & Lemanek, 1983; Hughes & Sullivan, 1988).

Several social skills treatment programs based on social learning theory have resulted in improvements in socially aberrant children's social behaviors and peer acceptance. For example, Ladd (1981) taught low-accepted third-grade children interactional skills that previous research had found differentiate popular and unpopular children: asking questions, leading, and offering support. Children were trained in dyads, and each dyad received eight 45- to 50-minute training sessions, conducted on alternating school days. The therapist provided verbal instructions regarding each skill, explaining why that skill helped children have fun, providing examples of the skill, and asking children to think of examples of the skill. Following verbal instructions, children were asked to try out the skill in a brief game session and then received feedback on their performance. In later sessions, children practiced the skills with untrained children in play situations and were asked to self-evaluate their skill performance. The therapist met with children individually and reviewed the child's performance of the skill, eliciting the child's perceptions of his or her performance, the peer's response to them, reasons for undesirable outcomes, and needed improvement. Trained children increased on measures of peer acceptance and engaged in the trained skills more often in naturalistic settings than children in the control groups. Furthermore, the gains were maintained at a 4-week follow-up.

In a more recent study, Bierman and Furman (1984) used verbal instructions and role plays to teach conversational skills to low-accepted fifth- and sixth-grade children. When conversational skills training was combined with opportunities for children to work with peers toward a shared goal, children improved on measures of conversational skills in the classroom as well as on measures of peer acceptance.

In summary, social skills training programs based on social-learning principles that incorporate coaching, practice opportunities, and performance evaluation are effective in improving children's social behaviors and peer acceptance. More research is needed to determine which children benefit from these programs as well as to establish the long-term benefits of training (Hughes & Sullivan, 1988).

BRIEF FAMILY THERAPY

The popularity family therapy enjoys today is a result, in part, of a paradigmatic shift in psychology away from intrapsychic explanations of behavior toward interpersonal and ecological explanations. Certainly, the family context is an important part of a child's ecology. Family therapists attempt to change family interactions in such a way that family influences on the child promote healthy development.

Although various schools of family therapy emphasize different aspects of family interaction, most family therapists are pragmatic eclectics, using those concepts that seem to fit a particular family situation rather than rigidly adhering to a single school or theory of family functioning. The following key concepts in family therapy are derived from literature on structural, strategic, and social-learning schools of family therapy. The brief family therapist uses these concepts to organize perceptions of family interaction and to formulate therapy goals.

1. The relational aspect of communication is central to the communication school of family therapy (Bateson, Jackson, Haley, & Weakland 1956; Satir, 1967). The communication theorist discriminates between the command, or relational function, of communication and the report function (Watzlawick, Beavin, & Jackson, 1967). The command aspect of a communication defines the relationship, and the report aspect carries the content of the communication. Most communications have both command and report functions. For example, a wife asks her husband if he picked up milk on his way home. In addition to the overt meaning of this question, this question also communicates something about the husband—wife relationship. Its relational message cannot be deciphered without knowledge of recurring husband—wife interactions. Thus, the wife may be saying that her husband does not care about the family or that she feels unappreciated. Because disturbed families do not talk about the relational aspect of communication, ambiguities are not clarified and family members have to guess about the relational aspect of their communication. The double-bind situation (Bateson et al., 1956) is an example of a single communication having contradictory command and report messages. For example, a mother tells her daughter to be independent and go to school, but she looks worried as the child prepares to leave for school and gives her detailed instructions on what to do that day.

   Another tenet of the communication theory of family therapy is that the symptom communicates something about family relationships. For example, a child's depression may communicate the child's desire for more affectionate interactions with parents or it may communicate something about the child's dependency on the mother.

2. The family is conceptualized as a rule-governed system. Although these rules are not articulated by family members, they define relationships and constrain individual members' behavior. For example, a wife and husband argue over the cost of the wife's new hobby, ceramics. The real conflict, however, is over the issue of de-

pendence and independence in the marital relationship. The family's rule has been that the husband and wife spend leisure time in joint activities.

3. It is assumed that the child's disturbed behavior serves a function in the family system. For example, when the parents argue and move toward a separation, the child's behavior worsens. The parents submerge their conflict as they work together to help the child. As the child improves, the parents once again move toward separation. Alternatively, the child may instigate conflict between the parents in order to maintain an alliance with one parent against the other.

4. Disturbed families are characterized by poor problem-solving skills, especially conflict resolution skills and negotiation skills. They tend to be rigid in their approach to problems and respond to conflict by either withdrawing or aggressing.

5. Boundaries are a special kind of interactional rule that defines who participates and how (Minuchin, 1974). Boundaries define the underlying structure of family interaction. A family system consists of several subsystems, separated by boundaries. Individuals are subsystems, as are dyads such as the husband–wife dyad and the mother–child dyad. The function of boundaraies is to protect the differentiation of the family system, defining individuals' relationships to others. Minuchin describes common boundary problems in families, including the parental child, overly rigid boundaries, enmeshment, and disengagement. Ideally, boundaries are clear to family members and change as the family passes through different developmental stages. For example, a disengaged father in a family with young children becomes more involved with the children as they grow up.

6. Triangulation is a special type of boundary problem in which a dyad involves a third person to stabilize the relationship. Frequently, the child serves an intermediary role in the marital relationship. For example, the parents may suppress their own conflict by blaming (scapegoating) the child.

These family therapy concepts help the therapist interpret the family history and interactions during the sessions. Certain interactional patterns characterize disturbed families, and the family therapist looks for patterns that may by symptomatic of particular boundary, communication, rules, or problem-solving problems. Brief family therapy demands that the therapist quickly diagnose key interactional problems, formulate desired changes in family interactional patterns, and develop strategies for helping the family change in the desired ways. Typically, the brief family therapist assumes a directive role, clearly articulating goals, issuing directives, coaching family members in new ways of communicating, blocking dysfunctional interactional patterns, modeling healthy functioning and good communication, and providing feedback on both functional and dysfunctional interactions. The therapist emphasizes communication in the present rather than historical accounts of the family and its problems.

The family therapist draws from a wide range of strategies in helping families. Techniques that are especially common in brief family therapy include joining and accommodating, reframing, issuing directives, emphasizing the complementarity of relationships, and enactment. These techniques are illustrated through the following case study.

Mrs. Ramos called to set up the initial appointment. Although she presented the older son, Keith, as the problem, she did not hesitate to make the first appointment for the entire family. Dr. R, age 41, is a university professor. Mrs. Ramos is a registered nurse. They have two sons, Keith, age 13, and Roger, age 8.

In the initial session, the therapist asked each family member to express their perceptions of the problems. Mr. R. stated that his relationship with Keith was poor and that his sons fight too much. Mrs. R. agreed that the children fight too much and that her husband's expectations for the boys are too high. She described herself as more lenient than her husband. The boys stated that they wanted more freedoms and that their father yelled at them too much. The therapist showed respect for each individual's perceptions, accepting similarities and differences in perceptions as normal. The therapist also modeled good communication skills, asking individuals to clarify vague statements, asking for examples, and checking each others' perceptions of what other family members were saying. The therapist obtained a brief chronology of significant events in the family's history. During this history taking, the boys interferred with their parents' communication with each other, and the parents allowed this interference. The therapist blocked the children's interference, saying "this concerns your parents and not you." When Roger misbehaved during the session, his parents verbally requested him to stop the misbehavior, with limited success. Near the end of the session, the father threatened to spank Roger, which resulted in a temporary improvement in his behavior. At the end of the first session, the therapist assumed that the boundary between the spouse and child subsystems was diffuse and that the mother was in alliance with the boys against the father, undermining his authority. Before the first session ended, the therapist and family members agreed on the following goals: decrease the boys' fighting, improve the family's problem-solving skills, and reduce arguing between the parents regarding child problems.

Over the next eight sessions, the therapist employed a range of strategies to accomplish these goals. For example, the therapist joined the family, accommodating her interpersonal style to resemble more closely that of the family. Because the Ramos family used humor to relieve tension, the therapist used humor and exaggeration to join with the family and to accomplish the goals of therapy. Another joining technique the therapist used is sharing anecdotes from her own family that emphasize the similarities between herself and the client family.

To strengthen the spouse subsystem, the therapist met with the parents alone for two sessions. She issued directives to the husband to plan an enjoyable evening out with his wife, keeping the plans a surprise. The wife was instructed to plan the child-care arrangements for the evening. The husband and wife were instructed not to discuss parenting during the evening, because they were spending an evening together as friends and lovers, not as parents.

The therapist served the roles of mediator, communication coach, and problem-solving coach in helping the family negotiate a family contract. The older boy was entering adolescence, and the family had not made the necessary changes in family rules to accommodate his greater needs for independence. The contract established privileges and responsibilities for both boys and served as a

vehicle for practicing family problem solving. In addition, the contract required the parents to treat the two boys differently. The parents had tried to treat the boys the same, in the name of fairness, which interferred with each boy's differentiation of self. The contract included a contingency management provision for hitting. Both boys were fined whenever they fought and sent to time out (regardless of who started the fight). Also, they could earn special privileges for settling their differences without personal violence.

The therapist asked family members to enact interactional sequences in the sessions. For example, if the husband and wife disagreed on their expectations for the boys, the therpiast directed the husband, "Talk to your wife about that."

The therapist emphasized complementarity of relationships and told the wife, "Your husband's temper causes you to side with the boys against their father." She told the husband, "Your wife's leniency causes you to yell at the children."

The wife and husband felt little appreciation from each other, and contributions to the family were viewed by the family as obligations rather than as gifts. Thus, the level of positive exchanges in the family was low and the parents complained that the children took them for granted. Thus, the therapist reframed family members' contributions as gifts and asked family members to accept the gifts graciously. "You need to teach your children to appreciate what you do for them. Thank your wife for cooking dinner."

At the eighth session, the therapist reviewed progress with the family. The incidence of the boys' fighting had decreased to one-tenth of its preintervention level. Substantial progress had been made toward the other goals. Consequently, therapy was terminated. Two months after termination, the parents reported in a telephone follow-up that the progress had been maintained.

EVALUATION OF BRIEF PSYCHOTHERAPY WITH CHILDREN

In the most comprehensive review of psychotherapy outcomes with children, Casey and Berman (1985) reviewed 75 studies published between 1952 and 1983 in which some form of psychotherapy was compared with a control group or another treatment. They found that therapy with children is similar in efficacy to therapy with adults and that children receiving psychotherapy achieved outcomes about two-thirds of a standard deviation better than untreated children. They concluded that doubts that the efficacy of psychotherapy with children can be put to rest.

Casey and Berman analyzed several factors that might be related to psychotherapy outcomes, including the length of treatment. Their results are summarized briefly here.

In the 75 studies reviewed, the mean treatment duration was just over 9 weeks, and treatment typically occurred once per week. With respect to the type of therapy, 42 (56%) used a form of behavior therapy. Of these, 16 (21%) used cognitive-behavior therapies, and the remainder used a range of common behavioral procedures (e.g., systematic desensitization, conditioning, modeling). A variety of nonbehavioral therapies were assessed in 36 (48%) studies, with client-centered therapy being the most common, used in 22 (29%) studies.

Across studies, the mean standardized measure of effect size was .71 with a standard deviation of .73. Casey and Berman compared the effect size for behavior therapies and nonbehavior therapies and found behavior therapies resulted in a larger effect size. However, they caution that the apparent superiority of behavior therapies may be a result of the fact that the two classes of therapy tended to study children with different problems and to use different measures of treatment efficacy.

A critical question in psychotherapy research is "How effective are different kinds of therapy for different child problems?" Due to the tendency for different problems to be treated with different approaches, only for problems in social adjustment were behavioral and nonbehavioral treatments used in sufficient numbers to permit a comparison between the two approaches. The resulting effect sizes for behavioral and nonbehavioral therapies were not significantly different.

Of particular importance to an evaluation of brief therapy is the finding of a negative correlation between the length of treatment and effect size. Casey and Berman suggest that this finding is a result of the tendency of shorter studies to use outcome measures that more closely resembled activities in therapy. Because the length of treatment is associated with therapy type, outcome measure, and child problem, one cannot conclude from these findings that brief psychotherapy is better than longer therapy. Nevertheless, the re-

sults support the conclusion that relatively short psychotherapy with children is effective.

REFERENCES

Asher, S. R., & Hymel, S. (1981). Children's social competence in peer relations: Sociometric and behavioral assessment. In J. D. Wine & M. D. Syme (Eds.), *Social competence.* New York: Guilford Press.

Bandura, A. (1977). *Social learning theory.* Englewood Cliffs, NJ: Prentice-Hall.

Bateson, G., Jackson, D. D., Haley, J., & Weakland, J. (1956). Toward a theory of schizophrenia. *Behavioral Science, 1,* 251–264.

Beck, A. T. (1976). *Cognitive therapy and emotional disorders.* New York: International Universities Press.

Bernard, M. E., & Joyce, M. R. (1984). *Rational-emotive therapy with children and adolescents.* New York: Wiley.

Bierman, K. L., & Furman, W. (1984). The effects of social skills training and peer involvement on the social adjustment of preadolescents. *Child Development, 55,* 151–162.

Bornstein, M., Bellack, A. S., & Hersen, B. (1977). Social skills training for unassertive children: A multiple-baseline analysis. *Journal of Applied Behavior Analysis, 10,* 183–195.

Bornstein, M., Bellack, A. S., & Hersen, M. (1980). Social skills training for highly aggressive children. *Behavior Modification, 4,* 173–186.

Camp, B. W., Blom, G., Hebert, F., & van Doorninck, W. (1977). "Think aloud": A program for developing self-control in young aggressive boys. *Journal of Abnormal Child Psychology, 5,* 157–168.

Caplan, G. (Ed.). (1961). *An approach to community mental health.* New York: Grune & Stratton.

Casey, R. J., & Berman, J. S. (1985). The outcome of psychotherapy with children. *Psychological Bulletin, 98,* 388–400.

Coats, K. I. (1979). Cognitive self-instructional training approach for reducing disruptive behavior of young children. *Psychological Reports, 44,* 127–134.

de Shazer, S. (1985). *Keys to solution in brief therapy.* New York: W. W. Norton.

Ellis, A. (1962). *Reason and emotion in psychotherapy.* New York: Lyle Stuart.

Ewing, C. P. (1978). *Crisis intervention as psychotherapy.* New York: Oxford University Press.

Feindler, E. L., Marriott, S. A., & Iwata, M. (1984). Group anger control training for junior high school delinquents. *Cognitive Therapy and Research, 8,* 299–311.

Fisher, S. (1980). The use of time limits in brief psychotherapy: A comparison of six sessions, twelve sessions, and unlimited treatment with families. *Family Process, 19,* 377–392.

Fisher, S. (1984). Time-limited brief therapy with families: A one-year follow-up study. *Family Process, 23,* 101–106.

Franco, P. P., Christoff, K. A., Crimmins, D. B., & Kelly, J. A. (1983). Social skills training for an extremely shy young adolescent: A case study. *Behavior Therapy, 14,* 568–575.

Gardner, R. A. (1973). *The talking, feeling and doing game.* Cresskill, NJ: Creative Therapeutics.

Goldstein, A. P. (Ed.). (1978). *Prescriptions for child mental health and education.* Elmsford, NY: Pergamon Press.

Goyette, C. H., Conners, C. K., & Ulrich, R. F. (1978). Normative data on revised Conners Parent and Teacher Rating Scales. *Journal of Abnormal Child Psychology, 6,* 221–236.

Graziano, A. M., & Mooney, K. C. (1980). Family self-control instruction for children's nighttime fear reduction. *Journal of Consulting and Clinical Psychology, 48,* 200–213.

Graziano, A. M., Mooney, K. C., Huber, C., & Ignasiak, D. (1979). Self-control instruction for children's fear reduction. *Journal of Behavior Therapy and Experimental Psychiatry, 10,* 221–227.

Gresham, F. M., & Lemanek, K. L. (1983). Social skills: A review of cognitive-behavioral training procedures with children. *Journal of Applied Developmental Psychology, 4,* 239–261.

Gurman, A. (1981). Integrative marital therapy: Toward the development of an interpersonal approach. In S. Budman (Ed.). *Forms of brief therapy* (pp. 415–457). New York: Guilford Press.

Hughes, J. (1986). Methods of skill selection in social skills training: A review. *Professional School Psychology, 1,* 235–248.

Hughes, J., & Sullivan, K. (1988). Outcome assessment in social skills training with children. *Journal of School Psychology, 26,* 167–183.

Jacobson, F. F. (1980). *Crisis intervention in the 1980s.* San Francisco: Jossey-Bass.

Kanfer, F. H. (1980). Self-management methods. In F. H. Kanfer & A. P. Goldstein (Eds.), *Helping people change.* Elmsford, NY: Pergamon Press.

Kanfer, F. H., Karoly, P., & Newman, A. (1975). Reduction of children's fear of the dark by competence-related and situational thought-related verbal cues. *Journal of Consulting and Clinical Psychology, 43,* 251–258.

Kendall, P. C., & Braswell, L. (1985). *Cognitive-behavioral therapy for impulsive children.* New York: Guilford Press.

Kinston, W., & Bentovim, A. (1981). Creating a focus for brief marital or family therapy. In S. H. Budman (Ed.), *Forms of brief therapy* (pp. 361–386). New York: Guilford Press.

Knaus, W. J. (1974). *Rational emotive education: A manual for elementary school teachers.* New York: Institute for Rational Living.

Knaus, W. J. (1977). Rational-emotive education. In A. Ellis and R. Grieger (Eds.), *Handbook of rational-emotive therapy.* New York: Springer.

Ladd, G. W. (1981). Effectiveness of a social learning model for enhancing children's social interaction

and peer acceptance. *Child Development, 52,* 171–178.

Ladd, G. W., & Mize, J. (1983). A cognitive-social learning model of social-skill training. *Psychological Review, 90,* 127–157.

Luria, A. (1961). *The role of speech in the regulation of normal and abnormal behaviors.* New York: Liveright.

Mahoney, M. J. (1974). *Cognition and behavior modification.* Cambridge, MA: Ballinger.

Mannario, A. P., Christy, M., Durlak, J. A., & Magnussen, M. G. (1982). Evaluation of social competence training in the schools. *Journal of School Psychology, 20,* 11–19.

Matson, J. L., Esveldt-Dawson, K., Andrasik, F., Ollendick, T. H., Petti, T., & Hersen, M. (1980). Direct, observational, and generalization effects of social skills training with emotionally disturbed children. *Behavior Therapy, 11,* 522–531.

Meichenbaum, D. (1975). Self-instructional methods. In F. H. Kanfer & A. P. Goldstein (Eds.), *Helping people change.* Elmsford, NY: Pergamon Press.

Meichenbaum, D., & Goodman, J. (1971). Training impulsive children to talk to themselves: A means of developing self-control. *Journal of Abnormal Psychology, 77,* 115–126.

Minuchin, S. (1974). *Families and family therapy.* Cambridge, MA: Harvard University Press.

Olexa, D. F., & Forman, A. (1984). Effects of social problem-solving training on classroom behavior or urban disadvantaged students. *Journal of School Psychology, 22,* 165–176.

Ornstein, R. E. (1972). *The psychology of consciousness.* San Francisco: W. H. Freeman.

Patterson, G. R. (1975). The aggressive child: Victim and architect of coercive system. In E. J. Mash, L. A. Hamerlynck, & L. C. Handy (Eds.), *Behavior modification and families* (pp. 267–316). New York: Brunner/Mazel.

Peterson, L., & Shigitomi, C. (1981). The use of coping techniques to minimize anxiety in hospitalized children. *Behavior Therapy, 12,* 1–14.

Phillips, E. L., & Johnston, M. S. (1973). Theoretical and clinical aspects of short-term parent-child psychotherapy. In H. H. Barten & J. S. Barten (Eds.), *Children and their parents in brief therapy* (pp. 22–39). New York: Behavioral Publications.

Platt, J. J., Spivack, G., Altman, N., Altman, D., & Peizer, S. B. (1974). Adolescent problem solving thinking. *Journal of Consulting and Clinical Psychology, 42,* 787–793.

Putallaz, M., & Gottman, J. (1982). Conceptualizing social competence in children. In P. Karoly & J. J. Steffen (Eds.), *Improving children's social competence.* Lexington, MA: Lexington Books.

Reynolds, C. R., & Richmond, B. O. (1978). "What I think and feel": A revised measure of children's manifest anxiety. *Journal of Abnormal Child Psychology, 6,* 271–280.

Rimm, D. C., & Masters, J. C. (1974). *Behavior therapy: Techniques and empirical findings.* New York: Academic Press.

Robin, A. L., Schneider, M., & Dolnick, M. (1976). The turtle technique: An extended case study of self-control in the classroom. *Psychology in the Schools, 13,* 449–453.

Ross, A. O. (1981). *Child behavior therapy: Principle, procedures, and empirical basis.* New York: Wiley.

Satir, V. (1967). *Conjoint family therapy: A guide to theory and technique.* Palo Alto, CA: Science & Behavior Books.

Schneider, M. (1974). Turtle technique in the classroom. *Teaching Exceptional Children, 8,* 22–24.

Schneider, M., & Robin, A. L. (1976). The turtle technique: A method for the self-control of impulsive behavior. In J. D. Krumboltz & C. E. Thoresen (Eds.), *Counseling methods.* New York: Holt, Rinehart and Winston.

Shure, M. B. (1981). Social competence as a problem solving skill. In J. D. Wine & M. D. Smye (Eds.), *Social competence* (pp. 158–185). New York: Guilford Press.

Shure, M. B., & Spivack, G. (1972). Means-end thinking, adjustment, and social class among elementary-school-aged children. *Journal of Consulting and Clinical Psychology, 38,* 348–353.

Shure, M. B., & Spivack, G. (1978). *Problem-solving techniques in childrearing.* San Francisco: Jossey-Bass.

Siegel, J. M., Platt, J. J., & Peizer, S. B. (1976). Emotional and social real-life problem-solving thinking in adolescent and adult psychiatric patients. *Journal of Clinical Psychology, 32,* 230–232.

Spivack, G., Platt, J., & Shure, M. (1976). *The problem-solving approach to adjustment.* San Francisco: Jossey-Bass.

Spivack, G., & Shure, M. B. (1974). *Social adjustment of young children: A cognitive approach to solving real-life problems.* San Francisco: Jossey-Bass.

Urbain, E. S., & Kendall, P. C. (1980). Review of social-cognitive problem-solving interventions with children. *Psychological Bulletin, 88,* 109–143.

Vygotsky, L. S. (1962). *Thought and language.* New York: Wiley.

Watzlawick, P., Beavin, J. H., & Jackson, D. D. (1967). *Pragmatics of human communication.* New York: W.W. Norton.

Weakland, J., Fisch, R., Watzlawick, P., & Bodin, A. (1974). Brief therapy: Focused problem resolution. *Family Process, 13,* 141–168.

Weissberg, R., Gesten, E., Carnrike, C., Toro, P., Rapkin, B., Davidson, E., & Cowen, E. (1981). Social problem-solving training: A competence building intervention with second to fourth grade children. *American Journal of Community Psychology, 9,* 411–423.

Werry, J. S., & Wollersheim, J. P. (1973). Behavior therapy with children: A broad overview. In H. H. Barten & S. S. Barten (Eds.), *Children and their parents in brief therapy* (pp. 263–291. New York: Behavioral Publications.

Young, H. S. (1983). Principles of assessment and methods of treatment with adolescents: Special considerations. In A. Ellis and M. E. Bernard (Eds.), *Rational-emotive approaches to the problems of childnood.* New York: Plenum Press.

Zahavi, S., & Asher, S. R. (1978). The effect of verbal instructions on preschool children's aggressive behavior. *Journal of School Psychology, 16,* 146–153.

30

HEALTH PROBLEMS IN SCHOOL-AGED CHILDREN

JENNIFER L. LAIL
CAROLYN S. SCHROEDER
University of North Carolina at Chapel Hill

As the correlation between good health and effective learning has become more apparent, the schools' interest in the health of their students and the involvement of health care professionals in the school setting have both increased. All 50 states have passed laws requiring documentation of immunization for school attendance, and many school systems now have in-school hearing, vision, dental, and scoliosis screenings, as well as on-site school nurses. Much of the impetus for this integration of health care and maintenance into the schools has come from the 1975 passage of Public Law 94-142, the Education for All Handicapped Children Act, which mandates appropriate education for children with physical, mental, and medical handicapping conditions. The implementation of this law demands communication and cooperation between the school and health care professionals. The school psychologist is often in an ideal position to serve as liaison with health care professionals as an educational plan is structured that takes a child's health needs into account. To optimize the drafting of such an integrated plan, the school psychologist must have a general knowledge of the diagnostic, therapeutic, and prognostic features of often-encountered diseases or disabilities. Similarly, the American Academy of Pediatrics (1987b) is strongly urging pediatricians to expand their knowledge of and involvement in children's psychosocial development and their learning processes. Physical therapists and occupational therapists are also becoming more involved in the schools, with many schools hiring them for staff positions or as regular consultants. It is obvious that the goals for *both* the schools and the health care professionals should be good health and good learning.

The purpose of this chapter is to provide a reference for school psychologists on the medical problems seen in the child from kindergarten through high school. First, there will be a brief overview of health problems during the elementary and adolescent years, followed by a section on health care maintenance. Then, diseases or disabilities will be addressed by body system, with a definition and information about their diagnosis, typical treatments, and expected outcomes. Finally, there will be a brief section on the effects of chronic illness. Clearly, in-depth coverage of medical conditions is not the intent of this chapter; those interested can find more information from the references in each section.

The elementary school years are often the healthiest period of one's life. Physical growth is at a steady rate, with an average of 7 pounds in weight and 2 to 3 inches in height per year, and there is a fine tuning of both gross and fine motor skills. Infectious illnesses tend to decrease with age, and injuries predominate as the reason to seek health care. Health problems often identified in the elementary age group are hearing impairment (3%), visual disorders (20 to 25%), speech and language defects (16 to 21%), and learning disabilities (5 to 15%) (American Academy of Pediatrics, 1987b). Evidence of suboptimal health care maintenance practices often emerges in the form of poor nutrition, obesity, inadequate hygiene, and dental decay. In some schools, even at the elementary level, cigarette smoking and alcohol and drug abuse pose serious health problems. Emotional and behavioral problems often emerge in the elementary school years as children learn to deal with new experiences and expectations, structure, peer pressure, and academic demands. It is estimated that in any one year, between 5 and 15% of the children will suffer from emotional or behavioral problems severe enough to interfere with their development and/or learning.

The changes experienced cognitively, emotionally, and socially are magnified in the adolescent years, with drastic physical changes in linear growth and sexual maturation. Common health issues during adolescence are scoliosis, acne, obesity and eating disorders, and perceived adequacy of sexual maturation when compared with peers. The heightened body awareness that accompanies the hormonal changes of adolescence also engenders many concerns (often unfounded) that trivial physical variations or abnormalities may signal life-threatening or disfiguring problems. Certainly, as sexual maturation occurs, problems with menstruation, birth control, and sexually transmitted diseases become critical health issues. Health concerns with alcohol and drug abuse also increase during the adolescent years. Another serious problem is suicide, with 5,000 adolescent suicides recorded per year, and between 50 and 200 attempts for each self-inflicted death. Females make more attempts than males (3.1 : 2), but males more often succeed, due to employing more lethal means (American Academy of Pediatrics, 1987a).

A child or adolescent who is chronically ill or has physical and/or mental handicaps has to deal not only with the unique features of his or her specific health problem but also with the already mentioned potential physical problems of "growing up." These children are additionally more vulnerable to psychosocial stresses and will generally need extra support in learning to negotiate the emotional hurdles posed by childhood.

Health Care Maintenance

Regular checkups by a student's personal physician are ideal for early detection and treatment of physical problems. The American Academy of Pediatrics (1985a) recommends routine "checkups" for school-aged children at least every 2 years, and more often if the child has an ongoing medical problem. A routine exam can evaluate the quality of their health practices and give information on the child's nutritional status, hygiene and dental care. The physical also offers a chance to screen vision and hearing, and often to check for anemia or diabetes with simple laboratory testing; adequacy of immunization can also be reviewed. As mentioned previously, documentation of immunization for school attendance is required in all 50 states. To maintain a high level of immunization among all students, schools must keep permanent files and perform annual surveillance of the adequacy of each student's immunization. A report of the recommended schedules for vaccines can be found in *School Health: a Guide for Health Professionals,* published by the American Academy of Pediatrics (1987b).

Nutritional Problems

In a typical physical examination, the height and weight of the child, plotted over time against age and sex appropriate standards, reflect his nutritional state. Weight is a good indicator of the present state of over-, under-, or normal nutrition, while height growth is more likely to be assessed in relationship to prior growth trends in order to reflect accurately the current growth status. Other useful assessments of nutritional state include serial head circumferences (a reflection of brain growth), triceps skinfold thickness (correlates with total body fat), and specific findings on a physical exam, such as rashes, pallor, or muscle wasting. When these evaluations are abnormal, biochemical testing may be in order to evaluate blood levels of protein, iron, and specific vitamins, as well as to screen for illnesses that may undermine nutritional status by calorie loss (diabetes), poor absorption of nutrients (parasites), or increased metabolic demands (thyroid disease, cardiac disease) (Suskind & Varma, 1984). Poor nutrition can also result when there is a variation from the recommended ratio of calories from fat (25%), protein (15%), and carbohydrates (60%) or when the diet does not include a balance of the four basic food groups (American Academy of Pediatrics, 1985b).

Malnutrition develops when the calorie and/or protein content of a child's diet is deficient, when the quantity of nutrients eaten is inadequate, or when the food ingested is poorly absorbed or digested. A child who has increased utilization of nutrients from thyroid, heart, lung, kidney, or gastrointestinal disease is at higher risk for malnutrition, as are those with malignancies such as childhood leukemia. Malnourished children may be more susceptible to infection, as their nutritional deficiencies often affect immune system function, and they may manifest lethargy or excessive fatigue in school activities (American Academy of Pediatrics, 1985b). Fortunately, malnutrition is a less common problem in the United States since the initiation of Food Assistance Programs such as the School Breakfast and Lunch Program, and the Food Stamp Program, which began in 1964. Almost 90% of the schools in the United States are participating in the School Lunch Program, which provides free and reduced-price school meals, whose quality and content is supervised by the U.S. Department of Agriculture (American Academy of Pediatrics, 1985b). Of the nutritional deficiencies seen in the United States, however, iron deficiency and its associated anemia are among the most common, with an estimated prevalence of 5 to 10% (Oski, 1985).

Definitions for obesity vary with the method by which it is measured (weight for age, weight/height ratio, triceps skinfold thickness), but is generally a diagnosis that can be made at a glance (American Academy of Pediatrics, 1985b). The prevalence of obesity in children varies from 10 to 30% and basically involves more energy intake in calories than expended in activity. The etiologies of obesity vary for each child, but it is rarely caused by metabolic or hormonal problems. More common contributing factors are physical inactivity, family eating patterns that include a preponderance of "fast foods," genetic tendencies toward the overweight state, and often boredom. Obesity has also been correlated with the inactivity associated with children's excessive watching of television (Dietz & Gortmaker, 1985).

A school child who is obese may demonstrate poor motor skills and is at risk for childhood hypertension, slipped capital femoral epiphysis (distortion of the growth plate of the thigh bone at the hip), heat intolerance, and in extreme cases, compromised breathing. The most significant effect is on self-esteem secondary to social isolation and ridicule. Dietary restriction and increased exercise are the cornerstones of therapy, but should be supervised by a physician or dietitian who is familiar with pediatric nutritional needs. The widely available commercial diet programs for adults are not appropriate for the growing child or adolescent. It is discouraging that the long-term prognosis for the obese child is poor; success in losing weight is rare, but is augmented when a combined program of exercise, psychological counseling, and dietary manipulation is employed, with in-depth involvement of the child's parents (American Academy of Pediatrics, 1985b).

Sensory Impairments

Acceptable school performance is a formidable task for the child who lacks the sensory capabilities to assimilate instructions and knowledge. Early detection and treatment are imperative, since repeatedly missing critical interactions in the classroom can only lead to poor school performance.

Hearing Disorders

A hearing deficit can be detected on routine screening either by a health professional or through in-school screening. The majority of children who are profoundly deaf, 1 in 1,000 infants (Ruben, 1987), are detected prior to school age, but those with less severe or unilateral hearing loss may not be detected until they begin formal schooling. Caplan (1987) found that the mean age at diagnosis of profound congenital deafness was 24 months of age, with the diagnosis for less striking hearing loss often being delayed until a mean of 48 months of age.

A hearing loss can be temporary or permanent, congenital or acquired. The location of the structural deficit in the middle ear, inner ear, auditory nerve, or in the auditory areas of the brain determines the type of hearing loss. Although screening is a valuable tool for detection of a hearing disorder, an evaluation by an audiologist and possibly an otolaryngologist is necessary to define the loss as conductive, sensorineural, or a mixed deficit. Conductive hearing losses involve impedance of sound transmission through the external ear canal and/or the three small bones of the middle ear. Those children with conductive hearing loss (often related to otitis media or a structural abnormality of the outer ear) can often be treated by giving louder auditory signals, and usually are not fitted with a hearing aid. The magnitude of these children's deficit may fluctuate, however, depending on the status of their middle ear disease or ear canal occlusion. Thus, teachers should be alerted that the child may require special seating in the classroom and/or repetition of instructions. The child also should be alerted to the fact that he may miss verbal cues and he should be given a method for acquiring help at those times (Fria, 1981). By contrast, children with sensorineural hearing loss often require hearing aids, because their disorder causes both decreased loudness of incoming auditory signals and blurred, distorted sounds. Sensorineural loss is, for the most part, irreversible, and although hearing aids may provide some amplification, they do not totally correct hearing (Fria, 1981). The child with sensorineural loss learns to depend heavily on lip reading, facial expressions, gestures, and body language to complete the task of hearing.

The use of Brainstem Auditory Evoked Responses (BAER) detects deficiencies in auditory processing and is valuable in assessing hearing in infants or children who cannot perform conventional audiometric testing. The BAER can also be used to confirm or clarify results from other methods of testing (Fria, 1981).

The severity of a child's hearing problem is expressed by the threshold of intensity of sound that is just audible. Inability to hear sounds of less than 15 decibels (dB) is considered within the normal range. Description of severity levels includes: mild (15 to 30 dB), moderate (31 to 50 dB), severe (51 to 80 dB), profound (81 to 100 dB), and total deafness. Generally, if a student's hearing cannot be corrected to better than a threshold of 60 to 70 dB, special educational programming is necessary (American Academy of Pediatrics, 1987b). It should be noted that the child with a unilateral hearing loss can be as impaired as one with a bilateral deficit, due to the constant effort required to localize and process sounds with the better ear.

Children likely to be at high risk for hearing deficits are those with chromosomal or genetic abnormalities, those with deformities of the external ear or lower jaw, or a family history of deafness. A high index of suspicion for hearing loss should also be maintained for the child who has had bacterial meningitis, prenatal rubella or cytomegalovirus infection (CMV), a complicated neonatal course, or been born prematurely (Caplan, 1987). Certainly, a history of otitis media, either acute or chronic, warrants careful observation and screening for intermittent or persistent hearing problems. It is also important to determine that the student's infection is being addressed medically, with good compliance with medications and follow-up visits. A subset of children with chronic otitis media will require surgical placement of ventilation tubes. Also called "grommets," "tubes," or "PE tubes," they are placed through the eardrum to remove old sticky middle-ear fluid and to prevent its reaccumulation by alleviating the vacuum that can develop in the middle-ear cavity from poor Eustachian tube function associated with upper respiratory illnesses or allergies.

Vision Disorders

It is estimated by the National Society for Prevention of Blindness that 1 in 5,000 school children in the United States has partial sight (Nelson, 1984). A Snellen eye chart test on a child with normal or near-normal vision would give a 20/20 to 20/70 result, meaning that the child can see at 20 feet what a normally sighted person can see at 20 feet or 70 feet, respectively. Abnormalities of vision are assessed as low vision or partial sight (20/70 to 20/200), or blindness (vision worse than 20/200 in the better, maximally corrected eye).

The American Academy of Pediatrics (1987b) recommends annual vision screening early in the school year from preschool through high school with the "E" chart, the Screening Test for Young Children and Retardates (STYCAR), or the Snellen chart. Generally, children older than age 5 should pass these tests with vision at 20/30 or better with each eye.

The most common causes of visual impairment are congenital conditions, including cataracts, glaucoma, hereditary conditions, structural malformations of the eye, metabolic diseases, and intrauterine infections. Trauma to the eye, retinopathy of prematurity, and eye tumors constitute the most common etiologies for acquired visual impairment. Seventy percent of blind children have associated disabilities, with mental retardation being the most common (American Academy of Pediatrics, 1987b).

Musculoskeletal Disorders

School-aged children are subject to a variety of disorders that affect the musculoskeletal system. Most are temporary and have symptoms such as localized pain, swelling, or limitation of motion, which can often be linked to recent exercise or trauma. Similar symptoms, especially if they are persistent, or have no apparent etiology, however, can herald more serious conditions and warrant medical evaluation. Without a definite recollection of trauma, a swollen joint or painful extremity can be an indicator of a bone infection (osteomyelitis), a joint infection (septic arthritis), or a myriad of diseases that involve joint inflammation (rheumatic fever, juvenile rheumatoid arthritis, systemic lupus erythematosus). Hemophilia or sickle cell anemia, along with a number of childhood malignancies (leukemia, osteogenic sarcoma) can present with a swollen joint, which may or may not be tender. Accordingly, ongoing complaints of bony or muscular discomforts or disabilities should be evaluated by a medical professional. Two musculoskeletal conditions, scoliosis and juvenile rheumatoid arthritis, are prevalent in school-aged children and will be presented in greater depth.

Scoliosis

Scoliosis is a spinal deformity seen most commonly in children 10 years or older, but can be found in its congenital form in about 5% of the cases. Scoliosis is defined as any lateral curvature of the spine; 85% of cases are idiopathic (of unknown cause). This curvature is estimated to develop in 5% of teenagers, with female children affected five times more frequently than male children (American Academy of Pediatrics, 1987b; Bunnell, 1986). Scoliosis, in its idiopathic form, often becomes evident during the rapid growth period of preadolescence and early adolescence, justifying in-school screening for scoliosis in grades 5 to 9. Scoliosis may remain undetected unless it is actively searched for, because the spinal curve is not always apparent in the standing position, and pain is not a symptom in a child with this curvature.

The diagnosis of scoliosis can be made by a simple exam, which can be performed effectively by specially trained teachers, nurses, or other health professionals. Key features of the exam are a search for shoulder height symmetry, shoulder blade symmetry, evenness of the hang of the arms, symmetry of the flanks and hips, and straight alignment of the rib cage. The screening exam will identify those children whose spine curvature is abnormal or equivocal; they will then require further evaluation by their personal physician or an orthopedic specialist to confirm the findings. Actual measurement of the degree of the curve is made from x-rays of the back.

Detection and early intervention are important, because the natural history of scoliosis involves a high risk of progression of the curve. Untreated scoliosis can result in cosmetic deformity, physiologic impairment secondary to compression, decreased linear height, and physiologic impairment secondary to compression of chest organs in cases with extreme curves.

Treatment varies according to the magnitude and site of the curve, and the child's proximity to skeletal maturity. Observation, with intermittent clinical and x-ray examinations, is part of the treatment for every case of scoliosis, but a percentage of the children will also require bracing and/or surgery. Those with curvatures documented on x-ray to be between 25 and 40 degrees are candidates for bracing, usually with the Milwaukee brace, which is worn 23 hours a day until bone maturity is reached. The brace fits tightly around the thorax, waist, and upper hips and is worn underneath clothing. Brace treatment for scoliosis has an estimated 85% success rate in preventing significant progression of the curve (American Academy of Pediatrics, 1987b; Bunnell, 1986).

Surgery is a treatment option for those whose curve is 40 to 50 degrees or greater on x-ray, or who have an unacceptable cosmetic appearance. Those children with congenital scoliosis or those with scoliosis in conjunction with a neuromuscular disorder are more likely to require surgery. The procedure involves fusing several bones of the spine, and surgical advances have obviated the need for lengthy body casting. Many children can return to school within 2 to 4 weeks of the procedure (American Academy of Pediatrics, 1987b; Bunnell, 1986).

Juvenile Rheumatoid Arthritis

Unlike rheumatoid arthritis in adults, juvenile rheumatoid arthritis (JRA) is characterized by a wide
spectrum of severity and the involvement of non-
joint organ systems. Its cause remains unknown,
and its onset may be anytime from infancy through
adolescence.

Three distinct types of JRA have been identified: systemic, polyarticular, and pauciarticular.
Systemic JRA makes up about 25% of reported
cases, with more boys affected than girls. It usually
has a sudden onset in very young children or in
late adolescence. Symptoms include spiking fevers, skin rash, and enlargement of the liver,
spleen, and lymph nodes. Sometimes these
symptoms precede the arthritis, which in 25% will
progress to crippling joint problems.

Polyarticular JRA occurs in about 40 to 50%
of children with JRA, with females predominating.
Joint pain, limitation of motion, and swelling involve at least five joints, usually symmetrically.
These children may also demonstrate lethargy,
poor appetite, irritability, and weight loss, with
about 20% developing disabling arthritis.

Pauciarticular JRA, which involves only one to
four joints, affects about one-third of affected
children, again mostly females. These children
seem otherwise healthy and rarely go on to severe
joint disease. However, this subgroup is at especially high risk for iridocyclitis, an insidious asymptomatic visual damage and loss, which can only be
detected by routine ophthalmological follow-up.

The diagnosis is made clinically, with no single
lab test being definitively diagnostic for JRA. A
number of lab tests are used to assess inflammation
and for follow-up purposes. Treatment goals are to
maintain the child's functional capacity and
prevent permanent crippling deformities. The drug
of choice is aspirin, effective in 40 to 60% of
patients with JRA, with doses given with each meal
and at bedtime. Nonsteroidal anti-inflammatory
drugs such as Motrin, Indocin, Tolectin, and others
are used as second-line drugs, both for their
anti-inflammatory properties and, especially, their
analgesic effects. Like aspirin, these may have
abdominal discomfort as a side effect, which can
be lessened if the medication is taken with meals
(Brewer & Arroyo, 1986). In the most refractory
cases of JRA, steroid injections or gold therapy
may be considered, but their higher toxicities
warrant evaluation of their risk–benefit ratio. Daily
physical therapy exercises are crucial for maintaining joint range of motion, but occasionally, orthopedic surgery is necessary to release crippled joints.
Occupational therapy is also of value for the
development of adaptive skills for routine activities
made difficult by the child's disease.

Infectious Diseases

The institution of immunization protocols and the
widespread use of antibiotic therapies have made
infectious illnesses in children milder in nature and
less likely to progress to severe complications.
They continue, however, to be a common cause of
school absences and visits to the physician. In the
United States, less than one child in 2,500 aged 5
to 14 dies each year; 20% of those deaths are from
infections such as influenza, pneumonia, tuberculosis, bacterial meningitis, and gastroenteritis
(American Academy of Pediatrics, 1987b). The
recent epidemic of AIDS may change these percentages as more children are infected neonatally.
Several typical childhood infections are discussed
briefly here, followed by an overview of practices
for infection control in schools. Further information
regarding specific infections can be found in textbooks of pediatric medicine and infectious disease.

Respiratory Infections

Acute respiratory infections are common in children. They can occur at a rate of 4 to 9 per year,
depending on a child's age and contacts. The
causative agent for upper respiratory infections
(colds, tonsillitis, pharyngitis) is rarely known, as
the overwhelming preponderance (90%) of these
illnesses are viral in origin (Denny, 1987). With the
exception of those caused by *group A streptococcus,* they usually require only supportive therapy
for their resolution (Denny, 1987). These diseases,
though, are strikingly communicable by droplet
transmission or exchange of secretions, so the
restricted environment of the classroom makes
passage to fellow students likely. Those children
with chronic disease, poor general health, or those
undergoing stress may be at particular risk for
acquisition of these infections. For example, an
immunosuppressed child with renal failure, leukemia, or AIDS is at an increased risk for complications from what appears to be a trivial illness. An
uncomplicated upper respiratory infection may
include a sore throat, runny nose, watery eyes,
malaise, or fever, and should last 3 to 5 days.
When the symptoms seem extreme or protracted,
the child should be evaluated for the possibility of a

complicating secondary bacterial infection such as otitis media or sinusitis. Antibiotics may be helpful in that circumstance, but otherwise serve no benefit for an upper respiratory infection. Treatment consists of rest, increased fluid intake, adequate humidification of ambient air, and medications to diminish fever and nasal congestion.

Lower respiratory infections (LRI) often present with fever, sore throat, cough, wheezing, or "croup" (a barky cough which sounds like a seal and is accompanied by a hoarse voice). Although the bacteria *Streptococcus pneumoniae* and *Hemophilus influenzae* are occasionally the agents in LRIs, lower-tract infections are caused predominantly by viruses and an agent called *Mycoplasma pneumoniae* (Denny, 1987), whose clinical syndrome is often called "walking pneumonia." The viral infections are usually self-limited, with the acute illness lasting 3 to 7 days, followed by a persistent, but lessening cough. Infections by *Mycoplasma* are characterized by a spasmodic, gagging cough, usually in a child who feels almost well. If untreated, the cough can last as long as 6 weeks, but specific antibiotic therapy can lessen the length of illness for this particular infection. Once again, therapy is, for the most part, supportive; the child should be seen by a physician if her illness seems out of character in severity or persistence of symptoms.

Influenza

Also a viral infection, influenza is marked by a sudden onset of fever, hacking cough, chills, headache, and muscle aches, often occurring within a community epidemic of similar illness. Influenza is most predominant in the months from December to April (Denny, 1987) has a short incubation period of 1 to 3 days, and high infectivity. The fevers associated with influenza may be high (103°) and respond somewhat poorly to the use of acetaminophen. Despite that fact, aspirin should *not* be used in influenza because of its association with the progression to Reye's syndrome, a life-threatening combination of brain swelling, severely low blood sugar, and liver failure (Kauffman & Roberts, 1987). Unless bacterial complications supervene, antibiotics are not helpful in influenza. The severity and the lengthy nature of influenza's symptoms often cause children to miss an entire week of school.

Otitis Media

Otitis media, or middle ear infection, is one of the most common diseases of childhood, with one-third of children having three or more episodes by age 3 (Klein, 1984). Although the incidence of otitis media is greatest in the first 2 years of life, these infections do occur in school-aged children, with 2 to 5% of early school-aged students developing otitis media after an upper respiratory infection (Denny, 1987). The most striking symptom is often pain in the affected ear, but can also present with decreased hearing acuity, irritability, or general malaise. The absence of fever or ear pain does not rule out the possibility of infection, especially in those children who have a past history of recurrent infection and so may have thickened or scarred eardrums. Approximately 70% of the infections are caused by bacteria, and usually show response to oral antibiotic therapy, but the remainder are of viral origin (P. F. Wright, 1984). Unfortunately, there are currently no noninvasive studies to determine which agents are causative, so most children with otitis media are treated with antibiotics.

The infection is triggered by any process that increases accumulation of respiratory secretions in the middle ear cavity or causes Eustachian tube blockage, such as upper respiratory infections or allergies. The fluid builds up in the tiny middle-ear compartment, and in that dark, wet, warm environment, bacteria and viruses are prone to grow. The stasis and infection of the fluid seems promoted if swelling or dysfunction of the eustachian tube prevents egress by normal drainage to the back of the throat. The ear drum stretches and becomes inflamed, causing symptoms. Occasionally, the ear drum will rupture (perforate) under this pressure, and spontaneously drain pus through the outer ear canal.

Prompt diagnosis and therapy are important to prevent chronic accumulation of sticky middle ear fluid and the associated temporary hearing loss. More life-threatening complications such as meningitis and mastoiditis can also be averted by appropriate and timely therapy. Typical treatment is a 10- to 14-day course of oral antibiotic, with or without decongestants, antihistamines, nosedrops, and ambient humidification. For children who suffer from intermittent bouts of otitis, no effects may be noted in school. However, for a subset of children who have recurrent or persistent fluid accumulations, fluctuating hearing abilities secondary to conductive losses may affect school attentiveness and performance. In the case of a persistent hearing deficit, active infection refractory to therapy, or long-standing fluid accumulation, the surgical placement of "tubes" is recommended. This outpatient procedure, performed by an otolaryngologist, serves to drain the middle ear cavity of old secretions and to ventilate that compartment to prevent new fluid collections. Other interventions, such as surgical removal of the adenoids or allergy workup may also be advised for children with unremitting ear disease. There is an increasing body of evidence that points to recurrent otitis media in preschool years as a risk factor for subsequent difficulties in the acquisition of language and academic skills (Public Health Reports, 1986).

Conjunctivitis

Conjunctivitis, also called "pinkeye," is a common contagious infection in school-aged children. Most acute conjunctivitis is bacterial in origin, but viruses, particularly the adenovirus, may account for as much as 20% of the infections (Hammerschlag, 1984). Allergic conjunctivitis can also present acutely on exposure to an allergic stimulus, but is more chronic and recurrent in nature than its bacterial or viral counterparts. Conjunctivitis is, for the most part, a mild infection lasting 3 to 4 days and having no lasting effect on the child's eye or vision. A persistent or particularly severe case of conjunctivitis could indicate inflammation of the cornea, or other important eye pathology, and should be medically evaluated. Additionally, conjunctivitis in the sexually active adolescent or sexually abused child could be caused by chlamydia or gonorrhea transferred from a genital site. These infections require aggressive treatment to prevent eye damage. It is obvious that in these cases there should also be some investigation into how the infection was acquired.

Conjunctivitis, both bacterial and viral, is easily transmissible because secretions from the eye can be passed from student to student on hands, towels, or other shared articles. The secretion can be either clear or purulent (puslike) and may cause eye discomfort and matting or crusting along the lashes. The inflammation of the conjunctiva itself induces swelling of the lids and redness of the white areas of the eye to give a "bloodshot" appearance. Although conjunctivitis is uncomfortable, it should not cause severe eye pain; in that event, the child should be checked for a foreign body, eye trauma, or a deeper structural problem of the eye. Otitis media may coexist in as many as 33% of children with bacterial conjunctivitis and requires oral rather than topical therapy (Hammerschlag, 1984). If the middle ear is not involved, some practitioners will obtain an eye culture to direct their choice of antibiotic therapy, while others may treat empirically with topical antibiotic drops or ointment.

Pharyngitis

Pharyngitis is a general term for infection or inflammation of the throat and its surrounding structures, and may be called tonsillitis. In the school-aged group, viruses cause 10 to 15% of the episodes of pharyngitis, with group A beta-hemolytic streptococcus accounting for 20 to 50% of the cases in ages 6 to 18. In cases of child sexual abuse or adolescent sexual activity, the gonorrhea bacteria can cause pharyngitis and requires a specific culture to detect it. Identification of and therapy for strep infections is also important, to avoid the complications of rheumatic fever or glomerulonephritis. These infections can, respectively, damage heart values and linings and the filtering systems of the kidneys.

A child with pharyngitis may complain of a sore throat, difficulty swallowing, and may or may not have fever or malaise. On examination, the throat may be red, with swollen tonsils, and may show white patches, ulcers, or blisters in the area. A child with a "strep throat" may present with rapid onset of fever, headache, sore throat, swollen glands in the neck, a nosebleed, and occasionally abdominal discomfort. Many viral infections have less impressive symptoms, but these infections cannot be differentiated by history or presentation alone. Even the most skilled clinicians are unable to tell a viral from a bacterial throat infection by mere examination, so it is imperative that testing (throat culture and/or a rapid test for the strep antigen) be performed for appropriate treatment. If the strep germ is identified, antibiotic therapy with penicillin or an appropriate substitution is indicated, usually for a 10-day course. The child is no longer contagious after 24 hours on the antibiotic, but may not feel well until 2 to 3 days after the treatment is begun. Viral infections are self-limited and their course is not altered by antibiotics, but measures such as pain control and cool liquids to drink are comforting. Strep and viral infections are highly contagious and often spread quickly through classrooms.

Diseases with Skin Manifestations

A large number of children's illnesses involve the skin, either primarily or as a component of a disease with multisystem involvement. Although many of these problems are trivial and self-limited, dermatologic findings may also herald serious infections, such as Rocky Mountain spotted fever, meningococcus infection, or other esoteric problems that require timely medical intervention. Accordingly, self-diagnosis of skin rashes by school professionals is not prudent, especially if they present with fever, bruising, or in an ill-appearing child. Only a few common skin rashes will be presented.

Impetigo

Impetigo is a superficial bacterial skin infection, most commonly caused by *Staphylococcus aureus* or *group A beta-hemolytic streptococcus* bacteria. This common skin infection is transmitted by direct contact with its characteristic blisters, and so is easily spread among children. It occurs more often in warm climates with high humidity; poor hygiene and crowding may increase the disease prevalence.

Impetigo, whether caused by staph or strep, is a crusted sore, the crust of which is often honey colored. Depending on which bacteria is involved, the lesion may be completely nontender despite its scablike appearance. The infection may present early with tiny blisters which rapidly progress to the crusted state and quickly spread in size.

The mildest forms of impetigo can respond to good hygiene and topical antibiotics. The treatment of choice, however, for both staph and strep impetigo is oral antibiotic therapy for 7 to 10 days, along with good cleaning of the lesions and the use of a light bandage to diminish transmission (Lookingbill, 1985). The lesions should heal in several days with treatment; medical attention should be sought if they are not responding to the treatment. Impetigo, in some cases, can be confused with herpes infections, scabies, or poison ivy.

Chickenpox

Chickenpox is an extremely contagious viral infection characterized by the progressive appearance of itchy skin blisters which increase in number and distribution over the first 2 to 3 days of the illness. The blisters initially contain clear fluid, which becomes cloudy and then forms a scab. The skin blisters may be accompanied by fever, malaise, and lack of appetite. A student with chickenpox is contagious the day prior to the eruption of the first skin blister and continues to be contagious until all the lesions are scabbed over, which is usually in 1 week. The incubation period is approximately 14 days, and the management of chickenpox consists of cool baths, medications for itching, fever control, and good hygiene to prevent secondary infection. The Food and Drug Administration has strongly urged that, as with influenza, children with chickenpox not be given aspirin-containing medication, to avoid Reye's syndrome (Kauffman & Roberts, 1987). Other rare complications have spurred the development of a chickenpox vaccine, which is especially helpful for those children who are being treated for cancer or are taking steroids.

Scarlet Fever

Scarlet fever is a strep infection accompanied by characteristic "sandpaper" rash, which occurs 1 or 2 days after fever, sore throat, and vomiting. The rash is rough to the touch, and appears as tiny red dots on the skin, especially of the abdomen, groin, and inner bends of the elbow. Like other strep infections, this illness responds well to penicillin therapy, and its treatment helps to prevent rheumatic fever and glomerulonephritis. The illness's incubation period is 2 to 4 days, and its contagious nature makes classroom epidemics likely.

Lice

The tiny parasites called lice are very contagious in group settings and can be found on the scalp, eyelashes, and even pubic hair of children and adolescents. The actual louse itself can occasionally be seen, especially at the nape of a child's neck or in the hair above the ears, but is more often diagnosed by the presence of the eggs (nits) clinging to the hair shaft. The nits are shaped like a miniature piece of white rice, and adhere tenaciously to the hair strand. Exclusion from school until treated is prudent (American Academy of Pediatrics, 1987b). Therapy involves treating the affected hair with a special shampoo or cream rinse, and combing the remaining nits from the hair with a fine-toothed comb. If the medication used is ovicidal (egg killing), the child may return to school with nits visible in the hair.

Gastrointestinal and Parasitic Infections
Infectious Gastroenteritis

Acute infectious gastroenteritis, better known as a "GI bug," is marked by various combinations of symptoms, including nausea, vomiting, abdominal cramps, and diarrhea. Fever is not always present. Although these illnesses can cause dehydration and electrolyte imbalance in infants and toddlers, they are often better tolerated by school-aged children, and resolve within 2 to 6 days without antibiotic therapy. The preponderance of these infections have viral causes. Viral gastroenteritis occurs in small outbreaks, especially in winter months, and treatment is aimed at preventing dehydration. When bacteria are the etiologic agent, the illness may be more lengthy, more severe, and accompanied by bloody diarrhea, often with dehydration. The illness must be distinguished from more severe abdominal problems, which may present with unrelenting, localized abdominal pain in a child who becomes progressively worse. In these instances the child should be assessed by a physician.

Giardia

Giardia is most commonly reported parasitic pathogen in the United States with prevalence rates from 3 to 13% (Turner, 1985). Although it is most often found in children in day care centers and in male homosexuals, it is also common in schoolchildren, who may have acquired parasites from younger siblings or from contaminated water sources such as creeks, streams, or even well water. Giardia infection occurs when the giardia cysts are ingested by food or water contamination, person-to-person transmission, or possibly from dogs and cats (Turner, 1985). The symptoms of giardia in a school-aged child are abdominal cramping, intermittent diarrhea, and flatulence. The child's stools may be particularly foul smelling, and the student may lose weight or have intermittent low-grade fevers. The best diagnostic test is a series of three fecal examinations to search for the parasite and its cysts. Although giardia can resolve spontaneously, treatment with specific oral therapy

for 5 to 10 days should be given to diminish symptoms and transmission. Good handwashing is critical in preventing spread in schools.

Urinary Tract Infections

Urinary tract infections (UTI) are a common acute illness of childhood, with approximately 3 to 5% of girls having one episode of UTI before puberty (Edelmann, 1988). Their importance, however, should not be underestimated. Irreversible kidney damage can occur from a seemingly simple infection, especially if the child has a functional or structural abnormality of the urinary tract. As many as 25% of school-aged girls with a urinary tract infection may have abnormal function of the bladder or ureters, called vesicoureteral reflux. Reflux causes urine to move backward through the system toward the kidneys, rather than being expelled through the bladder. Obstructions by abnormal structures, like reflux, increase the likelihood of kidney damage, which occurs in 1 to 2% of girls with UTI and in 10% of the boys who are infected (Edelmann, 1988).

Infected children often present with pain on urination, frequent voiding, an urgency to urinate, and lower abdominal discomfort. A low-grade fever may be present, and the child's urine may be foul smelling or contain blood. A urinalysis and urine culture are critical to determine the causative bacteria, which is often from the nearby gastrointestinal tract. The appropriate antibiotic is chosen on the basis of the bacterial culture results. A 10-day course of antibiotics is typical, with a repeat urine culture documenting bacterial clearing when the medication is completed. Due to the high incidence and serious implications of a structural or functional abnormality, when the infection is cleared a number of x-ray and/or ultrasound procedures are recommended to evaluate the urinary tract. Aggressive diagnosis and management of UTIs will aid in the prevention of chronic renal disease, which can progress to the need for a kidney transplant.

Control of Infections in the School Setting

Effective measures for prevention of and decrease of the spread of communicable diseases in schools include ensuring immunization, sanitation, surveillance for tuberculosis, and occasionally, mass treatment (American Academy of Pediatrics, 1987b). Basic sanitary practices include good handwashing, provision for proper food storage, preparatory facilities and waste disposal, clean drinking water supplies, and proper disposal methods for bodily secretions. Equally critical are readily available facilities for handwashing and laundering of gym and athletic clothing (American Academy of Pediatrics, 1987b). For some illnesses, such as infectious hepatitis, measles or chickenpox, immunization after exposure is valuable. In the event of exposure to a student with meningitis, the need for preventive treatment is assessed by the causative agent and proximity of exposure, and should be decided with the help of the health department and the child's personal physician.

Children with serious infectious diseases, impetigo, scabies, body or head lice, and conjunctivitis, should be excluded from school until they have received treatment (American Academy of Pediatrics, 1987b). In general, the exclusion from school activities during an illness is reasonable, but in many instances, the infection has already spread by the time a child's first symptoms appear. For most viral illnesses, the child can return to school when the symptoms are resolved. The communicability of a child's bacterial infection can be limited by prompt treatment of the child.

Chronic Respiratory Disease

Beyond the occasional respiratory infection, a number of children and adolescents in our schools will suffer from a chronic lung disease, which can be recurrent, disabling, and have major effects on school performance. Two such illnesses, asthma and cystic fibrosis, will be discussed.

Asthma

Asthma is one of the most common childhood illnesses. In school-aged children, prevalence rates for asthma in the United States are up to 12%, with the highest rates among blacks, Hispanics, and males (American Academy of Pediatrics, 1987b).

Asthma is a lung disorder which is marked by intermittent episodes of airway obstruction, brought on by airway narrowing, swelling of airway linings, and production of viscous secretions. These changes can be triggered by viral infection, exposure to an allergic agent, exercise, cold, or psychological stresses. The results are wheezing and shortness of breath, where the child has difficulty expiring and, possibly, inspiring, depending on the severity of the attack. A student with asthma may or may not have other allergic disorders, such as allergic rhinitis or eczema. Some asthmatics remain on medication year-round, but those whose attacks are more seasonal use their medications only when they have symptoms.

School professionals should be aware of the medications used for asthma therapy, because many of these drugs have side effects that are manifested in the classroom. Theophylline and its derivatives are used orally for asthmatics and can cause faster heart rate, hyperactivity, talkativeness, and decreased attentiveness, especially when the medication is just being started. Other agents, such as metaproterenol (Metaprel, Alupent) or albuterol (Ventolin, Proventil), can create similar behavioral changes when taken orally or by inhalation. Children with severe asthma may require inhaled steroids or Cromolyn, which aim at decreasing the inflammation and allergic response of the child's airways.

Asthma is a major cause of school absenteeism (Hen, 1986). Like any other chronic childhood disease, it can set the stage for pathologic interaction in the family, promote a "sick" role, and negatively affect school performance. It is ideal to have the child's asthma managed by a team of physicians who are familiar with the child and his family in order to maximize the child's medical stability, promote an attitude of wellness, and avoid relapses and hospitalizations.

Cystic Fibrosis

Cystic fibrosis (CF) is the most common lethal inherited disorder in the United States today, and is estimated to occur once per 1,500 to 2,000 live births (Denning, 1983). The cause of CF, with its chronic lung disease and poor pancreatic function is unknown, but is felt to be an inborn defect in metabolism that is genetically transmitted through family lines. The disease affects primarily white populations, with only 1 to 2% of cases in blacks (Denning, 1983). The child with CF, depending on the severity of the disease, may be quite thin and pale, with a barrel-shaped chest and protuberant abdomen. He may be cyanotic (blue) from a decreased blood oxygen level if the disease is advanced, and if so, rounding of the fingertips and nailbeds (clubbing) can be noted. Stamina and exercise tolerance are likely to be poor.

Cystic fibrosis mainly affects the respiratory and digestive systems, but also can involve the sinuses, liver, and reproductive systems. Accordingly, the disease can present with a wide range of manifestations, including chronic cough; recurrent infections; wheezing, rapid, or labored breathing; loose, foul-smelling stools; recurrent abdominal pain; or poor growth. The diagnosis of cystic fibrosis is confirmed by a specific test called a "sweat test" in which sodium and chloride levels are quantified in a sample of the child's sweat and found to be abnormally high (positive) in more than 99% of patients with CF. For a child with CF, respiratory mucus is thicker than normal and more prone to block airways and promote chronic infection. These students may have a deep, productive cough and usually require a rigorous daily program of chest physical therapy and medications to assist in thinning and clearing their secretions.

Eighty-five to 90% of children with CF have abnormal function of the pancreas, whose enzymes are essential to the digestion and absorption of food (Denning, 1983). As a result, fats and some vitamins are partially assimilated by the body, requiring that students with CF consume at least 50% more calories than are needed by their age- and sex-matched peers. A high-protein, low-fat diet, together with vitamin and enzyme supplements, helps prevent loss of nutrition in the stools.

School absences are higher than the norm, and many of these children will require intermittent hospitalizations to adjust medications, treat infection, and address the nutritional deficiencies that are inherent in CF. Needless to say, the physical disabilities of CF and its complex therapies are incredibly stressful to the child and the family, especially since there is presently no cure for the disease.

Allergic Disorders

Children's allergies have a broad range of causes and a similarly wide spectrum of clinical manifestations. Only a few of the most common disorders will be discussed.

"Hay Fever" or Allergic Rhinitis

The most common cause of chronic nasal congestion in children is allergic rhinitis. In the United States, this condition occurs in 6 million children and causes 2 million days of school absences per year (Shapiro, 1986). Allergic rhinitis may occur year round, or may affect a child only seasonally, with worsening in the spring, summer, or fall. There are endless numbers of allergens (allergic

triggers) but the most prevalent ones are the house dust mite, molds, and pet antigens found in dander and saliva; these are also the most difficult offending agents to remove from the environment. Food allergies are unlikely to present as allergic rhinitis alone.

A child with allergic rhinitis may show obvious symptoms, such as repeated sneezing, persistent clear nasal discharge, or nasal itching. An "allergic salute," the gesture of rubbing the hand upward to scratch an itchy nose, may be combined with puffy eyes or dark circles beneath the eyes, which are caused by swollen veins in the thin tissues below the eye. A student who suffers with the chronic nasal obstruction caused by allergic rhinitis may also breathe predominately through his mouth, creating a "fish-mouthed" facial appearance. Less classic presentations for children with allergic rhinitis can be repeated bouts of sinusitis or otitis, which may translate clinically into a chronic purulent rhinitis and persistent cough or wheezing. The palate of a child with allergic rhinitis is often itchy and may trigger clucking or throat-clearing mannerisms in an attempt to relieve the discomfort.

The aggressiveness of therapy for allergic rhinitis is proportional to the severity of the symptoms and can involve alteration of the child's environment, oral medications, nasal sprays, and/or a program of immunotherapy (allergy shots). It is helpful to diminish allergic challenges by changing features of the home, such as bedding and carpeting. Exposure to mold in basements, damp areas, or poorly ventilated buildings can be avoided, as can interaction with tobacco smoke and pets. For many children, environmental control may involve changes in both their primary residence and those of babysitters or a divorced parent. Medications are introduced if decreased exposure to allergens does not give adequate improvement of symptoms. It is important for a child's teacher to know if the student is taking oral antihistamines or decongestants, because the drowsiness or hyperactivity they can cause may drastically affect school performance. A trend toward the use of topical nasal sprays has been valuable in decreasing adverse effects. The child with the most refractory symptoms may require the input of a pediatric allergist who, with allergy testing, can pinpoint the child's worst allergies and consider immunotherapy. Also called desensitization, this ongoing series of allergy shots gradually exposes the child to those things to which she is most allergic, with the goal of building tolerance to those agents.

Eczema

Eczema is a chronic skin condition which may appear in infancy and persist through childhood, with relapses and remissions. It is more common in those children with food allergies, hay fever, or asthma. It can also appear without other allergic manifestations, especially if the child is bathed excessively or routinely has lengthy water exposure (i.e., swimmers) (Krafchik, 1983).

Redness, scaling, and dryness characterize the rash of eczema, which is often found on the elbows, knees, and face and neck of affected children. The rash is accompanied by intense itching and the child's scratching dries and thickens the skin, thus worsening the cycle. Eczema may worsen in the winter months and requires ongoing therapy of skin lubrication, medications to control itching, and steroid ointments to decrease inflammation.

Blood Disorders

Cancers of the blood system and abnormalities of blood cells are chronic diseases whose impact is clearly visible on the affected student. Leukemia, hemophilia, and sickle cell anemia will be discussed.

Leukemia

The most common malignancy of childhood, acute leukemia, is diagnosed in approximately 2,000 children per year in the United States. Prior to recent advances in chemotherapy, the affected child had a uniformly fatal disease, whereas 5-year survival in complete remission is presently at 55% (Diamond & Matthay, 1988). The disease occurs almost twice as often in white as in nonwhite children and is more common in boys than in girls (Poplack, 1985).

Leukemia is a cancer of the blood cells whose characteristic is uncontrolled growth and multiplication of young white blood cells, most commonly of the lymphocyte (acute lymphoblastic leukemia). The changes in the blood cells become apparent in the child because of the decreased number and poor function of the white blood cells, red blood cells, or platelets. Accordingly, a student might present with fatigue, weight loss, pallor, easy bruising, broken blood vessels in the skin (petechiae), bleeding, bone pain, or fever. If the disease has spread outside the bone marrow, the child may

have swollen lymph glands or an enlarged liver or spleen. The child's symptoms can appear suddenly or evolve over weeks to months, making the diagnosis difficult to pin down. Because other childhood diseases, such as infectious mononucleosis, can have a similar presentation, a complete blood count and bone marrow aspirate and biopsy are often used to be certain of the diagnosis of leukemia. Once the initial diagnosis is confirmed, other tests, such as x-rays, a lumbar puncture, and specific cell-type studies, will help determine the child's prognosis and treatment plan. Features that have been found to correlate with a favorable prognosis are a low white blood cell count at presentation and an age between 2 and 10 years at the time of the diagnosis (Diamond, 1988). Children with poorer prognostic features are treated with more aggressive therapeutic protocols. Combination chemotherapy and radiation are the main components of therapy, with remission (reduction and obliteration of tumor cells) being the goal of initial treatment. Thereafter, the child will likely have preventive therapy to avoid involvement of the brain and spinal cord, and a lengthy regimen of maintenance therapy to prevent reemergence of the tumor cells.

For a child with leukemia, the therapies involve side effects and, consequently, school absences. Chemotherapy is associated with nausea, vomiting, hair loss, and mouth ulcers. Radiation can also cause hair loss and superficial skin burns on the irradiated sites. Because the process of destroying tumor cells also damages healthy blood cells, the child in therapy is at high risk for infection, and a typical childhood disease (chickenpox, strep throat) can be life threatening.

Although survival has remarkably improved for children with leukemia, the responsible therapies may carry significant repercussions later. Chemotherapy can have long-term effects on liver function, and central nervous system preventive treatments can be associated with subtle neurologic and intellectual changes. At present, the reproductive capacities of children treated with conventional protocols appear intact. The risk of a second malignancy is somewhat increased in later life (Diamond and Matthay, 1988).

Hemophilia

Hemophilia is actually a pair of genetically inherited bleeding disorders, caused by decreased levels of blood clotting factors VIII and IX. Hemophilia is transmitted in an X-linked recessive genetic pattern; therefore, males are affected and females are carriers of the disease. The incidence rate is 1 : 10,000 males in the entire population (Karayalcin, 1985). The degree of deficit of clotting factors defines the disease as mild, moderate, or severe, and it helps predict the type and magnitude of hemorrhages. Children with mild hemophilia may not be diagnosed until later in life, when moderate to severe trauma or surgery elicits hemorrhage, whereas the 50 to 70% with severe hemophilia are usually detected prenatally or in infancy (Karayalcin, 1985). The diagnosis is confirmed by specific blood tests.

A schoolchild with hemophilia may have nosebleeds, bleeding of the gums or GI tract, blood in the urine, or more commonly, painful bleeding into muscles or joints. For children involved in active play, the joints involved (in order of frequency) are elbows, ankles, shoulders, hips, and wrists (Karayalcin, 1985). The bleeding may be spontaneous or associated with trauma, and it must be treated to avoid joint damage and scarring.

Treatment programs for children with hemophilia vary, but most involve replacement of the lacking clotting factors by administration of components of blood products, and the use of steroids to decrease inflammation. A relatively new risk to hemophiliacs is the exposure to blood-borne diseases such as hepatitis B and AIDS because of necessary repeated exposure to blood products. Advances being made in blood screening and alternate therapies will hopefully reduce this threat.

Sickle Cell Disease

Sickle cell disease is an inherited, presently incurable blood disorder caused by abnormal structure of the hemoglobin molecule in the red blood cell. Sickle cell disease occurs in one of every 500 to 800 black newborns but may not become clinically important until 4 to 6 months of age or older (Pearson, 1987). The abnormal red blood cells are fragile and have a short survival rate in the body, and their "sickle" shape blocks their routine passage through the body's small blood vessels. These aberrations lead to chronic anemia and to recurrent episodes of occluded blood supply to important organs, such as the liver, kidney, lungs, bone, spleen, eye, and brain. For a child with sickle cell disease, the triggers of these episodes of occluded

blood supply are unclear, but fever, dehydration, and viral infections have been associated with them (Pearson, 1987).

A child with sickle cell disease who complains of severe pain or develops fever should seek immediate medical attention. The splenic scarring from tangled sickle cells puts the affected child at high risk for severe bacterial infection and necessitates occasional hospitalization for intravenous fluids, transfusions, antibiotics, and pain control. Such setbacks contribute to school absenteeism and add stresses to these children, who are often small and have poor exercise tolerance and stamina.

Diabetes

As the third most common chronic illness in schoolchildren, diabetes mellitus (type I) affects 1.3 children per thousand in the United States (Chase, 1985). This disease results from decreased or absent production of insulin by the pancreas. Over the long term, the attendant fluctuations of blood sugar levels put the child at risk for growth failure, cataract formation, blood vessel damage to the eye and kidney, joint and skin changes, and early heart disease.

Treatment for diabetes includes insulin therapy, monitoring of blood and urine glucose levels, and the balancing of diet and exercise to keep blood sugar in a near-normal range. To implement this therapeutic plan, the child must have fairly regular meals, the equipment and skills to test blood sugar levels as much as three to four times per day, and must anticipate the amount of exercise to calculate an insulin dose for the day (Chase, 1985). In an attempt to simulate the second-to-second regulation of blood glucose by the normal pancreas' insulin, the child is administered insulin by subcutaneous injection intermittently throughout the day, or in some cases, by a small continuous infusion pump that the child wears on his belt. The child's diabetic diet avoids simple sugars, but most students can eat school lunches and can definitely participate in gym and sports by adjusting insulin doses. The management of this complex disease demands close communication between the child, the family, the school, and the child's health care team. Teachers should be educated to recognize signs of abnormally low or high blood sugar levels and have an emergency plan to handle these potential problems.

Cardiovascular Disorders

Children's heart disorders are of two types, congenital and acquired. The congenital defects are present at the time of birth, and occurred in the embryo, during the heart's formation at about the seventh week of gestation. Although these defects exist neonatally, they may become clinically apparent much later or only be detected on a physical examination, depending on the complexity of the abnormality. The acquired problems of the heart are much less common; they include rheumatic heart disease, hypertension, arteriosclerosis or damage to the heart function by infection, trauma, or systemic disease.

Congenital heart defects involve abnormalities of the structures of the heart which cause obstruction of blood flow through the normal paths of the heart or improper routing of the blood through the heart's chambers and blood vessels. No specific cause can be found for most inborn cardiac defects, but heart disease is known to be present in 40% of children with Down's syndrome and is also a component of fetal alcohol syndrome (Spicer, 1984). Advances in technology for diagnosis of congenital heart defects include prenatal ultrasound and echocardiography, along with Doppler, which permits study of the blood flow patterns in the heart. These advances, plus highly sophisticated surgical interventions, have greatly improved the prognosis for affected children, permitting many of them to attend school, play actively, and lead normal lives.

Congenital heart disease encompasses acyanotic defects (those that do not cause blueness or lack of oxygen) and cyanotic disease (which is marked by blueness of the lips, skin, and nailbeds). In general, the acyanotic abnormalities are less severe and include atrial septal or ventricular septal defects (opening in the wall between the two atria or ventricles), valve stenosis or insufficiency (tightness or leakage of a heart valve), or abnormalities of the blood vessels surrounding the heart. In infants born prematurely, persistence of a fetal blood vessel, called PDA, occurs in 20%, with the incidence increasing with the degree of prematurity (Dooley, 1984). Many children with acyanotic heart disease will not require cardiac surgery to repair their defect, but will require intermittent medical reevaluation and a special regimen of preventive antibiotics prior to dental or surgical procedures. These antibiotics help prevent endocarditis (i.e., bacterial infection within the heart).

A majority of children with cyanotic disease will require one or more surgical procedures to correct or improve the abnormal flow of blood within the heart. Children with cyanotic defects often have combinations of abnormalities, each of which must be repaired or palliated. These children require close medical follow-up, endocarditis prophylaxis, and, in a few cases, activity restriction.

A child with congenital heart disease may appear and function completely normally. Others, though, may have poor exercise tolerance or tire before their peers. They may have more lung or respiratory infections than their contemporaries and may take cardiac medications such as Digoxin or Lasix to improve their heart function. Most pediatric cardiologists will impose the fewest possible restrictions on their patient's activities but will ask that the child be permitted to self-restrict if he is having difficulty sustaining an activity.

Children with acquired heart disease usually have been born with healthy hearts. Rheumatic heart disease, which has been known to follow in the wake of an untreated strep infection, has shown a recent resurgence. The infection damages heart valves and linings and so can induce valve deformity, with obstruction or leakage across the valve. Antistreptococcal antibiotics, the treatment of choice, almost obliterated this disease, which was prevalent in the early part of the 20th century; its reemergence is not fully explained.

Another acquired cardiac problem that has been highlighted recently is the detection and management of abnormal cholesterol levels in children. High cholesterol levels along with risk factors such as diet, smoking, and lack of exercise are known precursors to arteriosclerosis and coronary artery disease. The American Academy of Pediatrics and American Heart Association are collaborating to make cogent recommendations regarding details of dietary and screening tenets (Strong & Dennison, 1988). In concert with these efforts, pediatricians are focusing efforts to detect elevations of blood pressure in children, especially those who have a strong family history of hypertension. Weight control, mild salt restriction and general life-style changes may prevent heart disease and blood vessel damage in these children.

AIDS

Since 1982, when the first case of AIDS was diagnosed in a pediatric patient, the number of infected children has steadily increased to a total of approximately 1,000 cases in the United States in children less than 13 years of age (Roger, 1988). For the majority of children, their infection is acquired from their infected mothers at birth or by the receipt of contaminated blood or blood products, although intravenous drug usage and sexual transmission are common sources of infection in the adolescent age group (Roger, 1988).

Children with AIDS are likely to present with failure to thrive, recurrent severe bacterial infections, and often with enlarged liver, spleen, or lymph nodes. Also, as many as 50 to 90% will have central nervous system dysfunction and developmental delays or regressions (Scott, 1988). The nature of the disease is to progress to multisystem involvement, and accordingly, the prognosis is grim. Present overall mortality is quoted at 61%, with those children diagnosed at less than 1 year of age having the poorest survival rate (Scott, 1988).

The estimates by the U.S. Public Health Service are that by 1991 there will be approximately 3,200 cases of AIDS in children; pediatric AIDS has currently been reported in 40 states (Roger, 1988). With those data in mind, it is critical for school personnel to know that "there have been no reported cases of transmission of HIV (human immunodeficiency virus) within the school or day care setting and no reports of casual transmission" (American Academy of Pediatrics, 1987b). Presently, the American Academy of Pediatrics (1987b) feels that the majority of school-aged children with AIDS who are neurologically intact can safely attend school without fear of transmission to class members (American Academy of Pediatrics, 1987b). The subset of infected children who are neurologically disabled, who drool, who control secretions poorly, or who have open wounds require more specific isolation. More information on this, and a list of precautions for the infected child, are presented in greater depth in the American Academy of Pediatrics publication on *School Health* (1987b).

Substance Abuse

Abuse of tobacco, alcohol, and drugs has emerged as major health risk for adolescents and preteens in the United States. National surveys done in 1984 showed that 66% of our young people regularly used alcohol, and 30% smoked cigarettes routinely (Macdonald, 1987). In 1985, 61% of high school seniors admitted to having used illicit drugs, with 40% identifying the use of an illegal drug other than marijuana (Macdonald, 1987). Efforts to combat substance abuse are being generated from many groups, but the school professional is in a unique position to detect drug use, abuse, and make the proper referrals to initiate therapy.

Cigarettes

From age 12 to 16 years, the risk of beginning to smoke cigarettes steadily increases (Silvis & Perry, 1987). The addictiveness of nicotine is so significant that two completely smoked cigarettes and the surmounting of smoking's initial noxious effects will convince 85% of experimenting teens to become regular smokers (Silvis & Perry, 1987). Cigarettes are used by teenagers more than any other class of drugs, with trials at smoking reported by over 50% of those between the ages of 12 and 17 years (Macdonald, 1987).

A causative link has been demonstrated between smoking and lung cancer, chronic lung disease, bladder cancer, heart disease, and growth retardation of infants whose mother smoked during pregnancy (Silvis & Perry, 1987). Adolescents who smoke are prone to develop bronchitis and sinusitis, and those with underlying allergies or asthma will find those problems exacerbated by smoking.

The influential predictors of adolescent smoking are first, peer influence, and second, parental smoking (Silvis & Perry, 1987). Smoking in students can be one of the earliest signals of upcoming behavioral difficulties, and may help identify the adolescent who is at risk for problems with self-esteem, rebelliousness, and future drug abuse. School professionals can be exceedingly valuable in educating students about the health risks of smoking and can decrease the amount of smoking done away from home by outlawing it on school grounds. For the student who is already addicted to smoking, "stop-smoking" courses can be offered through the schools, not only for students but also for teachers.

Alcohol

With the knowledge that two-thirds of our teenagers are using alcohol on at least an occasional basis, the identification of the problem user becomes a key issue. Certainly, the extent to which the student uses alcohol is important, but other factors to be considered are the magnitude of negative consequences in the student's life as a function of their alcohol abuse. Worrisome indicators are persistent alcohol-seeking behavior, changes in school attendance, performance or peer group, and abandonment of previous interests, such as sports or extracurricular activities. From a medical viewpoint, accidents occurring while intoxicated, gastrointestinal problems, and blackout episodes are red flags for alcohol abuse. Legal altercations, alcohol-related traffic violations, and family conflict regarding the student's alcohol use are still more convincing evidence of abuse. There is a genetic predisposition toward alcoholism, and this, combined with environmental stressors, can be a springboard for alcohol abuse. Thus, a family history of chemical dependency on alcohol or other drugs is important information for anyone who is trying to help the student who is abusing alcohol. School-based support groups, referral to inpatient or outpatient treatment programs, and programs to identify the student at risk are all feasible attacks on the very real problem of adolescent alcohol abuse.

Drug Abuse

In the mid-to-late 1970s, drug use and abuse in adolescents increased dramatically (Macdonald, 1987), as did the list of drugs involved. By 1979 the steady rise in drug abuse stabilized, and since then has shown a gradual overall decline (Macdonald, 1979), although it still represents a major source of psychological, behavioral, and physical pathology for adolescents. Marijuana remains the most commonly used illicit drug among teens (Macdonald, 1987), but cocaine has shown the most rapid increase in its prevalence of use (Mofenson, Copeland, & Caraccio, 1986). Amphetamines, LSD, PCP (phencyclidine), tranquilizers, opiates, methaqualone, and even jimson weed have been used as psychoactive drugs.

Of graduating high school seniors in the United States, 60% have smoked marijuana at least once, with as many as 5% using marijuana daily (Schwartz, 1987). Composed of the seeds, leaves, and stems of the hemp plant, marijuana has been cultured to an increased potency, with its active ingredient, Δ^9-tetrahydrocannabinol (Δ^9THC), almost tripled in amount since 1975 (Schwartz, 1987). Marijuana is usually smoked, although it is sometimes eaten in a food which has an oil base to utilize the drug's solubility in fat. The drug's psychoactive effects, which include euphoria, disinhibition, impaired short-term memory, and changes in perception of temporal, auditory,

and visual stimuli, usually begin in minutes after the drug is smoked, and in $\frac{1}{2}$ to 2 hours after the drug is ingested (Schwartz, 1987). Because of its fat solubility, marijuana is stored in body fats, so its breakdown products can be detected in the urine 2 to 3 days after one use, and weeks after long-term use of the drug (Schwartz, 1987).

The immediate physical findings of marijuana intoxication are irritation of the conjunctiva, increased heart rate, and increased appetite and thirst; chronic usage can lead to bronchitis and to sinus and nasal irritation. Marijuana, repeatedly used, can lead to "the amotivational syndrome" (Schwartz, 1987), which is marked by physical and mental lethargy, withdrawal from purposeful and social activities, decreased creativity and goal seeking, and a false sense of accomplishment. As with all substance abuse, psychological dysfunction, family conflict, and lags in normal adolescent development occur with the abuse of marijuana. Fifty percent of those adolescents who use marijuana as teens will progress to the use of other illicit drugs. Thus, marijuana, along with alcohol and tobacco, is considered a "gateway drug" (Macdonald, 1987).

Cocaine and "crack" (a purer, more concentrated form of cocaine) may be a next step for the adolescent using "gateway drugs." A 1985 study in Michigan reported that 17% of the high school senior class had tried cocaine (Tarr & Macklin, 1987). Cocaine, unlike marijuana, is physically addictive and has striking medical risks even with acute usage. Cocaine and crack are powerful stimulants of the central nervous system, and mimic the physiologic effects of adrenalin on the body, causing increases in heart rate, blood pressure, and body temperature. These changes can result in stroke, seizures, heart attack, rhythm disturbances of the heart, and/or cessation of breathing (Tarr & Macklin, 1987).

Cocaine hydrochloride (HC1) is usually taken intranasally ("snorted"), and crack is smoked, so their medical side effects differ. Cocaine HC1 causes upper respiratory symptoms, nasal congestion, nosebleed and sinus infections, whereas crack's effects on the lungs are apparent in a chronic cough, chest pain, and production of black or bloody secretions on coughing. When cocaine HC1 is used intravenously, infection at the injection site, bacterial infections in the bloodstream, endocarditis, hepatitis B, and AIDS can be added to the growing list of risks (Tarr & Macklin, 1987).

Along with the physical manifestations of these drugs' abuse, rapid mood swings, personality changes, and alterations in peer group structure and interaction can be apparent in the adolescent using cocaine or crack. With cocaine, the onset of exhilaration, euphoria, and marked self-confidence is within 1 to 5 minutes of its intranasal use and lasts 60 to 70 minutes; the adolescent smoking crack may sense these changes within seconds and be depressed and anxious 5 to 7 minutes after use (Mofenson et al., 1986). These striking mood alterations and their short duration are felt to contribute to the extraordinarily high addictive potential of cocaine and crack, and make these drugs particularly menacing to an adolescent suffering from depression, exogenous stresses, or psychological problems.

Eating Disorders

As many as 5 to 10% of adolescent girls and young women have anorexia nervosa or bulimia (Herzog & Copeland, 1985). Although both of these eating disorders involve weight fluctuations and preoccupation with food and eating, they differ in demography, natural history, clinical presentation, and psychological state.

Anorexia nervosa's essential features are marked weight loss, intense fears of becoming obese, altered body image, and usually amenorrhea (cessation of menstrual periods), when no medical illness can be found as a cause for these symptoms (Herzog & Copeland, 1985). Anorexia nervosa often begins in early teenage years, either acutely or gradually, with severe restriction of food intake and excessive and compulsive exercising with or without the use of self-induced vomiting, diuretics, or laxatives to attain a progressively lower weight. These girls (Herzog & Copeland, 1985, report that only 5 to 10% of patients with eating disorders are male) perceive their bodies as heavier than they are and may participate in sports such as ballet or track which reward thinness. They may show compulsive trends in their eating or exercising, counting calories and pushups meticulously, and often show similar attention to detail in school work and personal appearance. Classically, the anorectic girl has a history of being a model daughter, a good student, and has a sibling who has been the family "troublemaker." Common motifs in the anorectic's life are failure to attain normal developmental phases (especially in regard to sexuality), depression, and family dysfunction (Herzog & Copeland, 1985). These females are at psychological risk as well as physical risk from their disease, as 2 to 5% of those with chronic anorexia commit suicide (Herzog & Copeland, 1985).

Anorexia nervosa affects secretion of sexual hormones, resulting in amenorrhea and inhibition of ovulation, and also of growth and thyroid hormones. Other medical problems can be difficulty with temperature regulation, anemia, osteoporosis, slowed heart rate and irregular rhythms, and kidney dysfunction, resulting from starvation.

The therapy for anorexia nervosa is multifaceted and fraught with setbacks and denial from both the girl and her family. Clearly, her medical status must first be addressed to assure her immediate safety, but then a program of individual and family psychotherapy, along with dietary and medical input, must be pursued. Many anorectics will require inpatient therapy to address their difficulties.

Girls with bulimia are more likely to have periods and to be socially stable. Although their weight fluctuates, generally it does not drop to the critically low levels seen in anorexia nervosa. Typically, their disorder starts later in adolescence, often after attempts at traditional diets have failed (Herzog, 1982). The bulimic then discovers that laxative and diuretic abuse and self-induced vomiting (purging), alternating with episodes of "binging" (often on "junk food") serves to control weight while permitting out-of-control eating behaviors. The episodes of purging are usually associated with feelings of shame and poor self-esteem.

The bulimics' medical problems are usually related more to their vomiting behaviors than to their weight loss. These females may erode the enamel on their teeth from repeated exposure to stomach acid, develop esophageal inflammation and tears, and even suffer stomach rupture from recurrent vomiting. Laxatives and diuretics can cause abnormalities of sodium and potassium balance, and associated abnormal heart rhythms. As with anorexia, depression frequently accompanies bulimia, and a multidisciplinary approach is needed for treatment.

The school professional should be alert for subtle signals such as independent study projects chosen on eating disorders, intense interest in calories or nutrition, or repeated disparaging remarks by a student about her own body.

Sexually Transmitted Diseases

In 1984, a study of male and female adolescents stated that 70% of these teenagers had sexual intercourse by their 19th birthday (Shafer, 1984). These sexually active adolescents are in a high risk group for sexual infections because of multiple partners, and the females have been shown to be more prone than the adult woman to develop internal complications from their infections, such as pelvic inflammatory disease. It is not unusual for an adolescent to have several sexually transmitted diseases (STDs) at one time, so the suspicion or discovery of one infection should trigger a search for others. Although both males and females are infected with STDs, the female is often the symptomatic partner or the one who seeks health care, so males may remain untreated and continue to propagate their diseases with future partners.

The most prevalent STD in the United States today are those infections caused by the organism chlamydia (Centers for Disease Control, 1985, pp. 8–85). Estimates vary among groups tested, but incidence of infection with chlamydia in sexually active adolescents has been quoted at 4 to 37% (Frau & Alexander, 1985). The majority of cases of chlamydial infection, even those involving the uterus, fallopian tubes, or epididymis, are asymptomatic (Frau & Alexander, 1985). If untreated, this infection can scar fallopian tubes in females and the epididymis in males, causing later infertility. Because of the relative lack of symptoms, it is wise for sexually active adolescents to be checked routinely for chlamydia, and if found, to treat both partners with oral antibiotics.

Gonorrhea, too, can be asymptomatic, but may present with vaginal or penile discharge, or pain on urination. The incidence of gonorrhea again varies with the study population, but it is quoted at 1 at 10% (Frau & Alexander, 1985). Like chlamydia, gonorrhea can cause deeply damaging infections in the pelvic organs of the female, and the bacteria can spread to other parts of the body causing arthritis, heart valve damage, pharyngitis, and rectal and skin infections in both males and females. Both chlamydia and gonorrhea can be treated well orally if compliance with the medical regimen can be assured. Of the 5 to 25 million Americans infected with genital herpes virus, 25 to 50% are adolescents (Neinstein, 1984a). In contrast with chlamydia and gonorrhjea, herpes is a life-long infection that can not be cured. The herpes type II virus infects the skin of the genital organs and causes many painful blisters to form, which in the first episode, can last 10 to 14 days. Thereafter, the virus remains dormant in the nerve roots of the area and intermittently erupts again with similar vesicles which are smaller and fewer than in the initial bout. These recurrences can occur at any time, and are felt to have triggers, such as stress, menstrual periods, and local trauma. The blisters themselves are very infectious to sexual partners, so sexual intercourse with an active infection can lead to transmission of the disease.

One drug, acyclovir, has been used for the management of primary and secondary infections by the herpes virus. It does not cure the infection, but does decrease the duration of the attack and the magnitude of the symptoms during it (Neinstein, 1984a). Currently, research is in progress to find ways to reduce the recurrence rates of herpes outbreaks. Again, the sexual styles of adolescents—multiple partners, lack of abstinence during infection, and poor compliance with medical therapies—have contributed to the wide spread of herpes in young people.

It is important to note that each of the three STDs presented can have damaging effects on the fetus and newborn, so detection and management of the infections is especially critical in the pregnant adolescent. Other STDs, such as syphilis, trichomonas, and human papilloma virus infection, exist in adolescents and should be searched for in those who are sexually involved.

Adolescent Pregnancy and Contraception

More than 1 million teenagers become pregnant each year, with approximately one-half of those continuing their pregnancies to delivery (Weitzman, 1987). Almost three-fourths are unintentional pregnancies, and one-third are terminated in induced abortion (Neinstein, 1984b).

The education of teenagers about the available contraceptive methods, their acquisition, and use has been strongly encouraged by both the American Academy of Pediatrics and the American College of Obstetricians and Gynecologists (American Academy of Pediatrics, 1987a). Keys in addressing issues of pregnancy and contraception with adolescents are the same for health and school professionals. Confidentiality is critical, and knowledge of community resources for contraceptive counseling and pregnancy options is important for the teen who may want to avoid their conventional health care provider with regard to these topics. Good counseling skills are extremely important when communicating information about contraceptive use and their side effects and encouraging compliance with any contraceptive regimen.

At present, the major contraceptive methods available to and appropriate for adolescents include abstinence, condoms with spermicide or contraceptive sponges, diaphragms, and oral contraceptives. Abstinence should be listed as a feasible option when discussing pregnancy prevention with adolescents, especially as the incidence and implications of sexually transmitted diseases increase. Condoms, as marketed by the media to combat the recent AIDS crisis, are inexpensive, safe, and available to adolescents, and their efficacy as a contraceptive measure increases when used in conjunction with a spermicidal foam or jelly, or the newer intravaginal sponge, also permeated with spermicide. Condoms, foam, jelly, and sponges are all easily acquired by adolescents, because they can be obtained without a prescription or a visit to a health care professional. Diaphragms are workable for a small set of motivated teenage couples who are comfortable with the self-touching involved in their insertion. Again, the efficacy of the diaphragm is enhanced by the concomitant use of spermicide. Intrauterine devices are not recommended for use in adolescents secondary to their risk of pelvic inflammatory disease.

Oral contraceptives are effective in preventing pregnancy but offer no protection against STDs. Oral contraceptives do not require partner cooperation or advance planning, and so are widely accepted by adolescents. For a healthy teenage female, the oral contraceptives represent little risk of major side effects such as heart attack or stroke, but minor problems such as weight gain, bloating, and moodiness are quite common (Neinstein, 1984c). It should be noted that smokers who use oral contraceptives increase their risks of circulatory problems many fold over nonsmokers who take oral contraceptives (Neinstein, 1984c). All of these points must be discussed with an adolescent who is making a contraceptive decision.

For the adolescent who becomes pregnant, discussion of risks, benefits, and options is equally critical. The serious medical complication rate for legal abortion is quoted as .4%, but the risks associated with the procedure increase with each week of the advancing pregnancy (Biro & Wildey, 1986).

Feelings of depression, isolation, and guilt have been described by adolescents who have had abortions (Biro & Wildey, 1986). If this option is chosen for an unintended pregnancy, pre- and postprocedure counseling should be imperative for the girl, and for her partner if they have an ongoing relationship. The possibilities of having the baby, and allowing it to be adopted or of keeping the child herself should be given equal attention and pursued with investigation of the realistic implications of each decision.

Neurologic Disorders

The range of neurologic disorders is incredibly wide, encompassing many causes for retardation, movement disorders, developmental delays, and learning problems. One common neurological problem in the school-aged child is epilepsy, also called a seizure disorder. Epilepsy is diagnosed by the occurrence of repeated similar episodes of involuntary motor activity, associated with a change in consciousness or responsiveness, and unassociated with fever, trauma, or other disease (F. S. Wright, 1984). A seizure is a sudden electrical event in the brain's cells (neurons) which may or may not become clinically apparent, and when it does, may present in many fashions.

Although approximately 3% of children have epilepsy (F. S. Wright, 1984), their seizures can have diverse presentations, including a generalized, tonic-clonic seizure, with acute stiffening following by jerking of the limbs and trunk, or partial seizures, which may involve limited motor or sensory symptoms. In preschool children with fever, seizures can occur as a function of the fever, but are not considered to be epilepsy, and almost never occur after 5 years of age (Vining & Freeman, 1985a).

Any child with a first seizure requires immediate medical evaluation, and those with recurrent seizures will probably require therapy with a class of drugs called anticonvulsants, which calm the brain's electrical activity and increase the child's seizure threshold. A complex medical evaluation including a history, physical exam, and family history, along with tests such as an electroencephalogram, computerized tomography (CT scan), or a magnetic resonance imaging study will be used to define the child's seizure problem and choose appropriate medication.

Anticonvulsants are known to have a multitude of possible medical side effects, including liver and bone marrow dysfunction, rashes, allergic reactions, gum overgrowth, and increased body hair. The psychological, behavioral, and cognitive side effects of these medications are less clearly delineated, but phenobarbital specifically has been shown to interfere with learning (Vining & Freeman, 1985b). A child who is on anticonvulsant therapy will benefit both from intermittent medical and psychoeducational evaluations to assure that therapy is not impairing learning or triggering unacceptable behaviors.

If a schoolchild has a seizure disorder, his teachers and aides should be aware of his medications and possible side effects, and should have an emergency plan in the event that a seizure occurs during school. General management of a seizure includes calling for medical assistance, clearing the area around the child to prevent injury, and avoidance of restraint of the seizing child. Contrary to popular belief, a child does not "swallow his tongue" during a seizure, so no attempt should be made to put objects in the mouth. However, seizure activity can affect breathing, so oxygen may be administered by a health care team who arrives to attend to the child. Emotional, learning, and psychosocial problems often go hand in hand with seizure disorders in children, and it is equally important to address these issues for a child with epilepsy (American Academy of Pediatrics, 1987b).

Attention Deficit–Hyperactivity Disorder

Attention deficit–hyperactivity disorder (ADHD) is the diagnostic label currently being used to describe children who exhibit chronic and pervasive signs of inattention, impulsivity, physical restlessness, and deficiencies in rule-governed behavior which deviate significantly from age and gender expectations. It is a problem that cuts across all socioeconomic levels in an estimated 3 to 8% of the school-aged population, with the ratio of males to females being 4 to 1 (American Psychiatric Association, 1987). ADHD is also estimated to be present in 20% of children with learning disabilities. ADHD is generally viewed as a life-long problem but for one-third to one-half of the children the symptoms may decrease with age as they learn to compensate for the problems that this disorder presents.

Although no specific etiological mechanism has been identified, it appears that the etiology of ADHD is multidimensional and may stem from any one or combination of several causal factors. Anastopoulos and Barkley (1988) review research that supports a number of possible biological causes, including genetic transmission, biological variation of inborn temperamental difference, mesial frontal and frontal-limbic dysfunction, elevated blood levels and prenatal exposure to nicotine and alcohol. Research does not support other causes, such as neurological damage or the ingestion of food additives and sugar. Given the variety of potential causes, the degree and distribution of symptomatology may vary.

The Diagnostic and Statistical Manual of Mental Disorders–Revised (American Psychiatric Association, 1987) list the following criteria for making the diagnosis of ADHD:

A. The following characteristics should be considered only when the behavior is more frequent than most of the people the same age.
B. The symptoms should have been observed for at least 6 months, during which time at least eight of the following are present:
    1. Often fidgets with hands or feet or squirms in seat (in adolescents, may be limited to subjective feelings of restlessness)
    2. Has difficulty remaining seated when required to do so
    3. Is easily distracted by extraneous stimuli
    4. Has difficulty awaiting turn in games or group situations
    5. Often blurts out answers to questions before they have been completed
    6. Has difficulty following through on instructions from others (not due to oppositional behavior or failure of comprehension; e.g., fails to finish chores)
    7. Has difficulty sustaining attention in tasks or play activities
    8. Often shifts from one uncompleted activity to another
    9. Has difficulty playing quietly
    10. Often speaks excessively
    11. Often interrupts or intrudes on others (e.g., butts into other children's games)
    12. Often does not seem to listen to what is being said to him or her
    13. Often loses things necessary for tasks

or activities at school or at home (e.g., toys, pencils, books, assignments)

14. Often engages in physically dangerous activities without considering possible consequences (not for the purpose of thrill-seeking; e.g., runs into street without looking)

C. The onset of these is before age 7. This list does not apply to a second type of ADHD, called undifferentiated attention deficit disorder, wherein the main symptom is inattention.

It is important to differentiate children with ADHD from those who are displaying the symptoms of hyperactivity, distractibility, or impulsivity for other reasons, such as anxiety, depression, and negative/oppositional behavior. The diagnosis of ADHD should involve an examination by a physician to rule out medical or neurological factors, a psychological evaluation of the child's cognitive, educational, social, and emotional status, and observations by the parents and teacher using structured rating scales.

Due to the pervasive and developmental nature of ADHD, treatment usually must include a variety of therapies. These children are often very difficult to manage, so training parents and teachers in the use of behavior management techniques that focus on appropriate structure, consistency, and consequences is of prime importance. The child is also in need of information about his behavior and specific help in learning how to gain more control of this behavior. The use of stimulant medication such as Ritalin, Dexedrine, and Cylert can also be very helpful in decreasing impulsivity, activity level, and disruption while increasing concentration, attention span, and compliance. Side effects of these medications are usually minimal. The most common are appetite suppression and sleeplessness, which usually go away in a few days. While there has been some concern that weight and height growth are slowed with this medication, any such effects are usually corrected over time or reversed when medication is stopped. Medication should be used only after a behavior management program is in place. Further, the use of medication should be carefully monitored by a physician knowledgeable in the use of these drugs for ADHD. The initial drug trials and subsequent probe trials to determine its continued effectiveness should be done in a double-blind fashion with structured rating scales that are completed by the parents and teacher on a daily basis.

Accidents and Injuries

For elementary school children and adolescents, the primary cause of death is injuries (American Academy of Pediatrics, 1987a), with trauma causing 80% of all deaths in teenagers and young adults (Paulson, 1988). The leading causes of these accidental deaths are motor vehicle injuries, drowning, and burns, followed by poisoning, falls, firearms, and choking (Paulson, 1988).

For children and adolescents, the road represents their greatest risk, from injuries as a pedestrian, a bicyclist, motor cyclist, or a passenger or driver in a car. Teen drivers have been shown to have higher incidences of fatal crashes, and teen bicyclists' deaths peak in the age range from 10 to 14 years (Paulson, 1988). By contrast the school setting is a rare site for a fatal injury, but nonfatal injuries, especially from falls, represent a significant risk. These falls often result in head or extremity trauma, frequently connected with sports or playground activities.

At home or on the farm, poisoning, burns, and firearms play a major role in fatal accidents. Farm machinery, especially tractors, can be the culprits in trauma. It is significant that unintentional firearm injuries are the third-leading cause of death in the 10- to 19-year-old (Paulson, 1988).

Accordingly, our aim in prevention of injuries should be directed toward those identified high-risk areas. The American Academy of Pediatrics and the U.S. Division of Maternal and Child Health have both created a focus on accident prevention for children, and individual states are utilizing and assessing preventive strategies such as automobile safety restraint laws, bicycle safety classes, and poison and burn prevention programs in the classroom (Alpert & Guyer, 1985). Education throughout all grades about traffic safety and the risks of driving while intoxicated from alcohol or drugs is necessary as well. Schools can reevaluate play areas for safety, and consider such issues as the surface on which children play, the height of climbing apparatus, and the maintenance of playground equipment and playing fields. School sports programs should also enforce the maintenance and usage of all safety equipment and provide adequate personnel to supervise players. All students involved in sports should have a physical exam to document problems and identify contraindications to their participation (American Academy of Pediatrics, 1987a).

The Chronically Ill Child

Advances in modern medicine have increased our ability to sustain life but, unfortunately, not always to restore health. Chronic illness is part of the lives of many children and their families. A chronic or long-term illness refers to a "disorder with a protracted course which can be progressive and fatal, or associated with a relatively normal life span despite impaired physical or mental functioning" (Mattsson, 1972, p. 801). Often, such illnesses have acute exacerbations requiring intensive medical attention. The chronic disorder may be inherited, the result of a birth injury, an acute illness, or an injury. If one includes the disorders of vision, hearing, speech, learning, behavior disorders, mental retardation, and chronic disease such as asthma, diabetes, cystic fibrosis, leukemia, and muscular dystrophy, it is estimated that between 20 and 40% of children up to age 18 experience a chronic illness or handicap (Green & Haggerty, 1968). Excluding mental retardation and sensory disorders, surveys indicate that 7 to 10% of all children under age 18 have serious chronic illnesses, the most common being asthma (2%), cardiac conditions (0.5%), cerebral palsy (0.5%), orthopedic disorders (0.5%), and diabetes mellitus (0.1%) (Magrab & Calcagno, 1978).

Chronic diseases of childhood, especially life-threatening ones, can place inordinate stress on the child and his family. The medical treatment may be very long, painful, and intrusive, with some children left free of danger, others with severe limitations, and others with the threat of recurrence. As might be expected, these children generally have higher rates of maladjustment than those of their physically healthy peers (Sperling, 1968), but factors such as age of onset, severity and cause of illness, the personality of the child, the child's age, the family's adjustment to the problem, parent–child relationships, community resources, and support systems are all important in determining the child's response to an illness or handicap (Fife, Norton, & Groom, 1987; Pless & Pinkerton, 1975). The greatest psychological or social problems are likely to occur for the handicapped or chronically ill child whose family relationships are poor, whose parents' marriage is strained, and in the case of acute illnesses in the child who already has emotional problems. With more of these children in school the acceptance of peers and teachers is also a very important factor.

Treatment should include psychosocial strategies to help both the child and her family cope with the disease, its treatment, and the aftermath of treatment. Regardless of the particular disease, the child's needs are best met with a team approach that includes medical personnel, teachers, parents, and mental health professionals sharing knowledge and support. It is difficult if not impossible to replace the opportunities the school offers the chronically ill child to develop coping skills, friendships, and a sense of worth. In helping to meet the unique needs of these children, one must remember that the child's concepts of illness, health, and treatment are dependent on his or her level of cognitive development. A child under 3 years is not likely to understand the reasons given for his illness, but simple statements of fact or warning, such as "this will hurt," are understood and will help the child build a sense of trust. Children ages 3 to 7, with their increased vocabulary, often mislead adults into believing that they understand what and why things are happening to them. Words are usually parroted and visual imagery and fantasy can often distort even the simplest explanation. Children in this age range are likely to view their illness as a punishment for misbehavior. By ages 8 and 9 children are able to understand a variety of causalities for illness and handicaps, which makes explanations, verbally and visually, helpful in decreasing anxiety. Factual information can give them a sense of mastery over what is to happen. It is especially important that children of this age be given opportunities to care for themselves and master skills that might be more easily done by the adults around them. Magrab and Calcagno (1978) point out that the sense of difference generated by a chronic illness or handicap can be very difficult for the adolescent. This is a time when peers' reactions play an important role in the development of self-image. Schools should provide some discussion and education on the illness or handicapping condition to the non-handicapped peers.

REFERENCES

Alpert, J. J., & Guyer, B. (1985). Symposium on injuries and injury prevention. *Pediatric Clinics of North America, 32*(1), 2–4.

American Academy of Pediatrics. (1985a). *Guidelines for health supervision.* Elk Grove Village, IL: Author.

American Academy of Pediatrics. (1985b). *Pediatric nutrition handbook.* Elk Grove Village, IL: Author.

American Academy of Pediatrics. (1987a). *Health assessment and screening during adolescence.* Elk Grove Village, IL: Author.

American Academy of Pediatrics. (1987b). *School health: A guide for health professionals.* Elk Grove Village, IL: Author.

American Psychiatric Association. (1987). *Diagnostic and statistical manual of mental disorders* (3rd rev. ed.). Washington, DC: Author.

Anastopoulos, A. D., & Barkley, R. A. (1988). Biological factors in attention deficit–hyperactivity disorder. *The Behavior Therapist, 11*(3), 47–53.

Biro, F. M., & Wildey, L. S. (1986). Acute and long term consequences of adolescents who choose abortions. *Pediatric Annals, 15*(10), 667–674.

Brewer, E. J., & Arroyo, I. (1986). Use of nonsteroidal anti-inflammatory drugs in children. *Pediatric Annals, 15,* 575–582.

Bunnell, W. P. (1986). Spinal deformity. *Pediatric Clinics of North America, 33,* 1475–1488.

Caplan, J. (1987). Deafness: Ever heard of it? Delayed recognition of permanent hearing loss. *Pediatrics, 79,* 206–213.

Centers for Disease Control. (1985). Chlamydia infections. *Morbidity and Mortality Weekly Report, 34*(35), 8–85.

Chase, H. P. (1985). Avoiding the short and long term complications of juvenile diabetes. *Pediatrics in Review, 7,* 140–149.

Denning, C. R. (1983). Cystic fibrosis in the older child. *Pediatric Emergency Casebook, 1,* 1–12.

Denny, F. (1987). Acute respiratory infections: Etiology and epidemiology. *Pediatrics in Review, 9,* 135–146.

Diamond, C. A., & Matthay, K. (1988). Childhood acute lymphoblastic leukemia. *Pediatric Annals, 17,* 156–171.

Dietz, W. L., & Gortmaker, S. L. (1985). Do we fatten our children at the television set? Obesity and television viewing in children and adolescents. *Pediatrics, 5,* 807–812.

Dooley, K. J. (1984). Management of the premature infant with a patent ductus arteriosus. *Pediatric Clinics of North America, 31,* 1159–1174.

Edelmann, C. M., Jr. (1988). Urinary tract infection and vesicoureteral reflux. *Pediatric Annals, 17,* 568–583.

Fife, B., Norton, J., & Groom, G. (1987). The family's adaptation to childhood leukemia. *Social Science Medicine, 24*(2), 159–168.

Frau, L. M., & Alexander, E. R. (1985). Public health implications of sexually transmitted diseases in pediatric practices. *Pediatric Infectious Disease, 4*(5), 453–465.

Fria, T. J. (1981). Assessment of hearing. *Pediatric Clinics of North America, 28,* 757–776.

Hammerschlag, M. R. (1984). Conjunctivitis in infancy and childhood. *Pediatrics in Review, 5,* 285–290.

Hen, J., Jr. (1986). An overview of pediatric asthma. *Pediatric Annals, 15,* 92–98.

Herzog, D. B. (1982). Bulimia in the adolescent. *American Journal of Diseases of Children, 136,* 985–989.

Herzog, D. B., & Copeland, P. M. (1985). Eating disorders. *New England Journal of Medicine, 313*(5), 295–303.

Karayalcin, G. (1985). Current concepts in the management of hemophilia. *Pediatric Annals, 14,* 640–660.

Kauffmann, R. E., & Roberts, R. J. (1987). Aspirin use and Reye syndrome. *Pediatrics, 79*(6), 1049–1050.

Klein, J. O. (1984). Antimicrobial prophylaxis for recurrent acute otitis media. *Pediatric Annals, 13,* 398–404.

Lookingbill, D. P. (1985). Impetigo. *Pediatrics in Review, 7,* 177–181.

Macdonald, D. I. (1987). Patterns of alcohol and drug use among adolescents. *Pediatric Clinics of North America, 34,* 275–288.

Magrab, P. R., & Calcagno, P. L. (1978). Psychological impact of chronic pediatric conditions. In P. R. Magrab (Ed.), *Psychological management of pediatric problems: Early life conditions and chronic diseases* (Vol. 1). Baltimore: University Park Press.

Mattsson, A. (1972). Long term illness in children: A challenge to psychosocial adaptation. *Pediatrics, 50,* 801–805.

Mofenson, H. C., Copeland, P., & Caraccio, T. (1986). Cocaine and crack: The latest menace. *Contemporary Pediatrics, 3*(10), 44–50.

Neinstein, L. S. (1984a). Contraception. In L. S. Neinstein (Ed.), *Adolescent Health Care* (pp. 399–421). Baltimore: Urban and Schwarzenberg.

Neinstein, L. S. (1984b). Herpes genitalis. In L. S. Neinstein (Ed.), *Adolescent Health Care* (pp. 555–559). Baltimore: Urban and Schwarzenberg.

Neinstein, L. S. (1984c). Teenage pregnancy. In L. S. Neinstein (Ed.), *Adolescent Health Care* (pp. 387–397). Baltimore: Urban and Schwarzenberg.

Nelson, L. B. (1984). The visually handicapped child. *Pediatrics in Review, 6,* 173–182.

Oski, F. (1985). Iron deficiency: Facts and fallacies. *Pediatric Clinic of North America, 32,* 493–497.

Paulson, J. A. (1988). The epidemiology of injuries in adolescents. *Pediatric Annals, 17*(2), 84–98.

Pearson, H. A. (1987). Sickle cell diseases: Diagnosis and management in infancy and childhood. *Pediatrics in Review, 9,* 121–130.

Pless, I. B., & Pinkerton, P. (1975). *Chronic childhood disorder: Promoting patterns of adjustment.* London: Henry Kimpton.

Poplack, D. (1985). Acute lymphoblastic leukemia in childhood. *Pediatric Clinics of North America, 32,* 669–698.

Public Health Reports: NICHD Conference Summary. (1986). *101,* 289–293.

Roger, M. F. (1988). Pediatric HIV infection: Epidemology, etiopathogenesis and transmission. *Pediatric Annals, 17,* 324–331.

Ruben, R. J. (1987). Diagnosis of deafness in infancy. *Pediatrics in Review, 9,* 163–166.

Schwartz, R. H. (1987). Marijuana: An overview. *Pediatric Clinics of North America, 34*(2), 305–317.

Scott, G. B. (1988). Clinical manifestations of HIV infection in children. *Pediatric Annals, 17,* 365–370.

Shafer, M. A. (1984). *Chlamydia trachomatis:* Important relationships to race, contraception, lower genital tract infection and Papanicolaou smear. *Journal of Pediatrics, 104*(1), 141–146.

Silvis, G. L., & Perry, C. L. (1987). Understanding and deterring tobacco use among adolescents. *Pediatric Clinics of North America, 34,* 363–380.

Shapiro, G. G. (1986). Understanding allergic rhinitis: Differential diagnosis and management. *Pediatrics in Review, 7,* 212–218.

Sperling, E. (1978). Psychological issues in chronic illness and handicap. In E. Gellert (Ed.), *Psychosocial aspects of pediatric care.* New York: Grune & Stratton.

Spicer, R. L. (1984). Cardiovascular disease in Down syndrome. *Pediatric Clinics of North America, 31,* 1331–1344.

Strong, W. B., & Dennison, B. (1988). Pediatric preventive cardiology: Atherosclerosis and coronary heart disease. *Pediatrics in Review, 9,* 303–314.

Suskind, R. M., & Varma, R. (1984). Assessment of nutritional status of children, *Pediatrics in Review, 5,* 195–202.

Tarr, J. E. & Macklin, M. (1987). Cocaine. *Pediatric Clinics of North America, 34*(2), 319–332.

Turner, J. A. (1985). Giardiasis and infections with *Dientamoeba fragilis. Pediatric Clinics of North America, 32,* 865–880.

Vining, E. P. G., & Freeman, J. M. (1985a). Epilepsy and seizures: Where, why and what type of therapy. *Pediatric Annals, 14*(11), 741–746.

Vining, E. P. G., & Freeman, J. M. (1985b). Seizures which are not epilepsy. *Pediatric Annals, 14*(11), 711–726.

Weitzman, M. (1987). When pediatric patients become parents. *Pediatrics in Review, 9*(4), 99–100.

Wright, P. F. (1984). Indication and duration of antimicrobial agents for acute otitis media. *Pediatric Annals, 13,* 377–381.

Wright, F. S. (1984). Epilepsy in childhood. *Pediatric Clinics of North America, 31*(1), 177–188.

31

THE PRIMARY MENTAL HEALTH PROJECT: ALTERNATIVE APPROACHES IN SCHOOL-BASED PREVENTIVE INTERVENTION

EMORY L. COWEN
A. DIRK HIGHTOWER

University of Rochester

In this chapter we describe the development and current scope of the Primary Mental Health Project (PMHP), a program for the early detection and prevention of young children's school adjustment problems (Cowen, Trost, Lorion, Dorr, Izzo, & Isaacson, 1975). First, however, several comments on the place of prevention in the schools.

PREVENTION AND THE SCHOOLS

Prevention is a relatively new concept in mental health. Currently, only a small fraction of the field's resources is invested in such work (President's Commission on Mental Health, 1978; Prevention Task Panel Report, 1978). The same is true for school mental health (Shaw & Goodyear, 1984). From its inception, mental health has been guided by a fixed orientation and set of strategies. The orientation has been toward psychopathology and dysfunction. The strategies have been to minimize

or repair things that have gone wrong (Cowen, 1973, 1983; Zax & Cowen, 1976). That emphasis still prevails today. However responsive or humanitarian it may seem, the ultimate question is: How effective has it been for individuals and for society?

Concerns about inefficacies in the existing mental health system have grown substantially in the past several decades; indeed, they have fueled the development of entire new fields such as community mental health (Anderson et al, 1966), community psychology (Rappaport, 1977) and alternative concepts such as prevention (Felner, Jason, Moritsugu, & Farber, 1983; Roberts & Peterson, 1984). Those developments represent efforts to find solutions to vexing problems that the classically defined field of mental health has not been able to resolve. Given the extensive review of those problems in other sources (Cowen, 1977a, 1980, 1983; President's Commission Report, 1978; Zax & Cowen, 1976), only a brief summary is provided here. First, the mental health system, as defined, has lacked the resources needed to meet the demand for help, much less the underlying need. Moreover, its limited resources have been inequitably distributed and poorly suited to major segments of the population. Second, the mental health system has been singularly oriented to casualty and its repair. As a result of that "end-state" mentality, professionals typically come into play when evident deficit is brought forcibly to their attention. Prognostically, that is the poorest time to intervene, since rooted psychological dysfunction tends to resist change.

School mental health has been in much the same situation. Such approaches were conceived in the image of, and have to a considerable extent been imprisoned by, the parent mental health field's views of dysfunction and resultant ways of delivering services. Thus, school mental health services have not sufficiently capitalized on the special attributes and potentials of the young child or the special opportunities for constructive intervention that schools offer. Children spend major portions of their early lives in the schools, where they must meet two sets of demands. They must (a) master increasingly complex bodies of knowledge (i.e., they must *learn*) and (b) do so effectively within an existing framework of rules about appropriate behavior (i.e., they must *adapt*). Thus, for better or worse, schools are an important influence on children's personal and educational development (Task Panel Report: Learning Failure and Unused Learning Potential, 1978).

School mental health services, now nearly a century old, arose in problem contexts. Social workers, or visiting teachers as they were known, entered the schools when compulsory attendance laws were first passed. Their job was to establish family contacts and get children back in school, hopefully to reduce adverse social consequences of noneducation. School psychology, born in the psychometric tradition of the early 20th century, focused first on slow-learning or skill-deficient children, seeking to diagnose and then remediate such conditions.

Although there have been later, important liberalizations of those roles, current day-to-day practices still reflect the earlier imprimateur, that is, respond to trouble. Learning and adaptive problems in school are so widespread, and professional resources for dealing with them so thin (Glidewell & Swallow, 1969; Task Panel Report: Learning Failure and Unused Learning Potential, 1978), that

in most settings services are limited to a small fraction of children in dire need, that is, those with the most serious, vivid, nonpostponable problems. Many others whose difficulties are less apparent or socially disruptive are left to fend as best they can, or simply to sink into a swirling whirlpool of failure. Unfortunately, many early school difficulties, left unattended, mount and fan out as time passes (Cowen, Pedersen, Babigian, Izzo, & Trost, 1973; Ensminger, Kellam, & Rubin, 1983; Kellam, Simon, & Ensminger, 1983). Thus, microcosmically, school mental health services have been subject to the same difficulties as other mental health services: (a) too few resources to cope with problems as spontaneously defined, and (b) focusing on crystallized conditions that require the most time and have the poorest prognoses.

School failure, whether defined educationally and/or interpersonally, is a rampant destructive problem in America today (Task Panel Report: Learning Failure and Unused Learning Potential, 1978). Consistent with that observation, Glidewell and Swallow's (1969) survey for the Joint Commission on the Mental Health of Children (1969) concluded that 1 in 3 American schoolchildren had school adjustment problems, and 1 in 10 had sufficiently serious problems to need professional help. The problem is even more severe in the urban megalopolis. The Chicago-Woodlawn studies (Kellam, Branch, Agrawal, & Ensminger, 1975; Kellam, Branch, Agrawal, & Grabill, 1972), for example, reported a 7 in 10 school-maladjustment figure in one urban area. Namir and Weinstein (1982) provide more recent data confirming the widespread need for child mental health services. If, as Glidewell and Swallow (1969) suggest, education is a major national resource, the survey data cited indicate a tragic national waste.

The preceding analysis poses important questions of policy and tactics. How *should* finite school mental health energies and resources be allocated between those who are hurting visibly and the quietly suffering many, between older and younger children, between individual children and the systems that shape their well being, between restoration and prevention?

Prevention's basic rationale is well reflected in the aphorism that "an ounce of prevention is worth a pound of cure." Given the magnitude and cost of educational failure both to individuals and to society, the logic of prevention is impeccable and the need for such programs considerable. Schools are natural settings for conducting prevention programs (Cowen et al, 1975; Task Panel Report: Learning Failure and Unused Learning Potential, 1978). They are vital shaping forces in children's development, necessarily so in that children spend 30 to 35 hours a week in school for many years. Schools also bring together large numbers of children in a common geographical site within a consolidated administrative organization. Hence, they offer unique opportunities for actions and programs that can enhance children's cognitive and behavioral development. The challenge is less to justify the need for preventive programs in the schools and more to evolve effective technologies of prevention. The cluster of activities and programs that have been developed in the course of PMHP's evolution represent one systematic, persistent effort to do exactly that.

However appealing the word "prevention," it is in fact a relatively broad term that has been used to embrace many different types of activities (Cowen, 1977a, 1980, 1983). An important distinction, for example, can be made between primary prevention which seeks to forestall the development of pathology—better yet, to build health from the start—and ontogenetically early secondary prevention which seeks to identify early signs of dysfunction and to introduce prompt correctives to short-circuit negative outcomes (Zax & Cowen, 1976). Each of those two broad strategies offers a refreshing contrast to mental health's past rutted ways. Schools have done relatively little work using either approach; most of what has been done, including PMHP, has been early secondary prevention.

PRIMARY MENTAL HEALTH PROJECT

PMHP: Roots and Evolution

Among PMHP's most distinctive features is the simple fact that the project has survived 30 years. Although that fact is perhaps explainable by constructs such as rigidity and masochism, another possibility is that the project effectively addresses important problems that most schools face. Otherwise put, PMHP may have developed as it did because it is an approach for which the time was right (Klein & Goldston, 1977). In saying that PMHP has survived 30 years, we do not mean to imply that today's project is the same as its earliest ancestor. To the contrary, PMHP has been ever-

evolving rather than a static project, although changes within it have been more evolutionary than revolutionary (Cowen et al, 1975).

PMHP's start, as a small pilot project in one school in 1957, was prompted less by the preceding smoothed over, retrospective rationale and more by two earthy, clinical observations. First, classroom teachers often reported that 40 to 60% of their time was preempted by the problems of two, three, or four children, in a class of 25 to 30, to the detriment of those youngsters, the rest of the class, and the teacher's own sense of accomplishment and well-being. Second, and equally striking, was the observation of a sharp rise in mental health referrals during the transition between elementary and high school. Review of cumulative records of referred children often revealed problems dating back to the primary grades. Either helping resources had not been available to those youngsters or people had hoped that their troubles would disappear. Far from vanishing, many early problems rooted and spread to new areas. Those clinical observations or "regularites" (Sarason, 1971) led to the conclusion that help for early maladapting school children was not available either when, or in the amount, needed. They pointed to the need for proactive alternatives such as systematic early identification and prompt, preventive intervention. Through all the changes that define PMHP's evolutionary course, those two elements have remained central.

PMHP's basic program model emerged gradually over an 11-year period. In its earliest stage the project developed brief, objective methods for identifying primary graders at risk and showed that such youngsters, left alone, tended to decline in terms of academics and adjustment (Cowen, Zax, Izzo, & Trost, 1966). On that basis, a primitive secondary prevention program was developed and shown to have beneficial effects in terms of children's educational and personal development, how peers and teachers perceived them, how they saw themselves, and how they functioned (Cowen et al, 1975). But merely to identify children at risk is more frustrating than helpful for many school people (Bower, 1977, 1978; Keogh & Becker, 1973). The more basic question for them, understandably, is: "What can be done to make things better *now* and avert later unfortunate outcomes?"

Given that few schools had sufficient personnel to meet service demands, much less buried need, we began to consider changes in service-delivery patterns that might better meet children's needs. One intriguing possibility, suggested by then ongoing explorations of innovative uses of mental health personpower, was that human attributes such as commitment, interest, and relevant life-experience might be as, or more, important than education or advanced degrees, as qualities that could truly help young children in need (Holzberg, Knapp, & Turner, 1967; Rioch, 1967). That possibility led us to select and train nonprofessional help-agents, mostly homemakers, for roles as child-aides in the schools (Cowen, Dorr, & Pokracki, 1972; Sandler, 1972; Zax & Cowen, 1967).

Such people, following focused, time-limited training, have worked under professional supervision to promote the educational and personal development of children experiencing early school adjustment problems. Carefully selected for their life experiences, interest patterns, and helping reflexes (Cowen, Dorr, & Pokracki, 1972), subsequent research findings support their efficacy as help-agents with young schoolchildren in need. Although the initial use of child-aides was justified on grounds of professional shortages and fiscal austerity, we have since learned that they are often better suited than some professionals for child-helping in the schools, because of their naturalness, warmth, involvement, and belongingness in such work, and because of the continuing challenge that the job affords them. Child-aides are clearly a "motor force" in PMHP. Both project personnel and visitors have been impressed with their suitability for, and effectiveness in, this key child-serving role.

PMHP: Emphases and Practices

PMHP is best seen as a structural model, with four emphases. The approach (a) focuses on young, modifiable children before problems root; (b) uses an active, systematic screening process to identify children experiencing early school adjustment problems; (c) expands sharply the reach of early effective helping services to identified children through the use of carefully selected, trained, supervised child-aides; and (d) changes professional roles to "quarterbacking" activities such as selection, training, and supervision of nonprofessionals, and consultative and resource activities with school personnel, to increase geometrically the reach of preventive services.

Although the term "structural model" is used to convey PMHP's overarching emphases, the approach is flexible enough to accommodate substantial de facto variation in its literal defining practices. Actual school programs thus vary in such things as (a) specific measures used in early detection and screening; (b) depth and types of professional staffing patterns; (c) people who serve as child-aides (e.g., volunteer versus paid nonprofessionals; homemakers, students, retired persons, etc.); (d) ways of recruiting, training, and supervising aides; and (e) how aides actually work with children (e.g., individual versus group; relational versus behavioral orientations). Such variation is as it should, indeed must, be, since any school program, to be effective, must adapt to realities of its own "pond-ecology" (i.e., its specific needs, resources, belief systems, and prevailing practices). For similar ecological reasons no single program description fully captures how PMHP operates in all schools. The following step-by-step summary is, at best, a smoothed-over account of how the project works.

First, brief, objective screening measures were developed to provide profiles of young children's school problems (Lorion, Cowen, & Caldwell, 1975) and competencies (Gesten, 1976). Continuing efforts have been made to streamline these measures and strengthen their psychometric properties. Currently, three such measures are used: (a) the AML, a brief, quick screening or x-ray device that identifies young children's early aggressive, shy-anxious, and learning problems in the classroom (Cowen, Dorr, et al, 1973; Hightower, Spinell, & Lotyczewski, 1986), (b) the T-CRS, a teacher rating measure that assesses children's school problem behaviors and competencies (Hightower, Work, et al, 1986); and (c) the CRS, a child self-rating measure of socioemotional functioning (Hightower et al, 1987).

Second, most referrals are initiated when the teacher perceives initial ineffective functioning in the child: aggressive, acting-out, and disruptive behaviors; shy, anxious, withdrawn reactions; learning difficulties, and combinations of the preceding. Other school personnel and parents also make referrals.

Third, screening and referral data are reviewed at an assignment conference involving the principal, school mental health professionals, teachers, and child-aides (i.e., the PMHP "team"). That conference seeks to understand the child's situation and to establish appropriate intervention goals and strategies. Following receipt of parent permissions, aides begin to see referred children regularly. Collectively, the purpose of these steps is to identify early signs of dysfunction and to set the stage for doing something about them before such problems root and fan out.

Fourth, depending on size, PMHP schools have two to five half-time child-aides who serve as the program's direct help-agents. Although aides receive time-limited training to prepare them, PMHP depends more on selection than on training variables. Aides are supervised by the school mental health professionals. They get on-the-job training through school conferences and consultation sessions and are provided additional specialty training options over time. They are paid at a school district's prevailing hourly rates. By carrying caseloads of 13 to 14 children, they sharply expand the reach of early preventive services.

Fifth, teachers, aides, and PMHP team members exchange information and coordinate goals. Substitute time frees teachers to attend consultation and progress-review conferences. That step provides a formal communication mechanism that helps to increase teacher's sensitivity to relationships between psychological factors and a child's ability to learn. Some teachers have translated such learnings into more effective classroom handling, an important step toward primary prevention.

Sixth, midyear conferences take stock of children's progress to date and, when indicated, realign goals and procedures. End-of-year termination conferences evaluate children's overall progress and formulate recommendations for the next school year.

Seventh, PMHP consultants visit schools regularly to support professionals, provide enrichment and upgrading of skills for program participants, and consider interesting and challenging cases.

Eighth, the school professional's role in PMHP differs from the traditional one. Much less time is devoted to direct one-to-one services; much more goes into training, consultative, and resource activities for school personnel and aides. In that way, PMHP can get at many more problems, early, when they are still manageable and prevent future difficulties, rather than counterpunching after it is too late. The approach, far from implying professional obsolescence, points to new more socially utilitarian professional roles.

The parent PMHP in Rochester, New York, is located in 18 urban and suburban schools. Last year nearly 1,000 youngsters received an average of 22 helping contacts (i.e., a total of 22,000 child-serving contacts). Cost–benefit analysis (Dorr, 1972) suggests that a 40% increase in service costs expands the reach of services by about 1,000%.

Changes in the Basic PMHP Model

PMHP has been an evolving program. Changes has been catalyzed by a productive marriage between service and research. Thus research studies address live program issues and relevant findings are fed back to strengthen program services. In the next section we cite concrete examples of program modifications that have evolved from clinical findings.

At first, child-aides saw children only individually. However, the need to reach more children in some schools, and the fact that some children were face-valid candidates for groups, stimulated the development of a program to train aides to work with small groups (Terrell, McWilliams, & Cowen, 1972). That program has since been refined several times. Currently, about 10% of PMHP children are seen in groups. In some PMHP offshoot programs with different resource patterns and style preferences, that figure is much higher.

With grant support in its pilot period, PMHP had the atypical "luxury" of a full-time psychologist and social worker just for the primary grades of one school. That situation allowed for extensive family contact and close home–school liaison. When the pilot period ended and as school mental health professional time became scarcer, reductions in parent contact were inevitable. That gap led to the development of a new parent-aide program. Parent-aides are seasoned child-aides who receive additional specialized training. A curriculum was developed to prepare them for roles as mental health assistants in such activities as communication with parents about the project, feedback to and from families, and crisis management. That program too addressed a real project need and was warmly received by schools.

Program change has also grown out of research findings. For example, in refining its early detection procedures, PMHP developed a method for quantifying the predominant nature of children's school problems that made it possible first to identify acting-out, shy-withdrawn, and learning "pure-types" and then to evaluate program effectiveness with specific subgroups. The finding that PMHP was more effective with shy-anxious than with acting-out children (Lorion, Cowen, & Caldwell, 1974) led to the development of a program to train aides in the use of Ginnottian limit-setting methods with acting-out children. This new approach was found to improve outcomes with such youngsters (Cowen, Orgel, Gesten, & Wilson, 1979). It has since been more widely incorporated into the project's mainstream.

Several early PMHP studies (Felner, Ginter, Boike, & Cowen, 1981a; Felner, Stolberg, & Cowen, 1975) established that children who experience crises, such as parent divorce or death in the family, had more serious school adjustment problems than referred, noncrisis peers. Specifically, divorce was associated with acting-out problems and death with withdrawal and anxiety. Those findings led to the development of a pilot prevention program to train child-aides to work with children who had experienced recent life-crises. This focused, time-limited (12 sessions/6 weeks) program provided children with opportunities to identify and abreact to crisis-related feelings, and to develop relevant coping strategies. Program efficacy data (Felner, Norton, Cowen, & Farber, 1981) and the fact that school personnel found it to address important needs led to later important expansions of crisis intervention programming within PMHP.

PMHP has done several studies to assess the efficacy of specific program practices such as seeing children once versus several times a week and over the course of a single or several school years (Lorion, Cowen, & Kraus, 1974). One regularity noted was that children tended to be seen until the end of the school year. Although that practice can be viewed as a reflection of a natural nurturing tendency in aides, its net result, in a finite resource system, was to limit services to other youngsters in need. That consideration led to the development of a new training program for aides to work with youngsters in Planned Short-Term Intervention (PSI). PSI was developed for children with identifiable focal problems. It has a strong educational focus and is built around specific ways of dealing with target problems. Both aides and children know from the start that PSI has a 12-session limit. Contacts with parents and teachers are designed to maintain and support program gains. A pre–post follow-up study of PSI demonstrated the program's effectiveness, including significant reduc-

tions in the target classroom behaviors for which children had been referred (Winer, Weissberg, & Cowen, 1988). Because brief intervention expands the reach of resources, it can both increase program efficiency and make the approach more feasible to implement in underresourced systems.

Direct PMHP program extensions, such as those described above, come about in a low-key way. When clinical or research data identify potential ways of expanding the program's scope or enhancing its efficacy, a mini-pilot program is initiated to address the issue in question. Such "beachhead" programs are debugged with small pilot groups of aides to yield formative evaluation data. Promising programs are then more fully tested using an appropriate research design. As supporting research findings accrue, the new programs are more widely incorporated, through new rounds of aide training, on a solid base and in a receptive climate.

PMHP Research

Research on PMHP started when PMHP started; it has been a continuing, essential part of the program's fabric ever since. Indeed, PMHP may well be among the most extensively researched school mental health projects ever. Several PMHP research studies were cited in earlier specific contexts. The section that follows provides a broad overview of PMHP's principal domains of research focus.

Over the years, much effort has been invested in methodological and scale development work designed to produce measures that can be used both in conducting and evaluating the program. Beyond the usual psychometric requirements of such measures, everyday pressures of the "real" school world dictate that they be brief, understandable, easy to administer and score, and deal with relevant and important domains for teachers and children. With those objectives in mind, PMHP has developed and refined a number of measures of children's school problem behaviors and competencies, as assessed from the perspectives of teachers, parents, child-aides, and the children themselves (Cowen, Dorr, et al, 1973; Gesten, 1976; Hightower, Cowen, et al, 1987; Hightower, Work, et al, 1986; Lorion et al, 1975).

The bread-and-butter question for any program is whether it works. If that question cannot be answered positively, others become less interesting. Program efficacy data are essential both for accountability and dissemination purposes. PMHP has conducted some 25 separate program evaluations, including a recent composite evaluation for seven consecutive annual cohorts (Weissberg, Cowen, Lotyczewski, & Gesten, 1983). Those studies vary in scope, criteria, and rigor of design (e.g., use of control groups), reflecting in part the reality constraints of doing research in schools (Cowen & Gesten, 1980; Cowen, Lorion, & Dorr, 1974). Although no single outcome study provides once-and-forever evidence of program efficacy, the cumulated weight of many PMHP program outcome findings suggests that the program brings significant help to young maladapting schoolchildren (Cowen et al, 1975; Weissberg et al, 1983). Moreover, independent program evaluations done by other implementing groups support that conclusion (Cowen, Weissberg, et al, 1983; Durlak, 1977; Kirschenbaum, 1979; Kirschenbaum, DeVoge, Marsh, & Steffen, 1980; Rickel, Dyhdalo, & Smith, 1984; Sandler, Duricko, & Grande, 1975).

Follow-up, an important but often neglected aspect of program evaluation, is to assess the durability of the changes seen at the time the program ends. Sometimes short-term gains erode. In other cases gains not seen immediately become evident only with the passage of time. Several short-term (Lorion, Caldwell, & Cowen, 1976) and intermediate-term (Chandler, Weissberg, Cowen, & Guare, 1984; Cowen, Dorr, Trost, & Izzo, 1972) PMHP follow-up studies have shown that early program gains are maintained over time.

Because of the importance of the aide–child and aide–supervisor interaction processes in PMHP, several studies have been done to describe those processes. McWilliams (1972), for example, charted the frequency of occurrence of different types of aide–child activities (e.g., tutoring = 15%, cooperative activity = 21%, child active/aide passive = 29%) and found differences in activity patterns among different types of referral problems. Thus, academic activities were three times as frequent among children referred primarily for academic difficulties as for those referred for shy-anxious or acting-out problems; and problem-centered conversation occurred significantly more often with acting-out children. A later process study showed that aide satisfaction with a given session related to the child's predominant mood state in the session and the extent to which the session dealt with significant problems (Cowen, Gesten, Wilson, & Lorion, 1977). Ginsberg, Weissberg,

and Cowen (1985) reported that supervisor-judged satisfaction with the aide supervisory process related significantly to teacher judgments of reductions in children's problem behaviors and increases in their competence.

Related studies have sought to identify specific program elements or components that work well or represent sources of difficulty for program participants. Cowen, Lorion, and Caldwell (1975), for example, found that child aggression, family problems, and limit-testing problems produced greater discomfort in aides than the child's need to have an aide for him/herself or to be dependent. Parent interactions were more difficult for teachers to handle than child problems or class management problems (Gesten, Cowen, DeStefano, & Gallagher, 1978). Both child-aides and professionals judged shy-anxious children to be the easiest and most enjoyable children to work with and to have the best prognoses, and acting-out children to be the most difficult and to have the poorest prognoses (Cowen, Gesten, & DeStefano, 1977). Although teachers felt much the same way, they considered children with learning problems to be better candidates for PMHP than did aides or professionals (DeStefano, Gesten, & Cowen, 1977).

The child-aide's central place in PMHP has fueled extensive research on the characteristics of people selected for that role (Cowen, Dorr, Pokracki, 1972; Dorr, Cowen, Sandler, & Pratt, 1973; Sandler, 1972); how professionals view aides and their job functioning (Dorr, Cowen, & Kraus, 1973), and how aides develop over time on the job (Dorr, Cowen, & Sandler, 1973). Those studies have shown that aides are warm, interpersonally skilled, competent, child-oriented people, and that professionals are pleased with their performance in the program.

PMHP has also done extensive research to identify factors about children, their life situations, their family structure, and experiences that relate to good and poor school adjustment. The project's extensive use of early detection and screening measures and its many program evaluation studies have produced massive data banks that provide good entree points to such inquiry. One study, cited earlier (Felner et al, 1975), showed that (a) referred children who experienced parental divorce or death in the family had more serious school adjustment problems than did matched referred noncrisis peers, and (b) parental divorce related to acting-out problems and death to withdrawn-anxious behaviors in the child. Later studies generalized those findings to child-aide as well as teacher ratings, rural and nonreferred youngsters, and reductions in competence behaviors as well as increases in problem behaviors (Felner, Farber, Ginter, Boike, & Cowen, 1980; Felner, Ginter, Boike, & Cowen, 1981a, 1981b). Related studies have shown relationships between family structural characteristics (e.g., birth order, sibling similarity) and family orientations and styles (e.g., parental pressure on child to succeed, lack of educational stimulation, etc.) and children's school adjustment (Boike, Gesten, Cowen, Felner, & Francis, 1978; Gallagher & Cowen, 1976, 1977; Gesten, Scher, & Cowen, 1978; Lorion, Cowen, Kraus, & Milling, 1977; Searcy-Miller, Cowen, & Terrell, 1977).

Several recent studies help to round out that picture. Sterling, Cowen, Weissberg, Lotyczewski, and Boike (1985) found that children who experienced one or more recent (past 6 months) stressful life events had more serious school adjustment problems and fewer competencies than those who did not. Similarly, the more such events experienced, the more serious the problems and the greater the competence decrement. Lotyczewski, Cowen, and Weissberg (1986) reported similar findings for youngsters with physical health and illness problems. Brown (1985) found the same effects when children, rather than adults, were asked to report the frequency of stressful life events. Findings from these studies, consistent with Rutter's (1983) conjecture, suggest that the psychological toll exacted by multiple stressful events cumulates much as does lead poisoning.

Cowen, Weissberg, and Guare (1984) found that referred, compared to matched nonreferred, children experienced more stressful life events, were seen as less attractive physically, and had more serious health problems and poorer fine and gross motor coordination. Referred youngsters also required more "special services" in the schools, participated in fewer extracurricular activities, and had more serious family problems (e.g., natural father absent from home, father unemployed). Two composite risk indices were developed, one for problems and one for resources, based on items that significantly differentiated referred and nonreferred children (Cowen, Lotyczewski, & Weissberg, 1984). Both correlated significantly with teacher ratings of problem behaviors and

competencies. Among high-risk children, the presence of resources moderated the decrement in adjustment predisposed by stressful life events and familial disruption.

The preceding findings paint a clear, internally consistent picture. They suggest that the very occurrence of stressful life events and disruptive familial conditions can be taken as warning signs that school adjustment problems may ensue. One challenge they pose is how to intervene preventively to forestall the anticipated negative fallout from such circumstances.

The preceding "tip of the iceberg" summary is primarily to illustrate the breadth and depth of PMHP research activities. Research has been a core aspect of PMHP since its inception. Although program evaluation research has always been central, PMHP's total research effort has gone considerably beyond outcome studies to include in-depth study of program-relevant domains, such as the characteristics and functioning of child-aides, and factors that facilitate and impede young children's school adjustment. PMHP's research studies have been always mindful of the project's service roots and preventive mandate. Findings from research studies feed back into the program and structure the development and application of new, hopefully more effective modes of preventive intervention.

Recent Developments

PMHP has grown and changed more in the past decade than in its first two decades. Most of those recent changes fly under one of two banners: dissemination and primary prevention. We summarize those developments in the next sections.

Dissemination

In its first 15 years PMHP was limited to a small number of schools in a particular geographic area. The cumulation of program experience and effectiveness data during that period framed the challanege of how best to harness that information to promote constructive social change. Although we had written extensively about PMHP in the professional and scientific literature, the written word by itself does not appear to be an important factor in bringing about social change (Fairweather, 1972; Glaser, 1976; Shore, 1972). The National Institute of Mental Health (NIMH), which had funded PMHP's developmental stages, was strongly supportive of a dissemination thrust. A concern of NIMH and other funding agencies was that successful programs that ignored dissemination were at grave risk of early archival fates.

In that context, PMHP launched a three-pronged dissemination program in 1972. Compact sets of program descriptive materials, along with an announcement of a PMHP training workshop, were sent to school districts around the country. The workshop, directed to highly placed administrators from school districts with interest in implementation, provided detailed information about PMHP's rationale and operating practices and opportunities to mark-up implementation plans to fit a district's need and resource systems. Two other "hands-on" options were provided for districts that chose to implement (a) on-site visits by PMHP staff members, to provide concrete assistance around program start-up issues (e.g., aide selection and training, screening procedures), and (b) short-term internships in PMHP demonstration schools for personnel from new districts, to see the program in action and discuss program practices and issues with PMHP line personnel.

Over a 4-year period that approach helped to start a limited number of new programs around the country (Cowen, Davidson, & Gesten, 1980). To accelerate the pace of program dissemination, four PMHP Regional Dissemination Centers (RC), each based on its own successful program implementation, were established in Texas, Ohio, California, and North Carolina. Each replicated PMHP's dissemination activities with the goal of facilitating new implementations in its own geographic area. By the end of that second 4-year period, 87 PMHP-type, school-district-level programs were found to be in operation (Cowen, Spinell, Wright, & Weissberg, 1983). The RC development was constructive. It helped to start a number of new programs and further to identify elements in effective dissemination. Although that per se was gratifying, it was still a development with important reality limitations. RCs lacked the policy mandate, the clout, and the resources to bring about widespread program implementation.

Thus the RC thrust can be seen as an informative exercise in "demonstrational" innovation; it showed in an ad hoc way that new programs could be rooted in alert, favored, socially sensitive school environments. It did not (and could not) lead to "systematic" dissemination, that is, bringing effective preventive services to millions of youngsters in need, in thousands of school districts around the country. Moreover, at the time, the locus of re-

sponsibility for programming in education and mental health was shifting rapidly from the federal to the state level (Swift, 1980; Tableman, 1980). Given that trend, one that has continued to the present day, it became apparent that future systematic dissemination of a program such as PMHP could best proceed through an informed partnership involving those who were expert in the approach and duly empowered representatives of *state* agencies.

Accordingly, PMHP's next level of dissemination activity involved working directly with state agencies to promote program implementation. Interested state administrators were given detailed information about the program and its operation, within PMHP's workshop framework, as well as opportunities to discuss how an implementation program might work in their state. Concurrently, detailed guidelines for statewide program implementation were developed listing the concrete steps, commitments, and resources needed by states in that process, as well as the resources and support elements that PMHP staff could provide. Those efforts have borne significant fruit.

The single most extensive within-state PMHP development to date has, understandably, been in New York. With support from the New York State Department of Education, there are now approximately 100 implementing school districts in the state, ranging from the big city to highly rural areas. Within that broad development are subdevelopments of particular interest and potential modeling value. One example is the establishment of several effective rural PMHP program consortia (Farie, Cowen, & Smith, 1986), each consisting of six or seven rural districts with shared program resources for aide training, supervision, and consultation. The consortium approach has sharply expanded the reach of services and provided sources of interchange and stimulation that serve as antidotes to the discouragement and "burnout" that have long plagued personnel in isolated, underresourced systems.

Significant program expansion has taken place in other states as well. California, Washington, and Connecticut, for example, have passed specific PMHP enabling legislation, with a supporting budget leading to a rapid growth of district-level programs in those states. The California development is especially instructive. An initial piece of legislation authorized and provided seed money for the program; subsequent legislation designed to ensure the program's continuity and growth allocated to it proceeds from the sale of impounded merchandise (e.g., a yacht picked up in a drug "bust").

The rapid growth of new programs, both from the state thrust and the program's own internal ripple effects, makes it increasingly difficult to track the precise nature of program expansion. Our last formal, implementation survey was done in 1981 (Cowen, Spinell, et al, 1983). Presently, we estimate that there are 185 kindred district-level PMHP programs in the four states mentioned above and about 400 implementing school districts in all, around the world. The sum of those programs is considerable. Collectively, they screen and bring intensive effective helping services to thousands of young school children annually (Cowen, Hightower, Johnson, Sarno, & Weisberg, 1989).

PMHP's dissemination surveys (Cowen, Davidson, et al, 1980, Cowen, Spinell, et al, 1983) highlight several distinctive features of this development (i.e., its diversity and imaginativeness). Diversity means several things. Geographically, for example, programs range from Australia to the Wailing Wall in Jerusalem. Moreover, programs are located in large and small, urban, suburban and rural, and socioculturally, ethnically, and racially diverse districts. The latter include predominantly black and/or predominantly Hispanic school districts as well as complex, racially mixed groups such as those in Hawaii. Thus, one attribute of the model is its seeming adaptability to very diverse situations, including those involving historically neglected and underserved populations.

Diversity and imaginativeness were also apparent in the specific program defining elements reported. There was, for example, substantial variation in (a) extent and type of professional staffing (e.g., psychologists, social workers, guidance counselors), (b) types of nonprofessional help agents used (i.e., volunteer versus paid, full time versus part time, homemakers, retired people, students, businesspeople, and other community volunteers); (c) specific screening procedures; (d) methods of recruiting, training, and supervising help agents; (e) both formats for seeing children (e.g., group, individual) and approaches (e.g., relational versus behavioral) used; and (f) funding sources and patterns. Such variation is as it should, indeed *must*, be. To go back to an early metaphor, each new program must reflect its own defining

"pond ecology." Just as "flora and fauna" around a pond flourish to the extent that the pond offers certain environmental conditions, so must program "flora and fauna" (i.e., the specific defining practices of early detection and prevention programs) reflect the ecology of their host districts—their needs, resources, folkways, problems, skills, belief systems, and practices.

In summary, several aspects of the dissemination experience bear highlighting. The collective impact of the extended family of PMHP implementations is considerable: many, many thousands of youngsters screened and intensive effective preventive helping services brought to some 10,000 children, annually. Although the new programs follow PMHP's basic structural model, they range broadly in their literal program practices. Thus, it appears that the PMHP model can be adapted effectively to different environments and target populations. Progress in dissemination to date suggests that PMHP has had visible, constructive impact on how school mental health services are conceptualized and delivered, and has begun to crack the "tough nut" of bringing about constructive social change.

Primary Prevention Steps

The word "primary" in the Project's title is misleading. People have often assumed that that word was selected to connote primary *prevention* (Cowen, 1977b). That is not the case! Our initial intention in using that word was simply to highlight the project's focus on primary *graders*. Thus the PMHP we have so far described was, and remains, a project on ontogentically early secondary prevention.

The preceding explanation is to clarify, not apologize. To the contrary, we take pride in PMHP's accomplishments to date. It has been gratifying indeed to see consistent clinical and research evidence showing that young children can "turn it around" as a result of prompt, caring, and effective helping services. More broadly, it has also been rewarding to be part of a process whereby the PMHP alternative—an alternative that expands appreciably the reach and clout of school mental health services—has been adopted as a way of operating by other school districts.

Without discounting those accomplishments, it would be a mistake to be blinded by them. Whatever social gain PMHP offers, it is far from a perfect system. Although we have spoken of positive program outcomes, we use that term in a main-effects sense, knowing full well that not all children profit equally from the approach and that some youngsters fail to profit at all from it. Indeed, the many new project extensions that PMHP has developed over the years can individually and collectively be seen as an attempt to improve the project's batting average. Even so, it is clear that some children with seriously troubled early lives may enter PMHP's purview so late as to be largely immune even to the best of what it can offer.

As a program in ontogentically early secondary prevention, the classical PMHP, no matter how well it does its job, no matter how extensively it expands the reach of services, remains at best a more efficient and farther reaching route to (early) restoration. Although that per se is a bona fide alternative for mental health, it is not necessarily the only or best alternative. With that concern in mind, we have increasingly in recent years, within PMHP's broader framework, explored and developed true *primary* prevention programs for young school children. The latter differ qualitatively in assumptions and practices both from traditional mental health approaches and PMHP's basic approach as thus far described. Primary prevention programs are mass-oriented and before the fact of maladjustment (Cowen, 1982). They often seek to build health and competence from the start, rather than to counterpunch against entrenched problems, based on the assumption that the presence of competencies and resources can inoculate children against problems. Such programs are cast in an educational-building mode, not a rehabilitative-curative one. The very nature of primary prevention and its key tools suggest that working with young children in schools is an ideal route for such developments to follow. Moreover, working in a school context paves the way for other schools to adopt programs after evidence documenting their efficacy has been gathered.

PMHP's successful history in local area schools was a distinct plus in setting the stage for new primary prevention developments. Over many years, PMHP staff became well known to, and trusted by, school personnel, and a climate of close cordial working relationships was established. That PMHP has been widely accepted as a program that meets basic school needs and addresses important problems head-on and effectively, provided a currency of credibility for starting new programs. Beyond that, primary prevention pro-

gram extensions have been cast not as replacements for, but rather as "add-ons" to, the basic PMHP, which continues to meet school needs.

PMHP's school-based primary prevention thrust is still very much in process. Presently, these programs have neither the range nor depth of confirming outcome data of the basic PMHP. One reason for that difference, of course, is that these programs are much younger. Another is that they are time consuming and labor intensive, often requiring major changes both in the process of initial development and in later extensions to populations that differ, developmentally or socioculturally, from the original one (Cowen, 1984). With those constraints in mind, the next sections describe three directions that PMHP's recent primary prevention efforts have taken and cite program examples for each.

Competence Training. Generative knowledge bases (Cowen, 1980) demonstrate relationships between certain families of skills or competencies and adjustment in children; that is, their presence relates to adjustment, and deficiencies in them relate to maladjustment and/or are found in clinical groups. Accordingly, training children in those skills should, in principle, have adjustment enhancing effects. One area in which such linkages have been shown is social problem solving (SPS), a process that teaches children how, not what, to think in seeking to resolve interpersonal problems. Extensive work by the Hahnemann group (Shure & Spivack, 1978, 1982; Spivack, Platt, & Shure, 1976; Spivack & Shure, 1974) based on an interpersonal problem-solving training curriculum they developed, showed that children acquired the component program skills and, as they did, their adjustment improved. Both the cognitive and adjustment gains had short-term durability, and linkages between the two were established. Many attempts to replicate and extend that approach have since been made with different age and sociodemographic groups and modified training curricula and formats. Although some positive program findings have been reported (Elias et al, 1986), questions remain about the efficacy of the approach (Durlak, 1983).

PMHP has developed several SPS training curricula to teach young children such skills as alternative solution thinking, consequential thinking, means–end thinking, and taking the role of the other. Programs for younger and older children differ in level of complexity and specific exercises. All programs, however, are class-based and taught by the teacher much as any other academic subject. Detailed program training manuals provide goals and methods for each session. Teachers are trained in the curriculum's use and participate in discussion/supervisory sessions while the program is in progress. Separate curricula have been developed for second to fourth graders and for kindergarten and first-grade children. Those curricula, based on an approximate 15-week program, average about three sessions a week.

The basic curriculum for second- to fourth-grade children (Weissberg, Gesten, Liebenstein, Schmid, & Hutton, 1980) covers seven main steps: (a) recognizing feelings; (b) learning to formulate exactly what the problem is; (c) deciding on a goal; (d) impulse delay, (i.e., stopping to think before one acts); (e) generating as many different solutions as one can to solve the problem; (f) thinking ahead about possible consequences (i.e., what might happen next) of each solution; and (g) try a good solution; if that doesn't work, try another. A simplified version of the program for younger children (Winer, Hilpert, Gesten, Cowen, & Schubin, 1982) focuses ons teps 2, 5, and 6. Evaluations of various Rochester SPS programs (Gesten, Flores de Apodaca, Rains, Weissberg, & Cowen, 1979; Gesten et al, 1982; Weissberg et al, 1981a, 1981b; Winer et al, 1982) have shown that all trained groups have acquired the component SPS skills and that there have been some adjustment gains but fewer than those reported by the Hahnemann group. Linkages between skill and adjustment gains, however, have not been shown.

Teachers and children have found the program to be interesting and enjoyable; moreover, teachers have reported effective applications of program learnings in dealing with everyday interpersonal problems in the classroom. Hence SPS trained teachers often continue to teach the program, or portions of it, on their own, in subsequent years. Feedback from some teachers that the full program was time consuming and somewhat repetitive prompted the recent development of an abbreviated 20-session SPS program for fourth graders. An initial evaluation of its efficacy yielded positive skill acquisition and adjustment data (Work & Olsen, 1990).

Although SPS training well exemplifies a competence training approach in primary prevention with young children, it does not exhaust that strategy (Cowen & Work, 1988). Other conceptually related interventions have been developed to train children in such relevant skills as realistic goal setting (Stamps, 1975), curiosity behavior (Susskind, 1979), causal thinking (Ojemann, 1969), altruism (Jason, Robson, & Lipshutz, 1980), and relationship-forming behavior (Vogelsong, Most, & Yanchko, 1979). PMHP's recent primary prevention explorations have also included efforts to develop other types of skill enhancement programs, including programs to teach youngsters: (a) self-control skills (e.g., Stalonas et al., 1982; Rohrbeck, 1986) and (b) classroom coping skills such as appropriate assertiveness (Boike, 1987), based on a model shown to be effective by Rotheram, Armstrong, and Booraem (1982). The latter, still-evolving programs are based on generative knowledge bases linking their component skills to adjustment. Each therefore seeks to impart those skills as a way of enhancing adjustment.

Social System Analysis and Change. We are all, to a considerable extent, products of the environments in which we develop and have significant interactions. Environments are rarely neutral in their effects on people; they either facilitate or impede adaptation. That point is relevant for schools. Given the amount of time that children spend in schools, school environments and practices can enhance or restrict children's learning experiences and psychological wellness. Primary prevention's challenges are to identify elements or practices in school and class environments that favor positive outcomes and to develop structures that can enhance such outcomes.

Past studies have shown important relationships between school or class environments and the behavior of children/youth (Barker & Gump, 1964; Kelly, 1979; Moos, 1979; Stallings, 1975). Those studies demonstrate both main-effects relationships (e.g., children in small schools are involved in more activities and are more visible than children in large schools) (Barker & Gump, 1964) and person–environment interactions (e.g., distractible children do better in contained classes, whereas nondistractible children do better in open classrooms) (Reiss & Martell, 1974). Findings of that type prompted, within PMHP's framework, studies of the class environment and pilot interventions based on change in practice designed to enhance adjustment. With fifth- and sixth-grade children, for example, Wright and Cowen (1982) showed that in classes seen by children as high in Order and Organization, and Affiliation as measured by Moos's (1974) Class Environment Scale, teachers judged the children to be better adjusted. Similarly, teachers' self-control ratings of children were higher in classrooms that children judged to be high in Order and Organization, and Involvement (Humphrey, 1984).

To the extent that class attributes such as Affiliation and Involvement related to positive adjustment, a next logical step was to promote class practices that might strengthen those qualities. Peer teaching approaches have been used successfully in that context (Gump, 1980; Slavin, 1983; Sprinthall, 1984). One form of peer teaching, the so-called jigsaw group, was used by Aronson, Blaney, Stephan, Sikes, and Snapp (1978) in a program designed to reduce problems of violence and interracial tension following the forced busing of Texas school children. Aronson et al. (1978) created small, interdependent learning groups in which children taught each other in fifth-grade social studies classes. Jigsaw children learned the assigned social studies content as well as youngsters in traditional classes. They also came to like groupmates, classmates, and the school more and, interestingly, increased in self-esteem.

Wright and Cowen (1985) developed a similar program for fifth-grade social studies classes. Curriculum was prepared for two units covering 10 weeks. Classrooms were divided into five-person cross-sex jigsaw units. Each unit reflected diverse ability levels and excluded close friends. Each day's study unit was divided into five subunits and each group member was responsible for learning his or her assigned unit and teaching it to groupmates. Jigsaw students, compared to non-program controls, came to see their classes as more involved. They reported being happier in class and enjoying school work more. Teachers reported reductions in children's school problems and increases in their competencies. Importantly, jigsaw students did significantly better than controls on monthly social studies exams and report card grades; the greatest performance gains came from youngsers with initially low academic status.

Additional pilot work in the area of modified teaching practice now under way is based on a "Study Buddy" program (Hightower, Avery, & Levinson, 1988), a class-based preventive inter-vention for fourth to sixth graders. In this program children are paired with a same-sexed classmate for a 6-month period, to work collaboratively in two 45-minute units per week on academic and nonacademic tasks. Teacher training and consultation is provided to enhance teacher skills and support the new modality (Talmage, Pascarella, & Ford, 1984). Formal evaluation of this program has shown the leaders judged program children to have fewer problems and more competencies than controls. They reported greater satisfaction with their class environments and better relationships with peers. Their math skills improved more and they had fewer absences and days tardy (Hightower et al, 1988).

Stressful Life Events. Our own earlier findings cited above, and findings reported by others (Garmezy & Rutter, 1983; Honig, 1986a, 1986b; Johnson, 1986), support the conclusion that stressful life events and circumstances predispose adjustment problems in children. Because such effects often appear in the form of academic performance declines and behavior problems, they create vexing everyday problems for school personnel. If stressful events and circumstances can be taken as warning signs that adjustment and learning problems may follow, the challenge is to develop effective preventive interventions to forestall anticipated negative psychological consequences for children who experience those events.

An early pilot project with that goal was described previously (Felner, Norton, et al, 1981). In seeking to broaden that intervention, our attention turned both on epidemiological and substantive grounds to children of divorce. It is now estimated that 40 to 50% of today's marriages will end in divorce (Glick & Norton, 1979). Currently, more than 1 million American children experience parental separation or divorce annually (Report of the Select Committee on Children, Youth and Families, 1983). Those figures reflect signfiicant social change. Yoking that epidemiological data with consistent research findings, our own and others, documenting the damaging psychological effects of marital conflict and divorce on children (Guidubaldi, Cleminshaw, Perry, & Mcloughlin, 1983; Hetherington, Cox, & Cox, 1978; Wallerstein, 1983), provides a compelling rationale for preventive intervention. Indeed, given the stark nature of those findings it is surprising that there has been so little empirical study of preventive interventions for people affected by divorce. A case in point: Bloom, Asher, and White's (1978) review presented powerful evidence of divorce's adverse effects on many basic indicators of physical and psychological well-being in adults. Nothwithstanding the sledgehammer nature of those data, the authors noted ironically that not a single controlled, carefully evaluated preventive intervention for divorcing adults had been reported as of then. The same was true for children of divorce.

Important corrective steps have since been taken. Bloom, for example, reported an important preventive intervention for divorcing adults (Bloom, Hodges, Kern, & McFaddin, 1985). Re-follow-up data testifying to its positive effects (Bloom, Hodges, Kern, & McFaddin, 1985). Related explorations began for children of divorce (Cantor, 1977; Guerney & Jordon, 1979; Kalter, Pickar, & Lesowitz, 1984; Stolberg & Garrison, 1985). Those advances as well as our own prior work led to the development of the Children of Divorce Intervention Project—CODIP (Pedro-Carroll & Cowen, 1985). Its goal was to develop effective school-based preventive interventions for urban and suburban, elementary-aged children of divorce.

The first and most extensively tested CODIP program was targeted to fourth- to sixth-grade suburban children of divorce. Early program sessions seek to build a sense of support and to explore divorce-related feelings. A middle program unit teaches divorce-relevant problem-solving skills, including the important distinction between problems that are and are not within the child's control. The final sessions teach appropriate methods for the expression and control of anger and seek to build self-esteem. Program children are seen in mixed-sex groups of eight, for 12 one-hour sessions. The sessions are co-led, primarily by school-based personnel who receive extensive preprogram training both on children of divorce and group leadership techniques. Weekly discussion/supervisory meetings are held for leaders while the program is in progress.

Two separate, multiperspective, pre—post evaluations were completed for the suburban fourth- to sixth-grade program (Pedro-Carroll & Cowen, 1985; Pedro-Carroll, Cowen, Hightower, & Guare, 1986). In the first study, teachers reported significant decreases in participants' school problem behaviors and significant increases in their school competencies. Parents reported improved communication with their children about divorce-related matters and, more generally, about children's feelings, problems, experiences, and accomplishments. Children reported significantly lower anxiety scores and a better understanding of their parents' and their own feelings about the divorce. They learned to solve problems more effectively and came to feel less alone and/or different. Group leaders reported similarly positive program effects. Confirmation of those findings in the second study (Pedro-Carroll et al, 1986) led to the completion of a detailed program curriculum guide (Pedro-Carroll, 1985) and an integrative chapter summarizing CODIP procedures and findings to date (Pedro-Carroll & Cowen, 1987).

Notwithstanding those early, encouraging CODIP findings, generalizations about the program were restricted by the relatively small samples of suburban, white, late-latency, middle-class participants. Since them, our main goal has been to develop and evaluate CODIP variants for fourth- to sixth-grade urban, and second- to third-grade urban and suburban, children of divorce. Although the program's underlying goals have remained constant, major changes in program content and format were needed to make it developmentally and socioculturally relevant for these new groups. The translation of the program to younger children, for example, involved a greater use of play and expressive materials and less discussion, as well as a sharper tailoring to divorce-related concerns known to be developmentally relevant to younger children (Wallerstein, 1983). The program for younger children also required more sessions.

In like manner, moving from suburban to urban schools required more elastic definitions of family structures as well as program materials (e.g., books, dolls, puppets) that better reflected the racial diversity of urban groups. Modified CODIP programs have now been conducted with second- to third-grade suburban (Sterling, 1986) and urban (Alpert-Gillis, Pedro-Carroll, & Cowen, 1989) children, as well as fourth- to sixth-grade urban children. The ultimate goal of the CODIP thrust is to produce documented program intervention models that extend from second- to sixth-grade for urban and suburban school children. Current epidemiological data and the day-to-day experience of school personnel suggest that effective preventive intervention models of that type are needed.

Learnings from the CODIP experience can be

applied to other situations. Although divorce, to be sure, is *one* highly stressful life event for young children, there are other important ones as well (e.g., death of a close family member) for which appropriate preventive interventions can be gainfully developed. One step beyond, however, many children in modern society grow up under life conditions of profound and chronic adversity, described by Garmezy (1981) as "stressors of marked gravity." For most of those youngsters there are serious educational and psychological consequences. Some few, however, for reasons not yet clearly understood turn out to be competent and well adjusted in spite of chronic life adversities. Those youngsters have variously been called "invulnerable" (Garmezy & Neuchterlein, 1972), "invincible" (Werner & Smith, 1982), or highly "resilient." A fuller understanding of the wellsprings of that unusual type of resilience can both advance a needed psychology of wellness and help to frame early, school-based preventive interventions for children who enter the schools with high levels of exposure to stressors of marked gravity (Cowen & Work, 1988).

SUMMARY AND OVERVIEW

PMHP is a 30-year-old school-based program, built around the concepts of early detection and prevention of young children's adjustment problems. It has developed in slow, evolutionary ways and has approached the goal of prevention at different levels. PMHP's most basic structural features include its (a) focus on young children, (b) systematic use of screening and early detection procedures, (c) use of nonprofessional child-aides to provide prompt, effective preventive services, and (d) changing role for the school-based professional to support a geometric increase in the reach of needed services.

Multifaceted research on the program and on young schoolchildren has always been integral to PMHP's fabric. Research findings have been used to strengthen program practices and extend PMHP's range of applicability. Specifically, PMHP program evaluation studies have provided a basis for program dissemination. As part of that process, several states have enacted specific PMHP enabling legislation with supporting budgets in ways that have increased appreciably the numbers of school districts implementing this innovative pro-

gram model. Thus the PMHP experience has had some visible impact on how school mental health services are conceptualized and delivered, and on the difficult challenge of bringing about constructive social change.

Although the original PMHP development offers a useful, workable alternative to mental health's past traditional emphasis on repairing things that have gone seriously wrong, it remains at best, a more efficient, effective way of doing ontogenetically early secondary prevention. Awareness of that limitation has prompted recent efforts within PMHP's school-based framework, to develop programs in true primary prevention— programs based on the goals of promoting the well-being of all children from the start. This more recent, indeed still nascent, thrust has included three different strands: (a) mass-oriented, class-based educational programs designed to train adjustment mediating skills or competencies; (b) changes in class environments and practices designed to enhance learning and psychological wellness; and (c) preventive programs for children who have experienced stressful life events (e.g., children of divorce). The "book" on these new approaches remains open; certainly, supporting efficacy data for them are less extensive than for the basic PMHP.

Although the approaches described represent different levels or cross-cuts of prevention, individually and collectively they provide bona fide alternatives to mental health's established, after-the-fact restorative ways. Further development of these preventive pathways, pathways that put young children front and center, can advance the educational and psychological well-being of many young children—an entirely worthwhile and much needed goal.

REFERENCES

Alpert-Gillis, L. J., Pedro-Carroll, J. L., & Cowen, E. L. (1989). Children of Divorce Intervention Program: Development, implementation and evaluation of a program for young urban children. *Journal of Consulting and Clinical Psychology.* (in press)

Anderson, L. S., Cooper, S., Hassol, L., Klein, D. C., Rosenblum, G., & Bennett, C. C. (1966). *Community psychology: A report of the Boston Conference on the Education of Psychologists for Community Mental Health.* Boston: Boston University.

Aronson, E., Blaney, N., Stephan, C., Sikes, J., & Snapp,

M. (1978). *The jigsaw classroom.* Beverly Hills, CA: Sage.

Barker, R. G., & Gump, P. (1964). *Big school, small school.* Stanford, CA: Stanford University Press.

Bloom, B. L., Asher, S. J., & White, S. W. (1978). Marital disruption as a stressor: A review and analysis. *Psychological Bulletin, 85,* 867–894.

Bloom, B. L., Hodges, W. F., Kern, M. B., & McFaddin, preventive program for the newly separated. *American Journal of Community Psychology, 10,* 251–264.

Bloom, B. L., Hodges, W. F., Kern, M. B., & McFaddin, S. C. (1985). A preventive intervention program for the newly separated: Final report. *American Journal of Orthopsychiatry, 55,* 9–26.

Boike, M. F. (1987). *Classroom coping skills: Program curriculum.* Unpublished manual, University of Rochester, Center for Community Study, Rochseter, NY.

Boike, M. F., Gesten, E. L., Cowen, E. L., Felner, R. D., & Francis, R. (1978). Relationships between family background problems and school problems and competencies of young normal children. *Psychology in the Schools, 15,* 283–290.

Bower, E. M. (1977). Mythologies, realities and possibilities. In G. W. Albee & J. M. Joffe (Eds.), *Primary prevention of psychopathology: Vol. 1. The issues* (pp. 24–41). Hanover, NH; University Press of New England.

Bower, E. M. (1978). Early and periodic screening diagnosis and treatment: Realities, risks, and possibilities. *American Journal of Orthopsychiatry, 48,* 4–6.

Brown, L. P. (1985). *Stressful life events as perceived by children.* Unpublished Ph.D. dissertation, University of Rochester, Rochester, NY.

Cantor, D. W. (1977). School-based groups for children of divorce. *Journal of Divorce, 1,* 183–187.

Chandler, C., Weissberg, R. P., Cowen, E. L., & Guare, J. (1984). The long-term effects of a school-based secondary prevention program for young maladapting children. *Journal of Consulting and Clinical Psychology, 52,* 165–170.

Cowen, E. L. (1973). Social and community interventions. *Annual review of psychology, 24,* 423–472.

Cowen, E. L. (1977a). Baby-steps toward primary prevention. *American Journal of Community Psychology, 5,* 1–22.

Cowen, E. L. (1977b). Psychologists and primary prevention: Blowing the cover story. *American Journal of Community Psychology, 5,* 481–489.

Cowen, E. L. (1980). The wooing of primary prevention. *American Journal of Community Psychology, 8,* 258–284.

Cowen, E. L. (1982). The special number: A compleat roadmap. In E. L. Cowen (Ed.), *Research in primary prevention in mental health. American Journal of Community Psychology, 10,* 239–250.

Cowen, E. L. (1983). Primary prevention in mental health: Past, present and future. In R. D. Felner, L. Jason, J. Moritsugu, & S. S. Farber (Eds.), *Preventive psychology: Theory, research and practice in community interventions* (pp. 11–25). Elmsford, NY: Pergamon Press.

Cowen, E. L. (1984). A general structural model for primary prevention program development in mental health. *Personnel and Guidance Journal, 62,* 485–490.

Cowen, E. L., Davidson, E. R., & Gesten, E. L. (1980). Program dissemination and the modification of delivery practices in school mental health. *Professional Psychology, 11,* 36–47.

Cowen, E. L., Dorr, D. A., Clarfield, S. P., Kreling, B., McWilliams, S. A., Pokracki, F., Pratt, D. M., Terrell, D., & Wilson, A. (1973). The AML: A quick screening device for early detection of school maladaptation. *American Journal of Community Psychology, 1,* 12–35.

Cowen, E. L., Dorr, D. A., & Pokracki, F. (1972). Selection of nonprofessional child aides for a school mental health project. *Community Mental Health Journal, 121,* 145–154.

Cowen, E. L., Dorr, D. A., Trost, M. A., & Izzo, L. D. (1972). A follow-up study of maladapting school children seen by nonprofessionals. *Journal of Consulting and Clinical Psychology, 39,* 235–238.

Cowen, E. L., & Gesten, E. L. (1980). Evaluating community programs: Tough and tender perspectives. In M. Gibbs, J. R. Lachenmeyer, & J. Sigal (Eds.), *Community psychology: Theoretical and empirical approaches* (pp. 363–393). New York: Gardner Press.

Cowen, E. L., Gesten, E. L., & DeStefano, M. A. (1977). Nonprofessional and professional help agents' views of interventions with young maladapting school children. *American Journal of Community Psychology, 5,* 469–479.

Cowen, E. L., Gesten, E. L., Wilson, A. B., & Lorion, R. P. (1977). Helping contacts between nonprofessional child-aides and young children experiencing school adjustment problems. *Journal of School Psychology, 15,* 349–357.

Cowen, E. L., Hightower, A. D., Johnson, D. B., Sarno, M., & Weissberg, R. P. (1989). State level dissemination of a program for early detection and prevention of school maladaptation. *Professional Psychology, 20.* (In press)

Cowen, E. L., Lorion, R. P., & Caldwell, R. A. (1975). Nonprofessionals' judgments about clinical interaction problems. *Journal of Consulting and Clinical Psychology, 43,* 619–625.

Cowen, E. L., Lorion, R. P., & Dorr, D. (1974). Research in the community cauldron: A case history. *Canadian Psychologist, 15,* 313–325.

Cowen, E. L., Lotyczewski, B. S., & Weissberg, R. P. (1984). Risk and resource indicators and their relationship to young children's school adjustment. *American Journal of Community Psychology, 12,* 353–367.

Cowen, E. L., Orgel, A. R., Gesten, E. L., & Wilson, A. B. (1979). The evaluation of an intervention program for young school children with acting-out problems. *Journal of Abnormal Child Psychology, 7,* 381–396.

Cowen, E. L., Pedersen, A., Babigian, H., Izzo, L. D., & Trost, M. A. (1973). Long-term follow-up of early detected vulnerable children. *Journal of Consulting and Clinical Psychology, 41,* 438–446.

Cowen, E. L., Spinell, A., Wright, S., & Weissberg, R. P. (1983). Continuing dissemination of a school-based early detection and prevention model. *Professional Psychology, 14,* 118–127.

Cowen, E. L., Trost, M. A., Lorion, R. P., Dorr, D., Izzo, L. D., & Isaacson, R. V. (1975). *New ways in school mental health: Early detection and prevention of school maladaptation.* New York: Human Sciences Press.

Cowen, E. L., Weissberg, R. P., & Guare, J. (1984). Differentiating attributes of children referred to a school mental health program. *Journal of Abnormal Child Psychology, 12,* 397–409.

Cowen, E. L., Weissberg, R. P., Lotyczewski, B. S., Bromley, M. S., Gilliland-Mallo, G., DeMeis, J. L., Farago, J. P., Grassi, R. J., Haffey, W. G., Werner, M. J., & Woods, A. (1983). Validity generalization of school-based preventive mental health program. *Professional Psychology, 14,* 613–623.

Cowen, E. L., & Work, W. C. (1988). Resilient children, psychological wellness and primary prevention. *American Journal of Community Psychology, 16,* 591–607.

Cowen, E. L., Zax, M., Izzo, L. D., & Trost, M. A. (1966). Prevention of emotional disorders in the school setting: A further investigation. *Journal of Consulting Psychology, 30,* 381–387.

DeStefano, M. A., Gesten, E. L., & Cowen, E. L. (1977). Teachers' views of the treatability of children's school adjustment problems. *Journal of Special Education, 11,* 275–280.

Dorr, D. (1972). An ounce of prevention. *Mental Hygiene, 56,* 25–27.

Dorr, D., Cowen, E. L., & Kraus, R. (1973). Mental health professionals view nonprofessional mental health workers. *American Journal of Community Psychology, 1,* 258–265.

Dorr, D., Cowen, E. L., & Sandler, I. N. (1973). Changes in nonprofessional mental health workers' response preference and attitudes as a function of training and supervised field experience. *Journal of School Psychology, 11,* 118–122.

Dorr, D., Cowen, E. L., Sandler, I. N., & Pratt, D. M. (1973). Dimensionality of a test battery for nonprofessional mental health workers. *Journal of Consulting and Clinical Psychology, 41,* 181–185.

Durlak, J. A. (1977). Description and evaluation of a behaviorally oriented, school-based preventive mental health program. *Journal of Consulting and Clinical Psychology, 45,* 27–33.

Durlak, J. A. (1983). Social problem-solving as a primary prevention strategy. In R. D. Felner, L. A. Jason, J. N. Moritsugu, & S. S. Farber (Eds.), *Preventive psychology: Theory, research and practice* (pp. 31–48). Elmsford, NY: Pergamon Press.

Elias, M. J., Gara, M., Ubriaco, M., Rothbaum, P. A., Clabby, J. F., & Schuyler, T. (1986). Impact of a preventive social problem solving intervention on children's coping with middle school stressors. *American Journal of Community Psychology, 14,* 259–276.

Ensminger, M. E., Kellam, S. G., & Rubin, R. B. (1983). School and family origins of delinquency: Comparisons by sex. In K. T. VanDusen & S. A. Mednick (Eds.), *Prospective studies of crime and delinquency* (pp. 17–41). Boston: Kluwer Nijhoff.

Fairweather, G. W. (1972). *Social change: The challenge to survival.* Morristown, NJ: General Learning Press.

Farie, A. M., Cowen, E. L., & Smith, M. (1986). The development and implementation of a rural consortium program to provide early, preventive school mental health services. *Community Mental Health Journal, 22,* 94–103.

Felner, R. D., Farber, S. S., Ginter, M. A., Boike, M. F., & Cowen, E. L. (1980). Family stress and organization following parental divorce or death. *Journal of Divorce, 4,* 67–76.

Felner, R. D., Ginter, M. A., Boike, M. F., & Cowen, E. L. (1981a). Parental death or divorce and the school adjustment of young children. *American Journal of Community Psychology, 9,* 181–191.

Felner, R. D., Ginter, M. A., Boike, M. F., & Cowen, E. L. (1981b). Parental death or divorce in childhood: Problems, interventions and outcomes in a school-based project. *Journal of Prevention, 1,* 240–246.

Felner, R. D., Jason, L. A., Moritsugu, J. N., & Farber, S. S. (1983). *Preventive psychology: Theory, research and practice.* Elmsford, NY: Pergamon Press.

Felner, R. D., Norton, P. L., Cowen, E. L., & Farber, S. S. (1981). A prevention program for children experiencing life crisis. *Professional Psychology, 12,* 446–452.

Felner, R. D., Stolberg, A. L., & Cowen, E. L. (1975). Crisis events and school mental health referral patterns of young children. *Journal of Consulting and Clinical Psyhology, 43,* 305–310.

Gallagher, R., & Cowen, E. L. (1976). Similarity of referral problems in sibling and nonsibling pairs. *Journal of Consulting and Clinical Psychology, 44,* 873.

Gallagher, R., & Cowen, E. L. (1977). Birth order and school adjustment problems. *Journal of Individual Differences, 33,* 70–77.

Garmezy, N. (1981). Children under stress: Perspectives on antecedents and correlates of vulnerability and resistance to psychopathology. In A. I. Robin, J. Aronoff, A. M. Barclay, & R. A. Zucker (Eds.), *Further explorations in personality* (pp. 196–269). New York: Wiley.

Garmezy, N., & Neuchterlein, K. (1972). Invulnerable children: The fact and fiction of competence and disadvantage. *American Journal of Orthopsychiatry, 42,* 328–329.

Garmezy, N., & Rutter, M. (Eds.). (1983). *Stress, coping, and development in children.* New York: McGraw-Hill.

Gesten, E. L. (1976). A Health Resources Inventory: The development of a measure of the personal and social competence of primary grade children. *Journal of Consulting and Clinical Psychology, 44,* 775–786.

Gesten, E. L., Cowen, E. L., DeStefano, M. A., & Gallagher, R. (1978). Teachers' judgments of class-related and teaching-related problem situations. *Journal of Special Education, 12,* 171–181.

Gesten, E. L., Flores de Apodaca, R., Rains, M. H.,

Weissberg, R. P., & Cowen, E. L. (1979). Promoting peer related social competence in schools. In M. W. Kent & J. E. Rolf (Eds.), *The primary prevention of psychopathology: Vol. 3. Social competence in children* (pp. 220–247). Hanover, NH: University Press of New England.

Gesten, E. L., Rains, M. H., Rapkin, B. D., Weissberg, R. P., Flores de Apodaca, R., Cowen, E. L., & Bowen, R. (1982). Training children in social problem-solving competencies: A first and second look. *American Journal of Community Psychology, 10,* 95–115.

Gesten, E. L., Scher, K., & Cowen, E. L. (1978). Judged school problems and competencies of referred children with varying family background characteristics. *Journal of Abnormal Child Psychology, 6,* 247–255.

Ginsberg, M. R., Weissberg, R. P., & Cowen, E. L. (1985). The relationship between supervisor's satisfaction with supervision and client change in. *Journal of Community Psychology, 13,* 387–392.

Glaser, E. M. (Ed.). (1976). *Putting knowledge to use: A distillation of the literature regarding knowledge transfer and change.* Los Angeles: Human Interaction Research Institute.

Glick, P. C., & Norton, A. J. (1979). *Marrying, divorcing and living together in the U.S. today.* Washington, DC: Population Reference Bureau.

Glidewell, J. C., & Swallow, C. S. (1969). *The prevalence of maladjustment in elementary schools: A report prepared for the Joint Commission on the Mental Health of Children.* Chicago: University of Chicago Press.

Guerney, L., & Jordon, L. (1979). Children of divorce: A community support group. *Journal of Divorce, 2,* 283–294.

Guidubaldi, J., Cleminshaw, A. K., Perry, J. D., & Mcloughlin, C. S. (1983). The impact of parental divorce on children: Report of the nationwide NASP study. *School Psychology Review, 12,* 300–323.

Gump, P. V. (1980). The school as a social situation. *Annual Review of Psychology, 31,* 553–582.

Hetherington, E. M., Cox, M., & Cox, R. (1978). The aftermath of divorce. In J. H. Stevens & M. Mathews (Eds.), *Mother–child, father–child relationships* (pp. 149–176). Washington, DC: National Association for the Education of Young Children.

Hightower, A. D., Avery, R. R., & Levinson, H. R. (1988). An evaluation of the Study-Buddy Program: A preventive intervention for 4th and 5th grades. Paper presented at NASP Annual Meeting, Chicago.

Hightower, A. D., Cowen, E. L., Spinell, A. P., Lotyczewski, B. S., Guare, J. C., Rohrbeck, C. A., & Brown, L. P. (1987). The Child Rating Scale: The development and psychometric refinement of a socioemotional self-rating scale for young school children. *School Psychology Review, 16,* 239–255.

Hightower, A. D., Spinell, A. P., & Lotyczewski, B. S. (1986). *AML-R Behavior Rating Scale guidelines.* Unpublished manuscript, Primary Mental Health Project, Rochester, NY.

Hightower, A. D., Work, W. C., Cowen, E. L., Lotyczewski, B. S., Spinell, A. P., Guare, J. C., & Rohrbeck, C. A. (1986). The Teacher–Child Rating Scale: A brief objective measure of elementary children's school problem beahviors and competencies. *School Psychology Review, 15,* 393–409.

Holzberg, J. D., Knapp, R. H., & Turner, J. L. (1967). College students as companions to the mentally ill. In E. L. Cowen, E. A. Gardner, M. Zax (Eds.), *Emergent approaches to mental health problems* (pp. 91–109). New York: Appleton-Century-Crofts.

Honig, A. S. (1986a, May). Stress and coping in children: Part 1. *Young Children,* pp. 50–63.

Honig, A. S. (1986b, July). Stress and coping in children: Part 2. Interpersonal family relationships. *Young Children,* pp. 47–59.

Humphrey, L. L. (1984). Children's self control in relation to perceived environment. *Journal of Personality and Social Psychology, 46,* 178–188.

Jason, L. A., Robson, S. D., & Lipshutz, S. A. (1980). Enhancing sharing behaviors through the use of naturalistic contingencies. *Journal of Community Psychology, 8,* 237–244.

Johnson, J. H. (1986). *Life events as stressors in childhood and adolescence.* Newbury Park, CA: Sage.

Joint Commission on the Mental Health of Children. (1969). *Crisis in child mental health: Challenge for the 1970's.* New York: Harper & Row.

Kalter, N., Pickar, J., & Lesowitz, M. (1984). School-based developmental facilitation groups for children of divorce: A preventive intervention. *American Journal of Orthopsychiatry, 54,* 613–623.

Kellam, S. G., Branch, J. D., Agrawal, K. C., & Ensminger, M. E. (1975). *Mental health and going to school: The Woodlawn program of assessment, early intervention, and evaluation.* Chicago: University of Chicago Press.

Kellam, S. G., Branch, J. D., Agrawal, K. C., & Grabill, M. E. (1972). Woodlawn Mental Health Center: An evolving strategy for planning community mental health. In S. E. Golann & C. Eisdorfer (Eds.), *Handbook of community mental health* (pp. 711–727). New York: Appleton-Century-Crofts.

Kellam, S. G., Simon, M. B., & Ensminger, M. E. (1983). Antecedents in first grade of teenage substance use and psychological well being: A ten-year community-wide prospective study. In D. F. Ricks & B. S. Dohrenwend (Eds.), *Origins of psychopathology: Research and public policy* (pp. 73–97). New York: Cambridge University Press.

Kelly, J. G. (Ed.). (1979). *Adolescent boys in high school: A psychological study of coping and adaptation.* Hillsdale, NJ: Lawrence Erlbaum.

Keogh, B. K., & Becker, L. D. (1973). Early detection of learning problems: Questions, cautions and guidelines. *Exceptional Children, 40,* 5–11.

Kirschenbaum, D. (1979). Social competence intervention and evaluation in the inner city: Cincinnati's Social Skills Development Program. *Journal of Consulting and Clinical Psychology, 47,* 778–780.

Kirschenbaum, D., DeVoge, J. B., Marsh, M. E., & Steffen, J. J. (1980). Multimodal evaluation of therapy vs. consultation components in a large inner-city early intervention program. *American Journal of Community Psychology, 8,* 587–601.

Klein, D. C., & Goldstein, S. E. (Eds.). (1977). *Primary prevention: An idea whose time has come* (DHEW Publication No. ADM 77-447). Washington, DC: U.S. Government Printing Office.

Lorion, R. P., Caldwell, R. A., & Cowen, E. L. (1976). Effects of a school mental health project: A one-year follow-up. *Journal of School Psychology, 14,* 56–63.

Lorion, R. P., Cowen, E. L., & Caldwell, R. A. (1974). Problem types of children referred to a school based mental health program: Identification and outcome. *Journal of Consulting and Clinical Psychology, 42,* 491–496.

Lorion, R. P., Cowen, E. L., & Caldwell, R. A. (1975). Normative and parametric analyses of school maladjustment. *American Journal of Community Psychology, 3,* 291–301.

Lorion, R. P., Cowen, E. L., & Kraus, R. M. (1974). Some hidden "regularities" in a school mental health program and their relation to intended outcomes. *Journal of Consulting and Clinical Psychology, 42,* 346–352.

Lorion, R. P., Cowen, E. L., Kraus, R. M., & Milling, L. S. (1977). Family background characteristics and school adjustment problems. *Journal of Community Psychology, 5,* 142–148.

Lotyczewski, B. S., Cowen, E. L., & Weissberg, R. P. (1986). Adjustment correlates of physical and health problems in young children. *Journal of Special Education, 20,* 241–250.

McWilliams, S. A. (1972). A process analysis of nonprofessional intervention with children. *Journal of School Psychology, 10,* 367–377.

Moos, R. H. (1974). *Manual: Class Environment Scale.* Palo Alto, CA: Consulting Psychologists Press.

Moos, R. H. (1979). *Evaluating educational environments.* San Francisco: Jossey-Bass.

Namir, S., & Weinstein, R. S. (1982). Children: Facilitating new directions. In L. R. Snowden (Ed.), *Reaching the underserved: Mental health needs of neglected populations* (pp. 43–73). Beverly Hills, CA: Sage.

Ojemann, R. H. (1969). Incorporating psychological concepts in the school curriculum. In H. P. Clarizio (Ed.), *Mental health and the educative process* (pp. 360–368). Skokie, IL: Rand-McNally.

Pedro-Carroll, J. L. (1985). *The Children of Divorce Intervention Program: Procedures Manual.* Rochester, NY: University of Rochester Center for Community Study.

Pedro-Carroll, J. L., & Cowen, E. L. (1985). The Children of Divorce Intervention Project: An investigation of the efficacy of a school-based prevention program. *Journal of Consulting and Clinical Psychology, 53,* 603–611.

Pedro-Carroll, J. L., & Cowen, E. L. (1987). Preventive interventions for children of divorce. In J. P. Vincent (Ed.), *Advances in family intervention, assessment and theory* (Vol. 4, pp. 281–307). Greenwich, CT: JAI Press.

Pedro-Carroll, J. L., Cowen, E. L., Hightower, A. D., &

Guare, J. C. (1986). Preventive intervention with latency-aged children of divorce: A replication study. *American Journal of Community Psychology, 14,* 277–290.

President's Commission on Mental Health. (1978). *Report to the President* (Vol. 1). Washington, DC: U.S. Government Printing Office. (Stock No. 040-000-00390-8)

Prevention Task Panel Report. (1978). *Task Panel reports submitted to the President's Commission on Mental Health* (Vol. 4, pp. 1822–1863). Washington, DC: U.S. Government Printing Office. (Stock No. 040-000-00393-2)

Rappaport, J. (1977). *Community psychology: Values, research, and action.* New York: Holt, Rinehart and Winston.

Reiss, S., & Martell, R. (1974). *Educational and psychological effects of open space education in Oak Park, Illinois* [Final report to Board of Education, District 97, Oak Park, Illinois].

Report of the Select Committee on Children, Youth, and Families, 98th Congress. (1983). *U.S. children and their families: Current conditions and recent trends.* Washington, DC: Foundation for Child Development.

Rickel, A. U., Dyhdalo, L. L., & Smith, R. L. (1984). Prevention with preschoolers. In M. C. Roberts & L. Peterson (Eds.), *Prevention of problems in childhood: Psychological research and applications* (pp. 74–102). New York: Wiley.

Rioch, M. J. (1967). Pilot projects in training mental health counselors. In E. L. Cowen, E. A. Gardner, & M. Zax (Eds.), *Emergent approaches to mental health problems* (pp. 110–127). New York: Appleton-Century-Crofts.

Roberts, M. C., & Peterson, L. (Eds.), (1984). *Prevention of problems in childhood: Psychological research and applications.* New York: Wiley.

Rohrbeck, C. A. (1986). *An evaluation of a self-control skill-training program for urban third grade classes.* Unpublished Ph.D. dissertation, University of Rochester, Rochester, NY.

Rotheram, M. J., Armstrong, M., & Booraem, C. (1982). Assertiveness training in fourth- and fifth-grade children. *American Journal of Community Psychology, 10,* 567–582.

Rutter, M. (1983). Stress, coping and development: Some issues and some questions. In N. Garmezy & M. Rutter (Eds.), *Stress, coping and development in children* (pp. 1–41). New York: McGraw-Hill.

Sandler, I. N. (1972). Characteristics of women working as child-aides in a school based preventive mental health program. *Journal of Consulting and Clinical Psychology, 39,* 56–61.

Sandler, I. N., Duricko, A., & Grande, L. (1975). Effectiveness of an early secondary prevention program in an inner city elementary school. *American Journal of Community Psychology, 3,* 23–32.

Sarason, S. B. (1971). *The culture of the school and the problem of change.* Boston: Allyn and Bacon.

Searcy-Miller, M. L., Cowen, E. L., & Terrell, D. L. (1977). School adjustment problems of children from small vs. alrge families. *Journal of Community Psychology, 5,* 319–324.

Shaw, M. C., & Goodyear, R. K. (Eds.) (1984). Primary prevention in the schools. *Personnel and Guidance Journal, 62,* 443–495.

Shore, M. F. (1972). The federal scene. *Professional Psychology, 4,* 383–384.

Shure, M. B., & Spivack, G. (1978). *Problem-solving techniques in childrearing.* San Francisco: Jossey-Bass.

Shure, M. B., & Spivack, G. (1982). Interpersonal problem-solving in young children: A cognitive approach to prevention. *American Journal of Community Psychology, 10,* 341–356.

Slavin, R. E. (1983). When does cooperative learning increase student achievement? *Psychological Bulletin, 94,* 429–445.

Spivack, G., Platt, J. J., & Shure, M. B. (1976). *The problem-solving approach to adjustment.* San Francisco: Jossey-Bass.

Spivack, G., & Shure, M. B. (1974). *Social adjustment of young children: A cognitive approach to solving real-life problems.* San Francisco: Jossey-Bass.

Sprinthall, N. A. (1984). Primary prevention: A road paved with a plethora of promises and procrastinations. *Personnel and Guidance Journal, 62,* 491–495.

Stallings, J. (1975). Implementation and child effects of teaching practices in Follow-Through classrooms. *Monographs of the Society for Research on Child Development, 40* (Serial No. 163).

Stalonas, P. M., Toro, P. A., Cowen, E. L., Lamb, G., Spadofora, S., Thomassen, J., & Weissberg, R. P. (1982). *The evaluation of a preventively oriented self-improvement program for sixth-graders.* Unpublished manuscript, University of Rochester, Rochseter, NY.

Stamps, L. W. (1975). *Enhancing success in school for deprived children by teaching realistic goal setting.* Paper presented at the Society for Research in Child Development meeting, Denver, CO.

Sterling, S. E. (1986). *School-based intervention program for early latency-aged children of divorce.* Unpublished Ph.D. dissertation, University of Rochester, Rochester, NY.

Sterling, S., Cowen, E. L., Weissberg, R. P., Lotyczewski, B. S., & Boike, M. F. (1985). Recent stressful life events and young children's school adjustment. *American Journal of Community Psychology, 13,* 31–48.

Stolberg, A. L., & Garrison, K. M. (1985). Evaluating a primary prevention program for children of divorce: The Divorce Adjustment Project. *American Journal of Community Psychology, 13,* 111–124.

Susskind, E. (1979). Encouraging teachers to encourage children's curiosity: A pivotal competence. *Journal of Clinical Child Psychology, 8,* 101–106.

Swift, C. F. (1980). Prevention: Policy and practice. In R. H. Price, R. F. Ketterer, B. C. Bader, & J. Monahan (Eds.), *Prevention in mental health: Research, policy and practice* (pp. 207–236). Beverly Hills, CA: Sage.

Tableman, B. (1980). Prevention activities at the state level. In R. H. Price, R. F. Ketterer, B. C. Bader, & J. Monahan (Eds.), *Prevention in mental health: Research, policy and practice* (pp. 237–252). Beverly Hills, CA: Sage.

Talmage, H., Pascarella, E. T., & Ford, S. (1984). The influence of cooperative learning strategies on teacher practices, student perceptions of the learning environment and academic achievement. *American Educational Research Journal, 21,* 163–179.

Task Panel Report: Learning Failure and Unused Learning Potential. (1978). *Task panel reports submitted to the President's Commission on Mental Health* (Vol. 3, pp. 661–704). Washington, DC. U.S. Government Printing Office. (Stock No. 040-000-00392-4)

Terrell, D. L., McWilliams, S. A., & Cowen, E. L. (1972). Description and evaluation of group-work training for nonprofessional aides in a school mental health program. *Psychology in the Schools, 9,* 70–75.

Vogelsong, E. L., Most, R. K., & Yanchko, A. (1979). Relationship enhancement training for preadolescents in public schools. *Journal of Clinical Child Psychology, 8,* 97–100.

Wallerstein, J. S. (1983). Children of divorce: Stress and developmental tasks. In N. Garmezy & M. Rutter (Eds.), *Stress, coping and development in children* (pp. 265–302). New York: McGraw-Hill.

Weissberg, R. P., Cowen, E. L., Lotyczewski, B. S., & Gesten, E. L. (1983). The Primary Mental Health Project: Seven consecutive years of program outcome research. *Journal of Consulting and Clinical Psychology, 51,* 100–107.

Weissberg, R. P., Gesten, R. L., Carnrike, C. L., Toro, P. A., Rapkin, B. D., Davidson, E., & Cowen, E. L. (1981a). Social problem-solving skills training: A competence building intervention with 2nd–4th grade children. *American Journal of Community Psychology, 9,* 411–424.

Weissberg, R. P., Gesten, E. L., Liebenstein, N. L., Schmid, K. D., & Hutton, H. (1980). *The Rochester Social Problem Solving (SPS) Program: A training manual for teachers of 2nd–4th grade children* (p. 160). Rochester, NY: Primary Mental Health project.

Weissberg, R. P., Gesten, E. L., Rapkin, B. D., Cowen, E. L., Davidson, E., Flores de Apodaca, R., & McKim, B. J. (1981b). Evaluation of a social problem-solving training program for suburban and inner-city third grade children. *Journal of Consulting and Clinical Psychology, 49,* 251–261.

Wener, E. E., & Smith, R. S. (1982). *Vulnerable but invincible: A study of resilient children.* New York: McGraw-Hill.

Winer, J. I., Hilpert, P. L., Gesten, E. L., Cowen, E. L., & Schubin, W. E. (1982). The evaluation of a kindergarten social problem-solving program. *Journal of Primary Prevention, 2,* 205–216.

Winer, J. I., Weissberg, R. P., & Cowen, E. L. (1988). Evaluation of a planned short-term intervention for school children with focal adjustment problems. *Journal of Child Clinical Psychology, 17,* 106–115.

Work, W. C., & Olsen, K. H. (1990). Development and evaluation of a revised social problem solving curriculum for fourth graders *Journal of Primary Prevention, 10,* in press.

Wright, S., & Cowen, E. L. (1982). Student perception of school environment and its relationship to mood, achievement, popularity and adjustment. *American Journal of Community Psychology, 10,* 687–703.

Wright, S., & Cowen, E. L. (1985). The effects of peer teaching on student perceptions of class environment, adjustment and academic performance. *American Journal of Community Psychology, 13,* 413–427.

Zax, M., & Cowen, E. L. (1967). Early identification and prevention of emotional disturbance in a public school. In E. L. Cowen, E. A. Gardner, & M. Zax (Eds.), *Emergent approaches to mental health problems* (pp. 331–351). New York: Appleton-Century-Crofts.

Zax, M., & Cowen, E. L. (1976). *Abnormal psychology: Changing conceptions* (2nd ed.). New York: Holton, Rinehart and Winston.

SCHOOL PSYCHOLOGICAL INTERVENTIONAL: FOCUS ON STAFF, PROGRAMS, AND ORGANIZATIONS

32

AN OVERVIEW OF PRINCIPLES AND PROCEDURES OF PROGRAM PLANNING AND EVALUATION

ROBERT J. ILLBACK

Spalding University

JOSEPH E. ZINS

University of Cincinnati

CHARLES A. MAHER
RHONDA GREENBERG

Rutgers University

PROGRAM PLANNING AND EVALUATION

School psychologists have become involved in leadership roles in planning and evaluation of educational services and programs (Maher, 1978, 1981). To perform such functions in a competent manner, practitioners can benefit from possession of knowledge and skills in program planning and evaluation and planned organizational change (Illback & Maher, 1984; Maher & Illback, 1982). Such knowledge and skill can also enhance the practitioner's ability to function effectively in educational and related work settings by increasing awareness of program management and change processes within these human service organizations.

In this chapter we provide an overview of important principles and procedures of program planning and evaluation in the human services, arena, with particular reference to educational services, programs, and settings. We emphasize that planning and evaluation activities are related integrally to management and decision-making processes in human service organizations. Information gleaned from these activities is useful to the extent that it is used to inform decision makers and thereby improve decisions. Thus, central concepts, terminology, strategies, and methods from program planning and evaluation will be reviewed, followed by discussion of the relationship of planning and evaluation activities to planned organizational change. We conclude with an examination of the role and function of school psychologists relative to planning and evaluation functions, and discuss approaches to overcoming barriers and resistance which may occur when school psychologists seek to fulfill this role.

Historical Development of Program Planning and Evaluation

Few scientific and technical fields can trace their exact points of origin and the field of program evaluation is no exception. Some writers (e.g., Cronbach, 1980) trace origins of program evaluation to the 1680s, when Thomas Hobbs and his associates were involved in data collection to identify and address social problems of the day, particularly morbidity and mortality. However, it was not until the 1950s that program evaluation, conceived as a systematic method of empirical inquiry, came to the fore in education and human services.

Flaherty and Morell (1978) propose four reasons for the evolution of program planning and program evaluation during the last four decades: (a) greater requirements for accountability in publicly funded programs; (b) increased interest among social scientists in social relevance; (c) an increasing scarcity of resources for social science; and (d) expansion of methods appropriate for applied evaluative research. Thus, program evaluation began to grow rapidly during the period following World War II. During the 1950s, large-scale projects were initiated wherein federal monies were dedicated to developing and implementing projects such as urban and rural renewal, preventive health, housing, delinquency, and family planning approaches. With these large-scale social change efforts came demands for knowledge about outcomes and effectiveness of the programs. As such, the emerging technologies of evaluation, including survey research and multivariate statistical analysis techniques, were used to supply data on program efficiency and effectiveness to federal officials (Rossi & Freeman, 1985).

During the 1960s, a tremendous proliferation of social programs occurred in the United States. There was increased emphasis on developing highly specialized programs, targeted toward a broad range of social problems. This decade evidenced the birth of the categorical approach to funding and provision of service delivery in education and the human services; select populations of individuals were identified as needing intervention, categorized or classified in terms of diagnostic constructs or eligibility criteria, and then programs were designed and implemented to address the needs of a range of special interest groups, especially the oppressed, disadvantaged, and poverty stricken (Attkisson & Broskowski, 1978). It was also during this time that specialized services in community mental health, social services, and education (e.g., school psychology) became established. Also, social action programming became extensive, and program evaluation became a major growth industry as a function of increased concerns and demands for data by administrators, funders, and society as a whole. The evolution of program evaluation was thus tied to particular contemporary social, political, and financial circumstances.

Unfortunately, large-scale social programs often seemed to exacerbate social problems, and questions immediately arose regarding the wisdom of many of these endeavors. Problems of duplication of effort, overlapping of personnel responsibilities, maldistribution of human and financial resources, ineffective practices, and evaluation findings of nonsignificance called into question the continued expansion of government-mandated entitlement programs.

Nonetheless, significant contributions to promoting understanding of the impact of social programs during this period were seen, such as the pioneering work of Donald Campbell (see, e.g., Campbell, 1969). Campbell's conception of social reforms as experiments and the accompanying technology that he and others promoted, had a profound effect on the shape and evolution of social programs and their evaluation. Prior to this period, the majority of social and educational programs were evaluated using narrow and restrictive evaluation models within a traditional research perspective. Campbell, however, emphasized innovation in design, the use of quasi-experimental models, and the need for practicality and relevance in designing evaluations, thus linking social experimentation and societal improvement.

With the 1970s, the continued expansion of social and educational programs came under closer scrutiny. There was a continuing commitment on the part of legislators and professionals to strengthen and preserve the integrity of the programmatic movements implemented during the 1950s and 1960s. However, the convergence of social and political pressures (e.g., Vietnam war), combined with the huge inflationary crisis, proved to be powerful forces arguing for cost containment and the curtailment of large-scale social programs.

Program evaluation, and its interrelated area of program planning, became tools for the reexamination of programmatic efforts and the identification of new methods for attaining worthy goals. Increased attention was directed to fiscal responsibility, with the outcome that programs were designed, implemented, and evaluated with more modest target populations. Additionally, jurisdiction for programmatic efforts was gradually turned over to local and state governments and agencies, and with the resultant increase in interest among educational and human services administrators in planning programs, program planning, and evaluation became recognized as an essential management function.

The curricular reform movement of the late 1960s and early 1970s gave impetus to planning and evaluation in education (Borich & Jemelka, 1982). Beginning with the *Sputnick* launch in 1957, substantial changes were seen in curricular methods and materials across the content areas of education, particularly in mathematics and the sciences. Planning and evaluation of curricular materials became more closely linked, and the strategies used for program planning and evaluation became more available to local school districts (Scriven, 1967).

During the 1970s, a number of educational entitlement programs came into being, such as Title I (now Chapter I) of the Elementary and Secondary Education Act (ESEA) of 1965 and the Education for All Handicapped Children Act of 1975 (Public Law 94-142). These and similar landmark legislative initiatives mandated that school districts incorporate program planning and evaluation activities into their organizational routines. School professionals, including school psychologists, of necessity became involved in the data collection and analysis process. While initially much of the focus was on establishing the need for services and justifying reimbursement, interest in documenting services and relating these to outcomes has gradually increased (see, e.g., Phi Delta Kappa National Study Committee on Evaluation, authored by Stufflebeam et al., 1971).

Currently, program planning and evaluation activities are broad-based, diverse, and integrally related to management functions. Program evaluations do not focus exclusively on establishing cause–effect relationships between and among variables through controlled experimentation, but rather seek to make judgments about program effort, effectiveness, efficiency, and adequacy based on systematic data collection and analysis in the service of program planning (Attkisson & Broskowski, 1978).

Planning and Evaluation as Methods of Empirical Inquiry

An overview of program planning and program evaluation concepts, terminology, strategies, and methods, relative to the practice of school psychology, is presented in this section. The concept of "program" is first defined, and the need to conceptualize clearly and to specify services and programs is emphasized. Program planning approaches and their relationship to program evaluation is elucidated, followed by a discussion of implementation evaluation. Finally, the task of assessing programmatic outcomes is described.

The Concept of "Program"

For a program planning or program evaluation project to have focus, it must define the unit of analysis; that is, the program to be analyzed. Programs that can be reviewed range from individualized education programs (IEPs), through classroom-level programs, to building- or organizational-level programs. In order to address the somewhat vague question, "How effective is the special education resource room program at Sunnyville Elementary School?", a definition and some parameters must be established regarding what the special education resource room *program* encompasses; that is, what distinguishes it from other *programs* in the setting, and what are its constituent elements? Once the program has been defined and described, more specific evaluation questions can be derived.

All human services programs are embedded in complex social and community contexts. The decision to focus on a particular program or aspect of a program must take into account that it is difficult, if not impossible, to separate the program fully from its context in order to decide how to further develop it, improve it, or disseminate it to other sites. Therefore, the essential features of the program being examined must be delineated. For example, in studying the effectiveness of special education services, a question arises as to whether activities of handicapped students in "mainstream" classes should be categorized as part of the special or regular education program, and if these should be included in the evaluation. Similarly, should community awareness, attitudes, and involvement with handicapped persons be considered in the program evaluation? These issues need to be agreed upon prior to formulating more specific evaluation questions.

Decisions about how to categorize various services and programs in human service settings are aided by conceptual frameworks that serve to organize thinking about programs in the organizational context. One such framework, used for such purposes throughout the United States and internationally and clearly relevant to school psychology, is provided by Maher and Bennett (1984). Five domains of educational service delivery are defined within this model: assessment services, instructional services, related services, personnel development services, and administration services. Within each domain, specific programmatic efforts can be described.

Table 1, entitled Student Services Programs, provides a conceptual overview of how this model

TABLE 1   Student Services Programs

Assessment Services
  Pupil screening and child find program
  Prereferral intervention program
  Pupil evaluation and classification program
  Individualized education program design
  Individualized education program review
Instructional Services
  Speech and language program
  Learning disabilities program
  Educable mentally handicapped program
  Trainable mentally handicapped program
  Behavior disorders program
  Low-incidence handicap program
  Homebound instruction program
Related Services
  Physical therapy program
  Guidance and counseling program
  School psychology program
  School health services program
Personnel Development Services
  Inservice education and training
  Parent involvement program
  Community outreach program
Administrative Services
  Information management program
  Program planning and evaluation services
  Staff supervision program

---

has been applied within a department of student services in a school system, to include school psychological services. It can be seen that the activities or programs within each domain evidence similar characteristics. At the same time, there is some overlap between programs across the domains, and knowledge of such overlap is useful since it identifies areas where program coordination may be important. Within assessment services, programs such as IEP annual review and IEP design are described. They are placed in this domain because they focus on decision-oriented information gathering processes. The IEPs that result from these assessment programs are carried out through programs in the instructional services and related services domains.

Service delivery programs thus can be seen as distinct but interdependent entities. More specifically, they are organized configurations of resources—human, informational, financial, technological—which are designed to assist an individual, group, or organization to meet a specific need (Maher & Bennett, 1984). Stated differently, programs are interventions targeted toward specific aims.

In this context, programs may focus on either the prevention or remediation of problems experienced by various client groups or systems (e.g., children, families, teachers, school systems). The term "problems" as used here includes goals that have not been met, opportunities or resources that have not been fully utilized, and/or dysfunctional states in client systems.

Program Specification

The manner in which programmatic resources are configured or organized must be described by the evaluator prior to the formulation of specific evaluative questions; that is, in order for a program to be evaluated, it must be described in a form that is capable of being evaluated. Wholey (1979) calls this process "evaluability assessment." Determining program evaluability allows for (a) an examination of a program's logic, including whether causal links have been established between program goals and activities; (b) an analysis of program operations, including the plausability and measurability of expected events (activities); and (c) identification of program design options, such as new activities or products, and possible uses of program performance information.

Most fundamentally, evaluability assessment seeks well-defined programs that can be implemented and evaluated in a prescribed manner. Weiss (1973) notes:

> The sins of the program are often visited on the evaluation. When programs are well-conceptualized and developed, with clearly defined goals and consistent methods of work, the lot of evaluation is relatively easy. But when programs are disorganized, beset with disruptions, ineffectively designed, or poorly managed, the evaluation falls heir to the problems of the setting. (p. 54)

There are certain characteristics of a well-defined program which are derived from the concept of program described earlier.

Target Population. Well-conceived programs clearly specify the target audience toward whom the program is directed. The needs of the target population are stated based on a defensible rationale, and the defining characteristics of the population are described. For example, if the program to be evaluated is teacher consultation services offered by the school psychologist, the client system for the services would need to be stated (e.g., elementary school teachers with children experiencing specific types of learning and behavioral problems in the classroom).

Intended Outcomes. Well-defined programs also state the intended outcomes of the program in the form of goals or objectives. Thus, a particular reading program for students with learning disabilities may focus on goal areas such as phonic analysis, comprehension, reading speed and accuracy, and attitude toward reading. Causal links between program goals and program activities can only be established when goals are well-conceived and specified.

Resource Utilization. Another important element of program specification relates to use of resources: staffing, methods, and materials. Here, the explicit strategies, approaches, concepts, activities, materials, methods, and other resources that comprise the program are stated. Elements that are described include (a) number, type, and qualifications of required staff; (b) psychological or educational strategies which are central to the program's conception; (c) materials and equipment which are necessary for the implementation of the program; (d) financial resources which are required in the form of an operating budget; and (e) other temporal and physical resources needed (e.g., time, rooms, buildings, sites).

Program Plan. A final critical element of program design involves development of a plan for program operation, to include (a) policies, procedures, and practices which will be employed in organizing and operating the program; (b) roles, responsibilities, and relationships of staff members; (c) sequence and timing of programmatic activities; and (d) description of permissible variation of activities.

Table 2 provides a sample program description for a school district's Pupil Evaluation and Classification Program (part of assessment services), and Table 3 provides a similar program description for a learning disabilities resource room program.

TABLE 2   Pupil Evaluation and Classification Program

1.0 Target Population
　　1.1 Students who have recommended by the referral review committee as requiring a comprehensive and individualized evaluation to determine eligibility for specialized education and other forms of support or assistance.
　　1.2 Students already classified as educationally handicapped who require 3-year evaluations by state and federal statutes.
2.0 Major Goals
　　2.1 To gather reliable and meaningful (valid) information about a student's performance in areas of:
　　　　2.11　Academic Achievement
　　　　2.12　Adaptive and Functional Living

TABLE 2   (*continued*)

      2.13 Cognition and Problem Solving
      2.14 Verbal Communication
      2.15 Gross and Fine Motor Movement
      2.16 Social and Affective Development
      2.17 Physical and Health status
  2.2 To organize assessment information so that it may be analyzed in terms of a student educational strengths, range of normal functioning, and educational needs.
  2.3 To decide, based on the assessment information gathered, whether a student possesses an educational handicapping condition.
  2.4 To decide whether a student who possesses an educational handicapping condition is to be classified as handicapped pursuant to State Education Department Rules and Regulations.
  2.5 To determine the nature and scope of pupil difficulties for those children who are not eligible for special education and related services.
  2.6 To provide recommendations to regular educational personnel about how students who are not eligible for special education and resource services may be educated.
3.0 Pupil Evaluation and Classification Program Personnel
  3.1 Decisions about pupil evaluation and classification are made by the multidisciplinary team, as mandated by regulations. The multidisciplinary team is comprised of the principal (or designee), the counselor, the school psychologist, the referring teacher, a special education teacher, the speech and language clinician, a parent, and any other specialized personnel who may be required. These meetings are chaired by the counselors in most instances.
  3.2 For children whose needs cannot be met within the scope of building-level programs, the district-wide team will be constituted to assess the appropriateness of placement in a district-wide special program or in a contracted program with another school district. This team is chaired by the director of student services and is comprised of the referring teacher, a parent, a special education teacher, the principal, or designee the school psychologist, and the counselor. Related services personnel may be added, as necessary.
4.0 Pupil Evaluation and Classification Procedures and Activities
  4.1 Once the referral review committee has determined that a comprehensive and individualized evaluation is needed, a variety of components contribute to the multifactored, nondiscriminatory assessment process.
  4.2 The specific components of the evaluation will vary as a function of the suspected educational handicapping condition.
  4.3 Various members of the multidisciplinary team conduct different portions of the assessment.
  4.4 The steps in the assessment process are delineated in the handbook of student services and include systematic observations, educational assessment, psychoeducational assessment, speech and language assessment, gross and fine motor movement assessment, health assessment, and a range of other potential components.
  4.5 Once the required assessments are completed, the multidisciplinary team meets to review and integrate their findings.
  4.6 The admission and release committee then makes the necessary determination, based on state regulations.
5.0 Materials
  5.1 The team uses specific forms to record the nature of their deliberation and decisions that have been made.
  5.2 Members of the multidisciplinary team use materials and techniques intrinsic to their professions, including standardized tests, techniques of observation and assessment, and more informal materials.
6.0 Facilities and Equipment
  6.1 Multidisciplinary teams meet in various locations across all the school buildings.

TABLE 3   Learning Disabilities Resource Room

1.0 Target Population
   1.1 The resource room serves students in grades 1 through 5 at Sunnyville Elementary School who have been classified as learning disabled (LD) or educable mentally handicapped (EMH) using mandated identification and eligibility procedures. LD students are presumed to be experiencing substantial learning problems, including a severe discrepancy between ability and achievement, and deficits in one or more of the basic psychological processes involved in understanding or using language, spoken or written (as manifested in an imperfect ability to listen, think, read, write, spell, or do mathematical calculations). By definition, these difficulties are not attributable to visual, hearing, or motor handicaps, mental retardation, emotional disturbance, or cultural/economic disadvantage. EMH students are presumed to have significantly subaverage general intellectual functioning existing concurrently with deficits in adaptive behavior, and manifested during the developmental period. EMH students are functioning intellectually in the range 51 to 70 IQ.
   1.2 Students served in the resource room may be experiencing interpersonal problems, a low self-concept, and behavioral difficulties associated with their learning problems. For LD students, their general level of adaptive behavior appears to be similar to other children of their chronological age.
2.0 Major Educational Outcome Goals
   2.1 Students will acquire academic skills at a level and pace commensurate with their abilities
   2.2 Students will attain IEP goals in academic, social, behavioral, emotional, perceptual, and cognitive areas.
   2.3 Students will interact appropriately with peers and teachers in special and regular classroom placements.
   2.4 Students will communicate and behave in a manner that is understood and accepted by regular and special education classroom teachers.
3.0 Program Personnel
   3.1 The resource room is staffed by a full-time teacher certified by the state department of education to instruct learning-disabled children.
   3.2 A number of other persons at Sunnyville School contribute to the program on a regular basis, including the principal, the counselor, two other special education teachers, and an aide.
   3.3 Additionally, related service specialists are utilized on a case-by-case basis to resolve problems. These include the school psychologist, intern psychologist, physical therapist, speech clinician, school nurse, and the director of student services.
4.0 Methods and Materials
   4.1 Methods
      4.11 *SUCCESS Reading and Writing Program*
            SUCCESS is a language experience approach to teaching reading and writing. Daily lessons occur in one or more of four basis modules, listed below:
            Phonics/Spelling or Decoding in Context Module—students learn to decode words they wish to read with comprehension.
            Language Experience/Composition—students write about topics familiar care and strengthen skills in reading, writing, spelling, speaking, listening, and thinking.
            Research/Study Skills Module—students use newspapers, magazines, textbooks, maps, and catalogs to locate information related to a theme.
            Recreational Reading Module—students engage in uninterrupted, unrestricted silent reading from a wide selection fiction and nonfiction books and other materials.
      4.12 Affective education program—a program to help children understand themselves and others through discussion and activities.
      4.13 Group work—Many of the activities in the class occur in small groups to facilitate interaction and enhance the efficient delivery of instruction.

TABLE 3   (*continued*)

4.14 Seatwork—After group activities or individual instruction, students are given seatwork to apply what has been taught. This includes individual reading, writing, math, and spelling.

4.15 Individualized instruction—The instructional approach used in the resource room emphasizes the need to design tasks in relation to each child's idiosyncratic needs and goals. Individualization is accomplished through the language experience approach and careful monitoring of pupil progress toward goals.

4.2 Materials

4.21 Newspapers and Magazines

4.22 Textbooks

4.221 Macmillan English

4.222 Houghton Mifflin Mathematics

4.223 Follett Spelling

4.224 Ginn Reading Series

4.225 Barnell Loft Specific Skills/Multiple Reading Series

4.23 Kits

4.231 DLM Sound Foundations

4.232 DLM Capitalization and Punctuation,

4.233 DLM Sight Word Lab

4.234 GOAL Language

4.235 Peabody Language

4.236 DLM Moving Up in

4.237 DLM Moving Up in Money

4.238 DLM Moving Up in Number

4.239 DLM Moving Up in Story Problems

4.240 Individualized Mathematics Random House

4.241 SRA Schoolhouse Word Attack 1C

4.242 SYSTEM 80 Learning Letter Sounds C-H, Learning Number Facts, A-H

4.243 DLM Visual Kits (Eye–Hand, Memory, Tracking, Perception)

5.0 Organizational Structure of the Resource Room

5.1 The school day is comprised of:

8:40–9:40	Group 1—Spelling—Gr. 5/4
	Group 2—English—Gr. 4/5
9:10–9:40	Math
9:40–10:30	Reading, English, Spelling
10:30–11:45	Reading, Spelling, Individual Work—Gr. 2
11:45–12:05	Gr. 4/5 Special Reading
12:15–12:45	Lunch
12:45–3:00	Spelling (Gr. 2/3), Reading, Math, Language Arts

6.0 Facilities and Equipment

6.1 The resource room is located in Room 30 at Sunnyville Elementary School. The room is smaller than the size of a regular classroom.

6.2 Equipment

6.21 Apple II Computer

6.22 System 80 Machine

6.23 Tape Recorder

6.24 Language Master

Program Planning Strategies

Often, professionals with responsibility for program evaluation are asked to become involved in the initial stages of the design of new programs. Sometimes, this request may be in connection with submission of a state or federal grant application to seek funds for a new method or approach. More often, it is in connection with development of new or reconfigured programs using local resources, such as preschool education programs, a peer tutoring project, or a reorganized resource room for students with learning and behavior problems.

A number of strategies to assist in the planning of new programs, all of which are aimed toward development of responsive, evaluable, feasible, and cost-efficient programmatic efforts, are available. This aspect of planning and evaluation can be subdivided into three subareas: (a) contextual analysis and clarification of need, (b) providing initial structure to the intervention plan (program), and (c) preparing for implementation and evaluation of the program.

Problem Clarification. Presenting problems in service delivery, similar to those arising with the individual client system, can be seen as unsatisfactory states of affairs. Problem clarification activities are intended to gather systematic information to place the problem(s) in context and to assure that appropriate planning occurs based on a clear understanding of service needs.

Placing the problem in context involves initial data gathering regarding the nature and scope of the presenting problem(s). Through preliminary interviews with involved persons, records reviews, direct observation, and similar methods, the person with responsibilities for program planning and evaluation seeks, at this stage, to obtain a general sense of the history and development of the concern, to understand what the present state of affairs appears to be, to know which individuals perceive that there is a problem, and to recognize there are multiple perspectives from which the problem may be viewed. The task in the initial contact is largely to be heuristic in the formulation of hypotheses about problems and needs that may exist. Additionally, sensitivity to (a) limitations of available resources, (b) potential problems or sources of resistance to programmatic intervention, and (c) beliefs and attitudes of key persons is crucial at this stage.

Following the initial contextual analysis, evaluators may construct a more formal needs assessment strategy. The term "needs," in this context, is defined as a discrepancy between an unsatisfactory state of affairs and some desired state. Thus, needs assessment is the process of gathering information about actual conditions and comparing that to some desired state. The conduct of a needs assessment involves determining the client or service delivery systems which will be assessed, specifying the aspects (domains) of those systems that will be examined, designing appropriate methods (e.g., procedures, instrumentation) to obtain reliable and valid information about the relevant areas, and planning for data aggregation and analysis (Maher & Illback, 1981).

There are a number of systematic needs assessment methods available to the person with responsibility for program planning and evaluation. One such method is the *key informant approach* in which persons in central positions in the organization (relative to the presumed problem area) are identified and interviewed to obtain estimates of the problem. This approach has the advantage of obtaining essential information from persons who are assumed to be knowledgable and influential, and can also help form the basis for an effective intervention (program) by establishing the readiness of the organization for change and developing support for new initiatives. The approach has a disadvantage in that these persons have their own built-in biases and interests, which may not be representative of others in the organization. Also, individual key informants may not have full access to crucial information.

Another method for estimating need can be termed *indicators analysis.* Many federal, state, and local agencies, including schools, are required by regulation to maintain a broad base of statistical information on clients and products. For example, schools must collect information regarding racial balance, family socioeconomic status (for purposes such as free and reduced lunch), average daily attendance, types and severity of handicapping conditions, and the like. Often this information can serve to help formulate the nature and types of needs that may exist in a particular problem area, albeit at a global level. The ultimate utility of indicator analysis rests on the reliability and validity of the descriptive information, the logical and statistical appropriateness of the procedures used in data gathering, and the subjective perception developed about the problem on the basis of the data (Siegel, Attkisson, & Carson, 1978).

Related to indicator analysis approaches are methods involving *analysis of demands for services* (e.g., requests for consultation) and *analysis of service resources* (i.e., compiling, describing, and integrating available services or resources). Both are more passive approaches using already available data, which is less costly but may not be as valid or reliable as other approaches.

Another needs assessment approach, probably the most common, is the *questionnaire or survey.* This is the most direct and is usually a very accurate and representative approach. Here, a sample of respondents are asked central questions about the problem area, and findings are generalized to the target population as a whole. There is a well-developed science to survey construction and administration (see, e.g., Kosecoff & Fink, 1982; Sudman, 1976), and more sophisticated data analysis and interpretation can often result from the use of these measures.

Perhaps the most active and informative approaches to needs assessment are those that involve people in systematic analysis and/or discussion. In the *nominal group approach,* a broad-based sample is invited to generate their ideas about problems, needs, and possible solutions within a workshop format. Clients, external resource people, key administrators and resource controllers, and staff work together in a multistage process to explore problems and knowledge, set priorities, and develop and evaluate programs (Delbecq & Van de Ven, 1971). The *Delphi approach* (Dalkey, 1967) is also a carefully structured process, but focuses more on experts with presumed knowledge about the problem area, forecasting needs thorough a systematic questionnaire process. *Community forums* are more open-ended group discussions similar to town meetings in which anyone can express his or her opinions or ideas. These are often used in federally funded programs to give the public an opportunity to comment without imposing any constraints; this lack of structure is useful from an heuristic perspective but may lead to skewed or misleading findings.

The ultimate goal of problem clarification activities is to obtain a clear statement of the needs that exist in relation to contextual variables. Such a needs description specifies the individual, group, or service delivery system that is experiencing the problem and indicates the specific needs of this target(s) in the form of discrepancy statements (current versus desired states of affairs). The needs description also should place the identified needs in some priority or logical order. Some needs are of less importance than others, some are subsets of larger problems or issues, and some will not be amenable to direct intervention. The needs description thus forms the basis for program design.

Initial Program Organization. In this stage, the evaluator is concerned with designing a systematic course of action in response to a clarified problem. Crucial to the ultimate success of this stage is reaching agreement with key persons about the nature and priority of the needs to be addressed by the programmatic intervention. Activities at this level may include presenting the needs description to decision makers, negotiating about the needs which are to be addressed, and facilitation of group decision making. Evaluative methods to accomplish this task range from informal discussion to highly formalized means, such as decision-analytic techniques and voting procedures.

Once needs have been placed in priority order, a structure of goals for the prospective program must be established. Goals are statements of intent about what the program will accomplish and are derived directly from the statement of needs described earlier. Goals are specified in order that programmatic efforts can be directed logically and sequentially toward their attainment.

Program goals may be *general* or *specific,* with specific goals stated as subgoals of broader goals. Also, goals may be stated in terms of *outcomes* (intrinsically worthy occurrences, such as increased knowledge) or *outputs* (extrinsic indicators of change, such as successful completion of a task at 90% accuracy, as in behavioral objectives). Moreover, goals may be *primary,* in that they are valued for their own sake rather than as a means of obtaining other goals, or *instrumental.* To the extent possible, goals should be stated in terms that are measurable or observable, and it is often useful to attach goal indicators (performance criteria) to goal statements for this purpose.

A final component of program organization relates to intervention planning. For an effective intervention (program) to be planned, a systematic examination of solution requirements and solution alternatives must be employed. The specification of solution requirements should delineate the conditions or constraints under which the program must be planned and developed. The generation of solution alternatives is characterized initially by an heuristic and then subsequently a validating approach, resulting in a set of possible methods, materials, and resources for the program. It is thus possible to evaluate critically the advantages and disadvantages of available solution alternatives in light of established program goals. Available methods for this phase include brainstorming, logical analysis, site visitations, group discussion, literature review, and structured group decision making.

The ultimate intent of the program organization phase is to derive a logical goals and activities sequence which can serve to focus the program. Once these have been selected, they should be discussed and negotiated with decision makers to ensure their fit with environmental features and constraints.

Program Development. Once the structure of the program has been determined and agreed upon, resources to implement the program must be assembled and "packaged." Here, evaluative strategies are used to address questions about resource identification and utilization, packaging, personnel needs and issues, program routines and procedures, organizational readiness for the program, and program evaluation. Evaluative activities in this stage may include (a) writing a policy and procedure manual, (b) conducting training with staff on programmatic activities, (c) delineating permanent products (e.g., reports) of the program, (d) conducting pilot tests and simulations of the program, (e) developing descriptive material for clients and professionals, (f) acquiring materials and supplies, and (g) designing a program information system (programmatic, administrative, and financial information).

Program design can be evaluated in relation to five criteria suggested by Provus (1972). The first, clarity, refers to the extent to which the design is understandable and its components objectively measurable. Second, comprehensiveness relates to the extent to which the design fully describes the purpose, implementation, and expected outcomes of the effort. Third, the components of the design can be assessed to make certain they are logically interrelated, or internally consistent. Compatibility with the established need, with existing support conditions, and with other programs is a fourth

aspect to be evaluated. Finally, theoretical soundness in relation to the prevailing literature can be assessed.

A final element of program design involves actual preparations for implementation. Activities in this phase may include specifying implementation activities and timelines and developing a plan for program management and outcome evaluation.

Implementation Evaluation

The primary purpose of implementation evaluation is to determine the extent to which the program is operating as planned. This information can be used to document that there is compliance with important legal and ethical mandates, such as state and federal guidelines and regulations and the ethical and practice codes of professional organizations. Additionally, implementation evaluation facilitates program development and improvement by identifying problem areas that may require adaptation of program standards or operations and by highlighting program elements that are being effectively implemented. Finally, implementation evaluation increases confidence in the eventual assessment of program outcomes by ensuring that measured effects are attributable to an intervention that has been implemented as planned.

Implementation evaluation is especially crucial to program managers (e.g., director of special services) who are concerned with the fidelity and smooth operation of the program. Often, their concern is that problems be identified early so that they can be corrected. Unanticipated side effects (positive or negative) of the program may provide opportunities or threats to the program, and managers are also interested in these issues.

Relevant evaluative questions at the implementation phase included: (a) In what areas are program staff engaged in programmatic activities and to what extent? (b) How are program participants (client groups) involved in the program? (c) Are appropriate materials and facilities being utilized in the program? (d) What intended and unintended side effects do individuals perceive? (e) What types of services have been delivered to clients? (f) Is there a discrepancy between what was planned and what was actually delivered? (g) What permanent products (e.g., written documents) have resulted from programmatic activities?

Evaluative methods in implementation evaluation can be categorized into two areas: retrospective monitoring and naturalistic monitoring. Retrospective monitoring involves obtaining self-report information from program managers and staff about the extent to which the program has been operationalized. The evaluator may conduct a series of individual or small-group interviews or use paper-and-pencil measures to gather perceptual information about process variables such as the frequency of program sessions held relative to the number planned, the range of methods and materials used in the sessions, and any effects noted or problems. Record reviews or examination of other permanent products (e.g., staff activity logs, written reports) may also be employed.

In naturalistic monitoring, the evaluator observes the programmatic process directly using formal (e.g., systematic recording of behavior) and less formal means. In addition to systematic observation, checklists and rating scales may be used to obtain information on the nature and scope of the activities being provided and to compare that information to the program design. There is a complementarity between retrospective and naturalistic monitoring methods in that information derived from one approach can serve to supplement and enhance the other.

Perhaps the most well-researched approach to implementation evaluation in education is the concerns-based adoption model (CBAM) promulgated by Hall and Loucks (1977). Relying heavily on structured interviewing, CBAM views programs from a developmental perspective and postulates there are naturally occurring levels of use of any innovation (program), ranging from nonuse (in which the user has minimal knowledge or involvement with the innovation), through orientation and preparation stages, to mechanical and routine levels of use. Programs that are successful and effective may proceed through stages of refinement, integration, and renewal, depending on the nature of the program, strategies used to implement the program, characteristics of the adopting unit, and general organizational characteristics (Fullan & Pomfret, 1977).

Outcome Assessment

The purpose of outcome or impact assessment is to describe the effects that a program has had. It is critical to the design of an outcome assessment to specify clearly the evaluative questions that are of concern. This will largely be a function of the general decision area that is under consideration and of the decision maker who is involved.

For example, there are decisions to be made about the program which are in the domain of the program manager(s). These decisions focus on internal program operations and effects, such as judging the effectiveness of the program in addressing unmet needs of program clients, the extent to which client goals are attained, and client and staff perceptions of outcomes and appropriateness of services (consumer satisfaction).

Another level of decision making involves external accountability requirements, such as determining the extent to which the program complies with the intent of state and federal regulations. Evaluative information for external purposes may include cost-efficiency analysis, consumer reaction, and global outcome measures.

Decisions about program effectiveness may also be important in the service of contributing to scholarly knowledge and informing prospective adopting sites (dissemination and diffusion). In this regard, evaluative concerns may focus more on determining cause–effect relationships between independent and dependent variables. In making decisions about program effectiveness in field settings, such as schools, it is problematic to determine experimental validity due to difficulties in establishing adequate experimental controls. The use of quasi-experimental designs (Cook & Campbell, 1976) and single-subject methodology (Kratochwill, 1978) is therefore of increased relevance.

A range of evaluation questions may be addressed in the outcome assessment phase. The focus of the evaluation may be on one or more aspects, including (a) degree of goal attainment, (b) related program effects, (c) consumer reaction, (d) cause–effect relations, (e) cost-efficiency, and (f) need for program revision. The specific methods and strategies used to assess outcomes are thus a direct outcome of factors such as the evaluative question, the decision maker(s) who are seeking the information, the availability of methods and approaches (e.g., instrumentation) to investigate the problem area, and practical design considerations (e.g., cost, ability to randomize, time requirements).

A fundamental goal for any outcome assessment is to impose the greatest rigor practicable in order to achieve increased confidence in obtained findings. A major source of rigor in any experiment is the research design. Whereas traditional research methodology recognizes a rather limited number of designs, program evaluators tend to include a broader range of approaches, implicitly recognizing that the vagaries of conducting research in the "real" world will necessarily lead to weak and incomplete knowledge. Rossi and Freeman (1985) have therefore described a typology of potential research designs, including (a) "true" or randomized experiments, (b) quasi-experiments with nonrandom controls, (c) regression-discontinuity designs, (d) before-and-after studies, (e) retrospective before-and-after studies, (f) panel studies, (g) time-series analysis studies, (h) cross-sectional surveys, and (i) judgmental assessments. These are listed in descending order of control and power, and it remains for the evaluator to determine which design most appropriately fits the particular problem situation and provides the greatest possible rigor.

Another source of rigor stems from the instrumentation used for measurement. An array of information collection alternatives (instruments) such as observations (e.g., standard observations, time sampling observations), interview (e.g., face-to-face and telephone interviews), performance tests (e.g., work samples), record reviews, written ability tests (e.g., achievement tests), and written self-report measures (e.g., questionnaires, rating scales, ranking scales, semantic differentials, Q-sorts, diaries, and critical incidents) are available (Kosecoff & Fink, 1987). Each has advantages and disadvantages, both psychometrically and practically. Some will have established reliability and validity, but most will not. The evaluator is obligated to develop and employ measurement devices that can be shown to be internally consistent, reliable, valid, and relevant to the problem at hand. (For a summary review of the measurement technology for each of the approaches above, see Kosecoff & Fink, 1987).

Rigor can also be enhanced through the process of data collection and data analysis. In order to obtain accurate information, information collectors need to be identified and trained to ensure their proper use of procedures, potential sources of bias must be minimized through various methods of control and cross-checking, information collection must be monitored to ensure that information is not lost, and steps must be taken to be certain that client rights (e.g., confidentiality) are

not violated. In preparing data for analysis, systems for categorizing and coding a range of information can be delineated. The choice of statistical analysis derives from the research design used, the type(s) of data (e.g., ordinal, interval), the purposes of the evaluation (e.g., descriptive, comparative), and the availability of time and resources (e.g., expertise, computer access).

There are some outcome assessment methods specifically designed for program evaluation. Typical of these is Goal Attainment Scaling, a measurement approach formulated by Kiresuk and his associates (Kiresuk & Sherman, 1968) which has been used extensively in mental health, social service, and educational agencies. The centerpiece of Goal Attainment Scaling is the follow-up guide, on which expected outcomes of intervention plans are specified along a five-point continuum of potential outcomes. The actual degree of goal attainment over the predetermined time period is then compared to the predicted levels for each goal area, and results are aggregated across domains. This system allows for idiosyncratic assessment of client outcomes within a somewhat standardized approach, relative weighting of goal areas, and data aggregation across domains, clients, and even programs. However, it relies heavily on professional judgment in setting outcome levels and suffers from a number of design and statistical weaknesses. Nonetheless, when used appropriately, it can contribute significantly to data-based decision making.

Increasingly, schools and related agencies are utilizing management information systems to track relevant information about clients and programs. The most sophisticated of these systems can provide the basis for conducting periodic outcome assessments which are both descriptive and inferential in nature. The role of the evaluator is crucial in this regard to ensure that information is properly structured, analyzed, and interpreted.

EVALUATION IN THE SERVICE OF PLANNED ORGANIZATIONAL CHANGE

In this section we describe uses of evaluative information which facilitate the effective operation of educational services and programs, that is, how evaluation can provide leaders with "information to reduce decision uncertainties so as to increase their ability to predict the outcomes of programmatic activity and enhance their discretion as decision-makers" (Patton, 1978, p. 64). It is desirable that program evaluation become an integral, routine component of organizational operation. In fact, evaluation should be part of any change process that is initiated. At the same time, while organizational change should be planned, "change is not brought about by following a grand master plan [rigidly] but by continually readjusting direction and goals" (Beer & Walton, 1987, p. 356), and formative evaluation can assist in that adaptation process.

Other assumptions made with respect to the role of evaluation in planned organizational change are that it should be used to influence decision making, to provide accountability data to internal and external audiences, and to improve future organizational functioning by documenting information on the past performance of the program. Program development is a long, complex process—from initial adoption to implementation to eventual institutionalization—and evaluation should be a fundamental element that addresses both internal and environmental issues that may affect the functioning of the organization. However, as noted earlier, while evaluation should be built into the initial program design, it should not be attempted until the program has had sufficient time to become stabilized. Otherwise, spurious results may occur.

Systems Perspective

In relating evaluation to planned change, it is helpful to view schools from a systems perspective. Applying this viewpoint, schools are seen within the context of larger systems or the suprasystem (e.g., they are part of a community and of the state educational agency), as well as various subsystems operating within the school (e.g., administration, school psychological services, special education programs, English department). Each of these systems and subsystems is interrelated and interdependent on the others. The educational change literature (e.g., Fullan, Miles, & Taylor, 1980; Waugh & Punch, 1987) makes it clear that systems factors such as administrative support, school environment, and staff opportunity for involvement in the change process are all important to the success of any program.

A concept that help explain these interrelationships is that of *reciprocal interaction*. Operationally, this concept refers to the tendency for change in any system component to affect other components within the system as well as the organization as a whole. As Maher and Bennett (1984) note, each system, in whole and in part, both influences and is influenced by other systems, and their component parts also continuously interact with one another. For instance, a new principal can have dramatic effects on the communication patterns within every subsystem in the school; or, a school may develop such a widespread reputation for excellence that neighborhood property values rise. Similarly, change within the suprasystem affects the system and its subsystems. Higher credentialing requirements imposed by the state educational agency for teachers, for example, will affect the preservice training received by the teachers that the school system employs and this presumably will enhance the district's ability to offer a better education to its students. Consequently, program evaluation affects the school organization and the school affects evaluation efforts. Thus, evaluators must develop an understanding of all of the interrelated components of a school to be most effective.

Schools as Organizations

A related concept involves viewing schools as organizations, that is, complex and multidimensional structures which operate within broader social systems. One model for conceptualizing organizations is provided by Maher, Illback, and Zins (1984). It includes three essential organizational domains and their related elements: organizational structure, process, and behavior. These elements determine how effectively a school operates and meets its goals, and are illustrated in Figure 1. A brief explanation of that figure follows.

The first domain, organizational *structure*, includes the school's philosophy (ideals that it values and toward which it aspires), policies (written statements about its philosophy), and services and programs (these include instructional, assessment, related, administrative, and personnel development services). A district's philosophy, for instance, could emphasize that a primary goal is to promote students' personal and academic success and intellectual growth. Written policies might state that each student will know school standards for successful performance and will assume increasing responsibility for meeting the highest standards in each task undertaken. Inservice training in alternative teaching strategies, such as peer-mediated

Framework for Viewing Schools as Organizations

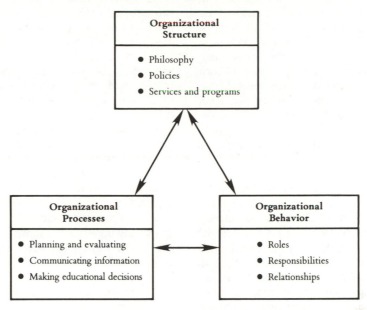

Figure 1. Framework for viewing schools as organizations. (From *Organizational Psychology in the Schools: A Handbook for Professionals* [p. 10] by C. A. Maher, R. J. Illback, and J. E. Zins, 1984, Springfield, IL: Charles C Thomas. Copyright 1984 by Charles C Thomas. Reprinted by permission.)

learning, might be provided to assist teachers in attaining district goals. To the extent that these elements of organizational structure are clear, valued, consistent, and coordinated, organizational processes will function effectively and organizational behaviors will be productive.

Organizational *processes* are the means that enable the school to enact the philosophies and policies and to design and deliver effective and efficient services. Included are planning and evaluating (e.g., developing new programs, altering those in existence to meet changing needs, and assessing the extent to which program outcomes are met), and communicating information about organizational structure in written (e.g., school handbook) and oral (e.g., faculty meetings) formats so that staff and consumers understand the school's philosophy. A third aspect of organizational processes is decision making, which is integrally related to planning, evaluation, and communication activities.

The third domain depicted in Figure 1, organizational *behavior*, represents the activities, skills,

efforts, and motivations of the school staff involved in providing educational services according to the organizational structure. Roles describe the functions of the school staff (e.g., history teacher), responsibilities are defined in job descriptions (e.g., develop daily lesson plans for four periods of tenth-grade U.S. history), and relationships describe how these persons work together in the performance of their roles and responsibilities (e.g., member of high school history department).

Relationship to Program Management
Program evaluation should be closely linked to the management of school programs. A primary purpose of the evaluative process "is to influence and guide, *but not determine*, management decisions, policies, and plans" (Broskowski, White, & Spector, 1979, p. 106; emphasis added). Furthermore, feedback mechanisms in the evaluation procedures that stimulate problem identification and decision making contribute to the success of program implementation. Data must be gathered continuously to assist in the problem-solving process

regarding operation of school programs. Further, evaluation procedures help to clarify issues in problem areas so that decision makers will be motivated to act upon them (Beer, 1980). Durable change is more likely to result when key persons in the organization view problem definitions similarly, and take "ownership" of the intervention (Illback & Zins, 1984). Ownership of organizational change may increase the commitment of school personnel and serve to encourage them to devote the necessary energy to change. Thus, evaluation should provide administrators with choices or alternative actions to pursue.

Assessing Need and Readiness for Change

Various trends in society in general and in schools in particular create a need for change (Lippitt, Langseth, & Mossop, 1986). In any educational organization, however, there are differential levels of readiness and willingness among individuals to attempt or accept change (Goodstein, 1978). Readiness refers to "the social, technological, or systemic ability of a[n] . . . organization to change or try new things. [Evaluation] programs need to identify where change is possible, rather than attempt to impose change on a highly resistant, unready system" (Beer & Walton, 1987, p. 36). There are numerous approaches for assessing organizational functioning (e.g., morale, cohesiveness, long-term planning) and desire for change. With each of them, a collaborative approach will help to ensure staff involvement, feelings of ownership, and commitment to the change program.

As an initial step, it is necessary to assess organizational receptivity to the planned change. Successful change programs are likely to be based on timely, relevant, and technically adequate organizational assessment data (Illback & Zins, 1984). Among the issues to be addressed is the congruence in the values of the proposed program and those currently in existence. Teachers are unlikely to be receptive to programs whose values are in direct conflict with those prevailing in the school (Waugh & Punch, 1987; Zins, Curtis, Graden, & Ponti, 1988). Feasibility must also be considered. A new program should require reasonable amounts of staff time, other resources, and minimal disruption of other operating programs (Maher & Bennett, 1984). The benefits must clearly outweigh the costs.

Among the most common methods of organizational assessment are (a) organizational flowcharts (graphic representations of organizational structure and the formal chain of command), (b) record reviews (e.g., minutes of school board meetings, attendance data, newspaper articles, financial statements), (c) direct observation (e.g., patterns of behavior, gatekeepers, interactions among staff members and among students), (d) questionnaires and surveys (developed to address specific information needs and usually administered anonymously), and (e) interviews (usually with a sample of organizational members to provide more in-depth information). Any one of these methods can be used to collect relevant information. Often, some combination of these approaches may be most appropriate. Again, a systems perspective remains important when attempting to understand a school's need and readiness for change as both internal and external forces can exert influence.

Dissemination and Utilization of Evaluation Results

Once a program is adopted, there is no assurance that it will be implemented as planned or that it eventually will become a permanent part of the organization. Effective and continuous communication of evaluation findings is one means to increase this probability.

The content, manner, and form in which evaluation results are disseminated are crucial factors that influence utilization. Throughout the evaluation process, open two-way lines of communication should be maintained and a participative style of interaction established. Frequent informal communication that is timely and appropriate is preferable to relying upon a single, formal summative report at the conclusion of a program. With ongoing communication patterns, formative information is readily provided. As a result, "surprise" findings, which tend not be utilized or to at least have little impact if they conflict with and disconfirm decision makers prevailing beliefs, can be avoided (Legge, 1984).

This is not to suggest that a final report and presentation be omitted, but rather that formal communication mechanisms are not always the most effective to ensure utilization of evaluation findings, and should not be relied on exclusively. When developing summative evaluation reports, decisions need to be made regarding how to communicate findings to facilitate utilization. For example: (a) to what extent should quantitative or qualitative data be included? (b) is it appropriate to use technical jargon? (c) is brevity or comprehensiveness more important? (d) is formality or informality called for? and (e) to what audience should the information be communicated (Legge, 1984)? Clearly, varying approaches are needed to reach different user groups, and there is no one "right" method.

Utilization is generally considered to occur if the findings influence decision making. A further aspect of utilization influence has to do with whether this information will have a "dramatic impact" or a "gradual influence" (Legge, 1984, p. 179). It seems more realistic to expect that it will exert a gradual influence or what Legge calls enlightenment, since evaluation findings are only one source of input into decision making and change always takes time. A frequently raised concern, however, is that evaluation information results in minimal influence on decision making or is even ignored by decision makers (e.g., Broskowski et al., 1979; Rein & White, 1977; Sproull & Larkey, 1979). Sproull and Larkey have referred to this outcome as a problem in "delivery," which describes the fact that while the evaluation information was produced, it was not delivered in such a way that it is actually used by decision makers.

Common reasons for the lack of utilization of evaluation results include the fact that evaluation results may "(a) reach the administrators/decision makers after decisions have been made, (b) speak to the wrong issues, or (c) may be incomprehensible to all but the most sophisticated methodologists" (Sproull & Larkey, 1979, p. 90). The extent to which evaluation procedures approach methodological rigor is also a consideration. The results may be equivocal or in some way qualified, thus becoming less persuasive, although methodological rigor does not in itself invariably appear strongly related to utilization (Legge, 1984).

Cousins, and Leithwood (1986) developed general guidelines regarding utilization. Following a review of 65 studies on evaluation use, they concluded that utilization of evaluation results was most apparent when "evaluations were appropriate in approach, methodological sophistication, and intensity; the decisions to be made were significant to users and of a sort considered appropriate for the application of formally collected data; users were involved in the evaluation process and had a prior commitment to the benefits of evaluation; users considered the data reported in the evaluation to be relevant to their problems; and a minimum amount of information from other sources conflicted with the results of the evaluation" (Cousins & Leithwood, 1986, p. 360).

These findings underscore the importance of collaborating with potential users to clarify the goals of the evaluation, thereby increasing their potential usefulness and enhancing user commitment to the overall evaluation. User involvement helps ensure that results are relevant and credible, and that they will meet the organization's information needs (Cousins & Leithwood, 1986).

Establishment of collaborative relationships fosters positive and productive interactions that are most conducive to effective program evaluation, which is important as a means of avoiding or resolving conflicts (Zins, 1985b). Evaluators, who possess more technical competence in this area than do most users, are in essence requesting that users develop trust in their judgments. Collaboration fosters this trust and emphasizes the "personal factor" that has been cited as important in utilization (e.g., Legge, 1984). Further, the interest that users have in the evaluation seems to be one of the best predictors of whether the knowledge will be utilized (Beer & Walton, 1987). However, Cousins and Leithwood (1986) caution that user involvement in the evaluation process can decrease objectivity and threaten the evaluator's integrity, although they also note that these potential costs must be weighed against those associated with the nonuse of the results.

INVOLVING THE SCHOOL PSYCHOLOGIST IN PROGRAM EVALUATION

School administrators usually delegate authority for conducting program evaluations to staff specialists because they do not have the technical training or the time to fulfill this responsibility themselves. School psychologists frequently are the primary (and often only) staff members who have expertise in research and program evaluation, and thus often are given responsibility for these tasks. However, evaluators must be cognizant of the fact that the major purpose of program evaluation usually is not to discover new knowledge, and that it is not always possible to implement strict experimental designs.

Role and Function Issues

The professional practice standards of both the American Psychological Association (1981) and the National Association of School Psychologists (NASP) (1984) both stress the importance of delivering and documenting effective school psychological services delivery. In addition, they note the importance of program evaluation activities in general. NASP (1984), for instance, states that "school psychologists provide program planning and evaluation services to assist in decision-making activities" (p. 19).

Despite the support and sanction provided by professional organizations for the school psychologist to participate in evaluation activities, there appears to be an incongruence between professional standards and daily practice. While there are no clear descriptions of the percentages of school psychologists who perform program evaluation activities or of how much time they devote to such efforts, it appears that this is not a major job function for most. For example, Smith (1984) found that his sample spent slightly over 2% of their time in "program development" and 1% in "developing and conducting research." While he did not include a category of program evaluation per se, it appears that program evaluation would be subsumed within these categories. It would be interesting to learn how frequently program evaluation is included in school psychologists' job descriptions.

A national survey of school psychologists' accountability practices was conducted by Zins and Fairchild (1986). Although they investigated only whether respondents collected data with regard to the evaluation of school psychological services, it is notable that only 60% reported currently collecting such information.

One reason for the lack of emphasis that appears to be given to program evaluation is that many school psychologists have not received preservice training in this area (Moore & Carlson, 1988; Zins & Fairchild, 1986). Both of these teams of researchers found that less than one-third of the respondents to their surveys had received related university coursework. Together, these studies suggest that program evaluation is not emphasized in graduate training programs, nor is it a major job function for school psychologists.

Overcoming Barriers and Resistance

Schools have a number of characteristics that make them resistant to change. Many writings in school psychology that address the issues of role expansion and the delivery of a broad range of services make mention of the need to overcome various barriers and resistance (e.g., Graden, Zins, & Curtis, 1988; Zins et al., 1988). The area of program evaluation is no exception.

Technical Expertise

Since many practitioners have not received training in program evaluation, it is understandable that they may resist involvement in these activities. They simply do not have the needed technical expertise. In fact, Gross, Giacquinta, and Berstein's (1971) sociological analysis of change found that lack of necessary skills and knowledge promoted blockage to change. When these persons do engage in evaluation efforts, there may be shortcomings in sampling, instrumentation, variable specification, and statistical analyses that lead to flawed results and questionable conclusions (Sproull & Larkey, 1979). Consequently, data that are generated may have limited usefulness for undertaking program alterations during the year, or for summatively determining whether or how the program should be maintained, modified, or discontinued. Simply put, reliable and convincing information is not developed that can be used in the decision-making process. It is no wonder, then, that many decision makers perceive evaluation as of limited utility. Unfortunately, such last-minute, technically inadequate methods are characteristic of evaluation efforts in many schools. Further, many are begun without clear, measurable objectives that can be assessed to detect change.

It is noteworthy that 22% of the respondents to the Zins and Fairchild (1986) survey desired more information about accountability techniques via methods such as thorough workshops, dissemination of sample formats and procedures, and expert consultation. There are numerous evaluation procedures and guidelines that are readily implementable in schools. Publications such as the Program Evaluation Kit (Herman, 1988) contain numerous ideas, methods, forms, and examples that help to guide the practitioner through the often complex evaluation process.

Evaluation Design

Evaluation need not be "high science" in order to be meaningful, significant, or useful. This statement does not imply that carefully designed studies are irrelevant to program evaluation. Without a doubt, the strongest evaluation designs are experimental ones (Campbell & Stanley, 1963). However, in the real world of the school, it often is difficult to conduct evaluations with direct control of the independent variable (the program), random assignment of subjects to different treatment groups, and so on (see Bennett, 1988, for further discussion). In fact, traditional research methods often are inappropriate. Consequently, quasi-experimental designs (e.g., comparison group and time series designs; see Barlow, Hayes, & Nelson, 1984, Campbell & Stanley, 1963, or Maher & Bennett, 1984, for further discussion) are more commonly used in schools.

Perceived Threat

It is also clear that evaluation activities can be perceived as threatening. Notwithstanding the positive outcomes that may result, there can be a "darker side" to evaluation as it requires much effort, has judgmental qualities, and may have unsettling consequences. Indeed, the Zins and Fairchild (1986) survey of accountability practices found that nearly one-fourth expressed concern about the potential negative consequences of such activities. As noted later, administrative support and reinforcement, both moral and resource related, are important means of dealing with this issue. Moreover, the means by which evaluation is presented, "packaged," and marketed to the organization is critical to its acceptance and utilization (Illback & Zins, 1984), as are incentives for engaging in program evaluation activities. Educators too often are not reinforced for their efforts.

Resource Requirements

Given the potential range of evaluation questions and goals, the design complexities and logistical requirements related to these efforts (particularly since evaluation must be an ongoing activity once a program is operational), and the time demands associated with continuous monitoring for quality control purposes, it is clear that virtually unlimited amounts of time can be devoted to evaluation activities. Indeed, Zins and Fairchild (1986) found that one-third of their respondents reported not collecting accountability data because it was too time consuming. Therefore, it is essential to establish arbitrary but realistic expectations about what is desirable to accomplish and to set corresponding limits on resource allocation.

There is, however, another side to consider. Evaluation endeavors can be an exciting avenue to facilitate professional growth and development, a critical means of establishing and demonstrating value and credibility to consumers and educational decision makers, and an effective way of managing services delivery options and procedures. Moreover, the risks of not evaluating educational programs can be great, ultimately even resulting in loss of employment (Zins, 1985a).

Funding is another issue that can lead to resistance. How will the costs associated with the evaluation be borne? With special services staff typically overextended in their time commitments, it may be difficult to ask them to take on an additional responsibility, particularly since there are multiple program evaluation demands within any school. Yet the alternative of hiring an additional staff member usually is prohibitive.

Administrative Support

Just as with any other organizational process, administrators must support program evaluation efforts. They must allocate sufficient time and resources to staff who conduct the evaluation to enable them to accomplish the task effectively and efficiently. However, as Bennett (1988) has noted, getting school officials to support evaluation is often a very difficult undertaking.

While administrators usually do not desire to become active participants in evaluation procedures (unless a new program is their "pet project"), making certain that they have some involvement in the process can help to ensure their commitment to it. Their participation helps to extinguish uncertainty and decrease estimations of risk (Giacquinta, 1975). Thus, it is important that they at least be kept appraised of the status of program evaluation efforts, and have the opportunity for input into the process.

Communicating Results

Administrators usually do not have extensive training in research and program evaluation, and in fact, some may be "bored" or overwhelmed by statistics and research (Broskowski et al., 1979). Reports of evaluation efforts must be communicated clearly and concisely, usually with minimal technical jargon, so that they are easily understood and take into consideration the fact that the audience may not be as technically sophisticated as the evaluator. The challenge is to present a simplified description of a complex situation. As Sproull and Larkey (1979) noted, "effective evaluation does not terminate with a technically correct design, proper execution, and publication of results" (p.

100). Moreover, since program evaluation can also be threatening as one possible outcome is identification of organizational or managerial deficiencies, results must be communicated sensitively and tactfully. Therefore, program evaluators must develop an understanding of these issues if they are to effectively influence the decision-making process and help administrators make full use of evaluative information.

Planning the Evaluation

It is common to find programs being developed without adequate consideration of the evaluation component. A concrete example exists with regard to alternative services delivery programs that are being implemented in many districts. Prereferral or intervention assistance programs (Zins et al., 1988) are designed, among other things, to provide support to all students and to reduce unnecessary referrals for special education by utilizing consultation as the basis for service delivery. A reasonable amount of research support for a consultative approach can be found in the literature. However, outcome data on this specific application of the consultative framework are sparse. Yet, in their haste to become involved in alternative services delivery programs and to overcome many of the current problems with special education assessment and decision making, many schools have begun implementing these programs because of their great *potential*, but often without building in an evaluation component. Such an approach to program development and implementation seems quite risky. As a result, intervention assistance programs are at risk of becoming another educational bandwagon that quickly fades away because "it doesn't work," when the real culprit is the fact that these programs were not implemented in a knowledgeable, responsible manner (see Zins et al., 1988, for further discussion). Relatedly, Porras and Berg (1978) examined 160 change interventions in business and found only 20 that assessed organizational and work group change. Clearly, evaluation is not always undertaken with competence, thoroughness, and commitment (Lippitt et al., 1986).

Furthermore, interest in evaluation often occurs only when it is required by some external agency, is paid for by an outside source, or is consistent with the political goals of the administration (Bennett, 1988). Similarly, consideration often is given to program evaluation only at the end of the school year, if at all, thereby prohibiting a thoughtful approach to the design of the evaluation. Many program developers simply do not seem to value or realize the contribution that program evaluation can have with respect to effective and efficient program operation.

Involving Schools in Evaluation Efforts

The various problems with program evaluation are relatively easy to identify. No doubt, most readers could add to the list. How, then, do we get schools involved in such efforts, ensure that the evaluations are of high quality, and increase the probabilities that the results will be utilized? Bennett (1988) suggests that program evaluation needs to be sold to administrators as being a cost-effective solution for improving various programs within the school so that they produce better outcomes. Without knowledge of how effectively a program operates and of how it might be improved, it is difficult to understand how resources could continually be directed toward that program. Evaluation attempts to provide some of this information.

Evaluation can be viewed as a type of insurance policy (Bennett, 1988). That is, it helps determine whether resources are being allocated and used wisely, thereby avoiding costly mistakes for the organization. Again, using the cost-effectiveness frame of reference should make evaluation more palatable to administrators.

As noted earlier, establishment of collaborative relationships is a critical aspect in developing support for program evaluation. When members of the organization have been involved in developing program evaluation goals and procedures, they will tend to feel ownership of the process, a commitment to ensuring that the evaluation is conducted according to plan, and also a vested interest in the outcomes. There also will be much higher probabilities that the results will meet their informational needs. Bennett (1988) referred to this approach as user-centered evaluation and noted that "these are the only evaluations that schools should be expected to fund and to cooperate fully with, and probably the only ones for which they will" (p. 523).

SUMMARY

In this chapter we have described the historical and conceptual development of program planning and evaluation within human services, including education. Salient concepts, terminology, strategies, and methods from this rapidly emerging field of empirical inquiry have been delineated in areas such as needs assessment, evaluability assessment, implementation evaluation, and outcome determination. The process of infusing evaluation into the routine of the organization and ensuring that evaluation findings are used to help organizations develop and improve has been discussed, and the need to identify and overcome barriers and resistance in utilization has been emphasized.

There is an increased sense of urgency within education regarding the importance of effective program planning and evaluation. The desire to establish and monitor the quality of educational programs and practices at individual, classroom, building, and school district levels occurs in part as a function of political and social pressures, as seen in the "educational reform" movement. However, this press is also attributable to recognition by school professionals of the contributions that systematic program planning and evaluation can make to developing and improving school organizations. School psychologists will increasingly be asked to participate in planning and evaluation activities, and thus need to prepare themselves to fulfill this role.

REFERENCES

American Psychological Association. (1981). *Ethical standards of psychologists*. Washington, DC: Author.

Attkisson, C. C., & Broskowski, A. (1978). Evaluation and the emerging human service concept. In C. C. Attkisson, W. A. Hargreaves, M. J. Horowitz, & J. E. Sorensen, (Eds.), *Evaluation of human services programs* (p. 523). New York: Academic Press.

Barlow, D. H., Hayes, S. C., & Nelson, R. O. (1984). *The scientist practitioner: Research and accountability in clinical and educational settings*. Elmsford, NY: Pergamon Press.

Beer, M. (1980). *Organizational change and development: A systems view*. Santa Monica, CA: Goodyear.

Beer, M., & Walton, A. E. (1987). Organization change and development. *Annual Review of Psychology, 36,* 339–367.

Bennett, R. E. (1988). Evaluating the effectiveness of alternative educational delivery systems. In J. L. Graden, J. E. Zins, & M. J. Curtis. (Eds.), *Alternative educational delivery systems*. Washington, DC: National Association of School Psychologists.

Borich, G. D., & Jemelka, R. P. (1982). *Programs and systems: An evaluation perspective*. New York: Academic Press.

Broskowski, A., White, S. L., & Spector, P. E. (1979). A management perspective on program evaluation. In H. C. Schulberg & J. M. Jerrell (Eds.), *The evaluator and management* (pp. 105–118). Beverly Hills, CA: Sage.

Campbell, D. T. (1969). Reforms as experiments. *American Psychologist, 24,* 409–429.

Campbell, D. T., & Stanley, J. C. (1963). *Experimental and quasi-experimental designs for research*. Skokie, IL: Rand McNally.

Cook, T. J., & Campbell, D. T. (1976) The design and conduct of quasi-experiments and true experiments in field settings. In M. D. Dunnette (Ed.), *Handbook of industrial and organizational psychology* (pp. 223–326). Skokie, IL: Rand McNally.

Cousins, J. B., & Leithwood, K. A. (1986). Current empirical research on evaluation utilization. *Review of Educational Research, 56,* 331–364.

Cronbach, L. J. (1980). *Toward reform of program evaluation*. San Francisco: Jossey-Bass.

Dalkey, N. C. (1967). *Delphi*. Santa Monica, CA: Rand Corporation.

Delbecq, A. L., & Van de Ven, A. H. (1971). A group process model for problem identification and program planning. *Journal of Applied Behavioral Science, 7,* 466–492.

Flaherty, E. W., & Morrell, J. A. (1978). Evaluation: Manifestations of a new field. *Evaluation and Program Planning, 1,* 1–10.

Fullan, M., Miles, M. B., & Taylor, G. (1980). Organization development in schools: The state of the art. *Review of Educational Research, 50,* 121–183.

Fullan, M., & Pomfret, A. (1977). Research on curriculum and instruction implementation. *Review of Educational Research, 47,* 335–397.

Giaquinta, J. B. (1975). Status risk-taking: A central issue in the initiation and implementation of public school innovations. *Journal of Research and Development in Education, 9*(1), 102–114.

Goodstein, L. D. (1978). *Consulting in human service organizations*. Reading, MA: Addison-Wesley.

Graden, J. L., Zins, J. E., & Curtis, M. J. (Eds.). (1988). *Alternative educational delivery systems*. Washington, DC: National Association of School Psychologists.

Gross, N., Giacquinta, J. B., & Bernstein, M. (1971). *Implementing organizational intervention*. New York: Basic Books.

Hall, G. E., & Loucks, S. F. (1977). A developmental model for determined whether the treatment is actually implemented. *American Educational Research Journal, 14,* 263–276.

Herman, J. L. (Ed.). (1988). *Program evaluation kit* (2nd ed.). Newbury Park, CA: Sage.

Illback, R. J., & Maher, C. A. (1984). The school psychologist as an organizational boundary role professional. *Journal of School Psychology, 22,* 63–72.

Illback, R. J., & Zins, J. E. (1984). In C. A. Maher, R. J. Illback, & J. E. Zins (Eds.), *Organizational psychology in the schools: A handbook for professionals* (pp. 21–52). Springfield, IL: Charles C Thomas.

Kiresuk, T. J., & Sherman, R. E. (1968). Goal attainment

scaling: A general method for evaluating comprehensive community mental health programs. *Community Mental Health Journal, 4,* 443–453.

Kosecoff, J., & Fink, A. (1982). *Evaluation basics: A practitioner's manual.* Beverly Hills, CA: Sage.

Kratochwill, T. R. (Ed.). (1978). *Single subject research: Strategies for evaluating change.* New York: Academic Press.

Legge, K. (1984). *Evaluating planned organization change.* London: Academic Press.

Lippitt, G. L., Langseth, P. M., & Mossop, J. (1986). *Implementing organizational change.* San Francisco: Jossey-Bass.

Maher, C. A. (1978). A synoptic framework for school program evaluation. *Journal of School Psychology, 16,* 322–333.

Maher, C. A. (1981). Program evaluation and school psychology: Perspectives, principles, procedures. In T. R. Kratochwill (Ed.), *Advances in School Psychology,* (Vol. 1, pp. 169–216). Hillsdale, NJ: Lawrence Erlbaum.

Maher, C. A., & Bennett, R. E. (1984). *Planning and evaluating special education services.* Englewood Cliffs, NJ: Prentice-Hall.

Maher, C. A., & Illback, R. J. (1981). Planning for the delivery of special services in public schools: A multidimensional needs assessment framework. *Evaluation and Program Planning, 4,* 249–259.

Maher, C. A., & Illback, R. J. (1982). Organizational school psychology: Issues and considerations. *Journal of School Psychology, 20,* 244–253.

Maher, C. A., Illback, R. J., & Zins, J. E. (Eds.). (1984). *Organizational psychology in the schools: A handbook for professionals.* Springfield, IL: Charles C Thomas.

Moore, C. M., & Carlsen, D. (1988, April). *Accountability: Practices and issues.* Paper presented at the annual meeting of the National Association of School Psychologists, Chicago.

National Association of School Psychologists. (1984). *Principles for professional ethics.* Washington, DC: Author.

Patton, M. Q. (1978). (1978). *Utilization-focused evaluation.* Beverly Hills, CA: Sage.

Porras, J. I., & Berg, P. O. (1978). The impact of organization development. *Academy of Management Review, 3,* 249–266.

Provus, M. M. (1972). *Discrepancy evaluation.* Berkeley, CA: McCutchan.

Rein, M., & White, S. (1977). Policy research: Belief in doubt. *Policy Analysis, 3,* 239–272.

Rossi, P. H., & Freeman, H. E. (1985). *Evaluation: A systematic approach.* Beverly Hills, CA: Sage.

Scriven, M. (1967). The methodology of evaluation. In *Perspective on curriculum evaluation.* (AERA Monograph Series on Curriculum Evaluation, No. 1). Skokie, IL: Rand McNally.

Siegel, L. M., Attkisson, C. C., & Carson, L. G. (1978). Need identification and program planning in the community context. In C. C. Attkisson, W. A. Hargreaves, M. J. Horowitz, & J. E. Sorensen, (Eds.), *Evaluation of human services programs* (pp. 215–252). New York: Academic Press.

Smith, D. K. (1984). Practicing school psychologists: Their characteristics, activities, and populations served. *Professional Psychology: Research and Practice, 15,* 798–810.

Sproull, L., & Larkey, P. (1979). Managerial behavior and evaluator effectiveness. In H. C. Schulberg & J. M. Jerrell (Eds.), *The evaluator and management* (pp. 89–104). Beverly Hills, CA: Sage.

Stufflebeam, D. L., Foley, W. J., Gephart, W. J., Guba, E. G., Hammond, H. D., Merriman, H. O., & Provus, M. M., (1971). *Educational evaluation and decision making.* Itasca, IL: Peacock.

Sudman, S. (1976). *Applied sampling.* New York: Academic Press.

Waugh, R. F., & Punch, K. F. (1987). Teacher receptivity to systemwide change in the implementation stage. *Review of Educational Research, 57,* 237–254.

Weiss, C. H. (1973). Between the cup and the lip. *Evaluation, 1,* 49–55.

Wholey, J. S. (1977). Evaluability assessment. In L. Rutman (Ed.), *Evaluation research methods: A basic guide* (pp. 39–56). Beverly Hills, CA: Sage.

Zins, J. E. (1985a). Best practices for improving school psychology through accountability. In A. Thomas & J. Grimes (Eds.), *Best practices in school psychology* (pp. 493–503). Washington, DC: National Association of School Psychologists.

Zins, J. E. (1985b). Work relations management. In C. A. Maher (Ed.), *Professional self-management* (pp. 105–127). Baltimore: Paul H. Brookes.

Zins, J. E., Curtis, M. J., Graden, J. L., & Ponti, C. R. (1988). *Helping students succeed in the regular classroom.* San Francisco: Jossey-Bass.

Zins, J. E., & Fairchild, T. N. (1986). An investigation of the accountability practices of school psychologists. *Professional School Psychology, 1*(3), 193–204.

33

EFFECTIVE TEACHING: A REVIEW OF INSTRUCTIONAL, AND ENVIRONMENTAL VARIABLES

WILLIAM T. MCKEE
JOSEPH C. WITT
Louisiana State University

This chapter is based on the following premise: that variables operative in the classroom environment, such as the specific behaviors of the teacher and the manner in which the classroom is arranged (e.g., seating arrangement, noise level), influence student behavior and student learning. This premise, in its most essential form, states merely that behavior is influenced by the environment, and this may seem trite to even the most naive students of human behavior. Nevertheless, despite what may be a nearly universal belief in the opening premise by school psychologists, there is an almost total disregard of this belief in their day-to-day functioning. Instead, service delivery activities of school psychologists (i.e., assessment, intervention, and consultation) focus almost exclusively on child variables. Thus, in a typical referral it is more common to assess the *child's* intelligence, the *child's* learning style, and the *child's* behavior than it is to assess what the *teacher* is doing and how the child is being instructed. It is also more common to talk of *child* deficits in learning rather than *teacher* deficits in teaching. And in situations where there is

a lack of fit between the child and the environment, the environment is often considered a constant and remediation activities focus on helping the child to change and to fit.

There exists in school psychology a lack of congruence between, on the one hand, our data-based assumptions and beliefs concerning the importance of the environment, and on the other hand, our practice where environmental variables are seldom seriously considered for the purpose of designing interventions. This discrepancy between beliefs and behaviors results from the enormously complex social and technical issues surrounding the assessment of instructional and other environmental variables. The social and political issues center around school psychologists entering the domain of the teacher and presuming to have the right and the knowledge to target instructional variables as appropriate subject matter for assessment and/or intervention. The technical problems are related to a lack of knowledge on the part of school psychologists about what to assess, how to assess it, and how to communicate that information to teachers in a way that is helpful and enabling.

Perhaps the most serious and fundamental impediment to school personnel giving any real consideration to environmental variables is an attitude or belief system that the locus of the problem must be *within* the child. The logic behind this belief goes something like this. A teacher has 26 children in a fourth-grade classroom, most of whom are at or above grade level in a subject such as math. One child is achieving at a second-grade level in math. Given that all children are exposed to exactly the same instructional environment, and given that most children are successful in this environment, the failure of the one child is more likely attributable to child variables (e.g., aptitude) than to instructional variables. If many children were failing, it might be appropriate to question how the children were being instructed.

Those interested in targeting the instructional environment as a focus for consultation will frequently encounter this argument in one form or another. The way to counter this argument is to attack the logic. Given that logic is only as strong as its assumptions, the critical assumption in this argument is the assumption that *the achievement of the children who were doing well was produced by the teacher*. There are rival hypotheses concerning factors that could account for the learning of the children who were achieving at or above expectation in the classroom. In this context Baer and Bushell (1981) observed that "schools do not teach very often, that they are not designed to do so, and that their personnel are neither inclined or taught how to do so . . ." (p. 264). Baer and Bushell (1981) go on to suggest:

> Public schooling is a series of hurdles. Those who figure out for themselves how to get over or around the hurdles, advance. The school provides a few resources, such as books and adults, that offer some help in getting over the hurdles, but only if the student figures out how to use them. Still, effective advancement requires more resources than those normally available in school; in particular, it requires many out-of-school aids. (pp. 262–263)

According to this view, a major difference between the children who advance and those who do not is the amount of instruction and support they receive

out of school, primarily from parents. The lack of parental support is one reason why many underprivileged children fail in school, whereas most children from suburbia succeed. Considering failure in school from this perspective provides an alternative to attributions typically made by school personnel. Even if 25 children in a classroom are successful and one child is not, it does not necessarily follow that instruction in the classroom is technically adequate. Perhaps it is the case that an effective teacher would be successful with all children in the class. Therefore, it is always useful to consider instructional and other environmental variables.

In consultative activities with teachers, a consideration of instructional variables presupposes a knowledge of those variables. A limiting factor in school psychologists' involvement in teacher consultation with a focus on environmental variables is a lack of knowledge and resources concerning what variables to assess, how to assess them, and how to translate assessment results into interventions. The literature on effective teaching (Wittrock, 1986) has identified a large number of teacher behaviors that make a difference in student achievement. These variables are reviewed in a later section of this chapter, but suffice it to say here that effective teachers do a lot. School psychologists have remained relatively unknowledgeable of the *specific components* of effective teaching.

The plight of the school psychologist who wants to consult about the quality of instruction but who does not know the teacher *effectiveness* literature is roughly analogous to a poorly trained physician who would undertake to diagnose the health of a person without a knowledge of anatomy and physiology. The physician must know how the system is *supposed* to work before a diagnosis can be made of what is not functioning properly. Similarly, for many school psychologists the "health" of a classroom system appears to be only a molar variable because there is a lack of knowledge of the *specific* underlying processes and behaviors that comprise an *effective* classroom. That is to say, the molar variable, "the environment," has not been broken down into the specific components so essential to the process of diagnosing instruction in a way that suggests not only what is wrong but what improvements can be made. For example, what teacher behaviors should occur to maintain effective classroom management? What types of questioning behavior should teachers use? How should chairs, learning centers, and other aspects of the physical environment be arranged? Although there exists a massive data base in response to such questions, surprisingly few teachers know the answers to these questions, although they may have extensive knowledge of how to design an attractive bulletin board or how to develop lesson plans. To be effective, school-based consultants need to be knowledgeable in how classrooms are supposed to operate.

In this chapter we review the literature pertaining to variables within the classroom environment that have been shown to have a marked impact on student achievement. The discussion will focus primarily on variables over which the teacher has control because school-based consultants are most interested in manipulable variables (i.e., those that can be changed) in the development of interventions that improve student learning. Our goal is to provide school psychologists with a list of variables that could be the foci of consultative interactions directed toward a comprehensive consideration of factors that impinge on student learning. Before reviewing the literature pertaining to these variables, we review three theoretical and conceptual models that help to provide a context with which instructional and environmental variables can be viewed relative to other factors that influence learning. A description of these models will also serve as an advanced organizer to facilitate understanding of the interrelationships of the many variables that follow.

THEORETICAL AND CONCEPTUAL FOUNDATIONS FOR ENVIRONMENTAL ASSESSMENT

To establish a proper context and foundation for understanding the process of environmental assessment, it will be useful to consider the theoretical and conceptual factors that have provided the impetus for our approach. In this section we elaborate briefly on three major domains of knowledge: (a) instructional theories, (b) recent developments in behavioral theory, and (c) ecological and systems theory.

Classroom Learning and Instructional Theories

The primary reason to conduct an assessment of instructional and other environmental variables is that these variables have been shown to impact student achievement. Hence, when student achievement in a particular case is below expectation it is appropriate to conduct a comprehensive assessment of all variables that potentially contribute to the problem. How specific instructional variables influence student achievement and how they interact with other variables have been subjects of considerable speculation. Often this speculation has evolved into the development of a theoretical model explicating the interrelationships between variables. One of the more comprehensive, yet practical models is that developed by Centra and Potter (1980), who proposed the interrelational model of school and teacher effects presented in Figure 1.

In the Centra and Potter model, school factors include those variables that characterize differences between schools or school districts and those that describe conditions within an individual school. Although this model highlights school and teacher factors, it does not disregard student peer-group influences or parental influences. Teacher factors include teacher characteristics, such as experience or verbal aptitude, and teachers' behaviors in the classroom. Three student-oriented factors complete the model: student behavior, student characteristics, and student learning outcomes.

The model contains two types of relationships: causal and correlational. A causal relationship exists if one variable or factor is thought to *cause* another. A correlational relationship is present when two variables are found to occur together, but one does not cause the other. For example, a child's height and reading ability are usually correlated because as children get taller, they also tend to become better readers. However, this is only a correlational relationship since neither variable causes the other. Instead, both variables are probably related to some third variables, such as getting older. In Figure 1 expected causal relationships are indicated by straight-line arrows. The curved arrow between teacher characteristics and within-school conditions represents a correlational rather than a causal relation. The double arrows going in opposite directions signify a causal relationship in either direction. For example, we would

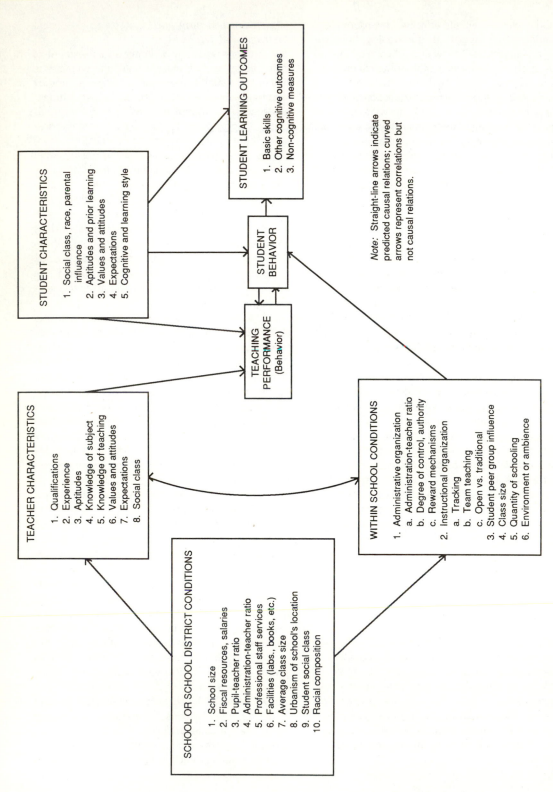

Figure 1. Structural model of school and teacher variables influencing student learning outcomes. (Reproduced by permission.)

expect that not only does teaching performance affect student behavior, but also the reverse is true; student behavior in response to what a teacher does probably causes many teachers to adjust their own behavior.

According to Centra and Potter (1980), their model indicates that "student behavior and student learning outcomes are most directly affected by student characteristics, teaching performance, and within-school conditions" (p. 275). Thus, when trying to solve a student's learning or behavior problem, an assessor would be wise to investigate the relationship among student characteristics, performance of the student's teachers, and within school conditions such as class size and school rules. For reasons stated above, school psychologists have typically overemphasized student characteristics in their assessment activities while almost completely ignoring teaching performance.

Behavioral Theories and Assumptions— Putting the "A" Back in A-B-C

A second force that has stimulated a focus on instructional and environmental variables is a new, or perhaps more accurately, a renewed interest in the *antecedent* component of the antecedent– behavior–consequence equation. This formulation, a fundamental mainstay of applied behavior analysis stipulates that behavior is a function of *both* antecedent and consequent events. Despite this fundamental assumption there is a growing recognition that assessment and intervention activities, even from a behavioral perspective, have not given proper emphasis to antecedent conditions. Seldom does assessment focus attention on physical conditions, elements of the instructional setting, or other potential "causes," and even less frequently are these manipulated in attempts to solve problems.

Even though it is clear that antecedent conditions are functionally related to learning and behavior problems, the "problem solving" of school personnel confronted with a child exhibiting a problem often overlooks this fact. This is partly a result of child-focused thinking mentioned earlier in this chapter and partly the result of ignorance. It is also just simply easier, when working with a child exhibiting a behavior problem, to think in terms of *consequences* (i.e., reinforcers, punishment) that could be applied to *correct* the problem. To think in terms of antecedent conditions that could be

altered to prevent the problem is often considerably more complex.

In this context it is useful to consider some of the antecedent conditions established by effective teachers to prevent learning and behavior problems. In an extensive investigation of 28 third-grade teachers, Emmer and Evertson (1981) reported the following:

> More effective managers spent considerable time during the first several weeks helping students learn how to behave in their classrooms. They had carefully thought out procedures for getting assistance, contacting the teacher, lining-up, turning work in, and standards for conduct during seatwork, group work, and whole class activities. Thus, these teachers knew what children needed to function in the classroom setting and in its activities, and they proceeded to teach these "survival" skills as part of the content at the beginning of the year. Better managers were also more careful monitors of student behavior and dealt with inappropriate behavior, when it occurred, more quickly than did less effective managers. The usefulness of this type of with-itness at the beginning of the year, before a pattern of inappropriate behavior becomes established, is evident. (p. 345)

This literature is reviewed more thoroughly in a later section of this chapter, but from this brief analysis it becomes apparent that effective teachers perform many activities that prevent problems. In fact, there are no differences between effective teachers and ineffective teachers in how they *react* to inappropriate student behavior, but there are large differences in terms of the antecedent conditions they establish to prevent inappropriate behavior (Kounin, 1970). The increased interest in an examination of these antecedent conditions from a behavioral perspective makes it imperative that school personnel know what to assess.

Behavioral Ecology and Person– Environment Fit

A third factor providing impetus for an increased interest in the study of environmental factors comes from attempts to apply *ecological* principles to human problems (Martens & Witt, in press-a; in press-b; Walker, 1985). The ecological analysis of human behavior has a major focus on *person–*

environment fit or *synomorphy*. A problem is conceptualized as a lack of congruence between a person and the environment rather than as necessarily a deficit or problem with either the person or the environment. More specifically, a concern with behavioral ecology has resulted in an increased focus on

(1) the degree of congruence between the individual's needs, capabilities, and aspirations and the environment's demands, resources, and response opportunities; (2) the manner in which different environmental conditions and arrangements force accommodations in the behavior of individuals within them; and (3) the reciprocal nature of individual-environment interactions and influence processes. (Walker, 1985, p. 33)

It follows that if the *fit* between person and environment is to be examined, there will be a necessity to assess not only the person but also the environment. Thus successful assessment should be able to identify the degree to which an individual is functioning "as we might predict" given the characteristics of the environment and the individual.

The mainstreaming of handicapped children and adults from more restrictive to more normal settings provides an example of how many problems are best conceptualized as person–environment fit problems rather than solely person or exclusively environmental problems. Walker (1985) cited data that the best predictor of adjustment in a community setting for developmentally disabled adults was a knowledge of the *setting* into which the individuals were going to be placed, not the personal characteristics of the individual or the individual's adjustment to the *institutional* environment. Thus, if the environment demands that an individual know how to ride a public bus to get to work and the individual has not been trained to perform this skill, the individual will not fit into the environment. Similarly, in mainstreaming handicapped children, Walker (1985) argues strongly from a position that failure to integrate handicapped children successfully into regular classrooms has come about because of "failures to properly match handicapped and disabled individuals with supportive environments, to provide the training and support they need to access the normalizing benefits of such environ-

ments, and to manage the transition process effectively" (p. 39).

THE CONTENT OF ENVIRONMENTAL ASSESSMENT: A REVIEW OF ENVIRONMENTAL AND INSTRUCTIONAL FACTORS

In previous sections of this chapter we have developed a rationale and a conceptual foundation for the conduct of environmental assessment. In other words, we have addressed the question *"Why conduct an assessment of the environment?"* In this section we review the literature relevant to important physical environmental, classroom organizational, and instructional variables. Thus, we are concerned with *what* to assess.

Physical Setting of the Classroom

The importance of the physical setting of the classroom has been acknowledged by ecological psychologists for some time (Barker & Gump, 1964). In particular, "behavior setting theory" (Barker & Wright, 1955; Gump, 1969; Wicker, 1968; Willems, 1967) posits that the successful operations of classroom settings depend on an adequate fit between the physical milieu and the program or standing patterns of behavior. This fit is labeled *synomorphy,* and the essential issue with respect to classroom is whether the milieu qualities will support the proposed program of behavior. Ecological psychologists such as Gump (1985) have stressed that the behavior setting is a multidimensional construct, encompassing ongoing patterns of behavior (e.g., the question–attend–answer sequence typical of recitation sessions), physical characteristics of the setting, and the number of inhabitants per environmental unit. All of these dimensions are interdependent, so changes in some physical characteristic of the classroom may affect standing patterns of behavior and further affect the distribution of individuals within the environment.

Illustrative of the interdependency of behavior setting elements is Weinstein's (1982) report of an "ecological" intervention in a preschool setting. This investigation found increased use of books and book-related materials by kindergarten children during free-play periods when a library corner was established in the classroom. The "packaged" environmental change in this situation included partitions and shelving, "soft" furniture and a variety of literature-related materials (cassette tape player, roll theater, etc.). Introducing this environmental change into the behavior setting led to new book-related activities (e.g., librarian role-playing games). Although the nature of interactions in any environment is complex and simple main effects are often difficult to isolate (Frank, 1984), a body of research evidence has accumulated which suggests that changes in some aspects of the physical environment can be related to changes in student academic performance, social behavior, and attitudes. In particular, Weinstein (1979) concluded in her review of research that manipulation of some aspects of the physical classroom environment result in differences in achievement, while impact on attitudes and a number of nonachievement behaviors such as use of materials, attendance, social interactions, number of interruptions, and level of questions is evident as well. Several of these areas are described below, including seating position, classroom design and furniture arrangement, spatial density and crowding, noise, and lighting.

Seating Position

Where a child sits in the classroom can have a significant effect on the student's performance and the nature of teacher–student interaction. For example, Weinstein (1979, 1985) cited evidence to support the notion of an "action zone" in conventional row-seating arrangements, both when seats are assigned and for self-selected seating positions (Adams & Biddle, 1970; Sommer, 1967). Those students who occupy front seats and those seated down the center of the room are recipients of more teacher-directed verbal interaction, questioning, and eye contact. Perhaps because of this they show increased attention and on-task behavior, greater participation, more positive attitudes, and improved achievement. In the studies reviewed by Weinstein (1985), students judged highly or moderately verbal were most affected by placement in or out of the action zone. Students characterized as low verbalizers did not vary their level of participation with changes in location. A study by Koneya (1976) further supports the notion that certain student characteristics will attenuate the degree of influence exerted by seating position. Presumably, these effects are the result of increased opportunities to respond to instruction, as well as increased attention, eye contact, and nonverbal commu-

nication between teacher and student (Weinstein, 1985). Brooks, Silvern, and Wooten (1978) substantiated these effects but described particular seating positions in the classroom as being in zones that are likely to receive different levels and types of teacher–student communications. They reported that students seated in the social-consultive zones (front and center) received more permissive and interactive styles of communication from their teachers. Students in the public zone (sides and back of the room) received more lectures and one-way communication (Doyle, 1985a).

Seating position effects are likely to be stronger in those classrooms where the teacher is tied to a single position for presentation and recitation. It is in such a situation that the two-way flow of instruction is most unequally distributed. Where a student sits relative to the teacher's "action zone" will be of particular concern when students who may benefit most from increased instructional contact are seated in positions least likely to receive such contact.

Classroom Design and Furniture Arrangement

In addition to evidence related to effects of seating position in traditional straight-row formation, effects of alternative spatial arrangements and classroom design issues have been investigated. The majority of research in this area has focused on preschool and playground settings (e.g., Brown & Burger, 1984; Kounin & Sherman, 1979), and open-space schools (Weinstein, 1979). The design of the physical setting as well as the type and arrangement of furnishings and materials within the setting can have reliable effects on student behaviors

Brown and Burger (1984), for example, studied preschool playground design and found that type of equipment available, zoning of playground areas (e.g., sand play in low-traffic areas), and availability of encapsulated (enclosed) play areas related to the amount of positive social interaction, language behavior, and vigorous and other desirable motor behaviors exhibited on the playground. Studies of open-space classrooms have provided considerable additional data to suggest that relatively minor modifications in classroom arrangement can affect not only traffic patterns but also time spent in transitions, number of interruptions, type and frequency of student questions, utilization of activities and materials, as well as overall level of student satisfaction and freedom from distraction (Ahrentzen & Evans, 1984; Cotterell, 1984; Evans & Lovell, 1979; Weinstein, 1977). Not only are student behaviors affected directly by such changes but teachers report having to develop and change rules, restrict activities, and modify curricula to adapt to design features and physical characteristics of specific classroom. Presumably, many problems result from teachers not being able to develop and implement modifications that promote adaption to the particular environmental conditions of their classrooms.

Weinstein (1979) reviewed a number of correlational and experimental studies that report similar behavior–design relationships (Evans & Lovell, 1979; Weinstein, 1977; Zifferblatt, 1972, cited in Weinstein, 1979). Zifferblatt (1972) compared two classrooms that differed primarily in the physical arrangement of furnishings. Despite similar instructional styles, curricular objectives and activities of the two teachers, the students in the first classroom were observed to have exhibited shorter periods of attention, as well as more loud conversation and non-task-oriented movement. A recent and more methodologically sound experiment by Rosenfield, Lambert, and Black (1985) compared the effects of row, cluster, and circle seating arrangements on pupil behavior during classroom discussion. They found that desk arrangement rather than student ability, student interest, or other architectural features significantly affected pupil behavior. More off-task behavior including disruption and withdrawal was noted in rows versus circle arrangements. Both cluster and circle patterns resulted in greater on-task than did rows. Students seated in clusters, while remaining on task and actively involved in discussions, had to raise their hand to get attention, whereas when students were seated in circles they simply made more on-task comments without waiting for recognition. Patterns of interaction, amount of participation, and development of leadership roles can also be affected by room arrangement and seating location. Data from several cooperative learning studies suggests that for some types of tasks at least, group seating arrangements can result in improved performance (Slavin, 1980). N. Bennett and Blundell (1983), in a single-case design study, found increased quantity of work, similar quality, and improved classroom behavior when students worked on independent seatwork in rows rather than in group desk arrangements. Although the

results of this research are not consistent in terms of the efficacy of specific types of arrangements, the clear implication from this and related studies (Steinzor, 1950; Wheldall, Morris, Vaughan, & Ng, 1981) is that the amount of on-task behavior is related not only to seating arrangement but also to the type of activities being undertaken. Clearly, instructional activities will be accomplished more efficiently when the physical arrangement of desks suits the kind of interaction necessary to the task. The classroom management research (Emmer, 1985) stresses that careful arrangement of classroom furnishings and materials can appreciably and positively affect student attention, access to materials and instruction, and can help facilitate teacher monitoring of student behavior. Although the physical arrangement of facilities may have an independent effect, when these are coupled with demands of ongoing activities, behavior is more profoundly affected.

Although the traditional straight-row formation appears to be most effective for traditional lesson presentation, lecture, demonstration, testing, and independent seatwork where no interaction is desired, such an arrangement may not be ideal or even effective for all activities. Where particular alternative arrangements are possible, the most appropriate will depend on a consideration of the type of activities desired in the situation, management of movement patterns, access to needed materials and work areas, and desired levels of pupil interaction. Krovetz (1977) and Musgrave (1975) have each described several ways in which teachers can match physical arrangement of the classroom to a variety of teaching and learning activities and styles so that the effects of different instructional methods are enhanced and potential problems minimized.

Spatial Density and Crowding

Classroom-based research of the effects of density and crowding on achievement is surprisingly scarce (Weinstein, 1979). Laboratory studies, however, indicate that detriments in performance are most evident in particular activity settings. Performance is most affected in those settings involving complex tasks requiring high information processing load (e.g., higher-level cognitive objectives), and tasks requiring physical interaction among subjects (e.g., lab partners completing a chemistry experiment). Performance in both of these types of activities is improved when conditions are less crowded. Although it has not been well demonstrated as yet, these findings would suggest that increased density may affect achievement in discussion groups more than in lecture situations (Lowey, cited in Weinstein, 1977).

The effects of classroom density and crowding on social behavior have been better documented (Weinstein, 1979). Greater classroom density has been associated with decreased attention (Krantz & Risley, 1972), increased social withdrawal (Hutt and Varzey, 1966), aggression, dissatisfaction, and nervousness (Weinstein, 1979). However, the demonstrated effects of density on student aggression in the classroom may be related to availability of resources, for example whether students have access to necessary and desirable work materials rather than the actual numbers of individuals. In those situations where there is both high density and needed or highly regarded resources are not equitably distributed, greater aggression is likely to be observed (Rohe & Patterson, 1974). Students become more aggressive when few required resources are available; this situation is exacerbated by increased student density. Density and availability of resources may be affected in turn by the use and arrangement of furnishings in the classroom, the distribution of materials, arrangement of activities and physical access to work areas.

Teachers can have significant effects on both achievement and social behavior through appropriate control of social density (i.e., by differing the size of groups in the same space in the classroom) and spatial density (i.e., by allocation of same-size groups to different-size spaces). Selection of the optimal group size for participation in activities should be based on the density requirements of the activity, and by selection and arrangement of furnishings with activity and interaction needs and access to necessary resources in mind.

Noise

Teachers report more problems from the effects of noise than do pupils (Brunetti, 1972, cited in Zentall, 1983), and certainly handling noise level within the classroom is a common management concern. Again, noise and other distractions are of more concern in certain situations than in others (e.g., open versus closed classrooms) and in particular activities (e.g., silent reading versus small group discussion) (S. N. Bennett, 1985). Weinstein (1979) is critical of most lab-based studies which

show detrimental effects of intense noise on complex learning tasks, and suggests uncertain relevance of these studies for educational settings. Weinstein reviews two other categories of studies however, considered to be more relevant: studies of short-term exposure to moderate (typical) noise originating within the school, and studies of long-term exposure to more severe noise from external sources such as airport or highway traffic.

Weinstein describes studies by Slater (1968) and Weinstein and Weinstein (1979) where performance on reading comprehension tasks or standardized reading test performance was not affected either "positively or negatively by the levels of noise which are typical of a normal school environment" (Slaterk, 1968, cited in Weinstein, 1979). Zentall (1983) reviewed several additional investigations which have failed to find normal levels of classroom noise to be detrimental to performance (Christie & Glichman, 1980; Ollila & Chamberlain, 1975). Zentall concludes, however, that studies by Hockey (1970) and Zentall and Shaw (1980) show *facilitation* of well-established responses with added classroom noise of moderate levels and *detrimental* effects of added noise on difficult tasks (Zentall, 1983). In particular, auditory linguistic stimulation (conversation) is thought to be more difficult to ignore than nonlinguistic stimulation, but these effects depend again on task difficulty (Zentall, 1983), with conversation being more intrusive for more difficult tasks. Collins-Eiland, Dansereau, Brooks, and Holley (1986), in a study of the effects of conversational noise on academic tasks, found significant individual effects (related to internal–external locus of control), suggesting (as in Zimmer & Brachlus-Raymond, 1978) the need for further study of individual differences in responses to conversational noise.

There is some evidence of detrimental effects on performance from long-term exposure to extreme noise (Weinstein, 1979). For example, Bronzaft and McCarthy (1975) found that reading scores of students attending an elementary school near an elevated train were lower for students on the near (noisy) side of the school building than for those on the far side. However, more recent work by Cohen and by Krantz, Evans, and Stokols (cited in Weinstein, 1979) does not support the general detrimental effects of high noise on achievement but did find "noisy school" students to have higher blood pressure, more distractibility and poorer performance, and less persistence on a puzzle-type learning task. These effects were observed to increased with increased number of years of exposure to high noise schooling.

With this and other studies investigating effects of noise on classroom processes (Cohen, Glass, & Singer, 1973; Crook & Langdon, 1974), several alternative hypotheses to explain these effects have been entertained: (a) noise may interfere with students hearing the teacher, thus missing essential instruction; (b) teaching is interrupted frequently, thus instructional time is affected; and (c) under constant or frequent high noise conditions children become generally inattentive. Research reviewed by Weinstein makes these all tenable and suggests multiple causes of effects of both short- and long-term exposure to classroom noise.

In creating ideal conditions for learning, teachers need be mindful of the differential effects of classroom noise on various types of tasks. It is likely that students will have differing tolerance levels for noise while learning, although almost all students will require less noise when performing more complex tasks. When teachers have little control over long-term student exposure to high noise, teaching will have to be adjusted to compensate for the decreased attention and instructional continuity.

Lighting

Several reports have suggested that classroom lighting effects children's overt behavior, cognitive performance, visual fatigue, and possibly their overall physical health (e.g., Fletcher, 1983). Unfortunately, lack of replication of results and methodological concerns in many of the studies make conclusions from this literature tentative. Studies in this area typically attempt to discover what differences in student behavior are to be observed under different lighting conditions. Frequently, student behavior in rooms lighted with standard cool-white fluorescent lamps is compared with student behavior under daylight fluorescent, or incandescent lamps. In the majority of the studies reviewed by Fletcher (1983), cool-white fluorescent lighting is associated with an increase in inappropriate behaviors (Colman, Frankel, Ritvo, & Freeman, 1976; Mayron, 1978). The hypothesized relation between lighting type and behavior has been criticized (Barkley, 1981), and some more rigorous studies found no significant differences in on-task behavior and activity levels of

behavior disordered and hyperactive children under different lighting conditions (O'Leary, Rosenbaum, & Hughes, 1978). Studies of achievement effects as well as visual acuity and fatigue have yielded mixed effects (Fletcher, 1983). In general, daylight fluorescent is favored over cool-white fluorescent. However, individual differences in behavior between and within classrooms have emerged. These differences are probably related to differences in lighting in different parts of classrooms. In particular, increases in natural light have been associated with improved visual acuity and decreases in visual fatigue (Fletcher, 1983). Work quality and attention appear not to be greatly affected by level of illumination (Fletcher, 1983), although at least one study reported increased quantity associated with higher intensity (Car-Gavrilovic, 1964). Level of illumination may affect social behavior as well. Decreased illumination in a college hallway was shown to be associated with decreases in student-generated noise level (Sanders, Gustanski, & Lawton, 1974).

Teachers generally have little control over lighting in school classrooms but should probably be aware of the need to restrict glare from natural or artificial light sources as well as potential differences in available illumination in different parts of the classroom resulting from type and placement of light sources. Some seating locations or arrangements may be more desirable than others given the availability of light sources in particular classrooms. Where source flexibility in light is possible, it may be desirable to vary the level of illumination in certain areas of the classroom to enhance particular kinds of activities.

Classroom Organization and Management

The learning environment created in a classroom, the established patterns of action and interaction, determine to a large extent what students do day after day in that classroom. Ultimately, of course, what students do, what behaviors they engage in, affects what they learn. Well-managed classrooms provide a learning environment with clearly articulated demands, where group activities, often several at one time, function smoothly, and where students are able to make productive use of instructional time.

Organization and management are usually defined in terms of group activities, although the scope is clearly much broader, including the management of the classroom as a unit, with management needs varying according to the nature of activities occurring at any time. At the classroom level, the goals of the teacher's management and organizational efforts are realized to the extent that students recognize and cooperate with the interactional demands of various classroom events (Doyle, 1985a). When attention is directed to what is required of individual students, however, cooperation with context demands might be realized with a variety of student behaviors, ranging from complete task engagement to at least passive noninvolvement. Most classroom activities can proceed if there is no obvious interference. Orderly group recitation, for example, requires active involvement on the part of some members of the group and at least passivity on the part of others. Thus, good management of the learning environment as it is described here is a "necessary, but not sufficient" condition for learning, particularly when learning is measured at the individual student level. However, the benefits of classroom instruction are certainly affected or moderated by the degree of order present and as a result learning is less likely to be optimal in poorly managed classroom (Hoge & Luce, 1979).

Classroom Management Skills

Reviews of classroom management literature (e.g., Brophy, 1983a) consistently acknowledge the work of Jacob Kounin and his colleagues as providing a leadership role in studying and understanding teacher classroom management efforts. Kounin produced one of the earliest and most important investigations of teacher management skills (Kounin, 1970). The initial focus of this work was an analysis of the ways in which teachers in a variety of settings handle student misbehavior. It was thought that teachers in well-managed classrooms, where everything seems to run smoothly, differed from their counterparts in comparison classrooms, where problems were more frequent, in the way they responded to disruptions and misconduct. The hypothesis was that the particular way teachers managed misbehavior affected not only the individuals involved but had a "ripple effect" on other students who observed but were not directly involved. Through observation of other's misbehavior and teacher management efforts students might be prevented from behaving in similar ways. Alternatively, if students "get away with" misbehavior or if the teacher does not manage problems effectively,

more inappropriate behavior would be expected to occur.

After videotaping and analyzing the interactions in 80 elementary classrooms, Kounin found no reliable differences in the methods of responding to misbehavior used by teachers in the more and less successfully managed classrooms. These results indicated that patterns of student behavior were not related to the way that problems were handled once they had happened. However, those teachers who had well-managed classrooms had far fewer occurrences of misbehavior in their classrooms. Although these teachers did not appear to have superior methods of dealing with problems when they arose, the more effective teachers were found to differ primarily in their use of group management skills, which in turn appeared to minimize the frequency and severity of disruptions that occurred in their classrooms. Kounin was able to identify a number of global management skills that were characteristic of these teachers.

With-itness. With-itness refers to the teacher's ability to be aware of, and be responsive to, student behavior at all times. With-it teachers not only knew what was going on in their classrooms all the time, but also communicated their awareness to students. By regularly monitoring activity in the classroom they were able to detect inappropriate behavior early, anticipate potential trouble spots, and manage problems before they could escalate and spread. The key elements here seemed to be their good timing and accuracy in identifying potential problems.

Overlapping. Good group management frequently necessitated teachers attending to and managing more than one activity at a time. For example, during whole-group instruction, momentary student inattention to task might be ignored, but the teacher would change voice tone to restore interest and attention while continuing lesson presentation. More serious inattention was handled in ways which in themselves were not disruptive, such as the use of eye contact, proximity, a touch on the shoulder, or other nonverbal cues. Examples of other nondisruptive measures included the use of instructional questions, brief directive comments, or merely using the student's name, any of which might serve to refocus a troublesome student while the flow of ongoing activities was maintained. Effective managers seemed to have learned ways to be "on top of" and respond to the demands of several situations at one time. To some extent this was the result of good planning, but it also required appropriate interactive decision making. Less effective managers were more likely to stop all instructional activities in order to respond to a problem situation.

Signal Continuity and Momentum. Well-planned, smooth, briskly paced instruction and clear activity demands present a continuous academic "signal" or task for students, which results in sustained momentum. Whether involved in group instruction or engaging in independent work, students were seldom interrupted and always had something to do. Effective managers were thoroughly prepared, had anticipated student needs, and had learned how to initiate, maintain, and terminate activities smoothly. Fragmentation, teacher attention to irrelevant details, or loss of focus was not allowed to interrupt instruction or students' active engagement with instructional activities. Moreover, students were always aware of task and activity requirements, so they were able to maintain task "momentum." Maintaining momentum appears to be important whether students are engaged in lectures, demonstrations, seatwork, or recitations and is particularly important when students are in transition between activities.

Group Alerting and Accountability in Lessons. During instruction effective managers used a variety of techniques which maintained student attention and engagement. In recitation, for example, attention of the entire group was maintained while one student was responding. The teacher maintained attention by making eye contact with everyone in the group before selecting someone, making selections randomly, and by asking students to respond to or expand on another student's response. These teachers also maintained interest in instruction by alerting students that something novel, interesting, or challenging could happen at any time, by mixing individual and choral responding, and by presenting exciting material. Further, by calling on individuals frequently and asking them to demonstrate understanding, the teachers maintained active student participation. using these procedures and by circulating to check work performance, teachers held students accountable for paying attention and engaging in instructional activities.

In a review of classroom management research, Brophy (1983a) noted that subsequent study of management skills (e.g., L. M. Anderson, Evertson & Brophy, 1979; Brophy & Evertson, 1976; Good & Grouws, 1977) has supported the finding that "with-itness," overlapping, and signal continuity and momentum are important to overall management and improved student learning. According to Brophy, however, the group alerting and accountability techniques described by Kounin do help maintain student attention, but are only appropriate for occasional use. The need for extensive use of these techniques may indicate a failure to implement more fundamental management strategies (Brophy, 1983a).

Summary. Kounin deserves and is given credit for providing the first wave of classroom research, which *described* the group management skills teachers use to prevent management problems from occurring (Brophy, 1983a; Evertson, 1987). The second wave of classroom management research has focused attention on *how teachers establish effective management systems* and *specific procedures* they implement. The importance of these findings has been investigated further through application in preservice and inservice teacher training programs. This second wave of classroom management research has elaborated on Kounin's work by describing which specific management procedures were important, how preventive management procedures were put in place by teachers, and whether effective management skills could be taught.

Findings across a wide range of studies provide evidence that preventive management results from "a systematic approach which starts with preparation and planning before the year begins, is implemented initially through systematic communication of expectations and establishment of procedures and routines at the beginning of the year and is maintained throughout the year" (Brophy, 1983a, p. 271). Observational studies in both elementary (Emmer, Evertson, & Anderson, 1980; Evertson & Anderson, 1979) and secondary schools (Evertson & Emmer, 1982; Sanford & Evertson, 1981) have identified several of the most important skills necessary to establishing an effective management system. These findings have in turn been developed into training materials for teachers (e.g., Emmer, Evertson, Sanford, Clements, & Worsham, 1982; Evertson et al., 1982). Evidence from subsequent experiments has demonstrated that teachers who implemented the management suggestions were able to establish in their classrooms better student engagement with less off-task, inappropriate, and disruptive behavior (Evertson, 1985; Evertson, Emmer, Sanford, & Clements, 1983).

Procedures for Establishing Effective Management

Establishing an effective management system involves considerable analysis by teachers of instructional activities and expected student behaviors before the year begins, as well as planning procedures to be implemented over the first few weeks of school. Since the kinds of activities engaged in will differ across subject areas and grade levels, teachers need to make explicit their expectations for student behavior for each activity. Thus, in addition to considering the content demands of each area of the curriculum, teachers need to be able to describe what information students will need and what skills will be required for them to function well in the classroom. For example, effective managers will let students know what different kinds of interactions are appropriate during lab experiments, small-group discussion, and teacher-directed whole-class instruction. Requirements must be considered for even the most basic of routines, such as the way handouts will be distributed, how students will be informed of assignments and work requirements, and what procedures are to be followed when students enter the room for the day or when class begins. During the first days of the school year much of instruction will focus on students learning and applying these "going to school" skills and on implementing the procedures that form the basis of classroom management for the remainder of the year. Maintaining an effective management system requires periodic review, careful monitoring, and consistent follow-through once the procedures are in place. An important part of maintenance is the use of consequences, including both positive consequences to reinforce appropriate actions and punishment to deter misbehavior. Evertson (1987) suggested that although management needs will vary for students at different grade levels and between classrooms, several basic concerns need to be addressed for any classroom to function effectively.

1. Determine classroom rules and decide what consequences will be imposed for infractions.
2. Plan procedures and establish requirements for everyday routines.
3. Provide procedures to maintain student accountability.
4. Manage inappropriate behavior.

Management needs in each of these areas are discussed below. In addition to the review by Evertson, this discussion draws heavily from a number of other sources (Doyle, 1985a, 1985b; Emmer, 1985; Emmer, Evertson, Sanford, Clements, & Worsham, 1984).

Classroom Rules. Effective classroom managers provide students with a clear set of standards for expected classroom behavior. Rules for the classroom establish a set of general expectations for student conduct and serve to promote the development of an orderly, cooperative, and purposeful environment. Evertson (1987) has suggested several general guidelines which are useful in developing classroom rules. First, classroom rules much be consistent with and enforce school-wide rules and policies. Second, rules should provide a clear statement of all major areas where there exist expectations for appropriate student behavior, with positive examples of appropriate conduct clearly specified. Third, whether rules are developed with or without student input, each rule should be supported by a rationale as to why the rule is both necessary and beneficial to positive classroom functioning. In particular, it is important that rules are not arbitrary or convey negative expectations. Finally, a few well-stated rules will be taught and enforced more effectively than will long lists of prohibited behaviors.

Although most students will follow stated rules most of the time without excessive use of incentives, teachers' management systems soon break down if rules are not enforced. Effective enforcement requires development of explicit consequences for compliance and noncompliance with expected norms of behavior, explanation of consequences ahead of time, and consistent application when rules are violated. The kind of consequences should fit the nature of the problem, should be realistic and simple enough so that the teacher can carry them through, and should be effective. Often "logical" consequences can be employed for violation of rules or for failing to follow procedures. For example, if work is to be completed in pen, work in pencil would be returned and not accepted until redone in pen. In many situations some form of penalty, such as detention or loss of a privilege, is more appropriate. Consequences that are extreme or require excessive teacher involvement may be applied inconsistently. Inconsistent application of consequences not only creates confusion but also detracts from teacher credibility.

One of the most important and yet frequently neglected tasks of the early weeks of school each year is to devote time to teaching students what is expected of them and what contingencies will be applied. This applies equally to teaching rules governing general behavioral expectations as well as to instruction in procedures related to specific student activities. Merely posting a set of rules or telling students what behaviors are prohibited, particularly after problems have occurred, is not effective in preventing management problems. Rules and procedures are taught in a manner similar to other important topics. Effective teachers provide a rationale for the use of particular rules and procedures by describing the purpose and need for each, provide examples of the desired behavior, give clear illustrations of inappropriate behavior, and describe consequences for violation of those rules that the teacher has emphasized. Importantly, effective managers provide frequent opportunities for students to rehearse and practice all of the components and give informative feedback. Rules and procedures are more likely to be followed when students have a clear understanding of what is expected of them and when they know that consequences will be applied consistently.

Finally, teachers should prepare and post a chart listing class rules. This can be displayed prominently to serve as a visual aid for review of rules and can also serve as a useful prop in day-to-day management. For example, the teacher could on observing misbehavior merely point to the rule chart as a nonverbal statement to desist, or ask the student to recite the pertinent rule. Posting of classroom rules is important but is only a part of implementation. Students will need *instruction* and *consistent enforcement of rules*.

Plan Classroom Procedures. Although rules help guide general classroom behavior, effective teachers also plan and teach all procedures required for the accomplishment of each major classroom routine. Established routines, for example, permit smooth transitions between activities thereby preventing disruptions that can lead to behavior problems. Thus in anticipating that transitions between learning centers is a time when problems occur, the effective teacher will instruct students in every aspect of the transition including how to put away materials, how to exit a chair quietly, where the next center is located, and how to walk quietly to that center. Training manuals for secondary and elementary school teachers (Emmer et al., 1984; Evertson et al., 1982) provide extensive checklists to focus attention on important areas in which procedures must be established.

1. *Student Use of Classroom Space and Facilities:* For many instructional activities students need to have access to a variety of materials and equipment, as well as to areas of the classroom away from their desks. Instruction in procedures will help students to know when and where they may move about the classroom, how to obtain needed materials, and how they are to perform with respect to different resources. Areas where established procedures are particularly important include requirements related to student access to storage of individual and class materials, use of equipment and materials, including responsibilities for cleanup, and procedures for the use of centers and other special areas of the class.

2. *Transitions In and Out of the Room:* Transitions in and out of the classroom provide an opportunity for students to waste instructional time, engage in misbehavior, and disrupt classroom activities. Thus, procedures need to be developed to deal with beginning and ending the school day, for class changes, for leaving and returning to the room, and for use of out-of-class areas such as the bathroom. For example, with younger students who frequently move to other areas of the school as a group, effective managers consider all the factors that interfere with efficient lining up and develop procedures to minimize these problems. This will involve the teacher specifying where and how students should line up, establishing a clear

signal to initiate student movement, and demonstration and practice of these procedures. Orderly transitions into and out of the classroom can also be problematic for older students who change classes throughout the day. In order to start classes on time and in an orderly way, expectations for beginning-of-period behavior must be planned (e.g., students in seat, started on a warm-up exercise when the tardy bell rings).

3. *Procedures During Teacher-Led Instruction and Seatwork:* Interruptions and distractions during teacher-led instruction and while students are engaged in independent seatwork interfere with student learning. To minimize these effects, procedures need to be developed that will ensure student attention and participation during instruction, and which decrease distractions during independent practice sessions. This might include deciding such issues as what materials should be on student desks during instruction, and establishing cues to signal students when they may call out and when to raise their hands to contribute to discussion. Students also need a means of indicating the need for assistance and a way of receiving help during independent work sessions without disrupting others. When teachers use group work and small-group instruction, procedures for student movement between locations in the classroom and expectations for student behavior in and out of the small group should also be identified. Students need to know, too, what to do when they have completed required seatwork, and what to do while waiting for teacher help.

4. *Planning Student Participation in Daily Routines:* Every day in every classroom, teachers have to manage a large number of noninstructional activities (e.g., taking roll, handing out and collecting materials, moving from small group to seatwork) which are vital to group functioning. Without well-established routines, management of these activities can consume valuable instructional time and create a sense of confusion. Teachers need to establish a consistent means for signaling student attention, develop efficient procedures for distributing and collecting materials, and provide a structure for transitions between instructional activities. Other important issues include procedures related to student use of other areas of the building (e.g., bathroom, library, office, or cafeteria), what to do during PA announcements and other interruptions, as well as fire and disaster drills.

5. *Communicating Assignments and Work Requirements:* Effective management of student academic work will require setting standards of form and neatness, providing a systematic means of posting assignments, and developing procedures for late and makeup work. When consistent requirements are stated and enforced, students can take more responsibility for the management of their own learning activities. For example, teachers might require students to maintain their own assignment records by copying assignments from the board as they are given and recording when they are completed. By providing explicit instruction in how students are to complete work and what responsibilities they need to assume, teachers help students develop better self-management of learning activities.

Provide Procedures for Student Accountability. Effective managers develop accountability procedures to communicate to students that they are interested in and will closely monitor student's activities. Accountability procedures include monitoring of (a) student behavior during instruction, (b) task engagement and success during independent work, and (c) compliance with required procedures. To ensure accountability, student work is checked regularly, feedback and corrective activities are provided, and work is rechecked for correctness. Teachers who check work promptly convey a sense of purposefulness which communicates to students that what they are doing is important. Consistent application of procedures and enforcement of work requirements for all students will help maintain a high level of accountability. Arbitrary and inconsistent procedures can lead to students losing a sense of accountability which frequently results in students testing the limits. An inability to maintain consistency is often an indication that requirements need to be reanalyzed and, if necessary procedures changed.

Manage Inappropriate Behavior. Preventive procedures can minimize problems; however, teachers need to act on prolonged inattention or work avoidance by students and obvious violations of classroom rules and procedures. Some problems can be ignored, for example, when the violation involves a minor deviation, which is of short duration, and which is unlikely to spread. Also, when an immediate teacher response would interrupt a lesson or would provide attention for an inappropriate behavior, it may be appropriate for the teacher to response to the behavior at another time. Other behaviors that interfere, or are likely to persist and escalate, must be acted upon immediately and directly. Appropriate teacher responses include asking the student to stop, reminding the student of the correct procedure, making eye contact, or redirecting the student to appropriate behavior.

Procedures for managing problems that persist or are very disruptive involve two phases. The first phase is to bring the behavior to an immediate halt with a minimum of disruption. During the second phase the teacher introduces procedures to prevent the problem from reoccurring. Prevention may involve activities such as identification and elimination of the "causes" of the incident (i.e., management of antecedents), providing consequences that will deter inappropriate responding in the future, or teaching more constructive means of behaving where students lack skills.

Brophy (1983a) reviewed a number of supplemental management techniques which can be used in addition to, but not in place of, the procedures described above. These include promoting prosocial behavior through group relationship activities such as the teams–games–tournaments (TGT) (Slavin, 1980) using individual counseling and therapy programs such as the Reality Therapy approaches suggested by Glasser (1977), or employing a variety of behavior modification techniques such as self-control training (Meichenbaum, 1977), the Response Cost Lottery (Witt & Elliott, 1982), or contingency contracting (Homme, Csanyi, Gonzales, & Rechs, 1970). As Doyle (1985a) suggested, however, recent emphasis has moved away from the use of elaborate token economy and contingency management procedures toward methods that focus on helping students learn to cope with classroom processes through preventive techniques that emphasize the teaching of social skills (Cartledge & Milburn, 1978), coping strategies (Spaulding, 1983), and self-monitoring and self-control strategies (L. Anderson & Prawat, 1983; Brophy, 1983a; McLaughlin, 1976).

Instruction

Lessons that proceed smoothly, that are well paced, and maintain high student engagement contribute to a well-managed classroom. Where instructions and directions for activities are clear, where students understand content presented and are able to complete assignments without confusion, students are more likely to use classroom time productively. In addition to the positive effects on classroom environment, however, good instruction also results in better student learning. In his *Synthesis of Research on Teaching,* Walberg (1985) provides substantial evidence for nine variables that appear to have causal influence on student academic outcomes. Seven of these relate to aptitude factors (i.e., developmental level, intellectual ability and prior achievement, and motivation) and elements of the student's own social-psychological environment (i.e., socioeconomic status, measures of home support and stimulation, exposure to mass media, and climate of the classroom). The final two constructs relate directly to what students do in the classroom and are factors primarily under teacher control: *quantity* and *quality* of instruction. The quantity and quality dimensions of instruction also hold a prominent place in many major models of educational performance, including the work of Carroll (1963), Cooley and Leinhardt (1975), Bloom (1976), Harnischfeger and Wiley (1976), and S. N. Bennett (1978). The major empirical evidence to support these findings has come from process–product research, where observational studies have been conducted in regular classroom settings to discover which teacher behaviors (process) are consistently related to student academic outcomes (product). A portion of this research has been dedicated to testing hypotheses derived from theoretical models. A second major emphasis of this research has involved testing the effects of instruction in "effective teaching procedures" on subsequent teacher and student behaviors. Typical of the kind of question posed in this research is: "Can teachers learn more effective ways of teaching which result in their students learning more?"

A number of recent reviews (Brophy, 1986; Brophy & Good, 1985; Rosenshine, 1987; Rosenshine & Stevens, 1985) have provided comprehensive documentation of those teacher behaviors which are related to the quantity or amount of instruction dimension as well as of those related to quality of instruction. In the following sections we review the most important of these variables.

Quantity or Amount of Instruction

Time is a complex variable in instruction. One consistent finding in this area has been a positive relation between amount of school exposure and student achievement (Wiley & Harnischfeger, 1974). This finding has led to the overly simplistic interpretation that in order to improve achievement, students merely need spend more hours in school; this isn't necessarily so. What does appear to be important is the amount of time dedicated to learning and, in particular, the amount of time that students are actively engaged with instruction and in practice relevant to curriculum objectives. Thus quantity of instruction is important only if it is the right type of instruction.

Allocated Time. To maximize attainment of worthwhile objectives, teachers have to maximize student opportunities to learn by allocating classroom time in proportion to objectives of the curriculum. Teachers maximize student achievement when more content is covered, when most available teaching time is allocated to academic activities, and when teachers have expectations that their students master the curriculum (Brophy, 1986). Most major decisions about curriculum, textbook selection, and required hours of instruction are made by individuals outside the classroom. Despite these efforts to ensure equivalence of educational experience, teachers vary tremendously in the "functional curriculum" they bring to the classroom (Berliner, 1987). Across classes and between schools students experience very different curricula despite outside attempts to standardize the content to which they are exposed. The Beginning Teacher Evaluation Study (BTES) (McDonald, 1977) found this to be the case (see Denham & Liberman, 1980, and Fisher & Berliner, 1985, for discussions of the findings of the BTES). Researchers carried out extensive observations and found the amount of classroom time allocated and degree of emphasis placed on given objectives varied as much as 100% for the same concepts

and curriculum areas. Berliner (1987) noted that teachers varied both in the amount of time they allocated to the teaching of reading and mathematics and varied as well in the amount of time dedicated to certain objectives within particular areas of the curriculum. Students in one classroom, for example, might get 29 minutes of instruction in linear measurement, while other classrooms devoted up to 400 minutes on the same topic over an essentially equivalent period of schooling.

The importance of these differences becomes acutely obvious when related to student learning. According to Leinhardt (1985), increasing reading time by 5 minutes each day would result in a 1-month achievement test gain on an end-of-year measure. Certainly, different objectives require different amounts of time for student attainment (Gettinger, 1985; Lyon & Gettinger, 1985) and some important areas of the curriculum will never be learned if enough time is not allocated to them (Berliner, 1987). Thus, the allocation of instructional time is a vital factor that places constraints on the amount of curricular content and instruction to which students are exposed.

Engaged Time. Even in classrooms where adequate time is allocated to instruction, students seldom spend all allocated time *actively engaged* in the appropriate academic activities. Engaged time refers to the amount of classroom time students are actually involved with instructional tasks such as attending to instruction, reading aloud, or completing seatwork. The amount of academic engaged time in classrooms ranges from less than 50% to 90% time on task by students, and within classes even greater variability may be observed (Brophy & Good, 1985; Graden, Thurlow, & Ysseldyke, 1983). In a study of engaged time with third and fourth graders, Graden, Thurlow, and Ysseldyke found 30% of each class day was allocated to academic instruction, but students were actively engaged in academic responding for only 12% of the day. Comparisons between pupils in this study revealed that some students spent 90 times as many minutes of class time engaged in instructional activities as other students. Summed over the school year, the differences between students ranged up to 76 more *hours* of silent reading time for one student than another. Further support for the importance of engagement rates was provided by Rossmiller (1982, cited in Berliner, 1987), where engaged time variables accounted for 10% of the variance in reading and math achievement for high-ability students and 73% for low-ability students.

Greater levels of engagement appear to be more easily attained in schools where the entire staff is concerned about this issue (Berliner, 1987). However, higher engagement rates and consequently the number of activities accomplished appear to be most related to the "teacher's ability to organize and manage the classroom as an efficient learning environment where academic activities run smoothly, transitions are brief and orderly, and little time is spent getting organized or dealing with inattention or resistance (Brophy & Good, 1985, p. 360). In addition to effective classroom management, improved instruction appears to result in improved student engaged time. The findings of the BTES (McDonald, 1977) suggest, for example, that substantive interaction (e.g., practice and correction) during group work and during seatwork led to increased engagement. Similarly, active teaching during instruction (questions, answers, feedback, explanations) correlated with higher overall engagement and higher engagement during seatwork (Rosenshine, 1980; 1987).

Academic Learning Time. Students learn more when they spend more time engaged in tasks they can perform with high success and that are directly relevant to academic outcomes. This combination of allocated time, student engagement, and high success rate is referred to as Academic Learning Time (ALT) (Fisher et al., 1978). The appropriateness of the tasks in which students are engaged and the degree of error-free performance students experience with these tasks are both important to the concept of ALT (Borg, 1980). Borg suggested that the goal of teaching is to create more curriculum and learner-appropriate instruction, which maximizes student success rate. According to Brophy and Good (1985), the necessity for high success rates varies with the type of learning activity (e.g., recitation versus independent seatwork), the stage of the learning process (i.e., acquisition of new skills versus practice for mastery), and the age and ability of the learners. With younger and less able learners, higher success rates are more important than with older and more able students (Fisher et al., 1978).

Quality of Instruction

Although quantity of instruction is important, recent research suggests that *quality* of instruction

during classroom lessons may be even more critical for student achievement and other important outcomes of schooling (e.g., establishing independent work habits, gaining appropriate social skills, developing appropriate learning strategies) (Brophy, 1986; Good, 1983; Rosenshine & Stevens, 1985). A number of authors have described what they see as the essential events and sequence of effective lessons (Block & Anderson, 1975; R. Gagné & Briggs, 1979; Hunter, 1976; Hunter & Russell, 1981). As a means of presenting these findings, Rosenshine and Stevens (1985) have developed what they call a "General Model of Effective Instruction," which includes six *fundamental instructional functions*. These functions include the following:

1. Daily review and checking homework
2. Presentation
3. Guided practice
4. Feedback and correctives
5. Independent practice
6. Weekly and monthly reviews

Daily Review and Checking Previous Work. Daily review of past learning is described as a critical component of classroom instruction in a number of descriptive as well as experimental studies (Becker, 1977; Emmer et al., 1982; Good & Grouws, 1979). Review of student work may involve correction of homework assignments, discussion of questions or problems that gave students difficulty, a short quiz, or oral questioning on material covered in the last class. Many effective teachers find choral review of main points of a previous lesson, or review of prerequisite skills, to be equally effective means of reviewing important prior learning. The checking of work not only provides accountability for completion, it also provides the teacher with feedback regarding student attainment of prior objectives and necessary direction for reteaching. In addition, review directs student attention to retrieve prerequisite skills, establishes the importance of past learning, and provides a meaningful context for new learning (Rosenshine & Stevens, 1985).

Presentation of Material to Be Learned. Rosenshine and Stevens (1985) suggested that in all classrooms some form of presentation occurs, but commonly students are not adequately prepared or "ready" to learn, and presentations are too short and are not well organized. In addition, too few examples are used and the samples used are often imprecise or unclear. Unfortunately, presentations in some classrooms consist merely of the teacher telling students what the daily assignment is and how to do it. Research reviewed by Rosenshine and Stevens and by others (Engliert, 1984; Good, 1983; Rosenshine, 1983, 1987) suggested that increases in active, teacher-led lessons result in more successful practice and higher achievement. The school psychologist interested in assessing classroom instruction can focus attention on the features of effective lessons identified by Rosenshine and Stevens (1985) and described briefly below.

Clarity of Goals. Student learning is enhanced when students have a clear understanding of what is to be learned, what outcomes are expected, and how this relates to prior learning (J. R. Anderson, 1985; Winne, 1985). To accommodate these needs, teachers have to know themselves what outcomes are expected, and transmit these goals to students. Without knowing why they are performing an activity, students are unlikely to derive any benefit from it, and merely follow what appear to be rather arbitrary steps (Johnston, 1985). Teachers can clarify the goals of learning by stating learning objectives, providing information about the organization of content, and making clear the relation of specific examples or steps to particular objectives.

Step-by-Step Presentations. Students learn more when information is well structured and sequenced and when it is sufficiently redundant (Brophy, 1986; Brophy & Good, 1985). Acquisition of new knowledge is thought to occur when new ideas are associated with the learner's existing network of knowledge (J. R. Anderson, 1976). Teachers can facilitate the formation of appropriate associations by providing cues for the retrieval of related prior knowledge and by making the organization of material explicit. Logical and purposeful development of the content helps establish a more meaningful body of learning and limits the development of inappropriate associations.

In general, effective presentations begin with overviews, statements of objectives, or some form of advanced organizer (Ausubel, 1960) which helps establish a learning set or cognitive structure into which students are able to assimilate lesson content (Johnston, 1985). Student learning is also enhanced when content is outlined, transitions

between parts of the presentation are indicated, key points are made salient, and internal and overall summaries are presented to help students integrate learning.

Specific and Concrete Procedures. Effective teachers provide active demonstrations, give clear, redundant explanations for complex material, and present specific and clear examples and analogies, while directing student attention to key ideas and relevant attributes. They also model appropriate responding and vary the pace and length of presentation with the nature of content. Which procedure is most appropriate depends on the kind of learning being promoted.

Checking for Student Understanding. Teachers can use a variety of methods to monitor student comprehension during instruction. They can ask questions, require students to repeat main points, or summarize a sequence of instruction in order to provide some measure of student comprehension. "With-it" teachers also use nonverbal information and ensure that students who are likely to have difficulty comprehending instruction are monitored most closely.

Guided Student Practice. Guided practice follows short segments of teacher presentation. The major reason to engage in guided practice is to afford students sufficient opportunities for practice of what is to be learned under controlled conditions while the teacher provides feedback and interactive instruction. In addition, guided practice provides the teacher with informative feedback about student understanding and ability to perform with respect to lesson objectives. Effective teachers devote more time to guided practice, whereas less effective teachers move more quickly to independent practice without adequate preparation or checking for understanding.

Frequent Practice. Across age levels and throughout the curriculum, frequent active student responding appears to be an important correlate of student learning. Frequent overt responding to teacher-directed factual questions and teacher-provided feedback are important (Brophy, 1986; Kulik & Kulik, 1979; Rosenshine & Stevens, 1985; Stallings & Kaskowitz, 1974). Considerable teacher ingenuity is required to design appropriate instructional activities, ensure that all students are actively practicing, provide feedback and check on student understanding.

Type of Task. No one type of guided practice activity has received universal acceptance as *the* way to promote active student responding, but the following methods have been implemented successfully in many classrooms: active verbal question-and-answer sequences where the teacher calls alternately on volunteers and nonvolunteers, participant modeling of appropriate responding, and group practice and recitation with choral responding. In addition, teachers use guided individual problem solving and application of algorithms as well as practice sessions where students supply verbal, written, or other nonverbal responses to problems posed by the teacher or fellow classmates. Importantly, practice must elicit student responding relevant to instructional objectives. For learning declarative knowledge students need to engage in tasks that help them organize and provide meaning to what is learned (Doyle, 1983; Winne, 1985). For procedural knowledge or knowing how, students need frequent opportunities to practice with feedback (E. D. Gagné, 1985).

Feedback and Correctives. Brophy's (1983b) review of teacher praise stresses that quality rather than quantity of teacher praise is important in determining its effectiveness and that the critical element is the feedback it provides the learner. Rather than being overly effusive in reacting to students, teachers should give students accurate feedback that extends and reinforces learning. The nature of student responses during presentation, guided practice, and review will determine what kinds of teacher feedback are necessary for effective learning (Brophy & Good, 1985; Rosenshine & Stevens, 1985).

Correct, Quick, Firm Responses. Then students answer correctly and confidently, the teacher can acknowledge the answer in some way so as to let all students know that it is correct but need not provide extensive praise. Occasional repetition and elaboration of answers is appropriate but not extensive use of these or effusive praise which might slow down lesson momentum.

Correct, but Hesitant. If students are able to provide correct responses but are tentative teachers may need not only to affirm correctness but also to provide more extensive feedback. Rosenshine and Stevens (1985) suggested the use of lots of process feedback, including review of the steps used to arrive at the answer. Other students will benefit as well from an explication of the procedures followed in arriving at the answer, explanations of why the answer is correct and review of the steps followed.

Incorrect Response. When a student provides a response that is partly correct or incomplete, the teacher can acknowledge the correct part and follow up with prompts or rephrasing. When students answer incorrectly, teachers can indicate that the answer is wrong and follow up by prompting, rephrasing, or by breaking down the task into steps or components. Incorrect responses can indicate the need to provide more extended feedback informing students how the answer was derived or why the correct answer is preferred. When the answer is incorrect because of a careless error, the teacher should correct the error and go to the next question.

Student-Initiated Questions and Comments. More effective teachers respond to student questions directly or redirect them back to the student or the class. Irrelevant questions and comments are discouraged, but the blending of relevant student-initiated content into lessons can have important motivational effects, particularly in the upper grades (Brophy, 1985, 1986; Brophy & Good, 1985).

Independent Practice, Seatwork, and Homework. To consolidate and maintain what is learned during instruction, students need to practice. It is important that students not only know how to find the answer, and be able to respond accurately, but they should practice learned skills and concepts to the point of overlearning. Repeated successful practice helps integrate newly learned material and develops automaticity where responses are consistent, correct, and fast. Here meaningful, interesting practice needs to be combined with high success rate (i.e., at or near 100% correct). Automaticity is particularly important in hierarchical content when facility with skills is prerequisite to future learning. Having to work hard to recall prerequisite knowledge or to apply only partially mastered skills interferes with performance of the intended higher-level objective (Calfee, 1981; Winne, 1985).

Two common problems that occur with independent seatwork are: (a) teachers do not adequately prepare students to be successful in independent practice, and (b) teachers not manage independent work sessions to ensure high rates of engagement.

Preparing Students for Practice. Frequently students are asked to engage in independently seatwork before they have learned the skill well enough to proceed independently (Duffy & McIntyre, 1982; Fisher et al., 1978). By engaging students in more active, explicit teaching, and providing adequate guided practice, teachers can ensure more successful independent practice and higher rates of engagement (Evertson, Anderson, Anderson, & Brophy, 1980). Another frequent problem is that students are not prepared adequately for the procedural requirements of independent seatwork assignments (Winne, 1985). For example, the kinds of performance required during seatwork may bear little relation to the lesson presented and skills demonstrated during instruction. Berliner (1983) notes further that instructional designers contribute to unsuccessful independent practice by providing poorly formatted and often unnecessarily complex workbook and textbook tasks. In this sort of situation, students require frequent reteaching and explaining in order to accomplish the task. To prevent this, teachers should make the procedural requirements explicit by demonstration and sample performance, and then require that the first few be completed as a group before students proceed independently (L. M. Anderson, Evertson, & Brophy, 1979).

Management of Independent Work. If students are adequately prepared to complete independent tasks, their performance can be facilitated by good teacher management of this phase of instruction. Once students are engaged in independent work they need an opportunity to work without interruption.

Students need clearly established routines, procedures, and rules to guide their behavior during independent work when the teacher is likely to have many competing demands for attention. Students need to know ahead of time what behavior is expected during the activity itself, what to do if they are "stuck," when to approach the teacher, and what to do when they finish.

Even if working with other groups, the teacher will need to monitor student performance during independent seatwork so that "with-itness" and accountability are maintained. According to Good and Grouws (1979), short active contacts with students during this phase increases engagement rate and enhances performance. If contacts are too frequent or protracted, this may indicate to the teacher that students need further guided practice or teaching before continuing with independent practice.

Finally, management of independent practice is enhanced when students know their work will be checked and they are provided with feedback on their performance. This is equally true for seatwork as well as for practice conducted at home. When feedback is delayed or does not follow from practice, the importance of practice is diminished and accountability is lost. In guiding teachers' selection of appropriate types of feedback, Brophy and Good (1985) suggest that performance feedback and follow up on seatwork and homework are more closely related to achievement than are praise or reward. However, for lower SES students and younger students, more warmth, support, and praise and symbolic rewards appear to be important adjuncts to performance feedback.

Periodic Reviews. Periodic review of learned material enhances retention, particularly when review lessons are scheduled and performance is assessed (Good, Grouws, & Ebmeier, 1983). Review lessons provide distributed practice of skills and information taught, give additional feedback to the teacher about student retention rates, and can indicate the need to reteach certain skills or provide extended practice. Periodic reviews, whether timed to coincide with content covered (i.e., objectives and content of a unit, chapter, or cumulative reviews) or provided weekly and monthly, have been endorsed as an important element in studies of effective teaching. Although this teaching function has not been studied as extensively in the instructional literature, review has been well established as a "necessary" learning condition for long-term retention and ease of retrieval (E. D. Gagné, 1985).

CONCLUSION

The purpose of school-based consultative activities is to solve problems. Traditionally, school psychology has considered relatively few variables as potential contributors to the problems exhibited by a particular child. It is frequently the case that school psychologists lack a clear *theoretical* understanding of the environment of schooling and the environments of individuals within schools. Consequently, practice has often been limited to a focus on what appear to be pragmatic and appealing elements rather than those based on sound theory and validated practice. The variables most often considered are those which can be assessed via the WISC-R, the WRAT-R, and the Bender-Gestalt administered by a psychologist sitting with a child in a room. Very often these child-based variables offer little information beyond that needed to make a classification decision.

Taking an ecological perspective assumes that the relatedness of assessment and intervention is extremely important. In fact, a major assumption underlying an ecological view is that some elements of the ecology may be adapted in order to better promote appropriate student performance. These elements, by necessity, will be limited to ones that are manipulable. Thus, student SES, IQ, perceptual skills, and other variables that are not easily changed are less relevant than are physical arrangement of the classroom, teacher–student interactions, and curriculum match with student instructional needs.

The proposed change in subject-matter emphasis to an ecological perspective demands the development and use of more appropriate methodological approaches to assessment. This methodology follows quite directly from the dynamic relation among elements in the classroom ecology. Thus, assessment cannot be restricted to the child alone; it must assume multiple and reciprocal causes, it must accept multiple potential targets for intervention, and finally, it must acknowledge that assessment, problem identification, and implementation of intervention will have multiple effects on the classroom ecology. If the present chapter has any value, it is as a compendium of a vast range of variables that do markedly affect the learning of schoolchildren. When properly understood and assessed, the variables described here, offer the school psychologist a road map of what *should* be occurring in classrooms. To the extent that these processes are not occurring, there is a need for intervention.

REFERENCES

Adams, R. S., & Biddle, B. J. (1970). *Realities of teaching: Explorations with videotape.* New York: Holt, Rinehart and Winston.

Ahrentzen, S., & Evans, G. W. (1984). Distraction, privacy and classroom design. *Environment and Behavior, 16*(4), 437–454.

Anderson, J. R. (1976). *Language, memory, and thought.* Hillsdale, NJ: Lawrence Erlbaum.

Anderson, J. R. (1985). Cognitive psychology and its implications (2nd ed.). San Francisco: W.H. Freeman.

Anderson, L. M., Evertson, C. M., & Brophy, J. E. (1979). An experimental study of effective teaching in first grade reading groups. *Elementary School Journal, 79,* 193–222.

Anderson, L., & Prawat, R. (1983). A synthesis of research on teaching self-control. *Educational Leadership, 40,* 62–66.

Ausubel, D. P. (1960). The use of advanced organizers in the learning and retention of meaningful verbal material. *Journal of Educational Psychology, 51,* 267–272.

Baer, D. M., & Bushell, D. (1981). The future of behavior analysis in the schools? Consider its recent past, and then ask a different question. *School Psychology Review, 10,* 259–270.

Barker, R. G., & Gump, P. V. (1964). *Big school, small school.* Stanford, CA: Stanford University Press.

Barker, R. G., & Wright, H. F. (1955). *Mid-west and it's children.* Evanston, IL: Row & Peterson.

Barkely, R. A. (1981). *Hyperactive children: A handbook for diagnosis and treatment.* New York: Guilford Press.

Becker. W. C. (1977). Teaching reading and language to the disadvantaged—What have we learned from field research. *Harvard Educational Review, 47,* 518–543.

Bennett, S. N. (1978). Recent research on teaching: A dream, a belief, and a model. *British Journal of Educational Psychology, 48,* 127–147.

Bennett, S. N. (1985). Instructional spaces, architecture of. In T. T. Husen & T. N. Postlethwaite (Eds.), *International encyclopedia of education.* Elmsford, NY: Pergamon Press.

Bennett, N., & Blundell, D. (1983). Quantity and quality of work in rows and classroom groups. *Educational Psychology, 3,* 93–105.

Berliner, D. C. (1987). Knowledge is power: A talk to teachers about a revolution in the teaching profession. In D. C. Berliner & B. V. Rosenshine (Eds.), *Talks to teachers.* New York: Random House.

Block, J. H., & Anderson, L. W. (1975). *Mastery learning in classroom instruction.* New York: Macmillan.

Bloom, B. S. (1976). *Human characteristics and school learning.* New York: McGraw-Hill.

Borg, W. (1980). Time and school learning. In C.

Denham & A. Lieberman (Eds.), *Time to learn* (pp. 33–72). Washington, DC: National Institute of Education.

Bronzaft, A. L., & McCarthy, D. P. (1975). The effect of elevated train noise on reading ability. *Environment and Behavior, 1*(4), 517–529.

Brooks, D. M., Silvern, S. B., & Wooten, M. (1978). The ecology of teacher-pupil verbal interaction. *Journal of Classroom Interaction, 14*, 39–45.

Brophy, J. E. (1983a). Classroom organization and management. *Elementary School Journal, 83*, 254–285.

Brophy, J. E. (1983b). Conceptualizing student motivation. *Educational Psychologist, 18*, 200–215.

Brophy, J. E. (1985). Teacher-student interaction. In J. B. Dusek (Ed.), *Teacher expectancies* (pp. 303–328). Hillsdale, NJ: Lawrence Earlbaum.

Brophy, J. (1986). Teacher influences on student achievement. *American Psychologist, 41*(1), 1069–1077.

Brophy, J., & Evertson, C. (1976). *Learning from teaching: A developmental perspective*. Boston: Allyn and Bacon.

Brophy, J., & Good, T. L. (1985). Teacher behavior and student achievement. In M. Wittrock (Ed.), *Handbook of research on teaching* (3rd ed., pp. 328–375). New York: Macmillan.

Brown, J. G., & Burger, C. (1984). Playground design and preschool children's behaviors. *Environment and Behavior, 16*(5), 599–626.

Brunetti, F. A. (1972). Noise, distraction, and privacy in conventional and open school environments. In W. Mitchell (Ed.), *Environmental design: Research and practice* (Proceedings of the EDRA conference). Washington, DC: American Institute of Architects.

Calfee, R. (1981). Cognitive psychology and educational practice. In D. C. Berliner (Ed.), *Review of research in education* (Vol. 9). Washington, DC: American Educational Research Association.

Car-Gavrilovic, I. (1964). Effect of the intensity of lighting on the simple mental work of school children. *Acta Instituti Psychologici*, 35–46, 59–64. (From *Psychological Abstracts*, 1965, *39*, Abstract No. 16296)

Carroll, J. (1963). A model for school learning. *Teachers College Record, 64*, 723–733.

Cartledge, G., & Milburn, J. (1978). The case for teaching social skills in the classroom: A review. *Review of Educational Research, 48*, 133–156.

Centra, J. A., & Potter, D. A. (1980). School and teacher effects: An interrelatinal model. *Review of Educational Research, 50*, 273–291.

Christie, D. J., & Glickman C. D. (1980). The effects of classroom noise on children: Evidence of sex differences. *Psychology in the Schools, 17*, 405–408.

Cohen, S., Glass, D., & Singer, J. (1973). Apartment noise, auditory discrimination and reading ability in children. *Journal of Experimental Social Psychology, 9*, 407–499.

Colman, R., Frankel, F., Ritvo, E., & Freeman, B. (1976). The effects of fluorescent and incandescent illumination upon repetitive behavior in autistic children. *Journal of Autism and Childhood Schizophrenia, 6*, 157–162.

Collins-Eiland, K., Danereau, D., Brooks, L., & Holley, C. (1986). Effects of conversational noise, locus of control, and field dependence/independence on the performance of academic tasks. *Contemporary Educational Psychology, 11*, 139–149.

Cooley, W. W., & Leinhardt, G. (1975). *The application of a model for investigating classroom processes*. Pittsburgh, PA: University of Pittsburgh, Learning Research and Development Center.

Cotterell, J. L. (1984). Effects of school architectural design on student and teacher anxiety. *Environment and Behavior, 16*, 455–479.

Crook, M. A., & Langdon, F. J. (1974). The effects of aircraft noise in schools around London airport. *Journal of Sound and Vibration, 34*(2), 221–232.

Denham, C., & Lieberman, A. (Eds.), (1980). *Time to learn*. Washington, DC: National Institute of Education.

Doyle, W. (1983). Academic work. *Review of Educational Research, 53*(2), 159–199.

Doyle, W. (1985a). Classroom organization and management. In M. C. Wittrock (Ed.), *Handbook of research on teaching* (3rd ed., pp. 392–431). New York: Macmillan.

Doyle, W. (1985b). Recent research on classroom management: Implications for teacher preparation. *Journal of Teacher Education, 36*(3), 31–35.

Duffy, G. G., & McIntyre, L. D. (1982). Naturalistic study of instructional assistance in primary grade reading. *Elementary School Journal, 83*, 14–23.

Emmer, E. T. (1985). Management in the classroom: Elementary grades. In T. T. Husen & T. N. Postlethwaite (Eds.), *International encyclopedia of education*. Elmsford, NY: Pergamon Press.

Emmer, E. T., & Evertson, C. M. (1981). Synthesis of research on classroom management. *Educational Leadership, 38*, 342–347.

Emmer, E., Evertson, C., & Anderson, L. (1980). Effective classroom management at the beginning of the school year. *Elementary School Journal, 80*, 219–231.

Emmer, E. T., Evertson, C. M., Sanford, J. P., Clements, B. S., & Worsham, M. E. (1982). *Organizing and managing the junior high classroom*. Austin, TX: Research and Development Center for Teacher Education.

Emmer, E. T., Evertson, C. M., Sanford, J. P., Clements, B. S., & Worsham, M. E. (1984). *Classroom management for secondary teachers*. Englewood Cliffs, NJ: Prentice-Hall.

Englert, C. S. (1984). Measuring teacher effectiveness from the teacher's point of view. *Focus on Exceptional Children. 17*(2), 1–15.

Evans, G., & Lovell, B. (1979). Design modification in an open-plan school. *Journal of Educational Psychology, 71*, 41–49.

Evertson, C. (1985). Training teachers in classroom management: An experiment in secondary school classrooms. *Journal of Educational Research, 79*(1), 51–58.

Evertson, C. M. (1987). Managing classrooms: A framework for teachers. In D. C. Berliner & B. V. Rosenshine (Eds.), *Talks to teachers* (pp. 54–74). New York: Random House.

Evertson, C. M., & Anderson, L. M. (1979). Beginning school. *Educational Horizons, 57,* 164–168.

Evertson, C., Anderson, C., Anderson, L., & Brophy, J. (1980). Relationships between classroom behaviors and student outcomes in junior high mathematics and English classes. *American Educational Research Journal, 17,* 43–60.

Evertson, C., & Emmer, E. (1982). Effective management at the beginning of the school year in junior high classes. *Journal of Educational Psychology, 74,* 485–498.

Evertson, C. M., Emmer, E. T., Clements, B. S., Sanford, J. P., Worsham, M. E., & Williams, E. L. (1982). *Organizing and managing the elementary school classroom.* Austin, TX: Research and Development Center for Teacher Education.

Evertson, C. M., Emmer, E. T., Sanford, J. P., & Clements, B. S. (1983). Improving classroom management: An experiment in elementary school classrooms. *Elementary School Journal, 84,* 173–188.

Fisher, C. W., & Berliner, D. C. (Eds.). (1985). *Perspectives on instructional time.* New York: Longman.

Fisher, C., Filby, N., Marliave, R., Cahen, L., Dishaw, M., Moore, J., & Berliner, D. (1978). *Teaching behaviors, academic learning time and student achievement: Final report of Phase III-B, Beginning Teacher Evaluation Study.* San Francisco: Far West Laboratory.

Fletcher, D. (1983). Effects of classroom lighting on the behavior of exceptional children. *Exceptional Education Quarterly, 4*(2), 75–89.

Frank, K. A. (1984). Exorcising the ghost of physical determinism. *Environment and Behavior, 16*(4), 411–436.

Gagné, E. D. (1985). *The cognitive psychology of school learning.* Boston: Little, Brown.

Gagné, R., & Briggs, L. (1979). *Principles of instructional design* (2nd ed.). New York: Holt, Rinehart and Winston.

Gettinger, M. (1985). Time allocated and time spent relative to time needed for learning as determinants of achievement. *Journal of Educational Psychology, 77*(11), 3–11.

Glasser, R. (1977). Ten steps to good discipline. *Today's Education, 66,* 61–63.

Good, T. L. (1983). Classroom research: A decade of progress. *Educational Psychologist, 18*(3), 127–144.

Good, T., & Grouws, D. (1977). Teaching effects: A process product study in fourth grade mathematics classrooms. *Journal of Teacher Education, 28,* 49–54.

Good, T., & Grouws, D. (1979). The Missouri mathematics effectiveness project: An experimental study in fourth grade classrooms. *Journal of Educational Psychology, 71,* 355–362.

Good, T., Grouws, D., & Ebmeier, H. (1983). *Active mathematics teaching.* New York: Longman.

Graden J., Thurlow, M., & Ysseldyke, J. (1983). Instructional ecology and academic responding time for students at three levels of teacher-perceived behavioral competence. *Journal of Experimental Child Psychology, 36,* 241–256.

Gump, P. V. (1969). Intra-setting analysis: The third grade classroom as a special but instructive case. In E. Williams & H. Raush (Eds.), *Naturalistic viewpoints in psychological research.* New York: Holt, Rinehart and Winston.

Gump, P. V. (1985). Structure and functioning: Class activities. In T. T. Husen & T. N. Postlethwaite (Eds.), *International encyclopedia of education.* Elmsford, NY: Pergamon Press.

Harnischfeger, A., & Wiley, D. E. (1976). The teaching–learning process in elementary schools: A synoptic view. *Curriculum Inquiry, 6,* 5–43.

Hockey, G. R. J. (1970). Effects of loud noise on attentional selectivity. *Quarterly Journal of Experimental Psychology, 22,* 28–36.

Hoge, R. D., & Luce, S. (1979). Predicting academic achievement from classroom behavior. *Review of Educational Research, 49*(3), 479–496.

Homme, L., Csanyi, A. P., Gonzales, M. A., & Rechs, J. R. (1970). *How to use contingency contracting in the classroom.* Champaign, IL: Research Press.

Hunter, M. (1976). *Improved instruction.* El Segundo, CA: TIP Publications.

Hunter, M., & Russell, D. (1981). Planning for effective instruction: Lesson design. In *Increasing your teaching effectiveness.* Palo Alto, CA: The Learning Institute.

Hutt, C., & Varzey, M. J. (1966). Differential effects of group density on social behavior. *Nature, 209,* 1371–1372.

Johnston, P. (1985). Teaching students to apply strategies that improve reading comprehension. *Elementary School Journal, 85*(5), 635–645.

Koneya, M. (1976). Location and interaction in row and column seating arrangements. *Environment and Behavior, 8*(2), 265.

Kounin, J. S. (1970). *Discipline and group management in classroom.* New York: Holt, Rinehart and Winston.

Kounin, J. S., & Sherman, L. W. (1979). School environments as behavior settings. *Theory into Practice, 13,* 145–151.

Krantz, P., & Risley, T. (1972). *The organization of group care environments: Behavioral ecology in the classroom.* Lawrence: Kansas University.

Krovetz, M. L. (1977). Who needs what when: Design of pluralistic learning environments. In D. Stohols (Ed.), *Perspectives on environment and behavior: Theory, research and application.* New York: Plenum Press.

Kulick, J. A., & Kulick, C. C. (1979). College teaching. In P. L. Peterson & H. J. Walberg (Eds.), *Research on teaching: Concepts, findings, and implications.* Berkeley, CA: McCutchan.

Leinhardt, G. (1985). Instructional time: A winged chariot? In C. W. Fishner & D. C. Berliner (Eds.), *Perspectives on instructional time* (pp. 263–282). New York: Longman.

Lyon, M. A., & Gettinger, M. (1985). Differences in school performance on knowledge, comprehension, and application tasks: Implications for school learning. *Journal of Educational Psychology, 77*(1), 12–19.

Martens, B. K., & Witt, J. C. (1988). Ecological behavior

analysis. In M. Hersen, R. M. Eisler, & P. M. Miller (Eds.), *Progress in behavior modification* (pp. 115–140). Newbury Park, CA: Sage.

Martens, B. K., & Witt, J. C. (1988). On the ecological validity of behavior modification. In J. C. Witt, S. N. Elliott, & F. M. Gresham (Eds.), *Handbook of behavior therapy in education* (pp. 325–342). New York: Plenum Press.

Mayron, L. W. (1978). Ecological factors in learning disabilities. *Journal of Learning Disabilities, 11,* 495–505.

McDonald, F. (1977). Research on teaching: Report on Phase II of the Beginning Teacher Evaluation Study. In G. Borich & K. Fenton (Eds.), *The appraisal of teaching: Concepts and processes.* Reading, MA: Addison-Wesley.

McLaughlin, T. F. (1976). Self-control in the classroom. *Review of Educational Research, 46,* 631–663.

Meichenbaum, D. (1977). *Cognitive behavior modification.* New York: Plenum Press.

Musgrave, G. R. (1975). *Individualized instruction: Teaching strategies focusing on the learner.* Boston: Allyn and Bacon.

O'Leary, K. D., Rosenbaum, A., & Hughes, P. C. (1978). Fluorescent lighting: A purported source of hyperactive behavior. *Journal of Abnormal Child Psychology, 6,* 285–289.

Ollila, L. O., & Chamberlain, L. A. (1975). The effects of noise and objects on acquisition of a sight vocabulary in kindergarten children. *Alberta Journal of Educational Research, 21,* 213–219.

Rohe, W., & Patterson, A. J. (1974). The effects of varied levels of resources and density on behavior in a day care center. In D. H. Carson (Ed.), *Man-environment interactions: The evaluations and applications* (Part 3, chap. 12). Stroudsburg, PA: Dowden, Hutchinson & Ross.

Rosenfield, P., Lambert, N. M., & Black, A. (1985). Desk arrangement effects on pupil classroom behavior. *Journal of Educational Psychology, 77*(1), 101–108.

Rosenshine, B. V. (1980). How time is spent in elementary classrooms. In C. Denham & A. Lieberman (Eds.), *Time to learn* (pp. 107–126). Washington, DC: National Institute of Education.

Rosenshine, B. (1983). Teaching functions in instructional programs. *Elementary School Journal, 83,* 335–351.

Rosenshine, B. (1987). Explicit teaching. In D. C. Berliner & B. V. Rosenshine (Eds.), *Talks to teachers* (pp. 75–92). New York: Random House.

Rosenshine, B., & Stevens, R. (1985). Teaching functions. In M. C. Wittrock (Ed.), *Handbook of research on teaching* (3rd ed., pp. 376–391). New York: Macmillan.

Sanders, M., Gustanski, J., & Lawton, M. (1974). Effect of ambient illumination on noise level of groups. *Journal of Applied Psychology, 59,* 527–528.

Sanford, J. P., & Evertson, C. M. (1981). Classroom management in a low SES junior high: Three case studies. *Journal of Teacher Education, 32*(1), 34–38.

Slater, B. (1968). Effects of noise on pupil performance. *Journal of Educational Psychology, 59,* 239–243.

Slavin, R. E. (1980). Cooperative learning. *Review of Educational Research, 50*(2), 315–342.

Sommer, R. (1967). Classroom ecology. *Journal of Applied Behavioral Science, 3,* 489–503.

Spaulding, R. L. (1983, December). Applications of low-inference observation in teacher education. In D. C. Smith (Ed.), *Essential knowledge for beginning educators* (pp. 80–100). Washington, DC: American Association of Colleges for Teacher Education.

Stallings, J., & Kaskowitz, D. (1974). *Follow through classroom observations, 1972–1973.* Menlo Park, CA: Stanford Research Institute.

Steinzor, B. (1950). The spatial factor in face-to-face discussion groups. *Journal of Abnormal Social Psychology, 45,* 552–555.

Walberg, H. J. (1985). Synthesis of research on teaching. In M. Wittrock (Ed.), *Handbook of research on teaching* (3rd ed., pp. 214–229). New York: Macmillan.

Walker, H. M. (1985). *Teacher social behavior standards and expectations as determinants of classroom ecology, teacher behavior and child outcomes.* Unpublished manuscript, University of Oregon, College of Education, Eugene.

Weinstein, C. S. (1977). Modifying student behavior in an open classroom through changes in the physical design. *American Education Research Journal, 14,* 249–262.

Weinstein, C. S. (1979). The physical environment of the school: A review of the research. *Review of Educational Research, 49,* 577–610.

Weinstein, C. S. (1982). Strategies for increasing the environmental competence of teachers. *New Jersey Journal of School Psychology, 5,* 25–38.

Weinstein, C. S. (1985). Seating arrangements in the classroom. In T. T. Husen & T. N. Postlethwaite (Eds.), *International encyclopedia of education.* Elmsford, NY: Pergamon Press.

Wheldell, K., Morris, M., Vaughn, P., & Ng, Y. Y. (1981). Rows versus tables: An example of the use of behavioral ecology in two classes of eleven-year-old children. *Educational Psychology, 1*(2), 171–184.

Wicker, A. W. (1968). Undermanning performances, and student's subjective experiences in behavior settings of large and small high schools. *Journal of Personality and Social Psychology, 10,* 255–261.

Wiley, D. E., & Harnischfeger, A. (1974). Explosion of a myth: Quantity of schooling and exposure to instruction, major educational vehicles. *Educational Researcher, 3,* 7–12.

Willems, E. P. (1967). Sense of obligation to high school activities as related to the size and marginality of student. *Child Development, 38,* 1247–1260.

Winne, P. H. (1985). Steps toward promoting cognitive achievements. *Elementary School Journal, 85*(5), 673–693.

Witt, J. C., & Elliott, S. N. (1982). The response cost lottery: A time efficient and effective intervention. *Journal of School Psychology, 20,* 155–161.

Wittrock, M. C. (Ed.), (1986). *Handbook of research on teaching* (3rd ed.). New York: Macmillan.

Zentall, S. S. (1983). Learning environments: A review of

physical and temporal factors. *Exceptional Education Quarterly, 4*(2), 91–115.

Zentall, S. S., & Shaw, J. H. (1980). Effects of classroom noise on performance and activity of second grade hyperactive and control children. *Journal of Educational Psychology, 72,* 830–840.

Zifferblatt, S. M. (1972). Architecture and human behav-ior: Toward increased understanding of a functional relationship. *Educational Technology, 12*(8), 54–57.

Zimmer, J. W., & Brachlus-Raymond, J. (1978). Effects of distracting stimuli on complex information processing. *Perceptual and Motor Skills, 46,* 791–794.

34

THE EFFECTIVE SCHOOLS LITERATURE: IMPLICATIONS FOR RESEARCH AND PRACTICE[1]

WILLIAM E. BICKEL

University of Pittsburgh

During the past decade, there has been a resurgence in interest at national, state, and local levels in the quality of education available in our public schools, and in how current practices can be improved. There are many contributing social, economic, and educational factors that have converged to stimulate this interest in educational reform. One important factor, and the subject of this chapter, is an area of educational research commonly referred to as the literature on "effective schools." This literature is having a direct and remarkable impact on the way educators and associated policy-shaping constituencies think about public schools and the means to improve educational practices within them.

This chapter is divided into four major sections. The first section offers a discussion of the origins of the first "wave" (1971–1979) of effective schools literature including some of the most salient results and criticisms associated with this body of work. The second section provides an

overview of the impact of the effective schools literature on school improvement initiatives. The third section contains a review of the influence this literature is having on contemporary programs of educational research. This is followed in the fourth section with an analysis of how the effective schools activity relates to another contemporary reform effort—the press for excellence. In the first three sections we generally will take a "review-of-reviews' approach in deference to the scope of the questions of interest and the space available. The reader is encouraged to consider specific articles and reviews cited for more details about any particular area of activity.

THE SEARCH FOR EFFECTIVE SCHOOLS

Origins
Work that is now associated with the effective schools literature had its beginnings in the early 1970s. An understanding of the origins of the effective schools literature requires a recollection of the status of schooling (especially urban schooling) and the central messages coming from educational

[1]The author would like to acknowledge gratefully the assistance of Terry A. Clark in critiquing early drafts of this chapter.

research, academe, and public commentators at that time about our nation's schools.

Education had been the focus of considerable attention and sustained criticism during the prior decade (the 1960s). The sources and types of criticism were many, but two critical streams were most telling. One rested with a series of what amounted to exposés of what were perceived to be intolerable conditions that characterized the reality of school life. Books such as *Death at an Early Age* (Kozol, 1967), *How Children Fail* (Holt, 1965), and *Crisis in the Classroom* (Silberman, 1970) presented a bleak (and well-publicized) picture of the social and intellectual conditions in schooling and their perceived negative impact on children.[2]

At this same time, some educators and many policymakers were becoming disenchanted with the ability of schools to serve as one of the central tools for breaking the "cycle of poverty" that was the focus of President Johnson's "War on Poverty." Early evaluations (Wolff & Stein, 1966) of major educational intervention efforts such as Head Start (a preschool program aimed at disadvantaged youth) were not promising. As resources at the national level were being stretched thin as a result of the Vietnam war; as the War on Poverty itself became more controversial from a political standpoint, the wisdom of pouring millions into education for social intervention was drawn increasingly into question.[3]

The impression of the *ineffectiveness* of schooling as it pertained to populations of at-risk children was dramatically reinforced by a nationally funded study investigating the issue of *Equality of Educational Opportunity* (Coleman et al., 1966). This study investigated the role of schooling as it related to performance outcomes in basic skills for students of various social classes and racial groups. The assumption was that variation in resource *inputs* such as age of the school building, instructional facilities, class size, teacher background, and so on, would account for differences in achievement outcomes. The critical result of the study in terms of this discussion was the much publicized finding that the traditional educational inputs measured had little relationship to achieve-

ment outcomes independent of the student's social, economic, and cultural background (Tesconi, 1975). There has been considerable criticism of the Coleman Report since its first population (see, e.g., the special issue of the *Harvard Education Review*, Volume 38, Winter 1968, devoted to an analysis of this study). However, the design quality of the study is not important to this discussion. What is critical is that this highly visible national report added considerable support to the notion that schooling in and of itself was an *ineffective* tool for addressing the inequity in achievement found among low-income populations.

The two streams of criticism of schooling reviewed briefly in the preceding paragraphs set a tone that the schools were, in effect, *guilty* of "cultural imperialism" (Carnoy, 1974) or largely *ineffective* in critical areas of educational and social needs (Jencks et al., 1972), or both. This perspective of the inadequacies of schooling, particularly as it related to redressing disparate needs between low and high income, and minority and majority student populations, was troubling to some in the educational practice and research communities. The concern was grounded in deep convictions about the need for improving social equality, and an intuitive response which suggested that, while many schools were indeed ineffective, not all were. Further, these reformers felt that holding the schools to be both "guilty" and "ineffective" had the functional effect of letting institutions off the hook, of allowing educators to avoid responsibility for improving current educational practices. In particular, it was felt that the image of an institution powerless to have an impact separate from family background provided an all-too-easy excuse for not making a serious effort in this regard.

The history of the effective schools literature begins with the kinds of concerns noted above. The following quotes from some early and central studies in this body of literature provide a flavor of the motivating factors and goals of those involved in this research.

> For some time before I began this project I had been intrigued by three facts. First, reading achievement in the early grades in almost all inner-city schools is both relatively and absolutely low. Second, most laymen and most school people believe that such low achievement is all that can be expected. Third, I have seen for myself one inner-city school

---

[2] See Schrag (1975), Troost (1973), and Rich (1985) for more complete discussions of the "romantic" and "radical" critics of education prevalent during the late 1960s and early 1970s.

[3] See Haney (1977) for an example of this kind of pressure as it pertained to the Follow-Through Program.

and had heard reports of several others in which reading achievement was *not* relatively low, in which it was, indeed, above the national average or better. (Weber, 1971, p. 1) We are surrounded and daily besieged by irresistible evidence of the social pathology that characterizes much of the life of our major institutions. Schools are no exception. Our national need to know of "things that work" has never been greater. It is at precisely this point in the public policy fray that this discussion seeks to enter. This discussion will describe the authors' efforts to identify and analyze city schools that are instructionally effective for poor and/or minority children. We are pleased to note that we have already developed unusually promising evidence of the thesis we seek to demonstrate in the research under discussion. Our thesis is that all children, excepting only those of certifiable handicap, are eminently educable, and the behavior of the school is critical in determining the quality of that education. (Edmonds & Frederiksen, undated, pp. 3–4)

The fundamental premises driving the first wave of effective schools research were that schools can be identified that are unusually effective in teaching poor and minority children basic skills as measured by standardized tests, that such successful schools may exhibit some common characteristics that are correlated with their success, that many of these correlates of effectiveness may well be within the domain of what educators can manipulate and improve, and that these correlates can be used to structure improvement efforts for schools not deemed to be effective (Bickel, 1983).

Results
The body of research associated with the effective schools literature is surprisingly diverse in its methods and findings (Purkey & Smith, 1983; Reynolds & Sullivan, 1981). The research base in what might be called the initial wave of research activity (1971–1979) includes case studies (e.g., Brookover & Lezotte, 1979; Rutter, Maughan, Morimore, Ouston & Smith, 1979; Venezky & Winfield, 1979; Weber, 1971), program evaluations (e.g., Armor et al., 1976), and outlier studies (e.g., Austin, 1979; Brookover & Schneider, 1975; Edmonds & Frederiksen, 1978).

What this diverse body of literature generally shared in common were criteria that tended to define "effectiveness" in terms of basic skills achievement in one or more of the following areas: reading, mathematics, language acquisition; as well as an interest in specific target populations (low-income and/or minority students). Further, there was a general presumption that the school culture and its organizational and educational manifestations were important correlates to school effectiveness. It is important to note that even along the dimensions of what is common in effective schools literature studies, any given single piece of research might differ in terms of which basic skills were observed and the precise cutoff points that were used as the determinants of effectiveness, as well as in the target populations that were of interest.

With the diversity in methods and criteria found in the effective schools literature, it is no small task to provide a detailed summary of results emanating from this work. Mackenzie (1983a) quite nicely captures the ambiguities built into the effective schools literature when he states that

the descriptive richness and the closely woven texture of the new applied research on schooling presents several paradoxes for the reviewer. There is broad agreement on the fundamental elements of effective schooling. Major constructs derive support from a variety of sources, such that the validity of many conclusions is stronger than would be warranted by the internal or external controls of any single study. At the same time, there is seldom clear agreement on the precise definition of constructs and variables in school effectiveness. The bright light of consensus around the central elements of a construct fades little by little into gray mists of uncertainty and unanswered questions at the edge. This is exactly the sort of picture one might expect [in an emerging literature], but it is also a picture that frustrates definitive summation, and resists being turned into specific recipies for school improvement (pp. 7–8)

The reader is encouraged to consider the several fine and comprehensive reviews that do exist (e.g., Bossert, Dwyer, Rowan, & Lee, 1982; Mackenzie, 1983a, 1983b; Purkey & Smith, 1983) for detailed discussions of results. For our purposes here, it is enough to focus on five key characteristics most often associated with effective schools:

- A school climate conducive to learning—one free of disciplinary problems and vandalism.
- The expectation among teachers that all students can achieve.
- An emphasis on basic skills instruction and high levels of student time-on-task.
- A system of clear instructional objectives for monitoring and assessing student performance.
- A school principal who is a strong programmatic leader and who sets school goals, maintains student discipline, frequently observes classrooms, and creates incentives for learning. (Bossert, 1985, p. 39)

Many additional characteristics could be added to this short list; however, these five, in one form or another, turn up again and again in the research and in the school improvement efforts stimulated by the effective schools literature. The image that emerges is coherent and intuitively logical. Effective schools exhibit a clear sense of mission. Students are expected to learn, and students, teachers, and administrators share a responsibility for creating a climate that supports learning processes. There is an emphasis on outcomes over procedure, with regularly monitored achievement in basic skills as the key performance measures.

Returning to the discussion of origin, the emerging effective schools literature sought to refute the notion that schools were powerless in having a positive influence on student achievement, even if the students being served happened to be poor or from minority populations. More fundamentally, the researchers sought to hold educational institutions responsible for positive student performance by finding examples of schools where this had been accomplished. In terms of the input—output studies typified by the Coleman Report (Coleman et al., 1966), effective schools literature researchers sought to identify school *process* variables (as opposed to more static school input factors) that mediated the school experience and that in turn affected student outcomes. In this sense, the effective schools literature work does not so much "refute" the Coleman data as ask a similar question with the different set of variables.

Taken as a whole, this first wave of effective schools literature is a powerful statement of the responsibilities and the possibilities that rest within the domains of actions manipulable by educators. Edmonds succinctly summarizes what was and is a central message found in the effective schools literature:

> Repudiation of the social science notion that family background is the principal cause of pupil acquisition of basic school skills is probably prerequisite to successful reform of public schooling for the children of the poor. . . . It seems to me, therefore, that what is left of this discussion [of effective schools literature results] are three declarative statements: We can, whenever we choose, successfully teach all children whose schooling is of interest to us. We already know more than we need to do that. Whether or not we do it must finally depend on how we feel about the fact that we haven't so far. (Edmonds, undated, p. 35)

Cautions to Interpretating the Effective Schools Literature

The literature on effective schools is divergent, recent, and dynamic. In interpreting the results that have and are emerging from this stream of research, it is important that the reader consider some of the fundamental criticisms and cautionary notes that have been sounded about the current knowledge base. Several recent analyses of the effective schools literature (e.g., Good & Brophy, 1986; Purkey & Smith, 1983; Rowan, Bossert & Dwyer, 1983) or related concepts (e.g., Madaus, Airasian, & Kellaghan, 1980; Rowan, 1985) that provide detailed discussions of inadequacies present in our ability to accurately identify and measure school effectiveness. These criticisms can be roughly sorted into three categories concerning philosophical/conceptual issues, methodological flaws, and gaps (unasked or as yet-to-be-answered questions) in this arena. Examples of several of the major concerns from each of these three categories of criticisms follow.

Philosophical/Conceptual Concerns

A basic philosophical concern raised by many (e.g., Bickel & Bickel, 1986; Good & Brophy, 1986; Purkey & Smith, 1983) concerns the criteria used by many studies to define "effectiveness." As noted earlier, a consistent and common theme in effective schools research has been on the measure of student achievement in basic skills areas, usually with performance on a standardized achievement test as the primary evidence of effectiveness.[4] This emphasis on basic skills leaves out many other important areas of intellectual and social growth that are legitimate domains in which schools might affect student performance. To take just one important example, the Wave I effective schools literature (1971–1979) leaves almost totally unexamined the issue of higher-order thinking skills, and how school-level characteristics might influence student outcomes. While the philosophical emphasis on basic skills can be readily understood in terms of the origins of the effective schools literature, the issues that early researchers were trying to address and the impression of school powerlessness they hoped to redress, the fact remains that the narrowly defined criteria of effectiveness is an important limitation of this body of research.

Related concerns involve the heavy emphasis on examining the effectiveness issue in elementary schools, particularly in urban settings. Again, the motivations of researchers involved explain these emphases. Nevertheless, serious questions have been raised about the applicability of results to other educational settings (Purkey & Smith, 1983; Rowan et al., 1983).

A fourth conceptual concern involves the concentration on school-level variables to the general exclusion of investigations of within-classroom instructional processes on the one hand, and on the other, an almost as pervasive disinterest in contextual variables outside the school setting (e.g., parental, district factors). In part, this focus on school process variables represented a focused attempt at correcting the social science research model that emphasized the examination of "school-level" inputs (albeit of a static nature). It also represented an intuitive conviction that this level was the right one for focusing reform energies. Yet, like the setting limitation, the sole emphasis on school variables leaves out such factors influence and are affected by variables at other levels in educational systems.

[4] This criticism is not uniformly true for a few important studies associated with the effective schools literature. For example, Rutter et al. (1979) also looked at "attendance, pupil behavior . . . and delinquency" (p. 66).

Methodological Concerns

A number of methodological criticisms also have been leveled at the effective schools literature. The most comprehensive statements can be found in Good & Brophy (1986) and Rowan et al. (1983). Effect size is one area of concern. The tendency to use "contrasted groups" research designs in which "hypotheses about organizational differences between effective and ineffective schools are tested one at a time" can lead to "spurious findings and provides no information on the magnitude of effects of a given variable . . . after the effects of other relevant variables have been controlled" (pp. 27–28, Rowan et al., 1983). Thus, these authors note that decisions about where to begin and what to emphasize in a school improvement effort based on the characteristics of effective schools has little information on which characteristics are more critical.

A second methodological concern involves a failure to adequately investigate whether discovered effects last over some reasonable length of time (Good & Brophy, 1986; Purkey & Smith, 1983). Some recent research (Rowan & Denk, 1982) documents that "the average stability of school effects on student achievement is low." This issue often went unexamined or investigated only over a limited time span in many effective schools literature studies. A lack of stability in student outcomes would seriously undercut the generalizability of school characteristics associated with the initial, if temporary, student performance data used to designate a school as being effective. An important confounding problem here is the high rate of student mobility in urban schools. This makes stable measures of achievement difficult even with the best designs.

Another serious methodological concern involves a lack of investigation of the causal ordering among school correlates of effectiveness. Rowan et al. (1983) asked "Do high performance expectations enhance effectiveness . . . or result from past success (p. 28)?" Wave I effective schools literature provides little insight into the causal ordering question.

Another criticism involves the general model in effective schools literature studies of comparing effective and ineffective schools in the search for correlates of effectiveness (Purkey & Smith, 1983). What is left out in this strategy is any information on what "average" schools look like when compared to either contrasted groups. Information on average schools would be particularly helpful in underscoring the critical differences that exist in highly effective schools and in aiding educators to develop plans to improve ineffective schools.

Unanswered Questions

A third major kind of criticism that has been leveled at effective schools literature involves gaps in our current knowledge. These gaps are the result of some of the philosophical/conceptual and methodological flaws noted in the previous paragraphs, as well as simply from the fact that the effective schools literature is a new and emerging research stream, one in which there is much work that remains to be done.

Clearly we need to know more about how effective schools literature findings (and questions) relate to school and educational processes for students at middle and secondary grade levels. Do similar school processes have the same impact when typically the school size, and the complicity of the curriculum, are significantly increased? How do school-level educational and organizational processes actually connect to teachers' instructional behaviors for students and teachers that affect achievement? What does an educational leader actually do during the school day that influences teacher and student behavior relevant to performance outcomes?

In a related area, how do findings emanating from the research on effective teaching (e.g., Berliner, 1984; Gage, 1983; Leinhardt & Bickel, in press; Shulman, 1986) connect to the effective schools literature? How are potentially powerful instructional strategies for affecting student achievement such as time on task facilitated (or hindered) by school-level processes? One can hope that an improvement effort focusing on correlates of effective schools would complement a program designed to stimulate changes needed within classrooms in instructional processes. However, without further understanding and evidence, this hope cannot change to presumption, much less a plan for action.

This leads to what is perhaps the most important gap in the knowledge base provided by the effective schools literature, namely, the absence of data on the relevance and efficacy of the characteristics of effective schools as a framework for improving schools not deemed to be effective. The assumption that the identification of effective schools could be an important stimulant to improv-

ing other schools was clearly in the mind of many effective schools researchers. This has clearly come to fruition. The actual use of characteristics as a blueprint for school improvement efforts was not as directly specified, but rather emanated from the positive, and responsive reform climate effective schools researchers confronted (and helped to stimulate) in the late 1970s as more and more results became available and well known. More will be said about this reform climate in the next section of this chapter. The important point here is that a serious gap in the Wave I effective schools knowledge base rested in basically unexamined questions of the relevance of results to programs of improvement.

Commenting on the Effective Schools Literature

The work manifested in the early effective schools literature represents a noteworthy period in American educational research. In what might be considered an extremely short period of time by almost anyone's standards, a new body of knowledge was created about what worked in some schools, and by implication, what could work in others. Further, this knowledge has provided a stimulus for reform action of considerable proportions. In all of this, the literature has had an important impact on many educators, politicians, and public constituencies in how they think about education and about improving educational practice. The relative balance between despair and optimism, between institutional denial and acceptance of responsibility for the education of poor and minority youth, at least has been shifted, if not entirely redressed. "The hopeful message of this literature is powerful and overdue. The ways schools are organized can make a difference in the education of students, even if those students happen to be poor [or] minority . . . while many . . . never lost this sense of hope (and responsibility) some had" (Bickel & Bickel, 1986, p. 491).

A second important contribution of the effective schools literature is the focus on school-level processes. While the exclusivity of this focus is indeed a drawback, we are reminded through this work that instruction and learning takes place "in a larger educational and social environment, and as an important expression of that social environment, the culture of the school has a significant role to play for good or ill" (Bickel & Bickel, 1986, p. 491). Several especially important aspects of the emphasis on school are noted by Purkey & Smith (1985) in their discussion of the school effectiveness movement stimulated by the effective schools literature: "It emphasizes that, whatever else schools can and should accomplish, their primary purpose is instructional . . . [and] schools are to be treated as organic units; improvement strategies that fragment the school's population or instructional program are likely to be unsuccessful" (p. 355).

In tracing the influence of the effective schools literature one sees two major areas of activity. The most obvious one lies in the domain of educational reform and the many efforts at school improvement that were directly spawned by or at least guided by the findings emerging from the effective schools literature. The school effectiveness movement is the subject of the next section of this chapter. A second major impact dimension of the effective schools literature in this writer's view, and one not often discussed, is the stimulus it has provided to the field of educational research, itself. This impact can be tracked along several paths, including the mounting of numerous new studies "wave II" in effective schools literature designed to address some of the methodological flaws of earlier work, or to fill in gaps in current knowledge; and "connections" analyses that seek to link emerging effective schools knowledge to potentially complementary understandings, or necessary extensions of current findings, drawn from other research streams (e.g., on instructional processes, organizational behavior, innovation/implementation processes). The research impact of the effective schools literature is discussed in a subsequent section of this chapter.

THE SCHOOL EFFECTIVENESS MOVEMENT

The impact of the effective schools literature on school improvement initiatives is a remarkable example of how research can contribute to educational reform and practice. As Purkey & Smith (1985) indicate:

This new literature has given rise to what has become a school effectiveness movement. According to the Education Commission of the States, at least eight states have incorporated the findings of the effective schools literature into their school improvement policies, and a number of other states have adopted aspects of the literature for their improvement programs (Odden & Dougherty 1982). Miles, Farrar, and Neufield (1983) located effective schools projects operating in 25 states and covering 875 school districts.

Why has this rapid application (some would say too rapid given our knowledge limitations) of effective schools results occurred? At least three factors have influenced the use of the effective schools literature in school improvement projects. One factor lies in the psychological climate prevalent among practitioners at the time effective schools results were receiving considerable publicity (mid-to-late 1970s). Teachers and administrators were ready to hear a more positive message about the capability of schools to influence the achievement performance of students within them. The years of extreme criticism emanating from campuses and the popular press, and the often despairing messages about the power of schooling to effect change, were wearing thin. Moreover, like the statement from Weber (1971) reported earlier in this chapter, many in the field had an intuitive sense that things were not as bad as they had been depicted in some of the literature. Many had their own personal examples of teachers and schools that seemed to be genuine success stories in precisely the domains, and with exactly those students who were thought to be beyond the reach of effective schooling. This climate provided fertile ground for research results that were saying "Some Schools Work and More Can" (Edmonds, 1979).

A second factor that influenced the rapid application of effective schools results to improvement initiatives was rooted in the specific findings emerging from the research. An orderly school climate, a press for basic skills achievement, strong instructional leadership, high expectations, and frequent monitoring of student performance had an intuitive appeal to most individuals knowledgeable about schools, and their social and organizational structures. The findings were sensible, tangible, and viewed as within domains that schools (and school reformers) could influence.

A third factor that influenced effective schools literature use involved the way researchers in this area framed the question, and in at least a few cases, the individual commitment to move beyond research to school change as an integral part of the effort. The fact that researchers were explicitly looking for what worked contrasted sharply with what apparently was the far more typical mode in research and writings about schooling, namely, the emphasis on identification of problems. The advantages of taking the "what works" approach was twofold. If one discovers an effective X (in this instance a school serving low-income and/or minority students), one already has the potential advantage of having ends-in-view, to guide reform processes in other settings not deemed to be effective. Further, such evidence provides direct challenges to institutional resisters to change who insist that the desired change cannot be accomplished. Edmonds (1979) had this in mind when he wrote: "How many effective schools would you have to see to be persuaded of the educability of poor children? If your answer is more than one, then I submit that you have reasons of your own for preferring to believe that basic pupil performance derives from family background instead of school response to family background (p. 23)."[5]

Complementing the emphasis on what works was the commitment of some prominent researchers associated with the effective schools literature to both publicize and in some cases actually take a leadership role in applying the findings. The most obvious example of this is Ron Edmonds, who not only contributed to critical original research but who also took a significant hand in using this work to guide school change efforts in New York City (Clark & McCarthy, 1983). Educational activism was inherent in the effective schools literature, given the goals and origins of the research. More than most research, this work was often explicitly designed to challenge and to stimulate change in existing educational practices.

The preceding three factors—the receptive psychological climate of the times, the characteristics of the findings, and the reasons and the ways the questions were formed—were critical factors that influenced the rapid stimulation of and application of effective schools literature results to school improvement initiatives. Evidence of the growth and visibility of interest in the school effectiveness movement at national levels can be found in a number of arenas. For example, in terms of the research community Mackenzie (1983b) reports that the 1983 annual meeting of the American Educational Research Association contained 25 entries in its program concerning topics directly related to school effectiveness movement activity. This number was four in 1978 and grew to 40 in the 1985 and 47 in the 1986 programs, respectively. Similarly, in the educational reform arena a national Council for Effective Schools was formed in 1984 with the explicit goal "to advocate, initiate, and support measures to make schools more effective" (*The Effective School Report,* Vol. 2, May 1984, p. 1). It is clear that the establishment of this National Council was in direct response to the numbers of improvement efforts already under way and the perceived need to establish "definitions, standards, and criteria . . . to preserve the basic philosophy" (p. 1) of the school effectiveness. This movement has even spawned a number of national publications devoted to tracking, reporting on improvement efforts and sharing information on implementation strategies and results. Perhaps the best known example of this is the *Effective School Report* started in 1983 and dedicated to the memory of Ron Edmonds.

These national indicators of interest in school improvement reflect the numerous state- and district-level school improvement efforts stimulated by the effective schools literature. A comprehensive inventory of these efforts can be found in the National Institute of Education's (now the Office of Educational Research and Improvement, OERI), publication: *Reaching for Excellence: An Effective Schools Sourcebook* (Kyle, 1985) and the directory of programs contained therein by Miles & Kaufman (1985). The directory includes information on:

> 39 programs; 13 of them were developed by local school districts, 9 of them by state departments of education, and 17 by other organizations, including regional laboratories, universities, and research institutes. These programs are in current use in 1,750 school districts, and a total of 5,228 elementary, 1,424 middle/junior high, and 824 high schools, or well over double the number of schools found by Miles, Farrar, Neufield (1983).

---

[5] It is interesting to note that the explicit emphasis on what works that is so characteristic of the effective schools literature is now a more common approach in research and written commentary about research. Nowhere is this trend more clearly evidenced than in recent national publications emanating from the federal government (e.g., U.S. Department of Education, 1986).

It is perhaps useful at this point to discuss in a little detail several examples of improvement efforts in order to provide the reader with a sense of the kinds of approaches that are being implemented in the school effectiveness movement. To this end a brief description follows of one state- and one district-level program.

Connecticut's Priority School District program was begun in 1984 as a Connecticut State Department of Education initiative designed "to assist school districts with the greatest demonstrated academic need to improve student achievement and enhance educational opportunities" (Sergi et al., 1985, p. 69). The focus was on basic skills achievement and instructional improvement. Districts identified by low student performance on ninth-grade proficiency tests were eligible. Ten districts were selected based on this criterion for inclusion in the first year of the program.

Each selected district works with a representative of the state department on the development of a locally designed, 3-year improvement plan employing a structured needs assessment process. New, as well as redirected state and local resources are made available in support of improvement activities. The entire process is the subject of local and state evaluations of progress. Initial information on district action plans in 10 locales indicated that the most frequently selected areas of district activity included:

- Improved basic skills curriculum and curriculum alignment with the district's testing program.
- Professional development for administrators, concentrating on improved supervision of teachers and instruction.
- Professional development for teachers, concentrating on more effective classroom instruction, with emphasis in the areas of mathematics, reading, and language arts.
- District management activities, such as comprehensive program planning, pupil information systems, and program evaluation—particularly of remedial education.
- School building effectiveness initiatives, including an improved school environment and efforts to improve student attendance, dropout prevention, discipline, and attitudes. (Sergi et al., 1985, p. 70)

The initial set of 10 districts has been increased. Early evaluations have provided "evidence that the schools involved have altered the school effectiveness characteristics that were the focus of their action plans" (Miles & Kaufman, 1985, p. 168). The "gap between the proportions of low income students and others scoring at the 30th percentile or below on standardized tests has narrowed in almost all schools over time" (p. 168). More complete evaluation data are due in 1987 (Sergi et al., 1985).

In contrast to the Connecticut effort, the New York City Public School's (NYCPS) School Improvement Project (SIP) was the result of district initiative.[6] In 1979, Ron Edmonds, then senior assistant to the chancellor for instruction, was responsible for addressing the problem of student achievement (Clark & McCarthy, 1983). Edmonds took the position that improving conditions related to the five correlates of effective schools would be critical in helping schools to become more effective (Clark & McCarthy, 1983).

SIP implementation processes included the following steps:

- A needs assessment conducted by the planning team using the five correlates.
- Formation of a school planning committee.
- Development of a school improvement plan based on the five school effectiveness factors.
- Plan review and approval.
- Implementation of the plan.
- Plan evaluation and revision.
- Maintenance, during which implementation, evaluation, and revision processes become cyclical and the liaison is no longer in the school, although he or she is available on request. (Clark & McCarthy, 1983, p. 18)

An important feature of the SIP was the use of a liaison/change agent role. This position was initially "to embody the system's capacity to respond to school requests for assistance" (Clark & McCarthy, 1983, p. 18). Eventually, liaisons were actually assigned to specific schools as a resource to a school's implementation process. Schools were invited to participate. Ten were selected in

---

[6] It is important to note that, once under way, the SIP initiative gathered support from a variety of sources, including the New York State Department of Education.

1979–1980 as the initial cohort based on three criteria: the voluntary participation of the principal, a match between school needs and SIP objectives, and absence of other developmental activity within the building. Nine additional schools joined the effort the following year and more joined in the third year.

One of the strengths of the SIP initiative was that its early years of implementation were documented by a district-based research team through funding provided by the Ford Foundation. This documentation work yielded considerable detail about initial implementation processes, planning strategies employed, and constraints encountered. Such process documentation is all too infrequent in most reform efforts.[7] Data reported (Clark & McCarthy, 1983) on the first two cohorts of SIP schools indicated that for two of three comparison years (1979–1982) SIP schools "showed greater improvement than other city schools in the percentage of students reading at or above grade level." The documentation effort uncovered a relationship between school commitment to SIP and increased student achievement. One result of this was the requirement that in more recent SIP cohorts principals, teachers (60 to 70%) and parents "agree to participate through a formal vote" (p. 23).

The Connecticut and New York City programs are but two of many example of the many initiatives under way as a result of the application of Effective schools literature results to school reform. They are illustrative of some of the most prominent characteristics of school effectiveness movement activities. While many objectives and strategies are encompassed by such efforts, all contain an emphasis on basic skills achievement and a school focus to their improvement initiatives. The effective schools literature findings are central "ends-in-view" that guide planning, assessment, and implementation processes. As this chapter goes to press, there is much that remains to be learned from the extensive network of school effectiveness movement activity currently in progress. The modest early data in hand tend to be promising (Eubanks & Levine, 1983; Purkey & Smith, 1985), but the data in hand represent only a small fraction of the improvement initiatives

under way and therefore the potential knowledge base in this area.

EFFECTIVE SCHOOLS LITERATURE: IMPACT ON RESEARCH

One of the most interesting, and potentially quite important outcomes of the widespread application of Wave I effective schools literature has been the stimuli this has provided for continuing research on and analysis of issues related to the effective schools agenda. That the effective schools literature has acted as a powerful impetus to further research can be understood in terms of two central features of its history. As noted earlier, the widespread dissemination of Wave I results occurred quite rapidly, before many questions were adequately addressed. So in one sense, current "wave II" activity can be thought of merely as representing a continuing research stream, part two. As important has been the critical impact of the level of acceptance of the effective shcools research agenda and the application of results to practice. In ways that have few comparable examples, the effective schools work represents an extremely important instance of the use of research to influence educational reform and practice. This research "opened" political and policy doors that traditionally were hard to budge. This receptivity in the world of practice had both a heady and a sobering impact on the research community. The experience was heady in the sense that the academic ideal (at least for some in academe) of research influencing practice was being met dramatically; sobering in that many felt that application was significantly ahead of the knowledge base. Both factors, the continuing agenda and the opportunity to influence practice, served as powerful stimulants to more work on related concerns.

One kind of research activity focused on addressing some of the methodological and conceptual flaws perceived to be in the effective schools literature. A second research activity has extended the implications of effective schools research to educational settings other than those of the elementary school, the primary focus of much of the Wave I work. Both of these recent research trends share some key elements with original work. They tend to focus on school-level variables and are concerned with the specific populations of interest to first-generation effective schools literature researchers. A third kind of activity, less

---

[7] For a discussion of the role of program documentation in the field of evaluation research, see Bickel (1984).

explicitly research than research synthesis and policy analysis, seeks to broaden the school improvement implications of Wave I work by drawing upon diverse sets of research knowledge that may or may not be school and population focused. In the case of one area, (organizational behavior) much of the knowledge was not even the result of work done in educational settings. These "connections" analyses seek to broaden the potential for educational reform and school improvement stimulated by the effective schools literature by crafting a network of understandings across a number of emerging knowledge bases. In this way, this area of activity of both filling gaps in knowledge and adding additional tools to the school effectiveness movement. Examples of each of the three kinds of Wave II activity follow.

Repairing Flaws
A number of important criticisms have been leveled at Wave I effective schools literature research. Several of the most important of these are summarized in the first section of this chapter. The reader will recall from that discussion that a serious flaw was the lack of specificity in effective schools studies about how important correlates of effective schools are operationalized in real behavior, policies, and practices. The correlate concerning the importance of a strong instructional leader is illustrative of this point. How does an instructional leader actually spend his/her time in an effective school setting in ways that make a difference (directly or indirectly) to student performance in basic skills? One has little to go on from the original research on these important questions.

Recent work has begun to address the leadership issue in the explicit context of the effective schools results. For example, Dwyer, Lee, Rowan, & Bossert (1983) report on a study of five successful principals and their instructional management behaviors. These authors note that

> [an] examination of the literature about effective schools and successful principals reveals that the usefulness of either is limited by noteworthy conceptual and methodological shortcomings (Bossert et al., 1982). While the leadership literature calls for principals to "structure" their organizations for effectiveness, little is said about what processes must be structured or what structures need to be imposed on these processes. (p. 1)

The goal of the case studies of exemplary principals was precisely to explore "the linkages between organizational variables [such as management behavior] and . . . concrete instructional processes" (p. 1). The five principals were "shadowed" during three full workdays over an 8-week period. In addition, observations were taken in the school of classroom processes, recesses, and lunchroom activity. Extensive debriefings with the principals as well as less formal interviews of teachers and students and document reviews were used to fill out the descriptive portraits. These data were used to prepare "models that illustrated the essential qualities of the organizations' contexts, the activities which best typified the essential qualities of the organizations' contexts, the activities which best typified the principals' management behaviors, and the expected outcomes of those actions as projected by the principals" (p. 5). In all of this, the authors were also interested in further testing of a theoretical framework for examining instructional management behaviors (Bossert, Dwyer, Roman, & Lee, 1982).

The Dwyer case studies (Dwyer et al., 1983) yielded a number of results, including the reshaping of the original theoretical model used to investigate management behavior in schools, methodological notes on the use of the "short field study" approach to research in this area, and examples of principals' management behavior. Findings in the latter domain are of interest here. The researchers note the importance of understanding principal behavior in part in relation to the primary leadership style or "mode" of the individual. Style was influenced both by the principals' characteristics, situational antecedents, and specific school/decision contexts. For example, some data suggest that the experience and the maturity of a faculty were important situational constraints on principals' leadership style, with more direct interventionalist management behavior needed in the presence of less senior faculties or faculties with high turnover. These researchers also noted the "routine" nature of management behavior: The "principals' most essential activities included forms of monitoring, information control and exchange, planning, direct interaction with students, staff development and hiring, and overseeing building maintenance (p. 53)." They document the principals' management responses to daily cycles in the life of the building, which in turn serve important "maintenance and development" functions within the school organization. In commenting on principals' routines, these researchers speculate that such behavior represents:

> acts through which principals can assess the working status of their organizations and the progress of their schools relative to long-term goals. They are the acts which allow principals to alter the course of events midstream: to return aberrant student behavior to acceptable norms; to suggest changes in teaching style or intervene to demonstrate a preferred form of instruction; to develop an awareness of changes in the organization that must be made in the future. . . . The effects of these routine acts on the quality of instruction and student experience in schools can be substantial. . . . Instructional leadership provides the overworked, out-of-time practitioner with a manageable alternative form of instructional leadership. These are the common acts of the principalship. They require no new program, no innovation, no extensive change. The success of these activities for instructional management hinges, instead, on the principal's capacity to connect them to the instructional system. (p. 54)

Other studies or policy papers can be cited that investigate principal leadership behavior as it pertains to school curriculum (e.g., Floden et al., 1984); the determinants of principal work, and key factors in influencing instructional management behavior (e.g., Duckworth, 1983); issues in other grade-level settings (e.g., Lee, 1984); and influencing program improvement (e.g., Leithwood & Montgomery, 1982). The central point here is that flaws in early research are beginning to be corrected through careful studies such as the Dwyer et al. (1983) work discussed above. This is quite a positive development. While the work on instructional leadership seems most advanced in this regard, other areas (e.g., school discipline, Duckworth, 1984; achievement monitoring, Cooley & Bickel, 1986) are also receiving attention. The promise is that early findings will be better understood and specified to the benefit of our collective knowledge about effective schools.

Extending Effectiveness to Other Settings

An important criticism of the first generation of effective schools research has been the emphasis on early-grades education to almost the exclusion of studies of secondary and middle school settings (Firestone & Herriott, 1982; Purkey & Smith, 1985). The Rutter et al. (1979) study is a notable exception to this general characteristic of the early work. Researchers such as Firestone & Herriott (1982) identify a number of key dimensions along which elementary and secondary schools differ, and variables that are likely to influence such central effectiveness correlates as instructional leadership and student–teacher expectations. Differences in a shared sense of purpose, departmentalization, curriculum complexity, staff size, and staff hierarchy are examples of how school organizations differ by the age of children and where high schools tend to show evidence of:

- Less consensus about goals.
- Fewer formal rules (except for noninstructional activities).
- Greater teacher autonomy.
- Less influence by principals over policy.
- Less communication among staff members.
- More administration–teacher conflict. (Firestone & Herriott, 1982, as reported in Corcoran, 1985, p. 77)

Recent research has begun to address this gap in the effective schools knowledge base. The new work has taken several forms. First, there are conceptual and theoretical analyses of the details of grade organizational differences and how these might impinge upon the ready transfer of effective schools literature findings to other settings (e.g., Firestone, Herriott, & Wilson, 1984; Corcoran, 1985). Second, there have been actual investigations of effective high and middle schools. This work is very much an area still in progress and the current status of the knowledge base is quite a bit short of providing "powerful generalizations to guide policy" (Corcoran, 1985). Nevertheless, these studies of secondary schools (e.g., Lightfoot, 1983; California Assembly Office of Research, 1984; Lipsitz, 1984) are offering important insights into "effectiveness" and how the effective schools literature analyses and correlates must be reexamined in new school organizational contexts. One of the most important features of many of these secondary efforts has been careful reappraisal and broadening of the original basic skills criteria. This change is captured nicely when authors such as Lipsitz (1984) and Lightfoot (1983) write of "good" schools for early adolescents and high school students, respectively. In their search for good schools, these researchers make clear distinctions between schools with high achievement scores and those that are also "developmentally appropriate" and that show evidence of "nurturance" and empathy among the children and adults in them. The Lipsitz (1984) study serves to illustrate both the search for effectiveness in nonelementary settings and the broadening of criteria that is taking place in many of theses studies.

Lipsitz (1984) describes a "central bias" in her study: "that to succeed with young adolescents, schools must be responsive to their developmental needs" (p. 6). Seven categories of needs serve to flesh out the researcher's notion of developmentally responsive: competence and achievement, self-exploration and definition, social interaction with peers and adults, physical activity, meaningful participation in school and community, routine/limits/structure, and diversity.[8]

The study reports on four case studies of successful middle-grades schools. The schools were selected based on an initial set of "threshold" criteria that included indices such as student achievement and absenteeism, parental satisfaction, and recognition for excellence. "Impressionistic case studies" were conducted in the four schools over a 7-day period of observation. Observations and inquiries focused on nine fundamental areas of school activity and structure: curriculum, purposes/goals, organization, leadership, and self-evaluation, climate, institutional practices, community context, and important public policy questions related to such issues as special education mainstreaming and desegregation.

Lipsitz reports on common themes across the four successful schools. Comments on leadership are illustrative. "Each of the four schools had a principal with a driving vision who imbues decisions and practices with meaning, placing powerful emphasis on why and how things are done. Decisions are made not just because they are practical, but for reasons of principle [connected to] a vision of what school should be for the age group" (p. 174). The researcher describes the principals as "authorative, not authoritarian." They see instructional leadership to be a critical function of their

role with real competence and opportunity to advise and evaluate within classrooms. These principals have also been able to develop considerable autonomy within the larger district context. Sometimes this is formally recognized (e.g., the designation of experimental status), at times it exists by default (a principal winning past battles with the central office). In either case, the impact is to provide opportunities to shape important curriculum and instructional decisions. Leadership included the ability to shape the makeup of their faculty. Through a variety of mechanisms, each of the four schools had principals with considerable input into who taught and who did not within their school. Interestingly, the principals clearly did not do it alone. Each had important colleagues in their work (e.g., assistant principal, or an administrative council, mechanisms for teacher input, etc.). In the researcher's own words:

> The major contribution of the principals is to make the schools larger than one person. They institutionalize their vision in program and organizational structure. The principals are good enough leaders to leave a legacy behind: their staff, a powerfully defined school, an educated community, and a tradition of excitement, sensitivity, and striving for excellence. (p. 178)

The work of Lipsitz (1984), Lightfoot (1983), and others is making contributions to our specific knowledge about school effectiveness in middle and secondary school settings. Further, this work illustrates the press for a broadening of original effective schools literature criteria in judging effectiveness. Both of these developments offer much promise for future school improvement efforts.

Making Connections Among Knowledge Bases

A third important "Wave II" activity under way involves analyses by prominent researchers of the implications of effective schools findings through lenses provided by other, relevant knowledge bases. This emergence of a "connections" literature nicely illustrates how interdisciplinary communication can be an important tool in advancing understanding of social (or for that matter, physical) phenomena. Analyses of the implications of research on effective schools have been done in relation to research on effective classroom instruc-

---

[8] Lipsitz draws these from earlier work done at the Center for Early Adolescence (Dorman, 1981).

tional practices, educational change processes, and through the latter models of organizational behavior (e.g., Bacharach & Conley, 1986; Cuban, 1985; Good & Brophy, 1986; Mackenzie, 1983a, 1983b; Purkey & Smith, 1985; Schlechty, 1985). Two analyses (Mackenzie, 1983a; Purkey & Smith, 1985) linking findings on effective schools to classroom instruction and educational change research, respectively, are discussed below as illustrations of the research synthesis activity under way.

Beginning with an analysis of first-generation effective schools research, Mackenzie (1983a) correctly concludes that this knowledge base becomes more powerful and indeed should only be understood in terms of a continuum of emerging knowl-edge that includes school-level processes, teaching strategies, and procedures for the organization of classroom instruction. Mackenzie's analysis purposely does not attempt "to distinguish sharply between the elements of social organization and those of instruction and curriculum . . . or between process-learning variables and organization-structure variables" (p. 8). Mackenzie reports on "dimensions of effective schooling" broken out along three continuums related to leadership, efficacy, and efficiency. The analysis identifies core (most frequently cited) and facilitating elements (less cited, also aiding in the implementation of core elements). Figure 1 reproduces Mackenzie's summary of emerging understandings across literatures. This type of analysis of effective schools

LEADERSHIP DIMENSIONS:

Core Elements
- Positive climate and overall atmosphere
- Goal-focused activities toward clear, attainable, relevant objectives
- Teacher-directed classroom management and decision making
- In-service staff training for effective teaching

Facilitating Elements
- Shared consensus on values and goals
- Long-range planning and coordination
- Stability and continuity of key staff
- District-level support for school improvement

EFFICACY DIMENSIONS:

Core Elements
- High and positive achievement expectations with a constant press for excellence
- Visible rewards for academic excellence and growth
- Cooperative activity and group interaction in the classroom
- Total staff involvement with school improvement
- Autonomy and flexibility to implement adaptive practices
- Appropriate levels of difficulty for learning tasks

- Teacher empathy, rapport, and personal interaction with students

Facilitating Elements
- Emphasis on homework and study
- Positive accountability; acceptance of responsibility for learning outcomes
- Strategies to avoid nonpromotion of students
- Deemphasis on strict ability grouping: interaction with more accomplished peers

EFFICIENCY DIMENSIONS:

Core Elements
- Effective use of instructional time; amount and intensity of engagement in school learning
- Orderly and disciplined school and classroom environments
- Continuous diagnosis, evaluation, and feedback
- Well-structures classroom activities
- Instruction guided by content coverage
- School-wide emphasis on basic and higher-order skills

Facilitating Elements
- Opportunities for individualized work
- Number and variety of opportunities to learn

Figure 1. Dimensions of effective schooling.

results in relation to findings emerging from research on classroom instruction (other examples include Good & Brophy, 1986; Kyle, 1985) suggests important structures for further research. Such new work can fill in our understanding of how school processes variables can be connected operationally to important within-classroom variables such as time-on task, direct instruction, grouping practices, and curriculum priorities, and so on.

In a second example of research synthesis activity, Purkey & Smith (1985) published an analysis of the implications of the literature on effective schools for district-level policies related to school reform. In doing so, these authors draw upon a diverse research literature focused on educational change and organizational behavior. They directly addressed one of the central criticisms raised, by themselves and others, about first-generation effective schools research, namely, the absence of knowledge about whether this work could be an effective tool for guiding school improvement initiatives. These writers take early effective schools research as a "springboard" and, combining new understandings about change processes (e.g., Berman, 1981; Fullan, 1982), "suggest local strategies and policies that will stimulate and facilitate school reform (p. 353).

They build on their earlier examination of the characteristics of an effective school, 13 in all (Purkey & Smith, 1983).[9] These authors employ a "backward mapping" analytical strategy (Elmore, 1979–1980) that focuses initially (in this case) on the school, and asks the following question: What conditions, internal resources, then external resources and influence patterns are needed to stimulate movement in the desired direction (i.e., an improving school)? This backward mapping strategy, in effect, allows the authors to describe necessary conditions for effectiveness and to analyze required district policies that will enable schools to move toward effectiveness. Four district-level policies are recommended:

---

[9] The 13 factors include 9 focused on setting the context (school site management and democratic decision making, leadership, staff development, parental involvement and support, school-wide recognition of academic success, maximized learning time, district support) and 4 that "define the school's culture and leads to the development of school climate" (collaborative planning and collegial relationships, sense of community, clear goals and high expectations, order and discipline).

- Make the school the focus of change, its culture the ultimate policy target.
- Encourage staff analysis of their school's conditions using the effective schools characteristics as a guide, concentrating on those most likely to produce an effective school culture in their situation.
- Provide resources (time, technical assistance) designed to nurture the process of collaboration necessary to change both people and school structures.
- Adopt a change process that maximizes local responsibility for school improvement. (pp. 362–364)

Each of these policy recommendations is grounded in analyses of relevant research about effective change processes and organizational constraints to change. In this way the authors advance our understanding about how the effective schools literature can be a basis for stimulating school improvement by setting this research in the context of a larger knowledge base about reform processes in organizations.

Commenting on the Impact on Research

The foregoing discussion illustrates the flowering that has occurred in a variety of research, research syntheses, and policy analyses activities that are in one way or another related to the important questions addressed and raised by the effective schools literature. Correcting flaws, filling in gaps in our knowledge, and connecting findings to other knowledge bases are illustrations of how our understandings about the nature of effective schools, and how to create more of them, is being deepened and expanded. It is perhaps overly "tidy" to refer to this diverse set of activity as "Wave II" or "second generation." Nevertheless, the relationships to earlier work are readily apparent. The point is much less what to call it than to note with expectancy the richness and breadth of activity under way.

In a similar spirit regarding classification schemes, it is important to state two caveats related to the structure used in describing Wave II activity. Our rough categories are intended for convenience of discussion rather than precision for categorization. For example, some research discussed as extending the effective schools research to other grade levels might also be thought of as efforts to correct conceptual flaws in earlier work. Finally, no order of importance is implied in the discussion of valuable "connections" analyses by linking it first to the development of the effective schools literature. For example, the literature on classroom teaching is clearly valuable in its own right, on its own terms, focused on its own questions. The position here is that both the effective schools literature and classroom instruction literature combined tell a larger and very important story (Bickel & Bickel, 1986). The focus of this chapter has been on the effective schools literature, and therefore the discussions come to other knowledge domains through this base; had this chapter been concerned with the literature on classroom instruction, we would arrive at the same point, albeit via a different route. Of course, the point is that in combination across various knowledge bases we know much about what works in education and how to improve what does not.

EDUCATIONAL REFORM: ALTERNATIVE PATHS

Research on effective schools began with five fundamental assumptions. The educational establishment has a significant responsibility in the education of poor and minority students. Some schools show evidence of the acceptance of this responsibility and the capability of stimulating measurable success in basic skills achievement. Effective schools have certain discernible school-level process characteristics that are correlated with their success. These correlates of effectiveness can be helpful in stimulating school improvement/reform initiatives and in serving as guides for school-focused improvement programs.

A careful reading of the record of effective schools-related research and reform activity provides evidence that these assumptions essentially were well founded. Of course, many questions remain, gaps in the knowledge base need to be explored (and hopefully filled in), implications of early results require further investigation as well as application to other settings, relationships to other knowledge bases need to be better understood and strengthened, and much more documentation of current school improvement efforts should occur. Yet having underscored these very considerable limitations and unfinished agenda, one can still agree with the assessment of Purkey & Smith (1985) when they write of a "cautious optimism"

and an "enthusiasm that is not inappropriate" in relation to this literature and the school improvement initiatives that it has stimulated.

Accepting that much remains to be accomplished, what can be said as an "interim report" about achievements that can reasonably be associated with the effective schools literature and related activity? First, this literature has played a significant role in reestablishing institutional responsibility for student progress, even if students come from poor or minority family backgrounds. Second, it has focused attention on the immediate context in which classroom instruction and learning takes place, the school. School process variables have a significant role to play in fostering a climate that supports instructional and learning processes. Third, this work has engendered optimism in some and, with an evidentiary base, sustained optimism in others who already knew that individual teachers and schools do make a difference. In this, the effective schools literature has served as a vital stimulant to reform energy within educational systems—a catalyst in generating considerable policy and resource momentum needed in any improvement effort. Finally, the first generation of research on effective schools has sparked a variety of further research and synthesis activities that promise to both broaden and deepen our understanding of how to organize schools and classrooms for effective instruction.

The foregoing are considerable accomplishments, indeed. What does the future hold for these important efforts well begun? Discerning paths of future reform efforts is a highly problematic task. There are a number of angles from which one could build an admittedly speculative discussion of the issue. Of particular interest for this writer is how future "school improvement efforts" will be influenced by another reform program that has gotten under way during the past several years. The "press for excellence" is a significant area of reform activity that may have a direct impact on educational improvement programs growing out of effective schools research. In the remainder of this section we examine briefly some of the connections, and areas of convergence and divergence, that may exist in these now-parallel reform efforts. An underlying assumption here is that understanding the future of effective schools–related reform activity is in part tied to whether the various reform energies under way will or will not complement each other.

"A Nation at Risk" (National Commission on Excellence in Education, 1983) was one of a number of national reports on the nation's schools released during the earlier part of this decade (Presseisien, 1985). This report, more than any other, has had a widespread impact on national educational circles. It stimulated a serious reexamination of how schools are fairing against internal and external (international) performance standards. As the title suggested, the judgment was clear—American schools were falling behind, and "the nation stands to lose its prominence as a world leader in industry and commerce."[10]

The flavor of the "At Risk" and many of the other reports was reminiscent of the kind of national attention education received in the era immediately following the USSR's launching of the first orbiting satellite (*Sputnik*). U.S. school performance represented a serious threat to the national well-being. The issue this time was less a deadly technological and scientific competition between competing superpowers than economic productivity among competing industrialized states. However, the central message was similar: U.S. schools needed to attain higher levels of proficiency as a tool for strengthening the nation in a time of crisis.

The "At Risk" report is an apt example of this most recent press for raising U.S. educational proficiency. First, it was one of the earliest of the national reports released in what has been called the "year of the reports," 1983. Second, it has received widespread public attention and the sustained support of the federal Department of Education, the commissioning source of the task force that released the report. Third, a number of the recommendations emanating from the "At Risk" document were been rapidly implemented through state and local educational policies.

The Commission's report recommended that a number of actions be taken to respond to the national threat. These included:

- Strengthening state and local high school graduation requirements and at a minimum recommendation that all students be required to lay the foundations in the "Five

New Basics" during their high school years by taking 4 years of English, 3 years of mathematics, 3 years of science, 3 years of social studies, and 1/2 year of computer science.
- Adopting "more rigorous and measurable standards, and higher expectations for academic performance and student conduct."
- Devoting more time to learning the "New Basics" through more effective use of the existing school day, a longer school day, or a lengthened school year.
- Raising standards for preparing and evaluating teachers, and modifying the workplace and career structures of teachers to attract outstanding new entries to the profession, and so on.

The Commission concludes its recommendations by pointing to the necessity for sustained local and national support to meet the crisis.

Reasons for the rapid influence of the Commission's recommendations most plausibly rested both with the nature of the "findings" (in this case suggestions for change) and in the social and political climate of the times. Commission recommendations in many instances lent themselves to quick implementation in that the likely reform mechanism was basically state legislative mandate. Thus, key "solutions" were readily available. The will to mandate educational reform rested with the political viability of such actions, justifiable in the "national economic defense" context that was perceived to be the central problem.

As one might expect, the press for excellence thus far has had its most profound impact in the areas of raising graduation standards and in modifying (toughening) curriculum offerings. These changes are affecting students graduating in the late 1980s. More units of academic coursework are being required; more state testing of students is occurring in order to determine student progress.

What are the implications of the press for excellence for the reform agenda associated with effective schools research and related school improvement activity? At first glance the raising of standards, with emphasis on "New Basics" and on the regular monitoring of student progress (although through state and district-level mechanisms), seem to complement the emphasis in effective schools research on higher expectations for students, frequent monitoring of student pro-

---

[10] This message of national school failure in relation to international industrial competitors has been strongly reinforced recently in studies comparing U.S. educational outcomes to those of Japan and other industrialized nations (e.g., Dorfman, 1987).

gress, and a concentration on basic skills. One interpretation of those apparently common themes is that the push for excellence activity is reinforcing at state and district levels some of the same goals that are of interest to the school improvement movement.

A closer inspection of the press for excellence movement, however, also reveals some quite divergent themes between the two sets of reform agenda. For example, the emphasis on target populations of students (e.g., poor and minority populations) is largely absent in many of the state-mandated excellence reforms. Fundamental goals related to educational equity are thus deemphasized in the new press. If "everyone" is the target of excellence, then, hopefully, all students will benefit. If on the other hand, "excellence" leaves currently low-achieving populations behind, the original gap in achievement noted by Edmonds and others will be widened. This question about possible tension between excellence and equity is already being raised (e.g., Cardenas & First, 1986; Natriello, McDill, & Pallas, 1986; Strike, 1985).

A second area of divergence in the two reform agendas involves the mechanisms or levers of change employed and the basis upon which these approaches to change are recommended. As has been noted above, the most immediate impact of the push for excellence has been a series of state-mandated changes in graduation policies and curriculum structures with little research evidence to support the validity that these changes will have the desired effect. While school improvement activity has also generated state-based and district-based reform efforts, these generally are aimed at stimulating *research-based, school-level* improvement processes whose substance is to be worked out by the educators, parents, and students involved (within broad guidelines drawn from the effective schools research). The emphasis on the engagement of educational personnel and the discovery of solutions close to the process of education in the latter case contrasts with the focus on centrally mandated solutions and accountability mechanisms implicit in much of the push for excellence reforms.

The two reform movements also differ markedly in their approach to stimulating educational change and in the primary targets of change. Like the pre-1970s critics of education, the press for excellence platform tends to emphasize problem identification linked with nongrounded recommendations for reform.[11] In contrast, while the effective schools movement does begin with an initial problem, the emphasis is then on the identification of what works and what these successful models exhibit that can be helpful in improving other schools. The danger in the excellence approach is that school personnel are left with (a) a serious problem, (b) the liability for past failure, and (c) centrally imposed (and largely untested) solutions. These are hardly the basis for serious engagement in the reform process.

Finally, and most fundamentally, the target of change has significantly shifted in the two reform agendas, at least in terms of what has already been implemented. While graduation requirements and curriculum structures are being manipulated, and perhaps "the" central point of the excellence movement is that the student must shape up. The alarm has been sounded, a danger threatens the nation, and we all, but especially students, must work harder. In contrast, the effective schools agenda places responsibility for change squarely at the feet of the schools. Students are a part of a school improvement process, but ultimately, the major responsibility for change rests with institutional environments that either foster or impede student learning. Both reform efforts emphasize improved student outcomes, it is the getting there that is different. In the press for excellence, some authors have noted that high-risk students may be left behind (e.g., Natriello et al., 1986). This may well be so, but what is also left behind is the institutional responsibility that effective schools researchers so clearly focused on in their work.

Equity and excellence should not necessarily be incompatible social and educational goals. However, as choices are made, and finite resources and political energy are allocated, serious questions must be addressed as to how reform policies can be crafted which ensure that both goals are met. Failure to address educational equity is no less a threat to the nation than failure to compete in the international marketplace; it is related to it directly. It would be the height of irony if at the very time that our knowledge base about

---

[11] The recent emphasis in studies of educational systems of other countries as part of the press for excellence reform process may be viewed as an attempt to redress this lack of evidence of what works in the centrally mandated solutions being debated. Of course, the many difficulties inherent in cross-cultural generalization are significant indeed.

how to improve achievement among students at risk is increasing, the nation turns from this toward policies that admittedly seek to raise standards but that are disconnected from our growing knowledge about how to reach them.

REFERENCES

Armor, D. J., Conry-Oseguera, P., Cox, M., King, N., McConnell, L., Pascal, A., Pauly, E., & Zellman, G. (1976). *Analysis of the school referred reading program in selected Los Angeles minority schools* (Report No. R-2007-LAUSD). Santa Monica, CA: Rand Corporation.

Austin, G. R. (1979). Exemplary schools and the search for efectiveness. *Educational Leadership, 37,* 10–14.

Bacharach, S. B., & Conley, S. C. (1986). Education reform: A managerial agenda. *Phi Delta Kappan, 67*(9), 641–645.

Berliner, D. C. (1984). The half-full glass: A review of research on teaching. In P. L. Hosford (Ed.), *Using what we know about teaching* (pp. 51–77). Alexandria, VA: Association for Supervision and Curriculum Development.

Berman, P. (1981). Educational change: An implementation paradigm. In R. Lehming & M. Kane (Eds.), *Improving schools.* Beverly Hills, CA: Sage.

Bickel, W. E. (1983). Effective schools: Knowledge, dissemination, inquiry. *Educational Researcher, 12*(4), 3.

Bickel, W. E. (1984). Evaluator in residence: New prospects for school district evaluation research. *Educational Evaluation and Policy Analysis, 6*(3), 297–306.

Bickel, W. E., & Bickel, D. D. (1986). Effective schools, classrooms, and instruction: Implications for special education. *Exceptional Children, 52*(6), 489–500.

Bossert, S. T. (1985). Effective elementary schools. In R. M. J. Kyle (Ed.), *Reaching for excellence: An effective schools sourcebook.* Washington, DC: E.H. White.

Bossert, S. T., Dwyer, D. C., Rowan, B., & Lee, G. U. (1982). The instructional management role of the principal. *Educational Administration Quarterly, 18,* 34–64.

Brookover, W. B., & Lezotte, L. W. (1979). *Changes in school characteristics coincident with changes in student achievement.* East Lansing: Michigan State University, Institute for Research on Teaching.

Brookover, W. B., & Schneider, J. M. (1975). Academic environments and elementary school achievement. *Journal of Research and Development in Education, 9*(1), 82–91.

California Assembly Office of Research. (1984). *Overcoming the odds: Making high school work.* Sacramento: Author.

Cardenas, J., & First, J. M. (1986). Children at risk. *Educational Leadership, 43*(1), 4–9.

Carnoy, M. (1974). *Education as cultural imperialism.* New York: David McKay.

Clark, T. S., & McCarthy, D. P. (1983). School improvement in New York City: The evolution of a project. *Educational Researcher, 12*(4), 17–23.

Coleman, J., Cambell, E., Hobson, C., McPartland, J., Mood, A., Weinfield, F., & York, R. (1966). *Equality of educational opportunity.* Washington, DC: U.S. Government Printing Office.

Cooley, W. W., & Bickel, W. E. (1986). *Decision-oriented educational research.* Boston: Kluwer.

Corcoran, T. B. (1985). Effective secondary schools. In R. M. J. Kyle (Ed.), *Reaching for excellence: An effective schools sourcebook.* Washington, DC: E.H. White.

Cuban, L. (1985). Effective schools research. In T. S. Sergi & J. Shoemaker (Eds.), *Improving student achievement.* Hartford: Connecticut State Department of Education.

Dorfman, C. H. (Ed.). (1987). *Japanese education today* (A report from the U.S. Study of Education in Japan). Washington, DC: U.S. Government Printing Office.

Dorman, G. (1981). *Middle grades assessment program.* Chapel Hill, NC: Center for Early Adolescence.

Duckworth, K. (1983). *Specifying determinants of teacher and principal work.* Eugene, OR: Center for Educational Policy and Management.

Duckworth, K. (1984). *School discipline policy: A problem of balance.* Eugene, OR: Center for Educational Policy and Management.

Dwyer, D. C., Lee, G. V., Rowan, B., & Bossert, S. T. (1983). *Five principals in action: Perspectives on instructional management.* San Francisco: Far West Laboratory.

Edmonds, R. (1979). Some schools work and more can. *Social Policy, 9*(2), 28–32.

Edmonds, R. R. (Undated) *A discussion of the literature and issues related to effective schooling.* Unpublished manuscript, New York City Public Schools, New York.

Edmonds, R., & Frederiksen, J. R. (1978). *Search for effective schools: The identification and analysis of city schools that are instructionally effective for poor children.* Cambridge, MA: Harvard University, Center for Urban Studies.

Edmonds, R. R., & Frederiksen, J. (Undated). *Search for effective schools.* Unpublished manuscript, Carnegie Corporation, New York.

Elmore, R. F. (1979–1980). Backward mapping: Implementation research and policy decision. *Political Science Quarterly, 94,* 601–616.

Eubanks, E. E., & Levine, D. U. (1983). A first look at effective schools projects in New York City and Milwaukee. *Education Leadership, 64*(10), 697–702.

Firestone, W. A., & Herriott, R. E. (1982). Prescription for effective elementary schools don't fit secondary schools. *Educational Leadership, 40*(3), 51–53.

Firestone, W. A., Herriott, R. E., & Wilson, B. L. (1984). *Explaining differences between elementary and secondary schools: Individual, organizational, and institutional perspectives.* Philadelphia: Research for Better Schools.

Floden, R. E., Alford, L., Freeman, D. J., Irwin, S., Porter, A. C., Schmidt, W. H., & Schwille, J. R.

(1984). *Elementary school principals' role in district and school curriculum change.* Paper presented at the American Educational Research Association meeting, New Orleans.

Fullan, M. (1982). *The meaning of educational change.* New York: Teachers College Press.

Gage, N. L. (1983). When does research on teaching yield implications for practice? *Elementary School Journal, 83,* 492–496.

Good, T. L., & Brophy, J. E. (1986). School effects. In M. C. Wittrock (Ed.), *Handbook of research on teaching* (3rd Ed.). New York: Macmillian.

Haney, W. (1977). *The follow-through planed variation experiments* (Vol. 5). Cambridge, MA: Huron Institute.

Holt, J. (1964). *How children fail.* New York: Pitman.

Jencks, C. S., Smith, M., Ackland, H., Bane, M. J., Cohen, D., Gintis, H., Heyns, B., & Michelson, S. (1972). *Inequality: A reassessment of the effect of family and schooling in America.* New York: Basic Books.

Kozol, J. (1967). *Death at an early age.* Boston: Houghton Mifflin.

Kyle, R. M. J. (Ed.). (1985). *Reaching for excellence: An effective schools sourcebook.* Washington, DC: E.H. White.

Lee, G. U. (1984). *Instructional management in the junior high school: The principal's role.* Paper presented at the American Educational Research Association meeting, New Orleans.

Leinhardt, G., & Bickel, W. E. (1987). (in press). Instruction's the thing wherein to catch the mind that falls behind. *Educational Psychologist, 22*(2), 177–207.

Leithwood, K. A., & Montgomery, D. J. (1982). The role of the elementary school principal in program, improvement. *Review of Educational Research, 52,* 309–339.

Lightfoot, S. L. (1983). *The good high school: Portraits of character and culture.* New York: Basic Books.

Lipsitz, J. (1984). *Successful schools for young adolescents.* New Brunswick, NJ: Transaction Books.

Mackenzie, D. E. (1983a). Research for school improvement: An appraisal of some recent trends. *Educational Researcher, 12*(4), 5–16.

Mackenzie, D. E. (1983b). School effectiveness research: A synthesis and assessment. In P. C. Duttweiler (Ed.), *Educational Productivity and school effectiveness.* Austin, TX: Southwest Educational Development Laboratory.

Madaus, G. F., Airasian, P. W., & Kellaghan, T. (1980). *A reassessment of the evidence: School effectiveness.* New York: McGraw-Hill.

Miles, M. B., Farrar, E., & Neufield, B. (1983). The extent of adoption of effective schools programs. *Vol. II of Review of effective schools programs.* Cambridge, MA: Huron Institute.

Miles, M. B., & Kaufman, T. (1985). A directory of programs. In R. M. J. Kyle (Ed.), *Reaching for excellence: An effective schools sourcebook.* Washington, DC: E.H. White.

National Commission on Excellence in Education. (1983). A nation at risk: The imperative for educational reform. Washington, DC: U.S. Department of Education.

Natriello, G., McDill, E. L., & Pallas, A. M. (1986). School reform and potential dropouts. *Educational Leadership, 43*(1), 10–15.

Odden, A., & Dougherty, U. (1982). State programs of school improvement: A 50-state survey. Denver, CO: Education Commission of the States.

Presseisien, B. Z. (1985). *Unlearned lessons.* Philadelphia, PA.: Palmer Press.

Purkey, S. C., & Smith, M. S. (1983). Effective schools: A review. *Elementary School Journal, 83,* 427–452.

Purkey, S. C., & Smith, M. S. (1985). School reform: The district policy implications of the effective schools literature. *Elementary School Journal, 85*(3), 353–389.

Reynolds, D., & Sullivan, M. (1981). The effects of school: A radical faith restated. In B. Hillham (Ed.), *Problem behavior in the secondary school.* London: Croom Helm.

Rich, J. M. (1985). *Innovations in education: Reformers and their ???.* Boston: Allyn and Bacon.

Rosenshine, B. V. (1983). Teaching functions in instructional programs. *Elementary School Journal, 83,* 335–352.

Rowan, B. (1985). The assessment of school effectiveness. In R. M. J. Kyle (Ed.), *Reaching for excellence: An effective schools sourcebook.* Washington, DC: E.H. White.

Rowen, B., Bossert, S. T., & Dwyer, D. C. (1983). Research on effective schools: A cautionary note. *Educational Researcher, 12*(4), 24–31.

Rowen, B., & Denk, C. E. (1982). Modeling the academic performance of schools. San Francisco: Far West Laboratory.

Rutter, M., Maughan, B., Morimore, P., Ouston, J., & Smith, A. (1979). *Fifteen thousand hours: Secondary schools and their effects on children.* Cambridge, MA: Harvard University Press.

Schlechty, P. C. (1985). District level policies and practices. In R. M. J. Kyle (Ed.), *Reaching for excellence: An effective schools sourcebook.* Washington, DC: E.H. White.

Schrag, P. (1975). Education's "romantic" critics. In S. Dropkin, H. Full, & E. Schwarcz (Eds.), *Contemporary American education.* New York: Macmillian.

Sergi, T. S., Brown, L., Burch, P., Gauthier, W., Speese, D., & Stewart, D. (1985). The role of the state education agency in school district improvement. In T. S. Sergi & J. Shoemaker (Eds.), *Improving student achievement.* Hartford: Connecticut State Department of Education.

Shulman, L. S. (1986). Paradigms and research programs in the study of teaching: A contemporary perspective. In M. C. Wittrock (Ed.), *Handbook of research on teaching* (3rd ed.). New York: Macmillan.

Silberman, C. (1970). *Crisis in the classroom.* New York: Random House.

Strike, K. (1985). Is there a conflict between equity and excellence? *Educational Evaluation and Policy Analysis, 7*(4), 409–416.

Tesconi, C. (1975). *Schooling in America.* Boston: Houghton Mifflin.

Troost, C. J. (1973). *Radical school reform.* Boston: Little, Brown.

U.S. Department of Education. (1986). *What works.* Washington, DC: Office of Educational Research and Improvement.

Venezky, R. L., & Winfield, L. F. (1979). *Schools that succeed beyond expectation in teaching* (Studies in Education Technical Report No. 1). Newark: University of Delaware.

Weber, G. (1971). *Inner-city children can be taught to read: Four successful schools.* Washington, DC: Council for Basic Education.

Wolff, M., & Stein, A. (1966). *Study I: Six months later, a comparison of children who had Head Start summer 1965 with their classmates in kindergarten* (EDO 15026). Washington, DC: Office of Educational Opportunity, Research and Evaluation Office.

35

EFFECTIVENESS OF SPECIAL EDUCATION

KEN KAVALE

University of Iowa

Special education is the segment of the education domain that deals with students experiencing difficulties in the regular system. To deal with these students, special education has developed a wide array of its own particular methods and materials. Although paralleling the regular education system, the promotion of an assortment of different procedures and techniques has caused special education to face continually a fundamental question: Is it effective? The purpose of this chapter is to explore that question.

THE HISTORY OF SPECIAL EDUCATION

Special education is not a new phenomenon. Its organized origins date back to the 18th century, with some isolated attempts to care for the handicapped dating back to the Stone Age (Hewett & Forness, 1984). Patton, Payne, Kauffman, Brown, and Payne (1987) partitioned the history of special education into chronological periods defined by the general social attitude prevalent at the time. They described eight periods: (a) period of abuse, neglect, ignorance, and benign acceptance (prior to 1700); (b) period of awareness and optimism (1740–1860); (c) period of skepticism (1860–

1900); (d) period of alarm (1900–1920); (e) period of limited progress (1920–1946); (f) period of renewed interest (1946–1960); (g) period of renewed optimism (1960–1970); and (h) period of reexamination (1970–present).

The plight of the handicapped was discussed by Hewett and Forness (1984) with respect to four critical aspects: (a) survival—the threat of harsh treatment or annihilation by the physical and social environments; (b) superstition—the wide range of beliefs related to the appearance and behavior of the handicapped; (c) science—attempts to understand and to approach the handicapped in a natural, lawful, and objective manner; and (d) service—the provision of humane treatment, care, education, and social acceptance.

Modern special education is usually traced to the work of Jean-Marc Gaspard Itard, a French physician who began the training of a feral child— Victor, the "wild boy of Aveyron"—in 1801. Although efforts to educate the deaf and the blind had been made before the beginning of the 19th century, it was Itard's work with Victor which marked the beginning of attempts to teach children with a variety of handicaps. Although the professional community acknowledged Itard's accomplishments, Itard was disappointed over his failure to make Victor more normal and the first controversy over "efficacy" was initiated.

Itard's work was continued by his student Edward O. Sequin, who published the classic *Idiocy and Its Treatment by the Physiological Method* in 1846. Sequin's influence can be seen in the modern classics, *Psychopathology and the Education of the Brain-Injured Child,* by Alfred Strauss and Laura Lehtinen published in 1947, and the 1960 volume by Newell Kephart entitled *The Slow Learner in the Classroom.* These volumes described particular programs and methods but also set the stage for questions about the effectiveness of these interventions. Although many of the issues surrounded basic philosophical concerns about treatment, the burgeoning special education literature found in professional journals (e.g., *Exceptional Children, Journal of Learning Disabilities, Journal of Special Education*) saw the debate rely increasingly upon empirical, scientific evidence to evaluate treatment effectiveness. This is not to say, however, that decisions about intervention efficacy have reached closure based on the empirical evidence. The data have not been unequivocal and have thus become entwined in political and ideological rhetoric associated with different "schools of thought" about special education.

Thus, special education possesses a relatively long history. Yet as Kauffman (1981) suggested, a review of special education history can lead to cynicism and despair because change, in the form of false hopes and easy solutions, has been more characteristic than has real progress. Many issues remain as points of controversy. Among the most prominent relates to the service aspect of special education and the question associated with it almost from the beginning: Is it effective?

THE MEANING OF SPECIAL EDUCATION

Special education may be defined as specially designed instruction that meets the unique needs of an exceptional child. An exceptional child is one who requires special education if his or her full human potential is to be realized. These common definitions (taken from Hallahan & Kauffman, 1986) suggest that special education can be conceived of as that subset of regular education that deals with children with special needs. But special education has also become an independent domain with its own philosophy and methodology. As such, special education experiences a tension between its natural science side, the scientific study of exceptional children and teaching, and its human science side, a helping profession aimed at improving the quality of life for exceptional children. Howell (1983) distinguished between special education as (a) the instruction of special pupils and (b) the use of special instruction. Although similar, these views differ; the first focuses on people while the second focuses on instruction. Special education appears to have emphasized the first view through a strong advocacy stance that has brought attention and resources to the education of exceptional children.

The desire to help people, however, has deflected attention away from the fact that the most effective help (i.e., instruction) should be based on scientific grounds. Without this scientific basis, special education becomes a variable enterprise that is sometimes effective but may also be ineffective. Special education possesses a respectable scientific base. The problem is that this base has never been communicated effectively and becomes confounded with the conventional wisdom whose overriding concern is helping. This tension between a humanistic spirit and a scientific reality has caused special education to become a target of those who question its value as a system separate from regular education. Periodically, special education is faced with a basic question: Is special education special (Milofsky, 1974)? Implied here is whether or not special education can be justified on a cost-benefit analysis basis. This represents a basic policy question and needs to be addressed through an analysis of the efficacy of the special practices that have come to be associated with the practice of special education.

The question of the effectiveness of special education is complicated by the growth of special education. In its early days, special education treated a relatively distinct population. The effectiveness of special education for the sensory handicapped, as an example, was relatively straightforward to document. The populations were relatively homogeneous and there was a continuous refinements of methods of treatment. Similar observations could be made for the physically handicapped and the severe levels of mental retardation and emotional disturbance. Although debate surrounded specific methods, there was a general belief that these populations were reasonably well served and that special education for these groups was a worthwhile and necessary enterprise.

Through advocacy efforts, however, special education grew and gradually encompassed less distinctive populations, such as the educable mentally retarded (EMR), the behaviorally disordered (BD), and the learning disabled (LD). The heterogeneity in these groups made it difficult to define the boundaries of these conditions with any precision (Hallahan & Kauffman, 1977). This mildly handicapped group continued to grow and now represents about 75% of the special education population. The interventions and practices used to treat this group also displayed significant growth. A situation developed wherein as the boundary conditions became less distinct, there was almost a concommitant increase in more special practices. Thus, questions about the effectiveness of special education became very real. The inability to provide any definitional precision in its terminology raised questions about the feasibility of special education which were only compounded by questions about the methods employed by special education: Are they effective? Has special education demonstrated enough efficacy in its unique procedures to warrant its continuation?

JUDGING THE EFFECTIVENESS OF SPECIAL EDUCATION

How does one judge the effectiveness of special education? Within the scientific context of special education, efficacy is best judged through an analysis of the existing research. The findings from special education research have not, however, provided a strong basis for making judgments about the efficacy of its practices. The reason is simple: Research in special education is a varied enterprise employing a variety of different paradigms, methods, and procedures. Special education presents a significant range in the types of research that can be found.

For example, both experimental and nonexperimental research can be found (Kerlinger, 1986). Nonexperimental research is usually associated with initial efforts to test clinically the efficacy of a new treatment. Although systematic, nonexperimental research possesses the basic flaw of not having the observer in direct control of independent variables making any conditional statement (i.e., If X, then Y) impossible. The lack of control in a nonexperimental study makes it difficult to determine whether the outcome was influenced by the treatment because of the possibility that a whole host of intervening variables may have influenced the outcome. The danger is in improper and erroneous interpretation, especially *post hoc, ergo propter hoc* (after this, therefore caused by this) even when seemingly plausible in light of occurring events.

The effectiveness of special education is best addressed through experimental research wherein it is possible to establish a cause-and-effect relationship. For example, when the question, "Does perceptual motor training improve academic performance?" is posed, it implies that when perceptual motor training is provided to students, their academic difficulties will be reduced *because* of the perceptual motor training. Three conditions are necessary, however, to establish cause and effect, including (a) a statistical relationship established through inferential tests, (b) a temporal sequence wherein the cause occurs before the effect, and (c) all other causes possible for the effect are ruled out. The unequivocal establishment of these three conditions is difficult and accounts for much of the difficulty encountered in interpreting research in special education.

The term *internal validity* (Campbell & Stanley, 1963) refers to the extent to which it can be claimed that the independent variable was responsible for or caused the dependent variable. The greater the internal validity, the more credible is the causal claim. Campbell and Stanley (1963) have discussed seven threats to internal validity which represent rival hypotheses or alternative explanations. These threats include history, maturation, testing, instrumentation, nonequivalence, regression, and mortality.

Resolution of the issues of internal validity permits the assumption that group differences were due to the treatment. This, however, leads to another task: To infer that the observed effect would also be observed in broader contexts. This is an issue of external validity and evolves around the question: How far can the experimental effect be generalized?

In a manner similar to that of Campbell and Stanley (1963), Bracht and Glass (1968) described threats to external validity. These threats may affect adversely population external validity (would the same effect be obtained with individuals other than those who participated directly as subjects?), ecological external validity (would the same effect be observed in other physical and social contexts?), and the external validity of operations (would other experimenters find the same effect?).

The effectiveness of special education has been investigated by a multitude of experimental research and has been a respectable form of disciplined inquiry (Cronbach & Suppes, 1969). The scientific method has been applied to studying the effectiveness of special education, yet controversy still rages over the question of the efficacy of interventions and practices falling under the rubric of special education. The problem resides in the fact that individual studies, because they have often not met unequivocally tenets of internal and external validity, have produced irresolute findings that are conflicting, inconstant, and sometimes paradoxical.

THE STATUS OF SPECIAL EDUCATION

The controversies surrounding research in special education led Andreski (1972) to argue that what passes as the scientific study of human behavior (e.g., special education) is little more than a form of sorcery. Instead of natural and predictable laws to explain phenomena, sorcery includes a primitive cause and effect termed sympathetic magic whereby events are assumed to exert influence on other events even though separated by space, time, and distance. One subset of sympathetic magic, homeopathic magic, is based on the principle of similarity ("like produces like"). When these magical principles are applied in the wrong places to the wrong events, they possess the irreparable flaw of unreliability (the magic neither produces nor influences the phenomenon). Unfortunately, some modern conceptions in special education evidence such magical thinking. For example, the assertion that patterning exercises to enhance neurological organization improves language and reading ability represents a form of homeopathic magic.

Special education's scientific method has been based on an approach termed "empiricism," defined as an emphasis on data collection and analysis. From an empiricist point of view, more is better. The primary difficulty is that these data are not joined theoretically and thus remain as isolated elements with no rational connection. Any individual study is not part of a logical research program

building knowledge cumulatively but rather is part of the search for the "perfect" study that will be the all-time true and unassailable fact about the effectiveness of some special education technique. But no single study approaches that perfectness and is thus subjected to criticism about its shortcomings and inconsistencies. The outcome is a variety of schools of thought that function on an ethnocentric basis wherein our ideas are sensible but theirs are not. The consequences are found in a separatism that characterizes special education and creates an unhealthy competition characterized by complexity, confusion, and chaos.

Decisions about the efficacy of special education might be aided if study data could be accumulated in a manner that makes it "usable knowledge" (Lindblom & Cohen, 1979). This is provided by the research review where results from independent studies are combined in an effort to show consistent and generalizable patterns. Traditionally, research has been combined through either narrative methods providing a verbal report of individual studies or numerical methods providing a "box score" tally based on statistical significance.

The inherent problems of traditional reviews is well illustrated by the debate over the effectiveness of psycholinguistic training which has raged for over 20 years in special education. If you were faced with deciding whether or not to include psycholinguistic training within the remedial curriculum, a reasonable approach would be based on "what the research says." The research has been combined in reviews and would reveal that the *Illinois Test of Psycholinguistic Abilities* (ITPA) (Kirk, McCarthy, & Kirk, 1968) has served as the clinical model for a variety of remedial and developmental language programs. These programs are based on the assumption that language is comprised of discrete components and that these components can be trained. It is this last assumption that has precipitated debate over the efficacy of psycholinguistic training. Further examination of the literature would identify reviews summarizing available primary research. At this point, however, knowledge becomes obscured and the decision process grows complex.

To illustrate, Hammill and Larsen (1974) constructed a table that paralleled statistical significance (.05 level) or nonsignificance and summarized the findings from 39 studies for either total ITPA score, ITPA subtests, or both. Two other aggregations, for subject groups and psycholinguistic constructs, were based on the percentage of positive analyses. Hammill and Larsen (1974) concluded that "researchers have been unsuccessful in developing those skills which would enable their subjects to do well on ITPA [and] the idea that psycholinguistic constructs, as measured by ITPA, can be trained by existing techniques remains nonvalidated" (pp. 10–11).

Minskoff (1975) offered a critique of Hammill and Larsen's (1974) review which suggested that "because of Hammill and Larsen's oversimplified approach, 39 studies with noncomparable subjects and treatments were grouped together. Moreover, for the most part, they reviewed methodologically inadequate studies in which there was short-term training using general approaches to treatment primarily with mentally retarded or disadvantaged subjects having no diagnosed learning disabilities" (p. 137). In effect, Minskoff (1975) suggested that Hammill and Larsen had compared "apples and oranges." Ten specific methodological errors were described that limited conclusions drawn from the studies. Minskoff (1975) then provided guidelines for research on psycholinguistic training and suggested that psycholinguistic disabilities can be trained, and a major criterion for evaluating effectiveness should be its relationship to various academic and social demands made upon a child at a particular age. Minskoff (1975) concluded by decrying the skepticism surrounding psycholinguistic training since, "it can be dangerous if it leads to the abolition of training methods that may be beneficial to some children with psycholinguistic disabilities" (p. 143).

Immediately following was a response by Newcomer, Larsen, and Hammill (1975) which contested the major points made by Minskoff (1975). Suffice it to say that the rhetoric became increasingly confusing and enmeshed in trivial controversy. Nevertheless, Newcomer et al. (1975) contended that "the reported literature raises doubts regarding the efficacy of presently available Kirk-Osgood psycholinguistic training programs. . ." (p. 147).

The debate lay dormant for some 3 years when Lund, Foster, and McCall-Perez (1978) offered a reevaluation of the 39 studies reviewed by Hammill and Larsen (1974). The studies were reexamined individually to determine the validity of negative conclusions regarding the effectiveness of psycholinguistic training. Six of the 24 studies clearly showed positive results for psycholinguistic

training and "contraindicate the conclusions that such training is nonvalidated" (p. 317). Of 10 studies showing negative results, only two were reported accurately. The remaining eight were either equivocal or showed positive results. Lund et al. (1978) thus reached conclusions markedly at variance with the statement that psycholinguistic training is nonvalidated:

> Our analysis indicates that some studies show significant positive results as measured by ITPA, some studies show positive results in the areas remediated, and some do not show results from which any conclusions can be drawn. It is, therefore, not logical to conclude either that all studies in psycholinguistic training are effective or that all studies in psycholinguistic training are not effective. (p. 317)

The special education community did not wait long for the debate to continue. Hammill and Larsen (1978) reaffirmed their original position. Their rebuttal concluded with the statement that

> the cumulative results of the pertinent research have failed to demonstrate that psycholinguistic training has value, at least with the ITPA as the criterion for successful training. It is important to note that, regardless of the reevaluations by propsycholinguistic educators, the current state of the research strongly questions the efficacy of psycholinguistic functioning need to be viewed cautiously and monitored with great care. (Hammill & Larsen, 1978, p. 413)

Thus, after some 5 years of feckless debate, polemics abounded but a nagging question remained: What is really known about the efficacy of psycholinguistic training? Increasingly, the principal issue had become entangled in a maze of extraneous detail only tangentially related to the major question. Because the clarity, explicitness, and openness required in the review process were lacking, reviewers were bound to see things differently. Consequently, trustworthy conclusions had not emerged.

The practitioner is offered little assistance in solving the riddles contained in conflicting research evidence through the traditional research review. In an effort to promote a point of view, traditional review methods are susceptible to a dismissal of scientific method. In the case of psycholinguistic training, it is not important that Hammill and Larsen, Minskoff, and Lund, Foster, and McCall-Perez disagreed, but rather that they did not approach the research review with a methodology so explicit, unambiguous, and well defined that even someone with only a cursory knowledge of special education could examine the same evidence and reach the same conclusion.

QUANTITATIVE METHODS OF RESEARCH SYNTHESIS

The theoretical and pragmatic difficulties of traditional methods led to the development of quantitative methods (e.g., Fisher, 1938; Jones & Fiske, 1953) which were reintroduced by Glass (1976, 1977), in what has come to be known as meta-analysis (the analysis of analyses). As a statistical analysis of the findings from many empirical studies, meta-analysis possesses the following advantages: (a) it is quantitative—it uses statistical methods for organizing and extracting information from large data bases; (b) it eliminates bias in study selection by not prejuding research quality; (c) it makes use of all information—study findings are transformed to commensurable expressions of magnitude of experimental effect or relationship; (d) it detects statistical interactions—study characteristics that mediate findings are defined, measured, and their covariation with findings is studied; and (e) it seeks general conclusions—practical implications require simplicity which does not do violence to important interactive conclusions. The satisfaction of these requirements allows for the systematic and statistical summarization of study findings necessary for discovering that knowledge that lies untapped in extant special education research.

The method of meta-analysis have been described and debated (see Glass, McGaw, & Smith, 1981), and while not universally accepted, are now an established means of summarizing statistically a research domain. Technical advances (see Hedges & Olkin, 1985; Hunter, Schmidt, & Jackson, 1982) in meta-analysis have served to increase the objectivity, verifiability, and replicability of the quantitative review process (Kavale, 1983).

Meta-analysis is based on a metric "effect size" which transforms individual study data into standard deviation units (z-scores). The effect size is defined by $ES = \overline{X}_e - \overline{X}_c/SD_c$, where $\overline{X}_e$ is the average score for the experimental group on an outcome measure, $\overline{X}_c$ the average score for the control group on an outcome measure, and SD_c the standard deviation of the control groups.

Individual ES calculations may then be combined and recombined into different aggregations representing average treatment effects (ES). The meaning of ES can be translated into notions of overlapping distributions and comparable percentiles. For example, suppose that a hypothetical study investigating the efficacy of Temporal Centripetal Therapy revealed an ES of +1.00. The ES of +1.00 obtained indicates an average superiority of one standard deviation for the treatment groups. If two separate distributions are drawn for those receiving therapy and those in the control condition, the distributions will be separated by one standard deviation at their means, as shown in Figure 1.

The average of the therapy curve is located above 84% of the area under the control group curve. This relationship suggests that the average child receiving therapy was better off than 84% of the control group, while only 16% of the control group were left better off than the average child receiving therapy.

In some instances, ES's are meaningful without comparison. For example, a zero ES or negative ES is categorically clear and meaningful in and of itself. Several other possibilities exist for interpreting the magnitude of ES. Comparison might be done within a single meta-analysis. Suppose that two innovative special teaching programs are compared with traditional classroom instruction: the ES for comparisons of method A and traditional instruction was .50 favoring method A,

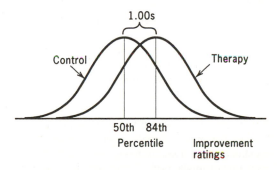

Figure 1. Findings from a hypothetical study assessing the efficacy of temporal centripetal therapy.

while method B produced an ES of .25 when compared to traditional instruction. Thus, method A was half again more beneficial than method B.

It is also possible to add meaning to ES by reference to known interventions. It is known, for example, that the average pupil will gain 10 months of achievement in a school year. Thus, the average third-grade pupil will score 3.0 in early September and 4.0 at the end of the school year. With the known standard deviation of 1.0 grade-equivalent unit of most elementary achievement tests, the ES for one year's instruction at the elementary school level is +1.00. This ES can then be used as a basis for comparison. Suppose that a new remedial technique (Intervention X) is introduced and the combined ES from a number of validation studies is .25. This ES is one-fourth as great as the effect of instruction itself (.25 versus 1.00). Hence, Intervention X benefits the average treated subject by the equivalent of one-fourth school year of teaching.

META-ANALYSIS AND SPECIAL EDUCATION

Kavale (1984) described the potential advantages of meta-analysis in terms of understanding and explanation. Meta-analysis, as an empirical and systematic form of applied epistemology, imparts a clarity, explicitness, and openness necessary to make research findings believeable. The findings of several meta-analyses will be presented so that they may be compared and contrasted with conclusions from traditional reviews.

PROCESS TRAINING

The issue of process training possesses a long and glorious history in special education (see Mann, 1979). Its intuitive appeal is great but its efficacy is the subject of both positive and negative interpretation. The empirical evidence, however, typically provides only equivocal findings.

Psycholinguistic Training

The long-standing debate over the efficacy of psycholinguistic training was outlined earlier. The inconclusiveness of both narrative and vote counting reviews discouraged any conclusive decisions and it remained unclear whether psycholinguistic training should be included in remedial programs.

Kavale (1981) performed a metal-analysis on 34 studies investigating the effectiveness of psycholinguistic training. The 34 studies yielded 240 ES's that produced an overall ES of .39. This finding was based on data representing approximately 1850 subjects who averaged 7.5 years of age with a mean IQ of 82 and who received an average of 50 hours of psycholinguistic training. Thus, the average subject receiving psycholinguistic training stands at approximately the 65th percentile of subjects receiving no special psycholinguistic training; the latter remain at the 50 percentile.

Table 1 presents ES's classified by ITPA subtest. These ES's are modest by most standards. If subtests where the data are thin (i.e., 5 or fewer ES's) are eliminated, five of the nine subtests show small, albeit positive, effects. It is questionable whether these psycholinguistic abilities respond to training and whether they should be subjected to training. The case is different for four abilities: Auditory and Visual Association, and Verbal and Manual Expression. For these psycholinguistic abilities, training improves functioning from 15 to 23 percentile ranks. Thus, the average trained subject would be better off than approximately 65 to 73% of untrained subjects in associative or expressive abilities.

Subtests of the ITPA were patterned upon psycholinguistic constructs derived from Osgood's (1957) model of communication. Table 2 presents an analysis of the effects of training upon theoretical psycholinguistic dimensions underlying the ITPA. Expressive Processes showed the greatest response to psycholinguistic training while such training produced small effects for Receptive Processes and Automatic Levels subtests. The box score analysis offered by Hammill and Larsen (1974) suggested that both Representational level and the Visual-Motor Modality were not particularly responsive to training. The ES's of .40 and .38, respectively, for these abilities belie such an interpretation. The ES data from meta-analysis are not confounded by elusive percentages of improvement but command a direct interpretation. Consequently, the 15- and 14-percentile-rank improvement shown by trained subjects in Representational Level and Visual-Motor Modalities subtest cannot be easily dismissed.

The ES data were next integrated by study features, and the findings are shown in Table 3. Not surprisingly, prescriptive/individualized ap-

TABLE 1   Average Effect Sizes for ITPA Subtests

ITPA Subtest	Mean Effect Size	Number of Effect Sizes
Auditory Reception	.21	20
Visual Reception	.21	20
Auditory Association	.44	24
Visual Association	.39	21
Verbal Expression	.63	24
Manual Expression	.54	23
Grammatic Closure	.30	21
Visual Closure	.48	5
Auditory Sequential Memory	.32	21
Visual Sequential Memory	.27	21
Auditory Closure	−.05	3
Sound Blending	.38	3

proaches were found superior to generalized/nonindividualized methods. As with many other educational approaches, individualized instruction proved superior. The next finding was surprising; the *Peabody Language Development Kits* (PDLK) (L. M. Dunn & Smith, 1967) demonstrated the largest $\overline{ES}$ when compared to both ITPA-related activities and other methods (sensory, perceptual, or motor training activities).

On the surface, the superiority of the PDLK appears contrary to expectation since ITPA-type activities should be most closely related to the criterion measure, the ITPA itself. Upon reflection, these findings are not surprising if viewed in terms of program structure. The PDLK represents a

highly structured sequence of lessons designed to increase general verbal ability. Although ITPA training procedures are based on the Osgood-Kirk model (Bush & Giles, 1977; Kirk & Kirk, 1971), they are only suggestions and guidelines for training activities. As such, they do not provide the sequential, structured activities found in the PDLK. Consequently, they do not represent a comprehensive training package but merely examples for psycholinguistic training activities which must

TABLE 2   Average Effect Size for ITPA Psycholinguistic Constructs

Dimension	Construct	Mean Effect Size
Level	Representational	.40
	Automatic	.21
Processes	Reception	.21
	Organization	.32
	Expression	.59
Modalities	Auditory-Verbal	.32
	Visual-Motor	.38

TABLE 3   Average Effect Size for Study Features

Feature	Mean Effect Size	Number of Effect Sizes
Approach		
General	.37	38
Prescriptive	.49	6
Method		
ITPA	.30	12
PDLK	.49	14
Other	.35	9
Subjects		
MR	.31	18
CD	.41	18
Level		
Preschool	.39	14
Elementary	.39	20

be structured and planned by individual teachers (Kavale, 1982b).

Comparisons of different subject populations' responses to psycholinguistic training indicated that disadvantaged (CD) children were more positively affected than were mentally retarded (MR) subjects. When the MR group was divided, however, differences emerged. The educable mentally retarded (EMR) subjects revealed an $\overline{ES}$ of .39, while trainable mentally retarded (TMR) subjects exhibited an $\overline{ES}$ of .22. Thus, EMR subjects showed training effects about equal to those found for CD subjects. Finally, age comparisons of psycholinguistic training yielded no differences between preschool and elementary-level subjects.

The validity of experimental designs has been a primary battleground in the psycholinguistic training question. By using the Campbell and Stanley (1963) criteria, it is possible to judge the internal validity of a study. Judgments about these factors resulted in a rating of internal validity as either low, medium, or high, which are then correlated with the ES that the study produces. The primary question is whether the domain studied contain "good" and "bad" studies which reveal different findings. If the quality of design (in the Campbell and Stanley sense) did correlate with ES, the "best" studies must be believed. In the case of no correlation between design quality and treatment effect (ES), no distinction between "good" and "bad" studies is necessary since the total picture would be unchanged because findings from both sets would be essentially the same. This was found to be the case for the psycholinguistic training literature. When internal validity was correlated with ES, a small positive correlation was found ($r = 0.22$). The conclusion by Newcomer et al. (1975) that "if the sources of error which exist in any of these studies were corrected, the results would be even bleaker regarding the merits of psycholinguistic training" (p. 45) was not supported by the resulting correlation. The absence of an association suggests that there is no basis for discarding poor-quality studies from the body of evidence since design considerations account for only 5% of the variance in the results of studies. Hence, indictment of the psycholinguistic training literature on the basis of design flaws is not warranted and the 34 studies reviewed reflect accurately the outcomes of such training.

The findings of this meta-analysis appear to provide an affirmative answer to the question of the effectiveness of psycholinguistic training. Serious doubt must be cast upon previous conclusions, such as "the overwhelming consensus of research evidence concerning the effectiveness of psycholinguistic training is that it remains essentially non-validated" (Hammill & Larsen, 1978, p. 412).

Findings for ITPA total score and subtest scores provided validation for the benefits of psycholinguistic training. Hammill and Larsen (1974) probably overstated their case when they concluded their review of the same literature with the statement that "neither the ITPA subtests nor their theoretical constructs are particularly ameliorative" (p. 12). Clearly, the findings regarding the receptiveness to intervention of the Expressive constructs, particularly Verbal Expression, and the Representational Level subtests are encouraging since they embody the "language" aspects of the ITPA and, ultimately, productive language behavior.

These findings, however, only fueled the debate over the efficacy of psycholinguistic training. Larsen, Parker, and Hammill (1982) suggested that the Kavale (1981) meta-analysis analyzed a body of literature that was more favorable to psycholinguistic training, and was thus different from that used by Hammill and Larsen (1974). The difference, however, was only four studies which would have added 28 ES measurements to the 240 obtained. These data would have led to a decline in $\overline{ES}$ of .04, on average, across subtests. Overall, the $\overline{ES}$ would decline from .39 to .35, which means that instead of 65% of children receiving psycholinguistic being better off than a control group (50%), 64% would now be better off. This is an inconsequential decline and hardly qualifies as an inflated estimate.

For a basic area such as language, the average elementary school pupil gains about one standard deviation ($\overline{ES} = +1.00$) over the school year and exceeds about 84% of the pupils' scores made on a language achievement measure at the beginning of the school year. The approximately 60% success rate for training Verbal Expression is thus substantial and is particularly important for EMR and CD children, who are likely to manifest difficulties in this area. In fact, roughly 50 hours of psycholinguistic training produce benefits on the Verbal Expression subtest ($\overline{ES} = .63$) exceeding that which would be expected from one-half year of schooling in language achievement ($\overline{ES} = .50$).

Larsen et al. (1982) as well as Sternberg and Taylor (1982) questioned the findings on a cost-benefit basis since the gains represented only about 15 to 20 items across ITPA subtests. A distinction was made between statistical significance and practical significance, with Sternberg and Taylor (1982) pursuing the question, "Does the increase of only two or three items per subtest within this instrument really made a *clinically significant* difference?" (p. 255).

The answer is affirmative and the example of Verbal Expression demonstrates why. In concrete terms, the $\overline{ES}$ obtained for Verbal Expression (.63) translates into improvement by perhaps an additional half-dozen correct responses on a test such as the ITPA. If these six items are considered proxies for hundreds of skills, abilities, and bits of information, an improvement in these seemingly few items is significant. Consider an analogous situation: A child with IQ 130 answers perhaps nine more Information questions or nine more Vocabulary items on the WISC-R than does a child with IQ 100. Does this suggest that the difference between IQ 100 and IQ 130 is nine bits of knowledge? Certainly the abilities involved transcend nine pieces of information or words. Similarly, improvement on a test of Verbal Expression represents more than the expected increase of six items since it comprises a complex amalgam of language abilities. Thus, for a child deficient in the areas enhanced by psycholinguistic training, remedial programs are likely to provide salutary effects and advantages for the child which probably surpass the abilities themselves.

Perceptual-Motor Training

Among the more popular intervention approaches in special education is perceptual-motor training. Its popularity is based partially on historical considerations as well as a variety of clinical reports attesting to the efficacy of perceptual-motor training (e.g., Arena, 1969; Ayres, 1972; Barsch, 1967; Chaney & Kephart, 1968; Cratty, 1969; Forstig & Horne, 1964; Getman, Kane, Halgren, & McKee, 1968; MacQuarrie, 1967; Van Witsen, 1967).

There have been, however, a number of experimental studies testing the validity of perceptual-motor interventions. Selected studies have been reviewed previously (e.g., Balow, 1971; Footlik, 1971; Goodman & Hammill, 1973; Hammill, Goodman, & Weiderholt, 1974; Keogh, 1978; Mann & Goodman, 1976). The conclusions

drawn did not favor perceptual-motor interventions but urged caution because of faulty reporting and unsound methodological procedures. There have also been philosophical attacks challenging the theoretical and empirical foundations of perceptual motor training programs (Mann, 1970, 1971a) but they have not gone unchallenged (Kephart, 1972).

Kavale and Mattson (1983) found 180 experiments assessing the efficacy of perceptual-motor training. A total of 637 $\underline{ES}$ measurements were obtained and represented about 13,000 subjects who averaged 8 years of age with an average IQ of 89 and received an average of 65 hours of perceptual-motor training. The $\overline{ES}$ across 637 $\underline{ES}$ measurements was .082, which in relative terms indicates that a child who is no better off than average (i.e., at the 50th percentile) rises to the 53rd percentile as a result of perceptual-motor interventions. At the end of treatment, the average trained subject was better off than 53% of control subjects, a gain only slightly better than no treatment at all. Additionally, of 637 $\underline{ES}$'s, 48% were negative, suggesting that the probability of obtaining a positive response to training is only slightly better than chance.

The overall effect of perceptual-motor training is thus negligible. Perhaps a single index may mask an important subset where perceptual-motor training is more effective. Consequently, $\underline{ES}$ data were aggregated into increasingly differentiated groupings of outcome measures and the findings are shown in Tables 4, 5, and 6.

These findings speak for themselves. Regardless of how global or discrete the aggregation, the effects of perceptual-motor training present an unbroken vista of disappointment. There are no positive effects and nothing indicative of an effective intervention.

TABLE 4   Average Effect Size for Perceptual Motor Outcome Classes

Outcome Class	Mean Effect Size	Number of Effect Sizes
Perceptual/Sensory Motor	.166	233
Academic Achievement	.013	283
Cognitive/Aptitude	.028	95
Adaptive Behavior	.267	26

TABLE 5   Average Effect Sizes for Perceptual Motor General Outcome Categories

General Outcome Categories	Mean Effect Size	Number of Effect Sizes
Perceptual/Sensory Motor		
Gross motor	.214	44
Fine motor	.178	28
Visual perception	.149	145
Auditory perception	.122	16
Academic Achievement		
Readiness	.076	69
Reading	−.039	142
Arithmetic	.095	26
Language	.031	18
Spelling	.021	16
Handwriting	.053	12
Cognitive/Aptitude		
Verbal IQ	−.007	53
Performance IQ	.068	34

TABLE 6   Average Effect Sizes for Perceptual Motor Specific Outcome Categories

General Outcome Categories	Mean Effect Size	Number of Effect Sizes
Gross Motor Skills		
Body awareness/image	.256	22
Balance/posture	.263	14
Locomotor skills	−.017	8
Visual Perceptual Skills		
Visual discrimination	.146	31
Figure–ground discrimination	.173	28
Visual-motor ability	.222	26
Visual integration	.086	17
Visual spatial perception	.144	16
Visual memory	.062	15
Reading Achievement		
Word recognition	−.016	36
Comprehension	−.055	33
Oral reading	−.037	17
Vocabulary	−.012	25
Speed/rate	−.038	8

TABLE 7   Average Effect Size for Subject Groups

Subject	Mean Effect Size	Number of Effect Sizes
Normal	.054	58
Educable Mentally Retarded (IQ = 50–75)	.132	143
Trainable Mentally Retarded (IQ = 25–50)	.147	66
Slow Learner (IQ = 75–90)	.098	14
Culturally Disadvantaged	.045	85
Learning Disabled	.018	77
Reading Disabled	−.007	74
Motor Disabled	.121	118

Tables 7 and 8 provide aggregated ES data for two study features: diagnostic category and grade level. Interpretation is unclouded: essentially zero effects are seen in all groups and at all grades. Nothing in these data suggest any selected benefits for perceptual-motor training. In no instance was perceptual-motor intervention effective; in fact, among the lowest ES's were those found for learning/reading disabled children for whom perceptual-motor training is a favored treatment approach.

Perceptual-motor training programs have taken a variety of forms and the names associated with these programs read like the roster from the Special Education Hall of Fame. The ES's for the various training methods are shown in Table 9. Again the findings offer a bleak picture; there is nothing even hinting at positive effects. The studies investigating the efficacy of individual programs included studies performed by both program advocates themselves and independent investigators. A single example will reveal the fragility of such empirical findings. The Delacato program (e.g., Delacato, 1959), based on the concept of neurological patterning, was assessed by both Delacato disciples (see Delacato, 1966) and more critical investigators (e.g., H. J. Cohen, Birch, & Taft, 1970; Glass & Robbins, 1967). The Delacato sources produced an ES of .723, while the non-Delacato sources revealed an ES of −.242.

Ratings of internal validity for the 180 studies reviewed found 83 (46%) rated low, 62 (35%) rated medium, and 35 (19%) were rated high. The largest ES was associated with low internal validity (ES = .198), while the medium and high

TABLE 8   Average Effect Sizes for Grade Level

Level	Mean Effect Size	Number of Effect Sizes
Preschool	.053	47
Kindergarten	.099	129
Primary (Grades 1–3)	.079	226
Middle (Grades 4–6)	.066	74
Junior high school	.085	94
High school	.088	67

TABLE 9   Average Effect Sizes for Perceptual Motor Training Programs

Training Program	Mean Effect Size	Number of Effect Sizes
Barsch	.157	18
Cratty	.113	27
Delacato	.161	79
Frostig	.096	173
Getman	.124	48
Kephart	.064	132
Combination	.057	78
Other	−.021	82

internal validity categories exhibited progressively smaller $\overline{ES}$ of .042 and $-.119$, respectively. The average effect for studies with many sources of invalidity translates into an 8-percentile-rank gain compared to the 2-percentile-rank loss for studies rated high on internal validity. On average, a trained subject in studies with adequate research design and control was worse off than 52% of control subjects receiving no perceptual-motor intervention.

Contrary to the suggestion that the available evidence does not allow either a positive or negative evaluation of perceptual-motor training (Hallahan & Cruickshank, 1973), this meta-analysis indicated that the necessary empirical evidence is presently available. It is not premature to draw definitive conclusions regarding the efficacy of perceptual-motor interventions since the available research offers the negative evidence necessary for questioning the value of perceptual-motor training. Yet the deep historical roots and strong clinical tradition will make difficult the removal of perceptual-motor training from its prominent position as a treatment technique.

Modality Training

The practice of assessing abilities and devising subsequent instruction in accord with assessed modality patterns possesses a long history and an intuitive appeal (e.g., R. S. Dunn, 1979). Arter and Jenkins (1977) found that 99% of teachers surveyed thought that a child's modality strengths and weaknesses should be considered and that a child learned more when instruction was modified to match modality patterns. Whether it is termed the modality model, aptitude $\times$ treatment interaction, differential programming or diagnostic-prescriptive teaching, the benefits are widely believed (e.g., R. S. Dunn & K. J. Dunn, 1978) even though the weight of the evidence suggests a negative evaluation (e.g., Cronbach & Snow, 1977; Tarver & Dawson, 1978). Yet the deep historical roots and strong clinical support has prevented the modality model from being dislodged from the repertoire of special education practices (Carbo, 1983).

Kavale and Forness (1987) synthesized data from 39 studies evaluating the modality model. The 39 studies yielded 318 $\underline{ES}$ measurements and represented about 3100 subjects whose average age was 8.66 years and average IQ was 98. Because the modality model includes two components, testing and teaching, no substantive insight is provided by a single index.

On the assessment side, the $\underline{ES}$ measurements indicate the level of group differentiation between subjects chosen because of assessed modal preferences and these demonstrating no such preferences. A total of 113 $\underline{ES}$ measurements were concerned with assessment and are shown in Table 10. The first $\overline{ES}$ column represents the magnitude of group differentiation as originally calculated. But one difficulty surrounds the reliability of the tests used to assess modality (Ysseldyke & Salvia, 1980), which suggests that these $\underline{ES}$ measurements need to be corrected for the influence of measurement error in order to provide a "true" level of group differentiation (see Hunter et al., 1982).

Across the 113 $\underline{ES}$ measurements, for example, the $\overline{ES}$, after correction, declined from .931 to .512. This means that, on average, 70% of subjects demonstrating a modality preference could be differentiated clearly on the basis of their test scores, while 30% could not be distinguished unequivocally. With the original $\overline{ES}$ (.931), the one standard deviation (SD) difference typically used to establish modality groups was approached but when corrected for measurement error, found that only 7 out of 10 subjects actually demonstrated a modality preference score different

TABLE 10   Effects of Modality Assessments

Modality	Number of Effect Sizes	Mean Effect Size (Uncorrected)	Mean Effect Size (Corrected)	Percent of Subjects Differentiated from Comparison Group
Auditory	47	.925	.552	71%
Visual	46	.899	.506	70%
Kinesthetic	20	.970	.430	67%

enough to warrant placement in a particular modality preference group, while 3 out of 10 would be misplaced in a modality preference group. For each modality area, the uncorrected $\overline{ES}$ approached the required one SD for modality group membership. Each modality area, however, declined by approximately four-tenths SD after correction for measurement error to an average of about 70% correct placement decisions.

Thus, although modality assessments were presumed to differentiate subjects on the basis of modality preferences, there was, in actuality, considerable overlap between preference and nonpreference groups. Much of the difficulty was the result of test unreliability, and when $\underline{ES}$ was corrected for test unreliability, it was found that measurement error reduced the distinction among modality groups to a level no better than, on average, two out of three correct placement decisions.

Besides assessing modality preferences, the 39 studies also evaluated the effect of matching instruction to preferred modalities. Of the 318 $\underline{ES}$ measurements, 205 assessed the effectiveness of modality teaching and the findings are displayed in Table 11. The 205 $\underline{ES}$ measurements produced an $\overline{ES}$ of .144, which translates into only a 6-percentile-rank improvement. This indicates that 56% of experimental subjects were better off after modality instruction, but this is only slightly above chance level (50%) and indicates conversely that 44% of experimental subjects did not reveal any gain. Furthermore, 72 $\underline{ES}$ measurements (35%) were negative, indicating that over one-third of subjects receiving instruction matched to their preferred learning modality actually scored less well than control subjects receiving no special instruction. These findings were similar across modalities.

Within the achievement domain, reading was a primary area where the effects of modality matched instruction was evaluated. Reading achievement data are displayed in Table 12. Across modalities, modality teaching produced gains of from 2 (comprehension) to 7 (vocabulary, spelling) percentile ranks. These levels of improvement are modest by any standard. Thus, modality teaching affects positively, albeit modestly, vocabulary and spelling, but only 57% of experimental subjects would show benefits, while 43% would not exhibit benefits from modality-based instruction. Individual modalities paralleled these overall findings.

Thus, modality instruction had only modest effects on improving reading abilities. Some differences in effectiveness emerged when instructional methods were matched to modality preferences but the positive effects were small. When modality instruction was evaluated across reading skills, 50% (6 out of 12) of the comparisons revealed effects that were not different from zero (as shown by a 95% confidence interval).

Arter and Jenkins (1977) suggested requirements for an "ideal" research design for modality model research. To determine if these methodological problems affected study outcomes, studies were rated on internal validity (low, medium, or high) according to criteria drawn from Arter and Jenkins (1977) as well as from Campbell and Stanley (1963). Of the 39 studies, 3 (8%) were rated high, 22 (56%) were rated medium, and 14 (35%) were rated low on internal validity.

Again, the primary question is whether the best designed studies yield evidence dramatically different than that from poorly designed studies. When $\underline{ES}$ data (for instruction only) were aggregated by internal validity rating, the low category

TABLE 11   Effects of Modality Matched Instruction

Method	Number of Effect Sizes	Mean Effect Size	Standard Error of Effect Size	Percentile Status of Experimental Subject in Control Group
Auditory	80	.184	.028	57
Visual	81	.086	.037	54
Kinesthetic	44	.175	.045	57

TABLE 12   Effects of Modality Matched Instruction on Reading Skills

	Modality														
	Total			Auditory			Visual			Kinesthetic		
	n^a	ES(SE)[b]	%[c]	n	ES(SE)	%	n	ES(SE)	%	n	ES(SE)	%
Word												
Recognition	75	.150(.039)	56	28	.203(.052)	58	33	.081(.072)	53	14	.197(.083)	58
Comprehension	38	.046(.051)	52	15	.062(.074)	52	16	.034(.081)	51	7	.041(.127)	52
Vocabulary	45	.174(.041)	57	18	.194(.060)	58	17	.141(.064)	56	10	.185(.097)	58
Spelling	47	.184(.037)	57	19	.249(.052)	60	15	.088(.066)	54	13	.216(.078)	59

[a]n = number of effect sizes.
[b]ES = mean effect size; (SE) = standard error of mean effect size.
[c]% = percentile status of experimental (modality matched) subject in comparison group.

(n = 66) produced the largest $\overline{ES}$ (.208), followed by the medium category (n = 121) with an $\overline{ES}$ of .125, and finally, the high category (n = 18) with the lowest $\overline{ES}$ (.037). The low-rated category $\overline{ES}$ was significantly greater than the $\overline{ES}$ of the high-rated category. Furthermore, a 95% confidence interval for the high-rated category spanned zero, suggesting that the best studies showed no positive effects for modality teaching. Although the poorest studies produced the largest effects, their instructional outcomes were quite modest, the inclusion of poor data did not appear to alter significantly the generally negative picture for modality teaching.

In providing answers to the question "Why teach through modality strengths?", Barbe and Milone (1981) suggested that (a) modality-based instruction is logical, (b) modality-based instruction is already practiced by teachers to some extent, and (c) research supports the contention that modality-based instruction works. The present findings contradict that last assumption since research evidence, when integrated statistically, did not render support for the effectiveness of the modality model.

Although the presumption of matching instructional strategies to individual modality preferences to enhance learning efficiency has great intuitive appeal, little empirical support for this proposition was found from the quantitative synthesis of the extant research. With respect to modality assessment, it was shown that groups seemingly differentiated on the basis of modality preferences actually revealed considerable overlap and it was doubtful whether any of the presumed preferences could really be deemed preferences.

On the teaching side, little (or no) gain in achievement was found when instructional methods were matched to preferred learning modality. Only modest improvement was demonstrated for either auditory, visual, or kinesthetic teaching methods.

The present negative findings contravene the conventional wisdom found in statements such as: "All children do not learn the same way. They relay on different sensory modes to help them. Some depend heavily on their sense of sight, other on their sense of hearing, and still others on their sense of touch. The mode they use influences their classroom behavior and achievement" (Barbe & Milone, 1980, p. 45).

Although the modality model has been long accepted as true, the present findings disclosed that the modality model is not effective and efforts would be better directed at improving more substantive aspects of the teaching–learning process. Both aspects of the modality model, testing and teaching, appeared problematic. No reliable assignment of subjects to preferred modality was found and no appreciable gain was found by differentiating instruction according to modality preference. Consequently, the modality concept appears to hold little promise for special education since learning appears to be really a matter of substance over style.

Conclusions About Process Training

The question of process training presents a vexing situation for special education practice. For psycholinguistic training, there existed benefits especially with regard to basic language skill areas. The selected benefits make psycholinguistic training not an all-or-none proposition and caution must be exercised lest "the baby gets thrown out with the bath water." The case for perceptual motor training and modality training is quite different. Here there were no selected benefits and they can rightly be judged in an all-or-none manner, with the judgment clearly being none. Yet they reveal a stubborn resistance because of the seductive statements found in clinical reports. When conjoined with their intuitive appeal and historical foundation, they remain as established practices in special education.

The attacks on process training (Mann, 1971b; Mann & Phillips, 1967) have been vigorous but apparently not convincing to a segment of special education practitioners. Why? Because processes are presumed to possess a reality which then assumes that they must be considered in remediation. For a process such as language, which is reasonably well understood and readily observed, this assumption is probably true and accounts for the selected benefits of psycholinguistic training. These assumptions, however, are not supported for perceptual-motor training and modality training, where perception, learning style, and the like are not well understood and certainly not obvious. Empirical evaluations of these methods were decidedly negative, yet are not enough to shake fundamental belief. This belief sets in motion an attitude of questioning about research findings typically centered around the notion "what if . . . ?" The tension between belief and reality provides a continuing sense of justification for process training. When historical considerations are included, process training becomes an entrenched element in special education. Debate about the efficacy of process training becomes centered on philosophical issues that are not so easily discussed. Regardless of the weight of the research evidence against it, process training, with its established clinical, historical, and philosophical base, has proven remarkably resistant, as suggested by Mann (1979):

> Process training has always made the phoenix look like a bedraggled sparrow. You cannot kill it. It simply bides its time in exile after being dislodged by one of history's periodic attacks upon it and then returns, wearing disguises or carrying new *noms de plume,* as it were, but consisting of the same old ideas, doing business much in the same old way. (p. 539)

SPECIAL VERSUS REGULAR CLASS PLACEMENT

The "efficacy question" is a long-standing one in special education. During the 1940s, it was possible to assemble and to summarize all the available literature (Shattuck, 1946), but the burgeoning literature in the area became difficult to harness (e.g., Guskin & Spicker, 1968; Kirk, 1964; Meyers, MacMillan, & Yoshida, 1980). With the research evidence seemingly inconclusive, legislation and litigation brought profound changes to special education with the advent of the mainstreaming movement (Kavale, 1979).

Its legislative mandate, P.L. 94-142, demanded placement in the "least restrictive environment," which for many exceptional children meant placement in the regular class instead of the previously favored special segregated class. Justification for the mandate was found in a series of efficacy studies suggesting that the special class may be inappropriate for the education of exceptional children. In the 1960s, there was an increased call for abandonment of segregated self-contained classes (L. M. Dunn, 1968; Johnson, 1962). Nevertheless, a nagging question remained: "Was the mainstreaming movement justified?" The most vocal advocates of mainstreaming (e.g., Christopolos & Renz, 1969) built their arguments on a philosophical rather than empirical founda-

tion. The philosophical commitment to mainstreaming, however, appears to be more steadfast than was warranted by the empirical evidence; the research literature has been criticized for a number of serious methodological flaws that confound interpretation (Guskin & Spicker, 1968; MacMillan, 1971). Consequently, research has provided little convincing evidence that either supports or disputes the efficacy of special or regular class placement for exceptional children.

Carlberg and Kavale (1980) performed a meta-analysis on 50 studies examining the efficacy question. The 50 studies produced 322 $\underline{ES}$ measurements and at the highest level of aggregation yielded an $\overline{ES}$ of $-.12$. (The $\underline{ES}$ statistic was arranged so that a positive $\underline{ES}$ favored the special class, while a negative $\underline{ES}$ favored the regular or mainstreamed class.) These data represented approximately 27,000 students, who averaged 11 years of age with a mean IQ of 74 and who remained in the special class for a little under 2 years. Approximately 58% of the $\underline{ES}$s were negative: in more than half the cases, special classes were less effective than regular classes. Since the average comparison regular class subject would be at the 50th percentile, the effect of approximately 2 years of special class placement was to reduce the relative standing of the average special class subject by 5 percentile ranks. In real terms, this reduction represents about 2 months' credit on most elementary achievement tests. Thus, special class students were worse off than if they had remained in regular classes.

Efficacy studies generally measured two outcomes. In the Carlberg and Kavale (1980) analysis, achievement and social-personality variables revealed $\overline{ES}$'s of $-.15$ and $-.11$, respectively. Thus, special class placement was inferior to regular class placement regardless of outcome measures. Special class subjects declined by 6 and 4 percentile ranks on achievement and social/personality measures, respectively.

These findings lend support for a significant, albeit small, negative effect for special class placement. The critics were apparently correct: special education placement produced no tangible benefits. When the $\underline{ES}$ measurements were classified and averaged in a number of different ways, the primary finding was not challenged: the special class was an inferior placement option.

Tindal (1985) suggested that this meta-analysis overlooked many methodological issues that may have had important influences on outcome. The variables suggested as important included (a) the nature of the program studied, (b) the population served, (c) the assignment of students to treatments, (d) the experimental design, and (e) outcome measures used to document affects. It must be understood that when synthesizing a body of literature, the basis is found in the information provided in the primary sources. To substantiate the findings, available features were correlated with ES to determine if any significant relationships existed. No significant relationships were found between ES and the following variables: IQ differences between regular and special classes, length of placement, age, interval between treatment and outcome assessment, attrition, sample size, blindness to treatment, reactivity of measurements, and teacher assignment.

This list of variables represents a respectable number of dimensions that may possibly have influenced outcomes. In fact, they had almost no bearing on the integrated findings. Nevertheless, special class placement, although statistically inferior, was practically, only slightly less efficacious than regular class placement. The modest ES suggested that the efficacy question is still open. Three plausible explanations may be appropriate for the lack of conclusive findings.

1. *No Treatment Effect*: It is possible that special classes are neither inferior nor superior to regular classes with respect to their effect on segregated students. Such a situation could be expected to cause a variety of findings, particularly in the event of selection bias influencing the assignment of students to classes (as would occur if, for example, more severely retarded students were assigned to special classes.)

2. *Power*: "Power" is a term used to describe the ability of statistical tests to detect significant treatment differences; the higher the power, the more sensitive the statistical test (J. Cohen, 1977). Power is not a quality of the statistical test itself, but rather of the data and the experimental design. If the variability among the classroom means is great, relative to the variability among the students, then the test has high power. If the variability among the classroom means is small relative to the variability among students, the power is low.

If many of the efficacy studies have low power, they might label small but real treatment differences as nonsignificant, thus leading the researcher to assume no real difference between special and regular classes.

3. *Internal Validity:* The *sine quo non* of a valid study is the comparison group. The situation is ideal when students have been randomly assigned to special and regular classes. Some form of random assignment is the best way of assuring that the two groups are, initially, equivalent. Because it is so difficult in practice, and often questionable ethically, to assign students randomly to different treatments, various techniques (matched pairs, analysis of covariance, residual gain scores, and wishful thinking) have been used in an attempt to approximate random assignment. None of these substitutes is entirely satisfactory, however, and the findings of most efficacy studies are weakened by the argument that one class or the other started out with an advantage that influenced the findings. A threat to internal validity such as selection bias could easily explain significant but contradictory findings.

Tindal (1985) questioned the efficacy literature with respect to the populations included in the studies. It was suggested that aggregations of ill-defined groups does not permit assessment of treatment effects in groups with similar problems. While definitions of specific categories and heterogenity within those categories are certainly problematic, it does not preclude aggregating studies by category of exceptionality. There exists enough distinction among these categories to include an analysis by category.

The analysis by category brought to light a significant and surprising finding. The ES measurements were classified into three categories: EMR (IQ 50 to 75), Slow Learner (IQ 75 to 90), and LD or BD/ED and the findings are shown in Table 13. Special class placement was most disadvantageous for exceptional children whose primary problem was lower IQ levels (EMR and SL). In comparison to regular class counterparts, SL's lost 13 percentile ranks while EMRs declined by 6 percentile ranks. For LD and BD/ED children in special classes, however, an improvement of 11

TABLE 13   Average Effect Size by Special Education Diagnosis

Diagnosis	Average Effect of Special vs. Regular Placement	Number of Effect Sizes
EMR (IQ 50–75)	−.14	249
SL (IQ 75–90)	−.34	38
LD and BD/ED	.29	35

percentile ranks results from that placement. The average LD or BD/ED pupil in a special class was better off than 61% of those placed in a regular class.

The $\overline{ES}$ for category were thus larger than those in the earlier findings. The differences between both EMR and SL and the LD/BD aggregation were significant, whereas there was no significant interaction between category and outcome. The lack of an interaction indicates no confounding between category and outcome, and that the advantage of the LD and BD/ED categories as well as the disadvantage of the EMR and SL categories was found in all three outcomes (achievement, social/personality, other [e.g., perceptual-motor measures, adaptive behavior]). This is shown in Figure 2.

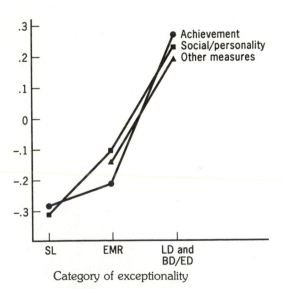

Figure 2. Graphic representation of category of exceptionality × type of outcome measure interaction.

It is thus difficult to agree with Tindal (1985) that differences in the populations included was a methodological problem that adversely influenced outcomes.

Yet the disturbing question remains as to why some pupils placed in special classes are slightly worse off (in terms of achievement and social/personality adjustment) than they would have been had they been left in regular classrooms remains. It is possible to speculate from these findings that the significant variable appears to be intelligence: If the child is placed in a special class because of a low IQ, it may lower teacher expectations for performance, which results in less effort on the teachers' part and less learning on the child's (e.g., Braun, 1976; Rosenthal & Jacobson, 1968; Rosenthal & Rubin, 1978). The lower expectancy, be it conscious or unconscious, may divert instructional efforts away from academic pursuits and toward solely a maintenance function. As such, the special class may become an instrument for preserving social order and not necessarily an arrangement for providing a better education.

On the other hand, the normal intelligence of LD and BD/ED pupils (at least, by definition) apparently does not dampen teacher expectation. Special class teachers apparently take an optimistic view and provide effort to improve academic functioning. Perhaps this effort represents the "real" special education, not a system seeking the status quo but a system focusing on individual learning needs and abilities in order to design the most effective program of *academic* remediation necessary to overcome *academic* deficits.

In general, these findings suggested that basic questions about the best placement for service delivery to exceptional children is complex and not easily answered. The studies surveyed included a multitude of different service delivery models under the general rubric of special education placement. Since no service arrangement proved more effective, it appears that the differences were related to indeterminate and imperceptible variables not easily assessed or controlled. Tindal (1985) suggested that special education must be evaluated with new methods that incorporate changes in experimental designs, outcome assessments, and data analysis procedures. These new models might include time series designs incorporating new metrics (e.g., slope of improvement on the IEP, goal mastery, absolute rate of improvement, relative rate of improvement) that focus on both the formative evaluation of special education as well as the summative evaluation of overall efficacy. New methodologies are certainly in order if the indeterminate and imperceptible variables are to be included in decisions about the efficacy question. As MacMillan (1971) suggested, however, "the real issue is not whether special classes or regular classes are better" (p. 9) but rather, where the best interests of the students might be. The answer of the efficacy question is obviously not an all-or-none response and unconditional judgments must be avoided until both new programs and new methods of evaluation are developed.

MEDICALLY BASED INTERVENTIONS

From its inception, special education has shown a fascination for medicine. Conversely, at times, medicine has sometimes shown a fascination for schools. The interface of this relationship has resulted in medically oriented interventions becoming an integral part of the special education repertoire of remedial techniques. Two meta-analysis have investigated medical treatments and provide information applicable for deciding policy about their inclusion in remedial programs.

Stimulant Drugs and Hyperactivity

The practice of treating hyperactive children with stimulant drugs is among the most controversial and emotionally loaded issues in special education. The medical community considers stimulant drugs to be the most efficacious treatment for hyperactivity (e.g., American Academy of Pediatrics, 1970, 1975). This conclusion has been challenged: first in the form of critical reviews suggesting that no positive interpretation could be drawn from extant literature because of numerous methodological flaws (e.g., Sprague & Werry, 1971; Sroufe,

1975), and second, in the form of ideological, political, and moral attacks on stimulant drug treatment (e.g., Schrag & Divoky, 1975).

Kavale (1982a) found 135 studies assessing the effectiveness of stimulant drug treatment for hyperactivity. The studies sampled represented approximately 5,300 subjects averaging 8.75 years of age with an average IQ of 102; subjects received medication for an average of 10 weeks. The $\overline{ES}$ across 984 $\underline{ES}$ measurements was .578, which indicates that the average drug-treated child moves from the 50th to the 72nd percentile as a result of drug intervention. This 22-percentile-rank gain suggests that an average drug-treated child would be expected to be better off than 72% of untreated control children.

The diverse assortment of outcomes measured in drug research makes it difficult to fully interpret a single index of drug efficacy. Three major outcome classes were identified: behavioral, cognitive, and physiological, and the findings are illustrated in Figure 3 in the form of normal distributions comparing hypothetical drug-treated and control populations. This more refined analysis revealed substantial positive effects on behavioral and cognitive outcomes. The negative effect for physiological outcomes indicated that drug intervention produced some negative consequences. (The physiological findings are, however, generally difficulty to interpret and are outside the province of this chapter.) Further refinement of the data in each outcome class is presented in Table 14.

Note (with the exception of anxiety) the impressive gains on behavioral outcomes. Substantial

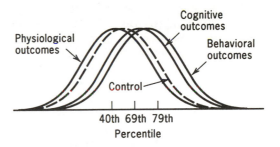

Behavioral $\overline{ES}$ = 0.804
Cognitive $\overline{ES}$ = 0.491
Physiological $\overline{ES}$ = –0.246

Figure 3. Effect of stimulant drug therapy on behavioral, cognitive, and physiological outcome classes.

TABLE 14   Average Effect Sizes for Outcome Categories

Category	Mean Effect Size	Number of Effect Sizes
Behavioral		
Global Improvement Ratings	.886	192
Rating Scales and Checklists	.837	113
Activity Level	.846	127
Attention and Concentration	.782	119
Behavior (Social and Classroom)	.634	92
Anxiety	.118	12
Cognitive		
Intelligence	.391	54
Achievement	.383	47
Drawing and Copying	.467	38
Perceptual, Memory, and Motor	.412	91
Learning Characteristics	.367	41
Physiological		
Biochemical	.558	7
Psychophysiological	−.275	51

benefits were found on ratings of behavioral functioning, lowered activity levels, and improved attending skills. Although not of the same magnitude as behavioral improvements, cognitive functioning also exhibited consequential improvement. With respect to cognitive tasks, the present findings were generally in accord with findings from laboratory studies (see Cantwell & Carlson, 1978, and Gittelman & Kanner, 1986, for reviews) regarding the salutary effects of stimulants on task that tap various aspects of attention and memory. Unlike past reviews (e.g., Aman, 1980; Barkley & Cunningham, 1978), the meta-analytic findings also showed stimulant medication to have a positive effect on academic performance. Children on stimulants could, in fact, be expected to gain the equivalent of a 15-percentile-rank increase in achievement, across these studies, when compared to nontreated children. To put these gains in perspective, other meta-analyses of certain classroom interventions deemed by some to be just as controversial as psychopharmacological treatment, such as perceptual-motor training or modality instruction, have only resulted in gains of 5 or 6 percentile ranks.

There appears to be, however, a resistance to acknowledging the positive effects of medication on academic achievement (e.g., Gadow, 1983; O'Leary, 1980). The improved academic performance is usually attributed to improved attention and reduced impulsivity. When the effects of attention are held constant in the meta-analysis (through partial correlation), however, the positive effect for achievement was reduced by only 20%, suggesting that factors other than simply attention were operating to enhance academic performance.

Pelham (1986) has also questioned the validity of the negative results obtained in studies of stimulant effects on achievement. It was suggested that the studies suffered from methodological difficulties that limit their findings, such as (a) insensitivity of achievement tests over the typically short (4 to 12 weeks) duration of medication studies, (b) lack of attention to drug-dose factors, (c) lack of compliance in administering medication, (d) lack of attention to the time course of stimulant effects, and (e) lack of attention to individual differences. Pelham (1986) then suggested that the presumed positive effects of behavioral interventions have resulted in an antimedication bias and different

TABLE 15 Average Effect Sizes for Achievement Measures

Measures	Mean Effect Size	Number of Effect Sizes
Wide Range Achievement Test		
Reading	.322	11
Arithmetic	.094	10
Spelling	.365	7
Iowa Test of Basic Skills	.628	6
Gray Oral Reading	.424	3
Language	.500	6
Handwriting	.437	4

evidential standards being applied to medication studies. It is also clear that relatively few systematic data on side effects of medication seem to be available in such studies, especially in relation to classroom functioning. These caveats and the present findings should be taken to suggest that previous negative findings should not necessarily be interpreted as evidence that stimulants have no beneficial effect on academic achievement. For example, the $\overline{ES}$'s for achievement measures are shown in Table 15. With the exception of arithmetic, the gains in academic achievement represent a level of improvement equal to approximately a half-year's worth of schooling ($\overline{ES}$ = .50). The effects of drug treatment exhibit a similar gain in achievement in only 10 weeks.

The overall $\overline{ES}$ of .578 for stimulant drugs was obtained from six major drugs as shown in Table 16. All major drugs with the exception of caffeine appear to be effective in the treatment of hyperactivity. The findings suggest little to choose from among the most popular stimulant drugs and provide support for stimulants being the most popular treatment for hyperactivity.

Drug research has been criticized on methodological grounds but no significant differences were found among the $\overline{ES}$'s for the low, medium, and high categories of internal validity ratings. Design problems thus appeared to play a subordinate role in drug research. In fact, design considerations accounted for only 1% of the variance in study findings for the behavioral and cognitive classes. Among the more important design considerations is the presence of placebo control. The control group is given an inert substance ("sugar pill") and if improvement is shown, the gain is attributed to the placebo effect and casts doubt on any observed drug effects. The difference between placebo-controlled studies ($\overline{ES}$ = .562) and studies without placebo control ($\overline{ES}$ = .628) was not significant. The $\overline{ES}$ difference (.066) can be considered an approximate index of the placebo effect, which is well below the standard value (around 35%) and indicates that the placebo effect accounted for only 7% of the improvement shown by drug-treated subjects.

Stimulant drug treatment appears to be an effective intervention for the treatment of hyperactivity. Compare this conclusion with this statement from a narrative review of the drug literature: "Our analysis of the literature in this area indicates that research findings do not indicate the general efficacy and therefore do not support the widespread use of stimulant drugs" (Adelman & Compas, 1977, p. 406). Quantitative synthesis methods provided a means to demonstrate that drug effects

TABLE 16 Average Effect Sizes for Stimulant Drugs

Drug	Mean Effect Size	Number of Effect Sizes
Methylphenidate (Ritalin)	.634	540
Dextroamphetamine (Dexedrine)	.585	276
Magnesium pemoline (Cylert)	.540	61
Levoamphetamine	.447	29
Amphetemine (Benzedrine)	.438	33
Caffeine	.111	45

produced positive outcomes that exceeded a half standard deviation and indicated that the average drug-treated subject would be better off than 72% of control subjects. No empirical analysis, however, can hope to elucidate the complex ideological questions associated with drug treatment. The beneficial effects of stimulant drug treatment have been demonstrated and it is now necessary to debate the ethical issues.

Diet Treatment and Hyperactivity

In 1975, Dr. Benjamin Feingold offered the hypothesis that the ingestion of artificial (synthetic) food additives (colors and flavors) results in hyperactivity in children (Feingold, 1976). The treatment suggested was based on the Feingold Kaiser-Permanente (K-P) diet designed to eliminate all foods containing artificial food additives from the diet (Feingold & Feingold, 1979).

Feingold (1976) reported that between 40 and 70% of hyperactive children who strictly adhered to the Feingold K-P diet demonstrated a marked reduction in hyperactive behavior. The available evidence, based on uncontrolled clinical trials and anecdotal accounts, was challenged; nevertheless, the diet received widespread media attention and a favorable and enthusiastic response from the general public. The question thus remained: Is there any justification for the major dietary changes required by the Feingold K-P diet in terms of reduced hyperactivity?

Kavale and Forness (1983) examined 23 experimental studies assessing the efficacy of the Feingold K-P diet in treating hyperactivity. The 23 studies produced 125 $\overline{ES}$ measurements and

yielded an $\overline{ES}$ of .118 but a median of $\underline{ES}$ of .045, suggesting a skewed distribution, with the $\overline{ES}$ probably overestimating the treatment effect. The average subject was 8.3 years of age, had an IQ of 99, and remained on the Feingold K-P diet for 39 weeks.

In relative terms, the $\overline{ES}$ of .118 indicates that a child no better off than average (i.e., at the 50th percentile) would rise to the 55th percentile as a result of the Feingold K-P diet. When compared to the 22-percentile rank gain for stimulant drug treatment, the 5-percentile-rank improvement for diet intervention is less than one-fourth as large. Although the average ages and IQ were similar for drug-treated and diet-treated subjects, the average duration of treatment differed: 39 weeks in a diet study and 10 weeks in a drug study. In relation to $\overline{ES}$ (.118 versus .578), these comparisons suggest that compared to Feingold K-P diet treatment, drug treatment is approximately five times as effective in about one-fourth the time. Thus, the Feingold K-P diet is cast in an unfavorable light since it produces a substantially lower treatment effect than stimulant drug treatment and approximates the negligible effects ($\overline{ES}$ = .082) of perceptual-motor training.

The $\underline{ES}$ data were next aggregated into descriptive outcome categories and the findings are shown in Table 17. The effects of the Feingold K-P diet ranged from a loss of 2 percentile ranks (learning ability) to a gain of 11 percentile ranks (*Conners Scale—Teachers,* and hyperkinesis ratings). Thus, the only obvious effect of diet treatment is upon overt behavior, specifically, a reduction in hyperactivity, with little influence on more

TABLE 17   Average Effect Size for Outcome Categories

Category	Mean Effect Size	Number of Effect Sizes
Conners Scale—Parents	.156	26
Conners Scale—Teachers	.268	9
Global Improvement	.128	23
Hyperkinesis Rating	.293	15
Attention	.015	36
Disruptive Behavior	.052	6
Impulsivity	.153	5
Learning Ability	−.055	10

cognitive aspects of behavior. This conclusion, however, must be tempered. Global ratings of improvement possess two major problems: objectivity in defining improvement, and psychometric deficiencies (reliability and validity). These problems influence the "reactivity" or subjectivity of outcome measures. Reactive measures are those which are under the control of observers who have an acknowledged interest in achieving predetermined outcomes (e.g., "improvement"). Nonreactive measures, on the other hand, are not easily influenced in any direction by observers. The correlation of ES and ratings of reactivity was significant ($r = .181$), suggesting the larger treatment effects were associated with more reactive measures. Additionally, aggregations of reactive versus nonreactive measures found $\overline{ES}$'s of .179 and .001, respectively, suggesting that in those instances where instruments paralleled the valued outcomes of observers, there was a tendency to view more improvement as revealed in larger treatment effects.

The initial evaluations of diet treatment by Dr. Feingold and associates were based on clinical trial and observation. The findings from such quasi-experimental designs are at variance with results from "better" studies, that is, those studies with more rigorous experimental control. Of the 23 studies, six were uncontrolled clinical trials and they yielded an $\overline{ES}$ .337 compared to the $\overline{ES}$ of .089 for the 17 controlled studies. There was, however, a significant relationship ($r = -.193$) between ES and ratings of design quality, which indicates that larger ES's were associated with studies rated low on internal validity.

The controlled studies used two primary experimental designs. A diet crossover study places groups of hyperactive children on two experimental diets; one follows the Feingold K-P diet strictly, while the other is disguised as the Feingold K-P diet but actually contains the substances supposedly eliminated. A challenge study selects groups of children who appear to respond to the Feingold K-P diet, who are then divided in experimental and control conditions. Both groups are given a strict Feingold K-P diet, but the experimental group is also given a challenge food (usually, a cookie or drink) that appears to meet the diet guidelines but actually contains eliminated substances.

Of the 17 controlled studies, seven used a diet crossover design and 10 were challenge studies. The diet crossover studies exhibited an $\overline{ES}$ of .196, while challenge studies revealed an $\overline{ES}$ of .045. Diet crossover studies, however, still possess methodological difficulties, which suggest caution in interpretation. Challenge studies, on the other hand, offer a methodology that permits the attribution of behavioral change to the substances eliminated in the Feingold K-P diet. Challenge studies can thus be considered the "best" studies in terms of design and control, and provide the strongest evidence for the efficacy of the Feingold K-P diet. The weight of this evidence is decidedly negative ($\overline{ES} = .045$) since at the end of diet treatment the average treatment subject was better off than 52% of control subjects, a gain only slightly better than no treatment at all.

These findings offer little support for the Feingold hypothesis. The modest and limited gains found suggest a more temperate view of the efficacy of the Feingold K-P diet than that asserted by the diet's proponents. The slight improvement shown by some children should not interfere with the critical examinations of the Feingold K-P diet, since it may postpone more appropriate medical, psychological, or educational intervention (Wender, 1977).

Although the Feingold diet offers an appealing treatment approach for hyperactivity since it offers an alternative to stimulant medication, it is not without pragmatic difficulties. The implementation of the Feingold K-P diet requires an abrupt lifestyle change since increased vigilance is necessary in grocery shopping and good preparation, families generally cannot eat at restaurants, and the child cannot eat school lunches (Sheridan & Meister, 1982). Lew (1977) conducted a 4-week trial of the Feingold K-P diet on her family and concluded that "the Feingold Diet is indeed a very different and very difficult diet to maintain in practice. The deprivations to the participants are real and is not the hyperactive child already set apart from his peers and family enough?" (p. 190). The negative empirical findings call into question the validity of the Feingold K-P diet as a treatment for hyperactivity, and suggest a cautious policy toward accepting the Feingold hypothesis.

Conclusions About Medically Based Interventions

Thus, the fascination with medical interventions by special education is not entirely warranted. The findings related to medically based treatment for hyperactivity presented an inconsistent picture:

one (stimulant medication) was effective while the other (diet modification) was not. These results suggest that medicine does not necessarily offer "better" treatments than those based on psycho-educational foundations. They require the same critical examination as treatments based on other disciplines.

IMPLICATIONS FOR SPECIAL EDUCATION

The findings from the reported meta-analysis paint a mixed picture of the efficacy of special education, it was shown to be both effective and not effective. This conclusion is further complicated by Swanson's (1984) findings that theory tends not to guide teaching practice. There was a significant discrepancy between what teachers say and what they do, which makes it likely that teachers are most comfortable with what they already know and what has intuitive appeal. Regardless of how exciting teachers may find new theoretically based strategies, there tends to be a resistance to implementing them in favor of existing interventions they find comfortable (such as those described in the meta-analysis). The difficulty however, is that

these favored interventions are problematic with respect to their efficacy. An efficacy summary is shown in Table 18 where, in addition to the meta-analysis reported, four others have been added.

Two observations about this table are important. One is that most of the $\overline{ES}$ are below .50 and represent less advantage than one-half year's worth of schooling. It may be that special education has taken its *special* adjective too seriously and placed too much faith in its unique interventions. There has always been a demand for instant and simple solutions in special education. Yet special education has never been able to provide *the* answer or *the* solution, and the meta-analytic findings cast doubt about any of the interventions reviewed here laying claim to being *the* answer or *the* solution.

Besides specific intervention techniques, special education has also wrestled with its fundamental concepts. These, too, have been subject to debate and also questioned as to whether they should be viewed as *the* answer or *the* solution. Consider, for example, a cornerstone of most special education models: individualized instruction and its mandate, the Individualized Education

TABLE 18   Summary of Meta-Analyses in Special Education Research

Intervention	Number of Studies	$\overline{ES}$	S.D.
Early Intervention	74	.40	62
Reducing Class Size	77	.31	.70
Special Class Placement	50	−.12	.65
Behavior Modification	41	.93	1.16
Psycholinguistic Training	34	.39	.54
Perceptual Motor Training	180	.08	.27
Modality Instruction	39	.15	.28
Stimulant Drugs	135	.58	.61
Psychotropic Drugs	70	.30	.75
Diet Intervention	23	.12	.42

Note. The following have been added to the efficacy summary:

Casto, G., & Mastropieri, M. A. (1986). The efficacy of early intervention programs: A meta-analysis. *Exceptional Children, 52*(5), 417–424. (Early Intervention).

Glass, G. V., & Smith, M. L. (1979). Meta-analysis of research in class size and achievement. *Educational Evaluation and Policy Analysis, 1,* 2–16. (Reducing Class Size).

Skiba, R., & Casey, A. (1985). Interventions for behaviorally disordered students: A quantitative review and methodological critique. *Behavioral Disorders, 10,* 239–252. (Behavior Modification).

Kavale, K.A., & Nye, C. (1984). The effectiveness of drug treatment for behavior disorders: A meta-analysis. *Behavioral Disorders, 9,* 117–130. (Psychotropic Drugs).

Program (Schenck, 1980). Lloyd (1984) questioned the validity of the assumption that some kinds of instruction are better for some students, while other kinds are better for other students. Based on three models of individualization (remedial, compensatory, and preferential) (Salomon, 1972), little evidence was found in support of any aptitude × treatment interaction hypotheses. Instead, Lloyd (1984) suggested that instruction be based on "skills students need to be taught."

Fuchs and Fuchs (1986) followed this suggestion with a call for systematic formative evaluation as the basis for individualization. Systematic formative evaluation focuses on ongoing evaluation and modification of proposed programs to provide a data base through which individualized programs may be developed. The advantages of systematic formative evaluation include the fact that (a) it is an inductive rather than a deductive approach to individualization, which avoids the pitfalls of formulating a diagnosis before the relationship between learner characteristics and educational intervention is fully established; (b) it is based on more psychometrically acceptable measurement procedures; and (c) it possesses more ecological validity because of repeated measurement in the classroom setting. Thus, even a fundamental concept such as individualization is open to varying interpretation and, depending on its conceptualization, may or may not possess utility for special education practice.

The second observation relates to the second column, illustrating the standard deviation (SD) associated with each $\overline{ES}$. The two statistics may be used to represent a form of expectation about an intervention. But the SD column reveals a disconcerting fact: the SD's reveal magnitudes two to three times greater than the $\overline{ES}$. In each case, the treatment exhibited greater variability than it did average effectiveness. This means that from one study to the next the effect of any intervention can vary from negative to zero to positive over a wide range. Thus, special education treatments are more variable in their effects than they are beneficial in their effects.

The variability makes special education treatments essentially unpredictable. In an effort to harness, at least, some of the variability, meta-analysis techniques attempt to determine if some features of studies (e.g., age, sex, treatment duration, setting, IQ, SES, severity, or the like) might correlate substantially with $\underline{ES}$. If some correlations were significant, it would be possible to predict, for example, that psycholinguistic training or stimulant drug treatment will be effective here but not there, and so on. Unfortunately, in no area of special education were there correlations of a magnitude that permitted useful predictions. Thus, special education interventions may produce benefits, but they do so in a manner that is essentially unpredictable.

The variability and unpredictability of special education treatments suggests that the system does not represent "perfect" knowledge (Brodbeck, 1962), which is characterized by a complete and closed set of input–output relationships (e.g., do A in circumstances X and Y, and do B in circumstance Z). Special education is thus "imperfect" knowledge, making it essentially indeterminate. What this implies is that special education cannot operate on the bases of prescriptive action, that is, a single course of action under a wide range of circumstances. Special education needs to be treated as an enterprise that is unlawful, unpredictable, and unknowable in a purely scientific sense.

The tacit acknowledgment of this view of special education can be seen in debates over the philosophical underpinnings of practice. Heshusius (1982) suggested that the foundation provided by a predominantly mechanistic (i.e., behavioral) special education approach serves only to reduce teaching and learning to the subordinate level of rules and instrumentality. The required measurement and quantification of instruction and student learning tend not to operate at those levels that are meaningful or worthwhile for the child. Heshusius (1982) warned that the mechanistic assumptions of current special education practices are too narrow or simplistic, and that the adequate descriptions of student behavior and behavior change are the ultimate consequences. Although recognizing that no one model holds ultimate truth or reality, Heshusius (1982) contended that special educators have been trying to do the impossible—"to force the innately unpredictable into the predictable, the unmeasurable into the measurable, and wholeness into fragmentation" (p. 12). Furthermore, the current predominant paradigm in special education demands that teachers become behavioral engineers or technicians, a transformation that serves to promote the reduction of complex reality into quantifiable triviality. A more holistic approach could allow for an understanding of "complexity in its own right and the relationship of the whole to its parts, rather than trying to understand complexity by fragmenting it and reducing it to small, statistically measurable units over which one things one has control" (Heshusius, 1986, p. 463). This view did not go unchallenged (Ulman & Rosenberg, 1986) and mechanistic approaches have been credited with being the primary agent for the efficient evaluation and modification of interventions (Nelson & Polsgove, 1984).

In a similar manner, Iano (1986) suggested that the natural science-technical model fails to capture the complexity of the teaching-learning process and has created an artificial distinction between researchers and practitioners. Researchers tend to reduce classroom behavior to controlled or defensible variables that fail to recognize classroom reality, while teachers view these as minor contributors and hence have little confidence in the generalizability of findings. Iano's (1986) view was followed by commentary (Carnine, 1987; Forness & Kavale, 1987; Lloyd, 1987) either criticizing, expanding, or clarifying specific points.

These debates have focused on the increased attention directed at model-based practice in special education. Presently, the validity and worth of any particular model is practically impossible to determine. It may be the case that special education will need to accept the fact that multiple models can be equally productive for studying the efficacy of special education (Labouvie, 1975). Although different models would lead to different interpretations of observed intervention effects, all would be retained for utilization in classroom situations. Nonetheless, this relativism, or belief that judgments concerning the adequacy of conflicting models cannot be made, has been challenged (Phillips, 1983). For example, Soltis (1984), while encouraging tolerance for all educational perspectives within an "associated community," emphasized that open-mindedness must not be mistakenly viewed as being synonymous with empty mindedness; special educators must exercise judgment when evaluating interventions. Donmoyer (1985) asserted that relativism has contributed to special education being a "solipsistic morass" where any single conclusion regarding the effectiveness of an intervention could be judged as being as positive as any other intervention, even when conflicting findings exist.

THE RELATIONSHIP BETWEEN SPECIAL AND REGULAR EDUCATION

The variability inherent in special education models is also apparent in general education models (i.e., programs of what to teach, when, how, and the like). These models reveal success to be highly variable (e.g., Dunkin & Biddle, 1974; Joyce & Weil, 1972; Peterson & Walberg, 1979). A simple truism emerges: what works in one place does not necessarily work someplace else. Consequently, special education must thus be viewed with uncertainty which introduces "risk" (Kaplan, 1964) since an intervention may or may not work.

The uncertainty and risk in special education does not preclude rationale program planning. Glass (1979) commented on the general principles necessary to cope sensibly with uncertainty: "Such systems must be monitored diligently; the actors within them must remain versatile and flexible, and the services must be highly decentralized. Persons must command options instead of eternal truths" (p. 14).

Where does the special education practitioner find these options? It is apparent that any model or even particular special intervention is not the answer. There exist a wide assortment of intervening variables that influence the teaching-learning process. Fortunately, formal knowledge about these variables has accumulated and has been commonly referred to as "effective schooling" research (e.g., Mackenzie, 1983; Purkey & Smith, 1983; Squires, 1983).

The effective schooling research has identified practices and characteristics associated with improvement in student achievement and excellence in student behavior. These practices include (a) elements associated with a clearly defined curriculum; (b) focused classroom instruction and management; (c) firm, consistent discipline; (d) close monitoring of student performance; and (e) strong instructional leadership. Of course, this list does not exhaust the possibilities surrounding school effects, teacher effects, curriculum alignment, program coupling, and educational change. Nevertheless, an integrated picture of effective schooling is emerging and its key elements are coming to the fore.

The implications of the effective schooling research for special education have been discussed (Bickel & Bickel, 1986; Samuels, 1986) and suggest the necessity of reconceptualizing how instructional services should be conceived and delivered.

One point seems clear: when it is realized that the success or failure of special education is contingent upon relatively uncontrolled (and unknown) factors, the key player then becomes the teacher, whose own skill and ability must interpose between the intricate concatenation of events involved in the special education teaching–learning process. This will best be achieved not through a dogmatic belief system, but rather, through an array of rational choices gleaned from the effective schooling literature.

Stevens and Rosenshine (1981) suggested characteristics of effective pedagogy, which included it being (a) teacher directed, (b) group based, (c) academically focused, and (d) individualized. It has been shown, however, that discrepancies exist between these suggestions for effective teaching and the observation of actual teaching practice in special education (Morsink, Soar, Soar, & Thomas, 1986). Specifically, there was only a small amount of time spent on activities that could be considered direct instruction with active learner involvement and teacher feedback (Englert, 1983), and students did not appear to receive frequent teacher attention (Gable, Hendrickson, Shores, Young, & Stowitschek, 1983). Thus, the effective schooling research needs to be better integrated into special education practice. It needs to be communicated clearly that schooling does make a difference and that teachers can substantially influence student outcomes.

The effectiveness of special education thus includes elements of both art and science. This is because the science (research) does not automatically apply in the real world. Phillips (1980) termed this distinction the *is/ought* dichotomy—research findings take an *is* form (i.e., X is Y), while practical implications take an *ought* form (i.e., A ought to do B)—that needs to be mediated through a mechanism such as the effective schooling literature which will ensure that the art (i.e., the individual teacher's interpretation of what is best practice) possesses a rational basis. The outcome can be enhanced quality of education for exceptional students because it will be based on the artful application of science.

REFERENCES

Adelman, H. S., & Compas, B. E. (1977). Stimulant drugs and learning problems. *Journal of Special Education, 11,* 377–416.

Aman, M. G. (1980). Psychotropic drugs and learning problems: A selective review. *Journal of Learning Disabilitis, 13,* 89–97.

American Academy of Pediatrics, Committee on Drugs. (1970). An examination of the pharmacologic approach to learning impediments. *Pediatrics, 46,* 142–144.

American Academic of Pediatrics, Council on Child Health. (1975). Medication for hyperkinetic children. *Pediatrics, 55,* 560–562.

Andreski, S. *Social sciences as sorcery.* (1972). London: André Deutsch.

Arena, J. I. (Ed.). (1969). *Teaching through sensory-motor experiences.* San Rafael, CA: Academic Therapy.

Arter, J. A., & Jenkins, J. R. (1977). Examining the benefits and prevalence of modality considerations in special education. *Journal of Special Education, 11,* 281–298.

Ayres, A. J. (1972). *Sensory integration and learning disorders.* Los Angeles: Western Psychological Services.

Balow, B. (1971). Perceptual-motor activities in the treatment of severe reading disability. *Reading Teacher, 25,* 513–525.

Barbe, W. B., & Milone, M. N. (1980). Modality. *Instructor, 89,* 44–47.

Barbe, W. B., & Milone, M. N. (1981). What we know about modality strengths. *Educational Leadership, 38,* 378–380.

Barkley, R. A., & Cunningham, C. E. (1978). Do stimulant drugs improve the academic performance of hyperactive children? *Clinical Pediatrics, 17,* 85–92.

Barsch, R. H. (1967). *Achieving perceptual-motor efficiency (Vol. 1).* Seattle, WA: Special Child Publications.

Bickel, W. E., & Bickel, D. D. (1986). Effective schools, classrooms, and instruction: Implications for special education. *Exceptional Children, 52*(6), 489–500.

Bracht, G. H., & Glass, G. V. (1968). The external validity of experiments. *American Educational Research Journal, 4,* 437–474.

Braun, C. (1976). Teacher expectations: Socio-psychological dynamics. *Review of Educational Research, 46,* 185–213.

Brodbeck, M. (1962). Explanation, prediction, and "imperfect" knowledge. In H. Feigl and G. Maxwell (Eds.), *Minnesota studies in the philosophy of science (Vol. 3).* Minneapolis: University of Minnesota Press.

Bush, W. J., & Giles, M. T. (1977). *Aids to psycholinguistic teaching* (2nd ed.). Columbus, OH: Charles E. Merrill.

Campbell, D. T., & Stanley, J. C. (1963). *Experimental and quasi-experimental designs for research.* Skokie, IL: Rand McNally.

Cantwell, D. P., & Carlson, G. A. (1978). Stimulants. In J. S. Werry (Ed.), *Pediatric pscyhopharmacology: The use of behavior modifying drugs in children* (pp. 171–207). New York: Brunner/Mazel.

Carlberg, C., & Kavale, K. (1980). The efficacy of special versus regular class placement for exceptional children: A meta-analysis. *Journal of Special Education, 14,* 295–309.

Carbo, M. (1983). Research in reading and learning style: Implications for exceptional children. *Exceptional Children, 49*(6), 486–494.

Carnine, D. (1987). A response to "False standards, a distorting and distintegrating effect on education, turning away from useful purposes, being inevitably unfilfilled, and remaining unrealistic and irrelevant." *Remedial and Special Education, 8*(1), 42–43.

Chaney, C. M., & Kephart, N. C. (1968). *Motoric aids to perceptual training.* Columbus, OH: Charles E. Merrill.

Christopolos, F., & Renz, P. (1969). A critical examination of special education programs. *Journal of Special Education, 3,* 371–379.

Cohen, H. J., Birch, H. G., & Taft, L. T. (1970). Some considerations for evaluating the Doman-Delacato "patterning" method. *Pediatrics, 45,* 302–314.

Cohen, J. (1977). *Statistical power analysis for the behavioral sciences.* New York: Academic Press.

Cratty, B. (1969). *Perceptual-motor behavior and educational processes.* Springfield, IL: Charles C Thomas.

Cronbach, L. J., & Snow, R. E. (1977). *Aptitudes and instructional methods: A handbook for research on interactions.* New York: Irvington.

Cronbach, L. J., & Suppes, P. (1969). *Research for tomorrow's school: Disciplined inquiry for education.* New York: Macmillan.

Delacato, C. H. (1959). *The treatment and prevention of reading problems: The neurological approach.* Springfield, IL: Charles C Thomas.

Delacato, C. H. (1966). *Neurological organization and reading.* Springfield, IL: Charles C Thomas.

Donmoyer, R. (1985). The rescue from relativism: Two failed attempts and an alternative strategy. *Educational Researcher, 14,* 13–20.

Dunkin, M. J., & Biddles, B. J. (1974). *The study of teaching.* New York: Holt, Rinehart and Winston.

Dunn, L. M. (1968). Special education for the mildly retarded—Is much of it justifiable? *Exceptional Children, 35,* 5–22.

Dunn, L. M., & Smith, J. O. (1967). *Peabody Language Development Kits.* Circle Pines, MN: American Guidance Serivce.

Dunn, R. S. (1979). Learning—A matter of style. *Educational Leadership, 36,* 430–432.

Dunn, R. S., & Dunn, K. J. (1978). *Teaching students through their individual learning style.* Reston, VA: Reston.

Englert, C. S. (1983). Measuring special education teacher effectiveness. *Exceptional Children, 50*(3), 247–254.

Feingold, B. F. (1976). Hyperkinesis and learning disabilities linked to the ingestion of artificial food colors and flavors. *Journal of Learning Disabilities, 9,* 551–559.

Feingold, B. F., & Feingold, H. S. (1979). *The Feingold cookbook for hyperactive children.* New York: Random House.

Fisher, R. A. (1938). *Statistical methods of research workers* (7th ed.). London: Oliver & Boyd.

Footlik, S. W. (1971). Perceptual-motor training and cognitive achievement: A survey of the literature. *Journal of Learning Disabilities, 3,* 40–49.

Forness, S. R., & Kavale, K. A. (1987). Holistic inquiry and the scientific challenge in special education: A reply to Iano. *Remedial and Specail Education, 8*(1), 47–51.

Frostig, M., & Horne, D. (1964). *The Forstig program for the development of visual perception.* Chicago: Follett Educational Corp.

Fuchs, L. S., & Fuchs, D. (1986). Effects of systematic formative evaluation: A meta-analysis. *Exceptional Children, 53*(3), 199–208.

Gable, R., Hendrickson, J., Shores, R., Young, C., & Stowitschek, J. (1983). A comparison of teacher approval statements across categories of exceptionality. *Journal of Special Education Technology, 6,* 15–22.

Gadow, K. D. (1983). Effects of stimulant drugs on academic performance in hyperactive and learning disabled children. *Journal of Learning Disabilities, 16,* 290–299.

Getman, G., Kane, E. R., Halgren, M. R., & McKee, G. W. (1968). *Developing learning readiness: A visual-motor tactile skills program.* Manchester, MO: Webster Divison, McGraw-Hill.

Gittleman, R., & Kanner, A. (1986). Psychopharmacology. In H. Quay & J. Werry (Eds.), *Psychopathological disorders of childhood* (3rd ed.). New York: Wiley.

Glass, G. V. (1976). Primary, secondary, and meta-analysis of research. *Educational Researcher, 5,* 3–8.

Glass, G. V. (1977). Integrating findings: The meta-analysis of research. In L. Shulman (Ed.), *Review of Research in Education, 5,* 351–379.

Glass, G. V. (1979). Policy for the unpredictable (uncertainty research and policy). *Educational Researcher, 8,* 12–14.

Glass, G. V., McGaw, B., & Smith, M. L. (1981). *Meta-analysis in social research.* Beverly Hills, CA: Sage.

Glass, G. V., & Robbins, M. P. (1967). A critique of experiments on the role of neurological organization in reading performance. *Reading Research Quarterly, 3,* 5–51.

Goodman, L., & Hammill, D. (1973). The effectiveness of the Kephart-Getman activities in developing peceptual-motor and cognitive skills. *Focus on Exceptional Children, 4,* 1–9.

Guskin, S. L., & Spicker, H. H. (1968). Educational research in mental retardation. In N. R. Ellis (Ed.), *International review of research in mental retardation* (Vol. 3). New York: Academic Press.

Hallahan, D. P., and Cruickshank, W. M. (1973). *Psychoeducational foundations of learning disabilities.* Englewood Cliffs, NJ: Prentice-Hall.

Hallahan, D. P., & Kauffman, J. M. (1977). Labels, categories, behaviors: ED, LD, and EMR reconsidered. *Journal of Special Education, 11,* 139–149.

Hallahan, D. P., & Kauffman, J. M. (1986). *Exceptional children: Introduction to special education* (3rd ed.). Englewood Cliffs, NJ: Prentice-Hall.

Hammill, D. D., Goodman, L., & Weiderholt, J. L. (1974). Visual-motor processes: Can we train them? *Reading Teacher, 27,* 469–478.

Hammill, D. D., & Larsen, S. C. (1974). The effectiveness of psycholinguistic training. *Exceptional Children, 41,* 5–14.

Hammill, D. D., & Larsen, S. C. (1978). The effectiveness of psycholinguistic training: A reaffirmation of position. *Exceptional Children, 44,* 402–414.

Hedges, L. V., & Olkin, I. (1985). *Statistical methods for meta-analysis.* New York: Academic Press.

Heshusius, L. (1982). At the heart of the advocacy dilemma: A mechanistic word view. *Exceptional Children, 49,* 6–13.

Heshusius, L. (1986). Paradigm shifts and special education: A response to Ulman and Rosenberg. *Exceptional Children, 52,* 461–465.

Hewett, L. M., & Forness, S. R. (1984). *Education of exceptional learners* (3rd ed.). Boston: Allyn and Bacon.

Howell, K. (1983). *Inside special education.* Columbus, OH: Charles E. Merrill.

Hunter, J. E., Schmidt, F. L., & Jackson, G. B. (1982). *Meta-analysis: Cumulating research findings across studies.* Beverly Hills, CA: Sage.

Iano, R. P. (1986). The study and development of teaching: With implications for the advancement of special education. *Remedial and Special Education, 7*(5), 50–61.

Johnson, G. O. (1962). Special education of the mentally handicapped—A paradox. *Exceptional Children, 29,* 62–69.

Jones, L. Y., & Fiske, D. W. (1953). Models for testing the significance of combined results. *Psychological Bulletin, 50,* 375–382.

Joyce, B., & Weil, M. (1972). *Models of teaching.* Englewood Cliffs, NJ: Prentice-Hall.

Kaplan, A. (1964). *The conduct of inquiry.* San Francisco: Chandler.

Kauffman, J. M. (1981). Historical trends and contemporary issues in special education in the United States. In J. M. Kauffman & D. P. Hallahan (Eds.), *Handbook of special education.* Englewood Cliffs, NJ: Prentice-Hall.

Kavale, K. A. (1979). Mainstreaming: The genesis of an idea. *Exceptional Child, 26,* 3–21.

Kavale, K. A. (1981). Functions of the Illinois Test of Psycholinguistic Abilities (ITPA): Are they trainable? *Exceptional Children, 47,* 496–510.

Kavale, K. A. (1982a). The efficacy of stimulant drug treatment for hyperactivity: A meta-analysis. *Journal of Learning Disabilities, 15,* 280–289.

Kavale, K. A. (1982b). Psycholinguistic training programs: Are there differential treatment effects? *Exceptional Child, 29,* 21–30.

Kavale, K. A. (1983). Fragile findings, complex conclusions, and meta-analysis in special education. *Exceptional Education Quarterly, 4*(3), 97–106.

Kavale, K. A. (1984). Potential advantages of the meta-analysis technique for research in special education. *Journal of Special Education, 18,* 61–72.

Kavale, K. A., & Forness, S. R. (1983). Hyperactivity and diet treatment: A meta-analysis of the Feingold hypothesis. *Journal of Learning Disabilities, 16,* 324–330.

Kavale, K. A., & Forness, S. R. (1987). A matter of substance over style: A quantitative synthesis assessing the efficacy of modality testing and teaching. *Exceptional Children, 54,* 228–239.

Kavale, K. A. & Mattson, P. D. (1983). "One jumped off the balance beam": Meta-analysis of perceptual-motor training. *Journal of Learning Disabilities, 16,* 165–173.

Keogh, B. (1978). Noncognitive aspects of learning disabilities: Another look at perceptual-motor approaches to assessment and remediation. In L. Oettinger (Ed.), *The psychologist, the school, and the child with MBD/LD.* New York: Grune & Stratton.

Kephart, N. C. (1972). On the value of empirical data in learning disability. *Journal of Learning Disabilities, 4,* 393–395.

Kerlinger, F. N. (1986). *Foundations of behavioral research* (3rd ed.). New York: Holt, Rinehart and Winston.

Kirk, S. A. (1964). Research in education. In H. A. Stevens & R. Heber (Eds.), *Mental retardation: A review of research.* Chicago: University of Chicago Press.

Kirk, S. A., & Kirk, W. D. (1971). *Psycholinguistic learning disabilities: Diagnosis and remediation.* Urbana: University of Illinois Press.

Kirk, S. A., McCarthy, J. J., & Kirk, W. D. (1968). *The Illinois Test of Psycholinguistic Abilities* (rev. ed.). Urbana: University of Illinois Press.

Labouvie, E. W. (1975). The dialetical nature of measurement activities in the behavioral sciences. *Human Development, 18,* 205–222.

Larsen, S. C., Parker, R. M., & Hammill, D. D. (1982). Effectiveness of psycholinguistic training: A response to Kavale. *Exceptional Children, 49*(1), 60–66.

Lew, F. (1977). The Feingold diet, experienced [letter]. *Medical Journal of Australia, 1,* 190.

Lindblom, C. E., & Cohen, D. K. (1979). *Usable knowledge: Social science and social problem solving.* New Haven, CT: Yale University Press.

Lloyd, J. W. (1984). How shall we individualize instruction—Or should we? *Remedial and Special Education, 5*(1), 7–15.

Lloyd, J. W. (1987). The art and science of research on teaching. *Remedial and Special Education, 8*(1), 44–46.

Lund, K. A., Foster, G. E., & McCall-Perez, G. C. (1978). The effectiveness of psycholinguistic training: A reevaluation. *Exceptional Children, 44,* 310–319.

Mackenzie, D. E. (1983). Research for school improvement: An appraisal of some recent trends. *Educational Researcher, 12*(4), 5–17.

MacMillan, D. L. (1971). Special education for the mildly retarded: Servant or savant? *Focus on Exceptional Children, 2,* 1–11.

MacQuarrie, C. W. (1967). *A perceptual testing and training guide for kindergarten teachers.* Winter Haven, FL: Lions Research Foundation.

Mann, L. (1970). Perceptual training: Misdirections and

redirections. *American Journal of Orthopsychiatry, 40,* 30–38.

Mann, L. (1971a). Perceptual training revisited: The training of nothing at all. *Rehabilitation Literature, 32,* 322–327, 335.

Mann, L. (1971b). Psychometric phrenology and the new faculty psychology: The case against ability assessment and training. *Journal of Special Education, 5,* 3–14.

Mann, L. (1979). *On the trail of process.* New York: Grune & Stratton.

Mann, L., & Goodman, L. (1976). Perceptual training: A critical retrospect. In E. Schopler & R. J. Reichler (Eds.), *Psychopathology and child development: Research and treatment.* New York: Plenum Press.

Mann, L., & Phillips, W. A. (1967). Fractional practices in special education: A critique. *Exceptional Children, 33*(44), 311–317.

Meyers, C. E., MacMillan, D. L., & Yoshida, R. K. (1980). Regular class education of EMR students, from efficacy to mainstreaming: A review of issues and research. In J. Gottlieb (Ed.), *Educating mentally retarded persons in the mainstream.* Baltimore: University Park Press.

Milofsky, C. D. (1974). Why special education isn't special. *Harvard Educational Review, 44*(4), 437–458.

Minskoff, R. (1975). Research on psycholinguistic training: Critique and guidelines. *Exceptional Children, 42,* 136–144.

Morsink, C. V., Soar, R. S., Soar, R. M., & Thomas, R. (1986). Research on teaching: Opening the door to special education classrooms. *Exceptional Children, 53*(1), 32–40.

Nelson, C. M., & Polsgrove, L. (1984). Behavior analysis in special education: White rabbit or white elephant. *Remedial and Special Education, 5,* 6–15.

Newcomer, P., Larsen, S., & Hammill, D. (1975). A response. *Exceptional Children, 42,* 144–148.

O'Leary, K. D. (1980). Pills or skills for hyperactive children. *Journal of Applied Behavior Analysis, 13,* 191–204.

Osgood, C. E. (1957). Motivational dynamics of language behavior. In M. R. Jones (Ed.), *Nebraska symposium on motivation.* Lincoln: University of Nebraska Press.

Patton, J. K., Payne, J. S., Kauffman, J. M., Brown, G. B., & Payne, R. A. (1987). *Exceptional children in focus* (4th ed.). Columbus, OH: Charles E. Merrill.

Pelham, W. E. (1986). The effects of psychostimulant drugs on learning and academic achievement in children with attention-deficit disorders and learning disabilities. In J. Torgesen & B. Wong (Eds.), *Psychological and educational perspectives on learning disabilities* (pp. 160–168). New York: Academic Press.

Peterson, P. L., & Walberg, H. J. (Eds.). (1979). *Research on teaching: Concepts, findings, and implications.* Berkeley, CA: McCutchan.

Phillips, D. (1983). After the wake: Post positivistic educational thought. *Educational Researcher, 12,* 4–12.

Phillips, D. C. (1980). What do the researcher and the practitioner have to offer each other? *Educational Researcher, 9,* 17–20, 24.

Purkey, S. C., & Smith, M. S. (1983). Effective schools: A review. *Elementary School Journal, 83,* 427–452.

Rosenthal, R., & Jacobson, L. (1968). *Pygmalion in the classroom.* New York: Holt, Rinehart and Winston.

Rosenthal, R., & Rubin, D. D. (1978). Interpersonal expectancy effects: The first 345 studies. *Behavioral and Brain Sciences, 3,* 377–415.

Salomon, G. (1972). Heuristic models for the generation of aptitude-treatment interaction hypotheses. *Review of Educational Research, 42,* 327–343.

Samuels, S. J. (1986). Why children fail to learn and what to do about it. *Exceptional Children, 53*(1), 7–16.

Schenck, S. J. (1980). The diagnostic-instructional link in individualized education programs. *Journal of Special Education, 14,* 337–345.

Schrag, P., & Divoky, D. (1975). *The myth of the hyperactive child.* New York: Pantheon Books.

Shattuck, M. (1946). Segregation versus non-segregation of exceptional children. *Journal of Exceptional Children, 12,* 235–240.

Sheridan, J. J., & Meister, K. A. (1982). *Food additives and hyperactivity.* New York: American Council on Science and Health.

Soltis, J. (1984). On the nature of educational research. *Educational Researcher, 13,* 5–10.

Sprague, R. L., & Werry, J. S. (1971). Methodology of psychopharmacological studies with the retarded. In N. R. Ellis (Ed.). *International review of research in mental retardation (Vol. 5).* New York: Academic Press.

Squires, D. (1983). *Effective schools and classrooms: A research-based perspective.* Alexandria, VA: Association for Supervision and Curriculum Development.

Sroufe, L. A. (1975). Drug treatment of children with behavior problems. In F. J. Horowitz (Ed.), *Review of child development research (Vol. 4).* Chicago: University of Chicago Press.

Sternberg, L., & Taylor, R. L. (1982). The insignificance of psycholinguistic training: A reply to Kavale. *Exceptional Children, 49*(3), 254–256.

Stevens, R., & Rosenshine, B. (1981). Advances in research on teaching. *Exceptional Education Quarterly, 2,* 1–9.

Swanson, H. L. (1984). Does theory guide practice? *Remedial and Special Education, 5*(5), 7–16.

Tarver, S. G., & Dawson, M. M. (1978). Modality preference and the teaching of reading: A review. *Journal of Learning Disabilities, 11,* 5–17.

Tindal, G. (1985). Investigating the effectiveness of special education: An analysis of methodology. *Journal of Learning Disabilities, 18*(2), 101–112.

Ulman, J. D., & Rosenberg, M. S. (1986). Science and superstition in special education. *Exceptional Children, 52,* 459–460.

Van Witsen, B. (1967). *Perceptual training activities handbook.* New York: Teachers College Press.

Wender, E. H. (1977). Food additives and hyperkinesis. *American Journal of Diseases of Children, 131,* 1204–1206.

Ysseldyke, J. E., & Salvia, J. (1980). Methodological considerations in aptitude-treatment interaction research with intact groups. *Diagnostique, 6,* 3–9.

36

ORGANIZATION DEVELOPMENT IN SCHOOLS: CONTEMPORARY CONCEPTS AND PRACTICES[1]

RICHARD A. SCHMUCK

University of Oregon

Schools are social organizations. Without interdependent and collaborative relationships among people, they are nothing but wood, concrete, and paper. Many of the difficulties experienced by staffs, during periods of change, may be traced to the nature of the organizational culture of the school. Thus, most deliberate efforts at school improvement affect not only the principal and the faculty, but also the relationships between them and their collective relationships with the students and parents. Unfortunately, school staffs are notoriously weak in their capabilities for productive collaboration. It is for those reasons that school psychologists have begun to add the theory and technology of organization development (OD) to their repertoires.

BASIC CONCEPTS OF ORGANIZATION DEVELOPMENT

Organization development is a planned and sustained effort at school self-study and improvement, focusing explicitly on change in both formal and

[1]More detail about the topics discussed in this chapter can be found in Schmuck and Runkel (1988).

informal norms, structures, and procedures, using behavioral science concepts and experiential learning. It involves the school participants themselves in the active assessment, diagnosis, and transformation of their own organization.

Assumptions of Organization Development

Organization development assumes that many efforts at educational reform have collapsed or have been absorbed without effect, precisely because of the limited attention given to the organizational context in which the reforms have been attempted. The assumption follows that innovation in curriculum or instructional techniques requires alterations in the school's behavioral and programmatic regularities, or to put it in another way, educational innovations require changes in the "culture" of the school. (For an in-depth discussion on the culture of the schools, *see* Sarason, 1982.)

Values of Organization Development

The most basic value of organization development is that of joining and working together collaboratively with educators, students, and parents to create democratic social structures and humanized interpersonal relationships. Attendant values include expanding all participants' consciousness about how others think and feel, as well as finding more and more choices for new action. Very important are (a) the valuing of I—thou interactions and authenticity in interpersonal relations; (b) a collaborative conception of freedom and control, and emphasis on participation with interpersonal respect; and (c) the valuing of internal commitment.

Goals of Organization Development

Organization development is a conceptual framework and a strategy to help schools meet the challenges of a pluralistic society. It encompasses a theory and a technology to help schools become self-renewing and self-correcting human systems. Organization development enables the school to monitor and respond to its environment, and to find, maintain, and use the human resources, ideas, and energy needed to respond to that environment. The tenacity of a school's culture lies in the power of norms, how well they are adhered to, and how resistant they are to change. Norms are shared expectations, usually implicit, that help guide the psychological dynamics and the group behaviors of members.

The Organization Development Perspective

When looking at the school through the lens of an organization-development perspective, the school psychologist considers a student's emotional problems, at least in part, as arising from the student's position in the school culture. Assigning a student to the psychologist often implies that the student is not adjusting to the school culture and that the student should make appropriate changes in behavior. In other words, a traditional psychologist's orientation is to help the deviant student to adjust to the school as it now exists. In contrast, the organization-development perspective teaches that personal, emotional problems are influenced by interpersonal environments and that the interpersonal relations of the staff can represent particularly potent social environments for students. The school psychologist with organization development in mind queries, "What are the deficiencies in the interpersonal and group dynamics of the staff?" before he or she asks, "What is psychologically wrong with the student?"

Instead of intervening primarily on a one-to-one basis, the school psychologist with an organization-development perspective works with most members of the faculty, or at least with key subsystems of the school such as academic departments, classroom groups, or the student government. The energy that school psychologists use on a few students is converted into working with groups of students and staff.

THEORY OF ORGANIZATION DEVELOPMENT IN SCHOOL

Organization development is based on human-systems theory. The theoretical foundations of organization development are in the Field Theory of Kurt Lewin (1976), and in the social-psychological systems theory as best delineated in D. Katz and Kahn (1978). The theory posits that acting on the educational system as a target for improvement offers a promising, indirect strategy for ameliorating the mental health and academic learning problems of individual students.

Characteristics of Social Systems

In attempting to understand human nature, psychologists typically have focused on the interrelationships among perceptions, cognitions, affect, motives, and actions of individuals. Their mental health interventions may, for example, aim at increasing veridicality of perceptions, organizing cognitive processes, clarifying affective states, integrating the cognitive with the affective, offering cognitive maps for satisfying motives and achieving self-esteem, and enhancing cognitive control over actions.

Norms, Structures, and Procedures

Compared to this psychological emphasis, the targets of social system interventions to enhance organization development require the analytic tools of the social psychologist. Groups and organizations are constituted of norms, structures, and procedures, a cluster of human events that do not simply grow out of the psychology of the individual actors.

Since norms are shared expectations about how a system member ought to think, feel, and behave toward a particular issue, the dynamics of sharedness must be assessed. Norms can not be measured by summing the individual attitudes of the participants in a social system, as one might attempt by polling each individual separately and by adding the responses. Assessing sharedness would require noting that two or more persons believe that the others hold expectations similar to theirs and that they expect one another to behave according to the content of those expectations. Thus, norms are constituted of implicit or explicit interpersonal exchanges between two or more system participants, with neophytes being socialized into the norms through listening, observing, modeling, venturing, and receiving feedback.

Structures entail visible networks of interdependencies, sequences of interaction, and behavioral exchanges that constitute a larger social reality than any individual participant brings to them. Structures may be more easily and directly assessed than norms because the latter so frequently are implicit or preconscious. System structures are physical and vivid; they can be assessed through observations of person-to-person interactions, group formations, routings of memos and correspondence, the paths of telephone calls, and the like. Even so, assessing system structures often is difficult, both because of the complex logistics required in monitoring the structures of complex bureaucracies and because of the not-so-obvious informal structures involving influence, friendship, and social support.

Procedures refer to the organization's formal activities for accomplishing tasks and for maintaining itself. They are analogous to the behavioral patterns of individuals, but have an existence based on law or tradition that is larger in time and scope than the unique ways in which individuals act in the organization. Meetings are called in a particular way and run according to some agreed-on patterns, records are kept in standard forms, travel vouchers must go through a number of steps to be bona fide, new members go through routines, job evaluations are carried out in certain fashions, and so on. Procedures are carried out through system structures and often are guided by strong norms.

Formal and Informal Aspects

In a workable social system, the subsystems are articulated and interrelated to accomplish the organization's primary tasks and to satisfy human needs sufficiently to keep the organization on course. The norms, structures, and procedures of the subsystems support the task focus by ensuring predictability, efficiency, and coordination of teachers, students, and administrators. But the formal organization of the school tells only part of the story.

In schools there inevitably arise conflicts between the instructional focus and the desires of the teachers, students, and administrators. Such divergent pulls reflect the rational and emotional sides of human nature. Rationality is highlighted by the norms, structures, and procedures of the subsystems, but the emotional aspects of human behavior frequently are deemphasized, even discouraged, by the school's curriculum and instructional arrangements. In the classroom, for example, the press for competition, getting the curriculum done on time, and performing learning tasks according to the teacher's standards can frustrate students' needs for friendship, autonomy, and creativity. Or, altering teachers' assignments to cut costs frequently frustrates their expectations and the informal routines they have established with colleagues. As a consequence, informal structures, which offer legitimate avenues for emotional expression, develop and exist along side of and within the formal subsystems. Moreover, informal structures take on norms and procedures of their own that frequently can oppose the smooth functioning of the formal subsystems.

For its basic ideas about the power of informal norms, structures, and procedures on formal organizational life, OD has relied on several seminal studies. The classic Hawthorne studies by Elton Mayo, as reported by Roethlisberger and Dickson (1939), did a great deal to turn attention from the formal to the informal. A fascinating study, too, in overcoming resistance to formal organizational change (Coch and French, 1948) demonstrated the power of informal group interaction in changing formal norms and procedures.

Linking the School Organization to Students

Lewin's Field Theory has been useful for tracing the social-psychological linkage between school and student, particularly the connections among informal organizational climate, student perception, and student learning. Lewin theorized that behavior is caused by a concatenation of the person's perceptions of the social environment and the person's personality structure. The theory was expressed in the form of an equation written as Behavior = $f(E$ and $P)$, where f stood for "function of," E stood for the social environment, and P stood for the psychological variables inside the person. OD theorists think of the school's formal structure and informal culture as offering stimuli for the E, whereas the student's motives, attitudes, cognitions, and values constitute important features of the P.

Field Theory Applied to OD

OD is guided by Lewin's equation, Behavior $= f(E$ and $P)$. The source of effective behavior in the school will be a function of organizational problem solving and subsystem effectiveness in the E, and self-actualization of the P.

Organizational Problem Solving

A healthy school goes beyond sheer survival to cope adequately over the long haul and to develop and extend its surviving and coping abilities. The "bottom line," of course, is the school's ability to educate successfully a continuously changing student body. Organizational problem solving means that the faculty is remaining open to information about students from both the environment and inside the organization, examining new instructional ideas, becoming aware of innovations in curriculum, and attempting to predict changes to come, both in the youth culture and in the area of school curriculum. That is no small order.

A healthy school uses many resources, both external and internal, to aid in solving problems and in being responsive to new demands. Buckley (1967) referred to an organization's repertoire of usable resources as its variety pool. A variety pool includes individuals' information, energy, and skills; and also norms, structures, and procedures in support of systematic and collaborative problem solving. Although many schools possess a rich variety pool, the healthy school makes use of much of the resourcefulness it has because it has established appropriate norms, structures, and procedures.

Subsystem Effectiveness

Schools engaging effectively in organization problem solving have subsystems that function effectively. Subsystem effectiveness may be determined in two ways: first by assessing healthiness of the subsystem's norms, structures, and procedures; and second by diagnosing the sorts of articulation, interdependence, and conflict management procedures connecting each subsystem with every other.

Subsystems that function effectively integrate the formal and informal lives of the participants in the service of both goal achievement and social-emotional maintenance. The effectiveness of subsystems can be assessed by checking on goal and role clarity, communication accuracy and clarity, efficient agenda setting and meeting procedures, resource identification and use, decision-making involvement and clarity, cohesiveness and morale, and the presence of evaluative feedback procedures up and down hierarchical levels. A diagnosis of system effectiveness must be concerned with the dovetailing of the formal and informal aspects of group life.

The process of subsystems may be conceived as the complex interplay of norms and roles. Norms when collected into a gestalt constitute the subsystem's culture, while an interrelated set of roles make up the subsystem's structure. Along with a focus on interpersonal skills, organization development looks to modifications in the school's culture and its structure for enhancing problem solving and effective change.

The social psychological character of norms is relevant to organization development in several ways. First, norms help to coordinate the school's structure by causing behavior to be guided by common expectations, attitudes, and understandings. Second, norms can facilitate both the school's viability and the individual staff member's sense of well-being. Third, norms can promote a clear division of labor by helping to specify the appropriate behaviors for each task. Finally, for the staff member, norms provide a basis for social reality, especially when objective reality is ambiguous, as it so often is for administrators and teachers.

Furthermore, although norms may act to resist school change, they can gradually be modified to facilitate changes in tasks, roles, and classroom procedures. They can be altered when staff members conjointly and simultaneously experiment with innovative ways of doing things, and sustain those new actions until enough members come to believe that their colleagues will accept and continue on with the new patterns of role behavior. Such sustained, conjoint action is particularly important when the norms to be changes are integrally associated with the competencies or skills of individuals. Many interpersonal patterns of a school can be modified if staff members make explicit formal agreements conjointly (and this is always a significant point for organization development), but many patterns of interaction characterized by strong ego involvement may require time-consuming, one-to-one agreements reached through private discussions. However agreements for new norms and roles are reached, they must be supported by other staff members and legitimized through formal, staff agreements.

Individuals as Self-Actualizing Participants
The work of Maslow (1954), McClelland (1975), and Rogers (1969) describe a central human motive as striving for self-actualization, and that striving typically takes place in at least three motivational domains: (a) the striving for achievement, also referred to as competency, efficacy, and curiosity; (b) the striving for affiliation, affection, and support; and (c) the striving for power and influence. Typical emotions resulting from frustrating those motives are feelings of inferiority and incompetence, of being put down, ignored, or losing control, and of rejection, loneliness, and distrust.

Teachers, students, and administrators will be more likely to remain motivated, have available more paths to further satisfaction, and become more productive if their achievement, power, and affiliation motives can be satisfied in school life. While collaborating and interacting with interdependent others in a variety of school settings can affect the satisfaction of these three motives and one's self-esteem, we look primarily to the classrooms to find achievement satisfactions, to peer and collegial relationships for affiliative satisfactions, and to hierarchical relationships both within the school and between the school and the district office for power satisfaction.

Formal Organizational Theories Applied to OD

In his history of schooling in Boston, M. B. Katz (1971) argued that urban schools began to display many of the attributes of a Weberian bureaucracy during the last quarter of the 19th century (for details on Weber's theory, see Weber and Parsons, 1947). In line with Weber, Katz enumerated the emerging features of school bureaucracy as (a) increased centralization of control, by way of a district office attempting to standardize programs across schools; (b) differentiation of function by formal job titles and role; (c) standardized qualifications for office; (d) objectivity and rationality in performance; and (e) precision and consistency in decision making along with a clear chain of command.

According to Katz, superintendents who came into authority at the turn of the century believed that rational bureaucracy represented an effective solution to the complexities of rapid growth in

student numbers. Specialization of teachers, clear division of labor, and the chain of accountability would help the school to overcome the intellectual and emotional limits of individuals, and to ensure a smooth-running, fair, and equitable educational experience for all students. From the point of view of OD, it is instructive to explore the theories of three sociologists, Merton, Selznick, and Gouldner, on the unanticipated dysfunctions of rational bureaucracy.

Merton's (1949) theory dealt with behavioral rigidity as an unplanned consequence of a chain of accountability. He argued that in bureaucracies administrators strive to establish both accountability and predictability of worker performance, and that three consequences often occur: (a) a reduction in personalized relationships as staff members interact with one another in terms of positions, (b) an increase in the internalization of rules of the organization, and (c) an increased use of standardized decision making, thus reducing creativity. All three consequences Merton viewed as increasing the behavioral rigidity of the staff.

Parallels to school organizations seem clear. As district administrators exert demands for control, stressing standardized action, they are unwittingly encouraging behavioral rigidity, thus reducing the innovativeness that would be risked by a staff member. The typical staff reaction becomes, "Don't rock the boat—Do it as they want it done—Do it according to the book." Filling out forms, having lesson plans prepared according to a format, writing narrow behavioral objectives, and the like can lead to a rigid, ritualistic adherence to administrative demands, and can also serve as a crutch to a staff member's defense against criticism from parents or students. Difficulties with students or parents can be written off as reactions from troublemakers or from those who are unsophisticated about the complexities of education.

In comparison with Merton's emphasis on rigidity, Selznick (1949) focused on the delegation of authority as a key variable of bureaucracies. In particular, he was concerned with the unplanned results that arise when delegation is employed for hierarchical control. Delegation results eventually in departmentalization and in what Selznick called a "bifurcation of interests" among the departments. Indeed, departmental maintenance dictates concern for departmental goals first and organizational purposes second. Moreover, as specialities increase, it becomes costly to move personnel from one department to another. Departments can become so entrenched that they will not change even in the face of demands on the organization for change.

Parallels of the school to Selznick's theory also seem familiar. The board delegates district responsibilities to the superintendent; the superintendent delegates site responsibility to the principals, and the principals delegate classroom authority to teachers. Moreover, staff members such as school psychologists are given authority to carry out their specialized functions. And, as in Selznick's analysis, the emergence of departments in district abounds, each with its own purposes and expertise. Each department establishes it own goals, competencies, and skills, making it difficult for a member of one department to function effectively in another. Organizational development becomes difficult as the separate departments solidify.

Finally, Gouldner (1954) argued that a bureaucracy maintains stability by establishing general and impersonal rules about how jobs should be executed. As a consequence, a norm of equality arises, which decreases the extent to which power differences in the organization are noticed. Such a norm facilitates work, because cooperation is enhanced in an equalitarian climate; however, the impersonal rules also provide cues for what is minimally acceptable performance. When administrators put pressure on the workers to upgrade their work, the increased closeness of supervision creates interpersonal tensions between hierarchical levels, culminating in new rules about what is appropriate behavior in the bureaucracy—and the cycle repeats itself.

Schools suffer from the bureaucratic dysfunctions noted by Gouldner. As Lortie (1975) theorized, a strong norm of equality exists among educators. Indeed, the elementary staff frequently is referred to as "one big, happy family," and in secondary schools, administrators strive to treat teachers alike, regardless of department and tenure. That equalitarian norm is violated, however, each time administrators give a negative evaluation of performance to teachers. In some schools, a new supervisory role has been introduced to upgrade teacher performance to take the principal "off the hook," but tensions still arise between supervisors and teachers, and new agreements must be reached to reduce the tension. Eventually, staff members learn how to live within the new norms and procedures, and to perform adequately. But again, performance that is only minimally adequate will be viewed as falling short of an ideal and the cycle can be reinstituted.

Although the theories of Merton, Selznick, and Gouldner can enhance our understanding of how organization development might reduce the dysfunctions of the school bureaucracy, they were developed primarily to explain problems of industrial organizations. Michaelsen (1977) offered another theory for understanding how the school works. He argued that the school is a nonprofit bureau, concerned more with politics than with sales and client responses. Thus, according to Michaelsen, school staffs seek to enlarge the scope of their activities, to gain prestige and credibility, to avoid conflict and tension, to control their daily activities, and finally, to survive. Administrators and teachers are viewed as striving to maximize politically related activities over which they might have some control. For the administrators, budgets rather than profits would be maximized. Larger budgets could help administrators to survive, to increase their prestige, and generally to gain control. For teachers, classroom space, materials, freedom of movement, autonomy, equality, and tenure would be emphasized.

Michaelsen's conceptualization of the school as a highly political system undergirds Kouzes and Mico's (1979) Domain Theory. Kouzes and Mico theorize that schools have political conflicts built into their structure and culture. They say that three kinds of subsystems are inevitably in conflict— those in the domains of policy, management, and service. In school districts, the policy domain is occupied primarily by the school board, while the administrators make up the management domain and the teachers the service domain.

Typically, people working in the policy domain are elected representatives, who measure success by whether they make just, impartial, and fair decisions. Their work modes involve negotiating, bargaining, and voting. Those in the management domain view the organization as hierarchy and bureaucracy. They measure their success by cost-efficiency and organizational effectiveness, and their modes are linear and rational. Those in the service domain operate by autonomy, collegiality, and self-regulation, measuring success by the quality of instruction and by whether they act according to professional standards. Their attention goes to process more than product, and their work modes are citizen specific and oriented to problem solving.

Management's insistence on conformity to

rules conflicts with the service domain's focus on the needs of students. The policy domain's norm of airing disagreements in public conflicts with management's norm of avoiding conflict. The norm of fair and equitable treatment among policymakers conflicts with the demand for cost-efficiency in management, and the latter conflicts with the maintenance of professional standards in the service domain.

Representation among policymakers, bureaucracy in the management, and collegiality for those in service require different kinds of interpersonal norms, and conflicts arise when a participant in one domain expects to be treated by norms that seem inappropriate to persons in another domain. The linear work modes in management, the individualized treatment of human problems in service, and negotiation and bargaining in policy call for different norms and values. It might be fruitless for participants in the three domains to try to adhere to the same norms and procedures.

One way to reduce the likelihood of conflict between domains is to arrange work so that people from different domains do not often interact with one another. Division of labor is the typical structure—among individuals, committees, departments, and so on, with specific resources allocated to each. To the extent that interdependence among persons or groups of diverse domains can be minimized, the occasions for conflict can be minimized. Weick (1976), in a classic article, called that reduced interdependence, "loose coupling." Schools are notoriously loosely coupled, thereby presenting a considerable challenge to the OD consultant.

To elaborate on the key points of formal organizational theory, schools are (a) vulnerable to conflicts between parts of their structure and consequently prone to a loosely coupled structure, (b) characterized by norms in support of accepting mediocre performances even in the face of contemporary cries for excellence, and (c) disposed to behavioral rigidity in their procedures even as they strive to be innovative and creative.

STAGES AND TECHNOLOGY OF OD

Consultation in OD aims to bridge the gaps between participants in the school and to make collaboration worthwhile and effective. It aims to help participants establish norms, structures, and procedures for problem solving about innovations that will lead to greater excellence in education. It works to arrive at those objectives through a systematic, sequential process involving five stages.

Contract Building

If organization development is to be built on a solid base of participant support, it is crucial to gain at least a publicly delivered, oral commitment from the key staff members that will be participating. To this end, the critical importance of establishing relaxed rapport, credibility, trust, and legitimacy at the outset, and of arriving at clear statements about goals, competencies, and shared expectations cannot be overemphasized. Organization-development consultants must be explicit about their role, the targets of change, the project's budget, and the time they are expecting to devote to the project. The first is very important since the school psychologist will have to be explicit about how taking the role of an organization-development consultant differs from the typical functions of the school psychologist. Also, the last is of supreme importance since organizational change requires time, often one or two years in many schools.

Although any staff member of a prospective target school may contact the school psychologist to ask for help in organization development, the introductory discussions should formally be carried out between the school's administrators and the consultant. While the principal, assistant principals, and department heads are usually the ones to meet with first, it must be remembered that gaining approval and collaboration of the managers alone will not necessarily win commitment from other staff members. Indeed, the implication of collusion between the consultant and the administrators can lead to the project's rapid demise. Remember that organization development works for school improvement through the instructional subsystems and that introductory, contract-building sessions should eventually be carried out with all key staff members.

While the characteristics of social systems, the strategy of organization development, the targets for change, consultative designs, and intervention techniques characterize the initial discussions, sound consultant-client relationships are not forged by agreement about consultative activities alone. The school psychologist should remain aware that the dynamics of start-up and contract building often arouse intense feelings of suspicion and distrust, defensiveness and dissatisfaction, investment and caution, and vulnerability and reserve. Even though improvements in the school's capability to do problem solving is the overriding target, individual staff members themselves will undergo changes with their own thoughts and feelings. Directly discussing staff member's thoughts and feelings about change in empathic ways can be a prime requisite for valid contract building and a successful design.

Frequently, a demonstration of how organization development works serves as a useful event as a prelude to contract building. A thorough demonstration requires 2 days, but one can be carried out in as little as 2 hours. The participating staff members are told that the demonstration is being offered to help them determine whether they would like to become involved in organization development.

Demonstration goals include (a) developing staff members' interest in the benefits of organization development; (b) presenting a picture of a self-renewing, problem-solving school; (c) helping staff members see how to confront current problems; (d) helping them understand the unique functions of organization development in contrast to those of management consultation or sensitivity training; (e) presenting a picture of the skills that might be gained through organization development; and (6) establishing the beginning of a collaborative relationship between "clients" and consultants.

Early in the demonstration the consultants present definitions, theory, an overview of technology, the stages, and the notion of organizational capacity for problem solving. Next, the demonstration proceeds to episodes that entail more active participation of staff members. Every remaining microaspect begins with experiential activity and is followed by debriefing with the help of client or consultant observer. Staff members are then asked to comment on the similarities and differences between the activity and their actual school experience. Finally, the consultant points out relevancies to the real school, presents concepts so that staff members can apply them to their school, and makes available more detailed readings.

Diagnosis
The consultants need some reliable scientific data on which to base their designs and they must also communicate to staff members of the target school that particular data on this specific school will be necessary for designing a tailored consultation. While collecting appropriate data on communication adequacy, goal agreement, conflicts, meeting skills, problem solving, and the like, consultants can communicate the focus of organization development and at the same time train staff members in what activities will follow.

Diagnosis should occur with even the most sophisticated faculty. Indeed, pessimistic comments by faculty members are important data in themselves. Special care should be taken with cautious or cynical faculty members to assess the amount of resistance to or readiness for organization development. The school psychologist should strive to discover the kinds of workshop events that occurred within the school before, the kinds of organizational problems that were worked on, and, why, from the staff members' point of view, previous change efforts were aborted. Problems that are attacked as part of the organization-development effort, such as ineffective meeting procedures, should take into account the frustrations or successes of previous problem-solving attempts.

The diagnosis should make use of multiple methods, of which self-report questionnaires, interview schedules, and systems for observation are the most typical. In addition to those formal methods, organizational memos and letters, informal conversations with staff members, and even observations made during casual visits with clients offer important information. Collecting formal data can strengthen staff members' views of the validity and legitimacy of the organization-development effort.

Design
Designs for implementing organization development can be divided into macroaspects and microaspects. A macrodesign comprises the overall structure and outline, sequence of parts, and general forms through which activities flow. An example would be a sequence in which interpersonal skills are upgraded, norms in support of collaborative goal setting are strengthened, and structures for improved organizational problem solving are established. Microaspects of a design refer to the specific activities played out during any limited period of consultation. Those could include specific skill-development activities, group exercises, and innovative organizational procedures. The most frequently used microaspect is a systematic

problem-solving sequence since it fits into most macrodesigns.

Four types of macrodesigns may be distinguished: training, data feedback, confrontation, and process observation and feedback—each calls for special sorts of skills on the part of the school psychologist. For staff members in the schools, it often is easier to classify these several types of interventions simply into just two, training and consultation, and then to contrast the highly structured pedagogical formats of training with the more immediately pragmatic features of data feedback, confrontation, and process observation and feedback.

In training, the consultant determines the learning goals for a scheduled time period, initiates structure, and directs activities. Training involves highly planned teaching and experience-based learning in structured formats that usually include lecturettes and assigned readings. It is similar to traditional classroom teaching except that in organization development the key members of a subsystem or of an entire school experience the training simultaneously with one another.

Training activities are made up of skills, exercises, and procedures. Skills denote ways in which interactions can be executed within a group. An exercise, or simulation, is a structured, gamelike activity designed to make prominent certain types of group processes that participants can easily conceptualize because they are related to their personal experience. Unlike exercises, whose content is determined by the consultant, procedures are content free and are used to make work more effective toward whatever goal has been chosen.

Data feedback, the systematic collecting of information that is reported back to key members of appropriate subsystems as a basis for diagnosis and subsequent action planning, is one of the most important intervention modes of organization development. At least three aspects of a data feedback strategy constitute the keys to its success. First, the consultant must be adept at collecting valid, relevant data and at putting the data into feedback formats that will be understandable and motivating to the participants. Second, the consultant must strive to elevate mundane data to a level of larger significance so that they are worthy of notice by the participants. Third, the consultant must find ways of incorporating data feedback into the ebb and flow of larger consultative designs and should look for opportunities to transfer the task of

data collection and feedback from the change project to the formal organization of the school itself.

In confrontation design, the consultant brings two or more bodies together to interact and to share the perceptions that each has of the other, to pinpoint areas where each is viewed as helpful or unhelpful to the other, to establish clear communication channels between the two groups, to introduce a problem-solving procedure that may facilitate collaborative inquiry into mutual problems, and finally, to specify the common concerns of all parties in the confrontation. In executing process observation and feedback, the purpose of which is to help group members become more aware of how they are working together, the consultant sits with the client group during its work sessions, observes the ongoing processes, and occasionally offers personal comments or observations.

Training, data feedback, confrontation, and process observation and feedback each in a different way set the stage for collaborative problem solving, plan making, and experimental trials.

Interventions

The OD skills of processing information, conceiving problems, and taking collective action are the fundamental ingredients of all interventions. Collaborative problem solving requires the gathering of diagnostic information, sharing and clarifying it, agreeing on the selection of a specific problem, conceiving and analyzing the problem, and having the ability to respond with experimental trials.

Giving relevant information about one's role and tasks, and eliciting task-related information from others, constitute the two sides of processing information. They offer the paths by which staff members can create the common reality needed for collaborative action and experimental change. However, when feelings run high, as they frequently do in schools when anxiety or disagreement surface, teachers and administrators tend to close off channels of communication that are ordinarily open when things are going smoothly. In such circumstances, those who withhold information about their skills, ideas, preferences, and other resources may deprive others of useful information and the potential means of solving problems.

Conceiving problems entails the search for available information about what is known of the present situation and the goals that are valued or preferred. In particular, it requires specifying a discrepancy between current aspects of a situation and an ideal state, and referring to that gap as the problem. Locating such gaps, acknowledging them, and accepting them as challenges requires time, energy, creativity, and discipline. Above all, successful problem solving requires norms that support taking risks in uncovering problems heretofore unknown or ignored. While there is no certain way for all participants at all times to think of the steps of problem solving, a school staff will be stronger to the extent that it has norms, structures, and procedures that are supportive of continuous, collaborative problem solving. The following skill areas are the primary ones on which the OD consultant focuses:

Clarifying Communication

Clarity of communication is an essential part of OD interventions. By developing more precision in the transmission and reception of information, ambiguity and conflict about norms and roles can be alleviated and interpersonal trust can be built, which can, in turn, reinforce a climate of openness and authenticity.

The OD consultant teaches participants to use six communication skills. Of the six skills, *paraphrasing* (checking your understanding of the other person's meaning) and *impression checking* (checking your impression of the other person's feelings) are ways of helping you understand the other person. *Describing the other's behavior, describing your own behavior, making clear statements of your ideas,* and *describing your own feelings* aim at helping others to understand you. Giving or receiving feedback, a central activity in OD, is not a single skill in the way the six are; rather all six come into play in giving or receiving feedback.

Feedback consists of information sent by the receiver; perhaps it is paraphrasing or feeling descriptions, for instance, back to the source of a message so that the original sender can gauge the effect of the message. By checking impressions or by describing behaviors, the original sender or the receiver can adjust their subsequent messages. One frequently used combination of two communication skills in feedback is for the sender to describe another's behavior and then to state how the sender felt when that behavior occurred. For detailed information about how to use commu-

nication skills during OD interventions, see Chapter 3 in Schmuck and Runkel (1988).

Establishing Clear Goals

Sharpening goal definitions can lead to exploring the differentiation and integration of effort needed to achieve them. Recognizing the pluralism of goals within the subsystem, organization, and environment can be a vital step toward acceptance of differences and greater ownership of common goals.

The Delphi method is one procedure used by OD consultants to help large groups of educators to establish clear goals. In the first step, participants are asked to write the goals they believe to be most suitable for the school or district. All those responses are collected and tabulated and a report is written, of which each participant is given a copy, telling which goals were chosen and how many participants either chose each goal or wrote very similar goals. Second, the participants are told to reconsider their previous answers for possible revision. New responses that deviate conspicuously from the goals recommended by the majority are noted and questioned for reasons; the reasons are reported to the others along with the statements of goals and their frequencies. Asking people who deviate from the majority to give reasons causes those without strong convictions to move toward the median; those who think they have good reason for deviant opinions are likely to maintain and defend them.

The consultant proceeds with two more rounds, repeating the previous round exactly and regarding the result of the fourth round as being as close to consensus as it is possible to get through purely rational processes. If after all that, the consensus is poor, participants will have to turn to group discussion, perhaps divide into subgroups to write up different goals, or the consultant might propose a list of goals after listening to all of the discussions.

Uncovering and Working with Conflict

Confronting conflict can help to clarify the norms and roles that will aid the organization in accomplishing its tasks. Norms for collaboration can replace norms for avoiding conflict. Individualized roles can satisfy diverse motivational patterns and capitalize on diverse abilities and value systems as well. OD consultants typically organize their tactics for resolving conflict into three steps: (a) distinguishing between miscommunication and conflict, (b) assessing the seriousness of the conflict, and (c) responding appropriately to the source of the conflict.

Miscommunications are not conflicts; they are gaps between intended messages and received messages. They occur when messages sent do not directly reflect intentions or when messages received are inaccurately understood. Miscommunications can be reduced by improved articulation and listening. OD consultants use the skills of paraphrasing and summarizing to enhance listening. When miscommunication might escalate into conflict, they seek face-to-face meetings with the parties involved. If clarifying the communication accentuates differences between the parties, the OD consultant assumes that there is conflict and proceeds to assess it.

OD consultants often classify the main sources of conflicts in schools as (a) power struggles between persons and groups, (b) role conflicts, and (c) differentiation of functions among parts of the school. They try to assess the source of the conflict and then respond accordingly. For example, with power struggles, the consultant talks separately with the conflicting parties about their perceptions of the conflict. Often just bringing an unconscious power struggle into the open with conversation can reduce its intensity and disruption. If, however, the struggle does not subside, the consultant recommends that a third party with authority be introduced to help resolve the conflict. That neutral party could, of course, be the consultant, or it could be a key administrator or a committee of trusted school participants who represent a legitimate advisory group (e.g., the department heads, an administrative cabinet, or a committee or teachers). Once the conflict has surfaced and the consultant has made a tentative assessment of its source, the consultant helps the participants seek ways in which they might become engaged in cooperative work toward ends they have in common.

When role conflict is the source, and the procedures above do not seem appropriate, the OD consultant asks each party to write three lists addressed to every other party in the conflict as follows: To help me carry out my role, I'd like you to do the following more or better _____; to help me . . . , I'd like you to do the following less often _____; and . . . , I'd like you to continue doing the following as you now are

_____. The consultant gives the responses to the parties, encouraging each to question others for clarification, but not to argue about the information. After the messages are understood, the consultant asks the parties to choose issues to negotiate, with each prepared to offer a temporary behavior change. The negotiation takes the form of an exchange: If I do _____, you will do _____. After the parties are satisfied that each will receive a return for what they are to give, the consultant records the agreement and moves to another issue.

When differentiation of function is the source, and the tactics above do not work, the consultant asks each of the conflicting parties to write descriptions, both favorable and unfavorable, of themself and of the other party. The consultant next convenes the parties to share their images with one another. Then the consultant separates the parties again and asks each to recall instances when its behavior supported the impressions of the other party. In other words, the OD consultant asks each party to confess that it did, at one time or another, behave in ways that might have exacerbated the conflict. The last stage is for the consultant to reconvene the parties to share the confessions and to specify the underlying issues that are pulling them apart. Although such a procedure will not resolve all differences, it can set the stage for collaborative problem solving.

Improving Procedures in Meetings

The face-to-face group meetings in which most organizational activity occurs in schools need not be frustrating or unproductive. Procedures aimed at facilitating task productivity and group maintenance can make such meetings more satisfying. At least four methods are available to the OD consultant to improve meetings: (a) modeling an effective group member, (b) providing information about effective meetings, (c) providing training, and (d) providing consultation and feedback.

For purposes of modeling, consultants may repeatedly paraphrase or at least clarify what others are saying, insist that particular agenda items be clarified, or volunteer to convene the meeting, organize its agenda, or reword and summarize agreements. Consultants can also help by providing information about effective meetings, especially guides for conveners, recorders, and process consultants. When participants are frustrated with their meetings, the consultant is in a good position to offer training in alternative modes and roles. Finally, since group members are often unaware of how they are influenced by group norms and processes, they could be helped by the OD consultant acting as a process consultant to the group by collecting and feeding back data about the meeting processes themselves so that members can perceive, understand, and act to improve their meetings.

Solving Problems

A school's adaptability implies continual engagement in problem-solving cycles for pinpointing, analyzing, and acting on goals that are not being reached. Since both the current situation and a preferred target are in flux, problem solving must be continual.

One procedure for resolving school-wide conflicts through collaborative problem solving is the quality circle. In school districts, quality circles are face-to-face discussion groups of from 6 to 12 staff members of the same school or the same central-office division. Such groups are formed voluntarily, meet regularly (once a week or once every 2 weeks), pinpoint problems that are keeping the school from being as effective as it might be, and make use of procedures, such as the S-T-P problem-solving method, to come up with tentative action ideas to resolve the problems.

In the S-T-P method, the "S" stands for the situation as it exists now, the "T" stands for the target toward which the group wishes to move, and the "P" stands for the plan needed to move from the current "S" to the ideal "T." The situation is analyzed through group discussion by enumerating the facilitating forces that are positive aspects of the situation vis-à-vis the target, and by enumerating the restraining forces that keep the situation from moving in the direction of the target. Once such a "force-field analysis" is prepared, the group brainstorms actions to reduce the restraining forces and to enhance the facilitating forces. The brainstormed ideas are then collected by the group into a larger action plan for changing the nature of the situation. The details of who will do what and when are constructed by the group and agreements are made about when to commence the actions. Finally, the quality circle reports its plan to the school's decision-making body for action.

Making Decisions

Effective subsystems, like adaptable organizations, must be capable of moving decisions into action, which can be done effectively only when staff members clearly understand a decision and are committed to it. Although it is not necessary for some to have less influence for others to have more, it is sometimes helpful to reduce authority if it is not based on knowledge and competence.

OD consultants strive to help participants use a decision-making procedure based on acquiescence and support of the total group after discussion and debate, known as consensus. Group consensus is a process in which (a) all members can paraphrase the issue under consideration to show that they understand it, (b) all members have a chance to voice their opinions on the issue, and (c) those who continue to doubt the decision or disagree are nevertheless willing to try it for a prescribed period without sabotaging it. Consensus does not mean that everyone agrees; rather, it means that enough people are in favor for it to be carried out and that those who remain doubtful nonetheless understand the decision and will not obstruct its implementation. A number of consensus exercises can be found in Chapter 6 of Schmuck and Runkel (1988).

Evaluating Interventions

There are at least three ways to evaluate interventions: to evaluate the design, the intervention itself, and the results of the intervention. Since the designs of organization development are tailored to fit the diagnostic data depicting the characteristics of the target group, the consultant can assess a design by scrutinizing the plan and trying to anticipate what could go wrong before it does go wrong. That may be done by asking how the macrodesign grows out of the diagnosis and how it furthers the goals of the target staff. Also, the consultant might invite two or three colleagues to examine and criticize the plan for possible weaknesses, and for purposes of comparison, to devise alternative plans that they think might work as well or better. Then, as each component of the microdesign is actually carried out, consultants are alert to any unwanted side effects during the play of the component and the first moments afterward. If the activity is relatively ineffective, compared with what was expected, the consultants would redesign the macrodesign.

Organizational change is sequential and usually requires reeducating staff members if the school is to move toward a heightened capacity for problem solving. Especially during a period of active intervention by the consultant and active change by the staff, it is vital for the consultant to make frequent formal or informal checks on progress to ascertain whether staff members are actually using new skills and procedures, following through on problem-solving steps, changing structures, and monitoring their own commitments.

Change for its own sake does not necessarily lead to an improved school with a heightened capacity to solve problems. School staffs must develop criteria for evaluating progress toward meeting short-range and long-range goals.

Diagnosing the conditions surrounding an organization-development project, assessing the project's design as it unfolds, and monitoring progress need not be highly technical or time consuming. The underlying strategy is reasonably simple, and the methods employed—interviewing, questionnaires, direct observation, poring over documents, and others—need not be sophisticated, provided that consultants obtain enough information to guide the change in self-conscious, systematic ways.

Two strategies of evaluation should be applied to an organization-development effort: formative and summative. When school people gather information to take timely action that will maximize the quality of a particular program, that information is labeled, informative. It helps to *form* the project, and its audience consists of those carrying out the project and their consultants. When someone gathers information to make a value judgment about the worth of a program, that information is called summative. It makes a *summation* of the project's value and is of use to many audiences concerned with setting policies and making decisions about programs.

In organization development, formative evaluation entails assessing the design and monitoring progress as the intervention proceeds. Careful consultants build their designs to match their diagnoses so that they can accurately predict the immediate effects of their design components as well as the cumulative effects of the sequenced components. At the same time, they invite colleagues to criticize their designs or to give them "dry runs," ceaselessly check as each component is carried through, and check immediately at its conclusion to be sure that the effect is close to that designed.

Monitoring progress means diagnosing the current functioning of the school and comparing that condition with plans for next steps. Consultants monitor progress to determine whether short-term and long-term goals are being met and whether the intervention is producing the knowledge, sensitivities, skills, and norms on which further advances can be built.

Summative evaluation involves evaluating outcomes. Here the strategy attempts to judge whether the intervention produced overall results to justify time and expense, whether the products or effects were superior to the old ways of doing things, and whether the intervention had produced any unexpected or undesirable side effects.

AN ILLUSTRATIVE SCHOOL-BASED OD EFFORT

In a large-scale survey of school-based OD efforts in North America, Miles, Fullan, and Taylor (1980) located 76 school districts where OD had gone on for at least 18 months. A subsequent survey by Schmuck and Runkel (1988) uncovered 12 school districts in which there were functioning cadres of OD consultants. Typically, a cadre is constituted of teachers, specialists, and administrators who act as OD consultants to schools other than their own. The following project demonstrates how a consultant outside the district can team up with members of an internal cadre to implement OD.

Communication Training for a Middle-School Faculty

After several years of becoming organized as a new middle school, the principal, assistant principal, and team coordinators decided to become involved in an OD effort for the whole faculty. The structure of the school was made up of six core teams of six teachers each; a large extended team made up of specialized teachers such as those in music, art, foreign language, and physical education; and a small administrative team made up of the principal, assistant principal, counselor, and librarian. The idea behind the project was to upgrade communication across teachers and administrators, and in particular to implement a closer working relationship between the core teams on the one hand, and between the core teams and the extended team on the other.

The assistant principal, who was also acting as temporary coordinator of a newly developing cadre of OD consultants in the district, joined the core-team coordinators in acting as a steering committee for the project. The steering committee reached an agreement with a university-based OD consultant to take leadership in the early stages of the macrodesign. At the same time, agreements were made with the cadre to lend consultative support as the design developed and ultimately to act as process consultants in the school after the outside consultant was gone.

With the assistance of the outside consultant, the steering committee created the initial stages of the macrodesign. Three periods of time were set aside by the entire faculty for OD: one day in each of January, March, and May from 3:00 to 9:00 P.M. The steering committee also put together an open-ended questionnaire to obtain data from the faculty on the particular communication problems that existed in the school. Those data revealed the following problems: (a) The core teams were not running efficient meetings; (b) there was infrequent communication between the core teams and members of the extended team; (c) the extended team had a weak identity as a team (it was not cohesive); and (d) a communication gap with some mistrust existed between the administrative team and the core teams.

The first OD event in January featured training the entire faculty in the communication skills of paraphrasing, stating ideas clearly, describing own behavior, describing others' behavior, describing own feelings, and impression checking. Handouts taken from Schmuck and Runkel (1988, pp. 100–107) were used to help staff members learn about the communication skills. Then the skills were practiced in the core teams, the extended team, and the administrative team by each of those units discussing ways to improve communication within the unit. Next, cross-team groups were formed to use the communication skills to discuss ways of improving communication across the teams. After dinner, all staff members filled out a questionnaire to assess their recognition of communication skills (see Schmuck and Runkel, 1988, pp. 116–117). Staff members formed into cross-team groups of four each to compare their answers and to discuss their differences. Next, the exercises described in

Schmuck and Runkel (1988, pp. 132–138) on the six communication skills were carried out in still another set of four-person cross-team groups. Finally, a discussion was held with the whole faculty about the communication gap between the core teams and the administrative team.

At the close of that first OD event, the coordinators of the core and extended teams agreed to meet with the outside consultant and the assistant principal the next morning before school to discuss how to keep practicing the communication skills in the school. That group agreed to make a concerted effort to use the communication skills during team meetings and at the once-each-month meeting of the whole faculty. The group also agreed to set aside 10 minutes at the end of each team meeting to discuss how well or poorly the communication skills were being used.

The next OD event in March featured the theme of running meetings effectively. The outside consultant started by stating that effective meetings are characterized by at least four features: (a) a balanced mixture of task and maintenance functions, with an edge given to sticking to the task; (b) many more group-oriented actions than self-oriented actions; (c) wide dispersal of leadership roles; and (d) adequate follow-through to permit decisions made at the meeting to result in the expected actions. Handouts taken from Schmuck and Runkel (1988, pp. 155–156) were used to help staff members understand the features of effective meetings. Then the core, extended, and administrative teams met to discuss how effective their meetings were. Next, the steering committee with the help of the outside consultant led the teams through a series of exercises on planning, conducting, and evaluating meetings (for details, see Schmuck and Runkel, 1988, pp. 172–181). Some of the topics were (a) planning and preparing, (b) organizing an agenda, (c) convening, (d) recording activities and decisions, (e) facilitating process, and (f) making group agreements. After dinner, each staff member filled out the Meetings Questionnaire taken from Schmuck and Runkel (1988, pp. 159–161). They focused on meetings of the whole faculty when completing that questionnaire. Next, cross-team groups of four met to discuss the similarities and differences of their answers on the questionnaire. Finally, members of the steering committee along with the outside consultant sat in a circle within a fishbowl arrangement with all other faculty members sitting in an outside circle surrounding them. The steering committee discussed how to improve whole-faculty meetings and came to some group agreements about setting clear agenda for the meetings, rotating the roles of convener and recorder, and holding regular evaluative discussions about how the meetings were going.

Again, the steering committee, the outside consultant, and the assistant principal met on the next morning before school to discuss how to keep the momentum of the previous evening going. The group agreed to implement new agenda procedures, to use convening and recording skills, and to evaluate their team meetings regularly. Members also agreed to use the meetings questionnaire in each of their teams.

The next OD event in May featured the theme of building trust and openness across the teams, particularly between the core teams and the administrative team. The initial activity was the Planners and Operators Exercise described by Schmuck and Runkel (1988, pp. 283–288). By simulating problems that arise when one team makes decisions about another team's work, this exercise demonstrates the difficulties of using a formal hierarchy in group problem solving. The outside consultant asked the newest teachers to act as planners and the administrators, coordinators, and most experienced teachers to act as operators. That is because typically in playing out the exercise, planners act like planners, regardless of their personalities or other life experiences, and operators act like operators. Thus, the staff members learned about the communication problems between a planning (or administrative) and an implementing (or a teaching) team, and about the frustrations an implementing team experiences when carrying out a plan that is not its own. After dinner, the outside consultant introduced four members of the district's OD cadre to the staff. Those cadre members, along with the assistant principal, lead the faculty through the rest of the program. They told about the Johari Awareness Model (see Schmuck and Runkel, 1988, pp. 94–95) and asked cross-team groups of four to discuss how to increase trust and openness between the core teams and the administrative team. After considerable discussion in small groups, the whole faculty made some agreements about using the cadre members regularly during the next fall (at least from September to December) to bridge the gap between hierarchical levels in the school. For

their part, the administrative team agreed to support a one-day workshop before the start of school in August to focus on establishing trust between administrators and teachers.

Other examples of school-based OD efforts can be found in the first edition of this *Handbook* (Schmuck, 1982) and in Schmuck and Runkel (1988, pp. 68–89 and 352–366). Examples in the latter are on such topics as team teaching, collegial supervision of teaching, desegregation, interpersonal conflict, group processes in the classroom, bringing parents and students into school management, and the like.

THE SCHOOL PSYCHOLOGIST AND ORGANIZATION DEVELOPMENT

In thinking about acting as an OD consultant, school psychologists should consider four roles: (a) action researcher, (b) staff developer, (c) social architect, and (d) political strategist.

Action Researcher

The school psychologist as action researcher, not unlike the formative evaluator, helps collect objective data—in the form of questionnaires, interviews, and observations—and then sees that the data are analyzed, discussed, and used for action planning. The school psychologist helps participants specify and clarify their shared problems, think of alternative actions to solve problems, use data in monitoring their success in implementing chosen actions, and use data to evaluate the outcomes of their actions.

For example, as action researcher the school psychologist could encourage principals to solicit feedback about their leadership styles as one way of modeling openness to change and of facilitating collaborative problems solving among teachers. The school psychologist could help principals create a questionnaire for teachers, and after the data are collected, the school psychologist could help the principals analyze them and design appropriate responses to their staffs. Or, the school psychologist might also lead a staff through the Delphi process for goal setting, use staff meetings questionnaires to facilitate meeting improvement, formally observe staff meetings and lead the group in problem solving about how they might be improved, and even offer to run a meeting or two as a demonstration.

Staff Developer

The school psychologist as staff developer seeks to help educators change the norms, structures, and procedures that are keeping the school from being effective. That can be accomplished by taking the role of an organizational trainer who directly teaches communication skills, goal-setting procedures, meetings skills, conflict resolution methods, problem-solving skills, and the like. As organizational trainer, the school psychologist determines the learning goals of the participants for a particular time period and organizes and directs the training activities. For example, as staff developer the school psychologist runs workshops, sees that other formal improvement efforts are integrated into the school culture, offers coaching to administrators and head teachers in their leadership roles, encourages administrators to participate with teachers in inservice workshops as a show of support, facilitates the work of teacher committees in setting up appropriate professional development experiences for the school, and the like.

Social Architect

The school psychologist as social architect seeks to build cooperation and collaboration among participants by discussing ideas about organizational improvement with key people outside formal meetings, by sounding out the group consensus, by pinpointing people who agree or disagree with various points of view, and by checking to see what the readiness is of the faculty for new ways of working together. One technique that the social architect might use, that of quality circles, was discussed above.

As social architect, the school psychologist might also help administrators articulate organizational tasks on which improvement is needed, go to individual teachers and subgroups to enlist interest in the tasks, listen carefully to the teachers' concerns about those tasks, and design formal faculty subgroups to work on the tasks. The school psychologist might also help administrators run more efficient and effective formal meetings. That means coaching them in building a clear agenda prior to the meeting, having someone act as a convener, seeing that all who speak are listened to, having the key decisions recorded, and having them follow-up the meeting to see that agreed-upon actions are implemented. Also, as social architect, the school psychologist could talk informally with teachers about how the meetings are going to increase their readiness for training in meeting improvement.

Political Strategist

The school psychologist as political strategist strives to build coalitions with key people, both inside and outside the school, to achieve a more effective school organization. That can be accomplished by taking on the roles of mediator, facilitator, and intergroup communicator. At times, it is appropriate for the political strategist to act as a third-party, neutral consultant to individuals and groups in conflict.

As political strategist, the school psychologist might help administrators initiate tactical messages with influential people, both within and outside the school. For example, principals could be coached to watch for informal coalitions on their staffs and to work with them on behalf of everyone's goals, whereas members of the superintendent's cabinet could be helped to design and manage more effective public relations by being reminded that the students and teachers are the most important public-relations agents in the community. Or, as political strategist, the school psychologist might persuade the superintendent's cabinet or even the school board to initiate their own participation in team building and meeting improvement to offer a model for others in the district to emulate.

RESEARCH ON ORGANIZATION DEVELOPMENT IN SCHOOLS

Much of the theory and research reported in this chapter emerged from 15 years of collaboration among more than 150 people working in a program of research, development, and dissemination on OD in schools at the University of Oregon. From 1967 to 1982, that program produced data, theory, practices, and techniques from work with over 2000 educators in more than 50 elementary and secondary schools. The results were summarized in the first edition of this *Handbook* and have been recently brought up to date in Runkel and Schmuck (1987) and Schmuck and Runkel (1988).

Separate from the Oregon program, Miles, Fullan, and Taylor (1980) produced a comprehensive assessment of the state of knowledge of educational OD and the nature and extent of its use in school districts in the United States and Canada. While the entire report is too large to summarize here, it is useful to present some of the results on consultants and programs.

Perhaps the most striking finding was that a great deal more organization development was discovered to be going on in school districts than the authors expected. For example, they located 308 consultants who have been doing extensive organization development with schools in the United States and Canada between 1973 and 1978. That number is approximately double those that were located in 1971 by Schmuck and Miles (1971/1975). Moreover, they amassed a sample of 76 school districts where organization development had gone on for at least 18 months. Surprisingly, more than 50% of the consultants involved in those projects were insiders with little or no formal training in organization development, and little or no linkage to OD experts.

Furthermore, the study indicated that about half the districts with organization development had district-level coordinators, a steering group for school improvement, and released time available to support the effort. Their results also indicated that the impact of organization development was most frequently reported to be associated with the implementation of instructional innovations, such as team teaching, individualization, and alternative schools. Many districts reported some negative effects, such as resistance or increased work load, but most of those annoyances did not result in terminating the organization-development project. Most programs did, on the whole, generate favorable attitudes toward organization development. Indeed, two-thirds of the districts thought that organization development should "definitely" be used more widely in the schools, and the majority had attended workshops and conferences in which they told others how organization development had helped their district. About a third of the districts had visited other districts to explain their work, had sent out reports, or had written articles. In other words, the users of organization development tend to proselytize. Finally, three-quarters of the districts predicted that organization development would become institutionalized in their district.

Miles, Fullan, and Taylor's (1980) case studies tended to confirm many findings of their questionnaires from districts, particularly the support required from top management to get organization development initiated, the need for a task emphasis, the importance of sustained consultation from participants inside the district, and the low money but high time costs that are involved. Other important themes also emerged: (a) Careful, early planning of an internal steering committee is important to future success; (b) organization-development efforts are probably easier to launch when the school environment is *not* turbulent; (c) success is accompanied by a close partnership between consultants inside the district and experts in organization development outside the district; (d) the idea that organization development is not a special add-on, but a core way of life in the district; and (e) the probability that true institutionalization will take up to 5 years for a moderately large school district.

Research since Miles, Fullan, and Taylor on OD in schools has been influenced by the effective schools movement. An important source of information on OD and effective schools in the urban environment is the April 1979 edition of *Theory Into Practice*. Along with contributions from the Oregon Program, taken from experiences in Oakland and New York, there are other significant contributions. The most notable are Bassin, Gross, and Jordan's (1979) work on self-renewal teams in New York high schools, Milstein's (1979) development of a cadre of organizational specialists to deal with desegregation of the Buffalo schools, Keys' (1979) successful use of OD in Catholic urban schools, and Scheinfeld's (1979) integration of OD with parent involvement and improved classroom instruction in the Chicago elementary schools.

Aside from that issue of *Theory Into Practice*, other sources of organization development programs and research in schools can be found in the annotated bibliography put together in 1975 for the updated, second printing of Schmuck and Miles (1971/1975), the *Review of Reviews* by Miles, Fullan, and Taylor (1980), the annotated bibliography on humanistic education by Schmuck and Schmuck (1976), the annotated bibliography on organizational change in schools by Runkel and Harris (1983), and the most extensive, up-to-date, annotated bibliography on OD in schools by Cooley (1986).

CONTEMPORARY CONCEPTS AND PRACTICES

The prospects for organization development theory and techniques to contribute to school improvement have never been stronger. Nowadays, most educators are concerned about healthy interpersonal and group processes. Teachers increasingly see the importance of supportive human relations and social support in their classes, while administrators increasingly understand the relevance of clear communication and positive school climate for staff effectiveness in instruction. I believe that we will begin to observe the following trends taking hold and coming to fruition during the next decade:

Institutionalization of OD

Although change in the role of the school psychologist can help bring organization development to many subsystems of a school district, it is unlikely in itself to influence the climate and problem-solving capabilities of the entire district. For a school district to achieve a renewing state and sustain a favorable impact on its participants, continuing attention must be given both to the interpersonal and group skills of district employees and to the district's group and organizational procedures. To achieve that requires the permanent maintenance of training and consultation by institutionalizing organization development through new norms, roles, and organizational structures.

Toward that end, our Center on OD in Schools located at the University of Oregon initiated and tested a design for establishing internal organizational specialists in school districts. That strategy calls for training district members to perform OD consulting part-time for school staffs and other district work groups. Cadre members are drawn from various roles and subsystems within the district to constitute a microcosm of the district. They do not consult with their own family groups and their role as organizational specialists is separated from their other functions.

Since cadre members are not full time, they bring to the consultative effort the skills and their place in the communication network that are parts of their regular jobs. Such collegial or peer consultation is fostered through horizontal interactions among "organizational cousins" (i.e., those who hold jobs within the same school district but who are not members of the same interdependent task

unit). In contrast to placing normative emphasis on expertise, typical of most school consultation, peer cadres for organization development become legitimized by norms that support collegial responsibility and helpfulness.

The Oregon Center has established peer cadres of organizational specialists within 12 school districts. Although the work of those cadres differs a good deal one from the other, the overall sequence of most organization-development projects include an initial period of start-up and contract building, followed by diagnosis and design. Then a series of sequential consultative sessions are interspersed with data collections for formative evaluation. A typical consultation lasts from a few months to a whole academic year. Evaluative data serve as springboards for redesign and more consultative sessions until the cadre and the clients believe that the necessary structures and procedures for self-renewal have been built into the client group.

The peer cadres emphasize building strong temporary teams for delivering the consultation. By understanding and supporting one another, the organizational specialists can more validly diagnose the organizational problems of their clients and design more effective interventions. Moreover, cadre members who feel comfortable working together learn from one another during the team planning and consultations. While specialists in the cadres occasionally work alone, their solo tasks have been listed and planned by a team. It is fairly typical, for example, for individual specialists to focus on particular functions such as designing interviews, training large groups, serving as process facilitators, or coaching individual clients. All team members share in providing one another with helpful feedback and in carrying out continual evaluation as the interventions move along. A cadre coordinator, typically a half-time position, plus representatives from each intervention team, form a steering committee to manage the overall cadre effort.

Infusing OD into Educator Functions

The concepts and techniques of OD will soon become integral to the functioning of most educators. As such, organization development will not just be implemented by change agents in temporary and expert roles. Ideas and activities about clear communication, shared goals, constructive conflict, effective meetings, joint problem solving, and collaborative decision making will become part and parcel of educators' roles. While it is likely that many educators will not use the words "organization development" to label what they are thinking and doing, they will be trying to act as effective organization developers nonetheless.

Distinctions Between Managing and Leading

A prominent theme in contemporary thought about effective school administration is that it takes both good leadership and good management to run a school well. Leadership entails influencing teachers to act toward values that are shared by all professional educators, while management entails seeing that institutional procedures are carried out efficiently and effectively. The concepts and techniques of OD can facilitate both good leadership and good management.

Organization development teaches that educational leaders must bring vision, excitement, energy, involvement, and a sense of pulling together to the staff. At the same time, OD teaches that managers must run the organization smoothly, seeing that laws, administrative rules, and ethics are followed, and that daily routines are executed to satisfy both institutional norms and human needs. OD techniques can help administrators act both as competent leaders and as efficient managers.

Distinctions Between Effective and Good Schools

Another important theme in current writing is a focus on effective and good schools. Effective-schools research has shown that certain organizational conditions in the school are correlated with the academic achievement of its students (for a review, see Austin and Garber, 1985). Those organizational conditions have to do broadly with school climate. When the teachers share high expectations for student performance; agree on master plans for homework, grading, and discipline; share a common vision of the centrality of academic performance; and show consistent psychological support for their students, the academic achievement of the students is high. The converse is also true; with little climate support in the school, students do poorly in academic achievement.

The effective schools' emphasis on academic achievement as the schools' raison d'être led to discussions about good schools (for an example,

see Lightfoot, 1983). Good schools are characterized, too, as having supportive climates, but less emphasis is placed on traditional achievement outcomes and more attention is given to student self-esteem and creativity; teacher–student playfulness and spontaneity; and humane, empathic, and respectful interpersonal relationships. Good schools' advocates wonder if a strong and narrow focus on academic achievement will not be dysfunctional for the development of moral character, civic responsibility, and mental health.

The concepts and techniques of OD can help resolve differences between effective and good schools. OD can help schools establish faculty agreements about how teachers will behave toward one another and about how they will relate to the students. The resulting product of OD can be a supportive climate for learning. But OD can also help staffs pinpoint school goals other than academic achievement, and through the techniques of survey data feedback and confrontation it can help maintain contact with the many yearnings and concerns of the students. The humane values of OD can help make effective schools good, while the data feedback and problem-solving techniques of OD can help make good schools more effective.

Integrating OD with Social Issues

Desegregation for both student bodies and faculties, an issue facing large numbers of schools, can be aided by attention to organization development and the introduction of third-party facilitators. Mainstreaming is another contemporary issue that can be enhanced by organization development. Scheinfeld (1979) has shown too how to use the concepts and techniques of organization development to bring teachers, administrators, and parents into joint problem solving and decision making. And the many projects that require school steering committees, parent advisory groups, and PTA committees can benefit significantly from the team-building strategies of organization development.

Perhaps the most pervasive contemporary issue facing public education for which organization development may make a significant contribution is that of bringing staff and students together for school improvement. The time when students—particularly secondary school students—adopted primarily a quiet and passive stance toward professionals is mostly in the past. There are several indications that times are changing for students. The growing number of alternative schools is evidence that students want to make choices about the sort of education they experience. Moreover, faculty–student conflict in some urban schools has led to increased power of students in the organizational functioning of the school. Still, the effort among organization-development practitioners to bring staff and students together to co-manage the secondary school is minuscule, and the knowledge and skill needed to do that is mostly lacking from educators' repertoires.

Three intervention strategies may be tried to help students increase their understandings of how the school organization works and to become skillful as "co-managers" of the school.

1. *Changing Classroom Norms:* The most common designs entail training the teacher and students simultaneously in the cognitive and behavioral aspects of interpersonal communication, steps and procedures for group problem solving, goal-setting methods, and in the procedures of process debriefing about the classroom group (for details, see Schmuck and Schmuck, 1988).

2. *Amending Curricula:* Arends, Schmuck, Wiseman, Milleman, and Arends (1981) have developed a series of experiential activities, readings, and group assignments to help secondary students understand how the school organization works through the study of organizational psychology. The students collect, analyze, and use data about their own school, attempting to make positive contributions to school improvements.

3. *Improving Student Governance:* Medina (1978) has developed and field tested a 30-hour design to train members of student councils to examine their own group behavior, to develop more effective interpersonal communication skills, and to consider new ways of conducting meetings in which collaborative problem solving and decision making occur. Because of the cultural complexities of the many adult and student subsystems of schools, efforts at planned change for desegregation, mainstreaming, parent involvement, or student involvement are much larger in scope than the typical organization-development con-

sultations that have been carried out in schools. Such school improvement efforts will no doubt call for further development of conflict resolution techniques, those which have received the smallest amount of attention in the past from consultants of organization development in schools.

Networks for OD in Schools

A few years ago, a new Center on Organization Development in Schools was formed at the University of Oregon under the sponsorship of the University Council for Educational Administration. The objectives of that center are to further training, research, development, and dissemination of OD in schools. The center stores and disseminates a collection of annotated bibliographies, sets up conferences, seminars, and workshops, and maintains networks of researchers, practitioners, and school districts involved with OD.

The researchers, practitioners, and representatives of the school districts convene for a conference once a year at the University of Oregon. Conference proceedings have focused on OD in the classroom; OD and racism, ageism, and sexism; OD for middle schools; OD and effective schools; OD and teacher supervision; and the like. For information about the Oregon Center on OD in Schools and the Oregon annual OD conference, write to the author.

SUMMARY

Organization development is a planned and sustained effort at school self-study and improvement. The focus is on the school as a social system and human culture. The process involves the school participants themselves in the active assessment, diagnosis, and transformation of their own organization. Our aim in this chapter was to help school psychologists understand why the concepts and techniques of organization development are important for their repertoires. We described the basic concepts of organization development and delineated the theory that undergirds it, summarized the generic stages of consultation in organization development, specified some of its current technology, described various roles that the school psychologist might take to implement organization development, and summarized research on OD in schools. The chapter ends with an overview of contemporary concepts and practices. School psychologists can make a major contribution to furthering organization development by redefining their role in the district to include membership in a cadre of OD specialists.

REFERENCES

Arends, R., Schmuck, R. A., Wiseman, J., Milleman, M., & Arends, J. (1981). *School life and organization psychology.* New York: Teachers College Press.

Austin, G. R., & Garber, H. (Eds.). (1985). *Research on exemplary schools.* New York: Academic Press.

Bassin, M., Gross, T., & Jordan, P. (1979). Developing renewal processes in urban high schools. *Theory into Practice, 18*(2), 73–81.

Buckley, W. (1967). *Sociology and modern systems theory.* Englewood Cliffs, NJ: Prentice-Hall.

Coch, L., & French, J. R. P. (1948). Overcoming resistance to change. *Human Relations, 1,* 512–532.

Cooley, F. E. (1986). *Bibliography on organization development in schools: Selected and annotated.* Eugene: University of Oregon, Division of Educational Policy and Management.

Gouldner, A. W. (1954). *Patterns of industrial bureaucracy.* Glencoe, IL: Free Press.

Katz, D., & Kahn, R. L. (1978). *The social psychology of organizations.* New York: Wiley.

Katz, M. B. (1971). *Class, bureaucracy, and schools: The illusion of educational changes in America.* New York: Praeger.

Keys, C. B. (1979). Renewal processes in urban parochial schools. *Theory into Practice, 18*(2), 97–105.

Kouzes, J. M., & Mico, P. (1979). Domain theory: An introduction to organizational behavior in human service organizations. *Journal of Applied Behavioral Science, 15*(4), 449–469.

Lewin, K. (1976). *Field theory as human science.* New York: Gardner Press.

Lightfoot, S. (1983). *The good high school: Portraits of character and culture.* New York: Basic Books.

Lortie, D. (1975). *School-teacher: A sociological study.* Chicago: University of Chicago Press.

Maslow, A. (1954). *Motivation and personality.* New York: Harper.

McClelland, D. C. (1975). *Power: The inner experience.* New York: Irvington.

Medina, G. (1978). *Student leadership skills: The development and testing of an instructional team.* Unpublished doctoral dissertation, University of Oregon, Eugene.

Merton, R. (1949). *Social theory and social structure.* Glencoe, IL: Free Press.

Michaelsen, J. (1977, February). Revision, bureaucracy, and school reform: A critique of Katz. *School Review, 50,* 121–183.

Miles, M., Fullan, M., & Taylor, G. (1980). OD in schools: The state of the art. *Review of Educational Research, 50,* 121–183.

Milstein, M. (1979). Developing a renewal team in an urban school district. *Theory into Practice, 18*(2), 106–113.

Roethlisberger, F. J., & Dickson, W. J. (1939). *Management and the worker.* Cambridge, MA: Harvard University Press.

Rogers, C. (1969). *Freedom to learn.* Columbus, OH: Charles E. Merrill.

Runkel, P. J., & Harris, P. (1983). *A bibliography on organizational change in schools.* Eugene: University of Oregon, Division of Educational Policy and Management.

Runkel, P. J., & Schmuck, R. A. (1987). *An account of studies of organization development in schools.* Eugene: University of Oregon, Division of Policy and Management.

Sarason, S. G. (1982). *The culture of the school and the problem of change* (2nd ed.). Boston: Allyn and Bacon.

Scheinfeld, D. (1979). A design for renewing urban elementary schools. *Theory into Practice, 18*(2), 114–125.

Schmuck, R. A. (1982). Organization development in the schools. In C. R. Reynolds and T. B. Gutkin (Eds.), *Handbook of school psychology.* New York: Wiley.

Schmuck, R. A., & Miles, M. B. (1975). *Organization development in schools.* La Jolla, CA: University Associates. (Original work published 1971).

Schmuck, R. A., & Runkel, P. J. (1988). *The handbook of organization development in schools* (3rd ed.). Prospect Heights, IL: Waveland Press.

Schmuck, R. A., & Schmuck, P. A. (1976). Humanistic education: A review of books since 1970. In J. W. Pfeiffer and J. E. Jones (Eds.), *Annual group facilitators handbook.* San Diego, CA: University Associates.

Schmuck, R. A., & Schmuck, P. A. (1988). *Group processes in the classroom* (5th ed.). Dubuque, IA: Wm. C. Brown.

Selznick, P. (1949). *TVA and the grass roots.* Berkeley: University of California Press.

Weber, M., & Parsons, T. (Eds.). (1947). *The theory of social and economic organizations.* Glencoe, IL: Free Press.

Weick, K. (1976). Educational organizations as loosely coupled systems. *Administrative Science Quarterly, 21*(1), 1–19.

37

SYSTEMS INTERVENTIONS IN SCHOOL SETTINGS: CASE STUDIES

MATTHEW SNAPP
Independent Practice, Austin, TX
JULIA A. HICKMAN
The University of Texas at Austin
JANE CLOSE CONOLEY
The University of Nebraska–Lincoln

Systems-level interventions by school psychologists have received significant attention in both the historical and contemporary literatures (Cutts, 1955; Fish & Jain, 1988; Kurplus, 1985; Levin, Trickett, & Kidder, 1986; Plas, 1986; Ysseldyke, 1986). For example, systems development and planning has been listed as one of 16 domains of school psychology practice in the recent proposal from the National School Psychology Inservice Network entitled *School Psychology: A Blueprint from Training and Practice* (Ysseldyke, Reynolds, & Weinberg, 1984). Despite professionals exalting the role of systems level interventions in schools, sound empirical research supporting such work

Dr. Snapp wishes to gratefully acknowledge the contribution made by Dr. Hickman to the revision of this chapter. Her assistance in coordinating the revision and in updating the literature significantly added to the chapter's present form. Appreciation is extended to Dr. Conoley for the additional case studies and to Olivia Miller Snapp for her suggestions.

remains a glaring gap in the mental health consultation literature in general (Levin, Trickett, & Kidder, 1986) and the school psychology literature specifically (e.g., Elliott & Witt, 1986).

Traditionally, school psychological services have emphasized the provision of psychoeducational assessments for children for the express purpose of determining their eligibility to receive special education services (Elliott & Witt, 1986). This "gatekeeper role" for school psychologists has not changed for many decades (Bardon, 1982) and is premised on the assumption that typically, dysfunctional behavior resides within the student and must be remediated by individualistic academic and/or behavioral strategies. Taking this perspective, a student is assessed, areas of strengths and, more specifically, weaknesses determined, and individual educational plans developed to remediate the weaknesses. The weaknesses, however, are almost without exception considered as residing within the child. Unfortunately, treatment of deficits has not been particularly effective in remediating academic or behavior problems in students (Reynolds, 1987).

Recently, an alternative model for the delivery of psychological services to schools has been proposed by Christenson, Abery, and Weinberg (1986). This model takes a developmental perspective, drawing heavily from ecological and transactional theories of human behavior and emphasizing a much more proactive and preventive stance than the traditional model. The first premise of the model proposed by Christenson et al. (1986) is that the individual is an actively developing system as opposed to a static organism. The emphasis then is on "systems" functioning and is addressed by considering "the nonlinear, interactive effect of genetic endowment, learning, and psychosituational demands of the child's environment" (p. 360).

In addition, this model views an individual's behavior from an ecological perspective (Bronfenbrenner, 1974; Gabarino, 1982; Lewin, 1951). In the ecological model of psychology, human behavior is seen as the product of the interaction of individuals with their environment(s), the latter being broadly defined (i.e., social, physical, psychological environments). Further, individuals develop within environments that are viewed as social systems that directly influence and are directly influenced by the individual's behavior. For example, interventions meant to effect a child's behavior should mobilize the complex ecosystems in which the student functions in order to maximize the probability that learning, adaptation, and development will proceed in a positive manner.

Christenson et al. (1986) takes an open systems perspective. Systems theory (von Bertalanffy, 1968) has been proposed as a theoretical basis for understanding an individual's behavior (Christensen et al., 1986), family functioning (e.g., Brassard, 1986; Fisher, 1986), organizational functioning in the schools (e.g., Curtis & Metz, 1986), and medical treatment (e.g., Engel, 1980). From an open systems perspective, social behavior is premised on two basic considerations:

1. Behavior occurs within a system, where *movement* in one part of the system results in certain movement in other interrelated parts of the system.
2. The system is open to environmental in-

fluences such that it is in a continual state of flux.

Typically, systems-level interventions in the schools have been defined in relation to traditional organizational development activities (e.g., Curtis & Metz, 1986). Richard Schmuck and his colleagues have done the most extensive work in the area of organizational development in the schools (Schmuck & Runkel, 1985). In organizational development models, schools are viewed as "open" rather than "closed" systems. Furthermore, schools are seen as composed not simply of a collection of individuals but rather interdependent subsystems characterized by both internal developmental trajectories and constant transaction with the larger environment. The reality of schools "openness" conflicts with the frequent misconception that somehow schools are "closed" or static and independent of the community or other societal pressures. Viewing schools from this perspective, the core issues for instituting any level of change are understanding and improving subsystem effectiveness and improving the interpersonal skills of the individuals (whose communication largely determines the effectiveness of the system and ultimately the adaptability of the organization). The primary goal of organizational development is improving the adaptability of the organization. Organizational adaptability refers to a system's ability to survive and remain effective in a constantly changing environment.

Individual human behaviors are the basic data of social psychology (Katz and Kahn, 1978). When these acts indicate dysfunction, it is assumed there needs to be a change in the individual's behavior. From an open systems perspective, desired behavioral changes at the microlevel (e.g., the individual or the organizational subsystem level) are more likely to occur and be maintained if concurrent changes also occur at the macrolevel(s) of the organization. For example, in schools, changing the behavior of individual students or educational staff are considered microlevel interventions. That is, if an individual's behavior is considerred aberrant, a microlevel change would involve some modification of that individual's behaviors, attitudes, or skills. Open systems perspectives would suggest that this microlevel change would most likely occur and be maintained if there were concurrent change in macrolevels of the organization

(Dollar & Klinger, 1975) and that changes in macrolevels of the organization would create changes in the individuals, or microlevel of the organization. The improvement of school-wide discipline procedures is an example.

The assumption is that relevant organizational subsystems and the organization's environment should be considered when attempting to implement change at microlevels. Chin and Benne (1976) assert that to reinforce an innovation, changes must be initiated in other subsystems within an organization that interact with the targeted subsystem. This principle suggests that change processes must consider the dynamics of the organization, particularly the interrelatedness of subsystems and the influence of the environment upon the organization. The following case study by Curtis and Metz (1986) illustrates this principle and is one of the few recent contributions to the literature of systems theory in the schools.

In this case study, one consultant internal to a school system (the school psychologist) and one consultant external to the school system (a university professor), conducted a series of traditional organizational development activities. These activities were effective in markedly improving communication between staff and the administration (between two of the organization's subsystems), among the staff (within a subsystem), and between parents and the staff (between an organizational subsystem and the environment). In addition, results indicated improvement in staff cohesiveness and trust. Staff problem solving skills, a major goal of school-based consultation, were also markedly improved. Perhaps most notable in this study was an increase in requests from school staff for psychological services. The results of this case study seem indicative of the system's openness to assistance in becoming more adaptable.

The use of case studies as a means to further advance conceptual and theoretical knowledge in a given area is widely accepted in various disciplines. According to Reynolds, Gutkin, Elliott, and Witt (1984), "the properly reported case study can provide a much needed beginning in the description and understanding of any particular human behavior not carefully documented in the past" (p. 285). Case studies are included in this chapter to illustrate ways of expanding the role of the school psychologist beyond that of "gatekeeping" for the special education subsystem of a school district.

In the following cases, the psychologist used an open systems approach to create and maintain changes at the microlevels of the organization, including participatory planning, problem solving, and group decision making. The psychologist intervened in the organization not only at the individual level, as is often the role for school psychologists, but also included interventions at the group and organization levels. Using an open systems approach, the role of the school psychologist expanded within the organization to include management, research and development, staff training, conflict management, and policy development. These are subsystem roles which directly influence the adaptability of an organization and consequently all the individuals in that organization as a system.

CASE STUDIES

During the time period in which case examples 1–6 occurred, the school district and the environment experienced a great deal of turbulence due to court-ordered busing. Additionally, the school superintendent who had been in the district for 20 years retired. A new superintendent was chosen to lead the district in its court-ordered desegregation process. The role of the superintendent is vital to the organization's adaptability because of its boundary position between the environment and the school district. Katz and Kahn (1978) state: "The ultimate decision to give or withhold the needed organizational inputs lies in the environment, and that the larger social environment in this way holds the power of life and death over every organization" (p. 238). The superintendent in this case was in a precarious position because of his unfamiliarity with both the specific organization and the environment at large. The school psychologist intervened in the organization during this time of great social and political flux in ways that assisted the organization in adapting to the turbulent environment. The psychologist's efforts helped ensure the system's efficiency, effectiveness, and survival. Following are case studies that illustrate open systems interventions by the psychologist.

Case Study 1

The school superintendent received a request for the long-term suspension of an eighth-grade junior high school student. Consistent with existing school board policy, the school suspended him for a "short term" for marijuana possession and requested that he be suspended for the remainder of the school term with the superintendent's approval. If the request was approved, the student would lose credit for the second half of the eighth grade and would be unable to go to ninth grade with his classmates. The school superintendent was new to the district. Upon receipt of the suspension request he sent a memorandum to the director of pupil personnel services, the director of secondary education, and other members of the administrative staff, including the school psychologist, requesting their opinions and suggestions for possible actions.

This was the first time the school psychologist had been asked to become involved with the administration's handling of a discipline problem. The school psychologist had been aware of frustration expressed by counselors that students they were working with might be suspended from school without counselors being given an opportunity to offer suggestions for handling the problem. Seeing an important opportunity in the superintendent's request for suggestions, the school psychologist quickly investigated the case. He determined a school counselor had developed an excellent relationship with the student in question and the student's friends. It was also apparent that this was not an isolated incident of drug abuse at the school. The problem, while not unique to this junior high school, was of great concern to the school's faculty and parents. Few people had much information about drugs and drug abuse, and no one was really sure how to deal with the problem. In similar situations throughout the school district the typical strategy had been to try to discover any drugs brought to school, identify anyone in possession, and suspend them permanently from school. The discipline policy established by the school board stated clearly that possession of marijuana would result in long-term suspension for the remainder of the school term and there would be a loss of credit for that term.

The psychologist also learned the suspended boy was one of a group of 8 to 10 eithth-grade students who were thought to be responsible for most of the drugs available at the school. The suspended student's peer group enjoyed high status among the other students in the school. Their influence and status seemed to be contributing to other students becoming interested in experimenting with drugs. Simply enforcing the suspension policy in this case would, at best, punish one student and be a warning to others. It might do little to affect the more general problem of drug abuse in the school. The school psychologist also realized that although the superintendent would be concerned with the handling of this individual suspension request, he would be more concerned with the larger issues of suspension policies and the problems of drugs in the schools.

The school psychologist began considering possible ways the superintendent could reduce the "drug problem" within the student population. In regard to the individual student, the suspension needed only to be examined as to the appropriateness of applying the policy. Administrators could certainly look to the eighth grader who was caught with the marijuana to determine what would be the most appropriate punishment and what would bring about the highest possibility for rehabilitation. They could view the punishment to be in the best interest for the overall development of the boy.

A more feasible option was to consider mental health interventions in addition to, or instead of, suspension, and ways to effect the group of students associated with the suspended student. Another consideration was to think of the entire school as a subsystem of the school district, and target that subsystem for intervention. As a whole, the use of illicit drugs by students and the way school administrators responded in the district was becoming a more critical problem. The question of primary interest for the school psychologist was how to intervene in order to reduce the use drugs at the school; that is, what could be done to change that subsystem within the school that provided status to those students modeling drug abuse to their peers? A feasible alternative seemed to exist in accepting the status of the students and modifying the way this status was being used.

The school psychologist presented to the superintendent a suggestion for an alternative to suspension that called for the school counselor bringing together the suspended student's friends thought to be responsible for bringing most of the drugs on campus. The psychologist intended to speak very directly with the students and, in effect, offer them a "deal." That is, that if those students were willing to "clean up" their school by removing all drugs from the campus through the end of the school year, the school psychologist would be willing to go back to the superintendent and argue for the reinstatement of their suspended friend. It would be made clear that the superintendent had given no guarantee of reinstatement from suspension but that he had agreed to listen to the argument. If the school psychologist could be convinced that the campus would be free of drugs, he would try to convince the superintendent to allow the student to return to school. It was also pointed out that everyone in the school would know that they were responsible for getting their friend back to junior high school. The students would continue to have high status, but the status would be for helping a friend and for "cleaning up the school" rather than for abusing and/or providing drugs. The students would have to develop a plan of action and convince the school psychologist that they would "clean up" the school. The superintendent agreed to the plan, seeming quite pleased to have an alternative to suspension and for a way to try to affect drug use at the school.

With the superintendent's support, the school psychologist had the counselor bring the students together for a meeting. At first, their reaction to the psychologist's plan consisted of denial, questions like "why us?", comments such as "we know nothing about drugs!" Not willing to argue with them, the school psychologist gave them the information they needed for their decision. If the students decided to go along with the plan, they would have to propose a way to convince the school psychologist that the school would be "clean." They were told, "you have 20 minutes, take it or leave it." At the end of the 20 minutes, the school psychologist returned to hear the decision. The students began by saying that some of the seventh graders were rather "immature," taking pills from home medicine cabinets without knowing what the drugs would do to them. They would not take responsibility for that. The school psychologist did not agree, reminding them that the seventh graders looked up to them and that they could convince the younger students to stop using those drugs. They agreed, accepted the terms, and convinced the school psychologist that they would clean the school of all drugs in order to help their friend get back into school.

The school psychologist went back to the superintendent and asked the suspended student be reinstated. The superintendent agreed and the boy was allowed to finish the school year having received only a short-term suspension. During the

following months, the counselors closely monitored the campus for drug usage. They believed that drugs were completely absent from the campus until the afternoon of the last school day, when one individual got "high." The boy graduated with his peers, went to high school, and has since successfully completed his public education.

Chin and Benne's (1976) assertations appear upheld by these data. The intervention in this case study was not directed at the suspended student. Instead, it involved responding very differently to a general discipline problem by intervening directly with a subsystem within a school system. In this case, the targeted subsystem included all those students directly or indirectly involved in giving status to the eighth graders primarily responsible for using and distributing drugs at that school. If intervention had been only aimed at an individual level, it might have changed the behavior of that one student, perhaps even a few others, but as it was, the patterns of drug usage of the individuals within that subsystem were apparently drastically reduced through the end of that school year. The organization (district) was also involved in the intervention and was affected by the outcome.

What were the results of this intervention? First, it had a significant impact on reducing drug usage in that school at that time. Second, the superintendent later sought the advice of the school psychologist on many other discipline cases. Third, the superintendent developed a reorganization plan for the administration which now included a role for the school psychologist in developing and implementing district discipline policy. This reorganization included the addition of an Office of Student Affairs, which would be charged with ensuring that students' rights were protected, especially the right to due process. The Office of Student Affairs was organized by the school psychologist with the direction of the superintendent. The office would be required to monitor discipline and develop alternatives to punishment.

Case Study 2

The next case involved an entire school district. It was precipitated by the concerns of four school board members, who constituted a majority of a seven-member board. The four board members began approaching the administration with their interest in eliminating, or at least severely limiting, the use of both corporal punishment and long-term suspension of students. They asked the administration to report on the different kinds of discipline (e.g., corporal punishment, long- and short-term suspension) used and the extent to which different discipline techniques were used. They also wanted information from staff and the community about recommendations for major changes in the school district's policies and procedures for discipline.

Following the board's request, the superintendent asked the school psychologist to design a study of discipline in the district and present it to the superintendent's cabinet. The original design was developed to ensure objectivity and generalizability of results. The school psychologist saw the study as an opportunity to assist in the overall discipline problem and provide a vehicle to distribute a teacher's manual (Phillips, 1980) that was being developed by the school psychological services staff. The manual described various discipline techniques presented in a step-by-step fashion.

The superintendent's cabinet was concerned about the reaction that local school administrators might have at the prospect of losing some of their usual punishment techniques. The school principals might even think some of their authority would be taken away, particularly in relation to the suspension of students. The cabinet decided to modify the design so that the data would be collected at each campus by the principal. This was avoided in the original design because of the school psychologist's concerns about objectivity. The schools and the community were included in order to obtain broad-based information about preferences and practices of discipline. The school psychologist pointed out that the evaluation design was no longer objective, that it allowed for a strong "principal" bias. However, the politics of the school district administration at that time outweighed the need for objectivity. The school psychologist's original design for the survey was modified.

Students, teachers, local school administrators, and parents were the subjects of the survey on current disciplinary practices and preferences for the management of student behavior. The results of the study produced a rather massive document, including the teacher's manual as an appendix. Upon receiving the report, the board reacted to its weaknesses, especially to the fact that principals were prime recipients of the information. The board considered it useless for decision making. The board president in particular indicated that the only thing of value was the appendix, calling the rest of the report a "hodgepodge." The board suggested disseminating the manual to every teacher along with staff training in the use of the classroom management techniques.

Despite the report's bad reviews, one issue clearly emerged. The survey consistently stated principal's and teachers' preferences to eliminate corporal punishment if they received training in other techniques for maintaining discipline. Following the report and the positive reception given to the teacher's manual, the school psychologist and his staff submitted a proposal to the National Institute of Mental Health (NIMH) for the purpose of funding personnel to be used exclusively for training teachers in classroom management techniques. The grant was obtained and teams of psychologists and master teachers were hired. The training occurred in large groups, small groups, and on a one-to-one basis with individual teachers.

Following the hodgepodge discipline study, many changes occurred. There was a drastic reduction in the use of corporal punishment in the school district and a significant reduction in long-term suspensions. In-school suspension centers, based on the principles of reality therapy (Glasser, 1969) and involving total faculty/staff development, were designed and used. A significant reduction in the disproportionate representation of black students among the number of disciplined students and a major reduction in suspensions of black students also resulted.

In this case, as far as the school psychologist was concerned, the question of the appropriateness or objectivity of the study dealt only with preferences for punishment. If he had been unyielding in trying to avoid the bias in the study, he would have missed an opportunity to modify the entire system's attitudes and practices. Doing the study provided a means to focus public attention on more positive approaches to discipline and ways to justify extensive staff development in alternatives to punishment.

Fortunately for the district and others concerned, the unscientific survey had beneficial side effects. It provided an opportunity for disseminating ideas about more effective ways to discipline students after infractions occurred. This case provided the school psychologist with an opportunity to implement an intervention that could have a major impact on the entire school district's system for managing student behavior.

Case Study 3

The school district was about to experience a series of major changes: desegregation, "back to basics," dramatic expansion of due process for students, increases in services for students with special needs, and so on. Generally, faculty and staff seemed very poorly prepared for these changes. Most of the administration had long histories in the school district, and many were close to retirement. These impending major changes precipitated the willingness of the "old guard" to listen to new ideas.

The school psychologist found an opportunity for systemic intervention in the midst of these changes when a group of Mexican-Americans, the Concerned Parents for Equal Education, presented the school board with 20 concerns for the education of their children. The superintendent was instructed by the school board to develop responses to the 20 concerns.

The school psychologist became involved when asked by the superintendent to develop a response to a question about the poor performance of Mexican-American children on academic achievement tests. The total written response was developed and given to the Concerned Parents for Equal Education. The response did not satisfy the committee and they returned to the board. The superintendent summoned his administrators together and asked for additional ideas for rephrasing or redeveloping the responses. Much consideration was given in developing the text of the response. However, the school psychologist suggested that a different approach to the problem might be advisable. He contended that trying to explain away the identified problems might only increase the frustration and anger of the Mexican-American parents. Furthermore, he believed that the parents were more interested in being heard and understood. Moreover, parents wanted some voice in attempting to remediate the problems they knew existed in the school district. The psychologist suggested that key problems be acknowledged. Even more important, he maintained that the parents' questions should be interpreted not as a criticism of the district but rather as a genuine expression of concern about such vital issues as low achievement scores of Mexican-American students and a disproportionately high incidence of Mexican-American students in special education.

Because the parents' committee included leaders of the Mexican-American community, the school psychologist recommended not writing any more responses. Instead, he proposed that some or all of the committee members attend a series of evening meetings to discuss different topics with representatives from different areas within the administration. For example, one night could be set aside for discussion of achievement test scores, another night for discussion of proposed bilingual education programs, another for disproportionate participation in special education programs, and so on.

This suggestion was based on certain assumptions that were explained to the superintendent and the other administrators present. The first assumption was that serious problems did exist. The second assumption was that the problems would be difficult to solve. The third assumption was that ongoing communication was essential. Showing that the administration was aware of the problems and planning changes to alleviate them would require continuing cooperation in examining, defining, and mutually attacking the problems. The suggestions and assumptions were acceptable to the superintendent. The task was delegated to the assistant superintendent, divisional directors, and the school psychologist, for scheduling, organizing, and holding the meetings. The parents committee very much appreciated the response, seeing it as a major positive shift in the attitude of the administration.

The school psychologist saw this crisis as an opportunity to modify the way in which the administration had been responding to demands placed on the school district. The approach used previously seemed dysfunctional and destined to keep the district in a mode of reacting to crisis generated by groups finding reason to criticize the schools. This intervention contributed to a proactive system that could develop more communication with various interest groups.

Responding directly to the persons involved defused anger and allowed for meaningful discussion. Many of the administrators were surprised to find how much understanding of the educational problems existed within the parent group. Their understanding was not only for the nature and causes of the problems but also for programs that had been used in other school districts to try to solve the problems. Parents' thoughts and feelings became an effective resource for the administration and motivated needed changes, especially in regard to minority group interests. Evening meetings were suggested in order to be convenient to the parents and to show willingness on the part of the administration to reach out to them. Effective conflict management involved openly confronting the issues rather than trying to negate or explain them away.

Case Study 4

The next case focused on a junior high school that was considered to be in "transition." The school was serving a neighborhood that had been all white and was gradually being integrated (Snapp & Sikes, 1977). During this time, the school staff noticed a dramatic increase in physical confrontations between students. The principal and one of the counselors requested a conference with the school psychologist for assistance in planning a program that might help prevent these physical confrontations.

The school staff had already made an assumption. Specifically, they believed that a systematic group counseling program, emphasizing counselor availability to intervene and induce controlled, verbal confrontation within a group, would be the way to avoid physical confrontations. The staff believed that the school psychologist was needed to train the counselors in small-group techniques. The school's faculty was supportive of the program since they too were very concerned about the increase in fighting. The faculty agreed to help free the counselors' time, so that they would be able to provide needed services (e.g., they were willing to take over all class scheduling responsibilities).

The school psychologist agreed to provide training in group skills for the counselors and students and to co-lead a group with each counselor during the school year. The school psychologist would provide supervision, using the group experiences as opportunities to focus on issues that co-leaders could discuss after each group session. He also agreed that beyond the first year, his supervision and/or consultation could be available on request.

In this case there was an opportunity to do more than simply reduce the high incidence of fighting. They might be able to provide a greater sense of pride and togetherness throughout the school, if they were to use the resources already being mobilized (i.e., counselors, students, and faculty). The focus would be on verbal and nonverbal communication as an alternative to dependence on physical altercations to settle disputes.

The school psychologist's plan for intervening into the school as a "system" was to train and supervise the teachers, counselors, and principal by setting up a group in which the adults in the school could participate on a voluntary basis. After each group, the counselors discussed with the school psychologist those issues and techniques that came up during the session. This ongoing group later became a support group for those who would be involved in the training program for students.

The program included the co-leading of an ethnically balanced group of 10 students. Each group of students, co-led by a teacher or an administrator and one of the counselors, focused on the development of communication skills, especially when strong feelings were involved. Students learned to describe their feelings, to state clearly their preferences, and to respond to each other's feelings. The groups had clearly defined socially acceptable ways for group members to behave. Fighting was absolutely *not* acceptable.

Initially, there were few instructions. However, this remarkable and energetic group of teachers and counselors was available for crisis group work. Any time there was a threat of a fight, any one of the students involved could initiate a contact with the counselor. In turn, the counselor invited any other students who might be involved in the potential fight to participate in small-group discussion in the group room. They would stay in the room and talk it out until there was no longer a threat of violence and until the students made an explicit agreement not to fight.

After the first year of this program actual numbers of fights were tabulated and a significant reduction was found. For the first time in 4 years there had not been an increase in the number of physical altercations. In comparison to the high school serving the same transitional area, desegregation in this junior high school progressed more smoothly and with little serious difficulty.

This program was continued for more than 8 years. Most of the teachers on the junior high school faculty were trained by the school psychologist during the first 3 years. Training beyond the first 3 years was provided to new faculty volunteers by the counselors themselves, with consultation from the psychologist as needed. The program became a regular part of the overall school program.

In addition to the success that was experienced in reducing fighting at that junior high school, the "game plan" developed by the counselors and teachers became a manual for group counseling activities in junior high schools. It was disseminated widely throughout the district and the state and received state and federal commendations for its usefulness in working on human relations. The manual included both activities for student groups as well as details for a 3-day training sessions for interested faculty.

From a broader perspective, this was an ideal opportunity to consult with, and intervene into a system. The system was in crisis and its resources were already being mobilized in an attempt at solution. The school psychologist needed only to help focus the efforts and identify more of the available resources to impact the system further. The program came to involve a large segment of the faculty in a way that promoted integration instead of merely diminishing some of the negative effects of desegregation.

Case Study 5

The following case study involves a crisis sitution of great proportions. This crisis was the most extreme act of violence in the school district's history—the shooting and killing of a teacher by a student. One morning, apparently without provocation, an eighth grader came to school with a .22-caliber rifle. He walked into the classroom, within 10 feet of his teacher, and fired three shots. The teacher died instantly in front of 32 of the boy's classmates.

The school psychologist had been visiting a nearby high school when a staff member heard about the shooting on a local radio station. Upon confirming the radio report, the school psychologist proceeded to the junior high school, arriving within 40 minutes of the shooting. Upon arrival, the psychologist discovered that all the student witnesses had been taken by bus to the police station, where they were giving their accounts of the shooting. He was asked to join them at the station and remained there until all of the students had returned to school or were taken home. After the questioning was finished and the students were taken care of, the psychologist went back to the junior high school to offer his help to the principal. The psychologist asked if there were something in particular that he could do with the students who had witnessed the violence and/or with the rest of the students in the school. At that time, the psychologist had not formulated a plan, but it was apparent that follow-up counseling services needed to be made available. The principal was in need of additional help. Calls from parents had

already begun coming in asking if the students would receive any help in dealing with the tragedy.

The school staff and the school psychologist designed a plan for intervention in this crisis. A doctoral-level counselor was assigned as a temporary part of the counseling staff at the junior high school. His function was to be available for individual students and teachers who might seek assistance in relation to the tragedy. He was also available to the regular school counselors for supervision, advice, or consultation. The principal was notified that a team of support personnel would be available to meet with parents having questions about the services and activities to be provided for the students. In addition, the team would discuss the kinds of reactions that parents might expect from their children, immediately following the crisis and thereafter.

The support team consisted of the teacher who had team taught with the deceased, a specially trained crisis intervention counselor, the school's social worker, and one of the school's counselors. All of these people joined the school psychologist in working with the students who had witnessed the violence. The team believed that the students needed to explore their feelings about the shooting, the student who had done the shooting, and the deceased teacher. Many of the students in the class were school leaders who had become a major source of information for the school and community.

The students were told what services would be offered and they were given some options. Group counseling sessions were available for questions and discussion regarding death, dying, and grieving. Students were also given opportunities to engage in activities in preparation for the funeral. In addition, some of the students had begun expressing an interest in becoming actively involved in a special project dedicated to their deceased teacher. About half of the students chose to participate in the discussion/counseling group, and most of the remaining became involved in tasks related to the funeral and the dedication to the teacher.

Parents requested a meeting with the school psychologist and the rest of the intervention team. Open discussion was held about what had gone on at school and what was done with the students and faculty. The parents asked questions about their own concerns and what they could expect from their sons and daughters. For example, the children's rather dramatic mood swings were puzzling to them. The team helped the parents plan ways to listen to, support their children, and to anticipate possible future reactions.

It is hard to evaluate the effectiveness of this intervention except in terms of the human experience. The gratitude of the eighth graders' classmates, their parents, and the school's faculty confirmed that the strategy met the expressed needs of those individuals, at least at that time. It is, however, an example of how the school psychologist can respond to a crisis situation and intervene at a systems level.

Case Study 6

This case study concerns the design and implementation of a system for delivering support services to a school district. The city in which this school district was located had within it a wide variety of mental health services. At the time of the intervention, many services existed within the city and school district but there was no systematic coordination of these services.

As a typical example, a principal called and was very concerned about the behavior of a fifth-grade boy in his school. The boy was described as difficult to control, generally disobedient, and frequently fighting. When the school psychologist asked about what had previously been done with the boy, the response was "we have tried everything." The boy had been referred at various times to the school counselor, to the school social worker, to the school nurse, and to the school psychologist assigned to that building. He had also been referred to the local mental health center for evaluation and treatment.

The supervising school psychologist asked if all people involved in the case had ever met to compare notes, exchange information, and develop a cooperative plan for intervention with the boy. Because no such meeting had occurred, a meeting was set up with all personnel involved. They identified strengths and weaknesses unique to that youngster, as well as relatively successful and unsuccessful strategies previously tried. They wanted to start a team effort that could circumvent the cycle of frustration which in the past had led to consideration of long-term suspension of the child from school.

This team effort occurred at a time when the concern about how resources were being utilized in the school paralleled concern that was being ex-

pressed by the staffs of mental health agencies. The agencies felt they had little access to the school staff with whom they needed to work cooperatively. Agency personnel were frustrated in attempts to provide information about what they thought a student might need in an educational setting. Neither could they obtain information or feedback from the school that would help them evaluate the effectiveness of their mental health interventions. Access to a school usually depended on the relationship developed with an individual principal. The agencies wanted to explore ways to coordinate with the school district to develop a delivery system designed to better meet students' needs and to mobilize existing resources to meet those needs. The school psychologist met with the superintendent and discussed the possible benefits to the school district. The superintendent responded favorably and committed staff time to the planning and coordination process. The school psychologist then began the process to develop a delivery system that would better serve the entire school district.

The first step in the process was to list possible representatives from the school district and community agencies that would serve on a planning committee. The School Community Consultation Committee (SCCC) was formed. It included representatives from support services within the school district and from community agencies (e.g., Mental Health-Mental Retardation Center, Child Guidance Center, Family Services Center, Police Department, Juvenile Court, etc.).

Representatives and agency heads of these support agencies were asked to meet and review existing referral procedures in an attempt to strengthen referrals and maximize the utilization of existing resources. Information about agency and interagency referral procedures was exchanged and the full spectrum of services available from all sources was outlined.

The SCCC held a series of meetings in which a total delivery system was designed. The committee met monthly for 2 years. During this time the referral procedures between the agencies were revised and refined. Considerable information regarding problems in the processing of referrals was shared and decisions were made to enhance the referral system. Consequently, communication and cooperation between the schools and various agencies within the community increased. Also, the agencies expressed a desire to aid the school district in one of its major priorities at that time— the desegregation of all schools in the system. The community agencies understood that desegregation of the district would create some disruption and require assistance from mental health and social service agencies.

The SCCC developed an overall service delivery system. The model for a Psychoeducational Services Delivery System (Snapp, Pells, Smith, & Gilmore, 1974) coordinated the services that were available to schools on an itinerant basis. The unit for coordination at the local level was called the Local Support Team (LST). It included a way for community agency personnel to directly serve schools. A referral to a community agency could originate from the LST. The community agency personnel would first contact the LST and request information about how agency personnel might work further with the school and/or with individual students. This freed agencies from the constraint of having to depend on individual personal relationships with the principals. A strong positive relationship with the school administrators was helpful, but that was not the only way to gain access to a school.

The school board approved the proposal for the Psychoeducational Services Delivery System. The approved proposal called for four levels of intervention. The first level was comprised of persons within the school itself (i.e., the teacher, the principal, and the parent). The second level incorporated the first and added personnel (LST) assigned on a regular and itinerant basis to the school. There were guidelines to facilitate the operation of the LST and its problem solving and planning for individuals and small groups of students. Also large, campus-wide problems could be brought to the resources on the LST for assistance in defining problems and planning solutions. Centrally assigned personnel, "on call" to the school, comprised the third-level intervention.

The fourth level was different from the previous three. It included a program designed by the SCCC as part of the total delivery system. This level, named the Diagnostic Intervention (D-I) Program, was designed as an additional resource for psychological services in the district. Community agency staff interfaced directly with this program as well as the LST.

The type of mutual planning between school and community agencies became a priority in the community (Pells, Sanford, Haug, & Snapp,

1974). Over a 6-year period, the local community mental health center paid the salaries of two staff persons, a psychologist, and a master teacher of emotionally disturbed children and youth, who were assigned full time to working with students in the school district and promoting interagency communications.

The D-I program provided a staff of master teachers, under the supervision of a school psychologist, to provide an assessment and planning model that was primarily educationally based. The diagnostic teaching technique was essentially that of developing hypotheses, testing them out with the referred students in an education environment, consulting with teachers about the results of the assessment, and planning ways to work with the students. The liaison developed between the school and the community mental health center provided for training mental health workers in school consultation techniques. This facilitated more effective planning between the two agencies.

The aforementioned case studies all illustrate the positive impact and aspects of systems level interventions. Viewing schools from an open systems perspective, it is also possible, and in fact probable, that interventions for individuals can have a negative impact on the system and in turn the individuals in the system and the systems themselves. Failing to remember this can result in a failed consultation effort overall even though change is obviously accomplished at the individual level. The following case study illustrates the results of failing to address systems-level issues accurately even though objective data indicated that the behavior of the individual child was significantly improved.

Case Study 7

Often when a systems-level change is attempted, the results may not go as planned or the impact may be even more far reaching than planned. In the following case, the psychologist was a psychologist working in a public school setting. As part of her role definition within the district, she was to serve as a member of the multidisciplinary team whose job it was to assess and determine a child's best educational plan. In one elementary school, the psychologist also was asked to attend special multidisciplinary committee meetings held expressly to determine students' eligibility for retention.

The school retention committee consisted of

the principal, the child's teacher, a special education teacher, and the psychologist. At the first meeting of this in-school retention committee, it was obvious that a decision whether or not to retain students was largely dependent on an individual teacher's and administrator's "experience" with such children rather than on any data showing that children below grade level who were retained actually performed better than similar children that were not retained.

Recognizing the opportunity to make a sub-systems-level change in the guise of decision making on an individual student, the psychologist attempted to facilitate change in the team's decision-making processes. She remembered a recent review of the literature on retention of children and she mentioned to the committee that research reported certain variables that were important to consider when deciding whether or not to retain a student. Generally, the literature suggests the students that are retained do not perform significantly better academically or behaviorally than students with similar academic problems who are not retained. The committee acknowledged the psychologist's suggestions but seemed not to consider the information in their final decisions to retain or not to retain the child being considered. The psychologist was disheartened that she had not been able to effect change in the subcommittee decision-making strategies.

The consultant was unaware at that time that the principal of the school had recently been appointed as chairperson of a district-wide committee established by the superintendent to study the problem of retention. Several weeks after the school retention committee meeting, the principal called the psychologist in and asked for more information on the research findings that were mentioned at the earlier meeting. The psychologist answered various questions and offered to bring in the particular research articles on retention for the principal to read. No specific followup was planned.

Later in the semester, the principal enthusiastically thanked the psychologist for the retention information and reported that many of the concepts presented therein directly affected the district committee's policy statements on retention. This is another case where what began as an attempt to effect change at the individual level (i.e., decision on child being retained) turned into a significant systems-level change. What is important is that the consultant recognized the potential for a systems-level change and had the withitness to attempt such a change. In this case, what began as a microsystems intervention (i.e., the school retention subcommittee) had turned into a much higher-level systems change (i.e., district retention policy).

Case Study 8

The psychologist in this case was an advanced doctoral student in school psychology. As part of a experiential component of her doctoral training program the student served as a consultant to one special education student teacher. She was asked by the student teacher to consult on a student, hereafter referred to as C., who was seen as a major behavior problem this year and who had a history of behavior problems since entering school. Quickly, the supervising teacher was included in the consultation sessions, as the student teacher had only two more weeks in that classroom. During the initial meeting it was evident that both consultees, but particularly the supervising teacher, felt hopeless and at the "end of her rope" regarding ways to improve C.'s behavior. In the first session, it was specified that the consultees considered C.'s failure to follow directions and negative interaction with peers (hitting, name calling, shoving) most apparent during transition times as the problems of greatest concern. The supervising teacher had previously contacted the school counselor and together they decided the student could be referred for placement in a class for the emotionally disturbed. The consultant did not agree with the view that the child was emotionally disturbed. She then suggested to the teacher that she (the consultant) work hard with her (the teacher) to help remediate the student's behavior, at least until more formal referral processes could begin.

The consultant used a collaborative, problem-solving consultation approach with the supervising teacher whereby she actively facilitated consultee participation in the problem-solving process. One primary goal of the consultant was to restore the consultee's hope that the problem could be solved or at least improved. For several weeks the consultant met with the consultee, problems were defined, baseline data were collected, and interventions were chosen, implemented, evaluated, and revised on two occasions. Throughout a 5-week period, the consultee reported feeling much more hopeful regarding problem remediation and was consistently cooperative and active in the problem-solving process. The student consultant was reminded by her university supervisor to include the counselor in all problem efforts when possible because she was a very important systems variable. The consultant did meet with the counselor early in the process to elicit her ideas and support regarding interventions with the child. The counselor volunteered to see the student with a group she had and to be a reinforcer to him when possible. At the end of the fifth week, the consultant checked to see how the revised interventions were working. Surprisingly, the consultee expressed considerable doubt that the intervention had been at all successful. The consultant then showed the consultee graphic representation of the data that the behavior had in fact significantly decreased since the baseline data were gathered. The consultee acknowledged that the undesirable behaviors had decreased, but she still seemed totally unwilling to invest any more time working on finding an even more optimal solution to the problem. The consultant was confused and disappointed that what appeared to be such a positive consultation outcome, both in terms of changes in consultee attitude and actual client behaviors, had taken such a negative turn. The consultant, however, continued to reinforce the consultee for her hard work and success, but left the school "scratching her head" over what happened.

The following week the consultant again contacted the consultee just to see what, if anything, had happened. The consultee was polite but very terse with the consultant. She (consultee) reported that the school counselor had agreed with her earlier suspicions that this child was a "hopeless" case and needed to be in a class for the emotionally disturbed. The teacher seemed quite relieved with the decision. The consultant was dumbfounded.

Analysis of the case suggests that possibly the consultant failed to properly involve an important school "gatekeeper" in the problem-solving process and that this gatekeeper was threatened by what to her appeared to be the consultant's success where she (the counselor) had failed in past years. The result was a psychological consultation intervention that worked on the individual level but failed to account for other systems variables (i.e., school counselor and in-house psychological intervention subsystems) and thus ultimately failed to ensure that the change was maintained.

Case Study 9

When careful retrospective analysis is possible, the signals of possible failure are often recognized as having occurred early in the consultation process. In the midst of implementing a strategy, however, such early-warning signs are often overlooked or misevaluated. The following case exemplifies one such failed intervention. In this case, the school psychologist attempted to improve the skills of special services staff so that children and other school personnel might receive more comprehensive psychological services. A post hoc analysis is offered, but obviously any "explanations" are merely hypotheses.

The special education director of a large metropolitan district was concerned about the functioning of her special services teams. These teams were composed of psychologists and social workers. Her primary concern was that interactions among the group members were often acrimonious and that certain individuals were performing at very low levels of productivity and expertise.

After a brief consultation with the group regarding her concerns, the director contacted a university-based school psychologist to serve as a conflict management consultant to the entire group. The consultant's name had been suggested by one of the team members (a former student of the consultant). Unknown to the consultant, he had not been the group's unanimous choice for a consultant; rather, his choice had been very controversial among the group.

The consultant began gathering premeeting assessment data by interviewing the special education director. He learned that the team members were polarized around a number of issues: some having to do with the personal characteristics of team members, some with recent changes in district policies that increased team accountability, and some with the different training orientations of the team members. In addition, the consultant spoke at length with his former student before the initial meeting with the entire team. Many "red flags" were raised through these conversations and the consultant planned accordingly.

The positive goals of the one-and-a-half-day consultation with the special services team were conceptualized as follows: (a) improve the communication and problem-solving skills of the team members (e.g., feedback, nondefensive communication, thorough problem identification and analysis), (b) increase the morale of the team by a focus on their strengths and positive accomplishements, and (c) improve the administrative skills of the director though modeling and didactic input.

The consultant's initial contact with the team members indicated that the team was unaware of the goals of the consultation and distrustful of the motives and expertise of the consultant. For example, several team members were very late in arriving for the opening meal. At the first session with the consultant this same group wanted to be "allowed" to drink wine during the meeting (the sessions were held in a nearby conference center, not in a school building). With no rapport built, the consultant worried about disallowing the drinking, but did so using the rationale that genuine encounter would be compromised if later people could "blame the alcohol" for what had been said. The dissatisfaction of the team with the consultant's plans was quite evident.

Following a reorienting of the goals of the consultation to meet the wishes of the team, the reminder of the meetings proceeded quite smoothly. The team members were complimentary and had participated actively in activities and interactions. The consultant felt the interactions had been difficult at times but had culminated successfully. In particular, the team members had given each other very positive feedback, they had disclosed personal information to each other that made each member feel more trusted and valued by the others, and several had confronted the special education director with their specific concerns about changing school district policy.

The consultant had not implemented all of his plans but was confident the director would see an improvement in the productivity, morale, and professionalism of the group. He was surprised, therefore, on a follow-up phone call 3 weeks later to hear from the director that nothing had changed for the better and, in fact, she thought her relationship with the staff was more tenous than ever before.

In retrospect it seems clear that the consultant had made errors throughout the consultation in terms of assessment, implementation, and evaluation. For example, he relied upon only two sources of information for his intervention planning. Each of these sources was probably unrepresentative of the entire team. The director's

insights were necessarily that of an outsider (and evaluator) looking in on the team process. The consultant's former student was probably prone to seeing group dynamics as taught by the consultant and perhaps unable to provide data that would create a need to plan innovative interventions. The former student would also be unable to gauge her contribution to the team's difficulties.

The inadequate assessment resulted in most team members feeling alienated and distrustful of the consultation process. In retrospect, their resistance to consultant-generated activities was predictable. The pressure they brought upon the consultant to revise the experience completely was successful in keeping the focus off their uncomfortable group dynamics. He facilitated "good feelings" among the group and confrontation of the director (outside the group, and perhaps, safe to criticize).

The consultant's assessment did not lead to careful identification of learning or behavioral objectives. He did not develop a mechanism for evaluating the effects of the consultation. This failure to idntify short- and long-term goals (and a method to measure attainment) made his work susceptible to "washing out" very quickly, as nothing specific was brought from the training back to the work environment.

CONCLUSION

The school psychologist continues to be seen too frequently as a "gatekeeper" for special education, that is, the provider of assessment services for the determination of students' eligibility for special education. Federal and state special education laws demand more resources for comprehensive appraisals. This legislative mandate has increased the difficulty of expanding the role of school psychologists beyond that of appraisal.

The preceding case studies illustrate how consultants, both internal and external to particular school systems, can greatly assist school organizations in adapting to the many complex environmental changes that affect them. In these examples, psychologists utilized the concept of a school as an open system where change at one level in one subsystem affects changes at many other levels in many other interrelated subsystems. The case studies illustrate the assertion of Chin and

Benne (1976) regarding any organizational change. That is, changes must be instituted in subsystems that interact with the targeted subsystem in which the change is desired to ensure that the change is reinforced and maintained. Unless the effects on any interrelated subsystems are considered and accounted for, the change will either not be initiated at all or, if initiated, the probability of it being maintained will be small. This perspective considers the intricate dynamics of the organization from an open systems perspective, namely the interrelatedness of the subsystems and the influence of the environment upon school organizational functioning.

REFERENCES

Bardon, J. I. (1982). The psychology of school psychology. In C. R. Reynolds & T. B. Gutkin (Eds.), *The handbook of school psychology* (pp. 3–13). New York: Wiley.

Brassard, M. R. (1986). Family assessment approaches and procedures. In H. M. Knoff (Ed.), *The assessment of child and adolescent personality*. New York: Guilford Press.

Bronfenbrenner, V. (1974). Is early intervention effective? In H. J. Leichter (Ed.), *The family as educator*. New York: Teachers College Press.

Chin, R., & Benne, K. D. (1976). General strategies for effecting changes in human systems. In W. G. Bennis, K. D. Benne, R. Chin, & K. D. Corey (Eds.), *The planning of change* (3rd ed., pp. 45–63). New York: Holt, Rinehart and Winston.

Christenson, T., Abery, B., & Weinberg, R. A. (1986). An alternative model for the delivery of psychological services in the school community. In S. N. Elliott & J. C. Witt (Eds.), *The delivery of psychological services in schools: Concepts, processes, and issues* (pp. 349, 392). Hillsdale, NJ: Lawrence Erlbaum.

Curtis, M. J., & Metz, L. W. (1986). Systems level intervention in a school for handicapped children. *School Psychology Review, 15*(4), 510–519.

Cutts, N. E. (Ed.). (1955). *School psychology at midcentury*. Washington, DC: American Psychological Association.

Dollar, B., & Klinger, R. (1975). A systems approach to improving teacher effectiveness: A triadic model of consultation and change. In C. A. Parker (Ed.), *Psychological consultation: Helping teachers meet special needs*. Minneapolis: University of Minnesota, Leadership Training Institute/Special Education.

Elliott, S. N., & Witt, J. G. (1986). *The delivery of psychological services in schools: Concepts, processes, and issues*. Hillsdale, NJ: Lawrence Erlbaum.

Engel, G. L. (1980). The clinical application of the biopsychosocial model. *American Journal of Psychiatry, 137*, 535–544.

Fish, M. C., & Jain, S. (1988). Using systems theory in school assessment and intervention: A structural model for school psychologists. *Professional School Psychology, 3*, 291–300.

Fisher, L. (1986). Systems-based consultation with schools. In L. C. Wynne, S. H. McDaniel, & T. T. Weber (Eds.), *Systems consultation: A new perspective for family therapy* (pp. 342–356). New York: Guilford Press.

Garbarino, J. (1982). *Children and families in the social environment*. Chicago: Aldine.

Glasser, W. (1969). *Schools without failure*. New York: Harper & Row.

Katz, D., & Kahn, R. L. (1978). *The social psychology of organizations* (2nd ed.). New York: Wiley.

Kurpius, D. J. (1985). Consultation interventions: Successes, failures, and proposals. *Counseling Psychologist, 13*(3), 368–389.

Levin, G., Trickett, E. J., & Kidder, M. G. (1986). The themes, promise, and challenges of mental health consultation. In F. V. Mannino, E. J. Trickett, M. F. Shore, M. G. Kidder, & G. Levin (Eds.), *Handbook of mental health consultation* (pp. 505–520). Rockville, MD: National Institute of Mental Health.

Lewin, K. (1951). *Field theory in social science*. New York: Harper & Row.

Pells, B., Sanford, G., Haug, D., & Snapp, M. (1974). A collaborative school mental health program. *International Journal of Mental Health, 3*, 177–194.

Phillips, B. W. (1980). *Management of behavior in the classroom*. Los Angeles: Western Psychological Services.

Plas, J. M. (1986). *Systems psychology in the schools*. Elmsford, NY: Pergamon Press.

Reynolds, C. R., (1987). Remediation, deficit-centered models of. In C. R. Reynolds & L. Mann (Eds.), *Encyclopedia of special education*. New York: Wiley-Interscience.

Reynolds, C. R., Gutkin, T. B., Elliot, S. N., & Witt, J. C. (1984). *School psychology: Essentials of theory and practice*. New York: Wiley.

Schmuck, R. A., & Runkel, P. J. (1985). *The handbook of organization development in the schools* (3rd ed.). Palo Alto, CA: Mayfield.

Snapp, M., Pells, B., Smith, J., & Gilmore, G. A. (1974). A district-wide psychoeducational services delivery system. *Journal of School Psychology, 12*, 60–69.

Snapp, M., & Sikes, J. N. (1977). Preventive counseling for teachers and students. In J. Meyers, R. Martin, & I. Hyman (Eds.), *School consultation*. Springfield, IL: Charles C Thomas.

von Bertalanffy, L. (1968). *General system theory*. New York: Braziller.

Ysseldyke, J. E. (1986). Current practices in school psychology. In S. N. Elliott & J. C. Witt (Eds.), *The delivery of psychological services in schools: Concepts, processes, and isuses* (pp. 27–52). Hillsdale, NJ: Lawrence Erlbaum.

Ysseldyke, J. E., Reynolds, M. C., & Weinberg, R. A. (1984). *School psychology: A blueprint for training and practice*. Minneapolis, MN: National School Psychology Inservice Training Network.

LEGAL, ETHICAL, AND LEGISLATIVE ISSUES IN THE PROVISION OF SCHOOL PSYCHOLOGICAL SERVICES

38

THE LEGAL REGULATION OF SCHOOL PSYCHOLOGY

DONALD N. BERSOFF
Jenner & Block
PAUL T. HOFER
Federal Judicial Center

The practice of school psychology has become highly regulated. In fact, it may seem that the courts, Congress, and the state legislators control school psychology rather than the professional organizations—the American Psychological Association or the National Association of School Psychologists—which one assumes would serve that function. In this chapter we seek to explore the ways in which the legal system affects our discipline and to analyze the reasons why there have been increasing constraints on the behavior of school psychologists.

As a threshold matter, one may ask whether the legal system should involve itself in school psychology at all. There was a time when the behavior of psychologists, indeed all school people, went virtually unexamined by the courts of law. Courts pleaded lack of expert knowledge and expressed concern about interfering in the discretion of educators. But ours has been called a "litigious society." Moral debates and value conflicts often become legal conflicts, as opposing groups lobby legislators and regulators or search the grandiloquent language of the Constitution for

support of their particular moral vision. American schools, especially our system of free public education, is seen as a central battleground for the shaping of our society's future. School psychologists should not be surprised that the legal system has established standards and exerted significant control over the practice of school psychology. The work of school psychologists' is so important, and so often implicates fundamental social values, that the legal system has been unwilling to keep its hands off.

The degree to which the legal system, particularly the courts, have been willing to involve themselves in the schools has fluctuated along with judicial activism in other areas of public life. In the case of schools, there is an especially strong case to be made for leaving control with the local school boards who are closest to the needs and values of their communities. The Supreme Court has warned that "judicial interposition in the operation of the public school system of the Nation raises problems requiring care and restraint . . . Courts do not and cannot intervene in the resolution of conflicts which arise in the daily operation of school

937

systems and which do not directly and sharply implicate basic constitutional values" (*Epperson v. Arkansas,* 1968, p. 104). In 1977, the Supreme Court reaffirmed its support for school administrators when it ruled that corporal punishment did not violate the U.S. Constitution and that a hearing was unnecessary before such discipline was inflicted. It reasoned:

> Assessment of the need for, and the appropriate means of maintaining, school discipline is committed generally to the discretion of school authorities subject to state law. The court has repeatedly emphasized the need for affirming the comprehensive authority of the States and of school officials, consistent with fundamental constitutional safeguards, to prescribe and control conduct in the schools (*Ingraham v. Wright,* 1977, pp. 681–682).

Despite these principles of judicial restraint, the courts have often become involved in educational matters. The example of the Board of Education of Topeka, Kansas, and other communities enforcing racial segregation in the 1950s emboldened judges to overrule local authorities and enforce constitutional values viewed as fundamental to the nation as a whole (*Brown v. Board of Education,* 1954). The Supreme Court has declared that "students in school as well as out of school are 'persons' under our constitution . . . possessed of fundamental rights which the State must respect" (*Tinker v. Des Moines Independent Community District,* 1969, p. 511). In the 1970s the Supreme Court decided such issues as the reach of compulsory education laws, the requirements of due process prior to the infliction of disciplinary and academic sanctions, the immunity of school officials from financial liability, the allocation of financial resources to pupils in poor school districts, the education of non-English-speaking children, the constitutionality of special admissions programs for minorities, the admission of handicapped persons to professional training programs, the breadth of remedies available to minorities when they seek to undo a past history of school segregation, and the right of schools to expel disruptive, handicapped students.

The tension between federal and local control of school policies has remained. The selection of books for the school library (*Board of Education v. Pico,* 1982), the ability of school officials to regulate student speech (*Bethel School District v.* *Fraser,* 1986), the authority of state legislators to require moments of silence (*Karcher v. May,* 1987), and the authority of school administrators to conduct warrantless searches of students (*New Jersey v. T.L.O.,* 1985) have all found their way to the Supreme Court in the last decade. Judicial decisions in the 1980s have left more discretion with local authorities than did the landmark decisions of preceding decades upholding constitutional rights of students against local administrators. The high court is in a period of transition, so predicting the future course of judicial involvement in school administration and school psychology is hazardous at best. But recent decisions such as *Hazelwood School District v. Kuhlmeier* (1988), where the Supreme Court refused to uphold student free press rights on the school newspaper, suggest that the court will keep its hands off school officials unless their behavior violates the most fundamental constitutional provisions without an adequate pedagogical reason.

The courts are not the only lawmakers involved in regulating school psychology. Congress and the federal administrative agencies have been equally energetic. In 1964, Congress passed the Civil Rights Act prohibiting many forms of discrimination in institutions receiving federal financial assistance. In 1965 it voted the Elementary and Secondary Education Act into law and 3 years later Congress began to exert extensive control over the development of local special education programs when it passed the Handicapped Children's Early Education Assistance Act. That was followed by the Rehabilitation Act of 1973, the Education for the Handicapped Amendments of 1974, the Family Education Rights and Privacy Act (the "Buckley Amendment") (P.L. 93-380), and most important, the Education for All Handicapped Children Act of 1975 (P.L. 94-142). In almost all instances, regulatory agencies published a series of complex, lengthy, often controversial regulations implementing these statutes.

In addition to the legal obligations created by the courts and legislatures, school psychologists also have ethical obligations imposed by their professional organizations, such as the American Psychological Association. These organizations promulgate standards of professional conduct that govern the behavior of their members. (see, e.g., the Specialty Guidelines for the Delivery of Services by School Psychologists [American Psychological Association, 1981]). Failure to abide by the standards subjects member psychologists to possible censure by the ethical committees of the organization. These standards do not, strictly speaking, have the force of law, but they do carry weight in some legal contexts.

CONSTITUTIONAL PRINCIPLES

Much that school psychologists do directly and sharply implicates the Constitution. Two basic values relevant to school systems appear in the Fourteenth Amendment. Generally, the amendment serves as a barrier to thoughtless and arbitrary actions by state officials (school systems and their employees are considered arms of the state for constitutional purposes). Section one of the Fourteenth Amendment forbids the state, among other things, to "deny to any person within its jurisdiction the equal protection of the laws" nor can it "deprive any persons of life, liberty, or property, without due process of law." These two quoted phrases comprise the equal protection and due process clauses of the Constitution.

The right to equal protection has been interpreted, in part, as the right to an equal educational opportunity. School systems cannot discriminate among groups of people when it provides an education unless there is a substantial and legitimate purpose for doing so. Advocates who fought for the right of previously excluded handicapped children to attend public school relied heavily on the equal protection clause to win their cases (e.g., *Mills v. Board of Education of the District of Columbia*, 1972; *Pa. Association for Retarded Children v. Commonwealth of Pa.* 1972). The courts, while acknowledging that admitting severely disturbed, profoundly retarded, and physically handicapped children would be administratively difficult and financially expensive, concluded that the interests sheltered by the equal protection clause outweighed problems created for schools by granting the right to education for all handicapped children. In like manner, many children classified as handicapped argued that they were not genuinely handicapped and to place them in special education programs denied them equal protection by precluding them from access to regular education with nonhandicapped youngsters (e.g., *P. v. Riles*, 1979).

The due process clause is also applicable to school systems. One major component of the clause is procedural due process. In that respect the Fourteenth Amendment requires the state to provide notice (e.g., information to the person concerning what action the state is proposing to take) and an opportunity for the person to be heard (e.g., as in a hearing) in a fair, impartial manner when it seeks to restrict or rescind interests protected by the Constitution. The requirements of due process depends on the precise nature of the government function as well as the private interest that has been affected by the governmental action. The clause is applied only when the state infringes on an individual's interest in life, liberty, or property.

One acknowledged interest is children's entitlement to a free public education. The Supreme Court has identified this as a property interest within the Fourteenth Amendment. Almost all states have created an entitlement to public schooling in their own constitutions or state statutes. "Protected interests in property are normally not created by the [U.S.] Constitution. Rather, they are created and their dimensions are defined by an independent source such as state statutes or rules entitling the citizen to certain benefits" (*Goss v. Lopez*, 1975, pp. 572–573). Once a state has extended the right to education it cannot withdraw that right from an individual without first affording the student access to fundamentally fair procedures. As an extension of that right, the school cannot remove children from the regular classroom environment unless it can substantiate the need to do so in an impartial forum in which all parties have the right to be heard.

The due process clause also forbids arbitrary deprivations of liberty. The constitutional meaning of liberty is broad. It does not mean only involuntary incarceration in a prison or commitment to a mental institution. Liberty can also mean the right to privacy, personal security, and reputation. "Where a person's good name, reputation, honor, or integrity is at stake because of what the government is doing to him, the minimal requirements of the clause must be satisfied" (*Goss v. Lopez*, 1975, p. 574). When applied to school psychology, this broad principle means that schools cannot label children as handicapped unless there is some form of impartial hearing to substantiate the stigmatization that may result. While children may enjoy some benefits by being labeled as retarded, emotionally disturbed, brain injured, or learning disabled (i.e., they may fall under statutes granting rights to such persons), such labeling by school systems is considered to be an "official branding" by the state because of the many long-term negative consequences that may result. For example, a record of impairment may prevent access to some forms of future employment, may increase insurance rates, or be used as evidence of incompetence to make one's own decisions. The Constitution thus prevents the school from unilaterally identifying children as handicapped.

A third constitutional principle that may trigger increased scrutiny of the behavior of school psychologists is the right of privacy. Defining the right of privacy has been difficult for the courts, legislatures, and legal scholars (e.g., Beaney, 1966; Parker, 1974; Westin, 1967). Because the word "privacy" does not appear in the text of the Constitution, it is not clear to many where one may discern a right to privacy. But the principles underlying the Bill of Rights have been used to establish a line of Supreme Court precedents guaranteeing a constitutionally protected right to privacy. Two somewhat overlapping interests have been identified as encompassed by that right. One is the interest in independence in making certain kinds of important decisions; the other, more relevant here, is "individual interests in avoiding disclosure of personal matters" (*Whalen v. Roe*, 1977, pp. 599–600). Over the past two decades, the Supreme Court has acknowledged the guarantee of personal privacy extended to conduct related to marriage, procreation, contraception, family relationships, child rearing, and education. It is unclear to what extent the constitutional right of privacy reaches other areas, but as we will see, it has been broadened to include freedom from unreasonable intrusion into family life by those providing mental health services in the public schools.

These three constitutional principles—equal protection, due process, and privacy—have been invoked to create significant limitations on the time-honored roles of school psychologists: (a) testing and evaluation, (b) intervention and therapy and (c) research. We will now turn to a discussion of each of these areas. Because of the extensive and significant legal involvement concerning the first topic, the bulk of the chapter is devoted to it.

TESTING AND EVALUATION

Nondiscriminatory Assessment

While every person in the United States probably has been affected in some way by tests, school-children are its most frequent targets. It has been estimated that more than 250 million standardized tests of academic ability, perceptual and motor skills, emotional and social characteristics, and vocational interests and talent are used each year in education (Holman & Docter, 1972). Undoubtedly, test results have been used to admit, advance, and employ, but for the majority of persons scores derived from psychometric instruments serve as exclusionary devices—to segregate, institutionalize, track, and deny access to desired goals. Because tests have been used in these ways, their critics charge that they have undermined "the American public school ideal promoted by educational reformers in the last century, whereby the school would serve as an object lesson in equality and brotherhood by drawing students from every social, economic and cultural background into close association of the classroom" (Sorgen, 1973, p. 1137).

While criticism of testing by social, political, and psychological commentators arose within the test industry itself, the legal system seriously began to examine the issue of nondiscriminatory assessment only since the mid-1960s. In part, judicial interest in testing may be explained by the Supreme Court's mandate in *Brown v. Board of Education* (1954) that the public schools must be desegregated. Civil rights advocates view educational and psychological tests as tools to hinder integration and, more broadly, as discriminatory instruments denying the full realization of the constitutional rights of racial and ethnic minorities. As a result, from the mid-1960s to the 1980s there was an explosion of litigation and legislation affecting the administration, interpretation, and use of psychological tests.

For a dozen years after *Brown,* southern school systems attempted to forestall the process of segregation by implementing innovative mechanisms that would preclude black children from attending previously all-white schools. Many of these tactics relied heavily on the use of intelligence and achievement tests. For example, in one major southern city black children were not permitted to transfer to a "white" school unless their grade-level score on an ability test was at least equal to the average of the class in the school to which the transfer was requested. Each of these dilatory mechanisms were challenged in the federal courts by minority plaintiffs and eventually struck down as unconstitutional.

In the process, tests were drawn into the national civil rights debate and were seen as a more subtle version of the blatant segregation of the pre-*Brown* era. In the early cases the validity of the tests themselves was not attacked. The only concern of the judiciary was whether standardized tests were administered only to blacks or were used to make decisions solely on racial grounds. But in the middle 1960s, charges that tests themselves were racist and culturally biased began to be heard. In the politically charged climate of the civil rights movement, sophisticated analysis of test validity became secondary to partisan rhetoric. Objective inquiry into test validity has been, and remains, difficult in the context of continuing and emotional debates about the heritability of racial differences in average test performance, the inadequacy of much of public schooling, and other political controversies that—although not strictly relevant to the validity of tests—understandably color any analysis of how test are used in the schools.

Hobson v. Hanson

Against this background, a federal district court in Washington, D.C. heard and decided *Hobson v. Hansen* (1967)—the first case in which a court directly ventured into the turgid waters of the controversy over test validity and cultural bias. This case primarily concerned the legality of disparities in financial and educational resources within the District of Columbia schools, whereby white children were receiving better education and more monetary support. But at the heart of the matter was the disproportionate number of black children in lower educational tracks, most of whom had been placed there on the basis of standardized groups tests.

Even though the District of Columbia had instituted ability grouping in a genuine attempt to remedy severe academic deficiencies of black children, the court ultimately condemned the system because it found significant racial disproportionality among the tracks. "As a general rule," the court said, "in those schools with a significant number of white and Negro students a higher proportion of Negroes will go into the Special Academic [EMR] Track than will white students" (p. 456). What also concerned the court was its finding that placement in groups was determined primarily on the basis of standardized tests results. While the stated criteria for entrance into any one of the tracks included teacher and counselor evaluation of maturity, stability, physical condition, and grades, the court found "that testing looms as the most important consideration in making track assignments" (p. 475). Thus it was this disproportional effect of the test—what is now called "adverse impact"— that triggered the court's extensive inquiry into the nature and limitations of standardized groups tests.

The only explanation the court would accept as legitimate for the racial disparities it found was that the tests upon which the classifications were based assessed children's innate endowment or capacity to learn, not their present level of skills. The court concluded that the evaluation instruments did not pass that test:

> The evidence shows that the method by which track assignments are made depends essentially on standardized aptitude tests which, although given on a system-wide basis, are completely inappropriate for use with a large segment of the student body. Because tests are standardized primarily on and are relevant to a white middle class group of students, they produce inaccurate and misleading test scores when given to lower class and Negro students . . . [T]hese students are in reality being classified . . . on factors which have nothing to do with innate ability. (p. 514)

The court's curious focus on "innate ability" as the only legitimate source of test score variance probably reflects the court's concern that prior educational deprivation, reflected in poor test performance, not be the basis for perpetuating further deprivation. But by insisting that tests not reflect cultural, economic, or motivational factors, the court contributed to the elevation of "cultural bias" as the primary criticism of educational tests.

Hobson, when read in its entirety, represents the condemnation of rigid, poorly conceived classification practices which adversely affect the educational opportunities of minority children. The court's major concern was not the test but the inflexibility of ability grouping as practiced by the school system, the tracking system's stigmatizing effect on blacks, and its failure to provide sufficient resources to those in the lower tracks, resulting in generally poor teaching. The result was to relegate students in EMR programs to permanent inequality. Swept within the ambit of those practices were ability tests, used as sole or primary decision-making devices to justify placement.

One of the significant findings by the court was that reliance on group measures contributed to the misclassification of approximately 820 of 1,272 students. Evidence of misclassification was provided by the school system itself. In 1965, two years prior to the *Hobson* decision, the superintendent of schools had ordered that no student could be assigned to the EMR track without an evaluation (usually an individual test) by a psychologist. It was when those clinicians reassessed the children in the special track that they concluded that almost two-thirds of them were not genuinely retarded. In that light, *Hobson* could be read as a vindication of the use of individual tests by school and clinical psychologists. However, soon after the case was decided, minority plaintiffs in California and several southwestern states began a round of cases of significant dimension. Despite *Hobson's* implicit approval of individual testing, these cases now began to attack the stately, revered, and venerated devices against which all other tests were measured—the individually administered intelligence scales such as the Stanford-Binet and WISC.

Larry P. (Phase One)

By far the most import of the post-Hobson cases is *P. v. Riles (1972, 1979, 1984, 1986), perhaps better known to readers as Larry P.* Phase One (or *Riles I* as it will also be called here) began in 1971 when black children attending the San Francisco school system filed suit in federal district court charging racial discrimination. All of them had been placed in EMR classes ostensibly because their IQ scores were lower than 75 on state-approved intelligence tests, predominately the Stanford-Binet and WISC. The plaintiffs claimed they were not mentally retarded and that the tests used to place them were culturally biased. They alleged that the resultant misclassification violated the equal protection clause of the U.S. Constitution. Consequently, they requested that the court grant an injunction temporarily restraining the school system from administering IQ tests to determine placement of black children in EMR classes until there was a full trial to decide the merits of their complaint.

The undisputed facts in the case were that while blacks constituted only 28.5% of all students in the San Francisco school system, 66% of all students in its EMR program were black. Similarly, while blacks comprised 9.1% of the California school population, 27.5% of all schoolchildren in the state in EMR classes were black. Thus, the contention of the plaintiffs was that although placement in EMR classes was based on intelligence, not race, the method of classification led to a disproportionate impact on black children.

To support their claim of misclassification the plaintiffs presented affidavits from several black psychologists who had retested the children. Although the psychologists administered the identical instruments initially given the plaintiffs, the examiners did so only after they made special attempts to establish rapport, took pains to reduce distraction, and reworded items in language considered more consistent with the children's cultural background. Scoring procedures were changed so that the children were given credit for nonstandard answers nevertheless judged to show an intelligent approach to solving the problem. The consequences of these efforts was that on retesting all of the plaintiffs scored above the cutoff point for EMR placement.

Although San Francisco was not classifying students explicitly on the basis of race, the court concluded there was a positive duty on the part of the defendants to avoid racial imbalance. In addition, the court concluded that disproportionality in EMR placement could not have occurred without discrimination given the presumption that intelligence is randomly distributed among all racial groups:

> Since it does not seem to be disputed that the qualification for placement in regular classes is the innate ability to learn at the pace which those classes proceed . . . such random distribution can be expected if there is in turn a random distribution of those learning abilities among members of all races. (*P. v. Riles,* 1972, p. 1310)

Here again the court, confronted with difficult and complex issues of test validity, relied on presumptions about "innate ability"—precisely the opposite presumptions than that used to justify much of the segregation at an earlier era. Once it is assumed that "innate ability to learn" is the only legitimate criterion for classifying students, and once we require tests to measure only this hypothetical "innate ability," it is a small step to declaring the tests inadequate for the task. If one adds the assumption that this "innate ability" is randomly distributed across all "racial" groups, it is easy to show that the tests are biased—since not all groups do equally well.

The court required that the plaintiffs make two showings before it would order the school system to shoulder the burden of proving that its practices were justified: (a) that racial imbalance existed in the composition of EMR classes, and (b) that the primary determinant for placement in those classes was test scores derived from the challenged intelligence tests. As we have seen, the data as to imbalance were undisputed and unequivocal. Satisfied that the first prong of the test was met, the court proceeded to analyze if the primary basis for EMR placement was the IQ test.

California's Education Code in existence at the time did, in fact, require a comprehensive evaluation. Children could not be placed in programs for the retarded unless their intelligence test score was at least two standard deviations below the mean and a credentialed school psychologist had assessed their developmental history, cultural background, school achievement, and adaptive behavior. Nevertheless, the court found that the district placed primary emphasis on IQ scores. It pointed to California's own statutes, which prohibited placement in programs for the retarded unless the IQ score was substantiated by other data, from which the court inferred that it was the score that served as the major placement determinant.

The plaintiffs in *Larry P.*, having satisfied both elements of the court's test, successfully shifted the burden to the defendants to justify their use of IQ scores and to "demonstrate the rational connection between the tests and the purpose for which they are allegedly used" (p. 1311). Faced with this task, the school system chose to concede that the tests were racially and culturally biased. But they justified their continued use on the fact that in the absence of suitable alternatives, they were the best means available for classifying students as retarded. The court retorted that "the absence of any rational means of identifying children in need of such treatment can hardly render acceptable on otherwise concededly irrational means, such as the IQ tests as it is presently administered to black students" (p. 1313).

In the end, the court held that the defendants failed to sustain "their burden of demonstrating that IQ tests are rationally related to the purpose of segregating students according to their ability to

learn in regular classes, at least insofar as those tests are applied to black students" (p. 1313). As a result, the school system's actions were judged to be in violation of the equal protection clause. The court issued the preliminary injunction requested by the plaintiffs enjoining, until the full trial, any future placement of black children in EMR classes on the basis of criteria which relied primarily on the results of intelligence tests as then administered. An appellate tribunal in 1974 affirmed the lower court's order. Then the lower court approved the plaintiffs' motion to broaden the injunction to prohibit the administration of individual intelligence tests to all black children in the state. Finally, California itself decided to go beyond that ban. In 1975 it issued a memorandum stating that until further notice none of the IQ tests then on its approved list could be used to place any child, regardless of race, in EMR classes in the state.

Between the granting of the preliminary injunction in 1972 and the court's opinion in 1979 (after the full trial on the merits in *Riles II*) both the Supreme Court and Congress took significant action which had an important effect on the court's decision. First, the Supreme Court decided *Washington v. Davis* (1976), a case which held that the *constitutional* standard for adjudicating claims of racial discrimination was not identical to the statutory standard under the 1964 Civil Rights Act. In the earlier case of *Griggs v. Duke Power Co.* (1971), the court had held that under the Civil Rights Act a statistical showing of a test's adverse impact upon a minority was sufficient to shift the burden onto the test givers to prove that a test was valid. In *Washington v. Davis,* the court held that because the claim was brought not under the Civil Rights Act but under the Constitution, the Constitution required a showing of a discriminatory *purpose* on the part of the test givers. Statistical disproportionality was not enough.

However, even under the rules of *Davis* a statute or practice need not explicitly reveal an intent to discriminate nor is adverse impact irrelevant. Under the Constitution invidious discriminatory purposes may be inferred from the totality of facts by demonstrating that disparities are difficult to explain on nonracial grounds, or that actions are taken that have the foreseeable and anticipated consequence of producing disproportionality. Thus, for the Court in *Riles II* to find a constitutional violation it would have to sift through the testimony to uncover evidence of intent, not merely discriminatory effect. This increased the burden on the plaintiffs for it is much more difficult to prove intent than it is to show statistical disparity.

The other significant activity affecting *Riles II* was by the legislative and executive branches of the federal government. In 1975 Congress passed P.L. 94-142 (20 U.S.C. §§ 1401–1461), the Education for All Handicapped Children Act (EAHCA). Two years earlier it had enacted § 504 of the Rehabilitation Act of 1973 (29 U.S.C. § 794). Implementing regulations for the EAHCA were drafted by the Department of Health, Education, and Welfare (now the Department of Education) and for § 504 by what is now the Department of Health and Human Services, both of which took effect in 1977.

P.L. 94-142 is essentially a grant-giving statute providing financial support to state and local education agencies for special education and related services if they meet certain detailed eligibility requirements. P.L. 94-142 and its implementing regulations reaffirmed earlier mandates concerning nondiscriminatory evaluation and fleshed out the meaning of this requirement. Section 300.532 of the regulations states:

(a) Tests and other evaluation materials:

(1) Are provided and administered in the child's native language or other mode of communication . . .

(2) Have been validated for the specific purpose for which they are used; and

(3) Are administered by trained personnel in conformance with the instructions provided by their producer. . . .

Other provisions also affect psychological and educational assessment. Children with sensory, manual, or speaking impairments are to be given tests that reflect genuine deficits in aptitude or achievement, not those impairments. Further, all assessment is to be comprehensive, multifaceted, and multidisciplinary. Evaluations for placement must be conducted by persons from education, medicine, and psychology who assess children "in all areas related to the suspected disability, including where appropriate, health, vision, hearing, social and emotional status, general intelligence, academic performance, communicative status, and motor abilities." Tests cannot be used which are "merely . . . designed to provide a single general intelligence quotient" nor can one single proce-dure be "used as the sole criterion for determining an appropriate educational program for a child." In making placement decisions the school is required to "draw upon information from a variety of sources, including aptitude and achievement tests, teacher recommendations, physical condition, social and cultural background and adaptive behavior." Thus, P.L. 94-142 makes it quite clear that assessment and placement decisions are the responsibility not of a school psychologist acting alone, but of a multidisciplinary team. The apparent reasons behind this diffusion of duty are to reduce individual bias and broaden accountability.

To ensure that all these provisions are effectuated, both the statute and the regulations provide mechanisms enabling parents "to present complaints with respect to any matter relating to the identification, evaluation, or educational placement" of their children. The complaints are presented in an impartial administrative hearing in which parents have the right to compel the attendance of, and to cross-examine, witnesses involved in the assessment and programming decisions. The consequence is that psychologists are vulnerable to intense scrutiny of their credentials and performance, including the reliability and validity of the evaluation measures they employ, the interpretations they make from the information gathered, or the recommendations they offer as a result of their evaluation (see Note, 1979).

With regard to the Rehabilitation Act, a multipurpose law to promote the education, employment, and training of handicapped persons, Congress declared in § 504 that "no otherwise qualified handicapped individual in the United States . . . shall, solely by reason of his handicap, be excluded from participation in, be denied the benefits, of, or be subjected to discrimination under any program or activity receiving federal financial assistance." This section thus represents the first federal civil rights law protecting the rights of handicapped persons and reflects a national commitment to end discrimination on the basis of handicap. Unlike P.L. 94-142, the requirements of § 504 are not triggered by receipt of funds under a specific statute but protect handicapped persons in all institutions receiving federal financial assistance. Thus, any school system, public or private, receiving federal monies for any program or activity whatsoever is bound by its mandates.

The regulations implementing the broad right-granting language of § 504 were published in

1977. In addition to general principles already established under P.L. 94-142, it sets forth regulations pertaining to the evaluation of children suspected of being handicapped. The language of those provisions, requiring preplacement evaluations, validated tests, multidisciplinary comprehensive assessment, and periodic reevaluations, are almost identical to that which now appear in the implementing regulations to P.L. 94-142 and thus will not be repeated here.

Larry P. (Phase Two)

Given the outcome in *Washington v. Davis* (1976) and the passage of federal legislation protecting handicapped persons, the plaintiffs in 1977 filed an amended complaint alleging, in addition to the equal protection claim under the Constitution, that the defendants had violated Title VI of the 1964 Civil Rights Act (where only discriminatory effect, not intent, would have to be proven). Later in that year the court also granted a motion permitting the U.S. Department of Justice to participate as a friend of the court. The government, siding with the plaintiffs, asserted that the state's conduct also violated P.L. 94-142 and § 504 of the Rehabilitation Act. The plaintiffs then filed a second amended complaint also alleging violation of P.L. 94-142.

Judge Peckham finally published his long, controversial opinion on the merits in October 1979. The court found for the plaintiffs on both statutory and constitutional grounds and permanently enjoined the defendants "from utilizing, permitting the use of, or approving the use of any standardized intelligence tests . . . for the identification of black E.M.R. children or their placement into E.M.R. classes, without securing prior approval by this court" (*P. v. Riles*, 1979, p. 989).

The court began its analysis by evaluating the defendant's conduct under Title VI of the 1964 Civil Rights Act, the Rehabilitation Act of 1973, and P.L. 94-142. In its scrutiny of defendant's behavior under Title VI, the court found no evidence that EMR classes "actually reflected and tapped a greater incidence of mild mental retardation" in black children or that the intelligence tests used for placement in those classes "had been validated for [that] purpose" (p. 966). The majority of the court's statutory analysis was under § 504 and P.L. 94-142. It began by stressing the least restrictive environment ["mainstreaming"] provisions of the acts, which require that "to the

maximum extent appropriate, handicapped children . . . are [to be] educated with children who are not handicapped" (20 U.S.C. § 1412). It chastised the state for adopting policies contrary to the philosophy expressed in those statutes: "Mainstreaming has become the theme of federal law, while California has opted to isolate E.M.R.'s in special day classes" (p. 966).

The court's primary focus, however, was on the nondiscriminatory assessment provisions of § 504 and P.L. 94-142, particularly that part of the implementing regulations requiring assessment instruments to be "validated for the specific purpose for which they are used" (34 CFR § 300.532). The court's interpretation of these provisions, of crucial importance in its holding and the shaping of the final remedy, broke new ground, for as the court recognized, "there are no cases applying validation criteria to test used for E.M.R. placement" (p. 969). Judge Peckham relied on analogous cases for guidance. In *Griggs v. Duke Power Co.,* (1971), the U.S. Supreme Court held that to rebut a prima facie case of discrimination brought by employees who claim employers' use of tests creates a disproportionate impact on minorities, employers must show that the test has a manifest relationship to the position for which the test is required. If this is done, the burden shifts to plaintiffs, who may then submit evidence that alternative selection procedures exist that would serve the employers' purposes as well without producing discriminatory effects. Following *Griggs,* the court held that the defendants should bear the burden of proving that the tests used for placement had been validated for black children. However, it would not merely accept proof that the tests used were able to predict school performance. It adopted the more stringent requirement that the tests be shown valid for selecting children who would be unable to profit from education in regular classes with remedial instruction. The tests would have to identify accurately those children who belonged in what the court characterized as isolated, dead-end, stigmatizing EMR programs. This kind of validation, the court found, had not been done. "[D]efendants must come forward and show that they [the tests] have been validated for each minority group with which they are used . . . This minimal burden has not been met for diagnosing the kind of mental retardation justifying the E.M.R. placement" (p. 971). The few studies that had been brought to the court's attention were not considered relevant. The court rejected validity studies correlating IQ scores with college grades or with other achievement tests. It was satisfied only with research relating IQ scores of black children with classroom grades, although the latter were admittedly subjective. The one relevant study cited yielded correlations between IQ scores and grades for white children of .25 and only .14 for blacks. The expert who testified about the study concluded that the WISC had "little or no validity for predicting the scholastic performance of black or brown children" (p. 972). Thus, the court concluded that "the IQ tests are differentially valid for black and white children . . . Differential validity means that more errors will be made for black children than whites, and that it unacceptable" (p. 973).

The court continued its analysis and found that alternative mechanisms for determining placement in EMR classes did exist. Between 1975 and the court's decision in 1979, there had been a state-wide moratorium on the use of IQ tests, and that there was no evidence to suggest that misplacements had occurred as a result. In fact, the court found that more time and care had been taken during this period in placing children in EMR classes:

> School psychologists, teachers, and others involved in the process are now making decisions based on a wide number of factors, and the evidence suggests that the results are less discriminatory than they were under the IQ-centered standards. Evaluations can and are taking place through *inter alia,* more thorough assessments of the child's personal history and development, adaptive behavior both inside and outside of the school environment, and classroom performance and academic achievement. (p. 973).

Nevertheless, the court warned, alternatives to IQ tests themselves had not been validated, and disproportionate placement, while less egregious than in the pre-1975 era, was still present. Continued use of tests would still be needed, not, however, for the purpose of labeling children as retarded, but for "the development of curricula that respond to specific educational needs" (p. 974). Thus, given the functional exclusion of black children under Title VI, and the failure to meet its burdens under the handicapped acts, the court

found the defendants in violation of the applicable statutes.

Judge Peckham was not content to rest his decision solely on statutory grounds. Testing for EMR placement had been preliminarily enjoined in *Riles I* on the basis of equal protection claims, and the court felt bound to determine whether the plaintiffs continued to warrant relief under the Constitution "where this litigation commenced" (p. 974), although to prevail the plaintiffs would now have to prove that the school system intended to discriminate. The court's ultimate conclusion was grounded in a detailed and lengthy analysis of California's education system generally, and its programs for retarded children specifically. It asserted that the state had been unable to meet the educational needs of disadvantaged children for most of its history and viewed placement of blacks in EMR classes as but one aspect of this failure. But is was the EMR program that received the brunt of the court's condemnation. Throughout the opinion, Judge Peckham labeled the program "dead-end," "isolating," "inferior," and "stigmatizing." Relying on either the testimony of the state's own witnesses or its printed material, the court concluded that EMR classes were "designed to separate out children who are *incapable* of learning in regular classes' (p. 941) [emphasis in the original] and were not meant to provide remedial instruction so that children could learn the skills necessary for eventual return to regular instruction. Given these characteristics, the court considered "the decision to place children in these classes . . . is a crucial one. Children wrongly placed in these classes are unlikely to escape as they inevitably lag farther and farther behind the children in regular classes" (p. 942). Coupled with this pejorative view of the EMR program was the undeniable substantial overrepresentation of black children in those classes, a fact essentially unchanged from *Riles I.*

The next step in the court's analysis was a review of the process by which a disproportionate number of black children were placed in EMR classes. Based on the testimony of the state's witnesses, it found that although California had acknowledged in 1969 that minorities were overrepresented in EMR classes, it chose for the first time in that year to mandate the use of specific standardized individual intelligence tests for EMR placement. The list had been developed by a state department of education official who was not an expert in IQ testing, and was formulated primarily by surveying which tests had been most frequently used by California's school psychologists and, by relying on the recommendations of test publishers. The court concluded that this "quick and unsystematic" process failed to consider "critical issues stemming from IQ testing" (p. 946), and its reaction was harsh: "[B]y relying on the most commonly used tests, they [the defendants] opted to perpetuate any discriminatory effects of those tests" (p. 947).

Before it would scrutinize whether the tests were indeed discriminatory, the court felt bound to determine, as it had in *Riles I,* whether IQ tests were the primary determinant in EMR placement. Once again, it concluded that they were. Of further importance, despite California's statutory scheme which required the consideration of other pertinent and specified data, the state's own investigation of the placement process revealed that about one-third of EMR pupils' records contained no estimates of adaptive behavior, and that over one-fourth were missing a history of physical and social development. In contrast, "the IQ score was clearly the most scrupulously kept record, and it appears to have been the most important one" (p. 950). Thus, the court hypothesized, "if the IQ tests are discriminatory, they inevitably must bias the entire process" (p. 950).

These initial analyses finally brought the court to the central issue—the nature of the intelligence tests themselves. Expert witnesses for both plaintiffs and defendants had agreed on two crucial facts. First, that it was impossible to "truly define, much less measure, intelligence"; and that instead, "IQ tests, like other ability tests, essentially measure achievement" (p. 952). Second, black children did significantly less well on intelligence tests than did their white counterparts. Only 2% of white students in California achieved IQ scores below 70, while 15% of black students did. The court's introductory question was why the tests had not been modified to remove this disparity in the same way that differences between males and females had been excised from early versions of the Stanford-Binet Intelligence Scale. While the court agreed that equalizing scores of minorities and whites might be difficult, it criticized testing experts for being "willing to tolerate or even encourage test that portray minorities, especially blacks, as intellectually inferior" (p. 955).

In sum, the court had constructed an analytic web from which the defendants could not extricate themselves. By defining purposeful discrimination to mean the intent to segregate minority children into special, isolated classes, the court laid the groundwork for vindication of the plaintiffs' claims. It judged California's EMR program to be a substandard, stigmatizing means of education, a virtual prison from which black children could not easily escape. It concluded that the state knew for a decade prior to 1979 that EMR classes were populated by a disproportionate number of minority children placed primarily on the basis of intelligence tests mandated by the state. The process by which these tests were chosen were haphazard, unthinking and suspect, making "the inference of discriminatory intent . . . inescapable" (p. 981).

The tests themselves were seen by both plaintiffs' and defendants' expert witnesses to be culturally biased since none of them had been specifically validated for black children:

> Defendants' complete failure to ascertain or attempt to ascertain the validity of the tests for minority children cannot be ignored. Rather defendants' actions resulting in the adoption of the IQ tests can only be explained as the product of the impermissible and scientifically dubious assumption that black children as a group are inherently less capable of academic achievement than white children. (pp. 981–982)

After finding for plaintiffs under both federal law and the Constitution (as well as the California Constitution), all that was left for the court was to forge proper remedies. In doing so it recognized the genuine changes initiated by California during the course of litigation and the complexity and risk of judicial interference in the administration of education. It also did not want its condemnation of intelligence tests to be seen as the final judgment on the scientific validity of such devices. But these concerns did not dissuade the court from holding the state responsible for its failure to assess and educate black children properly, and from fashioning remedies to halt both test abuse and disproportionate enrollment of blacks in EMR classes.

The court permanently enjoined the state from using any standardized intelligence tests to identify black children for EMR placement without first securing approval from the court. The state board of education would have to petition the court after determining that the test they sought to use were not racially or culturally discriminatory, that they would be administered in a nondiscriminatory manner, and that they had been validated for the purpose of placing black children in EMR classes. The petition would have to be supported by statistical evidence submitted under oath, and certification that public hearings had been held concerning the proposed tests.

With regard to disproportionate placement, the state was ordered to monitor and eliminate overrepresentation by obtaining annual data documenting enrollment in EMR classes by race and ethnicity, and by requiring each school district to prepare and adopt plans to correct significant imbalances. To remedy the harm to those children misidentified, the defendants were to reevaluate all black children then labeled as educably retarded without resort to any standardized intelligence tests that had not been approved by the court. Finally, schools would have to draft individual education plans designed to return all incorrectly identified children to regular classrooms.

Since Judge Peckham issued his opinion and orders in the second phase of *Larry P.* the case has been appealed to the U.S. Court of Appeals for the Ninth Circuit, which affirmed the district court's findings of violations of Title VI and P.L. 94-142 but reversed the findings of violation of both federal and state constitutions (1984). As part of a Coordinated Compliance Monitoring Review process, the state board of education has continued to gather data on minority enrollment in the special day classes that replaced the former EMR classes. The use of IQ tests for the assessment of black pupils for placement in any special education program continues to be prohibited. The board of education has directed that alternative means of assessment be used, such as "personal history and development, adaptive behavior, classroom performance, academic achievement, and evaluative instruments designed to point out specific information relative to a pupil's abilities and inabilities in specific skill areas." (Order Modifying Judgment, No. C-71-2270 RFP, Sept. 25, 1986). IQ tests may not be given to black students even with parental consent, and IQ scores obtained from other agencies are prohibited from becoming part of pupils' school records. (Ironically, a black parent is now suing in California to have her child tested.)

Subsequent Judicial Scrutiny of IQ Testing

Although Judge Peckham's analysis was the first of the new era of federal regulation, and although it alerted psychologists to the strict scrutiny that they might expect from some judges, his analysis was not the last word on the matter of IQ testing in the schools. Since *Larry P.* other noteworthy cases have reached the federal courts, and the judges in these cases have reached very different conclusions.

In *PASE v. Hannon* (1980) Judge Grady of the United States District Court for Illinois ruled that use of standard intelligence tests for placement of black students in classes for the educable mentally handicapped did not violate federal statutes or the Constitution. Examining the precedent in *Larry P.,* the judge decided that too little attention had been given to the threshold question of whether the test items were culturally biased. The judge was unimpressed with the testimony of the expert witnesses on both sides, so he reviewed the items himself and decided if the plaintiffs' arguments about cultural bias had face validity.

Judge Grady concluded that the Stanford-Binet, WISC, and WISC-R contained only a few items that were subject to suspicion for being culturally biased. These items had only a negligible affect on IQ scores. Questions concerning the meaning of "C.O.D.," the reasons for using checks instead of cash to pay bills, or the reasons for preferring organized charities over beggars had at least the appearance of being bound to middle-class values. "Aesthetic comparison" items involving only white faces were similarly suspect. But the judge found virtually no possibility that these few items alone would cause a child to be diverted from the regular classroom and placed in classes for the educable mentally handicapped.

Judge Grady did not share Judge Peckham's damning view of these special classes. Nor did he find that the tests were the sole determinant of placement. "First, the score itself is evaluated by the psychologist who administers the test. The child's responses are recorded verbatim, and the significance of his numerical score is a matter involving judgment and interpretation . . . The examiner who knows the milieu of the child can correct for cultural bias by asking the questions in a sensitive and intelligent way . . . Finally, the IQ test and the psychologist's evaluation of the child in the light of that test is only one component of several which form the basis for an EMR referral" (p. 840). In the context of the school psychologist's professional judgment concerning interpretation of the score, Judge Grady concluded that there was no need to prohibit use of the test.

In *Georgia State Conference of Branches of the NAACP v. State of Georgia* (1983) a major issue was the validity of achievement tests—not aptitude or intelligence tests—for placing black students in educational tracks. The lower federal district court had determined that for the purposes of achievement testing, the school district was "unitary"—a legal term indicating that the school had been desegregated under *Brown* and its progeny, and had worked toward eliminating all vestiges of past discrimination. Until a school is unitary, actions that have a racially discriminatory effect are prohibited, even if the school administrators have no intention to discriminate. The lower court had found that ability grouping was a useful educational practice, and that achievement tests were an appropriate method for making these track assignments, even though the tests resulted in a disproportionate number of black students in the remedial classes. Relying on the lower court's record of the testimony given by educators and psychologists, the court of appeals affirmed the lower court's ruling permitting use of the tests.

In *Montgomery v. Starkville Municipal Separate School System* (1987) the validity of achievement and intelligence tests for making track assignments was again the issue. Although the court was offered psychological testimony that achievement tests were without merit and that achievement grouping was detrimental to students' self-image, the court dismissed the testimony. (The court remarked that the plaintiff's expert "is a psychologist—not an educator" (p. 499). Given the persuasive testimony that achievement testing and grouping have important educational merit, that it was in place long before desegregation, and that there is a fair degree of mobility between tracks for both black and white students, the court permitted continuation of this testing.

But the court reached a different conclusion with regard to testing used to place students in the gifted program in the Starkville system. A combination of scores from the Stanford Achievement Test and the WISC-R were used to make these assignments. Despite testimony by an educational psychologist that the WISC-R represented the "state of the art," the judge could not accept that blacks typically represented less than 10% of the gifted program's students in a district that was approximately 50% black. He ordered a revision in the admissions criteria. The judge did not attempt an analysis of the WISC-R or enjoin its continued use, but he ordered that the district make some changes in use of the test so that more black students qualified for the gifted program.

Clearly, judicial scrutiny of testing must be considered within the context of historical, social, and political forces that shape our country's educational system. Although psychologists may argue that psychometric issues are within their unique expertise, these issues are not the sole criteria by which judges will evaluate the use of tests. School psychologists must be sensitive to the civil rights issues that necessarily touch on their work. They must be prepared to explain and defend their tests and procedures to the court. Better yet, they must be prepared to work with students, administrators, parents, and lawyers, to try to resolve complaints before they become lawsuits.

PROCEDURAL REQUIREMENTS

Justice Frankfurter remarked in one of his Supreme Court opinions that the history of constitutional guarantees was largely to be found in the history of procedure, that is, the process by which a government affords its citizens substantive rights may determine whether those rights are, in reality, exercised. For example, the right to nondiscriminatory assessment may be a hollow one if parents are never informed of their children's pending evaluation, if they are barred from reviewing test findings, if they are precluded from securing an independent evaluation to substantiate or refute the school's assessment, or if they have no opportunity to challenge the results of the assessment in a hearing before an impartial adjudicator. None of these are inherently part of the entitlement to unbiased evaluations but they are all aspects of the process of assessment. Because the courts and federal government have found it difficult to define precisely the substantive right itself, they have seized on procedural guarantees as one important way to help ensure that psychoeducational assessment will be performed fairly.

Notice and Consent

School psychologists must pay as much attention to the process as to the substance of assessment. Probably the most crucial procedural requirement is that of parental involvement concerning an impending psychoeducational evaluation. There are two somewhat separate aspects of this process—notice and consent.

The procedures for providing notice and obtaining consent for the evaluation of handicapped children, regardless of race or ethnicity, are found in the EAHCA, so it is to that law and its implementing regulations that we will turn for guidance. The pertinent provision is § 300.504 in Title 34 of those regulations:

(a) *Notice*. Written notice . . . must be given to the parents of a handicapped child a reasonable time before the public agency:

(1) Proposes to initiate or change the identification, evaluation, or educational placement of the child or the provisions of a free appropriate public education to the child, or

(2) Refuses to initiate or change [the above].

(b)*Consent*. (1) Parental consent must be obtained before:

(i) Conducting a preplacement evaluation; and

(ii) Initial placement of a handicapped child in a program providing special education and related services.

The intent of § 300.504 is to increase parent participation in educational decision making. It does so by requiring that school systems notify parents before they take certain actions and that they obtain consent before they engage in others. In that light it is important to understand the difference between notice and consent. Even the most comprehensive and accurate evaluation may be vitiated if it is performed without proper parent involvement.

Notice and consent are not equivalent. To notify is to *supply information* about impending actions. Consent requires *affirmative permission* before actions can be taken. This distinction raises three questions:

1. What is the legal definition of consent?
2. In what particular situations is notice sufficient; in which will consent be required?
3. In obtaining notice or consent, what information does the law require school systems give parents?

While the concept of informed consent is difficult to define, there is agreement that it possesses three basic characteristics: knowledge, voluntariness, and capacity.

1. *Knowledge:* The person seeking consent must disclose sufficient information in a manner that can be understood by the person from whom the consent is sought. The school need not inform parents of every possible detail with regard to the procedure for which consent is necessary. The regulations require only the communication "of all information relevant to the activity for which consent is sought" (§ 300.501[a]). What, then, is "relevant information?" In § 300.505 of the regulations, the Department of Education lists those items that it believes school systems must disclose to parents prior to obtaining their consent. We will discuss those items shortly. It is clear, however, that full disclosure of every conceivable aspect of an evaluation is not required, not because that is ethically undesirable, but because it is impossible to do so.

   This restriction on the duty to disclose does not excuse school psychologists for making every good-faith attempt to inform parents about those items they must disclose. The regulations indicate that a difference in language between the school psychologist and the parent cannot be a barrier to the communication of relevant information. Schools do not discharge their obligation to inform by exhaustive dissemination of facts in a language that parents cannot understand. Information must be imparted in the "native language" of the parent or in another mode of communication if the parents are unable to understand oral or written language of any sort. The term "native language" is defined, albeit vaguely, in the Elementary and Secondary Education Act of 1965 as "the language normally used by . . . individuals" (20 U.S.C. § 3223) of limited English-speaking ability.

2. *Voluntariness:* Communicating all necessary information in a comprehensive manner does not guarantee that the consent is voluntary. Consent must be obtained in the absence of coercion, duress, misrepresentation, or undue inducement. In short, the person giving consent must do so freely. From a philosophical perspective, it may be impossible to determine whether any decision is made freely, but as a practical matter, if school officials do not use unacceptable influence or interference, consent will be deemed voluntary. School psychologists do not use threats of violence or knowingly misinform parents to secure agreement to assessments, but it is possible for school officials to use subtle, unwitting, but undue influence to obtain permission (Rosen, 1977). While parents are becoming increasingly wary of school people, it is still true that many parents are frightened and intimidated by professional educators. There is nothing wrong with psychologists communicating the school's point of view and even attempting to influence a decision, but the means by which information is communicated should not destroy the parents' ability to weigh and consider that information.

3. *Capacity:* Persons must be legally competent to give consent. Children are considered incapable of making many legally binding decisions. Some adults, especially those in institutions, may also be judged incompetent. But when school personnel believe that a parent is incapable of consenting, they must be acutely sensitive to the civil and constitutional rights of that person. Adults are considered legally incompetent only after they been afforded a full hearing and an impartial factfinder, like a judge, decides that they meet the legal test of incompetency. Psychologists should be very wary of questioning the competency of those from whom they seek consent. The law presumes that every adult is competent and there is a heavy burden on those who seek to rebut that presumption.

The fact that a parent refuses to consent is not enough to trigger an adjudication of incompetency. On the other hand, consent from parents who clearly cannot comprehend any communication or who cannot respond in any manner to requests for consent does not meet legal standards. In those cases it would be appropriate for schools to initiate procedures for the appointment of a substitute decision maker who can represent meaningfully the interests of parents and their children.

Consent is mandated only when the school seeks to conduct a *preplacement evaluation* and when it proposes the *initial placement* of children in special education programs. Because the latter is not the direct responsibility of the school psychologist, we will restrict our discussion to the former situation.

A preplacement evaluation is defined as a "full and individual evaluation of the child's educational needs" (§300.531). Thus, large-scale screening of all children to identify those who might be handicapped and need individually focused assessment would fall outside this definition. Classroom observation designed to assess teacher–child interaction or for screening purposes would also fall outside the definition. Involvement of children in this kind of assessment is minimal and there is no immediate or direct negative effects on them. When an assessor observes members of a group acting in public, there is, at best, an inconsequential invasion of privacy. However, when a particular child becomes the focus of an assessment whose effect or intent will be to recommend placement in a special education program, parental consent must be secured for all procedures, including testing, interviewing, and observation. While the regulations do not require consent for evaluations once the child is placed, it is recommended that such consent be obtained for any evaluations the school performs, except where the instruments are used to assess academic performance only (e.g., reading, writing, spelling skills). To ensure compliance, school psychologists and other responsible for the assessment should not proceed with an evaluation without evidence of either a signed consent form (or some evidence of oral consent) or a legal order authorizing the evaluation when parents refuse to consent.

Of the three components of informed consent, knowledge is the most important. If parents do not receive sufficient information to make a decision, courts will look upon any consent as suspect. The EAHCA regulations provide guidance as to information that must be communicated. Section 300.505 states that parents are to be given:

(1) A full explanation of all of the procedure safeguards available to the parents . . .
(2) A description of the action proposed or refused by the agency, an explanation of why the agency proposes or refuses to take the action, and a description of any options the agency considered and the reasons why those options were rejected;
(3) A description of each evaluation procedure, test, record, or report the agency used as a basis for the proposal or refusal; and
(4) A description of any other factors which are relevant to the agency's proposal or refusal.

Thus, the knowledge component of consent can be satisfied if the school tells parents (a) that it proposes to assess their children with a comprehensive, individual educational evaluation; (b) why it believes the evaluation is necessary; and (c) what devices it proposes to use in the evaluation.

The operative word in § 300.505 is "description." To describe evaluation procedures is not merely to list them. At minimum, a brief characterization of each instrument that the psychologist plans to use should be given to parents. Further, any descriptions should not be framed in technical jargon. Section 300.505(b)(1) requires that any notice or consent form be "written in language understandable to the general public." While the rules with regard to notice and consent may place administrative burdens on school systems, in the long run there will be greater cooperation from parents, fewer challenges that tests are discriminatory, and fewer costly and time-consuming hearings if schools are open and informative.

Access to Records

The EAHCA regulations require that education institutions provide parents of handicapped children the right to inspect and review all education records pertaining to the identification, evaluation,

placement, and provisions of free appropriate education to their children. The relevant question for school psychologists is whether test protocols, scores, and reports are accessible under these rules. Section 300.562 of the EAHCA regulation grants access rights to parents "to inspect and review any education records relating to their children which are collected, maintained, or used by the agency under [EAHCA evaluation procedures]." Thus, not only documents bearing on education but any papers that schools have in their care (e.g., psychiatric and psychological reports received from other agencies) are accessible records. Beyond this, parents may have access to documents created by education agency employees such as the school psychologist. The only major exception is created by regulations promulgated under the Family Education Right and Privacy Act (FERPA, or the "Buckley Amendment"), on which the EAHCA regulations were based. They exclude from access papers that "are in the sole possession of the maker thereof, and are not accessible or revealed to any other individual . . ." (20 U.S.C. § 1232).

Test protocols themselves are usually not shown to anyone else. Test blanks and examinee answers have been guarded by publishers and users to prevent public disclosure. Most often the only tangible shared evidence of a psychological assessment is the report that follows testing. This report will typically include test scores and perhaps subscale scores. Psychologists in most instances attend a case conference of school personnel to discuss diagnoses and recommendations for placement and programming at which they disclose the results of testing. Even though psychologists may maintain the individual test records and responses in their offices, if particular information from them is communicated orally to others attending the case conferences, it would seem that these protocols or parts of the protocols might be considered records as they have been "revealed" to others. As such, they become accessible. Thus, test reports and scores, and in some cases even particular responses from the test protocols, might be accessible to parents exercising their full access rights under FERPA and EAHCA.

Finally, the accountability inherent in the complaint procedures under EAHCA makes disclosure of test questions possible in another way. Attorneys representing parents (or the school system if parents introduce the results of an independent evaluation) may not simply accept at face value the interpretations of test results presented in psychologists' reports. Under cross-examination, psychologists very likely will be asked for the factual bases underlying their conclusions. For example, assume that a psychologist is testifying that part of the evidence substantiating a diagnosis of mental retardation is a scale score of 5 on the Information subtest of the WISC-R. A sophisticated cross-examiner would inquire as to the student's separate responses in an attempt to cast doubt that those responses were the kind given by genuinely retarded children, but were more like those of a culturally different child with normal intelligence. In that process the questions themselves would have to be revealed. If psychologists refused to comply with the request, they could severely damage the position of the party for whom they are testifying, as the hearing examiner would be denied access to information useful in arriving at a decision. Perhaps recognizing the potential harm to clients if psychologists refused to testify, the APA's Code of Ethics, although reminding psychologists to "make every effort to maintain the security of tests" also cautions psychologists to "respect the client's right to know the results, the interpretations made, and the bases for their conclusions and recommendations" (APA, 1981, p. 637).

INTERVENTION AND THERAPY

As with assessments, issues concerning intervention in students' lives by school psychologists and other pupil personnel workers often center on the need to involve parents, whether it be for traditional psychotherapy, behavior modification, or counseling. The concern arises in its most difficult form when a student of high school age seeks the aid of a school psychologist but wants the psychologist to promise that the students' parents will not know of their interaction. Such a situation "surfaces the tension between the right of parents to be informed about and give permission for their children to enter counseling relationships and the right of adolescents to seek professional help when their interest may be adverse to those of their parents" (Bersoff, 1975, p. 370). That tension is the focus of this section.

To introduce the topic it may be helpful to describe a case in which many of the principles to be discussed are presented. The case *Merriken v.*

Cressman (1973) is a hybrid, presenting problems of assessment and research as well as intervention (Bersoff, 1975, 1978, 1979a). The case had its origins in 1970 when a survey ordered by the Commissioner of Montgomery County, Pennsylvania, and conducted by a company called Scientific Resources revealed that many children in the county were heavily involved with drugs. Most of the children who used drugs, the study claimed, possessed some common characteristics (e.g., estrangement from their families). On the basis of such data Scientific Resources proposed to the County Drug Commission that they sponsor a drug prevention program, later labeled CPI, for the Critical Period of Intervention. All three of the county school districts agreed to participate.

There were two phases to the study: identification and remediation. In the first phase, questionnaires were to be given to eight-grade students and their teachers so that certain students, deemed potential drug abusers, could become part of the remediation program. The teachers were asked to identify pupils who most and least fit eight descriptions of antisocial behavior, (e.g., "This pupil makes unusual or inappropriate responses during normal school activity"). The student form was to be somewhat lengthier. First, students would be asked to assess their own behavior, for example, to state which of the following statements was most like themselves: (a) someone who will probably be a success in life; (b) someone who gets upset when faced with a difficult school problem; (c) someone who has lost of self-confidence; (d) a student who has more problems than other students. In the next part of the questionnaire they would be asked questions about their relationships with their parents and the behavior of their parents (e.g., to indicate whether one or both parents "tell me how much they love me" or "make me feel unloved"). Finally, the students would select from their classmates those who fit certain descriptive statements similar in kind to the one given the teachers.

The second phase of the study was intervention. When the CPI staff had analyzed all the results, they would compile a list of children who would have significant potential for becoming drug abusers. This list would then be given to the school superintendent who would organize a joint effort among guidance counselors, teachers, school psychologists, and others to provide group therapeutic experiences. One of these experiences was called the Guided Group Interaction, a program to which the identified students would be involuntarily assigned. One of its stated purposes was to use the peer group as a leveler or equalizer ensuring that its members do not stray too far from its ranks.

When the program was first developed the school system did not intend to obtain the affirmative consent of the parents for their children to participate. They did plan to send a letter home to each parent as follows:

Dear Parent:

This letter is to inform you that, this fall, we are initiating a Drug Program called "Critical Period of Intervention" (CPI). The aim of this program is to identify children who may be susceptible to drug abuse and to intervene with concrete measures to help these children. Diagnostic testing will be part of this program and will provide data enabling the prevention program to be specific and positive . . .

We ask your support and cooperation in this program and assure you of the confidentiality of these studies. If you wish to examine or receive further information regarding the program, please feel free to contact the principal in your school. If you do not wish to participate in this program, please notify your principal of this decision. We will assume your cooperation unless otherwise notified by you . . .

Also, as originally proposed, the study contained no provision for student consent.

Sylvia Merriken, the mother of one of the intended participants in the study, who happened to be a therapist in a drug and alcoholic rehabilitation center, complained to the principal of the school where her son was enrolled and to the school board. The American Civil Liberties Union (ACLU) then announced that it would represent Mrs. Merriken in an attempt to enjoin permanently the school from carrying out its plans. The ACLU began by filing a complaint in federal district court claiming that the program would violate the constitutional rights of both Mrs. Merriken and her son. It quickly obtained a temporary injunction prohibiting the county from implementing its proposal until the litigation was completed. At that point, two of the three schools in Montgomery county decided

to discontinue their participation, but the Norristown system, which Mrs. Merriken's son attended, persisted, although it honored the temporary injunction.

When the suit itself began the school system offered to change the format of their letter so that affirmative written parental consent to participate would be required. In another attempt at compromise, the school modified the test so that students who did not want to be included could return an uncompleted protocol. But the proposal contained no provision for student consent and no data were to be provided whereby students could make an informed choice about participating.

Of the many constitutional challenges Mrs. Merriken made, the court entertained only one of them seriously—the right of privacy. The court found that the highly personal nature of the research instrument disrupted family associations and interfered with the right of the mother to rear her child. It said, "There is probably no more private a relationship, excepting marriage, which the Constitution safeguards than that between parent and child. This Court can look upon any invasion of that relationship as a direct violation of one's Constitutional right to privacy" (p. 918). The district court declared that privacy was entitled to as much constitutional protection as free speech. But who possessed this right—the student, the parents, or both? The court seemed ready to answer that question when it declared that "the fact that students are juveniles does not in any way invalidate their right to assert their Constitutional right to privacy" (p. 918). However, the court had not yet reached the essential question of whether the lack of consent by children to the invasion of their privacy would be sufficient to invalidate the program. Apparently reluctant to provide a definite answer it found a means to avoid doing so:

In the case at Bar, the children are never given the opportunity to consent to invasion of their privacy; only the opportunity to refuse to consent by returning a blank questionnaire. Whether this procedure is constitutional is questionable, but the Court does not have to face that issue because the facts presented show that the parents could not have been properly informed about the CPI Program and as a result could not have given informed consent for their children to take the CPI Test. (p. 919)

In essence, the court evaded two important issues; whether the failure to secure the child's consent was independently sufficient to discredit the CPI program constitutionally, and whether parents as guardians can waive their children's constitutional rights by consenting for them. Rather, the court concentrated on Mrs. Merriken's own right of privacy and found that she was unable to give genuinely informed consent to the invasion of her personal life because the parental permission letter was so inadequate. The court deridingly compared the letter to a Book-of-the Month Club solicitation in which parents' silence would be construed as acquiescence. The letter was also criticized as a selling device in which parents were convinced to allow children to participate. It was not, as it properly should be, an objective document telling parents of the potentially negative features and dangerous aspects of the program.

Persons may, of course, waive their constitutional rights but such waivers must be voluntary, knowing, intelligent, and done with sufficient awareness of the relevant consequences. Mrs. Merriken had the right to waive her right of privacy by consenting to the testing and intervention program. But because the request was little more than huckstering, it lacked the necessary substance to afford her the opprotunity to consent meaningfully to the exploration of her personal life. There were other infirmities to the program (e.g., no real assurance of confidentiality of the data obtained, lack of psychometric soundness of the instruments themselves, stigmatization of children inappropriately labeled) but they are relatively irrelevant in this chapter; for a full discussion of these problems, see Bersoff (1978).

A central issued raised by this case concerns the legal status of independent rights of children. Do children have an independent right to privacy that will enable school psychologists to intervene in students' lives without parental knowledge or consent? The question is part of a larger issue: How does the law allocate power among parents, children, and arms of the state, such as schools? That question has received considerable attention from legal scholars (e.g., Kleinfeld, 1970–1971; Mnookin, 1978; Wald, 1974) and from the courts. In *Tinker v. Des Moines Independent Community School* District (1969) the Supreme Court intimated that at least some rights were evenly distributed among children and adults: "First Amendment rights are available to teachers and students.

It can hardly be argued that either students or teachers shed their constitutional rights to freedom of speech or expression at the schoolhouse gate" (p. 506). However, the Court has also made it clear that children do not share equally in all provisions of the Constitution. In *In re Gault* (1967) children in juvenile court proceedings were afforded some, but not the entire range of due process protections granted adult criminals. In *Ginsberg v. New York* (1968) the Supreme Court said that it was rational for the state legislature to prohibit the sale of sexually related material to minors even though it would not allow to do so with regard to the sale of the same material to adults. And although it violates the Eight Amendment's cruel and inhuman punishment clause to physically discipline adult prisoners the Court ruled that corporal punishment of school children was constitutionally permissible (*Ingraham v. Wright*, 1977).

The Supreme Court's abortion-related decisions indicate that in some facets of personal life, certain children possess privacy rights that will be allowed expression even though to do so may conflict with parental wishes. In 1976 the Court declared unconstitutional a state statute requiring parental consent before a pregnant minor could obtain an abortion, saying: "Constitutional rights do not mature and come into being magically only when one attains the state-defined age of maturity. Minors, as well as adults are protected by the Constitution and possess constitutional rights" (*Planned Parenthood of Central Missouri v. Danforth*, 1976, p. 74). Thus it refused to uphold a blanket provision requiring the consent of a parent as a condition for all unmarried minors to obtain an abortion during the first trimester of pregnancy. A year later the Court was faced with a challenge to the constitutionality of a statute prohibiting the sale or distribution of contraceptives to children under 16. Given that it had previously concluded that minors could secure abortions without consent, it felt that an absolute ban against access to contraceptives was even more violative of children's independent rights to privacy. "The State's interests in protection of the mental and physical health of the pregnant minor, and in protection of potential life are clearly more implicated by the abortion decision than by the decision to use a nonhazardous contraceptive" (*Carey v. Population Services International Inc.*, 1977, p. 694).

The Court in 1979 once again ruled on a

minor's unencumbered right to abortion. In the light of the Supreme Court's decision in *Danforth,* Massachusetts amended its law so as to require parental consent for abortion but at the same time affording the child access to court if one or both parents refused to consent. Under the law judges would have the discretion to prohibit the abortion if they found that the adolescent insufficiently mature to make a decision or if the abortion was not in her best interest. The Court ultimately found even this potential judicial veto over the minor's own choice unduly burdened minors' rights to an abortion (*Bellotti v. Baird,* 1979).

Just two years later, however, the Court upheld a Utah statute requiring physicians to "notify, if possible" (p. 399) parents of minors before performing an abortion (*H.L. v. Matheson,* 1981). The case involved an unemancipated 15-year-old living at home and dependent on her parents. The Court expressed concern about the "unquestionable greater risks of inability to give informed consent" (p. 411) and upheld the notice requirement. Yet again 2 years later, the court struck down an Akron, Ohio, municipal ordinance that made a blanket determination that *all* minors under 15 years of age were too immature to make an abortion decision (*City of Akron v. Akron Ctr. for Reproductive Health,* 1983). The Court ruled that the city had to make a more individualized determination. It must provide an alternative procedure whereby a pregnant minor could demonstrate her maturity or show that an abortion without parental consent would be in her best interests despite her immaturity. As this is written, the Supreme Court is considering another abortion case involving minors. This time the question concerns the right of the state to require adolescents to wait 24 to 48 hours before receiving an abortion so as to inform both parents of the potential event.

Clearly, the courts have struggled with difficult questions of how to distribute decision making among children, parents, and professionals. In addition, we should be cautious about generalizing principles that arise in the abortion context to other domains. There is no reason to believe that any rights of children to choose abortion will be honored in other domains where their interests may also be at stake.

That this hypothesis has validity was borne out in *Parham v. J.L.* (1979). In *Parham,* the Court was called on to decide the constitutionality of a statute permitting parents to admit their children to mental institutions. When the state seeks to commit adults involuntarily they are afforded a number of procedural safeguards, including a hearing before an impartial decisionmaker and representation by an attorney. But in almost all states, when parents seek to place their children in mental hospitals it is considered a voluntary admission and children have no due process rights. In *Parham,* child advocates claimed that such admissions were voluntary in name only, that there were dangers of parents acting adversely to the interest of their children, and that as a result, children should be given procedural protections similar to those of adults.

In considering these claims the then-Chief Justice, writing for a five-member majority, balanced the children's interest, the state's interest, and the parents' interest. Justice Burger acknowledged that children have a substantial liberty interest in not being confined unnecessarily for medical treatment and in not being labeled erroneously by institutional authorities. The state had an interest in restricting use of costly mental health facilities to cases of genuine need. On the other hand, it also had an interest in not imposing unnecessary procedural obstacles that would discourage mentally ill children and their families from seeking psychiatric assistance. What the Court disparagingly called "time-consuming minuets" (what others could call an impartial due process hearing) not only would interfere with the treatment activities of professionals but would prove too onerous, too embarrassing, or too contentious for parents. In the end, the Court found the interests of the parents paramount. It reiterated its traditional concern for the family unit and of the primacy of the family over the state. While noting the incidence of child neglect and abuse, it relied on what it called the "pages of human experience" to undergird its conclusion that "parents generally do act in the child's best interest" (p. 2504).

Most important for our purposes, the court renewed its belief that children are incompetent to make decisions. It said, "The law's concept of the family rests on a presumption that parents possess what a child lacks in maturity, experience, and capacity for judgment required to making life's difficult decisions" (p. 2504) and concluded that "most children, even in adolescence, simply are not able to make sound judgments concerning many decisions, including their need for medical care or treatment" (p. 2505). "Parents," it declared, "can and must make those judgments" (p. 2505). The overall result of this tripartite interest analysis was to simply hold that a "neutral factfinder" (i.e., a staff physician at the admitting hospital) should review all available sources of information to determine that parental requests for institutionalization were not in error.

The legal system's solicitude for the family unit and the primacy of parental control does not mean, of course, that children are at the mercy of their mothers and fathers. "Parents may be free to become martyrs themselves. But it does not follow they are free . . . to make martyrs of their children . . ." *Prince v. Massachusetts,* 1944, p. 170). Courts will override parental prerogatives when parents are unable or refuse to care for their children's physical or emotional needs, when there is an abuse of parental authority, or when protectable property interests of children (e.g., inheritances) conflict with those of their parents. The most clear-cut example of state interference in family life is the passage of child abuse laws in all 50 of the United States (see Katz, Howe, & McGrath, 1975).

In sum, children generally are considered incapable of knowing what is best for themselves. The courts presume that parents, as preferred care givers, are competent to represent their children's interests and consequently protect the family from unreasonable interference by the state. However, the presumption may be rebutted by evidence of significant harm to the child and in those instances the courts replace parents—either permanently or for limited purposes—with alternative decision-makers.

Further, statutory and case law presently afford adolescents greater freedom to seek medical and psychological help without parental permission, a change advocated by many writers and legal scholars in recent years (Bersoff, 1976–1977; Foster & Freed, 1972; Holt, 1974; Kleinfeld, 1970–1971; Melton, Koocher, & Saks, 1983; Wald, 1974). Many states now have statutes permitting minors to give valid consent to treatment for venereal disease and other sex-related problems (Note, 1975). One state permits those 16 years of age or over to consent to treatment for emotional disorders, but potential clients are restricted receiving this help from medical personnel (Note, 1971). Despite these developments, the right of adolescents to seek aid by giving valid consent is far from universal and is presently confined to certain modes of intervention by certain classes of practitioners. There may be ample justification in the legal literature to support the right of young persons to secure treatment without parental permission, but in the light of the Supreme Court's overriding preference for parental control and its distrust of minors' ability to make mature judgments, it is presently very risky for school psychologists to agree to see children for any kind of therapeutic purpose without their parents' consent. Practitioners must be sensitive to the fact that the minor clients will be talking, in all probability, of family life. In that light, the clinician will be, in a sense, invading the privacy of the student's parents without their consent. Very few states afford school psychologists protection under privileged communications laws (see Bersoff & Jain, 1980; McDermott, 1972), and an unlimited guarantee against revelation is impossible for the practitioner to promise as a matter of law. Indeed, child abuse reporting statutes in all states require psychologists to divulge information concerning violence or sexual abuse, even if given to the psychologist in confidence. Thus, as an ethical and moral matter, it is disingenuous to ensure student clients of confidentiality. Perhaps the best approach to take is to clearly inform the student of the limits of privacy and confidentiality while at the same time attempting to secure the agreement of the parents that they will help protect their child's potential benefit from treatment if they permit the psychologist to see the student without being informed of information revealed during the course of intervention.

The recent case of *Pesce v. Morton High* (1987) illustrates the competing legal interest and professional obligations affecting school psychologists when they provide therapeutic and counseling services to students. Pesce was a school psychologist who was given by C.R., a student at the school, a note written by J.D., another student. The note included possible hints of suicide and expressions of guilt and confusion over J.D.'s sexual identity. C.R. also told Pesce that J.D. said he had visited the home of a faculty member when "something sexual" had happened. Pesce urged C.R. to have J.D. visit him, and also asked her to pass along the name of a professional therapist. Later that day J.D. visited Pesce in his office at school. Pesce assured him of the confidentiality of any information divulged and questioned him about the issues raised in the letter. J.D. denied suicidal intentions and also that any sexual acts had occurred, but he admitted that the teacher had shown him "pictures" when he visited the teacher's home.

Pesce considered the legal and psychological implications of honoring the confidentiality of the communication with J.D. He consulted with an attorney and another psychologist and considered the relevant state laws, school regulations and the specialty guidelines of the American Psychological Association. After due consideration and in good faith, Pesce decided not to notify any school officials nor J.D.'s parents at that time. Ten days later, Pesce learned that after attending two sessions, J.D. had canceled an appointment with his therapist. He met with J.D. and learned that the teacher had in fact engaged in a sexual act with him. He discussed the advantages and disadvantages of disclosing this fact and won J.D.'s agreement that it would be best to reveal the information to school authorities.

Among the state laws in effect at the time was the Illinois Abused and Neglected Child Reporting Act (Ill. Rev. Stat. ch. 23). It requires school personnel having reasonable cause to believe that a child may be abused to report the incident to the state Department of Child and Family Services. Another relevant law was the Mental Health and Development Disabilities Confidentiality Act (Ill. Rev. Stat. ch. 91). It protects confidential disclosures between psychologists and patients, with certain exceptions. Among these are disclosures with the consent of the parent or guardians and either the consent of the minor or a finding by the therapist that disclosure would be in the child's best interest. Also permitted are disclosures required under the Reporting Act.

There was an arguable ambiguity in the duties imposed by these two laws. The Reporting Act imposed obligations. The Confidentiality Act imposed countervailing obligations, with permissible exceptions that would cover the reporting of abuse. Pesce argued that he determined it would be in the best interest of J.D. to maintain his confidential communications.

When school officials learned of the matter, and of Pesce's 10-day delay in reporting the incident, they recommended to the school board that Pesce be suspended without pay for 5 days. They notified him of his right to a hearing, at which Pesce and his attorney presented evidence. The school board nevertheless voted to impose a 5-day suspension and to demote Pesce from "School Psychologist" to the "School Psychologist for the Behavior Disorders Program." They cited Pesce's employment contract, which permitted suspension for "misconduct," which was defined to include "any act or failure to act occurring during the course of an employee's duties which jeopardizes the health, safety, and welfare of any . . . student."

Pesce brought suit in federal court for an alleged violation of his constitutional due process and privacy rights. But the judge ruled that it was reasonable for the school board to conclude that Pesce's determination that nondisclosure of the information was in J.D.'s best interest was "misconduct" that jeopardized J.D.'s health. The court refused to interpose its judgment between the school board and its employees.

Clearly, psychologists who act as counselors and therapists in the schools face many of the same problems as adult therapists. But they are further complicated by the special relation of the school to parents and to its students. We must never forget that school psychologists are part of an encompassing institutional structure that affects many aspects of students' lives. The school psychologist is in many ways more similar to a hospital staff psychologist than to a 2-hour-a week counselor. Therapeutic intervention in the schools can be comparable to the design of comprehensive ward treatment plans. Sensitivity to issues of accurate record keeping, conscientious use of punishment or time-out procedures, and great care in designing interventions are required. (*See* Wherry, 1983, for a discussion of legal considerations in the use of behavior modification in the schools.)

RESEARCH

Like assessment and intervention, the third traditional role of the school psychologist—research—has also been subject to regulation by the legal system. Because of a series of disclosures concerning the unethical behavior of some researchers in a variety of settings (see Bersoff, 1979b; Annas, Glantz, & Katz, 1977; Katz, 1972) the courts and the federal government began to scrutinize carefully the conduct of biomedical and behavioral research. The year 1974 may be viewed as the watershed in that respect.

In mid-1974 the then-named DHEW (now DHHS) published regulations regarding the protection of human subjects. These regulations governed the activities of those organizations who receive research funds or are accountable to DHHS. First published in the Federal Register (39 Federal Register 18917, May 30, 1974) and now codified as federal regulations (45 CFR § 46), the rules explicitly declare that the department will not support by DHHS grants or contracts any research unless an institutional review board (IRB) of the organization has reviewed and approved such activity. These institutional review boards determine that the following requirements are satisfied:

1. Risks to subjects are minimized.

2. Risks to subjects are reasonable in relation to anticipated benefits, if any, to subjects, and the importance of the knowledge that may reasonably be expected to result.

3. Selection of subjects is equitable.

4. Informed consent will be sought from each prospective subject or the subject's legally authorized representative.

5. Informed consent will be appropriately documented.

6. Where appropriate, the research plan makes adequate provision for monitoring the data collected to insure the safety of subjects.

7. Where appropriate, there are adequate provisions to protect the privacy of subjects and to maintain the confidentiality of data. (45 CFR § 46.111, 1987).

The regulations give special emphasis to the requirements of informed consent. They call for providing to the subject information about the purposes of the research, the expected duration of the subject's participation, and a description of the research procedures. They require a description of reasonably foreseeable risks or discomforts, and any benefits that might be expected to the subject or to others. Researchers must make clear that participation is voluntary—refusal to participate must bring no penalty to the potential subject and cause no loss of benefits to which subjects are otherwise entitled. The names of persons to contact for more information about the research and about subject's rights must be part of the consent form.

The guidelines show special concern to prevent any coercion from influencing subjects' choices: "An investigator shall seek such consent only under circumstances that provide the prospective subject [or their legally authorized repre-

sentative] sufficient opportunity to consider whether or not to participate and that minimize the possibility of coercion or undue influence" (45 CFR § 46.116). The unusual situations of prisoners and children, whose circumstances affect their capacity to consent, is addressed in a special subpart of the regulations. Additional protections for children are found in Subpart D, 45 CFR § § 46.401—409.

Adequate provision must be made to solicit the *assent* of the minor subjects and the *permission* of their parents or legal guardians. The guidelines define children as persons "who have not attained the legal age for consent" (45 CFR § 46.402[a]) under the applicable law in the local jurisdiction where the research will be conducted. Assent means "a child's affirmative agreement to participate in research. Mere failure to object should not . . . be construed as assent" (45 CFR § 46.402[b]). Either the biological or adoptive parent of the child, or the child's legal guardian, must also give permission—that is, "agreement . . . to the participation of the child or ward" (45 CFR § 46.402[c]).

Assent is required "when in the judgment of the IRB the children are capable of assent" (45 CFR § 46.408[9]). IRB can make this determination for all potential subjects as a class or on a case-by-case basis. The age, maturity, and psychological state of the children should be evaluated to determine their capacity for assent. If the children are incapable of meaningful assent or if the research holds out the prospect of direct benefits to the subjects that are not available outside the context of the research, the assent of the children is not required. A few other rare exceptions are also listed in the regulations.

Research studies are categorized according to the risk they present to the subjects—more or less than minimal—and according to the types of benefits likely to result from the work. If there are more than minimal risks, the research can be justified in only two ways: (a) there are direct benefits to the subject that outweigh the risk, and no available alternative approaches would yield the same benefits; or (b) the research procedure "presents experiences to subjects that are reasonably commensurate with those inherent in their actual or expected . . . psychological, social, or educational situations" (45 CFR § 46.406[b]), and the research is likely to yield generalizable knowledge about the subject's disorder or condition which is of vital importance for the understanding or amelioration of [the condition] (45 CFR § 46.405[c]). Other studies that "present a reasonable opportunity to further the understanding, prevention, or alleviation of a serious problem affecting the health or welfare of children" (45 CFR § 46.407[a]) may be approved if it is conducted in accordance with sound ethical principles. In all cases, assent and permission must be obtained in accordance with the provisions discussed above.

With regard to parents' involvement, in less than minimally risky or in risky but directly beneficial research, the consent of only one parent would normally be required. In risky but not directly beneficial research the consent of both parents would be necessary unless one parent is deceased, unknown, incompetent, or not reasonably available. But the rules also take into account two special conditions. The requirement of parental permission may be waived by the IRB if neglected or abused children are asked to participate as research subjects. In those cases, DHHS recommends that children be protected by appropriate alternative mechanisms whose precise nature is to be defined by state or local law. The second special condition concerns children who are wards of the state, as is the case with many institutionalized or adjudicated youth. The regulations require appointment of an advocate for such participants.

Finally, school psychologists doing research may fall under one of the exceptions to the regulations. Certain research does not have to undergo full-scale IRB review. These kinds of research include the use of survey instruments, the observation of public behavior, and the study of documents and records. Perhaps most important, the regulations exempt from review the following:

1. Research conducted in established or commonly accepted educational settings, involving normal educational practices, such as (i) research on regular and special education instrumental strategies, or (ii) research on the effectiveness or the comparison among instructional techniques, curriculum, or classroom management.

2. Research involving the use of educational tests (cognitive, diagnostic, aptitude, or achievement) if information taken from these sources is recorded in such a manner that subjects cannot be identified, directly or through identifiers linked to the subjects (§ 46.101[b]).

CONCLUSION

It will be clear to any reader by this point that the practice of school psychology is no longer the unfettered province of academic department and professional organizations. Much of what school psychologists do is now guided, if not controlled, by statutes, regulations, case law, and the Constitution. In many respects, the constraints imposed by the legal system are onerous and overbearing, but that criticism should not overshadow the fact that much of this regulation was evoked by psychologists and educators who failed to understand fully the rights of children, parents, minorities, and the impoverished. What may at first be burdens or obstacles can be used as an opportunity for school psychologists to act as advocates for those they serve. It is our hope that school psychologists will look beyond the constraints described in this chapter and help in the furtherance of the rights of all those with whom they come in contact—parents, employers, and of course, children.

TABLE OF CASES

502 F.2d 963 (9th Cir. 1974); 495 F. Supp. 926 (N.D. Cal. 1979), *aff'd,* 793 F.2d 969 (9th Cir. 1984)

PARC v. C'wealth of Pa. 343 F. Supp 279 (E.D. Pa. 1972)

PASE v. Hannon, 506 F.2d 831 (N.D. Ill. 1980)

Parham v. J.L., 442 U.S. 584 (1979)

Pesce v. J. Sterling Morton High Sch. Dist., 651 F. Supp. 152 (N.D. Ill. 1986)

Planned Parenthood of Cent. Mo. v. Danforth, 428 U.S. 52 (1976)

Prince v. Massachusetts, 321 U.S. 158 (1944)

Roe v. Wade, 410 U.S. 113 (1973)

Tinker v. Des Moines Ind. Comm. Sch. Dist., 393 U.S. 503 (1969)

Washington v. Davis, 426 U.S. 229 (1976)

Whalen v. Roe, 423 U.S. 1313 (1977)

REFERENCES

American Psychological Association. (1981). Specialty guidelines for the delivery of services. *American Pscyhologist, 36,* 639–681.

Annas, G., Glantz, L., & Katz, B. (1977). *The law of informed consent to human experimentation.* Cambridge, MA: Ballinger.

Beaney, W. (1966). The right to privacy and American law. *Law and Contemporary Problems, 32,* 253–271.

Bersoff, D. (1975). Professional ethics and legal responsibilities: On the horns of a dilemma. *Journal of School Psychology, 13,* 359–376.

Bersoff, D. (1976–1977). Representation for children in custody proceedings: All that glitters is not Gault. *Journal of Family Law, 15,* 27–49.

Bersoff, D. (1978). Legal and ethical concerns in research. In L. Goldman (Ed.), *Research for the counselor.* New York: Wiley.

Bersoff, D. (1979a). Regarding psychologists testily: Legal constraints on psychological assessment in the public schools. *Maryland Law Review, 39,* 27–120.

Bersoff, D. (1979b). Handicapped persons as research subjects. *Amicus, 4,* 133–140.

Bersoff, D., & Jain, M. (1980). A practical guide to privileged communication for psychologists. In G. Cooke (Ed.), *The role of the forensic psychologist,* Springfield, IL: Charles C Thomas.

Foster, H., & Freed, D. (1972). A bill of rights for children. *Family Law Quarterly, 6,* 343–375.

Holman, M., & Docter, R. (1972). *Educational and psychological testing.* New York: Russell Sage.

Holt, J. (1974). *Escape from childhood.* New York: E.P. Dutton.

Katz, J. (1972). *Experimentation with human beings.* New York: Russell Sage.

Katz, S., Howe, R., & McGrath, M. (1975). Child neglect laws in America. *Family Law Quarterly, 9,* 1–372.

Kleinfeld, A. (1970–1971). Balance of power among infants, their parents, and the state (I, II, III). *Family Law Quarterly, 4, 5,* 320–349, 410–443, 64–107.

McDermott, P. A. (1972). Law, liability, and the school psychologist: Systems of law, privileged communication, and access to records. *Journal of School Psychology, 10,* 299–305.

Melton, G., Koocher, G., & Saks, M. (Eds.). (1983). *Children's competence to consent.* New York: Plenum Press.

Mnookin, R. (1978). *Child, family, and state.* Boston: Little, Brown.

Parker, H. C. (1974). Contingency management and concomitant changes in elementary school students' self-concepts. *Psychology in the Schools, 11,* 70–79.

Rosen, C. (1977). Why clients relinquish their rights to privacy under signaway pressures. *Professional Psychology, 8,* 17–24.

Sorgen, M. (1973). Testing and tracking in public school. *Hastings Law Journal, 14,* 1129–1190.

Wald, P. (1974). Making sense out of the rights of youth. *Human Rights, 4,* 13–29.

Westin, A. (1967). *Privacy and freedom.* New York: Atheneum.

Wherry, J. N. (1983). . Some legal considerations and implications for the use of behavior modification in the schools. *Psychology in the Schools, 20,* 46–51.

39

STUDENTS' RIGHTS IN PUBLIC SCHOOLS

THOMAS D. OVERCAST
Seattle, Washington
BRUCE SALES
DONAL M. SACKEN
University of Arizona

STUDENTS' RIGHTS IN ELEMENTARY AND SECONDARY PUBLIC SCHOOLS

It would be fair to assert that 50 years ago students in elementary and secondary public schools were recognized as having few, if any, legal rights. The teacher and school system were seen as standing *in loco parentis* to the child. From the time the child left home in the morning until returning in the evening, the school was viewed as the prime source of guidance, discipline, punishment, and control. Many early cases even recognized the right of the school to extend its influence over the child into the home, and to the child's behavior during nonschool hours.

However, beginning in the 1960s there was a recognition that the school's control over students should not be so prevasive. The courts have been willing to extend to students many of the legal rights taken for granted by other groups of individuals. A large part of the redefinition of the relationship between students and the school took place in cases that arose from the school officials' efforts to prohibit certain student activities. As a logical extension of the cases arising out of the civil rights movement, student rights case law initially focused more on racial inequality and the demand by minority groups for equal educational opportunity than it did on the assertions of the rights of individual students vis-à-vis the school. In addition, most of the earlier cases focusing on individual rights (as opposed to equal opportunity) were placed within the context of the college or university. The focus shifted to the individual rights of students in the elementary and secondary schools only at the end of the 1960s. Arguably, by the 1980s, courts had begun to respond to the schools' argument that their authority had been excessively eroded judicially.

In reading the existing case law and legal literature it is apparent that the issue of student rights arises only in relation to the duties and obligations imposed on the schools by state legislative or constitutional direction, with conflict between the student and the school potentially arising at any of a number of different points:

1. Before a person may be said to have the rights of a student, he or she must obtain access to the school and achieve the status of "student." Schools may prescribe rules and regulation controlling access to their facilities. They may attempt to restrict access based on a student's age, race, gender, residence, and physical or mental condition. Additionally, the school may attempt to regulate attendance by married students and pregnant females, although less than previously.

2. The school may have regulations regarding the assignment of students to particular schools or the transfer of students between schools.

3. The school may or may not have a duty to provide transportation for the student between his or her home and the school. If it does have such a duty, the school may attempt to regulate the eligibility of students to make use of transportation facilities.

4. Publicly supported schools generally may not charge tuition, but may assess incidental or supplemental fees. Special regulations may apply to nonresidents, indigent students, and students in institutions.

5. All states generally require a certain number of years of compulsory education for their citizens. Some students may be excused from compulsory attendance because of religious reasons, and others may be able to take advantage of acceptable alternatives to public schools.

6. Schools have the authority to assign students to particular grades or classes, and to establish criteria regarding promotion and demotion. Additionally, the school has control over the course of studies and the content of the curricula at each grade or class level.

7. The school has the general power to regulate the behavior and conduct of students. In varying degrees, this power exists regarding health regulations and the behavior of students both during and outside school hours. During school hours, the power exists over a wide variety of student behavior, including their freedom of speech and expression, and their right to privacy, and justifies a variety of disciplinary actions and punishments for student misconduct.

8. For a variety of violations of school rules and regulations, a student may be suspended or expelled from school. The school may provide any of a number of procedural protections to help ensure the justice of such an action.

9. Upon completion of a program of education, the student is entitled to a diploma certifying his or her skills. The school may not be held accountable to the student for the quality of the education the student has received.

In this chapter we describe the relationship outlined above by reviewing the existing law regarding the numerous topics under each of the foregoing headings. No attempt is made to advocate one position over another. The law presented here represents what "is," not necessarily what "ought to be." In several areas there is still little existing case law to guide the presentation. In such cases we have attempted to delineate what seem to be the important issues and to present a brief but balanced exposition of the arguments on both sides.

In this regard, three important points should be kept in mind. First, the legal rights of students often do not have an independent existence. They can only be understood against the framework of legislative and constitutional authority given to the school. Thus, much of the presentation in this chapter is phrased in terms of the discretionary authority of the school and the limits of that discretion, with the legal rights of students often being defined by those limits. Second, there may appear to be an incongruity in certain areas between the power of the school to regulate student behavior and the school's decision whether to exercise that power. The courts may have bestowed much more power on the schools than the school, for many reasons, may choose to exert. Thus, students in the schools may appear to have a right when, in fact, it is a privilege extended by the school. Finally, rights of schools and students will vary between states because state legislatures retain enormous discretion constitutionally to shape their educational systems and state educational codes vary quite broadly. The reader must use this chapter as a guide and not as the definitive answer for particular concerns that he or she may have.

Access to Education

Generally, the state has broad discretion in determining who may be eligible for a free public education.[1] Thus, in order to attend a state-supported public school, the student must meet the requirements prescribed by the state constitution and/or statutes, and the rules of state and local boards of education.[2] In this section we examine several general requirements affecting students' right of access to the public school system, including regulations relating to age, race, gender, handicapping conditions, and residency.

Minimum and maximum age requirements for attendance at public schools are generally expressly provided for either in a state's constitution or statutes, and normally have been upheld. However, the West Virginia Supreme Court required a local district to admit a child whose birthday fell only 3 days after the date for entry into kindergarten, declaring a contrary ruling to be arbitrary and capricious.[3] In the absence of express constitutional or statutory guidelines, a state-level official (i.e., state board of education) has the authority to establish age requirements for admission to the school system.[4]

It goes without saying that a school district may not withhold access to schooling based on the race of a particular student. It is not certain, however, whether a school may discriminate among applicants on the basis of their gender. The U.S. Supreme Court has affirmed without an opinion the decision of a lower court denying the admission of a female student to an all-male high school in the city of Philadelphia.[5] The lower court emphasized that both sexes were being treated similarly with respect to admissions policies in the female and male high schools, and that equal educational opportunities were available to both sexes in terms of the quality of school facilities. In a university-based case, the Supreme Court invalidated a policy of excluding men from a state nursing school at an all-women's university.[6] The Court indicated that gender-based discrimination in admission would require substantial justification. However, "separate but equal" educational facilities for the two sexes apparently does not infringe per se the Fourteenth Amendment's guarantee of equal protection under the laws.

Although a school district has an affirmative obligation to provide equal educational opportunities to all students within the district,[7] until recently such access was not ensured for handicapped students. Under some states' laws, certain handicapped persons were "exempt" from compulsory schooling based on the belief that they are incapable of benefiting from education. Now both federal and state laws prohibit a district from denying access to the school system and a free appropriate public education based solely on a student's handicapping condition.[8]

The final requirement that may bar a student's access to the school is residency status. Normally, the expense of providing a free public education is partially defrayed by a tax imposed on the residents of each school district. As a general rule, the privilege of a free public education in the district's schools is open only to residents of such district. In determining residency, the ordinary rules regarding legal residency are applied; it is sufficient if the student and his or her parent or guardian actually reside within the district without any present intention of leaving.

In 1982, the Supreme Court narrowly held unconstitutional a Texas statute that prevented children who were illegal aliens from attending public schools. Such a practice violated the equal protection clause because Texas could not demonstrate that its policy did not further a substantial, legitimate goal.[9] In a subsequent case, the Court specified that districts could enforce their normal residency standards (e.g., a requirement that a child reside with parents or legal guardians) without offending the Fourteenth Amendment.[10] Taken in sum, these developments indicate that a district is essentially responsible for providing a public education for any and all children of appropriate ages who happen to reside in that district.[11]

A public school district normally has no authority to admit nonresident students. Some statutes, however, allow such admissions if it would be more convenient for the student. Other statutes leave it to the discretion of the local district whether to admit a nonresident student. The student does not, however, acquire any right to admission under these statutes. The local district may accept or reject such admissions at its own discretion.[12]

Similar questions may arise regarding the residency status of children in public or private institutions or those committed to outside care. In such cases the institution to which the child is committed may be located outside the school district in which the parents reside. The courts have taken two positions on this issue. Some cases have held that such students, for purposes of school admission, are residents of the school district in which the institution is located.[13] Other courts have held that such students are not entitled to a free education within the district, but that either the institution or the parents must pay a nonresident's tuition fee to offset the cost of the student's schooling. Under P.L. 94-142, handicapped children placed in institutions are ensured a free public education.[14]

As noted above, the governing body of a local school district has the inherent power to determine who may be admitted into the schools, subject only to express statutory directives and to a standard of reasonableness in their decision making. Under these standards, children have been refused admission by reason of being determined to be morally deficient,[15] having[16] or having been exposed to an infectious disease,[17] or being insufficiently prepared to begin at a particular level in school, although these latter three criteria would seem to be limited by federal legislation, such as P.L. 94-142. Federal courts have so held with regard to serum hepatitis carriers and children with AIDS.[18] Since such decisions are subject to a standard of reasonableness, they are usually not subjected to judicial review if the particular decision was undertaken after fair and considered debate. In cases where a district's decision is reviewed, a court presumes that the district acted reasonably and properly, and the burden is on the person challenging the decision to affirmatively rebut that presumption. Although the power of the school district to exclude married students and unwed mothers from school, at least for a reasonable length of time, has been held to be within the discretion of the school district,[19] more courts have taken the position that school districts are never justified in excluding married students or unwed mothers solely on these bases.[20] School officials, after a fair hearing, might be able to show that such a person's presence in the school would significantly disrupt the education of other students.[21] However, efforts to exclude completely would appear to infringe students' constitutional right to privacy, an interest linked with both familial and procreative interests.[22]

Assignment

Once the student has been admitted to the district, the district has the responsibility of assigning the student to a particular school. Generally, a school district may, at its own discretion, assign a student to any school within the district.[23] Of course, the decisions of the district must be reasonable,[24] and not in violation of a student's civil rights.[25] The cases arising out of the civil rights arena have affirmed the power of the school district to make such intradistrict assignments. Although under no legal obligation, many school districts have endorsed the neighborhood school concept and have, within the limits imposed by the requirements of the Fourteenth Amendment, attempted to assign students to schools as close to their homes as is possible.[26]

As a general rule, students do not have the right to attend a school in a different district at the expense of the district in which they reside. They may have such a right, however, if the conditions for such transfer are specified in the state statutes, and the student comes within such provisions. These statutory conditions are much the same for both grade school and high school students. In order to establish a right to transfer outside his or her residence, the grade school pupil must show that there is no school or no adequate school within his or her home district,[27] that he or she can be better accommodated by the interdistrict transfer,[28] or that the desired transfer is more conveniently located by reason of distance from the student's residence.[29] Generally, interdistrict transfers can be arranged only with the consent of both the receiving and the sending districts.[30]

Under most state statutes, the power to accept or refuse an interdistrict transfer is vested in the local school board or with a county superintendent of schools. Additionally, some statutes provide that an appeal *de novo* may be taken to a local court. Under this procedure, the court will hear the same evidence presented to the board or superintendent. Under such schemes, the decisions of the board are subject to judicial review and reversal only if it can be shown that the board abused its discretion in refusing a requested transfer.[31]

Interdistrict transfers by high school students are subject to similar restrictions and procedures for judicial review. Within the terms of the controlling status, high school students may be transferred if the transfer is to a more "convenient" school. Convenience in this context has the same meaning as that described above relating to transfers by grade school students.[32]

Transportation

Provision of transportation to and from school is usually expressly provided for in state statutes, either as a mandatory or a discretionary district duty. In the absence of express authority, school districts may be permitted, but are not required, normally, to provide free transportation to students. Where free transportation is authorized, it is usually provided only for student living beyond a prescribed distance from the school.[33] Students not coming within the statutory conditions have been unsuccessful in challenging the validity of the statutes.[34] Students may also lose access to transportation through their misconduct.[35]

A statute requiring transportation of students only "to and from" school, however, may not authorize the use of buses for transportation to extracurricular activities. Thus, a district may not freely transport students to such outside activities as athletic events, spelling or speech contests, or to motion pictures. In some states, districts are authorized or required to transport children to nonpublic schools; such laws have withstood constitutional challenge.[36]

Tuition and Fees

Generally, students have the right to a free education within the public schools of a district. Thus the district cannot impose a tuition fee on students simply because private money has been used to finance portions of a school.[37] Note, however, that a free public education applies only to the regular course of schoolwork. A district may offer specialized courses, not within the normal curriculum, and require a fee for enrollment in such courses.[38]

Under most statutes, the district is authorized to charge incidental or supplemental fees which are used for purposes other than tuition. Thus, a student may be required to pay a fee for participation in athletics or other social events sponsored by the school, and for the use of textbooks,[39] but such fees must be reasonable and must be tied to the actual cost of the books.[40] A requirement that each student pay a registration fee, however, has been held invalid because it was an attempt to charge tuition in violation of a state statute.[41]

Nonresidents of a district are ordinarily not entitled to a free education within the district. They may be entitled to such privileges, however, if they are able to pay a nonresident tuition fee. Similarly, most residents of institutions are entitled to an education in the district in which the institution is located. Nearly all states require that the cost of the student's schooling be borne by the district in which he or she resided prior to coming to the institution.[42] Finally, students who are wards of the court or are otherwise maintained as public charges are considered to be residents of the

district in which they live and are entitled to full educational privileges.[43]

Compulsory Attendance

Compulsory education statutes are commonplace in the United States and everywhere regarded as valid exercises of a state's police power.[44] All statutes, however, allow certain exceptions; generally, the conditions of nonattendance are clearly specified in the statute. For instance, a student may be excused from secondary school attendance if employed. A familiar example is that of the child actor. A less familiar but certainly more widespread example of excused absence occurs in agricultural areas where children are excused to help with harvests. In addition, many statutes give the local school district discretionary power to excuse a student's absence due to some hardship based on his or her distance from school and the availability of transportation.[45] In such cases, the statutes provide rather strict guidelines that help ensure that the students maintain adequate educational progress.

Under certain conditions, absence from school also may be excused for religious reasons. If authorized by statute, a school district may excuse students from the public school for short periods of time to participate in religious or moral training off the public school grounds.[46] These "released time" programs, where students are excused from school in order to obtain religious instruction, withstood an early constitutional challenge, but such programs cannot be conducted in public schools.[47] However, a child normally may not be excused from school attendance on a certain day of every week because of his or her religious beliefs.[48]

In 1972, the Supreme Court granted a partial exemption to Amish children from compulsory attendance laws in Wisconsin. The Amish argued successfully that requiring their children to attend the last 2 years of high school would be in sharp conflict with their fundamental religious beliefs deeply rooted in their way of life. In *Wisconsin v. Yoder*,[49] the U.S. Supreme Court agreed, but in a carefully circumscribed decision. The Amish request had deep roots in their religious beliefs. The Court held that the state's interest in compulsory education was not so compelling that the religious practices of the Amish had to give way to it. The Court went to great lengths to detail the specific factors that made the Amish experience unique, referring to long-standing and deeply held religious beliefs that had been incorporated by the Amish into their educational and child-rearing practices. Given the very restrictive nature of the *Yoder* decision, it seemed unlikely that other groups would come easily under the *Yoder* rule. That has not prevented many groups and individuals from seeking to fit within the "Amish" exemption, however.[50]

Normally, compulsory attendance laws do not require that all students be sent to public schools. Indeed, such a requirement would be an unconstitutional interference with the right of the parent to freely choose a child's educational course.[51] There are several alternatives to public school attendance, with the two most important being parochial and private nonsectarian schools. State statutes vary considerably concerning what type of private school attendance fulfills the compulsory education requirement. Generally, however, the private school must receive the sanction of the state educational authorities. State regulation of private schools has generated a substantial volume of litigation, especially during the 1980s.[52]

Where no public or private school satisfies parents, they may engage in home education in most states. State statutes regulate this alternative in a quite divergent manner and litigation by disappointed parents is a common phenomenon.[53] Court responses have been so varied as to be without discernible pattern. These cases, along with challenges to regulation of private schools, are largely brought by parents and other groups under the Free Exercise clause of the First Amendment. As such, these cases represent serious constitutional dilemmas. Generalizations are quite difficult, beyond the observation that courts are likely to confront such challenges as long as state statutes prevent access to desired alternatives to public schooling.[54]

Classifications

Control over the classification of students and curricula is vested in the state and local boards of education. The state normally prescribes the broad outlines of the educational system, leaving control over specific details to individual school districts. Thus the state board of education may prescribe various courses of study for the different grades, but the local school may define the specific content of the courses as long as the coverage is not inconsistent with the intent of the state board.[55]

Implicit in the power to prescribe the necessary rules and regulations for the operation of the school system, the local school authorities may require the classification and assignment of students to classes or grades commensurate with their proficiency and ability.[56] To help make such a determination, school authorities may make use of any reasonable methods to test the fitness of a particular student for admission to a class or grade. For instance, the qualifications of a student may be tested by either a written or oral examination, or the school may presume a student's ability from the nature and reputation of his or her previous educational experiences. If such a determination is made fairly and with a sound basis, the school is within the boundaries of its discretion and neither the parent nor the student may overturn the decision.[57]

During the 1970s, the tradition of using standardized test scores to make educational decisions, including identification and placement of handicapped children, came under judicial scrutiny in a series of highly publicized cases.[58] In large part, these cases were tied to discriminatory effects associated with standardized tests. The best known case, *Larry P. v. Riles*,[59] was actively in litigation for over a decade. The plaintiffs successfully challenged the practice of using IQ tests to identify and place students in EMR classes, winning a statewide ban on such practices. This rather extraordinary outcome has not been duplicated in subsequent litigation.[60] Associated cases also challenged tracking practices,[61] as well as the testing, classification, and programs for language minorities.[62] It seems clear under both constitutional and statutory law that students have rights to appropriate assessment, as well as programs adequate to their educational needs. Courts have frequently expressed this concept as a right to "meaningful access" to the educational curriculum.[63]

Classification issues, particularly those affecting identifiable students populations, such as racial and ethnic minorities, are likely to continue creating periodic challenges to districts' authority.[64] The local school district has similar powers regarding the promotion, demotion, and retention of students. As long as they are reasonable, the school district may prescribe rules governing the tests and examinations, and the standards for promotion.[65] Even given the results of tests and examinations, promotion and demotion are largely at the discretion of the school authorities, and in the absence of evidence of abuse the courts generally will not intervene. Such discretion is given to the school to allow them to take account of factors other than academic performance in the decision to promote, demote, or retain a student. For instance, a student's level of physical and psychological maturity may play an important role in determining how well he or she will perform in a higher or lower grade. Such factors are not as easily quantifiable as academic skills; thus, there is reluctance to insist on a strictly objective set of standards for promotion.[66]

As noted earlier, the control over the curricula in the public schools is often vested jointly in both the state and local educational authorities. In the absence of specific directions from the state, the local schools have the authority to provide such content as they deem in the best interests of the students.[67] The local school district has no discretion, however, where a state constitutional provision or statute requires the adoption of a uniform statewide curriculum for the public school system. Under such a uniform system, usually neither the local districts, nor parents and students may require the courts to intervene in altering the established course of study.

A persistent controversy over control of public school curricula, however, has forced courts to play a role. The problem is not new[68] and centers on the teaching of competing theories of the origin of human life. Recent cases have challenged both the theories of divine creation[69] and general evolution.[70] The issues really are twofold: (a) science instruction and freedom of religion, and (b) the right of a parent to have his or her child excused from religiously or morally objectionable curriculum material.

In addition to court actions, state and local boards of education have been deluged with complaints from both parents and students protesting the content of a particular course of study involving the issue of the origin of life.[71] In response to lawsuits and public pressure, state legislatures have adopted various procedures for dealing with the problem. For instance, some states have prohibited the teaching of the theory of divine creation. Others have required the schools to present a balanced exposure of both viewpoints, couched in terms of competing theories. Balanced treatment statutes or policies are constitutionally vulnerable, however, if a court concludes that the policy constitutes an effort to inject sectarian beliefs into public schools. In 1987, the Supreme Court declared a Louisiana statute unconstitutional under this rationale.[72] These cases can be interpreted as protecting students' rights not to be subjected to religious indoctrination by the state while being a "captive audience."[73]

More generally, the courts also have become involved in litigating the right of a parent to have some control over the content of educational offerings made available to the student.[74] For example, recently parents have asserted their right to object to the nature of the values being taught by the school. Such protests have come from both ends of the political spectrum, raising claims of anti-American, anti-Christian, and obscene curricula and objecting to the "conservative" orientation of the schools that result in the teaching of gender bias, racism, and other stereotypes.[75] The conflict is between the power and interest of the state expressed through curriculum requirements, and the right of the parent to direct the education of his or her child. There is little question that the state, through curriculum requirements, is engaged in the process of the inculcation of values and the state legislature, as the representative of its citizens, may have an affirmative duty to engage in this process. On the other hand, parents may have a considerable stake in the moral and value training given to their children. The Supreme Court has long recognized the constitutional importance of this parental interest, and now describes parental interests as a component of the fundamental "privacy" rights.[76] The parent may have a legal right to protest a course of study that perpetuates or advocates a position morally reprehensible to him or her.[77] Recently, this issue has erupted in two cases involving parents seeking some judicial protection from "secular humanism" in public schools. In both instances, parents won at trial, but the verdicts were reversed by federal appellate courts. The parents claimed that the public curriculum was, in effect, indoctrination in a religion of secularism. It is likely that conflicts over school curricula are ineradicable as long as the "common schools" serve the distinctly heterogeneous clientele in this country.[78]

The Supreme Court also generated the basis for another ground for raising curricular objection: the student's right to receive information. In a case involving censorship of a public school library, the Court recognized that students have this First Amendment protection against unreasonable or improperly motivated censorship.[79] However, among an otherwise divided Court, there was agreement that students' rights were subordinate in formal curricular matters to the discretion and authority of the legislature or local board. In sum, official authority over the curriculum still firmly resides in the legislature, or its delegatee, the local boards, and parents or students who object have relatively small hope for obtaining judicial assistance.

School Regulation of Students

The courts have recognized that the establishment of an educational system requires the formation of rules and regulations to ensure an orderly learning process. Generally, in formulating rules and regulations, school authorities have broad discretion and courts are deferential toward educators' decisions. They are, however, bound by the requirement that their rules and regulations be reasonable.[80] Courts have adopted a general guideline for determining whether regulations are reasonable. School regulations must be within the authority of the school, and reasonably related to the goal of maintaining order and discipline within the educational system.[81] Moreover, there are other constraints that limit school authorities' discretion. The U.S. Supreme Court has noted that the vigilant protection of constitutional freedoms is nowhere more vital than in the schools. Thus the state may not impose and enforce unconstitutional conditions upon the right of a student to attend a public school. Students in the public schools are "persons" within the meaning of the constitution and have certain fundamental rights that the state and the schools must respect.[82]

The law does not require that every school regulation be formally adopted and publicized by school authorities before it may be enforced.[83] In addition, school officials are not prohibited from taking appropriate disciplinary action in confronting a problem simply because there is no preexisting rule on the books.[84] Some cases have held, however, that regulations governing the conduct of high school students must be sufficiently clear to provide meaningful notice to students that they must conform their conduct to its requirements.[85] This concern is heightened if the regulation involves students' basic personal freedoms (e.g., free speech or association).[86] In any event, the enforcement of school rules and regulations must be reasonable, giving due regard to all the circum-

stances surrounding the nature of each event, and the age, health, and mental condition of the student.

Although the local board is the policymaking body for schools, the control and discipline of students is effectively in the hands of teachers, principals, and superintendents of the local schools,[87] with rule-making power being given to each. In a sense, then, students may confront multiple-rule systems in the school, which should be congruent, yet distinctive. In exercising authority to control and maintain class discipline, a teacher may adopt reasonable rules and regulations if they are not inconsistent with other school or district rules and regulations. Each teacher's classroom rules normally will be supplemented by the principal, superintendent, and school board.[88] In the following subsections we examine the range of school regulations over student behavior.

Health Regulations

Nearly all states delegate the power to prescribe health regulations to the schools as a condition of school attendance. It has generally been held that health measures prescribed by the local school systems do not conflict either with compulsory attendance laws, or with statutory provisions permitting attendance at a particular age. For example, some school districts have adopted regulations requiring students to receive physical examinations as a condition of their admission to school. The courts have rules that such regulations are within the police power delegated to the schools by the state.[89] The school has the same power with regard to the formulation of regulations to control the introduction and spread of infectious or contagious diseases. Thus the school may prevent a student from attending if he or she has been exposed to such diseases.[90]

As a general rule, a state may require the vaccination of all students prior to their enrolling in school. Such statutes are a valid exercise of the police power and have been generally upheld.[91] It is uncertain, however, whether, in the absence of a state statute the local school district may legally require vaccination as a condition for school attendance. It is clear that when threatened by an epidemic, the local school district may require proof of vaccination before admitting a student. Many statutory provisions, however, provide for exemptions from the vaccination requirement. For instance, a student may be exempted on a showing that he or she is unfit for vaccination on medical grounds.[92] Additionally, statutes may provide exemptions for students who protest vaccination based on religious beliefs;[93] such exemptions are discretionary. Children are not constitutionally entitled to an exemption from uniform vaccination requirements.[94]

Behavior Outside School

Ordinarily, school officials have no right of control over students outside school, but where the acts or behavior of a student impacts on the school, the school officials may be able to regulate them. To penalize a student for such off-school behavior, however, there must be a direct and immediate connection between the prohibited behavior and the welfare of the school.[95] Thus, a student may be punished for acts done outside school if his or her behavior (a) could directly influence the conduct of other students in the classroom, (b) sets a bad disciplinary example for other students, or (c) impairs the authority of the teachers. Although broad discretion is granted to the school in determining when out-of-school behaviors can be regulated, the courts require that such regulations be linked with a direct need of the local school.[96]

In addition to these general guidelines for the regulation of out-of-school behavior, the courts have also addressed some specific issues. For instance, school regulations relating to policies toward homework have long been upheld,[97] although a school may not require that certain hours of the evening be set aside exclusively for the completion of homework assignments.[98]

Courts have also upheld state statutes and regulations relating to school-related extracurricular recreational and social activities of students, especially when such rules are for the purpose of promoting discipline within the school. In evaluating these rules, courts look to whether they are a reasonable exercise of the power and discretion of the school, not to whether they are wise or expedient.[99] Older cases intimated that a school could rightly prohibit any kind of outside social or recreational activities by students if those activities too greatly diverted students from school and their schoolwork. Today, it is probably very difficult for the school authorities to intrude into any aspect of a student's out-of-school life unless there is some very direct and immediate impact on the school.

School regulation of interscholastic athletics has raised two important issues regarding students'

participation rights. First, the courts have held that participation in school sponsored sports is not a right but a privilege, subject to any number of different conditions. The power of the school to regulate interscholastic athletics must be exercised reasonably, and the privilege of participation may not be arbitrarily extended or withheld.[100] Under this power, the school may prescribe rules relating to the eligibility of students who transfer into the district.[101] However, litigation over eligibility questions is persistent.[102] Students who were transferred involuntarily under a court-ordered desegregation plan, however, may not be subject to such interdistrict transfer rules. A recent controversy has been the adoption of increased academic standards as a condition of participation. A "no pass, no play" statute was upheld by the Texas Supreme Court as rationally related to the state's legitimate educational interests.[103]

A second area that has generated a great deal of controversy involves sex discrimination in the availability of athletic programs and the opportunity to participate in existing programs. Although still a litigated matter, these issues are substantially regulated by Title IX and its administrative regulations.[104] Title IX permits sex separation as long as team selection is based on competitive skill or the sport involves substantial contact. The overall statutory demand is that both sexes have comparable opportunities to enjoy athletics.[105] There has been recurrent litigation, however, focusing particularly on the right of girls to play on boys' teams.[106] The results are quite uneven, but girls have won a substantial number of victories, even involving contact sports.[107] Apart from Title IX, these cases have turned on equal protection, and state civil rights or equal rights laws.[108]

Under its authority to prescribe rules and regulations for the well-being of the school, a school may prohibit students from affiliating with a fraternal society without the permission of school authorities.[109] This is true even though the students have the consent of their parents and all of the meetings of the organization are held after school hours and off the school ground.[110] To exercise this power validly, however, the school must show that such organizations have a tendency to destroy good order, discipline, and scholarship among the students. In the absence of such evidence the school may not prohibit membership by students.

Regulating students' non-school-based associations will always be problematic because such school efforts directly affect students' associational rights, protected by the First Amendment. Decisions permitting the regulation of students' social organizations came for the more part before judicial recognition of students' constitutional rights. The current viability of these older decisions may be suspect. An effort to prevent students' participation based on the ideas promoted by an association would be especially dangerous.

Behavior During School

Generally, school officials have wide latitude in regulating the conduct, behavior, and appearance of students during school hours. Any number of such rules and regulations have been challenged and upheld by the courts. For instance, the school generally may require late students to report to the principal's office or to wait in the hall until the opening exercises of the school are completed,[111] require financially able students to pay a deposit to ensure proper care of free textbooks,[112] require students to return report cards with a parent or guardian's signature,[113] prohibit students from wearing metal heel plates on their shoes,[114] and prevent students from obtaining lunches except from home or from the school lunch program.[115] Generally, the rules and regulations of the school must be reasonable exercises of their discretion and must have a rational relationship to the orderly conduct of the educational process. There is a legal presumption in favor of the validity of school regulations and, as along as they are reasonable and proper, they will not be disturbed. However, certain areas of school regulation have received much attention, and are examined in detail.

Clothing and Hairstyle. School regulation of hair and clothing style is certainly not as important as issue as it was during the 1960s. During those years the school's authority to regulate the personal appearance of students was the subject of much litigation. Such litigation has diminished because school officials largely acquiesced to changing fashion trends. Cases involving student appearances will occasionally erupt, but such issues now appear to be resolved largely outside of the judicial system.[116] On the other hand, as a function of the schools' authority to reasonably regulate the conduct of students, schools can prescribe and enforce dress codes.[117] School officials do not, however, have unlimited

discretion in prescribing standards of personal appearance. For example, a dress code may violate a student's right to equal protection under the Fourteenth Amendment if it unduly restricts what clothing is acceptable in the school. This is especially likely if the dress code does not bear some rational relationship to orderly conduct of the school.[118] Where the school could not show that wearing blue dungarees disrupted the educational system, a dress code provision prohibiting them was held unconstitutional.[119] Also, clearly discriminatory rules, such as one prohibiting only females from wearing slacks, have been found invalid. The court noted that such a regulation was an attempt to control the style and taste of students and did not bear on the safety, order, or discipline of the students.[120]

The authority of the school to regulate hairstyles and lengths is not so clearly established. Courts again have come down on both sides of the issue. For instance, some cases have held that the right to wear one's hair at any length or in any fashion is an ingredient of personal freedom protected by the U.S. Constitution.[121] Other courts have held that a student's hair length is not a form of symbolic expression, and constitutional protections do not attach. Therefore, the school may validly regulate hairstyle.[122]

Restrictions on hairstyles have usually been upheld where the school can show that a legitimate interest was served by the rule, such as preventing the distraction of other students or the disruption of a proper classroom atmosphere.[123] Schools have cited incidents of harassment and violence directed against male students with long hair,[124] and argued that excessive hair length interfered with certain sports or that enforcement of hair length regulations was a legitimate means of building team morale, discipline, and spirit.[125] Where such restrictions have been held invalid, it is usually because the school failed to show that long hair would disrupt the educational process.[126]

Flag Salute and Pledge of Allegiance. School boards do not have the power to require all students to stand and recite the pledge of allegiance while saluting the flag. The U.S. Supreme Court held that such a requirement went beyond the bounds of the protections of the First Amendment.[127] The Court noted that students' nonparticipation in the flag ceremony did not interfere with or deny the rights of others, and did not disrupt the orderly conduct of the classroom. In addition to the right not to participate, the student cannot be forced to stand quietly while others do so.[128]

Married and Pregnant Students.

The courts are split over the question of how much control the school may exercise over married students. Some older cases generally upheld the right of the school to prohibit married students from participating in any extracurricular activities. These decisions were generally grounded on the power of the school to maintain discipline and regulate school activities.[129] In support of such restrictions, schools argued successfully that the policy both discourages student marriages and helps preserve existing marriages by avoiding the time-consuming and distracting activities.[130]

Rules interfering with married students are inherently problematic, however, because marriage is constitutionally protected as a "fundamental right."[131] Courts have rules more recently that the school has no power to prevent married students from participating in either interscholastic sports or other school-related activities.[132] In *Sturrup v. Mahan*,[133] the court stated that to justify such a rule the school must demonstrate some compelling interest in restricting married students from such activities. As with other regulations, the court required the school to show that the presence of married students would have a disruptive impact on the conduct of classes within the school. The school officials' desire to discourage student marriages or to show disapproval of such marriages is not sufficient to outweigh the infringement on the students. Finally, one court has simply held that such a rule denies married students equal protection of the laws under the Fourteenth Amendment[134] and that a school would never be justified in prohibiting married students from participating in any activity available to any other student.

School officials also have less regulatory power now with respect to pregnant students. Title IX regulations no longer permit schools to uniformly exclude pregnant students or those who have had an abortion.[135] To maintain discipline and to help ensure the orderly conduct of learning within the school, however, schools may make reasonable rules concerning such students. In addition, separate schools are permissible, but must be voluntary for the student.

Leaving School Grounds.

Questions regarding the right of school officials to operate "open" or "closed" campuses often arise, normally over whether students may leave the school grounds during the lunch hour or other blocks of time during when they are not in class. Schools again have substantial discretion in operating the school, and may prohibit students from leaving the grounds during school hours. Such rules may validly prevent some students from having their noon meals with their parents[136] or cause them difficulty in carrying on legitimate business they might have away from the school.[137] Similarly, the school can validly prevent students who drive to school from using their automobiles over the noon hour unless they receive special permission.[138] Even if the students are permitted to leave the grounds over noon, school officials may validly prohibit them from patronizing restaurants near the school.[139] Relevant to the issue of the "open" campus are issues of school liability for students. Schools have been found potentially liable for a student's injury, when he left the school without permission.[140] Relatedly, California now has a constitutional amendment creating a right for all students to a "safe, secure and peaceful" school.[141] School officials have supervisory responsibilities, then, which involve protecting students from injuries caused by other students or outsiders. School policies on students leaving campus will very likely be influenced by its possible liability and increasing attention to students' "rights to safety."[142]

Search and Seizure.

The issue of the legality of a search and seizure within the school usually arises when school officials search a student or his or her locker and find drugs or other contraband. The legal issue is whether the search was legally conducted so that the evidence found during the search may be used against the student either in criminal or school disciplinary proceedings. Under normal criminal procedure, if the search was illegal, the evidence is normally excluded. To show an illegal search and seizure, the person (defendant) must show both that the search was conducted by government action and that it was unreasonable. It is less clear that illegally seized evidence must be excluded in school disciplinary hearings.[143]

After substantial confusion and contrary judicial rulings had reigned for many years, the Supreme Court finally entered this arena, with the 1985 decision, *New Jersey v. T.L.O.*[144] The facts of the case were unextraordinary, involving a student turned over to the police after a school administrator's search revealed drugs and associated paraphernalia. The Supreme Court held that although students are protected by the Fourth Amendment, searches by school officials neither required a warrant nor would the "probable cause to search" standard apply. Instead, school personnel may rely on a "reasonable suspicion" standard to justify a search to discover violations of school rules or the law.

The *T.L.O.* decision resolves much of the prior confusion, but still makes discretionary judgment quite important at the school level.[145] For instance, some courts have reacted quite hostilely to schoolwide searches using dogs and to strip searches of students.[146] Any search involves invasion of the student's privacy; thus, the justification for a particularly search and the degree of invasiveness will be crucial in determining its reasonableness. A highly unreasonable search could well lead to individual and school liability.[147]

A new aspect of the schools' efforts to control drug-related behavior in schools is demanding urine samples from students, as well as employees. Courts have analyzed cases arising from such demands as involving a potential invasion of privacy. Where schools have sought urine samples, the standards of *T.L.O.* normally must be satisfied.[148]

Student Freedom of Speech. In *Tinker v. Des Moines Community School District*,[149] the U.S. Supreme Court spoke directly to the issue of the relationship between the school's right to regulate student conduct and the student's constitutionally protected freedom of speech and expression.[150] The Court specifically affirmed that such protections did extend to students in the public schools. Students may not be regarded by the schools as "closed circuit" receptors of only that information that the school wishes to expose them to, nor may students be prohibited from expressing viewpoints other than those accepted by the school. The Court noted that the principle of the vigilant protection of constitutional freedom is nowhere more vital than in the schools, and it is applicable both to orderly discussions in the classrooms and to communications among students. Finally, the right of free expression at-

taches beyond the classroom to other activities that occur during the school day. At any time, the student has a right to free expression as long as it does not materially and substantially interfere with the orderly conduct of the educational process.

The school can prohibit student expression only where the school can show that it may materially and substantially disrupt discipline in the school. The school must show that its action was motivated by more than an undifferentiated fear or apprehension that such expression would disrupt the school or a mere desire to avoid the discomfort and unpleasantness that accompanies the expression of an unpopular opinion. The school may, however, prohibit or punish any conduct by a student, in class or out, which materially disrupts classwork or involves substantial disorder of the school or an invasion of the rights of other students. *Tinker* has been an enormously important case, in part because it clearly accords constitutional protections to students; consequently, it has spawned a huge volume of cases. Two important concepts arose out of *Tinker* and its myriad progeny concerning freedom of speech and expression by students. First, the burden of proof as to the reasonableness of school regulations is on school *officials*. Thus, if a student chooses to litigate the validity of such a regulation, the court will require the school officials to demonstrate a reasonable basis for their interference with the student's life. In addition, the courts will not accept the bare testimony of school officials that student expressions would be disruptive.[151] Second, if a student is subject to disciplinary action because of a violation of such a regulation, the school must proceed carefully to ensure that justice is done. Because such actions involve the infringement of a basic constitutional right, disciplinary action must be considered on a case-by-case basis, taking into account the particular and often unique facts of each case.

In applying the principles of *Tinker* to specific activities of students in the schools, several distinctions arise in how the courts treat particular forms of expression. For instance, the courts have applied different standards to the production and distribution of printed material by students and the distribution of material not produced within the school.

Distribution of material not produced within the school may occur freely as long as it does not unreasonably disrupt normal school activities.

However, school officials can lawfully regulate the times and places where material may be distributed on the school grounds.[152] Thus, it has been held that the publication of off-campus newspapers and their distribution on or near school grounds cannot be prohibited where the school could show no disruptive influence on other students.[153] It has also been held that school officials may prohibit such material where its content goes beyond the bounds of decency, regardless of whether it is produced on or off school grounds.[154] School authority to regulate the use of facilities for non-school-related expressive activities will be influenced by prior conduct and current motives. That is, if a school generally encourages community use of the building, denying any group that use will raise the issue of improper motivation on the part of the school officials (e.g., a desire to avoid controversial topics).[155] If the school does not create an "open forum" on school facilities, regulation can be more extensive.

In terms of school-produced materials, it has been held that the school may validly establish a system of prior inspection and approval of material to be published by students.[156] The court did note, however, that such a procedure of prior restraint would be subject to very strict standards in order to guarantee the protection of students' rights. The school could prohibit distribution of material if it could show that either the material itself or the manner of its distribution would interfere with the operation of the school, cause violence or disorder, or would constitute an invasion of the rights of others. To be constitutionally permissible, however, the school must have a formal procedure whereby students can submit their material to school officials for prior approval. Specifically, the court noted that such a procedure would require (a) specifications of to whom such material would be submitted, (b) criteria by which school officials must make their decision, and (c) a stated period in which a decision would be made. In addition, the court required the regulation to define "distribution" and distinguish between public distribution or dissemination and simple passing of information between friends and acquaintances.[157]

In *Trachtman v. Anker*[158] the Court upheld the decision of the school to prohibit the distribution of a questionnaire to students in the school. The project had been undertaken by the student newspaper to prepare an article on the sexual attitudes and practices of high school students.

After reviewing the testimony of various witnesses (including several psychologists acting as expert witnesses), the *Trachtman* court agreed that the questionnaire should not be distributed because of the probability that it would result in psychological harm to some students. As with many other similar cases, the court balanced the infringement of the students' rights of expression against the potential harm that might arise as a result of the exercise of that right, particularly given the "captive audience" of the students.

Trachtman suggests two other points that should be made concerning students' right of expression. First, in regard to student-produced school newspapers, the school may not exert arbitrary control over the content of the publications. Courts have keyed the degree of permissible regulation to a preliminary determination whether the paper is intended as an "open forum" for student opinion.[159] If it is, substantially less regulation is permissible than for papers described as integrally part of the school's curriculum and subject to the school's comprehensive control of curriculum[160] Unfortunately, there is an absence of clear-cut standards for determining the character of the newspaper.

The second point derived from *Trachtman* is that censorship justified by a motive to protect students must take into account the students' age. In a recent case, censorship of articles involving divorce and student pregnancy on the grounds that the topics were inappropriate and that some students' privacy would be invaded was held unconstitutional, in part because the students were in high school.[161] The protective arguments of school officials were simply unpersuasive to the court.

That courts are still concerned about the special environment of the school and maintaining the authority of school officials is illustrated by the Supreme Court's 1986 decision, *Bethel School District v. Fraser*.[162] The Court upheld the school's decision to discipline a student whose speech at a school assembly was composed of unsubtle sexual innuendo. The Court emphasized the school's responsibility for inculcating norms of civility, as well as the disruption and invasion of other students' rights caused by the speech. These students were viewed as a "captive audience" to the student speaker, a concept that has earned *judicial solicitude* where the expressive conduct might be viewed as offensive or intrusive for other students. The decision can be interpreted as an application of the long-established principle that schools may reasonably enforce time, place, and manner restrictions on student expression.[163]

One final area of student speech activities ties into the multifaceted conflicts involving religious activities in public schools. Although the Supreme Court invalidated an Alabama statute that required a daily moment of "meditation or prayer," the decision in no way implied that students are prohibited from engaging individually in voluntary prayer during the school day.[164] On the other hand, as with other expressive acts, the prayer may not disrupt the educational process (e.g., an audible prayer during an examination).

A more complicated, unresolved issue is posed by groups of students requesting school recognition as an organization or use of school facilities for religious activities. The Supreme Court reviewed a federal appellate court's decision that such student groups should be denied recognition and other privileges accorded student groups by the school in order to preserve church state separation values.[165] Unfortunately, the Supreme Court's decision was on procedural matters only, leaving conflicts among lower court decisions.[166] Suffice it to say, regulation of student prayer (where no adult participation or school sponsorship is involved) raises very delicate constitutional concerns.[167]

In sum, *Tinker*, might be seen as loosing a cacophony of voices in the school by legitimating student speech under the First Amendment. It certainly precipitated a flood of interpretive cases, as new speech rights and new roles were renegotiated at the school level. Much remains tentative (and perhaps always will) respecting student expressive rights. Most recently, in *Bethel School District v. Fraser*, the Supreme Court apparently settled that the *texture* of speech, if not the ideational content, can be largely determined as a school prerogative. For example, a school could punish a student's vulgarity in protesting a school policy as unfair, but absent vulgarity, the protest might be constitutionally protected. Decisions also tend to indicate that mechanisms (or forums) for student speech, once created, still may be partially controllable, but rarely can be wholly constrained by the wishes and sensibilities of school authorities.

Privacy Issues. The issue of a student's right to privacy involves two related topics. The first

has to do with the files compiled on students throughout their academic careers. Of concern here is who is allowed access to these files, and to whom information contained in them is released. The second topic is the confidentiality of student actions when dealing with particular school officials. The rights that are accorded to students under these categories help define the relationship between the student and the school.

Traditionally, a student's academic files were closed to both the student and the parent. Schools' policies of keeping such information at least partly confidential were based on custom, not law. Many other individuals associated with the school were allowed to inspect a student's file at their convenience, even if they were not teaching the student or had no other close and direct contact with him or her. In addition, the schools often permitted outside organizations open access to student files, even organizations interested only for commercial or business purposes.

There were at least two very real problems with such a procedure. In the first place, fundamental educational decisions were often made for the student on the basis of information contained in his or her file. Because parents had no access to the file, they were unable to participate in making informed choices for their children's future. Relatedly, parents had no way of knowing what information the school kept in the file, and its accuracy. The second problem was that parents had absolutely no control over the dissemination of information from their children's educational files. They could not prohibit the school from releasing information about them and their children, and they did not know what individuals or organizations had obtained access and what information they had obtained.

These and other associated problems were finally addressed by the so-called "Buckley Amendment."[168] Although this law substantially changed school practices, it was apparently fully implemented without threatened federal enforcement. Its goals were undoubtedly reinforced by other legislation, such as P.L. 94-142, the Education for All Handicapped Children Act, which involved parents more fully in educational decisionmaking.

In the course of an educational career, a student may have many opportunities to interact with teachers and other school personnel on a basis other than that of student and teacher. For instance, a student may take advantage of a variety of counseling services offered by the school, may consult medical practitioners employed by the state, or may confide in a teacher regarding personal problems. A question that may often arise in these circumstances concerns the degree of confidentiality a student may expect regarding various communications with school personnel.

The first issue that needs to be addressed is the confused, frequently mistaken use of the terms "confidential" or "privileged." These terms are often incorrectly employed as synonyms to describe generally the nature of communications between a therapist and a client or patient. In fact, the confidentiality of a communication refers only to the therapist's ethical and/or legal duty to keep secret the information obtained from a client in the course of a professional relationship. A breach of this duty may be grounds for a civil lawsuit against the therapist. The therapist may, however, be forced to divulge confidential communications in the course of a legal proceeding unless such communications are privileged. Confidential communications become privileged only if a law provides that such information can not be disclosed in a legal proceeding without the client's express consent. Obviously, there would be no liability for information divulged during the course of a legal proceeding where the therapist was requested to testify and where the information was not privileged.

The degree of confidentiality may depend on the content of the communication and to whom it is made. If a communication involves information that may bear on the commission of a felony, nearly all states now require that recipients have a legal duty to report it to law enforcement officials. Thus, if a student confides in school officials concerning violations of drug laws, he or she should have no expectation that the information will be confidential. Even for attorneys and clients there is no confidentiality or privilege for information that may further a crime. Similarly, all states require all public officials, including school personnel, to report incidents of suspected child abuse. If a student communicates such information to school authorities, he or she cannot expect it to remain confidential.[169]

Student communications with a school counselor or psychologist may fall within a state law according a privilege to the interaction, although this would still not change the rule concerning the reporting of felonies. A word of caution is in order here regarding the coverage extended by such statutes. Some statutes cover only physicians and surgeons; others include licensed clinical psychologists; while still others include counselors and psychometrists. A student would be well advised to consider the legal status of the individual he or she intends to confide in if the information is potentially damaging. Additionally, states vary in the extent of the privilege extended by the statute. Some states extend the privilege only when the information was communicated in the course of a professional relationship to treat or diagnose a person's mental or emotional problem.[170] Other states specifically extend the privilege to counselors, psychologists, and psychological examiners in the schools and thus protect communications made to them by students. It should also be noted, however, that a counselor or psychologist may also have an independent duty to warn others if he or she feels that a client may be dangerous to some other person.[171]

In summary,[172] it is simply not clear how much confidentiality a student may expect in dealings with school personnel. It depends on the nature of the communication, to whom the communication is directed, and the particular status of the state law. It should be pointed out, however, that there is no student–teacher or student–school official privilege analogous to that of an attorney– or physician–client. For this reason, the student should not assume that any statements that he or she makes are privileged or confidential on any basis other than that of a personal relationship between the student and recipient. It is quite important that school personnel explain the limits of confidentiality clearly to students before a potentially damaging revelation occurs. As noted, some information must be divulged by a school official, even though a parent or other nonschool person could keep silent. It is unlikely that most students will be cognizant of such distinctions.[173]

Discipline and Punishment

Under the general mandate to operate the public school, school officials may exercise the necessary disciplinary authority to ensure that the school's educational purposes are achieved. In doing so, the school may delegate to teachers as much disciplinary power as necessary to ensure order in the classroom. It also is generally held that teachers may reasonably exercise their disciplinary power without seeking formal approval or sanction from school officials.[174] The authority of the school to discipline students certainly exists during school hours. There is also authority, albeit much older, that the school may exercise control over students between their homes and the school and may discipline or punish students for acts of misconduct occurring on the way to or from school.[175]

The justification for the school to discipline students for misconduct occurring outside school hours is not clear. Some cases have suggested that the school may discipline a student for such behavior if it directly affects the reputation, order, and welfare of the school.[176] On the other hand, it has also been argued that it does not make sense to extend the authority of the school to such lengths on the theory that such behavior interferes with the orderly process of education.[177] In *Sullivan* the Court noted that school officials did not have the authority to judge students' behavior either in their own homes or on the street corner. The student is subject to the same civil and criminal sanctions as other citizens, and a person's status as a student should not subject him or her to a higher standard of behavior than is applied to other citizens.

During school hours a teacher has the authority to punish a student for any behavior that is detrimental to the order and best interests of the school and for the breach of any rule or regulation that is within the power of the school to adopt. It is not necessary for the school to formally adopt and publish rules and regulations. In addition, a student may be punished for conduct that is technically not a violation of any explicit or recognized school rule. It is only necessary that the school have the power to adopt such a rule, not that the school has exercised its power.[178] Students cannot, however, be disciplined for the breach of an unreasonable regulation or one that was beyond his or her power of compliance. Nor should a student be disciplined for a breach of school rules committed at the request of his or her parents. For example, a student may refuse to participate in certain required school activities because of the directives of a parent. In such cases, disciplinary actions against the student are not appropriate.[179] What method school officials or teachers choose to discipline students is largely a matter of discretion. Students may be required to perform extra schoolwork, to consult with a principal or other school official about their misconduct, or have their parents come to the school for a disciplinary conference. A student may be excluded from attending a particu-lar class or may be detained after class. Students may also be subjected to corporal punishment administered by the teacher or other school official.[180] Subject to a general standard of reasonableness, the form of discipline or punishment is left to the discretion and creativity of the teacher or school official. Because discipline involves the invasion of various student interests (e.g., liberty, privacy), there is always a possibility that a particular disciplinary decision can be successfully challenged. By and large, courts remain quite deferential to schools' decisions though.[181] There are, however, three particular forms of discipline that have been the subject of concern. These involve detention, corporal punishment, and the use of drugs to control in-school behavior.

Detention after the dismissal of the rest of the students, as a penalty for misconduct, has long been an accepted and generally recognized method of enforcing school rules and regulations. If detention is imposed in good faith, without malicious motives, it does not constitute "false imprisonment" or "unlawful detention." This is true even though the teacher and school officials were completely mistaken as to the correctness of their decision.[182]

The use of corporal punishment as a means of enforcing discipline and punishing student misconduct increasingly has been a special concern. It has long been held that corporal punishment was a legitimate tool for a teacher or school official to employ. To allow the school to ensure order, the courts have held that corporal punishment was necessary for the prompt enforcement of the teacher's orders.[183]

However, the power of the school to use corporal punishment has come under attack. Lawsuits questioned whether the use of corporal punishment usurped a right belonging only to the parent. There were questions about what procedural rights must be afforded to a student and his or her parents before corporal punishment could be imposed (i.e., was the school required to give notice to the student and parent, and provide them an opportunity to be represented at a hearing before corporal punishment could be used?). Finally, teachers and school officials were concerned about their own personal civil liability arising out of the use of corporal punishment (i.e., for assault and battery for the wrongful imposition of corporal punishment).

The U.S. Supreme Court, in *Ingraham v.*

Wright,[184] affirmed the right of public school teachers and officials to use corporal punishment. The Court noted that the paddling of public school students as a means of maintaining school discipline does not constitute cruel and unusual punishment under the Eighth Amendment to the U.S. Constitution, because the Eighth Amendment was designed to protect those persons convicted of crimes. Extension of Eighth Amendment protections to ban corporal punishment in the schools was unwarranted as the schools are open to public scrutiny and are supervised by the community through local boards of education. In addition, the acts and behavior of teachers and school officials are subject to the same legal constraints as all other citizens. Thus, if they exceed their authority, they are subject to civil or criminal liability.[185]

In deciding *Ingraham,* the Court also resolved many of the questions posed about the use of corporal punishment. The Court ruled that procedural safeguards, including notice to parents or a hearing are not constitutionally required.[186] While the schools do have the authority to impose corporal punishment, it must be reasonable and within the bounds of moderation. It must not be cruel or excessive, and the teacher or school official must not act wantonly or from malice or passion.[187] The punishment, in each case, should be proportional to the seriousness of the offense,[188] the apparent motive and disposition of the student,[189] and the degree of his or her influence on the conduct of other students. Consideration must also be given to the age, size, sex, and physical strength of the student to be punished.[190]

The Court recognized the common law right of a student not to be subjected to excessive punishment in school. Teachers and school officials must exercise prudence and restraint in the initial decision to use corporal punishment. Under the circumstances of each incident, corporal punishment must have appeared to be reasonably necessary. If the punishment inflicted is later found by a court to have been excessive (i.e., not reasonably believed at the time to be necessary for the student's discipline or training), the teacher or school officials responsible for administering the punishment may be held liable for damages to the student.[191] Finally, if malice on the part of school officials or teacher can be shown, they may be subject to criminal penalties.[192]

In general, issues created by corporal punishment are state law matters.[193] One exception, after *Ingraham,* has been litigation brought in federal courts seeking relief under the Fourteenth Amendment's due process clause for particularly brutal or harmful acts. Students have occasionally claimed that an act of corporal punishment was so brutal and inhumane as to deprive the student of liberty without due process of law. Federal courts have split in resolving that question.[194] Otherwise, whether corporal punishment will be used is resolved usually by state legislatures. If corporal punishment is permitted, parental objections are not a barrier;[195] conversely, where prohibited, teachers have no right to use it for classroom control.[196]

A problematic disciplinary method employed with some students is the use of stimulant drugs, particularly Ritalin (methylphenidate). These amphetamines do not have the same effect on all people. For certain individuals, instead of being "speed" and accelerating the individual's behavioral activity, proponents claim that the drug slows the child down and makes him or her more controllable. This kind of drug therapy is claimed to work especially well for children who have been diagnosed as "hyperactive-hyperkinetic or minimally brain damaged."

The truly hyperkinetic child presents a serious disciplinary problem for the teacher and the school. In class, the child seems incapable of sitting still for the normal course of instruction. Such children are often singled out for their inability to cope with a structured classroom setting; and the school often recommends to the parent that some form of treatment be sought for the child. Frequently, school officials recommend some form of drug therapy to help the child conform to the expectations of the school setting. The problem arises when the parents resist or refuse to have such drugs administered to their child, and the school refuses to allow the child to attend classes until something is done to control the child's misbehavior. The issue is whether the school can lawfully refused to allow the child in classes until or unless the parents seek some form of drug or other therapy for the child. To our knowledge, the courts have not decided a case based on this issue, and it is difficult to predict how such a case would be decided.[197]

Certainly, the school has the authority to exercise those powers of control, restraint, and correction necessary to accomplish the purposes of education, including maintaining discipline and order in the classroom. To accomplish these purposes, as seen in the following section, the school may lawfully suspend or expel a student for violations of school rules and regulations. It seems likely, then, that a school could take whatever steps were necessary to control the behavior of a persistently misbehaving student. If the student's behavior could be shown to be a disruptive influence on other students such that a teacher could not perform his or her functions, the school would be within its right to exclude such a student from classes until the behavior was under control. On the other hand, it seems unclear how the school would justify excluding a student unless he or she obtained one particular kind of treatment (e.g., Ritalin therapy). This certainly seems like an usurpation of a parental right of control over the child. One legal commentator has argued at length that the school has absolutely no right to coerce the use of Ritalin as a behavior control method.[198]

Suspension and Expulsion

Generally, the right to attend a public school is conditioned on compliance with the reasonable rules and regulations established by school officials. Unless a student is willing to adhere to these school requirements, the school may legally suspend or expel the student.[199]

In most states local school officials are given the authority to determine which offenses merit suspension or expulsion and to determine whether such offenses have occurred. The school is limited, however, by the restriction that its actions in both instances be reasonable. The power of school officials to suspend or expel a student is not limited to those cases where a formally adopted rule has been violated. Subject to the restriction that they not be arbitrary, school officials may suspend or expel a student any time it is required by the best interests of the school as a whole.[200] Since teachers and principals also have a duty to maintain discipline and order within the classroom and school, they may have the power to suspend a student. In most cases, however, a teacher's recommendation to suspend or expel a student is subject to review by the principal or the local board of education. A principal may usually take some actions involving suspension without review by other school authorities.

As noted above, subject to a limitation of reasonableness, a student may be suspended or expelled for violating any rule or regulation, or for any other misconduct that is disruptive of the school purpose. Several specific grounds for suspension and expulsion have received the attention of the courts more frequently than others. For instance, the courts have consistently held that a student may be suspended or expelled for the use of profane or obscene language, particularly if directed at school personnel. Courts have held that "righting" words, and words that are lewd, obscene, profane, and libelous are not safeguarded by the constitution within the context of a public school.[201]

It is unclear whether a school may legally suspend or expel a student for failing to maintain a prescribed grade-point average, however; given a student's interests in education, a court might well be skeptical of such a policy. It is also uncertain whether the school may reduce grades to punish misconduct.[202] It is clear, however, that the school may refuse to promote a student to the next grade or may demote him or her to a lower grade. The best reasoning appears to be that it is the school's duty to attempt to educate a student, but the student's failure to achieve acceptable results is not a ground for suspension or expulsion.

In addition to these offenses, suspension or expulsion has been held proper in a variety of other circumstances. For instance, schools may take such action against a student because of excessive absence or tardiness without a satisfactory excuse,[203] gross disrespect and contempt for school officials, and being infested with head lice.[204] The most accurate generalization is that rulemaking is still largely a local function. Boards may regulate such student conduct as they believe is harmful to the school. They may also establish the magnitude of punishment for violence. Given appropriate procedures of application, these decisions will rarely be dislodged by a court, even if harsh or ultimately injurious to the punished student.[205]

An important element of the suspension and expulsion process is the provision of adequate procedural due process rights to the student. The U.S. Supreme Court, in *Goss v. Lopez*,[206] directly addressed this issue. In connection with a short suspension of a student (i.e., a 5-day suspension), due process requires that the student be given oral or written notice of the charges, an explanation of the evidence against the student and an opportunity to explain his or her side of the story. The

Court noted that at least these rudimentary protections where necessary to guard against unfair or mistaken charges of misconduct and arbitrary exclusion from school. To clarify its decision, the Court elaborated on the conditions appropriate to short suspensions: (a) There need be no time delay between giving "notice" to the student and holding the hearing—in the majority of cases, the school official may informally discuss the alleged violation with the student only moments after it has occurred; (b) in being given an opportunity to explain his or her version of the events, a student must first be told the nature and basis of the accusation; and (c) since the hearing may occur almost immediately following the incident, notice and hearing should normally precede removal of the student from school. The Court recognized that there were situations in which a student's continued presence in the school posed a danger to that student or to others or constituted an ongoing threat to the school process; if so, the student may be immediately removed from the school. In such cases, the necessary notice and rudimentary hearing should follow as soon as possible.

Many states now have statutes or administrative regulations that provide more extensive procedural protections for students subject to suspension or expulsion. These procedures will vary, but at the most formal level they include the rights to a preliminary hearing, notice of the charges, and a formal hearing at which the student may be represented by counsel and may confront and cross examine witnesses. It has been held, however, that a student may be suspended without these hearings if there is a clear and present danger to the student's physical or emotional safety and well-being or it is necessary for the safety of others. A student may also waive a required hearing and accept the suspension or expulsion. In such cases the school should require a written waiver signed by both the student and a parent or guardian.

If the school decides to seek a longer suspension or an expulsion, the student should be given a formal notice of the charges. Although it need not be drawn as precisely as a legal document, the notice of charges should contain a statement of the specific charges and the grounds on which suspension or expulsion will be based. Parents should be kept very closely informed of the proceedings against their children and given copies of all documents relating to the school's action.

Ample time should be allowed so that the student may examine the charges and prepare a defense by gathering evidence and witnesses. The time between notice and the formal hearing may be shortened at the request of the student.[207]

When a hearing is required, there is no agreement as to the exact format it must follow to satisfy constitutional requirements. Some courts have imposed close adherence to a judicial model, others have not. At a minimum, however, the student should have an adequate opportunity to present his or her own version of the incident. Many schools additionally require that witnesses against the student be present at the hearing and subject themselves to cross examination.[208] Issues arising from challenges to the adequacy of student hearings have generated persistent litigation. Given the enormous variability of factual contexts and the relative fluidity of due process concepts, it is very difficult to propose a generalization about judicial outcomes. Perhaps the best criterion to adopt as a guidepost is that students should have an opportunity to avoid unfair or erroneous deprivations of their educational interests. At bottom, procedures should comport with fundamental fairness.

In summary, although the school is required to provide due process under *Goss*, the nature of the hearing may vary as a function of the loss confronting the student. As the hearing moves from the principal's office to the district's board room, the degree of formality will increase commensurately. One issue yet to be resolved is whether "in-house" suspensions trigger due process requirements. If a loss of educational opportunity accompanies the in-house suspension, due process logically would be required.

Where it can be shown that a student was wrongfully suspended or expelled from school, the teacher and school officials responsible for the action can be civilly liable for damages.[209] Alternatively, a student may seek a court order requiring readmission.[210] In all such cases, there is a presumption that the school officials acted reasonably and in good faith, and the student will have the burden of showing that the school acted maliciously or unreasonably.[211]

Graduation and Diploma

When a student has completed the prescribed course of studies in a public school system, he or she is entitled to a diploma or certificate of graduation.[212] What the diploma or certificate indicates about the student, however, depends on whether the student lives in a state that has adopted a "minimum competency testing" ("MCT") program for the public school system. In a very general sense, competency testing involves the measurement (usually by test) of the degree of mastery of certain basic skills and satisfactory performance in functional literacy as designated by the state legislature or the state board of education. Upon completion of schooling, and based on the results of competency tests, students would be awarded differentiated diplomas or certificates of attendance to correspond with their various achievement levels and competencies.[213]

The initial surge of statutorily mandated competency tests may have peaked, and the accompanying response of litigative challenges has also largely ended.[214] The grounds for legally attacking MCTs were myriad.[215] For instance, such programs normally create racially discriminatory effects by virtue of the nature of the testing devices.[216] Those effects undergird a Fourteenth Amendment equal protection claim. Unless adequate phase-in periods are provided, students also do not have adequate notice of the change in educational requirements, which may give rise to a Fourteenth Amendment due process claim. The tests are difficult to properly validate and it is challenging to prove that school programs provide an appropriate match between the instruction and the knowledge demanded by the tests. Finally, plaintiffs could argue that the schools would not be able to provide adequate remedial instruction for those who failed to achieve the highest level of competency. Whatever the format of a competency testing program for a school, the students exposed to such tests had reasonable bases for mounting a legal assault.

Predictably, new MCT requirements were followed in virtually every instance by legal challenges. Although winning some partial victories, the challengers discovered that the courts were unwilling to resolve fully what was essentially a social or educational policy dispute. The keystone case arose in Florida.[217]

Plaintiffs did win an initial 5-year moratorium on the implementation of the MCT, based partially on due process and partially on the remaining effects of former *de jure* segregation. Moreover, the appellate court demanded that the state demonstrate "curricular validity" for its test (i.e., that the test covered subjects in the curriculum of Florida's public schools). This burden proved to be

costly, but not particularly difficult,[218] and in the last analysis, the court would not ban the MCT, as plaintiffs requested.

The more essential societal dilemma is the racial effects associated with MCT programs. Although the number of students who fail to pass the MCT normally has dropped off after a time, minority students still fail in disproportionate numbers.[219] Assuming the state can demonstrate "curricular validity," however, this outcome has not led to judicial declarations that the examination is unconstitutional. Where the state can demonstrate that students who fail receive adequate "remediation" opportunities, some judges have been positively predisposed to a program that prevents the high school diploma from being a "hollow certification."[220] As long as a court is persuaded that an MCT is fairly derived from the schools' curriculum and that all students have fair notice and access to the material covered by the test, racially discriminatory outcome data are not a sufficient basis for a court to prohibit a test.

A related problem that may arise after a student has graduated also concerns the basic competency level of the student. Several cases have been filed on behalf of students who have successfully completed all the requirements of a particular school, yet are found to be functionally illiterate on their graduation. Students with educational deficiencies have charged their teachers and their school officials with educational malpractice —the failure of the teacher and the school officials to demonstrate the skill, knowledge, and performance of a reasonable educator or administrator under similar circumstances. Educational malpractice is intended to redress the injuries suffered by students who have made a legitimate effort to meet the demands of coursework and the expectations of school officials, and who have been led by annual promotions and graduation to believe that they have performed in a satisfactory manner, but who are, in fact, inadequately prepared to succeed in society.[221]

The best known case directly addressing the issue of educational malpractice is *Peter W. v. San Francisco Unified School District.*[222] The plaintiff was an otherwise unremarkable student of normal intelligence. Upon his graduation, however, it was discovered that he could read at only the fifth-grade level despite the state statutory requirement of eighth-grade reading level for graduation. Upon appeal the court dismissed the suit. The court rules that teachers and school officials owed no duty of care to their students to ensure that they learn even minimal academic skills. The court also dismissed the claims that the school had breached a statutory duty for failing to require an eight-grade reading level, and for misrepresenting that *Peter W.* could read at the eighth-grade level by issuing him a diploma.

The *Peter W.* decision has proven prophetic of courts' reaction to such law suits. Even in cases involving factual situations harshly unfavorable to the school, courts have resisted taking jurisdiction in these disputes.[223] Among professional groups, then, educators alone avoid the prospect of litigation based on unsatisfactory outcomes from professional efforts and judgment.[224] The argument for malpractice cases remains alluring to legal scholars, who have continued to propose bases for judicial review.[225] Thus far, in public schools, although a student may have an enforceable right to appropriate care and supervision to prevent physical (and perhaps emotional) injuries, educational harms remain essentially noncompensable in legal forums.

CONCLUSION

When the legal rights of students in the public schools are viewed as a whole, contradictory patterns and trends emerge. There are indications that the courts are, at the same time, both expanding students' rights in particular areas and restricting them in others.

The expansion of rights can be seen in three particular areas. First, access to a free public education has been expanded by those cases and statutes that remove barriers based on race, ethnicity, or handicapping condition. For all the groups, the schools have been given an affirmative mandate to ensure that students are given meaningful access to educational opportunities. Additionally, the courts are unlikely to uphold regulations restricting full participation in educational activities by married or pregnant students. The courts have recognized that these students, along with all others, have a right to enjoy the full benefits of an education including participation in extracurricular, school-related activities.[226]

A second area of expansion can be seen in

regard to school regulation of a student's right of expression. The *Tinker* case was a dramatic affirmation of a student's right to hold and express a personal opinion, no matter how offensive it may be to school officials. *Tinker* placed an affirmative burden on the school to show that student expression would likely result in a serious disruption of school activities. Absent such a showing, the school may not suppress a student's right of speech or expression. It is important to note, however, that where school officials can show a strong likelihood of disruption or harm to other students (i.e., *Trachtman*),[227] courts are not reluctant to affirm such restrictions. *Bethel School District v. Fraser* also emphasizes that schools may regulate more extensively the *mode* of student expression (i.e., time, place, and manner), then the idea or content.

The students' right to some measure of privacy while in school also has been acknowledged. Reflected in the protection of married and pregnant students, this interest was focal in *T.L.O.*, where the Court imposed some limits on schools' authority to search students and their possessions. These limits must be put into perspective, however. Because of the school's interest in maintaining a safe and orderly environment, the Court granted more authority to school officials to search, then the police enjoy.

Finally, in a very limited sense, *Yoder* may be seen as an expansion of students' rights regarding state mandated compulsory attendance. At least for the Amish, the state's interest in compulsory attendance gave way to a small degree to deeply held and long-practiced religious and cultural practices. The *Yoder* opinion was narrowly written, however, and the precedent has not grown, despite the pressures of insistent litigation by parents and private schools. The state's interest in regulating the child's educational experience remains a powerful defense to constitutional challenges.

Just as these areas can be seen as expansions of students' rights, there are others in which courts have refused to enhance the degree of freedom a student (or parent) may exercise. In reference to access, when "separate but equal" facilities are available, the courts have refused to require equal access to the same educational opportunities for both sexes. It is highly likely that these issues will continue to evolve as a function of social change, rather than legal mandate.

A second area in which the courts have been

reluctant to intrude in granting greater freedom of choice is curricula selection. The legal system (and legislatures) are in a quandary as to how to resolve the conflict over parental and student objections about the nature and content of the courses offered by the school. The majority of cases have upheld the right of the school to select an appropriate curriculum. Objections have been heard with both increasing frequency and intensity, but to no avail. Courts have been unresponsive to parental claims rooted in religious belief and to student claims cast as a "right to learn."[228] This area continues to yield a significant number of bitterly contested lawsuits, but there is no evidence to predict that courts will become more receptive to arbitrating these disputes.

A third area where the legal rights of students are significantly limited concerns school discipline, particularly in the use of corporal punishment by school officials. While *Goss* ensured procedural protections for students confronting suspension or dismissal, courts have been loath to intrude on substantive concerns involving the type or degree of punishment meted out. *Ingraham* not only upheld the right of school officials to use corporal methods, but also eliminated any due process procedures that must precede its use. As to the exclusionary disciplines, school authorities' fidelity to minimally appropriate standards will normally insulate disciplinary judgment from judicial review.

In summary, the area of student rights is in a state of tension. The courts are recurrently faced with a variety of issues, many of which they are clearly uncomfortable resolving. School officials, students, and parents are each asserting their rights within the educational system. Courts are more receptive to requests to ensure fair procedures than to review outcomes for fairness or adequacy. A legacy of the 1960s and 1970s that remains, however, is the recognition that students have rights against school officials independent of their parents. Those rights are not as comprehensive as those of adults, nor as extensive *in* schools as out of them. In addition, the individual freedoms of each student are subordinate to the larger interests of society and the school in creating and maintaining a safe and efficient educational process. Thus it is not surprising that the balance between the rights of students and school officials inherent in a system of "ordered liberty" is constantly in a state of tension.

FOOTNOTES

1. State v. Hershberger, 144 N.E.2d 693, 103 Ohio App. 188 (1955). But see White v. Linkinogger, 344 S.E.2d 633 (W. Va. 1986).

2. Shuttlesworth v. Birmingham Board of Education of Jefferson County, 162 F. Supp, 372, *aff'd*, 79 S. Ct. 221, 358 U.S. 101, 3 L. Ed. 2d 145 (1958).

3. Blessing v. Macon County Board of Education, 34 S.E.2d 407 (W. Va. 1985). *Contra*, Hammond v. Marx, 406 F. Supp. 853 (D. Me. 1975).

4. Zweifel v. Joint District No. 1, Belleville, 251 N.W.2d 822, 76 Wis. 2d 648 (1977).

5. Vorchheimer v. School District of Philadelphia, 532 F.2d 880 (1976), *off'd by an equally divided Court*, 430 U.S. 703 (1977). But see Berkelman v. San Francisco Un. Sch. District, 501 F.2d 1264 (9th Cir. 1974).

6. Mississippi University for Women v. Hogan, 458 U.S. 718, 102 S. Ct. 3331 (1982).

7. The constitutional requirement that (the) public school system shall be "open" to all children . . . means that all children must have equal rights and opportunities to attend the grade or class of school for which they are suited by previous training or development. Lau v. Nichols, 418 U.S., 563, 94 S. Ct. 786 (1974).

8. *Pennsylvania Association for Retarded Children v. Commonwealth of Pennsylvania*, 334 F. Supp. 1257 (E.D. Pa. 1972); Education of All Handicapped Children Act of 1975, Pub. L. No. 94-142, 20 U.S.C. § 401 (Supp. 1975); Rehabilitation Act of 1973, § 504, 20 U.S.C. § 794-992 (Supp. 1975); *cf.*, B.D. Sales, D.M. Powell, & R. van Duizend (Eds.), *Disabled Persons and the Law*. New York: Plenum Press, 1982. For further discussion of the educational rights of handicapped persons, see Chapter 38.

9. Pylyer v. Doe, 457 U.S. 202, 102 S. Ct. 2382 (1982).

10. Martinez v. Bynum, 461 U.S. 321, 103 S. Ct. 1838 (1983). But see Horton v. Marshall Public Schools, 769 F.2d 1323 (8th Cir. 1985) (holding unconstitutional exclusion of children who resided with relatives other than parents or legal guardians).

11. Delgado v. Freeport Public School District, 499 N.Y.S.2d 606 (Sup. Ct. 1986).

12. Frazier v. Superintendent of Public Instruction, 795 P.2d 629 (Wash. 1986).

13. University Center, Inc. v. Ann Arbor Public Schools, 191 N.W.2d 302, 386 Mich. 210 (1971).

14. Because of the high educational costs for some handicapped children, complex financial questions have arisen respecting the obligation for children housed in state institutions located within a single district. Cf., Chapter 38.

15. Nutt v. Board of Education, 278 P. 1065, 128 Kan. 507 (1929).

16. Kennedy v. Gurley, 95 So. 34, 208 Ala. 623 (1923).

17. Bright v. Beard, 157 N.W. 501, 132 Minn. 375 (1916).

18. Mentally retarded children who were serum

hepatitis carriers could not be excluded from school under § 504 of the Rehabilitation Act. New York Association for Retarded Children v. Carey, 612 F.2d 644 (2d Cir. 1979). Courts sustained a board's policy that children with AIDS would not be excluded automatically, but instead reviewed on a case-by-case basis. District 27 Community School Board v. Board of Education, 502 N.Y.S.2d 325 (Sup. Ct. 1986); Thomas v. Atascadero Unified School District, 622 F. Supp. 376 (C.D. Cal. 1987).

19. State *ex rel.* Thompson v. Marion County Board of Education, 302 S.W.2d 57, 202 Tenn. 29 (1957).

20. Anderson v. Canyon Independent School District (Tex. Civ. App.) 412 S.W.2d 387 (1967); Board of Education v. Bentley, 383 S.W.2d 677 (1964).

21. McLeod v. State, 122 So. 737, 154 Miss. 468 (1929) Perry v. Grenada Municipal Separate School District, 300 F. Supp. 748 (1969).

22. *See, e.g.,* Planned Parenthood of Central Missouri v. Danforth, 428 U.S. 52, 96 S. Ct. 2831 (1976); Zablocki v. Redhail, 434 U.S. 374, 98 S. Ct. 673 (1978).

23. U.S. by Wheeler v. Choctaw County Board of Education, 310 F. Supp. 804 (1969); Wheeler v. Durham City Board of Education, 521 F.2d 1136 (1975).

24. Downs v. Board of Education of Kansas City, 336 F.2d 988 (1964); *Ex parte* Board of Education of Blount County, 84 S.2d 653, 264 Ala. 34 (1956).

25. Brown v. County School Board of Frederick County, 245 F. Supp. 549 (1965); Downs v. Board of Education of Kansas City, *supra* note 24; Harris v. Chrenshaw County Board of Education, 259 F. Supp. 167 (1966), Miller v. School District No. 2, 256 F. Supp. 370 (1966).

26. The neighborhood school concept, under which a student may attend the nearest school, is not in and of itself either constitutionally required nor forbidden, but it cannot be approved where it promotes or preserves *de jure* racial discrimination. Diaz v. San Jose Unified School District, 733 F.2d 660 (9th Cir. 1984), *cert. denied,* 105 S. Ct. 2140 (1985). See also Hobsen v. Hansen, 269 F. Supp. 401 (1967) and Smuck v. Hobsen, 408 F.2d 175 (D.C. Cir. 1969) where the court stated that "what appellants seek is assurance that a neighborhood school approach may be maintained by the Board. The decree (in *Hobsen v. Hansen*) permits retention of the neighborhood school approach where it does not result in relative overcrowding or other inequality of facilities." 408 F.2d at 186. Conversely, parents do not normally have a right to demand assignment to a neighborhood school. See Citizens Against Mandatory Bussing v. Palmason, 80 Wash. 2d 445, 495 P.2d 667 (1972).

27. School District of Soldier v. Moeller, 73 N.W.2d 43, 247 Iowa 239 (1955); School District of Mexico v. Maple Grove School District, 324 S.W.2d 369 (Mo. 1959).

28. Edwards v. State, 42 N.E. 525, 143 Ind. 84 (1895).

29. Otwell v. West, 137 S.E.2d 291, 220 Ga. 95 (1964); *In re* Hinze, 136 N.W.2d 434, 179 Neb. 69 (1965).

30. Delta Special School District No. 5 v. McGehee Special School District No. 17, 280 Ark. 489, 659 S.W.2d 508 (1983).

31. Dove v. Parham, 181 F. Supp. 504 (1960); Whitley v. Wilson City Board of Education, 457 F.2d 940 (1972); School Committee v. Board of Education, 287 N.E.2d 438 (Mass. 1972).

32. State *ex rel.* Seidl v. Jefferson County Board of Education Appeals, 548 S.W.2d 853 (1977).

33. Transportation may be required for handicapped children irrespective of their distance from the school. Section 504 of the Rehabilitation Act imposes duties on schools apart from state transportation law.

34. Cross v. Fisher, 177 S.W. 43, 132 Tenn. 31 (1951).

35. Rose v. Nashua Board of Education, 679 F.2d 279 (1st Cir. 1982).

36. Everson v. Board of Education, 330 U.S. 1, 67 S. Ct. 504 (1947). A handicapped child placed in a nonpublic school may well have a right to transportation to that pacement.

37. State v. Wilson, 297 S.W. 419, 221 Mo. App. 9 (1927).

38. Board of Education v. Sinclair, 222 N.W.2d 143, 65 Wis. 2d 179 (1974); Paulson v. Minidoka County School District, 463 P.2d 935, 93 Idaho 469 (1970).

39. Chandler v. South Bend Community School Corporation, 312 N.E.2d 915, 160 Ind. App. 592 (1974).

40. Board of Education v. Sinclair, *supra* note 38; Bond v. Public Schools of Ann Arbor School District, 178 N.W.2d 484, 383 Mich. 693 (1970).

41. Dowell v. School District No. 1, Boone County, 250 S.W.2d 127, 220 Ark. 828 (1952).

42. State *ex rel.* Gibbs v. Martin, 56 N.E.2d 148, 143 Ohio St. 491 (1944). States may assist local districts where the cost of a student's education is extraordinary (e.g., by increasing the state aid for that category of student).

43. Brown v. Union Free School, 398 N.Y.S.2d 710, 59 A.D.2d 761 (1977); Jeter v. Ellenville Central School District, 360 N.E.2d 1086, 392 N.Y.S.2d 403 (1977).

44. Hatch v. Goerke, 502 F.2d 1189 (1974); People v. Turner, 263 P.2d 685, 121 Cal. App. 2d 361, *appeal dismissed,* 347 U.S. 972, 74 S. Ct. 785 (1953); Snyder v. Town of Newton, 161 A.2d 770, 147 Conn. 374, *appeal dismissed,* 81 S. Ct. 692, 365 U.S. 299 (1960).

45. Berry v. Macon County Board of Education, 380 F. Supp. 1244 (1971); Roman Catholic Welfare Corporation of San Francisco v. City of Piedmont, 289 P.2d 438, 45 Cal. 2d 325 (1955).

46. Dilger v. School District, 352 P.2d 564, 222 Or. 108 (1960); Perry v. School District, 344 P.2d 1036, 54 Wash. 2d 886 (1959).

47. *Compare* Zorach v. Clausen, 343 U.S. 306, 72 S. Ct. 679 (1952) *with* McCollum v. Board of Education, 333 U.S. 203, 68 S. Ct. 461 (1948). Also, there are stringent, if inconsistent limits on providing public aid to private school students, particularly in parochial schools. Cf. T. van Geel, *The Courts and*

American Education. Buffalo, N.Y.: Prometheus Books, 1987, pp. 31–46.

48. Commonwealth v. Bey, 70 A.2d 693, 166 Pa. Super. Ct. 136 (1950); Commonwealth v. Smoker, 110 A.2d 740, 117 Pa. Super. Ct. 435 (1955). In *Bey* the parents were Mohammedans who refused to send their children to public school on Fridays.

49. 92 S. Ct. 1526, 406 U.S. 205 (1972).

50. See e.g., State v. Kasuboski, 275 N.W.2d 101 (Wis. App. 1978); Duro v. District Attorney, Second Judicial District of North Carolina, 712 F.2d 96 (1983); Hill v. State, 410 So. 2d 431 (Ala. App. 1981). Most but not all such efforts have been unsuccessful. Cf. R.D. Mawdsley, *Compulsory Attendance Laws under Attack,* 30 West's Educ. L. Rep. 627 (1986). Some states have created statutory "Amish" exemptions, also seeking to limit eligibility. At least one such statute has withstood constitutional attack. Fellowship Baptist Church v. Benton, 815 F.2d 485 (8th Cir. 1987).

51. Pierce v. Society of Sisters, 45 S. Ct. 571, 268 U.S. 510 (1925).

52. See J.G. Carpenter, *State Regulation of Religious Schools,* 14 J.L. & Educ. 229 (1985).

53. Cf. P.M. Lines, *Private Education Alternatives and State Regulation,* 12 J.L. & Educ. 189 (1983).

54. Many state laws have been modified, either in response to a lawsuit or in anticipation of one. Courts have been resistant to granting exemptions absent religious motivations, and have often attempted to preserve legislative standards, unsurprisingly. For a critical review of statutory and case law, as well as recommendations for a coherent judicial analysis, see D.M. Sacken, *Regulating Nonpublic Education: A Search for Just Law and Policy,* 98 Am. J. Educ. 394 (1988).

55. As part of recent educational reform agenda, some state legislatures have become more aggressive and preemptive in regulating local curricular choice. Cf. M.W. Kirst (Ed.), *The Vanishing Myth of Local Control,* Phi Delta Kappan (November 1984).

56. Miller v. School District No. 2, Clarendon County, 256 F. Supp. 370 (1966).

57. Of course, classroom assignments of individual students must be made in a racially nondiscriminatory fashion. Adams v. Rankin County Board of Education, 524 F.2d 928 (1976); Moore v. Tangipahoa Parish School Board; 304 F. Supp. 244, *appeal dismissed,* 421 F.2d 1407 (1969). In Hobsen v. Hansen, 269 F. Supp. 401 (1967) the court also held that "tracking" of students in the District of Columbia as practiced violated their constitutional rights. Students were divided into separate tracks ranging from "basic" for the slow students to "honors" for gifted students. Such a system was impermissible because disadvantaged children, primarily black, were relegated to lower tracks based on intelligence tests largely standardized on white middle-class children, where they received reduced and unequal educational opportunity.

58. Cf. D.N. Bersoff, *Reguarding Psychologists Testily: Legal Regulation of Psychological Assessment in the Public Schools,* 39 MD L. Rev. 27 (1979).

59. 793 F.2d 969 (9th Cir. 1984) (This is the last incarnation of a case that produced several voluminous opinions.)

60. See, e.g., PASE v. Hannon, 506 F. Supp. 831 (N.D. Ill. 1980). For a comprehensive discussion of "IQ test" litigation, see R. Elliott, *Litigating Intelligence.* Dover, Mass: Auburn House, 1987.

61. More recently, the Eleventh Circuit held that achievement grouping that remedied disadvantage through better educational opportunities was constitutionally permissible. Georgia State Conference of Branches of NAACP v. State of Georgia, 775 F.2d 1403 (11th Cir. 1985). Tracking remains a highly controversial, if pervasive educational practice; for a sharp critical analysis of tracking, see J. Oakes, *Keeping Track: How Schools Structure Inequality.* New Haven, CT: Yale Univeristy Press, 1985.

62. The seminal case here is Lau v. Nichols, 414 U.S. 563, 94 S. Ct. 786 (1974), where the Supreme Court required that schools "open" their curriculum to language minorities. Since that time, both assessment and appropriate programs for language minorities have become complex, disputations issues. For a recent case that captures both these qualities, see Castenda v. Pickard, 648 F.2d 989 (5th Cir. 1981). One federal court has treated speakers of "Black English" as a linguistic minority. Martin Luther King, Jr. Elementary School Children v. Michigan Board of Education, 451 F. Supp. 1324 (E.D. Mich, 1978), and 473 F. Supp. 1371 (E.D. Mich. 1979).

63. *See* Lau v. Nichols, id.; Board of Education v. Rowley, 458 U.S. 176 (1982).

64. Assessment practices in classifying students for educational placement are significantly affected by federal statutes. A good example is P.L. 94-142, which requires evaluation of children both in native language and using multiple procedures. See 34 C.F.R. § 300.532 (1985). *Cf.* K. Heller, W. Holtzman, & S. Messick, *Placing Children in Special Education: A Strategy for Equity.* Washington, D.C.: National Academy Press, 1982.

65. Morgan v. Board of Education, Trico Community School Unit School District No. 176, 317 N.E.2d 393, 22 Ill. App. 3d 241 (1974).

66. Board of Curators v. Horowitz, 98 S. Ct. 948 (1978). Courts are also reluctant to scrutinize carefully or "second guess" these educational judgments.

67. Bright v. Isenbarger, 314 F. Supp. 1382, *aff'd.* 445 F.2d 412 (1971). Cf. D. Shelton, *Legislative Control over Public School Curriculum,* 15 Williamette L. Rev. 473 (1979).

68. Scopes v. State, 289 S.W. 363, 154 Tenn. 105 (1927); Epperson v. Arkansas, 393 U.S. 97 (1968).

69. Daniel v. Waters, 515 F.2d 485 (1975).

70. Willoughby v. Stever, 504 F.2d 271, *cert. denied,* 420 U.S. 927 (1975); Wright v. Houston Independent School District, 366 F. Supp. 1208, *cert. denied,* 417 U.S. 969 (1974).

71. J. Hefley, *Textbooks on Trial.* Wheaton, Ill: Victor Books, 1976.

72. Edwards v. Aguillard, 107 S. Ct. 2573 (1987); *accord,* McLean v. Arkansas Board of Education, 529 F. Supp. 1255 (E.D. Ark. 1982). In both these cases, the key finding by the court was the improper motivation of the decision makers.

73. The Supreme Court articulated this interest in

Abington School District v. Schempp, 374 U.S. 203 (1963), which prohibited the prevasive practice of school-initiated religious instruction. Such practices were held to violate the establishment clause of the First Amendment. Parenthetically, teachers who introduce religious activities into public school classrooms are subject to dismissal. See, e.g., Lynch v. Indiana State University Board of Trustees, 378 N.E.2d 900 (Ind. App. 1978).

74. Mercer v. Michigan State Board of Education, 379 F. Supp. 580, aff'd., 95 S. Ct. 673, 419 U.S. 1081 (1974).

75. Cornwell v. State Board of Education, 314 F. Supp. 340 cert., denied, 400 U.S. 942 (1970); Todd v. Rochester Community Schools, 29 N.W.2d 90, 14 Mich. App. 320 (1970); Williams v. Board of Education, 388 F. Supp. 93, aff'd., 530 F.2d 972 (1975).

76. The Supreme Court recognized the constitutional quality of those parental interests over 60 years ago. See Pierce v. Society of Sisters, 268 U.S. 510 (1925). The Court currently describes this interest as a type of "highly personal relationship" that warrants "a substantial measure of sanctuary from unjustified interference by the State." Roberts v. United States Jaycees, 104 S. Ct. 3244, 3250 (1984).

77. See M. Hirschoof, Parents and the Public School Curriculum: Is There a Right to Have One's Child Excused from Objectionable Instruction? 50 S. Cal. L. Rev. 871 (1977).

78. The two "secular humanism" cases are Mozert v. Hawkins County Board of Education, 827 F.2d 1058 (6th Cir. 1987). reversing, 647 F. Supp. 1194 (E.D. Tenn. 1986), and Smith v. Board of School Commissioners, 827 F.2d 684 (11th Cir. 1987), reversing 655 F. Supp. 939 (S.D. Ala. 1987). See also Grove v. Mead School District No. 354, 753 F.2d 1528 (9th Cir. 1985).

79. Board of Education v. Pico, 457 U.S. 853 (1982). See also Seyfried v. Walton, 668 F.2d 214 (3d Cir. 1981) (school officials' decision to cancel a student performance of Pippin upheld because the production was an integral part of the educational program).

80. Baker v. Board of Education, 307 F. Supp. 517 (1969); Burnside v. Byars, 363 F.2d 744 (1966).

81. Johnson v. Joint School District No. 60, 508 P.2d 547 (Idaho 1973). Cf. S. Goldstein, The Scope of School Board Authority to Regulate Student Status and Conduct: A Nonconstitutional Analysis, 117 U. Pa. L. Rev. 403 (1969).

82. Tinker v. Des Moines Community School District, 89 S. Ct. 733, 393 U.S. 503 (1969).

83. Leonard v. School Committee of Attleboro, 212 N.E.2d 468, 349 Mass. 704 (1965).

84. Richards v. Thurston, 424 F.2d 1281 (1970).

85. Sullivan v. Houston Independent School District, 475 F.2d 1071, cert. denied, 94 S. Ct. 461, 414 U.S. 1032 (1973).

86. Eisner v. Stanford Board of Education, 440 F.2d 803 (2d Cir. 1971).

87. Melton v. Young, 328 F. Supp. 88, cert. denied, 93 S. Ct. 1926, 411 U.S. 951 (1973).

88. Citizens Against Mandatory Busing v. Palmason, 495 P.2d 657, 80 Wash. 2d 445 (1972).

89. Streich v. Board of Education, 147 N.W. 779, 34 S.D. 169 (1915).

90. Breese v. Smith, 510 P.2d 159 (1972). Such a policy necessarily involves an interference with the child's right to an education. It may also have implications under the Rehabilitation Act. See M. Welker, The Impact of AIDS upon Public Schools: A Problem for Jurisprudence, 33 Educ. L. Rep. 603 (1986).

91. Hanzel v. Arter, 625 F. Supp. 1259 (S.D. Ohio 1985); Mannis v. State ex rel DeWitt School District No. 1, 398 S.W.2d 206, 240 Ark. 42, cert. denied, 86 S. Ct. 1864, 384 U.S. 972 (1966).

92. Barber v. Rochester School Board, 135 A. 159, 82 N.H. 135 (1926).

93. In re Elwell, 284 N.Y.S.2d 924, 55 Misc. 2d 252 (1967); Maier v. Besser, 341 N.Y.S.2d 411, 73 Misc. 2d 241 (1972).

94. United States v. Ballard, 322 U.S. 78 (1944); Dalli v. Board of Education, 267 N.E.2d 219 (Mass. 1971).

95. Fenton v. Stear, 423 F. Supp. 767 (1976).

96. For instance, a court held that a student could not be disciplined for an obscene gesture to a teacher off school grounds and after school hours. Klein v. Smith, 635 F. Supp. 1440 (D. Me. 1986).

97. Bolding v. State, 4 S.W. 579, 23 Tex. App. 172 (1887).

98. Hobbs v. Germany, 49 So. 515, 94 Miss. 469 (1909).

99. Coggins v. Board of Education, 28 S.E.2d 527, 223 N.C. 763 (1944); Gentry v. Memphis Federation of Musicians, 151 S.W.2d 1081, 177 Tenn. 566 (1941); Starkey v. Board of Education, 381 P.2d 718, 14 Utah 2d 227 (1963).

100. Florida High School Activities Association v. Bryant, 313 So. 2d 57 (1975); Marino v. Waters, 220 So. 2d 802 (1969); State ex rel Missouri State High School Activities Association v. Schoenlaub, 507 S.W.2d 354 (1974); Wright v. Arkansas Athletic Association, 501 F.2d (1974).

101. State ex rel Ohio High School Athletics Association v. Judges of the Court of Common Pleas, 181 N.E.2d 261, 173 Ohio St. 239 (1962); Kampmeier v. Nyquist, 553 F.2d 296 (1977).

102. Although schools normally win such cases, the costs cannot be insignificant. Cf. C. Nolte, Judicial Intervention in School Athletics: The Changing Scene, 8 Educ. L. Rep. 1 (1983).

103. Spring Branch Independent School District v. Stamos, 695 S.W.2d 556 (1985), appeal dismissed, 106 S. Ct. 1170 (1986).

104. Title IX is 20 U.S.C. §1681 et seq. (1976); its implementing regulations are found at 34 C.F.R. § 106 (1985).

105. 34 CFR §106.41 (1985). The demand that schools provide comparable opportunities has not been translated into a requirement of equal expenditure levels.

106. See e.g., Yellow Springs v. Ohio High School Athletic Association, 647 F.2d 651 (6th Cir. 1981); O'Connor v. Board of Education District No. 23, 545 F. Supp. 376 (N.D. Ill. 1982). Parenthetically, boys seeking access to girls' teams have fared less well. Clark v. Arizona Interscholastic Association, 695 F.2d 1126 (9th Cir. 1982), cert. denied, 464 U.S. 818 (1983).

107. Hoover v. Meiklejohn, 430 F. Supp. 1117 (D. Colo. 1977) (soccer).

108. A school's success or failure may depend on the availability of a single gender team for that sport (i.e., a boys' and girls' basketball team) or the overall range of alternatives for both sexes. Also, state law may be important; schools in states with an equal rights amendment may have less discretion.

109. Holroyd v. Eibling, 188 N.E.2d 797, 116 Ohio App. 440 (1963); Satan Fraternity v. Board of Public Instruction, 22 So. 2d 892, 156 Fla. 222 (1945).

110. Passel v. Fort Worth Independent School District, 453 S.W.2d 888, *cert denied*, 91 S. Ct. 1667, 402 U.S. 968 (1970).

111. Fertich v. Michener, 11 N.E. 605, 111 Ind. 472 (1887).

112. Segar v. Rockford School District Board of Education, 148 N.E. 289, 317 Ill. 418 (1925).

113. Boume v. State, 52 N.W. 710, 35 Neb. 1 (1892).

114. Stromberg v. French, 236 N.W. 477, 60 N.D. 750 (1931).

115. Bishop v. Houston Independent School District, 29 S.W. 2d 312, 119 Tex. 403 (1930).

116. *Cf.* L. Bartlett, *Hair and Dress Codes Revisited*, 33 Educ. L. Rep. 7 (1986).

117. Jones v. Day, 89 So. 906, 127 Miss. 136 (1921); Pugsley v. Sellmeyer, 250 S.W. 538, 158 Ark. 247 (1923).

118. Miller v. Gillis, 315 F. Supp. 94 (1969).

119. Bannister v. Paradis, 316 F. Supp. 185 (1970).

120. Scott v. Board of Education, 305 N.Y.S.2d 601, 61 Misc. 333 (1969).

121. Breen v. Kahl, 419 F.2d 1034, *cert. denied*, 90 S. Ct. 1836, 398 U.S. 937 (1969).

122. Brownlee v. Bradley County Tennessee Board of Education, 311 F. Supp. 1360 (1970); Richards v. Thurston, 424 F.2d 1281 (1970); Jackson v. Dorrier, 424 F.2d 213, *cert. denied*, 91 S. Ct. 55, 400 U.S. 850 (1970).

123. Akin v. Board of Education, 262 Cal. App. 2d 162, 68 Cal. Rptr. 557, *cert. denied*, 89 S. Ct. 668, 393 U.S. 1041 (1968); Leonard v. School Committee of Atteboro, *supra* note 83; Mercer v. Board of Trustees, 538 S.W.2d 201 (1976).

124. Brick v. Board of Education, 305 F. Supp. 1316 (1969).

125. Neuhaus v. Torrey, 310 F. Supp. 192 (1970).

126. Black v. Cothren, 316 F. Supp. 468 (1970); Breen v. Kahl, *supra* note 121; Laine v. Dittman, 259 N.E.2d 824, 125 Ill App. 2d 136 (1974).

127. West Virginia State Board of Education v. Barnette, 63 S. Ct. 1178, 319 U.S. 624 (1942).

128. Banks v. Board of Public Instruction, 314 F. Supp. 285, S.D. Fla. (1970).

129. Board of Directors v. Green, 147 N.W.2d 854, 259 Iowa 1260 (1967); Estay v. Lafourche Parish School Board, 230 So. 2d 443 (1969).

130. Kissik v. Garland Independent School District, 330 S.W.2d 708 (1959); State *ex rel* Baker v. Stevenson, 189 N.E.2d 181, 27 Ohio App. 2d 223 (1962).

131. Zablocki v. Redhail, 434 U.S. 374 (1978).

132. Holt v. Shelton, 341 F. Supp. 821 (1972).

133. Sturrup v. Mahan, 305 N.E.2d 877, 261 Ind. 463 (1974).

134. Indiana High School Athletic Association v. Raike, 329 N.E.2d 66 (1975).

135. 45 CFR §83.37 (1988).

136. Ambroggio v. Board of Education, 427 N.E.2d 1029 (Ill. App. 1981).

137. Christian v. Jones, 100 So. 99, 211 Ala. 161 (1924).

138. McLean Independent School District v. Andres, 333 S.W.2d 886 (1960).

139. Casey County Board of Education v. Luster, 282 S.W.2d 333 (1955).

140. Hoyem v. Manhattan Beach City School District, 585 P.2d 851 (Cal. 1978).

141. Cal. Const. art. I, § 28(C).

142. *See, generally*, G. Nicholson, J. Rapp, & F. Carrington, *Campus Safety: A Legal Imperative*, 33 Educ. L. Rep. 981 (1986).

143. *Compare* Jones v. Latexo Independent School District, 499 F. Supp. 223 (E.D. Tex. 1980) (applying the exclusionary rule), *with* Morale v. Griegel, 422 F. Supp. 988 (D.N.H. 1976).

144. 105 S. Ct. 733 (1985).

145. For a thorough discussion of the complexities of school searches, see T. van Geel, *The Courts and American Education Law*. Buffalo, N.Y.: Prometheus Books, 1987, pp. 327–336.

146. *See, e.g.*, Jones v. Latexo Independent School District, *supra* notes 143; Doe v. Renfrow, 475 F. Supp. 1012 (N.D. 1979), *aff'd in part*, 631 F.2d 91 (7th Cir. 1980), *cert. denied*, 451 U.S. 1022 (1981).

147. Doe v. Renfrow, *id.* Justice Brennan, in dissenting to denial of *certiorari*, commented that a strip search of the 13-year-old female plaintiff violated not only her constitutional rights, but "any known standard of human decency." 451 U.S. 1022 (Brennan, J., dissenting).

148. Odenheim v. Carlstadt–East Rutherford Regional School District, 510 A.2d 709 (N.J. App. 1985); Anable v. Ford, 653 F. Supp. 22 (W.D. Ark, 1985).

149. 89 S. Ct. 733, 393 U.S. 503 (1968). High school students, however, may be treated differently than students in elementary schools or in college. Thus, high school students are seen as more adolescent and in a more immature stage of life and less able than college students to screen fact from propaganda. Baker v. Board of Education, 307 F. Supp. 517 (1969); Widmar v. Vincent, 454 U.S. 263 (1981).

150. In discussing students' expressive activities, courts have included under the First Amendment's protection direct speech acts, both written and oral, and "symbolic" speech acts, such as Tinker's black armband, buttons, and other emblems, even remaining silent as a communicative act.

151. Burnside v. Byars, 363 F.2d 744 (1966); Eisner v. Stamford Board of Education, 440 F.2d 803 (1971); Tinker v. Des Moines Community School District, *supra* note 82.

152. Fujishima v. Board of Education, 460 F.2d 1355 (1972); Nitzberg v. Parks, 525 F.2d 378 (1975); Peterson v. Board of Education, 370 F. Supp 1208 (1973); Sullivan v. Houston Independent School District, 333 F. Supp. 1149 (1971). The court noted that the school may lawfully prohibit students from reading such material during class periods.

153. Scoville v. Board of Education, 425 F.2d 10, *cert. denied,* 91 S. Ct. 51, 400 U.S. 826 (1970).

154. Baker v. Board of Education, *supra* note 149.

155. Zuker v. Panitz, 299 F. Supp. 102 (1969).

156. Eisner v. Stamford Board of Education, *supra* note 151.

157. Given such broad principles, case outcomes are necessarily inconsistent, driven by contextual circumstances. Suffice it to say, prior restraint is possible in schools, but a reviewing court must be persuaded that school officials acted in good faith and from proper motivations (i.e., to protect the education or safety of students).

158. 563 F.2d 512 (1977).

159. Kuhlmeier v. Hazelwood School District, 108 S. Ct. 562 (1988); Gambino v. Fairfax County School, 429 F. Supp. 731 (E.D.Va.), *aff'd,* 564 F.2d 157 (4th Cir. 1977).

160. *Id.* Even if a school newspaper is explicitly curricular and subject to substantial school regulation, a school would still be subject to the restrained standard that it cannot act in a wholly arbitrary and capricious manner.

161. Kuhlmeier v. Hazelwood School District, *supra* note 159. This does not imply that there are no limits; some material or expression is unsuitable to a student at any level of public schools.

162. 106 S. Ct. 3159 (1986).

163. See e.g., Sullivan v. School District, 307 F. Supp. 1322 (S.D. Tex. 1969).

164. Wallace v. Jaffee, 105 S. Ct. 2479 (1985). Any effort to regulate a student's prayer should be subject to free speech analysis under Tinker v. Des Moines. Cf. Widmar v. Vincent, *supra* note 149 (applying free speech analysis in a college setting).

165. Bender v. Williamsport Area High School, 741 F.2d 538 (3d Cir. 1984). *Accord,* Lubbock Civil Liberties Union v. Lubbock Independent School District, 669 F.2d 1038 (5th Cir. 1982).

166. 106 S. Ct. 1326 (1986). The Court reversed the prohibition of the student group, but on the ground that the school board member who appealed the trial court's decision did not have standing to appeal. The substantive question of school-recognized, student religious groups remains unanswered.

167. In 1984, Congress passed the Equal Access Act, assuring student groups and others to hold religious, political and philosophical meetings in public schools. 20 U.S.C. §4071 (1984). See R. Brandley & F. Delon, *Influence of the Equal Access Act on School Facilities Usage Policies,* 34 Educ. L. Rep. 653 (1987).

168. 20 U.S.C.A. § 1232g et seq. The accompanying regulations are set down in 34 C.F.R. pt. 99 (1985).

169. Interest in controlling child abuse has made those statutes a pervasive reality in educators' lives. There is little research which evaluates the statutes' effects. Cf. F. Lombard, M. Michlak, & T. Pearlman, *Identifying the Abused Child: A Study of Reporting Practices of Teachers,* 63 U. Detroit L. Rev. 657 (1986).

170. Under such a statute it is unclear whether a communication between a student and a school psychologist or counselor would be protected.

171. Tarasoff v. Regents of the University of California, 33 Cal. App. 3d 275 (1973).

172. A relatively recent federal law attempts to protect student and parental privacy by regulating school use of psychological and psychiatric testing and requiring parental access to curricular materials. 20 U.S.C. § 1232h (1985).

173. Cf. L. Fischer & G. Sorensen, *School Law for Counselors, Psychologists and Social Workers.* New York: Longman, 1985.

174. Leonard v. School Committee of Attleboro, *supra* note 83; People v. Jackson, 319 N.Y.S.2d 731 (1971).

175. Kinzer v. Independent School District, 105 N.W. 686, 129 Iowa 441 (1906); Jones v. Cody, 92 N.W. 495, 132 Mich. 13 (1902).

176. R.R. v. Board of Education, 263 A.2d 180, 109 N.J. Super. 337 (1970).

177. Sullivan v. Houston Independent School District, *supra* note 152.

178. Sims v. Board of Education, 329 F. Supp. 678 (1971). Of course, most school policies will contain some broadly phrased language, such as prohibiting behavior detrimental to the order of the school. A wide variety of behavior can be punished under such language.

179. It is not clear, however, that in such circumstances, the student cannot legally be punished. If the misconduct is *by* the parent, the child may not be punished for parental actions. St. Ann v. Palisi, 495 F.2d 423 (5th Cir. 1974).

180. Discipline should not be excessive or humiliating. School officials are subject to liability for assault and battery or for intentional infliction of emotional distress. Mott v. Endicott School District, 713 P.2d 98 (Wash. 1986); Jefferson v. Ysleta Independent School District, 817 F.2d 303 (5th Cir. 1987).

181. Board of Education of Rogers, Arkansas v. McCluskey, 102 S. Ct. 3469 (1982); Petry v. Flaughter, 505 F. Supp. 1087 (E.D. Ky. 1981).

182.. Fertich v. Michener, *supra* note 111.

183. Carr v. Wright, 423 S.W.2d 521 (1968); Drum v. Miller, 47 S.E. 421, 135 N.C. 204 (1904); Marlar v. Bill, 178 S.W.2d 634, 181 Tenn. 100 (1944).

184. 97 S. Ct. 1401, 430 U.S. 651 (1976).

185. They are also subject to dismissal. Mott v. Endicott School District, *supra* note 180.

186. The court took judicial notice that the purposes to be served by corporal punishment would be long past if formal notice, hearings, and representation were required, and that due process interests were protected by the availability of state law remedies (i.e., civil liability).

187. Carr v. Wright, *supra* note 183; Houeye v. St. Helena Parish School Board, 67 So. 2d 553, La. 966 (1953); Suits v. Glover, 71 So. 2d 49, 260 Ala. 449 (1954); Tinkham v. Kole, 110 N.W.2d 258, 252 Iowa 1303 (1961).

188. Lander v. Seaver, 32 Vt. 114 (1859); State v. Mizner, 50 Iowa 145 (1878).

189. Calway v. Williamson, 36 A.2d 377, 130 Conn. 575 (1944); Patterson v. Nutter, 7 A. 273, 78 Me. 509 (1886).

190. Boyd v. State, 7 So. 268, 88 Ala. 169 (1890); Calaway v. Williamson, *supra* note 189; Melen v. McLaughlin, 176 A. 297, 107 Vt. 111 (1935); Suits v. Glover, *supra* note 187.

191. Wood v. Strickland, 95 S. Ct. 992, 420 U.S. 308 (1975).

192. People v. Wehmeyer, 108 Ill. Dec. 909, 509 N.E.2d 605 (Ill. App. 1987).

193. A few state legislatures have prohibited corporal punishment in all public schools. *See, e.g.,* Mass. Gen. Laws Ann., c. 71 § 37G (1985); N.J. Stat. Ann. 18A:6–1 (1968). Most states permit local boards to choose whether their schools will use corporal punishment.

194. The Fifth Circuit has decided that *all* such cases will be handled under state law. Ingraham v. Wright, 498 F.2d 248 (5th Cir. 1974). The Fourth and Tenth Circuits will allow federal courts to hear claims involving school acts which "shock the conscience." Hall v. Tawney, 621 F.2d 607 (4th Cir. 1980); Garcia v. Miera, 817 F.2d 650 (10th Cir. 1987).

195. Baker v. Owen, 395 F. Supp. 294 (M.D.N.C.), *aff'd mem.,* 423 U.S. 907 (1975).

196. Belasco v. Board of Education, 486 A.2d 358 (Pa. Commw. Ct. 1985).

197. Cole v. Greenfield-Central Community Schools, 657 F. Supp. 56 (S.D. Ind. 1986), might be suggestive of some courts' attitude. There, a 9-year old hyperactive, emotionally disturbed child's conduct was controlled by a variety of techniques, including paddling, isolation in the classroom, denial of field trips, and taping the child's mouth shut. All but the last were approved by the court, which observed that a school "cannot be subjugated by the tyrannical behavior of a nine-year-old child." 657 F. Supp. at 63. Normally, such a child now will be protected by the procedures of P.L. 94–142.

198. J.E. Jackson, *The Coerced Use of Ritalin for Behavior Control in Public Schools:* Legal Challenges, Clearinghouse Rev. 181–193 (1976). This chapter does not cover the legal limitations placed on the use of other intervention techniques since that topic is covered in Bersoff's chapter in this volume. To the extent that a child was protected under P.L. 94–142, the school's discretion to exclude would be significantly reduced.

199. Board of Education v. Bentley, 383 S.W.2d 677 (1964); Flory v. Smith, 134 S.E. 360, 145 Va. 164 (1926); Nicholls v. Lynn 7 N.E.2d 577, 297 Mass. 65 (1973); Texarkana Independent School District v. Lewis, 470 S.W.2d 727 (1971).

200. Board of Education v. Booth, 62 S.W. 872, 110 Ky. 807 (1901); Douglass v. Campbell, 116 S.W. 211, 89 Ark. 254 (1909); State *ex rel* Dresser v. District Board, 116 N.W. 232, 135 Wis. 619 (1908). The age of these cases should be noted. Suspension of students in the absence of their knowledge of the particular rule would raise procedural due process concerns today.

201. Fenton v. Stear, *supra* note 95; Bethel School District v. Fraser, *supra* note 162.

202. Courts have split on this issue. *Compare* New Braunfels Independent School District v. Armke, 658 S.W.2d 330 (Tex. Civ. App. 1983) (upholding reduction) *with* Gutierrez v. School District 4-1, 585 P.2d 935 (Col. App. 1978) (disallowing).

203. Courts have tolerated both suspensions and expulsions, as well as grade reductions based on absences and truancy, but not with consistency. Raymon v. Alvord Independent School District, 639 F.2d 257 (5th Cir. 1981); Dorsey v. Bale, 521 S.W.2d 76 (Ky. 1975).

204. Holman v. School District No. 5, 43 N.W. 996, 71 Mich. 605 (1889).

205. In Board of Education of Rogers, Arkansas v. McCluskey, *supra* note 181, the Supreme Court reminded lower federal courts to grant broad discretion to local boards in determining the needs of individual students and schools. When a board expels a child, called "academic capital punishment," by Mark Yudof, it is hardly acting on the "best interest of the child."

206. 95 S. Ct. 729, 419 U.S. 565 (1974).

207. Texarkana Independent School District v. Lewis, *supra* note 199.

208. Tibbs v. Board of Education, 276 A.2d 165, 114 N.J. Super. 287 (1971). Although the court noted that questioning should be carefully controlled by the person in charge of the hearing to prevent abuse of the witnesses.

209. Such liability would normally occur in a suit involving a claim of civil rights violation. See Carey v. Piphus, 98 S. Ct. 1042 (1978). Such litigation involves substantial complexities.

210. Cooley v. Board of School Commissioners of Mobile County, 341 F. Supp. 1375 (1972); R.R. v. Board of Education of Shore Regional High School District, 263 A.2d 180, 109 N.J. Super. 237 (1970).

211. Presumptions of good faith are powerful protections for local boards, but certain factual components can erode favorable presumptions. An example might be an extensive pattern of discriminatory outcomes. Hawkins v. Coleman, 376 F. Supp. 1330 (N.D. Tex. 1974).

212. Board of Elementary and Secondary Education v. Nix, 347 So. 2d 147 (1977); Clark v. Board of Education, 367 N.E.2d 69, 51 Ohio Misc. 71 (1977); U.S. by Marshall v. Choctaw County Board of Education, 310 F. Supp. 804 (1969).

213. For a description of the prevalence of state enacted competency testing programs, see M. McClung, *Competency Testing: Legal and Educational Issues,* 47 Fordham L. Rev. 651 (1979).

214. *Cf.* A. Logar, *Minimum Competency Testing in Schools: Legislative Action and Judicial Review,* 13 J.L. & Educ. 35 (1984).

215. *See* M. McCarthy, *Minimum Competency Testing for Students: Educational and Legal Issues,* Educ. Horizons 103–110 (1983).

216. McNeal v. Tate County School District, 508 F.2d 1017 (1975); Moses v. Washington Parish School Board, 456 F.2d 1285 (1972).

217. Debra P. v. Turlington, 474 F. Supp. 244 (M.D. Fla. 1979). *aff'd in part, vacated in part and remanded,* 644 F.2d 397 (5th Cir. 1981), *on remand* 564 F. Supp. 177 (M.D. Fla. 1983), *aff'd* 730 F.2d 1405 (11th Cir. 1984). See also Anderson v. Banks, 520 F. Supp. 472 (S.D. Ga. 1981).

218. Florida hired a consulting firm, IOX Associates, to conduct the validity study. They pursued an elaborate, wide-ranging survey process that ultimately

satisfied the courts. For a description of that process, see Debra P. v. Turlington, 564 F. Supp. 177 et seq.

219. See Debra P. v. Turlington, *supra* note 217; Anderson v. Banks, *supra* note 217. Cf. McClung, *supra* note 213.

220. This observation was made by a Fifth Circuit judge in an exchange of opinions over the equal educational opportunity implications of MCTs. He argued that to compel Florida to issue diplomas to students who failed its MCT was to "perpetuate the hollow certification that accompanied graduation pre-*Brown*." Debra P. v. Turlington, 654 F.2d 1079, 1985 (5th Cir. 1981) (denying a petition for rehearing).

221. For a presentation of the logic of the legal cause of action for educational malpractice, see Note, *Educational Malpractice: Can the Judiciary Remedy the Growing Problem of Functional Illiteracy?* 13 Suffolk U.L. Rev. 27 (1979).

222. 60 Cal. App. 3d 814, 131 Cal. Rptr. 854 (1976).

223. See Hoffman v. Board of Education, 400 N.E.2d 317, 424 N.Y.S.2d 376 (1979). Plaintiff was able to win a $750,000 jury verdict for injuries caused by a misdiagnosis and misplacement that was undiscovered for 12 years. An appellate court reversed the jury verdict, refusing to permit the cause of action.

224. Because educators operate solely in a "corporate environment," across many years, finding the "guilty party" would be quite difficult, especially as the standard of minimally adequate professional instruction is unclear. *See* Peter W., *supra* note 222.

225. See, e.g., G. Ratner, A New Legal Duty for Urban Public Schools: Effective Education in Basic Skills, 63 Tex. L. Rev. 777 (1985); L. Rothstein, Accountability for Professional Misconduct in Providing Education to Handicapped Children, 14 J.L. & Educ. 349 (1985).

226. Although nondiscriminatory enjoyment of all school opportunities is required, extracurricular activities are not considered a "right." This distinction has procedural due process consequences. See text at notes 99–103.

227. It will be recalled that the *Trachtman* court was willing to limit student speech that interfered with the privacy rights of other students. The *Kuhlmeier* court took a quite different tack, substantially limiting a school's paternalistic authority, at least for secondary students. The Supreme Court may soon address this issue, but it justified its decision to permit restriction of "lewd" speech in *Bethel School District*, in part, on the school's paternalistic powers to protect other students' sensibilities. See text *supra* at note 158 et seq.

228. *Pico* approached the identification of "learning" or "inquiry" rights for students, but only in a noncurricular context. Courts have been completely resistant to compensating students who have finished school disappointed with their aggregate learning. See text *supra* at note 221 et seq.

40

PROFESSIONAL REGULATION AND TRAINING IN SCHOOL PSYCHOLOGY

DOUGLAS T. BROWN

James Madison University

This chapter deals with the mechanisms employed by professional psychology and education for the regulation of the practice of school psychology. These mechanisms are highly diverse and are administered by both public and private agencies. School psychology, unlike other areas in psychology, emerged as a profession from a variety of subfields including clinical psychology, educational psychology, special education, and counseling. Because of this hybrid parenthood, school psychology is regulated by agencies in both psychology and education. The nature of graduate training programs in school psychology and the curriculum contained theirein also function to influence the development of standards for quality control in the profession. The purpose of this chapter is to clarify the relationships among various regulatory agencies and to provide the reader with an understanding of the interactive nature of those agencies exercising authority over training and practice in school psychology.

The lines of power and authority in the regulation of school psychology are complex and often ill-defined. As Fagan (1986) has astutely observed,

it is necessary to understand the differences between agencies which have legal regulatory power and those that exercise political/professional power. In this regard we examine graduate training, accreditation, and credentialing as they relate to the governance of school psychology. We will also examine the interaction between graduate training and credentialing. It is the interplay between these two forces that ultimately determines the nature of entry-level practice in school psychology.

HISTORICAL PERSPECTIVE

The fundamental basis for regulation in school psychology resides in the ethical principles published by the American Psychological Association (APA) (1981b) and the National Association of School Psychologists (NASP) (1985). Of particular importance to regulation is the fact that ethical standards broadly outline the requirements for competence to practice as a psychologist. More specifically, behaviors that are mandatory for effective functioning are described by these ethical principles. There is a tendency for ethical principles to be updated periodically to conform to revisions of law or to subsume an issue not previously addressed (e.g., the 1985 NASP ethics promulgate principles regarding computerized assessment and instruction). In many states ethics are recognized legally as appropriate codes of behavior for psychologists. Typically, this recognition is found in the regulations for individual licensure and/or certification laws.

The practice of psychology and, therefore, school psychology is legally regulated in most states by the state board of psychology and, in the case of school psychology, the state department of education. Most state legislatures view such regulation as a means to protect the public welfare through the imposition of quality control standards for the practice of psychology (Herbsleb, Sales, & Overcast, 1985). For the purpose of this discussion, *licensure* will be designated as that process which is administered by the state board of psychology and leads to a credential permitting the private or nonpublic practice of psychology. Conversely, the term *certification* will be used to describe that process administered by the state department of education which leads to a credential for the practice of school psychology in the public sector. Historically, most states have had statutes which permit the licensure of psychologists and, in some instances, school psychologists (Brown, Horn, & Lindstrom, 1980). The certification of school psychologists, however, has been a more recent development with significant increases in the number of states certifying school psychologists occurring within the past 15 years. Some state certification requirements are statutory in that they are written into law while others are in the form of regulations promulgated by the state department of education. This is in contrast with licensure regulations, which are almost always statutory in nature. It should be noted, however, that the specific regulations which govern the review process for candidates seeking licensure have changed considerably over the past 20 years. These regulations are generally not written into law but may be modified by the board of psychology from time to time as part of its statutory functioning.

Both the American Psychological Association (APA) and the National Association of School Psychologists (NASP) have traditionally been in-

volved in promulgating standards which are designed to have an impact on the practice of psychology and school psychology. Both organizations publish standards for the accreditation of graduate training programs (APA, 1981a; NASP, 1985). In addition, both associations publish specialty standards for the practice of school psychology. These are the *Standards for the Provision of School Psychological Services* in the case of NASP (NASP, 1984b), the *Standards for Providers of Psychological Services* (APA, 1977), and the *APA Guidelines for the Delivery of Services by School Psychologists* (1981a) in the case of APA. Cross-organizational standards also exist such as the *Joint Accreditation Standards for School Psychology* developed by APA, NASP, and the National Council for Accreditation of Teacher Education (NCATE).

As will be seen below, a review of the APA and NASP accreditation standards clearly demonstrates that their intent is to establish a uniform core curriculum in which all school psychologists can receive training. In effect, by establishing a core curriculum, NASP and APA have suggested an *entry* or minimum level of training necessary to graduate from a school psychology graduate training program. Both national associations promote their accreditation standards by requiring that programs wishing to be accredited through APA or NASP meet the minimum *core* requirements. Many states require that candidates for school psychology certification graduate from nationally accredited programs. Thus the authority link between program accreditation and the right to practice as a school psychologist is clearly established in those states.

Content of Service Provision Standards

The purpose of the NASP and APA standards for service provision (cited above) has been somewhat different from that of accreditation standards. These standards are designed to influence more directly the design and implementation of certification and licensure policies within individual states. They are also designed to promote quality control in the provision of psychological services at the local, state, and regional levels. Within that framework, the standards suggest dimensions for optimal practice as a school psychologist and define the specific skills required for practice as a school psychologist. In this regard service provision standards are more competency based, while accreditation standards tend to be more curriculum or course area/knowledge based. Clearly, the intent of both APA and NASP is to influence the nature of licensure and certification legislation regulations by promulgating credentialing and service provision standards. Put more succinctly, standards of this type attempt to designate who may use the title School Psychologist and what constitutes the minimum acceptable quality level for the provision of services.

The NASP standards focus on a variety of areas, including professional evaluation and supervision, conditions for effective service delivery, the organizational structure for psychological service units, minimum quality levels for psychological service provision, the conditions for independent practice, continuing professional development requirements, accountability requirements, the conditions for private practice, and the use of professional ethics and guidelines. The NASP standards tend also to be aimed at federal and state legislative bodies in that they encourage the inclusion of many of the service provision standards in state and federal law.

The APA standards are divided into four parts: (a) requirements for providers of school psychological services, (b) requirements for school psychological service programs, (c) accountability requirements, and (d) environmental requirements. Within these general areas the APA standards stipulate the minimum levels of staffing for quality psychological services. Also stipulated are the supervisory relationships among various psychologists in a school system. For example, the term "professional school psychologist" is used to describe the entry level for independent school-based practice. Persons not meeting this requirement must be supervised. The APA standards also require "periodic, systematic, and effective evaluations of school psychological services." They also require that the structure of a school psychology unit be clearly defined and retain a certain amount of professional autonomy from other professional groups functioning in the schools.

Both the APA and NASP service provision standards defer to each organization's accreditation and ethical standards. With the exception of the entry-level issue, both sets of standards are highly complementary with the NASP standards being somewhat more specific regarding nondiscriminatory assessment, parent/child/administrator/school psychologist interactions, and the use of assessment and intervention techniques. The APA standards specify the educational content for school psychologists. These education and training requirements are similar to the NASP accreditation standards discussed above, with the exception of requiring the doctoral degree as the entry level.

Wenger and Pryzwansky (1987) examined the impact of the *APA Guidelines for Delivery of Services by School Psychologists.* They surveyed directors of psychological services in a cross section of school districts and determined the extent to which they had implemented the service provision guidelines. Results of this survey indicated broad support for standards dealing with the structure of programs and accountability. The guidelines requiring the doctorate for entry level and those guidelines specifying the staffing levels for school psychological services were seen as more difficult, if not impossible, to implement. Care should be taken in interpreting Wenger and Pryzwansky's data since they are based on a very small return rate.

Two other recent studies (Brown, 1985; Smith, 1984) have examined the perception of school psychologists regarding the priority of services that are provided. Currently, most time is spent in assessment activities, with the least time devoted to research. Smith found that school psychologists wish to decrease significantly their assessment activities and to increase the time devoted to intervention and consultation. The need to spend substantially more time in counseling and consultation activities has also been identified. It appears that a discrepancy exists between the relatively broad roles and skills described in the NASP and APA service provision standards and those day-to-day activities described by practicing school psychologists. However, additional research will be necessary in order to clarify the relationship of service provision standards to the actual practice of school psychology.

Jurisdictional Issues

A variety of private and public agencies are involved in the regulation of school psychology. Among the private agencies the most notable are the American Psychological Association (APA), the National Association of School Psychologists (NASP), the National Council for the Accreditation of Teacher Education (NCATE), and the Council on Post-Secondary Accreditation (COPA). The public organizations most directly involved in regulation include the American Association of State Psychology Boards (AASPB), and the National Association of State Directors of Teacher Education and Certification (NASDTEC). AASPB and NASDTEC are national groups that represent state licensure boards and state teacher certification offices, respectively. Both private and public groups promote policies that protect the welfare of the consumer of psychological services. Private agencies tend also to protect the welfare of the profession. Within both types of agencies considerable debate has occurred regarding the basic competencies for school psychology training and practice. At the core of this debate are conflicting positions held by APA and NASP with regard to entry-level training. The APA specialty standards essentially require the doctoral degree as the entry-level criterion for practice as a school psychologist. In fact, APA accreditation standards are currently designed to accredit only doctoral level programs. NASP accreditation standards specify the specialist degree as the entry level for practice as a school psychologist. NASP standards recognize also the doctorate as an additional level of training possible for school psychologists. It can be seen easily that with such a fundamental discrepancy in policy, that conflict over a number of public policy issues arises between the two associations. This conflict has been well summarized by a number of researchers (Bardon, 1983; Brown, 1979; Hilke & Brantley, 1982; Lambert, 1981; Phillips, 1985; Trachtman, 1981, 1985). These issues include:

1. The presence of two parallel accreditation systems for school psychology, one directed at doctoral programs and administered by APA, and the other directed at doctoral and specialist programs and administered by NASP through NCATE. This obviously creates redundancy in the accreditation process.

2. Discrepancies between APA and NASP policy exist with regard to the balance of various core areas in graduate training. Specifically, the amount of training devoted to core psychology course work versus specialized course work in school psychology has been a focus of debate. Another area of disagreement surrounds the level of specificity in course requirements and, therefore, the degree of uniformity in core curriculum across training programs nationally.

3. The existence of conflicting standards for entry-level practice in school psychology has created considerable friction at the state level in the development of school psychology and school psychology licensure statutes. Generally, this debate has focused around attempts by state school psychological associations to establish licensure bills with an entry level at the master's or specialist level. As a result of such conflicts, a variety of training models and licensure statutes are now employed throughout the country. While specialist programs are reasonably uniform in their curricular content, doctoral programs tend to show greater heterogeneity (Brown & Minke, 1986). Approximately 20 states license nondoctoral psychologists or school psychologists, while the remaining states require the doctorate for entry level. The diversity of licensure laws enacted for school psychologists nationally has tended to restrict the role and function permitted for school psychologists when compared with other specialties in psychology. As will be discussed below, the resolution to much of this controversy may be forthcoming as NASP and APA begin to recognize the concept of specialist and doctoral programs as an interlocking continuum in the training of school psychologists (Hilke & Brantley, 1982). It must be emphasized, however, that credentialing is a state-level process and is not nationally controlled per se. While conflicting national standards exacerbate conflict in credentialing legislation, they are often not the primary impetus for conflict within a particular state. For example, sunset legislation (legislation that requires the review of licensure laws periodically) has promoted considerable interprofessional conflict in states such as Florida (Lazarus & Jackson, 1983).

CHARACTERISTICS OF GRADUATE TRAINING

In this section we present information on the nature of graduate education in school psychology. Curricular and demographic information will be reviewed as well as the major theoretical models employed to train school psychologists.

Models of Training

Two basic models of training have been employed for the training of school psychologists. These include the scientist-practitioner and the applied professional psychologist models. In the early stages of psychology a third model, scientist/researcher, was also in evidence. This model existed predominantly in doctoral programs developed within departments of educational or developmental psychology. The scientist/researcher model assumed that graduates of doctoral programs would enter academic positions and function primarily as academicians and researchers. In 1973 the Vail Conference (Korman, 1974) recommended that alternative models of training for applied psychologists be explored. As a result, the scientist/professional model was espoused as the major model for the training of applied psychologists. The scientist/professional model assumes that all psychologists receive basic training in *core* areas of psychology, including quantitative methods; personality theory; history and systems of psychology; developmental psychology; learning, motivation, and cognition; social psychology; and biological bases of behavior. Under this model other specialized course work in school or clinical psychology is added to the core psychology content. This course work tends to be idiosyncratic to the individual doctoral training program. This fact is underscored by data (Brown & Rooney, 1987) suggesting considerable heterogeneity among doctoral programs espousing the scientist/professional model with regard to *applied* course work in school psychology.

The applied professional psychologist model (Peterson, 1985) has been employed in a number of recently developed doctoral programs and in most master's and educational specialist training programs. This mdoel tends to focus more on the applied course work than core theoretical courses in psychology. Typical course work for programs espousing this model includes intelligence assessment, learning problems assessment, consultation, social problems assessment, general education, special education, behavioral intervention, personality theory, history and systems of psychology, developmental psychology, learning theory, neuropsychology, and abnormal psychology. A number of variants of the applied professional psychologist model have been developed over the years. These include the following. The professional child psychology model developed by Carboy and Curley (1976) was designed to train

practitioners in a set of specific skills presumed to be applicable with children in a variety of institutional settings. Training areas within this model include physiological development, child development, motivation, sensory processes, learning, adjustment, exceptional behavior, socialization, and research methodology. The consultation model (Dinkmeyer, 1973; Gallessich, 1974) is currently employed in a number of doctoral and specialist programs in school psychology. This model assumes that the school psychologist functions as a consultant to the school system. The emphasis in training programs employing this model tends to be more on the techniques for effective consultation than on specific psychometric or intervention technqiues. Finally, the clinical/diagnostic model (Bardon, 1965) is employed in a large number of specialist programs. This model emphasizes course work in assessment and psychotherapeutic intervention. It tends to deemphasize the theoretical aspects of psychology.

The trend in school psychology has tended away from the scientist/practitioner model and toward the applied professional psychologist model (Brown, 1987; Brown and Minke, 1986; Brown & Rooney, 1988). This is especially true in specialist-level programs. At the doctoral level, established programs tend to employ the scientist/practitioner model while newly developed programs employ the applied professional psychologist model. New specialist programs have modeled themselves after the NASP accreditation standards (1978, 1984c). A number of new doctoral programs have been developed based on the PsyD (Doctor of Psychology) model of training. This model (Peterson, 1985) assumes considerably more applied course work than is contained in the typical PhD program.

Demographic Characteristics of Graduate Programs

The number of graduate institutions offering education in school psychology has expanded considerably during the past 15 years. In 1956 only nine training programs existed (Moore, 1956). Studies have shown a continued increase in numbers of programs especially from 1965 to the present. In 1962 (Ross, 1962) 45 programs existed while in 1972 (Bardon & Walker, 1972) 112 programs were reported. By 1977 that number had climbed to 203 programs (Brown & Lindstrom, 1977). From 1977 to the present the number of programs has tended to reach an asymptote with 211 programs being identified by Brown and Minke in 1984.

Corresponding to the increase in the number of training programs has been an increase in the number of students being trained. White (1963) determined that approximately 1,055 students were in training in school psychology. Bardon and Walker (1972) estimated that approximately 3,633 students were in training. In 1977, Brown and Lindstrom calculated that 7,450 students were in training across all degree levels. From 1977 to the present the number of students entering school psychology has leveled off and may be declining.

An inspection of the degrees awarded for training for school psychology at various points in history reveals some interesting trends. In the 1960s approximately half of all students in training were at the nondoctoral level increasing steadily to about 60% by the early 1970s (Bardon & Walker, 1972; Cardon & French, 1969; White, 1963). In the Brown and Lindstrom (1977) study students were subdivided into master's, specialist, and doctoral levels. Using these criteria, 24% of the students in training were at the master's level while 53% were being trained at the specialist level. Brown and Lindstrom employed the NASP accreditation criteria to identify programs that were training students at the specialist level. At the doctoral level the number of students being trained remained relatively constant during the late 1960s and early 1970s. Brown and Minke (1984) report an increase in the number of students being trained at the doctoral level between 1977 and 1984. This increase was approximately 1% per year. Current data (Brown & Rooney, 1987) indicate that approximately 40% of the students in training in school psychology are being trained at the doctoral level. If the general trend toward increased doctoral training continues, then by the early 1990s approximately half of all students in training could be in doctoral programs. Table 1 presents demographic data summarizing the nature of graduate training in school psychology. These data were collected in 1984 (Brown & Minke).

In summary, graduate training in school psychology experienced a significant growth spurt from 1970 to 1980. In this period of time the number of programs approximately doubled as did the number of students in training. The size and complexity of training programs has increased consistently since the early 1970s with the majority of current programs training at the specialist or doctoral levels. A wide array of training models are

TABLE 1   Data Summary of School Psychology Training Programs

	1984	
	Frequency	Program[a] Response Level
States training school psychologists	42	
Training programs (total)	211	
Master's	80	
Specialist	174	
Doctoral	79	
Students in training (total)	7,293	211
Master's	1,466	80
Specialist	2,526	174
Doctoral (total)	2,301	79
EdD	421	26
PhD	1,644	57
PsyD	236	6
Total students graduated		
1981	2,131	
1982	2,350	

[a] This column contains the number of programs providing data in a given category. Some programs award more than one type of degree.

employed in school psychology graduate programs. However, programs have tended to increase in uniformity with regard to their core content with many programs meeting NASP/NCATE standards. The amount of training in applied research has tended to increase also at both the specialist and doctoral levels during the past 10 years (French & Raykovitz, 1984). In general, specialist programs in school psychology tend to be remarkable similar to their doctoral counterparts with regard to applied training. The major differences between these two levels of training are found in curriculum dealing with quantitative methods, biological bases of behavior, and areas of specialization such as psychotherapeutic intervention. While differences between doctoral and specialist level training obviously exist, further research needs to be completed in order to ascertain the relationship of these curricular differences to the practice of school psychology. This is especially important since the majority of both specialist and doctoral graduates enter public school practice (Brown & Minke, 1984).

Levels of Training

School psychology training programs are offered at three basic degree levels. These include the master's degree, the education specialist or sixth-year degree, and the doctoral degree (EdD, PhD, PsyD). The Master of Science, Master of Arts, and Master of Education degrees account for the majority of master's degrees awarded. The majority of master's degree programs are in the range 30 to 59 semester credit hours. The sixth-year degree or specialist degree is awarded in a variety of forms including the Educational Specialist, Specialist of Arts, and Advanced Graduate Specialist. Generally, programs offering this degree require from 60 to 80 graduate semester hours of course work. Doctoral degrees are offered in basically four types, the PhD, EdD, DEd, and PsyD. The PhD is clearly the most common degree awarded at the doctoral level, followed by the EdD and the PsyD. Typical doctoral programs require from 80 to 100 graduate semester hours of course work. Table 2 summarizes the distribution of credit hour requirements across various degree levels in school psychology training programs nationally. As can be seen by inspection of this table, specialist and doctoral programs show wide variation in their credit hour requirements.

Wide variation is also found among programs when examining practicum and internship hour requirements. A significant percentage of programs, particularly at the master's level, require no minimum practicum hours. Specialist programs typically require from 200 to 600 hours of practicum experience, while doctoral programs typically require from 300 to 600 hours of practicum experience. Fifty percent of master's programs require no internship. Of those requiring an internship, the range is typically from 400 to 700 clock hours of experience. At the specialist level most programs, 90%, require an internship. The typical range of hours required for this experience is from 400 to 1,300 hours. Virtually all doctoral programs require an internship with the typical range being from 1,000 to 1,600 clock hours of experience.

Curricular Characteristics of Graduate Programs

Brown and Minke (1986) have comprehensively reviewed the curriculum of specialist- and doctoral-level programs in school psychology. They per-

formed an analysis of all known school psychology programs in terms of the frequency and distribution of curricular areas across various levels of training. As a result, they isolated 26 course areas utilized by graduate training programs. These include assessment of intelligence; assessment of learning problems; assessment of social and emotional problems; other specialized assessment techniques; general education courses; exceptional education courses; quantitative methods; behavioral intervention; psychotherapeutic intervention; school-based consultation; other consultation courses; professional issues; program development; supervision/administration; personality theory; history and systems of psychology; human development; learning, motivation, and cognition; biological bases of behavior; social psychology; neuropsychology; abnormal psychology; cross-cultural spychology; electives external to psychology; specialty area courses; and other courses which were highly idiosyncratic to a particular program. In comparing curriculum between specialist and doctoral programs, Brown and Minke (1986) found that 13 course areas could be used to discriminate doctoral from specialist training. These include quantitative methods, biological bases of behavior, cross-cultural psychology, professional issues, other consultation, social psychology, psychotherapeutic intervention, program development, supervision/administration, school-based consultation, and other assessment courses as well as elective courses and specialty areas. In each of these course areas doctoral programs tended to contain more course work. Of special note were significant differences in the amount of course work in quantitative methods, biological bases of behavior, and professional issues. No differences in the amount of course work in doctoral and specialist programs was found for areas such as intelligence assessment, learning problems assessment, social/emotional assessment, general and special education, behavioral interventions, personality theory, history and systems, developmental psychology, learning theory, neuropsychology, and abnormal psychology. On the basis of this curricular analysis, Brown and Minke (1986) concluded that specialist and doctoral programs are comparable in much of the core course work recommended by NASP and APA. Doctoral programs contain much more comprehensive course work in quantitative methods, biological bases of behavior, and professional issues. Doctoral programs also contained specialty areas concentrations (e.g.,

TABLE 2   Graduate Credit Hours Required Across Degree Levels

	Required Credit Hours										
Degree Awarded	29 or Fewer	30–45	46–59	60–66	67–79	80–89	90–99	100–109	110–119	120–129	130 or More
Master's											
N	1	78	20	37							
%	0.7	57	15	27							
Specialist											
N		1	6	96	28	3	2	1			
%		0.7	4	70	20	2	1.5	0.7			
Doctorate											
N				6	7	7	36	11	7	4	1
%				7	9	9	46	14	9	5	1.2

counseling, consultation, and program evaluation) which are not typically found in specialist programs. Furthermore, almost all doctoral programs require a dissertation or its equivalent. Only about 25% of the specialist programs have a research requirement.

On the basis of the major studies conducted on graduate training in school psychology, a number of conclusions can be drawn (Bardon & Walker, 1972; Brown & Minke, 1984; Cardon & French, 1969; French & McCloskey, 1980; Teglasi & Pumroy, 1982).

1. Doctoral programs contain a much more comprehensive research and quantitative methods component than do specialist programs. Recent data collected by Brown and Rooney (1987) suggest that this component often outweighs many applied aspects of doctoral training programs.

2. The ratio of applied to theoretical course work differs in specialist versus doctoral-level training programs with specialist programs containing relatively more applied course work. A study by Smith (1984) indicates that school psychologists devote 54% of their time to assessment, 23% to intervention, 19% to consultation, and 1% to research. Ideally they would prefer to spend equal amounts of time in assessment, intervention, and consultation, and approximately 4% of their time doing research. On the basis of these data the match between specialist training and field practice appears more congruent than between doctoral training and practice. Brown and Minke (1986) conclude that the extensive training and research acquired by doctoral graduates does not appear to be used appropriately in applied practice. However, this training has great potential value to school systems.

3. Training in school psychology has increased considerably in uniformity during the past 15 years. This is especially true at the specialist level, probably a result of the imposition of NASP accreditation standards. The notion that school psychology training can be conceived along a master's/doctoral dichotomy is clearly not supported by the data. Specialist programs appear to predominate with doctoral pro-

grams having gradually increased in numbers during the past 10 years.

4. Training in school psychology appears to be moving gradually toward the doctoral level. While the specialist degree is widely accepted as the current entry level for school psychologists, the amount and diversity of training required of school psychology graduate students has increased consistently over the years. Current data suggest that this trend will continue and that new degree structures may be necessary in order to adequately compensate students for this higher level of training. The use of the PsyD degree, for example, might be an appropriate alternative to the awarding of the specialist degree in the future.

Professional Issues Surrounding Graduate Education

No issue in the history of school psychology has produced more rancorous debate than that surrounding entry level. "Entry level" refers to the minimum amount of training necessary to enter the profession of school psychology. Historically, the debate has several dimensions. First, school psychology grew out of education and psychology, and as Fagan (1986) has indicated, this bifurcated structure produced significant differences in the training of early school psychologists. As a result, early school psychologists tended to identify themselves either with education or psychology. Second, the American Psychological Association has maintained for a number of years that the doctoral degree is the appropriate minimum entry-level credential for the practice of psychology. This position and the historical antecedents described above produced the formation of the National Association of School Psychologists (NASP) in 1969. NASP, since its inception, has maintained the position that the appropriate entry level for the practice of school psychology is at the nondoctoral level. Initially, NASP endorsed the master's degree as the appropriate entry-level credential. In 1978 NASP revised its training standards and changed the entry level to the specialist or sixth-year degree. Third, school psychologists are credentialed by two agencies. State Departments of Education are responsible for certification of school psychologists while Board of Psychology are responsible for the licensure of school psychologists. This has tended to create systems of credentialing which often are contradictory, redundant, or at odds with one another.

The presence of the above conditions has created significant differences in the orientation of various graduate programs in school psychology. Those programs which grew out of departments of education, departments of special education, departments of educational psychology, or counselor education tend to have more content related to education than do programs which grew out of departments of psychology. In 1978 NASP standards for accreditation had a significant impact on the core curriculum of many training programs. In this respect, it is easier to identify a common thread in the training of school psychologists today than it was in 1970. Substantial differences in emphasis, however, continue to exist among programs. The differences in these emphases can be conceptualized roughly across an applied versus scientist continuum. Programs exist at both ends of this continuum with a greater number of doctoral programs espousing a pure scientist model, and a greater number of specialist and master's programs espousing the purely applied model. The presence of NASP standards has tended to move programs at the extremes toward the middle of this continuum. Other dimensions found in training programs include specialization in counseling, special education, consultation, program evaluation, administration, and advanced assessment techniques.

To some extent, the variation among training programs in school psychology can be attributed to perceived differences between the accreditation standards of APA and NASP. This issue has been discussed extensively (Bardon, 1982; Brown, 1979; Fagan, 1985; Phillips, 1985). In the early stages of the debate, the issue of school psychology's *autonomy* was predominate. That is, the notion of school psychology being a part of American psychology or existing as a profession in its own right (Brown, 1979). Later the issue became one of the appropriateness of NASP versus APA accreditation standards for the training of school psychologists. APA standards tend to be generic in nature and are applied equally to each specialty (school, clinical, and counseling). Conversely, NASP standards incorporate both generic or core areas and areas of specialization deemed necessary for school psychology. Philosophically, at the root of APA's standards is the belief that one is first trained as a psychologist and then specializes. At

the core of NASP standards is the notion that a cluster of skills, specific to the profession of school psychology, can be identified and should be part of all training programs. Thus APA standards tend to produce training programs which have highly variable applied content but very consistent core psychology content. NASP standards tend to produce programs which have more consistent applied content but somewhat more variable core psychology content.

Phillips (1985) has examined the entry-level issue in some depth. He concludes that no empirical evidence exists which demonstrates the efficacy of any particular entry level for school psychology. The reliance on accreditation standards for defining entry level is seen as problematic since the differences between doctoral and nondoctoral training are not well defined. Phillips (1985) believes that an empirically valid procedure for defining entry level would include an analysis of the job-related behaviors of school psychologists coupled with a study of the characteristics of psychology as a profession. That is, a relationship must be drawn between the curricular standards of the training of school psychologists and the job-related behaviors required by practice in the schools. Phillips (1985) is suggesting that under the current system of accreditation, standards of training and practice are imposed on the field rather than being reciprocally developed on the basis of models of job-related practice.

Bardon (1982, 1983) presented a means for resolving the entry-level issue. He proposed that the title school psychologist be dropped by APA. This would leave the title solely in the possession of NASP. APA would develop a new professional field in applied educational psychology. Thus school psychology would continue as a nondoctoral field with Division 16 of the American Psychological Association representing applied educational psychology at the doctoral level. Much discussion has surrounded Bardon's proposal (Fagan, 1986; Goldwasser, 1982; Kratochwill, 1982; Reschly, 1982). But as Fagan (1986) has observed, it is doubtful that either national organization would permit this kind of resolution because of the major changes in credentialing policy necessary to allow the emergence of a new professional title. It is clear that the highly interactive matrix of existing controls on school psychology training imposed by APA, NASP, and other organizations will continue to perpetuate the existing bifurcated system of standards. Attempts at reconciling differences in accreditation techniques such as that of the APA/NASP Task Force on Joint Accreditation (APA/NASP, 1986) should ultimately aid in reconciling these issues, at least at the doctoral level. While it is unlikely that APA will accept the specialist degree as the entry level for school psychology, the reality of the situation suggests that this *is* the current entry level endorsed by the majority of organizations exierting power and authority over school psychology. As Brown (1989) has suggested, the whole issue of doctoral versus nondoctoral training eventually will be moot as the majority of students in training shift to the doctoral level. Of much greater consequence is the issue of models of training and their relationship to the practice of school psychology in the field. This coupled with the need for the development of specializations within school psychology (e.g., vocational school psychology, cross-cultural school psychology, curriculum-based assessment) represents the major challenge to the profession in the future.

Employment Trends

Very little information on employment trends in school psychology is available. Brown and Minke (1984) examined the placement of graduates from school psychology training programs throughout the United States. School psychologists enter six types of practice including public schools, private schools, research, university faculty positions, administrative positions, and private practice. Of those students graduating in 1980–1984 the vast majority (92%) enter either public or private applied practice. Of particular note is the fact that this is true for doctoral-level graduates. Other data (Anderson, 1982) indicate that school psychologists in the public sector enjoy a high degree of job satisfaction and a relatively low level of mobility out of the profession to other occupations. Recent data on the employable of school psychologists nationally (Brown, 1985) indicate an expanding job market for school psychologists with the demand consistently exceeding the number of students being supplied annually by training programs.

Accreditation

This section is designed to acquaint the reader with the nature of program accreditation in school psychology and to review the curriculum standards published by NASP and APA. The role of accreditation traditionally has been that of providing quality control in the training of various professionals. Accreditation by its nature is a voluntary process administered predominantly by private organizations. The exception to this rule is found in school psychology in which many state departments of education (public agencies) accredit school psychology training programs within their state. Accreditation standards are usually written to reflect the *minimum* levels of training necessary to gain entry to a profession. The level of specificity in standards tends to vary from organization to organization. For example, NASP standards have greater specificity for curriculum content than do APA standards. In addition to quality control, accreditation standards often are designed to promote a process of *self-study* within training programs seeking accreditation. Presumably this process aids programs in identifying the strengths and weaknesses and in modifying curriculum on the basis of some formative evaluation plan.

Several agencies are involved in the accreditation of school psychology programs. First, the Council of Post-Secondary Accreditation (COPA) is the body that accredits accrediting agencies. Thus COPA (a private organization) identifies those organizations which will be permitted to accredit under its umbrella. Two major organizations which are members of COPA accredit in school psychology. The National Council for Accreditation of Teacher Education (NCATE) has accredited school psychology training programs since 1956. In 1977 NASP became a constituent member of NCATE, and thereafter NCATE adopted NASP's curriculum standards for the accreditation of school psychology training programs. NASP and NCATE accredit training programs at the specialist and doctoral levels. The American Psychological Association is a member of COPA and is authorized to accredit programs in psychology at the doctoral level only. Thus, APA accredits doctoral programs in school, clinical, and counseling psychology. APA began accrediting doctoral-level school psychology programs in the early 1970s. NASP/NCATE and APA are the national accrediting bodies for school psycology. As has been mentioned above, at the state level, some state departments of education accredit school psychology training programs within their jurisdiction. The standards adopted by the state departments of education have been influenced by standards adopted by the National Association of

State Directors of Teacher Education and Certification (NASDTEC). State departments of education have the authority to impose standards on training programs as a requirement for gaining certification to practice school psychology in a given state. On the other hand, national accrediting bodies provide a voluntary vehicle for accreditation. This *voluntary* accreditation, however, is misleading since in a number of states NCATE accreditation is required for certification as a school psychologist. Also, implied in many state licensure laws is a requirement that a student graduate from an APA-accredited psychology program. Other groups associated with accreditation who do not have direct authority include the Council of Directors of School Psychology Programs (CDSPP), the Trainers of School Psychology (TSP), and the APA/NASP Interorganizational Committee (IOC).

NASP and APA Training Standards

The NASP Standards for Training Programs (1984c) are divided into five major sections. These include (a) the structure of training programs in school psychology; (b) criteria for program faculty; (c) cirteria for students; (d) institutional resources and facilities; and (e) evaluation of graduates, program, and planning. Within this structure, NASP standards specify two levels of training: the specialist and doctoral levels. Other than the degrees awarded and the number of hours contained in each of these programs (minimum of 84 for doctoral and 60 graduate semester hours for specialist), no differentiation is made in the curricular content of these two levels of training. NASP standards are divided into six curriculum catagories: (a) psychological foundations, (b) educational foundations, (c) assessment, (d) interventions, (e) statistics and research design, and (f) professional school psychology. Other specific course area requirements include biological bases of behavior, cultural diversity, child and adolescent development, human exceptionality, learning, social bases of behavior, education of exceptional learners, instruction and remedial techniques, organization and operation of the schools, consultation, counseling, behavior management, history and foundations of school psychology, legal and ethical issues, professional issues and standards, and roles and functions of the school psychologist.

Within this curriculum framework NASP standards require that the program have an articulated set of goals and objectives in that they be able to relate these goals and objectives to the components of the curriculum. The curriculum of doctoral-level programs is assumed to be an upward extension of the specialist level. The NASP standards, at least tacitly, promote the concept of interlock between specialist and doctoral programs suggested by Hilke and Brantley (1982).

NASP standards require that students be oriented to the nature of schools and the educational process. They also require comprehensive preinternship practicum experiences associated with applied course work. An internship of at least 1,200 clock hours is required also at both the specialist and doctoral levels. Finally, NASP standards require that programs engage in a systematic plan to evaluate the quality of their graduates and to use this information for program review and revision.

APA *Criteria for Accreditation of Doctoral Training Programs and Internships in Professional Psychology* (1979) (hereafter known as APA Accreditation Standards) are divided into seven categories: (a) institutional setting, (b) cultural and individual differences, (c) training models and curricula, (d) faculty, (e) students, (f) facilities, and (g) practicum and internship training. APA curriculum standards require the following areas: (a) biological bases of behavior (e.g., physiological psychology, comparative psychology, neuropsychology, sensation, psychopharmacology), (b) cognitive/affective bases of behavior (e.g., learning, memory, perception, cognition, thinking, motivation, emotion), (c) social bases of behavior (e.g., social psychology; cultural, ethnic, and group processes; sex roles; organizational and systems theory), and (d) individual behavior (e.g., personality theory, human development, individual differences, abnormal psychology). In order to be competent professionals students are also expected to receive training in areas such as psychodiagnosis, psychological assessment (group and individual), intervention procedures (group and individual psychotherapy and behavior therapy), consultation, and program evaluation. Students must also be familiar with ethical standards, APA standards for educational and psychological tests, and the APA standards for the providers of psychological services. Finally, the APA curriculum standard requires a comprehensive research training component. All curriculum within the APA accreditation standards is assumed to be at the doctoral level.

APA faculty standards generally require that

faculty in training programs have appropriate education and experience in the specialty in which they are teaching. This is similar to the NASP faculty standards which require that faculty have experience as a school psychologist. The APA standards specify criteria for the admission and retention of students and require nondiscrimination in the selection of students. APA standards require both practicum and internship components. The minimum required practicum experience is 400 clock hours, of which at least 150 hours must be direct service. Seventy-five hours must be formally scheduled supervision. The internship in school psychology is one academic year in length. In this regard it is similar to the NASP requirement for internships. The APA requirements are highly specific with regard to the setting of the internship, the number of hours of on-site supervision, and quality of the supervision provided. Thus, NASP and APA standards are, in many respects, quite similar. This fact was underscored by the report of the APA/NASP Joint Task Force that compared the accreditation standards of NASP and APA.

Aside from the doctoral/nondoctoral issue, however, some important differences do exist. APA standards are more critical with regard to the institutional setting of psychology programs. The preference is clearly for the existence of psychology programs within psychology departments. The departments housing psychology programs must be clearly designated as such and must have a core of duly credentialed psychology faculty. In the curricular area, APA standards are much more specific with regard to the core psychology content of programs than they are with regard to applied content specific to a given subspecialty. Thus APA standards do not address with any specificity required areas of concentration within school, clinical, or counseling psychology. On the other hand, NASP standards are highly specific in this area. With regard to practicum and internship experience, APA and NASP standards are congruent. The exception is in the area of practicum experience in which APA standards are more explicit in terms of the number of hours required. Finally, NASP standards tend to require more extensive review of graduates and their success as psychologists as a means of program evaluation than do APA standards.

In summary, it can be seen that in many ways APA and NASP standards are complementary.

Very little conflict exists with regard to substantive requirements with the exception of the entry-level issue. The major difficulty facing the field of school psychology is the fact that both APA and NASP/NCATE accredit at the doctoral level. This process is seen by some as redundant. Attempts to encourage APA to collaborate in nondoctoral accreditation, as of yet, have not been successful (APA, NASP, & NCATE, 1982; Annis, Tucker, & Baker, 1984). The joint process developed by APA and NASP for doctoral-level accreditation, however, has been successfully employed on a pilot basis. Inspection of the *Joint Accreditation Program in School Psychology Handbook* (APA, NASP, & NCATE, 1982) suggests that a merged set of standards among APA, NASP, and NCATE would facilitate a comprehensive and credible accreditation process that could be implemented as a single accreditation procedure. Brown and Minke (1986) have suggested that

> adoption of a uniform core curriculum is an especially critical issue at the doctoral level, because APA standards do not specify the content of the school psychology specialty at that level. A hybrid set of standards containing elements of both the NASP and APA accreditation standards might best serve to promote consistent quality control among programs. (p. 1337)

CERTIFICATION AND LICENSURE REQUIREMENTS

Certification

Historically, school psychologists have been certified by state departments of education under a variety of titles, including psychometrist, educational evaluator, psychologial evaluator, psychological technician, educational diagnostician, associate psychologist, and school psychologist. During the past 10 years, the title has been standardized, principally through NASP efforts, with the title of school psychologist emerging as the msot common type of certification.

The number of states certifying school psychologists has increased steadily from 1946 to the present. In 1946 (Horrocks, 1946) only seven states certified school psychologists. By 1963 (Gray, 1963), 32 states were certifying school psychologists. By 1976 (Sewall & Brown, 1976)

50 states certified school psychologists. The most recent studies on certification indicate that (Brown, 1988; Brown, Horn, & Lindstrom, 1980) all 50 states certify some form of school psychologist. Currently, most states certify school psychologists based on requirements that are either course based or course-area based. In a number of instances, states will also certify based on the applicants having graduated from an NCATE-accredited program. The existence of the NASP/NCATE accreditation procedure appears to have provided a vehicle for reciprocity among states with regard to certification. Approximately 24 states currently hold reciprocity under the NASP/NCATE reciprocity agreement. The number of states participating in this reciprocity agreement has tended to increase over time as more and more school psychology programs have been accredited.

States certify one or more levels of school psychologists. For example, Virginia certifies one level of school psychologist, the educational specialist level. South Carolina certifies school psychologists at three levels, the master's, specialist, and doctorate. Each carries the title school psychologist. By contrast, Texas certifies three levels of three psychologists, but titles them differently, with level I being the Educational Diagnostician (master's degree), Level II being the Associate School Psychologist (master's degree), and Level III being the School Psychologist (doctoral degree). Three other states require the doctorate for use of the term "school psychologist."

Aside from reciprocity agreements, states certify based on a variety of specific requirements, some of which are course based and others which are competency based. The majority of states certify using course-based requirements. That is, they indicate specific courses or areas in which training must be received in order to gain certification. The most common areas used for certification are psychological foundations of education, consultation and intervention, tests and measurements, and special education. The most common specific courses included in certification requirements include abnormal psychology, developmental psychology, educational psychology, personality theory, psychology of learning, psychology of the exceptional child, education of the exceptional child, curriculum development, teaching techniques, counseling and guidance, individual and group intelligence testing, personality assessment, and general psychological assessment.

Most states require specific training in one or more areas of special education (e.g., mental retardation, learning disabilities). An increasing number of states require training in counseling and psychotherapeutic techniques. While many states employ course-based accreditation, few states define the content of these courses. Thus, certification decisions are made strictly on the basis of an individual applicant's transcript having the appropriate course titles.

Several states (e.g., Florida, North Carolina, Tennessee, West Virginia) have certification requirements that specify competency areas rather than specific courses. Each competency area is described in detail with standards and criteria for evaluating the presence of that competency. Generally, states that employ competency-based requirements also require graduation from an NCATE- or APA-accredited program.

Most states require some form of field experience (practicum and/or internship) for certification. However, the nature of these requirements varies considerably from state to state. Some practicum hours are specified in credit hours, while others are specified in clock hours of supervised experience. Internships may be specified in either clock hours or in months of full-time service. A number of states require that the internship experience be primarily in a school setting (required by NASP standards) while others allow a diversity of settings. A few states, including Illinois and Kentucky, specify the content of the internship in considerable detail. In some instances a percentage of supervised experience can be substituted for an internship. Supervised experience is typically defined as nonacademically related experience in a school setting. A few states require that a school psychologist be certified initially at the lowest level of certification and that he/she serve an apprenticeship in order to qualify for higher levels of certification. Clearly, there is more heterogeneity among states with regard to field experience requirements than course area requirements. In this regard, the NASP *Standards for Field Experience* (1984) have had less apparent impact on certification policy than have the course area accreditation standards.

A review of the data on certification practices nationally[1] suggests the following trends:

---

[1]A detailed summary of state certification requirements may be obtained from the author upon request.

1. An increasing number of states are adopting the sixth year or specialist level of training as the entry level for the title school psychologist. Only 12 states currently allow the use of the title school psychologist based on the master's level of training.

2. As school psychology has developed, more states have attempted to clarify the basic role dimensions of the school psychologist by developing competency statements or extensive role descriptions.

3. There has been a considerable increase in the number of states requiring field experience (practicum and/or internship) for certification. There has also been a consistent increase over the past 10 years in the length of this experience.

4. The introduction of the NASP accreditation standards in 1978 and their revision in 1984 appears to have influenced state certification requirements considerably with many states adopting the NASP standards as their model for certification.

5. No particular trend seems to exist with regard to the adoption of single- versus multilevel certification systems. Of the most recent states developing certification requirements, both models are equally in evidence.

Licensure

Licensure for private practice in school psychology has not enjoyed the consistent evolutionary gains seen in certification. As numerous authors have pointed out (Bardon, 1983; Fagan, 1986; Howard & Lowman, 1985), APA has had a primary influence on the development of licensure requirements in psychology. In fact, licensure statutes for the practice of psychology predate the strong emergence of school psychology in the 1970s and 1980s. Licensure is principally controlled by the American Association of State Psychology Boards (AASPB). This group is composed of representatives from each state board of psychology. AASPB develops examination procedures for psychology and its various specialties. For example, a common multiple-choice exam is employed by virtually every state for the initial evaluation of psychologists for licensure. AASPB currently has in development a number of specialty-area license exams for school, clinical, and counseling psychologists.

Most states require the doctoral degree for the practice of psychology or to be titled "psychologist." A number of states traditionally have licensed nondoctoral practitioners under other titles, such as associate psychologist, psychological examiner, and psychological associate. In the late 1970s a trend began in which school psychologists sought private practice licensure in order to perform activities in the private sector which they currently performed in the public sector under the certification statutes. The first states to grant licensure for the title school psychologist included Virginia, California, Kentucky, and Wisconsin. Later, in 1980s, a number of additional states have acquired nondoctoral licensure (e.g., Connecticut, Michigan, Florida) but have encountered significant resistance from state psychological associations in this process. The general trend has been toward increased numbers of states specifying the title school psychologist for licensure but with substantial restrictions on the nature of practice encompassed by this title as compared to licensure at the doctoral level. For example, in the state of Florida, a person licensed as a school psychologist has a considerably more restricted role than a person licensed as a psychologist at the doctoral level.

The advent of school psychology specialty licensure has brought into focus a long-standing debate within the American Psychological Association surrounding generic versus specialty-area licensure. APA's current position is that licensure shuld be generic and that specializations (clinical, counseling, industrial, school) should be based on training, competencies, and experience. Most states license generically. A few states (e.g., Virginia, California) license specialty areas directly. In those states that license generically, movements to add a separate specialty for school psychology are often seen as oppositional to the basic licensure structure and, of course, clearly in violation of APA standards.

At the core of the debate surrounding nondoctoral licensure is the purely guild issue of who shall receive third-party or mental health payments from insurance carriers. The American Psychological Association and Division 12 (Division of Clinical Psychology) of APA have consistently maintained that licensure at the doctoral level is necessary to maintain parity with medical professionals (Bardon, 1983). Thus, nondoctoral licensure is considered a direct affront to the credibility of doctoral level psychologists seeking reimbursement through medical channels. This includes some doctoral-level school psychologists (designated by APA as health service providers) who see nondoctoral licensure as threatening that status.

As with all professions (Herbsleb, Sales, & Overcast, 1985), the development of licensure laws for psychology has been essentially a guild issue. Licensure laws in psychology have tended to become more and more restrictive over the years. To the author's knowledge no substantive data has ever been presented suggesting that the current licensure procedures lead to protection of the public. Rather, licensure laws appear to be a means through which professional groups restrict the number of individuals entering practice in order to maximize the economic rewards accorded that profession. The resistance of American psychology to the intrusion of other licensed mental health practitioners is well documented (Herbsleb, Sales & Overcast, 1985; Snow, 1982). The involvement of school psychologists in this debate is intriguing since the majority of school psychologists at doctoral and nondoctoral levels enter public rather than private practice. A reasonable conclusion regarding this matter is that school psychologists seek licensure more as additional evidence of their competence than as a means to primary employment. This would be in contrast to mental health counselors and social workers who seek licensure as a means of obtaining third-party payments and who are clearly employed in private practice full-time.

Perhaps there is a need for school psychology to recognize an appropriate balance between its educational and mental health orientations. While its mental health orientation is increasing substantially in the public sector, no conclusive evidence suggests that any significant number of nondoctoral school psychologists will be in private practice in the future. The fact that school psychology is gradually moving to the doctoral level should produce caution in moves by state and national associations to engage significant resources in obtaining nondoctoral licensure bills.

National Register

The National Register of Health Service Providers in Psychology is a private organization that identifies psychologists qualified to practice as health service providers in a variety of settings. The register was established to provide consumers of psychological services (e.g., government agencies, medical insurance companies) with a listing of qualified psychologists. Application to be included in the register is voluntary. Criteria for inclusion include (a) current licensure as a psychologist by the state board of psychology, (b) a doctoral degree in psychology from a regionally accredited university, and (c) 2 years of supervised experience in health services in psychology, one of which must be postdoctoral. The register is housed with APA but not affiliated with it.

NASP is in the process of developing a national register for school psychologists. Listing in the NASP register will be voluntary and based on meeting certain education and experience requirements. In addition, NASP is developing a national exam in school psychology to be used in licensure, certification, and for listing in the registry.

CONCLUSION

After reading this chapter it is easy to conclude that the interactive complexity of the organizations governing school psychology produces more heterogeneity than homogeneity in standards. Before the late 1970s, this was certainly true. In the late 1970s and throughout the 1980s, however, considerable consensus has been reached regarding the content of training programs, and the basic structure of certification laws. Indications of an emerging consensus are found in the APA/NASP Interorganizational Committee (IOC) report entitled *Accreditation of School Psychology Programs at the Doctoral Level: A Joint Summary Statement* (APA/NASP, 1986). This document outlines areas in accreditation in which APA and NASP have been able to agree and disagree. While there is disagreement with regard to the entry level in school psychology, both organizations have agreed upon a framework for the joint accreditation of doctoral-level programs in school psychology. In examining NASP and APA accreditation standards, the IOC determined that the standards and criteria of both associations have no major substantive areas of conflict. In fact, the two sets of standards tend to complement one another, with each set adding strengths to the other. With regard to the education of school psychologists, the IOC produced the following statement:

The education of school psychologists encompasses the equivalent of at least three years of full-time graduate academic study. While instructional formats and course titles may vary from program to program, each program has didactic and experiential instruction (a) in scientific and professional areas common to all professional psychology programs, such as ethics and standards, research design and methodology, statistics, and psychometric methods, and (b) in such substantive areas such as the biological bases of behavior, the cognitive and affective bases of behavior, the social, cultural, ethnic, and sexual bases of behavior, and individual differences. Course work includes social and philosophical bases of education, curriculum theory and practice, etiology of learning and behavior disorders, exceptional children, and special education. Organization theory and administrative practice should also be included in the program. . . .

The experiential preparation of school psychologists includes practicum and field experience in conjunction with the academic program. In addition to the academic program of three years, the program includes a supervised internship experience beyond practicum and field work, equivalent to at least one academic school year, with at least half the hours of the internship in a school setting. (APA/NASP, 1986, p. 4)

This statement provides a framework through which joint accreditation may occur at the doctoral level in school psychology. It also provides substantive theoretical agreement with regard to the core conceptual content of school psychology training programs.

For the present at least, APA and NASP have agreed to disagree about the entry level for school psychology. While debate surrounding this issue continues (Bardon, 1983; Fagan, 1986; Trachtman, 1985), it does so with reduced vigor when compared with the adversarial relationship between NASP and APA in the late 1970s. School psychology finds itself in the paradoxical situation of politically being an autonomous profession while simultaneously drawing its knowledge base and theoretical orientation from American psychology. School psychology is not unique in this

regard. Industrial/organizational psychology is straddled between psychology and business with departments of industrial/organizational psychology often found in schools of business (Howard & Lowman, 1985).

In summary, the issues discussed in this chapter require a reasoned approach to their solution. Historically, as research has been done, the focus has shifted away from parochial or guild issues and toward those professional issues effecting the quality of practice in schools. This suggests that school psychology has moved out of its "adolescence" and is beginning to grapple with more substantive matters. There is every reason to believe that this trend will continue with vigor in the future.

REFERENCES

American Psychological Association. (1977). *Standards for providers of psychological services.* Washington, DC: Author.

American Psychological Association. (1979). *Criteria for accreditation of doctoral training programs and internships in professional psychology.* Washington, DC: Author.

American Psychological Association. (1981a). *Specialty guidelines for the delivery of services by school psychologists.* Washington, DC: Author.

American Psychological Association. (1981b). *Ethical standards of psychologists.* Washington, DC: Author.

American Psychological Association & National Association of School Psychologists. (1986). *Accreditation of school psychology programs at the doctoral level: A joint summary statement.* Washington, DC: Author.

American Psychological Association, National Association of School Psychologists, & National Council for Accreditation of Teacher Education. (1982). *Joint accreditation program in school psychology handbook.* Washington, DC: Author.

Anderson, T. (1982). *Job satisfaction among school psychologists.* Unpublished doctoral dissertation, Virginia Polytechnic Institute and State University, Blacksburg.

Annis, L. V., Tucker, G. H., & Baker, C. A. (1984). APA certification of terminal master's degree programs. *American Psychologist, 39,* 563–566.

Bardon, J. I. (1965). Problems and issues in school psychology. *Journal of School Psychology, 3*(2), 1–14.

Bardon, J. I. (1982). School psychology's dilemma: A proposal for its resolution. *Professional Psychology, 13*(6), 955–968.

Bardon, J. I. (1983). Psychology applied to education: A specialty in search of an identity. *American Psychologist, 38*(2), 185–196.

Bardon, J. I., & Walker, N. W. (1972). Characteristics of graduate training in school psychology. *American psychologist, 27,* 652–656.

Brown, D. T. (1979). Debate: Will the real school psychologist please stand up? II. The drive for independence. *School Psychology Review, 8,* 168–173.

Brown, D. T. (1985, March). *Analysis of school psychology employment trends for the coming decade.* Paper presented at the annual convention of the National Association of School Psychologists, Las Vegas, NV.

Brown, D. T. (1987). Response to Fagan's view on the future of school psychology. *American Psychologist, 41,* 756–757.

Brown, D. T. (1988). *An analysis of state certification requirements in school psychology.* Unpublished manuscript.

Brown, D. T. (1989). The evolution of entry level training in school psychology: Are we approaching the doctoral level. *School Psychology Review, 18,* 11–16.

Brown, D. T., Horn, A. J., & Lindstrom, J. P. (1980). *The handbook of certification/licensure requirements for school psychologists.* Washington, DC: National Association of School Psychologists.

Brown, D. T., & Lindstrom, J. P. (1977). *Directory of school psychology training programs in the United States and Canada.* Stratford, CT: National Association of School Psychologists.

Brown, D. T., & Minke, K. M. (1984). *Directory of school psychology training programs in the United States.* Stratford, CT: National Association of School Psychologists.

Brown, D. T., & Minke, K. M. (1986). School psychology graduate training: A comprehensive analysis. *American Psychologist, 41,* 1328–1338.

Brown, D. T., & Rooney, E. F. (1988). *Doctoral training in school psychology: A comparative analysis.* Unpublished manuscript.

Carboy, J. J., & Curley, J. F. (1976). A new training model: Professional child psychology. *Psychology in the Schools, 8,* 152–156.

Cardon, B. W., & French, J. L. (1969). Organization and content of graduate programs in school psychology. *Journal of School Psychology, 7,* 28–32.

Dinkmeyer, D. C. (1973). *Consulting: Facilitating human potential and change processes.* Columbus, OH: Charles E. Merrill.

Fagan, T. K. (1985). Further on the development of school psychology. *American Psychologist, 40,* 1262–1264.

Fagan, T. K. (1986). School psychology's dilemma: Reappraising solutions and directing attention to the future. *American Psychologist, 41,* 851–861.

French, J. T., & McCloskey, G. (1980). Characteristics of doctoral and nondoctoral programs: Their implications for the entry-level doctorate. *Journal of School Psychology, 18,* 247–255.

French, J. L., & Raykovitz, J. (1984). Dissertation research in school psychology, 1978–1980. *Journal of School Psychology, 22,* 73–82.

Gallessich, J. (1974). Training the school psychologist for consultation. *Journal of School Psychology, 12,* 95–101.

Goldwasser, E. B. (1982). The emperor's used clothes. *Professional Psychology, 13,* 969–976.

Gray, S. W. (1963). *The psychologist in the schools.* New York: Holt, Rinehart and Winston.

Herbsleb, J. D., Sales, B. D., & Overcast, T. D. (1985). Challenging licensure and certification. *American Psychologist, 40,* 1165–1178.

Hilke, J. L., & Brantley, J. C. (1982). The specialist–doctoral controversy: Some realities of training, practice, and advocacy. *Professional Psychology, 13,* 634–638.

Horrocks, J. E. (1946). State certification requirements for school psychologists. *American Psychologist, 1,* 399–401.

Howard, A., & Lowman, R. L. (1985). Should industrial/organizational psychologists be licensed? *American Psychologist, 40,* 40–47.

Korman, M. (1974). National conference on levels and patterns of professional training in psychology. *American psychologist, 29,* 441–449.

Kratochwill, T. R. (1982). School psychology: Dimensions of its dilemmas and future directions. *Professional Psychology, 13,* 977–989.

Lambert, N. (1981). School psychology training for the decades ahead, or rivers, streams, and creeks—currents and tributaries to the sea. *School Psychology Review, 10,* 194–205.

Lazarus, P. J., & Jackson, J. (1983). Sunset–sunrise: The history of school psychology licensure in Florida. *School Psychology Review, 12,* 62–70.

Moore, B. V. (1956). Educational facilities and financial assistance for graduate students in psychology: 1957–1958. *American Psychologist, 11,* 689–709.

National Association of School Psychologists. (1978). *Standards for training programs.* Washington, DC: Author.

National Association of School Psychologists. (1984a). *Standards for field placement programs.* Washington, DC: Author.

National Association of School Psychologists. (1984b). *Standards for the provision of school psychological services.* Washington, DC: Author.

National Association of School Psychologists. (1984c). *Standards for training programs.* Washington, DC: Author.

National Association of School Psychologists. (1985). *Principles for professional ethics.* Washington, DC: Author.

Peterson, D. R. (1985). Twenty years of practitioner training in psychology. *American Psychologist, 40,* 441–451.

Phillips, B. N. (1985). Toward an empirically derivable definition of entry level. *Professional Psychology: Research and Practice, 16,* 138–147.

Reschly, D. J. (1982). School psychology today: progress, not impasse. *Professional Psychology, 13,* 990–998.

Ross, S. (1962). Educational facilities and financial assistance for graduate students in psychology: 1963–64. *American Psychologist, 17,* 901–922.

Sewall, T. J., & Brown, D. T. (1976). *Handbook for*

certification/licensure requirements for school psychologists. Washington, DC: National Association of School Psychologists.

Smith, D. K. (1984). Practicing school psychologists: Their characteristics, activities, and populations served. *Professional Psychology: Research and Practice, 15,* 798–810.

Snow, B. (1982, March). Counselor licensure: What activities should be allowed? *Counselor Education and Supervision, 21,* 237–244.

Teglasi, H., & Pumroy, D. K. (1982). Field experiences in school psychology training programs. *Journal of School Psychology, 20,* 188–197.

Trachtman, G. (1981). On such a full sea. *School Psychology Review, 10*(2), 138–181.

Trachtman, G. (1985). Repressers, sensitizers and the politics of school psychology. *School Psychology Review, 14,* 108–117.

Wenger, R. D., & Pryzwansky, W. B. (1987). Implementation status of the APA Guidelines for the delivery of Services by School Psychologists. *Professional Psychology, 18,* 461–467.

White, M. A. (1963). Graduate training in school psychology. *Journal of School Psychology, 2,* 34–42.

APPENDIX A

AMERICAN PSYCHOLOGICAL ASSOCIATION ETHICAL PRINCIPLES OF PSYCHOLOGISTS[1,2]

(1981 Revision)

PREAMBLE

Psychologists respect the dignity and worth of the individual and strive for the preservation and protection of fundamental human rights. They are committed to increasing knowledge of human behavior and of people's understanding of themselves and others and to the utilization of such knowledge for the promotion of human welfare.

[1]Approved by the Council of Representatives (January 1981).

[2]These Ethical Principles apply to psychologists, to students of psychology and others who do work of a psychological nature under the supervision of a psychologist. They are also intended for the guidance of non-members of the Association who are engaged in psychological research or practice.

Copyright © American Psychological Association, Inc. Reprinted by permission.

This version of the Ethical Principles of Psychologists (formerly entitled: Ethical Standards of Psychologists) was adopted by the American Psychological Association's Council of Representatives on January 24, 1981. The Ethical Principles of Psychologists (1981 Revision) contains both substantive and grammatical changes in each of the nine ethical principles which comprised the Ethical Standards of Psychologists previously adopted by the Council of Representatives in 1979, plus a new tenth principle entitled: Care and Use of Animals. Inquiries concerning the Ethical Principles of Psychologists should be addressed to the Administrative Officer for Ethics; American Psychological Association; 1200 Seventeenth Street, N.W.; Washington, D.C. 20036.

While pursuing these objectives, they make every effort to protect the welfare of those who seek their services and of the research participants that may be the object of study. They use their skills only for purposes consistent with these values and do not knowingly permit their misuse by others. While demanding for themselves freedom of inquiry and communication, psychologists accept the responsibility this freedom requires: competence, objectivity in the application of skills, and concern for the best interests of clients, colleagues, students, research participants and society. In the pursuit of these ideals, psychologists subscribe to principles in the following areas: 1. Responsibility, 2. Competence, 3. Moral and Legal Standards, 4. Public Statements, 5. Confidentiality, 6. Welfare of the Consumer, 7. Professional Relationships, 8. Assessment Techniques, 9. Research with Human Participants, and 10. Care and Use of Animals.

Acceptance of membership in the American Psychological Association commits the member to adherence to these principles.

Psychologists cooperate with duly constituted committees of the American Psychological Association, in particular, the Committee on Scientific and Professional Ethics and Conduct, by responding to inquiries promptly and completely. Members also respond promptly and completely to inquiries from duly constituted state association ethics committees and professional standards review committees.

PRINCIPLE 1.
RESPONSIBILITY

In providing services, psychologists maintain the highest standards of their profession. They accept responsibility for the consequences of their acts and make every effort to insure that their services are used appropriately.

    a. As scientists, psychologists accept responsibility for the selection of their research topics and the methods used in investigation, analysis, and reporting. They plan their research in ways to minimize the possibility that their findings will be misleading. They provide thorough discussion of the limitations of their data, especially where their work touches on social policy or might be construed to the detriment of persons in specific age, sex, ethnic, socioeconomic or other social groups. In publishing reports of their work, they never suppress disconfirming data, and they acknowledge the existence of alternative hypotheses and explanations of their findings. Psychologists take credit only for work they have actually done.

    b. Psychologists clarify in advance with all appropriate persons and agencies the expectations for sharing and utilizing research data. They avoid relationships which may limit their objectivity or create a conflict of interest. Interference with the milieu in which the data are collected is kept to a minimum.

    c. Psychologists have the responsibility to attempt to prevent distortion, misuse, or suppression of psychological findings by the institution or agency of which they are employees.

    d. As members of governmental or other organizational bodies, psychologists remain accountable as individuals to the highest standards of their profession.

    e. As teachers, psychologists recognize their primary obligation to help others acquire knowledge and skill. They maintain high standards of scholarship by presenting psychological information objectively, fully, and accurately.

    f. As practitioners, psychologists know that they bear a heavy social responsibility because their recommendations and professional actions may alter the lives of others. They are alert to personal, social, organizational, financial, or political situations and pressures that might lead to misuse of their influence.

PRINCIPLE 2.
COMPETENCE

The maintenance of high standards of competence is a responsibility shared by all psychologists in the interest of the public and the profession as a whole. Psychologists recognize the boundaries of their competence and the limitations of their techniques. They only provide services and only use techniques for which they are qualified by training and experience. In those areas in which recognized standards do not yet exist, psychologists take whatever precautions are necessary to protect the welfare of their clients. They maintain knowledge of current scientific and professional information related to the services they render.

    a. Psychologists accurately represent their competence, education, training, and experience. They claim as evidence of educational qualifications only those degrees obtained from institutions acceptable under the Bylaws and Rules of Council of the American Psychological Association.

    b. As teachers, psychologists perform their duties on the basis of careful preparation so that their instruction is accurate, current, and scholarly.

    c. Psychologists recognize the need for continuing education and are open to new procedures and changes in expectations and values over time.

    d. Psychologists recognize differences among people, such as those that may be associated with age, sex, socioeconomic, and ethnic backgrounds. When necessary, they obtain training, experience or counsel to assure competent service or research relating to such persons.

e. Psychologists responsible for decisions involving individuals or policies based on test results have an understanding of psychological or educational measurement, validation problems, and test research.

f. Psychologists recognize that personal problems and conflicts may interfere with professional effectiveness. Accordingly, they refrain from undertaking any activity in which their personal problems are likely to lead to inadequate performance or harm to a client, colleague, student, or research participant. If engaged in such activity when they become aware of their personal problems, they seek competent professional assistance to determine whether they should suspend, terminate, or limit the scope of their professional and/or scientific activities.

PRINCIPLE 3.
MORAL AND LEGAL STANDARDS

Psychologists' moral and ethical standards of behavior are a personal matter to the same degree as they are for any other citizen, except as these may compromise the fulfillment of their professional responsibilities, or reduce the public trust in psychology and psychologists. Regarding their own behavior, psychologists are sensitive to prevailing community standards and to the possible impact that conformity to or deviation from these standards may have upon the quality of their performance as psychologists. Psychologists are also aware of the possible impact of their public behavior upon the ability of colleagues to perform their professional duties.

a. As teachers, psychologists are aware of the fact that their personal values may affect the selection and presentation of instructional materials. When dealing with topics that may give offense, they recognize and respect the diverse attitudes that students may have toward such materials.

b. As employees or employers, psychologists do not engage in or condone practices that are inhumane or that result in illegal or unjustifiable actions. Such practices include but are not limited to those based on considerations of race, handicap, age, gender, sexual preferences, religion, or national origin in hiring, promotion, or training.

c. In their professional roles, psychologists avoid any action that will violate or diminish the legal and civil rights of clients or of others who may be affected by their actions.

d. As practitioners and researchers, psychologists act in accord with Association standards and guidelines related to the practice and to the conduct of research with human beings and animals. In the ordinary course of events psychologists adhere to relevant governmental laws and institutional regulations. When federal, state, provincial, organization, or institutional laws, regulations, or practices are in conflict with Association standards and guidelines, psychologists make known their commitment to Association standards and guidelines, and wherever possible work toward a resolution of the conflict. Both practitioners and researchers are concerned with the development of such legal and quasi-legal regulations as best serve the public interest, and they work toward changing existing regulations that are not beneficial to the public interest.

PRINCIPLE 4.
PUBLIC STATEMENTS

Public statements, announcements of services, advertising, and promotional activities of psychologists serve the purpose of helping the public make informed judgments and choices. Psychologists represent accurately and objectively their professional qualifications, affiliations, and functions, as well as those of the institutions or organizations with which they or the statements may be associated. In public statements providing psychological information or professional opinions or providing information about the availability of psychological products, publications, and services, psychologists base their statements on scientifically acceptable psychological findings and techniques with full recognition of the limits and uncertainties of such evidence.

a. When announcing or advertising professional services, psychologists may list the following information to describe the provider and services provided: name, highest relevant academic degree earned from a regionally accredited institution, date, type and level of certification or licensure, diplomate status, APA membership status, address, telephone number, office hours, a brief listing of the type of psychological services offered, an appropriate presentation of fee information, foreign languages spoken, and policy with regard to third-party payments. Additional relevant or important consumer information may be included if not prohibited by other sections of these Ethical Principles.

b. In announcing or advertising the availability of psychological products, publications, or services, psychologists do not present their affiliation with any organization in a manner that falsely implies sponsorship or certification by that organization. In particular and for example, psychologists do not state APA membership or fellow status in a way to suggest that such status implies specialized professional competence or qualifications. Public statements include, but are not limited to, communication by means of periodical, book, list, directory, television, radio, or motion picture. They do not contain: (i) a false, fraudulent, misleading, deceptive, or unfair statement; (ii) a misinterpretation of fact, or a statement likely to mislead or deceive because in context it makes only a partial disclosure of relevant facts; (iii) a testimonial from a patient regarding the quality of a psychologist's services or products; (iv) a statement intended or likely to create false or unjustified expectations of favorable results; (v) a statement implying unusual, unique, or one-of-a-kind abilities; (vi) a statement intended or likely to appeal to a client's fears, anxieties, or emotions concerning the possible results of a failure to obtain the offered services; (vii) a statement concerning the comparative desirability of offered service; (viii) a statement of direct solicitation of individual clients.

c. Psychologists do not compensate or give anything of value to a representative of the press, radio, television, or other communication medium in anticipation of or in return for professional publicity in a news item. A paid advertisement must be identified as such, unless it is apparent from the context that it is a paid advertisement. If communicated to the public by use of radio or television, an advertisement shall be prerecorded and approved for broadcast by the psychologist, and a recording of the actual transmission shall be retained by the psychologist.

d. Announcements or advertisements of "personal growth groups," clinics, and agencies give a clear statement of purpose and a clear description of the experiences to be provided. The education, training, and experience of the staff members are appropriately specified.

e. Psychologists associated with the development or promotion of psychological devices, books, or other products offered for commercial sale make reasonable efforts to insure that announcements and advertisements are presented in a professional, scientifically acceptable, and factually informative manner.

f. Psychologists do not participate for personal gain in commercial announcements or advertisements recommending to the public the purchase or use of proprietary or single-source products or services when that participation is based solely upon their identification as psychologists.

g. Psychologists present the science of psychology and offer their services, products, and publications fairly and accurately, avoiding misrepresentation through sensationalism, exaggeration, or superficiality. Psychologists are guided by the primary obligation to aid the public in developing informed judgments, opinions, and choices.

h. As teachers, psychologists insure that statements in catalogs and course outlines are accurate and not misleading, particularly in terms of subject matter to be covered, bases for evaluating progress, and the nature of course experiences. Announcements, brochures, or advertisements describing workshops, seminars, or other educational programs accurately describe the audience for which the program is intended as well as eligibility requirements, educational objectives, and nature of the materials to be covered. These announcements also accurately represent the education, training, and experience of the psychologists presenting the programs, and any fees involved.

i. Public announcements or advertisements soliciting research participants in which clinical services or other professional services are offered as an inducement, make clear the nature of the services as well as the costs and other obligations to be accepted by the participants of the research.

j. Psychologists accept the obligation to correct others who represent that psychologist's professional qualifications, or associations with products or services, in a manner incompatible with these guidelines.

k. Individual diagnostic and therapeutic services are provided only in the context of a professional psychological relationship. When personal advice is given by means of public lecture or demonstration, newspaper or magazine articles, radio or television programs, mail, or similar media, the psychologist utilizes the most current relevant data and exercises the highest level of professional judgment.

l. Products that are described or presented by means of public lectures or demonstrations, newspaper or magazine articles, radio or television programs, or similar media meet the same recognized standards as exist for use in the context of a professional relationship.

PRINCIPLE 5.
CONFIDENTIALITY

Psychologists have a primary obligation to respect the confidentiality of information obtained from persons in the course of their work as psychologists. They reveal such information to others only with the consent of the person or the person's legal representative, except in those unusual circumstances in which not to do so would result in clear danger to the person or to others. Where appro-

priate, psychologists inform their clients of the legal limits of confidentiality.

a. Information obtained in clinical or consulting relationships, or evaluative data concerning children, students, employees, and others, are discussed only for professional purposes and only with persons clearly concerned with the case. Written and oral reports present only data germane to the purposes of the evaluation and every effort is made to avoid undue invasion of privacy.

b. Psychologists who present personal information obtained during the course of professional work in writings, lectures, or other public forums either obtain adequate prior consent to do so or adequately disguise all identifying information.

c. Psychologists make provisions for maintaining confidentiality in the storage and disposal of records.

d. When working with minors or other persons who are unable to give voluntary informed consent, psychologists take special care to protect these persons' best interests.

PRINCIPLE 6.
WELFARE OF THE CONSUMER

Psychologists respect the integrity and protect the welfare of the people and groups with whom they work. When there is a conflict of interest between a client and the psychologist's employing institution, psychologists clarify the nature and direction of their loyalties and responsibilities and keep all parties informed of their commitments. Psychologists fully inform consumers as to the purpose and nature of an evaluative, treatment, educational or training procedure, and they freely acknowledge that clients, students, or participants in research have freedom of choice with regard to participation.

a. Psychologists are continually cognizant of their own needs and of their potentially influential position vis-à-vis persons such as clients, students, and subordinates. They avoid exploiting the trust and dependency of such persons. Psychologists make every effort to avoid dual relationships which could impair their professional judgment or increase the risk of exploitation. Examples of such dual relationships included but are not limited to research with and treatment of employees, students, supervisees, close friends, or relatives. Sexual intimacies with clients are unethical.

b. When a psychologist agrees to provide services to a client at the request of a third party, the psychologist assumes the responsibility of clarifying the nature of the relationships to all parties concerned.

c. Where the demands of an organization require psychologists to violate these Ethical Principles, psychologists clarify the nature of the conflict between the demand and these principles. They inform all parties of psychologists' ethical responsibilities, and take appropriate action.

d. Psychologists make advance financial arrangements that safeguard the best interests of and are clearly understood by their clients. They neither give nor receive any remuneration for referring clients for professional services. They contribute a portion of their services to work for which they receive little or no financial return.

e. Psychologists terminate a clinical or consulting relationship when it is reasonably clear that the consumer is not benefitting from it. They offer to help the consumer locate alternative sources of assistance.

PRINCIPLE 7.
PROFESSIONAL RELATIONSHIP

Psychologists act with due regard for the needs, special competencies, and obligations of their colleagues in psychology and other professions. They respect the prerogatives and obligations of the institutions or organizations with which these other colleagues are associated.

a. Psychologists understand the areas of competence of related professions. They make full use of all the professional, technical, and administrative resources that serve the best interests of consumers. The absence of formal relationships with other professional workers does not relieve psy-

chologists of the responsibility of securing for their clients the best possible professional service nor does it relieve them of the obligation to exercise foresight, diligence, and tact in obtaining the complementary or alternative assistance needed by clients.

b. Psychologists know and take into account the traditions and practices of other professional groups with whom they work and cooperate fully with such groups. If a person is receiving similar services from another professional, psychologists do not offer their own services directly to such a person. If a psychologist is contacted by a person who is already receiving similar services from another professional, the psychologist carefully considers that professional relationship and proceeds with caution and sensitivity to the therapeutic issues as well as the client's welfare. The psychologist discusses these issues with the client so as to minimize the risk of confusion and conflict.

c. Psychologists who employ or supervise other professionals or professionals in training accept the obligation to facilitate the further professional development of these individuals. They provide appropriate working conditions, timely evaluations, constructive consultation and experience opportunities.

d. Psychologists do not exploit their professional relationships with clients, supervisees, students, employees, or research participants sexually or otherwise. Psychologists do not condone nor engage in sexual harassment. Sexual harassment is defined as deliberate or repeated comments, gestures, or physical contacts of a sexual nature that are unwanted by the recipient.

e. In conducting research in institutions or organizations, psychologists secure appropriate authorization to conduct such research. They are aware of their obligation to future research workers and insure that host institutions receive adequate information about the research and proper acknowledgment of their contributions.

f. Publication credit is assigned to those who have contributed to a publication in proportion to their professional contribution.

Major contributions of a professional character made by several persons to a common project are recognized by joint authorship, with the individual who made the principal contribution listed first. Minor contributions of a professional character and extensive clerical or similar non-professional assistance may be acknowledged in footnotes or in an introductory statement. Acknowledgement through specific citations is made for unpublished as well as published material that has directly influenced the research or writing. A psychologist who compiles and edits material of others for publication publishes the material in the name of the originating group, if appropriate, with his/her own name appearing as chairperson or editor. All contributors are to be acknowledged and named.

g. When psychologists know of an ethical violation by another psychologist, and it seems appropriate, they informally attempt to resolve the issue by bringing the behavior to the attention of the psychologist. If the misconduct is of a minor nature and/or appears to be due to a lack of sensitivity, knowledge, or experience, such an informal solution is usually appropriate. Such informal corrective efforts are made with sensitivity to any rights to confidentiality involved. If the violation does not seem amenable to an informal solution, or is of a more serious nature, psychologists bring it to the attention of the appropriate local, state, and/or national committee on professional ethics and conduct.

PRINCIPLE 8.
ASSESSMENT TECHNIQUES

In the development, publication, and utilization of psychological assessment techniques, psychologists make every effort to promote the welfare and best interests of the client. They guard against the misuse of assessment results. They respect the client's right to know the results, the interpretations made and the bases for their conclusions and recommendations. Psychologists make every effort to maintain the security of tests and other assessment techniques within limits of legal man-
dates. They strive to assure the appropriate use of assessment techniques by others.

a. In using assessment techniques, psychologists respect the right of clients to have a full explanation of the nature and purpose of the techniques in language that the client can understand, unless an explicit exception to this right has been agreed upon in advance. When the explanations are to be provided by others, the psychologist establishes procedures for insuring the adequacy of these explanations.

b. Psychologists responsible for the development and standardization of psychological tests and other assessment techniques utilize established scientific procedures and observe the relevant APA standards.

c. In reporting assessment results, psychologists indicate any reservations that exist regarding validity or reliability because of the circumstances of the assessment or the inappropriateness of the norms for the person tested. Psychologists strive to insure that the results of assessments and their interpretations are not misused by others.

d. Psychologists recognize that assessment results may become obsolete. They make every effort to avoid and prevent the misuse of obsolete measures.

e. Psychologists offering scoring and interpretation services are able to produce appropriate evidence for the validity of the programs and procedures used in arriving at interpretations. The public offering of an automated interpretation service is considered as a professional-to-professional consultation. The psychologist makes every effort to avoid misuse of assessment reports.

f. Psychologists do not encourage or promote the use of psychological assessment techniques by inappropriately trained or otherwise unqualified persons through teaching, sponsorship, or supervision.

PRINCIPLE 9.
RESEARCH WITH HUMAN PARTICIPANTS

The decision to undertake research rests upon a considered judgment by the individual psychologist about how best to contribute to psychological science and human welfare. Having made the decision to conduct research, the psychologist considers alternative directions in which research energies and resources might be invested. On the basis of this consideration, the psychologist carries out the investigation with respect and concern for the dignity and welfare of the people who participate, and with cognizance of federal and state regulations and professional standards governing the conduct of research with human participants.

a. In planning a study, the investigator has the responsibility to make a careful evaluation of its ethical acceptability. To the extent that the weighing of scientific and human values suggests a compromise to any principle, the investigator incurs a correspondingly serious obligation to seek ethical advice and to observe stringent safeguards to protect the rights of human participants.

b. Considering whether a participant in a planned study will be a "subject at risk" or a "subject at minimal risk," according to recognized standards, is of primary ethical concern to the investigator.

c. The investigator always retains the responsibility for insuring ethical practice in research. The investigator is also responsible for the ethical treatment of research participants by collaborators, assistants, students, and employees, all of whom, however, incur similar obligations.

d. Except for minimal risk research, the investigator establishes a clear and fair agreement with the research participants, prior to their participation, that clarifies the obligations and responsibilities of each. The investigator has the obligation to honor all promises and commitments included in that agreement. The investigator informs the participant of all aspects of the research that might reasonably be expected to influence willingness to participate, and explains all other aspects of the research about which the participant inquires. Failure to make full disclosure prior to obtaining informed consent requires additional safeguards to protect the welfare and dignity of the research participant. Research with children or participants who have impairments which would limit under-

standing and/or communication requires special safeguard procedures.

e. Methodological requirements of a study may make the use of concealment or deception necessary. Before conducting such a study, the investigator has a special responsibility to: (i) determine whether the use of such techniques is justified by the study's prospective scientific, educational, or applied value; (ii) determine whether alternative procedures are available that do not utilize concealment or deception; and (iii) insure that the participants are provided with sufficient explanation as soon as possible.

f. The investigator respects the individual's freedom to decline to participate in or to withdraw from the research at any time. The obligation to protect this freedom requires careful thought and consideration when the investigator is in a position of authority or influence over the participant. Such positions of authority include but are not limited to situations when research participation is required as part of employment or when the participant is a student, client, or employee of the investigator.

g. The investigator protects the participants from physical and mental discomfort, harm, and danger that may arise from research procedures. If risks of such consequences exist, the investigator informs the participant of that fact. Research procedures likely to cause serious or lasting harm to a participant are not used unless the failure to use these procedures might expose the participant to risk of greater harm, or unless the research has great potential benefit and fully informed and voluntary consent is obtained from each participant. The participant should be informed of procedures for contacting the investigator within a reasonable time period following participation should stress, potential harm, or related questions or concerns arise.

h. After the data are collected, the investigator provides the participant with information about the nature of the study and attempts to remove any misconceptions that may have arisen. Where scientific or humane values justify delaying or withholding information, the investigator incurs a special responsibility to monitor the research and to assure that there are no damaging consequences for the participant.

i. Where research procedures result in undesirable consequences for the individual participant, the investigator has the responsibility to detect and remove or correct these consequences, including long-term effects.

j. Information obtained about the research participant during the course of an investigation is confidential unless otherwise agreed upon in advance. When the possibility exists that others may obtain access to such information, this possibility, together with the plans for protecting confidentiality, is explained to the participant as part of the procedure for obtaining informed consent.

PRINCIPLE 10.
CARE AND USE OF ANIMALS

An investigator of animal behavior strives to advance our understanding of basic behavioral principles and/or to contribute to the improvement of human health and welfare. In seeking these ends, the investigator insures the welfare of the animals and treats them humanely. Laws and regulations notwithstanding, the animal's immediate protection depends upon the scientist's own conscience.

a. The acquisition, care, use, and disposal of all animals is in compliance with current federal, state or provincial, and local laws and regulations.

b. A psychologist trained in research methods and experienced in the care of laboratory animals closely supervises all procedures involving animals and is responsible for insuring appropriate consideration of their comfort, health, and humane treatment.

c. Psychologists insure that all individuals using animals under their supervision have received explicit instruction in experimental methods and in the care, maintenance, and handling of the species being used. Responsibilities and activities of individuals participating in a research project are consistent with their respective competencies.

d. Psychologists make every effort to minimize discomfort, illness, and pain of animals. A procedure subjecting animals to pain, stress, or privation is used only when an alternative procedure is unavailable and the goal is justified by its prospective scientific, educational, or applied value. Surgical procedures are performed under appropriate anesthesia; techniques to avoid infection and minimize pain are followed during and after surgery.

e. When it is appropriate that the animal's life be terminated, it is done rapidly and painlessly.

APPENDIX B

NATIONAL ASSOCIATION OF SCHOOL PSYCHOLOGISTS' PRINCIPLES FOR PROFESSIONAL ETHICS

I. INTRODUCTION

Standards for professional conduct, usually referred to as ethics, recognize the obligation of professional persons to provide services and to conduct themselves so as to place the highest esteem on human rights and individual dignity. A code of ethics is an additional professional technique which seeks to ensure that each person served will receive the highest quality of service. Even though ethical behavior involves interactions between the professional, the person served and employing institutions, responsibility for ethical conduct must rest with the professional.

School psychologists are a specialized segment within a larger group of professional psychologists. The school psychologist works in situations where circumstances may develop which are not clearly dealt with in other ethical guidelines. This possibility is heightened by intense concern for such issues as due process, protection of individual rights, record keeping, accountability and equal access to opportunity.

The most basic ethical principle is that of the responsibility to perform only those services for which that person has acquired a recognized level of competency. Recognition must be made of the uncertainties associated with delivery of psychological services in a situation where rights of the student, the parent, the school and society may conflict.

The intent of these guidelines is to supply clarification which will facilitate the delivery of high quality psychological services in the school or community. Thus they acknowledge the fluid and expanding functions of the school and community. In addition to these ethical standards, there is the ever present necessity to differentiate between legal mandate and ethical responsibility. The school psychologist is urged to become familiar with applicable legal requirements.

The ethical standards in this guide are organized into several sections representing the multifaceted concerns with which school psychologists must deal. The grouping arrangement is a matter of convenience, and principles discussed in one section may also apply to other areas and situations. The school psychologist should consult with other experienced psychologists and seek advice from the appropriate professional organization when a situation is encountered for which there is no clearly indicated course of action.

II. PROFESSIONAL COMPETENCY

A. General

1. The school psychologist's role mandates a mastery of skills in both education and psychology. In the interest of children and adults served in both the public and private sector, school psychologists strive to maintain high standards of competence. School psychologists recognize the strengths, as well as limitations, of their training and experience, and only provide services in areas of competence. They must be professional in the on-going pursuit of knowledge, training and research with the welfare of children, families and other individuals in mind.

2. School psychologists offer only those services which are within their individual area of training and experience. Competence levels, education, training and experience are accurately represented to schools and clients in a professional manner. School psychologists do not use affiliations with other professional persons or with institutions to imply a level of professional competence which exceeds that which has actually been achieved.

3. School psychologists are aware of their limitations and enlist the assistance of other specialists in supervisory, consultative or referral roles as appropriate in providing services competently.

4. School psychologists recognize the need for continuing professional development and pursue opportunities to learn new procedures, become current with new research and technology, and advance with changes with benefit children and families.

5. School psychologists refrain from involvement in any activity in which their personal problems or conflicts may interfere with professional effectiveness. Competent professional assistance is sought to alleviate such problems and conflicts in professional relationships.

III. PROFESSIONAL RELATIONSHIPS AND RESPONSIBILITIES

A. General

1. School psychologists take responsibility for their actions in a multitude of areas of service, and in so doing, maintain the highest standards of their profession. They are committed to the application of professional expertise for promoting improvement in the quality of life available to the student, family, school, and community. This objective is pursued in ways that protect the dignity and rights of those served. School psychologists accept responsibility for the consequences of their acts and ensure that professional skills, position and influence are applied only for purposes which are consistent with these values.

2. School psychologists respect each person with whom they are working and deal justly and impartially with each regardless of his/her physical, mental, emotional, political, economic, social, cultural, racial or religious characteristics.

3. School psychologists apply influence, position and professional skills in ways that protect the dignity and rights of those served. They promote the improvement of the quality of education and of life in general when determining assessment, counseling and intervention.

4. School psychologists define the direction and the nature of personal loyalties, objectives and competencies, and advise and inform all persons concerned of these commitments.

5. School psychologists working in both public schools and private settings maintain professional relationships with students, parents, the school and community. They understand the importance of informing students/clients of all aspects of the potential professional relationship prior to beginning psychological services of any type. School psychologists recognize the need for parental involvement and the significant influence the parent has on the student/client's growth.

6. In a situation where there are divided or

conflicting interests (as between parents, school, student, supervisor, trainer) school psychologists are responsible for attempting to work out a plan of action which protects the rights and encourages mutual benefit and protection of rights.

7. School psychologists do not exploit their professional relationships with students, employees, clients or research participants sexually or otherwise. School psychologists do not engage in, nor condone, deliberate comments, gestures or physical contacts of a sexual nature.

B. Students

1. School psychologists are guided by an awareness of the intimate nature of the examination of personal aspects of an individual. School psychologists use an approach which reflects a humanistic concern for dignity and personal integrity.

2. School psychologists inform the student/ client about important aspects of their relationship in a manner that is understood by the student. The explanation includes the uses to be made of information, persons who will receive specific information and possible implications of results.

3. School psychologists recognize the obligation to the student/client and respect the student's/client's right of choice to enter, or to participate, in services voluntarily.

4. School psychologists inform the student/ client of the outcomes of assessment, counseling or other services. Contemplated changes in program, plans for further services and other pertinent information are discussed with the student as a result of services. An account of alternatives available to the student/client is included.

5. The student/client is informed by the school psychologist of those who will receive information regarding the services and the type of information that they will receive. The sharing of information is formulated to fit the age and maturity of the student/client and the nature of the information.

C. Parents

1. School psychologists confer with parents regarding assessment, counseling and intervention plans in language understandable to the parent. They strive to establish a set of alternatives and suggestions which match the values and skills of each parent.

2. School psychologists recognize the importance of parental support and seek to obtain this by assuring that there is direct parent contact prior to seeing the student/ client. They secure continuing parental involvement by a frank and prompt reporting to the parent of findings and progress.

3. School psychologists continue to maintain contact with the parent even though the parent objects to having their child receive services. Alternatives are described which will enable the student to get needed help.

4. School psychologists discuss recommendations and plans for assisting the student/ client with the parent. The discussion includes alternatives associated with each set of plans. The parents are advised as to sources of help available at school and in the community.

5. School psychologists inform parents of the nature of records made of parent conferences and evaluations of the student/ client. Rights of confidentiality and content of reports are shared.

D. Service—Delivery

1. School psychologists employed by school districts prepare by becoming knowledgeable of the organization, philosophy, goals, objectives and methodology of the school.

2. School psychologists recognize that a working understanding of the goals, processes and legal requirements of the educational system is essential for an effective relationship with the school.

3. Familiarization with organization, instructional materials and teaching strategies of the school are basic to enable school psychologists to contribute to the common objective of fostering maximum self development opportunities for each student/ client.

4. School psychologists accept the responsibility of being members of the staff of those schools. They recognize the need to establish an integral role within the school system and familiarize themselves with the system and community.

E. Community

1. Although enjoying professional identity as a school psychologist, school psychologists are also citizens, thereby accepting the same responsibilities and duties expected of all members of society. School psychologists are free to pursue individual interests, except to the degree that these may compromise fulfillment of their professional responsibilities and have negative impact on the profession. Awareness of such impact guides public behavior.

2. As citizens, school psychologists may exercise their constitutional rights as the basis for procedures and practices designed to bring about social change. Such activities are conducted as involved citizens and not as representatives of school psychologists.

3. As employees or employers, in public or private domains, school psychologists do not engage in or condone practices based on race, handicap, age, gender, sexual preference, religion or national origin.

4. School psychologists avoid any action that could violate or diminish civil and legal rights of clients.

5. School psychologists in public and private practice have the responsibility of adhering to federal, state and local laws and ordinances governing their practice. If such laws are in conflict with existing ethical guidelines, school psychologists proceed toward resolution of such conflict through positive, respected and legal channels.

F. Related Professions

1. School psychologists respect and understand the areas of competence of other professions. They work in full cooperation with other professional disciplines in a relationship based on mutual respect and recognition of the multidisciplinary service needed to meet the needs of students and clients. They recognize the role and obligation of the institution or agency with which other professionals are associated.

2. School psychologists recognize the areas of competence of related professions and other professionals in the field of school psychology. They encourage and support use of all the resources that best serve the interests of their students/clients. They are obligated to have prior knowledge of the competency and qualifications of a referral source. Professional services, as well as technical and administrative resources, are sought in the effort of providing the best possible professional service.

3. School psychologists working within the school system explain their professional competencies to other professionals including role descriptions, assignment of services and the working relationships among varied professionals within the system.

4. School psychologists cooperate with other professionals and agencies with the rights and needs of their student/client in mind. If a student/client is receiving similar services from another professional, school psychologists assure coordination of services. Private practice school psychologists do not offer their own services to those already receiving services. As school psychologists working within the school system, a need to serve a student may arise as dictated by the student's special program. In this case, consultation with another professional serving the student takes place to assure coordination of services for the welfare of the student.

5. When school psychologists suspect the existence of detrimental or unethical practices, the appropriate professional organization is contacted for assistance and procedures established for questioning ethical practice are followed.

G. Other School Psychologists

1. School psychologists who employ, supervise and train other professionals accept the obligation of providing experiences to further their professional development.

Appropriate working conditions, fair and timely evaluation and constructive consultation are provided.

2. School psychologists acting as supervisors to interns review and evaluate assessment results, conferences, counseling strategies and documents. They assure the profession that training in the field is supervised adequately.

3. When school psychologists are aware of a possible ethical violation by another school psychologist, they attempt to resolve the issue on an informal level. If such informal efforts are not productive and a violation appears to be enacted, steps for filling an ethical complaint as outlined by the appropriate professional association are followed.

IV. PROFESSIONAL PRACTICES— PUBLIC SETTINGS

A. Advocacy

1. School psychologists consider the pupils/clients to be their primary responsibility and act as advocates of their rights and welfare. Course of action takes into account the rights of the student, rights of the parent, the responsibilities of the school personnel, and the expanding self-independence and mature status of the student.

2. School psychologists outline and interpret services to be provided. Their concern for protecting the interests and rights of students is communicated to the school administration and staff. Human advocacy is the number one priority.

B. Assessment and Intervention

1. School psychologists strive to maintain the highest standard of service by an objective collecting of appropriate data and information necessary to effectively work with students. In conducting a psychoeducational evaluation or counseling/consultation services, due consideration is given to individual integrity and individual differences. School psychologists recognize differences in age, sex, socioeconomic and ethnic backgrounds and strive to select and use appropriate procedures, techniques and strategies relevant to such differences.

2. School psychologists insist on collecting relevant data for an evaluation that includes the use of valid and reliable instruments and techniques that are applicable and appropriate for the student.

3. School psychologists combine observations, background information, multi-disciplinary results and other pertinent data to present the most comprehensive and valid picture possible of the student. School psychologists utilize assessment, counseling procedures, consultation techniques and other intervention methods that are consistent with responsible practice, recent research and professional judgment.

4. School psychologists do not promote the use of psychoeducational assessment techniques by inappropriately trained or otherwise unqualified persons through teaching, sponsorship or supervision.

5. School psychologists develop interventions which are appropriate to the presenting problems of the referred student/client, and which are consistent with the data collected during the assessment of the referral situation.

6. The student/client is referred to another professional for services when a condition is identified which is outside the treatment competencies or scope of the school psychologist.

7. When transferring the intervention responsibility for a student/client to another professional, school psychologists ensure that all relevant and appropriate individuals, including the student/client when appropriate, are notified of the change and reasons for the change.

C. Use of Materials and Computers

1. School psychologists are responsible for maintaining security of psychological tests which might be rendered useless by revealing the underlying principles or specific content. Every attempt is made by school psychologists to protect test security and copyright restrictions.

2. Copyright laws are adhered to regarding reproduction of tests or any parts thereof. Permission is obtained from authors of noncopyrighted published instruments.
3. School psychologists who utilize student/client information in lectures or publications, either obtain prior consent in writing or remove all identifying data.
4. When publishing, school psychologists acknowledge the sources of their ideas and materials. Credit is given to those who have contributed.
5. School psychologists do not promote or encourage inappropriate use of computer-generated test analysis or reports.
6. School psychologist maintain full responsibility for computerized or any other technological services used by them for diagnostic, consultative or information management purposes. Such services, if used, should be regarded as tools to be used judiciously without abdiction of any responsibility of the psychologist to the tool or to the people who make its operation possible.
7. In the utilization of technological data management services, school psychologists apply the same ethical standards for use, intepretation and maintenance of data as for any other information. They are assured that the computer programs are accurate in all areas of information produced prior to using the results.

D. School-Based Research and Evaluation

1. School psychologists continually assess the impact of any treatment/intervention/counseling plan and terminate or modify the plan when the data indicates that the plan is not achieving the desired goals.
2. In performing research, school psychologists accept responsibility for selection of topics and research methodology to be used in subject selection, data gathering, analysis and reporting. In publishing reports of their research, they provide discussion of limitations of their data and acknowledge existence of confirming data, as well as alternate hypotheses and explanations of their findings.

E. Reporting Data and Conferencing Results

1. School psychologists ascertain that student/client information reaches responsible and authorized persons and is adequately interpreted for their use in helping the student/client. This involves establishing procedures which safeguard the personal and confidential interests of those concerned.
2. School psychologists communicate findings and recommendations in language readily understood by the school staff. These communications describe possible favorable and unfavorable consequences associated with the alternative proposals.
3. When reporting data which are to be representative of a student/client, school psychologists take the responsibility for preparing information that is written in terms that are understandable to all involved. It is made certain that information is in such form and style as to assure that the recipient of the report will be able to give maximum assistance to the individual. The emphasis is on the interpretations and recommendations rather than the simple passing along of test scores, and will include an appraisal of the degree of reliance and confidence which can be placed on the information.
4. School psychologists ensure the accuracy of their reports, letters and other written documents through reviewing and signing such.
5. School psychologists comply with all laws, regulations and policies pertaining to the adequate storage and disposal of records to maintain appropriate confidentiality of information.

V. PROFESSIONAL PRACTICES— PRIVATE SETTINGS

A. Relationship with School Districts

1. Many school psychologists are employed in both the public and private sector, and in so doing, create a possible conflict of services if they do not adhere to standards of professional ethics. School psychologists operating in both sectors recognize the

importance of separation of roles and the necessity of adherence to all ethical standards.

2. School psychologists engaged in employment in a public school setting and in private practice, may not accept a fee, or any other form of remuneration, for professional work with clients who are entitled to such service through the schools where the school psychologists are currently assigned.

3. School psychologists in private practice have an obligation to inform parents of free and/or mandated services available from the public school system before providing services for pay.

4. School psychologists engaged in employment in a public, as well as private, practice setting, maintain such practice outside the hours of contracted employment in their school district.

5. School psychologists engaged in private practice do not utilize tests, materials or services belonging to the school district without authorization.

6. School psychologists carefully evaluate the appropriateness of the use of public school facilities for part-time private practice. Such use can be confusing to the client and may be criticized as improper. Before the facility is utilized, school psychologists enter into a rental agreement with the school district and clearly define limits of use to the district and the client.

B. Service—Delivery

1. School psychologists clarify financial arrangements in advance of services to ensure to the best of their ability that they are clearly understood by the client. They neither give nor receive any remuneration for referring clients for professional services.

2. School psychologists in private practice adhere to the conditions of a contract with the school district, other agency, or individual until service thereunder has been performed, the contract has been terminated by mutual consent or the contract has otherwise been legally terminated. They have responsibility to follow-up a completed contract to assure that conclusions

are understood, interpreted and utilized effectively.

3. School psychologists in private practice guard against any misunderstanding occuring from recommendations, advice or information given a parent or child which a school may not be prepared to carry out, or which is in conflict with what the district is doing for the child. Such conflicts are not avoided where the best interests of those served require consideration of different opinion. Direct consultation between the school psychologist in private practice and the school psychologist assigned to the case at the school level may avoid confusing parents by resolving at the professional level any difference of interpretation of clinical data.

4. School psychologists provide individual diagnostic and therapeutic services only within the context of a professional psychological relationship. Personal diagnosis and therapy are not given by means of public lectures, newspaper columns, magazine articles, radio and television programs or mail. Any information shared through such media activities is general in nature and utilizes only current relevant data and professional judgment.

C. Announcements/Advertising

1. Considerations of appropriate announcement of services, advertising and public media statements are necessary in the role of the school psychologist in private practice. Such activities are necessary in assisting the public to make appropriate and knowledgeable decisions and choices regarding services. Accurate representation of training, experience, services provided and affiliation are made by school psychologists. Public statements must be based on sound and accepted theory, research and practice.

2. Individual, agency or clinical listings in telephone directories are limited to the following: name/names, highest relevant degree, certification status, address, telephone number, brief identification of major areas of practice, office hours, appropriate fee information, foreign languages spoken,

policy with regard to third party payments and license number.

3. Announcements of services by school psychologists in private practice, agency or clinic are made in a formal, professional manner limited to the same information as is included in a telephone listing. Clear statements of purposes with clear descriptions of the experiences to be provided are given. The education, training and experience of the staff members are appropriately specified.

4. School psychologists in private practice may utilize brochures in the announcement of services. The brochures may be sent to professional persons, schools, business firms, governmental agencies and other similar organizations.

5. Announcements and advertisements of the availability of publications, products and services for sale are presented in a professional, scientific and factual manner. Information may be communicated by means of periodical, book, list, directory, television, radio or motion picture and must not include any false, misleading or comparative statements.

6. School psychologists in private practice do not directly solicit clients for individual diagnosis or therapy.

7. School psychologists do not compensate in any manner a representative of the press, radio or television in return for personal professional publicity in a news item.

8. School psychologists do not participate for personal gain in commercial announcements or advertisements recommending to the public the purchase or use of products or services.

APPENDIX C

ABRIDGED RULES AND REGULATIONS FOR THE IMPLEMENTATION OF P.L. 94–142 (THE EDUCATION FOR ALL HANDICAPPED CHILDREN ACT OF 1975)

SUBPART A—GENERAL

Purpose, Applicability, and General Provisions Regulations

§ 300.1 Purpose

The purpose of this part is:

(a) To insure that all handicapped children have available to them a free appropriate public education which includes special education and related services to meet their unique needs,

(b) To insure that the rights of handicapped children and their parents are protected,

(c) To assist States and localities to provide for the education of all handicapped children, and

(d) To assess and insure the effectiveness of efforts to educate those children.

§ 300.2 Applicability to State, Local, and Private Agencies

(a) *States.* This part applies to each State which receives payments under Part B of the Education of the Handicapped Act.

(b) *Public agencies within the State.* The annual program plan is submitted by the State educational agency on behalf of the State as a whole. Therefore, the provisions of this part apply to all political subdivisions of the State that are involved in the education of handicapped children. These would include: (1) The State educational agency, (2) local educational agencies and intermediate educational units, (3) other State agencies and schools (such as Departments of Mental Health and Welfare and State schools for the deaf or blind), and (4) State correctional facilities.

(c) *Private schools and facilities.* Each public agency in the State is responsible for insuring that the rights and protections under this part are given to children referred to or placed in private schools and facilities by that public agency.

Comment. The requirements of this part are binding on each public agency that has direct or delegated authority to provide special education and related services in a State that receives funds under Part B of the Act, regardless of whether that agency is receiving funds under Part B.

§ 300.4   Free Appropriate Public Education

As used in this part, the term "free appropriate public education" means special education and related services which:

(a) Are provided at public expense, under public supervision and direction, and without charge.

(b) Meet the standards of the State educational agency, including the requirements of this part,

(c) Include preschool, elementary school, or secondary school education in the State involved, and

(d) Are provided in conformity with an individualized education program which meets the requirements under §§300.340–300.349 of Subpart C.

§ 300.5   Handicapped Children

(a) As used in this part, the term "handicapped children" means those children evaluated in accordance with §§300.530–300.534 as being mentally retarded, hard of hearing, deaf, speech impaired, visually handicapped, seriously emotionally disturbed, orthopedically impaired, other health impaired, deaf-blind, multi-handicapped, or as having specific learning disabilities, who because of those impairments need special education and related services.

(b) The terms used in this definition are defined as follows:

(1) "Deaf" means a hearing impairment which is so severe that the child is impaired in processing linguistic information through hearing, with or without amplification, which adversely affects educational performance.

(2) "Deaf-blind" means concomitant hearing and visual impairments, the combination of which causes such severe communication and other developmental and educational problems that they cannot be accommodated in special education programs solely for deaf or blind children.

(3) "Hard of hearing" means a hearing impairment, whether permanent or fluctuating, which adversely affects a child's educational performance but which is not included under the definition of "deaf" in this section.

(4) "Mentally retarded" means significantly subaverage general intellectual functioning existing concurrently with deficits in adaptive behavior and manifested during the developmental period,

which adversely affects a child's educational performance.

(5) "Multihandicapped" means concomitant impairments (such as mentally retarded-blind, mentally retarded-orthopedically impaired, etc.), the combination of which causes such severe educational problems that they cannot be accommodated in special education programs solely for one of the impairments. The term does not include deaf-blind children.

(6) "Orthopedically impaired" means a severe orthopedic impairment which adversely affects a child's educational performance. The term includes impairments caused by congenital anomaly (e.g., clubfoot, absence of some member, etc.), impairments caused by disease (e.g., poliomyelitis, bone tuberculosis, etc.), and impairments from other causes (e.g., cerebral palsy, amputations, and fractures or burns which cause contractures).

(7) "Other health impaired" means limited strength, vitality or alertness, due to chronic or acute health problems such as a heart condition, tuberculosis, rheumatic fever, nephritis, asthma, sickle cell anemia, hemophilia, epilepsy, lead poisoning, leukemia, or diabetes, which adversely affects a child's educational performance.

(8) "Seriously emotionally disturbed" is defined as follows:

(i) The term means a condition exhibiting one or more of the following characteristics over a long period of time and to a marked degree, which adversely affects educational performance:

(A) An inability to learn which cannot be explained by intellectual, sensory, or health factors;

(B) An inability to build or maintain satisfactory interpersonal relationships with peers and teachers;

(C) Inappropriate types of behavior or feelings under normal circumstances;

(D) A general pervasive mood of unhappiness or depression; or

(E) A tendency to develop physical symptoms or fears associated with personal or school problems.

(ii) The term includes children who are schizophrenic or autistic. The term does not include children who are socially maladjusted, unless it is determined that they are seriously emotionally disturbed.

(9) "Specific learning disability" means a dis-

order in one or more of the basic psychological processes involved in understanding or in using language, spoken or written, which may manifest itself in an imperfect ability to listen, think, speak, read, write, spell, or to do mathematical calculations. The term includes such conditions as perceptual handicaps, brain injury, minimal brain disfunction, dyslexia, and developmental aphasia. The term does not include children who have learning problems which are primarily the result of visual, hearing, or motor handicaps, of mental retardation, or of environmental, cultural, or economic disadvantage.

(10) "Speech impaired" means a communication disorder, such as stuttering, impaired articulation, a language impairment, or a voice impairment, which adversely affects a child's educational performance.

(11) "Visually handicapped" means a visual impairment which, even with correction, adversely affects a child's educational performance. The term includes both partially seeing and blind children.

§ 300.9   Native Language

As used in this part, the term "native language" has the meaning given that term by section 703(a)(2) of the Bilingual Education Act, which provides as follows:

> The term "native language," when used with reference to a person of limited English-speaking ability, means the language normally used by that person, or in the case of a child, the language normally used by the parents of the child.

Comment. Section 602(21) of the Education of the Handicapped Act states that the term "native language" has the same meaning as the definition from the Bilingual Education Act. In using the term, the Act does not prevent the following means of communication:

(1) In all direct contact with a child (including evaluation of the child), communication would be in the language normally used by the child and not that of the parents, if there is a difference between the two.

(2) If a person is deaf or blind, or has no written language, the mode of communication would be that normally used by the person (such as sign language, braille, or oral communication).

§ 300.13   Related Services

(a) As used in this part, the term "related services" means transportation and such developmental, corrective, and other supportive services as are required to assist a handicapped child to benefit from special education, and includes speech pathology and audiology, psychological services, physical and occupational therapy, recreation, early identification and assessment of disabilities in children, counseling services, and medical services for diagnostic or evaluation purposes. The term also includes school health services, social work services in schools, and parent counseling and training.

(b) The terms used in this definition are defined as follow:

(1) "Audiology" includes:

(i)   Identification of children with hearing loss;

(ii) Determination of the range, nature, and degree of hearing loss, including referral for medical or other professional attention for the habilitation of hearing;

(iii) Provision of habilitative activities, such as language habilitation, auditory training, speech reading (lip-reading), hearing evaluation, and speech conservation;

(iv) Creation and administration of programs for prevention of hearing loss;

(v)   Counseling and guidance of pupils, parents, and teachers regarding hearing loss; and

(vi) Determination of the child's need for group and individual amplification, selecting and fitting an appropriate aid, and evaluating the effectiveness of amplification.

(2) "Counseling services" means services provided by qualified social workers, psychologists, guidance counselors, or other qualified personnel.

(3) "Early identification" means the implementation of a formal plan for identifying a disability as early as possible in a child's life.

(4) "Medical services" means services provided by a licensed physician to determine a child's medically related handicapping condition which results in the child's need for special education and related services.

(5) "Occupational therapy" includes:

(i)   Improving, developing or restoring functions impaired or lost through illness, injury, or deprivation;

(ii) Improving ability to perform tasks for independent functioning when functions are impaired or lost; and

(iii) Preventing, through early intervention, initial or further impairment or loss of function.

(6) "Parent counseling and training" means assisting parents in understanding the special needs of their child and providing parents with information about child development.

(7) "Physical therapy" means services provided by a qualified physical therapist.

(8) "Psychological services" include:

(i) Administering psychological and educational tests, and other assessment procedures;

(ii) Interpreting assessment results;

(iii) Obtaining, integrating, and interpreting information about child behavior and conditions relating to learning;

(iv) Consulting with other staff members in planning school programs to meet the special needs of children as indicated by psychological tests, interviews, and behavioral evaluations; and

(v) Planning and managing a program of psychological services, including psychological counseling for children and parents.

(9) "Recreation" includes:

(i) Assessment of leisure function;

(ii) Therapeutic recreation services;

(iii) Recreation programs in schools and community agencies; and

(iv) Leisure education.

(10) "School health services" means services provided by a qualified school nurse or other qualified person.

(11) "Social work services in schools" include:

(i) Preparing a social or developmental history on a handicapped child;

(ii) Group and individual counseling with the child and family;

(iii) Working with those problems in a child's living situation (home, school, and community) that affect the child's adjustment in school; and

(iv) Mobilizing school and community resources to enable the child to receive maximum benefit from his or her educational program.

(12) "Speech pathology" includes:

(i) Identification of children with speech or language disorders;

(ii) Diagnosis and appraisal of specific speech or language disorders;

(iii) Referral for medical or other professional attention necessary for the habilitation of speech or language disorders;

(iv) Provisions of speech and language services for the habilitation or prevention of communicative disorders; and

(v) Counseling and guidance of parents, children, and teachers regarding speech and language disorders.

(13) "Transportation" includes

(i) Travel to and from school and between schools,

(ii) Travel in and around school buildings, and

(iii) Specialized equipment (such as special or adapted buses, lifts, and ramps), if required to provide special transportation for a handicapped child.

Comment. There are certain kinds of services which might be provided by persons from varying professional backgrounds and with a variety of operational titles, depending upon requirements in individual States. For example, counseling services might be provided by social workers, psychologists, or guidance counselors; and psychological testing might be done by qualified psychological examiners, psychometrists, or psychologists, depending upon State standards.

§ 300.14 Special Education

(a)(1) As used in this part, the term "special education" means specially designed instruction, at no cost to the parent, to meet the unique needs of a handicapped child, including classroom instruction in physical education, home instruction, and instruction in hospitals and institutions.

(2) The term includes speech pathology, or any other related service, if the service consists of specially designed instruction, at no cost to the parents, to meet the unique needs of a handicapped child, and is considered "special education" rather than a "related service" under State standards.

(3) The term also includes vocational education if it consists of specially designed instruction, at

no cost to the parents, to meet the unique needs of a handicapped child.

(b) The terms in this definition are defined as follows:

(1) "At no cost" means that all specially designed instruction is provided without charge, but does not preclude incidental fees which are normally charged to non-handicapped students or their parents as a part of the regular education program.

(2) "Physical education" is defined as follows:

(i) The term means the development of

(A) Physical and motor fitness;

(B) Fundamental motor skills and patterns; and

(C) Skills in aquatics, dance, and individual and group games and sports (including intramural and lifetime sports).

(ii) The term includes special physical education, adapted physical education, movement education, and motor development.

(3) "Vocational education" means organized educational programs which are directly related to the preparation of individuals for paid or unpaid employment, or for additional preparation for a career requiring other than a baccalaureate or advanced degree.

Comment. (1) The definition of "special education" is a particularly important one under these regulations, since a child is not handicapped unless he or she needs special education. (See the definition of "handicapped children" in section 300.5) The definition of "related services" (section 300.13) also depends on this definition, since a related service must be necessary for a child to benefit from special education. Therefore, if a child does not need special education, there can be no "related services," and the child (because not "handicapped") is not covered under the Act.

SUBPART C—SERVICES

Free Appropriate Public Education

§ 300.300 Timelines for Free Appropriate Public Education

(a) General. Each State shall insure that free appropriate public education is available to all handicapped children aged three through eighteen within the State not later than September 1, 1978, and to all handicapped children aged three through twenty-one within the State not later than September 1, 1980.

(b) Age ranges 3–5 and 18–21. This paragraph provides rules for applying the requirement in paragraph (a) of this section to handicapped children aged three, four, five, eighteen, nineteen, twenty, and twenty-one:

(1) If State law or a court order requires the State to provide education for handicapped children in any disability category in any of these age groups, the State must make a free appropriate public education available to all handicapped children of the same age who have that disability.

(2) If a public agency provides education to non-handicapped children in any of these age groups, it must make a free appropriate public education available to at least a proportionate number of handicapped children of the same age.

(3) If a public agency provides education to 50 percent or more of its handicapped children in any disability category in any of these age groups, it must make a free appropriate public education available to all of its handicapped children of the same age who have that disability.

(4) If a public agency provides education to a handicapped child in any of these age groups, it must make a free appropriate public education available to that child and provide that child and his or her parents all of the rights under Part B of the Act and this part.

(5) A State is not required to make a free appropriate public education available to a handicapped child in one of these age groups if:

(i) State law expressly prohibits, or does not authorize, the expenditure of public funds to provide education to non-handicapped children in that age group; or

(ii) The requirement is inconsistent with a court order which governs the provision of free public education to handicapped children in that State.

§ 300.305 Program Options

Each public agency shall take steps to insure that its handicapped children have available to them the variety of educational programs and services available to non-handicapped children in the area served by the agency, including art, music, industrial arts, consumer and homemaking education, and vocational education.

§ 300.306   Nonacademic Services

(a) Each public agency shall take steps to provide nonacademic and extracurricular services and activities in such manner as is necessary to afford handicapped children an equal opportunity for participation in those services and activities.

(b) Nonacademic and extracurricular services and activities may include counseling services, athletics, transportation, health services, recreational activities, special interest groups or clubs sponsored by the public agency, referrals to agencies which provide assistance to handicapped persons, and employment of students, including both employment by the public agency and assistance in making outside employment available.

§ 300.307   Physical Education

(a) *General.* Physical education services, specially designed if necessary, must be made available to every handicapped child receiving a free appropriate public education.

(b) *Regular physical education.* Each handicapped child must be afforded the opportunity to participate in the regular physical education program available to non-handicapped children unless:

(1) The child is enrolled full time in a separate facility; or

(2) The child needs specially designed physical education, as prescribed in the child's individualized education program.

(c) *Special physical education.* If specially designed physical education is prescribed in a child's individualized education program, the public agency responsible for the education of that child shall provide the services directly, or make arrangements for it to be provided through other public or private programs.

(d) *Education in separate facilities.* The public agency responsible for the education of a handicapped child who is enrolled in a separate facility shall insure that the child receives appropriate physical education services in compliance with paragraphs (a) and (c) of this section.

Priorities in the Use of Part B Funds

§ 300.320   Definitions of "First Priority Children" and "Second Priority Children"

For the purposes of §§300.321–300.324, the term:

(a) "First priority children" means handicapped children who:

(1) Are in an age group for which the State must make available free appropriate public education under §300.300; and

(2) Are not receiving any education.

(b) "Second priority children" means handicapped children, within each disability, with the most severe handicaps who are receiving an inadequate education.

Comment. After September 1, 1978, there should be no second priority children, since States must insure, as a condition of receiving Part B funds for fiscal year 1979, that all handicapped children will have available a free appropriate public education by that date.

New "First priority children" will continue to be found by the State after September 1, 1978 through on-going efforts to identify, locate, and evaluate all handicapped children.

§ 300.321   Priorities

(a) Each State and local educational agency shall use funds provided under Part B of the Act in the following order of priorities:

(1) To provide free appropriate public education to first priority children, including the identification, location, and evaluation of first priority children.

(2) To provide free appropriate public education to second priority children, including the identification, location, and evaluation of second priority children.

§ 300.323   Services to Other Children

If a state or a local educational agency is providing free appropriate public education to all of its first priority children, that State or agency may use funds provided under Part B of the Act:

(a) To provide free appropriate public education to handicapped children who are not receiving any education and who are in the age groups not covered under §300.300 in that State; or

(b) To provide free appropriate public education to second priority children; or

(c) Both.

§ *300.324   Application of Local Educational Agency to Use Funds for the Second Priority*

A local educational agency may use funds provided under Part B of the Act for second priority children, if it provides assurance satisfactory to the State educational agency in its application (or an amendment to its application):

(a) That all first priority children have a free appropriate public education available to them;

(b) That the local educational agency has a system for the identification, location, and evaluation of handicapped children, as described in its application; and

(c) That whenever a first priority child is identified, located, and evaluated, the local educational agency makes available a free appropriate public education to the child.

Individualized Education Programs

§ *300.340   Definition*

As used in this part, the term "individualized education program" means a written statement for a handicapped child that is developed and implemented in accordance with §§300.341–300.349.

§ *300.341   State Educational Agency Responsibility*

(a) *Public agencies.* The State educational agency shall insure that each public agency develops and implements an individualized education program for each of its handicapped children.

(b) *Private schools and facilities.* The State educational agency shall insure that an individualized education program is developed and implemented for each handicapped child who:

(1) Is placed in or referred to a private school or facility by a public agency; or

(2) Is enrolled in a parochial or other private school and receives special education or related services from a public agency.

§ *300.342   When Individualized Education Programs Must be in Effect*

(a) On October 1, 1977, and at the beginning of each school year thereafter, each public agency shall have in effect an individualized education program for every handicapped child who is receiving special education from that agency.

(b) An individualized education program must:

(1) Be in effect before special education and related services are provided to a child; and

(2) Be implemented as soon as possible following the meetings under § 300.343.

§ *300.343   Meetings*

(a) *General.* Each public agency is responsible for initiating and conducting meetings for the purpose of developing, reviewing, and revising a handicapped child's individualized education program.

(b) *Handicapped children currently served.* If the public agency has determined that a handicapped child will receive special education during school year 1977–1978, a meeting must be held early enough to insure than an individualized education program is developed by October 1, 1977.

(c) *Other handicapped children.* For a handicapped child who is not included under paragraph (b) of this action, a meeting must be held within thirty calendar days of a determination that the child needs special education and related services.

(d) *Review.* Each public agency shall initiate and conduct meetings to periodically review each child's individualized education program and if appropriate revise its provisions. A meeting must be held for this purpose at least once a year.

Comment. The dates on which agencies must have individualized education programs (IEPs) in effect are specified in §300.342 (October 1, 1977, and the beginning of each school year thereafter). However, except for new handicapped children (i.e., those evaluated and determined to need special education after October 1, 1977), the timing of meetings to develop, review, and revise IEPs is left to the discretion of each agency.

In order to have IEPs in effect by the dates in § 300.342, agencies could hold meetings at the end of the school year or during the summer preceding those dates. In meeting the October 1, 1977 timeline, meeting could be conducted up through the October 1 date. Thereafter, meetings may be held any time throughout the year, as long as IEPs are in effect at the beginning of each school year.

The statute requires agencies to hold a meeting at least once each year in order to review, and if appropriate revise, each child's IEP. The timing of those meetings could be on the anniversary date of the last IEP meeting on the child, but this is left to the discretion of the agency.

§ 300.344   Participants in Meetings

(a) *General.* The public agency shall insure that each meeting includes the following participants: (1) A representative of the public agency, other than the child's teacher, who is qualified to provide, or supervise the provision of, special education.

(2) The child's teacher.

(3) One or both of the child's parents, subject to §300.345.

(4) The child, where appropriate.

(5) Other individuals at the discretion of the parent or agency.

(b) *Evaluation personnel.* For a handicapped child who has been evaluated for the first time, the public agency shall insure:

(1) That a member of the evaluation team participates in the meeting, or

(2) That the representative of the public agency, the child's teacher, or some other person is present at the meeting, who is knowledgeable about the evaluation procedures used with the child and is familiar with the results of the evaluation.

§ 300.345   Parent Participation

(a) Each public agency shall take steps to insure that one or both of the parents of the handicapped child are present at each meeting or are afforded the opportunity to participate, including:

(1) Notifying parents of the meeting early enough to insure that they will have an opportunity to attend; and

(2) Scheduling the meeting at a mutually agreed on time and place.

(b) The notice under paragraph (a)(1) of this section must indicate the purpose, time, and location of the meeting, and who will be in attendance.

(c) If neither parent can attend, the public agency shall use other methods to insure parent participation, including individual or conference telephone calls.

(d) A meeting may be conducted without a parent in attendance if the public agency is unable to convince the parents that they should attend. In this case the public agency must have a record of

its attempts to arrange a mutually agreed on time and place such as:

(1) Detailed records of telephone calls made or attempted and the results of those calls.

(2) Copies of correspondence sent to the parents and any responses received, and

(3) Detailed records of visits made to the parent's homes or place of employment and the result of those visits.

(e) The public agency shall take whatever action is necessary to ensure that the parent understands the proceedings at a meeting, including arranging for an interpreter for parents who are deaf or whose native language is other than English.

(f) The public agency shall give the parent, on request, a copy of the individualized education program.

§ 300.346   Contents of Individualized Education Program

The individualized education program for each child must include:

(a) A statement of the child's present levels of educational performance;

(b) A statement of annual goals, including short term instructional objectives;

(c) A statement of the specific special education and related services to be provided to the child, and the extent to which the child will be able to participate in regular educational programs;

(d) The projected dates for initiation of services and the anticipated duration of the services; and

(e) Appropriate objective criteria and evaluation procedures and schedules for determining, or at least an annual basis, whether the short term instructional objectives are being achieved.

§ 300.349   Individualized Education Program-Accountability

Each public agency must provide special education and related services to a handicapped child in accordance with an individual education program. However, Part B of the Act does not require that any agency, teacher, or other person be held accountable if a child does not achieve the growth projected in the annual goals and objectives.

Comment. This section is intended to relieve concerns that the individualized education program constitutes a guarantee by the public agency and the teacher that a child will progress at a specified rate. However, this section does not relieve agencies and teachers from making good faith efforts to assist the child in achieving the objectives and goals listed in the individualized education program. Further, the section does not limit a parent's right to complain and ask for revisions of the child's program, or to invoke due process procedures, if the parent feels that these efforts are not being made.

SUBPART D—PRIVATE SCHOOLS

Handicapped Children in Private Schools Placed or Referred by Public Agencies

§ 300.401   Responsibility of State Educational Agency

Each State educational agency shall insure that a handicapped child who is placed in or referred to a private school or facility by a public agency:

(a) Is provided special education and related services:

(1) In conformance with an individualized education program which meets the requirements under §§300.340–300.349 of Subpart C;

(2) At not cost to the parents; and

(3) At a school or facility which meets the standards that apply to State and local educational agencies (including the requirements in this part); and

(b) Has all of the rights of a handicapped child who is served by a public agency.

§ 300.403   Placement of Children by Parents

(a) If a handicapped child has available a free appropriate public education and the parents choose to place the child in a private school or facility, the public agency is not required by this part to pay for the child's education at the private school or facility. However, the public agency shall make services available to the child as provided under §§300.450–300.460.

(b) Disagreements between a parent and a public agency regarding the availability of a program appropriate for the child, and the question of financial responsibility, are subject to the due process procedures under §§300.500–300.514 of Subpart E.

Handicapped Children in Private Schools Not Placed or Referred by Public Agencies

§ 300.452   Local Educational Agency Responsibility

(a) Each local educational agency shall provide special education and related services designed to meet the needs of private school handicapped children residing in the jurisdiction of the agency.

(b) Each local educational agency shall provide private school handicapped children with genuine opportunities to participate in special education and related services consistent with the number of those children and their needs.

§ 300.453   Determination of Needs, Number of Children, and Types of Services

The needs of private school handicapped children, the number of them who will participate under this part, and the types of special education and related services which the local educational agency will provide for them must be determined after consultation with persons knowledgeable of the needs of these children, on a basis comparable to that used in providing for the participation under this part of handicapped children enrolled in public schools.

SUBPART E—PROCEDURAL SAFEGUARDS

Due Process Procedures for Parents and Children

§ 300.500   Definitions of "Consent," "Evaluation," and "Personally Identifiable"

As used in this part: "Consent" means that

(a) The parent has been fully informed of all information relevant to the activity for which consent is sought, in his or her native language, or other mode of communication.

(b) The parent understands and agrees in writing to the carrying out of the activity for which his or her consent is sought, and the consent describes that activity and lists the records (if any) which will be released and to whom; and

(c) The parent understands that the granting of consent is voluntary on the part of the parent and may be revoked at any time.

"Evaluation" means procedures used in accordance with §§300.530–300.534 to determine whether a child is handicapped and the nature and extent of the special education and related services that the child needs. The term means procedures used selectively with an individual child and does not include basic tests administered to or procedures used with all children in a school, grade, or class.

"Personally identifiable" means that information includes:

(a) The name of the child, the child's parent, or other family member;

(b) The address of the child;

(c) A personal identifier, such as the child's social security number or student number; or

(d) A list of personal characteristics or other information which would make it possible to identify the child with reasonable certainty.

§ 300.502 Opportunity to Examine Records

The parents of a handicapped child shall be afforded, in accordance with the procedures in §§300.562–300.569 an opportunity to inspect and review all education records with respect to:

(a) The identification, evaluation, and educational placement of the child, and

(b) The provision of a free appropriate public education to the child.

§ 300.503 Independent Educational Evaluation

(a) *General.* (1) The parents of a handicapped child have the right under this part to obtain an independent educational evaluation of the child, subject to paragraphs (b) through (e) of this section.

(2) Each public agency shall provide to parents, on request, information about where an independent educational evaluation may be obtained.

(3) For the purposes of this part:

(i) "Independent educational evaluation" means an evaluation conducted by a qualified examiner who is not employed by the public agency responsible for the education of the child in question.

(ii) "Public expense" means that the public agency either pays for the full cost of the evaluation or insures that the evaluation is otherwise provided at no cost to the parent, consistent with §300.301 of Subpart C.

(b) *Parent right to evaluation at public expense.* A parent has the right to an independent educational evaluation at public expense if the parent disagrees with an evaluation obtained by the public agency. However, the public agency may initiate a hearing under §300.506 of this subpart to show that its evaluation is appropriate. If the final decision is that the evaluation is appropriate, the parent still has the right to an independent educational evaluation, but not at public expense.

(c) *Parent initiated evaluations.* If the parent obtains an independent educational evaluation at private expense, the results of the evaluation:

(1) Must be considered by the public agency in any decision made with respect to the provision of a free appropriate public education to the child, and

(2) May be presented as evidence at a hearing under this subpart regarding that child.

(d) *Requests for evaluations by hearing officers.* If a hearing officer requests an independent educational evaluation as part of a hearing, the cost of the evaluation must be at public expense.

(e) *Agency criteria.* Whenever an independent evaluation is at public expense, the criteria under which the evaluation is obtained, including the location of the evaluation and the qualifications of the examiner, must be the same as the criteria which the public agency uses when it initiates an evaluation.

§ 300.504 Prior Notice: Parent Consent

(a) *Notice.* Written notice which meets the requirements under §300.505 must be given to the parents of a handicapped child a reasonable time before the public agency:

(1) Proposes to initiate or change the identification, evaluation, or educational placement of the child or the provision of a free appropriate public education to the child, or

(2) Refuses to initiate or change the identification, evaluation, or educational placement of the child or the provision of a free appropriate public education to the child, or

(b) *Consent.* (1) Parental consent must be obtained before:

(i) Conducting a preplacement evaluation; and

(ii) Initial placement of a handicapped child in a program providing special education and related services.

(2) Except for preplacement evaluation and initial placement, consent may not be required as a condition of any benefit to the parent or child.

(c) *Procedures where parent refuses consent.*
(1) Where State law requires parental consent before a handicapped child is evaluated or initially provided special education and related services. State procedures govern the public agency in overriding a parent's refusal to consent.

(2)(i) Where there is no State law requiring consent before a handicapped child is evaluated or initially provided special education and related services, the public agency may use the hearing procedures in §§300.506–300.508 to determine if the child may be evaluated or initially provided special education and related services without parental consent.

(ii) If the hearing officer upholds the agency, the agency may evaluate or initially provide special education and related services to the child without the parent's consent, subject to the parent's rights under §§300.510–300.513.

Comment. 1. Any changes in a child's special education program, after the initial placement, are not subject to the prior notice requirement in paragraph (a) and the individualized education program requirements in Subpart C.

2. Paragraph (c) means that where State law requires parental consent before evaluation or before special education and related services are initially provided, and the parent refuses (or otherwise withholds) consent. State procedures, such as obtaining a court order authorizing the public agency to conduct the evaluation or provide the education and related services, must be followed.

If, however, there is no legal requirement for consent outside of these regulations, the public agency may use the due process procedures under this subpart to obtain a decision to allow the evaluation or services without parental consent. The agency must notify the parent of its actions, and the parent has appeal rights as well as rights at the hearing itself.

§ 300.505   Content of Notice

(a) The notice under §300.504 must include:

(1) A full explanation of all of the procedural safeguards available to the parents under Subpart E;

(2) A description of the action proposed or refused by the agency, an explanation of why the agency proposes or refuses to take the action, and a description of any options the agency considered and the reasons why those options were rejected;

(3) A description of each evaluation procedure, test, record, or report the agency uses as a basis for the proposal or refusal; and

(4) A description of any other factors which are relevant to the agency's proposal or refusal.

(b) The notice must be:

(1) Written in language understandable to the general public, and

(2) Provided in the native language of the parent or other mode of communication used by the parent, unless it is clearly not feasible to do so.

(c) If the native language or other mode of communication of the parent is not a written language, the State or local educational agency shall take steps to insure:

(1) That the notice is translated orally or by other means to the parent in his or her native language or other mode of communication;

(2) That the parent understands the content of the notice, and

(3) That there is written evidence that the requirements in paragraph (c) (1) and (2) of this section have been met.

§ 300.506   Impartial Due Process Hearing

(a) A parent or a public educational agency may initiate a hearing on any of the matters described in §300.504(a)(1) and (2).

(b) The hearing must be conducted by the State educational agency or the public agency directly responsible for the education of the child, as determined under State statute, State regulation, or a written policy of the State educational agency.

(c) The public agency shall inform the parent of any free or low-cost legal and other relevant services available in the area if:

(1) The parent requests the information; or

(2) The parent or the agency initiates a hearing under this section.

§ 300.507   Impartial Hearing Officer

(a) A hearing may not be conducted:

(1) By a person who is an employee of a public agency which is involved in the education or care of the child, or

(2) By any person having a personal or professional interest which would conflict with his or her objectivity in the hearing.

(b) A person who otherwise qualifies to conduct a hearing under paragraph (a) of this section is not an employee of the agency solely because he or she is paid by the agency to serve as a hearing officer.

(c) Each public agency shall keep a list of the persons who serve as hearing officers. The list must include a statement of the qualifications of each of those persons.

§ 300.508   Hearing Rights

(a) Any party to a hearing has the right to:

(1) Be accompanied and advised by counsel and by individuals with special knowledge or training with respect to the problems of handicapped children;

(2) Present evidence and confront, cross-examine, and compel the attendance of witnesses;

(3) Prohibit the introduction of any evidence at the hearing that has not been disclosed to that party at least five days before the hearing;

(4) Obtain a written or electronic verbatim record of the hearing;

(5) Obtain written findings of fact and decisions. (The public agency shall transmit those findings and decisions, after deleting any personally identifiable information, to the State advisory panel established under Subpart F).

(b) Parents involved in hearings must be given the right to:

(1) Have the child who is the subject of the hearing present; and

(2) Open the hearing to the public.

§ 300.509   Hearing Decision: Appeal

A decision made in a hearing conducted under this subpart is final, unless a party to the hearing appeals the decision under §300.510 or §300.511.

§ 300.510   Administrative Appeal; Impartial Review

(a) If the hearing is conducted by a public agency other than the State educational agency, any party aggrieved by the findings and decision in the hearing may appeal to the State educational agency.

(b) If there is an appeal, the State educational agency shall conduct an impartial review of the hearing. The official conducting the review shall:

(1) Examine the entire hearing record;

(2) Insure that the procedures at the hearing were consistent with the requirements of due process;

(3) Seek additional evidence if necessary. If a hearing is held to receive additional evidence, the rights in §300.508 apply;

(4) Afford the parties an opportunity for oral or written argument, or both, at the discretion of the reviewing official;

(5) Make an independent decision on completion of the review; and

(6) Give a copy of written findings and the decision to the parties.

(c) The decision made by the reviewing official is final, unless a party brings a civil action under §300.512.

§ 300.511   Civil Action

Any party aggrieved by the findings and decision made in a hearing who does not have the right to appeal under §300.510 of this subpart, and any party aggrieved by the decision of a reviewing officer under §300.510 has the right to bring a civil action under section 615(e)(2) of the Act.

§ 300.512   Timeliness and Convenience of Hearings and Reviews

(a) The public agency shall insure that not later than 45 days after the receipt of a request for hearing:

(1) A final decision is reached in the hearing; and

(2) A copy of the decision is mailed to each of the parties.

(b) The State educational agency shall insure that not later than 30 days after the receipt of a request for a review:

(1) A final decision is reached in the review; and

(2) A copy of the decision is mailed to each of the parties.

(c) A hearing or reviewing officer may grant specific extensions of time beyond the periods set out in paragraphs (a) and (b) of this section at the request of either party.

(d) Each hearing and each review involving oral arguments must be conducted at a time and place which is reasonably convenient to the parents and child involved.

§ 300.513   Child's Status During Proceedings

(a) During the pendency of any administrative or judicial proceeding regarding a complaint, unless the public agency and the parents of the child agree otherwise, the child involved in the complaint must remain in his or her present educational placement.

(b) If the complaint involves an application for initial admission to public school, the child, with the consent of the parents, must be placed in the public school program until the completion of all the proceedings.

Comment. Section 300.513 does not permit a child's placement to be changed during a complaint proceeding, unless the parents and agency agree otherwise. While the placement may not be changed, this does not preclude the agency from using its normal procedures for dealing with children who are endangering themselves or others.

§ 300.514   Surrogate Parents

(a) *General.* Each public agency shall insure that the rights of a child are protected when:

(1) No parent (as defined in §300.10) can be identified;

(2) The public agency, after reasonable efforts, cannot discover the whereabouts of a parent; or

(3) The child is a ward of the State under the laws of that State.

(b) *Duty of public agency.* The duty of a public agency under paragraph (a) of this section includes the assignment of an individual to act as a surrogate for the parents. This must include a method (1) for determining whether a child needs a surrogate parent, and (2) for assigning a surrogate parent to the child.

(c) *Criteria for selection of surrogates.*

(1) The public agency may select a surrogate parent in any way permitted under State law.

(2) Public agencies shall insure that a person selected as a surrogate:

(i) Has no interest that conflicts with the interests of the child he or she represents; and

(ii) Has knowledge and skills, that insure adequate representation of the child.

(d) *Non-employee requirement; compensation.*

(1) A person assigned as a surrogate may not be an employee of a public agency which is involved in the education or care of the child.

(2) A person who otherwise qualifies to be a surrogate parent under paragraph (c) and (d)(1) of this section is not an employee of the agency solely because he or she is paid by the agency to serve as a surrogate parent.

(e) *Responsibilities.* The surrogate parent may represent the child in all matters relating to:

(1) The identification, evaluation, and educational placement of the child, and

(2) The provision of a free appropriate public education to the child.

Protection in Evaluation Procedures
§ 300.530   General

(a) Each State educational agency shall insure that each public agency establishes and implements procedures which meet the requirements of §§300.530–300.534.

(b) Testing and evaluation materials and procedures used for the purposes of evaluation and placement of handicapped children must be selected and administered so as not to be racially or culturally discriminatory.

§ 300.531   Preplacement Evaluation

Before any action is taken with respect to the initial placement of a handicapped child in a special education program, a full and individual evaluation of the child's educational needs must be conducted in accordance with the requirements of §300.532.

§ 300.532   Evaluation Procedures

State and local educational agencies shall insure, at a minimum, that:

(a) Tests and other evaluation materials:

(1) Are provided and administered in the child's native language or other mode of communication, unless it is clearly not feasible to do so;

(2) Have been validated for the specific purpose for which they are used; and

(3) Are administered by training personnel in conformance with the instructions provided by their producer:

(b) Tests and other evaluation materials include those tailored to assess specific areas of educational need and not merely those which are designed to provide a single general intelligence quotient;

(c) Tests are selected and administered so as best ensure that when a test is administered to a child with impaired sensory, manual, or speaking skills, the test results accurately reflect the child's aptitude or achievement level or whatever other factors the test purports to measure, rather than reflecting the child's impaired sensory, manual, or speaking skills (except where those skills are the factors which the test purports to measure);

(d) No single procedure is used as the sole criterion for determining an appropriate educational program for a child; and

(e) The evaluation is made by a multidisciplinary team or group of persons, including at least one teacher or other specialist with knowledge in the area of suspected disability.

(f) The child is assessed in all areas related to the suspected disability, including, where appropriate, health, vision, hearing, social and emotional status, general intelligence, academic performance, communicative status, and motor abilities.

§ 300.533   Placement Procedures

(a) In interpreting evaluation data and in making placement decisions, each public agency shall:

(1) Draw upon information from a variety of sources, including aptitude and achievement tests, teacher recommendations, physical condition, social or cultural background, and adaptive behavior;

(2) Insure that information obtained from all of these sources is documented and carefully considered;

(3) Insure that the placement decision is made by a group of persons, including persons knowledgeable about the child, the meaning of the evaluation data, and the placement options; and

(4) Insure that the placement decision is made in conformity with the least restrictive environment rules in §§300.550–300.554.

(b) If a determination is made that a child is handicapped and needs special education and related services, an individualized education program must be developed for the child in accordance with §§300.340–300.349 of Subpart C.

§ 300.534   Reevaluation

Each State and local educational agency shall insure:

(a) That each handicapped child's individualized education program is reviewed in accordance with §§300.340–300.349 of Subpart C, and

(b) That an evaluation of the child, based on procedures which meet the requirements under §300.532 is conducted every three years or more frequently if conditions warrant or if the child's parent or teacher requests an evaluation.

Least Restrictive Environment

§ 300.550   General

(a) Each State educational agency shall insure that each public agency establishes and implements procedures which meet the requirements of §§300.550–300.556.

(b) Each public agency shall insure:

(1) That to the maximum extent appropriate, handicapped children, including children in public or private institutions or other care facilities, are educated with children who are not handicapped, and

(2) That special classes, separate schooling or other removal of handicapped children from the regular educational environment occurs only when the nature or severity of the handicap is such that education in regular classes with the use of supplementary aids and services cannot be achieved satisfactorily.

§ 300.551   Continuum of Alternative Placements

(a) Each public agency shall insure that a continuum of alternative placements is available to meet the needs of handicapped children for special education and related services.

(b) The continuum required under paragraph (a) of this section must:

(1) Include the alternative placements listed in the definition of special education under §300.13 of Subpart A (instruction in regular classes, special classes, special schools, home instruction, and instruction in hospitals and institutions), and

(2) Make provision for supplementary services (such as resource room or itinerant instruction) to be provided in conjunction with regular class placement.

§ 300.552   Placements

Each public agency shall insure that:

(a) Each handicapped child's educational placement:

(1) Is determined at least annually,

(2) Is based on his or her individualized education program, and

(3) Is as close as possible to the child's home;

(b) The various alternative placements included under §300.551 are available to the extent necessary to implement the individualized education program for each handicapped child;

(c) Unless a handicapped child's individualized education program requires some other arrangement, the child is educated in the school which he or she would attend if not handicapped; and

(d) In selecting the least restrictive environment, consideration is given to any potential harmful effect on the child or on the quality of services which he or she needs.

Comment. It should be stressed that, where a handicapped child is so disruptive in a regular classroom that the education of other students is significantly impaired, the needs of the handicapped child cannot be met in that environment. Therefore regular placement would not be appropriate to his or her needs . . ."

Confidentiality of Information
§ 300.560   *Definitions*
As used in this subpart:

"Destruction" means physical destruction or removal of personal identifiers from information so that the information is no longer personally identifiable.

"Education records" means the type of records covered under the definition of "education records" in Part 99 of this title (the regulations implementing the Family Educational Rights and Privacy Act of 1974).

"Participating agency" means any agency or institution which collects, maintains, or uses personally identifiable information, or from which information is obtained, under this part.

§ 300.561   *Notice to parents*
(a) The State educational agency shall give notice which is adequate to fully inform parents about the requirements under §300.128 of Subpart B including:

(1) A description of the extent to which the notice is given in the native languages of the various population groups in the State;

(2) A description of the children on whom personally identifiable information is maintained, the types of information sought, the methods of State intends to use in gathering the information (including the sources from whom information is gathered), and the uses to be made of the information;

(3) A summary of the policies and procedures which participating agencies must follow regarding storage, disclosure to third parties, retention, and destruction of personally identifiable information; and

(4) A description of all of the rights of parents and children regarding this information, including the rights under section 438 of the General Education Provisions Act and Part 99 of this title (the Family Educational Rights and Privacy Act of 1974, and implementing regulations).

(b) Before any major identification, location, or evaluation activity, the notice must be published or announced in newspapers or other media, or both, with circulation adequate to notify parents throughout the State of the activity.

§ 300.562   *Access Rights*
(a) Each participating agency shall permit parents to inspect and review any education records relating to their children which are collected, maintained, or used by the agency under this part. The agency shall comply with a request without unnecessary delay and before any meeting regarding an individualized education program or hearing relating to the identification, evaluation, or placement of the child, and in no case more than 45 days after the request has been made.

(b) The right to inspect and review education records under this section includes:

(1) The right to a response from the participating agency to reasonable requests for explanations and interpretations of the records;

(2) The right to request that the agency provide copies of the records containing the information if failure to provide those copies would effectively prevent the parent from exercising the right to inspect and review the records; and

(3) The right to have a representative of the parent inspect and review the records.

(c) An agency may presume that the parent has authority to inspect and review records relating to his or her child unless the agency has been advised that the parent does not have the authority under applicable State law governing such matters as guardianship, separation, and divorce.

§ 300.563   *Record of Access*
Each participating agency shall keep a record of parties obtaining access to education records collected, maintained, or used under this part (except access by parents and authorized employees of the participating agency), including the name of the

party, the date access was given, and the purpose for which the party is authorized to use the records.

§ 300.564   Records on More Than One Child

If any education record includes information on more than one child, the parents of those children shall have the right to inspect and review only the information relating to their child or to be informed of that specific information.

§ 300.565   List of Types and Locations of Information

Each participating agency shall provide parents on request a list of the types and locations of education records collected, maintained, or used by the agency.

§ 300.567   Amendment of Records at Parent's Request

(a) A parent who believes that information in education records collected, maintained, or used under this part is inaccurate or misleading or violates the privacy or other rights of the child, may request the participating agency which maintains the information to amend the information.

(b) The agency shall decide whether to amend the information in accordance with the request within a reasonable period of time of receipt of the request.

(c) If the agency decides to refuse to amend the information in accordance with the request it shall inform the parent of the refusal, and advise the parent of the right of a hearing under §300.568.

§ 300.568   Opportunity for a Hearing

The agency shall, on request, provide an opportunity for a hearing to challenge information in education records to insure that it is not inaccurate, misleading, or otherwise in violation of the privacy or other rights of the child.

§ 300.571   Consent

(a) Parental consent must be obtained before personally identifiable information is:

(1) Disclosed to anyone other than officials of participating agencies collecting or using the information under this part, subject to paragraph (b) of this section; or

(2) Used for any purpose other than meeting a requirement under this part.

(b) An educational agency or institution subject to Part 99 of this title may not release information from education records to participating agencies without parental consent unless authorized to do so under Part 99 of this title.

(c) The State educational agency shall include policies and procedures in its annual program plan which are used in the event that a parent refuses to provide consent under this section.

§ 300.572   Safeguards

(a) Each participating agency shall protect the confidentiality of personally identifiable information at collection, storage, disclosure, and destruction stages.

(b) One official at each participating agency shall assume responsibility for insuring the confidentiality of any personally identifiable information.

(c) All persons collecting or using personally identifiable information must receive training or instruction regarding the State's policies and procedures under §300.129 of Subpart B and Part 99 of this title.

(d) Each participating agency shall maintain, for public inspection, a current listing of the names and positions of those employees within the agency who may have access to personally identifiable information.

§ 300.573   Destruction of Information

(a) The public agency shall inform parents when personally identifiable information collected, maintained, or used under this part is not longer needed to provide educational services to the child.

(b) The information must be destroyed at the request of the parents. However, a permanent record of a student's name, address, and phone number, his or her grades, attendance record, classes attended, grade level completed, and year completed may be maintained without time limitation.

Comment. Under section 300.573, the personally identifiable information on a handicapped child may be retained permanently unless the parents request that it be destroyed. Destruction of records is the best protection against improper and unauthorized disclosure. However, the records may be needed for other purposes. In informing parents about their rights under this section, the agency should remind them that the records may be needed by the child or the parents for social security benefits or other purposes. If the parents request that the information be destroyed, the agency may retain the information in paragraph (b).

SUBPART G—ALLOCATION OF FUNDS; REPORTS

Allocations

§ 300.701 *State Entitlement; Formula*

(a) The maximum amount of the grant to which a State is entitled under section 611 of the Act in any fiscal year is equal to the number of handicapped children aged three through 21 in the State who are receiving special education and related services, multiplied by the applicable percentage, under paragraph (b) of this section, of the average per pupil expenditure in public elementary and secondary schools in the United States.

(b) For the purposes of the formula in paragraph (a) of this section, the applicable percentage of the average per pupil expenditure in public elementary and secondary schools in the United States for each fiscal year is:

(1) 1978—5 percent,

(2) 1979—10 percent,

(3) 1980—20 percent,

(4) 1981—30 percent, and

(5) 1982, and for each fiscal year after 1982, 40 percent.

(c) For the purposes of this section, the average per pupil expenditure in public elementary and secondary schools in the United States, means the aggregate expenditures during the second fiscal year preceding the fiscal year for which the computation is made (or if satisfactory data for that year are not available at the time of computation, then during the most recent preceding fiscal year for which satisfactory data are available) of all local educational agencies in the United States (which, for the purpose of this section, means the fifty States and the District of Columbia), plus any direct expenditures by the State for operation of those agencies (without regard to the source of funds from which either of those expenditures are made), divided by the aggregate number of children in average daily attendance to whom those

agencies provided free public education during that preceding year.

§ 300.702 *Limitations and Exclusions*

(a) In determining the amount of a grant under §300.701 of this subpart, the Commissioner may not count:

(1) Handicapped children in a State to the extent that the number of those children is greater than 12 percent of the number of all children aged five through 17 in the State;

(3) Handicapped children who are counted under section 300 of the Elementary and Secondary Education Act of 1965.

(b) For the purposes of paragraph (a) of this section, the number of children aged five through 17 in any State shall be determined by the Commissioner on the basis of the most recent satisfactory data available to him.

§ 300.707 *Local Educational Agency Entitlements; Formula*

From the total amount of funds available to all local educational agencies, each local educational agency is entitled to an amount which bears the same ratio to the total amount as the number of handicapped children aged three through 21 in that agency who are receiving special education and related services bears to the aggregate number of handicapped children aged three through 21 receiving special education and related services in all local educational agencies which apply to the State educational agency for funds under Part B of the Act.

AMENDED LEARNING DISABILITIES REGUALTIONS

§ 300.5 *Handicapped Children*

(b) . . .

(9) "Specific learning disability" means a disorder in one or more of the basic psychological processes involved in understanding or in using language, spoken or written, which may manifest itself in an imperfect ability to listen, think, speak, read, write, spell, or to do mathematical calculations. The term includes such conditions as perceptual handicaps, brain injury, minimal brain dysfunction, dyslexia, and developmental aphasia. The term does not include children who have

learning problems which are primarily the result of visual, hearing, or motor handicaps, of mental retardation, of emotional disturbance, or of environmental, cultural, or economic disadvantage.

Additional Procedures for Evaluating Specific Learning Disabilities

§ 300.540   Additional Team Members

In evaluating a child suspected of having a specific learning disability, in addition to the requirements of §300.532, each public agency shall include on the multidisciplinary evaluation team:

(a)(1) The child's regular teacher; or

(2) If the child does not have a regular teacher, a regular classroom teacher qualified to teach a child of his or her age; or

(3) For a child of less than school age, an individual qualified by the State educational agency to teach a child of his or her age; and

(4) At least one person qualified to conduct individual diagnostic examinations of children, such as a school psychologist, speech-language pathologist, or remedial reading teacher.

§ 300.541   Criteria for Determining the Existence of a Specific Learning Disability

(a) A team may determine that a child has a specific learning disability if:

(1) The child does not achieve commensurate with his or her age and ability levels in one or more of the areas listed in paragraph (a) (2) of this section, when provided with learning experiences appropriate for the child's age and ability levels; and

(2) The team finds that a child has a severe discrepancy between achievement and intellectual ability in one or more of the following areas:

(i)   Oral expression;

(ii)   Listening comprehension;

(iii) Written expression;

(iv)   Basic reading skill;

(v)   Reading comprehension;

(vi)   Mathematics calculation; or

(vii) Mathematics reasoning.

(b)   The team may not identify a child as having a specific learning disability if the severe discrepancy between ability and achievement is primarily the result of:

(1) A visual, hearing, or motor handicap;

(2) Mental retardation;

(3) Emotional disturbnce; or

(4) Environmental, cultural or economic disadvantage.

§ 300.542   Observation

(a) At least one team member other than the child's regular teacher shall observe the child's academic performance in the regular classroom setting.

(b) In the case of a child of less than school age or out of school, a team member shall observe the child in an environment appropriate for a child of that age.

§ 300.543   Written report

(a) The team shall prepare a written report of the results of the evaluation.

(b) The report must include a statement of:

(1) Whether the child has a specific learning disability;

(2) The basis for making the determination;

(3) The relevant behavior noted during the observation of the child;

(4) The relationship of that behavior to the child's academic functioning;

(5) The educationally relevant medical findings, if any;

(6) Whether there is a severe discrepancy between achievement and ability which is not correctable without special education and related services; and

(7) The determination of the team concerning the effects of environmental, cultural, or economic disadvantage.

(c) Each team member shall certify in writing whether the report reflects his or her conclusion. If it does not reflect his or her conclusion, the team member must submit a separate statement presenting his or her conclusions.

APPENDIX **D**

RULES AND REGULATIONS FOR P.L. 93-380 IMPLEMENTING SECTION 438 (THE FAMILY EDUCATIONAL RIGHTS AND PRIVACY ACT)

SUBPART A—GENERAL

§ 99.1 Applicability of Part

(a) This part applies to all educational agencies or institutions to which funds are made available under any Federal [program for which the U.S. Commissioner of Education has administrative responsibility, as specified by law or by delegation of authority pursuant to law.]

(b) This part does not apply to an educational agency or institution solely because students attending that nonmonetary agency or institution receive benefits under one or more of the Federal programs referenced in paragraph (a) of this section, if no funds under those programs are made available to the agency or institution itself.

(c) For the purposes of this part, funds will be considered to have been made available to an agency or institution when funds under one or more of the programs referenced in paragraph (a) of this section: (1) Are provided to the agency or institution by grant, contract, subgrant, or subcontract, or (2) are provided to students attending the agency or institution and the funds may be paid to the agency or institution by those students for educational purposes, such as under the Basic Educational Opportunity Grants Program and the Guaranteed Student Loan Program (Titles IV-A-1 and IV-B, respectively of the Higher Education Act of 1965, as amended).

(d) Except as otherwise specifically provided, this part applies to education records of students who are or have been in attendance at the educational agency or institution which maintains the records.

§ 99.2 Purpose

The purpose of this part is to set forth requirements governing the protection of privacy of parents and students under section 438 of the General Educational Provisions Act, as amended.

§ 99.3 Definitions

As used in this Part:

"Act" means the General Education Provisions Act, Title IV of Pub. 1. 90-247, as amended.

"Attendance" at an agency or institution includes, but is not limited to: (a) attendance in person and by correspondence, and (b) the period during which a person is working under a work-study program.

"Commissioner" means the U.S. Commissioner of Education.

"Directory information" includes the following information relating to a student: the student's name, address, telephone number, date and place of birth, major field of study, participation in officially recognized activities and sports, weight and height of members of athletic teams, dates of attendance, degrees and awards received, the most recent previous educational agency or institution attended by the student, and other similar information.

"Disclosure" means permitting access or the release, transfer, or other communication of education records of the student or the personally identifiable information contained therein, orally or in writing, or by electronic means, or by any other means to any party.

"Educational institution" or "educational agency or institution" means any public or private agency or institution which is the recipient of funds under any Federal program referenced in §99.1 (a). The term refers to the agency or institution recipient as a whole, including all of its components (such as schools or departments in a university) and shall not be read to refer to one or more of these components separate from that agency or institution.

"Education records" (a) means those records which: (1) Are directly related to a student and (2) are maintained by an educational agency or institution or by a party acting for the agency or institution.

(b) The term does not include:

(1) Records of instructional, supervisory, and administrative personnel and educational personnel ancillary thereto which:

(i) Are in the sole possession of the maker thereof, and

(ii) Are not accessible or revealed to any other individual except a substitute. For the purpose of this definition a "substitute" means an individual who performs on a temporary basis the duties of the individual who made the record, and does not refer to an individual who permanently succeeds the maker of the record in his or her position.

(2) Records of a law enforcement unit of an educational agency or institution which are:

(i) Maintained apart from the records described in paragraph (a) of this definition;

(ii) Maintained solely for law enforcement purposes, and

(iii) Not disclosed to individuals other than law enforcement officials of the same jurisdiction; *Provided,* That education records maintained by the educational agency or institution are not disclosed to the personnel of the law enforcement unit.

(3) (i) Records relating to an individual who is employed by an educational agency or institution which:

(A) Are made and maintained in the normal course of business;

(B) Relate exclusively to the individual in that individual's capacity as an employee, and

(C) Are not available for use for any other purpose.

(ii) This paragraph does not apply to records relating to an individual in attendance at the agency or institution who is employed as a result of his or her status as a student.

(4) Records relating to an eligible student which are:

(i) Created or maintained by a physician, psychiatrist, psychologist, or other recognized professional or paraprofessional acting in his or her professional or paraprofessional capacity, or assisting in that capacity;

(ii) Created, maintained, or used only in connection with the provision of treatment to the student, and

(iii) Not disclosed to anyone other than individuals providing the treatment; *Provided,* That the records can be personally reviewed by a physician or other appropriate professional of the student's choice. For the purpose of this definition, "treatment" does not include remedial educational activities or activities which are part of the program of instruction at the educational agency or institution.

(5) Records of an educational agency or institution which contain only information relating to a person after that person was no longer a student at the educational agency or institution. An example would be information collected by an educational agency or institution pertaining to the accomplishments of its alumni.

"Eligible student" means a student who has attained eighteen years of age, or is attending an institution of post-secondary education.

"Financial Aid," as used in §99.31 (a) (4),

means a payment of funds provided to an individual (or a payment in kind of tangible or intangible property to the individual) which is conditioned on the individual's attendance at an educational agency or institution.

"Institution of postsecondary education" means an institution which provides education to students beyond the secondary school level; "secondary school level" means the educational level (not beyond grade 12) at which secondary education is provided, as determined under State law.

"Panel" means the body which will adjudicate cases under procedures set forth in §§99.65–99.67.

"Parent" includes a parent, a guardian, or an individual acting as a parent of a student in the absence of a parent or guardian. An educational agency or institution may presume the parent has the authority to exercise the rights inherent in the Act unless the agency or institution has been provided with evidence that there is a State law or court order governing such matters as divorce, separation or custody, or a legally binding instrument which provides to the contrary.

"Party" means an individual, agency, institution or organization.

"Personally identifiable" means that the data or information includes (a) the name of the student, the student's parent, or other family member, (b) the address of the student, (c) a personal identifier, such as the student's social security number or student number, (d) a list of personal characteristics which would make the student's identity easily traceable, or (e) other information which would make the student's identity easily traceable.

"Record" means any information or data recorded in any medium, including, but not limited to: handwriting, print, tapes, film, microfilm, and microfiche.

"Secretary" means the Secretary of the U.S. Department of Health, Education, and Welfare.

"Student" (a) includes any individual with respect to whom an educational agency or institution maintains education records.

(b) The term does not include an individual who has not been in attendance at an educational agency or institution. A person who has applied for admission to, but has never been in attendance at a component unit of an institution of postsecondary education (such as the various colleges or schools which comprise a university), even if that individual is or has been in attendance at another component unit of that institution of postsecondary education, is not considered to be a student with respect to the component to which an application for admission has been made.

§ 99.4   Student Rights

(a) For the purposes of this part, whenever a student has attained eighteen years of age, or is attending an institution of postsecondary education, the rights accorded to and the consent required of the parent of the student shall thereafter only be accorded to and required of the eligible student.

(b) The status of an eligible student as a dependent of his or her parents for the purposes of §99.31(a)(8) does not otherwise affect the rights accorded to and the consent required of the eligible student by paragraph (a) of this section.

(c) Section 438 of the Act and the regulations in this part shall not be construed to preclude educational agencies or institutions from according to students rights in addition to those accorded to parents of students.

§ 99.5   Formulation of Institutional Policy and Procedures

(a) Each educational agency or institution shall, consistent with the minimum requirements of section 438 of the Act and this part, formulate and adopt a policy of—

(1) Informing parents of students or eligible students of their rights under §99.6;

(2) Permitting parents of students or eligible students to inspect and review the education records of the student in accordance with §99.11, including at least:

(i) A statement of the procedure to be followed by a parent or an eligible student who requests to inspect and review the education records of the student;

(ii) With an understanding that it may not deny access to an education record, a description of the circumstances in which the agency or institution feels it has a legitimate cause to deny a request for a copy of such records;

(iii) A schedule of fees for copies, and

(iv) A listing of the types and locations of education records maintained by the educational agency or institution and the titles and the addresses of the officials responsible for those records;

(3) Not disclosing personally identifiable information from the education records of a student without the prior written consent of the parent of the student or the eligible student, except as otherwise permitted by §§99.31 and 99.37; the policy shall include, at least: (i) A statement of whether the educational agency or institution will disclose personally identifiable information from the education records of a student under §99.31 (a) (1) and, if so, a specification of the criteria for determining which parties are "school officials" and what the educational agency or institution consider to be a "legitimate educational interest," and (ii) a specification of the personally identifiable information to be designated as directory information to be designated as directory information under §99.37;

(4) Maintaining the record of disclosures of personally identifiable information from the education records of a student required to be maintained by §99.32, and permitting a parent or an eligible student to inspect that record;

(5) Providing a parent of the student or an eligible student with an opportunity to seek the correction of education records of the student through a request to amend the records or a hearing under Subpart C, and permitting the parent of a student or an eligible student to place a statement in the education records of the student as provided in §99.21(c);

(b) The policy required to be adopted by paragraph (a) of this section shall be in writing and copies shall be made available upon request to parents of students and to eligible students.

§ 99.6   Annual Notification of Rights

(a) Each educational agency or institution shall give parents of students in attendance or eligible students in attendance at the agency or institution annual notice by such means as are reasonably likely to inform them of the following:

(1) Their rights under section 438 of the Act, the regulations in this part, and the policy adopted under §99.5; the notice shall also inform parents of students or eligible students of the locations where copies of the policy may be obtained; and

(2) The right to file complaints under §99.63 concerning alleged failures by the educational agency or institution to comply with the requirements of section 438 of the Act and this part.

(b) Agencies and institutions of elementary and secondary education shall provide for the need to effectively notify parents of students identified as having a primary or home language other than English.

§ 99.7   Limitations on Waivers

(a) Subject to the limitations in this section and §99.12, a parent of a student or a student may waive any of his or her rights under section 438 of the Act or this part. A waiver shall not be valid unless in writing and signed by the parent or student, as appropriate.

(b) An educational agency or institution may not require that a parent of a student or student waive his or her rights under section 438 of the Act or this part. This paragraph does not preclude an educational agency or institution from requesting such a waiver.

(c) An individual who is an applicant for admission to an institution of postsecondary education or is a student in attendance at an institution of postsecondary education may waive his or her right to inspect and review confidential letters and confidential statements of recommendation described in §99.12(a)(3) except that the waiver may apply to confidential letters and statements only if: (1) The applicant or student is, upon request, notified of the names of all individuals providing the letters or statements; (2) the letters or statements are used only for the purpose for which they were originally intended, and (3) such waiver is not required by the agency or institution as a condition of admission to or receipt of any other service or benefit from the agency or institution.

(d) All waivers under paragraph (c) of this section must be executed by the individual, regardless of age, rather than by the parent of the individual.

(e) A waiver under this section may be made with respect to specified classes of: (1) Education records, and (2) persons or institutions.

(f)(1) A waiver under this section may be revoked with respect to any actions occurring after the revocation.

(2) A revocation under this paragraph must be in writing.

(3) If a parent of a student executes a waiver under this section, that waiver may be revoked by the student at any time after he or she becomes an eligible student.

§ 99.8   Fees

(a) An educational agency or institution may charge a fee for copies of education records which are made for the parents of students, students, and eligible students under section 438 of the Act and this part: *Provided,* That the fee does not effectively prevent the parents and students from exercising their right to inspect and review those records.

(b) An educational agency or institution may not charge a fee to search for or to retrieve the education records of a student.

SUBPART B—INSPECTION AND REVIEW OF EDUCATION RECORDS

§ 99.11   Rights to Inspect and Review Education Records

(a) Each educational agency or institution, except as may be provided by §99.12, shall permit the parent of a student or an eligible student who is or has been in attendance at the agency or institution, to inspect and review the education records of the student. The agency or institution shall comply with a request within a reasonable period of time, but in no case more than 45 days after the request has been made.

(b) The right to inspect and review education records under paragraph (a) of this section includes:

(1) The right to a response from the educational agency or institution to reasonable requests for explanations and interpretations of the records; and

(2) The right to obtain copies of the records from the educational agency or institution where failure of the agency or institution to provide the copies would effectively prevent a parent or eligible student from exercising the right to inspect and review the education records.

(c) An educational agency or institution may presume that either parent of the student has authority to inspect and review the education records of the student unless the agency or institution has been provided with evidence that there is a legally binding instrument, or a State law or court order governing such matters as divorce, separation or custody, which provides to the contrary.

§ 99.12   Limitations on Right to Inspect and Review Education Records at the Postsecondary Level

(a) An institution of postsecondary education is not required by section 438 of the Act or this part to permit a student to inspect and review the following records:

(1) Financial records and statements of their parents or any information contained therein;

(2) Confidential letters and confidential statements of recommendation which were placed in the education records of a student prior to January 1, 1975; *Provided,* That:

(i) The letters and statements were solicited with a written assurance of confidentiality, or sent and retained with a documented understanding of confidentiality, and

(ii) The letters and statements are used only for the purposes for which they were specifically intended;

(3) Confidential letters of recommendation and confidential statements of recommendation which were placed in the education records of the student after January 1, 1975:

(i) Respecting admission to an educational institution;

(ii) Respecting an application for employment, or

(iii) Respecting the receipt of an honor or honorary recognition; *Provided,* That the student has waived his or her right to inspect and review those letters and statements of recommendation under §99.7(c).

(b) If the education records of a student contain information on more than one student, the parent of the student or the eligible student may inspect and review or be informed of only the specific information which pertains to that student.

§ 99.13   Limitation on Destruction of Education Records

An educational agency or institution is not precluded by section 438 of the Act or this part from destroying education records, subject to the following exceptions:

(a) The agency or institution may not destroy any education records if there is an outstanding request to inspect and review them under §99.11;

(b) Explanations placed in the education record under §99.21 shall be maintained as provided in §99.21(d), and

(c) The record of access required under §99.32 shall be maintained for as long as the education record to which it pertains is maintained.

SUBPART C—AMENDMENT OF EDUCATION RECORDS

§ 99.20   Request to Amend Education Records

(a) The parent of a student or an eligible student who believes that information contained in the education records of the student is inaccurate or misleading or violates the privacy or other rights of the student may request that the educational agency or institution which maintains the records amend them.

(b) The educational agency or institution shall decide whether to amend the education records of the student in accordance with the request within a reasonable period of time of receipt of the request.

(c) If the educational agency or institution decides to refuse to amend the education records of the student in accordance with the request it shall so inform the parent of the student or the eligible student of the refusal, and advise the parent or the eligible student of the right to a hearing under §99.21.

§ 99.21   Right to a Hearing

(a) An educational agency or institution shall, on request, provide an opportunity for a hearing in order to challenge the content of a student's education records to insure that information in the education records of the student is not inaccurate, misleading or otherwise in violation of the privacy or other rights of students. The hearing shall be conducted in accordance with §99.22.

(b) If, as a result of the hearing, the educational agency or institution decides that the information is inaccurate, misleading or otherwise in violation of the privacy or other rights of students, it shall amend the education records of the student accordingly and so inform the parent of the student or the eligible student in writing.

(c) If, as a result of the hearing, the educational agency or institution decides that the information is not accurate, misleading or otherwise in violation of the privacy or other rights of students, it shall inform the parent or eligible student of the right to place in the education records of the student a statement commenting upon the information in the education records and/or setting forth any reasons for disagreeing with the decision of the agency or institution.

(d) Any explanation placed in the education records of the student under paragraph (c) of this section shall:

(1) Be maintained by the educational agency or institution as part of the education records of the student as long as the record or contested portion thereof is maintained by the agency or institution, and

(2) If the education records of the student or the contested portion thereof is disclosed by the educational agency or institution to any party, the explanation shall also be disclosed to that party.

§ 99.22   Conduct of the Hearing

The hearing required to be held by §99.21(a) shall be conducted according to procedures which shall include at least the following elements:

(a) The hearing shall be held within a reasonable period of time after the educational agency or institution has received the request, and the parent of the student or the eligible student shall be given notice of the date, place and time reasonably in advance of the hearing;

(b) The hearing may be conducted by any party, including an official of the educational agency or institution, who does not have a direct interest in the outcome of the hearing;

(c) The parent of the student or the eligible student shall be afforded a full and fair opportunity to present evidence relevant to the issues raised under §99.21, and may be assisted or represented by individuals of his or her choice at his or her own expense, including an attorney;

(d) The educational agency or institution shall make its decision in writing within a reasonable period of time after the conclusion of the hearing; and

(e) The decision of the agency or institution shall be based solely upon the evidence presented at the hearing and shall include a summary of the evidence and the reasons for the decision.

SUBPART D—DISCLOSURE OF PERSONALLY IDENTIFIABLE INFORMATION FROM EDUCATION RECORDS

§ 99.30   Prior Consent for Disclosure Required

(a)(1) An educational agency or institution shall obtain the written consent of the parent of a student or the eligible student before disclosing personally identifiable information from the education records of a student, other than directory information, except as provided in §99.31.

(2) Consent is not required under this section where the disclosure is to (i) the parent of a student who is not an eligible student, or (ii) the student himself or herself.

(b) Whenever written consent is required, an educational agency or institution may presume that the parent of the student or the eligible student giving consent has the authority to do so unless the agency or institution has been provided with evidence that there is a legally binding instrument, or a State law or court order governing such matters as divorce, separation or custody, which provides to the contrary.

(c) The written consent required by paragraph (a) of this section must be signed and dated by the parent of the student or the eligible student giving the consent and shall include:

(1) A specification of the records to be disclosed,

(2) The purpose or purposes of the dislosure, and

(3) The party or class of parties to whom the disclosure may be made.

(d) When a disclosure is made pursuant to paragraph (a) of this section, the educational agency or institution shall, upon request, provide a copy of the record which is disclosed to the parent of the student or the eligible student, and to the student who is not an eligible student if so requested by the student's parents.

§ 99.31   Prior Consent for Disclosure Not Required

(a) An educational agency or institution may disclose personally identifiable information from the education records of a student without the written consent of the parent of the student or the eligible student if the disclosure is—

(1) To other school officials, including teachers, within the educational institution or local educational agency who have been determined by the agency or institution to have legitimate educational interests;

(2) To officials of another school or school system in which the student seeks or intends to enroll, subject to the requirements set forth in §99.34;

(3) Subject to the conditions set forth in §99.35, to authorized representatives of:

   (i)   The Comptroller General of the United States,

   (ii) The Secretary,

   (iii) The Commissioner, the Director of the National Institute of Education, or the Assistant Secretary for Education, or

   (iv) State educational authorities;

(4) In connection with financial aid for which a student has applied or which a student has received; *Provided,* That personally identifiable information from the education records of the student may be disclosed only as may be necessary for such purposes as:

   (i)   To determine the eligibility of the student for financial aid,

   (ii) To determine the amount of the financial aid,

   (iii) To determine the conditions which will be imposed regarding the financial aid, or

   (iv) To enforce the terms or conditions which will be imposed regarding the financial aid, or

(5) To State and local officials or authorities to whom information is specifically required to be reported or disclosed pursuant to State statute adopted prior to November 19, 1974. This subparagraph applies only to statutes which require that specific information be disclosed to State or local officials and does not apply to statutes which permit but do not require disclosure. Nothing in this paragraph shall prevent a State from further limiting the number or type of State or local officials to whom disclosures are made under this subparagraph;

(6) To organizations conducting studies for, or on behalf of, educational agencies or institutions for the purpose of developing, validating, or administering predictive tests, administering student aid programs, and improving instruction; *Provided,* That the studies are conducted in a manner which will not permit the personal identification of students and their parents by individuals other than representatives of the organization and the infor-

mation will be destroyed when no longer needed for the purposes for which the study was conducted; the term "organizations" includes, but is not limited to, Federal, State and local agencies, and independent organizations;

(7) To accrediting organizations in order to carry out their accrediting functions;

(8) To parents of a dependent student as defined in section 152 of the Internal Revenue Code of 1954;

(9) To comply with a judicial order or lawfully issued supoena; *Provided,* That the educational agency or institution makes a reasonable effort to notify the parent of the student or the eligible student of the order or subpoena in advance of compliance therewith; and

(10) To appropriate parties in a health or safety emergency subject to the conditions set forth in §99.36.

(b) This section shall not be construed to require or preclude disclosure of any personally identifiable information from the education records of a student by an educational agency or institution to the parties set forth in paragraph (a) of this section.

§ 99.32   Record of Disclosures Required to be Maintained

(a) An educational agency or institution shall for each request for and each disclosure of personally identifiable information from the education records of a student, maintain a record kept with the education records of the student which indicates:

(1) The parties who have requested or obtained personally identifiable information from the education records of the student, and

(2) The legitimate interests these parties had in requesting or obtaining the information.

(b) Paragraph (a) of this section does not apply to disclosures to a parent of a student or an eligible student, disclosures pursuant to the written consent of a parent of a student or an eligible student when the consent is specific with respect to the party or parties to whom the disclosure is to be made, disclosures to school officials under §99.31(a)(1), or to disclosures of directory information under §99.37.

(c) The record of disclosures may be inspected;

(1) By the parent of the student or the eligible student,

(2) By the school official and his or her assistants who are responsible for the custody of the records, and

(3) For the purpose of auditing the record-keeping procedures of the educational agency or institution by the parties authorized in, and under the conditions set forth in §99.31(a)(1) and (3).

§ 99.33   Limitation on Redisclosure

(a) An educational agency or institution may disclose personally identifiable information from the education records of a student only on the condition that the party to whom the information is disclosed will not disclose the information to any other party without the prior written consent of the parent of the student or the eligible student, except that the personally identifiable information which is disclosed to an institution, agency or organization may be used by its officers, employees and agents, but only for the purposes for which the disclosure was made.

(b) Paragraph (a) of this section does not preclude an agency or institution from disclosing personally identifiable information under §99.31 with the understanding that the information will be redisclosed to other parties under that section; *Provided,* That the recordkeeping requirements of §99.32 are met with respect to each of those parties.

(c) An educational agency or institution shall, except for the disclosure of directory information under §99.37, inform the party to whom a disclosure is made of the requirement set forth in paragraph (a) of this section.

§ 99.34   Conditions for Disclosure to Officials of Other Schools and School Systems

(a) An educational agency or institution transferring the education records of a student pursuant to §99.31(a)(2) shall:

(1) Make a reasonable attempt to notify the parent of the student or the eligible student of the transfer of the records at the last known address of the parent or eligible student, except:

　(i) When the transfer of the records is initiated by the parent or eligible student at the sending agency or institution, or

　(ii) When the agency or institution includes a notice in its policies and procedures formulated under §99.5 that it forwards education records on request to a school in which a student seeks or intends to enroll; the agency or institution does not have to provide any further notice of the transfer;

(2) Provide the parent of the student or the eligible student, upon request, with a copy of the education records which have been transferred; and

(3) Provide the parent of the student or the eligible student, upon request, with an opportunity for a hearing under Subpart C of this part.

(b) If a student is enrolled in more than one school, or receives services from more than one school, the schools may disclose information from the education records of the student to each other without obtaining the written consent of the parent of the student or the eligible student; *Provided,* That the disclosure meets the requirements of paragraph (a) of this section.

§ 99.35   Disclosure to Certain Federal and State Officials for Federal Program Purposes

(a) Nothing in section 438 of the Act or this part shall preclude authorization representatives of officials listed in §99.31(a)(3) from having access to student and other records which may be necessary in connection with the audit and evaluation of Federally supported education programs, or in connection with the enforcement of or compliance with the Federal legal requirements which relate to these programs.

(b) Except when the consent of the parent of a student or an eligible student has been obtained under §99.30, or when the collection of personally identifiable information is specifically authorized by Federal law, any data collected by officials listed in §99.31(a)(3) shall be protected in a manner which will not permit the personal identification of students and their parents by other than those officials, and personally identifiable data shall be destroyed when no longer needed for such audit, evaluation, or enforcement of or compliance with Federal legal requirements.

§ 99.36   Conditions for Disclosure in Health and Safety Emergencies

(a) An educational agency or institution may disclose personally identifiable information from the education records of a student to appropriate parties in connection with an emergency if knowl-edge of the information is necessary to protect the health or safety of the student or other individuals.

(b) The factors to be taken into account in determining whether personally identifiable information from the education records of a student may be disclosed under this section shall include the following:

(1) The seriousness of the threat to the health or safety of the student or other individuals;

(2) The need for the information to meet the emergency;

(3) Whether the parties to whom the information is disclosed are in a position to deal with the emergency; and

(4) The extent to which time is of the essence in dealing with the emergency.

(c) Paragraph (a) of this section shall be strictly construed.

§ 99.37   Conditions for Disclosure of Directory Information

(a) An educational agency or institution may disclose personally identifiable information from the education records of a student who is in attendance at the institution or agency if that information has been designated as directory information (as defined in §99.3) under paragraph (c) of this section.

(b) An educational agency or institution may disclose directory information from the education records of an individual who is no longer in attendance at the agency or institution without following the procedures under paragraph (c) of this section.

(c) An educational agency or institution which wishes to designate directory information shall give public notice of the following:

(1) The categories of personally identifiable information which the institution has designated as directory information;

(2) The right of the parent of the student or the eligible student to refuse to permit the designation of any or all of the categories of personally identifiable information with respect to that student as directory information; and

(3) The period of time within which the parent of the student or the eligible student must inform the agency or institution in writing that such personally identifiable information is not to be designated as directory information with respect to that student.

SUBPART E—ENFORCEMENT

§ 99.60   Office and Review Board

(a) The Secretary is required to establish or designate an office and a review board under section 438(g) of the Act. The office will investigate, process, and review violations, and complaints which may be filed concerning alleged violations of the provisions of section 438 of the Act and the regulations in this part. The review board will adjudicate cases referred to it by the office under the procedures set forth in §§99.65–99.67.

(b) The following is the address of the office which has been designated under paragraph (a) of this section: The Family Educational Rights and Privacy Act Office (FERPA), Department of Health, Education, and Welfare, 330 Independence Ave. SW., Washington, D.C. 20201.

§ 99.61   Conflict with State or Local Law

An educational agency or institution which determines that it cannot comply with the requirements of section 438 of the Act or of this part because of State or local law conflicts with the provisions of section 438 of the Act or the regulations in this part shall so advise the office designated under §99.60(b) within 45 days of any such determination, giving the text and legal citation of the conflicting law.

§ 99.62   Reports and Records

Each educational agency or institution shall (a) submit reports in the form and containing such information as the Office of the Review Board may require to carry out their functions under this part, and (b) keep the records and afford access thereto as the Office or the Review Board may find necessary to assure the correctness of those reports and compliance with the provisions of sections 438 of the Act and this part.

§ 99.63   Complaint Procedure

(a) Complaints regarding violations of rights accorded parents and eligible students by section 438 of the Act or the regulations in this part shall be submitted to the Office in writing.

(b)(1) The Office will notify each complainant and the educational agency or institution against which the violation has been alleged, in writing, that the complaint has been received.

(2) The notification to the agency or institution under paragraph (b)(1) of this section shall include the substance of the alleged violation and the agency or institution shall be given an opportunity to submit a written response.

(c) (1) The Office will investigate all timely complaints received to determine whether there has been a failure to comply with the provisions of section 438 of the Act or the regulations in this part, and may permit further written or oral submissions by both parties.

(2) Following its investigation the Office will provide written notification of its findings and the basis for such findings to the complainant and the agency or institution involved.

(3) If the Office finds that there has been a failure to comply, it will include in its notification under paragraph (c) (2) of this section, the specific steps which must be taken by the agency or institution into compliance. The notification shall also set forth a reasonable period of time, given all of the circumstances of the case, for the agency or institution to voluntarily comply.

(d) If the educational agency or institution does not come into compliance within the period of time set under paragraph (c)(3) of this section, the matter will be referred to the Review Board for a hearing under §§99.64–99.67, inclusive.

§ 99.64   Termination of Funding

If the Secretary, after reasonable notice and opportunity for a hearing by the Review Board, (1) finds that an educational agency or institution has failed to comply with the provisions of section 438 of the Act, or the regulations in this part, and (2) determines that compliance cannot be secured by voluntary means, he shall issue a decision, in writing, that no funds under any of the Federal programs referenced in §99.1(a) shall be made available to that educational agency or institution (or, at the Secretary's discretion, to the unit of the educational agency or institution affected by the failure to comply) until there is no longer any such failure to comply.

§ 99.65   Hearing Procedures

(a) *Panels.* The Chairman of the Review Board shall designate Hearing Panels to conduct one or more hearings under §99.64. Each Panel shall consist of not less than three members of the Review Board. The Review Board may, at its discretion, sit for any hearing or class of hearings. The Chairman of the Review Board shall designate himself or any other member of a Panel to serve as Chairman.

(b) *Procedural rules.* (1) With respect to hearings involving, in the opinion of the Panel, no dispute as to a material fact the resolution of which would be materially assisted by oral testimony, the Panel shall take appropriate steps to afford to each party to the proceeding an opportunity for presenting his case at the option of the Panel (i) in whole or in part in writing or (ii) in an informal conference before the Panel which shall afford each party: (A) Sufficient notice of the issues to be considered (where such notice has not previously been afforded); and (B) an opportunity to be represented by counsel.

(2) With respect to hearings involving a dispute as to a material fact the resolution of which would be materially assisted by oral testimony, the Panel shall afford each party an opportunity, which shall include, in addition to provisions required by subparagraph (1)(ii) of this paragraph, provisions designed to assure to each party the following:

(i) An opportunity for a record of the proceedings;

(ii) An opportunity to present witnesses on the party's behalf; and

(iii) An opportunity to cross-examine other witnesses either orally or through written interrogatories.

§ 99.66   Hearing before Panel or a Hearing Officer

A hearing pursuant to §99.65(b)(2) shall be conducted, as determined by the Panel Chairman, either before the Panel or a hearing officer. The hearing officer may be (a) one of the members of the Panel or (b) a nonmember who is appointed as a hearing examiner under 5 U.S.C. 3105.

§ 99.67   Initial Decision; Final Decision

(a) The Panel shall prepare an initial written decision, which shall include findings of fact and conclusions based thereon. When a hearing is conducted before a hearing officer alone, the hearing officer shall separately find and state the facts and conclusions which shall be incorporated in the initial decision prepared by the Panel.

(b) Copies of the initial decision shall be mailed promptly by the Panel to each party (or to the party's counsel), and to the Secretary with a notice affording the party an opportunity to submit written comments thereon to the Secretary within a specified reasonable time.

(c) The initial decision of the Panel transmitted to the Secretary shall become the final decision of the Secretary, unless, within 25 days after the expiration of the time for receipt of written comments, the Secretary advises the Review Board in writing of his determination to review the decision.

(d) In any case in which the Secretary modifies or reverses the initial decision of the Panel, he shall accompany that action with a written statement of the grounds for the modification or reversal, which shall promptly be filed with the Review Board.

(e) Review of any initial decision by the Secretary shall be based upon the decision, the written record, if any, of the Panel's proceedings, and written comments or oral arguments by the parties, or by their counsel, to the proceedings.

(f) No decision under this section shall become final until it is served upon the educational agency or institution involved or its attorney.

AUTHOR INDEX

SUBJECT INDEX

f school